ECONOMETRICS

ECONOMETRICS

BRUCE E. HANSEN

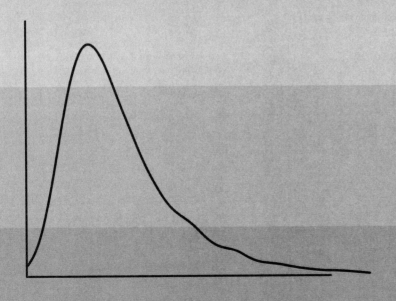

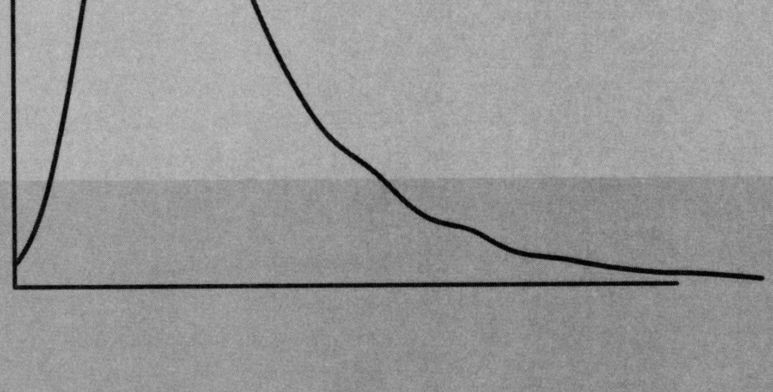

Princeton University Press
Princeton and Oxford

Published by Princeton University Press
41 William Street, Princeton, New Jersey 08540
99 Banbury Road, Oxford OX2 6JX

press.princeton.edu

Library of Congress Cataloging-in-Publication Data

Names: Hansen, Bruce E., 1962- author.
Title: Econometrics / Bruce E. Hansen.
Description: Princeton : Princeton University Press, 2022. | Includes bibliographical references and index.
Identifiers: LCCN 2021049283 (print) | LCCN 2021049284 (ebook) | ISBN 9780691235899 (hardcover) | ISBN 9780691236155 (ebook)
Subjects: LCSH: Econometrics.
Classification: LCC HB139 .H3636 2022 (print) | LCC HB139 (ebook) | DDC 330.01/5195¯dc23/eng/20211112
LC record available at https://lccn.loc.gov/2021049283
LC ebook record available at https://lccn.loc.gov/2021049284

British Library Cataloging-in-Publication Data is available

Editorial: Joe Jackson, Josh Drake
Production Editorial: Terri O'Prey
Text Design: Wanda España
Cover Design: Wanda España
Production: Jacqueline Poirier
Publicity: Kate Hensley, Charlotte Coyne
Copyeditor: Cyd Westmoreland

This book has been composed in Minion Pro

Printed on acid-free paper. ∞

Printed in the United States of America

10 9 8 7 6 5 4 3 2

CONTENTS

8 RESTRICTED ESTIMATION 199

9 HYPOTHESIS TESTING 225

28 MODEL SELECTION, STEIN SHRINKAGE, AND MODEL AVERAGING 889

29 MACHINE LEARNING 941

APPENDIX B: USEFUL INEQUALITIES 999

PREFACE

This textbook is the second in a two-part series covering the core material typically taught in a one-year Ph.D. course in econometrics. The sequence is:

1. *Probability and Statistics for Economists* (first volume);
2. *Econometrics* (this volume).

Econometrics assumes that students have a background in multivariate calculus, probability theory, linear algebra, and mathematical statistics. A prior course in undergraduate econometrics would be helpful but is not required. Two excellent undergraduate textbooks are Stock and Watson (2019) and Wooldridge (2020). The relevant background in probability theory and mathematical statistics is provided in *Probability and Statistics for Economists.*

For reference, the basic tools of matrix algebra and probability inequalites are reviewed in Appendixes A and B.

This textbook contains more material than can be covered in a one-semester course. This is intended to provide instructors flexibility concerning which topics to cover, which to cover in depth, and which to cover briefly. Some material is suitable for second-year Ph.D. instruction. At the University of Wisconsin, where this material was developed, in the first half of the fall semester, we cover *Probability and Statistics for Economists.* In the second half of the fall semester, we cover Chapters 1–9 of *Econometrics.* In the first half of the spring semester, we cover Chapters 10–17, with some chapters covered briefly. In the second half of the spring semester, we cover Chapters 18–29, with many details only covered briefly. We revisit much of the latter material in our second-year curriculum, with greater focus on the econometric theory.

For students wishing to deepen their knowledge of matrix algebra in relation to econometrics, I recommend *Matrix Algebra* by Abadir and Magnus (2005).

For further study in econometrics beyond this text, I recommend Davidson (1994) for asymptotic theory, Hamilton (1994) and Kilian and Lütkepohl (2017) for time series methods, Cameron and Trivedi (2005) and Wooldridge (2010) for panel data and discrete response models, and Li and Racine (2007) for nonparametric and semiparametric econometrics. Beyond these texts, the *Handbook of Econometrics* series provides advanced summaries of contemporary econometric methods and theory.

Alternative Ph.D.-level econometrics textbooks include Theil (1971), Amemiya (1985), Judge, Griffiths, Hill, Lütkepohl, and Lee (1985), Goldberger (1991), Davidson and MacKinnon (1993, 2004), Johnston and DiNardo (1997), Davidson (2000), Hayashi (2000), Ruud (2000), Greene (2018), and Magnus (2017). For a focus on applied issues, see Angrist and Pischke (2009) and Cunningham (2021).

The end-of-chapter exercises are important parts of the text and are meant to help teach students of econometrics.

ACKNOWLEDGMENTS

This book and its companion, *Probability and Statistics for Economists*, would not have been possible without the amazing flow of volunteered advice, corrections, comments, and questions I have received from students, faculty, and other readers over the 20 years I have worked on this project. I have received emailed corrections and comments from so many individuals that I have completely lost track of the list. So rather than publish an incomplete list, I simply give a grateful and sincere *Thank You* to every single one of them.

I thank Ying-Ying Lee and Wooyoung Kim for providing research assistance in preparing some of the numerical analysis, graphics, and empirical examples presented in the text.

My most heartfelt thanks go to my family: Korinna, Zoe, and Nicholas. Without their love and support over these years, this project would not have been possible.

All of the author's royalties will be gifted to charitable causes.

NOTATION

Real numbers (elements of the real line $\mathbb{R}$, also called **scalars**) are written using lowercase italics, such as x.

Vectors (elements of $\mathbb{R}^k$) are typically written using lowercase italics, such as x, and sometimes using lowercase bold italics, such as $\boldsymbol{x}$ (for matrix algebra expressions). For example, we write

$$x = \begin{pmatrix} x_1 \\ x_2 \\ \vdots \\ x_k \end{pmatrix}.$$

Vectors by default are written as column vectors. The **transpose** of x is the row vector

$$x' = \begin{pmatrix} x_1 & x_2 & \cdots & x_m \end{pmatrix}.$$

There is diversity across fields concerning the choice of notation for the transpose. The notation x' is the most common in econometrics. In statistics and mathematics, the notation $x^\top$ is typically used, or occasionally x^t.

Matrices are written using uppercase bold italics, for example,

$$\boldsymbol{A} = \begin{bmatrix} a_{11} & a_{12} \\ a_{21} & a_{22} \end{bmatrix}.$$

Random variables and vectors are written using uppercase italics, such as X.

Typically, Greek letters, such as β, θ, and σ^2, are used to denote parameters of a probability model. Estimators are typically denoted by putting a hat "^", tilde "~" or bar "-" over the corresponding letter, for example, $\widehat{\beta}$ and $\widetilde{\beta}$ are estimators of β.

COMMON SYMBOLS

a	scalar
a or $\boldsymbol{a}$	vector
$\boldsymbol{A}$	matrix
X	random variable or vector
$\mathbb{R}$	real line
$\mathbb{R}_+$	positive real line
$\mathbb{R}^k$	Euclidean k space
$\mathbb{P}[A]$	probability

$\mathbb{P}[A \mid B]$	conditional probability
$F(x)$	cumulative distribution function
$f(x)$	probability density function
$\mathbb{E}[X]$	mathematical expectation
$\mathbb{E}[Y \mid X=x]$, $\mathbb{E}[Y \mid X]$	conditional expectation
$\operatorname{var}[X]$	variance or covariance matrix
$\operatorname{var}[Y \mid X=x]$, $\operatorname{var}[Y \mid X]$	conditional variance
$\operatorname{cov}(X, Y)$	covariance
$\mathscr{P}[Y \mid X=x]$, $\mathscr{P}[Y \mid X]$	best linear predictor
$\operatorname{corr}(X, Y)$	correlation
$\overline{X}$	sample mean
$\widehat{\sigma}^2$	sample variance
s^2	biased-corrected sample variance
$\widehat{\theta}$	estimator
$s(\widehat{\theta})$	standard error of estimator
$\lim_{n\to\infty}$	limit
$\operatorname{plim}_{n\to\infty}$	probability limit
$\longrightarrow$	convergence
$\underset{p}{\longrightarrow}$	convergence in probability
$\underset{d}{\longrightarrow}$	convergence in distribution
$L_n(\theta)$	likelihood function
$\ell_n(\theta)$	log-likelihood function
$\mathscr{I}_\theta$	information matrix
$\mathrm{N}(0, 1)$	standard normal distribution
$\mathrm{N}(\mu, \sigma^2)$	normal distribution with mean μ and variance σ^2
χ^2_k	chi-square distribution with k degrees of freedom
$\boldsymbol{I}_n$	$n \times n$ identity matrix
$\mathbf{1}_n$	$n \times 1$ vector of ones
$\operatorname{tr} \boldsymbol{A}$	trace of matrix $\boldsymbol{A}$
$\boldsymbol{a}'$ or $\boldsymbol{A}'$	vector or matrix transpose
$\boldsymbol{A}^{-1}$	matrix inverse
$\boldsymbol{A} > 0$	positive definite
$\boldsymbol{A} \geq 0$	positive semi-definite
$\lVert \boldsymbol{a} \rVert$	Euclidean norm
$\lVert \boldsymbol{A} \rVert$	matrix norm

$\stackrel{\text{def}}{=}$	definitional equality
$\mathbb{1}\{a\}$	indicator function (1 if a is true, else 0)
$\simeq$	approximate equality
$\sim$	is distributed as
$\log(x)$	natural logarithm
$\exp(x)$	exponential function
$\sum_{i=1}^{n}$	summation from $i=1$ to $i=n$

GREEK ALPHABET

It is common in economics and econometrics to use Greek characters to augment the Latin alphabet. The following table lists the various Greek characters and their pronunciations in English. The second character, when listed, is the uppercase character (except for ϵ, which is an alternative script for ε.)

Greek Character	**Name**	**Latin Keyboard Equivalent**
α	alpha	a
β	beta	b
γ, Γ	gamma	g
δ, Δ	delta	d
ε, ϵ	epsilon	e
ζ	zeta	z
η	eta	h
θ, Θ	theta	y
ι	iota	i
κ	kappa	k
λ, Λ	lambda	l
μ	mu	m
ν	nu	n
ξ, Ξ	xi	x
π, Π	pi	p
ρ	rho	r
σ, Σ	sigma	s
τ	tau	t
υ	upsilon	u
ϕ, Φ	phi	f
χ	chi	x
ψ, Ψ	psi	c
ω, Ω	omega	w

ECONOMETRICS

CHAPTER 1
INTRODUCTION

1.1 WHAT IS ECONOMETRICS?

The term "econometrics" is believed to have been crafted by Ragnar Frisch (1895–1973) of Norway, one of the three principal founders of the Econometric Society, first editor of the journal *Econometrica*, and co-winner of the first Nobel Memorial Prize in Economic Sciences in 1969. It is therefore fitting that we turn to Frisch's own words in the introduction to the first issue of *Econometrica* to describe the discipline.

> A word of explanation regarding the term econometrics may be in order. Its definition is implied in the statement of the scope of the [Econometric] Society, in Section I of the Constitution, which reads: "The Econometric Society is an international society for the advancement of economic theory in its relation to statistics and mathematics. . . . Its main object shall be to promote studies that aim at a unification of the theoretical-quantitative and the empirical-quantitative approach to economic problems. . . ."
>
> But there are several aspects of the quantitative approach to economics, and no single one of these aspects, taken by itself, should be confounded with econometrics. Thus, econometrics is by no means the same as economic statistics. Nor is it identical with what we call general economic theory, although a considerable portion of this theory has a defininitely quantitative character. Nor should econometrics be taken as synonomous with the application of mathematics to economics. Experience has shown that each of these three view-points, that of statistics, economic theory, and mathematics, is a necessary, but not by itself a sufficient, condition for a real understanding of the quantitative relations in modern economic life. It is the *unification* of all three that is powerful. And it is this unification that constitutes econometrics. (Frisch, 1933, pp. 1–2).

This definition remains valid today, although some terms have evolved somewhat in their usage. Today, we would say that econometrics is the unified study of economic models, mathematical statistics, and economic data.

In the field of econometrics there are subdivisions and specializations. **Econometric theory** concerns the development of tools and methods, and the study of the properties of econometric methods. **Applied econometrics** is a term describing the development of quantitative economic models and the application of econometric methods to these models using economic data.

1.2 THE PROBABILITY APPROACH TO ECONOMETRICS

The unifying methodology of modern econometrics was articulated by Trygve Haavelmo (1911–1999) in his seminal paper "The probability approach in econometrics" (1944). Haavelmo argued that quantitative economic models must necessarily be *probability models* (by which today we would mean *stochastic*). Deterministic models are blatently inconsistent with observed economic quantities, and it is incoherent to apply deterministic models to nondeterministic data. Economic models should be explicitly designed to incorporate randomness; stochastic errors should not be simply added to deterministic models to make them random. Once we acknowledge that an economic model is a probability model, it follows naturally that an appropriate tool to quantify, estimate, and conduct inferences about the economy is the powerful theory of mathematical statistics. The appropriate method for a quantitative economic analysis follows from the probabilistic construction of the economic model. Haavelmo's probability approach was quickly embraced by the economics profession. Today, no quantitative work in economics shuns its fundamental vision.

While all economists embrace the probability approach, there has been some evolution in its implementation.

The **structural approach** is the closest to Haavelmo's original idea. A probabilistic economic model is specified, and the quantitative analysis performed under the assumption that the economic model is correctly specified. Researchers often describe this as "taking their model seriously." The structural approach typically leads to likelihood-based analysis, including maximum likelihood and Bayesian estimation.

A criticism of the structural approach is that it is misleading to treat an economic model as correctly specified. Instead, it is more accurate to view a model as a useful abstraction or approximation. In this case, how should we interpret structural econometric analysis? The **quasi-structural approach** to inference views a structural economic model as an approximation rather than the truth. This theory has led to the concepts of the pseudo-true value (the parameter value defined by the estimation problem), the quasi-likelihood function, quasi–maximum likelihood estimate (quasi-MLE), and quasi-likelihood inference.

Closely related is the **semiparametric approach**. A probabilistic economic model is partially specified but some features are left unspecified. This approach typically leads to estimation methods, such as least squares and the generalized method of moments. The semiparametric approach dominates contemporary econometrics and is the main focus of this textbook.

Another branch of quantitative structural economics is the **calibration approach.** Similar to the quasi-structural approach, the calibration approach interprets structural models as approximations and hence inherently false. The difference is that the calibrationist literature rejects mathematical statistics (deeming classical theory as inappropriate for approximate models) and instead selects parameters by matching model and data moments using nonstatistical ad hoc[1] methods.

Trygve Haavelmo

The founding ideas of the field of econometrics are largely due to the Norweigen econometrician Trygve Haavelmo (1911–1999). His advocacy of probability models revolutionized the field, and his use of formal mathematical reasoning laid the foundation for subsequent generations. He was awarded the Nobel Memorial Prize in Economic Sciences in 1989.

1.3 ECONOMETRIC TERMS

In a typical application, an econometrician has a set of repeated measurements on a set of variables. For example, in a labor application, the variables could include weekly earnings, educational attainment, age, and other descriptive characteristics. We call this information the **data, dataset**, or **sample**.

[1] *Ad hoc* means "for this purpose"—a method designed for a specific problem—and not based on a generalizable principle.

We use the term **observations** to refer to distinct repeated measurements on the variables. An individual observation often corresponds to a specific economic unit, such as a person, household, corporation, firm, organization, country, state, city, or other geographical region. An individual observation could also be a measurement at a point in time, such as quarterly gross domestic product (GDP) or a daily interest rate.

Economists typically denote variables by the italicized roman characters Y, X, and/or Z. The convention in econometrics is to use the character Y to denote the variable to be explained, while the characters X and Z are used to denote the conditioning (explanatory) variables. Following mathematical practice, random variables and vectors are denoted by uppercase roman characters, such as Y and X. We make an exception for equation errors, which we typically denote by the lowercase letters e, u, or v.

Real numbers (elements of the real line $\mathbb{R}$, also called **scalars**) are written using lowercase italics, such as x. Vectors (elements of $\mathbb{R}^k$) are typically also written using lowercase italics, such as x, or using lowercase bold italics, such as $\boldsymbol{x}$. We use bold in matrix algebraic expressions for compatibility with matrix notation.

Matrices are written using uppercase bold italics, such as $\boldsymbol{X}$. Our notation will not make a distinction between random and nonrandom matrices. Typically we use $\boldsymbol{U}$, $\boldsymbol{V}$, $\boldsymbol{X}$, $\boldsymbol{Y}$, $\boldsymbol{Z}$ to denote random matrices and use $\boldsymbol{A}$, $\boldsymbol{B}$, $\boldsymbol{C}$, $\boldsymbol{W}$ to denote nonrandom matrices.

We denote the number of observations by the natural number n, and subscript the variables by the index i to denote the individual observation (e.g., Y_i). In some contexts, we use indices other than i, such as in time series applications where the index t is common. In panel studies, we typically use the double index it to refer to individual i at time period t.

We typically use Greek letters, such as β, θ, and σ^2, to denote unknown parameters (scalar or vectors). Parameter matrices are written using uppercase Latin boldface (e.g., $\boldsymbol{A}$). Estimators are typically denoted by putting a hat "$\wedge$," tilde "$\sim$," or bar "–" over the corresponding letter (e.g., $\widehat{\beta}$ and $\widetilde{\beta}$ are estimators of β, and $\widehat{\boldsymbol{A}}$ is an estimator of $\boldsymbol{A}$).

The covariance matrix of an econometric estimator will typically be written using the uppercase boldface $\boldsymbol{V}$, often with a subscript to denote the estimator (e.g., $\boldsymbol{V}_{\widehat{\beta}} = \operatorname{var}\left[\widehat{\beta}\right]$ as the covariance matrix for $\widehat{\beta}$). Hopefully without causing confusion, we will use the notation $\boldsymbol{V}_\beta = \operatorname{avar}\left[\widehat{\beta}\right]$ to denote the asymptotic covariance matrix of $\sqrt{n}\left(\widehat{\beta} - \beta\right)$ (the variance of the asymptotic distribution). Covariance matrix estimators will be denoted by appending hats or tildes (e.g., $\widehat{\boldsymbol{V}}_\beta$ is an estimator of $\boldsymbol{V}_\beta$).

1.4 OBSERVATIONAL DATA

A common econometric question is to quantify the causal impact of one set of variables on another variable. For example, a concern in labor economics is the returns to schooling–the change in earnings induced by increasing a worker's education, holding other variables constant. Another issue of interest is the earnings gap between men and women.

Ideally, we would use **experimental** data to answer these questions. To measure the returns to schooling, an experiment might randomly divide children into groups, mandate different levels of education to the different groups, and then follow the children's wage path after they mature and enter the labor force. The differences between the groups would be direct measurements of the effects of different levels of education. However, experiments such as this would be widely condemned as immoral! Consequently, in economics, experimental data sets are typically narrow in scope.

Instead, most economic data is **observational**. To continue the above example, through data collection we can record the level of a person's education and their wage. With such data, we can measure the joint distribution of these variables and assess their joint dependence. But from observational data, it is difficult to infer **causality** as we are not able to manipulate one variable to see the direct effect on the other. For example, a person's level of education is (at least partially) determined by that person's choices. These factors are likely to be affected by their personal abilities and attitudes toward work. The fact that a person is highly educated suggests a high level of ability, which suggests a high relative wage. This is an alternative explanation for an observed positive correlation between educational levels and wages. High ability individuals do better in school, and therefore choose to attain higher levels of education, and their high ability is the fundamental reason for their high wages. The point is that multiple explanations are consistent with a positive correlation between schooling levels and education. Knowledge of the joint distribution alone may not be able to distinguish between these explanations.

> Most economic data sets are observational, not experimental. Thus, all variables must be treated as random and possibly jointly determined.

This discussion shows that it is difficult to infer causality from observational data alone. Causal inference requires identification, which is based on strong assumptions. We will discuss these issues on occasion throughout the text.

1.5 STANDARD DATA STRUCTURES

There are five major types of economic data sets: cross-sectional, time series, panel, clustered, and spatial. They are distinguished by the dependence structure across observations.

Cross-sectional data sets have one observation per individual. Surveys and administrative records are a typical source for cross-sectional data. In typical applications, the individuals surveyed are persons, households, firms, or other economic agents. In many contemporary econometric cross-sectional studies, the sample size n is quite large. It is conventional to assume that cross-sectional observations are mutually independent. Most of this text is devoted to the study of cross-sectional data.

Time series data are indexed by time. Typical examples include macroeconomic aggregates, prices, and interest rates. This type of data is characterized by serial dependence. Most aggregate economic data are only available at a low frequency (annual, quarterly, or monthly), so the sample size is typically much smaller than in cross-sectional studies. An exception is financial data, where data are available at a high frequency (daily, hourly, or by transaction), so sample sizes can be quite large.

Panel data combines elements of cross-sectional and time series. These data sets consist of a set of individuals (typically persons, households, or corporations) measured repeatedly over time. The common modeling assumption is that the individuals are mutually independent of one another, but a given individual's observations are mutually dependent. In some panel data contexts, the number of time series observations T per individual is small, while the number of individuals n is large. In other panel data contexts (for example when countries or states are taken as the unit of measurement), the number of individuals n can be small, while the number of time series observations T can be moderately large. An important issue in econometric panel data is the treatment of error components.

Clustered samples are becoming increasingly popular in applied economics and are related to panel data. In clustered sampling, the observations are grouped into "clusters" which are treated as mutually independent yet allowed to be dependent within the cluster. The major difference from panel data is that clustered sampling typically does not explicitly model error component structures, nor the dependence within clusters, but is instead concerned with inference which is robust to arbitrary forms of within-cluster correlation.

Spatial dependence is another model of interdependence. The observations are treated as mutually dependent according to a spatial measure (for example, geographic proximity). Unlike clustering, spatial models allow all observations to be mutually dependent and typically rely on explicit modeling of the dependence relationships. Spatial dependence can also be viewed as a generalization of time series dependence.

Data Structures

- Cross-section
- Time series
- Panel
- Clustered
- Spatial

As mentioned above, most of this text will be devoted to cross-sectional data under the assumption of mutually independent observations. By mutual independence, we mean that the ith observation (Y_i, X_i) is independent of the jth observation (Y_j, X_j) for $i \neq j$. In this case, we say that the data are **independently distributed**. (Sometimes the label "independent" is misconstrued. It is a statement about the relationship between observations i and j, not a statement about the relationship between Y_i and X_i.)

Furthermore, if the data are randomly gathered, it is reasonable to model each observation as a draw from the same probability distribution. In this case, we say that the data are **identically distributed**. If the observations are mutually independent and identically distributed, we say that the observations are **independent and identically distributed (i.i.d.)** or a **random sample**. For most of this text, we will assume that our observations come from a random sample.

Definition 1.1 The variables (Y_i, X_i) are a **sample** from the distribution F if they are identically distributed with distribution F.

Definition 1.2 The variables (Y_i, X_i) are a **random sample** if they are mutually independent and identically distributed (i.i.d.) across $i = 1, \ldots, n$.

In the random sampling framework, we think of an individual observation (Y_i, X_i) as a realization from a joint probability distribution $F(y, x)$, which we call the **population**. This "population" is infinitely large. This abstraction can be a source of confusion, as it does not correspond to a physical population in the real world. It is an abstraction because the distribution F is unknown, and the goal of statistical inference is to learn about features of F from the sample. The *assumption* of random sampling provides the mathematical foundation for treating economic statistics with the tools of mathematical statistics.

The random sampling framework was a major intellectual breakthrough of the late nineteenth century, allowing the application of mathematical statistics to the social sciences. Before this conceptual development, methods from mathematical statistics had not been applied to economic data, as the latter were viewed as nonrandom. The random sampling framework enabled economic samples to be treated as random, a necessary precondition for the application of statistical methods.

1.6 ECONOMETRIC SOFTWARE

Economists use a variety of econometric, statistical, and programming software. Stata is a powerful statistical program with a broad set of pre-programmed econometric and statistical tools. It is quite popular among economists and is continuously being updated with new methods. It is an excellent package for most econometric analysis but is limited when you want to use new or less-common econometric methods which have not yet been programed. At many points in this textbook, specific Stata estimation methods and commands are described. These commands are valid for Stata version 16.

MATLAB, GAUSS, and OxMetrics are high-level matrix programming languages with a wide variety of built-in statistical functions. Many econometric methods have been programed in these languages and are available on the web. The advantage of these packages is that you are in complete control of your analysis, and it is easier to program new methods than it is in Stata. Some disadvantages are that you have to do much of the programming yourself, programming complicated procedures takes significant time, and programming errors are hard to prevent and difficult to detect and eliminate. Of these languages, GAUSS used to be quite popular among econometricians, but currently MATLAB is more popular.

An intermediate choice is R. R has the capabilities of the above high-level matrix programming languages, but it also has many built-in statistical environments which can replicate much of the functionality of Stata. R is the dominant programming language in the statistics field, so methods developed in that arena are most commonly available in R. Uniquely, R is open source, user contributed, and best of all, completely free! A growing group of econometricians are enthusiastic fans of R.

For highly intensive computational tasks, some economists write their programs in a standard programming language, such as Fortran or C. This can lead to major gains in computational speed, at the cost of increased time in programming and debugging.

Many other packages are used by econometricians, including Eviews, Gretl, PcGive, Python, Julia, RATS, and SAS.

As the packages described above have distinct advantages, many empirical economists use multiple packages. As a student of econometrics, you will learn at least one of these packages and probably more than one. My advice is that all students of econometrics should develop a basic level of familiarity with Stata, MATLAB, and R.

1.7 REPLICATION

Scientific research needs to be documented and replicable. For social science research using observational data, this requires careful documentation and archiving of the research methods, data manipulations, and coding.

The best practice is as follows. Accompanying each published paper, an author should create a complete replication package (set of data files, documentation, and program code files). This package should contain the source (raw) data used for analysis and code which executes the empirical analysis and other numerical work reported in the paper. In most cases, this code is a set of programs which may need to be executed sequentially. (For example, there may be an initial program which "cleans" and manipulates the data, and then a second set of programs which estimate the reported models.) The ideal is full documentation and clarity. This package should be posted on the author(s) website and posted on the journal website when that is an option.

A complicating factor is that many current economic data sets have restricted access and cannot be shared without permission. In these cases, the data cannot be posted or shared. The computed code, however, can and should be posted.

Most journals in economics require authors of published papers to make their datasets generally available. For example:

Econometrica states:

> *Econometrica* has the policy that all empirical, experimental and simulation results must be replicable. Therefore, authors of accepted papers must submit data sets, programs, and information on empirical analysis, experiments and simulations that are needed for replication and some limited sensitivity analysis.

The *American Economic Review* states (on its webpage):

> It is the policy of the American Economic Association to publish papers only if the data and code used in the analysis are clearly and precisely documented and access to the data and code is non-exclusive to the authors. Authors of accepted papers that contain empirical work, simulations, or experimental work must provide, prior to acceptance, information about the data, programs, and other details of the computations sufficient to permit replication, as well as information about access to data and programs.

The *Journal of Political Economy* states:

> It is the policy of the *Journal of Political Economy* to publish papers only if the data used in the analysis are clearly and precisely documented and are readily available to any researcher for purposes of replication.

If you are interested in using the data from a published paper, first check the journal's website, as many journals archive data and replication programs online. Second, check the website(s) of the paper's author(s). Most academic economists maintain webpages, and some make available replication files complete with data and programs. If these investigations fail, email the author(s), politely requesting the data. You may need to be persistent.

As a matter of professional etiquette, all authors absolutely have the obligation to make their data and programs available. Unfortunately, many fail to do so, and typically for poor reasons. The irony of the situation is that it is typically in the best interests of a scholar to make as much of their work (including all data and programs) freely available, as this only increases the likelihood of their work being cited and having an impact.

Keep this in mind as you start your own empirical project. Remember that as part of your end product, you will need (and want) to provide all data and programs to the community of scholars. The greatest form of flattery is to learn that another scholar has read your paper, wants to extend your work, or wants to use your empirical methods. In addition, public openness provides a healthy incentive for transparency and integrity in empirical analysis.

1.8 DATA FILES FOR TEXTBOOK

On the textbook webpage https://press.princeton.edu/books/econometrics are posted files containing data sets which are used in this textbook both for illustration and for end-of-chapter empirical exercises. Most of the datasets have four files: (1) Description (pdf format); (2) Excel data file; (3) Text data file; and (4) Stata data file. The three data files are identical in content: the observations and variables are listed in the same order in each, and all have variable labels.

For example, the text makes frequent reference to a wage dataset extracted from the Current Population Survey. This dataset is named `cps09mar`, and is represented by the files `cps09mar_description.pdf`, `cps09mar.xlsx`, `cps09mar.txt`, and `cps09mar.dta`.

The datasets currently included are

- `AB1991`
  —Data file from Arellano and Bond (1991)
- `AJR2001`
  —Data file from Acemoglu, Johnson, and Robinson (2001)
- `AK1991`
  —Data file from Angrist and Krueger (1991)
- `AL1999`
  —Data file from Angrist and Lavy (1999)
- `BMN2016`
  —Data file from Bernheim, Meer, and Novarro (2016)
- `cps09mar`
  —household survey data extracted from the March 2009 Current Population Survey
- `Card1995`
  —Data file from Card (1995)
- `CHJ2004`
  —Data file from Cox, Hansen, and Jimenez (2004)
- `CK1994`
  —Data file from Card and Krueger (1994)
- `CMR2008`
  —Date file from Card, Mas, and Rothstein (2008)
- `DDK2011`
  —Data file from Duflo, Dupas, and Kremer (2011)
- `DS2004`
  —Data file from DiTella and Schargrodsky (2004)
- `FRED-MD` and `FRED-QD`
  —U.S. monthly and quarterly macroeconomic databases from McCracken and Ng (2016, 2021)
- `Invest1993`
  —Data file from B. Hall and R. Hall (1993)
- `LM2007`
  —Data file from Ludwig and Miller (2007) and Cattaneo, Titiunik, and Vazquez-Bare (2017)
- `Kilian2009`
  —Data file from Kilian (2009)

- `Koppelman`
  —Data file from Forinash and Koppelman (1993), Koppelman and Wen (2000), and Wen and Koppelman (2001)
- `MRW1992`
  —Data file from Mankiw, Romer, and Weil (1992)
- `Nerlove1963`
  —Data file from Nerlov (1963)
- `PSS2017`
  —Data file from Papageorgiou, Saam, and Schulte (2017)
- `RR2010`
  —Data file from Reinhard and Rogoff (2010)

1.9 READING THE BOOK

I have endeavored to use a unified notation and nomenclature. The development of the material is cumulative, with later chapters building on the earlier ones. Nevertheless, every attempt has been made to make each chapter self-contained, so readers can pick and choose topics according to their interests.

To fully understand econometric methods, it is necessary to have a mathematical understanding of its mechanics, and this includes the mathematical proofs of the main results. Consequently, this text is self-contained with nearly all results proved with full mathematical rigor. The mathematical development and proofs aim at brevity and conciseness (sometimes described as mathematical elegance), but also at pedagogy. To understand a mathematical proof, it is not sufficient to simply *read* the proof, you need to follow it and re-create it for yourself.

Nevertheless, many readers will not be interested in each mathematical detail, explanation, or proof. This is okay. To use a method, it may not be necessary to understand the mathematical details. Accordingly, I have placed the more technical mathematical proofs and details in chapter appendices. These appendices and other technical sections are marked with an asterisk (*). These sections can be skipped without any loss in exposition.

Key concepts in matrix algebra and a set of useful inequalities are reviewed in Appendices A and B. It may be useful to read or review Appendix A.1–A.11 before starting Chapter 3, and review Appendix B before Chapter 6. It is not necessary to understand all the material in the appendices. They are intended to be reference material, and some of the results are not used in this textbook.

PART I

REGRESSION

CHAPTER 2
CONDITIONAL EXPECTATION AND PROJECTION

2.1 INTRODUCTION

The most commonly applied econometric tool is least squares estimation, also known as **regression**. Least squares is a tool to estimate the conditional mean of one variable (the **dependent variable**) given another set of variables (the **regressors**, **conditioning variables**, or **covariates**).

In this chapter, we abstract from estimation and focus on the probabilistic foundation of the conditional expectation model and its projection approximation. This includes a review of probability theory. For a background in intermediate probability theory, see Chapters 1–5 of *Probability and Statistics for Economists*.

2.2 THE DISTRIBUTION OF WAGES

Suppose that we are interested in wage rates in the United States. Since wage rates vary across workers, we cannot describe wage rates by a single number. Instead, we can describe wages using a probability distribution. Formally, we view the wage of an individual worker as a random variable *wage* with the **probability distribution**

$$F(y) = \mathbb{P}\left[wage \leq y\right].$$

When we say that a person's wage is random, we mean that we do not know their wage before it is measured, and we treat observed wage rates as realizations from the distribution F. Treating unobserved wages as random variables and observed wages as realizations is a powerful mathematical abstraction which allows us to use the tools of mathematical probability.

A useful thought experiment is to imagine dialing a telephone number selected at random, and then asking the person who responds to tell us their wage rate. (Assume for simplicity that all workers have equal access to telephones and that the person who answers your call will answer honestly.) In this thought experiment, the wage of the person you have called is a single draw from the distribution F of wages in the population. By making many such phone calls, we can learn the full distribution.

When a distribution function F is differentiable, we define the **probability density function**

$$f(y) = \frac{d}{dy}F(y).$$

The density contains the same information as the distribution function, but the density is typically easier to visually interpret.

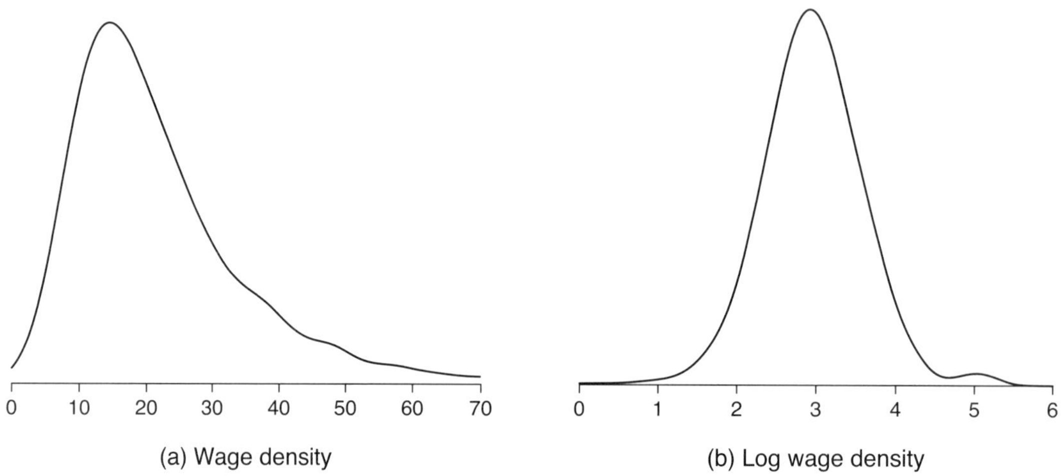

FIGURE 2.1 Density of wages and log wages

Figure 2.1(a) displays an estimate[1] of the probability density function of U.S. wage rates in 2009. We see that the density peaks around \$15, and most of the probability mass appears to lie between \$10 and \$40. These are ranges for typical wage rates in the U.S. population.

Important measures of central tendency are the median and the mean. The **median** m of a continuous distribution F is the unique solution to

$$F(m) = \frac{1}{2}.$$

The median U.S. wage is \$19.23. The median is a robust[2] measure of central tendency, but it is tricky to use for many calculations, as it is not a linear operator.

The **mean** or **expectation** of a random variable Y with discrete support is

$$\mu = \mathbb{E}[Y] = \sum_{j=1}^{\infty} \tau_j \mathbb{P}[Y = \tau_j].$$

For a continuous random variable with density $f(y)$, the expectation is

$$\mu = \mathbb{E}[Y] = \int_{-\infty}^{\infty} y f(y) dy.$$

Here we have used the common and convenient convention of using the single character Y to denote a random variable, rather than the more cumbersome label *wage*. An alternative notation which includes both discrete and continuous random variables as special cases is to write the integral as $\int_{-\infty}^{\infty} y dF(y)$.

The expectation is a convenient measure of central tendency, because it is a linear operator and arises naturally in many economic models. A disadvantage of the expectation is that it is not robust,[3] especially in the presence of substantial skewness or thick tails, both of which are features of the wage distribution, as can

[1]The distribution and density are estimated nonparametrically from the sample of 50,742 full-time non-military wage earners reported in the March 2009 Current Population Survey. The wage rate is constructed as annual individual wage and salary earnings divided by hours worked.

[2]The median is not sensitive to pertubations in the tails of the distribution.

[3]The expectation is sensitive to pertubations in the tails of the distribution.

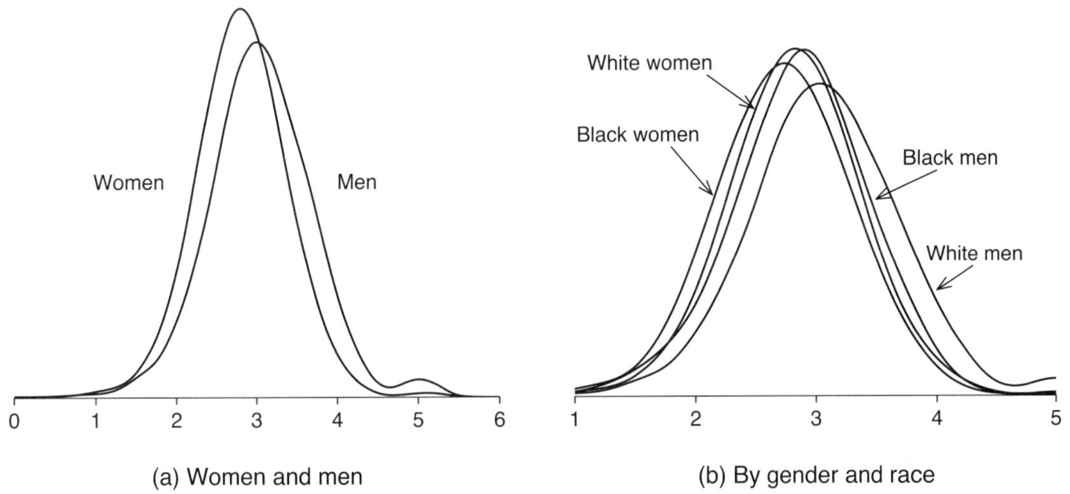

FIGURE 2.2 Log wage density by gender and race

be seen in Figure 2.1(a). Another way of viewing this is that 64% of workers earn less than the mean wage of \$23.90, suggesting that it is incorrect to describe the mean \$23.90 as a "typical" wage rate.

In this context, it is useful to transform the data by taking the natural logarithm.[4] Figure 2.1(b) shows the density of log hourly wages log(*wage*) for the same population. The density of log wages is less skewed and fat-tailed than the density of the level of wages, so its mean

$$\mathbb{E}\left[\log(wage)\right] = 2.95$$

is a better (more robust) measure[5] of central tendency of the distribution. For this reason, wage regressions typically use log wages as a dependent variable rather than the level of wages.

Another useful way to summarize the probability distribution $F(y)$ is in terms of its **quantiles**. For any $\alpha \in (0,1)$, the αth quantile of the continuous[6] distribution F is the real number q_α which satisfies $F\left(q_\alpha\right) = \alpha$. The quantile function q_α, viewed as a function of α, is the inverse of the distribution function F. The most commonly used quantile is the median, that is, $q_{0.5} = m$. We sometimes refer to quantiles by the percentile representation of α, and in this case, they are called **percentiles** (e.g., the median is the 50th percentile).

2.3 CONDITIONAL EXPECTATION

We saw in Figure 2.1(b) the density of log wages. Is this distribution the same for all workers, or does the wage distribution vary across subpopulations? To answer this question, we can compare wage distributions for different groups—for example, men and women. To investigate, we plot in Figure 2.2(a) the densities of log wages for U.S. men and women. We can see that the two wage densities take similar shapes but the density for men is somewhat shifted to the right.

---

[4]Throughout the text, we will use $\log(y)$ or $\log y$ to denote the natural logarithm of y.

[5]More precisely, the geometric mean $\exp\left(\mathbb{E}\left[\log W\right]\right) = \$19.11$ is a robust measure of central tendency.

[6]If F is not continuous, the definition is $q_\alpha = \inf\{y : F(y) \geq \alpha\}$.

The values 3.05 and 2.81 are the mean log wages, respectively, in the subpopulations of men and women workers. They are called the **conditional expectation** (or **conditional mean**) of log wages given gender. We can write their specific values as

$$\mathbb{E}\left[\log(wage) \mid gender = man\right] = 3.05$$
$$\mathbb{E}\left[\log(wage) \mid gender = woman\right] = 2.81.$$

We call these expectations "conditional," as they are conditioning on a fixed value of the variable *gender*. While you might not think of a person's gender as a random variable, it is random from the viewpoint of econometric analysis. If you randomly select an individual, the gender of the individual is unknown and thus random. (In the population of U.S. workers, the probability that a worker is a woman happens to be 43%.) In observational data, it is most appropriate to view all measurements as random variables, and the means of subpopulations are then conditional means.

It is important to mention at this point that we in no way attribute causality or interpretation to the difference in the conditional expectation of log wages between men and women. There are multiple potential explanations.

As the two densities in Figure 2.2(a) appear similar, a hasty inference might be that there is no meaningful difference between the wage distributions of men and women. Before jumping to this conclusion, let us examine the differences in the distributions more carefully. As mentioned above, the primary difference between the two densities appears to be their means. This difference equals

$$\begin{aligned}\mathbb{E}\left[\log(wage) \mid gender = man\right] - \mathbb{E}\left[\log(wage) \mid gender = woman\right] &= 3.05 - 2.81 \\ &= 0.24. \end{aligned} \tag{2.1}$$

A difference in expected log wages of 0.24 is often interpreted as an average 24% difference between the wages of men and women, which is quite substantial. (For a more complete explanation, see Section 2.4.)

Consider further splitting the male and female subpopulations by race, dividing the population into whites, Blacks, and other races. We display the log wage density functions of four of these groups in Figure 2.2(b). Again we see that the primary difference between the four density functions is their central tendency.

Focusing on the means of these distributions, Table 2.1 reports the mean log wage for each of the six subpopulations.

Once again we stress that we in no way attribute causality or interpretation to the differences across the entries of the table. The reason we use these particular subpopulations to illustrate conditional expectation is because differences in economic outcomes between gender and racial groups in the United States (and elsewhere) are widely discussed; part of the role of social science is to carefully document such patterns, and part of its role is to craft models and explanations. Conditional expectations (by themselves) can help

Table 2.1
Mean log wages by gender and race

	Men	Women
White	3.07	2.82
Black	2.86	2.73
Other	3.03	2.86

in the documentation and description; conditional expectations by themselves are neither a model nor an explanation.

The entries in Table 2.1 are the conditional means of log(*wage*) given *gender* and *race*. For example,

$$\mathbb{E}\left[\log(wage) \mid gender = man,\ race = white\right] = 3.07$$

and

$$\mathbb{E}\left[\log(wage) \mid gender = woman,\ race = Black\right] = 2.73.$$

One benefit of focusing on conditional means is that they reduce complicated distributions to a single summary measure and thereby facilitate comparisons across groups. Because of this simplifying property, conditional means are the primary interest of regression analysis and are a major focus in econometrics.

Table 2.1 allows us to easily calculate average wage differences between groups. For example, we can see that the wage gap between men and women continues after disaggregation by race, as the average gap between white men and white women is 25%, and that between Black men and Black women is 13%. We also can see that there is a race gap, as the average wages of Blacks are substantially less than the other race categories. In particular, the average wage gap between white men and Black men is 21%, and that between white women and Black women is 9%.

2.4 LOGS AND PERCENTAGES

This section motivates and clarifies the use of the logarithm in regression analysis by making two observations. First, when applied to numbers, the difference of logarithms approximately equals the percentage difference. Second, when applied to averages, the difference in logarithms approximately equals the percentage difference in the geometric mean. We now explore these ideas and the nature of the approximations involved.

Take two positive numbers a and b. The percentage difference between a and b is

$$p = 100\left(\frac{a-b}{b}\right).$$

Rewriting,

$$\frac{a}{b} = 1 + \frac{p}{100}.$$

Taking natural logarithms,

$$\log a - \log b = \log\left(1 + \frac{p}{100}\right). \tag{2.2}$$

A useful approximation for small x is

$$\log(1+x) \simeq x. \tag{2.3}$$

This can be derived from the infinite series expansion of $\log(1+x)$:

$$\log(1+x) = x - \frac{x^2}{2} + \frac{x^3}{3} - \frac{x^4}{4} + \cdots = x + O(x^2).$$

The symbol $O(x^2)$ means that the remainder is bounded by Ax^2 as $x \to 0$ for some $A < \infty$. Numerically, the approximation $\log(1+x) \simeq x$ is within 0.001 for $|x| \leq 0.1$, and the approximation error increases with $|x|$.

Applying (2.3) to (2.2) and multiplying by 100, we find

$$p \simeq 100 \left(\log a - \log b\right).$$

This shows that 100 multiplied by the difference in logarithms is approximately the percentage difference. Numerically, the approximation error is less than 0.1 percentage points for $|p| \leq 10$.

Now consider the difference in the expectation of log transformed random variables. Take two random variables $X_1, X_2 > 0$. Define their geometric means $\theta_1 = \exp\left(\mathbb{E}\left[\log X_1\right]\right)$ and $\theta_2 = \exp\left(\mathbb{E}\left[\log X_2\right]\right)$ and their percentage difference

$$p = 100\left(\frac{\theta_2 - \theta_1}{\theta_1}\right).$$

The difference in the expectation of the log transforms (multiplied by 100) is

$$100\left(\mathbb{E}\left[\log X_2\right] - \mathbb{E}\left[\log X_1\right]\right) = 100\left(\log\theta_2 - \log\theta_1\right) \simeq p$$

the percentage difference between θ_2 and θ_1. In words, the difference between the average of the log transformed variables is (approximately) the percentage difference in the geometric means.

The reason this latter observation is important is because many econometric equations take the semi-log form

$$\mathbb{E}\left[\log Y \mid group = 1\right] = \mu_1$$
$$\mathbb{E}\left[\log Y \mid group = 2\right] = \mu_2$$

and considerable attention is given to the difference $\mu_1 - \mu_2$. For example, in Section 2.3, we compared the average log wages for men and women and found that the difference is 0.24. In that section, we stated that this difference is often interpreted as the average percentage difference. This is not quite right, but is not quite wrong, either. What the above calculation shows is that this difference is approximately the percentage difference in the geometric mean. So $\mu_1 - \mu_2$ is an average percentage difference, where "average" refers to the geometric rather than arithmetic mean.

To compare different measures of percentage difference, see Table 2.2. The first two columns report average wages for men and women in the CPS population using four "averages": arithmetic mean, median, geometric mean, and mean log. For both groups the arithmetic mean is higher than the median and geometric mean, and the latter two are similar to one another. This is a common feature of skewed distributions, such as the wage distribution. The third column reports the percentage difference between the first two columns (using men's wages as the base). For example, the first entry of 34% states that the mean wage for men is 34% higher than the mean wage for women. The next entries show that the median and geometric mean for men is 26% higher than those for women. The final entry in this column is 100 times the simple difference

Table 2.2
Average wages and percentage differences

	Men	Women	% Difference
Arithmetic mean	\$26.80	\$20.00	34%
Median	\$21.14	\$16.83	26%
Geometric mean	\$21.03	\$16.64	26%
Mean log wage	3.05	2.81	24%

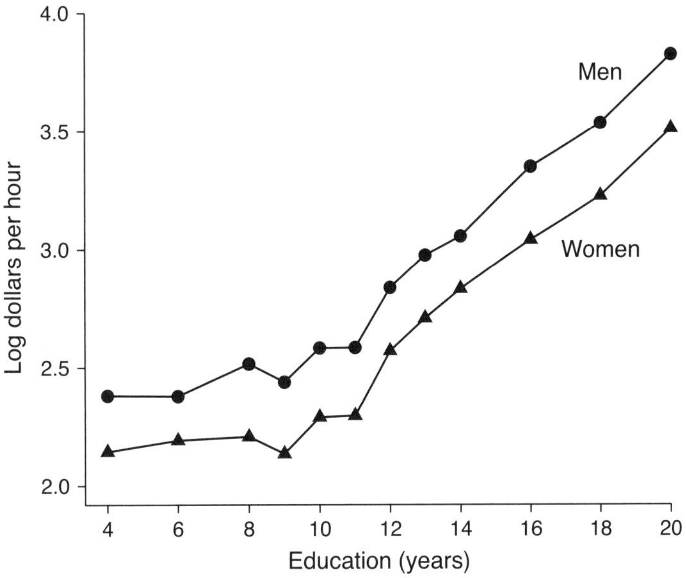

FIGURE 2.3 Expected log wage as a function of education

between the mean log wage, which is 24%. As shown above, the difference in the mean of the log transformation is approximately the percentage difference in the geometric mean, and this approximation is excellent for differences under 10%.

Let's summarize this analysis. It is common to take logarithms of variables and make comparisons between conditional means. We have shown that these differences are measures of the percentage difference in the geometric mean. Thus, the common description that the difference between expected log transforms (such as the 0.24 difference between those for men and women's wages) is an approximate percentage difference (e.g., a 24% difference in men's wages relative to women's) is correct, so long as we realize that we are implicitly comparing geometric means.

2.5 CONDITIONAL EXPECTATION FUNCTION

An important determinant of wages is education. In many empirical studies economists measure educational attainment by the number of years[7] of schooling. We will write this variable as *education*.

The conditional expectation of log(*wage*) given *gender*, *race*, and *education* is a single number for each category. For example,

$$\mathbb{E}\left[\log(wage) \mid gender = man,\ race = white,\ education = 12\right] = 2.84.$$

Figure 2.3 shows the conditional expectation of log(*wage*) as a function of *education*, separately for (white) men and women. The plot is quite revealing. We see that the conditional expectation is increasing in years of education, but at a different rate for schooling levels above and below 9 years. Another striking feature of

[7]Here, *education* is defined as years of schooling beyond kindergarten. A high school graduate has *education* = 12, a college graduate has *education* = 16, a Master's degree has *education* = 18, and a professional degree (medical, law, or Ph.D.) has *education* = 20.

Figure 2.3 is that the gap between men and women is roughly constant for all education levels. As the variables are measured in logs, this implies a constant average percentage gap between men and women regardless of educational attainment.

In many cases it is convenient to simplify the notation by writing variables using single characters, typically Y, X, and/or Z. It is conventional in econometrics to denote the dependent variable (e.g. $\log(wage)$) by the letter Y, a conditioning variable (such as *gender*) by the letter X, and multiple conditioning variables (such as *race*, *education*, and *gender*) by the subscripted letters $X_1, X_2, \ldots, X_k$.

Conditional expectations can be written with the generic notation

$$\mathbb{E}\left[Y \mid X_1 = x_1, X_2 = x_2, \ldots, X_k = x_k\right] = m(x_1, x_2, \ldots, x_k).$$

We call this the **conditional expectation function** (CEF). The CEF is a function of $(x_1, x_2, \ldots, x_k)$ as it varies with the variables. For example, the conditional expectation of $Y = \log(wage)$ given $(X_1, X_2) = (gender, race)$ is given by the six entries in Table 2.1.

For greater compactness, we typically write the conditioning variables as a vector in $\mathbb{R}^k$:

$$X = \begin{pmatrix} X_1 \\ X_2 \\ \vdots \\ X_k \end{pmatrix}. \tag{2.4}$$

Given this notation, the CEF can be compactly written as

$$\mathbb{E}\left[Y \mid X = x\right] = m\left(x\right).$$

The CEF $m(x) = \mathbb{E}\left[Y \mid X = x\right]$ is a function of $x \in \mathbb{R}^k$. It says: "When X takes the value x, then the average value of Y is $m(x)$." Sometimes it is useful to view the CEF as a function of the random variable X. In this case, we evaluate the function $m(x)$ at X, and write $m(X)$ or $\mathbb{E}\left[Y \mid X\right]$. This is random, as it is a function of the random variable X.

2.6 CONTINUOUS VARIABLES

In the previous sections, we implicitly assumed that the conditioning variables are discrete. However, many conditioning variables are continuous. In this section, we take up this case and assume that the variables (Y, X) are continuously distributed with a joint density function $f(y, x)$.

As an example, take $Y = \log(wage)$ and $X = experience$, the latter being the number of years of potential labor market experience.[8] The contours of their joint density are plotted in Figure 2.4(a) for the population of white men with 12 years of education.

Given the joint density $f(y, x)$, the variable x has the marginal density

$$f_X(x) = \int_{-\infty}^{\infty} f(y, x)dy.$$

For any x such that $f_X(x) > 0$, the conditional density of Y given X is defined as

$$f_{Y|X}\left(y \mid x\right) = \frac{f(y, x)}{f_X(x)}. \tag{2.5}$$

[8] As there is no direct measure for experience, we instead define *experience* as *age* − *education* − 6.

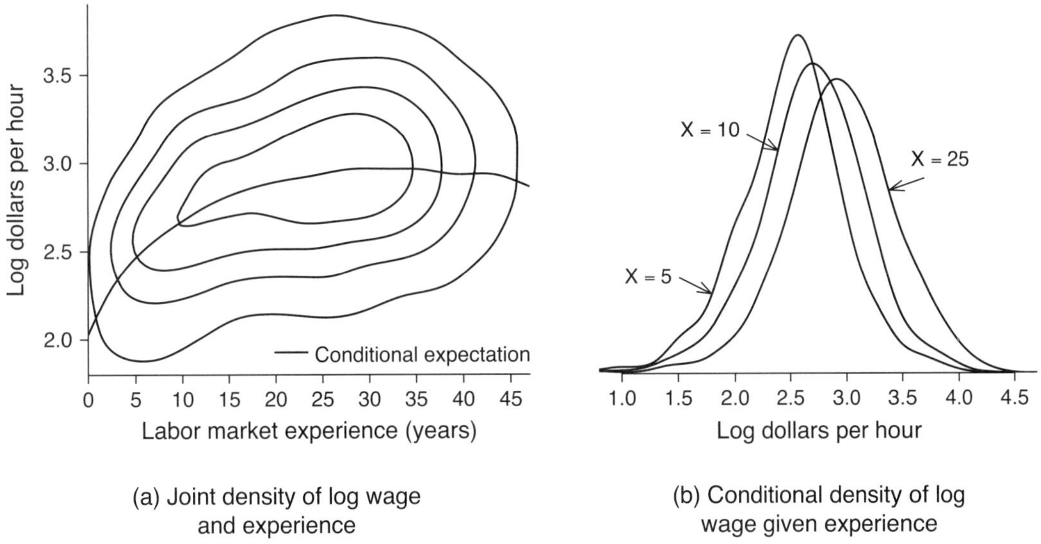

FIGURE 2.4 Log wage and experience

The conditional density is a renormalized slice of the joint density $f(y, x)$ holding x fixed. The slice is renormalized (divided by $f_X(x)$ so that it integrates to 1) and is thus a density. We can visualize this by slicing the joint density function at a specific value of x parallel to the y-axis. For example, take the density contours in Figure 2.4(a) and slice through the contour plot at a specific value of *experience*, and then renormalize the slice so that it is a proper density. This gives us the conditional density of log(*wage*) for white men with 12 years of education and this level of experience. We do this for three levels of *experience* (5, 10, and 25 years) and plot these densities in Figure 2.4(b). We can see that the distribution of wages shifts to the right and becomes more diffuse as experience increases.

The CEF of Y given $X = x$ is the expectation of the conditional density (2.5)

$$m(x) = \mathbb{E}[Y \mid X = x] = \int_{-\infty}^{\infty} y f_{Y|X}(y \mid x)\, dy. \tag{2.6}$$

Intuitively, $m(x)$ is the expectation of Y for the idealized subpopulation where the conditioning variables are fixed at x. When X is continuously distributed, this subpopulation is infinitely small.

This definition (2.6) is appropriate when the conditional density (2.5) is well defined. However, Theorem 2.13 in Section 2.31 will show that $m(x)$ can be defined for any random variables (Y, X) so long as $\mathbb{E}|Y| < \infty$.

In Figure 2.4(a) the CEF of log(*wage*) given *experience* is plotted as the solid line. We can see that the CEF is a smooth but nonlinear function. The CEF is initially increasing in *experience*, flattens out around *experience* $= 30$, and then decreases for high levels of *experience*.

2.7 LAW OF ITERATED EXPECTATIONS

An extremely useful tool from probability theory is the **law of iterated expectations**. An important special case is known as the simple law.

Theorem 2.1 Simple Law of Iterated Expectations
If $\mathbb{E}|Y| < \infty$, then for any random vector X,

$$\mathbb{E}[\mathbb{E}[Y \mid X]] = \mathbb{E}[Y].$$

This theorem states that the expectation of the conditional expectation is the unconditional expectation. In other words, the average of the conditional averages is the unconditional average. For discrete X,

$$\mathbb{E}[\mathbb{E}[Y \mid X]] = \sum_{j=1}^{\infty} \mathbb{E}\left[Y \mid X = x_j\right] \mathbb{P}\left[X = x_j\right].$$

For continuous X,

$$\mathbb{E}[\mathbb{E}[Y \mid X]] = \int_{\mathbb{R}^k} \mathbb{E}[Y \mid X = x] f_X(x) dx.$$

Going back to our investigation of average log wages for men and women, the simple law states that

$$\begin{aligned} &\mathbb{E}\left[\log(wage) \mid gender = man\right] \mathbb{P}\left[gender = man\right] \\ &\quad + \mathbb{E}\left[\log(wage) \mid gender = woman\right] \mathbb{P}\left[gender = woman\right] \\ &= \mathbb{E}\left[\log(wage)\right]. \end{aligned}$$

Or numerically,

$$3.05 \times 0.57 + 2.81 \times 0.43 = 2.95.$$

The general law of iterated expectations allows two sets of conditioning variables.

Theorem 2.2 Law of Iterated Expectations
If $\mathbb{E}|Y| < \infty$, then for any random vectors X_1 and X_2,

$$\mathbb{E}[\mathbb{E}[Y \mid X_1, X_2] \mid X_1] = \mathbb{E}[Y \mid X_1].$$

Notice the way that the law is applied. The inner expectation conditions on X_1 and X_2, while the outer expectation conditions only on X_1. The iterated expectation yields the simple answer $\mathbb{E}[Y \mid X_1]$, the expectation conditional on X_1 alone. Sometimes we phrase this as: "The smaller information set wins."

As an example

$$\begin{aligned} &\mathbb{E}\left[\log(wage) \mid gender = man,\ race = white\right] \mathbb{P}\left[race = white \mid gender = man\right] \\ &\quad + \mathbb{E}\left[\log(wage) \mid gender = man,\ race = Black\right] \mathbb{P}\left[race = Black \mid gender = man\right] \\ &\quad + \mathbb{E}\left[\log(wage) \mid gender = man,\ race = other\right] \mathbb{P}\left[race = other \mid gender = man\right] \\ &= \mathbb{E}\left[\log(wage) \mid gender = man\right] \end{aligned}$$

or numerically,

$$3.07 \times 0.84 + 2.86 \times 0.08 + 3.03 \times 0.08 = 3.05.$$

A property of conditional expectations is that when you condition on a random vector X, you can effectively treat it as if it were constant. For example, $\mathbb{E}[X \mid X] = X$ and $\mathbb{E}\left[g(X) \mid X\right] = g(X)$ for any function $g(\cdot)$. The general property is known as the conditioning theorem.

Theorem 2.3 Conditioning Theorem
If $\mathbb{E}|Y| < \infty$, then

$$\mathbb{E}\left[g(X)\, Y \mid X\right] = g(X)\, \mathbb{E}[Y \mid X]. \tag{2.7}$$

If in addition, $\mathbb{E}\left|g(X)\right| < \infty$, then

$$\mathbb{E}\left[g(X)\, Y\right] = \mathbb{E}\left[g(X)\, \mathbb{E}[Y \mid X]\right]. \tag{2.8}$$

The proofs of Theorems 2.1, 2.2, and 2.3 are given in Section 2.33.

2.8 CEF ERROR

The CEF error e is defined as the difference between Y and the CEF evaluated at X:

$$e = Y - m(X).$$

By construction, this yields the formula

$$Y = m(X) + e. \tag{2.9}$$

In (2.9) it is useful to understand that the error e is derived from the joint distribution of (Y, X), and so its properties are derived from this construction.

Many authors in econometrics denote the CEF error using the Greek letter ε. I do not follow this convention, because the error e is a random variable similar to Y and X, and it is customary to use Latin characters for random variables.

A key property of the CEF error is that it has a conditional expectation of 0. To see this, by the linearity of expectations, the definition $m(X) = \mathbb{E}[Y \mid X]$, and the conditioning theorem (Theorem 2.3),

$$\begin{aligned}
\mathbb{E}[e \mid X] &= \mathbb{E}[(Y - m(X)) \mid X] \\
&= \mathbb{E}[Y \mid X] - \mathbb{E}[m(X) \mid X] \\
&= m(X) - m(X) = 0.
\end{aligned}$$

This fact can be combined with the law of iterated expectations to show that the unconditional expectation is also 0.

$$\mathbb{E}[e] = \mathbb{E}[\mathbb{E}[e \mid X]] = \mathbb{E}[0] = 0.$$

We state this and some other results formally.

Theorem 2.4 Properties of the CEF error
If $\mathbb{E}|Y| < \infty$, then

1. $\mathbb{E}[e \mid X] = 0$.
2. $\mathbb{E}[e] = 0$.

3. If $\mathbb{E}|Y|^r < \infty$ for $r \geq 1$, then $\mathbb{E}|e|^r < \infty$.
4. For any function $h(x)$ such that $\mathbb{E}|h(X)e| < \infty$, then $\mathbb{E}[h(X)e] = 0$.

The proof of the third result is deferred to Section 2.33. The fourth result, whose proof is left to Exercise 2.3, implies that e is uncorrelated with any function of the regressors.

The equations

$$Y = m(X) + e$$

$$\mathbb{E}[e \mid X] = 0$$

together imply that $m(X)$ is the CEF of Y given X. It is important to understand that this is not a restriction. These equations hold true by definition.

The condition $\mathbb{E}[e \mid X] = 0$ is implied by the definition of e as the difference between Y and the CEF $m(X)$. The equation $\mathbb{E}[e \mid X] = 0$ is sometimes called a "conditional mean restriction," because the conditional mean of the error e is restricted to equal 0. The property is also sometimes called **mean independence**, for the conditional mean of e is 0 and thus is independent of X. However, it does not imply that the distribution of e is independent of X. Sometimes the assumption "e is independent of X" is added as a convenient simplification, but it is not generic feature of the conditional mean. Typically and generally, e and X are jointly dependent, even though the conditional mean of e is 0.

As an example, the contours of the joint density of the regression error e and *experience* are plotted in Figure 2.5 for the same population as Figure 2.4. Notice that the shape of the conditional distribution varies with the level of *experience*.

As a simple example of a case where X and e are mean independent yet dependent, let $e = Xu$, where X and u are independent N(0, 1). Then conditional on X, the error e has the distribution $\mathrm{N}(0, X^2)$. Thus $\mathbb{E}[e \mid X] = 0$,

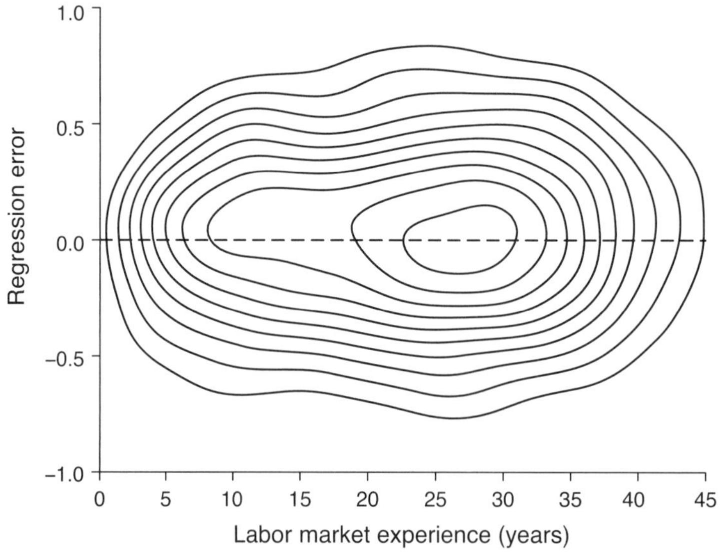

FIGURE 2.5 Joint density of regression error and experience

and e is mean independent of X, yet e is not fully independent of X. Mean independence does not imply full independence.

2.9 INTERCEPT-ONLY MODEL

A special case of the regression model is when there are no regressors X. In this case, $m(X) = \mathbb{E}[Y] = \mu$, the unconditional expectation of Y. We can still write an equation for Y in the regression format:

$$Y = \mu + e$$
$$\mathbb{E}[e] = 0.$$

This is useful, because it unifies the notation.

2.10 REGRESSION VARIANCE

An important measure of the dispersion about the CEF function is the unconditional variance of the CEF error e. We write this as

$$\sigma^2 = \operatorname{var}[e] = \mathbb{E}\left[(e - \mathbb{E}[e])^2\right] = \mathbb{E}\left[e^2\right].$$

Theorem 2.4.3 implies the following simple but useful result.

Theorem 2.5 If $\mathbb{E}\left[Y^2\right] < \infty$, then $\sigma^2 < \infty$.

We can call σ^2 the **regression variance** or the variance of the regression error. The magnitude of σ^2 measures the amount of variation in Y which is not "explained" or accounted for in the conditional expectation $\mathbb{E}[Y \mid X]$.

The regression variance depends on the regressors X. Consider two regressions

$$Y = \mathbb{E}[Y \mid X_1] + e_1$$
$$Y = \mathbb{E}[Y \mid X_1, X_2] + e_2.$$

We write the two errors distinctly as e_1 and e_2, as they are different—changing the conditioning information changes the conditional expectation and therefore the regression error as well.

In our discussion of iterated expectations we have seen that by increasing the conditioning set, the conditional expectation reveals greater detail about the distribution of Y. What is the implication for the regression error?

It turns out that there is a simple relationship. We can think of the conditional expectation $\mathbb{E}[Y \mid X]$ as the "explained portion" of Y. The remainder $e = Y - \mathbb{E}[Y \mid X]$ is the "unexplained portion." The simple relationship we now derive shows that the variance of this unexplained portion decreases when we condition on more variables. This relationship is monotonic in the sense that increasing the amount of information always decreases the variance of the unexplained portion.

Theorem 2.6 If $\mathbb{E}\left[Y^2\right] < \infty$, then

$$\operatorname{var}[Y] \geq \operatorname{var}[Y - \mathbb{E}[Y \mid X_1]] \geq \operatorname{var}[Y - \mathbb{E}[Y \mid X_1, X_2]].$$

Theorem 2.6 says that the variance of the difference between Y and its conditional expectation (weakly) decreases whenever an additional variable is added to the conditioning information. The proof of Theorem 2.6 is given in Section 2.33.

2.11 BEST PREDICTOR

Suppose that given a random vector X, we want to predict or forecast Y. We can write any predictor as a function $g(X)$ of X. The (ex post) prediction error is the realized difference $Y - g(X)$. A nonstochastic measure of the magnitude of the prediction error is the expectation of its square:

$$\mathbb{E}\left[(Y - g(X))^2\right]. \tag{2.10}$$

We can define the best predictor as the function $g(X)$ which minimizes (2.10). What function is the best predictor? It turns out that the answer is the CEF $m(X)$. This holds regardless of the joint distribution of (Y, X).

To see this, note that the mean-squared error of a predictor $g(X)$ is

$$\begin{aligned}
\mathbb{E}\left[(Y - g(X))^2\right] &= \mathbb{E}\left[(e + m(X) - g(X))^2\right] \\
&= \mathbb{E}\left[e^2\right] + 2\mathbb{E}\left[e\left(m(X) - g(X)\right)\right] + \mathbb{E}\left[\left(m(X) - g(X)\right)^2\right] \\
&= \mathbb{E}\left[e^2\right] + \mathbb{E}\left[\left(m(X) - g(X)\right)^2\right] \\
&\geq \mathbb{E}\left[e^2\right] \\
&= \mathbb{E}\left[(Y - m(X))^2\right].
\end{aligned}$$

The first equality makes the substitution $Y = m(X) + e$, and the third equality uses Theorem 2.4.4. The right-hand side after the third equality is minimized by setting $g(X) = m(X)$, yielding the inequality in the fourth line. The minimum is finite under the assumption $\mathbb{E}\left[Y^2\right] < \infty$, as shown by Theorem 2.5.

We state this formally in the following result.

Theorem 2.7 Conditional Expectation as Best Predictor
If $\mathbb{E}\left[Y^2\right] < \infty$, then for any predictor $g(X)$,

$$\mathbb{E}\left[(Y - g(X))^2\right] \geq \mathbb{E}\left[(Y - m(X))^2\right]$$

where $m(X) = \mathbb{E}[Y \mid X]$.

It may be helpful to consider this result in the context of the intercept-only model:

$$Y = \mu + e$$
$$\mathbb{E}[e] = 0.$$

Theorem 2.7 shows that the best predictor for Y (in the class of constants) is the unconditional mean $\mu = \mathbb{E}[Y]$, in the sense that the mean minimizes the mean-squared prediction error.

2.12 CONDITIONAL VARIANCE

While the conditional mean is a good measure of the location of a conditional distribution, it does not provide information about the spread of the distribution. A common measure of the dispersion is the **conditional variance**. We first give the general definition of the conditional variance of a random variable Y.

Definition 2.1 If $\mathbb{E}\left[Y^2\right] < \infty$, the **conditional variance** of Y given $X = x$ is

$$\sigma^2(x) = \text{var}[Y \mid X = x] = \mathbb{E}\left[(Y - \mathbb{E}[Y \mid X = x])^2 \mid X = x\right].$$

The conditional variance treated as a random variable is $\text{var}[Y \mid X] = \sigma^2(X)$.

The conditional variance is distinct from the **unconditional** variance $\text{var}[Y]$. The difference is that the conditional variance is a function of the conditioning variables. Notice that the conditional variance is the conditional second moment, centered around the conditional first moment.

Given this definition, we define the conditional variance of the regression error.

Definition 2.2 If $\mathbb{E}\left[e^2\right] < \infty$, the **conditional variance** of the regression error e given $X = x$ is

$$\sigma^2(x) = \text{var}[e \mid X = x] = \mathbb{E}\left[e^2 \mid X = x\right].$$

The conditional variance of e treated as a random variable is $\text{var}[e \mid X] = \sigma^2(X)$.

Again, the conditional variance $\sigma^2(x)$ is distinct from the unconditional variance σ^2. The conditional variance is a function of the regressors; the unconditional variance is not. Generally, $\sigma^2(x)$ is a nontrivial function of x and can take any form subject to the restriction that it is nonnegative. One way to think about $\sigma^2(x)$ is that it is the conditional mean of e^2 given X. Notice as well that $\sigma^2(x) = \text{var}[Y \mid X = x]$, so it is equivalently the conditional variance of the dependent variable.

The variance of Y is in a different unit of measurement than Y. To convert the variance to the same unit of measure, define the **conditional standard deviation** as its square root: $\sigma(x) = \sqrt{\sigma^2(x)}$.

As an example of how the conditional variance depends on observables, compare the conditional log wage densities for men and women displayed in Figure 2.2. The difference between the densities is not purely a location shift but is also a difference in spread. Specifically, we can see that the density for men's log wages is somewhat more spread out than that for women, while the density for women's wages is somewhat more peaked. Indeed, the conditional standard deviation for men's wages is 3.05 and that for women is 2.81. So while men have higher average wages, they are also somewhat more dispersed.

The unconditional variance is related to the conditional variance by the following identity.

Theorem 2.8 If $\mathbb{E}\left[Y^2\right] < \infty$, then

$$\operatorname{var}[Y] = \mathbb{E}[\operatorname{var}[Y \mid X]] + \operatorname{var}[\mathbb{E}[Y \mid X]].$$

See Theorem 4.14 in *Probability and Statistics for Economists*. Theorem 2.8 decomposes the unconditional variance into what are sometimes called the "within group variance" and the "across group variance." For example, if X is education level, then the first term is the expected variance of the conditional expectation by education level. The second term is the variance after controlling for education.

The regression error has a conditional mean of 0, so its unconditional error variance equals the expected conditional variance, or equivalently, it can be found by the law of iterated expectations:

$$\sigma^2 = \mathbb{E}\left[e^2\right] = \mathbb{E}\left[\mathbb{E}\left[e^2 \mid X\right]\right] = \mathbb{E}\left[\sigma^2(X)\right].$$

That is, the unconditional error variance is the average conditional variance.

Given the conditional variance, we can define a rescaled error:

$$u = \frac{e}{\sigma(X)}. \tag{2.11}$$

We calculate that since $\sigma(X)$ is a function of X,

$$\mathbb{E}[u \mid X] = \mathbb{E}\left[\frac{e}{\sigma(X)} \,\middle|\, X\right] = \frac{1}{\sigma(X)}\mathbb{E}[e \mid X] = 0$$

and

$$\operatorname{var}[u \mid X] = \mathbb{E}\left[u^2 \mid X\right] = \mathbb{E}\left[\frac{e^2}{\sigma^2(X)} \,\middle|\, X\right] = \frac{1}{\sigma^2(X)}\mathbb{E}\left[e^2 \mid X\right] = \frac{\sigma^2(X)}{\sigma^2(X)} = 1.$$

Thus u has a conditional expectation of 0 and a conditional variance of 1.

Notice that (2.11) can be rewritten as

$$e = \sigma(X)u.$$

and substituting this for e in the CEF equation (2.9), we find that

$$Y = m(X) + \sigma(X)u.$$

This is an alternative (mean-variance) representation of the CEF equation.

Many econometric studies focus on the conditional expectation $m(x)$ and either ignore the conditional variance $\sigma^2(x)$, treat it as a constant $\sigma^2(x) = \sigma^2$, or treat it as a nuisance parameter (a parameter not of primary interest). This approach is appropriate when the primary variation in the conditional distribution is in the mean, but it can be short-sighted in other cases. Dispersion is relevant to many economic topics, including income and wealth distribution, economic inequality, and price dispersion. Conditional dispersion (variance) can be a fruitful subject for investigation.

The perverse consequences of a narrow-minded focus on the mean is parodied in a classic joke:

> An economist was standing with one foot in a bucket of boiling water and the other foot in a bucket of ice. When asked how he felt, he replied, "On average I feel just fine."

Clearly, the economist in question ignored variance!

2.13 HOMOSKEDASTICITY AND HETEROSKEDASTICITY

An important special case obtains when the conditional variance $\sigma^2(x)$ is a constant and independent of x. This is called **homoskedasticity**.

> **Definition 2.3** The error is **homoskedastic** if $\sigma^2(x) = \sigma^2$ does not depend on x.

In the general case where $\sigma^2(x)$ depends on x, we say that the error e is **heteroskedastic**.

> **Definition 2.4** The error is **heteroskedastic** if $\sigma^2(x)$ depends on x.

It is helpful to understand that the concepts homoskedasticity and heteroskedasticity concern the conditional variance, not the unconditional variance. By definition, the unconditional variance σ^2 is a constant and is independent of the regressors X. So when we talk about the variance as a function of the regressors, we are talking about the conditional variance $\sigma^2(x)$.

Some older or introductory textbooks describe heteroskedasticity as the case where "the variance of e varies across observations." This is a poor and confusing definition. It is more constructive to understand that heteroskedasticity means that the conditional variance $\sigma^2(x)$ depends on observables.

Older textbooks also tend to describe homoskedasticity as a component of a correct regression specification and describe heteroskedasticity as an exception or deviance. This description has influenced many generations of economists, but it is unfortunately backwards. The correct view is that heteroskedasticity is generic and "standard," while homoskedasticity is unusual and exceptional. The default in empirical work should be to assume that the errors are heteroskedastic, not homoskedastic.

In apparent contradiction to the above statement, we will still frequently impose the homoskedasticity assumption when making theoretical investigations into the properties of estimation and inference methods. The reason is that in many cases, homoskedasticity greatly simplifies the theoretical calculations, and it is therefore quite advantageous for teaching and learning. It should always be remembered, however, that homoskedasticity is never imposed because it is believed to be a correct feature of an empirical model but rather because of its simplicity.

> **Heteroskedastic or Heteroscedastic?**
>
> The spelling of the words *homoskedastic* and *heteroskedastic* have been somewhat controversial. Early econometrics textbooks were split, with some using a "c" as in *heteroscedastic* and some "k" as in

heteroskedastic. McCulloch (1985) pointed out that the word is derived from Greek roots. $o\mu o\iota o\varsigma$ means "same." $\varepsilon\tau\varepsilon\rho o$ means "other" or "different." $\sigma\kappa\varepsilon\delta\alpha\nu\nu\upsilon\mu\iota$ means "to scatter." Since the proper transliteration of the Greek letter κ in $\sigma\kappa\varepsilon\delta\alpha\nu\nu\upsilon\mu\iota$ is "k," the correct English spelling of the two words is with a "k": *homoskedastic* and *heteroskedastic*.

2.14 REGRESSION DERIVATIVE

One way to interpret the CEF $m(x) = \mathbb{E}[Y \mid X = x]$ is in terms of how marginal changes in the regressors X imply changes in the conditional expectation of the response variable Y. It is typical to consider marginal changes in a single regressor, say, X_1, holding the remainder fixed. When a regressor X_1 is continuously distributed, we define the marginal effect of a change in X_1, holding the variables $X_2, \ldots, X_k$ fixed, as the partial derivative of the CEF:

$$\frac{\partial}{\partial x_1} m(x_1, \ldots, x_k).$$

When X_1 is discrete, we define the marginal effect as a discrete difference. For example, if X_1 is binary, then the marginal effect of X_1 on the CEF is

$$m(1, x_2, \ldots, x_k) - m(0, x_2, \ldots, x_k).$$

We can unify the continuous and discrete cases with the following notation:

$$\nabla_1 m(x) = \begin{cases} \dfrac{\partial}{\partial x_1} m(x_1, \ldots, x_k), & \text{if } X_1 \text{ is continuous} \\ m(1, x_2, \ldots, x_k) - m(0, x_2, \ldots, x_k), & \text{if } X_1 \text{ is binary.} \end{cases}$$

Collecting the k effects into one $k \times 1$ vector, we define the **regression derivative** with respect to X:

$$\nabla m(x) = \begin{bmatrix} \nabla_1 m(x) \\ \nabla_2 m(x) \\ \vdots \\ \nabla_k m(x) \end{bmatrix}.$$

When all elements of X are continuous, then we have the simplification $\nabla m(x) = \frac{\partial}{\partial x} m(x)$, the vector of partial derivatives.

There are two important points to remember concerning our definition of the regression derivative. First, the effect of each variable is calculated holding the other variables constant. This is the **ceteris paribus** concept commonly used in economics. But in the case of a regression derivative, the conditional expectation does not literally hold *all else* constant. It only holds constant the variables included in the conditional expectation. Thus the regression derivative depends on which regressors are included. For example, in a regression of wages on education, experience, race, and gender, the regression derivative with respect to education shows the marginal effect of education on expected wages, holding constant experience, race, and gender. But it does not hold constant an individual's unobservable characteristics (such as ability), nor variables not included in the regression (such as the quality of education).

Second, the regression derivative is the change in the conditional expectation of Y, not the change in the actual value of Y for an individual. It is tempting to think of the regression derivative as the change in the actual value of Y, but this interpretation is not correct. The regression derivative $\nabla m(x)$ is the change in the actual value of Y only if the error e is unaffected by the change in the regressor X. We return to a discussion of causal effects in Section 2.30.

2.15 LINEAR CEF

An important special case is when the CEF $m(x) = \mathbb{E}[Y \mid X = x]$ is linear in x. In this case, we can write the mean equation as

$$m(x) = x_1\beta_1 + x_2\beta_2 + \cdots + x_k\beta_k + \beta_{k+1}.$$

Notationally it is convenient to write this as a simple function of the vector x. An easy way to do so is to augment the regressor vector X by listing the number "1" as an element. We call this the "constant," and the corresponding coefficient is called the "intercept." Equivalently, specify that the final element[9] of the vector x is $x_k = 1$. Thus (2.4) has been redefined as the $k \times 1$ vector

$$X = \begin{pmatrix} X_1 \\ X_2 \\ \vdots \\ X_{k-1} \\ 1 \end{pmatrix}. \tag{2.12}$$

With this redefinition, the CEF is

$$m(x) = x_1\beta_1 + x_2\beta_2 + \cdots + \beta_k = x'\beta \tag{2.13}$$

where

$$\beta = \begin{pmatrix} \beta_1 \\ \vdots \\ \beta_k \end{pmatrix}$$

is a $k \times 1$ coefficient vector. This is the **linear CEF model**. It is also often called the **linear regression model**, or the regression of Y on X.

In the linear CEF model, the regression derivative is simply the coefficient vector. That is, $\nabla m(x) = \beta$. This is one of the appealing features of the linear CEF model. The coefficients have simple and natural interpretations as the marginal effects of changing one variable, holding the others constant.

Linear CEF Model

$$Y = X'\beta + e$$

$$\mathbb{E}[e \mid X] = 0.$$

[9] The order doesn't matter. It could be any element.

If in addition the error is homoskedastic, we call this the **homoskedastic linear CEF model**.

Homoskedastic Linear CEF Model

$$Y = X'\beta + e$$
$$\mathbb{E}[e \mid X] = 0$$
$$\mathbb{E}\left[e^2 \mid X\right] = \sigma^2.$$

2.16 LINEAR CEF WITH NONLINEAR EFFECTS

The linear CEF model of Section 2.15 is less restrictive than it might appear, as we can include as regressors nonlinear transformations of the original variables. In this sense, the linear CEF framework is flexible and can capture many nonlinear effects.

For example, suppose we have two scalar variables X_1 and X_2. The CEF could take the quadratic form

$$m(x_1, x_2) = x_1\beta_1 + x_2\beta_2 + x_1^2\beta_3 + x_2^2\beta_4 + x_1x_2\beta_5 + \beta_6. \tag{2.14}$$

This equation is quadratic in the regressors (x_1, x_2) yet linear in the coefficients $\beta = (\beta_1, \ldots, \beta_6)'$. We still call (2.14) a linear CEF, because it is a linear function of the coefficients. At the same time, it has nonlinear effects, because it is nonlinear in the underlying variables x_1 and x_2. The key is to understand that (2.14) is quadratic in the variables (x_1, x_2) yet linear in the coefficients β.

To simplify the expression, we define the transformations $x_3 = x_1^2$, $x_4 = x_2^2$, $x_5 = x_1x_2$, and $x_6 = 1$, and redefine the regressor vector as $x = (x_1, \ldots, x_6)'$. With this redefinition, $m(x_1, x_2) = x'\beta$, which is linear in β. For most econometric purposes (estimation and inference on β), the linearity in β is all that is important.

An exception is in the analysis of regression derivatives. In nonlinear equations such as (2.14), the regression derivative should be defined with respect to the original variables, not with respect to the transformed variables. Thus

$$\frac{\partial}{\partial x_1} m(x_1, x_2) = \beta_1 + 2x_1\beta_3 + x_2\beta_5$$

$$\frac{\partial}{\partial x_2} m(x_1, x_2) = \beta_2 + 2x_2\beta_4 + x_1\beta_5.$$

We see that in the model (2.14), the regression derivatives are not simple coefficients, but are functions of several coefficients plus the levels of (x_1, x_2). Consequently, it is difficult to interpret the coefficients individually. It is more useful to interpret them as a group.

We typically call β_5 the **interaction effect**. Notice that it appears in both regression derivative equations and has a symmetric interpretation in each. If $\beta_5 > 0$, then the regression derivative with respect to x_1 is increasing in the level of x_2 (and the regression derivative with respect to x_2 is increasing in the level of x_1), while if $\beta_5 < 0$, the reverse is true.

2.17 LINEAR CEF WITH DUMMY VARIABLES

When all regressors take a finite set of values, it turns out that the CEF can be written as a linear function of regressors. This simplest example is a **binary** variable which takes only two distinct values. For example, in traditional datasets, the variable *gender* takes only the values *man* and *woman* (or male and female). Binary variables are extremely common in econometric applications and are alternatively called **dummy variables** or **indicator variables**.

Consider the simple case of a single binary regressor. In this case, the conditional expectation can only take two distinct values. For example,

$$\mathbb{E}\left[Y \mid gender\right] = \begin{cases} \mu_0, & \text{if} \quad gender = man \\ \mu_1, & \text{if} \quad gender = woman. \end{cases}$$

To facilitate a mathematical treatment, we record dummy variables with the values $\{0, 1\}$. For example,

$$X_1 = \begin{cases} 0, & \text{if} \quad gender = man \\ 1, & \text{if} \quad gender = woman. \end{cases} \tag{2.15}$$

Given this notation, we write the conditional expectation as a linear function of the dummy variable X_1. Thus $\mathbb{E}\left[Y \mid X_1\right] = \beta_1 X_1 + \beta_2$, where $\beta_1 = \mu_1 - \mu_0$ and $\beta_2 = \mu_0$. In this simple regression equation, the intercept β_2 is equal to the conditional expectation of Y for the $X_1 = 0$ subpopulation (men) and the slope β_1 is equal to the difference in the conditional expectations between the two subpopulations.

Alternatively, we could have defined X_1 as

$$X_1 = \begin{cases} 1, & \text{if} \quad gender = man \\ 0, & \text{if} \quad gender = woman. \end{cases} \tag{2.16}$$

In this case, the regression intercept is the expectation for women (rather than for men) and the regression slope has switched signs. The two regressions are equivalent but the interpretation of the coefficients has changed. Therefore it is always important to understand the precise definitions of the variables, and illuminating labels are helpful. For example, labeling X_1 as "gender" does not help distinguish between definitions (2.15) and (2.16). Instead, it is better to label X_1 as "women" or "female" if definition (2.15) is used, or as "men" or "male" if (2.16) is used.

Now suppose we have two dummy variables X_1 and X_2. For example, $X_2 = 1$ if the person is married, else $X_2 = 0$. The conditional expectation given X_1 and X_2 takes at most four possible values:

$$\mathbb{E}\left[Y \mid X_1, X_2\right] = \begin{cases} \mu_{00}, & \text{if} \quad X_1 = 0 \text{ and } X_2 = 0 \quad \text{(unmarried men)} \\ \mu_{01}, & \text{if} \quad X_1 = 0 \text{ and } X_2 = 1 \quad \text{(married men)} \\ \mu_{10}, & \text{if} \quad X_1 = 1 \text{ and } X_2 = 0 \quad \text{(unmarried women)} \\ \mu_{11}, & \text{if} \quad X_1 = 1 \text{ and } X_2 = 1 \quad \text{(married women).} \end{cases}$$

In this case, we can write the conditional mean as a linear function of X, X_2, and their product $X_1 X_2$:

$$\mathbb{E}\left[Y \mid X_1, X_2\right] = \beta_1 X_1 + \beta_2 X_2 + \beta_3 X_1 X_2 + \beta_4$$

where $\beta_1 = \mu_{10} - \mu_{00}$, $\beta_2 = \mu_{01} - \mu_{00}$, $\beta_3 = \mu_{11} - \mu_{10} - \mu_{01} + \mu_{00}$, and $\beta_4 = \mu_{00}$.

We can view the coefficient β_1 as the effect of gender on expected log wages for unmarried wage earners, the coefficient β_2 as the effect of marriage on expected log wages for men wage earners, and the coefficient β_3 as the difference between the effects of marriage on expected log wages among women and among men.

Alternatively, it can also be interpreted as the difference between the effects of gender on expected log wages among married and unmarried wage earners. Both interpretations are equally valid. We often describe β_3 as measuring the **interaction** between the two dummy variables, or the **interaction effect**, and describe $\beta_3 = 0$ as the case when the interaction effect is 0.

In this setting, we can see that the CEF is linear in the three variables (X_1, X_2, X_1X_2). To put the model in the framework of Section 2.15, we define the regressor $X_3 = X_1X_2$ and the regressor vector as

$$X = \begin{pmatrix} X_1 \\ X_2 \\ X_3 \\ 1 \end{pmatrix}.$$

So while we started with two dummy variables, the number of regressors (including the intercept) is four.

If there are three dummy variables X_1, X_2, X_3, then $\mathbb{E}[Y \mid X_1, X_2, X_3]$ takes at most $2^3 = 8$ distinct values and can be written as the linear function

$$\mathbb{E}[Y \mid X_1, X_2, X_3] = \beta_1 X_1 + \beta_2 X_2 + \beta_3 X_3 + \beta_4 X_1 X_2 + \beta_5 X_1 X_3 + \beta_6 X_2 X_3 + \beta_7 X_1 X_2 X_3 + \beta_8$$

which has eight regressors including the intercept.

In general, if there are p dummy variables $X_1, \ldots, X_p$, then the CEF $\mathbb{E}\left[Y \mid X_1, X_2, \ldots, X_p\right]$ takes at most 2^p distinct values and can be written as a linear function of the 2^p regressors including $X_1, X_2, \ldots, X_p$ and all cross-products. A linear regression model which includes all 2^p binary interactions is called a **saturated dummy variable regression model**. It is a complete model of the conditional expectation. In contrast, a model with no interactions equals

$$\mathbb{E}\left[Y \mid X_1, X_2, \ldots, X_p\right] = \beta_1 X_1 + \beta_2 X_2 + \cdots + \beta_p X_p + \beta_p.$$

This model has $p + 1$ coefficients instead of 2^p.

We started this section by saying that the conditional expectation is linear when all regressors take only a finite number of possible values. How can we see this? Take a **categorical** variable, such as *race*. For example, we earlier divided *race* into three categories. We can record categorical variables using numbers to indicate each category, for example

$$X_3 = \begin{cases} 1, & \text{if } \textit{white} \\ 2, & \text{if } \textit{Black} \\ 3, & \text{if } \textit{other.} \end{cases}$$

When doing so, the values of X_3 have no meaning in terms of magnitude, they simply indicate the relevant category.

When the regressor is categorical, the conditional expectation of Y given X_3 takes a distinct value for each possibility:

$$\mathbb{E}[Y \mid X_3] = \begin{cases} \mu_1, & \text{if } X_3 = 1 \\ \mu_2, & \text{if } X_3 = 2 \\ \mu_3, & \text{if } X_3 = 3. \end{cases}$$

This is not a linear function of X_3 itself, but it can be made a linear function by constructing dummy variables for two of the three categories. For example,

$$X_4 = \begin{cases} 1, & \text{if } \textit{Black} \\ 0, & \text{if } \textit{not Black} \end{cases}$$

$$X_5 = \begin{cases} 1, & \text{if} \quad \textit{other} \\ 0, & \text{if} \quad \textit{not other.} \end{cases}$$

In this case, the categorical variable X_3 is equivalent to the pair of dummy variables (X_4, X_5). The explicit relationship is

$$X_3 = \begin{cases} 1, & \text{if} \quad X_4 = 0 \text{ and } X_5 = 0 \\ 2, & \text{if} \quad X_4 = 1 \text{ and } X_5 = 0 \\ 3, & \text{if} \quad X_4 = 0 \text{ and } X_5 = 1. \end{cases}$$

Given these transformations, we can write the conditional expectation of Y as a linear function of X_4 and X_5:

$$\mathbb{E}[Y \mid X_3] = \mathbb{E}[Y \mid X_4, X_5] = \beta_1 X_4 + \beta_2 X_5 + \beta_3.$$

We can write the CEF as either $\mathbb{E}[Y \mid X_3]$ or $\mathbb{E}[Y \mid X_4, X_5]$ (they are equivalent), but it is only linear as a function of X_4 and X_5.

This setting is similar to the case of two dummy variables, the difference being that we have not included the interaction term X_4X_5. This is because the event $\{X_4 = 1 \text{ and } X_5 = 1\}$ is empty by construction, so $X_4X_5 = 0$ by definition.

2.18 BEST LINEAR PREDICTOR

While the conditional expectation $m(X) = \mathbb{E}[Y \mid X]$ is the best predictor of Y among all functions of X, its functional form is typically unknown. In particular, the linear CEF model is empirically unlikely to be accurate unless X is discrete and low-dimensional so all interactions are included. Consequently, in most cases, it is more realistic to view the linear specification (2.13) as an approximation. In this section, we derive a specific approximation with a simple interpretation.

Theorem 2.7 showed that the conditional expectation $m(X)$ is the best predictor in the sense that it has the lowest mean-squared error among all predictors. By extension, we can define an approximation to the CEF by the linear function with the lowest mean-squared error among all linear predictors.

For this derivation, we require the following regularity condition:

Assumption 2.1

1. $\mathbb{E}\left[Y^2\right] < \infty$.
2. $\mathbb{E}\,\|X\|^2 < \infty$.
3. $\boldsymbol{Q}_{XX} = \mathbb{E}\left[XX'\right]$ is positive definite.

In Assumption 2.1.2, we use $\|x\| = \left(x'x\right)^{1/2}$ to denote the Euclidean length of the vector x.

The first two parts of Assumption 2.1 imply that the variables Y and X have finite means, variances, and covariances. The third part of the assumption is more technical, and its role will become apparent shortly. It is equivalent to imposing the condition that the columns of the matrix $\boldsymbol{Q}_{XX} = \mathbb{E}\left[XX'\right]$ are linearly independent and that the matrix is invertible.

A linear predictor for Y is a function $X'\beta$ for some $\beta \in \mathbb{R}^k$. The mean-squared prediction error is

$$S(\beta) = \mathbb{E}\left[\left(Y - X'\beta\right)^2\right]. \tag{2.17}$$

The **best linear predictor** of Y given X, written $\mathscr{P}[Y \mid X]$, is found by selecting the β which minimizes $S(\beta)$.

Definition 2.5 The **best linear predictor** of Y given X is

$$\mathscr{P}[Y \mid X] = X'\beta$$

where β minimizes the mean-squared prediction error

$$S(\beta) = \mathbb{E}\left[\left(Y - X'\beta\right)^2\right].$$

The minimizer

$$\beta = \underset{b \in \mathbb{R}^k}{\operatorname{argmin}}\, S(b) \tag{2.18}$$

is called the **linear projection coefficient**.

We now calculate an explicit expression for its value. The mean-squared prediction error (2.17) can be written out as a quadratic function of β:

$$S(\beta) = \mathbb{E}\left[Y^2\right] - 2\beta'\mathbb{E}[XY] + \beta'\mathbb{E}\left[XX'\right]\beta. \tag{2.19}$$

The quadratic structure of $S(\beta)$ means that we can solve explicitly for the minimizer. The first-order condition for minimization (from Appendix A.20) is

$$0 = \frac{\partial}{\partial \beta} S(\beta) = -2\mathbb{E}[XY] + 2\mathbb{E}\left[XX'\right]\beta. \tag{2.20}$$

Rewriting (2.20) as

$$2\mathbb{E}[XY] = 2\mathbb{E}\left[XX'\right]\beta$$

and dividing by 2, this equation takes the form

$$\boldsymbol{Q}_{XY} = \boldsymbol{Q}_{XX}\beta \tag{2.21}$$

where $\boldsymbol{Q}_{XY} = \mathbb{E}[XY]$ is $k \times 1$, and $\boldsymbol{Q}_{XX} = \mathbb{E}\left[XX'\right]$ is $k \times k$. The solution is found by inverting the matrix $\boldsymbol{Q}_{XX}$ and is written

$$\beta = \boldsymbol{Q}_{XX}^{-1}\boldsymbol{Q}_{XY}$$

or

$$\beta = \left(\mathbb{E}\left[XX'\right]\right)^{-1}\mathbb{E}[XY]. \tag{2.22}$$

It is worth taking the time to understand the notation involved in the expression (2.22). $\boldsymbol{Q}_{XX}$ is a $k \times k$ matrix, and $\boldsymbol{Q}_{XY}$ is a $k \times 1$ column vector. Therefore, alternative expressions, such as $\frac{\mathbb{E}[XY]}{\mathbb{E}[XX']}$ or $\mathbb{E}[XY]\left(\mathbb{E}\left[XX'\right]\right)^{-1}$ are incoherent and incorrect. We also can now see the role of Assumption 2.1.3. It is equivalent to assuming that $\boldsymbol{Q}_{XX}$ has an inverse $\boldsymbol{Q}_{XX}^{-1}$, which is necessary for the solution to the normal equations (2.21) to be unique, and equivalently for (2.22) to be uniquely defined. In the absence of Assumption 2.1.3, there could be multiple solutions to (2.21).

We now have an explicit expression for the best linear predictor:

$$\mathscr{P}[Y \mid X] = X'\left(\mathbb{E}\left[XX'\right]\right)^{-1}\mathbb{E}[XY].$$

This expression is also referred to as the **linear projection** of Y on X.

The **projection error** is

$$e = Y - X'\beta. \tag{2.23}$$

This equals the error (2.9) from the regression equation when (and only when) the conditional expectation is linear in X; otherwise, they are distinct.

Rewriting, we obtain a decomposition of Y into linear predictor and error:

$$Y = X'\beta + e. \tag{2.24}$$

In general, we call equation (2.24) or $X'\beta$ the best linear predictor of Y given X, or the linear projection of Y on X. Equation (2.24) is also often called the **regression** of Y on X, but this can sometimes be confusing, as economists use the term "regression" in many contexts. (Recall that we said in Section 2.15 that the linear CEF model is also called the linear regression model.)

An important property of the projection error e is

$$\mathbb{E}[Xe] = 0. \tag{2.25}$$

To see this, using the definitions (2.23) and (2.22) and the matrix properties $\boldsymbol{A}\boldsymbol{A}^{-1} = \boldsymbol{I}$ and $\boldsymbol{I}\boldsymbol{a} = \boldsymbol{a}$,

$$\begin{aligned}
\mathbb{E}[Xe] &= \mathbb{E}\left[X\left(Y - X'\beta\right)\right] \\
&= \mathbb{E}[XY] - \mathbb{E}\left[XX'\right]\left(\mathbb{E}\left[XX'\right]\right)^{-1}\mathbb{E}[XY] \\
&= 0
\end{aligned} \tag{2.26}$$

as claimed.

Equation (2.25) is a set of k equations, one for each regressor. In other words, (2.25) is equivalent to

$$\mathbb{E}\left[X_j e\right] = 0 \tag{2.27}$$

for $j = 1, \ldots, k$. As in (2.12), the regressor vector X typically contains a constant (e.g., $X_k = 1$). In this case, (2.27) for $j = k$ is the same as

$$\mathbb{E}[e] = 0. \tag{2.28}$$

Thus the projection error has a mean of 0 when the regressor vector contains a constant. (When X does not have a constant, (2.28) is not guaranteed. As it is desirable for e to have a 0 mean, this is a good reason to always include a constant in any regression model.)

It is also useful to observe that because $\operatorname{cov}(X_j, e) = \mathbb{E}\left[X_j e\right] - \mathbb{E}\left[X_j\right]\mathbb{E}[e]$, then (2.27)–(2.28) together imply that the variables X_j and e are uncorrelated.

This completes the derivation of the model. Let us now summarize some of the most important properties.

Theorem 2.9 Properties of the Linear Projection Model
Under Assumption 2.1,

1. The moments $\mathbb{E}\left[XX'\right]$ and $\mathbb{E}[XY]$ exist with finite elements.
2. The linear projection coefficient (2.18) exists, is unique, and equals

$$\beta = \left(\mathbb{E}\left[XX'\right]\right)^{-1}\mathbb{E}[XY].$$

3. The best linear predictor of Y given X is

$$\mathscr{P}(Y \mid X) = X'\left(\mathbb{E}\left[XX'\right]\right)^{-1}\mathbb{E}[XY].$$

4. The projection error $e = Y - X'\beta$ exists. It satisfies $\mathbb{E}\left[e^2\right] < \infty$ and $\mathbb{E}[Xe] = 0$.
5. If X contains an constant, then $\mathbb{E}[e] = 0$.
6. If $\mathbb{E}|Y|^r < \infty$ and $\mathbb{E}\|X\|^r < \infty$ for $r \geq 2$, then $\mathbb{E}|e|^r < \infty$.

A complete proof of Theorem 2.9 is given in Section 2.33.

It is useful to reflect on the generality of Theorem 2.9. The only restriction is Assumption 2.1. Thus for any random variables (Y, X) with finite variances, we can define a linear equation (2.24) with the properties listed in Theorem 2.9. Stronger assumptions (such as the linear CEF model) are not necessary. In this sense, the linear model (2.24) exists quite generally. However, it is important not to misinterpret the generality of this statement. The linear equation (2.24) is defined as the best linear predictor. It is not necessarily a conditional mean, nor is it a parameter of a structural or causal economic model.

Linear Projection Model

$$Y = X'\beta + e$$

$$\mathbb{E}[Xe] = 0$$

$$\beta = \left(\mathbb{E}\left[XX'\right]\right)^{-1}\mathbb{E}[XY].$$

Invertibility and Identification

The linear projection coefficient $\beta = \left(\mathbb{E}\left[XX'\right]\right)^{-1}\mathbb{E}[XY]$ exists and is unique as long as the $k \times k$ matrix $\boldsymbol{Q}_{XX} = \mathbb{E}\left[XX'\right]$ is invertible. The matrix $\boldsymbol{Q}_{XX}$ is often called the **design matrix**, because in experimental settings, the researcher is able to control $\boldsymbol{Q}_{XX}$ by manipulating the distribution of the regressors X.

Observe that for any nonzero $\alpha \in \mathbb{R}^k$,

$$\alpha'\boldsymbol{Q}_{XX}\alpha = \mathbb{E}\left[\alpha'XX'\alpha\right] = \mathbb{E}\left[\left(\alpha'X\right)^2\right] \geq 0$$

so $\boldsymbol{Q}_{XX}$ by construction is positive semi-definite, conventionally written as $\boldsymbol{Q}_{XX} \geq 0$. The assumption that it is positive definite means that this is a strict inequality, $\mathbb{E}\left[\left(\alpha'X\right)^2\right] > 0$, conventionally written as $\boldsymbol{Q}_{XX} > 0$. This condition means that there is no nonzero vector α such that $\alpha'X = 0$ identically. Positive definite matrices are invertible. Thus when $\boldsymbol{Q}_{XX} > 0$, then $\beta = \left(\mathbb{E}\left[XX'\right]\right)^{-1}\mathbb{E}[XY]$ exists and is uniquely defined. In other words, if we can exclude the possibility that a linear function of X is degenerate, then β is uniquely defined.

Theorem 2.5 shows that the linear projection coefficient β is **identified** (uniquely determined) under Assumption 2.1. The key is invertibility of $\boldsymbol{Q}_{XX}$. Otherwise, there is no unique solution to the equation

$$\boldsymbol{Q}_{XX}\beta = \boldsymbol{Q}_{XY}. \tag{2.29}$$

When $\boldsymbol{Q}_{XX}$ is not invertible, there are multiple solutions to (2.29). In this case, the coefficient β is **not identified**, as it does not have a unique value.

Minimization

The mean-squared prediction error (2.19) is a function with vector argument of the form

$$f(x) = a - 2b'x + x'\boldsymbol{C}x$$

where $\boldsymbol{C} > 0$. For any function of this form, the unique minimizer is

$$x = \boldsymbol{C}^{-1}b. \tag{2.30}$$

To see that this is the unique minimizer, I present two proofs. The first uses matrix calculus. From Appendix A.20

$$\frac{\partial}{\partial x}\left(b'x\right) = b \tag{2.31}$$

$$\frac{\partial}{\partial x}\left(x'\boldsymbol{C}x\right) = 2\boldsymbol{C}x \tag{2.32}$$

$$\frac{\partial^2}{\partial x \partial x'}\left(x'\boldsymbol{C}x\right) = 2\boldsymbol{C}. \tag{2.33}$$

Using (2.31) and (2.32), we find

$$\frac{\partial}{\partial x} f(x) = -2b + 2\boldsymbol{C}x.$$

The first-order condition for minimization sets this derivative equal to zero. Thus the solution satisfies $-2b + 2\boldsymbol{C}x = 0$. Solving for x, we find (2.30). Using (2.33), we also find

$$\frac{\partial^2}{\partial x \partial x'} f(x) = 2\boldsymbol{C} > 0$$

which is the second-order condition for minimization. Thus (2.30) is the unique minimizer of $f(x)$.

Our second proof is algebraic. Rewrite $f(x)$ as

$$f(x) = \left(a - b'\boldsymbol{C}^{-1}b\right) + \left(x - \boldsymbol{C}^{-1}b\right)'\boldsymbol{C}\left(x - \boldsymbol{C}^{-1}b\right).$$

The first term does not depend on x so does not affect the minimizer. The second term is a quadratic form in a positive definite matrix. This means that for any nonzero α, $\alpha'\boldsymbol{C}\alpha > 0$. Thus for $x \neq \boldsymbol{C}^{-1}b$, the second term is strictly positive, yet for $x = \boldsymbol{C}^{-1}b$, this term equals zero. It is therefore minimized at $x = \boldsymbol{C}^{-1}b$, as claimed.

2.19 ILLUSTRATIONS OF BEST LINEAR PREDICTOR

We illustrate the best linear predictor (projection) using three log wage equations introduced in earlier sections. For our first example, consider a model with the two dummy variables for gender and race similar to Table 2.1. As we learned in Section 2.17, the entries in this table can be equivalently expressed by a linear CEF. For simplicity, let's consider the CEF of $\log(wage)$ as a function of *Black* and *female*:

$$\mathbb{E}\left[\log(wage) \mid Black, female\right] = -0.20 Black - 0.24 female + 0.10 Black \times female + 3.06. \tag{2.34}$$

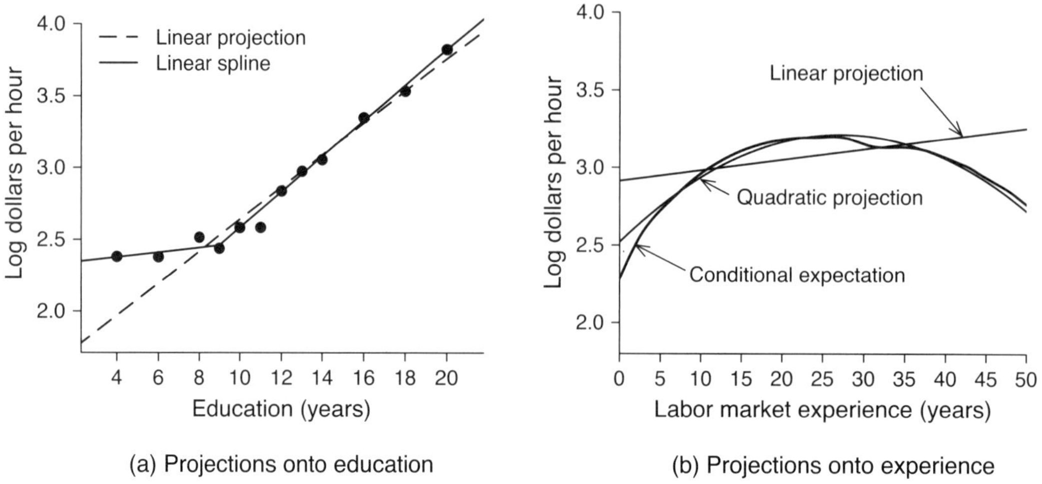

FIGURE 2.6 Projections of log wage onto education and experience

This is a CEF, as the variables are binary and all interactions are included.

Now consider a simpler model omitting the interaction effect: the linear projection on the variables *Black* and *female*:

$$\mathscr{P}\left[\log(wage) \mid Black, female\right] = -0.15Black - 0.23female + 3.06. \tag{2.35}$$

What is the difference? The full CEF (2.34) shows that the race gap is differentiated by gender: it is 20% for Black men (relative to non-Black men) and 10% for Black women (relative to non-Black women). The projection model (2.35) simplifies this analysis, calculating an average 15% wage gap for Black wage earners, ignoring the role of gender. Notice that this is true even though *gender* is included in (2.35).

For our second example, consider the CEF of log wages as a function of years of education for white men, which was illustrated in Figure 2.3 and is replotted in Figure 2.6(a). Superimposed on the figure are two projections. The first (given by the dashed line) is the linear projection of log wages on years of education:

$$\mathscr{P}\left[\log(wage) \mid education\right] = 0.11education + 1.5.$$

This simple equation indicates an average of 11% increase in wages for every year of education. An inspection of the figure shows that this approximation works well for $education \geq 9$, but it underpredicts wages for individuals with lower levels of education. To correct this imbalance, we use a linear spline equation, which allows different rates of return above and below 9 years of education:

$$\begin{aligned}&\mathscr{P}\left[\log(wage) \mid education, (education - 9) \times \mathbb{1}\{education > 9\}\right]\\&= 0.02education + 0.10 \times (education - 9) \times \mathbb{1}\{education > 9\} + 2.3.\end{aligned}$$

This equation is displayed in Figure 2.6(a) using the solid line, and appears to fit much better. It indicates a 2% increase in mean wages for every year of education below 9, and a 12% increase in mean wages for every year of education above 9. It is still an approximation to the conditional mean, but it appears to be fairly reasonable.

For our third example, let us take the CEF of log wages as a function of years of experience for white men with 12 years of education, which is graphed in Figure 2.4 and is repeated as the thick line in Figure 2.6(b). Superimposed on the latter figure are two projections. The first (labeled "Linear Projection") is the linear projection on experience

$$\mathscr{P}\left[\log(wage) \mid experience\right] = 0.011 experience + 2.5$$

and the second (labeled "Quadratic Projection") is the linear projection on experience and its square

$$\mathscr{P}\left[\log(wage) \mid experience\right] = 0.046 experience - 0.0007 experience^2 + 2.3.$$

It is fairly clear from an examination of Figure 2.6(b) that the first linear projection is a poor approximation. It overpredicts wages for young and old workers, underpredicts for the rest, and misses the strong downturn in expected wages for older wage earners. The second projection fits much better. We can call this equation a **quadratic projection**, because the function is quadratic in *experience*.

2.20 LINEAR PREDICTOR ERROR VARIANCE

Assume that X contains an intercept. As in the CEF model, we define the error variance as $\sigma^2 = \mathbb{E}\left[e^2\right]$. Setting $Q_{YY} = \mathbb{E}\left[Y^2\right]$ and $\boldsymbol{Q}_{YX} = \mathbb{E}\left[YX'\right]$, we can write σ^2 as

$$\begin{aligned}
\sigma^2 &= \mathbb{E}\left[\left(Y - X'\beta\right)^2\right] \\
&= \mathbb{E}\left[Y^2\right] - 2\mathbb{E}\left[YX'\right]\beta + \beta'\mathbb{E}\left[XX'\right]\beta \\
&= Q_{YY} - 2\boldsymbol{Q}_{YX}\boldsymbol{Q}_{XX}^{-1}\boldsymbol{Q}_{XY} + \boldsymbol{Q}_{YX}\boldsymbol{Q}_{XX}^{-1}\boldsymbol{Q}_{XX}\boldsymbol{Q}_{XX}^{-1}\boldsymbol{Q}_{XY} \\
&= Q_{YY} - \boldsymbol{Q}_{YX}\boldsymbol{Q}_{XX}^{-1}\boldsymbol{Q}_{XY} \\
&\stackrel{\text{def}}{=} Q_{YY \cdot X}.
\end{aligned} \tag{2.36}$$

One useful feature of this formula is that it shows that $Q_{YY \cdot X} = Q_{YY} - \boldsymbol{Q}_{YX}\boldsymbol{Q}_{XX}^{-1}\boldsymbol{Q}_{XY}$ equals the variance of the error from the linear projection of Y on X.

2.21 REGRESSION COEFFICIENTS

Sometimes it is useful to separate the constant from the other regressors and write the linear projection equation in the format

$$Y = X'\beta + \alpha + e \tag{2.37}$$

where α is the intercept, and X does not contain a constant.

Taking expectations of this equation, we find

$$\mathbb{E}\left[Y\right] = \mathbb{E}\left[X'\beta\right] + \mathbb{E}\left[\alpha\right] + \mathbb{E}\left[e\right]$$

or $\mu_Y = \mu_X'\beta + \alpha$, where $\mu_Y = \mathbb{E}\left[Y\right]$ and $\mu_X = \mathbb{E}\left[X\right]$, since $\mathbb{E}\left[e\right] = 0$ from (2.28). (While X does not contain a constant, the equation does, so (2.28) still applies.) Rearranging, we find $\alpha = \mu_Y - \mu_X'\beta$. Subtracting this equation from (2.37), we find

$$Y - \mu_Y = \left(X - \mu_X\right)'\beta + e \tag{2.38}$$

which is a linear equation between the centered variables $Y - \mu_Y$ and $X - \mu_X$. (They are centered at their means, so are mean-zero random variables.) Because $X - \mu_X$ is uncorrelated with e, (2.38) is also a linear projection. Thus by the formula for the linear projection model,

$$\begin{aligned}\beta &= \left(\mathbb{E}\left[(X-\mu_X)(X-\mu_X)'\right]\right)^{-1}\mathbb{E}\left[(X-\mu_X)(Y-\mu_Y)\right]\\ &= \operatorname{var}[X]^{-1}\operatorname{cov}(X,Y)\end{aligned}$$

a function only of the covariances[10] of X and Y.

Theorem 2.10 In the linear projection model $Y = X'\beta + \alpha + e$,

$$\alpha = \mu_Y - \mu_X'\beta \tag{2.39}$$

and

$$\beta = \operatorname{var}[X]^{-1}\operatorname{cov}(X,Y). \tag{2.40}$$

2.22 REGRESSION SUBVECTORS

Let the regressors be partitioned as

$$X = \begin{pmatrix} X_1 \\ X_2 \end{pmatrix}. \tag{2.41}$$

We can write the projection of Y on X as

$$\begin{aligned} Y &= X'\beta + e \\ &= X_1'\beta_1 + X_2'\beta_2 + e \\ \mathbb{E}[Xe] &= 0. \end{aligned} \tag{2.42}$$

In this section, we derive formulas for the subvectors β_1 and β_2.

Partition $\boldsymbol{Q}_{XX}$ conformably with X:

$$\boldsymbol{Q}_{XX} = \begin{bmatrix} \boldsymbol{Q}_{11} & \boldsymbol{Q}_{12} \\ \boldsymbol{Q}_{21} & \boldsymbol{Q}_{22} \end{bmatrix} = \begin{bmatrix} \mathbb{E}\left[X_1X_1'\right] & \mathbb{E}\left[X_1X_2'\right] \\ \mathbb{E}\left[X_2X_1'\right] & \mathbb{E}\left[X_2X_2'\right] \end{bmatrix}$$

and similarly,

$$\boldsymbol{Q}_{XY} = \begin{bmatrix} \boldsymbol{Q}_{1Y} \\ \boldsymbol{Q}_{2Y} \end{bmatrix} = \begin{bmatrix} \mathbb{E}[X_1Y] \\ \mathbb{E}[X_2Y] \end{bmatrix}.$$

By the partitioned matrix inversion formula (A.3)

$$\boldsymbol{Q}_{XX}^{-1} = \begin{bmatrix} \boldsymbol{Q}_{11} & \boldsymbol{Q}_{12} \\ \boldsymbol{Q}_{21} & \boldsymbol{Q}_{22} \end{bmatrix}^{-1} \stackrel{\text{def}}{=} \begin{bmatrix} \boldsymbol{Q}^{11} & \boldsymbol{Q}^{12} \\ \boldsymbol{Q}^{21} & \boldsymbol{Q}^{22} \end{bmatrix} = \begin{bmatrix} \boldsymbol{Q}_{11\cdot 2}^{-1} & -\boldsymbol{Q}_{11\cdot 2}^{-1}\boldsymbol{Q}_{12}\boldsymbol{Q}_{22}^{-1} \\ -\boldsymbol{Q}_{22\cdot 1}^{-1}\boldsymbol{Q}_{21}\boldsymbol{Q}_{11}^{-1} & \boldsymbol{Q}_{22\cdot 1}^{-1} \end{bmatrix} \tag{2.43}$$

[10]The **covariance matrix** between vectors X and Z is $\operatorname{cov}(X,Z) = \mathbb{E}\left[(X - \mathbb{E}[X])(Z - \mathbb{E}[Z])'\right]$. The covariance matrix of the vector X is $\operatorname{var}[X] = \operatorname{cov}(X,X) = \mathbb{E}\left[(X - \mathbb{E}[X])(X - \mathbb{E}[X])'\right]$.

where $\boldsymbol{Q}_{11\cdot 2} \stackrel{\text{def}}{=} \boldsymbol{Q}_{11} - \boldsymbol{Q}_{12}\boldsymbol{Q}_{22}^{-1}\boldsymbol{Q}_{21}$, and $\boldsymbol{Q}_{22\cdot 1} \stackrel{\text{def}}{=} \boldsymbol{Q}_{22} - \boldsymbol{Q}_{21}\boldsymbol{Q}_{11}^{-1}\boldsymbol{Q}_{12}$. Thus

$$
\begin{aligned}
\beta &= \begin{pmatrix} \beta_1 \\ \beta_2 \end{pmatrix} \\
&= \begin{bmatrix} \boldsymbol{Q}_{11\cdot 2}^{-1} & -\boldsymbol{Q}_{11\cdot 2}^{-1}\boldsymbol{Q}_{12}\boldsymbol{Q}_{22}^{-1} \\ -\boldsymbol{Q}_{22\cdot 1}^{-1}\boldsymbol{Q}_{21}\boldsymbol{Q}_{11}^{-1} & \boldsymbol{Q}_{22\cdot 1}^{-1} \end{bmatrix} \begin{bmatrix} \boldsymbol{Q}_{1Y} \\ \boldsymbol{Q}_{2Y} \end{bmatrix} \\
&= \begin{pmatrix} \boldsymbol{Q}_{11\cdot 2}^{-1}\left(\boldsymbol{Q}_{1y} - \boldsymbol{Q}_{12}\boldsymbol{Q}_{22}^{-1}\boldsymbol{Q}_{2Y}\right) \\ \boldsymbol{Q}_{22\cdot 1}^{-1}\left(\boldsymbol{Q}_{2y} - \boldsymbol{Q}_{21}\boldsymbol{Q}_{11}^{-1}\boldsymbol{Q}_{1Y}\right) \end{pmatrix} \\
&= \begin{pmatrix} \boldsymbol{Q}_{11\cdot 2}^{-1}\boldsymbol{Q}_{1Y\cdot 2} \\ \boldsymbol{Q}_{22\cdot 1}^{-1}\boldsymbol{Q}_{2Y\cdot 1} \end{pmatrix}.
\end{aligned}
$$

We have shown that $\beta_1 = \boldsymbol{Q}_{11\cdot 2}^{-1}\boldsymbol{Q}_{1Y\cdot 2}$ and $\beta_2 = \boldsymbol{Q}_{22\cdot 1}^{-1}\boldsymbol{Q}_{2Y\cdot 1}$.

2.23 COEFFICIENT DECOMPOSITION

In Section 2.22, we derived formulas for the coefficient subvectors β_1 and β_2. We now use these formulas to give a useful interpretation of the coefficients in terms of an iterated projection.

Take equation (2.42) for the case $\dim(X_1) = 1$ so that $\beta_1 \in \mathbb{R}$.

$$
Y = X_1\beta_1 + X_2'\beta_2 + e. \tag{2.44}
$$

Now consider the projection of X_1 on X_2:

$$
\begin{aligned}
X_1 &= X_2'\gamma_2 + u_1 \\
\mathbb{E}\left[X_2 u_1\right] &= 0.
\end{aligned}
$$

From (2.22) and (2.36), $\gamma_2 = \boldsymbol{Q}_{22}^{-1}\boldsymbol{Q}_{21}$, and $\mathbb{E}\left[u_1^2\right] = \boldsymbol{Q}_{11\cdot 2} = \boldsymbol{Q}_{11} - \boldsymbol{Q}_{12}\boldsymbol{Q}_{22}^{-1}\boldsymbol{Q}_{21}$. We can also calculate that

$$
\mathbb{E}\left[u_1 Y\right] = \mathbb{E}\left[\left(X_1 - \gamma_2' X_2\right) Y\right] = \mathbb{E}\left[X_1 Y\right] - \gamma_2'\mathbb{E}\left[X_2 Y\right] = \boldsymbol{Q}_{1Y} - \boldsymbol{Q}_{12}\boldsymbol{Q}_{22}^{-1}\boldsymbol{Q}_{2Y} = \boldsymbol{Q}_{1Y\cdot 2}.
$$

We have found that

$$
\beta_1 = \boldsymbol{Q}_{11\cdot 2}^{-1}\boldsymbol{Q}_{1Y\cdot 2} = \frac{\mathbb{E}\left[u_1 Y\right]}{\mathbb{E}\left[u_1^2\right]}
$$

the coefficient from the simple regression of Y on u_1.

What this means is that in the multivariate projection equation (2.44), the coefficient β_1 equals the projection coefficient from a regression of Y on u_1, the error from a projection of X_1 on the other regressors X_2. The error u_1 can be thought of as the component of X_1 which is not linearly explained by the other regressors. Thus the coefficient β_1 equals the linear effect of X_1 on Y after stripping out the effects of the other variables.

There was nothing special in the choice of the variable X_1. This derivation applies symmetrically to all coefficients in a linear projection. Each coefficient equals the simple regression of Y on the error from a projection of that regressor on all the other regressors. Each coefficient equals the linear effect of that variable on Y after linearly controlling for all the other regressors.

2.24 OMITTED VARIABLE BIAS

Again, let the regressors be partitioned as in (2.41). Consider the projection of Y on X_1 only. Perhaps this is done because the variables X_2 are not observed. This is the equation

$$Y = X_1'\gamma_1 + u \tag{2.45}$$
$$\mathbb{E}[X_1 u] = 0.$$

Notice that we have written the coefficient as γ_1 rather than β_1 and the error as u rather than e. This is because (2.45) is different than (2.42). Goldberger (1991) introduced the catchy labels **long regression** for (2.42) and **short regression** for (2.45) to emphasize the distinction.

Typically, $\beta_1 \neq \gamma_1$, except in special cases. To see this, we calculate

$$\begin{aligned}
\gamma_1 &= \left(\mathbb{E}\left[X_1X_1'\right]\right)^{-1}\mathbb{E}\left[X_1Y\right] \\
&= \left(\mathbb{E}\left[X_1X_1'\right]\right)^{-1}\mathbb{E}\left[X_1\left(X_1'\beta_1 + X_2'\beta_2 + e\right)\right] \\
&= \beta_1 + \left(\mathbb{E}\left[X_1X_1'\right]\right)^{-1}\mathbb{E}\left[X_1X_2'\right]\beta_2 \\
&= \beta_1 + \Gamma_{12}\beta_2
\end{aligned}$$

where $\Gamma_{12} = \boldsymbol{Q}_{11}^{-1}\boldsymbol{Q}_{12}$ is the coefficient matrix from a projection of X_2 on X_1, where we use the notation from Section 2.22.

Observe that $\gamma_1 = \beta_1 + \Gamma_{12}\beta_2 \neq \beta_1$ unless $\Gamma_{12} = 0$ or $\beta_2 = 0$. Thus the short and long regressions have different coefficients. They are the same only under one of two conditions. First, if the projection of X_2 on X_1 yields a set of zero coefficients (they are uncorrelated), or second, if the coefficient on X_2 in (2.42) is zero. The difference $\Gamma_{12}\beta_2$ between γ_1 and β_1 is known as **omitted variable bias**. It is the consequence of the omission of a relevant correlated variable.

To avoid omitted variables bias, the standard advice is to include all potentially relevant variables in estimated models. By construction, the general model will be free of such bias. Unfortunately in many cases, it is not feasible to completely follow this advice, as many desired variables are not observed. In this case, the possibility of omitted variables bias should be acknowledged and discussed in the course of an empirical investigation.

For example, suppose Y is log wages, X_1 is education, and X_2 is intellectual ability. Suppose that education and intellectual ability are positively correlated (highly able individuals attain higher levels of education), which means $\Gamma_{12} > 0$. Also suppose that conditional on education, individuals with higher intelligence earn higher wages on average, so that $\beta_2 > 0$. In this case, $\Gamma_{12}\beta_2 > 0$ and $\gamma_1 = \beta_1 + \Gamma_{12}\beta_2 > \beta_1$. Therefore, under these assumptions, in a regression of wages on education with intelligence omitted (as the latter is not measured), the coefficient on education will be higher than in a regression where intelligence is included. In other words, in this context, the omitted variable biases the regression coefficient upward. It is possible, for example, that $\beta_1 = 0$, so that education has no direct effect on wages, yet $\gamma_1 = \Gamma_{12}\beta_2 > 0$, meaning that the regression coefficient on education alone is positive but is a consequence of the unmodeled correlation between education and intellectual ability.

Unfortunately, the above simple characterization of omitted variable bias does not immediately carry over to more complicated settings, as discovered by De Luca, Magnus, and Peracchi (2018). For example, suppose we compare three nested projections:

$$Y = X_1'\gamma_1 + u_1$$

$$Y = X_1'\delta_1 + X_2'\delta_2 + u_2$$
$$Y = X_1'\beta_1 + X_2'\beta_2 + X_3'\beta_3 + e.$$

We can call them "short," "medium," and "long" regressions. Suppose that the parameter of interest is β_1 in the long regression. We are interested in the consequences of omitting X_3 when estimating the medium regression, and of omitting both X_2 and X_3 when estimating the short regression. In particular, we are interested in the question: Is it better to estimate the short or medium regression, given that both omit X_3? Intuition suggests that the medium regression should be "less biased," but it is worth investigating in greater detail. By similar calculations to those above, we find that

$$\gamma_1 = \beta_1 + \Gamma_{12}\beta_2 + \Gamma_{13}\beta_3$$
$$\delta_1 = \beta_1 + \Gamma_{13\cdot 2}\beta_3$$

where $\Gamma_{13\cdot 2} = \boldsymbol{Q}_{11\cdot 2}^{-1}\boldsymbol{Q}_{13\cdot 2}$ using the notation from Section 2.22.

We see that the bias in the short regression coefficient is $\Gamma_{12}\beta_2 + \Gamma_{13}\beta_3$, which depends on both β_2 and β_3, while that for the medium regression coefficient is $\Gamma_{13\cdot 2}\beta_3$, which only depends on β_3. So the bias for the medium regression is less complicated and intuitively seems more likely to be smaller than that for the short regression. However, it is impossible to strictly rank the two. It is quite possible that γ_1 is less biased than δ_1. Thus as a general rule, it is unknown whether estimation of the medium regression will be less biased than estimation of the short regression.

2.25 BEST LINEAR APPROXIMATION

There are alternative ways we could construct a linear approximation $X'\beta$ to the conditional expectation $m(X)$. In this section, we show that one alternative approach turns out to yield the same answer as the best linear predictor.

We start by defining the mean-square approximation error of $X'\beta$ to $m(X)$ as the expected squared difference between $X'\beta$ and the conditional expectation $m(X)$:

$$d(\beta) = \mathbb{E}\left[\left(m(X) - X'\beta\right)^2\right].$$

The function $d(\beta)$ is a measure of the deviation of $X'\beta$ from $m(X)$. If the two functions are identical, then $d(\beta) = 0$, otherwise $d(\beta) > 0$. We can also view the mean-squared difference $d(\beta)$ as a density-weighted average of the function $\left(m(X) - X'\beta\right)^2$, since

$$d(\beta) = \int_{\mathbb{R}^k} \left(m(x) - x'\beta\right)^2 f_X(x)dx$$

where $f_X(x)$ is the marginal density of X.

We can then define the best linear approximation to the conditional expectation $m(X)$ as the function $X'\beta$ obtained by selecting β to minimize $d(\beta)$:

$$\beta = \underset{b\in\mathbb{R}^k}{\operatorname{argmin}}\, d(b). \tag{2.46}$$

Similar to the best linear predictor, we are measuring accuracy by the expected squared error. The difference is that the best linear predictor (2.18) selects β to minimize the expected squared prediction error, while the best linear approximation (2.46) selects β to minimize the expected squared approximation error.

Despite the different definitions, it turns out that the best linear predictor and the best linear approximation are identical. By the same steps as in (2.18) plus an application of conditional expectations, we can find that

$$\beta = \left(\mathbb{E}\left[XX'\right]\right)^{-1} \mathbb{E}\left[Xm(X)\right] \tag{2.47}$$

$$= \left(\mathbb{E}\left[XX'\right]\right)^{-1} \mathbb{E}\left[XY\right] \tag{2.48}$$

(see Exercise 2.19). Thus (2.46) equals (2.18). We conclude that the definition (2.46) can be viewed as an alternative motivation for the linear projection coefficient.

2.26 REGRESSION TO THE MEAN

The term **regression** originated in an influential paper by Francis Galton (1886), where he examined the joint distribution of the stature (height) of parents and children. Effectively, he was estimating the conditional expectation of children's height given their parent's height. Galton discovered that this conditional expectation was approximately linear with a slope of 2/3. This implies that *on average*, a child's height is more mediocre (average) than his or her parent's height. Galton called this phenomenon **regression to the mean**, and the label **regression** has stuck to this day to describe most conditional relationships.

One of Galton's fundamental insights was to recognize that if the marginal distributions of Y and X are the same (e.g., the heights of children and parents in a stable environment), then the regression slope in a linear projection is always less than 1.

To be more precise, take the simple linear projection

$$Y = X\beta + \alpha + e \tag{2.49}$$

where Y equals the height of the child, and X equals the height of the parent. Assume that Y and X have the same expectation, so that $\mu_Y = \mu_X = \mu$. Then from (2.39), $\alpha = (1-\beta)\,\mu$, so we can write the linear projection (2.49) as

$$\mathscr{P}\,(Y \mid X) = (1-\beta)\,\mu + X\beta.$$

This shows that the projected height of the child is a weighted average of the population expectation μ and the parent's height X with weights $1-\beta$ and β. When the height distribution is stable across generations so that $\operatorname{var}[Y] = \operatorname{var}[X]$, then this slope is the simple correlation of Y and X. Using (2.40), we have

$$\beta = \frac{\operatorname{cov}(X, Y)}{\operatorname{var}[X]} = \operatorname{corr}(X, Y).$$

By the Cauchy-Schwarz inequality (B.32), $-1 \le \operatorname{corr}(X, Y) \le 1$, with $\operatorname{corr}(X, Y) = 1$ only in the degenerate case $Y = X$. Thus if we exclude degeneracy, β is strictly less than 1. Thus on average, a child's height is more mediocre (closer to the population average) than the parent's.

A common error—known as the **regression fallacy**—is to infer from $\beta < 1$ that the population is **converging**, meaning that its variance is declining toward 0. This is a fallacy, because we derived the implication $\beta < 1$ under the assumption of constant means and variances. So certainly $\beta < 1$ does not imply that the variance Y is less than than the variance of X.

Another way of seeing this is to examine the conditions for convergence in the context of equation (2.49). Since X and e are uncorrelated, it follows that

$$\operatorname{var}[Y] = \beta^2 \operatorname{var}[X] + \operatorname{var}[e].$$

Then $\operatorname{var}[Y] < \operatorname{var}[X]$ if and only if

$$\beta^2 < 1 - \frac{\operatorname{var}[e]}{\operatorname{var}[X]}$$

which is not implied by the simple condition $|\beta| < 1$.

The regression fallacy arises in related empirical situations. Suppose you sort families into groups by the heights of the parents, and then plot the average heights of each subsequent generation over time. If the population is stable, the regression property implies that the plots lines will converge—children's heights will be more average than their parents'. The regression fallacy is to incorrectly conclude that the population is converging. A message to be learned from this example is that such plots are misleading for inferences about convergence.

The regression fallacy is subtle. It is easy for intelligent economists to succumb to its temptation. A famous example is *The Triumph of Mediocrity in Business* by Horace Secrist published in 1933. In this book, Secrist carefully and with great detail documented that in a sample of department stores during 1920–1930, when he divided the stores into groups based on 1920–1921 profits and plotted the average profits of these groups for the subsequent 10 years, he found clear and persuasive evidence for convergence "toward mediocrity." Of course, this was no discovery—regression to the mean is a necessary feature of stable distributions.

2.27 REVERSE REGRESSION

Galton noticed another interesting feature of the bivariate distribution. There is nothing special about a regression of Y on X. We can also regress X on Y. (In Galton's heredity example, this is the best linear predictor of the height of parents given the height of their children.) This regression takes the form

$$X = Y\beta^* + \alpha^* + e^*. \tag{2.50}$$

This is sometimes called the **reverse regression**. In this equation, the coefficients α^*, β^*, and error e^* are defined by linear projection. In a stable population, we find that

$$\beta^* = \operatorname{corr}(X, Y) = \beta$$
$$\alpha^* = (1 - \beta)\,\mu = \alpha$$

which are exactly the same as in the projection of Y on X! The intercept and slope have exactly the same values in the forward and reverse projections! [This equality is not particularly imporant; it is an artifact of the assumption that X and Y have the same variances.]

While this algebraic discovery is quite simple, it is counterintuitive. Instead, a common yet mistaken guess for the form of the reverse regression is to take equation (2.49), divide through by β, and rewrite to find the equation

$$X = Y\frac{1}{\beta} - \frac{\alpha}{\beta} - \frac{1}{\beta}e \tag{2.51}$$

suggesting that the projection of X on Y should have a slope coefficient of $1/\beta$ instead of β, and intercept of $-\alpha/\beta$ rather than α. What went wrong? Equation (2.51) is perfectly valid, because it is a simple manipulation of the valid equation (2.49). The trouble is that (2.51) is neither a CEF nor a linear projection. Inverting a projection (or CEF) does not yield a projection (or CEF). Instead, (2.50) is a valid projection, not (2.51).

In any event, Galton's finding was that when the variables are standardized, the slope in both projections (Y on X, and X on Y) equals the correlation, and both equations exhibit regression to the mean. It is not a causal relation, but a natural feature of joint distributions.

2.28 LIMITATIONS OF THE BEST LINEAR PROJECTION

Let's compare the linear projection and linear CEF models. From Theorem 2.4.4, we know that the CEF error has the property $\mathbb{E}[Xe] = 0$. Thus a linear CEF is the best linear projection. However, the converse is not true, as the projection error does not necessarily satisfy $\mathbb{E}[e \mid X] = 0$. Furthermore, the linear projection may be a poor approximation to the CEF.

To see these points in a simple example, suppose that the true process is $Y = X + X^2$ with $X \sim \mathrm{N}(0, 1)$. In this case, the true CEF is $m(x) = x + x^2$, and there is no error. Now consider the linear projection of Y on X and a constant, namely, the model $Y = \beta X + \alpha + e$. Since $X \sim \mathrm{N}(0, 1)$, X and X^2 are uncorrelated and the linear projection takes the form $\mathscr{P}[Y \mid X] = X + 1$. This is quite different from the true CEF $m(X) = X + X^2$. The projection error equals $e = X^2 - 1$ which is a deterministic function of X yet is uncorrelated with X. We see in this example that a projection error need not be a CEF error, and a linear projection can be a poor approximation to the CEF.

Another defect of linear projection is that it is sensitive to the marginal distribution of the regressors when the conditional mean is nonlinear. We illustrate the issue in Figure 2.7 for a constructed[11] joint distribution of Y and X. The thick line is the nonlinear CEF of Y given X. The data are divided into two groups—Group 1 and Group 2—which have different marginal distributions for the regressor X, and Group 1 has a lower mean value of X than Group 2. The separate linear projections of Y on X for these two groups are displayed in the figure by the thin lines. These two projections are distinct approximations to the CEF. A defect with linear projection is that it leads to the incorrect conclusion that the effect of X on Y is different for individuals in the two groups. This conclusion is incorrect, because in fact there is no difference in the conditional expectation function. The apparent difference is a by-product of linear approximations to a nonlinear expectation combined with different marginal distributions for the conditioning variables.

2.29 RANDOM COEFFICIENT MODEL

A model which is notationally similar to but conceptually distinct from the linear CEF model is the linear random coefficient model. It takes the form $Y = X'\eta$, where the individual-specific coefficient η is random and independent of X. For example, if X is years of schooling and Y is log wages, then η is the individual-specific returns to schooling. If a person obtains an extra year of schooling, η is the actual change in their wage. The random coefficient model allows the returns to schooling to vary in the population. Some individuals might have a high return to education (a high η) and others a low return, possibly 0, or even negative.

[11] The X in Group 1 are $\mathrm{N}(2, 1)$, those in Group 2 are $\mathrm{N}(4, 1)$, and the conditional distribution of Y given X is $\mathrm{N}(m(X), 1)$, where $m(x) = 2x - x^2/6$. The functions are plotted over $0 \le x \le 6$.

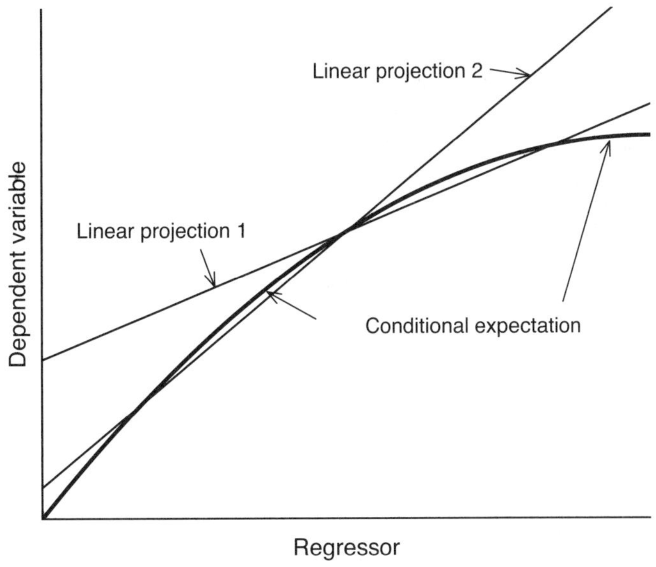

FIGURE 2.7 Conditional expectation and two linear projections

In the linear CEF model, the regressor coefficient equals the regression derivative—the change in the conditional expectation due to a change in the regressors, $\beta = \nabla m(X)$. This is not the effect on a given individual; it is the effect on the population average. In contrast, in the random coefficient model, the random vector $\eta = \nabla \left(X'\eta\right)$ is the true causal effect—the change in the response variable Y itself due to a change in the regressors.

It is interesting, however, to discover that the linear random coefficient model implies a linear CEF. To see this, let $\beta = \mathbb{E}[\eta]$ and $\Sigma = \operatorname{var}[\eta]$ denote the mean and covariance matrix of η, respectively, and then decompose the random coefficient as $\eta = \beta + u$, where u is distributed independently of X with mean 0 and covariance matrix Σ. Then we can write

$$\mathbb{E}[Y \mid X] = X'\mathbb{E}[\eta \mid X] = X'\mathbb{E}[\eta] = X'\beta$$

so the CEF is linear in X, and the coefficient β equals the expectation of the random coefficient η.

We can thus write the equation as a linear CEF $Y = X'\beta + e$, where $e = X'u$ and $u = \eta - \beta$. The error is conditionally mean 0: $\mathbb{E}[e \mid X] = 0$. Furthermore

$$\operatorname{var}[e \mid X] = X' \operatorname{var}[\eta]\, X = X'\Sigma X$$

so the error is conditionally heteroskedastic with its variance a quadratic function of X.

Theorem 2.11 In the linear random coefficient model $Y = X'\eta$ with η independent of X, $\mathbb{E}\|X\|^2 < \infty$, and $\mathbb{E}\|\eta\|^2 < \infty$, then

$$\mathbb{E}[Y \mid X] = X'\beta$$
$$\operatorname{var}[Y \mid X] = X'\Sigma X$$

where $\beta = \mathbb{E}[\eta]$ and $\Sigma = \operatorname{var}[\eta]$.

2.30 CAUSAL EFFECTS

So far we have avoided the concept of causality, yet often the underlying goal of an econometric analysis is to measure a causal relationship between variables. It is often of great interest to understand the causes and effects of decisions, actions, and policies. For example, we may be interested in the effect of class sizes on test scores, police expenditures on crime rates, climate change on economic activity, years of schooling on wages, institutional structure on growth, the effectiveness of rewards on behavior, the consequences of medical procedures for health outcomes, or any variety of possible causal relationships. In each case, the goal is to understand what the actual effect is on the outcome due to a change in an input. We are not just interested in the conditional expectation or linear projection, we would like to know the actual change.

Two inherent barriers are: (1) the causal effect is typically specific to an individual; and (2) the causal effect is typically unobserved.

Consider the effect of schooling on wages. The causal effect is the actual difference a person would receive in wages if we could change their level of education *holding all else constant*. This is specific to each individual, as their employment outcomes in these two distinct situations are individual. The causal effect is unobserved, because the most we can observe is their actual level of education and their actual wage, but not the counterfactual wage if their education had been different.

To be concrete, suppose that there are two individuals, Jennifer and George, and both have the possibility of being high school graduates or college graduates, and both would have received different wages given their choices. For example, suppose that Jennifer would have earned \$10 an hour as a high school graduate and \$20 an hour as a college graduate, while George would have earned \$8 as a high school graduate and \$12 as a college graduate. In this example, the causal effect of schooling is \$10 a hour for Jennifer and \$4 an hour for George. The causal effects are specific to the individual, and neither causal effect is observed.

Rubin (1974) developed the **potential outcomes** framework (also known as the **Rubin causal model**) to clarify the issues. Let Y be a scalar outcome (for example, wages) and D be a binary **treatment** (for example, college attendence). The specification of treatment as binary is not essential, but it simplifies the notation. A flexible model describing the impact of the treatment on the outcome is

$$Y = h(D, U) \tag{2.52}$$

where U is an $\ell \times 1$ unobserved random factor, and h is a functional relationship. It is also common to use the simplified notation $Y(0) = h(0, U)$ and $Y(1) = h(1, U)$ for the potential outcomes associated with nontreatment and treatment, respectively. The notation implicitly holds U fixed. The potential outcomes are specific to each individual, as they depend on U. For example, if Y is an individual's wage, the unobservables U could include characteristics such as the individual's abilities, skills, work ethic, interpersonal connections, and preferences, all of which potentially influence their wage. In our example, these factors are summarized by the labels "Jennifer" and "George."

Rubin described the effect as **causal** when we vary D while holding U constant. In our example, this means changing an individual's education while holding constant their other attributes.

Definition 2.6 In the model (2.52) the **causal effect** of D on Y is

$$C(U) = Y(1) - Y(0) = h(1, U) - h(0, U) \tag{2.53}$$

which is the change in Y due to treatment while holding U constant.

It may be helpful to understand that (2.53) is a definition and does not necessarily describe causality in a fundamental or experimental sense. Perhaps it would be more appropriate to label (2.53) as a **structural effect** (the effect within the structural model).

The causal effect of treatment $C(U)$ defined in (2.53) is heterogeneous and random, as the potential outcomes $Y(0)$ and $Y(1)$ vary across individuals. Also, we do not observe both $Y(0)$ and $Y(1)$ for a given individual, but rather only the realized value:

$$Y = \begin{cases} Y(0) & \text{if} \quad D=0 \\ Y(1) & \text{if} \quad D=1. \end{cases}$$

Consequently, the causal effect $C(U)$ is unobserved.

Rubin's goal was to learn features of the distribution of $C(U)$, including its expected value, which he called the average causal effect. He defined it as follows.

Definition 2.7 In the model (2.52), the **average causal effect** (ACE) of D on Y is

$$\text{ACE} = \mathbb{E}[C(U)] = \int_{\mathbb{R}^\ell} C(u) f(u) du$$

where $f(u)$ is the density of U.

The ACE is the population average of the causal effect. Extending our Jennifer and George example, suppose that half of the population is like Jennifer and the other half is like George. Then the average causal effect of college on wages is $(10+4)/2 = \$7$ an hour.

To estimate the ACE, a reasonable starting place is to compare average Y for treated and untreated individuals. In our example, this is the difference between the average wage among college graduates and high school graduates, which is the same as the coefficient in a regression of the outcome Y on the treatment D. Does this equal the ACE?

The answer depends on the relationship between treatment D and the unobserved component U. If D is randomly assigned as in an experiment, then D and U are independent, and the regression coefficient equals the ACE. However, if D and U are dependent, then the regression coefficient and ACE are different. To see this, observe that the difference between the average outcomes of the treated and untreated populations are

$$\mathbb{E}[Y \mid D=1] - \mathbb{E}[Y \mid D=0] = \int_{\mathbb{R}^\ell} h(1,u) f(u \mid D=1)\, du - \int_{\mathbb{R}^\ell} h(1,u) f(u \mid D=0)\, du$$

where $f(u \mid D)$ is the conditional density of U given D. If U is independent of D, then $f(u \mid D) = f(u)$, and the above expression equals $\int_{\mathbb{R}^\ell} (h(1,u) - h(0,u)) f(u)\, du = \text{ACE}$. However, if U and D are dependent, this equality fails.

To illustrate, let's return to our example of Jennifer and George. Suppose that all high school students take an aptitude test. If a student gets a high (H) score, they go to college with probability 3/4, and if a student gets a low (L) score, they go to college with probability 1/4. Suppose further that Jennifer gets an aptitude score of H with probability 3/4, while George gets a score of H with probability 1/4. Given this situation, 62.5% of Jennifers will go to college, while 37.5% of George's will go to college.[12]

[12] $\mathbb{P}[college \mid Jennifer] = \mathbb{P}[college \mid H]\mathbb{P}[H \mid Jennifer] + \mathbb{P}[college \mid L]\mathbb{P}[L \mid Jennifer] = (3/4)^2 + (1/4)^2$; $\mathbb{P}[college \mid George] = \mathbb{P}[college \mid H]\mathbb{P}[H \mid George] + \mathbb{P}[college \mid L]\mathbb{P}[L \mid George] = (3/4)(1/4) + (1/4)(3/4)$.

Table 2.3
Example distribution

	\$8	\$10	\$12	\$20	Mean
High school graduate	10	6	0	0	\$8.75
College graduate	0	0	6	10	\$17.00
Difference					\$8.25

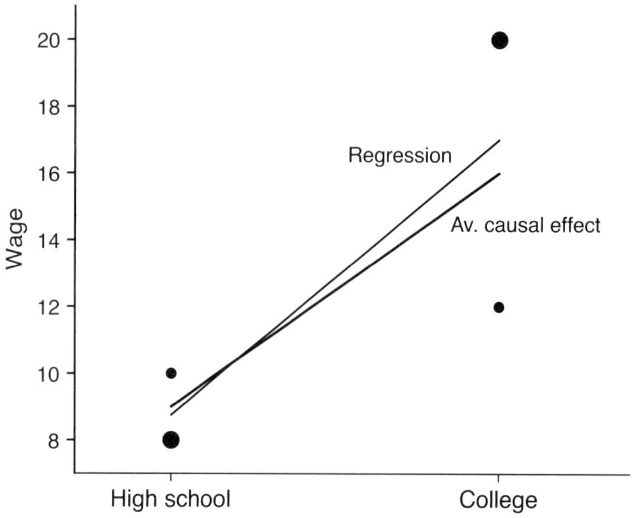

FIGURE 2.8 Average causal effect vs. regression

An econometrician who randomly samples 32 individuals and collects data on educational attainment and wages will find the wage distribution displayed in Table 2.3.

Our econometrician finds that the average wage among high school graduates is \$8.75, while the average wage among college graduates is \$17.00. The difference of \$8.25 is the econometrician's regression coefficient for the effect of college on wages. But \$8.25 overstates the true ACE of \$7. The reason is that college attendence is determined by an aptitude test, which is correlated with an individual's causal effect. Jennifer has both a high causal effect and is more likely to attend college, so the observed difference in wages overstates the causal effect of college.

To visualize Table 2.3, examine Figure 2.8. The four points are the four education/wage pairs from the table, with the size of the points calibrated to the wage distribution. The two lines are the econometrician's regression line and the average causal effect. The Jennifers in the population correspond to the points above the two lines, the Georges in the population correspond to the points below the two lines. Because most Jennifer's go to college and most Georges do not, the regression line is tilted away from the average causal effect toward the two large points.

Our first lesson from this analysis is that we need to be cautious about interpreting regression coefficients as causal effects. Unless the regressors (e.g., education attainment) can be interpreted as randomly assigned, it is inappropriate to interpret the regression coefficients causally.

Our second lesson will be that a causal interpretation can be obtained if we condition on a sufficiently rich set of covariates. We now explore this issue.

Suppose that the observables include a set of covariates X in addition to the outcome Y and treatment D. We extend the potential outcomes model (2.52) to include X:

$$Y = h(D, X, U). \tag{2.54}$$

We also extend the definition of a causal effect to allow conditioning on X.

Definition 2.8 In the model (2.54), the **causal effect** of D on Y is

$$C(X, U) = h(1, X, U) - h(0, X, U)$$

which is the change in Y due to treatment holding X and U constant.

The **conditional average causal effect** of D on Y conditional on $X = x$ is

$$\text{ACE}(x) = \mathbb{E}[C(X, U) \mid X = x] = \int_{\mathbb{R}^\ell} C(x, u) f(u \mid x) du$$

where $f(u \mid x)$ is the conditional density of U given X.

The **unconditional average causal effect** of D on Y is

$$\text{ACE} = \mathbb{E}[C(X, U)] = \int \text{ACE}(x) f(x) dx$$

where $f(x)$ is the density of X.

The conditional average causal effect ACE(x) is the ACE for the subpopulation with characteristics $X = x$. Given observations on (Y, D, X), we want to measure the causal effect of D on Y and are interested if this can be obtained by a regression of Y on (D, X). We would like to interpret the coefficient on D as a causal effect. Is this appropriate?

Our previous analysis showed that a causal interpretation obtains when U is independent of the regressors. While this condition is sufficient, it is stronger than necessary. Instead, the following is sufficient.

Definition 2.9 Conditional Independence Assumption (CIA). Conditional on X, the random variables D and U are statistically independent.

The CIA implies that the conditional density of U given (D, X) only depends on X, thus $f(u \mid D, X) = f(u \mid X)$. This implies that the regression of Y on (D, X) equals

$$\begin{aligned} m(d, x) &= \mathbb{E}[Y \mid D = d, X = x] \\ &= \mathbb{E}[h(d, x, U) \mid D = d, X = x] \\ &= \int h(d, x, u) f(u \mid x) du. \end{aligned}$$

Under the CIA, the treatment effect measured by the regression is

$$\begin{aligned} \nabla m(d, x) &= m(1, x) - m(0, x) \\ &= \int h(1, x, u) f(u \mid x) du - \int h(0, x, u) f(u \mid x) du \end{aligned}$$

$$= \int C(x,u) f(u \mid x) du$$

$$= \text{ACE}(x). \tag{2.55}$$

This is the conditional ACE. Thus under the CIA, the regression coefficient equals the ACE.

We deduce that the regression of Y on (D, X) reveals the causal impact of treatment when the CIA holds. Thus a regression analysis can be interpreted causally when we can make the case that the regressors X are sufficient to control for factors which are correlated with treatment.

Theorem 2.12 In the structural model (2.54), the CIA implies $\nabla m(d,x) = \text{ACE}(x)$; that is, the regression derivative with respect to treatment equals the conditional ACE.

This is a fascinating result. It shows that when the unobservable is independent of the treatment variable after conditioning on appropriate regressors, the regression derivative equals the conditional causal effect. This means the CEF has causal economic meaning, giving strong justification to estimation of the CEF.

It is important to understand the critical role of the CIA. If the CIA fails, then the equality (2.55) of the regression derivative and the ACE fails. The CIA states that conditional on X, the variables U and D are independent. This means that treatment D is not affected by the unobserved individual factors U and is effectively random. It is a strong assumption. In the wage/education example, it means that education is not selected by individuals based on their unobserved characteristics.

However, it is also helpful to understand that the CIA is weaker than full independence of U from the regressors (D, X). What is required is only that U and D are independent after conditioning on X. If X is sufficiently rich, this condition may not be restrictive.

Returning to our example, we require a variable X which breaks the dependence between D and U. In our example, this variable is the aptitude test score, because the decision to attend college was based on the test score. It follows that educational attainment and type are independent once we condition on the test score.

To see this, observe that if a student's test score is H, the probability they go to college ($D = 1$) is 3/4 for both Jennifers and Georges. Similarly, if their test score is L, the probability they go to college is 1/4 for both types. Thus college attendence is independent of type, conditional on the aptitude test score.

The conditional ACE depends on the test score. Among students who receive a high test score, 3/4 are Jennifers and 1/4 are Georges. Thus the conditional ACE for students with a score of H is $(3/4) \times 10 + (1/4) \times 4 = \$8.50$. Among students who receive a low test score, 1/4 are Jennifers and 3/4 are Georges. Thus the ACE for students with a score of L is $(1/4) \times 10 + (3/4) \times 4 = \$5.50$. The unconditional ACE is the average, ACE $= (8.50 + 5.50)/2 = \$7$, because 50% of students each receive scores of H and L.

Theorem 2.12 shows that the conditional ACE is revealed by a regression which includes test scores. To see this in the wage distribution, suppose that the econometrician collects data on the aptitude test score as well as education and wages. Given a random sample of 32 individuals, we would expect to find the wage distribution shown in Table 2.4.

Define a dummy *highscore* to indicate students who received a high test score. The regression of wages on college attendance and test scores with their interaction is

$$\mathbb{E}\left[wage \mid college, highscore\right] = 1.00 highscore + 5.50 college + 3.00 highscore \times college + 8.50. \tag{2.56}$$

The coefficient on *college*, \$5.50, is the regression derivative of college attendance for those with low test scores, and the sum of this coefficient with the interaction coefficient \$3.00 equals \$8.50, which is the

Table 2.4
Example distribution 2

	\$8	\$10	\$12	\$20	Mean
High school graduate + high test score	1	3	0	0	\$9.50
College graduate + high test score	0	0	3	9	\$18.00
High school graduate + low test score	9	3	0	0	\$8.50
College graduate + low test score	0	0	3	1	\$14.00

regression derivative for college attendance for those with high test scores. The values \$5.50 and \$8.50 equal the conditional causal effects as calculated above.

Thus we see that from the regression (2.56), an econometrician will find that the effect of college on wages is \$8.50 for those with high test scores and \$5.50 for those with low test scores with an average effect of \$7 (because 50% of students receive high and 50% low test scores). This is the true average causal effect of college on wages. Thus the regression coefficient on *college* in (2.56) can be interpreted causally, while a regression omitting the aptitude test score does not reveal the causal effect of education.

To summarize our findings, we have shown how it is possible that a simple regression will give a false measurement of a causal effect, but a more careful regression can reveal the true causal effect. The key is to condition on a suitably rich set of covariates, such that the remaining unobserved factors affecting the outcome are independent of the treatment variable.

2.31 EXISTENCE AND UNIQUENESS OF THE CONDITIONAL EXPECTATION*

In Sections 2.3 and 2.6, we defined the conditional expectation when the conditioning variables X are discrete and when the variables (Y, X) have a joint density. We have explored these cases because these are the situations where the conditional mean is easiest to describe and understand. However, the conditional mean exists quite generally without appealing to the properties of either discrete or continuous random variables.

To justify this claim, I now present a deep result from probability theory. What it says is that the conditional mean exists for all joint distributions (Y, X) for which Y has a finite mean.

Theorem 2.13 Existence of the Conditional Expectation
If $\mathbb{E}|Y| < \infty$, then there exists a function $m(x)$ such that for all sets $\mathscr{X}$ for which $\mathbb{P}[X \in \mathscr{X}]$ is defined,

$$\mathbb{E}[\mathbb{1}\{X \in \mathscr{X}\} Y] = \mathbb{E}[\mathbb{1}\{X \in \mathscr{X}\} m(X)]. \tag{2.57}$$

The function $m(X)$ is almost everywhere unique, in the sense that if $h(x)$ satisfies (2.57), then there is a set S such that $\mathbb{P}[S] = 1$ and $m(x) = h(x)$ for $x \in S$. The function $m(x)$ is called the **conditional expectation** and is written $m(x) = \mathbb{E}[Y \mid X = x]$.

See, for example, Ash (1972), Theorem 6.3.3.

The conditional expectation $m(x)$ defined by (2.57) specializes to (2.6) when (Y, X) have a joint density. The usefulness of definition (2.57) is that Theorem 2.13 shows that the conditional expectation $m(X)$ exists for all finite-mean distributions. This definition allows Y to be discrete or continuous, for X to be scalar or vector valued, and for the components of X to be discrete or continuously distributed.

You may have noticed that Theorem 2.13 applies only to sets $\mathscr{X}$ for which $\mathbb{P}[X \in \mathscr{X}]$ is defined. This is a technical issue—measurability—which we largely side step in this textbook. Formal probability theory only applies to sets which are measurable—for which probabilities are defined—as it turns out that not all sets satisfy measurability. This is not a practical concern for applications, so we defer such distinctions to formal theoretical treatments.

2.32 IDENTIFICATION*

A critical and important issue in structural econometric modeling is identification, meaning that a parameter is uniquely determined by the distribution of the observed variables. Identification is relatively straightforward in the context of the unconditional and conditional expectation, but it is worthwhile to introduce and explore the concept at this point for clarity.

Let F denote the distribution of the observed data, for example, the distribution of the pair (Y, X). Let $\mathscr{F}$ be a collection of distributions F. Let θ be a parameter of interest (e.g., the expectation $\mathbb{E}[Y]$).

Definition 2.10 A parameter $\theta \in \mathbb{R}$ is identified on $\mathscr{F}$ if for all $F \in \mathscr{F}$, there is a uniquely determined value of θ.

Equivalently, θ is identified if we can write it as a mapping $\theta = g(F)$ on the set $\mathscr{F}$. The restriction to the set $\mathscr{F}$ is important. Most parameters are identified only on a strict subset of the space of all distributions. Take, for example, the expectation $\mu = \mathbb{E}[Y]$. It is uniquely determined if $\mathbb{E}|Y| < \infty$, so μ is identified for the set $\mathscr{F} = \{F : \mathbb{E}|Y| < \infty\}$.

Next, consider the conditional expectation. Theorem 2.13 demonstrates that $\mathbb{E}|Y| < \infty$ is a sufficient condition for identification.

Theorem 2.14 Identification of the Conditional Expectation
If $\mathbb{E}|Y| < \infty$, the conditional expectation $m(x) = \mathbb{E}[Y \mid X = x]$ is identified almost everywhere.

It might seem as if identification is a general property for parameters so long as we exclude degenerate cases. This is true for moments of observed data, but not necessarily for more complicated models. As a case in point, consider the context of censoring. Let Y be a random variable with distribution F. Instead of observing Y, we observe Y^* defined by the censoring rule

$$Y^* = \begin{cases} Y, & \text{if } Y \leq \tau \\ \tau, & \text{if } Y > \tau. \end{cases}$$

That is, Y^* is capped at the value τ. A common example is income surveys, where income responses are "top-coded," meaning that incomes above the top code τ are recorded as the top code. The observed variable Y^* has distribution

$$F^*(u) = \begin{cases} F(u), & \text{for } u \leq \tau \\ 1, & \text{for } u \geq \tau. \end{cases}$$

We are interested in features of the distribution F, not the censored distribution F^*. For example, we are interested in the expected wage $\mu = \mathbb{E}[Y]$. The difficulty is that we cannot calculate μ from F^* except in the trivial case where there is no censoring: $\mathbb{P}[Y \geq \tau] = 0$. Thus the expectation μ is not generically identified from the censored distribution.

A typical solution to the identification problem is to assume a parametric distribution. For example, let $\mathscr{F}$ be the set of normal distributions $Y \sim \mathrm{N}(\mu, \sigma^2)$. It is possible to show that the parameters (μ, σ^2) are identified for all $F \in \mathscr{F}$. That is, if we know that the uncensored distribution is normal, we can uniquely determine the parameters from the censored distribution. This is often called **parametric identification**, as identification is restricted to a parametric class of distributions. In modern econometrics, this is generally viewed as a second-best solution, because identification has been achieved only through the use of an arbitrary and unverifiable parametric assumption.

A pessimistic conclusion might be that it is impossible to identify parameters of interest from censored data without parametric assumptions. Interestingly, this pessimism is unwarranted. It turns out that we can identify the quantiles q_α of F for $\alpha \leq \mathbb{P}[Y \leq \tau]$. For example, if 20% of the distribution is censored, we can identify all quantiles for $\alpha \in (0, 0.8)$. This is often called **nonparametric identification**, because the parameters are identified without restriction to a parametric class.

What we have learned from this little exercise is that in the context of censored data, moments can only be parametrically identified, while noncensored quantiles are nonparametrically identified. Part of the message is that a study of identification can help focus attention on what can be learned from the data distributions available.

2.33 TECHNICAL PROOFS*

Proof of Theorem 2.1 For convenience, assume that the variables have a joint density $f(y, x)$. Since $\mathbb{E}[Y \mid X]$ is a function of the random vector X only, to calculate its expectation, we integrate with respect to the density $f_X(x)$ of X, that is,

$$\mathbb{E}[\mathbb{E}[Y \mid X]] = \int_{\mathbb{R}^k} \mathbb{E}[Y \mid X] f_X(x)\, dx.$$

Substituting in (2.6) and noting that $f_{Y|X}(y \mid x) f_X(x) = f(y, x)$, we find that the above expression equals

$$\int_{\mathbb{R}^k} \left(\int_{\mathbb{R}} y f_{Y|X}(y \mid x)\, dy \right) f_X(x)\, dx = \int_{\mathbb{R}^k} \int_{\mathbb{R}} y f(y, x)\, dy dx = \mathbb{E}[Y]$$

which is the unconditional expectation of Y. ■

Proof of Theorem 2.2 Again assume that the variables have a joint density. It is useful to observe that

$$f(y \mid x_1, x_2) f(x_2 \mid x_1) = \frac{f(y, x_1, x_2)}{f(x_1, x_2)} \frac{f(x_1, x_2)}{f(x_1)} = f(y, x_2 \mid x_1) \tag{2.58}$$

the density of (Y, X_2) given X_1. Here we have abused notation and used a single symbol f to denote the various unconditional and conditional densities to reduce notational clutter.

Note that

$$\mathbb{E}[Y \mid X_1 = x_1, X_2 = x_2] = \int_{\mathbb{R}} y f(y \mid x_1, x_2)\, dy. \tag{2.59}$$

Integrating (2.59) with respect to the conditional density of X_2 given X_1, and applying (2.58), we find that

$$\begin{aligned}
\mathbb{E}\left[\mathbb{E}\left[Y \mid X_1, X_2\right] \mid X_1 = x_1\right] &= \int_{\mathbb{R}^{k_2}} \mathbb{E}\left[Y \mid X_1 = x_1, X_2 = x_2\right] f\left(x_2 \mid x_1\right) dx_2 \\
&= \int_{\mathbb{R}^{k_2}} \left(\int_{\mathbb{R}} y f\left(y \mid x_1, x_2\right) dy\right) f\left(x_2 \mid x_1\right) dx_2 \\
&= \int_{\mathbb{R}^{k_2}} \int_{\mathbb{R}} y f\left(y \mid x_1, x_2\right) f\left(x_2 \mid x_1\right) dy dx_2 \\
&= \int_{\mathbb{R}^{k_2}} \int_{\mathbb{R}} y f\left(y, x_2 \mid x_1\right) dy dx_2 \\
&= \mathbb{E}\left[Y \mid X_1 = x_1\right].
\end{aligned}$$

This implies $\mathbb{E}\left[\mathbb{E}\left[Y \mid X_1, X_2\right] \mid X_1\right] = \mathbb{E}\left[Y \mid X_1\right]$, as stated. ■

Proof of Theorem 2.3

$$\mathbb{E}\left[g(X) Y \mid X = x\right] = \int_{\mathbb{R}} g(x) y f_{Y \mid X}\left(y \mid x\right) dy = g(x) \int_{\mathbb{R}} y f_{Y \mid X}\left(y \mid x\right) dy = g(x) \mathbb{E}\left[Y \mid X = x\right]$$

This implies $\mathbb{E}\left[g(X) Y \mid X\right] = g(X) \mathbb{E}\left[Y \mid X\right]$, which is (2.7). Equation (2.8) follows by applying the simple law of iterated expectations (Theorem 2.1) to (2.7). ■

Proof of Theorem 2.4 Applying Minkowski's inequality (B.34) to $e = Y - m(X)$, we have

$$\left(\mathbb{E}\left|e\right|^r\right)^{1/r} = \left(\mathbb{E}\left|Y - m(X)\right|^r\right)^{1/r} \leq \left(\mathbb{E}\left|Y\right|^r\right)^{1/r} + \left(\mathbb{E}\left|m(X)\right|^r\right)^{1/r} < \infty,$$

where the two parts on the right-hand side are finite, because $\mathbb{E}\left|Y\right|^r < \infty$ by assumption, and $\mathbb{E}\left|m(X)\right|^r < \infty$ by the conditional expectation inequality (B.29). The fact that $\left(\mathbb{E}\left|e\right|^r\right)^{1/r} < \infty$ implies $\mathbb{E}\left|e\right|^r < \infty$. ■

Proof of Theorem 2.6 The assumption that $\mathbb{E}\left[Y^2\right] < \infty$ implies that all the conditional expectations mentioned below exist. Using the law of iterated expectations (Theorem 2.2) $\mathbb{E}\left[Y \mid X_1\right] = \mathbb{E}\left(\mathbb{E}\left[Y \mid X_1, X_2\right] \mid X_1\right)$ and the conditional Jensen's inequality (B.28), we have

$$\left(\mathbb{E}\left[Y \mid X_1\right]\right)^2 = \left(\mathbb{E}\left(\mathbb{E}\left[Y \mid X_1, X_2\right] \mid X_1\right)\right)^2 \leq \mathbb{E}\left[\left(\mathbb{E}\left[Y \mid X_1, X_2\right]\right)^2 \mid X_1\right].$$

Taking unconditional expectations, this implies

$$\mathbb{E}\left[\left(\mathbb{E}\left[Y \mid X_1\right]\right)^2\right] \leq \mathbb{E}\left[\left(\mathbb{E}\left[Y \mid X_1, X_2\right]\right)^2\right].$$

Similarly,

$$\left(\mathbb{E}\left[Y\right]\right)^2 \leq \mathbb{E}\left[\left(\mathbb{E}\left[Y \mid X_1\right]\right)^2\right] \leq \mathbb{E}\left[\left(\mathbb{E}\left[Y \mid X_1, X_2\right]\right)^2\right]. \tag{2.60}$$

The variables $Y, \mathbb{E}\left[Y \mid X_1\right]$, and $\mathbb{E}\left[Y \mid X_1, X_2\right]$ all have the same expectation $\mathbb{E}\left[Y\right]$, so the inequality (2.60) implies that the variances are ranked monotonically:

$$0 \leq \operatorname{var}\left(\mathbb{E}\left[Y \mid X_1\right]\right) \leq \operatorname{var}\left(\mathbb{E}\left[Y \mid X_1, X_2\right]\right). \tag{2.61}$$

Define $e = Y - \mathbb{E}\left[Y \mid X\right]$ and $u = \mathbb{E}\left[Y \mid X\right] - \mu$, so that we have the decomposition $Y - \mu = e + u$. Notice that $\mathbb{E}\left[e \mid X\right] = 0$ and u is a function of X. Thus by the conditioning theorem (Theorem 2.3), $\mathbb{E}\left[eu\right] = 0$, so e

and u are uncorrelated. It follows that

$$\operatorname{var}[Y]=\operatorname{var}[e]+\operatorname{var}[u]=\operatorname{var}[Y-\mathbb{E}[Y\mid X]]+\operatorname{var}[\mathbb{E}[Y\mid X]]. \tag{2.62}$$

The monotonicity of the variances of the conditional expectation (2.61) applied to the variance decomposition (2.62) implies the reverse monotonicity of the variances of the differences, completing the proof. ■

Proof of Theorem 2.9 For part 1, by the expectation inequality (B.30), (A.17), and Assumption 2.1,

$$\left\|\mathbb{E}\left[XX'\right]\right\| \leq \mathbb{E}\left\|XX'\right\| = \mathbb{E}\left\|X\right\|^2 < \infty.$$

Similarly, using the expectation inequality (B.30), the Cauchy-Schwarz inequality (B.32), and Assumption 2.1,

$$\|\mathbb{E}[XY]\| \leq \mathbb{E}\|XY\| \leq \left(\mathbb{E}\|X\|^2\right)^{1/2}\left(\mathbb{E}\left[Y^2\right]\right)^{1/2} < \infty.$$

Thus the moments $\mathbb{E}[XY]$ and $\mathbb{E}\left[XX'\right]$ are finite and well defined.

For part 2, the coefficient $\beta=\left(\mathbb{E}\left[XX'\right]\right)^{-1}\mathbb{E}[XY]$ is well defined, because $\left(\mathbb{E}\left[XX'\right]\right)^{-1}$ exists under Assumption 2.1.

Part 3 follows from Definition 2.5 and part 2.

For part 4, first note that

$$\begin{aligned}
\mathbb{E}\left[e^2\right] &= \mathbb{E}\left[\left(Y-X'\beta\right)^2\right] \\
&= \mathbb{E}\left[Y^2\right]-2\mathbb{E}\left[YX'\right]\beta+\beta'\mathbb{E}\left[XX'\right]\beta \\
&= \mathbb{E}\left[Y^2\right]-\mathbb{E}\left[YX'\right]\left(\mathbb{E}\left[XX'\right]\right)^{-1}\mathbb{E}[XY] \\
&\leq \mathbb{E}\left[Y^2\right] < \infty.
\end{aligned}$$

The first inequality holds because $\mathbb{E}\left[YX'\right]\left(\mathbb{E}\left[XX'\right]\right)^{-1}\mathbb{E}[XY]$ is a quadratic form and therefore necessarily nonnegative. Second, by the expectation inequality (B.30), the Cauchy-Schwarz inequality (B.32), and Assumption 2.1,

$$\|\mathbb{E}[Xe]\| \leq \mathbb{E}\|Xe\| = \left(\mathbb{E}\|X\|^2\right)^{1/2}\left(\mathbb{E}\left[e^2\right]\right)^{1/2} < \infty.$$

It follows that the expectation $\mathbb{E}[Xe]$ is finite and is 0 by the calculation (2.26).

For part 6, applying Minkowski's inequality (B.34) to $e=Y-X'\beta$ gives

$$\begin{aligned}
\left(\mathbb{E}|e|^r\right)^{1/r} &= \left(\mathbb{E}\left|Y-X'\beta\right|^r\right)^{1/r} \\
&\leq \left(\mathbb{E}|Y|^r\right)^{1/r}+\left(\mathbb{E}\left|X'\beta\right|^r\right)^{1/r} \\
&\leq \left(\mathbb{E}|Y|^r\right)^{1/r}+\left(\mathbb{E}\|X\|^r\right)^{1/r}\|\beta\| < \infty,
\end{aligned}$$

the final inequality by assumption. ■

2.34 EXERCISES

Exercise 2.1 Find $\mathbb{E}[\mathbb{E}[\mathbb{E}[Y\mid X_1,X_2,X_3]\mid X_1,X_2]\mid X_1]$.

Exercise 2.2 If $\mathbb{E}[Y\mid X]=a+bX$, find $\mathbb{E}[YX]$ as a function of moments of X.

Exercise 2.3 Prove Theorem 2.4.4 using the law of iterated expectations.

Exercise 2.4 Suppose that the random variables Y and X only take the values 0 and 1, and they have the following joint probability distribution:

	$X=0$	$X=1$
$Y=0$	.1	.2
$Y=1$	.4	.3

Find $\mathbb{E}[Y \mid X]$, $\mathbb{E}\left[Y^2 \mid X\right]$, and $\operatorname{var}[Y \mid X]$ for $X=0$ and $X=1$.

Exercise 2.5 Show that $\sigma^2(X)$ is the best predictor of e^2 given X:

(a) Write down the mean-squared error of a predictor $h(X)$ for e^2.

(b) What does it mean to be predicting e^2?

(c) Show that $\sigma^2(X)$ minimizes the mean-squared error and is thus the best predictor.

Exercise 2.6 Use $Y=m(X)+e$ to show that $\operatorname{var}[Y]=\operatorname{var}[m(X)]+\sigma^2$.

Exercise 2.7 Show that the conditional variance can be written as $\sigma^2(X)=\mathbb{E}\left[Y^2 \mid X\right]-(\mathbb{E}[Y \mid X])^2$.

Exercise 2.8 Suppose that Y is discrete valued, taking values only on the nonnegative integers, and the conditional distribution of Y given $X=x$ is Poisson:

$$\mathbb{P}\left[Y=j \mid X=x\right]=\frac{\exp\left(-x'\beta\right)\left(x'\beta\right)^j}{j!}, \qquad j=0,1,2,\ldots.$$

Compute $\mathbb{E}[Y \mid X]$ and $\operatorname{var}[Y \mid X]$. Does this justify a linear regression model of the form $Y=X'\beta+e$?

Hint: If $\mathbb{P}\left[Y=j\right]=\dfrac{\exp(-\lambda)\lambda^j}{j!}$, then $\mathbb{E}[Y]=\lambda$, and $\operatorname{var}[Y]=\lambda$.

Exercise 2.9 Suppose you have two regressors: X_1 is binary (takes values 0 and 1), and X_2 is categorical with three categories (A, B, C). Write $\mathbb{E}[Y \mid X_1, X_2]$ as a linear regression.

Exercise 2.10 True or False. If $Y=X\beta+e$, $X \in \mathbb{R}$, and $\mathbb{E}[e \mid X]=0$, then $\mathbb{E}\left[X^2 e\right]=0$.

Exercise 2.11 True or False. If $Y=X\beta+e$, $X \in \mathbb{R}$, and $\mathbb{E}[Xe]=0$, then $\mathbb{E}\left[X^2 e\right]=0$.

Exercise 2.12 True or False. If $Y=X'\beta+e$ and $\mathbb{E}[e \mid X]=0$, then e is independent of X.

Exercise 2.13 True or False. If $Y=X'\beta+e$ and $\mathbb{E}[Xe]=0$, then $\mathbb{E}[e \mid X]=0$.

Exercise 2.14 True or False. If $Y=X'\beta+e$, $\mathbb{E}[e \mid X]=0$, and $\mathbb{E}\left[e^2 \mid X\right]=\sigma^2$, then e is independent of X.

Exercise 2.15 Consider the intercept-only model $Y=\alpha+e$ with α the best linear predictor. Show that $\alpha=\mathbb{E}[Y]$.

Exercise 2.16 Let X and Y have the joint density $f(x,y) = \frac{3}{2}\left(x^2 + y^2\right)$ on $0 \le x \le 1$, $0 \le y \le 1$. Compute the coefficients of the best linear predictor $Y = \alpha + \beta X + e$. Compute the conditional expectation $m(x) = \mathbb{E}[Y \mid X = x]$. Are the best linear predictor and conditional expectation different?

Exercise 2.17 Let X be a random variable with $\mu = \mathbb{E}[X]$ and $\sigma^2 = \operatorname{var}[X]$. Define

$$g\left(x, \mu, \sigma^2\right) = \begin{pmatrix} x - \mu \\ (x - \mu)^2 - \sigma^2 \end{pmatrix}.$$

Show that $\mathbb{E}\left[g(X, m, s)\right] = 0$ if and only if $m = \mu$ and $s = \sigma^2$.

Exercise 2.18 Suppose that $X = (1, X_2, X_3)$, where $X_3 = \alpha_1 + \alpha_2 X_2$ is a linear function of X_2.

(a) Show that $\boldsymbol{Q}_{XX} = \mathbb{E}\left[XX'\right]$ is not invertible.

(b) Use a linear transformation of X to find an expression for the best linear predictor of Y given X. (Be explicit, do not just use the generalized inverse formula.)

Exercise 2.19 Show (2.47)–(2.48), namely, that for

$$d(\beta) = \mathbb{E}\left[\left(m(X) - X'\beta\right)^2\right]$$

then

$$\beta = \underset{b \in \mathbb{R}^k}{\operatorname{argmin}}\, d(b) = \left(\mathbb{E}\left[XX'\right]\right)^{-1} \mathbb{E}\left[Xm(X)\right] = \left(\mathbb{E}\left[XX'\right]\right)^{-1} \mathbb{E}\left[XY\right].$$

Hint: To show $\mathbb{E}[Xm(X)] = \mathbb{E}[XY]$, use the law of iterated expectations.

Exercise 2.20 Verify that (2.57) holds with $m(X)$ defined in (2.6) when (Y, X) have a joint density $f(y, x)$.

Exercise 2.21 Consider the short and long projections

$$Y = X\gamma_1 + e$$
$$Y = X\beta_1 + X^2\beta_2 + u.$$

(a) Under what condition does $\gamma_1 = \beta_1$?

(b) Take the long projection to be $Y = X\theta_1 + X^3\theta_2 + v$. Is there a condition under which $\gamma_1 = \theta_1$?

Exercise 2.22 Take the homoskedastic model

$$\begin{aligned} Y &= X_1'\beta_1 + X_2'\beta_2 + e \\ \mathbb{E}\left[e \mid X_1, X_2\right] &= 0 \\ \mathbb{E}\left[e^2 \mid X_1, X_2\right] &= \sigma^2 \\ \mathbb{E}\left[X_2 \mid X_1\right] &= \Gamma X_1. \end{aligned}$$

Assume $\Gamma \neq 0$. Suppose the parameter β_1 is of interest. We know that the exclusion of X_2 creates omited variable bias in the projection coefficient on X_2. It also changes the equation error. The question is: What is the effect on the homoskedasticity property of the induced equation error? Does the exclusion of X_2 induce heteroskedasticity or not? Be specific.

CHAPTER 3

THE ALGEBRA OF LEAST SQUARES

3.1 INTRODUCTION

In this chapter, we introduce the popular least squares estimator. Most of the discussion will be algebraic, with questions of distribution and inference deferred to later chapters.

3.2 SAMPLES

In Section 2.18, we derived and discussed the best linear predictor of Y given X for a pair of random variables $(Y,X) \in \mathbb{R} \times \mathbb{R}^k$ and called this predictor the linear projection model. We are now interested in estimating the parameters of this model, in particular, the projection coefficient

$$\beta = \left(\mathbb{E}\left[XX'\right]\right)^{-1} \mathbb{E}\left[XY\right]. \tag{3.1}$$

We can estimate β from samples which include joint measurements of (Y,X). For example, supposing we are interested in estimating a wage equation, we would use a dataset with observations on wages (or weekly earnings), education, experience (or age), and demographic characteristics (gender, race, location). One possible dataset is the Current Population Survey (CPS), a survey of U.S. households which includes questions on employment, income, education, and demographic characteristics.

Notationally we wish to distinguish observations (realizations) from the underlying random variables. The random variables are (Y,X). The observations are (Y_i, X_i). From the vantage of the researcher, the latter are numbers. From the vantage of statistical theory, we view them as realizations of random variables. For individual observations, we append a subscript i which runs from 1 to n, thus the ith observation is (Y_i, X_i). The number n is the sample size. The **dataset** or **sample** is $\{(Y_i, X_i) : i = 1, \ldots, n\}$.

From the viewpoint of empirical analysis, a dataset is an array of numbers. It is typically organized as a table in which each column is a variable and each row is an observation. For empirical analysis the dataset is fixed in the sense that they are numbers presented to the researcher. For statistical analysis we view the dataset as random, or more precisely, as a realization of a random process.

The individual observations could be draws from a common (homogeneous) distribution or draws from heterogeneous distributions. The simplest approach is to assume homogeneity—the observations are realizations from an identical underlying population F.

Assumption 3.1 The variables $\{(Y_1, X_1), \ldots, (Y_i, X_i), \ldots, (Y_n, X_n)\}$ are **identically distributed**; they are draws from a common distribution F.

This assumption does not need to be viewed as literally true. Instead it is a useful modeling device to ensure that parameters such as β are well defined. This assumption should be interpreted as how we view an observation a priori, before we actually observe it. If I tell you that we have a sample with $n = 59$ observations set in no particular order, then it makes sense to view two observations (say, 17 and 58) as draws from the same distribution. We have no reason to expect anything special about either observation.

In econometric theory we refer to the underlying common distribution F as the **population**. Some authors prefer the label **data-generating process**. You can think of it as a theoretical concept or an infinitely large potential population. In contrast, we refer to the observations available to us $\{(Y_i, X_i) : i = 1, \dots, n\}$ as the **sample** or **dataset**. In some contexts, the dataset consists of all potential observations; for example, administrative tax records may contain every single taxpayer in a political unit. Even in this case, we can view the observations as if they were random draws from an underlying infinitely large population, as this will allow us to apply the tools of statistical theory.

The linear projection model applies to the random variables (Y, X). This is the probability model described in Section 2.18. The model is

$$Y = X'\beta + e \tag{3.2}$$

where the linear projection coefficient β is defined as

$$\beta = \underset{b \in \mathbb{R}^k}{\operatorname{argmin}}\, S(b) \tag{3.3}$$

which is the minimizer of the expected squared error

$$S(\beta) = \mathbb{E}\left[\left(Y - X'\beta\right)^2\right]. \tag{3.4}$$

The coefficient has the explicit solution (3.1).

3.3 MOMENT ESTIMATORS

We want to estimate the coefficient β defined in (3.1) from the sample of observations. Notice that β is written as a function of certain population expectations. In this context, an appropriate estimator is the same function of the sample moments. Let's examine this in detail.

To start, suppose that we are interested in the population mean μ of a random variable Y with distribution function F

$$\mu = \mathbb{E}[Y] = \int_{-\infty}^{\infty} y\,dF(y). \tag{3.5}$$

The expectation μ is a function of the distribution F. To estimate μ given n random variables Y_i from F, a natural estimator is the sample mean

$$\widehat{\mu} = \overline{Y} = \frac{1}{n}\sum_{i=1}^{n} Y_i.$$

Notice that we have written this using two types of notation. The notation $\overline{Y}$ with the bar on top is conventional for a sample mean. The notation $\widehat{\mu}$ with the hat "∧" is conventional in econometrics to denote an estimator of the parameter μ. In this case, $\overline{Y}$ is the estimator of μ, so $\widehat{\mu}$ and $\overline{Y}$ are the same. The sample mean $\overline{Y}$ can be viewed as the natural analog of the population mean (3.5), because $\overline{Y}$ equals the expectation (3.5) with respect to the empirical distribution—the discrete distribution which puts weight $1/n$ on each observation Y_i. There are other justifications for $\overline{Y}$ as an estimator for μ. We will defer these discussions for now. Suffice it to say that $\overline{Y}$ is the conventional estimator.

Now suppose that we are interested in a set of population expectations of possibly nonlinear functions of a random vector Y, say, $\mu = \mathbb{E}[h(Y)]$. For example, we may be interested in the first two moments of Y, $\mathbb{E}[Y]$ and $\mathbb{E}\left[Y^2\right]$. In this case, the natural estimator is the vector of sample means:

$$\widehat{\mu} = \frac{1}{n}\sum_{i=1}^{n} h(Y_i).$$

We call $\widehat{\mu}$ the **moment estimator** for μ. For example, if $h(y) = (y, y^2)'$, then $\widehat{\mu}_1 = n^{-1}\sum_{i=1}^{n} Y_i$ and $\widehat{\mu}_2 = n^{-1}\sum_{i=1}^{n} Y_i^2$.

Now suppose that we are interested in a nonlinear function of a set of moments. For example, consider the variance of Y:

$$\sigma^2 = \operatorname{var}[Y] = \mathbb{E}\left[Y^2\right] - (\mathbb{E}[Y])^2.$$

In general, many parameters of interest can be written as a function of moments of Y. Notationally, $\beta = g(\mu)$ and $\mu = \mathbb{E}[h(Y)]$. Here, the Y are the random variables, $h(Y)$ are functions (transformations) of the random variables, and μ is the expectation of these functions. β is the parameter of interest, and is the (nonlinear) function $g(\cdot)$ of these expectations.

In this context, a natural estimator of β is obtained by replacing μ with $\widehat{\mu}$. Thus $\widehat{\beta} = g(\widehat{\mu})$. The estimator $\widehat{\beta}$ is often called a **plug-in estimator**. We also call $\widehat{\beta}$ a moment, or moment-based, estimator of β, since it is a natural extension of the moment estimator $\widehat{\mu}$.

Take the example of the variance $\sigma^2 = \operatorname{var}[Y]$. Its moment estimator is

$$\widehat{\sigma}^2 = \widehat{\mu}_2 - \widehat{\mu}_1^2 = \frac{1}{n}\sum_{i=1}^{n} Y_i^2 - \left(\frac{1}{n}\sum_{i=1}^{n} Y_i\right)^2.$$

This is not the only possible estimator for σ^2 (there is also the well-known bias-corrected estimator), but $\widehat{\sigma}^2$ is a straightforward and simple choice.

3.4 LEAST SQUARES ESTIMATOR

The linear projection coefficient β is defined in (3.3) as the minimizer of the expected squared error $S(\beta)$ defined in (3.4). For a given β, the expected squared error is the expectation of the squared error $\left(Y - X'\beta\right)^2$. The moment estimator of $S(\beta)$ is the sample average:

$$\widehat{S}(\beta) = \frac{1}{n}\sum_{i=1}^{n}\left(Y_i - X_i'\beta\right)^2 = \frac{1}{n}\mathrm{SSE}(\beta) \tag{3.6}$$

where

$$\mathrm{SSE}(\beta) = \sum_{i=1}^{n}\left(Y_i - X_i'\beta\right)^2$$

is called the **sum of squared errors** function.

Since $\widehat{S}(\beta)$ is a sample average, we can interpret it as an estimator of the expected squared error $S(\beta)$. Examining $\widehat{S}(\beta)$ as a function of β is informative about how $S(\beta)$ varies with β. Since the projection coefficient minimizes $S(\beta)$, an analog estimator minimizes (3.6).

We define the estimator $\widehat{\beta}$ as the minimizer of $\widehat{S}(\beta)$.

Definition 3.1 The **least squares estimator** is $\widehat{\beta} = \underset{\beta\in\mathbb{R}^k}{\operatorname{argmin}}\, \widehat{S}(\beta)$, where $\widehat{S}(\beta) = \frac{1}{n}\sum_{i=1}^{n}\left(Y_i - X_i'\beta\right)^2$.

As $\widehat{S}(\beta)$ is a scale multiple of $\mathrm{SSE}(\beta)$, we may equivalently define $\widehat{\beta}$ as the minimizer of $\mathrm{SSE}(\beta)$. Hence $\widehat{\beta}$ is commonly called the **least squares** estimator of β. The estimator is also commonly refered to as the **ordinary least squares (OLS)** estimator. For the origin of this label, see the historical discussion on Adrien-Marie Legendre near the end of Section 3.6. Here, as is common in econometrics, we put a hat "∧" over the parameter β to indicate that $\widehat{\beta}$ is a sample estimator of β. This convention is helpful. Just by seeing the symbol $\widehat{\beta}$, we can immediately interpret it as an estimator (because of the hat) of the parameter β. Sometimes when we want to be explicit about the estimation method, we will write $\widehat{\beta}_{\mathrm{ols}}$ to signify that it is the OLS estimator. It is also common to see the notation $\widehat{\beta}_n$, where the subscript "n" indicates that the estimator depends on the sample size n.

It is important to understand the distinction between population parameters (such as β) and sample estimators (such as $\widehat{\beta}$). The population parameter β is a nonrandom feature of the population, while the sample estimator $\widehat{\beta}$ is a random feature of a random sample. β is fixed, while $\widehat{\beta}$ varies across samples.

3.5 SOLVING FOR LEAST SQUARES WITH ONE REGRESSOR

For simplicity, we start by considering the case $k = 1$, so that there is a scalar regressor X and a scalar coefficient β. To illustrate, Figure 3.1(a) displays a scatter plot[1] of 20 pairs (Y_i, X_i).

The sum of squared errors $\mathrm{SSE}(\beta)$ is a function of β. Given β, we calculate the "error" $Y_i - X_i\beta$ by taking the vertical distance between Y_i and $X_i\beta$. This can be seen in Figure 3.1(a) by the vertical lines which connect the observations to the straight line. These vertical lines are the errors $Y_i - X_i\beta$. The sum of squared errors is the sum of the 20 squared lengths.

The sum of squared errors is the function

$$\mathrm{SSE}(\beta) = \sum_{i=1}^{n}(Y_i - X_i\beta)^2 = \left(\sum_{i=1}^{n} Y_i^2\right) - 2\beta\left(\sum_{i=1}^{n} X_iY_i\right) + \beta^2\left(\sum_{i=1}^{n} X_i^2\right).$$

This is a quadratic function of β. The sum of squared errors function is displayed in Figure 3.1(b) over the range $[2, 4]$. The coefficient β ranges along the x-axis, and $\mathrm{SSE}(\beta)$ as a function of β is displayed on the y-axis.

The OLS estimator $\widehat{\beta}$ minimizes this function. From elementary algebra, we know that the minimizer of the quadratic function $a - 2bx + cx^2$ is $x = b/c$. Thus the minimizer of $\mathrm{SSE}(\beta)$ is

$$\widehat{\beta} = \frac{\sum_{i=1}^{n} X_iY_i}{\sum_{i=1}^{n} X_i^2}. \tag{3.7}$$

[1]The observations were generated by simulation as $X \sim U[0, 1]$ and $Y \sim \mathrm{N}[3X, 1]$.

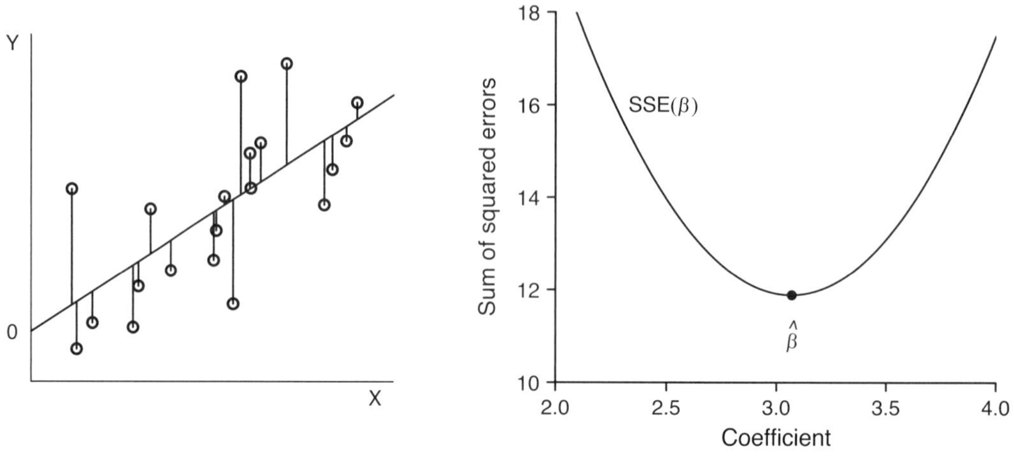

(a) Deviation from fitted line (b) Sum of squared errors function

FIGURE 3.1 Regression with one regressor

For example, the minimizer of the sum of squared errors function displayed in Figure 3.1(b) is $\widehat{\beta}=3.07$, as marked.

The intercept-only model is the special case $X_i=1$. In this case, we find

$$\widehat{\beta}=\frac{\sum_{i=1}^{n} 1Y_i}{\sum_{i=1}^{n} 1^2}=\frac{1}{n}\sum_{i=1}^{n} Y_i=\overline{Y} \tag{3.8}$$

the sample mean of Y_i. Here, as is common, we put a bar over Y to indicate that the quantity is a sample mean. This shows that the OLS estimator in the intercept-only model is the sample mean.

Technically, the estimator $\widehat{\beta}$ in (3.7) only exists if the denominator is nonzero. Since it is a sum of squares, it is necessarily nonnegative. Thus $\widehat{\beta}$ exists if $\sum_{i=1}^{n} X_i^2>0$.

3.6 SOLVING FOR LEAST SQUARES WITH MULTIPLE REGRESSORS

We now consider the case with $k>1$ so that the coefficient $\beta\in\mathbb{R}^k$ is a vector. To illustrate, Figure 3.2 displays a scatter plot of 100 triples (Y_i, X_{1i}, X_{2i}). The regression function $x'\beta=x_1\beta_1+x_2\beta_2$ is a two-dimensional surface and is shown as the plane in Figure 3.2.

The $\mathrm{SSE}(\beta)$ is a function of the vector β. For any β, the error $Y_i-X_i'\beta$ is the vertical distance between Y_i and $X_i'\beta$. These distances are depicted in Figure 3.2 by the vertical lines which connect the observations to the plane. As in the single regressor case, these vertical lines are the errors $e_i=Y_i-X_i'\beta$. The sum of squared errors is the sum of the 100 squared lengths.

The sum of squared errors can be written as

$$\mathrm{SSE}(\beta)=\sum_{i=1}^{n} Y_i^2-2\beta'\sum_{i=1}^{n} X_iY_i+\beta'\sum_{i=1}^{n} X_iX_i'\beta.$$

As in the single regressor case, this is a quadratic function in β. The difference is that in the multiple regressor case, it is a vector-valued quadratic function. To visualize the sum of squared errors function, Figure 3.3(a)

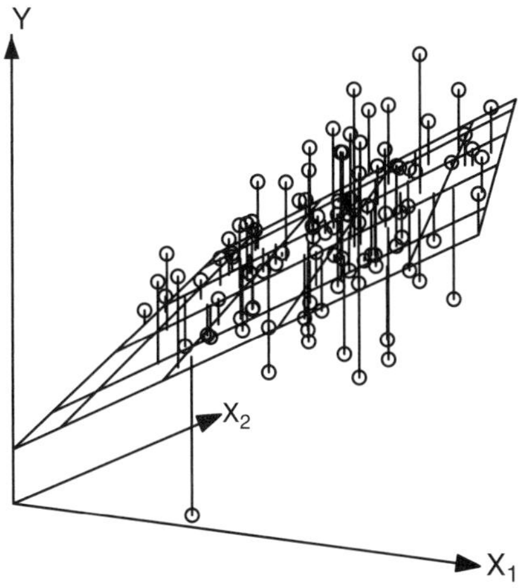

FIGURE 3.2 Regression with two variables

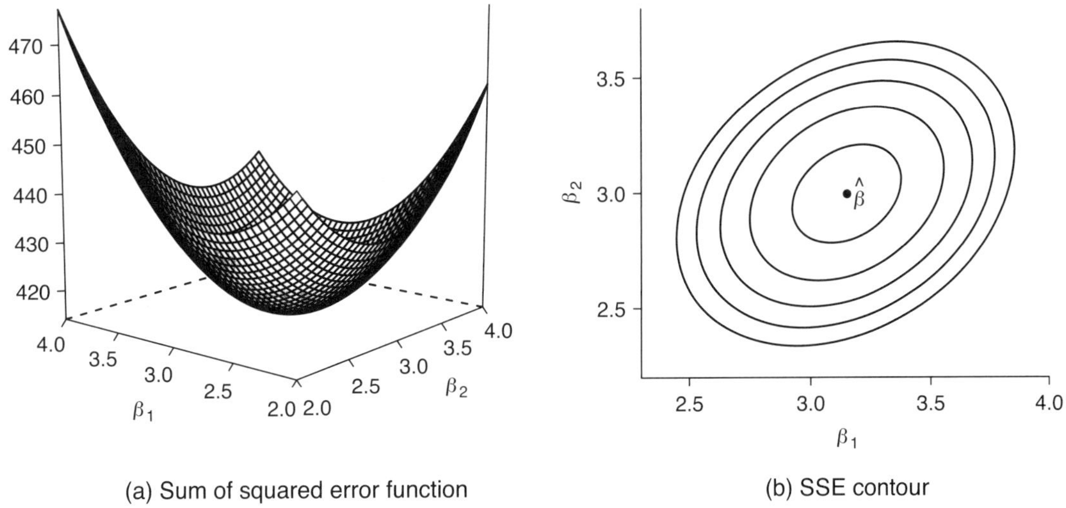

FIGURE 3.3 SSE with two regressors

displays SSE(β). Another way to visualize a three-dimensional surface is by a contour plot. A contour plot of the same SSE(β) function is shown in Figure 3.3(b). The contour lines are points in the (β_1, β_2) space where SSE(β) takes the same value. The contour lines are elliptical, because SSE(β) is quadratic.

The least squares estimator $\widehat{\beta}$ minimizes SSE(β). A simple way to find the minimum is by solving the first-order conditions. The latter are

$$0 = \frac{\partial}{\partial \beta} \text{SSE}(\widehat{\beta}) = -2 \sum_{i=1}^{n} X_i Y_i + 2 \sum_{i=1}^{n} X_i X_i' \widehat{\beta}. \tag{3.9}$$

I have written this using a single expression, but it is actually a system of k equations with k unknowns (the elements of $\widehat{\beta}$).

The solution for $\widehat{\beta}$ may be found by solving the system of k equations in (3.9). We can write this solution compactly using matrix algebra. Dividing (3.9) by 2, we obtain

$$\sum_{i=1}^{n} X_i X_i' \widehat{\beta} = \sum_{i=1}^{n} X_i Y_i. \tag{3.10}$$

This is a system of equations of the form $\boldsymbol{A}\boldsymbol{b} = \boldsymbol{c}$, where $\boldsymbol{A}$ is $k \times k$ and $\boldsymbol{b}$ and $\boldsymbol{c}$ are $k \times 1$. The solution is $\boldsymbol{b} = \boldsymbol{A}^{-1}\boldsymbol{c}$ and can be obtained by pre-multiplying $\boldsymbol{A}\boldsymbol{b} = \boldsymbol{c}$ by $\boldsymbol{A}^{-1}$ and using the matrix inverse property $\boldsymbol{A}^{-1}\boldsymbol{A} = \boldsymbol{I}_k$. Applied to (3.10), we find an explicit formula for the least squares estimator:

$$\widehat{\beta} = \left(\sum_{i=1}^{n} X_i X_i' \right)^{-1} \left(\sum_{i=1}^{n} X_i Y_i \right). \tag{3.11}$$

This is the natural estimator of the best linear projection coefficient β defined in (3.3) and could also be called the **linear projection estimator**.

Recall that we claimed that $\widehat{\beta}$ in (3.11) is the minimizer of $\mathrm{SSE}(\beta)$ and found it by solving the first-order conditions. To be thorough, we should verify the second-order conditions. We calculate that

$$\frac{\partial^2}{\partial \beta \partial \beta'} \mathrm{SSE}(\beta) = 2 \sum_{i=1}^{n} X_i X_i'$$

which is a positive semi-definite matrix. If actually positive definite, then the second-order condition for minimization is satisfied, in which case, $\widehat{\beta}$ is the unique minimizer of $\mathrm{SSE}(\beta)$.

Returning to the example $\mathrm{SSE}(\beta)$ displayed in Figure 3.3, the least squares estimator $\widehat{\beta}$ is the the pair $(\widehat{\beta}_1, \widehat{\beta}_2)$ which minimize this function; visually it is the low spot in the three-dimensional graph and is marked in Figure 3.3(b) as the center point of the contour plots.

Consider equation (3.11) and suppose that $k = 1$. In this case, X_i is scalar, so $X_i X_i' = X_i^2$. Then (3.11) simplifies to the expression (3.7) previously derived. The expression (3.11) is a notationally simple generalization but requires careful attention to vector and matrix manipulations.

Alternatively, equation (3.1) writes the projection coefficient β as an explicit function of the population moments $\boldsymbol{Q}_{XY}$ and $\boldsymbol{Q}_{XX}$. Their moment estimators are the sample moments

$$\widehat{\boldsymbol{Q}}_{XY} = \frac{1}{n} \sum_{i=1}^{n} X_i Y_i$$

$$\widehat{\boldsymbol{Q}}_{XX} = \frac{1}{n} \sum_{i=1}^{n} X_i X_i'.$$

The moment estimator of β replaces the population moments in (3.1) with the sample moments:

$$\begin{aligned}
\widehat{\beta} &= \widehat{\boldsymbol{Q}}_{XX}^{-1} \widehat{\boldsymbol{Q}}_{XY} \\
&= \left(\frac{1}{n} \sum_{i=1}^{n} X_i X_i' \right)^{-1} \left(\frac{1}{n} \sum_{i=1}^{n} X_i Y_i \right) \\
&= \left(\sum_{i=1}^{n} X_i X_i' \right)^{-1} \left(\sum_{i=1}^{n} X_i Y_i \right)
\end{aligned}$$

which is identical to (3.11).

Technically, the estimator $\widehat{\beta}$ is unique and equals (3.11) only if the inverted matrix is actually invertible, which holds if (and only if) this matrix is positive definite. This excludes the case that X_i contains redundant regressors. This will be discussed further in Section 3.24.

Theorem 3.1 If $\sum_{i=1}^n X_i X_i' > 0$, the least squares estimator is unique and equals

$$\widehat{\beta} = \left(\sum_{i=1}^n X_i X_i'\right)^{-1} \left(\sum_{i=1}^n X_i Y_i\right).$$

Adrien-Marie Legendre

The method of least squares was published in 1805 by the French mathematician Adrien-Marie Legendre (1752–1833). Legendre proposed least squares as a solution to the algebraic problem of solving a system of equations when the number of equations exceeded the number of unknowns. This was a vexing and common problem in astronomical measurement. As viewed by Legendre, (3.2) is a set of n equations with k unknowns. As the equations cannot be solved exactly, Legendre's goal was to select β to make the set of errors as small as possible. He proposed the sum of squared error criterion and derived the algebraic solution presented in the text. As he noted, the first-order conditions (3.9) form a system of k equations with k unknowns which can be solved by "ordinary" methods. Hence the method became known as **Ordinary Least Squares** and to this day, we still use the abbreviation OLS to refer to Legendre's estimation method.

3.7 ILLUSTRATION

We illustrate the least squares estimator in practice with the dataset used to calculate the estimates reported in Chapter 2. This is the March 2009 Current Population Survey, which has extensive information on the U.S. population. This dataset is described in more detail in Section 3.22. For this illustration, we use the subsample of married (spouse present) Black female wage earners with 12 years potential work experience. This subsample has 20 observations.[2]

Table 3.1 displays the observations for reference. Each row is an individual observation which consists of the data for an individual person. The columns correspond to the variables (measurements) for the individuals. The second column is the reported *wage* (total annual earnings divided by hours worked). The third column is the natural logarithm of the wage. The fourth column is years of *education*. The fifth and six columns are further transformations, specifically the square of *education* and the product of *education* and log(*wage*). The bottom row lists the sums of the elements in that column.

Putting the variables into the standard regression notation, let Y_i be log(*wage*) and X_i be years of *education* and an intercept. Then from the column sums in Table 3.1, we have

$$\sum_{i=1}^n X_i Y_i = \begin{pmatrix} 995.86 \\ 62.64 \end{pmatrix}$$

[2]This sample was selected specifically so that it has a small number of observations, facilitating exposition.

Table 3.1
Observations from CPS dataset

Observation	Wage	Log(Wage)	Education	Education^2	Education × Log(Wage)
1	37.93	3.64	18	324	65.44
2	40.87	3.71	18	324	66.79
3	14.18	2.65	13	169	34.48
4	16.83	2.82	16	256	45.17
5	33.17	3.50	16	256	56.03
6	29.81	3.39	18	324	61.11
7	54.62	4.00	16	256	64.00
8	43.08	3.76	18	324	67.73
9	14.42	2.67	12	144	32.03
10	14.90	2.70	16	256	43.23
11	21.63	3.07	18	324	55.44
12	11.09	2.41	16	256	38.50
13	10.00	2.30	13	169	29.93
14	31.73	3.46	14	196	48.40
15	11.06	2.40	12	144	28.84
16	18.75	2.93	16	256	46.90
17	27.35	3.31	14	196	46.32
18	24.04	3.18	16	256	50.76
19	36.06	3.59	18	324	64.53
20	23.08	3.14	16	256	50.22
Sum	515	62.64	314	5010	995.86

and

$$\sum_{i=1}^{n} X_i X_i' = \begin{pmatrix} 5010 & 314 \\ 314 & 20 \end{pmatrix}.$$

Taking the inverse, we obtain

$$\left(\sum_{i=1}^{n} X_i X_i'\right)^{-1} = \begin{pmatrix} 0.0125 & -0.196 \\ -0.196 & 3.124 \end{pmatrix}.$$

Thus by matrix multiplication

$$\widehat{\beta} = \begin{pmatrix} 0.0125 & -0.196 \\ -0.196 & 3.124 \end{pmatrix} \begin{pmatrix} 995.86 \\ 62.64 \end{pmatrix} = \begin{pmatrix} 0.155 \\ 0.698 \end{pmatrix}.$$

In practice, the regression estimates $\widehat{\beta}$ are computed by computer software without the user taking the explicit steps listed above. However, it is useful to understand that the least squares estimator can be calculated by simple algebraic operations. If your data are in a spreadsheet similar to Table 3.1, then the listed transformations (logarithm, squares, cross-products, column sums) can be computed by spreadsheet operations. $\widehat{\beta}$ could then be calculated by matrix inversion and multiplication. Once again, this is rarely done by applied economists, because computer software is available to facilitate the process.

We often write the estimated equation using the format

$$\widehat{\log(wage)} = 0.155\ education + 0.698. \tag{3.12}$$

An interpretation of the estimated equation is that each year of education is associated with a 16% increase in mean wages.

Another use of the estimated equation (3.12) is for prediction. Suppose one individual has 12 years of education and a second has 16. Using (3.12), we find that the first's expected log wage is

$$\widehat{\log(wage)} = 0.155 \times 12 + 0.698 = 2.56$$

and for the second

$$\widehat{\log(wage)} = 0.155 \times 16 + 0.698 = 3.18.$$

Equation (3.12) is called a **bivariate regression** as there are two variables. It is also called a **simple regression** as there is a single regressor. A **multiple regression** has two or more regressors and allows a more detailed investigation. Let's take an example similar to (3.12) but include all levels of experience. This time we use the subsample of single (never married) Asian men which has 268 observations. Including as regressors the years of potential work experience (*experience*) and its square ($experience^2/100$) (we divide by 100 to simplify reporting), we obtain the estimates

$$\widehat{\log(wage)} = 0.143\ education + 0.036\ experience - 0.071\ experience^2/100 + 0.575. \tag{3.13}$$

These estimates suggest a 14% increase in mean wages per year of education, holding experience constant.

3.8 LEAST SQUARES RESIDUALS

As a by-product of estimation, we define the **fitted value** $\widehat{Y}_i = X_i'\widehat{\beta}$ and the **residual**

$$\widehat{e}_i = Y_i - \widehat{Y}_i = Y_i - X_i'\widehat{\beta}. \tag{3.14}$$

Sometimes $\widehat{Y}_i$ is called the predicted value, but this is a misleading label. The fitted value $\widehat{Y}_i$ is a function of the entire sample, including Y_i, and thus cannot be interpreted as a valid prediction of Y_i. It is thus more accurate to describe $\widehat{Y}_i$ as a *fitted* rather than a *predicted* value.

Note that $Y_i = \widehat{Y}_i + \widehat{e}_i$, and

$$Y_i = X_i'\widehat{\beta} + \widehat{e}_i. \tag{3.15}$$

We make a distinction between the **error** e_i and the **residual** $\widehat{e}_i$. The error e_i is unobservable, while the residual $\widehat{e}_i$ is an estimator. These two variables are frequently mislabeled, which can cause confusion.

Equation (3.9) implies that

$$\sum_{i=1}^{n} X_i\widehat{e}_i = 0. \tag{3.16}$$

To see this by a direct calculation, use (3.14) and (3.11):

$$\begin{aligned}
\sum_{i=1}^{n} X_i\widehat{e}_i &= \sum_{i=1}^{n} X_i\left(Y_i - X_i'\widehat{\beta}\right) \\
&= \sum_{i=1}^{n} X_iY_i - \sum_{i=1}^{n} X_iX_i'\widehat{\beta}
\end{aligned}$$

$$= \sum_{i=1}^{n} X_i Y_i - \sum_{i=1}^{n} X_i X_i' \left(\sum_{i=1}^{n} X_i X_i' \right)^{-1} \left(\sum_{i=1}^{n} X_i Y_i \right)$$

$$= \sum_{i=1}^{n} X_i Y_i - \sum_{i=1}^{n} X_i Y_i = 0.$$

When X_i contains a constant, an implication of (3.16) is

$$\frac{1}{n} \sum_{i=1}^{n} \widehat{e}_i = 0. \tag{3.17}$$

Thus the residuals have a sample mean of 0 and the sample correlation between the regressors and the residual is 0. These are algebraic results and hold true for all linear regression estimates.

3.9 DEMEANED REGRESSORS

Sometimes it is useful to separate the constant from the other regressors and write the linear projection equation in the format

$$Y_i = X_i' \beta + \alpha + e_i$$

where α is the intercept, and X_i does not contain a constant. The least squares estimates and residuals can be written as $Y_i = X_i' \widehat{\beta} + \widehat{\alpha} + \widehat{e}_i$.

In this case, (3.16) can be written as the equation system

$$\sum_{i=1}^{n} \left(Y_i - X_i' \widehat{\beta} - \widehat{\alpha} \right) = 0$$

$$\sum_{i=1}^{n} X_i \left(Y_i - X_i' \widehat{\beta} - \widehat{\alpha} \right) = 0.$$

The first equation implies

$$\widehat{\alpha} = \overline{Y} - \overline{X}' \widehat{\beta}.$$

Subtracting from the second, we obtain

$$\sum_{i=1}^{n} X_i \left(\left(Y_i - \overline{Y} \right) - \left(X_i - \overline{X} \right)' \widehat{\beta} \right) = 0.$$

Solving for $\widehat{\beta}$, we find

$$\widehat{\beta} = \left(\sum_{i=1}^{n} X_i \left(X_i - \overline{X} \right)' \right)^{-1} \left(\sum_{i=1}^{n} X_i \left(Y_i - \overline{Y} \right) \right)$$

$$= \left(\sum_{i=1}^{n} \left(X_i - \overline{X} \right) \left(X_i - \overline{X} \right)' \right)^{-1} \left(\sum_{i=1}^{n} \left(X_i - \overline{X} \right) \left(Y_i - \overline{Y} \right) \right). \tag{3.18}$$

Thus the OLS estimator for the slope coefficients is OLS with demeaned data and no intercept.

The representation (3.18) is known as the demeaned formula for the least squares estimator.

3.10 MODEL IN MATRIX NOTATION

For many purposes, including computation, it is convenient to write the model and statistics in matrix notation. The n linear equations $Y_i = X_i'\beta + e_i$ make a system of n equations. We can stack these n equations together as

$$\begin{aligned} Y_1 &= X_1'\beta + e_1 \\ Y_2 &= X_2'\beta + e_2 \\ &\vdots \\ Y_n &= X_n'\beta + e_n. \end{aligned}$$

Define

$$\boldsymbol{Y} = \begin{pmatrix} Y_1 \\ Y_2 \\ \vdots \\ Y_n \end{pmatrix}, \qquad \boldsymbol{X} = \begin{pmatrix} X_1' \\ X_2' \\ \vdots \\ X_n' \end{pmatrix}, \qquad \boldsymbol{e} = \begin{pmatrix} e_1 \\ e_2 \\ \vdots \\ e_n \end{pmatrix}.$$

Observe that $\boldsymbol{Y}$ and $\boldsymbol{e}$ are $n \times 1$ vectors and $\boldsymbol{X}$ is an $n \times k$ matrix. The system of n equations can be compactly written in the single equation

$$\boldsymbol{Y} = \boldsymbol{X}\beta + \boldsymbol{e}. \tag{3.19}$$

Sample sums can be written in matrix notation. For example,

$$\begin{aligned} \sum_{i=1}^{n} X_i X_i' &= \boldsymbol{X}'\boldsymbol{X} \\ \sum_{i=1}^{n} X_i Y_i &= \boldsymbol{X}'\boldsymbol{Y}. \end{aligned}$$

Therefore the least squares estimator can be written as

$$\widehat{\beta} = \left(\boldsymbol{X}'\boldsymbol{X}\right)^{-1}\left(\boldsymbol{X}'\boldsymbol{Y}\right).$$

The matrix version of (3.15) and estimated version of (3.19) is

$$\boldsymbol{Y} = \boldsymbol{X}\widehat{\beta} + \widehat{\boldsymbol{e}}.$$

Equivalently, the residual vector is

$$\widehat{\boldsymbol{e}} = \boldsymbol{Y} - \boldsymbol{X}\widehat{\beta}.$$

Using the residual vector, we can write (3.16) as

$$\boldsymbol{X}'\widehat{\boldsymbol{e}} = 0.$$

It can also be useful to write the sum of squared error criterion as

$$\mathrm{SSE}(\beta) = (\boldsymbol{Y} - \boldsymbol{X}\beta)'(\boldsymbol{Y} - \boldsymbol{X}\beta).$$

Using matrix notation, we have simple expressions for most estimators. This is particularly convenient for computer programming, as most languages allow matrix notation and manipulation.

Theorem 3.2 Important Matrix Expressions

$$\widehat{\beta} = \left(X'X\right)^{-1}\left(X'Y\right)$$
$$\widehat{e} = Y - X\widehat{\beta}$$
$$X'\widehat{e} = 0.$$

Early Use of Matrices

The earliest known treatment of the use of matrix methods to solve simultaneous systems is found in Chapter 8 of the Chinese text *The Nine Chapters on the Mathematical Art*, written by several generations of scholars from the tenth to second century BCE.

3.11 PROJECTION MATRIX

Define the matrix

$$\boldsymbol{P} = \boldsymbol{X}\left(\boldsymbol{X}'\boldsymbol{X}\right)^{-1}\boldsymbol{X}'.$$

Observe that

$$\boldsymbol{P}\boldsymbol{X} = \boldsymbol{X}\left(\boldsymbol{X}'\boldsymbol{X}\right)^{-1}\boldsymbol{X}'\boldsymbol{X} = \boldsymbol{X}.$$

This is a property of a **projection matrix**. More generally, for any matrix $\boldsymbol{Z}$ which can be written as $\boldsymbol{Z} = \boldsymbol{X}\boldsymbol{\Gamma}$ for some matrix $\boldsymbol{\Gamma}$ (we say that $\boldsymbol{Z}$ lies in the **range space** of $\boldsymbol{X}$), then

$$\boldsymbol{P}\boldsymbol{Z} = \boldsymbol{P}\boldsymbol{X}\boldsymbol{\Gamma} = \boldsymbol{X}\left(\boldsymbol{X}'\boldsymbol{X}\right)^{-1}\boldsymbol{X}'\boldsymbol{X}\boldsymbol{\Gamma} = \boldsymbol{X}\boldsymbol{\Gamma} = \boldsymbol{Z}.$$

As an important example, if we partition the matrix $\boldsymbol{X}$ into two matrices $\boldsymbol{X}_1$ and $\boldsymbol{X}_2$ so that $\boldsymbol{X} = [\boldsymbol{X}_1 \quad \boldsymbol{X}_2]$, then $\boldsymbol{P}\boldsymbol{X}_1 = \boldsymbol{X}_1$. (See Exercise 3.7.)

The projection matrix $\boldsymbol{P}$ has the algebraic property that it is **idempotent**: $\boldsymbol{P}\boldsymbol{P} = \boldsymbol{P}$. (See Theorem 3.3.2 below.) For the general properties of projection matrices, see Appendix A, Section A.11.

The matrix $\boldsymbol{P}$ creates the fitted values in a least squares regression:

$$\boldsymbol{P}\boldsymbol{Y} = \boldsymbol{X}\left(\boldsymbol{X}'\boldsymbol{X}\right)^{-1}\boldsymbol{X}'\boldsymbol{Y} = \boldsymbol{X}\widehat{\beta} = \widehat{\boldsymbol{Y}}.$$

Because of this property, $\boldsymbol{P}$ is also known as the **hat matrix**.

A special example of a projection matrix occurs when $\boldsymbol{X} = \mathbf{1}_n$ is an n-vector of 1s. Then

$$\boldsymbol{P} = \mathbf{1}_n\left(\mathbf{1}_n'\mathbf{1}_n\right)^{-1}\mathbf{1}_n' = \frac{1}{n}\mathbf{1}_n\mathbf{1}_n'.$$

Note that in this case,

$$\boldsymbol{P}\boldsymbol{Y} = \mathbf{1}_n \left(\mathbf{1}_n'\mathbf{1}_n\right)^{-1}\mathbf{1}_n'\boldsymbol{Y} = \mathbf{1}_n\overline{Y}$$

creates an n-vector whose elements are the sample mean $\overline{Y}$.

The projection matrix $\boldsymbol{P}$ appears frequently in algebraic manipulations in least squares regression. The matrix has the following important properties.

Theorem 3.3 The projection matrix $\boldsymbol{P} = \boldsymbol{X}\left(\boldsymbol{X}'\boldsymbol{X}\right)^{-1}\boldsymbol{X}'$ for any full rank $n \times k$ $\boldsymbol{X}$ with $n \geq k$ has the following algebraic properties.

1. $\boldsymbol{P}$ is symmetric ($\boldsymbol{P}' = \boldsymbol{P}$).
2. $\boldsymbol{P}$ is idempotent ($\boldsymbol{P}\boldsymbol{P} = \boldsymbol{P}$).
3. $\operatorname{tr} \boldsymbol{P} = k$.
4. The eigenvalues of $\boldsymbol{P}$ are 1 and 0.
5. $\boldsymbol{P}$ has k eigenvalues equaling 1 and $n - k$ equaling 0.
6. $\operatorname{rank}(\boldsymbol{P}) = k$.

We close this section by proving the claims in Theorem 3.3. Part 1 holds because

$$\begin{aligned}
\boldsymbol{P}' &= \left(\boldsymbol{X}\left(\boldsymbol{X}'\boldsymbol{X}\right)^{-1}\boldsymbol{X}'\right)' \\
&= \left(\boldsymbol{X}'\right)'\left(\left(\boldsymbol{X}'\boldsymbol{X}\right)^{-1}\right)'\left(\boldsymbol{X}\right)' \\
&= \boldsymbol{X}\left(\left(\boldsymbol{X}'\boldsymbol{X}\right)'\right)^{-1}\boldsymbol{X}' \\
&= \boldsymbol{X}\left(\left(\boldsymbol{X}\right)'\left(\boldsymbol{X}'\right)'\right)^{-1}\boldsymbol{X}' = \boldsymbol{P}.
\end{aligned}$$

To establish part 2, the fact that $\boldsymbol{P}\boldsymbol{X} = \boldsymbol{X}$ implies that

$$\boldsymbol{P}\boldsymbol{P} = \boldsymbol{P}\boldsymbol{X}\left(\boldsymbol{X}'\boldsymbol{X}\right)^{-1}\boldsymbol{X}' = \boldsymbol{X}\left(\boldsymbol{X}'\boldsymbol{X}\right)^{-1}\boldsymbol{X}' = \boldsymbol{P}$$

as claimed. For part 3,

$$\operatorname{tr} \boldsymbol{P} = \operatorname{tr}\left(\boldsymbol{X}\left(\boldsymbol{X}'\boldsymbol{X}\right)^{-1}\boldsymbol{X}'\right) = \operatorname{tr}\left(\left(\boldsymbol{X}'\boldsymbol{X}\right)^{-1}\boldsymbol{X}'\boldsymbol{X}\right) = \operatorname{tr}\left(\boldsymbol{I}_k\right) = k.$$

See Appendix A.5 for definition and properties of the trace operator.

Appendix A.11 shows that part 4 holds for any idempotent matrix. For part 5, since $\operatorname{tr} \boldsymbol{P}$ equals the sum of the n eigenvalues and $\operatorname{tr} \boldsymbol{P} = k$ by part 3, it follows that there are k eigenvalues equaling 1 and the remainder $n - k$ equaling 0.

For part 6, observe that $\boldsymbol{P}$ is positive semi-definite, because its eigenvalues are all nonnegative. By Theorem A.4.5, its rank equals the number of positive eigenvalues, which is k, as claimed.

3.12 ANNIHILATOR MATRIX

Define

$$\boldsymbol{M}=\boldsymbol{I}_n-\boldsymbol{P}=\boldsymbol{I}_n-\boldsymbol{X}\left(\boldsymbol{X}'\boldsymbol{X}\right)^{-1}\boldsymbol{X}'$$

where $\boldsymbol{I}_n$ is the $n \times n$ identity matrix. Note that

$$\boldsymbol{M}\boldsymbol{X}=(\boldsymbol{I}_n-\boldsymbol{P})\,\boldsymbol{X}=\boldsymbol{X}-\boldsymbol{P}\boldsymbol{X}=\boldsymbol{X}-\boldsymbol{X}=0. \tag{3.21}$$

Thus $\boldsymbol{M}$ and $\boldsymbol{X}$ are orthogonal. We call $\boldsymbol{M}$ the **annihilator matrix** due to the property that for any matrix $\boldsymbol{Z}$ in the range space of $\boldsymbol{X}$,

$$\boldsymbol{M}\boldsymbol{Z}=\boldsymbol{Z}-\boldsymbol{P}\boldsymbol{Z}=0.$$

For example, $\boldsymbol{M}\boldsymbol{X}_1=0$ for any subcomponent $\boldsymbol{X}_1$ of $\boldsymbol{X}$, and $\boldsymbol{M}\boldsymbol{P}=0$ (see Exercise 3.7).

The annihilator matrix $\boldsymbol{M}$ has similar properties with $\boldsymbol{P}$, including that $\boldsymbol{M}$ is symmetric ($\boldsymbol{M}'=\boldsymbol{M}$) and idempotent ($\boldsymbol{M}\boldsymbol{M}=\boldsymbol{M}$). It is thus a projection matrix. Similarly to Theorem 3.3.3, we can calculate

$$\operatorname{tr}\boldsymbol{M}=n-k. \tag{3.22}$$

(See Exercise 3.9.) One implication is that the rank of $\boldsymbol{M}$ is $n-k$.

While $\boldsymbol{P}$ creates fitted values, $\boldsymbol{M}$ creates least squares residuals:

$$\boldsymbol{M}\boldsymbol{Y}=\boldsymbol{Y}-\boldsymbol{P}\boldsymbol{Y}=\boldsymbol{Y}-\boldsymbol{X}\widehat{\beta}=\widehat{\boldsymbol{e}}. \tag{3.23}$$

As discussed in Section 3.11, a special example of a projection matrix occurs when $\boldsymbol{X}=\mathbf{1}_n$ is an n-vector of 1s, so that $\boldsymbol{P}=\mathbf{1}_n\left(\mathbf{1}_n'\mathbf{1}_n\right)^{-1}\mathbf{1}_n'$. The associated annihilator matrix is

$$\boldsymbol{M}=\boldsymbol{I}_n-\boldsymbol{P}=\boldsymbol{I}_n-\mathbf{1}_n\left(\mathbf{1}_n'\mathbf{1}_n\right)^{-1}\mathbf{1}_n'.$$

While $\boldsymbol{P}$ creates a vector of sample means, $\boldsymbol{M}$ creates demeaned values:

$$\boldsymbol{M}\boldsymbol{Y}=\boldsymbol{Y}-\mathbf{1}_n\overline{Y}.$$

For simplicity, we will often write the right-hand side as $\boldsymbol{Y}-\overline{Y}$. The ith element is $Y_i-\overline{Y}$, the **demeaned** value of Y_i.

We can also use (3.23) to write an alternative expression for the residual vector. Substituting $\boldsymbol{Y}=\boldsymbol{X}\beta+\boldsymbol{e}$ into $\widehat{\boldsymbol{e}}=\boldsymbol{M}\boldsymbol{Y}$ and using $\boldsymbol{M}\boldsymbol{X}=\mathbf{0}$, we find

$$\widehat{\boldsymbol{e}}=\boldsymbol{M}\boldsymbol{Y}=\boldsymbol{M}\left(\boldsymbol{X}\beta+\boldsymbol{e}\right)=\boldsymbol{M}\boldsymbol{e} \tag{3.24}$$

which is free of dependence on the regression coefficient β.

3.13 ESTIMATION OF ERROR VARIANCE

The error variance $\sigma^2=\mathbb{E}\left[e^2\right]$ is a moment, so a natural estimator is a moment estimator. If e_i were observed, we would estimate σ^2 by

$$\widetilde{\sigma}^2=\frac{1}{n}\sum_{i=1}^{n}e_i^2. \tag{3.25}$$

However, this is infeasible, as e_i is not observed. In this case it is common to take a two-step approach to estimation. The residuals $\widehat{e}_i$ are calculated in the first step, and then we substitute $\widehat{e}_i$ for e_i in expression (3.25) to obtain the feasible estimator

$$\widehat{\sigma}^2 = \frac{1}{n}\sum_{i=1}^{n}\widehat{e}_i^2. \tag{3.26}$$

In matrix notation, we can write (3.25) and (3.26) as $\widetilde{\sigma}^2 = n^{-1}\boldsymbol{e}'\boldsymbol{e}$ and

$$\widehat{\sigma}^2 = n^{-1}\widehat{\boldsymbol{e}}'\widehat{\boldsymbol{e}}. \tag{3.27}$$

Recall the expressions $\widehat{\boldsymbol{e}} = \boldsymbol{M}\boldsymbol{Y} = \boldsymbol{M}\boldsymbol{e}$ from (3.23) and (3.24). Applied to (3.27), we find

$$\widehat{\sigma}^2 = n^{-1}\widehat{\boldsymbol{e}}'\widehat{\boldsymbol{e}} = n^{-1}\boldsymbol{e}'\boldsymbol{M}\boldsymbol{M}\boldsymbol{e} = n^{-1}\boldsymbol{e}'\boldsymbol{M}\boldsymbol{e} \tag{3.28}$$

the third equality holds because $\boldsymbol{M}\boldsymbol{M} = \boldsymbol{M}$.

An interesting implication is that

$$\widetilde{\sigma}^2 - \widehat{\sigma}^2 = n^{-1}\boldsymbol{e}'\boldsymbol{e} - n^{-1}\boldsymbol{e}'\boldsymbol{M}\boldsymbol{e} = n^{-1}\boldsymbol{e}'\boldsymbol{P}\boldsymbol{e} \geq 0.$$

The final inequality holds because $\boldsymbol{P}$ is positive semi-definite, and $\boldsymbol{e}'\boldsymbol{P}\boldsymbol{e}$ is a quadratic form. This shows that the feasible estimator $\widehat{\sigma}^2$ is numerically smaller than the idealized estimator (3.25).

3.14 ANALYSIS OF VARIANCE

Another way of writing (3.23) is

$$\boldsymbol{Y} = \boldsymbol{P}\boldsymbol{Y} + \boldsymbol{M}\boldsymbol{Y} = \widehat{\boldsymbol{Y}} + \widehat{\boldsymbol{e}}. \tag{3.29}$$

This decomposition is **orthogonal**, that is,

$$\widehat{\boldsymbol{Y}}'\widehat{\boldsymbol{e}} = (\boldsymbol{P}\boldsymbol{Y})'(\boldsymbol{M}\boldsymbol{Y}) = \boldsymbol{Y}'\boldsymbol{P}\boldsymbol{M}\boldsymbol{Y} = 0. \tag{3.30}$$

It follows that

$$\boldsymbol{Y}'\boldsymbol{Y} = \widehat{\boldsymbol{Y}}'\widehat{\boldsymbol{Y}} + 2\widehat{\boldsymbol{Y}}'\widehat{\boldsymbol{e}} + \widehat{\boldsymbol{e}}'\widehat{\boldsymbol{e}} = \widehat{\boldsymbol{Y}}'\widehat{\boldsymbol{Y}} + \widehat{\boldsymbol{e}}'\widehat{\boldsymbol{e}}$$

or

$$\sum_{i=1}^{n} Y_i^2 = \sum_{i=1}^{n}\widehat{Y}_i^2 + \sum_{i=1}^{n}\widehat{e}_i^2.$$

Subtracting $\overline{Y}$ from both sides of (3.29), we obtain

$$\boldsymbol{Y} - \mathbf{1}_n\overline{Y} = \widehat{\boldsymbol{Y}} - \mathbf{1}_n\overline{Y} + \widehat{\boldsymbol{e}}.$$

This decomposition is also orthogonal when $\boldsymbol{X}$ contains a constant, as

$$\left(\widehat{\boldsymbol{Y}} - \mathbf{1}_n\overline{Y}\right)'\widehat{\boldsymbol{e}} = \widehat{\boldsymbol{Y}}'\widehat{\boldsymbol{e}} - \overline{Y}\mathbf{1}_n'\widehat{\boldsymbol{e}} = 0$$

using (3.17). It follows that

$$\left(\boldsymbol{Y} - \mathbf{1}_n\overline{Y}\right)'\left(\boldsymbol{Y} - \mathbf{1}_n\overline{Y}\right) = \left(\widehat{\boldsymbol{Y}} - \mathbf{1}_n\overline{Y}\right)'\left(\widehat{\boldsymbol{Y}} - \mathbf{1}_n\overline{Y}\right) + \widehat{\boldsymbol{e}}'\widehat{\boldsymbol{e}}$$

or

$$\sum_{i=1}^{n}\left(Y_i-\overline{Y}\right)^2=\sum_{i=1}^{n}\left(\widehat{Y}_i-\overline{Y}\right)^2+\sum_{i=1}^{n}\widehat{e}_i^2.$$

This is commonly called the **analysis-of-variance** formula for least squares regression.

A commonly reported statistic is the **coefficient of determination** or **R-squared**:

$$R^2=\frac{\sum_{i=1}^{n}\left(\widehat{Y}_i-\overline{Y}\right)^2}{\sum_{i=1}^{n}\left(Y_i-\overline{Y}\right)^2}=1-\frac{\sum_{i=1}^{n}\widehat{e}_i^2}{\sum_{i=1}^{n}\left(Y_i-\overline{Y}\right)^2}.$$

It is often described as "the fraction of the sample variance of Y which is explained by the least squares fit." R^2 is a crude measure of regression fit. We have better measures of fit, but these require a statistical (not just algebraic) analysis, and we will return to these issues later. One deficiency with R^2 is that it increases when regressors are added to a regression (see Exercise 3.16), so the "fit" can be always increased by increasing the number of regressors.

The coefficient of determination was introduced by Sewell Wright (1921).

3.15 PROJECTIONS

One way to visualize least squares fitting is as a projection operation. Write the regressor matrix as $\boldsymbol{X}=[\boldsymbol{X}_1\ \boldsymbol{X}_2 \ldots \boldsymbol{X}_k]$, where $\boldsymbol{X}_j$ is the jth column of $\boldsymbol{X}$. The range space $\mathscr{R}(\boldsymbol{X})$ of $\boldsymbol{X}$ is the space consisting of all linear combinations of the columns $\boldsymbol{X}_1, \boldsymbol{X}_2, \ldots, \boldsymbol{X}_k$. $\mathscr{R}(\boldsymbol{X})$ is a k-dimensional surface contained in $\mathbb{R}^n$. If $k=2$, then $\mathscr{R}(\boldsymbol{X})$ is a plane. The operator $\boldsymbol{P}=\boldsymbol{X}\left(\boldsymbol{X}'\boldsymbol{X}\right)^{-1}\boldsymbol{X}'$ projects vectors onto $\mathscr{R}(\boldsymbol{X})$. The fitted values $\widehat{\boldsymbol{Y}}=\boldsymbol{P}\boldsymbol{Y}$ are the projection of $\boldsymbol{Y}$ onto $\mathscr{R}(\boldsymbol{X})$.

To visualize, examine Figure 3.4, which displays the case $n=3$ and $k=2$. Displayed are three vectors $\boldsymbol{Y}$, $\boldsymbol{X}_1$, and $\boldsymbol{X}_2$, which are each elements of $\mathbb{R}^3$. The plane created by $\boldsymbol{X}_1$ and $\boldsymbol{X}_2$ is the range space $\mathscr{R}(\boldsymbol{X})$. Regression fitted values are linear combinations of $\boldsymbol{X}_1$ and $\boldsymbol{X}_2$ and so lie in this plane. The fitted value $\widehat{\boldsymbol{Y}}$ is the vector in this plane closest to $\boldsymbol{Y}$. The residual $\widehat{\boldsymbol{e}}=\boldsymbol{Y}-\widehat{\boldsymbol{Y}}$ is the difference between the two. The angle between the vectors $\widehat{\boldsymbol{Y}}$ and $\widehat{\boldsymbol{e}}$ is 90°, and therefore they are orthogonal, as shown.

3.16 REGRESSION COMPONENTS

Partition $\boldsymbol{X}=[\boldsymbol{X}_1 \quad \boldsymbol{X}_2]$ and $\beta=(\beta_1,\beta_2)$. The regression model can be written as

$$\boldsymbol{Y}=\boldsymbol{X}_1\beta_1+\boldsymbol{X}_2\beta_2+\boldsymbol{e}. \tag{3.31}$$

The OLS estimator of $\beta=(\beta_1',\beta_2')'$ is obtained by regression of $\boldsymbol{Y}$ on $\boldsymbol{X}=[\boldsymbol{X}_1\ \boldsymbol{X}_2]$ and can be written as

$$\boldsymbol{Y}=\boldsymbol{X}\widehat{\beta}+\widehat{\boldsymbol{e}}=\boldsymbol{X}_1\widehat{\beta}_1+\boldsymbol{X}_2\widehat{\beta}_2+\widehat{\boldsymbol{e}}. \tag{3.32}$$

We are interested in algebraic expressions for $\widehat{\beta}_1$ and $\widehat{\beta}_2$.

Let's first focus on $\widehat{\beta}_1$. By definition, the least squares estimator is found by the joint minimization

$$\left(\widehat{\beta}_1,\widehat{\beta}_2\right)=\underset{\beta_1,\beta_2}{\operatorname{argmin}}\ \mathrm{SSE}\left(\beta_1,\beta_2\right) \tag{3.33}$$

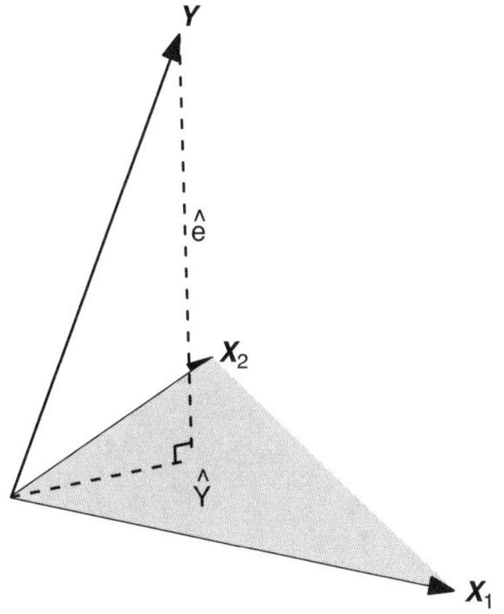

FIGURE 3.4 Projection of Y onto X_1 and X_2

where

$$\mathrm{SSE}(\beta_1, \beta_2) = (Y - X_1\beta_1 - X_2\beta_2)'(Y - X_1\beta_1 - X_2\beta_2).$$

An equivalent expression for $\widehat{\beta}_1$ can be obtained by concentration (nested minimization). The solution (3.33) can be written as

$$\widehat{\beta}_1 = \underset{\beta_1}{\operatorname{argmin}} \left(\min_{\beta_2} \mathrm{SSE}(\beta_1, \beta_2) \right). \tag{3.34}$$

The inner expression, $\min_{\beta_2} \mathrm{SSE}(\beta_1, \beta_2)$, minimizes over β_2 while holding β_1 fixed. It is the smallest possible sum of squared errors given β_1. The outer minimization $\operatorname{argmin}_{\beta_1}$ finds the coefficient β_1 which minimizes the "smallest possible sum of squared errors given β_1". Thus, $\widehat{\beta}_1$ as defined in (3.33) and (3.34) are algebraically identical.

Examine the inner minimization problem in (3.34). This is simply the least squares regression of $Y - X_1\beta_1$ on X_2, which has solution

$$\underset{\beta_2}{\operatorname{argmin}} \mathrm{SSE}(\beta_1, \beta_2) = \left(X_2'X_2\right)^{-1}\left(X_2'(Y - X_1\beta_1)\right)$$

with residuals

$$\begin{aligned} Y - X_1\beta_1 - X_2\left(X_2'X_2\right)^{-1}\left(X_2'(Y - X_1\beta_1)\right) &= (M_2Y - M_2X_1\beta_1) \\ &= M_2(Y - X_1\beta_1) \end{aligned}$$

where

$$M_2 = I_n - X_2\left(X_2'X_2\right)^{-1}X_2' \tag{3.35}$$

is the annihilator matrix for X_2. Thus the inner minimization problem (3.34) has minimized value

$$\begin{aligned} \min_{\beta_2} \mathrm{SSE}(\beta_1, \beta_2) &= (Y - X_1\beta_1)' M_2 M_2 (Y - X_1\beta_1) \\ &= (Y - X_1\beta_1)' M_2 (Y - X_1\beta_1) \end{aligned}$$

where the second equality holds because M_2 is idempotent. Substituting this into (3.34), we find

$$\begin{aligned}\widehat{\beta}_1 &= \underset{\beta_1}{\operatorname{argmin}} \left(Y - X_1\beta_1\right)' M_2 \left(Y - X_1\beta_1\right) \\ &= \left(X_1' M_2 X_1\right)^{-1} \left(X_1' M_2 Y\right).\end{aligned}$$

By a similar argument, we find

$$\widehat{\beta}_2 = \left(X_2' M_1 X_2\right)^{-1} \left(X_2' M_1 Y\right)$$

where

$$M_1 = I_n - X_1 \left(X_1' X_1\right)^{-1} X_1' \tag{3.36}$$

is the annihilator matrix for X_1.

Theorem 3.4 The least squares estimator $\left(\widehat{\beta}_1, \widehat{\beta}_2\right)$ for (3.32) has the algebraic solution

$$\widehat{\beta}_1 = \left(X_1' M_2 X_1\right)^{-1} \left(X_1' M_2 Y\right) \tag{3.37}$$

$$\widehat{\beta}_2 = \left(X_2' M_1 X_2\right)^{-1} \left(X_2' M_1 Y\right) \tag{3.38}$$

where M_1 and M_2 are defined in (3.36) and (3.35), respectively.

3.17 REGRESSION COMPONENTS (ALTERNATIVE DERIVATION)*

An alternative proof of Theorem 3.4 uses an algebraic argument based on the population calculations from Section 2.22. Since this is a classic derivation, I present it here for completeness.

Partition $\widehat{Q}_{XX}$ as

$$\widehat{Q}_{XX} = \begin{bmatrix} \widehat{Q}_{11} & \widehat{Q}_{12} \\ \widehat{Q}_{21} & \widehat{Q}_{22} \end{bmatrix} = \begin{bmatrix} \frac{1}{n} X_1' X_1 & \frac{1}{n} X_1' X_2 \\ \frac{1}{n} X_2' X_1 & \frac{1}{n} X_2' X_2 \end{bmatrix}$$

and similarly $\widehat{Q}_{XY}$ as

$$\widehat{Q}_{XY} = \begin{bmatrix} \widehat{Q}_{1Y} \\ \widehat{Q}_{2Y} \end{bmatrix} = \begin{bmatrix} \frac{1}{n} X_1' Y \\ \frac{1}{n} X_2' Y \end{bmatrix}.$$

By the partitioned matrix inversion formula (A.3),

$$\widehat{Q}_{XX}^{-1} = \begin{bmatrix} \widehat{Q}_{11} & \widehat{Q}_{12} \\ \widehat{Q}_{21} & \widehat{Q}_{22} \end{bmatrix}^{-1} \overset{\text{def}}{=} \begin{bmatrix} \widehat{Q}^{11} & \widehat{Q}^{12} \\ \widehat{Q}^{21} & \widehat{Q}^{22} \end{bmatrix} = \begin{bmatrix} \widehat{Q}_{11\cdot 2}^{-1} & -\widehat{Q}_{11\cdot 2}^{-1} \widehat{Q}_{12} \widehat{Q}_{22}^{-1} \\ -\widehat{Q}_{22\cdot 1}^{-1} \widehat{Q}_{21} \widehat{Q}_{11}^{-1} & \widehat{Q}_{22\cdot 1}^{-1} \end{bmatrix} \tag{3.39}$$

where $\widehat{Q}_{11\cdot 2} = \widehat{Q}_{11} - \widehat{Q}_{12} \widehat{Q}_{22}^{-1} \widehat{Q}_{21}$, and $\widehat{Q}_{22\cdot 1} = \widehat{Q}_{22} - \widehat{Q}_{21} \widehat{Q}_{11}^{-1} \widehat{Q}_{12}$. Thus

$$
\begin{aligned}
\widehat{\beta} &= \begin{pmatrix} \widehat{\beta}_1 \\ \widehat{\beta}_2 \end{pmatrix} \\
&= \begin{bmatrix} \widehat{Q}_{11\cdot 2}^{-1} & -\widehat{Q}_{11\cdot 2}^{-1}\widehat{Q}_{12}\widehat{Q}_{22}^{-1} \\ -\widehat{Q}_{22\cdot 1}^{-1}\widehat{Q}_{21}\widehat{Q}_{11}^{-1} & \widehat{Q}_{22\cdot 1}^{-1} \end{bmatrix} \begin{bmatrix} \widehat{Q}_{1Y} \\ \widehat{Q}_{2Y} \end{bmatrix} \\
&= \begin{pmatrix} \widehat{Q}_{11\cdot 2}^{-1}\widehat{Q}_{1Y\cdot 2} \\ \widehat{Q}_{22\cdot 1}^{-1}\widehat{Q}_{2Y\cdot 1} \end{pmatrix}.
\end{aligned}
$$

Now

$$
\begin{aligned}
\widehat{Q}_{11\cdot 2} &= \widehat{Q}_{11} - \widehat{Q}_{12}\widehat{Q}_{22}^{-1}\widehat{Q}_{21} \\
&= \frac{1}{n}\boldsymbol{X}_1'\boldsymbol{X}_1 - \frac{1}{n}\boldsymbol{X}_1'\boldsymbol{X}_2\left(\frac{1}{n}\boldsymbol{X}_2'\boldsymbol{X}_2\right)^{-1}\frac{1}{n}\boldsymbol{X}_2'\boldsymbol{X}_1 \\
&= \frac{1}{n}\boldsymbol{X}_1'\boldsymbol{M}_2\boldsymbol{X}_1
\end{aligned}
$$

and

$$
\begin{aligned}
\widehat{Q}_{1y\cdot 2} &= \widehat{Q}_{1Y} - \widehat{Q}_{12}\widehat{Q}_{22}^{-1}\widehat{Q}_{2Y} \\
&= \frac{1}{n}\boldsymbol{X}_1'\boldsymbol{Y} - \frac{1}{n}\boldsymbol{X}_1'\boldsymbol{X}_2\left(\frac{1}{n}\boldsymbol{X}_2'\boldsymbol{X}_2\right)^{-1}\frac{1}{n}\boldsymbol{X}_2'\boldsymbol{Y} \\
&= \frac{1}{n}\boldsymbol{X}_1'\boldsymbol{M}_2\boldsymbol{Y}.
\end{aligned}
$$

Equation (3.38) follows.

Similarly to the calculation for $\widehat{Q}_{11\cdot 2}$ and $\widehat{Q}_{1Y\cdot 2}$, you can show that $\widehat{Q}_{2Y\cdot 1} = \frac{1}{n}\boldsymbol{X}_2'\boldsymbol{M}_1\boldsymbol{Y}$ and $\widehat{Q}_{22\cdot 1} = \frac{1}{n}\boldsymbol{X}_2'\boldsymbol{M}_1\boldsymbol{X}_2$. This establishes (3.37). Together, these equations are Theorem 3.4.

3.18 RESIDUAL REGRESSION

As first recognized by Frisch and Waugh (1933) and extended by Lovell (1963), expressions (3.37) and (3.38) can be used to show that the least squares estimators $\widehat{\beta}_1$ and $\widehat{\beta}_2$ can be found by a two-step regression procedure.

Take (3.38). Since $\boldsymbol{M}_1$ is idempotent, $\boldsymbol{M}_1 = \boldsymbol{M}_1\boldsymbol{M}_1$ and thus

$$
\begin{aligned}
\widehat{\beta}_2 &= \left(\boldsymbol{X}_2'\boldsymbol{M}_1\boldsymbol{X}_2\right)^{-1}\left(\boldsymbol{X}_2'\boldsymbol{M}_1\boldsymbol{Y}\right) \\
&= \left(\boldsymbol{X}_2'\boldsymbol{M}_1\boldsymbol{M}_1\boldsymbol{X}_2\right)^{-1}\left(\boldsymbol{X}_2'\boldsymbol{M}_1\boldsymbol{M}_1\boldsymbol{Y}\right) \\
&= \left(\widetilde{\boldsymbol{X}}_2'\widetilde{\boldsymbol{X}}_2\right)^{-1}\left(\widetilde{\boldsymbol{X}}_2'\widetilde{\boldsymbol{e}}_1\right)
\end{aligned}
$$

where $\widetilde{\boldsymbol{X}}_2 = \boldsymbol{M}_1\boldsymbol{X}_2$ and $\widetilde{\boldsymbol{e}}_1 = \boldsymbol{M}_1\boldsymbol{Y}$.

Thus the coefficient estimator $\widehat{\beta}_2$ is algebraically equal to the least squares regression of $\widetilde{\boldsymbol{e}}_1$ on $\widetilde{\boldsymbol{X}}_2$. Notice that these two are $\boldsymbol{Y}$ and $\boldsymbol{X}_2$, respectively, pre-multiplied by $\boldsymbol{M}_1$. But we know that pre-multiplication by $\boldsymbol{M}_1$ creates least squares residuals. Therefore, $\widetilde{\boldsymbol{e}}_1$ is simply the least squares residual from a regression of $\boldsymbol{Y}$ on $\boldsymbol{X}_1$, and the columns of $\widetilde{\boldsymbol{X}}_2$ are the least squares residuals from the regressions of the columns of $\boldsymbol{X}_2$ on $\boldsymbol{X}_1$.

We have proven the following theorem.

Theorem 3.5 Frisch-Waugh-Lovell (FWL)
In the model (3.31), the OLS estimator of β_2 and the OLS residuals $\widehat{\boldsymbol{e}}$ may be computed by either the OLS regression (3.32) or by the following algorithm:

1. Regress $\boldsymbol{Y}$ on $\boldsymbol{X}_1$, obtain residuals $\widetilde{\boldsymbol{e}}_1$;
2. Regress $\boldsymbol{X}_2$ on $\boldsymbol{X}_1$, obtain residuals $\widetilde{\boldsymbol{X}}_2$;
3. Regress $\widetilde{\boldsymbol{e}}_1$ on $\widetilde{\boldsymbol{X}}_2$, obtain OLS estimates $\widehat{\beta}_2$ and residuals $\widehat{\boldsymbol{e}}$.

In some contexts (such as panel data models, to be introduced in Chapter 17), the FWL theorem can be used to greatly speed computation.

The FWL theorem is a direct analog of the coefficient representation obtained in Section 2.23. The result obtained in that section concerned the population projection coefficients; the result obtained here concerns the least squares estimators. The key message is the same. In the least squares regression (3.32), the estimated coefficient $\widehat{\beta}_2$ algebraically equals the regression of $\boldsymbol{Y}$ on the regressors $\boldsymbol{X}_2$ after the regressors $\boldsymbol{X}_1$ have been linearly projected out. Similarly, the coefficient estimate $\widehat{\beta}_1$ algebraically equals the regression of $\boldsymbol{Y}$ on the regressors $\boldsymbol{X}_1$ after the regressors $\boldsymbol{X}_2$ have been linearly projected out. This result can be insightful when interpreting regression coefficients.

A common application of the FWL theorem is the demeaning formula for regression obtained in (3.18). Partition $\boldsymbol{X} = [\boldsymbol{X}_1\ \boldsymbol{X}_2]$ where $\boldsymbol{X}_1 = \mathbf{1}_n$ is a vector of 1s and $\boldsymbol{X}_2$ is a matrix of observed regressors. In this case, $\boldsymbol{M}_1 = \boldsymbol{I}_n - \mathbf{1}_n\left(\mathbf{1}_n'\mathbf{1}_n\right)^{-1}\mathbf{1}_n'$. Observe that $\widetilde{\boldsymbol{X}}_2 = \boldsymbol{M}_1\boldsymbol{X}_2 = \boldsymbol{X}_2 - \overline{\boldsymbol{X}}_2$ and $\boldsymbol{M}_1\boldsymbol{Y} = \boldsymbol{Y} - \overline{\boldsymbol{Y}}$ are the "demeaned" variables. The FWL theorem says that $\widehat{\beta}_2$ is the OLS estimate from a regression of $Y_i - \overline{Y}$ on $X_{2i} - \overline{X}_2$:

$$\widehat{\beta}_2 = \left(\sum_{i=1}^{n}\left(X_{2i} - \overline{X}_2\right)\left(X_{2i} - \overline{X}_2\right)'\right)^{-1}\left(\sum_{i=1}^{n}\left(X_{2i} - \overline{X}_2\right)\left(Y_i - \overline{Y}\right)\right).$$

This is (3.18).

Ragnar Frisch

Ragnar Frisch (1895–1973) was co-winner with Jan Tinbergen of the first Nobel Memorial Prize in Economic Sciences in 1969 for their work on developing and applying dynamic models for the analysis of economic problems. Frisch made other foundational contributions to modern economics beyond the Frisch-Waugh-Lovell Theorem, including formalizing consumer theory, production theory, and business cycle theory.

3.19 LEVERAGE VALUES

The **leverage** values for the regressor matrix $\boldsymbol{X}$ are the diagonal elements of the projection matrix $\boldsymbol{P} = \boldsymbol{X}\left(\boldsymbol{X}'\boldsymbol{X}\right)^{-1}\boldsymbol{X}'$. There are n leverage values, typically written as h_{ii} for $i = 1, \ldots, n$. Since

$$\boldsymbol{P} = \begin{pmatrix} X_1' \\ X_2' \\ \vdots \\ X_n' \end{pmatrix} \left(\boldsymbol{X}'\boldsymbol{X}\right)^{-1} \begin{pmatrix} X_1 & X_2 & \cdots & X_n \end{pmatrix}$$

they are

$$h_{ii} = X_i' \left(\boldsymbol{X}'\boldsymbol{X}\right)^{-1} X_i. \tag{3.40}$$

The leverage value h_{ii} is a normalized length of the observed regressor vector X_i. They appear frequently in the algebraic and statistical analysis of least squares regression, including leave-one-out regression, influential observations, robust covariance matrix estimation, and cross-validation.

A few properties of the leverage values are listed in Theorem 3.6.

Theorem 3.6

1. $0 \le h_{ii} \le 1$.
2. $h_{ii} \ge 1/n$ if X includes an intercept.
3. $\sum_{i=1}^{n} h_{ii} = k$.

We prove Theorem 3.6 below.

The leverage value h_{ii} measures how unusual the ith observation X_i is relative to the other observations in the sample. A large h_{ii} occurs when X_i is quite different from the other sample values. A measure of overall unusualness is the maximum leverage value

$$\overline{h} = \max_{1 \le i \le n} h_{ii}. \tag{3.41}$$

It is common to say that a regression design is **balanced** when the leverage values are all roughly equal to one another. From Theorem 3.6.3, we deduce that complete balance occurs when $h_{ii} = \overline{h} = k/n$. An example of complete balance is when the regressors are all orthogonal dummy variables, each of which has equal occurrance of 0s and 1s.

A regression design is **unbalanced** if some leverage values are highly unequal from the others. The most extreme case is $\overline{h} = 1$. An example where this occurs is when a dummy regressor takes the value 1 for only one observation in the sample.

The maximal leverage value (3.41) will change, depending on the choice of regressors. For example, consider equation (3.13), the wage regression for single Asian men, which has $n = 268$ observations. This regression has $\overline{h} = 0.33$. If the squared experience regressor is omitted, the leverage drops to $\overline{h} = 0.10$. If a cubic in experience is added, it increases to $\overline{h} = 0.76$. And if a fourth and fifth power are added, it increases to $\overline{h} = 0.99$.

Some inference procedures (such as robust covariance matrix estimation and cross-validation) are sensitive to high leverage values. We will return to these issues in Chapter 4.

We now prove Theorem 3.6. For part 1, let s_i be an $n \times 1$ unit vector with a 1 in the ith place and 0s elsewhere, so that $h_{ii} = s_i' \boldsymbol{P} s_i$. Then applying the Quadratic Inequality (B.18) and Theorem 3.3.4,

$$h_{ii} = s_i' \boldsymbol{P} s_i \leq s_i' s_i \lambda_{\max}(\boldsymbol{P}) = 1$$

as claimed.

For part 2, partition $X_i = (1, Z_i')'$. Without loss of generality, we can replace Z_i with the demeaned values $Z_i^* = Z_i - \overline{Z}$. Then since Z_i^* and the intercept are orthgonal

$$\begin{aligned} h_{ii} &= (1, Z_i^{*\prime}) \begin{bmatrix} n & 0 \\ 0 & \boldsymbol{Z}^{*\prime}\boldsymbol{Z}^* \end{bmatrix}^{-1} \begin{pmatrix} 1 \\ Z_i^* \end{pmatrix} \\ &= \frac{1}{n} + Z_i^{*\prime} \left(\boldsymbol{Z}^{*\prime}\boldsymbol{Z}^*\right)^{-1} Z_i^* \geq \frac{1}{n}. \end{aligned}$$

For part 3, $\sum_{i=1}^n h_{ii} = \operatorname{tr} \boldsymbol{P} = k$, where the second equality is Theorem 3.3.3.

3.20 LEAVE-ONE-OUT REGRESSION

Some statistical procedures—residual analysis, jackknife variance estimation, cross-validation, two-step estimation, hold-out sample evaluation—make use of estimators constructed on subsamples. Of particular importance is the case where we exclude a single observation and then repeat this for all observations. This is called **leave-one-out** regression.

Specifically, the leave-one-out estimator of the regression coefficient β is the least squares estimator constructed using the full sample excluding a single observation i. This can be written as

$$\begin{aligned} \widehat{\beta}_{(-i)} &= \left(\sum_{j \neq i} X_j X_j'\right)^{-1} \left(\sum_{j \neq i} X_j Y_j\right) \\ &= \left(\boldsymbol{X}'\boldsymbol{X} - X_i X_i'\right)^{-1} \left(\boldsymbol{X}'\boldsymbol{Y} - X_i Y_i\right) \\ &= \left(\boldsymbol{X}_{(-i)}'\boldsymbol{X}_{(-i)}\right)^{-1} \boldsymbol{X}_{(-i)}'\boldsymbol{Y}_{(-i)}. \end{aligned} \tag{3.42}$$

Here, $\boldsymbol{X}_{(-i)}$ and $\boldsymbol{Y}_{(-i)}$ are the data matrices omitting the ith row. The notation $\widehat{\beta}_{(-i)}$ or $\widehat{\beta}_{-i}$ is commonly used to denote an estimator with the ith observation omitted. There is a leave-one-out estimator for each observation, $i = 1, \ldots, n$, so we have n such estimators.

The leave-one-out predicted value for Y_i is $\widetilde{Y}_i = X_i' \widehat{\beta}_{(-i)}$. This is the predicted value obtained by estimating β on the sample without observation i and then using the covariate vector X_i to predict Y_i. Notice that $\widetilde{Y}_i$ is an authentic prediction, because Y_i is not used to construct $\widetilde{Y}_i$. This is in contrast to the fitted values $\widehat{Y}_i$, which are functions of Y_i.

The **leave-one-out residual**, **prediction error**, or **prediction residual** is $\widetilde{e}_i = Y_i - \widetilde{Y}_i$. The prediction errors may be used as estimators of the errors instead of the residuals. The prediction errors are better estimators than the residuals, because the former are based on authentic predictions.

The leave-one-out formula (3.42) gives the unfortunate impression that the leave-one-out coefficients and errors are computationally cumbersome, requiring n separate regressions. In the context of linear regression, this is fortunately not the case. There are simple linear expressions for $\widehat{\beta}_{(-i)}$ and $\widetilde{e}_i$.

Theorem 3.7 The leave-one-out estimator and prediction error equal:

$$\widehat{\beta}_{(-i)} = \widehat{\beta} - \left(\boldsymbol{X}'\boldsymbol{X}\right)^{-1} X_i\widetilde{e}_i \tag{3.43}$$

and

$$\widetilde{e}_i = (1-h_{ii})^{-1}\widehat{e}_i \tag{3.44}$$

where h_{ii} are the leverage values as defined in (3.40).

We prove Theorem 3.7 at the end of this section.

Equation (3.43) shows that the leave-one-out coefficients can be calculated by a simple linear operation and do not need to be calculated using n separate regressions. An interesting feature of equation (3.44) is that the prediction errors $\widetilde{e}_i$ are a simple scaling of the least squares residuals $\widehat{e}_i$ with the scaling dependent on the leverage values h_{ii}. If h_{ii} is small, then $\widetilde{e}_i \simeq \widehat{e}_i$. However if h_{ii} is large, then $\widetilde{e}_i$ can be quite different from $\widehat{e}_i$. Thus the difference between the residuals and predicted values depends on the leverage values, that is, how unusual X_i is.

To write (3.44) in vector notation, define

$$\begin{aligned}\boldsymbol{M}^* &= \left(\boldsymbol{I}_n - \operatorname{diag}\{h_{11},\ldots,h_{nn}\}\right)^{-1}\\ &= \operatorname{diag}\{(1-h_{11})^{-1},\ldots,(1-h_{nn})^{-1}\}.\end{aligned}$$

Then (3.44) is equivalent to

$$\widetilde{\boldsymbol{e}} = \boldsymbol{M}^*\widehat{\boldsymbol{e}}. \tag{3.45}$$

One use of the prediction errors is to estimate the out-of-sample mean squared error:

$$\widetilde{\sigma}^2 = \frac{1}{n}\sum_{i=1}^{n}\widetilde{e}_i^2 = \frac{1}{n}\sum_{i=1}^{n}(1-h_{ii})^{-2}\widehat{e}_i^2. \tag{3.46}$$

This is known as the **sample mean squared prediction error**. Its square root $\widetilde{\sigma} = \sqrt{\widetilde{\sigma}^2}$ is the **prediction standard error**.

We complete the section with a proof of Theorem 3.7. The leave-one-out estimator (3.42) can be written as

$$\widehat{\beta}_{(-i)} = \left(\boldsymbol{X}'\boldsymbol{X} - X_iX_i'\right)^{-1}\left(\boldsymbol{X}'\boldsymbol{Y} - X_iY_i\right). \tag{3.47}$$

Multiply (3.47) by $\left(\boldsymbol{X}'\boldsymbol{X}\right)^{-1}\left(\boldsymbol{X}'\boldsymbol{X} - X_iX_i'\right)$. We obtain

$$\widehat{\beta}_{(-i)} - \left(\boldsymbol{X}'\boldsymbol{X}\right)^{-1} X_iX_i'\widehat{\beta}_{(-i)} = \left(\boldsymbol{X}'\boldsymbol{X}\right)^{-1}\left(\boldsymbol{X}'\boldsymbol{Y} - X_iY_i\right) = \widehat{\beta} - \left(\boldsymbol{X}'\boldsymbol{X}\right)^{-1} X_iY_i.$$

Rewriting gives

$$\widehat{\beta}_{(-i)} = \widehat{\beta} - \left(\boldsymbol{X}'\boldsymbol{X}\right)^{-1} X_i\left(Y_i - X_i'\widehat{\beta}_{(-i)}\right) = \widehat{\beta} - \left(\boldsymbol{X}'\boldsymbol{X}\right)^{-1} X_i\widetilde{e}_i$$

which is (3.43). Premultiplying this expression by X_i' and using definition (3.40), we obtain

$$X_i'\widehat{\beta}_{(-i)} = X_i'\widehat{\beta} - X_i'\left(\boldsymbol{X}'\boldsymbol{X}\right)^{-1} X_i\widetilde{e}_i = X_i'\widehat{\beta} - h_{ii}\widetilde{e}_i.$$

Using the definitions for $\widehat{e}_i$ and $\widetilde{e}_i$, we obtain $\widetilde{e}_i = \widehat{e}_i + h_{ii}\widetilde{e}_i$. Rewriting, we obtain (3.44).

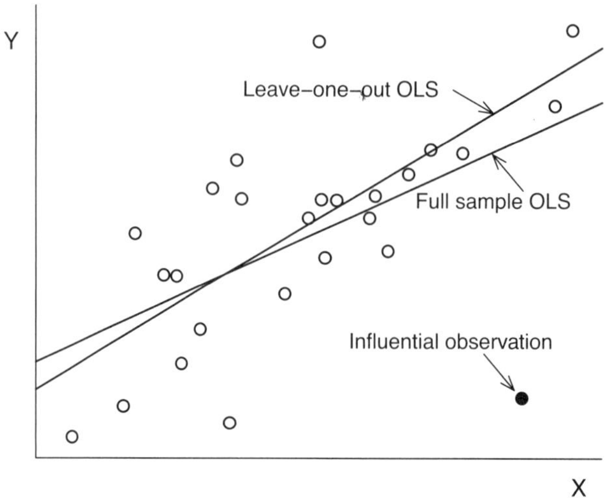

FIGURE 3.5 Impact of an influential observation on the least squares estimator

3.21 INFLUENTIAL OBSERVATIONS

Another use of the leave-one-out estimator is to investigate the impact of **influential observations**, sometimes called **outliers**. We say that observation i is influential if its omission from the sample induces a substantial change in a parameter estimate of interest.

For illustration, consider Figure 3.5, which shows a scatter plot of realizations (Y_i, X_i). The 25 observations shown with the open circles are generated by $X_i \sim U[1, 10]$ and $Y_i \sim \mathrm{N}(X_i, 4)$. The 26th observation shown with the filled circle is $X_{26} = 9$, $Y_{26} = 0$. (Imagine that $Y_{26} = 0$ was incorrectly recorded due to a mistaken key entry.) The figure shows both the least squares fitted line from the full sample and that obtained after deletion of the 26th observation from the sample. In this example, we can see how the 26th observation (the "outlier") greatly tilts the least squares fitted line toward the 26th observation. In fact, the slope coefficient decreases from 0.97 (which is close to the true value of 1.00) to 0.56, which is substantially reduced. Neither Y_{26} nor X_{26} are unusual values relative to their marginal distributions, so this outlier would not have been detected from examination of the marginal distributions of the data. The change in the slope coefficient of -0.41 is meaningful and should be of concern to an applied economist.

From (3.43), we know that

$$\widehat{\beta} - \widehat{\beta}_{(-i)} = \left(\boldsymbol{X}'\boldsymbol{X}\right)^{-1} X_i \widetilde{e}_i. \tag{3.48}$$

By direct calculation of this quantity for each observation i, we can directly discover if a specific observation i is influential for a coefficient estimate of interest.

For a general assessment, we can focus on the predicted values. The difference between the full-sample and leave-one-out predicted values is

$$\widehat{Y}_i - \widetilde{Y}_i = X_i'\widehat{\beta} - X_i'\widehat{\beta}_{(-i)} = X_i' \left(\boldsymbol{X}'\boldsymbol{X}\right)^{-1} X_i \widetilde{e}_i = h_{ii}\widetilde{e}_i$$

which is a simple function of the leverage values h_{ii} and prediction errors $\widetilde{e}_i$. Observation i is influential for the predicted value if $|h_{ii}\widetilde{e}_i|$ is large, which requires that both h_{ii} and $|\widetilde{e}_i|$ are large.

One way to think about this is that a large leverage value h_{ii} gives the potential for observation i to be influential. A large h_{ii} means that observation i is unusual in the sense that the regressor X_i is far from its sample mean. We call an observation with large h_{ii} a **leverage point**. A leverage point is not necessarily influential, as the latter also requires that the prediction error $\widetilde{e}_i$ is large.

To determine if any individual observations are influential in this sense, several diagnostics have been proposed (some names include DFITS, Cook's Distance, and Welsch Distance). Unfortunately, from a statistical perspective, it is difficult to recommend these diagnostics for applications, as they are not based on statistical theory. Probably the most relevant measure is the change in the coefficient estimates given in (3.48). The ratio of these changes to the coefficient's standard error is called its "DFBETA," and is a postestimation diagnostic available in Stata. While there is no magic threshold, the concern is whether an individual observation meaningfully changes an estimated coefficient of interest. A simple diagnostic for influential observations is to calculate

$$\text{Influence} = \max_{1\le i\le n} \left|\widehat{Y}_i - \widetilde{Y}_i\right| = \max_{1\le i\le n} \left|h_{ii}\widetilde{e}_i\right| .$$

This is the largest (absolute) change in the predicted value due to a single observation. If this diagnostic is large relative to the distribution of Y, it may indicate that that observation is influential.

If an observation is determined to be influential, what should be done? As a common cause of influential observations is data error, the influential observations should be examined for evidence that the observation was incorrectly recorded. Perhaps the observation falls outside of permitted ranges, or some observables are inconsistent (for example, a person is listed as having a job but receives earnings of \$0). If it is determined that an observation is incorrectly recorded, then the observation is typically deleted from the sample. This process is often called "cleaning the data." The decisions made in this process involve a fair amount of individual judgment. When this is done, the proper practice is to retain the source data in its original form and create a program file which executes all cleaning operations (for example deletion of individual observations). The cleaned data file can be saved at this point, and then used for the subsequent statistical analysis. The point of retaining the source data and a specific program file which cleans the data is twofold: so that all decisions are documented, and so that modifications can be made in revisions and future research. It is also possible that an observation is correctly measured but is unusual and influential. In this case, it is unclear how to proceed. Some researchers will try to alter the specification to properly model the influential observation. Other researchers will delete the observation from the sample. The motivation for this choice is to prevent the results from being skewed or determined by individual observations. This latter practice is viewed skeptically by many researchers who believe it reduces the integrity of reported empirical results.

For an empirical illustration, consider the log wage regression (3.13) for single Asian men. This regression, which has 268 observations, has Influence = 0.29. This means that the most influential observation, when deleted, changes the predicted (fitted) value of the dependent variable log(*wage*) by 0.29, or equivalently, the average wage by 29%. This change is meaningful and suggests that further investigation is warranted. We examine the influential observation, and find that its leverage h_{ii} is 0.33. It is a moderately large leverage value, meaning that the regressor X_i is somewhat unusual. Examining further, we find that this individual is 65 years old with 8 years of education, so that his potential work experience is 51 years. This is the highest experience in the subsample—the next highest is 41 years. The large leverage is due to his unusual characteristics (very low education and very high experience) in this sample. Essentially, regression (3.13) is attempting to estimate the conditional mean at *experience*= 51 with only one observation. It is not surprising that this observation determines the fit and is thus influential. A reasonable conclusion is that the regression function can only be estimated over a smaller range of *experience*. We restrict the sample to individuals with less than 45 years experience, re-estimate, and obtain the following estimates:

$$\widehat{\log(wage)} = 0.144\, education + 0.043\, experience - 0.095\, experience^2/100 + 0.531. \tag{3.49}$$

For this regression, we calculate that Influence = 0.11, which is greatly reduced relative to the regression (3.13). Comparing (3.49) with (3.13), the slope coefficient for education is essentially unchanged, but the coefficients for experience and its square have slightly increased.

By eliminating the influential observation, equation (3.49) can be viewed as a more robust estimate of the conditional mean for most levels of *experience*. Whether to report (3.13) or (3.49) in an application is largely a matter of judgment.

3.22 CPS DATASET

In this section we describe the dataset used in the empirical illustrations.

The Current Population Survey (CPS) is a monthly survey of about 57,000 U.S. households conducted by the Bureau of the Census of the Bureau of Labor Statistics. The CPS is the primary source of information on the labor force characteristics of the U.S. population. The survey covers employment, earnings, educational attainment, income, poverty, health insurance coverage, job experience, voting and registration, computer usage, veteran status, and other variables. Details can be found at www.census.gov/program-surveys/cps.html.

From the March 2009 survey, we extracted the individuals with nonallocated variables who were employed full-time (defined as those who had worked at least 36 hours per week for at least 48 weeks the past year), and excluded those in the military. This sample has 50,742 individuals. We extracted 14 variables from the CPS on these individuals and created the dataset `cps09mar`. This dataset, and all others used in this textbook, are available at https://press.princeton.edu/books/econometrics.

3.23 NUMERICAL COMPUTATION

Modern econometric estimation involves large samples and many covariates. Consequently, calculation of even simple statistics, such as the least squares estimator, requires a large number (millions) of arithmetic operations. In practice, most economists don't need to think much about this as it is done swiftly and effortlessly on personal computers. Nevertheless it is useful to understand the underlying calculation methods, as choices can occasionally make substantive differences.

While today nearly all statistical computations are made using statistical software running on electronic computers, this was not always the case. In the nineteenth and early twentieth centuries, "computer" was a job label for workers who made computations by hand. Computers were employed by astronomers and statistical laboratories. This fascinating job (and the fact that most computers employed in laboratories were women) has entered popular culture. For example, the lives of several computers who worked for the early U.S. space program is described in the book and popular movie *Hidden Figures*, a fictional computer/astronaut is the protagonist of the novel *The Calculating Stars*, and the life of computer/astronomer Henrietta Swan Leavitt is dramatized in the play *Silent Sky*.

Until programmable electronic computers became available in the 1960s, economics graduate students were routinely employed as computers. Sample sizes were considerably smaller than those seen today, but still the effort required to calculate by hand a regression with even $n = 100$ observations and $k = 5$ variables is considerable! If you are a current graduate student, you should feel fortunate that the profession has moved on from the era of human computers! (Now research assistants do more elevated tasks, such as writing Stata, R, and MATLAB code.)

To obtain the least squares estimate $\widehat{\beta} = \left(\boldsymbol{X}'\boldsymbol{X}\right)^{-1}\left(\boldsymbol{X}'\boldsymbol{Y}\right)$, we need to either invert $\boldsymbol{X}'\boldsymbol{X}$ or solve a system of equations. To be specific, let $\boldsymbol{A} = \boldsymbol{X}'\boldsymbol{X}$ and $\boldsymbol{c} = \boldsymbol{X}'\boldsymbol{Y}$, so that the least squares estimate can be written as either the solution to

$$\boldsymbol{A}\widehat{\beta} = \boldsymbol{c} \tag{3.50}$$

or as

$$\widehat{\beta} = \boldsymbol{A}^{-1}\boldsymbol{c}. \tag{3.51}$$

Equations (3.50) and (3.51) are algebraically identical, but they suggest two distinct numerical approaches to obtain $\widehat{\beta}$. Equation (3.50) suggests solving a system of k equations, whereas (3.51) suggests finding $\boldsymbol{A}^{-1}$ and then multiplying by $\boldsymbol{c}$. While the two expressions are algebraically identical, the implied numerical approaches are different.

In a nutshell, solving the system of equations (3.50) is numerically preferred to the matrix inversion problem (3.51). Directly solving (3.50) is faster and produces a solution with a higher degree of numerical accuracy. Thus (3.50) is generally recommended over (3.51). However, in most practical applications, the choice will not make any practical difference. Contexts where the choice may make a difference are when the matrix $\boldsymbol{A}$ is ill-conditioned (to be discussed in Section 3.24) or of extremely high dimension.

Numerical methods to solve the system of equations (3.50) and calculate $\boldsymbol{A}^{-1}$ are discussed in Sections A.18 and A.19, respectively.

Statistical packages use a variety of matrix methods to solve (3.50). Stata uses the sweep algorithm, which is a variant of the Gauss-Jordan algorithm discussed in Section A.18. (For the sweep algorithm, see Goodnight 1979.) In R, `solve(A,b)` uses the QR decomposition. In MATLAB, `A\b` uses the Cholesky decomposition when $\boldsymbol{A}$ is positive definite and the QR decomposition otherwise.

3.24 COLLINEARITY ERRORS

For the least squares estimator to be uniquely defined, the regressors cannot be linearly dependent. However, it is quite easy to *attempt* to calculate a regression with linearly dependent regressors. This can occur for many reasons, including the following:

1. Including the same regressor twice.
2. Including regressors which are a linear combination of one another, such as *education*, *experience*, and *age* in the CPS dataset example (recall, *experience* is defined as *age–education–6*).
3. Including a dummy variable and its square.
4. Estimating a regression on a subsample for which a dummy variable is either all 0s or all 1s.
5. Including a dummy variable interaction which yields all 0s.
6. Including more regressors than observations.

In any of the above cases, the regressors are linearly dependent, so $\boldsymbol{X}'\boldsymbol{X}$ is singular and the least squares estimator is not unique. If you attempt to estimate the regression, you are likely to encounter an error message. (A possible exception is MATLAB using "`A\b`", as discussed later in this section.) The message may be that "system is exactly singular," "system is computationally singular," a variable is "omitted because of collinearity," or a coefficient is listed as "NA." In some cases (such as estimation in R using explicit matrix computation or MATLAB using the `regress` command), the program will stop execution. In other cases, the program will continue to run. In Stata (and in the `lm` package in R), a regression will be reported but one or more variables will be omitted.

If any of these warnings or error messages appear, the correct response is to stop and examine the regression coding and data. Did you make a mistake? Have you included a linearly dependent regressor? Are you estimating on a subsample for which the variables (in particular, dummy variables) have no variation? If you can determine that one of these scenarios caused the error, the solution is immediately apparent. You need to respecify your model (either sample or regressors) so that the redundancy is eliminated. All empirical researchers encounter this error in the course of empirical work. You should not, however, simply accept output if the package has selected variables for omission. It is the researcher's job to understand the underlying cause and enact a suitable remedy.

There is also a possibility that the statistical package will not detect and report the matrix singularity. If you compute in MATLAB using explicit matrix operations and use the recommended `A\b` command to compute the least squares estimator, MATLAB may return a numerical solution without an error message, even when the regressors are algebraically dependent. It is therefore recommended that you perform a numerical check for matrix singularity when using explicit matrix operations in MATLAB.

How can we numerically check whether a matrix $\boldsymbol{A}$ is singular? A standard diagnostic is the **reciprocal condition number**

$$C=\frac{\lambda_{\min}(\boldsymbol{A})}{\lambda_{\max}(\boldsymbol{A})}.$$

If $C=0$, then $\boldsymbol{A}$ is singular. If $C=1$, then $\boldsymbol{A}$ is perfectly balanced. If C is extremely small, we say that $\boldsymbol{A}$ is **ill-conditioned**. The reciprocal condition number can be calculated in MATLAB or R by the `rcond` command. Unfortunately, there is no accepted tolerance for how small C should be before regarding $\boldsymbol{A}$ as numerically singular, in part since `rcond(A)` can return a positive (but small) result even if $\boldsymbol{A}$ is algebraically singular. However, in double precision (which is typically used for computation), numerical accuracy is bounded by $2^{-52}\simeq$ 2e-16, suggesting the minimum bound $C\geq$ 2e-16.

Checking for numerical singularity is complicated by the fact that low values of C can also be caused by unbalanced or highly correlated regressors.

To illustrate, consider a wage regression using the sample from (3.13) on powers of experience X from 1 through k (i.e., $X, X^2, X^3, \ldots, X^k$). We calculated the reciprocal condition number C for each k, and found that C is decreasing as k increases, indicating increasing ill-conditioning. Indeed, for $k=5$, we find $C=$ 6e-17, which is lower than double precision accuracy. This means that a regression on (X, X^2, X^3, X^4, X^5) is ill-conditioned. The regressor matrix, however, is not singular. The low value of C is not due to algebraic singularity but rather is due to a lack of balance and to high collinearity.

Ill-conditioned regressors have the potential problem that the numerical results (the reported coefficient estimates) will be inaccurate. It may not be a concern in most applications, as this only occurs in extreme cases. Nevertheless, we should try and avoid ill-conditioned regressions when possible.

There are strategies which can reduce or even eliminate ill-conditioning. Often it is sufficient to rescale the regressors. A simple rescaling which often works for nonnegative regressors is to divide each by its sample mean, thus replacing X_{ji} with $X_{ji}/\overline{X}_j$. In the above example with the powers of experience, this means replacing X_i^2 with $X_i^2/\left(n^{-1}\sum_{i=1}^n X_i^2\right)$, and so forth. Doing so dramatically reduces the ill-conditioning. With this scaling, regressions for $k\leq 11$ satisfy $C\geq$ 1e-15. Another rescaling specific to a regression with powers is to first rescale the regressor to lie in $[-1, 1]$ before taking powers. With this scaling, regressions for $k \leq 16$ satisfy $C \geq$ 1e-15. A simpler scaling option is to rescale the regressor to lie in $[0, 1]$ before taking powers. With this scaling, regressions for $k \leq 9$ satisfy $C \geq$ 1e-15, which is sufficient for most applications.

Ill-conditioning can often be eliminated by orthogonalization of the regressors. This is achieved by sequentially regressing each variable (each column in $\boldsymbol{X}$) on the preceeding variables (each preceeding column), taking the residual, and then rescaling to have a unit variance. This procedure will produce regressors which algebraically satisfy $\boldsymbol{X}'\boldsymbol{X} = n\boldsymbol{I}_n$ and have a condition number of $C = 1$. If we apply this method to the above example, we obtain a condition number close to 1 for $k \leq 20$.

What this discussion shows is that when a regression has a small condition number, it is important to examine the specification carefully. It is possible that the regressors are linearly dependent, in which case one or more regressors will need to be omitted. It is also possible that the regressors are badly scaled, in which case it may be useful to rescale some of the regressors. It is also possible that the variables are highly collinear, in which case a possible solution is orthogonalization. These choices should be made by the researcher, not by an automated software program.

3.25 PROGRAMMING

Most software packages allow both interactive programming (you enter commands one-by-one) and batch programming (you run a pre-written sequence of commands from a file). Interactive programming can be useful for exploratory analysis, but eventually all work should be executed in batch mode. This is the best way to control and document your work.

Batch programs are text files where each line executes a single command. For Stata, this file needs to have the filename extension ".do", and for MATLAB ".m". For R there is no specific naming requirements, though it is typical to use the extension ".r". When writing batch files, it is useful to include comments for documentation and readability. To execute a program file, you type a command in the program.

Stata: `do chapter3` executes the file `chapter3.do`.
MATLAB: `run chapter3` executes the file `chapter3.m`.
R: `source('chapter3.r')` executes the file `chapter3.r`.

There are similarities and differences between the commands used in these packages. For example:

1. Different symbols are used to create comments. `*` in Stata, # in R, and `%` in MATLAB.
2. MATLAB uses the symbol `;` to separate lines. Stata and R use a hard return.
3. Stata uses `ln()` to compute natural logarithms. R and MATLAB use `log()`.
4. The symbol = is used to define a variable. R prefers `<-`. Double equality == is used to test equality.

Let us now look at some programming files for Stata, R, and MATLAB, which execute a portion of the empirical illustrations from Sections 3.7 and 3.21. For the R and MATLAB code we consider explicit matrix operations. Alternatively, R and MATLAB have built-in functions which implement least squares regression without the need for explicit matrix operations. In R, the standard function is `lm`. In MATLAB, the standard function is `regress`. The advantage of using explicit matrix operations as shown below is that you know exactly what computations are done and it is easier to go "out of the box" to execute new procedures. The advantage of using built-in functions is that coding is simplified and you are much less likely to make a coding error.

Stata do File

```
*	Clear memory and load the data
clear
use cps09mar.dta
*	Generate transformations
gen wage = ln(earnings/(hours*week))
gen experience = age - education - 6
gen exp2 = (experience^2)/100
*	Create indicator for subsamples
gen mbf = (race == 2) & (marital <= 2) & (female == 1)
gen mbf12 = (mbf == 1) & (experience == 12)
gen sam = (race == 4) & (marital == 7) & (female == 0)
*	Regressions
reg wage education if mbf12 == 1
reg wage education experience exp2 if sam == 1
*	Leverage and influence
predict leverage, hat
predict e, residual
gen d=e*leverage/(1-leverage)
summarize d if sam ==1
```

R Program File

```
#	Load the data and create subsamples
dat <- read.table("cps09mar.txt")
experience <- dat[,1]-dat[,4]-6
mbf <- (dat[,11]==2)&(dat[,12]<=2)&(dat[,2]==1)&(experience==12)
sam <- (dat[,11]==4)&(dat[,12]==7)&(dat[,2]==0)
dat1 <- dat[mbf,]
dat2 <- dat[sam,]
#	First regression
y <- as.matrix(log(dat1[,5]/(dat1[,6]*dat1[,7])))
x <- cbind(dat1[,4],matrix(1,nrow(dat1),1))
xx <- t(x)%*%x
xy <- t(x)%*%y
beta <- solve(xx,xy)
print(beta)
#	Second regression
y <- as.matrix(log(dat2[,5]/(dat2[,6]*dat2[,7])))
experience <- dat2[,1]-dat2[,4]-6
exp2 <- (experience^2)/100
x <- cbind(dat2[,4],experience,exp2,matrix(1,nrow(dat2),1))
xx <- t(x)%*%x
```

```
xy <- t(x)%*%y
beta <- solve(xx,xy)
print(beta)
#       Create leverage and influence
e <- y-x%*%beta
xxi <- solve(xx)
leverage <- rowSums(x*(x%*%xxi))
r <- e/(1-leverage)
d <- leverage*e/(1-leverage)
print(max(abs(d)))
```

MATLAB Program File

```
% Load the data and create subsamples
dat = load cps09mar.txt;
# An alternative to load the data from an excel file is
# dat = xlsread('cps09mar.xlsx');
experience = dat(:,1)-dat(:,4)-6;
mbf = (dat(:,11)==2)&(dat(:,12)<=2)&(dat(:,2)==1)&(experience==12);
sam = (dat(:,11)==4)&(dat(:,12)==7)&(dat(:,2)==0);
dat1 = dat(mbf,:);
dat2 = dat(sam,:);
%       First regression
y = log(dat1(:,5)./(dat1(:,6).*dat1(:,7)));
x = [dat1(:,4),ones(length(dat1),1)];
xx = x'*x
xy = x'*y
beta = xx\xy;
display(beta);
%       Second regression
y = log(dat2(:,5)./(dat2(:,6).*dat2(:,7)));
experience = dat2(:,1)-dat2(:,4)-6;
exp2 = (experience.^2)/100;
x = [dat2(:,4),experience,exp2,ones(length(dat2),1)];
xx = x'*x
xy = x'*y
beta = xx\xy;display(beta);
%       Create leverage and influence
e = y-x*beta;
xxi = inv(xx)
leverage = sum((x.*(x*xxi))')';
d = leverage.*e./(1-leverage);
influence = max(abs(d));
display(influence);
```

3.26 EXERCISES

Exercise 3.1 Let Y be a random variable with $\mu = \mathbb{E}[Y]$ and $\sigma^2 = \text{var}[Y]$. Define

$$g(y, \mu, \sigma^2) = \begin{pmatrix} y - \mu \\ (y-\mu)^2 - \sigma^2 \end{pmatrix}.$$

Let $(\widehat{\mu}, \widehat{\sigma}^2)$ be the values such that $\overline{g}_n(\widehat{\mu}, \widehat{\sigma}^2) = 0$, where $\overline{g}_n(m, s) = n^{-1} \sum_{i=1}^n g(y_i, m, s)$. Show that $\widehat{\mu}$ and $\widehat{\sigma}^2$ are the sample mean and variance.

Exercise 3.2 Consider the OLS regression of the $n \times 1$ vector $\boldsymbol{Y}$ on the $n \times k$ matrix $\boldsymbol{X}$. Consider an alternative set of regressors $\boldsymbol{Z} = \boldsymbol{X}\boldsymbol{C}$, where $\boldsymbol{C}$ is a $k \times k$ nonsingular matrix. Thus, each column of $\boldsymbol{Z}$ is a mixture of some of the columns of $\boldsymbol{X}$. Compare the OLS estimates and residuals from the regression of $\boldsymbol{Y}$ on $\boldsymbol{X}$ to the OLS estimates from the regression of $\boldsymbol{Y}$ on $\boldsymbol{Z}$.

Exercise 3.3 Using matrix algebra, show $\boldsymbol{X}'\widehat{\boldsymbol{e}} = 0$.

Exercise 3.4 Let $\widehat{\boldsymbol{e}}$ be the OLS residual from a regression of $\boldsymbol{Y}$ on $\boldsymbol{X} = [\boldsymbol{X}_1 \ \boldsymbol{X}_2]$. Find $\boldsymbol{X}_2'\widehat{\boldsymbol{e}}$.

Exercise 3.5 Let $\widehat{\boldsymbol{e}}$ be the OLS residual from a regression of $\boldsymbol{Y}$ on $\boldsymbol{X}$. Find the OLS coefficient from a regression of $\widehat{\boldsymbol{e}}$ on $\boldsymbol{X}$.

Exercise 3.6 Let $\widehat{\boldsymbol{Y}} = \boldsymbol{X}(\boldsymbol{X}'\boldsymbol{X})^{-1}\boldsymbol{X}'\boldsymbol{Y}$. Find the OLS coefficient from a regression of $\widehat{\boldsymbol{Y}}$ on $\boldsymbol{X}$.

Exercise 3.7 Show that if $\boldsymbol{X} = [\boldsymbol{X}_1 \ \boldsymbol{X}_2]$, then $\boldsymbol{P}\boldsymbol{X}_1 = \boldsymbol{X}_1$ and $\boldsymbol{M}\boldsymbol{X}_1 = 0$.

Exercise 3.8 Show that $\boldsymbol{M}$ is idempotent: $\boldsymbol{M}\boldsymbol{M} = \boldsymbol{M}$.

Exercise 3.9 Show that $\text{tr}\,\boldsymbol{M} = n - k$.

Exercise 3.10 Show that if $\boldsymbol{X} = [\boldsymbol{X}_1 \ \boldsymbol{X}_2]$ and $\boldsymbol{X}_1'\boldsymbol{X}_2 = 0$, then $\boldsymbol{P} = \boldsymbol{P}_1 + \boldsymbol{P}_2$.

Exercise 3.11 Show that when $\boldsymbol{X}$ contains a constant, $n^{-1}\sum_{i=1}^n \widehat{Y}_i = \overline{Y}$.

Exercise 3.12 A dummy variable takes on only the values 0 and 1. It is used for categorical variables. Let $\boldsymbol{D}_1$ and $\boldsymbol{D}_2$ be vectors of 1's and 0's, with the ith element of $\boldsymbol{D}_1$ equaling 1 and that of $\boldsymbol{D}_2$ equaling 0 if the person is a man, and the reverse if the person is a woman. Suppose that there are n_1 men and n_2 women in the sample. Consider fitting the following three equations by OLS:

$$\boldsymbol{Y} = \mu + \boldsymbol{D}_1\alpha_1 + \boldsymbol{D}_2\alpha_2 + \boldsymbol{e} \tag{3.52}$$

$$\boldsymbol{Y} = \boldsymbol{D}_1\alpha_1 + \boldsymbol{D}_2\alpha_2 + \boldsymbol{e} \tag{3.53}$$

$$\boldsymbol{Y} = \mu + \boldsymbol{D}_1\phi + \boldsymbol{e}. \tag{3.54}$$

Can all three equations (3.52), (3.53), and (3.54) be estimated by OLS? Explain if not.

(a) Compare regressions (3.53) and (3.54). Is one more general than the other? Explain the relationship between the parameters in (3.53) and (3.54).

(b) Compute $\mathbf{1}_n' \boldsymbol{D}_1$ and $\mathbf{1}_n' \boldsymbol{D}_2$, where $\mathbf{1}_n$ is an $n \times 1$ vector of 1s.

Exercise 3.13 Let $\boldsymbol{D}_1$ and $\boldsymbol{D}_2$ be defined as in the previous exercise.

(a) In the OLS regression

$$\boldsymbol{Y} = \boldsymbol{D}_1 \widehat{\gamma}_1 + \boldsymbol{D}_2 \widehat{\gamma}_2 + \widehat{\boldsymbol{u}}$$

show that $\widehat{\gamma}_1$ is the sample mean of the dependent variable among the men of the sample ($\overline{Y}_1$), and that $\widehat{\gamma}_2$ is the sample mean among the women ($\overline{Y}_2$).

(b) Let $\boldsymbol{X}$ $(n \times k)$ be an additional matrix of regressors. Describe in words the transformations

$$\boldsymbol{Y}^* = \boldsymbol{Y} - \boldsymbol{D}_1 \overline{Y}_1 - \boldsymbol{D}_2 \overline{Y}_2$$

$$\boldsymbol{X}^* = \boldsymbol{X} - \boldsymbol{D}_1 \overline{X}_1' - \boldsymbol{D}_2 \overline{X}_2'$$

where $\overline{X}_1$ and $\overline{X}_2$ are the $k \times 1$ means of the regressors for men and women, respectively.

(c) Compare $\widetilde{\beta}$ from the OLS regression

$$\boldsymbol{Y}^* = \boldsymbol{X}^* \widetilde{\boldsymbol{\beta}} + \widetilde{\boldsymbol{e}}$$

with $\widehat{\beta}$ from the OLS regression

$$\boldsymbol{Y} = \boldsymbol{D}_1 \widehat{\alpha}_1 + \boldsymbol{D}_2 \widehat{\alpha}_2 + \boldsymbol{X} \widehat{\boldsymbol{\beta}} + \widehat{\boldsymbol{e}}.$$

Exercise 3.14 Let $\widehat{\beta}_n = \left(\boldsymbol{X}_n' \boldsymbol{X}_n\right)^{-1} \boldsymbol{X}_n' \boldsymbol{Y}_n$ denote the OLS estimate when $\boldsymbol{Y}_n$ is $n \times 1$ and $\boldsymbol{X}_n$ is $n \times k$. A new observation (Y_{n+1}, X_{n+1}) becomes available. Prove that the OLS estimate computed using this additional observation is

$$\widehat{\beta}_{n+1} = \widehat{\beta}_n + \frac{1}{1 + X_{n+1}' \left(\boldsymbol{X}_n' \boldsymbol{X}_n\right)^{-1} X_{n+1}} \left(\boldsymbol{X}_n' \boldsymbol{X}_n\right)^{-1} X_{n+1} \left(Y_{n+1} - X_{n+1}' \widehat{\beta}_n\right).$$

Exercise 3.15 Prove that R^2 is the square of the sample correlation between $\boldsymbol{Y}$ and $\widehat{\boldsymbol{Y}}$.

Exercise 3.16 Consider two least squares regressions

$$\boldsymbol{Y} = \boldsymbol{X}_1 \widetilde{\beta}_1 + \widetilde{\boldsymbol{e}}$$

and

$$\boldsymbol{Y} = \boldsymbol{X}_1 \widehat{\beta}_1 + \boldsymbol{X}_2 \widehat{\beta}_2 + \widehat{\boldsymbol{e}}.$$

Let R_1^2 and R_2^2 be the R-squared from the two regressions. Show that $R_2^2 \geq R_1^2$. Is there a case when equality holds: $R_2^2 = R_1^2$? If so, explain the case.

Exercise 3.17 For $\widetilde{\sigma}^2$ defined in (3.46), show that $\widetilde{\sigma}^2 \geq \widehat{\sigma}^2$. Is equality possible?

Exercise 3.18 For which observations will $\widehat{\beta}_{(-i)} = \widehat{\beta}$?

Exercise 3.19 For the intercept-only model $Y_i = \beta + e_i$, show that the leave-one-out prediction error is

$$\widetilde{e}_i = \left(\frac{n}{n-1}\right)\left(Y_i - \overline{Y}\right).$$

Exercise 3.20 Define the leave-one-out estimator of σ^2,

$$\widehat{\sigma}^2_{(-i)} = \frac{1}{n-1}\sum_{j\neq i}\left(Y_j - X_j'\widehat{\beta}_{(-i)}\right)^2.$$

This is the estimator obtained from the sample with observation i omitted. Show that

$$\widehat{\sigma}^2_{(-i)} = \frac{n}{n-1}\widehat{\sigma}^2 - \frac{\widehat{e}_i^2}{(n-1)(1-h_{ii})}.$$

Exercise 3.21 Consider the least squares regression estimators

$$Y_i = X_{1i}\widehat{\beta}_1 + X_{2i}\widehat{\beta}_2 + \widehat{e}_i$$

and the "one regressor at a time" regression estimators

$$Y_i = X_{1i}\widetilde{\beta}_1 + \widetilde{e}_{1i}, \qquad Y_i = X_{2i}\widetilde{\beta}_2 + \widetilde{e}_{2i}.$$

Under what condition does $\widetilde{\beta}_1 = \widehat{\beta}_1$ and $\widetilde{\beta}_2 = \widehat{\beta}_2$?

Exercise 3.22 You estimate a least squares regression

$$Y_i = X_{1i}'\widetilde{\beta}_1 + \widetilde{u}_i$$

and then regress the residuals on another set of regressors

$$\widetilde{u}_i = X_{2i}'\widetilde{\beta}_2 + \widetilde{e}_i.$$

Check whether this second regression gives you the same estimated coefficients as from estimation of a least squares regression on both set of regressors

$$Y_i = X_{1i}'\widehat{\beta}_1 + X_{2i}'\widehat{\beta}_2 + \widehat{e}_i.$$

In other words, is it true that $\widetilde{\beta}_2 = \widehat{\beta}_2$? Explain your reasoning.

Exercise 3.23 The data matrix is $(\boldsymbol{Y}, \boldsymbol{X})$ with $\boldsymbol{X} = [\boldsymbol{X}_1, \boldsymbol{X}_2]$. Consider the transformed regressor matrix $\boldsymbol{Z} = [\boldsymbol{X}_1, \boldsymbol{X}_2 - \boldsymbol{X}_1]$. Suppose you do a least squares regression of $\boldsymbol{Y}$ on $\boldsymbol{X}$, and a least squares regression of $\boldsymbol{Y}$ on $\boldsymbol{Z}$. Let $\widehat{\sigma}^2$ and $\widetilde{\sigma}^2$ denote the residual variance estimates from the two regressions. Give a formula relating $\widehat{\sigma}^2$ and $\widetilde{\sigma}^2$. Explain your reasoning.

Exercise 3.24 Use the `cps09mar` dataset described in Section 3.22 and available on the textbook website. Take the subsample used for equation (3.49) for data construction,

(a) Estimate equation (3.49), and compute the equation R^2 and sum of squared errors.

(b) Re-estimate the slope on education using the residual regression approach. Regress log(wage) on experience and its square, regress education on experience and its square, and the residuals on the residuals. Report the estimates from this final regression, along with the equation R^2 and sum of squared errors. Does the slope coefficient equal the value in (3.49)? Explain.

(c) Are the R^2 and sum of squared errors from parts (a) and (b) equal? Explain.

Exercise 3.25 Estimate equation (3.49) as in part (a) of Exercise 3.24. Let $\widehat{e}_i$ be the OLS residual, $\widehat{Y}_i$ the predicted value from the regression, X_{1i} be education, and X_{2i} be experience. Numerically calculate the following:

(a) $\sum_{i=1}^{n} \widehat{e}_i$.
(b) $\sum_{i=1}^{n} X_{1i}\widehat{e}_i$.
(c) $\sum_{i=1}^{n} X_{2i}\widehat{e}_i$.
(d) $\sum_{i=1}^{n} X_{1i}^2\widehat{e}_i$.
(e) $\sum_{i=1}^{n} X_{2i}^2\widehat{e}_i$.
(f) $\sum_{i=1}^{n} \widehat{Y}_i\widehat{e}_i$.
(g) $\sum_{i=1}^{n} \widehat{e}_i^2$.

Are these calculations consistent with the theoretical properties of OLS? Explain.

Exercise 3.26 Use the `cps09mar` dataset.

(a) Estimate a log wage regression for the subsample of white male Hispanics. In addition to education, experience, and its square, include a set of binary variables for regions and marital status. For regions, create dummy variables for Northeast, South, and West, so that Midwest is the excluded group. For marital status, create variables for married, widowed, or divorced, and separated, so that single (never married) is the excluded group.

(b) Repeat using a different econometric package. Compare your results. Do you obtain the same results?

CHAPTER 4

LEAST SQUARES REGRESSION

4.1 INTRODUCTION

In this chapter, we investigate some finite-sample properties of the least squares estimator in the linear regression model. In particular, we calculate its finite-sample expectation and covariance matrix and propose standard errors for the coefficient estimators.

4.2 RANDOM SAMPLING

Assumption 3.1 specified that the observations have identical distributions. To derive the finite-sample properties of the estimators, we will need to additionally specify the dependence structure across the observations.

The simplest context is when the observations are mutually independent, in which case we say that they are **independent and identically distributed** or **i.i.d.** It is also common to describe i.i.d. observations as a **random sample**. Traditionally, random sampling has been the default assumption in cross-section (e.g., survey) contexts. It is quite convenient, as i.i.d. sampling leads to straightforward expressions for estimation variance. The assumption seems appropriate (meaning that it should be approximately valid) when samples are small and relatively dispersed. That is, if you randomly sample 1000 people from a large country such as the United States it seems reasonable to model their responses as mutually independent.

Assumption 4.1 The random variables $\{(Y_1, X_1), \ldots, (Y_i, X_i), \ldots, (Y_n, X_n)\}$ are i.i.d.

For most of this chapter, we will use Assumption 4.1 to derive properties of the OLS estimator.

Assumption 4.1 means that if you take any two individuals $i \neq j$ in a sample, the values (Y_i, X_i) are independent of the values (Y_j, X_j) yet have the same distribution. Independence means that the decisions and choices of individual i do not affect the decisions of individual j and conversely.

This assumption may be violated if individuals in the sample are connected in some way, for example, if they are neighbors, members of the same village, classmates at a school, or even firms in a specific industry. In this case, it seems plausible that decisions may be interconnected and thus mutually dependent rather than independent. Allowing for such interactions complicates inference and requires specialized treatment. A currently popular approach which allows for mutual dependence is known as **clustered dependence**, which assumes that that observations are grouped into "clusters" (for example, schools). We will discuss clustering in more detail in Section 4.21.

4.3 SAMPLE MEAN

We start with the simplest setting of the intercept-only model:

$$Y = \mu + e$$
$$\mathbb{E}[e] = 0$$

which is equivalent to the regression model with $k = 1$ and $X = 1$. In the intercept model, $\mu = \mathbb{E}[Y]$ is the expectation of Y (see Exercise 2.15). The least squares estimator $\widehat{\mu} = \overline{Y}$ equals the sample mean, as shown in equation (3.8).

We now calculate the expectation and variance of the estimator $\overline{Y}$. Since the sample mean is a linear function of the observations, its expectation is simple to calculate:

$$\mathbb{E}\left[\overline{Y}\right] = \mathbb{E}\left[\frac{1}{n}\sum_{i=1}^{n} Y_i\right] = \frac{1}{n}\sum_{i=1}^{n} \mathbb{E}[Y_i] = \mu.$$

Thus the expected value of the least squares estimator (the sample mean) equals the projection coefficient (the population expectation). An estimator with the property that its expectation equals the parameter it is estimating is called **unbiased**.

Definition 4.1 An estimator $\widehat{\theta}$ for θ is **unbiased** if $\mathbb{E}\left[\widehat{\theta}\right] = \theta$.

We next calculate the variance of the estimator $\overline{Y}$ under Assumption 4.1. Making the substitution $Y_i = \mu + e_i$, we find

$$\overline{Y} - \mu = \frac{1}{n}\sum_{i=1}^{n} e_i.$$

Then

$$\begin{aligned}
\operatorname{var}\left[\overline{Y}\right] &= \mathbb{E}\left[\left(\overline{Y} - \mu\right)^2\right] \\
&= \mathbb{E}\left[\left(\frac{1}{n}\sum_{i=1}^{n} e_i\right)\left(\frac{1}{n}\sum_{j=1}^{n} e_j\right)\right] \\
&= \frac{1}{n^2}\sum_{i=1}^{n}\sum_{j=1}^{n} \mathbb{E}\left[e_i e_j\right] \\
&= \frac{1}{n^2}\sum_{i=1}^{n} \sigma^2 \\
&= \frac{1}{n}\sigma^2.
\end{aligned}$$

The second-to-last equality is because $\mathbb{E}\left[e_i e_j\right] = \sigma^2$ for $i = j$, yet $\mathbb{E}\left[e_i e_j\right] = 0$ for $i \neq j$ due to independence.

We have shown that $\operatorname{var}\left[\overline{Y}\right] = \frac{1}{n}\sigma^2$. This is the familiar formula for the variance of the sample mean.

4.4 LINEAR REGRESSION MODEL

We now consider the linear regression model. Throughout this chapter, we maintain the following assumptions.

Assumption 4.2 Linear Regression Model
The variables (Y, X) satisfy the linear regression equation

$$Y = X'\beta + e \tag{4.1}$$

$$\mathbb{E}[e \mid X] = 0. \tag{4.2}$$

The variables have finite second moments

$$\mathbb{E}\left[Y^2\right] < \infty,$$

$$\mathbb{E}\,\|X\|^2 < \infty,$$

and an invertible design matrix

$$\boldsymbol{Q}_{XX} = \mathbb{E}\left[XX'\right] > 0.$$

We will consider both the general case of heteroskedastic regression, where the conditional variance $\mathbb{E}\left[e^2 \mid X\right] = \sigma^2(X)$ is unrestricted, and the specialized case of homoskedastic regression, where the conditional variance is constant. In the latter case, we add the following assumption.

Assumption 4.3 Homoskedastic Linear Regression Model
In addition to Assumption 4.2,

$$\mathbb{E}\left[e^2 \mid X\right] = \sigma^2(X) = \sigma^2 \tag{4.3}$$

is independent of X.

4.5 EXPECTATION OF LEAST SQUARES ESTIMATOR

In this section, we show that the OLS estimator is unbiased in the linear regression model. This calculation can be done using either summation notation or matrix notation. We will use both.

First take summation notation. Observe that under (4.1) and (4.2)

$$\mathbb{E}[Y_i \mid X_1, \ldots, X_n] = \mathbb{E}[Y_i \mid X_i] = X_i'\beta. \tag{4.4}$$

The first equality states that the conditional expectation of Y_i given $\{X_1, \ldots, X_n\}$ only depends on X_i, because the observations are independent across i. The second equality is the assumption of a linear conditional expectation.

Using Definition (3.1), the conditioning theorem (Theorem 2.3), the linearity of expectations (4.4), and properties of the matrix inverse, we find

$$\begin{aligned}
\mathbb{E}\left[\widehat{\beta} \mid X_1, \ldots, X_n\right] &= \mathbb{E}\left[\left(\sum_{i=1}^n X_i X_i'\right)^{-1}\left(\sum_{i=1}^n X_i Y_i\right) \middle| X_1, \ldots, X_n\right] \\
&= \left(\sum_{i=1}^n X_i X_i'\right)^{-1} \mathbb{E}\left[\left(\sum_{i=1}^n X_i Y_i\right) \middle| X_1, \ldots, X_n\right] \\
&= \left(\sum_{i=1}^n X_i X_i'\right)^{-1} \sum_{i=1}^n \mathbb{E}\left[X_i Y_i \mid X_1, \ldots, X_n\right] \\
&= \left(\sum_{i=1}^n X_i X_i'\right)^{-1} \sum_{i=1}^n X_i \mathbb{E}\left[Y_i \mid X_i\right] \\
&= \left(\sum_{i=1}^n X_i X_i'\right)^{-1} \sum_{i=1}^n X_i X_i' \beta \\
&= \beta.
\end{aligned}$$

Now let's show the same result using matrix notation. Equation (4.4) implies

$$\mathbb{E}[\boldsymbol{Y} \mid \boldsymbol{X}] = \begin{pmatrix} \vdots \\ \mathbb{E}[Y_i \mid \boldsymbol{X}] \\ \vdots \end{pmatrix} = \begin{pmatrix} \vdots \\ X_i'\beta \\ \vdots \end{pmatrix} = \boldsymbol{X}\beta. \tag{4.5}$$

Similarly,

$$\mathbb{E}[\boldsymbol{e} \mid \boldsymbol{X}] = \begin{pmatrix} \vdots \\ \mathbb{E}[e_i \mid \boldsymbol{X}] \\ \vdots \end{pmatrix} = \begin{pmatrix} \vdots \\ \mathbb{E}[e_i \mid X_i] \\ \vdots \end{pmatrix} = 0.$$

Using $\widehat{\beta} = \left(\boldsymbol{X}'\boldsymbol{X}\right)^{-1}\left(\boldsymbol{X}'\boldsymbol{Y}\right)$, the conditioning theorem, the linearity of expectations, (4.5), and the properties of the matrix inverse, we have

$$\begin{aligned}
\mathbb{E}\left[\widehat{\beta} \mid \boldsymbol{X}\right] &= \mathbb{E}\left[\left(\boldsymbol{X}'\boldsymbol{X}\right)^{-1}\boldsymbol{X}'\boldsymbol{Y} \mid \boldsymbol{X}\right] \\
&= \left(\boldsymbol{X}'\boldsymbol{X}\right)^{-1}\boldsymbol{X}'\mathbb{E}[\boldsymbol{Y} \mid \boldsymbol{X}] \\
&= \left(\boldsymbol{X}'\boldsymbol{X}\right)^{-1}\boldsymbol{X}'\boldsymbol{X}\beta \\
&= \beta.
\end{aligned}$$

At the risk of belaboring the derivation, another way to calculate the same result is as follows. Insert $\boldsymbol{Y} = \boldsymbol{X}\beta + \boldsymbol{e}$ into the formula for $\widehat{\beta}$ to obtain

$$\begin{aligned}
\widehat{\beta} &= \left(\boldsymbol{X}'\boldsymbol{X}\right)^{-1}\left(\boldsymbol{X}'\left(\boldsymbol{X}\beta + \boldsymbol{e}\right)\right) \\
&= \left(\boldsymbol{X}'\boldsymbol{X}\right)^{-1}\boldsymbol{X}'\boldsymbol{X}\beta + \left(\boldsymbol{X}'\boldsymbol{X}\right)^{-1}\left(\boldsymbol{X}'\boldsymbol{e}\right) \\
&= \beta + \left(\boldsymbol{X}'\boldsymbol{X}\right)^{-1}\boldsymbol{X}'\boldsymbol{e}.
\end{aligned} \tag{4.6}$$

This is a useful linear decomposition of the estimator $\widehat{\beta}$ into the true parameter β and the stochastic component $\left(\boldsymbol{X}'\boldsymbol{X}\right)^{-1}\boldsymbol{X}'\boldsymbol{e}$. Once again, we can calculate that

$$\begin{aligned}\mathbb{E}\left[\widehat{\beta}-\beta \mid \boldsymbol{X}\right] &= \mathbb{E}\left[\left(\boldsymbol{X}'\boldsymbol{X}\right)^{-1}\boldsymbol{X}'\boldsymbol{e} \mid \boldsymbol{X}\right] \\ &= \left(\boldsymbol{X}'\boldsymbol{X}\right)^{-1}\boldsymbol{X}'\mathbb{E}\left[\boldsymbol{e} \mid \boldsymbol{X}\right] = 0.\end{aligned}$$

Regardless of the method used, we have shown that $\mathbb{E}\left[\widehat{\beta} \mid \boldsymbol{X}\right] = \beta$. We have shown the following theorem.

> **Theorem 4.1 Expectation of Least Squares Estimator**
> In the linear regression model (Assumption 4.2) with i.i.d. sampling (Assumption 4.1), we have
>
> $$\mathbb{E}\left[\widehat{\beta} \mid \boldsymbol{X}\right] = \beta. \tag{4.7}$$

Equation (4.7) says that the estimator $\widehat{\beta}$ is unbiased for β, conditional on $\boldsymbol{X}$. Thus the conditional distribution of $\widehat{\beta}$ is centered at β. "Conditional on $\boldsymbol{X}$" means that the distribution is unbiased for any realization of the regressor matrix $\boldsymbol{X}$. In conditional models, we simply refer to this as saying "$\widehat{\beta}$ is unbiased for β."

It is worth mentioning that Theorem 4.1, and all finite sample results in this chapter, make the implicit assumption that $\boldsymbol{X}'\boldsymbol{X}$ is full rank with probability 1.

4.6 VARIANCE OF LEAST SQUARES ESTIMATOR

In this section, we calculate the conditional variance of the OLS estimator.

For any $r \times 1$ random vector Z, define the $r \times r$ covariance matrix

$$\operatorname{var}[Z] = \mathbb{E}\left[(Z-\mathbb{E}[Z])(Z-\mathbb{E}[Z])'\right] = \mathbb{E}\left[ZZ'\right] - (\mathbb{E}[Z])(\mathbb{E}[Z])'$$

and for any pair (Z, X), define the conditional covariance matrix

$$\operatorname{var}[Z \mid X] = \mathbb{E}\left[(Z-\mathbb{E}[Z \mid X])(Z-\mathbb{E}[Z \mid X])' \mid X\right].$$

We define $\boldsymbol{V}_{\widehat{\beta}} \overset{\text{def}}{=} \operatorname{var}\left[\widehat{\beta} \mid \boldsymbol{X}\right]$ as the conditional covariance matrix of the regression coefficient estimators. Let us now derive its form.

The conditional covariance matrix of the $n \times 1$ regression error $\boldsymbol{e}$ is the $n \times n$ matrix

$$\operatorname{var}[\boldsymbol{e} \mid \boldsymbol{X}] = \mathbb{E}\left[\boldsymbol{e}\boldsymbol{e}' \mid \boldsymbol{X}\right] \overset{\text{def}}{=} \boldsymbol{D}.$$

The ith diagonal element of $\boldsymbol{D}$ is

$$\mathbb{E}\left[e_i^2 \mid \boldsymbol{X}\right] = \mathbb{E}\left[e_i^2 \mid X_i\right] = \sigma_i^2$$

while the ijth off-diagonal element of $\boldsymbol{D}$ is

$$\mathbb{E}\left[e_i e_j \mid \boldsymbol{X}\right] = \mathbb{E}\left(e_i \mid X_i\right)\mathbb{E}\left[e_j \mid X_j\right] = 0$$

where the first equality uses independence of the observations (Assumption 4.1) and the second is (4.2). Thus $\boldsymbol{D}$ is a diagonal matrix with ith diagonal element σ_i^2:

$$\boldsymbol{D} = \operatorname{diag}\left(\sigma_1^2, \ldots, \sigma_n^2\right) = \begin{pmatrix} \sigma_1^2 & 0 & \cdots & 0 \\ 0 & \sigma_2^2 & \cdots & 0 \\ \vdots & \vdots & \ddots & \vdots \\ 0 & 0 & \cdots & \sigma_n^2 \end{pmatrix}. \tag{4.8}$$

In the special case of the linear homoskedastic regression model (4.3), then $\mathbb{E}\left[e_i^2 \mid X_i\right] = \sigma_i^2 = \sigma^2$, and we have the simplification $\boldsymbol{D} = \boldsymbol{I}_n \sigma^2$. In general, however, $\boldsymbol{D}$ need not necessarily take this simplified form.

For any $n \times r$ matrix $\boldsymbol{A} = \boldsymbol{A}(\boldsymbol{X})$,

$$\operatorname{var}\left[\boldsymbol{A}'\boldsymbol{Y} \mid \boldsymbol{X}\right] = \operatorname{var}\left[\boldsymbol{A}'\boldsymbol{e} \mid \boldsymbol{X}\right] = \boldsymbol{A}'\boldsymbol{D}\boldsymbol{A}. \tag{4.9}$$

In particular, we can write $\widehat{\beta} = \boldsymbol{A}'\boldsymbol{Y}$, where $\boldsymbol{A} = \boldsymbol{X}\left(\boldsymbol{X}'\boldsymbol{X}\right)^{-1}$ and thus

$$\boldsymbol{V}_{\widehat{\beta}} = \operatorname{var}\left[\widehat{\beta} \mid \boldsymbol{X}\right] = \boldsymbol{A}'\boldsymbol{D}\boldsymbol{A} = \left(\boldsymbol{X}'\boldsymbol{X}\right)^{-1} \boldsymbol{X}'\boldsymbol{D}\boldsymbol{X} \left(\boldsymbol{X}'\boldsymbol{X}\right)^{-1}.$$

It is useful to note that

$$\boldsymbol{X}'\boldsymbol{D}\boldsymbol{X} = \sum_{i=1}^{n} X_i X_i' \sigma_i^2$$

which is a weighted version of $\boldsymbol{X}'\boldsymbol{X}$.

In the special case of the linear homoskedastic regression model, $\boldsymbol{D} = \boldsymbol{I}_n \sigma^2$, so $\boldsymbol{X}'\boldsymbol{D}\boldsymbol{X} = \boldsymbol{X}'\boldsymbol{X}\sigma^2$, and the covariance matrix simplifies to $\boldsymbol{V}_{\widehat{\beta}} = \left(\boldsymbol{X}'\boldsymbol{X}\right)^{-1} \sigma^2$.

Theorem 4.2 Variance of Least Squares Estimator
In the linear regression model (Assumption 4.2) with i.i.d. sampling (Assumption 4.1),

$$\boldsymbol{V}_{\widehat{\beta}} = \operatorname{var}\left[\widehat{\beta} \mid \boldsymbol{X}\right] = \left(\boldsymbol{X}'\boldsymbol{X}\right)^{-1} \left(\boldsymbol{X}'\boldsymbol{D}\boldsymbol{X}\right) \left(\boldsymbol{X}'\boldsymbol{X}\right)^{-1} \tag{4.10}$$

where $\boldsymbol{D}$ is defined in (4.8). If in addition the error is homoskedastic (Assumption 4.3), then (4.10) simplifies to $\boldsymbol{V}_{\widehat{\beta}} = \sigma^2 \left(\boldsymbol{X}'\boldsymbol{X}\right)^{-1}$.

4.7 UNCONDITIONAL MOMENTS

The previous sections derived the form of the conditional expectation and variance of the least squares estimator where we conditioned on the regressor matrix $\boldsymbol{X}$. What about the unconditional expectation and variance?

Indeed, it is not obvious whether $\widehat{\beta}$ has a finite expectation or variance. Take the case of a single dummy variable regressor D_i with no intercept. Assume $\mathbb{P}\left[D_i = 1\right] = p < 1$. Then

$$\widehat{\beta} = \frac{\sum_{i=1}^{n} D_i Y_i}{\sum_{i=1}^{n} D_i}$$

is well defined if $\sum_{i=1}^{n} D_i > 0$. However, $\mathbb{P}\left[\sum_{i=1}^{n} D_i = 0\right] = (1-p)^n > 0$. Thus, with positive (but small) probability, $\widehat{\beta}$ does not exist. Consequently, $\widehat{\beta}$ has no finite moments! We ignore this complication in practice, but it does pose a conundrum for theory. This existence problem arises whenever there are discrete regressors.

This dilemma is avoided when the regressors have continuous distributions. A clean statement was obtained by Kinal (1980) under the assumption of normal regressors and errors.

Theorem 4.3 Kinal (1980)
In the linear regression model with i.i.d. sampling, if in addition the (X,e) have a joint normal distribution, then for any r, $\mathbb{E}\left\|\widehat{\beta}\right\|^r < \infty$ if and only if $r < n-k+1$.

This theorem shows that when the errors and regressors are normally distributed, the least squares estimator possesses all moments up to $n-k$, which includes all moments of practical interest. The normality assumption is not critical for this result. What is key is the assumption that the regressors are continuously distributed.

The law of iterated expectations (Theorem 2.1) combined with Theorems 4.1 and 4.3 allow us to deduce that the least squares estimator is unconditionally unbiased. Under the normality assumption, Theorem 4.3 allows us to apply the law of iterated expectations, and thus using Theorem 4.1, we deduce that if $n > k$

$$\mathbb{E}\left[\widehat{\beta}\right] = \mathbb{E}\left[\mathbb{E}\left[\widehat{\beta} \mid \boldsymbol{X}\right]\right] = \beta.$$

Hence $\widehat{\beta}$ is unconditionally unbiased, as asserted.

Furthermore, if $n-k > 1$, then $\mathbb{E}\left\|\widehat{\beta}\right\|^2 < \infty$, and $\widehat{\beta}$ has a finite unconditional variance. Using Theorem 2.8, we can calculate explicitly that

$$\operatorname{var}\left[\widehat{\beta}\right] = \mathbb{E}\left[\operatorname{var}\left[\widehat{\beta} \mid \boldsymbol{X}\right]\right] + \operatorname{var}\left[\mathbb{E}\left[\widehat{\beta} \mid \boldsymbol{X}\right]\right] = \mathbb{E}\left[\left(\boldsymbol{X}'\boldsymbol{X}\right)^{-1}\left(\boldsymbol{X}'\boldsymbol{D}\boldsymbol{X}\right)\left(\boldsymbol{X}'\boldsymbol{X}\right)^{-1}\right]$$

the second equality because $\mathbb{E}\left[\widehat{\beta} \mid \boldsymbol{X}\right] = \beta$ has zero variance. In the homoskedastic case, this simplifies to

$$\operatorname{var}\left[\widehat{\beta}\right] = \sigma^2 \mathbb{E}\left[\left(\boldsymbol{X}'\boldsymbol{X}\right)^{-1}\right].$$

In both cases, the expectation cannot pass through the matrix inverse, because this is a nonlinear function. Thus there is not a simple expression for the unconditional variance, other than stating that is it the expectation of the conditional variance.

4.8 GAUSS-MARKOV THEOREM

The Gauss-Markov Theorem is one of the most celebrated results in econometric theory. It provides a classical justification for the least squares estimator, showing that it has the lowest variance among unbiased estimators.

Under Assumption 4.2, we know that the least squares estimator is unbiased for β. Under Assumption 4.3, it has covariance matrix $\sigma^2\left(\boldsymbol{X}'\boldsymbol{X}\right)^{-1}$. The question raised in this section is whether there exists an alternative unbiased estimator $\widetilde{\beta}$ which has a smaller covariance matrix.

The following version of the theorem is due to B. E. Hansen (2022a).

Theorem 4.4 Gauss-Markov
Take the linear regression model (Assumption 4.2). Assume $\widetilde{\beta}$ is an unbiased estimator of β. Then under homoskedasticity (Assumption 4.3),

$$\operatorname{var}\left[\widetilde{\beta} \mid \boldsymbol{X}\right] \geq \sigma^2 \left(\boldsymbol{X}'\boldsymbol{X}\right)^{-1}.$$

Theorem 4.4 provides a lower bound on the covariance matrix of unbiased estimators under the assumption of homoskedasticity. It says that no unbiased estimator can have a variance matrix smaller (in the positive definite sense) than $\sigma^2 \left(\boldsymbol{X}'\boldsymbol{X}\right)^{-1}$. Since the variance of the OLS estimator is exactly equal to this bound, no unbiased estimator has a lower variance than OLS. Consequently, we describe OLS as **efficient** in the class of unbiased estimators.

The earliest version of Theorem 4.4 was articulated by Carl Friedrich Gauss in 1823. Andreĭ Andreevich Markov provided a textbook treatment of the theorem in 1912 and clarified the central role of unbiasedness, which Gauss had only assumed implicitly.

Their versions of the Theorem restricted attention to **linear** estimators of β, which are estimators that can be written as $\widetilde{\beta} = \boldsymbol{A}'\boldsymbol{Y}$, where $\boldsymbol{A} = \boldsymbol{A}(\boldsymbol{X})$ is an $m \times n$ function of the regressors $\boldsymbol{X}$. Linearity in this context means "linear in $\boldsymbol{Y}$." This restriction simplifies variance calculations, but greatly limits the class of estimators.This classical version of the theorem gave rise to the description of OLS as the **best linear unbiased estimator (BLUE)**. However, Theorem 4.4 as stated above shows that OLS is the **best unbiased estimator (BUE)**.

The derivation of the Gauss-Markov Theorem under the restriction to linear estimators is straightforward, so we now provide this demonstration. For $\widetilde{\beta} = \boldsymbol{A}'\boldsymbol{Y}$, we have

$$\mathbb{E}\left[\widetilde{\beta} \mid \boldsymbol{X}\right] = \boldsymbol{A}'\mathbb{E}\left[\boldsymbol{Y} \mid \boldsymbol{X}\right] = \boldsymbol{A}'\boldsymbol{X}\beta$$

where the second equality holds because $\mathbb{E}\left[\boldsymbol{Y} \mid \boldsymbol{X}\right] = \boldsymbol{X}\beta$. Then $\widetilde{\beta}$ is unbiased for all β if (and only if) $\boldsymbol{A}'\boldsymbol{X} = \boldsymbol{I}_k$. Furthermore, we saw in (4.9) that

$$\operatorname{var}\left[\widetilde{\beta} \mid \boldsymbol{X}\right] = \operatorname{var}\left[\boldsymbol{A}'\boldsymbol{Y} \mid \boldsymbol{X}\right] = \boldsymbol{A}'\boldsymbol{D}\boldsymbol{A} = \boldsymbol{A}'\boldsymbol{A}\sigma^2$$

the last equality using the homoskedasticity assumption. To establish Theorem 4.4, we need to show that for any such matrix $\boldsymbol{A}$,

$$\boldsymbol{A}'\boldsymbol{A} \geq \left(\boldsymbol{X}'\boldsymbol{X}\right)^{-1}. \tag{4.11}$$

Set $\boldsymbol{C} = \boldsymbol{A} - \boldsymbol{X}\left(\boldsymbol{X}'\boldsymbol{X}\right)^{-1}$. Note that $\boldsymbol{X}'\boldsymbol{C} = 0$. We calculate that

$$\begin{aligned}
\boldsymbol{A}'\boldsymbol{A} - \left(\boldsymbol{X}'\boldsymbol{X}\right)^{-1} &= \left(\boldsymbol{C} + \boldsymbol{X}\left(\boldsymbol{X}'\boldsymbol{X}\right)^{-1}\right)'\left(\boldsymbol{C} + \boldsymbol{X}\left(\boldsymbol{X}'\boldsymbol{X}\right)^{-1}\right) - \left(\boldsymbol{X}'\boldsymbol{X}\right)^{-1} \\
&= \boldsymbol{C}'\boldsymbol{C} + \boldsymbol{C}'\boldsymbol{X}\left(\boldsymbol{X}'\boldsymbol{X}\right)^{-1} + \left(\boldsymbol{X}'\boldsymbol{X}\right)^{-1}\boldsymbol{X}'\boldsymbol{C}
\end{aligned}$$

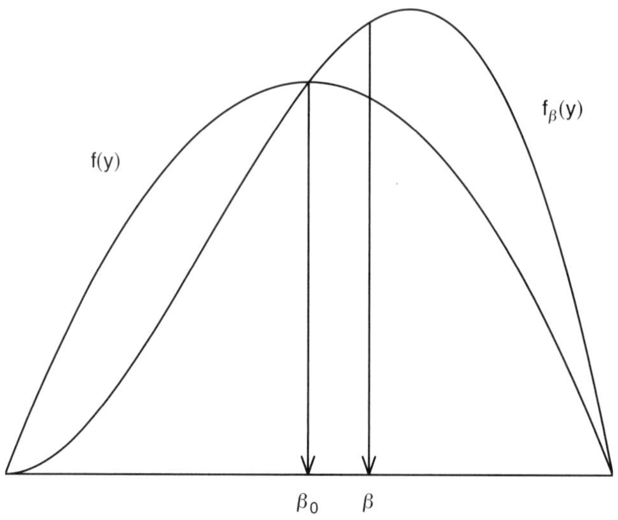

FIGURE 4.1 Original and auxiliary density

$$+\left(\boldsymbol{X}'\boldsymbol{X}\right)^{-1}\boldsymbol{X}'\boldsymbol{X}\left(\boldsymbol{X}'\boldsymbol{X}\right)^{-1}-\left(\boldsymbol{X}'\boldsymbol{X}\right)^{-1}$$
$$=\boldsymbol{C}'\boldsymbol{C}\geq 0.$$

The final inequality states that the matrix $\boldsymbol{C}'\boldsymbol{C}$ is positive semi-definite, which is a property of quadratic forms (see Appendix A.10). We have shown (4.11), as required.

The above derivation imposed the restriction that the estimator $\widetilde{\beta}$ is linear in $\boldsymbol{Y}$. The proof of Theorem 4.4 in the general case is considerably more advanced. Here I provide a simplified sketch of the argument for interested readers.

For simplicity, treat the regressors X as fixed, and suppose that Y has a density $f(y)$ with bounded support $\mathscr{Y}$. Without loss of generality, assume that the true coefficient equals $\beta_0 = 0$.

Since Y has bounded support $\mathscr{Y}$, there is a set $B \subset \mathbb{R}^m$ such that $\left|yX'\beta/\sigma^2\right| < 1$ for all $\beta \in B$ and $y \in \mathscr{Y}$. For such values of β, define the auxiliary density function

$$f_\beta(y) = f(y)\left(1 + yX'\beta/\sigma^2\right). \tag{4.12}$$

Under the assumptions, $0 \leq f_\beta(y) \leq 2f(y)$, $f_\beta(y)$ has support $\mathscr{Y}$, and $\int_{\mathscr{Y}} f_\beta(y)dy = 1$. To see the last statement, observe that $\int_{\mathscr{Y}} yf(y)dy = X'\beta_0 = 0$ under the normalization $\beta_0 = 0$, and thus

$$\int_{\mathscr{Y}} f_\beta(y)dy = \int_{\mathscr{Y}} f(y)dy + \int_{\mathscr{Y}} f(y)ydyX'\beta/\sigma^2 = 1$$

because $\int_{\mathscr{Y}} f(y)dy = 1$. Thus f_β is a parametric family of density functions. Evaluated at β_0, we see that $f_0 = f$, which means that f_β is a correctly specified parametric family with true parameter value $\beta_0 = 0$.

To illustrate, take the case $X = 1$. Figure 4.1 displays an example density $f(y) = (3/4)(1 - y^2)$ on $[-1, 1]$ with auxiliary density $f_\beta(y) = f(y)\left(1 + y\right)$. We can see how the auxiliary density is a tilted version of the original density $f(y)$.

Let $\mathbb{E}_\beta$ denote expectation with respect to the auxiliary distribution. Since $\int_{\mathscr{Y}} yf(y)dy = 0$ and $\int_{\mathscr{Y}} y^2 f(y)dy = \sigma^2$, we find

$$\mathbb{E}_\beta[Y] = \int_{\mathscr{Y}} yf_\beta(y)dy = \int_{\mathscr{Y}} yf(y)dy + \int_{\mathscr{Y}} y^2 f(y)dyX'\beta/\sigma^2 = X'\beta.$$

This shows that f_β is a regression model with regression coefficient β.

In Figure 4.1, the means of the two densities are indicated by the arrows to the x-axis. In this example, we can see how the auxiliary density has a larger expected value, because the density has been tilted to the right.

The parametric family f_β over $\beta \in B$ has the following properties: Its expectation is $X'\beta$, its variance is finite, the true value β_0 lies in the interior of B, and the support of the distribution does not depend on β.

The likelihood score of the auxiliary density function for an observation, using the fact that $Y_i = e_i$, is

$$S_i = \frac{\partial}{\partial\beta}\left(\log f_\beta(Y_i)\right)\Big|_{\beta=0} = \frac{\partial}{\partial\beta}\left(\log f(e_i) + \log\left(1 + e_i X_i'\beta/\sigma^2\right)\right)\Big|_{\beta=0} = X_i e_i/\sigma^2. \tag{4.13}$$

Therefore the information matrix is

$$\mathscr{I} = \sum_{i=1}^{n} \mathbb{E}\left[S_i S_i'\right] = \sum_{i=1}^{n} X_i X_i' \mathbb{E}\left[e_i^2\right]/\sigma^4 = \left(\boldsymbol{X}'\boldsymbol{X}\right)/\sigma^2.$$

By assumption, $\widetilde{\beta}$ is unbiased. The Cramér-Rao lower bound (see Theorem 10.6 of *Probability and Statistics for Economists*) states that

$$\operatorname{var}\left[\widetilde{\beta}\right] \geq \mathscr{I}^{-1} = \sigma^2\left(\boldsymbol{X}'\boldsymbol{X}\right)^{-1}.$$

This is the variance lower bound, completing the proof of Theorem 4.4.

The above argument is rather tricky. At its core is the observation that the model f_β is a submodel of the set of all linear regression models. The Cramér-Rao bound over any regular parametric submodel is a lower bound on the variance of any unbiased estimator. Thus the Cramér-Rao bound over f_β is a lower bound for unbiased estimation of the regression coefficient. The model f_β was selected judiciously so that its Cramér-Rao bound equals the variance of the least squares estimator, which sufficient to establish the bound.

4.9 GENERALIZED LEAST SQUARES

Take the linear regression model in matrix format:

$$\boldsymbol{Y} = \boldsymbol{X}\beta + \boldsymbol{e}. \tag{4.14}$$

Consider a generalized situation where the observation errors are possibly correlated and/or heteroskedastic. Specifically, suppose that

$$\mathbb{E}[\boldsymbol{e} \mid \boldsymbol{X}] = 0 \tag{4.15}$$

$$\operatorname{var}[\boldsymbol{e} \mid \boldsymbol{X}] = \Sigma\sigma^2 \tag{4.16}$$

for some $n \times n$ matrix $\Sigma > 0$, possibly a function of $\boldsymbol{X}$, and some scalar σ^2. This includes the independent sampling framework where Σ is diagonal but allows for nondiagonal covariance matrices as well. As a scaled covariance matrix, Σ is necessarily symmetric and positive semi-definite.

Under these assumptions, by arguments similar to those in Sections 4.5 and 4.6, we can calculate the expectation and variance of the OLS estimator:

$$\mathbb{E}\left[\widehat{\beta} \mid X\right] = \beta \tag{4.17}$$

$$\operatorname{var}\left[\widehat{\beta} \mid X\right] = \sigma^2 \left(X'X\right)^{-1} \left(X'\Sigma X\right) \left(X'X\right)^{-1} \tag{4.18}$$

(see Exercise 4.5).

Aitken (1935) established a generalization of the Gauss-Markov Theorem. The following statement is due to B. E. Hansen (2022a).

> **Theorem 4.5** Take the linear regression model (4.14)–(4.16). If $\widetilde{\beta}$ is an unbiased estimator of β, then
>
> $$\operatorname{var}\left[\widetilde{\beta} \mid X\right] \geq \sigma^2 \left(X'\Sigma^{-1}X\right)^{-1}.$$

We defer the proof to Section 4.24. See also Exercise 4.6.

Theorem 4.5 provides a lower bound on the covariance matrix of unbiased estimators.

When Σ is known, Aitken (1935) constructed an estimator which achieves the lower bound in Theorem 4.5. Take the linear model (4.14) and pre-multiply by $\Sigma^{-1/2}$. This produces the equation $\widetilde{Y} = \widetilde{X}\beta + \widetilde{e}$, where $\widetilde{Y} = \Sigma^{-1/2}Y$, $\widetilde{X} = \Sigma^{-1/2}X$, and $\widetilde{e} = \Sigma^{-1/2}e$. Consider OLS estimation of β in this equation:

$$\begin{aligned}
\widetilde{\beta}_{\text{gls}} &= \left(\widetilde{X}'\widetilde{X}\right)^{-1} \widetilde{X}'\widetilde{Y} \\
&= \left(\left(\Sigma^{-1/2}X\right)'\left(\Sigma^{-1/2}X\right)\right)^{-1} \left(\Sigma^{-1/2}X\right)'\left(\Sigma^{-1/2}Y\right) \\
&= \left(X'\Sigma^{-1}X\right)^{-1} X'\Sigma^{-1}Y.
\end{aligned} \tag{4.19}$$

This is called the **Generalized Least Squares** (GLS) estimator of β.

You can calculate that

$$\mathbb{E}\left[\widetilde{\beta}_{\text{gls}} \mid X\right] = \beta \tag{4.20}$$

$$\operatorname{var}\left[\widetilde{\beta}_{\text{gls}} \mid X\right] = \sigma^2 \left(X'\Sigma^{-1}X\right)^{-1}. \tag{4.21}$$

This shows that the GLS estimator is unbiased and has a covariance matrix equal to the lower bound from Theorem 4.5. Thus the lower bound is sharp. GLS is thus efficient in the class of unbiased estimators.

In the linear regression model with independent observations and known conditional variances, so that $\Sigma = D = \operatorname{diag}\left(\sigma_1^2, \ldots, \sigma_n^2\right)$, the GLS estimator takes the form

$$\begin{aligned}
\widetilde{\beta}_{\text{gls}} &= \left(X'D^{-1}X\right)^{-1} X'D^{-1}Y \\
&= \left(\sum_{i=1}^{n} \sigma_i^{-2} X_i X_i'\right)^{-1} \left(\sum_{i=1}^{n} \sigma_i^{-2} X_i Y_i\right).
\end{aligned}$$

The assumption $\Sigma > 0$ in this case reduces to $\sigma_i^2 > 0$ for $i = 1, \ldots, n$.

In most settings, the matrix Σ is unknown, so the GLS estimator is not feasible. However, the form of the GLS estimator motivates feasible versions, effectively by replacing Σ with a suitable estimator.

4.10 RESIDUALS

What are some properties of the residuals $\widehat{e}_i = Y_i - X_i'\widehat{\beta}$ and prediction errors $\widetilde{e}_i = Y_i - X_i'\widehat{\beta}_{(-i)}$ in the context of the linear regression model?

Recall from (3.24) that we can write the residuals in vector notation as $\widehat{\boldsymbol{e}} = \boldsymbol{M}\boldsymbol{e}$, where $\boldsymbol{M} = \boldsymbol{I}_n - \boldsymbol{X}\left(\boldsymbol{X}'\boldsymbol{X}\right)^{-1}\boldsymbol{X}'$ is the orthogonal projection matrix. Using the properties of conditional expectation

$$\mathbb{E}\left[\widehat{\boldsymbol{e}} \mid \boldsymbol{X}\right] = \mathbb{E}\left[\boldsymbol{M}\boldsymbol{e} \mid \boldsymbol{X}\right] = \boldsymbol{M}\mathbb{E}\left[\boldsymbol{e} \mid \boldsymbol{X}\right] = 0$$

and

$$\operatorname{var}\left[\widehat{\boldsymbol{e}} \mid \boldsymbol{X}\right] = \operatorname{var}\left[\boldsymbol{M}\boldsymbol{e} \mid \boldsymbol{X}\right] = \boldsymbol{M}\operatorname{var}\left[\boldsymbol{e} \mid \boldsymbol{X}\right]\boldsymbol{M} = \boldsymbol{M}\boldsymbol{D}\boldsymbol{M} \tag{4.22}$$

where $\boldsymbol{D}$ is defined in (4.8).

We can simplify this expression under the assumption of conditional homoskedasticity

$$\mathbb{E}\left[e^2 \mid X\right] = \sigma^2.$$

In this case, (4.22) simplifies to

$$\operatorname{var}\left[\widehat{\boldsymbol{e}} \mid \boldsymbol{X}\right] = \boldsymbol{M}\sigma^2. \tag{4.23}$$

In particular, for a single observation i, we can find the variance of $\widehat{e}_i$ by taking the ith diagonal element of (4.23). Since the ith diagonal element of $\boldsymbol{M}$ is $1 - h_{ii}$, as defined in (3.40), we obtain

$$\operatorname{var}\left[\widehat{e}_i \mid \boldsymbol{X}\right] = \mathbb{E}\left[\widehat{e}_i^2 \mid \boldsymbol{X}\right] = (1 - h_{ii})\,\sigma^2. \tag{4.24}$$

As this variance is a function of h_{ii} and hence X_i, the residuals $\widehat{e}_i$ are heteroskedastic even if the errors e_i are homoskedastic. Notice as well that (4.24) implies that $\widehat{e}_i^2$ is a biased estimator of σ^2.

Similarly, recall from (3.45) that the prediction errors $\widetilde{e}_i = (1 - h_{ii})^{-1}\widehat{e}_i$ can be written in vector notation as $\widetilde{\boldsymbol{e}} = \boldsymbol{M}^*\widehat{\boldsymbol{e}}$, where $\boldsymbol{M}^*$ is a diagonal matrix with ith diagonal element $(1 - h_{ii})^{-1}$. Thus $\widetilde{\boldsymbol{e}} = \boldsymbol{M}^*\boldsymbol{M}\boldsymbol{e}$. We can calculate that

$$\mathbb{E}\left[\widetilde{\boldsymbol{e}} \mid \boldsymbol{X}\right] = \boldsymbol{M}^*\boldsymbol{M}\mathbb{E}\left[\boldsymbol{e} \mid \boldsymbol{X}\right] = 0$$

and

$$\operatorname{var}\left[\widetilde{\boldsymbol{e}} \mid \boldsymbol{X}\right] = \boldsymbol{M}^*\boldsymbol{M}\operatorname{var}\left[\boldsymbol{e} \mid \boldsymbol{X}\right]\boldsymbol{M}\boldsymbol{M}^* = \boldsymbol{M}^*\boldsymbol{M}\boldsymbol{D}\boldsymbol{M}\boldsymbol{M}^*$$

which simplifies under homoskedasticity to

$$\operatorname{var}\left[\widetilde{\boldsymbol{e}} \mid \boldsymbol{X}\right] = \boldsymbol{M}^*\boldsymbol{M}\boldsymbol{M}\boldsymbol{M}^*\sigma^2 = \boldsymbol{M}^*\boldsymbol{M}\boldsymbol{M}^*\sigma^2.$$

The variance of the ith prediction error is then

$$\begin{aligned}\operatorname{var}\left[\widetilde{e}_i \mid \boldsymbol{X}\right] &= \mathbb{E}\left[\widetilde{e}_i^2 \mid \boldsymbol{X}\right] \\ &= (1 - h_{ii})^{-1}(1 - h_{ii})(1 - h_{ii})^{-1}\sigma^2 \\ &= (1 - h_{ii})^{-1}\sigma^2.\end{aligned}$$

A residual with constant conditional variance can be obtained by rescaling. The **standardized residuals** are

$$\bar{e}_i = (1 - h_{ii})^{-1/2}\widehat{e}_i \tag{4.25}$$

and in vector notation,

$$\overline{\boldsymbol{e}} = (\bar{e}_1, \ldots, \bar{e}_n)' = \boldsymbol{M}^{*1/2}\boldsymbol{M}\boldsymbol{e}. \tag{4.26}$$

From the above calculations, under homoskedasticity,

$$\operatorname{var}\left[\overline{\boldsymbol{e}} \mid \boldsymbol{X}\right] = \boldsymbol{M}^{*1/2}\boldsymbol{M}\boldsymbol{M}^{*1/2}\sigma^2$$

and

$$\operatorname{var}\left[\bar{e}_i \mid \boldsymbol{X}\right] = \mathbb{E}\left[\bar{e}_i^2 \mid \boldsymbol{X}\right] = \sigma^2$$

and thus these standardized residuals have the same bias and variance as the original errors when the latter are homoskedastic.

4.11 ESTIMATION OF ERROR VARIANCE

The error variance $\sigma^2 = \mathbb{E}\left[e^2\right]$ can be a parameter of interest even in a heteroskedastic regression or a projection model. The error variance σ^2 measures the variation in the "unexplained" part of the regression. Its method of moments estimator is the sample average of the squared residuals:

$$\widehat{\sigma}^2 = \frac{1}{n}\sum_{i=1}^{n}\widehat{e}_i^2.$$

In the linear regression model, we can calculate the expectation of $\widehat{\sigma}^2$. From (3.28) and the properties, of the trace operator, observe that

$$\widehat{\sigma}^2 = \frac{1}{n}\boldsymbol{e}'\boldsymbol{M}\boldsymbol{e} = \frac{1}{n}\operatorname{tr}\left(\boldsymbol{e}'\boldsymbol{M}\boldsymbol{e}\right) = \frac{1}{n}\operatorname{tr}\left(\boldsymbol{M}\boldsymbol{e}\boldsymbol{e}'\right).$$

Then

$$\begin{aligned}
\mathbb{E}\left[\widehat{\sigma}^2 \mid \boldsymbol{X}\right] &= \frac{1}{n}\operatorname{tr}\left(\mathbb{E}\left[\boldsymbol{M}\boldsymbol{e}\boldsymbol{e}' \mid \boldsymbol{X}\right]\right) \\
&= \frac{1}{n}\operatorname{tr}\left(\boldsymbol{M}\mathbb{E}\left[\boldsymbol{e}\boldsymbol{e}' \mid \boldsymbol{X}\right]\right) \\
&= \frac{1}{n}\operatorname{tr}\left(\boldsymbol{M}\boldsymbol{D}\right) \qquad (4.27) \\
&= \frac{1}{n}\sum_{i=1}^{n}\left(1 - h_{ii}\right)\sigma_i^2.
\end{aligned}$$

The final equality holds because the trace is the sum of the diagonal elements of $\boldsymbol{M}\boldsymbol{D}$, and because $\boldsymbol{D}$ is diagonal, the diagonal elements of $\boldsymbol{M}\boldsymbol{D}$ are the product of the diagonal elements of $\boldsymbol{M}$ and $\boldsymbol{D}$, which are $1 - h_{ii}$ and σ_i^2, respectively.

Adding the assumption of conditional homoskedasticity $\mathbb{E}\left[e^2 \mid X\right] = \sigma^2$ so that $\boldsymbol{D} = \boldsymbol{I}_n\sigma^2$, then (4.27) simplifies to

$$\mathbb{E}\left[\widehat{\sigma}^2 \mid \boldsymbol{X}\right] = \frac{1}{n}\operatorname{tr}\left(\boldsymbol{M}\sigma^2\right) = \sigma^2\left(\frac{n-k}{n}\right)$$

the final equality by (3.22). This calculation shows that $\widehat{\sigma}^2$ is biased toward 0. The order of the bias depends on k/n, the ratio of the number of estimated coefficients to the sample size.

Another way to see this is to use (4.24). Note that

$$\mathbb{E}\left[\widehat{\sigma}^2 \mid \boldsymbol{X}\right] = \frac{1}{n}\sum_{i=1}^{n}\mathbb{E}\left[\widehat{e}_i^2 \mid \boldsymbol{X}\right] = \frac{1}{n}\sum_{i=1}^{n}(1-h_{ii})\,\sigma^2 = \left(\frac{n-k}{n}\right)\sigma^2.$$

The last equality is obtained by using Theorem 3.6.

Since the bias takes a scale form, a classic method to obtain an unbiased estimator is by rescaling. Define

$$s^2 = \frac{1}{n-k}\sum_{i=1}^{n}\widehat{e}_i^2. \tag{4.28}$$

By the above calculation, $\mathbb{E}\left[s^2 \mid \boldsymbol{X}\right] = \sigma^2$, and $\mathbb{E}\left[s^2\right] = \sigma^2$. Hence the estimator s^2 is unbiased for σ^2. Consequently, s^2 is known as the **bias-corrected estimator** for σ^2 and in empirical practice, s^2 is the most widely used estimator for σ^2.

Interestingly, this is not the only method to construct an unbiased estimator for σ^2. An estimator constructed with the standardized residuals $\overline{e}_i$ from (4.25) is

$$\overline{\sigma}^2 = \frac{1}{n}\sum_{i=1}^{n}\overline{e}_i^2 = \frac{1}{n}\sum_{i=1}^{n}(1-h_{ii})^{-1}\widehat{e}_i^2.$$

You can show (see Exercise 4.9) that

$$\mathbb{E}\left[\overline{\sigma}^2 \mid \boldsymbol{X}\right] = \sigma^2 \tag{4.29}$$

and thus $\overline{\sigma}^2$ is unbiased for σ^2 (in the homoskedastic linear regression model).

When k/n is small, the estimators $\widehat{\sigma}^2$, s^2, and $\overline{\sigma}^2$ are likely to be similar to one another. However, if k/n is large, then s^2 and $\overline{\sigma}^2$ are generally preferred to $\widehat{\sigma}^2$. Consequently it is best to use one of the bias-corrected variance estimators in applications.

4.12 MEAN-SQUARED FORECAST ERROR

One use of an estimated regression is to predict out-of-sample. Consider an out-of-sample realization (Y_{n+1}, X_{n+1}) where X_{n+1} is observed but not Y_{n+1}. Given the coefficient estimator $\widehat{\beta}$, the standard point estimator of $\mathbb{E}\left[Y_{n+1} \mid X_{n+1}\right] = X_{n+1}'\beta$ is $\widetilde{Y}_{n+1} = X_{n+1}'\widehat{\beta}$. The forecast error is the difference between the actual value Y_{n+1} and the point forecast $\widetilde{Y}_{n+1}$. This is the forecast error $\widetilde{e}_{n+1} = Y_{n+1} - \widetilde{Y}_{n+1}$. The mean-squared forecast error (MSFE) is its expected squared value $\mathrm{MSFE}_n = \mathbb{E}\left[\widetilde{e}_{n+1}^2\right]$. In the linear regression model, $\widetilde{e}_{n+1} = e_{n+1} - X_{n+1}'\left(\widehat{\beta} - \beta\right)$, so

$$\mathrm{MSFE}_n = \mathbb{E}\left[e_{n+1}^2\right] - 2\mathbb{E}\left[e_{n+1}X_{n+1}'\left(\widehat{\beta}-\beta\right)\right] + \mathbb{E}\left[X_{n+1}'\left(\widehat{\beta}-\beta\right)\left(\widehat{\beta}-\beta\right)'X_{n+1}\right]. \tag{4.30}$$

The first term in (4.30) is σ^2. The second term in (4.30) is 0, because $e_{n+1}X_{n+1}'$ is independent of $\widehat{\beta}-\beta$ and both are mean 0. Using the properties of the trace operator, the third term in (4.30) is

$$\begin{aligned}
&\operatorname{tr}\left(\mathbb{E}\left[X_{n+1}X_{n+1}'\right]\mathbb{E}\left[\left(\widehat{\beta}-\beta\right)\left(\widehat{\beta}-\beta\right)'\right]\right)\\
&=\operatorname{tr}\left(\mathbb{E}\left[X_{n+1}X_{n+1}'\right]\mathbb{E}\left[\mathbb{E}\left[\left(\widehat{\beta}-\beta\right)\left(\widehat{\beta}-\beta\right)' \mid \boldsymbol{X}\right]\right]\right)
\end{aligned}$$

$$
\begin{aligned}
&= \operatorname{tr}\left(\mathbb{E}\left[X_{n+1}X_{n+1}'\right]\mathbb{E}\left[\boldsymbol{V}_{\widehat{\beta}}\right]\right) \\
&= \mathbb{E}\left[\operatorname{tr}\left(\left(X_{n+1}X_{n+1}'\right)\boldsymbol{V}_{\widehat{\beta}}\right)\right] \\
&= \mathbb{E}\left[X_{n+1}'\boldsymbol{V}_{\widehat{\beta}}X_{n+1}\right] \qquad (4.31)
\end{aligned}
$$

where we use the fact that X_{n+1} is independent of $\widehat{\beta}$, the definition $\boldsymbol{V}_{\widehat{\beta}} = \mathbb{E}\left[\left(\widehat{\beta}-\beta\right)\left(\widehat{\beta}-\beta\right)' \mid \boldsymbol{X}\right]$, and the fact that X_{n+1} is independent of $\boldsymbol{V}_{\widehat{\beta}}$. Thus

$$
\mathrm{MSFE}_n = \sigma^2 + \mathbb{E}\left[X_{n+1}'\boldsymbol{V}_{\widehat{\beta}}X_{n+1}\right].
$$

Under conditional homoskedasticity, this simplifies to

$$
\mathrm{MSFE}_n = \sigma^2\left(1 + \mathbb{E}\left[X_{n+1}'\left(\boldsymbol{X}'\boldsymbol{X}\right)^{-1}X_{n+1}\right]\right).
$$

A simple estimator for the MSFE is obtained by averaging the squared prediction errors (3.46)

$$
\widetilde{\sigma}^2 = \frac{1}{n}\sum_{i=1}^{n}\widetilde{e}_i^2
$$

where $\widetilde{e}_i = Y_i - X_i'\widehat{\beta}_{(-i)} = \widehat{e}_i(1-h_{ii})^{-1}$. Indeed, we can calculate that

$$
\begin{aligned}
\mathbb{E}\left[\widetilde{\sigma}^2\right] &= \mathbb{E}\left[\widetilde{e}_i^2\right] \\
&= \mathbb{E}\left[\left(e_i - X_i'\left(\widehat{\beta}_{(-i)}-\beta\right)\right)^2\right] \\
&= \sigma^2 + \mathbb{E}\left[X_i'\left(\widehat{\beta}_{(-i)}-\beta\right)\left(\widehat{\beta}_{(-i)}-\beta\right)'X_i\right].
\end{aligned}
$$

By a similar calculation as in (4.31), we find

$$
\mathbb{E}\left[\widetilde{\sigma}^2\right] = \sigma^2 + \mathbb{E}\left[X_i'\boldsymbol{V}_{\widehat{\beta}_{(-i)}}X_i\right] = \mathrm{MSFE}_{n-1}.
$$

This is the MSFE based on a sample of size $n-1$ rather than size n. The difference arises because the in-sample prediction errors $\widetilde{e}_i$ for $i \le n$ are calculated using an effective sample size of $n-1$, while the out-of-sample prediction error $\widetilde{e}_{n+1}$ is calculated from a sample with the full n observations. Unless n is very small, we should expect MSFE_{n-1} (the MSFE based on $n-1$ observations) to be close to MSFE_n (the MSFE based on n observations). Thus $\widetilde{\sigma}^2$ is a reasonable estimator for MSFE_n.

Theorem 4.6 MSFE
In the linear regression model (Assumption 4.2) and i.i.d. sampling (Assumption 4.1),

$$
\mathrm{MSFE}_n = \mathbb{E}\left[\widetilde{e}_{n+1}^2\right] = \sigma^2 + \mathbb{E}\left[X_{n+1}'\boldsymbol{V}_{\widehat{\beta}}X_{n+1}\right]
$$

where $\boldsymbol{V}_{\widehat{\beta}} = \operatorname{var}\left[\widehat{\beta} \mid \boldsymbol{X}\right]$. Furthermore, $\widetilde{\sigma}^2$ defined in (3.46) is an unbiased estimator of MSFE_{n-1}, because $\mathbb{E}\left[\widetilde{\sigma}^2\right] = \mathrm{MSFE}_{n-1}$.

4.13 COVARIANCE MATRIX ESTIMATION UNDER HOMOSKEDASTICITY

For inference, we need an estimator of the covariance matrix $\boldsymbol{V}_{\widehat{\beta}}$ of the least squares estimator. In this section, we consider the homoskedastic regression model (Assumption 4.3).

Under homoskedasticity, the covariance matrix takes the simple form

$$\boldsymbol{V}^0_{\widehat{\beta}} = \left(\boldsymbol{X}'\boldsymbol{X}\right)^{-1}\sigma^2$$

which is known up to the scale σ^2. In Section 4.11, we discussed three estimators of σ^2. The most commonly used choice is s^2, leading to the classic covariance matrix estimator

$$\widehat{\boldsymbol{V}}^0_{\widehat{\beta}} = \left(\boldsymbol{X}'\boldsymbol{X}\right)^{-1}s^2. \tag{4.32}$$

Since s^2 is conditionally unbiased for σ^2, it is simple to calculate that $\widehat{\boldsymbol{V}}^0_{\widehat{\beta}}$ is conditionally unbiased for $\boldsymbol{V}_{\widehat{\beta}}$ under the assumption of homoskedasticity:

$$\mathbb{E}\left[\widehat{\boldsymbol{V}}^0_{\widehat{\beta}} \mid \boldsymbol{X}\right] = \left(\boldsymbol{X}'\boldsymbol{X}\right)^{-1}\mathbb{E}\left[s^2 \mid \boldsymbol{X}\right] = \left(\boldsymbol{X}'\boldsymbol{X}\right)^{-1}\sigma^2 = \boldsymbol{V}_{\widehat{\beta}}.$$

This was the dominant covariance matrix estimator in applied econometrics for many years and is still the default method in most regression packages. For example, Stata uses the covariance matrix estimator (4.32) by default in linear regression unless an alternative is specified.

If the estimator (4.32) is used but the regression error is heteroskedastic, it is possible for $\widehat{\boldsymbol{V}}^0_{\widehat{\beta}}$ to be quite biased for the correct covariance matrix $\boldsymbol{V}_{\widehat{\beta}} = \left(\boldsymbol{X}'\boldsymbol{X}\right)^{-1}\left(\boldsymbol{X}'\boldsymbol{D}\boldsymbol{X}\right)\left(\boldsymbol{X}'\boldsymbol{X}\right)^{-1}$. For example, suppose $k=1$ and $\sigma_i^2 = X_i^2$ with $\mathbb{E}[X]=0$. The ratio of the true variance of the least squares estimator to the expectation of the variance estimator is

$$\frac{\boldsymbol{V}_{\widehat{\beta}}}{\mathbb{E}\left[\widehat{\boldsymbol{V}}^0_{\widehat{\beta}} \mid \boldsymbol{X}\right]} = \frac{\sum_{i=1}^n X_i^4}{\sigma^2\sum_{i=1}^n X_i^2} \simeq \frac{\mathbb{E}\left[X^4\right]}{\left(\mathbb{E}\left[X^2\right]\right)^2} \stackrel{\text{def}}{=} \kappa.$$

(Notice that we use the fact that $\sigma_i^2 = X_i^2$ implies $\sigma^2 = \mathbb{E}\left[\sigma_i^2\right] = \mathbb{E}\left[X^2\right]$.) The constant κ is the standardized fourth moment (or kurtosis) of the regressor X and can be any number greater than 1. For example, if $X \sim \mathrm{N}\left(0,\sigma^2\right)$, then $\kappa=3$, so the true variance $\boldsymbol{V}_{\widehat{\beta}}$ is three times larger than the expected homoskedastic estimator $\widehat{\boldsymbol{V}}^0_{\widehat{\beta}}$. But κ can be much larger. Take, for example, the variable *wage* in the CPS dataset. It satisfies $\kappa=30$, so that if the conditional variance equals $\sigma_i^2 = X_i^2$, then the true variance $\boldsymbol{V}_{\widehat{\beta}}$ is 30 times larger than the expected homoskedastic estimator $\widehat{\boldsymbol{V}}^0_{\widehat{\beta}}$. While this is an extreme case, the point is that the classic covariance matrix estimator (4.32) may be quite biased when the homoskedasticity assumption fails.

4.14 COVARIANCE MATRIX ESTIMATION UNDER HETEROSKEDASTICITY

In Section 4.13, we showed that that the classic covariance matrix estimator can be highly biased if homoskedasticity fails. In this section, we show how to construct covariance matrix estimators which do not require homoskedasticity.

Recall that the general form for the covariance matrix is

$$\boldsymbol{V}_{\widehat{\beta}} = \left(\boldsymbol{X}'\boldsymbol{X}\right)^{-1}\left(\boldsymbol{X}'\boldsymbol{D}\boldsymbol{X}\right)\left(\boldsymbol{X}'\boldsymbol{X}\right)^{-1}.$$

with $\boldsymbol{D}$ defined in (4.8). This depends on the unknown matrix $\boldsymbol{D}$, which we can write as

$$\boldsymbol{D} = \operatorname{diag}\left(\sigma_1^2, \ldots, \sigma_n^2\right) = \mathbb{E}\left[\boldsymbol{e}\boldsymbol{e}' \mid \boldsymbol{X}\right] = \mathbb{E}\left[\widetilde{\boldsymbol{D}} \mid \boldsymbol{X}\right]$$

where $\widetilde{\boldsymbol{D}} = \operatorname{diag}\left(e_1^2, \ldots, e_n^2\right)$. Thus $\widetilde{\boldsymbol{D}}$ is a conditionally unbiased estimator for $\boldsymbol{D}$. If the squared errors e_i^2 were observable, we could construct an unbiased estimator for $\boldsymbol{V}_{\widehat{\beta}}$ as

$$\begin{aligned}
\widehat{\boldsymbol{V}}_{\widehat{\beta}}^{\text{ideal}} &= \left(\boldsymbol{X}'\boldsymbol{X}\right)^{-1}\left(\boldsymbol{X}'\widetilde{\boldsymbol{D}}\boldsymbol{X}\right)\left(\boldsymbol{X}'\boldsymbol{X}\right)^{-1} \\
&= \left(\boldsymbol{X}'\boldsymbol{X}\right)^{-1}\left(\sum_{i=1}^n X_i X_i' e_i^2\right)\left(\boldsymbol{X}'\boldsymbol{X}\right)^{-1}.
\end{aligned}$$

Indeed,

$$\begin{aligned}
\mathbb{E}\left[\widehat{\boldsymbol{V}}_{\widehat{\beta}}^{\text{ideal}} \mid \boldsymbol{X}\right] &= \left(\boldsymbol{X}'\boldsymbol{X}\right)^{-1}\left(\sum_{i=1}^n X_i X_i' \mathbb{E}\left[e_i^2 \mid \boldsymbol{X}\right]\right)\left(\boldsymbol{X}'\boldsymbol{X}\right)^{-1} \\
&= \left(\boldsymbol{X}'\boldsymbol{X}\right)^{-1}\left(\sum_{i=1}^n X_i X_i' \sigma_i^2\right)\left(\boldsymbol{X}'\boldsymbol{X}\right)^{-1} \\
&= \left(\boldsymbol{X}'\boldsymbol{X}\right)^{-1}\left(\boldsymbol{X}'\boldsymbol{D}\boldsymbol{X}\right)\left(\boldsymbol{X}'\boldsymbol{X}\right)^{-1} = \boldsymbol{V}_{\widehat{\beta}}
\end{aligned}$$

verifying that $\widehat{\boldsymbol{V}}_{\widehat{\beta}}^{\text{ideal}}$ is unbiased for $\boldsymbol{V}_{\widehat{\beta}}$.

Since the errors e_i^2 are unobserved, $\widehat{\boldsymbol{V}}_{\widehat{\beta}}^{\text{ideal}}$ is not a feasible estimator. However, we can replace e_i^2 with the squared residuals $\widehat{e}_i^2$. Making this substitution, we obtain the estimator

$$\widehat{\boldsymbol{V}}_{\widehat{\beta}}^{\text{HC0}} = \left(\boldsymbol{X}'\boldsymbol{X}\right)^{-1}\left(\sum_{i=1}^n X_i X_i' \widehat{e}_i^2\right)\left(\boldsymbol{X}'\boldsymbol{X}\right)^{-1}. \tag{4.33}$$

The label "HC" refers to "heteroskedasticity-consistent." The label "HC0" refers to this being the baseline heteroskedasticity-consistent covariance matrix estimator.

We know, however, that $\widehat{e}_i^2$ is biased toward 0 (recall equation (4.24)). To estimate the variance σ^2, the unbiased estimator s^2 scales the moment estimator $\widehat{\sigma}^2$ by $n/(n-k)$. Making the same adjustment, we obtain the estimator

$$\widehat{\boldsymbol{V}}_{\widehat{\beta}}^{\text{HC1}} = \left(\frac{n}{n-k}\right)\left(\boldsymbol{X}'\boldsymbol{X}\right)^{-1}\left(\sum_{i=1}^n X_i X_i' \widehat{e}_i^2\right)\left(\boldsymbol{X}'\boldsymbol{X}\right)^{-1}. \tag{4.34}$$

While the scaling by $n/(n-k)$ is ad hoc, HC1 is often recommended over the unscaled HC0 estimator:

Alternatively, we could use the standardized residuals $\bar{e}_i$ or the prediction errors $\widetilde{e}_i$, yielding the "HC2" and "HC3" estimators:

$$\begin{aligned}
\widehat{\boldsymbol{V}}_{\widehat{\beta}}^{\text{HC2}} &= \left(\boldsymbol{X}'\boldsymbol{X}\right)^{-1}\left(\sum_{i=1}^n X_i X_i' \bar{e}_i^2\right)\left(\boldsymbol{X}'\boldsymbol{X}\right)^{-1} \\
&= \left(\boldsymbol{X}'\boldsymbol{X}\right)^{-1}\left(\sum_{i=1}^n \left(1-h_{ii}\right)^{-1} X_i X_i' \widehat{e}_i^2\right)\left(\boldsymbol{X}'\boldsymbol{X}\right)^{-1}
\end{aligned} \tag{4.35}$$

and

$$\widehat{\boldsymbol{V}}_{\widehat{\beta}}^{\mathrm{HC3}} = \left(\boldsymbol{X}'\boldsymbol{X}\right)^{-1}\left(\sum_{i=1}^{n} X_i X_i' \widetilde{e}_i^2\right)\left(\boldsymbol{X}'\boldsymbol{X}\right)^{-1}$$
$$= \left(\boldsymbol{X}'\boldsymbol{X}\right)^{-1}\left(\sum_{i=1}^{n} (1-h_{ii})^{-2} X_i X_i' \widehat{e}_i^2\right)\left(\boldsymbol{X}'\boldsymbol{X}\right)^{-1}. \tag{4.36}$$

The four estimators HC0, HC1, HC2, and HC3 are collectively called **robust**, **heteroskedasticity-consistent**, or **heteroskedasticity-robust** covariance matrix estimators. The HC0 estimator was first developed by Eicker (1963) and introduced to econometrics by White (1980) and is sometimes called the **Eicker-White** or **White** covariance matrix estimator. The degree-of-freedom adjustment in HC1 was recommended by Hinkley (1977) and is the default robust covariance matrix estimator implemented in Stata. It is implement by the "`, r`" option. In current applied econometric practice this is the most popular covariance matrix estimator. The HC2 estimator was introduced by Horn, Horn, and Duncan (1975) and is implemented using the `vce(hc2)` option in Stata. The HC3 estimator was derived by MacKinnon and White (1985) from the jackknife principle (see Section 10.3), and by Andrews (1991a) based on the principle of leave-one-out cross-validation, and is implemented using the `vce(hc3)` option in Stata.

Since $(1-h_{ii})^{-2} > (1-h_{ii})^{-1} > 1$, it is straightforward to show that

$$\widehat{\boldsymbol{V}}_{\widehat{\beta}}^{\mathrm{HC0}} < \widehat{\boldsymbol{V}}_{\widehat{\beta}}^{\mathrm{HC2}} < \widehat{\boldsymbol{V}}_{\widehat{\beta}}^{\mathrm{HC3}}. \tag{4.37}$$

(See Exercise 4.10.) The inequality $\boldsymbol{A} < \boldsymbol{B}$ when applied to matrices means that the matrix $\boldsymbol{B} - \boldsymbol{A}$ is positive definite.

In general, the bias of the covariance matrix estimators is complicated but simplifies under the assumption of homoskedasticity (4.3). For example, using (4.24),

$$\mathbb{E}\left[\widehat{\boldsymbol{V}}_{\widehat{\beta}}^{\mathrm{HC0}} \mid \boldsymbol{X}\right] = \left(\boldsymbol{X}'\boldsymbol{X}\right)^{-1}\left(\sum_{i=1}^{n} X_i X_i' \mathbb{E}\left[\widehat{e}_i^2 \mid \boldsymbol{X}\right]\right)\left(\boldsymbol{X}'\boldsymbol{X}\right)^{-1}$$
$$= \left(\boldsymbol{X}'\boldsymbol{X}\right)^{-1}\left(\sum_{i=1}^{n} X_i X_i' (1-h_{ii})\,\sigma^2\right)\left(\boldsymbol{X}'\boldsymbol{X}\right)^{-1}$$
$$= \left(\boldsymbol{X}'\boldsymbol{X}\right)^{-1}\sigma^2 - \left(\boldsymbol{X}'\boldsymbol{X}\right)^{-1}\left(\sum_{i=1}^{n} X_i X_i' h_{ii}\right)\left(\boldsymbol{X}'\boldsymbol{X}\right)^{-1}\sigma^2$$
$$< \left(\boldsymbol{X}'\boldsymbol{X}\right)^{-1}\sigma^2 = \boldsymbol{V}_{\widehat{\beta}}.$$

This calculation shows that $\widehat{\boldsymbol{V}}_{\widehat{\beta}}^{\mathrm{HC0}}$ is biased toward 0.

By a similar calculation (again under homoskedasticity), we can calculate that the HC2 estimator is unbiased

$$\mathbb{E}\left[\widehat{\boldsymbol{V}}_{\widehat{\beta}}^{\mathrm{HC2}} \mid \boldsymbol{X}\right] = \left(\boldsymbol{X}'\boldsymbol{X}\right)^{-1}\sigma^2. \tag{4.38}$$

(See Exercise 4.11.)

It might seem rather odd to compare the bias of heteroskedasticity-robust estimators under the assumption of homoskedasticity, but it does give us a baseline for comparison.

Another interesting calculation shows that in general (that is, without assuming homoskedasticity), the HC3 estimator is biased away from 0. Indeed, using the definition of the prediction errors (3.44)

$$\widetilde{e}_i = Y_i - X_i'\widehat{\beta}_{(-i)} = e_i - X_i'\left(\widehat{\beta}_{(-i)} - \beta\right)$$

so

$$\widetilde{e}_i^2 = e_i^2 - 2X_i'\left(\widehat{\beta}_{(-i)} - \beta\right)e_i + \left(X_i'\left(\widehat{\beta}_{(-i)} - \beta\right)\right)^2.$$

Note that e_i and $\widehat{\beta}_{(-i)}$ are functions of non-overlapping observations and are thus independent. Hence $\mathbb{E}\left[\left(\widehat{\beta}_{(-i)} - \beta\right)e_i \mid \boldsymbol{X}\right] = 0$, and

$$\begin{aligned}\mathbb{E}\left[\widetilde{e}_i^2 \mid \boldsymbol{X}\right] &= \mathbb{E}\left[e_i^2 \mid \boldsymbol{X}\right] - 2X_i'\mathbb{E}\left[\left(\widehat{\beta}_{(-i)} - \beta\right)e_i \mid \boldsymbol{X}\right] + \mathbb{E}\left[\left(X_i'\left(\widehat{\beta}_{(-i)} - \beta\right)\right)^2 \mid \boldsymbol{X}\right] \\ &= \sigma_i^2 + \mathbb{E}\left[\left(X_i'\left(\widehat{\beta}_{(-i)} - \beta\right)\right)^2 \mid \boldsymbol{X}\right] \\ &\geq \sigma_i^2.\end{aligned}$$

It follows that

$$\begin{aligned}\mathbb{E}\left[\widehat{\boldsymbol{V}}_{\widehat{\beta}}^{\mathrm{HC3}} \mid \boldsymbol{X}\right] &= \left(\boldsymbol{X}'\boldsymbol{X}\right)^{-1}\left(\sum_{i=1}^n X_iX_i'\mathbb{E}\left[\widetilde{e}_i^2 \mid \boldsymbol{X}\right]\right)\left(\boldsymbol{X}'\boldsymbol{X}\right)^{-1} \\ &\geq \left(\boldsymbol{X}'\boldsymbol{X}\right)^{-1}\left(\sum_{i=1}^n X_iX_i'\sigma_i^2\right)\left(\boldsymbol{X}'\boldsymbol{X}\right)^{-1} = \boldsymbol{V}_{\widehat{\beta}}.\end{aligned}$$

Thus the HC3 estimator is conservative in the sense that it is weakly larger (in expectation) than the correct variance for any realization of $\boldsymbol{X}$.

We have introduced five covariance matrix estimators, including the homoskedastic estimator $\widehat{\boldsymbol{V}}_{\widehat{\beta}}^0$ and the four HC estimators. Which should you use? The classic estimator $\widehat{\boldsymbol{V}}_{\widehat{\beta}}^0$ is typically a poor choice, as it is only valid under the unlikely homoskedasticity restriction. For this reason, it is not typically used in contemporary econometric research. Unfortunately, standard regression packages set their default choice as $\widehat{\boldsymbol{V}}_{\widehat{\beta}}^0$, so users must intentionally select a robust covariance matrix estimator.

Of the four robust estimators, HC1 is the most commonly used, as it is the default robust covariance matrix option in Stata. However, HC2 and HC3 are preferred. HC2 is unbiased (under homoskedasticity), and HC3 is conservative for any $\boldsymbol{X}$. In most applications, HC1, HC2, and HC3 will be similar, so this choice will not matter. The context where the estimators can differ substantially is when the sample has a large leverage value h_{ii} for at least one observation. You can see this by comparing formulas (4.34), (4.35), and (4.36) and noting that the only difference is the scaling by the leverage values h_{ii}. If there is an observation with h_{ii} close to 1, then $(1 - h_{ii})^{-1}$ and $(1 - h_{ii})^{-2}$ will be large, giving this observation much greater weight in the covariance matrix formula.

Halbert L. White

Hal White (1950–2012) of the United States was an influential econometrician of recent years. His 1980 paper on heteroskedasticity-consistent covariance matrix estimation is one of the most cited papers in economics. His research was central to the movement to view econometric models as approximations, and to the drive for increased mathematical rigor in the discipline. He also pioneered the introduction of neural network methods into econometrics. In addition to being a highly prolific and influential scholar, he also co-founded the economic consulting firm Bates White.

4.15 STANDARD ERRORS

A variance estimator such as $\widehat{\boldsymbol{V}}_{\widehat{\beta}}$ is an estimator of the variance of the distribution of $\widehat{\beta}$. A more easily interpretable measure of spread is its square root—the standard deviation. This is so important when discussing the distribution of parameter estimators that we have a special name for estimates of their standard deviation.

Definition 4.2 A **standard error** $s(\widehat{\beta})$ for a real-valued estimator $\widehat{\beta}$ is an estimator of the standard deviation of the distribution of $\widehat{\beta}$.

When β is a vector with estimator $\widehat{\beta}$ and covariance matrix estimator $\widehat{\boldsymbol{V}}_{\widehat{\beta}}$, standard errors for individual elements are the square roots of the diagonal elements of $\widehat{\boldsymbol{V}}_{\widehat{\beta}}$. That is,

$$s(\widehat{\beta}_j) = \sqrt{\widehat{V}_{\widehat{\beta}_j}} = \sqrt{\left[\widehat{\boldsymbol{V}}_{\widehat{\beta}}\right]_{jj}}.$$

When the classical covariance matrix estimator (4.32) is used, the standard error takes the simple form

$$s(\widehat{\beta}_j) = s\sqrt{\left[\left(\boldsymbol{X}'\boldsymbol{X}\right)^{-1}\right]_{jj}}. \tag{4.39}$$

As we discussed in Section 4.14, there are multiple possible covariance matrix estimators, so standard errors are not unique. It is therefore important to understand what formula and method is used by an author when studying their work. It is also important to understand that a particular standard error may be relevant under one set of model assumptions but not under another set of assumptions.

To illustrate, we return to the log wage regression (3.12) of Section 3.7. We calculate that $s^2 = 0.160$. Therefore the homoskedastic covariance matrix estimate is

$$\widehat{\boldsymbol{V}}^0_{\widehat{\beta}} = \begin{pmatrix} 5010 & 314 \\ 314 & 20 \end{pmatrix}^{-1} 0.160 = \begin{pmatrix} 0.002 & -0.031 \\ -0.031 & 0.499 \end{pmatrix}.$$

We also calculate that

$$\sum_{i=1}^{n} (1 - h_{ii})^{-1} X_i X_i' \widehat{e}_i^2 = \begin{pmatrix} 763.26 & 48.513 \\ 48.513 & 3.1078 \end{pmatrix}.$$

Therefore the HC2 covariance matrix estimate is

$$\begin{aligned} \widehat{\boldsymbol{V}}^{\mathrm{HC2}}_{\widehat{\beta}} &= \begin{pmatrix} 5010 & 314 \\ 314 & 20 \end{pmatrix}^{-1} \begin{pmatrix} 763.26 & 48.513 \\ 48.513 & 3.1078 \end{pmatrix} \begin{pmatrix} 5010 & 314 \\ 314 & 20 \end{pmatrix}^{-1} \\ &= \begin{pmatrix} 0.001 & -0.015 \\ -0.015 & 0.243 \end{pmatrix}. \end{aligned} \tag{4.40}$$

Table 4.1
Standard errors

	Education	Intercept
Homoskedastic (4.32)	0.045	0.707
HC0 (4.33)	0.029	0.461
HC1 (4.34)	0.030	0.486
HC2 (4.35)	0.031	0.493
HC3 (4.36)	0.033	0.527

The standard errors are the square roots of the diagonal elements of these matrices. A conventional format to write the estimated equation with standard errors is

$$\widehat{\log(wage)} = \underset{(0.031)}{0.155} \quad education + \underset{(0.493)}{0.698}. \tag{4.41}$$

Alternatively, standard errors could be calculated using the other formulas. The different standard errors are reported in the Table 4.1.

The homoskedastic standard errors are noticeably different (larger in this case) than the others. The robust standard errors are reasonably close to one another, though the HC3 standard errors are larger than the others.

4.16 ESTIMATION WITH SPARSE DUMMY VARIABLES

The heteroskedasticity-robust covariance matrix estimators can be quite imprecise in some contexts. One is in the presence of **sparse dummy variables**—when a dummy variable only takes the value 1 or 0 for very few observations. In these contexts, one component of the covariance matrix is estimated on just those few observations and will be imprecise. This imprecision is effectively hidden from the user.

To see the problem, let D be a dummy variable (i.e., it takes on the values 1 and 0), and consider the dummy variable regression

$$Y = \beta_1 D + \beta_2 + e. \tag{4.42}$$

The number of observations for which $D_i = 1$ is $n_1 = \sum_{i=1}^{n} D_i$. The number of observations for which $D_i = 0$ is $n_2 = n - n_1$. We say the design is **sparse** if n_1 or n_2 is small.

To simplify our analysis, take the extreme case $n_1 = 1$. The ideas extend to the case of $n_1 > 1$ but small, though with less dramatic effects.

In the regression model (4.42), we can calculate that the true covariance matrix of the least squares estimator for the coefficients under the simplifying assumption of conditional homoskedasticity is

$$\boldsymbol{V}_{\widehat{\beta}} = \sigma^2 \left(\boldsymbol{X}'\boldsymbol{X}\right)^{-1} = \sigma^2 \begin{pmatrix} 1 & 1 \\ 1 & n \end{pmatrix}^{-1} = \frac{\sigma^2}{n-1} \begin{pmatrix} n & -1 \\ -1 & 1 \end{pmatrix}.$$

In particular, the variance of the estimator for the coefficient on the dummy variable is

$$V_{\widehat{\beta}_1} = \sigma^2 \frac{n}{n-1}.$$

Essentially, the coefficient β_1 is estimated from a single observation, so its variance is roughly unaffected by sample size. An important conclusion is that certain coefficient estimators in the presence of sparse dummy variables will be imprecise, regardless of the sample size. A large sample alone is not sufficient to ensure precise estimation.

Now let's examine the standard HC1 covariance matrix estimator (4.34). The regression has perfect fit for the observation for which $D_i = 1$, so the corresponding residual is $\widehat{e}_i = 0$. It follows that $D_i\widehat{e}_i = 0$ for all i (either $D_i = 0$ or $\widehat{e}_i = 0$). Hence

$$\sum_{i=1}^{n} X_i X_i' \widehat{e}_i^2 = \begin{pmatrix} 0 & 0 \\ 0 & \sum_{i=1}^{n} \widehat{e}_i^2 \end{pmatrix} = \begin{pmatrix} 0 & 0 \\ 0 & (n-2)s^2 \end{pmatrix}$$

where $s^2 = (n-2)^{-1} \sum_{i=1}^{n} \widehat{e}_i^2$ is the bias-corrected estimator of σ^2. We find that

$$\begin{aligned}\widehat{\boldsymbol{V}}_{\widehat{\beta}}^{\mathrm{HC1}} &= \left(\frac{n}{n-2}\right) \frac{1}{(n-1)^2} \begin{pmatrix} n & -1 \\ -1 & 1 \end{pmatrix} \begin{pmatrix} 0 & 0 \\ 0 & (n-2)s^2 \end{pmatrix} \begin{pmatrix} n & -1 \\ -1 & 1 \end{pmatrix} \\ &= s^2 \frac{n}{(n-1)^2} \begin{pmatrix} 1 & -1 \\ -1 & 1 \end{pmatrix}.\end{aligned}$$

In particular, the estimator for $V_{\widehat{\beta}_1}$ is

$$\widehat{V}_{\widehat{\beta}_1}^{\mathrm{HC1}} = s^2 \frac{n}{(n-1)^2}.$$

It has expectation

$$\mathbb{E}\left[\widehat{V}_{\widehat{\beta}_1}^{\mathrm{HC1}}\right] = \sigma^2 \frac{n}{(n-1)^2} = \frac{V_{\widehat{\beta}_1}}{n-1} << V_{\widehat{\beta}_1}.$$

The variance estimator $\widehat{V}_{\widehat{\beta}_1}^{\mathrm{HC1}}$ is extremely biased for $V_{\widehat{\beta}_1}$. It is too small by a multiple of n! The reported variance—and standard error—is misleadingly small. The variance estimate erroneously misstates the precision of $\widehat{\beta}_1$. The fact that $\widehat{V}_{\widehat{\beta}_1}^{\mathrm{HC1}}$ is biased is unlikely to be noticed by an applied researcher. Nothing in the reported output will alert a researcher to the problem.

Another way to see the issue is to consider the estimator $\widehat{\theta} = \widehat{\beta}_1 + \widehat{\beta}_2$ for the sum of the coefficients $\theta = \beta_1 + \beta_2$. This estimator has true variance σ^2. The variance estimator, however, is $\widehat{\boldsymbol{V}}_{\widehat{\theta}}^{\mathrm{HC1}} = 0$! (It equals the sum of the four elements in $\widehat{\boldsymbol{V}}_{\widehat{\beta}}^{\mathrm{HC1}}$). Clearly, the estimator "0" is biased for the true value σ^2.

Another insight is to examine the leverage values. The (single) observation with $D_i = 1$ has

$$h_{ii} = \frac{1}{n-1} \begin{pmatrix} 1 & 1 \end{pmatrix} \begin{pmatrix} n & -1 \\ -1 & 1 \end{pmatrix} \begin{pmatrix} 1 \\ 1 \end{pmatrix} = 1.$$

This is an extreme leverage value.

A possible solution is to replace the biased covariance matrix estimator $\widehat{V}_{\widehat{\beta}_1}^{\mathrm{HC1}}$ with the unbiased estimator $\widehat{V}_{\widehat{\beta}_1}^{\mathrm{HC2}}$ (unbiased under homoskedasticity) or the conservative estimator $\widehat{V}_{\widehat{\beta}_1}^{\mathrm{HC3}}$. Neither approach can be used in the extreme sparse case $n_1 = 1$ (because $\widehat{V}_{\widehat{\beta}_1}^{\mathrm{HC2}}$ and $\widehat{V}_{\widehat{\beta}_1}^{\mathrm{HC3}}$ cannot be calculated if $h_{ii} = 1$ for any observation) but applies otherwise. When $h_{ii} = 1$ for an observation, then $\widehat{V}_{\widehat{\beta}_1}^{\mathrm{HC2}}$ and $\widehat{V}_{\widehat{\beta}_1}^{\mathrm{HC3}}$ cannot be calculated. In this case, unbiased covariance matrix estimation appears to be impossible.

It is unclear if there is a best practice to avoid this situation. Once possibility is to calculate the maximum leverage value. If it is very large, calculate the standard errors using several methods to see whether variation occurs.

4.17 COMPUTATION

We illustrate methods to compute standard errors for equation (3.13), extending the code of Section 3.25.

Stata do File (continued)

```
*      Homoskedastic formula (4.32):
reg wage education experience exp2 if (mnwf == 1)
*      HC1 formula (4.34):
reg wage education experience exp2 if (mnwf == 1), r
*      HC2 formula (4.35):
reg wage education experience exp2 if (mnwf == 1), vce(hc2)
*      HC3 formula (4.36):
reg wage education experience exp2 if (mnwf == 1), vce(hc3)
```

R Program File (continued)

```
n <- nrow(y)
k <- ncol(x)
a <- n/(n-k)
sig2 <- (t(e) %*% e)/(n-k)
u1 <- x*(e%*%matrix(1,1,k))
u2 <- x*((e/sqrt(1-leverage))%*%matrix(1,1,k))
u3 <- x*((e/(1-leverage))%*%matrix(1,1,k))
xx <- solve(t(x)%*%x)
v0 <- xx*sig2
v1 <- xx %*% (t(u1)%*%u1) %*% xx
v1a <- a * xx %*% (t(u1)%*%u1) %*% xx
v2 <- xx %*% (t(u2)%*%u2) %*% xx
v3 <- xx %*% (t(u3)%*%u3) %*% xx
s0 <- sqrt(diag(v0))        # Homoskedastic formula
s1 <- sqrt(diag(v1))        # HC0
s1a <- sqrt(diag(v1a))      # HC1
s2 <- sqrt(diag(v2))        # HC2
s3 <- sqrt(diag(v3))        # HC3
```

MATLAB Program File (continued)

```
[n,k]=size(x);
a=n/(n-k);
sig2=(e'*e)/(n-k);
u1=x.*e;u2=x.*(e./sqrt(1-leverage));
```

```
u3=x.*(e./(1-leverage));
xx=inv(x'*x);
v0=xx*sig2;
v1=xx*(u1'*u1)*xx;
v1a=a*xx*(u1'*u1)*xx;
v2=xx*(u2'*u2)*xx;
v3=xx*(u3'*u3)*xx;
s0=sqrt(diag(v0));          # Homoskedastic formula
s1=sqrt(diag(v1));          # HC0 formula
s1a=sqrt(diag(v1a));        # HC1 formula
s2=sqrt(diag(v2));          # HC2 formula
s3=sqrt(diag(v3));          # HC3 formula
```

4.18 MEASURES OF FIT

As described in Chapter 3, a commonly reported measure of regression fit is the regression R^2, defined as

$$R^2 = 1 - \frac{\sum_{i=1}^n \widehat{e}_i^2}{\sum_{i=1}^n \left(Y_i - \overline{Y}\right)^2} = 1 - \frac{\widehat{\sigma}^2}{\widehat{\sigma}_Y^2}$$

where $\widehat{\sigma}_Y^2 = n^{-1}\sum_{i=1}^n \left(Y_i - \overline{Y}\right)^2$. R^2 is an estimator of the population parameter

$$\rho^2 = \frac{\operatorname{var}\left[X'\beta\right]}{\operatorname{var}[Y]} = 1 - \frac{\sigma^2}{\sigma_Y^2}.$$

However, $\widehat{\sigma}^2$ and $\widehat{\sigma}_Y^2$ are biased. Theil (1961) proposed replacing these by the unbiased versions s^2 and $\widetilde{\sigma}_Y^2 = (n-1)^{-1}\sum_{i=1}^n \left(Y_i - \overline{Y}\right)^2$, yielding what is known as **R-bar-squared** or **adjusted R-squared**:

$$\overline{R}^2 = 1 - \frac{s^2}{\widetilde{\sigma}_Y^2} = 1 - \frac{(n-1)^{-1}\sum_{i=1}^n \widehat{e}_i^2}{(n-k)^{-1}\sum_{i=1}^n \left(Y_i - \overline{Y}\right)^2}.$$

While $\overline{R}^2$ is an improvement on R^2, a much better improvement is

$$\widetilde{R}^2 = 1 - \frac{\sum_{i=1}^n \widetilde{e}_i^2}{\sum_{i=1}^n \left(Y_i - \overline{Y}\right)^2} = 1 - \frac{\widetilde{\sigma}^2}{\widehat{\sigma}_Y^2}$$

where $\widetilde{e}_i$ are the prediction errors (3.44), and $\widetilde{\sigma}^2$ is the MSPE from (3.46). As described in Section 4.12, $\widetilde{\sigma}^2$ is a good estimator of the out-of-sample mean-square forecast error, so $\widetilde{R}^2$ is a good estimator of the percentage of the forecast variance which is explained by the regression forecast. In this sense, $\widetilde{R}^2$ is a good measure of fit.

One problem with R^2, which is partially corrected by $\overline{R}^2$ and fully corrected by $\widetilde{R}^2$, is that R^2 necessarily increases when regressors are added to a regression model. This occurs because R^2 is a negative function of the sum of squared residuals, which cannot increase when a regressor is added. In contrast, $\overline{R}^2$ and $\widetilde{R}^2$ are non-monotonic in the number of regressors. $\widetilde{R}^2$ can even be negative, which occurs when an estimated model predicts worse than a constant-only model.

In the statistical literature, the MSPE $\widetilde{\sigma}^2$ is known as the **leave-one-out cross validation** criterion and is popular for model comparison and selection, especially in high-dimensional and nonparametric contexts. It is equivalent to using $\widetilde{R}^2$ or $\widetilde{\sigma}^2$ to compare and select models. Models with high $\widetilde{R}^2$ (or low $\widetilde{\sigma}^2$) are better models in terms of expected out-of-sample squared error. In contrast, R^2 cannot be used for model selection, as it necessarily increases when regressors are added to a regression model. $\overline{R}^2$ is also an inappropriate choice for model selection (it tends to select models with too many parameters), though a justification of this assertion requires a study of the theory of model selection. Unfortunately, $\overline{R}^2$ is routinely used by some economists, possibly as a hold-over from previous generations.

In summary, it is recommended to omit R^2 and $\overline{R}^2$. If a measure of fit is desired, report $\widetilde{R}^2$ or $\widetilde{\sigma}^2$.

Henri Theil

Henri Theil (1924–2000) of the Netherlands invented $\overline{R}^2$ and two-stage least squares, both of which are routinely seen in applied econometrics. He also wrote an early influential advanced textbook on econometrics (Theil 1971).

4.19 EMPIRICAL EXAMPLE

We again return to our wage equation but use a much larger sample of all individuals with at least 12 years of education. For regressors, we include years of education, potential work experience, experience squared, and dummy variable indicators for the following: female, female union member, male union member, married female,[1] married male, formerly married female,[2] formerly married male, Hispanic, Black, American Indian, Asian, and mixed race.[3] The available sample is 46,943, so the parameter estimates are quite precise and are reported in Table 4.2. For standard errors, we use the unbiased HC2 formula.

Table 4.2 displays the parameter estimates in a standard tabular format. Parameter estimates and standard errors are reported for all coefficients. In addition to the coefficient estimates, the table also reports the estimated error standard deviation and the sample size. These are useful summary measures of fit which aid readers.

As a general rule, it is advisable to always report standard errors along with parameter estimates. This allows readers to assess the precision of the parameter estimates, and as we will discuss in later chapters, form confidence intervals and t-tests for individual coefficients if desired.

The results in Table 4.2 confirm our earlier findings that the return to a year of education is approximately 12%, the return to experience is concave, single women earn approximately 10% less than single men, and Blacks earn about 10% less than whites. In addition, we see that Hispanics earn about 11% less than whites, American Indians 14% less, and Asians and Mixed races about 4% less. We also see there are wage premiums for men who are members of a labor union (about 10%), married (about 21%), or formerly married (about 8%), but no similar premiums are apparent for women.

[1] Defining "married" as marital code 1, 2, or 3.

[2] Defining "formerly married" as marital code 4, 5, or 6.

[3] Race code 6 or higher.

Table 4.2
OLS estimates of linear equation for log(wage)

	$\widehat{\beta}$	$s(\widehat{\beta})$
Education	0.117	0.001
Experience	0.033	0.001
Experience^2/100	−0.056	0.002
Female	−0.098	0.011
Female union member	0.023	0.020
Male union member	0.095	0.020
Married female	0.016	0.010
Married male	0.211	0.010
Formerly married female	−0.006	0.012
Formerly married male	0.083	0.015
Hispanic	−0.108	0.008
Black	−0.096	0.008
American Indian	−0.137	0.027
Asian	−0.038	0.013
Mixed race	−0.041	0.021
Intercept	0.909	0.021
$\widehat{\sigma}$	0.565	
Sample size	46,943	

Note: Standard errors are heteroskedasticity-consistent (Horn-Horn-Duncan formula)

4.20 MULTICOLLINEARITY

As discussed in Section 3.24, if $X'X$ is singular, then $(X'X)^{-1}$ and $\widehat{\beta}$ are not defined. This situation is called **strict multicollinearity**, as the columns of X are linearly dependent (i.e., there is some $\alpha \neq 0$ such that $X\alpha = 0$). Most commonly, this arises when sets of regressors are included which are identically related. In Section 3.24, we discussed possible causes of strict multicollinearity and discussed the related problem of ill-conditioning, which can cause numerical inaccuracies in severe cases.

A related common situation is **near multicollinearity**, which is often called "multicollinearity" for brevity. (In this situation, the regressors are highly correlated. An implication of near multicollinearity is that individual coefficient estimates will be imprecise. This is not necessarily a problem for econometric analysis, if the reported standard errors are accurate. However, robust standard errors can be sensitive to large leverage values, which can occur under near multicollinearity. This leads to the undesirable situation in which the coefficient estimates are imprecise, yet the standard errors are misleadingly small.

We can see the impact of near multicollinearity on precision in a simple homoskedastic linear regression model with two regressors:

$$Y = X_1\beta_1 + X_2\beta_2 + e$$

and

$$\frac{1}{n}X'X = \begin{pmatrix} 1 & \rho \\ \rho & 1 \end{pmatrix}.$$

In this case,

$$\operatorname{var}\left[\widehat{\beta} \mid X\right] = \frac{\sigma^2}{n}\begin{pmatrix} 1 & \rho \\ \rho & 1 \end{pmatrix}^{-1} = \frac{\sigma^2}{n\left(1-\rho^2\right)}\begin{pmatrix} 1 & -\rho \\ -\rho & 1 \end{pmatrix}.$$

The correlation ρ indexes collinearity, since as ρ approaches 1, the matrix becomes singular. We can see the effect of collinearity on precision by observing that the variance of a coefficient estimate $\sigma^2\left[n\left(1-\rho^2\right)\right]^{-1}$ approaches infinity as ρ approaches 1. Thus the more "collinear" the regressors are, the worse the precision of the individual coefficient estimates will be.

What is happening is that when the regressors are highly dependent, it is statistically difficult to disentangle the impact of β_1 from that of β_2. As a consequence, the precision of individual estimates are reduced.

Many early textbooks overemphasized multicollinearity. An amusing parody of these texts is "Micronumerosity," Chapter 23.3 of Goldberger's *A Course in Econometrics* (1991). Among the witty remarks of his chapter are the following:

> The extreme case, 'exact micronumerosity', arises when $n = 0$, in which case the sample estimate of μ is not unique. (Technically, there is a violation of the rank condition $n > 0$: the matrix 0 is singular.)
>
> Tests for the presence of micronumerosity require the judicious use of various fingers. Some researchers prefer a single finger, others use their toes, still others let their thumbs rule.
>
> A generally reliable guide may be obtained by counting the number of observations. Most of the time in econometric analysis, when n is close to zero, it is also far from infinity.
>
> Arthur S. Goldberger, *A Course in Econometrics* (1991, p. 249).

To understand Goldberger's basic point, you should notice that the estimation variance $\sigma^2\left[n\left(1-\rho^2\right)\right]^{-1}$ depends equally and symmetrically on the correlation ρ and the sample size n. He was pointing out that the only statistical implication of multicollinearity in the homoskedastic model is a lack of precision. Small sample sizes have the very same implication.

Arthur S. Goldberger

Art Goldberger (1930–2009) was one of the most distinguished members of the Department of Economics at the University of Wisconsin. His Ph.D. thesis developed a pioneering macroeconometric forecasting model (the Klein-Goldberger model). Most of his remaining career focused on microeconometric issues. He was the leading pioneer of what has been called the Wisconsin Tradition of empirical work—a combination of formal econometric theory and careful critical analysis of empirical work. Goldberger wrote a series of highly regarded and influential graduate econometric textbooks, including *Econometric Theory* (1964), *Topics in Regression Analysis* (1968), and *A Course in Econometrics* (1991).

4.21 CLUSTERED SAMPLING

Section 4.2 briefly mentioned clustered sampling as an alternative to the assumption of random sampling. Let us now consider the framework in more detail and extend the primary results of this chapter to encompass clustered dependence.

It might be easiest to understand the idea of clusters by considering a concrete example. Duflo, Dupas, and Kremer (2011) investigate the impact of tracking (assigning students based on initial test score) on educational attainment in a randomized experiment. An extract of their dataset is available on the textbook webpage in the file `DDK2011`.

In 2005, 140 primary schools in Kenya received funding to hire an extra first grade teacher to reduce class sizes. In half of the schools (selected randomly), students were assigned to classrooms based on an initial test score ("tracking"); in the remaining schools, the students were randomly assigned to classrooms. For their analysis, the authors restricted attention to the 121 schools which initially had a single first-grade class.

The key regression[4] in the paper is

$$TestScore_{ig} = -0.071 + 0.138 Tracking_g + e_{ig} \tag{4.43}$$

where $TestScore_{ig}$ is the standardized test score (normalized to have mean 0 and variance 1) of student i in school g, and $Tracking_g$ is a dummy equal to 1 if school g was tracking. The OLS estimates indicate that schools which tracked the students had an overall increase in test scores by about 0.14 standard deviations, which is meaningful. More general versions of this regression are estimated, many of which take the form

$$TestScore_{ig} = \alpha + \gamma\, Tracking_g + X'_{ig}\beta + e_{ig} \tag{4.44}$$

where X_{ig} is a set of controls specific to the student (including age, gender, and initial test score).

A difficulty with applying the classical regression framework is that student achievement is likely to be correlated within a given school. Student achievement may be affected by local demographics, individual teachers, and classmates, all of which imply dependence. These concerns, however, do not suggest that achievement will be correlated across schools, so it seems reasonable to model achievement across schools as mutually independent. We call such dependence **clustered**.

In clustering contexts, it is convenient to double index the observations as (Y_{ig}, X_{ig}), where $g = 1, \ldots, G$ indexes the cluster, and $i = 1, \ldots, n_g$ indexes the individual in the gth cluster. The number of observations per cluster n_g may vary across clusters. The number of clusters is G. The total number of observations is $n = \sum_{g=1}^{G} n_g$. In the Kenyan schooling example, the number of clusters (schools) in the estimation sample is $G = 121$, the number of students per school varies from 19 to 62, and the total number of observations is $n = 5,795$.

While it is typical to write the observations using the double index notation (Y_{ig}, X_{ig}), it is also useful to use cluster-level notation. Let $\boldsymbol{Y}_g = (Y_{1g}, \ldots, Y_{n_g g})'$ and $\boldsymbol{X}_g = (X_{1g}, \ldots, X_{n_g g})'$ denote the $n_g \times 1$ vector of dependent variables and $n_g \times k$ matrix of regressors for the gth cluster. A linear regression model can be written by individual as

$$Y_{ig} = X'_{ig}\beta + e_{ig}$$

and using cluster notation as

$$\boldsymbol{Y}_g = \boldsymbol{X}_g\beta + \boldsymbol{e}_g \tag{4.45}$$

where $\boldsymbol{e}_g = (e_{1g}, \ldots, e_{n_g g})'$ is a $n_g \times 1$ error vector. We can also stack the observations into full sample matrices and write the model as

$$\boldsymbol{Y} = \boldsymbol{X}\beta + \boldsymbol{e}.$$

[4] See their Table 2, column (1). Duflo, Dupas, and Kremer (2011) report a coefficient estimate of 0.139, perhaps due to a slightly different calculation to standardize the test score.

Using this notation, we can write the sums over the observations using the double sum $\sum_{g=1}^{G}\sum_{i=1}^{n_g}$. This is the sum across clusters of the sum across observations in each cluster. The OLS estimator can be written as

$$\begin{aligned}\widehat{\beta} &= \left(\sum_{g=1}^{G}\sum_{i=1}^{n_g} X_{ig}X_{ig}'\right)^{-1}\left(\sum_{g=1}^{G}\sum_{i=1}^{n_g} X_{ig}Y_{ig}\right)\\ &= \left(\sum_{g=1}^{G}\boldsymbol{X}_g'\boldsymbol{X}_g\right)^{-1}\left(\sum_{g=1}^{G}\boldsymbol{X}_g'\boldsymbol{Y}_g\right)\\ &= \left(\boldsymbol{X}'\boldsymbol{X}\right)^{-1}\left(\boldsymbol{X}'\boldsymbol{Y}\right).\end{aligned} \tag{4.46}$$

The residuals are $\widehat{e}_{ig} = Y_{ig} - X_{ig}'\widehat{\beta}$ in individual level notation and $\widehat{\boldsymbol{e}}_g = \boldsymbol{Y}_g - \boldsymbol{X}_g\widehat{\beta}$ in cluster level notation.

The standard clustering assumption is that the clusters are known to the researcher and that the observations are independent across clusters.

Assumption 4.4 The clusters $(\boldsymbol{Y}_g, \boldsymbol{X}_g)$ are mutually independent across clusters g.

In our example, clusters are schools. In other common applications, cluster dependence has been assumed within individual classrooms, families, villages, regions, and within larger units (such as industries and states). This choice is up to the researcher, though the justification will depend on the context and the nature of the data, and it will reflect information and assumptions about the dependence structure across observations.

The model is a linear regression under the assumption

$$\mathbb{E}\left[\boldsymbol{e}_g \mid \boldsymbol{X}_g\right] = 0. \tag{4.47}$$

This is the same as assuming that the individual errors are conditionally mean 0:

$$\mathbb{E}\left[e_{ig} \mid \boldsymbol{X}_g\right] = 0$$

or that the conditional expectation of $\boldsymbol{Y}_g$ given $\boldsymbol{X}_g$ is linear. As in the independent case, equation (4.47) means that the linear regression model is correctly specified. In the clustered regression model, this requires that all interaction effects within clusters have been accounted for in the specification of the individual regressors X_{ig}.

In the regression (4.43), the conditional expectation is necessarily linear and satisfies (4.47), since the regressor $Tracking_g$ is a dummy variable at the cluster level. In the regression (4.44) with individual controls, (4.47) requires that the achievement of any student is unaffected by the individual controls (e.g., age, gender, and initial test score) of other students in the same school.

Given (4.47), we can calculate the expectation of the OLS estimator. Substituting (4.45) into (4.46), we find

$$\widehat{\beta} - \beta = \left(\sum_{g=1}^{G}\boldsymbol{X}_g'\boldsymbol{X}_g\right)^{-1}\left(\sum_{g=1}^{G}\boldsymbol{X}_g'\boldsymbol{e}_g\right).$$

The mean of $\widehat{\beta} - \beta$ conditioning on all the regressors is

$$\mathbb{E}\left[\widehat{\beta} - \beta \mid \boldsymbol{X}\right] = \left(\sum_{g=1}^{G}\boldsymbol{X}_g'\boldsymbol{X}_g\right)^{-1}\left(\sum_{g=1}^{G}\boldsymbol{X}_g'\mathbb{E}\left[\boldsymbol{e}_g \mid \boldsymbol{X}\right]\right)$$

$$= \left(\sum_{g=1}^{G} X_g' X_g \right)^{-1} \left(\sum_{g=1}^{G} X_g' \mathbb{E}\left[e_g \mid X_g \right] \right)$$

$$= 0.$$

The first equality holds by linearity, the second by Assumption 4.4, and the third by (4.47). Thus, OLS is unbiased under clustering if the conditional expectation is linear.

Theorem 4.7 In the clustered linear regression model (Assumption 4.4 and (4.47)), $\mathbb{E}\left[\widehat{\beta} \mid X\right] = \beta$.

Now consider the covariance matrix of $\widehat{\beta}$. Let $\Sigma_g = \mathbb{E}\left[e_g e_g' \mid X_g \right]$ denote the $n_g \times n_g$ conditional covariance matrix of the errors in the gth cluster. Since the observations are independent across clusters,

$$\begin{aligned} \operatorname{var}\left[\left(\sum_{g=1}^{G} X_g' e_g \right) \middle| X \right] &= \sum_{g=1}^{G} \operatorname{var}\left[X_g' e_g \mid X_g \right] \\ &= \sum_{g=1}^{G} X_g' \mathbb{E}\left[e_g e_g' \mid X_g \right] X_g \\ &= \sum_{g=1}^{G} X_g' \Sigma_g X_g \\ &\stackrel{\text{def}}{=} \Omega_n. \end{aligned} \tag{4.48}$$

It follows that

$$V_{\widehat{\beta}} = \operatorname{var}\left[\widehat{\beta} \mid X\right] = \left(X'X\right)^{-1} \Omega_n \left(X'X\right)^{-1}. \tag{4.49}$$

Equation (4.49) differs from the formula in the independent case due to the correlation between observations within clusters. The magnitude of the difference depends on the degree of correlation between observations within clusters and the number of observations within clusters. To see this, suppose that all clusters have the same number of observations $n_g = N$, $\mathbb{E}\left[e_{ig}^2 \mid X_g \right] = \sigma^2$, $\mathbb{E}\left[e_{ig} e_{\ell g} \mid X_g \right] = \sigma^2 \rho$ for $i \neq \ell$, and the regressors X_{ig} do not vary within a cluster. In this case, the exact variance of the OLS estimator equals[5] (after some calculations)

$$V_{\widehat{\beta}} = \left(X'X\right)^{-1} \sigma^2 \left(1 + \rho \left(N - 1\right)\right). \tag{4.50}$$

If $\rho > 0$, the exact variance is appropriately a multiple ρN of the conventional formula. In the Kenyan school example, the average cluster size is 48. If $\rho = 0.25$, this means the exact variance exceeds the conventional formula by a factor of about 12. In this case, the correct standard errors (the square root of the variance) are a multiple of about three times the conventional formula. This is a substantial difference and should not be neglected.

[5]This formula is due to Moulton (1990).

Arellano (1987) proposed a cluster-robust covariance matrix estimator which is an extension of the White estimator. Recall that the insight of the White covariance estimator is that the squared error e_i^2 is unbiased for $\mathbb{E}\left[e_i^2 \mid X_i\right] = \sigma_i^2$. Similarly, with cluster dependence, the matrix $\boldsymbol{e}_g\boldsymbol{e}_g'$ is unbiased for $\mathbb{E}\left[\boldsymbol{e}_g\boldsymbol{e}_g' \mid \boldsymbol{X}_g\right] = \Sigma_g$. Thus an unbiased estimator for (4.48) is $\widetilde{\Omega}_n = \sum_{g=1}^G \boldsymbol{X}_g'\boldsymbol{e}_g\boldsymbol{e}_g'\boldsymbol{X}_g$. This is not feasible, but we can replace the unknown errors by the OLS residuals to obtain Arellano's estimator:

$$\begin{aligned}
\widehat{\Omega}_n &= \sum_{g=1}^{G} \boldsymbol{X}_g'\widehat{\boldsymbol{e}}_g\widehat{\boldsymbol{e}}_g'\boldsymbol{X}_g \\
&= \sum_{g=1}^{G}\sum_{i=1}^{n_g}\sum_{\ell=1}^{n_g} X_{ig}X_{\ell g}'\widehat{e}_{ig}\widehat{e}_{\ell g} \\
&= \sum_{g=1}^{G}\left(\sum_{i=1}^{n_g} X_{ig}\widehat{e}_{ig}\right)\left(\sum_{\ell=1}^{n_g} X_{\ell g}\widehat{e}_{\ell g}\right)'.
\end{aligned} \tag{4.51}$$

The three expressions in (4.51) give three equivalent formulas which could be used to calculate $\widehat{\Omega}_n$. The final expression writes $\widehat{\Omega}_n$ in terms of the cluster sums $\sum_{\ell=1}^{n_g} X_{\ell g}\widehat{e}_{\ell g}$, which is the basis for our example R and MATLAB codes shown near the end of this section.

Given the expressions (4.48)–(4.49), a natural cluster covariance matrix estimator takes the form

$$\widehat{\boldsymbol{V}}_{\widehat{\beta}} = a_n\left(\boldsymbol{X}'\boldsymbol{X}\right)^{-1}\widehat{\Omega}_n\left(\boldsymbol{X}'\boldsymbol{X}\right)^{-1} \tag{4.52}$$

where a_n is a possible finite-sample adjustment. The Stata `cluster` command uses

$$a_n = \left(\frac{n-1}{n-k}\right)\left(\frac{G}{G-1}\right). \tag{4.53}$$

The factor $G/(G-1)$ was derived by Chris Hansen (2007) in the context of equal-sized clusters to improve performance when the number G of clusters is small. The factor $(n-1)/(n-k)$ is an ad hoc generalization which nests the adjustment used in (4.34), since $G = n$ implies the simplification $a_n = n/(n-k)$.

Alternative cluster-robust covariance matrix estimators can be constructed using cluster-level prediction errors, such as $\widetilde{\boldsymbol{e}}_g = \boldsymbol{Y}_g - \boldsymbol{X}_g\widehat{\beta}_{(-g)}$, where $\widehat{\beta}_{(-g)}$ is the least squares estimator omitting cluster g. As in Section 3.20, we can show that

$$\widetilde{\boldsymbol{e}}_g = \left(\boldsymbol{I}_{n_g} - \boldsymbol{X}_g\left(\boldsymbol{X}'\boldsymbol{X}\right)^{-1}\boldsymbol{X}_g'\right)^{-1}\widehat{\boldsymbol{e}}_g \tag{4.54}$$

and

$$\widehat{\beta}_{(-g)} = \widehat{\beta} - \left(\boldsymbol{X}'\boldsymbol{X}\right)^{-1}\boldsymbol{X}_g'\widetilde{\boldsymbol{e}}_g. \tag{4.55}$$

We then have the robust covariance matrix estimator

$$\widehat{\boldsymbol{V}}_{\widehat{\beta}}^{\mathrm{CR3}} = \left(\boldsymbol{X}'\boldsymbol{X}\right)^{-1}\left(\sum_{g=1}^{G}\boldsymbol{X}_g'\widetilde{\boldsymbol{e}}_g\widetilde{\boldsymbol{e}}_g'\boldsymbol{X}_g\right)\left(\boldsymbol{X}'\boldsymbol{X}\right)^{-1}. \tag{4.56}$$

The label "CR" refers to "cluster-robust," and "CR3" refers to the analogous formula for the HC3 estimator.

Similarly to the heteroskedastic-robust case, you can show that CR3 is a conservative estimator for $\boldsymbol{V}_{\widehat{\beta}}$ in the sense that the conditional expectation of $\widehat{\boldsymbol{V}}_{\widehat{\beta}}^{\mathrm{CR3}}$ exceeds $\boldsymbol{V}_{\widehat{\beta}}$. This covariance matrix estimator is more cumbersome to implement, however, as the cluster-level prediction errors (4.54) cannot be calculated in a simple linear operation and requires a loop across clusters to calculate.

To illustrate the estimator in the context of the Kenyan schooling example, consider the regression of student test scores on the school-level tracking dummy with two standard errors displayed. The first (in parenthesis) is the conventional robust standard error. The second [in square brackets] is the clustered standard error (4.52)–(4.53), where clustering is at the level of the school.

$$\begin{array}{rccl} \mathit{TestScore}_{ig} = & -\underset{\substack{(0.019)\\ [0.054]}}{0.071} & + & \underset{\substack{(0.026)\\ [0.078]}}{0.138}\ \mathit{Tracking}_g + e_{ig}. \end{array} \tag{4.57}$$

We can see that the cluster-robust standard errors are roughly three times the conventional robust standard errors. Consequently, confidence intervals for the coefficients are greatly affected by the choice.

For illustration, we list here the commands needed to produce the regression results with clustered standard errors in Stata, R, and MATLAB.

Stata do File

```
*      Load data:
use "DDK2011.dta"
*      Standard the test score variable to have mean zero and unit variance:
egen testscore = std(totalscore)
*      Regression with standard errors clustered at the school level:
reg testscore tracking, cluster(schoolid)
```

You can see that clustered standard errors are simple to calculate in Stata.

R Program File

```
# Load the data and create variables
data <- read.table("DDK2011.txt",header=TRUE,sep="\ t")
y <- scale(as.matrix(data$totalscore))
n <- nrow(y)
x <- cbind(as.matrix(data$tracking),matrix(1,n,1))
schoolid <- as.matrix(data$schoolid)
k <- ncol(x)
xx <- t(x)%*%x
invx <- solve(xx)
beta <- solve(xx,t(x)%*%y)
xe <- x*rep(y-x%*%beta,times=k)
# Clustered robust standard error
xe_sum <- rowsum(xe,schoolid)
G <- nrow(xe_sum)
```

```
omega <- t(xe_sum)%*%xe_sum
scale <- G/(G-1)*(n-1)/(n-k)
V_clustered <- scale*invx%*%omega%*%invx
se_clustered <- sqrt(diag(V_clustered))
print(beta)
print(se_clustered)
```

Programming clustered standard errors in R is also relatively easy due to the convenient `rowsum` command, which sums variables within clusters.

MATLAB Program File

```
% Load the data and create variables
data = xlsread('DDK2011.xlsx');
schoolid = data(:,2);
tracking = data(:,7);
totalscore = data(:,62);
y = (totalscore - mean(totalscore))./std(totalscore);
x = [tracking,ones(size(y,1),1)];
[n,k] = size(x);
xx = x'*x;
invx = inv(xx);
beta = xx\(x'*y)
e = y - x*beta;
% Clustered robust standard error
[schools,~,schoolidx] = unique(schoolid);
G = size(schools,1);
cluster_sums = zeros(G,k);
for j = 1:k
cluster_sums(:,j) = accumarray(schoolidx,x(:,j).*e);
end
omega = cluster_sums'*cluster_sums;
scale = G/(G-1)*(n-1)/(n-k);
V_clustered = scale*invx*omega*invx;
se_clustered = sqrt(diag(V_clustered));
display(beta);
display(se_clustered);
```

Here we see that programming clustered standard errors in MATLAB is less convenient than in the other packages but still can be executed with just a few lines of code. This example uses the `accumarray` command, which is similar to the `rowsum` command in R but can be applied only to vectors (hence the loop across the regressors) and works best if the *clusterid* variable are indices (which is why the original *schoolid* variable is transformed into indices in *schoolidx*). Application of these commands requires care and attention.

4.22 INFERENCE WITH CLUSTERED SAMPLES

This section covers some cautionary remarks and general advice about cluster-robust inference in econometric practice. Remarkably little theoretical research has been done on the properties of cluster-robust methods—until quite recently.

In many respects, cluster-robust inference should be viewed similarly to heteroskedaticity-robust inference where a "cluster" in the cluster-robust case is interpreted similarly to an "observation" in the heteroskedasticity-robust case. In particular, the effective sample size should be viewed as the number of clusters, not the "sample size" n. This is because the cluster-robust covariance matrix estimator effectively treats each cluster as a single observation and estimates the covariance matrix based on the variation across cluster means. Hence if there are only $G=50$ clusters, inference should be viewed as (at best) similar to heteroskedasticity-robust inference with $n=50$ observations. This is a bit unsettling when the number of regressors is large (say $k=20$), because then the covariance matrix will be estimated imprecisely.

Furthermore, most cluster-robust theory (for example, the work of Chris Hansen 2007) assumes that the clusters are homogeneous, including the assumption that the cluster sizes are all identical. This simplification turns out to be very important. When it is violated—when, for example, cluster sizes are highly heterogeneous—the regression should be viewed as roughly equivalent to the heteroskedastic case with an extremely high degree of heteroskedasticity. Cluster sums have variances which are proportional to the cluster sizes, so if the latter is heterogeneous, so will be the variances of the cluster sums. This also has a large effect on finite sample inference. When clusters are heterogeneous, then cluster-robust inference is similar to heteroskedasticity-robust inference with highly heteroskedastic observations.

Put together, if the number of clusters G is small and the number of observations per cluster is highly varied, then we should interpret inferential statements with a great degree of caution. Unfortunately, small G with heterogeneous cluster sizes is commonplace. Many empirical studies on U.S. data cluster at the "state" level, meaning that there are 50 or 51 clusters (the District of Columbia is typically treated as a state). The number of observations varies considerably across states, since the populations are highly unequal. Thus when you read empirical papers with individual-level data but clustered at the "state" level, you should be cautious and recognize that this is equivalent to inference with a small number of extremely heterogeneous observations.

A further complication occurs when we are interested in treatment, as in the tracking example given in Section 4.21. In many cases (including Duflo, Dupas, and Kremer, 2011) the interest is in the effect of a treatment applied at the cluster level (e.g., schools). In many cases (not, however, in Duflo, Dupas, and Kremer, 2011), the number of treated clusters is small relative to the total number of clusters; in an extreme case, there is just a single treated cluster. Based on the reasoning given above, these applications should be interpreted as equivalent to heteroskedasticity-robust inference with a sparse dummy variable, as discussed in Section 4.16. As discussed there, standard error estimates can be erroneously small. In the extreme of a single treated cluster (in the example, if only a single school were tracked), the estimated coefficient on *tracking* will be very imprecisely estimated yet will have a misleadingly small cluster standard error. In general, reported standard errors will greatly understate the imprecision of parameter estimates.

4.23 AT WHAT LEVEL TO CLUSTER?

A practical question which arises in the context of cluster-robust inference is: "At what level should we cluster?" In some examples, you could cluster at a very fine level, such as families or classrooms, or at higher levels of aggregation, such as neighborhoods, schools, towns, counties, or states. What is the correct level at which to cluster? Rules of thumb have been advocated by practitioners but at present there is little formal analysis to provide useful guidance. What do we know?

First, suppose cluster dependence is ignored or imposed at too fine a level (e.g., clustering by households instead of villages). Then variance estimators will be biased, because they will omit covariance terms. As correlation is typically positive, this suggests that standard errors will be too small, giving rise to spurious indications of significance and precision.

Second, suppose cluster dependence is imposed at too aggregate a measure (e.g., clustering by states rather than by villages). This does not cause bias. But the variance estimators will contain many extra components, so the precision of the covariance matrix estimator will be poor. Thus reported standard errors will be imprecise—more random—than if clustering had been less aggregate.

These considerations show that there is a trade-off between bias and variance in the estimation of the covariance matrix by cluster-robust methods. It is not at all clear—based on current theory—what to do. I state this emphatically. We really do not know what the "correct" level is at which to do cluster-robust inference. This question is very interesting and should certainly be explored by econometric research.

One challenge is that in empirical practice, many researchers have observed: "Clustering is important. Standard errors change a lot whether or not we cluster. Therefore we should only report clustered standard errors." The flaw in this reasoning is that we do not know why, in a specific empirical example, the standard errors change under clustering. One possibility is that clustering reduces bias and thus is more accurate. The other possibility is that clustering adds sampling noise and is thus less accurate. In reality, it is likely that both factors are present.

In any event, a researcher should be aware of the number of clusters used in the reported calculations and should treat the number of clusters as the effective sample size for assessing inference. If the number of clusters is, say, $G=20$, this should be treated as a very small sample.

To illustrate by a thought experiment, consider the empirical example of Duflo, Dupas, and Kremer (2011). They reported standard errors clustered at the school level, and the application uses 111 schools. Thus $G=111$ is the effective sample size. The number of observations (students) ranges from 19 to 62, which is reasonably homogeneous. This seems like a well-balanced application of clustered variance estimation. However, one could imagine clustering at a different level of aggregation. We might consider clustering at a less aggregate level, such as the classroom level, but this cannot be done in this particular application, as there was only one classroom per school. Clustering at a more aggregate level could be done in this application at the level of the "zone." However, there are only nine zones. Thus if we cluster by zone, $G=9$ is the effective sample size, which would lead to imprecise standard errors. In this particular example, clustering at the school level (as done by the authors) is indeed the prudent choice.

4.24 TECHNICAL PROOFS*

Proof of Theorem 4.5 This argument is taken from B. E. Hansen (2022a).

Our approach is to calculate the Cramér-Rao bound for a carefully crafted parametric model. This is based on an insight of Newey (1990, Appendix B) for the simpler context of a population expectation.

Without loss of generality, assume that the true coefficient equals $\beta_0=0$ and that $\sigma^2=1$. These are merely normalizations which simplify the notation. Also assume that $\boldsymbol{Y}$ has a joint density $f(\boldsymbol{y})$. This assumption simplifies the argument but is not essential.

Define the truncation function $\mathbb{R}^n \to \mathbb{R}^n$:

$$\psi_c(\boldsymbol{y}) = \boldsymbol{y}\mathbb{1}\{\|\boldsymbol{y}\| \le c\} - \mathbb{E}\left[\boldsymbol{Y}\mathbb{1}\{\|\boldsymbol{y}\| \le c\}\right].$$

Notice that it satisfies $|\psi_c(\boldsymbol{y})| \le 2c$, $\mathbb{E}[\psi_c(\boldsymbol{Y})] = 0$, and

$$\mathbb{E}\left[\boldsymbol{Y}\psi_c(\boldsymbol{Y})'\right] = \mathbb{E}\left[\boldsymbol{Y}\boldsymbol{Y}'\mathbb{1}\{\|\boldsymbol{y}\| \le c\}\right] \stackrel{\text{def}}{=} \Sigma_c.$$

As $c \to \infty$, $\Sigma_c \to \mathbb{E}\left[\boldsymbol{Y}\boldsymbol{Y}'\right] = \Sigma$. Pick c sufficiently large so that $\Sigma_c > 0$, which is feasible because $\Sigma > 0$.

Define the auxiliary joint density function

$$f_\beta(\boldsymbol{y}) = f(\boldsymbol{y})\left(1 + \psi_c(\boldsymbol{y})'\Sigma_c^{-1}\boldsymbol{X}\beta\right)$$

for parameters β in the set

$$B = \left\{\beta \in \mathbb{R}^m : \left\|\Sigma_c^{-1}\boldsymbol{X}\beta\right\| \le \frac{1}{4c}\right\}.$$

The bounds imply that for $\beta \in B$ and all $\boldsymbol{y}$,

$$\left|\psi_c(\boldsymbol{y})'\Sigma_c^{-1}\boldsymbol{X}\beta\right| \le \frac{1}{2}.$$

Thus, f_β has the same support as f and satisfies the bounds

$$0 < f_\beta(\boldsymbol{y}) < 2f(\boldsymbol{y}). \tag{4.58}$$

We calculate that

$$\begin{aligned}
\int f_\beta(\boldsymbol{y})\,d\boldsymbol{y} &= \int f(\boldsymbol{y})\,d\boldsymbol{y} + \int \psi_c(\boldsymbol{y})'\Sigma_c^{-1}\boldsymbol{X}\beta f_\beta(\boldsymbol{y})\,d\boldsymbol{y} \\
&= 1 + \mathbb{E}[\psi_c(\boldsymbol{Y})]'\,\Sigma_c^{-1}\boldsymbol{X}\beta \\
&= 1
\end{aligned}$$

the last equality because $\mathbb{E}[\psi_c(\boldsymbol{Y})] = 0$. Together, these facts imply that f_β is a valid density function, and over $\beta \in B$ is a parametric family for $\boldsymbol{Y}$. Evaluated at $\beta_0 = 0$, which is in the interior of B, we see that $f_0 = f$. Thus f_β is a correctly specified parametric family with the true parameter value β_0.

Let $\mathbb{E}_\beta$ denote expectation under the density f_β. The expectation of $\boldsymbol{Y}$ in this model is

$$\begin{aligned}
\mathbb{E}_\beta[\boldsymbol{Y}] &= \int \boldsymbol{y} f_\beta(\boldsymbol{y})\,d\boldsymbol{y} \\
&= \int \boldsymbol{y} f(\boldsymbol{y})\,d\boldsymbol{y} + \int \boldsymbol{y}\psi_c(\boldsymbol{y})'\Sigma_c^{-1}\boldsymbol{X}\beta f_\beta(\boldsymbol{y})\,d\boldsymbol{y} \\
&= \mathbb{E}[\boldsymbol{Y}] + \mathbb{E}\left[\boldsymbol{Y}\psi_c(\boldsymbol{Y})'\right]\Sigma_c^{-1}\boldsymbol{X}\beta \\
&= \boldsymbol{X}\beta
\end{aligned}$$

because $\mathbb{E}[\boldsymbol{Y}] = 0$ and $\mathbb{E}\left[\boldsymbol{Y}\psi_c(\boldsymbol{Y})'\right] = \Sigma_c$. Thus, the model f_β is a linear regression with regression coefficient β.

The bound (4.58) implies

$$\mathbb{E}_\beta\left[\|\boldsymbol{Y}\|^2\right] = \int \|\boldsymbol{y}\|^2 f_\beta(\boldsymbol{y})\,d\boldsymbol{y} \le 2\int \|\boldsymbol{y}\|^2 f(\boldsymbol{y})\,d\boldsymbol{y} = 2\mathbb{E}\left[\|\boldsymbol{Y}\|^2\right] = 2\operatorname{tr}(\Sigma) < \infty.$$

Thus, f_β has a finite variance for all $\beta \in B$.

The likelihood score for f_β is

$$
\begin{aligned}
S &= \frac{\partial}{\partial \beta} \log f_\beta\,(\boldsymbol{Y})\bigg|_{\beta=0} \\
&= \frac{\partial}{\partial \beta} \log\left(1 + \psi_c(\boldsymbol{Y})'\Sigma_c^{-1}\boldsymbol{X}\beta\right)\bigg|_{\beta=0} \\
&= \boldsymbol{X}'\Sigma_c^{-1}\psi_c(\boldsymbol{Y}).
\end{aligned}
$$

The information matrix is

$$
\begin{aligned}
\mathscr{I}_c &= \mathbb{E}\left[SS'\right] \\
&= \boldsymbol{X}'\Sigma_c^{-1}\mathbb{E}\left[\psi_c(\boldsymbol{Y})\psi_c(\boldsymbol{Y})'\right]\Sigma_c^{-1}\boldsymbol{X} \\
&\leq \boldsymbol{X}'\Sigma_c^{-1}\boldsymbol{X} \qquad (4.59)
\end{aligned}
$$

where the inequality is

$$
\mathbb{E}\left[\psi_c(\boldsymbol{Y})\psi_c(\boldsymbol{Y})'\right] = \Sigma_c - \mathbb{E}\left[\boldsymbol{Y}\mathbb{1}\left\{\left|\boldsymbol{X}'\Sigma^{-1}\boldsymbol{Y}\right| \leq c\right\}\right]\mathbb{E}\left[\boldsymbol{Y}\mathbb{1}\left\{\left|\boldsymbol{X}'\Sigma^{-1}\boldsymbol{Y}\right| \leq c\right\}\right]' \leq \Sigma_c.
$$

By assumption, the estimator $\widetilde{\beta}$ is unbiased for β. The model f_β is regular (it is correctly specified, as it contains the true density f, the support of $\boldsymbol{Y}$ does not depend on β, and the true value $\beta_0 = 0$ lies in the interior of B). Thus by the Cramér-Rao Theorem (Theorem 10.6 of *Probability and Statistics for Economists*),

$$
\operatorname{var}\left[\widetilde{\beta}\right] \geq \mathscr{I}_c^{-1} \geq \left(\boldsymbol{X}'\Sigma_c^{-1}\boldsymbol{X}\right)^{-1}
$$

where the second inequality is (4.59). Since this holds for all c, and $\Sigma_c \to \Sigma$ as $c \to \infty$,

$$
\operatorname{var}\left[\widetilde{\beta}\right] \geq \limsup_{c\to\infty} \left(\boldsymbol{X}'\Sigma_c^{-1}\boldsymbol{X}\right)^{-1} = \left(\boldsymbol{X}'\Sigma^{-1}\boldsymbol{X}\right)^{-1}.
$$

This is the variance lower bound. ■

4.25 EXERCISES

Exercise 4.1 For some integer k, set $\mu_k = \mathbb{E}[Y^k]$.

(a) Construct an estimator $\widehat{\mu}_k$ for μ_k.

(b) Show that $\widehat{\mu}_k$ is unbiased for μ_k.

(c) Calculate the variance of $\widehat{\mu}_k$, say, $\operatorname{var}[\widehat{\mu}_k]$. What assumption is needed for $\operatorname{var}[\widehat{\mu}_k]$ to be finite?

(d) Propose an estimator of $\operatorname{var}[\widehat{\mu}_k]$.

Exercise 4.2 Calculate $\mathbb{E}\left[\left(\overline{Y} - \mu\right)^3\right]$, the skewness of $\overline{Y}$. Under what condition is it 0?

Exercise 4.3 Explain the difference between $\overline{Y}$ and μ. Explain the difference between $n^{-1}\sum_{i=1}^{n} X_i X_i'$ and $\mathbb{E}\left[X_i X_i'\right]$.

Exercise 4.4 True or False: If $Y = X'\beta + e$, $X \in \mathbb{R}$, $\mathbb{E}[e \mid X] = 0$, and $\widehat{e}_i$ is the OLS residual from the regression of Y_i on X_i, then $\sum_{i=1}^{n} X_i^2 \widehat{e}_i = 0$.

Exercise 4.5 Prove (4.17) and (4.18).

Exercise 4.6 Prove Theorem 4.5 under the restriction to linear estimators.

Exercise 4.7 Let $\widetilde{\beta}$ be the GLS estimator (4.19) under the assumptions (4.15) and (4.16). Assume that Σ is known and σ^2 is unknown. Define the residual vector $\widetilde{\boldsymbol{e}} = \boldsymbol{Y} - \boldsymbol{X}\widetilde{\beta}$, and an estimator for σ^2:

$$\widetilde{\sigma}^2 = \frac{1}{n-k}\widetilde{\boldsymbol{e}}'\Sigma^{-1}\widetilde{\boldsymbol{e}}.$$

(a) Show (4.20).

(b) Show (4.21).

(c) Prove that $\widetilde{\boldsymbol{e}} = \boldsymbol{M}_1\boldsymbol{e}$, where $\boldsymbol{M}_1 = \boldsymbol{I} - \boldsymbol{X}\left(\boldsymbol{X}'\Sigma^{-1}\boldsymbol{X}\right)^{-1}\boldsymbol{X}'\Sigma^{-1}$.

(d) Prove that $\boldsymbol{M}_1'\Sigma^{-1}\boldsymbol{M}_1 = \Sigma^{-1} - \Sigma^{-1}\boldsymbol{X}\left(\boldsymbol{X}'\Sigma^{-1}\boldsymbol{X}\right)^{-1}\boldsymbol{X}'\Sigma^{-1}$.

(e) Find $\mathbb{E}\left[\widetilde{\sigma}^2 \mid \boldsymbol{X}\right]$.

(f) Is $\widetilde{\sigma}^2$ a reasonable estimator for σ^2?

Exercise 4.8 Let (Y_i, X_i) be a random sample with $\mathbb{E}[Y \mid X] = X'\beta$. Consider the **weighted least squares** estimator $\widetilde{\beta}_{\text{wls}} = \left(\boldsymbol{X}'\boldsymbol{W}\boldsymbol{X}\right)^{-1}\left(\boldsymbol{X}'\boldsymbol{W}\boldsymbol{Y}\right)$, where $\boldsymbol{W} = \text{diag}(w_1, \ldots, w_n)$ and $w_i = X_{ji}^{-2}$, where X_{ji} is one of the X_i.

(a) In which contexts would $\widetilde{\beta}_{\text{wls}}$ be a good estimator?

(b) Using your intuition, in which situations do you expect $\widetilde{\beta}_{\text{wls}}$ to perform better than OLS?

Exercise 4.9 Show that (4.29) in the homoskedastic regression model.

Exercise 4.10 Prove (4.37).

Exercise 4.11 Show that (4.38) holds in the homoskedastic regression model.

Exercise 4.12 Let $\mu = \mathbb{E}[Y]$, $\sigma^2 = \mathbb{E}\left[(Y-\mu)^2\right]$, and $\mu_3 = \mathbb{E}\left[(Y-\mu)^3\right]$, and consider the sample mean $\overline{Y} = \frac{1}{n}\sum_{i=1}^n Y_i$. Find $\mathbb{E}\left[\left(\overline{Y}-\mu\right)^3\right]$ as a function of μ, σ^2, μ_3, and n.

Exercise 4.13 Take the simple regression model $Y = X\beta + e$, $X \in \mathbb{R}$, $\mathbb{E}[e \mid X] = 0$. Define $\sigma_i^2 = \mathbb{E}\left[e_i^2 \mid X_i\right]$ and $\mu_{3i} = \mathbb{E}\left[e_i^3 \mid X_i\right]$, and consider the OLS coefficient $\widehat{\beta}$. Find $\mathbb{E}\left[\left(\widehat{\beta}-\beta\right)^3 \mid \boldsymbol{X}\right]$.

Exercise 4.14 Take a regression model $Y = X\beta + e$ with $\mathbb{E}[e \mid X] = 0$ and i.i.d. observations (Y_i, X_i) and scalar X. The parameter of interest is $\theta = \beta^2$. Consider the OLS estimators $\widehat{\beta}$ and $\widehat{\theta} = \widehat{\beta}^2$.

(a) Find $\mathbb{E}\left[\widehat{\theta} \mid \boldsymbol{X}\right]$, using your knowledge of $\mathbb{E}\left[\widehat{\beta} \mid \boldsymbol{X}\right]$ and $V_{\widehat{\beta}} = \text{var}\left[\widehat{\beta} \mid \boldsymbol{X}\right]$. Is $\widehat{\theta}$ biased for θ?

(b) Suggest an (approximate) biased-corrected estimator $\widehat{\theta}^*$ using an estimator $\widehat{V}_{\widehat{\beta}}$ for $V_{\widehat{\beta}}$.

(c) For $\widehat{\theta}^*$ to be potentially unbiased, which estimator of $V_{\widehat{\beta}}$ is most appropriate? Under which conditions is $\widehat{\theta}^*$ unbiased?

Exercise 4.15 Consider an i.i.d. sample $\{Y_i, X_i\}$ $i = 1, \ldots, n$, where X is $k \times 1$. Assume the linear conditional expectation model $Y = X'\beta + e$ with $\mathbb{E}[e \mid X] = 0$. Assume that $n^{-1}\boldsymbol{X}'\boldsymbol{X} = \boldsymbol{I}_k$ (orthonormal regressors). Consider the OLS estimator $\widehat{\beta}$.

(a) Find $\boldsymbol{V}_{\widehat{\beta}} = \operatorname{var}\left[\widehat{\beta}\right]$.

(b) In general, are $\widehat{\beta}_j$ and $\widehat{\beta}_\ell$ for $j \neq \ell$ correlated or uncorrelated?

(c) Find a sufficient condition so that $\widehat{\beta}_j$ and $\widehat{\beta}_\ell$ for $j \neq \ell$ are uncorrelated.

Exercise 4.16 Take the linear homoskedastic conditional expectation function (CEF):

$$Y^* = X'\beta + e \tag{4.60}$$
$$\mathbb{E}[e \mid X] = 0$$
$$\mathbb{E}\left[e^2 \mid X\right] = \sigma^2$$

and suppose that Y^* is measured with error. Instead of Y^*, we observe $Y = Y^* + u$, where u is measurement error. Suppose that e and u are independent and

$$\mathbb{E}[u \mid X] = 0$$
$$\mathbb{E}\left[u^2 \mid X\right] = \sigma_u^2(X).$$

(a) Derive an equation for Y as a function of X. Be explicit and write the error term as a function of the structural errors e and u. What is the effect of this measurement error on the model (4.60)?

(b) Describe the effect of this measurement error on OLS estimation of β in the feasible regression of the observed Y on X.

(c) Describe the effect (if any) of this measurement error on standard error calculation for $\widehat{\beta}$.

Exercise 4.17 Suppose that for the random variables (Y, X) with $X > 0$, an economic model implies

$$\mathbb{E}[Y \mid X] = (\gamma + \theta X)^{1/2}. \tag{4.61}$$

A friend suggests that you estimate γ and θ by the linear regression of Y^2 on X, that is, to estimate the equation

$$Y^2 = \alpha + \beta X + e. \tag{4.62}$$

(a) Investigate your friend's suggestion. Define $u = Y - (\gamma + \theta X)^{1/2}$. Show that $\mathbb{E}[u \mid X] = 0$ is implied by (4.61).

(b) Use $Y = (\gamma + \theta X)^{1/2} + u$ to calculate $\mathbb{E}\left[Y^2 \mid X\right]$. What does this tell you about the implied equation (4.62)?

(c) Can you recover either γ and/or θ from estimation of (4.62)? Are additional assumptions required?

(d) Is this a reasonable suggestion?

Exercise 4.18 Take the model

$$Y = X_1'\beta_1 + X_2'\beta_2 + e$$
$$\mathbb{E}[e \mid X] = 0$$
$$\mathbb{E}\left[e^2 \mid X\right] = \sigma^2$$

where $X = (X_1, X_2)$, with X_1 $k_1 \times 1$ and X_2 $k_2 \times 1$. Consider the short regression $Y_i = X_{1i}'\widehat{\beta}_1 + \widehat{e}_i$, and define the error variance estimator $s^2 = (n - k_1)^{-1} \sum_{i=1}^n \widehat{e}_i^2$. Find $\mathbb{E}\left[s^2 \mid \boldsymbol{X}\right]$.

Exercise 4.19 Let $\boldsymbol{Y}$ be $n \times 1$, $\boldsymbol{X}$ be $n \times k$, and $\boldsymbol{X}^* = \boldsymbol{X}\boldsymbol{C}$, where $\boldsymbol{C}$ is $k \times k$ and full rank. Let $\widehat{\beta}$ be the least squares estimator from the regression of $\boldsymbol{Y}$ on $\boldsymbol{X}$, and let $\widehat{\boldsymbol{V}}$ be the estimate of its asymptotic covariance matrix. Let $\widehat{\beta}^*$ and $\widehat{\boldsymbol{V}}^*$ be those from the regression of $\boldsymbol{Y}$ on $\boldsymbol{X}^*$. Derive an expression for $\widehat{\boldsymbol{V}}^*$ as a function of $\widehat{\boldsymbol{V}}$.

Exercise 4.20 Consider the model in vector notation:

$$\boldsymbol{Y} = \boldsymbol{X}\beta + \boldsymbol{e}$$
$$\mathbb{E}[\boldsymbol{e} \mid \boldsymbol{X}] = 0$$
$$\mathbb{E}\left[\boldsymbol{e}\boldsymbol{e}' \mid \boldsymbol{X}\right] = \Sigma.$$

Assume for simplicity that Σ is known. Consider the OLS and GLS estimators $\widehat{\beta} = \left(\boldsymbol{X}'\boldsymbol{X}\right)^{-1}\left(\boldsymbol{X}'\boldsymbol{Y}\right)$ and $\widetilde{\beta} = \left(\boldsymbol{X}'\Sigma^{-1}\boldsymbol{X}\right)^{-1}\left(\boldsymbol{X}'\Sigma^{-1}\boldsymbol{Y}\right)$, respectively. Compute the (conditional) covariance between $\widehat{\beta}$ and $\widetilde{\beta}$:

$$\mathbb{E}\left[\left(\widehat{\beta} - \beta\right)\left(\widetilde{\beta} - \beta\right)' \mid \boldsymbol{X}\right].$$

Find the (conditional) covariance matrix for $\widehat{\beta} - \widetilde{\beta}$:

$$\mathbb{E}\left[\left(\widehat{\beta} - \widetilde{\beta}\right)\left(\widehat{\beta} - \beta\right)' \mid \boldsymbol{X}\right].$$

Exercise 4.21 Consider the model

$$Y_i = X_i'\beta + e_i$$
$$\mathbb{E}[e_i \mid X_i] = 0$$
$$\mathbb{E}\left[e_i^2 \mid X_i\right] = \sigma_i^2$$
$$\Sigma = \operatorname{diag}\{\sigma_1^2, \ldots, \sigma_n^2\}.$$

The parameter β is estimated by OLS $\widehat{\beta} = \left(\boldsymbol{X}'\boldsymbol{X}\right)^{-1}\boldsymbol{X}'\boldsymbol{Y}$, and GLS $\widetilde{\beta} = \left(\boldsymbol{X}'\Sigma^{-1}\boldsymbol{X}\right)^{-1}\boldsymbol{X}'\Sigma^{-1}\boldsymbol{Y}$. Let $\widehat{\boldsymbol{e}} = \boldsymbol{Y} - \boldsymbol{X}\widehat{\beta}$ and $\widetilde{\boldsymbol{e}} = \boldsymbol{Y} - \boldsymbol{X}\widetilde{\beta}$ denote the residuals. Let $\widehat{R}^2 = 1 - \widehat{\boldsymbol{e}}'\widehat{\boldsymbol{e}}/(\boldsymbol{Y}^{*\prime}\boldsymbol{Y}^*)$ and $\widetilde{R}^2 = 1 - \widetilde{\boldsymbol{e}}'\widetilde{\boldsymbol{e}}/(\boldsymbol{Y}^{*\prime}\boldsymbol{Y}^*)$ denote the equation R^2, where $\boldsymbol{Y}^* = \boldsymbol{Y} - \overline{Y}$. If the error e_i is truly heteroskedastic, will $\widehat{R}^2$ or $\widetilde{R}^2$ be smaller?

Exercise 4.22 An economist friend tells you that the assumption that the observations (Y_i, X_i) are i.i.d. implies that the regression $Y = X'\beta + e$ is homoskedastic. Do you agree with your friend? How would you explain your position?

Exercise 4.23 Take the linear regression model with $\mathbb{E}[\boldsymbol{Y} \mid \boldsymbol{X}] = \boldsymbol{X}\beta$. Define the **ridge regression** estimator

$$\widehat{\beta} = \left(\boldsymbol{X}'\boldsymbol{X} + \boldsymbol{I}_k\lambda\right)^{-1}\boldsymbol{X}'\boldsymbol{Y}$$

where $\lambda > 0$ is a fixed constant. Find $E\left[\widehat{\beta} \mid \boldsymbol{X}\right]$. Is $\widehat{\beta}$ biased for β?

Exercise 4.24 Continue the empirical analysis in Exercise 3.24.

(a) Calculate standard errors using the homoskedasticity formula and using the four covariance matrices from Section 4.14.

(b) Repeat in a second programming language. Are the results identical?

Exercise 4.25 Continue the empirical analysis in Exercise 3.26. Calculate standard errors using the HC3 method. Repeat in your second programming language. Are they identical?

Exercise 4.26 Extend the empirical analysis reported in Section 4.21 using the `DDK2011` dataset on the textbook website. Do a regression of standardized test score (*totalscore* normalized to have 0 mean and variance 1) on tracking, age, gender, being assigned to the contract teacher, and student's percentile in the initial distribution. (The sample size will be reduced, as some observations have missing variables.) Calculate standard errors using both the conventional robust formula and clustering based on the school.

(a) Compare the two sets of standard errors. Which standard error changes the most by clustering? Which changes the least?

(b) How does the coefficient on *tracking* change by inclusion of the individual controls (in comparison to the results from (4.57))?

CHAPTER 5

NORMAL REGRESSION

5.1 INTRODUCTION

This chapter introduces the normal regression model, which is a special case of the linear regression model. This model is important, as normality allows precise distributional characterizations and sharp inferences. It also provides a baseline for comparison with alternative inference methods, such as asymptotic approximations and the bootstrap.

The normal regression model is a fully parametric setting where maximum likelihood estimation is appropriate. Therefore in this chapter, we introduce likelihood methods. The method of maximum likelihood is a powerful statistical method for parametric models (such as the normal regression model) and is widely used in econometric practice.

We start the chapter with a review of the definition and properties of the normal distribution. For detail and mathematical proofs, see Chapter 5 of this book's companion volume, *Probability and Statistics for Economists*.

5.2 THE NORMAL DISTRIBUTION

We say that a random variable Z has the **standard normal distribution**, or **Gaussian**, written $Z \sim \mathrm{N}(0, 1)$, if it has the density

$$\phi(x) = \frac{1}{\sqrt{2\pi}} \exp\left(-\frac{x^2}{2}\right), \qquad -\infty < x < \infty.$$

The standard normal density is typically written as $\phi(x)$ and the corresponding distribution function as $\Phi(x)$. Plots of the standard normal density function $\phi(x)$ and distribution function $\Phi(x)$ are displayed in Figure 5.1.

Theorem 5.1 If $Z \sim \mathrm{N}(0, 1)$ then

1. All integer moments of Z are finite.
2. All odd moments of Z equal 0.
3. For any positive integer m,

$$\mathbb{E}\left[Z^{2m}\right] = (2m-1)!! = (2m-1) \times (2m-3) \times \cdots \times 1.$$

4. For any $r > 0$,

$$\mathbb{E}\left|Z\right|^r = \frac{2^{r/2}}{\sqrt{\pi}} \Gamma\left(\frac{r+1}{2}\right)$$

where $\Gamma(t) = \int_0^\infty u^{t-1} e^{-u} du$ is the gamma function.

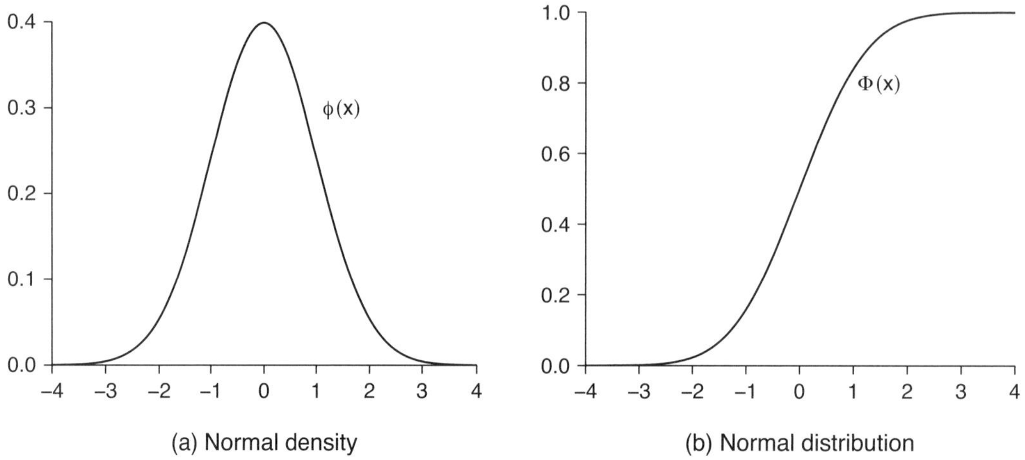

FIGURE 5.1 Standard normal density and distribution

Table 5.1
Numerical cumulative distribution functions

	To calculate $\mathbb{P}[Z \le x]$ for given x		
	MATLAB	R	Stata
N (0, 1)	`normcdf(x)`	`pnorm(x)`	`normal(x)`
χ_r^2	`chi2cdf(x,r)`	`pchisq(x,r)`	`chi2(r,x)`
t_r	`tcdf(x,r)`	`pt(x,r)`	`1-ttail(r,x)`
$F_{r,k}$	`fcdf(x,r,k)`	`pf(x,r,k)`	`F(r,k,x)`
$\chi_r^2(d)$	`ncx2cdf(x,r,d)`	`pchisq(x,r,d)`	`nchi2(r,d,x)`
$F_{r,k}(d)$	`ncfcdf(x,r,k,d)`	`pf(x,r,k,d)`	`1-nFtail(r,k,d,x)`

If $Z \sim \mathrm{N}(0,1)$ and $X = \mu + \sigma Z$ for $\mu \in \mathbb{R}$ and $\sigma \ge 0$, then X has the **univariate normal distribution**, written $X \sim \mathrm{N}\left(\mu, \sigma^2\right)$. By a change of variables, X has the density

$$f(x) = \frac{1}{\sqrt{2\pi\sigma^2}} \exp\left(-\frac{(x-\mu)^2}{2\sigma^2}\right), \qquad -\infty < x < \infty.$$

The expectation and variance of X are μ and σ^2, respectively.

The normal distribution and its relatives (the chi-square, student t, F, non-central chi-square, and F) are frequently used for inference to calculate critical values and p-values. This involves evaluating the normal cumulative distribution function (CDF) $\Phi(x)$ and its inverse. Since the CDF $\Phi(x)$ is not available in closed form, statistical textbooks have traditionally provided tables for this purpose. Such tables are not used currently, as these calculations are embedded in modern statistical software. For convenience, the appropriate commands in MATLAB, R, and Stata to compute the cumulative distribution function of commonly used statistical distributions are listed in Table 5.1.

Table 5.2 lists the appropriate commands to compute the inverse probabilities (quantiles) of the same distributions.

Table 5.2
Numerical quantile functions

	To calculate x which solves $p = \mathbb{P}[Z \le x]$ for given p		
	MATLAB	R	Stata
$\mathrm{N}(0,1)$	`norminv(p)`	`qnorm(p)`	`invnormal(p)`
χ^2_r	`chi2inv(p,r)`	`qchisq(p,r)`	`invchi2(r,p)`
t_r	`tinv(p,r)`	`qt(p,r)`	`invttail(r,1-p)`
$F_{r,k}$	`finv(p,r,k)`	`qf(p,r,k)`	`invF(r,k,p)`
$\chi^2_r(d)$	`ncx2inv(p,r,d)`	`qchisq(p,r,d)`	`invnchi2(r,d,p)`
$F_{r,k}(d)$	`ncfinv(p,r,k,d)`	`qf(p,r,k,d)`	`invnFtail(r,k,d,1-p)`

5.3 MULTIVARIATE NORMAL DISTRIBUTION

We say that the k-vector Z has a **multivariate standard normal distribution**, written $Z \sim \mathrm{N}(0, \boldsymbol{I}_k)$, if it has the joint density

$$f(x) = \frac{1}{(2\pi)^{k/2}} \exp\left(-\frac{x'x}{2}\right), \qquad x \in \mathbb{R}^k.$$

The mean and covariance matrix of Z are 0 and $\boldsymbol{I}_k$, respectively. The multivariate joint density factors into the product of univariate normal densities, so the elements of Z are mutually independent standard normals.

If $Z \sim \mathrm{N}(0, \boldsymbol{I}_k)$ and $X = \mu + \boldsymbol{B}Z$, then the k-vector X has a **multivariate normal distribution**, written $X \sim \mathrm{N}(\mu, \Sigma)$, where $\Sigma = \boldsymbol{B}\boldsymbol{B}' \ge 0$. If $\Sigma > 0$, then by change of variables, X has the joint density function

$$f(x) = \frac{1}{(2\pi)^{k/2} \det(\Sigma)^{1/2}} \exp\left(-\frac{(x-\mu)' \Sigma^{-1} (x-\mu)}{2}\right), \qquad x \in \mathbb{R}^k.$$

The expectation and covariance matrix of X are μ and Σ, respectively. By setting $k = 1$, you can check that the multivariate normal simplifies to the univariate normal.

An important property of normal random vectors is that affine functions are multivariate normal.

Theorem 5.2 If $X \sim \mathrm{N}(\mu, \Sigma)$ and $Y = \boldsymbol{a} + \boldsymbol{B}X$, then $Y \sim \mathrm{N}\left(\boldsymbol{a} + \boldsymbol{B}\mu, \boldsymbol{B}\Sigma\boldsymbol{B}'\right)$.

One simple implication of Theorem 5.2 is that if X is multivariate normal, then each component of X is univariate normal. Another useful property of the multivariate normal distribution is that uncorrelatedness is the same as independence. That is, if a vector is multivariate normal, subsets of variables are independent if and only if they are uncorrelated.

Theorem 5.3 Properties of the Multivariate Normal Distribution

1. The expectation and covariance matrix of $X \sim \mathrm{N}(\mu, \Sigma)$ are $\mathbb{E}[X] = \mu$ and $\operatorname{var}[X] = \Sigma$.
2. If (X, Y) are multivariate normal, X and Y are uncorrelated if and only if they are independent.
3. If $X \sim \mathrm{N}(\mu, \Sigma)$ and $Y = \boldsymbol{a} + \boldsymbol{B}X$, then $Y \sim \mathrm{N}\left(\boldsymbol{a} + \boldsymbol{B}\mu, \boldsymbol{B}\Sigma\boldsymbol{B}'\right)$.

4. If $X \sim \mathrm{N}(0, \boldsymbol{I}_k)$, then $X'X \sim \chi_k^2$, chi-square with k degrees of freedom.
5. If $X \sim \mathrm{N}(0, \Sigma)$ with $\Sigma > 0$, then $X'\Sigma^{-1}X \sim \chi_k^2$, where $k = \dim(X)$.
6. If $X \sim \mathrm{N}(\mu, \Sigma)$ with $\Sigma > 0$, $r \times r$, then $X'\Sigma^{-1}X \sim \chi_r^2(\lambda)$, where $\lambda = \mu'\Sigma^{-1}\mu$.
7. If $Z \sim \mathrm{N}(0,1)$ and $Q \sim \chi_k^2$ are independent, then $Z/\sqrt{Q/k} \sim t_k$, student t with k degrees of freedom.
8. If (Y, X) are multivariate normal

$$\begin{pmatrix} Y \\ X \end{pmatrix} \sim \mathrm{N}\left(\begin{pmatrix} \mu_Y \\ \mu_X \end{pmatrix}, \begin{pmatrix} \Sigma_{YY} & \Sigma_{YX} \\ \Sigma_{XY} & \Sigma_{XX} \end{pmatrix}\right)$$

with $\Sigma_{YY} > 0$ and $\Sigma_{XX} > 0$, then the conditional distributions are

$$Y \mid X \sim \mathrm{N}\left(\mu_Y + \Sigma_{YX}\Sigma_{XX}^{-1}(X - \mu_X), \Sigma_{YY} - \Sigma_{YX}\Sigma_{XX}^{-1}\Sigma_{XY}\right)$$

$$X \mid Y \sim \mathrm{N}\left(\mu_X + \Sigma_{XY}\Sigma_{YY}^{-1}(Y - \mu_Y), \Sigma_{XX} - \Sigma_{XY}\Sigma_{YY}^{-1}\Sigma_{YX}\right).$$

5.4 JOINT NORMALITY AND LINEAR REGRESSION

Suppose the variables (Y, X) are jointly normally distributed. Consider the best linear predictor of Y given X:

$$Y = X'\beta + \alpha + e.$$

By the properties of the best linear predictor, $\mathbb{E}[Xe] = 0$ and $\mathbb{E}[e] = 0$, so X and e are uncorrelated. Since (e, X) is an affine transformation of the normal vector (Y, X), it follows that (e, X) is jointly normal (Theorem 5.2). Since (e, X) is jointly normal and uncorrelated, X and e are independent (Theorem 5.3). Independence implies that

$$\mathbb{E}[e \mid X] = \mathbb{E}[e] = 0$$

and

$$\mathbb{E}\left[e^2 \mid X\right] = \mathbb{E}\left[e^2\right] = \sigma^2$$

which are properties of a homoskedastic linear CEF.

We have shown that when (Y, X) are jointly normally distributed they satisfy a normal linear CEF

$$Y = X'\beta + \alpha + e$$

where

$$e \sim \mathrm{N}(0, \sigma^2)$$

is independent of X. This result can also be deduced from Theorem 5.3.7.

This is a classical motivation for the linear regression model.

5.5 NORMAL REGRESSION MODEL

The normal regression model is the linear regression model with an independent normal error:

$$Y = X'\beta + e \tag{5.1}$$
$$e \sim \mathrm{N}(0, \sigma^2).$$

As we learned in Section 5.4, the normal regression model holds when (Y, X) are jointly normally distributed. Normal regression, however, does not require joint normality. All that is required is that the conditional distribution of Y given X is normal (the marginal distribution of X is unrestricted). In this sense, the normal regression model is broader than joint normality. Notice that for notational convenience, we have written (5.1) so that X contains the intercept.

Normal regression is a parametric model, so that likelihood methods can be used for estimation, testing, and distribution theory. The **likelihood** is the name for the joint probability density of the data, evaluated at the observed sample, and viewed as a function of the parameters. The maximum likelihood estimator is the value that maximizes this likelihood function. Let us now derive the likelihood of the normal regression model.

First, observe that model (5.1) is equivalent to the statement that the conditional density of Y given X takes the form:

$$f(y \mid x) = \frac{1}{(2\pi\sigma^2)^{1/2}} \exp\left(-\frac{1}{2\sigma^2}(y - x'\beta)^2\right).$$

Under the assumption that the observations are mutually independent, this implies that the conditional density of $(Y_1, \ldots, Y_n)$ given $(X_1, \ldots, X_n)$ is

$$\begin{aligned} f(y_1, \ldots, y_n \mid x_1, \ldots, x_n) &= \prod_{i=1}^n f(y_i \mid x_i) \\ &= \prod_{i=1}^n \frac{1}{(2\pi\sigma^2)^{1/2}} \exp\left(-\frac{1}{2\sigma^2}(y_i - x_i'\beta)^2\right) \\ &= \frac{1}{(2\pi\sigma^2)^{n/2}} \exp\left(-\frac{1}{2\sigma^2}\sum_{i=1}^n (y_i - x_i'\beta)^2\right) \\ &\stackrel{\text{def}}{=} L_n(\beta, \sigma^2). \end{aligned}$$

This is called the **likelihood function** when evaluated at the sample data.

For convenience, it is typical to work with the natural logarithm

$$\log L_n(\beta, \sigma^2) = -\frac{n}{2}\log(2\pi\sigma^2) - \frac{1}{2\sigma^2}\sum_{i=1}^n (Y_i - X_i'\beta)^2 \stackrel{\text{def}}{=} \ell_n(\beta, \sigma^2) \tag{5.2}$$

which is called the **log-likelihood function**.

The **maximum likelihood estimator (MLE)** $(\widehat{\beta}_{\mathrm{mle}}, \widehat{\sigma}^2_{\mathrm{mle}})$ is the value that maximizes the log-likelihood. We can write the maximization problem as

$$(\widehat{\beta}_{\mathrm{mle}}, \widehat{\sigma}^2_{\mathrm{mle}}) = \underset{\beta \in \mathbb{R}^k,\, \sigma^2 > 0}{\operatorname{argmax}} \ \ell_n(\beta, \sigma^2). \tag{5.3}$$

In most applications of maximum likelihood, the MLE must be found by numerical methods. However, in the case of the normal regression model, we can find an explicit expression for $\widehat{\beta}_{\mathrm{mle}}$ and $\widehat{\sigma}^2_{\mathrm{mle}}$.

The maximizers $(\widehat{\beta}_{\mathrm{mle}}, \widehat{\sigma}^2_{\mathrm{mle}})$ of (5.3) jointly solve the first-order conditions:

$$0 = \frac{\partial}{\partial \beta} \ell_n(\beta, \sigma^2)\bigg|_{\beta=\widehat{\beta}_{\mathrm{mle}}, \sigma^2=\widehat{\sigma}^2_{\mathrm{mle}}} = \frac{1}{\widehat{\sigma}^2_{\mathrm{mle}}} \sum_{i=1}^{n} X_i \left(Y_i - X_i'\widehat{\beta}_{\mathrm{mle}}\right) \tag{5.4}$$

$$0 = \frac{\partial}{\partial \sigma^2} \ell_n(\beta, \sigma^2)\bigg|_{\beta=\widehat{\beta}_{\mathrm{mle}}, \sigma^2=\widehat{\sigma}^2_{\mathrm{mle}}} = -\frac{n}{2\widehat{\sigma}^2_{\mathrm{mle}}} + \frac{1}{2\widehat{\sigma}^4_{\mathrm{mle}}} \sum_{i=1}^{n} \left(Y_i - X_i'\widehat{\beta}_{\mathrm{mle}}\right)^2. \tag{5.5}$$

The first-order condition (5.4) is proportional to the first-order conditions for the least squares minimization problem of Section 3.6. It follows that the MLE satisfies

$$\widehat{\beta}_{\mathrm{mle}} = \left(\sum_{i=1}^{n} X_i X_i'\right)^{-1} \left(\sum_{i=1}^{n} X_i Y_i\right) = \widehat{\beta}_{\mathrm{ols}}.$$

That is, the MLE for β is algebraically identical to the OLS estimator.

Solving the second first-order condition (5.5) for $\widehat{\sigma}^2_{\mathrm{mle}}$, we find

$$\widehat{\sigma}^2_{\mathrm{mle}} = \frac{1}{n}\sum_{i=1}^{n}\left(Y_i - X_i'\widehat{\beta}_{\mathrm{mle}}\right)^2 = \frac{1}{n}\sum_{i=1}^{n}\left(Y_i - X_i'\widehat{\beta}_{\mathrm{ols}}\right)^2 = \frac{1}{n}\sum_{i=1}^{n}\widehat{e}_i^2 = \widehat{\sigma}^2_{\mathrm{ols}}.$$

Thus the MLE for σ^2 is identical to the OLS/moment estimator from (3.26).

Since the OLS estimator and MLE under normality are equivalent, $\widehat{\beta}$ is described by some authors as the maximum likelihood estimator, and by other authors as the least squares estimator. It is important to remember, however, that $\widehat{\beta}$ is only the MLE when the error e has a known normal distribution and not otherwise.

Plugging the estimators into (5.2), we obtain the maximized log-likelihood:

$$\ell_n\left(\widehat{\beta}_{\mathrm{mle}}, \widehat{\sigma}^2_{\mathrm{mle}}\right) = -\frac{n}{2}\log\left(2\pi\widehat{\sigma}^2_{\mathrm{mle}}\right) - \frac{n}{2}. \tag{5.6}$$

The log-likelihood is typically reported as a measure of fit.

It may seem surprising that the MLE $\widehat{\beta}_{\mathrm{mle}}$ is algebraically equal to the OLS estimator, despite emerging from quite different motivations. It is not completely accidental. The least squares estimator minimizes a particular sample loss function—the sum of squared error criterion—and most loss functions are equivalent to the likelihood of a specific parametric distribution, in this case the normal regression model. In this sense, it is not surprising that the least squares estimator can be motivated as either the minimizer of a sample loss function or as the maximizer of a likelihood function.

Carl Friedrich Gauss

Carl Friedrich Gauss (1777–1855) was one of the most influential mathematicians in history. His contributions impact many topics of importance to economics and econometrics, including the Gauss-Markov Theorem, the Gauss-Newton algorithm, and Gaussian elimination. In a 1809 paper, he put the regression model on probabilistic foundations by proposing that the equation errors be treated as random variables. He showed that if the error distribution takes the form we now call normal (or "Gaussian"), then the MLE for the coefficients equals the least squares estimator.

5.6 DISTRIBUTION OF OLS COEFFICIENT VECTOR

In the normal linear regression model, we can derive exact sampling distributions for the OLS/MLE estimator, residuals, and variance estimator. In this section, we derive the distribution of the OLS coefficient estimator.

The normality assumption $e \mid X \sim \mathrm{N}\left(0, \sigma^2\right)$ combined with independence of the observations has the multivariate implication

$$\boldsymbol{e} \mid \boldsymbol{X} \sim \mathrm{N}\left(0, \boldsymbol{I}_n \sigma^2\right).$$

That is, the error vector $\boldsymbol{e}$ is independent of $\boldsymbol{X}$ and is normally distributed.

Recall that the OLS estimator satisfies

$$\widehat{\beta} - \beta = \left(\boldsymbol{X}'\boldsymbol{X}\right)^{-1} \boldsymbol{X}'\boldsymbol{e}$$

which is a linear function of $\boldsymbol{e}$. Since linear functions of normals are also normal (Theorem 5.2), this implies that conditional on $\boldsymbol{X}$,

$$\begin{aligned} \widehat{\beta} - \beta \mid \boldsymbol{X} &\sim \left(\boldsymbol{X}'\boldsymbol{X}\right)^{-1} \boldsymbol{X}'\mathrm{N}\left(0, \boldsymbol{I}_n \sigma^2\right) \\ &\sim \mathrm{N}\left(0, \sigma^2 \left(\boldsymbol{X}'\boldsymbol{X}\right)^{-1} \boldsymbol{X}'\boldsymbol{X} \left(\boldsymbol{X}'\boldsymbol{X}\right)^{-1}\right) \\ &= \mathrm{N}\left(0, \sigma^2 \left(\boldsymbol{X}'\boldsymbol{X}\right)^{-1}\right). \end{aligned}$$

Thus, under the assumption of normal errors, the OLS estimator has an exact normal distribution.

Theorem 5.4 In the normal regression model,

$$\widehat{\beta} \mid \boldsymbol{X} \sim \mathrm{N}\left(\beta, \sigma^2 \left(\boldsymbol{X}'\boldsymbol{X}\right)^{-1}\right).$$

Theorems 5.2 and 5.4 imply that any affine function of the OLS estimator is also normally distributed, including individual components. Letting β_j and $\widehat{\beta}_j$ denote the jth elements of β and $\widehat{\beta}$, we have

$$\widehat{\beta}_j \mid \boldsymbol{X} \sim \mathrm{N}\left(\beta_j, \sigma^2 \left[\left(\boldsymbol{X}'\boldsymbol{X}\right)^{-1}\right]_{jj}\right). \tag{5.7}$$

Theorem 5.4 is a statement about the conditional distribution. What about the unconditional distribution? In Section 4.7, we presented Kinal's theorem (Theorem 4.3) about the existence of moments for the joint normal regression model. We restate the result here.

Theorem 5.5 Kinal (1980)
If (Y, X) are jointly normal, then for any r, $\mathbb{E}\left\|\widehat{\beta}\right\|^r < \infty$ if and only if $r < n - k + 1$.

5.7 DISTRIBUTION OF OLS RESIDUAL VECTOR

Consider the OLS residual vector. Recall from (3.24) that $\widehat{\boldsymbol{e}} = \boldsymbol{M}\boldsymbol{e}$, where $\boldsymbol{M} = \boldsymbol{I}_n - \boldsymbol{X}\left(\boldsymbol{X}'\boldsymbol{X}\right)^{-1}\boldsymbol{X}'$. Thus, $\widehat{\boldsymbol{e}}$ is linear in $\boldsymbol{e}$. So conditional on $\boldsymbol{X}$,

$$\widehat{\boldsymbol{e}} = \boldsymbol{M}\boldsymbol{e} \mid \boldsymbol{X} \sim \mathrm{N}\left(0, \sigma^2 \boldsymbol{M}\boldsymbol{M}\right) = \mathrm{N}\left(0, \sigma^2 \boldsymbol{M}\right)$$

where the final equality holds because $\boldsymbol{M}$ is idempotent (see Section 3.12). Thus, the residual vector has an exact normal distribution.

Furthermore, it is useful to find the joint distribution of $\widehat{\beta}$ and $\widehat{\boldsymbol{e}}$. This is easiest done by writing the two as a stacked linear function of the error $\boldsymbol{e}$. Indeed,

$$\begin{pmatrix} \widehat{\beta} - \beta \\ \widehat{\boldsymbol{e}} \end{pmatrix} = \begin{pmatrix} \left(\boldsymbol{X}'\boldsymbol{X}\right)^{-1}\boldsymbol{X}'\boldsymbol{e} \\ \boldsymbol{M}\boldsymbol{e} \end{pmatrix} = \begin{pmatrix} \left(\boldsymbol{X}'\boldsymbol{X}\right)^{-1}\boldsymbol{X}' \\ \boldsymbol{M} \end{pmatrix} \boldsymbol{e}$$

which is a linear function of $\boldsymbol{e}$. The vector has a joint normal distribution with covariance matrix

$$\begin{pmatrix} \sigma^2\left(\boldsymbol{X}'\boldsymbol{X}\right)^{-1} & 0 \\ 0 & \sigma^2 \boldsymbol{M} \end{pmatrix}.$$

The off-diagonal block is 0, because $\boldsymbol{X}'\boldsymbol{M} = 0$ from (3.21). Since this is 0, it follows that $\widehat{\beta}$ and $\widehat{\boldsymbol{e}}$ are statistically independent (Theorem 5.3.2).

> **Theorem 5.6** In the normal regression model, $\widehat{\boldsymbol{e}} \mid \boldsymbol{X} \sim \mathrm{N}\left(0, \sigma^2 \boldsymbol{M}\right)$ and is independent of $\widehat{\beta}$.

The fact that $\widehat{\beta}$ and $\widehat{\boldsymbol{e}}$ are independent implies that $\widehat{\beta}$ is independent of any function of the residual vector, including individual residuals $\widehat{e}_i$ and the variance estimators s^2 and $\widehat{\sigma}^2$.

5.8 DISTRIBUTION OF VARIANCE ESTIMATOR

Next, consider the variance estimator s^2 from (4.28). Using (3.28), it satisfies $(n-k)s^2 = \widehat{\boldsymbol{e}}'\widehat{\boldsymbol{e}} = \boldsymbol{e}'\boldsymbol{M}\boldsymbol{e}$. The spectral decomposition of $\boldsymbol{M}$ (equation (A.4)) is $\boldsymbol{M} = \boldsymbol{H}\Lambda\boldsymbol{H}'$, where $\boldsymbol{H}'\boldsymbol{H} = \boldsymbol{I}_n$, and Λ is diagonal with the eigenvalues of $\boldsymbol{M}$ on the diagonal. Since $\boldsymbol{M}$ is idempotent with rank $n-k$ (see Section 3.12), it has $n-k$ eigenvalues equaling 1 and k eigenvalues equaling 0, so

$$\Lambda = \begin{bmatrix} \boldsymbol{I}_{n-k} & \boldsymbol{0} \\ \boldsymbol{0} & \boldsymbol{0}_k \end{bmatrix}.$$

Let $\boldsymbol{u} = \boldsymbol{H}'\boldsymbol{e} \sim \mathrm{N}\left(\boldsymbol{0}, \boldsymbol{I}_n\sigma^2\right)$ (see Exercise 5.2), and partition $\boldsymbol{u} = \left(\boldsymbol{u}_1', \boldsymbol{u}_2'\right)'$, where $\boldsymbol{u}_1 \sim \mathrm{N}\left(0, \boldsymbol{I}_{n-k}\sigma^2\right)$. Then

$$\begin{aligned}
(n-k)s^2 &= \boldsymbol{e}'\boldsymbol{M}\boldsymbol{e} \\
&= \boldsymbol{e}'\boldsymbol{H}\begin{bmatrix} \boldsymbol{I}_{n-k} & \boldsymbol{0} \\ \boldsymbol{0} & \boldsymbol{0} \end{bmatrix}\boldsymbol{H}'\boldsymbol{e} \\
&= \boldsymbol{u}'\begin{bmatrix} \boldsymbol{I}_{n-k} & \boldsymbol{0} \\ \boldsymbol{0} & \boldsymbol{0} \end{bmatrix}\boldsymbol{u}
\end{aligned}$$

$$= \boldsymbol{u}_1' \boldsymbol{u}_1$$
$$\sim \sigma^2 \chi^2_{n-k}.$$

We see that in the normal regression model, the exact distribution of s^2 is a scaled chi-square.

Since $\widehat{\boldsymbol{e}}$ is independent of $\widehat{\beta}$, it follows that s^2 is independent of $\widehat{\beta}$ as well.

Theorem 5.7 In the normal regression model,

$$\frac{(n-k)\, s^2}{\sigma^2} \sim \chi^2_{n-k}$$

and is independent of $\widehat{\beta}$.

5.9 *t*-STATISTIC

An alternative way of writing (5.7) is

$$\frac{\widehat{\beta}_j - \beta_j}{\sqrt{\sigma^2 \left[\left(\boldsymbol{X}'\boldsymbol{X} \right)^{-1} \right]_{jj}}} \sim \mathrm{N}\left(0, 1\right).$$

This is sometimes called a **standardized** statistic, because the distribution is the standard normal.

Now take the standardized statistic and replace the unknown variance σ^2 with its estimator s^2. We call this a ***t*-ratio** or ***t*-statistic**:

$$T = \frac{\widehat{\beta}_j - \beta_j}{\sqrt{s^2 \left[\left(\boldsymbol{X}'\boldsymbol{X} \right)^{-1} \right]_{jj}}} = \frac{\widehat{\beta}_j - \beta_j}{s(\widehat{\beta}_j)}$$

where $s(\widehat{\beta}_j)$ is the classical (homoskedastic) standard error for $\widehat{\beta}_j$ from (4.39). We will sometimes write the t-statistic as $T(\beta_j)$ to explicitly indicate its dependence on the parameter value β_j, and sometimes will simplify notation and write the t-statistic as T when the dependence is clear from the context.

Using algebraic rescaling, we can write the t-statistic as the ratio of the standardized statistic and the square root of the scaled variance estimator. Since the distributions of these two components are normal and chi-square, respectively, and independent, we deduce that the t-statistic has the distribution

$$\begin{aligned} T &= \frac{\widehat{\beta}_j - \beta_j}{\sqrt{\sigma^2 \left[\left(\boldsymbol{X}'\boldsymbol{X} \right)^{-1} \right]_{jj}}} \Bigg/ \sqrt{\frac{(n-k)s^2}{\sigma^2} \Big/ (n-k)} \\ &\sim \frac{\mathrm{N}\left(0, 1\right)}{\sqrt{\chi^2_{n-k} / \left(n-k\right)}} \\ &\sim t_{n-k} \end{aligned}$$

that is, a student t distribution with $n-k$ degrees of freedom.

This derivation shows that the t-ratio has a sampling distribution that depends only on the quantity $n-k$. The distribution does not depend on any other features of the data. In this context, we say that the distribution of the t-ratio is **pivotal**, meaning that it does not depend on unknowns.

The trick behind this result is scaling the centered coefficient by its standard error, and recognizing that each depends on the unknown σ only through scale. Thus the ratio of the two does not depend on σ. This trick (scaling to eliminate dependence on unknowns) is known as **studentization**.

Theorem 5.8 In the normal regression model, $T \sim t_{n-k}$.

An important caveat about Theorem 5.8 is that it only applies to the t-statistic constructed with the homoskedastic (old-fashioned) standard error. It does not apply to a t-statistic constructed with any of the robust standard errors. In fact, the robust t-statistics can have finite sample distributions that deviate considerably from t_{n-k} even when the regression errors are independent $\mathrm{N}(0, \sigma^2)$. Thus the distributional result in Theorem 5.8 and the use of the t distribution in finite samples is only exact when applied to classical t-statistics under the normality assumption.

5.10 CONFIDENCE INTERVALS FOR REGRESSION COEFFICIENTS

The OLS estimator $\widehat{\beta}$ is a **point estimator** for a coefficient β. A broader concept is a **set** or **interval estimator**, which takes the form $\widehat{C} = [\widehat{L}, \widehat{U}]$. The goal of an interval estimator $\widehat{C}$ is to contain the true value (e.g., $\beta \in \widehat{C}$), with high probability. The interval estimator $\widehat{C}$ is a function of the data and hence is random.

An interval estimator $\widehat{C}$ is called a $1-\alpha$ **confidence interval** when $\mathbb{P}\left[\beta \in \widehat{C}\right] = 1-\alpha$ for a selected value of α. The value $1-\alpha$ is called the **coverage probability**. Typical choices for the coverage probability $1-\alpha$ are 0.95 or 0.90.

The probability calculation $\mathbb{P}\left[\beta \in \widehat{C}\right]$ is easily misinterpreted as treating β as random and $\widehat{C}$ as fixed. (The probability that β is in $\widehat{C}$.) This is not the appropriate interpretation. Instead, the correct interpretation is that the probability $\mathbb{P}\left[\beta \in \widehat{C}\right]$ treats the point β as fixed and the set $\widehat{C}$ as random. It is the probability that the random set $\widehat{C}$ covers (or contains) the fixed true coefficient β.

No unique method exists for constructing confidence intervals. For example, one simple (yet silly) interval is

$$\widehat{C} = \begin{cases} \mathbb{R} & \text{with probability } 1-\alpha \\ \{\widehat{\beta}\} & \text{with probability } \alpha. \end{cases}$$

If $\widehat{\beta}$ has a continuous distribution, then by construction, $\mathbb{P}\left[\beta \in \widehat{C}\right] = 1-\alpha$, so this confidence interval has perfect coverage. However, $\widehat{C}$ is uninformative about $\widehat{\beta}$ and is therefore not useful.

Instead, a good choice for a confidence interval for the regression coefficient β is obtained by adding and subtracting from the estimator $\widehat{\beta}$ a fixed multiple of its standard error:

$$\widehat{C} = \left[\widehat{\beta} - c \times s(\widehat{\beta}), \quad \widehat{\beta} + c \times s(\widehat{\beta})\right] \tag{5.8}$$

where $c > 0$ is a pre-specified constant. This confidence interval is symmetric about the point estimator $\widehat{\beta}$, and its length is proportional to the standard error $s(\widehat{\beta})$.

Equivalently, $\widehat{C}$ is the set of parameter values for β such that the t-statistic $T(\beta)$ is smaller (in absolute value) than c, that is,

$$\widehat{C}=\{\beta:|T(\beta)|\leq c\}=\left\{\beta:-c\leq\frac{\widehat{\beta}-\beta}{s(\widehat{\beta})}\leq c\right\}.$$

The coverage probability of this confidence interval is

$$\begin{aligned}\mathbb{P}\left[\beta\in\widehat{C}\right]&=\mathbb{P}\left[|T(\beta)|\leq c\right]\\&=\mathbb{P}\left[-c\leq T(\beta)\leq c\right].\end{aligned}\tag{5.9}$$

Since the t-statistic $T(\beta)$ has the t_{n-k} distribution, (5.9) equals $F(c)-F(-c)$, where $F(u)$ is the student t distribution function with $n-k$ degrees of freedom. Since $F(-c)=1-F(c)$ (see Exercise 5.8), we can write (5.9) as

$$\mathbb{P}\left[\beta\in\widehat{C}\right]=2F(c)-1.$$

This is the **coverage probability** of the interval $\widehat{C}$, and it only depends on the constant c.

As mentioned before, a confidence interval has the coverage probability $1-\alpha$. This requires selecting the constant c so that $F(c)=1-\alpha/2$, which holds if c equals the $1-\alpha/2$ quantile of the t_{n-k} distribution. As there is no closed-form expression for these quantiles, we compute their values numerically, for example, by using `tinv(1-alpha/2,n-k)` in MATLAB. With this choice, the confidence interval (5.8) has exact coverage probability $1-\alpha$. By default, Stata reports 95% confidence intervals $\widehat{C}$ for each estimated regression coefficient, using the same formula.

Theorem 5.9 In the normal regression model, (5.8) with $c=F^{-1}(1-\alpha/2)$ has coverage probability $\mathbb{P}\left[\beta\in\widehat{C}\right]=1-\alpha$.

When the degree of freedom is large, the distinction between the student t and the normal distribution is negligible. In particular, for $n-k\geq 61$, we have $c\leq 2.00$ for a 95% interval. Using this value, we obtain the most commonly used confidence interval in applied econometric practice:

$$\widehat{C}=\left[\widehat{\beta}-2s(\widehat{\beta}),\quad \widehat{\beta}+2s(\widehat{\beta})\right].\tag{5.10}$$

This is a useful rule-of-thumb. This 95% confidence interval $\widehat{C}$ is simple to compute and can be easily calculated from coefficient estimates and standard errors.

Theorem 5.10 In the normal regression model, if $n-k\geq 61$, then (5.10) has coverage probability $\mathbb{P}\left[\beta\in\widehat{C}\right]\geq 0.95$.

Confidence intervals are a simple yet effective tool to assess estimation uncertainty. When reading a set of empirical results, look at the estimated coefficient estimates and the standard errors. For a parameter of interest, compute the confidence interval $\widehat{C}$, and consider the meaning of the spread of the suggested values. If the range of values in the confidence interval is too wide to learn about β, then do not jump to a conclusion about β based on the point estimate alone.

5.11 CONFIDENCE INTERVALS FOR ERROR VARIANCE

We can also construct a confidence interval for the regression error variance σ^2 using the sampling distribution of s^2 from Theorem 5.7. This theorem states that in the normal regression model,

$$\frac{(n-k)\,s^2}{\sigma^2} \sim \chi^2_{n-k}. \tag{5.11}$$

Let $F(u)$ denote the χ^2_{n-k} distribution function, and for some α, set $c_1 = F^{-1}(\alpha/2)$ and $c_2 = F^{-1}(1-\alpha/2)$ (the $\alpha/2$ and $1-\alpha/2$ quantiles of the χ^2_{n-k} distribution). Equation (5.11) implies that

$$\mathbb{P}\left[c_1 \le \frac{(n-k)\,s^2}{\sigma^2} \le c_2\right] = F(c_2) - F(c_1) = 1-\alpha.$$

Rewriting the inequalities, we find

$$\mathbb{P}\left[\frac{(n-k)\,s^2}{c_2} \le \sigma^2 \le \frac{(n-k)\,s^2}{c_1}\right] = 1-\alpha.$$

Thus, an exact $1-\alpha$ confidence interval for σ^2 is

$$\widehat{C} = \left[\frac{(n-k)\,s^2}{c_2}, \quad \frac{(n-k)\,s^2}{c_1}\right]. \tag{5.12}$$

Theorem 5.11 In the normal regression model, (5.12) has coverage probability $\mathbb{P}\left[\sigma^2 \in \widehat{C}\right] = 1-\alpha$.

The confidence interval (5.12) for σ^2 is asymmetric about the point estimate s^2 due to the latter's asymmetric sampling distribution.

5.12 *t*-TEST

A typical goal in an econometric exercise is to assess whether a coefficient β equals a specific value β_0. Often the specific value to be tested is $\beta_0 = 0$, but this is not essential. This is called **hypothesis testing**, a subject explored in detail in Chapter 9. This section and Section 5.13 give a short introduction specific to the normal regression model.

For simplicity, write the coefficient to be tested as β. The **null hypothesis** is

$$\mathbb{H}_0 : \beta = \beta_0. \tag{5.13}$$

This states that the hypothesis is that the true value of β equals the hypothesized value β_0.

The alternative hypothesis is the complement of $\mathbb{H}_0$ and is written as

$$\mathbb{H}_1 : \beta \ne \beta_0.$$

This states that the true value of β does not equal the hypothesized value.

We are interested in testing $\mathbb{H}_0$ against $\mathbb{H}_1$. The method is to design a statistic that is informative about $\mathbb{H}_1$. If the observed value of the statistic is consistent with random variation under the assumption that $\mathbb{H}_0$ is true, then we deduce that there is no evidence against $\mathbb{H}_0$ and consequently do not reject $\mathbb{H}_0$. However, if the statistic takes a value that is unlikely to occur under the assumption that $\mathbb{H}_0$ is true, then we deduce that there is evidence against $\mathbb{H}_0$ and consequently reject $\mathbb{H}_0$ in favor of $\mathbb{H}_1$. The main steps are to design a test statistic and to characterize its sampling distribution.

The standard statistic to test $\mathbb{H}_0$ against $\mathbb{H}_1$ is the absolute value of the t-statistic:

$$|T| = \left| \frac{\widehat{\beta} - \beta_0}{s(\widehat{\beta})} \right|. \tag{5.14}$$

If $\mathbb{H}_0$ is true, then we expect $|T|$ to be small; but if $\mathbb{H}_1$ is true, then we would expect $|T|$ to be large. Hence the standard rule is to reject $\mathbb{H}_0$ in favor of $\mathbb{H}_1$ for large values of the t-statistic $|T|$ and otherwise fail to reject $\mathbb{H}_0$. Thus the hypothesis test takes the form

$$\text{Reject } \mathbb{H}_0 \text{ if } |T| > c.$$

The constant c in the statement of the test is called the **critical value**. Its value is selected to control the probability of false rejections. When the null hypothesis is true, T has an exact t_{n-k} distribution in the normal regression model. Thus for a given value of c, the probability of false rejection is

$$\begin{aligned}
\mathbb{P}\left[\text{Reject } \mathbb{H}_0 \mid \mathbb{H}_0\right] &= \mathbb{P}\left[|T| > c \mid \mathbb{H}_0\right] \\
&= \mathbb{P}\left[T > c \mid \mathbb{H}_0\right] + \mathbb{P}\left[T < -c \mid \mathbb{H}_0\right] \\
&= 1 - F(c) + F(-c) \\
&= 2(1 - F(c))
\end{aligned}$$

where $F(u)$ is the t_{n-k} distribution function. This is the probability of false rejection and is decreasing in the critical value c. We select the value c so that this probability equals a pre-selected value called the **significance level**, which is typically written as α. It is conventional to set $\alpha = 0.05$, though this is not a hard rule. We then select c so that $F(c) = 1 - \alpha/2$, which means that c is the $1 - \alpha/2$ quantile (inverse CDF) of the t_{n-k} distribution, the same as used for confidence intervals. With this choice, the decision rule "Reject $\mathbb{H}_0$ if $|T| > c$" has a significance level (false rejection probability) of α.

Theorem 5.12 In the normal regression model, if the null hypothesis (5.13) is true, then for $|T|$ defined in (5.14), $T \sim t_{n-k}$. If c is set so that $\mathbb{P}\left[\left|t_{n-k}\right| \geq c\right] = \alpha$, then the test "Reject $\mathbb{H}_0$ in favor of $\mathbb{H}_1$ if $|T| > c$" has significance level α.

To report the result of a hypothesis test, we need to pre-determine the significance level α to calculate the critical value c. This can be inconvenient and arbitrary. A simplification is to report what is known as the **p-value** of the test. In general, when a test takes the form "Reject $\mathbb{H}_0$ if $S > c$" and S has null distribution $G(u)$, then the p-value of the test is $p = 1 - G(S)$. A test with significance level α can be restated as "Reject $\mathbb{H}_0$ if $p < \alpha$." It is sufficient to report the p-value p, and we can interpret the value of p as indexing the test's strength of rejection of the null hypothesis. Thus a p-value of 0.07 might be interpreted as "nearly significant," 0.05 as "borderline significant," and 0.001 as "highly significant." In the context of the normal regression model, the p-value of a t-statistic $|T|$ is $p = 2(1 - F_{n-k}(|T|))$, where F_{n-k} is the t_{n-k} CDF. For example, in MATLAB the calculation is `2*(1-tcdf(abs(t),n-k))`. In Stata, the default is that for any estimated regression, t-statistics for each estimated coefficient are reported along with their p-values calculated using this same formula. These t-statistics test the hypotheses that each coefficient is 0.

A p-value reports the strength of evidence against $\mathbb{H}_0$ but is not itself a probability. A common misunderstanding is that the p-value is the "probability that the null hypothesis is true." This interpretation is incorrect. It is a statistic, is random, and is a measure of the evidence against $\mathbb{H}_0$. Nothing more.

5.13 LIKELIHOOD RATIO TEST

Section 5.12 described the t-test as the standard method to test a hypothesis on a single coefficient in a regression. In many contexts, however, we want to simultaneously assess a set of coefficients. In the normal regression model, this can be done by an F test, which can be derived from the likelihood ratio test.

Partition the regressors as $X=(X_1', X_2')$ and similarly, partition the coefficient vector as $\beta=(\beta_1', \beta_2')'$. The regression model can be written as

$$Y = X_1'\beta_1 + X_2'\beta_2 + e. \tag{5.15}$$

Let $k=\dim(X)$, $k_1=\dim(X_1)$, and $q=\dim(X_2)$, so that $k=k_1+q$. Partition the variables so that the hypothesis is that the second set of coefficients equals 0, or

$$\mathbb{H}_0 : \beta_2 = 0. \tag{5.16}$$

If $\mathbb{H}_0$ is true, then the regressors X_2 can be omitted from the regression. In this case, we can write (5.15) as

$$Y = X_1'\beta_1 + e. \tag{5.17}$$

We call (5.17) the "null model." The alternative hypothesis is that at least one element of β_2 is nonzero and is written as $\mathbb{H}_1 : \beta_2 \neq 0$.

When models are estimated by maximum likelihood, a well-accepted testing procedure is to reject $\mathbb{H}_0$ in favor of $\mathbb{H}_1$ for large values of the likelihood ratio—the ratio of the maximized likelihood function under $\mathbb{H}_1$ and $\mathbb{H}_0$, respectively. We now construct this statistic in the normal regression model. Recall from (5.6) that the maximized log-likelihood equals

$$\ell_n\left(\widehat{\beta}, \widehat{\sigma}^2\right) = -\frac{n}{2}\log\left(2\pi\widehat{\sigma}^2\right) - \frac{n}{2}.$$

We similarly calculate the maximized log-likelihood for the constrained model (5.17). By the same steps for derivation of the unconstrained MLE, we find that the MLE for (5.17) is OLS of Y on X_1. We can write this estimator as

$$\widetilde{\beta}_1 = \left(\boldsymbol{X}_1'\boldsymbol{X}_1\right)^{-1}\boldsymbol{X}_1'\boldsymbol{Y}$$

with residual $\widetilde{e}_i = Y_i - X_{1i}'\widetilde{\beta}_1$ and error variance estimate $\widetilde{\sigma}^2 = \frac{1}{n}\sum_{i=1}^n \widetilde{e}_i^2$. We use tildes "$\sim$" rather than hats "$\wedge$" above the constrained estimates to distinguish them from the unconstrained estimates. Similarly to (5.6), we can calculate that the maximized constrained log-likelihood is

$$\ell_n\left(\widetilde{\beta}_1, \widetilde{\sigma}^2\right) = -\frac{n}{2}\log\left(2\pi\widetilde{\sigma}^2\right) - \frac{n}{2}.$$

A classic testing procedure is to reject $\mathbb{H}_0$ for large values of the ratio of the maximized likelihoods. Equivalently, the test rejects $\mathbb{H}_0$ for large values of twice the difference in the log-likelihood functions. (Multiplying the likelihood difference by 2 turns out to be a useful scaling.) This equals

$$\begin{aligned}
\mathrm{LR} &= 2\left(\ell_n\left(\widehat{\beta},\widehat{\sigma}^2\right) - \ell_n\left(\widetilde{\beta}_1,\widetilde{\sigma}^2\right)\right) \\
&= 2\left(\left(-\frac{n}{2}\log\left(2\pi\widehat{\sigma}^2\right) - \frac{n}{2}\right) - \left(-\frac{n}{2}\log\left(2\pi\widetilde{\sigma}^2\right) - \frac{n}{2}\right)\right) \\
&= n\log\left(\frac{\widetilde{\sigma}^2}{\widehat{\sigma}^2}\right). \qquad (5.18)
\end{aligned}$$

The likelihood ratio test rejects $\mathbb{H}_0$ for large values of LR, or equivalently (see Exercise 5.10), for large values of

$$F = \frac{\left(\widetilde{\sigma}^2 - \widehat{\sigma}^2\right)/q}{\widehat{\sigma}^2/(n-k)}. \qquad (5.19)$$

This is known as the F statistic for the test of hypothesis $\mathbb{H}_0$ against $\mathbb{H}_1$.

To develop an appropriate critical value, we need the null distribution of F. Recall from (3.28) that $n\widehat{\sigma}^2 = \boldsymbol{e}'\boldsymbol{M}\boldsymbol{e}$, where $\boldsymbol{M} = \boldsymbol{I}_n - \boldsymbol{P}$ with $\boldsymbol{P} = \boldsymbol{X}\left(\boldsymbol{X}'\boldsymbol{X}\right)^{-1}\boldsymbol{X}'$. Similarly, under $\mathbb{H}_0$, $n\widetilde{\sigma}^2 = \boldsymbol{e}'\boldsymbol{M}_1\boldsymbol{e}$, where $\boldsymbol{M} = \boldsymbol{I}_n - \boldsymbol{P}_1$ with $\boldsymbol{P}_1 = \boldsymbol{X}_1\left(\boldsymbol{X}_1'\boldsymbol{X}_1\right)^{-1}\boldsymbol{X}_1'$. You can calculate that $\boldsymbol{M}_1 - \boldsymbol{M} = \boldsymbol{P} - \boldsymbol{P}_1$ is idempotent with rank q. Furthermore, $\left(\boldsymbol{M}_1 - \boldsymbol{M}\right)\boldsymbol{M} = 0$. It follows that $\boldsymbol{e}'\left(\boldsymbol{M}_1 - \boldsymbol{M}\right)\boldsymbol{e} \sim \chi^2_q$ and is independent of $\boldsymbol{e}'\boldsymbol{M}\boldsymbol{e}$. Hence,

$$\mathrm{F} = \frac{\boldsymbol{e}'\left(\boldsymbol{M}_1 - \boldsymbol{M}\right)\boldsymbol{e}/q}{\boldsymbol{e}'\boldsymbol{M}\boldsymbol{e}/(n-k)} \sim \frac{\chi^2_q/q}{\chi^2_{n-k}/(n-k)} \sim F_{q,n-k}$$

which is an exact F distribution with degrees of freedom q and $n-k$, respectively. Thus under $\mathbb{H}_0$, the F statistic has an exact F distribution.

The critical values are selected from the upper tail of the F distribution. For a given significance level α (typically $\alpha = 0.05$), we select the critical value c so that $\mathbb{P}\left[F_{q,n-k} \geq c\right] = \alpha$. For example, in MATLAB, the expression is `finv(1-α,q,n-k)`. The test rejects $\mathbb{H}_0$ in favor of $\mathbb{H}_1$ if $F > c$ and does not reject $\mathbb{H}_0$ otherwise. The p-value of the test is $p = 1 - G_{q,n-k}(F)$, where $G_{q,n-k}(u)$ is the $F_{q,n-k}$ distribution function. In MATLAB, the p-value is computed as `1-fcdf(f,q,n-k)`. We reject $\mathbb{H}_0$ if $F > c$, or equivalently, if $p < \alpha$.

In Stata, the command to test multiple coefficients takes the form "`test X1 X2`" where `X1` and `X2` are the names of the variables whose coefficients are tested. Stata then reports the F statistic for the hypothesis that the coefficients are jointly 0 along with the p-value calculated using the F distribution.

Theorem 5.13 In the normal regression model, if the null hypothesis (5.16) is true, then for F defined in (5.19), $F \sim F_{q,n-k}$. If c is set so that $\mathbb{P}\left[F_{q,n-k} \geq c\right] = \alpha$, then the test "Reject $\mathbb{H}_0$ in favor of $\mathbb{H}_1$ if $F > c$" has significance level α.

Theorem 5.13 justifies the F test in the normal regression model with critical values from the F distribution.

5.14 INFORMATION BOUND FOR NORMAL REGRESSION

This section requires a familiarity with the theory of the Cramér-Rao Lower Bound. See Chapter 10 of *Probability and Statistics for Economists.*

The likelihood scores for the normal regression model are

$$\frac{\partial}{\partial \beta} \ell_n(\beta, \sigma^2) = \frac{1}{\sigma^2} \sum_{i=1}^{n} X_i \left(Y_i - X_i'\beta\right) = \frac{1}{\sigma^2} \sum_{i=1}^{n} X_i e_i$$

and

$$\frac{\partial}{\partial \sigma^2} \ell_n(\beta, \sigma^2) = -\frac{n}{2\sigma^2} + \frac{1}{2\sigma^4} \sum_{i=1}^{n} \left(Y_i - X_i'\beta\right)^2 = \frac{1}{2\sigma^4} \sum_{i=1}^{n} \left(e_i^2 - \sigma^2\right).$$

It follows that the information matrix is

$$\mathscr{I} = \operatorname{var}\left[\begin{array}{c} \frac{\partial}{\partial \beta} \ell(\beta, \sigma^2) \\ \frac{\partial}{\partial \sigma^2} \ell(\beta, \sigma^2) \end{array} \middle| \boldsymbol{X} \right] = \begin{pmatrix} \frac{1}{\sigma^2} \boldsymbol{X}'\boldsymbol{X} & 0 \\ 0 & \dfrac{2\sigma^4}{n} \end{pmatrix} \tag{5.20}$$

(see Exercise 5.11). The Cramér-Rao lower bound is

$$\mathscr{I}^{-1} = \begin{pmatrix} \sigma^2 \left(\boldsymbol{X}'\boldsymbol{X}\right)^{-1} & 0 \\ 0 & \dfrac{2\sigma^4}{n} \end{pmatrix}.$$

Thus, the lower bound for estimation of β is $\sigma^2 \left(\boldsymbol{X}'\boldsymbol{X}\right)^{-1}$, and the lower bound for σ^2 is $2\sigma^4/n$.

The unbiased variance estimator s^2 of σ^2 has variance $2\sigma^4/(n-k)$ (see Exercise 5.12), which is larger than the Cramér-Rao lower bound $2\sigma^4/n$. Thus in contrast to the coefficient estimator, the variance estimator is not Cramér-Rao efficient.

5.15 EXERCISES

Exercise 5.1 Show that if $Q \sim \chi_r^2$, then $\mathbb{E}[Q] = r$ and $\operatorname{var}[Q] = 2r$.

Hint: Use the representation $Q = \sum_{i=1}^{n} Z_i^2$ with Z_i independent $\mathrm{N}(0,1)$.

Exercise 5.2 Show that if $\boldsymbol{e} \sim \mathrm{N}\left(0, \boldsymbol{I}_n \sigma^2\right)$ and $\boldsymbol{H}'\boldsymbol{H} = \boldsymbol{I}_n$, then $\boldsymbol{u} = \boldsymbol{H}'\boldsymbol{e} \sim \mathrm{N}\left(0, \boldsymbol{I}_n \sigma^2\right)$.

Exercise 5.3 Show that if $\boldsymbol{e} \sim \mathrm{N}(0, \Sigma)$ and $\Sigma = \boldsymbol{A}\boldsymbol{A}'$, then $\boldsymbol{u} = \boldsymbol{A}^{-1}\boldsymbol{e} \sim \mathrm{N}(0, \boldsymbol{I}_n)$.

Exercise 5.4 Show that $\operatorname{argmax}_{\theta \in \Theta} \ell_n(\theta) = \operatorname{argmax}_{\theta \in \Theta} L_n(\theta)$.

Exercise 5.5 For the regression in-sample predicted values $\widehat{Y}_i$, show that $\widehat{Y}_i \mid \boldsymbol{X} \sim \mathrm{N}\left(X_i'\beta, \sigma^2 h_{ii}\right)$, where the h_{ii} are the leverage values (3.40).

Exercise 5.6 In the normal regression model, show that the leave-one-out prediction errors $\widetilde{e}_i$ and the standardized residuals $\bar{e}_i$ are independent of $\widehat{\beta}$, conditional on $\boldsymbol{X}$.

Hint: Use (3.45) and (4.26).

Exercise 5.7 In the normal regression model, show that the robust covariance matrices $\widehat{\boldsymbol{V}}_{\widehat{\beta}}^{\mathrm{HC0}}$, $\widehat{\boldsymbol{V}}_{\widehat{\beta}}^{\mathrm{HC1}}$, $\widehat{\boldsymbol{V}}_{\widehat{\beta}}^{\mathrm{HC2}}$, and $\widehat{\boldsymbol{V}}_{\widehat{\beta}}^{\mathrm{HC3}}$ are independent of the OLS estimator $\widehat{\beta}$, conditional on $\boldsymbol{X}$.

Exercise 5.8 Let $F(u)$ be the distribution function of a random variable X whose density is symmetric about 0. (This includes the standard normal and the student t.) Show that $F(-u) = 1 - F(u)$.

Exercise 5.9 Let $\widehat{C}_\beta = [L, U]$ be a $1 - \alpha$ confidence interval for β, and consider the transformation $\theta = g(\beta)$, where $g(\cdot)$ is monotonically increasing. Consider the confidence interval $\widehat{C}_\theta = [g(L), g(U)]$ for θ. Show that $\mathbb{P}\left[\theta \in \widehat{C}_\theta\right] = \mathbb{P}\left[\beta \in \widehat{C}_\beta\right]$. Use this result to develop a confidence interval for σ.

Exercise 5.10 Show that the test "Reject $\mathbb{H}_0$ if $\text{LR} \geq c_1$" for LR defined in (5.18), and the test "Reject $\mathbb{H}_0$ if $\text{F} \geq c_2$" for F defined in (5.19), yield the same decisions if $c_2 = \left(\exp(c_1/n) - 1\right)(n-k)/q$. Does this mean that the two tests are equivalent?

Exercise 5.11 Show (5.20).

Exercise 5.12 In the normal regression model, let s^2 be the unbiased estimator of the error variance σ^2 from (4.28).

(a) Show that $\text{var}\left[s^2\right] = 2\sigma^4/(n-k)$.
(b) Show that $\text{var}\left[s^2\right]$ is strictly larger than the Cramér-Rao lower bound for σ^2.

PART II

LARGE SAMPLE METHODS

CHAPTER 6

A REVIEW OF LARGE SAMPLE ASYMPTOTICS

6.1 INTRODUCTION

The most widely used tool in sampling theory is large sample asymptotics. "Asymptotics" means approximating a finite-sample sampling distribution by taking its limit as the sample size diverges to infinity. This chapter provides a brief review of the main results of large sample asymptotics. It is meant as a reference, not as a teaching guide. Asymptotic theory is covered in detail in Chapters 7–9 of *Probability and Statistics for Economists.* If you have not previously studied asymptotic theory in detail, you should study these chapters before proceeding.

6.2 MODES OF CONVERGENCE

Definition 6.1 A sequence of random vectors $Z_n \in \mathbb{R}^k$ **converges in probability** to Z as $n \to \infty$, denoted $Z_n \underset{p}{\longrightarrow} Z$ or alternatively, $\operatorname{plim}_{n\to\infty} Z_n = Z$, if for all $\delta > 0$,

$$\lim_{n\to\infty} \mathbb{P}\left[\|Z_n - Z\| \leq \delta\right] = 1. \tag{6.1}$$

We call Z the **probability limit** (or **plim**) of Z_n.

Definition 6.1 treats random variables and random vectors simultaneously by using the vector norm. It is useful to know that for a random vector, (6.1) holds if and only if each element in the vector converges in probability to its limit.

Definition 6.2 Let Z_n be a sequence of random vectors with distributions $F_n(u) = \mathbb{P}\left[Z_n \leq u\right]$. We say that Z_n **converges in distribution** to Z as $n \to \infty$, denoted $Z_n \underset{d}{\longrightarrow} Z$, if for all u at which $F(u) = \mathbb{P}\left[Z \leq u\right]$ is continuous, $F_n(u) \to F(u)$ as $n \to \infty$. We refer to Z and its distribution $F(u)$ as the **asymptotic distribution, large sample distribution**, or **limit distribution** of Z_n.

6.3 WEAK LAW OF LARGE NUMBERS

Theorem 6.1 Weak Law of Large Numbers (WLLN)
If $Y_i \in \mathbb{R}^k$ are i.i.d. and $\mathbb{E}\|Y\| < \infty$, then as $n \to \infty$,

$$\overline{Y} = \frac{1}{n}\sum_{i=1}^{n} Y_i \underset{p}{\longrightarrow} \mathbb{E}[Y].$$

The WLLN shows that the sample mean $\overline{Y}$ converges in probability to the true population expectation μ. The result applies to any transformation of a random vector with a finite mean.

Theorem 6.2 If $Y_i \in \mathbb{R}^k$ are i.i.d., $h(y): \mathbb{R}^k \to \mathbb{R}^q$, and $\mathbb{E}\|h(Y)\| < \infty$, then $\widehat{\mu} = \frac{1}{n}\sum_{i=1}^{n} h(Y_i) \underset{p}{\longrightarrow} \mu = \mathbb{E}[h(Y)]$ as $n \to \infty$.

An estimator that converges in probability to the population value is called **consistent**.

Definition 6.3 An estimator $\widehat{\theta}$ of θ is **consistent** if $\widehat{\theta} \underset{p}{\longrightarrow} \theta$ as $n \to \infty$.

6.4 CENTRAL LIMIT THEOREM

Theorem 6.3 Multivariate Lindeberg-Lévy Central Limit Theorem (CLT). If $Y_i \in \mathbb{R}^k$ are i.i.d. and $\mathbb{E}\|Y\|^2 < \infty$, then as $n \to \infty$,

$$\sqrt{n}\left(\overline{Y} - \mu\right) \underset{d}{\longrightarrow} \mathrm{N}(0, \boldsymbol{V})$$

where $\mu = \mathbb{E}[Y]$ and $\boldsymbol{V} = \mathbb{E}\left[(Y-\mu)(Y-\mu)'\right]$.

The central limit theorem shows that the distribution of the sample mean is approximately normal in large samples. For some applications, it may be useful to notice that Theorem 6.3 does not impose any restrictions on $\boldsymbol{V}$ other than that the elements are finite. Therefore, this result allows for the possibility of singular $\boldsymbol{V}$.

The following two generalizations allow for heterogeneous random variables.

Theorem 6.4 Multivariate Lindeberg CLT. Suppose that for all n, $Y_{ni} \in \mathbb{R}^k$, $i = 1, \ldots, r_n$, are independent but not necessarily identically distributed with expectations $\mathbb{E}[Y_{ni}] = 0$ and variance matrices

$\boldsymbol{V}_{ni} = \mathbb{E}\left[Y_{ni}Y_{ni}'\right]$. Set $\overline{\boldsymbol{V}}_n = \sum_{i=1}^{n} \boldsymbol{V}_{ni}$. Suppose $\nu_n^2 = \lambda_{\min}(\overline{\boldsymbol{V}}_n) > 0$ and for all $\epsilon > 0$,

$$\lim_{n\to\infty} \frac{1}{\nu_n^2} \sum_{i=1}^{r_n} \mathbb{E}\left[\|Y_{ni}\|^2 \mathbb{1}\left\{\|Y_{ni}\|^2 \geq \epsilon \nu_n^2\right\}\right] = 0. \tag{6.2}$$

Then as $n \to \infty$,

$$\overline{\boldsymbol{V}}_n^{-1/2} \sum_{i=1}^{r_n} Y_{ni} \underset{d}{\longrightarrow} \mathrm{N}\left(0, \boldsymbol{I}_k\right).$$

Theorem 6.5 Suppose $Y_{ni} \in \mathbb{R}^k$ are independent but not necessarily identically distributed with expectations $\mathbb{E}\left[Y_{ni}\right] = 0$ and variance matrices $\boldsymbol{V}_{ni} = \mathbb{E}\left[Y_{ni}Y_{ni}'\right]$. Suppose

$$\frac{1}{n}\sum_{i=1}^{n} \boldsymbol{V}_{ni} \to \boldsymbol{V} > 0$$

and for some $\delta > 0$,

$$\sup_{n,i} \mathbb{E}\left\|Y_{ni}\right\|^{2+\delta} < \infty. \tag{6.3}$$

Then as $n \to \infty$,

$$\sqrt{n}\,\overline{Y} \underset{d}{\longrightarrow} \mathrm{N}\left(0, \boldsymbol{V}\right).$$

6.5 CONTINUOUS MAPPING THEOREM AND DELTA METHOD

Continuous functions are limit-preserving. There are two forms of the continuous mapping theorem, for convergence in probability and convergence in distribution.

Theorem 6.6 Continuous Mapping Theorem (CMT). Let $Z_n \in \mathbb{R}^k$ and $g(u) : \mathbb{R}^k \to \mathbb{R}^q$. If $Z_n \underset{p}{\longrightarrow} c$ as $n \to \infty$ and $g(u)$ is continuous at c, then $g(Z_n) \underset{p}{\longrightarrow} g(c)$ as $n \to \infty$.

Theorem 6.7 Continuous Mapping Theorem. If $Z_n \underset{d}{\longrightarrow} Z$ as $n \to \infty$ and $g : \mathbb{R}^m \to \mathbb{R}^k$ has the set of discontinuity points D_g such that $\mathbb{P}\left[Z \in D_g\right] = 0$, then $g(Z_n) \underset{d}{\longrightarrow} g(Z)$ as $n \to \infty$.

Differentiable functions of asymptotically normal random estimators are asymptotically normal.

Theorem 6.8 Delta Method. Let $\mu \in \mathbb{R}^k$ and $g(u): \mathbb{R}^k \to \mathbb{R}^q$. If $\sqrt{n}(\widehat{\mu} - \mu) \underset{d}{\longrightarrow} \xi$, where $g(u)$ is continuously differentiable in a neighborhood of μ, then as $n \to \infty$,

$$\sqrt{n}\left(g(\widehat{\mu}) - g(\mu)\right) \underset{d}{\longrightarrow} \boldsymbol{G}'\xi \tag{6.4}$$

where $\boldsymbol{G}(u) = \frac{\partial}{\partial u} g(u)'$ and $\boldsymbol{G} = \boldsymbol{G}(\mu)$. In particular, if $\xi \sim \mathrm{N}(0, \boldsymbol{V})$, then as $n \to \infty$,

$$\sqrt{n}\left(g(\widehat{\mu}) - g(\mu)\right) \underset{d}{\longrightarrow} \mathrm{N}\left(0, \boldsymbol{G}'\boldsymbol{V}\boldsymbol{G}\right). \tag{6.5}$$

6.6 SMOOTH FUNCTION MODEL

The smooth function model is $\theta = g(\mu)$, where $\mu = \mathbb{E}[h(Y)]$, and $g(\mu)$ is smooth in a suitable sense. The parameter $\theta = g(\mu)$ is not a population moment, so it does not have a direct moment estimator. Instead, it is common to use a **plug-in estimator** formed by replacing the unknown μ with its point estimator $\widehat{\mu}$ and then "plugging" this into the expression for θ. The first step is to calculate the sample mean $\widehat{\mu} = n^{-1}\sum_{i=1}^n h(Y_i)$. The second step is the transformation $\widehat{\theta} = g(\widehat{\mu})$. The hat "^" indicates that $\widehat{\theta}$ is a sample estimator of θ. The smooth function model includes a broad class of estimators, including sample variances and the least squares estimator.

Theorem 6.9 If $Y_i \in \mathbb{R}^m$ are i.i.d., $h(u): \mathbb{R}^m \to \mathbb{R}^k$, $\mathbb{E}\|h(Y)\| < \infty$, and $g(u): \mathbb{R}^k \to \mathbb{R}^q$ is continuous at μ, then $\widehat{\theta} \underset{p}{\longrightarrow} \theta$ as $n \to \infty$.

Theorem 6.10 If $Y_i \in \mathbb{R}^m$ are i.i.d., $h(u): \mathbb{R}^m \to \mathbb{R}^k$, $\mathbb{E}\|h(Y)\|^2 < \infty$, $g(u): \mathbb{R}^k \to \mathbb{R}^q$, and $\boldsymbol{G}(u) = \dfrac{\partial}{\partial u} g(u)'$ is continuous in a neighborhood of μ, then as $n \to \infty$,

$$\sqrt{n}\left(\widehat{\theta} - \theta\right) \underset{d}{\longrightarrow} \mathrm{N}(0, \boldsymbol{V}_\theta)$$

where $\boldsymbol{V}_\theta = \boldsymbol{G}'\boldsymbol{V}\boldsymbol{G}$, $\boldsymbol{V} = \mathbb{E}\left[(h(Y) - \mu)(h(Y) - \mu)'\right]$, and $\boldsymbol{G} = \boldsymbol{G}(\mu)$.

Theorem 6.9 establishes the consistency of $\widehat{\theta}$ for θ, and Theorem 6.10 establishes its asymptotic normality. It is instructive to compare the conditions. Consistency requires that $h(Y)$ has a finite expectation; asymptotic normality requires that $h(Y)$ has a finite variance. Consistency requires that $g(u)$ be continuous; asymptotic normality requires that $g(u)$ is continuously differentiable.

6.7 STOCHASTIC ORDER SYMBOLS

It is convenient to have simple symbols for random variables and vectors that converge in probability to 0 or are stochastically bounded. This Section introduces some of the most common notation.

Let Z_n and a_n, $n = 1, 2, \ldots$ be sequences of random variables and constants, respectively. The notation

$$Z_n = o_p(1)$$

("small oh-P-one") means that $Z_n \underset{p}{\longrightarrow} 0$ as $n \to \infty$. We also write

$$Z_n = o_p(a_n)$$

if $a_n^{-1} Z_n = o_p(1)$.

Similarly, the notation $Z_n = O_p(1)$ ("big oh-P-one") means that Z_n is bounded in probability. Precisely, for any $\epsilon > 0$, there is a constant $M_\epsilon < \infty$ such that

$$\limsup_{n \to \infty} \mathbb{P}\left[|Z_n| > M_\epsilon\right] \leq \epsilon.$$

Furthermore, we write

$$Z_n = O_p(a_n)$$

if $a_n^{-1} Z_n = O_p(1)$.

$O_p(1)$ is weaker than $o_p(1)$ in the sense that $Z_n = o_p(1)$ implies $Z_n = O_p(1)$ but not the reverse. However, if $Z_n = O_p(a_n)$, then $Z_n = o_p(b_n)$ for any b_n such that $a_n/b_n \to 0$.

A random sequence with a bounded moment is stochastically bounded.

Theorem 6.11 If Z_n is a random vector that satisfies $\mathbb{E}\|Z_n\|^\delta = O(a_n)$ for some sequence a_n and $\delta > 0$, then $Z_n = O_p(a_n^{1/\delta})$. Similarly, $\mathbb{E}\|Z_n\|^\delta = o(a_n)$ implies $Z_n = o_p(a_n^{1/\delta})$.

Many simple rules for manipulating $o_p(1)$ and $O_p(1)$ sequences can be deduced from the Continuous Mapping Theorem. For example,

$$\begin{aligned} o_p(1) + o_p(1) &= o_p(1) \\ o_p(1) + O_p(1) &= O_p(1) \\ O_p(1) + O_p(1) &= O_p(1) \\ o_p(1) o_p(1) &= o_p(1) \\ o_p(1) O_p(1) &= o_p(1) \\ O_p(1) O_p(1) &= O_p(1). \end{aligned}$$

6.8 CONVERGENCE OF MOMENTS

We give a sufficient condition for the existence of the mean of the asymptotic distribution, define uniform integrability, provide a primitive condition for uniform integrability, and show that uniform integrability is the key condition under which $\mathbb{E}[Z_n]$ converges to $\mathbb{E}[Z]$.

Theorem 6.12 If $Z_n \underset{d}{\longrightarrow} Z$ and $\mathbb{E}\|Z_n\| \leq C$, then $\mathbb{E}\|Z\| \leq C$.

Definition 6.4 The random vector Z_n is **uniformly integrable** as $n \to \infty$ if

$$\lim_{M\to\infty} \limsup_{n\to\infty} \mathbb{E}\left[\|Z_n\| \mathbb{1}\left\{\|Z_n\| > M\right\}\right] = 0.$$

Theorem 6.13 If for some $\delta > 0$, $\mathbb{E}\|Z_n\|^{1+\delta} \le C < \infty$, then Z_n is uniformly integrable.

Theorem 6.14 If $Z_n \underset{d}{\longrightarrow} Z$ and Z_n is uniformly integrable, then $\mathbb{E}[Z_n] \longrightarrow \mathbb{E}[Z]$.

The following is a uniform stochastic bound.

Theorem 6.15 If $|Y_i|^r$ is uniformly integrable, then as $n \to \infty$,

$$n^{-1/r} \max_{1\le i\le n} |Y_i| \underset{p}{\longrightarrow} 0. \tag{6.6}$$

Equation (6.6) implies that if Y has r finite moments, then the largest observation will diverge at a rate slower than $n^{1/r}$. The higher the moments, the slower the rate of divergence will be.

CHAPTER 7

ASYMPTOTIC THEORY FOR LEAST SQUARES

7.1 INTRODUCTION

It turns out that the asymptotic theory of least squares estimation applies equally to the projection model and the linear CEF model. Therefore, the results in this chapter will be stated for the broader projection model described in Section 2.18. Recall that the model is $Y = X'\beta + e$ with the linear projection coefficient $\beta = \left(\mathbb{E}\left[XX'\right]\right)^{-1} \mathbb{E}\left[XY\right]$.

Maintained assumptions in this chapter will be random sampling and finite second moments. We restate these assumptions here for clarity.

> **Assumption 7.1**
>
> 1. The variables (Y_i, X_i), $i = 1, \ldots, n$, are i.i.d.
> 2. $\mathbb{E}\left[Y^2\right] < \infty$.
> 3. $\mathbb{E}\left\|X\right\|^2 < \infty$.
> 4. $\boldsymbol{Q}_{XX} = \mathbb{E}\left[XX'\right]$ is positive definite.

The distributional results will require a strengthening of these assumptions to finite fourth moments. We discuss the specific conditions in Section 7.3.

7.2 CONSISTENCY OF LEAST SQUARES ESTIMATOR

In this section, we use the weak law of large numbers (WLLN, Theorem 6.1 and Theorem 6.2) and the Continuous Mapping Theorem (CMT, Theorem 6.6) to show that the least squares estimator $\widehat{\beta}$ is consistent for the projection coefficient β.

This derivation is based on three key components. First, the OLS estimator can be written as a continuous function of a set of sample moments. Second, the WLLN shows that sample moments converge in probability to population moments. And third, the CMT states that continuous functions preserve convergence in probability. We now discuss each step in brief and then in greater detail.

First, observe that the OLS estimator

$$\widehat{\beta} = \left(\frac{1}{n}\sum_{i=1}^{n} X_i X_i'\right)^{-1} \left(\frac{1}{n}\sum_{i=1}^{n} X_i Y_i\right) = \widehat{\boldsymbol{Q}}_{XX}^{-1} \widehat{\boldsymbol{Q}}_{XY}$$

is a function of the sample moments $\widehat{\boldsymbol{Q}}_{XX} = \frac{1}{n}\sum_{i=1}^{n} X_i X_i'$ and $\widehat{\boldsymbol{Q}}_{XY} = \frac{1}{n}\sum_{i=1}^{n} X_i Y_i$.

Second, by an application of the WLLN, these sample moments converge in probability to their population expectations. Specifically, the fact that (Y_i, X_i) are mutually i.i.d. implies that any function of (Y_i, X_i) is i.i.d., including $X_i X_i'$ and $X_i Y_i$. These variables also have finite expectations under Assumption 7.1. Under these conditions, the WLLN implies that as $n \to \infty$,

$$\widehat{\boldsymbol{Q}}_{XX} = \frac{1}{n}\sum_{i=1}^{n} X_i X_i' \underset{p}{\longrightarrow} \mathbb{E}\left[XX'\right] = \boldsymbol{Q}_{XX} \tag{7.1}$$

and

$$\widehat{\boldsymbol{Q}}_{XY} = \frac{1}{n}\sum_{i=1}^{n} X_i Y_i \underset{p}{\longrightarrow} \mathbb{E}\left[XY\right] = \boldsymbol{Q}_{XY}.$$

Third, the CMT allows us to combine these equations to show that $\widehat{\beta}$ converges in probability to β. Specifically, as $n \to \infty$,

$$\widehat{\beta} = \widehat{\boldsymbol{Q}}_{XX}^{-1} \widehat{\boldsymbol{Q}}_{XY} \underset{p}{\longrightarrow} \boldsymbol{Q}_{XX}^{-1} \boldsymbol{Q}_{XY} = \beta. \tag{7.2}$$

We have shown that $\widehat{\beta} \underset{p}{\longrightarrow} \beta$ as $n \to \infty$. In words, the OLS estimator converges in probability to the projection coefficient vector β as the sample size n gets large.

To fully understand the application of the CMT, let us walk through it in detail. We can write

$$\widehat{\beta} = \boldsymbol{g}\left(\widehat{\boldsymbol{Q}}_{XX}, \widehat{\boldsymbol{Q}}_{XY}\right)$$

where $\boldsymbol{g}(\boldsymbol{A}, \boldsymbol{b}) = \boldsymbol{A}^{-1}\boldsymbol{b}$ is a function of $\boldsymbol{A}$ and $\boldsymbol{b}$. The function $\boldsymbol{g}(\boldsymbol{A}, \boldsymbol{b})$ is a continuous function of $\boldsymbol{A}$ and $\boldsymbol{b}$ at all values of the arguments such that $\boldsymbol{A}^{-1}$ exists. Assumption 7.1 specifies that $\boldsymbol{Q}_{XX}$ is positive definite, which means that $\boldsymbol{Q}_{XX}^{-1}$ exists. Thus $\boldsymbol{g}(\boldsymbol{A}, \boldsymbol{b})$ is continuous at $\boldsymbol{A} = \boldsymbol{Q}_{XX}$. This justifies the application of the CMT in (7.2).

For a slightly different demonstration of (7.2), recall that (4.6) implies that

$$\widehat{\beta} - \beta = \widehat{\boldsymbol{Q}}_{XX}^{-1} \widehat{\boldsymbol{Q}}_{Xe} \tag{7.3}$$

where

$$\widehat{\boldsymbol{Q}}_{Xe} = \frac{1}{n}\sum_{i=1}^{n} X_i e_i.$$

The WLLN and (2.25) imply that

$$\widehat{\boldsymbol{Q}}_{Xe} \underset{p}{\longrightarrow} \mathbb{E}\left[Xe\right] = 0.$$

Therefore,

$$\widehat{\beta} - \beta = \widehat{\boldsymbol{Q}}_{XX}^{-1} \widehat{\boldsymbol{Q}}_{Xe} \underset{p}{\longrightarrow} \boldsymbol{Q}_{XX}^{-1} 0 = 0$$

which is the same as $\widehat{\beta} \underset{p}{\longrightarrow} \beta$.

Theorem 7.1 Consistency of Least Squares. Under Assumption 7.1, $\widehat{\boldsymbol{Q}}_{XX} \underset{p}{\longrightarrow} \boldsymbol{Q}_{XX}$, $\widehat{\boldsymbol{Q}}_{XY} \underset{p}{\longrightarrow} \boldsymbol{Q}_{XY}$, $\widehat{\boldsymbol{Q}}_{XX}^{-1} \underset{p}{\longrightarrow} \boldsymbol{Q}_{XX}^{-1}$, $\widehat{\boldsymbol{Q}}_{Xe} \underset{p}{\longrightarrow} 0$, and $\widehat{\beta} \underset{p}{\longrightarrow} \beta$ as $n \to \infty$.

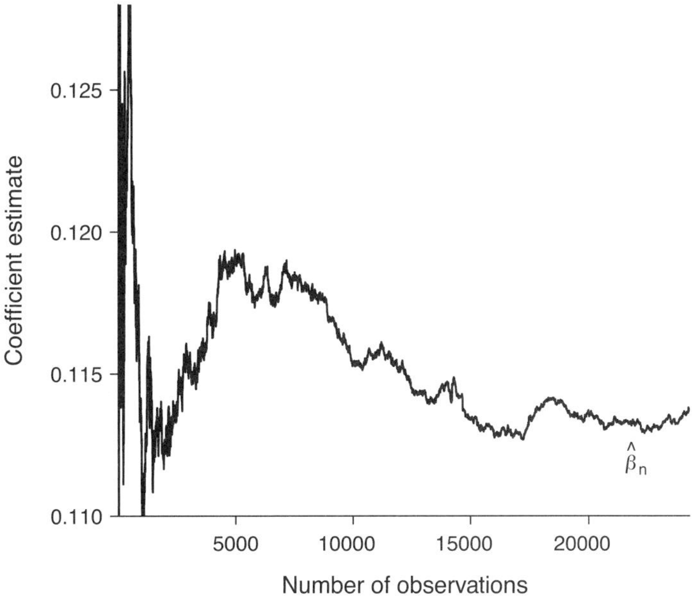

FIGURE 7.1 The least squares estimator as a function of sample size

Theorem 7.1 states that the OLS estimator $\widehat{\beta}$ converges in probability to β as n increases and thus, $\widehat{\beta}$ is consistent for β. In the stochastic order notation, Theorem 7.1 can be equivalently written as

$$\widehat{\beta} = \beta + o_p(1). \tag{7.4}$$

To illustrate the effect of sample size on the least squares estimator, consider the least squares regression

$$\log(wage) = \beta_1 education + \beta_2 experience + \beta_3 experience^2 + \beta_4 + e.$$

Let us use the sample of 24,344 white men from the March 2009 Current Population Survey (CPS). We randomly sort the observations and sequentially estimate the model by least squares starting with the first five observations and continuing until the full sample is used. The sequence of estimates is displayed in Figure 7.1. You can see how the least squares estimate changes with the sample size. As the number of observations increases, it settles down to the full-sample estimate $\widehat{\beta}_1 = 0.114$.

7.3 ASYMPTOTIC NORMALITY

We started this chapter by discussing the need for an approximation to the distribution of the OLS estimator $\widehat{\beta}$. In Section 7.2, we showed that $\widehat{\beta}$ converges in probability to β. Consistency is a good first step, but in itself does not describe the distribution of the estimator. In this section, we derive an approximation typically called the **asymptotic distribution**.

The derivation starts by writing the estimator as a function of sample moments. One of the moments must be written as a sum of 0-mean random vectors and normalized so that the central limit theorem (Theorem 6.3) can be applied. The steps are as follows.

Take equation (7.3) and multiply it by $\sqrt{n}$. This yields the expression

$$\sqrt{n}\left(\widehat{\beta}-\beta\right)=\left(\frac{1}{n}\sum_{i=1}^{n}X_iX_i'\right)^{-1}\left(\frac{1}{\sqrt{n}}\sum_{i=1}^{n}X_ie_i\right). \tag{7.5}$$

Thus the normalized and centered estimator $\sqrt{n}\left(\widehat{\beta}-\beta\right)$ is a function of the sample average $n^{-1}\sum_{i=1}^{n}X_iX_i'$ and the normalized sample average $n^{-1/2}\sum_{i=1}^{n}X_ie_i$.

The random pairs (Y_i, X_i) are i.i.d., meaning that they are independent across i and identically distributed. Any function of (Y_i, X_i) is also i.i.d., which includes $e_i = Y_i - X_i'\beta$ and the product X_ie_i. The latter has mean-0 ($\mathbb{E}[Xe]=0$) and has $k\times k$ covariance matrix

$$\Omega=\mathbb{E}\left[(Xe)(Xe)'\right]=\mathbb{E}\left[XX'e^2\right].$$

We show below that Ω has finite elements under a strengthening of Assumption 7.1. Since X_ie_i is i.i.d., mean 0, and finite variance, the central limit theorem (Theorem 6.3) implies

$$\frac{1}{\sqrt{n}}\sum_{i=1}^{n}X_ie_i \underset{d}{\longrightarrow} \mathrm{N}(0,\Omega).$$

The required conditions are listed in Assumption 7.2.

Assumption 7.2

1. The variables (Y_i, X_i), $i=1,\ldots,n$, are i.i.d.
2. $\mathbb{E}\left[Y^4\right]<\infty$.
3. $\mathbb{E}\|X\|^4<\infty$.
4. $\boldsymbol{Q}_{XX}=\mathbb{E}\left[XX'\right]$ is positive definite.

Assumption 7.2 implies that $\Omega<\infty$. To see this, take its $j\ell$th element, $\mathbb{E}\left[X_jX_\ell e^2\right]$. Theorem 2.9.6 shows that $\mathbb{E}\left[e^4\right]<\infty$. By the expectation inequality (B.30), the $j\ell$th element of Ω is bounded by

$$\left|\mathbb{E}\left[X_jX_\ell e^2\right]\right|\le\mathbb{E}\left|X_jX_\ell e^2\right|=\mathbb{E}\left[\left|X_j\right|\left|X_\ell\right|e^2\right].$$

By two applications of the Cauchy-Schwarz inequality (B.32), this is smaller than

$$\left(\mathbb{E}\left[X_j^2X_\ell^2\right]\right)^{1/2}\left(\mathbb{E}\left[e^4\right]\right)^{1/2}\le\left(\mathbb{E}\left[X_j^4\right]\right)^{1/4}\left(\mathbb{E}\left[X_\ell^4\right]\right)^{1/4}\left(\mathbb{E}\left[e^4\right]\right)^{1/2}<\infty$$

where the finiteness holds under Assumptions 7.2.2 and 7.2.3. Thus $\Omega<\infty$.

An alternative way to show that the elements of Ω are finite is by using a matrix norm $\|\cdot\|$ (See Appendix A.23). Then by the expectation inequality, the Cauchy-Schwarz inequality, Assumption 7.2.3, and $\mathbb{E}\left[e^4\right]<\infty$,

$$\|\Omega\|\le\mathbb{E}\left\|XX'e^2\right\|=\mathbb{E}\left[\|X\|^2e^2\right]\le\left(\mathbb{E}\|X\|^4\right)^{1/2}\left(\mathbb{E}\left[e^4\right]\right)^{1/2}<\infty.$$

This is a more compact argument (often described as more *elegant*), but such manipulations should not be done without understanding the notation and the applicability of each step of the argument.

Regardless, the finiteness of the covariance matrix means that we can apply the multivariate CLT (Theorem 6.3).

Theorem 7.2 Assumption 7.2 implies that

$$\Omega < \infty \tag{7.6}$$

and

$$\frac{1}{\sqrt{n}} \sum_{i=1}^{n} X_i e_i \underset{d}{\longrightarrow} \mathrm{N}(0, \Omega) \tag{7.7}$$

as $n \to \infty$.

Putting together (7.1), (7.5), and (7.7), we have

$$\sqrt{n}\left(\widehat{\beta} - \beta\right) \underset{d}{\longrightarrow} \boldsymbol{Q}_{XX}^{-1} \mathrm{N}(0, \Omega) = \mathrm{N}\left(0, \boldsymbol{Q}_{XX}^{-1} \Omega \boldsymbol{Q}_{XX}^{-1}\right)$$

as $n \to \infty$. The final equality follows from the property that linear combinations of normal vectors are also normal (Theorem 5.2).

We have derived the asymptotic normal approximation to the distribution of the least squares estimator.

Theorem 7.3 Asymptotic Normality of Least Squares Estimator
Under Assumption 7.2, as $n \to \infty$,

$$\sqrt{n}\left(\widehat{\beta} - \beta\right) \underset{d}{\longrightarrow} \mathrm{N}\left(0, \boldsymbol{V}_{\beta}\right)$$

where $\boldsymbol{Q}_{XX} = \mathbb{E}\left[XX'\right]$, $\Omega = \mathbb{E}\left[XX'e^2\right]$, and

$$\boldsymbol{V}_{\beta} = \boldsymbol{Q}_{XX}^{-1} \Omega \boldsymbol{Q}_{XX}^{-1}. \tag{7.8}$$

In the stochastic order notation, Theorem 7.3 implies that $\widehat{\beta} = \beta + O_p(n^{-1/2})$ which is stronger than (7.4).

The matrix $\boldsymbol{V}_{\beta} = \boldsymbol{Q}_{XX}^{-1} \Omega \boldsymbol{Q}_{XX}^{-1}$ is the variance of the asymptotic distribution of $\sqrt{n}\left(\widehat{\beta} - \beta\right)$. Consequently, $\boldsymbol{V}_{\beta}$ is often referred to as the **asymptotic covariance matrix** of $\widehat{\beta}$. The expression $\boldsymbol{V}_{\beta} = \boldsymbol{Q}_{XX}^{-1} \Omega \boldsymbol{Q}_{XX}^{-1}$ is called a **sandwich** form, as the matrix Ω is sandwiched between two copies of $\boldsymbol{Q}_{XX}^{-1}$.

It is useful to compare the variance of the asymptotic distribution given in (7.8) and the finite-sample conditional variance in the CEF model as given in (4.10):

$$\boldsymbol{V}_{\widehat{\beta}} = \operatorname{var}\left[\widehat{\beta} \mid \boldsymbol{X}\right] = \left(\boldsymbol{X}'\boldsymbol{X}\right)^{-1} \left(\boldsymbol{X}'\boldsymbol{D}\boldsymbol{X}\right) \left(\boldsymbol{X}'\boldsymbol{X}\right)^{-1}. \tag{7.9}$$

Notice that $\boldsymbol{V}_{\widehat{\beta}}$ is the exact conditional variance of $\widehat{\beta}$, and $\boldsymbol{V}_{\beta}$ is the asymptotic variance of $\sqrt{n}\left(\widehat{\beta} - \beta\right)$. Thus $\boldsymbol{V}_{\beta}$ should be (roughly) n times as large as $\boldsymbol{V}_{\widehat{\beta}}$, or $\boldsymbol{V}_{\beta} \approx n\boldsymbol{V}_{\widehat{\beta}}$. Indeed, multiplying (7.9) by n and distributing, we find

$$n\boldsymbol{V}_{\widehat{\beta}} = \left(\frac{1}{n}\boldsymbol{X}'\boldsymbol{X}\right)^{-1} \left(\frac{1}{n}\boldsymbol{X}'\boldsymbol{D}\boldsymbol{X}\right) \left(\frac{1}{n}\boldsymbol{X}'\boldsymbol{X}\right)^{-1}$$

which looks like an estimator of $\boldsymbol{V}_{\beta}$. Indeed, as $n \to \infty$, $n\boldsymbol{V}_{\widehat{\beta}} \underset{p}{\longrightarrow} \boldsymbol{V}_{\beta}$. The expression $\boldsymbol{V}_{\widehat{\beta}}$ is useful for practical inference (such as computation of standard errors and tests), as it is the variance of the estimator $\widehat{\beta}$, while $\boldsymbol{V}_{\beta}$ is useful for asymptotic theory, as it is well defined in the limit as n goes to infinity. We make use of both symbols, and it will be advisable to adhere to this convention.

There is a special case where Ω and $\boldsymbol{V}_\beta$ simplify. Suppose that

$$\operatorname{cov}(XX', e^2) = 0. \tag{7.10}$$

Condition (7.10) holds in the homoskedastic linear regression model but is somewhat broader. Under (7.10), the asymptotic variance formulas simplify as

$$\begin{aligned}\Omega &= \mathbb{E}\left[XX'\right]\mathbb{E}\left[e^2\right] = \boldsymbol{Q}_{XX}\sigma^2 \\ \boldsymbol{V}_\beta &= \boldsymbol{Q}_{XX}^{-1}\Omega\boldsymbol{Q}_{XX}^{-1} = \boldsymbol{Q}_{XX}^{-1}\sigma^2 \equiv \boldsymbol{V}_\beta^0.\end{aligned} \tag{7.11}$$

In (7.11), we define $\boldsymbol{V}_\beta^0 = \boldsymbol{Q}_{XX}^{-1}\sigma^2$ whether (7.10) is true, or false. When (7.10) is true then $\boldsymbol{V}_\beta = \boldsymbol{V}_\beta^0$; otherwise, $\boldsymbol{V}_\beta \neq \boldsymbol{V}_\beta^0$. We call $\boldsymbol{V}_\beta^0$ the **homoskedastic asymptotic covariance matrix**.

Theorem 7.3 states that the sampling distribution of the least squares estimator, after rescaling, is approximately normal when the sample size n is sufficiently large. This holds true for all joint distributions of (Y, X) that satisfy the conditions of Assumption 7.2. Consequently, asymptotic normality is routinely used to approximate the finite sample distribution of $\sqrt{n}\left(\widehat{\beta} - \beta\right)$.

A difficulty is that for any fixed n, the sampling distribution of $\widehat{\beta}$ can be arbitrarily far from the normal distribution. The normal approximation improves as n increases, but how large should n be for the approximation to be useful? Unfortunately, there is no simple answer to this reasonable question. The trouble is that no matter how large the sample size is the normal approximation is arbitrarily poor for some data distribution satisfying the assumptions. We illustrate this problem using a simulation. Let $Y = \beta_1 X + \beta_2 + e$, where X is $\mathrm{N}(0,1)$, and e is independent of X with the Double Pareto density $f(e) = \frac{\alpha}{2}|e|^{-\alpha-1}$, $|e| \geq 1$. If $\alpha > 2$ the error e has 0 mean and variance $\alpha/(\alpha-2)$. As α approaches 2, however, its variance diverges to infinity. In this context, the normalized least squares slope estimator $\sqrt{n\frac{\alpha-2}{\alpha}}\left(\widehat{\beta}_1 - \beta_1\right)$ has the $\mathrm{N}(0,1)$ asymptotic distribution for any $\alpha > 2$. Figure 7.2(a) displays the finite sample densities of the normalized estimator $\sqrt{n\frac{\alpha-2}{\alpha}}\left(\widehat{\beta}_1 - \beta_1\right)$, setting $n = 100$ and varying the parameter α. For $\alpha = 3.0$, the density is very close to the $\mathrm{N}(0,1)$ density. As α diminishes, the density changes significantly, concentrating most of the probability mass around 0.

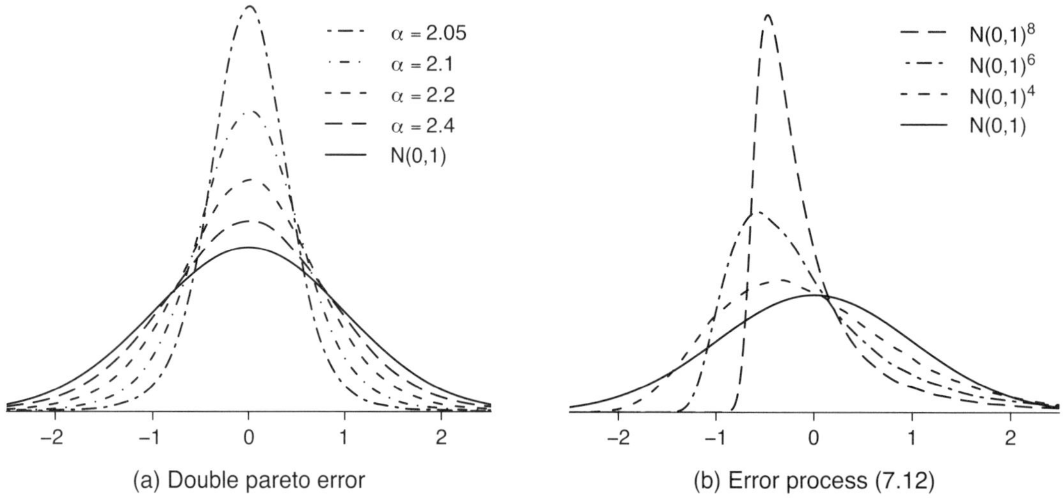

FIGURE 7.2 Density of normalized OLS estimator

Another example is shown in Figure 7.2(b). Here the model is $Y = \beta + e$, where

$$e = \frac{u^r - \mathbb{E}[u^r]}{\left(\mathbb{E}\left[u^{2r}\right] - (\mathbb{E}[u^r])^2\right)^{1/2}} \tag{7.12}$$

and $u \sim \mathrm{N}(0,1)$. We show the sampling distribution of $\sqrt{n}\left(\widehat{\beta} - \beta\right)$ for $n = 100$, for various $r = 1, 4, 6$, and 8. As r increases, the sampling distribution becomes highly skewed and non-normal. The lesson from Figure 7.2 is that the $\mathrm{N}(0,1)$ asymptotic approximation is never guaranteed to be accurate.

7.4 JOINT DISTRIBUTION

Theorem 7.3 gives the joint asymptotic distribution of the coefficient estimators. We can use the result to study the covariance between the coefficient estimators. For simplicity, take the case of two regressors, no intercept, and homoskedastic error. Assume the regressors are mean 0, variance 1, with correlation ρ. Then using the formula for inversion of a 2×2 matrix,

$$\boldsymbol{V}_{\beta}^{0} = \sigma^2 \boldsymbol{Q}_{XX}^{-1} = \frac{\sigma^2}{1-\rho^2}\left[\begin{array}{cc} 1 & -\rho \\ -\rho & 1 \end{array}\right].$$

Thus if X_1 and X_2 are positively correlated ($\rho > 0$), then $\widehat{\beta}_1$ and $\widehat{\beta}_2$ are negatively correlated (and vice versa).

For illustration, Figure 7.3(a) displays the probability contours of the joint asymptotic distribution of $\widehat{\beta}_1 - \beta_1$ and $\widehat{\beta}_2 - \beta_2$ when $\beta_1 = \beta_2 = 0$ and $\rho = 0.5$. The coefficient estimators are negatively correlated, because the regressors are positively correlated. Thus if $\widehat{\beta}_1$ is unusually negative, it is likely that $\widehat{\beta}_2$ is unusually positive, and conversely. It is also unlikely that we will observe both $\widehat{\beta}_1$ and $\widehat{\beta}_2$ unusually large and of the same sign.

This finding that the correlation of the regressors is of opposite sign of the correlation of the coefficient estimates is sensitive to the assumption of homoskedasticity. If the errors are heteroskedastic, then this relationship is not guaranteed.

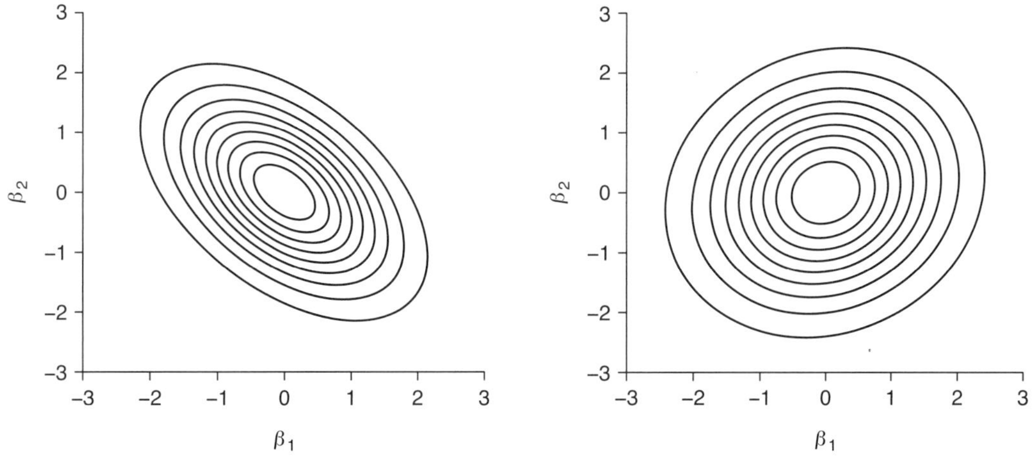

(a) Homoskedastic case (b) Heteroskedastic case

FIGURE 7.3 Contours of joint distribution of $\hat{\beta}_1$ and $\hat{\beta}_2$

This sensitivity can be seen through a simple constructed example. Suppose that X_1 and X_2 only take the values $\{-1,+1\}$, symmetrically, with $\mathbb{P}[X_1=X_2=1]=\mathbb{P}[X_1=X_2=-1]=3/8$, and $\mathbb{P}[X_1=1,X_2=-1]=\mathbb{P}[X_1=-1,X_2=1]=1/8$. You can check that the regressors are mean 0, unit variance, and correlation 0.5, which is identical with the setting displayed in Figure 7.3(a).

Now suppose that the error is heteroskedastic. Specifically, suppose that $\mathbb{E}\left[e^2 \mid X_1=X_2\right]=5/4$, and $\mathbb{E}\left[e^2 \mid X_1\neq X_2\right]=1/4$. You can check that $\mathbb{E}\left[e^2\right]=1$, $\mathbb{E}\left[X_1^2e^2\right]=\mathbb{E}\left[X_2^2e^2\right]=1$, and $\mathbb{E}\left[X_1X_2e^2\right]=7/8$. Therefore,

$$\begin{aligned}
\boldsymbol{V}_\beta &= \boldsymbol{Q}_{XX}^{-1}\Omega\boldsymbol{Q}_{XX}^{-1} \\
&= \frac{16}{9}\begin{bmatrix} 1 & -\frac{1}{2} \\ -\frac{1}{2} & 1 \end{bmatrix}\begin{bmatrix} 1 & \frac{7}{8} \\ \frac{7}{8} & 1 \end{bmatrix}\begin{bmatrix} 1 & -\frac{1}{2} \\ -\frac{1}{2} & 1 \end{bmatrix} \\
&= \frac{2}{3}\begin{bmatrix} 1 & \frac{1}{4} \\ \frac{1}{4} & 1 \end{bmatrix}.
\end{aligned}$$

Thus the coefficient estimators $\widehat{\beta}_1$ and $\widehat{\beta}_2$ are positively correlated (their correlation is 1/4.) The joint probability contours of their asymptotic distribution is displayed in Figure 7.3(b). We can see how the two estimators are positively associated. What we have found through this example is that in the presence of heteroskedasticity, there is no simple relationship between the correlation of the regressors and the correlation of the parameter estimators.

We can extend the above analysis to study the covariance between coefficient subvectors. For example, partitioning $X'=\left(X_1',X_2'\right)$ and $\beta'=\left(\beta_1',\beta_2'\right)$, we can write the general model as

$$Y=X_1'\beta_1+X_2'\beta_2+e$$

and the coefficient estimates as $\widehat{\beta}'=\left(\widehat{\beta}_1',\widehat{\beta}_2'\right)$. Make the partitions

$$\boldsymbol{Q}_{XX}=\begin{bmatrix} \boldsymbol{Q}_{11} & \boldsymbol{Q}_{12} \\ \boldsymbol{Q}_{21} & \boldsymbol{Q}_{22} \end{bmatrix}, \qquad \Omega=\begin{bmatrix} \Omega_{11} & \Omega_{12} \\ \Omega_{21} & \Omega_{22} \end{bmatrix}.$$

From (2.43), we have

$$\boldsymbol{Q}_{XX}^{-1}=\begin{bmatrix} \boldsymbol{Q}_{11\cdot 2}^{-1} & -\boldsymbol{Q}_{11\cdot 2}^{-1}\boldsymbol{Q}_{12}\boldsymbol{Q}_{22}^{-1} \\ -\boldsymbol{Q}_{22\cdot 1}^{-1}\boldsymbol{Q}_{21}\boldsymbol{Q}_{11}^{-1} & \boldsymbol{Q}_{22\cdot 1}^{-1} \end{bmatrix}$$

where $\boldsymbol{Q}_{11\cdot 2}=\boldsymbol{Q}_{11}-\boldsymbol{Q}_{12}\boldsymbol{Q}_{22}^{-1}\boldsymbol{Q}_{21}$, and $\boldsymbol{Q}_{22\cdot 1}=\boldsymbol{Q}_{22}-\boldsymbol{Q}_{21}\boldsymbol{Q}_{11}^{-1}\boldsymbol{Q}_{12}$. Thus when the error is homoskedastic,

$$\operatorname{cov}\left(\widehat{\beta}_1,\widehat{\beta}_2\right)=-\sigma^2\boldsymbol{Q}_{11\cdot 2}^{-1}\boldsymbol{Q}_{12}\boldsymbol{Q}_{22}^{-1}$$

which is a matrix generalization of the two-regressor case.

In general, you can show that (Exercise 7.5)

$$\boldsymbol{V}_\beta=\begin{bmatrix} \boldsymbol{V}_{11} & \boldsymbol{V}_{12} \\ \boldsymbol{V}_{21} & \boldsymbol{V}_{22} \end{bmatrix} \tag{7.13}$$

where

$$\boldsymbol{V}_{11}=\boldsymbol{Q}_{11\cdot 2}^{-1}\left(\Omega_{11}-\boldsymbol{Q}_{12}\boldsymbol{Q}_{22}^{-1}\Omega_{21}-\Omega_{12}\boldsymbol{Q}_{22}^{-1}\boldsymbol{Q}_{21}+\boldsymbol{Q}_{12}\boldsymbol{Q}_{22}^{-1}\Omega_{22}\boldsymbol{Q}_{22}^{-1}\boldsymbol{Q}_{21}\right)\boldsymbol{Q}_{11\cdot 2}^{-1} \tag{7.14}$$

$$\boldsymbol{V}_{21}=\boldsymbol{Q}_{22\cdot 1}^{-1}\left(\Omega_{21}-\boldsymbol{Q}_{21}\boldsymbol{Q}_{11}^{-1}\Omega_{11}-\Omega_{22}\boldsymbol{Q}_{22}^{-1}\boldsymbol{Q}_{21}+\boldsymbol{Q}_{21}\boldsymbol{Q}_{11}^{-1}\Omega_{12}\boldsymbol{Q}_{22}^{-1}\boldsymbol{Q}_{21}\right)\boldsymbol{Q}_{11\cdot 2}^{-1} \tag{7.15}$$

$$\boldsymbol{V}_{22}=\boldsymbol{Q}_{22\cdot 1}^{-1}\left(\Omega_{22}-\boldsymbol{Q}_{21}\boldsymbol{Q}_{11}^{-1}\Omega_{12}-\Omega_{21}\boldsymbol{Q}_{11}^{-1}\boldsymbol{Q}_{12}+\boldsymbol{Q}_{21}\boldsymbol{Q}_{11}^{-1}\Omega_{11}\boldsymbol{Q}_{11}^{-1}\boldsymbol{Q}_{12}\right)\boldsymbol{Q}_{22\cdot 1}^{-1}. \tag{7.16}$$

Unfortunately, these expressions are not easily interpretable.

7.5 CONSISTENCY OF ERROR VARIANCE ESTIMATORS

Using the methods of Section 7.2, we can show that the estimators $\widehat{\sigma}^2=n^{-1}\sum_{i=1}^n \widehat{e}_i^2$ and $s^2=(n-k)^{-1}\sum_{i=1}^n \widehat{e}_i^2$ are consistent for σ^2. The trick is to write the residual $\widehat{e}_i$ as equal to the error e_i plus a deviation:

$$\widehat{e}_i=Y_i-X_i'\widehat{\beta}=e_i-X_i'\left(\widehat{\beta}-\beta\right).$$

Thus the squared residual equals the squared error plus a deviation:

$$\widehat{e}_i^2=e_i^2-2e_iX_i'\left(\widehat{\beta}-\beta\right)+\left(\widehat{\beta}-\beta\right)'X_iX_i'\left(\widehat{\beta}-\beta\right). \tag{7.17}$$

So when we take the average of the squared residuals, we obtain the average of the squared errors, plus two terms that are (hopefully) asymptotically negligible. This average is:

$$\widehat{\sigma}^2=\frac{1}{n}\sum_{i=1}^n e_i^2-2\left(\frac{1}{n}\sum_{i=1}^n e_iX_i'\right)\left(\widehat{\beta}-\beta\right)+\left(\widehat{\beta}-\beta\right)'\left(\frac{1}{n}\sum_{i=1}^n X_iX_i'\right)\left(\widehat{\beta}-\beta\right). \tag{7.18}$$

The WLLN implies that

$$\frac{1}{n}\sum_{i=1}^n e_i^2 \underset{p}{\longrightarrow} \sigma^2$$

$$\frac{1}{n}\sum_{i=1}^n e_iX_i' \underset{p}{\longrightarrow} \mathbb{E}\left[eX'\right]=0$$

$$\frac{1}{n}\sum_{i=1}^n X_iX_i' \underset{p}{\longrightarrow} \mathbb{E}\left[XX'\right]=\boldsymbol{Q}_{XX}.$$

Theorem 7.1 shows that $\widehat{\beta}\underset{p}{\longrightarrow}\beta$. Hence, (7.18) converges in probability to σ^2, as desired.

Finally, since $n/(n-k)\to 1$ as $n\to\infty$, it follows that $s^2=\left(\frac{n}{n-k}\right)\widehat{\sigma}^2\underset{p}{\longrightarrow}\sigma^2$. Thus both estimators are consistent.

Theorem 7.4 Under Assumption 7.1, $\widehat{\sigma}^2\underset{p}{\longrightarrow}\sigma^2$ and $s^2\underset{p}{\longrightarrow}\sigma^2$ as $n\to\infty$.

7.6 HOMOSKEDASTIC COVARIANCE MATRIX ESTIMATION

Theorem 7.3 shows that $\sqrt{n}\left(\widehat{\beta}-\beta\right)$ is asymptotically normal with asymptotic covariance matrix $\boldsymbol{V}_{\beta}$. For asymptotic inference (confidence intervals and tests), we need a consistent estimator of $\boldsymbol{V}_{\beta}$. Under homoskedasticity, $\boldsymbol{V}_{\beta}$ simplifies to $\boldsymbol{V}_{\beta}^{0}=\boldsymbol{Q}_{XX}^{-1}\sigma^{2}$ and in this section, we consider the simplified problem of estimating $\boldsymbol{V}_{\beta}^{0}$.

The standard moment estimator of $\boldsymbol{Q}_{XX}$ is $\widehat{\boldsymbol{Q}}_{XX}$ defined in (7.1), and thus an estimator for $\boldsymbol{Q}_{XX}^{-1}$ is $\widehat{\boldsymbol{Q}}_{XX}^{-1}$. The standard estimator of σ^2 is the unbiased estimator s^2 defined in (4.28). Thus a natural plug-in estimator for $\boldsymbol{V}_{\beta}^{0}=\boldsymbol{Q}_{XX}^{-1}\sigma^{2}$ is $\widehat{\boldsymbol{V}}_{\beta}^{0}=\widehat{\boldsymbol{Q}}_{XX}^{-1}s^{2}$.

Consistency of $\widehat{\boldsymbol{V}}_{\beta}^{0}$ for $\boldsymbol{V}_{\beta}^{0}$ follows from consistency of the moment estimators $\widehat{\boldsymbol{Q}}_{XX}$ and s^2 and an application of the Continuous Mapping Theorem (Theorem 6.6). Specifically, Theorem 7.1 established that $\widehat{\boldsymbol{Q}}_{XX}\underset{p}{\longrightarrow}\boldsymbol{Q}_{XX}$, and Theorem 7.4 established that $s^2\underset{p}{\longrightarrow}\sigma^2$. The function $\boldsymbol{V}_{\beta}^{0}=\boldsymbol{Q}_{XX}^{-1}\sigma^{2}$ is a continuous function of $\boldsymbol{Q}_{XX}$ and σ^2 so long as $\boldsymbol{Q}_{XX}>0$, which holds true under Assumption 7.1.4. It follows by the CMT that

$$\widehat{\boldsymbol{V}}_{\beta}^{0}=\widehat{\boldsymbol{Q}}_{XX}^{-1}s^{2}\underset{p}{\longrightarrow}\boldsymbol{Q}_{XX}^{-1}\sigma^{2}=\boldsymbol{V}_{\beta}^{0}$$

so that $\widehat{\boldsymbol{V}}_{\beta}^{0}$ is consistent for $\boldsymbol{V}_{\beta}^{0}$.

Theorem 7.5 Under Assumption 7.1, $\widehat{\boldsymbol{V}}_{\beta}^{0}\underset{p}{\longrightarrow}\boldsymbol{V}_{\beta}^{0}$ as $n\rightarrow\infty$.

It is instructive to notice that Theorem 7.5 does not require the assumption of homoskedasticity. That is, $\widehat{\boldsymbol{V}}_{\beta}^{0}$ is consistent for $\boldsymbol{V}_{\beta}^{0}$, regardless of whether the regression is homoskedastic or heteroskedastic. However, $\boldsymbol{V}_{\beta}^{0}=\boldsymbol{V}_{\beta}=\operatorname{avar}\left[\widehat{\beta}\right]$ only under homoskedasticity. Thus, in the general case, $\widehat{\boldsymbol{V}}_{\beta}^{0}$ is consistent for a well-defined but non-useful object.

7.7 HETEROSKEDASTIC COVARIANCE MATRIX ESTIMATION

Theorem 7.3 established that the asymptotic covariance matrix of $\sqrt{n}\left(\widehat{\beta}-\beta\right)$ is $\boldsymbol{V}_{\beta}=\boldsymbol{Q}_{XX}^{-1}\Omega\boldsymbol{Q}_{XX}^{-1}$. We now consider estimation of this covariance matrix without imposing homoskedasticity. The standard approach is to use a plug-in estimator that replaces the unknowns with sample moments.

As described in Section 7.6, a natural estimator for $\boldsymbol{Q}_{XX}^{-1}$ is $\widehat{\boldsymbol{Q}}_{XX}^{-1}$, where $\widehat{\boldsymbol{Q}}_{XX}$ defined in (7.1).

The moment estimator for Ω is

$$\widehat{\Omega}=\frac{1}{n}\sum_{i=1}^{n}X_iX_i'\widehat{e}_i^{2},$$

leading to the plug-in covariance matrix estimator

$$\widehat{\boldsymbol{V}}_{\beta}^{\mathrm{HC0}}=\widehat{\boldsymbol{Q}}_{XX}^{-1}\widehat{\Omega}\widehat{\boldsymbol{Q}}_{XX}^{-1}. \tag{7.19}$$

You can check that $\widehat{\boldsymbol{V}}_{\beta}^{\mathrm{HC0}}=n\widehat{\boldsymbol{V}}_{\widehat{\beta}}^{\mathrm{HC0}}$, where $\widehat{\boldsymbol{V}}_{\widehat{\beta}}^{\mathrm{HC0}}$ is the HC0 covariance matrix estimator from (4.33).

As shown in Theorem 7.1, $\widehat{\boldsymbol{Q}}_{XX}^{-1} \underset{p}{\longrightarrow} \boldsymbol{Q}_{XX}^{-1}$, so we just need to verify the consistency of $\widehat{\Omega}$. The key is to replace the squared residual $\widehat{e}_i^2$ with the squared error e_i^2, and then show that the difference is asymptotically negligible.

Specifically, observe that

$$\begin{aligned}\widehat{\Omega} &= \frac{1}{n}\sum_{i=1}^{n} X_i X_i' \widehat{e}_i^2 \\ &= \frac{1}{n}\sum_{i=1}^{n} X_i X_i' e_i^2 + \frac{1}{n}\sum_{i=1}^{n} X_i X_i' \left(\widehat{e}_i^2 - e_i^2\right).\end{aligned}$$

The first term is an average of the i.i.d. random variables $X_i X_i' e_i^2$, and therefore by the WLLN, it converges in probability to its expectation, namely,

$$\frac{1}{n}\sum_{i=1}^{n} X_i X_i' e_i^2 \underset{p}{\longrightarrow} \mathbb{E}\left[XX'e^2\right] = \Omega.$$

Technically, this requires that Ω has finite elements, which was shown in (7.6).

To establish that $\widehat{\Omega}$ is consistent for Ω, it remains to show that

$$\frac{1}{n}\sum_{i=1}^{n} X_i X_i' \left(\widehat{e}_i^2 - e_i^2\right) \underset{p}{\longrightarrow} 0. \tag{7.20}$$

There are multiple ways to do this. A reasonably straightforward yet slightly tedious derivation is to start by applying the triangle inequality (B.16) using a matrix norm:

$$\begin{aligned}\left\| \frac{1}{n}\sum_{i=1}^{n} X_i X_i' \left(\widehat{e}_i^2 - e_i^2\right) \right\| &\le \frac{1}{n}\sum_{i=1}^{n} \left\| X_i X_i' \left(\widehat{e}_i^2 - e_i^2\right) \right\| \\ &= \frac{1}{n}\sum_{i=1}^{n} \|X_i\|^2 \left|\widehat{e}_i^2 - e_i^2\right|. \end{aligned} \tag{7.21}$$

Then recalling the expression for the squared residual (7.17), apply the triangle inequality (B.1) and then the Schwarz inequality (B.12) twice:

$$\begin{aligned}\left|\widehat{e}_i^2 - e_i^2\right| &\le 2\left|e_i X_i' \left(\widehat{\beta} - \beta\right)\right| + \left(\widehat{\beta} - \beta\right)' X_i X_i' \left(\widehat{\beta} - \beta\right) \\ &= 2\left|e_i\right| \left|X_i' \left(\widehat{\beta} - \beta\right)\right| + \left|\left(\widehat{\beta} - \beta\right)' X_i\right|^2 \\ &\le 2\left|e_i\right| \|X_i\| \left\|\widehat{\beta} - \beta\right\| + \|X_i\|^2 \left\|\widehat{\beta} - \beta\right\|^2. \end{aligned} \tag{7.22}$$

Combining (7.21) and (7.22), we find

$$\begin{aligned}\left\| \frac{1}{n}\sum_{i=1}^{n} X_i X_i' \left(\widehat{e}_i^2 - e_i^2\right) \right\| &\le 2\left(\frac{1}{n}\sum_{i=1}^{n} \|X_i\|^3 \left|e_i\right|\right) \left\|\widehat{\beta} - \beta\right\| + \left(\frac{1}{n}\sum_{i=1}^{n} \|X_i\|^4\right) \left\|\widehat{\beta} - \beta\right\|^2 \\ &= o_p(1). \end{aligned} \tag{7.23}$$

The expression is $o_p(1)$, because $\left\|\widehat{\beta}-\beta\right\| \underset{p}{\longrightarrow} 0$ and both averages in parenthesis are averages of random variables with finite expectation under Assumption 7.2 (and are thus $O_p(1)$). Indeed, by Hölder's inequality (B.31)

$$\mathbb{E}\left[\|X\|^3 |e|\right] \le \left(\mathbb{E}\left[\left(\|X\|^3\right)^{4/3}\right]\right)^{3/4} \left(\mathbb{E}\left[e^4\right]\right)^{1/4} = \left(\mathbb{E}\|X\|^4\right)^{3/4} \left(\mathbb{E}\left[e^4\right]\right)^{1/4} < \infty.$$

We have established (7.20), as desired.

Theorem 7.6 Under Assumption 7.2, as $n \to \infty$, $\widehat{\Omega} \underset{p}{\longrightarrow} \Omega$ and $\widehat{\boldsymbol{V}}_{\beta}^{\mathrm{HC0}} \underset{p}{\longrightarrow} \boldsymbol{V}_{\beta}$.

For an alternative proof of this result, see Section 7.20.

7.8 SUMMARY OF COVARIANCE MATRIX NOTATION

The notation we have introduced may be somewhat confusing, so it is helpful to write it down in one place.

The exact variance of $\widehat{\beta}$ (under the assumptions of the linear regression model) and the asymptotic variance of $\sqrt{n}\,(\widehat{\beta}-\beta)$ (under the more general assumptions of the linear projection model) are

$$\boldsymbol{V}_{\widehat{\beta}} = \operatorname{var}\left[\widehat{\beta} \mid \boldsymbol{X}\right] = \left(\boldsymbol{X}'\boldsymbol{X}\right)^{-1}\left(\boldsymbol{X}'\boldsymbol{D}\boldsymbol{X}\right)\left(\boldsymbol{X}'\boldsymbol{X}\right)^{-1}$$
$$\boldsymbol{V}_{\beta} = \operatorname{avar}\left[\sqrt{n}\,(\widehat{\beta}-\beta)\right] = \boldsymbol{Q}_{XX}^{-1}\Omega\boldsymbol{Q}_{XX}^{-1}.$$

The HC0 estimators of these two covariance matrices are

$$\widehat{\boldsymbol{V}}_{\widehat{\beta}}^{\mathrm{HC0}} = \left(\boldsymbol{X}'\boldsymbol{X}\right)^{-1}\left(\sum_{i=1}^{n} X_i X_i' \widehat{e}_i^2\right)\left(\boldsymbol{X}'\boldsymbol{X}\right)^{-1}$$
$$\widehat{\boldsymbol{V}}_{\beta}^{\mathrm{HC0}} = \widehat{\boldsymbol{Q}}_{XX}^{-1}\widehat{\Omega}\widehat{\boldsymbol{Q}}_{XX}^{-1}$$

and satisfy the simple relationship $\widehat{\boldsymbol{V}}_{\beta}^{\mathrm{HC0}} = n\widehat{\boldsymbol{V}}_{\widehat{\beta}}^{\mathrm{HC0}}$.

Similarly, under the assumption of homoskedasticity, the exact and asymptotic variances simplify to

$$\boldsymbol{V}_{\widehat{\beta}}^{0} = \left(\boldsymbol{X}'\boldsymbol{X}\right)^{-1}\sigma^2$$
$$\boldsymbol{V}_{\beta}^{0} = \boldsymbol{Q}_{XX}^{-1}\sigma^2.$$

Their standard estimators are

$$\widehat{\boldsymbol{V}}_{\widehat{\beta}}^{0} = \left(\boldsymbol{X}'\boldsymbol{X}\right)^{-1}s^2$$
$$\widehat{\boldsymbol{V}}_{\beta}^{0} = \widehat{\boldsymbol{Q}}_{XX}^{-1}s^2$$

which also satisfy the relationship $\widehat{\boldsymbol{V}}_{\beta}^{0} = n\widehat{\boldsymbol{V}}_{\widehat{\beta}}^{0}$.

The exact formula and estimators are useful when constructing test statistics and standard errors. However, for theoretical purposes, the asymptotic formula (variances and their estimates) are more useful as these retain nondegenerate limits as the sample sizes diverge. That is why both sets of notation are useful.

7.9 ALTERNATIVE COVARIANCE MATRIX ESTIMATORS*

Section 7.7 introduced $\widehat{V}_{\beta}^{\mathrm{HC0}}$ as an estimator of V_{β}. $\widehat{V}_{\beta}^{\mathrm{HC0}}$ is a scaled version of $\widehat{V}_{\widehat{\beta}}^{\mathrm{HC0}}$ from Section 4.14, where we also introduced the alternative HC1, HC2, and HC3 heteroskedasticity-robust covariance matrix estimators. We now discuss the consistency properties of these estimators.

To do so, we introduce their scaled versions, that is, $\widehat{V}_{\beta}^{\mathrm{HC1}} = n\widehat{V}_{\widehat{\beta}}^{\mathrm{HC1}}$, $\widehat{V}_{\beta}^{\mathrm{HC2}} = n\widehat{V}_{\widehat{\beta}}^{\mathrm{HC2}}$, and $\widehat{V}_{\beta}^{\mathrm{HC3}} = n\widehat{V}_{\widehat{\beta}}^{\mathrm{HC3}}$. These are (alternative) estimators of the asymptotic covariance matrix V_{β}.

First, consider $\widehat{V}_{\beta}^{\mathrm{HC1}}$. Notice that $\widehat{V}_{\beta}^{\mathrm{HC1}} = n\widehat{V}_{\widehat{\beta}}^{\mathrm{HC1}} = \frac{n}{n-k}\widehat{V}_{\beta}^{\mathrm{HC0}}$, where $\widehat{V}_{\beta}^{\mathrm{HC0}}$ was defined in (7.19) and shown to be consistent for V_{β} in Theorem 7.6. If k is fixed as $n \to \infty$, then $\frac{n}{n-k} \to 1$, and thus

$$\widehat{V}_{\beta}^{\mathrm{HC1}} = (1+o(1))\widehat{V}_{\beta}^{\mathrm{HC0}} \underset{p}{\longrightarrow} V_{\beta}.$$

Thus, $\widehat{V}_{\beta}^{\mathrm{HC1}}$ is consistent for V_{β}.

The alternative estimators $\widehat{V}_{\beta}^{\mathrm{HC2}}$ and $\widehat{V}_{\beta}^{\mathrm{HC3}}$ take the form (7.19) but with $\widehat{\Omega}$ replaced by

$$\widetilde{\Omega} = \frac{1}{n}\sum_{i=1}^{n}(1-h_{ii})^{-2} X_i X_i' \widehat{e}_i^2$$

and

$$\overline{\Omega} = \frac{1}{n}\sum_{i=1}^{n}(1-h_{ii})^{-1} X_i X_i' \widehat{e}_i^2,$$

respectively. To show that these estimators also consistent for V_{β} given $\widehat{\Omega} \underset{p}{\longrightarrow} \Omega$, it is sufficient to show that the differences $\widetilde{\Omega} - \widehat{\Omega}$ and $\overline{\Omega} - \widehat{\Omega}$ converge in probability to 0 as $n \to \infty$.

The trick is to use the fact that the leverage values are asymptotically negligible:

$$h_n^* = \max_{1\le i\le n} h_{ii} = o_p(1). \tag{7.24}$$

(See Theorem 7.17 in Section 7.21.) Then using the triangle inequality (B.16),

$$\begin{aligned}\left\|\overline{\Omega} - \widehat{\Omega}\right\| &\le \frac{1}{n}\sum_{i=1}^{n}\left\|X_i X_i'\right\| \widehat{e}_i^2 \left|(1-h_{ii})^{-1} - 1\right| \\ &\le \left(\frac{1}{n}\sum_{i=1}^{n}\|X_i\|^2 \widehat{e}_i^2\right)\left|\left(1-h_n^*\right)^{-1} - 1\right|.\end{aligned}$$

The sum in parenthesis can be shown to be $O_p(1)$ under Assumption 7.2 by the same argument as in the proof of Theorem 7.6. (In fact, it can be shown to converge in probability to $\mathbb{E}\left[\|X\|^2 e^2\right]$.) The term in absolute values is $o_p(1)$ by (7.24). Thus the product is $o_p(1)$, which means that $\overline{\Omega} = \widehat{\Omega} + o_p(1) \underset{p}{\longrightarrow} \Omega$.

Similarly,

$$\begin{aligned}\left\|\widetilde{\Omega} - \widehat{\Omega}\right\| &\le \frac{1}{n}\sum_{i=1}^{n}\left\|X_i X_i'\right\| \widehat{e}_i^2 \left|(1-h_{ii})^{-2} - 1\right| \\ &\le \left(\frac{1}{n}\sum_{i=1}^{n}\|X_i\|^2 \widehat{e}_i^2\right)\left|\left(1-h_n^*\right)^{-2} - 1\right| \\ &= o_p(1).\end{aligned}$$

Theorem 7.7 Under Assumption 7.2, as $n \to \infty$, $\widetilde{\Omega} \underset{p}{\longrightarrow} \Omega$, $\overline{\Omega} \underset{p}{\longrightarrow} \Omega$, $\widehat{\boldsymbol{V}}_{\beta}^{\mathrm{HC1}} \underset{p}{\longrightarrow} \boldsymbol{V}_{\beta}$, $\widehat{\boldsymbol{V}}_{\beta}^{\mathrm{HC2}} \underset{p}{\longrightarrow} \boldsymbol{V}_{\beta}$, and $\widehat{\boldsymbol{V}}_{\beta}^{\mathrm{HC3}} \underset{p}{\longrightarrow} \boldsymbol{V}_{\beta}$.

Theorem 7.7 shows that the alternative covariance matrix estimators are also consistent for the asymptotic covariance matrix.

To simplify notation, for the remainder of the chapter, let us use the notation $\widehat{\boldsymbol{V}}_{\beta}$ and $\widehat{\boldsymbol{V}}_{\widehat{\beta}}$ to refer to any of the heteroskedasticity-consistent covariance matrix estimators HC0, HC1, HC2, and HC3, as they all have the same asymptotic limits.

7.10 FUNCTIONS OF PARAMETERS

In most serious applications, a researcher is actually interested in a specific transformation of the coefficient vector $\beta = (\beta_1, \ldots, \beta_k)$. For example, the researcher may be interested in a single coefficient β_j or a ratio β_j/β_l. More generally, interest may focus on a quantity such as consumer surplus, which could be a complicated function of the coefficients. In any of these cases, we can write the parameter of interest θ as a function of the coefficients, for example, $\theta = r(\beta)$ for some function $r : \mathbb{R}^k \to \mathbb{R}^q$. The estimate of θ is

$$\widehat{\theta} = r(\widehat{\beta}).$$

By the continuous mapping theorem (Theorem 6.6) and the fact $\widehat{\beta} \underset{p}{\longrightarrow} \beta$, we can deduce that $\widehat{\theta}$ is consistent for θ if the function $r(\cdot)$ is continuous.

Theorem 7.8 Under Assumption 7.1, if $r(\beta)$ is continuous at the true value of β, then as $n \to \infty$, $\widehat{\theta} \underset{p}{\longrightarrow} \theta$.

Furthermore, if the transformation is sufficiently smooth, by the Delta Method (Theorem 6.8), we can show that $\widehat{\theta}$ is asymptotically normal.

Assumption 7.3 $r(\beta) : \mathbb{R}^k \to \mathbb{R}^q$ is continuously differentiable at the true value of β, and $\boldsymbol{R} = \frac{\partial}{\partial \beta} r(\beta)'$ has rank q.

Theorem 7.9 Asymptotic Distribution of Functions of Parameters
Under Assumptions 7.2 and 7.3, as $n \to \infty$,

$$\sqrt{n}\left(\widehat{\theta} - \theta\right) \underset{d}{\longrightarrow} \mathrm{N}\left(0, \boldsymbol{V}_{\theta}\right) \tag{7.25}$$

where $\boldsymbol{V}_{\theta} = \boldsymbol{R}' \boldsymbol{V}_{\beta} \boldsymbol{R}$.

In many cases, the function $r(\beta)$ is linear:

$$r(\beta) = \boldsymbol{R}'\beta$$

for some $k \times q$ matrix $\boldsymbol{R}$. In particular, if $\boldsymbol{R}$ is a "selector matrix"

$$\boldsymbol{R} = \begin{pmatrix} \boldsymbol{I} \\ 0 \end{pmatrix}$$

then we can partition $\beta = (\beta_1', \beta_2')'$ so that $\boldsymbol{R}'\beta = \beta_1$. Then

$$\boldsymbol{V}_{\boldsymbol{\theta}} = \begin{pmatrix} \boldsymbol{I} & 0 \end{pmatrix} \boldsymbol{V}_\beta \begin{pmatrix} \boldsymbol{I} \\ 0 \end{pmatrix} = \boldsymbol{V}_{11},$$

the upper-left sub-matrix of $\boldsymbol{V}_{11}$ given in (7.14). In this case, (7.25) states that

$$\sqrt{n}\left(\widehat{\beta}_1 - \beta_1\right) \underset{d}{\longrightarrow} \mathrm{N}\left(0, \boldsymbol{V}_{11}\right).$$

That is, subsets of $\widehat{\beta}$ are approximately normal with variances given by the conformable subcomponents of $\boldsymbol{V}$.

To illustrate the case of a nonlinear transformation, take the example $\theta = \beta_j/\beta_l$ for $j \neq l$. Then

$$\boldsymbol{R} = \frac{\partial}{\partial\beta} r(\beta) = \begin{pmatrix} \frac{\partial}{\partial\beta_1}\left(\beta_j/\beta_l\right) \\ \vdots \\ \frac{\partial}{\partial\beta_j}\left(\beta_j/\beta_l\right) \\ \vdots \\ \frac{\partial}{\partial\beta_\ell}\left(\beta_j/\beta_l\right) \\ \vdots \\ \frac{\partial}{\partial\beta_k}\left(\beta_j/\beta_l\right) \end{pmatrix} = \begin{pmatrix} 0 \\ \vdots \\ 1/\beta_l \\ \vdots \\ -\beta_j/\beta_l^2 \\ \vdots \\ 0 \end{pmatrix} \tag{7.26}$$

so

$$\boldsymbol{V}_\theta = \boldsymbol{V}_{jj}/\beta_l^2 + \boldsymbol{V}_{ll}\beta_j^2/\beta_l^4 - 2\boldsymbol{V}_{jl}\beta_j/\beta_l^3$$

where $\boldsymbol{V}_{ab}$ denotes the abth element of $\boldsymbol{V}_\beta$.

For inference, we need an estimator of the asymptotic covariance matrix $\boldsymbol{V}_\theta = \boldsymbol{R}'\boldsymbol{V}_\beta\boldsymbol{R}$. It is typical to use the plug-in estimator

$$\widehat{\boldsymbol{R}} = \frac{\partial}{\partial\beta} r(\widehat{\beta})'. \tag{7.27}$$

The derivative in (7.27) may be calculated analytically or numerically. By "analytically," we mean working out the formula for the derivative and replacing the unknowns by point estimates. For example, if $\theta = \beta_j/\beta_l$, then $\frac{\partial}{\partial\beta} r(\beta)$ is (7.26). However, in some cases, the function $r(\beta)$ may be extremely complicated, and a formula for the analytic derivative may not be easily available. In this case, numerical differentiation may be preferable. Let $\delta_l = (0 \ \cdots \ 1 \ \cdots \ 0)'$ be the unit vector with the "1" in the lth place. The jlth element of a numerical derivative $\widehat{\boldsymbol{R}}$ is

$$\widehat{\boldsymbol{R}}_{jl} = \frac{r_j(\widehat{\beta} + \delta_l\epsilon) - r_j(\widehat{\beta})}{\epsilon}$$

for some small ϵ.

The estimator of $\boldsymbol{V}_\theta$ is

$$\widehat{\boldsymbol{V}}_\theta = \widehat{\boldsymbol{R}}'\widehat{\boldsymbol{V}}_\beta\widehat{\boldsymbol{R}}. \tag{7.28}$$

Alternatively, the homoskedastic covariance matrix estimator could be used, leading to a homoskedastic covariance matrix estimator for θ:

$$\widehat{\boldsymbol{V}}_\theta^0 = \widehat{\boldsymbol{R}}'\widehat{\boldsymbol{V}}_\beta^0\widehat{\boldsymbol{R}} = \widehat{\boldsymbol{R}}'\widehat{\boldsymbol{Q}}_{XX}^{-1}\widehat{\boldsymbol{R}}s^2. \tag{7.29}$$

Given (7.27), equations (7.28) and (7.29) are simple to calculate using matrix operations.

As the primary justification for $\widehat{\boldsymbol{V}}_\theta$ is the asymptotic approximation (7.25), $\widehat{\boldsymbol{V}}_\theta$ is often called an **asymptotic covariance matrix estimator**. The estimator $\widehat{\boldsymbol{V}}_\theta$ is consistent for $\boldsymbol{V}_\theta$ under the conditions of Theorem 7.9, because $\widehat{\boldsymbol{V}}_\beta \underset{p}{\longrightarrow} \boldsymbol{V}_\beta$ by Theorem 7.6, and

$$\widehat{\boldsymbol{R}} = \frac{\partial}{\partial\beta} r(\widehat{\beta})' \underset{p}{\longrightarrow} \frac{\partial}{\partial\beta} r(\beta)' = \boldsymbol{R}$$

because $\widehat{\beta} \underset{p}{\longrightarrow} \beta$ and the function $\frac{\partial}{\partial\beta} r(\beta)'$ is continuous in β.

Theorem 7.10 Under Assumptions 7.2 and 7.3, as $n \to \infty$, $\widehat{\boldsymbol{V}}_\theta \underset{p}{\longrightarrow} \boldsymbol{V}_\theta$.

Theorem 7.10 shows that $\widehat{\boldsymbol{V}}_\theta$ is consistent for $\boldsymbol{V}_\theta$ and thus may be used for asymptotic inference. In practice, we may set

$$\widehat{\boldsymbol{V}}_{\widehat{\theta}} = \widehat{\boldsymbol{R}}'\widehat{\boldsymbol{V}}_{\widehat{\beta}}\widehat{\boldsymbol{R}} = n^{-1}\widehat{\boldsymbol{R}}'\widehat{\boldsymbol{V}}_\beta\widehat{\boldsymbol{R}} \tag{7.30}$$

as an estimator of the variance of $\widehat{\theta}$.

7.11 ASYMPTOTIC STANDARD ERRORS

As described in Section 4.15, a standard error is an estimator of the standard deviation of the distribution of an estimator. Thus if $\widehat{\boldsymbol{V}}_{\widehat{\beta}}$ is an estimator of the covariance matrix of $\widehat{\beta}$, then the standard errors are the square roots of the diagonal elements of this matrix. These take the form

$$s(\widehat{\beta}_j) = \sqrt{\widehat{\boldsymbol{V}}_{\widehat{\beta}_j}} = \sqrt{\left[\widehat{\boldsymbol{V}}_{\widehat{\beta}}\right]_{jj}}.$$

Standard errors for $\widehat{\theta}$ are constructed similarly. Supposing that $\theta = h(\beta)$ is real-valued, then the standard error for $\widehat{\theta}$ is the square root of (7.30):

$$s(\widehat{\theta}) = \sqrt{\widehat{\boldsymbol{R}}'\widehat{\boldsymbol{V}}_{\widehat{\beta}}\widehat{\boldsymbol{R}}} = \sqrt{n^{-1}\widehat{\boldsymbol{R}}'\widehat{\boldsymbol{V}}_\beta\widehat{\boldsymbol{R}}}.$$

When the justification is based on asymptotic theory, we call $s(\widehat{\beta}_j)$ or $s(\widehat{\theta})$ an **asymptotic standard error** for $\widehat{\beta}_j$ or $\widehat{\theta}$. When reporting your results, it is good practice to report standard errors for each reported estimate, and this includes functions and transformations of your parameter estimates. To do so helps users of the work (including yourself) assess the estimation precision.

We illustrate using the log wage regression

$$\log(wage) = \beta_1\ education + \beta_2\ experience + \beta_3\ experience^2/100 + \beta_4 + e.$$

Consider the following three parameters of interest.

1. Percentage return to education:

$$\theta_1 = 100\beta_1$$

(100 times the partial derivative of the conditional expectation of log(wage) with respect to education.)

2. Percentage return to experience for individuals with 10 years of experience:

$$\theta_2 = 100\beta_2 + 20\beta_3$$

(100 times the partial derivative of the conditional expectation of log wages with respect to experience, evaluated at experience = 10.)

3. Experience level that maximizes expected log wages:

$$\theta_3 = -50\beta_2/\beta_3$$

(The level of experience at which the partial derivative of the conditional expectation of log(wage) with respect to experience equals 0.)

The 4×1 vector $\boldsymbol{R}$ for these three parameters is

$$\boldsymbol{R} = \begin{pmatrix} 100 \\ 0 \\ 0 \\ 0 \end{pmatrix}, \quad \begin{pmatrix} 0 \\ 100 \\ 20 \\ 0 \end{pmatrix}, \quad \begin{pmatrix} 0 \\ -50/\beta_3 \\ 50\beta_2/\beta_3^2 \\ 0 \end{pmatrix},$$

respectively.

We use the subsample of married Black women (all experience levels), which has 982 observations. The point estimates and standard errors are

$$\widehat{\log(wage)} = \underset{(0.008)}{0.118}\ education + \underset{(0.006)}{0.016}\ experience - \underset{(0.012)}{0.022}\ experience^2/100 + \underset{(0.157)}{0.947}. \tag{7.31}$$

The standard errors are the square roots of the HC2 covariance matrix estimate:

$$\overline{\boldsymbol{V}}_{\widehat{\beta}} = \begin{pmatrix} 0.632 & 0.131 & -0.143 & -11.1 \\ 0.131 & 0.390 & -0.731 & -6.25 \\ -0.143 & -0.731 & 1.48 & 9.43 \\ -11.1 & -6.25 & 9.43 & 246 \end{pmatrix} \times 10^{-4}. \tag{7.32}$$

We calculate that

$$\widehat{\theta}_1 = 100\widehat{\beta}_1 = 100 \times 0.118 = 11.8$$

$$s(\widehat{\theta}_1) = \sqrt{100^2 \times 0.632 \times 10^{-4}} = 0.8$$

$$\widehat{\theta}_2 = 100\widehat{\beta}_2 + 20\widehat{\beta}_3 = 100 \times 0.016 - 20 \times 0.022 = 1.16$$

$$s(\widehat{\theta}_2) = \sqrt{\begin{pmatrix} 100 & 20 \end{pmatrix} \begin{pmatrix} 0.390 & -0.731 \\ -0.731 & 1.48 \end{pmatrix} \begin{pmatrix} 100 \\ 20 \end{pmatrix} \times 10^{-4}} = 0.55$$

$$\widehat{\theta}_3 = -50\widehat{\beta}_2/\widehat{\beta}_3 = 50 \times 0.016/0.022 = 35.2$$

$$s(\widehat{\theta}_3) = \sqrt{\begin{pmatrix} -50/\widehat{\beta}_3 & 50\widehat{\beta}_2/\widehat{\beta}_3^2 \end{pmatrix} \begin{pmatrix} 0.390 & -0.731 \\ -0.731 & 1.48 \end{pmatrix} \begin{pmatrix} -50/\widehat{\beta}_3 \\ 50\widehat{\beta}_2/\widehat{\beta}_3^2 \end{pmatrix} \times 10^{-4}} = 7.0.$$

The calculations show that the estimate of the percentage return to education is 12% per year with a standard error of 0.8. The estimate of the percentage return to experience for those with 10 years of experience is 1.2% per year with a standard error of 0.6. The estimate of the experience level that maximizes expected log wages is 35 years with a standard error of 7.

In Stata, the `nlcom` command can be used after estimation to perform the same calculations. To illustrate, after estimation of (7.31), use the commands given below. In each case, Stata reports the coefficient estimate, asymptotic standard error, and 95% confidence interval.

Stata Commands

```
nlcom 100*_b[education]
nlcom 100*_b[experience]+20*_b[exp2]
nlcom -50*_b[experience]/_b[exp2]
```

7.12 *t*-STATISTIC

Let $\theta = r(\beta) : \mathbb{R}^k \to \mathbb{R}$ be a parameter of interest, $\widehat{\theta}$ its estimator, and $s(\widehat{\theta})$ its asymptotic standard error. Consider the statistic

$$T(\theta) = \frac{\widehat{\theta} - \theta}{s(\widehat{\theta})}. \tag{7.33}$$

Different writers call (7.33) a ***t*-statistic**, a ***t*-ratio**, a ***z*-statistic**, or a **studentized statistic**, sometimes using the different labels to distinguish between finite-sample and asymptotic inference. As the statistics themselves are always (7.33) we won't make this distinction and will simply refer to $T(\theta)$ as a t-statistic or a t-ratio. We also often suppress the parameter dependence, writing it as T. The t-statistic is a function of the estimator, its standard error, and the parameter.

By Theorems 7.9 and 7.10, $\sqrt{n}\left(\widehat{\theta} - \theta\right) \underset{d}{\longrightarrow} \mathrm{N}\left(0, V_\theta\right)$, and $\widehat{V}_\theta \underset{p}{\longrightarrow} V_\theta$. Thus

$$\begin{aligned} T(\theta) &= \frac{\widehat{\theta} - \theta}{s(\widehat{\theta})} \\ &= \frac{\sqrt{n}\left(\widehat{\theta} - \theta\right)}{\sqrt{\widehat{V}_\theta}} \\ &\underset{d}{\longrightarrow} \frac{\mathrm{N}\left(0, V_\theta\right)}{\sqrt{V_\theta}} \\ &= Z \sim \mathrm{N}\left(0, 1\right). \end{aligned}$$

The last equality is the property that affine functions of normal variables are normal (Theorem 5.2).

This calculation requires that $V_\theta > 0$; otherwise, the Continuous Mapping Theorem cannot be employed. In practice, this requirement is innocuous, as it only excludes degenerate sampling distributions. Formally, we add the following assumption.

Assumption 7.4 $\boldsymbol{V}_\theta = \boldsymbol{R}'\boldsymbol{V}_\beta \boldsymbol{R} > 0.$

Assumption 7.4 states that $\boldsymbol{V}_\theta$ is positive definite. Since $\boldsymbol{R}$ is full rank under Assumption 7.3, a sufficient condition is that $\boldsymbol{V}_\beta > 0$. Since $\boldsymbol{Q}_{XX} > 0$, a sufficient condition is $\Omega > 0$. Thus Assumption 7.4 could be replaced by the assumption $\Omega > 0$. Assumption 7.4 is weaker, so this is what we use.

Thus the asymptotic distribution of the t-ratio $T(\theta)$ is standard normal. Since this distribution does not depend on the parameters, we say that $T(\theta)$ is **asymptotically pivotal**. In finite samples, $T(\theta)$ is not necessarily pivotal, but the property means that the dependence on unknowns diminishes as n increases.

It is also useful to consider the distribution of the **absolute *t*-ratio** $|T(\theta)|$. Since $T(\theta) \underset{d}{\longrightarrow} Z$, the Continuous Mapping Theorem yields $|T(\theta)| \underset{d}{\longrightarrow} |Z|$. Letting $\Phi(u) = \mathbb{P}[Z \le u]$ denote the standard normal distribution function, we calculate that the distribution of $|Z|$ is

$$\begin{aligned}
\mathbb{P}[|Z| \le u] &= \mathbb{P}[-u \le Z \le u] \\
&= \mathbb{P}[Z \le u] - \mathbb{P}[Z < -u] \\
&= \Phi(u) - \Phi(-u) \\
&= 2\Phi(u) - 1. \qquad (7.34)
\end{aligned}$$

Theorem 7.11 Under Assumptions 7.2, 7.3, and 7.4, $T(\theta) \underset{d}{\longrightarrow} Z \sim \mathrm{N}(0,1)$, and $|T(\theta)| \underset{d}{\longrightarrow} |Z|$.

The asymptotic normality of Theorem 7.11 is used to justify confidence intervals and tests for the parameters.

7.13 CONFIDENCE INTERVALS

The estimator $\widehat{\theta}$ is a **point estimator** for θ, meaning that $\widehat{\theta}$ is a single value in $\mathbb{R}^q$. A broader concept is a **set estimator** $\widehat{C}$, which is a collection of values in $\mathbb{R}^q$. When the parameter θ is real-valued, then it is common to focus on sets of the form $\widehat{C} = [\widehat{L}, \widehat{U}]$, which is called an **interval estimator** for θ.

An interval estimator $\widehat{C}$ is a function of the data and hence is random. The **coverage probability** of the interval $\widehat{C} = [\widehat{L}, \widehat{U}]$ is $\mathbb{P}\left[\theta \in \widehat{C}\right]$. The randomness comes from $\widehat{C}$, as the parameter θ is treated as fixed. In Section 5.10, we introduced confidence intervals for the normal regression model, which used the finite sample distribution of the t-statistic. When we are outside the normal regression model, we cannot rely on the exact normal distribution theory but instead often use asymptotic approximations. A benefit is that we can construct confidence intervals for general parameters of interest θ, not just regression coefficients.

An interval estimator $\widehat{C}$ is called a **confidence interval** when the goal is to set the coverage probability to equal a pre-specified target, such as 90% or 95%. $\widehat{C}$ is called a $1-\alpha$ confidence interval if $\inf_\theta \mathbb{P}_\theta\left[\theta \in \widehat{C}\right] = 1 - \alpha$.

When $\widehat{\theta}$ is asymptotically normal with standard error $s(\widehat{\theta})$, the conventional confidence interval for θ takes the form

$$\widehat{C} = \left[\widehat{\theta} - c \times s(\widehat{\theta}), \quad \widehat{\theta} + c \times s(\widehat{\theta})\right] \tag{7.35}$$

where c equals the $1-\alpha$ quantile of the distribution of $|Z|$. Using (7.34), we calculate that c is equivalently the $1-\alpha/2$ quantile of the standard normal distribution. Thus, c solves

$$2\Phi(c) - 1 = 1 - \alpha.$$

This can be computed by, for example, `norminv(1-α/2)` in MATLAB. The confidence interval (7.35) is symmetric about the point estimator $\widehat{\theta}$, and its length is proportional to the standard error $s(\widehat{\theta})$.

Equivalently, (7.35) is the set of parameter values for θ such that the t-statistic $T(\theta)$ is smaller (in absolute value) than c; that is,

$$\widehat{C} = \{\theta : |T(\theta)| \le c\} = \left\{\theta : -c \le \frac{\widehat{\theta} - \theta}{s(\widehat{\theta})} \le c\right\}.$$

The coverage probability of this confidence interval is

$$\mathbb{P}\left[\theta \in \widehat{C}\right] = \mathbb{P}\left[|T(\theta)| \le c\right] \to \mathbb{P}\left[|Z| \le c\right] = 1 - \alpha$$

where the limit is taken as $n \to \infty$, and it holds because $T(\theta)$ is asymptotically $|Z|$ by Theorem 7.11. We call the limit the **asymptotic coverage probability** and call $\widehat{C}$ an asymptotic $1-\alpha\%$ confidence interval for θ. Since the t-ratio is asymptotically pivotal, the asymptotic coverage probability is independent of the parameter θ.

It is useful to contrast the confidence interval (7.35) with (5.8) for the normal regression model. They are similar, but there are differences. The normal regression interval (5.8) only applies to regression coefficients β, not to functions θ of the coefficients. The normal interval (5.8) also is constructed with the homoskedastic standard error, while (7.35) can be constructed with a heteroskedastic-robust standard error. Furthermore, the constants c in (5.8) are calculated using the student t distribution, while c values in (7.35) are calculated using the normal distribution. The difference between the student t and normal values are typically small in practice (since sample sizes are large in typical economic applications). However, since the student t values are larger, it results in slightly larger confidence intervals, which is reasonable. (A practical rule of thumb is that if the sample sizes are sufficiently small that it makes a difference, then neither (5.8) nor (7.35) should be trusted.) Despite these differences, the coincidence of the intervals means that inference on regression coefficients is generally robust to using either the exact normal sampling assumption or the asymptotic large-sample approximation, at least in large samples.

Stata by default reports 95% confidence intervals for each coefficient, where the critical values c are calculated using the t_{n-k} distribution. This is done for all standard error methods, even though it is only exact for homoskedastic standard errors and under normality.

The standard coverage probability for confidence intervals is 95%, leading to the choice $c = 1.96$ for the constant in (7.35). Rounding 1.96 to 2, we obtain the most commonly used confidence interval in applied econometric practice:

$$\widehat{C} = \left[\widehat{\theta} - 2s(\widehat{\theta}), \quad \widehat{\theta} + 2s(\widehat{\theta})\right].$$

This is a useful rule-of thumb. This asymptotic 95% confidence interval $\widehat{C}$ is simple to compute and can be roughly calculated from tables of coefficient estimates and standard errors. (Technically, it is an asymptotic 95.4% interval, due to the substitution of 2.0 for 1.96, but this distinction is overly precise.)

Theorem 7.12 Under Assumptions 7.2, 7.3, and 7.4, for $\widehat{C}$ defined in (7.35) with $c = \Phi^{-1}(1-\alpha/2)$, $\mathbb{P}\left[\theta \in \widehat{C}\right] \to 1-\alpha$. For $c = 1.96$, $\mathbb{P}\left[\theta \in \widehat{C}\right] \to 0.95$.

Confidence intervals are a simple yet effective tool to assess estimation uncertainty. When reading a set of empirical results, look at the estimated coefficient estimates and the standard errors. For a parameter of interest, compute the confidence interval $\widehat{C}$, and consider the meaning of the spread of the suggested values. If the range of values in the confidence interval is too wide to learn about θ, then do not jump to a conclusion about θ based on the point estimate alone.

For illustration, consider the three examples presented in Section 7.11 based on the log wage regression for married Black women.

1. Percentage return to education. A 95% asymptotic confidence interval is $11.8 \pm 1.96 \times 0.8 = [10.2, 13.3]$. This is reasonably tight.
2. Percentage return to experience (per year) for individuals with 10 years experience. A 90% asymptotic confidence interval is $1.1 \pm 1.645 \times 0.4 = [0.5, 1.8]$. The interval is positive but broad. This indicates that the return to experience is positive, but of uncertain magnitude.
3. Experience level, which maximizes expected log wages. An 80% asymptotic confidence interval is $35 \pm 1.28 \times 7 = [26, 44]$. This is rather imprecise, indicating that the estimates are not very informative regarding this parameter.

7.14 REGRESSION INTERVALS

In the linear regression model, the conditional expectation of Y given $X = x$ is

$$m(x) = \mathbb{E}\left[Y \mid X = x\right] = x'\beta.$$

In some cases, we want to estimate $m(x)$ at a particular point x. Notice that this is a linear function of β. Letting $r(\beta) = x'\beta$ and $\theta = r(\beta)$, we see that $\widehat{m}(x) = \widehat{\theta} = x'\widehat{\beta}$ and $\boldsymbol{R} = x$, so $s(\widehat{\theta}) = \sqrt{x'\widehat{\boldsymbol{V}}_{\widehat{\beta}}x}$. Thus an asymptotic 95% confidence interval for $m(x)$ is

$$\left[x'\widehat{\beta} \pm 1.96\sqrt{x'\widehat{\boldsymbol{V}}_{\widehat{\beta}}x}\right].$$

It is interesting to observe that if this is viewed as a function of x, the width of the confidence interval is dependent on x.

To illustrate, let us return to the log wage regression (3.12) of Section 3.7. The estimated regression equation is

$$\widehat{\log(wage)} = x'\widehat{\beta} = 0.155x + 0.698$$

where $x = education$. The covariance matrix estimate from (4.40) is

$$\widehat{\boldsymbol{V}}_{\widehat{\beta}} = \begin{pmatrix} 0.001 & -0.015 \\ -0.015 & 0.243 \end{pmatrix}.$$

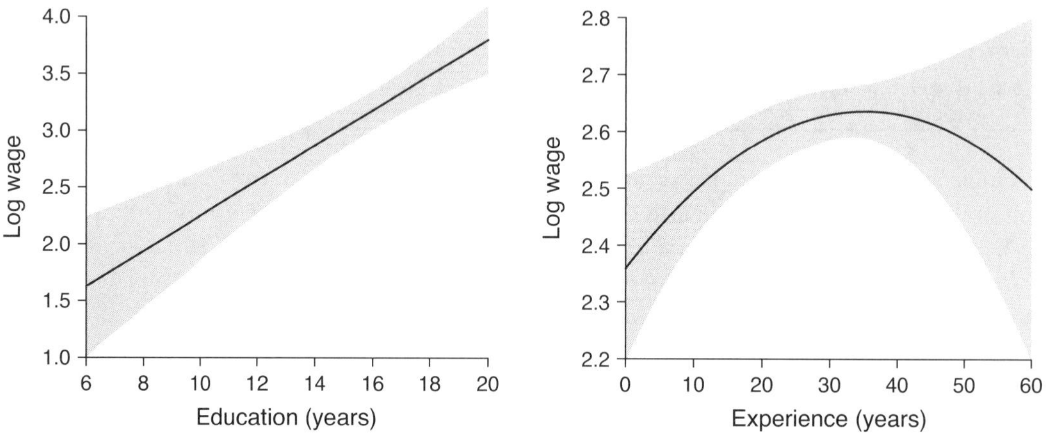

(a) Wage on education (b) Wage on experience

FIGURE 7.4 Regression intervals

Thus the 95% confidence interval for the regression is

$$0.155x + 0.698 \pm 1.96\sqrt{0.001x^2 - 0.030x + 0.243}.$$

The estimated regression and 95% intervals are shown in Figure 7.4(a). Notice that the confidence bands take a hyperbolic shape, which means that the regression line is less precisely estimated for large and small values of *education*.

Plots of the estimated regression line and confidence intervals are especially useful when the regression includes nonlinear terms. To illustrate, consider the log wage regression (7.31), which includes experience and its square, and covariance matrix estimate (7.32). We are interested in plotting the regression estimate and regression intervals as a function of *experience*. Since the regression also includes *education*, to plot the estimates in a simple graph, we fix *education* at a specific value: *education* = 12. This only affects the level of the estimated regression, since *education* enters without an interaction. Define the points of evaluation:

$$z(x) = \begin{pmatrix} 12 \\ x \\ x^2/100 \\ 1 \end{pmatrix}$$

where $x = experience$.

The 95% regression interval for *education* = 12 as a function of $x = experience$ is

$$\begin{aligned} & 0.118 \times 12 + 0.016\,x - 0.022\,x^2/100 + 0.947 \\ & \pm 1.96 \sqrt{z(x)' \begin{pmatrix} 0.632 & 0.131 & -0.143 & -11.1 \\ 0.131 & 0.390 & -0.731 & -6.25 \\ -0.143 & -0.731 & 1.48 & 9.43 \\ -11.1 & -6.25 & 9.43 & 246 \end{pmatrix} z(x) \times 10^{-4}} \\ & = 0.016\,x - .00022\,x^2 + 2.36 \\ & \pm 0.0196\sqrt{70.608 - 9.356\,x + 0.54428\,x^2 - 0.01462\,x^3 + 0.000148\,x^4}. \end{aligned}$$

The estimated regression and 95% intervals are shown in Figure 7.4(b). The regression interval widens greatly for small and large values of experience, indicating considerable uncertainty about the effect of experience on mean wages for this population. The confidence bands take a more complicated shape than in Figure 7.4(a) due to the nonlinear specification.

7.15 FORECAST INTERVALS

Suppose we are given a value of the regressor vector X_{n+1} for an individual outside the sample, and we want to forecast (guess) Y_{n+1} for this individual. This is equivalent to forecasting Y_{n+1} given $X_{n+1}=x$, which will generally be a function of x. A reasonable forecasting rule is the conditional expectation $m(x)$, as it is the mean-square minimizing forecast. A point forecast is the estimated conditional expectation $\widehat{m}(x)=x'\widehat{\beta}$. We would also like a measure of uncertainty for the forecast.

The forecast error is $\widehat{e}_{n+1}=Y_{n+1}-\widehat{m}(x)=e_{n+1}-x'\left(\widehat{\beta}-\beta\right)$. As the out-of-sample error e_{n+1} is independent of the in-sample estimator $\widehat{\beta}$, this has conditional variance

$$
\begin{aligned}
\mathbb{E}\left[\widehat{e}_{n+1}^2 \mid X_{n+1}=x\right] &= \mathbb{E}\left[e_{n+1}^2-2x'\left(\widehat{\beta}-\beta\right)e_{n+1}+x'\left(\widehat{\beta}-\beta\right)\left(\widehat{\beta}-\beta\right)'x \mid X_{n+1}=x\right] \\
&= \mathbb{E}\left[e_{n+1}^2 \mid X_{n+1}=x\right]+x'\mathbb{E}\left[\left(\widehat{\beta}-\beta\right)\left(\widehat{\beta}-\beta\right)'\right]x \\
&= \sigma^2(x)+x'\boldsymbol{V}_{\widehat{\beta}}x. \qquad (7.36)
\end{aligned}
$$

Under homoskedasticity, $\mathbb{E}\left[e_{n+1}^2 \mid X_{n+1}\right]=\sigma^2$. In this case, a simple estimator of (7.36) is $\widehat{\sigma}^2+x'\boldsymbol{V}_{\widehat{\beta}}x$, so a standard error for the forecast is $\widehat{s}(x)=\sqrt{\widehat{\sigma}^2+x'\boldsymbol{V}_{\widehat{\beta}}x}$. Notice that this is different from the standard error for the conditional expectation.

The conventional 95% forecast interval for Y_{n+1} uses a normal approximation and equals $\left[x'\widehat{\beta}\pm 2\widehat{s}(x)\right]$. It is difficult, however, to fully justify this choice. It would be correct if we have a normal approximation to the ratio

$$
\frac{e_{n+1}-x'\left(\widehat{\beta}-\beta\right)}{\widehat{s}(x)}.
$$

The difficulty is that the equation error e_{n+1} is generally non-normal, and asymptotic theory cannot be applied to a single observation. The only special exception is the case where e_{n+1} has the exact distribution $\mathrm{N}(0,\sigma^2)$, which is generally invalid.

An accurate forecast interval would use the conditional distribution of e_{n+1} given $X_{n+1}=x$, which is more challenging to estimate. Due to this difficulty, many applied forecasters use the simple approximate interval $\left[x'\widehat{\beta}\pm 2\widehat{s}(x)\right]$, despite the lack of a convincing justification.

7.16 WALD STATISTIC

Let $\theta=r(\beta):\mathbb{R}^k\rightarrow\mathbb{R}^q$ be any parameter vector of interest, $\widehat{\theta}$ its estimator, and $\widehat{\boldsymbol{V}}_{\widehat{\theta}}$ its covariance matrix estimator. Consider the quadratic form

$$
W(\theta)=\left(\widehat{\theta}-\theta\right)'\widehat{\boldsymbol{V}}_{\widehat{\theta}}^{-1}\left(\widehat{\theta}-\theta\right)=n\left(\widehat{\theta}-\theta\right)'\widehat{\boldsymbol{V}}_{\theta}^{-1}\left(\widehat{\theta}-\theta\right) \qquad (7.37)
$$

where $\widehat{\boldsymbol{V}}_{\theta}=n\widehat{\boldsymbol{V}}_{\widehat{\theta}}$. When $q=1$, then $W(\theta)=T(\theta)^2$ is the square of the t-ratio. When $q>1$, $W(\theta)$ is typically called a **Wald statistic**, as it was proposed by Wald (1943). We are interested in its sampling distribution.

The asymptotic distribution of $W(\theta)$ is simple to derive, given Theorem 7.9 and Theorem 7.10. They show that $\sqrt{n}\left(\widehat{\theta}-\theta\right) \underset{d}{\longrightarrow} Z \sim \mathrm{N}\left(0, \boldsymbol{V}_{\theta}\right)$, and $\widehat{\boldsymbol{V}}_{\theta} \underset{p}{\longrightarrow} \boldsymbol{V}_{\theta}$. It follows that

$$W(\theta)=\sqrt{n}\left(\widehat{\theta}-\theta\right)' \widehat{\boldsymbol{V}}_{\theta}^{-1} \sqrt{n}\left(\widehat{\theta}-\theta\right) \underset{d}{\longrightarrow} Z' \boldsymbol{V}_{\theta}^{-1} Z$$

which is a quadratic in the normal random vector Z. As shown in Theorem 5.3.5, the distribution of this quadratic form is χ_q^2, a chi-square random variable with q degrees of freedom.

Theorem 7.13 Under Assumptions 7.2, 7.3, and 7.4, as $n \rightarrow \infty$, $W(\theta) \underset{d}{\longrightarrow} \chi_q^2$.

Theorem 7.13 is used to justify multivariate confidence regions and multivariate hypothesis tests.

7.17 HOMOSKEDASTIC WALD STATISTIC

Under the conditional homoskedasticity assumption $\mathbb{E}\left[e^2 \mid X\right]=\sigma^2$, we can construct the Wald statistic using the homoskedastic covariance matrix estimator $\widehat{\boldsymbol{V}}_{\theta}^{0}$ defined in (7.29). This yields a homoskedastic Wald statistic:

$$W^0(\theta)=\left(\widehat{\theta}-\theta\right)'\left(\widehat{\boldsymbol{V}}_{\widehat{\theta}}^{0}\right)^{-1}\left(\widehat{\theta}-\theta\right)=n\left(\widehat{\theta}-\theta\right)'\left(\widehat{\boldsymbol{V}}_{\theta}^{0}\right)^{-1}\left(\widehat{\theta}-\theta\right). \tag{7.38}$$

Under the assumption of conditional homoskedasticity, it has the same asymptotic distribution as $W(\theta)$.

Theorem 7.14 Under Assumptions 7.2, 7.3, and $\mathbb{E}\left[e^2 \mid X\right]=\sigma^2>0$, as $n \rightarrow \infty$, $W^0(\theta) \underset{d}{\longrightarrow} \chi_q^2$.

7.18 CONFIDENCE REGIONS

A confidence region $\widehat{C}$ is a set estimator for $\theta \in \mathbb{R}^q$ when $q>1$. A confidence region $\widehat{C}$ is a set in $\mathbb{R}^q$ intended to cover the true parameter value with a pre-selected probability $1-\alpha$. Thus an ideal confidence region has the coverage probability $\mathbb{P}\left[\theta \in \widehat{C}\right]=1-\alpha$. In practice, it is typically not possible to construct a region with exact coverage, but we can calculate its asymptotic coverage.

When the parameter estimator satisfies the conditions of Theorem 7.13, a good choice for a confidence region is the ellipse

$$\widehat{C}=\left\{\theta: W(\theta) \leq c_{1-\alpha}\right\}$$

with $c_{1-\alpha}$ the $1-\alpha$ quantile of the χ_q^2 distribution. (Thus $F_q(c_{1-\alpha})=1-\alpha$.) It can be computed by, for example, `chi2inv(1-α,q)` in MATLAB.

Theorem 7.13 implies that

$$\mathbb{P}\left[\theta \in \widehat{C}\right] \rightarrow \mathbb{P}\left[\chi_q^2 \leq c_{1-\alpha}\right]=1-\alpha$$

which shows that $\widehat{C}$ has asymptotic coverage $1-\alpha$.

To illustrate the construction of a confidence region, consider the estimated regression (7.31) of

$$\widehat{\log(wage)} = \beta_1 \, education + \beta_2 \, experience + \beta_3 \, experience^2/100 + \beta_4.$$

Suppose that the two parameters of interest are the percentage return to education, $\theta_1 = 100\beta_1$, and the percentage return to experience for individuals with 10 years of experience, $\theta_2 = 100\beta_2 + 20\beta_3$. These two parameters are a linear transformation of the regression parameters with point estimates:

$$\widehat{\theta} = \begin{pmatrix} 100 & 0 & 0 & 0 \\ 0 & 100 & 20 & 0 \end{pmatrix} \widehat{\beta} = \begin{pmatrix} 11.8 \\ 1.2 \end{pmatrix}$$

and they have the covariance matrix estimate

$$\widehat{\boldsymbol{V}}_{\widehat{\theta}} = \begin{pmatrix} 0 & 100 & 0 & 0 \\ 0 & 0 & 100 & 20 \end{pmatrix} \widehat{\boldsymbol{V}}_{\widehat{\beta}} \begin{pmatrix} 0 & 0 \\ 100 & 0 \\ 0 & 100 \\ 0 & 20 \end{pmatrix} = \begin{pmatrix} 0.632 & 0.103 \\ 0.103 & 0.157 \end{pmatrix}$$

with inverse

$$\widehat{\boldsymbol{V}}_{\widehat{\theta}}^{-1} = \begin{pmatrix} 1.77 & -1.16 \\ -1.16 & 7.13 \end{pmatrix}.$$

Thus the Wald statistic is

$$\begin{aligned} W(\theta) &= \left(\widehat{\theta} - \theta\right)' \widehat{\boldsymbol{V}}_{\widehat{\theta}}^{-1} \left(\widehat{\theta} - \theta\right) \\ &= \begin{pmatrix} 11.8 - \theta_1 \\ 1.2 - \theta_2 \end{pmatrix}' \begin{pmatrix} 1.77 & -1.16 \\ -1.16 & 7.13 \end{pmatrix} \begin{pmatrix} 11.8 - \theta_1 \\ 1.2 - \theta_2 \end{pmatrix} \\ &= 1.77\,(11.8 - \theta_1)^2 - 2.32\,(11.8 - \theta_1)\,(1.2 - \theta_2) + 7.13\,(1.2 - \theta_2)^2. \end{aligned}$$

The 90% quantile of the χ_2^2 distribution is 4.605 (we use the χ_2^2 distribution, because the dimension of θ is 2), so an asymptotic 90% confidence region for the two parameters is the interior of the ellipse $W(\theta) = 4.605$, which is displayed in Figure 7.5. Since the estimated correlation of the two coefficient estimates is modest (about 0.3), the region is modestly elliptical.

7.19 EDGEWORTH EXPANSION*

Theorem 7.11 showed that the t-ratio $T(\theta)$ is asymptotically normal. In practice, this means that we can use the normal distribution to approximate the finite sample distribution of T. How good is this approximation? Some insight into the accuracy of the normal approximation can be obtained by an Edgeworth expansion, which is a higher-order approximation to the distribution of T. The following result is an application of Theorem 9.11 from *Probability and Statistics for Economists.*

Theorem 7.15 Assume Assumptions 7.2, 7.3, $\Omega > 0$, $\mathbb{E}\,\|e\|^{16} < \infty$, $\mathbb{E}\,\|X\|^{16} < \infty$, $g(\beta)$ has five continuous derivatives in a neighborhood of β, and $\mathbb{E}\left[\exp\left(t\left(\|e\|^4 + \|X\|^4\right)\right)\right] \le B < 1$, then as $n \to \infty$,

$$\mathbb{P}\left[T(\theta) \le x\right] = \Phi(x) + n^{-1/2} p_1(x)\phi(x) + n^{-1} p_2(x)\phi(x) + o\left(n^{-1}\right)$$

uniformly in x, where $p_1(x)$ is an even polynomial of order 2, and $p_2(x)$ is an odd polynomial of degree 5 with coefficients depending on the moments of e and X up to order 16.

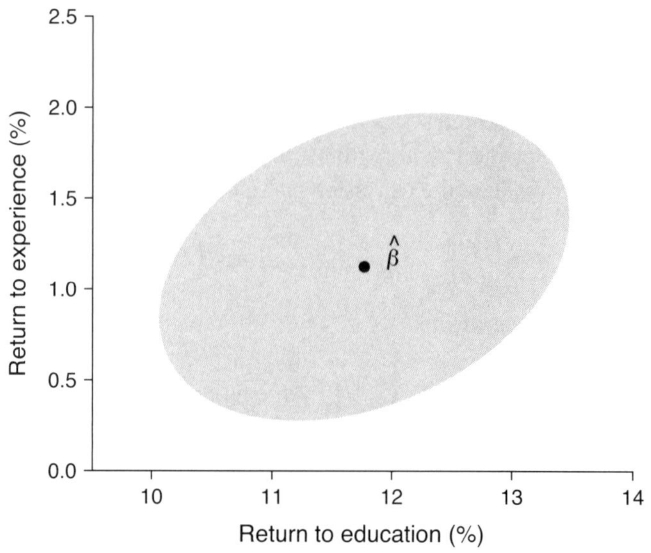

FIGURE 7.5 Confidence region for return to experience and return to education

Theorem 7.15 shows that the finite sample distribution of the t-ratio can be approximated up to $o(n^{-1})$ by the sum of three terms, the first being the standard normal distribution, the second a $O\left(n^{-1/2}\right)$ adjustment, and the third a $O\left(n^{-1}\right)$ adjustment.

Consider a one-sided confidence interval $\widehat{C} = \left[\widehat{\theta} - z_{1-\alpha} s(\widehat{\theta}), \infty\right)$, where $z_{1-\alpha}$ is the $1-\alpha$th quantile of $Z \sim \mathrm{N}(0,1)$, so that $\Phi(z_{1-\alpha}) - 1 - \alpha$. Then

$$\begin{aligned}\mathbb{P}\left[\theta \in \widehat{C}\right] &= \mathbb{P}\left[T(\theta) \leq z_{1-\alpha}\right] \\ &= \Phi(z_{1-\alpha}) + n^{-1/2} p_1(z_{1-\alpha})\phi(z_{1-\alpha}) + O\left(n^{-1}\right) \\ &= 1 - \alpha + O\left(n^{-1/2}\right).\end{aligned}$$

Thus the actual coverage is within $O\left(n^{-1/2}\right)$ of the desired $1-\alpha$ level.

Now consider a two-sided interval $\widehat{C} = \left[\widehat{\theta} - z_{1-\alpha/2} s(\widehat{\theta}), \widehat{\theta} + z_{1-\alpha/2} s(\widehat{\theta})\right]$. It has coverage

$$\begin{aligned}\mathbb{P}\left[\theta \in \widehat{C}\right] &= \mathbb{P}\left[|T(\theta)| \leq z_{1-\alpha/2}\right] \\ &= 2\Phi(z_{1-\alpha/2}) - 1 + n^{-1} 2 p_2(z_{1-\alpha/2})\phi(z_{1-\alpha/2}) + o\left(n^{-1}\right) \\ &= 1 - \alpha + O\left(n^{-1}\right).\end{aligned}$$

Thus the actual coverage is within $O\left(n^{-1}\right)$ of the desired $1-\alpha$ level. The accuracy is better than the one-sided interval, because the $O\left(n^{-1/2}\right)$ term in the Edgeworth expansion has offsetting effects in the two tails of the distribution.

7.20 UNIFORMLY CONSISTENT RESIDUALS*

It seems natural to view the residuals $\widehat{e}_i$ as estimators of the unknown errors e_i. Are they consistent? In this section, we develop a convergence result.

We can write the residual as

$$\widehat{e}_i = Y_i - X_i'\widehat{\beta} = e_i - X_i'\left(\widehat{\beta} - \beta\right). \tag{7.39}$$

Since $\widehat{\beta} - \beta \underset{p}{\longrightarrow} 0$, it seems reasonable to guess that $\widehat{e}_i$ will be close to e_i if n is large.

We can bound the difference in (7.39) by using the Schwarz inequality (B.12) to find

$$\left|\widehat{e}_i - e_i\right| = \left|X_i'\left(\widehat{\beta} - \beta\right)\right| \le \|X_i\| \left\|\widehat{\beta} - \beta\right\|. \tag{7.40}$$

To bound (7.40), we can use $\left\|\widehat{\beta} - \beta\right\| = O_p\left(n^{-1/2}\right)$ from Theorem 7.3. We also need to bound the random variable $\|X_i\|$. If the regressor is bounded (that is, $\|X_i\| \le B < \infty$), then $\left|\widehat{e}_i - e_i\right| \le B\left\|\widehat{\beta} - \beta\right\| = O_p\left(n^{-1/2}\right)$. However if the regressor does not have bounded support, then we have to be more careful.

The key is Theorem 6.15, which shows that $\mathbb{E}\|X\|^r < \infty$ implies $X_i = o_p\left(n^{1/r}\right)$ uniformly in i, or

$$n^{-1/r} \max_{1\le i\le n} \|X_i\| \underset{p}{\longrightarrow} 0.$$

Applied to (7.40), we obtain

$$\max_{1\le i\le n} \left|\widehat{e}_i - e_i\right| \le \max_{1\le i\le n} \|X_i\| \left\|\widehat{\beta} - \beta\right\| = o_p\left(n^{-1/2+1/r}\right).$$

We have shown the following.

Theorem 7.16 Under Assumption 7.2 and $\mathbb{E}\|X\|^r < \infty$,

$$\max_{1\le i\le n} \left|\widehat{e}_i - e_i\right| = o_p\left(n^{-1/2+1/r}\right). \tag{7.41}$$

The rate of convergence in (7.41) depends on r. Assumption 7.2 requires $r \ge 4$, so the rate of convergence is at least $o_p\left(n^{-1/4}\right)$. As r increases, the rate improves.

We mentioned in Section 7.7 that there are multiple ways to prove the consistency of the covariance matrix estimator $\widehat{\Omega}$. We now show that Theorem 7.16 provides one simple method to establish (7.23) and thus Theorem 7.6. Let $q_n = \max_{1\le i\le n}\left|\widehat{e}_i - e_i\right| = o_p\left(n^{-1/4}\right)$. Since $\widehat{e}_i^2 - e_i^2 = 2e_i\left(\widehat{e}_i - e_i\right) + \left(\widehat{e}_i - e_i\right)^2$, then

$$\begin{aligned}
\left\|\frac{1}{n}\sum_{i=1}^n X_iX_i'\left(\widehat{e}_i^2 - e_i^2\right)\right\| &\le \frac{1}{n}\sum_{i=1}^n \left\|X_iX_i'\right\| \left|\widehat{e}_i^2 - e_i^2\right| \\
&\le \frac{2}{n}\sum_{i=1}^n \|X_i\|^2 |e_i| \left|\widehat{e}_i - e_i\right| + \frac{1}{n}\sum_{i=1}^n \|X_i\|^2 \left|\widehat{e}_i - e_i\right|^2 \\
&\le \frac{2}{n}\sum_{i=1}^n \|X_i\|^2 |e_i| q_n + \frac{1}{n}\sum_{i=1}^n \|X_i\|^2 q_n^2 \\
&\le o_p\left(n^{-1/4}\right).
\end{aligned}$$

7.21 ASYMPTOTIC LEVERAGE*

Recall the definition of leverage from (3.40): $h_{ii} = X_i' \left(\boldsymbol{X}'\boldsymbol{X}\right)^{-1} X_i$. These are the diagonal elements of the projection matrix $\boldsymbol{P}$ and appear in the formula for leave-one-out prediction errors and HC2 and HC3 covariance matrix estimators. We can show that under i.i.d. sampling, the leverage values are uniformly asymptotically small.

Let $\lambda_{\min}(\boldsymbol{A})$ and $\lambda_{\max}(\boldsymbol{A})$ denote the smallest and largest eigenvalues, respectively, of a symmetric square matrix $\boldsymbol{A}$, and note that $\lambda_{\max}(\boldsymbol{A}^{-1}) = (\lambda_{\min}(\boldsymbol{A}))^{-1}$.

Since $\frac{1}{n}\boldsymbol{X}'\boldsymbol{X} \underset{p}{\longrightarrow} \boldsymbol{Q}_{XX} > 0$, by the CMT, $\lambda_{\min}\left(\frac{1}{n}\boldsymbol{X}'\boldsymbol{X}\right) \underset{p}{\longrightarrow} \lambda_{\min}\left(\boldsymbol{Q}_{XX}\right) > 0$. (The latter is positive, since $\boldsymbol{Q}_{XX}$ is positive definite and thus all its eigenvalues are positive.) Then by the Quadratic Inequality (B.18),

$$\begin{aligned} h_{ii} &= X_i' \left(\boldsymbol{X}'\boldsymbol{X}\right)^{-1} X_i \\ &\le \lambda_{\max}\left(\left(\boldsymbol{X}'\boldsymbol{X}\right)^{-1}\right)\left(X_i'X_i\right) \\ &= \left(\lambda_{\min}\left(\frac{1}{n}\boldsymbol{X}'\boldsymbol{X}\right)\right)^{-1} \frac{1}{n}\|X_i\|^2 \\ &\le \left(\lambda_{\min}\left(\boldsymbol{Q}_{XX}\right) + o_p(1)\right)^{-1} \frac{1}{n} \max_{1\le i\le n} \|X_i\|^2. \end{aligned} \tag{7.42}$$

Theorem 6.15 shows that $\mathbb{E}\|X\|^r < \infty$ implies $\max_{1\le i\le n}\|X_i\|^2 = \left(\max_{1\le i\le n}\|X_i\|\right)^2 = o_p\left(n^{2/r}\right)$, and thus (7.42) is $o_p\left(n^{2/r-1}\right)$.

Theorem 7.17 If X_i is i.i.d., $\boldsymbol{Q}_{XX} > 0$, and $\mathbb{E}\|X\|^r < \infty$ for some $r \ge 2$, then $\max_{1\le i\le n} h_{ii} = o_p\left(n^{2/r-1}\right)$.

For any $r \ge 2$, then $h_{ii} = o_p(1)$ (uniformly in $i \le n$). Larger r implies a faster rate of convergence. For example, $r = 4$ implies $h_{ii} = o_p\left(n^{-1/2}\right)$. Theorem (7.17) implies that under random sampling with finite variances and large samples, no individual observation should have a large leverage value. Consequently, individual observations should not be influential, unless one of these conditions is violated.

7.22 EXERCISES

Exercise 7.1 Take the model $Y = X_1'\beta_1 + X_2'\beta_2 + e$ with $\mathbb{E}[Xe] = 0$. Suppose that β_1 is estimated by regressing Y on X_1 only. Find the probability limit of this estimator. In general, is it consistent for β_1? If not, under what conditions is this estimator consistent for β_1?

Exercise 7.2 Take the model $Y = X'\beta + e$ with $\mathbb{E}[Xe] = 0$. Define the **ridge regression** estimator

$$\widehat{\beta} = \left(\sum_{i=1}^n X_iX_i' + \lambda \boldsymbol{I}_k\right)^{-1}\left(\sum_{i=1}^n X_iY_i\right) \tag{7.43}$$

where $\lambda > 0$ is a fixed constant. Find the probability limit of $\widehat{\beta}$ as $n \to \infty$. Is $\widehat{\beta}$ consistent for β?

Exercise 7.3 For the ridge regression estimator (7.43), set $\lambda = cn$, where $c > 0$ is fixed as $n \to \infty$. Find the probability limit of $\widehat{\beta}$ as $n \to \infty$.

Exercise 7.4 Verify some of the calculations reported in Section 7.4. Specifically, suppose that X_1 and X_2 only take the values $\{-1, +1\}$, symmetrically, with

$$\begin{aligned}
\mathbb{P}[X_1 = X_2 = 1] = \mathbb{P}[X_1 = X_2 = -1] &= 3/8 \\
\mathbb{P}[X_1 = 1, X_2 = -1] = \mathbb{P}[X_1 = -1, X_2 = 1] &= 1/8 \\
\mathbb{E}\left[e^2 \mid X_1 = X_2\right] &= \frac{5}{4} \\
\mathbb{E}\left[e^2 \mid X_1 \neq X_2\right] &= \frac{1}{4}.
\end{aligned}$$

Verify the following:

(a) $\mathbb{E}[X_1] = 0$

(b) $\mathbb{E}\left[X_1^2\right] = 1$

(c) $\mathbb{E}[X_1 X_2] = \frac{1}{2}$

(d) $\mathbb{E}\left[e^2\right] = 1$

(e) $\mathbb{E}\left[X_1^2 e^2\right] = 1$

(f) $\mathbb{E}\left[X_1 X_2 e^2\right] = \frac{7}{8}$.

Exercise 7.5 Show (7.13)–(7.16).

Exercise 7.6 The model is

$$\begin{aligned}
Y &= X'\beta + e \\
\mathbb{E}[Xe] &= 0 \\
\Omega &= \mathbb{E}\left[XX'e^2\right].
\end{aligned}$$

Find the method of moments estimators $(\widehat{\beta}, \widehat{\Omega})$ for (β, Ω).

Exercise 7.7 Of the variables (Y^*, Y, X), only the pair (Y, X) are observed. In this case, we say that Y^* is a **latent variable**. Suppose

$$\begin{aligned}
Y^* &= X'\beta + e \\
\mathbb{E}[Xe] &= 0 \\
Y &= Y^* + u
\end{aligned}$$

where u is a measurement error satisfying

$$\begin{aligned}
\mathbb{E}[Xu] &= 0 \\
\mathbb{E}\left[Y^* u\right] &= 0.
\end{aligned}$$

Let $\widehat{\beta}$ denote the OLS coefficient from the regression of Y on X.

(a) Is β the coefficient from the linear projection of Y on X?

(b) Is $\widehat{\beta}$ consistent for β as $n \to \infty$?

(c) Find the asymptotic distribution of $\sqrt{n}\left(\widehat{\beta}-\beta\right)$ as $n \to \infty$.

Exercise 7.8 Find the asymptotic distribution of $\sqrt{n}\left(\widehat{\sigma}^2-\sigma^2\right)$ as $n \to \infty$.

Exercise 7.9 The model is $Y = X\beta + e$ with $\mathbb{E}[e \mid X] = 0$ and $X \in \mathbb{R}$. Consider the two estimators

$$\widehat{\beta} = \frac{\sum_{i=1}^n X_i Y_i}{\sum_{i=1}^n X_i^2}$$

$$\widetilde{\beta} = \frac{1}{n}\sum_{i=1}^n \frac{Y_i}{X_i}.$$

(a) Under the stated assumptions, are both estimators consistent for β?

(b) Are there conditions under which either estimator is efficient?

Exercise 7.10 In the homoskedastic regression model $Y = X'\beta + e$ with $\mathbb{E}[e \mid x] = 0$ and $\mathbb{E}\left[e^2 \mid X\right] = \sigma^2$, suppose $\widehat{\beta}$ is the OLS estimator of β with covariance matrix estimator $\widehat{\boldsymbol{V}}_{\widehat{\beta}}$ based on a sample of size n. Let $\widehat{\sigma}^2$ be the estimator of σ^2. You wish to forecast an out-of-sample value of Y_{n+1}, given that $X_{n+1} = x$. Thus the available information is the sample, the estimates $(\widehat{\beta}, \widehat{\boldsymbol{V}}_{\widehat{\beta}}, \widehat{\sigma}^2)$, the residuals $\widehat{e}_i$, and the out-of-sample value of the regressors X_{n+1}.

(a) Find a point forecast of Y_{n+1}.

(b) Find an estimator of the variance of this forecast.

Exercise 7.11 Take a regression model with i.i.d. observations (Y_i, X_i) with $X \in \mathbb{R}$:

$$Y = X\beta + e$$

$$\mathbb{E}[e \mid X] = 0$$

$$\Omega = \mathbb{E}\left[X^2 e^2\right].$$

Let $\widehat{\beta}$ be the OLS estimator of β with residuals $\widehat{e}_i = Y_i - X_i\widehat{\beta}$. Consider the estimators of Ω:

$$\widetilde{\Omega} = \frac{1}{n}\sum_{i=1}^n X_i^2 e_i^2$$

$$\widehat{\Omega} = \frac{1}{n}\sum_{i=1}^n X_i^2 \widehat{e}_i^2.$$

(a) Find the asymptotic distribution of $\sqrt{n}\left(\widetilde{\Omega}-\Omega\right)$ as $n \to \infty$.

(b) Find the asymptotic distribution of $\sqrt{n}\left(\widehat{\Omega}-\Omega\right)$ as $n \to \infty$.

(c) How do you use the regression assumption $\mathbb{E}[e \mid X] = 0$ in your answer to (b)?

Exercise 7.12 Consider the model

$$Y = \alpha + \beta X + e$$
$$\mathbb{E}[e] = 0$$
$$\mathbb{E}[Xe] = 0$$

with both Y and X scalar. Assuming $\alpha > 0$ and $\beta < 0$, suppose the parameter of interest is the area under the regression curve (e.g., consumer surplus), which is $A = -\alpha^2/2\beta$. Let $\widehat{\theta} = (\widehat{\alpha}, \widehat{\beta})'$ be the least squares estimators of $\theta = (\alpha, \beta)'$, so that $\sqrt{n}\left(\widehat{\theta} - \theta\right) \to_d N(0, \boldsymbol{V}_\theta)$, and let $\widehat{\boldsymbol{V}}_\theta$ be a standard estimator for $\boldsymbol{V}_\theta$.

(a) Describe an estimator of A.

(b) Construct an asymptotic $1 - \eta$ confidence interval for A.

Exercise 7.13 Consider an i.i.d. sample $\{Y_i, X_i\}$ $i = 1, \ldots, n$, where Y and X are scalar. Consider the reverse projection model $X = Y\gamma + u$ with $\mathbb{E}[Yu] = 0$, and define the parameter of interest as $\theta = 1/\gamma$.

(a) Propose an estimator $\widehat{\gamma}$ of γ.

(b) Propose an estimator $\widehat{\theta}$ of θ.

(c) Find the asymptotic distribution of $\widehat{\theta}$.

(d) Find an asymptotic standard error for $\widehat{\theta}$.

Exercise 7.14 Take the model

$$Y = X_1\beta_1 + X_2\beta_2 + e$$
$$\mathbb{E}[Xe] = 0$$

with both $\beta_1 \in \mathbb{R}$ and $\beta_2 \in \mathbb{R}$, and define the parameter $\theta = \beta_1\beta_2$.

(a) What is the appropriate estimator $\widehat{\theta}$ for θ?

(b) Find the asymptotic distribution of $\widehat{\theta}$ under standard regularity conditions.

(c) Show how to calculate an asymptotic 95% confidence interval for θ.

Exercise 7.15 Take the linear model $Y = X\beta + e$ with $\mathbb{E}[e \mid X] = 0$ and $X \in \mathbb{R}$. Consider the estimator

$$\widehat{\beta} = \frac{\sum_{i=1}^n X_i^3 Y_i}{\sum_{i=1}^n X_i^4}.$$

Find the asymptotic distribution of $\sqrt{n}\left(\widehat{\beta} - \beta\right)$ as $n \to \infty$.

Exercise 7.16 From an i.i.d. sample (Y_i, X_i) of size n, you randomly take half the observations. You estimate a least squares regression of Y on X using only this subsample. Is the estimated slope coefficient $\widehat{\beta}$ consistent for the population projection coefficient? Explain your reasoning.

Exercise 7.17 An economist reports a set of parameter estimates, including the coefficient estimates $\widehat{\beta}_1 = 1.0$, $\widehat{\beta}_2 = 0.8$, and standard errors $s(\widehat{\beta}_1) = 0.07$ and $s(\widehat{\beta}_2) = 0.07$. The author writes: "The estimates show that β_1 is larger than β_2."

(a) Write down the formula for an asymptotic 95% confidence interval for $\theta = \beta_1 - \beta_2$, expressed as a function of $\widehat{\beta}_1$, $\widehat{\beta}_2$, $s(\widehat{\beta}_1)$, $s(\widehat{\beta}_2)$, and $\widehat{\rho}$, where $\widehat{\rho}$ is the estimated correlation between $\widehat{\beta}_1$ and $\widehat{\beta}_2$.

(b) Can $\widehat{\rho}$ be calculated from the reported information?

(c) Is the author correct? Does the reported information support the author's claim?

Exercise 7.18 Suppose an economic model suggests

$$m(x) = \mathbb{E}[Y \mid X = x] = \beta_0 + \beta_1 x + \beta_2 x^2$$

where $X \in \mathbb{R}$. You have a random sample (Y_i, X_i), $i = 1, \ldots, n$.

(a) Describe how to estimate $m(x)$ at a given value x.

(b) Describe (be specific) an appropriate confidence interval for $m(x)$.

Exercise 7.19 Take the model $Y = X'\beta + e$ with $\mathbb{E}[Xe] = 0$, and suppose you have observations $i = 1, \ldots, 2n$. (The number of observations is $2n$.) You randomly split the sample in half (each half has n observations), calculate $\widehat{\beta}_1$ by least squares on the first sample, and $\widehat{\beta}_2$ by least squares on the second sample. What is the asymptotic distribution of $\sqrt{n}\left(\widehat{\beta}_1 - \widehat{\beta}_2\right)$?

Exercise 7.20 The variables $\{Y_i, X_i, W_i\}$ are a random sample. The parameter β is estimated by minimizing the criterion function

$$S(\beta) = \sum_{i=1}^{n} W_i \left(Y_i - X_i'\beta\right)^2.$$

That is $\widehat{\beta} = \operatorname{argmin}_\beta S(\beta)$.

(a) Find an explicit expression for $\widehat{\beta}$.

(b) What population parameter β is $\widehat{\beta}$ estimating? Be explicit about any assumptions you need to impose. Do not make more assumptions than necessary.

(c) Find the probability limit for $\widehat{\beta}$ as $n \to \infty$.

(d) Find the asymptotic distribution of $\sqrt{n}\left(\widehat{\beta} - \beta\right)$ as $n \to \infty$.

Exercise 7.21 Take the model

$$Y = X'\beta + e$$
$$\mathbb{E}[e \mid X] = 0$$
$$\mathbb{E}\left[e^2 \mid X\right] = Z'\gamma$$

where Z is a (vector) function of X. The sample is $i = 1, \ldots, n$ with i.i.d. observations. Assume that $Z'\gamma > 0$ for all Z. Suppose you want to forecast Y_{n+1} given $X_{n+1} = x$ and $Z_{n+1} = z$ for an out-of-sample observation $n + 1$. Describe how you would construct a point forecast and a forecast interval for Y_{n+1}.

Exercise 7.22 Take the model

$$Y = X'\beta + e$$
$$\mathbb{E}[e \mid X] = 0$$

$$Z = X'\beta\gamma + u$$
$$\mathbb{E}[u \mid X] = 0$$

where X is a k-vector and Z is scalar. Your goal is to estimate the scalar parameter γ. You use a two-step estimator:

- Estimate $\widehat{\beta}$ by least squares of Y on X.
- Estimate $\widehat{\gamma}$ by least squares of Z on $X'\widehat{\beta}$.

(a) Show that $\widehat{\gamma}$ is consistent for γ.

(b) Find the asymptotic distribution of $\widehat{\gamma}$ when $\gamma = 0$.

Exercise 7.23 The model is $Y = X + e$ with $\mathbb{E}[e \mid X] = 0$ and $X \in \mathbb{R}$. Consider the estimator

$$\widetilde{\beta} = \frac{1}{n}\sum_{i=1}^{n}\frac{Y_i}{X_i}.$$

Find conditions under which $\widetilde{\beta}$ is consistent for β as $n \to \infty$.

Exercise 7.24 The parameter β is defined in the model $Y = X^*\beta + e$, where e is independent of $X^* \geq 0$, $\mathbb{E}[e] = 0$, $\mathbb{E}\left[e^2\right] = \sigma^2$. The observables are (Y, X), where $X = X^* v$, and $v > 0$ is a random scale measurement error, independent of X^* and e. Consider the least squares estimator $\widehat{\beta}$ for β.

(a) Find the plim of $\widehat{\beta}$ expressed in terms of β and moments of (X, v, e).

(b) Can you find a nontrivial condition under which $\widehat{\beta}$ is consistent for β? (By nontrivial is meant something other than $v = 1$.)

Exercise 7.25 Take the projection model $Y = X'\beta + e$ with $\mathbb{E}[Xe] = 0$. For a positive function $w(x)$, let $W_i = w(X_i)$. Consider the estimator

$$\widetilde{\beta} = \left(\sum_{i=1}^{n} W_i X_i X_i'\right)^{-1}\left(\sum_{i=1}^{n} W_i X_i Y_i\right).$$

Find the probability limit (as $n \to \infty$) of $\widetilde{\beta}$. Do you need to add an assumption? Is $\widetilde{\beta}$ consistent for $\widetilde{\beta}$? If not, under what assumption is $\widetilde{\beta}$ consistent for β?

Exercise 7.26 Take the regression model

$$Y = X'\beta + e$$
$$\mathbb{E}[e \mid X] = 0$$
$$\mathbb{E}\left[e^2 \mid X = x\right] = \sigma^2(x)$$

with $X \in \mathbb{R}^k$. Assume that $\mathbb{P}[e = 0] = 0$. Consider the infeasible estimator

$$\widetilde{\beta} = \left(\sum_{i=1}^{n} e_i^{-2} X_i X_i'\right)^{-1}\left(\sum_{i=1}^{n} e_i^{-2} X_i Y_i\right).$$

This is a weighted least squares estimator using the weights e_i^{-2}.

(a) Find the asymptotic distribution of $\widetilde{\beta}$.

(b) Contrast your result with the asymptotic distribution of infeasible GLS.

Exercise 7.27 The model is $Y = X'\beta + e$ with $\mathbb{E}[e \mid X] = 0$. An econometrician is worried about the impact of some unusually large values of the regressors. The model is thus estimated on the subsample for which $|X_i| \le c$ for some fixed c. Let $\widetilde{\beta}$ denote the OLS estimator on this subsample. It equals

$$\widetilde{\beta} = \left(\sum_{i=1}^{n} X_i X_i' \mathbb{1}\{|X_i| \le c\} \right)^{-1} \left(\sum_{i=1}^{n} X_i Y_i \mathbb{1}\{|X_i| \le c\} \right).$$

(a) Show that $\widetilde{\beta} \underset{p}{\longrightarrow} \beta$.

(b) Find the asymptotic distribution of $\sqrt{n}\left(\widetilde{\beta} - \beta\right)$.

Exercise 7.28 As in Exercise 3.26, use the `cps09mar` dataset and the subsample of white male Hispanics. Estimate the regression

$$\widehat{\log(wage)} = \beta_1\, education + \beta_2\, experience + \beta_3\, experience^2/100 + \beta_4.$$

(a) Report the coefficient estimates and robust standard errors.

(b) Let θ be the ratio of the return to 1 year of education to the return to 1 year of experience for $experience = 10$. Write θ as a function of the regression coefficients and variables. Compute $\widehat{\theta}$ from the estimated model.

(c) Write out the formula for the asymptotic standard error for $\widehat{\theta}$ as a function of the covariance matrix for $\widehat{\beta}$. Compute $s(\widehat{\theta})$ from the estimated model.

(d) Construct a 90% asymptotic confidence interval for θ from the estimated model.

(e) Compute the regression function at $education = 12$ and $experience = 20$. Compute a 95% confidence interval for the regression function at this point.

(f) Consider an out-of-sample individual with 16 years of education and 5 years of experience. Construct an 80% forecast interval for their log wage and wage. (To obtain the forecast interval for the wage, apply the exponential function to both endpoints.)

CHAPTER 8
RESTRICTED ESTIMATION

8.1 INTRODUCTION

In the linear projection model,

$$Y = X'\beta + e$$
$$\mathbb{E}[Xe] = 0$$

a common task is to impose a constraint on the coefficient vector β. For example, partitioning $X' = (X_1', X_2')$ and $\beta' = (\beta_1', \beta_2')$, a typical constraint is an exclusion restriction of the form $\beta_2 = 0$. In this case, the constrained model is

$$Y = X_1'\beta_1 + e$$
$$\mathbb{E}[Xe] = 0.$$

At first glance, this appears to be the same as the linear projection model, but there is one important difference: The error e is uncorrelated with the entire regressor vector $X' = (X_1', X_2')$ not just the included regressor X_1.

In general, a set of q linear constraints on β takes the form

$$\boldsymbol{R}'\beta = \boldsymbol{c} \tag{8.1}$$

where $\boldsymbol{R}$ is $k \times q$, $\operatorname{rank}(\boldsymbol{R}) = q < k$, and $\boldsymbol{c}$ is $q \times 1$. The assumption that $\boldsymbol{R}$ is full rank means that the constraints are linearly independent (there are no redundant or contradictory constraints). Define the restricted parameter space B as the set of values of β that satisfy (8.1), that is,

$$B = \left\{\beta : \boldsymbol{R}'\beta = \boldsymbol{c}\right\}.$$

Sometimes we will call (8.1) a **constraint** and sometimes a **restriction**. The terms mean the same thing. Similarly, sometimes we will call estimators that satisfy (8.1) **constrained estimators** and sometimes **restricted estimators**. They also mean the same thing.

The constraint $\beta_2 = 0$ discussed above is a special case of the constraint (8.1) with

$$\boldsymbol{R} = \begin{pmatrix} 0 \\ \boldsymbol{I}_{k_2} \end{pmatrix}, \tag{8.2}$$

a selector matrix, and $\boldsymbol{c} = 0$.

Another common restriction is that a set of coefficients sum to a known constant (e.g., $\beta_1 + \beta_2 = 1$). For example, this constraint arises in a constant-return-to-scale production function. Other common restrictions include the equality of coefficients $\beta_1 = \beta_2$, and equal and offsetting coefficients $\beta_1 = -\beta_2$.

A typical reason to impose a constraint is that we believe (or have information) that the constraint is true. By imposing the constraint, we hope to improve estimation efficiency. The goal is to obtain consistent estimates with reduced variance relative to the unconstrained estimator.

The questions then arise: How should we estimate the coefficient vector β imposing the linear restriction (8.1)? If we impose such constraints, what is the sampling distribution of the resulting estimator? How should we calculate standard errors? These are the questions explored in this chapter.

8.2 CONSTRAINED LEAST SQUARES

An intuitively appealing method to estimate a constrained linear projection is to minimize the least squares criterion subject to the constraint $\boldsymbol{R}'\beta = \boldsymbol{c}$. The constrained least squares estimator is

$$\widetilde{\beta}_{\text{cls}} = \underset{\boldsymbol{R}'\beta=\boldsymbol{c}}{\operatorname{argmin}}\ \text{SSE}(\beta) \tag{8.3}$$

where

$$\text{SSE}(\beta) = \sum_{i=1}^{n} \left(Y_i - X_i'\beta\right)^2 = \boldsymbol{Y}'\boldsymbol{Y} - 2\boldsymbol{Y}'\boldsymbol{X}\beta + \beta'\boldsymbol{X}'\boldsymbol{X}\beta. \tag{8.4}$$

The estimator $\widetilde{\beta}_{\text{cls}}$ minimizes the sum of squared errors over all $\beta \in B$, or equivalently, such that the restriction (8.1) holds. We call $\widetilde{\beta}_{\text{cls}}$ the **constrained least squares** (CLS) estimator. We use the convention that a tilde "$\sim$" rather than a hat "$\wedge$" indicates that $\widetilde{\beta}_{\text{cls}}$ is a restricted estimator, in contrast to the unrestricted least squares estimator $\widehat{\beta}$, and write it as $\widetilde{\beta}_{\text{cls}}$ to be clear that the estimation method is CLS.

One method for finding the solution to (8.3) is the technique of Lagrange multipliers. The problem (8.3) is equivalent to finding the critical points of the Lagrangian

$$\mathscr{L}(\beta, \lambda) = \frac{1}{2}\text{SSE}(\beta) + \lambda' \left(\boldsymbol{R}'\beta - \boldsymbol{c}\right) \tag{8.5}$$

over (β, λ), where λ is an $s \times 1$ vector of Lagrange multipliers. The solution is a saddlepoint. The Lagrangian is minimized over β while maximized over λ. The first-order conditions for the solution of (8.5) are

$$\frac{\partial}{\partial \beta}\mathscr{L}(\widetilde{\beta}_{\text{cls}}, \widetilde{\lambda}_{\text{cls}}) = -\boldsymbol{X}'\boldsymbol{Y} + \boldsymbol{X}'\boldsymbol{X}\widetilde{\beta}_{\text{cls}} + \boldsymbol{R}\widetilde{\lambda}_{\text{cls}} = 0 \tag{8.6}$$

and

$$\frac{\partial}{\partial \lambda}\mathscr{L}(\widetilde{\beta}_{\text{cls}}, \widetilde{\lambda}_{\text{cls}}) = \boldsymbol{R}'\widetilde{\beta}_{\text{cls}} - \boldsymbol{c} = 0. \tag{8.7}$$

Premultiplying (8.6) by $\boldsymbol{R}'\left(\boldsymbol{X}'\boldsymbol{X}\right)^{-1}$, we obtain

$$-\boldsymbol{R}'\widehat{\beta} + \boldsymbol{R}'\widetilde{\beta}_{\text{cls}} + \boldsymbol{R}'\left(\boldsymbol{X}'\boldsymbol{X}\right)^{-1}\boldsymbol{R}\widetilde{\lambda}_{\text{cls}} = 0$$

where $\widehat{\beta} = \left(\boldsymbol{X}'\boldsymbol{X}\right)^{-1}\boldsymbol{X}'\boldsymbol{Y}$ is the unrestricted least squares estimator. Imposing $\boldsymbol{R}'\widetilde{\beta}_{\text{cls}} - \boldsymbol{c} = 0$ from (8.7) and solving for $\widetilde{\lambda}_{\text{cls}}$, we find

$$\widetilde{\lambda}_{\text{cls}} = \left[\boldsymbol{R}'\left(\boldsymbol{X}'\boldsymbol{X}\right)^{-1}\boldsymbol{R}\right]^{-1}\left(\boldsymbol{R}'\widehat{\beta} - \boldsymbol{c}\right).$$

Notice that $\left(\boldsymbol{X}'\boldsymbol{X}\right)^{-1} > 0$ and $\boldsymbol{R}$ full rank imply that $\boldsymbol{R}'\left(\boldsymbol{X}'\boldsymbol{X}\right)^{-1}\boldsymbol{R} > 0$ and is hence invertible. (See Section A.10.)

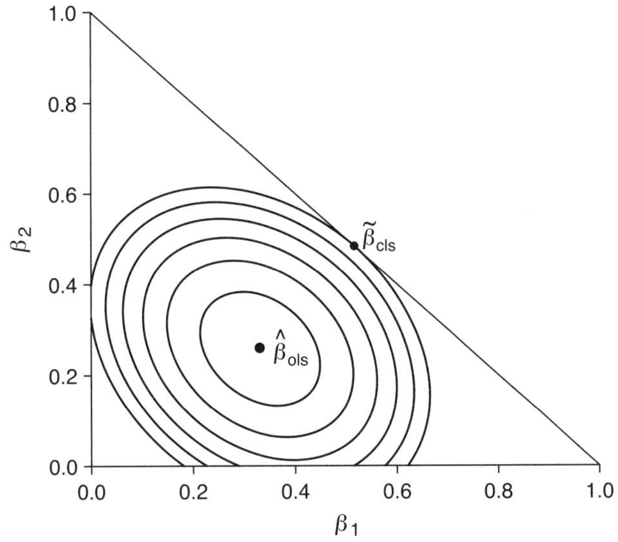

FIGURE 8.1 Constrained least squares criterion

Substituting this expression into (8.6) and solving for $\widetilde{\beta}_{\text{cls}}$, we find the solution to the constrained minimization problem (8.3):

$$\widetilde{\beta}_{\text{cls}} = \widehat{\beta}_{\text{ols}} - \left(\boldsymbol{X}'\boldsymbol{X}\right)^{-1} \boldsymbol{R}\left[\boldsymbol{R}'\left(\boldsymbol{X}'\boldsymbol{X}\right)^{-1}\boldsymbol{R}\right]^{-1}\left(\boldsymbol{R}'\widehat{\beta}_{\text{ols}} - \boldsymbol{c}\right). \tag{8.8}$$

(See Exercise 8.5 to verify that (8.8) satisfies (8.1).)

This is a general formula for the CLS estimator. It also can be written as

$$\widetilde{\beta}_{\text{cls}} = \widehat{\beta}_{\text{ols}} - \widehat{\boldsymbol{Q}}_{XX}^{-1}\boldsymbol{R}\left(\boldsymbol{R}'\widehat{\boldsymbol{Q}}_{XX}^{-1}\boldsymbol{R}\right)^{-1}\left(\boldsymbol{R}'\widehat{\beta}_{\text{ols}} - \boldsymbol{c}\right). \tag{8.9}$$

The CLS residuals are $\widetilde{e}_i = Y_i - X_i'\widetilde{\beta}_{\text{cls}}$ and are written in vector notation as $\widetilde{\boldsymbol{e}}$.

To illustrate, consider a random sample of 100 observations for the variables (Y, X_1, X_2) and the sum of squared errors function for the regression of Y on X_1 and X_2. Figure 8.1 displays contour plots of the sum of squared errors function. The center of the contour plots is the least squares minimizer $\widehat{\beta}_{\text{ols}} = (0.33, 0.26)$. Suppose we want to estimate the coefficients subject to the constraint $\beta_1 + \beta_2 = 1$. This constraint is displayed in the figure by the straight line. The constrained least squares estimator is the point on this straight line that yields the smallest sum of squared errors. This is the point that intersects the lowest contour plot. The solution is the point where a contour plot is tangent to the constraint line and is marked as $\widetilde{\beta}_{\text{cls}} = (0.52, 0.48)$.

In Stata, constrained least squares is implemented using the `cnsreg` command.

8.3 EXCLUSION RESTRICTION

While (8.8) is a general formula for CLS, in most cases, the estimator can be found by applying least squares to a reparameterized equation. To illustrate, let us return to the first example presented at the beginning of this chapter—a simple exclusion restriction. Recall that the unconstrained model is

$$Y = X_1'\beta_1 + X_2'\beta_2 + e \tag{8.10}$$

the exclusion restriction is $\beta_2 = 0$, and the constrained equation is

$$Y = X_1'\beta_1 + e. \tag{8.11}$$

In this setting, the CLS estimator is OLS of Y on X_1. (See Exercise 8.1.) We can write this as

$$\widetilde{\beta}_1 = \left(\sum_{i=1}^{n} X_{1i}X_{1i}'\right)^{-1}\left(\sum_{i=1}^{n} X_{1i}Y_i\right). \tag{8.12}$$

The CLS estimator of the entire vector $\beta' = (\beta_1', \beta_2')$ is

$$\widetilde{\beta} = \begin{pmatrix} \widetilde{\beta}_1 \\ 0 \end{pmatrix}. \tag{8.13}$$

It is not immediately obvious, but (8.8) and (8.13) are algebraically identical. To see this, the first component of (8.8) using the constraint (8.2) is

$$\widetilde{\beta}_1 = \begin{pmatrix} \boldsymbol{I}_{k_2} & 0 \end{pmatrix}\left[\widehat{\beta} - \widehat{\boldsymbol{Q}}_{XX}^{-1}\begin{pmatrix} 0 \\ \boldsymbol{I}_{k_2} \end{pmatrix}\left[\begin{pmatrix} 0 & \boldsymbol{I}_{k_2} \end{pmatrix}\widehat{\boldsymbol{Q}}_{XX}^{-1}\begin{pmatrix} 0 \\ \boldsymbol{I}_{k_2} \end{pmatrix}\right]^{-1}\begin{pmatrix} 0 & \boldsymbol{I}_{k_2} \end{pmatrix}\widehat{\beta}\right].$$

Using (3.39), this equals

$$\begin{aligned}
\widetilde{\beta}_1 &= \widehat{\beta}_1 - \widehat{\boldsymbol{Q}}^{12}\left(\widehat{\boldsymbol{Q}}^{22}\right)^{-1}\widehat{\beta}_2 \\
&= \widehat{\beta}_1 + \widehat{\boldsymbol{Q}}_{11\cdot 2}^{-1}\widehat{\boldsymbol{Q}}_{12}\widehat{\boldsymbol{Q}}_{22}^{-1}\widehat{\boldsymbol{Q}}_{22\cdot 1}\widehat{\beta}_2 \\
&= \widehat{\boldsymbol{Q}}_{11\cdot 2}^{-1}\left(\widehat{\boldsymbol{Q}}_{1Y} - \widehat{\boldsymbol{Q}}_{12}\widehat{\boldsymbol{Q}}_{22}^{-1}\widehat{\boldsymbol{Q}}_{2Y}\right) \\
&\quad + \widehat{\boldsymbol{Q}}_{11\cdot 2}^{-1}\widehat{\boldsymbol{Q}}_{12}\widehat{\boldsymbol{Q}}_{22}^{-1}\widehat{\boldsymbol{Q}}_{22\cdot 1}\widehat{\boldsymbol{Q}}_{22\cdot 1}^{-1}\left(\widehat{\boldsymbol{Q}}_{2y} - \widehat{\boldsymbol{Q}}_{21}\widehat{\boldsymbol{Q}}_{11}^{-1}\widehat{\boldsymbol{Q}}_{1Y}\right) \\
&= \widehat{\boldsymbol{Q}}_{11\cdot 2}^{-1}\left(\widehat{\boldsymbol{Q}}_{1Y} - \widehat{\boldsymbol{Q}}_{12}\widehat{\boldsymbol{Q}}_{22}^{-1}\widehat{\boldsymbol{Q}}_{21}\widehat{\boldsymbol{Q}}_{11}^{-1}\widehat{\boldsymbol{Q}}_{1Y}\right) \\
&= \widehat{\boldsymbol{Q}}_{11\cdot 2}^{-1}\left(\widehat{\boldsymbol{Q}}_{11} - \widehat{\boldsymbol{Q}}_{12}\widehat{\boldsymbol{Q}}_{22}^{-1}\widehat{\boldsymbol{Q}}_{21}\right)\widehat{\boldsymbol{Q}}_{11}^{-1}\widehat{\boldsymbol{Q}}_{1Y} \\
&= \widehat{\boldsymbol{Q}}_{11}^{-1}\widehat{\boldsymbol{Q}}_{1Y}
\end{aligned}$$

which is (8.13), as originally claimed.

8.4 FINITE SAMPLE PROPERTIES

In this section, we explore some of the properties of the CLS estimator in the linear regression model:

$$Y = X'\beta + e \tag{8.14}$$

$$\mathbb{E}\left[e \mid X\right] = 0. \tag{8.15}$$

First, it is useful to write the estimator and the residuals as linear functions of the error vector. These are algebraic relationships and do not rely on the linear regression assumptions.

Theorem 8.1 The CLS estimator satisfies

1. $\boldsymbol{R}'\widehat{\beta} - \boldsymbol{c} = \boldsymbol{R}'\left(\boldsymbol{X}'\boldsymbol{X}\right)^{-1}\boldsymbol{X}'\boldsymbol{e}$
2. $\widetilde{\beta}_{\text{cls}} - \beta = \left(\left(\boldsymbol{X}'\boldsymbol{X}\right)^{-1}\boldsymbol{X}' - \boldsymbol{A}\boldsymbol{X}'\right)\boldsymbol{e}$
3. $\widetilde{\boldsymbol{e}} = \left(\boldsymbol{I} - \boldsymbol{P} + \boldsymbol{X}\boldsymbol{A}\boldsymbol{X}'\right)\boldsymbol{e}$
4. $\boldsymbol{I}_n - \boldsymbol{P} + \boldsymbol{X}\boldsymbol{A}\boldsymbol{X}'$ is symmetric and idempotent
5. $\operatorname{tr}\left(\boldsymbol{I}_n - \boldsymbol{P} + \boldsymbol{X}\boldsymbol{A}\boldsymbol{X}'\right) = n - k + q$

where $\boldsymbol{P} = \boldsymbol{X}\left(\boldsymbol{X}'\boldsymbol{X}\right)^{-1}\boldsymbol{X}'$, and $\boldsymbol{A} = \left(\boldsymbol{X}'\boldsymbol{X}\right)^{-1}\boldsymbol{R}\left(\boldsymbol{R}'\left(\boldsymbol{X}'\boldsymbol{X}\right)^{-1}\boldsymbol{R}\right)^{-1}\boldsymbol{R}'\left(\boldsymbol{X}'\boldsymbol{X}\right)^{-1}$.

You are asked to prove Theorem 8.1 in Exercise 8.6. Given the linearity of Theorem 8.1.2, it is not hard to show that the CLS estimator is unbiased for β.

Theorem 8.2 In the linear regression model (8.14)–(8.15) under (8.1), $\mathbb{E}\left[\widetilde{\beta}_{\text{cls}} \mid \boldsymbol{X}\right] = \beta$.

For a proof, see Exercise 8.7.

We can also calculate the covariance matrix of $\widetilde{\beta}_{\text{cls}}$. First, for simplicity, take the case of conditional homoskedasticity.

Theorem 8.3 In the homoskedastic linear regression model (8.14)–(8.15) with $\mathbb{E}\left[e^2 \mid X\right] = \sigma^2$, under (8.1),

$$\begin{aligned}\boldsymbol{V}^0_{\widetilde{\beta}} &= \operatorname{var}\left[\widetilde{\beta}_{\text{cls}} \mid \boldsymbol{X}\right] \\ &= \left(\left(\boldsymbol{X}'\boldsymbol{X}\right)^{-1} - \left(\boldsymbol{X}'\boldsymbol{X}\right)^{-1}\boldsymbol{R}\left(\boldsymbol{R}'\left(\boldsymbol{X}'\boldsymbol{X}\right)^{-1}\boldsymbol{R}\right)^{-1}\boldsymbol{R}'\left(\boldsymbol{X}'\boldsymbol{X}\right)^{-1}\right)\sigma^2.\end{aligned}$$

For a proof, see Exercise 8.8. The $\boldsymbol{V}^0_{\widetilde{\beta}}$ notation is used to emphasize that this is the covariance matrix under the assumption of conditional homoskedasticity.

For inference, we need an estimate of $\boldsymbol{V}^0_{\widetilde{\beta}}$. A natural estimator is

$$\widehat{\boldsymbol{V}}^0_{\widetilde{\beta}} = \left(\left(\boldsymbol{X}'\boldsymbol{X}\right)^{-1} - \left(\boldsymbol{X}'\boldsymbol{X}\right)^{-1}\boldsymbol{R}\left(\boldsymbol{R}'\left(\boldsymbol{X}'\boldsymbol{X}\right)^{-1}\boldsymbol{R}\right)^{-1}\boldsymbol{R}'\left(\boldsymbol{X}'\boldsymbol{X}\right)^{-1}\right)s^2_{\text{cls}}$$

where

$$s^2_{\text{cls}} = \frac{1}{n-k+q}\sum_{i=1}^{n}\widetilde{e}_i^2 \tag{8.16}$$

is a biased-corrected estimator of σ^2. Standard errors for the components of β are then found by taking the squares roots of the diagonal elements of $\widehat{\boldsymbol{V}}_{\widetilde{\beta}}$, for example,

$$s(\widehat{\beta}_j) = \sqrt{\left[\widehat{\boldsymbol{V}}^0_{\widetilde{\beta}}\right]_{jj}}.$$

The estimator (8.16) has the property that it is unbiased for σ^2 under conditional homoskedasticity. To see this, using the properties of Theorem 8.1, we have

$$\begin{aligned}(n-k+q)\, s_{\text{cls}}^2 &= \widetilde{\boldsymbol{e}}'\widetilde{\boldsymbol{e}} \\ &= \boldsymbol{e}'\left(\boldsymbol{I}_n - \boldsymbol{P} + \boldsymbol{X}\boldsymbol{A}\boldsymbol{X}'\right)\left(\boldsymbol{I}_n - \boldsymbol{P} + \boldsymbol{X}\boldsymbol{A}\boldsymbol{X}'\right)\boldsymbol{e} \\ &= \boldsymbol{e}'\left(\boldsymbol{I}_n - \boldsymbol{P} + \boldsymbol{X}\boldsymbol{A}\boldsymbol{X}'\right)\boldsymbol{e}. \end{aligned} \tag{8.17}$$

We defer the remainder of the proof to Exercise 8.9.

Theorem 8.4 In the homoskedastic linear regression model (8.14)–(8.15) with $\mathbb{E}\left[e^2 \mid X\right] = \sigma^2$, under (8.1), $\mathbb{E}\left[s_{\text{cls}}^2 \mid \boldsymbol{X}\right] = \sigma^2$ and $\mathbb{E}\left[\widehat{\boldsymbol{V}}_{\widetilde{\beta}}^0 \mid \boldsymbol{X}\right] = \boldsymbol{V}_{\widetilde{\beta}}^0$.

Now consider the distributional properties in the normal regression model $Y = X'\beta + e$ with $e \sim \mathrm{N}(0, \sigma^2)$. By the linearity of Theorem 8.1.2, conditional on $\boldsymbol{X}$, $\widetilde{\beta}_{\text{cls}} - \beta$ is normal. Given Theorems 8.2 and 8.3, we deduce that $\widetilde{\beta}_{\text{cls}} \sim \mathrm{N}\left(\beta, \boldsymbol{V}_{\widetilde{\beta}}^0\right)$.

Similarly, from Exericise 8.1, we know $\widetilde{\boldsymbol{e}} = \left(\boldsymbol{I}_n - \boldsymbol{P} + \boldsymbol{X}\boldsymbol{A}\boldsymbol{X}'\right)\boldsymbol{e}$ is linear in $\boldsymbol{e}$, so it is also conditionally normal. Furthermore, since $\left(\boldsymbol{I}_n - \boldsymbol{P} + \boldsymbol{X}\boldsymbol{A}\boldsymbol{X}'\right)\left(\boldsymbol{X}\left(\boldsymbol{X}'\boldsymbol{X}\right)^{-1} - \boldsymbol{X}\boldsymbol{A}\right) = 0$, $\widetilde{\boldsymbol{e}}$ and $\widetilde{\beta}_{\text{cls}}$ are uncorrelated and thus independent. Thus s_{cls}^2 and $\widetilde{\beta}_{\text{cls}}$ are independent.

From (8.17) and the fact that $\boldsymbol{I}_n - \boldsymbol{P} + \boldsymbol{X}\boldsymbol{A}\boldsymbol{X}'$ is idempotent with rank $n-k+q$, it follows that

$$s_{\text{cls}}^2 \sim \sigma^2 \chi_{n-k+q}^2 / (n-k+q).$$

It follows that the t-statistic has the exact distribution

$$T = \frac{\widehat{\beta}_j - \beta_j}{s(\widehat{\beta}_j)} \sim \frac{\mathrm{N}(0,1)}{\sqrt{\chi_{n-k+q}^2 / (n-k+q)}} \sim t_{n-k+q}$$

which is a student t distribution with $n-k+q$ degrees of freedom.

The relevance of this calculation is that the "degrees of freedom" for CLS regression equal $n-k+q$ rather than $n-k$ as in OLS. Essentially, the model has $k-q$ free parameters instead of k. Another way of thinking about this is that estimation of a model with k coefficients and q restrictions is equivalent to estimation with $k-q$ coefficients.

Theorem 8.5 summarizes the properties of the normal regression model.

Theorem 8.5 In the normal linear regression model (8.14)–(8.15) with constraint (8.1),

$$\widetilde{\beta}_{\text{cls}} \sim \mathrm{N}\left(\beta, \boldsymbol{V}_{\widetilde{\beta}}^0\right)$$

$$\frac{(n-k+q)\, s_{\text{cls}}^2}{\sigma^2} \sim \chi_{n-k+q}^2$$

$$T \sim t_{n-k+q}.$$

An interesting relationship is that in the homoskedastic regression model,

$$\begin{aligned}\operatorname{cov}\left(\widehat{\beta}_{\text{ols}}-\widetilde{\beta}_{\text{cls}},\widetilde{\beta}_{\text{cls}}\mid \boldsymbol{X}\right) &= \mathbb{E}\left[\left(\widehat{\beta}_{\text{ols}}-\widetilde{\beta}_{\text{cls}}\right)\left(\widetilde{\beta}_{\text{cls}}-\beta\right)'\mid \boldsymbol{X}\right] \\ &= \mathbb{E}\left[\boldsymbol{A}\boldsymbol{X}'\boldsymbol{e}\boldsymbol{e}'\left(\boldsymbol{X}\left(\boldsymbol{X}'\boldsymbol{X}\right)^{-1}-\boldsymbol{X}\boldsymbol{A}\right)\mid \boldsymbol{X}\right] \\ &= \boldsymbol{A}\boldsymbol{X}'\left(\boldsymbol{X}\left(\boldsymbol{X}'\boldsymbol{X}\right)^{-1}-\boldsymbol{X}\boldsymbol{A}\right)\sigma^2 = 0.\end{aligned}$$

Thus, $\widehat{\beta}_{\text{ols}}-\widetilde{\beta}_{\text{cls}}$ and $\widetilde{\beta}_{\text{cls}}$ are conditionally uncorrelated and hence independent. A corollary is

$$\operatorname{cov}\left(\widehat{\beta}_{\text{ols}},\widetilde{\beta}_{\text{cls}}\mid \boldsymbol{X}\right)=\operatorname{var}\left[\widetilde{\beta}_{\text{cls}}\mid \boldsymbol{X}\right].$$

A second corollary is

$$\begin{aligned}\operatorname{var}\left[\widehat{\beta}_{\text{ols}}-\widetilde{\beta}_{\text{cls}}\mid \boldsymbol{X}\right] &= \operatorname{var}\left[\widehat{\beta}_{\text{ols}}\mid \boldsymbol{X}\right]-\operatorname{var}\left[\widetilde{\beta}_{\text{cls}}\mid \boldsymbol{X}\right] \\ &= \left(\boldsymbol{X}'\boldsymbol{X}\right)^{-1}\boldsymbol{R}\left(\boldsymbol{R}'\left(\boldsymbol{X}'\boldsymbol{X}\right)^{-1}\boldsymbol{R}\right)^{-1}\boldsymbol{R}'\left(\boldsymbol{X}'\boldsymbol{X}\right)^{-1}\sigma^2.\end{aligned} \tag{8.18}$$

Equation (8.18) also shows that the difference between the CLS and OLS variances matrices equals

$$\operatorname{var}\left[\widehat{\beta}_{\text{ols}}\mid \boldsymbol{X}\right]-\operatorname{var}\left[\widetilde{\beta}_{\text{cls}}\mid \boldsymbol{X}\right]=\left(\boldsymbol{X}'\boldsymbol{X}\right)^{-1}\boldsymbol{R}\left(\boldsymbol{R}'\left(\boldsymbol{X}'\boldsymbol{X}\right)^{-1}\boldsymbol{R}\right)^{-1}\boldsymbol{R}'\left(\boldsymbol{X}'\boldsymbol{X}\right)^{-1}\sigma^2\geq 0$$

the final equality meaning that the difference is positive semi-definite. It follows that $\operatorname{var}\left[\widehat{\beta}_{\text{ols}}\mid \boldsymbol{X}\right]\geq \operatorname{var}\left[\widetilde{\beta}_{\text{cls}}\mid \boldsymbol{X}\right]$ in the positive definite sense, and thus CLS is more efficient than OLS. Both estimators are unbiased (in the linear regression model), and CLS has a lower covariance matrix (in the linear homoskedastic regression model).

The relationship (8.18) is rather interesting and will appear again. The expression says that the variance of the difference between the estimators is equal to the difference between the variances. This is rather special. It occurs generically when we are comparing an efficient and an inefficient estimator. We call (8.18) the **Hausman Equality**, as it was first pointed out in econometrics by Hausman (1978).

8.5 MINIMUM DISTANCE

Section 8.4 explored the finite sample distribution theory under the assumptions of the linear regression model, homoskedastic regression model, and normal regression model. We now return to the general projection model, where we do not impose linearity, homoskedasticity, or normality. We are interested in the question: Can we do better than CLS in this setting?

A minimum distance estimator tries to find a parameter value satisfying the constraint that is as close as possible to the unconstrained estimator. Let $\widehat{\beta}$ be the unconstrained least squares estimator, and for some $k\times k$ positive definite weight matrix $\widehat{\boldsymbol{W}}$, define the quadratic criterion function:

$$J(\beta)=n\left(\widehat{\beta}-\beta\right)'\widehat{\boldsymbol{W}}\left(\widehat{\beta}-\beta\right). \tag{8.19}$$

This is a (squared) weighted Euclidean distance between $\widehat{\beta}$ and β. $J(\beta)$ is small if β is close to $\widehat{\beta}$, and is minimized at 0 only if $\beta=\widehat{\beta}$. A **minimum distance estimator** $\widetilde{\beta}_{\text{md}}$ for β minimizes $J(\beta)$ subject to the constraint (8.1), that is,

$$\widetilde{\beta}_{\text{md}}=\underset{\boldsymbol{R}'\beta=\boldsymbol{c}}{\operatorname{argmin}}\, J(\beta).$$

The CLS estimator is the special case when $\widehat{\boldsymbol{W}}=\widehat{\boldsymbol{Q}}_{XX}$, and we write this criterion function as

$$J^0(\beta)=n\left(\widehat{\beta}-\beta\right)'\widehat{\boldsymbol{Q}}_{XX}\left(\widehat{\beta}-\beta\right). \tag{8.20}$$

To see the equality of CLS and minimum distance, rewrite the least squares criterion as follows. Substitute the unconstrained least squares fitted equation $Y_i=X_i'\widehat{\beta}+\widehat{e}_i$ into $\mathrm{SSE}(\beta)$ to obtain

$$\begin{aligned}
\mathrm{SSE}(\beta)&=\sum_{i=1}^{n}\left(Y_i-X_i'\beta\right)^2\\
&=\sum_{i=1}^{n}\left(X_i'\widehat{\beta}+\widehat{e}_i-X_i'\beta\right)^2\\
&=\sum_{i=1}^{n}\widehat{e}_i^2+\left(\widehat{\beta}-\beta\right)'\left(\sum_{i=1}^{n}X_iX_i'\right)\left(\widehat{\beta}-\beta\right)\\
&=n\widehat{\sigma}^2+J^0(\beta)
\end{aligned} \tag{8.21}$$

where the third equality uses the fact that $\sum_{i=1}^{n}X_i\widehat{e}_i=0$, and the last line uses $\sum_{i=1}^{n}X_iX_i'=n\widehat{\boldsymbol{Q}}_{XX}$. The expression (8.21) only depends on β through $J^0(\beta)$. Thus minimization of $\mathrm{SSE}(\beta)$ and $J^0(\beta)$ are equivalent, and hence $\widetilde{\beta}_{\mathrm{md}}=\widetilde{\beta}_{\mathrm{cls}}$ when $\widehat{\boldsymbol{W}}=\widehat{\boldsymbol{Q}}_{XX}$.

We can solve for $\widetilde{\beta}_{\mathrm{md}}$ explicitly by the method of Lagrange multipliers. The Lagrangian is

$$\mathscr{L}(\beta,\lambda)=\frac{1}{2}J\left(\beta,\widehat{\boldsymbol{W}}\right)+\lambda'\left(\boldsymbol{R}'\beta-\boldsymbol{c}\right).$$

The solution to the pair of first order conditions is

$$\widetilde{\lambda}_{\mathrm{md}}=n\left(\boldsymbol{R}'\widehat{\boldsymbol{W}}^{-1}\boldsymbol{R}\right)^{-1}\left(\boldsymbol{R}'\widehat{\boldsymbol{\beta}}-\boldsymbol{c}\right) \tag{8.22}$$

$$\widetilde{\beta}_{\mathrm{md}}=\widehat{\boldsymbol{\beta}}-\widehat{\boldsymbol{W}}^{-1}\boldsymbol{R}\left(\boldsymbol{R}'\widehat{\boldsymbol{W}}^{-1}\boldsymbol{R}\right)^{-1}\left(\boldsymbol{R}'\widehat{\beta}-\boldsymbol{c}\right). \tag{8.23}$$

(See Exercise 8.10.) Comparing (8.23) with (8.9), we can see that $\widetilde{\beta}_{\mathrm{md}}$ specializes to $\widetilde{\beta}_{\mathrm{cls}}$ when we set $\widehat{\boldsymbol{W}}=\widehat{\boldsymbol{Q}}_{XX}$.

An obvious question is which weight matrix $\widehat{\boldsymbol{W}}$ is best. We will address this question after we derive the asymptotic distribution for a general weight matrix.

8.6 ASYMPTOTIC DISTRIBUTION

We first show that the class of minimum distance estimators is consistent for the population parameters when the constraints are valid.

Assumption 8.1 $\boldsymbol{R}'\beta=\boldsymbol{c}$, where $\boldsymbol{R}$ is $k\times q$ with $\mathrm{rank}(\boldsymbol{R})=q$.

Assumption 8.2 $\widehat{W} \underset{p}{\longrightarrow} W > 0$.

Theorem 8.6 Consistency
Under Assumptions 7.1, 8.1, and 8.2, $\widetilde{\beta}_{\text{md}} \underset{p}{\longrightarrow} \beta$ as $n \to \infty$.

For a proof, see Exercise 8.11. Theorem 8.6 shows that consistency holds for any weight matrix with a positive definite limit so includes the CLS estimator.

Similarly, the constrained estimators are asymptotically normally distributed.

Theorem 8.7 Asymptotic Normality
Under Assumptions 7.2, 8.1, and 8.2,

$$\sqrt{n}\left(\widetilde{\beta}_{\text{md}} - \beta\right) \underset{d}{\longrightarrow} \mathrm{N}\left(0, \boldsymbol{V}_\beta(\boldsymbol{W})\right)$$

as $n \to \infty$, where

$$\begin{aligned}\boldsymbol{V}_\beta(\boldsymbol{W}) = \boldsymbol{V}_\beta &- \boldsymbol{W}^{-1}\boldsymbol{R}\left(\boldsymbol{R}'\boldsymbol{W}^{-1}\boldsymbol{R}\right)^{-1}\boldsymbol{R}'\boldsymbol{V}_\beta \\ &- \boldsymbol{V}_\beta\boldsymbol{R}\left(\boldsymbol{R}'\boldsymbol{W}^{-1}\boldsymbol{R}\right)^{-1}\boldsymbol{R}'\boldsymbol{W}^{-1} \\ &+ \boldsymbol{W}^{-1}\boldsymbol{R}\left(\boldsymbol{R}'\boldsymbol{W}^{-1}\boldsymbol{R}\right)^{-1}\boldsymbol{R}'\boldsymbol{V}_\beta\boldsymbol{R}\left(\boldsymbol{R}'\boldsymbol{W}^{-1}\boldsymbol{R}\right)^{-1}\boldsymbol{R}'\boldsymbol{W}^{-1}\end{aligned} \tag{8.24}$$

and $\boldsymbol{V}_\beta = \boldsymbol{Q}_{XX}^{-1}\Omega\boldsymbol{Q}_{XX}^{-1}$.

For a proof, see Exercise 8.12. Theorem 8.7 shows that the minimum distance estimator is asymptotically normal for all positive definite weight matrices. The asymptotic variance depends on $\boldsymbol{W}$. The theorem includes the CLS estimator as a special case by setting $\boldsymbol{W} = \boldsymbol{Q}_{XX}$.

Theorem 8.8 Asymptotic Distribution of CLS Estimator
Under Assumptions 7.2 and 8.1, as $n \to \infty$,

$$\sqrt{n}\left(\widetilde{\beta}_{\text{cls}} - \beta\right) \underset{d}{\longrightarrow} \mathrm{N}\left(0, \boldsymbol{V}_{\text{cls}}\right)$$

where

$$\begin{aligned}\boldsymbol{V}_{\text{cls}} = \boldsymbol{V}_\beta &- \boldsymbol{Q}_{XX}^{-1}\boldsymbol{R}\left(\boldsymbol{R}'\boldsymbol{Q}_{XX}^{-1}\boldsymbol{R}\right)^{-1}\boldsymbol{R}'\boldsymbol{V}_\beta \\ &- \boldsymbol{V}_\beta\boldsymbol{R}\left(\boldsymbol{R}'\boldsymbol{Q}_{XX}^{-1}\boldsymbol{R}\right)^{-1}\boldsymbol{R}'\boldsymbol{Q}_{XX}^{-1} \\ &+ \boldsymbol{Q}_{XX}^{-1}\boldsymbol{R}\left(\boldsymbol{R}'\boldsymbol{Q}_{XX}^{-1}\boldsymbol{R}\right)^{-1}\boldsymbol{R}'\boldsymbol{V}_\beta\boldsymbol{R}\left(\boldsymbol{R}'\boldsymbol{Q}_{XX}^{-1}\boldsymbol{R}\right)^{-1}\boldsymbol{R}'\boldsymbol{Q}_{XX}^{-1}.\end{aligned}$$

For a proof, see Exercise 8.13.

8.7 VARIANCE ESTIMATION AND STANDARD ERRORS

In Section 3.4, we introduced the covariance matrix estimator under the assumption of conditional homoskedasticity. We now introduce an estimator that does not impose homoskedasticity.

The asymptotic covariance matrix $\boldsymbol{V}_{\text{cls}}$ may be estimated by replacing $\boldsymbol{V}_\beta$ with a consistent estimator, such as $\widehat{\boldsymbol{V}}_\beta$. A more efficient estimator can be obtained by using the restricted coefficient estimator, which we now show. Given the constrained least squares residuals $\widetilde{e}_i = Y_i - X_i'\widetilde{\beta}_{\text{cls}}$, we can estimate the matrix $\Omega = \mathbb{E}\left[XX'e^2\right]$ by

$$\widetilde{\Omega} = \frac{1}{n-k+q}\sum_{i=1}^{n} X_i X_i' \widetilde{e}_i^2.$$

Notice that we have used an adjusted degrees of freedom. This is an ad hoc adjustment designed to mimic that used for estimation of the error variance σ^2. The moment estimator of $\boldsymbol{V}_\beta$ is

$$\widetilde{\boldsymbol{V}}_\beta = \widehat{\boldsymbol{Q}}_{XX}^{-1}\widetilde{\Omega}\widehat{\boldsymbol{Q}}_{XX}^{-1}$$

and that for $\boldsymbol{V}_{\text{cls}}$ is

$$\begin{aligned}\widetilde{\boldsymbol{V}}_{\text{cls}} = {} & \widetilde{\boldsymbol{V}}_\beta - \widehat{\boldsymbol{Q}}_{XX}^{-1}\boldsymbol{R}\left(\boldsymbol{R}'\widehat{\boldsymbol{Q}}_{XX}^{-1}\boldsymbol{R}\right)^{-1}\boldsymbol{R}'\widetilde{\boldsymbol{V}}_\beta \\ & - \widetilde{\boldsymbol{V}}_\beta\boldsymbol{R}\left(\boldsymbol{R}'\widehat{\boldsymbol{Q}}_{XX}^{-1}\boldsymbol{R}\right)^{-1}\boldsymbol{R}'\widehat{\boldsymbol{Q}}_{\boldsymbol{xx}}^{-1} \\ & + \widehat{\boldsymbol{Q}}_{XX}^{-1}\boldsymbol{R}\left(\boldsymbol{R}'\widehat{\boldsymbol{Q}}_{XX}^{-1}\boldsymbol{R}\right)^{-1}\boldsymbol{R}'\widetilde{\boldsymbol{V}}_\beta\boldsymbol{R}\left(\boldsymbol{R}'\widehat{\boldsymbol{Q}}_{XX}^{-1}\boldsymbol{R}\right)^{-1}\boldsymbol{R}'\widehat{\boldsymbol{Q}}_{XX}^{-1}.\end{aligned}$$

We can calculate standard errors for any linear combination $h'\widetilde{\beta}_{\text{cls}}$ such that h does not lie in the range space of $\boldsymbol{R}$. A standard error for $h'\widetilde{\beta}$ is

$$s\left(h'\widetilde{\boldsymbol{\beta}}_{\text{cls}}\right) = \left(n^{-1}h'\widetilde{\boldsymbol{V}}_{\text{cls}}h\right)^{1/2}.$$

8.8 EFFICIENT MINIMUM DISTANCE ESTIMATOR

Theorem 8.7 shows that minimum distance estimators, which include CLS as a special case, are asymptotically normal with an asymptotic covariance matrix that depends on the weight matrix $\boldsymbol{W}$. The asymptotically optimal weight matrix is the one that minimizes the asymptotic variance $\boldsymbol{V}_\beta(\boldsymbol{W})$. This turns out to be $\boldsymbol{W} = \boldsymbol{V}_\beta^{-1}$, as shown in Theorem 8.9 below. Since $\boldsymbol{V}_\beta^{-1}$ is unknown, this weight matrix cannot be used for a feasible estimator, but we can replace $\boldsymbol{V}_\beta^{-1}$ with a consistent estimator $\widehat{\boldsymbol{V}}_\beta^{-1}$, and the asymptotic distribution (and efficiency) are unchanged. We call the minimum distance estimator with $\widehat{\boldsymbol{W}} = \widehat{\boldsymbol{V}}_\beta^{-1}$ the **efficient minimum distance (EMD) estimator**, and it takes the form:

$$\widetilde{\beta}_{\text{emd}} = \widehat{\beta} - \widehat{\boldsymbol{V}}_\beta\boldsymbol{R}\left(\boldsymbol{R}'\widehat{\boldsymbol{V}}_\beta\boldsymbol{R}\right)^{-1}\left(\boldsymbol{R}'\widehat{\beta} - \boldsymbol{c}\right). \tag{8.25}$$

The asymptotic distribution of (8.25) can be deduced from Theorem 8.7. (See Exercises 8.14 and 8.15, and the proof for Theorem 8.9 in Section 8.16.)

Theorem 8.9 Efficient Minimum Distance Estimator
Under Assumptions 7.2 and 8.1,

$$\sqrt{n}\left(\widetilde{\beta}_{\text{emd}} - \beta\right) \underset{d}{\longrightarrow} \mathrm{N}\left(0, \boldsymbol{V}_{\beta,\text{emd}}\right)$$

as $n \to \infty$, where

$$\boldsymbol{V}_{\beta,\text{emd}} = \boldsymbol{V}_{\beta} - \boldsymbol{V}_{\beta}\boldsymbol{R}\left(\boldsymbol{R}'\boldsymbol{V}_{\beta}\boldsymbol{R}\right)^{-1}\boldsymbol{R}'\boldsymbol{V}_{\beta}. \tag{8.26}$$

Since

$$\boldsymbol{V}_{\beta,\text{emd}} \leq \boldsymbol{V}_{\beta} \tag{8.27}$$

the estimator (8.25) has lower asymptotic variance than the unrestricted estimator. Furthermore, for any $\boldsymbol{W}$,

$$\boldsymbol{V}_{\beta,\text{emd}} \leq \boldsymbol{V}_{\beta}(\boldsymbol{W}) \tag{8.28}$$

so (8.25) is asymptotically efficient in the class of minimum distance estimators.

Theorem 8.9 shows that the minimum distance estimator with the smallest asymptotic variance is (8.25). One implication is that the CLS estimator is generally inefficient. The interesting exception for conditional homoskedasticity, in which case the optimal weight matrix is $\boldsymbol{W} = \left(\boldsymbol{V}_{\beta}^{0}\right)^{-1}$ and the CLS is an EMD estimator. Otherwise when the error is conditionally heteroskedastic, there are asymptotic efficiency gains by using minimum distance rather than least squares.

The fact that CLS is generally inefficient is counterintuitive and requires some reflection. Standard intuition suggests applying the same estimation method (least squares) to the unconstrained and constrained models, which is the common empirical practice. But Theorem 8.9 shows that this is inefficient. Why? Because the least squares estimator does not make use of the regressor X_2. It ignores the information $\mathbb{E}\left[X_2 e\right] = 0$. This information is relevant when the error is heteroskedastic and the excluded regressors are correlated with the included regressors.

Inequality (8.27) shows that the EMD estimator $\widetilde{\beta}_{\text{emd}}$ has a smaller asymptotic variance than the unrestricted least squares estimator $\widehat{\beta}$. Thus efficient estimation is attained by imposing correct restrictions when we use the minimum distance method.

8.9 EXCLUSION RESTRICTION REVISITED

Let us return to the example of estimation with a simple exclusion restriction. The model is

$$Y = X_1'\beta_1 + X_2'\beta_2 + e$$

with the exclusion restriction $\beta_2 = 0$. We have introduced three estimators of β_1. The first is unconstrained least squares applied to (8.10), which can be written as $\widehat{\beta}_1 = \widehat{\boldsymbol{Q}}_{11\cdot 2}^{-1}\widehat{\boldsymbol{Q}}_{1Y\cdot 2}$. From Theorem 6.8 and equation (7.14), its asymptotic variance is

$$\operatorname{avar}\left[\widehat{\beta}_1\right] = \boldsymbol{Q}_{11\cdot 2}^{-1}\left(\Omega_{11} - \boldsymbol{Q}_{12}\boldsymbol{Q}_{22}^{-1}\Omega_{21} - \Omega_{12}\boldsymbol{Q}_{22}^{-1}\boldsymbol{Q}_{21} + \boldsymbol{Q}_{12}\boldsymbol{Q}_{22}^{-1}\Omega_{22}\boldsymbol{Q}_{22}^{-1}\boldsymbol{Q}_{21}\right)\boldsymbol{Q}_{11\cdot 2}^{-1}.$$

The second estimator of β_1 is CLS, which can be written as $\widetilde{\beta}_1 = \widehat{\boldsymbol{Q}}_{11}^{-1} \widehat{\boldsymbol{Q}}_{1Y}$. Its asymptotic variance can be deduced from Theorem 8.8, but it is simpler to apply the CLT directly to show that

$$\operatorname{avar}\left[\widetilde{\beta}_1\right] = \boldsymbol{Q}_{11}^{-1} \Omega_{11} \boldsymbol{Q}_{11}^{-1}. \tag{8.29}$$

The third estimator of β_1 is efficient minimum distance. Applying (8.25), it equals

$$\overline{\beta}_1 = \widehat{\beta}_1 - \widehat{\boldsymbol{V}}_{12} \widehat{\boldsymbol{V}}_{22}^{-1} \widehat{\beta}_2 \tag{8.30}$$

where we have partitioned

$$\widehat{\boldsymbol{V}}_\beta = \begin{bmatrix} \widehat{\boldsymbol{V}}_{11} & \widehat{\boldsymbol{V}}_{12} \\ \widehat{\boldsymbol{V}}_{21} & \widehat{\boldsymbol{V}}_{22} \end{bmatrix}.$$

From Theorem 8.9, its asymptotic variance is

$$\operatorname{avar}\left[\overline{\beta}_1\right] = \boldsymbol{V}_{11} - \boldsymbol{V}_{12} \boldsymbol{V}_{22}^{-1} \boldsymbol{V}_{21}. \tag{8.31}$$

Exercise 8.16 asks you to verify equations (8.29), (8.30), and (8.31).

In general, the three estimators are different, and they have different asymptotic variances. It is instructive to compare the variances to assess whether the constrained estimator is more efficient than the unconstrained estimator.

First, assume conditional homoskedasticity. In this case, the two covariance matrices simplify to $\operatorname{avar}\left[\widehat{\beta}_1\right] = \sigma^2 \boldsymbol{Q}_{11\cdot 2}^{-1}$ and $\operatorname{avar}\left[\widetilde{\beta}_1\right] = \sigma^2 \boldsymbol{Q}_{11}^{-1}$. If $\boldsymbol{Q}_{12} = 0$ (so X_1 and X_2 are uncorrelated), then these two variance matrices are equal, and the two estimators have equal asymptotic efficiency. Otherwise, since $\boldsymbol{Q}_{12} \boldsymbol{Q}_{22}^{-1} \boldsymbol{Q}_{21} \geq 0$, then $\boldsymbol{Q}_{11} \geq \boldsymbol{Q}_{11} - \boldsymbol{Q}_{12} \boldsymbol{Q}_{22}^{-1} \boldsymbol{Q}_{21}$, and consequently,

$$\boldsymbol{Q}_{11}^{-1} \sigma^2 \leq \left(\boldsymbol{Q}_{11} - \boldsymbol{Q}_{12} \boldsymbol{Q}_{22}^{-1} \boldsymbol{Q}_{21}\right)^{-1} \sigma^2.$$

Thus under conditional homoskedasticity, $\widetilde{\beta}_1$ has a lower asymptotic covariance matrix than $\widehat{\beta}_1$. Therefore in this context, constrained least squares is more efficient than unconstrained least squares. This finding is consistent with our intuition that imposing a correct restriction (excluding an irrelevant regressor) improves estimation efficiency.

However, in the general case of conditional heteroskedasticity, this ranking is not guaranteed. In fact what is really amazing is that the variance ranking can be reversed. The CLS estimator can have a larger asymptotic variance than the unconstrained least squares estimator.

To see this, let's use the simple heteroskedastic example from Section 7.4. In that example, $Q_{11} = Q_{22} = 1$, $Q_{12} = \frac{1}{2}$, $\Omega_{11} = \Omega_{22} = 1$, and $\Omega_{12} = \frac{7}{8}$. We can calculate (see Exercise 8.17) that $Q_{11\cdot 2} = \frac{3}{4}$ and

$$\operatorname{avar}\left[\widehat{\beta}_1\right] = \frac{2}{3} \tag{8.32}$$

$$\operatorname{avar}\left[\widetilde{\beta}_1\right] = 1 \tag{8.33}$$

$$\operatorname{avar}\left[\overline{\beta}_1\right] = \frac{5}{8}. \tag{8.34}$$

Thus the CLS estimator $\widetilde{\beta}_1$ has a larger variance than the unrestricted least squares estimator $\widehat{\beta}_1$! The minimum distance estimator has the smallest variance of the three, as expected.

What we have found is that when the estimation method is least squares, deleting the irrelevant variable X_2 can actually increase estimation variance, or equivalently, adding an irrelevant variable can decrease the estimation variance.

To repeat this unexpected finding, we have shown that it is possible for least squares applied to the short regression (8.11) to be less efficient for estimation of β_1 than least squares applied to the long regression (8.10), even though the constraint $\beta_2 = 0$ is valid! This result is strongly counterintuitive. It seems to contradict our initial motivation for pursuing constrained estimation—to improve estimation efficiency.

It turns out that a more refined answer is appropriate. Constrained estimation is desirable but not necessarily CLS. While least squares is asymptotically efficient for estimation of the unconstrained projection model, it is not an efficient estimator of the constrained projection model.

8.10 VARIANCE AND STANDARD ERROR ESTIMATION

We have discussed covariance matrix estimation for CLS but not yet for the EMD estimator.

The asymptotic covariance matrix (8.26) may be estimated by replacing $\boldsymbol{V}_\beta$ with a consistent estimator. It is best to construct the variance estimate using $\widetilde{\beta}_{\mathrm{emd}}$. The EMD residuals are $\widetilde{e}_i = Y_i - X_i'\widetilde{\beta}_{\mathrm{emd}}$. Using these, we can estimate the matrix $\Omega = \mathbb{E}\left[XX'e^2\right]$ by

$$\widetilde{\Omega} = \frac{1}{n-k+q}\sum_{i=1}^{n} X_i X_i' \widetilde{e}_i^2.$$

Following the formula for CLS, I recommend an adjusted degrees of freedom. Given $\widetilde{\Omega}$, the moment estimator of $\boldsymbol{V}_\beta$ is $\widetilde{\boldsymbol{V}}_\beta = \widehat{\boldsymbol{Q}}_{XX}^{-1}\widetilde{\Omega}\widehat{\boldsymbol{Q}}_{XX}^{-1}$. Given this, we can construct the variance estimator

$$\widetilde{\boldsymbol{V}}_{\beta,\mathrm{emd}} = \widetilde{\boldsymbol{V}}_\beta - \widetilde{\boldsymbol{V}}_\beta \boldsymbol{R}\left(\boldsymbol{R}'\widetilde{\boldsymbol{V}}_\beta\boldsymbol{R}\right)^{-1}\boldsymbol{R}'\widetilde{\boldsymbol{V}}_\beta. \tag{8.35}$$

A standard error for $h'\widetilde{\beta}$ is then

$$s\left(h'\widetilde{\beta}\right) = \left(n^{-1}h'\widetilde{\boldsymbol{V}}_{\beta,\mathrm{emd}}h\right)^{1/2}. \tag{8.36}$$

8.11 HAUSMAN EQUALITY

From (8.25), we have

$$\begin{aligned}\sqrt{n}\left(\widehat{\beta}_{\mathrm{ols}} - \widetilde{\beta}_{\mathrm{emd}}\right) &= \widehat{\boldsymbol{V}}_\beta\boldsymbol{R}\left(\boldsymbol{R}'\widehat{\boldsymbol{V}}_\beta\boldsymbol{R}\right)^{-1}\sqrt{n}\left(\boldsymbol{R}'\widehat{\beta}_{\mathrm{ols}} - \boldsymbol{c}\right)\\ &\underset{d}{\longrightarrow} \mathrm{N}\left(0, \boldsymbol{V}_\beta\boldsymbol{R}\left(\boldsymbol{R}'\boldsymbol{V}_\beta\boldsymbol{R}\right)^{-1}\boldsymbol{R}'\boldsymbol{V}_\beta\right).\end{aligned}$$

It follows that the asymptotic variances of the estimators satisfy the relationship

$$\operatorname{avar}\left[\widehat{\beta}_{\mathrm{ols}} - \widetilde{\beta}_{\mathrm{emd}}\right] = \operatorname{avar}\left[\widehat{\beta}_{\mathrm{ols}}\right] - \operatorname{avar}\left[\widetilde{\beta}_{\mathrm{emd}}\right]. \tag{8.37}$$

We call (8.37) the **Hausman Equality**: The asymptotic variance of the difference between an efficient and another estimator is the difference in the asymptotic variances.

8.12 EXAMPLE: MANKIW, ROMER, AND WEIL (1992)

Let us illustrate the methods by replicating some of the estimates reported in a well-known paper by Mankiw, Romer, and Weil (1992). The paper investigates the implications of the Solow growth model using cross-country regressions. A key equation in their paper regresses the change between 1960 and 1985 in log GDP per capita on (1) log GDP in 1960; (2) the log of the ratio of aggregate investment to GDP; (3) the log of the sum of the population growth rate n, the technological growth rate g, and the rate of depreciation δ; and (4) the log of the percentage of the working-age population that is in secondary school (*School*), the latter a proxy for human-capital accumulation.

The data are available on the textbook webpage in the file `MRW1992`.

The sample is 98 non-oil-producing countries, and the data were reported in the published paper. As g and δ were unknown, the authors set $g+\delta=0.05$. Table 8.1 reports least squares estimates in the first column of the Table. The estimates are consistent with the Solow theory, due to the positive coefficients on investment and human capital and negative coefficient for population growth. The estimates are also consistent with the convergence hypothesis (that income levels tend toward a common mean over time), as the coefficient on intial GDP is negative.

The authors show that in the Solow model, the 2nd, 3rd, and 4th coefficients sum to 0. They re-estimated the equation imposing this constraint. The constrained least squares estimates are presented in the second column of Table 8.1 and efficient minimum distance estimates in the third column. Most of the coefficients and standard errors exhibit only small changes by imposing the constraint. The one exception is the coefficient on log population growth, which increases in magnitude and its standard error decreases substantially. The differences between the CLS and EMD estimates are modest.

The Stata, R, and MATLAB codes that implement these estimates are displayed below.

You may notice that the Stata code has a section that uses the Mata matrix programming language. This is used because Stata does not implement the efficient minimum distance estimator, so this function needs to be separately programmed. As illustrated here, the Mata language allows a Stata user to implement methods using commands that are quite similar to MATLAB.

Table 8.1
Estimates of Solow growth model

	$\widehat{\beta}_{\text{ols}}$	$\widehat{\beta}_{\text{cls}}$	$\widehat{\beta}_{\text{emd}}$
$\log GDP_{1960}$	−0.29	−0.30	−0.30
	(0.05)	(0.05)	(0.05)
$\log \frac{I}{GDP}$	0.52	0.50	0.46
	(0.11)	(0.09)	(0.08)
$\log(n+g+\delta)$	−0.51	−0.74	−0.71
	(0.24)	(0.08)	(0.07)
$\log(School)$	0.23	0.24	0.25
	(0.07)	(0.07)	(0.06)
Intercept	3.02	2.46	2.48
	(0.74)	(0.44)	(0.44)

Note: Standard errors are heteroskedasticity-consistent

Stata do File

```
use "MRW1992.dta", clear
gen lndY = log(Y85)-log(Y60)
gen lnY60 = log(Y60)
gen lnI = log(invest/100)
gen lnG = log(pop_growth/100+0.05)
gen lnS = log(school/100)
* Unrestricted regression
reg lndY lnY60 lnI lnG lnS if N==1, r
* Store result for efficient minimum distance
mat b = e(b)'
scalar k = e(rank)
mat V = e(V)
* Constrained regression
constraint define 1 lnI+lnG+lnS=0
cnsreg lndY lnY60 lnI lnG lnS if N==1, constraints(1) r
* Efficient minimum distance
mata{
    data = st_data(.,("lnY60","lnI","lnG","lnS","lndY","N"))
    data_select = select(data,data[.,6]:==1)
    y = data_select[.,5]
    n = rows(y)
    x = (data_select[.,1..4],J(n,1,1))
    k = cols(x)
    invx = invsym(x'*x)
    b_ols = st_matrix("b")
    V_ols = st_matrix("V")
    R = (0 \ 1 \ 1 \ 1 \ 0)
    b_emd = b_ols-V_ols*R*invsym(R'*V_ols*R)*R'*b_ols
    e_emd = J(1,k,y-x*b_emd)
    xe_emd = x:*e_emd
    xe_emd'*xe_emd
    V2 = (n/(n-k+1))*invx*(xe_emd'*xe_emd)*invx
    V_emd = V2 - V2*R*invsym(R'*V2*R)*R'*V2
    se_emd = diagonal(sqrt(V_emd))
    st_matrix("b_emd",b_emd)
    st_matrix("se_emd",se_emd)}
mat list b_emd
mat list se_emd
```

R Program File

```
data <- read.table("MRW1992.txt",header=TRUE)
N <- matrix(data$N,ncol=1)
lndY <- matrix(log(data$Y85)-log(data$Y60),ncol=1)
lnY60 <- matrix(log(data$Y60),ncol=1)
lnI <- matrix(log(data$invest/100),ncol=1)
lnG <- matrix(log(data$pop_growth/100+0.05),ncol=1)
lnS <- matrix(log(data$school/100),ncol=1)
xx <- as.matrix(cbind(lnY60,lnI,lnG,lnS,matrix(1,nrow(lndY),1)))
x <- xx[N==1,]
y <- lndY[N==1]
n <- nrow(x)
k <- ncol(x)
# Unrestricted regression
invx <-solve(t(x)%*%x)
b_ols <- solve((t(x)%*%x),(t(x)%*%y))
e_ols <- rep((y-x%*%beta_ols),times=k)
xe_ols <- x*e_ols
V_ols <- (n/(n-k))*invx%*%(t(xe_ols)%*%xe_ols)%*%invx
se_ols <- sqrt(diag(V_ols))
print(beta_ols)
print(se_ols)
# Constrained regression
R <- c(0,1,1,1,0)
iR <- invx%*%R%*%solve(t(R)%*%invx%*%R)%*%t(R)
b_cls <- b_ols - iR%*%b_ols
e_cls <- rep((y-x%*%b_cls),times=k)
xe_cls <- x*e_cls
V_tilde <- (n/(n-k+1))*invx%*%(t(xe_cls)%*%xe_cls)%*%invx
V_cls <- V_tilde - iR%*%V_tilde - V_tilde%*%t(iR) +iR%*%V_tilde%*%t(iR)
print(b_cls)print(se_cls)
# Efficient minimum distance
Vr <- V_ols%*%R%*%solve(t(R)%*%V_ols%*%R)%*%t(R)
b_emd <- b_ols - Vr%*%b_ols
e_emd <- rep((y-x%*%b_emd),times=k)
xe_emd <- x*e_emd
V2 <- (n/(n-k+1))*invx%*%(t(xe_emd)%*%xe_emd)%*%invx
V_emd <- V2 - V2%*%R%*%solve(t(R)%*%V2%*%R)%*%t(R)%*%V2
se_emd <- sqrt(diag(V_emd))
```

MATLAB Program File

```
data = xlsread('MRW1992.xlsx');
N = data(:,1);
Y60 = data(:,4);
Y85 = data(:,5);
pop_growth = data(:,7);
invest = data(:,8);
school = data(:,9);
lndY = log(Y85)-log(Y60);
lnY60 = log(Y60);
lnI = log(invest/100);
lnG = log(pop_growth/100+0.05);
lnS = log(school/100);
xx = [lnY60,lnI,lnG,lnS,ones(size(lndY,1),1)];
x = xx(N==1,:);
y = lndY(N==1);
[n,k] = size(x);
% Unrestricted regression
invx = inv(x'*x);
beta_ols = (x'*x)\(x'*y);
xe_ols = x.*(y-x*beta_ols);
V_ols = (n/(n-k))*invx*(xe_ols'*xe_ols)*invx;
se_ols = sqrt(diag(V_ols));
display(beta_ols);
display(se_ols);
% Constrained regression
R = [0;1;1;1;0];
iR = invx*R*inv(R'*invx*R)*R';
beta_cls = beta_ols - iR*beta_ols;
xe_cls = x.*(y-x*beta_cls);
V_tilde = (n/(n-k+1))*invx*(xe_cls'*xe_cls)*invx;
V_cls = V_tilde - iR*V_tilde - V_tilde*(iR') + iR*V_tilde*(iR');
se_cls = sqrt(diag(V_cls));
display(beta_cls);display(se_cls);
% Efficient minimum distance
beta_emd = beta_ols-V_ols*R*inv(R'*V_ols*R)*R'*beta_ols;
xe_emd = x.*(y-x*beta_emd);
V2 = (n/(n-k+1))*invx*(xe_emd'*xe_emd)*invx;
V_emd = V2 - V2*R*inv(R'*V2*R)*R'*V2;
se_emd = sqrt(diag(V_emd));
display(beta_emd);display(se_emd);
```

8.13 MISSPECIFICATION

What are the consequences for a constrained estimator $\widetilde{\beta}$ if the constraint (8.1) is incorrect? To be specific, suppose that the truth is

$$\boldsymbol{R}'\beta = \boldsymbol{c}^*$$

where $\boldsymbol{c}^*$ is not necessarily equal to $\boldsymbol{c}$.

This situation is a generalization of the analysis of "omitted variable bias" in Section 2.24, where we found that the short regression (i.e., (8.12)) is estimating a different projection coefficient than the long regression (i.e., (8.10)).

One answer is to apply formula (8.23) to find

$$\widetilde{\beta}_{\mathrm{md}} \underset{p}{\longrightarrow} \beta^*_{\mathrm{md}} = \beta - \boldsymbol{W}^{-1}\boldsymbol{R}\left(\boldsymbol{R}'\boldsymbol{W}^{-1}\boldsymbol{R}\right)^{-1}\left(\boldsymbol{c}^* - \boldsymbol{c}\right). \tag{8.38}$$

The second term, $\boldsymbol{W}^{-1}\boldsymbol{R}\left(\boldsymbol{R}'\boldsymbol{W}^{-1}\boldsymbol{R}\right)^{-1}(\boldsymbol{c}^* - \boldsymbol{c})$, shows that imposing an incorrect constraint leads to inconsistency—an asymptotic bias. We can call the limiting value β^*_{md} the "minimum-distance projection coefficient" or the "pseudo-true value" implied by the restriction.

However, we can say more. For example, we can describe some characteristics of the approximating projections. The CLS estimator projection coefficient has the representation

$$\beta^*_{\mathrm{cls}} = \underset{\boldsymbol{R}'\beta=\boldsymbol{c}}{\operatorname{argmin}}\, \mathbb{E}\left[\left(Y - X'\beta\right)^2\right]$$

which is the best linear predictor subject to the constraint (8.1). The minimum distance estimator converges in probability to

$$\beta^*_{\mathrm{md}} = \underset{\boldsymbol{R}'\beta=\boldsymbol{c}}{\operatorname{argmin}}\, (\beta - \beta_0)'\, \boldsymbol{W}\, (\beta - \beta_0)$$

where β_0 is the true coefficient. That is, β^*_{md} is the coefficient vector satisfying (8.1) closest to the true value in the weighted Euclidean norm. These calculations show that the constrained estimators are still reasonable, in the sense that they produce good approximations to the true coefficient conditional on being required to satisfy the constraint.

We can also show that $\widetilde{\beta}_{\mathrm{md}}$ has an asymptotic normal distribution. The trick is to define the pseudo-true value

$$\beta^*_n = \beta - \widehat{\boldsymbol{W}}^{-1}\boldsymbol{R}\left(\boldsymbol{R}'\widehat{\boldsymbol{W}}^{-1}\boldsymbol{R}\right)^{-1}\left(\boldsymbol{c}^* - \boldsymbol{c}\right). \tag{8.39}$$

(Note that (8.38) and (8.39) are different!) Then

$$\begin{aligned}
\sqrt{n}\left(\widetilde{\beta}_{\mathrm{md}} - \beta^*_n\right) &= \sqrt{n}\left(\widehat{\beta} - \beta\right) - \widehat{\boldsymbol{W}}^{-1}\boldsymbol{R}\left(\boldsymbol{R}'\widehat{\boldsymbol{W}}^{-1}\boldsymbol{R}\right)^{-1}\sqrt{n}\left(\boldsymbol{R}'\widehat{\beta} - \boldsymbol{c}^*\right) \\
&= \left(\boldsymbol{I}_k - \widehat{\boldsymbol{W}}^{-1}\boldsymbol{R}\left(\boldsymbol{R}'\widehat{\boldsymbol{W}}^{-1}\boldsymbol{R}\right)^{-1}\boldsymbol{R}'\right)\sqrt{n}\left(\widehat{\beta} - \beta\right) \\
&\underset{d}{\longrightarrow} \left(\boldsymbol{I}_k - \boldsymbol{W}^{-1}\boldsymbol{R}\left(\boldsymbol{R}'\boldsymbol{W}^{-1}\boldsymbol{R}\right)^{-1}\boldsymbol{R}'\right)\mathrm{N}\left(0, \boldsymbol{V}_\beta\right) \\
&= \mathrm{N}\left(0, \boldsymbol{V}_\beta(\boldsymbol{W})\right).
\end{aligned} \tag{8.40}$$

In particular,

$$\sqrt{n}\left(\widetilde{\beta}_{\mathrm{emd}}-\beta_n^*\right)\underset{d}{\longrightarrow}\mathrm{N}\left(0,\boldsymbol{V}_\beta^*\right).$$

Thus even when the constraint (8.1) is misspecified, the conventional covariance matrix estimator (8.35) and standard error (8.36) are appropriate measures of the sampling variance, though the distributions are centered at the pseudo-true values (projections) β_n^* rather than at β. That the estimators are biased is an unavoidable consequence of misspecification.

An alternative approach to the asymptotic distribution theory under misspecification uses the concept of local alternatives. It is a technical device that might seem a bit artificial, but it is a powerful method to derive useful distributional approximations in a wide variety of contexts. The idea is to index the true coefficient β_n by n via the relationship

$$\boldsymbol{R}'\beta_n=\boldsymbol{c}+\delta n^{-1/2}. \tag{8.41}$$

for some $\delta\in\mathbb{R}^q$. Equation (8.41) specifies that β_n violates (8.1), and thus the constraint is misspecified. However, the constraint is "close" to correct, as the difference $\boldsymbol{R}'\beta_n-\boldsymbol{c}=\delta n^{-1/2}$ is "small" in the sense that it decreases with the sample size n. We call (8.41) **local misspecification**.

The asymptotic theory is derived as $n\rightarrow\infty$ under the sequence of probability distributions with the coefficients β_n. The way to think about this is that the true value of the parameter is β_n and it is "close" to satisfying (8.1). The deviation is proportional to $n^{-1/2}$ because this is the only choice for which the localizing parameter δ appears in the asymptotic distribution but does not dominate it. The best way to see this is to work through the asymptotic approximation.

Since β_n is the true coefficient value, then $Y=X'\beta_n+e$, and we have the standard representation for the unconstrained estimator, namely,

$$\sqrt{n}\left(\widehat{\beta}-\beta_n\right)=\left(\frac{1}{n}\sum_{i=1}^n X_iX_i'\right)^{-1}\left(\frac{1}{\sqrt{n}}\sum_{i=1}^n X_ie_i\right)\underset{d}{\longrightarrow}\mathrm{N}\left(0,\boldsymbol{V}_\beta\right). \tag{8.42}$$

There is no difference under fixed (classical) or local asymptotics, since the right-hand side is independent of the coefficient β_n.

A difference arises for the constrained estimator. Using (8.41), $\boldsymbol{c}=\boldsymbol{R}'\beta_n-\delta n^{-1/2}$, so

$$\boldsymbol{R}'\widehat{\beta}-\boldsymbol{c}=\boldsymbol{R}'\left(\widehat{\beta}-\beta_n\right)+\delta n^{-1/2}$$

and

$$\begin{aligned}\widetilde{\beta}_{\mathrm{md}}&=\widehat{\beta}-\widehat{\boldsymbol{W}}^{-1}\boldsymbol{R}\left(\boldsymbol{R}'\widehat{\boldsymbol{W}}^{-1}\boldsymbol{R}\right)^{-1}\left(\boldsymbol{R}'\widehat{\beta}-\boldsymbol{c}\right)\\&=\widehat{\beta}-\widehat{\boldsymbol{W}}^{-1}\boldsymbol{R}\left(\boldsymbol{R}'\widehat{\boldsymbol{W}}^{-1}\boldsymbol{R}\right)^{-1}\boldsymbol{R}'\left(\widehat{\beta}-\beta_n\right)+\widehat{\boldsymbol{W}}^{-1}\boldsymbol{R}\left(\boldsymbol{R}'\widehat{\boldsymbol{W}}^{-1}\boldsymbol{R}\right)^{-1}\delta n^{-1/2}.\end{aligned}$$

It follows that

$$\sqrt{n}\left(\widetilde{\beta}_{\mathrm{md}}-\beta_n\right)=\left(\boldsymbol{I}_k-\widehat{\boldsymbol{W}}^{-1}\boldsymbol{R}\left(\boldsymbol{R}'\widehat{\boldsymbol{W}}^{-1}\boldsymbol{R}\right)^{-1}\boldsymbol{R}'\right)\sqrt{n}\left(\widehat{\beta}-\beta_n\right)+\widehat{\boldsymbol{W}}^{-1}\boldsymbol{R}\left(\boldsymbol{R}'\widehat{\boldsymbol{W}}^{-1}\boldsymbol{R}\right)^{-1}\delta.$$

The first term is asymptotically normal (from (8.42)). The second term converges in probability to a constant. This is because the $n^{-1/2}$ local scaling in (8.41) is exactly balanced by the $\sqrt{n}$ scaling of the estimator. No alternative rate would have produced this result.

Consequently, we find that the asymptotic distribution equals

$$\sqrt{n}\left(\widetilde{\beta}_{\mathrm{md}}-\beta_n\right) \underset{d}{\longrightarrow} \mathrm{N}\left(0, \boldsymbol{V}_\beta\right)+\boldsymbol{W}^{-1}\boldsymbol{R}\left(\boldsymbol{R}'\boldsymbol{W}^{-1}\boldsymbol{R}\right)^{-1}\delta=\mathrm{N}\left(\delta^*, \boldsymbol{V}_\beta(\boldsymbol{W})\right) \tag{8.43}$$

where $\delta^*=\boldsymbol{W}^{-1}\boldsymbol{R}\left(\boldsymbol{R}'\boldsymbol{W}^{-1}\boldsymbol{R}\right)^{-1}\delta$.

The asymptotic distribution (8.43) is an approximation of the sampling distribution of the restricted estimator under misspecification. The distribution (8.43) contains an asymptotic bias component δ^*. The approximation is not fundamentally different from (8.40)—they both have the same asymptotic variances and both reflect the bias due to misspecification. The difference is that (8.40) puts the bias on the left side of the convergence arrow, while (8.43) has the bias on the right side. There is no substantive difference between the two. However, (8.43) is more convenient for some purposes, such as the analysis of the power of tests, as we will explore in Chapter 9.

8.14 NONLINEAR CONSTRAINTS

In some cases, it is desirable to impose nonlinear constraints on the parameter vector β. They can be written as

$$r(\beta)=0 \tag{8.44}$$

where $r:\mathbb{R}^k\rightarrow\mathbb{R}^q$. Equation (8.44) includes the linear constraints (8.1) as a special case. An example of (8.44) that cannot be written as (8.1) is $\beta_1\beta_2=1$, which is (8.44) with $r(\beta)=\beta_1\beta_2-1$.

The constrained least squares and minimum distance estimators of β subject to (8.44) solve the minimization problems

$$\widetilde{\beta}_{\mathrm{cls}}=\underset{r(\beta)=0}{\operatorname{argmin}}\ \mathrm{SSE}(\beta) \tag{8.45}$$

$$\widetilde{\beta}_{\mathrm{md}}=\underset{r(\beta)=0}{\operatorname{argmin}}\ J(\beta) \tag{8.46}$$

where $\mathrm{SSE}(\beta)$ and $J(\beta)$ are defined in (8.4) and (8.19), respectively. The solutions solve the Lagrangians

$$\mathscr{L}(\beta,\lambda)=\frac{1}{2}\mathrm{SSE}(\beta)+\lambda' r(\beta)$$

or

$$\mathscr{L}(\beta,\lambda)=\frac{1}{2}J(\beta)+\lambda' r(\beta) \tag{8.47}$$

over (β,λ).

Computationally, there is no general closed-form solution, so the solutions must be found numerically. Algorithms to numerically solve (8.45) and (8.46) are known as **constrained optimization** methods and are available in programming languages including MATLAB and R. See Chapter 12 of *Probability and Statistics for Economists*.

Assumption 8.3

1. $r(\beta)=0$.
2. $r(\beta)$ is continuously differentiable at the true β.
3. $\mathrm{rank}(\boldsymbol{R})=q$, where $\boldsymbol{R}=\frac{\partial}{\partial\beta}r(\beta)'$.

The asymptotic distribution is a simple generalization of the case of a linear constraint, but the proof is more delicate.

Theorem 8.10 Under Assumptions 7.2, 8.2, and 8.3, for $\widetilde{\beta} = \widetilde{\beta}_{\text{md}}$ and $\widetilde{\beta} = \widetilde{\beta}_{\text{cls}}$ defined in (8.45) and (8.46),

$$\sqrt{n}\left(\widetilde{\beta} - \beta\right) \underset{d}{\longrightarrow} \mathrm{N}\left(0, \boldsymbol{V}_{\beta}(\boldsymbol{W})\right)$$

as $n \to \infty$, where $\boldsymbol{V}_{\beta}(\boldsymbol{W})$ is defined in (8.24). For $\widetilde{\beta}_{\text{cls}}$, $\boldsymbol{W} = \boldsymbol{Q}_{XX}$ and $\boldsymbol{V}_{\beta}(\boldsymbol{W}) = \boldsymbol{V}_{\text{cls}}$, as defined in Theorem 8.8. $\boldsymbol{V}_{\beta}(\boldsymbol{W})$ is minimized with $\boldsymbol{W} = \boldsymbol{V}_{\beta}^{-1}$, in which case the asymptotic variance is

$$\boldsymbol{V}_{\beta}^{*} = \boldsymbol{V}_{\beta} - \boldsymbol{V}_{\beta}\boldsymbol{R}\left(\boldsymbol{R}'\boldsymbol{V}_{\beta}\boldsymbol{R}\right)^{-1}\boldsymbol{R}'\boldsymbol{V}_{\beta}.$$

The asymptotic covariance matrix for the efficient minimum distance estimator can be estimated by

$$\widehat{\boldsymbol{V}}_{\beta}^{*} = \widehat{\boldsymbol{V}}_{\beta} - \widehat{\boldsymbol{V}}_{\beta}\widehat{\boldsymbol{R}}\left(\widehat{\boldsymbol{R}}'\widehat{\boldsymbol{V}}_{\beta}\widehat{\boldsymbol{R}}\right)^{-1}\widehat{\boldsymbol{R}}'\widehat{\boldsymbol{V}}_{\beta}$$

where

$$\widehat{\boldsymbol{R}} = \frac{\partial}{\partial \beta} r(\widetilde{\beta}_{\text{md}})'. \tag{8.48}$$

Standard errors for the elements of $\widetilde{\beta}_{\text{md}}$ are the square roots of the diagonal elements of $\widehat{\boldsymbol{V}}_{\widetilde{\beta}}^{*} = n^{-1}\widehat{\boldsymbol{V}}_{\beta}^{*}$.

8.15 INEQUALITY RESTRICTIONS

Inequality constraints on the parameter vector β take the form

$$r(\beta) \geq 0 \tag{8.49}$$

for some function $r: \mathbb{R}^k \to \mathbb{R}^q$. The most common example is a nonnegative constraint $\beta_1 \geq 0$.

The constrained least squares and minimum distance estimators can be written as

$$\widetilde{\beta}_{\text{cls}} = \underset{r(\beta)\geq 0}{\operatorname{argmin}}\, \mathrm{SSE}(\beta) \tag{8.50}$$

and

$$\widetilde{\beta}_{\text{md}} = \underset{r(\beta)\geq 0}{\operatorname{argmin}}\, J(\beta). \tag{8.51}$$

Except in special cases, the constrained estimators do not have simple algebraic solutions. An important exception is when there is a single nonnegativity constraint (e.g., $\beta_1 \geq 0$ with $q = 1$). In this case, the constrained estimator can be found by the following approach. Compute the uncontrained estimator $\widehat{\beta}$. If $\widehat{\beta}_1 \geq 0$, then $\widetilde{\beta} = \widehat{\beta}$. Otherwise if $\widehat{\beta}_1 < 0$, then impose $\beta_1 = 0$ (eliminate the regressor X_1) and re-estimate. This method yields the constrained least squares estimator. While this method works when there is a single nonnegativity constraint, it does not immediately generalize to other contexts.

Inference on inequality-constrained estimators is unfortunately quite challenging. The conventional asymptotic theory gives rise to the following dichotomy. If the true parameter satisfies the strict inequality

$r(\beta) > 0$, then asymptotically, the estimator is not subject to the constraint and the inequality-constrained estimator has an asymptotic distribution equal to the unconstrained case. However, if the true parameter is on the boundary (e.g., $r(\beta) = 0$), then the estimator has a truncated structure. This is easiest to see in the one-dimensional case. If we have an estimator $\widehat{\beta}$ that satisfies $\sqrt{n}\left(\widehat{\beta} - \beta\right) \underset{d}{\longrightarrow} Z = \mathrm{N}\left(0, V_\beta\right)$ and $\beta = 0$, then the constrained estimator $\widetilde{\beta} = \max[\widehat{\beta}, 0]$ will have the asymptotic distribution $\sqrt{n}\widetilde{\beta} \underset{d}{\longrightarrow} \max[Z, 0]$, a "half-normal" distribution.

8.16 TECHNICAL PROOFS*

Proof of Theorem 8.9, equation (8.28) Let $\boldsymbol{R}_\perp$ be a full rank $k \times \left(k - q\right)$ matrix satisfying $\boldsymbol{R}_\perp' \boldsymbol{V}_\beta \boldsymbol{R} = 0$, and then set $\boldsymbol{C} = [\boldsymbol{R}, \boldsymbol{R}_\perp]$, which is full rank and invertible. Then we can calculate that

$$\boldsymbol{C}'\boldsymbol{V}_\beta^*\boldsymbol{C} = \begin{bmatrix} \boldsymbol{R}'\boldsymbol{V}_\beta^*\boldsymbol{R} & \boldsymbol{R}'\boldsymbol{V}_\beta^*\boldsymbol{R}_\perp \\ \boldsymbol{R}_\perp'\boldsymbol{V}_\beta^*\boldsymbol{R} & \boldsymbol{R}_\perp'\boldsymbol{V}_\beta^*\boldsymbol{R}_\perp \end{bmatrix} = \begin{bmatrix} 0 & 0 \\ 0 & \boldsymbol{R}_\perp'\boldsymbol{V}_\beta\boldsymbol{R}_\perp \end{bmatrix}$$

and

$$\begin{aligned} &\boldsymbol{C}'\boldsymbol{V}_\beta(\boldsymbol{W})\boldsymbol{C} \\ &= \begin{bmatrix} \boldsymbol{R}'\boldsymbol{V}_\beta^*(\boldsymbol{W})\boldsymbol{R} & \boldsymbol{R}'\boldsymbol{V}_\beta^*(\boldsymbol{W})\boldsymbol{R}_\perp \\ \boldsymbol{R}_\perp'\boldsymbol{V}_\beta^*(\boldsymbol{W})\boldsymbol{R} & \boldsymbol{R}_\perp'\boldsymbol{V}_\beta^*(\boldsymbol{W})\boldsymbol{R}_\perp \end{bmatrix} \\ &= \begin{bmatrix} 0 & 0 \\ 0 & \boldsymbol{R}_\perp'\boldsymbol{V}_\beta\boldsymbol{R}_\perp + \boldsymbol{R}_\perp'\boldsymbol{W}\boldsymbol{R}\left(\boldsymbol{R}'\boldsymbol{W}\boldsymbol{R}\right)^{-1}\boldsymbol{R}'\boldsymbol{V}_\beta\boldsymbol{R}\left(\boldsymbol{R}'\boldsymbol{W}\boldsymbol{R}\right)^{-1}\boldsymbol{R}'\boldsymbol{W}\boldsymbol{R}_\perp \end{bmatrix}. \end{aligned}$$

Thus,

$$\begin{aligned} &\boldsymbol{C}'\left(\boldsymbol{V}_\beta(\boldsymbol{W}) - \boldsymbol{V}_\beta^*\right)\boldsymbol{C} \\ &= \boldsymbol{C}'\boldsymbol{V}_\beta(\boldsymbol{W})\boldsymbol{C} - \boldsymbol{C}'\boldsymbol{V}_\beta^*\boldsymbol{C} \\ &= \begin{bmatrix} 0 & 0 \\ 0 & \boldsymbol{R}_\perp'\boldsymbol{W}\boldsymbol{R}\left(\boldsymbol{R}'\boldsymbol{W}\boldsymbol{R}\right)^{-1}\boldsymbol{R}'\boldsymbol{V}_\beta\boldsymbol{R}\left(\boldsymbol{R}'\boldsymbol{W}\boldsymbol{R}\right)^{-1}\boldsymbol{R}'\boldsymbol{W}\boldsymbol{R}_\perp \end{bmatrix} \\ &\geq 0 \end{aligned}$$

Since $\boldsymbol{C}$ is invertible, it follows that $\boldsymbol{V}_\beta(\boldsymbol{W}) - \boldsymbol{V}_\beta^* \geq 0$, which is (8.28). ■

Proof of Theorem 8.10 We show the result for the minimum distance estimator $\widetilde{\beta} = \widetilde{\beta}_{\mathrm{md}}$, because the proof for the constrained least squares estimator is similar. For simplicity, assume that the constrained estimator is consistent $\widetilde{\beta} \underset{p}{\longrightarrow} \beta$. This can be shown with more effort but requires a deeper treatment than is appropriate for this textbook.

For each element $r_j(\beta)$ of the q-vector $r(\beta)$, by the Mean Value Theorem (Theorem A.14 in *Probability and Statistics for Economists*), there exists a β_j^* on the line segment joining $\widetilde{\beta}$ and β such that

$$r_j(\widetilde{\beta}) = r_j(\beta) + \frac{\partial}{\partial \beta} r_j(\beta_j^*)'\left(\widetilde{\beta} - \beta\right). \tag{8.52}$$

Let $\boldsymbol{R}_n^*$ be the $k \times q$ matrix:

$$\boldsymbol{R}^* = \left[\frac{\partial}{\partial \beta} r_1(\beta_1^*) \quad \frac{\partial}{\partial \beta} r_2(\beta_2^*) \quad \cdots \quad \frac{\partial}{\partial \beta} r_q(\beta_q^*) \right].$$

Since $\widetilde{\beta} \underset{p}{\longrightarrow} \beta$, it follows that $\beta_j^* \underset{p}{\longrightarrow} \beta$, and by the CMT, $\boldsymbol{R}^* \underset{p}{\longrightarrow} \boldsymbol{R}$. Stacking (8.52), we obtain

$$r(\widetilde{\beta}) = r(\beta) + \boldsymbol{R}^{*\prime} \left(\widetilde{\beta} - \beta \right).$$

Since $r\left(\widetilde{\beta}\right) = 0$ by construction and $r(\beta) = 0$ by Assumption 8.1, this implies

$$0 = \boldsymbol{R}^{*\prime} \left(\widetilde{\beta} - \beta \right). \tag{8.53}$$

The first-order condition for (8.47) is $\widehat{\boldsymbol{W}} \left(\widehat{\beta} - \widetilde{\beta} \right) = \widehat{\boldsymbol{R}} \widetilde{\lambda}$, where $\widehat{\boldsymbol{R}}$ is defined in (8.48). Premultiplying by $\boldsymbol{R}^{*\prime} \widehat{\boldsymbol{W}}^{-1}$, inverting, and using (8.53), we find

$$\widetilde{\lambda} = \left(\boldsymbol{R}^{*\prime} \widehat{\boldsymbol{W}}^{-1} \widehat{\boldsymbol{R}} \right)^{-1} \boldsymbol{R}^{*\prime} \left(\widehat{\beta} - \widetilde{\beta} \right) = \left(\boldsymbol{R}^{*\prime} \widehat{\boldsymbol{W}}^{-1} \widehat{\boldsymbol{R}} \right)^{-1} \boldsymbol{R}^{*\prime} \left(\widehat{\beta} - \beta \right).$$

Thus,

$$\widetilde{\beta} - \beta = \left(\boldsymbol{I}_k - \widehat{\boldsymbol{W}}^{-1} \widehat{\boldsymbol{R}} \left(\boldsymbol{R}_n^{*\prime} \widehat{\boldsymbol{W}}^{-1} \widehat{\boldsymbol{R}} \right)^{-1} \boldsymbol{R}_n^{*\prime} \right) \left(\widehat{\beta} - \beta \right). \tag{8.54}$$

From Theorem 7.3 and Theorem 7.6, we find

$$\begin{aligned}
\sqrt{n} \left(\widetilde{\beta} - \beta \right) &= \left(\boldsymbol{I}_k - \widehat{\boldsymbol{W}}^{-1} \widehat{\boldsymbol{R}} \left(\boldsymbol{R}_n^{*\prime} \widehat{\boldsymbol{W}}^{-1} \widetilde{\boldsymbol{R}} \right)^{-1} \boldsymbol{R}_n^{*\prime} \right) \sqrt{n} \left(\widehat{\beta} - \beta \right) \\
&\underset{d}{\longrightarrow} \left(\boldsymbol{I}_k - \boldsymbol{W}^{-1} \boldsymbol{R} \left(\boldsymbol{R}' \boldsymbol{W}^{-1} \boldsymbol{R} \right)^{-1} \boldsymbol{R}' \right) \mathrm{N}\left(0, \boldsymbol{V}_\beta\right) \\
&= \mathrm{N}\left(0, \boldsymbol{V}_\beta(\boldsymbol{W})\right).
\end{aligned}$$

■

8.17 EXERCISES

Exercise 8.1 In the model $Y = X_1'\beta_1 + X_2'\beta_2 + e$, show directly from equation (8.3) that the CLS estimator of $\beta = (\beta_1, \beta_2)$ subject to the constraint that $\beta_2 = 0$ is the OLS regression of Y on X_1.

Exercise 8.2 In the model $Y = X_1'\beta_1 + X_2'\beta_2 + e$, show directly from equation (8.3) that the CLS estimator of $\beta = (\beta_1, \beta_2)$ subject to the constraint $\beta_1 = \boldsymbol{c}$ (where $\boldsymbol{c}$ is some given vector) is OLS of $Y - X_1'\boldsymbol{c}$ on X_2.

Exercise 8.3 In the model $Y = X_1'\beta_1 + X_2'\beta_2 + e$, with β_1 and β_2 each $k \times 1$, find the CLS estimator of $\beta = (\beta_1, \beta_2)$ subject to the constraint that $\beta_1 = -\beta_2$.

Exercise 8.4 In the linear projection model $Y = \alpha + X'\beta + e$, consider the restriction $\beta = 0$.

(a) Find the CLS estimator of α under the restriction $\beta = 0$.

(b) Find an expression for the efficient minimum distance estimator of α under the restriction $\beta = 0$.

Exercise 8.5 Verify that for $\widetilde{\beta}_{\text{cls}}$ defined in (8.8), $\boldsymbol{R}'\widetilde{\beta}_{\text{cls}} = \boldsymbol{c}$.

Exercise 8.6 Prove Theorem 8.1.

Exercise 8.7 Prove Theorem 8.2, that is, $\mathbb{E}\left[\widetilde{\beta}_{\text{cls}} \mid \boldsymbol{X}\right] = \beta$, under the assumptions of the linear regression regression model and (8.1). (Hint: Use Theorem 8.1.)

Exercise 8.8 Prove Theorem 8.3.

Exercise 8.9 Prove Theorem 8.4. That is, show that $\mathbb{E}\left[s^2_{\text{cls}} \mid \boldsymbol{X}\right] = \sigma^2$ under the assumptions of the homoskedastic regression model and (8.1).

Exercise 8.10 Verify (8.22), (8.23), and that the minimum distance estimator $\widetilde{\beta}_{\text{md}}$ with $\widehat{\boldsymbol{W}} = \widehat{\boldsymbol{Q}}_{XX}$ equals the CLS estimator.

Exercise 8.11 Prove Theorem 8.6.

Exercise 8.12 Prove Theorem 8.7.

Exercise 8.13 Prove Theorem 8.8. (Hint: Use that CLS is a special case of Theorem 8.7.)

Exercise 8.14 Verify that (8.26) is $\boldsymbol{V}_{\beta}(\boldsymbol{W})$ with $\boldsymbol{W} = \boldsymbol{V}_{\beta}^{-1}$.

Exercise 8.15 Prove (8.27). Hint: Use (8.26).

Exercise 8.16 Verify (8.29), (8.30), and (8.31).

Exercise 8.17 Verify (8.32), (8.33), and (8.34).

Exercise 8.18 Suppose you have two independent samples each with n observations that satisfy the models $Y_1 = X_1'\beta_1 + e_1$ with $\mathbb{E}[X_1 e_1] = 0$ and $Y_2 = X_2'\beta_2 + e_2$ with $\mathbb{E}[X_2 e_2] = 0$, where β_1 and β_2 are both $k \times 1$. You estimate β_1 and β_2 by OLS on each sample, with consistent asymptotic covariance matrix estimators $\widehat{\boldsymbol{V}}_{\beta_1}$ and $\widehat{\boldsymbol{V}}_{\beta_2}$. Consider efficient minimum distance estimation under the restriction $\beta_1 = \beta_2$.

(a) Find the estimator $\widetilde{\beta}$ of $\beta = \beta_1 = \beta_2$.

(b) Find the asymptotic distribution of $\widetilde{\beta}$.

(c) How would you approach the problem if the sample sizes were different, say, n_1 and n_2?

Exercise 8.19 Use the `cps09mar` dataset and the subsample of white male Hispanics.

(a) Estimate the regression

$$\widehat{\log(wage)} = \beta_1\, education + \beta_2\, experience + \beta_3\, experience^2/100 + \beta_4 married_1$$
$$+ \beta_5 married_2 + \beta_6 married_3 + \beta_7 widowed + \beta_8 divorced + \beta_9 separated + \beta_{10}$$

where $married_1$, $married_2$, and $married_3$ are the first three marital codes listed in the dataset description file.

(b) Estimate the equation by CLS, imposing the constraints $\beta_4 = \beta_7$ and $\beta_8 = \beta_9$. Report the estimates and standard errors.

(c) Estimate the equation using efficient minimum distance and imposing the same constraints as in part (b). Report the estimates and standard errors.

(d) Under what constraint on the coefficients is the wage equation nondecreasing in experience for experience up to 50?

(e) Estimate the equation imposing $\beta_4 = \beta_7$, $\beta_8 = \beta_9$, and the inequality from part (d).

Exercise 8.20 Take the model

$$Y = m(X) + e$$
$$m(x) = \beta_0 + \beta_1 x + \beta_2 x^2 + \cdots + \beta_p x^p$$
$$\mathbb{E}\left[X^j e\right] = 0, \qquad j = 0, \ldots, p$$
$$g(x) = \frac{d}{dx} m(x)$$

with i.i.d. observations (Y_i, X_i), $i = 1, \ldots, n$. The order of the polynomial p is known.

(a) How should we interpret the function $m(x)$ given the projection assumption? How should we interpret $g(x)$? (Briefly explain)

(b) Describe an estimator $\widehat{g}(x)$ of $g(x)$.

(c) Find the asymptotic distribution of $\sqrt{n}\left(\widehat{g}(x) - g(x)\right)$ as $n \to \infty$.

(d) Show how to construct an asymptotic 95% confidence interval for $g(x)$ (for a single x).

(e) Assume $p = 2$. Describe how to estimate $g(x)$ imposing the constraint that $m(x)$ is concave.

(f) Assume $p = 2$. Describe how to estimate $g(x)$ imposing the constraint that $m(u)$ is increasing on the region $u \in [x_L, x_U]$.

Exercise 8.21 Take the linear model with restrictions $Y = X'\beta + e$ with $\mathbb{E}[Xe] = 0$ and $\boldsymbol{R}'\beta = \boldsymbol{c}$. Consider three estimators for β:

- $\widehat{\beta}$ the unconstrained least squares estimator,
- $\widetilde{\beta}$ the constrained least squares estimator, and
- $\overline{\beta}$ the constrained efficient minimum distance estimator.

For the three estimators, define the residuals $\widehat{e}_i = Y_i - X_i'\widehat{\beta}$, $\widetilde{e}_i = Y_i - X_i'\widetilde{\beta}$, $\overline{e}_i = Y_i - X_i'\overline{\beta}$, and variance estimators $\widehat{\sigma}^2 = n^{-1}\sum_{i=1}^n \widehat{e}_i^2$, $\widetilde{\sigma}^2 = n^{-1}\sum_{i=1}^n \widetilde{e}_i^2$, and $\overline{\sigma}^2 = n^{-1}\sum_{i=1}^n \overline{e}_i^2$.

(a) As $\overline{\beta}$ is the most efficient estimator and $\widehat{\beta}$ the least, do you expect $\overline{\sigma}^2 < \widetilde{\sigma}^2 < \widehat{\sigma}^2$ in large samples?

(b) Consider the statistic

$$T_n = \widehat{\sigma}^{-2} \sum_{i=1}^n \left(\widehat{e}_i - \widetilde{e}_i\right)^2.$$

Find the asymptotic distribution for T_n when $\boldsymbol{R}'\beta = \boldsymbol{c}$ is true.

(c) Does the result of part (b) simplify when the error e_i is homoskedastic?

Exercise 8.22 Take the linear model $Y = X_1\beta_1 + X_2\beta_2 + e$ with $\mathbb{E}[Xe] = 0$. Consider the restriction $\frac{\beta_1}{\beta_2} = 2$.

(a) Find an explicit expression for the CLS estimator $\widetilde{\beta} = (\widetilde{\beta}_1, \widetilde{\beta}_2)$ of $\beta = (\beta_1, \beta_2)$ under the restriction. Your answer should be specific to the restriction. It should not be a generic formula for an abstract general restriction.

(b) Derive the asymptotic distribution of $\widetilde{\beta}_1$ under the assumption that the restriction is true.

CHAPTER 9

HYPOTHESIS TESTING

9.1 INTRODUCTION

In Chapter 5, we briefly discussed hypothesis testing in the context of the normal regression model. In this chapter, we explore hypothesis testing in greater detail with a particular emphasis on asymptotic inference. For more detail on the foundations, see Chapter 13 of *Probability and Statistics for Economists*.

In Chapter 8, we discussed estimation subject to restrictions, including linear restrictions (8.1), nonlinear restrictions (8.44), and inequality restrictions (8.49). In this chapter, we discuss **tests** of such restrictions.

9.2 HYPOTHESES

Hypothesis tests attempt to assess whether there is evidence contrary to a proposed restriction. Let $\theta = r(\beta)$ be a $q \times 1$ parameter of interest, where $r : \mathbb{R}^k \to \Theta \subset \mathbb{R}^q$ is some transformation. For example, θ may be a single coefficient (e.g., $\theta = \beta_j$), the difference between two coefficients (e.g., $\theta = \beta_j - \beta_\ell$), or the ratio of two coefficients (e.g., $\theta = \beta_j / \beta_\ell$).

A point hypothesis concerning θ is a proposed restriction, such as

$$\theta = \theta_0 \tag{9.1}$$

where θ_0 is a hypothesized (known) value.

More generally, letting $\beta \in B \subset \mathbb{R}^k$ be the parameter space, a hypothesis is a restriction $\beta \in B_0$, where B_0 is a proper subset of B. This definition specializes to (9.1) by setting $B_0 = \{\beta \in B : r(\beta) = \theta_0\}$.

In this chapter, we focus exclusively on point hypotheses of the form (9.1), as they are the most common and are relatively simple to handle.

The hypothesis to be tested is called the null hypothesis.

Definition 9.1 The **null hypothesis** $\mathbb{H}_0$ is the restriction $\theta = \theta_0$ or $\beta \in B_0$.

We often write the null hypothesis as $\mathbb{H}_0 : \theta = \theta_0$ or $\mathbb{H}_0 : r(\beta) = \theta_0$.

The complement of the null hypothesis (the collection of parameter values that do not satisfy the null hypothesis) is called the alternative hypothesis.

Definition 9.2 The **alternative hypothesis** $\mathbb{H}_1$ is the set $\{\theta \in \Theta : \theta \neq \theta_0\}$ or $\{\beta \in B : \beta \notin B_0\}$.

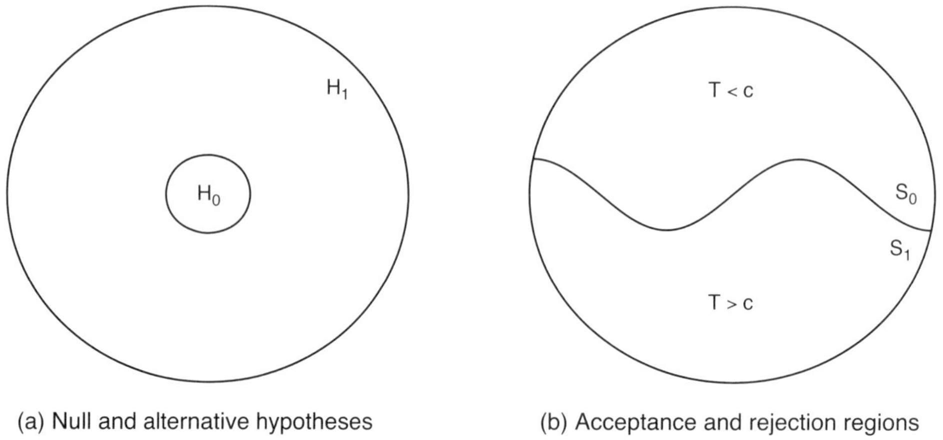

FIGURE 9.1 Hypothesis testing

We often write the alternative hypothesis as $\mathbb{H}_1 : \theta \neq \theta_0$ or $\mathbb{H}_1 : r(\beta) \neq \theta_0$. For simplicity, we often refer to the hypotheses as "the null" and "the alternative." Figure 9.1(a) illustrates the division of the parameter space into null and alternative hypotheses.

In hypothesis testing, we assume that there is a true (but unknown) value of θ, and this value either satisfies $\mathbb{H}_0$ or does not satisfy $\mathbb{H}_0$. The goal of hypothesis testing is to assess whether $\mathbb{H}_0$ is true by asking whether $\mathbb{H}_0$ is consistent with the observed data.

To be specific, take our example of wage determination and consider the question: Does union membership affect wages? We can turn this into a hypothesis test by specifying the null as the restriction that a coefficient on union membership is 0 in a wage regression. Consider, for example, the estimates reported in Table 4.2. The coefficient for "Male Union Member" is 0.095 (a wage premium of 9.5%) and the coefficient for "Female Union Member" is 0.023 (a wage premium of 2.3%). These are estimates, not the true values. The question is: Are the true coefficients 0? To answer this question, the testing method asks the question: Are the observed estimates compatible with the hypothesis, in the sense that the deviation from the hypothesis can be reasonably explained by stochastic variation? Or are the observed estimates incompatible with the hypothesis, in the sense that the observed estimates would be highly unlikely if the hypothesis were true?

9.3 ACCEPTANCE AND REJECTION

A hypothesis test either accepts the null hypothesis or rejects the null hypothesis in favor of the alternative hypothesis. We can describe these two decisions as "Accept $\mathbb{H}_0$" and "Reject $\mathbb{H}_0$." In the example given in Section 9.2, the decision is either to accept the hypothesis that union membership does not affect wages, or to reject the hypothesis in favor of the alternative that union membership does affect wages.

The decision is based on the data and so is a mapping from the sample space to the decision set. This splits the sample space into two regions, S_0 and S_1, such that if the observed sample falls into S_0, we accept $\mathbb{H}_0$, while if the sample falls into S_1, we reject $\mathbb{H}_0$. The set S_0 is called the **acceptance region** and the set S_1 the **rejection** or **critical region**.

It is convenient to express this mapping as a real-valued function called a **test statistic**:

$$T = T\left((Y_1, X_1), \ldots, (Y_n, X_n)\right)$$

relative to a **critical value** c. The hypothesis test then consists of the decision rule:

1. Accept $\mathbb{H}_0$ if $T \le c$.
2. Reject $\mathbb{H}_0$ if $T > c$.

Figure 9.1(b) illustrates the division of the sample space into acceptance and rejection regions.

A test statistic T should be designed so that small values are likely when $\mathbb{H}_0$ is true and large values are likely when $\mathbb{H}_1$ is true. There is a well developed statistical theory concerning the design of optimal tests. We will not review that theory here, but instead refer the reader to Lehmann and Romano (2005). In this chapter, we summarize the main approaches to the design of test statistics.

The most commonly used test statistic is the absolute value of the t-statistic:

$$T = |T(\theta_0)| \tag{9.2}$$

where

$$T(\theta) = \frac{\widehat{\theta} - \theta}{s(\widehat{\theta})} \tag{9.3}$$

is the t-statistic from (7.33), $\widehat{\theta}$ is a point estimator, and $s(\widehat{\theta})$ its standard error. T is an appropriate statistic when testing hypotheses on individual coefficients or real-valued parameters $\theta = h(\beta)$, and θ_0 is the hypothesized value. Quite typically $\theta_0 = 0$, as interest focuses on whether a coefficient equals 0, but this is not the only possibility. For example, interest may focus on whether an elasticity θ equals 1, in which case, we may wish to test $\mathbb{H}_0 : \theta = 1$.

9.4 TYPE I ERROR

A false rejection of the null hypothesis $\mathbb{H}_0$ (rejecting $\mathbb{H}_0$ when $\mathbb{H}_0$ is true) is called a **Type I error**. The probability of a Type I error is called the **size** of the test.

$$\mathbb{P}\left[\text{Reject } \mathbb{H}_0 \mid \mathbb{H}_0 \text{ true}\right] = \mathbb{P}\left[T > c \mid \mathbb{H}_0 \text{ true}\right]. \tag{9.4}$$

The **uniform size** of the test is the supremum of (9.4) across all data distributions that satisfy $\mathbb{H}_0$. A primary goal of test construction is to limit the incidence of Type I error by bounding the size of the test.

For the reasons discussed in Chapter 7, in typical econometric models, the exact sampling distributions of estimators and test statistics are unknown, and hence we cannot explicitly calculate (9.4). Instead, we typically rely on asymptotic approximations. Suppose that the test statistic has an asymptotic distribution under $\mathbb{H}_0$. That is, when $\mathbb{H}_0$ is true,

$$T \underset{d}{\longrightarrow} \xi \tag{9.5}$$

as $n \to \infty$ for some continuously distributed random variable ξ. This is not a substantive restriction, as most conventional econometric tests satisfy (9.5). Let $G(u) = \mathbb{P}[\xi \le u]$ denote the distribution of ξ. We call ξ (or G) the **asymptotic null distribution**.

It is desirable to design test statistics T whose asymptotic null distribution G is known and does not depend on unknown parameters. In this case, we say that T is **asymptotically pivotal**.

For example, if the test statistic equals the absolute t-statistic from (9.2), then we know from Theorem 7.11 that if $\theta = \theta_0$ (that is, the null hypothesis holds), then $T \underset{d}{\longrightarrow} |Z|$ as $n \to \infty$, where $Z \sim \mathrm{N}(0, 1)$. This means that $G(u) = \mathbb{P}[|Z| \leq u] = 2\Phi(u) - 1$, the distribution of the absolute value of the standard normal, as shown in (7.34). This distribution does not depend on unknowns and is pivotal.

We define the **asymptotic size** of the test as the asymptotic probability of a Type I error:

$$\lim_{n\to\infty} \mathbb{P}[T > c \mid \mathbb{H}_0 \text{ true}] = \mathbb{P}[\xi > c] = 1 - G(c).$$

We see that the asymptotic size of the test is a simple function of the asymptotic null distribution G and the critical value c. For example, the asymptotic size of a test based on the absolute t-statistic with critical value c is $2(1 - \Phi(c))$.

In the dominant approach to hypothesis testing, the researcher pre-selects a **significance level** $\alpha \in (0, 1)$ and then selects c so the asymptotic size is no larger than α. When the asymptotic null distribution G is pivotal, we accomplish this selection by setting c equal to the $1 - \alpha$ quantile of the distribution G. (If the distribution G is not pivotal, more complicated methods must be used.) We call c the **asymptotic critical value**, because it has been selected from the asymptotic null distribution. For example, since $2(1 - \Phi(1.96)) = 0.05$, it follows that the 5% asymptotic critical value for the absolute t-statistic is $c = 1.96$. Calculation of normal critical values is done numerically in statistical software. For example, in MATLAB, the command is `norminv(1-α/2)`.

9.5 *t*-TESTS

As mentioned earlier, the most common test of the one-dimensional hypothesis $\mathbb{H}_0 : \theta = \theta_0 \in \mathbb{R}$ against the alternative $\mathbb{H}_1 : \theta \neq \theta_0$ is the absolute value of the t-statistic (9.3). We now formally state its asymptotic null distribution, which is a simple application of Theorem 7.11.

Theorem 9.1 Under Assumptions 7.2, 7.3, and $\mathbb{H}_0 : \theta = \theta_0 \in \mathbb{R}$, $T(\theta_0) \underset{d}{\longrightarrow} Z \sim \mathrm{N}(0, 1)$. For c satisfying $\alpha = 2(1 - \Phi(c))$, $\mathbb{P}[|T(\theta_0)| > c \mid \mathbb{H}_0] \to \alpha$, and the test "Reject $\mathbb{H}_0$ if $|T(\theta_0)| > c$" has asymptotic size α.

Theorem 9.1 shows that asymptotic critical values can be taken from the normal distribution. As in our discussion of asymptotic confidence intervals (Section 7.13), the critical value could alternatively be taken from the student t distribution, which would be the exact test in the normal regression model (Section 5.12). Indeed, t critical values are the default in packages, such as Stata. Since the critical values from the student t distribution are (slightly) larger than those from the normal distribution, student t critical values slightly decrease the rejection probability of the test. In practical applications, the difference is typically unimportant, unless the sample size is quite small (in which case the asymptotic approximation should be questioned as well).

The alternative hypothesis $\theta \neq \theta_0$ is sometimes called a "two-sided" alternative. In contrast, sometimes we are interested in testing for one-sided alternatives, such as $\mathbb{H}_1 : \theta > \theta_0$ or $\mathbb{H}_1 : \theta < \theta_0$. Tests of $\theta = \theta_0$ against $\theta > \theta_0$ or $\theta < \theta_0$ are based on the signed t-statistic $T = T(\theta_0)$. The hypothesis $\theta = \theta_0$ is rejected in favor of $\theta > \theta_0$ if $T > c$, where c satisfies $\alpha = 1 - \Phi(c)$. Negative values of T are not taken as evidence against $\mathbb{H}_0$, as point estimates $\widehat{\theta}$ less than θ_0 do not point to $\theta > \theta_0$. Since the critical values are taken from the single tail of the normal distribution, they are smaller than for two-sided tests. Specifically, the asymptotic 5% critical value is $c = 1.645$. Thus, we reject $\theta = \theta_0$ in favor of $\theta > \theta_0$ if $T > 1.645$.

Conversely, tests of $\theta = \theta_0$ against $\theta < \theta_0$ reject $\mathbb{H}_0$ for negative t-statistics (e.g., if $T < -c$). Large positive values of T are not evidence for $\mathbb{H}_1 : \theta < \theta_0$. An asymptotic 5% test rejects if $T < -1.645$.

There seems to be an ambiguity. Should we use the two-sided critical value 1.96 or the one-sided critical value 1.645? The answer is that in most cases, the two-sided critical value is appropriate. We should use the one-sided critical values only when the parameter space is known to satisfy a one-sided restriction, such as $\theta \geq \theta_0$. This is when the test of $\theta = \theta_0$ against $\theta > \theta_0$ makes sense. If the restriction $\theta \geq \theta_0$ is not known a priori then imposing this restriction to test $\theta = \theta_0$ against $\theta > \theta_0$ does not makes sense. Since linear regression coefficients typically do not have a priori sign restrictions, the standard convention is to use two-sided critical values.

This choice may seem contrary to the way testing is presented in statistical textbooks, which often focus on one-sided alternative hypotheses. The latter focus is primarily for pedagogy, as the one-sided theoretical problem is cleaner and easier to understand.

9.6 TYPE II ERROR AND POWER

A false acceptance of the null hypothesis $\mathbb{H}_0$ (accepting $\mathbb{H}_0$ when $\mathbb{H}_1$ is true) is called a **Type II error**. The rejection probability under the alternative hypothesis is called the **power** of the test, and equals 1 minus the probability of a Type II error:

$$\pi(\theta) = \mathbb{P}\left[\text{Reject } \mathbb{H}_0 \mid \mathbb{H}_1 \text{ true}\right] = \mathbb{P}\left[T > c \mid \mathbb{H}_1 \text{ true}\right].$$

We call $\pi(\theta)$ the **power function** and write it as a function of θ to indicate its dependence on the true value of the parameter θ.

In the dominant approach to hypothesis testing, the goal of test construction is to have high power subject to the constraint that the size of the test is lower than the pre-specified significance level. Generally, the power of a test depends on the true value of the parameter θ, and for a well-behaved test, the power is increasing both as θ moves away from the null hypothesis θ_0 and as the sample size n increases.

Given the two possible states of the world ($\mathbb{H}_0$ or $\mathbb{H}_1$) and the two possible decisions (Accept $\mathbb{H}_0$ or Reject $\mathbb{H}_0$), there are four possible pairings of states and decisions, as depicted in Table 9.1.

Given a test statistic T, increasing the critical value c increases the acceptance region S_0 while decreasing the rejection region S_1. This decreases the likelihood of a Type I error (decreases the size) but increases the likelihood of a Type II error (decreases the power). Thus the choice of c involves a trade-off between size and the power. This is why the significance level α of the test cannot be set arbitrarily small. Otherwise, the test will not have meaningful power.

It is important to consider the power of a test when interpreting hypothesis tests, as an overly narrow focus on size can lead to poor decisions. For example, it is easy to design a test that has perfect size yet has trivial power. Specifically, for any hypothesis, we can use the following test: Generate a random variable $U \sim U[0, 1]$, and reject $\mathbb{H}_0$ if $U < \alpha$. This test has an exact size of α. Yet the test also has power precisely equal to α. When the power of a test equals the size, we say that the test has **trivial power**. Nothing is learned from such a test.

Table 9.1
Hypothesis testing decisions

	Accept $\mathbb{H}_0$	Reject $\mathbb{H}_0$
$\mathbb{H}_0$ true	Correct decision	Type I error
$\mathbb{H}_1$ true	Type II error	Correct decision

9.7 STATISTICAL SIGNIFICANCE

Testing requires a pre-selected choice of significance level α, yet there is no objective scientific basis for the choice of α. Nevertheless, the common practice is to set $\alpha = 0.05$ (5%). Alternative common values are $\alpha = 0.10$ (10%) and $\alpha = 0.01$ (1%). These choices are somewhat the by-product of traditional tables of critical values and statistical software.

The informal reasoning behind the 5% critical value is to ensure that Type I errors should be relatively unlikely—that the decision "Reject $\mathbb{H}_0$" has scientific strength—yet the test retains power against reasonable alternatives. The decision "Reject $\mathbb{H}_0$" means that the evidence is inconsistent with the null hypothesis in the sense that it is relatively unlikely (1 in 20) that data generated by the null hypothesis would yield the observed test result.

In contrast, the decision "Accept $\mathbb{H}_0$" is not a strong statement. It does not mean that the evidence supports $\mathbb{H}_0$, only that there is insufficient evidence to reject $\mathbb{H}_0$. Because of this, it is more accurate to use the label "Do not Reject $\mathbb{H}_0$" instead of "Accept $\mathbb{H}_0$."

When a test rejects $\mathbb{H}_0$ at the 5% significance level, it is common to say that the statistic is **statistically significant** and if the test accepts $\mathbb{H}_0$ it is common to say that the statistic is **not statistically significant** or that it is **statistically insignificant**. It is helpful to remember that this is simply a compact way of saying "Using the statistic T, the hypothesis $\mathbb{H}_0$ can [cannot] be rejected at the asymptotic 5% level." Furthermore, when the null hypothesis $\mathbb{H}_0 : \theta = 0$ is rejected, it is common to say that the coefficient θ is statistically significant, because the test has rejected the hypothesis that the coefficient is equal to 0.

Let us return to the example about the union wage premium as measured in Table 4.2. The absolute t-statistic for the coefficient on "Male Union Member" is $0.095/0.020 = 4.7$, which is greater than the 5% asymptotic critical value of 1.96. Therefore we reject the hypothesis that union membership does not affect wages for men. In this case, we can say that union membership is statistically significant for men. However, the absolute t-statistic for the coefficient on "Female Union Member" is $0.023/0.020 = 1.2$, which is less than 1.96, and therefore we do not reject the hypothesis that union membership does not affect wages for women. In this case, we find that membership for women is not statistically significant.

When a test accepts a null hypothesis (when a test is not statistically significant) a common misinterpretation is that this is evidence that the null hypothesis is true. This is incorrect. Failure to reject is by itself not evidence. Without an analysis of power, we do not know the likelihood of making a Type II error and thus are uncertain. In our wage example, it would be a mistake to write that "the regression finds that female union membership has no effect on wages." This is an incorrect and most unfortunate interpretation. The test has failed to reject the hypothesis that the coefficient is 0 but that does not mean that the coefficient is actually 0.

When a test rejects a null hypothesis (when a test is statistically significant) it is strong evidence against the hypothesis (because if the hypothesis were true, then rejection is an unlikely event). Rejection should be taken as evidence against the null hypothesis. However, we can never conclude that the null hypothesis is indeed false, as we cannot exclude the possibility that we are making a Type I error.

Perhaps more importantly, there is an important distinction between statistical and economic significance. If we correctly reject the hypothesis $\mathbb{H}_0 : \theta = 0$, it means that the true value of θ is nonzero. This includes the possibility that θ may be nonzero but close to 0 in magnitude. This only makes sense if we interpret the parameters in the context of their relevant models. In our wage regression example, we might consider wage effects of 1% magnitude or less as being "close to 0." In a log wage regression, this corresponds to a dummy variable with a coefficient less than 0.01. If the standard error is sufficiently small (less than 0.005), then a coefficient estimate of 0.01 will be statistically significant but not economically significant. This occurs frequently in applications with very large sample sizes, where standard errors can be quite small.

The solution is to focus whenever possible on confidence intervals and the economic meaning of the coefficients. For example, if the coefficient estimate is 0.005 with a standard error of 0.002, then a 95% confidence interval would be [0.001, 0.009], indicating that the true effect is likely between 0% and 1%, and hence is slightly positive but small. This conclusion is much more informative than the misleading statement "the effect is statistically positive."

9.8 p-VALUES

Continuing with the wage regression estimates reported in Table 4.1, consider another question: Does marriage status affect wages? To test the hypothesis that marriage status has no effect on wages, we examine the t-statistics for the coefficients on "Married Male" and "Married Female" in Table 4.2, which are $0.211/0.010 = 22$ and $0.016/0.010 = 1.7$, respectively. The first exceeds the asymptotic 5% critical value of 1.96, so we reject the hypothesis for men. The second is smaller than 1.96, so we fail to reject the hypothesis for women. Taking a second look at the statistics, we see that the statistic for men (22) is exceptionally high and that for women (1.7) is only slightly below the critical value. Suppose that the t-statistic for women were slightly increased to 2.0. This is larger than the critical value and so would lead to the decision "Reject $\mathbb{H}_0$" rather than "Accept $\mathbb{H}_0$." Should we really be making a different decision if the t-statistic is 2.0 rather than 1.7? The difference in values is small. Shouldn't the difference in the decision be also small? Thinking through these examples, it seems unsatisfactory to simply report "Accept $\mathbb{H}_0$" or "Reject $\mathbb{H}_0$." These two decisions do not summarize the evidence. Instead, the magnitude of the statistic T suggests a "degree of evidence" against $\mathbb{H}_0$. How can we take this into account?

The answer is to report what is known as the **asymptotic p-value**:

$$p = 1 - G(T).$$

Since the distribution function G is monotonically increasing, the p-value is a monotonically decreasing function of T and is an equivalent test statistic. Instead of rejecting $\mathbb{H}_0$ at the significance level α if $T > c$, we can reject $\mathbb{H}_0$ if $p < \alpha$. Thus it is sufficient to report p, and let the reader decide. In practice, the p-value is calculated numerically. For example, in MATLAB, the command is `2*(1-normalcdf(abs(t)))`.

It is instructive to interpret p as the **marginal significance level**: the smallest value of α for which the test T "rejects" the null hypothesis. That is, $p = 0.11$ means that T rejects $\mathbb{H}_0$ for all significance levels greater than 0.11 but fails to reject $\mathbb{H}_0$ for significance levels less than 0.11.

Furthermore, the asymptotic p-value has a very convenient asymptotic null distribution. Since $T \underset{d}{\longrightarrow} \xi$ under $\mathbb{H}_0$, then $p = 1 - G(T) \underset{d}{\longrightarrow} 1 - G(\xi)$, which has the distribution

$$\begin{aligned}
\mathbb{P}\left[1 - G(\xi) \le u\right] &= \mathbb{P}\left[1 - u \le G(\xi)\right] \\
&= 1 - \mathbb{P}\left[\xi \le G^{-1}(1-u)\right] \\
&= 1 - G\left(G^{-1}(1-u)\right) \\
&= 1 - (1-u) \\
&= u
\end{aligned}$$

which is the uniform distribution on $[0,1]$. (This calculation assumes that $G(u)$ is strictly increasing, which is true for conventional asymptotic distributions, such as the normal.) Thus $p \underset{d}{\longrightarrow} U[0,1]$. Thus the "unusualness" of p is easier to interpret than the "unusualness" of T.

An important caveat is that the p-value p should not be interpreted as the probability that either hypothesis is true. A common misinterpretation is that p is the probability "that the null hypothesis is true." This is incorrect. Instead, p is the marginal significance level—a measure of the strength of information against the null hypothesis.

For a t-statistic, the p-value can be calculated either using the normal distribution or the student t distribution. p-values calculated using the student t will be slightly larger, though the difference is small when the sample size is large.

Returning to our empirical example, for the test that the coefficient on "Married Male" is 0, the p-value is 0.000. Thus it would be nearly impossible to observe a t-statistic as large as 22 when the true value of the coefficient is 0. When presented with such evidence, we can say that we "strongly reject" the null hypothesis, that the test is "highly significant," or that "the test rejects at any conventional critical value." In contrast, the p-value for the coefficient on "Married Female" is 0.094. In this context, it is typical to say that the test is "close to significant," meaning that the p-value is larger than 0.05 but not too much larger.

A related but inferior empirical practice is to append asterisks (*) to coefficient estimates or test statistics to indicate the level of significance. A common practice to to append a single asterisk (*) for an estimate or test statistic that exceeds the 10% critical value (i.e., is significant at the 10% level), append a double asterisk (**) for a test that exceeds the 5% critical value, and append a triple asterisk (***) for a test exceeding the 1% critical value. Such a practice can be better than a table of raw test statistics, as the asterisks permit a quick interpretation of significance. However, asterisks are inferior to p-values, which are also easy and quick to interpret. The goal is essentially the same; it is wiser to report p-values whenever possible and avoid the use of asterisks.

My recommendation is that the best empirical practice is to compute and report the asymptotic p-value p rather than simply the test statistic T, the binary decision Accept/Reject, or appending asterisks. The p-value is a simple statistic, easy to interpret, and contains more information than the other choices.

Let us now summarize the main features of hypothesis testing:

1. Select a significance level α.
2. Select a test statistic T with asymptotic distribution $T \xrightarrow[d]{} \xi$ under $\mathbb{H}_0$.
3. Set the asymptotic critical value c, so that $1 - G(c) = \alpha$, where G is the distribution function of ξ.
4. Calculate the asymptotic p-value $p = 1 - G(T)$.
5. Reject $\mathbb{H}_0$ if $T > c$, or equivalently, if $p < \alpha$.
6. Accept $\mathbb{H}_0$ if $T \le c$, or equivalently, if $p \ge \alpha$.
7. Report p to summarize the evidence concerning $\mathbb{H}_0$ versus $\mathbb{H}_1$.

9.9 t-RATIOS AND THE ABUSE OF TESTING

In Section 4.19 we argued that a good applied practice is to report coefficient estimates $\widehat{\theta}$ and standard errors $s(\widehat{\theta})$ for all coefficients of interest in estimated models. With $\widehat{\theta}$ and $s(\widehat{\theta})$, the reader can easily construct confidence intervals $[\widehat{\theta} \pm 2s(\widehat{\theta})]$ and t-statistics $\left(\widehat{\theta} - \theta_0\right)/s(\widehat{\theta})$ for hypotheses of interest.

Some applied papers (especially older ones) report t-ratios $T = \widehat{\theta}/s(\widehat{\theta})$ instead of standard errors. This is poor econometric practice. Although the same information is being reported (you can back out standard errors by division, e.g., $s(\widehat{\theta}) = \widehat{\theta}/T$), standard errors are generally more helpful to readers than t-ratios. Standard errors help the reader focus on the estimation precision and confidence intervals, while t-ratios focus attention on statistical significance. Statistical significance is important, but it is less important that the parameter estimates themselves and their confidence intervals. The focus should be on the meaning of the parameter estimates, their magnitudes, and their interpretation, not on listing which variables have significant (e.g., nonzero) coefficients. In many modern applications, sample sizes are very large, so standard errors can be very small. Consequently t-ratios can be large even if the coefficient estimates are economically small. In such contexts, it may not be interesting to announce "The coefficient is nonzero!" Instead, what is interesting to announce is that "The coefficient estimate is economically interesting!"

In particular, some applied papers report coefficient estimates and t-ratios and limit their discussion of the results to describing which variables are "significant" (meaning that their t-ratios exceed 2) and the signs of the coefficient estimates. This approach indicates very poor empirical work and should be studiously avoided. It is also a recipe for banishment of your work to lower tier economics journals.

Fundamentally, the common t-ratio is a test for the hypothesis that a coefficient equals 0. This ratio should be reported and discussed when this hypothesis is an interesting economic hypothesis. But if this is not the case, it is distracting.

One problem is that standard packages, such as Stata, by default report t-statistics and p-values for every estimated coefficient. Although this can be useful (as a user doesn't need to explicitly ask to test a desired coefficient), it can be misleading, as it may unintentionally suggest that the entire list of t-statistics and p-values are important. Instead, a user should focus on tests of scientifically motivated hypotheses.

In general, when a coefficient θ is of interest, it is constructive to focus on the point estimate, its standard error, and its confidence interval. The point estimate gives our "best guess" for the value. The standard error is a measure of precision. The confidence interval gives us the range of values consistent with the data. If the standard error is large, then the point estimate is not a good summary of θ. The endpoints of the confidence interval describe the bounds on the likely possibilities. If the confidence interval embraces too broad a set of values for θ, then the dataset is not sufficiently informative to render useful inferences about θ. But if the confidence interval is tight, then the data have produced an accurate estimate, and the focus should be on the value and interpretation of this estimate. In contrast, the statement "the t-ratio is highly significant" has little interpretive value.

The above discussion requires that the researcher should know what the coefficient θ means (in terms of the economic problem) and can interpret values and magnitudes, not just signs. This is critical for good applied econometric practice.

For example, consider the question about the effect of marriage status on mean log wages. We had found that the effect is "highly significant" for men and "close to significant" for women. Now, let's construct asymptotic 95% confidence intervals for the coefficients. The one for men is [0.19, 0.23] and that for women is [−0.00, 0.03]. This shows that average wages for married men are about 19–23% higher than for unmarried men, which is substantial, while the difference for women is about 0–3%, which is small. These *magnitudes* are more informative than the results of the hypothesis tests.

9.10 WALD TESTS

The t-test is appropriate when the null hypothesis is a real-valued restriction. More generally, there may be multiple restrictions on the coefficient vector β. Suppose that we have $q > 1$ restrictions that can be written in the form (9.1). It is natural to estimate $\theta = r(\beta)$ by the plug-in estimator $\widehat{\theta} = r\left(\widehat{\beta}\right)$. To test $\mathbb{H}_0 : \theta = \theta_0$ against $\mathbb{H}_1 : \theta \neq \theta_0$, one approach is to measure the magnitude of the discrepancy $\widehat{\theta} - \theta_0$. As this is a vector, there is more than one measure of its length. One simple measure is the weighted quadratic form known as the **Wald**

statistic, which is (7.37) evaluated at the null hypothesis:

$$W = W(\theta_0) = \left(\widehat{\theta} - \theta_0\right)' \widehat{\boldsymbol{V}}_{\widehat{\theta}}^{-1} \left(\widehat{\theta} - \theta_0\right) \tag{9.6}$$

where $\widehat{\boldsymbol{V}}_{\widehat{\theta}} = \widehat{\boldsymbol{R}}' \widehat{\boldsymbol{V}}_{\widehat{\beta}} \widehat{\boldsymbol{R}}$ is an estimator of $\boldsymbol{V}_{\widehat{\theta}}$, and $\widehat{\boldsymbol{R}} = \frac{\partial}{\partial \beta} r(\widehat{\beta})'$. Notice that we can write W alternatively as

$$W = n\left(\widehat{\theta} - \theta_0\right)' \widehat{\boldsymbol{V}}_{\theta}^{-1} \left(\widehat{\theta} - \theta_0\right)$$

using the asymptotic variance estimator $\widehat{\boldsymbol{V}}_{\theta}$, or we can write it directly as a function of $\widehat{\beta}$:

$$W = \left(r(\widehat{\beta}) - \theta_0\right)' \left(\widehat{\boldsymbol{R}}' \widehat{\boldsymbol{V}}_{\widehat{\beta}} \widehat{\boldsymbol{R}}\right)^{-1} \left(r(\widehat{\beta}) - \theta_0\right).$$

Also, when $r(\beta) = \boldsymbol{R}'\beta$ is a linear function of β, then the Wald statistic simplifies to

$$W = \left(\boldsymbol{R}'\widehat{\beta} - \theta_0\right)' \left(\boldsymbol{R}' \widehat{\boldsymbol{V}}_{\widehat{\beta}} \boldsymbol{R}\right)^{-1} \left(\boldsymbol{R}'\widehat{\beta} - \theta_0\right).$$

The Wald statistic W is a weighted Euclidean measure of the length of the vector $\widehat{\theta} - \theta_0$. When $q = 1$, then $W = T^2$, the square of the t-statistic, so hypothesis tests based on W and $|T|$ are equivalent. The Wald statistic (9.6) is a generalization of the t-statistic to the case of multiple restrictions. As the Wald statistic is symmetric in the argument $\widehat{\theta} - \theta_0$, it treats positive and negative alternatives symmetrically. Thus the inherent alternative is always two-sided.

As shown in Theorem 7.13, when β satisfies $r(\beta) = \theta_0$ then $W \underset{d}{\longrightarrow} \chi_q^2$, a chi-square random variable with q degrees of freedom. Let $G_q(u)$ denote the χ_q^2 distribution function. For a given significance level α, the asymptotic critical value c satisfies $\alpha = 1 - G_q(c)$. For example, the 5% critical values for $q = 1$, $q = 2$, and $q = 3$ are 3.84, 5.99, and 7.82, respectively, and in general, the level α critical value can be calculated in MATLAB as `chi2inv(1-α,q)`. An asymptotic test rejects $\mathbb{H}_0$ in favor of $\mathbb{H}_1$ if $W > c$. As with t-tests, it is conventional to describe a Wald test as "significant" if W exceeds the 5% asymptotic critical value.

Theorem 9.2 Under Assumptions 7.2, 7.3, 7.4, and $\mathbb{H}_0 : \theta = \theta_0 \in \mathbb{R}^q$, then $W \underset{d}{\longrightarrow} \chi_q^2$. For c satisfying $\alpha = 1 - G_q(c)$, $\mathbb{P}\left[W > c \mid \mathbb{H}_0\right] \longrightarrow \alpha$, so the test "Reject $\mathbb{H}_0$ if $W > c$" has asymptotic size α.

Notice that the asymptotic distribution in Theorem 9.2 depends solely on q, the number of restrictions being tested. It does not depend on k, the number of parameters estimated.

The asymptotic p-value for W is $p = 1 - G_q(W)$, which is particularly useful when testing multiple restrictions. For example, if you write that a Wald test on eight restrictions ($q = 8$) has the value $W = 11.2$, it is difficult for a reader to assess the magnitude of this statistic unless they have quick access to a statistical table or software. Instead, if you write that the p-value is $p = 0.19$ (as is the case for $W = 11.2$ and $q = 8$), then it is simple for a reader to interpret its magnitude as "insignificant." To calculate the asymptotic p-value for a Wald statistic in MATLAB, use the command `1-chi2cdf(w,q)`.

Some packages (including Stata) and papers report F versions of Wald statistics. For any Wald statistic W that tests a q-dimensional restriction, the F version of the test is

$$F = W/q.$$

When F is reported, it is conventional to use $F_{q,n-k}$ critical values and p-values rather than χ_q^2 values. The connection between Wald and F statistics is demonstrated in Section 9.15, where we show that when Wald statistics are calculated using a homoskedastic covariance matrix then $F = W/q$ is identicial to the F statistic of (5.19). While there is no formal justification for using the $F_{q,n-k}$ distribution for non-homoskedastic covariance matrices, the $F_{q,n-k}$ distribution provides continuity with the exact distribution theory under normality and is a bit more conservative than the χ^2_q distribution. (Furthermore, the difference is small when $n-k$ is moderately large.)

To implement a test of zero restrictions in Stata, an easy method is to use the command `test X1 X2`, where `X1` and `X2` are the names of the variables whose coefficients are hypothesized to equal 0. The F version of the Wald statistic is reported using the covariance matrix calculated by the method specified in the regression command. A p-value is reported, calculated using the $F_{q,n-k}$ distribution.

To illustrate, consider the empirical results presented in Table 4.2. The hypothesis "Union membership does not affect wages" is the joint restriction that both coefficients on "Male Union Member" and "Female Union Member" are 0. We calculate the Wald statistic for this joint hypothesis and find $W = 23$ (or $F = 12.5$) with a p-value of $p = 0.000$. Thus we reject the null hypothesis in favor of the alternative that at least one of the coefficients is nonzero. This does not mean that both coefficients are nonzero, just that one of the two is. Therefore examining both the joint Wald statistic and the individual t-statistics is useful for interpretation.

As a second example from the same regression, take the hypothesis that married status has no effect on mean wages for women. This is the joint restriction that the coefficients on "Married Female" and "Formerly Married Female" are 0. The Wald statistic for this hypothesis is $W = 6.4$ ($F = 3.2$) with a p-value of 0.04. Such a p-value is typically called "marginally significant" in the sense that it is slightly smaller than 0.05.

The Wald statistic was proposed by Wald (1943).

Abraham Wald

The Hungarian mathematician/statistician/econometrician Abraham Wald (1902–1950) developed an optimality property for the Wald test in terms of weighted average power. He also developed the field of sequential testing, the design of experiments, and one of the first instrumental variable estimators.

9.11 HOMOSKEDASTIC WALD TESTS

If the error is known to be homoskedastic, then it is appropriate to use the homoskedastic Wald statistic (7.38), which replaces $\widehat{\boldsymbol{V}}_{\widehat{\theta}}$ with the homoskedastic estimator $\widehat{\boldsymbol{V}}^0_{\widehat{\theta}}$. This statistic equals

$$\begin{aligned} W^0 &= \left(\widehat{\theta} - \theta_0\right)' \left(\widehat{\boldsymbol{V}}^0_{\widehat{\theta}}\right)^{-1} \left(\widehat{\theta} - \theta_0\right) \\ &= \left(r(\widehat{\beta}) - \theta_0\right)' \left(\boldsymbol{R}' \left(\boldsymbol{X}'\boldsymbol{X}\right)^{-1} \widehat{\boldsymbol{R}}\right)^{-1} \left(r(\widehat{\beta}) - \theta_0\right) / s^2. \end{aligned}$$

In the case of linear hypotheses $\mathbb{H}_0 : \boldsymbol{R}'\beta = \theta_0$, we can write this as

$$W^0 = \left(\boldsymbol{R}'\widehat{\beta} - \theta_0\right)' \left(\boldsymbol{R}' \left(\boldsymbol{X}'\boldsymbol{X}\right)^{-1} \boldsymbol{R}\right)^{-1} \left(\boldsymbol{R}'\widehat{\beta} - \theta_0\right) / s^2. \tag{9.7}$$

We call W^0 a **homoskedastic Wald statistic**, as it is appropriate when the errors are conditionally homoskedastic.

When $q = 1$, then $W^0 = T^2$, the square of the t-statistic, where the latter is computed with a homoskedastic standard error.

Theorem 9.3 Under Assumptions 7.2 and 7.3, $\mathbb{E}\left[e^2 \mid X\right] = \sigma^2 > 0$, and $\mathbb{H}_0 : \theta = \theta_0 \in \mathbb{R}^q$, then $W^0 \underset{d}{\longrightarrow} \chi_q^2$. For c satisfying $\alpha = 1 - G_q(c)$, $\mathbb{P}\left[W^0 > c \mid \mathbb{H}_0\right] \longrightarrow \alpha$, so the test "Reject $\mathbb{H}_0$ if $W^0 > c$" has asymptotic size α.

9.12 CRITERION-BASED TESTS

The Wald statistic is based on the length of the vector $\widehat{\theta} - \theta_0$: the discrepancy between the estimator $\widehat{\theta} = r(\widehat{\beta})$ and the hypothesized value θ_0. An alternative class of tests is based on the discrepancy between the criterion function minimized with and without the restriction.

Criterion-based testing applies when we have a criterion function, say, $J(\beta)$ with $\beta \in B$, which is minimized for estimation, and the goal is to test $\mathbb{H}_0 : \beta \in B_0$ versus $\mathbb{H}_1 : \beta \notin B_0$, where $B_0 \subset \beta$. Minimizing the criterion function over B and B_0, we obtain the unrestricted and restricted estimators:

$$\widehat{\beta} = \underset{\beta \in B}{\operatorname{argmin}}\ J(\beta)$$

$$\widetilde{\beta} = \underset{\beta \in B_0}{\operatorname{argmin}}\ J(\beta).$$

The **criterion-based statistic** for $\mathbb{H}_0$ versus $\mathbb{H}_1$ is proportional to

$$J = \min_{\beta \in B_0} J(\beta) - \min_{\beta \in B} J(\beta) = J(\widetilde{\beta}) - J(\widehat{\beta}).$$

The criterion-based statistic J is sometimes called a **distance** statistic, a **minimum-distance** statistic, or a **likelihood-ratio-like** statistic.

Since B_0 is a subset of B, $J(\widetilde{\beta}) \geq J(\widehat{\beta})$ and thus $J \geq 0$. The statistic J measures the cost on the criterion of imposing the null restriction $\beta \in B_0$.

9.13 MINIMUM DISTANCE TESTS

The minimum distance test is based on the minimum distance criterion (8.19),

$$J(\beta) = n\left(\widehat{\beta} - \beta\right)' \widehat{\boldsymbol{W}} \left(\widehat{\beta} - \beta\right) \tag{9.8}$$

with $\widehat{\beta}$ the unrestricted least squares estimator. The restricted estimator $\widetilde{\beta}_{\text{md}}$ minimizes (9.8) subject to $\beta \in B_0$. Observing that $J(\widehat{\beta}) = 0$, the minimum distance statistic simplifies to

$$J = J(\widetilde{\beta}_{\text{md}}) = n\left(\widehat{\beta} - \widetilde{\beta}_{\text{md}}\right)' \widehat{\boldsymbol{W}} \left(\widehat{\beta} - \widetilde{\beta}_{\text{md}}\right). \tag{9.9}$$

The efficient minimum distance estimator $\widetilde{\beta}_{\text{emd}}$ is obtained by setting $\widehat{\boldsymbol{W}} = \widehat{\boldsymbol{V}}_{\beta}^{-1}$ in (9.8) and (9.9). The efficient minimum distance statistic for $\mathbb{H}_0 : \beta \in B_0$ is therefore

$$J^* = n\left(\widehat{\beta} - \widetilde{\beta}_{\text{emd}}\right)' \widehat{\boldsymbol{V}}_{\beta}^{-1} \left(\widehat{\beta} - \widetilde{\beta}_{\text{emd}}\right). \tag{9.10}$$

Consider the class of linear hypotheses $\mathbb{H}_0 : \boldsymbol{R}'\beta = \theta_0$. In this case, we know from (8.25) that the efficient minimum distance estimator $\widetilde{\beta}_{\text{emd}}$ subject to the constraint $\boldsymbol{R}'\beta = \theta_0$ is

$$\widetilde{\beta}_{\text{emd}} = \widehat{\beta} - \widehat{\boldsymbol{V}}_\beta \boldsymbol{R}\left(\boldsymbol{R}'\widehat{\boldsymbol{V}}_\beta \boldsymbol{R}\right)^{-1}\left(\boldsymbol{R}'\widehat{\beta} - \theta_0\right)$$

and thus

$$\widehat{\beta} - \widetilde{\beta}_{\text{emd}} = \widehat{\boldsymbol{V}}_\beta \boldsymbol{R}\left(\boldsymbol{R}'\widehat{\boldsymbol{V}}_\beta \boldsymbol{R}\right)^{-1}\left(\boldsymbol{R}'\widehat{\beta} - \theta_0\right).$$

Substituting into (9.10), we find

$$\begin{aligned} J^* &= n\left(\boldsymbol{R}'\widehat{\beta} - \theta_0\right)'\left(\boldsymbol{R}'\widehat{\boldsymbol{V}}_\beta \boldsymbol{R}\right)^{-1} \boldsymbol{R}'\widehat{\boldsymbol{V}}_\beta \widehat{\boldsymbol{V}}_{\boldsymbol{\beta}}^{-1} \widehat{\boldsymbol{V}}_\beta \boldsymbol{R}\left(\boldsymbol{R}'\widehat{\boldsymbol{V}}_\beta \boldsymbol{R}\right)^{-1}\left(\boldsymbol{R}'\widehat{\beta} - \theta_0\right) \\ &= n\left(\boldsymbol{R}'\widehat{\beta} - \theta_0\right)'\left(\boldsymbol{R}'\widehat{\boldsymbol{V}}_\beta \boldsymbol{R}\right)^{-1}\left(\boldsymbol{R}'\widehat{\beta} - \theta_0\right) \\ &= W \end{aligned}$$

which is the Wald statistic (9.6).

Thus for linear hypotheses $\mathbb{H}_0 : \boldsymbol{R}'\beta = \theta_0$, the efficient minimum distance statistic J^* is identical to the Wald statistic (9.6). For nonlinear hypotheses, however, the Wald and minimum distance statistics are different.

Newey and West (1987a) established the asymptotic null distribution of J^*.

> **Theorem 9.4** Under Assumptions 7.2, 7.3, 7.4, and $\mathbb{H}_0 : \theta = \theta_0 \in \mathbb{R}^q$, $J^* \underset{d}{\longrightarrow} \chi^2_q$.

Testing using the minimum distance statistic J^* is similar to testing using the Wald statistic W. Critical values and p-values are computed using the χ^2_q distribution. $\mathbb{H}_0$ is rejected in favor of $\mathbb{H}_1$ if J^* exceeds the level α critical value, which can be calculated in MATLAB as `chi2inv(1-α,q)`. The asymptotic p-value is $p = 1 - G_q(J^*)$. In MATLAB, use the command `1-chi2cdf(J,q)`.

Let us now demonstrate Theorem 9.4. The conditions of Theorem 8.10 hold, because $\mathbb{H}_0$ implies Assumption 8.1. From (8.54) with $\widehat{\boldsymbol{W}} = \widehat{\boldsymbol{V}}_\beta$, we see that

$$\begin{aligned} \sqrt{n}\left(\widehat{\beta} - \widetilde{\beta}_{\text{emd}}\right) &= \widehat{\boldsymbol{V}}_\beta \widehat{\boldsymbol{R}}\left(\boldsymbol{R}_n^{*\prime}\widehat{\boldsymbol{V}}_\beta \widehat{\boldsymbol{R}}\right)^{-1} \boldsymbol{R}_n^{*\prime}\sqrt{n}\left(\widehat{\beta} - \beta\right) \\ &\underset{d}{\longrightarrow} \boldsymbol{V}_\beta \boldsymbol{R}\left(\boldsymbol{R}'\boldsymbol{V}_\beta \boldsymbol{R}\right)^{-1} \boldsymbol{R}'\mathrm{N}(0, \boldsymbol{V}_\beta) = \boldsymbol{V}_\beta \boldsymbol{R}\, Z \end{aligned}$$

where $Z \sim \mathrm{N}(0, \left(\boldsymbol{R}'\boldsymbol{V}_\beta \boldsymbol{R}\right)^{-1})$. Thus

$$J^* = n\left(\widehat{\beta} - \widetilde{\beta}_{\text{emd}}\right)'\widehat{\boldsymbol{V}}_\beta^{-1}\left(\widehat{\beta} - \widetilde{\beta}_{\text{emd}}\right) \underset{d}{\longrightarrow} Z'\boldsymbol{R}'\boldsymbol{V}_\beta \boldsymbol{V}_\beta^{-1} \boldsymbol{V}_\beta \boldsymbol{R}\, Z = Z'\left(\boldsymbol{R}'\boldsymbol{V}_\beta \boldsymbol{R}\right) Z = \chi^2_q$$

as claimed.

9.14 MINIMUM DISTANCE TESTS UNDER HOMOSKEDASTICITY

If we set $\widehat{\boldsymbol{W}} = \widehat{\boldsymbol{Q}}_{XX}/s^2$ in (9.8), we obtain a criterion similar to (8.20):

$$J^0(\beta) = n\left(\widehat{\beta} - \beta\right)'\widehat{\boldsymbol{Q}}_{XX}\left(\widehat{\beta} - \beta\right)/s^2.$$

A minimum distance statistic for $\mathbb{H}_0 : \beta \in B_0$ is

$$J^0 = \min_{\beta \in B_0} J^0(\beta).$$

Equation (8.21) showed that $\mathrm{SSE}(\beta) = n\widehat{\sigma}^2 + s^2 J^0(\beta)$. So the minimizers of $\mathrm{SSE}(\beta)$ and $J^0(\beta)$ are identical. Thus the constrained minimizer of $J^0(\beta)$ is constrained least squares

$$\widetilde{\beta}_{\mathrm{cls}} = \underset{\beta \in B_0}{\operatorname{argmin}}\, J^0(\beta) = \underset{\beta \in B_0}{\operatorname{argmin}}\, \mathrm{SSE}(\beta) \tag{9.11}$$

and therefore

$$J_n^0 = J_n^0(\widetilde{\beta}_{\mathrm{cls}}) = n\left(\widehat{\beta} - \widetilde{\beta}_{\mathrm{cls}}\right)' \widehat{\boldsymbol{Q}}_{XX}\left(\widehat{\beta} - \widetilde{\beta}_{\mathrm{cls}}\right)/s^2.$$

In the special case of linear hypotheses $\mathbb{H}_0 : \boldsymbol{R}'\beta = \theta_0$, the constrained least squares estimator subject to $\boldsymbol{R}'\beta = \theta_0$ has the solution (8.9):

$$\widetilde{\beta}_{\mathrm{cls}} = \widehat{\beta} - \widehat{\boldsymbol{Q}}_{XX}^{-1}\boldsymbol{R}\left(\boldsymbol{R}'\widehat{\boldsymbol{Q}}_{XX}^{-1}\boldsymbol{R}\right)^{-1}\left(\boldsymbol{R}'\widehat{\beta} - \theta_0\right)$$

and solving, we find

$$J^0 = n\left(\boldsymbol{R}'\widehat{\beta} - \theta_0\right)'\left(\boldsymbol{R}'\widehat{\boldsymbol{Q}}_{XX}^{-1}\boldsymbol{R}\right)^{-1}\left(\boldsymbol{R}'\widehat{\beta} - \theta_0\right)/s^2 = W^0.$$

This is the homoskedastic Wald statistic (9.7). Thus for testing linear hypotheses, homoskedastic minimum distance and Wald statistics agree.

For nonlinear hypotheses, they disagree but have the same null asymptotic distribution.

Theorem 9.5 Under Assumptions 7.2 and 7.3, $\mathbb{E}\left[e^2 \mid X\right] = \sigma^2 > 0$, and $\mathbb{H}_0 : \theta = \theta_0 \in \mathbb{R}^q$, then $J^0 \underset{d}{\longrightarrow} \chi_q^2$.

9.15 *F*-TESTS

In Section 5.13, we introduced the F test for exclusion restrictions in the normal regression model. In this section, we generalize this test to a broader set of restrictions. Let $B_0 \subset \mathbb{R}^k$ be a constrained parameter space that imposes q restrictions on β.

Let $\widehat{\beta}_{\mathrm{ols}}$ be the unrestricted least squares estimator, and let $\widehat{\sigma}^2 = n^{-1}\sum_{i=1}^n \left(Y_i - X_i'\widehat{\beta}_{\mathrm{ols}}\right)^2$ be the associated estimator of σ^2. Let $\widetilde{\beta}_{\mathrm{cls}}$ be the CLS estimator (9.11) satisfying $\widetilde{\beta}_{\mathrm{cls}} \in B_0$, and let $\widetilde{\sigma}^2 = n^{-1}\sum_{i=1}^n \left(Y_i - X_i'\widetilde{\beta}_{\mathrm{cls}}\right)^2$ be the associated estimator of σ^2. The F statistic for testing $\mathbb{H}_0 : \beta \in B_0$ is

$$F = \frac{\left(\widetilde{\sigma}^2 - \widehat{\sigma}^2\right)/q}{\widehat{\sigma}^2/(n-k)}. \tag{9.12}$$

We can alternatively write

$$F = \frac{\mathrm{SSE}(\widetilde{\beta}_{\mathrm{cls}}) - \mathrm{SSE}(\widehat{\beta}_{\mathrm{ols}})}{qs^2} \tag{9.13}$$

where $\mathrm{SSE}(\beta) = \sum_{i=1}^n \left(Y_i - X_i'\beta\right)^2$ is the sum-of-squared errors.

Equation (9.13) shows that F is a criterion-based statistic. Using (8.21), we can also write $F = J^0/q$, so the F statistic is identical to the homoskedastic minimum distance statistic divided by the number of restrictions q.

As we discussed in Section 9.13, in the special case of linear hypotheses $\mathbb{H}_0 : \boldsymbol{R}'\beta = \theta_0$, $J^0 = W^0$. It follows that in this case, $F = W^0/q$. Thus for linear restrictions, the F statistic equals the homoskedastic Wald statistic divided by q. It follows that they are equivalent tests for $\mathbb{H}_0$ against $\mathbb{H}_1$.

> **Theorem 9.6** For tests of linear hypotheses $\mathbb{H}_0 : \boldsymbol{R}'\beta = \theta_0 \in \mathbb{R}^q$, the F statistic equals $F = W^0/q$, where W^0 is the homoskedastic Wald statistic. Thus under 7.2, $\mathbb{E}\left[e^2 \mid X\right] = \sigma^2 > 0$, and $\mathbb{H}_0 : \theta = \theta_0$, then $F \underset{d}{\longrightarrow} \chi_q^2/q$.

When using an F statistic, it is conventional to use the $F_{q,n-k}$ distribution for critical values and p-values. Critical values are given in MATLAB by `finv(1-α,q,n-k)` and p-values by `1-fcdf(F,q,n-k)`. Alternatively, the χ_q^2/q distribution can be used, using `chi2inv(1-α,q)/q` and `1-chi2cdf(F*q,q)`, respectively. Using the $F_{q,n-k}$ distribution is a prudent small sample adjustment that yields exact answers if the errors are normal and otherwise slightly increases the critical values and p-values relative to the asymptotic approximation. Once again, if the sample size is small enough that the choice makes a difference, then probably we shouldn't be trusting the asymptotic approximation anyway!

An elegant feature of (9.12) or (9.13) is that they are directly computable from the standard output from two simple OLS regressions, as the sum of squared errors (or regression variance) is a typical printed output from statistical packages and is often reported in applied tables. Thus F can be calculated by hand from standard reported statistics even if you don't have the original data—or if you are sitting in a seminar and listening to a presentation!

If you are presented with an F statistic (or a Wald statistic, as you can just divide by q) but don't have access to critical values, a useful rule of thumb is to know that for large n, the 5% asymptotic critical value is decreasing as q increases and is less than 2 for $q \geq 7$.

A word of warning: In many statistical packages when an OLS regression is estimated, an "F-statistic" is automatically reported, even though no hypothesis test was requested. What the package is reporting is an F statistic of the hypothesis that all slope coefficients[1] are 0. This statistic was popular in the early days of econometric reporting, when sample sizes were very small and researchers wanted to know if there was "any explanatory power" to their regression. This is rarely an issue today, as sample sizes are typically sufficiently large that this F statistic is nearly always highly significant. While in special cases, this F statistic is useful, these cases are not typical. As a general rule, there is no reason to report this F statistic.

9.16 HAUSMAN TESTS

Hausman (1978) introduced a general idea about how to test a hypothesis $\mathbb{H}_0$. If you have two estimators, one that is efficient under $\mathbb{H}_0$ but inconsistent under $\mathbb{H}_1$, and another that is consistent under $\mathbb{H}_1$, then construct a test as a quadratic form in the differences of the estimators. In the case of testing a hypothesis $\mathbb{H}_0 : r(\beta) = \theta_0$, let $\widehat{\beta}_{\text{ols}}$ denote the unconstrained least squares estimator, and let $\widetilde{\beta}_{\text{emd}}$ denote the efficient minimum distance estimator that imposes $r(\beta) = \theta_0$. Both estimators are consistent under $\mathbb{H}_0$, but $\widetilde{\beta}_{\text{emd}}$ is asymptotically efficient.

[1] All coefficients except the intercept.

Under $\mathbb{H}_1$, $\widehat{\beta}_{\text{ols}}$ is consistent for β, but $\widetilde{\beta}_{\text{emd}}$ is inconsistent. The difference has the asymptotic distribution

$$\sqrt{n}\left(\widehat{\beta}_{\text{ols}}-\widetilde{\beta}_{\text{emd}}\right)\underset{d}{\longrightarrow}\mathrm{N}\left(0, \boldsymbol{V}_{\beta}\boldsymbol{R}\left(\boldsymbol{R}'\boldsymbol{V}_{\beta}\boldsymbol{R}\right)^{-1}\boldsymbol{R}'\boldsymbol{V}_{\beta}\right).$$

Let $\boldsymbol{A}^{-}$ denote the Moore-Penrose generalized inverse. The Hausman statistic for $\mathbb{H}_0$ is

$$\begin{aligned} H &= \left(\widehat{\beta}_{\text{ols}}-\widetilde{\beta}_{\text{emd}}\right)'\widehat{\text{avar}}\left(\widehat{\beta}_{\text{ols}}-\widetilde{\beta}_{\text{emd}}\right)^{-}\left(\widehat{\beta}_{\text{ols}}-\widetilde{\beta}_{\text{emd}}\right) \\ &= n\left(\widehat{\beta}_{\text{ols}}-\widetilde{\beta}_{\text{emd}}\right)'\left(\widehat{\boldsymbol{V}}_{\beta}\widehat{\boldsymbol{R}}\left(\widehat{\boldsymbol{R}}'\widehat{\boldsymbol{V}}_{\beta}\widehat{\boldsymbol{R}}\right)^{-1}\widehat{\boldsymbol{R}}'\widehat{\boldsymbol{V}}_{\beta}\right)^{-}\left(\widehat{\beta}_{\text{ols}}-\widetilde{\beta}_{\text{emd}}\right). \end{aligned}$$

The matrix $\widehat{\boldsymbol{V}}_{\beta}^{1/2}\widehat{\boldsymbol{R}}\left(\widehat{\boldsymbol{R}}'\widehat{\boldsymbol{V}}_{\beta}\widehat{\boldsymbol{R}}\right)^{-1}\widehat{\boldsymbol{R}}'\widehat{\boldsymbol{V}}_{\beta}^{1/2}$ idempotent, so its generalized inverse is itself. (See Section A.11.) It follows that

$$\begin{aligned} \left(\widehat{\boldsymbol{V}}_{\beta}\widehat{\boldsymbol{R}}\left(\widehat{\boldsymbol{R}}'\widehat{\boldsymbol{V}}_{\beta}\widehat{\boldsymbol{R}}\right)^{-1}\widehat{\boldsymbol{R}}'\widehat{\boldsymbol{V}}_{\beta}\right)^{-} &= \widehat{\boldsymbol{V}}_{\beta}^{-1/2}\left(\widehat{\boldsymbol{V}}_{\beta}^{1/2}\widehat{\boldsymbol{R}}\left(\widehat{\boldsymbol{R}}'\widehat{\boldsymbol{V}}_{\beta}\widehat{\boldsymbol{R}}\right)^{-1}\widehat{\boldsymbol{R}}'\widehat{\boldsymbol{V}}_{\beta}^{1/2}\right)^{-}\widehat{\boldsymbol{V}}_{\beta}^{-1/2} \\ &= \widehat{\boldsymbol{V}}_{\beta}^{-1/2}\widehat{\boldsymbol{V}}_{\beta}^{1/2}\widehat{\boldsymbol{R}}\left(\widehat{\boldsymbol{R}}'\widehat{\boldsymbol{V}}_{\beta}\widehat{\boldsymbol{R}}\right)^{-1}\widehat{\boldsymbol{R}}'\widehat{\boldsymbol{V}}_{\beta}^{1/2}\widehat{\boldsymbol{V}}_{\beta}^{-1/2} \\ &= \widehat{\boldsymbol{R}}\left(\widehat{\boldsymbol{R}}'\widehat{\boldsymbol{V}}_{\beta}\widehat{\boldsymbol{R}}\right)^{-1}\widehat{\boldsymbol{R}}'. \end{aligned}$$

Thus the Hausman statistic is

$$H = n\left(\widehat{\beta}_{\text{ols}}-\widetilde{\beta}_{\text{emd}}\right)'\widehat{\boldsymbol{R}}\left(\widehat{\boldsymbol{R}}'\widehat{\boldsymbol{V}}_{\beta}\widehat{\boldsymbol{R}}\right)^{-1}\widehat{\boldsymbol{R}}'\left(\widehat{\beta}_{\text{ols}}-\widetilde{\beta}_{\text{emd}}\right).$$

In the context of linear restrictions, $\widehat{\boldsymbol{R}}=\boldsymbol{R}$ and $\boldsymbol{R}'\widetilde{\beta}=\theta_0$, so the statistic takes the form

$$H = n\left(\boldsymbol{R}'\widehat{\beta}_{\text{ols}}-\theta_0\right)'\widehat{\boldsymbol{R}}\left(\boldsymbol{R}'\widehat{\boldsymbol{V}}_{\beta}\boldsymbol{R}\right)^{-1}\left(\boldsymbol{R}'\widehat{\beta}_{\text{ols}}-\theta_0\right)$$

which is precisely the Wald statistic. With nonlinear restrictions, W and H can differ.

In either case, we see that that the asymptotic null distribution of the Hausman statistic H is χ^2_q, so the appropriate test is to reject $\mathbb{H}_0$ in favor of $\mathbb{H}_1$ if $H > c$, where c is a critical value taken from the χ^2_q distribution.

Theorem 9.7 For general hypotheses, the Hausman test statistic is

$$H = n\left(\widehat{\beta}_{\text{ols}}-\widetilde{\beta}_{\text{emd}}\right)'\widehat{\boldsymbol{R}}\left(\widehat{\boldsymbol{R}}'\widehat{\boldsymbol{V}}_{\beta}\widehat{\boldsymbol{R}}\right)^{-1}\widehat{\boldsymbol{R}}'\left(\widehat{\beta}_{\text{ols}}-\widetilde{\beta}_{\text{emd}}\right).$$

Under Assumptions 7.2, 7.3, and 7.4, and $\mathbb{H}_0: r(\beta)=\theta_0\in\mathbb{R}^q$, $H\underset{d}{\longrightarrow}\chi^2_q$.

9.17 SCORE TESTS

Score tests are traditionally derived in likelihood analysis but can more generally be constructed from first-order conditions evaluated at restricted estimates. We focus on the likelihood derivation. Given the log likelihood function $\ell_n(\beta,\sigma^2)$, a restriction $\mathbb{H}_0: r(\beta)=\theta_0$, and restricted estimators $\widetilde{\beta}$ and $\widetilde{\sigma}^2$, the **score**

statistic for $\mathbb{H}_0$ is defined as

$$S = \left(\frac{\partial}{\partial \beta}\ell_n(\widetilde{\beta},\widetilde{\sigma}^2)\right)'\left(-\frac{\partial^2}{\partial\beta\partial\beta'}\ell_n(\widetilde{\beta},\widetilde{\sigma}^2)\right)^{-1}\left(\frac{\partial}{\partial \beta}\ell_n(\widetilde{\beta},\widetilde{\sigma}^2)\right).$$

The idea is that if the restriction is true, then the restricted estimators should be close to the maximum of the log-likelihood where the derivative is 0. However if the restriction is false, then the restricted estimators should be distant from the maximum, and the derivative should be large. Hence small values of S are expected under $\mathbb{H}_0$ and large values under $\mathbb{H}_1$. Tests of $\mathbb{H}_0$ reject for large values of S.

We explore the score statistic in the context of the normal regression model and linear hypotheses $r(\beta) = \boldsymbol{R}'\beta$. Recall that in the normal regression, the log-likelihood function is

$$\ell_n(\beta,\sigma^2) = -\frac{n}{2}\log(2\pi\sigma^2) - \frac{1}{2\sigma^2}\sum_{i=1}^{n}\left(Y_i - X_i'\beta\right)^2.$$

The constrained MLE under linear hypotheses is constrained least squares:

$$\begin{aligned}
\widetilde{\beta} &= \widehat{\beta} - \left(\boldsymbol{X}'\boldsymbol{X}\right)^{-1}\boldsymbol{R}\left[\boldsymbol{R}'\left(\boldsymbol{X}'\boldsymbol{X}\right)^{-1}\boldsymbol{R}\right]^{-1}\left(\boldsymbol{R}'\widehat{\beta} - \boldsymbol{c}\right)\\
\widetilde{e}_i &= Y_i - X_i'\widetilde{\beta}\\
\widetilde{\sigma}^2 &= \frac{1}{n}\sum_{i=1}^{n}\widetilde{e}_i^2.
\end{aligned}$$

We can calculate that the derivative and Hessian are

$$\begin{aligned}
\frac{\partial}{\partial\beta}\ell_n(\widetilde{\beta},\widetilde{\sigma}^2) &= \frac{1}{\widetilde{\sigma}^2}\sum_{i=1}^{n}X_i\left(Y_i - X_i'\widetilde{\beta}\right) = \frac{1}{\widetilde{\sigma}^2}\boldsymbol{X}'\widetilde{\boldsymbol{e}}\\
-\frac{\partial^2}{\partial\beta\partial\beta'}\ell_n(\widetilde{\beta},\widetilde{\sigma}^2) &= \frac{1}{\widetilde{\sigma}^2}\sum_{i=1}^{n}X_iX_i' = \frac{1}{\widetilde{\sigma}^2}\boldsymbol{X}'\boldsymbol{X}.
\end{aligned}$$

Since $\widetilde{\boldsymbol{e}} = \boldsymbol{Y} - \boldsymbol{X}\widetilde{\beta}$, we can further calculate that

$$\begin{aligned}
\frac{\partial}{\partial\beta}\ell_n(\widetilde{\beta},\widetilde{\sigma}^2) &= \frac{1}{\widetilde{\sigma}^2}\left(\boldsymbol{X}'\boldsymbol{X}\right)\left(\left(\boldsymbol{X}'\boldsymbol{X}\right)^{-1}\boldsymbol{X}'\boldsymbol{Y} - \left(\boldsymbol{X}'\boldsymbol{X}\right)^{-1}\boldsymbol{X}'\boldsymbol{X}\widetilde{\beta}\right)\\
&= \frac{1}{\widetilde{\sigma}^2}\left(\boldsymbol{X}'\boldsymbol{X}\right)\left(\widehat{\beta} - \widetilde{\beta}\right)\\
&= \frac{1}{\widetilde{\sigma}^2}\boldsymbol{R}\left[\boldsymbol{R}'\left(\boldsymbol{X}'\boldsymbol{X}\right)^{-1}\boldsymbol{R}\right]^{-1}\left(\boldsymbol{R}'\widehat{\beta} - \boldsymbol{c}\right).
\end{aligned}$$

Taken together, we find that the score statistic is

$$S = \left(\boldsymbol{R}'\widehat{\boldsymbol{\beta}} - \boldsymbol{c}\right)'\left(\boldsymbol{R}'\left(\boldsymbol{X}'\boldsymbol{X}\right)^{-1}\boldsymbol{R}\right)^{-1}\left(\boldsymbol{R}'\widehat{\boldsymbol{\beta}} - \boldsymbol{c}\right)/\widetilde{\sigma}^2.$$

This is identical to the homoskedastic Wald statistic with s^2 replaced by $\widetilde{\sigma}^2$. We can also write S as a monotonic transformation of the F statistic:

$$S = n\frac{\left(\widetilde{\sigma}^2 - \widehat{\sigma}^2\right)}{\widetilde{\sigma}^2} = n\left(1 - \frac{\widehat{\sigma}^2}{\widetilde{\sigma}^2}\right) = n\left(1 - \frac{1}{1 + \frac{q}{n-k}F}\right).$$

The test "Reject $\mathbb{H}_0$ for large values of S" is identical to the test "Reject $\mathbb{H}_0$ for large values of F," so they are identical tests. Since for the normal regression model, the exact distribution of F is known, it is better to use the F statistic with F p-values.

In more complicated settings, a potential advantage of score tests is that they are calculated using the restricted parameter estimates $\widetilde{\beta}$ rather than the unrestricted estimates $\widehat{\beta}$. Thus when $\widetilde{\beta}$ is relatively easy to calculate, there can be a preference for score statistics. This is not a concern for linear restrictions.

More generally, score and score-like statistics can be constructed from first-order conditions evaluated at restricted parameter estimates. Also, when test statistics are constructed using covariance matrix estimators that are calculated using restricted parameter estimates (e.g., restricted residuals), then these are often described as score tests.

An example of the latter is the Wald-type statistic,

$$W = \left(r(\widehat{\beta}) - \theta_0\right)' \left(\widehat{\boldsymbol{R}}' \widetilde{\boldsymbol{V}}_{\widehat{\beta}} \widehat{\boldsymbol{R}}\right)^{-1} \left(r(\widehat{\beta}) - \theta_0\right)$$

where the covariance matrix estimate $\widetilde{\boldsymbol{V}}_{\widehat{\beta}}$ is calculated using the restricted residuals $\widetilde{e}_i = Y_i - X_i'\widetilde{\beta}$. This may be a good choice when β and θ are high-dimensional, as in this context, there may be concerns that the estimator $\widehat{\boldsymbol{V}}_{\widehat{\beta}}$ is imprecise.

9.18 PROBLEMS WITH TESTS OF NONLINEAR HYPOTHESES

Although the t and Wald tests work well when the hypothesis is a linear restriction on β, they can work quite poorly when the restrictions are nonlinear. This can be seen by a simple example introduced by Lafontaine and White (1986). Take the model $Y \sim \mathrm{N}(\beta, \sigma^2)$, and consider the hypothesis $\mathbb{H}_0 : \beta = 1$. Let $\widehat{\beta}$ and $\widehat{\sigma}^2$ be the sample mean and variance of Y, respectively. The standard Wald statistic to test $\mathbb{H}_0$ is

$$W = n\frac{\left(\widehat{\beta} - 1\right)^2}{\widehat{\sigma}^2}.$$

Notice that $\mathbb{H}_0$ is equivalent to the hypothesis $\mathbb{H}_0(s) : \beta^s = 1$ for any positive integer s. Letting $r(\beta) = \beta^s$, and noting $\boldsymbol{R} = s\beta^{s-1}$, we find that the Wald statistic to test $\mathbb{H}_0(s)$ is

$$W_s = n\frac{\left(\widehat{\beta}^s - 1\right)^2}{\widehat{\sigma}^2 s^2 \widehat{\beta}^{2s-2}}.$$

While the hypothesis $\beta^s = 1$ is unaffected by the choice of s, the statistic W_s varies with s, which is an unfortunate feature of the Wald statistic.

To demonstrate this effect, Figure 9.2 plots the Wald statistic W_s as a function of s, setting $n/\widehat{\sigma}^2 = 10$. The increasing curve is for the case $\widehat{\beta} = 0.8$. The decreasing curve is for the case $\widehat{\beta} = 1.6$. It is easy to see that in each case, there are values of s for which the test statistic is significant relative to asymptotic critical values, while there are other values of s for which the test statistic is insignificant. This is distressing, because the choice of s is arbitrary and irrelevant to the actual hypothesis.

Our first-order asymptotic theory is not useful for picking s, as $W_s \underset{d}{\longrightarrow} \chi_1^2$ under $\mathbb{H}_0$ for any s. This is a context where **Monte Carlo simulation** can be quite useful as a tool to study and compare the exact distributions of statistical procedures in finite samples. The method uses random simulation to create artificial datasets, to which we apply the statistical tools of interest. This produces random draws from the statistic's sampling distribution. Through repetition, features of this distribution can be calculated.

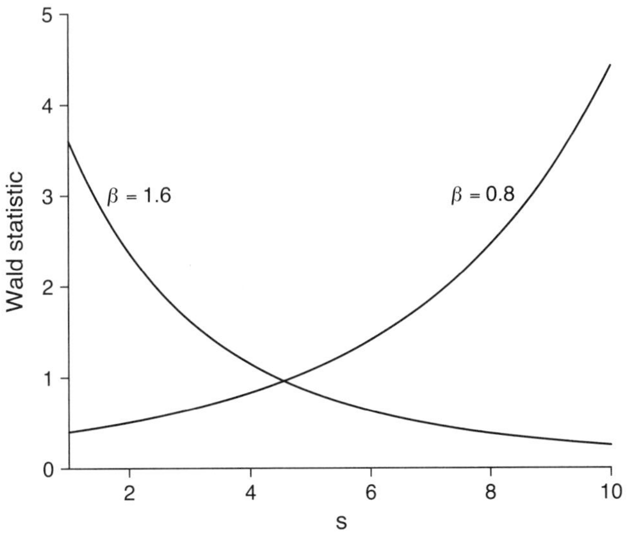

FIGURE 9.2 Wald statistic as a function of s

Table 9.2
Type I error probability of asymptotic 5% $W(s)$ test

	$\sigma=1$			$\sigma=3$		
s	$n=20$	$n=100$	$n=500$	$n=20$	$n=100$	$n=500$
1	0.05	0.05	0.05	0.05	0.05	0.05
2	0.07	0.06	0.05	0.14	0.08	0.06
3	0.09	0.06	0.05	0.21	0.12	0.07
4	0.12	0.07	0.05	0.25	0.15	0.08
5	0.14	0.08	0.06	0.27	0.18	0.10
6	0.16	0.09	0.06	0.30	0.20	0.12
7	0.18	0.10	0.06	0.32	0.22	0.13
8	0.20	0.12	0.07	0.33	0.24	0.14
9	0.21	0.13	0.07	0.34	0.25	0.16
10	0.23	0.14	0.08	0.35	0.26	0.17

Note: Rejection frequencies from 50,000 simulated random samples

In the present context of the Wald statistic, one feature of importance is the Type I error of the test using the asymptotic 5% critical value 3.84—the probability of a false rejection, $\mathbb{P}[W_s > 3.84 \mid \beta = 1]$. Given the simplicity of the model, this probability depends only on s, n, and σ^2. Table 9.2 reports the results of a Monte Carlo simulation that varies these three parameters. The value of s is varied from 1 to 10, n is varied among 20, 100, and 500, and σ is varied between 1 and 3. The table reports the simulation estimate of the Type I error probability from 50,000 random samples. Each row of the table corresponds to a different value of s—and thus corresponds to a particular choice of test statistic. The second through seventh columns contain the Type I error probabilities for different combinations of n and σ. These probabilities are calculated as the percentage of the 50,000 simulated Wald statistics W_s that are larger than 3.84. The null hypothesis $\beta^s = 1$ is true, so these probabilities are Type I error.

To interpret the table, remember that the ideal Type I error probability is 5% (.05) with deviations indicating distortion. Type I error rates between 3% and 8% are considered reasonable. Error rates above 10% are considered excessive. Rates above 20% are unacceptable. When comparing statistical procedures, we compare the rates row by row, looking for tests for which rejection rates are close to 5% and rarely fall outside of the 3–8% range. For this particular example, the only test that meets this criterion is the conventional $W = W_1$ test. Any other s leads to a test with unacceptable Type I error probabilities.

In Table 9.2, you can also see the impact of variation in sample size. In each case, the Type I error probability improves toward 5% as the sample size n increases. There is, however, no magic choice of n for which all tests perform uniformly well. Test performance deteriorates as s increases, which is not surprising, given the dependence of W_s on s as shown in Figure 9.2.

In this example, it is not surprising that the choice $s = 1$ yields the best test statistic. Other choices are arbitrary and would not be used in practice. Although this is clear in this particular example, in other examples natural choices are not obvious and the best choices may be counterintuitive.

This point can be illustrated through an example based on Gregory and Veall (1985). Take the model

$$Y = \beta_0 + X_1\beta_1 + X_2\beta_2 + e \tag{9.14}$$

$$\mathbb{E}[Xe] = 0$$

and the hypothesis $\mathbb{H}_0 : \frac{\beta_1}{\beta_2} = \theta_0$, where θ_0 is a known constant. Equivalently, define $\theta = \beta_1/\beta_2$, so the hypothesis can be stated as $\mathbb{H}_0 : \theta = \theta_0$.

Let $\widehat{\beta} = (\widehat{\beta}_0, \widehat{\beta}_1, \widehat{\beta}_2)$ be the least squares estimator of (9.14), let $\widehat{\boldsymbol{V}}_{\widehat{\beta}}$ be an estimator of the covariance matrix for $\widehat{\beta}$, and set $\widehat{\theta} = \widehat{\beta}_1/\widehat{\beta}_2$. Define

$$\widehat{\boldsymbol{R}}_1 = \begin{pmatrix} 0 \\ \dfrac{1}{\widehat{\beta}_2} \\ -\dfrac{\widehat{\beta}_1}{\widehat{\beta}_2^2} \end{pmatrix}$$

so that the standard error for $\widehat{\theta}$ is $s(\widehat{\theta}) = \left(\widehat{\boldsymbol{R}}_1' \widehat{\boldsymbol{V}}_{\widehat{\beta}} \widehat{\boldsymbol{R}}_1\right)^{1/2}$. In this case, a t-statistic for $\mathbb{H}_0$ is

$$T_1 = \frac{\left(\frac{\widehat{\beta}_1}{\widehat{\beta}_2} - \theta_0\right)}{s(\widehat{\theta})}.$$

An alternative statistic can be constructed by reformulating the null hypothesis as

$$\mathbb{H}_0 : \beta_1 - \theta_0\beta_2 = 0.$$

A t-statistic based on this formulation of the hypothesis is

$$T_2 = \frac{\widehat{\beta}_1 - \theta_0\widehat{\beta}_2}{\left(\boldsymbol{R}_2' \widehat{\boldsymbol{V}}_{\widehat{\beta}} \boldsymbol{R}_2\right)^{1/2}}$$

where

$$\boldsymbol{R}_2 = \begin{pmatrix} 0 \\ 1 \\ -\theta_0 \end{pmatrix}.$$

Table 9.3
Type I error probability of asymptotic 5% t-tests

	$n=100$				$n=500$			
	$\mathbb{P}(T<-1.645)$		$\mathbb{P}(T>1.645)$		$\mathbb{P}(T<-1.645)$		$\mathbb{P}(T>1.645)$	
β_2	T_1	T_2	T_1	T_2	T_1	T_2	T_1	T_2
0.10	0.47	0.05	0.00	0.05	0.28	0.05	0.00	0.05
0.25	0.27	0.05	0.00	0.05	0.16	0.05	0.00	0.05
0.50	0.14	0.05	0.00	0.05	0.12	0.05	0.00	0.05
0.75	0.03	0.05	0.00	0.05	0.08	0.05	0.01	0.05
1.00	0.00	0.05	0.00	0.05	0.03	0.05	0.03	0.05

Note: Rejection frequencies from 50,000 simulated random samples.

To compare T_1 and T_2, we perform another simple Monte Carlo simulation. Let X_1 and X_2 be mutually independent N$(0,1)$ variables, e be an independent N$(0,\sigma^2)$ draw with $\sigma=3$, and normalize $\beta_0=0$ and $\beta_1=1$. This leaves β_2 as a free parameter along with sample size n. We vary β_2 among 0.1, 0.25, 0.50, 0.75, and 1.0 and n among 100 and 500.

The one-sided Type I error probabilities $\mathbb{P}[T<-1.645]$ and $\mathbb{P}[T>1.645]$ are calculated from 50,000 simulated samples. The results are presented in Table 9.3. Ideally, the entries in the table should be 0.05. However, the rejection rates for the T_1 statistic diverge greatly from this value, especially for small values of β_2. The left tail probabilities $\mathbb{P}[T_1<-1.645]$ greatly exceed 5%, while the right tail probabilities $\mathbb{P}[T_1>1.645]$ are close to 0 in most cases. In contrast, the rejection rates for the T_2 statistic are invariant to the value of β_2 and equal 5% for both sample sizes. The implication of Table 9.3 is that the two t-ratios have dramatically different sampling behavior.

The common message from both examples is that Wald statistics are sensitive to the algebraic formulation of the null hypothesis.

A simple solution is to use the minimum distance statistic J, which equals W with $r=1$ in the first example, and $|T_2|$ in the second example. The minimum distance statistic is invariant to the algebraic formulation of the null hypothesis and so is immune to this problem. Whenever possible, the Wald statistic should not be used to test nonlinear hypotheses.

Theoretical investigations of these issues include Park and Phillips (1988a) and Dufour (1997).

9.19 MONTE CARLO SIMULATION

Section 9.18 introduced the method of Monte Carlo simulation to illustrate the small sample problems with tests of nonlinear hypotheses. In this section, we describe the method in more detail.

Recall that our data consist of observations (Y_i, X_i), which are random draws from a population distribution F. Let θ be a parameter, and let $T=T((Y_1,X_1),\ldots,(Y_n,X_n),\theta)$ be a statistic of interest, for example, an estimator $\widehat{\theta}$ or a t-statistic $(\widehat{\theta}-\theta)/s(\widehat{\theta})$. The exact distribution of T is

$$G(u,F)=\mathbb{P}[T\le u\mid F].$$

Although the asymptotic distribution of T might be known, the exact (finite sample) distribution G is generally unknown.

Monte Carlo simulation uses numerical simulation to compute $G(u,F)$ for selected choices of F. This is useful for investigating the performance of the statistic T in reasonable situations and sample sizes. The basic idea is that for any given F, the distribution function $G(u, F)$ can be calculated numerically through simulation. The name **Monte Carlo** derives from the Mediterranean gambling resort where games of chance are played.

The method of Monte Carlo is simple to describe. The researcher chooses F (the distribution of the pseudodata) and the sample size n. A "true" value of θ is implied by this choice, or equivalently, the value θ is selected directly by the researcher, which implies restrictions on F.

Then the following experiment is conducted by computer simulation:

1. n independent random pairs $\left(Y_i^*, X_i^*\right)$, $i=1,\ldots,n$, are drawn from the distribution F using the computer's random number generator.
2. The statistic $T=T\left(\left(Y_1^*, X_1^*\right),\ldots,\left(Y_n^*, X_n^*\right),\theta\right)$ is calculated on this pseudodata.

For step 1, computer packages have built-in random number procedures including U[0, 1] and N(0, 1). From these, most random variables can be constructed. (For example, a chi-square can be generated by sums of squares of normals.)

For step 2, it is important that the statistic be evaluated at the "true" value of θ corresponding to the choice of F.

The above experiment creates one random draw T from the distribution $G(u, F)$. This is one observation from an unknown distribution. Clearly, from one observation, very little can be said. So the researcher repeats the experiment B times, where B is a large number. Typically, we set $B \geq 1000$. We will discuss this choice later.

Notationally, let the bth experiment result in the draw T_b, $b=1,\ldots,B$. These results are stored. After all B experiments have been calculated, these results constitute a random sample of size B from the distribution of $G(u, F)=\mathbb{P}\left[T_b \leq u\right]=\mathbb{P}\left[T \leq u \mid F\right]$.

From a random sample we can estimate any feature of interest using (typically) a method of moments estimator. We now describe some specific examples.

Suppose we are interested in the bias, mean-squared error (MSE), and/or variance of the distribution of $\widehat{\theta}-\theta$. We then set $T=\widehat{\theta}-\theta$, run the above experiment, and calculate

$$\widehat{\text{bias}}\left[\widehat{\theta}\right]=\frac{1}{B}\sum_{b=1}^{B} T_b=\frac{1}{B}\sum_{b=1}^{B}\widehat{\theta}_b-\theta$$

$$\widehat{\text{mse}}\left[\widehat{\theta}\right]=\frac{1}{B}\sum_{b=1}^{B}\left(T_b\right)^2=\frac{1}{B}\sum_{b=1}^{B}\left(\widehat{\theta}_b-\theta\right)^2.$$

$$\widehat{\text{var}}\left[\widehat{\theta}\right]=\widehat{\text{mse}}\left[\widehat{\theta}\right]-\left(\widehat{\text{bias}}\left[\widehat{\theta}\right]\right)^2.$$

Suppose we are interested in the Type I error associated with an asymptotic 5% two-sided t-test. We would then set $T=\left|\widehat{\theta}-\theta\right|/s(\widehat{\theta})$ and calculate

$$\widehat{P}=\frac{1}{B}\sum_{b=1}^{B}\mathbb{1}\left\{T_b \geq 1.96\right\} \tag{9.15}$$

the percentage of the simulated t-ratios that exceed the asymptotic 5% critical value.

Suppose we are interested in the 5% and 95% quantile of $T=\widehat{\theta}$ or $T=\left(\widehat{\theta}-\theta\right)/s(\widehat{\theta})$. We then compute the 5% and 95% sample quantiles of the sample $\{T_b\}$. For details on quantile estimation, see Section 11.13 of *Probability and Statistics for Economists*.

The typical purpose of a Monte Carlo simulation is to investigate the performance of a statistical procedure in realistic settings. Generally, the performance will depend on n and F. In many cases, an estimator or test may perform wonderfully for some values and poorly for others. It is therefore useful to conduct a variety of experiments for various choices of n and F.

As discussed above, the researcher must select the number of experiments B. Often this is called the number of **replications**. Quite simply, a larger B results in more precise estimates of the features of interest of G but requires more computational time. In practice, therefore, the choice of B is often guided by the computational demands of the statistical procedure. Since the results of a Monte Carlo experiment are estimates computed from a random sample of size B, it is straightforward to calculate standard errors for any quantity of interest. If the standard error is too large to make a reliable inference, then B will have to be increased. A useful rule-of-thumb is to set $B = 10,000$ when possible.

In particular, it is simple to make inferences about rejection probabilities from statistical tests, such as the percentage estimate reported in (9.15). The random variable $\mathbb{1}\{T_b \geq 1.96\}$ is i.i.d. Bernoulli, equaling 1 with probability $p = \mathbb{E}[\mathbb{1}\{T_b \geq 1.96\}]$. The average (9.15) is therefore an unbiased estimator of p with standard error $s(\widehat{p}) = \sqrt{p(1-p)/B}$. As p is unknown, this may be approximated by replacing p with $\widehat{p}$ or with a hypothesized value. For example, if we are assessing an asymptotic 5% test, then we can set $s(\widehat{p}) = \sqrt{(.05)(.95)/B} \simeq .22/\sqrt{B}$. Hence, standard errors for $B = 100$, 1000, and 5000, are, respectively, $s(\widehat{p}) = .022$, .007, and .003.

Most papers in econometric methods and some empirical papers include the results of Monte Carlo simulations to illustrate the performance of their methods. When extending existing results, it is good practice to start by replicating existing (published) results. This may not be exactly possible in the case of simulation results, as they are inherently random. For example, suppose a paper investigates a statistical test and reports a simulated rejection probability of 0.07 based on a simulation with $B = 100$ replications. Suppose you attempt to replicate this result and find a rejection probability of 0.03 (again using $B = 100$ simulation replications). Should you conclude that you have failed in your attempt? Absolutely not! Under the hypothesis that both simulations are identical, you have two independent estimates, $\widehat{p}_1 = 0.07$ and $\widehat{p}_2 = 0.03$, of a common probability p. The asymptotic (as $B \to \infty$) distribution of their difference is $\sqrt{B}(\widehat{p}_1 - \widehat{p}_2) \underset{d}{\longrightarrow} \mathrm{N}(0, 2p(1-p))$, so a standard error for $\widehat{p}_1 - \widehat{p}_2 = 0.04$ is $\widehat{s} = \sqrt{2\overline{p}(1-\overline{p})/B} \simeq 0.03$, using the estimate $\overline{p} = (\widehat{p}_1 + \widehat{p}_2)/2$. Since the t-ratio $0.04/0.03 = 1.3$ is not statistically significant, it is incorrect to reject the null hypothesis that the two simulations are identical. The difference between the results $\widehat{p}_1 = 0.07$ and $\widehat{p}_2 = 0.03$ is consistent with random variation.

What should be done? The first mistake was to copy the previous paper's choice of $B = 100$. Instead, suppose you set $B = 10,000$ and now obtain $\widehat{p}_2 = 0.04$. Then $\widehat{p}_1 - \widehat{p}_2 = 0.03$, and a standard error is $\widehat{s} = \sqrt{\overline{p}(1-\overline{p})(1/100 + 1/10000)} \simeq 0.02$. Still we cannot reject the hypothesis that the two simulations are different. Even though the estimates (0.07 and 0.04) appear to be quite different, the difficulty is that the original simulation used a very small number of replications ($B = 100$), so the reported estimate is quite imprecise. In this case, it is appropriate to conclude that your results "replicate" the previous study, as there is no statistical evidence to reject the hypothesis that they are equivalent.

Most journals have policies requiring authors to make available their datasets and computer programs required for empirical results. Most do not have similar policies regarding simulations. Nevertheless, it is good professional practice to make your simulations available. The best practice is to post your simulation code on your webpage. This invites others to build on and use your results, leading to possible collaboration, citation, and/or advancement.

9.20 CONFIDENCE INTERVALS BY TEST INVERSION

There is a close relationship between hypothesis tests and confidence intervals. We observed in Section 7.13 that the standard 95% asymptotic confidence interval for a parameter θ is

$$\widehat{C} = \left[\widehat{\theta} - 1.96 \times s(\widehat{\theta}), \quad \widehat{\theta} + 1.96 \times s(\widehat{\theta})\right] = \{\theta : |T(\theta)| \leq 1.96\}. \tag{9.16}$$

That is, we can describe $\widehat{C}$ as "the point estimate plus or minus 2 standard errors" or "the set of parameter values not rejected by a two-sided t-test." The second definition, known as **test statistic inversion**, is a general method for finding confidence intervals, and it typically produces confidence intervals with excellent properties.

Given a test statistic $T(\theta)$ and critical value c, the acceptance region "Accept if $T(\theta) \le c$" is identical to the confidence interval $\widehat{C} = \{\theta : T(\theta) \le c\}$. Since the regions are identical, the probability of coverage $\mathbb{P}\left[\theta \in \widehat{C}\right]$ equals the probability of correct acceptance $\mathbb{P}\left[\text{Accept} \mid \theta\right]$, which is exactly 1 minus the Type I error probability. Thus inverting a test with good Type I error probabilities yields a confidence interval with good coverage probabilities.

Now suppose that the parameter of interest $\theta = r(\beta)$ is a nonlinear function of the coefficient vector β. In this case, the standard confidence interval for θ is the set $\widehat{C}$ as in (9.16), where $\widehat{\theta} = r(\widehat{\beta})$ is the point estimator, and $s(\widehat{\theta}) = \sqrt{\widehat{\boldsymbol{R}}' \widehat{\boldsymbol{V}}_{\widehat{\beta}} \widehat{\boldsymbol{R}}}$ is the delta method standard error. This confidence interval is inverting the t-test based on the nonlinear hypothesis $r(\beta) = \theta$. The trouble is that in Section 9.18, we learned that there is no unique t-statistic for tests of nonlinear hypotheses and that the choice of parameterization matters greatly.

For example, if $\theta = \beta_1/\beta_2$, then the coverage probability of the standard interval (9.16) is 1 minus the probability of the Type I error, which, as shown in Table 9.3, can be far from the nominal 5%.

In this example, a good solution is the same as that discussed in Section 9.18—to rewrite the hypothesis as a linear restriction. The hypothesis $\theta = \beta_1/\beta_2$ is the same as $\theta\beta_2 = \beta_1$. The t-statistic for this restriction is

$$T(\theta) = \frac{\widehat{\beta}_1 - \widehat{\beta}_2\theta}{\left(\boldsymbol{R}'\widehat{\boldsymbol{V}}_{\widehat{\beta}}\boldsymbol{R}\right)^{1/2}}$$

where

$$\boldsymbol{R} = \begin{pmatrix} 1 \\ -\theta \end{pmatrix}$$

and $\widehat{\boldsymbol{V}}_{\widehat{\beta}}$ is the covariance matrix for $(\widehat{\beta}_1\ \widehat{\beta}_2)$. A 95% confidence interval for $\theta = \beta_1/\beta_2$ is the set of values of θ such that $|T(\theta)| \le 1.96$. Since $T(\theta)$ is a nonlinear function of θ, one method to find the confidence set is grid search over θ.

For example, in the wage equation

$$\log(wage) = \beta_1 experience + \beta_2 experience^2/100 + \cdots$$

the highest expected wage occurs at $experience = -50\beta_1/\beta_2$. From Table 4.2, we have the point estimate $\widehat{\theta} = 29.8$, and we can calculate the standard error $s(\widehat{\theta}) = 0.022$ for a 95% confidence interval [29.8, 29.9]. However, if we instead invert the linear form of the test, we numerically find the interval [29.1, 30.6], which is much larger. From the evidence presented in Section 9.18, we know the first interval can be quite inaccurate, and the second interval is greatly preferred.

9.21 MULTIPLE TESTS AND BONFERRONI CORRECTIONS

In most applications, economists examine a large number of estimates, test statistics, and p-values. What does it mean (if anything) if one statistic appears to be "significant" after examining a large number of statistics? This is known as the problem of **multiple testing** or **multiple comparisons**.

To be specific, suppose we examine a set of k coefficients, standard errors and t-ratios, and consider the "significance" of each statistic. Based on conventional reasoning, for each coefficient, we would reject the hypothesis that the coefficient is 0 with asymptotic size α if the absolute t-statistic exceeds the $1-\alpha$ critical value of the normal distribution, or equivalently, if the p-value for the t-statistic is smaller than α. If we observe that one of the k statistics is "significant" based on this criterion, this means that one of the p-values is smaller than α, or equivalently, that the smallest p-value is smaller than α. We can then rephrase the question: Under the joint hypothesis that a set of k hypotheses are all true, what is the probability that the smallest p-value is smaller than α? In general, we cannot provide a precise answer to this quesion, but the Bonferroni correction bounds this probability by αk. The Bonferroni method furthermore suggests that if we want the **familywise error probability** (the probability that one of the tests falsely rejects) to be bounded below α, then an appropriate rule is to reject only if the smallest p-value is smaller than α/k. Equivalently, the Bonferroni familywise p-value is $k \min_{j\le k} p_j$.

Formally, suppose we have k hypotheses $\mathbb{H}_j, j=1,\dots,k$. For each we have a test and associated p-value p_j with the property that when $\mathbb{H}_j$ is true, $\lim_{n\to\infty} \mathbb{P}\left[p_j < \alpha\right] = \alpha$. We then observe that among the k tests, one of the k is "significant" if $\min_{j\le k} p_j < \alpha$. This event can be written as

$$\left\{\min_{j\le k} p_j < \alpha\right\} = \bigcup_{j=1}^{k} \left\{p_j < \alpha\right\}.$$

Boole's inequality states that for any k events A_j, $\mathbb{P}\left[\bigcup_{j=1}^{k} A_j\right] \le \sum_{j=1}^{k} \mathbb{P}\left[A_k\right]$. Thus

$$\mathbb{P}\left[\min_{j\le k} p_j < \alpha\right] \le \sum_{j=1}^{k} \mathbb{P}\left[p_j < \alpha\right] \to k\alpha$$

as stated. This demonstates that the asymptotic familywise rejection probability is at most k times the individual rejection probability.

Furthermore,

$$\mathbb{P}\left[\min_{j\le k} p_j < \frac{\alpha}{k}\right] \le \sum_{j=1}^{k} \mathbb{P}\left[p_j < \frac{\alpha}{k}\right] \to \alpha$$

which demonstrates that the asymptotic familywise rejection probability can be controlled (bounded below α) if each individual test is subjected to the stricter standard that a p-value must be smaller than α/k to be labeled as "significant."

To illustrate, suppose we have two coefficient estimates with individual p-values of 0.04 and 0.15. Based on a conventional 5% level, the standard individual tests would suggest that the first coefficient estimate is "significant" but not the second. A Bonferroni 5% test, however, does not reject, as it would require that the smallest p-value be smaller than 0.025, which is not the case in this example. Alternatively, the Bonferroni familywise p-value is $0.04 \times 2 = 0.08$, which is not significant at the 5% level.

In contrast, if the two p-values were 0.01 and 0.15, then the Bonferroni familywise p-value would be $0.01 \times 2 = 0.02$, which is significant at the 5% level.

9.22 POWER AND TEST CONSISTENCY

The **power** of a test is the probability of rejecting $\mathbb{H}_0$ when $\mathbb{H}_1$ is true. For simplicity, suppose that Y_i is i.i.d. $\mathrm{N}(\theta, \sigma^2)$ with σ^2 known, consider the t-statistic $T(\theta) = \sqrt{n}\left(\overline{Y} - \theta\right)/\sigma$, and tests of $\mathbb{H}_0 : \theta = 0$ against $\mathbb{H}_1 : \theta > 0$. We reject $\mathbb{H}_0$ if $T = T(0) > c$. Note that

$$T = T(\theta) + \sqrt{n}\theta/\sigma$$

and $T(\theta)$ has an exact $\mathrm{N}(0, 1)$ distribution. This is because $T(\theta)$ is centered at the true mean θ, while the test statistic $T(0)$ is centered at the (false) hypothesized mean of 0.

The power of the test is

$$\mathbb{P}\left[T > c \mid \theta\right] = \mathbb{P}\left[Z + \sqrt{n}\theta/\sigma > c\right] = 1 - \Phi\left(c - \sqrt{n}\theta/\sigma\right).$$

This function is monotonically increasing in μ and n, and decreasing in σ and c.

Notice that for any c and $\theta \neq 0$, the power increases to 1 as $n \to \infty$. Thus for $\theta \in \mathbb{H}_1$, the test will reject $\mathbb{H}_0$ with probability approaching 1 as the sample size gets large. We call this property **test consistency**.

Definition 9.3 A test of $\mathbb{H}_0 : \theta \in \Theta_0$ is **consistent against fixed alternatives** if for all $\theta \in \Theta_1$, $\mathbb{P}\left[\text{Reject } \mathbb{H}_0 \mid \theta\right] \to 1$ as $n \to \infty$.

For tests of the form "Reject $\mathbb{H}_0$ if $T > c$," a sufficient condition for test consistency is that the T diverges to positive infinity with probability one for all $\theta \in \Theta_1$.

Definition 9.4 We say that $T \xrightarrow[p]{} \infty$ as $n \to \infty$ if for all $M < \infty$, $\mathbb{P}\left[T \leq M\right] \to 0$ as $n \to \infty$. Similarly, we say that $T \xrightarrow[p]{} -\infty$ as $n \to \infty$ if for all $M < \infty$, $\mathbb{P}\left[T \geq -M\right] \to 0$ as $n \to \infty$.

In general, t-tests and Wald tests are consistent against fixed alternatives. Take a t-statistic for a test of $\mathbb{H}_0 : \theta = \theta_0$, $T = \left(\widehat{\theta} - \theta_0\right)/s(\widehat{\theta})$, where θ_0 is a known value, and $s(\widehat{\theta}) = \sqrt{n^{-1}\widehat{V}_\theta}$. Note that

$$T = \frac{\widehat{\theta} - \theta}{s(\widehat{\theta})} + \frac{\sqrt{n}\left(\theta - \theta_0\right)}{\sqrt{\widehat{V}_\theta}}.$$

The first term on the right-hand side converges in distribution to $\mathrm{N}(0, 1)$. The second term on the right-hand side equals 0 if $\theta = \theta_0$, converges in probability to $+\infty$ if $\theta > \theta_0$, and converges in probability to $-\infty$ if $\theta < \theta_0$. Thus the two-sided t-test is consistent against $\mathbb{H}_1 : \theta \neq \theta_0$, and one-sided t-tests are consistent against the alternatives for which they are designed.

Theorem 9.8 Under Assumptions 7.2, 7.3, and 7.4, for $\theta = r(\beta) \neq \theta_0$ and $q = 1$, $|T| \xrightarrow[p]{} \infty$. For any $c < \infty$, the test "Reject $\mathbb{H}_0$ if $|T| > c$" is consistent against fixed alternatives.

The Wald statistic for $\mathbb{H}_0 : \theta = r(\beta) = \theta_0$ against $\mathbb{H}_1 : \theta \neq \theta_0$ is $W = n\left(\widehat{\theta} - \theta_0\right)' \widehat{\boldsymbol{V}}_\theta^{-1} \left(\widehat{\theta} - \theta_0\right)$. Under $\mathbb{H}_1$, $\widehat{\theta} \underset{p}{\longrightarrow} \theta \neq \theta_0$. Thus, $\left(\widehat{\theta} - \theta_0\right)' \widehat{\boldsymbol{V}}_\theta^{-1} \left(\widehat{\theta} - \theta_0\right) \underset{p}{\longrightarrow} (\theta - \theta_0)' \boldsymbol{V}_\theta^{-1} (\theta - \theta_0) > 0$. Hence under $\mathbb{H}_1$, $W \underset{p}{\longrightarrow} \infty$. Again, this implies that Wald tests are consistent.

Theorem 9.9 Under Assumptions 7.2, 7.3, and 7.4, for $\theta = r(\beta) \neq \theta_0$, $W \underset{p}{\longrightarrow} \infty$. For any $c < \infty$, the test "Reject $\mathbb{H}_0$ if $W > c$" is consistent against fixed alternatives.

9.23 ASYMPTOTIC LOCAL POWER

Consistency is a good property for a test, but it does not provided a tool to calculate test power. To approximate the power function, we need a distributional approximation.

The standard asymptotic method for power analysis uses what are called **local alternatives**. This is similar to our analysis of restricted estimation under misspecification (Section 8.13). The technique is to index the parameter by sample size, so that the asymptotic distribution of the statistic is continuous in a localizing parameter. In this section, we consider t-tests on real-valued parameters and in the next section, Wald tests. Specifically, we consider parameter vectors β_n that are indexed by sample size n and satisfy the real-valued relationship

$$\theta_n = r(\beta_n) = \theta_0 + n^{-1/2} h \tag{9.17}$$

where the scalar h is called a **localizing parameter**. We index β_n and θ_n by sample size to indicate their dependence on n. The way to think of (9.17) is that the true value of the parameters are β_n and θ_n. The parameter θ_n is close to the hypothesized value θ_0, with deviation $n^{-1/2}h$.

The specification (9.17) states that for any fixed h, θ_n approaches θ_0 as n gets large. Thus θ_n is "close" or "local" to θ_0. The concept of a localizing sequence (9.17) might seem odd, since in the actual world, the sample size cannot mechanically affect the value of the parameter. Thus (9.17) should not be interpreted literally. Instead, it should be interpreted as a technical device that allows the asymptotic distribution to be continuous in the alternative hypothesis.

To evaluate the asymptotic distribution of the test statistic, we start by examining the scaled estimator centered at the hypothesized value θ_0. Breaking it into a term centered at the true value θ_n and a remainder, we find

$$\sqrt{n}\left(\widehat{\theta} - \theta_0\right) = \sqrt{n}\left(\widehat{\theta} - \theta_n\right) + \sqrt{n}\left(\theta_n - \theta_0\right) = \sqrt{n}\left(\widehat{\theta} - \theta_n\right) + h$$

where the second equality is (9.17). The first term is asymptotically normal:

$$\sqrt{n}\left(\widehat{\theta} - \theta_n\right) \underset{d}{\longrightarrow} \sqrt{V_\theta} Z$$

where $Z \sim \mathrm{N}(0, 1)$. Therefore,

$$\sqrt{n}\left(\widehat{\theta} - \theta_0\right) \underset{d}{\longrightarrow} \sqrt{V_\theta} Z + h \sim \mathrm{N}(h, V_\theta).$$

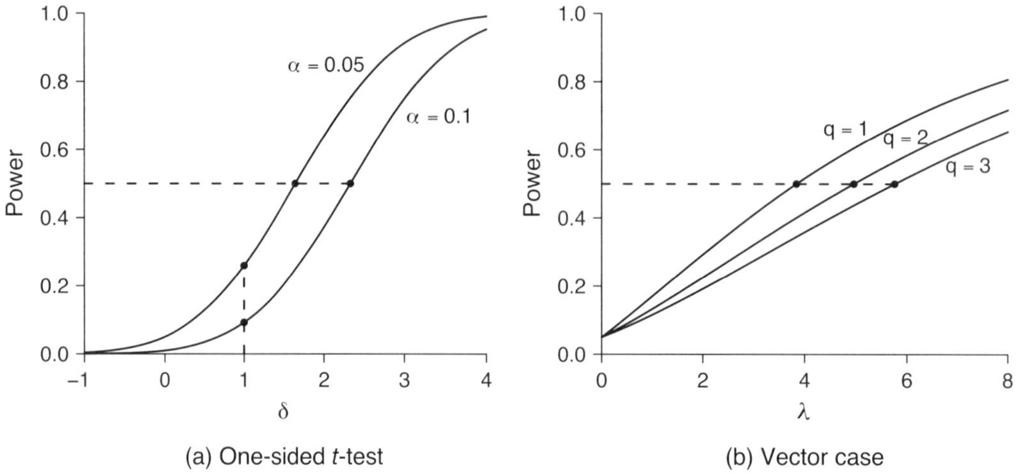

FIGURE 9.3 Asymptotic local power function

This asymptotic distribution depends continuously on the localizing parameter h. Applied to the t statistic we find

$$T = \frac{\widehat{\theta} - \theta_0}{s(\widehat{\theta})} \underset{d}{\longrightarrow} \frac{\sqrt{V_\theta} Z + h}{\sqrt{V_\theta}} \sim Z + \delta \tag{9.18}$$

where $\delta = h/\sqrt{V_\theta}$. This generalizes Theorem 9.1 (which assumes $\mathbb{H}_0$ is true) to allow for local alternatives of the form (9.17).

Consider a t-test of $\mathbb{H}_0$ against the one-sided alternative $\mathbb{H}_1 : \theta > \theta_0$, which rejects $\mathbb{H}_0$ for $T > c$, where $\Phi(c) = 1 - \alpha$. The **asymptotic local power** of this test is the limit (as the sample size diverges) of the rejection probability under the local alternative (9.17):

$$\begin{aligned}
\lim_{n\to\infty} \mathbb{P}\left[\text{Reject } \mathbb{H}_0\right] &= \lim_{n\to\infty} \mathbb{P}\left[T > c\right] \\
&= \mathbb{P}\left[Z + \delta > c\right] \\
&= 1 - \Phi\left(c - \delta\right) \\
&= \Phi\left(\delta - c\right) \\
&\overset{\text{def}}{=} \pi(\delta).
\end{aligned}$$

We call $\pi(\delta)$ the **asymptotic local power function**.

Figure 9.3(a) plots the local power function $\pi(\delta)$ as a function of $\delta \in [-1, 4]$ for tests of asymptotic size $\alpha = 0.05$ and $\alpha = 0.01$. $\delta = 0$ corresponds to the null hypothesis, so $\pi(\delta) = \alpha$. The power functions are monotonically increasing in δ. Note that the power is lower than α for $\delta < 0$, due to the one-sided nature of the test.

We can see that the power functions are ranked by α, so that the test with $\alpha = 0.05$ has higher power than the test with $\alpha = 0.01$. This is the inherent trade-off between size and power. Decreasing size induces a decrease in power, and conversely.

The coefficient δ can be interpreted as the parameter deviation measured as a multiple of the standard error $s(\widehat{\theta})$. To see this, recall that $s(\widehat{\theta}) = n^{-1/2}\sqrt{\widehat{V}_\theta} \simeq n^{-1/2}\sqrt{V_\theta}$, and then note that

$$\delta = \frac{h}{\sqrt{V_\theta}} \simeq \frac{n^{-1/2}h}{s(\widehat{\theta})} = \frac{\theta_n - \theta_0}{s(\widehat{\theta})}.$$

Thus δ approximately equals the deviation $\theta_n - \theta_0$ expressed as multiples of the standard error $s(\widehat{\theta})$. So as we examine Figure 9.3(a), we can interpret the power function at $\delta = 1$ (e.g., 26% for a 5% size test) as the power when the parameter θ_n is one standard error above the hypothesized value. For example, from Table 4.2, the standard error for the coefficient on "Married Female" is 0.010. Thus, in this example, $\delta = 1$ corresponds to $\theta_n = 0.010$ or an 1.0% wage premium for married females. Our calculations show that the asymptotic power of a one-sided 5% test against this alternative is about 26%.

The difference between power functions can be measured either vertically or horizontally. For example, in Figure 9.3(a), there is a vertical dashed line at $\delta = 1$, showing that the asymptotic local power function $\pi(\delta)$ equals 26% for $\alpha = 0.0$, and 9% for $\alpha = 0.01$. This is the difference in power across tests of differing size, holding fixed the parameter in the alternative.

A horizontal comparison can also be illuminating. To illustrate, in Figure 9.3(a) there is a horizontal dashed line at 50% power, which is a useful benchmark, as it is the point where the test has equal odds of rejection and acceptance. The dotted line crosses the two power curves at $\delta = 1.65$ ($\alpha = 0.05$) and $\delta = 2.33$ ($\alpha = 0.01$). Thus the parameter θ must be at least 1.65 standard errors above the hypothesized value for a one-sided 5% test to have 50% (approximate) power, and 2.33 standard errors for a one-sided 1% test.

The ratio of these values (e.g., $2.33/1.65 = 1.41$) measures the relative parameter magnitude needed to achieve the same power. (Thus, for a 1% size test to achieve 50% power, the parameter must be 41% larger than for a 5% size test.) Even more interesting, the square of this ratio (e.g., $1.41^2 = 2$) is the increase in sample size needed to achieve the same power under fixed parameters. That is, to achieve 50% power, a 1% size test needs twice as many observations as a 5% size test. This interpretation follows by the following informal argument. By definition and (9.17), $\delta = h/\sqrt{V_\theta} = \sqrt{n}\left(\theta_n - \theta_0\right)/\sqrt{V_\theta}$. Thus, holding θ and V_θ fixed, δ^2 is proportional to n.

The analysis of a two-sided t test is similar. Equation (9.18) implies that

$$T = \left|\frac{\widehat{\theta} - \theta_0}{s(\widehat{\theta})}\right| \underset{d}{\longrightarrow} |Z + \delta|$$

and thus the local power of a two-sided t test is

$$\lim_{n\to\infty} \mathbb{P}\left[\text{Reject } \mathbb{H}_0\right] = \lim_{n\to\infty} \mathbb{P}\left[T > c\right] = \mathbb{P}\left[|Z + \delta| > c\right] = \Phi\left(\delta - c\right) + \Phi\left(-\delta - c\right)$$

which is monotonically increasing in $|\delta|$.

Theorem 9.10 Under Assumptions 7.2, 7.3, 7.4, and $\theta_n = r(\beta_n) = r_0 + n^{-1/2}h$,

$$T(\theta_0) = \frac{\widehat{\theta} - \theta_0}{s(\widehat{\theta})} \underset{d}{\longrightarrow} Z + \delta$$

where $Z \sim \mathrm{N}(0,1)$, and $\delta = h/\sqrt{V_\theta}$. For c such that $\Phi(c) = 1 - \alpha$,

$$\mathbb{P}\left[T(\theta_0) > c\right] \longrightarrow \Phi\left(\delta - c\right).$$

Furthermore, for c such that $\Phi(c) = 1 - \alpha/2$,

$$\mathbb{P}\left[|T(\theta_0)| > c\right] \longrightarrow \Phi\left(\delta - c\right) + \Phi\left(-\delta - c\right).$$

9.24 ASYMPTOTIC LOCAL POWER, VECTOR CASE

This section extends the local power analysis Section 9.22 to the case of vector-valued alternatives. We generalize (9.17) to vector-valued θ_n. The local parameterization is

$$\theta_n = r(\beta_n) = \theta_0 + n^{-1/2} h \tag{9.19}$$

where h is $q \times 1$.

Under (9.19),

$$\sqrt{n}\left(\widehat{\theta} - \theta_0\right) = \sqrt{n}\left(\widehat{\theta} - \theta_n\right) + h \underset{d}{\longrightarrow} Z_h \sim \mathrm{N}(h, \boldsymbol{V}_\theta)$$

which is a normal random vector with mean h and covariance matrix $\boldsymbol{V}_\theta$. Applied to the Wald statistic, we find

$$W = n\left(\widehat{\theta} - \theta_0\right)' \widehat{\boldsymbol{V}}_\theta^{-1} \left(\widehat{\theta} - \theta_0\right) \underset{d}{\longrightarrow} Z_h' \boldsymbol{V}_\theta^{-1} Z_h \sim \chi_q^2(\lambda) \tag{9.20}$$

where $\lambda = h'\boldsymbol{V}^{-1}h$. $\chi_q^2(\lambda)$ is a non-central chi-square random variable with non-centrality parameter λ. (Theorem 5.3.6.)

The convergence (9.20) shows that under the local alternatives (9.19), $W \underset{d}{\longrightarrow} \chi_q^2(\lambda)$. This generalizes the null asymptotic distribution, which obtains as the special case $\lambda = 0$. We can use this result to obtain a continuous asymptotic approximation to the power function. For any significance level $\alpha > 0$, set the asymptotic critical value c so that $\mathbb{P}\left[\chi_q^2 > c\right] = \alpha$. Then as $n \to \infty$,

$$\mathbb{P}\left[W > c\right] \longrightarrow \mathbb{P}\left[\chi_q^2(\lambda) > c\right] \stackrel{\text{def}}{=} \pi(\lambda).$$

The asymptotic local power function $\pi(\lambda)$ depends only on α, q, and λ.

Theorem 9.11 Under Assumptions 7.2, 7.3, 7.4, and $\theta_n = r(\beta_n) = \theta_0 + n^{-1/2}h$, $W \underset{d}{\longrightarrow} \chi_q^2(\lambda)$, where $\lambda = h'\boldsymbol{V}_\theta^{-1}h$. Furthermore, for c such that $\mathbb{P}\left[\chi_q^2 > c\right] = \alpha$, $\mathbb{P}\left[W > c\right] \longrightarrow \mathbb{P}\left[\chi_q^2(\lambda) > c\right]$.

Figure 9.3(b) plots $\pi(\lambda)$ as a function of λ for $q = 1$, $q = 2$, and $q = 3$, and $\alpha = 0.05$. The asymptotic power functions are monotonically increasing in λ and asymptote to 1.

Figure 9.3(b) also shows the power loss for fixed non-centrality parameter λ as the dimensionality of the test increases. The power curves shift to the right as q increases, resulting in a decrease in power. This is illustrated by the dashed line at 50% power. The dashed line crosses the three power curves at $\lambda = 3.85$ $(q = 1)$, $\lambda = 4.96$ $(q = 2)$, and $\lambda = 5.77$ $(q = 3)$. The ratios of these λ values correspond to the relative sample sizes needed to obtain the same power. Thus increasing the dimension of the test from $q = 1$ to $q = 2$ requires a 28% increase in sample size, or an increase from $q = 1$ to $q = 3$ requires a 50% increase in sample size, to maintain 50% power.

9.25 EXERCISES

Exercise 9.1 Prove that if an additional regressor $\boldsymbol{X}_{k+1}$ is added to $\boldsymbol{X}$, Theil's adjusted $\overline{R}^2$ (see Section 4.18) increases if and only if $\left|T_{k+1}\right| > 1$, where $T_{k+1} = \widehat{\beta}_{k+1}/s(\widehat{\beta}_{k+1})$ is the t-ratio for $\widehat{\beta}_{k+1}$, and

$$s(\widehat{\beta}_{k+1}) = \left(s^2[(\boldsymbol{X}'\boldsymbol{X})^{-1}]_{k+1,k+1}\right)^{1/2}$$

is the homoskedastic standard error.

Exercise 9.2 You have two independent samples (Y_{1i}, X_{1i}) and (Y_{2i}, X_{2i}), both with sample sizes n, that satisfy $Y_1 = X_1'\beta_1 + e_1$ and $Y_2 = X_2'\beta_2 + e_2$, where $\mathbb{E}[X_1 e_1] = 0$ and $\mathbb{E}[X_2 e_2] = 0$. Let $\widehat{\beta}_1$ and $\widehat{\beta}_2$ be the OLS estimators of $\beta_1 \in \mathbb{R}^k$ and $\beta_2 \in \mathbb{R}^k$.

(a) Find the asymptotic distribution of $\sqrt{n}\left(\left(\widehat{\beta}_2 - \widehat{\beta}_1\right) - (\beta_2 - \beta_1)\right)$ as $n \to \infty$.

(b) Find an appropriate test statistic for $\mathbb{H}_0 : \beta_2 = \beta_1$.

(c) Find the asymptotic distribution of this statistic under $\mathbb{H}_0$.

Exercise 9.3 Let T be a t-statistic for $\mathbb{H}_0 : \theta = 0$ versus $\mathbb{H}_1 : \theta \neq 0$. Since $|T| \to_d |Z|$ under $\mathbb{H}_0$, someone suggests the test "Reject $\mathbb{H}_0$ if $|T| < c_1$ or $|T| > c_2$, where c_1 is the $\alpha/2$ quantile of $|Z|$ and c_2 is the $1 - \alpha/2$ quantile of $|Z|$."

(a) Show that the asymptotic size of the test is α.

(b) Is this a good test of $\mathbb{H}_0$ versus $\mathbb{H}_1$? Why or why not?

Exercise 9.4 Let W be a Wald statistic for $\mathbb{H}_0 : \theta = 0$ versus $\mathbb{H}_1 : \theta \neq 0$, where θ is $q \times 1$. Since $W \underset{d}{\longrightarrow} \chi^2_q$ under H_0, someone suggests the test "Reject $\mathbb{H}_0$ if $W < c_1$ or $W > c_2$, where c_1 is the $\alpha/2$ quantile of χ^2_q and c_2 is the $1 - \alpha/2$ quantile of χ^2_q."

(a) Show that the asymptotic size of the test is α.

(b) Is this a good test of $\mathbb{H}_0$ versus $\mathbb{H}_1$? Why or why not?

Exercise 9.5 Take the linear model $Y = X_1'\beta_1 + X_2'\beta_2 + e$ with $\mathbb{E}[Xe] = 0$, where both X_1 and X_2 are $q \times 1$. Show how to test the hypotheses $\mathbb{H}_0 : \beta_1 = \beta_2$ against $\mathbb{H}_1 : \beta_1 \neq \beta_2$.

Exercise 9.6 Suppose a researcher wants to know which of a set of 20 regressors has an effect on a variable *testscore*. He regresses *testscore* on the 20 regressors and reports the results. One of the 20 regressors (*studytime*) has a large t-ratio (about 2.5), while the other t-ratios are insignificant (smaller than 2 in absolute value). He argues that the data show that *studytime* is the key predictor for *testscore*. Do you agree with this conclusion? Is there a deficiency in his reasoning?

Exercise 9.7 Take the model $Y = X\beta_1 + X^2\beta_2 + e$ with $\mathbb{E}[e \mid X] = 0$, where Y is wages (dollars per hour) and X is age. Describe how you would test the hypothesis that the expected wage for a 40-year-old worker is \$20 an hour.

Exercise 9.8 You want to test $\mathbb{H}_0 : \beta_2 = 0$ against $\mathbb{H}_1 : \beta_2 \neq 0$ in the model $Y = X_1'\beta_1 + X_2'\beta_2 + e$ with $\mathbb{E}[Xe] = 0$. You read a paper that estimates the model

$$Y = X_1'\widehat{\gamma}_1 + (X_2 - X_1)'\,\widehat{\gamma}_2 + u$$

and reports a test of $\mathbb{H}_0 : \gamma_2 = 0$ against $\mathbb{H}_1 : \gamma_2 \neq 0$. Is this related to the test you want to conduct?

Exercise 9.9 Suppose a researcher uses one dataset to test a specific hypothesis $\mathbb{H}_0$ against $\mathbb{H}_1$ and finds that he can reject $\mathbb{H}_0$. A second researcher gathers a similar but independent dataset, uses similar methods, and finds that she cannot reject $\mathbb{H}_0$. How should we (as interested professionals) interpret these mixed results?

Exercise 9.10 In Exercise 7.8 you showed that $\sqrt{n}\left(\widehat{\sigma}^2 - \sigma^2\right) \underset{d}{\longrightarrow} \mathrm{N}(0, V)$ as $n \to \infty$ for some V. Let $\widehat{V}$ be an estimator of V.

(a) Using this result, construct a t-statistic for $\mathbb{H}_0 : \sigma^2 = 1$ against $\mathbb{H}_1 : \sigma^2 \neq 1$.
(b) Using the Delta Method, find the asymptotic distribution of $\sqrt{n}\,(\widehat{\sigma} - \sigma)$.
(c) Use the result in (b) to construct a t-statistic for $\mathbb{H}_0 : \sigma = 1$ against $\mathbb{H}_1 : \sigma \neq 1$.
(d) Are the null hypotheses in (a) and (c) the same, or are they different? Are the tests in (a) and (c) the same or are they different? If they are different, describe a context in which the two tests would give contradictory results.

Exercise 9.11 Consider a regression such as that shown in Table 4.2 where both *experience* and its square are included. A researcher wants to test the hypothesis that *experience* does not affect mean wages and does this by computing the t-statistic for *experience*. Is this the correct approach? If not, what is the appropriate testing method?

Exercise 9.12 A researcher estimates a regression and computes a test of $\mathbb{H}_0$ against $\mathbb{H}_1$ and finds a p-value of $p = 0.08$, or "not significant." She says "I need more data. If I had a larger sample, the test will have more power and then the test will reject." Is this interpretation correct?

Exercise 9.13 A common view is that "If the sample size is large enough, any hypothesis will be rejected." What does this mean? Interpret and comment.

Exercise 9.14 Take the model $Y = X'\beta + e$ with $\mathbb{E}[Xe] = 0$ and parameter of interest $\theta = \boldsymbol{R}'\beta$ with $\boldsymbol{R}$ $k \times 1$. Let $\widehat{\beta}$ be the least squares estimator and $\widehat{\boldsymbol{V}}_{\widehat{\beta}}$ its variance estimator.

(a) Write down $\widehat{C}$, the 95% asymptotic confidence interval for θ, in terms of $\widehat{\beta}$, $\widehat{\boldsymbol{V}}_{\widehat{\beta}}$, $\boldsymbol{R}$, and $z = 1.96$ (the 97.5% quantile of $\mathrm{N}(0, 1)$).
(b) Show that the decision "Reject $\mathbb{H}_0$ if $\theta_0 \notin \widehat{C}$" is an asymptotic 5% test of $\mathbb{H}_0 : \theta = \theta_0$.

Exercise 9.15 You are at a seminar where a colleague presents a simulation study of a test of a hypothesis $\mathbb{H}_0$ with nominal size 5%. Based on $B = 100$ simulation replications under $\mathbb{H}_0$, the estimated size is 7%. Your colleague says: "Unfortunately, the test over-rejects."

(a) Do you agree or disagree with your colleague? Explain. Hint: Use an asymptotic (large B) approximation.

(b) Suppose that the number of simulation replications were $B = 1000$ yet the estimated size is still 7%. Does your answer change?

Exercise 9.16 Consider two alternative regression models:

$$Y = X_1'\beta_1 + e_1 \tag{9.21}$$
$$\mathbb{E}[X_1 e_1] = 0$$

and

$$Y = X_2'\beta_2 + e_2 \tag{9.22}$$
$$\mathbb{E}[X_2 e_2] = 0$$

where X_1 and X_2 have at least some different regressors. (For example, (9.21) is a wage regression on geographic variables, and (2) is a wage regression on personal appearance measurements.) You want to know whether model (9.21) or model (9.22) fits the data better. Define $\sigma_1^2 = \mathbb{E}\left[e_1^2\right]$ and $\sigma_2^2 = \mathbb{E}\left[e_2^2\right]$. You decide that the model with the smaller variance fit (e.g., model (9.21)) fits better if $\sigma_1^2 < \sigma_2^2$. You decide to test for this by testing the hypothesis of equal fit $\mathbb{H}_0 : \sigma_1^2 = \sigma_2^2$ against the alternative of unequal fit $\mathbb{H}_1 : \sigma_1^2 \neq \sigma_2^2$. For simplicity, suppose that e_{1i} and e_{2i} are observed.

(a) Construct an estimator $\widehat{\theta}$ of $\theta = \sigma_1^2 - \sigma_2^2$.
(b) Find the asymptotic distribution of $\sqrt{n}\left(\widehat{\theta} - \theta\right)$ as $n \to \infty$.
(c) Find an estimator of the asymptotic variance of $\widehat{\theta}$.
(d) Propose a test of asymptotic size α of $\mathbb{H}_0$ against $\mathbb{H}_1$.
(e) Suppose the test accepts $\mathbb{H}_0$. Briefly, what is your interpretation?

Exercise 9.17 You have two regressors, X_1 and X_2, and estimate a regression with all quadratic terms included:

$$Y = \alpha + \beta_1 X_1 + \beta_2 X_2 + \beta_3 X_1^2 + \beta_4 X_2^2 + \beta_5 X_1 X_2 + e.$$

One of your advisors asks: Can we exclude the variable X_2 from this regression? How do you translate this question into a statistical test? When answering these questions, be specific, not general.

(a) What is the relevant null and alternative hypotheses?
(b) What is an appropriate test statistic?
(c) What is the appropriate asymptotic distribution for the statistic?
(d) What is the rule for acceptance/rejection of the null hypothesis?

Exercise 9.18 The observed data are $\{Y_i, X_i, Z_i\} \in \mathbb{R} \times \mathbb{R}^k \times \mathbb{R}^\ell$, $k > 1$ and $\ell > 1$, $i = 1, \ldots, n$. An econometrician first estimates $Y_i = X_i'\widehat{\beta} + \widehat{e}_i$ by least squares. The econometrician next regresses the residual $\widehat{e}_i$ on Z_i, which can be written as $\widehat{e}_i = Z_i'\widetilde{\gamma} + \widetilde{u}_i$.

(a) Define the population parameter γ being estimated in this second regression.
(b) Find the probability limit for $\widetilde{\gamma}$.
(c) Suppose the econometrician constructs a Wald statistic W for $\mathbb{H}_0 : \gamma = 0$ from the second regression, ignoring the two-stage estimation process. Write down the formula for W.

(d) Assume $\mathbb{E}\left[ZX'\right] = 0$. Find the asymptotic distribution for W under $\mathbb{H}_0 : \gamma = 0$.

(e) If $\mathbb{E}\left[ZX'\right] \neq 0$, will your answer to (d) change?

Exercise 9.19 An economist estimates $Y = X_1'\beta_1 + X_2\beta_2 + e$ by least squares and tests the hypothesis $\mathbb{H}_0 : \beta_2 = 0$ against $\mathbb{H}_1 : \beta_2 \neq 0$. Assume $\beta_1 \in \mathbb{R}^k$ and $\beta_2 \in \mathbb{R}$. She obtains a Wald statistic $W = 0.34$. The sample size is $n = 500$.

(a) What is the correct degrees of freedom for the χ^2 distribution to evaluate the significance of the Wald statistic?

(b) The Wald statistic W is very small. Indeed, is it less than the 1% quantile of the appropriate χ^2 distribution? If so, should you reject $\mathbb{H}_0$? Explain your reasoning.

Exercise 9.20 You are reading a paper, and it reports the results from two nested OLS regressions:

$$Y_i = X_{1i}'\widetilde{\beta}_1 + \widetilde{e}_i$$
$$Y_i = X_{1i}'\widehat{\beta}_1 + X_{2i}'\widehat{\beta}_2 + \widehat{e}_i.$$

Some summary statistics are reported:

Short Regression	Long Regression
$R^2 = .20$	$R^2 = .26$
$\sum_{i=1}^{n} \widetilde{e}_i^2 = 106$	$\sum_{i=1}^{n} \widehat{e}_i^2 = 100$
# of coefficients $= 5$	# of coefficients $= 8$
$n = 50$	$n = 50$

You are curious as to whether the estimate $\widehat{\beta}_2$ is statistically different from the zero vector. Is there a way to determine an answer from this information? Do you have to make any assumptions (beyond the standard regularity conditions) to justify your answer?

Exercise 9.21 Take the model $Y = X_1\beta_1 + X_2\beta_2 + X_3\beta_3 + X_4\beta_4 + e$ with $\mathbb{E}[Xe] = 0$. Describe how to test

$$\mathbb{H}_0 : \frac{\beta_1}{\beta_2} = \frac{\beta_3}{\beta_4}$$

against

$$\mathbb{H}_1 : \frac{\beta_1}{\beta_2} \neq \frac{\beta_3}{\beta_4}.$$

Exercise 9.22 You have a random sample from the model $Y = X\beta_1 + X^2\beta_2 + e$ with $\mathbb{E}[e \mid X] = 0$, where Y is wages (dollars per hour) and X is age. Describe how you would test the hypothesis that the expected wage for a 40-year-old worker is \$20 an hour.

Exercise 9.23 Let T be a test statistic such that under $\mathbb{H}_0$, $T \xrightarrow[d]{} \chi_3^2$. Since $\mathbb{P}\left[\chi_3^2 > 7.815\right] = 0.05$, an asymptotic 5% test of $\mathbb{H}_0$ rejects when $T > 7.815$. An econometrician is interested in the Type I error of this test when $n = 100$ and the data structure is well specified. She performs the following Monte Carlo experiment.

- $B = 200$ samples of size $n = 100$ are generated from a distribution satisfying $\mathbb{H}_0$.
- On each sample, the test statistic T_b is calculated.
- She calculates $\widehat{p} = B^{-1} \sum_{b=1}^{B} \mathbb{1}\{T_b > 7.815\} = 0.070$.
- The econometrician concludes that the test T is oversized in this context—it rejects too frequently under $\mathbb{H}_0$.

Is her conclusion correct, incorrect, or incomplete? Be specific in your answer.

Exercise 9.24 Do a Monte Carlo simulation. Take the model $Y = \alpha + X\beta + e$ with $\mathbb{E}[Xe] = 0$, where the parameter of interest is $\theta = \exp(\beta)$. Your data generating process for the simulation is: X is $U[0,1]$, $e \sim \mathrm{N}(0,1)$ is independent of X, and $n = 50$. Set $\alpha = 0$ and $\beta = 1$. Generate $B = 1000$ independent samples with α. On each, estimate the regression by least squares, calculate the covariance matrix using a standard (heteroskedasticity-robust) formula, and similarly estimate θ and its standard error. For each replication, store $\widehat{\beta}$, $\widehat{\theta}$, $T_\beta = \left(\widehat{\beta} - \beta\right) / s\left(\widehat{\beta}\right)$, and $T_\theta = \left(\widehat{\theta} - \theta\right) / s\left(\widehat{\theta}\right)$.

(a) Does the value of α matter? Explain why the described statistics are **invariant** to α and thus setting $\alpha = 0$ is irrelevant.

(b) From the 1000 replications, estimate $\mathbb{E}\left[\widehat{\beta}\right]$ and $\mathbb{E}\left[\widehat{\theta}\right]$. Discuss whether you see evidence that either estimator is biased or unbiased.

(c) From the 1000 replications, estimate $\mathbb{P}\left[T_\beta > 1.645\right]$ and $\mathbb{P}\left[T_\theta > 1.645\right]$. What does asymptotic theory predict these probabilities should be in large samples? What do your simulation results indicate?

Exercise 9.25 The dataset `Invest1993` on the textbook website contains data on 1962 U.S. firms extracted from Compustat, assembled by Bronwyn Hall, and used in B. Hall and B. Hall (1993).

The variables used in this exercise are given in the table below. The flow variables are annual sums. The stock variables are beginning of year.

	year	year of the observation
I	inva	Investment to Capital Ratio
Q	vala	Total Market Value to Asset Ratio (Tobin's Q)
C	cfa	Cash Flow to Asset Ratio
D	debta	Long Term Debt to Asset Ratio

(a) Extract the subsample of observations for 1987. There should be 1028 observations. Estimate a linear regression of I (investment to capital ratio) on the other variables. Calculate appropriate standard errors.

(b) Calculate asymptotic confidence intervals for the coefficients.

(c) This regression is related to Tobin's q theory of investment, which suggests that investment should be predicted solely by Q (Tobin's Q). This theory predicts that the coefficient on Q should be positive, and the others should be 0. Test the joint hypothesis that the coefficients on cash flow (C) and debt (D) are 0. Test the hypothesis that the coefficient on Q is 0. Are the results consistent with the predictions of the theory?

(d) Now try a nonlinear (quadratic) specification. Regress I on $Q, C, D, Q^2, C^2, D^2, Q \times C, Q \times D, C \times D$. Test the joint hypothesis that the six interaction and quadratic coefficients are 0.

Exercise 9.26 In a paper in 1963, Marc Nerlove analyzed a cost function for 145 American electric companies. Nerlov was interested in estimating a *cost function*: $C = f(Q, PL, PF, PK)$, where the variables are listed in the table below. His dataset `Nerlove1963` is on the textbook website.

C	Total cost
Q	Output
PL	Unit price of labor
PK	Unit price of capital
PF	Unit price of fuel

(a) First, estimate an unrestricted Cobb-Douglass specification

$$\log C = \beta_1 + \beta_2 \log Q + \beta_3 \log PL + \beta_4 \log PK + \beta_5 \log PF + e. \tag{9.23}$$

Report parameter estimates and standard errors.

(b) What is the economic meaning of the restriction $\mathbb{H}_0 : \beta_3 + \beta_4 + \beta_5 = 1$?

(c) Estimate (9.23) by constrained least squares, imposing $\beta_3 + \beta_4 + \beta_5 = 1$. Report your parameter estimates and standard errors.

(d) Estimate (9.23) by efficient minimum distance, imposing $\beta_3 + \beta_4 + \beta_5 = 1$. Report your parameter estimates and standard errors.

(e) Test $\mathbb{H}_0 : \beta_3 + \beta_4 + \beta_5 = 1$ using a Wald statistic.

(f) Test $\mathbb{H}_0 : \beta_3 + \beta_4 + \beta_5 = 1$ using a minimum distance statistic.

Exercise 9.27 Section 8.12 reported estimates from Mankiw, Romer, and Weil (1992). The section reported estimation both by unrestricted least squares and by constrained estimation, imposing the constraint that three coefficients (2nd, 3rd, and 4th coefficients) sum to 0, as implied by the Solow growth theory. Using the same dataset `MRW1992`, estimate the unrestricted model, and test the hypothesis that the three coefficients sum to 0.

Exercise 9.28 Using the `cps09mar` dataset and the subsample of non-Hispanic Black individuals (race code = 2), test the hypothesis that marriage status does not affect mean wages.

(a) Take the regression reported in Table 4.2. Which variables will need to be omitted to estimate a regression for this subsample?

(b) Express the hypothesis "marriage status does not affect mean wages" as a restriction on the coefficients. How many restrictions is this?

(c) Find the Wald (or F) statistic for this hypothesis. What is the appropriate distribution for the test statistic? Calculate the p-value of the test.

(d) What do you conclude?

Exercise 9.29 Using the `cps09mar` dataset and the subsample of non-Hispanic Black individuals (race code = 2) and white individuals (race code = 1) test the hypothesis that the returns to education is common across groups.

(a) Allow the return to education to vary across the four groups (white male, white female, Black male, Black female) by interacting dummy variables with education. Estimate an appropriate version of the regression reported in Table 4.2.

(b) Find the Wald (or F) statistic for this hypothessis. What is the appropriate distribution for the test statistic? Calculate the p-value of the test.

(c) What do you conclude?

CHAPTER 10
RESAMPLING METHODS

10.1 INTRODUCTION

So far in this textbook, we have discussed two approaches to inference: exact and asymptotic. Both have their strengths and weaknesses. Exact theory provides a useful benchmark but is based on the unrealistic and stringent assumption of the homoskedastic normal regression model. Asymptotic theory provides a more flexible distribution theory but is an approximation with uncertain accuracy.

In this chapter, we consider a set of alternative inference methods that are based on the concept of resampling—which means using sampling information extracted from the empirical distribution of the data. These methods are powerful, widely applicable, and often more accurate than exact methods and asymptotic approximations. Two disadvantages, however, are (1) resampling methods typically require more computation power; and (2) the theory is considerably more challenging. A consequence of the computation requirement is that most empirical researchers use asymptotic approximations for routine calculations, while resampling approximations are used for final reporting.

We discuss two categories of resampling methods used in statistical and econometric practice: jackknife and bootstrap. Most of our attention will be given to the bootstrap, as it is the most commonly used resampling method in econometric practice.

The **jackknife** is the distribution obtained from the n leave-one-out estimators (see Section 3.20). The jackknife is most commonly used for variance estimation.

The **bootstrap** is the distribution obtained by estimation on samples created by i.i.d. sampling with replacement from the dataset. (There are other variants of bootstrap sampling, including parametric sampling and residual sampling.) The bootstrap is commonly used for variance estimation, confidence interval construction, and hypothesis testing.

A third category of resampling methods is known as **subsampling**, which we will not cover in this textbook. Subsampling is the distribution obtained by estimation on subsamples (sampling without replacement) of the dataset. Subsampling can be used for most of same purposes as the bootstrap. See the excellent monograph by Politis, Romano, and Wolf (1999).

10.2 EXAMPLE

To motivate our discussion, we focus on the application presented in Section 3.7, which is a bivariate regression applied to the CPS subsample of married Black female wage earners with 12 years of potential work experience and displayed in Table 3.1. The regression equation is

$$\log(wage) = \beta_1 education + \beta_2 + e.$$

The estimates as reported in (4.41) are

$$\begin{aligned}\log(\mathit{wage}) &= \underset{(0.031)}{0.155}\ \mathit{education} + \underset{(0.493)}{0.698} + \widehat{e} \\ \widehat{\sigma}^2 &= \underset{(0.043)}{0.144} \\ n &= 20.\end{aligned}$$

We focus on four estimates constructed from this regression. The first two are the coefficient estimates $\widehat{\beta}_1$ and $\widehat{\beta}_2$. The third is the variance estimate $\widehat{\sigma}^2$. The fourth is an estimate of the expected level of wages for an individual with 16 years of education (a college graduate), which turns out to be a nonlinear function of the parameters. Under the simplifying assumption that the error e is independent of the level of education and is normally distributed, we find that the expected level of wages is

$$\begin{aligned}\mu &= \mathbb{E}\left[\mathit{wage} \mid \mathit{education} = 16\right] \\ &= \mathbb{E}\left[\exp\left(16\beta_1 + \beta_2 + e\right)\right] \\ &= \exp\left(16\beta_1 + \beta_2\right)\mathbb{E}\left[\exp(e)\right] \\ &= \exp\left(16\beta_1 + \beta_2 + \sigma^2/2\right).\end{aligned}$$

The final equality is $\mathbb{E}\left[\exp(e)\right] = \exp\left(\sigma^2/2\right)$, which can be obtained from the normal moment generating function. The parameter μ is a nonlinear function of the coefficients. The natural estimator of μ replaces the unknowns by the point estimators. Thus,

$$\widehat{\mu} = \exp\left(16\widehat{\beta}_1 + \widehat{\beta}_2 + \widehat{\sigma}^2/2\right) = \underset{(2.29)}{25.80}$$

The standard error for $\widehat{\mu}$ can be found by extending Exercise 7.8 to find the joint asymptotic distribution of $\widehat{\sigma}^2$ and the slope estimates, and then applying the delta method.

We are interested in calculating standard errors and confidence intervals for the four estimates described in this section.

10.3 JACKKNIFE ESTIMATION OF VARIANCE

The jackknife estimates moments of estimators using the distribution of the leave-one-out estimators. The jackknife estimators of bias and variance were introduced by Quenouille (1949) and Tukey (1958), respectively. The idea was expanded further in the monographs of Efron (1982) and Shao and Tu (1995).

Let $\widehat{\theta}$ be any estimator of a vector-valued parameter θ that is a function of a random sample of size n. Let $\boldsymbol{V}_{\widehat{\theta}} = \operatorname{var}\left[\widehat{\theta}\right]$ be the variance of $\widehat{\theta}$. Define the leave-one-out estimators $\widehat{\theta}_{(-i)}$, which are computed using the formula for $\widehat{\theta}$ except that observation i is deleted. Tukey's jackknife estimator for $\boldsymbol{V}_{\widehat{\theta}}$ is defined as a scale of the sample variance of the leave-one-out estimators:

$$\widehat{\boldsymbol{V}}_{\widehat{\theta}}^{\text{jack}} = \frac{n-1}{n}\sum_{i=1}^{n}\left(\widehat{\theta}_{(-i)} - \overline{\theta}\right)\left(\widehat{\theta}_{(-i)} - \overline{\theta}\right)' \tag{10.1}$$

where $\overline{\theta}$ is the sample mean of the leave-one-out estimators $\overline{\theta} = n^{-1} \sum_{i=1}^{n} \widehat{\theta}_{(-i)}$. For scalar estimators $\widehat{\theta}$, the jackknife standard error is the square root of (10.1): $s_{\widehat{\theta}}^{\text{jack}} = \sqrt{\widehat{\boldsymbol{V}}_{\widehat{\theta}}^{\text{jack}}}$.

A convenient feature of the jackknife estimator $\widehat{\boldsymbol{V}}_{\widehat{\theta}}^{\text{jack}}$ is that the formula (10.1) is quite general and does not require any technical (exact or asymptotic) calculations. A downside is that it can require n separate estimations, which in some cases can be computationally costly.

In most cases, $\widehat{\boldsymbol{V}}_{\widehat{\theta}}^{\text{jack}}$ is similar to a robust asymptotic covariance matrix estimator. The main attractions of the jackknife estimator are that it can be used when an explicit asymptotic variance formula is not available and it can be used as a check on the reliability of an asymptotic formula.

The formula (10.1) is not immediately intuitive, so it may benefit from some motivation. We start by examining the sample mean $\overline{Y} = \frac{1}{n} \sum_{i=1}^{n} Y_i$ for $Y \in \mathbb{R}^m$. The leave-one-out estimator is

$$\overline{Y}_{(-i)} = \frac{1}{n-1} \sum_{j \neq i} Y_j = \frac{n}{n-1} \overline{Y} - \frac{1}{n-1} Y_i. \tag{10.2}$$

The sample mean of the leave-one-out estimators is

$$\frac{1}{n} \sum_{i=1}^{n} \overline{Y}_{(-i)} = \frac{n}{n-1} \overline{Y} - \frac{1}{n-1} \overline{Y} = \overline{Y}.$$

The difference is

$$\overline{Y}_{(-i)} - \overline{Y} = \frac{1}{n-1} \left(\overline{Y} - Y_i \right).$$

The jackknife estimate of variance (10.1) is then

$$\begin{aligned} \widehat{\boldsymbol{V}}_{\overline{Y}}^{\text{jack}} &= \frac{n-1}{n} \sum_{i=1}^{n} \left(\frac{1}{n-1} \right)^2 \left(\overline{Y} - Y_i \right) \left(\overline{Y} - Y_i \right)' \\ &= \frac{1}{n} \left(\frac{1}{n-1} \right) \sum_{i=1}^{n} \left(\overline{Y} - Y_i \right) \left(\overline{Y} - Y_i \right)'. \end{aligned} \tag{10.3}$$

This result is identical to the conventional estimator for the variance of $\overline{Y}$. Indeed, Tukey proposed the $(n-1)/n$ scaling in (10.1) so that $\widehat{\boldsymbol{V}}_{\overline{Y}}^{\text{jack}}$ precisely equals the conventional estimator.

We next examine the case of the least squares regression coefficient estimator. Recall from (3.43) that the leave-one-out OLS estimator equals

$$\widehat{\beta}_{(-i)} = \widehat{\beta} - \left(\boldsymbol{X}'\boldsymbol{X} \right)^{-1} X_i \widetilde{e}_i \tag{10.4}$$

where $\widetilde{e}_i = (1 - h_{ii})^{-1} \widehat{e}_i$, and $h_{ii} = X_i' \left(\boldsymbol{X}'\boldsymbol{X} \right)^{-1} X_i$. The sample mean of the leave-one-out estimators is $\overline{\beta} = \widehat{\beta} - \left(\boldsymbol{X}'\boldsymbol{X} \right)^{-1} \widetilde{\mu}$, where $\widetilde{\mu} = n^{-1} \sum_{i=1}^{n} X_i \widetilde{e}_i$. Thus $\widehat{\beta}_{(-i)} - \overline{\beta} = - \left(\boldsymbol{X}'\boldsymbol{X} \right)^{-1} (X_i \widetilde{e}_i - \widetilde{\mu})$. The jackknife estimate of variance for $\widehat{\beta}$ is

$$\begin{aligned} \widehat{\boldsymbol{V}}_{\widehat{\beta}}^{\text{jack}} &= \frac{n-1}{n} \sum_{i=1}^{n} \left(\widehat{\beta}_{(-i)} - \overline{\beta} \right) \left(\widehat{\beta}_{(-i)} - \overline{\beta} \right)' \\ &= \frac{n-1}{n} \left(\boldsymbol{X}'\boldsymbol{X} \right)^{-1} \left(\sum_{i=1}^{n} X_i X_i' \widetilde{e}_i^2 - n \widetilde{\mu} \widetilde{\mu}' \right) \left(\boldsymbol{X}'\boldsymbol{X} \right)^{-1} \\ &= \frac{n-1}{n} \widehat{\boldsymbol{V}}_{\widehat{\beta}}^{\text{HC3}} - (n-1) \left(\boldsymbol{X}'\boldsymbol{X} \right)^{-1} \widetilde{\mu} \widetilde{\mu}' \left(\boldsymbol{X}'\boldsymbol{X} \right)^{-1} \end{aligned} \tag{10.5}$$

where $\widehat{V}_{\widehat{\beta}}^{\mathrm{HC3}}$ is the HC3 covariance estimator (4.36) based on prediction errors. The second term in (10.5) is typically quite small, since $\widetilde{\mu}$ is typically small in magnitude. Thus $\widehat{V}_{\widehat{\beta}}^{\mathrm{jack}} \simeq \widehat{V}_{\widehat{\beta}}^{\mathrm{HC3}}$. Indeed, the HC3 estimator was originally motivated as a simplification of the jackknife estimator. Thus, for regression coefficients, the jackknife estimator of variance is similar to a conventional robust estimator. This is accomplished without the user "knowing" the form of the asymptotic covariance matrix, which is further confirmation that the jackknife is making a reasonable calculation.

Now, consider the jackknife estimator for a function $\widehat{\theta} = r(\widehat{\beta})$ of a least squares estimator. The leave-one-out estimator of θ is

$$\begin{aligned}\widehat{\theta}_{(-i)} &= r(\widehat{\beta}_{(-i)}) \\ &= r\left(\widehat{\beta} - \left(\boldsymbol{X}'\boldsymbol{X}\right)^{-1} X_i\widetilde{e}_i\right) \\ &\simeq \widehat{\theta} - \widehat{\boldsymbol{R}}'\left(\boldsymbol{X}'\boldsymbol{X}\right)^{-1} X_i\widetilde{e}_i.\end{aligned}$$

The second equality is (10.4). The final approximation is obtained by a mean-value expansion, using $r(\widehat{\beta}) = \widehat{\theta}$ and setting $\widehat{\boldsymbol{R}} = (\partial/\partial\beta)\, r(\widehat{\beta})'$. This approximation holds in large samples, because the $\widehat{\beta}_{(-i)}$ are uniformly consistent for β. The jackknife variance estimator for $\widehat{\theta}$ thus equals

$$\begin{aligned}\widehat{V}_{\widehat{\theta}}^{\mathrm{jack}} &= \frac{n-1}{n}\sum_{i=1}^{n}\left(\widehat{\theta}_{(-i)} - \overline{\theta}\right)\left(\widehat{\theta}_{(-i)} - \overline{\theta}\right)' \\ &\simeq \frac{n-1}{n}\widehat{\boldsymbol{R}}'\left(\boldsymbol{X}'\boldsymbol{X}\right)^{-1}\left(\sum_{i=1}^{n} X_iX_i'\widetilde{e}_i^2 - n\widetilde{\mu}\widetilde{\mu}'\right)\left(\boldsymbol{X}'\boldsymbol{X}\right)^{-1}\widehat{\boldsymbol{R}} \\ &= \widehat{\boldsymbol{R}}'\widehat{\boldsymbol{V}}_{\widehat{\beta}}^{\mathrm{jack}}\widehat{\boldsymbol{R}} \\ &\simeq \widehat{\boldsymbol{R}}'\widetilde{\boldsymbol{V}}_{\widehat{\beta}}\widehat{\boldsymbol{R}}.\end{aligned}$$

The final line equals a delta-method estimator for the variance of $\widehat{\theta}$ constructed with the covariance estimator (4.36). This shows that the jackknife estimator of variance for $\widehat{\theta}$ is approximately an asymptotic delta-method estimator. Although this is an asymptotic approximation, it again shows that the jackknife produces an estimator that is asymptotically similar to one produced by asymptotic methods, even though the jackknife estimator is calculated without reference to asymptotic theory and does not require calculation of the derivatives of $r(\beta)$.

This argument extends directly to any "smooth function" estimator. Most of the estimators discussed so far in this textbook take the form $\widehat{\theta} = g\left(\overline{W}\right)$, where $\overline{W} = n^{-1}\sum_{i=1}^{n} W_i$, and W_i is some vector-valued function of the data. For any such estimator $\widehat{\theta}$, the leave-one-out estimator equals $\widehat{\theta}_{(-i)} = g\left(\overline{W}_{(-i)}\right)$, and its jackknife estimator of variance is (10.1). Using (10.2) and a mean-value expansion, we have the large-sample approximation:

$$\begin{aligned}\widehat{\theta}_{(-i)} &= g\left(\overline{W}_{(-i)}\right) \\ &= g\left(\frac{n}{n-1}\overline{W} - \frac{1}{n-1}W_i\right) \\ &\simeq g\left(\overline{W}\right) - \frac{1}{n-1}\boldsymbol{G}\left(\overline{W}\right)' W_i\end{aligned}$$

where $\boldsymbol{G}(x) = (\partial/\partial x)\, g(x)'$. Thus

$$\widehat{\theta}_{(-i)} - \overline{\theta} \simeq -\frac{1}{n-1}\boldsymbol{G}\left(\overline{W}\right)'\left(W_i - \overline{W}\right)$$

and the jackknife estimator of the variance of $\widehat{\theta}$ approximately equals

$$\begin{aligned}\widehat{\boldsymbol{V}}_{\widehat{\theta}}^{\text{jack}} &= \frac{n-1}{n}\sum_{i=1}^{n}\left(\widehat{\theta}_{(-i)}-\widehat{\theta}_{(\cdot)}\right)\left(\widehat{\theta}_{(-i)}-\widehat{\theta}_{(\cdot)}\right)' \\ &\simeq \frac{n-1}{n}\boldsymbol{G}\left(\overline{W}\right)'\left(\frac{1}{(n-1)^2}\sum_{i=1}^{n}\left(W_i-\overline{W}\right)\left(W_i-\overline{W}\right)'\right)\boldsymbol{G}\left(\overline{W}\right) \\ &= \boldsymbol{G}\left(\overline{W}\right)'\widehat{\boldsymbol{V}}_{\overline{W}}^{\text{jack}}\boldsymbol{G}\left(\overline{W}\right)\end{aligned}$$

where $\widehat{\boldsymbol{V}}_{\overline{W}}^{\text{jack}}$ as defined in (10.3) is the conventional (and jackknife) estimator for the variance of $\overline{W}$. Thus $\widehat{\boldsymbol{V}}_{\widehat{\theta}}^{\text{jack}}$ is approximately the delta-method estimator. Once again, we see that the jackknife estimator automatically calculates what is effectively the delta-method variance estimator, but without requiring the user to explicitly calculate the derivative of $g(x)$.

10.4 EXAMPLE

We illustrate by reporting the asymptotic and jackknife standard errors for the four parameter estimates discussed in Section 10.2. Table 10.1 reports the actual values of the leave-one-out estimates for each of the 20 observations in the sample. The jackknife standard errors are calculated as the scaled square roots of the

Table 10.1
Leave-one-out estimators and jackknife standard errors

Observation	$\widehat{\beta}_{1(-i)}$	$\widehat{\beta}_{2(-i)}$	$\widehat{\sigma}^2_{(-i)}$	$\widehat{\mu}_{(-i)}$
1	0.150	0.764	0.150	25.63
2	0.148	0.798	0.149	25.48
3	0.153	0.739	0.151	25.97
4	0.156	0.695	0.144	26.31
5	0.154	0.701	0.146	25.38
6	0.158	0.655	0.151	26.05
7	0.152	0.705	0.114	24.32
8	0.146	0.822	0.147	25.37
9	0.162	0.588	0.151	25.75
10	0.157	0.693	0.139	26.40
11	0.168	0.510	0.141	26.40
12	0.158	0.691	0.118	26.48
13	0.139	0.974	0.141	26.56
14	0.169	0.451	0.131	26.26
15	0.146	0.852	0.150	24.93
16	0.156	0.696	0.148	26.06
17	0.165	0.513	0.140	25.22
18	0.155	0.698	0.151	25.90
19	0.152	0.742	0.151	25.73
20	0.155	0.697	0.151	25.95
s^{jack}	0.032	0.514	0.046	2.39
s^{asy}	0.031	0.493	0.043	2.29

sample variances of these leave-one-out estimates and are reported in the second-to-last row. For comparison, the asymptotic standard errors are reported in the final row.

For all estimates, the jackknife and asymptotic standard errors are quite similar. This reinforces the credibility of both standard error estimates. The largest differences arise for $\widehat{\beta}_2$ and $\widehat{\mu}$, whose jackknife standard errors are about 5% larger than the asymptotic standard errors.

The takeaway from this presentation is that the jackknife is a simple and flexible method for variance and standard error calculations. Circumventing technical asymptotic and exact calculations, the jackknife produces estimates that in many cases are similar to their asymptotic delta-method counterparts. The jackknife is especially appealing in cases where asymptotic standard errors are not available or are difficult to calculate. They can also be used as a double-check on the reasonableness of asymptotic delta-method calculations.

In Stata, jackknife standard errors for coefficient estimates in many models are obtained by the `vce(jackknife)` option. For nonlinear functions of the coefficients or other estimators, the `jackknife` command can be combined with any other command to obtain jackknife standard errors.

To illustrate, below are listed the Stata commands that calculate the jackknife standard errors given above. The first line is least squares estimation with standard errors calculated by the jackknife. The second line calculates the error variance estimate $\widehat{\sigma}^2$ with a jackknife standard error. The third line does the same for the estimate $\widehat{\mu}$.

Stata Commands

```
reg wage education if mbf12 == 1, vce(jackknife)
jackknife (e(rss)/e(N)): reg wage education if mbf12 == 1
jackknife exp(16*_b[education]+_b[_cons]+e(rss)/e(N)/2): reg wage education if mbf12 == 1
```

10.5 JACKKNIFE FOR CLUSTERED OBSERVATIONS

In Section 4.21, we introduced the clustered regression model, cluster-robust variance estimators, and cluster-robust standard errors. Jackknife variance estimation can also be used for clustered samples but with some natural modifications. Recall that the least squares estimator in the clustered sample context can be written as

$$\widehat{\beta} = \left(\sum_{g=1}^{G} \boldsymbol{X}_g' \boldsymbol{X}_g \right)^{-1} \left(\sum_{g=1}^{G} \boldsymbol{X}_g' \boldsymbol{Y}_g \right)$$

where $g = 1, \ldots, G$ indexes the cluster. Instead of leave-one-out estimators, it is natural to use delete-cluster estimators, which delete one cluster at a time. They take the form (4.55):

$$\widehat{\beta}_{(-g)} = \widehat{\beta} - \left(\boldsymbol{X}'\boldsymbol{X} \right)^{-1} \boldsymbol{X}_g' \widetilde{\boldsymbol{e}}_g$$

where

$$\widetilde{\boldsymbol{e}}_g = \left(\boldsymbol{I}_{n_g} - \boldsymbol{X}_g \left(\boldsymbol{X}'\boldsymbol{X} \right)^{-1} \boldsymbol{X}_g' \right)^{-1} \widehat{\boldsymbol{e}}_g$$

$$\widehat{\boldsymbol{e}}_g = \boldsymbol{Y}_g - \boldsymbol{X}_g \widehat{\beta}.$$

The delete-cluster jackknife estimator of the variance of $\widehat{\beta}$ is

$$\widehat{\boldsymbol{V}}_{\widehat{\beta}}^{\text{jack}} = \frac{G-1}{G}\sum_{g=1}^{G}\left(\widehat{\beta}_{(-g)} - \overline{\beta}\right)\left(\widehat{\beta}_{(-g)} - \overline{\beta}\right)'$$

$$\overline{\beta} = \frac{1}{G}\sum_{g=1}^{G}\widehat{\beta}_{(-g)}.$$

We call $\widehat{\boldsymbol{V}}_{\widehat{\beta}}^{\text{jack}}$ a **cluster-robust jackknife estimator of variance.**

Using the same approximations as in the Section 10.4, we can show that the delete-cluster jackknife estimator is asymptotically equivalent to the cluster-robust covariance matrix estimator (4.56) calculated with the delete-cluster prediction errors. This verifies that the delete-cluster jackknife is the appropriate jackknife approach for clustered dependence.

For parameters that are functions $\widehat{\theta} = r(\widehat{\beta})$ of the least squares estimator, the delete-cluster jackknife estimator of the variance of $\widehat{\theta}$ is

$$\widehat{\boldsymbol{V}}_{\widehat{\theta}}^{\text{jack}} = \frac{G-1}{G}\sum_{g=1}^{G}\left(\widehat{\theta}_{(-g)} - \overline{\theta}\right)\left(\widehat{\theta}_{(-g)} - \overline{\theta}\right)'$$

$$\widehat{\theta}_{(-i)} = r(\widehat{\beta}_{(-g)})$$

$$\overline{\theta} = \frac{1}{G}\sum_{g=1}^{G}\widehat{\theta}_{(-g)}.$$

Using a mean-value expansion, we can show that this estimator is asymptotically equivalent to the delta-method cluster-robust covariance matrix estimator for $\widehat{\theta}$. Thus the jackknife estimator is appropriate for covariance matrix estimation.

As in the context of i.i.d. samples, one advantage of the jackknife covariance matrix estimators is that they do not require the user to make a technical calculation of the asymptotic distribution. A downside is an increase in computational cost, as G separate regressions are effectively estimated.

In Stata, jackknife standard errors for coefficient estimates with clustered observations are obtained by using the options `cluster(id) vce(jackknife)`, where "`id`" denotes the cluster variable.

10.6 THE BOOTSTRAP ALGORITHM

The bootstrap is a powerful approach to inference and is due to the pioneering work of Efron (1979). There are many textbook and monograph treatments of the bootstrap, including Efron (1982), P. Hall (1992), Efron and Tibshirani (1993), Shao and Tu (1995), and Davison and Hinkley (1997). Reviews for econometricians are provided by P. Hall (1994) and Horowitz (2001).

There are several ways to describe or define the bootstrap and there are several forms of the bootstrap. We start in this section by discussing the basic nonparametric bootstrap algorithm. Subsequent sections give more formal definitions of the bootstrap as well as theoretical justifications.

Briefly, the bootstrap distribution is obtained by estimation on independent samples created by i.i.d. sampling (sampling with replacement) from the original dataset.

To understand this, it is useful to start with the concept of sampling with replacement from the dataset. To continue the empirical example used earlier in the chapter, we focus on the dataset displayed in Table 3.1, which has $n = 20$ observations. Sampling from this distribution means randomly selecting one row from this table. Mathematically this is the same as randomly selecting an integer from the set $\{1, 2, \ldots, 20\}$. To illustrate, MATLAB has a random integer generator (the function `randi`). Using the random number seed of 13 (an arbitrary choice), we obtain the random draw 16. This means that we draw observation number 16 from Table 3.1. Examining the table, we can see that this observation describes an individual with wage \$18.75 and education of 16 years. We repeat by drawing another random integer on the set $\{1, 2, \ldots, 20\}$, and this time obtain 5. Thus we take observation 5 from Table 3.1, which is an individual with wage \$33.17 and education of 16 years. We continue until we have $n = 20$ such draws. This random set of observations are {16, 5, 17, 20, 20, 10, 13, 16, 13, 15, 1, 6, 2, 18, 8, 14, 6, 7, 1, 8}. We call this the **bootstrap sample**.

Notice that the observations 1, 6, 8, 13, 16, 20 each appear twice in the bootstrap sample, and the observations 3, 4, 9, 11, 12, 19 do not appear at all. That is okay. In fact, it is necessary for the bootstrap to work, because we are **drawing with replacement**. (If we instead made draws without replacement, then the constructed dataset would have exactly the same observations as in Table 3.1, only in different order.) We can also ask the question: "What is the probability that an individual observation will appear at least once in the bootstrap sample?" The answer is

$$\mathbb{P}\left[\text{Observation in Bootstrap Sample}\right] = 1 - \left(1 - \frac{1}{n}\right)^n \rightarrow 1 - e^{-1} \simeq 0.632. \tag{10.6}$$

The limit holds as $n \rightarrow \infty$. The approximation 0.632 is excellent even for small n. For example, when $n = 20$, the probability (10.6) is 0.641. These calculations show that an individual observation is in the bootstrap sample with probability near 2/3.

Once again, the bootstrap sample is the constructed dataset with the 20 observations drawn randomly from the original sample. Notationally, we write the ith bootstrap observation as (Y_i^*, X_i^*) and the bootstrap sample as $\{(Y_1^*, X_1^*), \ldots, (Y_n^*, X_n^*)\}$. In our present example, with Y denoting the log wage, the bootstrap sample is

$$\{(Y_1^*, X_1^*), \ldots, (Y_n^*, X_n^*)\} = \{(2.93, 16), (3.50, 16) \ldots, (3.76, 18)\}.$$

The bootstrap estimate $\widehat{\beta}^*$ is obtained by applying the least squares estimation formula to the bootstrap sample. Thus we regress Y^* on X^*. The other bootstrap estimates (in our example, $\widehat{\sigma}^{2*}$ and $\widehat{\mu}^*$) are obtained by applying their estimation formulas to the bootstrap sample as well. Writing $\widehat{\theta}^* = \left(\widehat{\beta}_1^*, \widehat{\beta}_2^*, \widehat{\sigma}^{*2}, \widehat{\mu}^*\right)'$, we have the bootstrap estimate of the parameter vector $\theta = \left(\beta_1, \beta_2, \sigma^2, \mu\right)'$. In our example (the bootstrap sample described above), $\widehat{\theta}^* = (0.195, 0.113, 0.107, 26.7)'$. This is one draw from the bootstrap distribution of the estimates.

The estimate $\widehat{\theta}^*$ as described is one random draw from the distribution of estimates obtained by i.i.d. sampling from the original data. With one draw, we can say relatively little. But we can repeat this exercise to obtain multiple draws from this bootstrap distribution. To distinguish between these draws, we index the bootstrap samples by $b = 1, \ldots, B$, and write the bootstrap estimates as $\widehat{\theta}_b^*$ or $\widehat{\theta}^*(b)$.

To continue our illustration, we draw 20 more random integers {19, 5, 7, 19, 1, 2, 13, 18, 1, 15, 17, 2, 14, 11, 10, 20, 1, 5, 15, 7} and construct a second bootstrap sample. On this sample, we again estimate the parameters and obtain $\widehat{\theta}^*(2) = (0.175, 0.52, 0.124, 29.3)'$. This is a second random draw from the distribution of $\widehat{\theta}^*$. We repeat this B times, storing the parameter estimates $\widehat{\theta}^*(b)$. We have thus created a new dataset of

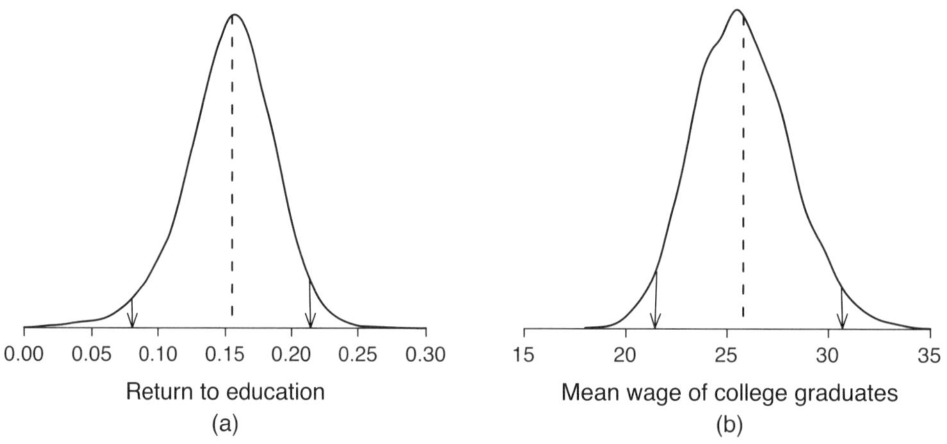

FIGURE 10.1 Bootstrap distributions of (a) $\hat{\beta}_1^*$ and (b) $\hat{\mu}^*$

bootstrap draws $\{\widehat{\theta}^*(b) : b = 1, \ldots, B\}$. By construction, the draws are independent across b and identically distributed.

The number of bootstrap draws, B, is often called the "number of bootstrap replications." Typical choices for B are 1000, 5000, and 10,000. We discuss selecting B later, but roughly speaking, larger B results in a more precise estimate at an increased computational cost. For our application, we set $B = 10,000$.

To illustrate, Figure 10.1 displays the densities of the distributions of the bootstrap estimates $\widehat{\beta}_1^*$ and $\widehat{\mu}^*$ across 10,000 draws. The dashed lines show the point estimate. You can notice that the density for $\widehat{\beta}_1^*$ is slightly skewed to the left.

10.7 BOOTSTRAP VARIANCE AND STANDARD ERRORS

Given the bootstrap draws, we can estimate features of the bootstrap distribution. The **bootstrap estimator of variance** of an estimator $\widehat{\theta}$ is the sample variance across the bootstrap draws $\widehat{\theta}^*(b)$. It equals

$$\widehat{\boldsymbol{V}}_{\widehat{\theta}}^{\text{boot}} = \frac{1}{B-1} \sum_{b=1}^{B} \left(\widehat{\theta}^*(b) - \overline{\theta}^*\right) \left(\widehat{\theta}^*(b) - \overline{\theta}^*\right)' \tag{10.7}$$

$$\overline{\theta}^* = \frac{1}{B} \sum_{b=1}^{B} \widehat{\theta}^*(b).$$

For a scalar estimator $\widehat{\theta}$, the **bootstrap standard error** is the square root of the bootstrap estimator of variance:

$$s_{\widehat{\theta}}^{\text{boot}} = \sqrt{\widehat{\boldsymbol{V}}_{\widehat{\theta}}^{\text{boot}}}.$$

This is a very simple statistic to calculate and is the most common use of the bootstrap in applied econometric practice. A caveat (discussed in more detail in Section 10.15) is that in many cases, it is better to use a trimmed estimator.

Standard errors are conventionally reported to convey the precision of the estimator. They are also commonly used to construct confidence intervals. Bootstrap standard errors can be used for this purpose.

Table 10.2
Comparison of methods

	$\widehat{\beta}_1$	$\widehat{\beta}_2$	$\widehat{\sigma}^2$	$\widehat{\mu}$
Estimate	0.155	0.698	0.144	25.80
Asymptotic standard error	(0.031)	(0.493)	(0.043)	(2.29)
Jackknife standard error	(0.032)	(0.514)	(0.046)	(2.39)
Bootstrap standard error	(0.034)	(0.548)	(0.041)	(2.38)
95% Percentile interval	[0.08, 0.21]	[−0.27, 1.91]	[0.06, 0.22]	[21.4, 30.7]
95% BC percentile interval	[0.08, 0.21]	[−0.25, 1.93]	[0.09, 0.28]	[22.0, 31.5]
95% BC$_a$ percentile interval	[0.08, 0.21]	[−0.25, 1.93]	[0.09, 0.28]	[22.0, 31.5]
95% Percentile-t interval	[0.09, 0.21]	[−0.20, 1.81]	[0.08, 0.34]	[21.6, 32.2]

The **normal-approximation bootstrap confidence interval** is

$$C^{\mathrm{nb}} = \left[\widehat{\theta} - z_{1-\alpha/2} s_{\widehat{\theta}}^{\mathrm{boot}}, \quad \widehat{\theta} + z_{1-\alpha/2} s_{\widehat{\theta}}^{\mathrm{boot}}\right]$$

where $z_{1-\alpha/2}$ is the $1-\alpha/2$ quantile of the $\mathrm{N}(0,1)$ distribution. This interval C^{nb} is identical in format to an asymptotic confidence interval, but with the bootstrap standard error replacing the asymptotic standard error. C^{nb} is the default confidence interval reported by Stata when the bootstrap has been used to calculate standard errors. However, the normal-approximation interval is in general a poor choice for confidence interval construction, as it relies on the normal approximation to the t-ratio, which can be inaccurate in finite samples. There are other methods—such as the bias-corrected percentile method to be discussed in Section 10.17—that are just as simple to compute but have better performance. In general, bootstrap standard errors should be used as estimates of precision rather than as tools to construct confidence intervals.

Since B is finite, all bootstrap statistics, such as $\widehat{\boldsymbol{V}}_{\widehat{\theta}}^{\mathrm{boot}}$, are estimates and hence random. Their values will vary across different choices for B and simulation runs (depending on how the simulation seed is set). Thus you should not expect to obtain identical bootstrap standard errors as other researchers when replicating their results. They should be similar (up to simulation sampling error) but not precisely the same.

Table 10.2 reports the four parameter estimates introduced in Section 10.2 along with asymptotic, jackknife, and bootstrap standard errors. Also reported are four bootstrap confidence intervals that will be introduced in subsequent sections.

For these four estimators, we can see that the bootstrap standard errors are quite similar to the asymptotic and jackknife standard errors. The most noticeable difference arises for $\widehat{\beta}_2$, where the bootstrap standard error is about 10% larger than the asymptotic standard error.

In Stata, bootstrap standard errors for coefficient estimates in many models are obtained by the `vce(bootstrap, reps(#))` option, where # is the number of bootstrap replications. For nonlinear functions of the coefficients or other estimators, the `bootstrap` command can be combined with any other command to obtain bootstrap standard errors. Synonyms for `bootstrap` are `bstrap` and `bs`.

To illustrate, below are listed the Stata commands that will calculate[1] the bootstrap standard errors listed above.

[1]They will not *exactly* replicate the standard errors, since those in Table 10.2 were produced in Matlab, which uses a different random number sequence.

Stata Commands

```
reg wage education if mbf12 == 1, vce(bootstrap, reps(10000))
bs (e(rss)/e(N)), reps(10000): reg wage education if mbf12 == 1
bs (exp(16*_b[education]+_b[_cons]+e(rss)/e(N)/2)), reps(10000): ///
    reg wage education if mbf12 == 1
```

10.8 PERCENTILE INTERVAL

The second most common use of bootstrap methods is for confidence intervals. There are multiple bootstrap methods to form confidence intervals. A popular and simple method is called the **percentile interval**. It is based on the quantiles of the bootstrap distribution.

Section 10.6 described the bootstrap algorithm that creates an i.i.d. sample of bootstrap estimates $\{\widehat{\theta}_1^*, \widehat{\theta}_2^*, \ldots, \widehat{\theta}_B^*\}$ corresponding to an estimator $\widehat{\theta}$ of a parameter θ. We focus on the case of a scalar parameter θ.

For any $0 < \alpha < 1$, we can calculate the empirical quantile q_α^* of these bootstrap estimates. This is the number such that $n\alpha$ bootstrap estimates are smaller than q_α^*, and it is typically calculated by taking the $n\alpha$th order statistic of the $\widehat{\theta}_b^*$. See Section 11.13 of *Probability and Statistics for Economists* for a precise discussion of empirical quantiles and common quantile estimators.

The percentile bootstrap $100(1-\alpha)\%$ confidence interval is

$$C^{\mathrm{pc}} = \left[q_{\alpha/2}^*, q_{1-\alpha/2}^*\right]. \tag{10.8}$$

For example, if $B = 1000$, $\alpha = 0.05$, and the empirical quantile estimator is used, then $C^{\mathrm{pc}} = \left[\widehat{\theta}_{(25)}^*, \widehat{\theta}_{(975)}^*\right]$. To illustrate, the 0.025 and 0.975 quantiles of the bootstrap distributions of $\widehat{\beta}_1^*$ and $\widehat{\mu}^*$ are indicated in Figure 10.1 by the arrows. The intervals between the arrows are the 95% percentile intervals.

The percentile interval has the convenience that it does not require calculation of a standard error. This is particularly convenient in contexts where asymptotic standard error calculation is complicated, burdensome, or unknown. C^{pc} is a simple by-product of the bootstrap algorithm and does not require meaningful computational cost above that required to calculate the bootstrap standard error.

The percentile interval has the useful property that it is **transformation-respecting**. Take a monotone parameter transformation $m(\theta)$. The percentile interval for $m(\theta)$ is simply the percentile interval for θ mapped by $m(\theta)$. That is, if $\left[q_{\alpha/2}^*, q_{1-\alpha/2}^*\right]$ is the percentile interval for θ, then $\left[m\left(q_{\alpha/2}^*\right), m\left(q_{1-\alpha/2}^*\right)\right]$ is the percentile interval for $m(\theta)$. This property follows directly from the equivariance property of sample quantiles. Many confidence-interval methods, such as the delta-method asymptotic interval and the normal-approximation interval C^{nb}, do not share this property.

To illustrate the usefulness of the transformation-respecting property, consider the variance σ^2. In some cases, it is useful to report the variance σ^2 and in other cases, it is useful to report the standard deviation σ. Thus we may be interested in confidence intervals for σ^2 or σ. For example, the asymptotic 95% normal confidence interval for σ^2, which we calculate from Table 10.2, is [0.060, 0.228]. Taking square roots, we obtain an interval for σ of [0.244, 0.477]. Alternatively, the delta method standard error for $\widehat{\sigma} = 0.379$ is 0.057, leading to an asymptotic 95% confidence interval for σ of [0.265, 0.493], which is different. This shows that the delta method is not transformation-respecting. In contrast, the 95% percentile interval for σ^2 is [0.062, 0.220] and that for σ is [0.249, 0.469], which is identical to the square roots of the interval for σ^2.

The bootstrap percentile intervals for the four estimators are reported in Table 10.2.

In Stata, percentile confidence intervals can be obtained by using the command `estat bootstrap, percentile` or the command `estat bootstrap, all` after an estimation command that calculates standard errors via the bootstrap.

10.9 THE BOOTSTRAP DISTRIBUTION

For applications, it is often sufficient if one understands the bootstrap as an algorithm. However, for theory, it is more useful to view the bootstrap as a specific estimator of the sampling distribution. For this it is useful to introduce some additional notation. The key is that the distribution of any estimator or statistic is determined by the distribution of the data. While the latter is unknown, it can be estimated by the empirical distribution of the data. This is what the bootstrap does.

To fix the notation, let F denote the distribution of an individual observation W. (In regression, W is the pair (Y, X).) Let $G_n(u, F)$ denote the distribution of an estimator $\widehat{\theta}$. That is,

$$G_n(u, F) = \mathbb{P}\left[\widehat{\theta} \le u \mid F\right].$$

We write the distribution G_n as a function of n and F, since the latter (generally) affect the distribution of $\widehat{\theta}$. We are interested in the distribution G_n. For example, we want to know its variance to calculate a standard error or its quantiles to calculate a percentile interval.

In principle, if we knew the distribution F, we should be able to determine the distribution G_n. In practice, there are two barriers to implementation. The first barrier is that the calculation of $G_n(u, F)$ is generally infeasible except in certain special cases, such as the normal regression model. The second barrier is that in general, we do not know F.

The bootstrap simultaneously circumvents these two barriers by two clever ideas. First, the bootstrap proposes estimation of F by the empirical distribution function (EDF) F_n, which is the simplest nonparametric estimator of the joint distribution of the observations. The EDF is $F_n(w) = n^{-1} \sum_{i=1}^{n} \mathbb{1}\left\{W_i \le w\right\}$. (See Section 11.2 of *Probability and Statistics for Economists* for details and properties.) Replacing F with F_n, we obtain the idealized bootstrap estimator of the distribution of $\widehat{\theta}$:

$$G_n^*(u) = G_n(u, F_n). \tag{10.9}$$

The bootstrap's second clever idea is to estimate G_n^* by simulation. This is the bootstrap algorithm described in Section 10.6. The essential idea is that simulation from F_n is sampling with replacement from the original data, which is computationally simple. Applying the estimation formula for $\widehat{\theta}$, we obtain i.i.d. draws from the distribution $G_n^*(u)$. By making a large number B of such draws, we can estimate any feature of G_n^* of interest. The bootstrap combines these two ideas: (1) estimate $G_n(u, F)$ by $G_n(u, F_n)$; (2) estimate $G_n(u, F_n)$ by simulation. These ideas are intertwined. Only by considering these steps together do we obtain a feasible method.

The connection between G_n and G_n^* can be thought about as follows. G_n is the distribution of the estimator $\widehat{\theta}$ obtained when the observations are sampled i.i.d. from the population distribution F. G_n^* is the distribution of the same statistic, denoted by $\widehat{\theta}^*$, obtained when the observations are sampled i.i.d. from the empirical distribution F_n. It is useful to conceptualize the "universe" that separately generates the dataset and the bootstrap sample. The "sampling universe" is the population distribution F. In this universe, the true parameter is θ.

The "bootstrap universe" is the empircal distribution F_n. When drawing from the bootstrap universe, we are treating F_n as if it were the true distribution. Thus anything that is true about F_n should be treated as true in the bootstrap universe. In the bootstrap universe, the "true" value of the parameter θ is the value determined by the EDF F_n. In most cases, this is the estimate $\widehat{\theta}$. It is the true value of the coefficient when the true distribution is F_n.

Let us now carefully explore the connection with the bootstrap algorithm as previously described. First, observe that sampling with replacement from the sample $\{Y_1, \ldots, Y_n\}$ is identical to sampling from the EDF F_n, because the EDF is the probability distribution that puts probability mass $1/n$ on each observation. Thus sampling from F_n means sampling an observation with probability $1/n$, which is sampling with replacement.

Second, observe that the bootstrap estimator $\widehat{\theta}^*$ described here is identical to the bootstrap algorithm described in Section 10.6. That is, $\widehat{\theta}^*$ is the random vector generated by applying the estimator formula $\widehat{\theta}$ to samples obtained by random sampling from F_n.

Third, observe that the distribution of these bootstrap estimators is the bootstrap distribution (10.9). This is a precise equality. That is, the bootstrap algorithm generates i.i.d. samples from F_n, and when the estimators are applied, we obtain random variables $\widehat{\theta}^*$ with the distribution G_n^*.

Fourth, observe that the bootstrap statistics described earlier—bootstrap variance, standard error, and quantiles—are estimators of the corresponding features of the bootstrap distribution G_n^*.

This discussion is meant to carefully describe why the notation $G_n^*(u)$ is useful to help understand the properties of the bootstrap algorithm. Since F_n is the natural nonparametric estimator of the unknown distribution F, $G_n^*(u) = G_n(u, F_n)$ is the natural plug-in estimator of the unknown $G_n(u, F)$. Furthermore, because F_n is uniformly consistent for F by the Glivenko-Cantelli Lemma (Theorem 18.1 in *Probability and Statistics for Economists*), we also can expect $G_n^*(u)$ to be consistent for $G_n(u)$. Making this notion precise is a bit challenging, since F_n and G_n are functions. In the next several sections, we develop an asymptotic distribution theory for the bootstrap distribution based on extending asymptotic theory to the case of conditional distributions.

10.10 THE DISTRIBUTION OF THE BOOTSTRAP OBSERVATIONS

Let Y^* be a random draw from the sample $\{Y_1, \ldots, Y_n\}$. What is the distribution of Y^*? Since we are fixing the observations, the correct question is: What is the *conditional* distribution of Y^*, conditional on the observed data? The empirical distribution function F_n summarizes the information in the sample, so equivalently, we are talking about the distribution conditional on F_n. Consequently, let us write the bootstrap probability function and expectation as

$$\mathbb{P}^*\left[Y^* \le x\right] = \mathbb{P}\left[Y^* \le x \mid F_n\right]$$
$$\mathbb{E}^*\left[Y^*\right] = \mathbb{E}\left[Y^* \mid F_n\right].$$

Notationally, the starred distribution and expectation are conditional given the data.

The (conditional) distribution of Y^* is the empirical distribution function F_n, which is a discrete distribution with mass points $1/n$ on each observation Y_i. Thus even if the original data come from a continuous distribution, the bootstrap data distribution is discrete.

The (conditional) mean and variance of Y^* are calculated from the EDF and equal the sample mean and variance of the data. The mean is

$$\mathbb{E}^*\left[Y^*\right] = \sum_{i=1}^{n} Y_i \mathbb{P}^*\left[Y^* = Y_i\right] = \sum_{i=1}^{n} Y_i \frac{1}{n} = \overline{Y} \tag{10.10}$$

and the variance is

$$\begin{aligned}\operatorname{var}^*\left[Y^*\right] &= \mathbb{E}^*\left[Y^*Y^{*\prime}\right] - \left(\mathbb{E}^*\left[Y^*\right]\right)\left(\mathbb{E}^*\left[Y^*\right]\right)' \\ &= \sum_{i=1}^n Y_i Y_i' \mathbb{P}^*\left[Y^* = Y_i\right] - \overline{Y}\,\overline{Y}' \\ &= \sum_{i=1}^n Y_i Y_i' \frac{1}{n} - \overline{Y}\,\overline{Y}' \\ &= \widehat{\Sigma}. \end{aligned} \tag{10.11}$$

To summarize, the conditional distribution of Y^*, given F_n, is the discrete distribution on $\{Y_1, \ldots, Y_n\}$ with mean $\overline{Y}$ and covariance matrix $\widehat{\Sigma}$.

We can extend this analysis to any integer moment r. Assume Y is scalar. The rth moment of Y^* is

$$\mu_r^{*\prime} = \mathbb{E}^*\left[Y^{*r}\right] = \sum_{i=1}^n Y_i^r \mathbb{P}^*\left[Y^* = Y_i\right] = \frac{1}{n}\sum_{i=1}^n Y_i^r = \widehat{\mu}_r',$$

which is the rth sample moment. The rth central moment of Y^* is

$$\mu_r^* = \mathbb{E}^*\left[\left(Y^* - \overline{Y}\right)^r\right] = \frac{1}{n}\sum_{i=1}^n \left(Y_i - \overline{Y}\right)^r = \widehat{\mu}_r,$$

which is the rth central sample moment. Similarly, the rth cumulant of Y^* is $\kappa_r^* = \widehat{\kappa}_r$, which is the rth sample cumulant.

10.11 THE DISTRIBUTION OF THE BOOTSTRAP SAMPLE MEAN

The bootstrap sample mean is

$$\overline{Y}^* = \frac{1}{n}\sum_{i=1}^n Y_i^*.$$

We can calculate its (conditional) mean and variance. The mean is

$$\mathbb{E}^*\left[\overline{Y}^*\right] = \mathbb{E}^*\left[\frac{1}{n}\sum_{i=1}^n Y_i^*\right] = \frac{1}{n}\sum_{i=1}^n \mathbb{E}^*\left[Y_i^*\right] = \frac{1}{n}\sum_{i=1}^n \overline{Y} = \overline{Y} \tag{10.12}$$

using (10.10). Thus the bootstrap sample mean $\overline{Y}^*$ has a distribution centered at the sample mean $\overline{Y}$. This is because the bootstrap observations Y_i^* are drawn from the bootstrap universe, which treats the EDF as the truth, and the mean of the latter distribution is $\overline{Y}$.

The (conditional) variance of the bootstrap sample mean is

$$\operatorname{var}^*\left[\overline{Y}^*\right] = \operatorname{var}^*\left[\frac{1}{n}\sum_{i=1}^n Y_i^*\right] = \frac{1}{n^2}\sum_{i=1}^n \operatorname{var}^*\left[Y_i^*\right] = \frac{1}{n^2}\sum_{i=1}^n \widehat{\Sigma} = \frac{1}{n}\widehat{\Sigma} \tag{10.13}$$

using (10.11). In the scalar case, $\operatorname{var}^*\left[\overline{Y}^*\right]=\widehat{\sigma}^2/n$. Thus the bootstrap variance of $\overline{Y}^*$ is precisely described by the sample variance of the original observations. Again, this is because the bootstrap observations Y_i^* are drawn from the bootstrap universe.

We can extend this process to any integer moment r. Assume Y is scalar. Define the normalized bootstrap sample mean $Z_n^*=\sqrt{n}\left(\overline{Y}^*-\overline{Y}\right)$. Using expressions from Section 6.17 of *Probability and Statistics for Economists*, the 3rd through 6th conditional moments of Z_n^* are

$$\begin{aligned}
\mathbb{E}^*\left[Z_n^{*3}\right] &= \widehat{\kappa}_3/n^{1/2} \\
\mathbb{E}^*\left[Z_n^{*4}\right] &= \widehat{\kappa}_4/n+3\widehat{\kappa}_2^2 \\
\mathbb{E}^*\left[Z_n^{*5}\right] &= \widehat{\kappa}_5/n^{3/2}+10\widehat{\kappa}_3\widehat{\kappa}_2/n^{1/2} \\
\mathbb{E}^*\left[Z_n^{*6}\right] &= \widehat{\kappa}_6/n^2+\left(15\widehat{\kappa}_4\kappa_2+10\widehat{\kappa}_3^2\right)/n+15\widehat{\kappa}_2^3
\end{aligned} \tag{10.14}$$

where $\widehat{\kappa}_r$ is the rth sample cumulant. Similar expressions can be derived for higher moments. The moments (10.14) are exact, not approximations.

10.12 BOOTSTRAP ASYMPTOTICS

The bootstrap mean $\overline{Y}^*$ is a sample average over n i.i.d. random variables, so we might expect it to converge in probability to its expectation. Indeed, this is the case, but we have to be a bit careful, since the bootstrap mean has a conditional distribution (given the data), so we need to define convergence in probability for conditional distributions.

Definition 10.1 We say that a random vector Z_n^* **converges in bootstrap probability** to Z as $n\to\infty$, denoted $Z_n^* \underset{p^*}{\longrightarrow} Z$, if for all $\epsilon>0$,

$$\mathbb{P}^*\left[\left\|Z_n^*-Z\right\|>\epsilon\right] \underset{p}{\longrightarrow} 0.$$

To understand this definition, recall that conventional convergence in probability $Z_n \underset{p}{\longrightarrow} Z$ means that for a sufficiently large sample size n, the probability is high that Z_n is arbitrarily close to its limit Z. In contrast, Definition 10.1 says $Z_n^* \underset{p^*}{\longrightarrow} Z$ means that for a sufficiently large n, the probability is high that the conditional probability that Z_n^* is close to its limit Z is high. Note that there are two uses of probability—both unconditional and conditional.

Our label "convergence in bootstrap probability" is a bit unusual. The label used in much of the statistical literature is "convergence in probability, in probability" but that seems like a mouthful. That literature more often focuses on the related concept of "convergence in probability, almost surely," which holds if we replace the "$\underset{p}{\longrightarrow}$" convergence with almost sure convergence. We do not use this concept in this chapter, as it is an unnecessary complication.

While we have stated Definition 10.1 for the specific conditional probability distribution $\mathbb{P}^*$, the idea is more general and can be used for any conditional distribution and any sequence of random vectors.

The following may seem obvious, but it is useful to state for clarity. Its proof is given in Section 10.31.

Theorem 10.1 If $Z_n \underset{p}{\longrightarrow} Z$ as $n \to \infty$, then $Z_n \underset{p^*}{\longrightarrow} Z$.

Given Definition 10.1, we can establish a law of large numbers for the bootstrap sample mean.

Theorem 10.2 **Bootstrap WLLN**. If Y_i are independent and uniformly integrable, then $\overline{Y}^* - \overline{Y} \underset{p^*}{\longrightarrow} 0$ and $\overline{Y}^* \underset{p^*}{\longrightarrow} \mu = \mathbb{E}[Y]$ as $n \to \infty$.

The proof (presented in Section 10.31) is somewhat different from the classical case, as it is based on the Marcinkiewicz WLLN (Theorem 10.20, presented in Section 10.31).

Notice that the conditions for the bootstrap WLLN are the same as for the conventional WLLN. Notice as well that we state two related but slightly different results. The first is that the difference between the bootstrap sample mean $\overline{Y}^*$ and the sample mean $\overline{Y}$ diminishes as the sample size diverges. The second result is that the bootstrap sample mean converges to the population mean μ. The latter is not surprising (since the sample mean $\overline{Y}$ converges in probability to μ), but it is constructive to be precise, since we are dealing with a new convergence concept.

Theorem 10.3 **Bootstrap Continuous Mapping Theorem**. If $Z_n^* \underset{p^*}{\longrightarrow} c$ as $n \to \infty$ and $g(\cdot)$ is continuous at c, then $g(Z_n^*) \underset{p^*}{\longrightarrow} g(c)$ as $n \to \infty$.

The proof is essentially identical to that of Theorem 6.6, so is omitted here.

We next show that the bootstrap sample mean is asymptotically normally distributed, but for that, we need a definition of convergence for conditional distributions.

Definition 10.2 Let Z_n^* be a sequence of random vectors with conditional distributions $G_n^*(x) = \mathbb{P}^*\left[Z_n^* \leq x\right]$. We say that Z_n^* **converges in bootstrap distribution** to Z as $n \to \infty$, denoted $Z_n^* \underset{d^*}{\longrightarrow} Z$, if for all x at which $G(x) = \mathbb{P}[Z \leq x]$ is continuous, $G_n^*(x) \underset{p}{\longrightarrow} G(x)$ as $n \to \infty$.

The difference between this and the conventional definition is that Definition 10.2 treats the conditional distribution as random. An alternative label for Definition 10.2 is "convergence in distribution, in probability."

The following is a CLT for the bootstrap sample mean, with a proof given in Section 10.31.

Theorem 10.4 **Bootstrap CLT**. If the Y_i are i.i.d., $\mathbb{E}\|Y\|^2 < \infty$, and $\Sigma = \operatorname{var}[Y] > 0$, then as $n \to \infty$, $\sqrt{n}\left(\overline{Y}^* - \overline{Y}\right) \underset{d^*}{\longrightarrow} \mathrm{N}(0, \Sigma)$.

Theorem 10.4 shows that the normalized bootstrap sample mean has the same asymptotic distribution as the sample mean. Thus the bootstrap distribution is asymptotically the same as the sampling distribution. A notable difference, however, is that the bootstrap sample mean is normalized by centering at the sample mean, not at the population mean. This is because $\overline{Y}$ is the true mean in the bootstrap universe.

The next theorems state the distributional form of the continuous mapping theorem for bootstrap distributions and the Bootstrap Delta Method.

Theorem 10.5 Bootstrap Continuous Mapping Theorem
If $Z_n^* \underset{d^*}{\longrightarrow} Z$ as $n \to \infty$ and $g : \mathbb{R}^m \to \mathbb{R}^k$ has the set of discontinuity points D_g such that $\mathbb{P}^* \left[Z^* \in D_g\right] = 0$, then $g(Z_n^*) \underset{d^*}{\longrightarrow} g(Z)$ as $n \to \infty$.

Theorem 10.6 Bootstrap Delta Method
If $\widehat{\mu} \underset{p}{\longrightarrow} \mu$, $\sqrt{n}\,(\widehat{\mu}^* - \widehat{\mu}) \underset{d^*}{\longrightarrow} \xi$, and $g(u)$ is continuously differentiable in a neighborhood of μ, then as $n \to \infty$,

$$\sqrt{n}\left(g\left(\widehat{\mu}^*\right) - g(\widehat{\mu})\right) \underset{d^*}{\longrightarrow} \boldsymbol{G}'\xi$$

where $\boldsymbol{G}(x) = \frac{\partial}{\partial x} g(x)'$ and $\boldsymbol{G} = \boldsymbol{G}(\mu)$. In particular, if $\xi \sim \mathrm{N}\,(0, \boldsymbol{V})$, then as $n \to \infty$,

$$\sqrt{n}\left(g\left(\widehat{\mu}^*\right) - g(\widehat{\mu})\right) \underset{d^*}{\longrightarrow} \mathrm{N}\left(0, \boldsymbol{G}'\boldsymbol{V}\boldsymbol{G}\right).$$

For a proof, see Exercise 10.7.

We state an analog of Theorem 6.10, which presented the asymptotic distribution for general smooth functions of sample means, which covers most econometric estimators.

Theorem 10.7 Under the assumptions of Theorem 6.10, that is, if Y_i is i.i.d., $\mu = \mathbb{E}\left[h\,(Y)\right], \theta = g\,(\mu)$, $\mathbb{E}\left\|h\,(Y)\right\|^2 < \infty$, and $\boldsymbol{G}\,(x) = \dfrac{\partial}{\partial x} g\,(x)'$ is continuous in a neighborhood of μ, for $\widehat{\theta} = g\,(\widehat{\mu})$ with $\widehat{\mu} = \frac{1}{n}\sum_{i=1}^n h\,(Y_i)$ and $\widehat{\theta}^* = g\,(\widehat{\mu}^*)$ with $\widehat{\mu}^* = \frac{1}{n}\sum_{i=1}^n h\left(Y_i^*\right)$, as $n \to \infty$,

$$\sqrt{n}\left(\widehat{\theta}^* - \widehat{\theta}\right) \underset{d^*}{\longrightarrow} \mathrm{N}\,(0, \boldsymbol{V}_\theta)$$

where $\boldsymbol{V}_\theta = \boldsymbol{G}'\boldsymbol{V}\boldsymbol{G}$, $\boldsymbol{V} = \mathbb{E}\left[(h\,(Y) - \mu)\,(h\,(Y) - \mu)'\right]$, and $\boldsymbol{G} = \boldsymbol{G}\,(\mu)$.

For a proof, see Exercise 10.8.

Theorem 10.7 shows that the asymptotic distribution of the bootstrap estimator $\widehat{\theta}^*$ is identical to that of the sample estimator $\widehat{\theta}$. Thus we can learn the distribution of $\widehat{\theta}$ from the bootstrap distribution, and hence perform asymptotically correct inference.

For some bootstrap applications, we use bootstrap estimates of variance. The plug-in estimator of $\boldsymbol{V}_\theta$ is $\widehat{\boldsymbol{V}}_\theta = \widehat{\boldsymbol{G}}'\widehat{\boldsymbol{V}}\widehat{\boldsymbol{G}}$, where $\widehat{\boldsymbol{G}} = \boldsymbol{G}\,(\widehat{\mu})$ and

$$\widehat{\boldsymbol{V}} = \frac{1}{n}\sum_{i=1}^n (h\,(Y_i) - \widehat{\mu})\,(h\,(Y_i) - \widehat{\mu})'.$$

The bootstrap version is

$$\widehat{\boldsymbol{V}}_{\theta}^{*} = \widehat{\boldsymbol{G}}^{*\prime}\widehat{\boldsymbol{V}}^{*}\widehat{\boldsymbol{G}}^{*}$$

$$\widehat{\boldsymbol{G}}^{*} = \boldsymbol{G}\left(\widehat{\mu}^{*}\right)$$

$$\widehat{\boldsymbol{V}}^{*} = \frac{1}{n}\sum_{i=1}^{n}\left(h\left(Y_i^{*}\right)-\widehat{\mu}^{*}\right)\left(h\left(Y_i^{*}\right)-\widehat{\mu}^{*}\right)'.$$

Application of the bootstrap WLLN and bootstrap CMT show that $\widehat{\boldsymbol{V}}_{\theta}^{*}$ is consistent for $\boldsymbol{V}_{\theta}$.

Theorem 10.8 Under the assumptions of Theorem 10.7, $\widehat{\boldsymbol{V}}_{\theta}^{*} \underset{p^*}{\longrightarrow} \boldsymbol{V}_{\theta}$ as $n \to \infty$.

For a proof, see Exercise 10.9.

10.13 CONSISTENCY OF THE BOOTSTRAP ESTIMATE OF VARIANCE

Recall the definition (10.7) of the bootstrap estimator of variance $\widehat{\boldsymbol{V}}_{\widehat{\theta}}^{\text{boot}}$ of an estimator $\widehat{\theta}$. In this section, we explore conditions under which $\widehat{\boldsymbol{V}}_{\widehat{\theta}}^{\text{boot}}$ is consistent for the asymptotic variance of $\widehat{\theta}$. To do so, it is useful to focus on a normalized version of the estimator so that the asymptotic variance is not degenerate. Suppose that for some sequence a_n we have

$$Z_n = a_n\left(\widehat{\theta}-\theta\right) \underset{d}{\longrightarrow} \xi \tag{10.15}$$

and

$$Z_n^{*} = a_n\left(\widehat{\theta}^{*}-\widehat{\theta},\right) \underset{d^*}{\longrightarrow} \xi \tag{10.16}$$

for some limit distribution ξ. That is, for some normalization, both $\widehat{\theta}$ and $\widehat{\theta}^{*}$ have the same asymptotic distribution. This property is quite general, as it includes the smooth function model. The conventional bootstrap estimator of the variance of Z_n is the sample variance of the bootstrap draws $\left\{Z_n^{*}(b) : b = 1, \ldots, B\right\}$. This equals the estimator (10.7) multiplied by a_n^2. Thus it is equivalent (up to scale) whether we discuss estimating the variance of $\widehat{\theta}$ or Z_n.

The bootstrap estimator of variance of Z_n is

$$\widehat{\boldsymbol{V}}_{\theta}^{\text{boot,B}} = \frac{1}{B-1}\sum_{b=1}^{B}\left(Z_n^{*}(b)-Z_n^{*}\right)\left(Z_n^{*}(b)-Z_n^{*}\right)'$$

$$\overline{Z}_n^{*} = \frac{1}{B}\sum_{b=1}^{B} Z_n^{*}(b).$$

Notice that we index the estimator by the number of bootstrap replications B. Since Z_n^{*} converges in bootstrap distribution to the same asymptotic distribution as Z_n, it seems reasonable to guess that the variance of Z_n^{*} will converge to that of ξ. However, convergence in distribution is not sufficient for convergence in moments. For the variance to converge, it is also necessary for the sequence Z_n^{*} to be uniformly square integrable.

Theorem 10.9 If (10.15) and (10.16) hold for some sequence a_n, and $\left\|Z_n^*\right\|^2$ is uniformly integrable, then as $B \to \infty$

$$\widehat{V}_\theta^{\text{boot,B}} \underset{p^*}{\longrightarrow} \widehat{V}_\theta^{\text{boot}} = \text{var}\left[Z_n^*\right]$$

and as $n \to \infty$

$$\widehat{V}_\theta^{\text{boot}} \underset{p^*}{\longrightarrow} V_\theta = \text{var}\left[\xi\right].$$

This raises the question: Is the normalized sequence Z_n uniformly integrable? We spend the remainder of this section exploring this question and in Section 10.14 turn to trimmed variance estimators that do not require uniform integrability.

This condition is reasonably straightforward to verify for the case of a scalar sample mean with a finite variance. That is, suppose $Z_n^* = \sqrt{n}\left(\overline{Y}^* - \overline{Y}\right)$ and $\mathbb{E}\left[Y^2\right] < \infty$. In (10.14), we calculated the exact fourth central moment of Z_n^*:

$$\mathbb{E}^*\left[Z_n^{*4}\right] = \frac{\widehat{\kappa}_4}{n} + 3\widehat{\sigma}^4 = \frac{\widehat{\mu}_4 - 3\widehat{\sigma}^4}{n} + 3\widehat{\sigma}^4$$

where $\widehat{\sigma}^2 = n^{-1}\sum_{i=1}^n \left(Y_i - \overline{Y}\right)^2$ and $\widehat{\mu}_4 = n^{-1}\sum_{i=1}^n \left(Y_i - \overline{Y}\right)^4$. The assumption $\mathbb{E}\left[Y^2\right] < \infty$ implies that $\mathbb{E}\left[\widehat{\sigma}^2\right] = O(1)$, so $\widehat{\sigma}^2 = O_p(1)$. Furthermore, $n^{-1}\widehat{\mu}_4 = n^{-2}\sum_{i=1}^n \left(Y_i - \overline{Y}\right)^4 = o_p(1)$ by the Marcinkiewicz WLLN (Theorem 10.20). It follows that

$$\mathbb{E}^*\left[Z_n^{*4}\right] = n^2\mathbb{E}^*\left[\left(\overline{Y}^* - \overline{Y}\right)^4\right] = O_p(1). \tag{10.17}$$

Theorem 6.13 shows that (10.17) implies that Z_n^{*2} is uniformly integrable. Thus if Y has a finite variance, the normalized bootstrap sample mean is uniformly square integrable and the bootstrap estimate of variance is consistent by Theorem 10.9.

Now consider the smooth function model of Theorem 10.7. We can establish the following result.

Theorem 10.10 In the smooth function model of Theorem 10.7, if for some $p \geq 1$ the pth-order derivatives of $g(x)$ are bounded, then $Z_n^* = \sqrt{n}\left(\widehat{\theta}^* - \widehat{\theta}\right)$ is uniformly square integrable and the bootstrap estimator of variance is consistent, as in Theorem 10.9.

For a proof, see Section 10.31.

This theorem shows that the bootstrap estimate of variance is consistent for a reasonably broad class of estimators. The class of functions $g(x)$ covered by this result includes all pth-order polynomials.

10.14 TRIMMED ESTIMATOR OF BOOTSTRAP VARIANCE

Theorem 10.10 shows that the bootstrap estimator of variance is consistent for smooth functions with a bounded pth-order derivative. This is a fairly broad class but excludes many important applications. An example is $\theta=\mu_1/\mu_2$, where $\mu_1=\mathbb{E}[Y_1]$ and $\mu_2=\mathbb{E}[Y_2]$. This function does not have a bounded derivative (unless μ_2 is bounded away from 0) so is not covered by Theorem 10.10.

This is more than a technical issue. When (Y_1, Y_2) are jointly normally distributed, then it is known that $\widehat{\theta}=\overline{Y}_1/\overline{Y}_2$ does not possess a finite variance. Consequently, we cannot expect the bootstrap estimator of variance to perform well. (It is attempting to estimate the variance of $\widehat{\theta}$, which is infinity.)

In these cases, it is preferred to use a trimmed estimator of bootstrap variance. Let $\tau_n \to \infty$ be a sequence of positive trimming numbers satisfying $\tau_n^4 = O\left(e^{n^{1/2}}\right)$. Define the trimmed statistic

$$Z_n^{**} = Z_n^* \mathbb{1}\left\{\left\|Z_n^*\right\| \le \tau_n\right\}.$$

The trimmed bootstrap estimator of variance is

$$\widehat{V}_\theta^{\text{boot,B},\tau} = \frac{1}{B-1}\sum_{b=1}^{B}\left(Z_n^{**}(b)-\overline{Z_n^{**}}\right)\left(Z_n^{**}(b)-\overline{Z_n^{**}}\right)'$$

$$\overline{Z_n^{**}} = \frac{1}{B}\sum_{b=1}^{B} Z_n^{**}(b).$$

We first examine the behavior of $\widehat{V}_\theta^{\text{boot,B}}$ as the number of bootstrap replications B grows to infinity. It is a sample variance of independent bounded random vectors. Thus by the bootstrap WLLN (Theorem 10.2), $\widehat{V}_\theta^{\text{boot,B},\tau}$ converges in bootstrap probability to the variance of Z_n^{**}.

Theorem 10.11 As $B\to\infty$, $\widehat{V}_\theta^{\text{boot,B},\tau} \underset{p^*}{\longrightarrow} \widehat{V}_\theta^{\text{boot},\tau} = \operatorname{var}\left[Z_n^{**}\right]$.

We next examine the behavior of the bootstrap estimator $\widehat{V}_\theta^{\text{boot},\tau}$ as n grows to infinity. Let us focus on the smooth function model of Theorem 10.7, which showed that $Z_n^* = \sqrt{n}\left(\widehat{\theta}^* - \widehat{\theta}\right) \underset{d^*}{\longrightarrow} Z \sim \mathrm{N}(0, V_\theta)$. Since the trimming is asymptotically negligible, it follows that $Z_n^{**} \underset{d^*}{\longrightarrow} Z$. If we can show that Z_n^{**} is uniformly square integrable, Theorem 10.9 shows that $\operatorname{var}\left[Z_n^{**}\right] \to \operatorname{var}[Z] = V_\theta$ as $n\to\infty$. This is shown in the following result, whose proof is presented in Section 10.31.

Theorem 10.12 Under the assumptions of Theorem 10.7, $\widehat{V}_\theta^{\text{boot},\tau} \underset{p^*}{\longrightarrow} V_\theta$.

Theorems 10.11 and 10.12 show that the trimmed bootstrap estimator of variance is consistent for the asymptotic variance in the smooth function model, which includes most econometric estimators. This justifies bootstrap standard errors as consistent estimators for the asymptotic distribution.

An important caveat is that these results critically rely on the trimmed variance estimator. This caveat is critical, as conventional statistical packages (e.g., Stata) calculate bootstrap standard errors using the untrimmed estimator (10.7). Thus there is no guarantee that the reported standard errors are consistent. The untrimmed variance estimator works in the context of Theorem 10.10 and whenever the bootstrap statistic is uniformly square integrable, but not necessarily in general applications.

Table 10.3
Experience level that maximizes expected log wages

Estimate	35.2
Asymptotic s.e.	(7.0)
Jackknife s.e.	(7.0)
Bootstrap s.e. (standard)	(825)
Bootstrap s.e. (repeat)	(544)
Bootstrap s.e. (trimmed)	(10.1)

In practice, it may be difficult to know how to select the trimming sequence τ_n. The rule $\tau_n^4 = O\left(e^{n^{1/2}}\right)$ does not provide practical guidance. Instead, it may be useful to think about trimming in terms of percentages of the bootstrap draws. Thus we can set τ_n so that a given small percentage γ_n is trimmed. For theoretical interpretation we would set $\gamma_n \to 0$ as $n \to \infty$. In practice, we might set $\gamma_n = 1\%$.

10.15 UNRELIABILITY OF UNTRIMMED BOOTSTRAP STANDARD ERRORS

Section 10.14 we presented a trimmed bootstrap variance estimator that should be used to form bootstrap standard errors for nonlinear estimators. Otherwise, the untrimmed estimator is potentially unreliable. This is an unfortunate situation, because reporting of bootstrap standard errors is commonplace in contemporary applied econometric practice, and standard applications (including Stata) use the untrimmed estimator. To illustrate the seriousness of the problem, let us use the simple wage regression (7.31), which is repeated here. This is the subsample of married Black women with 982 observations. The point estimates and standard errors are

$$\widehat{\log(wage)} = \underset{(0.008)}{0.118}\ education + \underset{(0.006)}{0.016}\ experience - \underset{(0.012)}{0.022}\ experience^2/100 + \underset{(0.157)}{0.947}.$$

We are interested in the experience level that maximizes expected log wages $\theta_3 = -50\beta_2/\beta_3$. The point estimate and standard errors calculated with different methods are reported in Table 10.3.

The point estimate of the experience level with maximum earnings is $\widehat{\theta}_3 = 35$. The asymptotic and jackknife standard errors are about 7. The bootstrap standard error, however, is 825! Confused by this unusual value, we rerun the bootstrap and obtain a standard error of 544. Each was computed with 10,000 bootstrap replications. The fact that the two bootstrap standard errors are considerably different when recomputed (with different starting seeds) is indicative of moment failure. When an enormous discrepancy like this exists between the asymptotic and bootstrap standard errors, and between bootstrap runs, it is a signal that there may be moment failure, and consequently bootstrap standard errors are unreliable. A trimmed bootstrap with $\tau = 25$ (set to slightly exceed three asymptotic standard errors) produces a more reasonable standard error of 10.

One message from this application is that when different methods produce very different standard errors, we should be cautious about trusting any single method. The large discrepancies indicate poor asymptotic approximations, rendering all methods inaccurate. Another message is to be cautious about reporting conventional bootstrap standard errors. Trimmed versions are preferred, especially for nonlinear functions of estimated coefficients.

10.16 CONSISTENCY OF THE PERCENTILE INTERVAL

Recall the percentile interval (10.8). We now provide conditions under which it has asymptotically correct coverage.

Theorem 10.13 Assume that for some sequence a_n,

$$a_n\left(\widehat{\theta}-\theta\right) \underset{d}{\longrightarrow} \xi \tag{10.18}$$

and

$$a_n\left(\widehat{\theta}^*-\widehat{\theta}\right) \underset{d^*}{\longrightarrow} \xi \tag{10.19}$$

where ξ is continuously distributed and symmetric about 0. Then $\mathbb{P}\left[\theta \in C^{\mathrm{pc}}\right] \rightarrow 1-\alpha$ as $n \rightarrow \infty$.

The assumptions (10.18) and (10.19) hold for the smooth function model of Theorem 10.7, so this result incorporates many applications. The beauty of Theorem 10.13 is that the simple confidence interval C^{pc}—which does not require technical calculation of asymptotic standard errors—has asymptotically valid coverage for any estimator that falls in the smooth function class, as well as any other estimator satisfying the convergence results (10.18) and (10.19) with ξ symmetrically distributed. The conditions are weaker than those required for consistent bootstrap variance estimation (and normal-approximation confidence intervals), because it is not necessary to verify that $\widehat{\theta}^*$ is uniformly integrable nor necessary to employ trimming.

The proof of Theorem 10.13 is not difficult. The convergence assumption (10.19) implies that the αth quantile of $a_n\left(\widehat{\theta}^*-\widehat{\theta}\right)$, which is $a_n\left(q_\alpha^*-\widehat{\theta}\right)$ by quantile equivariance, converges in probability to the αth quantile of ξ, which we can denote as $\bar{q}_\alpha$. Thus

$$a_n\left(q_\alpha^*-\widehat{\theta}\right) \underset{p}{\longrightarrow} \bar{q}_\alpha. \tag{10.20}$$

Let $H(x)=\mathbb{P}[\xi \leq x]$ be the distribution function of ξ. The assumption of symmetry implies $H(-x)=1-H(x)$. Then the percentile interval has coverage

$$\begin{aligned}
\mathbb{P}\left[\theta \in C^{\mathrm{pc}}\right] &= \mathbb{P}\left[q_{\alpha/2}^* \leq \theta \leq q_{1-\alpha/2}^*\right] \\
&= \mathbb{P}\left[-a_n\left(q_{\alpha/2}^*-\widehat{\theta}\right) \geq a_n\left(\widehat{\theta}-\theta\right) \geq -a_n\left(q_{1-\alpha/2}^*-\widehat{\theta}\right)\right] \\
&\rightarrow \mathbb{P}\left[-\bar{q}_{\alpha/2} \geq \xi \geq -\bar{q}_{1-\alpha/2}\right] \\
&= H\left(-\bar{q}_{\alpha/2}\right)-H\left(-\bar{q}_{1-\alpha/2}\right) \\
&= H\left(\bar{q}_{1-\alpha/2}\right)-H\left(\bar{q}_{\alpha/2}\right) \\
&= 1-\alpha.
\end{aligned}$$

The convergence holds by (10.18) and (10.20). The following equality uses the definition of H, the next-to-last is the symmetry of H, and the final equality is the definition of $\bar{q}_\alpha$. This establishes Theorem 10.13.

Theorem 10.13 seems quite general, but it critically rests on the assumption that the asymptotic distribution ξ is symmetrically distributed about 0. This may seem innocuous since conventional asymptotic distributions are normal and hence symmetric, but it deserves further scrutiny. It is not merely a technical assumption—an examination of the steps in the preceeding argument isolate quite clearly that if the symmetry assumption is violated, then the asymptotic coverage will not be $1-\alpha$. While Theorem 10.13 does show that the percentile interval is asymptotically valid for a conventional asymptotically normal estimator, the reliance on symmetry in the argument suggests that the percentile method will work poorly when the finite sample distribution is asymmetric. This turns out to be the case and leads us to consider alternative methods in the following sections.

It is also worthwhile to investigate a finite sample justification for the percentile interval based on a heuristic analogy due to Efron (1987). Assume that there exists an unknown but strictly increasing transformation $\psi(\theta)$ such that $\psi(\widehat{\theta})-\psi(\theta)$ has a pivotal distribution $H(u)$ (does not vary with θ) that is symmetric about 0. For example, if $\widehat{\theta} \sim \mathrm{N}(\theta, \sigma^2)$, we can set $\psi(\theta)=\theta/\sigma$. Alternatively, if $\widehat{\theta}=\exp(\widehat{\mu})$ and $\widehat{\mu} \sim \mathrm{N}(\mu, \sigma^2)$, then we can set $\psi(\theta)=\log(\theta)/\sigma$.

To assess the coverage of the percentile interval, observe that since the distribution H is pivotal, the bootstrap distribution $\psi(\widehat{\theta}^*)-\psi(\widehat{\theta})$ also has distribution $H(u)$. Let $\overline{q}_\alpha$ be the αth quantile of the distribution H. Since q^*_α is the αth quantile of the distribution of $\widehat{\theta}^*$ and $\psi(\widehat{\theta}^*)-\psi(\widehat{\theta})$ is a monotonic transformation of $\widehat{\theta}^*$, by the quantile equivariance property, we deduce that $\overline{q}_\alpha+\psi(\widehat{\theta})=\psi(q^*_\alpha)$. The percentile interval has coverage

$$
\begin{aligned}
\mathbb{P}\left[\theta \in C^{\mathrm{pc}}\right] &= \mathbb{P}\left[q^*_{\alpha/2} \le \theta \le q^*_{1-\alpha/2}\right] \\
&= \mathbb{P}\left[\psi(q^*_{\alpha/2}) \le \psi(\theta) \le \psi(q^*_{1-\alpha/2})\right] \\
&= \mathbb{P}\left[\psi(\widehat{\theta}) - \psi(q^*_{\alpha/2}) \ge \psi(\widehat{\theta}) - \psi(\theta) \ge \psi(\widehat{\theta}) - \psi(q^*_{1-\alpha/2})\right] \\
&= \mathbb{P}\left[-\overline{q}_{\alpha/2} \ge \psi(\widehat{\theta}) - \psi(\theta) \ge -\overline{q}_{1-\alpha/2}\right] \\
&= H\left(-\overline{q}_{\alpha/2}\right) - H\left(-\overline{q}_{1-\alpha/2}\right) \\
&= H\left(\overline{q}_{1-\alpha/2}\right) - H\left(\overline{q}_{\alpha/2}\right) \\
&= 1-\alpha.
\end{aligned}
$$

The second equality applies the monotonic transformation $\psi(u)$ to all elements. The fourth uses the relationship $\overline{q}_\alpha+\psi(\widehat{\theta})=\psi(q^*_\alpha)$. The fifth uses the defintion of H. The sixth uses the symmetry property of H, and the final is by the definition of $\overline{q}_\alpha$ as the αth quantile of H.

This calculation shows that under these assumptions, the percentile interval has exact coverage $1-\alpha$. The nice thing about this argument is the introduction of the unknown transformation $\psi(u)$ for which the percentile interval automatically adapts. The unpleasant feature is the assumption of symmetry. Similar to the asymptotic argument, the calculation strongly relies on the symmetry of the distribution $H(x)$. Without symmetry, the coverage will be incorrect.

Intuitively, we expect that when the assumptions are approximately true, then the percentile interval will have approximately correct coverage. Thus so long as there is a transformation $\psi(u)$ such that $\psi(\widehat{\theta})-\psi(\theta)$ is approximately pivotal and symmetric about 0, then the percentile interval should work well.

This argument has the following application. Suppose that the parameter of interest is $\theta=\exp(\mu)$, where $\mu=\mathbb{E}[Y]$, and suppose Y has a pivotal symmetric distribution about μ. Then even though $\widehat{\theta}=\exp(\overline{Y})$ does not have a symmetric distribution, the percentile interval applied to $\widehat{\theta}$ will have the correct coverage, because the monotonic transformation $\log\left(\widehat{\theta}\right)$ has a pivotal symmetric distribution.

10.17 BIAS-CORRECTED PERCENTILE INTERVAL

The accuracy of the percentile interval depends critically on the assumption that the sampling distribution is approximately symmetrically distributed. This excludes finite sample bias, because an estimator that is biased cannot be symmetrically distributed. Many contexts in which we want to apply bootstrap methods (rather than asymptotic) are when the parameter of interest is a nonlinear function of the model parameters, and nonlinearity typically induces estimation bias. Consequently, it is difficult to expect the percentile method to generally have accurate coverage.

To reduce the bias problem, Efron (1982) introduced the **bias-corrected (BC) percentile interval**. The justification is heuristic, but there is considerable evidence that the bias-corrected method is an important improvement on the percentile interval.

The construction is based on the assumption is that there is a an unknown but strictly increasing transformation $\psi(\theta)$ and unknown constant z_0 such that

$$Z = \psi(\widehat{\theta}) - \psi(\theta) + z_0 \sim \mathrm{N}(0,1). \tag{10.21}$$

(The assumption that Z is normal is not critical. It could be replaced by any known symmetric and invertible distribution.) Let $\Phi(x)$ denote the normal distribution function, $\Phi^{-1}(p)$ its quantile function, and $z_\alpha = \Phi^{-1}(\alpha)$ the normal critical values. Then the BC interval can be constructed from the bootstrap estimators $\widehat{\theta}_b^*$ and bootstrap quantiles q_α^* as follows. Set

$$p^* = \frac{1}{B}\sum_{b=1}^{B} \mathbb{1}\left\{\widehat{\theta}_b^* \le \widehat{\theta}\right\} \tag{10.22}$$

and

$$z_0 = \Phi^{-1}(p^*) \tag{10.23}$$

where p^* is a measure of median bias, and z_0 is p^* transformed into normal units. If the bias of $\widehat{\theta}$ is 0, then $p^* = 0.5$ and $z_0 = 0$. If $\widehat{\theta}$ is upward biased, then $p^* < 0.5$ and $z_0 < 0$. Conversely, if $\widehat{\theta}$ is downward biased, then $p^* > 0.5$ and $z_0 > 0$. Define for any α an adjusted version

$$x(\alpha) = \Phi(z_\alpha + 2z_0). \tag{10.24}$$

If $z_0 = 0$, then $x(\alpha) = \alpha$. If $z_0 > 0$, then $x(\alpha) > \alpha$, and conversely when $x(\alpha) < 0$. The BC interval is

$$C^{\mathrm{bc}} = \left[q^*_{x(\alpha/2)}, q^*_{x(1-\alpha/2)}\right]. \tag{10.25}$$

Essentially, rather than going from the 2.5% to 97.5% quantile, the BC interval uses adjusted quantiles, with the degree of adjustment depending on the extent of the bias.

The construction of the BC interval is not intuitive. We now show that assumption (10.21) implies that the BC interval has exact coverage. Equation (10.21) implies that

$$\mathbb{P}\left[\psi(\widehat{\theta}) - \psi(\theta) + z_0 \le x\right] = \Phi(x).$$

Since the distribution is pivotal, the result carries over to the bootstrap distribution:

$$\mathbb{P}^*\left[\psi(\widehat{\theta}^*) - \psi(\widehat{\theta}) + z_0 \le x\right] = \Phi(x). \tag{10.26}$$

Evaluating (10.26) at $x = z_0$, we find $\mathbb{P}^*\left[\psi(\widehat{\theta}^*) - \psi(\widehat{\theta}) \le 0\right] = \Phi(z_0)$, which implies $\mathbb{P}^*\left[\widehat{\theta}^* \le \widehat{\theta}\right] = \Phi(z_0)$. Inverting, we obtain

$$z_0 = \Phi^{-1}\left(\mathbb{P}^*\left[\widehat{\theta}^* \le \widehat{\theta}\right]\right) \tag{10.27}$$

which is the probability limit of (10.23) as $B \to \infty$. Thus the unknown z_0 is recoved by (10.23), and we can treat z_0 as if it were known.

From (10.26), we deduce that

$$\begin{aligned} x(\alpha) &= \Phi(z_\alpha + 2z_0) \\ &= \mathbb{P}^*\left[\psi(\widehat{\theta}^*) - \psi(\widehat{\theta}) \le z_\alpha + z_0)\right] \\ &= \mathbb{P}^*\left[\widehat{\theta}^* \le \psi^{-1}\left(\psi(\widehat{\theta}) + z_0 + z_\alpha\right)\right]. \end{aligned}$$

This equation shows that $\psi^{-1}\left(\psi(\widehat{\theta}) + z_0 + z_\alpha\right)$ equals the $x(\alpha)$th bootstrap quantile. That is, $q^*_{x(\alpha)} = \psi^{-1}\left(\psi(\widehat{\theta}) + z_0 + z_\alpha\right)$. Hence we can write (10.25) as

$$C^{\mathrm{bc}} = \left[\psi^{-1}\left(\psi(\widehat{\theta}) + z_0 + z_{\alpha/2}\right), \psi^{-1}\left(\psi(\widehat{\theta}) + z_0 + z_{1-\alpha/2}\right)\right].$$

It has coverage probability

$$\begin{aligned} \mathbb{P}\left[\theta \in C^{\mathrm{bc}}\right] &= \mathbb{P}\left[\psi^{-1}\left(\psi(\widehat{\theta}) + z_0 + z_{\alpha/2}\right) \le \theta \le \psi^{-1}\left(\psi(\widehat{\theta}) + z_0 + z_{1-\alpha/2}\right)\right] \\ &= \mathbb{P}\left[\psi(\widehat{\theta}) + z_0 + z_{\alpha/2} \le \psi(\theta) \le \psi(\widehat{\theta}) + z_0 + z_{1-\alpha/2}\right] \\ &= \mathbb{P}\left[-z_{\alpha/2} \ge \psi(\widehat{\theta}) - \psi(\theta) + z_0 \ge -z_{1-\alpha/2}\right] \\ &= \mathbb{P}\left[z_{1-\alpha/2} \ge Z \ge z_{\alpha/2}\right] \\ &= \Phi\left(z_{1-\alpha/2}\right) - \Phi\left(z_{\alpha/2}\right) \\ &= 1 - \alpha. \end{aligned}$$

The second equality applies the transformation $\psi(\theta)$. The fourth equality uses the model (10.21) and the fact $z_\alpha = -z_{1-\alpha}$. This shows that the BC interval (10.25) has exact coverage under the assumption (10.21). Furthermore, under the assumptions of Theorem 10.13, the BC interval has asymptotic coverage probability $1 - \alpha$, since the bias correction is asymptotically negligible.

An important property of the BC percentile interval is that it is transformation-respecting (like the percentile interval). To see this, observe that p^* is invariant to transformations, because it is a probability, and thus z_0^* and $x(\alpha)$ are invariant. Since the interval is constructed from the $x(\alpha/2)$ and $x(1-\alpha/2)$ quantiles, the quantile equivariance property shows that the interval is transformation-respecting.

The bootstrap BC percentile intervals for the four estimators are reported in Table 10.2. They are generally similar to the percentile intervals, though the intervals for σ^2 and μ are somewhat shifted to the right.

In Stata, BC percentile confidence intervals can be obtained by using the command `estat bootstrap` after an estimation command that calculates standard errors via the bootstrap.

10.18 BC_a PERCENTILE INTERVAL

A further improvement on the BC interval was made by Efron (1987) to account for the skewness in the sampling distribution, which can be modeled by specifying that the variance of the estimator depends on the parameter. The resulting **bootstrap accelerated bias-corrected percentile interval** (BC_a) has improved performance on the BC interval, but it requires a bit more computation and is less intuitive.

The construction is a generalization of that for the BC intervals. The assumption is that there is an unknown but strictly increasing transformation $\psi(\theta)$ and unknown constants a and z_0 such that

$$Z = \frac{\psi(\widehat{\theta}) - \psi(\theta)}{1 + a\psi(\theta)} + z_0 \sim \mathrm{N}(0,1). \tag{10.28}$$

(As before, the assumption that Z is normal could be replaced by any known symmetric and invertible distribution.)

The constant z_0 is estimated by (10.23) just as for the BC interval. There are several possible estimators of a. Efron's suggestion is a scaled jackknife estimator of the skewness of $\widehat{\theta}$:

$$\widehat{a} = \frac{\sum_{i=1}^{n}\left(\overline{\theta} - \widehat{\theta}_{(-i)}\right)^3}{6\left(\sum_{i=1}^{n}\left(\overline{\theta} - \widehat{\theta}_{(-i)}\right)^2\right)^{3/2}}$$

$$\overline{\theta} = \frac{1}{n}\sum_{i=1}^{n}\widehat{\theta}_{(-i)}.$$

The jackknife estimator of $\widehat{a}$ makes the BC_a interval more computationally costly than other intervals.

Define for any α the adjusted version

$$x(\alpha) = \Phi\left(z_0 + \frac{z_\alpha + z_0}{1 - a(z_\alpha + z_0)}\right).$$

The BC_a percentile interval is

$$C^{\mathrm{bca}} = \left[q^*_{x(\alpha/2)}, q^*_{x(1-\alpha/2)}\right].$$

Note that $x(\alpha)$ simplifies to (10.24), and C^{bca} simplies to C^{bc} when $a = 0$. While C^{bc} improves on C^{pc} by correcting the median bias, C^{bca} makes a further correction for skewness.

The BC_a interval is only well defined for values of α such that $a(z_\alpha + z_0) < 1$. (Or equivalently, if $\alpha < \Phi\left(a^{-1} - z_0\right)$ for $a > 0$, and $\alpha > \Phi\left(a^{-1} - z_0\right)$ for $a < 0$.)

The BC_a interval, like the BC and percentile intervals, is transformation-respecting. Thus if $\left[q^*_{x(\alpha/2)}, q^*_{x(1-\alpha/2)}\right]$ is the BC_a interval for θ, then $\left[m\left(q^*_{x(\alpha/2)}\right), m\left(q^*_{x(1-\alpha/2)}\right)\right]$ is the BC_α interval for $\phi = m(\theta)$ when $m(\theta)$ is monotone.

I now give a justification for the BC_a interval. The most difficult feature to understand is the estimator $\widehat{a}$ for a. This involves higher-order approximations that are too advanced for our treatment, so I instead refer readers to chapter 4.1.4 of Shao and Tu (1995) and simply assume that a is known.

Let us now show that assumption (10.28) with a known implies that C^{bca} has exact coverage. The argument is essentially the same as that given in Section 10.17. Assumption (10.28) implies that the bootstrap distribution satisfies

$$\mathbb{P}^*\left[\frac{\psi(\widehat{\theta}^*) - \psi(\widehat{\theta})}{1 + a\psi(\widehat{\theta})} + z_0 \le x\right] = \Phi(x). \tag{10.29}$$

Evaluating at $x = z_0$ and inverting, we obtain (10.27), which is the same as for the BC interval. Thus the estimator (10.23) is consistent as $B \to \infty$, and we can treat z_0 as if it were known.

From (10.29) we deduce that

$$x(\alpha) = \mathbb{P}^*\left[\frac{\psi(\widehat{\theta}^*) - \psi(\widehat{\theta})}{1 + a\psi(\widehat{\theta})} \le \frac{z_\alpha + z_0}{1 - a(z_\alpha + z_0)}\right]$$
$$= \mathbb{P}^*\left[\widehat{\theta}^* \le \psi^{-1}\left(\frac{\psi(\widehat{\theta}) + z_\alpha + z_0}{1 - a(z_\alpha + z_0)}\right)\right].$$

This shows that $\psi^{-1}\left(\frac{\psi(\widehat{\theta})+z_\alpha+z_0}{1-a(z_\alpha+z_0)}\right)$ equals the $x(\alpha)$th bootstrap quantile. Hence we can write C^{bca} as

$$C^{\text{bca}} = \left[\psi^{-1}\left(\frac{\psi(\widehat{\theta}) + z_{\alpha/2} + z_0}{1 - a\left(z_{\alpha/2} + z_0\right)}\right), \quad \psi^{-1}\left(\frac{\psi(\widehat{\theta}) + z_{1-\alpha/2} + z_0}{1 - a\left(z_{1-\alpha/2} + z_0\right)}\right)\right].$$

It has coverage probability

$$\mathbb{P}\left[\theta \in C^{\text{bca}}\right] = \mathbb{P}\left[\psi^{-1}\left(\frac{\psi(\widehat{\theta}) + z_{\alpha/2} + z_0}{1 - a\left(z_{\alpha/2} + z_0\right)}\right) \le \theta \le \psi^{-1}\left(\frac{\psi(\widehat{\theta}) + z_{1-\alpha/2} + z_0}{1 - a\left(z_{1-\alpha/2} + z_0\right)}\right)\right]$$
$$= \mathbb{P}\left[\frac{\psi(\widehat{\theta}) + z_{\alpha/2} + z_0}{1 - a\left(z_{\alpha/2} + z_0\right)} \le \psi(\theta) \le \frac{\psi(\widehat{\theta}) + z_{1-\alpha/2} + z_0}{1 - a\left(z_{1-\alpha/2} + z_0\right)}\right]$$
$$= \mathbb{P}\left[-z_{\alpha/2} \ge \frac{\psi(\widehat{\theta}) - \psi(\theta)}{1 + a\psi(\theta)} + z_0 \ge -z_{1-\alpha/2}\right]$$
$$= \mathbb{P}\left[z_{1-\alpha/2} \ge Z \ge z_{\alpha/2}\right]$$
$$= 1 - \alpha.$$

The second equality applies the transformation $\psi(\theta)$. The fourth equality uses the model (10.28) and the fact $z_\alpha = -z_{1-\alpha}$. This shows that the BC_a interval C^{bca} has exact coverage under assumption (10.28) with a known.

The bootstrap BC_a percentile intervals for the four estimators are reported in Table 10.2. They are generally similar to the BC intervals, though the intervals for σ^2 and μ are slightly shifted to the right.

In Stata, BC_a intervals can be obtained by using the command `estat bootstrap, bca` or the command `estat bootstrap, all` after an estimation command that calculates standard errors via the bootstrap using the `bca` option.

10.19 PERCENTILE-t INTERVAL

In many cases, we can obtain improvement in accuracy by bootstrapping a studentized statistic such as a t-ratio. Let $\widehat{\theta}$ be an estimator of a scalar parameter θ and $s(\widehat{\theta})$ a standard error. The sample t-ratio is

$$T = \frac{\widehat{\theta} - \theta}{s(\widehat{\theta})}.$$

The bootstrap t-ratio is

$$T^* = \frac{\widehat{\theta}^* - \widehat{\theta}}{s(\widehat{\theta}^*)}$$

where $s(\widehat{\theta}^*)$ is the standard error calculated on the bootstrap sample. Notice that the bootstrap t-ratio is centered at the parameter estimator $\widehat{\theta}$. This is because $\widehat{\theta}$ is the "true value" in the bootstrap universe.

The percentile-t interval is formed using the distribution of T^*. This can be calculated via the bootstrap algorithm. On each bootstrap sample, the estimator $\widehat{\theta}^*$ and its standard error $s(\widehat{\theta}^*)$ are calculated, and the t-ratio $T^* = \left(\widehat{\theta}^* - \widehat{\theta}\right) / s(\widehat{\theta}^*)$ calculated and stored. This is repeated B times. The αth quantile q^*_α is estimated by the αth empirical quantile (or any quantile estimator) from the B bootstrap draws of T^*.

The bootstrap percentile-t confidence interval is defined as

$$C^{\mathrm{pt}} = \left[\widehat{\theta} - s(\widehat{\theta})q^*_{1-\alpha/2}, \widehat{\theta} - s(\widehat{\theta})q^*_{\alpha/2}\right].$$

The form may appear unusual compared to the percentile interval. The left endpoint is determined by the upper quantile of the distribution of T^*, and the right endpoint is determined by the lower quantile. As we show below, this construction is important for the interval to have correct coverage when the distribution is not symmetric.

When the estimator is asymptotically normal and the standard error a reliable estimator of the standard deviation of the distribution, we would expect the t-ratio T to be roughly approximated by the normal distribution. In this case, we would expect $q^*_{0.975} \approx -q^*_{0.025} \approx 2$. Departures from this baseline occur as the distribution becomes skewed or fat-tailed. If the bootstrap quantiles depart substantially from this baseline, it is evidence of substantial departure from normality. (It may also indicate a programming error, so in these cases it is wise to triple-check!)

The percentile-t has the following advantages. First, when the standard error $s(\widehat{\theta})$ is reasonably reliable, the percentile-t bootstrap makes use of the information in the standard error, thereby reducing the role of the bootstrap. This can improve the precision of the method relative to other methods. Second, as we show later, the percentile-t intervals achieve higher-order accuracy than the percentile and BC percentile intervals. Third, the percentile-t intervals correspond to the set of parameter values "not rejected" by one-sided t-tests using bootstrap critical values (bootstrap tests are presented in Section 10.21).

The percentile-t interval has the following disadvantages. First, it may be infeasible when standard error formulas are unknown. Second, they may be practically infeasible when standard error calculations are computationally costly (since the standard error calculation needs to be performed on each bootstrap sample). Third, the percentile-t may be unreliable if the standard errors $s(\widehat{\theta})$ are unreliable and thus add more noise than clarity. Fourth, the percentile-t interval is not translation preserving, unlike the percentile, BC percentile, and BC$_a$ percentile intervals.

It is typical to calculate percentile-t intervals with t-ratios constructed with conventional asymptotic standard errors. But this is not the only possible implementation. The percentile-t interval can be constructed with any data-dependent measure of scale. For example, if $\widehat{\theta}$ is a two-step estimator for which it is unclear how to construct a correct asymptotic standard error, but we know how to calculate a standard error $s(\widehat{\theta})$ appropriate for the second step alone, then $s(\widehat{\theta})$ can be used for a percentile-t-type interval as described above. It will not possess the higher-order accuracy properties of Section 10.20, but it will satisfy the conditions for first-order validity.

Furthermore, percentile-t intervals can be constructed using bootstrap standard errors. That is, the statistics T and T^* can be computed using bootstrap standard errors $s^{\mathrm{boot}}_{\widehat{\theta}}$. This is computationally costly, as it requires what we call a "nested bootstrap." Specifically, for each bootstrap replication, a random sample is drawn, the bootstrap estimate $\widehat{\theta}^*$ computed, and then B additional bootstrap subsamples drawn from the bootstrap sample to compute the bootstrap standard error for the bootstrap estimate $\widehat{\theta}^*$. Effectively, B^2 bootstrap samples are drawn and estimated, which increases the computational requirement by an order of magnitude.

Let us now discuss the distribution theory for first-order validity of the percentile-t bootstrap. First, consider the smooth function model, where $\widehat{\theta} = g(\widehat{\mu})$ and $s(\widehat{\theta}) = \sqrt{\frac{1}{n}\widehat{\boldsymbol{G}}'\widehat{\boldsymbol{V}}\widehat{\boldsymbol{G}}}$ with bootstrap analogs $\widehat{\theta}^* = g(\widehat{\mu}^*)$ and $s(\widehat{\theta}^*) = \sqrt{\frac{1}{n}\widehat{\boldsymbol{G}}^{*\prime}\widehat{\boldsymbol{V}}^*\widehat{\boldsymbol{G}}^*}$. From Theorems 6.10, 10.7, and 10.8, we have

$$T = \frac{\sqrt{n}\left(\widehat{\theta} - \theta\right)}{\sqrt{\widehat{\boldsymbol{G}}'\widehat{\boldsymbol{V}}\widehat{\boldsymbol{G}}}} \underset{d}{\longrightarrow} Z$$

and

$$T^* = \frac{\sqrt{n}\left(\widehat{\theta}^* - \widehat{\theta}\right)}{\sqrt{\widehat{\boldsymbol{G}}^{*\prime}\widehat{\boldsymbol{V}}^*\widehat{\boldsymbol{G}}^*}} \underset{d^*}{\longrightarrow} Z$$

where $Z \sim \mathrm{N}(0, 1)$. This shows that the sample and bootstrap t-ratios have the same asymptotic distribution.

This result motivates considering the broader situation where the sample and bootstrap t-ratios have the same asymptotic distribution but are not necessarily normal. Thus assume that

$$T \underset{d}{\longrightarrow} \xi \tag{10.30}$$

$$T^* \underset{d^*}{\longrightarrow} \xi \tag{10.31}$$

for some continuous distribution ξ. Expression (10.31) implies that the quantiles of T^* converge in probability to those of ξ, that is, $q^*_\alpha \underset{p}{\longrightarrow} q_\alpha$, where q_α is the αth quantile of ξ. This and (10.30) imply

$$\begin{aligned}
\mathbb{P}\left[\theta \in C^{\mathrm{pt}}\right] &= \mathbb{P}\left[\widehat{\theta} - s(\widehat{\theta})q^*_{1-\alpha/2} \le \theta \le \widehat{\theta} - s(\widehat{\theta})q^*_{\alpha/2}\right] \\
&= \mathbb{P}\left[q^*_{\alpha/2} \le T \le q^*_{1-\alpha/2}\right] \\
&\to \mathbb{P}\left[q_{\alpha/2} \le \xi \le q_{1-\alpha/2}\right] \\
&= 1 - \alpha.
\end{aligned}$$

Thus the percentile-t is asymptotically valid.

Theorem 10.14 If (10.30) and (10.31) hold where ξ is continuously distributed, then $\mathbb{P}\left[\theta \in C^{\mathrm{pt}}\right] \to 1 - \alpha$ as $n \to \infty$.

The bootstrap percentile-t intervals for the four estimators are reported in Table 10.2. They are similar but somewhat different from the percentile-type intervals, and generally wider. The largest difference arises with the interval for σ^2, which is noticeably wider than the other intervals.

10.20 PERCENTILE-t ASYMPTOTIC REFINEMENT

This section uses the theory of Edgeworth and Cornish-Fisher expansions introduced in Sections 9.8–9.10 of *Probability and Statistics for Economists*. This theory will not be familiar to most students. If you are interested in the following refinement theory, it is advisable to start by reading these sections of *Probability and Statistics for Economists*.

The percentile-t interval can be viewed as the intersection of two one-sided confidence intervals. In our discussion of Edgeworth expansions for the coverage probability of one-sided asymptotic confidence intervals (following Theorem 7.15 in the context of functions of regression coefficients), we found that one-sided asymptotic confidence intervals have accuracy to order $O\left(n^{-1/2}\right)$. We now show that the percentile-t interval has improved accuracy.

Theorem 9.13 of *Probability and Statistics for Economists* showed that the Cornish-Fisher expansion for the quantile q_α of a t-ratio T in the smooth function model takes the form

$$q_\alpha = z_\alpha + n^{-1/2} p_{11}(z_\alpha) + O\left(n^{-1}\right)$$

where $p_{11}(x)$ is an even polynomial of order 2 with coefficients depending on the moments up to order 8. The bootstrap quantile q_α^* has a similar Cornish-Fisher expansion:

$$q_\alpha^* = z_\alpha + n^{-1/2} p_{11}^*(z_\alpha) + O_p\left(n^{-1}\right)$$

where $p_{11}^*(x)$ is the same as $p_{11}(x)$, except that the population moments are replaced by the corresponding sample moments. Sample moments are estimated at the rate $n^{-1/2}$. Thus we can replace p_{11}^* with p_{11} without affecting the order of this expansion:

$$q_\alpha^* = z_\alpha + n^{-1/2} p_{11}(z_\alpha) + O_p\left(n^{-1}\right) = q_\alpha + O_p\left(n^{-1}\right).$$

This shows that the bootstrap quantiles q_α^* of the studentized t-ratio are within $O_p\left(n^{-1}\right)$ of the exact quantiles q_α.

By the Edgeworth expansion Delta method (Theorem 9.12 of *Probability and Statistics for Economists*), T and $T + (q_\alpha - q_\alpha^*) = T + O_p\left(n^{-1}\right)$ have the same Edgeworth expansion to order $O(n^{-1})$. Thus

$$\begin{aligned}
\mathbb{P}\left[T \le q_\alpha^*\right] &= \mathbb{P}\left[T + (q_\alpha - q_\alpha^*) \le q_\alpha\right] \\
&= \mathbb{P}\left[T \le q_\alpha\right] + O(n^{-1}) \\
&= \alpha + O(n^{-1}).
\end{aligned}$$

Thus the coverage of the percentile-t interval is

$$\begin{aligned}
\mathbb{P}\left[\theta \in C^{\mathrm{pt}}\right] &= \mathbb{P}\left[q_{\alpha/2}^* \le T \le q_{1-\alpha/2}^*\right] \\
&= \mathbb{P}\left[q_{\alpha/2} \le T \le q_{1-\alpha/2}\right] + O(n^{-1}) \\
&= 1 - \alpha + O(n^{-1}).
\end{aligned}$$

This is an improved rate of convergence relative to the one-sided asymptotic confidence interval.

Theorem 10.15 Under the assumptions of Theorem 9.11 of *Probability and Statistics for Economists*, $\mathbb{P}\left[\theta \in C^{\mathrm{pt}}\right] = 1 - \alpha + O(n^{-1})$.

The following definition of the accuracy of a confidence interval is useful.

Definition 10.3 A confidence set C for θ is kth-order accurate if

$$\mathbb{P}\left[\theta \in C\right] = 1 - \alpha + O\left(n^{-k/2}\right).$$

Examining our results, we find that one-sided asymptotic confidence intervals are first-order accurate, but percentile-t intervals are second-order accurate. When a bootstrap confidence interval (or test) achieves higher-order accuracy than the analogous asymptotic interval (or test), we say that the bootstrap method achieves an **asymptotic refinement**. Here we have shown that the percentile-t interval achieves an asymptotic refinement.

To achieve this asymptotic refinement, it is important that the t-ratio T (and its bootstrap counterpart T^*) are constructed with asymptotically valid standard errors. This is because the first term in the Edgeworth expansion is the standard normal distribution, which requires that the t-ratio is asymptotically normal. It also has the practical finite-sample implication that the accuracy of the percentile-t interval in practice depends on the accuracy of the standard errors used to construct the t-ratio.

We will not go through the details, but normal-approximation bootstrap intervals, percentile bootstrap intervals, and bias-corrected percentile bootstrap intervals are all first-order accurate and do not achieve an asymptotic refinement.

The BC_a interval, however, can be shown to be asymptotically equivalent to the percentile-t interval, and thus it achieves an asymptotic refinement. We do not make this demonstration here, as it is an advanced topic. See section 3.10.4 of P. Hall (1992).

Peter Hall

Peter Gavin Hall (1951–2016) of Australia was one of the most influential and prolific theoretical statisticians in history. He made wide-ranging contributions. Some of the most relevant for econometrics are his theoretical investigations of bootstrap methods and nonparametric kernel methods.

10.21 BOOTSTRAP HYPOTHESIS TESTS

To test the hypothesis $\mathbb{H}_0 : \theta = \theta_0$ against $\mathbb{H}_1 : \theta \neq \theta_0$, the most common approach is a t-test. We reject $\mathbb{H}_0$ in favor of $\mathbb{H}_1$ for large absolute values of the t-statistic $T = \left(\widehat{\theta} - \theta_0\right) / s(\widehat{\theta})$, where $\widehat{\theta}$ is an estimator of θ, and $s(\widehat{\theta})$ is a standard error for $\widehat{\theta}$. For a bootstrap test, we use the bootstrap algorithm to calculate the critical value.

The bootstrap algorithm samples with replacement from the dataset. Given a bootstrap sample, the bootstrap estimator $\widehat{\theta}^*$ and standard error $s(\widehat{\theta}^*)$ are calculated. Given these values, the bootstrap t-statistic is $T^* = \left(\widehat{\theta}^* - \widehat{\theta}\right) / s(\widehat{\theta}^*)$. There are two important features about the bootstrap t-statistic. First, T^* is centered at the sample estimate $\widehat{\theta}$, not at the hypothesized value θ_0. This is done because $\widehat{\theta}$ is the true value in the bootstrap universe, and the distribution of the t-statistic must be centered at the true value in the bootstrap sampling framework. Second, T^* is calculated using the bootstrap standard error $s(\widehat{\theta}^*)$. This allows the bootstrap to incorporate the randomness in standard error estimation.

The failure to properly center the bootstrap statistic at $\widehat{\theta}$ is a common error in applications. Often this is because the hypothesis to be tested is $\mathbb{H}_0 : \theta = 0$, so the test statistic is $T = \widehat{\theta}/s(\widehat{\theta})$. This intuitively suggests the bootstrap statistic $T^* = \widehat{\theta}^*/s(\widehat{\theta}^*)$, but this choice is wrong. The correct bootstrap statistic is $T^* = \left(\widehat{\theta}^* - \widehat{\theta}\right) / s(\widehat{\theta}^*)$.

The bootstrap algorithm creates B draws $T^*(b) = \left(\widehat{\theta}^*(b) - \widehat{\theta}\right) / s(\widehat{\theta}^*(b))$, $b = 1, \ldots, B$. The bootstrap $100\alpha\%$ critical value is $q^*_{1-\alpha}$, where q^*_α is the αth quantile of the absolute values of the bootstrap t-ratios $|T^*(b)|$. For a $100\alpha\%$ test, we reject $\mathbb{H}_0 : \theta = \theta_0$ in favor of $\mathbb{H}_1 : \theta \neq \theta_0$ if $|T| > q^*_{1-\alpha}$ and fail to reject if $|T| \leq q^*_{1-\alpha}$.

It is generally better to report p-values rather than critical values. Recall that a p-value is $p = 1 - G_n(|T|)$, where $G_n(u)$ is the null distribution of the statistic $|T|$. The bootstrap p-value is defined as $p^* = 1 - G_n^*(|T|)$, where $G_n^*(u)$ is the bootstrap distribution of $|T^*|$. This is estimated from the bootstrap algorithm as

$$p^* = \frac{1}{B}\sum_{b=1}^{B} \mathbb{1}\left\{\left|T^*(b)\right| > |T|\right\},$$

the percentage of bootstrap t-statistics that are larger than the observed t-statistic. Intuitively, we want to know how "unusual" the observed statistic T is when the null hypothesis is true. The bootstrap algorithm generates a large number of independent draws from the distribution T^* (which is an approximation to the unknown distribution of T). If the percentage of the $|T^*|$ that exceed $|T|$ is very small (say, 1%), this tells us that $|T|$ is an unusually large value. However, if the percentage is larger (say, 15%), then we cannot interpret $|T|$ as unusually large.

If desired, the bootstrap test can be implemented as a one-sided test. In this case, the statistic is the signed version of the t-ratio, and bootstrap critical values are calculated from the upper tail of the distribution for the alternative $\mathbb{H}_1 : \theta > \theta_0$, and from the lower tail for the alternative $\mathbb{H}_1 : \theta < \theta_0$. There is a connection between the one-sided tests and the percentile-t confidence interval. The latter is the set of parameter values θ that are not rejected by either one-sided $100\alpha/2\%$ bootstrap t-test.

Bootstrap tests can also be conducted with other statistics. When standard errors are not available or are not reliable, we can use the non-studentized statistic $T = \widehat{\theta} - \theta_0$. The bootstrap version is $T^* = \widehat{\theta}^* - \widehat{\theta}$. Let q_α^* be the αth quantile of the bootstrap statistics $\left|\widehat{\theta}^*(b) - \widehat{\theta}\right|$. A bootstrap $100\alpha\%$ test rejects $\mathbb{H}_0 : \theta = \theta_0$ if $\left|\widehat{\theta} - \theta_0\right| > q_{1-\alpha}^*$. The bootstrap p-value is

$$p^* = \frac{1}{B}\sum_{b=1}^{B} \mathbb{1}\left\{\left|\widehat{\theta}^*(b) - \widehat{\theta}\right| > \left|\widehat{\theta} - \theta_0\right|\right\}.$$

Theorem 10.16 If (10.30) and (10.31) hold where ξ is continuously distributed, then the bootstrap critical value satisfies $q_{1-\alpha}^* \underset{p}{\longrightarrow} q_{1-\alpha}$, where $q_{1-\alpha}$ is the $1-\alpha$th quantile of $|\xi|$. The bootstrap test "Reject $\mathbb{H}_0$ in favor of $\mathbb{H}_1$ if $|T| > q_{1-\alpha}^*$" has asymptotic size α: $\mathbb{P}\left[|T| > q_{1-\alpha}^* \mid \mathbb{H}_0\right] \longrightarrow \alpha$ as $n \to \infty$.

In the smooth function model, the t-test (with correct standard errors) has the following performance.

Theorem 10.17 Under the assumptions of Theorem 9.11 of *Probability and Statistics for Economists*,

$$q_{1-\alpha}^* = \bar{z}_{1-\alpha} + o_p\left(n^{-1}\right)$$

where $\bar{z}_\alpha = \Phi^{-1}\left((1+\alpha)/2\right)$ is the αth quantile of $|Z|$. The asymptotic test "Reject $\mathbb{H}_0$ in favor of $\mathbb{H}_1$ if $|T| > \bar{z}_{1-\alpha}$" has accuracy

$$\mathbb{P}\left[|T| > \bar{z}_{1-\alpha} \mid \mathbb{H}_0\right] = 1 - \alpha + O\left(n^{-1}\right)$$

and the bootstrap test "Reject $\mathbb{H}_0$ in favor of $\mathbb{H}_1$ if $|T| > q_{1-\alpha}^*$" has accuracy

$$\mathbb{P}\left[|T| > q_{1-\alpha}^* \mid \mathbb{H}_0\right] = 1 - \alpha + o\left(n^{-1}\right).$$

Theorem 10.17 shows that the bootstrap test achieves a refinement relative to the asymptotic test. The reasoning is as follows. We have shown that the Edgeworth expansion for the absolute t-ratio takes the form

$$\mathbb{P}\left[|T| \leq x\right] = 2\Phi(x) - 1 + n^{-1} 2p_2(x) + o(n^{-1}).$$

Thus the asymptotic test has accuracy of order $O(n^{-1})$.

Given the Edgeworth expansion, the Cornish-Fisher expansion for the αth quantile q_α of the distribution of $|T|$ takes the form

$$q_\alpha = \overline{z}_\alpha + n^{-1} p_{21}(\overline{z}_\alpha) + o\left(n^{-1}\right).$$

The bootstrap quantile q_α^* has the Cornish-Fisher expansion

$$\begin{aligned} q_\alpha^* &= \overline{z}_\alpha + n^{-1} p_{21}^*(\overline{z}_\alpha) + o\left(n^{-1}\right) \\ &= \overline{z}_\alpha + n^{-1} p_{21}(\overline{z}_\alpha) + o_p\left(n^{-1}\right) \\ &= q_\alpha + o_p\left(n^{-1}\right) \end{aligned}$$

where $p_{21}^*(x)$ is the same as $p_{21}(x)$, except that the population moments are replaced by the corresponding sample moments. The bootstrap test has rejection probability, using the Edgeworth expansion Delta method (Theorem 11.12 of of *Probability and Statistics for Economists*), of

$$\begin{aligned} \mathbb{P}\left[|T| > q_{1-\alpha}^* | \mathbb{H}_0\right] &= \mathbb{P}\left[|T| + (q_{1-\alpha} - q_{1-\alpha}^*) > q_{1-\alpha}\right] \\ &= \mathbb{P}\left[|T| > q_{1-\alpha}\right] + o(n^{-1}) \\ &= 1 - \alpha + o(n^{-1}) \end{aligned}$$

as claimed.

10.22 WALD-TYPE BOOTSTRAP TESTS

If θ is a vector, then to test $\mathbb{H}_0 : \theta = \theta_0$ against $\mathbb{H}_1 : \theta \neq \theta_0$ at size α, a common test is based on the Wald statistic $W = \left(\widehat{\theta} - \theta_0\right)' \widehat{\boldsymbol{V}}_{\widehat{\theta}}^{-1} \left(\widehat{\theta} - \theta_0\right)$, where $\widehat{\theta}$ is an estimator of θ, and $\widehat{\boldsymbol{V}}_{\widehat{\theta}}$ is a covariance matrix estimator. For a bootstrap test, we use the bootstrap algorithm to calculate the critical value.

The bootstrap algorithm samples with replacement from the dataset. Given a bootstrap sample, the bootstrap estimator $\widehat{\theta}^*$ and covariance matrix estimator $\widehat{\boldsymbol{V}}_{\widehat{\theta}}^*$ are calculated. Given these values, the bootstrap Wald statistic is

$$W^* = \left(\widehat{\theta}^* - \widehat{\theta}\right)' \widehat{\boldsymbol{V}}_{\widehat{\theta}}^{*-1} \left(\widehat{\theta}^* - \widehat{\theta}\right).$$

As for the t-test, it is essential that the bootstrap Wald statistic W^* is centered at the sample estimator $\widehat{\theta}$ instead of the hypothesized value θ_0. This is because $\widehat{\theta}$ is the true value in the bootstrap universe.

Based on B bootstrap replications, we calculate the αth quantile q_α^* of the distribution of the bootstrap Wald statistics W^*. The bootstrap test rejects $\mathbb{H}_0$ in favor of $\mathbb{H}_1$ if $W > q_{1-\alpha}^*$. More commonly, we calculate a bootstrap p-value:

$$p^* = \frac{1}{B} \sum_{b=1}^{B} \mathbb{1}\left\{W^*(b) > W\right\}.$$

The asymptotic performance of the Wald test mimics that of the t-test. In general, the bootstrap Wald test is first-order correct (achieves the correct size asymptotically) and under conditions for which an Edgeworth expansion exists, has accuracy

$$\mathbb{P}\left[W > q^*_{1-\alpha} \mid \mathbb{H}_0\right] = 1 - \alpha + o(n^{-1})$$

and thus achieves a refinement relative to the asymptotic Wald test.

If a reliable covariance matrix estimator $\widehat{\boldsymbol{V}}_{\widehat{\theta}}$ is not available, a Wald-type test can be implemented with any positive-definite weight matrix instead of $\widehat{\boldsymbol{V}}_{\widehat{\theta}}$. This includes simple choices, such as the identity matrix. The bootstrap algorithm can be used to calculate critical values and p-values for the test. So long as the estimator $\widehat{\theta}$ has an asymptotic distribution, this bootstrap test will be asymptotically first-order valid. The test will not achieve an asymptotic refinement but provides a simple method to test hypotheses when covariance matrix estimates are not available.

10.23 CRITERION-BASED BOOTSTRAP TESTS

A criterion-based estimator takes the form

$$\widehat{\beta} = \underset{\beta}{\operatorname{argmin}}\ J(\beta)$$

for some criterion function $J(\beta)$. This includes least squares, maximum likelihood, and minimum distance. Given a hypothesis $\mathbb{H}_0 : \theta = \theta_0$ where $\theta = r(\beta)$, the restricted estimator that satisfies $\mathbb{H}_0$ is

$$\widetilde{\beta} = \underset{r(\beta)=\theta_0}{\operatorname{argmin}}\ J(\beta).$$

A criterion-based statistic to test $\mathbb{H}_0$ is

$$J = \min_{r(\beta)=\theta_0} J(\beta) - \min_{\beta} J(\beta) = J(\widetilde{\beta}) - J(\widehat{\beta}).$$

A criterion-based test rejects $\mathbb{H}_0$ for large values of J. A bootstrap test uses the bootstrap algorithm to calculate the critical value.

In this context, we need to be a bit thoughtful about how to construct bootstrap versions of J. It might seem natural to construct the same statistic on the bootstrap samples as on the original sample, but this approach is incorrect. It makes the same error as calculating a t-ratio or Wald statistic centered at the hypothesized value. In the bootstrap universe, the true value of θ is not θ_0; instead it is $\widehat{\theta} = r\left(\widehat{\beta}\right)$. Thus when using the nonparametric bootstrap, we want to impose the constraint $r(\beta) = r\left(\widehat{\beta}\right) = \widehat{\theta}$ to obtain the bootstrap version of J.

Thus, the correct way to calculate a bootstrap version of J is as follows. Generate a bootstrap sample by random sampling from the dataset. Let $J^*(\beta)$ be the the bootstrap version of the criterion. On a bootstrap sample, calculate the unrestricted estimator $\widehat{\beta}^* = \underset{\beta}{\operatorname{argmin}}\ J^*(\beta)$ and the restricted version $\widetilde{\beta}^* = \underset{r(\beta)=\widehat{\theta}}{\operatorname{argmin}}\ J^*(\beta)$, where $\widehat{\theta} = r\left(\widehat{\beta}\right)$. The bootstrap statistic is

$$J^* = \min_{r(\beta)=\widehat{\theta}} J^*(\beta) - \min_{\beta} J^*(\beta) = J^*(\widetilde{\beta}^*) - J^*(\widehat{\beta}^*).$$

Calculate J^* on each bootstrap sample. Take the $1-\alpha$th quantile $q^*_{1-\alpha}$. The bootstrap test rejects $\mathbb{H}_0$ in favor of $\mathbb{H}_1$ if $J > q^*_{1-\alpha}$. The bootstrap p-value is

$$p^* = \frac{1}{B}\sum_{b=1}^{B} \mathbb{1}\left\{J^*(b) > J\right\}.$$

Special cases of criterion-based tests are minimum distance tests, F tests, and likelihood ratio tests. Take the F test for a linear hypothesis $\boldsymbol{R}'\beta = \theta_0$. The F statistic is

$$\mathrm{F} = \frac{\left(\widetilde{\sigma}^2 - \widehat{\sigma}^2\right)/q}{\widehat{\sigma}^2/(n-k)}$$

where $\widehat{\sigma}^2$ is the unrestricted estimator of the error variance, $\widetilde{\sigma}^2$ is the restricted estimator, q is the number of restrictions, and k is the number of estimated coefficients. The bootstrap version of the F statistic is

$$\mathrm{F}^* = \frac{\left(\widetilde{\sigma}^{*2} - \widehat{\sigma}^{*2}\right)/q}{\widehat{\sigma}^{*2}/(n-k)}$$

where $\widehat{\sigma}^{*2}$ is the unrestricted estimator on the bootstrap sample, and $\widetilde{\sigma}^{*2}$ is the restricted estimator, which imposes the restriction $\widehat{\theta} = \boldsymbol{R}'\widehat{\beta}$.

Take the likelihood ratio (LR) test for the hypothesis $r(\beta) = \theta_0$. The LR test statistic is

$$\mathrm{LR} = 2\left(\ell_n\left(\widehat{\beta}\right) - \ell_n\left(\widetilde{\beta}\right)\right)$$

where $\widehat{\beta}$ is the unrestricted MLE, and $\widetilde{\beta}$ is the restricted MLE (imposing $r(\beta) = \theta_0$). The bootstrap version is

$$\mathrm{LR}^* = 2\left(\ell^*_n\left(\widehat{\beta}^*\right) - \ell^*_n\left(\widetilde{\beta}^*\right)\right)$$

where $\ell^*_n(\beta)$ is the log-likelihood function calculated on the bootstrap sample, $\widehat{\beta}^*$ is the unrestricted maximizer, and $\widetilde{\beta}^*$ is the restricted maximizer imposing the restriction $r(\beta) = r\left(\widehat{\beta}\right)$.

10.24 PARAMETRIC BOOTSTRAP

Throughout this chapter, we have described the most popular form of the bootstrap known as the nonparametric bootstrap. However, there are other forms of the bootstrap algorithm, including the parametric bootstrap. This form is appropriate when there is a full parametric model for the distribution, as in likelihood estimation.

First, consider the context where the model specifies the full distribution of the random vector Y (e.g., $Y \sim F(y \mid \beta)$), where the distribution function F is known but the parameter β is unknown. Let $\widehat{\beta}$ be an estimator of β, such as the maximum likelihood estimator. The parametric bootstrap algorithm generates bootstrap observations Y^*_i by drawing random vectors from the distribution function $F(y \mid \widehat{\beta})$. When this is done, the true value of β in the bootstrap universe is $\widehat{\beta}$. Everything that has been discussed in this chapter also applies when using this bootstrap algorithm.

Second, consider the context where the model specifies the conditional distribution of the random vector Y given the random vector X (i.e., $Y \mid X \sim F(y \mid X, \beta)$). An example is the normal linear regression model, where $Y \mid X \sim \mathrm{N}\left(X'\beta, \sigma^2\right)$. In this context, we can hold the regressors X_i fixed and then draw the bootstrap observations Y^*_i from the conditional distribution $F(y \mid X_i, \widehat{\beta})$. In the example of the normal regression model, this is equivalent to drawing a normal error $e^*_i \sim \mathrm{N}\left(0, \widehat{\sigma}^2\right)$ and then setting $Y^*_i = X'_i\widehat{\beta} + e^*_i$. Again, in this algorithm, the true value of β is $\widehat{\beta}$ and everything discussed in this chapter can be applied as before.

Third, consider tests of the hypothesis $r(\beta)=\theta_0$. In this context, we can also construct a restricted estimator $\widetilde{\beta}$ (e.g., the restricted MLE) that satisfies the hypothesis $r\left(\widetilde{\beta}\right)=\theta_0$. Then we can generate bootstrap samples by simulating from the distribution $Y_i^* \sim F(y \mid \widetilde{\beta})$, or in the conditional context from $Y_i^* \sim F(y \mid X_i, \widetilde{\beta})$. When this is done, the true value of β in the bootstrap is $\widetilde{\beta}$, which satisfies the hypothesis. So in this context, the correct values of the bootstrap statistics are

$$T^* = \frac{\widehat{\theta}^* - \theta_0}{s(\widehat{\theta}^*)}$$

$$W^* = \left(\widehat{\theta}^* - \theta_0\right)' \widehat{\boldsymbol{V}}_{\widehat{\theta}}^{*-1} \left(\widehat{\theta}^* - \theta_0\right)$$

$$J^* = \min_{r(\beta)=\theta_0} J^*(\beta) - \min_{\beta} J^*(\beta)$$

$$\mathrm{LR}^* = 2\left(\max_{\beta} \ell_n^*(\beta) - \max_{r(\beta)=\theta_0} \ell_n^*(\beta)\right)$$

and

$$\mathrm{F}^* = \frac{\left(\widetilde{\sigma}^{*2} - \widehat{\sigma}^{*2}\right)/q}{\widehat{\sigma}^{*2}/(n-k)}$$

where $\widehat{\sigma}^{*2}$ is the unrestricted estimator on the bootstrap sample, and $\widetilde{\sigma}^{*2}$ is the restricted estimator that imposes the restriction $\boldsymbol{R}'\beta=\theta_0$.

The primary advantage of the parametric bootstrap (relative to the nonparametric bootstrap) is that it will be more accurate when the parametric model is correct, which may be quite important in small samples. The primary disadvantage of the parametric bootstrap is that it can be inaccurate when the parametric model is incorrect.

10.25 HOW MANY BOOTSTRAP REPLICATIONS?

How many bootstrap replications should be used? No universally correct answer is available, as there is a trade-off between accuracy and computation cost. Computation cost is essentially linear in B. Accuracy (either standard errors or p-values) is proportional to $B^{-1/2}$. Improved accuracy can be obtained, but only at a higher computational cost.

In most empirical research, most calculations are quick and investigatory, not requiring full accuracy. But final results (those going into the final version of the paper) should be accurate. Thus it seems reasonable to use asymptotic and/or bootstrap methods with a modest number of replications for daily calculations, but use a much larger B for the final version.

In particular, for final calculations, $B=10,000$ is desired, with $B=1000$ a minimal choice. In contrast, for daily quick calculations, values as low as $B=100$ may be sufficient for rough estimates.

A useful way to think about the accuracy of bootstrap methods stems from the calculation of p-values. The bootstrap p-value p^* is an average of B Bernoulli draws. The variance of the simulation estimator of p^* is $p^*(1-p^*)/B$, which is bounded above by $1/4B$. To calculate the p-value within, say, 0.01 of the true value with 95% probability requires a standard error below 0.005. This is ensured if $B \geq 10,000$.

Stata by default sets $B=50$. This is useful for verification that a program runs but is a poor choice for empirical reporting. Make sure that you set B to the value you want.

10.26 SETTING THE BOOTSTRAP SEED

Computers do not generate true random numbers but rather pseudo-random numbers generated by a deterministic algorithm. The algorithms generate sequences that are indistinguishable from random sequences, so this is not a worry for bootstrap applications.

The methods, however, necessarily require a starting value known as a "seed." Some packages (including Stata and MATLAB) implement this with a default seed that is reset each time the statistical package is started. Thus if you start the package fresh, run a bootstrap program (e.g., a "do" file in Stata), exit the package, restart the package and then rerun the bootstrap program, you should obtain exactly the same results. If you instead run the bootstrap program (e.g., "do" file) twice sequentially without restarting the package, the seed is not reset, so a different set of pseudo-random numbers will be generated, and the results from the two runs will be different.

The R package has a different implementation. When R is loaded, the random number seed is generated based on the computer's clock (which results in an essentially random starting seed). Therefore, if you run a bootstrap program in R, exit, restart, and rerun, you will obtain a different set of random draws and thus a different bootstrap result.

Packages allow users to set their own seed. (In Stata, the command is `set seed #`. In MATLAB, the command is `rng(#)`. In R, the command is `set.seed(#)`.) If the seed is set to a specific number at the start of a file, then the same pseudo-random numbers will be generated each time the program is run. If this is the case, the results of a bootstrap calculation (standard error or test) will be identical across computer runs.

The fact that the bootstrap results can be fixed by setting the seed in the replication file has motivated many researchers to follow this choice. They set the seed at the start of the replication file, so that repeated executions result in the same numerical findings.

Fixing seeds, however, should be done cautiously. It may be a wise choice for a final calculation (when a paper is finished) but is an unwise choice for daily calculations. If you use a small number of replications in your preliminary work (say, $B = 100$) then the bootstrap calculations will be inaccurate. But as you run your results again and again (as is typical in empirical projects), you will obtain the same numerical standard errors and test results, giving you a false sense of stability and accuracy. If instead a different seed is used each time the program is run, then the bootstrap results will vary across runs, and you will observe that the results vary across these runs, giving you important and meaningful information about the (lack of) accuracy in your results. One way to ensure this is to set the seed according to the current clock. In MATLAB, use the command `rng('shuffle')`. In R, use `set.seed(seed=NULL)`. Stata does not have this option.

These considerations lead to a recommended hybrid approach. For daily empirical investigations, do not fix the bootstrap seed in your program unless you have it set by the clock. For your final calculations, set the seed to a specific arbitrary choice, and set $B = 10,000$, so that the results are insensitive to the seed.

10.27 BOOTSTRAP REGRESSION

A major focus of this textbook has been on the least squares estimator $\widehat{\beta}$ in the projection model. The bootstrap can be used to calculate standard errors and confidence intervals for smooth functions of the coefficient estimates.

The nonparametric bootstrap algorithm, as described in Section 10.6, samples observations randomly with replacement from the dataset, creating the bootstrap sample $\{(Y_1^*, X_1^*), \ldots, (Y_n^*, X_n^*)\}$, or in matrix notation, $(\boldsymbol{Y}^*, \boldsymbol{X}^*)$. It is important to recognize that entire observations (pairs of Y_i and X_i) are sampled. This is often called the **pairs bootstrap**.

Given this bootstrap sample, we calculate the regression estimator

$$\widehat{\beta}^* = \left(\boldsymbol{X}^{*\prime}\boldsymbol{X}^*\right)^{-1}\left(\boldsymbol{X}^{*\prime}\boldsymbol{Y}^*\right). \tag{10.32}$$

This is repeated B times. The bootstrap standard errors are the standard deviations across the draws, and confidence intervals are constructed from the empirical quantiles across the draws.

What is the nature of the bootstrap distribution of $\widehat{\beta}^*$? It is useful to start with the distribution of the bootstrap observations $\left(Y_i^*, X_i^*\right)$, which is the discrete distribution that puts weight $1/n$ on each observation pair (Y_i, X_i). The bootstrap universe can be thought of as the empirical scatter plot of the observations. The true value of the projection coefficient in this bootstrap universe is

$$\left(\mathbb{E}^*\left[X_i^* X_i^{*\prime}\right]\right)^{-1}\left(\mathbb{E}^*\left[X_i^* Y_i^*\right]\right) = \left(\frac{1}{n}\sum_{i=1}^n X_i X_i'\right)^{-1}\left(\frac{1}{n}\sum_{i=1}^n X_i Y_i\right) = \widehat{\beta}.$$

We see that the true value in the bootstrap distribution is the least squares estimator $\widehat{\beta}$.

The bootstrap observations satisfy the projection equation

$$\begin{aligned} Y_i^* &= X_i^{*\prime}\widehat{\beta} + e_i^* \\ \mathbb{E}^*\left[X_i^* e_i^*\right] &= 0. \end{aligned} \tag{10.33}$$

For each bootstrap pair $\left(Y_i^*, X_i^*\right) = \left(Y_j, X_j\right)$, the true error $e_i^* = \widehat{e}_j$ equals the least squares residual from the original dataset. This is because each bootstrap pair corresponds to an actual observation.

A technical problem (which is typically ignored) is that it is possible for $\boldsymbol{X}^{*\prime}\boldsymbol{X}^*$ to be singular in a simulated bootstrap sample, in which case, the least squares estimator $\widehat{\beta}^*$ is not uniquely defined. Indeed, the probability is positive that $\boldsymbol{X}^{*\prime}\boldsymbol{X}^*$ is singular. For example, the probability that a bootstrap sample consists entirely of one observation repeated n times is $n^{-(n-1)}$. This is a small probability, but it is positive. A more significant example is sparse dummy variable designs, where it is possible to draw an entire sample with only one observed value for the dummy variable. For example, if a sample has $n = 20$ observations with a dummy variable with treatment (equals 1) for only 3 of the 20 observations, the probability is 4% that a bootstrap sample contains entirely nontreated values (all 0s). 4% is quite high!

The standard approach to circumvent this problem is to compute $\widehat{\beta}^*$ only if $\boldsymbol{X}^{*\prime}\boldsymbol{X}^*$ is nonsingular, as defined by a conventional numerical tolerance, and treat it as missing otherwise. A better solution is to define a tolerance that bounds $\boldsymbol{X}^{*\prime}\boldsymbol{X}^*$ away from nonsingularity. Define the ratio of the smallest eigenvalue of the bootstrap design matrix to that of the data design matrix:

$$\lambda^* = \frac{\lambda_{\min}\left(\boldsymbol{X}^{*\prime}\boldsymbol{X}^*\right)}{\lambda_{\min}\left(\boldsymbol{X}'\boldsymbol{X}\right)}.$$

If, in a given bootstrap replication, $\lambda^* < \tau$ is smaller than a given tolerance (Shao and Tu (1995, p. 291) recommend $\tau = 1/2$), then the estimator can be treated as missing, or we can define the trimming rule:

$$\widehat{\beta}^* = \begin{cases} \widehat{\beta}^* & \text{if } \lambda^* \geq \tau \\ \widehat{\beta} & \text{if } \lambda^* < \tau. \end{cases} \tag{10.34}$$

This ensures that the bootstrap estimator $\widehat{\beta}^*$ will be well behaved.

10.28 BOOTSTRAP REGRESSION ASYMPTOTIC THEORY

Define the least squares estimator $\widehat{\beta}$, its bootstrap version $\widehat{\beta}^*$ as in (10.32), and the transformations $\widehat{\theta} = g(\widehat{\beta})$ and $\widehat{\theta}^* = r(\widehat{\beta}^*)$ for some smooth transformation r. Let $\widehat{\boldsymbol{V}}_\beta$ and $\widehat{\boldsymbol{V}}_\theta$ denote heteroskedasticity-robust covariance matrix estimators for $\widehat{\beta}$ and $\widehat{\theta}$, and let $\widehat{\boldsymbol{V}}^*_\beta$ and $\widehat{\boldsymbol{V}}^*_\theta$ be their bootstrap versions. When θ is scalar, define the standard errors $s(\widehat{\theta}) = \sqrt{n^{-1}\widehat{\boldsymbol{V}}_\theta}$ and $s(\widehat{\theta}^*) = \sqrt{n^{-1}\widehat{\boldsymbol{V}}_{\theta^*}}$. Define the t-ratios $T = \left(\widehat{\theta} - \theta\right)/s(\widehat{\theta})$ and the bootstrap version $T^* = \left(\widehat{\theta}^* - \widehat{\theta}\right)/s(\widehat{\theta}^*)$. We are interested in the asymptotic distributions of $\widehat{\beta}^*$, $\widehat{\theta}^*$, and T^*.

Since the bootstrap observations satisfy the model (10.33), we see by standard calculations that

$$\sqrt{n}\left(\widehat{\beta}^* - \widehat{\beta}\right) = \left(\frac{1}{n}\sum_{i=1}^n X_i^* X_i^{*\prime}\right)^{-1}\left(\frac{1}{\sqrt{n}}\sum_{i=1}^n X_i^* e_i^*\right).$$

By the bootstrap WLLN,

$$\frac{1}{n}\sum_{i=1}^n X_i^* X_i^{*\prime} \underset{p^*}{\longrightarrow} \mathbb{E}\left[X_i X_i'\right] = \boldsymbol{Q}$$

and by the bootstrap CLT,

$$\frac{1}{\sqrt{n}}\sum_{i=1}^n X_i^* e_i^* \underset{d^*}{\longrightarrow} \mathrm{N}(0, \Omega)$$

where $\Omega = \mathbb{E}\left[XX'e^2\right]$. Again applying the bootstrap WLLN, we obtain

$$\widehat{\boldsymbol{V}}_\beta \underset{p^*}{\longrightarrow} \boldsymbol{V}_\beta = \boldsymbol{Q}^{-1}\Omega\boldsymbol{Q}^{-1}$$

and

$$\widehat{\boldsymbol{V}}_\theta \underset{p^*}{\longrightarrow} \boldsymbol{V}_\theta = \boldsymbol{R}'\boldsymbol{V}_\beta\boldsymbol{R}$$

where $\boldsymbol{R} = \boldsymbol{R}(\beta)$.

Combining with the bootstrap CMT and delta method, we establish the asymptotic distribution of the bootstrap regression estimator.

Theorem 10.18 Under Assumption 7.2, as $n \to \infty$

$$\sqrt{n}\left(\widehat{\theta}^* - \widehat{\theta}\right) \underset{d^*}{\longrightarrow} \mathrm{N}\left(0, \boldsymbol{V}_\beta\right).$$

If Assumption 7.3 also holds, then

$$\sqrt{n}\left(\widehat{\theta}^* - \widehat{\theta}\right) \underset{d^*}{\longrightarrow} \mathrm{N}(0, \boldsymbol{V}_\theta).$$

If Assumption 7.4 also holds, then

$$T^* \underset{d^*}{\longrightarrow} \mathrm{N}(0, 1).$$

Thus the bootstrap confidence interval and testing methods all apply for inference on β and θ. This includes the percentile, BC percentile, BC_a, and percentile-t intervals, and hypothesis tests based on t-tests, Wald tests, MD tests, LR tests, and F tests.

To justify bootstrap standard errors, we also need to verify the uniform square integrability of $\widehat{\beta}^*$ and $\widehat{\theta}^*$. This is technically challenging, because the least squares estimator involves matrix inversion, which is not globally continuous. A partial solution is to use the trimmed estimator (10.34). This bounds the moments of $\widehat{\beta}^*$ by those of $n^{-1}\sum_{i=1}^{n} X_i^* e_i^*$. Since this is a sample mean, Theorem 10.10 applies, and $\widehat{\boldsymbol{V}}_\beta^*$ is bootstrap consistent for $\boldsymbol{V}_\beta$. However, this does not ensure that $\widehat{\boldsymbol{V}}_\theta^*$ will be consistent for $\widehat{\boldsymbol{V}}_\theta$ unless the function $r(x)$ satisfies the conditions of Theorem 10.10. For general applications, use a trimmed estimator for the bootstrap variance. For some $\tau_n = O\left(e^{n/8}\right)$, define

$$Z_n^* = \sqrt{n}\left(\widehat{\theta}^* - \widehat{\theta}\right)$$
$$Z^{**} = z^* \mathbb{1}\left\{\left\|Z_n^*\right\| \le \tau_n\right\}$$
$$Z^{**} = \frac{1}{B}\sum_{b=1}^{B} Z^{**}(b)$$
$$\widehat{\boldsymbol{V}}_\theta^{\text{boot},\tau} = \frac{1}{B-1}\sum_{b=1}^{B}\left(Z^{**}(b) - Z^{**}\right)\left(Z^{**}(b) - Z^{**}\right)'.$$

The matrix $\widehat{\boldsymbol{V}}_\theta^{\text{boot}}$ is a trimmed bootstrap estimator of the variance of $Z_n = \sqrt{n}\left(\widehat{\theta} - \theta\right)$. The associated bootstrap standard error for $\widehat{\theta}$ (in the scalar case) is $s(\widehat{\theta}) = \sqrt{n^{-1}\widehat{\boldsymbol{V}}_\theta^{\text{boot}}}$.

By an application of Theorems 10.11 and 10.12, we find that this estimator $\widehat{\boldsymbol{V}}_\theta^{\text{boot}}$ is consistent for the asymptotic variance.

Theorem 10.19 Under Assumptions 7.2 and 7.3, as $n \to \infty$, $\widehat{\boldsymbol{V}}_\theta^{\text{boot},\tau} \underset{p^*}{\longrightarrow} \boldsymbol{V}_\theta$.

Programs such as Stata use the untrimmed estimator $\widehat{\boldsymbol{V}}_\theta^{\text{boot}}$ rather than the trimmed estimator $\widehat{\boldsymbol{V}}_\theta^{\text{boot},\tau}$. Thus we should be cautious about interpreting reported bootstrap standard errors, especially for nonlinear functions, such as ratios.

10.29 WILD BOOTSTRAP

Take the linear regression model

$$Y = X'\beta + e$$
$$\mathbb{E}\left[e \mid X\right] = 0.$$

What is special about this model is the conditional mean restriction. The nonparametric bootstrap (which samples the pairs $\left(Y_i^*, X_i^*\right)$ i.i.d. from the original observations) does not make use of this restriction. Consequently, the bootstrap distribution for (Y^*, X^*) does not satisfy the conditional mean restriction and therefore does not satisfy the linear regression assumption. To improve precision, it seems reasonable to impose the conditional mean restriction on the bootstrap distribution.

A natural approach is to hold the regressors X_i fixed and then draw the errors e_i^* in some way that imposes a conditional mean of 0. The simplest approach is to draw the errors independent from the regressors, perhaps from the empirical distribution of the residuals. This procedure is known as the **residual bootstrap**. However, this approach imposes independence of the errors from the regressors, which is much stronger than the conditional mean assumption. This is generally undesirable.

A method that imposes the conditional mean restriction while allowing general heteroskedasticity is the **wild bootstrap**. It was proposed by Liu (1988) and extended by Mammen (1993). The method uses auxiliary random variables ξ^*, which are i.i.d., mean 0, and variance 1. The bootstrap observations are then generated as $Y_i^* = X_i'\widehat{\beta} + e_i^*$ with $e_i^* = \widehat{e}_i \xi_i^*$, where the regressors X_i are held fixed at their sample values, $\widehat{\beta}$ is the sample least squares estimator, and $\widehat{e}_i$ are the least squares residuals, which are also held fixed at their sample values.

This algorithm generates bootstrap errors e_i^* that are conditionally mean 0. Thus the bootstrap pairs (Y_i^*, X_i) satisfy a linear regression with the "true" coefficient of $\widehat{\beta}$. The conditional variance of the wild bootstrap errors e_i^* are $\mathbb{E}^*\left[e_i^{*2} \mid X_i\right] = \widehat{e}_i^2$. Thus the conditional variance of the bootstrap estimator $\widehat{\beta}^*$ is

$$\mathbb{E}^*\left[\left(\widehat{\beta}^* - \widehat{\beta}\right)\left(\widehat{\beta}^* - \widehat{\beta}\right)' \mid \boldsymbol{X}\right] = \left(\boldsymbol{X}'\boldsymbol{X}\right)^{-1}\left(\sum_{i=1}^{n} X_i X_i' \widehat{e}_i^2\right)\left(\boldsymbol{X}'\boldsymbol{X}\right)^{-1}$$

which is the White estimator of the variance of $\widehat{\beta}$. Thus the wild bootstrap replicates the appropriate first and second moments of the distribution.

Two distributions have been proposed for the auxilary variables ξ_i^*, both of which are two-point discrete distributions. The first are **Rademacher** random variables, which satisfy $\mathbb{P}\left[\xi^* = 1\right] = \frac{1}{2}$ and $\mathbb{P}\left[\xi^* = -1\right] = \frac{1}{2}$. The second is the Mammen (1993) two-point distribution:

$$\mathbb{P}\left[\xi^* = \frac{1+\sqrt{5}}{2}\right] = \frac{\sqrt{5}-1}{2\sqrt{5}}$$

$$\mathbb{P}\left[\xi^* = \frac{1-\sqrt{5}}{2}\right] = \frac{\sqrt{5}+1}{2\sqrt{5}}.$$

The reasoning behind the Mammen distribution is that this choice implies $\mathbb{E}\left[\xi^{*3}\right] = 1$, which implies that the third central moment of $\widehat{\beta}^*$ matches the natural nonparametric estimator of the third central moment of $\widehat{\beta}$. Since the wild bootstrap matches the first three moments, the percentile-t interval and one-sided t-tests can be shown to achieve asymptotic refinements.

The reasoning behind the Rademacher distribution is that this choice implies $\mathbb{E}\left[\xi^{*4}\right] = 1$, which implies that the fourth central moment of $\widehat{\beta}^*$ matches the natural nonparametric estimator of the fourth central moment of $\widehat{\beta}$. If the regression errors e are symmetrically distributed (so the third moment is 0), then the first four moments are matched. In this case, the wild bootstrap should have even better performance, and additionally two-sided t-tests can be shown to achieve an asymptotic refinement. When the regression error is not symmetrically distributed, these asymptotic refinements are not achieved. Limited simulation evidence for one-sided t-tests presented in Davidson and Flachaire (2008) suggests that the Rademacher distribution (used with the restricted wild bootstrap) has better performance and is their recommendation.

For hypothesis testing, improved precision can be obtained by the **restricted wild bootstrap**. Consider tests of the hypothesis $\mathbb{H}_0 : r(\beta) = 0$. Let $\widetilde{\beta}$ be a CLS or EMD estimator of β subject to the restriction $r\left(\widetilde{\beta}\right) = 0$. Let $\widetilde{e}_i = Y_i - X_i'\widetilde{\beta}$ be the constrained residuals. The restricted wild bootstrap algorithm generates observations as $Y_i^* = X_i'\widetilde{\beta} + e_i^*$, with $e_i^* = \widetilde{e}_i \xi_i^*$. With this modification, $\widetilde{\beta}$ is the true value in the bootstrap universe, so the null hypothesis $\mathbb{H}_0$ holds. Thus bootstrap tests are constructed in the same way as for the parametric bootstrap using a restricted parameter estimator.

10.30 BOOTSTRAP FOR CLUSTERED OBSERVATIONS

Bootstrap methods can also be applied in to clustered samples, though the methodological literature is relatively thin. Here we review methods discussed in Cameron, Gelbach, and Miller (2008).

Let $\boldsymbol{Y}_g = (Y_{1g}, \ldots, Y_{n_g g})'$ and $\boldsymbol{X}_g = (X_{1g}, \ldots, X_{n_g g})'$ denote the $n_g \times 1$ vector of dependent variables and $n_g \times k$ matrix of regressors for the gth cluster, respectively. A linear regression model using cluster notation is $\boldsymbol{Y}_g = \boldsymbol{X}_g \beta + \boldsymbol{e}_g$, where $\boldsymbol{e}_g = (e_{1g}, \ldots, e_{n_g g})'$ is an $n_g \times 1$ error vector. The sample has G cluster pairs $(\boldsymbol{Y}_g, \boldsymbol{X}_g)$.

The **pairs cluster bootstrap** samples G cluster pairs $(\boldsymbol{Y}_g, \boldsymbol{X}_g)$ to create the bootstrap sample. Least squares is applied to the bootstrap sample to obtain the coefficient estimators. By repeating B times, bootstrap standard errors for coefficients estimates, or functions of the coefficient estimates, can be calculated. Percentile, BC percentile, and BC_a confidence intervals can be calculated.

The BC_a interval requires an estimator of the acceleration coefficient a, which is a scaled jackknife estimate of the third moment of the estimator. In the context of clustered observations, the delete-cluster jackknife should be used for estimation of a.

Furthermore, for each bootstrap sample, the cluster-robust standard errors can be calculated and used to compute bootstrap t-ratios, from which percentile-t confidence intervals can be calculated.

The **wild cluster bootstrap** fixes the clusters and regressors, and it generates the bootstrap observations as

$$\boldsymbol{Y}_g^* = \boldsymbol{X}_g \widehat{\beta} + \boldsymbol{e}_g^*$$

$$\boldsymbol{e}_g^* = \widehat{\boldsymbol{e}}_g \xi_g^*$$

where ξ_g^* is a scalar auxilary random variable, as described in Section 10.29. Notice that ξ_g^* is interacted with the entire vector of residuals from cluster g. Cameron, Gelbach, and Miller (2008) follow the recommendation of Davidson and Flachaire (2008) and use Rademacher random variables for ξ_g^*.

For hypothesis testing, Cameron, Gelbach, and Miller (2008) recommend the **restricted wild cluster bootstrap**. For tests of $\mathbb{H}_0 : r(\beta) = 0$, let $\widetilde{\beta}$ be a CLS or EMD estimator of β subject to the restriction $r\left(\widetilde{\beta}\right) = 0$. Let $\widetilde{\boldsymbol{e}}_g = \boldsymbol{Y}_g - \boldsymbol{X}_g \widetilde{\beta}$ be the constrained cluster-level residuals. The restricted wild cluster bootstrap algorithm generates observations as

$$\boldsymbol{Y}_g^* = \boldsymbol{X}_g \widetilde{\beta} + \boldsymbol{e}_g^*$$

$$\boldsymbol{e}_g^* = \widetilde{\boldsymbol{e}}_g \xi_g^*.$$

On each bootstrap sample, the test statistic for $\mathbb{H}_0$ (t-ratio, Wald, LR, or F) is applied. Since the bootstrap algorithm satisfies $\mathbb{H}_0$, these statistics are centered at the hypothesized value. p-Values are then calculated conventionally and used to assess the significance of the test statistic.

Conventional asymptotic approximations may work poorly with clustered observations for several reasons. First, while the sample size n may be large, the effective sample size is the number of clusters G. This is because when the dependence structure in each cluster is unconstrained, the central limit theorem effectively treats each cluster as a single observation. Thus, if G is small, we should treat inference as a small-sample problem. Second, cluster-robust covariance matrix estimation explicitly treats each cluster as a single observation. Consequently, the accuracy of normal approximations to t-ratios and Wald statistics is more accurately viewed as a small-sample distribution problem. Third, when cluster sizes n_g are heterogeneous, the estimation problems just described also involve heterogeneous variances. Specifically, heterogeneous cluster sizes induce a high degree of effective heteroskedasticity (since the variance of a within-cluster sum is proportional to n_g). When G is small, this means that cluster-robust inference is similar to finite-sample inference with a small heteroskedastic sample. Fourth, interest is often focused on treatment that is applied at the level of a cluster

Table 10.4
Comparison of methods for estimate of effect of tracking

Coefficient on *Tracking*	0.138
Asymptotic cluster s.e.	(0.078)
Jackknife cluster s.e.	(0.078)
Cluster bootstrap s.e.	(0.078)
95% percentile interval	[−0.013, 0.291]
95% BC percentile interval	[−0.015, 0.289]
95% BC$_a$ percentile interval	[−0.018, 0.286]

(such as the effect of tracking, discussed in Section 4.21). If the number of treated clusters is small, this is equivalent to estimation with a highly sparse dummy variable design, in which case cluster-robust covariance matrix estimation can be unreliable.

These concerns suggest that conventional normal approximations may be poor in the context of clustered observations with a small number of groups G, motivating the use of bootstrap methods. However, these concerns also can cause challenges with the accuracy of bootstrap approximations. When the number of clusters G is small, the cluster sizes n_g heterogeneous, or the number of treated clusters small, bootstrap methods may be inaccurate. In such cases, inference should proceed cautiously.

To illustrate the use of the pairs cluster bootstrap, Table 10.4 reports the estimates of the example from Section 4.21 of the effect of tracking on test scores from Duflo, Dupas, and Kremer (2011). In addition to the asymptotic cluster standard error, we report the cluster jackknife and cluster bootstrap standard errors, as well as three percentile-type confidence intervals. We use 10,000 bootstrap replications. In this example, the asymptotic, jackknife, and cluster bootstrap standard errors are identical, which reflects the good balance of this particular regression design.

In Stata, to obtain cluster bootstrap standard errors and confidence intervals, use the options `cluster(id) vce(bootstrap, reps(#))`, where `id` is the cluster variable, and # is the number of replications.

10.31 TECHNICAL PROOFS*

Some of the asymptotic results in this chapter are facilitated by the following convergence result.

> **Theorem 10.20 Marcinkiewicz WLLN**
> If u_i are independent and uniformly integrable, then for any $r > 1$, as $n \to \infty$, $n^{-r} \sum_{i=1}^{n} |u_i|^r \underset{p}{\longrightarrow} 0$.

Proof of Theorem 10.20

$$n^{-r} \sum_{i=1}^{n} |u_i|^r \leq \left(n^{-1} \max_{1 \leq i \leq n} |u_i| \right)^{r-1} \frac{1}{n} \sum_{i=1}^{n} |u_i| \underset{p}{\longrightarrow} 0$$

by the WLLN, Theorem 6.15, and $r > 1$. ∎

Proof of Theorem 10.1 Fix $\epsilon > 0$. Since $Z_n \underset{p}{\longrightarrow} Z$, there is an n sufficiently large such that

$$\mathbb{P}\left[\|Z_n - Z\| > \epsilon\right] < \epsilon.$$

Since the event $\|Z_n - Z\| > \epsilon$ is nonrandom under the conditional probability $\mathbb{P}^*$, for such n,

$$\mathbb{P}^*\left[\|Z_n - Z\| > \epsilon\right] = \begin{cases} 0 & \text{with probability exceeding } 1-\epsilon \\ 1 & \text{with probability less than } \epsilon. \end{cases}$$

Since ε is arbitrary, we conclude that $\mathbb{P}^*\left[\|Z_n - Z\| > \epsilon\right] \underset{p}{\longrightarrow} 0$, as required. ∎

Proof of Theorem 10.2 Fix $\epsilon > 0$. By Markov's inequality (B.36), equations (10.12) and (10.13), and finally the Marcinkiewicz WLLN (Theorem 10.20) with $r = 2$ and $u_i = \|Y_i\|$,

$$\begin{aligned}
\mathbb{P}^*\left[\left\|\overline{Y}^* - \overline{Y}\right\| > \epsilon\right] &\leq \epsilon^{-2}\mathbb{E}^*\left\|\overline{Y}^* - \overline{Y}\right\|^2 \\
&= \epsilon^{-2}\operatorname{tr}\left(\operatorname{var}^*\left[\overline{Y}^*\right]\right) \\
&= \epsilon^{-2}\operatorname{tr}\left(\frac{1}{n}\widehat{\Sigma}\right) \\
&\leq \epsilon^{-2}n^{-2}\sum_{i=1}^{n} Y_i' Y_i \\
&\underset{p}{\longrightarrow} 0.
\end{aligned}$$

This establishes that $\overline{Y}^* - \overline{Y} \underset{p^*}{\longrightarrow} 0$.

Since $\overline{Y} - \mu \underset{p}{\longrightarrow} 0$ by the WLLN, $\overline{Y} - \mu \underset{p^*}{\longrightarrow} 0$ by Theorem 10.1. Since $\overline{Y}^* - \mu = \overline{Y}^* - \overline{Y} + \overline{Y} - \mu$, we deduce that $\overline{Y}^* - \mu \underset{p^*}{\longrightarrow} 0$. ∎

Proof of Theorem 10.4 We verify conditions for the multivariate Lindeberg CLT (Theorem 6.4). (We cannot use the Lindeberg–Lévy CLT, because the conditional distribution depends on n.) Conditional on F_n, the bootstrap draws $Y_i^* - \overline{Y}$ are i.i.d. with mean 0 and covariance matrix $\widehat{\Sigma}$. Set $\nu_n^2 = \lambda_{\min}(\widehat{\Sigma})$. Note that by the WLLN, $\nu_n^2 \underset{p}{\longrightarrow} \nu^2 = \lambda_{\min}(\Sigma) > 0$. Thus for n sufficiently large, $\nu_n^2 > 0$ with high probability. Fix $\epsilon > 0$. Equation (6.2) equals

$$\begin{aligned}
\frac{1}{n\nu_n^2}\sum_{i=1}^{n}\mathbb{E}^*\left[\left\|Y_i^* - \overline{Y}\right\|^2 \mathbb{1}\left\{\left\|Y_i^* - \overline{Y}\right\|^2 \geq \epsilon n \nu_n^2\right\}\right] &= \frac{1}{\nu_n^2}\mathbb{E}^*\left[\left\|Y_i^* - \overline{Y}\right\|^2 \mathbb{1}\left\{\left\|Y_i^* - \overline{Y}\right\|^2 \geq \epsilon n \nu_n^2\right\}\right] \\
&\leq \frac{1}{\epsilon n \nu_n^4}\mathbb{E}^*\left\|Y_i^* - \overline{Y}\right\|^4 \\
&\leq \frac{2^4}{\epsilon n \nu_n^4}\mathbb{E}^*\left\|Y_i^*\right\|^4 \\
&= \frac{2^4}{\epsilon n^2 \nu_n^4}\sum_{i=1}^{n}\|Y_i\|^4 \\
&\underset{p}{\longrightarrow} 0.
\end{aligned}$$

The second inequality uses Minkowski's inequality (B.34), Lyapunov's inequality (B.35), and the c_r inequality (B.7). The following equality is $\mathbb{E}^* \left\| Y_i^* \right\|^4 = n^{-1} \sum_{i=1}^n \| Y_i \|^4$, which is similar to (10.10). The final convergence holds by the Marcinkiewicz WLLN (Theorem 10.20) with $r = 2$ and $u_i = \| Y_i \|^2$. The conditions for Theorem 6.4 hold, and we conclude that

$$\widehat{\Sigma}^{-1/2} \sqrt{n} \left(\overline{Y}^* - \overline{Y} \right) \underset{d^*}{\longrightarrow} \mathrm{N}\left(0, \boldsymbol{I}\right).$$

Since $\widehat{\Sigma} \underset{p^*}{\longrightarrow} \Sigma$, we deduce that $\sqrt{n} \left(\overline{Y}^* - \overline{Y} \right) \underset{d^*}{\longrightarrow} \mathrm{N}\left(0, \Sigma\right)$, as claimed. ■

Proof of Theorem 10.10 For notational simplicity, assume θ and μ are scalar. Set $h_i = h(Y_i)$. The assumption that the pth derivative of $g(u)$ is bounded implies $\left| g^{(p)}(u) \right| \le C$ for some $C < \infty$. Taking a pth-order Taylor series expansion, we have

$$\widehat{\theta}^* - \widehat{\theta} = g(\overline{h}^*) - g(\overline{h}) = \sum_{j=1}^{p-1} \frac{g^{(j)}\left(\overline{h}\right)}{j!} \left(\overline{h}^* - \overline{h} \right)^j + \frac{g^{(p)}\left(\zeta_n^*\right)}{p!} \left(\overline{h}^* - \overline{h} \right)^p$$

where ζ_n^* lies between $\overline{h}^*$ and $\overline{h}$. This implies

$$\left| z_n^* \right| = \sqrt{n} \left| \widehat{\theta}^* - \widehat{\theta} \right| \le \sqrt{n} \sum_{j=1}^{p} c_j \left| \overline{h}^* - \overline{h} \right|^j$$

where $c_j = \left| g^{(j)}\left(\overline{h}\right) \right| / j!$ for $j < p$ and $c_p = C/p!$. The fourth central moment of the normalized bootstrap estimator $Z_n^* = \sqrt{n}\left(\widehat{\theta}^* - \widehat{\theta} \right)$ satisfies the bound

$$\mathbb{E}^*\left[Z_n^{*4} \right] \le \sum_{r=4}^{4p} a_r n^2 \mathbb{E}^* \left| \overline{h}^* - \overline{h} \right|^r \tag{10.35}$$

where the coefficients a_r are products of the coefficients c_j and hence each $O_p(1)$. Thus, $\mathbb{E}^*\left[Z_n^{*4} \right] = O_p(1)$ if $n^2 \mathbb{E}^* \left| \overline{h}^* - \overline{h} \right|^r = O_p(1)$ for $r = 4, \ldots, 4p$.

We show this holds for any $r \ge 4$ using Rosenthal's inequality (B.50), which states that for each r, there is a constant $R_r < \infty$ such that

$$\begin{aligned} n^2 \mathbb{E}^* \left| \overline{h}^* - \overline{h} \right|^r &= n^{2-r} \mathbb{E}^* \left| \sum_{i=1}^n \left(h_i^* - \overline{h} \right) \right|^r \\ &\le n^{2-r} R_r \left\{ \left(n \mathbb{E}^* \left(h_i^* - \overline{h} \right)^2 \right)^{r/2} + n \mathbb{E}^* \left| h_i^* - \overline{h} \right|^r \right\} \\ &= R_r \left\{ n^{2-r/2} \widehat{\sigma}^r + \frac{1}{n^{r-2}} \sum_{i=1}^n \left| h_i - \overline{h} \right|^r \right\}. \end{aligned} \tag{10.36}$$

Since $\mathbb{E}\left[h_i^2 \right] < \infty$, $\widehat{\sigma}^2 = O_p(1)$, so the first term in (10.36) is $O_p(1)$. Also, by the Marcinkiewicz WLLN (Theorem 10.20), $n^{-r/2} \sum_{i=1}^n \left| h_i - \overline{h} \right|^r = o_p(1)$ for any $r \ge 1$, so the second term in (10.36) is $o_p(1)$ for $r \ge 4$. Thus for all $r \ge 4$, (10.36) is $O_p(1)$ and thus (10.35) is $O_p(1)$. We deduce that Z_n^* is uniformly square integrable, and the bootstrap estimate of variance is consistent.

This argument can be extended to vector-valued means and estimates. ■

Proof of Theorem 10.12 We show that $\mathbb{E}^* \left\| Z_n^{**} \right\|^4 = O_p(1)$. Theorem 6.13 shows that Z_n^{**} is uniformly square integrable. Since $Z_n^{**} \underset{d^*}{\longrightarrow} Z$, Theorem 6.14 implies that $\operatorname{var}\left[Z_n^{**}\right] \to \operatorname{var}[Z] = \boldsymbol{V}_\beta$, as stated.

Set $h_i = h(Y_i)$. Since $\boldsymbol{G}(x) = \frac{\partial}{\partial x} g(x)'$ is continuous in a neighborhood of μ, there exists $\eta > 0$ and $M < \infty$ such that $\|x - \mu\| \le 2\eta$ implies $\operatorname{tr}\left(\boldsymbol{G}(x)' \boldsymbol{G}(x)\right) \le M$. By the WLLN and bootstrap WLLN, there is an n sufficiently large such that $\left\|\overline{h}_n - \mu\right\| \le \eta$ and $\left\|\overline{h}_n^* - \overline{h}_n\right\| \le \eta$ with probability exceeding $1 - \eta$. In this event, $\left\|x - \overline{h}_n\right\| \le \eta$ implies $\operatorname{tr}\left(\boldsymbol{G}(x)' \boldsymbol{G}(x)\right) \le M$. Using the mean-value theorem at a point ζ_n^* intermediate between $\overline{h}_n^*$ and $\overline{h}_n$, we have

$$\begin{aligned}
\left\|Z_n^{**}\right\|^4 \mathbb{1}\left\{\left\|\overline{h}_n^* - \overline{h}_n\right\| \le \eta\right\} &\le n^2 \left\| g\left(\overline{h}_n^*\right) - g\left(\overline{h}_n\right)\right\|^4 \mathbb{1}\left\{\left\|\overline{h}_n^* - \overline{h}_n\right\| \le \eta\right\} \\
&\le n^2 \left\| \boldsymbol{G}\left(\zeta_n^*\right)' \left(\overline{h}_n^* - \overline{h}_n\right)\right\|^4 \\
&\le M^2 n^2 \left\|\overline{h}_n^* - \overline{h}_n\right\|^4.
\end{aligned}$$

Then

$$\begin{aligned}
\mathbb{E}^* \left\|Z_n^{**}\right\|^4 &\le \mathbb{E}^*\left[\left\|Z_n^{**}\right\|^4 \mathbb{1}\left\{\left\|\overline{h}_n^* - \overline{h}_n\right\| \le \eta\right\}\right] + \tau_n^4 \mathbb{E}^*\left[\mathbb{1}\left\{\left\|\overline{h}_n^* - \overline{h}_n\right\| > \eta\right\}\right] \\
&\le M^2 n^2 \mathbb{E}^* \left\|\overline{h}_n^* - \overline{h}_n\right\|^4 + \tau_n^4 \mathbb{P}^*\left(\left\|\overline{h}_n^* - \overline{h}_n\right\| > \eta\right). \qquad (10.37)
\end{aligned}$$

In (10.17), we showed that the first term in (10.37) is $O_p(1)$ in the scalar case. The vector case follows by element-by-element expansion.

Now take the second term in (10.37). We apply Bernstein's inequality for vectors (B.41). Note that $\overline{h}_n^* - \overline{h}_n = n^{-1}\sum_{i=1}^n u_i^*$ with $u_i^* = h_i^* - \overline{h}_n$ and jth element $u_{ji}^* = h_{ji}^* - \overline{h}_{jn}$. The u_i^* are i.i.d., mean 0, $\mathbb{E}^*\left[u_{ji}^{*2}\right] = \widehat{\sigma}_j^2 = O_p(1)$, and satisfy the bound $\left|u_{ji}^*\right| \le 2\max_{i,j}\left|h_{ji}\right| = B_n$, say. Bernstein's inequality states that

$$\mathbb{P}^*\left[\left\|\overline{h}_n^* - \overline{h}_n\right\| > \eta\right] \le 2m \exp\left(-n^{1/2} \frac{\eta^2}{4m^2 n^{-1/2} \max_j \widehat{\sigma}_j^2 + 4mn^{-1/2} B_n \eta}\right). \qquad (10.38)$$

Theorem 6.15 shows that $n^{-1/2} B_n = o_p(1)$. Thus the expression in the denominator of the parentheses in (10.38) is $o_p(1)$ as $n \to \infty$. It follows that for n sufficiently large, (10.38) is $o_p\left(\exp\left(-n^{1/2}\right)\right)$. Hence the second term in (10.37) is $O\left(\exp\left(n^{1/2}\right)\right) o_p\left(\exp\left(-n^{1/2}\right)\right) = o_p(1)$ by the assumption on τ_n.

We have shown that the two terms in (10.37) are each $O_p(1)$. This completes the proof. ■

10.32 EXERCISES

Exercise 10.1 Find the jackknife estimator of variance of the estimator $\widehat{\mu}_r = n^{-1}\sum_{i=1}^n Y_i^r$ for $\mu_r = \mathbb{E}\left[Y_i^r\right]$.

Exercise 10.2 Show that if the jackknife estimator of variance of $\widehat{\beta}$ is $\widehat{\boldsymbol{V}}_{\widehat{\beta}}^{\text{jack}}$, then the jackknife estimator of variance of $\widehat{\theta} = \boldsymbol{a} + \boldsymbol{C}\widehat{\beta}$ is $\widehat{\boldsymbol{V}}_{\widehat{\theta}}^{\text{jack}} = \boldsymbol{C}\widehat{\boldsymbol{V}}_{\widehat{\beta}}^{\text{jack}}\boldsymbol{C}'$.

Exercise 10.3 A two-step estimator such as (12.49) is $\widehat{\beta}=\left(\sum_{i=1}^{n}\widehat{W}_i\widehat{W}_i'\right)^{-1}\left(\sum_{i=1}^{n}\widehat{W}_iY_i\right)$, where $\widehat{W}_i=\widehat{\boldsymbol{A}}'Z_i$ and $\widehat{\boldsymbol{A}}=\left(\boldsymbol{Z}'\boldsymbol{Z}\right)^{-1}\boldsymbol{Z}'\boldsymbol{X}$. Describe how to construct the jackknife estimator of variance of $\widehat{\beta}$.

Exercise 10.4 Show that if the bootstrap estimator of variance of $\widehat{\beta}$ is $\widehat{\boldsymbol{V}}_{\widehat{\beta}}^{\text{boot}}$, then the bootstrap estimator of variance of $\widehat{\theta}=\boldsymbol{a}+\boldsymbol{C}\widehat{\beta}$ is $\widehat{\boldsymbol{V}}_{\widehat{\theta}}^{\text{boot}}=\boldsymbol{C}\widehat{\boldsymbol{V}}_{\widehat{\beta}}^{\text{boot}}\boldsymbol{C}'$.

Exercise 10.5 Show that if the percentile interval for β is $[L,U]$, then the percentile interval for $a+c\beta$ is $[a+cL, a+cU]$.

Exercise 10.6 Consider the following bootstrap procedure. Using the nonparametric bootstrap, generate bootstrap samples, calculate the estimate $\widehat{\theta}^*$ on these samples, and then calculate

$$T^*=(\widehat{\theta}^*-\widehat{\theta})/s(\widehat{\theta})$$

where $s(\widehat{\theta})$ is the standard error in the original data. Let $q_{\alpha/2}^*$ and $q_{1-\alpha/2}^*$ denote the $\alpha/2$th and $1-\alpha/2$th quantiles of T^*, and define the bootstrap confidence interval

$$C=\left[\widehat{\theta}+s(\widehat{\theta})q_{\alpha/2}^*,\quad \widehat{\theta}+s(\widehat{\theta})q_{1-\alpha/2}^*\right].$$

Show that C exactly equals the percentile interval.

Exercise 10.7 Prove Theorem 10.6.

Exercise 10.8 Prove Theorem 10.7.

Exercise 10.9 Prove Theorem 10.8.

Exercise 10.10 Let Y_i be i.i.d., $\mu=\mathbb{E}[Y]>0$, and $\theta=\mu^{-1}$. Let $\widehat{\mu}=\overline{Y}_n$ be the sample mean, and $\widehat{\theta}=\widehat{\mu}^{-1}$.

(a) Is $\widehat{\theta}$ unbiased for θ?

(b) If $\widehat{\theta}$ is biased, can you determine the direction of the bias $\mathbb{E}\left[\widehat{\theta}-\theta\right]$ (up or down)?

(c) Is the percentile interval appropriate in this context for confidence interval construction?

Exercise 10.11 Consider the following bootstrap procedure for a regression of Y on X. Let $\widehat{\beta}$ denote the OLS estimator and $\widehat{e}_i=Y_i-X_i'\widehat{\beta}$ the OLS residuals.

(a) Draw a random vector (X^*, e^*) from the pair $\{(X_i,\widehat{e}_i): i=1,\ldots,n\}$. That is, draw a random integer i' from $[1,2,\ldots,n]$, and set $X^*=X_{i'}$ and $e^*=\widehat{e}_{i'}$. Set $Y^*=X^{*\prime}\widehat{\beta}+e^*$. Draw (with replacement) n such vectors, creating a random bootstrap dataset $(\boldsymbol{Y}^*,\boldsymbol{X}^*)$.

(b) Regress $\boldsymbol{Y}^*$ on $\boldsymbol{X}^*$, yielding OLS estimator $\widehat{\beta}^*$ and any other statistic of interest.

Show that this bootstrap procedure is (numerically) identical to the nonparametric bootstrap.

Exercise 10.12 Take p^* as defined in (10.22) for the BC percentile interval. Show that it is invariant to replacing θ with $g(\theta)$ for any strictly monotonically increasing transformation $g(\theta)$. Does this extend to z_0^* as defined in (10.23)?

Exercise 10.13 Show that if the percentile-t interval for β is $[L, U]$, then the percentile-t interval for $a + c\beta$ is $[a + bL, a + bU]$.

Exercise 10.14 You want to test $\mathbb{H}_0 : \theta = 0$ against $\mathbb{H}_1 : \theta > 0$. The test for $\mathbb{H}_0$ is to reject if $T_n = \widehat{\theta}/s(\widehat{\theta}) > c$, where c is picked so that the Type I error is α. You do this as follows. Using the nonparametric bootstrap, you generate bootstrap samples, calculate the estimates $\widehat{\theta}^*$ on these samples, and then calculate $T^* = \widehat{\theta}^*/s(\widehat{\theta}^*)$. Let $q^*_{1-\alpha}$ denote the $1-\alpha$th quantile of T^*. You replace c with $q^*_{1-\alpha}$, and thus reject $\mathbb{H}_0$ if $T_n = \widehat{\theta}/s(\widehat{\theta}) > q^*_{1-\alpha}$. What is wrong with this procedure?

Exercise 10.15 Suppose that in an application, $\widehat{\theta} = 1.2$ and $s(\widehat{\theta}) = 0.2$. Using the nonparametric bootstrap, 1000 samples are generated from the bootstrap distribution, and $\widehat{\theta}^*$ is calculated on each sample. The $\widehat{\theta}^*$ are sorted, and the 0.025th and 0.975th quantiles of the $\widehat{\theta}^*$ are .75 and 1.3, respectively.

(a) Report the 95% percentile interval for θ.

(c) With the given information, can you calculate the 95% BC percentile interval or percentile-t interval for θ?

Exercise 10.16 Take the normal regression model $Y = X'\beta + e$ with $e \mid X \sim \mathrm{N}(0, \sigma^2)$, where we know the MLE equals the least squares estimators $\widehat{\beta}$ and $\widehat{\sigma}^2$.

(a) Describe the parametric regression bootstrap for this model. Show that the conditional distribution of the bootstrap observations is $Y_i^* \mid F_n \sim \mathrm{N}\left(X_i'\widehat{\beta}, \widehat{\sigma}^2\right)$.

(b) Show that the distribution of the bootstrap least squares estimator is $\widehat{\beta}^* \mid F_n \sim \mathrm{N}\left(\widehat{\beta}, \left(\boldsymbol{X}'\boldsymbol{X}\right)^{-1}\widehat{\sigma}^2\right)$.

(c) Show that the distribution of the bootstrap t-ratio with a homoskedastic standard error is $T^* \sim t_{n-k}$.

Exercise 10.17 Consider the model $Y = X'\beta + e$ with $\mathbb{E}[e \mid X] = 0$, Y scalar, and X a k-vector. You have a random sample $(Y_i, X_i : i = 1, \ldots, n)$. You are interested in estimating the regression function $m(x) = \mathbb{E}[Y \mid X = x]$ at a fixed vector x and constructing a 95% confidence interval.

(a) Write down the standard estimator and asymptotic confidence interval for $m(x)$.

(b) Describe the percentile bootstrap confidence interval for $m(x)$.

(c) Describe the percentile-t bootstrap confidence interval for $m(x)$.

Exercise 10.18 The observed data are $\{Y_i, X_i\} \in \mathbb{R} \times \mathbb{R}^k$, $k > 1$, $i = 1, \ldots, n$. Take the model $Y = X'\beta + e$ with $\mathbb{E}[Xe] = 0$.

(a) Write down an estimator for $\mu_3 = \mathbb{E}\left[e^3\right]$.

(b) Explain how to use the percentile method to construct a 90% confidence interval for μ_3 in this specific model.

Exercise 10.19 Take the model $Y = X'\beta + e$ with $\mathbb{E}[Xe] = 0$. Describe the bootstrap percentile confidence interval for $\sigma^2 = \mathbb{E}\left[e^2\right]$.

Exercise 10.20 The model is $Y = X_1'\beta_1 + X_2'\beta_2 + e$ with $\mathbb{E}[Xe] = 0$ and X_2 scalar. Describe how to test $\mathbb{H}_0 : \beta_2 = 0$ against $\mathbb{H}_1 : \beta_2 \neq 0$ using the nonparametric bootstrap.

Exercise 10.21 The model is $Y = X_1'\beta_1 + X_2'\beta_2 + e$ with $\mathbb{E}[Xe] = 0$, and both X_1 and X_2 are $k \times 1$. Describe how to test $\mathbb{H}_0 : \beta_1 = \beta_2$ against $\mathbb{H}_1 : \beta_1 \neq \beta_2$ using the nonparametric bootstrap.

Exercise 10.22 Suppose a Ph.D. student has a sample $(Y_i, X_i, Z_i : i = 1, \ldots, n)$ and estimates by OLS the equation $Y = Z\alpha + X'\beta + e$, where α is the coefficient of interest. She is interested in testing $\mathbb{H}_0 : \alpha = 0$ against $\mathbb{H}_1 : \alpha \neq 0$. She obtains $\widehat{\alpha} = 2.0$ with standard error $s(\widehat{\alpha}) = 1.0$, so the value of the t-ratio for $\mathbb{H}_0$ is $T = \widehat{\alpha}/s(\widehat{\alpha}) = 2.0$. To assess significance, the student decides to use the bootstrap. She uses the following algorithm:

1. Samples (Y_i^*, X_i^*, Z_i^*) randomly from the observations. (Random sampling with replacement). Creates a random sample with n observations.
2. On this pseudo-sample, estimates the equation $Y_i^* = Z_i^*\alpha + X_i^{*\prime}\beta + e_i^*$ by OLS and computes standard errors, including $s(\widehat{\alpha}^*)$. The t-ratio for $\mathbb{H}_0$, $T^* = \widehat{\alpha}^*/s(\widehat{\alpha}^*)$, is computed and stored.
3. Steps 1–2 are repeated $B = 10{,}000$ times.
4. The 0.95th empirical quantile $q^*_{.95} = 3.5$ of the bootstrap absolute t-ratios $|T^*|$ is computed.
5. The student notes that while $|T| = 2 > 1.96$ (and thus an asymptotic 5% size test rejects $\mathbb{H}_0$), $|T| = 2 < q^*_{.95} = 3.5$, and thus the bootstrap test does not reject $\mathbb{H}_0$. As the bootstrap is more reliable, the student concludes that $\mathbb{H}_0$ cannot be rejected in favor of $\mathbb{H}_1$.

Question: Do you agree with the student's method and reasoning? Do you see an error in her method?

Exercise 10.23 Take the model $Y = X_1\beta_1 + X_2\beta_2 + e$ with $\mathbb{E}[Xe] = 0$ and scalar X_1 and X_2. The parameter of interest is $\theta = \beta_1\beta_2$. Show how to construct a confidence interval for θ using the following three methods:

(a) Asymptotic Theory.
(b) Percentile Bootstrap.
(c) Percentile-t Bootstrap.

Your answer should be specific to this problem, not general.

Exercise 10.24 Take the model $Y = X_1\beta_1 + X_2\beta_2 + e$ with i.i.d observations, $\mathbb{E}[Xe] = 0$, and scalar X_1 and X_2. Describe how you would construct the percentile-t bootstrap confidence interval for $\theta = \beta_1/\beta_2$.

Exercise 10.25 The model is i.i.d. data, $i = 1, \ldots, n$, $Y = X'\beta + e$ and $\mathbb{E}[e \mid X] = 0$. Does the presence of conditional heteroskedasticity invalidate the application of the nonparametric bootstrap? Explain.

Exercise 10.26 The RESET specification test for nonlinearity in a random sample (due to Ramsey (1969)) is the following. The null hypothesis is a linear regression $Y = X'\beta + e$ with $\mathbb{E}[e \mid X] = 0$. The parameter β is estimated by OLS, yielding predicted values $\widehat{Y}_i$. Then a second-stage least squares regression is estimated including both X_i and $\widehat{Y}_i$:

$$Y_i = X_i'\widetilde{\beta} + \left(\widehat{Y}_i\right)^2 \widetilde{\gamma} + \widetilde{e}_i$$

The RESET test statistic R is the squared t-ratio on $\widetilde{\gamma}$.

A colleague suggests obtaining the critical value for the test using the bootstrap. He proposes the following bootstrap implementation:

- Draw n observations (Y_i^*, X_i^*) randomly from the observed sample pairs (Y_i, X_i) to create a bootstrap sample.
- Compute the statistic R^* on this bootstrap sample as described above.
- Repeat this B times. Sort the bootstrap statistics R^*, take the 0.95th quantile, and use this as the critical value.
- Reject the null hypothesis if R exceeds this critical value, otherwise do not reject.

Is this procedure a correct implementation of the bootstrap in this context? If not, propose a modification.

Exercise 10.27 The model is $Y = X'\beta + e$ with $\mathbb{E}[Xe] \neq 0$. We know that in this case, the least squares estimator may be biased for the parameter β. We also know that the nonparametric BC percentile interval is (generally) a good method for confidence interval construction in the presence of bias. Explain whether or not you expect the BC percentile interval applied to the least squares estimator will have accurate coverage in this context.

Exercise 10.28 In Exercise 9.26, you estimated a cost function for 145 electric companies and tested the restriction $\theta = \beta_3 + \beta_4 + \beta_5 = 1$.

(a) Estimate the regression by unrestricted least squares, and report standard errors calculated by asymptotic, jackknife, and the bootstrap.
(b) Estimate $\theta = \beta_3 + \beta_4 + \beta_5$, and report standard errors calculated by asymptotic, jackknife, and the bootstrap.
(c) Report confidence intervals for θ using the percentile and BC_a methods.

Exercise 10.29 In Exercise 9.27 you estimated the Mankiw, Romer, and Weil (1992) unrestricted regression. Let θ be the sum of the second, third, and fourth coefficients.

(a) Estimate the regression by unrestricted least squares, and report standard errors calculated by asymptotic, jackknife, and the bootstrap.
(b) Estimate θ and report standard errors calculated by asymptotic, jackknife, and the bootstrap.
(c) Report confidence intervals for θ using the percentile and BC methods.

Exercise 10.30 In Exercise 7.28, you estimated a wage regression with the `cps09mar` dataset and the subsample of white male Hispanics. Further restrict the sample to those never married and who live in the Midwest region. (This sample has 99 observations.) Let θ be the ratio of the return to 1 year of education to the return of 1 year of experience.

(a) Estimate θ, and report standard errors calculated by asymptotic, jackknife, and the bootstrap.
(b) Explain the discrepancy between the standard errors.
(c) Report confidence intervals for θ using the BC percentile method.

Exercise 10.31 In Exercise 4.26, you extended the work from Duflo, Dupas, and Kremer (2011). Repeat that regression, now calculating the standard error by cluster bootstrap. Report a BC_a confidence interval for each coefficient.

PART III
MULTIPLE EQUATION MODELS

CHAPTER 11
MULTIVARIATE REGRESSION

11.1 INTRODUCTION

Multivariate regression is a system of regression equations. Multivariate regression is used as reduced form models for instrumental variable estimation (Chaper 12), vector autoregressions (Chapter 15), demand systems (demand for multiple goods), and in other contexts. Multivariate regression is also called **systems of regression equations**. Closely related is the method of **Seemingly Unrelated Regressions** (SUR) introduced in Section 11.7.

Most of the tools of single equation regression generalize to multivariate regression. A major difference is a new set of notation to handle matrix estimators.

11.2 REGRESSION SYSTEMS

A univariate linear regression equation equals $Y = X'\beta + e$, where Y is scalar and X is a vector. **Multivariate regression** is a system of m linear regressions

$$Y_j = X_j'\beta_j + e_j \tag{11.1}$$

for $j = 1, \ldots, m$. Here we use the subscript j to denote the jth dependent variable, not the jth individual. As an example, Y_j could be expenditures by a household on goods category j (e.g., food, housing, transportation, clothing, recreation). The regressor vectors X_j are $k_j \times 1$, and e_j is an error. The coefficient vectors β_j are $k_j \times 1$. The total number of coefficients are $\overline{k} = \sum_{j=1}^m k_j$. The regressors can be common across j or can vary across j. In the household expenditure example, the regressors X_j are typically common across j and include such variables as household income, number and ages of family members, and demographic characteristics. The regression system specializes to univariate regression when $m = 1$.

Define the $m \times 1$ error vector $e = (e_1, \ldots, e_m)'$ and its $m \times m$ covariance matrix $\Sigma = \mathbb{E}\left[ee'\right]$. The diagonal elements are the variances of the errors e_j, and the off-diagonals are the covariances across variables.

We can group the m equations (11.1) into a single equation as follows. Let $Y = (Y_1, \ldots, Y_m)'$ be the $m \times 1$ vector of dependent variables. Define the $m \times \overline{k}$ matrix of regressors

$$\overline{X} = \begin{pmatrix} X_1' & 0 & \cdots & 0 \\ \vdots & X_2' & & \vdots \\ 0 & 0 & \cdots & X_m' \end{pmatrix}$$

and the $\overline{k} \times 1$ stacked coefficient vector

$$\beta = \begin{pmatrix} \beta_1 \\ \vdots \\ \beta_m \end{pmatrix}.$$

The m regression equations can be jointly written as

$$Y = \overline{X}\beta + e. \tag{11.2}$$

This is a system of m equations.

For n observations, the joint system can be written in matrix notation by stacking. Define

$$\boldsymbol{Y} = \begin{pmatrix} Y_1 \\ \vdots \\ Y_n \end{pmatrix}, \quad \boldsymbol{e} = \begin{pmatrix} e_1 \\ \vdots \\ e_n \end{pmatrix}, \quad \overline{\boldsymbol{X}} = \begin{pmatrix} \overline{X}_1 \\ \vdots \\ \overline{X}_n \end{pmatrix}$$

which are $mn \times 1$, $mn \times 1$, and $mn \times \overline{k}$, respectively. The system can be written as $\boldsymbol{Y} = \overline{\boldsymbol{X}}\beta + \boldsymbol{e}$.

In many applications, the regressor vectors X_j are common across the variables j, so $X_j = X$ and $k_j = k$. By this we mean that the same variables enter each equation with no exclusion restrictions. Several important simplifications occur in this context. One is that we can write (11.2) using the notation

$$Y = \boldsymbol{B}'X + e \tag{11.3}$$

where $\boldsymbol{B} = (\beta_1, \beta_2, \cdots, \beta_m)$ is $k \times m$. Another is that we can write the joint system of observations in the $n \times m$ matrix notation $\boldsymbol{Y} = \boldsymbol{X}\boldsymbol{B} + \boldsymbol{E}$, where

$$\boldsymbol{Y} = \begin{pmatrix} Y_1' \\ \vdots \\ Y_n' \end{pmatrix}, \quad \boldsymbol{E} = \begin{pmatrix} e_1' \\ \vdots \\ e_n' \end{pmatrix}, \quad \boldsymbol{X} = \begin{pmatrix} X_1' \\ \vdots \\ X_n' \end{pmatrix}.$$

Another convenient implication of common regressors is that we have the simplification

$$\overline{X} = \begin{pmatrix} X' & 0 & \cdots & 0 \\ 0 & X' & & 0 \\ \vdots & \vdots & & \vdots \\ 0 & 0 & \cdots & X' \end{pmatrix} = \boldsymbol{I}_m \otimes X'$$

where $\otimes$ is the Kronecker product (see Appendix A.21).

11.3 LEAST SQUARES ESTIMATOR

The equations (11.1) can be estimated by least squares. This takes the form

$$\widehat{\beta}_j = \left(\sum_{i=1}^{n} X_{ji}X_{ji}'\right)^{-1}\left(\sum_{i=1}^{n} X_{ji}Y_{ji}\right).$$

An estimator of β is the stacked vector

$$\widehat{\beta} = \begin{pmatrix} \widehat{\beta}_1 \\ \vdots \\ \widehat{\beta}_m \end{pmatrix}.$$

We can alternatively write this estimator using the systems notation:

$$\widehat{\beta} = \left(\overline{\boldsymbol{X}}'\overline{\boldsymbol{X}}\right)^{-1}\left(\overline{\boldsymbol{X}}'\boldsymbol{Y}\right) = \left(\sum_{i=1}^{n} \overline{X}_i'\overline{X}_i\right)^{-1}\left(\sum_{i=1}^{n} \overline{X}_i' Y_i\right). \tag{11.4}$$

To see this, observe that

$$\begin{aligned}
\overline{\boldsymbol{X}}'\overline{\boldsymbol{X}} &= \begin{pmatrix} \overline{X}_1' & \cdots & \overline{X}_n' \end{pmatrix} \begin{pmatrix} \overline{X}_1 \\ \vdots \\ \overline{X}_n \end{pmatrix} \\
&= \sum_{i=1}^{n} \overline{X}_i'\overline{X}_i \\
&= \sum_{i=1}^{n} \begin{pmatrix} X_{1i} & 0 & \cdots & 0 \\ \vdots & X_{2i} & & \vdots \\ 0 & 0 & \cdots & X_{mi} \end{pmatrix} \begin{pmatrix} X_{1i}' & 0 & \cdots & 0 \\ \vdots & X_{2i}' & & \vdots \\ 0 & 0 & \cdots & X_{mi}' \end{pmatrix} \\
&= \begin{pmatrix} \sum_{i=1}^{n} X_{1i}X_{1i}' & 0 & \cdots & 0 \\ \vdots & \sum_{i=1}^{n} X_{2i}X_{2i}' & & \vdots \\ 0 & 0 & \cdots & \sum_{i=1}^{n} X_{mi}X_{mi}' \end{pmatrix}
\end{aligned}$$

and

$$\begin{aligned}
\overline{\boldsymbol{X}}'\boldsymbol{Y} &= \begin{pmatrix} \overline{X}_1' & \cdots & \overline{X}_n' \end{pmatrix} \begin{pmatrix} Y_1 \\ \vdots \\ Y_n \end{pmatrix} \\
&= \sum_{i=1}^{n} \overline{X}_i' Y_i \\
&= \sum_{i=1}^{n} \begin{pmatrix} X_{1i} & 0 & \cdots & 0 \\ \vdots & X_{2i} & & \vdots \\ 0 & 0 & \cdots & X_{mi} \end{pmatrix} \begin{pmatrix} Y_{1i} \\ \vdots \\ Y_{mi} \end{pmatrix} \\
&= \begin{pmatrix} \sum_{i=1}^{n} X_{1i}Y_{1i} \\ \vdots \\ \sum_{i=1}^{n} X_{mi}Y_{mi} \end{pmatrix}.
\end{aligned}$$

Hence

$$\left(\overline{\boldsymbol{X}}'\overline{\boldsymbol{X}}\right)^{-1}\left(\overline{\boldsymbol{X}}'\boldsymbol{Y}\right)=\left(\sum_{i=1}^{n}\overline{X}_i\overline{X}_i'\right)^{-1}\left(\sum_{i=1}^{n}\overline{X}_iY_i\right)$$
$$=\begin{pmatrix}\left(\sum_{i=1}^{n}X_{1i}X_{1i}'\right)^{-1}\left(\sum_{i=1}^{n}X_{1i}Y_{1i}\right)\\ \vdots\\ \left(\sum_{i=1}^{n}X_{mi}X_{mi}'\right)^{-1}\left(\sum_{i=1}^{n}X_{mi}Y_{mi}\right)\end{pmatrix}$$
$$=\widehat{\beta}$$

as claimed.

The $m\times 1$ residual vector for the ith observation is $\widehat{e}_i=Y_i-\overline{\boldsymbol{X}}_i'\widehat{\beta}$. The least squares estimator of the $m\times m$ error covariance matrix is

$$\widehat{\Sigma}=\frac{1}{n}\sum_{i=1}^{n}\widehat{e}_i\widehat{e}_i'. \tag{11.5}$$

In the case of common regressors, the least squares coefficients can be written as

$$\widehat{\beta}_j=\left(\sum_{i=1}^{n}X_iX_i'\right)^{-1}\left(\sum_{i=1}^{n}X_iY_{ji}\right)$$

and

$$\widehat{\boldsymbol{B}}=(\widehat{\beta}_1,\widehat{\beta}_2,\cdots,\widehat{\beta}_m)=\left(\boldsymbol{X}'\boldsymbol{X}\right)^{-1}\left(\boldsymbol{X}'\boldsymbol{Y}\right). \tag{11.6}$$

In Stata, multivariate regression can be implemented using the `mvreg` command.

11.4 EXPECTATION AND VARIANCE OF SYSTEMS LEAST SQUARES

We can calculate the finite-sample expectation and variance of $\widehat{\beta}$ under the conditional expectation assumption

$$\mathbb{E}\left[e\mid X\right]=0 \tag{11.7}$$

where X is the union of the regressors X_j. Equation (11.7) is equivalent to $\mathbb{E}\left[Y_j\mid X\right]=X_j'\beta_j$, which means that the regression model is correctly specified.

We can center the estimator as

$$\widehat{\beta}-\beta=\left(\overline{\boldsymbol{X}}'\overline{\boldsymbol{X}}\right)^{-1}\left(\overline{\boldsymbol{X}}'\boldsymbol{e}\right)=\left(\sum_{i=1}^{n}\overline{X}_i'\overline{X}_i\right)^{-1}\left(\sum_{i=1}^{n}\overline{X}_i'e_i\right).$$

Taking conditional expectations, we find $\mathbb{E}\left[\widehat{\beta}\mid\boldsymbol{X}\right]=\beta$. Consequently, systems least squares is unbiased under correct specification.

To compute the variance of the estimator, define the conditional covariance matrix of the errors of the ith observation $\mathbb{E}\left[e_ie_i'\mid X_i\right]=\Sigma_i$, which in general is a function of X_i. If the observations are mutually independent, then

$$\mathbb{E}\left[\boldsymbol{e}\boldsymbol{e}' \mid \boldsymbol{X}\right]=\mathbb{E}\left[\left(\begin{array}{cccc} e_1e_1' & e_1e_2' & \cdots & e_1e_n' \\ \vdots & \ddots & & \vdots \\ e_ne_1' & e_ne_2' & \cdots & e_ne_n' \end{array}\right) \middle| \boldsymbol{X}\right]=\left(\begin{array}{cccc} \Sigma_1 & 0 & \cdots & 0 \\ \vdots & \ddots & & \vdots \\ 0 & 0 & \cdots & \Sigma_n \end{array}\right).$$

Also, by independence across observations,

$$\operatorname{var}\left[\sum_{i=1}^n \overline{X}_i' e_i \middle| \boldsymbol{X}\right]=\sum_{i=1}^n \operatorname{var}\left[\overline{X}_i' e_i \middle| X_i\right]=\sum_{i=1}^n \overline{X}_i' \Sigma_i \overline{X}_i.$$

It follows that

$$\operatorname{var}\left[\widehat{\beta} \mid \boldsymbol{X}\right]=\left(\overline{\boldsymbol{X}}'\overline{\boldsymbol{X}}\right)^{-1}\left(\sum_{i=1}^n \overline{X}_i' \Sigma_i \overline{X}_i\right)\left(\overline{\boldsymbol{X}}'\overline{\boldsymbol{X}}\right)^{-1}.$$

When the regressors are common, so that $\overline{X}_i=\boldsymbol{I}_m \otimes X_i'$, then the covariance matrix can be written as

$$\operatorname{var}\left[\widehat{\beta} \mid \boldsymbol{X}\right]=\left(\boldsymbol{I}_m \otimes \left(\boldsymbol{X}'\boldsymbol{X}\right)^{-1}\right)\left(\sum_{i=1}^n \left(\Sigma_i \otimes X_i X_i'\right)\right)\left(\boldsymbol{I}_m \otimes \left(\boldsymbol{X}'\boldsymbol{X}\right)^{-1}\right).$$

If the errors are conditionally homoskedastic

$$\mathbb{E}\left[ee' \mid X\right]=\Sigma \tag{11.8}$$

then the covariance matrix simplifies to

$$\operatorname{var}\left[\widehat{\beta} \mid \boldsymbol{X}\right]=\left(\overline{\boldsymbol{X}}'\overline{\boldsymbol{X}}\right)^{-1}\left(\sum_{i=1}^n \overline{X}_i' \Sigma \overline{X}_i\right)\left(\overline{\boldsymbol{X}}'\overline{\boldsymbol{X}}\right)^{-1}.$$

If both simplifications (common regressors and conditional homoskedasticity) hold, then we have considerable simplication:

$$\operatorname{var}\left[\widehat{\beta} \mid \boldsymbol{X}\right]=\Sigma \otimes \left(\boldsymbol{X}'\boldsymbol{X}\right)^{-1}.$$

11.5 ASYMPTOTIC DISTRIBUTION

For an asymptotic distribution, it is sufficient to consider the equation-by-equation projection model, in which case

$$\mathbb{E}\left[X_j e_j\right]=0. \tag{11.9}$$

First, consider consistency. Since the $\widehat{\beta}_j$ are the standard least squares estimators, they are consistent for the projection coefficients β_j.

Second, consider the asymptotic distribution. Our single equation theory implies that the $\widehat{\beta}_j$ are asymptotically normal. But this theory does not provide a joint distribution of the $\widehat{\beta}_j$ across j, which we now derive.

Since the vector

$$\overline{X}_i' e_i = \begin{pmatrix} X_{1i}e_{1i} \\ \vdots \\ X_{mi}e_{mi} \end{pmatrix}$$

is i.i.d. across i and has mean 0 under (11.9), the central limit theorem implies

$$\frac{1}{\sqrt{n}} \sum_{i=1}^{n} \overline{X}_i' e_i \underset{d}{\longrightarrow} \mathrm{N}(0, \Omega)$$

where

$$\Omega = \mathbb{E}\left[\overline{X}_i' e_i e_i' \overline{X}_i\right] = \mathbb{E}\left[\overline{X}_i' \Sigma_i \overline{X}_i\right].$$

The matrix Ω is the covariance matrix of the variables $X_{ji}e_{ji}$ across equations. Under conditional homoskedasticity (11.8), the matrix Ω simplifies to

$$\Omega = \mathbb{E}\left[\overline{X}_i' \Sigma \overline{X}_i\right] \tag{11.10}$$

(see Exercise 11.1). When the regressors are common, it simplies to

$$\Omega = \mathbb{E}\left[ee' \otimes XX'\right] \tag{11.11}$$

(see Exercise 11.2). Under both conditions (homoskedasticity and common regressors), it simplifies to

$$\Omega = \Sigma \otimes \mathbb{E}\left[XX'\right] \tag{11.12}$$

(see Exercise 11.3).

Applied to the centered and normalized estimator, we obtain the asymptotic distribution.

Theorem 11.1 Under Assumption 7.2, $\sqrt{n}\left(\widehat{\beta} - \beta\right) \underset{d}{\longrightarrow} \mathrm{N}\left(0, \boldsymbol{V}_\beta\right)$, where $\boldsymbol{V}_\beta = \boldsymbol{Q}^{-1}\Omega\boldsymbol{Q}^{-1}$ and

$$\boldsymbol{Q} = \mathbb{E}\left[\overline{X}'\overline{X}\right] = \begin{pmatrix} \mathbb{E}\left[X_1X_1'\right] & 0 & \cdots & 0 \\ \vdots & & \ddots & \vdots \\ 0 & 0 & \cdots & \mathbb{E}\left[X_mX_m'\right] \end{pmatrix}.$$

You are asked to prove this theorem in Exercise 11.4.

When the regressors are common, the matrix $\boldsymbol{Q}$ simplifies to

$$\boldsymbol{Q} = \boldsymbol{I}_m \otimes \mathbb{E}\left[XX'\right] \tag{11.13}$$

(See Exercise 11.5). If both the regressors are common and the errors are conditionally homoskedastic (as in (11.8)), then we have the simplification

$$\boldsymbol{V}_\beta = \Sigma \otimes \left(\mathbb{E}\left[XX'\right]\right)^{-1}. \tag{11.14}$$

Sometimes we are interested in parameters $\theta = r(\beta_1, \ldots, \beta_m) = r(\beta)$, which are functions of the coefficients from multiple equations. In this case, the least squares estimator of θ is $\widehat{\theta} = r(\widehat{\beta})$. The asymptotic distribution of $\widehat{\theta}$ can be obtained from Theorem 11.1 by the delta method.

Theorem 11.2 Under Assumptions 7.2 and 7.3, $\sqrt{n}\left(\widehat{\theta}-\theta\right) \underset{d}{\longrightarrow} \mathrm{N}\left(0, \boldsymbol{V}_{\theta}\right)$, where $\boldsymbol{V}_{\theta}=\boldsymbol{R}' \boldsymbol{V}_{\beta} \boldsymbol{R}$ and $\boldsymbol{R}=\frac{\partial}{\partial \beta} r(\beta)'$.

Exercise 11.7 asks you to prove this theorem. Theorem 11.2 is an example where multivariate regression is fundamentally distinct from univariate regression. Only by treating least squares as a joint estimator can we obtain a distributional theory for a function of multiple equations. We can thereby construct standard errors, confidence intervals, and hypothesis tests.

11.6 COVARIANCE MATRIX ESTIMATION

From the finite sample and asymptotic theory, we can construct appropriate estimators for the variance of $\widehat{\beta}$. In the general case, we have

$$\widehat{\boldsymbol{V}}_{\widehat{\beta}}=\left(\overline{\boldsymbol{X}}'\overline{\boldsymbol{X}}\right)^{-1}\left(\sum_{i=1}^{n} \overline{X}_i'\widehat{e}_i\widehat{e}_i'\overline{X}_i\right)\left(\overline{\boldsymbol{X}}'\overline{\boldsymbol{X}}\right)^{-1}.$$

Under conditional homoskedasticity (11.8), an appropriate estimator is

$$\widehat{\boldsymbol{V}}_{\widehat{\beta}}^{0}=\left(\overline{\boldsymbol{X}}'\overline{\boldsymbol{X}}\right)^{-1}\left(\sum_{i=1}^{n} \overline{X}_i'\widehat{\Sigma}\overline{X}_i\right)\left(\overline{\boldsymbol{X}}'\overline{\boldsymbol{X}}\right)^{-1}.$$

When the regressors are common, these estimators equal

$$\widehat{\boldsymbol{V}}_{\widehat{\beta}}=\left(\boldsymbol{I}_m \otimes\left(\boldsymbol{X}'\boldsymbol{X}\right)^{-1}\right)\left(\sum_{i=1}^{n}\left(\widehat{e}_i\widehat{e}_i' \otimes X_i X_i'\right)\right)\left(\boldsymbol{I}_m \otimes\left(\boldsymbol{X}'\boldsymbol{X}\right)^{-1}\right)$$

and $\widehat{\boldsymbol{V}}_{\widehat{\beta}}^{0}=\widehat{\Sigma} \otimes\left(\boldsymbol{X}'\boldsymbol{X}\right)^{-1}$, respectively.

Covariance matrix estimators for $\widehat{\theta}$ are found as

$$\widehat{\boldsymbol{V}}_{\widehat{\theta}}=\widehat{\boldsymbol{R}}'\widehat{\boldsymbol{V}}_{\widehat{\beta}}\widehat{\boldsymbol{R}}$$

$$\widehat{\boldsymbol{V}}_{\widehat{\theta}}^{0}=\widehat{\boldsymbol{R}}'\widehat{\boldsymbol{V}}_{\widehat{\beta}}^{0}\widehat{\boldsymbol{R}}$$

$$\widehat{\boldsymbol{R}}=\frac{\partial}{\partial \beta} r\left(\widehat{\beta}\right)'.$$

Theorem 11.3 Under Assumption 7.2, $n\widehat{\boldsymbol{V}}_{\widehat{\beta}} \underset{p}{\longrightarrow} \boldsymbol{V}_{\beta}$, and $n\widehat{\boldsymbol{V}}_{\widehat{\beta}}^{0} \underset{p}{\longrightarrow} \boldsymbol{V}_{\beta}^{0}$.

Exercise 11.8 asks you to prove this theorem.

11.7 SEEMINGLY UNRELATED REGRESSION

Consider the systems regression model under the conditional expectation and homoskedasticity assumptions:

$$Y = \overline{X}\beta + e \tag{11.15}$$

$$\mathbb{E}\left[e \mid X\right] = 0$$

$$\mathbb{E}\left[ee' \mid X\right] = \Sigma.$$

Since the errors are correlated across equations, we consider estimation by Generalized Least Squares (GLS). To derive the estimator, premultiply (11.15) by $\Sigma^{-1/2}$, so that the transformed error vector is i.i.d. with covariance matrix $\boldsymbol{I}_m$. Then apply least squares and rearrange to find:

$$\widehat{\beta}_{\text{gls}} = \left(\sum_{i=1}^{n} \overline{X}_i' \Sigma^{-1} \overline{X}_i\right)^{-1} \left(\sum_{i=1}^{n} \overline{X}_i' \Sigma^{-1} Y_i\right). \tag{11.16}$$

(see Exercise 11.9). Another approach is to take the vector representation

$$\boldsymbol{Y} = \overline{\boldsymbol{X}}\beta + \boldsymbol{e}$$

and calculate that the equation error $\boldsymbol{e}$ has variance $\mathbb{E}\left[\boldsymbol{ee}'\right] = \boldsymbol{I}_n \otimes \Sigma$. Premultiply the equation by $\boldsymbol{I}_n \otimes \Sigma^{-1/2}$, so that the transformed error has covariance matrix $\boldsymbol{I}_{nm}$, and then apply least squares to find

$$\widehat{\beta}_{\text{gls}} = \left(\overline{\boldsymbol{X}}' \left(\boldsymbol{I}_n \otimes \Sigma^{-1}\right) \overline{\boldsymbol{X}}\right)^{-1} \left(\overline{\boldsymbol{X}}' \left(\boldsymbol{I}_n \otimes \Sigma^{-1}\right) \boldsymbol{Y}\right) \tag{11.17}$$

(see Exercise 11.10).

Expressions (11.16) and (11.17) are algebraically equivalent. To see the equivalence, observe that

$$\begin{aligned}
\overline{\boldsymbol{X}}' \left(\boldsymbol{I}_n \otimes \Sigma^{-1}\right) \overline{\boldsymbol{X}} &= \begin{pmatrix} \overline{X}_1' & \cdots & \overline{X}_n' \end{pmatrix} \begin{pmatrix} \Sigma^{-1} & 0 & \cdots & 0 \\ \vdots & \Sigma^{-1} & & \vdots \\ 0 & 0 & \cdots & \Sigma^{-1} \end{pmatrix} \begin{pmatrix} \overline{X}_1 \\ \vdots \\ \overline{X}_n \end{pmatrix} \\
&= \sum_{i=1}^{n} \overline{X}_i' \Sigma^{-1} \overline{X}_i
\end{aligned}$$

and

$$\begin{aligned}
\overline{\boldsymbol{X}}' \left(\boldsymbol{I}_n \otimes \Sigma^{-1}\right) \boldsymbol{Y} &= \begin{pmatrix} \overline{X}_1' & \cdots & \overline{X}_n' \end{pmatrix} \begin{pmatrix} \Sigma^{-1} & 0 & \cdots & 0 \\ \vdots & \Sigma^{-1} & & \vdots \\ 0 & 0 & \cdots & 0^{-1} \end{pmatrix} \begin{pmatrix} Y_1 \\ \vdots \\ Y_n \end{pmatrix} \\
&= \sum_{i=1}^{n} \overline{X}_i' \Sigma^{-1} Y_i.
\end{aligned}$$

Since Σ is unknown, it must be replaced by an estimator. Using $\widehat{\Sigma}$ from (11.5), we obtain a feasible GLS estimator:

$$\widehat{\beta}_{\text{sur}} = \left(\sum_{i=1}^{n} \overline{X}_i' \widehat{\Sigma}^{-1} \overline{X}_i\right)^{-1} \left(\sum_{i=1}^{n} \overline{X}_i' \widehat{\Sigma}^{-1} Y_i\right)$$

$$= \left(\overline{\boldsymbol{X}}' \left(\boldsymbol{I}_n \otimes \widehat{\Sigma}^{-1} \right) \overline{\boldsymbol{X}} \right)^{-1} \left(\overline{\boldsymbol{X}}' \left(\boldsymbol{I}_n \otimes \widehat{\Sigma}^{-1} \right) \boldsymbol{Y} \right). \tag{11.18}$$

This is the **Seemingly Unrelated Regression (SUR)** estimator as introduced by Zellner (1962).

The estimator $\widehat{\Sigma}$ can be updated by calculating the SUR residuals $\widehat{e}_i = Y_i - \overline{X}_i' \widehat{\beta}_{\text{sur}}$ and the covariance matrix estimator $\widehat{\Sigma} = \frac{1}{n} \sum_{i=1}^{n} \widehat{e}_i \widehat{e}_i'$. Substituted into (11.18), we obtain an iterated SUR estimator. This can be iterated until convergence.

Under conditional homoskedasticity (11.8), we can derive its asymptotic distribution.

Theorem 11.4 Under Assumption 7.2 and (11.8),

$$\sqrt{n} \left(\widehat{\beta}_{\text{sur}} - \beta \right) \underset{d}{\longrightarrow} \mathrm{N}\left(0, \boldsymbol{V}_\beta^* \right)$$

where $\boldsymbol{V}_\beta^* = \left(\mathbb{E}\left[\overline{X}' \Sigma^{-1} \overline{X} \right] \right)^{-1}$.

Exercise 11.11 asks you to prove this theorem.

Under these assumptions, SUR is more efficient than least squares.

Theorem 11.5 Under Assumption 7.2 and (11.8),

$$\boldsymbol{V}_\beta^* = \left(\mathbb{E}\left[\overline{X}' \Sigma^{-1} \overline{X} \right] \right)^{-1} \leq \left(\mathbb{E}\left[\overline{X}' \overline{X} \right] \right)^{-1} \mathbb{E}\left[\overline{X}' \Sigma \overline{X} \right] \left(\mathbb{E}\left[\overline{X}' \overline{X} \right] \right)^{-1} = \boldsymbol{V}_\beta$$

and thus $\widehat{\beta}_{\text{sur}}$ is asymptotically more efficient than $\widehat{\beta}_{\text{ols}}$.

Exercise 11.12 asks you to prove this theorem.

An appropriate estimator of the variance of $\widehat{\beta}_{\text{sur}}$ is

$$\widehat{\boldsymbol{V}}_{\widehat{\beta}} = \left(\sum_{i=1}^{n} \overline{X}_i' \widehat{\Sigma}^{-1} \overline{X}_i \right)^{-1}.$$

Theorem 11.6 Under Assumption 7.2 and (11.8), $n \widehat{\boldsymbol{V}}_{\widehat{\beta}} \underset{p}{\longrightarrow} \boldsymbol{V}_\beta$.

See Exercise 11.13.

In Stata, the seemingly unrelated regressions estimator is implemented using the `sureg` command.

Arnold Zellner

Arnold Zellner (1927–2010) of the United States was a founding father of the econometrics field. He was a pioneer in Bayesian econometrics. One of his core contributions was the method of Seemingly Unrelated Regressions.

11.8 EQUIVALENCE OF SUR AND LEAST SQUARES

When the regressors are common across equations $X_j = X$, it turns out that the SUR estimator simplifies to least squares. To see this, recall that when regressors are common, this implies that $\overline{X} = \boldsymbol{I}_m \otimes X'$. Then

$$\begin{aligned}\overline{X}_i' \widehat{\Sigma}^{-1} &= (\boldsymbol{I}_m \otimes X_i)\, \widehat{\Sigma}^{-1} \\ &= \widehat{\Sigma}^{-1} \otimes X_i \\ &= \left(\widehat{\Sigma}^{-1} \otimes \boldsymbol{I}_k\right) (\boldsymbol{I}_m \otimes X_i) \\ &= \left(\widehat{\Sigma}^{-1} \otimes \boldsymbol{I}_k\right) \overline{X}_i'.\end{aligned}$$

Thus

$$\begin{aligned}\widehat{\beta}_{\text{sur}} &= \left(\sum_{i=1}^{n} \overline{X}_i' \widehat{\Sigma}^{-1} \overline{X}_i\right)^{-1} \left(\sum_{i=1}^{n} \overline{X}_i' \widehat{\Sigma}^{-1} Y_i\right) \\ &= \left(\left(\widehat{\Sigma}^{-1} \otimes \boldsymbol{I}_k\right) \sum_{i=1}^{n} \overline{X}_i' \overline{X}_i\right)^{-1} \left(\left(\widehat{\Sigma}^{-1} \otimes \boldsymbol{I}_k\right) \sum_{i=1}^{n} \overline{X}_i' Y_i\right) \\ &= \left(\sum_{i=1}^{n} \overline{X}_i' \overline{X}_i\right)^{-1} \left(\sum_{i=1}^{n} \overline{X}_i' Y_i\right) = \widehat{\beta}_{\text{ols}}.\end{aligned}$$

A model where regressors are not common across equations is nested within a model with the union of all regressors included in all equations. Thus the model with regressors common across equations is a fully unrestricted model, and a model where the regressors differ across equations is a restricted model. Thus the above result shows that the SUR estimator reduces to least squares in the absence of restrictions, but SUR can differ from least squares otherwise.

Another context where SUR = OLS is when the variance matrix is diagonal: $\Sigma = \operatorname{diag}\left\{\sigma_1^2, \ldots, \sigma_m^2\right\}$. In this case, $\Sigma^{-1/2}\overline{X}_i = \overline{X}_i \operatorname{diag}\left\{\boldsymbol{I}_{k_1}\sigma_1^{-1/2}, \ldots, \boldsymbol{I}_{k_m}\sigma_m^{-1/2}\right\}$, from which you can calculate that $\widehat{\beta}_{\text{sur}} = \widehat{\beta}_{\text{ols}}$. The intuition is that there is no difference in systems estimation when the equations are uncorrelated, which occurs when Σ is diagonal.

11.9 MAXIMUM LIKELIHOOD ESTIMATOR

Consider the linear model under the assumption that the error is independent of the regressors and multivariate normally distributed. Thus $Y = \overline{X}\beta + e$, with $e \sim \mathrm{N}(0, \Sigma)$. In this case, we can consider the maximum likelihood estimator (MLE) of the coefficients.

It is convenient to reparameterize the covariance matrix in terms of its inverse $\boldsymbol{S} = \Sigma^{-1}$. With this reparameterization, the conditional density of Y given $X = x$ equals

$$f(y \mid x) = \frac{\det(\boldsymbol{S})^{1/2}}{(2\pi)^{m/2}} \exp\left(-\frac{1}{2}(y - x\beta)' \boldsymbol{S} (y - x\beta)\right).$$

The log-likelihood function for the sample is

$$\ell_n(\beta, \boldsymbol{S}) = -\frac{nm}{2}\log(2\pi) + \frac{n}{2}\log(\det(\boldsymbol{S})) - \frac{1}{2}\sum_{i=1}^{n}\left(Y_i - \overline{X}_i\beta\right)' \boldsymbol{S}\left(Y_i - \overline{X}_i\beta\right).$$

The maximum likelihood estimator $(\widehat{\beta}_{\text{mle}}, \widehat{\boldsymbol{S}}_{\text{mle}})$ maximizes the log-likelihood function. The first-order conditions are

$$0 = \frac{\partial}{\partial \beta} \ell_n(\beta, \boldsymbol{S}) \bigg|_{\beta=\widehat{\beta}, \boldsymbol{S}=\widehat{\boldsymbol{S}}} = \sum_{i=1}^{n} \overline{X}_i \widehat{\boldsymbol{S}} \left(Y_i - \overline{X}_i \widehat{\beta}\right)$$

and

$$0 = \frac{\partial}{\partial \boldsymbol{S}} \ell_n(\beta, \Sigma) \bigg|_{\beta=\widehat{\beta}, \boldsymbol{S}=\widehat{\boldsymbol{S}}} = \frac{n}{2} \widehat{\boldsymbol{S}}^{-1} - \frac{1}{2} \operatorname{tr}\left(\sum_{i=1}^{n} \left(Y_i - \overline{X}_i \widehat{\beta}\right) \left(Y_i - \overline{X}_i \widehat{\beta}\right)'\right).$$

The second equation uses the matrix results $\frac{\partial}{\partial \boldsymbol{S}} \log(\det(\boldsymbol{S})) = \boldsymbol{S}^{-1}$, and $\frac{\partial}{\partial \boldsymbol{B}} \operatorname{tr}(\boldsymbol{AB}) = \boldsymbol{A}'$ from Appendix A.20.

Solving and making the substitution $\widehat{\Sigma} = \widehat{\boldsymbol{S}}^{-1}$, we obtain

$$\widehat{\beta}_{\text{mle}} = \left(\sum_{i=1}^{n} \overline{X}_i' \widehat{\Sigma}^{-1} \overline{X}_i\right)^{-1} \left(\sum_{i=1}^{n} \overline{X}_i' \widehat{\Sigma}^{-1} Y_i\right)$$

$$\widehat{\Sigma}_{\text{mle}} = \frac{1}{n} \sum_{i=1}^{n} \left(Y_i - \overline{X}_i \widehat{\beta}\right) \left(Y_i - \overline{X}_i \widehat{\beta}\right)'.$$

Notice that each equation refers to the other. Hence these are not closed-form expressions but can be solved via iteration. The solution is identical to the iterated SUR estimator. Thus the iterated SUR estimator is identical to MLE under normality.

Recall that the SUR estimator simplifies to OLS when the regressors are common across equations. The same occurs for the MLE. Thus when $\overline{X}_i = \boldsymbol{I}_m \otimes X_i'$, we find that $\widehat{\beta}_{\text{mle}} = \widehat{\beta}_{\text{ols}}$ and $\widehat{\Sigma}_{\text{mle}} = \widehat{\Sigma}_{\text{ols}}$.

11.10 RESTRICTED ESTIMATION

In many multivariate regression applications, it is desired to impose restrictions on the coefficients. In particular, cross-equation restrictions (for example, imposing Slutsky symmetry on a demand system) can be quite important and can only be imposed by a multivariate estimation method. Estimation subject to restrictions can be done by minimum distance, maximum likelihood, or the generalized method of moments.

Minimum distance is a straightforward application of the methods of Chapter 8 to the estimators presented in this chapter, as such methods apply to any asymptotically normal estimator. Imposing restrictions on maximum likelihood is also straightforward. The likelihood is maximized subject to the imposed restrictions. One important example is explored in detail in Section 11.11. Generalized method of moments estimation of multivariate regression subject to restrictions will be explored in Section 13.18. This is a particularly simple and straightforward way to estimate restricted multivariate regression models and is our generally preferred approach.

11.11 REDUCED RANK REGRESSION

One context where systems estimation is important is when it is desired to impose or test restrictions across equations. Restricted systems are commonly estimated by maximum likelihood under normality. In this section, we explore one important special case of restricted multivariate regression known as reduced rank regression. The model was originally proposed by Anderson (1951) and extended by Johansen (1995).

The unrestricted model is

$$Y = \boldsymbol{B}'X + \boldsymbol{C}'Z + e \tag{11.19}$$
$$\mathbb{E}\left[ee' \mid X, Z\right] = \Sigma$$

where $\boldsymbol{B}$ is $k \times m$, $\boldsymbol{C}$ is $\ell \times m$, $Y \in \mathbb{R}^m$, $X \in \mathbb{R}^k$, and $Z \in \mathbb{R}^\ell$. We separate the regressors as X and Z, because the coefficient matrix $\boldsymbol{B}$ will be restricted, while $\boldsymbol{C}$ will be unrestricted.

The matrix $\boldsymbol{B}$ is full rank if

$$\operatorname{rank}(\boldsymbol{B}) = \min(k, m).$$

The reduced rank restriction is $\operatorname{rank}(\boldsymbol{B}) = r < \min(k, m)$for some known r. The reduced rank restriction implies that we can write the coefficient matrix $\boldsymbol{B}$ in the factored form $\boldsymbol{B} = \boldsymbol{G}\boldsymbol{A}'$, where $\boldsymbol{A}$ is $m \times r$ and $\boldsymbol{G}$ is $k \times r$. This representation is not unique, as we can replace $\boldsymbol{G}$ with $\boldsymbol{G}\boldsymbol{Q}$ and $\boldsymbol{A}$ with $\boldsymbol{A}\boldsymbol{Q}^{-1\prime}$ for any invertible $\boldsymbol{Q}$ and the same relation holds. Identification therefore requires a normalization of the coefficients. A conventional normalization is $\boldsymbol{G}'\boldsymbol{D}\boldsymbol{G} = \boldsymbol{I}_r$ for a given $\boldsymbol{D}$.

Equivalently, the reduced rank restriction can be imposed by requiring that $\boldsymbol{B}$ satisfy the restriction $\boldsymbol{B}\boldsymbol{A}_\perp = \boldsymbol{G}\boldsymbol{A}'\boldsymbol{A}_\perp = 0$ for some $m \times (m - r)$ coefficient matrix $\boldsymbol{A}_\perp$. Since $\boldsymbol{G}$ is full rank, this requires that $\boldsymbol{A}'\boldsymbol{A}_\perp = 0$; hence $\boldsymbol{A}_\perp$ is the orthogonal complement of $\boldsymbol{A}$. Note that $\boldsymbol{A}_\perp$ is not unique, as it can be replaced by $\boldsymbol{A}_\perp\boldsymbol{Q}$ for any $(m - r) \times (m - r)$ invertible $\boldsymbol{Q}$. Thus if $\boldsymbol{A}_\perp$ is to be estimated, it requires a normalization.

We discuss methods for estimation of $\boldsymbol{G}$, $\boldsymbol{A}$, Σ, $\boldsymbol{C}$, and $\boldsymbol{A}_\perp$. The standard approach is maximum likelihood under the assumption that $e \sim \mathrm{N}(0, \Sigma)$. The log-likelihood function for the sample is

$$\ell_n(\boldsymbol{G}, \boldsymbol{A}, \boldsymbol{C}, \Sigma) = -\frac{nm}{2}\log(2\pi) - \frac{n}{2}\log(\det(\Sigma))$$
$$-\frac{1}{2}\sum_{i=1}^{n}\left(Y_i - \boldsymbol{A}\boldsymbol{G}'X_i - \boldsymbol{C}'Z_i\right)'\Sigma^{-1}\left(Y_i - \boldsymbol{A}\boldsymbol{G}'X_i - \boldsymbol{C}'Z_i\right).$$

Anderson (1951) derived the MLE by imposing the constraint $\boldsymbol{B}\boldsymbol{A}_\perp = 0$ via the method of Lagrange multipliers. This turns out to be algebraically cumbersome. Johansen (1995) instead proposed the following straightforward concentration method. Treating $\boldsymbol{G}$ as if it were known, maximize the log-likelihood with respect to the other parameters. Resubstituting these estimators, we obtain the concentrated log-likelihood function with respect to $\boldsymbol{G}$. This can be maximized to find the MLE for $\boldsymbol{G}$. The other parameter estimators are then obtained by substitution. We now describe these steps in detail.

Given $\boldsymbol{G}$, the likelihood is a normal multivariate regression in the variables $\boldsymbol{G}'X$ and Z, so the MLE for $\boldsymbol{A}$, $\boldsymbol{C}$, and Σ are least squares. In particular, using the Frisch-Waugh-Lovell residual regression formula (Theorem 3.5), we can write the estimators for $\boldsymbol{A}$ and Σ as

$$\widehat{\boldsymbol{A}}(\boldsymbol{G}) = \left(\widetilde{\boldsymbol{Y}}'\widetilde{\boldsymbol{X}}\boldsymbol{G}\right)\left(\boldsymbol{G}'\widetilde{\boldsymbol{X}}'\widetilde{\boldsymbol{X}}\boldsymbol{G}\right)^{-1}$$

and

$$\widehat{\Sigma}(\boldsymbol{G}) = \frac{1}{n}\left(\widetilde{\boldsymbol{Y}}'\widetilde{\boldsymbol{Y}} - \widetilde{\boldsymbol{Y}}'\widetilde{\boldsymbol{X}}\boldsymbol{G}\left(\boldsymbol{G}'\widetilde{\boldsymbol{X}}'\widetilde{\boldsymbol{X}}\boldsymbol{G}\right)^{-1}\boldsymbol{G}'\widetilde{\boldsymbol{X}}'\widetilde{\boldsymbol{Y}}\right)$$

where $\widetilde{\boldsymbol{Y}} = \boldsymbol{Y} - \boldsymbol{Z}\left(\boldsymbol{Z}'\boldsymbol{Z}\right)^{-1}\boldsymbol{Z}'\boldsymbol{Y}$, and $\widetilde{\boldsymbol{X}} = \boldsymbol{X} - \boldsymbol{Z}\left(\boldsymbol{Z}'\boldsymbol{Z}\right)^{-1}\boldsymbol{Z}'\boldsymbol{X}$.

Substituting these estimators into the log-likelihood function, we obtain the concentrated likelihood function, which is a function of $\boldsymbol{G}$ only:

$$\begin{aligned}\widetilde{\ell}_n(\boldsymbol{G}) &= \ell_n\left(\boldsymbol{G}, \widehat{\boldsymbol{A}}(\boldsymbol{G}), \widehat{\boldsymbol{C}}(\boldsymbol{G}), \widehat{\Sigma}(\boldsymbol{G})\right) \\ &= \frac{m}{2}\left(n\log(2\pi)-1\right) - \frac{n}{2}\log\left[\det\left(\widetilde{\boldsymbol{Y}}'\widetilde{\boldsymbol{Y}} - \widetilde{\boldsymbol{Y}}'\widetilde{\boldsymbol{X}}\boldsymbol{G}\left(\boldsymbol{G}'\widetilde{\boldsymbol{X}}'\widetilde{\boldsymbol{X}}\boldsymbol{G}\right)^{-1}\boldsymbol{G}'\widetilde{\boldsymbol{X}}'\widetilde{\boldsymbol{Y}}\right)\right] \\ &= \frac{m}{2}\left(n\log(2\pi)-1\right) - \frac{n}{2}\log\left(\det\left(\widetilde{\boldsymbol{Y}}'\widetilde{\boldsymbol{Y}}\right)\right) - \frac{n}{2}\log\left[\frac{\det\left(\boldsymbol{G}'\left(\widetilde{\boldsymbol{X}}'\widetilde{\boldsymbol{X}} - \widetilde{\boldsymbol{X}}'\widetilde{\boldsymbol{Y}}\left(\widetilde{\boldsymbol{Y}}'\widetilde{\boldsymbol{Y}}\right)^{-1}\boldsymbol{Y}'\widetilde{\boldsymbol{X}}\right)\boldsymbol{G}\right)}{\det\left(\boldsymbol{G}'\widetilde{\boldsymbol{X}}'\widetilde{\boldsymbol{X}}\boldsymbol{G}\right)}\right].\end{aligned}$$

The third equality uses Theorem A.1.8. The MLE $\widehat{\boldsymbol{G}}$ for $\boldsymbol{G}$ is the maximizer of $\widetilde{\ell}_n(\boldsymbol{G})$, or equivalently equals

$$\begin{aligned}\widehat{\boldsymbol{G}} &= \underset{\boldsymbol{G}}{\operatorname{argmin}} \frac{\det\left(\boldsymbol{G}'\left(\widetilde{\boldsymbol{X}}'\widetilde{\boldsymbol{X}} - \widetilde{\boldsymbol{X}}'\widetilde{\boldsymbol{Y}}\left(\widetilde{\boldsymbol{Y}}'\widetilde{\boldsymbol{Y}}\right)^{-1}\boldsymbol{Y}'\widetilde{\boldsymbol{X}}\right)\boldsymbol{G}\right)}{\det\left(\boldsymbol{G}'\widetilde{\boldsymbol{X}}'\widetilde{\boldsymbol{X}}\boldsymbol{G}\right)} \qquad (11.20) \\ &= \underset{\boldsymbol{G}}{\operatorname{argmax}} \frac{\det\left(\boldsymbol{G}'\widetilde{\boldsymbol{X}}'\widetilde{\boldsymbol{Y}}\left(\widetilde{\boldsymbol{Y}}'\widetilde{\boldsymbol{Y}}\right)^{-1}\boldsymbol{Y}'\widetilde{\boldsymbol{X}}\boldsymbol{G}\right)}{\det\left(\boldsymbol{G}'\widetilde{\boldsymbol{X}}'\widetilde{\boldsymbol{X}}\boldsymbol{G}\right)} \\ &= \{v_1, \ldots, v_r\}\end{aligned}$$

which are the generalized eigenvectors of $\widetilde{\boldsymbol{X}}'\widetilde{\boldsymbol{Y}}\left(\widetilde{\boldsymbol{Y}}'\widetilde{\boldsymbol{Y}}\right)^{-1}\boldsymbol{Y}'\widetilde{\boldsymbol{X}}$ with respect to $\widetilde{\boldsymbol{X}}'\widetilde{\boldsymbol{X}}$ corresponding to the r largest generalized eigenvalues. (Generalized eigenvalues and eigenvectors are discussed in Section A.14.) The estimator satisfies the normalization $\widehat{\boldsymbol{G}}'\widetilde{\boldsymbol{X}}'\widetilde{\boldsymbol{X}}\widehat{\boldsymbol{G}} = \boldsymbol{I}_r$. Letting v_j^* denote the eigenvectors of (11.20), we can also express $\widehat{\boldsymbol{G}} = \left\{v_m^*, \ldots, v_{m-r+1}^*\right\}$.

This is computationally straightforward. In MATLAB, for example, the generalized eigenvalues and eigenvectors of a matrix $\boldsymbol{A}$ with respect to $\boldsymbol{B}$ are found using the command `eig(A,B)`.

Given $\widehat{\boldsymbol{G}}$, the MLE $\widehat{\boldsymbol{A}}$, $\widehat{\boldsymbol{C}}$, $\widehat{\Sigma}$ are found by least squares regression of Y on $\widehat{\boldsymbol{G}}'X$ and Z. In particular, $\widehat{\boldsymbol{A}} = \widehat{\boldsymbol{G}}'\widetilde{\boldsymbol{X}}'\widetilde{\boldsymbol{Y}}$, because $\widehat{\boldsymbol{G}}'\widetilde{\boldsymbol{X}}'\widetilde{\boldsymbol{X}}\widehat{\boldsymbol{G}} = \boldsymbol{I}_r$.

We now discuss the estimator $\widehat{\boldsymbol{A}}_\perp$ of $\boldsymbol{A}_\perp$. It turns out that

$$\begin{aligned}\widehat{\boldsymbol{A}}_\perp &= \underset{\boldsymbol{A}}{\operatorname{argmax}} \frac{\det\left(\boldsymbol{A}'\left(\widetilde{\boldsymbol{Y}}'\widetilde{\boldsymbol{Y}} - \widetilde{\boldsymbol{Y}}'\widetilde{\boldsymbol{X}}\left(\widetilde{\boldsymbol{X}}'\widetilde{\boldsymbol{X}}\right)^{-1}\widetilde{\boldsymbol{X}}'\widetilde{\boldsymbol{Y}}\right)\boldsymbol{A}\right)}{\det\left(\boldsymbol{A}'\widetilde{\boldsymbol{Y}}'\widetilde{\boldsymbol{Y}}\boldsymbol{A}\right)} \qquad (11.21) \\ &= \{w_1, \ldots, w_{m-r}\}\end{aligned}$$

which are the eigenvectors of $\widetilde{\boldsymbol{Y}}'\widetilde{\boldsymbol{Y}} - \widetilde{\boldsymbol{Y}}'\widetilde{\boldsymbol{X}}\left(\widetilde{\boldsymbol{X}}'\widetilde{\boldsymbol{X}}\right)^{-1}\widetilde{\boldsymbol{X}}'\widetilde{\boldsymbol{Y}}$ with respect to $\widetilde{\boldsymbol{Y}}'\widetilde{\boldsymbol{Y}}$ associated with the largest $m-r$ eigenvalues.

By the dual eigenvalue relation (Theorem A.5), equations (11.20) and (11.21) have the same nonzero eigenvalues λ_j, and the associated eigenvectors v_j^* and w_j satisfy the relationship

$$w_j = \lambda_j^{-1/2}\left(\widetilde{\boldsymbol{Y}}'\widetilde{\boldsymbol{Y}}\right)^{-1}\widetilde{\boldsymbol{Y}}'\widetilde{\boldsymbol{X}}v_j^*.$$

Letting $\Lambda = \operatorname{diag}\{\lambda_m, \dots, \lambda_{m-r+1}\}$, this implies

$$\{w_m, \dots, w_{m-r+1}\} = \left(\widetilde{\boldsymbol{Y}}'\widetilde{\boldsymbol{Y}}\right)^{-1} \widetilde{\boldsymbol{Y}}'\widetilde{\boldsymbol{X}} \left\{v_m^*, \dots, v_{m-r+1}^*\right\} \Lambda = \left(\widetilde{\boldsymbol{Y}}'\widetilde{\boldsymbol{Y}}\right)^{-1} \widehat{\boldsymbol{A}}\Lambda.$$

The second equality holds because $\widehat{\boldsymbol{G}} = \left\{v_m^*, \dots, v_{m-r+1}^*\right\}$ and $\widehat{\boldsymbol{A}} = \widetilde{\boldsymbol{Y}}'\widetilde{\boldsymbol{X}}\widehat{\boldsymbol{G}}$. Since the eigenvectors w_j satisfy the orthogonality property $w_j'\widetilde{\boldsymbol{Y}}'\widetilde{\boldsymbol{Y}}w_\ell = 0$ for $j \neq \ell$, it follows that

$$0 = \widehat{\boldsymbol{A}}_\perp' \widetilde{\boldsymbol{Y}}'\widetilde{\boldsymbol{Y}} \{w_m, \dots, w_{m-r+1}\} = \widehat{\boldsymbol{A}}_\perp' \widehat{\boldsymbol{A}}\Lambda.$$

Since $\Lambda > 0$ we conclude that $\widehat{\boldsymbol{A}}_\perp' \widehat{\boldsymbol{A}} = 0$, as desired.

The solution $\widehat{\boldsymbol{A}}_\perp$ in (11.21) can be represented several ways. One that is computationally convenient is to observe that

$$\widetilde{\boldsymbol{Y}}'\widetilde{\boldsymbol{Y}} - \widetilde{\boldsymbol{Y}}'\widetilde{\boldsymbol{X}} \left(\widetilde{\boldsymbol{X}}'\widetilde{\boldsymbol{X}}\right)^{-1} \widetilde{\boldsymbol{Y}}'\widetilde{\boldsymbol{X}} = \boldsymbol{Y}'\boldsymbol{M}_{X,Z}\boldsymbol{Y} = \widetilde{\boldsymbol{E}}'\widetilde{\boldsymbol{E}}$$

where $\boldsymbol{M}_{X,Z} = \boldsymbol{I}_n - (\boldsymbol{X}, \boldsymbol{Z}) \left((\boldsymbol{X}, \boldsymbol{Z})' (\boldsymbol{X}, \boldsymbol{Z})\right)^{-1} (\boldsymbol{X}, \boldsymbol{Z})'$, and $\widetilde{\boldsymbol{E}} = \boldsymbol{M}_{X,Z}\boldsymbol{Y}$ is the residual matrix from the unrestricted multivariate least squares regression of $\boldsymbol{Y}$ on $\boldsymbol{X}$ and $\boldsymbol{Z}$. The first equality follows by the Frisch-Waugh-Lovell theorem (Theorem 3.5). This shows that $\widehat{\boldsymbol{A}}_\perp$ consists of the generalized eigenvectors of $\widetilde{\boldsymbol{E}}'\widetilde{\boldsymbol{E}}$ with respect to $\widetilde{\boldsymbol{Y}}'\widetilde{\boldsymbol{Y}}$ corresponding to the $m - r$ largest eigenvalues. In MATLAB, for example, these can be computed using the `eig(A,B)` command. Another representation is to write $\boldsymbol{M}_Z = \boldsymbol{I}_n - \boldsymbol{Z}\left(\boldsymbol{Z}'\boldsymbol{Z}\right)^{-1} \boldsymbol{Z}'$, so that

$$\widehat{\boldsymbol{A}}_\perp = \underset{A}{\operatorname{argmax}} \frac{\det\left(\boldsymbol{A}'\boldsymbol{Y}'\boldsymbol{M}_{X,Z}\boldsymbol{Y}\boldsymbol{A}\right)}{\det\left(\boldsymbol{A}'\boldsymbol{Y}'\boldsymbol{M}_Z\boldsymbol{Y}\boldsymbol{A}\right)} = \underset{A}{\operatorname{argmin}} \frac{\det\left(\boldsymbol{A}'\boldsymbol{Y}'\boldsymbol{M}_Z\boldsymbol{Y}\boldsymbol{A}\right)}{\det\left(\boldsymbol{A}'\boldsymbol{Y}'\boldsymbol{M}_{X,Z}\boldsymbol{Y}\boldsymbol{A}\right)}.$$

We summarize our findings in the following theorem.

Theorem 11.7 The MLE for the reduced rank model (11.19) under $e \sim \mathrm{N}(0, \Sigma)$ is given as follows. Let $\widetilde{\boldsymbol{Y}}$ and $\widetilde{\boldsymbol{X}}$ be the residual matrices from multivariate regression of $\boldsymbol{Y}$ and $\boldsymbol{X}$ on $\boldsymbol{Z}$, respectively. Then $\widehat{\boldsymbol{G}}_{\text{mle}} = \{v_1, \dots, v_r\}$, the generalized eigenvectors of $\widetilde{\boldsymbol{X}}'\widetilde{\boldsymbol{Y}} \left(\widetilde{\boldsymbol{Y}}'\widetilde{\boldsymbol{Y}}\right)^{-1} \boldsymbol{Y}'\widetilde{\boldsymbol{X}}$ with respect to $\widetilde{\boldsymbol{X}}'\widetilde{\boldsymbol{X}}$ corresponding to the r largest eigenvalues $\widehat{\lambda}_j$. $\widehat{\boldsymbol{A}}_{\text{mle}}$, $\widehat{\boldsymbol{C}}_{\text{mle}}$ and $\widehat{\Sigma}_{\text{mle}}$ are obtained by the least squares regression

$$Y_i = \widehat{\boldsymbol{A}}_{\text{mle}}\widehat{\boldsymbol{G}}_{\text{mle}}'X_i + \widehat{\boldsymbol{C}}_{\text{mle}}'Z_i + \widehat{e}_i$$

$$\widehat{\Sigma}_{\text{mle}} = \frac{1}{n}\sum_{i=1}^n \widehat{e}_i\widehat{e}_i'.$$

Let $\widetilde{\boldsymbol{E}}$ be the residual matrix from a multivariate regression of $\boldsymbol{Y}$ on $\boldsymbol{X}$ and $\boldsymbol{Z}$. Then $\widehat{\boldsymbol{A}}_\perp$ equals the generalized eigenvectors of $\widetilde{\boldsymbol{E}}'\widetilde{\boldsymbol{E}}$ with respect to $\widetilde{\boldsymbol{Y}}'\widetilde{\boldsymbol{Y}}$ corresponding to the $m - r$ smallest eigenvalues. The maximized likelihood equals

$$\ell_n = \frac{m}{2}\left(n \log(2\pi) - 1\right) - \frac{n}{2}\log\left(\det\left(\widetilde{\boldsymbol{Y}}'\widetilde{\boldsymbol{Y}}\right)\right) - \frac{n}{2}\sum_{j=1}^r \log\left(1 - \widehat{\lambda}_j\right).$$

An R package for reduced rank regression is “RRR.” I am unaware of a Stata command.

11.12 PRINCIPAL COMPONENT ANALYSIS

Section 4.21 described the Duflo, Dupas, and Kremer (2011) dataset, which is a sample of Kenyan first grade test scores. Following the authors, we focused on the variable *totalscore*, which is each student's composite test score. If you examine the data file, you will find other pieces of information about the students' performance, including each student's score on separate sections of the test, with the labels *wordscore* (word recognition), *sentscore* (sentence recognition), *letterscore* (letter recognition), *spellscore* (spelling), *additions_score* (addition), *substractions_score* (subtraction), and *multiplications_score* (multiplication). The total score sums the scores from the individual sections. Perhaps there is more information in the section scores. How can we learn about this from the data?

Principal component analysis (PCA) addresses this issue by ordering linear combinations by their contribution to variance.

Definition 11.1 Let X be a $k \times 1$ random vector.
The **first principal component** is $U_1 = h_1'X$, where h_1 satisfies

$$h_1 = \underset{h'h=1}{\operatorname{argmax}} \quad \operatorname{var}\left[h'X\right].$$

The **second principal component** is $U_2 = h_2'X$, where

$$h_2 = \underset{h'h=1,h'h_1=0}{\operatorname{argmax}} \quad \operatorname{var}\left[h'X\right].$$

In general, the jth **principal component** is $U_j = h_j'X$, where

$$h_j = \underset{h'h=1,h'h_1=0,\ldots,h'h_{j-1}=0}{\operatorname{argmax}} \quad \operatorname{var}\left[h'X\right].$$

The principal components of X are linear combinations $h'X$ ranked by contribution to variance. By the properties of quadratic forms (Section A.15), the weight vectors h_j are the eigenvectors of $\Sigma = \operatorname{var}[X]$.

Theorem 11.8 The principal components of X are $U_j = h_j'X$, where h_j is the eigenvector of Σ associated with the jth ordered eigenvalue λ_j of Σ.

Another way to see the PCA construction is as follows. Since Σ is symmetric the spectral decomposition, Theorem A.3, states that $\Sigma = \boldsymbol{H}\boldsymbol{D}\boldsymbol{H}'$, where $\boldsymbol{H} = [h_1, \ldots, h_k]$ and $\boldsymbol{D} = \operatorname{diag}(d_1, \ldots, d_k)$ are the eigenvectors and eigenvalues of Σ. Since Σ is positive semi-definite, the eigenvalues are real, nonnegative, and ordered $d_1 \geq d_2 \geq \cdots \geq d_k$. Let $U = (U_1, \ldots, U_k)$ be the principal components of X. By Theorem 11.8, $U = \boldsymbol{H}'X$. The covariance matrix of U is

$$\operatorname{var}[U] = \operatorname{var}\left[\boldsymbol{H}'X\right] = \boldsymbol{H}'\Sigma\boldsymbol{H} = \boldsymbol{D}$$

which is diagonal. Thus, $\operatorname{var}\left[U_j\right] = d_j$, and the principal components are mutually uncorrelated. The relative variance contribution of the jth principal component is $d_j / \operatorname{tr}(\Sigma)$.

Principal components are sensitive to the scaling of X. Consequently, it is recommended to first scale each element of X to have mean 0 and unit variance. In this case, Σ is a correlation matrix.

Table 11.1
Eigenvalue decomposition of sample correlation matrix

	Eigenvalue	Proportion
1	4.02	0.57
2	1.04	0.15
3	0.57	0.08
4	0.52	0.08
5	0.37	0.05
6	0.29	0.04
7	0.19	0.03

Table 11.2
Principal component weight vectors

	First	Second
Words	0.41	−0.32
Sentences	0.32	−0.49
Letters	0.40	−0.13
Spelling	0.43	−0.28
Addition	0.38	0.41
Subtraction	0.35	0.52
Multiplication	0.33	0.36

The sample principal components are obtained by replacing the unknowns by sample estimators. Let $\widehat{\Sigma}$ be the sample covariance or correlation matrix and $\widehat{h}_1, \widehat{h}_2, \ldots, \widehat{h}_k$ its ordered eigenvectors. The sample principal components are $\widehat{h}_j' X_i$.

To illustrate, we use the Duflo, Dupas, and Kremer (2011) dataset. Table 11.1 displays the seven eigenvalues of the sample correlation matrix for the seven test scores described above. The seven eigenvalues sum to 7, because we have applied PCA to the correlation matrix. The first eigenvalue is 4.0, implying that the first principal component explains 57% of the variance of the seven test scores. The second eigenvalue is 1.0, implying that the second principal component explains 15% of the variance. Together the first two components explain 72% of the variance of the seven test scores.

Table 11.2 displays the weight vectors (eigenvectors) for the first two principal components. The weights for the first component are all positive and similar in magnitude. Thus the first principal component is similar to a simple average of the seven test scores, which is quite fascinating. It is consistent with our intuition that a simple average (e.g., the variable *totalscore*) captures most of the information contained in the seven test scores. The weights for the second component have a different pattern. The four literacy scores receive negative weight, and the three math scores receive positive weight with similar magnitudes. Thus the second principal component is similar to the difference between a student's math and verbal test scores. Taken together, the information in the first two principal components is equivalent to "average verbal" and "average math" test scores. What this shows is that 57% of the variation in the seven section test scores can be explained by a simple average (e.g., *totalscore*), and 72% can be explained by averages for the verbal and math halves of the test.

In Stata, principal components analysis can be implemented with the `pca` command. In R, use `prcomp` or `princomp`. All three commands can be applied to either covariance matrices (unscaled data) or correlation matrices (normalized data), but they have different default settings. The Stata `pca` command by default normalizes the observations. The R commands by default do not normalize the observations.

11.13 FACTOR MODELS

Closely related to principal components are factor models. These are statistical models that decompose random vectors into common factors and idiosyncratic errors. Factor models are popular throughout the social sciences. Consequently, a variety of estimation methods have been developed. In the next few sections, we focus on methods that are popular among economists.

Let $X = (X_1, \ldots, X_k)'$ be a $k \times 1$ random vector (e.g., the seven test scores described in Section 11.12). Assume that the elements of X are scaled to have mean 0 and unit variance.

A **single factor model** for X is

$$X = \lambda F + u \tag{11.22}$$

where $\lambda \in \mathbb{R}^k$ are **factor loadings**, $F \in \mathbb{R}$ is a **common factor**, and $u \in \mathbb{R}^k$ is a random error. The factor F is individual-specific, while the coefficient λ is common across individuals. The model (11.22) specifies that correlation between the elements of X is due to the common factor F. In the student test score example, it is intuitive to think of F as a student's scholastic "aptitude;" in this case, the vector λ describes how scholastic aptitude affects the seven subject scores.

A multiple factor model has $r < k$ factors. We write the model as

$$X = \Lambda F + u \tag{11.23}$$

where Λ is a $k \times r$ matrix of factor loadings, and $F = (F_1, \ldots, F_r)'$ is an $r \times 1$ vector of factors. In the student test score example, possible factors could be "math aptitude," "language skills," "social skills," "artistic ability," "creativity," and so forth. The factor loading matrix Λ indicates the effect of each factor on each test score. The number of factors r is taken as known. We discuss selection of r later.

The error vector u is assumed to be mean 0, uncorrelated with F, and (under correct specification) to have mutually uncorrelated elements. We write its covariance matrix as $\Psi = \mathbb{E}\left[uu'\right]$. The factor vector F can either be treated as random or as a regressor. In this section we treat F as random; in Section 11.14, we treat F as a regressor. The random factors F are assumed to have mean 0 and are normalized, so that $\mathbb{E}\left[FF'\right] = \boldsymbol{I}_r$.

The assumptions imply that the correlation matrix $\Sigma = \mathbb{E}\left[XX'\right]$ equals

$$\Sigma = \Lambda\Lambda' + \Psi. \tag{11.24}$$

The factor analysis literature often describes $\Lambda\Lambda'$ as the **communality** and the idiosyncratic error matrix Ψ as the **uniqueness**. The former is the portion of the variance that is explained by the factor model and the latter is the unexplained portion of the variance.

The model is often[1] estimated by **maximum likelihood**. Under joint normality of (F, u), the distribution of X is $\mathrm{N}\left(0, \Lambda\Lambda' + \Psi\right)$. The parameters are Λ and $\Psi = \operatorname{diag}(\psi_1, \ldots, \psi_k)$. The log-likelihood function of a random sample $(X_1, \ldots, X_n)$ is

$$\ell_n(\Lambda, \Psi) = -\frac{nk}{2}\log(2\pi) - \frac{n}{2}\log\det\left(\Lambda\Lambda' + \Psi\right) - \frac{n}{2}\operatorname{tr}\left(\left(\Lambda\Lambda' + \Psi\right)^{-1}\widehat{\Sigma}\right). \tag{11.25}$$

[1]Other estimators are used in applied factor analysis. However, there is little reason to consider estimators beyond the MLE of this section and the principal components estimator of Section 11.14.

The MLE $\left(\widehat{\Lambda}, \widehat{\Psi}\right)$ maximizes $\ell_n(\Lambda, \Psi)$. There is not an algebraic solution so the estimator is found using numerical methods. Fortunately, computational algorithms are available in standard packages. A detailed description and analysis can be found in Anderson (2003, chapter 14).

The form of the log likelihood is intriguing. Notice that the log likelihood is only a function of the observations through its correlation matrix $\widehat{\Sigma}$, and only a function of the parameters through the population correlation matrix $\Lambda\Lambda' + \Psi$. The final term in (11.25) is a measure of the match between $\widehat{\Sigma}$ and $\Lambda\Lambda' + \Psi$. Together, we see that the Gaussian log likelihood is essentially a measure of the fit of the model and sample correlation matrices. It is therefore not reliant on the normality assumption.

It is often of interest to estimate the factors F_i. Given Λ, the equation $X_i = \Lambda F_i + u_i$ can be viewed as a regression with coefficient F_i. Its least squares estimator is $\widehat{F}_i = \left(\Lambda'\Lambda\right)^{-1}\Lambda' X_i$. The GLS estimator (taking into account the covariance matrix of u_i) is $\widehat{F}_i = \left(\Lambda'\Psi^{-1}\Lambda\right)^{-1}\Lambda'\Psi^{-1}X_i$. This motivates the **Bartlett scoring** estimator:

$$\widetilde{F}_i = \left(\widehat{\Lambda}'\widehat{\Psi}^{-1}\widehat{\Lambda}\right)^{-1}\widehat{\Lambda}'\widehat{\Psi}^{-1}X_i.$$

The idealized version satisfies

$$\widehat{F}_i = \left(\Lambda'\Psi^{-1}\Lambda\right)^{-1}\Lambda'\Psi^{-1}\left(\Lambda F_i + u_i\right) = F_i + \left(\Lambda'\Psi^{-1}\Lambda\right)^{-1}\Lambda'\Psi^{-1}u_i$$

which is unbiased for F_i and has variance $\left(\Lambda'\Psi^{-1}\Lambda\right)^{-1}$. Thus the Barlett scoring estimator is typically described as "unbiased," though this is actually a property of its idealized version $\widehat{F}_i$.

A second estimator for the factors can be constructed from the multivariate linear projection of F on X. This is $F = \boldsymbol{A}X + \xi$, where the coefficient matrix $\boldsymbol{A}$ is $r \times k$. The coefficient matrix equals

$$\boldsymbol{A} = \mathbb{E}\left[FX'\right]\mathbb{E}\left[XX'\right]^{-1} = \Lambda'\Sigma^{-1}$$

where the second equation uses $\mathbb{E}\left[FX'\right] = \mathbb{E}\left[F\left(\Lambda F + u\right)'\right] = \mathbb{E}\left[FF'\right]\Lambda' + \mathbb{E}\left[Fu'\right] = \Lambda'$. The predicted value of F_i is $F_i^* = \boldsymbol{A}X_i = \Lambda'\Sigma^{-1}X_i$. This motivates the **regression scoring** estimator:

$$\overline{F}_i = \widehat{\Lambda}'\widehat{\Sigma}^{-1}X_i.$$

The idealized version F_i^* has conditional expectation $\Lambda'\Sigma^{-1}\Lambda F_i$ and is thus biased for F_i. Hence the regression scoring estimator $\overline{F}_i$ is often described as "biased." Some algebraic manipulations reveal that F_i^* has MSE $\boldsymbol{I}_r - \Lambda'\left(\Lambda'\Lambda + \Psi\right)^{-1}\Lambda$, which is smaller (in a positive definite sense) than the MSE of the idealized Bartlett estimator $\widehat{F}_i$.

Which estimator is preferred, Bartlett or regression scoring? The differences diminish when k is large, so the choice is most relevant for small to moderate k. The regression scoring estimator has lower approximate MSE, meaning that it is a more precise estimator. So based on estimation precision, this is our recommended choice.

The factor loadings Λ and factors F are not separately identified. To see this, notice that if you replace (Λ, F) with $\Lambda^* = \Lambda\boldsymbol{G}$ and $F^* = \boldsymbol{G}'F$, where $\boldsymbol{G}$ is $r \times r$ and orthonormal, then the regression model is identical. Such replacements are called "rotations" in the factor analysis literature. Any orthogonal rotation of the factor loadings is an equally valid representation. The default MLE outputs are one specific rotation; others can be obtained by a variety of algorithms (which we do not review here). Consequently it is unwise to attribute meaning to the individual factor loading estimates.

Another important and tricky issue is selection of the number of factors r. There is no clear guideline. One approach is to examine the principal component decomposition, look for a division between the "large" and "small" eigenvalues, and set r to equal to the number of "large" eigenvalues. Another approach is based on testing. As a by-product of the MLE (and standard package implementations), we obtain the LR test for the null hypothesis of r factors against the alternative hypothesis of k factors. If the LR test rejects (has a small p-value), this is evidence that the given r may be too small.

In Stata, the MLE $\left(\widehat{\Lambda}, \widehat{\Psi}\right)$ can be calculated with the `factor, ml factors(r)` command. The factor estimates $\widetilde{F}_i$ and $\overline{F}_i$ can be calculated by the `predict` command with either the `barlett` or `regression` option, respectively. In R, the command `factanal(X,factors=r,rotation="none")` calculates the MLE $\left(\widehat{\Lambda}, \widehat{\Psi}\right)$ and also calculates the factor estimates $\widetilde{F}_i$ and/or $\overline{F}_i$ using the `scores` option.

11.14 APPROXIMATE FACTOR MODELS

The MLE of Section 11.13 is a good choice for factor estimation when the number of variables k is small and the factor model is believed to be correctly specified. In many economic applications of factor analysis, however, the number k of variables is large. In such contexts, the MLE can be computationally costly and/or unstable. Furthermore, it is typically not credible to believe that the model is correctly specified; instead it is more reasonable to view the factor model as a useful approximation. In this section, we explore an approach known as the approximate factor model with estimation by principal components. The estimation method is justified by an asymptotic framework where the number of variables $k \to \infty$.

The **approximate factor model** was introduced by Chamberlain and Rothschild (1983). It is the same as (11.23) but relaxes the assumption on the idiosyncratic error u, so that the covariance matrix $\Psi = \mathbb{E}\left[uu'\right]$ is left unrestricted. In this context, the Gaussian MLE of Section 11.13 is misspecified.

Chamberlain and Rothschild (and the literature which followed) proposed estimation by least squares. The idea is to treat the factors as unknown regressors and simultaneously estimate the factors F_i and factor loadings Λ. We first discuss the estimation method.

Let $(X_1, \ldots, X_n)$ be a sample centered at sample means. The least squares criterion is

$$\frac{1}{n}\sum_{i=1}^{n}\left(X_i - \Lambda F_i\right)'\left(X_i - \Lambda F_i\right).$$

Let $\left(\widehat{\Lambda}, \widehat{F}_1, \ldots, \widehat{F}_n\right)$ be the joint minimizers. As Λ and F_i are not separately identified, a normalization is needed. For compatibility with the notation of Section 11.13, we use $n^{-1}\sum_{i=1}^{n}\widehat{F}_i\widehat{F}_i' = \boldsymbol{I}_r$.

Let us use a concentration argument to find the solution. As described in Section 11.13, each observation satisfies the multivariate equation $X_i = \Lambda F_i + u_i$. For fixed Λ, this is a set of k equations with r unknowns F_i. The least squares solution is $\widehat{F}_i(\Lambda) = \left(\Lambda'\Lambda\right)^{-1}\Lambda' X_i$. Substituting this expression into the least squares criterion, the concentrated least squares criterion for Λ is

$$\begin{aligned}\frac{1}{n}\sum_{i=1}^{n}\left(X_i - \Lambda\widehat{F}_i(\Lambda)\right)'\left(X_i - \Lambda\widehat{F}_i(\Lambda)\right) &= \frac{1}{n}\sum_{i=1}^{n}\left(X_i - \Lambda\left(\Lambda'\Lambda\right)^{-1}\Lambda' X_i\right)'\left(X_i - \Lambda\left(\Lambda'\Lambda\right)^{-1}\Lambda' X_i\right)\\ &= \frac{1}{n}\sum_{i=1}^{n}\left(X_i'X_i - X_i'\Lambda\left(\Lambda'\Lambda\right)^{-1}\Lambda' X_i\right)\\ &= \operatorname{tr}\left[\widehat{\Sigma}\right] - \operatorname{tr}\left[\left(\Lambda'\Lambda\right)^{-1}\Lambda'\widehat{\Sigma}\Lambda\right]\end{aligned}$$

where $\widehat{\Sigma} = n^{-1}\sum_{i=1}^{n}X_iX_i'$ is the sample covariance matrix. The least squares estimator $\widehat{\Lambda}$ minimizes this criterion. Let $\widehat{\boldsymbol{D}}$ and $\widehat{\boldsymbol{H}}$ be first r eigenvalues and eigenvectors of $\widehat{\Sigma}$. Using the normalization $\Lambda'\Lambda = \boldsymbol{I}_r$, from the extrema results of Section A.15, the minimizer of the least squares criterion is $\widehat{\Lambda} = \widehat{\boldsymbol{H}}$. More broadly, any rotation of $\widehat{\boldsymbol{H}}$ is valid. Consider $\widehat{\Lambda}=\widehat{\boldsymbol{H}}\widehat{\boldsymbol{D}}^{1/2}$. Recall the expression for the factors $\widehat{F}_i(\Lambda)=\left(\Lambda'\Lambda\right)^{-1}\Lambda' X_i$. We find that the estimated factors are

$$\widehat{F}_i=\left(\widehat{\boldsymbol{D}}^{1/2}\widehat{\boldsymbol{H}}'\widehat{\boldsymbol{H}}\widehat{\boldsymbol{D}}^{1/2}\right)^{-1}\widehat{\boldsymbol{D}}^{1/2}\widehat{\boldsymbol{H}}' X_i=\widehat{\boldsymbol{D}}^{-1/2}\widehat{\boldsymbol{H}}' X_i.$$

We calculate that

$$n^{-1}\sum_{i=1}^{n}\widehat{F}_i\widehat{F}_i'=\widehat{\boldsymbol{D}}^{-1/2}\widehat{\boldsymbol{H}}'\widehat{\Sigma}\widehat{\boldsymbol{H}}\widehat{\boldsymbol{D}}^{-1/2\prime}=\widehat{\boldsymbol{D}}^{-1/2}\widehat{\boldsymbol{D}}\widehat{\boldsymbol{D}}^{-1/2\prime}=\boldsymbol{I}_r$$

which is the desired normalization. Thus the rotation $\widehat{\Lambda}=\widehat{\boldsymbol{H}}\widehat{\boldsymbol{D}}^{1/2}$ produces factor estimates satisfying this normalization.

We have proven the following result.

Theorem 11.9 The least squares estimator of the factor model (11.23) under the normalization $n^{-1}\sum_{i=1}^{n}\widehat{F}_i\widehat{F}_i'=\boldsymbol{I}_r$ has the following solution:

1. Let $\widehat{\boldsymbol{D}}=\operatorname{diag}\left[\widehat{d}_1,\ldots,\widehat{d}_r\right]$ and $\widehat{\boldsymbol{H}}=\left[\widehat{h}_1,\ldots,\widehat{h}_r\right]$ be the first r eigenvalues and eigenvectors of the sample covariance matrix $\widehat{\Sigma}$.
2. $\widehat{\Lambda}=\widehat{\boldsymbol{H}}\widehat{\boldsymbol{D}}^{1/2}$.
3. $\widehat{F}_i=\widehat{\boldsymbol{D}}^{-1/2}\widehat{\boldsymbol{H}}' X_i$.

Theorem 11.9 shows that the least squares estimator is based on an eigenvalue decomposition of the covariance matrix. This is computationally stable even in high dimensions.

The factor estimates are the principal components scaled by the eigenvalues of $\widehat{\Sigma}$. Specifically, the jth factor estimate is $\widehat{F}_{ji}=\widehat{d}_j^{-1/2}\widehat{h}_j' X$. Consequently, many authors call this estimator the "principal-component method."

Unfortunately, $\widehat{\Lambda}$ is inconsistent for Λ if k is fixed, as we now show. By the WLLN and CMT, $\widehat{\Sigma}\underset{p}{\longrightarrow}\Sigma$ and $\widehat{\boldsymbol{H}}\underset{p}{\longrightarrow}\boldsymbol{H}$, the latter the first r eigenvectors of Σ. When Ψ is diagonal, the eigenvectors of $\Sigma=\Lambda\Lambda'+\Psi$ do not lie in the range space of Λ except in the special case $\Psi=\sigma^2\boldsymbol{I}_k$. Consequently, the estimator $\widehat{\Lambda}$ is inconsistent.

This inconsistency should not be viewed as surprising. The sample has a total of nk observations, and the model has a total of $nr+kr-r(r+1)/2$ parameters. Since the number of estimated pararameters is proportional to sample size, we should not expect estimator consistency.

As first recognized by Chamberlain and Rothschild, this deficiency diminishes as k increases. Specifically, assume that $k\to\infty$ as $n\to\infty$. One implication is that the number of observations nk increases at a rate faster than n, while the number of parameters increases at a rate proportional to n. Another implication is that as k increases, there is increasing information about the factors.

To make this observation precise, we add the following assumption. Let $\lambda_{\min}(\boldsymbol{A})$ and $\lambda_{\max}(\boldsymbol{A})$ denote the smallest and largest eigenvalues of a positive semi-definite matrix $\boldsymbol{A}$.

Assumption 11.1 As $k\to\infty$

1. $\lambda_{\max}(\Psi)\le B<\infty$.
2. $\lambda_{\min}\left(\Lambda'\Lambda\right)\to\infty$ as $k\to\infty$.

Assumption 11.1.1 bounds the covariance matrix of the idiosyncratic errors. When $\Psi = \text{diag}\left(\sigma_1^2, \ldots, \sigma_k^2\right)$, this is the same as bounding the individual variances. Effectively, Assumption 11.1.1 means that while the elements of u can be correlated, they cannot have a correlation structure similar to that of a factor model. Assumption 11.1.2 requires the factor loading matrix to increase in magnitude as the number of variables increases. This is a fairly mild requirement. When the factor loadings are of similar magnitude across variables, $\lambda_{\min}\left(\Lambda'\Lambda\right) \sim k \to \infty$. Conceptually, Assumption 11.1.2 requires additional variables to add information about the unobserved factors.

Assumption 11.1 implies that for the covariance matrix factorization $\Sigma = \Lambda\Lambda' + \Psi$, the component $\Lambda\Lambda'$ dominates as k increases. Thus for large k, the first r eigenvectors of Σ are equivalent to those of $\Lambda\Lambda'$, which are in the range space of Λ. This observation led Chamberlain and Rothschild (1983) to deduce that the principal components estimator is an asymptotic (large k) analog estimator for the factor loadings and factors. Bai (2003) demonstrated that the estimator is consistent as $n, k \to \infty$ jointly. The conditions and proofs are technical and so are not reviewed here.

Now consider the estimated factors

$$\widehat{F}_i = \boldsymbol{D}^{-1/2}\boldsymbol{H}'X_i = \boldsymbol{D}^{-1}\Lambda'X_i$$

where for simplicity we ignore estimation error. Since $X_i = \Lambda F_i + u_i$ and $\Lambda'\Lambda = \boldsymbol{D}$, we can write this as

$$\widehat{F}_i = F_i + \boldsymbol{D}^{-1}\Lambda'u_i.$$

Thus $\widehat{F}_i$ is an unbiased estimator for F_i and has variance $\text{var}\left[\widehat{F}_i\right] = \boldsymbol{D}^{-1}\Lambda'\Psi\Lambda\boldsymbol{D}^{-1}$. Under Assumption 11.1, $\left\|\text{var}\left[\widehat{F}_i\right]\right\| \leq B/\lambda_{\min}\left(\Lambda'\Lambda\right) \to 0$. Thus $\widehat{F}_i$ is consistent for F_i as $k \to \infty$. Bai (2003) shows that this result extends to the feasible estimator as $n, k \to \infty$.

In Stata, the least squares estimator $\widehat{\Lambda}$ and factors $\widehat{F}_i$ can be calculated with the `factor, pcf factors(r)` command followed by `predict`. In R, a feasible estimation approach is to calculate the factors by eigenvalue decomposition.

11.15 FACTOR MODELS WITH ADDITIONAL REGRESSORS

Consider the model

$$X = \Lambda F + \boldsymbol{B}Z + e$$

where X and e are $k \times 1$, Λ is $k \times r$, F is $r \times 1$, $\boldsymbol{B}$ is $k \times \ell$, and Z is $\ell \times 1$. The coefficients Λ and $\boldsymbol{B}$ can be estimated by a combination of factor regression (either MLE or principal components) and least squares. The key is the following two observations:

1. Given $\boldsymbol{B}$, the coefficient Λ can be estimated by factor regression applied to $X - \boldsymbol{B}Z$.
2. Given the factors F, the coefficients Λ and $\boldsymbol{B}$ can be estimated by multivariate least squares of X on F and Z.

Estimation iterates between these two steps. Start with a preliminary estimator of $\boldsymbol{B}$ obtained by multivariate least squares of X on Z. Then apply the above two steps and iterate until convergence.

11.16 FACTOR-AUGMENTED REGRESSION

In the previous sections, we considered factor models that decompose a set of variables into common factors and idiosyncratic errors. In this section, we consider factor-augmented regression, which uses such common factors as regressors for dimension reduction.

Suppose we have the variables (Y, Z, X), where $Y \in \mathbb{R}$, $Z \in \mathbb{R}^{\ell}$, and $X \in \mathbb{R}^{k}$. In practice, k may be large and the elements of X may be highly correlated. The **factor-augmented regression** model is

$$
\begin{aligned}
Y &= F'\beta + Z'\gamma + e \\
X &= \Lambda F + u \\
\mathbb{E}[Fe] &= 0 \\
\mathbb{E}[Ze] &= 0 \\
\mathbb{E}\left[Fu'\right] &= 0 \\
\mathbb{E}[ue] &= 0
\end{aligned}
$$

The random variables are $e \in \mathbb{R}$, $F \in \mathbb{R}^{r}$, and $u \in \mathbb{R}^{k}$. The regression coefficients are $\beta \in \mathbb{R}^{k}$ and $\gamma \in \mathbb{R}^{\ell}$. The matrix Λ consists of the factor loadings.

This model specifies that the influence of X on Y is through the common factors F. The idea is that the variation in the regressors is mostly captured by the variation in the factors, so the influence of the regressors can be captured through these factors. This can be viewed as a dimension-reduction technique, as we have reduced the k-dimensional X to the r-dimensional F. Interest typically focuses on the regressors Z and their coefficients γ. The factors F are included in the regression as "controls" and their coefficient β is less typically of interest. Since it is difficult to interpret the factors F, only their range space is identified, and it is generally prudent to avoid intrepreting the coefficients β.

The model is typically estimated in multiple steps. First, the factor loadings Λ and factors F_i are estimated by factor regression. In the case of principal-components estimation, the factor estimates are the scaled[2] principal components $\widehat{F}_i = \widehat{\boldsymbol{D}}^{-1}\widehat{\Lambda}'X_i$. Second, Y is regressed on the estimated factors and the other regressors to obtain the estimator of β and γ. This second-step estimator equals (for simplicity, assume there is no Z)

$$
\begin{aligned}
\widehat{\beta} &= \left(\sum_{i=1}^{n} \widehat{F}_i \widehat{F}_i'\right)^{-1} \left(\sum_{i=1}^{n} \widehat{F}_i Y_i\right) \\
&= \left(\widehat{\boldsymbol{D}}^{-1}\widehat{\Lambda}' \frac{1}{n}\sum_{i=1}^{n} X_i X_i' \widehat{\Lambda}\widehat{\boldsymbol{D}}^{-1}\right)^{-1} \left(\widehat{\boldsymbol{D}}^{-1}\widehat{\Lambda}' \frac{1}{n}\sum_{i=1}^{n} X_i Y_i\right).
\end{aligned}
$$

Now let's investigate its asymptotic behavior. As $n \to \infty$, $\widehat{\Lambda} \underset{p}{\longrightarrow} \Lambda$ and $\widehat{\boldsymbol{D}} \underset{p}{\longrightarrow} \boldsymbol{D}$, so

$$
\widehat{\beta} \underset{p}{\longrightarrow} \beta^* = \left(\boldsymbol{D}^{-1}\Lambda'\mathbb{E}\left[XX'\right]\Lambda\boldsymbol{D}^{-1}\right)^{-1}\left(\boldsymbol{D}^{-1}\Lambda'\mathbb{E}[XY]\right). \tag{11.26}
$$

Recall that $\mathbb{E}\left[XX'\right] = \Lambda\Lambda' + \Psi$ and $\Lambda'\Lambda = \boldsymbol{D}$. We calculate that

$$
\mathbb{E}[XY] = \mathbb{E}\left[(\Lambda F + u)\left(F'\beta + e\right)\right] = \Lambda\beta.
$$

[2] The unscaled principal components can equivalently be used if the coefficients $\widehat{\beta}$ are not reported. The coefficient estimates $\widehat{\gamma}$ are unaffected by the choice of factor scaling.

We find that the right-hand side of (11.26) equals

$$\beta^* = \left(D^{-1}\Lambda'\left(\Lambda\Lambda'+\Psi\right)\Lambda D^{-1}\right)^{-1}\left(D^{-1}\Lambda'\Lambda\beta\right) = \left(I_r + D^{-1}\Lambda'\Psi\Lambda D^{-1}\right)^{-1}\beta$$

which does not equal β. Thus $\widehat{\beta}$ has a probability limit but is inconsistent for β as $n\to\infty$.

This deficiency diminishes as $k\to\infty$. Indeed,

$$\left\| D^{-1}\Lambda'\Psi\Lambda D^{-1}\right\| \le B\left\| D^{-1}\right\| \to 0$$

as $k\to\infty$, which implies $\beta^*\to\beta$. Hence, if we take the sequential asymptotic limit $n\to\infty$ followed by $k\to\infty$, we find $\widehat{\beta}\underset{p}{\longrightarrow}\beta$. This implies that the estimator is consistent. Bai (2003) demonstrated consistency under the more rigorous but technically challenging setting where $n,k\to\infty$ jointly. The implication of this result is that factor-augmented regression is consistent if both the sample size and dimension of X are large.

For asymptotic normality of $\widehat{\beta}$, it turns out that we need to strengthen Assumption 11.1.2. The relevant condition is $n^{-1/2}\lambda_{\min}\left(\Lambda'\Lambda\right)\to\infty$, which is similar to the condition that $k^2/n\to\infty$. This is technical but can be interpreted as meaning that k is large relative to $\sqrt{n}$. Intuitively, this condition requires that the dimension of X be larger than sample size n.

In Stata, estimation takes the following steps. First, the `factor` command is used to estimate the factor model. Either MLE or principal components estimation can be used. Second, the `predict` command is used to estimate the factors, either by Barlett or regression scoring. Third, the factors are treated as regressors in an estimated regression.

11.17 MULTIVARIATE NORMAL*

Some interesting sampling results hold for matrix-valued normal variates. Let $\boldsymbol{Y}$ be an $n\times m$ matrix whose rows are independent and distributed $\mathrm{N}(\mu,\Sigma)$. We say that $\boldsymbol{Y}$ is **multivariate matrix normal**, and write $\boldsymbol{Y}\sim\mathrm{N}(\overline{\mu},\boldsymbol{I}_n\otimes\Sigma)$, where $\overline{\mu}$ is $n\times m$ with each row equal to μ'. The notation is due to the fact that $\operatorname{vec}\left((\boldsymbol{Y}-\mu)'\right)\sim\mathrm{N}(0,\boldsymbol{I}_n\otimes\Sigma)$.

Definition 11.2 If $n\times m$ $\boldsymbol{Y}\sim\mathrm{N}(\overline{\mu},\boldsymbol{I}_n\otimes\Sigma)$, then $W=\boldsymbol{Y}'\boldsymbol{Y}$ is distributed **Wishart** with n degress of freedom and covariance matrix $\boldsymbol{\Sigma}$, and is written as $W\sim W_m(n,\Sigma)$.

The Wishart is a multivariate generalization of the chi-square. If $W\sim W_1\left(n,\sigma^2\right)$, then $W\sim\sigma^2\chi^2_n$. The Wishart arises as the exact distribution of a sample covariance matrix in the normal sampling model. The bias-corrected estimator of Σ is

$$\widehat{\Sigma}=\frac{1}{n-1}\sum_{i=1}^{n}\left(Y_i-\overline{Y}\right)\left(Y_i-\overline{Y}\right)'.$$

Theorem 11.10 If $Y_i\sim\mathrm{N}(\mu,\Sigma)$ are independent, then $\widehat{\Sigma}\sim W_m\left(n-1,\frac{1}{n-1}\Sigma\right)$.

The following manipulation is useful.

Theorem 11.11 If $W \sim W_m(n, \Sigma)$, then for $m \times 1$ α, $\left(\alpha' W^{-1} \alpha\right)^{-1} \sim \frac{\chi^2_{n-m+1}}{\alpha' \Sigma^{-1} \alpha}$.

To prove this, note that without loss of generality, we can take $\Sigma = \boldsymbol{I}_m$ and $\alpha'\alpha = 1$. Let $\boldsymbol{H}$ be $m \times m$ orthonormal with first row equal to α, so that $\boldsymbol{H}\alpha = \begin{pmatrix} 1 \\ 0 \end{pmatrix}$. Since the distribution of $\boldsymbol{Y}$ and $\boldsymbol{Y}\boldsymbol{H}$ are identical, we can without loss of generality set $\alpha = \begin{pmatrix} 1 \\ 0 \end{pmatrix}$. Partition $\boldsymbol{Y} = [\boldsymbol{Y}_1, \boldsymbol{Y}_2]$, where $\boldsymbol{Y}_1$ is $n \times 1$, $\boldsymbol{Y}_2$ is $n \times (m-1)$, and they are independent. Then

$$
\begin{aligned}
\left(\alpha' W^{-1} \alpha\right)^{-1} &= \left(\begin{pmatrix} 1 & 0 \end{pmatrix} \begin{pmatrix} \boldsymbol{Y}_1'\boldsymbol{Y}_1 & \boldsymbol{Y}_1'\boldsymbol{Y}_2 \\ \boldsymbol{Y}_2'\boldsymbol{Y}_1 & \boldsymbol{Y}_2'\boldsymbol{Y}_2 \end{pmatrix}^{-1} \begin{pmatrix} 1 \\ 0 \end{pmatrix} \right)^{-1} \\
&= \boldsymbol{Y}_1'\boldsymbol{Y}_1 - \boldsymbol{Y}_1'\boldsymbol{Y}_2 \left(\boldsymbol{Y}_2'\boldsymbol{Y}_2\right)^{-1} \boldsymbol{Y}_2'\boldsymbol{Y}_1 \\
&= \boldsymbol{Y}_1'\boldsymbol{M}_2\boldsymbol{Y}_1 \sim \chi^2_{n-(m-1)}
\end{aligned}
$$

where $\boldsymbol{M}_2 = \boldsymbol{I}_{m-1} - \boldsymbol{Y}_2\left(\boldsymbol{Y}_2'\boldsymbol{Y}_2\right)^{-1}\boldsymbol{Y}_2'$. The final distributional equality holds conditional on $\boldsymbol{Y}_2$ by the same argument as in the proof of Theorem 5.7. Since this does not depend on $\boldsymbol{Y}_2$, it is the unconditional distribution as well. This establishes the stated result.

To test hypotheses about μ, a classical statistic known as **Hotelling's** T^2 can be used:

$$
T^2 = n\left(\overline{Y} - \mu\right)' \widehat{\Sigma}^{-1} \left(\overline{Y} - \mu\right).
$$

Theorem 11.12 If $Y \sim \mathrm{N}(\mu, \Sigma)$, then

$$
T^2 \sim \frac{m}{(n-m)(n-1)} F(m, n-m)
$$

a scaled F distribution.

To prove this, recall that $\overline{Y}$ is independent of $\widehat{\Sigma}$. Apply Theorem 11.11 with $\alpha = \overline{Y} - \mu$. Conditional on $\overline{Y}$ and using the fact that $\widehat{\Sigma} \sim W_m\left(n-1, \frac{1}{n-1}\Sigma\right)$,

$$
\begin{aligned}
\frac{n}{T^2} &= \left(\left(\overline{Y} - \Sigma\right)' \widehat{\Sigma}^{-1} \left(\overline{Y} - \Sigma\right)\right)^{-1} \\
&\sim \frac{\chi^2_{n-1-m+1}}{\left(\overline{Y} - \mu\right)' \left(\frac{1}{n-1}\Sigma\right)^{-1} \left(\overline{Y} - \mu\right)} \\
&\sim n(n-1)\frac{\chi^2_{n-m}}{\chi^2_m}.
\end{aligned}
$$

Since the two chi-square variables are independent, this is the stated result. A very interesting property of this result is that the T^2 statistic is a multivariate quadratic form in normal random variables, yet it has the exact F distribution.

11.18 EXERCISES

Exercise 11.1 Show (11.10) when the errors are conditionally homoskedastic (see (11.8)).

Exercise 11.2 Show (11.11) when the regressors are common across equations $X_j = X$.

Exercise 11.3 Show (11.12) when the regressors are common across equations $X_j = X$ and the errors are conditionally homoskedastic (see (11.8)).

Exercise 11.4 Prove Theorem 11.1.

Exercise 11.5 Show (11.13) when the regressors are common across equations $X_j = X$.

Exercise 11.6 Show (11.14) when the regressors are common across equations $X_j = X$ and the errors are conditionally homoskedastic, as in (11.8).

Exercise 11.7 Prove Theorem 11.2.

Exercise 11.8 Prove Theorem 11.3.

Exercise 11.9 Show that (11.16) follows from the steps described.

Exercise 11.10 Show that (11.17) follows from the steps described.

Exercise 11.11 Prove Theorem 11.4.

Exercise 11.12 Prove Theorem 11.5.

Hint: First, show that it is sufficient to show that

$$\mathbb{E}\left[\overline{X}'\overline{X}\right]\left(\mathbb{E}\left[\overline{X}'\Sigma^{-1}\overline{X}\right]\right)^{-1}\mathbb{E}\left[\overline{X}'\overline{X}\right] \leq \mathbb{E}\left[\overline{X}'\Sigma\overline{X}\right].$$

Second, rewrite this equation using the transformations $U = \Sigma^{1/2}\overline{X}$ and $V = \Sigma^{1/2}\overline{X}$, and then apply the matrix Cauchy-Schwarz inequality (B.33).

Exercise 11.13 Prove Theorem 11.6.

Exercise 11.14 Take the model

$$Y = \pi'\beta + e$$
$$\pi = \mathbb{E}[X \mid Z] = \Gamma' Z$$
$$\mathbb{E}[e \mid Z] = 0$$

where Y is scalar, X is a k vector, and Z is an ℓ vector; β and π are $k \times 1$, and Γ is $\ell \times k$. The sample is $(Y_i, X_i, Z_i : i = 1, \ldots, n)$ with π_i unobserved. Consider the estimator $\widehat{\beta}$ for β by OLS of Y on $\widehat{\pi} = \widehat{\Gamma}' Z$, where $\widehat{\Gamma}$ is the OLS coefficient from the multivariate regression of X on Z.

(a) Show that $\widehat{\beta}$ is consistent for β.

(b) Find the asymptotic distribution $\sqrt{n}\left(\widehat{\beta}-\beta\right)$ as $n \to \infty$, assuming that $\beta = 0$.

(c) Why is the assumption $\beta = 0$ an important simplifying condition in part (b)?

(d) Using the result in part (c), construct an appropriate asymptotic test for the hypothesis $\mathbb{H}_0 : \beta = 0$.

Exercise 11.15 The observations are i.i.d., $(Y_{1i}, Y_{2i}, X_i : i = 1, \ldots, n)$. The dependent variables Y_1 and Y_2 are real-valued. The regressor X is a k-vector. The model is the two-equation system

$$Y_1 = X'\beta_1 + e_1$$
$$\mathbb{E}[Xe_1] = 0$$
$$Y_2 = X'\beta_2 + e_2$$
$$\mathbb{E}[Xe_2] = 0.$$

(a) What are the appropriate estimators $\widehat{\beta}_1$ and $\widehat{\beta}_2$ for β_1 and β_2?

(b) Find the joint asymptotic distribution of $\widehat{\beta}_1$ and $\widehat{\beta}_2$.

(c) Describe a test for $\mathbb{H}_0 : \beta_1 = \beta_2$.

CHAPTER 12
INSTRUMENTAL VARIABLES

12.1 INTRODUCTION

The concepts of **endogeneity** and **instrumental variable** are fundamental to econometrics and mark a substantial departure from other branches of statistics. The ideas of endogeneity arise naturally in economics from models of simultaneous equations, most notably the classic supply/demand model of price determination.

The identification problem in simultaneous equations dates back to Philip Wright (1915) and Working (1927). The method of instrumental variables first appears in an Appendix of a 1928 book by Philip Wright, though the authorship is sometimes credited to his son Sewell Wright. The label "instrumental variables" was introduced by Reiersøl (1945). An excellent review of the history of instrumental variables is Stock and Trebbi (2003).

12.2 OVERVIEW

We say that there is **endogeneity** in the linear model

$$Y = X'\beta + e \tag{12.1}$$

if β is the parameter of interest and

$$\mathbb{E}[Xe] \neq 0. \tag{12.2}$$

This is a core problem in econometrics and largely differentiates the field from statistics. To distinguish (12.1) from the regression and projection models, we will call (12.1) a **structural equation** and β a **structural parameter**. When (12.2) holds, it is typical to say that X is **endogenous** for β.

Endogeneity cannot happen if the coefficient is defined by linear projection. Indeed, we can define the linear projection coefficient $\beta^* = \mathbb{E}\left[XX'\right]^{-1}\mathbb{E}[XY]$ and linear projection equation

$$\begin{aligned} Y &= X'\beta^* + e^* \\ \mathbb{E}\left[Xe^*\right] &= 0. \end{aligned}$$

However, under endogeneity (12.2), the projection coefficient β^* does not equal the structural parameter β. Indeed,

$$\begin{aligned} \beta^* &= \left(\mathbb{E}\left[XX'\right]\right)^{-1}\mathbb{E}[XY] \\ &= \left(\mathbb{E}\left[XX'\right]\right)^{-1}\mathbb{E}\left[X\left(X'\beta + e\right)\right] \\ &= \beta + \left(\mathbb{E}\left[XX'\right]\right)^{-1}\mathbb{E}[Xe] \neq \beta \end{aligned}$$

where the final relation holds because $\mathbb{E}[Xe] \neq 0$. Thus endogeneity requires that the coefficient be defined differently than projection. We describe such definitions as **structural**. Section 12.3 presents three examples.

Endogeneity implies that the least squares estimator is inconsistent for the structural parameter. Indeed, under i.i.d. sampling, least squares is consistent for the projection coefficient:

$$\widehat{\beta} \underset{p}{\longrightarrow} \left(\mathbb{E}\left[XX'\right]\right)^{-1} \mathbb{E}[XY] = \beta^* \neq \beta.$$

The inconsistency of least squares is typically referred to as **endogeneity bias** or **estimation bias** due to endogeneity. This label is imperfect, as the actual issue is inconsistency, not bias.

As the structural parameter β is the parameter of interest, endogeneity requires the development of alternative estimation methods. We discuss those in later sections.

12.3 EXAMPLES

The concept of endogeneity may be easiest to understand by example. We discuss three. In each case, it is important to see how the structural parameter β is defined independently from the linear projection model.

Example: Measurement error in the regressor. Suppose that (Y, Z) are joint random variables, $\mathbb{E}[Y \mid Z] = Z'\beta$ is linear, and β is the structural parameter. Z is not observed. Instead we observe $X = Z + u$, where u is a $k \times 1$ measurement error, independent of e and Z. This is an example of a latent variable model, where "latent" refers to an unobserved structural variable.

The model $X = Z + u$ with Z and u independent and $\mathbb{E}[u] = 0$ is known as **classical measurement error**, which means that X is a noisy but unbiased measure of Z.

By substitution, we can express Y as a function of the observed variable X:

$$Y = Z'\beta + e = (X - u)'\beta + e = X'\beta + v$$

where $v = e - u'\beta$. Thus (Y, X) satisfies the linear equation

$$Y = X'\beta + v$$

with an error v. But this error is not a projection error. Indeed,

$$\mathbb{E}[Xv] = \mathbb{E}\left[(Z+u)\left(e - u'\beta\right)\right] = -\mathbb{E}\left[uu'\right]\beta \neq 0$$

if $\beta \neq 0$ and $\mathbb{E}\left[uu'\right] \neq 0$. As we learned in Section 12.2, if $\mathbb{E}[Xv] \neq 0$, then least squares estimation will be inconsistent.

We can calculate the form of the projection coefficient (which is consistently estimated by least squares). For simplicity, suppose that $k = 1$. We find

$$\beta^* = \beta + \frac{\mathbb{E}[Xv]}{\mathbb{E}\left[X^2\right]} = \beta\left(1 - \frac{\mathbb{E}\left[u^2\right]}{\mathbb{E}\left[X^2\right]}\right).$$

Since $\mathbb{E}\left[u^2\right]/\mathbb{E}\left[X^2\right] < 1$, the projection coefficient shrinks the structural parameter β toward 0. This is called **measurement error bias** or **attenuation bias**.

To illustrate, Figure 12.1(a) displays the impact of measurement error on the regression line. The three solid circles are pairs (Y, Z) which are measured without error. The regression function drawn through these three points is marked as "No Measurement Error." The six open circles mark pairs (Y, X) where $X = Z + u$

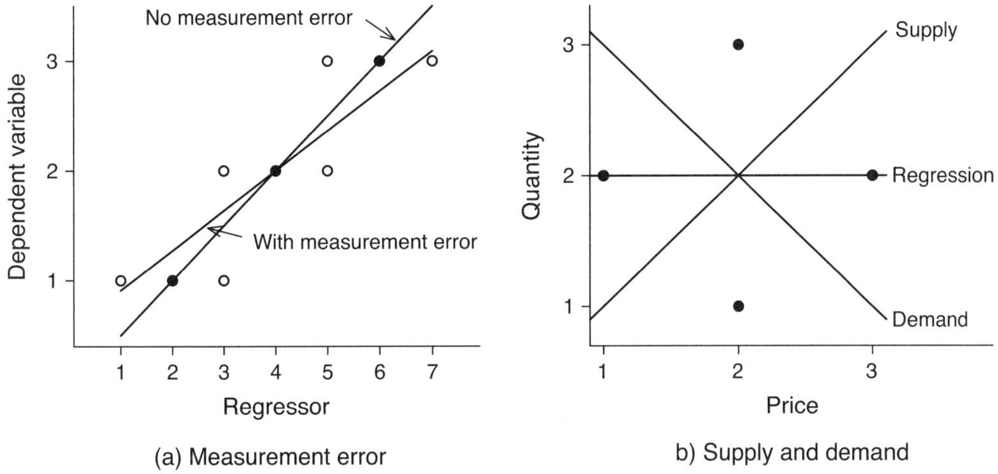

FIGURE 12.1 Examples of endogeneity

with $u = \{+1, -1\}$. Thus X is a mismeasured version of Z. The six open circles spread the joint distribution along the x-axis, but not along the y-axis. The regression line drawn for these six points is marked as "With Measurement Error." You can see that the latter regression line is flattened relative to the original regression function. This is the attenuation bias due to measurement error.

Example: Supply and demand. The variables Q and P (quantity and price) are determined jointly by the demand equation

$$Q = -\beta_1 P + e_1$$

and the supply equation

$$Q = \beta_2 P + e_2.$$

Assume that $e = (e_1, e_2)$ satisfies $\mathbb{E}[e] = 0$ and $\mathbb{E}\left[ee'\right] = \boldsymbol{I}_2$ (the latter for simplicity). The question is: If we regress Q on P, what happens?

It is helpful to solve for Q and P in terms of the errors. In matrix notation,

$$\begin{bmatrix} 1 & \beta_1 \\ 1 & -\beta_2 \end{bmatrix} \begin{pmatrix} Q \\ P \end{pmatrix} = \begin{pmatrix} e_1 \\ e_2 \end{pmatrix}$$

so

$$\begin{aligned} \begin{pmatrix} Q \\ P \end{pmatrix} &= \begin{bmatrix} 1 & \beta_1 \\ 1 & -\beta_2 \end{bmatrix}^{-1} \begin{pmatrix} e_1 \\ e_2 \end{pmatrix} \\ &= \begin{bmatrix} \beta_2 & \beta_1 \\ 1 & -1 \end{bmatrix} \begin{pmatrix} e_1 \\ e_2 \end{pmatrix} \left(\frac{1}{\beta_1 + \beta_2} \right) \\ &= \begin{pmatrix} (\beta_2 e_1 + \beta_1 e_2) / (\beta_1 + \beta_2) \\ (e_1 - e_2) / (\beta_1 + \beta_2) \end{pmatrix}. \end{aligned}$$

The projection of Q on P yields $Q = \beta^* P + e^*$ with $\mathbb{E}[Pe^*] = 0$, and the projection coefficient is

$$\beta^* = \frac{\mathbb{E}[PQ]}{\mathbb{E}[P^2]} = \frac{\beta_2 - \beta_1}{2}.$$

The projection coefficient β^* equals neither the demand slope β_1 nor the supply slope β_2, but it equals an average of the two. (The fact that it is a simple average is an artifact of the covariance structure.)

The OLS estimator satisfies $\widehat{\beta} \underset{p}{\longrightarrow} \beta^*$, and the limit does not equal either β_1 or β_2. This is called **simultaneous equations bias**. This occurs generally when Y and X are jointly determined, as in a market equilibrium.

Generally, when both the dependent variable and a regressor are simultaneously determined, then the regressor should be treated as endogenous. To illustrate, Figure 12.1(b) draws a supply/demand model with Quantity on the y-axis and Price on the x-axis. The supply and demand equations are $Q = P + \varepsilon_1$ and $Q = 4 - P - \varepsilon_2$, respectively. Suppose that the errors each have the Rademacher distribution $\varepsilon \in \{-1, +1\}$. This model has four equilibrium outcomes, marked by the four solid circles in the figure. The regression line through these four circles has a slope of 0 and is marked "Regression." This is what would be measured by a least squares regression of observed quantity on observed price. This is endogeneity bias due to simultaneity.

Example: Choice variables as regressors. Take the classic wage equation

$$\log(wage) = \beta education + e$$

with β the average causal effect of education on wages. If wages are affected by unobserved ability, and individuals with high ability self-select into higher education, then e contains unobserved ability, so *education* and e will be positively correlated. Hence *education* is endogenous. The positive correlation means that the linear projection coefficient β^* will be upward biased relative to the structural coefficient β. Thus least squares (which is estimating the projection coefficient) will tend to overestimate the causal effect of education on wages.

This type of endogeneity occurs generally when Y and X are both choices made by an economic agent, even if they are made at different points in time. Generally, when both the dependent variable and a regressor are choice variables made by the same agent, the variables should be treated as endogenous. This example was illustrated in Figure 2.8, which displayed the joint distribution of wages and education of the population of Jennifers and Georges. In Figure 2.8, the plotted average causal effect is the structural impact (on average in the population) of college education on wages. The plotted regression line has a larger slope, as it adds the endogeneity bias, because education is a choice variable.

12.4 ENDOGENOUS REGRESSORS

We have defined endogeneity as the context in which a regressor is correlated with the equation error. The converse of endogeneity is exogeneity. That is, we say a regressor X is **exogenous** for β if $\mathbb{E}[Xe] = 0$. In general, the distinction in an economic model is that a regressor X is endogenous if it is jointly determined with Y, while a regressor X is exogenous if it is determined separately from Y.

In most applications only a subset of the regressors are treated as endogenous. Partition $X = (X_1, X_2)$ with dimensions (k_1, k_2) so that X_1 contains the **exogenous** regressors and X_2 contains the **endogenous** regressors. As the dependent variable Y is also endogenous, we sometimes differentiate X_2 by calling it the **endogenous**

right-hand-side variable. Similarly partition $\beta = (\beta_1, \beta_2)$. With this notation the **structural equation** is

$$Y = X_1'\beta_1 + X_2'\beta_2 + e. \tag{12.3}$$

An alternative notation is as follows. Let $Y_2 = X_2$ be the endogenous regressors, and rename the dependent variable Y as Y_1. Then the structural equation is

$$Y_1 = X_1'\beta_1 + Y_2'\beta_2 + e. \tag{12.4}$$

This is especially useful, because the notation clarifies which variables are endogenous and which exogenous. We also write $\vec{Y} = (Y_1, Y_2)$ as the set of endogenous variables. We use the notation $\vec{Y}$, so that there is no confusion with Y as defined in (12.3).

The assumptions regarding the regressors and regression error are

$$\mathbb{E}[X_1 e] = 0$$
$$\mathbb{E}[Y_2 e] \neq 0.$$

The endogenous regressors Y_2 are the critical variables discussed in the examples of Section 12.3—simultaneous variables, choice variables, mismeasured regressors—that are potentially correlated with the equation error e. In many applications, k_2 is small (1 or 2). The exogenous variables X_1 are the remaining regressors (including the equation intercept) and can be low or high dimensional.

12.5 INSTRUMENTS

To consistently estimate β, we require additional information. One type of information that is commonly used in economic applications are what we call **instruments**.

Definition 12.1 The $\ell \times 1$ random vector Z is an **instrumental variable** for (12.3) if

$$\mathbb{E}[Ze] = 0 \tag{12.5}$$
$$\mathbb{E}\left[ZZ'\right] > 0 \tag{12.6}$$
$$\operatorname{rank}\left(\mathbb{E}\left[ZX'\right]\right) = k. \tag{12.7}$$

There are three components to the definition as given. The first, (12.5), is that the instruments are uncorrelated with the regression error. The second, (12.6), is a normalization that excludes linearly redundant instruments. The third, (12.7), is often called the **relevance condition** and is essential for the identification of the model, as we discuss later. A necessary condition for (12.7) is that $\ell \geq k$.

Condition (12.5)—that the instruments are uncorrelated with the equation error—is often described as that they are **exogenous** in the sense that they are determined outside the model for Y. Notice that the regressors X_1 satisfy condition (12.5) and thus should be included as instrumental variables. They are therefore a subset of the variables Z. Notationally, we make the partition

$$Z = \begin{pmatrix} Z_1 \\ Z_2 \end{pmatrix} = \begin{pmatrix} X_1 \\ Z_2 \end{pmatrix} \begin{matrix} k_1 \\ \ell_2 \end{matrix}. \tag{12.8}$$

Here, the $X_1 = Z_1$ are the **included exogenous variables**, and the Z_2 are the **excluded exogenous variables**. That is, Z_2 are variables that could be included in the equation for Y (in the sense that they are uncorrelated with e) yet can be excluded, as they have true 0 coefficients in the equation. With this notation, we can also write the structural equation (12.4) as

$$Y_1 = Z_1'\beta_1 + Y_2'\beta_2 + e. \tag{12.9}$$

This notation is useful as it clarifies that the variable Z_1 is exogenous and the variable Y_2 is endogenous.

Many authors describe Z_1 as the "exogenous variables," Y_2 as the "endogenous variables," and Z_2 as the "instrumental variables."

We say that the model is **just-identified** if $\ell = k$ and **overidentified** if $\ell > k$.

What variables can be used as instrumental variables? From the definition $\mathbb{E}[Ze] = 0$, the instrument must be uncorrelated with the equation error, meaning that it is excluded from the structural equation, as mentioned above. From the rank condition (12.7), it is also important that the instrumental variables be correlated with the endogenous variables Y_2 after controlling for the other exogenous variables Z_1. These two requirements are typically interpreted as requiring that the instruments be determined outside the system for $\vec{Y}$, causally determine Y_2, but do not causally determine Y_1 except through Y_2.

Let's take the three examples given above.

Measurement error in the regressor. When X is a mismeasured version of Z, a common choice for an instrument Z_2 is an alternative measurement of Z. For this Z_2 to satisfy the property of an instrumental variable, the measurement error in Z_2 must be independent of that in X.

Supply and Demand. An appropriate instrument for price P in a demand equation is a variable Z_2 that influences supply but not demand. Such a variable affects the equilibrium values of P and Q but does not directly affect price except through quantity. Variables that affect supply but not demand are typically related to production costs.

An appropriate instrument for price in a supply equation is a variable that influences demand but not supply. Such a variable affects the equilibrium values of price and quantity but only affects price through quantity.

Choice Variable as Regressor. An ideal instrument affects the choice of the regressor (e.g., education) but does not directly influence the dependent variable (e.g., wages) except through the indirect effect on the regressor. We discuss an example in Section 12.6.

12.6 EXAMPLE: COLLEGE PROXIMITY

In a influential paper, David Card (1995) suggested that if a potential student lives close to a college, this reduces the cost of attendence and thereby raises the likelihood that the student will attend college. However, college proximity does not directly affect a student's skills or abilities, so it should not have a direct effect on his or her market wage. These considerations suggest that college proximity can be used as an instrument for education in a wage regression. We use the simplest model reported in Card's paper to illustrate the concepts of instrumental variables throughout this chapter.

Card used data from the National Longitudinal Survey of Young Men for 1976. A baseline least squares wage regression for his dataset is reported in the first column of Table 12.1. The dependent variable is the log of weekly earnings. The regressors are *education* (years of schooling), *experience* (years of work experience, calculated as *age* (years) less *education*+6), *experience*^{2}/100, *Black*, *south* (an indicator for residence in the

Table 12.1
Instrumental variable wage regressions

	OLS	IV(a)	IV(b)	2SLS(a)	2SLS(b)	LIML
education	0.074	0.132	0.133	0.161	0.160	0.164
	(0.004)	(0.049)	(0.051)	(0.040)	(0.041)	(0.042)
experience	0.084	0.107	0.056	0.119	0.047	0.120
	(0.007)	(0.021)	(0.026)	(0.018)	(0.025)	(0.019)
experience^2/100	−0.224	−0.228	−0.080	−0.231	−0.032	−0.231
	(0.032)	(0.035)	(0.133)	(0.037)	(0.127)	(0.037)
Black	−0.190	−0.131	−0.103	−0.102	−0.064	−0.099
	(0.017)	(0.051)	(0.075)	(0.044)	(0.061)	(0.045)
south	−0.125	−0.105	−0.098	−0.095	−0.086	−0.094
	(0.015)	(0.023)	(0.0284)	(0.022)	(0.026)	(0.022)
urban	0.161	0.131	0.108	0.116	0.083	0.115
	(0.015)	(0.030)	(0.049)	(0.026)	(0.041)	(0.027)
Sargan				0.82	0.52	0.82
p-value				0.37	0.47	0.37

Note: IV(a) uses *college* as an instrument for *education*. IV(b) uses *college*, *age*, and *age*^{2}/100 as instruments for *education*, *experience*, and *experience*^{2}/100. 2SLS(a) uses *public* and *private* as instruments for *education*. 2SLS(b) uses *public*, *private*, *age*, and *age*^{2} as instruments for *education*, *experience*, and *experience*^{2}/100. LIML uses *public* and *private* as instruments for *education*.

southern region of the United States), and *urban* (an indicator for residence in a standard metropolitan statistical area). We drop observations for which *wage* is missing. The remaining sample has 3,010 observations. His data are in the file `Card1995` on the textbook website.

The point estimate obtained by least squares suggests a 7% increase in earnings for each year of education.

As discussed in the previous sections, it is reasonable to view years of education as a choice made by an individual and thus it is likely endogenous for the structural return to education. Thus least squares is an estimate of a linear projection but is inconsistent for coefficient of a structural equation representing the causal impact of years of education on expected wages. Labor economics predicts that ability, education, and wages will be positively correlated. This suggests that the population projection coefficient estimated by least squares will be higher than the structural parameter (and hence upward biased). However, the sign of the bias is uncertain, because there are multiple regressors and other potential sources of endogeneity.

To instrument for the endogeneity of education, Card suggested that a reasonable instrument is a dummy variable indicating whether the individual grew up near a college. We consider three measures:

college	Grew up in same county as a 4-year college
public	Grew up in same county as a 4-year public college
private	Grew up in same county as a 4-year private college.

12.7 REDUCED FORM

The reduced form is the relationship between the endogenous regressors Y_2 and the instruments Z. A linear reduced form model for Y_2 is

$$Y_2 = \Gamma' Z + u_2 = \Gamma'_{12} Z_1 + \Gamma'_{22} Z_2 + u_2 \tag{12.10}$$

This is a multivariate regression introduced in Chapter 11. The $\ell \times k_2$ coefficient matrix Γ is defined by linear projection:

$$\Gamma = \mathbb{E}\left[ZZ'\right]^{-1} \mathbb{E}\left[ZY_2'\right] \tag{12.11}$$

which implies $\mathbb{E}\left[Zu_2'\right] = 0$. The projection coefficient (12.11) is well defined and unique under (12.6).

We can also construct the reduced form for Y_1. Substitute (12.10) into (12.9) to obtain

$$\begin{aligned} Y_1 &= Z_1'\beta_1 + \left(\Gamma_{12}'Z_1 + \Gamma_{22}'Z_2 + u_2\right)'\beta_2 + e \\ &= Z_1'\lambda_1 + Z_2'\lambda_2 + u_1 && (12.12) \\ &= Z'\lambda + u_1 && (12.13) \end{aligned}$$

where

$$\begin{aligned} \lambda_1 &= \beta_1 + \Gamma_{12}\beta_2 && (12.14) \\ \lambda_2 &= \Gamma_{22}\beta_2 && (12.15) \\ u_1 &= u_2'\beta_2 + e. \end{aligned}$$

We can also write

$$\lambda = \overline{\Gamma}\beta \tag{12.16}$$

where

$$\overline{\Gamma} = \begin{bmatrix} \boldsymbol{I}_{k_1} & \Gamma_{12} \\ 0 & \Gamma_{22} \end{bmatrix} = \begin{bmatrix} \boldsymbol{I}_{k_1} & \Gamma \\ 0 & \end{bmatrix}.$$

Together, the reduced form equations for the system are

$$\begin{aligned} Y_1 &= \lambda' Z + u_1 \\ Y_2 &= \Gamma' Z + u_2. \end{aligned}$$

or

$$\vec{Y} = \begin{bmatrix} \lambda_1' & \lambda_2' \\ \Gamma_{12}' & \Gamma_{22}' \end{bmatrix} Z + u \tag{12.17}$$

where $u = (u_1, u_2)$.

The relationships (12.14)–(12.16) are critically important for understanding the identification of the structural parameters β_1 and β_2, as we discuss below. These equations show the tight relationship between the structural parameters (β_1 and β_2) and the reduced form parameters (Γ and λ).

The reduced form equations are projections, so the coefficients may be estimated by least squares (see Chapter 11). The least squares estimators of (12.11) and (12.13) are

$$\widehat{\Gamma} = \left(\sum_{i=1}^{n} Z_i Z_i'\right)^{-1} \left(\sum_{i=1}^{n} Z_i Y_{2i}'\right) \tag{12.18}$$

$$\widehat{\lambda} = \left(\sum_{i=1}^{n} Z_i Z_i'\right)^{-1} \left(\sum_{i=1}^{n} Z_i Y_{1i}\right). \tag{12.19}$$

12.8 IDENTIFICATION

A parameter is **identified** if it is a unique function of the probability distribution of the observables. One way to show that a parameter is identified is to write it as an explicit function of population moments. For example, the reduced form coefficient matrices Γ and λ are identified, because they can be written as explicit functions of the moments of the variables (Y, X, Z). That is,

$$\Gamma = \mathbb{E}\left[ZZ'\right]^{-1}\mathbb{E}\left[ZY_2'\right] \tag{12.20}$$

$$\lambda = \mathbb{E}\left[ZZ'\right]^{-1}\mathbb{E}\left[ZY_1\right]. \tag{12.21}$$

These are uniquely determined by the probability distribution of (Y_1, Y_2, Z) if Definition 12.1 holds, because this includes the requirement that $\mathbb{E}\left[ZZ'\right]$ is invertible.

We are interested in the structural parameter β. It relates to (λ, Γ) through (12.16). β is identified if it is uniquely determined by this relation, which is a set of ℓ equations with k unknowns with $\ell \geq k$. From linear algebra, we know that there is a unique solution if and only if $\overline{\Gamma}$ has full rank k:

$$\operatorname{rank}\left(\overline{\Gamma}\right) = k. \tag{12.22}$$

If (12.22) holds, then β can be uniquely solved from (12.16). If (12.22) fails, then (12.16) has fewer equations than coefficients, so there is no unique solution.

Equation (12.16) can be written as

$$\mathbb{E}\left[ZZ'\right]^{-1}\mathbb{E}\left[ZY_1\right] = \mathbb{E}\left[ZZ'\right]^{-1}\mathbb{E}\left[ZX'\right]\beta$$

which simplifies to

$$\mathbb{E}\left[ZY_1\right] = \mathbb{E}\left[ZX'\right]\beta$$

which is a set of ℓ equations with k unknowns. This has a unique solution if (and only if)

$$\operatorname{rank}\left(\mathbb{E}\left[ZX'\right]\right) = k \tag{12.23}$$

which was listed in (12.7) as a condition of Definition 12.1. (Indeed, this is why it was listed as part of the definition.) We deduce that (12.22) and (12.23) are equivalent ways of expressing the same requirement. If this condition fails, then β will not be identified. The condition (12.22)–(12.23) is called the **relevance condition**.

It is useful to have explicit expressions for the solution β. The easiest case is when $\ell = k$. Then (12.22) implies $\overline{\Gamma}$ is invertible, so the structural parameter equals $\beta = \overline{\Gamma}^{-1}\lambda$. It is a unique solution, because $\overline{\Gamma}$ and λ are unique and $\overline{\Gamma}$ is invertible.

When $\ell > k$, we can solve for β by applying least squares to the system of equations $\lambda = \overline{\Gamma}\beta$. This is ℓ equations with k unknowns and no error. The least squares solution is $\beta = \left(\overline{\Gamma}'\overline{\Gamma}\right)^{-1}\overline{\Gamma}'\lambda$. Under (12.22), the matrix $\overline{\Gamma}'\overline{\Gamma}$ is invertible, so the solution is unique.

β is identified if $\operatorname{rank}(\overline{\Gamma}) = k$, which is true if and only if $\operatorname{rank}(\Gamma_{22}) = k_2$ (by the upper-diagonal structure of $\overline{\Gamma}$). Thus the key to identification of the model rests on the $\ell_2 \times k_2$ matrix Γ_{22} in (12.10). To see this, recall the reduced form relationships (12.14)–(12.15). We can see that β_2 is identified from (12.15) alone, and the necessary and sufficient condition is $\operatorname{rank}(\Gamma_{22}) = k_2$. If this is satisfied, then the solution equals $\beta_2 = \left(\Gamma_{22}'\Gamma_{22}\right)^{-1}\Gamma_{22}'\lambda_2$. β_1 is identified from this and (12.14), with the explicit solution $\beta_1 = \lambda_1 - \Gamma_{12}\left(\Gamma_{22}'\Gamma_{22}\right)^{-1}\Gamma_{22}'\lambda_2$. In the just-identified case ($\ell_2 = k_2$), these equations simplify to $\beta_2 = \Gamma_{22}^{-1}\lambda_2$ and $\beta_1 = \lambda_1 - \Gamma_{12}\Gamma_{22}^{-1}\lambda_2$.

12.9 INSTRUMENTAL VARIABLES ESTIMATOR

In this section, we consider the special case where the model is just-identified, so that $\ell = k$.

The assumption that Z is an instrumental variable implies that $\mathbb{E}[Ze] = 0$. Making the substitution $e = Y_1 - X'\beta$, we find $\mathbb{E}\left[Z\left(Y_1 - X'\beta\right)\right] = 0$. Expanding,

$$\mathbb{E}[ZY_1] - \mathbb{E}\left[ZX'\right]\beta = 0.$$

This is a system of $\ell = k$ equations and k unknowns. Solving for β, we find

$$\beta = \left(\mathbb{E}\left[ZX'\right]\right)^{-1}\mathbb{E}[ZY_1]$$

which requires that the matrix $\mathbb{E}\left[ZX'\right]$ is invertible, which holds under (12.7) or equivalently, (12.23).

The **instrumental variables (IV)** estimator β replaces population by sample moments. We find

$$\begin{aligned}\widehat{\beta}_{\text{iv}} &= \left(\frac{1}{n}\sum_{i=1}^{n} Z_i X_i'\right)^{-1}\left(\frac{1}{n}\sum_{i=1}^{n} Z_i Y_{1i}\right)\\ &= \left(\sum_{i=1}^{n} Z_i X_i'\right)^{-1}\left(\sum_{i=1}^{n} Z_i Y_{1i}\right).\end{aligned} \tag{12.24}$$

More generally, given any variable $W \in \mathbb{R}^k$, it is common to refer to the estimator

$$\widehat{\beta}_{\text{iv}} = \left(\sum_{i=1}^{n} W_i X_i'\right)^{-1}\left(\sum_{i=1}^{n} W_i Y_{1i}\right)$$

as the IV estimator for β using the instrument W.

Alternatively, recall that when $\ell = k$, the structural parameter can be written as a function of the reduced form parameters as $\beta = \overline{\Gamma}^{-1}\lambda$. Replacing $\overline{\Gamma}$ and λ by their least squares estimators (12.18)–(12.19), we can construct what is called the **Indirect Least Squares (ILS)** estimator. Using the matrix algebra representations

$$\begin{aligned}\widehat{\beta}_{\text{ils}} &= \widehat{\overline{\Gamma}}^{-1}\widehat{\lambda}\\ &= \left(\left(\boldsymbol{Z}'\boldsymbol{Z}\right)^{-1}\left(\boldsymbol{Z}'\boldsymbol{X}\right)\right)^{-1}\left(\left(\boldsymbol{Z}'\boldsymbol{Z}\right)^{-1}\left(\boldsymbol{Z}'\boldsymbol{Y}_1\right)\right)\\ &= \left(\boldsymbol{Z}'\boldsymbol{X}\right)^{-1}\left(\boldsymbol{Z}'\boldsymbol{Z}\right)\left(\boldsymbol{Z}'\boldsymbol{Z}\right)^{-1}\left(\boldsymbol{Z}'\boldsymbol{Y}_1\right)\\ &= \left(\boldsymbol{Z}'\boldsymbol{X}\right)^{-1}\left(\boldsymbol{Z}'\boldsymbol{Y}_1\right)\end{aligned}$$

we see that this equals the IV estimator (12.24). Thus the ILS and IV estimators are identical.

Given the IV estimator, we define the residual $\widehat{e}_i = Y_{1i} - X_i'\widehat{\beta}_{\text{iv}}$. It satisfies

$$\boldsymbol{Z}'\widehat{\boldsymbol{e}} = \boldsymbol{Z}'\boldsymbol{Y}_1 - \boldsymbol{Z}'\boldsymbol{X}\left(\boldsymbol{Z}'\boldsymbol{X}\right)^{-1}\left(\boldsymbol{Z}'\boldsymbol{Y}_1\right) = 0. \tag{12.25}$$

Since Z includes an intercept, the residuals sum to 0 and are uncorrelated with the included and excluded instruments.

To illustrate IV regression, let us estimate the reduced form equations, treating *education* as endogenous and using *college* as an instrumental variable. The reduced form equations for log(*wage*) and *education* are reported in the first and second columns of Table 12.2.

Table 12.2
Reduced form regressions

	log(*wage*)	*education*	*education*	*experience*	*experience*^{2}/100	*education*
experience	0.053	−0.410				−0.413
	(0.007)	(0.032)				(0.032)
experience^2/100	−0.219	0.073				0.093
	(0.033)	(0.170)				(0.171)
black	−0.264	−1.006	−1.468	1.468	0.282	−1.006
	(0.018)	(0.088)	(0.115)	(0.115)	(0.026)	(0.088)
south	−0.143	−0.291	−0.460	0.460	0.112	−0.267
	(0.017)	(0.078)	(0.103)	(0.103)	(0.022)	(0.079)
urban	0.185	0.404	0.835	−0.835	−0.176	0.400
	(0.017)	(0.085)	(0.112)	(0.112)	(0.025)	(0.085)
college	0.045	0.337	0.347	−0.347	−0.073	
	(0.016)	(0.081)	(0.109)	(0.109)	(0.023)	
public						0.430
						(0.086)
private						0.123
						(0.101)
age			1.061	−0.061	−0.555	
			(0.296)	(0.296)	(0.065)	
age^2/100			−1.876	1.876	1.313	
			(0.516)	(0.516)	(0.116)	
F		17.51	8.22	1581	1112	13.87

Of particular interest is the equation for the endogenous regressor *education*, and the coefficients for the excluded instruments—in this case, *college*. The estimated coefficient equals 0.337 with a small standard error. Thus growing up near a 4-year college increases average educational attainment by 0.3 years. This seems to be a reasonable magnitude.

Since the structural equation is just-identified with one right-hand-side endogenous variable, the ILS/IV estimate for the education coefficient is the ratio of the coefficient estimates for the instrument *college* in the two equations (e.g., $0.045/0.337 = 0.13$), implying a 13% return to each year of education. This is substantially greater than the 7% least squares estimate from the first column of Table 12.1. The IV estimates of the full equation are reported in the second column of Table 12.1. One first reaction is surprise that the IV estimate is larger than the OLS estimate. The endogeneity of educational choice should lead to upward bias in the OLS estimator, which predicts that the IV estimate should have been smaller than the OLS estimator. An alternative explanation may be needed. One possibility is heterogeneous education effects (when the education coefficient β is heterogenous across individuals). In Section 12.34, we show that in this context, the IV estimator picks up this treatment effect for a subset of the population, which may explain why IV estimation results in a larger estimated coefficient.

Card (1995) also points out that if *education* is endogenous, then so is our measure of *experience*, as it is calculated by subtracting *education* from *age*. He suggests that we can use the variables *age* and *age*^{2} as instruments for *experience* and *experience*^{2}. The age variables are exogenous (not choice variables) yet are highly correlated with *experience* and *experience*^{2}. Notice that this approach treats *experience*^{2} as a variable separate from *experience*. Indeed, this is the correct approach.

Following this recommendation, we now have three endogenous regressors and three instruments. We present the three reduced form equations for the three endogenous regressors in the third through fifth columns of Table 12.2. It is interesting to compare the equations for *education* and *experience*. The two sets of coefficients are simply the sign change of the other with the exception of the coefficient on *age*. Indeed this must be the case because the three variables are linearly related. Does this cause a problem for 2SLS? Fortunately, no. The fact that the coefficient on age is not simply a sign change means that the equations are not linearly singular. Hence Assumption (12.22) is not violated.

The IV estimates using the three instruments *college*, *age*, and *age*^{2} for the endogenous regressors *education*, *experience*, and *experience*^{2} are presented in the third column of Table 12.1. The estimate of the returns to schooling is not affected by this change in the instrument set, but the estimated return to experience profile flattens (the quadratic effect diminishes).

The IV estimator may be calculated in Stata using the `ivregress 2sls` command.

12.10 DEMEANED REPRESENTATION

Does the well-known demeaned representation for linear regression (3.18) carry over to the IV estimator? To see, write the linear projection equation in the format $Y_1 = X'\beta + \alpha + e$, where α is the intercept and X does not contain a constant. Similarly, partition the instrument as $(1, Z)$, where Z does not contain a constant. We can write the IV estimator for the ith equation as

$$Y_{1i} = X_i'\widehat{\beta}_{\mathrm{iv}} + \widehat{\alpha}_{\mathrm{iv}} + \widehat{e}_i.$$

The orthogonality condition (12.25) implies the two-equation system:

$$\sum_{i=1}^{n} \left(Y_{1i} - X_i'\widehat{\beta}_{\mathrm{iv}} - \widehat{\alpha}_{\mathrm{iv}}\right) = 0$$

$$\sum_{i=1}^{n} Z_i \left(Y_{1i} - X_i'\widehat{\beta}_{\mathrm{iv}} - \widehat{\alpha}_{\mathrm{iv}}\right) = 0.$$

The first equation implies $\widehat{\alpha}_{\mathrm{iv}} = \overline{Y_1} - \overline{X}'\widehat{\beta}_{\mathrm{iv}}$. Substituting into the second equation

$$\sum_{i=1}^{n} Z_i \left(\left(Y_{1i} - \overline{Y_1}\right) - \left(X_i - \overline{X}\right)'\widehat{\beta}_{\mathrm{iv}}\right)$$

and solving for $\widehat{\beta}_{\mathrm{iv}}$, we find

$$\begin{aligned} \widehat{\beta}_{\mathrm{iv}} &= \left(\sum_{i=1}^{n} Z_i \left(X_i - \overline{X}\right)'\right)^{-1} \left(\sum_{i=1}^{n} Z_i \left(Y_{1i} - \overline{Y_1}\right)\right) \\ &= \left(\sum_{i=1}^{n} \left(Z_i - \overline{Z}\right)\left(X_i - \overline{X}\right)'\right)^{-1} \left(\sum_{i=1}^{n} \left(Z_i - \overline{Z}\right)\left(Y_{1i} - \overline{Y_1}\right)\right). \end{aligned} \tag{12.26}$$

Thus the demeaning equations for least squares carry over to the IV estimator. The coefficient estimator $\widehat{\beta}_{\mathrm{iv}}$ is a function only of the demeaned data.

12.11 WALD ESTIMATOR

In many cases, including the Card proximity example, the excluded instrument is a binary (dummy) variable. Let's focus on that case and suppose that the model has just one endogenous regressor and no other regressors beyond the intercept. The model can be written as $Y = X\beta + \alpha + e$, with $\mathbb{E}[e \mid Z] = 0$ and Z binary.

Take expectations of the structural equation given $Z = 1$ and $Z = 0$, respectively. We obtain

$$\mathbb{E}[Y \mid Z=1] = \mathbb{E}[X \mid Z=1]\,\beta + \alpha$$

$$\mathbb{E}[Y \mid Z=0] = \mathbb{E}[X \mid Z=0]\,\beta + \alpha.$$

Subtracting and dividing, we obtain an expression for the slope coefficient:

$$\beta = \frac{\mathbb{E}[Y \mid Z=1] - \mathbb{E}[Y \mid Z=0]}{\mathbb{E}[X \mid Z=1] - \mathbb{E}[X \mid Z=0]}. \tag{12.27}$$

The natural moment estimator replaces the expectations by the averages within the "grouped data" where $Z_i = 1$ and $Z_i = 0$, respectively. That is, define the group means

$$\overline{Y}_1 = \frac{\sum_{i=1}^n Z_i Y_i}{\sum_{i=1}^n Z_i}, \qquad \overline{Y}_0 = \frac{\sum_{i=1}^n (1 - Z_i) Y_i}{\sum_{i=1}^n (1 - Z_i)}$$

$$\overline{X}_1 = \frac{\sum_{i=1}^n Z_i X_i}{\sum_{i=1}^n Z_i}, \qquad \overline{X}_0 = \frac{\sum_{i=1}^n (1 - Z_i) X_i}{\sum_{i=1}^n (1 - Z_i)}$$

and the moment estimator

$$\widehat{\beta} = \frac{\overline{Y}_1 - \overline{Y}_0}{\overline{X}_1 - \overline{X}_0}. \tag{12.28}$$

This is the "Wald estimator" of Wald (1940).

These expressions are rather insightful. Equation (12.27) shows that the structural slope coefficient is the expected change in Y due to changing the instrument divided by the expected change in X due to changing the instrument. Informally, it is the change in Y (due to Z) over the change in X (due to Z). Equation (12.28) shows that the slope coefficient can be estimated by the ratio of differences in means.

The expression (12.28) may appear to be a distinct estimator from the IV estimator $\widehat{\beta}_{\text{iv}}$, but it turns out that they are the same. That is, $\widehat{\beta} = \widehat{\beta}_{\text{iv}}$. To see this, use (12.26) to find

$$\widehat{\beta}_{\text{iv}} = \frac{\sum_{i=1}^n Z_i \left(Y_i - \overline{Y}\right)}{\sum_{i=1}^n Z_i \left(X_i - \overline{X}\right)} = \frac{\overline{Y}_1 - \overline{Y}}{\overline{X}_1 - \overline{X}}.$$

Then notice

$$\overline{Y}_1 - \overline{Y} = \overline{Y}_1 - \left(\frac{1}{n} \sum_{i=1}^n Z_i \overline{Y}_1 + \frac{1}{n} \sum_{i=1}^n (1 - Z_i) \overline{Y}_0 \right) = \left(1 - \overline{Z}\right)\left(\overline{Y}_1 - \overline{Y}_0\right)$$

and similarly,

$$\overline{X}_1 - \overline{X} = \left(1 - \overline{Z}\right)\left(\overline{X}_1 - \overline{X}_0\right)$$

and hence

$$\widehat{\beta}_{\text{iv}} = \frac{\left(1 - \overline{Z}\right)\left(\overline{Y}_1 - \overline{Y}_0\right)}{\left(1 - \overline{Z}\right)\left(\overline{X}_1 - \overline{X}_0\right)} = \widehat{\beta}$$

as defined in (12.28). Thus the Wald estimator equals the IV estimator.

We can illustrate using the Card proximity example. If we estimate a simple IV model with no covariates, we obtain the estimate $\widehat{\beta}_{\text{iv}} = 0.19$. If we estimate the group mean of log wages and education based on the instrument *college*, we find

	near college	not near college	difference
log(*wage*)	6.311	6.156	0.155
education	13.527	12.698	0.829
ratio			0.19

Based on these estimates, the Wald estimator of the slope coefficient is (6.311 − 6.156) / (13.527 − 12.698) = 0.155/0.829 = 0.19, the same as the IV estimator.

12.12 TWO-STAGE LEAST SQUARES

The IV estimator described in Section 12.11 presumed $\ell = k$. Now we allow the general case of $\ell \geq k$. Examining the reduced-form equation (12.13), we see

$$\begin{aligned} Y_1 &= Z'\overline{\Gamma}\beta + u_1 \\ \mathbb{E}[Zu_1] &= 0. \end{aligned}$$

Defining $W = \overline{\Gamma}'Z$, we can write this as

$$\begin{aligned} Y_1 &= W'\beta + u_1 \\ \mathbb{E}[Wu_1] &= 0. \end{aligned}$$

One way of thinking about this is that Z is the set of candidate instruments. The instrument vector $W = \overline{\Gamma}'Z$ is a k-dimentional set of linear combinations.

Suppose that $\overline{\Gamma}$ were known. Then we would estimate β by least squares of Y_1 on $W = \overline{\Gamma}'Z$:

$$\widehat{\beta} = (\boldsymbol{W}'\boldsymbol{W})^{-1}(\boldsymbol{W}'\boldsymbol{Y}_1) = \left(\overline{\Gamma}'\boldsymbol{Z}'\boldsymbol{Z}\overline{\Gamma}\right)^{-1}\left(\overline{\Gamma}'\boldsymbol{Z}'\boldsymbol{Y}_1\right).$$

While this is infeasible, we can estimate $\overline{\Gamma}$ from the reduced form regression. Replacing $\overline{\Gamma}$ with its estimator $\widehat{\Gamma} = (\boldsymbol{Z}'\boldsymbol{Z})^{-1}(\boldsymbol{Z}'\boldsymbol{X})$, we obtain

$$\begin{aligned} \widehat{\beta}_{2\text{sls}} &= \left(\widehat{\Gamma}'\boldsymbol{Z}'\boldsymbol{Z}\widehat{\Gamma}\right)^{-1}\left(\widehat{\Gamma}'\boldsymbol{Z}'\boldsymbol{Y}_1\right) \\ &= \left(\boldsymbol{X}'\boldsymbol{Z}(\boldsymbol{Z}'\boldsymbol{Z})^{-1}\boldsymbol{Z}'\boldsymbol{Z}(\boldsymbol{Z}'\boldsymbol{Z})^{-1}\boldsymbol{Z}'\boldsymbol{X}\right)^{-1}\boldsymbol{X}'\boldsymbol{Z}(\boldsymbol{Z}'\boldsymbol{Z})^{-1}\boldsymbol{Z}'\boldsymbol{Y}_1 \\ &= \left(\boldsymbol{X}'\boldsymbol{Z}(\boldsymbol{Z}'\boldsymbol{Z})^{-1}\boldsymbol{Z}'\boldsymbol{X}\right)^{-1}\boldsymbol{X}'\boldsymbol{Z}(\boldsymbol{Z}'\boldsymbol{Z})^{-1}\boldsymbol{Z}'\boldsymbol{Y}_1. \end{aligned} \tag{12.29}$$

This is called the **two-stage least squares (2SLS)** estimator. It was originally proposed by Theil (1953) and Basmann (1957) and is a standard estimator for linear equations with instruments.

If the model is just-identified, so that $k=\ell$, then 2SLS simplifies to the IV estimator of Section 12.11. Since the matrices $\boldsymbol{X}'\boldsymbol{Z}$ and $\boldsymbol{Z}'\boldsymbol{X}$ are square, we can factor

$$\begin{aligned}\left(\boldsymbol{X}'\boldsymbol{Z}\left(\boldsymbol{Z}'\boldsymbol{Z}\right)^{-1}\boldsymbol{Z}'\boldsymbol{X}\right)^{-1} &= \left(\boldsymbol{Z}'\boldsymbol{X}\right)^{-1}\left(\left(\boldsymbol{Z}'\boldsymbol{Z}\right)^{-1}\right)^{-1}\left(\boldsymbol{X}'\boldsymbol{Z}\right)^{-1}\\ &= \left(\boldsymbol{Z}'\boldsymbol{X}\right)^{-1}\left(\boldsymbol{Z}'\boldsymbol{Z}\right)\left(\boldsymbol{X}'\boldsymbol{Z}\right)^{-1}.\end{aligned}$$

(Once again, this only works when $k=\ell$.) Then

$$\begin{aligned}\widehat{\beta}_{2\text{sls}} &= \left(\boldsymbol{X}'\boldsymbol{Z}\left(\boldsymbol{Z}'\boldsymbol{Z}\right)^{-1}\boldsymbol{Z}'\boldsymbol{X}\right)^{-1}\boldsymbol{X}'\boldsymbol{Z}\left(\boldsymbol{Z}'\boldsymbol{Z}\right)^{-1}\boldsymbol{Z}'\boldsymbol{Y}_1\\ &= \left(\boldsymbol{Z}'\boldsymbol{X}\right)^{-1}\left(\boldsymbol{Z}'\boldsymbol{Z}\right)\left(\boldsymbol{X}'\boldsymbol{Z}\right)^{-1}\boldsymbol{X}'\boldsymbol{Z}\left(\boldsymbol{Z}'\boldsymbol{Z}\right)^{-1}\boldsymbol{Z}'\boldsymbol{Y}_1\\ &= \left(\boldsymbol{Z}'\boldsymbol{X}\right)^{-1}\left(\boldsymbol{Z}'\boldsymbol{Z}\right)\left(\boldsymbol{Z}'\boldsymbol{Z}\right)^{-1}\boldsymbol{Z}'\boldsymbol{Y}_1\\ &= \left(\boldsymbol{Z}'\boldsymbol{X}\right)^{-1}\boldsymbol{Z}'\boldsymbol{Y}_1=\widehat{\beta}_{\text{iv}}\end{aligned}$$

as claimed. Thus the 2SLS estimator as defined in (12.29) is a generalization of the IV estimator defined in (12.24).

We now discuss several alternative representations of the 2SLS estimator. First, defining the projection matrix

$$\boldsymbol{P}_Z=\boldsymbol{Z}\left(\boldsymbol{Z}'\boldsymbol{Z}\right)^{-1}\boldsymbol{Z}', \tag{12.30}$$

we can write the 2SLS estimator more compactly as

$$\widehat{\beta}_{2\text{sls}}=\left(\boldsymbol{X}'\boldsymbol{P}_Z\boldsymbol{X}\right)^{-1}\boldsymbol{X}'\boldsymbol{P}_Z\boldsymbol{Y}_1. \tag{12.31}$$

This is useful for representation and derivations but is not useful for computation, as the $n\times n$ matrix $\boldsymbol{P}_Z$ is too large to compute when n is large.

Second, define the fitted values for $\boldsymbol{X}$ from the reduced form $\widehat{\boldsymbol{X}}=\boldsymbol{P}_Z\boldsymbol{X}=\boldsymbol{Z}\widehat{\Gamma}$. Then the 2SLS estimator can be written as

$$\widehat{\beta}_{2\text{sls}}=\left(\widehat{\boldsymbol{X}}'\boldsymbol{X}\right)^{-1}\widehat{\boldsymbol{X}}'\boldsymbol{Y}_1.$$

This is an IV estimator as defined in Section 12.11 using $\widehat{X}$ as an instrument for X.

Third, because $\boldsymbol{P}_Z$ is idempotent, we can also write the 2SLS estimator as

$$\widehat{\beta}_{2\text{sls}}=\left(\boldsymbol{X}'\boldsymbol{P}_Z\boldsymbol{P}_Z\boldsymbol{X}\right)^{-1}\boldsymbol{X}'\boldsymbol{P}_Z\boldsymbol{Y}_1=\left(\widehat{\boldsymbol{X}}'\widehat{\boldsymbol{X}}\right)^{-1}\widehat{\boldsymbol{X}}'\boldsymbol{Y}_1$$

which is the least squares estimator obtained by regressing Y_1 on the fitted values $\widehat{X}$.

This is the source of the "two-stage" name, as this estimation can be computed as follows.

- Regress X on Z to obtain the fitted $\widehat{X}$: $\widehat{\Gamma}=\left(\boldsymbol{Z}'\boldsymbol{Z}\right)^{-1}\left(\boldsymbol{Z}'\boldsymbol{X}\right)$ and $\widehat{\boldsymbol{X}}=\boldsymbol{Z}\widehat{\Gamma}=\boldsymbol{P}_Z\boldsymbol{X}$.
- Regress Y_1 on $\widehat{X}$: $\widehat{\beta}_{2\text{sls}}=\left(\widehat{\boldsymbol{X}}'\widehat{\boldsymbol{X}}\right)^{-1}\widehat{\boldsymbol{X}}'\boldsymbol{Y}_1$.

It is useful to scrutinize the projection $\widehat{\boldsymbol{X}}$. Recall that $\boldsymbol{X}=[\boldsymbol{Z}_1,\boldsymbol{Y}_2]$ and $\boldsymbol{Z}=[\boldsymbol{Z}_1,\boldsymbol{Z}_2]$. Notice that $\widehat{\boldsymbol{X}}_1=\boldsymbol{P}_Z\boldsymbol{Z}_1=\boldsymbol{Z}_1$, because $\boldsymbol{Z}_1$ lies in the span of $\boldsymbol{Z}$. Then $\widehat{\boldsymbol{X}}=\left[\widehat{\boldsymbol{X}}_1,\widehat{\boldsymbol{Y}}_2\right]=\left[\boldsymbol{Z}_1,\widehat{\boldsymbol{Y}}_2\right]$. This shows that in the second stage, we regress Y_1 on Z_1 and $\widehat{Y}_2$, which means that only the endogenous variables Y_2 are replaced by their fitted values: $\widehat{Y}_2=\widehat{\Gamma}'_{12}Z_1+\widehat{\Gamma}'_{22}Z_2$.

A fourth representation of 2SLS can be obtained using the FWL theorem (see Theorem 3.5). The third representation and following discussion showed that 2SLS is obtained as least squares of Y_1 on the fitted values $(Z_1, \widehat{Y}_2)$. Hence the coefficient $\widehat{\beta}_2$ on the endogenous variables can be found by residual regression. Set $\boldsymbol{P}_1 = \boldsymbol{Z}_1 \left(\boldsymbol{Z}_1'\boldsymbol{Z}_1\right)^{-1} \boldsymbol{Z}_1'$. Applying the FWL theorem, we obtain

$$
\begin{aligned}
\widehat{\beta}_2 &= \left(\widehat{\boldsymbol{Y}}_2' (\boldsymbol{I}_n - \boldsymbol{P}_1) \widehat{\boldsymbol{Y}}_2\right)^{-1} \left(\widehat{\boldsymbol{Y}}_2' (\boldsymbol{I}_n - \boldsymbol{P}_1) \boldsymbol{Y}_1\right) \\
&= \left(\boldsymbol{Y}_2' \boldsymbol{P}_Z (\boldsymbol{I}_n - \boldsymbol{P}_1) \boldsymbol{P}_Z \boldsymbol{Y}_2\right)^{-1} \left(\boldsymbol{Y}_2' \boldsymbol{P}_Z (\boldsymbol{I}_n - \boldsymbol{P}_1) \boldsymbol{Y}_1\right) \\
&= \left(\boldsymbol{Y}_2' (\boldsymbol{P}_Z - \boldsymbol{P}_1) \boldsymbol{Y}_2\right)^{-1} \left(\boldsymbol{Y}_2' (\boldsymbol{P}_Z - \boldsymbol{P}_1) \boldsymbol{Y}_1\right)
\end{aligned}
$$

because $\boldsymbol{P}_Z \boldsymbol{P}_1 = \boldsymbol{P}_1$.

A fifth representation can be obtained by a further projection. The projection matrix $\boldsymbol{P}_Z$ can be replaced by the projection onto the pair $[\boldsymbol{Z}_1, \widetilde{\boldsymbol{Z}}_2]$, where $\widetilde{\boldsymbol{Z}}_2 = (\boldsymbol{I}_n - \boldsymbol{P}_1) \boldsymbol{Z}_2$ is $\boldsymbol{Z}_2$ projected orthogonal to $\boldsymbol{Z}_1$. Since $\boldsymbol{Z}_1$ and $\widetilde{\boldsymbol{Z}}_2$ are orthogonal, $\boldsymbol{P}_Z = \boldsymbol{P}_1 + \boldsymbol{P}_2$, where $\boldsymbol{P}_2 = \widetilde{\boldsymbol{Z}}_2 \left(\widetilde{\boldsymbol{Z}}_2'\widetilde{\boldsymbol{Z}}_2\right)^{-1} \widetilde{\boldsymbol{Z}}_2'$. Thus $\boldsymbol{P}_Z - \boldsymbol{P}_1 = \boldsymbol{P}_2$ and

$$
\begin{aligned}
\widehat{\beta}_2 &= \left(\boldsymbol{Y}_2' \boldsymbol{P}_2 \boldsymbol{Y}_2\right)^{-1} \left(\boldsymbol{Y}_2' \boldsymbol{P}_2 \boldsymbol{Y}_1\right) \\
&= \left(\boldsymbol{Y}_2' \widetilde{\boldsymbol{Z}}_2 \left(\widetilde{\boldsymbol{Z}}_2'\widetilde{\boldsymbol{Z}}_2\right)^{-1} \widetilde{\boldsymbol{Z}}_2' \boldsymbol{Y}_2\right)^{-1} \left(\boldsymbol{Y}_2' \widetilde{\boldsymbol{Z}}_2 \left(\widetilde{\boldsymbol{Z}}_2'\widetilde{\boldsymbol{Z}}_2\right)^{-1} \widetilde{\boldsymbol{Z}}_2' \boldsymbol{Y}_1\right). \qquad (12.32)
\end{aligned}
$$

Given the 2SLS estimator, we define the residual $\widehat{e}_i = Y_{1i} - X_i'\widehat{\beta}_{2\text{sls}}$. When the model is overidentified, the instruments and residuals are not orthogonal. That is, $\boldsymbol{Z}'\widehat{\boldsymbol{e}} \neq 0$. It does, however, satisfy

$$
\begin{aligned}
\widehat{\boldsymbol{X}}'\widehat{\boldsymbol{e}} &= \widehat{\boldsymbol{\Gamma}}'\boldsymbol{Z}'\widehat{\boldsymbol{e}} \\
&= \boldsymbol{X}'\boldsymbol{Z}\left(\boldsymbol{Z}'\boldsymbol{Z}\right)^{-1}\boldsymbol{Z}'\widehat{\boldsymbol{e}} \\
&= \boldsymbol{X}'\boldsymbol{Z}\left(\boldsymbol{Z}'\boldsymbol{Z}\right)^{-1}\boldsymbol{Z}'\boldsymbol{Y}_1 - \boldsymbol{X}'\boldsymbol{Z}\left(\boldsymbol{Z}'\boldsymbol{Z}\right)^{-1}\boldsymbol{Z}'\boldsymbol{X}\widehat{\beta}_{2\text{sls}} = 0.
\end{aligned}
$$

Returning to Card's college proximity example, suppose that we treat experience as exogeneous but that instead of using the single instrument *college* (grew up near a 4-year college), we use the two instruments (*public, private*) (grew up near a public/private 4-year college, respectively). In this case, we have one endogenous variable (*education*) and two instruments (*public, private*). The estimated reduced form equation for *education* is presented in the sixth column of Table 12.2. In this specification, the coefficient on *public*—growing up near a public 4-year college—is somewhat larger than that found for the variable *college* in the previous specification (column 2). Furthermore, the coefficient on *private*—growing up near a private 4-year college—is much smaller. This indicates that the key impact of proximity on education is via public colleges rather than private colleges.

The 2SLS estimates obtained using these two instruments are presented in the fourth column of Table 12.1. The coefficient on *education* increases to 0.161, indicating a 16% return to a year of education. This is roughly twice as large as the estimate obtained by least squares in the first column.

Additionally, if we follow Card and treat *experience* as endogenous and use *age* as an instrument, we now have three endogenous variables (*education, experience, experience*$^2/100$) and four instruments (*public, private, age, age*^{2}). The 2SLS estimates using this specification is given in the fifth column of Table 12.1. The estimate of the return to education remains 16% and the return to experience flattens.

You might wonder if we could use all three instruments—*college*, *public*, and *private*. The answer is no, because *college* = *public* + *private*, so the three variables are colinear. Since the instruments are linearly related, the three together would violate the full-rank condition (12.6).

The 2SLS estimator may be calculated in Stata using the `ivregress 2sls` command.

12.13 LIMITED INFORMATION MAXIMUM LIKELIHOOD

An alternative method to estimate the parameters of the structural equation is by maximum likelihood. Anderson and Rubin (1949) derived the maximum likelihood estimator for the joint distribution of $\vec{Y} = (Y_1, Y_2)$. The estimator is known as **limited information maximum likelihood (LIML)**.

This estimator is called "limited information" because it is based on the structural equation for Y combined with the reduced form equation for X_2. If maximum likelihood is derived based on a structural equation for X_2 as well this leads to what is known as **full information maximum likelihood (FIML)**. The advantage of LIML relative to FIML is that the former does not require a structural model for X_2 and thus allows the researcher to focus on the structural equation of interest—that for Y. We do not further discuss the FIML estimator, as it is not commonly used in applied econometrics.

While the LIML estimator is less widely used among economists than 2SLS, it has received a resurgence of attention from econometric theorists.

To derive the LIML estimator, recall the definition $\vec{Y} = (Y_1, Y_2)$ and the reduced form (12.17):

$$\begin{aligned} \vec{Y} &= \begin{bmatrix} \lambda_1' & \lambda_2 \\ \Gamma_{12}' & \Gamma_{22}' \end{bmatrix} \begin{pmatrix} Z_1 \\ Z_2 \end{pmatrix} + u \\ &= \Pi_1' Z_1 + \Pi_2' Z_2 + u \end{aligned} \tag{12.33}$$

where $\Pi_1 = \begin{bmatrix} \lambda_1 & \Gamma_{12} \end{bmatrix}$ and $\Pi_2 = \begin{bmatrix} \lambda_2 & \Gamma_{22} \end{bmatrix}$. The LIML estimator is derived under the assumption that u is multivariate normal.

Define $\gamma' = \begin{bmatrix} 1 & -\beta_2' \end{bmatrix}$. From (12.15), we find

$$\Pi_2 \gamma = \lambda_2 - \Gamma_{22}\beta_2 = 0.$$

Thus the $\ell_2 \times (k_2 + 1)$ coefficient matrix Π_2 in (12.33) has deficient rank. Indeed, its rank must be k_2, because Γ_{22} has full rank. Thus the model (12.33) is precisely the reduced rank regression model of Section 11.11. Theorem 11.7 presents the MLEs for the reduced rank parameters. In particular, the MLE for γ is

$$\widehat{\gamma} = \underset{\gamma}{\operatorname{argmin}} \frac{\gamma' \vec{\boldsymbol{Y}}' \boldsymbol{M}_1 \vec{\boldsymbol{Y}} \gamma}{\gamma' \vec{\boldsymbol{Y}}' \boldsymbol{M}_Z \vec{\boldsymbol{Y}} \gamma} \tag{12.34}$$

where $\boldsymbol{M}_1 = \boldsymbol{I}_n - \boldsymbol{Z}_1 \left(\boldsymbol{Z}_1'\boldsymbol{Z}_1\right)^{-1} \boldsymbol{Z}_1'$ and $\boldsymbol{M}_Z = \boldsymbol{I}_n - \boldsymbol{Z}\left(\boldsymbol{Z}'\boldsymbol{Z}\right)^{-1}\boldsymbol{Z}'$. The minimization (12.34) is sometimes called the "least variance ratio" problem.

The minimization problem (12.34) is invariant to the scale of γ (that is, $\widehat{\gamma} c$ is equivalently the argmin for any c), so normalization is required. A convenient choice is $\gamma' \vec{\boldsymbol{Y}}' \boldsymbol{M}_Z \vec{\boldsymbol{Y}} \gamma = 1$. Using this normalization and the theory of the minimum of quadratic forms (Section A.15), $\widehat{\gamma}$ is the generalized eigenvector of $\vec{\boldsymbol{Y}}' \boldsymbol{M}_1 \vec{\boldsymbol{Y}}$ with respect to $\vec{\boldsymbol{Y}}' \boldsymbol{M}_Z \vec{\boldsymbol{Y}}$ associated with the smallest generalized eigenvalue. (See Section A.14 for the definition of generalized eigenvalues and eigenvectors.) Computationally, this is straightforward. For example, in MATLAB, the generalized eigenvalues and eigenvectors of the matrix $\boldsymbol{A}$ with respect to $\boldsymbol{B}$ are found by the command `eig(A, B)`. Once this $\widehat{\gamma}$ is found, any other normalization can be obtained by rescaling. For example, to obtain the MLE for β_2, make the partition $\widehat{\gamma}' = [\ \widehat{\gamma}_1 \quad \widehat{\gamma}_2'\ ]$ and set $\widehat{\beta}_2 = -\widehat{\gamma}_2/\widehat{\gamma}_1$.

To obtain the MLE for β_1 recall the structural equation $Y_1 = Z_1'\beta_1 + Y_2'\beta_2 + e$. Replace β_2 with the MLE $\widehat{\beta}_2$, and apply regression. This yields

$$\widehat{\beta}_1 = \left(\boldsymbol{Z}_1'\boldsymbol{Z}_1\right)^{-1}\boldsymbol{Z}_1'\left(\boldsymbol{Y}_1 - \boldsymbol{Y}_2\widehat{\beta}_2\right). \tag{12.35}$$

These solutions are the MLE for the structural parameters β_1 and β_2.

Previous econometrics textbooks did not present a derivation of the LIML estimator, as the original derivation by Anderson and Rubin (1949) is lengthy and not particularly insightful. In contrast, the derivation given here based on reduced rank regression is simple.

There is an alternative (and traditional) expression for the LIML estimator. Define the minimum obtained in (12.34):

$$\widehat{\kappa} = \min_{\gamma} \frac{\gamma'\vec{\boldsymbol{Y}}'\boldsymbol{M}_1\vec{\boldsymbol{Y}}\gamma}{\gamma'\vec{\boldsymbol{Y}}'\boldsymbol{M}_Z\vec{\boldsymbol{Y}}\gamma} \tag{12.36}$$

which is the smallest generalized eigenvalue of $\vec{\boldsymbol{Y}}'\boldsymbol{M}_1\vec{\boldsymbol{Y}}$ with respect to $\vec{\boldsymbol{Y}}'\boldsymbol{M}_Z\vec{\boldsymbol{Y}}$. The LIML estimator can be written as

$$\widehat{\beta}_{\text{liml}} = \left(\boldsymbol{X}'\left(\boldsymbol{I}_n - \widehat{\kappa}\boldsymbol{M}_Z\right)\boldsymbol{X}\right)^{-1}\left(\boldsymbol{X}'\left(\boldsymbol{I}_n - \widehat{\kappa}\boldsymbol{M}_Z\right)\boldsymbol{Y}_1\right). \tag{12.37}$$

We defer the derivation of (12.37) until the end of this section. Expression (12.37) does not simplify computation (because $\widehat{\kappa}$ requires solving the same eigenvector problem that yields $\widehat{\beta}_2$). However, (12.37) is important for the distribution theory. It also helps reveal the algebraic connection between LIML, least squares, and 2SLS.

The estimator (12.37) with arbitrary κ is known as a **k-class estimator** of β. While the LIML estimator obtains by setting $\kappa = \widehat{\kappa}$, the least squares estimator is obtained by setting $\kappa = 0$, and 2SLS is obtained by setting $\kappa = 1$. It is worth observing that the LIML solution satisfies $\widehat{\kappa} \geq 1$.

When the model is just-identified, the LIML estimator is identical to the IV and 2SLS estimators. They are only different in the overidentified setting. (One corollary is that under just-identification and normal errors, the IV estimator is MLE.)

For inference, it is useful to observe that (12.37) shows that $\widehat{\beta}_{\text{liml}}$ can be written as an IV estimator

$$\widehat{\beta}_{\text{liml}} = \left(\widetilde{\boldsymbol{X}}'\boldsymbol{X}\right)^{-1}\left(\widetilde{\boldsymbol{X}}'\boldsymbol{Y}_1\right)$$

using the instrument

$$\widetilde{\boldsymbol{X}} = \left(\boldsymbol{I}_n - \widehat{\kappa}\boldsymbol{M}_Z\right)\boldsymbol{X} = \begin{pmatrix} \boldsymbol{X}_1 \\ \boldsymbol{X}_2 - \widehat{\kappa}\widehat{\boldsymbol{U}}_2 \end{pmatrix}$$

where $\widehat{\boldsymbol{U}}_2 = \boldsymbol{M}_Z\boldsymbol{X}_2$ are the reduced-form residuals from the multivariate regression of the endogenous regressors Y_2 on the instruments Z. Expressing LIML using this IV formula is useful for variance estimation.

The LIML estimator has the same asymptotic distribution as 2SLS. However, they have quite different behaviors in finite samples. There is considerable evidence that the LIML estimator has reduced finite sample bias relative to 2SLS when there are many instruments or the reduced form is weak. (We review these cases in later sections.) However, LIML has wider finite sample dispersion.

Let us now derive the expression (12.37). Use the normalization $\gamma' = \begin{bmatrix} 1 & -\beta_2' \end{bmatrix}$ to write (12.34) as

$$\widehat{\beta}_2 = \underset{\beta_2}{\operatorname{argmin}} \frac{(\boldsymbol{Y}_1 - \boldsymbol{Y}_2\beta_2)' \boldsymbol{M}_1 (\boldsymbol{Y}_1 - \boldsymbol{Y}_2\beta_2)}{(\boldsymbol{Y}_1 - \boldsymbol{Y}\beta_2)' \boldsymbol{M}_{\boldsymbol{Z}} (\boldsymbol{Y}_1 - \boldsymbol{Y}_2\beta_2)}.$$

The first-order condition for minimization is $2/\left(\boldsymbol{Y}_1 - \boldsymbol{Y}_2\widehat{\beta}_2\right)' \boldsymbol{M}_{\boldsymbol{Z}} \left(\boldsymbol{Y}_1 - \boldsymbol{Y}_2\widehat{\beta}_2\right)$ times

$$\begin{aligned} 0 &= \boldsymbol{Y}_2'\boldsymbol{M}_1 \left(\boldsymbol{Y}_1 - \boldsymbol{Y}_2\widehat{\beta}_2\right) - \frac{\left(\boldsymbol{Y}_1 - \boldsymbol{Y}_2\widehat{\beta}_2\right)' \boldsymbol{M}_1 \left(\boldsymbol{Y}_1 - \boldsymbol{Y}_2\widehat{\beta}_2\right)}{\left(\boldsymbol{Y}_1 - \boldsymbol{Y}_2\widehat{\beta}_2\right)' \boldsymbol{M}_{\boldsymbol{Z}} \left(\boldsymbol{Y}_1 - \boldsymbol{Y}_2\widehat{\beta}_2\right)} \boldsymbol{X}_2'\boldsymbol{M}_{\boldsymbol{Z}} \left(\boldsymbol{Y}_1 - \boldsymbol{Y}_2\widehat{\beta}_2\right) \\ &= \boldsymbol{Y}_2'\boldsymbol{M}_1 \left(\boldsymbol{Y}_1 - \boldsymbol{Y}_2\widehat{\beta}_2\right) - \widehat{\kappa}\boldsymbol{X}_2'\boldsymbol{M}_{\boldsymbol{Z}} \left(\boldsymbol{Y}_1 - \boldsymbol{Y}_2\widehat{\beta}_2\right) \end{aligned}$$

using definition (12.36). Rewriting,

$$\boldsymbol{Y}_2' (\boldsymbol{M}_1 - \widehat{\kappa}\boldsymbol{M}_{\boldsymbol{Z}}) \boldsymbol{X}_2\widehat{\beta}_2 = \boldsymbol{X}_2' (\boldsymbol{M}_1 - \widehat{\kappa}\boldsymbol{M}_{\boldsymbol{Z}}) \boldsymbol{Y}_1. \tag{12.38}$$

Equation (12.37) is the same as the two-equation system:

$$\begin{aligned} \boldsymbol{Z}_1'\boldsymbol{Z}_1\widehat{\beta}_1 + \boldsymbol{Z}_1'\boldsymbol{Y}_2\widehat{\beta}_2 &= \boldsymbol{Z}_1'\boldsymbol{Y}_1 \\ \boldsymbol{Y}_2'\boldsymbol{Z}_1\widehat{\beta}_1 + \left(\boldsymbol{Y}_2' (\boldsymbol{I}_n - \widehat{\kappa}\boldsymbol{M}_{\boldsymbol{Z}}) \boldsymbol{Y}_2\right) \widehat{\beta}_2 &= \boldsymbol{Y}_2' (\boldsymbol{I}_n - \widehat{\kappa}\boldsymbol{M}_{\boldsymbol{Z}}) \boldsymbol{Y}_1. \end{aligned}$$

The first equation is (12.35). Using (12.35), the second is

$$\boldsymbol{Y}_2'\boldsymbol{Z}_1 \left(\boldsymbol{Z}_1'\boldsymbol{Z}_1\right)^{-1} \boldsymbol{Z}_1' \left(\boldsymbol{Y}_1 - \boldsymbol{Y}_2\widehat{\beta}_2\right) + \left(\boldsymbol{Y}_2' (\boldsymbol{I}_n - \widehat{\kappa}\boldsymbol{M}_{\boldsymbol{Z}}) \boldsymbol{Y}_2\right) \widehat{\beta}_2 = \boldsymbol{Y}_2' (\boldsymbol{I}_n - \widehat{\kappa}\boldsymbol{M}_{\boldsymbol{Z}}) \boldsymbol{Y}_1$$

which is (12.38) when rearranged. We have thus shown that (12.37) is equivalent to (12.35) and (12.38) and is thus a valid expression for the LIML estimator.

Returning to the Card college proximity example, we now present the LIML estimates of the equation with the two instruments (*public, private*). They are reported in the final column of Table 12.1. They are quite similar to the 2SLS estimates.

The LIML estimator may be calculated in Stata using the `ivregress liml` command.

> **Theodore Anderson**
>
> Theodore (Ted) Anderson (1918–2016) was a American statistician and econometrician who made fundamental contributions to multivariate statistical theory. Important contributions include the Anderson-Darling distribution test, the Anderson-Rubin statistic, the method of reduced rank regression, and his most famous econometrics contribution—the LIML estimator. He continued working throughout his long life, even publishing theoretical work at the age of 97!

12.14 SPLIT-SAMPLE IV AND JIVE

The ideal instrument for estimation of β is $W = \overline{\Gamma}'Z$. We can write the ideal IV estimator as

$$\widehat{\beta}_{\text{ideal}} = \left(\sum_{i=1}^{n} W_i X_i'\right)^{-1} \left(\sum_{i=1}^{n} W_i Y_i\right).$$

This estimator is not feasible since Γ is unknown. The 2SLS estimator replaces Γ with the multivariate least squares estimator $\widehat{\Gamma}$ and W_i with $\widehat{W}_i = \widehat{\Gamma}' Z_i$ leading to the following representation for 2SLS:

$$\widehat{\beta}_{\text{2sls}} = \left(\sum_{i=1}^{n} \widehat{W}_i X_i' \right)^{-1} \left(\sum_{i=1}^{n} \widehat{W}_i Y_i \right).$$

Since $\widehat{\Gamma}$ is estimated on the full sample, including observation i, it is a function of the reduced form error u, which is correlated with the structural error e. It follows that $\widehat{W}$ and e are correlated, which means that $\widehat{\beta}_{\text{2sls}}$ is biased for β. This correlation and bias disappears asymptotically, but it can be important in applications.

A possible solution to this problem is to replace $\widehat{W}$ with a predicted value that is uncorrelated with the error e. One method is the **split-sample IV (SSIV)** estimator of Angrist and Krueger (1995). Divide the sample randomly into two independent halves A and B. Use A to estimate the reduced form and B to estimate the structural coefficient. Specifically, use sample A to construct $\widehat{\Gamma}_A = \left(\boldsymbol{Z}_A' \boldsymbol{Z}_A\right)^{-1} \left(\boldsymbol{Z}_A' \boldsymbol{X}_A\right)$. Combine this with sample B to create the predicted values $\widehat{\boldsymbol{W}}_B = \boldsymbol{Z}_B \widehat{\Gamma}_A$. The SSIV estimator is $\widehat{\beta}_{\text{ssiv}} = \left(\widehat{\boldsymbol{W}}_B' \boldsymbol{X}_B\right)^{-1} \left(\widehat{\boldsymbol{W}}_B' \boldsymbol{Y}_B\right)$. This has lower bias than $\widehat{\beta}_{\text{2sls}}$.

A limitation of SSIV is that the results will be sensitive to the sample spliting. One split will produce one estimator; another split will produce a different estimator. Any specific split is arbitrary, so the estimator depends on the specific random sorting of the observations into the samples A and B. A second limitation of SSIV is that it is unlikely to work well when the sample size n is small.

A much better solution is obtained by a leave-one-out estimator for Γ. Specifically, let

$$\widehat{\Gamma}_{(-i)} = \left(\boldsymbol{Z}'\boldsymbol{Z} - Z_i Z_i'\right)^{-1} \left(\boldsymbol{Z}'\boldsymbol{X} - Z_i X_i'\right)$$

be the least squares leave-one-out estimator of the reduced form matrix Γ, and let $\widehat{W}_i = \widehat{\Gamma}_{(-i)}' Z_i$ be the reduced form predicted values. Using $\widehat{W}_i = \widehat{\Gamma}_{(-i)}' Z_i$ as an instrument, we obtain the estimator

$$\widehat{\beta}_{\text{jive1}} = \left(\sum_{i=1}^{n} \widehat{W}_i X_i' \right)^{-1} \left(\sum_{i=1}^{n} \widehat{W}_i Y_i \right) = \left(\sum_{i=1}^{n} \widehat{\Gamma}_{(-i)}' Z_i X_i' \right)^{-1} \left(\sum_{i=1}^{n} \widehat{\Gamma}_{(-i)}' Z_i Y_i \right).$$

This was called the **jackknife instrumental variables (JIVE1)** estimator by Angrist, Imbens, and Krueger (1999). It first appeared in G. Phillips and Hale (1977).

Angrist, Imbens, and Krueger (1999) pointed out that a somewhat simpler adjustment also removes the correlation and bias. Define the estimator and predicted value

$$\widetilde{\Gamma}_{(-i)} = \left(\boldsymbol{Z}'\boldsymbol{Z}\right)^{-1} \left(\boldsymbol{Z}'\boldsymbol{X} - Z_i X_i'\right)$$
$$\widetilde{W}_i = \widetilde{\Gamma}_{(-i)}' Z_i$$

which only adjusts the $\boldsymbol{Z}'\boldsymbol{X}$ component. Their **JIVE2** estimator is

$$\widehat{\beta}_{\text{jive2}} = \left(\sum_{i=1}^{n} \widetilde{W}_i X_i' \right)^{-1} \left(\sum_{i=1}^{n} \widetilde{W}_i Y_i \right) = \left(\sum_{i=1}^{n} \widetilde{\Gamma}_{(-i)}' Z_i X_i' \right)^{-1} \left(\sum_{i=1}^{n} \widetilde{\Gamma}_{(-i)}' Z_i Y_i \right).$$

Using the formula for leave-one-out estimators (Theorem 3.7), the JIVE1 and JIVE2 estimators use two linear operations: the first to create the predicted values $\widehat{W}_i$ or $\widetilde{W}_i$, and the second to calculate the IV estimator. Thus the estimators do not require significantly more computation than 2SLS.

An asymptotic distribution theory for JIVE1 and JIVE2 was developed by Chao, Swanson, Hausman, Newey, and Woutersen (2012).

The JIVE1 and JIVE2 estimators may be calculated in Stata using the `jive` command. It is not a part of the standard package but can be easily added.

12.15 CONSISTENCY OF 2SLS

We now demonstrate the consistency of the 2SLS estimator for the structural parameter. Assumption 12.1 defines a set of regularity conditions.

Assumption 12.1

1. The variables (Y_{1i}, X_i, Z_i), $i = 1, \ldots, n$, are i.i.d.
2. $\mathbb{E}\left[Y_1^2\right] < \infty$.
3. $\mathbb{E}\|X\|^2 < \infty$.
4. $\mathbb{E}\|Z\|^2 < \infty$.
5. $\mathbb{E}\left[ZZ'\right]$ is positive definite.
6. $\mathbb{E}\left[ZX'\right]$ has full rank k.
7. $\mathbb{E}[Ze] = 0$.

Assumptions 12.1.2–4 state that all variables have finite variances. Assumption 12.1.5 states that the instrument vector has an invertible design matrix, which is identical to the core assumption about regressors in the linear regression model. This excludes linearly redundant instruments. Assumptions 12.1.6 and 12.1.7 are the key identification conditions for instrumental variables. Assumption 12.1.6 states that the instruments and regressors have a full-rank cross-moment matrix. This is often called the "relevance" condition. Assumption 12.1.7 states that the instrumental variables and structural error are uncorrelated. Assumptions 12.1.5–7 are identical to Definition 12.1.

Theorem 12.1 Under Assumption 12.1, $\widehat{\beta}_{2\text{sls}} \underset{p}{\longrightarrow} \beta$ as $n \to \infty$.

The proof of the theorem is provided below. This theorem shows that the 2SLS estimator is consistent for the structural coefficient β under similar moment conditions as the least squares estimator. The key differences are the instrumental variables assumption $\mathbb{E}[Ze] = 0$ and the relevance condition $\operatorname{rank}\left(\mathbb{E}\left[ZX'\right]\right) = k$. The result includes the IV estimator (when $\ell = k$) as a special case.

The proof of this consistency result is similar to that for least squares. Take the structural equation $\boldsymbol{Y} = \boldsymbol{X}\beta + \boldsymbol{e}$ in matrix format and substitute it into the expression for the estimator. We obtain

$$\begin{aligned}
\widehat{\beta}_{2\text{sls}} &= \left(\boldsymbol{X}'\boldsymbol{Z}\left(\boldsymbol{Z}'\boldsymbol{Z}\right)^{-1}\boldsymbol{Z}'\boldsymbol{X}\right)^{-1}\boldsymbol{X}'\boldsymbol{Z}\left(\boldsymbol{Z}'\boldsymbol{Z}\right)^{-1}\boldsymbol{Z}'\left(\boldsymbol{X}\beta + \boldsymbol{e}\right) \\
&= \beta + \left(\boldsymbol{X}'\boldsymbol{Z}\left(\boldsymbol{Z}'\boldsymbol{Z}\right)^{-1}\boldsymbol{Z}'\boldsymbol{X}\right)^{-1}\boldsymbol{X}'\boldsymbol{Z}\left(\boldsymbol{Z}'\boldsymbol{Z}\right)^{-1}\boldsymbol{Z}'\boldsymbol{e}. \qquad (12.39)
\end{aligned}$$

This separates out the stochastic component. Rewriting and applying the WLLN and CMT,

$$\widehat{\beta}_{2\text{sls}} - \beta = \left(\left(\frac{1}{n}\boldsymbol{X}'\boldsymbol{Z}\right)\left(\frac{1}{n}\boldsymbol{Z}'\boldsymbol{Z}\right)^{-1}\left(\frac{1}{n}\boldsymbol{Z}'\boldsymbol{X}\right)\right)^{-1}$$

$$\times \left(\frac{1}{n}\boldsymbol{X}'\boldsymbol{Z}\right)\left(\frac{1}{n}\boldsymbol{Z}'\boldsymbol{Z}\right)^{-1}\left(\frac{1}{n}\boldsymbol{Z}'\boldsymbol{e}\right)$$

$$\underset{p}{\longrightarrow} \left(\boldsymbol{Q}_{XZ}\boldsymbol{Q}_{ZZ}^{-1}\boldsymbol{Q}_{ZX}\right)^{-1}\boldsymbol{Q}_{XZ}\boldsymbol{Q}_{ZZ}^{-1}\mathbb{E}\left[Ze\right]=0$$

where

$$\boldsymbol{Q}_{XZ}=\mathbb{E}\left[XZ'\right]$$
$$\boldsymbol{Q}_{ZZ}=\mathbb{E}\left[ZZ'\right]$$
$$\boldsymbol{Q}_{ZX}=\mathbb{E}\left[ZX'\right].$$

The WLLN holds under Assumptions 12.1.1 and 12.1.2–4. The CMT applies if the matrices $\boldsymbol{Q}_{ZZ}$ and $\boldsymbol{Q}_{XZ}\boldsymbol{Q}_{ZZ}^{-1}\boldsymbol{Q}_{ZX}$ are invertible, which hold under Assumptions 12.1.5 and 12.1.6. The final equality uses Assumption 12.1.7.

12.16 ASYMPTOTIC DISTRIBUTION OF 2SLS

We can now show that the 2SLS estimator satisfies a central limit theorem (CLT). We first state a set of sufficient regularity conditions.

Assumption 12.2 In addition to Assumption 12.1:

1. $\mathbb{E}\left[Y_1^4\right]<\infty$.
2. $\mathbb{E}\left\|X\right\|^4<\infty$.
3. $\mathbb{E}\left\|Z\right\|^4<\infty$.
4. $\Omega=\mathbb{E}\left[ZZ'e^2\right]$ is positive definite.

Assumption 12.2 strengthens Assumption 12.1 by requiring that the dependent variable and instruments have finite fourth moments. This is used to establish the central limit theorem.

Theorem 12.2 Under Assumption 12.2, as $n\to\infty$,

$$\sqrt{n}\left(\widehat{\beta}_{\text{2sls}}-\beta\right)\underset{d}{\longrightarrow}\mathrm{N}\left(0,\boldsymbol{V}_\beta\right)$$

where

$$\boldsymbol{V}_\beta=\left(\boldsymbol{Q}_{XZ}\boldsymbol{Q}_{ZZ}^{-1}\boldsymbol{Q}_{ZX}\right)^{-1}\left(\boldsymbol{Q}_{XZ}\boldsymbol{Q}_{ZZ}^{-1}\Omega\boldsymbol{Q}_{ZZ}^{-1}\boldsymbol{Q}_{ZX}\right)\left(\boldsymbol{Q}_{XZ}\boldsymbol{Q}_{ZZ}^{-1}\boldsymbol{Q}_{ZX}\right)^{-1}.$$

This theorem shows that the 2SLS estimator converges at a $\sqrt{n}$ rate to a normal random vector. It shows as well the form of the covariance matrix. The latter takes a substantially more complicated form than the least squares estimator.

As in the case of least squares estimation, the asymptotic variance simplifies under a conditional homoskedasticity condition. For 2SLS, the simplification occurs when $\mathbb{E}\left[e^2\mid Z\right]=\sigma^2$, which holds when Z

and e are independent. It may be reasonable in some contexts to conceive that the error e is independent of the excluded instruments Z_2, since by assumption, the impact of Z_2 on Y is only through X, but there is no reason to expect e to be independent of the included exogenous variables X_1. Hence heteroskedasticity should be equally expected in 2SLS and least squares regression. Nevertheless, under homoskedasticity, we have the simplifications $\Omega = \boldsymbol{Q}_{ZZ}\sigma^2$ and $\boldsymbol{V}_\beta = \boldsymbol{V}_\beta^0 \stackrel{\text{def}}{=} \left(\boldsymbol{Q}_{XZ}\boldsymbol{Q}_{ZZ}^{-1}\boldsymbol{Q}_{ZX}\right)^{-1}\sigma^2$.

The derivation of the asymptotic distribution builds on the proof of consistency. Using equation (12.39), we have

$$\sqrt{n}\left(\widehat{\beta}_{2\text{sls}} - \beta\right) = \left(\left(\frac{1}{n}\boldsymbol{X}'\boldsymbol{Z}\right)\left(\frac{1}{n}\boldsymbol{Z}'\boldsymbol{Z}\right)^{-1}\left(\frac{1}{n}\boldsymbol{Z}'\boldsymbol{X}\right)\right)^{-1}\left(\frac{1}{n}\boldsymbol{X}'\boldsymbol{Z}\right)\left(\frac{1}{n}\boldsymbol{Z}'\boldsymbol{Z}\right)^{-1}\left(\frac{1}{\sqrt{n}}\boldsymbol{Z}'\boldsymbol{e}\right).$$

We apply the WLLN and CMT for the moment matrices involving $\boldsymbol{X}$ and $\boldsymbol{Z}$ in the same way as in the proof of consistency. In addition, by the CLT for i.i.d. observations,

$$\frac{1}{\sqrt{n}}\boldsymbol{Z}'\boldsymbol{e} = \frac{1}{\sqrt{n}}\sum_{i=1}^{n} Z_i e_i \underset{d}{\longrightarrow} \mathrm{N}(0, \Omega)$$

because the vector $Z_i e_i$ is i.i.d. and mean 0 under Assumptions 12.1.1 and 12.1.7, and it has a finite second moment, as we verify below. We obtain

$$\begin{aligned}\sqrt{n}\left(\widehat{\beta}_{2\text{sls}} - \beta\right) &= \left(\left(\frac{1}{n}\boldsymbol{X}'\boldsymbol{Z}\right)\left(\frac{1}{n}\boldsymbol{Z}'\boldsymbol{Z}\right)^{-1}\left(\frac{1}{n}\boldsymbol{Z}'\boldsymbol{X}\right)\right)^{-1}\left(\frac{1}{n}\boldsymbol{X}'\boldsymbol{Z}\right)\left(\frac{1}{n}\boldsymbol{Z}'\boldsymbol{Z}\right)^{-1}\left(\frac{1}{\sqrt{n}}\boldsymbol{Z}'\boldsymbol{e}\right)\\ &\underset{d}{\longrightarrow} \left(\boldsymbol{Q}_{XZ}\boldsymbol{Q}_{ZZ}^{-1}\boldsymbol{Q}_{ZX}\right)^{-1}\boldsymbol{Q}_{XZ}\boldsymbol{Q}_{ZZ}^{-1}\mathrm{N}(0, \Omega) = \mathrm{N}\left(0, \boldsymbol{V}_\beta\right)\end{aligned}$$

as stated.

To complete the proof, we demonstrate that Ze has a finite second moment under Assumption 12.2. To see this, note that by Minkowski's inequality (B.34),

$$\left(\mathbb{E}\left[e^4\right]\right)^{1/4} = \left(\mathbb{E}\left[\left(Y_1 - X'\beta\right)^4\right]\right)^{1/4} \leq \left(\mathbb{E}\left[Y_1^4\right]\right)^{1/4} + \|\beta\|\left(\mathbb{E}\|X\|^4\right)^{1/4} < \infty$$

under Assumptions 12.2.1 and 12.2.2. Then by the Cauchy-Schwarz inequality (B.32)

$$\mathbb{E}\|Ze\|^2 \leq \left(\mathbb{E}\|Z\|^4\right)^{1/2}\left(\mathbb{E}\left[e^4\right]\right)^{1/2} < \infty$$

using Assumptions 12.2.3.

12.17 DETERMINANTS OF 2SLS VARIANCE

It is instructive to examine the asymptotic variance of the 2SLS estimator to understand the factors that determine the precision (or lack thereof) of the estimator. As in the least squares case, it is more transparent to examine the variance under the assumption of homoskedasticity. In this case, the asymptotic variance takes the form

$$\begin{aligned}\boldsymbol{V}_\beta^0 &= \left(\boldsymbol{Q}_{XZ}\boldsymbol{Q}_{ZZ}^{-1}\boldsymbol{Q}_{ZX}\right)^{-1}\sigma^2\\ &= \left(\mathbb{E}\left[XZ'\right]\left(\mathbb{E}\left[ZZ'\right]\right)^{-1}\mathbb{E}\left[ZX'\right]\right)^{-1}\mathbb{E}\left[e^2\right].\end{aligned}$$

As in the least squares case, we can see that the variance of $\widehat{\beta}_{2\text{sls}}$ is increasing in the variance of the error e and decreasing in the variance of X. What is different is that the variance is decreasing in the (matrix-valued) correlation between X and Z.

It is also useful to observe that the variance expression is not affected by the variance structure of Z. Indeed, $\boldsymbol{V}_{\beta}^{0}$ is invariant to rotations of Z (if you replace Z with $\boldsymbol{C}Z$ for invertible $\boldsymbol{C}$, the expression does not change). Thus the variance expression is not affected by the scaling of Z and is not directly affected by correlation among the Z.

We can also use this expression to examine the impact of increasing the instrument set. Suppose we partition $Z=(Z_a, Z_b)$, where $\dim(Z_a) \geq k$, so we can construct a 2SLS estimator using Z_a alone. Let $\widehat{\beta}_a$ and $\widehat{\beta}$ denote the 2SLS estimators constructed using the instrument sets Z_a and (Z_a, Z_b), respectively. Without loss of generality we can assume that Z_a and Z_b are uncorrelated (if not, replace Z_b with the projection error after projecting onto Z_a). In this case, both $\mathbb{E}\left[ZZ'\right]$ and $\left(\mathbb{E}\left[ZZ'\right]\right)^{-1}$ are block diagonal, so

$$
\begin{aligned}
\operatorname{avar}\left[\widehat{\beta}\right] &= \left(\mathbb{E}\left[XZ'\right]\left(\mathbb{E}\left[ZZ'\right]\right)^{-1}\mathbb{E}\left[ZX'\right]\right)^{-1}\sigma^2 \\
&= \left(\mathbb{E}\left[XZ_a'\right]\left(\mathbb{E}\left[Z_aZ_a'\right]\right)^{-1}\mathbb{E}\left[Z_aX'\right]+\mathbb{E}\left[XZ_b'\right]\left(\mathbb{E}\left[Z_bZ_b'\right]\right)^{-1}\mathbb{E}\left[Z_bX'\right]\right)^{-1}\sigma^2 \\
&\leq \left(\mathbb{E}\left[XZ_a'\right]\left(\mathbb{E}\left[Z_aZ_a'\right]\right)^{-1}\mathbb{E}\left[Z_aX'\right]\right)^{-1}\sigma^2 \\
&= \operatorname{avar}\left[\widehat{\beta}_a\right]
\end{aligned}
$$

with strict inequality if $\mathbb{E}\left[XZ_b'\right] \neq 0$. Thus the 2SLS estimator with the full instrument set has a smaller asymptotic variance than the estimator with the smaller instrument set.

What we have shown is that the asymptotic variance of the 2SLS estimator is decreasing as the number of instruments increases. From the viewpoint of asymptotic efficiency, this means that it is better to use more instruments (when they are available and are all known to be valid instruments).

Unfortunately, there is a catch. It turns out that the finite sample bias of the 2SLS estimator (which cannot be calculated exactly but can be approximated using asymptotic expansions) is generally increasing linearly as the number of instruments increases. We will see some calculations illustrating this phenomenon in Section 12.37. Thus the choice of instruments in practice induces a trade-off between bias and variance.

12.18 COVARIANCE MATRIX ESTIMATION

Estimation of the asymptotic covariance matrix $\boldsymbol{V}_{\beta}$ is done using similar techniques as for least squares estimation. The estimator is constructed by replacing the population moment matrices by sample counterparts. Thus

$$
\widehat{\boldsymbol{V}}_{\beta}=\left(\widehat{\boldsymbol{Q}}_{XZ}\widehat{\boldsymbol{Q}}_{ZZ}^{-1}\widehat{\boldsymbol{Q}}_{ZX}\right)^{-1}\left(\widehat{\boldsymbol{Q}}_{XZ}\widehat{\boldsymbol{Q}}_{ZZ}^{-1}\widehat{\Omega}\widehat{\boldsymbol{Q}}_{ZZ}^{-1}\widehat{\boldsymbol{Q}}_{ZX}\right)\left(\widehat{\boldsymbol{Q}}_{XZ}\widehat{\boldsymbol{Q}}_{ZZ}^{-1}\widehat{\boldsymbol{Q}}_{ZX}\right)^{-1} \tag{12.40}
$$

where

$$
\widehat{\boldsymbol{Q}}_{ZZ}=\frac{1}{n}\sum_{i=1}^{n} Z_iZ_i'=\frac{1}{n}\boldsymbol{Z}'\boldsymbol{Z}
$$

$$
\widehat{\boldsymbol{Q}}_{XZ}=\frac{1}{n}\sum_{i=1}^{n} X_iZ_i'=\frac{1}{n}\boldsymbol{X}'\boldsymbol{Z}
$$

$$\widehat{\Omega} = \frac{1}{n}\sum_{i=1}^{n} Z_i Z_i' \widehat{e}_i^2$$

$$\widehat{e}_i = Y_i - X_i'\widehat{\beta}_{2\text{sls}}.$$

The homoskedastic covariance matrix can be estimated by

$$\widehat{\boldsymbol{V}}_\beta^0 = \left(\widehat{\boldsymbol{Q}}_{XZ}\widehat{\boldsymbol{Q}}_{ZZ}^{-1}\widehat{\boldsymbol{Q}}_{ZX}\right)^{-1}\widehat{\sigma}^2$$

$$\widehat{\sigma}^2 = \frac{1}{n}\sum_{i=1}^{n}\widehat{e}_i^2.$$

Standard errors for the coefficients are obtained as the square roots of the diagonal elements of $n^{-1}\widehat{\boldsymbol{V}}_\beta$. Confidence intervals, t-tests, and Wald tests may all be constructed from the coefficient and covariance matrix estimates exactly as for least squares regression.

In Stata, the `ivregress` command by default calculates the covariance matrix estimator using the homoskedastic covariance matrix. To obtain covariance matrix estimation and standard errors with the robust estimator $\widehat{\boldsymbol{V}}_\beta$, use the "`, r`" option.

Theorem 12.3 Under Assumption 12.2, as $n \to \infty$, $\widehat{\boldsymbol{V}}_\beta^0 \underset{p}{\longrightarrow} \boldsymbol{V}_\beta^0$ and $\widehat{\boldsymbol{V}}_\beta \underset{p}{\longrightarrow} \boldsymbol{V}_\beta$.

To prove Theorem 12.3 the key is to show $\widehat{\Omega} \underset{p}{\longrightarrow} \Omega$, as the other convergence results were established in the proof of consistency. We defer this proof to Exercise 12.6.

It is important that the covariance matrix be constructed using the correct residual formula $\widehat{e}_i = Y_i - X_i'\widehat{\beta}_{2\text{sls}}$. This is different than what would be obtained if the "two-stage" computation method were used. To see this, let's walk through the two-stage method. First, we estimate the reduced form $X_i = \widehat{\Gamma}'Z_i + \widehat{u}_i$ to obtain the predicted values $\widehat{X}_i = \widehat{\Gamma}'Z_i$. Second, we regress Y on $\widehat{X}$ to obtain the 2SLS estimator $\widehat{\beta}_{2\text{sls}}$. This latter regression takes the form

$$Y_i = \widehat{X}_i'\widehat{\beta}_{2\text{sls}} + \widehat{v}_i \tag{12.41}$$

where $\widehat{v}_i$ are least squares residuals. The covariance matrix (and standard errors) reported by this regression are constructed using the residual $\widehat{v}_i$. For example, the homoskedastic formula is

$$\widehat{\boldsymbol{V}}_\beta = \left(\frac{1}{n}\widehat{\boldsymbol{X}}'\widehat{\boldsymbol{X}}\right)^{-1}\widehat{\sigma}_v^2 = \left(\widehat{\boldsymbol{Q}}_{XZ}\widehat{\boldsymbol{Q}}_{ZZ}^{-1}\widehat{\boldsymbol{Q}}_{ZX}\right)^{-1}\widehat{\sigma}_v^2$$

$$\widehat{\sigma}_v^2 = \frac{1}{n}\sum_{i=1}^{n}\widehat{v}_i^2$$

which is proportional to the variance estimator $\widehat{\sigma}_v^2$ rather than $\widehat{\sigma}^2$. This difference is important, because the residual $\widehat{v}$ differs from $\widehat{e}$. We can see this because the regression (12.41) uses the regressor $\widehat{X}$ rather than X. Indeed, we calculate that

$$\widehat{v}_i = Y_i - X_i'\widehat{\beta}_{2\text{sls}} + \left(X_i - \widehat{X}_i\right)'\widehat{\beta}_{2\text{sls}} = \widehat{e}_i + \widehat{u}_i'\widehat{\beta}_{2\text{sls}} \neq \widehat{e}_i.$$

Thus the standard errors reported by the regression (12.41) will be incorrect.

This problem is avoided if the 2SLS estimator is constructed directly and the standard errors calculated with the correct formula rather than taking the "two-step" shortcut.

12.19 LIML ASYMPTOTIC DISTRIBUTION

This section shows that the LIML estimator is asymptotically equivalent to the 2SLS estimator. I recommend, however, a different covariance matrix estimator based on the IV representation. We start by deriving the asymptotic distribution. Recall that the LIML estimator has several representations, including

$$\widehat{\beta}_{\text{liml}} = \left(\boldsymbol{X}'\left(\boldsymbol{I}_n - \widehat{\kappa}\boldsymbol{M}_Z\right)\boldsymbol{X}\right)^{-1}\left(\boldsymbol{X}'\left(\boldsymbol{I}_n - \widehat{\kappa}\boldsymbol{M}_Z\right)\boldsymbol{Y}_1\right)$$

where

$$\widehat{\kappa} = \min_{\gamma} \frac{\gamma'\vec{\boldsymbol{Y}}'\boldsymbol{M}_1\vec{\boldsymbol{Y}}\gamma}{\gamma'\vec{\boldsymbol{Y}}'\boldsymbol{M}_Z\vec{\boldsymbol{Y}}\gamma}$$

and $\gamma = (1, -\beta_2')'$. For the distribution theory, it is useful to rewrite the slope coefficient as

$$\widehat{\beta}_{\text{liml}} = \left(\boldsymbol{X}'\boldsymbol{P}_Z\boldsymbol{X} - \widehat{\mu}\boldsymbol{X}'\boldsymbol{M}_Z\boldsymbol{X}\right)^{-1}\left(\boldsymbol{X}'\boldsymbol{P}_Z\boldsymbol{Y}_1 - \widehat{\mu}\boldsymbol{X}'\boldsymbol{M}_Z\boldsymbol{Y}_1\right)$$

where

$$\widehat{\mu} = \widehat{\kappa} - 1 = \min_{\gamma} \frac{\gamma'\vec{\boldsymbol{Y}}'\boldsymbol{M}_1\boldsymbol{Z}_2\left(\boldsymbol{Z}_2'\boldsymbol{M}_1\boldsymbol{Z}_2\right)^{-1}\boldsymbol{Z}_2'\boldsymbol{M}_1\vec{\boldsymbol{Y}}\gamma}{\gamma'\vec{\boldsymbol{Y}}'\boldsymbol{M}_Z\vec{\boldsymbol{Y}}\gamma}.$$

This second equality holds because the span of $\boldsymbol{Z} = [\boldsymbol{Z}_1, \boldsymbol{Z}_2]$ equals the span of $[\boldsymbol{Z}_1, \boldsymbol{M}_1\boldsymbol{Z}_2]$, which implies

$$\boldsymbol{P}_Z = \boldsymbol{Z}\left(\boldsymbol{Z}'\boldsymbol{Z}\right)^{-1}\boldsymbol{Z}' = \boldsymbol{Z}_1\left(\boldsymbol{Z}_1'\boldsymbol{Z}_1\right)^{-1}\boldsymbol{Z}_1' + \boldsymbol{M}_1\boldsymbol{Z}_2\left(\boldsymbol{Z}_2'\boldsymbol{M}_1\boldsymbol{Z}_2\right)^{-1}\boldsymbol{Z}_2'\boldsymbol{M}_1.$$

We now show that $n\widehat{\mu} = O_p(1)$. The reduced form (12.33) implies that

$$\boldsymbol{Y} = \boldsymbol{Z}_1\Pi_1 + \boldsymbol{Z}_2\Pi_2 + \boldsymbol{e}.$$

It will be important to note that

$$\Pi_2 = [\lambda_2, \Gamma_{22}] = [\Gamma_{22}\beta_2, \Gamma_{22}]$$

using (12.15). It follows that $\Pi_2\gamma = 0$. Note $\boldsymbol{U}\gamma = \boldsymbol{e}$. Then $\boldsymbol{M}_Z\boldsymbol{Y}\gamma = \boldsymbol{M}_Z\boldsymbol{e}$ and $\boldsymbol{M}_1\boldsymbol{Y}\gamma = \boldsymbol{M}_1\boldsymbol{e}$. Hence

$$\begin{aligned}
n\widehat{\mu} &= \min_{\gamma} \frac{\gamma'\vec{\boldsymbol{Y}}'\boldsymbol{M}_1\boldsymbol{Z}_2\left(\boldsymbol{Z}_2'\boldsymbol{M}_1\boldsymbol{Z}_2\right)^{-1}\boldsymbol{Z}_2'\boldsymbol{M}_1\vec{\boldsymbol{Y}}\gamma}{\gamma'\frac{1}{n}\vec{\boldsymbol{Y}}'\boldsymbol{M}_Z\vec{\boldsymbol{Y}}\gamma} \\
&\le \frac{\left(\frac{1}{\sqrt{n}}\boldsymbol{e}'\boldsymbol{M}_1\boldsymbol{Z}_2\right)\left(\frac{1}{n}\boldsymbol{Z}_2'\boldsymbol{M}_1\boldsymbol{Z}_2\right)^{-1}\left(\frac{1}{\sqrt{n}}\boldsymbol{Z}_2'\boldsymbol{M}_1\boldsymbol{e}\right)}{\frac{1}{n}\boldsymbol{e}'\boldsymbol{M}_Z\boldsymbol{e}} \\
&= O_p(1).
\end{aligned}$$

It follows that

$$\sqrt{n}\left(\widehat{\beta}_{\text{liml}} - \beta\right) = \left(\frac{1}{n}\boldsymbol{X}'\boldsymbol{P}_Z\boldsymbol{X} - \widehat{\mu}\frac{1}{n}\boldsymbol{X}'\boldsymbol{M}_Z\boldsymbol{X}\right)^{-1}\left(\frac{1}{\sqrt{n}}\boldsymbol{X}'\boldsymbol{P}_Z\boldsymbol{e} - \sqrt{n}\widehat{\mu}\frac{1}{n}\boldsymbol{X}'\boldsymbol{M}_Z\boldsymbol{e}\right)$$

$$= \left(\frac{1}{n}\boldsymbol{X}'\boldsymbol{P}_Z\boldsymbol{X} - o_p(1)\right)^{-1}\left(\frac{1}{\sqrt{n}}\boldsymbol{X}'\boldsymbol{P}_Z\boldsymbol{e} - o_p(1)\right)$$
$$= \sqrt{n}\left(\widehat{\beta}_{\mathrm{2sls}} - \beta\right) + o_p(1)$$

which means that LIML and 2SLS have the same asymptotic distribution. This holds under the same assumptions as for 2SLS.

Consequently, one method to obtain an asymptotically valid covariance estimator for LIML is to use the 2SLS formula. However, this is not the best choice. Instead, consider the IV representation for LIML

$$\widehat{\beta}_{\mathrm{liml}} = \left(\widetilde{\boldsymbol{X}}'\boldsymbol{X}\right)^{-1}\left(\widetilde{\boldsymbol{X}}'\boldsymbol{Y}_1\right)$$

where

$$\widetilde{\boldsymbol{X}} = \begin{pmatrix} \boldsymbol{X}_1 \\ \boldsymbol{X}_2 - \widehat{\kappa}\widehat{\boldsymbol{U}}_2 \end{pmatrix}$$

and $\widehat{\boldsymbol{U}}_2 = \boldsymbol{M}_Z\boldsymbol{X}_2$. The asymptotic covariance matrix formula for an IV estimator is

$$\widehat{\boldsymbol{V}}_\beta = \left(\frac{1}{n}\widetilde{\boldsymbol{X}}'\boldsymbol{X}\right)^{-1}\widehat{\Omega}\left(\frac{1}{n}\boldsymbol{X}'\widetilde{\boldsymbol{X}}\right)^{-1} \tag{12.42}$$

where

$$\widehat{\Omega} = \frac{1}{n}\sum_{i=1}^{n}\widetilde{X}_i\widetilde{X}_i\widehat{e}_i^2$$
$$\widehat{e}_i = Y_{1i} - X_i'\widehat{\beta}_{\mathrm{liml}}.$$

This expression simplifies to the 2SLS formula when $\widehat{\kappa} = 1$ but otherwise differs. The estimator (12.42) is a better choice than the 2SLS formula for covariance matrix estimation, as it takes advantage of the LIML estimator structure.

12.20 FUNCTIONS OF PARAMETERS

Given the distribution theory in Theorems 12.2 and 12.3, it is straightforward to derive the asymptotic distribution of smooth nonlinear functions of the coefficient estimators. Specifically, given a function $r(\beta): \mathbb{R}^k \to \Theta \subset \mathbb{R}^q$, define the parameter $\theta = r(\beta)$. Given $\widehat{\beta}_{\mathrm{2sls}}$, a natural estimator of θ is $\widehat{\theta}_{\mathrm{2sls}} = r\left(\widehat{\beta}_{\mathrm{2sls}}\right)$.

Consistency follows from Theorem 12.1 and the CMT.

> **Theorem 12.4** Under Assumptions 12.1 and 7.3, as $n \to \infty$, $\widehat{\theta}_{\mathrm{2sls}} \xrightarrow[p]{} \theta$.

If $r(\beta)$ is differentiable, then an estimator of the asymptotic covariance matrix for $\widehat{\theta}_{\mathrm{2sls}}$ is

$$\widehat{\boldsymbol{V}}_\theta = \widehat{\boldsymbol{R}}'\widehat{\boldsymbol{V}}_\beta\widehat{\boldsymbol{R}}$$
$$\widehat{\boldsymbol{R}} = \frac{\partial}{\partial\beta}r(\widehat{\beta}_{\mathrm{2sls}})'.$$

We similarly define the homoskedastic variance estimator as $\widehat{\boldsymbol{V}}_\theta^0 = \widehat{\boldsymbol{R}}'\widehat{\boldsymbol{V}}_\beta^0\widehat{\boldsymbol{R}}$.

The asymptotic distribution theory follows from Theorems 12.2 and 12.3 and the delta method.

Theorem 12.5 Under Assumptions 12.2 and 7.3, as $n \to \infty$,

$$\sqrt{n}\left(\widehat{\theta}_{2\text{sls}} - \theta\right) \underset{d}{\longrightarrow} \mathrm{N}\left(0, \boldsymbol{V}_{\theta}\right)$$

and $\widehat{\boldsymbol{V}}_{\theta} \underset{p}{\longrightarrow} \boldsymbol{V}_{\theta}$ where $\boldsymbol{V}_{\theta} = \boldsymbol{R}' \boldsymbol{V}_{\beta} \boldsymbol{R}$ and $\boldsymbol{R} = \frac{\partial}{\partial \beta} r(\beta)'$.

When $q = 1$, a standard error for $\widehat{\theta}_{2\text{sls}}$ is $s(\widehat{\theta}_{2\text{sls}}) = \sqrt{n^{-1} \widehat{\boldsymbol{V}}_{\theta}}$.

For example, let's take the parameter estimates from the fifth column of Table 12.1, which are the 2SLS estimates with three endogenous regressors and four excluded instruments. Suppose we are interested in the return to experience, which depends on the level of experience. The estimated return at $\textit{experience} = 10$ is $0.047 - 0.032 \times 2 \times 10/100 = 0.041$ and its standard error is 0.003. This implies a 4% increase in wages per year of experience and is precisely estimated. Or suppose we are interested in the level of experience at which the function maximizes. The estimate is $50 \times 0.047/0.032 = 73$, which has a standard error of 249. The large standard error implies that the estimate (73 years of experience) is without precision and is thus uninformative.

12.21 HYPOTHESIS TESTS

As in Section 12.20, for a given function $r(\beta) : \mathbb{R}^k \to \Theta \subset \mathbb{R}^q$, we define the parameter $\theta = r(\beta)$ and consider tests of hypotheses of the form $\mathbb{H}_0 : \theta = \theta_0$ against $\mathbb{H}_1 : \theta \neq \theta_0$. The Wald statistic for $\mathbb{H}_0$ is

$$W = n\left(\widehat{\theta} - \theta_0\right)' \widehat{\boldsymbol{V}}_{\widehat{\theta}}^{-1} \left(\widehat{\theta} - \theta_0\right).$$

From Theorem 12.5, we deduce that W is asymptotically chi-square distributed. Let $G_q(u)$ denote the χ_q^2 distribution function.

Theorem 12.6 Under Assumption 12.2, Assumption 7.3, and $\mathbb{H}_0$, then as $n \to \infty$, $W \underset{d}{\longrightarrow} \chi_q^2$. For c satisfying $\alpha = 1 - G_q(c)$, $\mathbb{P}\left[W > c \mid \mathbb{H}_0\right] \longrightarrow \alpha$, so the test "Reject $\mathbb{H}_0$ if $W > c$" has asymptotic size α.

In linear regression, we often report the F version of the Wald statistic (by dividing by degrees of freedom) and use the F distribution for inference, as this is justified in the normal sampling model. For 2SLS estimation, however, this is not done, as there is no finite sample F justification for the F version of the Wald statistic.

To illustrate, once again let's take the parameter estimates from the fifth column of Table 12.1 and again consider the return to experience, which is determined by the coefficients on *experience* and $\textit{experience}^2/100$. Neither coefficient is statisticially significant at the 5% level, and it is unclear if the overall effect is statistically significant. We can assess this by testing the joint hypothesis that both coefficients are 0. The Wald statistic for this hypothesis is $W = 244$, which is highly significant with an asymptotic p-value of 0.0000. Thus by examining the joint test in contrast to the individual tests, is quite clear that experience has a nonzero effect.

12.22 FINITE SAMPLE THEORY

In Chapter 5, we reviewed the rich exact distribution available for the linear regression model under the assumption of normal innovations. There is a similarly rich literature in econometrics for IV, 2SLS, and LIML estimators. An excellent review of the theory, mostly developed in the 1970s and early 1980s, is provided by Peter Phillips (1983).

This theory was developed under the assumption that the structural error vector e and reduced form error u_2 are multivariate normally distributed. Even though the errors are normal, IV-type estimators are nonlinear functions of these errors and are thus non-normally distributed. Formulas for the exact distributions have been derived but are, unfortunately, functions of model parameters and hence are not directly useful for finite sample inference.

One important implication of this literature is that even in this optimal context of exact normal innovations, the finite sample distributions of the IV estimators are non-normal, and the finite sample distributions of test statistics are not chi-squared. The normal and chi-squared approximations hold asymptotically, but there is no reason to expect these approximations to be accurate in finite samples.

A second important result is that under the assumption of normal errors, most of the estimators do not have finite moments in any finite sample. A clean statement concerning the existence of moments for the 2SLS estimator was obtained by Kinal (1980) for the case of joint normality. Let $\widehat{\beta}_{2\text{sls},2}$ be the 2SLS estimators of the coefficients on the endogeneous regressors.

Theorem 12.7 If (Y, X, Z) are jointly normal, then for any r, $\mathbb{E}\left\|\widehat{\beta}_{2\text{sls},2}\right\|^r < \infty$ if and only if $r < \ell_2 - k_2 + 1$.

This result states that in the just-identified case the IV estimator does not have any finite order integer moments. In the overidentified case, the number of finite moments corresponds to the number of overidentifying restrictions $(\ell_2 - k_2)$. Thus if there is one overidentifying restriction, 2SLS has a finite expectation; and if there are two overidentifying restrictions, then the 2SLS estimator has a finite variance.

The LIML estimator has a more severe moment problem, as it has no finite integer moments (Mariano, 1982) regardless of the number of overidentifying restrictions. Due to this lack of moments, Fuller (1977) proposed the following modification of LIML. His estimator is

$$\widehat{\beta}_{\text{Fuller}} = \left(\boldsymbol{X}'\left(\boldsymbol{I}_n - K\boldsymbol{M}_Z\right)\boldsymbol{X}\right)^{-1}\left(\boldsymbol{X}'\left(\boldsymbol{I}_n - K\boldsymbol{M}_Z\right)\boldsymbol{Y}_1\right)$$

$$K = \widehat{\kappa} - \frac{C}{n-k}$$

for some $C \geq 1$. Fuller showed that his estimator has all moments finite under suitable conditions.

Hausman et al. (2012) propose an estimator they call HFUL, which combines the ideas of JIVE and Fuller, and has excellent finite sample properties.

12.23 BOOTSTRAP FOR 2SLS

The standard bootstrap algorithm for IV, 2SLS, and GMM generates bootstrap samples by sampling the triplets (Y_{1i}^*, X_i^*, Z_i^*) independently and with replacement from the original sample $\{(Y_{1i}, X_i, Z_i) : i = 1, \ldots, n\}$.

Sampling n such observations and stacking into observation matrices $(\boldsymbol{Y}_1^*, \boldsymbol{X}^*, \boldsymbol{Z}^*)$, the bootstrap 2SLS estimator is

$$\widehat{\beta}^*_{2\text{sls}} = \left(\boldsymbol{X}^{*\prime}\boldsymbol{Z}^*\left(\boldsymbol{Z}^{*\prime}\boldsymbol{Z}^*\right)^{-1}\boldsymbol{Z}^{*\prime}\boldsymbol{X}^*\right)^{-1}\boldsymbol{X}^{*\prime}\boldsymbol{Z}^*\left(\boldsymbol{Z}^{*\prime}\boldsymbol{Z}^*\right)^{-1}\boldsymbol{Z}^{*\prime}\boldsymbol{Y}_1^*.$$

This is repeated B times to create a sample of B bootstrap draws. Given these draws, bootstrap statistics can be calculated, including the bootstrap estimate of variance, standard errors, and confidence intervals (including percentile, BC percentile, BC_a and percentile-t).

We now show that the bootstrap estimator has the same asymptotic distribution as the sample estimator. For overidentified cases, this demonstration requires a bit of extra care. This was first shown by Hahn (1996).

The sample observations satisfy the model $Y_1 = X'\beta + e$ with $\mathbb{E}[Ze] = 0$. The true value of β in the population can be written as

$$\beta = \left(\mathbb{E}\left[XZ'\right]\mathbb{E}\left[ZZ'\right]^{-1}\mathbb{E}\left[ZX'\right]\right)^{-1}\mathbb{E}\left[XZ'\right]\mathbb{E}\left[ZZ'\right]^{-1}\mathbb{E}\left[ZY_1\right].$$

The true value in the bootstrap universe is obtained by replacing the population moments by the sample moments, which equal the 2SLS estimator:

$$\begin{aligned}
&\left(\mathbb{E}^*\left[X^*Z^{*\prime}\right]\mathbb{E}^*\left[Z^*Z^{*\prime}\right]^{-1}\mathbb{E}^*\left[Z^*X^{*\prime}\right]\right)^{-1}\mathbb{E}^*\left[X^*Z^{*\prime}\right]\mathbb{E}^*\left[Z^*Z^{*\prime}\right]^{-1}\mathbb{E}^*\left[Z^*Y_1^*\right]\\
&=\left(\left(\frac{1}{n}\boldsymbol{X}'\boldsymbol{Z}\right)\left(\frac{1}{n}\boldsymbol{Z}'\boldsymbol{Z}\right)^{-1}\left(\frac{1}{n}\boldsymbol{Z}'\boldsymbol{X}\right)\right)^{-1}\left(\frac{1}{n}\boldsymbol{X}'\boldsymbol{Z}\right)\left(\frac{1}{n}\boldsymbol{Z}'\boldsymbol{Z}\right)^{-1}\left[\frac{1}{n}\boldsymbol{Z}'\boldsymbol{Y}_1\right]\\
&=\widehat{\beta}_{2\text{sls}}.
\end{aligned}$$

The bootstrap observations thus satisfy the equation $Y_{1i}^* = X_i^{*\prime}\widehat{\beta}_{2\text{sls}} + e_i^*$. In matrix notation, for the sample, this is

$$\boldsymbol{Y}_1^* = \boldsymbol{X}^{*\prime}\widehat{\beta}_{2\text{sls}} + \boldsymbol{e}^*. \tag{12.43}$$

Given a bootstrap triple $(Y_{1i}^*, X_i^*, Z_i^*) = (Y_{1j}, X_j, Z_j)$ for some observation j, the true bootstrap error is

$$e_i^* = Y_{1j} - X_j'\widehat{\beta}_{2\text{sls}} = \widehat{e}_j.$$

It follows that

$$\mathbb{E}^*\left[Z^*e^*\right] = n^{-1}\boldsymbol{Z}'\widehat{\boldsymbol{e}}. \tag{12.44}$$

This is generally not equal to 0 in the overidentified case, which is an important complication. In overidentified models, the true observations satisfy the population condition $\mathbb{E}[Ze] = 0$, but in the bootstrap sample, $\mathbb{E}^*[Z^*e^*] \neq 0$. Thus to apply the CLT to the bootstrap estimator, we first have to recenter the moment condition. That is, (12.44) and the bootstrap CLT imply:

$$\frac{1}{\sqrt{n}}\left(\boldsymbol{Z}^{*\prime}\boldsymbol{e}^* - \boldsymbol{Z}'\widehat{\boldsymbol{e}}\right) = \frac{1}{\sqrt{n}}\sum_{i=1}^{n}\left(Z_i^*e_i^* - \mathbb{E}^*\left[Z^*e^*\right]\right) \underset{d^*}{\longrightarrow} \mathrm{N}(0, \Omega) \tag{12.45}$$

where

$$\Omega = \mathbb{E}\left[ZZ'e^2\right].$$

Using (12.43), we can normalize the bootstrap estimator as

$$\begin{aligned}\sqrt{n}\left(\widehat{\boldsymbol{\beta}}^*_{2\text{sls}}-\widehat{\boldsymbol{\beta}}_{2\text{sls}}\right) &= \sqrt{n}\left(\boldsymbol{X}^{*\prime}\boldsymbol{Z}^*\left(\boldsymbol{Z}^{*\prime}\boldsymbol{Z}^*\right)^{-1}\boldsymbol{Z}^{*\prime}\boldsymbol{X}^*\right)^{-1}\boldsymbol{X}^{*\prime}\boldsymbol{Z}^*\left(\boldsymbol{Z}^{*\prime}\boldsymbol{Z}^*\right)^{-1}\boldsymbol{Z}^{*\prime}\boldsymbol{e}^* \\
&= \left(\left(\frac{1}{n}\boldsymbol{X}^{*\prime}\boldsymbol{Z}^*\right)\left(\frac{1}{n}\boldsymbol{Z}^{*\prime}\boldsymbol{Z}^*\right)^{-1}\left(\frac{1}{n}\boldsymbol{Z}^{*\prime}\boldsymbol{X}^*\right)\right)^{-1} \\
&\quad\times\left(\frac{1}{n}\boldsymbol{X}^{*\prime}\boldsymbol{Z}^*\right)\left(\frac{1}{n}\boldsymbol{Z}^{*\prime}\boldsymbol{Z}^*\right)^{-1}\frac{1}{\sqrt{n}}\left(\boldsymbol{Z}^{*\prime}\boldsymbol{e}^*-\boldsymbol{Z}'\widehat{\boldsymbol{e}}\right) \qquad (12.46)\\
&\quad+\left(\left(\frac{1}{n}\boldsymbol{X}^{*\prime}\boldsymbol{Z}^*\right)\left(\frac{1}{n}\boldsymbol{Z}^{*\prime}\boldsymbol{Z}^*\right)^{-1}\left(\frac{1}{n}\boldsymbol{Z}^{*\prime}\boldsymbol{X}^*\right)\right)^{-1} \\
&\quad\times\left(\frac{1}{n}\boldsymbol{X}^{*\prime}\boldsymbol{Z}^*\right)\left(\frac{1}{n}\boldsymbol{Z}^{*\prime}\boldsymbol{Z}^*\right)^{-1}\left(\frac{1}{\sqrt{n}}\boldsymbol{Z}'\widehat{\boldsymbol{e}}\right). \qquad (12.47)\end{aligned}$$

Using the bootstrap WLLN,

$$\begin{aligned}\frac{1}{n}\boldsymbol{X}^{*\prime}\boldsymbol{Z}^* &= \frac{1}{n}\boldsymbol{X}'\boldsymbol{Z}+o_p(1)\\ \frac{1}{n}\boldsymbol{Z}^{*\prime}\boldsymbol{Z}^* &= \frac{1}{n}\boldsymbol{Z}'\boldsymbol{Z}+o_p(1)\end{aligned}$$

which implies that (12.47) is equal to

$$\sqrt{n}\left(\boldsymbol{X}'\boldsymbol{Z}\left(\boldsymbol{Z}'\boldsymbol{Z}\right)^{-1}\left(\boldsymbol{Z}'\boldsymbol{X}\right)\right)^{-1}\boldsymbol{X}'\boldsymbol{Z}\left(\boldsymbol{Z}'\boldsymbol{Z}\right)^{-1}\boldsymbol{Z}'\widehat{\boldsymbol{e}}+o_p(1)=0+o_p(1).$$

The equality holds because the 2SLS first-order condition implies $\boldsymbol{X}'\boldsymbol{Z}\left(\boldsymbol{Z}'\boldsymbol{Z}\right)^{-1}\boldsymbol{Z}'\widehat{\boldsymbol{e}}=0$. Also, combined with (12.45), we see that (12.46) converges in bootstrap distribution to

$$\left(\boldsymbol{Q}_{XZ}\boldsymbol{Q}_{ZZ}^{-1}\boldsymbol{Q}_{ZX}\right)^{-1}\boldsymbol{Q}_{XZ}\boldsymbol{Q}_{ZZ}^{-1}\mathrm{N}\left(0,\Omega\right)=\mathrm{N}\left(0,\boldsymbol{V}_\beta\right)$$

where $\boldsymbol{V}_\beta$ is the 2SLS asymptotic variance from Theorem 12.2. This is the asymptotic distribution of $\sqrt{n}\left(\widehat{\beta}^*_{2\text{sls}}-\widehat{\beta}_{2\text{sls}}\right)$.

By standard calculations, we can also show that bootstrap t-ratios are asymptotically normal.

Theorem 12.8 Under Assumption 12.2, as $n\to\infty$

$$\sqrt{n}\left(\widehat{\beta}^*_{2\text{sls}}-\widehat{\beta}_{2\text{sls}}\right)\underset{d^*}{\longrightarrow}\mathrm{N}\left(0,\boldsymbol{V}_\beta\right)$$

where $\boldsymbol{V}_\beta$ is the 2SLS asymptotic variance from Theorem 12.2. Furthermore,

$$T^*=\frac{\sqrt{n}\left(\widehat{\beta}^*_{2\text{sls}}-\widehat{\beta}_{2\text{sls}}\right)}{s\left(\widehat{\beta}^*_{2\text{sls}}\right)}\underset{d^*}{\longrightarrow}\mathrm{N}\left(0,1\right).$$

Theorem 12.8 shows that percentile-type and percentile-t confidence intervals are asymptotically valid.

One might expect that the asymptotic refinement arguments extend to the BC_a and percentile-t methods, but this does not appear to be the case. While $\sqrt{n}\left(\widehat{\beta}^*_{\mathrm{2sls}} - \widehat{\beta}_{\mathrm{2sls}}\right)$ and $\sqrt{n}\left(\widehat{\beta}_{\mathrm{2sls}} - \beta\right)$ have the same asymptotic distribution, they differ in finite samples by an $O_p\left(n^{-1/2}\right)$ term. Thus they have distinct Edgeworth expansions. Consequently, unadjusted bootstrap methods will not achieve an asymptotic refinement.

An alternative suggested by P. Hall and Horowitz (1996) is to recenter the bootstrap 2SLS estimator so that it satisfies the correct orthogonality condition. Define

$$\widehat{\beta}^{**}_{\mathrm{2sls}} = \left(\boldsymbol{X}^{*\prime}\boldsymbol{Z}^*\left(\boldsymbol{Z}^{*\prime}\boldsymbol{Z}^*\right)^{-1}\boldsymbol{Z}^{*\prime}\boldsymbol{X}^*\right)^{-1}\boldsymbol{X}^{*\prime}\boldsymbol{Z}^*\left(\boldsymbol{Z}^{*\prime}\boldsymbol{Z}^*\right)^{-1}\left(\boldsymbol{Z}^{*\prime}\boldsymbol{Y}_1^* - \boldsymbol{Z}'\widehat{\boldsymbol{e}}\right).$$

We can see that

$$\sqrt{n}\left(\widehat{\beta}^{**}_{\mathrm{2sls}} - \widehat{\beta}_{\mathrm{2sls}}\right) = \left(\frac{1}{n}\boldsymbol{X}^{*\prime}\boldsymbol{Z}^*\left(\frac{1}{n}\boldsymbol{Z}^{*\prime}\boldsymbol{Z}^*\right)^{-1}\frac{1}{n}\boldsymbol{Z}^{*\prime}\boldsymbol{X}^*\right)^{-1}$$
$$\times\left(\frac{1}{n}\boldsymbol{X}^{*\prime}\boldsymbol{Z}^*\right)\left(\frac{1}{n}\boldsymbol{Z}^{*\prime}\boldsymbol{Z}^*\right)^{-1}\left(\frac{1}{\sqrt{n}}\sum_{i=1}^{n}\left(Z_i^* e_i^* - \mathbb{E}^*\left[Z^* e^*\right]\right)\right)$$

which converges to the $\mathrm{N}\left(0, \boldsymbol{V}_\beta\right)$ distribution without special handling. P. Hall and Horowitz (1996) show that percentile-t methods applied to $\widehat{\beta}^{**}_{\mathrm{2sls}}$ achieve an asymptotic refinement and are thus preferred to the unadjusted bootstrap estimator. This recentered estimator, however, is not the standard implementation of the bootstrap for 2SLS as used in empirical practice.

12.24 THE PERIL OF BOOTSTRAP 2SLS STANDARD ERRORS

It is tempting to use the bootstrap algorithm to estimate variance matrices and standard errors for the 2SLS estimator. In fact, this is one of the most common uses of bootstrap methods in current econometric practice. Unfortunately, this idea is a unjustified and ill-conceived and should not be done. In finite samples, the 2SLS estimator may not have a finite second moment, meaning that bootstrap variance estimates are unstable and unreliable.

Theorem 12.7 shows that under joint normality, the 2SLS estimator will have a finite variance if and only if the number of overidentifying restrictions is two or larger. Thus for just-identified IV, and 2SLS with one degree of overidentification, the finite sample variance is infinite. The bootstrap will be attempting to estimate this value—infinity—and will yield nonsensical answers. When the observations are not jointly normal, there is no finite sample theory (so it is possible that the finite sample variance is actually finite, but this is unknown and unverifiable).

In overidentified settings when the number of overidentifying restrictions is two or larger, the bootstrap can be applied for standard error estimation. However this is not the most common application of IV methods in econometric practice and thus should be viewed as the exception rather than the norm.

To understand what is going on, consider the simplest case of a just-identified model with a single endogenous regressor and no included exogenous regressors. In this case, the estimator can be written as a ratio of means:

$$\widehat{\beta}_{\mathrm{iv}} - \beta = \frac{\sum_{i=1}^{n} Z_i e_i}{\sum_{i=1}^{n} Z_i X_i}.$$

Table 12.3
Instrumental variable return to education for Black men

Estimate	0.11
Asymptotic standard error	(0.11)
Jackknife standard error	(0.11)
Bootstrap standard error (standard)	(1.42)
Bootstrap standard error (repeat)	(4.79)

Under joint normality of (e, X), this has a Cauchy-like distribution that does not possess any finite integer moments. The trouble is that the denominator can be either positive or negative, and can be arbitrarily close to 0, so the ratio can take arbitrarily large values.

To illustrate, let us return to the basic Card IV wage regression from column 2 of Table 12.1, which uses *college* as an instrument for *education*. We estimate this equation for the subsample of Black men, which has $n = 703$ observations, and focus on the coefficient for the return to education. The coefficient estimate is reported in Table 12.3, along with asymptotic, jackknife, and two bootstrap standard errors each calculated with 10,000 bootstrap replications.

The bootstrap standard errors are an order of magnitude larger than the asymptotic standard errors, and vary substantially across the bootstrap runs despite using 10,000 bootstrap replications, which indicates moment failure and unreliability of the bootstrap standard errors. This is a strong message that **bootstrap standard errors should not be computed for IV estimators**. Instead, report percentile-type confidence intervals.

12.25 CLUSTERED DEPENDENCE

Section 4.21 introduced clustered dependence. We can also use the methods of clustered dependence for 2SLS estimation. Recall that the gth cluster has the observations $\boldsymbol{Y}_g = (Y_{1g}, \dots, Y_{n_g g})'$, $\boldsymbol{X}_g = (X_{1g}, \dots, X_{n_g g})'$, and $\boldsymbol{Z}_g = (Z_{1g}, \dots, Z_{n_g g})'$. The structural equation for the gth cluster can be written as the matrix system $\boldsymbol{Y}_g = \boldsymbol{X}_g \beta + \boldsymbol{e}_g$. Using this notation, the centered 2SLS estimator can be written as

$$\widehat{\beta}_{2\text{sls}} - \beta = \left(\boldsymbol{X}'\boldsymbol{Z}\left(\boldsymbol{Z}'\boldsymbol{Z}\right)^{-1}\boldsymbol{Z}'\boldsymbol{X}\right)^{-1}\boldsymbol{X}'\boldsymbol{Z}\left(\boldsymbol{Z}'\boldsymbol{Z}\right)^{-1}\boldsymbol{Z}'\boldsymbol{e}$$
$$= \left(\boldsymbol{X}'\boldsymbol{Z}\left(\boldsymbol{Z}'\boldsymbol{Z}\right)^{-1}\boldsymbol{Z}'\boldsymbol{X}\right)^{-1}\boldsymbol{X}'\boldsymbol{Z}\left(\boldsymbol{Z}'\boldsymbol{Z}\right)^{-1}\left(\sum_{g=1}^{G}\boldsymbol{Z}_g'\boldsymbol{e}_g\right).$$

The cluster-robust covariance matrix estimator for $\widehat{\beta}_{2\text{sls}}$ thus takes the form

$$\widehat{\boldsymbol{V}}_\beta = \left(\boldsymbol{X}'\boldsymbol{Z}\left(\boldsymbol{Z}'\boldsymbol{Z}\right)^{-1}\boldsymbol{Z}'\boldsymbol{X}\right)^{-1}\boldsymbol{X}'\boldsymbol{Z}\left(\boldsymbol{Z}'\boldsymbol{Z}\right)^{-1}\widehat{\boldsymbol{S}}\left(\boldsymbol{Z}'\boldsymbol{Z}\right)^{-1}\boldsymbol{Z}'\boldsymbol{X}\left(\boldsymbol{X}'\boldsymbol{Z}\left(\boldsymbol{Z}'\boldsymbol{Z}\right)^{-1}\boldsymbol{Z}'\boldsymbol{X}\right)^{-1}$$

with

$$\widehat{\boldsymbol{S}} = \sum_{g=1}^{G}\boldsymbol{Z}_g'\widehat{\boldsymbol{e}}_g\widehat{\boldsymbol{e}}_g'\boldsymbol{Z}_g$$

and the clustered residuals $\widehat{\boldsymbol{e}}_g = \boldsymbol{Y}_g - \boldsymbol{X}_g\widehat{\beta}_{2\text{sls}}$.

The difference between the heteroskedasticity-robust estimator and the cluster-robust estimator is the covariance estimator $\widehat{\boldsymbol{S}}$.

12.26 GENERATED REGRESSORS

The "two-stage" form of the 2SLS estimator is an example of what is called "estimation with generated regressors." We say a regressor is a **generated** if it is an estimate of an idealized regressor or if it is a function of estimated parameters. Typically, a generated regressor $\widehat{W}$ is an estimate of an unobserved ideal regressor W. As an estimate, $\widehat{W}_i$ is a function of the full sample, not just observation i. Hence it is not i.i.d., as it is dependent across observations, which invalidates the conventional regression assumptions. Consequently, the sampling distribution of regression estimates is affected. Unless this is incorporated into our inference methods, covariance matrix estimates and standard errors will be incorrect.

The econometric theory of generated regressors was developed by Pagan (1984) for linear models and extended to nonlinear models and more general two-step estimators by Pagan (1986). Independently, similar results were obtained by Murphy and Topel (1985). Here we focus on the linear model:

$$Y = W'\beta + v \tag{12.48}$$

$$W = \boldsymbol{A}'Z$$

$$\mathbb{E}[Zv] = 0.$$

The observables are (Y, Z). We also have an estimate $\widehat{\boldsymbol{A}}$ of $\boldsymbol{A}$.

Given $\widehat{\boldsymbol{A}}$, we construct the estimate $\widehat{W}_i = \widehat{\boldsymbol{A}}'Z_i$ of W_i, replace W_i in (12.48) with $\widehat{W}_i$, and then estimate β by least squares, resulting in the estimator

$$\widehat{\beta} = \left(\sum_{i=1}^{n} \widehat{W}_i \widehat{W}_i'\right)^{-1} \left(\sum_{i=1}^{n} \widehat{W}_i Y_i\right). \tag{12.49}$$

The regressors $\widehat{W}_i$ are called **generated regressors**. The properties of $\widehat{\beta}$ are different from those for least squares with i.i.d. observations, because the generated regressors are themselves estimates.

This framework includes 2SLS as well as other common estimators. The 2SLS model can be written as (12.48) by looking at the reduced form equation (12.13), with $W = \Gamma'Z$, $\boldsymbol{A} = \Gamma$, and $\widehat{\boldsymbol{A}} = \widehat{\Gamma}$.

The examples that motivated Pagan (1984) and Murphy and Topel (1985) emerged from the macroeconomics literature, in particular, the work of Barro (1977), which examined the impact of inflation expectations and expectation errors on economic output. Let π denote realized inflation and Z be variables available to economic agents. A model of inflation expectations sets $W = \mathbb{E}[\pi \mid Z] = \gamma'Z$, and a model of expectation error sets $W = \pi - \mathbb{E}[\pi \mid Z] = \pi - \gamma'Z$. Since expectations and errors are not observed, they are replaced in applications with the fitted values $\widehat{W}_i = \widehat{\gamma}'Z_i$ and residuals $\widehat{W}_i = \pi_i - \widehat{\gamma}'Z_i$, where $\widehat{\gamma}$ is the coefficient from a regression of π on Z.

The generated regressor framework includes all of these examples.

The goal is to obtain a distributional approximation for $\widehat{\beta}$ to construct standard errors, confidence intervals, and tests. Start by substituting equation (12.48) into (12.49). We obtain

$$\widehat{\beta} = \left(\sum_{i=1}^{n} \widehat{W}_i \widehat{W}_i'\right)^{-1} \left(\sum_{i=1}^{n} \widehat{W}_i \left(W_i'\beta + v_i\right)\right).$$

Next, substitute $W_i'\beta = \widehat{W}_i'\beta + \left(W_i - \widehat{W}_i\right)'\beta$:

$$\widehat{\beta} - \beta = \left(\sum_{i=1}^{n} \widehat{W}_i \widehat{W}_i'\right)^{-1} \left(\sum_{i=1}^{n} \widehat{W}_i \left(\left(W_i - \widehat{W}_i\right)'\beta + v_i\right)\right). \tag{12.50}$$

Effectively, (12.50) shows that the distribution of $\widehat{\beta}-\beta$ has two random components, one due to the conventional regression component and the second due to the generated regressor. Conventional variance estimators do not address this second component and thus will be biased.

Interestingly, the distribution in (12.50) dramatically simplifies in the special case that the "generated regressor term" $\left(W_i-\widehat{W}_i\right)'\beta$ disappears. This occurs when the slope coefficients on the generated regressors are 0. To be specific, partition $W_i=(W_{1i},W_{2i})$, $\widehat{W}_i=\left(W_{1i},\widehat{W}_{2i}\right)$, and $\beta=(\beta_1,\beta_2)$, so that the W_{1i} are the conventional observed regressors, and $\widehat{W}_{2i}$ are the generated regressors. Then $\left(W_i-\widehat{W}_i\right)'\beta=\left(W_{2i}-\widehat{W}_{2i}\right)'\beta_2$. Thus if $\beta_2=0$, this term disappears. In this case, (12.50) equals

$$\widehat{\beta}-\widehat{\beta}=\left(\sum_{i=1}^n\widehat{W}_i\widehat{W}_i'\right)^{-1}\left(\sum_{i=1}^n\widehat{W}_i v_i\right).$$

This is a dramatic simplification.

Furthermore, since $\widehat{W}_i=\widehat{\boldsymbol{A}}'Z_i$ we can write the estimator as a function of sample moments:

$$\sqrt{n}\left(\widehat{\beta}-\beta\right)=\left(\widehat{\boldsymbol{A}}'\left(\frac{1}{n}\sum_{i=1}^n Z_iZ_i'\right)\widehat{\boldsymbol{A}}\right)^{-1}\widehat{\boldsymbol{A}}'\left(\frac{1}{\sqrt{n}}\sum_{i=1}^n Z_i v_i\right).$$

If $\widehat{\boldsymbol{A}}\underset{p}{\longrightarrow}\boldsymbol{A}$, we find from standard manipulations that $\sqrt{n}\left(\widehat{\beta}-\beta\right)\underset{d}{\longrightarrow}\mathrm{N}\left(0,\boldsymbol{V}_\beta\right)$, where

$$\boldsymbol{V}_{\boldsymbol{\beta}}=\left(\boldsymbol{A}'\mathbb{E}\left[ZZ'\right]\boldsymbol{A}\right)^{-1}\left(\boldsymbol{A}'\mathbb{E}\left[ZZ'v^2\right]\boldsymbol{A}\right)\left(\boldsymbol{A}'\mathbb{E}\left[ZZ'\right]\boldsymbol{A}\right)^{-1}. \tag{12.51}$$

The conventional asymptotic covariance matrix estimator for $\widehat{\beta}$ takes the form

$$\widehat{\boldsymbol{V}}_\beta=\left(\frac{1}{n}\sum_{i=1}^n\widehat{W}_i\widehat{W}_i'\right)^{-1}\left(\frac{1}{n}\sum_{i=1}^n\widehat{W}_i\widehat{W}_i'\widehat{v}_i^2\right)\left(\frac{1}{n}\sum_{i=1}^n\widehat{W}_i\widehat{W}_i'\right)^{-1} \tag{12.52}$$

where $\widehat{v}_i=Y_i-\widehat{W}_i'\widehat{\beta}$. Under the given assumptions, $\widehat{\boldsymbol{V}}_\beta\underset{p}{\longrightarrow}\boldsymbol{V}_\beta$. Thus inference using $\widehat{\boldsymbol{V}}_\beta$ is asymptotically valid, which is useful when we are interested in tests of $\beta_2=0$. Often this is of major interest in applications.

To test $\mathbb{H}_0:\beta_2=0$, we partition $\widehat{\beta}=\left(\widehat{\beta}_1,\widehat{\beta}_2\right)$ and construct a conventional Wald statistic

$$W=n\widehat{\beta}_2'\left(\left[\widehat{\boldsymbol{V}}_\beta\right]_{22}\right)^{-1}\widehat{\beta}_2.$$

Theorem 12.9 Take model (12.48) with $\mathbb{E}\left[Y^4\right]<\infty$, $\mathbb{E}\left\|Z\right\|^4<\infty$, $\boldsymbol{A}'\mathbb{E}\left[ZZ'\right]\boldsymbol{A}>0$, $\widehat{\boldsymbol{A}}\underset{p}{\longrightarrow}\boldsymbol{A}$, and $\widehat{W}_i=\left(W_{1i},\widehat{W}_{2i}\right)$. Under $\mathbb{H}_0:\beta_2=0$, as $n\to\infty$, $\sqrt{n}\left(\widehat{\beta}-\beta\right)\underset{d}{\longrightarrow}\mathrm{N}\left(0,\boldsymbol{V}_\beta\right)$, where $\boldsymbol{V}_\beta$ is given in (12.51). For $\widehat{\boldsymbol{V}}_\beta$ given in (12.52), $\widehat{\boldsymbol{V}}_\beta\underset{p}{\longrightarrow}\boldsymbol{V}_\beta$. Furthermore, $W\underset{d}{\longrightarrow}\chi_q^2$, where $q=\dim(\beta_2)$. For c satisfying $\alpha=1-G_q(c)$, $\mathbb{P}\left[W>c\mid\mathbb{H}_0\right]\to\alpha$, so the test "Reject $\mathbb{H}_0$ if $W>c$" has asymptotic size α.

In the special case when $\widehat{\boldsymbol{A}}=\boldsymbol{A}\left(\boldsymbol{X},\boldsymbol{Z}\right)$ and $v\mid X,Z\sim\mathrm{N}\left(0,\sigma^2\right)$, there is a finite sample version of the previous result. Let W^0 be the Wald statistic constructed with a homoskedastic covariance matrix estimator, and let

$$F=W/q \tag{12.53}$$

be the the F statistic, where $q=\dim(\beta_2)$.

Theorem 12.10 Take model (12.48) with $\widehat{\boldsymbol{A}} = \boldsymbol{A}(\boldsymbol{X}, \boldsymbol{Z})$, $v \mid X, Z \sim \mathrm{N}(0, \sigma^2)$, and $\widehat{W} = (W_1, \widehat{W}_2)$. Under $\mathbb{H}_0 : \beta_2 = 0$, t-statistics have exact $\mathrm{N}(0,1)$ distributions, and the F statistic (12.53) has an exact $F_{q,n-k}$ distribution, where $q = \dim(\beta_2)$ and $k = \dim(\beta)$.

To summarize, in the model $Y = W_1'\beta_1 + W_2'\beta_2 + v$, where W_2 is not observed but is replaced with an estimate $\widehat{W}_2$, conventional significance tests for $\mathbb{H}_0 : \beta_2 = 0$ are asymptotically valid without adjustment.

While this theory allows tests of $\mathbb{H}_0 : \beta_2 = 0$, it unfortunately does not justify conventional standard errors or confidence intervals. For this, we need to work out the distribution without imposing the simplification $\beta_2 = 0$, which often needs to be worked out case-by-case or by using methods based on the generalized method of moments (to be introduced in Chapter 13). However, in one important set of examples, it is straightforward to work out the asymptotic distribution.

For the remainder of this section, we examine the setting where the estimators $\widehat{\boldsymbol{A}}$ take a least squares form and so for some $\boldsymbol{X}$ can be written as $\widehat{\boldsymbol{A}} = (\boldsymbol{Z}'\boldsymbol{Z})^{-1}(\boldsymbol{Z}'\boldsymbol{X})$. Such estimators correspond to the multivariate projection model

$$X = \boldsymbol{A}'Z + u \tag{12.54}$$
$$\mathbb{E}[Zu'] = 0.$$

This class of estimators includes 2SLS and the expectation model described above. We can write the matrix of generated regressors as $\widehat{\boldsymbol{W}} = \boldsymbol{Z}\widehat{\boldsymbol{A}}$ and then (12.50) as

$$\begin{aligned}
\widehat{\beta} - \beta &= \left(\widehat{\boldsymbol{W}}'\widehat{\boldsymbol{W}}\right)^{-1}\left(\widehat{\boldsymbol{W}}'\left(\left(\boldsymbol{W} - \widehat{\boldsymbol{W}}\right)\beta + \boldsymbol{v}\right)\right) \\
&= \left(\widehat{\boldsymbol{A}}'\boldsymbol{Z}'\boldsymbol{Z}\widehat{\boldsymbol{A}}\right)^{-1}\left(\widehat{\boldsymbol{A}}'\boldsymbol{Z}'\left(-\boldsymbol{Z}(\boldsymbol{Z}'\boldsymbol{Z})^{-1}(\boldsymbol{Z}'\boldsymbol{U})\beta + \boldsymbol{v}\right)\right) \\
&= \left(\widehat{\boldsymbol{A}}'\boldsymbol{Z}'\boldsymbol{Z}\widehat{\boldsymbol{A}}\right)^{-1}\left(\widehat{\boldsymbol{A}}'\boldsymbol{Z}'(-\boldsymbol{U}\beta + \boldsymbol{v})\right) \\
&= \left(\widehat{\boldsymbol{A}}'\boldsymbol{Z}'\boldsymbol{Z}\widehat{\boldsymbol{A}}\right)^{-1}\left(\widehat{\boldsymbol{A}}'\boldsymbol{Z}'\boldsymbol{e}\right)
\end{aligned}$$

where

$$e = v - u'\beta = Y - X'\beta. \tag{12.55}$$

This estimator has the asymptotic distribution $\sqrt{n}\left(\widehat{\beta} - \beta\right) \underset{d}{\longrightarrow} \mathrm{N}(0, \boldsymbol{V}_\beta)$, where

$$\boldsymbol{V}_\beta = \left(\boldsymbol{A}'\mathbb{E}[ZZ']\boldsymbol{A}\right)^{-1}\left(\boldsymbol{A}'\mathbb{E}[ZZ'e^2]\boldsymbol{A}\right)\left(\boldsymbol{A}'\mathbb{E}[ZZ']\boldsymbol{A}\right)^{-1}. \tag{12.56}$$

Under conditional homoskedasticity, the covariance matrix simplifies to

$$\boldsymbol{V}_\beta = \left(\boldsymbol{A}'\mathbb{E}[ZZ']\boldsymbol{A}\right)^{-1}\mathbb{E}[e^2].$$

An appropriate estimator of $\boldsymbol{V}_\beta$ is

$$\widehat{\boldsymbol{V}}_\beta = \left(\frac{1}{n}\widehat{\boldsymbol{W}}'\widehat{\boldsymbol{W}}\right)^{-1}\left(\frac{1}{n}\sum_{i=1}^n \widehat{W}_i\widehat{W}_i'\widehat{e}_i^2\right)\left(\frac{1}{n}\widehat{\boldsymbol{W}}'\widehat{\boldsymbol{W}}\right)^{-1} \tag{12.57}$$
$$\widehat{e}_i = Y_i - X_i'\widehat{\beta}.$$

Under the assumption of conditional homoskedasticity, this estimator can be simplified as usual.

This appears to be the usual covariance matrix estimator, but it is not, because the least squares residuals $\widehat{v}_i = Y_i - \widehat{W}_i'\widehat{\beta}$ have been replaced with $\widehat{e}_i$, which is exactly the substitution made by the 2SLS covariance matrix formula. Indeed, the covariance matrix estimator $\widehat{\boldsymbol{V}}_\beta$ precisely equals (12.40).

Theorem 12.11 Take model (12.48) and (12.54) with $\mathbb{E}\left[Y^4\right] < \infty$, $\mathbb{E}\,\|Z\|^4 < \infty$, $\boldsymbol{A}'\mathbb{E}\left[ZZ'\right]\boldsymbol{A} > 0$, and $\widehat{\boldsymbol{A}} = \left(\boldsymbol{Z}'\boldsymbol{Z}\right)^{-1}\left(\boldsymbol{Z}'\boldsymbol{X}\right)$. As $n \to \infty$, $\sqrt{n}\left(\widehat{\beta} - \beta\right) \underset{d}{\longrightarrow} \mathrm{N}\left(0, \boldsymbol{V}_\beta\right)$, where $\boldsymbol{V}_\beta$ is given in (12.56) with e defined in (12.55). For $\widehat{\boldsymbol{V}}_\beta$ given in (12.57), $\widehat{\boldsymbol{V}}_\beta \underset{p}{\longrightarrow} \boldsymbol{V}_\beta$.

Since the parameter estimators are asymptotically normal and the covariance matrix is consistently estimated, standard errors and test statistics constructed from $\widehat{\boldsymbol{V}}_\beta$ are asymptotically valid with conventional interpretations.

To summarize the results of this section, in general, care needs to be exercised when estimating models with generated regressors. As a general rule, generated regressors and two-step estimation affect sampling distributions and variance matrices. An important simplication occurs for tests that the generated regressors have 0 slopes. In this case, conventional tests have conventional distributions, both asymptotically and in finite samples. Another important special case occurs when the generated regressors are least squares fitted values. In this case, the asymptotic distribution takes a conventional form, but the conventional residual needs to be replaced by one constructed with the forecasted variable. With this one modification, asymptotic inference using the generated regressors is conventional.

12.27 REGRESSION WITH EXPECTATION ERRORS

In this section, we examine a generated regressor model that includes expectation errors in the regression. This is an important class of generated regressor models and is relatively straightforward to characterize. The model is

$$
\begin{aligned}
Y &= X'\beta + u'\alpha + v \\
W &= \boldsymbol{A}'Z \\
X &= W + u \\
\mathbb{E}\left[Zv\right] &= 0 \\
\mathbb{E}\left[uv\right] &= 0 \\
\mathbb{E}\left[Zu'\right] &= 0.
\end{aligned}
$$

The observables are (Y, X, Z). This model states that W is the expectation of X (or more generally, the projection of X on Z), and u is its expectation error. The model allows for exogenous regressors as in the standard IV model if they are listed in W, X, and Z. This model is used, for example, to decompose the effect of expectations from expectation errors. In some cases, it is desired to include only the expectation error u, not the expectation W. This does not change the results described here.

The model is estimated as follows. First, $\boldsymbol{A}$ is estimated by multivariate least squares of X on Z, $\widehat{\boldsymbol{A}} = \left(\boldsymbol{Z}'\boldsymbol{Z}\right)^{-1}\left(\boldsymbol{Z}'\boldsymbol{X}\right)$, which yields as by-products the fitted values $\widehat{W}_i = \widehat{\boldsymbol{A}}' Z_i$ and residuals $\widehat{u}_i = \widehat{X}_i - \widehat{W}_i$. Second, the coefficients are estimated by least squares of Y on the fitted values $\widehat{W}$ and residuals $\widehat{u}$:

$$Y_i = \widehat{W}_i'\widehat{\beta} + \widehat{u}_i'\widehat{\alpha} + \widehat{v}_i.$$

We now examine the asymptotic distributions of these estimators.

By the first-step regression, $\boldsymbol{Z}'\widehat{\boldsymbol{U}} = 0$, $\widehat{\boldsymbol{W}}'\widehat{\boldsymbol{U}} = 0$ and $\boldsymbol{W}'\widehat{\boldsymbol{U}} = 0$. Thus $\widehat{\beta}$ and $\widehat{\alpha}$ can be computed separately. Notice that

$$\widehat{\beta} = \left(\widehat{\boldsymbol{W}}'\widehat{\boldsymbol{W}}\right)^{-1}\widehat{\boldsymbol{W}}'\boldsymbol{Y}$$

and

$$\boldsymbol{Y} = \widehat{\boldsymbol{W}}\beta + \boldsymbol{U}\alpha + \left(\boldsymbol{W} - \widehat{\boldsymbol{W}}\right)\beta + \boldsymbol{v}.$$

Substituting, using $\widehat{\boldsymbol{W}}'\widehat{\boldsymbol{U}} = 0$ and $\boldsymbol{W} - \widehat{\boldsymbol{W}} = -\boldsymbol{Z}\left(\boldsymbol{Z}'\boldsymbol{Z}\right)^{-1}\boldsymbol{Z}'\boldsymbol{U}$, we find

$$\begin{aligned}
\widehat{\beta} - \beta &= \left(\widehat{\boldsymbol{W}}'\widehat{\boldsymbol{W}}\right)^{-1}\widehat{\boldsymbol{W}}'\left(\boldsymbol{U}\alpha + \left(\boldsymbol{W} - \widehat{\boldsymbol{W}}\right)\beta + \boldsymbol{v}\right) \\
&= \left(\widehat{\boldsymbol{A}}'\boldsymbol{Z}'\boldsymbol{Z}\widehat{\boldsymbol{A}}\right)^{-1}\widehat{\boldsymbol{A}}'\boldsymbol{Z}'\left(\boldsymbol{U}\alpha - \boldsymbol{U}\beta + \boldsymbol{v}\right) \\
&= \left(\widehat{\boldsymbol{A}}'\boldsymbol{Z}'\boldsymbol{Z}\widehat{\boldsymbol{A}}\right)^{-1}\widehat{\boldsymbol{A}}'\boldsymbol{Z}'\boldsymbol{e}
\end{aligned}$$

where

$$e_i = v_i + u_i'(\alpha - \beta) = Y_i - X_i'\beta.$$

We also find

$$\widehat{\alpha} = \left(\widehat{\boldsymbol{U}}'\widehat{\boldsymbol{U}}\right)^{-1}\widehat{\boldsymbol{U}}'\boldsymbol{Y}.$$

Since $\widehat{\boldsymbol{U}}'\boldsymbol{W} = 0$, $\boldsymbol{U} - \widehat{\boldsymbol{U}} = \boldsymbol{Z}\left(\boldsymbol{Z}'\boldsymbol{Z}\right)^{-1}\boldsymbol{Z}'\boldsymbol{U}$ and $\widehat{\boldsymbol{U}}'\boldsymbol{Z} = 0$, then

$$\begin{aligned}
\widehat{\alpha} - \alpha &= \left(\widehat{\boldsymbol{U}}'\widehat{\boldsymbol{U}}\right)^{-1}\widehat{\boldsymbol{U}}'\left(\boldsymbol{W}\beta + \left(\boldsymbol{U} - \widehat{\boldsymbol{U}}\right)\alpha + \boldsymbol{v}\right) \\
&= \left(\widehat{\boldsymbol{U}}'\widehat{\boldsymbol{U}}\right)^{-1}\widehat{\boldsymbol{U}}'\boldsymbol{v}.
\end{aligned}$$

Taken together, these results establish the following theorem.

Theorem 12.12 For the model and estimators described in this section, with $\mathbb{E}\left[Y^4\right] < \infty$, $\mathbb{E}\|Z\|^4 < \infty$, $\mathbb{E}\|X\|^4 < \infty$, $\boldsymbol{A}'\mathbb{E}\left[ZZ'\right]\boldsymbol{A} > 0$, and $\mathbb{E}\left[uu'\right] > 0$, as $n \to \infty$,

$$\sqrt{n}\begin{pmatrix} \widehat{\beta} - \beta \\ \widehat{\alpha} - \alpha \end{pmatrix} \underset{d}{\longrightarrow} \mathrm{N}(0, \boldsymbol{V}) \tag{12.58}$$

where

$$\boldsymbol{V} = \begin{pmatrix} \boldsymbol{V}_{\beta\beta} & \boldsymbol{V}_{\beta\alpha} \\ \boldsymbol{V}_{\alpha\beta} & \boldsymbol{V}_{\alpha\alpha} \end{pmatrix}$$

and

$$\boldsymbol{V}_{\beta\beta} = \left(\boldsymbol{A}'\mathbb{E}\left[ZZ'\right]\boldsymbol{A}\right)^{-1}\left(\boldsymbol{A}'\mathbb{E}\left[ZZ'e^2\right]\boldsymbol{A}\right)\left(\boldsymbol{A}'\mathbb{E}\left[ZZ'\right]\boldsymbol{A}\right)^{-1}$$
$$\boldsymbol{V}_{\alpha\beta} = \left(\mathbb{E}\left[uu'\right]\right)^{-1}\left(\mathbb{E}\left[uZ'ev\right]\boldsymbol{A}\right)\left(\boldsymbol{A}'\mathbb{E}\left[ZZ'\right]\boldsymbol{A}\right)^{-1}$$
$$\boldsymbol{V}_{\alpha\alpha} = \left(\mathbb{E}\left[uu'\right]\right)^{-1}\mathbb{E}\left[uu'v^2\right]\left(\mathbb{E}\left[uu'\right]\right)^{-1}.$$

The asymptotic covariance matrix is estimated by

$$\widehat{\boldsymbol{V}}_{\beta\beta} = \left(\frac{1}{n}\widehat{\boldsymbol{W}}'\widehat{\boldsymbol{W}}\right)^{-1}\left(\frac{1}{n}\sum_{i=1}^{n}\widehat{W}_i\widehat{W}_i'\widehat{e}_i^2\right)\left(\frac{1}{n}\widehat{\boldsymbol{W}}'\widehat{\boldsymbol{W}}\right)^{-1}$$
$$\widehat{\boldsymbol{V}}_{\alpha\beta} = \left(\frac{1}{n}\widehat{\boldsymbol{U}}'\widehat{\boldsymbol{U}}\right)^{-1}\left(\frac{1}{n}\sum_{i=1}^{n}\widehat{u}_i\widehat{W}_i'\widehat{e}_i\widehat{v}_i\right)\left(\frac{1}{n}\widehat{\boldsymbol{W}}'\widehat{\boldsymbol{W}}\right)^{-1}$$
$$\widehat{\boldsymbol{V}}_{\alpha\alpha} = \left(\frac{1}{n}\widehat{\boldsymbol{U}}'\widehat{\boldsymbol{U}}\right)^{-1}\left(\frac{1}{n}\sum_{i=1}^{n}\widehat{U}_i\widehat{U}_i'\widehat{v}_i^2\right)\left(\frac{1}{n}\widehat{\boldsymbol{U}}'\widehat{\boldsymbol{U}}\right)^{-1}$$

where

$$\widehat{W}_i = \widehat{\boldsymbol{A}}'Z_i$$
$$\widehat{u}_i = \widehat{X}_i - \widehat{W}_i$$
$$\widehat{e}_i = Y_i - X_i'\widehat{\beta}$$
$$\widehat{v}_i = Y_i - \widehat{W}_i'\widehat{\beta} - \widehat{u}_i'\widehat{\alpha}.$$

Under conditional homoskedasticity, specifically,

$$\mathbb{E}\left[\left(\begin{array}{cc} e_i^2 & e_i v_i \\ e_i v_i & v_i^2 \end{array}\right)\middle| Z_i\right] = \boldsymbol{C}$$

then $\boldsymbol{V}_{\alpha\beta} = 0$ and the coefficient estimates $\widehat{\beta}$ and $\widehat{\alpha}$ are asymptotically independent. The variance components also simplify to

$$\boldsymbol{V}_{\beta\beta} = \left(\boldsymbol{A}'\mathbb{E}\left[ZZ'\right]\boldsymbol{A}\right)^{-1}\mathbb{E}\left[e_i^2\right]$$
$$\boldsymbol{V}_{\alpha\alpha} = \left(\mathbb{E}\left[uu'\right]\right)^{-1}\mathbb{E}\left[v^2\right].$$

In this case, we have the covariance matrix estimators

$$\widehat{\boldsymbol{V}}_{\beta\beta}^0 = \left(\frac{1}{n}\widehat{\boldsymbol{W}}'\widehat{\boldsymbol{W}}\right)^{-1}\left(\frac{1}{n}\sum_{i=1}^{n}\widehat{e}_i^2\right)$$
$$\widehat{\boldsymbol{V}}_{\alpha\alpha}^0 = \left(\frac{1}{n}\widehat{\boldsymbol{U}}'\widehat{\boldsymbol{U}}\right)^{-1}\left(\frac{1}{n}\sum_{i=1}^{n}\widehat{v}_i^2\right)$$

and $\widehat{\boldsymbol{V}}_{\alpha\beta}^0 = 0$.

12.28 CONTROL FUNCTION REGRESSION

In this section, we discuss an alternative way of computing the 2SLS estimator by least squares. It is useful in nonlinear contexts and also in the linear model to construct tests for endogeneity.

The structural and reduced form equations for the standard IV model are

$$\begin{aligned} Y &= X_1'\beta_1 + X_2'\beta_2 + e \\ X_2 &= \Gamma_{12}'Z_1 + \Gamma_{22}'Z_2 + u_2. \end{aligned}$$

Since the instrumental variable assumption specifies that $\mathbb{E}[Ze] = 0$, X_2 is endogenous (correlated with e) if u_2 and e are correlated. We can therefore consider the linear projection of e on u_2:

$$\begin{aligned} e &= u_2'\alpha + \nu \\ \alpha &= \left(\mathbb{E}\left[u_2u_2'\right]\right)^{-1}\mathbb{E}[u_2e] \\ \mathbb{E}[u_2\nu] &= 0. \end{aligned}$$

Substituting this into the structural form equation, we find

$$\begin{aligned} Y &= X_1'\beta_1 + X_2'\beta_2 + u_2'\alpha + \nu \qquad (12.59) \\ \mathbb{E}[X_1\nu] &= 0 \\ \mathbb{E}[X_2\nu] &= 0 \\ \mathbb{E}[u_2\nu] &= 0. \end{aligned}$$

Notice that X_2 is uncorrelated with ν, because X_2 is correlated with e only through u_2, and ν is the error after e has been projected orthogonal to u_2.

If u_2 were observed, we could then estimate (12.59) by least squares. Since it is not observed, we estimate it by the reduced-form residual $\widehat{u}_{2i} = X_{2i} - \widehat{\Gamma}_{12}'Z_{1i} - \widehat{\Gamma}_{22}'Z_{2i}$. Then the coefficients $(\beta_1, \beta_2, \alpha)$ can be estimated by least squares of Y on $(X_1, X_2, \widehat{u}_2)$. We can write this as

$$Y_i = X_i'\widehat{\beta} + \widehat{u}_{2i}'\widehat{\alpha} + \widehat{\nu}_i \qquad (12.60)$$

or in matrix notation as

$$\boldsymbol{Y} = \boldsymbol{X}\widehat{\beta} + \widehat{\boldsymbol{U}}_2\widehat{\alpha} + \widehat{\boldsymbol{\nu}}$$

which turns out to be an alternative algebraic expression for the 2SLS estimator.

Indeed, we now show that $\widehat{\beta} = \widehat{\beta}_{2\text{sls}}$. First, note that the reduced form residual can be written as

$$\widehat{\boldsymbol{U}}_2 = (\boldsymbol{I}_n - \boldsymbol{P}_Z)\,\boldsymbol{X}_2$$

where $\boldsymbol{P}_Z$ is defined in (12.30). By the FWL representation

$$\widehat{\beta} = \left(\widetilde{\boldsymbol{X}}'\widetilde{\boldsymbol{X}}\right)^{-1}\left(\widetilde{\boldsymbol{X}}'\boldsymbol{Y}\right) \qquad (12.61)$$

where $\widetilde{\boldsymbol{X}} = \left[\widetilde{\boldsymbol{X}}_1, \widetilde{\boldsymbol{X}}_2\right]$, with

$$\widetilde{\boldsymbol{X}}_1 = \boldsymbol{X}_1 - \widehat{\boldsymbol{U}}_2\left(\widehat{\boldsymbol{U}}_2'\widehat{\boldsymbol{U}}_2\right)^{-1}\widehat{\boldsymbol{U}}_2'\boldsymbol{X}_1 = \boldsymbol{X}_1$$

(since $\widehat{U}_2'X_1 = 0$), and

$$\begin{aligned}\widetilde{X}_2 &= X_2 - \widehat{U}_2\left(\widehat{U}_2'\widehat{U}_2\right)^{-1}\widehat{U}_2'X_2 \\ &= X_2 - \widehat{U}_2\left(X_2'\left(I_n - P_Z\right)X_2\right)^{-1}X_2'\left(I_n - P_Z\right)X_2 \\ &= X_2 - \widehat{U}_2 \\ &= P_Z X_2.\end{aligned}$$

Thus $\widetilde{X} = [X_1, P_Z X_2] = P_Z X$. Substituted into (12.61), we find

$$\widehat{\beta} = \left(X' P_Z X\right)^{-1}\left(X' P_Z Y\right) = \widehat{\beta}_{2\mathrm{sls}}$$

which is (12.31), as claimed.

Again, what we have found is that OLS estimation of equation (12.60) yields algebraically the 2SLS estimator $\widehat{\beta}_{2\mathrm{sls}}$.

We now consider the distribution of the control function estimator $(\widehat{\beta}, \widehat{\alpha})$. It is a generated regression model, and in fact is covered by the model examined in Section 12.27 after a slight reparametrization. Let $W = \overline{\Gamma}' Z$. Note that $u = X - W$. Then the main equation (12.59) can be written as $Y = W'\beta + u_2'\gamma + v$, where $\gamma = \alpha + \beta_2$. This is the model in Section 12.27.

Set $\widehat{\gamma} = \widehat{\alpha} + \widehat{\beta}_2$. It follows from (12.58) that as $n \to \infty$, we have the joint distribution

$$\sqrt{n}\begin{pmatrix} \widehat{\beta}_2 - \beta_2 \\ \widehat{\gamma} - \gamma \end{pmatrix} \underset{d}{\longrightarrow} \mathrm{N}(0, V)$$

where

$$V = \begin{pmatrix} V_{22} & V_{2\gamma} \\ V_{\gamma 2} & V_{\gamma\gamma} \end{pmatrix}$$

$$\begin{aligned}V_{22} &= \left[\left(\overline{\Gamma}'\mathbb{E}\left[ZZ'\right]\overline{\Gamma}\right)^{-1}\overline{\Gamma}'\mathbb{E}\left[ZZ'e^2\right]\overline{\Gamma}\left(\overline{\Gamma}'\mathbb{E}\left[ZZ'\right]\overline{\Gamma}\right)^{-1}\right]_{22} \\ V_{\gamma 2} &= \left[\left(\mathbb{E}\left[u_2u_2'\right]\right)^{-1}\mathbb{E}\left[uZ'ev\right]\overline{\Gamma}\left(\overline{\Gamma}'\mathbb{E}\left[ZZ'\right]\overline{\Gamma}\right)^{-1}\right]_{\cdot 2} \\ V_{\gamma\gamma} &= \left(\mathbb{E}\left[u_2u_2'\right]\right)^{-1}\mathbb{E}\left[u_2u_2'v^2\right]\left(\mathbb{E}\left[u_2u_2'\right]\right)^{-1} \\ e &= Y - X'\beta.\end{aligned}$$

The asymptotic distribution of $\widehat{\gamma} = \widehat{\alpha} - \widehat{\beta}_2$ can be deduced.

Theorem 12.13 If $\mathbb{E}\left[Y^4\right] < \infty$, $\mathbb{E}\|Z\|^4 < \infty$, $\mathbb{E}\|X\|^4 < \infty$, $A'\mathbb{E}\left[ZZ'\right]A > 0$, and $\mathbb{E}\left[uu'\right] > 0$, as $n \to \infty$,

$$\sqrt{n}\left(\widehat{\alpha} - \alpha\right) \underset{d}{\longrightarrow} \mathrm{N}\left(0, V_\alpha\right)$$

where

$$V_\alpha = V_{22} + V_{\gamma\gamma} - V_{\gamma 2} - V_{\gamma 2}'.$$

Under conditional homoskedasticity, we have the important simplifications

$$\begin{aligned}
\boldsymbol{V}_{22} &= \left[\left(\overline{\Gamma}'\mathbb{E}\left[ZZ'\right]\overline{\Gamma}\right)^{-1}\right]_{22}\mathbb{E}\left[e^2\right] \\
\boldsymbol{V}_{\gamma\gamma} &= \left(\mathbb{E}\left[u_2u_2'\right]\right)^{-1}\mathbb{E}\left[\nu^2\right] \\
\boldsymbol{V}_{\gamma 2} &= 0 \\
\boldsymbol{V}_{\alpha} &= \boldsymbol{V}_{22} + \boldsymbol{V}_{\gamma\gamma}.
\end{aligned}$$

An estimator for $\boldsymbol{V}_\alpha$ in the general case is

$$\widehat{\boldsymbol{V}}_{\alpha} = \widehat{\boldsymbol{V}}_{22} + \widehat{\boldsymbol{V}}_{\gamma\gamma} - \widehat{\boldsymbol{V}}_{\gamma 2} - \widehat{\boldsymbol{V}}'_{\gamma 2} \tag{12.62}$$

where

$$\begin{aligned}
\widehat{\boldsymbol{V}}_{22} &= \left[\frac{1}{n}\left(\boldsymbol{X}'\boldsymbol{P}_Z\boldsymbol{X}\right)^{-1}\boldsymbol{X}'\boldsymbol{Z}\left(\boldsymbol{Z}'\boldsymbol{Z}\right)^{-1}\left(\sum_{i=1}^n Z_iZ_i'\widehat{e}_i^2\right)\left(\boldsymbol{Z}'\boldsymbol{Z}\right)^{-1}\boldsymbol{Z}'\boldsymbol{X}\left(\boldsymbol{X}'\boldsymbol{P}_Z\boldsymbol{X}\right)^{-1}\right]_{22} \\
\widehat{\boldsymbol{V}}_{\gamma 2} &= \left[\frac{1}{n}\left(\widehat{\boldsymbol{U}}'\widehat{\boldsymbol{U}}\right)^{-1}\left(\sum_{i=1}^n \widehat{u}_i\widehat{W}_i'\widehat{e}_i\widehat{\nu}_i\right)\left(\boldsymbol{X}'\boldsymbol{P}_Z\boldsymbol{X}\right)^{-1}\right]_{\cdot 2} \\
\widehat{e}_i &= Y_i - X_i'\widehat{\beta} \\
\widehat{\nu}_i &= Y_i - X_i'\widehat{\beta} - \widehat{u}_{2i}'\widehat{\gamma}.
\end{aligned}$$

Under the assumption of conditional homoskedasticity, we have the estimator

$$\begin{aligned}
\widehat{\boldsymbol{V}}_{\alpha}^0 &= \widehat{\boldsymbol{V}}_{\beta\beta}^0 + \widehat{\boldsymbol{V}}_{\gamma\gamma}^0 \\
\widehat{\boldsymbol{V}}_{\beta\beta} &= \left[\left(\boldsymbol{X}'\boldsymbol{P}_Z\boldsymbol{X}\right)^{-1}\right]_{22}\left(\sum_{i=1}^n \widehat{e}_i^2\right) \\
\widehat{\boldsymbol{V}}_{\gamma\gamma} &= \left(\widehat{\boldsymbol{U}}'\widehat{\boldsymbol{U}}\right)^{-1}\left(\sum_{i=1}^n \widehat{\nu}_i^2\right).
\end{aligned}$$

12.29 ENDOGENEITY TESTS

The 2SLS estimator allows the regressor X_2 to be endogenous, meaning that X_2 is correlated with the structural error e. If this correlation is 0, then X_2 is exogenous and the structural equation can be estimated by least squares. This is a testable restriction. Effectively, the null hypothesis is

$$\mathbb{H}_0 : \mathbb{E}\left[X_2 e\right] = 0$$

with the alternative

$$\mathbb{H}_1 : \mathbb{E}\left[X_2 e\right] \neq 0.$$

The maintained hypothesis is $\mathbb{E}\left[Ze\right] = 0$. Since X_1 is a component of Z, this implies $\mathbb{E}\left[X_1 e\right] = 0$. Consequently, we could alternatively write the null as $\mathbb{H}_0 : \mathbb{E}\left[Xe\right] = 0$ (and some authors do so).

Recall the control function regression (12.59):

$$Y = X_1'\beta_1 + X_2'\beta_2 + u_2'\alpha + \nu$$
$$\alpha = \left(\mathbb{E}\left[u_2 u_2'\right]\right)^{-1} \mathbb{E}\left[u_2 e\right].$$

Notice that $\mathbb{E}[X_2 e] = 0$ if and only if $\mathbb{E}[u_2 e] = 0$, so the hypothesis can be restated as $\mathbb{H}_0 : \alpha = 0$ against $\mathbb{H}_1 : \alpha \neq 0$. Thus a natural test is based on the Wald statistic W for $\alpha = 0$ in the control function regression (12.59). Under Theorem 12.9, Theorem 12.10, and $\mathbb{H}_0$, W is asymptotically chi-square with k_2 degrees of freedom. In addition, under the normal regression assumption, the F statistic has an exact $F(k_2, n - k_1 - 2k_2)$ distribution. We accept the null hypothesis that X_2 is exogenous if W (or F) is smaller than the critical value, and reject in favor of the hypothesis that X_2 is endogenous if the statistic is larger than the critical value.

Specifically, estimate the reduced form by least squares

$$X_{2i} = \widehat{\Gamma}_{12}' Z_{1i} + \widehat{\Gamma}_{22}' Z_{2i} + \widehat{u}_{2i}$$

to obtain the residuals. Then estimate the control function by least squares

$$Y_i = X_i'\widehat{\beta} + \widehat{u}_{2i}'\widehat{\alpha} + \widehat{\nu}_i. \tag{12.63}$$

Let W, W^0, and $F = W^0/k_2$ denote the Wald, homoskedastic Wald, and F statistics for $\alpha = 0$ respectively.

Theorem 12.14 Under $\mathbb{H}_0$, $W \underset{d}{\longrightarrow} \chi^2_{k_2}$. Let $c_{1-\alpha}$ solve $\mathbb{P}\left[\chi^2_{k_2} \leq c_{1-\alpha}\right] = 1 - \alpha$. The test "Reject $\mathbb{H}_0$ if $W > c_{1-\alpha}$" has asymptotic size α.

Theorem 12.15 Suppose $e \mid X, Z \sim \mathrm{N}\left(0, \sigma^2\right)$. Under $\mathbb{H}_0$, $\mathrm{F} \sim F(k_2, n - k_1 - 2k_2)$. Let $c_{1-\alpha}$ solve $\mathbb{P}\left[F(k_2, n - k_1 - 2k_2) \leq c_{1-\alpha}\right] = 1 - \alpha$. The test "Reject $\mathbb{H}_0$ if $\mathrm{F} > c_{1-\alpha}$" has exact size α.

Since in general we do not want to impose homoskedasticity, these results suggest that the most appropriate test is the Wald statistic constructed with the robust heteroskedastic covariance matrix. It can be computed in Stata using the command `estat endogenous` after `ivregress`, when the latter uses a robust covariance option. Stata reports the Wald statistic in F form (and thus uses the F distribution to calculate the p-value) as "Robust regression F." Using the F rather than the χ^2 is not formally justified but is a reasonable finite sample adjustment. If the command `estat endogenous` is applied after `ivregress` without a robust covariance option, Stata reports the F statistic as "Wu-Hausman F."

There is an alternative (and traditional) way to derive a test for endogeneity. Under $\mathbb{H}_0$, both OLS and 2SLS are consistent estimators. But under $\mathbb{H}_1$, they converge to different values. Thus the difference between the OLS and 2SLS estimators is a valid test statistic for endogeneity. It also measures what we often care most about—the impact of endogeneity on the parameter estimates. This literature was developed under the assumption of conditional homoskedasticity (and it is important for these results), so we assume this condition for the development of the statistic.

Let $\widehat{\beta}=(\widehat{\beta}_1,\widehat{\beta}_2)$ be the OLS estimator, and let $\widetilde{\beta}=(\widetilde{\beta}_1,\widetilde{\beta}_2)$ be the 2SLS estimator. Under $\mathbb{H}_0$ and homoskedasticity, the OLS estimator is Gauss-Markov efficient, so by the Hausman equality

$$\begin{aligned}\operatorname{var}\left[\widehat{\beta}_2-\widetilde{\beta}_2\right]&=\operatorname{var}\left[\widetilde{\beta}_2\right]-\operatorname{var}\left[\widehat{\beta}_2\right]\\&=\left(\left(\boldsymbol{X}_2'\left(\boldsymbol{P}_{\boldsymbol{Z}}-\boldsymbol{P}_1\right)\boldsymbol{X}_2\right)^{-1}-\left(\boldsymbol{X}_2'\boldsymbol{M}_1\boldsymbol{X}_2\right)^{-1}\right)\sigma^2\end{aligned}$$

where $\boldsymbol{P}_{\boldsymbol{Z}}=\boldsymbol{Z}\left(\boldsymbol{Z}'\boldsymbol{Z}\right)^{-1}\boldsymbol{Z}'$, $\boldsymbol{P}_1=\boldsymbol{X}_1\left(\boldsymbol{X}_1'\boldsymbol{X}_1\right)^{-1}\boldsymbol{X}_1'$, and $\boldsymbol{M}_1=\boldsymbol{I}_n-\boldsymbol{P}_1$. Thus a valid test statistic for $\mathbb{H}_0$ is

$$T=\frac{(\widehat{\beta}_2-\widetilde{\beta}_2)'\left(\left(\boldsymbol{X}_2'\left(\boldsymbol{P}_{\boldsymbol{Z}}-\boldsymbol{P}_1\right)\boldsymbol{X}_2\right)^{-1}-\left(\boldsymbol{X}_2'\boldsymbol{M}_1\boldsymbol{X}_2\right)^{-1}\right)^{-1}(\widehat{\beta}_2-\widetilde{\beta}_2)}{\widehat{\sigma}^2} \tag{12.64}$$

for some estimator $\widehat{\sigma}^2$ of σ^2. Durbin (1954) first proposed T as a test for endogeneity in the context of IV estimation, setting $\widehat{\sigma}^2$ to be the least squares estimator of σ^2. Wu (1973) proposed T as a test for endogeneity in the context of 2SLS estimation, considering a set of possible estimators $\widehat{\sigma}^2$, including the regression estimator from (12.63). Hausman (1978) proposed a version of T based on the full contrast $\widehat{\beta}-\widetilde{\beta}$, and observed that it equals the regression Wald statistic W^0 described earlier. In fact, when $\widehat{\sigma}^2$ is the regression estimator from (12.63), the statistic (12.64) algebraically equals both W^0 and the version of (12.64) based on the full contrast $\widehat{\beta}-\widetilde{\beta}$. We show these equalities below. Thus these three approaches yield the same statistic except for possible differences regarding the choice of $\widehat{\sigma}^2$. Since the regression F test described earlier has an exact F distribution in the normal sampling model and thus can exactly control test size, this is the preferred version of the test. The general class of tests are called **Durbin-Wu-Hausman** tests, **Wu-Hausman** tests, or **Hausman** tests, depending on the author.

When $k_2=1$ (there is one right-hand-side endogenous variable), which is quite common in applications, the endogeneity test can be equivalently expressed at the t-statistic for $\widehat{\alpha}$ in the estimated control function. Thus it is sufficient to estimate the control function regression and check the t-statistic for $\widehat{\alpha}$. If $|\widehat{\alpha}|>2$, then we can reject the hypothesis that X_2 is exogenous for β.

Let us illustrate using the Card proximity example with the two instruments *public* and *private*. We first estimate the reduced form for *education*, obtain the residual, and then estimate the control function regression. The residual has a coefficient -0.088 with a standard error of 0.037 and a t-statistic of 2.4. Since the latter exceeds the 5% critical value (its p-value is 0.017), we reject exogeneity. Thus the 2SLS estimates are statistically different from the least squares estimates of the structural equation, which supports our decision to treat education as an endogenous variable. (Alternatively, the F statistic is $2.4^2=5.7$ with the same p-value).

Let us now show the equality of the various statistics.

We first show that the statistic (12.64) is not altered if based on the full contrast $\widehat{\beta}-\widetilde{\beta}$. Indeed, $\widehat{\beta}_1-\widetilde{\beta}_1$ is a linear function of $\widehat{\beta}_2-\widetilde{\beta}_2$, so there is no extra information in the full contrast. To see this, observe that given $\widehat{\beta}_2$, we can solve by least squares to find

$$\widehat{\beta}_1=\left(\boldsymbol{X}_1'\boldsymbol{X}_1\right)^{-1}\left(\boldsymbol{X}_1'\left(\boldsymbol{Y}-\boldsymbol{X}_2\widehat{\beta}_2\right)\right)$$

and similarly,

$$\widetilde{\beta}_1=\left(\boldsymbol{X}_1'\boldsymbol{X}_1\right)^{-1}\left(\boldsymbol{X}_1'\left(\boldsymbol{Y}-\boldsymbol{P}_{\boldsymbol{Z}}\boldsymbol{X}_2\widetilde{\beta}\right)\right)=\left(\boldsymbol{X}_1'\boldsymbol{X}_1\right)^{-1}\left(\boldsymbol{X}_1'\left(\boldsymbol{Y}-\boldsymbol{X}_2\widetilde{\beta}\right)\right)$$

the second equality follows because $\boldsymbol{P}_{\boldsymbol{Z}}\boldsymbol{X}_1=\boldsymbol{X}_1$. Thus

$$\begin{aligned}\widehat{\beta}_1-\widetilde{\beta}_1&=\left(\boldsymbol{X}_1'\boldsymbol{X}_1\right)^{-1}\boldsymbol{X}_1'\left(\boldsymbol{Y}-\boldsymbol{X}_2\widehat{\beta}_2\right)-\left(\boldsymbol{X}_1'\boldsymbol{X}_1\right)^{-1}\boldsymbol{X}_1'\left(\boldsymbol{Y}-\boldsymbol{P}_{\boldsymbol{Z}}\boldsymbol{X}_2\widetilde{\beta}\right)\\&=\left(\boldsymbol{X}_1'\boldsymbol{X}_1\right)^{-1}\boldsymbol{X}_1'\boldsymbol{X}_2\left(\widetilde{\beta}_2-\widehat{\beta}_2\right)\end{aligned}$$

as claimed.

We next show that T in (12.64) equals the homoskedastic Wald statistic W^0 for $\widehat{\alpha}$ from the regression (12.63). Consider the latter regression. Since $\boldsymbol{X}_2$ is contained in $\boldsymbol{X}$, the coefficient estimate $\widehat{\alpha}$ is invariant to replacing $\widehat{\boldsymbol{U}}_2 = \boldsymbol{X}_2 - \widehat{\boldsymbol{X}}_2$ with $-\widehat{\boldsymbol{X}}_2 = -\boldsymbol{P}_Z \boldsymbol{X}_2$. By the FWL representation, setting $\boldsymbol{M}_X = \boldsymbol{I}_n - \boldsymbol{X}\left(\boldsymbol{X}'\boldsymbol{X}\right)^{-1}\boldsymbol{X}'$,

$$\widehat{\alpha} = -\left(\widehat{\boldsymbol{X}}_2'\boldsymbol{M}_X\widehat{\boldsymbol{X}}_2\right)^{-1}\widehat{\boldsymbol{X}}_2'\boldsymbol{M}_X\boldsymbol{Y} = -\left(\boldsymbol{X}_2'\boldsymbol{P}_Z\boldsymbol{M}_X\boldsymbol{P}_Z\boldsymbol{X}_2\right)^{-1}\boldsymbol{X}_2'\boldsymbol{P}_Z\boldsymbol{M}_X\boldsymbol{Y}.$$

It follows that

$$W^0 = \frac{\boldsymbol{Y}'\boldsymbol{M}_X\boldsymbol{P}_Z\boldsymbol{X}_2\left(\boldsymbol{X}_2'\boldsymbol{P}_Z\boldsymbol{M}_X\boldsymbol{P}_Z\boldsymbol{X}_2\right)^{-1}\boldsymbol{X}_2'\boldsymbol{P}_Z\boldsymbol{M}_X\boldsymbol{Y}}{\widehat{\sigma}^2}.$$

Our goal is to show that $T = W^0$. Define $\widetilde{\boldsymbol{X}}_2 = (\boldsymbol{I}_n - \boldsymbol{P}_1)\boldsymbol{X}_2$, so $\widehat{\beta}_2 = \left(\widetilde{\boldsymbol{X}}_2'\widetilde{\boldsymbol{X}}_2\right)^{-1}\widetilde{\boldsymbol{X}}_2'\boldsymbol{Y}$. Then using $(\boldsymbol{P}_Z - \boldsymbol{P}_1)(\boldsymbol{I}_n - \boldsymbol{P}_1) = (\boldsymbol{P}_Z - \boldsymbol{P}_1)$ and defining $\boldsymbol{Q} = \widetilde{\boldsymbol{X}}_2\left(\widetilde{\boldsymbol{X}}_2'\widetilde{\boldsymbol{X}}_2\right)^{-1}\widetilde{\boldsymbol{X}}_2'$, we find

$$\begin{aligned}
\boldsymbol{\Delta} &\stackrel{\text{def}}{=} \left(\boldsymbol{X}_2'(\boldsymbol{P}_Z - \boldsymbol{P}_1)\boldsymbol{X}_2\right)\left(\widetilde{\beta}_2 - \widehat{\beta}_2\right) \\
&= \boldsymbol{X}_2'(\boldsymbol{P}_Z - \boldsymbol{P}_1)\boldsymbol{Y} - \left(\boldsymbol{X}_2'(\boldsymbol{P}_Z - \boldsymbol{P}_1)\boldsymbol{X}_2\right)\left(\widetilde{\boldsymbol{X}}_2'\widetilde{\boldsymbol{X}}_2\right)^{-1}\widetilde{\boldsymbol{X}}_2'\boldsymbol{Y} \\
&= \boldsymbol{X}_2'(\boldsymbol{P}_Z - \boldsymbol{P}_1)(\boldsymbol{I}_n - \boldsymbol{Q})\boldsymbol{Y} \\
&= \boldsymbol{X}_2'(\boldsymbol{P}_Z - \boldsymbol{P}_1 - \boldsymbol{P}_Z\boldsymbol{Q})\boldsymbol{Y} \\
&= \boldsymbol{X}_2'\boldsymbol{P}_Z(\boldsymbol{I}_n - \boldsymbol{P}_1 - \boldsymbol{Q})\boldsymbol{Y} \\
&= \boldsymbol{X}_2'\boldsymbol{P}_Z\boldsymbol{M}_X\boldsymbol{Y}.
\end{aligned}$$

The third-to-last equality is $\boldsymbol{P}_1\boldsymbol{Q} = 0$, and the final uses $\boldsymbol{M}_X = \boldsymbol{I}_n - \boldsymbol{P}_1 - \boldsymbol{Q}$. We also calculate that

$$\begin{aligned}
\boldsymbol{Q}^* &\stackrel{\text{def}}{=} \left(\boldsymbol{X}_2'(\boldsymbol{P}_Z - \boldsymbol{P}_1)\boldsymbol{X}_2\right)\left(\left(\boldsymbol{X}_2'(\boldsymbol{P}_Z - \boldsymbol{P}_1)\boldsymbol{X}_2\right)^{-1} - \left(\boldsymbol{X}_2'\boldsymbol{M}_1\boldsymbol{X}_2\right)^{-1}\right)\left(\boldsymbol{X}_2'(\boldsymbol{P}_Z - \boldsymbol{P}_1)\boldsymbol{X}_2\right) \\
&= \boldsymbol{X}_2'\left(\boldsymbol{P}_Z - \boldsymbol{P}_1 - (\boldsymbol{P}_Z - \boldsymbol{P}_1)\boldsymbol{Q}(\boldsymbol{P}_Z - \boldsymbol{P}_1)\right)\boldsymbol{X}_2 \\
&= \boldsymbol{X}_2'\left(\boldsymbol{P}_Z - \boldsymbol{P}_1 - \boldsymbol{P}_Z\boldsymbol{Q}\boldsymbol{P}_Z\right)\boldsymbol{X}_2 \\
&= \boldsymbol{X}_2'\boldsymbol{P}_Z\boldsymbol{M}_X\boldsymbol{P}_Z\boldsymbol{X}_2.
\end{aligned}$$

Thus

$$\begin{aligned}
T &= \frac{\boldsymbol{\Delta}'\boldsymbol{Q}^{*-1}\boldsymbol{\Delta}}{\widehat{\sigma}^2} \\
&= \frac{\boldsymbol{Y}'\boldsymbol{M}_X\boldsymbol{P}_Z\boldsymbol{X}_2\left(\boldsymbol{X}_2'\boldsymbol{P}_Z\boldsymbol{M}_X\boldsymbol{P}_Z\boldsymbol{X}_2\right)^{-1}\boldsymbol{X}_2'\boldsymbol{P}_Z\boldsymbol{M}_X\boldsymbol{Y}}{\widehat{\sigma}^2} \\
&= W^0
\end{aligned}$$

as claimed.

12.30 SUBSET ENDOGENEITY TESTS

In some cases, we may only wish to test the endogeneity of a subset of the variables. In the Card proximity example, we may wish to test the exogeneity of *education* separately from *experience* and its square. To execute a subset endogeneity test, it is useful to partition the regressors into three groups, so that the structural model is

$$Y = X_1'\beta_1 + X_2'\beta_2 + X_3'\beta_3 + e$$
$$\mathbb{E}[Ze] = 0.$$

As before, the instrument vector Z includes X_1. The vector X_3 is treated as endogenous, and X_2 is treated as potentially endogenous. The hypothesis to test is that X_2 is exogenous, or $\mathbb{H}_0 : \mathbb{E}[X_2 e] = 0$ against $\mathbb{H}_1 : \mathbb{E}[X_2 e] \neq 0$.

Under homoskedasticity, a straightfoward test can be constructed by the Durbin-Wu-Hausman principle. Under $\mathbb{H}_0$, the appropriate estimator is 2SLS using the instruments (Z, X_2). Let this estimator of β_2 be denoted $\widehat{\beta}_2$. Under $\mathbb{H}_1$, the appropriate estimator is 2SLS using the smaller instrument set Z. Let this estimator of β_2 be denoted $\widetilde{\beta}_2$. A Durbin-Wu-Hausman statistic for $\mathbb{H}_0$ against $\mathbb{H}_1$ is

$$T = \left(\widehat{\beta}_2 - \widetilde{\beta}_2\right)' \left(\widehat{\operatorname{var}}\left[\widetilde{\beta}_2\right] - \widehat{\operatorname{var}}\left[\widehat{\beta}_2\right]\right)^{-1} \left(\widehat{\beta}_2 - \widetilde{\beta}_2\right).$$

The asymptotic distribution under $\mathbb{H}_0$ is $\chi^2_{k_2}$, where $k_2 = \dim(X_2)$, so we reject the hypothesis that the variables X_2 are exogenous if T exceeds an upper critical value from the $\chi^2_{k_2}$ distribution.

Instead of using the Wald statistic, one could use the F version of the test by dividing by k_2 and using the F distribution for critical values. There is no finite sample justification for this modification, however, since X_3 is endogenous under the null hypothesis.

In Stata, the command `estat endogenous` (adding the variable name to specify which variable to test for exogeneity) after `ivregress` without a robust covariance option reports the F version of this statistic as "Wu-Hausman F." For example, in the Card proximity example using the four instruments *public*, *private*, *age*, and *age*^{2}, if we estimate the equation by 2SLS with a non-robust covariance matrix and then compute the endogeneity test for education, we find $F = 272$ with a p-value of 0.0000; but if we compute the test for experience and its square, we find $F = 2.98$ with a p-value of 0.051. In this model, the assumption of exogeneity with homogenous coefficients is rejected for education, but the result for experience is unclear.

A heteroskedasticity or cluster-robust test cannot be constructed easily by the Durbin-Wu-Hausman approach, since the covariance matrix does not take a simple form. To allow for non-homoskedastic errors, it is recommended to use GMM estimation. See Section 13.24.

12.31 OVERIDENTIFICATION TESTS

When $\ell > k$, the model is **overidentified**, meaning that there are more moments than free parameters. This is a restriction and is testable. Such tests are called **overidentification tests**.

The IV model specifies $\mathbb{E}[Ze] = 0$. Equivalently, since $e = Y - X'\beta$, this is

$$\mathbb{E}[ZY] - \mathbb{E}\left[ZX'\right]\beta = 0$$

which is an $\ell \times 1$ vector of restrictions on the moment matrices $\mathbb{E}[ZY]$ and $\mathbb{E}\left[ZX'\right]$. Since β is of dimension k, which is less than ℓ, it is not certain if indeed such a β exists.

To make things a bit more concrete, suppose there is a single endogenous regressor X_2, no X_1, and two instruments Z_1 and Z_2. Then the model specifies that

$$\mathbb{E}[Z_1 Y] = \mathbb{E}[Z_1 X_2]\beta$$

and

$$\mathbb{E}\left[Z_2Y\right] = \mathbb{E}\left[Z_2X_2\right]\beta.$$

Thus β solves both equations. This is rather special.

Alternatively, we could solve for β using either one equation or the other. In terms of estimation, this is equivalent to estimating by IV using just the instrument Z_1 or instead just using the instrument Z_2. These two estimators (in finite samples) are different. If the overidentification hypothesis is correct, both are estimating the same parameter and both are consistent for β. In contrast, if the overidentification hypothesis is false, then the two estimators will converge to different probability limits and it is unclear if either probability limit is interesting.

For example, take the 2SLS estimates in the fourth column of Table 12.1, which use *public* and *private* as instruments for *education*. Suppose we instead estimate by IV using just *public* as an instrument and then repeat using *private*. The IV coefficient for *education* in the first case is 0.16 and in the second case 0.27. These appear to be quite different. However, the second estimate has a large standard error (0.16), so the difference may be sampling variation. An overidentification test addresses this question.

For a general overidentification test, the null and alternative hypotheses are $\mathbb{H}_0 : \mathbb{E}\left[Ze\right] = 0$ against $\mathbb{H}_1 : \mathbb{E}\left[Ze\right] \neq 0$. We will also add the conditional homoskedasticity assumption:

$$\mathbb{E}\left[e^2 \mid Z\right] = \sigma^2. \tag{12.65}$$

To avoid (12.65), it is best to take a GMM approach, which we defer until Chapter 13.

To implement a test of $\mathbb{H}_0$, consider a linear regression of the error e on the instruments Z,

$$e = Z'\alpha + v \tag{12.66}$$

with $\alpha = \left(\mathbb{E}\left[ZZ'\right]\right)^{-1}\mathbb{E}\left[Ze\right]$. We can rewrite $\mathbb{H}_0$ as $\alpha = 0$. While e is not observed, we can replace it with the 2SLS residual $\widehat{e}_i$ and estimate α by least squares regression (e.g., $\widehat{\alpha} = \left(\boldsymbol{Z}'\boldsymbol{Z}\right)^{-1}\boldsymbol{Z}'\widehat{\boldsymbol{e}}$). Sargan (1958) proposed testing $\mathbb{H}_0$ via a score test, which equals

$$S = \widehat{\alpha}'\left(\widehat{\operatorname{var}}\left[\widehat{\alpha}\right]\right)^{-}\widehat{\alpha} = \frac{\widehat{\boldsymbol{e}}'\boldsymbol{Z}\left(\boldsymbol{Z}'\boldsymbol{Z}\right)^{-1}\boldsymbol{Z}'\widehat{\boldsymbol{e}}}{\widehat{\sigma}^2} \tag{12.67}$$

where $\widehat{\sigma}^2 = \frac{1}{n}\widehat{\boldsymbol{e}}'\widehat{\boldsymbol{e}}$. Basmann (1960) independently proposed a Wald statistic for $\mathbb{H}_0$, which is S with $\widehat{\sigma}^2$ replaced with $\widetilde{\sigma}^2 = n^{-1}\widehat{\boldsymbol{v}}'\widehat{\boldsymbol{v}}$, where $\widehat{\boldsymbol{v}} = \widehat{\boldsymbol{e}} - \boldsymbol{Z}\widehat{\alpha}$. By the equivalence of homoskedastic score and Wald tests (see Section 9.17), Basmann's statistic is a monotonic function of Sargan's statistic and hence they yield equivalent tests. Sargan's version is more typically reported.

The Sargan test rejects $\mathbb{H}_0$ in favor of $\mathbb{H}_1$ if $S > c$ for some critical value c. An asymptotic test sets c as the $1-\alpha$ quantile of the $\chi^2_{\ell-k}$ distribution. This is justified by the asymptotic null distribution of S, which we now derive.

> **Theorem 12.16** Under Assumption 12.2 and $\mathbb{E}\left[e^2 \mid Z\right] = \sigma^2$, then as $n \to \infty$, $S \xrightarrow[d]{} \chi^2_{\ell-k}$. For c satisfying $\alpha = 1 - G_{\ell-k}(c)$, $\mathbb{P}\left[S > c \mid \mathbb{H}_0\right] \to \alpha$, so the test "Reject $\mathbb{H}_0$ if $S > c$" has asymptotic size α.

We prove Theorem 12.16 below.

The Sargan statistic S is an asymptotic test of the overidentifying restrictions under the assumption of conditional homoskedasticity. It has some limitations. First, it is an asymptotic test and does not have a finite sample (e.g., F) counterpart. Simulation evidence suggests that the test can be oversized (reject too frequently) in small and moderate sample sizes. Consequently, p-values should be interpreted cautiously. Second, the assumption of conditional homoskedasticity is unrealistic in applications. The best way to generalize the Sargan statistic to allow heteroskedasticity is to use the GMM overidentification statistic, which we will examine in Chapter 13. For 2SLS, Wooldridge (1995) suggested a robust score test, but Baum, Schaffer and Stillman (2003) point out that it is numerically equivalent to the GMM overidentification statistic. Hence the bottom line appears to be that to allow heteroskedasticity or clustering, it is best to use a GMM approach.

In overidentified applications, it is always prudent to report an overidentification test. If the test is insignificant, it means that the overidentifying restrictions are not rejected, supporting the estimated model. If the overidentifying test statistic is highly significant (if the p-value is very small), this is evidence that the overidentifying restrictions are violated. In this case we should be concerned that the model is misspecified, and interpreting the parameter estimates should be done cautiously.

When reporting the results of an overidentification test, it seems reasonable to focus on very small significance levels, such as 1%. Thus we should only treat a model as "rejected" if the Sargan p-value is very small (e.g., less than 0.01). The reason to focus on very small significance levels is because it is very difficult to interpret the result "The model is rejected." Stepping back a bit, it does not seem credible that any overidentified model is literally true; instead what seems potentially credible is that an overidentified model is a reasonable approximation. A test is asking the question: "Is there evidence that a model is not true?" But we really want to know the answer to: "Is there evidence that the model is a poor approximation?" Consequently it seems reasonable to require strong evidence to lead to the conclusion "Let's reject this model." The recommendation is that mild rejections (p-values between 1% and 5%) should be viewed as mildly worrisome but not critical evidence against a model. The results of an overidentification test should be integrated with other information before making a strong decision.

We illustrate the methods with the Card college proximity example (see Section 12.6). We have estimated two overidentified models by 2SLS in columns 4 and 5 of Table 12.1. In each case, the number of overidentifying restrictions is 1. We report the Sargan statistic and its asymptotic p-value (calculated using the χ_1^2 distribution) in the table. Both p-values (0.37 and 0.47) are far from significant, indicating that there is no evidence that the models are misspecified.

Let us now prove Theorem 12.16. The statistic S is invariant to rotations of $\boldsymbol{Z}$ (replacing $\boldsymbol{Z}$ with $\boldsymbol{ZC}$), so without loss of generality, we assume $\mathbb{E}\left[ZZ'\right] = \boldsymbol{I}_\ell$. As $n \to \infty$, $n^{-1/2}\boldsymbol{Z}'\boldsymbol{e} \underset{d}{\longrightarrow} \sigma \mathrm{Z}$, where $\mathrm{Z} \sim \mathrm{N}\left(0, \boldsymbol{I}_\ell\right)$. Also $\frac{1}{n}\boldsymbol{Z}'\boldsymbol{Z} \underset{p}{\longrightarrow} \boldsymbol{I}_\ell$ and $\frac{1}{n}\boldsymbol{Z}'\boldsymbol{X} \underset{p}{\longrightarrow} \boldsymbol{Q}$, say. Then

$$
\begin{aligned}
n^{-1/2}\boldsymbol{Z}'\widehat{\boldsymbol{e}} &= \left(\boldsymbol{I}_\ell - \left(\frac{1}{n}\boldsymbol{Z}'\boldsymbol{X}\right)\left(\frac{1}{n}\boldsymbol{X}'\boldsymbol{P}_Z\boldsymbol{X}\right)^{-1}\left(\frac{1}{n}\boldsymbol{X}'\boldsymbol{Z}\right)\left(\frac{1}{n}\boldsymbol{Z}'\boldsymbol{Z}\right)^{-1}\right) n^{-1/2}\boldsymbol{Z}'\boldsymbol{e} \\
&\underset{d}{\longrightarrow} \sigma\left(\boldsymbol{I}_\ell - \boldsymbol{Q}\left(\boldsymbol{Q}'\boldsymbol{Q}\right)^{-1}\boldsymbol{Q}'\right)\mathrm{Z}.
\end{aligned}
$$

Since $\widehat{\sigma}^2 \underset{p}{\longrightarrow} \sigma^2$, it follows that

$$
S \underset{d}{\longrightarrow} \mathrm{Z}'\left(\boldsymbol{I}_\ell - \boldsymbol{Q}\left(\boldsymbol{Q}'\boldsymbol{Q}\right)^{-1}\boldsymbol{Q}'\right)\mathrm{Z} \sim \chi^2_{\ell-k}.
$$

The distribution is $\chi^2_{\ell-k}$, because $\boldsymbol{I}_\ell - \boldsymbol{Q}\left(\boldsymbol{Q}'\boldsymbol{Q}\right)^{-1}\boldsymbol{Q}'$ is idempotent with rank $\ell - k$.

The Sargan statistic test can be implemented in Stata using the command `estat overid` after `ivregress 2sls` or `ivregres liml` if a standard (non-robust) covariance matrix has been specified (that is, without the '`, r`' option), or otherwise by the command `estat overid, forcenonrobust`.

Denis Sargan

The British econometrician John Denis Sargan (1924–1996) was a pioneer in the field of econometrics. He made a range of fundamental contributions, including the overidentification test, Edgeworth expansions, and unit root theory. He was also influential in his role as dissertation advisor for many students of econometrics.

12.32 SUBSET OVERIDENTIFICATION TESTS

Tests of $\mathbb{H}_0 : \mathbb{E}[Ze] = 0$ are typically interpreted as tests of model specification. The alternative $\mathbb{H}_1 : \mathbb{E}[Ze] \neq 0$ means that at least one element of Z is correlated with the error e and is thus an invalid instrumental variable. In some cases, it may be reasonable to test only a subset of the moment conditions.

As in Section 12.31, we restrict attention to the homoskedastic case $\mathbb{E}\left[e^2 \mid Z\right] = \sigma^2$.

Partition $Z = (Z_a, Z_b)$ with dimensions ℓ_a and ℓ_b, respectively, where Z_a contains the instruments that are believed to be uncorrelated with e, and Z_b contains the instruments that may be correlated with e. It is necessary to select this partition so that $\ell_a > k$, or equivalently, $\ell_b < \ell - k$. Thus the model with just the instruments Z_a is overidentified, or ℓ_b is smaller than the number of overidentifying restrictions. (If $\ell_a = k$, then the tests described here exist but reduce to the Sargan test, so are not interesting.) Hence the tests require that $\ell - k > 1$, that the number of overidentifying restrictions exceeds 1.

Given this partition the maintained hypothesis is $\mathbb{E}[Z_a e] = 0$. The null and alternative hypotheses are $\mathbb{H}_0 : \mathbb{E}[Z_b e] = 0$ against $\mathbb{H}_1 : \mathbb{E}[Z_b e] \neq 0$. That is, the null hypothesis is that the full set of moment conditions are valid, while the alternative hypothesis is that the instrument subset Z_b is correlated with e and thus is an invalid instrument. Rejection of $\mathbb{H}_0$ in favor of $\mathbb{H}_1$ is then interpreted as evidence that Z_b is misspecified as an instrument.

Based on the same reasoning as described in Section 12.3, to test $\mathbb{H}_0$ against $\mathbb{H}_1$ we consider a partitioned version of the regression (12.66),

$$e = Z_a'\alpha_a + Z_b'\alpha_b + \nu$$

but now focus on the coefficient α_b. Given $\mathbb{E}[Z_a e] = 0$, $\mathbb{H}_0$ is equivalent to $\alpha_b = 0$. The equation is estimated by least squares replacing the unobserved e_i with the 2SLS residual $\widehat{e}_i$. The estimate of α_b is

$$\widehat{\alpha}_b = \left(\boldsymbol{Z}_b'\boldsymbol{M}_a\boldsymbol{Z}_b\right)^{-1}\boldsymbol{Z}_b'\boldsymbol{M}_a\widehat{\boldsymbol{e}}$$

where $\boldsymbol{M}_a = \boldsymbol{I}_n - \boldsymbol{Z}_a\left(\boldsymbol{Z}_a'\boldsymbol{Z}_a\right)^{-1}\boldsymbol{Z}_a'$. Newey (1985) showed that an optimal (asymptotically most powerful) test of $\mathbb{H}_0$ against $\mathbb{H}_1$ is to reject for large values of the score statistic

$$N = \widehat{\alpha}_b'\left(\widehat{\operatorname{var}}[\widehat{\alpha}_b]\right)^{-}\widehat{\alpha}_b = \frac{\widehat{\boldsymbol{e}}'\boldsymbol{R}\left(\boldsymbol{R}'\boldsymbol{R} - \boldsymbol{R}'\widehat{\boldsymbol{X}}\left(\widehat{\boldsymbol{X}}'\widehat{\boldsymbol{X}}\right)^{-1}\widehat{\boldsymbol{X}}'\boldsymbol{R}\right)^{-1}\boldsymbol{R}'\widehat{\boldsymbol{e}}}{\widehat{\sigma}^2}$$

where $\widehat{\boldsymbol{X}} = \boldsymbol{P}\boldsymbol{X}$, $\boldsymbol{P} = \boldsymbol{Z}\left(\boldsymbol{Z}'\boldsymbol{Z}\right)^{-1}\boldsymbol{Z}'$, $\boldsymbol{R} = \boldsymbol{M}_a\boldsymbol{Z}_b$, and $\widehat{\sigma}^2 = \frac{1}{n}\widehat{\boldsymbol{e}}'\widehat{\boldsymbol{e}}$.

Independently from Newey (1985), Eichenbaum, Hansen, and Singleton (1988) proposed a test based on the difference of Sargan statistics. Let S be the Sargan test statistic (12.67) based on the full instrument set and S_a be the Sargan statistic based on the instrument set Z_a. The Sargan difference statistic is $C = S - S_a$. Specifically, let $\widetilde{\beta}_{2\text{sls}}$ be the 2SLS estimator using the instruments Z_a only, set $\widetilde{e}_i = Y_i - X_i'\widetilde{\beta}_{2\text{sls}}$, and set $\widetilde{\sigma}^2 = \frac{1}{n}\widetilde{\boldsymbol{e}}'\widetilde{\boldsymbol{e}}$. Then

$$S_a = \frac{\widetilde{\boldsymbol{e}}'\boldsymbol{Z}_a\left(\boldsymbol{Z}_a'\boldsymbol{Z}_a\right)^{-1}\boldsymbol{Z}_a'\widetilde{\boldsymbol{e}}}{\widetilde{\sigma}^2}.$$

An advantage of the C statistic is that it is quite simple to calculate from the standard regression output.

At this point, it is useful to reflect on our stated requirement that $\ell_a > k$. Indeed, if $\ell_a < k$, then Z_a fails the order condition for identification and $\widetilde{\beta}_{2\text{sls}}$ cannot be calculated. Thus $\ell_a \geq k$ is necessary to compute S_a and hence S. Furthermore, if $\ell_a = k$, then model a is just identified so while $\widetilde{\beta}_{2\text{sls}}$ can be calculated, the statistic $S_a = 0$, so $C = S$. Thus when $\ell_a = k$, the subset test equals the full overidentification test, so there is no gain from considering subset tests.

The C statistic is asymptotically equivalent to replacing $\widetilde{\sigma}^2$ in S_a with $\widehat{\sigma}^2$, yielding the statistic

$$C^* = \frac{\widehat{\boldsymbol{e}}'\boldsymbol{Z}\left(\boldsymbol{Z}'\boldsymbol{Z}\right)^{-1}\boldsymbol{Z}'\widehat{\boldsymbol{e}}}{\widehat{\sigma}^2} - \frac{\widetilde{\boldsymbol{e}}'\boldsymbol{Z}_a\left(\boldsymbol{Z}_a'\boldsymbol{Z}_a\right)^{-1}\boldsymbol{Z}_a'\widetilde{\boldsymbol{e}}}{\widehat{\sigma}^2}.$$

It turns out that this is Newey's statistic N. These tests have chi-square asymptotic distributions.

Let c satisfy $\alpha = 1 - G_{\ell_b}(c)$.

Theorem 12.17 Algebraically, $N = C^*$. Under Assumption 12.2 and $\mathbb{E}\left[e^2 \mid Z\right] = \sigma^2$, as $n \to \infty$, $N \underset{d}{\longrightarrow} \chi^2_{\ell_b}$ and $C \underset{d}{\longrightarrow} \chi^2_{\ell_b}$. Thus the tests "Reject $\mathbb{H}_0$ if $N > c$" and "Reject $\mathbb{H}_0$ if $C > c$" are asymptotically equivalent and have asymptotic size α.

Theorem 12.17 shows that N and C^* are identical and are near equivalents to the convenient statistic C. The appropriate asymptotic distribution is $\chi^2_{\ell_b}$. Computationally, the easiest method to implement a subset overidentification test is to estimate the model twice by 2SLS, first using the full instrument set Z and the second time using the partial instrument set Z_a. Compute the Sargan statistics for both 2SLS regressions, and compute C as the difference in the Sargan statistics. In Stata, for example, this is simple to implement with a few lines of code.

We illustrate using the Card college proximity example from Section 12.6. Our reported 2SLS estimates have $\ell - k = 1$, so there is no role for a subset overidentification test. (Recall that the number of overidentifying restrictions must exceed one.) To illustrate, we add extra instruments to the estimates in column 5 of Table 12.1 (the 2SLS estimates using *public*, *private*, *age*, and *age*^{2} as instruments for *education*, *experience*, and *experience*$^2/100$). We add two instruments: the years of education of the *father* and the *mother* of the worker. These variables had been used in the earlier labor economics literature as instruments, but Card did not use them. (He used them as regression controls in some specifications.) The motivation for using parent's education as instruments is the hypothesis that parental education influences children's educational attainment but does not directly influence their ability. The more modern labor economics literature has disputed this idea, arguing that children are educated in part at home and thus parent's education has a direct impact on the skill attainment of children (and not just an indirect impact via educational attainment). The older view was that parent's education is a valid instrument, the modern view is that it is not valid. We can test this dispute using a overidentification subset test.

We do this by estimating the wage equation by 2SLS using *public*, *private*, *age*, *age*^{2}, *father*, and *mother*, as instruments for *education*, *experience*, and *experience*$^2/100$. We do not report the parameter estimates here but observe that this model is overidentified with three overidentifying restrictions. We calculate the Sargan overidentification statistic. It is 7.9 with an asymptotic p-value (calculated using χ_3^2) of 0.048. This is a mild rejection of the null hypothesis of correct specification. As we argued in Section 12.31, this by itself is not reason to reject the model. Now we consider a subset overidentification test. We are interested in testing the validity of the two instruments *father* and *mother*, not the instruments *public*, *private*, *age*, *age*^{2}. To test the hypothesis that these two instruments are uncorrelated with the structural error, we compute the difference in Sargan statistic, $C = 7.9 - 0.5 = 7.4$, which has a p-value (calculated using χ_2^2) of 0.025. This value is marginally statistically significant, meaning that there is evidence that *father* and *mother* are not valid instruments for the wage equation. Since the p-value is not smaller than 1%, it is not overwhelming evidence, but it still supports Card's decision to not use parental education as instruments for the wage equation.

We now prove the results in Theorem 12.17.

We first show that $N = C^*$. Define $\boldsymbol{P}_a = \boldsymbol{Z}_a \left(\boldsymbol{Z}_a'\boldsymbol{Z}_a\right)^{-1} \boldsymbol{Z}_a'$ and $\boldsymbol{P}_{\boldsymbol{R}} = \boldsymbol{R}\left(\boldsymbol{R}'\boldsymbol{R}\right)^{-1}\boldsymbol{R}'$. Since $[\boldsymbol{Z}_a, \boldsymbol{R}]$ span $\boldsymbol{Z}$, we find $\boldsymbol{P} = \boldsymbol{P}_{\boldsymbol{R}} + \boldsymbol{P}_a$ and $\boldsymbol{P}_{\boldsymbol{R}}\boldsymbol{P}_a = 0$. It will be useful to note that

$$\boldsymbol{P}_{\boldsymbol{R}}\widehat{\boldsymbol{X}} = \boldsymbol{P}_{\boldsymbol{R}}\boldsymbol{P}\boldsymbol{X} = \boldsymbol{P}_{\boldsymbol{R}}\boldsymbol{X}$$

$$\widehat{\boldsymbol{X}}'\widehat{\boldsymbol{X}} - \widehat{\boldsymbol{X}}'\boldsymbol{P}_{\boldsymbol{R}}\widehat{\boldsymbol{X}} = \boldsymbol{X}'\left(\boldsymbol{P} - \boldsymbol{P}_{\boldsymbol{R}}\right)\boldsymbol{X} = \boldsymbol{X}'\boldsymbol{P}_a\boldsymbol{X}.$$

The fact that $\boldsymbol{X}'\boldsymbol{P}\widehat{\boldsymbol{e}} = \widehat{\boldsymbol{X}}'\widehat{\boldsymbol{e}} = 0$ implies $\boldsymbol{X}'\boldsymbol{P}_{\boldsymbol{R}}\widehat{\boldsymbol{e}} = -\boldsymbol{X}'\boldsymbol{P}_a\widehat{\boldsymbol{e}}$. Finally, since $\boldsymbol{Y} = \boldsymbol{X}\widehat{\beta} + \widehat{\boldsymbol{e}}$,

$$\widetilde{\boldsymbol{e}} = \left(\boldsymbol{I}_n - \boldsymbol{X}\left(\boldsymbol{X}'\boldsymbol{P}_a\boldsymbol{X}\right)^{-1}\boldsymbol{X}'\boldsymbol{P}_a\right)\widehat{\boldsymbol{e}}$$

so

$$\widetilde{\boldsymbol{e}}'\boldsymbol{P}_a\widetilde{\boldsymbol{e}} = \widehat{\boldsymbol{e}}'\left(\boldsymbol{P}_a - \boldsymbol{P}_a\boldsymbol{X}\left(\boldsymbol{X}'\boldsymbol{P}_a\boldsymbol{X}\right)^{-1}\boldsymbol{X}'\boldsymbol{P}_a\right)\widehat{\boldsymbol{e}}.$$

Applying the Woodbury matrix equality to the definition of N and the above algebraic relationships,

$$\begin{aligned}
N &= \frac{\widehat{\boldsymbol{e}}'\boldsymbol{P}_{\boldsymbol{R}}\widehat{\boldsymbol{e}} + \widehat{\boldsymbol{e}}'\boldsymbol{P}_{\boldsymbol{R}}\widehat{\boldsymbol{X}}\left(\widehat{\boldsymbol{X}}'\widehat{\boldsymbol{X}} - \widehat{\boldsymbol{X}}'\boldsymbol{P}_{\boldsymbol{R}}\widehat{\boldsymbol{X}}\right)^{-1}\widehat{\boldsymbol{X}}'\boldsymbol{P}_{\boldsymbol{R}}\widehat{\boldsymbol{e}}}{\widehat{\sigma}^2} \\
&= \frac{\widehat{\boldsymbol{e}}'\boldsymbol{P}\widehat{\boldsymbol{e}} - \widehat{\boldsymbol{e}}'\boldsymbol{P}_a\widehat{\boldsymbol{e}} + \widehat{\boldsymbol{e}}'\boldsymbol{P}_a\boldsymbol{X}\left(\boldsymbol{X}'\boldsymbol{P}_a\boldsymbol{X}\right)^{-1}\boldsymbol{X}'\boldsymbol{P}_a\widehat{\boldsymbol{e}}}{\widehat{\sigma}^2} \\
&= \frac{\widehat{\boldsymbol{e}}'\boldsymbol{P}\widehat{\boldsymbol{e}} - \widetilde{\boldsymbol{e}}'\boldsymbol{P}_a\widetilde{\boldsymbol{e}}}{\widehat{\sigma}^2} \\
&= C^*
\end{aligned}$$

as claimed.

We next establish the asymptotic distribution. Since $\boldsymbol{Z}_a$ is a subset of $\boldsymbol{Z}$, $\boldsymbol{P}\boldsymbol{M}_a = \boldsymbol{M}_a\boldsymbol{P}$, thus $\boldsymbol{P}\boldsymbol{R} = \boldsymbol{R}$ and $\boldsymbol{R}'\boldsymbol{X} = \boldsymbol{R}'\widehat{\boldsymbol{X}}$. Consequently,

$$\begin{aligned}
\frac{1}{\sqrt{n}}\boldsymbol{R}'\widehat{\boldsymbol{e}} &= \frac{1}{\sqrt{n}}\boldsymbol{R}'\left(\boldsymbol{Y} - \boldsymbol{X}\widehat{\boldsymbol{\beta}}\right) \\
&= \frac{1}{\sqrt{n}}\boldsymbol{R}'\left(\boldsymbol{I}_n - \boldsymbol{X}\left(\widehat{\boldsymbol{X}}'\widehat{\boldsymbol{X}}\right)^{-1}\widehat{\boldsymbol{X}}'\right)\boldsymbol{e}
\end{aligned}$$

$$= \frac{1}{\sqrt{n}} \boldsymbol{R}' \left(\boldsymbol{I}_n - \widehat{\boldsymbol{X}} \left(\widehat{\boldsymbol{X}}' \widehat{\boldsymbol{X}} \right)^{-1} \widehat{\boldsymbol{X}}' \right) \boldsymbol{e}$$

$$\underset{d}{\longrightarrow} \mathrm{N}\left(0, \boldsymbol{V}_2\right)$$

where

$$\boldsymbol{V}_2 = \operatorname*{plim}_{n\to\infty} \left(\frac{1}{n} \boldsymbol{R}'\boldsymbol{R} - \frac{1}{n} \boldsymbol{R}' \widehat{\boldsymbol{X}} \left(\frac{1}{n} \widehat{\boldsymbol{X}}' \widehat{\boldsymbol{X}} \right)^{-1} \frac{1}{n} \widehat{\boldsymbol{X}}' \boldsymbol{R} \right).$$

It follows that $N = C^* \underset{d}{\longrightarrow} \chi^2_{\ell_b}$, as claimed. Since $C = C^* + o_p(1)$, it has the same limiting distribution.

12.33 BOOTSTRAP OVERIDENTIFICATION TESTS

In small to moderate sample sizes, the overidentification tests are not well approximated by the asymptotic chi-square distributions. For improved accuracy it is advised to use bootstrap critical values. The bootstrap for 2SLS (Section 12.23) can be used for this purpose, but the bootstrap version of the overidentification statistic must be adjusted. This is because in the bootstrap universe, the overidentified moment conditions are not satisfied. One solution is to center the moment conditions.

For the 2SLS estimator, the standard overidentification test is based on the Sargan statistic:

$$S = n \frac{\widehat{\boldsymbol{e}}' \boldsymbol{Z} \left(\boldsymbol{Z}'\boldsymbol{Z}\right)^{-1} \boldsymbol{Z}' \widehat{\boldsymbol{e}}}{\widehat{\boldsymbol{e}}' \widehat{\boldsymbol{e}}}$$

$$\widehat{\boldsymbol{e}} = \boldsymbol{Y} - \boldsymbol{X} \widehat{\beta}_{2\text{sls}}.$$

The recentered bootstrap analog is

$$S^{**} = n \frac{\left(\widehat{\boldsymbol{e}}^{*\prime} \boldsymbol{Z}^* - \boldsymbol{Z}' \widehat{\boldsymbol{e}}\right) \left(\boldsymbol{Z}^{*\prime}\boldsymbol{Z}^*\right)^{-1} \left(\boldsymbol{Z}^{*\prime} \widehat{\boldsymbol{e}}^* - \boldsymbol{Z}' \widehat{\boldsymbol{e}}\right)}{\widehat{\boldsymbol{e}}^{*\prime} \widehat{\boldsymbol{e}}^*}$$

$$\widehat{\boldsymbol{e}}^* = \boldsymbol{Y}^* - \boldsymbol{X}^* \widehat{\beta}^*_{2\text{sls}}.$$

On each bootstrap sample, $S^{**}(b)$ is calculated and stored. The bootstrap p-value is

$$p^* = \frac{1}{B} \sum_{b=1}^{B} \mathbb{1}\left\{S^{**}(b) > S\right\}.$$

This bootstrap p-value is valid, because the statistic S^{**} satisfies the overidentified moment conditions.

12.34 LOCAL AVERAGE TREATMENT EFFECTS

In a pair of influential papers, Imbens, and Angrist (1994) and Angrist, Imbens, and Rubin (1996) proposed an new interpretation of the instrumental variables estimator using the potential outcomes model introduced in Section 2.30.

We will restrict attention to the case that the endogenous regressor X and excluded instrument Z are binary variables. We write the model as a pair of potential outcome functions. The dependent variable Y is a function of the regressor and an unobservable vector U, $Y = h(X, U)$, and the endogenous regressor X is a function of the instrument Z and U, $X = g(Z, U)$. By specifying U as a vector, there is no loss of generality in letting both equations depend on U.

In this framework, the outcomes are determined by the random vector U and the exogenous instrument Z. This determines X, which determines Y. In the context of the college proximity example, the variable U is everything specific about an individual. Given college proximity Z, the person decides to attend college or not. The person's wage is determined by individual attributes U as well as college attendence X but is not directly affected by college proximity Z.

We can omit the random variable U from the notation as follows. An individual has a realization U. We then set $Y(x) = h(x, U)$ and $X(z) = g(z, U)$. Also, given a realization Z, the observables are $X = X(Z)$ and $Y = Y(X)$.

In this model, the causal effect of college for an individual is $C = Y(1) - Y(0)$. As discussed in Section 2.30, this is individual-specific and random.

We would like to learn about the distribution of the causal effects, or at least features of the distribution. A common feature of interest is the average treatment effect (ATE):

$$\text{ATE} = \mathbb{E}[C] = \mathbb{E}[Y(1) - Y(0)].$$

This effect, however, is typically not feasible to estimate allowing for endogenous X without strong assumptions (such as that the causal effect C is constant across individuals). The treatment effect literature has explored what features of the distribution of C can be estimated.

One particular feature of interest emphasized by Imbens and Angrist (1994) is the local average treatment effect (LATE). Roughly, it is the average effect upon those affected by the instrumental variable. To understand LATE, consider the college proximity example. In the potential outcomes framework, each person is fully characterized by their individual unobservable U. Given U, their decision to attend college is a function of the proximity indicator Z. For some students, proximity has no effect on their decision. For other students, it has an effect in the specific sense that given $Z = 1$, they choose to attend college, while if $Z = 0$, they choose to not attend. We can summarize the possibilites with the following chart, which is based on labels developed by Angrist, Imbens, and Rubin (1996).

	$X(0) = 0$	$X(0) = 1$
$X(1) = 0$	Never Takers	Defiers
$X(1) = 1$	Compliers	Always Takers

The columns indicate the college attendence decision given $Z = 0$ (not close to a college). The rows indicate the college attendence decision given $Z = 1$ (close to a college). The four entries are labels for the four types of individuals based on these decisions. The upper-left entry defines the individuals who do not attend college regardless of Z. They are called "Never Takers." The lower-right entry defines the individuals who, conversely, attend college regardless of Z. They are called "Always Takers." The bottom left describes the individuals who only attend college if they live close to one. They are called "Compliers." The upper right entry is a bit of a challenge. These are individuals who attend college only if they do not live close to one. They are called "Defiers." Imbens and Angrist discovered that to identify the parameters of interest, we need to assume that there are no Defiers, or equivalently, that $X(1) \geq X(0)$. They call this "monotonicity"—increasing the instrument does not decrease X for any individual.

As another example, suppose we are interested in the effect of wearing a face mask X on health Y during a virus pandemic. Wearing a face mask is a choice made by the individual, so it should be viewed as endogenous. For an instrument Z, consider a government policy that requires face masks to be worn in public. The "Compliers" are those who wear a face mask if there is a policy but otherwise do not. The "Defiers" are those who do the converse. That is, these individuals would have worn a face mask based on the evidence of a pandemic but rebel against a government policy. Once again, identification requires that there are no Defiers.

We can distinguish the types in the table by the relative values of $X(1) - X(0)$. For Never-Takers and Always-Takers, $X(1) - X(0) = 0$, while for Compliers, $X(1) - X(0) = 1$.

We are interested in the causal effect $C = h(1, U) - h(0, U)$ of college on wages. The average causal effect (ACE) is its expectation $\mathbb{E}[Y(1) - Y(0)]$. To estimate the ACE, we need observations of both $Y(0)$ and $Y(1)$, which means we need to observe some individuals who attend college and some who do not attend college. Consider the group "Never-Takers." They never attend college, so we only observe $Y(0)$. It is thus impossible to estimate the ACE of college for this group. Similarly, consider the group "Always-Takers." They always attend college, so we only observe $Y(1)$ and again we cannot estimate the ACE of college for this group. The group for which we can estimate the ACE are the "Compliers." The ACE for this group is

$$\text{LATE} = \mathbb{E}[Y(1) - Y(0) \mid X(1) > X(0)].$$

Imbens and Angrist call this the **local average treatment effect (LATE)**, as it is the average treatment effect for the subpopulation whose endogenous regressor is affected by the instrument. Examining the definition, LATE is the average causal effect of college attendence on wages for the subsample of individuals who choose to attend college if (and only if) they live close to one.

Interestingly, we show below that

$$\text{LATE} = \frac{\mathbb{E}[Y \mid Z=1] - \mathbb{E}[Y \mid Z=0]}{\mathbb{E}[X \mid Z=1] - \mathbb{E}[X \mid Z=0]}. \tag{12.68}$$

That is, LATE equals the Wald expression (12.27) for the slope coefficient in the IV regression model. So the standard IV estimator is an estimator of LATE. Thus when treatment effects are potentially heterogeneous, we can interpret IV as an estimator of LATE. The equality (12.68) occurs under the following conditions.

Assumption 12.3 U and Z are independent, and $\mathbb{P}[X(1) - X(0) < 0] = 0$.

One interesting feature about LATE is that its value can depend on the instrument Z and the distribution of causal effects C in the population. To make this concrete, suppose that instead of the Card proximity instrument, we consider an instrument based on the financial cost of local college attendence. It is reasonable to expect that while the set of students affected by these two instruments are similar, the two sets of students will not be the same. That is, some students may be responsive to proximity but not finances, and conversely. If the causal effect C has a different average in these two groups of students, then LATE will be different when calculated with these two instruments. Thus LATE can vary by the choice of instrument.

How can that be? How can a well-defined parameter depend on the choice of instrument? Doesn't this contradict the basic IV regression model? The answer is that the basic IV regression model is restrictive—it specifies that the causal effect β is common across all individuals. Its value is the same regardless of the choice of specific instrument (so long as it satisfies the instrumental variables assumptions). In contrast, the potential outcomes framework is more general, allowing for the causal effect to vary across individuals. What this analysis shows us is that in this context, it is quite possible for the LATE coefficient to vary by instrument. This occurs when causal effects are heterogeneous.

One implication of the LATE framework is that IV estimates should be interpreted as causal effects only for the population of compliers. Interpretation should focus on the population of potential compliers, and extension to other populations should be done with caution. For example, in the Card proximity model, the

IV estimates of the causal return to schooling presented in Table 12.1 should be interpreted as applying to the population of students who are incentivized to attend college by the presence of a college in their home county. The estimates should not be applied to other students.

Formally, the analysis of this section examines the case of a binary instrument and endogenous regressor. How does this generalize? Suppose that the regressor X is discrete, taking $J+1$ discrete values. We can then rewrite the model as one with J binary endogenous regressors. If we then have J binary instruments, we are back in the Imbens-Angrist framework (assuming the instruments have a monotonic impact on the endogenous regressors). A benefit is that with a larger set of instruments, it is plausible that the set of compliers in the population is expanded.

Let us close this section by showing (12.68) under Assumption 12.3. The realized value of X can be written as

$$X = (1-Z)\,X(0) + ZX(1) = X(0) + Z\,(X(1) - X(0)).$$

Similarly,

$$Y = Y(0) + X\,(Y(1) - Y(0)) = Y(0) + XC.$$

Combining,

$$Y = Y(0) + X(0)C + Z\,(X(1) - Y(0))\,C.$$

The independence of u and Z implies independence of $(Y(0), Y(1), X(0), X(1), C)$ and Z. Thus

$$\mathbb{E}\,[Y \mid Z=1] = \mathbb{E}\,[Y(0)] + \mathbb{E}\,[X(0)C] + \mathbb{E}\,[(X(1) - X(0))\,C]$$

and

$$\mathbb{E}\,[Y \mid Z=0] = \mathbb{E}\,[Y(0)] + \mathbb{E}\,[X(0)C].$$

Subtracting, we obtain

$$\begin{aligned}
\mathbb{E}\,[Y \mid Z=1] - \mathbb{E}\,[Y \mid Z=0] &= \mathbb{E}\,[(X(1) - X(0))\,C] \\
&= 1 \times \mathbb{E}\,[C \mid X(1) - X(0) = 1]\,\mathbb{P}\,[X(1) - X(0) = 1] \\
&\quad + 0 \times \mathbb{E}\,[C \mid X(1) - X(0) = 0]\,\mathbb{P}\,[X(1) - X(0) = 0] \\
&\quad + (-1) \times \mathbb{E}\,[C \mid X(1) - X(0) = -1]\,\mathbb{P}\,[X(1) - X(0) = -1] \\
&= \mathbb{E}\,[C \mid X(1) - X(0) = 1]\,(\mathbb{E}\,[X \mid X=1] - \mathbb{E}\,[X \mid Z=0])
\end{aligned}$$

where the final equality uses $\mathbb{P}\,[X(1) - X(0) < 0] = 0$ and

$$\mathbb{P}\,[X(1) - X(0) = 1] = \mathbb{E}\,[X(1) - X(0)] = \mathbb{E}\,[X \mid Z=1] - \mathbb{E}\,[X \mid Z=0].$$

Rearranging, we have

$$\text{LATE} = \mathbb{E}\,[C \mid X(1) - X(0) = 1] = \frac{\mathbb{E}\,[Y \mid Z=1] - \mathbb{E}\,[Y \mid Z=0]}{\mathbb{E}\,[X \mid Z=1] - \mathbb{E}\,[X \mid Z=0]}$$

as claimed.

12.35 IDENTIFICATION FAILURE

Recall the reduced form equation

$$X_2 = \Gamma_{12}' Z_1 + \Gamma_{22}' Z_2 + u_2.$$

The parameter β fails to be identified if Γ_{22} has deficient rank. The consequences of identification failure for inference are quite severe.

Take the simplest case, where $k_1 = 0$ and $k_2 = \ell_2 = 1$. Then the model may be written as

$$Y = X\beta + e \tag{12.69}$$

$$X = Z\gamma + u$$

and $\Gamma_{22} = \gamma = \mathbb{E}[ZX] / \mathbb{E}[Z^2]$. We see that β is identified if and only if $\gamma \neq 0$, which occurs when $\mathbb{E}[XZ] \neq 0$. Thus identification hinges on the existence of correlation between the excluded exogenous variable and the included endogenous variable.

Suppose this condition fails. In this case, $\gamma = 0$, and $\mathbb{E}[XZ] = 0$. We now analyze the distribution of the least squares and IV estimators of β. For simplicity, we assume conditional homoskedasticity and normalize the variances of e, u, and Z to unity. Thus,

$$\operatorname{var}\left[\left(\begin{array}{c} e \\ u \end{array}\right) \middle| Z\right] = \left(\begin{array}{cc} 1 & \rho \\ \rho & 1 \end{array}\right). \tag{12.70}$$

The errors have nonzero correlation $\rho \neq 0$ when the variables are endogenous.

By the CLT, we have the joint convergence

$$\frac{1}{\sqrt{n}} \sum_{i=1}^{n} \left(\begin{array}{c} Z_i e_i \\ Z_i u_i \end{array}\right) \underset{d}{\longrightarrow} \left(\begin{array}{c} \xi_1 \\ \xi_2 \end{array}\right) \sim \mathrm{N}\left(0, \left(\begin{array}{cc} 1 & \rho \\ \rho & 1 \end{array}\right)\right).$$

It is convenient to define $\xi_0 = \xi_1 - \rho\xi_2$, which is normal and independent of ξ_2.

As a benchmark it is useful to observe that the least squares estimator of β satisfies

$$\widehat{\beta}_{\mathrm{ols}} - \beta = \frac{n^{-1}\sum_{i=1}^{n} u_i e_i}{n^{-1}\sum_{i=1}^{n} u_i^2} \underset{p}{\longrightarrow} \rho \neq 0$$

so endogeneity causes $\widehat{\beta}_{\mathrm{ols}}$ to be inconsistent for β.

Under identification failure $\gamma = 0$, the asymptotic distribution of the IV estimator is

$$\widehat{\beta}_{\mathrm{iv}} - \beta = \frac{\frac{1}{\sqrt{n}}\sum_{i=1}^{n} Z_i e_i}{\frac{1}{\sqrt{n}}\sum_{i=1}^{n} Z_i X_i} \underset{d}{\longrightarrow} \frac{\xi_1}{\xi_2} = \rho + \frac{\xi_0}{\xi_2}.$$

This asymptotic convergence result uses the CMT, which applies since the function ξ_1/ξ_2 is continuous everywhere except at $\xi_2 = 0$, which occurs with probability equal to 0.

This limiting distribution has several notable features.

First, $\widehat{\beta}_{\mathrm{iv}}$ does not converge in probability to a limit, instead it converges in distribution to a random variable. Thus the IV estimator is inconsistent. Indeed, it is not possible to consistently estimate an unidentified parameter, and β is not identified when $\gamma = 0$.

Second, the ratio ξ_0/ξ_2 is symmetrically distributed about 0, so the median of the limiting distribution of $\widehat{\beta}_{\mathrm{iv}}$ is $\beta + \rho$. So the IV estimator is median biased under endogeneity. Thus under identification failure, the IV estimator does not correct the centering (median bias) of least squares.

Third, the ratio ξ_0/ξ_2 of two independent normal random variables is Cauchy distributed. This property is particularly nasty, as the Cauchy distribution does not have a finite mean. The distribution has thick tails, meaning that extreme values occur with higher frequency than for the normal. Inferences based on the normal distribution can be quite incorrect.

Together, these results show that $\gamma = 0$ renders the IV estimator particularly poorly behaved—it is inconsistent, median biased, and non-normally distributed.

We can also examine the behavior of the t-statistic. For simplicity, consider the classical (homoskedastic) t-statistic. The error variance estimate has the asymptotic distribution

$$\begin{aligned}\widehat{\sigma}^2 &= \frac{1}{n}\sum_{i=1}^{n}\left(Y_i - X_i\widehat{\beta}_{\mathrm{iv}}\right)^2 \\ &= \frac{1}{n}\sum_{i=1}^{n} e_i^2 - \frac{2}{n}\sum_{i=1}^{n} e_i X_i\left(\widehat{\beta}_{\mathrm{iv}} - \beta\right) + \frac{1}{n}\sum_{i=1}^{n} X_i^2\left(\widehat{\beta}_{\mathrm{iv}} - \beta\right)^2 \\ &\underset{d}{\longrightarrow} 1 - 2\rho\frac{\xi_1}{\xi_2} + \left(\frac{\xi_1}{\xi_2}\right)^2.\end{aligned}$$

Thus the t-statistic has the asymptotic distribution

$$T = \frac{\widehat{\beta}_{\mathrm{iv}} - \beta}{\sqrt{\widehat{\sigma}^2 \sum_{i=1}^{n} Z_i^2 / \left|\sum_{i=1}^{n} Z_i X_i\right|}} \underset{d}{\longrightarrow} \frac{\xi_1/\xi_2}{\sqrt{1 - 2\rho\frac{\xi_1}{\xi_2} + \left(\frac{\xi_1}{\xi_2}\right)^2}}.$$

The limiting distribution is non-normal, meaning that inference using the normal distribution will be (considerably) incorrect. This distribution depends on the correlation ρ. The distortion is increasing in ρ. Indeed as $\rho \to 1$, we have $\xi_1/\xi_2 \to_p 1$ and the unexpected finding $\widehat{\sigma}^2 \to_p 0$. The latter means that the conventional standard error $s(\widehat{\beta}_{\mathrm{iv}})$ for $\widehat{\beta}_{\mathrm{iv}}$ also converges in probability to 0. Thus the t-statistic diverges in the sense $|T| \to_p \infty$. In this situation, users may incorrectly interpret estimates as precise despite the fact that they are highly imprecise.

12.36 WEAK INSTRUMENTS

In Section 12.35, we examined the extreme consequences of full identification failure. Similar problems occur when identification is weak in the sense that the reduced form coefficients are of small magnitude. In this section, we derive the asymptotic distribution of the OLS, 2SLS, and LIML estimators when the reduced form coefficients are treated as weak. We show that the estimators are inconsistent and the 2SLS and LIML estimators remain random in large samples.

To simplify the exposition, we assume that there are no included exogenous variables (no X_1), so we write X_2, Z_2, and β_2 simply as X, Z, and β. The model is

$$\begin{aligned}Y &= X'\beta + e \\ X &= \Gamma' Z + u_2.\end{aligned}$$

Recall the reduced form error vector $u = (u_1, u_2)$ and its covariance matrix:

$$\mathbb{E}\left[uu'\right] = \Sigma = \begin{bmatrix} \Sigma_{11} & \Sigma_{12} \\ \Sigma_{21} & \Sigma_{22} \end{bmatrix}.$$

Recall that the structural error is $e = u_1 - \beta' u_2 = \gamma' u$, where $\gamma = (1, -\beta)$, which has variance $\mathbb{E}\left[e^2 \mid Z\right] = \gamma' \Sigma \gamma$. Also define the covariance $\Sigma_{2e} = \mathbb{E}\left[u_2 e \mid Z\right] = \Sigma_{21} - \Sigma_{22}\beta$.

In Section 12.35, we assumed complete identification failure in the sense that $\Gamma = 0$. We now want to assume that identification does not completely fail but is weak in the sense that Γ is small. A rich asymptotic distribution theory has been developed to understand this setting by modeling Γ as "local-to-zero." The seminal contribution is Staiger and Stock (1997). The theory was extended to nonlinear GMM estimation by Stock and Wright (2000).

The technical device introduced by Staiger and Stock (1997) is to assume that the reduced form parameter is **local-to-zero**, specifically,

$$\Gamma = n^{-1/2} \boldsymbol{C} \tag{12.71}$$

where $\boldsymbol{C}$ is a free matrix. The $n^{-1/2}$ scaling is picked because it provides just the right balance to allow a useful distribution theory. The local-to-zero assumption (12.71) is not meant to be taken literally but instead is meant to be a useful distributional approximation. The parameter $\boldsymbol{C}$ indexes the degree of identification. Larger $\|\boldsymbol{C}\|$ implies stronger identification; smaller $\|\boldsymbol{C}\|$ implies weaker identification.

We now derive the asymptotic distribution of the least squares, 2SLS, and LIML estimators under the local-to-zero assumption (12.71).

The least squares estimator satisfies

$$\begin{aligned}
\widehat{\beta}_{\text{ols}} - \beta &= \left(n^{-1}\boldsymbol{X}'\boldsymbol{X}\right)^{-1}\left(n^{-1}\boldsymbol{X}'\boldsymbol{e}\right) \\
&= \left(n^{-1}\boldsymbol{U}_2'\boldsymbol{U}_2\right)^{-1}\left(n^{-1}\boldsymbol{U}_2'\boldsymbol{e}\right) + o_p(1) \\
&\underset{p}{\longrightarrow} \Sigma_{22}^{-1}\Sigma_{2e}.
\end{aligned}$$

Thus the least squares estimator is inconsistent for β.

To examine the 2SLS estimator, by the CLT,

$$\frac{1}{\sqrt{n}}\sum_{i=1}^{n} Z_i u_i' \underset{d}{\longrightarrow} \xi = [\xi_1, \xi_2]$$

where

$$\operatorname{vec}(\xi) \sim \mathrm{N}\left(0, \mathbb{E}\left[uu' \otimes ZZ'\right]\right).$$

This implies

$$\frac{1}{\sqrt{n}}\boldsymbol{Z}'\boldsymbol{e} \underset{d}{\longrightarrow} \xi_e = \xi\gamma.$$

We also find that

$$\frac{1}{\sqrt{n}}\boldsymbol{Z}'\boldsymbol{X} = \frac{1}{n}\boldsymbol{Z}'\boldsymbol{Z}\boldsymbol{C} + \frac{1}{\sqrt{n}}\boldsymbol{Z}'\boldsymbol{U}_2 \underset{d}{\longrightarrow} \boldsymbol{Q}_{ZZ}\boldsymbol{C} + \xi_2.$$

Thus,

$$\boldsymbol{X}'\boldsymbol{P}_Z\boldsymbol{X} = \left(\frac{1}{\sqrt{n}}\boldsymbol{X}'\boldsymbol{Z}\right)\left(\frac{1}{n}\boldsymbol{Z}'\boldsymbol{Z}\right)^{-1}\left(\frac{1}{\sqrt{n}}\boldsymbol{Z}'\boldsymbol{X}\right) \underset{d}{\longrightarrow} \left(\boldsymbol{Q}_{ZZ}\boldsymbol{C} + \xi_2\right)' \boldsymbol{Q}_{ZZ}^{-1}\left(\boldsymbol{Q}_{ZZ}\boldsymbol{C} + \xi_2\right)$$

and

$$X'P_Z e = \left(\frac{1}{\sqrt{n}}X'Z\right)\left(\frac{1}{n}Z'Z\right)^{-1}\left(\frac{1}{\sqrt{n}}Z'e\right) \underset{d}{\longrightarrow} \left(Q_{ZZ}C + \xi_2\right)' Q_{ZZ}^{-1}\xi_e.$$

We find that the 2SLS estimator has the asymptotic distribution

$$\begin{aligned}\widehat{\beta}_{2\text{sls}} - \beta &= \left(X'P_Z X\right)^{-1}\left(X'P_Z e\right)\\ &\underset{d}{\longrightarrow} \left(\left(Q_{ZZ}C+\xi_2\right)' Q_{ZZ}^{-1}\left(Q_{ZZ}C+\xi_2\right)\right)^{-1}\left(Q_{ZZ}C+\xi_2\right)' Q_{ZZ}^{-1}\xi_e. \qquad (12.72)\end{aligned}$$

As in the case of complete identification failure, we find that $\widehat{\beta}_{2\text{sls}}$ is inconsistent for β, it is asymptotically random, and its asymptotic distribution is non-normal. The distortion is affected by the coefficient C. As $\|C\| \to \infty$, the distribution in (12.72) converges in probability to 0, suggesting that $\widehat{\beta}_{2\text{sls}}$ is consistent for β. This corresponds to the classic "strong identification" context.

Now consider the LIML estimator. The reduced form is $\vec{Y} = Z\Pi + U$, which implies $M_Z\vec{Y} = M_Z U$ and by standard asymptotic theory

$$\frac{1}{n}\vec{Y}' M_Z \vec{Y} = \frac{1}{n}U' M_Z U \underset{p}{\longrightarrow} \Sigma = \mathbb{E}\left[uu'\right].$$

Define $\overline{\beta} = [\beta, I_k]$ so that the reduced form coefficients equal $\Pi = [\Gamma\beta, \Gamma] = n^{-1/2}C\overline{\beta}$. Then

$$\frac{1}{\sqrt{n}}Z'\vec{Y} = \frac{1}{n}Z'ZC\overline{\beta} + \frac{1}{\sqrt{n}}Z'U \underset{d}{\longrightarrow} Q_{ZZ}C\overline{\beta} + \xi$$

and

$$\vec{Y}'Z\left(Z'Z\right)^{-1}Z'\vec{Y} \underset{d}{\longrightarrow} \left(Q_{ZZ}C\overline{\beta}+\xi\right)' Q_{ZZ}^{-1}\left(Q_{ZZ}C\overline{\beta}+\xi\right).$$

This allows us to calculate that, by the CMT,

$$\begin{aligned} n\widehat{\mu} &= \min_{\gamma} \frac{\gamma'\vec{Y}'Z\left(Z'Z\right)^{-1}Z'\vec{Y}\gamma}{\gamma'\frac{1}{n}\vec{Y}'M_Z\vec{Y}\gamma}\\ &\underset{d}{\longrightarrow} \min_{\gamma} \frac{\gamma'\left(Q_{ZZ}C\overline{\beta}+\xi\right)' Q_{ZZ}^{-1}\left(Q_{ZZ}C\overline{\beta}+\xi\right)\gamma}{\gamma'\Sigma\gamma}\\ &= \mu^* \end{aligned}$$

say, which is a function of ξ and thus random. We deduce that the asymptotic distribution of the LIML estimator is

$$\begin{aligned}\widehat{\beta}_{\text{liml}} - \beta &= \left(X'P_Z X - n\widehat{\mu}\frac{1}{n}X'M_Z X\right)^{-1}\left(X'P_Z e - n\widehat{\mu}\frac{1}{n}X'M_Z e\right)\\ &\underset{d}{\longrightarrow} \left(\left(Q_{ZZ}C+\xi_2\right)' Q_{ZZ}^{-1}\left(Q_{ZZ}C+\xi_2\right) - \mu^*\Sigma_{22}\right)^{-1}\left(\left(Q_{ZZ}C+\xi_2\right)' Q_{ZZ}^{-1}\xi_e - \mu^*\Sigma_{2e}\right).\end{aligned}$$

Similarly to 2SLS, the LIML estimator is inconsistent for β, is asymptotically random, and non-normally distributed.

We summarize.

Theorem 12.18 Under (12.71),

$$\widehat{\beta}_{\text{ols}} - \beta \underset{p}{\longrightarrow} \Sigma_{22}^{-1}\Sigma_{2e}$$

$$\widehat{\beta}_{\text{2sls}} - \beta \underset{d}{\longrightarrow} \left(\left(\boldsymbol{Q}_{ZZ}\boldsymbol{C} + \xi_2 \right)' \boldsymbol{Q}_{ZZ}^{-1} \left(\boldsymbol{Q}_{ZZ}\boldsymbol{C} + \xi_2 \right) \right)^{-1} \left(\boldsymbol{Q}_{ZZ}\boldsymbol{C} + \xi_2 \right)' \boldsymbol{Q}_{ZZ}^{-1}\xi_e$$

and

$$\widehat{\beta}_{\text{liml}} - \beta \underset{d}{\longrightarrow} \left(\left(\boldsymbol{Q}_{ZZ}\boldsymbol{C} + \xi_2 \right)' \boldsymbol{Q}_{ZZ}^{-1} \left(\boldsymbol{Q}_{ZZ}\boldsymbol{C} + \xi_2 \right) - \mu^* \Sigma_{22} \right)^{-1}$$
$$\times \left(\left(\boldsymbol{Q}_{ZZ}\boldsymbol{C} + \xi_2 \right)' \boldsymbol{Q}_{ZZ}^{-1}\xi_e - \mu^* \boldsymbol{\Sigma}_{2e} \right)$$

where

$$\mu^* = \min_{\gamma} \frac{\gamma' \left(\boldsymbol{Q}_{ZZ}\boldsymbol{C}\overline{\beta} + \xi \right)' \boldsymbol{Q}_{ZZ}^{-1} \left(\boldsymbol{Q}_{ZZ}\boldsymbol{C}\overline{\beta} + \xi \right) \gamma}{\gamma' \Sigma \gamma}$$

and $\overline{\beta} = [\beta, \boldsymbol{I}_k]$.

All three estimators are inconsistent. The 2SLS and LIML estimators are asymptotically random with non-standard distributions, similar to the asymptotic distribution of the IV estimator under complete identification failure explored in Section 12.35. The difference under weak identification is the presence of the coefficient matrix $\boldsymbol{C}$.

12.37 MANY INSTRUMENTS

Some applications have available a large number ℓ of instruments. If they are all valid, using a large number should reduce the asymptotic variance relative to estimation with a smaller number of instruments. Is it then good practice to use many instruments? Or is there a cost to this practice? Bekker (1994) initiated a large literature investigating this question by formalizing the idea of "many instruments." Bekker proposed an asymptotic approximation that treats the number of instruments ℓ as proportional to the sample size, that is $\ell = \alpha n$, or equivalently, $\ell/n \to \alpha \in [0, 1)$. The distributional theory obtained is similar in many respects to the weak instrument theory outlined in Section 12.36. Consequently, the impact of "weak" and "many" instruments is similar.

Again for simplicity, we assume that there are no included exogenous regressors, so that the model is

$$Y = X'\beta + e \tag{12.73}$$
$$X = \Gamma' Z + u_2$$

with Z $\ell \times 1$. We also make the simplifying assumption that the reduced form errors are conditionally homoskedastic. Specifically,

$$\mathbb{E}\left[uu' \mid Z \right] = \Sigma = \begin{bmatrix} \Sigma_{11} & \Sigma_{12} \\ \Sigma_{21} & \Sigma_{22} \end{bmatrix}. \tag{12.74}$$

In addition, we assume that the conditional fourth moments are bounded:

$$\mathbb{E}\left[\|u\|^4 \mid Z\right] \le B < \infty. \tag{12.75}$$

The idea that there are "many instruments" is formalized by the assumption that the number of instruments is increasing proportionately with the sample size

$$\frac{\ell}{n} \longrightarrow \alpha. \tag{12.76}$$

The best way to think about this is to view α as the ratio of ℓ to n in a given sample. Thus if an application has $n = 100$ observations and $\ell = 10$ instruments, then we should treat $\alpha = 0.10$.

Suppose that there is a single endogenous regressor X. Calculate its variance using the reduced form: $\operatorname{var}[X] = \operatorname{var}\left[Z'\Gamma\right] + \operatorname{var}[u]$. Suppose as well that $\operatorname{var}[X]$ and $\operatorname{var}[u]$ are unchanging as ℓ increases, which implies that $\operatorname{var}\left[Z'\Gamma\right]$ is unchanging, even though the dimension ℓ is increasing. This is a useful assumption, as it implies that the population R^2 of the reduced form is not changing with ℓ. We don't need this exact condition; instead we simply assume that the sample version converges in probability to a fixed constant. Specifically, we assume that

$$\frac{1}{n}\sum_{i=1}^{n} \Gamma' Z_i Z_i' \Gamma \underset{p}{\longrightarrow} \boldsymbol{H} \tag{12.77}$$

for some matrix $\boldsymbol{H} > 0$. Again, this essentially implies that the R^2 of the reduced form regressions for each component of X converge to constants.

As a baseline, it is useful to examine the behavior of the least squares estimator of β. First, observe that the variance of $\operatorname{vec}\left(n^{-1}\sum_{i=1}^{n}\Gamma' Z_i u_i'\right)$, conditional on $\boldsymbol{Z}$, is

$$\Sigma \otimes n^{-2} \sum_{i=1}^{n} \Gamma' Z_i Z_i' \Gamma \underset{p}{\longrightarrow} 0$$

by (12.77). Thus it converges in probability to 0:

$$n^{-1}\sum_{i=1}^{n} \Gamma' Z_i u_i' \underset{p}{\longrightarrow} 0. \tag{12.78}$$

Combined with (12.77) and the WLLN, we find

$$\frac{1}{n}\sum_{i=1}^{n} X_i e_i = \frac{1}{n}\sum_{i=1}^{n} \Gamma' Z_i e_i + \frac{1}{n}\sum_{i=1}^{n} u_{2i} e_i \underset{p}{\longrightarrow} \Sigma_{2e}$$

and

$$\frac{1}{n}\sum_{i=1}^{n} X_i X_i' = \frac{1}{n}\sum_{i=1}^{n} \Gamma' Z_i Z_i' \Gamma + \frac{1}{n}\sum_{i=1}^{n} \Gamma' Z_i u_{2i}' + \frac{1}{n}\sum_{i=1}^{n} u_{2i} Z_i' \Gamma + \frac{1}{n}\sum_{i=1}^{n} u_{2i} u_{2i}' \underset{p}{\longrightarrow} \boldsymbol{H} + \Sigma_{22}.$$

Hence

$$\widehat{\beta}_{\text{ols}} = \beta + \left(\frac{1}{n}\sum_{i=1}^{n} X_i X_i'\right)^{-1} \left(\frac{1}{n}\sum_{i=1}^{n} X_i e_i\right) \underset{p}{\longrightarrow} \beta + \left(\boldsymbol{H} + \Sigma_{22}\right)^{-1} \Sigma_{2e}.$$

Thus least squares is inconsistent for β.

Now consider the 2SLS estimator. In matrix notation, setting $\boldsymbol{P}_Z = \boldsymbol{Z}\left(\boldsymbol{Z}'\boldsymbol{Z}\right)^{-1}\boldsymbol{Z}'$,

$$\begin{aligned}
\widehat{\beta}_{2\text{sls}} - \beta &= \left(\frac{1}{n}\boldsymbol{X}'\boldsymbol{P}_Z\boldsymbol{X}\right)^{-1}\left(\frac{1}{n}\boldsymbol{X}'\boldsymbol{P}_Z\boldsymbol{e}\right) \\
&= \left(\frac{1}{n}\overline{\Gamma}'\boldsymbol{Z}'\boldsymbol{Z}\overline{\Gamma} + \frac{1}{n}\overline{\Gamma}'\boldsymbol{Z}'\boldsymbol{u}_2 + \frac{1}{n}\boldsymbol{u}_2'\boldsymbol{Z}\overline{\Gamma} + \frac{1}{n}\boldsymbol{u}_2'\boldsymbol{P}_Z\boldsymbol{u}_2\right)^{-1}\left(\frac{1}{n}\Gamma'\boldsymbol{Z}'\boldsymbol{e} + \frac{1}{n}\boldsymbol{u}_2'\boldsymbol{P}_Z\boldsymbol{e}\right). \qquad (12.79)
\end{aligned}$$

In the expression on the right side of (12.79), several of the components have been examined in (12.77) and (12.78). We now examine the remaining components $\frac{1}{n}\boldsymbol{u}_2'\boldsymbol{P}_Z\boldsymbol{e}$ and $\frac{1}{n}\boldsymbol{u}_2'\boldsymbol{P}_Z\boldsymbol{u}_2$, which are subcomponents of the matrix $\frac{1}{n}\boldsymbol{u}'\boldsymbol{P}_Z\boldsymbol{u}$. Take the jkth element $\frac{1}{n}\boldsymbol{u}_j'\boldsymbol{P}_Z\boldsymbol{u}_k$.

First, take its expectation. We have (given the conditional homoskedasticity assumption (12.74))

$$\mathbb{E}\left[\frac{1}{n}\boldsymbol{u}_j'\boldsymbol{P}_Z\boldsymbol{u}_k\middle|\,\boldsymbol{Z}\right] = \frac{1}{n}\operatorname{tr}\left(\mathbb{E}\left[\boldsymbol{P}_Z\boldsymbol{u}_k\boldsymbol{u}_j'\middle|\,\boldsymbol{Z}\right]\right) = \frac{1}{n}\operatorname{tr}\left(\boldsymbol{P}_Z\right)\Sigma_{jk} = \frac{\ell}{n}\Sigma_{jk} \to \alpha\Sigma_{jk} \qquad (12.80)$$

using $\operatorname{tr}\left(\boldsymbol{P}_Z\right) = \ell$.

Second, we calculate its variance, which is a more cumbersome exercise. Let $P_{im} = Z_i'\left(\boldsymbol{Z}'\boldsymbol{Z}\right)^{-1}Z_m$ be the imth element of $\boldsymbol{P}_Z$. Then $\boldsymbol{u}_j'\boldsymbol{P}_Z\boldsymbol{u}_k = \sum_{i=1}^n\sum_{m=1}^n u_{ji}u_{km}P_{im}$. The matrix $\boldsymbol{P}_Z$ is idempotent. It therefore has the properties $\sum_{i=1}^n P_{ii} = \operatorname{tr}\left(\boldsymbol{P}_Z\right) = \ell$ and $0 \le P_{ii} \le 1$. The property $\boldsymbol{P}_Z\boldsymbol{P}_Z = \boldsymbol{P}_Z$ also implies $\sum_{m=1}^n P_{im}^2 = P_{ii}$. Then

$$\begin{aligned}
\operatorname{var}\left[\frac{1}{n}\boldsymbol{u}_j'\boldsymbol{P}_Z\boldsymbol{u}_k\middle|\,\boldsymbol{Z}\right] &= \frac{1}{n^2}\mathbb{E}\left[\sum_{i=1}^n\sum_{m=1}^n\left(u_{ji}u_{km} - \mathbb{E}\left[u_{ji}u_{km}\right]\mathbb{1}\left\{i=m\right\}\right)P_{im}\middle|\,\boldsymbol{Z}\right]^2 \\
&= \frac{1}{n^2}\mathbb{E}\left[\sum_{i=1}^n\sum_{m=1}^n\sum_{q=1}^n\sum_{r=1}^n\left(u_{ji}u_{km} - \Sigma_{jk}\mathbb{1}\left\{i=m\right\}\right)P_{im}\left(u_{jq}u_{kr} - \Sigma_{jk}\mathbb{1}\left\{q=r\right\}\right)P_{qr}\right] \\
&= \frac{1}{n^2}\sum_{i=1}^n\mathbb{E}\left[\left(u_{ji}u_{ki} - \Sigma_{jk}\right)^2\right]P_{ii}^2 \\
&\quad + \frac{1}{n^2}\sum_{i=1}^n\sum_{m\neq i}\mathbb{E}\left[u_{ji}^2u_{km}^2\right]P_{im}^2 + \frac{1}{n^2}\sum_{i=1}^n\sum_{m\neq i}\mathbb{E}\left[u_{ji}u_{km}u_{jm}u_{ki}\right]P_{im}^2 \\
&\le \frac{B}{n^2}\left(\sum_{i=1}^n P_{ii}^2 + 2\sum_{i=1}^n\sum_{m=1}^n P_{im}^2\right) \\
&\le \frac{3B}{n^2}\sum_{i=1}^n P_{ii} \\
&= 3B\frac{\ell}{n^2} \to 0.
\end{aligned}$$

The third equality holds because the remaining cross-products have zero expectation as the observations are independent and the errors have zero mean. The first inequality is (12.75). The second uses $P_{ii}^2 \le P_{ii}$ and $\sum_{m=1}^n P_{im}^2 = P_{ii}$. The final equality is $\sum_{i=1}^n P_{ii} = \ell$.

Using (12.76), (12.80), Markov's inequality (B.36), and combining across all j and k, we deduce that

$$\frac{1}{n}\boldsymbol{u}'\boldsymbol{P}_Z\boldsymbol{u} \underset{p}{\longrightarrow} \alpha\Sigma. \qquad (12.81)$$

Returning to the 2SLS estimator (12.79) and combining (12.77), (12.78), and (12.81), we find

$$\widehat{\beta}_{2\text{sls}} - \beta \underset{p}{\longrightarrow} \left(\boldsymbol{H} + \alpha \Sigma_{22}\right)^{-1} \alpha \Sigma_{2e}.$$

Thus 2SLS is also inconsistent for β. The limit, however, depends on the magnitude of α.

We finally examine the LIML estimator. Expression (12.81) implies

$$\frac{1}{n}\boldsymbol{Y}'\boldsymbol{M}_Z\boldsymbol{Y} = \frac{1}{n}\boldsymbol{u}'\boldsymbol{u} - \frac{1}{n}\boldsymbol{u}'\boldsymbol{P}_Z\boldsymbol{u} \underset{p}{\longrightarrow} (1-\alpha)\,\Sigma.$$

Similarly,

$$\begin{aligned}\frac{1}{n}\boldsymbol{Y}'\boldsymbol{Z}\left(\boldsymbol{Z}'\boldsymbol{Z}\right)^{-1}\boldsymbol{Z}'\boldsymbol{Y} &= \overline{\beta}'\Gamma'\left(\frac{1}{n}\boldsymbol{Z}'\boldsymbol{Z}\right)\Gamma\overline{\beta} + \overline{\beta}'\Gamma'\left(\frac{1}{n}\boldsymbol{Z}'\boldsymbol{u}\right) + \left(\frac{1}{n}\boldsymbol{u}'\boldsymbol{Z}\right)\Gamma\overline{\beta} + \frac{1}{n}\boldsymbol{u}'\boldsymbol{P}_Z\boldsymbol{u} \\ &\underset{d}{\longrightarrow} \overline{\beta}'\boldsymbol{H}\overline{\beta} + \alpha\Sigma.\end{aligned}$$

Hence

$$\widehat{\mu} = \min_{\gamma} \frac{\gamma'\boldsymbol{Y}'\boldsymbol{Z}\left(\boldsymbol{Z}'\boldsymbol{Z}\right)^{-1}\boldsymbol{Z}'\boldsymbol{Y}\gamma}{\gamma'\boldsymbol{Y}'\boldsymbol{M}_Z\boldsymbol{Y}\gamma} \underset{d}{\longrightarrow} \min_{\gamma} \frac{\gamma'\left(\overline{\beta}'\boldsymbol{H}\overline{\beta} + \alpha\Sigma\right)\gamma}{\gamma'(1-\alpha)\,\Sigma\gamma} = \frac{\alpha}{1-\alpha}$$

and

$$\begin{aligned}\widehat{\beta}_{\text{liml}} - \beta &= \left(\frac{1}{n}\boldsymbol{X}'\boldsymbol{P}_Z\boldsymbol{X} - \widehat{\mu}\frac{1}{n}\boldsymbol{X}'\boldsymbol{M}_Z\boldsymbol{X}\right)^{-1}\left(\frac{1}{n}\boldsymbol{X}'\boldsymbol{P}_Z\boldsymbol{e} - \widehat{\mu}\frac{1}{n}\boldsymbol{X}'\boldsymbol{M}_Z\boldsymbol{e}\right) \\ &\underset{d}{\longrightarrow} \left(\boldsymbol{H} + \alpha\Sigma_{22} - \frac{\alpha}{1-\alpha}(1-\alpha)\,\Sigma_{22}\right)^{-1}\left(\alpha\Sigma_{2e} - \frac{\alpha}{1-\alpha}(1-\alpha)\,\Sigma_{2e}\right) \\ &= \boldsymbol{H}^{-1}0 \\ &= 0.\end{aligned}$$

Thus LIML is consistent for β, unlike 2SLS.

Theorem 12.19 states these results formally.

> **Theorem 12.19** In the model (12.73), under assumptions (12.74), (12.75), and (12.76), as $n \to \infty$,
>
> $$\widehat{\beta}_{\text{ols}} \underset{p}{\longrightarrow} \beta + \left(\boldsymbol{H} + \Sigma_{22}\right)^{-1}\Sigma_{2e}$$
>
> $$\widehat{\beta}_{2\text{sls}} \underset{p}{\longrightarrow} \beta + \left(\boldsymbol{H} + \alpha\Sigma_{22}\right)^{-1}\alpha\Sigma_{2e}$$
>
> $$\widehat{\beta}_{\text{liml}} \underset{p}{\longrightarrow} \beta.$$

This result is quite insightful. It shows that while endogeneity ($\Sigma_{2e} \neq 0$) renders the least squares estimator inconsistent, the 2SLS estimator is also inconsistent if the number of instruments diverges proportionately with n. The limit in Theorem 12.19 shows a continuity between least squares and 2SLS. The probability limit of the 2SLS estimator is continuous in α, with the extreme case ($\alpha = 1$) implying that 2SLS and least squares have the same probability limit. The general implication is that the distortion in 2SLS is increasing in α.

The theorem also shows that unlike 2SLS, the LIML estimator is consistent under the many instruments assumption. Effectively, LIML makes a bias correction.

Theorems 12.18 (weak instruments) and 12.19 (many instruments) tell a cautionary tale. They show that when instruments are weak and/or many, the 2SLS estimator is inconsistent. The degree of inconsistency depends on the weakness of the instruments (the magnitude of the matrix $\boldsymbol{C}$ in Theorem 12.18) and the degree of overidentification (the ratio α in Theorem 12.19). The theorems also show that the LIML estimator is inconsistent under the weak instrument assumption but with a bias-correction, and is consistent under the many instrument assumption. This suggests that LIML is more robust than 2SLS to weak and many instruments.

An important limitation of the results in Theorem 12.19 is the assumption of conditional homoskedasticity. It appears likely that the consistency of LIML fails in the many instrument setting if the errors are heteroskedastic.

In applications, users should be aware of the potential consequences of the many instrument framework. It is useful to calculate the "many instrument ratio" $\alpha = \ell/n$. While there is no specific rule-of-thumb for α that leads to acceptable inference, a minimum criterion is that if $\alpha \geq 0.05$, you should be seriously concerned about the many-instrument problem. In general, when α is large, it seems preferable to use LIML instead of 2SLS.

12.38 TESTING FOR WEAK INSTRUMENTS

In the previous sections, we found that weak instruments results in non-standard asymptotic distributions for the 2SLS and LIML estimators. In practice, how do we know if this is a problem? Is there a way to check if the instruments are weak?

This question was addressed in an influential paper by Stock and Yogo (2005) as an extension of Staiger and Stock (1997). Stock-Yogo focus on two implications of weak instruments: (1) estimation bias and (2) inference distortion. They show how to test the hypothesis that these distortions are not "too big." They propose F tests for the excluded instruments in the reduced form regressions with non-standard critical values. In particular, when there is one endogenous regressor and a single instrument, the Stock-Yogo test rejects the null of weak instruments when this F statistic exceeds 10. While Stock and Yogo explore two types of distortions, we focus exclusively on inference, as that is the more challenging problem. In this section, we describe the Stock-Yogo theory and tests for the case of a single endogenous regressor ($k_2 = 1$). In Section 12.39, we describe their method for the case of multiple endogeneous regressors.

While the theory in Stock and Yogo allows for an arbitrary number of exogenous regressors and instruments, for the sake of clear exposition, let us focus on the very simple case of no included exogenous variables ($k_1 = 0$), and just one exogenous instrument ($\ell_2 = 1$), which is model (12.69) from Section 12.35:

$$Y = X\beta + e$$
$$X = Z\Gamma + u.$$

Furthermore, as in Section 12.35, we assume conditional homoskedasticity and normalize the variances as in (12.70). Since the model is just-identified, the 2SLS, LIML, and IV estimators are all equivalent.

The question of primary interest is to determine conditions on the reduced form under which the IV estimator of the structural equation is well behaved, and secondly, what statistical tests can be used to learn whether these conditions are satisfied. As in Section 12.36, we assume that the reduced form coefficient Γ is **local-to-zero**, specifically, $\Gamma = n^{-1/2}\mu$. The asymptotic distribution of the IV estimator is presented in

Theorem 12.18. Given the simplifying assumptions, the result is

$$\widehat{\beta}_{\mathrm{iv}} - \beta \underset{d}{\longrightarrow} \frac{\xi_e}{\mu + \xi_2}$$

where (ξ_e, ξ_2) are bivariate normal. For inference, we also examine the behavior of the classical (homoskedastic) t-statistic for the IV estimator. Note that

$$\begin{aligned}\widehat{\sigma}^2 &= \frac{1}{n}\sum_{i=1}^{n}\left(Y_i - X_i\widehat{\beta}_{\mathrm{iv}}\right)^2 \\ &= \frac{1}{n}\sum_{i=1}^{n} e_i^2 - \frac{2}{n}\sum_{i=1}^{n} e_i X_i\left(\widehat{\beta}_{\mathrm{iv}} - \beta\right) + \frac{1}{n}\sum_{i=1}^{n} X_i^2\left(\widehat{\beta}_{\mathrm{iv}} - \beta\right)^2 \\ &\underset{d}{\longrightarrow} 1 - 2\rho\frac{\xi_e}{\mu + \xi_2} + \left(\frac{\xi_e}{\mu + \xi_2}\right)^2.\end{aligned}$$

Thus

$$T = \frac{\widehat{\beta}_{\mathrm{iv}} - \beta}{\sqrt{\widehat{\sigma}^2 \sum_{i=1}^{n} z_i^2 / \left|\sum_{i=1}^{n} z_i x_i\right|}} \underset{d}{\longrightarrow} \frac{\xi_1}{\sqrt{1 - 2\rho\frac{\xi_1}{\mu+\xi_2} + \left(\frac{\xi_1}{\mu+\xi_2}\right)^2}} \stackrel{\mathrm{def}}{=} S. \tag{12.82}$$

In general, S is non-normal, and its distribution depends on the parameters ρ and μ.

Can we use the distribution S for inference on β? The distribution depends on two unknown parameters, and neither is consistently estimable. This means we cannot use the distribution in (12.82) with ρ and μ replaced with estimates. To eliminate the dependence on ρ, one possibility is to use the "worst case" value, which turns out to be $\rho = 1$. By "worst case," we mean the value that causes the greatest distortion away from normal critical values. Setting $\rho = 1$, we have the considerable simplification

$$S = S_1 = \xi\left|1 + \frac{\xi}{\mu}\right| \tag{12.83}$$

where $\xi \sim \mathrm{N}(0, 1)$. When the model is strongly identified (so $|\mu|$ is very large), then $S_1 \approx \xi$ is standard normal, consistent with classical theory. However, when $|\mu|$ is very small (but nonzero), $|S_1| \approx \xi^2/\mu$ (in the sense that this term dominates), which is a scaled χ_1^2 and quite far from normal. As $|\mu| \to 0$ we find the extreme case $|S_1| \to_p \infty$.

While (12.83) is a convenient simplification, it does not yield a useful approximation for inference, as the distribution in (12.83) is highly dependent on the unknown μ. If we take the worst-case value of μ, which is $\mu = 0$, we find that $|S_1|$ diverges and all distributional approximations fail.

To break this impasse, Stock and Yogo (2005) recommended a constructive alternative. Rather than using the worst-case μ, they suggested finding a threshold such that if μ exceeds this threshold, then the distribution (12.83) is not "too badly" distorted from the normal distribution.

Specifically, the Stock-Yogo recommendation can be summarized by two steps. First, the distribution result (12.83) can be used to find a threshold value τ^2 such that if $\mu^2 \geq \tau^2$, then the size of the nominal[1] 5% test "Reject if $|T| \geq 1.96$" has asymptotic size $\mathbb{P}\left[|S_1| \geq 1.96\right] \leq 0.15$. Thus while the goal is to obtain a test with size 5%, we recognize that there may be size distortion due to weak instruments and are willing to tolerate a

[1]The term "nominal size" of a test is the official intended size—the size that would obtain under ideal circumstances. In this context, the test "Reject if $|T| \geq 1.96$" has nominal size 0.05, as this would be the asymptotic rejection probability in the ideal context of strong instruments.

specific distortion. For example, a 10% distortion means we allow the actual size to be up to 15%. Second, they use the asymptotic distribution of the reduced-form (first stage) F statistic to test whether the actual unknown value of μ^2 exceeds the threshold τ^2. These two steps together give rise to the rule-of-thumb that the first-stage F statistic should exceed 10 in order to achieve reliable IV inference. (This is for the case of one instrumental variable. If there is more than one instrument, then the rule-of-thumb changes.) We now describe the steps behind this reasoning in more detail.

The first step is to use the distribution (12.82) to determine the threshold τ^2. Formally, the goal is to find the value of $\tau^2 = \mu^2$ at which the asymptotic size of a nominal 5% test is actually a given r (e.g., $r = 0.15$), thus $\mathbb{P}\left[|S_1| \geq 1.96\right] \leq r$. By some algebra and the quadratic formula, the event $|\xi\,(1 + \xi/\mu)| < x$ is the same as

$$\frac{\mu^2}{4} - x\mu < \left(\xi + \frac{\mu}{2}\right)^2 < \frac{\mu^2}{4} + x\mu.$$

The random variable between the inequalities is distributed $\chi_1^2(\mu^2/4)$, a non-central chi-square with one degree of freedom and non-centrality parameter $\mu^2/4$. Thus,

$$\begin{aligned}\mathbb{P}\left[|S_1| \geq x\right] &= \mathbb{P}\left[\chi_1^2\left(\frac{\mu^2}{4}\right) \geq \frac{\mu^2}{4} + x\mu\right] + \mathbb{P}\left[\chi_1^2\left(\frac{\mu^2}{4}\right) \leq \frac{\mu^2}{4} - x\mu\right] \\ &= 1 - G\left(\frac{\mu^2}{4} + x\mu, \frac{\mu^2}{4}\right) + G\left(\frac{\mu^2}{4} - x\mu, \frac{\mu^2}{4}\right) \qquad (12.84)\end{aligned}$$

where $G(u, \lambda)$ is the distribution function of $\chi_1^2(\lambda)$. Hence the desired threshold τ^2 solves

$$1 - G\left(\frac{\tau^2}{4} + 1.96\tau, \frac{\tau^2}{4}\right) + G\left(\frac{\tau^2}{4} - 1.96\tau, \frac{\tau^2}{4}\right) = r$$

or effectively,

$$G\left(\frac{\tau^2}{4} + 1.96\tau, \frac{\tau^2}{4}\right) = 1 - r$$

because $\tau^2/4 - 1.96\tau < 0$ for relevant values of τ. The numerical solution (computed with the non-central chi-square distribution function, e.g. `ncx2cdf` in MATLAB) is $\tau^2 = 1.70$ when $r = 0.15$. (That is, the command

```
ncx2cdf(1.7/4 + 1.96 * sqrt(1.7), 1, 1.7/4)
```

yields the answer `0.8500`. Stock and Yogo (2005) approximate the same calculation using simulation methods and report $\tau^2 = 1.82$.)

This calculation means that if the reduced form satisfies $\mu^2 \geq 1.7$, or equivalently, if $\Gamma^2 \geq 1.7/n$, then the asymptotic size of a nominal 5% test on the structural parameter is no larger than 15%.

To summarize the Stock-Yogo first step, we calculate the minimum value τ^2 for μ^2 sufficient to ensure that the asymptotic size of a nominal 5% t-test does not exceed r, and find that $\tau^2 = 1.70$ for $r = 0.15$.

The Stock-Yogo second step is to find a critical value for the first-stage F statistic sufficient to reject the hypothesis that $\mathbb{H}_0 : \mu^2 = \tau^2$ against $\mathbb{H}_1 : \mu^2 > \tau^2$. We now describe this procedure.

They suggest testing $\mathbb{H}_0 : \mu^2 = \tau^2$ at the 5% size using the first stage F statistic. If the F statistic is small so that the test does not reject, then we should be worried that the true value of μ^2 is small and there is a weak instrument problem. However, if the F statistic is large, so that the test rejects, then we can have some confidence that the true value of μ^2 is sufficiently large that the weak instrument problem is not too severe.

To implement the test, we need to calculate an appropriate critical value. It should be calculated under the null hypothesis $\mathbb{H}_0 : \mu^2 = \tau^2$. This is different from a conventional F test, which is calculated under $\mathbb{H}_0 : \mu^2 = 0$.

We start by calculating the asymptotic distribution of F. Since there is one regressor and one instrument in our simplified setting, the first-stage F statistic is the squared t-statistic from the reduced form. Given our previous calculations, it has the asymptotic distribution

$$\mathrm{F}=\frac{\widehat{\gamma}^2}{s(\widehat{\gamma})^2}=\frac{\left(\sum_{i=1}^n Z_i X_i\right)^2}{\left(\sum_{i=1}^n X_i^2\right)\widehat{\sigma}_u^2}\underset{d}{\longrightarrow}(\mu+\xi_2)^2\sim\chi_1^2\left(\mu^2\right).$$

This is a non-central chi-square distribution $G(u,\mu^2)$ with one degree of freedom and non-centrality parameter μ^2.

To test $\mathbb{H}_0:\mu^2=\tau^2$ against $\mathbb{H}_1:\mu^2>\tau^2$, we reject for $\mathrm{F}\geq c$, where c is selected so that the asymptotic rejection probability satisfies

$$\mathbb{P}\left[\mathrm{F}\geq c\mid\mu^2=\tau^2\right]\to\mathbb{P}\left[\chi_1^2\left(\tau^2\right)\geq c\right]=1-G\left(c,\tau^2\right)=0.05$$

for $\tau^2=1.70$, or equivalently, $G(c,1.7)=0.95$. This is found by inverting the non-central chi-square quantile function, that is, the function $Q(p,d)$ that solves $G(Q(p,d),d)=p$. We find that $c=Q(0.95,1.7)=8.7$. In MATLAB, this can be computed by `ncx2inv(.95,1.7)`. Stock and Yogo (2005) report $c=9.0$, because they used $\tau^2=1.82$.

Thus if $\mathrm{F}>8.7$, we can reject $\mathbb{H}_0:\mu^2=1.7$ against $\mathbb{H}_1:\mu^2>1.7$ with an asymptotic 5% test. In this context, we should expect the IV estimator and tests to be reasonably well behaved. However, if $\mathrm{F}<8.7$, then we should be cautious about the IV estimator, confidence intervals, and tests. This finding led Staiger and Stock (1997) to propose the informal "rule of thumb" that the first stage F statistic should exceed 10. Notice that F exceeding 8.7 (or 10) is equivalent to the reduced form t-statistic exceeding 2.94 (or 3.16), which is considerably larger than a conventional check if the t-statistic is "significant." Equivalently, the recommended rule-of-thumb for the case of a single instrument is to estimate the reduced form and verify that the t-statistic for exclusion of the instrumental variable exceeds 3 in absolute value.

Does the proposed procedure control the asymptotic size of a 2SLS test? The first step has asymptotic size bounded below r (e.g., 15%). The second step has asymptotic size 5%. By the Bonferroni bound (see Section 9.21), the two steps together have asymptotic size bounded below $r+0.05$ (i.e., 20%). We can thus call the Stock-Yogo procedure a rigorous test with asymptotic size $r+0.05$ (or 20%).

Our analysis has been confined to the case $k_2=\ell_2=1$. Stock and Yogo (2005) also examine the case $\ell_2>1$ (which requires numerical simulation to solve) and both the 2SLS and LIML estimators. They show that the F statistic critical values depend on the number of instruments ℓ_2 as well as the estimator. Their critical values (calculated by simulation) are in their paper and are posted on Motohiro Yogo's webpage. We report a subset in Table 12.4.

One striking feature about these critical values is that those for the 2SLS estimator are strongly increasing in ℓ_2, while those for the LIML estimator are decreasing in ℓ_2. Thus when the number of instruments ℓ_2 is large, 2SLS requires a much stronger reduced form (larger μ^2) for inference to be reliable, but this is not the case for LIML. This is direct evidence that LIML inference is less sensitive to weak instruments than 2SLS, which makes a strong case for LIML over 2SLS, especially when ℓ_2 is large or the instruments are potentially weak.

We now summarize the recommended Staiger-Stock/Stock-Yogo procedure for $k_1\geq 1$, $k_2=1$, and $\ell_2\geq 1$. The structural equation and reduced form equations are

$$Y_1=Z_1'\beta_1+Y_2\beta_2+e$$

$$Y_2=Z_1'\gamma_1+Z_2'\gamma_2+u.$$

Table 12.4
5% Critical value for weak instruments, $k_2 = 1$

	Maximal size r							
	2SLS				LIML			
ℓ_2	0.10	0.15	0.20	0.25	0.10	0.15	0.20	0.25
1	16.4	9.0	6.7	5.5	16.4	9.0	6.7	5.5
2	19.9	11.6	8.7	7.2	8.7	5.3	4.4	3.9
3	22.3	12.8	9.5	7.8	6.5	4.4	3.7	3.3
4	24.6	14.0	10.3	8.3	5.4	3.9	3.3	3.0
5	26.9	15.1	11.0	8.8	4.8	3.6	3.0	2.8
6	29.2	16.2	11.7	9.4	4.4	3.3	2.9	2.6
7	31.5	17.4	12.5	9.9	4.2	3.2	2.7	2.5
8	33.8	18.5	13.2	10.5	4.0	3.0	2.6	2.4
9	36.2	19.7	14.0	11.1	3.8	2.9	2.5	2.3
10	38.5	20.9	14.8	11.6	3.7	2.8	2.5	2.2
15	50.4	26.8	18.7	12.2	3.3	2.5	2.2	2.0
20	62.3	32.8	22.7	17.6	3.2	2.3	2.1	1.9
25	74.2	38.8	26.7	20.6	3.8	2.2	2.0	1.8
30	86.2	44.8	30.7	23.6	3.9	2.2	1.9	1.7

Source: `https://sites.google.com/site/motohiroyogo/research/econometrics`

The structural equation is estimated by either 2SLS or LIML. Let F be the F statistic for $\mathbb{H}_0 : \gamma_2 = 0$ in the reduced form equation. Let $s(\widehat{\beta}_2)$ be a standard error for β_2 in the structural equation. The procedure is:

1. Compare F with the critical values c in Table 12.4 with the row selected to match the number of excluded instruments ℓ_2 and the columns to match the estimation method (2SLS or LIML) and the desired size r.
2. If $\mathrm{F} > c$, then report the 2SLS or LIML estimates with conventional inference.

The Stock-Yogo test can be implemented in Stata using the command `estat firststage` after `ivregress 2sls` or `ivregres liml` if a standard (non-robust) covariance matrix has been specified (that is, without the '`, r`' option).

There are possible extensions to the Stock-Yogo procedure.

One modest extension is to use the information to convey the degree of confidence in the accuracy of a confidence interval. Suppose in an application, you have $\ell_2 = 5$ excluded instruments and have estimated your equation by 2SLS. Now suppose that your reduced form F statistic equals 12. You check Table 12.4 and find that $\mathrm{F} = 12$ is significant with $r = 0.20$. Thus we can interpret the conventional 2SLS confidence interval as having coverage of 80% (or 75% if we make the Bonferroni correction). However, if $\mathrm{F} = 27$, we would conclude that the test for weak instruments is significant with $r = 0.10$, meaning that the conventional 2SLS confidence interval can be interpreted as having coverage of 90% (or 85% after Bonferroni correction). Thus the value of the F statistic can be used to calibrate the coverage accuracy.

A more substantive extension, which we now discuss, reverses the steps. Unfortunately this discussion will be limited to the case $\ell_2 = 1$. First, use the reduced form F statistic to find a one-sided confidence interval for μ^2 of the form $[\mu_L^2, \infty)$. Second, use the lower bound μ_L^2 to calculate a critical value c for S_1 such that the 2SLS test has asymptotic size bounded below 0.05. This produces better size control than the Stock-Yogo procedure and produces more informative confidence intervals for β_2. We now describe the steps in detail.

The first goal is to find a one-sided confidence interval for μ^2, which is found by test inversion. As we described earlier, for any τ^2, we reject $\mathbb{H}_0 : \mu^2 = \tau^2$ in favor of $\mathbb{H}_1 : \mu^2 > \tau^2$ if $F > c$, where $G(c, \tau^2) = 0.95$. Equivalently, we reject if $G(F, \tau^2) > 0.95$. By the test inversion principle, an asymptotic 95% confidence interval $[\mu_L^2, \infty)$ is the set of all values of τ^2 that are not rejected. Since $G(F, \tau^2) \geq 0.95$ for all τ^2 in this set, the lower bound μ_L^2 satisfies $G(F, \mu_L^2) = 0.95$ and is found numerically. In MATLAB, the solution is `mu2` when `ncx2cdf(F,1,mu2)` returns `0.95`.

The second goal is to find the critical value c such that $\mathbb{P}[|S_1| \geq c] = 0.05$ when $\mu^2 = \mu_L^2$. From (12.84) this goal is achieved when

$$1 - G\left(\frac{\mu_L^2}{4} + c\mu_L, \frac{\mu_L^2}{4}\right) + G\left(\frac{\mu_L^2}{4} - c\mu_L, \frac{\mu_L^2}{4}\right) = 0.05. \tag{12.85}$$

This can be solved as

$$G\left(\frac{\mu_L^2}{4} + c\mu_L, \frac{\mu_L^2}{4}\right) = 0.95.$$

(The third term on the left-hand side of (12.85) is 0 for all solutions, so it can be ignored.) Using the non-central chi-square quantile function $Q(p, d)$, this c equals

$$c = \frac{Q\left(0.95, \frac{\mu_L^2}{4}\right) - \frac{\mu_L^2}{4}}{\mu_L}.$$

For example, in MATLAB, this is found as `c=(ncx2inv(.95,1,mu2/4)-mu2/4)/sqrt(mu2)`. Then 95% confidence intervals for β_2 are calculated as $\widehat{\beta}_{\text{iv}} \pm cs(\widehat{\beta}_{\text{iv}})$.

We can also calculate a p-value for the t-statistic T for β_2:

$$p = 1 - G\left(\frac{\mu_L^2}{4} + |T|\,\mu_L, \frac{\mu_L^2}{4}\right) + G\left(\frac{\mu_L^2}{4} - |T|\,\mu_L, \frac{\mu_L^2}{4}\right)$$

where the third term equals 0 if $|T| \geq \mu_L/4$. In MATLAB, for example, this can be calculated by the commands

```
T1 = mu2/4 + abs(T) * sqrt(mu2);
T2 = mu2/4 - abs(T) * sqrt(mu2);
p = -ncx2cdf(T1,1,mu2/4) + ncx2cdf(T2,1,mu2/4);
```

These confidence intervals and p-values will be larger than the conventional intervals and p-values, reflecting the incorporation of information about the strength of the instruments through the first-stage F statistic. Also, by the Bonferroni bound, these tests have asymptotic size bounded below 10% and the confidence intervals have asymptotic converage exceeding 90%, unlike the Stock-Yogo method, which has size of 20% and coverage of 80%.

The augmented procedure suggested here, only for the $\ell_2 = 1$ case, is

1. Find μ_L^2 that solves $G\left(F, \mu_L^2\right) = 0.95$. In MATLAB, the solution is `mu2` when `ncx2cdf(F,1,mu2)` returns `0.95`.
2. Find c that solves $G\left(\mu_L^2/4 + c\mu_L, \mu_L^2/4\right) = 0.95$. In MATLAB, the command is
   `c=(ncx2inv(.95,1,mu2/4)-mu2/4)/sqrt(mu2)`
3. Report the confidence interval $\widehat{\beta}_2 \pm cs(\widehat{\beta}_2)$ for β_2.
4. For the t-statistic $T = \left(\widehat{\beta}_2 - \beta_2\right)/s(\widehat{\beta}_2)$, the asymptotic p-value is

$$p = 1 - G\left(\frac{\mu_L^2}{4} + |T|\,\mu_L, \frac{\mu_L^2}{4}\right) + G\left(\frac{\mu_L^2}{4} - |T|\,\mu_L, \frac{\mu_L^2}{4}\right)$$

which is computed in MATLAB by `T1=mu2/4+abs(T)*sqrt(mu2); T2=mu2/4-abs(T)*sqrt(mu2);` and `p=1-ncx2cdf(T1,1,mu2/4)+ncx2cdf(T2,1,mu2/4)`.

We have described an extension to the Stock-Yogo procedure for the case of one instrumental variable $\ell_2 = 1$. This restriction was due to the use of the analytic formula (12.85) for the asymptotic distribution, which is only available when $\ell_2 = 1$. In principle the procedure could be extended using simulation or bootstrap methods, but this has not been done to my knowledge.

To illustrate the Stock-Yogo and extended procedures, let us return to the Card proximity example. Take the IV estimates reported in the second column of Table 12.1, which used *college* as a single instrument. The reduced form estimates for the endogenous variable *education* are reported in the second column of Table 12.2. The excluded instrument *college* has a t-ratio of 4.2, which implies an F statistic of 17.8. The F statistic exceeds the rule-of thumb of 10, so the structural estimates pass the Stock-Yogo threshold. Based on their recommendation, we can interpret the estimates conventionally. However, the conventional confidence interval (e.g., for the returns to education $0.132 \pm 0.049 \times 1.96 = [0.04, 0.23]$) has an asymptotic coverage of 80% rather than the nominal 95% rate.

Now consider the extended procedure. Given $\mathrm{F} = 17.8$, we calculate the lower bound $\mu_L^2 = 6.6$. This implies a critical value of $C = 2.7$. Hence an improved confidence interval for the returns to education in this equation is $0.132 \pm 0.049 \times 2.7 = [0.01, 0.26]$, which is a wider confidence interval but has improved asymptotic coverage of 90%. The p-value for $\beta_2 = 0$ is $p = 0.012$.

Next, take the 2SLS estimates reported in the fourth column of Table 12.1, which use the two instruments *public* and *private*. The reduced form equation is reported in column six of Table 12.2. An F statistic for exclusion of the two instruments is $\mathrm{F} = 13.9$, which exceeds the 15% size threshold for 2SLS and all thresholds for LIML, indicating that the structural estimates pass the Stock-Yogo threshold test and can be interpreted conventionally.

The weak instrument methods described here are important for applied econometrics, as they discipline researchers to assess the quality of their reduced form relationships before reporting structural estimates. The theory, however, has limitations and shortcomings, in particular, the strong assumption of conditional homoskedasticity. Despite this limitation, in practice, researchers apply the Stock-Yogo recommendations to estimates computed with heteroskedasticity-robust standard errors. This is an active area of research, so the recommended methods may change in the years ahead.

12.39 WEAK INSTRUMENTS WITH $k_2 > 1$

When there is more than one endogenous regressor ($k_2 > 1$), it is better to examine the reduced form as a system. Staiger and Stock (1997) and Stock and Yogo (2005) provided an analysis of this case and constructed a test for weak instruments. The theory is considerably more involved than the $k_2 = 1$ case, so let us briefly summarize it here excluding many details, emphasizing their suggested methods.

The structural equation and reduced form equations are

$$Y_1 = Z_1'\beta_1 + Y_2'\beta_2 + e$$
$$Y_2 = \Gamma_{12}'Z_1 + \Gamma_{22}'Z_2 + u_2.$$

As in Section 12.38, we assume that the errors are conditionally homoskedastic.

Identification of β_2 requires the matrix Γ_{22} to be full rank. A necessary condition is that each row of Γ_{22}' is nonzero, but this is not sufficient.

We focus on the size performance of the homoskedastic Wald statistic for the 2SLS estimator of β_2. For simplicity, assume that the variance of e is known and normalized to 1. Using representation (12.32), the Wald statistic can be written as

$$W = e'\widetilde{Z}_2\left(\widetilde{Z}_2'\widetilde{Z}_2\right)^{-1}\widetilde{Z}_2'Y_2\left(Y_2'\widetilde{Z}_2\left(\widetilde{Z}_2'\widetilde{Z}_2\right)^{-1}\widetilde{Z}_2'Y_2\right)^{-1}\left(Y_2'\widetilde{Z}_2\left(\widetilde{Z}_2'\widetilde{Z}_2\right)^{-1}\widetilde{Z}_2'e\right)$$

where $\widetilde{Z}_2 = (I_n - P_1) Z_2$ and $P_1 = Z_1\left(Z_1'Z_1\right)^{-1} Z_1'$.

Recall from Section 12.36 that Stock and Staiger model the excluded instruments Z_2 as weak by setting $\Gamma_{22} = n^{-1/2}C$ for some matrix C. In this framework, we have the asymptotic distribution results

$$\frac{1}{n}\widetilde{Z}_2'\widetilde{Z}_2 \underset{p}{\longrightarrow} Q = \mathbb{E}\left[Z_2Z_2'\right] - \mathbb{E}\left[Z_2Z_1'\right]\left(\mathbb{E}\left[Z_1Z_1'\right]\right)^{-1}\mathbb{E}\left[Z_1Z_2'\right]$$

and

$$\frac{1}{\sqrt{n}}\widetilde{Z}_2'e \underset{d}{\longrightarrow} Q^{1/2}\xi_0$$

where ξ_0 is a matrix normal variate whose columns are independent $\mathrm{N}(0, I)$. Furthermore, setting $\Sigma = \mathbb{E}\left[u_2u_2'\right]$ and $\overline{C} = Q^{1/2}C\Sigma^{-1/2}$,

$$\frac{1}{\sqrt{n}}\widetilde{Z}_2'Y_2 = \frac{1}{n}\widetilde{Z}_2'\widetilde{Z}_2C + \frac{1}{\sqrt{n}}\widetilde{Z}_2'U_2 \underset{d}{\longrightarrow} Q^{1/2}\overline{C}\Sigma^{1/2} + Q^{1/2}\xi_2\Sigma^{1/2}$$

where ξ_2 is a matrix normal variate whose columns are independent $\mathrm{N}(0, I)$. The variables ξ_0 and ξ_2 are correlated. Combining, we obtain the asymptotic distribution of the Wald statistic:

$$W \underset{d}{\longrightarrow} S = \xi_0'\left(\overline{C} + \xi_2\right)\left(\overline{C}'\overline{C}\right)^{-1}\left(\overline{C} + \xi_2\right)'\xi_0.$$

Using the spectral decomposition, $\overline{C}'\overline{C} = H'\Lambda H$, where $H'H = I$ and Λ is diagonal. Thus we can write $S = \xi_0'\overline{\xi}_2\Lambda^{-1}\overline{\xi}_2'\xi_0$, where $\overline{\xi}_2 = \overline{C}H' + \xi_2 H'$. The matrix $\xi^* = (\xi_0, \overline{\xi}_2)$ is multivariate normal, so $\xi^{*\prime}\xi^*$ has what is called a non-central Wishart distribution. It only depends on the matrix $\overline{C}$ through $H\overline{C}'\overline{C}H' = \Lambda$, which are the eigenvalues of $\overline{C}'\overline{C}$. Since S is a function of ξ^* only through $\overline{\xi}_2'\xi_0$, we conclude that S is a function of $\overline{C}$ only through these eigenvalues.

This is a very quick sketch of a rather involved derivation, but the conclusion drawn by Stock and Yogo is that the asymptotic distribution of the Wald statistic is non-standard and is a function of the model parameters only through the eigenvalues of $\overline{C}'\overline{C}$ and the correlations between the normal variates ξ_0 and $\overline{\xi}_2$. The worst-case scenario can be summarized by the maximal correlation between ξ_0 and $\overline{\xi}_2$ and the smallest eigenvalue of $\overline{C}'\overline{C}$. For convenience, Stock and Yogo rescale the latter by dividing by the number of endogenous variables. Define

$$G = \overline{C}'\overline{C}/k_2 = \Sigma^{-1/2}C'QC\Sigma^{-1/2}/k_2$$

and

$$g = \lambda_{\min}(G) = \lambda_{\min}\left(\Sigma^{-1/2}C'QC\Sigma^{-1/2}\right)/k_2.$$

This can be estimated from the reduced-form regression:

$$X_{2i} = \widehat{\Gamma}_{12}'Z_{1i} + \widehat{\Gamma}_{22}'Z_{2i} + \widehat{u}_{2i}.$$

The estimator is

$$\widehat{G} = \widehat{\Sigma}^{-1/2}\widehat{\Gamma}'_{22}\left(\widetilde{Z}'_2\widetilde{Z}_2\right)\widehat{\Gamma}_{22}\widehat{\Sigma}^{-1/2}/k_2 = \widehat{\Sigma}^{-1/2}\left(X'_2\widetilde{Z}_2\left(\widetilde{Z}'_2\widetilde{Z}_2\right)^{-1}\widetilde{Z}'_2X_2\right)\widehat{\Sigma}^{-1/2}/k_2$$

$$\widehat{\Sigma} = \frac{1}{n-k}\sum_{i=1}^{n}\widehat{u}_{2i}\widehat{u}'_{2i}$$

$$\widehat{g} = \lambda_{\min}\left(\widehat{G}\right).$$

$\widehat{G}$ is a matrix F-type statistic for the coefficient matrix $\widehat{\Gamma}_{22}$.

The statistic $\widehat{g}$ was proposed by Cragg and Donald (1993) as a test for underidentification. Stock and Yogo (2005) use it as a test for weak instruments. Using simulation methods, they determined critical values for $\widehat{g}$ similar to those for $k_2 = 1$. For given size $r > 0.05$, there is a critical value c (reported in Table 12.5) such that if $\widehat{g} > c$ then the 2SLS (or LIML) Wald statistic W for $\widehat{\beta}_2$ has asymptotic size bounded below r. In contrast, if $\widehat{g} \leq c$, then we cannot bound the asymptotic size below r, and we cannot reject the hypothesis of weak instruments.

Critical values (calculated by simulation) are reported in the Stock and Yogo paper and posted on Motohiro Yogo's webpage. Table 12.5 reports a subset for the case $k_2 = 2$. The methods and theory apply to the cases $k_2 > 2$ as well, but those critical values have not been calculated. As for the $k_2 = 1$ case, the critical values for 2SLS are dramatically increasing in ℓ_2. Thus when the model is overidentified, we need a large value of $\widehat{g}$ to reject the hypothesis of weak instruments. This is a strong cautionary message to check the $\widehat{g}$ statistic in applications. Furthermore, the critical values for LIML are generally decreasing in ℓ_2 (except for $r = 0.10$, where the critical values are increasing for large ℓ_2). Thus for overidentified models, LIML inference is less sensitive to weak instruments than 2SLS and may be the preferred estimation method.

The Stock-Yogo test can be implemented in Stata using the command `estat firststage` after `ivregress 2sls` or `ivregres liml` if a standard (non-robust) covariance matrix has been specified (that is, without the '`, r`' option). Critical values that control for size are only available for $k_2 \leq 2$. For $k_2 > 2$, critical values that control for relative bias are reported.

Robust versions of the test have been proposed by Kleibergen and Paap (2006). These can be implemented in Stata using the downloadable command `ivreg2`.

12.40 EXAMPLE: ACEMOGLU, JOHNSON, AND ROBINSON (2001)

One particularly well-cited instrumental variable regression is Acemoglu, Johnson, and Robinson (2001) with additional details published their in 2012 paper. They are interested in the effect of political institutions on economic performance. The theory is that good institutions (rule-of-law, property rights) should result in a country having higher long-term economic output than if the same country had poor institutions. To investigate this question, they focus on a sample of 64 former European colonies. Their data are in the file `AJR2001` on the textbook website.

The authors' premise is that modern political institutions have been influenced by colonization. In particular, they argue that colonizing countries tended to set up colonies as either an "extractive state" or as a "migrant colony." An extractive state was used by the colonizer to extract resources for the colonizing country but was not largely settled by the European colonists. In this case, the colonists had no incentive to set up good political institutions. In contrast, if a colony was set up as a "migrant colony," then large numbers of European settlers migrated to the colony to live. These settlers desired institutions similar to those in their home country and hence had an incentive to set up political institutions with strong protections for private property. The nature of institutions is quite persistent over time, so these nineteenth-century foundations affect the nature

Table 12.5
5% Critical value for weak instruments, $k_2 = 2$

	Maximal size r							
	2SLS				LIML			
ℓ_2	0.10	0.15	0.20	0.25	0.10	0.15	0.20	0.25
2	7.0	4.6	3.9	3.6	7.0	4.6	3.9	3.6
3	13.4	8.2	6.4	5.4	5.4	3.8	3.3	3.1
4	16.9	9.9	7.5	6.3	4.7	3.4	3.0	2.8
5	19.4	11.2	8.4	6.9	4.3	3.1	2.8	2.6
6	21.7	12.3	9.1	7.4	4.1	2.9	2.6	2.5
7	23.7	13.3	9.8	7.9	3.9	2.8	2.5	2.4
8	25.6	14.3	10.4	8.4	3.8	2.7	2.4	2.3
9	27.5	15.2	11.0	8.8	3.7	2.7	2.4	2.2
10	29.3	16.2	11.6	9.3	3.6	2.6	2.3	2.1
15	38.0	20.6	14.6	11.6	3.5	2.4	2.1	2.0
20	46.6	25.0	17.6	13.8	3.6	2.4	2.0	1.9
25	55.1	29.3	20.6	16.1	3.6	2.4	1.97	1.8
30	63.5	33.6	23.5	18.3	4.1	2.4	1.95	1.7

Source: `https://sites.google.com/site/motohiroyogo/research/econometrics`

of modern institutions. The authors conclude that the nineteenth-century nature of the colony is predictive of the nature of modern institutions and hence modern economic growth.

To start the investigation, they report an OLS regression of log GDP per capita in 1995 on a measure of political institutions they call "*risk*," which is a measure of legal protection against expropriation. This variable ranges from 0 to 10, with 0 the lowest protection against expropriation and 10 the highest. For each country, the authors take the average value of the index over 1985 to 1995 (the mean is 6.5 with a standard deviation of 1.5). Their reported OLS estimates (intercept omitted) are

$$\log(\widehat{GDP\ per\ Capita}) = \underset{(0.06)}{0.52}\ risk. \tag{12.86}$$

These estimates imply a 52% difference in GDP between countries with a 1-unit difference in *risk*.

The authors argue that the *risk* is endogenous, since economic output influences political institutions and because the variable *risk* is undoubtedly measured with error. These issues induce least-square bias in different directions and thus the overall bias effect is unclear.

To correct for endogeneity bias, the authors argue for the need for an instrumental variable that does not directly affect economic performance yet is associated with political institutions. Their innovative suggestion was to use the mortality rate that faced potential European settlers in the nineteenth century. Colonies with high expected mortality were less attractive to European settlers, resulting in lower levels of European migrants. As a consequence, the authors expect such colonies to be more likely structured as an extractive state rather than a migrant colony. To measure the expected mortality rate, the authors use estimates provided by historical research of the annualized deaths per 1000 soldiers, labeled *mortality*. (They used military mortality rates, as the military maintained high-quality records.) The first-stage regression is

$$risk = \underset{(0.13)}{-0.61}\ \log(mortality) + \widehat{u}. \tag{12.87}$$

These estimates confirm that nineteenth-century high mortality rates are associated with lower quality modern institutions. Using log(*mortality*) as an instrument for *risk*, they estimate the structural equation using 2SLS and report

$$\log(\widehat{GDP\ per\ Capita}) = \underset{(0.16)}{0.94}\ risk. \tag{12.88}$$

This estimate is much higher than the OLS estimate from (12.86). The estimate is consistent with a near doubling of GDP due to a 1-unit difference in the risk index.

These are simple regressions involving just one right-hand-side variable. The authors considered a range of other models. Included in these results are a reversal of a traditional finding. In a conventional least squares regression, two relevant variables for output are *latitude* (distance from the equator) and *africa* (a dummy variable for countries from Africa), both of which are difficult to interpret causally. But in the proposed instrumental variables regression, the variables *latitude* and *africa* have much smaller—and statistically insignificant—coefficients.

To assess the specification, we can use the Stock and Yogo (2005) and endogeneity tests. The Stock-Yogo test is from the reduced form (12.87). The instrument has a t-ratio of 4.8 (or $F = 23$), which exceeds the Stock-Yogo critical value and hence can be treated as strong. For an endogeneity test, we take the least squares residual $\widehat{u}$ from this equation and include it in the structural equation and estimate by least squares. The result is a coefficient on $\widehat{u}$ of -0.57 with a t-ratio of 4.7, which is highly significant. We conclude that the least squares and 2SLS estimates are statistically different and reject the hypothesis that the variable *risk* is exogenous for the GDP structural equation.

In Exercise 12.22, you will replicate and extend these results using the authors' data.

The Acemoglu, Johnson, and Robinson (2001) paper is a creative and careful use of instrumental variables. The creativity stems from the historical analysis, which led to the focus on mortality as a potential predictor of migration choices. The care comes in the implementation, as the authors needed to gather country-level data on political institutions and mortality from distinct sources. Putting these pieces together is the art of the project.

12.41 EXAMPLE: ANGRIST AND KRUEGER (1991)

Another influential instrument variable regression is Angrist and Krueger (1991). Their concern, similar to that of Card (1995), is estimation of the structural returns to education while treating educational attainment as endogenous. Like Card, their goal is to find an instrument that is exogenous for wages yet has an impact on education. A subset of their data in the file `AK1991` on the textbook website.

Their creative suggestion was to focus on compulsory school attendance policies and their interaction with birthdates. Compulsory schooling laws vary across states in the United States, but typically require that youth remain in school until their sixteenth or seventeenth birthday. Angrist and Krueger argue that compulsory schooling has a causal effect on wages—youth who would have chosen to drop out of school stay in school for more years—and thus have more education, which causally impacts their earnings as adults.

Angrist and Krueger observe that these policies have differential impact on youth who are born early or late in the school year. Students who are born early in the calendar year are typically older when they enter school. Consequently when they attain the legal dropout age, they have attended less school than those born near the end of the year. So birthdate (early in the calendar year versus late) exogenously impacts educational attainment and thus wages through education. Yet birthdate must be exogenous for the structural wage equation, as there is no reason to believe that birthdate itself has a causal impact on a person's ability or wages.

These considerations together suggest that birthdate is a valid instrumental variable for education in a causal wage equation.

Typical wage datasets include age but not birthdates. To obtain information on birthdate, Angrist and Krueger used U.S. Census data, which includes an individual's quarter of birth (January–March, April–June, etc.). They use this variable to construct 2SLS estimates of the return to education.

Their paper carefully documents that educational attainment varies by quarter of birth (as predicted by the above discussion) and reports a large set of least squares and 2SLS estimates. We focus on two estimates at the core of their analysis, reported in column (6) of their Tables V and VII. These involve data from the 1980 census for men born in 1930–1939, with 329,509 observations. The first equation is

$$\widehat{\log(wage)} = \underset{(0.016)}{0.081}\ edu - \underset{(0.026)}{0.230}\ Black + \underset{(0.017)}{0.158}\ urban + \underset{(0.005)}{0.244}\ married \tag{12.89}$$

where *edu* is years of education, and *Black*, *urban*, and *married* are dummy variables indicating race (1 if Black, 0 otherwise), lives in a metropolitan area, and if married. In addition to the reported coefficients, the equation also includes as regressors nine year-of-birth dummies and eight region-of-residence dummies. The equation is estimated by 2SLS. The instrumental variables are the 30 interactions of three quarter-of-birth times ten year-of-birth dummy variables.

This equation indicates an 8% increase in wages due to each year of education.

Angrist and Krueger observe that the effect of compulsory education laws are likely to vary across states, so they expand the instrument set to include interactions with state-of-birth. They estimate the following equation by 2SLS:

$$\widehat{\log(wage)} = \underset{(0.009)}{0.083}\ edu - \underset{(0.011)}{0.233}\ Black + \underset{(0.009)}{0.151}\ urban + \underset{(0.004)}{0.244}\ married. \tag{12.90}$$

This equation also adds 50 state-of-birth dummy variables as regressors. The instrumental variables are the 180 interactions of quarter-of-birth times year-of-birth dummy variables, plus quarter-of-birth times state-of-birth interactions.

This equation shows a similar estimated causal effect of education on wages as in (12.89). More notably, the standard error is smaller in (12.90), suggesting improved precision by the expanded instrumental variable set.

However, these estimates seem excellent candidates for weak instruments and many instruments. Indeed, this paper (published in 1991) helped spark these two literatures. We can use the Stock-Yogo tools to explore the instrument strength and the implications for the Angrist-Krueger estimates.

First consider equation (12.89). Using the original Angrist-Krueger data, we estimate the corresponding reduced form and calculate the *F* statistic for the 30 excluded instruments. We find $F = 4.8$. It has an asymptotic p-value of 0.000, suggesting that we can reject (at any significance level) the hypothesis that the coefficients on the excluded instruments are 0. Thus Angrist and Krueger appear to be correct that quarter of birth helps explain educational attainment and thus form a valid instrumental variable set. However, using the Stock-Yogo test, $F = 4.8$ is not high enough to reject the hypothesis that the instruments are weak. Specifically, for $\ell_2 = 30$ and 15% size, the critical value for the *F* statistic is 45. The actual value of 4.8 is far below 45. Since we cannot reject that the instruments are weak, this indicates that we cannot interpret the 2SLS estimates and test statistics in (12.89) as reliable.

Second, take (12.90) with the expanded regressor and instrument set. Estimating the corresponding reduced form, we find the *F* statistic for the 180 excluded instruments is $F = 2.43$, which also has an asymptotic p-value of 0.000, indicating that we can reject at any significance level the hypothesis that the excluded instruments have no effect on educational attainment. However, using the Stock-Yogo test, we also cannot reject the hypothesis that the instruments are weak. While Stock and Yogo did not calculate the critical values for $\ell_2 = 180$, the 2SLS critical values are increasing in ℓ_2, so we can use those for $\ell_2 = 30$ as a lower bound. The observed value of F = 2.43 is far below the level needed for significance. Consequently the results in (12.90) cannot be viewed as reliable. In particular, the observation that the standard errors in (12.90) are smaller than those in (12.89) should not be interpreted as evidence of greater precision. Instead, they should be viewed as evidence of unreliability due to weak instruments.

When instruments are weak, one constructive suggestion is to use LIML estimation rather than 2SLS. Another constructive suggestion is to alter the instrument set. While Angrist and Krueger used a large number of instrumental variables, we can consider a smaller set. Take equation (12.89). Rather than estimating it using the 30 interaction instruments, consider using only the three quarter-of-birth dummy variables. We report the reduced form estimates here:

$$\widehat{edu} = -\underset{(0.02)}{1.57}\ Black + \underset{(0.01)}{1.05}\ urban + \underset{(0.016)}{0.225}\ married + \underset{(0.016)}{0.050}\ Q_2 + \underset{(0.016)}{0.101}\ Q_3 + \underset{(0.016)}{0.142}\ Q_4 \tag{12.91}$$

where Q_2, Q_3, and Q_4 are dummy variables for birth in the 2nd, 3rd, and 4th quarters. The regression also includes nine year-of-birth and eight region-of-residence dummy variables.

The reduced form coefficients in (12.91) on the quarter-of-birth dummies are instructive. The coefficients are positive and increasing, consistent with the Angrist-Krueger hypothesis that individuals born later in the year achieve higher average education. Focusing on the weak instrument problem, the *F* test for exclusion of these three variables is F = 31. The Stock-Yogo critical value is 12.8 for $\ell_2 = 3$ and a size of 15%, and is 22.3 for a size of 10%. Since F = 31 exceeds both these thresholds, we can reject the hypothesis that this reduced form is weak. Estimating the model by 2SLS with these three instruments, we find

$$\widehat{\log(wage)} = \underset{(0.021)}{0.099}\ edu - \underset{(0.033)}{0.201}\ Black + \underset{(0.022)}{0.139}\ urban + \underset{(0.006)}{0.240}\ married. \tag{12.92}$$

These estimates indicate a slightly larger (10%) causal impact of education on wages but with a larger standard error. The Stock-Yogo analysis indicates that we can interpret the confidence intervals from these estimates as having asymptotic coverage of 85%.

While the original Angrist-Krueger estimates suffer due to weak instruments, their paper is a very creative and thoughtful application of the **natural experiment** methodology. They discovered a completely exogenous variation present in the world—birthdate—and showed how this has a small but measurable effect on educational attainment and thereby on earnings. Their crafting of this natural experiment regression is clever and demonstrates a style of analysis that can successfully underpin an effective instrumental variables empirical analysis.

12.42 PROGRAMMING

We now present Stata code for some of the empirical work reported in this chapter.

Stata do File for Card Example

```
use Card1995.dta, clear
set more off
gen exp = age76 - ed76 - 6
```

```
gen exp2 = (exp^2)/100
* Drop observations with missing wage
drop if lwage76==.
* Table 12.1 regressions
reg lwage76 ed76 exp exp2 black reg76r smsa76r, r
ivregress 2sls lwage76 exp exp2 black reg76r smsa76r (ed76=nearc4), r
ivregress 2sls lwage76 black reg76r smsa76r (ed76 exp exp2 = nearc4 age76 age2), r perfect
ivregress 2sls lwage76 exp exp2 black reg76r smsa76r (ed76=nearc4a nearc4b), r
ivregress 2sls lwage76 black reg76r smsa76r (ed76 exp exp2 = nearc4a nearc4b age76 age2), r perfect
ivregress liml lwage76 exp exp2 black reg76r smsa76r (ed76=nearc4a nearc4b), r
* Table 12.2 regressions
reg lwage76 exp exp2 black reg76r smsa76r nearc4, r
reg ed76 exp exp2 black reg76r smsa76r nearc4, r
reg ed76 black reg76r smsa76r nearc4 age76 age2, r
reg exp black reg76r smsa76r nearc4 age76 age2, r
reg exp2 black reg76r smsa76r nearc4 age76 age2, r
reg ed76 exp exp2 black reg76r smsa76r nearc4a nearc4b, r
reg lwage76 ed76 exp exp2 smsa76r reg76r, r
reg lwage76 nearc4 exp exp2 smsa76r reg76r, r
reg ed76 nearc4 exp exp2 smsa76r reg76r, r
```

Stata do File for Acemoglu-Johnson-Robinson Example

```
use AJR2001.dta, clear
reg loggdp risk
reg risk logmort0
predict u, residual
ivregress 2sls loggdp (risk=logmort0)
reg loggdp risk u
```

Stata do File for Angrist-Krueger Example

```
use AK1991.dta, clear
ivregress 2sls logwage black smsa married i.yob i.region (edu = i.qob#i.yob)
ivregress 2sls logwage black smsa married i.yob i.region i.state (edu = i.qob#i.yob i.qob#i.state)
reg edu black smsa married i.yob i.region i.qob#i.yob
testparm i.qob#i.yob
reg edu black smsa married i.yob i.region i.state i.qob#i.yob i.qob#i.state
testparm i.qob#i.yob i.qob#i.state
reg edu black smsa married i.yob i.region i.qob
testparm i.qob
ivregress 2sls logwage black smsa married i.yob i.region (edu = i.qob)
```

12.43 EXERCISES

Exercise 12.1 Consider the single equation model $Y = Z\beta + e$, where Y and Z are both real-valued (1×1). Let $\widehat{\beta}$ denote the IV estimator of β using as an instrument a dummy variable D (taking only the values 0 and 1). Find a simple expression for the IV estimator in this context.

Exercise 12.2 Consider the linear model $Y = X'\beta + e$ with $\mathbb{E}[e \mid X] = 0$. Suppose $\sigma^2(x) = \mathbb{E}\left[e^2 \mid X = x\right]$ is known. Show that the GLS estimator of β can be written as an IV estimator using some instrument Z. (Find an expression for Z.)

Exercise 12.3 Consider the linear model $Y = X'\beta + e$. Let the OLS estimator for β be $\widehat{\beta}$ with OLS residual $\widehat{e}_i$. Let the IV estimator for β using some instrument Z be $\widetilde{\beta}$ with IV residual $\widetilde{e}_i = Y_i - X_i'\widetilde{\beta}$. If X is indeed endogenous, will IV "fit" better than OLS in the sense that $\sum_{i=1}^n \widetilde{e}_i^2 < \sum_{i=1}^n \widehat{e}_i^2$, at least in large samples?

Exercise 12.4 The reduced form between the regressors X and instruments Z takes the form $X = \Gamma' Z + u$, where X is $k \times 1$, Z is $\ell \times 1$, and Γ is $\ell \times k$. The parameter Γ is defined by the population moment condition $\mathbb{E}\left[Zu'\right] = 0$. Show that the method of moments estimator for Γ is $\widehat{\Gamma} = \left(\boldsymbol{Z}'\boldsymbol{Z}\right)^{-1}\left(\boldsymbol{Z}'\boldsymbol{X}\right)$.

Exercise 12.5 In the structural model $Y = X'\beta + e$ with $X = \Gamma' Z + u$ and Γ $\ell \times k$, $\ell \geq k$, we claim that a necessary condition for β to be identified (i.e., can be recovered from the reduced form) is $\operatorname{rank}(\Gamma) = k$. Explain why this is true. That is, show that if $\operatorname{rank}(\Gamma) < k$, then β is not identified.

Exercise 12.6 For Theorem 12.3, establish that $\widehat{\boldsymbol{V}}_\beta \underset{p}{\longrightarrow} \boldsymbol{V}_\beta$.

Exercise 12.7 Consider the linear model $Y = X'\beta + e$ with $\mathbb{E}[e \mid X] = 0$, where X and β are 1×1.

(a) Show that $\mathbb{E}[Xe] = 0$ and $\mathbb{E}\left[X^2 e\right] = 0$. Is $Z = (X \quad X^2)'$ a valid instrument for estimation of β?

(b) Define the 2SLS estimator of β using Z as an instrument for X. How does this differ from OLS?

Exercise 12.8 Suppose that price and quantity are determined by the intersection of the linear demand and supply curves:

$$\begin{aligned} \text{Demand}: \quad & Q = a_0 + a_1 P + a_2 Y + e_1 \\ \text{Supply}: \quad & Q = b_0 + b_1 P + b_2 W + e_2 \end{aligned}$$

where income (Y) and wage (W) are determined outside the market. In this model, are the parameters identified?

Exercise 12.9 Consider the model $Y = X'\beta + e$ with $\mathbb{E}[e \mid Z] = 0$, with Y scalar and X and Z each a k vector. You have a random sample $(Y_i, X_i, Z_i : i = 1, \ldots, n)$.

(a) Assume that X is exogenous in the sense that $\mathbb{E}[e \mid Z, X] = 0$. Is the IV estimator $\widehat{\beta}_{\text{iv}}$ unbiased?

(b) Continuing to assume that X is exogenous, find the conditional covariance matrix $\operatorname{var}\left[\widehat{\beta}_{\text{iv}} \mid \boldsymbol{X}, \boldsymbol{Z}\right]$.

Exercise 12.10 Consider the model

$$\begin{aligned} Y &= X'\beta + e \\ X &= \Gamma' Z + u \end{aligned}$$

$$\mathbb{E}[Ze] = 0$$
$$\mathbb{E}\left[Zu'\right] = 0$$

with Y scalar and X and Z each a k vector. You have a random sample $(Y_i, X_i, Z_i : i = 1, \ldots, n)$. Take the control function equation to be $e = u'\gamma + v$ with $\mathbb{E}[uv] = 0$, and assume for simplicity that u is observed. Inserting into the structural equation, we find $Y = Z'\beta + u'\gamma + v$. The control function estimator $(\widehat{\beta}, \widehat{\gamma})$ is OLS estimation of this equation.

(a) Show that $\mathbb{E}[Xv] = 0$ (algebraically).

(b) Derive the asymptotic distribution of $(\widehat{\beta}, \widehat{\gamma})$.

Exercise 12.11 Consider the structural equation

$$Y = \beta_0 + \beta_1 X + \beta_2 X^2 + e \tag{12.93}$$

with $X \in \mathbb{R}$ treated as endogenous, so that $\mathbb{E}[Xe] \neq 0$. We have an instrument $Z \in \mathbb{R}$ that satisfies $\mathbb{E}[e \mid Z] = 0$, so in particular, $\mathbb{E}[e] = 0$, $\mathbb{E}[Ze] = 0$, and $\mathbb{E}\left[Z^2 e\right] = 0$.

(a) Should X^2 be treated as endogenous or exogenous?

(b) Suppose we have a scalar instrument Z that satisfies

$$X = \gamma_0 + \gamma_1 Z + u \tag{12.94}$$

with u independent of Z and mean 0.

Consider using $(1, Z, Z^2)$ as instruments. Is this a sufficient number of instruments? Is (12.93) just-identified, overidentified, or underidentified?

(c) Write out the reduced form equation for X^2. Under what condition on the reduced form parameters (12.94) are the parameters in (12.93) identified?

Exercise 12.12 Consider the structural equation and reduced form

$$Y = \beta X^2 + e$$
$$X = \gamma Z + u$$
$$\mathbb{E}[Ze] = 0$$
$$\mathbb{E}[Zu] = 0$$

with X^2 treated as endogenous so that $\mathbb{E}\left[X^2 e\right] \neq 0$. For simplicity, assume no intercepts. Y, Z, and X are scalar. Assume $\gamma \neq 0$. Consider the following estimator. First, estimate γ by OLS of X on Z and construct the fitted values $\widehat{X}_i = \widehat{\gamma} Z_i$. Second, estimate β by OLS of Y_i on $\left(\widehat{X}_i\right)^2$.

(a) Write out this estimator $\widehat{\beta}$ explicitly as a function of the sample.

(b) Find its probability limit as $n \to \infty$.

(c) In general, is $\widehat{\beta}$ consistent for β? Is there a reasonable condition under which $\widehat{\beta}$ is consistent?

Exercise 12.13 Consider the structural equation $Y_1 = Z_1'\beta_1 + Y_2'\beta_2 + e$ with $\mathbb{E}[Ze] = 0$, where Y_2 is $k_2 \times 1$ and is treated as endogenous. The variables $Z = (Z_1, Z_2)$ are treated as exogenous, where Z_2 is $\ell_2 \times 1$ and $\ell_2 \geq k_2$. You are interested in testing the hypothesis $\mathbb{H}_0 : \beta_2 = 0$.

Consider the reduced form equation for Y_1:

$$Y_1 = Z_1'\lambda_1 + Z_2'\lambda_2 + u_1. \tag{12.95}$$

Show how to test $\mathbb{H}_0$ using only the OLS estimates of (12.95).

Hint: This will require an analysis of the reduced form equations and their relation to the structural equation.

Exercise 12.14 Consider the linear instrumental variables equation $Y_1 = Z_1'\beta_1 + Y_2'\beta_2 + e$ with $\mathbb{E}[Ze] = 0$, where Z_1 is $k_1 \times 1$, Y_2 is $k_2 \times 1$, and Z is $\ell \times 1$, with $\ell \geq k = k_1 + k_2$. The sample size is n. Assume that $\boldsymbol{Q}_{ZZ} = \mathbb{E}[ZZ'] > 0$, and $Q_{ZX} = \mathbb{E}[ZX']$ has full rank k. Suppose that only (Y_1, Z_1, Z_2) are available and Y_2 is missing from the dataset. Consider the 2SLS estimator $\widehat{\beta}_1$ of β_1 obtained from the misspecified IV regression of Y_1 on Z_1 only, using Z_2 as an instrument for Z_1.

(a) Find a stochastic decomposition $\widehat{\beta}_1 = \beta_1 + b_{1n} + r_{1n}$, where r_{1n} depends on the error e, and b_{1n} does not depend on the error e.

(b) Show that $r_{1n} \to_p 0$ as $n \to \infty$.

(c) Find the probability limit of b_{1n} and $\widehat{\beta}_1$ as $n \to \infty$.

(d) Does $\widehat{\beta}_1$ suffer from "omitted variables bias"? Explain. Under what conditions is there no omitted variables bias?

(e) Find the asymptotic distribution as $n \to \infty$ of $\sqrt{n}\left(\widehat{\beta}_1 - \beta_1 - b_{1n}\right)$.

Exercise 12.15 Take the linear instrumental variables equation $Y_1 = Z\beta_1 + Y_2\beta_2 + e$ with $\mathbb{E}[e \mid Z] = 0$, where both X and Z are scalar 1×1.

(a) Can the coefficients (β_1, β_2) be estimated by 2SLS using Z as an instrument for Y_2?
Why or why not?

(b) Can the coefficients (β_1, β_2) be estimated by 2SLS using Z and Z^2 as instruments?

(c) For the 2SLS estimator suggested in (b), what is the implicit exclusion restriction?

(d) In (b), what is the implicit assumption about instrument relevance?
Hint: Write down the implied reduced form equation for Y_2.

(e) In a generic application, would you be comfortable with the assumptions in (c) and (d)?

Exercise 12.16 Consider a linear equation with endogeneity and a just-identified linear reduced form $Y = X\beta + e$ with $X = \gamma Z + u_2$, where both X and Z are scalar 1×1. Assume that $\mathbb{E}[Ze] = 0$ and $\mathbb{E}[Zu_2] = 0$.

(a) Derive the reduced form equation $Y = Z\lambda + u_1$. Show that $\beta = \lambda/\gamma$ if $\gamma \neq 0$, and that $\mathbb{E}[Zu] = 0$.

(b) Let $\widehat{\lambda}$ denote the OLS estimate from linear regression of Y on Z, and let $\widehat{\gamma}$ denote the OLS estimate from linear regression of X on Z. Write $\theta = (\lambda, \gamma)'$ and let $\widehat{\theta} = (\widehat{\lambda}, \widehat{\gamma})'$. Define $u = (u_1, u_2)$. Write $\sqrt{n}\left(\widehat{\theta} - \theta\right)$ using a single expression as a function of the error u.

(c) Show that $\mathbb{E}[Zu] = 0$.

(d) Derive the joint asymptotic distribution of $\sqrt{n}\left(\widehat{\theta} - \theta\right)$ as $n \to \infty$. Hint: Define $\Omega_u = \mathbb{E}\left[Z^2 uu'\right]$.

(e) Using the previous result and the delta method, find the asymptotic distribution of the indirect least squares estimator $\widehat{\beta} = \widehat{\lambda}/\widehat{\gamma}$.

(f) Is the answer in (e) the same as the asymptotic distribution of the 2SLS estimator in Theorem 12.2?

Hint: Show that $\begin{pmatrix} 1 & -\beta \end{pmatrix} u = e$ and $\begin{pmatrix} 1 & -\beta \end{pmatrix} \Omega_u \begin{pmatrix} 1 \\ -\beta \end{pmatrix} = \mathbb{E}\left[Z^2 e^2\right]$.

Exercise 12.17 Take the model $Y = X'\beta + e$ with $\mathbb{E}[Ze] = 0$, and consider the two-stage least squares estimator. The first-stage estimate is least squares of X on Z with least squares fitted values $\widehat{X}$. The second-stage is least squares of Y on $\widehat{X}$ with coefficient estimator $\widehat{\beta}$ and least squares residuals $\widehat{e}_i = Y_i - \widehat{X}_i\widehat{\beta}$. Consider $\widehat{\sigma}^2 = \frac{1}{n}\sum_{i=1}^n \widehat{e}_i^2$ as an estimator for $\sigma^2 = \mathbb{E}\left[e_i^2\right]$. Is this appropriate? If not, propose an alternative estimator.

Exercise 12.18 You have two independent i.i.d. samples $(Y_{1i}, X_{1i}, Z_{1i} : i = 1, \ldots, n)$ and $(Y_{2i}, X_{2i}, Z_{2i} : i = 1, \ldots, n)$. The dependent variables Y_1 and Y_2 are real-valued. The regressors X_1 and X_2 and instruments Z_1 and Z_2 are k-vectors. The model is standard just-identified linear instrumental variables:

$$
\begin{aligned}
Y_1 &= X_1'\beta_1 + e_1 \\
\mathbb{E}[Z_1 e_1] &= 0 \\
Y_2 &= X_2'\beta_2 + e_2 \\
\mathbb{E}[Z_2 e_2] &= 0.
\end{aligned}
$$

For concreteness, sample 1 consists of women and sample 2 consists of men. You want to test $\mathbb{H}_0 : \beta_1 = \beta_2$, that is, that the two samples have the same coefficients.

(a) Develop a test statistic for $\mathbb{H}_0$.

(b) Derive the asymptotic distribution of the test statistic.

(c) Describe (in brief) the testing procedure.

Exercise 12.19 You want to use household data to estimate β in the model $Y = X\beta + e$ with X scalar and endogenous, using as an instrument the state of residence.

(a) What are the assumptions needed to justify this choice of instrument?

(b) Is the model just-identified or overidentified?

Exercise 12.20 The model is $Y = X'\beta + e$ with $\mathbb{E}[Ze] = 0$. An economist wants to obtain the 2SLS estimates and standard errors for β. He uses the following steps:

- Regresses X on Z, obtains the predicted values $\widehat{X}$.
- Regresses Y on $\widehat{X}$, obtains the coefficient estimate $\widehat{\beta}$ and standard error $s(\widehat{\beta})$ from this regression.

Is this correct? Does this produce the 2SLS estimates and standard errors?

Exercise 12.21 In the linear model $Y = X\beta + e$ with $X \in \mathbb{R}$, suppose $\sigma^2(x) = \mathbb{E}\left[e^2 \mid X = x\right]$ is known. Show that the GLS estimator of β can be written as an instrumental variables estimator using some instrument Z. (Find an expression for Z.)

Exercise 12.22 You will replicate and extend the work reported in Acemoglu, Johnson, and Robinson (2001). The authors provided an expanded set of controls when they published their 2012 extension and posted the data on the AER website. This dataset is `AJR2001` on the textbook website.

(a) Estimate the OLS regression (12.86), the reduced form regression (12.87), and the 2SLS regression (12.88). (Which point estimate is different by 0.01 from the reported values? This is a common phenomenon in empirical replication).

(b) For the above estimates, calculate both homoskedastic and heteroskedastic-robust standard errors. Which were used by the authors (as reported in (12.86)–(12.88)?)

(c) Calculate the 2SLS estimates by the indirect least squares formula. Are they the same?

(d) Calculate the 2SLS estimates by the two-stage approach. Are they the same?

(e) Calculate the 2SLS estimates by the control variable approach. Are they the same?

(f) Acemoglu, Johnson, and Robinson (2001) reported many specifications including alternative regressor controls, for example, *latitude* and *africa*. Estimate by least squares the equation for logGDP adding *latitude* and *africa* as regressors. Does this regression suggest that *latitude* and *africa* are predictive of the level of GDP?

(g) Now estimate the same equation as in (f) but by 2SLS using log(mortality) as an instrument for *risk*. How does the interpretation of the effect of *latitude* and *africa* change?

(h) Return to our baseline model (without including *latitude* and *africa*). The authors' reduced form equation uses log(*mortality*) as the instrument, rather than, say, the level of mortality. Estimate the reduced form for risk with *mortality* as the instrument. (This variable is not provided in the dataset, so you need to take the exponential of log(*mortality*).) Can you explain why the authors preferred the equation with log(*mortality*)?

(i) Try an alternative reduced form including both log(*mortality*) and the square of log(*mortality*). Interpret the results. Re-estimate the structural equation by 2SLS using both log(*mortality*) and its square as instruments. How do the results change?

(j) For the estimates in (i), are the instruments strong or weak using the Stock-Yogo test?

(k) Calculate and interpret a test for exogeneity of the instruments.

(l) Estimate the equation by LIML using the instruments log(*mortality*) and the square of log(*mortality*).

Exercise 12.23 In Exercise 12.22, you extended the work reported in Acemoglu, Johnson, and Robinson (2001). Consider the 2SLS regression (12.88). Compute the standard errors both by the asymptotic formula and by the bootstrap using a large number (10,000) of bootstrap replications. Recalculate the bootstrap standard errors. Comment on the reliability of bootstrap standard errors for IV regression.

Exercise 12.24 You will replicate and extend the work reported in the chapter relating to Card (1995). The data are from the Card's website and are posted as `Card1995` on the textbook website. The model we focus on is labeled 2SLS(a) in Table 12.1, which uses *public* and *private* as instruments for *edu*. The variables you will need for this exercise include *lwage76*, *ed76* , *age76*, *smsa76r*, *reg76r*, *nearc2*, *nearc4*, *nearc4a*, *nearc4b*. See the description file for definitions. Experience is not in the dataset, so it needs to be generated as $age - edu - 6$.

(a) First, replicate the reduced form regression presented in the final column of Table 12.2, and the 2SLS regression described above (using *public* and *private* as instruments for *edu*) to verify that you have the same variable defintions.

(b) Try a different reduced form model. The variable *nearc2* means "grew up near a 2-year college." See if adding it to the reduced form equation is useful.

(c) Try more interactions in the reduced form. Create the interactions *nearc4a*age76* and *nearc4a* age76*$^2/100$, and add them to the reduced form equation. Estimate this by least squares. Interpret the coefficients on the two new variables.

(d) Estimate the structural equation by 2SLS using the expanded instrument set

$\{nearc4a, nearc4b, nearc4a{*}age76, nearc4a{*}age76^2/100\}$.
What is the impact on the structural estimate of the return to schooling?

(e) Using the Stock-Yogo test, are the instruments strong or weak?

(f) Test the hypothesis that *edu* is exogenous for the structural return to schooling.

(g) Re-estimate the last equation by LIML. Do the results change meaningfully?

Exercise 12.25 In Exercise 12.24, you extended the work reported in Card (1995). Now, estimate the IV equation corresponding to the IV(a) column of Table 12.1, which is the baseline specification considered in Card. Use the bootstrap to calculate a BC percentile confidence interval. In this example, should you also report the bootstrap standard error?

Exercise 12.26 You will extend Angrist and Krueger (1991) using the data file `AK1991` on the textbook website. Their Table VIII reports estimates of an analog of (12.90) for the subsample of 26,913 Black men. Use this subsample for the following analysis.

(a) Estimate an equation which is identical in form to (12.90) with the same additional regressors (year-of-birth, region-of-residence, and state-of-birth dummy variables) and 180 excluded instrumental variables (the interactions of quarter-of-birth times year-of-birth dummy variables, and quarter-of-birth times state-of-birth interactions), but use the subsample of Black men. One regressor must be omitted to achieve identification. Which variable is this?

(b) Estimate the reduced form for part (a) by least squares. Calculate the F statistic for the excluded instruments. What do you conclude about the strength of the instruments?

(c) Repeat part (b), estimating the reduced form for the analog of (12.89), which has 30 excluded instrumental variables and does not include the state-of-birth dummy variables in the regression. What do you conclude about the strength of the instruments?

(d) Repeat part (c), estimating the reduced form for the analog of (12.92), which has only three excluded instrumental variables. Are the instruments sufficiently strong for 2SLS estimation? For LIML estimation?

(e) Estimate the structural wage equation using what you believe is the most appropriate set of regressors, instruments, and the most appropriate estimation method. What is the estimated return to education (for the subsample of Black men) and its standard error? Without doing a formal hypothesis test, do these results appear meaningfully different from the results for the full sample? If they do appear to be different, in which way do they differ?

Exercise 12.27 In Exercise 12.26, you extended the work reported in Angrist and Krueger (1991) by estimating wage equations for the subsample of Black men. Re-estimate equation (12.92) for this group using as instruments only the three quarter-of-birth dummy variables. Calculate the standard error for the return to education by asymptotic and bootstrap methods. Calculate a BC percentile interval. In this application of 2SLS, is it appropriate to report the bootstrap standard error?

CHAPTER 13

GENERALIZED METHOD OF MOMENTS

13.1 INTRODUCTION

One of the most popular estimation methods in applied econometrics is the generalized method of moments (GMM). GMM generalizes the classical method of moments by allowing for more equations than unknown parameters (so they are overidentified) and by allowing general nonlinear functions of the observations and parameters. Together, these generalizations allow for a fairly rich and flexible estimation framework. GMM includes as special cases OLS, IV, multivariate regression, and 2SLS. It includes both linear and nonlinear models. In this chapter, we focus primarily on linear models.

The GMM label and methods were introduced to econometrics in a seminal paper by Lars Hansen (1982). The ideas and methods build on the work of Amemiya (1974, 1977), Gallant (1977), and Gallant and Jorgenson (1979). The ideas are closely related to the contemporaneous work of Halbert White (1980, 1982) and White and Domowitz (1984). The methods are also related to what are called **estimating equations** in the statistics literature. For a review of the latter, see Godambe (1991).

13.2 MOMENT EQUATION MODELS

All of the models that have been introduced so far can be written as **moment equation models**, where the population parameters solve a system of moment equations. Moment equation models are broader than the models so far considered, and understanding their common structure opens up straightforward techniques to handle new econometric models.

Moment equation models take the following form. Let $g_i(\beta)$ be a known $\ell \times 1$ function of the ith observation and a $k \times 1$ parameter β. A moment equation model is summarized by the moment equations

$$\mathbb{E}\left[g_i(\beta)\right] = 0 \tag{13.1}$$

and a parameter space $\beta \in B$. For example, in the instrumental variables model, $g_i(\beta) = Z_i\left(Y_i - X_i'\beta\right)$.

In general, we say that a parameter β is **identified** if there is a unique mapping from the data distribution to β. In the context of the model (13.1), this means that there is a unique β satisfying (13.1). Since (13.1) is a system of ℓ equations with k unknowns, it is necessary that $\ell \geq k$ for there to be a unique solution. If $\ell = k$, we say that the model is **just-identified**, meaning that there is just enough information to identify the parameters. If $\ell > k$, we say that the model is **overidentified**, meaning that there is excess information. If $\ell < k$ we say that the model is **underidentified**, meaning that there is insufficient information to identify the parameters. In general, we assume that $\ell \geq k$, so the model is either just-identified or overidentified.

13.3 METHOD OF MOMENTS ESTIMATORS

In this section, we consider the just-identified case $\ell = k$.

Define the sample analog of (13.1)

$$\overline{g}_n(\beta) = \frac{1}{n}\sum_{i=1}^{n} g_i(\beta). \tag{13.2}$$

The **method of moments estimator (MME)** $\widehat{\beta}_{\mathrm{mm}}$ is the parameter value that sets $\overline{g}_n(\beta) = 0$. Thus

$$\overline{g}_n(\widehat{\beta}_{\mathrm{mm}}) = \frac{1}{n}\sum_{i=1}^{n} g_i(\widehat{\beta}_{\mathrm{mm}}) = 0. \tag{13.3}$$

The equations (13.3) are known as the **estimating equations**, as they are the equations that determine the estimator $\widehat{\beta}_{\mathrm{mm}}$.

In some contexts (such as those discussed in the examples below), there is an explicit solution for $\widehat{\beta}_{\mathrm{mm}}$. In other cases, the solution must be found numerically.

We now show how most of the estimators discussed so far in the textbook can be written as MMEs.

Mean: Set $g_i(\mu) = Y_i - \mu$. The MME is $\widehat{\mu} = \frac{1}{n}\sum_{i=1}^{n} Y_i$.

Mean and variance: Set

$$g_i\left(\mu, \sigma^2\right) = \begin{pmatrix} Y_i - \mu \\ (Y_i - \mu)^2 - \sigma^2 \end{pmatrix}.$$

The MME are $\widehat{\mu} = \frac{1}{n}\sum_{i=1}^{n} Y_i$ and $\widehat{\sigma}^2 = \frac{1}{n}\sum_{i=1}^{n}(Y_i - \widehat{\mu})^2$.

OLS: Set $g_i(\beta) = X_i\left(Y_i - X_i'\beta\right)$. The MME is $\widehat{\beta} = \left(\boldsymbol{X}'\boldsymbol{X}\right)^{-1}\left(\boldsymbol{X}'\boldsymbol{Y}\right)$.

OLS and variance: Set

$$g_i\left(\beta, \sigma^2\right) = \begin{pmatrix} X_i\left(Y_i - X_i'\beta\right) \\ \left(Y_i - X_i'\beta\right)^2 - \sigma^2 \end{pmatrix}.$$

The MME is $\widehat{\beta} = \left(\boldsymbol{X}'\boldsymbol{X}\right)^{-1}\left(\boldsymbol{X}'\boldsymbol{Y}\right)$, and $\widehat{\sigma}^2 = \frac{1}{n}\sum_{i=1}^{n}\left(Y_i - X_i'\widehat{\beta}\right)^2$.

Multivariate least squares, vector form: Set $g_i(\beta) = \overline{X}_i'\left(Y_i - \overline{X}_i\beta\right)$. The MME is $\widehat{\beta} = \left(\sum_{i=1}^{n}\overline{X}_i'\overline{X}_i\right)^{-1}\left(\sum_{i=1}^{n}\overline{X}_i Y_i\right)$, which is (11.4).

Multivariate least squares, matrix form: Set $g_i(\boldsymbol{B}) = \operatorname{vec}\left(X_i\left(Y_i' - X_i'\boldsymbol{B}\right)\right)$. The MME is $\widehat{\boldsymbol{B}} = \left(\sum_{i=1}^{n} X_i X_i'\right)^{-1}\left(\sum_{i=1}^{n} X_i Y_i'\right)$, which is (11.6).

Seemingly unrelated regression: Set

$$g_i(\beta, \Sigma) = \begin{pmatrix} \overline{X}_i\Sigma^{-1}\left(Y_i - \overline{X}_i'\beta\right) \\ \operatorname{vec}\left(\Sigma - \left(Y_i - \overline{X}_i'\beta\right)\left(Y_i - \overline{X}_i'\beta\right)'\right) \end{pmatrix}.$$

The MME is $\widehat{\beta}=\left(\sum_{i=1}^{n}\overline{X}_i\widehat{\Sigma}^{-1}\overline{X}_i'\right)^{-1}\left(\sum_{i=1}^{n}\overline{X}_i\widehat{\Sigma}^{-1}Y_i\right)$, and $\widehat{\Sigma}=n^{-1}\sum_{i=1}^{n}\left(Y_i-\overline{X}_i'\widehat{\beta}\right)\left(Y_i-\overline{X}_i'\widehat{\beta}\right)'$.

IV: Set $g_i(\beta)=Z_i\left(Y_i-X_i'\beta\right)$. The MME is $\widehat{\beta}=\left(\boldsymbol{Z}'\boldsymbol{X}\right)^{-1}\left(\boldsymbol{Z}'\boldsymbol{Y}\right)$.

Generated regressors: Set

$$g_i(\beta,\boldsymbol{A})=\begin{pmatrix}\boldsymbol{A}'Z_i\left(Y_i-Z_i'\boldsymbol{A}\beta\right)\\ \operatorname{vec}\left(Z_i\left(X_i'-Z_i'\boldsymbol{A}\right)\right)\end{pmatrix}.$$

The MME is $\widehat{\boldsymbol{A}}=\left(\sum_{i=1}^{n}Z_iZ_i'\right)^{-1}\left(\sum_{i=1}^{n}Z_iX_i'\right)$, and $\widehat{\beta}=\left(\widehat{\boldsymbol{A}}'\boldsymbol{Z}'\boldsymbol{Z}\widehat{\boldsymbol{A}}\right)^{-1}\left(\widehat{\boldsymbol{A}}'\boldsymbol{Z}'\boldsymbol{Y}\right)$.

A common feature of these examples is that the estimator can be written as the solution to a set of estimating equations (13.3). This provides a common framework, which enables a convenient development of a unified distribution theory.

13.4 OVERIDENTIFIED MOMENT EQUATIONS

In the instrumental variables model, $g_i(\beta)=Z_i\left(Y_i-X_i'\beta\right)$. Thus (13.2) is

$$\overline{g}_n(\beta)=\frac{1}{n}\sum_{i=1}^{n}g_i(\beta)=\frac{1}{n}\sum_{i=1}^{n}Z_i\left(Y_i-X_i'\beta\right)=\frac{1}{n}\left(\boldsymbol{Z}'\boldsymbol{Y}-\boldsymbol{Z}'\boldsymbol{X}\beta\right).\tag{13.4}$$

We have defined the method of moments estimator for β as the parameter value that sets $\overline{g}_n(\beta)=0$. However, when the model is overidentified (if $\ell>k$), this is generally impossible, as there are more equations than free parameters. Equivalently, there is no choice of β that sets (13.4) to 0. Thus the method of moments estimator is not defined for the overidentified case.

While we cannot find an estimator that sets $\overline{g}_n(\beta)$ equal to 0, we can try to find an estimator that makes $\overline{g}_n(\beta)$ as close to 0 as possible.

One way to think about this is to define the vector $\mu=\boldsymbol{Z}'\boldsymbol{Y}$, the matrix $\boldsymbol{G}=\boldsymbol{Z}'\boldsymbol{X}$, and the "error" $\eta=\mu-\boldsymbol{G}\beta$. Then we can write (13.4) as $\mu=\boldsymbol{G}\beta+\eta$. This looks like a regression equation with the $\ell\times 1$ dependent variable μ, the $\ell\times k$ regressor matrix $\boldsymbol{G}$, and the $\ell\times 1$ error vector η. The goal is to make the error vector η as small as possible. Recalling our knowledge about least squares, we deduce that a simple method is to regress μ on $\boldsymbol{G}$, obtaining $\widehat{\beta}=\left(\boldsymbol{G}'\boldsymbol{G}\right)^{-1}\left(\boldsymbol{G}'\mu\right)$, which minimizes the sum-of-squares $\eta'\eta$. This is certainly one way to make η "small."

More generally, we know that when errors are nonhomogeneous, it can be more efficient to estimate by weighted least squares. Thus for some weight matrix $\boldsymbol{W}$, consider the estimator

$$\widehat{\beta}=\left(\boldsymbol{G}'\boldsymbol{W}\boldsymbol{G}\right)^{-1}\left(\boldsymbol{G}'\boldsymbol{W}\mu\right)=\left(\boldsymbol{X}'\boldsymbol{Z}\boldsymbol{W}\boldsymbol{Z}'\boldsymbol{X}\right)^{-1}\left(\boldsymbol{X}'\boldsymbol{Z}\boldsymbol{W}\boldsymbol{Z}'\boldsymbol{Y}\right).$$

This minimizes the weighted sum of squares $\eta'\boldsymbol{W}\eta$. This solution is known as the **generalized method of moments (GMM)**.

The estimator is typically defined as follows. Given a set of moment equations (13.2) and an $\ell\times\ell$ weight matrix $\boldsymbol{W}>0$, the GMM criterion function is defined as

$$J(\beta)=n\,\overline{g}_n(\beta)'\boldsymbol{W}\,\overline{g}_n(\beta).$$

The factor "n" is not important for the definition of the estimator but is convenient for the distribution theory. The criterion $J(\beta)$ is the weighted sum of squared moment equation errors. When $\boldsymbol{W}=\boldsymbol{I}_{\ell}$, then $J(\beta)=n\overline{g}_n(\beta)'\overline{g}_n(\beta)=n\left\|\overline{g}_n(\beta)\right\|^2$, the square of the Euclidean length. Since we restrict attention to positive definite weight matrices $\boldsymbol{W}$, the criterion $J(\beta)$ is nonnegative.

Definition 13.1 The **Generalized Method of Moments (GMM)** estimator is

$$\widehat{\beta}_{\mathrm{gmm}}=\underset{\beta}{\operatorname{argmin}}\, J(\beta).$$

Recall that in the just-identified case $k=\ell$, the method of moments estimator $\widehat{\beta}_{\mathrm{mm}}$ solves $\overline{g}_n(\widehat{\beta}_{\mathrm{mm}})=0$. Hence in this case, $J(\widehat{\beta}_{\mathrm{mm}})=0$, which means that $\widehat{\beta}_{\mathrm{mm}}$ minimizes $J(\beta)$ and equals $\widehat{\beta}_{\mathrm{gmm}}=\widehat{\beta}_{\mathrm{mm}}$. Thus GMM includes MME as a special case, which implies that all of our results for GMM apply to any method of moments estimator.

In the overidentified case, the GMM estimator depends on the choice of weight matrix $\boldsymbol{W}$, and so this is an important focus of the theory. In the just-identified case, the GMM estimator simplifies to the MME, which does not depend on $\boldsymbol{W}$.

The method and theory of GMM was developed in an influential paper by Lars Hansen (1982). This paper introduced the method, its asymptotic distribution, the form of the efficient weight matrix, and tests for overidentification.

13.5 LINEAR MOMENT MODELS

One of the great advantages of the moment equation framework is that it allows both linear and nonlinear models. However, when the moment equations are linear in the parameters, then we have explicit solutions for the estimates and a straightforward asymptotic distribution theory. Hence we start by confining our attention to linear moment equations and will return to nonlinear moment equations later. In the examples listed earlier, the estimators that have linear moment equations include the sample mean, OLS, multivariate least squares, IV, and 2SLS. The estimates that have nonlinear moment equations include the sample variance, SUR, and generated regressors.

In particular, we focus on the overidentified IV model with moment equations

$$g_i(\beta)=Z_i(Y_i-X_i'\beta) \tag{13.5}$$

where Z_i is $\ell\times 1$, and X_i is $k\times 1$.

13.6 GMM ESTIMATOR

Given (13.5), the sample moment equations are (13.4). The GMM criterion can be written as

$$J(\beta)=n\left(\boldsymbol{Z}'\boldsymbol{Y}-\boldsymbol{Z}'\boldsymbol{X}\beta\right)'\boldsymbol{W}\left(\boldsymbol{Z}'\boldsymbol{Y}-\boldsymbol{Z}'\boldsymbol{X}\beta\right).$$

The GMM estimator minimizes $J(\beta)$. The first order conditions are

$$0=\frac{\partial}{\partial\beta}J(\widehat{\beta})$$

$$= 2n\frac{\partial}{\partial\beta}\overline{g}_n(\widehat{\beta})'\boldsymbol{W}\overline{g}_n(\widehat{\beta})$$

$$= -2n\left(\frac{1}{n}\boldsymbol{X}'\boldsymbol{Z}\right)\boldsymbol{W}\left(\frac{1}{n}\boldsymbol{Z}'\left(\boldsymbol{Y}-\boldsymbol{X}\widehat{\beta}\right)\right).$$

The solution is given as follows.

Theorem 13.1 For the overidentified IV model,

$$\widehat{\beta}_{\mathrm{gmm}} = \left(\boldsymbol{X}'\boldsymbol{Z}\boldsymbol{W}\boldsymbol{Z}'\boldsymbol{X}\right)^{-1}\left(\boldsymbol{X}'\boldsymbol{Z}\boldsymbol{W}\boldsymbol{Z}'\boldsymbol{Y}\right). \tag{13.6}$$

While the estimator depends on $\boldsymbol{W}$, the dependence is only up to scale. This is because if $\boldsymbol{W}$ is replaced by $c\boldsymbol{W}$ for some $c > 0$, $\widehat{\beta}_{\mathrm{gmm}}$ does not change. When $\boldsymbol{W}$ is fixed by the user, we call $\widehat{\beta}_{\mathrm{gmm}}$ a **one-step GMM** estimator. The formula (13.6) applies for the overidentified ($\ell > k$) and the just-identified ($\ell = k$) cases. When the model is just-identified, then $\boldsymbol{X}'\boldsymbol{Z}$ is $k \times k$, so expression (13.6) simplifies to

$$\widehat{\beta}_{\mathrm{gmm}} = \left(\boldsymbol{Z}'\boldsymbol{X}\right)^{-1}\boldsymbol{W}^{-1}\left(\boldsymbol{X}'\boldsymbol{Z}\right)^{-1}\left(\boldsymbol{X}'\boldsymbol{Z}\boldsymbol{W}\boldsymbol{Z}'\boldsymbol{Y}\right) = \left(\boldsymbol{Z}'\boldsymbol{X}\right)^{-1}\left(\boldsymbol{Z}'\boldsymbol{Y}\right) = \widehat{\beta}_{\mathrm{iv}}$$

the IV estimator.

The GMM estimator (13.6) resembles the 2SLS estimator (12.29). In fact, they are equal when $\boldsymbol{W} = \left(\boldsymbol{Z}'\boldsymbol{Z}\right)^{-1}$. Thus the 2SLS estimator is a one-step GMM estimator for the linear model.

Theorem 13.2 If $\boldsymbol{W} = \left(\boldsymbol{Z}'\boldsymbol{Z}\right)^{-1}$, then $\widehat{\beta}_{\mathrm{gmm}} = \widehat{\beta}_{\mathrm{2sls}}$. Furthermore, if $k = \ell$, then $\widehat{\beta}_{\mathrm{gmm}} = \widehat{\beta}_{\mathrm{iv}}$.

13.7 DISTRIBUTION OF GMM ESTIMATOR

Let $\boldsymbol{Q} = \mathbb{E}\left[ZX'\right]$ and $\Omega = \mathbb{E}\left[ZZ'e^2\right]$. Then

$$\left(\frac{1}{n}\boldsymbol{X}'\boldsymbol{Z}\right)\boldsymbol{W}\left(\frac{1}{n}\boldsymbol{Z}'\boldsymbol{X}\right) \underset{p}{\longrightarrow} \boldsymbol{Q}'\boldsymbol{W}\boldsymbol{Q}$$

and

$$\left(\frac{1}{n}\boldsymbol{X}'\boldsymbol{Z}\right)\boldsymbol{W}\left(\frac{1}{\sqrt{n}}\boldsymbol{Z}'\boldsymbol{e}\right) \underset{d}{\longrightarrow} \boldsymbol{Q}'\boldsymbol{W}\,\mathrm{N}\left(0,\Omega\right).$$

We conclude that the following theorem is true.

Theorem 13.3 Asymptotic Distribution of GMM Estimator. Under Assumption 12.2, as $n \to \infty$, $\sqrt{n}\left(\widehat{\beta}_{\mathrm{gmm}} - \beta\right) \underset{d}{\longrightarrow} \mathrm{N}\left(0, \boldsymbol{V}_{\beta}\right)$, where

$$\boldsymbol{V}_{\beta} = \left(\boldsymbol{Q}'\boldsymbol{W}\boldsymbol{Q}\right)^{-1}\left(\boldsymbol{Q}'\boldsymbol{W}\Omega\boldsymbol{W}\boldsymbol{Q}\right)\left(\boldsymbol{Q}'\boldsymbol{W}\boldsymbol{Q}\right)^{-1}. \tag{13.7}$$

The GMM estimator is asymptotically normal with a “sandwich form” asymptotic variance.

Our derivation treated the weight matrix $\boldsymbol{W}$ as if it were nonrandom, but Theorem 13.3 applies to the random weight matrix case so long as $\widehat{\boldsymbol{W}}$ converges in probability to a positive definite limit $\boldsymbol{W}$. This may require scaling the weight matrix, for example, replacing $\widehat{\boldsymbol{W}} = \left(\boldsymbol{Z}'\boldsymbol{Z}\right)^{-1}$ with $\widehat{\boldsymbol{W}} = \left(n^{-1}\boldsymbol{Z}'\boldsymbol{Z}\right)^{-1}$. Since rescaling the weight matrix does not affect the estimator, this rescaling is ignored in implementation.

13.8 EFFICIENT GMM

The asymptotic distribution of the GMM estimator $\widehat{\beta}_{\text{gmm}}$ depends on the weight matrix $\boldsymbol{W}$ through the asymptotic variance $\boldsymbol{V}_\beta$. The asymptotically optimal weight matrix $\boldsymbol{W}_0$ is that which minimizes $\boldsymbol{V}_\beta$, which turns out to be $\boldsymbol{W}_0 = \Omega^{-1}$. The proof is left to Exercise 13.4.

When the GMM estimator $\widehat{\beta}$ is constructed with $\boldsymbol{W} = \boldsymbol{W}_0 = \Omega^{-1}$ (or a weight matrix that is a consistent estimator of $\boldsymbol{W}_0$), we call it the **efficient GMM** estimator:

$$\widehat{\beta}_{\text{gmm}} = \left(\boldsymbol{X}'\boldsymbol{Z}\Omega^{-1}\boldsymbol{Z}'\boldsymbol{X}\right)^{-1}\left(\boldsymbol{X}'\boldsymbol{Z}\Omega^{-1}\boldsymbol{Z}'\boldsymbol{Y}\right).$$

Its asymptotic distribution takes a simpler form than in Theorem 13.3. By substituting $\boldsymbol{W} = \boldsymbol{W}_0 = \Omega^{-1}$ into (13.7), we find

$$\boldsymbol{V}_\beta = \left(\boldsymbol{Q}'\Omega^{-1}\boldsymbol{Q}\right)^{-1}\left(\boldsymbol{Q}'\Omega^{-1}\Omega\Omega^{-1}\boldsymbol{Q}\right)\left(\boldsymbol{Q}'\Omega^{-1}\boldsymbol{Q}\right)^{-1} = \left(\boldsymbol{Q}'\Omega^{-1}\boldsymbol{Q}\right)^{-1}.$$

This is the asymptotic variance of the efficient GMM estimator.

Theorem 13.4 Asymptotic Distribution of GMM with Efficient Weight Matrix. Under Assumption 12.2 and $\boldsymbol{W} = \Omega^{-1}$, as $n \to \infty$, $\sqrt{n}\left(\widehat{\beta}_{\text{gmm}} - \beta\right) \underset{d}{\longrightarrow} \mathrm{N}\left(0, \boldsymbol{V}_\beta\right)$, where $\boldsymbol{V}_\beta = \left(\boldsymbol{Q}'\Omega^{-1}\boldsymbol{Q}\right)^{-1}$.

Theorem 13.5 Efficient GMM. Under Assumption 12.2, for any $\boldsymbol{W} > 0$,

$$\left(\boldsymbol{Q}'\boldsymbol{W}\boldsymbol{Q}\right)^{-1}\left(\boldsymbol{Q}'\boldsymbol{W}\Omega\boldsymbol{W}\boldsymbol{Q}\right)\left(\boldsymbol{Q}'\boldsymbol{W}\boldsymbol{Q}\right)^{-1} - \left(\boldsymbol{Q}'\Omega^{-1}\boldsymbol{Q}\right)^{-1} \geq 0.$$

Thus if $\widehat{\beta}_{\text{gmm}}$ is the efficient GMM estimator and $\widetilde{\beta}_{\text{gmm}}$ is another GMM estimator, then

$$\operatorname{avar}\left[\widehat{\beta}_{\text{gmm}}\right] \leq \operatorname{avar}\left[\widetilde{\beta}_{\text{gmm}}\right].$$

For a proof, see Exercise 13.4.

Thus the smallest possible GMM covariance matrix (in the positive definite sense) is achieved by the efficient GMM weight matrix.

$\boldsymbol{W}_0 = \Omega^{-1}$ is not known in practice, but it can be estimated consistently, as we discuss in Section 13.10. For any $\widehat{\boldsymbol{W}} \underset{p}{\longrightarrow} \boldsymbol{W}_0$, the asymptotic distribution in Theorem 13.4 is unaffected. Consequently, we call any $\widehat{\beta}_{\text{gmm}}$ constructed with an estimate of the efficient weight matrix an efficient GMM estimator.

By "efficient" we mean that this estimator has the smallest asymptotic variance in the class of GMM estimators with this set of moment conditions. This is a weak concept of optimality, as we are only considering alternative weight matrices $\widehat{\boldsymbol{W}}$. However, it turns out that the GMM estimator is semiparametrically efficient, as shown by Gary Chamberlain (1987). If it is known that $\mathbb{E}\left[g_i(\beta)\right]=0$ and this is all that is known, this is a semiparametric problem, because the distribution of the data is unknown. Chamberlain showed that in this context, no semiparametric estimator (one that is consistent globally for the class of models considered) can have a smaller asymptotic variance than $\left(\boldsymbol{G}'\Omega^{-1}\boldsymbol{G}\right)^{-1}$, where $\boldsymbol{G}=\mathbb{E}\left[\frac{\partial}{\partial\beta'}g_i(\beta)\right]$. Since the GMM estimator has this asymptotic variance, it is semiparametrically efficient.

The results in this section show that in the linear model, no estimator has better asymptotic efficiency than the efficient linear GMM estimator. No estimator can do better (in this first-order asymptotic sense) without imposing additional assumptions.

13.9 EFFICIENT GMM VERSUS 2SLS

For the linear model, we introduced 2SLS as a standard estimator for β. Now we have introduced GMM, which includes 2SLS as a special case. Is there a context where 2SLS is efficient?

To answer this question, recall that 2SLS is GMM given the weight matrix $\widehat{\boldsymbol{W}}=\left(\boldsymbol{Z}'\boldsymbol{Z}\right)^{-1}$ or equivalently, $\widehat{\boldsymbol{W}}=\left(n^{-1}\boldsymbol{Z}'\boldsymbol{Z}\right)^{-1}$, since scaling doesn't matter. Since $\widehat{\boldsymbol{W}}\underset{p}{\longrightarrow}\left(\mathbb{E}\left[ZZ'\right]\right)^{-1}$, this is asymptotically equivalent to the weight matrix $\boldsymbol{W}=\left(\mathbb{E}\left[ZZ'\right]\right)^{-1}$. In contrast, the efficient weight matrix takes the form $\left(\mathbb{E}\left[ZZ'e^2\right]\right)^{-1}$. Now suppose that the structural equation error e is conditionally homoskedastic in the sense that $\mathbb{E}\left[e^2\mid Z\right]=\sigma^2$. Then the efficient weight matrix equals $\boldsymbol{W}=\left(\mathbb{E}\left[ZZ'\right]\right)^{-1}\sigma^{-2}$ or equivalently, $\boldsymbol{W}=\left(\mathbb{E}\left[ZZ'\right]\right)^{-1}$, since scaling doesn't matter. The latter weight matrix is the same as the 2SLS asymptotic weight matrix. Thus the 2SLS weight matrix is the efficient weight matrix under conditional homoskedasticity.

Theorem 13.6 Under Assumption 12.2 and $\mathbb{E}\left[e^2\mid Z\right]=\sigma^2$, $\widehat{\beta}_{\text{2sls}}$ is efficient GMM.

Theorem 13.6 shows that 2SLS is efficient under homoskedasticity. When homoskedasticity holds, there is no reason to use efficient GMM over 2SLS. More broadly, when homoskedasticity is a reasonable approximation, then 2SLS will be a reasonable estimator. However, this result also shows that in the general case where the error is conditionally heteroskedastic, 2SLS is inefficient relative to efficient GMM.

13.10 ESTIMATION OF THE EFFICIENT WEIGHT MATRIX

To construct the efficient GMM estimator, we need a consistent estimator $\widehat{\boldsymbol{W}}$ of $\boldsymbol{W}_0=\Omega^{-1}$. The convention is to form an estimator $\widehat{\Omega}$ of Ω and then set $\widehat{\boldsymbol{W}}=\widehat{\Omega}^{-1}$.

The **two-step GMM estimator** proceeds by using a one-step consistent estimator of β to construct the weight matrix estimator $\widehat{\boldsymbol{W}}$. In the linear model, the natural one-step estimator for β is 2SLS. Set $\widetilde{e}_i=Y_i-X_i'\widehat{\beta}_{\text{2sls}}$, $\widetilde{g}_i=g_i(\widetilde{\beta})=Z_i\widetilde{e}_i$, and $\overline{g}_n=n^{-1}\sum_{i=1}^n\widetilde{g}_i$. Two moment estimators of Ω are

$$\widehat{\Omega}=\frac{1}{n}\sum_{i=1}^n\widetilde{g}_i\widetilde{g}_i' \tag{13.8}$$

and

$$\widehat{\Omega}^*=\frac{1}{n}\sum_{i=1}^n\left(\widetilde{g}_i-\overline{g}_n\right)\left(\widetilde{g}_i-\overline{g}_n\right)'. \tag{13.9}$$

The estimator (13.8) is an uncentered covariance matrix estimator, while the estimator (13.9) is a centered version. Either is consistent when $\mathbb{E}[Ze]=0$, which holds under correct specification. However, under misspecification, we may have $\mathbb{E}[Ze]\neq 0$. In the latter context, $\widehat{\Omega}^*$ remains an estimator of $\operatorname{var}[Ze]$, while $\widehat{\Omega}$ is an estimator of $\mathbb{E}\left[ZZ'e^2\right]$. In this sense, $\widehat{\Omega}^*$ is a robust variance estimator. For some testing problems, it turns out to be preferable to use a covariance matrix estimator, which is robust to the alternative hypothesis. For these reasons, estimator (13.9) is generally preferred. The uncentered estimator (13.8) is more commonly seen in practice, since it is the default choice by most software packages. It is also worth observing that when the model is just-identified, then $\overline{g}_n=0$, so the two are algebraically identical. The choice of weight matrix may also impact covariance matrix estimation, as discussed in Section 13.12.

Given the choice of covariance matrix estimator, we set $\widehat{\boldsymbol{W}}=\widehat{\Omega}^{-1}$ or $\widehat{\boldsymbol{W}}=\widehat{\Omega}^{*-1}$. Given this weight matrix, we construct the **two-step GMM estimator** as (13.6) using the weight matrix $\widehat{\boldsymbol{W}}$.

Since the 2SLS estimator is consistent for β, by arguments nearly identical to those used for covariance matrix estimation, we can show that $\widehat{\Omega}$ and $\widehat{\Omega}^*$ are consistent for Ω, and thus $\widehat{\boldsymbol{W}}$ is consistent for Ω^{-1}. See Exercise 13.3.

As a result, the two-step GMM estimator satisfies the conditions for Theorem 13.4.

Theorem 13.7 Under Assumption 12.2 and $\Omega>0$, if $\widehat{\boldsymbol{W}}=\widehat{\Omega}^{-1}$ or $\widehat{\boldsymbol{W}}=\widehat{\Omega}^{*-1}$ where the latter are defined in (13.8) and (13.9), then as $n\to\infty$, $\sqrt{n}\left(\widehat{\beta}_{\text{gmm}}-\beta\right)\underset{d}{\longrightarrow}\mathrm{N}\left(0,\boldsymbol{V}_\beta\right)$, where $\boldsymbol{V}_\beta=\left(\boldsymbol{Q}'\Omega^{-1}\boldsymbol{Q}\right)^{-1}$.

This shows that the two-step GMM estimator is asymptotically efficient.

The two-step GMM estimator of the IV regression equation can be computed in Stata using the `ivregress gmm` command. By default it uses formula (13.8). The centered version (13.9) may be selected using the `center` option.

13.11 ITERATED GMM

The asymptotic distribution of the two-step GMM estimator does not depend on the choice of the preliminary one-step estimator. However, the actual value of the estimator depends on this choice, and so will the finite sample distribution. This is undesirable and likely inefficient. To remove this dependence, we can iterate the estimation sequence. Specifically, given $\widehat{\beta}_{\text{gmm}}$, we can construct an updated weight matrix estimate $\widehat{\boldsymbol{W}}$ and then re-estimate $\widehat{\beta}_{\text{gmm}}$. This updating can be iterated until convergence.[1] The result is called the **iterated GMM estimator** and is a common implementation of efficient GMM.

Interestingly, B. Hansen and Lee (2021) show that the iterated GMM estimator is unaffected if the weight matrix is computed with or without centering. Standard errors and test statistics, however, will be affected by the choice.

The iterated GMM estimator of the IV regression equation can be computed in Stata using the `ivregress gmm` command using the `igmm` option.

[1]In practice, "convergence" obtains when the difference between the estimates at subsequent steps is smaller than a prespecified tolerance. A sufficient condition for convergence is that the sequence is a contraction mapping. Indeed, B. Hansen and Lee (2021) have shown that the iterated GMM estimator generally satisfies this condition in large samples.

13.12 COVARIANCE MATRIX ESTIMATION

An estimator of the asymptotic variance of $\widehat{\beta}_{\text{gmm}}$ can be obtained by replacing the matrices in the asymptotic variance formula by consistent estimators.

For the one-step or two-step GMM estimator, the covariance matrix estimator is

$$\widehat{\boldsymbol{V}}_\beta = \left(\widehat{\boldsymbol{Q}}'\widehat{\boldsymbol{W}}\widehat{\boldsymbol{Q}}\right)^{-1}\left(\widehat{\boldsymbol{Q}}'\widehat{\boldsymbol{W}}\widehat{\Omega}\widehat{\boldsymbol{W}}\widehat{\boldsymbol{Q}}\right)\left(\widehat{\boldsymbol{Q}}'\widehat{\boldsymbol{W}}\widehat{\boldsymbol{Q}}\right)^{-1} \tag{13.10}$$

where $\widehat{\boldsymbol{Q}} = \frac{1}{n}\sum_{i=1}^n Z_i X_i'$. The weight matrix is constructed using either the uncentered estimator (13.8) or centered estimator (13.9) with the residuals $\widehat{e}_i = Y_i - X_i'\widehat{\beta}_{\text{gmm}}$.

For the efficient iterated GMM estimator, the covariance matrix estimator is

$$\widehat{\boldsymbol{V}}_\beta = \left(\widehat{\boldsymbol{Q}}'\widehat{\Omega}^{-1}\widehat{\boldsymbol{Q}}\right)^{-1} = \left(\left(\frac{1}{n}\boldsymbol{X}'\boldsymbol{Z}\right)\widehat{\Omega}^{-1}\left(\frac{1}{n}\boldsymbol{Z}'\boldsymbol{X}\right)\right)^{-1}. \tag{13.11}$$

$\widehat{\Omega}$ can be computed using either the uncentered estimator (13.8) or centered estimator (13.9). Based on the asymptotic approximation, the estimator (13.11) can be used as well for the two-step estimator but should use the final residuals $\widehat{e}_i = Y_i - X_i'\widehat{\beta}_{\text{gmm}}$.

Asymptotic standard errors are given by the square roots of the diagonal elements of $n^{-1}\widehat{\boldsymbol{V}}_\beta$.

It is unclear whether it is preferable to use the covariance matrix estimator based on the centered or the uncentered estimator of Ω to construct the covariance matrix estimator. Using the centered estimator results in a smaller covariance matrix and standard errors, and thus more "significant" tests based on asymptotic critical values. In contrast, the uncentered estimator of Ω will result in larger standard errors and will thus be more "conservative."

In Stata, the default covariance matrix estimation method is determined by the choice of weight matrix. Thus if the centered estimator (13.9) is used for the weight matrix, it is also used for the covariance matrix estimator.

13.13 CLUSTERED DEPENDENCE

Section 4.21 introduced clustered dependence, and Section 12.25 described covariance matrix estimation for 2SLS under clustering. The methods extend naturally to GMM but with the additional complication of potentially altering the weight matrix calculation.

The structural equation for the gth cluster can be written as the matrix system $\boldsymbol{Y}_g = \boldsymbol{X}_g\beta + \boldsymbol{e}_g$. Using this notation, the centered GMM estimator with weight matrix $\boldsymbol{W}$ can be written as

$$\widehat{\beta}_{\text{gmm}} - \beta = \left(\boldsymbol{X}'\boldsymbol{Z}\boldsymbol{W}\boldsymbol{Z}'\boldsymbol{X}\right)^{-1}\boldsymbol{X}'\boldsymbol{Z}\boldsymbol{W}\left(\sum_{g=1}^G \boldsymbol{Z}_g'\boldsymbol{e}_g\right).$$

The cluster-robust covariance matrix estimator for $\widehat{\beta}_{\text{gmm}}$ is

$$\widehat{\boldsymbol{V}}_\beta = \left(\boldsymbol{X}'\boldsymbol{Z}\boldsymbol{W}\boldsymbol{Z}'\boldsymbol{X}\right)^{-1}\boldsymbol{X}'\boldsymbol{Z}\boldsymbol{W}\widehat{\boldsymbol{S}}\boldsymbol{W}\boldsymbol{Z}'\boldsymbol{X}\left(\boldsymbol{X}'\boldsymbol{Z}\boldsymbol{W}\boldsymbol{Z}'\boldsymbol{X}\right)^{-1} \tag{13.12}$$

with

$$\widehat{\boldsymbol{S}} = \sum_{g=1}^G \boldsymbol{Z}_g'\widehat{\boldsymbol{e}}_g\widehat{\boldsymbol{e}}_g'\boldsymbol{Z}_g \tag{13.13}$$

and the clustered residuals

$$\widehat{\boldsymbol{e}}_g = \boldsymbol{Y}_g - \boldsymbol{X}_g \widehat{\beta}_{\mathrm{gmm}}. \tag{13.14}$$

The cluster-robust estimator (13.12) is appropriate for the one-step or two-step GMM estimator. It is also appropriate for the iterated estimator when the latter uses a conventional (nonclustered) efficient weight matrix. However in the clustering context, it is more natural to use a cluster-robust weight matrix, such as $\boldsymbol{W} = \widehat{\boldsymbol{S}}^{-1}$, where $\widehat{\boldsymbol{S}}$ is a cluster-robust covariance estimator as in (13.13) based on a one-step or iterated residual. This gives rise to the cluster-robust GMM estimator:

$$\widehat{\beta}_{\mathrm{gmm}} = \left(\boldsymbol{X}'\boldsymbol{Z}\widehat{\boldsymbol{S}}^{-1}\boldsymbol{Z}'\boldsymbol{X}\right)^{-1}\boldsymbol{X}'\boldsymbol{Z}\widehat{\boldsymbol{S}}^{-1}\boldsymbol{Z}'\boldsymbol{Y}. \tag{13.15}$$

An appropriate cluster-robust covariance matrix estimator is

$$\widehat{\boldsymbol{V}}_\beta = \left(\boldsymbol{X}'\boldsymbol{Z}\widehat{\boldsymbol{S}}^{-1}\boldsymbol{Z}'\boldsymbol{X}\right)^{-1}$$

where $\widehat{\boldsymbol{S}}$ is calculated using the final residuals.

To implement a cluster-robust weight matrix, use the 2SLS estimator for first step. Compute the cluster residuals (13.14) and covariance matrix (13.13). Then (13.15) is the two-step GMM estimator. Iterating the residuals and covariance matrix until convergence, we obtain the iterated GMM estimator.

In Stata, using the `ivregress gmm` command with the `cluster` option implements the two-step GMM estimator using the cluster-robust weight matrix and cluster-robust covariance matrix estimator. To use the centered covariance matrix, use the `center` option, and to implement the iterated GMM estimator, use the `igmm` option. Alternatively, you can use the `wmatrix` and `vce` options to separately specify the weight matrix and covariance matrix estimation methods.

13.14 WALD TEST

For a given function $r(\beta): \mathbb{R}^k \to \Theta \subset \mathbb{R}^q$, we define the parameter $\theta = r(\beta)$. The GMM estimator of θ is $\widehat{\theta}_{\mathrm{gmm}} = r\left(\widehat{\beta}_{\mathrm{gmm}}\right)$. By the delta method, it is asymptotically normal with covariance matrix $\boldsymbol{V}_\theta = \boldsymbol{R}'\boldsymbol{V}_\beta\boldsymbol{R}$, where $\boldsymbol{R} = \frac{\partial}{\partial\beta}r(\beta)'$. An estimator of the asymptotic covariance matrix is $\widehat{\boldsymbol{V}}_\theta = \widehat{\boldsymbol{R}}'\widehat{\boldsymbol{V}}_\beta\widehat{\boldsymbol{R}}$, where $\widehat{\boldsymbol{R}} = \frac{\partial}{\partial\beta}r(\widehat{\beta}_{\mathrm{gmm}})'$. When θ is scalar then an asymptotic standard error for $\widehat{\theta}_{\mathrm{gmm}}$ is formed as $\sqrt{n^{-1}\widehat{\boldsymbol{V}}_\theta}$.

A standard test of the hypothesis $\mathbb{H}_0: \theta = \theta_0$ against $\mathbb{H}_1: \theta \neq \theta_0$ is based on the Wald statistic:

$$W = n\left(\widehat{\theta} - \theta_0\right)'\widehat{\boldsymbol{V}}_{\widehat{\theta}}^{-1}\left(\widehat{\theta} - \theta_0\right).$$

Let $G_q(u)$ denote the χ_q^2 distribution function.

Theorem 13.8 Under Assumption 12.2, Assumption 7.3, and $\mathbb{H}_0$, as $n \to \infty$, $W \underset{d}{\longrightarrow} \chi_q^2$. For c satisfying $\alpha = 1 - G_q(c)$, $\mathbb{P}\left[W > c \mid \mathbb{H}_0\right] \longrightarrow \alpha$, so the test "Reject $\mathbb{H}_0$ if $W > c$" has asymptotic size α.

Exercise 13.5 asks that you prove this theorem.

In Stata, the commands `test` and `testparm` can be used after `ivregress gmm` to implement Wald tests of linear hypotheses. The commands `nlcom` and `testnl` can be used after `ivregress gmm` to implement Wald tests of nonlinear hypotheses.

13.15 RESTRICTED GMM

It is often desirable to impose restrictions on the coefficients. In this section, we consider estimation subject to the linear constraints $\boldsymbol{R}'\beta = \boldsymbol{c}$. In Section 13.16, we consider nonlinear constraints.

The constrained GMM estimator minimizes the GMM criterion subject to the constraint. It is

$$\widehat{\beta}_{\text{cgmm}} = \underset{\boldsymbol{R}'\beta=\boldsymbol{c}}{\operatorname{argmin}}\, J(\beta).$$

This is the parameter vector that makes the estimating equations as close to 0 as possible with respect to the weighted quadratic distance while imposing the restriction on the parameters.

Suppose the weight matrix $\boldsymbol{W}$ is fixed. Using the methods of Chapter 8, it is straightforward to derive that the constrained GMM estimator is

$$\widehat{\beta}_{\text{cgmm}} = \widehat{\beta}_{\text{gmm}} - \left(\boldsymbol{X}'\boldsymbol{Z}\boldsymbol{W}\boldsymbol{Z}'\boldsymbol{X}\right)^{-1}\boldsymbol{R}\left(\boldsymbol{R}'\left(\boldsymbol{X}'\boldsymbol{Z}\boldsymbol{W}\boldsymbol{Z}'\boldsymbol{X}\right)^{-1}\boldsymbol{R}\right)^{-1}\left(\boldsymbol{R}'\widehat{\beta}_{\text{gmm}} - \boldsymbol{c}\right). \tag{13.16}$$

(For details, see Exercise 13.6.)

We derive the asymptotic distribution under the assumption that the restriction is true. Make the substitution $\boldsymbol{c} = \boldsymbol{R}'\beta$ in (13.16) and reorganize to find

$$\sqrt{n}\left(\widehat{\beta}_{\text{cgmm}} - \beta\right) = \left(\boldsymbol{I}_k - \left(\boldsymbol{X}'\boldsymbol{Z}\boldsymbol{W}\boldsymbol{Z}'\boldsymbol{X}\right)^{-1}\boldsymbol{R}\left(\boldsymbol{R}'\left(\boldsymbol{X}'\boldsymbol{Z}\boldsymbol{W}\boldsymbol{Z}'\boldsymbol{X}\right)^{-1}\boldsymbol{R}\right)^{-1}\boldsymbol{R}'\right)\sqrt{n}\left(\widehat{\beta}_{\text{gmm}} - \beta\right). \tag{13.17}$$

This is a linear function of $\sqrt{n}\left(\widehat{\beta}_{\text{gmm}} - \beta\right)$. Since the asymptotic distribution of the latter is known, the asymptotic distribution of $\sqrt{n}\left(\widehat{\beta}_{\text{cgmm}} - \beta\right)$ is a linear function of the former.

Theorem 13.9 Under Assumptions 12.2 and 8.3, for the constrained GMM estimator (13.16), $\sqrt{n}\left(\widehat{\beta}_{\text{cgmm}} - \beta\right) \underset{d}{\longrightarrow} \mathrm{N}\left(0, \boldsymbol{V}_{\text{cgmm}}\right)$ as $n \to \infty$, where

$$\begin{aligned}\boldsymbol{V}_{\text{cgmm}} = \boldsymbol{V}_\beta &- \left(\boldsymbol{Q}'\boldsymbol{W}\boldsymbol{Q}\right)^{-1}\boldsymbol{R}\left(\boldsymbol{R}'\left(\boldsymbol{Q}'\boldsymbol{W}\boldsymbol{Q}\right)^{-1}\boldsymbol{R}\right)^{-1}\boldsymbol{R}'\boldsymbol{V}_\beta \\ &- \boldsymbol{V}_\beta\boldsymbol{R}\left(\boldsymbol{R}'\left(\boldsymbol{Q}'\boldsymbol{W}\boldsymbol{Q}\right)^{-1}\boldsymbol{R}\right)^{-1}\boldsymbol{R}'\left(\boldsymbol{Q}'\boldsymbol{W}\boldsymbol{Q}\right)^{-1} \\ &+ \left(\boldsymbol{Q}'\boldsymbol{W}\boldsymbol{Q}\right)^{-1}\boldsymbol{R}\left(\boldsymbol{R}'\left(\boldsymbol{Q}'\boldsymbol{W}\boldsymbol{Q}\right)^{-1}\boldsymbol{R}\right)^{-1}\boldsymbol{R}'\boldsymbol{V}_\beta\boldsymbol{R}\left(\boldsymbol{R}'\left(\boldsymbol{Q}'\boldsymbol{W}\boldsymbol{Q}\right)^{-1}\boldsymbol{R}\right)^{-1}\boldsymbol{R}'\left(\boldsymbol{Q}'\boldsymbol{W}\boldsymbol{Q}\right)^{-1}.\end{aligned} \tag{13.18}$$

Exercise 13.8 asks you to prove this theorem. Unfortunately, the asymptotic covariance matrix formula (13.18) is quite tedious!

Now suppose that the weight matrix is set to $\boldsymbol{W} = \widehat{\Omega}^{-1}$, the efficient weight matrix from the unconstrained estimation. In this case, the constrained GMM estimator can be written as

$$\widehat{\beta}_{\text{cgmm}} = \widehat{\beta}_{\text{gmm}} - \widehat{\boldsymbol{V}}_\beta\boldsymbol{R}\left(\boldsymbol{R}'\widehat{\boldsymbol{V}}_\beta\boldsymbol{R}\right)^{-1}\left(\boldsymbol{R}'\widehat{\beta}_{\text{gmm}} - \boldsymbol{c}\right) \tag{13.19}$$

which is the same as the efficient minimum distance estimator (8.25). (For details, see Exercise 13.7.) We find that the asymptotic covariance matrix simplifies considerably.

Theorem 13.10 Under Assumptions 12.2 and 8.3, for the efficient constrained GMM estimator (13.19), $\sqrt{n}\left(\widehat{\beta}_{\mathrm{cgmm}}-\beta\right) \underset{d}{\longrightarrow} \mathrm{N}\left(0, \boldsymbol{V}_{\mathrm{cgmm}}\right)$ as $n \rightarrow \infty$, where

$$\boldsymbol{V}_{\mathrm{cgmm}}=\boldsymbol{V}_{\beta}-\boldsymbol{V}_{\beta} \boldsymbol{R}\left(\boldsymbol{R}^{\prime} \boldsymbol{V}_{\beta} \boldsymbol{R}\right)^{-1} \boldsymbol{R}^{\prime} \boldsymbol{V}_{\beta}. \tag{13.20}$$

Exercise 13.9 asks you to prove this theorem.

The asymptotic covariance matrix (13.20) can be estimated by

$$\widehat{\boldsymbol{V}}_{\mathrm{cgmm}}=\widetilde{\boldsymbol{V}}_{\beta}-\widetilde{\boldsymbol{V}}_{\beta} \boldsymbol{R}\left(\boldsymbol{R}^{\prime} \widetilde{\boldsymbol{V}}_{\beta} \boldsymbol{R}\right)^{-1} \boldsymbol{R}^{\prime} \widetilde{\boldsymbol{V}}_{\beta}. \tag{13.21}$$

$$\widetilde{\boldsymbol{V}}_{\beta}=\left(\widehat{\boldsymbol{Q}}^{\prime} \widetilde{\Omega}^{-1} \widehat{\boldsymbol{Q}}\right)^{-1}$$

$$\widetilde{\Omega}=\frac{1}{n} \sum_{i=1}^{n} Z_{i} Z_{i}^{\prime} \widetilde{e}_{i}^{2} \tag{13.22}$$

$$\widetilde{e}_{i}=Y_{i}-X_{i}^{\prime} \widehat{\beta}_{\mathrm{cgmm}}.$$

The covariance matrix (13.18) can be estimated similarly, by using (13.10) to estimate $\boldsymbol{V}_{\beta}$. The covariance matrix estimator $\widetilde{\Omega}$ can also be replaced with a centered version.

A constrained iterated GMM estimator can be implemented by setting $\boldsymbol{W}=\widetilde{\Omega}^{-1}$, where $\widetilde{\Omega}$ is defined in (13.22), and then iterating until convergence. This is a natural estimator, as it is the appropriate implementation of iterated GMM.

Since both $\widehat{\Omega}$ and $\widetilde{\Omega}$ converge to the same limit Ω under the assumption that the constraint is true, the constrained iterated GMM estimator has the asymptotic distribution given in Theorem 13.10.

13.16 NONLINEAR RESTRICTED GMM

Nonlinear constraints on the parameters can be written as $r(\beta)=0$ for some function $r: \mathbb{R}^{k} \rightarrow \mathbb{R}^{q}$. The constraint is nonlinear if $r(\beta)$ cannot be written as a linear function of β. Least squares estimation subject to nonlinear constraints was explored in Section 8.14. In this section, we introduce GMM estimation subject to nonlinear constraints.

The constrained GMM estimator minimizes the GMM criterion subject to the constraint. It is

$$\widehat{\beta}_{\mathrm{cgmm}}=\underset{r(\beta)=0}{\operatorname{argmin}} J(\beta). \tag{13.23}$$

This parameter vector makes the estimating equations as close to 0 as possible with respect to the weighted quadratic distance while imposing the restriction on the parameters.

In general there is no explicit solution for $\widehat{\beta}_{\mathrm{cgmm}}$. Instead the solution is found numerically. Fortunately, there are excellent nonlinear constrained optimization solvers implemented in standard software packages.

For the asymptotic distribution, assume that the restriction $r(\beta)=0$ is true. Using the same methods as in the proof of Theorem 8.10, we can show that (13.17) approximately holds in the sense that

$$\sqrt{n}\left(\widehat{\beta}_{\text{cgmm}}-\beta\right)=\left(\boldsymbol{I}_k-\left(\boldsymbol{X}'\boldsymbol{Z}\boldsymbol{W}\boldsymbol{Z}'\boldsymbol{X}\right)^{-1}\boldsymbol{R}\left(\boldsymbol{R}'\left(\boldsymbol{X}'\boldsymbol{Z}\boldsymbol{W}\boldsymbol{Z}'\boldsymbol{X}\right)^{-1}\boldsymbol{R}\right)^{-1}\boldsymbol{R}'\right)\sqrt{n}\left(\widehat{\beta}_{\text{gmm}}-\beta\right)+o_p(1)$$

where $\boldsymbol{R}=\frac{\partial}{\partial\beta}r(\beta)'$. Thus the asymptotic distribution of the constrained estimator takes the same form as in the linear case.

Theorem 13.11 Under Assumptions 12.2 and 8.3, for the constrained GMM estimator (13.23), $\sqrt{n}\left(\widehat{\beta}_{\text{cgmm}}-\beta\right)\underset{d}{\longrightarrow}\mathrm{N}\left(0,\boldsymbol{V}_{\text{cgmm}}\right)$ as $n\to\infty$, where $\boldsymbol{V}_{\text{cgmm}}$ equals (13.18). If $\boldsymbol{W}=\widehat{\Omega}^{-1}$, then $\boldsymbol{V}_{\text{cgmm}}$ equals (13.20).

The asymptotic covariance matrix in the efficient case is estimated by (13.21) with $\boldsymbol{R}$ replaced by $\widehat{\boldsymbol{R}}=\frac{\partial}{\partial\beta}r\left(\widehat{\beta}_{\text{cgmm}}\right)'$. The asymptotic covariance matrix (13.18) in the general case is estimated similarly.

To implement an iterated restricted GMM estimator, the weight matrix may be set to $\boldsymbol{W}=\widetilde{\Omega}^{-1}$, where $\widetilde{\Omega}$ is defined in (13.22), and then iterated until convergence.

13.17 CONSTRAINED REGRESSION

Consider the conventional projection model $Y=X'\beta+e$ with $\mathbb{E}[Xe]=0$. This is a special case of GMM, as it is model (13.5) with $Z=X$. The just-identified GMM estimator equals least squares $\widehat{\beta}_{\text{gmm}}=\widehat{\beta}_{\text{ols}}$.

In Chapter 8, we discussed estimation of the projection model subject to linear constraints $\boldsymbol{R}'\beta=\boldsymbol{c}$, which includes exclusion restrictions. Since the projection model is a special case of GMM, the constrained projection model is also constrained GMM. From the results of Section 13.15, we find that the efficient constrained GMM estimator is

$$\widehat{\beta}_{\text{cgmm}}=\widehat{\beta}_{\text{ols}}-\widehat{\boldsymbol{V}}_{\beta}\boldsymbol{R}\left(\boldsymbol{R}'\widehat{\boldsymbol{V}}_{\beta}\boldsymbol{R}\right)^{-1}\left(\boldsymbol{R}'\widehat{\beta}_{\text{ols}}-\boldsymbol{c}\right)=\widehat{\beta}_{\text{emd}}$$

which is the efficient minimum distance estimator. Thus for linear constraints on the linear projection model, efficient GMM equals efficient minimum distance. So one convenient method to implement efficient minimum distance is GMM.

13.18 MULTIVARIATE REGRESSION

GMM methods can simplify estimation and inference for multivariate regressions such as those introduced in Chapter 11.

The general multivariate regression (projection) model is

$$Y_j=X_j'\beta_j+e_j$$
$$\mathbb{E}\left[X_je_j\right]=0$$

for $j = 1, \ldots, m$. Using the notation from Section 11.2, the equations can be written jointly as $Y = \overline{X}\beta + e$ and for the full sample as $\boldsymbol{Y} = \overline{\boldsymbol{X}}\beta + \boldsymbol{e}$. The $\overline{k}$ moment conditions are

$$\mathbb{E}\left[\overline{X}'\left(Y - \overline{X}\beta\right)\right] = 0. \tag{13.24}$$

Given a $\overline{k} \times \overline{k}$ weight matrix $\boldsymbol{W}$, the GMM criterion is

$$J(\beta) = n\left(\boldsymbol{Y} - \overline{\boldsymbol{X}}\beta\right)'\overline{\boldsymbol{X}}\boldsymbol{W}\overline{\boldsymbol{X}}'\left(\boldsymbol{Y} - \overline{\boldsymbol{X}}\beta\right).$$

The GMM estimator $\widehat{\beta}_{\text{gmm}}$ minimizes $J(\beta)$. Since this is a just-identified model, the estimator solves the sample equations

$$\overline{\boldsymbol{X}}'\left(\boldsymbol{Y} - \overline{\boldsymbol{X}}\widehat{\beta}_{\text{gmm}}\right) = 0.$$

The solution is

$$\widehat{\beta}_{\text{gmm}} = \left(\sum_{i=1}^{n} \overline{X}_i'\overline{X}_i\right)^{-1}\left(\sum_{i=1}^{n} \overline{X}_i'Y_i\right) = \left(\overline{\boldsymbol{X}}'\overline{\boldsymbol{X}}\right)^{-1}\left(\overline{\boldsymbol{X}}'\boldsymbol{Y}\right) = \widehat{\beta}_{\text{ols}},$$

the multivariate least squares estimator.

Thus the unconstrained GMM estimator of the multivariate regression model is least squares. The estimator does not depend on the weight matrix, since the model is just-identified.

A important advantage of the GMM framework is the ability to incorporate cross-equation constraints. Consider the class of restrictions $\boldsymbol{R}'\beta = \boldsymbol{c}$. Minimization of the GMM criterion subject to this restriction has solutions as described by (13.15). The restricted GMM estimator is

$$\widehat{\beta}_{\text{gmm}} = \widehat{\beta}_{\text{ols}} - \left(\overline{\boldsymbol{X}}'\overline{\boldsymbol{X}}\boldsymbol{W}\overline{\boldsymbol{X}}'\overline{\boldsymbol{X}}\right)^{-1}\boldsymbol{R}\left(\boldsymbol{R}'\left(\overline{\boldsymbol{X}}'\overline{\boldsymbol{X}}\boldsymbol{W}\overline{\boldsymbol{X}}'\overline{\boldsymbol{X}}\right)^{-1}\boldsymbol{R}\right)^{-1}\left(\boldsymbol{R}'\widehat{\beta}_{\text{ols}} - \boldsymbol{c}\right).$$

This estimator depends on the weight matrix, because it is overidentified.

A simple choice for the weight matrix is $\boldsymbol{W} = \overline{\boldsymbol{X}}'\overline{\boldsymbol{X}}$, which leads to the one-step estimator

$$\widehat{\beta}_1 = \widehat{\beta}_{\text{ols}} - \left(\overline{\boldsymbol{X}}'\overline{\boldsymbol{X}}\right)^{-1}\boldsymbol{R}\left(\boldsymbol{R}'\left(\overline{\boldsymbol{X}}'\overline{\boldsymbol{X}}\right)^{-1}\boldsymbol{R}\right)^{-1}\left(\boldsymbol{R}'\widehat{\beta}_{\text{ols}} - \boldsymbol{c}\right).$$

The asymptotically efficient choice sets $\boldsymbol{W} = \widehat{\Omega}^{-1}$, where $\widehat{\Omega} = n^{-1}\sum_{i=1}^{n}\overline{X}_i'\widehat{e}_i\widehat{e}_i'\overline{X}_i$ and $\widehat{e}_i = Y_i - \overline{X}_i\widehat{\beta}_1$. This leads to the two-step estimator:

$$\widehat{\beta}_2 = \widehat{\beta}_{\text{ols}} - \left(\overline{\boldsymbol{X}}'\overline{\boldsymbol{X}}\widehat{\Omega}^{-1}\overline{\boldsymbol{X}}'\overline{\boldsymbol{X}}\right)^{-1}\boldsymbol{R}\left(\boldsymbol{R}'\left(\overline{\boldsymbol{X}}'\overline{\boldsymbol{X}}\widehat{\Omega}^{-1}\overline{\boldsymbol{X}}'\overline{\boldsymbol{X}}\right)^{-1}\boldsymbol{R}\right)^{-1}\left(\boldsymbol{R}'\widehat{\beta}_{\text{ols}} - \boldsymbol{c}\right).$$

When the regressors X are common across all equations, the multivariate regression model can be written conveniently as in (11.3): $Y = \boldsymbol{B}'X + e$, with $\mathbb{E}\left[Xe'\right] = 0$. The moment restrictions can be written as the matrix system $\mathbb{E}\left[X\left(Y' - X'\boldsymbol{B}\right)\right] = 0$. Written as a vector system, this is (13.24) and leads to the same restricted GMM estimators.

These are general formulas for imposing restrictions. In specific cases (such as an exclusion restriction), direct methods may be more convenient. In all cases, the solution is found by minimization of the GMM criterion $J(\beta)$ subject to the restriction.

13.19 DISTANCE TEST

Section 13.14 introduced Wald tests of the hypothesis $\mathbb{H}_0 : \theta = \theta_0$, where $\theta = r(\beta)$ for a given function $r(\beta) : \mathbb{R}^k \to \Theta \subset \mathbb{R}^q$. When $r(\beta)$ is nonlinear, an alternative is to use a criterion-based statistic. This is sometimes called the GMM distance statistic and sometimes called an LR-like statistic (the LR stands for "likelihood ratio"). The idea was first put forward by Newey and West (1987a).

The idea is to compare the unrestricted and restricted estimators by contrasting the criterion functions. The unrestricted estimator takes the form

$$\widehat{\beta}_{\text{gmm}} = \underset{\beta}{\operatorname{argmin}}\, \widehat{J}(\beta)$$

where

$$\widehat{J}(\beta) = n\,\overline{g}_n(\beta)'\widehat{\Omega}^{-1}\overline{g}_n(\beta)$$

is the unrestricted GMM criterion with an efficient weight matrix estimate $\widehat{\Omega}$. The minimized value of the criterion is $\widehat{J} = \widehat{J}(\widehat{\beta}_{\text{gmm}})$.

As in Section 13.15, the estimator subject to $r(\beta) = \theta_0$ is

$$\widehat{\beta}_{\text{cgmm}} = \underset{r(\beta)=\theta_0}{\operatorname{argmin}}\, \widetilde{J}(\beta)$$

where

$$\widetilde{J}(\beta) = n\,\overline{g}_n(\beta)'\widetilde{\Omega}^{-1}\,\overline{g}_n(\beta)$$

which depends on an efficient weight matrix estimator, either $\widehat{\Omega}$ (the same as the unrestricted estimator) or $\widetilde{\Omega}$ (the iterated weight matrix from constrained estimation). The minimized value of the criterion is $\widetilde{J} = \widetilde{J}\left(\widehat{\beta}_{\text{cgmm}}\right)$.

The GMM distance (or LR-like) statistic is the difference in the criterion functions: $D = \widetilde{J} - \widehat{J}$. The distance test shares the useful feature of LR tests in that it is a natural by-product of the computation of alternative models.

The test has the following large sample distribution.

Theorem 13.12 Under Assumption 12.2, Assumption 7.3, and $\mathbb{H}_0$, then as $n \to \infty$, $D \underset{d}{\longrightarrow} \chi^2_q$. For c satisfying $\alpha = 1 - G_q(c)$, $\mathbb{P}\left[D > c \mid \mathbb{H}_0\right] \longrightarrow \alpha$. The test "Reject $\mathbb{H}_0$ if $D > c$" has asymptotic size α.

The proof is given in Section 13.28.

Theorem 13.12 shows that the distance statistic has the same asymptotic distribution as Wald and likelihood ratio statistics and can be interpreted similarly. Small values of D mean that imposing the restriction does not result in a large value of the moment equations. Hence the restriction appears to be compatible with the data. In contrast, large values of D mean that imposing the restriction results in a much larger value of the moment equations, implying that the restriction is not compatible with the data. The finding that the asymptotic distribution is chi-squared allows the calculation of asymptotic critical values and p-values.

We now discuss the choice of weight matrix. One simple choice is to set $\widetilde{\Omega} = \widehat{\Omega}$. In this case, we have the following result.

Theorem 13.13 If $\widetilde{\Omega} = \widehat{\Omega}$, then $D \geq 0$. Furthermore, if r is linear in β, then D equals the Wald statistic.

The statement that $\widetilde{\Omega} = \widehat{\Omega}$ implies $D \geq 0$ follows from the fact that in this case, the criterion functions $\widehat{J}(\beta) = \widetilde{J}(\beta)$ are identical, so the constrained minimum cannot be smaller than the unconstrained minimum. The statement that linear hypotheses and $\widetilde{\Omega} = \widehat{\Omega}$ implies $D = W$ follows from applying the expression for the constrained GMM estimator (13.19) and using the covariance matrix formula (13.11).

The fact that $D \geq 0$ when $\widetilde{\Omega} = \widehat{\Omega}$ motivated Newey and West (1987a) to recommend this choice. However, $\widetilde{\Omega} = \widehat{\Omega}$ is not necessary. Instead, setting $\widetilde{\Omega}$ to equal the constrained efficient weight matrix is natural for efficient estimation of $\widehat{\beta}_{\text{cgmm}}$. In the event that $D < 0$, the test simply fails to reject $\mathbb{H}_0$ at any significance level.

As discussed in Section 9.18, for tests of nonlinear hypotheses, the Wald statistic can work quite poorly. In particular, the Wald statistic is affected by how the hypothesis $r(\beta)$ is formulated. In contrast, the distance statistic D is not affected by the algebraic formulation of the hypothesis. Current evidence suggests that the D statistic appears to have good sampling properties and is a preferred test statistic relative to the Wald statistic for nonlinear hypotheses. See B. Hansen (2006).

In Stata, the command `estat overid` after `ivregress gmm` can be used to report the value of the GMM criterion J. By estimating the two nested GMM regressions, the values $\widehat{J}$ and $\widetilde{J}$ can be obtained and D computed.

13.20 CONTINUOUSLY UPDATED GMM

An alternative to the two-step GMM estimator can be constructed by letting the weight matrix be an explicit function of β, which leads to the criterion function

$$J(\beta) = n\overline{g}_n(\beta)' \left(\frac{1}{n} \sum_{i=1}^{n} g_i(\beta) g_i(\beta)' \right)^{-1} \overline{g}_n(\beta).$$

The $\widehat{\beta}$ that minimizes this function is called the **continuously updated GMM (CU-GMM) estimator** and was introduced by L. Hansen, Heaton, and Yaron (1996).

A complication is that the continuously updated criterion $J(\beta)$ is not quadratic in β. Thus minimization requires numerical methods. It may appear that the CU-GMM estimator is the same as the iterated GMM estimator, but this is not the case at all. They solve distinct first-order conditions and can be quite different in applications.

Relative to traditional GMM, the CU-GMM estimator has lower bias but thicker distributional tails. While it has received considerable theoretical attention, it is not used commonly in applications.

13.21 OVERIDENTIFICATION TEST

In Section 12.31, we introduced the Sargan (1958) overidentification test for the 2SLS estimator under the assumption of homoskedasticity. L. Hansen (1982) generalized the test to cover the GMM estimator allowing for general heteroskedasticity.

Recall that overidentified models ($\ell > k$) are special in the sense that there may not be a parameter value β such that the moment condition $\mathbb{H}_0 : \mathbb{E}[Ze] = 0$ holds. Thus the model—the overidentifying restrictions—are testable.

For example, take the linear model $Y=\beta_1'X_1+\beta_2'X_2+e$ with $\mathbb{E}[X_1e]=0$ and $\mathbb{E}[X_2e]=0$. It is possible that $\beta_2=0$, so that the linear equation may be written as $Y=\beta_1'X_1+e$. However, it is possible that $\beta_2\neq 0$. In this case, it is impossible to find a value of β_1 such that both $\mathbb{E}\left[X_1\left(Y-X_1'\beta_1\right)\right]=0$ and $\mathbb{E}\left[X_2\left(Y-X_1'\beta_1\right)\right]=0$ hold simultaneously. In this sense, an exclusion restriction can be seen as an overidentifying restriction.

Note that $\overline{g}_n \underset{p}{\longrightarrow} \mathbb{E}[Ze]$, and thus $\overline{g}_n$ can be used to assess the hypothesis $\mathbb{E}[Ze]=0$. Assuming that an efficient weight matrix estimator is used, the criterion function at the parameter estimator is $J=J(\widehat{\beta}_{\mathrm{gmm}})=n\,\overline{g}_n'\widehat{\Omega}^{-1}\overline{g}_n$. This is a quadratic form in $\overline{g}_n$ and is thus a natural test statistic for $\mathbb{H}_0:\mathbb{E}[Ze]=0$. Note that we assume that the criterion function is constructed with an efficient weight matrix estimator. This construction is important for the distribution theory.

Theorem 13.14 Under Assumption 12.2, as $n\to\infty$, $J=J\left(\widehat{\beta}_{\mathrm{gmm}}\right)\underset{d}{\longrightarrow}\chi^2_{\ell-k}$. For c satisfying $\alpha=1-G_{\ell-k}(c)$, $\mathbb{P}\left[J>c\mid\mathbb{H}_0\right]\longrightarrow\alpha$, so the test "Reject $\mathbb{H}_0$ if $J>c$" has asymptotic size α.

The proof of the theorem is left to Exercise 13.13.

The degrees of freedom of the asymptotic distribution are the number of overidentifying restrictions. If the statistic J exceeds the chi-square critical value, we can reject the model. Based on this information alone, it is unclear what is wrong, but it is typically cause for concern. The GMM overidentification test is a useful by-product of the GMM methodology, and it is advisable to report the statistic J when GMM is the estimation method. When overidentified models are estimated by GMM, it is customary to report the J statistic as a general test of model adequacy.

In Stata, the command `estat overid` afer `ivregress gmm` can be used to implement the overidentification test. The GMM criterion J and its asymptotic p-value using the $\chi^2_{\ell-k}$ distribution are reported.

13.22 SUBSET OVERIDENTIFICATION TESTS

Section 12.32 introduced subset overidentification tests for the 2SLS estimator under the assumption of homoskedasticity. In this section, we describe how to construct analogous tests for the GMM estimator under general heteroskedasticity.

Recall that subset overidentification tests are used when it is desired to focus attention on a subset of instruments whose validity is questioned. Partition $Z=(Z_a,Z_b)$ with dimensions ℓ_a and ℓ_b, respectively, where Z_a contains the instruments believed to be uncorrelated with e, and Z_b contains the instruments that may be correlated with e. It is necessary to select this partition so that $\ell_a>k$, and so the instruments Z_a alone identify the parameters.

Given this partition, the maintained hypothesis is $\mathbb{E}[Z_ae]=0$. The null and alternative hypotheses are $\mathbb{H}_0:\mathbb{E}[Z_be]=0$ and $\mathbb{H}_1:\mathbb{E}[Z_be]\neq 0$, respectively. The GMM test is constructed as follows. First, estimate the model by efficient GMM with only the smaller set Z_a of instruments. Let $\widetilde{J}$ denote the resulting GMM criterion. Second, estimate the model by efficient GMM with the full set $Z=(Z_a,Z_b)$ of instruments. Let $\widehat{J}$ denote the resulting GMM criterion. The test statistic is the difference in the criterion functions: $C=\widehat{J}-\widetilde{J}$, which is similar to the GMM distance statistic presented in Section 13.19. The difference is that the distance statistic compares models that differ based on the parameter restrictions, while the C statistic compares models based on different instrument sets.

Typically $C\geq 0$. However, this is not necessary, and $C<0$ can arise. If this occurs, it leads to a non-rejection of $\mathbb{H}_0$.

If the smaller instrument set Z_a is just-identified so that $\ell_a = k$, then $\widetilde{J} = 0$ and so $C = \widehat{J}$ is simply the standard overidentification test. This is why we have restricted attention to the case $\ell_a > k$.

The test has the following large sample distribution.

Theorem 13.15 Under Assumption 12.2 and $\mathbb{E}\left[Z_a X'\right]$ has full rank k, then as $n \to \infty$, $C \underset{d}{\longrightarrow} \chi^2_{\ell_b}$. For c satisfying $\alpha = 1 - G_{\ell_b}(c)$, $\mathbb{P}\left[C > c \mid \mathbb{H}_0\right] \longrightarrow \alpha$. The test "Reject $\mathbb{H}_0$ if $C > c$" has asymptotic size α.

The proof of Theorem 13.15 is presented in Section 13.28.

In Stata the command `estat overid zb` afer `ivregress gmm` can be used to implement a subset overidentification test where `zb` is the name(s) of the instruments(s) tested for validity. The statistic C and its asymptotic p-value using the $\chi^2_{\ell_2}$ distribution are reported.

13.23 ENDOGENEITY TEST

Section 12.29 introduced tests for endogeneity in the context of 2SLS estimation. Endogeneity tests are simple to implement in the GMM framework as a subset overidentification test. The model is $Y = Z_1'\beta_1 + Y_2'\beta_2 + e$, where the maintained assumption is that the regressors Z_1 and excluded instruments Z_2 are exogenous, so that $\mathbb{E}\left[Z_1 e\right] = 0$ and $\mathbb{E}\left[Z_2 e\right] = 0$. The question is whether Y_2 is endogenous. The null hypothesis is $\mathbb{H}_0 : \mathbb{E}\left[Y_2 e\right] = 0$ with the alternative $\mathbb{H}_1 : \mathbb{E}\left[Y_2 e\right] \neq 0$.

The GMM test is constructed as follows. First, estimate the model by efficient GMM using (Z_1, Z_2) as instruments for (Z_1, Y_2). Let $\widetilde{J}$ denote the resulting GMM criterion. Second, estimate the model by efficient GMM[2] using (Z_1, Z_2, Y_2) as instruments for (Z_1, Y_2). Let $\widehat{J}$ denote the resulting GMM criterion. The test statistic is the difference in the criterion functions: $C = \widehat{J} - \widetilde{J}$.

The distribution theory for the test is a special case of overidentification testing.

Theorem 13.16 Under Assumption 12.2 and $\mathbb{E}\left[Z_2 Y_2'\right]$ has full rank k_2, then as $n \to \infty$, $C \underset{d}{\longrightarrow} \chi^2_{k_2}$. For c satisfying $\alpha = 1 - G_{k_2}(c)$, $\mathbb{P}\left[C > c \mid \mathbb{H}_0\right] \to \alpha$. The test "Reject $\mathbb{H}_0$ if $C > c$" has asymptotic size α.

In Stata the command `estat endogenous` afer `ivregress gmm` can be used to implement the test for endogeneity. The statistic C and its asymptotic p-value using the $\chi^2_{k_2}$ distribution are reported.

13.24 SUBSET ENDOGENEITY TEST

Section 12.30 introduced subset endogeneity tests for 2SLS estimation. GMM tests are simple to implement as subset overidentification tests. The model is $Y = Z_1'\beta_1 + Y_2'\beta_2 + Y_3'\beta_3 + e$ with $\mathbb{E}\left[Ze\right] = 0$, where the instrument vector is $Z = (Z_1, Z_2)$. The $k_3 \times 1$ variables Y_3 are treated as endogenous, and the $k_2 \times 1$ variables Y_2 are treated as potentially endogenous. The hypothesis to test is that Y_2 is exogenous, or $\mathbb{H}_0$:

[2]If the homoskedastic weight matrix is used, this GMM estimator equals least squares, but when the weight matrix allows for heteroskedasticity, the efficient GMM estimator does not equal least squares as the model is overidentified.

$\mathbb{E}[Y_2 e] = 0$ against $\mathbb{H}_1 : \mathbb{E}[Y_2 e] \neq 0$. The test requires that $\ell_2 \geq (k_2 + k_3)$ so that the model can be estimated under $\mathbb{H}_1$.

The GMM test is constructed as follows. First, estimate the model by efficient GMM using (Z_1, Z_2) as instruments for (Z_1, Y_2, Y_3). Let $\widetilde{J}$ denote the resulting GMM criterion. Second, estimate the model by efficient GMM using (Z_1, Z_2, Y_2) as instruments for (Z_1, Y_2, Y_3). Let $\widehat{J}$ denote the resulting GMM criterion. The test statistic is the difference in the criterion functions: $C = \widehat{J} - \widetilde{J}$.

The distribution theory for the test is a special case of the theory of overidentification testing.

Theorem 13.17 Under Assumption 12.2 and $\mathbb{E}\left[Z_2 \left(Y_2', Y_3'\right)\right]$ has full rank $k_2 + k_3$, then as $n \to \infty$, $C \underset{d}{\longrightarrow} \chi^2_{k_2}$. For c satisfying $\alpha = 1 - G_{k_2}(c)$, $\mathbb{P}[C > c \mid \mathbb{H}_0] \longrightarrow \alpha$. The test "Reject $\mathbb{H}_0$ if $C > c$" has asymptotic size α.

In Stata, the command `estat endogenous x2` afer `ivregress gmm` can be used to implement the test for endogeneity, where `x2` is the name(s) of the variable(s) tested for endogeneity. The statistic C and its asymptotic p-value using the $\chi^2_{k_2}$ distribution are reported.

13.25 NONLINEAR GMM

GMM applies when an economic or statistical model implies the $\ell \times 1$ moment condition

$$\mathbb{E}\left[g_i(\beta)\right] = 0$$

where $g_i(\beta)$ is a possibly nonlinear function of the parameters β. Often, this is all that is known. Identification requires $\ell \geq k = \dim(\beta)$. The GMM estimator minimizes

$$J(\beta) = n\, \overline{g}_n(\beta)' \widehat{\boldsymbol{W}}\, \overline{g}_n(\beta)$$

for some weight matrix $\widehat{\boldsymbol{W}}$, where

$$\overline{g}_n(\beta) = \frac{1}{n} \sum_{i=1}^{n} g_i(\beta).$$

The efficient GMM estimator can be constructed by setting

$$\widehat{\boldsymbol{W}} = \left(\frac{1}{n} \sum_{i=1}^{n} \widehat{g}_i \widehat{g}_i' - \overline{g}_n \overline{g}_n'\right)^{-1}$$

with $\widehat{g}_i = g_i(\widetilde{\beta})$ constructed using a preliminary consistent estimator $\widetilde{\beta}$, perhaps obtained with $\widehat{\boldsymbol{W}} = \boldsymbol{I}_\ell$. As in the case of the linear model, the weight matrix can be iterated until convergence to obtain the iterated GMM estimator.

Proposition 13.1 Distribution of Nonlinear GMM Estimator
Under general regularity conditions, $\sqrt{n}\left(\widehat{\beta}_{\mathrm{gmm}} - \beta\right) \underset{d}{\longrightarrow} \mathrm{N}\left(0, \boldsymbol{V}_\beta\right)$, where

$$\boldsymbol{V}_\beta = \left(\boldsymbol{Q}' \boldsymbol{W} \boldsymbol{Q}\right)^{-1} \left(\boldsymbol{Q}' \boldsymbol{W} \Omega \boldsymbol{W} \boldsymbol{Q}\right) \left(\boldsymbol{Q}' \boldsymbol{W} \boldsymbol{Q}\right)^{-1}$$

with $\Omega = \mathbb{E}\left[g_i g_i'\right]$ and

$$\boldsymbol{Q} = \mathbb{E}\left[\frac{\partial}{\partial \beta'} g_i(\beta)\right].$$

If the efficient weight matrix is used, then $\boldsymbol{V}_\beta = \left(\boldsymbol{Q}'\Omega^{-1}\boldsymbol{Q}\right)^{-1}$.

The proof of this result is omitted, as it uses more advanced techniques.

The asymptotic covariance matrices can be estimated by sample counterparts of the population matrices. For the case of a general weight matrix,

$$\widehat{\boldsymbol{V}}_\beta = \left(\widehat{\boldsymbol{Q}}'\widehat{\boldsymbol{W}}\widehat{\boldsymbol{Q}}\right)^{-1}\left(\widehat{\boldsymbol{Q}}'\widehat{\boldsymbol{W}}\widehat{\Omega}\widehat{\boldsymbol{W}}\widehat{\boldsymbol{Q}}\right)\left(\widehat{\boldsymbol{Q}}'\widehat{\boldsymbol{W}}\widehat{\boldsymbol{Q}}\right)^{-1}$$

where

$$\widehat{\Omega} = \frac{1}{n}\sum_{i=1}^{n}\left(g_i(\widehat{\beta}) - \overline{g}\right)\left(g_i(\widehat{\beta}) - \overline{g}\right)'$$

$$\overline{g} = n^{-1}\sum_{i=1}^{n} g_i(\widehat{\beta})$$

and

$$\widehat{\boldsymbol{Q}} = \frac{1}{n}\sum_{i=1}^{n}\frac{\partial}{\partial \beta'} g_i(\widehat{\beta}).$$

For the case of the iterated efficient weight matrix,

$$\widehat{\boldsymbol{V}}_\beta = \left(\widehat{\boldsymbol{Q}}'\widehat{\Omega}^{-1}\widehat{\boldsymbol{Q}}\right)^{-1}.$$

All of the methods discussed in this chapter—Wald tests, constrained estimation, distance tests, overidentification tests, endogeneity tests—apply similarly to the nonlinear GMM estimator.

13.26 BOOTSTRAP FOR GMM

The bootstrap for 2SLS (Section 12.23) can be used for GMM estimation. The standard bootstrap algorithm generates bootstrap samples by sampling the triplets (Y_i^*, X_i^*, Z_i^*) independently and with replacement from the original sample. The GMM estimator is applied to the bootstrap sample to obtain the bootstrap estimates $\widehat{\beta}^*_{\mathrm{gmm}}$. This procedure is repeated B times to create a sample of B bootstrap draws. Given these draws, bootstrap confidence intervals, including percentile, BC percentile, BC$_a$ and percentile-t, are calculated conventionally.

For variance and standard error estimation, the same cautions apply as for 2SLS. It is difficult to know whether the GMM estimator has a finite variance in a given application. It is best to avoid using the bootstrap to calculate standard errors. Instead, use the bootstrap for percentile and percentile-t confidence intervals.

When the model is overidentified, as discussed for 2SLS, bootstrap GMM inference will not achieve an asymptotic refinement unless the bootstrap estimator is recentered to satisfy the orthogonality condition. We now discuss the recentering recommended by P. Hall and Horowitz (1996).

For linear GMM with weight matrix $\boldsymbol{W}$, the recentered GMM bootstrap estimator is

$$\widehat{\beta}^{**}_{\mathrm{gmm}} = \left(\boldsymbol{X}^{*\prime}\boldsymbol{Z}^*\boldsymbol{W}^*\boldsymbol{Z}^{*\prime}\boldsymbol{X}^*\right)^{-1}\left(\boldsymbol{X}^{*\prime}\boldsymbol{Z}^*\boldsymbol{W}^*\left(\boldsymbol{Z}^{*\prime}\boldsymbol{Y}^* - \boldsymbol{Z}'\widehat{\boldsymbol{e}}\right)\right)$$

where $\boldsymbol{W}^*$ is the bootstrap version of $\boldsymbol{W}$, and $\widehat{\boldsymbol{e}} = \boldsymbol{Y} - \boldsymbol{X}\widehat{\beta}_{\text{gmm}}$. For efficient GMM,

$$\boldsymbol{W}^* = \left(\frac{1}{n}\sum_{i=1}^{n} Z_i^* Z_i^{*\prime} \left(Y_i^* - X_i^{*\prime}\widetilde{\beta}^*\right)^2\right)^{-1}$$

for preliminary estimator $\widetilde{\beta}^*$.

For nonlinear GMM (Section 13.25), the bootstrap criterion function is modified. The recentered bootstrap criterion is

$$J^{**}(\beta) = n\left(\overline{g}_n^*(\beta) - \overline{g}_n(\widehat{\beta}_{\text{gmm}})\right)' \boldsymbol{W}^* \left(\overline{g}_n^*(\beta) - \overline{g}_n(\widehat{\beta}_{\text{gmm}})\right)$$

$$\overline{g}_n^*(\beta) = \frac{1}{n}\sum_{i=1}^{n} g_i^*(\beta)$$

where $\overline{g}_n(\widehat{\beta}_{\text{gmm}})$ is from the sample, not from the bootstrap data. The bootstrap estimator is

$$\widehat{\beta}_{\text{gmm}}^{**} = \operatorname{argmin} J^{**}(\beta).$$

The bootstrap can be used to calculate the p-value of the GMM overidentification test. For the GMM estimator with an efficient weight matrix, the standard overidentification test is the Hansen J statistic:

$$J = n\,\overline{g}_n(\widehat{\beta}_{\text{gmm}})'\widehat{\Omega}^{-1}\overline{g}_n(\widehat{\beta}_{\text{gmm}}).$$

The recentered bootstrap analog is

$$J^{**} = n\left(\overline{g}_n^*(\widehat{\beta}_{\text{gmm}}^{**}) - \overline{g}_n(\widehat{\beta}_{\text{gmm}})\right)' \widehat{\Omega}^{*-1} \left(\overline{g}_n^*(\widehat{\beta}_{\text{gmm}}^{**}) - \overline{g}_n(\widehat{\beta}_{\text{gmm}})\right).$$

On each bootstrap sample, $J^{**}(b)$ is calculated and stored. The bootstrap p-value is

$$p^* = \frac{1}{B}\sum_{b=1}^{B} \mathbb{1}\left\{J^{**}(b) > S\right\}.$$

This bootstrap p-value is asymptotically valid since J^{**} satisfies the overidentified moment conditions.

13.27 CONDITIONAL MOMENT EQUATION MODELS

In many contexts, an economic model implies a conditional moment restriction of the form

$$\mathbb{E}\left[e_i(\beta) \mid Z_i\right] = 0$$

where $e_i(\beta)$ is some $s \times 1$ function of the observation and the parameters. In many cases, $s = 1$. It turns out that this conditional moment restriction is more powerful than the unconditional moment equation model discussed throughout this chapter.

For example, the linear model $Y = X'\beta + e$ with instruments Z falls into this class under the assumption $\mathbb{E}\left[e \mid Z\right] = 0$. In this case, $e_i(\beta) = Y_i - X_i'\beta$.

It is also helpful to realize that conventional regression models also fall into this class, except that in this case, $X = Z$. For example, for a linear regression, $e_i(\beta) = Y_i - X_i'\beta$, while for a nonlinear regression model, $e_i(\beta) = Y_i - m(X_i, \beta)$. In a joint model of the conditional expectation $\mathbb{E}[Y \mid X = x] = x'\beta$ and variance $\operatorname{var}[Y \mid X = x] = f(x)'\gamma$, then

$$e_i(\beta, \gamma) = \begin{cases} Y_i - X_i'\beta \\ \left(Y_i - X_i'\beta\right)^2 - f(X_i)'\gamma \end{cases}.$$

Here $s = 2$.

Given a conditional moment restriction, an unconditional moment restriction can always be constructed. That is, for any $\ell \times 1$ function $\phi(Z, \beta)$, we can set $g_i(\beta) = \phi(Z_i, \beta)\, e_i(\beta)$ which satisfies $\mathbb{E}\left[g_i(\beta)\right] = 0$ and hence defines an unconditional moment equation model. The obvious problem is that the class of functions ϕ is infinite. Which should be selected?

This is equivalent to the problem of selection of the best instruments. If $Z \in \mathbb{R}$ is a valid instrument satisfying $\mathbb{E}[e \mid Z] = 0$, then $Z, Z^2, Z^3, \ldots,$ are all valid instruments. Which should be used?

One solution is to construct an infinite list of potential instruments and then use the first ℓ of them. How is ℓ to be determined? This is an area of theory still under development. One study of this problem is Donald and Newey (2001).

Another approach is to construct the **optimal instrument** that minimizes the asymptotic variance. The form was uncovered by Chamberlain (1987). Take the case $s = 1$. Let

$$R_i = \mathbb{E}\left[\frac{\partial}{\partial \beta} e_i(\beta) \middle| Z_i\right]$$

and $\sigma_i^2 = \mathbb{E}\left[e_i(\beta)^2 \mid Z_i\right]$. Then the optimal instrument is $A_i = -\sigma_i^{-2} R_i$. The optimal moment is $g_i(\beta) = A_i e_i(\beta)$. Setting $g_i(\beta)$ to be this choice (which is $k \times 1$, so is just-identified) yields the GMM estimator with lowest asymptotic variance. In practice A_i is unknown, but its form helps us think about construction of good instruments.

In the linear model $e_i(\beta) = Y_i - X_i'\beta$, note that $R_i = -\mathbb{E}[X_i \mid Z_i]$ and $\sigma_i^2 = \mathbb{E}\left[e_i^2 \mid Z_i\right]$. Thus the optimal instrument is $A_i = \sigma_i^{-2}\mathbb{E}[X_i \mid Z_i]$. In the case of linear regression, $X_i = Z_i$ so $A_i = \sigma_i^{-2} Z_i$. Hence efficient GMM is equivalent to GLS!

In the case of endogenous variables, note that the efficient instrument A_i involves the estimation of the conditional mean of X given Z. In other words, to get the best instrument for X, we need the best conditional mean model for X given Z and not just an arbitrary linear projection. The efficient instrument is also inversely proportional to the conditional variance of e. This is the same as the GLS estimator, namely, that improved efficiency can be obtained if the observations are weighted inversely by the conditional variance of the errors.

13.28 TECHNICAL PROOFS*

Proof of Theorem 13.12 Set $\widetilde{e}_i = Y_i - X_i'\widehat{\beta}_{\text{cgmm}}$ and $\widehat{e}_i = Y_i - X_i'\widehat{\beta}_{\text{gmm}}$. By standard covariance matrix analysis, $\widehat{\Omega} \underset{p}{\longrightarrow} \Omega$ and $\widetilde{\Omega} \underset{p}{\longrightarrow} \Omega$. Thus we can replace $\widehat{\Omega}$ and $\widetilde{\Omega}$ in the criteria without affecting the asymptotic distribution. In particular,

$$\begin{aligned} \widetilde{J}(\widehat{\beta}_{\text{cgmm}}) &= \frac{1}{n}\widetilde{\boldsymbol{e}}'\boldsymbol{Z}\widetilde{\Omega}^{-1}\boldsymbol{Z}'\widetilde{\boldsymbol{e}} \\ &= \frac{1}{n}\widetilde{\boldsymbol{e}}'\boldsymbol{Z}\widehat{\Omega}^{-1}\boldsymbol{Z}'\widetilde{\boldsymbol{e}} + o_p(1). \end{aligned} \tag{13.25}$$

Now observe that

$$\boldsymbol{Z}'\widetilde{\boldsymbol{e}} = \boldsymbol{Z}'\widehat{\boldsymbol{e}} - \boldsymbol{Z}'\boldsymbol{X}\left(\widehat{\beta}_{\text{cgmm}} - \widehat{\beta}_{\text{gmm}}\right).$$

Thus

$$\begin{aligned}\frac{1}{n}\widetilde{\boldsymbol{e}}'\boldsymbol{Z}\widehat{\Omega}^{-1}\boldsymbol{Z}'\widetilde{\boldsymbol{e}} &= \frac{1}{n}\widehat{\boldsymbol{e}}'\boldsymbol{Z}\widehat{\Omega}^{-1}\boldsymbol{Z}'\widehat{\boldsymbol{e}} - \frac{2}{n}\left(\widehat{\beta}_{\text{cgmm}} - \widehat{\beta}_{\text{gmm}}\right)'\boldsymbol{X}'\boldsymbol{Z}\widehat{\Omega}^{-1}\boldsymbol{Z}'\widehat{\boldsymbol{e}} \\ &\quad + \frac{1}{n}\left(\widehat{\beta}_{\text{cgmm}} - \widehat{\beta}_{\text{gmm}}\right)'\boldsymbol{X}'\boldsymbol{Z}\widehat{\Omega}^{-1}\boldsymbol{Z}'\boldsymbol{X}\left(\widehat{\beta}_{\text{cgmm}} - \widehat{\beta}_{\text{gmm}}\right) \\ &= \widehat{J}(\widehat{\beta}_{\text{gmm}}) + \frac{1}{n}\left(\widehat{\beta}_{\text{cgmm}} - \widehat{\beta}_{\text{gmm}}\right)'\boldsymbol{X}'\boldsymbol{Z}\widehat{\Omega}^{-1}\boldsymbol{Z}'\boldsymbol{X}\left(\widehat{\beta}_{\text{cgmm}} - \widehat{\beta}_{\text{gmm}}\right) \qquad (13.26)\end{aligned}$$

where the second equality holds because $\boldsymbol{X}'\boldsymbol{Z}\widehat{\Omega}^{-1}\boldsymbol{Z}'\widehat{\boldsymbol{e}} = 0$ is the first-order condition for $\widehat{\beta}_{\text{gmm}}$. By (13.16) and Theorem 13.4, under $\mathbb{H}_0$

$$\begin{aligned}\sqrt{n}\left(\widehat{\beta}_{\text{cgmm}} - \widehat{\beta}_{\text{gmm}}\right) &= -\left(\boldsymbol{X}'\boldsymbol{Z}\Omega^{-1}\boldsymbol{Z}'\boldsymbol{X}\right)^{-1}\boldsymbol{R}\left(\boldsymbol{R}'\left(\boldsymbol{X}'\boldsymbol{Z}\Omega^{-1}\boldsymbol{Z}'\boldsymbol{X}\right)^{-1}\boldsymbol{R}\right)^{-1}\boldsymbol{R}'\sqrt{n}\left(\widehat{\beta}_{\text{gmm}} - \beta\right) + o_p(1) \\ &\underset{d}{\longrightarrow} \left(\boldsymbol{Q}'\Omega^{-1}\boldsymbol{Q}\right)^{-1}\boldsymbol{R}Z \qquad (13.27)\end{aligned}$$

where

$$Z \sim \mathrm{N}(0, \boldsymbol{V}_{\boldsymbol{R}}) \qquad (13.28)$$

$$\boldsymbol{V}_{\boldsymbol{R}} = \left(\boldsymbol{R}\boldsymbol{V}'\left(\boldsymbol{Q}'\Omega^{-1}\boldsymbol{Q}\right)^{-1}\boldsymbol{R}\right)^{-1}.$$

Putting together (13.25), (13.26), (13.27) and (13.28),

$$\begin{aligned}D &= \widetilde{J}(\widehat{\beta}_{\text{cgmm}}) - \widehat{J}(\widehat{\beta}_{\text{gmm}}) \\ &= \sqrt{n}\left(\widehat{\beta}_{\text{cgmm}} - \widehat{\beta}_{\text{gmm}}\right)'\frac{1}{n}\boldsymbol{X}'\boldsymbol{Z}\widehat{\Omega}^{-1}\frac{1}{n}\boldsymbol{Z}'\boldsymbol{X}\sqrt{n}\left(\widehat{\beta}_{\text{cgmm}} - \widehat{\beta}_{\text{gmm}}\right) \\ &\underset{d}{\longrightarrow} Z'\boldsymbol{V}_{\boldsymbol{R}}^{-1}Z \sim \chi_q^2\end{aligned}$$

because $\boldsymbol{V}_{\boldsymbol{R}} > 0$ and Z is $q \times 1$. ■

Proof of Theorem 13.15 Let $\widetilde{\beta}$ denote the GMM estimator obtained with the instrument set Z_a, and let $\widehat{\beta}$ denote the GMM estimator obtained with the instrument set Z. Set $\widetilde{e}_i = Y_i - X_i'\widetilde{\beta}$, $\widehat{e}_i = Y_i - X_i'\widehat{\beta}$,

$$\widetilde{\Omega} = n^{-1}\sum_{i=1}^{n} Z_{ai}Z_{ai}'\widetilde{e}_i^2$$

$$\widehat{\Omega} = n^{-1}\sum_{i=1}^{n} Z_iZ_i'\widehat{e}_i^2.$$

Let $\boldsymbol{R}$ be the $\ell \times \ell_a$ selector matrix, so that $Z_a = \boldsymbol{R}'Z$. Note that

$$\widetilde{\Omega} = \boldsymbol{R}'n^{-1}\sum_{i=1}^{n} Z_iZ_i'\widetilde{e}_i^2\boldsymbol{R}.$$

By standard covariance matrix analysis, $\widehat{\Omega} \underset{p}{\longrightarrow} \Omega$ and $\widetilde{\Omega} \underset{p}{\longrightarrow} \boldsymbol{R}'\Omega\boldsymbol{R}$. Also, $\frac{1}{n}\boldsymbol{Z}'\boldsymbol{X} \underset{p}{\longrightarrow} \boldsymbol{Q}$, say. By the CLT, $n^{-1/2}\boldsymbol{Z}'\boldsymbol{e} \underset{d}{\longrightarrow} Z$, where $Z \sim \mathrm{N}(0, \Omega)$. Then

$$\begin{aligned} n^{-1/2}\boldsymbol{Z}'\widehat{\boldsymbol{e}} &= \left(\boldsymbol{I}_\ell - \left(\frac{1}{n}\boldsymbol{Z}'\boldsymbol{X}\right)\left(\frac{1}{n}\boldsymbol{X}'\boldsymbol{Z}\widehat{\Omega}^{-1}\frac{1}{n}\boldsymbol{Z}'\boldsymbol{X}\right)^{-1}\left(\frac{1}{n}\boldsymbol{X}'\boldsymbol{Z}\right)\widehat{\Omega}^{-1}\right) n^{-1/2}\boldsymbol{Z}'\boldsymbol{e} \\ &\underset{d}{\longrightarrow} \left(\boldsymbol{I}_\ell - \boldsymbol{Q}\left(\boldsymbol{Q}'\Omega^{-1}\boldsymbol{Q}\right)^{-1}\boldsymbol{Q}'\Omega^{-1}\right) Z \end{aligned}$$

and

$$\begin{aligned} n^{-1/2}\boldsymbol{Z}_a'\widetilde{\boldsymbol{e}} &= \boldsymbol{R}'\left(\boldsymbol{I}_\ell - \left(\frac{1}{n}\boldsymbol{Z}'\boldsymbol{X}\right)\left(\frac{1}{n}\boldsymbol{X}'\boldsymbol{Z}\boldsymbol{R}\widetilde{\Omega}^{-1}\boldsymbol{R}'\frac{1}{n}\boldsymbol{Z}'\boldsymbol{X}\right)^{-1}\left(\frac{1}{n}\boldsymbol{X}'\boldsymbol{Z}\right)\boldsymbol{R}\widetilde{\Omega}^{-1}\boldsymbol{R}'\right) n^{-1/2}\boldsymbol{Z}'\boldsymbol{e} \\ &\underset{d}{\longrightarrow} \boldsymbol{R}'\left(\boldsymbol{I}_\ell - \boldsymbol{Q}\left(\boldsymbol{Q}'\boldsymbol{R}\left(\boldsymbol{R}'\Omega\boldsymbol{R}\right)^{-1}\boldsymbol{R}'\boldsymbol{Q}\right)^{-1}\boldsymbol{Q}'\boldsymbol{R}\left(\boldsymbol{R}'\Omega\boldsymbol{R}\right)^{-1}\boldsymbol{R}'\right) Z \end{aligned}$$

jointly.

By linear rotations of Z and $\boldsymbol{R}$, we can set $\Omega = \boldsymbol{I}_\ell$ to simplify the notation. Thus setting $\boldsymbol{P}_Q = \boldsymbol{Q}\left(\boldsymbol{Q}'\boldsymbol{Q}\right)^{-1}\boldsymbol{Q}'$, $\boldsymbol{P}_R = \boldsymbol{R}\left(\boldsymbol{R}'\boldsymbol{R}\right)^{-1}\boldsymbol{R}'$, and $Z \sim \mathrm{N}(0, \boldsymbol{I}_\ell)$, we have

$$\widehat{J} \underset{d}{\longrightarrow} Z'\left(\boldsymbol{I}_\ell - \boldsymbol{P}_Q\right) Z$$

and

$$\widetilde{J} \underset{d}{\longrightarrow} Z'\left(\boldsymbol{P}_R - \boldsymbol{P}_R\boldsymbol{Q}\left(\boldsymbol{Q}'\boldsymbol{P}_R\boldsymbol{Q}\right)^{-1}\boldsymbol{Q}'\boldsymbol{P}_R\right) Z.$$

It follows that

$$C = \widehat{J} - \widetilde{J} \underset{d}{\longrightarrow} Z'\boldsymbol{A}Z$$

where

$$\boldsymbol{A} = \left(\boldsymbol{I}_\ell - \boldsymbol{P}_Q - \boldsymbol{P}_R + \boldsymbol{P}_R\boldsymbol{Q}\left(\boldsymbol{Q}'\boldsymbol{P}_R\boldsymbol{Q}\right)^{-1}\boldsymbol{Q}'\boldsymbol{P}_R\right).$$

This is a quadratic form in a standard normal vector, and the matrix $\boldsymbol{A}$ is idempotent (this is straightforward to check). Thus $Z'\boldsymbol{A}Z$ is distributed χ^2_d with degrees of freedom d equal to

$$\begin{aligned} \operatorname{rank}(\boldsymbol{A}) &= \operatorname{tr}\left(\boldsymbol{I}_\ell - \boldsymbol{P}_Q - \boldsymbol{P}_R + \boldsymbol{P}_R\boldsymbol{Q}\left(\boldsymbol{Q}'\boldsymbol{P}_R\boldsymbol{Q}\right)^{-1}\boldsymbol{Q}'\boldsymbol{P}_R\right) \\ &= \ell - k - \ell_a + k = \ell_b. \end{aligned}$$

Thus the asymptotic distribution of C is $\chi^2_{\ell_b}$, as claimed. ■

13.29 EXERCISES

Exercise 13.1 Consider the model

$$Y = X'\beta + e$$

$$\mathbb{E}[Xe] = 0$$

$$e^2 = Z'\gamma + \eta$$
$$\mathbb{E}[Z\eta] = 0.$$

Find the method of moments estimators $(\widehat{\beta}, \widehat{\gamma})$ for (β, γ).

Exercise 13.2 Consider the model $Y = X'\beta + e$ with $\mathbb{E}[e \mid Z] = 0$. Let $\widehat{\beta}_{\text{gmm}}$ be the GMM estimator using the weight matrix $\boldsymbol{W}_n = (\boldsymbol{Z}'\boldsymbol{Z})^{-1}$. Under the assumption $\mathbb{E}[e^2 \mid Z] = \sigma^2$, show that

$$\sqrt{n}(\widehat{\beta} - \beta) \underset{d}{\longrightarrow} \mathrm{N}\left(0, \sigma^2 (\boldsymbol{Q}'\boldsymbol{M}^{-1}\boldsymbol{Q})^{-1}\right)$$

where $\boldsymbol{Q} = \mathbb{E}[ZX']$ and $\boldsymbol{M} = \mathbb{E}[ZZ']$.

Exercise 13.3 Consider the model $Y = X'\beta + e$ with $\mathbb{E}[Ze] = 0$. Let $\widetilde{e}_i = Y_i - X_i'\widetilde{\beta}$, where $\widetilde{\beta}$ is consistent for β (e.g., a GMM estimator with some weight matrix). An estimator of the optimal GMM weight matrix is

$$\widehat{\boldsymbol{W}} = \left(\frac{1}{n}\sum_{i=1}^{n} Z_i Z_i' \widetilde{e}_i^2\right)^{-1}.$$

Show that $\widehat{\boldsymbol{W}} \underset{p}{\longrightarrow} \Omega^{-1}$, where $\Omega = \mathbb{E}[ZZ'e^2]$.

Exercise 13.4 In the linear model estimated by GMM with general weight matrix $\boldsymbol{W}$, the asymptotic variance of $\widehat{\beta}_{\text{gmm}}$ is

$$\boldsymbol{V} = (\boldsymbol{Q}'\boldsymbol{W}\boldsymbol{Q})^{-1}\boldsymbol{Q}'\boldsymbol{W}\Omega\boldsymbol{W}\boldsymbol{Q}(\boldsymbol{Q}'\boldsymbol{W}\boldsymbol{Q})^{-1}.$$

(a) Let $\boldsymbol{V}_0$ be this matrix when $\boldsymbol{W} = \Omega^{-1}$. Show that $\boldsymbol{V}_0 = (\boldsymbol{Q}'\Omega^{-1}\boldsymbol{Q})^{-1}$.

(b) We want to show that for any $\boldsymbol{W}$, $\boldsymbol{V} - \boldsymbol{V}_0$ is positive semi-definite (because then $\boldsymbol{V}_0$ is the smallest possible covariance matrix, and $\boldsymbol{W} = \Omega^{-1}$ is the efficient weight matrix). To do this, start by finding matrices $\boldsymbol{A}$ and $\boldsymbol{B}$ such that $\boldsymbol{V} = \boldsymbol{A}'\Omega\boldsymbol{A}$ and $\boldsymbol{V}_0 = \boldsymbol{B}'\Omega\boldsymbol{B}$.

(c) Show that $\boldsymbol{B}'\Omega\boldsymbol{A} = \boldsymbol{B}'\Omega\boldsymbol{B}$ and therefore that $\boldsymbol{B}'\Omega(\boldsymbol{A} - \boldsymbol{B}) = 0$.

(d) Use the expressions $\boldsymbol{V} = \boldsymbol{A}'\Omega\boldsymbol{A}$, $\boldsymbol{A} = \boldsymbol{B} + (\boldsymbol{A} - \boldsymbol{B})$, and $\boldsymbol{B}'\Omega(\boldsymbol{A} - \boldsymbol{B}) = 0$ to show that $\boldsymbol{V} \geq \boldsymbol{V}_0$.

Exercise 13.5 Prove Theorem 13.8.

Exercise 13.6 Derive the constrained GMM estimator (13.16).

Exercise 13.7 Show that the constrained GMM estimator (13.16) with the efficient weight matrix is (13.19).

Exercise 13.8 Prove Theorem 13.9.

Exercise 13.9 Prove Theorem 13.10.

Exercise 13.10 The equation of interest is $Y = m(X, \beta) + e$ with $\mathbb{E}[Ze] = 0$, where $m(x, \beta)$ is a known function, β is $k \times 1$, and Z is $\ell \times 1$. Show how to construct an efficient GMM estimator for β.

Exercise 13.11 As a continuation of Exercise 12.7, derive the efficient GMM estimator using the instrument $Z = (X \quad X^2)'$. Does this differ from 2SLS and/or OLS?

Exercise 13.12 In the linear model $Y = X'\beta + e$ with $\mathbb{E}[Xe] = 0$, the GMM criterion function for β is

$$J(\beta) = \frac{1}{n}(\boldsymbol{Y} - \boldsymbol{X}\beta)' \boldsymbol{X}\widehat{\Omega}^{-1}\boldsymbol{X}'(\boldsymbol{Y} - \boldsymbol{X}\beta) \tag{13.29}$$

where $\widehat{\Omega} = n^{-1}\sum_{i=1}^{n} X_i X_i' \widehat{e}_i^2$, $\widehat{e}_i = Y_i - X_i'\widehat{\beta}$ are the OLS residuals, and $\widehat{\beta} = (\boldsymbol{X}'\boldsymbol{X})^{-1}\boldsymbol{X}'\boldsymbol{Y}$ is least squares. The GMM estimator of β, subject to the restriction $r(\beta) = 0$, is

$$\widetilde{\beta} = \underset{r(\beta)=0}{\operatorname{argmin}}\, J_n(\beta).$$

The GMM test statistic (the distance statistic) of the hypothesis $r(\beta) = 0$ is

$$D = J(\widetilde{\beta}) = \min_{r(\beta)=0} J(\beta). \tag{13.30}$$

(a) Show that you can rewrite $J(\beta)$ in (13.29) as

$$J(\beta) = n\left(\beta - \widehat{\beta}\right)' \widehat{\boldsymbol{V}}_{\beta}^{-1}\left(\beta - \widehat{\beta}\right)$$

and thus $\widetilde{\beta}$ is the same as the minimum distance estimator.

(b) Show that under linear hypotheses, the distance statistic D in (13.30) equals the Wald statistic.

Exercise 13.13 Take the linear model $Y = X'\beta + e$ with $\mathbb{E}[Ze] = 0$. Consider the GMM estimator $\widehat{\beta}$ of β. Let $J = n\overline{g}_n(\widehat{\beta})'\widehat{\Omega}^{-1}\overline{g}_n(\widehat{\beta})$ denote the test of overidentifying restrictions. Show that $J \underset{d}{\longrightarrow} \chi^2_{\ell-k}$ as $n \to \infty$ by demonstrating each of the following.

(a) Since $\Omega > 0$, we can write $\Omega^{-1} = \boldsymbol{C}\boldsymbol{C}'$ and $\Omega = \boldsymbol{C}'^{-1}\boldsymbol{C}^{-1}$ for some matrix $\boldsymbol{C}$.

(b) $J = n\left(\boldsymbol{C}'\overline{g}_n(\widehat{\beta})\right)'\left(\boldsymbol{C}'\widehat{\Omega}\boldsymbol{C}\right)^{-1}\boldsymbol{C}'\overline{g}_n(\widehat{\beta})$.

(c) $\boldsymbol{C}'\overline{g}_n(\widehat{\beta}) = \boldsymbol{D}_n\boldsymbol{C}'\overline{g}_n(\beta)$, where $\overline{g}_n(\beta) = \frac{1}{n}\boldsymbol{Z}'\boldsymbol{e}$, and

$$\boldsymbol{D}_n = \boldsymbol{I}_\ell - \boldsymbol{C}'\left(\frac{1}{n}\boldsymbol{Z}'\boldsymbol{X}\right)\left(\left(\frac{1}{n}\boldsymbol{X}'\boldsymbol{Z}\right)\widehat{\Omega}^{-1}\left(\frac{1}{n}\boldsymbol{Z}'\boldsymbol{X}\right)\right)^{-1}\left(\frac{1}{n}\boldsymbol{X}'\boldsymbol{Z}\right)\widehat{\Omega}^{-1}\boldsymbol{C}'^{-1}.$$

(d) $\boldsymbol{D}_n \underset{p}{\longrightarrow} \boldsymbol{I}_\ell - \boldsymbol{R}\left(\boldsymbol{R}'\boldsymbol{R}\right)^{-1}\boldsymbol{R}'$, where $\boldsymbol{R} = \boldsymbol{C}'\mathbb{E}\left[ZX'\right]$.

(e) $n^{1/2}\boldsymbol{C}'\overline{g}_n(\beta) \underset{d}{\longrightarrow} u \sim \mathrm{N}(0, \boldsymbol{I}_\ell)$.

(f) $J \underset{d}{\longrightarrow} u'\left(\boldsymbol{I}_\ell - \boldsymbol{R}\left(\boldsymbol{R}'\boldsymbol{R}\right)^{-1}\boldsymbol{R}'\right)u$.

(g) $u'\left(\boldsymbol{I}_\ell - \boldsymbol{R}\left(\boldsymbol{R}'\boldsymbol{R}\right)^{-1}\boldsymbol{R}'\right)u \sim \chi^2_{\ell-k}$.
Hint: $\boldsymbol{I}_\ell - \boldsymbol{R}\left(\boldsymbol{R}'\boldsymbol{R}\right)^{-1}\boldsymbol{R}'$ is a projection matrix.

Exercise 13.14 Use the model $Y = X'\beta + e$ with $\mathbb{E}[Ze] = 0$, $Y \in \mathbb{R}$, $X \in \mathbb{R}^k$, $Z \in \mathbb{R}^\ell$, $\ell \geq k$. Consider the statistic

$$J(\beta) = n\overline{m}_n(\beta)'\boldsymbol{W}\overline{m}_n(\beta)$$

$$\overline{m}_n(\beta) = \frac{1}{n}\sum_{i=1}^{n} Z_i\left(Y_i - X_i'\beta\right)$$

for some weight matrix $\boldsymbol{W} > 0$.

(a) Take the hypothesis $\mathbb{H}_0 : \beta = \beta_0$. Derive the asymptotic distribution of $J(\beta_0)$ under $\mathbb{H}_0$ as $n \to \infty$.

(b) What choice for $\boldsymbol{W}$ yields a known asymptotic distribution in part (a)? (Be specific about degrees of freedom.)

(c) Write down an appropriate estimator $\widehat{\boldsymbol{W}}$ for $\boldsymbol{W}$ that takes advantage of $\mathbb{H}_0$. (You do not need to demonstrate consistency or unbiasedness.)

(d) Describe an asymptotic test of $\mathbb{H}_0$ against $\mathbb{H}_1 : \beta \neq \beta_0$ based on this statistic.

(e) Use the result in part (d) to construct a confidence region for β. What can you say about the form of this region? For example, does the confidence region take the form of an ellipse, similar to conventional confidence regions?

Exercise 13.15 Consider the model $Y = X'\beta + e$ with $\mathbb{E}[Ze] = 0$ and

$$\boldsymbol{R}'\beta = 0 \tag{13.31}$$

with $Y \in \mathbb{R}, X \in \mathbb{R}^k, Z \in \mathbb{R}^\ell, \ell > k$. The matrix $\boldsymbol{R}$ is $k \times q$ with $1 \leq q < k$. You have a random sample $(Y_i, X_i, Z_i : i = 1, \ldots, n)$.
For simplicity, assume the efficient weight matrix $\boldsymbol{W} = \left(\mathbb{E}\left[ZZ'e^2\right]\right)^{-1}$ is known.

(a) Write out the GMM estimator $\widehat{\beta}$ ignoring constraint (13.31).

(b) Write out the GMM estimator $\widetilde{\beta}$ adding the constraint (13.31).

(c) Find the asymptotic distribution of $\sqrt{n}\left(\widetilde{\beta} - \beta\right)$ as $n \to \infty$ assuming (13.31).

Exercise 13.16 The observed data are $\{Y_i, X_i, Z_i\} \in \mathbb{R} \times \mathbb{R}^k \times \mathbb{R}^\ell$, $k > 1$ and $\ell > k > 1$, $i = 1, \ldots, n$. The model is $Y = X'\beta + e$ with $\mathbb{E}[Ze] = 0$.

(a) Given a weight matrix $\boldsymbol{W} > 0$, write down the GMM estimator $\widehat{\beta}$ for β.

(b) Suppose the model is misspecified. Specifically, assume that for some $\delta \neq 0$,

$$e = \delta n^{-1/2} + u \tag{13.32}$$

$$\mathbb{E}[u \mid Z] = 0$$

with $\mu_Z = \mathbb{E}[Z] \neq 0$. Show that (13.32) implies $\mathbb{E}[Ze] \neq 0$.

(c) Express $\sqrt{n}\left(\widehat{\beta} - \beta\right)$ as a function of $\boldsymbol{W}$, n, δ, and the variables (X_i, Z_i, u_i).

(d) Find the asymptotic distribution of $\sqrt{n}\left(\widehat{\beta} - \beta\right)$ assuming (13.32).

Exercise 13.17 The model is $Y = Z\beta + X\gamma + e$ with $\mathbb{E}[e \mid Z] = 0$, $X \in \mathbb{R}$, and $Z \in \mathbb{R}$. X is potentially endogenous, and Z is exogenous. Someone suggests estimating (β, γ) by GMM using the pair (Z, Z^2) as instruments. Is this feasible? Under what conditions is this a valid estimator?

Exercise 13.18 The observations are i.i.d., $(Y_i, X_i, Q_i : i = 1, \ldots, n)$, where X is $k \times 1$ and Q is $m \times 1$. The model is $Y = X'\beta + e$ with $\mathbb{E}[Xe] = 0$ and $\mathbb{E}[Qe] = 0$. Find the efficient GMM estimator for β.

Exercise 13.19 You want to estimate $\mu = \mathbb{E}[Y]$ under the assumption that $\mathbb{E}[X] = 0$, where Y and X are scalar and observed from a random sample. Find an efficient GMM estimator for μ.

Exercise 13.20 Consider the model $Y = X'\beta + e$, given $\mathbb{E}[Ze] = 0$ and $\boldsymbol{R}'\beta = 0$. The dimensions are $X \in R^k$ and $Z \in R^\ell$ with $\ell > k$. The matrix $\boldsymbol{R}$ is $k \times q$, $1 \le q < k$. Derive an efficient GMM estimator for β.

Exercise 13.21 Take the linear equation $Y = X'\beta + e$, and consider the following estimators of β:

1. $\widehat{\beta}$: 2SLS using the instruments Z_1.
2. $\widetilde{\beta}$: 2SLS using the instruments Z_2.
3. $\overline{\beta}$: GMM using the instruments $Z = (Z_1, Z_2)$ and the weight matrix

$$\boldsymbol{W} = \begin{pmatrix} \left(\boldsymbol{Z}_1'\boldsymbol{Z}_1\right)^{-1}\lambda & 0 \\ 0 & \left(\boldsymbol{Z}_2'\boldsymbol{Z}_2\right)^{-1}(1-\lambda) \end{pmatrix}$$

for $\lambda \in (0, 1)$.

Find an expression for $\overline{\beta}$ showing that it is a specific weighted average of $\widehat{\beta}$ and $\widetilde{\beta}$.

Exercise 13.22 Consider the just-identified model $Y = X_1'\beta_1 + X_2'\beta_2 + e$ with $\mathbb{E}[Ze] = 0$, where $X = (X_1'\ X_2')' \in \mathbb{R}^k$ and $Z \in \mathbb{R}^k$. We want to test $\mathbb{H}_0 : \beta_1 = 0$. Three econometricians are called for advice.

- Econometrician 1 proposes testing $\mathbb{H}_0$ by a Wald statistic.
- Econometrician 2 suggests testing $\mathbb{H}_0$ by the GMM distance statistic.
- Econometrician 3 suggests testing $\mathbb{H}_0$ using the test of overidentifying restrictions.

You are asked to settle this dispute. Explain the advantages and/or disadvantages of the different procedures in this specific context.

Exercise 13.23 Consider the model $Y = X'\beta + e$ with $\mathbb{E}[Xe] = 0$ and $\beta = \boldsymbol{Q}\theta$, where β is $k \times 1$, $\boldsymbol{Q}$ is $k \times m$ with $m < k$, $\boldsymbol{Q}$ is known, and θ is $m \times 1$. The observations (Y_i, X_i) are i.i.d. across $i = 1, \ldots, n$. Under these assumptions what is the efficient estimator of θ?

Exercise 13.24 Consider the model $Y = \theta + e$ with $\mathbb{E}[Xe] = 0$, $Y \in \mathbb{R}$, $X \in \mathbb{R}^k$, and (Y_i, X_i) a random sample.

(a) Find the efficient GMM estimator of θ.

(b) Is this model overidentified or just-identified?

(c) Find the GMM test statistic for overidentification.

Exercise 13.25 Consider the model $Y = X'\beta + e$ with $\mathbb{E}[Xe] = 0$, where X contains an intercept, so $\mathbb{E}[e] = 0$. An enterprising econometrician notices that the following n moment conditions are implied:

$$\mathbb{E}[e_i] = 0, \; i = 1, \ldots, n.$$

Given an $n \times n$ weight matrix $\boldsymbol{W}$, this implies a GMM criterion

$$J(\beta) = (\boldsymbol{Y} - \boldsymbol{X}\beta)'\,\boldsymbol{W}\,(\boldsymbol{Y} - \boldsymbol{X}\beta).$$

(a) Under i.i.d. sampling, show that the efficient weight matrix is $\boldsymbol{W} = \sigma^{-2}\boldsymbol{I}_n$, where $\sigma^2 = \mathbb{E}\left[e^2\right]$.

(b) Using the weight matrix $\boldsymbol{W}=\sigma^{-2}\boldsymbol{I}_n$, find the GMM estimator $\widehat{\beta}$ that minimizes $J(\beta)$.

(c) Find a simple expression for the minimized criteria $J(\widehat{\beta})$.

(d) Theorem 13.14 says that criteria such as $J(\widehat{\beta})$ are asymptotically $\chi^2_{\ell-k}$, where ℓ is the number of moments. While the assumptions of Theorem 13.14 do not apply to this context, what is ℓ here? That is, which χ^2 distribution is the asserted asymptotic distribution?

(e) Does the answer in (d) make sense? Explain your reasoning.

Exercise 13.26 Consider the model $Y=X'\beta+e$ with $\mathbb{E}[e \mid X]=0$ and $\mathbb{E}\left[e^2 \mid X\right]=\sigma^2$. An econometrician more enterprising than the one in Exercise 13.25 notices that this model implies the nk moment conditions

$$\mathbb{E}[X_i e_i]=0, \quad i=1,\ldots,n.$$

We can write the moments using matrix notation as $\mathbb{E}\left[\overline{\boldsymbol{X}}'(\boldsymbol{Y}-\boldsymbol{X}\beta)\right]$, where

$$\overline{\boldsymbol{X}}=\begin{pmatrix} X_1' & 0 & \cdots & 0 \\ 0 & X_2' & & 0 \\ \vdots & \vdots & & \vdots \\ 0 & 0 & \cdots & X_n' \end{pmatrix}.$$

Given an $nk \times nk$ weight matrix $\boldsymbol{W}$, this implies a GMM criterion

$$J(\beta)=(\boldsymbol{Y}-\boldsymbol{X}\beta)'\overline{\boldsymbol{X}}\boldsymbol{W}\overline{\boldsymbol{X}}'(\boldsymbol{Y}-\boldsymbol{X}\beta).$$

The econometrician decides to set $\boldsymbol{W}=\Omega^-$, the Moore-Penrose generalized inverse of Ω. (See Section A.6.) Note: A useful fact is that for a vector $\boldsymbol{a}$, $(\boldsymbol{a}\boldsymbol{a}')^-=\boldsymbol{a}\boldsymbol{a}'(\boldsymbol{a}'\boldsymbol{a})^{-2}$.

(a) Calculate $\Omega=\mathbb{E}\left[\overline{\boldsymbol{X}}'\boldsymbol{e}\boldsymbol{e}'\overline{\boldsymbol{X}}\right]$.

(b) Find the GMM estimator $\widehat{\beta}$ that minimizes $J(\beta)$.

(c) Find a simple expression for the minimized criterion $J(\widehat{\beta})$.

(d) Comment on whether the χ^2 approximation from Theorem 13.14 is appropriate for $J(\widehat{\beta})$.

Exercise 13.27 This exercise is a continuation of Exercise 12.22, based on the empirical work reported in Acemoglu, Johnson, and Robinson (2001).

(a) Re-estimate the model estimated in part (j) by efficient GMM. Use the 2SLS estimates as the first step for the weight matrix, and then calculate the GMM estimator using this weight matrix without further iteration. Report the estimates and standard errors.

(b) Calculate and report the J statistic for overidentification.

(c) Compare the GMM and 2SLS estimates. Discuss your findings.

Exercise 13.28 This exercise is a continuation of Exercise 12.24, which involved estimation of a wage equation by 2SLS.

(a) Re-estimate the model in part (a) by efficient GMM. Do the results change meaningfully?

(b) Re-estimate the model in part (d) by efficient GMM. Do the results change meaningfully?

(c) Report the J statistic for overidentification.

PART IV

DEPENDENT AND PANEL DATA

CHAPTER 14

TIME SERIES

14.1 INTRODUCTION

A **time series** $Y_t \in \mathbb{R}^m$ is a process that is sequentially ordered over time. In this textbook, we focus on discrete time series, where t is an integer, though there is also a considerable literature on continuous-time processes. To denote the time period, it is typical to use the subscript t. The time series is **univariate** if $m = 1$ and **multivariate** if $m > 1$. This chapter is primarily focused on univariate time series models, though we describe the concepts for the multivariate case when the added generality does not add extra complication.

Most economic time series are recorded at discrete intervals such as annual, quarterly, monthly, weekly, or daily intervals. The number of observed periods s per year is called the **frequency**. In most cases, we denote the observed sample by the periods $t = 1, \dots, n$.

Because of the sequential nature of time series, we expect that observations close in calender time, (e.g., Y_t and its **lagged** value Y_{t-1}) will be dependent. This type of dependence structure requires a different distributional theory than for cross-sectional and clustered observations, since we cannot divide the sample into independent groups. Many of the issues that distinguish time series from cross-section econometrics concern the modeling of these dependence relationships.

There are many excellent textbooks for time series analysis. The encyclopedic standard is Hamilton (1994). Others include Harvey (1990), Tong (1990), Brockwell and Davis (1991), Fan and Yao (2003), Lütkepohl (2005), Enders (2014), and Kilian and Lütkepohl (2017). For textbooks on the related subject of forecasting see Granger and Newbold (1986), Granger (1989), and Elliott and Timmermann (2016).

14.2 EXAMPLES

Many economic time series are macroeconomic variables. An excellent resource for U.S. macroeconomic data are the FRED-MD and FRED-QD databases, which contain a wide set of monthly and quarterly variables, assembled and maintained by the St. Louis Federal Reserve Bank. See McCracken and Ng (2016, 2021). The datasets FRED-MD and FRED-QD for 1959–2017 are posted on the textbook website. FRED-MD has 129 variables over 708 months. FRED-QD has 248 variables over 236 quarters.

When working with time series data, one of the first tasks is to plot the series against time. Figures 14.1 and 14.2 plot eight example time series from FRED-QD and FRED-MD. As is conventional, the x-axis displays calendar dates (in this case years), and the y-axis displays the level of the series. The series plotted are: (1a) Real U.S. GDP (*gdpc1*); (1b) U.S.-Canada exchange rate (*excausx*); (1c) Interest rate on U.S. 10-year Treasury bond (*gs10*); (1d) Real crude oil price (*oilpricex*); (2a) U.S. unemployment rate (*unrate*); (2b) U.S. real nondurables consumption growth rate (growth rate of *pcndx*); (2c) U.S. CPI inflation rate (growth rate of *cpiaucsl*); (2d) S&P 500 return (growth rate of *sp500*). Panels (1a) and (2b) are quarterly series, the rest are monthly.

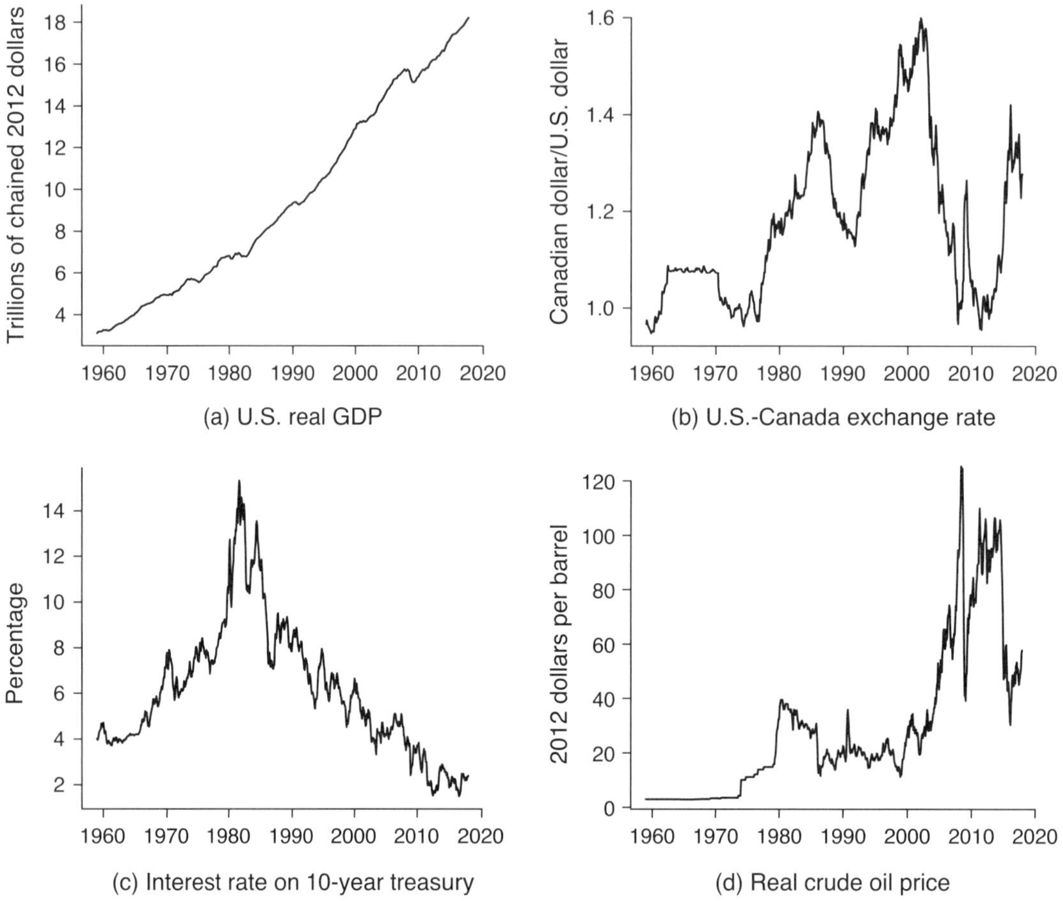

FIGURE 14.1 GDP, exchange rate, interest rate, and oil price

Many of the plots are smooth, meaning that the neighboring values (in calendar time) are similar to one another and hence are serially correlated. Some of the plots are not smooth, meaning that the neighboring values are less similar and hence less correlated. At least one plot (real GDP) displays an upward trend.

14.3 DIFFERENCES AND GROWTH RATES

It is common to transform series by taking logarithms, differences, and/or growth rates. Three of the series in Figure 14.2 (consumption growth, inflation [growth rate of CPI index], and S&P 500 return) are displayed as growth rates. This may be done for various reasons. The most credible is that this is the suitable transformation for the desired analysis. Many aggregate series such as real GDP are transformed by taking natural logarithms, which flattens the apparent exponential growth and makes fluctuations proportionate.

The first difference of a series Y_t is

$$\Delta Y_t = Y_t - Y_{t-1}.$$

The second difference is

$$\Delta^2 Y_t = \Delta Y_t - \Delta Y_{t-1}.$$

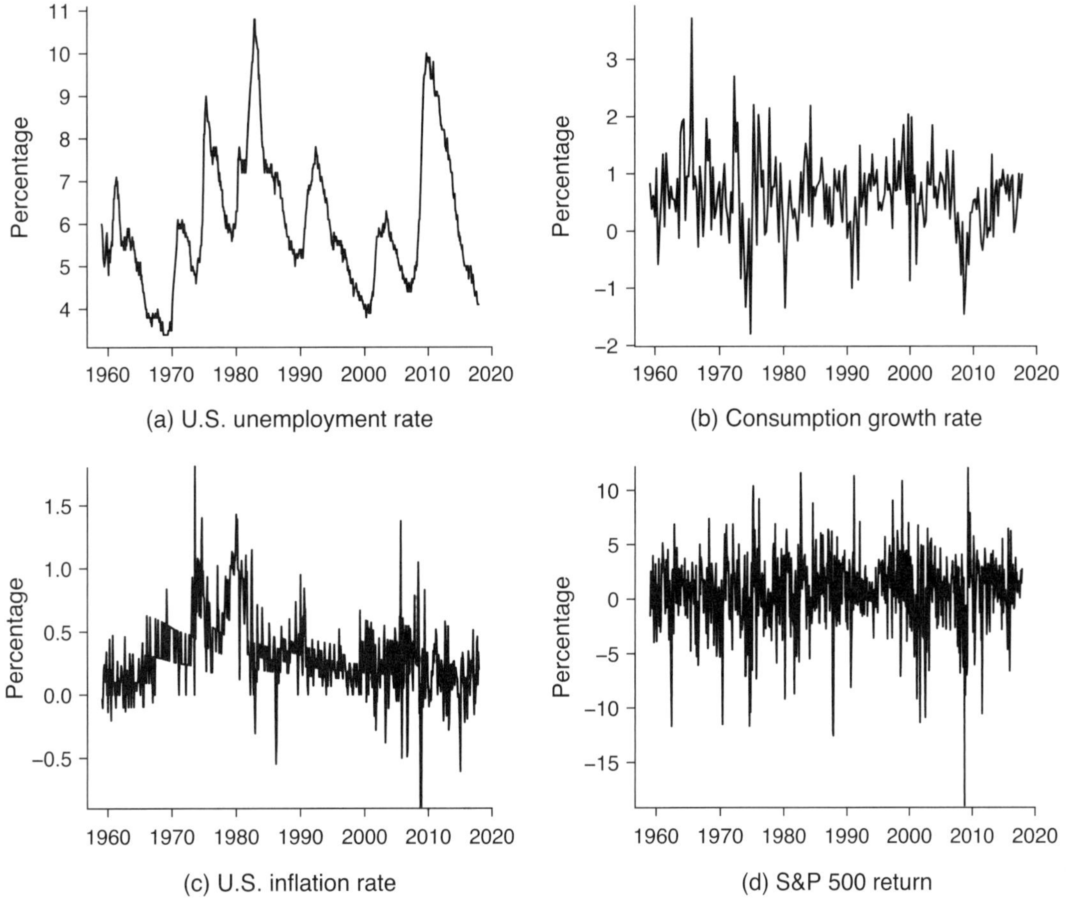

FIGURE 14.2 Unemployment rate, consumption growth rate, inflation rate, and S&P 500 return

Higher-order differences can be defined similarly but are not used in practice. The annual, or year-on-year, change of a series Y_t with frequency s is

$$\Delta_s Y_t = Y_t - Y_{t-s}.$$

Several methods can be used to calculate growth rates. The one-period growth rate is the percentage change from period $t-1$ to period t:

$$Q_t = 100\left(\frac{\Delta Y_t}{Y_{t-1}}\right) = 100\left(\frac{Y_t}{Y_{t-1}} - 1\right). \tag{14.1}$$

The multiplication by 100 is not essential but scales Q_t so that it is a percentage. This transformation is used for the plots in Figure 14.2(b)–(d). For quarterly data, Q_t is the quarterly growth rate. For monthly data, Q_t is the monthly growth rate.

For non-annual data, the one-period growth rate (14.1) may be unappealing for interpretation. Consequently, statistical agencies commonly report an "annualized" growth rate, which is the annual growth that would occur if the one-period growth rate is compounded for a full year. For a series with frequency s, the annualized growth rate is

$$A_t = 100\left(\left(\frac{Y_t}{Y_{t-1}}\right)^s - 1\right). \tag{14.2}$$

Notice that A_t is a nonlinear function of Q_t.

Year-on-year growth rates are

$$G_t = 100\left(\frac{\Delta_s Y_t}{Y_{t-s}}\right) = 100\left(\frac{Y_t}{Y_{t-s}} - 1\right).$$

These rates do not need annualization.

Growth rates are closely related to logarithmic transformations. For small growth rates, Q_t, A_t, and G_t are approximately first differences in logarithms:

$$Q_t \simeq 100\Delta \log Y_t$$
$$A_t \simeq s \times 100\Delta \log Y_t$$
$$G_t \simeq 100\Delta_s \log Y_t.$$

For analysis using growth rates, I recommend the one-period growth rates (14.1) or differenced logarithms rather than the annualized growth rates (14.2). While annualized growth rates are preferred for reporting, they are a highly nonlinear transformation, which is unnatural for statistical analysis. Differenced logarithms are the most common choice and are recommended for models that combine log-levels and growth rates, because then the models are linear in all variables.

14.4 STATIONARITY

Recall that cross-sectional observations are conventionally treated as random draws from an underlying population. This is not an appropriate model for time series processes due to serial dependence. Instead, we treat the observed sample $\{Y_1, \ldots, Y_n\}$ as a realization of a dependent stochastic process. It is often useful to view $\{Y_1, \ldots, Y_n\}$ as a subset of an underlying doubly infinite sequence $\{\ldots, Y_{t-1}, Y_t, Y_{t+1}, \ldots\}$.

A random vector Y_t can be characterized by its distribution. A set such as $(Y_t, Y_{t+1}, \ldots, Y_{t+\ell})$ can be characterized by its joint distribution. Important features of these distributions are their means, variances, and covariances. Since there is only one observed time series sample, to learn about these distributions, some sort of constancy is needed. This may only hold after a suitable transformation such as growth rates (as discussed in Section 14.3).

The most commonly assumed form of constancy is **stationarity**. There are two definitions. The first is sufficient for the construction of linear models.

Definition 14.1 $\{Y_t\}$ is **covariance or weakly stationary** if the expectation $\mu = \mathbb{E}[Y_t]$ and covariance matrix $\Sigma = \operatorname{var}[Y_t] = \mathbb{E}\left[(Y_t - \mu)(Y_t - \mu)'\right]$ are finite and are independent of t, and the **autocovariances**

$$\Gamma(k) = \operatorname{cov}\left(Y_t, Y_{t-k}\right) = \mathbb{E}\left[(Y_t - \mu)\left(Y_{t-k} - \mu\right)'\right]$$

are independent of t for all k.

In the univariate case, we typically write the variance as σ^2 and autocovariances as $\gamma(k)$.

The expectation μ and variance Σ are features of the marginal distribution of Y_t (the distribution of Y_t at a specific time period t). Their constancy as stated in Definition 14.1 means that these features of the distribution are stable over time.

The autocovariances $\Gamma(k)$ are features of the bivariate distributions of (Y_t, Y_{t-k}). Their constancy as stated in the definition means that the correlation patterns between adjacent Y_t are stable over time and only depend on the number of time periods k separating the variables. By symmetry, we have $\Gamma(-k) = \Gamma(k)'$. In the univariate case, this simplifies to $\gamma(-k) = \gamma(k)$. The autocovariances $\Gamma(k)$ are finite under the assumption that the covariance matrix Σ is finite by the Cauchy-Schwarz inequality.

The autocovariances summarize the linear dependence between Y_t and its lags. A scale-free measure of linear dependence in the univariate case are the **autocorrelations**

$$\rho(k) = \operatorname{corr}\left(Y_t, Y_{t-k}\right) = \frac{\operatorname{cov}\left(Y_t, Y_{t-k}\right)}{\sqrt{\operatorname{var}\left[Y_t\right] \operatorname{var}\left[Y_{t-1}\right]}} = \frac{\gamma(k)}{\sigma^2} = \frac{\gamma(k)}{\gamma(0)}.$$

Notice by symmetry that $\rho(-k) = \rho(k)$.

The second definition of stationarity concerns the entire joint distribution.

Definition 14.2 $\{Y_t\}$ is **strictly stationary** if the joint distribution of $(Y_t, \ldots, Y_{t+\ell})$ is independent of t for all ℓ.

Definition 14.2 is the natural generalization of the cross-section definition of identical distributions. Strict stationarity implies that the (marginal) distribution of Y_t does not vary over time. It also implies that the bivariate distributions of (Y_t, Y_{t+1}) and multivariate distributions of $(Y_t, \ldots, Y_{t+\ell})$ are stable over time. Under the assumption of a bounded variance, a strictly stationary process is covariance stationary.[1]

For formal statistical theory, we generally require the stronger assumption of strict stationarity. Therefore if we label a process as "stationary," you should interpret it as meaning "strictly stationary."

The core meaning of both weak and strict stationarity is the same—that the distribution of Y_t is stable over time. To understand the concept, it may be useful to review the plots in Figures 14.1 and 14.2. Are these stationary processes? If so, we would expect that the expectation and variance to be stable over time. This seems unlikely to apply to the series in Figure 14.1, as in each case, it is difficult to describe what the "typical" value of the series is. Stationarity may be appropriate for the series in Figure 14.2, as each oscillates with a fairly regular pattern. It is difficult, however, to know whether a given time series is stationary simply by examining a time series plot.

A straightforward but essential relationship is that an i.i.d. process is strictly stationary.

Theorem 14.1 If Y_t is i.i.d., then it strictly stationary.

Here are some examples of strictly stationary scalar processes. In each, e_t is i.i.d. and $\mathbb{E}[e_t] = 0$.

Example 14.1 $Y_t = e_t + \theta e_{t-1}$.

Example 14.2 $Y_t = Z$ for some random variable Z.

[1]More generally, the two classes are non-nested, since strictly stationary infinite variance processes are not covariance stationary.

Example 14.3 $Y_t = (-1)^t Z$ for a random variable Z, which is symmetrically distributed about 0.

Here are some examples of processes that are not stationary.

Example 14.4 $Y_t = t$.

Example 14.5 $Y_t = (-1)^t$.

Example 14.6 $Y_t = \cos(\theta t)$.

Example 14.7 $Y_t = \sqrt{t}\, e_t$.

Example 14.8 $Y_t = e_t + t^{-1/2} e_{t-1}$.

Example 14.9 $Y_t = Y_{t-1} + e_t$ with $Y_0 = 0$.

From the examples, we can see that stationarity means that the distribution is constant over time. It does not mean, however, that the process has some sort of limited dependence, nor does it mean that periodic patterns are absent. These restrictions are associated with the concepts of ergodicity and mixing, which we shall introduce in subsequent sections.

14.5 TRANSFORMATIONS OF STATIONARY PROCESSES

One of the important properties of strict stationarity is that it is preserved by transformation. That is, transformations of strictly stationary processes are also strictly stationary. This includes transformations that include the full history of Y_t.

Theorem 14.2 If Y_t is strictly stationary and $X_t = \phi(Y_t, Y_{t-1}, Y_{t-2}, \ldots) \in \mathbb{R}^q$ is a random vector, then X_t is strictly stationary.

Theorem 14.2 is extremely useful both for the study of stochastic processes that are constructed from underlying errors and for the study of sample statistics, such as linear regression estimators, that are functions of sample averages of squares and cross-products of the original data.

The proof of Theorem 14.2 is in Section 14.47.

14.6 CONVERGENT SERIES

A transformation that includes the full past history is an infinite-order moving average. For scalar Y and coefficients a_j, define the vector process

$$X_t = \sum_{j=0}^{\infty} a_j Y_{t-j}. \tag{14.3}$$

Many time series models involve representations and transformations of the form (14.3).

The infinite series (14.3) exists if it is convergent, meaning that the sequence $\sum_{j=0}^{N} a_j Y_{t-j}$ has a finite limit as $N \to \infty$. Since the inputs Y_t are random, we define this as a probability limit.

Definition 14.3 The infinite series (14.3) **converges almost surely** if $\sum_{j=0}^{N} a_j Y_{t-j}$ has a finite limit as $N \to \infty$ with probability 1. In this case, we describe X_t as **convergent**.

Theorem 14.3 If Y_t is strictly stationary, $\mathbb{E}|Y| < \infty$, and $\sum_{j=0}^{\infty} |a_j| < \infty$, then (14.3) converges almost surely. Furthermore, X_t is strictly stationary.

The proof of Theorem 14.3 is provided in Section 14.47.

14.7 ERGODICITY

Stationarity alone is not sufficient for the WLLN, as there are strictly stationary processes with no time series variation. As described earlier, an example of a stationary process is $Y_t = Z$ for some random variable Z. This is random but constant over all time. An implication is that the sample mean of $Y_t = Z$ will be inconsistent for the population expectation.

What is a minimal assumption beyond stationarity so that the law of large numbers applies? This topic is called **ergodicity**. It is sufficiently important that it is treated as a separate area of study. We mention only a few highlights here. For a rigorous treatment, see a standard textbook, such as Walters (1982).

A time series Y_t is **ergodic** if all time invariant events are trivial, meaning that any event that is unaffected by time shifts has probability either 0 or 1. This definition is rather abstract and difficult to grasp, but fortunately it is not needed by most economists.

A useful intuition is that if Y_t is ergodic, then its sample paths will pass through all parts of the sample space, never getting "stuck" in a subregion.

Let us first discuss the properties of ergodic series that are relevant for our needs and follow with the more rigorous technical definitions. For proofs of the results, see Section 14.47.

First, many standard time series processes can be shown to be ergodic. A useful starting point is the observation that an i.i.d. sequence is ergodic.

Theorem 14.4 If $Y_t \in \mathbb{R}^m$ is i.i.d., then it strictly stationary and ergodic.

Second, ergodicity, like stationarity, is preserved by transformation.

Theorem 14.5 If $Y_t \in \mathbb{R}^m$ is strictly stationary and ergodic and $X_t = \phi(Y_t, Y_{t-1}, Y_{t-2}, \ldots)$ is a random vector, then X_t is strictly stationary and ergodic.

As an example, the infinite-order moving average transformation (14.3) is ergodic if the input is ergodic and the coefficients are absolutely convergent.

Theorem 14.6 If Y_t is strictly stationary, ergodic, $\mathbb{E}|Y| < \infty$, and $\sum_{j=0}^{\infty} |a_j| < \infty$, then $X_t = \sum_{j=0}^{\infty} a_j Y_{t-j}$ is strictly stationary and ergodic.

We now consider a useful property. It is that the Cesàro sum of the autocovariances limits to 0.

Theorem 14.7 If $Y_t \in \mathbb{R}$ is strictly stationary, ergodic, and $\mathbb{E}\left[Y^2\right] < \infty$, then

$$\lim_{n\to\infty} \frac{1}{n} \sum_{\ell=1}^{n} \operatorname{cov}(Y_t, Y_{t+\ell}) = 0. \tag{14.4}$$

The result (14.4) can be interpreted as that the autocovariances "on average" tend to 0. Some authors have misstated ergodicity as implying that the covariances tend to 0, but this is not correct, as (14.4) allows, for example, the nonconvergent sequence $\operatorname{cov}(Y_t, Y_{t+\ell}) = (-1)^{\ell}$. The reason (14.4) is particularly useful is because it is sufficient for the WLLN, as we discover later in Theorem 14.9.

I now give the formal definition of ergodicity for interested readers. As the concepts will not be used again, most readers can safely skip this discussion.

As stated above, by definition, the series $Y_t \in \mathbb{R}^m$ is ergodic if all time invariant events are trivial. To understand this, we introduce some technical definitions. First, we can write an event as $A = \left\{\widetilde{Y}_t \in G\right\}$, where $\widetilde{Y}_t = (\ldots, Y_{t-1}, Y_t, Y_{t+1}, \ldots)$ is an infinite history and $G \subset \mathbb{R}^{m\infty}$. Second, the ℓth **time-shift** of $\widetilde{Y}_t$ is defined as $\widetilde{Y}_{t+\ell} = (\ldots, Y_{t-1+\ell}, Y_{t+\ell}, Y_{t+1+\ell}, \ldots)$. Thus $\widetilde{Y}_{t+\ell}$ replaces each observation in $\widetilde{Y}_t$ by its ℓth shifted value $Y_{t+\ell}$. A time-shift of the event $A = \left\{\widetilde{Y}_t \in G\right\}$ is $A_\ell = \left\{\widetilde{Y}_{t+\ell} \in G\right\}$. Third, an event A is called **invariant** if it is unaffected by a time-shift, so that $A_\ell = A$. Thus replacing any history $\widetilde{Y}_t$ with its shifted history $\widetilde{Y}_{t+\ell}$ doesn't change the event. Invariant events are rather special. An example of an invariant event is $A = \{\max_{-\infty<t<\infty} Y_t \le 0\}$. Fourth, an event A is called **trivial** if either $\mathbb{P}[A] = 0$ or $\mathbb{P}[A] = 1$. You can think of trivial events as essentially nonrandom. Recall that by definition, Y_t is ergodic if all invariant events are trivial. Thus any event that is unaffected by a time shift is trivial—is essentially nonrandom. For example, again consider the invariant event $A = \{\max_{-\infty<t<\infty} Y_t \le 0\}$. If $Y_t = Z \sim \mathrm{N}(0, 1)$ for all t, then $\mathbb{P}[A] = \mathbb{P}[Z \le 0] = 0.5$. Since this does not equal 0 or 1, then $Y_t = Z$ is not ergodic. However, if Y_t is i.i.d. $\mathrm{N}(0, 1)$, then $\mathbb{P}[\max_{-\infty<t<\infty} Y_t \le 0] = 0$. This event is trivial. For Y_t to be ergodic (it is in this case), all such invariant events must be trivial.

An important technical result is that ergodicity is equivalent to the following property.

Theorem 14.8 A stationary series $Y_t \in \mathbb{R}^m$ is ergodic iff for all events A and B

$$\lim_{n\to\infty} \frac{1}{n} \sum_{\ell=1}^{n} \mathbb{P}[A_\ell \cap B] = \mathbb{P}[A]\, \mathbb{P}[B]. \tag{14.5}$$

This result is rather deep, so we do not prove it here. See Walters (1982, Corollary 1.14.2), or Davidson (1994, Theorem 14.7). The limit in (14.5) is the Cesàro sum of $\mathbb{P}[A_\ell \cap B]$. The Theorem of Cesàro Means (Theorem A.4 of *Probability and Statistics for Economists*) shows that a sufficient condition for (14.5) is that $\mathbb{P}[A_\ell \cap B] \to \mathbb{P}[A]\, \mathbb{P}[B]$, which is known as **mixing**. Thus mixing implies ergodicity. Mixing, roughly, means that separated events are asymptotically independent. Ergodicity is weaker, only requiring that the events are asymptotically independent "on average." We discuss mixing in Section 14.12.

14.8 ERGODIC THEOREM

The ergodic theorem is one of the most famous results in time series theory. There are actually several forms of the theorem, most of which concern almost sure convergence. For simplicity, we consider the theorem in terms of convergence in probability.

Theorem 14.9 Ergodic Theorem.
If $Y_t \in \mathbb{R}^m$ is strictly stationary, ergodic, and $\mathbb{E}\,\|Y\| < \infty$, then as $n \to \infty$,

$$\mathbb{E}\left\|\overline{Y} - \mu\right\| \longrightarrow 0 \tag{14.6}$$

and

$$\overline{Y} \underset{p}{\longrightarrow} \mu \tag{14.7}$$

where $\mu = \mathbb{E}[Y]$.

The ergodic theorem shows that ergodicity is sufficient for consistent estimation. The moment condition $\mathbb{E}\,\|Y\| < \infty$ is the same as in the WLLN for i.i.d. observations.

I now provide a proof of the ergodic theorem for the scalar case under the additional assumption that $\operatorname{var}[Y] = \sigma^2 < \infty$. A proof that relaxes this assumption is provided in Section 14.47.

By direct calculation

$$\operatorname{var}\left[\overline{Y}\right] = \frac{1}{n^2}\sum_{t=1}^{n}\sum_{j=1}^{n}\gamma\left(t-j\right)$$

where $\gamma(\ell) = \operatorname{cov}(Y_t, Y_{t+\ell})$. The double sum is over all elements of an $n \times n$ matrix whose tjth element is $\gamma\left(t-j\right)$. The diagonal elements are $\gamma(0) = \sigma^2$, the first off-diagonal elements are $\gamma(1)$, the second off-diagonal elements are $\gamma(2)$, and so on. Thus there are precisely n diagonal elements equaling σ^2, $2(n-1)$ equaling $\gamma(1)$, and so forth. Thus the above equals

$$\begin{aligned}\operatorname{var}\left[\overline{Y}\right] &= \frac{1}{n^2}\left(n\sigma^2 + 2(n-1)\gamma(1) + 2(n-2)\gamma(2) + \cdots + 2\gamma(n-1)\right)\\ &= \frac{\sigma^2}{n} + \frac{2}{n}\sum_{\ell=1}^{n}\left(1 - \frac{\ell}{n}\right)\gamma(\ell).\end{aligned} \tag{14.8}$$

This expression is rather intruiging. It shows that the variance of the sample mean precisely equals σ^2/n (which is the variance of the sample mean under i.i.d. sampling) plus a weighted Cesàro mean of the autocovariances. The latter is 0 under i.i.d. sampling but is nonzero otherwise. Theorem 14.7 shows that the Cesàro mean of the autocovariances converges to 0. Let $w_{n\ell} = 2(\ell/n^2)$, which satisfy the conditions of the Toeplitz

Lemma (Theorem A.5 of *Probability and Statistics for Economists*). Then

$$\frac{2}{n}\sum_{\ell=1}^{n}\left(1-\frac{\ell}{n}\right)\gamma(\ell)=\frac{2}{n^2}\sum_{\ell=1}^{n-1}\sum_{j=1}^{\ell}\gamma(j)=\sum_{\ell=1}^{n-1}w_{n\ell}\left(\frac{1}{\ell}\sum_{j=1}^{\ell}\gamma(j)\right)\longrightarrow 0. \tag{14.9}$$

Thus we have shown that (14.8) is $o(1)$ under ergodicity. Hence $\operatorname{var}\left[\overline{Y}\right]\to 0$. Markov's inequality establishes that $\overline{Y}\underset{p}{\longrightarrow}\mu$.

14.9 CONDITIONING ON INFORMATION SETS

The past few sections have introduced the concept of infinite histories. We now consider conditional expectations given infinite histories.

First, some basics. Recall from probability theory that an **outcome** is an element of a sample space. An **event** is a set of outcomes. A probability law is a rule that assigns nonnegative real numbers to events. When outcomes are infinite histories, then events are collections of such histories and a probability law is a rule that assigns numbers to collections of infinite histories.

Now we wish to define a conditional expectation given an infinite past history. Specifically, we wish to define

$$\mathbb{E}_{t-1}\left[Y_t\right]=\mathbb{E}\left[Y_t\mid Y_{t-1},Y_{t-2},\ldots\right] \tag{14.10}$$

which is the expected value of Y_t given the history $\widetilde{Y}_{t-1}=(Y_{t-1},Y_{t-2},\ldots)$ up to time t. Intuitively, $\mathbb{E}_{t-1}\left[Y_t\right]$ is the mean of the conditional distribution, the latter reflecting the information in the history. Mathematically, this cannot be defined using (2.6), as the latter requires a joint density for $(Y_t,Y_{t-1},Y_{t-2},\ldots)$, which does not make much sense. Instead, we can appeal to Theorem 2.13, which states that the conditional expectation (14.10) exists if $\mathbb{E}\left|Y_t\right|<\infty$ and the probabilities $\mathbb{P}\left[\widetilde{Y}_{t-1}\in A\right]$ are defined. The latter events are discussed in the previous paragraph. Thus the conditional expectation is well defined.

In this textbook, we have avoided measure-theoretic terminology to keep the presentation accessible, and because it is my belief that measure theory is more distracting than helpful. However, it is standard in the time series literature to follow the measure-theoretic convention of writing (14.10) as the conditional expectation given a σ-field. So at the risk of being overly technical, we will follow this convention and write the expectation (14.10) as $\mathbb{E}\left[Y_t\mid\mathscr{F}_{t-1}\right]$, where $\mathscr{F}_{t-1}=\sigma\left(\widetilde{Y}_{t-1}\right)$ is the σ-field generated by the history $\widetilde{Y}_{t-1}$. A **σ-field** (also known as a σ-algebra) is a collection of sets satisfying certain regularity conditions.[2] See *Probability and Statistics for Economists*, Section 1.14. The σ-field generated by a random variable Y is the collection of measurable events involving Y. Similarly, the σ-field generated by an infinite history is the collection of measurable events involving this history. Intuitively, $\mathscr{F}_{t-1}$ contains all the information available in the history $\widetilde{Y}_{t-1}$. Consequently, economists typically call $\mathscr{F}_{t-1}$ an **information set** rather than a σ-field. As I said, in this textbook, I endeavor to avoid measure-theoretic complications, so will follow the economists' label rather than the probabilists', but use the latter's notation, as it is conventional. To summarize, let us write $\mathscr{F}_t=\sigma\left(Y_t,Y_{t-1},\ldots\right)$ to indicate the information set generated by an infinite history $(Y_t,Y_{t-1},\ldots)$, and write (14.10) as $\mathbb{E}\left[Y_t\mid\mathscr{F}_{t-1}\right]$.

We now discuss some properties of information sets $\mathscr{F}_t$.

First, they are nested: $\mathscr{F}_{t-1}\subset\mathscr{F}_t$. Thus information accumulates over time. Information is not lost.

[2] A σ-field contains the universal set, is closed under complementation, and closed under countable unions.

Second, it is important to be precise about which variables are contained in the information set. Some economists are sloppy and refer to "the information set at time t" without specifying which variables are in the information set. It is better to be specific. For example, the information sets $\mathscr{F}_{1t} = \sigma(Y_t, Y_{t-1}, \ldots)$ and $\mathscr{F}_{2t} = \sigma(Y_t, X_t, Y_{t-1}, X_{t-1} \ldots)$ are distinct, even though they are both dated at time t.

Third, the conditional expectations (14.10) follow the law of iterated expectations and the conditioning theorem, thus

$$\mathbb{E}\left[\mathbb{E}\left[Y_t \mid \mathscr{F}_{t-1}\right] \mid \mathscr{F}_{t-2}\right] = \mathbb{E}\left[Y_t \mid \mathscr{F}_{t-2}\right]$$
$$\mathbb{E}\left[\mathbb{E}\left[Y_t \mid \mathscr{F}_{t-1}\right]\right] = \mathbb{E}\left[Y_t\right]$$

and

$$\mathbb{E}\left[Y_{t-1} Y_t \mid \mathscr{F}_{t-1}\right] = Y_{t-1}\mathbb{E}\left[Y_t \mid \mathscr{F}_{t-1}\right].$$

14.10 MARTINGALE DIFFERENCE SEQUENCES

An important concept in economics is unforecastability, meaning that the conditional expectation is the unconditional expectation. This is similar to the properties of a regression error. An unforecastable process is called a **martingale difference sequence (MDS)**.

A MDS e_t is defined with respect to a specific sequence of information sets $\mathscr{F}_t$. Most commonly the latter are the **natural filtration** $\mathscr{F}_t = \sigma(e_t, e_{t-1}, \ldots)$ (the past history of e_t), but it could be a larger information set. The only requirement is that e_t is adapted to $\mathscr{F}_t$, meaning that $\mathbb{E}\left[e_t \mid \mathscr{F}_t\right] = e_t$.

Definition 14.4 The process $(e_t, \mathscr{F}_t)$ is a **Martingale Difference Sequence (MDS)** if e_t is adapted to $\mathscr{F}_t$, $\mathbb{E}|e_t| < \infty$, and $\mathbb{E}\left[e_t \mid \mathscr{F}_{t-1}\right] = 0$.

In words, a MDS e_t is unforecastable in the mean. It is useful to notice that if we apply iterated expectations, $\mathbb{E}\left[e_t\right] = \mathbb{E}\left[\mathbb{E}\left[e_t \mid \mathscr{F}_{t-1}\right]\right] = 0$. Thus a MDS is mean 0.

The definition of a MDS requires the information sets $\mathscr{F}_t$ to contain the information in e_t, but is broader in the sense that it can contain more information. When no explicit definition is given, it is standard to assume that $\mathscr{F}_t$ is the natural filtration. However, it is best to explicitly specify the information, sets, so there is no confusion.

The term "martingale difference sequence" refers to the fact that the summed process $S_t = \sum_{j=1}^{t} e_j$ is a martingale and e_t is its first difference. A **martingale** S_t is a process that has a finite mean and $\mathbb{E}\left[S_t \mid \mathscr{F}_{t-1}\right] = S_{t-1}$.

If e_t is i.i.d. and mean 0, it is a MDS, but the reverse is not the case. To see this, first suppose that e_t is i.i.d. and mean 0. It is then independent of $\mathscr{F}_{t-1} = \sigma(e_{t-1}, e_{t-2}, \ldots)$, so $\mathbb{E}\left[e_t \mid \mathscr{F}_{t-1}\right] = \mathbb{E}\left[e_t\right] = 0$. Thus an i.i.d. shock is a MDS, as claimed.

To show that the reverse is not true, let u_t be i.i.d. $\mathrm{N}(0, 1)$ and set

$$e_t = u_t u_{t-1}. \tag{14.11}$$

By the conditioning theorem,

$$\mathbb{E}\left[e_t \mid \mathscr{F}_{t-1}\right] = u_{t-1}\mathbb{E}\left[u_t \mid \mathscr{F}_{t-1}\right] = 0$$

so e_t is a MDS. The process (14.11) is not, however, i.i.d. One way to see this is to calculate the first autocovariance of e_t^2, which is

$$\begin{aligned}\operatorname{cov}\left(e_t^2, e_{t-1}^2\right) &= \mathbb{E}\left[e_t^2 e_{t-1}^2\right] - \mathbb{E}\left[e_t^2\right]\mathbb{E}\left[e_{t-1}^2\right] \\ &= \mathbb{E}\left[u_t^2\right]\mathbb{E}\left[u_{t-1}^4\right]\mathbb{E}\left[u_{t-2}^2\right] - 1 \\ &= 2 \neq 0.\end{aligned}$$

Since the covariance is nonzero, e_t is not an independent sequence. Thus e_t is a MDS but not i.i.d.

An important property of a square integrable MDS is that it is serially uncorrelated. To see this, observe that by iterated expectations, the conditioning theorem, and the definition of a MDS, for $k > 0$,

$$\begin{aligned}\operatorname{cov}\left(e_t, e_{t-k}\right) &= \mathbb{E}\left[e_t e_{t-k}\right] \\ &= \mathbb{E}\left[\mathbb{E}\left[e_t e_{t-k} \mid \mathscr{F}_{t-1}\right]\right] \\ &= \mathbb{E}\left[\mathbb{E}\left[e_t \mid \mathscr{F}_{t-1}\right] e_{t-k}\right] \\ &= \mathbb{E}\left[0 e_{t-k}\right] \\ &= 0.\end{aligned}$$

Thus the autocovariances and autocorrelations are 0.

A process that is serially uncorrelated, however, is not necessarily a MDS. Take the process $e_t = u_t + u_{t-1}u_{t-2}$ with u_t i.i.d. N(0, 1). The process e_t is not a MDS, because $\mathbb{E}\left[e_t \mid \mathscr{F}_{t-1}\right] = u_{t-1}u_{t-2} \neq 0$. However,

$$\begin{aligned}\operatorname{cov}\left(e_t, e_{t-1}\right) &= \mathbb{E}\left[e_t e_{t-1}\right] \\ &= \mathbb{E}\left[\left(u_t + u_{t-1}u_{t-2}\right)\left(u_{t-1} + u_{t-2}u_{t-3}\right)\right] \\ &= \mathbb{E}\left[u_t u_{t-1} + u_t u_{t-2} u_{t-3} + u_{t-1}^2 u_{t-2} + u_{t-1} u_{t-2}^2 u_{t-3}\right] \\ &= \mathbb{E}\left[u_t\right]\mathbb{E}\left[u_{t-1}\right] + \mathbb{E}\left[u_t\right]\mathbb{E}\left[u_{t-2}\right]\mathbb{E}\left[u_{t-3}\right] \\ &\quad + \mathbb{E}\left[u_{t-1}^2\right]\mathbb{E}\left[u_{t-2}\right] + \mathbb{E}\left[u_{t-1}\right]\mathbb{E}\left[u_{t-2}^2\right]\mathbb{E}\left[u_{t-3}\right] \\ &= 0.\end{aligned}$$

Similarly, $\operatorname{cov}\left(e_t, e_{t-k}\right) = 0$ for $k \neq 0$. Thus e_t is serially uncorrelated. We have proved the following.

Theorem 14.10 If $(e_t, \mathscr{F}_t)$ is a MDS and $\mathbb{E}\left[e_t^2\right] < \infty$, then e_t is serially uncorrelated.

Another important special case is a homoskedastic martingale difference sequence.

Definition 14.5 The MDS $(e_t, \mathscr{F}_t)$ is a **Homoskedastic Martingale Difference Sequence** if $\mathbb{E}\left[e_t^2 \mid \mathscr{F}_{t-1}\right] = \sigma^2$.

A homoskedastic MDS should more properly be called a "conditionally homoskedastic MDS," because the property concerns the conditional distribution rather than the unconditional. That is, any strictly stationary

MDS satisfies a constant variance $\mathbb{E}\left[e_t^2\right]$, but only a homoskedastic MDS has a constant conditional variance $\mathbb{E}\left[e_t^2 \mid \mathscr{F}_{t-1}\right]$.

A homoskedatic MDS is analogous to a conditionally homoskedastic regression error. It is intermediate between a MDS and an i.i.d. sequence. Specifically, a square integrable and mean 0 i.i.d. sequence is a homoskedastic MDS, and the latter is a MDS.

The reverse is not the case. First, a MDS is not necessarily conditionally homoskedastic. Consider the example $e_t = u_t u_{t-1}$ given previously, which we showed to be a MDS. It is not conditionally homoskedastic, however, because

$$\mathbb{E}\left[e_t^2 \mid \mathscr{F}_{t-1}\right] = u_{t-1}^2 \mathbb{E}\left[u_t^2 \mid \mathscr{F}_{t-1}\right] = u_{t-1}^2$$

which is time varying. Thus this MDS e_t is conditionally heteroskedastic. Second, a homoskedastic MDS is not necessarily i.i.d. Consider the following example. Set $e_t = \sqrt{1 - 2/\eta_{t-1}}\,T_t$, where T_t is distributed as student t with a degree of freedom parameter $\eta_{t-1} = 2 + e_{t-1}^2$. This is scaled so that $\mathbb{E}\left[e_t \mid \mathscr{F}_{t-1}\right] = 0$ and $\mathbb{E}\left[e_t^2 \mid \mathscr{F}_{t-1}\right] = 1$, and is thus a homoskedastic MDS. The conditional distribution of e_t depends on e_{t-1} through the degree of freedom parameter. Hence, e_t is not an independent sequence.

One way to think about the difference between MDS and i.i.d. shocks is in terms of forecastability. An i.i.d. process is fully unforecastable, because no function of an i.i.d. process is forecastable. A MDS is unforecastable in the mean, but other moments may be forecastable.

As mentioned above, the definition of a MDS e_t allows for **conditional heteroskedasticity**, meaning that the **conditional variance** $\sigma_t^2 = \mathbb{E}\left[e_t^2 \mid \mathscr{F}_{t-1}\right]$ may be time varying. In financial econometrics, there are many models for conditional heteroskedasticity, including autoregressive conditional heteroskedasticity (ARCH), generalized ARCH (GARCH), and stochastic volatility. A good reference for this class of models is Campbell, Lo, and MacKinlay (1997).

14.11 CLT FOR MARTINGALE DIFFERENCES

We are interested in an asymptotic approximation for the distribution of the normalized sample mean

$$S_n = \frac{1}{\sqrt{n}} \sum_{t=1}^{n} u_t \tag{14.12}$$

where u_t is mean 0 with variance $\mathbb{E}\left[u_t u_t'\right] = \Sigma < \infty$. In this section, we discuss a CLT for the case where u_t is a martingale difference sequence.

Theorem 14.11 **MDS CLT**. If u_t is a strictly stationary and ergodic martingale difference sequence and $\mathbb{E}\left[u_t u_t'\right] = \Sigma < \infty$, then as $n \to \infty$,

$$S_n = \frac{1}{\sqrt{n}} \sum_{t=1}^{n} u_t \underset{d}{\longrightarrow} \mathrm{N}(0, \Sigma).$$

The conditions for Theorem 14.11 are similar to those for the Lindeberg-Lévy CLT. The only difference is that the i.i.d. assumption has been replaced by the assumption of a strictly stationary and ergodic MDS.

The proof of Theorem 14.11 is technically advanced, so I do not present the full details, but instead refer readers to Theorem 3.2 of P. Hall and Heyde (1980) or Theorem 25.3 of Davidson (1994) (which are more general than Theorem 14.11, not requiring strict stationarity). To illustrate the role of the MDS assumption, a sketch of the proof appears in Section 14.47.

14.12 MIXING

For many results, including a CLT for correlated (non-MDS) series, we need a stronger restriction than ergodicity on the dependence between observations. Recalling the property (14.5) of ergodic sequences, we can measure the dependence between two events A and B by the discrepancy

$$\alpha(A, B) = |\mathbb{P}[A \cap B] - \mathbb{P}[A]\,\mathbb{P}[B]| \tag{14.13}$$

Which equals 0 when A and B are independent and is positive otherwise. In general, $\alpha(A, B)$ can be used to measure the degree of dependence between the events A and B.

Now consider the two information sets (σ-fields)

$$\mathscr{F}_{-\infty}^{t} = \sigma(\ldots, Y_{t-1}, Y_t)$$
$$\mathscr{F}_{t}^{\infty} = \sigma(Y_t, Y_{t+1}, \ldots).$$

The first is the history of the series up until period t, and the second is the history of the series starting in period t and going forward. We then separate the information sets by ℓ periods, that is, take $\mathscr{F}_{-\infty}^{t-\ell}$ and $\mathscr{F}_{t}^{\infty}$. We can measure the degree of dependence between the information sets by taking all events in each and then taking the largest discrepancy (14.13), which is

$$\alpha(\ell) = \sup_{A \in \mathscr{F}_{-\infty}^{t-\ell},\, B \in \mathscr{F}_{t}^{\infty}} \alpha(A, B).$$

The constants $\alpha(\ell)$ are known as the **strong mixing coefficients**. We say that Y_t is **strong mixing** if $\alpha(\ell) \to 0$ as $\ell \to \infty$. This means that as the time separation increases between the information sets, the degree of dependence decreases, eventually reaching independence.

From the Theorem of Cesàro Means (Theorem A.4 of *Probability and Statistics for Economists*), strong mixing implies (14.5), which is equivalent to ergodicity. Thus a mixing process is ergodic.

An intuition concerning mixing can be colorfully illustrated by the following example due to Halmos (1956). A martini is a drink consisting of a large portion of gin and a small part of vermouth. Suppose that you pour a serving of gin into a martini glass, pour a small amount of vermouth on top, and then stir the drink with a swizzle stick. If your stirring process is mixing, with each turn of the stick the vermouth will become more evenly distributed throughout the gin, and asymptotically (as the number of stirs tends to infinity), the vermouth and gin distributions will become independent.[3] If so, this is a mixing process.

For applications, mixing is often useful when we can characterize the rate at which the coefficients $\alpha(\ell)$ decline to 0. Two types of conditions are seen in asymptotic theory: rates and summation. Rate conditions take the form $\alpha(\ell) = O(\ell^{-r})$ or $\alpha(\ell) = o(\ell^{-r})$. Summation conditions take the form $\sum_{\ell=0}^{\infty} \alpha(\ell)^r < \infty$ or $\sum_{\ell=0}^{\infty} \ell^s \alpha(\ell)^r < \infty$.

[3] Of course, if you really make an asymptotic number of stirs, you will never finish stirring and you won't be able to enjoy the martini. Hence in practice it is advised to stop stirring before the number of stirs reaches infinity.

There are alternative measures of dependence beyond (14.13), and many have been proposed. Strong mixing is one of the weakest (and thus embraces a wide set of time series processes) but is insufficiently strong for some applications. Another popular dependence measure is known as **absolute regularity** or **β-mixing**. The β-mixing coefficients are

$$\beta(\ell) = \sup_{A \in \mathscr{F}_t^{\infty}} \mathbb{E}\left|\mathbb{P}\left[A \mid \mathscr{F}_{-\infty}^{t-\ell}\right] - \mathbb{P}[A]\right|.$$

Absolute regularity is stronger than strong mixing in the sense that $\beta(\ell) \to 0$ implies $\alpha(\ell) \to 0$, and rate conditions for the β-mixing coefficients imply the same rates for the strong mixing coefficients.

One reason mixing is useful for applications is that it is preserved by transformations.

Theorem 14.12 If Y_t has mixing coefficients $\alpha_Y(\ell)$ and $X_t = \phi(Y_t, Y_{t-1}, Y_{t-2}, \ldots, Y_{t-q})$, then X_t has mixing coefficients $\alpha_X(\ell) \le \alpha_Y(\ell - q)$ (for $\ell \ge q$). The coefficients $\alpha_X(\ell)$ satisfy the same summation and rate conditions as $\alpha_Y(\ell)$.

A limitation of the above result is that it is confined to a finite number of lags, unlike the transformation results for stationarity and ergodicity.

Mixing can be a useful tool because of the following inequalities.

Theorem 14.13 Let $\mathscr{F}_{-\infty}^{t}$ and $\mathscr{F}_t^{\infty}$ be constructed from the pair (X_t, Z_t).

1. If $|X_t| \le C_1$ and $|Z_t| \le C_2$, then
$$|\operatorname{cov}(X_{t-\ell}, Z_t)| \le 4C_1C_2\alpha(\ell).$$
2. If $\mathbb{E}|X_t|^r < \infty$ and $\mathbb{E}|Z_t|^q < \infty$ for $1/r + 1/q < 1$, then
$$|\operatorname{cov}(X_{t-\ell}, Z_t)| \le 8\left(\mathbb{E}|X_t|^r\right)^{1/r}\left(\mathbb{E}|Z_t|^q\right)^{1/q}\alpha(\ell)^{1-1/r-1/q}.$$
3. If $\mathbb{E}[Z_t] = 0$ and $\mathbb{E}|Z_t|^r < \infty$ for $r \ge 1$, then
$$\mathbb{E}\left|\mathbb{E}\left[Z_t \mid \mathscr{F}_{-\infty}^{t-\ell}\right]\right| \le 6\left(\mathbb{E}|Z_t|^r\right)^{1/r}\alpha(\ell)^{1-1/r}.$$

The proof is given in Section 14.47. Our next result follows fairly directly from the definition of mixing.

Theorem 14.14 If Y_t is i.i.d., then it is strong mixing and ergodic.

14.13 CLT FOR CORRELATED OBSERVATIONS

In this section, we develop a CLT for the normalized mean S_n defined in (14.12) allowing the variables u_t to be serially correlated.

In (14.8), we found that in the scalar case,

$$\operatorname{var}[S_n]=\sigma^2+2\sum_{\ell=1}^{n}\left(1-\frac{\ell}{n}\right)\gamma(\ell)$$

where $\sigma^2=\operatorname{var}[u_t]$ and $\gamma(\ell)=\operatorname{cov}(u_t,u_{t-\ell})$. Since $\gamma(-\ell)=\gamma(\ell)$, this can be written as

$$\operatorname{var}[S_n]=\sum_{\ell=-n}^{n}\left(1-\frac{|\ell|}{n}\right)\gamma(\ell). \tag{14.14}$$

In the vector case, define the variance $\Sigma=\mathbb{E}\left[u_t u_t'\right]$ and the matrix covariance $\Gamma(\ell)=\mathbb{E}\left[u_t u_{t-\ell}'\right]$, which satisfies $\Gamma(-\ell)=\Gamma(\ell)'$. By a calculation analogous to (14.14), we obtain

$$\operatorname{var}[S_n]=\Sigma+\sum_{\ell=1}^{n}\left(1-\frac{\ell}{n}\right)\left(\Gamma(\ell)+\Gamma(\ell)'\right)=\sum_{\ell=-n}^{n}\left(1-\frac{|\ell|}{n}\right)\Gamma(\ell). \tag{14.15}$$

A necessary condition for S_n to converge to a normal distribution is that the variance (14.15) converges to a limit. Indeed, as $n\to\infty$,

$$\sum_{\ell=1}^{n}\left(1-\frac{\ell}{n}\right)\Gamma(\ell)=\frac{1}{n}\sum_{\ell=1}^{n-1}\sum_{j=1}^{\ell}\Gamma(j)\to\sum_{\ell=0}^{\infty}\Gamma(\ell) \tag{14.16}$$

where the convergence holds by the Theorem of Cesàro Means if the limit in (14.16) is convergent. A necessary condition for this to hold is that the covariances $\Gamma(\ell)$ decline to 0 as $\ell\to\infty$. A sufficient condition is that the covariances are absolutely summable, which can be verified using a mixing inequality. Using the triangle inequality (B.16) and Theorem 14.13, part 2, for any $r>2$,

$$\sum_{\ell=0}^{\infty}\|\Gamma(\ell)\|\leq 8\left(\mathbb{E}\|u_t\|^r\right)^{2/r}\sum_{\ell=0}^{\infty}\alpha(\ell)^{1-2/r}.$$

Thus (14.15) converges if $\mathbb{E}\|u_t\|^r<\infty$, and $\sum_{\ell=0}^{\infty}\alpha(\ell)^{1-2/r}<\infty$. We conclude that under these assumptions,

$$\operatorname{var}[S_n]\to\sum_{\ell=-\infty}^{\infty}\Gamma(\ell)\stackrel{\text{def}}{=}\Omega. \tag{14.17}$$

The matrix Ω plays a special role in the inference theory for tme series. It is often called the **long-run variance** of u_t as it is the variance of sample means in large samples.

It turns out that these conditions are sufficient for the CLT.

Theorem 14.15 If u_t is strictly stationary with mixing coefficients $\alpha(\ell)$, $\mathbb{E}[u_t]=0$, for some $r>2$, $\mathbb{E}\|u_t\|^r<\infty$ and $\sum_{\ell=0}^{\infty}\alpha(\ell)^{1-2/r}<\infty$, then (14.17) is convergent, and $S_n=n^{-1/2}\sum_{t=1}^{n}u_t\underset{d}{\longrightarrow}\mathrm{N}(0,\Omega)$.

The proof is in Section 14.47.

The theorem requires $r>2$ finite moments, which is stronger than the MDS CLT. This r does not need to be an integer, meaning that the theorem holds under slightly more than two finite moments. The summability condition on the mixing coefficients in Theorem 14.15 is considerably stronger than ergodicity. There is a tradeoff involving the choice of r. A larger r means more moments are required to be finite, but a slower decay in the coefficients $\alpha(\ell)$ is allowed. Smaller r is less restrictive regarding moments but requires a faster decay rate in the mixing coefficients.

14.14 LINEAR PROJECTION

In Chapter 2, we extensively studied the properties of linear projection models. In the context of stationary time series, we can use similar tools here. An important extension is to allow for projections onto infinite dimensional random vectors. For this analysis, let us assume that Y_t is covariance stationary.

Recall that when (Y,X) have a joint distribution with bounded variances, the linear projection of Y onto X (the best linear predictor) is the minimizer of $S(\beta)=\mathbb{E}\left[\left(Y-\beta'X\right)^2\right]$ and has the solution

$$\mathscr{P}[Y \mid X]=X'\left(\mathbb{E}\left[XX'\right]\right)^{-1}\mathbb{E}[XY].$$

This projection is unique and has a unique projection error $e=Y-\mathscr{P}[Y \mid X]$.

This idea extends to any Hilbert space including the infinite past history $\widetilde{Y}_{t-1}=(\ldots,Y_{t-2},Y_{t-1})$. From the projection theorem for Hilbert spaces (see Theorem 2.3.1 of Brockwell and Davis (1991)), the projection $\mathscr{P}_{t-1}[Y_t]=\mathscr{P}\left[Y_t \mid \widetilde{Y}_{t-1}\right]$ of Y_t onto $\widetilde{Y}_{t-1}$ is unique and has a unique projection error:

$$e_t=Y_t-\mathscr{P}_{t-1}[Y_t]. \tag{14.18}$$

The projection error is mean 0, has finite variance $\sigma^2=\mathbb{E}\left[e_t^2\right]\leq\mathbb{E}\left[Y_t^2\right]<\infty$, and is serially uncorrelated. By Theorem 14.2, if Y_t is strictly stationary, then $\mathscr{P}_{t-1}[Y_t]$ and e_t are strictly stationary.

The property (14.18) implies that the projection errors are serially uncorrelated. Theorem 14.16 states these results formally.

Theorem 14.16 If $Y_t\in\mathbb{R}$ is covariance stationary, it has the projection equation

$$Y_t=\mathscr{P}_{t-1}[Y_t]+e_t.$$

The projection error e_t satisfies

$$\mathbb{E}[e_t]=0$$

$$\mathbb{E}\left[e_{t-j}e_t\right]=0 \qquad j\geq 1$$

and

$$\sigma^2=\mathbb{E}\left[e_t^2\right]\leq\mathbb{E}\left[Y_t^2\right]<\infty. \tag{14.19}$$

If Y_t is strictly stationary, then e_t is strictly stationary.

14.15 WHITE NOISE

The projection error e_t is mean 0, has a finite variance, and is serially uncorrelated. This describes what is known as a white noise process.

Definition 14.6 The process e_t is **white noise** if $\mathbb{E}[e_t]=0$, $\mathbb{E}\left[e_t^2\right]=\sigma^2<\infty$, and $\operatorname{cov}\left(e_t, e_{t-k}\right)=0$ for $k\neq 0$.

A MDS is white noise (Theorem 14.10), but the reverse is not true, as shown by the example $e_t=u_t+u_{t-1}u_{t-2}$ given in Section 14.10, which is white noise but not a MDS. Therefore, the following types of shocks are nested: i.i.d., MDS, and white noise, with i.i.d. being the most narrow class and white noise the broadest. It is helpful to observe that a white noise process can be conditionally heteroskedastic, as the conditional variance is unrestricted.

14.16 THE WOLD DECOMPOSITION

In Section 14.14, we showed that a covariance stationary process has a white noise projection error. This result can be used to express the series as an infinite linear function of the projection errors. This famous result is known as the Wold decomposition.

Theorem 14.17 The Wold Decomposition. If Y_t is covariance stationary and $\sigma^2>0$, where σ^2 is the projection error variance (14.19), then Y_t has the linear representation

$$Y_t=\mu_t+\sum_{j=0}^{\infty} b_j e_{t-j} \tag{14.20}$$

where the e_t are the white noise projection errors (14.18), $b_0=1$,

$$\sum_{j=1}^{\infty} b_j^2<\infty \tag{14.21}$$

and

$$\mu_t=\lim_{m\to\infty}\mathscr{P}_{t-m}\left[Y_t\right]. \tag{14.22}$$

The Wold decomposition shows that Y_t can be written as a linear function of the white noise projection errors plus μ_t. The infinite sum in (14.20) is also known as a **linear process**. The Wold decomposition is a foundational result for linear time series analysis. Since any covariance stationary process can be written in this format, this justifies linear models as approximations.

The series μ_t is the projection of Y_t on the history from the infinite past. It is the part of Y_t that is perfectly predictable from its past values and is called the **deterministic component**. In most cases, $\mu_t=\mu$, the unconditional mean of Y_t. However, it is possible for stationary processes to have more substantive deterministic components. An example is

$$\mu_t=\begin{cases}(-1)^t & \text{with probability } 1/2\\ (-1)^{t+1} & \text{with probability } 1/2.\end{cases}$$

This series is strictly stationary, mean 0, and variance 1. However, it is perfectly predictable, given the previous history, as it simply oscillates between -1 and 1.

In practical applied time series analysis, deterministic components are typically excluded by assumption. We call a stationary time series **nondeterministic**[4] if $\mu_t = \mu$, a constant. In this case, the Wold decomposition has a simpler form.

Theorem 14.18 If Y_t is covariance stationary and nondeterministic, then Y_t has the linear representation

$$Y_t = \mu + \sum_{j=0}^{\infty} b_j e_{t-j}$$

where the b_j satisfy (14.21) and the e_t are the white noise projection errors (14.18).

A limitation of the Wold decomposition is the restriction to linearity. While it shows that there is a valid linear approximation, it may be that a nonlinear model provides a better approximation.

For a proof of Theorem 14.17, see Section 14.47.

14.17 LAG OPERATOR

An algebraic construct that is useful for the analysis of time series models is the lag operator.

Definition 14.7 The **lag operator** L satisfies $\mathrm{L}Y_t = Y_{t-1}$.

Defining $\mathrm{L}^2 = \mathrm{LL}$, we see that $\mathrm{L}^2 Y_t = \mathrm{L}Y_{t-1} = Y_{t-2}$. In general, $\mathrm{L}^k Y_t = Y_{t-k}$.

Using the lag operator, the Wold decomposition can be written in the format

$$\begin{aligned} Y_t &= \mu + b_0 e_t + b_1 \mathrm{L} e_t + b_2 \mathrm{L}^2 e_t + \cdots \\ &= \mu + \left(b_0 + b_1 \mathrm{L} + b_2 \mathrm{L}^2 + \cdots\right) e_t \\ &= \mu + b(\mathrm{L}) e_t \end{aligned}$$

where $b(z) = b_0 + b_1 z + b_2 z^2 + \cdots$ is an infinite-order polynomial. The expression $Y_t = \mu + b(\mathrm{L}) e_t$ is a compact way to write the Wold representation.

14.18 AUTOREGRESSIVE WOLD REPRESENTATION

From Theorem 14.16, Y_t satisfies a projection onto its infinite past. Theorem 14.18 shows that this projection equals a linear function of the lagged projection errors. An alternative way to write the projection is as a linear function of the lagged Y_t. It turns out that to obtain a unique and convergent representation, we need a strengthening of the conditions.

[4]Most authors define purely nondeterministic as the case $\mu_t = 0$. We allow for a nonzero mean to accomodate practical time series applications.

Theorem 14.19 If Y_t is covariance stationary, nondeterministic, with Wold representation $Y_t = b(\mathrm{L})e_t$, such that $|b(z)| \geq \delta > 0$ for all complex $|z| \leq 1$, and for some integer $s \geq 0$ the Wold coefficients satisfy $\sum_{j=0}^{\infty} \left(\sum_{k=0}^{\infty} k^s b_{j+k}\right)^2 < \infty$, then Y_t has the representation

$$Y_t = \mu + \sum_{j=1}^{\infty} a_j Y_{t-j} + e_t \tag{14.23}$$

for some coefficients μ and a_j. The coefficients satisfy $\sum_{k=0}^{\infty} k^s |a_k| < \infty$, so (14.23) is convergent.

Equation (14.23) is known as an infinite-order **autoregressive** representation with autoregressive coefficients a_j.

A solution to the equation $b(z) = 0$ is a **root** of the polynomial $b(z)$. The assumption $|b(z)| > 0$ for $|z| \leq 1$ means that the roots of $b(z)$ lie outside the unit circle $|z| = 1$ (the circle in the complex plane with radius 1). Theorem 14.19 makes the stronger restriction that $|b(z)|$ is bounded away from 0 for z on or within the unit circle. The need for this strengthening is less intuitive but essentially excludes the possibility of an infinite number of roots outside but arbitrarily close to the unit circle. The summability assumption on the Wold coefficients ensures convergence of the autoregressive coefficients a_j.

To understand the restriction on the roots of $b(z)$, consider the simple case $b(z) = 1 - b_1 z$. (In Section 14.20, we call this an MA(1) model.) The requirement $|b(z)| \geq \delta$ for $|z| \leq 1$ means[5] $|b_1| \leq 1 - \delta$. Thus the assumption in Theorem 14.19 bounds the absolute value of the coefficient strictly below 1. Now consider an infinite polynomial case $b(z) = \prod_{j=1}^{\infty} \left(1 - b_j z\right)$. The assumption in Theorem 14.19 requires $\sup_j \left|b_j\right| < 1$.

Theorem 14.19 is attributed to Wiener and Masani (1958). For a recent treatment and proof, see Corollary 6.1.17 of Politis and McElroy (2020). These authors (as is common in the literature) state their assumptions differently than is done in Theorem 14.19. First, instead of the condition on $b(z)$, they bound from below the spectral density function $f(\lambda)$ of Y_t. The spectral density is not defined in this text, so here their condition is restated in terms of the linear process polynomial $b(z)$. Second, instead of the condition on the Wold coefficients, they require that the autocovariances satisfy $\sum_{k=0}^{\infty} k^s |\gamma(k)| < \infty$. This is implied by our stated summability condition on the b_j (using the expression for $\gamma(k)$ in Section 14.21 below and simplifying).

14.19 LINEAR MODELS

In the Sections 14.17 and 14.18, we showed that any nondeterministic covariance stationary time series has the projection representation

$$Y_t = \mu + \sum_{j=0}^{\infty} b_j e_{t-j}$$

[5]To see this, focus on the case $b_1 \geq 0$. The requirement $|1 - b_1 z| \geq \delta$ for $|z| \leq 1$ means $\min_{|z| \leq 1} |1 - b_1 z| = 1 - b_1 \geq \delta$, or $b_1 \leq 1 - \delta$.

and under a restriction on the projection coefficients satisfies the autoregressive representation

$$Y_t = \mu + \sum_{j=1}^{\infty} a_j Y_{t-j} + e_t.$$

In both equations, the errors e_t are white noise projection errors. These representations help us understand that linear models can be used as approximations for stationary time series.

For the next several sections, we reverse the analysis. We will assume a specific linear model and then study the properties of the resulting time series. In particular, we will be seeking conditions under which the stated process is stationary. This helps us understand the properties of linear models. Throughout, we assume that the error e_t is a strictly stationary and ergodic white noise process. This allows as a special case the stronger assumption that e_t is i.i.d. but is less restrictive. In particular, it allows for conditional heteroskedasticity.

14.20 MOVING AVERAGE PROCESS

The **first-order moving average process**, denoted **MA(1)**, is

$$Y_t = \mu + e_t + \theta e_{t-1}$$

where e_t is a strictly stationary and ergodic white noise process with $\operatorname{var}[e_t] = \sigma^2$. The model is called a "moving average," because Y_t is a weighted average of the shocks e_t and e_{t-1}.

It is straightforward to calculate that a MA(1) has the following moments:

$$\begin{aligned}
\mathbb{E}[Y_t] &= \mu \\
\operatorname{var}[Y_t] &= \left(1+\theta^2\right)\sigma^2 \\
\gamma(1) &= \theta\sigma^2 \\
\rho(1) &= \frac{\theta}{1+\theta^2} \\
\gamma(k) &= \rho(k) = 0, \quad k \geq 2.
\end{aligned}$$

Thus the MA(1) process has a nonzero first autocorrelation with the remainder being 0.

A MA(1) process with $\theta \neq 0$ is serially correlated, with each pair of adjacent observations (Y_{t-1}, Y_t) correlated. If $\theta > 0$, the pair is positively correlated, while if $\theta < 0$, it is negatively correlated. The serial correlation is limited in that observations separated by multiple periods are mutually independent.

The **q**th-**order moving average process**, denoted **MA(q)**, is

$$Y_t = \mu + \theta_0 e_t + \theta_1 e_{t-1} + \theta_2 e_{t-2} + \cdots + \theta_q e_{t-q}$$

where $\theta_0 = 1$. It is straightforward to calculate that a MA(q) has the following moments:

$$\begin{aligned}
\mathbb{E}[Y_t] &= \mu \\
\operatorname{var}[Y_t] &= \left(\sum_{j=0}^{q} \theta_j^2\right)\sigma^2
\end{aligned}$$

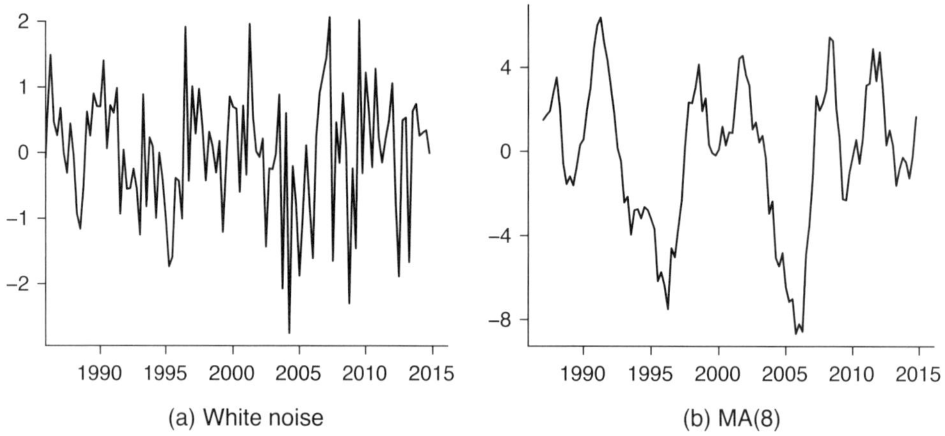

FIGURE 14.3 White noise and MA(8)

$$\gamma(k)=\left(\sum_{j=0}^{q-k}\theta_{j+k}\theta_j\right)\sigma^2,\quad k\leq q$$

$$\rho(k)=\frac{\sum_{j=0}^{q-k}\theta_{j+k}\theta_j}{\sum_{j=0}^{q}\theta_j^2}$$

$$\gamma(k)=\rho(k)=0,\quad k>q.$$

In particular, a MA(q) has q nonzero autocorrelations with the remainder being 0.

An MA(q) process Y_t is strictly stationary and ergodic.

An MA(q) process with moderately large q can have considerably more complicated dependence relations than an MA(1) process. One specific pattern that can be induced by a MA process is smoothing. Suppose that the coefficients θ_j all equal 1. Then Y_t is a smoothed version of the shocks e_t.

To illustrate, Figure 14.3(a) displays a plot of a simulated white noise (i.i.d. N(0, 1)) process with $n=120$ observations. Figure 14.3(b) displays a plot of a MA(8) process constructed with the same innovations, with $\theta_j=1, j=1,\ldots,8$. You can see that the white noise has no predictable behavior, while the MA(8) is smooth.

14.21 INFINITE-ORDER MOVING AVERAGE PROCESS

An **infinite-order moving average process**, denoted **MA(∞)**, also known as a **linear process**, is

$$Y_t=\mu+\sum_{j=0}^{\infty}\theta_j e_{t-j} \tag{14.24}$$

where e_t is a strictly stationary and ergodic white noise process, $\text{var}[e_t]=\sigma^2$, and $\sum_{j=0}^{\infty}\left|\theta_j\right|<\infty$. From Theorem 14.6, Y_t is strictly stationary and ergodic. A linear process has the following moments:

$$\mathbb{E}[Y_t]=\mu$$

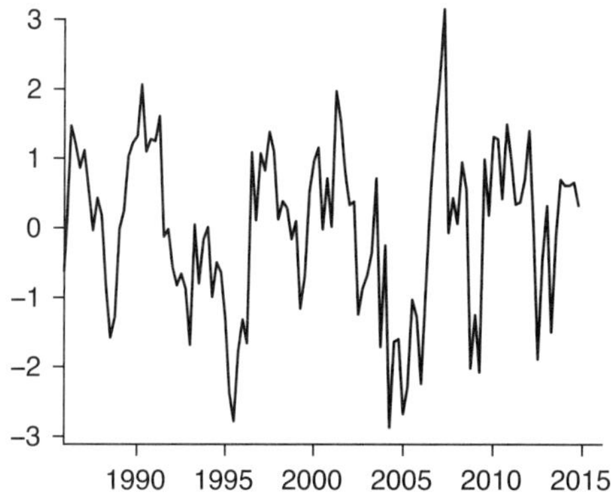

(a) AR(1) with $\alpha_1 = 0.5$

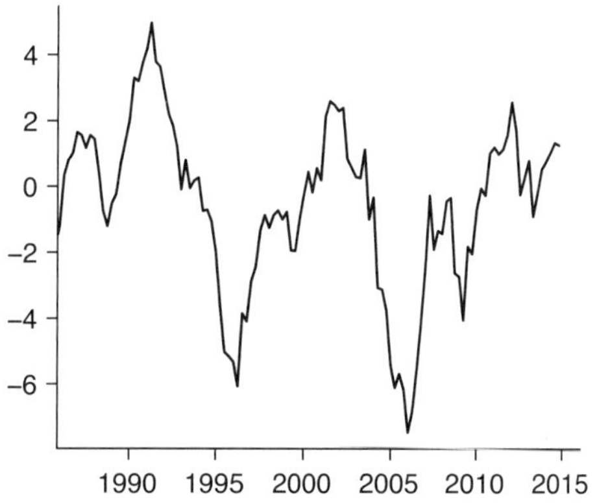

(b) AR(1) with $\alpha_1 = 0.95$

FIGURE 14.4 AR(1) processes

$$\operatorname{var}[Y_t] = \left(\sum_{j=0}^{\infty} \theta_j^2\right)\sigma^2$$

$$\gamma(k) = \left(\sum_{j=0}^{\infty} \theta_{j+k}\theta_j\right)\sigma^2$$

$$\rho(k) = \frac{\sum_{j=0}^{\infty} \theta_{j+k}\theta_j}{\sum_{j=0}^{\infty} \theta_j^2}.$$

14.22 FIRST-ORDER AUTOREGRESSIVE PROCESS

The **first-order autoregressive process**, denoted **AR(1)**, is

$$Y_t = \alpha_0 + \alpha_1 Y_{t-1} + e_t \tag{14.25}$$

where e_t is a strictly stationary and ergodic white noise process with $\operatorname{var}[e_t] = \sigma^2$. The AR(1) model is probably the single most important model in econometric time series analysis.

As a simple motivating example, let Y_t be the employment level (number of jobs) in an economy. Suppose that a fixed fraction $1 - \alpha_1$ of employees lose their job and a random number u_t of new employees are hired each period. Setting $\alpha_0 = \mathbb{E}[u_t]$ and $e_t = u_t - \alpha_0$, this implies the law of motion (14.25).

To illustrate the behavior of the AR(1) process, Figure 14.4 plots two simulated AR(1) processes. Each is generated using the white noise process e_t displayed in Figure 14.3(a). The plot in Figure 14.4(a) sets $\alpha_1 = 0.5$, and the plot in Figure 14.4(b) sets $\alpha_1 = 0.95$. You can see how both are more smooth than the white noise process and that the smoothing increases with α.

Our first goal is to obtain conditions under which (14.25) is stationary. We can do so by showing that Y_t can be written as a convergent linear process and then appealing to Theorem 14.5. To find a linear process representation for Y_t, we can use backward recursion. Notice that Y_t in (14.25) depends on its previous value Y_{t-1}. If we take (14.25) and lag it one period, we find $Y_{t-1} = \alpha_0 + \alpha_1 Y_{t-2} + e_{t-1}$. Substituting this into (14.25), we find

$$\begin{aligned} Y_t &= \alpha_0 + \alpha_1 (\alpha_0 + \alpha_1 Y_{t-2} + e_{t-1}) + e_t \\ &= \alpha_0 + \alpha_1\alpha_0 + \alpha_1^2 Y_{t-2} + \alpha_1 e_{t-1} + e_t. \end{aligned}$$

Similarly we can lag (14.25) twice to find $Y_{t-2} = \alpha_0 + \alpha_1 Y_{t-3} + e_{t-2}$, which can be used to substitute out Y_{t-2}. Continuing recursively t times, we find

$$\begin{aligned} Y_t &= \alpha_0 \left(1 + \alpha_1 + \alpha_1^2 + \cdots + \alpha_1^{t-1}\right) + \alpha_1^t Y_0 + \alpha_1^{t-1} e_1 + \alpha_1^{t-2} e_2 + \cdots + e_t \\ &= \alpha_0 \sum_{j=0}^{t-1} \alpha_1^j + \alpha_1^t Y_0 + \sum_{j=0}^{t-1} \alpha_1^j e_{t-j}. \end{aligned} \tag{14.26}$$

Thus Y_t equals an intercept plus the scaled initial condition $\alpha_1^t Y_0$ and the moving average $\sum_{j=0}^{t-1} \alpha_1^j e_{t-j}$.

Now suppose we continue this recursion into the infinite past. By Theorem 14.3, this recursion converges if $\sum_{j=0}^{\infty} |\alpha_1|^j < \infty$. The limit is provided by the following well-known result.

Theorem 14.20 $\sum_{k=0}^{\infty} \beta^k = \frac{1}{1-\beta}$ is absolutely convergent if $|\beta| < 1$.

The series converges by the ratio test (see Theorem A.3 of *Probability and Statistics for Economists*). To find the limit, note that

$$A = \sum_{k=0}^{\infty} \beta^k = 1 + \sum_{k=1}^{\infty} \beta^k = 1 + \beta \sum_{k=0}^{\infty} \beta^k = 1 + \beta A.$$

Solving, we find $A = 1/(1-\beta)$.

Thus the intercept in (14.26) converges to $\alpha_0/(1-\alpha_1)$. We deduce the following:

Theorem 14.21 If $\mathbb{E}|e_t| < \infty$ and $|\alpha_1| < 1$, then the AR(1) process (14.25) has the convergent representation

$$Y_t = \mu + \sum_{j=0}^{\infty} \alpha_1^j e_{t-j} \tag{14.27}$$

where $\mu = \alpha_0 / (1-\alpha_1)$. The AR(1) process Y_t is strictly stationary and ergodic.

We can compute the moments of Y_t from (14.27):

$$\mathbb{E}[Y_t] = \mu + \sum_{k=0}^{\infty} \alpha_1^k \mathbb{E}[e_{t-k}] = \mu$$

$$\operatorname{var}[Y_t] = \sum_{k=0}^{\infty} \alpha_1^{2k} \operatorname{var}[e_{t-k}] = \frac{\sigma^2}{1-\alpha_1^2}.$$

One way to calculate the moments is as follows. Apply expectations to both sides of (14.25):

$$\mathbb{E}[Y_t] = \alpha_0 + \alpha_1 \mathbb{E}[Y_{t-1}] + \mathbb{E}[e_t] = \alpha_0 + \alpha_1 \mathbb{E}[Y_{t-1}].$$

Stationarity implies $\mathbb{E}[Y_{t-1}] = \mathbb{E}[Y_t]$. Solving, we find $\mathbb{E}[Y_t] = \alpha_0/(1-\alpha_1)$. Similarly,

$$\operatorname{var}[Y_t] = \operatorname{var}[\alpha Y_{t-1} + e_t] = \alpha_1^2 \operatorname{var}[Y_{t-1}] + \operatorname{var}[e_t] = \alpha_1^2 \operatorname{var}[Y_{t-1}] + \sigma^2.$$

Stationarity implies $\operatorname{var}[Y_{t-1}] = \operatorname{var}[Y_t]$. Solving, we find $\operatorname{var}[Y_t] = \sigma^2/(1-\alpha_1^2)$. This method is useful for calculation of autocovariances and autocorrelations. For simplicity, set $\alpha_0 = 0$ so that $\mathbb{E}[Y_t] = 0$ and $\mathbb{E}\left[Y_t^2\right] = \operatorname{var}[Y_t]$. We find

$$\gamma(1) = \mathbb{E}[Y_{t-1}Y_t] = \mathbb{E}[Y_{t-1}(\alpha_1 Y_{t-1} + e_t)] = \alpha_1 \operatorname{var}[Y_t]$$

so

$$\rho(1) = \gamma(1)/\operatorname{var}[Y_t] = \alpha_1.$$

Furthermore,

$$\gamma(k) = \mathbb{E}[Y_{t-k}Y_t] = \mathbb{E}[Y_{t-k}(\alpha_1 Y_{t-1} + e_t)] = \alpha_1 \gamma(k-1).$$

By recursion we obtain

$$\gamma(k) = \alpha_1^k \operatorname{var}[Y_t]$$
$$\rho(k) = \alpha_1^k.$$

Thus the AR(1) process with $\alpha_1 \neq 0$ has nonzero autocorrelations of all orders which decay to 0 geometrically as k increases. For $\alpha_1 > 0$, the autocorrelations are all positive. For $\alpha_1 < 0$, the autocorrelations alternate in sign.

We can also express the AR(1) process using the lag operator notation:

$$(1 - \alpha_1 \mathrm{L})\, Y_t = \alpha_0 + e_t. \tag{14.28}$$

We can write this as $\alpha(\mathrm{L}) Y_t = \alpha_0 + e_t$, where $\alpha(\mathrm{L}) = 1 - \alpha_1 \mathrm{L}$. We call $\alpha(z) = 1 - \alpha_1 z$ the **autoregressive polynomial** of Y_t.

This suggests an alternative way of obtaining the representation (14.27). We can invert the operator $(1 - \alpha_1 \mathrm{L})$ to write Y_t as a function of lagged e_t. That is, suppose that the inverse operator $(1 - \alpha_1 \mathrm{L})^{-1}$ exists. Then we can use this operator on (14.28) to find

$$Y_t = (1 - \alpha_1 \mathrm{L})^{-1}(1 - \alpha_1 \mathrm{L})\, Y_t = (1 - \alpha_1 \mathrm{L})^{-1}(\alpha_0 + e_t). \tag{14.29}$$

What is the operator $(1 - \alpha_1 \mathrm{L})^{-1}$? Recall from Theorem 14.20 that for $|x| < 1$,

$$\sum_{j=0}^{\infty} x^j = \frac{1}{1-x} = (1-x)^{-1}.$$

Evaluate this expression at $x = \alpha_1 z$. We find

$$(1 - \alpha_1 z)^{-1} = \sum_{j=0}^{\infty} \alpha_1^j z^j. \tag{14.30}$$

Setting $z = \mathrm{L}$, this is

$$(1-\alpha_1 \mathrm{L})^{-1} = \sum_{j=0}^{\infty} \alpha_1^j \mathrm{L}^j.$$

Substituted into (14.29), we obtain

$$\begin{aligned} Y_t &= (1-\alpha_1 \mathrm{L})^{-1}(\alpha_0 + e_t) \\ &= \left(\sum_{j=0}^{\infty} \alpha^j \mathrm{L}^j\right)(\alpha_0 + e_t) \\ &= \sum_{j=0}^{\infty} \alpha_1^j \mathrm{L}^j (\alpha_0 + e_t) \\ &= \sum_{j=0}^{\infty} \alpha_1^j \left(\alpha_0 + e_{t-j}\right) \\ &= \frac{\alpha_0}{1-\alpha_1} + \sum_{j=0}^{\infty} \alpha_1^j e_{t-j} \end{aligned}$$

which is (14.27). This result is valid for $|\alpha_1| < 1$.

This illustrates another important concept. We say that a polynomial $\alpha(z)$ is **invertible** if

$$\alpha(z)^{-1} = \sum_{j=0}^{\infty} a_j z^j$$

is absolutely convergent. In particular, the AR(1) autoregressive polynomial $\alpha(z) = 1 - \alpha_1 z$ is invertible if $|\alpha_1| < 1$. This condition is the same as that for stationarity of the AR(1) process. Invertibility turns out to be a useful property.

14.23 UNIT ROOT AND EXPLOSIVE AR(1) PROCESSES

The AR(1) process (14.25) is stationary if $|\alpha_1| < 1$. What happens otherwise?

If $\alpha_0 = 0$ and $\alpha_1 = 1$, the model is known as a **random walk**:

$$Y_t = Y_{t-1} + e_t.$$

This is also called a **unit root process**, a **martingale**, or an **integrated process**. By back-substitution, we find

$$Y_t = Y_0 + \sum_{j=1}^{t} e_j.$$

Thus the initial condition does not disappear for large t. Consequently, the series is nonstationary. The autoregressive polynomial $\alpha(z) = 1 - z$ is not invertible, meaning that Y_t cannot be written as a convergent function of the infinite past history of e_t.

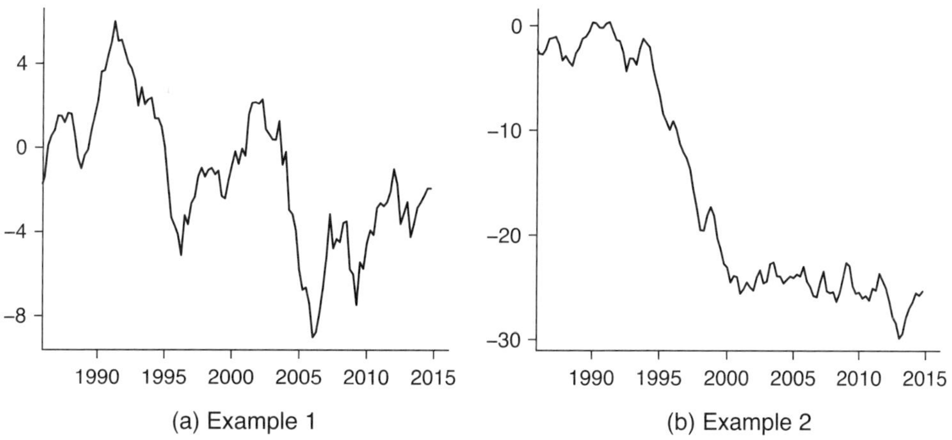

FIGURE 14.5 Random walk processes

The stochastic behavior of a random walk is noticeably different from a stationary AR(1) process. It wanders up and down with equal likelihood and is not mean-reverting. While it has no tendency to return to its previous values, the wandering nature of a random walk can give the illusion of mean reversion. The difference is that a random walk will take a very large number of time periods to "revert."

To illustrate, Figure 14.5 plots two independent random walk processes. The plot in panel (a) uses the innovations from Figure 14.3(a). The plot in panel (b) uses an independent set of i.i.d. N(0, 1) errors. You can see that the plot in panel (a) appears similar to the MA(8) and AR(1) plots in the sense that the series is smooth with long swings, but the difference is that the series does not return to a long-term mean. It appears to have drifted down over time. The plot in panel (b) appears to have quite different behavior, falling dramatically over a 5-year period, and then appearing to stabilize. These are both common behaviors of random walk processes.

If $\alpha_1 > 1$ the process is **explosive**. The model (14.25) with $\alpha_1 > 1$ exhibits exponential growth and high sensitivity to initial conditions. Explosive autoregressive processes do not seem to be good descriptions for most economic time series. While aggregate time series, such as the GDP process displayed in Figure 14.1(a), exhibits a similar exponential growth pattern, the exponential growth can typically be removed by taking logarithms.

The case $\alpha_1 < -1$ induces explosive oscillating growth and does not appear to be empirically relevant for economic applications.

14.24 SECOND-ORDER AUTOREGRESSIVE PROCESS

The **second-order autoregressive process**, denoted **AR(2)**, is

$$Y_t = \alpha_0 + \alpha_1 Y_{t-1} + \alpha_2 Y_{t-2} + e_t \tag{14.31}$$

where e_t is a strictly stationary and ergodic white noise process. The dynamic patterns of an AR(2) process are more complicated than those of an AR(1) process.

As a motivating example, consider the multiplier-accelerator model of Samuelson (1939). It might be a bit dated as a model, but it is simple and so hopefully makes the point. Aggregate output (in an economy with no trade) is defined as $Y_t = Consumption_t + Investment_t + Gov_t$. Suppose that individuals make their consumption decisions based on the previous period's income, $Consumption_t = bY_{t-1}$; firms make their investment decisions on the change in consumption, $Investment_t = d\Delta C_t$; and government spending is random, $Gov_t = a + e_t$. Then aggregate output follows

$$Y_t = a + b(1+d)Y_{t-1} - bdY_{t-2} + e_t \tag{14.32}$$

which is an AR(2) process.

Using the lag operator, we can write (14.31) as

$$Y_t - \alpha_1 \mathrm{L} Y_t - \alpha_2 \mathrm{L}^2 Y_t = \alpha_0 + e_t,$$

or $\alpha(\mathrm{L})Y_t = \alpha_0 + e_t$, where $\alpha(\mathrm{L}) = 1 - \alpha_1\mathrm{L} - \alpha_2\mathrm{L}^2$. We call $\alpha(z)$ the **autoregressive polynomial** of Y_t.

We would like to find the conditions for the stationarity of Y_t. It turns out that it is convenient to transform the process (14.31) into a vector autoregressive (VAR) process (to be studied in Chapter 15). Set $\widetilde{Y}_t = (Y_t, Y_{t-1})'$, which is stationary if and only if Y_t is stationary. Equation (14.31) implies that $\widetilde{Y}_t$ satisfies

$$\begin{pmatrix} Y_t \\ Y_{t-1} \end{pmatrix} = \begin{pmatrix} \alpha_1 & \alpha_2 \\ 1 & 0 \end{pmatrix} \begin{pmatrix} Y_{t-1} \\ Y_{t-2} \end{pmatrix} + \begin{pmatrix} a_0 + e_t \\ 0 \end{pmatrix}$$

or

$$\widetilde{Y}_t = \boldsymbol{A}\widetilde{Y}_{t-1} + \widetilde{e}_t \tag{14.33}$$

where $\boldsymbol{A} = \begin{pmatrix} \alpha_1 & \alpha_2 \\ 1 & 0 \end{pmatrix}$, and $\widetilde{e}_t = (a_0 + e_t, 0)'$. Equation (14.33) falls in the class of VAR models studied in Section 15.6. Theorem 15.6 shows that the VAR process is strictly stationary and ergodic if the innovations satisfy $\mathbb{E}\,\|\widetilde{e}_t\| < \infty$ and all eigenvalues λ of $\boldsymbol{A}$ are less than 1 in absolute value. The eigenvalues satisfy $\det(\boldsymbol{A} - \boldsymbol{I}_2\lambda) = 0$, where

$$\det(\boldsymbol{A} - \boldsymbol{I}_2\lambda) = \det\begin{pmatrix} \alpha_1 - \lambda & \alpha_2 \\ 1 & -\lambda \end{pmatrix} = \lambda^2 - \lambda\alpha_1 - \alpha_2 = \lambda^2\alpha(1/\lambda)$$

and $\alpha(z) = 1 - \alpha_1 z - \alpha_2 z^2$ is the autoregressive polynomial. Thus the eigenvalues satisfy $\alpha(1/\lambda) = 0$. Factoring the autoregressive polynomial as $\alpha(z) = (1 - \lambda_1 z)(1 - \lambda_2 z)$, the solutions $\alpha(1/\lambda) = 0$ must equal λ_1 and λ_2. The quadratic formula shows that these equal

$$\lambda_j = \frac{\alpha_1 \pm \sqrt{\alpha_1^2 + 4\alpha_2}}{2}. \tag{14.34}$$

These eigenvalues are real if $\alpha_1^2 + 4\alpha_2 \geq 0$ and are complex conjugates otherwise. The AR(2) process is stationary if the solutions (14.34) satisfy $|\lambda_j| < 1$.

Using (14.34) to solve for the AR coefficients in terms of the eigenvalues, we find $\alpha_1 = \lambda_1 + \lambda_2$ and $\alpha_2 = -\lambda_1\lambda_2$. With some algebra (the details are deferred to Section 14.47), we can show that $|\lambda_1| < 1$ and $|\lambda_2| < 1$ iff the following restrictions hold on the autoregressive coefficients:

$$\alpha_1 + \alpha_2 < 1 \tag{14.35}$$

$$\alpha_2 - \alpha_1 < 1 \tag{14.36}$$

$$\alpha_2 > -1. \tag{14.37}$$

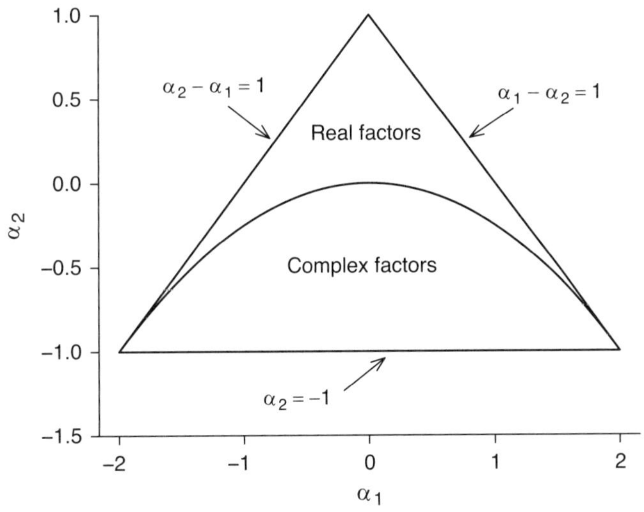

FIGURE 14.6 Stationarity region for AR(2)

These restrictions describe a triangle in (α_1, α_2) space, which is shown in Figure 14.6. Coefficients within this triangle correspond to a stationary AR(2) process.

Consider the Samuelson multiplier-accelerator model (14.32). You can calculate that (14.35)–(14.37) are satisfied (and thus the process is strictly stationary) if $0 \le b < 1$ and $0 \le d \le 1$, which are reasonable restrictions on the model parameters. The most important restriction is $b < 1$, which in the language of old-school macroeconomics is that the marginal propensity to consume out of income is less than 1.

Furthermore, the triangle is divided into two regions, as marked in Figure 14.6: the region above the parabola $\alpha_1^2 + 4\alpha_2 = 0$ producing real eigenvalues λ_j, and the region below the parabola producing complex eigenvalues λ_j. This behavior is interesting, because when the eigenvalues are complex, the autocorrelations of Y_t display damped oscillations. For this reason, the dynamic patterns of an AR(2) can be much more complicated than those of an AR(1).

Again, consider the Samuelson multiplier-accelerator model (14.32). You can calculate that if $b \ge 0$, the model has real eigenvalues iff $b \ge 4d/(1+d)^2$, which holds for b large and d small, which are "stable" parameterizations. In contrast, the model has complex eigenvalues (and thus oscillations) for sufficiently small b and large d.

Theorem 14.22 If $\mathbb{E}|e_t| < \infty$ and $|\lambda_j| < 1$ for λ_j defined in (14.34), or equivalently, if the inequalities (14.35)–(14.37) hold, then the AR(2) process (14.31) is absolutely convergent, strictly stationary, and ergodic.

The proof is presented in Section 14.47.

To illustrate, Figure 14.7 displays two simulated AR(2) processes. The plot in panel (a) sets $\alpha_1 = \alpha_2 = 0.4$. These coefficients produce real factors, so the process displays behavior similar to that of AR(1) processes. The plot in panel (b) sets $\alpha_1 = 1.3$ and $\alpha_2 = -0.8$. These coefficients produce complex factors, so the process displays oscillations.

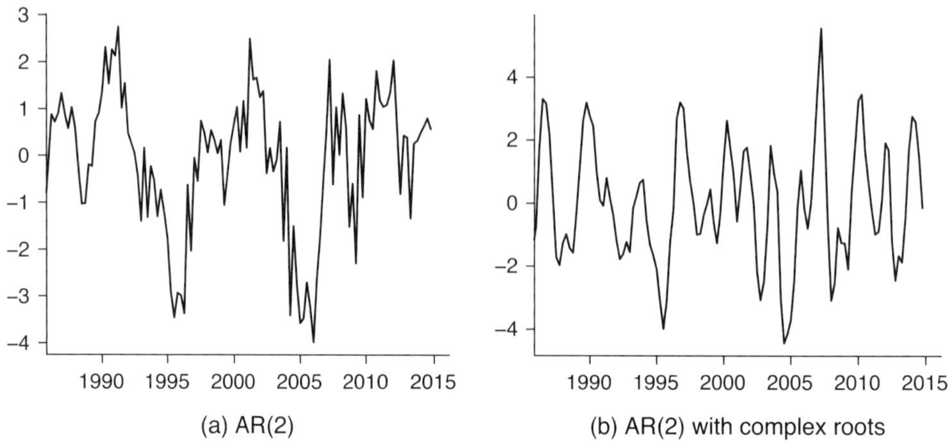

FIGURE 14.7 AR(2) processes

14.25 AR(P) PROCESS

The **pth-order autoregressive process**, denoted **AR(p)**, is

$$Y_t = \alpha_0 + \alpha_1 Y_{t-1} + \alpha_2 Y_{t-2} + \cdots + \alpha_p Y_{t-p} + e_t \tag{14.38}$$

where e_t is a strictly stationary and ergodic white noise process.

Using the lag operator,

$$Y_t - \alpha_1 \mathrm{L} Y_t - \alpha_2 \mathrm{L}^2 Y_t - \cdots - \alpha_p \mathrm{L}^p Y_t = \alpha_0 + e_t,$$

or $\alpha(\mathrm{L}) Y_t = \alpha_0 + e_t$, where

$$\alpha(\mathrm{L}) = 1 - \alpha_1 \mathrm{L} - \alpha_2 \mathrm{L}^2 - \cdots - \alpha_p \mathrm{L}^p. \tag{14.39}$$

We call $\alpha(z)$ the "autoregressive polynomial" of Y_t.

We find conditions for the stationarity of Y_t by a technique similar to that used for the AR(2) process. Set $\widetilde{Y}_t = (Y_t, Y_{t-1}, \ldots, Y_{t-p+1})'$ and $\widetilde{e}_t = (a_0 + e_t, 0, \ldots, 0)'$. Equation (14.38) implies that $\widetilde{Y}_t$ satisfies the VAR(1) equation (14.33) with

$$\boldsymbol{A} = \begin{pmatrix} \alpha_1 & \alpha_2 & \cdots & \alpha_{p-1} & \alpha_p \\ 1 & 0 & \cdots & 0 & 0 \\ 0 & 1 & \cdots & 0 & 0 \\ \vdots & \vdots & \ddots & \vdots & \vdots \\ 0 & 0 & \cdots & 1 & 0 \end{pmatrix}. \tag{14.40}$$

As shown in the proof of Theorem 14.23 below, the eigenvalues λ_j of $\boldsymbol{A}$ are the reciprocals of the roots r_j of the autoregressive polynomial (14.39). The roots r_j are the solutions to $\alpha(r) = 0$. Theorem 15.6 in Chapter 15 shows that stationarity of the VAR process $\widetilde{Y}_t$ holds if the eigenvalues λ_j are less than 1 in absolute value, or equivalently, when the roots r_j are greater than 1 in absolute value. For complex numbers, the equation $|z| = 1$ defines the **unit circle** (the circle with radius of unity). We therefore say that "z lies outside the unit circle" if $|z| > 1$.

Theorem 14.23 If $\mathbb{E}|e_t| < \infty$ and all roots of $\alpha(z)$ lie outside the unit circle, then the AR(p) process (14.38) is absolutely convergent, strictly stationary, and ergodic.

When the roots of $\alpha(z)$ lie outside the unit circle, then the polynomial $\alpha(z)$ is invertible. Inverting the autoregressive representation $\alpha(\mathrm{L})Y_t = \alpha_0 + e_t$, we obtain an infinite-order moving average representation

$$Y_t = \mu + b(\mathrm{L})e_t$$

where

$$b(z) = \alpha(z)^{-1} = \sum_{j=0}^{\infty} b_j z^j \tag{14.41}$$

and $\mu = \alpha(1)^{-1}a_0$.

We have the following characterization of the moving average coefficients.

Theorem 14.24 If all roots r_j of the autoregressive polynomial $\alpha(z)$ satisfy $|r_j| > 1$, then (14.41) holds with $|b_j| \le (j+1)^p \lambda^j$ and $\sum_{j=0}^{\infty} |b_j| < \infty$, where $\lambda = \max_{1\le j\le p} \left|r_j^{-1}\right| < 1$.

The proof is presented in Section 14.47.

14.26 IMPULSE RESPONSE FUNCTION

The coefficients of the moving average representation

$$\begin{aligned} Y_t &= b(\mathrm{L})e_t \\ &= \sum_{j=0}^{\infty} b_j e_{t-j} \\ &= b_0 e_t + b_1 e_{t-1} + b_2 e_{t-2} + \cdots \end{aligned}$$

are known among economists as the **impulse response function (IRF)**. Often the IRF is scaled by the standard deviation of e_t. We discuss this scaling at the end of the section. In linear models, the IRF is defined as the change in Y_{t+j} due to a shock at time t:

$$\frac{\partial}{\partial e_t} Y_{t+j} = b_j.$$

Thus the coefficient b_j can be interpreted as the magnitude of the impact of a time t shock on the time $t+j$ variable. Plots of b_j can be used to assess the time-propagation of shocks.

It is desirable to have a convenient method to calculate the impulse responses b_j from the coefficients of an autoregressive model (14.38). There are two methods, which we now discuss.

The first uses a simple recursion. In the linear AR(p) model, we can see that the coefficient b_j is the simple derivative

$$b_j = \frac{\partial}{\partial e_t} Y_{t+j} = \frac{\partial}{\partial e_0} Y_j.$$

We can calculate b_j by generating a history and perturbing the shock e_0. Since this calculation is unaffected by all other shocks, we can simply set $e_t = 0$ for $t \neq 0$ and set $e_0 = 1$. This implies the recursion

$$\begin{aligned}
b_0 &= 1 \\
b_1 &= \alpha_1 b_0 \\
b_2 &= \alpha_1 b_1 + \alpha_2 b_0 \\
&\vdots \\
b_j &= \alpha_1 b_{j-1} + \alpha_2 b_{j-2} + \cdots + \alpha_p b_{j-p}.
\end{aligned}$$

This recursion is conveniently calculated by the following simulation. Set $Y_t = 0$ for $t \leq 0$. Set $e_0 = 1$ and $e_t = 0$ for $t \geq 1$. Generate Y_t for $t \geq 0$ by $Y_t = \alpha_1 Y_{t-1} + \alpha_2 Y_{t-2} + \cdots + \alpha_p Y_{t-p} + e_t$. Then $Y_j = b_j$.

A second method uses the vector representation (14.33) of the AR(p) model with coefficient matrix (14.40). By recursion,

$$\widetilde{Y}_t = \sum_{j=0}^{\infty} \boldsymbol{A}^j \widetilde{e}_{t-j}.$$

Here, $\boldsymbol{A}^j = \boldsymbol{A} \cdots \boldsymbol{A}$ means the jth matrix product of $\boldsymbol{A}$ with itself. Setting $S = (1, 0, \ldots 0)'$, we find

$$Y_t = \sum_{j=0}^{\infty} S' \boldsymbol{A}^j S e_{t-j}.$$

By linearity,

$$b_j = \frac{\partial}{\partial e_t} Y_{t+j} = S' \boldsymbol{A}^j S. \tag{14.42}$$

Thus the coefficient b_j can be calculated by forming the matrix $\boldsymbol{A}$, its j-fold product $\boldsymbol{A}^j$, and then taking the upper-left element.

As mentioned at the beginning of the section, it is often desirable to scale the IRF so that it is the response to a one-deviation shock. Let $\sigma^2 = \operatorname{var}[e_t]$, and define $\varepsilon_t = e_t / \sigma$, which has unit variance. Then the IRF at lag j is

$$\mathrm{IRF}_j = \frac{\partial}{\partial \varepsilon_t} Y_{t+j} = \sigma b_j.$$

14.27 ARMA AND ARIMA PROCESSES

The **autoregressive-moving-average process**, denoted **ARMA(p,q)**, is

$$Y_t = \alpha_0 + \alpha_1 Y_{t-1} + \alpha_2 Y_{t-2} + \cdots + \alpha_p Y_{t-p} + \theta_0 e_t + \theta_1 e_{t-1} + \theta_2 e_{t-2} + \cdots + \theta_q e_{t-q} \tag{14.43}$$

where e_t is a strictly stationary and erogodic white noise process. It can be written using lag operator notation as $\alpha(\mathrm{L})Y_t = \alpha_0 + \theta(\mathrm{L})e_t$.

Theorem 14.25 The ARMA(p,q) process (14.43) is strictly stationary and ergodic if all roots of $\alpha(z)$ lie outside the unit circle. In this case, we can write

$$Y_t = \mu + b(\mathrm{L})e_t$$

where $b_j = O\left(j^p \beta^j\right)$ and $\sum_{j=0}^{\infty} |b_j| < \infty$.

The process Y_t follows an **autoregressive-integrated moving-average process**, denoted **ARIMA(p,d,q)**, if $\Delta^d Y_t$ is ARMA(p,q). It can be written using lag operator notation as $\alpha(\mathrm{L})(1-\mathrm{L})^d Y_t = \alpha_0 + \theta(\mathrm{L})e_t$.

14.28 MIXING PROPERTIES OF LINEAR PROCESSES

There is a considerable probability literature investigating the mixing properties of time series processes. One challenge is that as autoregressive processes depend on the infinite past sequence of innovations e_t, it is not immediately obvious if they satisfy the mixing conditions.

In fact, a simple AR(1) is not necessarily mixing. A counterexample was developed by Andrews (1984). He showed that if the error e_t has a two-point discrete distribution, then an AR(1) is not strong mixing. The reason is that a discrete innovation combined with the autoregressive structure means that by observing Y_t, you can deduce with near certainty the past history of the shocks e_t. The example seems rather special but shows the need to be careful with the theory. The intuition stemming from Andrews' example is that for an autoregressive process to be mixing, it is necessary for the errors e_t to be continuous.

A useful characterization was provided by Pham and Tran (1985).

Theorem 14.26 Suppose that $Y_t = \mu + \sum_{j=0}^{\infty} \theta_j e_{t-j}$ satisfies the following conditions:

1. e_t is i.i.d. with $\mathbb{E}|e_t|^r < \infty$ for some $r > 0$ and density $f(x)$ that satisfies
$$\int_{-\infty}^{\infty} \left|f(x-u) - f(x)\right| dx \le C|u| \tag{14.44}$$
for some $C < \infty$.
2. All roots of $\theta(z) = 0$ lie outside the unit circle, and $\sum_{j=0}^{\infty} |\theta_j| < \infty$.
3. $\sum_{k=1}^{\infty} \left(\sum_{j=k}^{\infty} |\theta_j|\right)^{r/(1+r)} < \infty$.

Then for some $B < \infty$,
$$\alpha(\ell) \le 4\beta(\ell) \le B \sum_{k=\ell}^{\infty} \left(\sum_{j=k}^{\infty} |\theta_j|\right)^{r/(1+r)}$$
and Y_t is absolutely regular and strong mixing.

The condition (14.44) is rather unusual, but it specifies that e_t has a smooth density, which rules out Andrews' counterexample.

The summability condition on the coefficients in part 3 of the theorem involves a tradeoff with the number of moments r. If e_t has all moments finite (e.g., normal errors), then we can set $r=\infty$, and this condition simplifies to $\sum_{k=1}^{\infty} k\,|\theta_k| < \infty$. For any finite r, the summability condition holds if θ_j has geometric decay.

It is instructive to deduce how the decay in the coefficients θ_j affects the rate for the mixing coefficients $\alpha(\ell)$. If $|\theta_j| \le O\left(j^{-\eta}\right)$, then $\sum_{j=k}^{\infty} |\theta_j| \le O\left(k^{-(\eta-1)}\right)$, so the rate is $\alpha(\ell) \le 4\beta(\ell) \le O\left(\ell^{-s}\right)$ for $s = (\eta-1)\,r/(1+r) - 1$. Mixing requires $s>0$, which holds for sufficiently large η. For example, if $r=4$, it holds for $\eta > 9/4$.

The primary message from this section is that linear processes, including autoregressive and ARMA processes, are mixing if the innovations satisfy suitable conditions. The mixing coefficients decay at rates related to the decay rates of the moving average coefficients.

14.29 IDENTIFICATION

The parameters of a model are identified if the parameters are uniquely determined by the probability distribution of the observations. In the case of linear time series analysis, we typically focus on the first two moments of the observations (means, variances, covariances). We therefore say that the coefficients of a stationary MA, AR, or ARMA model are **identified** if they are uniquely determined by the autocorrelation function. That is, given the autocorrelation function $\rho(k)$, are the coefficients unique?

It turns out that the answer is that MA and ARMA models are generally not identified. Identification is achieved by restricting the class of polynomial operators. In contrast, AR models are generally identified.

Let us start with the MA(1) model:

$$Y_t = e_t + \theta e_{t-1}.$$

It has first-order autocorrelation

$$\rho(1) = \frac{\theta}{1+\theta^2}.$$

Set $\omega = 1/\theta$. Then

$$\frac{\omega}{1+\omega^2} = \frac{1/\omega}{1+(1/\omega)^2} = \frac{\theta}{1+\theta^2} = \rho(1).$$

Thus the MA(1) model with coefficient $\omega = 1/\theta$ produces the same autocorrelations as the MA(1) model with coefficient θ. For example, $\theta = 1/2$ and $\omega = 2$ each yield $\rho(1) = 2/5$. There is no empirical way to distinguish between the models $Y_t = e_t + \theta e_{t-1}$ and $Y_t = e_t + \omega e_{t-1}$. Thus the coefficient θ is not identified.

The standard solution is to select the parameter that produces an invertible moving average polynomial. Since there is only one such choice, this yields a unique solution. This may be sensible when there is reason to believe that shocks have their primary impact in the contemporaneous period and secondary (lesser) impact in the second period.

Now consider the MA(2) model

$$Y_t = e_t + \theta_1 e_{t-1} + \theta_2 e_{t-2}.$$

The moving average polynomial can be factored as

$$\theta(z) = (1-\beta_1 z)(1-\beta_2 z)$$

so that $\beta_1\beta_2 = \theta_2$ and $\beta_1 + \beta_2 = -\theta_1$. The process has first- and second-order autocorrelations:

$$\rho(1) = \frac{\theta_1 + \theta_1\theta_2}{1 + \theta_1^2 + \theta_2^2} = \frac{-\beta_1 - \beta_2 - \beta_1^2\beta_2 - \beta_1\beta_2^2}{1 + \beta_1^2 + \beta_2^2 + 2\beta_1\beta_2 + \beta_1^2\beta_2^2}$$

$$\rho(2) = \frac{\theta_2}{1 + \theta_1^2 + \theta_2^2} = \frac{\beta_1\beta_2}{1 + \beta_1^2 + \beta_2^2 + 2\beta_1\beta_2 + \beta_1^2\beta_2^2}.$$

If we replace β_1 with $\omega_1 = 1/\beta_1$, we obtain

$$\rho(1) = \frac{-1/\beta_1 - \beta_2 - \beta_2/\beta_1^2 - \beta_2^2/\beta_1}{1 + 1/\beta_1^2 + \beta_2^2 + 2\beta_2/\beta_1 + \beta_2^2/\beta_1^2} = \frac{-\beta_1 - \beta_2\beta_1^2 - \beta_2 - \beta_2^2\beta_1}{\beta_1^2 + 1 + \beta_2^2\beta_1^2 + 2\beta_2\beta_1 + \beta_2^2}$$

$$\rho(2) = \frac{\beta_2/\beta_1}{1 + 1/\beta_1^2 + \beta_2^2 + 2\beta_2/\beta_1 + \beta_2^2/\beta_1^2} = \frac{\beta_1\beta_2}{\beta_1^2 + 1 + \beta_1^2\beta_2^2 + 2\beta_1\beta_2 + \beta_2^2}$$

which is unchanged. Similarly, if we replace β_2 with $\omega_2 = 1/\beta_2$, we obtain unchanged first- and second-order autocorrelations. It follows that in the MA(2) model, neither the factors β_1 and β_2 nor the coefficients θ_1 and θ_2 are identified. Consequently, there are four distinct MA(2) models that are identifiably indistinguishable.

This analysis extends to the MA(q) model. The factors of the MA polynomial can be replaced by their inverses, and consequently the coefficients are not identified.

The standard solution is to confine attention to MA(q) models with invertible roots. This technically solves the identification dilemma. This solution corresponds to the Wold decomposition, as it is defined in terms of the projection errors that correspond to the invertible representation.

A deeper identification failure occurs in ARMA models. Consider an ARMA(1,1) model:

$$Y_t = \alpha Y_{t-1} + e_t + \theta e_{t-1}.$$

Written in lag operator notation, we have

$$(1 - \alpha \mathrm{L})\, Y_t = (1 + \theta \mathrm{L})\, e_t.$$

The identification failure is that when $\alpha = -\theta$, then the model simplifies to $Y_t = e_t$. Thus the continuum of models with $\alpha = -\theta$ are all identical and the coefficients are not identified.

This behavior extends to higher order ARMA models. Take the ARMA(2,2) model written in factored lag operator notation:

$$(1 - \alpha_1 \mathrm{L})\,(1 - \alpha_2 \mathrm{L})\, Y_t = (1 + \theta_1 \mathrm{L})\,(1 + \theta_2 \mathrm{L})\, e_t.$$

The models with $\alpha_1 = -\theta_1$, $\alpha_1 = -\theta_2$, $\alpha_2 = -\theta_1$, or $\alpha_2 = -\theta_2$ all simplify to an ARMA(1,1). Thus all these models are identical, and hence the coefficients are not identified.

The problem is called "canceling roots," because it arises when there are two identical lag polynomial factors in the AR and MA polynomials.

The standard solution in the ARMA literature is to *assume* that there are no canceling roots. The trouble with this solution is that it is an assumption about the true process, which is unknown. Thus it is not really a solution to the identification problem. One recommendation is to be careful when using ARMA models and be aware that highly parameterized models may not have unique coefficients.

Now consider the AR(p) model (14.38). It can be written as

$$Y_t = X_t'\alpha + e_t \tag{14.45}$$

where $\alpha = (\alpha_0, \alpha_1, \ldots \alpha_p)'$, and $X_t = (1, Y_{t-1}, \ldots, Y_{t-p})'$. The MDS assumption implies that $\mathbb{E}[e_t] = 0$ and $\mathbb{E}[X_t e_t] = 0$. Thus the coefficient α satisfies

$$\alpha = \left(\mathbb{E}\left[X_t X_t'\right]\right)^{-1} \left(\mathbb{E}[X_t Y_t]\right). \tag{14.46}$$

This equation is unique if $\boldsymbol{Q} = \mathbb{E}\left[X_t X_t'\right]$ is positive definite. It turns out that this is generically true, so α is unique and identified.

> **Theorem 14.27** In the AR(p) model (14.38), if $0 < \sigma^2 < \infty$, then $\boldsymbol{Q} > 0$ and α is unique and identified.

The assumption $\sigma^2 > 0$ means that Y_t is not purely deterministic.

We can extend this result to approximating AR(p) models. That is, consider the equation (14.45) without the assumption that Y_t is necessarily a true AR(p) with a MDS error. Instead, suppose that Y_t is a nondeterministic stationary process. (Recall that nondeterministic means that $\sigma^2 > 0$, where σ^2 is the projection error variance (14.19).) Define the coefficient α as the best linear predictor, which is (14.46). The error e_t is defined by the equation (14.45). This is a linear projection model.

As in the case of any linear projection, the error e_t satisfies $\mathbb{E}[X_t e_t] = 0$. Thus $\mathbb{E}[e_t] = 0$ and $\mathbb{E}\left[Y_{t-j} e_t\right] = 0$ for $j = 1, \ldots, p$. However, the error e_t is not necessarily a MDS or white noise.

The coefficient α is identified if $\boldsymbol{Q} > 0$. The proof of Theorem 14.27 (presented in Section 14.47) does not make use of the assumption that Y_t is an AR(p) with a MDS error. Instead, it only uses the assumption that $\sigma^2 > 0$. This holds in the approximate AR(p) model as well under the assumption that Y_t is nondeterministic. We conclude that any approximating AR(p) is identified.

> **Theorem 14.28** If Y_t is strictly stationary, not purely deterministic, and $\mathbb{E}\left[Y_t^2\right] < \infty$, then for any p, $\boldsymbol{Q} = \mathbb{E}\left[X_t X_t'\right] > 0$, and thus the coefficient vector (14.46) is identified.

14.30 ESTIMATION OF AUTOREGRESSIVE MODELS

Consider the estimation of an AR(p) model for stationary, ergodic, and nondeterministic Y_t. The model is (14.45), where $X_t = (1, Y_{t-1}, \ldots, Y_{t-p})'$. The coefficient α is defined by projection in (14.46). The error is defined by (14.45) and has variance $\sigma^2 = \mathbb{E}\left[e_t^2\right]$. This allows Y_t to follow a true AR(p) process but it is not necessary.

The least squares estimator is

$$\widehat{\alpha} = \left(\sum_{t=1}^{n} X_t X_t'\right)^{-1} \left(\sum_{t=1}^{n} X_t Y_t\right).$$

This notation presumes that there are $n + p$ total observations on Y_t, from which the first p are used as initial conditions so that $X_1 = (1, Y_0, Y_{-1}, \ldots, Y_{-p+1})$ is defined. Effectively, this choice redefines the sample period. (An alternative notational choice is to define the periods so the sums range from observations $p + 1$ to n.)

The least squares residuals are $\widehat{e}_t = Y_t - X_t'\widehat{\alpha}$. The error variance can be estimated by $\widehat{\sigma}^2 = n^{-1} \sum_{t=1}^{n} \widehat{e}_t^2$ or $s^2 = (n - p - 1)^{-1} \sum_{t=1}^{n} \widehat{e}_t^2$.

If Y_t is strictly stationary and ergodic, then so are X_tX_t' and X_tY_t. They have finite means if $\mathbb{E}\left[Y_t^2\right] < \infty$. Under these assumptions, the ergodic theorem implies that

$$\frac{1}{n}\sum_{t=1}^{n} X_tY_t \underset{p}{\longrightarrow} \mathbb{E}\left[X_tY_t\right] \tag{14.47}$$

and

$$\frac{1}{n}\sum_{t=1}^{n} X_tX_t' \underset{p}{\longrightarrow} \mathbb{E}\left[X_tX_t'\right] = \boldsymbol{Q}.$$

Theorem 14.28 shows that $\boldsymbol{Q} > 0$. Combined with the continuous mapping theorem, we see that

$$\widehat{\alpha} = \left(\frac{1}{n}\sum_{t=1}^{n} X_tX_t'\right)^{-1}\left(\frac{1}{n}\sum_{t=1}^{n} X_tY_t\right) \underset{p}{\longrightarrow} \left(\mathbb{E}\left[X_tX_t'\right]\right)^{-1}\mathbb{E}\left[X_tY_t\right] = \alpha.$$

It is straightforward to show that $\widehat{\sigma}^2$ is consistent as well.

Theorem 14.29 If Y_t is strictly stationary, ergodic, not purely deterministic, and $\mathbb{E}\left[Y_t^2\right] < \infty$, then for any p, $\widehat{\alpha} \underset{p}{\longrightarrow} \alpha$ and $\widehat{\sigma}^2 \underset{p}{\longrightarrow} \sigma^2$ as $n \to \infty$.

This theorem shows that under very mild conditions, the coefficients of an AR(p) model can be consistently estimated by least squares. Once again, this does not require that the series Y_t is actually an AR(p) process. It holds for any stationary process with the coefficient defined by projection.

14.31 ASYMPTOTIC DISTRIBUTION OF LEAST SQUARES ESTIMATOR

The asymptotic distribution of the least squares estimator $\widehat{\alpha}$ depends on the stochastic assumptions. In this section, we derive the asymptotic distribution under the assumption of correct specification.

Specifically, let us assume that the error e_t is a MDS. An important implication of the MDS assumption is that since $X_t = (1, Y_{t-1}, \ldots, Y_{t-p})'$ is part of the information set $\mathscr{F}_{t-1}$, by the conditioning theorem,

$$\mathbb{E}\left[X_te_t \mid \mathscr{F}_{t-1}\right] = X_t\mathbb{E}\left[e_t \mid \mathscr{F}_{t-1}\right] = 0.$$

Thus X_te_t is a MDS. It has a finite variance if e_t has a finite fourth moment. To see this, by Theorem 14.24, $Y_t = \mu + \sum_{j=0}^{\infty} b_je_{t-j}$ with $\sum_{j=0}^{\infty}\left|b_j\right| < \infty$. Using Minkowski's inequality,

$$\left(\mathbb{E}\left|Y_t\right|^4\right)^{1/4} \leq \sum_{j=0}^{\infty}\left|b_j\right|\left(\mathbb{E}\left|e_{t-j}\right|^4\right)^{1/4} < \infty.$$

Thus $\mathbb{E}\left[Y_t^4\right] < \infty$. The Cauchy-Schwarz inequality then shows that $\mathbb{E}\left\|X_te_t\right\|^2 < \infty$. We can then apply the martingale difference CLT (Theorem 14.11) to see that

$$\frac{1}{\sqrt{n}}\sum_{t=1}^{n} X_te_t \underset{d}{\longrightarrow} \mathrm{N}\left(0, \Sigma\right)$$

where $\Sigma = \mathbb{E}\left[X_tX_t'e_t^2\right]$.

Theorem 14.30 If Y_t follows the AR(p) model (14.38), all roots of $a(z)$ lie outside the unit circle, $\mathbb{E}[e_t \mid \mathscr{F}_{t-1}] = 0$, $\mathbb{E}[e_t^4] < \infty$, and $\mathbb{E}[e_t^2] > 0$, then as $n \to \infty$, $\sqrt{n}(\widehat{\alpha} - \alpha) \underset{d}{\longrightarrow} \mathrm{N}(0, \boldsymbol{V})$, where $\boldsymbol{V} = \boldsymbol{Q}^{-1} \Sigma \boldsymbol{Q}^{-1}$.

This limit distribution is identical in form to the asymptotic distribution of least squares in cross-section regression. The implication is that asymptotic inference is the same. In particular, the asymptotic covariance matrix is estimated just as in the cross-section case.

14.32 DISTRIBUTION UNDER HOMOSKEDASTICITY

In cross-section regression, we found that the covariance matrix simplifies under the assumption of conditional homoskedasticity. The same occurs in the time series context. Assume that the error is a homoskedastic MDS:

$$\mathbb{E}[e_t \mid \mathscr{F}_{t-1}] = 0$$
$$\mathbb{E}[e_t^2 \mid \mathscr{F}_{t-1}] = \sigma^2.$$

In this case,

$$\Sigma = \mathbb{E}\left[X_t X_t' \mathbb{E}\left[e_t^2 \mid \mathscr{F}_{t-1}\right]\right] = \boldsymbol{Q}\sigma^2$$

and the asymptotic distribution simplifies.

Theorem 14.31 Under the assumptions of Theorem 14.30, if in addition $\mathbb{E}[e_t^2 \mid \mathscr{F}_{t-1}] = \sigma^2$, then as $n \to \infty$, $\sqrt{n}(\widehat{\alpha} - \alpha) \underset{d}{\longrightarrow} \mathrm{N}(0, \boldsymbol{V}^0)$, where $\boldsymbol{V}^0 = \sigma^2 \boldsymbol{Q}^{-1}$.

These results show that under correct specification (a MDS error), the format of the asymptotic distribution of the least squares estimator exactly parallels the cross-section case. In general, the covariance matrix takes a sandwich form with components exactly equal to the cross-section case. Under conditional homoskedasticity, the covariance matrix simplifies exactly as in the cross-section case.

A particularly useful insight that can be derived from Theorem 14.31 is to focus on the simple AR(1) with no intercept. In this case, $Q = \mathbb{E}[Y_t^2] = \sigma^2/(1 - \alpha_1^2)$, so the asymptotic distribution simplifies to

$$\sqrt{n}(\widehat{\alpha}_1 - \alpha_1) \underset{d}{\longrightarrow} \mathrm{N}(0, 1 - \alpha_1^2).$$

Thus the asymptotic variance depends only on α_1 and is decreasing with α_1^2. An intuition is that larger α_1^2 means greater signal and hence greater estimation precision. This result also shows that the asymptotic distribution is nonsimilar: the variance is a function of the parameter of interest. Thus we can expect (from advanced statistical theory) asymptotic inference to be less accurate than indicated by nominal levels.

In the context of cross-section data, we argued that the homoskedasticity assumption was dubious except for occasional theoretical insight. For practical applications, it is recommended to use heteroskedasticity-robust theory and methods when possible. The same argument applies to the time series case. While the distribution theory simplifies under conditional homoskedasticity, there is no reason to expect homoskedasticity to hold in practice. Therefore in applications, it is better to use the heteroskedasticity-robust distributional theory when possible.

Unfortunately, many existing time series textbooks report the distribution theory from (14.31). This choice has influenced computer software packages, many of which also by default (or exclusively) use the homoskedastic distribution theory. This is unfortunate.

14.33 ASYMPTOTIC DISTRIBUTION UNDER GENERAL DEPENDENCE

Whether the AR(p) model (14.38) holds with white noise errors or if the AR(p) is an approximation with α defined as the best linear predictor, the MDS CLT does not apply. Instead, if Y_t is strong mixing, we can use the CLT for mixing processes (Theorem 14.15).

Theorem 14.32 Assume that Y_t is strictly stationary, ergodic, and for some $r > 4$, $\mathbb{E}\left|Y_t\right|^r < \infty$ and the mixing coefficients satisfy $\sum_{\ell=1}^{\infty} \alpha(\ell)^{1-4/r} < \infty$. Let α be defined as the best linear projection coefficients (14.46) from an AR(p) model with projection errors e_t. Let $\widehat{\alpha}$ be the least squares estimator of α. Then

$$\Omega = \sum_{\ell=-\infty}^{\infty} \mathbb{E}\left[X_{t-\ell} X_t' e_t e_{t-\ell}\right]$$

is convergent, and $\sqrt{n}\left(\widehat{\alpha} - \alpha\right) \underset{d}{\longrightarrow} \mathrm{N}\left(0, \boldsymbol{V}\right)$ as $n \to \infty$, where $\boldsymbol{V} = \boldsymbol{Q}^{-1} \Omega \boldsymbol{Q}^{-1}$.

This result is substantially different from the cross-section case. It shows that model misspecification (including misspecifying the order of the autoregression) renders invalid the conventional "heteroskedasticity-robust" covariance matrix formula. Misspecified models do not have unforecastable (martingale difference) errors, so the regression scores $X_t e_t$ are potentially serially correlated. The asymptotic variance takes a sandwich form with the central component Ω being the long-run variance (recall Section 14.13) of the regression scores $X_t e_t$.

14.34 COVARIANCE MATRIX ESTIMATION

Under the assumption of correct specification, covariance matrix estimation is identical to the cross-section case. The asymptotic covariance matrix estimator under homoskedasticity is

$$\widehat{\boldsymbol{V}}^0 = \widehat{\sigma}^2 \widehat{\boldsymbol{Q}}^{-1}$$

$$\widehat{\boldsymbol{Q}} = \frac{1}{n} \sum_{t=1}^{n} X_t X_t'$$

The estimator s^2 may be used instead of $\widehat{\sigma}^2$.

The heteroskedasticity-robust asymptotic covariance matrix estimator is

$$\widehat{\boldsymbol{V}} = \widehat{\boldsymbol{Q}}^{-1} \widehat{\Sigma} \widehat{\boldsymbol{Q}}^{-1} \tag{14.48}$$

where

$$\widehat{\Sigma} = \frac{1}{n}\sum_{t=1}^{n} X_t X_t' \widehat{e}_t^2.$$

Degree-of-freedom adjustments may be made as in the cross-section case, though a theoretical justification has not been developed.

Standard errors $s\left(\widehat{\alpha}_j\right)$ for individual coefficient estimates can be formed by taking the scaled diagonal elements of $\widehat{\boldsymbol{V}}$.

Theorem 14.33 Under the assumptions of Theorem 14.30, as $n \to \infty$, $\widehat{\boldsymbol{V}} \underset{p}{\longrightarrow} \boldsymbol{V}$ and $\left(\widehat{\alpha}_j - \alpha_j\right)/s(\widehat{\alpha}_j) \underset{d}{\longrightarrow} \mathrm{N}(0,1)$.

Theorem 14.33 shows that standard covariance matrix estimation is consistent and the resulting t-ratios are asymptotically normal. Thus for stationary autoregressions, inference can proceed using conventional regression methods.

14.35 COVARIANCE MATRIX ESTIMATION UNDER GENERAL DEPENDENCE

Under the assumptions of Theorem 14.32, the conventional covariance matrix estimators are inconsistent, as they do not capture the serial dependence in the regression scores $X_t e_t$. To consistently estimate the covariance matrix, we need an estimator of the long-run variance Ω. The appropriate class of estimators are called **heteroskedasticity and autocorrelation consistent (HAC)** or **heteroskedasticity and autocorrelation robust (HAR)** covariance matrix estimators.

To understand the methods, it is helpful to define the vector series $u_t = X_t e_t$ and autocovariance matrices $\Gamma(\ell) = \mathbb{E}\left[u_{t-\ell} u_t'\right]$ so that

$$\Omega = \sum_{\ell=-\infty}^{\infty} \Gamma(\ell).$$

Since this sum is convergent, the autocovariance matrices converge to 0 as $\ell \to \infty$. Therefore, Ω can be approximated by taking a finite sum of autocovariances, such as

$$\Omega_M = \sum_{\ell=-M}^{M} \Gamma(\ell).$$

The number M is sometimes called the **lag truncation** number. Other authors call it the **bandwidth**. An estimator of $\Gamma(\ell)$ is

$$\widehat{\Gamma}(\ell) = \frac{1}{n}\sum_{1 \le t-\ell \le n} \widehat{u}_{t-\ell}\widehat{u}_t'$$

where $\widehat{u}_t = X_t \widehat{e}_t$. By the ergodic theorem, we can show that for any ℓ, $\widehat{\Gamma}(\ell) \underset{p}{\longrightarrow} \Gamma(\ell)$. Thus for any fixed M, the estimator

$$\widehat{\Omega}_M = \sum_{\ell=-M}^{M} \widehat{\Gamma}(\ell) \tag{14.49}$$

is consistent for Ω_M.

If the serial correlation in $X_t e_t$ is known to be 0 after M lags, then $\Omega_M = \Omega$, and the estimator (14.49) is consistent for Ω. This estimator was proposed by L. Hansen and Hodrick (1980) in the context of multiperiod forecasts and by L. Hansen (1982) for the generalized method of moments.

In the general case, we can select M to increase with sample size n. If the rate at which M increases is sufficiently slow, then $\widehat{\Omega}_M$ will be consistent for Ω, as first shown by White and Domowitz (1984).

Once we view the lag truncation number M as a choice, the estimator (14.49) has two potential deficiencies. One is that $\widehat{\Omega}_M$ can change nonsmoothly with M, which makes estimation results sensitive to the choice of M. The other is that $\widehat{\Omega}_M$ may not be positive semi-definite and is therefore not a valid covariance matrix estimator. We can see this in the simple case of scalar u_t and $M = 1$. In this case, $\widehat{\Omega}_1 = \widehat{\gamma}(0)\,(1 + 2\widehat{\rho}(1))$, which is negative when $\widehat{\rho}(1) < -1/2$. Thus if the data are strongly negatively autocorrelated, the variance estimator can be negative. A negative variance estimator means that standard errors are ill defined. (A naïve computation will produce a complex standard error, which makes no sense.[6])

These two deficiencies can be resolved if we amend (14.49) by a weighted sum of autocovariances. Newey and West (1987b) proposed

$$\widehat{\Omega}_{\mathrm{nw}} = \sum_{\ell=-M}^{M} \left(1 - \frac{|\ell|}{M+1}\right) \widehat{\Gamma}(\ell) \tag{14.50}$$

which is a weighted sum of the autocovariances. Other weight functions can be used; the one in (14.50) is known as the Bartlett kernel.[7] Newey and West (1987b) showed that this estimator has the algebraic property that $\widehat{\Omega}_{\mathrm{nw}} \geq 0$ (it is positive semi-definite), solving the negative variance problem, and it is also a smooth function of M. Thus this estimator solves the two problems described above.

For $\widehat{\Omega}_{\mathrm{nw}}$ to be consistent for Ω, the lag truncion number M must increase to infinity with n. Sufficient conditions were established by B. Hansen (1992).

Theorem 14.34 Under the assumptions of Theorem 14.32 plus $\sum_{\ell=1}^{\infty} \alpha(\ell)^{1/2-4/r} < \infty$, if $M \to \infty$ yet $M^3/n = O(1)$, then as $n \to \infty$, $\widehat{\Omega}_{\mathrm{nw}} \underset{p}{\longrightarrow} \Omega$.

The assumption $M^3/n = O(1)$ technically means that M grows no faster than $n^{1/3}$, but this does not have a practical counterpart other than the implication that "M should be much smaller than n." The assumption on the mixing coefficients is slightly stronger than in Theorem 14.32, due to the technical nature of the derivation.

A important practical issue is how to select M. One way to think about it is that M impacts the precision of the estimator $\widehat{\Omega}_{\mathrm{nw}}$ through its bias and variance. Since $\widehat{\Gamma}(\ell)$ is a sample average, its variance is $O(1/n)$, so

[6] A common computational mishap is a complex standard error. This occurs when a covariance matrix estimator has negative elements on the diagonal.

[7] See Andrews (1991b) for a description of popular options. In practice, the choice of weight function is much less important than the choice of lag truncation number M.

we expect the variance of $\widehat{\Omega}_M$ to be of order $O(M/n)$. The bias of $\widehat{\Omega}_{\text{nw}}$ for Ω is harder to calculate but depends on the rate at which the covariances $\Gamma(\ell)$ decay to 0. Andrews (1991b) found that the M that minimizes the mean squared error of $\widehat{\Omega}_{\text{nw}}$ satisfies the rate $M = Cn^{1/3}$, where the constant C depends on the autocovariances. Practical rules to estimate and implement this optimal lag truncation parameter have been proposed by Andrews (1991b) and Newey and West (1994). Andrews' rule for the Newey-West estimator (14.50) can be written as

$$M = \left(6\frac{\rho^2}{\left(1-\rho^2\right)^2}\right)^{1/3} n^{1/3} \tag{14.51}$$

where ρ is a serial correlation parameter. When u_t is scalar, ρ is the first autocorrelation of u_t. Andrews suggested using an estimator of ρ to plug into this formula to find M. An alternative is to use a default value of ρ. For example, if we set $\rho = 0.5$, then the Andrews rule is $M = 1.4n^{1/3}$, which is a useful benchmark.

14.36 TESTING THE HYPOTHESIS OF NO SERIAL CORRELATION

In some cases, it may be of interest to test the hypothesis that the series Y_t is serially uncorrelated against the alternative that it is serially correlated. There have been many proposed tests of this hypothesis. The most appropriate is based on the least squares regression of an AR(p) model. Take the model

$$Y_t = \alpha_0 + \alpha_1 Y_{t-1} + \alpha_2 Y_{t-2} + \cdots + \alpha_p Y_{t-p} + e_t$$

with e_t a MDS. In this model, the series Y_t is serially uncorrelated if the slope coefficients are all 0. Thus the hypothesis of interest is

$$\mathbb{H}_0 : \alpha_1 = \cdots = \alpha_p = 0$$
$$\mathbb{H}_1 : \alpha_j \neq 0 \text{ for some } j \geq 1.$$

The test can be implemented by a Wald or F test. Estimate the AR(p) model by least squares. Form the Wald or F statistic using the variance estimator (14.48). (The Newey-West estimator should not be used, as there is no serial correlation under the null hypothesis.) Accept the hypothesis if the test statistic is smaller than a conventional critical value (or if the p-value exceeds the significance level), and reject the hypothesis otherwise.

Implementation of this test requires a choice of autoregressive order p. This choice affects the power of the test. A sufficient number of lags should be included so as to pick up potential serial correlation patterns but not so many that the power of the test is diluted. A reasonable choice in many applications is to set p to equals s, the seasonal periodicity. Thus include four lags for quarterly data or 12 lags for monthly data.

14.37 TESTING FOR OMITTED SERIAL CORRELATION

When using an AR(p) model, it may be of interest to know whether there is any remaining serial correlation. This can be expressed as a test for serial correlation in the error or equivalently, as a test for a higher-order autogressive model.

Consider the AR(p) model

$$Y_t = \alpha_0 + \alpha_1 Y_{t-1} + \alpha_2 Y_{t-2} + \cdots + \alpha_p Y_{t-p} + u_t. \tag{14.52}$$

The null hypothesis is that u_t is serially uncorrelated, and the alternative hypothesis is that it is serially correlated. We can model the latter as a mean-0 autoregressive process:

$$u_t = \theta_1 u_{t-1} + \cdots + \theta_q u_{t-q} + e_t. \tag{14.53}$$

The hypothesis is

$$\mathbb{H}_0 : \theta_1 = \cdots = \theta_q = 0$$
$$\mathbb{H}_1 : \theta_j \neq 0 \text{ for some } j \geq 1.$$

A seemingly natural test for $\mathbb{H}_0$ uses a two-step method. First estimate (14.52) by least squares and obtain the residuals $\widehat{u}_t$. Second, estimate (14.53) by least squares by regressing $\widehat{u}_t$ on its lagged values and obtain the Wald or F test for $\mathbb{H}_0$. This seems like a natural approach, but it is muddled by the fact that the distribution of the Wald statistic is distorted by the two-step procedure. The Wald statistic is not asymptotically chi-square, so it is inappropriate to make a decision based on the conventional critical values. One approach to obtaining the correct asymptotic distribution is to use the generalized method of moments, treating (14.52) and (14.53) as a two-equation just-identified system.

An easier solution is to rewrite (14.52) and (14.53) as a higher-order autoregression, so that we can use a standard test statistic. To illustrate how this works, take the case $q = 1$. Take (14.52) and lag the equation once:

$$Y_{t-1} = \alpha_0 + \alpha_1 Y_{t-2} + \alpha_2 Y_{t-3} + \cdots + \alpha_p Y_{t-p-1} + u_{t-1}.$$

Multiply this by θ_1 and subtract from (14.52) to find

$$\begin{aligned} Y_t - \theta_1 Y_{t-1} = {} & \alpha_0 + \alpha_1 Y_{t-1} + \alpha_2 Y_{t-2} + \cdots + \alpha_p Y_{t-p} + u_t \\ & - \theta_1 \alpha_0 - \theta_1 \alpha_1 Y_{t-2} - \theta_1 \alpha_2 Y_{t-3} - \cdots - \theta_1 \alpha_p Y_{t-p-1} - \theta_1 u_{t-1} \end{aligned}$$

or

$$Y_t = \alpha_0 (1 - \theta_1) + (\alpha_1 + \theta_1) Y_{t-1} + (\alpha_2 - \theta_1 \alpha_1) Y_{t-2} + \cdots - \theta_1 \alpha_p Y_{t-p-1} + e_t.$$

This is an AR(p+1). It simplifies to an AR(p) when $\theta_1 = 0$. Thus $\mathbb{H}_0$ is equivalent to the restriction that the coefficient on Y_{t-p-1} is 0.

Thus testing the null hypothesis of an AR(p) (14.52) against the alternative that the error is an AR(1) is equivalent to testing an AR(p) against an AR(p+1). The latter test is implemented as a t test on the coefficient on Y_{t-p-1}.

More generally, testing the null hypothesis of an AR(p) (14.52) against the alternative that the error is an AR(q) is equivalent to testing that Y_t is an AR(p) against the alternative that Y_t is an AR(p+q). The latter test is implemented as a Wald (or F) test on the coefficients on $Y_{t-p-1}, \ldots, Y_{t-p-q}$. If the statistic is smaller than the critical values (or the p-value is larger than the significance level), then we reject the hypothesis that the AR(p) is correctly specified in favor of the alternative that there is omitted serial correlation. Otherwise we accept the hypothesis that the AR(p) model is correctly specified.

Another way of deriving the test is as follows. Write (14.52) and (14.53) using lag operator notation $\alpha(\mathrm{L}) Y_t = \alpha_0 + u_t$ with $\theta(\mathrm{L}) u_t = e_t$. Applying the operator $\theta(\mathrm{L})$ to the first equation, we obtain $\theta(\mathrm{L})\alpha(\mathrm{L}) Y_t = \alpha_0^* + e_t$, where $\alpha_0^* = \theta(1)\alpha_0$. The product $\theta(\mathrm{L})\alpha(\mathrm{L})$ is a polynomial of order $p + q$, so Y_t is an AR(p+q).

While this discussion is all good fun, it is unclear whether there is good reason to use the test described in this section. Economic theory does not typically produce hypotheses concerning the autoregressive order. Consequently, rarely is there scientific interest in testing, say, the hypothesis that a series is an AR(4) or any other specific autoregressive order. Instead, practitioners tend to use hypothesis tests for another purpose—model selection. That is, in practice, users want to know "what autoregressive model should be used" in a specific application and resort to hypothesis tests to aid in this decision. This is an inappropriate use of hypothesis tests, because tests are designed to provide answers to scientific questions rather than being designed to select models with good approximation properties. Instead, model selection should be based on model selection tools. One is described in the following section.

14.38 MODEL SELECTION

What is an appropriate choice of autoregressive order p? This is the problem of model selection.

A good choice is to minimize the Akaike information criterion (AIC)

$$\mathrm{AIC}(p) = n \log \widehat{\sigma}^2(p) + 2p$$

where $\widehat{\sigma}^2(p)$ is the estimated residual variance from an AR(p). The AIC is a penalized version of the Gaussian log-likelihood function for the estimated regression model. It is an estimator of the divergence between the fitted model and the true conditional density (see Section 28.4). By selecting the model with the smallest value of the AIC, you select the model with the smallest estimated divergence—the best estimated fit between the estimated and true densities.

The AIC is also a monotonic transformation of an estimator of the one-step-ahead forecast mean squared error. Thus by selecting the model with the smallest value of the AIC, you are selecting the model with the smallest estimated forecast error.

One hiccup in computing the AIC criterion for multiple models is that the sample size available for estimation changes as p changes. (If you increase p, you need more initial conditions.) This renders AIC comparisons inappropriate. The same sample—the same number of observations—should be used for estimation of all models. This is because AIC is a penalized likelihood, and if the samples are different, then the likelihoods are not the same. The appropriate remedy is to fix an upper value $\overline{p}$ and then reserve the first $\overline{p}$ as initial conditions. Then estimate the models AR(1), AR(2), ..., AR($\overline{p}$) on this (unified) sample.

The AIC of an estimated regression model can be displayed in Stata by using the `estimates stats` command.

14.39 ILLUSTRATIONS

I illustrate autoregressive estimation with three empirical examples using U.S. quarterly time series from the FRED-QD data file.

The first example is real GDP growth rates (growth rate of *gdpc1*). We estimate autoregressive models of order 0 through 4 using the sample from 1980 to 2017.[8] This is a commonly estimated model in applied macroeconomic practice and is the empirical version of the Samuelson multiplier-accelerator model discussed

[8]This subsample was used for estimation, as it has been argued that the growth rate of U.S. GDP slowed around this period. The goal was to estimate the model over a period of time when the series is plausibly stationary.

Table 14.1
U.S. GDP AR models

	AR(0)	AR(1)	AR(2)	AR(3)	AR(4)
α_0	0.65	0.40	0.34	0.34	0.34
	(0.06)	(0.08)	(0.10)	(0.10)	(0.11)
	[0.09]	[0.08]	[0.09]	[0.09]	[0.09]
α_1		0.39	0.34	0.33	0.34
		(0.09)	(0.10)	(0.10)	(0.10)
		[0.10]	[0.10]	[0.10]	[0.10]
α_2			0.14	0.13	0.13
			(0.11)	(0.13)	(0.14)
			[0.10]	[0.10]	[0.11]
α_3				0.02	0.03
				(0.11)	(0.12)
				[0.07]	[0.09]
α_4					−0.02
					(0.12)
					[0.13]
AIC	329	306	305	307	309

Standard errors robust to heteroskedasticity are in parenthesis. Newey-West standard errors are in square brackets, with $M = 5$.

in Section 14.24. The coefficient estimates, conventional (heteroskedasticity-robust) standard errors, Newey-West (with $M = 5$) standard errors, and AIC are displayed in Table 14.1. This sample has 152 observations. The model selected by the AIC criterion is the AR(2). The estimated model has positive and small values for the first two autoregressive coefficients. Thus quarterly output growth rates are positively correlated from quarter to quarter, but only mildly so, and most of the correlation is captured by the first lag. The coefficients of this model are in the real section of Figure 14.6, meaning that the dynamics of the estimated model do not display oscillations. The coefficients of the estimated AR(4) model are nearly identical to those of the AR(2) model. The conventional and Newey-West standard errors are somewhat different from one another for the AR(0) and AR(4) models, but are nearly identical to one another for the AR(1) and AR(2) models

Our second example is real nondurables consumption growth rates C_t (growth rate of *pcndx*). This is motivated by an influential paper by Robert Hall (1978), who argued that the permanent income hypothesis implies that changes in consumption should be unpredictable (martingale differences). To test this model, Hall (1978) estimated an AR(4) model. Our estimated regression using the full sample ($n = 231$) is reported in the following equation:

$$\widehat{C}_t = \underset{(0.07)}{0.15}\ C_{t-1} + \underset{(0.07)}{0.11}\ C_{t-2} + \underset{(0.07)}{0.13}\ C_{t-3} + \underset{(0.08)}{0.02}\ C_{t-4} + \underset{(0.09)}{0.35}.$$

Here, we report heteroskedasticity-robust standard errors. Hall's hypothesis is that all autoregressive coefficients should be 0. We test this joint hypothesis with an F statistic and find $F = 3.32$ with a p-value of $p = 0.012$. This is significant at the 5% level and close to the 1% level. The first three autoregressive coefficients appear to be positive, but small, indicating positive serial correlation. This evidence is (mildly) inconsistent with Hall's hypothesis. We report heteroskedasticity-robust standard errors (not Newey-West standard errors), since the purpose was to test the hypothesis of no serial correlation.

Table 14.2
U.S. Inflation AR Models

	AR(1)	AR(2)	AR(3)	AR(4)	AR(5)
α_0	0.004	0.003	0.003	0.003	0.003
	(0.034)	(0.032)	(0.032)	(0.032)	(0.032)
	[0.023]	[0.028]	[0.029]	[0.031]	[0.032]
α_1	−0.26	−0.36	−0.36	−0.36	−0.37
	(0.08)	(0.07)	(0.07)	(0.07)	(0.07)
	[0.05]	[0.07]	[0.07]	[0.07]	[0.07]
α_2		−0.36	−0.37	−0.42	−0.43
		(0.07)	(0.06)	(0.06)	(0.06)
		[0.06]	[0.05]	[0.07]	[0.07]
α_3			−0.00	−0.06	−0.08
			(0.09)	(0.10)	(0.11)
			[0.09]	[0.12]	[0.13]
α_4				−0.16	−0.18
				(0.08)	(0.08)
				[0.09]	[0.09]
α_5					−0.04
					(0.07)
					[0.06]
AIC	342	312	314	310	312

Standard errors are robust to heteroskedasticity in parenthesis. Newey-West standard errors are in square brackets, with $M = 5$.

The third example is the first difference of CPI inflation (first difference of growth rate of *cpiaucsl*). This is motivated by Stock and Watson (2007), who examined forecasting models for inflation rates. We estimate autoregressive models of order 1 through 8 using the full sample ($n = 226$); we report models 1 through 5 in Table 14.2. The model with the lowest AIC is the AR(4). All four estimated autoregressive coefficients are negative, most particularly the first two. The two sets of standard errors are quite similar for the AR(4) model. There are meaningful differences only for the lower order AR models.

14.40 TIME SERIES REGRESSION MODELS

Least squares regression methods can be used broadly with stationary time series. Interpretation and usefulness can depend, however, on constructive dynamic specifications. Furthermore, it is necessary to be aware of the serial correlation properties of the series involved, and to use the appropriate covariance matrix estimator when the dynamics have not been explicitly modeled.

Let (Y_t, X_t) be paired observations, with Y_t the dependent variable and X_t a vector of regressors including an intercept. The regressors can contain lagged Y_t, so this framework includes the autoregressive model as a special case. A linear regression model takes the form

$$Y_t = X_t'\beta + e_t. \tag{14.54}$$

The coefficient vector is defined by projection and therefore equals

$$\beta = \left(\mathbb{E}\left[X_t X_t'\right]\right)^{-1} \mathbb{E}\left[X_t Y_t\right]. \tag{14.55}$$

The error e_t is defined by (14.54) and thus its properties are determined by that relationship. Implicitly the model assumes that the variables have finite second moments and $\mathbb{E}\left[X_t X_t'\right] > 0$, otherwise the model is not uniquely defined, and a regressor could be eliminated. By the property of projection, the error is uncorrelated with the regressors $\mathbb{E}\left[X_t e_t\right] = 0$.

The least squares estimator of β is

$$\widehat{\beta} = \left(\sum_{t=1}^{n} X_t X_t'\right)^{-1} \left(\sum_{t=1}^{n} X_t Y_t\right).$$

Under the assumption that the joint series (Y_t, X_t) is strictly stationary and ergodic, the estimator is consistent. Under the mixing and moment conditions of Theorem 14.32, the estimator is asymptotically normal with a general covariance matrix

However, under the stronger assumption that the error is a MDS, the asymptotic covariance matrix simplifies. It is worthwhile investigating this condition further. The necessary condition is $\mathbb{E}\left[e_t \mid \mathscr{F}_{t-1}\right] = 0$, where $\mathscr{F}_{t-1}$ is an information set to which (e_{t-1}, X_t) is adapted. This notation may appear somewhat odd, but recall in the autoregessive context that $X_t = (1, Y_{t-1}, \ldots, Y_{t-p})$ contains variables dated time $t-1$ and previously, thus X_t in this context is a "time $t-1$" variable. The reason we need (e_{t-1}, X_t) to be adapted to $\mathscr{F}_{t-1}$ is that for the regression function $X_t'\beta$ to be the conditional mean of Y_t given $\mathscr{F}_{t-1}$, X_t must be part of the information set $\mathscr{F}_{t-1}$. Under this assumption,

$$\mathbb{E}\left[X_t e_t \mid \mathscr{F}_{t-1}\right] = X_t \mathbb{E}\left[e_t \mid \mathscr{F}_{t-1}\right] = 0$$

so $(X_t e_t, \mathscr{F}_t)$ is a MDS. Thus we can apply the MDS CLT to obtain the asymptotic distribution.

We summarize this discussion with the following formal statement.

Theorem 14.35 If (Y_t, X_t) is strictly stationary, ergodic, with finite second moments, and $\boldsymbol{Q} = \mathbb{E}\left[X_t X_t'\right] > 0$, then β in (14.55) is uniquely defined, and the least squares estimator is consistent: $\widehat{\beta} \underset{p}{\longrightarrow} \beta$.

If in addition, $\mathbb{E}\left[e_t \mid \mathscr{F}_{t-1}\right] = 0$, where $\mathscr{F}_{t-1}$ is an information set to which (e_{t-1}, X_t) is adapted, $\mathbb{E}\left|Y_t\right|^4 < \infty$, and $\mathbb{E}\left\|X_t\right\|^4 < \infty$, then

$$\sqrt{n}\left(\widehat{\beta} - \beta\right) \underset{d}{\longrightarrow} \mathrm{N}\left(0, \boldsymbol{Q}^{-1} \Omega \boldsymbol{Q}^{-1}\right) \tag{14.56}$$

as $n \to \infty$, where $\Omega = \mathbb{E}\left[X_t X_t' e_t^2\right]$.

Alternatively, if for some $r > 4$, $\mathbb{E}\left|Y_t\right|^r < \infty$, $\mathbb{E}\left\|X_t\right\|^r < \infty$, and the mixing coefficients for (Y_t, X_t) satisfy $\sum_{\ell=1}^{\infty} \alpha(\ell)^{1-4/r} < \infty$, then (14.56) holds with

$$\Omega = \sum_{\ell=-\infty}^{\infty} \mathbb{E}\left[X_{t-\ell} X_t' e_t e_{t-\ell}\right].$$

14.41 STATIC, DISTRIBUTED LAG, AND AUTOREGRESSIVE DISTRIBUTED LAG MODELS

In this section, we discuss standard linear time series regression models.

Let (Y_t, Z_t) be paired observations with Y_t the dependent variable and Z_t an observed regressor vector, which does not include lagged Y_t.

The simplest regression model is the static equation

$$Y_t = \alpha + Z_t'\beta + e_t$$

which becomes (14.54) by setting $X_t = (1, Z_t')'$. Static models are motivated to describe how Y_t and Z_t co-move. Their advantage is their simplicity. The disadvantage is that they are difficult to interpret. The coefficient is the best linear predictor (14.55) but almost certainly is dynamically misspecified. The regression of Y_t on contemporaneous Z_t is difficult to interpret without a causal framework, since the two may be simultaneous. If this regression is estimated, it is important that the standard errors be calculated using the Newey-West method to account for serial correlation in the error.

A model that allows the regressor to have impact over several periods is called a **distributed lag (DL)** model. It takes the form

$$Y_t = \alpha + Z_{t-1}'\beta_1 + Z_{t-2}'\beta_2 + \cdots + Z_{t-q}'\beta_q + e_t.$$

It is also possible to include the contemporaneous regressor Z_t. In this model, the leading coefficient β_1 represents the initial impact of Z_t on Y_t, β_2 represents the impact in the second period, and so on. The cumulative impact is the sum of the coefficients $\beta_1 + \cdots + \beta_q$, which is called the **long-run multiplier**.

The DL model falls in the class (14.54) by setting $X_t = (1, Z_{t-1}', Z_{t-2}', \ldots, Z_{t-q}')'$. While it allows for a lagged impact of Z_t on Y_t, the model does not incorporate serial correlation, so the error e_t should be expected to be serially correlated. Thus the model is (typically) dynamically misspecified, which can make interpretation difficult. It is also necessary to use Newey-West standard errors to account for the serial correlation.

A more complete model combines autoregressive and distributed lags. It takes the form

$$Y_t = \alpha_0 + \alpha_1 Y_{t-1} + \cdots + \alpha_p Y_{t-p} + Z_{t-1}'\beta_1 + \cdots + Z_{t-q}'\beta_q + e_t.$$

This is called an **autoregressive distributed lag (AR-DL)** model. It nests both the autoregressive and distributed lag models, thereby combining serial correlation and dynamic impact. The AR-DL model falls in the class (14.54) by setting $X_t = (1, Y_{t-1}, \ldots, Y_{t-p}, Z_{t-1}', \ldots, Z_{t-q}')'$.

If the lag orders p and q are selected to be sufficiently large, the AR-DL model will have an error that is approximately white noise, in which case the model can be interpreted as dynamically well specified, and so conventional standard error methods can be used.

In an AR-DL specification, the long-run multiplier is

$$\frac{\beta_1 + \cdots + \beta_q}{1 - \alpha_1 - \cdots - \alpha_p}$$

which is a nonlinear function of the coefficients.

14.42 TIME TRENDS

Many economic time series have means that change over time. A useful way to think about this is the components model,

$$Y_t = T_t + u_t$$

where T_t is the trend component, and u_t is the stochastic component. The latter can be modeled by a linear process or autoregression:

$$\alpha(\mathrm{L}) u_t = e_t.$$

The trend component is often modeled as a linear function in the time index,

$$T_t = \beta_0 + \beta_1 t$$

or a quadratic function in time,

$$T_t = \beta_0 + \beta_1 t + \beta_2 t^2.$$

These models are typically not thought of as being literally true but rather as useful approximations.

When we write down time series models, we write the index as $t = 1, \ldots, n$. But in practical applications, the time index corresponds to a date (e.g., $t = 1960, 1961, \ldots, 2017$). Furthermore, if the data are at a higher frequency than annual, then they are incremented in fractional units. This is not of fundamental importance; it merely changes the meaning of the intercept β_0 and slope β_1. Consequently, these values should not be interpreted outside of how the time index is defined.

One traditional way of dealing with time trends is to "detrend" the data, which means using an estimation method to estimate the trend and subtract it off. The simplest method is least squares linear detrending. Given the linear model,

$$Y_t = \beta_0 + \beta_1 t + u_t \tag{14.57}$$

the coefficients are estimated by least squares. The detrended series is the residual $\widehat{u}_t$. More intricate methods can be used, but they have a similar flavor.

To understand the properties of the detrending method, we can apply an asymptotic approximation. A time trend is not a stationary process, so we should be thoughtful before applying standard theory. We will study asymptotics for nonstationary processes in more detail in Chapter 16, so our treatment here will be brief. It turns out that most of our conventional procedures work just fine with time trends (and quadratics in time) as regressors. The rates of convergence change, but this does not affect anything of practical importance.

Let us demonstrate that the least squares estimator of the coefficients in (14.57) is consistent. We can write the estimator as

$$\begin{pmatrix} \widehat{\beta}_0 - \beta_0 \\ \widehat{\beta}_1 - \beta_1 \end{pmatrix} = \begin{pmatrix} n & \sum_{t=1}^n t \\ \sum_{t=1}^n t & \sum_{t=1}^n t^2 \end{pmatrix}^{-1} \begin{pmatrix} \sum_{t=1}^n u_t \\ \sum_{t=1}^n t u_t \end{pmatrix}.$$

We need to study the behavior of the sums in the design matrix. For this the following result is useful, which follows by taking the limit of the Riemann sum for the integral $\int_0^1 x^r dx = 1/(1+r)$.

Theorem 14.36 For any $r > 0$, as $n \to \infty$, $n^{-1-r} \sum_{t=1}^n t^r \longrightarrow 1/(1+r)$.

Theorem 14.36 implies that

$$\frac{1}{n^2} \sum_{t=1}^n t \to \frac{1}{2}$$

and

$$\frac{1}{n^3} \sum_{t=1}^n t^2 \to \frac{1}{3}.$$

What is interesting about these results is that the sums require normalizations other than n^{-1}!

To handle this in multiple regression, it is convenient to define a scaling matrix that normalizes each element in the regression by its convergence rate. Define the matrix $D_n = \begin{bmatrix} 1 & 0 \\ 0 & n \end{bmatrix}$. The first diagonal element is the intercept and second is for the time trend. Then

$$\begin{aligned} D_n \begin{pmatrix} \widehat{\beta}_0 - \beta_0 \\ \widehat{\beta}_1 - \beta_1 \end{pmatrix} &= D_n \begin{pmatrix} n & \sum_{t=1}^n t \\ \sum_{t=1}^n t & \sum_{t=1}^n t^2 \end{pmatrix}^{-1} D_n D_n^{-1} \begin{pmatrix} \sum_{t=1}^n u_t \\ \sum_{t=1}^n t u_t \end{pmatrix} \\ &= \left(D_n^{-1} \begin{pmatrix} n & \sum_{t=1}^n t \\ \sum_{t=1}^n t & \sum_{t=1}^n t^2 \end{pmatrix} D_n^{-1} \right)^{-1} \begin{pmatrix} \sum_{t=1}^n u_t \\ \frac{1}{n} \sum_{t=1}^n t u_t \end{pmatrix} \\ &= \begin{pmatrix} n & \frac{1}{n} \sum_{t=1}^n t \\ \frac{1}{n} \sum_{t=1}^n t & \frac{1}{n^2} \sum_{t=1}^n t^2 \end{pmatrix}^{-1} \begin{pmatrix} \sum_{i=1}^n u_t \\ \frac{1}{n} \sum_{i=1}^n t u_t \end{pmatrix}. \end{aligned}$$

Multiplying by $n^{1/2}$, we obtain

$$\begin{pmatrix} n^{1/2} \left(\widehat{\beta}_0 - \beta_0 \right) \\ n^{3/2} \left(\widehat{\beta}_1 - \beta_1 \right) \end{pmatrix} = \begin{pmatrix} 1 & \frac{1}{n^2} \sum_{t=1}^n t \\ \frac{1}{n^2} \sum_{t=1}^n t & \frac{1}{n^3} \sum_{t=1}^n t^2 \end{pmatrix}^{-1} \begin{pmatrix} \frac{1}{n^{1/2}} \sum_{t=1}^n u_t \\ \frac{1}{n^{3/2}} \sum_{t=1}^n t u_t \end{pmatrix}.$$

The denominator matrix satisfies

$$\begin{pmatrix} 1 & \frac{1}{n^2} \sum_{t=1}^n t \\ \frac{1}{n^2} \sum_{t=1}^n t & \frac{1}{n^3} \sum_{t=1}^n t^2 \end{pmatrix} \to \begin{pmatrix} 1 & \frac{1}{2} \\ \frac{1}{2} & \frac{1}{3} \end{pmatrix}$$

which is invertible. Setting $X_{nt} = (t/n, 1)$, the numerator vector can be written as $n^{-1/2} \sum_{t=1}^n X_{nt} u_t$. It has variance

$$\begin{aligned} \left\| \operatorname{var} \left[\frac{1}{n^{1/2}} \sum_{t=1}^n X_{nt} u_t \right] \right\| &= \left\| \frac{1}{n} \sum_{t=1}^n \sum_{j=1}^n X_{nt} X_{nj}' \mathbb{E} \left[u_t u_j \right] \right\| \\ &\le \sqrt{2} \sum_{\ell=-\infty}^{\infty} \left\| \mathbb{E} \left[u_t u_j \right] \right\| < \infty \end{aligned}$$

by Theorem 14.15, if u_t satisfies the mixing and moment conditions for the CLT, which means that the numerator vector is $O_p(1)$. (It is also asymptotically normal, but we defer this demonstration for now.) We conclude that

$$\begin{pmatrix} n^{1/2} \left(\widehat{\beta}_0 - \beta_0 \right) \\ n^{3/2} \left(\widehat{\beta}_1 - \beta_1 \right) \end{pmatrix} = O_p(1).$$

This shows that both coefficients are consistent, $\widehat{\beta}_0$ converges at the standard $n^{1/2}$ rate, and $\widehat{\beta}_1$ converges at the faster $n^{3/2}$ rate.

The consistency of the coefficient estimators (and their rates of convergence) can be used to show that linear detrending (regression of Y_t on an intercept and time trend to obtain a residual $\widehat{u}_t$) is consistent for the error u_t in (14.57).

An alternative is to include a time trend in the estimated regression. If we have an autoregression, a distributed lag, or an AR-DL model, we add a time index to obtain a model of the form

$$Y_t = \alpha_0 + \alpha_1 Y_{t-1} + \cdots + \alpha_p Y_{t-p} + Z_{t-1}' \beta_1 + \cdots + Z_{t-q}' \beta_q + \gamma t + e_t.$$

Estimation by least squares is equivalent to estimation after linear detrending by the FWL theorem (Theorem 3.5). Inclusion of a linear (and possibly quadratic) time trend in a regression model is typically the easiest method to incorporate time trends.

14.43 ILLUSTRATION

Let us illustrate the models described in Section 14.42 using a classical Phillips curve for inflation prediction. A. W. Phillips (1958) famously observed that the unemployment rate and the wage inflation rate are negatively correlated over time. Equations relating the inflation rate, or the change in the inflation rate, to macroeconomic indicators (such as the unemployment rate) are typically described as "Phillips curves." A simple Phillips curve takes the form

$$\Delta \pi_t = \alpha + \beta U_t + e_t \tag{14.58}$$

where π_t is price inflation, and U_t is the unemployment rate. This specification relates the change in inflation in a given period to the level of the unemployment rate.

The least squares estimate of (14.58) using U.S. quarterly series from FRED-QD is reported in the first column of Table 14.3. Both heteroskedasticity-robust and Newey-West standard errors are reported. The Newey-West standard errors are the appropriate choice, since the estimated equation is static (no modeling of the serial correlation). In this example, the measured impact of the unemployment rate on inflation appears minimal. The estimate is consistent with a small effect of the unemployment rate on the inflation rate, but it is not precisely estimated.

A distributed lag (DL) model takes the form

$$\Delta \pi_t = \alpha + \beta_1 U_{t-1} + \beta_2 U_{t-2} + \cdots + \beta_q U_{t-q} + e_t. \tag{14.59}$$

The least squares estimate of (14.59) is reported in the second column of Table 14.3. The estimates are quite different from the static model. We see large negative impacts in the first and third periods, countered by a large positive impact in the second period. The model suggests that the unemployment rate has a strong impact on the inflation rate, but the long-run impact is mitigated. The long-run multiplier is reported at the bottom of the column. The point estimate of -0.022 is quite small and similar to the static estimate. It implies that an increase in the unemployment rate by 5 percentage points (a typical recession) decreases the long-run annual inflation rate by about a half of a percentage point.

An AR-DL takes the form

$$\Delta \pi_t = \alpha_0 + \alpha_1 \Delta \pi_{t-1} + \cdots + \alpha_p \Delta \pi_{t-p} + \beta_1 U_{t-1} + \cdots + \beta_q U_{t-q} + e_t. \tag{14.60}$$

The least squares estimate of (14.60) is reported in the third column of Table 14.3. The coefficient estimates are similar to those from the distributed lag model. The point estimate of the long-run multiplier is also nearly identical but with a smaller standard error.

14.44 GRANGER CAUSALITY

In the AR-DL model (14.60), the unemployment rate has no predictive impact on the inflation rate under the coefficient restriction $\beta_1 = \cdots = \beta_q = 0$. This restriction is called **Granger non-causality**. When the coefficients are nonzero, we say that the unemployment rate "Granger causes" the inflation rate. This definition of causality was developed by Granger (1969) and Sims (1972).

Table 14.3
Phillips curve regressions

	Static model	DL model	AR-DL model
U_t	−0.023		
	(0.025)		
	[0.017]		
U_{t-1}		−0.59	−0.62
		(0.20)	(0.16)
		[0.16]	[0.12]
U_{t-2}		1.14	0.88
		(0.29)	(0.25)
		[0.28]	[0.21]
U_{t-3}		−0.68	−0.36
		(0.22)	(0.25)
		[0.25]	[0.24]
U_{t-4}		0.12	0.05
		(0.11)	(0.12)
		[0.11]	[0.12]
π_{t-1}			−0.43
			(0.08)
			[0.08]
π_{t-2}			−0.47
			(0.10)
			[0.09]
π_{t-3}			−0.14
			(0.10)
			[0.11]
π_{t-4}			−0.19
			(0.08)
			[0.09]
Multiplier	−0.023	−0.022	−0.021
	[0.017]	[0.012]	[0.008]

Note: Standard errors robust to heteroskedasticity in parenthesis. Newey-West standard errors in square brackets with $M = 5$.

The reason we call this "Granger causality" rather than "causality" is because this is not a structural definition. An alternative label is "predictive causality."

To be precise, assume that we have two series (Y_t, Z_t). Consider the projection of Y_t onto the lagged history of both series:

$$\begin{aligned} Y_t &= \mathscr{P}_{t-1}(Y_t) + e_t \\ &= \alpha_0 + \sum_{j=1}^{\infty} \alpha_j Y_{t-j} + \sum_{j=1}^{\infty} \beta_j Z_{t-j} + e_t. \end{aligned}$$

We say that Z_t does not Granger-cause Y_t if $\beta_j = 0$ for all j. If $\beta_j \neq 0$ for some j, then we say that Z_t Granger-causes Y_t.

It is important that the definition includes the projection on the past history of Y_t. Granger causality means that Z_t helps predict Y_t even after the past history of Y_t has been accounted for.

The definition can alternatively be written in terms of conditional expectations rather than projections. We can say that Z_t does not Granger-cause Y_t if

$$\mathbb{E}\left[Y_t \mid Y_{t-1}, Y_{t-2} \ldots ; Z_{t-1}, Z_{t-2}, \ldots\right] = \mathbb{E}\left[Y_t \mid Y_{t-1}, Y_{t-2}, \ldots\right].$$

Granger causality can be tested in AR-DL models using a standard Wald or F test. In the context of model (14.60), we report the F statistic for $\beta_1 = \cdots = \beta_q = 0$. The test rejects the hypothesis (and thus finds evidence of Granger causality) if the statistic is larger than the critical value (if the p-value is small) and fails to reject the hypothesis (and thus finds no evidence of causality) if the statistic is smaller than the critical value.

For example, in the results presented in Table 14.3, the F statistic for the hypothesis $\beta_1 = \cdots = \beta_4 = 0$ using the Newey-West covariance matrix is $F = 6.98$ with a p-value of 0.000. This is statistically significant at any conventional level, so we can conclude that the unemployment rate has a predictively causal impact on inflation.

Granger causality should not be interpreted structurally outside the context of an economic model. For example, consider the regression of GDP growth rates Y_t on stock price growth rates R_t. Let us use the quarterly series from FRED-QD, estimating an AR-DL specification with two lags:

$$\begin{array}{lllllllll} Y_t = & \underset{(0.09)}{0.22} & Y_{t-1} & + & \underset{(0.10)}{0.14} & Y_{t-2} + & \underset{(0.01)}{0.03} & R_{t-1} + & \underset{(0.01)}{0.01} \; R_{t-2}. \end{array}$$

The coefficients on the lagged stock price growth rates are small in magnitude, but the first lag appears to be statistically significant. The F statistic for exclusion of (R_{t-1}, R_{t-2}) is $F = 9.3$ with a p-value of 0.0002, which is highly significant. We can therefore reject the hypothesis of no Granger causality and deduce that stock prices Granger-cause GDP growth. We should be wary of concluding that this is structurally causal—that stock market movements cause output fluctuations. A more reasonable explanation from economic theory is that stock prices are forward-looking measures of expected future profits. When corporate profits are forecasted to rise, the value of corporate stock rises, bidding up stock prices. Thus stock prices move in advance of actual economic activity but are not necessarily structurally causal.

Clive W. J. Granger

Clive Granger (1934–2009) of England was one of the leading figures in time-series econometrics, and co-winner of the 2003 Nobel Memorial Prize in Economic Sciences. In addition to formalizing the definition of causality known as Granger causality, he invented the concept of cointegration, introduced spectral methods into econometrics, and formalized methods for the combination of forecasts.

14.45 TESTING FOR SERIAL CORRELATION IN REGRESSION MODELS

Consider the problem of testing for omitted serial correlation in an AR-DL model such as

$$Y_t = \alpha_0 + \alpha_1 Y_{t-1} + \cdots + \alpha_p Y_{t-p} + \beta_1 Z_{t-1} + \cdots + \beta_q Z_{t-q} + u_t. \tag{14.61}$$

The null hypothesis is that u_t is serially uncorrelated, and the alternative hypothesis is that it is serially correlated. We can model the latter as a mean-0 autoregressive process:

$$u_t = \theta_1 u_{t-1} + \cdots + \theta_r u_{t-r} + e_t. \tag{14.62}$$

The hypothesis is

$$\mathbb{H}_0 : \theta_1 = \cdots = \theta_r = 0$$
$$\mathbb{H}_1 : \theta_j \neq 0 \text{ for some } j \geq 1.$$

There are two ways to implement a test of $\mathbb{H}_0$ against $\mathbb{H}_1$. The first is to estimate equations (14.61) and (14.62) sequentially by least squares and construct a test for $\mathbb{H}_0$ on the second equation. This test is complicated by the two-step estimation. Therefore, this approach is not recommended.

The second approach is to combine equations (14.61) and (14.62) into a single model and execute the test as a restriction within this model. One way to make this combination is by using lag operator notation. Write (14.61) and (14.62) as

$$\alpha(\mathrm{L})Y_t = \alpha_0 + \beta(\mathrm{L})Z_{t-1} + u_t$$
$$\theta(\mathrm{L})u_t = e_t$$

Applying the operator $\theta(\mathrm{L})$ to the first equation, we obtain

$$\theta(\mathrm{L})\alpha(\mathrm{L})Y_t = \theta(\mathrm{L})\alpha_0 + \theta(\mathrm{L})\beta(\mathrm{L})Z_{t-1} + \theta(\mathrm{L})u_t$$

or

$$\alpha^*(\mathrm{L})Y_t = \alpha_0^* + \beta^*(\mathrm{L})Z_{t-1} + e_t$$

where $\alpha^*(\mathrm{L})$ is a $p+r$ order polynomial, and $\beta^*(\mathrm{L})$ is a $q+r$ order polynomial. The restriction $\mathbb{H}_0$ is that these are p and q order polynomials. Thus we can implement a test of $\mathbb{H}_0$ against $\mathbb{H}_1$ by estimating an AR-DL model with $p+r$ and $q+r$ lags, and testing the exclusion of the final r lags of Y_t and Z_t. This test has a conventional asymptotic distribution and so is simple to implement.

The basic message is that testing for omitted serial correlation can be implemented in regression models by estimating and contrasting different dynamic specifications.

14.46 BOOTSTRAP FOR TIME SERIES

Recall that the bootstrap approximates the sampling distribution of estimators and test statistics by the empirical distribution of the observations. The traditional nonparametric bootstrap is appropriate for independent observations. For dependent observations, alternative methods should be used.

Bootstrapping for time series is considerably more complicated than the crosssection case. Many methods have been proposed. One of the challenges is that theoretical justifications are more difficult to establish than in the independent observation case.

In this section, we discuss the most popular methods to implement bootstrap resampling for time series data.

Recursive Bootstrap.

1. Estimate a complete model, such as an AR(p), producing coefficient estimates $\widehat{\alpha}$ and residuals $\widehat{e}_t$.
2. Fix the initial condition $(Y_{-p+1}, Y_{-p+2}, \ldots, Y_0)$.
3. Simulate i.i.d. draws e_t^* from the empirical distribution of the residuals $\{\widehat{e}_1, \ldots, \widehat{e}_n\}$.

4. Create the bootstrap series Y_t^* by the recursive formula

$$Y_t^* = \widehat{\alpha}_0 + \widehat{\alpha}_1 Y_{t-1}^* + \widehat{\alpha}_2 Y_{t-2}^* + \cdots + \widehat{\alpha}_p Y_{t-p}^* + e_t^*.$$

This construction creates bootstrap samples Y_t^* with the stochastic properties of the estimated AR(p) model, including the auxiliary assumption that the errors are i.i.d. This method can work well if the true process is an AR(p). One flaw is that it imposes homoskedasticity on the errors e_t^*, which may be different than the properties of the actual e_t. Another limitation is that it is inappropriate for AR-DL models unless the conditioning variables are strictly exogenous.

There are alternative versions of this basic method. First, instead of fixing the initial conditions at the sample values, a random block can be drawn from the sample. The difference is that this produces an unconditional distribution rather than a conditional one. Second, instead of drawing the errors from the residuals, a parametric (typically normal) distribution can be used. This can improve precision when sample sizes are small but otherwise is not recommended.

Pairwise Bootstrap.

1. Write the sample as $\{Y_t, X_t\}$, where $X_t = (Y_{t-1}, \ldots, Y_{t-p})'$ contains the lagged values used in estimation.
2. Apply the traditional nonparametric bootstrap, which samples pairs (Y_t^*, X_t^*) i.i.d. from $\{Y_t, X_t\}$ with replacement to create the bootstrap sample.
3. Create the bootstrap estimates on this bootstrap sample (i.e., regress Y_t^* on X_t^*).

This construction is essentially the traditional nonparametric bootstrap but applied to the paired sample $\{Y_t, X_t\}$. It does not mimic the time series correlations across observations. However, it does produce bootstrap statistics with the correct first-order asymptotic distribution under MDS errors. This method may be useful when we are interested in the distribution of nonlinear functions of the coefficient estimates and therefore desire an improvement on the delta method approximation.

Fixed Design Residual Bootstrap.

1. Write the sample as $\{Y_t, X_t, \widehat{e}_t\}$, where $X_t = (Y_{t-1}, \ldots, Y_{t-p})'$ contains the lagged values used in estimation, and $\widehat{e}_t$ are the residuals.
2. Fix the regressors X_t at their sample values.
3. Simulate i.i.d. draws e_t^* from the empirical distribution of the residuals $\{\widehat{e}_1, \ldots, \widehat{e}_n\}$.
4. Set $Y_t^* = X_t'\widehat{\beta} + e_t^*$.

This construction is similar to the pairwise bootstrap but imposes an i.i.d. error. It is therefore only valid when the errors are i.i.d. (and thus excludes heteroskedasticity).

Fixed Design Wild Bootstrap.

1. Write the sample as $\{Y_t, X_t, \widehat{e}_t\}$, where $X_t = (Y_{t-1}, \ldots, Y_{t-p})'$ contains the lagged values used in estimation, and $\widehat{e}_t$ are the residuals.
2. Fix the regressors X_t and residuals $\widehat{e}_t$ at their sample values.
3. Simulate i.i.d. auxiliary random variables ξ_t^* with mean 0 and variance 1. See Section 10.29 for a discussion of choices.
4. Set $e_t^* = \xi_t^* \widehat{e}_t$ and $Y_t^* = X_t'\widehat{\beta} + e_t^*$.

This construction is similar to the pairwise and fixed design bootstrap combined with the wild bootstrap. It imposes the conditional mean assumption on the error but allows heteroskedasticity.

Block Bootstrap.

1. Write the sample as $\{Y_t, X_t\}$, where $X_t = (Y_{t-1}, \ldots, Y_{t-p})'$ contains the lagged values used in estimation.
2. Divide the sample of paired observations $\{Y_t, X_t\}$ into n/m blocks of length m.
3. Resample complete blocks. For each simulated sample, draw n/m blocks.
4. Paste the blocks together to create the bootstrap time series $\{Y_t^*, X_t^*\}$.

This construction allows for arbitrary stationary serial correlation, heteroskedasticity, and model misspecification. One challenge is that the block bootstrap is sensitive to the block length and the way that the data are partitioned into blocks. The method may also work less well for small samples. Notice that the block bootstrap with $m = 1$ is equal to the pairwise bootstrap, and the latter is the traditional nonparametric bootstrap. Thus the block bootstrap is a natural generalization of the nonparametric bootstrap.

14.47 TECHNICAL PROOFS*

Proof of Theorem 14.2 Define $\widetilde{Y}_t = (Y_t, Y_{t-1}, Y_{t-2}, \ldots) \in \mathbb{R}^{m\times\infty}$ as the history of Y_t up to time t. Write $X_t = \phi(\widetilde{Y}_t)$. Let B be the pre-image of $\{X_t \leq x\}$ (the vectors $\widetilde{Y} \in \mathbb{R}^{m\times\infty}$ such that $\phi(\widetilde{Y}) \leq x$). Then

$$\mathbb{P}\left[X_t \leq x\right] = \mathbb{P}\left[\phi(\widetilde{Y}_t) \leq x\right] = \mathbb{P}\left[\widetilde{Y}_t \in B\right].$$

Since Y_t is strictly stationary, $\mathbb{P}\left[\widetilde{Y}_t \in B\right]$ is independent[9] of t. Thus the distribution of X_t is independent of t. This argument can be extended to show that the distribution of $(X_t, \ldots, X_{t+\ell})$ is independent of t. This means that X_t is strictly stationary, as claimed. ■

Proof of Theorem 14.3 By the Cauchy criterion for convergence (see Theorem A.2 of *Probability and Statistics for Economists*), $S_N = \sum_{j=0}^{N} a_j Y_{t-j}$ converges almost surely if for all $\epsilon > 0$,

$$\inf_N \sup_{j>N} \left|S_{N+j} - S_N\right| \leq \epsilon.$$

Let A_ϵ be this event. Its complement is

$$A_\epsilon^c = \bigcap_{N=1}^{\infty} \left\{ \sup_{j>N} \left| \sum_{i=N+1}^{N+j} a_i Y_{t-i} \right| > \epsilon \right\}$$

which has probability

$$\mathbb{P}\left[A_\epsilon^c\right] \leq \lim_{N\to\infty} \mathbb{P}\left[\sup_{j>N} \left| \sum_{i=N+1}^{N+j} a_i Y_{t-i} \right| > \epsilon\right] \leq \lim_{N\to\infty} \frac{1}{\epsilon}\mathbb{E}\left[\sup_{j>N} \left| \sum_{i=N+1}^{N+j} a_i Y_{t-i} \right|\right] \leq \frac{1}{\epsilon} \lim_{N\to\infty} \sum_{i=N+1}^{\infty} |a_i|\, \mathbb{E}\left|Y_{t-i}\right| = 0.$$

[9]An astute reader may notice that the independence of $\mathbb{P}\left[\widetilde{Y}_t \in B\right]$ from t does not follow directly from the definition of strict stationarity. Indeed, a full derivation requires a measure-theoretic treatment. See Section 1.2.B of Petersen (1983) or Section 3.5 of Stout (1974).

The second inequality is Markov's inequality (B.36), and the following one is the triangle inequality (B.1). The limit is 0 because $\sum_{i=0}^{\infty}|a_i| < \infty$ and $\mathbb{E}|Y_t| < \infty$. Hence for all $\epsilon > 0$, $\mathbb{P}\left[A_\epsilon^c\right] = 0$ and $\mathbb{P}\left[A_\epsilon\right] = 1$. Thus S_N converges with probability 1, as claimed.

Since Y_t is strictly stationary, then X_t is as well by Theorem 14.2. ■

Proof of Theorem 14.4 See Theorem 14.14. ■

Proof of Theorem 14.5 Strict stationarity follows from Theorem 14.2. Let $\widetilde{Y}_t$ and $\widetilde{X}_t$ be the histories of Y_t and X_t. Write $X_t = \phi\left(\widetilde{Y}_t\right)$. Let A be an invariant event for X_t. We want to show $\mathbb{P}[A] = 0$ or 1. The event A is a collection of $\widetilde{X}_t$ histories, and occurs if and and only if an associated collection of $\widetilde{Y}_t$ histories occur. That is, for some sets G and H,

$$A = \left\{\widetilde{X}_t \in G\right\} = \left\{\phi\left(\widetilde{Y}_t\right) \in G\right\} = \left\{\widetilde{Y}_t \in H\right\}.$$

The assumption that A is invariant means it is unaffected by the time shift, thus can be written as

$$A = \left\{\widetilde{X}_{t+\ell} \in G\right\} = \left\{\widetilde{Y}_{t+\ell} \in H\right\}.$$

This means the event $\left\{\widetilde{Y}_{t+\ell} \in H\right\}$ is invariant. Since Y_t is ergodic the event has probability 0 or 1. Hence $\mathbb{P}[A] = 0$ or 1, as desired. ■

Proof of Theorem 14.7 Suppose Y_t is discrete with support on $(\tau_1, \ldots, \tau_N)$ and without loss of generality assume $\mathbb{E}[Y_t] = 0$. Then by Theorem 14.8

$$\begin{aligned}
\lim_{n\to\infty} \frac{1}{n}\sum_{\ell=1}^{n} \operatorname{cov}(Y_t, Y_{t+\ell}) &= \lim_{n\to\infty} \frac{1}{n}\sum_{\ell=1}^{n} \mathbb{E}[Y_t Y_{t+\ell}] \\
&= \lim_{n\to\infty} \frac{1}{n}\sum_{\ell=1}^{n}\sum_{j=1}^{N}\sum_{k=1}^{N} \tau_j\tau_k \mathbb{P}\left[Y_t = \tau_j, Y_{t+\ell} = \tau_k\right] \\
&= \sum_{j=1}^{N}\sum_{k=1}^{N} \tau_j\tau_k \lim_{n\to\infty} \frac{1}{n}\sum_{\ell=1}^{n} \mathbb{P}\left[Y_t = \tau_j, Y_{t+\ell} = \tau_k\right] \\
&= \sum_{j=1}^{N}\sum_{k=1}^{N} \tau_j\tau_k \mathbb{P}\left[y_t = \tau_j\right]\mathbb{P}\left[Y_{t+\ell} = \tau_k\right] \\
&= \mathbb{E}[Y_t]\,\mathbb{E}[Y_{t+\ell}] \\
&= 0
\end{aligned}$$

which is (14.4). This can be extended to the case of continuous distributions using the monotone convergence theorem. See Corollary 14.8 of Davidson (1994). ■

Proof of Theorem 14.9 We show (14.6). The limit (14.7) follows by Markov's inequality (B.36).

Without loss of generality, we focus on the scalar case and assume $\mathbb{E}[Y_t] = 0$. Fix $\epsilon > 0$. Pick B large enough such that

$$\mathbb{E}\left|Y_t \mathbb{1}\{|Y_t| > B\}\right| \leq \frac{\epsilon}{4} \tag{14.63}$$

which is feasible, because $\mathbb{E}|Y_t| < \infty$. Define

$$W_t = Y_t \mathbb{1}\{|Y_t| \le B\} - \mathbb{E}[Y_t \mathbb{1}\{|Y_t| \le B\}]$$
$$Z_t = Y_t \mathbb{1}\{|Y_t| > B\} - \mathbb{E}[Y_t \mathbb{1}\{|Y_t| > B\}].$$

Notice that W_t is a bounded transformation of the ergodic series Y_t. Thus by (14.4) and (14.9), there is an n sufficiently large so that

$$\frac{\operatorname{var}[W_t]}{n} + \frac{2}{n}\sum_{m=1}^{n}\left(1-\frac{m}{n}\right)\operatorname{cov}\left(W_t, W_j\right) \le \frac{\epsilon^2}{4}. \tag{14.64}$$

By the triangle inequality (B.1),

$$\mathbb{E}\left|\overline{Y}\right| = \mathbb{E}\left|\overline{W}+\overline{Z}\right| \le \mathbb{E}\left|\overline{W}\right| + \mathbb{E}\left|\overline{Z}\right|. \tag{14.65}$$

By another application of the triangle inequality and (14.63),

$$\mathbb{E}\left|\overline{Z}\right| \le \mathbb{E}|Z_t| \le 2\mathbb{E}\left|Y_t \mathbb{1}(|Y_t| > B)\right| \le \frac{\epsilon}{2}. \tag{14.66}$$

By Jensen's inequality (B.27), direct calculation, and (14.64),

$$\begin{aligned}
\left(\mathbb{E}\left|\overline{W}\right|\right)^2 &\le \mathbb{E}\left[\left|\overline{W}\right|^2\right] \\
&= \frac{1}{n^2}\sum_{t=1}^{n}\sum_{j=1}^{n}\mathbb{E}\left[W_t W_j\right] \\
&= \frac{\operatorname{var}[W_t]}{n} + \frac{2}{n}\sum_{m=1}^{n}\left(1-\frac{m}{n}\right)\operatorname{cov}\left(W_t, W_j\right) \\
&\le \frac{\epsilon^2}{4}.
\end{aligned}$$

Thus

$$\mathbb{E}\left|\overline{W}\right| \le \frac{\epsilon}{2}. \tag{14.67}$$

Together, (14.65), (14.66) and (14.67) show that $\mathbb{E}\left|\overline{Y}\right| \le \epsilon$. Since ε is arbitrary, this establishes (14.6), as claimed. ■

Proof of Theorem 14.11 (sketch) By the Cramér-Wold device (Theorem 8.4 from *Probability and Statistics for Economists*), it is sufficient to establish the result for scalar u_t. Let $\sigma^2 = \mathbb{E}\left[u_t^2\right]$. By a Taylor series expansion, for x small, $\log(1+x) \simeq x - x^2/2$. Taking exponentials and rearranging, we obtain the approximation

$$\exp(x) \simeq (1+x)\exp\left(\frac{x^2}{2}\right). \tag{14.68}$$

Fix λ. Define

$$T_j = \prod_{i=1}^{j}\left(1+\frac{\lambda}{\sqrt{n}}u_t\right)$$

$$V_n = \frac{1}{n}\sum_{t=1}^{n}u_t^2.$$

Since u_t is strictly stationary and ergodic, $V_n \xrightarrow{p} \sigma^2$ by the ergodic theorem (Theorem 14.9). Since u_t is a MDS,

$$\mathbb{E}\left[T_n\right] = 1. \tag{14.69}$$

To see this, define $\mathscr{F}_t = \sigma\left(\ldots, u_{t-1}, u_t\right)$. Note that $T_j = T_{j-1}\left(1+\frac{\lambda}{\sqrt{n}}u_j\right)$. By iterated expectations,

$$\begin{aligned}
\mathbb{E}\left[T_n\right] &= \mathbb{E}\left[\mathbb{E}\left[T_n \mid \mathscr{F}_{n-1}\right]\right] \\
&= \mathbb{E}\left[T_{n-1}\mathbb{E}\left[1+\frac{\lambda}{\sqrt{n}}u_n \,\middle|\, \mathscr{F}_{n-1}\right]\right] \\
&= \mathbb{E}\left[T_{n-1}\right] = \cdots = \mathbb{E}\left[T_1\right] \\
&= 1.
\end{aligned}$$

This is (14.69).

The moment generating function of S_n is

$$\begin{aligned}
\mathbb{E}\left[\exp\left(\frac{\lambda}{\sqrt{n}}\sum_{t=1}^{n}u_t\right)\right] &= \mathbb{E}\left[\prod_{i=1}^{n}\exp\left(\frac{\lambda}{\sqrt{n}}u_t\right)\right] \\
&\simeq \mathbb{E}\left[\prod_{i=1}^{n}\left[1+\frac{\lambda}{\sqrt{n}}u_t\right]\exp\left(\frac{\lambda^2}{2n}u_t^2\right)\right] && (14.70) \\
&= \mathbb{E}\left[T_n\exp\left(\frac{\lambda^2 V_n}{2}\right)\right] \\
&\simeq \mathbb{E}\left[T_n\exp\left(\frac{\lambda^2\sigma^2}{2}\right)\right] && (14.71) \\
&= \exp\left(\frac{\lambda^2\sigma^2}{2}\right).
\end{aligned}$$

The approximation in (14.70) is (14.68). The approximation (14.71) is $V_n \underset{p}{\longrightarrow} \sigma^2$. (A rigorous justification that allows this substitution in the expectation is technical.) The final equality is (14.69). This shows that the moment generating function of S_n is approximately that of $\mathrm{N}\left(0, \sigma^2\right)$, as claimed.

The assumption that u_t is a MDS is critical for (14.69). T_n is a nonlinear function of the errors u_t, so a white noise assumption cannot be used instead. The MDS assumption is exactly the minimal condition needed to obtain (14.69). This is why the MDS assumption cannot be easily replaced by a milder assumption, such as white noise. ■

Proof of Theorem 14.13.1 Without loss of generality, suppose $\mathbb{E}[X_t]=0$ and $\mathbb{E}[Z_t]=0$. Set $\eta_{t-m}=\operatorname{sgn}\left(\mathbb{E}\left[Z_t \mid \mathscr{F}_{-\infty}^{t-m}\right]\right)$. By iterated expectations, $|X_t| \le C_1$, $\left|\mathbb{E}\left[Z_t \mid \mathscr{F}_{-\infty}^{t-m}\right]\right| = \eta_{t-m}\mathbb{E}\left[Z_t \mid \mathscr{F}_{-\infty}^{t-m}\right]$, and again using iterated expectations,

$$\begin{aligned}
|\operatorname{cov}(X_{t-m}, Z_t)| &= \left|\mathbb{E}\left[\mathbb{E}\left[X_{t-m}Z_t \mid \mathscr{F}_{-\infty}^{t-m}\right]\right]\right| \\
&= \left|\mathbb{E}\left(X_{t-m}\mathbb{E}\left[Z_t \mid \mathscr{F}_{-\infty}^{t-m}\right]\right)\right| \\
&\le C_1\mathbb{E}\left|\mathbb{E}\left[Z_t \mid \mathscr{F}_{-\infty}^{t-m}\right]\right| \\
&= C_1\mathbb{E}\left[\eta_{t-m}\mathbb{E}\left[Z_t \mid \mathscr{F}_{-\infty}^{t-m}\right]\right] \\
&= C_1\mathbb{E}\left[\mathbb{E}\left[\eta_{t-m}Z_t \mid \mathscr{F}_{-\infty}^{t-m}\right]\right] \\
&= C_1\mathbb{E}\left[\eta_{t-m}Z_t\right] \\
&= C_1 \operatorname{cov}\left(\eta_{t-m}, Z_t\right). \qquad (14.72)
\end{aligned}$$

Setting $\xi_t = \operatorname{sgn}\left(\mathbb{E}\left[X_{t-m} \mid \mathscr{F}_t^{\infty}\right]\right)$, by a similar argument, (14.72) is bounded by $C_1C_2 \operatorname{cov}(\eta_{t-m}, \xi_t)$. Set $A_1 = \mathbb{1}\{\eta_{t-m}=1\}$, $A_2=\mathbb{1}\{\eta_{t-m}=-1\}$, $B_1=\mathbb{1}\{\xi_t=1\}$, $B_2=\mathbb{1}\{\xi_t=-1\}$. We calculate

$$\begin{aligned}
|\operatorname{cov}(\eta_{t-m}, \xi_t)| = &\,|\mathbb{P}[A_1\cap B_1] + \mathbb{P}[A_2\cap B_2] - \mathbb{P}[A_2\cap B_1] - \mathbb{P}[A_1\cap B_2] \\
&- \mathbb{P}[A_1]\mathbb{P}[B_1] - \mathbb{P}[A_2]\mathbb{P}[B_2] + \mathbb{P}[A_2]\mathbb{P}[B_1] + \mathbb{P}[A_1]\mathbb{P}[B_2]| \\
\le &\, 4\alpha(m).
\end{aligned}$$

Together, $|\operatorname{cov}(X_{t-m}, z_t)| \le 4C_1C_2\alpha(m)$, as claimed. ■

Proof of Theorem 14.13.2 Assume $\mathbb{E}[X_t]=0$ and $\mathbb{E}[Z_t]=0$. We first show that if $|X_t|\le C$, then

$$|\operatorname{cov}(X_{t-\ell}, Z_t)| \le 6C\left(\mathbb{E}|Z_t|^r\right)^{1/r}\alpha(\ell)^{1-1/r}. \qquad (14.73)$$

Indeed, if $\alpha(\ell)=0$, the result is immediate, so assume $\alpha(\ell)>0$. Set $D=\alpha(\ell)^{-1/r}\left(\mathbb{E}|Z_t|^r\right)^{1/r}$, $V_t = Z_t\mathbb{1}\{|Z_t|\le D\}$, and $W_t = Z_t\mathbb{1}\{|Z_t|>D\}$. Using the triangle inequality (B.1) and then part 1 of Theorem 14.13, because $|X_t|\le C$ and $|V_t|\le D$,

$$|\operatorname{cov}(X_{t-\ell}, Z_t)| \le |\operatorname{cov}(X_{t-\ell}, V_t)| + |\operatorname{cov}(X_{t-\ell}, W_t)| \le 4CD\alpha(\ell) + 2C\mathbb{E}|w_t|.$$

Also,

$$\mathbb{E}|W_t| = \mathbb{E}|Z_t\mathbb{1}\{|Z_t|>D\}| = \mathbb{E}\left|\frac{|Z_t|^r}{|Z_t|^{r-1}}\mathbb{1}\{|Z_t|>D\}\right| \le \frac{\mathbb{E}|Z_t|^r}{D^{r-1}} = \alpha(\ell)^{(r-1)/r}\left(\mathbb{E}|Z_t|^r\right)^{1/r}$$

using the definition of D. Together we have

$$|\operatorname{cov}(X_{t-\ell}, Z_t)| \le 6C\left(\mathbb{E}|X_t|^r\right)^{1/r}\alpha(\ell)^{1-1/r}$$

which is (14.73) as claimed.

Now set $C=\alpha(\ell)^{-1/r}\left(\mathbb{E}|X_t|^r\right)^{1/r}$, $V_t = X_t\mathbb{1}\{|X_t|\le C\}$ and $W_t = X_t\mathbb{1}\{|X_t|>C\}$. Using the triangle inequality and (14.73)

$$|\operatorname{cov}(X_{t-\ell}, Z_t)| \le |\operatorname{cov}(V_{t-\ell}, Z_t)| + |\operatorname{cov}(W_{t-\ell}, Z_t)|.$$

Since $|V_t|\le C$, using (14.73) and the definition of C, we have

$$|\operatorname{cov}(V_{t-\ell}, Z_t)| \le 6C\left(\mathbb{E}|Z_t|^q\right)^{1/q}\alpha(\ell)^{1-1/q} = 6\left(\mathbb{E}|X_t|^r\right)^{1/r}\left(\mathbb{E}|Z_t|^q\right)^{1/q}\alpha(\ell)^{1-1/q-1/r}.$$

Using Hölder's inequality (B.31) and the definition of C:

$$
\begin{aligned}
|\operatorname{cov}(W_{t-\ell}, Z_t)| &\leq 2\left(\mathbb{E}|W_t|^{q/(q-1)}\right)^{(q-1)/q}\left(\mathbb{E}|Z_t|^q\right)^{1/q} \\
&= 2\left(\mathbb{E}\left[|X_t|^{q/(q-1)}\mathbb{1}\{|X_t|>C\}\right]\right)^{(q-1)/q}\left(\mathbb{E}|Z_t|^q\right)^{1/q} \\
&= 2\left(\mathbb{E}\left[\frac{|X_t|^r}{|X_t|^{r-q/(q-1)}}\mathbb{1}\{|X_t|>C\}\right]\right)^{(q-1)/q}\left(\mathbb{E}|Z_t|^q\right)^{1/q} \\
&\leq \frac{2}{C^{r(q-1)/q-1}}\left(\mathbb{E}|X_t|^r\right)^{(q-1)/q}\left(\mathbb{E}|Z_t|^q\right)^{1/q} \\
&= 2\left(\mathbb{E}|X_t|^r\right)^{1/r}\left(\mathbb{E}|Z_t|^q\right)^{1/q}\alpha(\ell)^{1-1/q-1/r}.
\end{aligned}
$$

Taking these results together, we have

$$
|\operatorname{cov}(X_{t-\ell}, Z_t)| \leq 8\left(\mathbb{E}|X_t|^r\right)^{1/r}\left(\mathbb{E}|Z_t|^q\right)^{1/q}\alpha(\ell)^{1-1/r-1/q}
$$

as claimed. ∎

Proof of Theorem 14.13.3 Set $\eta_{t-\ell} = \operatorname{sgn}\left(\mathbb{E}\left[Z_t \mid \mathscr{F}_{-\infty}^{t-\ell}\right]\right)$, which satisfies $|\eta_{t-\ell}| \leq 1$. Since $\eta_{t-\ell}$ is $\mathscr{F}_{-\infty}^{t-\ell}$-measurable, iterated expectations, using (14.73) with $C = 1$, the conditional Jensen's inequality (B.28), and iterated expectations,

$$
\begin{aligned}
\mathbb{E}\left|\mathbb{E}\left[Z_t \mid \mathscr{F}_{-\infty}^{t-\ell}\right]\right| &= \mathbb{E}\left[\eta_{t-\ell}\mathbb{E}\left[Z_t \mid \mathscr{F}_{-\infty}^{t-\ell}\right]\right] \\
&= \mathbb{E}\left[\mathbb{E}\left[\eta_{t-\ell}Z_t \mid \mathscr{F}_{-\infty}^{t-\ell}\right]\right] \\
&= \mathbb{E}\left[\eta_{t-\ell}Z_t\right] \\
&\leq 6\left(\mathbb{E}\left|\mathbb{E}\left[Z_t \mid \mathscr{F}_{-\infty}^{t-\ell}\right]\right|^r\right)^{1/r}\alpha(\ell)^{1-1/r} \\
&\leq 6\left(\mathbb{E}\left(\mathbb{E}\left[|Z_t|^r \mid \mathscr{F}_{-\infty}^{t-\ell}\right]\right)\right)^{1/r}\alpha(\ell)^{1-1/r} \\
&= 6\left(\mathbb{E}\,|Z_t|^r\,|\right)^{1/r}\alpha(\ell)^{1-1/r}
\end{aligned}
$$

as claimed. ∎

Proof of Theorem 14.15 By the Cramér-Wold device (Theorem 8.4 of *Probability and Statistics for Economists*), it is sufficient to prove the result for the scalar case. Our proof method is based on a MDS approximation. The trick is to establish the relationship

$$
u_t = e_t + Z_t - Z_{t+1} \tag{14.74}
$$

where e_t is a strictly stationary and ergodic MDS with $\mathbb{E}\left[e_t^2\right] = \Omega$ and $\mathbb{E}|Z_t| < \infty$. Defining $S_n^e = \frac{1}{\sqrt{n}}\sum_{t=1}^n e_t$, we have

$$
S_n = \frac{1}{\sqrt{n}}\sum_{t=1}^n (e_t + Z_t - Z_{t+1}) = S_n^e + \frac{Z_1}{\sqrt{n}} - \frac{Z_{n+1}}{\sqrt{n}}. \tag{14.75}
$$

The first component on the right side is asymptotically $\mathrm{N}(0,\Omega)$ by the MDS CLT (Theorem 14.11). The second and third terms are $o_p(1)$ by Markov's inequality (B.36).

The desired relationship (14.74) holds as follows. Set $\mathscr{F}_t = \sigma(\ldots, u_{t-1}, u_t)$,

$$e_t = \sum_{\ell=0}^{\infty} \left(\mathbb{E}\left[u_{t+\ell} \mid \mathscr{F}_t\right] - \mathbb{E}\left[u_{t+\ell} \mid \mathscr{F}_{t-1}\right]\right) \tag{14.76}$$

and

$$Z_t = \sum_{\ell=0}^{\infty} \mathbb{E}\left[u_{t+\ell} \mid \mathscr{F}_{t-1}\right].$$

You can verify that these definitions satisfy (14.74) given $\mathbb{E}\left[u_t \mid \mathscr{F}_t\right] = u_t$. The variable Z_t has a finite expectation, because by the triangle inequality (B.1), Theorem 14.13 part 3, and the moment assumptions

$$\mathbb{E}\left|Z_t\right| = \mathbb{E}\left|\sum_{\ell=0}^{\infty} \mathbb{E}\left[u_{t+\ell} \mid \mathscr{F}_{t-1}\right]\right| \le 6\left(\mathbb{E}\left|u_t\right|^r\right)^{1/r} \sum_{\ell=0}^{\infty} \alpha(\ell)^{1-1/r} < \infty$$

the final inequality, because $\sum_{\ell=0}^{\infty} \alpha(\ell)^{1-2/r} < \infty$ implies $\sum_{\ell=0}^{\infty} \alpha(\ell)^{1-1/r} < \infty$.

The series e_t in (14.76) has a finite expectation by the same calculation as for Z_t. It is a MDS since by iterated expectations,

$$\begin{aligned}
\mathbb{E}\left[e_t \mid \mathscr{F}_{t-1}\right] &= \mathbb{E}\left[\sum_{\ell=0}^{\infty} \left(\mathbb{E}\left[u_{t+\ell} \mid \mathscr{F}_t\right] - \mathbb{E}\left[u_{t+\ell} \mid \mathscr{F}_{t-1}\right]\right) \mid \mathscr{F}_{t-1}\right] \\
&= \sum_{\ell=0}^{\infty} \left(\mathbb{E}\left[\mathbb{E}\left[u_{t+\ell} \mid \mathscr{F}_t\right] \mid \mathscr{F}_{t-1}\right] - \mathbb{E}\left[\mathbb{E}\left[u_{t+\ell} \mid \mathscr{F}_{t-1}\right] \mid \mathscr{F}_{t-1}\right]\right) \\
&= \sum_{\ell=0}^{\infty} \left(\mathbb{E}\left[u_{t+\ell} \mid \mathscr{F}_{t-1}\right] - \mathbb{E}\left[u_{t+\ell} \mid \mathscr{F}_{t-1}\right]\right) \\
&= 0.
\end{aligned}$$

It is strictly stationary and ergodic by Theorem 14.2, because it is a function of the history $(\ldots, u_{t-1}, u_t)$.

The proof is completed by showing that e_t has a finite variance that equals Ω. The trickiest step is to show that $\operatorname{var}\left[e_t\right] < \infty$. Since

$$\mathbb{E}\left|S_n\right| \le \sqrt{\operatorname{var}\left[S_n\right]} \to \sqrt{\Omega}$$

(as shown in (14.17)), it follows that $\mathbb{E}\left|S_n\right| \le 2\sqrt{\Omega}$ for n sufficiently large. Using (14.75) and $\mathbb{E}\left|Z_t\right| < \infty$, for n sufficiently large,

$$\mathbb{E}\left|S_n^e\right| \le \mathbb{E}\left|S_n\right| + \frac{\mathbb{E}\left|Z_1\right|}{\sqrt{n}} + \frac{\mathbb{E}\left|Z_{n+1}\right|}{\sqrt{n}} \le 3\sqrt{\Omega}. \tag{14.77}$$

Now define $e_{Bt} = e_t \mathbb{1}\left\{\left|e_t\right| \le B\right\} - \mathbb{E}\left[e_t \mathbb{1}\left\{\left|e_t\right| \le B\right\} \mid \mathscr{F}_{t-1}\right]$, which is a bounded MDS. By Theorem 14.11, $\frac{1}{\sqrt{n}} \sum_{t=1}^{n} e_{Bt} \xrightarrow{d} \mathrm{N}\left(0, \sigma_B^2\right)$, where $\sigma_B^2 = \mathbb{E}\left[e_{Bt}^2\right]$. Since the sequence is uniformly integrable, this implies

$$\mathbb{E}\left|\frac{1}{\sqrt{n}} \sum_{t=1}^{n} e_{Bt}\right| \longrightarrow \mathbb{E}\left|\mathrm{N}\left(0, \sigma_B^2\right)\right| = \sqrt{\frac{2}{\pi}}\sigma_B \tag{14.78}$$

using $\mathbb{E}\left|\mathrm{N}(0,1)\right| = 2/\pi$. We want to show that $\text{var}[e_t] < \infty$. Suppose not. Then $\sigma_B \to \infty$ as $B \to \infty$, so there will be some B sufficiently large such that the right side of (14.78) exceeds the right side of (14.77). This is a contradiction. We deduce that $\text{var}[e_t] < \infty$.

Examining (14.75), we see that since $\text{var}[S_n] \to \Omega < \infty$ and $\text{var}\left[S_n^e\right] = \text{var}[e_t] < \infty$, then $\text{var}[Z_1 - Z_{n+1}]/n < \infty$. Since Z_t is stationary, we deduce that $\text{var}[Z_1 - Z_{n+1}] < \infty$. Equation (14.75) implies $\text{var}[e_t] = \text{var}\left[S_n^e\right] = \text{var}[S_n] + o(1) \to \Omega$. We deduce that $\text{var}[e_t] = \Omega$, as claimed. ■

Proof of Theorem 14.17 (Sketch) Consider the projection of Y_t onto $(\ldots, e_{t-1}, e_t)$. Since the projection errors e_t are uncorrelated, the coefficients of this projection are the bivariate projection coefficients $b_j = \mathbb{E}\left[Y_t e_{t-j}\right]/\mathbb{E}\left[e_{t-j}^2\right]$. The leading coefficient is

$$b_0 = \frac{\mathbb{E}[Y_t e_t]}{\sigma^2} = \frac{\sum_{j=1}^{\infty} \alpha_j \mathbb{E}\left[Y_{t-j} e_t\right] + \mathbb{E}\left[e_t^2\right]}{\sigma^2} = 1$$

using Theorem 14.16. By Bessel's Inequality (Brockwell and Davis, 1991, Corollary 2.4.1),

$$\sum_{j=1}^{\infty} b_j^2 = \sigma^{-4} \sum_{j=1}^{\infty} \left(\mathbb{E}[Y_t e_t]\right)^2 \le \sigma^{-4}\left(\mathbb{E}\left[Y_t^2\right]\right)^2 < \infty$$

because $\mathbb{E}\left[Y_t^2\right] < \infty$ by the assumption of covariance stationarity.

The error from the projection of Y_t onto $(\ldots, e_{t-1}, e_t)$ is $\mu_t = Y_t - \sum_{j=0}^{\infty} b_j e_{t-j}$. The fact that this can be written as (14.22) is technical. See Theorem 5.7.1 of Brockwell and Davis (1991). ■

Proof of Theorem 14.22 In the text, we showed that $\left|\lambda_j\right| < 1$ is sufficient for Y_t to be strictly stationary and ergodic. Let us now verify that $\left|\lambda_j\right| < 1$ is equivalent to (14.35)–(14.37). The roots λ_j are defined in (14.34). Consider separately the cases of real roots and complex roots.

Suppose that the roots are real, which occurs when $\alpha_1^2 + 4\alpha_2 \ge 0$. Then $\left|\lambda_j\right| < 1$ iff $|\alpha_1| < 2$ and

$$\frac{\alpha_1 + \sqrt{\alpha_1^2 + 4\alpha_2}}{2} < 1 \qquad \text{and} \qquad -1 < \frac{\alpha_1 - \sqrt{\alpha_1^2 + 4\alpha_2}}{2}.$$

Equivalently, this holds iff

$$\alpha_1^2 + 4\alpha_2 < (2-\alpha_1)^2 = 4 - 4\alpha_1 + \alpha_1^2 \qquad \text{and} \qquad \alpha_1^2 + 4\alpha_2 < (2+\alpha_1)^2 = 4 + 4\alpha_1 + \alpha_1^2$$

or equivalently, iff

$$\alpha_2 < 1 - \alpha_1 \qquad \text{and} \qquad \alpha_2 < 1 + \alpha_1$$

which are (14.35) and (14.36). In addition, $\alpha_1^2 + 4\alpha_2 \ge 0$ and $|\alpha_1| < 2$ imply $\alpha_2 \ge -\alpha_1^2/4 \ge -1$, which is (14.37).

Now suppose the roots are complex, which occurs when $\alpha_1^2 + 4\alpha_2 < 0$. The squared modulus of the roots $\lambda_j = \left(\alpha_1 \pm \sqrt{\alpha_1^2 + 4\alpha_2}\right)/2$ is

$$\left|\lambda_j\right|^2 = \left(\frac{\alpha_1}{2}\right)^2 - \left(\frac{\sqrt{\alpha_1^2 + 4\alpha_2}}{2}\right)^2 = -\alpha_2.$$

Thus the requirement $|\lambda_j| < 1$ is satisfied iff $\alpha_2 > -1$, which is (14.37). $\alpha_1^2 + 4\alpha_2 < 0$ and $\alpha_2 > -1$ imply $\alpha_1^2 < -4\alpha_2 < 4$, so $|\alpha_1| < 2$. $\alpha_1^2 + 4\alpha_2 < 0$ and $|\alpha_1| < 2$ imply $\alpha_1 + \alpha_2 < \alpha_1 - \alpha_1^2/4 < 1$ and $\alpha_2 - \alpha_1 < -\alpha_1^2/4 - \alpha_1 < 1$ which are (14.35) and (14.36). ■

Proof of Theorem 14.23 To complete the proof, we need to establish that the eigenvalues λ_j of $\boldsymbol{A}$ defined in (14.40) equal the reciprocals of the roots r_j of the autoregressive polynomial $\alpha(z)$ of (14.39). Our goal is therefore to show that if λ satisfies $\det\left(\boldsymbol{A} - \boldsymbol{I}_p\lambda\right) = 0$ then it satisfies $\alpha(1/\lambda) = 0$.

Notice that

$$\boldsymbol{A} - \boldsymbol{I}_p\lambda = \begin{pmatrix} -\lambda + \alpha_1 & \widetilde{\alpha}' \\ a & \boldsymbol{B} \end{pmatrix}$$

where $\widetilde{\alpha}' = (\alpha_2, \ldots, \alpha_p)$, $a' = (1, 0, \ldots, 0)$, and $\boldsymbol{B}$ is a lower-diagonal matrix with $-\lambda$ on the diagonal and 1 immediately below the diagonal. Notice that $\det(\boldsymbol{B}) = (-\lambda)^{p-1}$ and by direct calculation

$$\boldsymbol{B}^{-1} = -\begin{pmatrix} \lambda^{-1} & 0 & \cdots & 0 & 0 \\ \lambda^{-2} & \lambda^{-1} & \cdots & 0 & 0 \\ \lambda^{-3} & \lambda^{-2} & \cdots & 0 & 0 \\ \vdots & \vdots & \ddots & \vdots & \vdots \\ \lambda^{-p+1} & \lambda^{-p+2} & \cdots & \lambda^{-2} & \lambda^{-1} \end{pmatrix}.$$

Using the properties of the determinant (Theorem A.1.5)

$$\begin{aligned} \det\left(\boldsymbol{A} - \boldsymbol{I}_p\lambda\right) &= \det\begin{pmatrix} -\lambda + \alpha_1 & \widetilde{\alpha}' \\ a & \boldsymbol{B} \end{pmatrix} \\ &= \det(\boldsymbol{B})\left(-\lambda + \alpha_1 - \widetilde{\alpha}'\boldsymbol{B}^{-1}a\right) \\ &= (-\lambda)^p\left(1 - \alpha_1\lambda^{-1} - \alpha_2\lambda^{-2} - \alpha_3\lambda^{-3} - \cdots - \alpha_p\lambda^{-p}\right) \\ &= (-\lambda)^p\,\alpha\,(1/\lambda). \end{aligned}$$

Thus if λ satisfies $\det\left(\boldsymbol{A} - \boldsymbol{I}_p\lambda\right) = 0$ then $\alpha\,(1/\lambda) = 0$ as required. ■

Proof of Theorem 14.24 By the Fundamental Theorem of Algebra, we can factor the autoregressive polynomial as $\alpha(z) = \prod_{\ell=1}^{p}(1 - \lambda_\ell z)$, where $\lambda_\ell = r_\ell^{-1}$. By assumption, $|\lambda_\ell| < 1$. Inverting the autoregressive polynomial, we obtain

$$\begin{aligned} \alpha(z)^{-1} &= \prod_{\ell=1}^{p}(1 - \lambda_\ell z)^{-1} \\ &= \prod_{\ell=1}^{p}\left(\sum_{j=0}^{\infty}\lambda_\ell^j z^j\right) \end{aligned}$$

$$= \sum_{j=0}^{\infty} \left(\sum_{i_1+\cdots+i_p=j} \lambda_1^{i_1} \cdots \lambda_p^{i_p} \right) z^j$$

$$= \sum_{j=0}^{\infty} b_j z^j$$

with $b_j = \sum_{i_1+\cdots+i_p=j} \lambda_1^{i_1} \cdots \lambda_p^{i_p}$.

Using the triangle inequality and the stars and bars theorem (Theorem 1.12 of *Probability and Statistics for Economists*), we have

$$\begin{aligned} \left|b_j\right| &\le \sum_{i_1+\cdots+i_p=j} |\lambda_1|^{i_1} \cdots \left|\lambda_p\right|^{i_p} \\ &\le \sum_{i_1+\cdots+i_p=j} \lambda^j \\ &\le \binom{p+j-1}{j} \lambda^j \\ &= \frac{(p+j-1)!}{(p-1)!j!} \lambda^j \\ &\le (j+1)^p \lambda^j \end{aligned}$$

as claimed. We next verify the convergence of $\sum_{j=0}^{\infty} \left|b_j\right| \le \sum_{j=0}^{\infty} (j+1)^p \lambda^j$. Note that

$$\lim_{j\to\infty} \frac{(j+1)^p \lambda^j}{(j)^p \lambda^{j-1}} = \lambda < 1.$$

By the ratio test (Theorem A.3 part 2, of *Probability and Statistics for Economists*), $\sum_{j=0}^{\infty} (j+1)^p \lambda^j$ is convergent. ■

Proof of Theorem 14.27 If $\boldsymbol{Q}$ is singular, then there is some γ such that $\gamma' \boldsymbol{Q} \gamma = 0$. We can normalize γ to have a unit coefficient on Y_{t-1} (or the first nonzero coefficient other than the intercept). We then have that $\mathbb{E}\left[\left(Y_{t-1} - \left(1, Y_{t-2}, \ldots, Y_{t-p)}\right)' \phi\right)^2\right] = 0$ for some ϕ, or equivalently, $\mathbb{E}\left[\left(Y_t - \left(1, Y_{t-1}, \ldots, Y_{t-p+1)}\right)' \phi\right)^2\right] = 0$. Setting $\beta = (\phi', 0)'$, this implies $\mathbb{E}\left[\left(Y_t - \beta' X_t\right)^2\right] = 0$. Since α is the best linear predictor, we must have $\beta = \alpha$, which implies $\sigma^2 = \mathbb{E}\left[\left(Y_t - \alpha' X_t\right)^2\right] = 0$. This contradicts the assumption $\sigma^2 > 0$. We conclude that $\boldsymbol{Q}$ is not singular. ■

14.48 EXERCISES

Exercise 14.1 For a scalar time series Y_t define the sample autocovariance and autocorrelation:

$$\widehat{\gamma}(k) = n^{-1} \sum_{t=k+1}^{n} \left(Y_t - \overline{Y}\right) \left(Y_{t-k} - \overline{Y}\right)$$

$$\widehat{\rho}(k) = \frac{\widehat{\gamma}(k)}{\widehat{\gamma}(0)} = \frac{\sum_{t=k+1}^{n} \left(Y_t - \overline{Y}\right)\left(Y_{t-k} - \overline{Y}\right)}{\sum_{t=1}^{n} \left(Y_t - \overline{Y}\right)^2}.$$

Assume the series is strictly stationary, ergodic, strictly stationary, and $\mathbb{E}\left[Y_t^2\right] < \infty$. Show that $\widehat{\gamma}(k) \underset{p}{\longrightarrow} \gamma(k)$ and $\widehat{\rho}(k) \underset{p}{\longrightarrow} \gamma(k)$ as $n \to \infty$. (Use the Ergodic Theorem.)

Exercise 14.2 Show that if $(e_t, \mathscr{F}_t)$ is a MDS and X_t is $\mathscr{F}_t$-measurable, then $u_t = X_{t-1}e_t$ is a MDS.

Exercise 14.3 Let $\sigma_t^2 = \mathbb{E}\left[e_t^2 \mid \mathscr{F}_{t-1}\right]$. Show that $u_t = e_t^2 - \sigma_t^2$ is a MDS.

Exercise 14.4 Continuing the previous exercise, show that if $\mathbb{E}\left[e_t^4\right] < \infty$, then

$$n^{-1/2} \sum_{t=1}^{n} \left(e_t^2 - \sigma_t^2\right) \underset{d}{\longrightarrow} \mathrm{N}\left(0, v^2\right).$$

Express v^2 in terms of the moments of e_t.

Exercise 14.5 A stochastic volatility model is

$$Y_t = \sigma_t e_t$$
$$\log \sigma_t^2 = \omega + \beta \log \sigma_{t-1}^2 + u_t$$

where e_t and u_t are independent i.i.d. $\mathrm{N}(0,1)$ shocks.

(a) Write down an information set for which Y_t is a MDS.
(b) Show that if $|\beta| < 1$, then Y_t is strictly stationary and ergodic.

Exercise 14.6 Verify the formula $\rho(1) = \theta / \left(1 + \theta^2\right)$ for a MA(1) process.

Exercise 14.7 Verify the formula $\rho(k) = \left(\sum_{j=0}^{\infty} \theta_{j+k}\theta_j\right) / \left(\sum_{j=0}^{q} \theta_j^2\right)$ for a MA(∞) process.

Exercise 14.8 Suppose $Y_t = Y_{t-1} + e_t$ with e_t i.i.d. $(0,1)$ and $Y_0 = 0$. Find $\operatorname{var}[Y_t]$. Is Y_t stationary?

Exercise 14.9 Consider the AR(1) model with no intercept: $Y_t = \alpha_1 Y_{t-1} + e_t$.

(a) Find the impulse response function $b_j = \frac{\partial}{\partial e_t} Y_{t+j}$.
(b) Let $\widehat{\alpha}_1$ be the least squares estimator of α_1. Find an estimator of b_j.
(c) Let $s(\widehat{\alpha}_1)$ be a standard error for $\widehat{\alpha}_1$. Use the delta method to find a 95% asymptotic confidence interval for b_j.

Exercise 14.10 Consider the AR(2) model $Y_t = \alpha_1 Y_{t-1} + \alpha_2 Y_{t-1} + e_t$.

(a) Find expressions for the impulse responses b_1, b_2, b_3, and b_4.
(b) Let $(\widehat{\alpha}_1, \widehat{\alpha}_2)$ be the least squares estimator. Find an estimator of b_2.
(c) Let $\widehat{\boldsymbol{V}}$ be the estimated covariance matrix for the coefficients. Use the delta method to find a 95% asymptotic confidence interval for b_2.

Exercise 14.11 Show that the models

$$\alpha(\mathrm{L})Y_t = \alpha_0 + e_t$$

and

$$\alpha(\mathrm{L})Y_t = \mu + u_t$$
$$\alpha(\mathrm{L})u_t = e_t$$

are identical. Find an expression for μ in terms of α_0 and $\alpha(\mathrm{L})$.

Exercise 14.12 Consider the model

$$\alpha(\mathrm{L})Y_t = u_t$$
$$\beta(\mathrm{L})u_t = e_t$$

where $\alpha(\mathrm{L})$ and $\beta(\mathrm{L})$ are p and q order lag polynomials. Show that these equations imply that

$$\gamma(\mathrm{L})Y_t = e_t$$

for some lag polynomial $\gamma(\mathrm{L})$. What is the order of $\gamma(\mathrm{L})$?

Exercise 14.13 Suppose that $Y_t = e_t + u_t + \theta u_{t-1}$, where u_t and e_t are mutually independent i.i.d. $(0,1)$ processes.

(a) Show that Y_t is a MA(1) process $Y_t = \eta_t + \psi\eta_{t-1}$ for a white noise error η_t.
Hint: Calculate the autocorrelation function of Y_t.

(b) Find an expression for ψ in terms of θ.

(c) Suppose $\theta = 1$. Find ψ.

Exercise 14.14 Suppose that

$$Y_t = X_t + e_t$$
$$X_t = \alpha X_{t-1} + u_t$$

where the errors e_t and u_t are mutually independent i.i.d. processes. Show that Y_t is an ARMA(1,1) process.

Exercise 14.15 A Gaussian AR model is an autoregression with i.i.d. $\mathrm{N}(0,\sigma^2)$ errors. Consider the Gaussian AR(1) model,

$$Y_t = \alpha_0 + \alpha_1 Y_{t-1} + e_t$$
$$e_t \sim \mathrm{N}\left(0,\sigma^2\right)$$

with $|\alpha_1| < 1$. Show that the marginal distribution of Y_t is also normal:

$$Y_t \sim \mathrm{N}\left(\frac{\alpha_0}{1-\alpha_1}, \frac{\sigma^2}{1-\alpha_1^2}\right).$$

Hint: Use the MA representation of Y_t.

Exercise 14.16 Assume that Y_t is a Gaussian AR(1) as in exercise 14.15. Calculate the moments

$$\mu = \mathbb{E}[Y_t]$$
$$\sigma_Y^2 = \mathbb{E}\left[(Y_t - \mu)^2\right]$$
$$\kappa = \mathbb{E}\left[(Y_t - \mu)^4\right]$$

A colleague suggests estimating the parameters $(\alpha_0, \alpha_1, \sigma^2)$ of the Gaussian AR(1) model by GMM applied to the corresponding sample moments. He points out that there are three moments and three parameters, so it should be identified. Can you find a flaw in his approach?

Hint: This is subtle.

Exercise 14.17 Consider the nonlinear process

$$Y_t = Y_{t-1}^{\alpha} u_t^{1-\alpha}$$

where u_t is i.i.d. with strictly positive support.

(a) Find the condition under which Y_t is strictly stationary and ergodic.
(b) Find an explicit expression for Y_t as a function of $(u_t, u_{t-1}, \ldots)$.

Exercise 14.18 Consider the quarterly series *pnfix* (nonresidential real private fixed investment) from FRED-QD.

(a) Transform the series into quarterly growth rates.
(b) Estimate an AR(4) model. Report using heteroskedastic-consistent standard errors.
(c) Repeat using the Newey-West standard errors, using $M = 5$.
(d) Comment on the magnitude and interpretation of the coefficients.
(e) Calculate (numerically) the impulse responses for $j = 1, \ldots, 10$.

Exercise 14.19 Consider the quarterly series *oilpricex* (real price of crude oil) from FRED-QD.

(a) Transform the series by taking first differences.
(b) Estimate an AR(4) model. Report using heteroskedastic-consistent standard errors.
(c) Test the hypothesis that the real oil price is a random walk by testing that the four AR coefficients jointly equal 0.
(d) Interpret the coefficient estimates and test result.

Exercise 14.20 Consider the monthly series *unrate* (unemployment rate) from FRED-MD.

(a) Estimate AR(1) through AR(8) models, using the sample starting in 1960m1, so that all models use the same observations.
(b) Compute the AIC for each AR model and report.
(c) Which AR model has the lowest AIC?
(d) Report the coefficient estimates and standard errors for the selected model.

Exercise 14.21 Take the quarterly series *unrate* (unemployment rate) and *claimsx* (initial claims) from `FRED-QD`. "Initial claims" are the number of individuals who file for unemployment insurance.

(a) Estimate a distributed lag regression of the unemployment rate on initial claims. Use lags 1 through 4. Which standard error method is appropriate?

(b) Estimate an autoregressive distributed lag regression of the unemployment rate on initial claims. Use lags 1 through 4 for both variables.

(c) Test the hypothesis that initial claims does not Granger cause the unemployment rate.

(d) Interpret your results.

Exercise 14.22 Take the quarterly series *gdpc1* (real GDP) and *houst* (housing starts) from `FRED-QD`. "Housing starts" are the number of new houses on which construction is started.

(a) Transform the real GDP series into its one quarter growth rate.

(b) Estimate a distributed lag regression of GDP growth on housing starts. Use lags 1 through 4. Which standard error method is appropriate?

(c) Estimate an autoregressive distributed lag regression of GDP growth on housing starts. Use lags 1 through 2 for GDP growth and 1 through 4 for housing starts.

(d) Test the hypothesis that housing starts do not Granger cause GDP growth.

(e) Interpret your results.

CHAPTER 15

MULTIVARIATE TIME SERIES

15.1 INTRODUCTION

A multivariate time series $Y_t = (Y_{1t}, \ldots, Y_{mt})'$ is an $m \times 1$ vector process observed in sequence over time, $t = 1, \ldots, n$. Multivariate time series models primarily focus on the joint modeling of the vector series Y_t. The most common multivariate time series models used by economists are vector autoregressions (VARs). VARs were introduced to econometrics by Sims (1980).

Some excellent textbooks and review articles on multivariate time series include Hamilton (1994), Watson (1994), Canova (1995), Lütkepohl (2005), Ramey (2016), Stock and Watson (2016), and Kilian and Lütkepohl (2017).

15.2 MULTIPLE EQUATION TIME SERIES MODELS

To motivate vector autoregressions, let us start by reviewing the autoregressive distributed lag model of Section 14.41 for the case of two series $Y_t = (Y_{1t}, Y_{2t})'$ with a single lag. An AR-DL model for Y_{1t} is

$$Y_{1t} = \alpha_0 + \alpha_1 Y_{1,t-1} + \beta_1 Y_{2,t-1} + e_{1t}.$$

Similarly, an AR-DL model for Y_{2t} is

$$Y_{2t} = \gamma_0 + \gamma_1 Y_{2,t-1} + \delta_1 Y_{1,t-1} + e_{2t}.$$

These two equations specify that each variable is a linear function of its own lag and the lag of the other variable. In so doing, we find that the variables on the right hand side of each equation are Y_{t-1}.

We can simplify the equations by combining the regressors, stacking the two equations together, and writing the vector error as $e_t = (e_{1t}, e_{2t})'$ to find

$$Y_t = a_0 + \boldsymbol{A}_1 Y_{t-1} + e_t$$

where a_0 is 2×1, and $\boldsymbol{A}_1$ is 2×2. This is a bivariate vector autoregressive model for Y_t. It specifies that the multivariate process Y_t is a linear function of its own lag Y_{t-1} plus e_t. It is the combination of two equations, each of which is an autoregressive distributed lag model. Thus a multivariate autoregression is a set of autoregressive distributed lag models.

The above derivation assumed a single lag. If the equations include p lags of each variable, we obtain the pth order **vector autoregressive (VAR)** model:

$$Y_t = a_0 + \boldsymbol{A}_1 Y_{t-1} + \boldsymbol{A}_2 Y_{t-2} + \cdots + \boldsymbol{A}_p Y_{t-p} + e_t. \tag{15.1}$$

Furthermore, there is nothing special about the two-variable case. The notation in (15.1) allows $Y_t = (Y_{1t}, \ldots, Y_{mt})'$ to be a vector of dimension m, in which case the matrices $\boldsymbol{A}_\ell$ are $m \times m$, and the error e_t is $m \times 1$. Let us denote the elements of $\boldsymbol{A}_\ell$ using the notation

$$\boldsymbol{A}_\ell = \begin{bmatrix} a_{11,\ell} & a_{12,\ell} & \cdots & a_{1m,\ell} \\ a_{21,\ell} & a_{22,\ell} & \cdots & a_{2m,\ell} \\ \vdots & \vdots & & \vdots \\ a_{m1,\ell} & a_{m2,\ell} & \cdots & a_{mm,\ell} \end{bmatrix}.$$

The error $e_t = (e_{1t}, \ldots, e_{mt})'$ is the component of Y_t that is unforecastable at time $t-1$. However, the components of Y_t are contemporaneously correlated. Therefore, the contemporaneous covariance matrix $\Sigma = \mathbb{E}\left[ee'\right]$ is nondiagonal.

The VAR model falls in the class of multivariate regression models studied in Chapter 11.

In the following several sections, we take a step back and provide a rigorous foundation for vector autoregressions for stationary time series.

15.3 LINEAR PROJECTION

In Section 14.14, we derived the linear projection of the univariate series Y_t on its infinite past history. We now extend this to the multivariate case. Define the multivariate infinite past history $\widetilde{Y}_{t-1} = (\ldots, Y_{t-2}, Y_{t-1})$. The projection of Y_t onto $\widetilde{Y}_{t-1}$, written $\mathscr{P}_{t-1}[Y_t] = \mathscr{P}\left[Y_t \mid \widetilde{Y}_{t-1}\right]$, is unique and has a unique projection error

$$e_t = Y_t - \mathscr{P}_{t-1}[Y_t]. \tag{15.2}$$

We will call the projection errors e_t the "innnovations."

The innovations e_t are mean 0 and serially uncorrelated. We state this formally.

Theorem 15.1 If Y_t is covariance stationary, it has the projection equation

$$Y_t = \mathscr{P}_{t-1}[Y_t] + e_t.$$

The innovations e_t satisfy $\mathbb{E}[e_t] = 0$, $\mathbb{E}\left[e_{t-\ell}e_t'\right] = 0$ for $\ell \geq 1$, and $\Sigma = \mathbb{E}\left[ee'\right] < \infty$. If Y_t is strictly stationary, then e_t is strictly stationary.

The uncorrelatedness of the projection errors is a property of a multivariate white noise process.

Definition 15.1 The vector process e_t is **multivariate white noise** if $\mathbb{E}[e_t] = 0$, $\mathbb{E}\left[e_te_t'\right] = \Sigma < \infty$, and $\mathbb{E}\left[e_te_{t-\ell}'\right] = 0$ for $\ell \neq 0$.

15.4 MULTIVARIATE WOLD DECOMPOSITION

By projecting Y_t onto the past history of the white noise innovations e_t, we obtain a multivariate version of the Wold decomposition.

Theorem 15.2 If Y_t is covariance stationary and nondeterministic, then it has the linear representation

$$Y_t = \mu + \sum_{\ell=0}^{\infty} \Theta_\ell e_{t-\ell} \tag{15.3}$$

where the e_t are the white noise projection errors and $\Theta_0 = \boldsymbol{I}_m$. The coefficient matrices Θ_ℓ are $m \times m$.

Using the lag operator notation, we can write the moving average representation as

$$Y_t = \mu + \Theta(\mathrm{L})\, e_t$$

where

$$\Theta(z) = \sum_{\ell=0}^{\infty} \Theta_\ell z^\ell.$$

A multivariate version of Theorem 14.19 can also be established.

Theorem 15.3 If Y_t is covariance stationary, nondeterministic, with Wold representation $Y_t = \Theta(\mathrm{L})\, e_t$, such that $\lambda_{\min}(\Theta^*(z)\Theta(z)) \geq \delta > 0$ for all complex $|z| \leq 1$, and for some integer $s \geq 0$, the Wold coefficients satisfy $\sum_{j=0}^{\infty} \left\| \sum_{k=0}^{\infty} k^s \Theta_{j+k} \right\|^2 < \infty$, then Y_t has an infinite-order autoregressive representation

$$\boldsymbol{A}(\mathrm{L})\, Y_t = a_0 + e_t$$

where

$$\boldsymbol{A}(z) = \boldsymbol{I}_m - \sum_{\ell=1}^{\infty} \boldsymbol{A}_\ell z^\ell \tag{15.4}$$

and the coefficients satisfy $\sum_{k=1}^{\infty} k^s \|\boldsymbol{A}_k\| < \infty$. The series in (15.4) is convergent.

For a proof, see Section 2 of Meyer and Kreiss (2015).

We can also provide an analog of Theorem 14.6.

Theorem 15.4 If $e_t \in \mathbb{R}^m$ is strictly stationary, ergodic, $\mathbb{E}\|e_t\| < \infty$, and $\sum_{\ell=0}^{\infty} \|\Theta_\ell\| < \infty$, then $Y_t = \sum_{\ell=0}^{\infty} \Theta_\ell e_{t-\ell}$ is strictly stationary and ergodic.

The proof of Theorem 15.4 is a straightforward extension of Theorem 14.6 so is omitted.

The moving average and autoregressive lag polynomials satisfy the relationship $\Theta(z) = \boldsymbol{A}(z)^{-1}$.

For some purposes (such as impulse response calculations), we need to calculate the moving average coefficient matrices Θ_ℓ from the autoregressive coefficient matrices $\boldsymbol{A}_\ell$. While no closed-form solution exists, there is a simple recursion by which the coefficients may be calculated.

Theorem 15.5 For $j \geq 1$, $\Theta_j = \sum_{\ell=1}^{j} \boldsymbol{A}_\ell \Theta_{j-\ell}$.

To see this, suppose for simplicity that $a_0 = 0$ and that the innovations satisfy $e_t = 0$ for $t \neq 0$. Then $Y_t = 0$ for $t < 0$. Using the regression equation (15.4) for $t \geq 0$, we can solve for each Y_t. For $t = 0$,

$$Y_0 = e_0 = \Theta_0 e_0$$

where $\Theta_0 = \boldsymbol{I}_m$. For $t = 1$,

$$Y_1 = \boldsymbol{A}_1 Y_0 = \boldsymbol{A}_1 \Theta_0 e_0 = \Theta_1 e_0$$

where $\Theta_1 = \boldsymbol{A}_1 \Theta_0$. For $t = 2$,

$$Y_2 = \boldsymbol{A}_1 Y_1 + \boldsymbol{A}_2 Y_0 = \boldsymbol{A}_1 \Theta_1 e_0 + \boldsymbol{A}_2 \Theta_0 e_0 = \Theta_2 e_0$$

where $\Theta_2 = \boldsymbol{A}_1 \Theta_1 + \boldsymbol{A}_2 \Theta_0$. For $t = 3$,

$$Y_3 = \boldsymbol{A}_1 Y_2 + \boldsymbol{A}_2 Y_1 + \boldsymbol{A}_3 Y_0 = \boldsymbol{A}_1 \Theta_2 e_0 + \boldsymbol{A}_2 \Theta_1 e_0 + \boldsymbol{A}_3 \Theta_0 e_0 = \Theta_3 e_0$$

where $\Theta_3 = \boldsymbol{A}_1 \Theta_2 + \boldsymbol{A}_2 \Theta_2 + \boldsymbol{A}_2 \Theta_0$. The coefficients satisfy the stated recursion, as claimed.

15.5 IMPULSE RESPONSE

One of the most important concepts in applied multivariate time series is the **impulse response function (IRF)**, which is defined as the change in Y_t due to a change in an innovation or shock. In this section, we define the baseline IRF—the unnormalized non-orthogonalized impulse response function—which is the change in Y_t due to a change in an innovation e_t. Specifically, let us define the impulse response of variable i with respect to innovation j as the change in the time t projection of the ith variable $Y_{i,t+h}$ due to the jth innovation e_{jt}:

$$\text{IRF}_{ij}(h) = \frac{\partial}{\partial e_{jt}} \mathscr{P}_t \left[Y_{i,t+h} \right].$$

There are m^2 such responses for each horizon h. We can write them as an $m \times m$ matrix:

$$\text{IRF}(h) = \frac{\partial}{\partial e_t'} \mathscr{P}_t \left[Y_{t+h} \right].$$

Recall the multivariate Wold representation

$$Y_t = \mu + \sum_{\ell=0}^{\infty} \Theta_\ell e_{t-\ell}.$$

We can calculate that the projection onto the history at time t is

$$\mathscr{P}_t \left[Y_{t+h} \right] = \mu + \sum_{\ell=h}^{\infty} \Theta_\ell e_{t+h-\ell} = \mu + \sum_{\ell=0}^{\infty} \Theta_{h+\ell} e_{t-\ell}.$$

We deduce that the impulse response matrix is $\text{IRF}(h) = \Theta_h$, the hth moving average coefficient matrix. The individual impulse response is $\text{IRF}_{ij}(h) = \Theta_{h,ij}$, the ijth element of Θ_h.

Here we have defined the impulse response in terms of the linear projection operator. An alternative is to define the impulse response in terms of the conditional expectation operator. The two coincide when the innovations e_t are a martingale difference sequence (and thus when the true process is linear) but otherwise will not coincide.

Typically we view impulse responses as a function of the horizon h and plot them as a function of h for each pair (i,j). The impulse response function $\mathrm{IRF}_{ij}(h)$ is interpreted as how the ith variable responds over time to the jth innovation.

In a linear vector autoregression, the impulse response function is symmetric in negative and positive innovations. That is, the impact on Y_{it+h} of a positive innovation $e_{jt}=1$ is $\mathrm{IRF}_{ij}(h)$ and the impact of a negative innovation $e_{jt}=-1$ is $-\mathrm{IRF}_{ij}(h)$. Furthermore, the magnitude of the impact is linear in the magnitude of the innovation. Thus the impact of the innovation $e_{jt}=2$ is $2\times\mathrm{IRF}_{ij}(h)$, and the impact of the innovation $e_{jt}=-2$ is $-2\times\mathrm{IRF}_{ij}(h)$. So the shape of the impulse response function is unaffected by the magnitude of the innovation. (These are consequences of the linearity of the VAR model, not necessarily features of the true world.)

The IRFs can be scaled as desired. One standard choice is to scale so that the innovations correspond to one unit of the impulse variable. Thus if the impulse variable is measured in dollars, the impulse response can be scaled to correspond to a change in \$1 or some multiple, such as a million dollars. If the impulse variable is measured in percentage points (e.g., an interest rate) then the impulse response can be scaled to correspond to a change of one percentage point (e.g., from 3% to 4%) or to correspond to a change of one basis point (e.g., from 3.05% to 3.06%). Another standard choice is to scale the impulse responses to correspond to a "one standard deviation" innovation. This occurs when the innovations have been scaled to have unit variances. In this case, IRFs can be interpreted as responses due to a "typical" sized (one standard deviation) innovation.

Closely related to the IRF is the **cumulative impulse response function (CIRF)**, defined as

$$\mathrm{CIRF}(h)=\sum_{\ell=1}^{h}\frac{\partial}{\partial e_t'}\mathscr{P}_t\left[Y_{t+\ell}\right]=\sum_{\ell=1}^{h}\Theta_\ell.$$

The cumulative impulse response is the accumulated (summed) responses on Y_t from time t to $t+h$. The limit of the cumulative impulse response as $h\to\infty$ is the **long-run impulse response matrix**:

$$\boldsymbol{C}=\lim_{h\to\infty}\mathrm{CIRF}(h)=\sum_{\ell=1}^{\infty}\Theta_\ell=\Theta\,(1)=\boldsymbol{A}\,(1)^{-1}.$$

This is the full (summed) effect of the innovation over all time.

It is useful to observe that when a VAR is estimated on differenced observations ΔY_t, then the cumulative impulse response is

$$\mathrm{CIRF}(h)=\frac{\partial}{\partial e_t'}\mathscr{P}_t\left[\sum_{\ell=1}^{h}\Delta Y_{t+\ell}\right]=\frac{\partial}{\partial e_t'}\mathscr{P}_t\left[Y_{t+h}\right]$$

which is the impulse response for the variable Y_t in levels. More generally, when a VAR is estimated with some variables in levels and some in differences, then the cumulative impulse response for the second group will coincide with the impulse responses for the same variables measured in levels.

It is typical to report CIRFs for variables that enter a VAR in differences. In fact, in this context, many authors label the cumulative impulse response as "the impulse response."

15.6 VAR(1) MODEL

The **first-order vector autoregressive process**, denoted **VAR(1)**, is

$$Y_t=a_0+\boldsymbol{A}_1Y_{t-1}+e_t$$

where e_t is a strictly stationary and ergodic white noise process.

We are interested in conditions under which Y_t is a stationary process. Let $\lambda_i(\boldsymbol{A})$ denote the ith eigenvalue of $\boldsymbol{A}$.

Theorem 15.6 If e_t is strictly stationary, ergodic, $\mathbb{E}\|e_t\| < \infty$, and $|\lambda_i(\boldsymbol{A}_1)| < 1$ for $i = 1, \ldots, m$, then the VAR(1) process Y_t is strictly stationary and ergodic.

The proof is given in Section 15.31.

15.7 VAR(P) MODEL

The **pth-order vector autoregressive process**, denoted **VAR(p)**, is

$$Y_t = a_0 + \boldsymbol{A}_1 Y_{t-1} + \cdots + \boldsymbol{A}_p Y_{t-p} + e_t$$

where e_t is a strictly stationary and ergodic white noise process.

Using the lag operator notation, we can write the model as

$$\boldsymbol{A}(\mathrm{L})\, Y_t = a_0 + e_t$$

where

$$\boldsymbol{A}(z) = \boldsymbol{I}_m - \boldsymbol{A}_1 z - \cdots - \boldsymbol{A}_p z^p.$$

The condition for stationarity of the system can be expressed as a restriction on the roots of the determinant equation of the autoregressive polynomial. Recall, a **root** r of $\det(\boldsymbol{A}(z))$ is a solution to $\det(\boldsymbol{A}(r)) = 0$.

Theorem 15.7 If all roots r of $\det(\boldsymbol{A}(z))$ satisfy $|r| > 1$, then the VAR(p) process Y_t is strictly stationary and ergodic.

The proof is structurally identical to that of Theorem 14.23 and so is omitted.

15.8 REGRESSION NOTATION

Define the $(mp+1) \times 1$ vector

$$X_t = \begin{pmatrix} 1 \\ Y_{t-1} \\ Y_{t-2} \\ \vdots \\ Y_{t-p} \end{pmatrix}$$

and the $m \times (mp+1)$ matrix $\boldsymbol{A}' = \begin{pmatrix} a_0 & \boldsymbol{A}_1 & \boldsymbol{A}_2 & \cdots & \boldsymbol{A}_p \end{pmatrix}$. Then the VAR system of equations can be written as

$$Y_t = \boldsymbol{A}' X_t + e_t. \tag{15.5}$$

This is a multivariate regression model. The error has covariance matrix

$$\Sigma = \mathbb{E}\left[e_t e_t'\right]. \tag{15.6}$$

We can also write the coefficient matrix as $\boldsymbol{A} = \begin{pmatrix} a_1 & a_2 & \cdots & a_m \end{pmatrix}$, where a_j is the vector of coefficients for the jth equation. Thus $Y_{jt} = a_j' X_t + e_{jt}$.

In general, if Y_t is strictly stationary, we can define the coefficient matrix $\boldsymbol{A}$ by linear projection.

$$\boldsymbol{A} = \left(\mathbb{E}\left[X_t X_t'\right]\right)^{-1} \mathbb{E}\left[X_t Y_t'\right].$$

This holds whether or not Y_t is actually a VAR(p) process. By the properties of projection errors,

$$\mathbb{E}\left[X_t e_t'\right] = 0. \tag{15.7}$$

The projection coefficient matrix $\boldsymbol{A}$ is identified if $\mathbb{E}\left[X_t X_t'\right]$ is invertible.

Theorem 15.8 If Y_t is strictly stationary and $0 < \Sigma < \infty$ for Σ defined in (15.6), then $\boldsymbol{Q} = \mathbb{E}\left[X_t X_t'\right] > 0$, and the coefficient vector (14.46) is identified.

The proof is given in Section 15.31.

15.9 ESTIMATION

From Chapter 11, we know that the systems estimator of a multivariate regression is least squares. The estimator can be written as

$$\widehat{\boldsymbol{A}} = \left(\sum_{t=1}^{n} X_t X_t'\right)^{-1} \left(\sum_{t=1}^{n} X_t Y_t'\right).$$

Alternatively, the coefficient estimator for the jth equation is

$$\widehat{a}_j = \left(\sum_{t=1}^{n} X_t X_t'\right)^{-1} \left(\sum_{t=1}^{n} X_t Y_{jt}\right).$$

The least squares residual vector is $\widehat{e}_t = Y_t - \widehat{\boldsymbol{A}}' X_t$. The estimator of the covariance matrix is

$$\widehat{\Sigma} = \frac{1}{n} \sum_{t=1}^{n} \widehat{e}_t \widehat{e}_t'. \tag{15.8}$$

(This may be adjusted for degrees-of-freedom if desired, but there is no established finite-sample justification for a specific adjustment.)

If Y_t is strictly stationary and ergodic with finite variances, then we can apply the ergodic theorem (Theorem 14.9) to deduce that

$$\frac{1}{n} \sum_{t=1}^{n} X_t Y_t' \underset{p}{\longrightarrow} \mathbb{E}\left[X_t Y_t'\right]$$

and

$$\sum_{t=1}^{n} X_t X_t' \xrightarrow[p]{} \mathbb{E}\left[X_t X_t'\right].$$

Since the latter is positive definite by Theorem 15.8, we conclude that $\widehat{\boldsymbol{A}}$ is consistent for $\boldsymbol{A}$. Standard manipulations show that $\widehat{\Sigma}$ is consistent as well.

Theorem 15.9 If Y_t is strictly stationary, ergodic, and $0 < \Sigma < \infty$, then $\widehat{\boldsymbol{A}} \xrightarrow[p]{} \boldsymbol{A}$ and $\widehat{\Sigma} \xrightarrow[p]{} \Sigma$ as $n \to \infty$.

VAR models can be estimated in Stata using the `var` command.

15.10 ASYMPTOTIC DISTRIBUTION

Set

$$a = \operatorname{vec}(\boldsymbol{A}) = \begin{pmatrix} a_1 \\ \vdots \\ a_m \end{pmatrix}, \qquad \widehat{a} = \operatorname{vec}\left(\widehat{\boldsymbol{A}}\right) = \begin{pmatrix} \widehat{a}_1 \\ \vdots \\ \widehat{a}_m \end{pmatrix}.$$

By the same analysis as used for Theorem 14.30 combined with Theorem 11.1, we obtain the following.

Theorem 15.10 Suppose that Y_t follows the VAR(p) model, all roots r of $\det(\boldsymbol{A}(z))$ satisfy $|r| > 1$, $\mathbb{E}[e_t \mid \mathscr{F}_{t-1}] = 0$, $\mathbb{E}\|e_t\|^4 < \infty$, and $\Sigma > 0$. Then as $n \to \infty$, $\sqrt{n}(\widehat{a} - a) \xrightarrow[d]{} \mathrm{N}(0, \boldsymbol{V})$, where

$$\begin{aligned}
\boldsymbol{V} &= \overline{\boldsymbol{Q}}^{-1} \Omega \overline{\boldsymbol{Q}}^{-1} \\
\overline{\boldsymbol{Q}} &= \boldsymbol{I}_m \otimes \boldsymbol{Q} \\
\boldsymbol{Q} &= \mathbb{E}\left[X_t X_t'\right] \\
\Omega &= \mathbb{E}\left[e_t e_t' \otimes X_t X_t'\right].
\end{aligned}$$

Notice that the theorem uses the strong assumption that the innovation is a martingale difference sequence $\mathbb{E}[e_t \mid \mathscr{F}_{t-1}] = 0$. Thus the VAR(p) model is the correct conditional expectation for each variable. In words, these are the correct lags, and there is no omitted nonlinearity.

If we further strengthen the MDS assumption to conditional homoskedasticity,

$$\mathbb{E}\left[e_t e_t' \mid \mathscr{F}_{t-1}\right] = \Sigma$$

then the asymptotic variance simplifies to

$$\begin{aligned}
\Omega &= \Sigma \otimes \boldsymbol{Q} \\
\boldsymbol{V} &= \Sigma \otimes \boldsymbol{Q}^{-1}.
\end{aligned}$$

In contrast, if the VAR(p) is an approximation, then the MDS assumption is not appropriate. In this case, the asymptotic distribution can be derived under mixing conditions.

Theorem 15.11 Assume that Y_t is strictly stationary, ergodic, and for some $r > 4$, $\mathbb{E}\|Y_t\|^r < \infty$ and the mixing coefficients satisfy $\sum_{\ell=1}^{\infty} \alpha(\ell)^{1-4/r} < \infty$. Let a be the projection coefficient vector and e_t the projection error. Then as $n \to \infty$, $\sqrt{n}(\widehat{a} - a) \underset{d}{\longrightarrow} \mathrm{N}(0, \boldsymbol{V})$, where

$$\boldsymbol{V} = \left(\boldsymbol{I}_m \otimes \boldsymbol{Q}^{-1}\right) \Omega \left(\boldsymbol{I}_m \otimes \boldsymbol{Q}^{-1}\right)$$

$$\boldsymbol{Q} = \mathbb{E}\left[X_t X_t'\right]$$

$$\Omega = \sum_{\ell=-\infty}^{\infty} \mathbb{E}\left[e_{t-\ell} e_t' \otimes X_{t-\ell} X_t'\right].$$

This theorem does not require that the true process be a VAR. Instead, the coefficients are defined as those that produce the best (mean square) approximation, and the only requirements on the true process are general dependence conditions. The theorem shows that the coefficient estimators are asymptotically normal with a covariance matrix that takes a "long-run" sandwich form.

15.11 COVARIANCE MATRIX ESTIMATION

The classic homoskedastic estimator of the covariance matrix for $\widehat{a}$ equals

$$\widehat{\boldsymbol{V}}_{\widehat{a}}^{0} = \widehat{\Sigma} \otimes \left(\boldsymbol{X}'\boldsymbol{X}\right)^{-1}. \tag{15.9}$$

Estimators adjusted for degree-of-freedom can also be used, though there is no established finite-sample justification. This variance estimator is appropriate under the assumption that the conditional expectation is correctly specified as a VAR(p) and the innovations are conditionally homoskedastic.

The heteroskedasticity-robust estimator equals

$$\widehat{\boldsymbol{V}}_{\widehat{a}} = \left(\boldsymbol{I}_n \otimes \left(\boldsymbol{X}'\boldsymbol{X}\right)^{-1}\right) \left(\sum_{t=1}^{n} \left(\widehat{e}_t \widehat{e}_t' \otimes X_t X_t'\right)\right) \left(\boldsymbol{I}_n \otimes \left(\boldsymbol{X}'\boldsymbol{X}\right)^{-1}\right). \tag{15.10}$$

This variance estimator is appropriate under the assumption that the conditional expectation is correctly specified as a VAR(p) but does not require that the innovations are conditionally homoskedastic.

The Newey-West estimator equals

$$\widehat{\boldsymbol{V}}_{\widehat{a}} = \left(\boldsymbol{I}_n \otimes \left(\boldsymbol{X}'\boldsymbol{X}\right)^{-1}\right) \widehat{\Omega}_M \left(\boldsymbol{I}_n \otimes \left(\boldsymbol{X}'\boldsymbol{X}\right)^{-1}\right) \tag{15.11}$$

$$\widehat{\Omega}_M = \sum_{\ell=-M}^{M} w_\ell \sum_{1 \le t-\ell \le n} \left(\widehat{e}_{t-\ell} \otimes X_{t-\ell}\right) \left(\widehat{e}_t' \otimes X_t'\right)$$

$$w_\ell = 1 - \frac{|\ell|}{M+1}.$$

The number M is called the "lag truncation number." An unweighted version sets $w_\ell = 1$. The Newey-West estimator does not require that the VAR(p) is correctly specified.

Traditional textbooks have only used the homoskedastic variance estimation formula (15.9), and consequently, existing software follows the same convention. For example, the `var` command in Stata displays only homoskedastic standard errors. Some researchers use the heteroskedasticity-robust estimator (15.10). The Newey-West estimator (15.11) is not commonly used for VAR models.

Asymptotic approximations tend to be much less accurate for time series dependence than for independent observations. Therefore, bootstrap methods are popular. Section 14.46 describes several bootstrap methods for time series observations. While Section 14.46 focused on univariate time series, the extension to multivariate observations is straightforward.

15.12 SELECTION OF LAG LENGTH IN A VAR

For a data-dependent rule to pick the lag length p, it is recommended to minimize an information criterion. The formula for the AIC is

$$\mathrm{AIC}(p) = n \log \det \widehat{\Sigma}(p) + 2K(p)$$

$$\widehat{\Sigma}(p) = \frac{1}{n} \sum_{t=1}^{n} \widehat{e}_t(p) \widehat{e}_t(p)'$$

$$K(p) = m(pm + 1)$$

where $K(p)$ is the number of parameters, and $\widehat{e}_t(p)$ is the OLS residual vector from the model with p lags. The log determinant is the criterion from the multivariate normal likelihood.

In Stata, the AIC for a set of estimated VAR models can be compared using the `varsoc` command. It should be noted, however, that the Stata routine actually displays $\mathrm{AIC}(p)/n = \log \det \widehat{\Sigma}(p) + 2K(p)/n$. This does not affect the ranking of the models, but it makes the differences between models appear misleadingly small.

15.13 ILLUSTRATION

We estimate a three-variable system that is a simplified version of a model often used to study the impact of monetary policy. The three variables are quarterly from FRED-QD: real GDP growth rate ($100\Delta \log(GDP_t)$, denoted GDP), GDP inflation rate ($100\Delta \log(P_t)$, denoted INF), and the Federal funds interest rate (denoted FF). VARs from lags 1 through 8 were estimated by least squares. The model with the smallest AIC is the VAR(6). The coefficient estimates and (homoskedastic) standard errors for the VAR(6) are reported in Table 15.1.

Examining the coefficients in the table, we can see that GDP displays a moderate degree of serial correlation and shows a large response to the federal funds rate, especially at lags 2 and 3. Inflation also displays serial correlation, shows minimal response to GDP, and also has meaningful response to the federal funds rate. The federal funds rate has the strongest serial correlation. Overall, it is difficult to read too much meaning into the coefficient estimates due to the complexity of the interactions. Because of this difficulty, it is typical to focus on other representations of the coefficient estimates, such as impulse responses, which we discuss in the upcoming sections.

15.14 PREDICTIVE REGRESSIONS

In some contexts (including prediction), it is useful to consider models where the dependent variable is dated multiple periods ahead of the right-hand-side variables. These equations can be a single equation or multivariate; we can consider both as special cases of a VAR (because a single equation model can be written

Table 15.1
Vector autoregression

	GDP	INF	FF
GDP_{t-1}	0.25	0.01	0.08
	(0.07)	(0.02)	(0.02)
GDP_{t-2}	0.23	−0.02	0.04
	(0.07)	(0.02)	(0.02)
GDP_{t-3}	0.00	0.03	0.01
	(0.07)	(0.02)	(0.02)
GDP_{t-4}	0.14	0.04	−0.02
	(0.07)	(0.02)	(0.02)
GDP_{t-5}	−0.02	−0.03	0.04
	(0.07)	(0.02)	(0.02)
GDP_{t-6}	0.05	−0.00	−0.01
	(0.06)	(0.02)	(0.02)
INF_{t-1}	0.11	0.57	0.01
	(0.20)	(0.07)	(0.05)
INF_{t-2}	−0.17	0.10	0.17
	(0.23)	(0.08)	(0.06)
INF_{t-3}	0.01	0.09	−0.05
	(0.23)	(0.08)	(0.06)
INF_{t-4}	0.16	0.14	−0.05
	(0.23)	(0.08)	(0.06)
INF_{t-5}	0.12	−0.05	−0.05
	(0.24)	(0.08)	(0.06)
INF_{t-6}	−0.14	0.10	0.09
	(0.21)	(0.07)	(0.05)
FF_{t-1}	0.13	0.28	1.14
	(0.26)	(0.08)	(0.07)
FF_{t-2}	−1.50	−0.27	−0.53
	(0.38)	(0.12)	(0.10)
FF_{t-3}	1.40	0.12	0.53
	(0.40)	(0.13)	(0.10)
FF_{t-4}	−0.57	−0.13	−0.28
	(0.41)	(0.13)	(0.11)
FF_{t-5}	0.01	0.25	0.28
	(0.40)	(0.13)	(0.10)
FF_{t-6}	0.47	−0.27	−0.24
	(0.26)	(0.08)	(0.07)
Intercept	1.15	0.22	−0.33
	(0.54)	(0.18)	(0.14)

as one equation taken from a VAR system). An h-step predictive VAR(p) takes the form

$$Y_{t+h} = b_0 + \boldsymbol{B}_1 Y_t + \cdots + \boldsymbol{B}_p Y_{t-p+1} + u_t. \tag{15.12}$$

The integer $h \geq 1$ is the **horizon**. A one-step predictive VAR equals a standard VAR. The coefficients should be viewed as the best linear predictors of Y_{t+h} given $(Y_t, \ldots, Y_{t-p+1})$.

There is an interesting relationship between a VAR model and the corresponding h-step predictive VAR model.

Theorem 15.12 If Y_t is a VAR(p) process, then its h-step predictive regression is a predictive VAR(p) with u_t a MA(h-1) process and $\boldsymbol{B}_1 = \Theta_h = \mathrm{IRF}(h)$.

The proof of Theorem 15.12 is presented in Section 15.31.

This theorem has several implications. First, if Y_t is a VAR(p) process, then the correct number of lags for an h-step predictive regression is also p lags. Second, the error in a predictive regression is a MA process and is thus serially correlated. The linear dependence, however, is capped by the horizon. Third, the leading coefficient matrix corresponds to the hth moving average coefficient matrix, which also equals the hth impulse response matrix.

The predictive regression (15.12) can be estimated by least squares. We can write the estimates as

$$Y_{t+h} = \widehat{b}_0 + \widehat{\boldsymbol{B}}_1 Y_t + \cdots + \widehat{\boldsymbol{B}}_p Y_{t-p+1} + \widehat{u}_t. \tag{15.13}$$

For a distribution theory, we need to apply Theorem 15.11, since the innovations u_t are a moving average and thus violate the MDS assumption. In addition, it follows that the covariance matrix for the estimators should be estimated by the Newey-West (15.11) estimator. There is a difference, however. Since u_t is known to be a MA(h-1), a reasonable choice is to set $M = h - 1$ and use the simple weights $w_\ell = 1$. Indeed, this was the original suggestion by L. Hansen and Hodrick (1980).

For a distributional theory, we can apply Theorem 15.11. Let b be the vector of coefficients in (15.12) and $\widehat{b}$ the corresponding least squares estimator. Let X_t be the vector of regressors in (15.12).

Theorem 15.13 If Y_t is strictly stationary, ergodic, $\Sigma > 0$, and for some $r > 4$, $\mathbb{E}\|Y_t\|^r < \infty$ and the mixing coefficients satisfy $\sum_{\ell=1}^{\infty} \alpha(\ell)^{1-4/r} < \infty$, then as $n \to \infty$, $\sqrt{n}\left(\widehat{b} - b\right) \underset{d}{\longrightarrow} \mathrm{N}(0, \boldsymbol{V})$, where

$$\boldsymbol{V} = \left(\boldsymbol{I}_m \otimes \boldsymbol{Q}^{-1}\right) \Omega \left(\boldsymbol{I}_m \otimes \boldsymbol{Q}^{-1}\right)$$
$$\boldsymbol{Q} = \mathbb{E}\left[X_t X_t'\right]$$
$$\Omega = \sum_{\ell=-\infty}^{\infty} \mathbb{E}\left[\left(u_{t-\ell} \otimes X_{t-\ell}\right)\left(u_t' \otimes X_t'\right)\right].$$

15.15 IMPULSE RESPONSE ESTIMATION

Reporting impulse response estimates is one of the most common applications of vector autoregressive modeling. There are several methods for estimating the impulse response function. In this section, we review the most common estimator based on the estimated VAR parameters.

In a VAR(p) model, the impulse responses are determined by the VAR coefficients. We can write this mapping as $\Theta_h = g_h(\boldsymbol{A})$. The plug-in approach suggests the estimator $\widehat{\Theta}_h = g_h(\widehat{\boldsymbol{A}})$ given the VAR(p) coefficient estimator $\widehat{\boldsymbol{A}}$. These are the impulse responses implied by the estimated VAR coefficients. While it is possible to explicitly write the function $g_h(\boldsymbol{A})$, a computationally simple approach is to use Theorem 15.5, which shows that the impulse response matrices can be written as a simple recursion in the VAR coefficients. Thus the impulse response estimator satisfies the recursion

$$\widehat{\Theta}_h = \sum_{\ell=1}^{\min[h,p]} \widehat{\boldsymbol{A}}_\ell \widehat{\Theta}_{h-\ell}.$$

We then set $\widehat{\mathrm{IRF}}(h) = \widehat{\Theta}_h$.

This is the the most commonly used method for impulse response estimation, and it is the method implemented in standard packages.

Since $\widehat{\boldsymbol{A}}$ is random, so is $\widehat{\mathrm{IRF}}(h)$, as it is a nonlinear function of $\widehat{\boldsymbol{A}}$. Using the delta method, we deduce that the elements of $\widehat{\mathrm{IRF}}(h)$ (the impulse responses) are asymptotically normally distributed. With some messy algebra, explicit expressions for the asymptotic variances can be obtained. Sample versions can be used to calculate asymptotic standard errors. These can be used to form asymptotic confidence intervals for the impulse responses.

The asymptotic approximations, however, can be poor. The asymptotic approximations for the distribution of the coefficients $\widehat{\boldsymbol{A}}$ can be poor due to the serial dependence in the observations. The asymptotic approximations for $\widehat{\mathrm{IRF}}(h)$ can be significantly worse, because the impulse responses are highly nonlinear functions of the coefficients. For example, in the simple AR(1) model with coefficient estimate $\widehat{\alpha}$, the hth impulse response is $\widehat{\alpha}^h$, which is highly nonlinear for even moderate horizons h.

Consequently, asymptotic approximations are less popular than bootstrap approximations. The most popular bootstrap approximation uses the recursive bootstrap (see Section 14.46) using the fitted VAR model and calculates confidence intervals for the impulse responses with the percentile method. An unfortunate feature of this choice is that the percentile bootstrap confidence interval is biased, since the nonlinear impulse response estimates are biased, and the percentile bootstrap accentuates bias.

Some advantages of the estimation method as described is that it produces impulse response estimates that are directly related to the estimated VAR(p) model and are internally consistent with one another. The method is also numerically stable. It is efficient when the true process is a true VAR(p) with conditionally homoskedastic MDS innovations. When the true process is not a VAR(p), the method can be thought of as a nonparametric estimator of the impulse response if p is large (or selected appropriately in a data-dependent fashion, such as by the AIC).

A disadvantage of this estimator is that it is a highly nonlinear function of the VAR coefficient estimators. Therefore the distribution of the impulse response estimator is unlikely to be well approximated by the normal distribution. When the VAR(p) is not the true process, then it is possible that the nonlinear transformation accentuates the misspecification bias.

Impulse response functions can be calculated and displayed in Stata using the `irf` command. The command `irf create` is used to calculate IRFs and confidence intervals. The default confidence intervals are asymptotic (delta method). Bootstrap (recursive method) standard errors can be substituted using the `bs` option. The command `irf graph irf` produces graphs of the IRF along with 95% asymptotic confidence intervals. The command `irf graph cirf` produces the CIRF. It may be useful to know that the impulse response estimates are unscaled and so represent the response due to a one-unit change in the impulse variable. A limitation of the Stata `irf` command is that there are limited options for standard error and confidence interval construction. The asymptotic standard errors are calculated using the homoskedastic formula, not the correct heteroskedastic formula. The bootstrap confidence intervals are calculated using the normal approximation bootstrap confidence interval, which is the least reliable bootstrap confidence interval method. Better options, such as the bias-corrected percentile confidence interval, are not provided as options.

15.16 LOCAL PROJECTION ESTIMATOR

Jordà (2005) observed that the impulse response can be estimated by a least squares predictive regression. The key is Theorem 15.12, which establishes that $\Theta_h = \boldsymbol{B}_1$, the leading coefficient matrix in the h-step predictive regression.

The method is as follows. For each horizon h, estimate a predictive regression (15.12) to obtain the leading coefficient matrix estimator $\widehat{\boldsymbol{B}}_1$. The estimator is $\widehat{\mathrm{IRF}}(h) = \widehat{\boldsymbol{B}}_1$ and is known as the **local projection** estimator.

Theorem 15.13 shows that the local projection impulse response estimator is asymptotically normal. Newey-West methods must be used for calculation of asymptotic standard errors, since the regression errors are serially correlated.

Jordà (2005) speculates that the local projection estimator will be less sensitive to misspecification, since it is a straightforward linear estimator. This is intuitive but unclear. Theorem 15.12 relies on the assumption that Y_t is a VAR(p) process, and fails otherwise. Thus if the true process is not a VAR(p), then the coefficient matrix $\boldsymbol{B}_1$ in (15.12) does not correspond to the desired impulse response matrix Θ_h and hence will be misspecified. The accuracy (in the sense of low bias) of both the conventional and the local projection estimator relies on p being sufficiently large so that the VAR(p) model is a good approximation to the true infinite-order regression (15.4). Without a formal theory, it is difficult to know which estimator is more robust.

One implementation challenge is the choice of p. While the method allows for p to vary across horizon h, there is no well-established method for selection of the VAR order for predictive regressions. (Standard selection criteria, such as AIC, are inappropriate under serially correlated errors, just as conventional standard errors are inappropriate.) Therefore the seemingly natural choice is to use the same p for all horizons and base this choice on the one-step VAR model, where AIC can be used for model selection.

An advantage of the local projection method is that it is a linear estimator of the impulse response and thus is likely to have a better-behaved sampling distribution.

A disadvantage is that the method relies on a regression (15.12), which has serially correlated errors. The latter are highly correlated at long horizons, and this renders the estimator imprecise. Local projection estimators tend to be less smooth and more erratic than those produced by the conventional estimator, reflecting a possible lack of precision.

15.17 REGRESSION ON RESIDUALS

If the innovations e_t were observed, it would be natural to directly estimate the coefficients of the multivariate Wold decomposition. We would pick a maximum horizon h and then estimate the equation

$$Y_t = \mu + \Theta_1 e_{t-1} + \Theta_2 e_{t-2} + \cdots + \Theta_h e_{t-h} + u_t$$

where

$$u_t = e_t + \sum_{\ell=h+1}^{\infty} \Theta_\ell e_{t-\ell}.$$

The variables $(e_{t-1}, \ldots, e_{t-h})$ are uncorrelated with u_t, so the least squares estimator of the coefficients is consistent and asymptotically normal. Since u_t is serially correlated, the Newey-West method should be used to calculate standard errors.

In practice, the innovations e_t are not observed. If they are replaced by the residuals $\widehat{e}_t$ from an estimated VAR(p), then we can estimate the coefficients by least squares applied to the equation

$$Y_t = \mu + \Theta_1 \widehat{e}_{t-1} + \Theta_2 \widehat{e}_{t-2} + \cdots + \Theta_h \widehat{e}_{t-h} + \widehat{u}_t.$$

This idea originated with Durbin (1960).

This is a two-step estimator with generated regressors. (See Section 12.26.) The impulse response estimators are consistent and asymptotically normal but with a nonstandard covariance matrix due to the two-step estimation. Conventional, robust, and Newey-West standard errors do not account for this without modification.

Chang and Sakata (2007) proposed a simplified version of the Durbin regression. Notice that for any horizon h, we can rewrite the Wold decomposition as

$$Y_{t+h} = \mu + \Theta_h e_t + v_{t+h}$$

where

$$v_t = \sum_{\ell=0}^{h-1} \Theta_\ell e_{t-\ell} + \sum_{\ell=h+1}^{\infty} \Theta_\ell e_{t-\ell}.$$

The regressor e_t is uncorrelated with v_{t+h}. Thus Θ_h can be estimated by a regression of Y_{t+h} on e_t. In practice, we can replace e_t by the least squares residual $\widehat{e}_t$ from an estimated VAR(p) to estimate the regression

$$Y_{t+h} = \mu + \Theta_h \widehat{e}_t + \widehat{v}_{t+h}. \tag{15.14}$$

Similar to the Durbin regression, the Chang-Sakata estimator is a two-step estimator with a generated regressor. However, as it takes the form studied in Section 12.27, it can be shown that the Chang-Sakata two-step estimator has the same asymptotic distribution as the idealized one-step estimator as if e_t were observed. Thus the standard errors do not need to be adjusted for generated regressors, which is an advantage. The errors are serially correlated, so Newey-West standard errors should be used. The variance of the error v_{t+h} is larger than the variance of the error u_t in the Durbin regression, so the Chang-Sakata estimator may be less precise than the Durbin estimator.

Chang and Sakata (2007) also point out the following implication of the FWL theorem. The least squares slope estimator in (15.14) is algebraically identical[1] to the slope estimator $\widehat{\boldsymbol{B}}_1$ in a predictive regression with $p-1$ lags. Thus the Chang-Sakata estimator is similar to a local projection estimator.

[1] Technically, only if the sample lengths are adjusted.

15.18 ORTHOGONALIZED SHOCKS

We can use the impulse response function to examine how the innnovations impact the time-paths of the variables. A difficulty in interpretation, however, is that the elements of the innovation vector e_t are contemporaneously correlated. Thus e_{jt} and e_{it} are (in general) not independent, so consequently, it does not make sense to treat e_{jt} and e_{it} as fundamental "shocks." Another way of describing the problem is that it does not make sense, for example, to describe the impact of e_{jt} while "holding" e_{it} constant.

The natural solution is to orthogonalize the innovations so that they are uncorrelated and then view the orthogonalized errors as the fundamental "shocks." Recall that e_t is mean 0 with covariance matrix Σ. We can factor Σ into the product of an $m \times m$ matrix $\boldsymbol{B}$ with its transpose $\Sigma = \boldsymbol{B}\boldsymbol{B}'$. The matrix $\boldsymbol{B}$ is called a "square root" of Σ. (See Section A.13.) Define $\varepsilon_t = \boldsymbol{B}^{-1} e_t$. The random vector ε_t has mean zero and covariance matrix $\boldsymbol{B}^{-1}\Sigma\boldsymbol{B}^{-1\prime} = \boldsymbol{B}^{-1}\boldsymbol{B}\boldsymbol{B}'\boldsymbol{B}^{-1\prime} = \boldsymbol{I}_m$. The elements $\varepsilon_t = (\varepsilon_{1t}, \ldots, \varepsilon_{mt})$ are mutually uncorrelated. We can write the innovations as a function of the orthogonalized errors as

$$e_t = \boldsymbol{B}\varepsilon_t. \tag{15.15}$$

To distinguish ε_t from e_t, we will typically call ε_t the "orthogonalized shocks" or more simply, the "shocks" and continue to call e_t the "innovations."

When $m > 1$, there is no unique square root matrix $\boldsymbol{B}$, so there is no unique orthogonalization. The most common choice (which was originally advocated by Sims (1980)) is the Cholesky decomposition (see Section A.16). This sets $\boldsymbol{B}$ to be **lower triangular**, meaning that it takes the form

$$\boldsymbol{B} = \begin{bmatrix} b_{11} & 0 & 0 \\ b_{21} & b_{22} & 0 \\ b_{31} & b_{32} & b_{33} \end{bmatrix}$$

with nonnegative diagonal elements. We can write the Cholesky decomposition of a matrix $\boldsymbol{A}$ as $\boldsymbol{C} = \text{chol}(\boldsymbol{A})$, which means that $\boldsymbol{A} = \boldsymbol{C}\boldsymbol{C}'$ with $\boldsymbol{C}$ lower triangular. We thus set

$$\boldsymbol{B} = \text{chol}(\Sigma). \tag{15.16}$$

Equivalently, the innovations are related to the orthogonalized shocks by the equations

$$\begin{aligned} e_{1t} &= b_{11}\varepsilon_{1t} \\ e_{2t} &= b_{21}\varepsilon_{1t} + b_{22}\varepsilon_{2t} \\ e_{3t} &= b_{31}\varepsilon_{1t} + b_{31}\varepsilon_{2t} + b_{33}\varepsilon_{3t}. \end{aligned}$$

This structure is **recursive**. The innovation e_{1t} is a function only of the single shock ε_{1t}. The innovation e_{2t} is a function of the shocks ε_{1t} and ε_{2t}, and the innovation e_{3t} is a function of all three shocks. Another way of looking at the structure is that the first shock ε_{1t} affects all three innovations, the second shock ε_{2t} affects e_{2t} and e_{3t}, and the third shock ε_{3t} only affects e_{3t}.

A recursive structure is an exclusion restriction. The recursive structure excludes ε_{2t} and ε_{3t} contemporaneously affecting e_{1t}, and it excludes ε_{3t} contemporaneously affecting e_{2t}.

When using the Cholesky decomposition, the recursive structure is determined by the ordering of the variables in the system. The order matters and is the key identifying assumption.

Finally, note that the system (15.15) is equivalent to the system

$$\boldsymbol{A}e_t = \varepsilon_t \tag{15.17}$$

where $\boldsymbol{A} = \boldsymbol{B}^{-1}$ is lower triangular when $\boldsymbol{B}$ is lower triangular. The representation (15.15) is more convenient, however, for most of our purposes.

15.19 ORTHOGONALIZED IMPULSE RESPONSE FUNCTION

We have defined the impulse response function as the change in the time t projection of the variables Y_{t+h} due to the innovation e_t. As discussed in Section 15.18, since the innovations are contemporaneously correlated, it makes better sense to focus on changes due to the orthogonalized shocks ε_t. Consequently, let us define the **orthgonalized impulse response function (OIRF)** as

$$\mathrm{OIRF}(h) = \frac{\partial}{\partial \varepsilon_t'} \mathscr{P}_t\left[Y_{t+h}\right].$$

We can write the multivariate Wold representation as

$$Y_t = \mu + \sum_{\ell=0}^{\infty} \Theta_\ell e_{t-\ell} = \mu + \sum_{\ell=0}^{\infty} \Theta_\ell \boldsymbol{B} \varepsilon_{t-\ell}$$

where $\boldsymbol{B}$ is from (15.16). We deduce that

$$\mathrm{OIRF}(h) = \Theta_h \boldsymbol{B} = \mathrm{IRF}(h) \boldsymbol{B}.$$

This is the non-orthogonalized impulse response matrix multiplied by the matrix square root $\boldsymbol{B}$.

Write the rows of the matrix Θ_h as

$$\Theta_h = \begin{bmatrix} \theta_{1h}' \\ \\ \theta_{mh}' \end{bmatrix}$$

and the columns of the matrix $\boldsymbol{B}$ as $\boldsymbol{B} = [b_1, \ldots, b_m]$. We can see that

$$\mathrm{OIRF}_{ij}(h) = [\Theta_h \boldsymbol{B}]_{ij} = \theta_{ih}' b_j.$$

There are m^2 such responses for each horizon h.

The **cumulative orthogonalized impulse response function** is

$$\mathrm{COIRF}(h) = \sum_{\ell=1}^{h} \mathrm{OIRF}(\ell) = \sum_{\ell=1}^{h} \Theta_\ell \boldsymbol{B}.$$

15.20 ORTHOGONALIZED IMPULSE RESPONSE ESTIMATION

We have discussed estimation of the moving average matrices Θ_ℓ. We need an estimator of $\boldsymbol{B}$.

First let us estimate the VAR(p) model by least squares. This gives us the coefficient matrices $\widehat{\boldsymbol{A}}$ and the error covariance matrix $\widehat{\Sigma}$. From the latter, we apply the Cholesky decomposition $\widehat{\boldsymbol{B}} = \mathrm{chol}\left(\widehat{\Sigma}\right)$, so that $\widehat{\Sigma} = \widehat{\boldsymbol{B}}\widehat{\boldsymbol{B}}'$. (See Section A.16 for the algorithm.) The orthogonalized impulse response estimators are

$$\widehat{\mathrm{OIRF}}(h) = \widehat{\Theta}_h \widehat{\boldsymbol{B}} = \widehat{\theta}_{ih}' \widehat{b}_j.$$

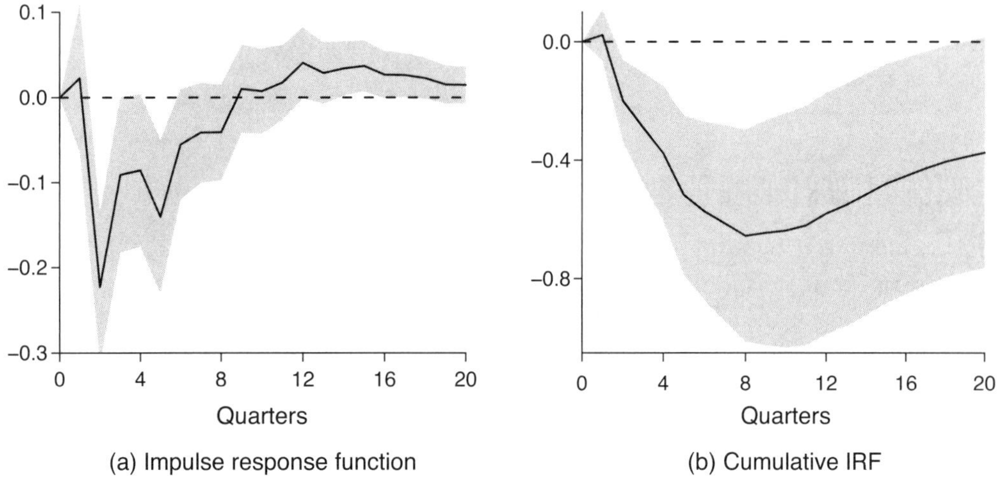

FIGURE 15.1 Response of GDP growth to orthogonalized fed funds shock

The estimator $\widehat{\mathrm{OIRF}}(h)$ is a nonlinear function of $\widehat{\boldsymbol{A}}$ and $\widehat{\Sigma}$. It is asymptotically normally distributed by the delta method, which allows for explicit calculation of asymptotic standard errors. These can be used to form asymptotic confidence intervals for the impulse responses.

As discussed earlier, the asymptotic approximations can be quite poor. Consequently, bootstrap approximations are more widely used than asymptotic methods.

Orthogonalized IRFs can be displayed in Stata using the `irf` command. The command `irf graph oirf` produces graphs of the OIRF along with 95% asymptotic confidence intervals. The command `irf graph coirf` produces the cumulative OIRF. It may also be useful to know that the OIRFs are scaled for a one-standard deviation shock, so the impulse response represents the response due to a one-standard-deviation change in the impulse variable. As discussed earlier, the Stata `irf` command has limited options for standard error and confidence interval construction. The asymptotic standard errors are calculated using the homoskedastic formula, not the correct heteroskedastic formula. The bootstrap confidence intervals are calculated using the normal approximation bootstrap confidence interval.

15.21 ILLUSTRATION

To illustrate, consider the three-variable system from Section 15.13. We use the ordering (1) real GDP growth rate, (2) inflation rate, and (3) Federal funds interest rate. We discuss the choice later, when discussing identification. We use the estimated VAR(6) and calculate the orthogonalized IRFs using the standard VAR estimator.

Figure 15.1 displays the estimated orthogonalized impulse response of the GDP growth rate in response to a one standard deviation increase in the federal funds rate. Panel (a) shows the IRF and panel (b) the CIRF. As discussed earlier, the interpretation of the impulse response and the cumulative impulse response depends on whether the variable enters the VAR in differences or in levels. In this case, GDP growth is the first difference of the natural logarithm. Thus panel (a) (the IRF) shows the effect of interest rates on the growth rate of GDP. Panel (b) (the cumulative impulse response) shows the effect on the log-level of GDP. The IRF shows that the GDP growth rate is negatively affected in the second quarter after an interest rate increase (a drop of about

0.2%, nonannualized), and the negative effects continue for several quarters following. The CIRF shows the effect on the level of GDP measured as percentage changes. It shows that an interest rate increase causes GDP to fall for about 8 quarters, reducing GDP by about 0.6%.

15.22 FORECAST ERROR DECOMPOSITION

An alternative tool to investigate an estimated VAR is the **forecast error decomposition**, which decomposes multi-step forecast error variances by the component shocks. The forecast error decomposition indicates which shocks contribute to the fluctuations of each variable in the system.

It is defined as follows. Take the moving average representation of the ith variable $Y_{i,t+h}$ written as a function of the orthogonalized shocks:

$$Y_{i,t+h} = \mu_i + \sum_{\ell=0}^{\infty} \theta_i(\ell)' \boldsymbol{B}\varepsilon_{t+h-\ell}.$$

The best linear forecast of Y_{t+h} at time t is

$$Y_{i,t+h|t} = \mu_i + \sum_{\ell=h}^{\infty} \theta_i(\ell)' \boldsymbol{B}\varepsilon_{t+h-\ell}.$$

The h-step forecast error is the difference:

$$Y_{i,t+h} - Y_{i,t+h|t} = \sum_{\ell=0}^{h-1} \theta_i(\ell)' \boldsymbol{B}\varepsilon_{t+h-\ell}.$$

The variance of this forecast error is

$$\operatorname{var}\left[Y_{i,t+h} - Y_{i,t+h|t}\right] = \sum_{\ell=0}^{h-1} \operatorname{var}\left[\theta_i(\ell)' \boldsymbol{B}\varepsilon_{t+h-\ell}\right] = \sum_{\ell=0}^{h-1} \theta_i(\ell)' \boldsymbol{B}\boldsymbol{B}'\theta_i(\ell). \tag{15.18}$$

To isolate the contribution of the jth shock, notice that

$$e_t = \boldsymbol{B}\varepsilon_t = b_1\varepsilon_{1t} + \cdots + b_m\varepsilon_{mt}.$$

Thus the contribution of the jth shock is $b_j\varepsilon_{jt}$. Now imagine replacing $\boldsymbol{B}\varepsilon_t$ in the variance calculation by the jth contribution $b_j\varepsilon_{jt}$:

$$\operatorname{var}\left[Y_{it+h} - Y_{i,t+h|t}\right] = \sum_{\ell=0}^{h-1} \operatorname{var}\left[\theta_i(\ell)' b_j\varepsilon_{jt+h-\ell}\right] = \sum_{\ell=0}^{h-1} \left(\theta_i(\ell)' b_j\right)^2. \tag{15.19}$$

Examining (15.18) and using $\boldsymbol{B} = [b_1, \ldots, b_m]$ we can write (15.18) as

$$\operatorname{var}\left[Y_{i,t+h} - Y_{i,t+h|t}\right] = \sum_{j=1}^{m}\sum_{\ell=0}^{h-1} \left(\theta_i(\ell)' b_j\right)^2. \tag{15.20}$$

The forecast error decomposition is defined as the ratio of the jth contribution to the total, which is the ratio of (15.19) to (15.20):

$$\mathrm{FE}_{ij}(h) = \frac{\sum_{\ell=0}^{h-1} \left(\theta_i(\ell)' b_j\right)^2}{\sum_{j=1}^{m}\sum_{\ell=0}^{h-1} \left(\theta_i(\ell)' b_j\right)^2}.$$

The $FE_{ij}(h)$ lies in [0,1] and varies across h. Small values indicate that ε_{jt} contributes only a small amount to the variance of Y_{it}. Large values indicate that ε_{jt} contributes a major amount of the variance of ε_{it}.

A forecast error decomposition requires orthogonalized innovations. There is no non-orthogonalized version.

The forecast error decomposition can be calculated and displayed in Stata using the `irf` command. The command `irf graph fevd` produces graphs of the forecast error decomposition along with 95% asymptotic confidence intervals.

15.23 IDENTIFICATION OF RECURSIVE VARs

As we have discussed, a common method to orthogonalize the VAR errors is the lower triangular Cholesky decomposition, which implies a recursive structure. The ordering of the variables is critical to this recursive structure. Unless the errors are uncorrelated, different orderings will lead to different IRFs and forecast error decompositions. The ordering must be selected by the user; there is no data-dependent choice.

For impulse responses and forecast error decompositions to be interpreted causally, the orthogonalization must be identified by the user based on a structural economic argument. The choice is similar to the exclusion restrictions necessary for specification of an instrumental variables regression. By ordering the variables recursively, we are effectively imposing exclusion restrictions. Recall that in our empirical example, we used the ordering: (1) real GDP growth rate, (2) inflation rate, (3) Federal funds interest rate. Thus in the equation for GDP, we excluded the contemporaneous inflation rate and interest rate, and in the equation for inflation, we excluded the contemporaneous interest rate. These are exclusion restrictions. Are they justified?

One approach is to order first the variables that are believed to be contemporaneously affected by the fewest number of shocks. One way of thinking about it is that they are the variables that are "most sticky" within a period. The variables listed last are those believed to be contemporaneously affected by the greatest number of shocks. These are able to respond within a single period to the shocks or are the most flexible. Our example listed output first, prices second, and interest rates last. This is consistent with the view that output is effectively predetermined (within a period) and does not (within a period) respond to price and interest rate movements. Prices are allowed to respond within a period to output changes but not to interest rate changes. The latter could be justified if interest rate changes affect investment decisions but the latter take at least one period to implement. By listing the federal funds rate last, the model allows monetary policy to respond within a period to contemporaneous information about output and prices.

In general, this line of reasoning suggests that production measures should be listed first, goods prices second, and financial prices last. This reasoning is more credible when the time periods are short and less credible for longer time periods.

Further justifications for possible recursive orderings can include: (1) information delays, (2) implementation delays, (3) institutions, (4) market structure, (5) homogeneity, and (6) imposing estimates from other sources. In most cases, such arguments can be made but will be viewed as debatable and restrictive. In any situation, it is best to be explicit about your choice and reasoning.

Returning to the empirical illustration, it is fairly conventional to order the fed funds rate last. This allows the fed funds rate to respond to contemporaneous information about output and price growth and identifies the fed funds **policy shock** by the assumption that it does not have a contemporaneous impact on the other variables. It is not clear, however, how to order the other two variables. For simplicity, consider a traditional aggregate supply/aggregate demand model of the determination of output and the price level. If the aggregate supply curve is perfectly inelastic in the short run (one quarter), then output is effectively fixed (sticky), so changes in aggregate demand affect prices but not output. Changes in aggregate supply affect both output and prices. Thus we would want to order GDP first and inflation second. This choice would identify the GDP error as the **aggregate supply shock**. This is the ordering used in our example.

In contrast, suppose that the aggregate supply curve is perfectly elastic in the short run. Then prices are fixed, and output is flexible. Changes in aggregate supply affect both price and output, but changes in aggregate demand only affect output. In this case, we would want to order inflation first and GDP second. This choice identifies the inflation error as the aggregate supply shock, the opposite case from the previous assumption!

If the choice between perfectly elastic and perfectly inelastic aggregate supply is not credible, then the supply and demand shocks cannot be separately identified based on ordering alone. In this case, the full set of impulse responses and error decompositions are not identified. However, a subset may be identified. In general, if the shocks can be ordered in groups, then we can identify any shock for which a group has a single variable. In our example, consider the ordering (1) GDP and inflation and (2) federal funds rate. Thus the model assumes that GDP and inflation do not contemporaneously respond to interest rate movements, but no other restrictions are imposed. In this case, the fed funds policy shock is identified. Thus impulse responses of all three variables with respect to the policy shock are identified and similarly, the forecast error composition of the effect of the fed funds shock on each variable is identified. These can be estimated by a VAR using the ordering (GDP, inflation, federal funds rate), as done in our example, or by using the ordering (inflation, GDP, federal funds rate). Both choices will lead to the same estimated impulse responses, as described. The remaining impulse responses (responses to GDP and inflation shocks), however, will differ across these two orderings.

15.24 OIL PRICE SHOCKS

To further illustrate the identification of impulse response functions by recursive structural assumptions, we repeat here some of the analysis from Kilian (2009). His paper concerns the identification of the factors affecting crude oil prices, in particular, separating supply and demand shocks. The goal is to determine how oil prices respond to economic shocks and how the responses differ by the type of shock.

To answer these questions, Kilian uses a three-variable VAR with monthly measures of global oil production, global economic activity, and the global price of crude oil for 1973m2–2007m12. He uses global variables, since the price of crude oil is globally determined. One innovation in the paper is that Kilian develops a new index of global economic activity based on ocean freight rates. His motivation is that shipping rates are directly related to the global demand for industrial commodities. This dataset is posted on the textbook webpage as `Kilian2009`.

Kilian argues that these three variables are determined by three economic shocks: oil supply, aggregate demand, and oil demand. He suggests that oil supply shocks should be thought of as disruptions in production, processing, or shipping. Aggregate demand is global economic activity. Kilian also argues that oil demand shocks are primarily due to the precautionary demand for oil driven by uncertainty about future oil supply shortfalls.

To identify the shocks, Kilian makes the following exclusion restrictions. First, he assumes that the short-run (1 month) supply of crude oil is inelastic with respect to price. Equivalently, oil production takes at least 1 month to respond to price changes. This restriction is believed to be plausible because of technological factors in crude oil production. It is costly to open new oil fields; and it is nearly impossible to cap an oil well once tapped. Second, Kilian assumes that in the short run (1 month), global real economic activity does not respond to changes in oil prices (due to shocks specific to the oil market), while economic activity is

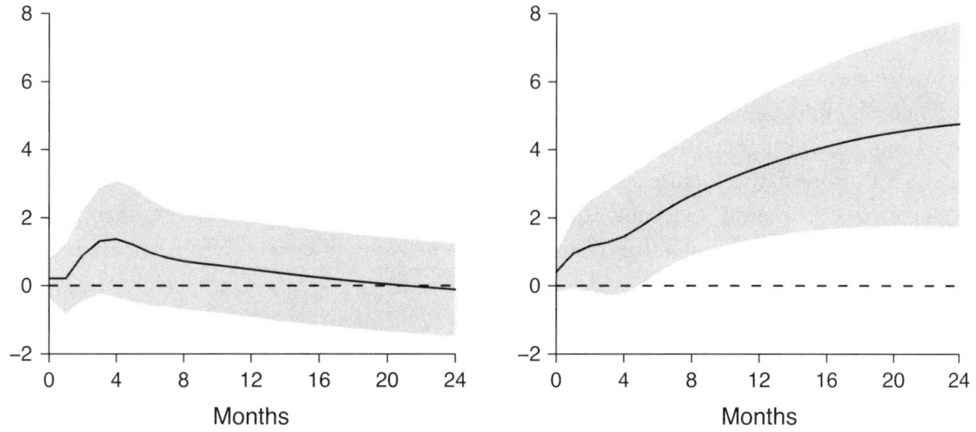

(a) Supply shock

(b) Aggregate demand shock

FIGURE 15.2 Response of oil prices to orthogonalized shocks

allowed to respond to oil production shocks. This assumption is viewed by Kilian as plausible due to the sluggishness in the response of economic activity to price changes. Crude oil prices, however, are allowed to respond simultaneously to all three shocks.

Kilian's identification strategy is similar to that described in Section 15.23 for the simple aggregate demand/aggregate supply model. The separation of supply and demand shocks is achieved by exclusion restrictions that imply short-run inelasticities. The plausibility of these assumptions rests in part on the monthly frequency of the data. While it is plausible that oil production and economic activity may not respond within 1 month to price shocks, it is much less plausible that there is no response for a full quarter. Kilian's least convincing identifying assumption (in my opinion) is that economic activity does not respond simultaneously to oil price changes. While much economic activity is preplanned and hence sluggish to respond, some economic activity (recreational driving, for example) may immediately respond to price changes.

Kilian estimates the three-variable VAR using 24 lags and calculates the orthogonalized IRFs using the ordering implied by these assumptions. He does not discuss the choice of 24 lags but presumably, this is intended to allow for flexible dynamic responses. If the AIC is used for model selection, three lags would be selected. For the analysis reported here, I used four lags. The results are qualitatively similar to those obtained using 24 lags. For ease of interpretation, oil supply is entered negatively (multiplied by -1), so that all three shocks are scaled to increase oil prices. Two IRFs for the price of crude oil are displayed in Figure 15.2 for 1–24 months. Panel (a) displays the response of crude oil prices to an oil supply shock; panel (b) displays the response to an aggregate demand shock. Notice that both panels have been displayed using the same y-axis scalings, so that the figures are comparable.

What is noticeable about the figures is how differently crude oil prices respond to the two shocks. Panel (a) shows that oil prices are only minimally affected by oil production shocks. There is an estimated small short-term increase in oil prices, but it is not statistically significant, and it reverses within 1 year. In contrast, panel (b) shows that oil prices are significantly affected by aggregate demand shocks, and the effect cumulatively increases over 2 years. Presumaby, this is because economic activity relies on crude oil, and output growth is positively serially correlated.

The Kilian (2009) paper is an excellent example of how recursive orderings can be used to identify an orthogonalized VAR through a careful discussion of the causal system and the use of monthly observations.

15.25 STRUCTURAL VARS

Recursive models do not allow for simultaneity between the elements of e_t, and thus the variables Y_t cannot be contemporaneously endogenous. This is highly restrictive and may not credibly describe many economic systems. There is a general preference in the economics community for **structural vector autoregressive models** (SVARs), which use alternative identification restrictions that do not rely exclusively on recursiveness. Two popular categories of structural VAR models are those based on short-run (contemporaneous) restrictions and those based on long-run (cumulative) restrictions. In this section we review SVARs based on short-run restrictions.

When discussing methods to orthogonalize the VAR errors, I pointed out that we can represent the relationship between the errors and shocks using either the equation $e_t = \boldsymbol{B}\varepsilon_t$ (15.15) or the equation $\boldsymbol{A}e_t = \varepsilon_t$ (15.17). Equation (15.15) writes the errors as a function of the shocks. Equation (15.17) writes the errors as a simultaneous system. A broader class of models can be captured by the equation system

$$\boldsymbol{A}e_t = \boldsymbol{B}\varepsilon_t \tag{15.21}$$

where (in the 3×3 case)

$$\boldsymbol{A} = \begin{bmatrix} 1 & a_{12} & a_{13} \\ a_{21} & 1 & a_{23} \\ a_{31} & a_{32} & 1 \end{bmatrix}, \qquad \boldsymbol{B} = \begin{bmatrix} b_{11} & b_{12} & b_{13} \\ b_{21} & b_{22} & b_{23} \\ b_{31} & b_{32} & b_{33} \end{bmatrix}. \tag{15.22}$$

(Note: This matrix $\boldsymbol{A}$ has nothing to do with the regression coefficient matrix $\boldsymbol{A}$. I apologize for the double use of $\boldsymbol{A}$, but I use the notation (15.21) to be consistent with the notation elsewhere in the literature.)

Written out,

$$\begin{aligned} e_{1t} &= -a_{12}e_{2t} - a_{13}e_{3t} + b_{11}\varepsilon_{1t} + b_{12}\varepsilon_{2t} + b_{13}\varepsilon_{3t} \\ e_{2t} &= -a_{21}e_{1t} - a_{23}e_{3t} + b_{21}\varepsilon_{1t} + b_{22}\varepsilon_{2t} + b_{23}\varepsilon_{3t} \\ e_{3t} &= -a_{31}e_{1t} - a_{32}e_{2t} + b_{31}\varepsilon_{1t} + b_{32}\varepsilon_{2t} + b_{33}\varepsilon_{3t}. \end{aligned}$$

The diagonal elements of the matrix $\boldsymbol{A}$ are set to 1 as normalizations. This normalization allows the shocks ε_{it} to have unit variance, which is convenient for impulse response calculations.

The system as written is underidentified. In this three-equation example, the matrix Σ provides only six moments, but the above system has 15 free parameters! To achieve identification, we need nine restrictions.

In most applications, it is common to start with the restriction that for each common nondiagonal element of $\boldsymbol{A}$ and $\boldsymbol{B}$, at most one can be nonzero. That is, for any pair $i \neq j$, either $b_{ji} = 0$ or $a_{ji} = 0$.

I will illustrate by using a simplified version of the model employed by Blanchard and Perotti (2002) who were interested in decomposing the effects of government spending and taxes on GDP. They proposed a three-variable system consisting of real government spending (net of transfers), real tax revenues (including transfer payments as negative taxes), and real GDP. All variables are measured in logs. They start with the restrictions $a_{21} = a_{12} = b_{31} = b_{32} = b_{13} = b_{23} = 0$, or

$$\boldsymbol{A} = \begin{bmatrix} 1 & 0 & a_{13} \\ 0 & 1 & a_{23} \\ a_{31} & a_{32} & 1 \end{bmatrix}, \qquad \boldsymbol{B} = \begin{bmatrix} b_{11} & b_{12} & 0 \\ b_{21} & b_{22} & 0 \\ 0 & 0 & b_{33} \end{bmatrix}.$$

This is done so that the relationship between the shocks ε_{1t} and ε_{2t} is treated as reduced-form but the coefficients in the $\boldsymbol{A}$ matrix can be interpreted as contemporaneous elasticities between the variables. For example,

a_{23} is the within-quarter elasticity of tax revenue with respect to GDP, a_{31} is the within-quarter elasticity of GDP with respect to government spending, and so forth.

We just described six restrictions, while nine are required for identification. Blanchard and Perotti (2002) made a strong case for two additional restrictions. First, the within-quarter elasticity of government spending with respect to GDP is 0: $a_{13} = 0$. This is because government fiscal policy does not (and cannot) respond to news about GDP within the same quarter. Since the authors defined government spending as net of transfer payments, there is no "automatic stabilizer" component of spending. Second, the within-quarter elasticity of tax revenue with respect to GDP can be estimated from existing microeconometric studies. The authors survey the available literature and set $a_{23} = -2.08$. To fully identify the model, we need one final restriction. The authors argue that there is no clear case for any specific restriction, and so they impose a recursive $\boldsymbol{B}$ matrix (setting $b_{12} = 0$) and experiment with the alternative $b_{21} = 0$, finding that the two specifications are nearly equivalent, since the two shocks are nearly uncorrelated. In summary, the estimated model takes the form

$$\boldsymbol{A} = \begin{bmatrix} 1 & 0 & 0 \\ 0 & 1 & -2.08 \\ a_{31} & a_{32} & 1 \end{bmatrix}, \qquad \boldsymbol{B} = \begin{bmatrix} b_{11} & 0 & 0 \\ b_{21} & b_{22} & 0 \\ 0 & 0 & b_{33} \end{bmatrix}.$$

Blanchard and Perotti (2002) make use of both matrices $\boldsymbol{A}$ and $\boldsymbol{B}$. Other authors use either the simpler structure $\boldsymbol{A}e_t = \varepsilon_t$ or $e_t = \boldsymbol{B}\varepsilon_t$. In general, either of the two simpler structures are easier to compute and interpret.

Taking the variance of the variables on each side of (15.21), we find

$$\boldsymbol{A}\Sigma\boldsymbol{A}' = \boldsymbol{B}\boldsymbol{B}'. \tag{15.23}$$

This is a system of quadratic equations in the free parameters. If the model is just-identified, it can be solved numerically to find the coefficients of $\boldsymbol{A}$ and $\boldsymbol{B}$ given Σ. Similarly, given the least squares error covariance matrix $\widehat{\Sigma}$, we can numerically solve for the coefficients of $\widehat{\boldsymbol{A}}$ and $\widehat{\boldsymbol{B}}$.

While most applications use just-identified models, if the model is overidentified (if there are fewer free parameters than estimated components of Σ), then the coefficients of $\widehat{\boldsymbol{A}}$ and $\widehat{\boldsymbol{B}}$ can be found using minimum distance. The implementation in Stata uses MLE (which simultaneously estimates the VAR coefficients). The latter is appropriate when the model is correctly specified (including normality) but is otherwise an unclear choice.

Given the parameter estimates, the **structural impulse response function** is

$$\widehat{\text{SIRF}}(h) = \widehat{\Theta}(h)\widehat{\boldsymbol{A}}^{-1}\widehat{\boldsymbol{B}}.$$

The structural forecast error decompositions are calculated as before but with b_j replaced by the jth column of $\widehat{\boldsymbol{A}}^{-1}\widehat{\boldsymbol{B}}$.

The structural impulse responses are nonlinear functions of the VAR coefficient and covariance matrix estimators, so by the delta method, they are asymptotically normal. Thus asymptotic standard errors can be calculated (using numerical derivatives if convenient). As for orthogonalized impulse responses, the asymptotic normal approximation is unlikely to be a good approximation, so bootstrap methods are an attractive alternative.

Structural VARs should be interpreted similarly to instrumental variable estimators. Their interpretation relies on valid exclusion restrictions, which can only be justified by external information.

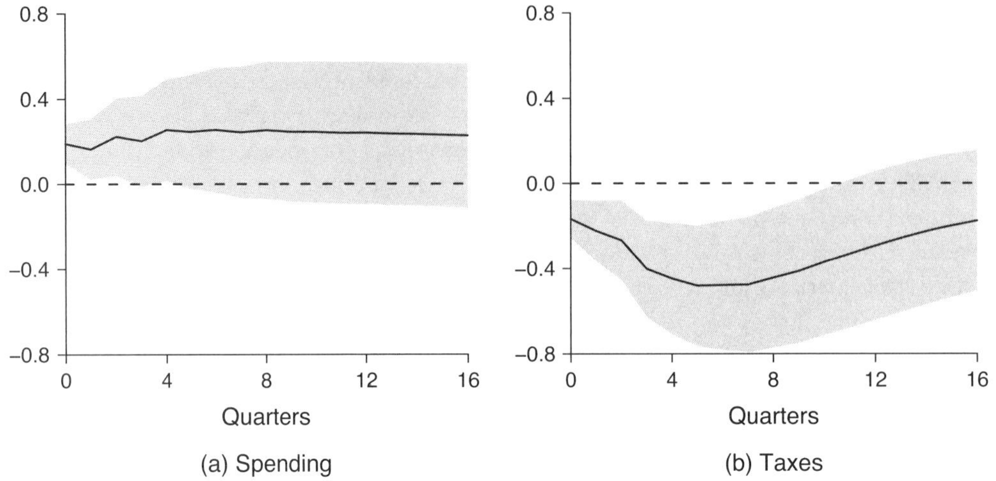

FIGURE 15.3 Response of GDP to government spending and tax shocks

Let us replicate a simplified version of Blanchard and Perotti (2002). We use[2] quarterly variables from FRED-QD for 1959–2017: real GDP (*gdpc1*), real tax revenue (*fgrecptx*), and real government spending (*gcec1*), all in natural logarithms. Using the AIC for lag length selection, we estimate VARs from one to eight lags and select a VAR(5). The model also includes a linear and quadratic function of time.[3] Figure 15.3 displays the estimated structural impulse responses of GDP with respect to government spending (panel (a)) and tax shocks (panel (b)). The estimated impulse responses are similar to those reported by Blanchard-Perotti.

In panel (a) we see that the effect of a 1% government spending shock on GDP is positive, small (around 0.2%), but persistent, remaining stable at 0.2% for 4 years. In panel (b) we see that the effect of a 1% tax revenue shock is quite different. The effect on GDP is negative and persistent, and more substantial than the effect of a spending shock, reaching about −0.5% at six quarters. Together, the impulse response estimates show that changes in government spending and tax revenue have meaningful economic impacts. Increased spending has a positive effect on GDP, while increased taxes has a negative effect.

The Blanchard and Perotti (2002) paper is an excellent example of how credible exclusion restrictions can be used to identify a nonrecursive structural system and help answer an important economic question. The within-quarter exogeneity of government spending is compelling, and the use of external information to fix the elasticity of tax revenue with respect to GDP is clever.

Structural vector autoregressions can be estimated in Stata using the `svar` command. Short-run restrictions of the form (15.21) can be imposed using the `aeq` and `beq` options. Structural impulse responses can be displayed using `irf graph sirf`, and structural forecast error decompositions by using `irf graph sfevd`. Unfortunately, Stata does not provide a convenient way to display cumulative structural impulse response functions. The same limitations for standard error and confidence interval construction in Stata hold for structural impulse responses as for nonstructural impulse responses.

[2] These are similar to, but not the same as, the variables used by Blanchard and Perotti.

[3] The authors detrend their data using a quadratic function of time. By the FWL theorem (Theorem 3.5), this is equivalent to including a quadratic in time in the regression.

15.26 IDENTIFICATION OF STRUCTURAL VARS

The coefficient matrices $\boldsymbol{A}$ and $\boldsymbol{B}$ in (15.21) are identified if they can be uniquely solved from (15.23). This is a set of $m(m+1)/2$ unique equations, so the total number of free coefficients in $\boldsymbol{A}$ and $\boldsymbol{B}$ cannot be larger than $m(m+1)/2$ (e.g., 6 when $m=3$). This is the order condition for identification. It is necessary, but not sufficient. It is easy to write down restrictions that satisfy the order condition but do not produce an identified system.

It is difficult to see whether the system is identified simply by looking at the restrictions (except in the recursive case, which is relatively straightforward to identify). An intuitive way of verifying identification is to use our knowledge of instrumental variables. We can identify the equations sequentially, one at a time, or in blocks, using the metaphor of instrumental variables.

The general technique is as follows. Start by writing out the system by imposing all restrictions and absorbing the diagonal elements of $\boldsymbol{B}$ into the shocks (so that they are still uncorrelated but have non-unit variances). For the Blanchard and Perotti (2002) example, the result is

$$e_{1t} = \varepsilon_{1t}$$

$$e_{2t} = 2.08 e_{3t} + b_{21}\varepsilon_{1t} + \varepsilon_{2t}$$

$$e_{3t} = -a_{31}e_{1t} - a_{32}e_{2t} + \varepsilon_{3t}.$$

Take the equations one at a time, and ask whether they can be estimated by instrumental variables using the excluded variables as instruments. Once an equation has been verified as identified, then its shock is identified and can be used as an instrument, because it is uncorrelated with the shocks in the other equations.

In this example, take the equations as ordered. The first equation is identified, as there are no coefficients to estimate. Thus ε_{1t} is identified. For the second equation, there is one free parameter, which can be estimated by least squares of $e_{2t} - 2.08e_{3t}$ on ε_{1t}, which is valid because ε_{1t} and ε_{2t} are uncorrelated. This identifies the second equation and the shock ε_{2t}. The third equation has two free parameters and two endogenous regressors, so we need two instruments. We can use the shocks ε_{1t} and ε_{2t} as they are uncorrelated with ε_{3t} and are correlated with the variables e_{1t} and e_{2t}. Thus this equation is identified. We deduce that the system is identified.

Consider another example based on Keating (1992). He estimated a four-variable system with prices, the fed funds rate, M2, and GDP. His model for the errors takes the form $\boldsymbol{A}e_t = \varepsilon_t$. Written out explicitly:

$$e_P = \varepsilon_{AS}$$

$$e_{FF} = a_{23}e_M + \varepsilon_{MS}$$

$$e_M = a_{31}\left(e_P + e_{GDP}\right) + a_{32}e_{FF} + \varepsilon_{MD}$$

$$e_{GDP} = a_{41}e_P + a_{42}e_{FF} + a_{43}e_M + \varepsilon_{IS}$$

where the four shocks are "aggregate supply," "money supply," "money demand," and "IS". This structure can be based on the following assumptions: an elastic short-run aggregate supply curve (prices do not respond within the a quarter); a simple monetary supply policy (the fed funds rate only responds within the quarter to the money supply); money demand only responds to nominal output (log price plus log real output) and fed funds rate within a quarter; and unrestricted IS curve (from a classical IS-LM model).

To analyze conditions for identification, we start by checking the order condition. There are 10 coefficients in the system (including the four variances), which equals $m(m+1)/2$ because $m=4$. Thus the order condition is exactly satisfied.

Let us check the equations for identification. We start with the first equation. It has no coefficients, so is identified, and thus so is ε_{AS}. The second equation has one coefficient. We can use ε_{AS} as an instrument because it is uncorrelated with ε_{MS}. The relevance condition will hold if ε_{AS} is correlated with e_M. From the third equation, we see that this will hold if $a_{31} \neq 0$. Given this assumption, a_{23} and ε_{MS} are identified. The third equation has two coefficients, so we can use $(\varepsilon_{AS}, \varepsilon_{MS})$ as instruments, because they are uncorrelated with ε_{MD}. ε_{MS} is correlated with e_{FF}, and ε_{AS} is correlated with e_P. Thus the relevance condition is satisfied. The final equation has three coefficients, so we use $(\varepsilon_{AS}, \varepsilon_{MS}, \varepsilon_{MD})$ as instruments. They are uncorrelated with ε_{IS} and correlated with the variables (e_P, e_{FF}, e_M), so this equation is identified.

We find that the system is identified if $a_{31} \neq 0$. This requires that money demand responds to nominal GDP, which is a prediction from standard monetary economics. This condition seems reasonable. Regardless, the point of this exercise is to determine specific conditions for identification and articulate them in your analysis.

15.27 LONG-RUN RESTRICTIONS

To review, the algebraic identification problem for impulse response estimation is that we require a square root matrix $\boldsymbol{B} = \Sigma^{1/2}$, yet the latter is not unique and the results are sensitive to the choice. The non-uniqueness arises because $\boldsymbol{B}$ has m^2 elements while Σ has $m(m+1)/2$ free elements. The recursive solution is to set $\boldsymbol{B}$ to equal the Cholesky decomposition of Σ, or equivalently, to specify $\boldsymbol{B}$ as lower triangular. Structural VARs based on short-run (contemporaneous) restrictions generalize this idea by allowing general restrictions on $\boldsymbol{B}$ based on economic assumptions about contemporaneous causal relations and prior knowledge about $\boldsymbol{B}$. Identification requires $m(m-1)/2$ restrictions. Even more generally, a structural VAR can be constructed by imposing $m(m-1)/2$ restrictions due to any known structure or features of the IRFs.

One important class of such structural VARs are those based on long-run restrictions. Some economic hypotheses imply restrictions on long-run impulse responses. These can provide a compelling case for identification.

An influential example of a structural VAR based on a long-run restriction is Blanchard and Quah (1989). They were interested in decomposing the effects of demand and supply shocks on output. Their hypothesis is that demand shocks are long-run neutral, meaning that the long-run impact of a demand shock on output is 0. Thus the long-run impulse response of output with respect to demand is 0. This can be used as an identifying restriction.

The long-run structural impulse response is the cumulative sum of all impulse responses:

$$\boldsymbol{C} = \sum_{\ell=1}^{\infty} \Theta_\ell \boldsymbol{B} = \Theta(1)\boldsymbol{B} = \boldsymbol{A}(1)^{-1}\boldsymbol{B}.$$

A long-run restriction is a restriction placed on the matrix $\boldsymbol{C}$. Since the sum $\boldsymbol{A}(1)$ is identified, this provides identifying information on the matrix $\boldsymbol{B}$.

Blanchard and Quah (1989) suggest a bivariate VAR for the first-differenced logarithm of real GDP and the unemployment rate. Blanchard and Quah assume that the structural shocks are aggregate supply and aggregate demand. They adopt the hypothesis that aggregate demand has no long-run impact on GDP. Thus the long-run impulse response matrix satisfies

$$\boldsymbol{C} = \begin{bmatrix} c_{11} & 0 \\ c_{21} & c_{22} \end{bmatrix}. \tag{15.24}$$

Another way of thinking about this is that Blanchard and Quah label "aggregate supply" as the long-run component of GDP and label "aggregate demand" as the transitory component of GDP.

The relations $\boldsymbol{C} = \boldsymbol{A}(1)^{-1}\boldsymbol{B}$ and $\boldsymbol{B}\boldsymbol{B}' = \Sigma$ imply

$$\boldsymbol{C}\boldsymbol{C}' = \boldsymbol{A}(1)^{-1}\boldsymbol{B}\boldsymbol{B}'\boldsymbol{A}(1)^{-1\prime} = \boldsymbol{A}(1)^{-1}\Sigma\boldsymbol{A}(1)^{-1\prime}. \tag{15.25}$$

This is a set of m^2 equations, but because the matrices are positive semi-definite, there are $m(m+1)/2$ independent equations. If the matrix $\boldsymbol{C}$ has $m(m+1)/2$ free coefficients, then the system is identified. This requires $m(m-1)/2$ restrictions. In the Blanchard-Quah example, $m=2$, so one restriction is sufficient for identification.

In many applications, including Blanchard-Quah, the matrix $\boldsymbol{C}$ is lower triangular, which permits the following elegant solution. Examining (15.25), we see that $\boldsymbol{C}$ is a matrix square root of $\boldsymbol{A}(1)^{-1}\Sigma\boldsymbol{A}(1)^{-1\prime}$, and because $\boldsymbol{C}$ is lower triangular, it is the Cholesky decomposition. We deduce $\boldsymbol{C} = \text{chol}\left(\boldsymbol{A}(1)^{-1}\Sigma\boldsymbol{A}(1)^{-1}\right)$.

The plug-in estimator for $\boldsymbol{C}$ is $\widehat{\boldsymbol{C}} = \text{chol}\left(\widehat{\boldsymbol{A}}(1)^{-1}\widehat{\Sigma}\widehat{\boldsymbol{A}}(1)^{-1}\right)$, where $\widehat{\boldsymbol{A}}(1) = \boldsymbol{I}_m - \widehat{\boldsymbol{A}}_1 - \cdots - \widehat{\boldsymbol{A}}_p$. By construction, the solution $\widehat{\boldsymbol{C}}$ will be lower triangular and satisfy the desired restriction.

More generally, if the restrictions on $\boldsymbol{C}$ do not take a lower triangular form, then the estimator can be found by numerically solving the system of quadratic equations

$$\widehat{\boldsymbol{C}}\widehat{\boldsymbol{C}}' = \widehat{\boldsymbol{A}}(1)^{-1}\widehat{\Sigma}\widehat{\boldsymbol{A}}(1)^{-1\prime}.$$

In either case the estimator is $\widehat{\boldsymbol{B}} = \widehat{\boldsymbol{A}}(1)\widehat{\boldsymbol{C}}$, and the estimator of the structural impulse response is

$$\widehat{\text{SIRF}}(h) = \widehat{\Theta}_h\widehat{\boldsymbol{B}} = \widehat{\Theta}_h\widehat{\boldsymbol{A}}(1)\widehat{\boldsymbol{C}}.$$

Notice that by construction, the long-run impulse response is

$$\sum_{\ell=1}^{\infty}\widehat{\text{SIRF}}(h) = \sum_{\ell=1}^{\infty}\widehat{\Theta}_h\widehat{\boldsymbol{A}}(1)\widehat{\boldsymbol{C}} = \widehat{\boldsymbol{A}}(1)^{-1}\widehat{\boldsymbol{A}}(1)\widehat{\boldsymbol{C}} = \widehat{\boldsymbol{C}}$$

so indeed $\widehat{\boldsymbol{C}}$ is the estimated long-run impulse response and satisfies the desired restriction.

Long-run structural vector autoregressions can be estimated in Stata using the `svar` command with the `lreq` option. Structural impulse responses can be displayed using `irf graph sirf` and structural forecast error decompositions using `irf graph sfevd`. This Stata option does not produce asymptotic standard errors when imposing long-run restrictions, so for confidence intervals, bootstrapping is recommended. The same limitations for such intervals constructed in Stata hold for structural impulse response functions as for the other cases discussed.

Unfortunately, a limitation of the Stata `svar` command is that it does not display cumulative structural impulse response functions. To display these, one needs to cumulate the impulse response estimates. This can be done, but then standard errors and confidence intervals are not available. Thus for serious applied work, programming needs to be done outside of Stata.

15.28 BLANCHARD AND QUAH (1989) ILLUSTRATION

As discussed in Section 15.27, Blanchard and Quah (1989) estimated a bivariate VAR in GDP growth and the unemployment rate assuming that the the structural shocks are aggregate supply and aggregate demand and imposing that the long-run response of GDP with respect to aggregate demand is 0. Their original application used U.S. data for 1950–1987. We revisit using FRED-QD (1959–2017). While Blanchard and Quah used a

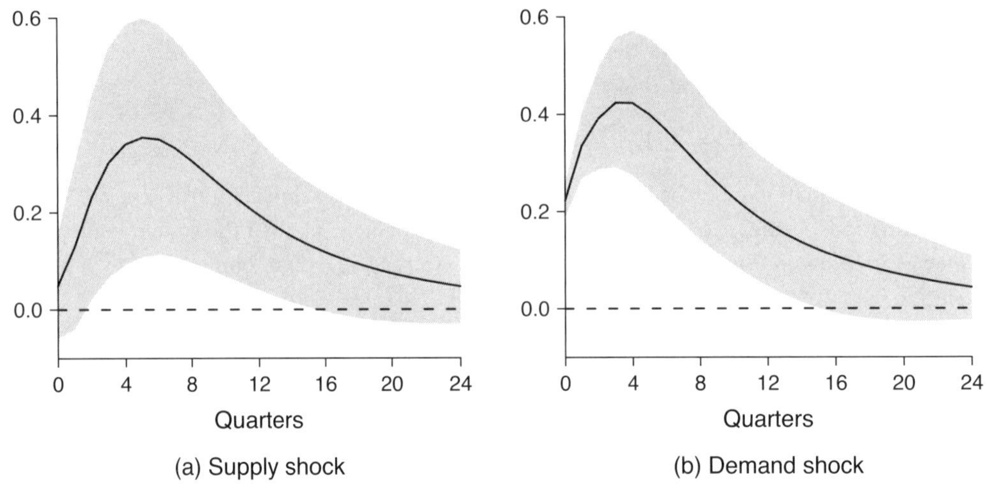

FIGURE 15.4 Response of unemployment rate

VAR(8) model, the AIC selects a VAR(3). We use a VAR(4). To ease the interpretation of the impulse responses, the unemployment rate is entered negatively (multiplied by -1), so that both series are pro-cyclical and positive shocks increase output. Blanchard and Quah used a careful detrending method; instead, we include a linear time trend in the estimated VAR.

The fitted reduced form model coefficients satisfy

$$\widehat{\boldsymbol{A}}(1)=\boldsymbol{I}_m-\sum_{j=1}^{4}\widehat{\boldsymbol{A}}_j=\begin{pmatrix}0.42 & 0.05\\ -0.15 & 0.04\end{pmatrix}$$

and the residual covariance matrix is

$$\widehat{\Sigma}=\begin{pmatrix}0.531 & 0.095\\ 0.095 & 0.053\end{pmatrix}.$$

We calculate

$$\widehat{\boldsymbol{C}}=\operatorname{chol}\left(\widehat{\boldsymbol{A}}(1)^{-1}\,\widehat{\Sigma}\widehat{\boldsymbol{A}}(1)^{-1\prime}\right)=\begin{pmatrix}1.00 & 0\\ 4.75 & 5.42\end{pmatrix}$$

$$\widehat{\boldsymbol{B}}=\widehat{\boldsymbol{A}}(1)\widehat{\boldsymbol{C}}=\begin{pmatrix}0.67 & 0.28\\ 0.05 & 0.23\end{pmatrix}.$$

Examining $\widehat{\boldsymbol{B}}$, the unemployment rate is contemporaneously mostly affected by the aggregate demand shock, while GDP growth is affected by both shocks.

Using this square root of $\widehat{\Sigma}$, let us construct the structural impulse response functions as a function of the two shocks (aggregate supply and aggregate demand). Figure 15.4 displays the estimated structural impulse responses of the (negative) unemployment rate. Panel (a) displays the impulse response of the unemployment rate with respect to the aggregate supply shock, while panel (b) displays the impulse response of the unemployment rate with respect to the aggregate demand shock. Displayed are 95% normal approximation bootstrap intervals, calculated from 10,000 bootstrap replications. The estimated impulse responses have similar hump shapes with a peak around four quarters and are similar to those found by Blanchard and Quah (1989).

Let's examine and contrast panels (a) and (b) of Figure 15.4. The response to a supply shock (panel (a)) takes several quarters to take effect, peaks around 5 quarters, and then decays. The response to a demand

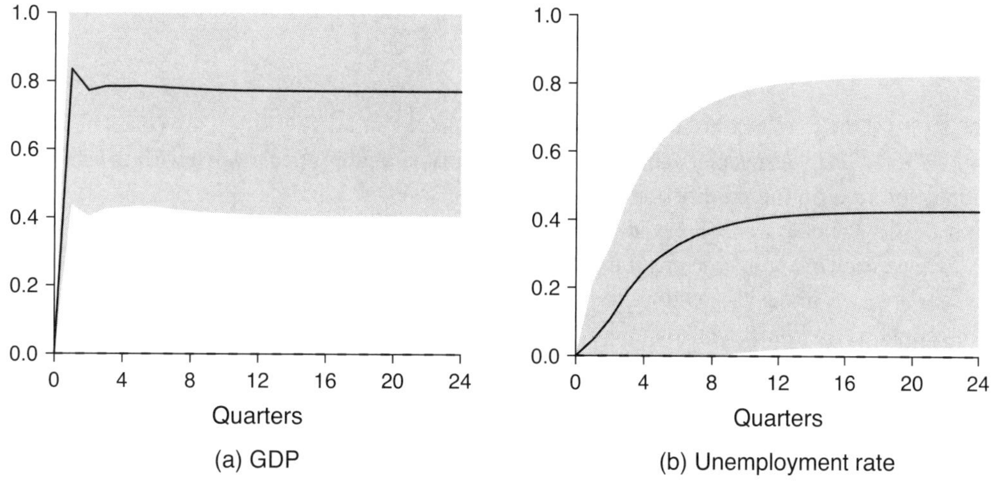

FIGURE 15.5 Forecast error decomposition, percent due to supply shock

shock (panel (b)) is more immediate, peaks around 4 quarters, and then decays. Both are near 0 by 6 years. The confidence intervals for the supply shock impulse responses are wider than those for the demand shocks, indicating that the estimates of the impulse responses due to supply shocks are not precisely estimated.

Figure 15.5 displays the estimated structural forecast error decompositions. Since there are only two errors, we only display the percentage squared error due to the supply shock. Panel (a) displays the forecast error decomposition for GDP, and panel (b) shows the forecast error decomposition for the unemployment rate. We can see that about 80% of the fluctuations in GDP are attributed to the supply shock. For the unemployment rate, the short-term fluctuations are mostly attributed to the demand shock, but the long-run impact is about 40% due to the supply shock. The confidence intervals are very wide, however, indicating that these estimates are not precise.

It is fascinating that the structural impulse response estimates shown here are nearly identical to those found by Blanchard and Quah (1989), even though we have used a considerably different sample period.

15.29 EXTERNAL INSTRUMENTS

Structural VARs can also be identified and estimated using **external instrumental variables**. This method is also called **Proxy SVARs**. Consider the three-variable system for the innovations:

$$e_{1t} + a_{12}e_{2t} + a_{13}e_{3t} = \varepsilon_{1t} \tag{15.26}$$

$$a_{21}e_{1t} + e_{2t} = \varepsilon_{2t} + b_{23}\varepsilon_{3t} = u_{2t} \tag{15.27}$$

$$a_{31}e_{1t} + e_{3t} = b_{32}\varepsilon_{2t} + \varepsilon_{3t} = u_{3t}. \tag{15.28}$$

In this system, we have used the normalization $b_{11} = b_{22} = b_{33} = 1$ rather than normalizing the variances of the shocks.

Suppose we have an external instrumental variable Z_t that satisfies the properties

$$\mathbb{E}\left[Z_t\varepsilon_{1t}\right] \neq 0 \tag{15.29}$$

$$\mathbb{E}\left[Z_t \varepsilon_{2t}\right] = 0 \tag{15.30}$$

$$\mathbb{E}\left[Z_t \varepsilon_{3t}\right] = 0. \tag{15.31}$$

Equation (15.29) is the relevance condition—that the instrument and the shock ε_{1t} are correlated. Equations (15.30) and (15.31) are the exogeneity condition—that the instrument is uncorrelated with the shocks ε_{2t} and ε_{3t}. Identification rests on the validity of these assumptions.

Suppose e_{1t}, e_{2t}, and e_{3t} were observed. Then the coefficient a_{21} in (15.27) can be estimated by instrumental variables regression of e_{2t} on e_{1t} using the instrumental variable Z_t. This is valid, because Z_t is uncorrelated with $u_{2t} = \varepsilon_{2t} + b_{23}\varepsilon_{3t}$ under the assumptions (15.30) and (15.31) yet is correlated with e_{1t} under (15.29). Given this estimator, we obtain a residual $\widehat{u}_{2t}$. Similarly, we can estimate a_{31} in (15.27) by instrumental variables regression of e_{3t} on e_{1t} using the instrumental variable Z_t and obtaining a residual $\widehat{u}_{3t}$. We can then estimate a_{12} and a_{13} in (15.26) by instrumental variables regression of e_{1t} on (e_{2t}, e_{3t}) using the instrumental variables $(\widehat{u}_{2t}, \widehat{u}_{3t})$. The latter are valid instruments because $\mathbb{E}\left[u_{2t}\varepsilon_{1t}\right] = 0$ and $\mathbb{E}\left[u_{3t}\varepsilon_{1t}\right] = 0$ as the structural errors are uncorrelated, and because (u_{2t}, u_{3t}) is correlated with (e_{2t}, e_{3t}) by construction. This regression also produces a residual $\widehat{\varepsilon}_{1t}$, which is an appropriate estimator for the shock ε_{1t}.

This estimation method is not specific to a three-variable system; it can be applied for any m. The identified coefficients are those in the first equation (15.26), the structural shock ε_{1t}, and the impacts (a_{21} and α_{31}) of this shock on the other variables. The other shocks, ε_{2t} and ε_{3t}, are not separately identified, and their correlation structure (b_{23} and b_{32}) is not identified. An exception arises when $m = 2$, in which case all coefficients and shocks are identified.

While e_{1t}, e_{2t}, and e_{3t} are not observed, we can replace their values by the residuals $\widehat{e}_{1t}$, $\widehat{e}_{2t}$, and $\widehat{e}_{3t}$ from the estimated VAR(p) model. All of the coefficient estimates are then two-step estimators with generated regressors. This substitution affects the asymptotic distribution, so conventional asymptotic standard errors should not be used. Bootstrap confidence intervals are appropriate.

The structure (15.26)–(15.28) is convenient, as four coefficients can be identified. Other structures can also be used. Consider the structure

$$e_{1t} = \varepsilon_{1t} + b_{12}\varepsilon_{2t} + b_{23}\varepsilon_{3t}$$

$$e_{2t} = b_{21}\varepsilon_{1t} + \varepsilon_{2t} + b_{23}\varepsilon_{3t}$$

$$e_{3t} = b_{31}\varepsilon_{1t} + b_{32}\varepsilon_{2t} + \varepsilon_{3t}.$$

If the same procedure is applied, we can identify the coefficients b_{21} and b_{31} and the shock ε_{1t} but no other coefficients or shocks. In this structure, the coefficients b_{12} and b_{23} cannot be separately identified, because the shocks ε_{2t} and ε_{3t} are not separately identified.

For more details, see Stock and Watson (2012) and Mertens and Ravn (2013).

15.30 DYNAMIC FACTOR MODELS

Dynamic factor models are increasingly popular in applied time series, in particular for forecasting. For a detailed review of the methods, see Stock and Watson (2016) and the references therein. For some of the foundational theory, see Bai (2003) and Bai and Ng (2002, 2006).

In Sections 11.13–11.16, we discussed the standard multifactor model (11.23):

$$X_t = \Lambda F_t + u_t \tag{15.32}$$

where X_t and u_t are $k \times 1$, Λ is $k \times r$ with $r < k$, and F_t is $r \times 1$. The elements of F_t are called the "common factors," as they affect all elements of X_t. The columns of Λ are called the "factor loadings." The variables u_t are the idiosyncratic errors. It is often assumed that the elements of X_t have been transformed to be mean 0 and have common variances.

In the time series case, it is natural to augment the model to allow for dynamic relationships. In particular, we would like to allow F_t and u_t to be serially correlated. It is convenient to consider VAR models that can be written using lag operator notation as

$$\boldsymbol{A}\,(\mathrm{L})\,F_t = v_t \tag{15.33}$$

$$\boldsymbol{B}\,(\mathrm{L})\,u_t = e_t \tag{15.34}$$

where $\boldsymbol{A}\,(\mathrm{L})$ and $\boldsymbol{B}\,(\mathrm{L})$ are lag polynomials with p and q lags, respectively. Equations (15.32)–(15.34) together make the standard **dynamic factor model**. To simplify the model and aid identification, further restrictions are often imposed, in particular, that the lag polynomial $\boldsymbol{B}\,(\mathrm{L})$ is diagonal.

Furthermore, we may wish to generalize (15.32) to allow F_t to impact X_t via a distributed lag relationship. This generalization can be written as

$$X_t = \Lambda\,(\mathrm{L})\,F_t + u_t \tag{15.35}$$

where $\Lambda\,(\mathrm{L})$ is an ℓth-order distributed lag of dimension $k \times r$. Equation (15.35), however, is not fundamentally different from (15.32). That is, if we define the stacked factor vector $\overline{F}_t = \left(F_t', F_{t-1}', \ldots, F_{t-\ell}'\right)'$, then (15.35) can be written in the form (15.32) with $\overline{F}_t$ replacing F_t and the matrix Λ replaced by $(\Lambda_1, \Lambda_2, \ldots, \Lambda_\ell)$. Hence we will focus on the standard model (15.32)–(15.34).

Define the inverse lag operators $\boldsymbol{D}\,(\mathrm{L}) = \boldsymbol{A}\,(\mathrm{L})^{-1}$ and $\boldsymbol{C}\,(\mathrm{L}) = \boldsymbol{B}\,(\mathrm{L})^{-1}$. Then by applying $\boldsymbol{C}\,(\mathrm{L})$ to (15.32) and $\boldsymbol{D}\,(\mathrm{L})$ to (15.33), we obtain

$$\begin{aligned}\boldsymbol{C}\,(\mathrm{L})\,X_t &= \boldsymbol{C}\,(\mathrm{L})\,\Lambda F_t + \boldsymbol{C}\,(\mathrm{L})\,u_t \\ &= \boldsymbol{C}\,(\mathrm{L})\,\Lambda \boldsymbol{D}\,(\mathrm{L})\,v_t + e_t \\ &= \Lambda\,(\mathrm{L})\,v_t + e_t\end{aligned}$$

where $\Lambda\,(\mathrm{L}) = \boldsymbol{C}\,(\mathrm{L})\,\Lambda\boldsymbol{D}\,(\mathrm{L})$. For simplicity, treat this lag polynomial as if it had ℓ lags. Using the same stacking trick from the previous paragraph and defining $V_t = \left(v_t', v_{t-1}', \ldots, v_{t-\ell}'\right)'$, we find that this model can be written as

$$\boldsymbol{C}\,(\mathrm{L})\,X_t = \boldsymbol{H}\,V_t + e_t \tag{15.36}$$

for some $k \times r\ell$ matrix $\boldsymbol{H}$. Equation (15.36) is known as the **static form** of the dynamic factor model. It shows that X_t can be written as a function of its own lags plus a linear function of the serially uncorrelated factors V_t and a serially uncorrelated error e_t.

The static form (15.36) is convenient, as factor regression can be used for estimation. The model is identical to factor regression with additional regressors, as described in Section 11.15. (The additional regressors are the lagged values of X_t.) That section describes how to estimate the coefficients and factors by iterating between multivariate least squares and factor regression.

To estimate the explicit dynamic model (15.32)–(15.34), state-space methods are convenient. For details and references, see Stock and Watson (2016).

The dynamic factor model (15.32)–(15.34) can be estimated in Stata using `dfactor`.

15.31 TECHNICAL PROOFS*

Proof of Theorem 15.6 Without loss of generality, assume $a_0 = 0$. By the Jordan matrix decomposition (see Section A.13), $\boldsymbol{A} = \boldsymbol{P}\boldsymbol{J}\boldsymbol{P}^{-1}$, where $\boldsymbol{J} = \operatorname{diag}\{\boldsymbol{J}_1, \dots, \boldsymbol{J}_r\}$ is in Jordan normal form. The dimension of each Jordan block $\boldsymbol{J}_i$ is determined by the multiplicity of the eigenvalues λ_i of $\boldsymbol{A}$. For unique eigenvalues λ_i, $\boldsymbol{J}_i = \lambda_i$. For eigenvalues λ_i with double multiplicity, the Jordan blocks take the form

$$\boldsymbol{J}_i = \begin{bmatrix} \lambda_i & 1 \\ 0 & \lambda_i \end{bmatrix}.$$

For eigenvalues with multiplicity $s > 2$, the Jordan blocks are $s \times s$ upper diagonal with the eigenvalue on the diagonal and 1 immediately above the diagonal (see A.7).

Define $X_t = \boldsymbol{P}^{-1} Y_t$ and $u_t = \boldsymbol{P}^{-1} e_t$, which satisfy $X_t = \boldsymbol{J} X_{t-1} + u_t$. Partition X_t and u_t conformably with $\boldsymbol{J}$. The ith set satisfies $X_{it} = \boldsymbol{J}_i X_{i,t-1} + u_{it}$. We now show that X_{it} is strictly stationary and ergodic, from which we deduce that $Y_t = \boldsymbol{P} X_t$ is strictly stationary and ergodic.

For single dimension blocks, $\boldsymbol{J}_i = \lambda_i$, so $X_{it} = \lambda_i X_{i,t-1} + u_{it}$, which is an AR(1) model with coefficient λ_i and innovation u_{it}. The assumptions imply $|\lambda_i| < 1$ and $\mathbb{E}|u_{it}| < \infty$, so the conditions of Theorem 14.21 are satisfied, implying that X_{it} is strictly stationary and ergodic.

For blocks with dimension two, by back-substitution, we find $X_{it} = \sum_{\ell=0}^{\infty} \boldsymbol{J}_i^{\ell} u_{i,t-\ell}$. By direct calculation, we find that

$$\boldsymbol{J}_i^{\ell} = \begin{bmatrix} \lambda_i^{\ell} & \ell\lambda_i^{\ell-1} \\ 0 & \lambda_i^{\ell} \end{bmatrix}.$$

Partitioning $X_{it} = (X_{1it}, X_{2it})$ and $u_{it} = (u_{1it}, u_{2it})$, this means that

$$X_{1it} = \sum_{\ell=0}^{\infty} \lambda_i^{\ell} u_{1i,t-\ell} + \sum_{\ell=0}^{\infty} \ell\lambda_i^{\ell} u_{2i,t-\ell}$$

$$X_{2it} = \sum_{\ell=0}^{\infty} \lambda_i^{\ell} u_{2i,t-\ell}.$$

The series $\sum_{\ell=0}^{\infty} \lambda_i^{\ell}$ and $\sum_{\ell=0}^{\infty} \ell\lambda_i^{\ell}$ are convergent by the ratio test (Theorem A.3 of *Probability and Statistics for Economists*), because $|\lambda_i| < 1$. Thus the above sums satisfy the conditions of Theorem 14.6 and so are strictly stationary and ergodic, as required.

Blocks with multiplicity $s > 2$ are handled by similar but more tedious calculations. ■

Proof of Theorem 15.8 The assumption that $\Sigma > 0$ means that if we regress Y_{1t} on $Y_{2t}, \dots, Y_{pt}$ and $Y_{t-1}, \dots, Y_{t-p}$, then the error will have positive variance. If $\boldsymbol{Q}$ is singular, then there is some γ such that $\gamma' \boldsymbol{Q} \gamma = 0$. As in the proof of Theorem 14.28, this means that the regression of Y_{1t} on $Y_{2t}, \dots, Y_{pt}, Y_{t-1}, \dots, Y_{t-p+1}$ has a zero variance. This is a contradiction. We conclude that $\boldsymbol{Q}$ is not singular. ■

Proof of Theorem 15.12 The first part of the theorem is established by back-substitution. Since Y_t is a VAR(p) process,

$$Y_{t+h} = a_0 + \boldsymbol{A}_1 Y_{t+h-1} + \boldsymbol{A}_2 Y_{t+h-2} + \cdots + \boldsymbol{A}_p Y_{t+h-p} + e_t.$$

We then substitute out the first lag. We find:

$$
\begin{aligned}
&Y_{t+h} \\
&= a_0 + A_1\left(a_0 + A_1 Y_{t+h-2} + A_2 Y_{t+h-3} + \cdots + A_p Y_{t+h-p-1} + e_{t-1}\right) + A_2 Y_{t+h-2} + \cdots + A_p Y_{t+h-p} + e_t \\
&= a_0 + A_1 a_0 + (A_1 A_1 + A_2)\, Y_{t+h-2} + (A_1 A_2 + A_3)\, Y_{t+h-3} + \cdots + A_p A_p Y_{t+h-p-1} + A_1 e_{t-1} + e_t.
\end{aligned}
$$

We continue making substitutions. With each substitution, the error increases its MA order. After $h-1$ substitutions, the equation takes the form (15.12) with u_t an MA(h-1) process.

To see that $\boldsymbol{B}_1 = \Theta_h$, notice that the deduction that u_t is an MA(h-1) process means that we can equivalently write (15.12) as

$$
Y_{t+h} = b_0 + \sum_{j=1}^{\infty} \boldsymbol{B}_j Y_{t+1-j} + u_t
$$

with $\boldsymbol{B}_j = 0$ for $j > p$. That is, the equation (15.12) includes all relevant lags. By the projection properties of regression coefficients, this means that the coefficient $\boldsymbol{B}_1$ is invariant to replacing the regressor Y_t by the innovation from its regression on the other lags. This is the VAR(p) model itself, which has innovation e_t. We have deduced that the coefficient $\boldsymbol{B}_1$ is equivalent to that in the regression

$$
Y_{t+h} = b_0 + \boldsymbol{B}_1 e_t + \sum_{j=2}^{\infty} \boldsymbol{B}_j Y_{t+1-j} + u_t.
$$

Notice that e_t is uncorrelated with the other regressors. Thus, $\boldsymbol{B}_1 = \frac{\partial}{\partial e_t'} \mathscr{P}_t\left[Y_{t+h}\right] = \Theta_h$, as claimed. This completes the proof. ■

15.32 EXERCISES

Exercise 15.1 Consider the VAR(1) model $Y_t = \boldsymbol{A} Y_{t-1} + e_t$. Assume e_t is i.i.d. For each specified matrix $\boldsymbol{A}$ below, check whether Y_t is strictly stationary. Use mathematical software to compute eigenvalues if needed.

(a) $\boldsymbol{A} = \begin{bmatrix} 0.7 & 0.2 \\ 0.2 & 0.7 \end{bmatrix}$

(b) $\boldsymbol{A} = \begin{bmatrix} 0.8 & 0.4 \\ 0.4 & 0.8 \end{bmatrix}$

(c) $\boldsymbol{A} = \begin{bmatrix} 0.8 & 0.4 \\ -0.4 & 0.8 \end{bmatrix}$

Exercise 15.2 Consider the VAR(2) model $Y_t = \boldsymbol{A}_1 Y_{t-1} + \boldsymbol{A}_2 Y_{t-2} + e_t$ with $\boldsymbol{A}_1 = \begin{bmatrix} 0.3 & 0.2 \\ 0.2 & 0.3 \end{bmatrix}$ and $\boldsymbol{A}_2 = \begin{bmatrix} 0.4 & -0.1 \\ -0.1 & 0.4 \end{bmatrix}$. Assume e_t is i.i.d. Is Y_t strictly stationary? Use mathematical software if needed.

Exercise 15.3 Suppose $Y_t = \boldsymbol{A} Y_{t-1} + u_t$ and $u_t = \boldsymbol{B} u_{t-1} + e_t$. Show that Y_t is a VAR(2), and derive the coefficient matrices and equation error.

Exercise 15.4 Suppose Y_{it}, $i = 1, \ldots, m$, are independent AR(p) processes. Derive the form of their joint VAR representation.

Exercise 15.5 For the VAR(1) model $Y_t = \boldsymbol{A}_1 Y_{t-1} + e_t$, find an explicit expression for the h-step moving average matrix Θ_h from (15.3).

Exercise 15.6 In the VAR(2) model $Y_t = \boldsymbol{A}_1 Y_{t-1} + \boldsymbol{A}_2 Y_{t-2} + e_t$, find explicit expressions for the moving average matrix Θ_h from (15.3) for $h = 1, \ldots, 4$.

Exercise 15.7 Derive a VAR(1) representation of a VAR(p) process analogous to equation (14.33) for autoregressions. Use this to derive an explicit formula for the h-step impulse response IRF(h) analogous to (14.42).

Exercise 15.8 Let $Y_t = (Y_{1t}, Y_{2t})'$ be 2×1, and consider a VAR(2) model. Suppose Y_{2t} does not Granger-cause Y_{1t}. What are the implications for the VAR coefficient matrices $\boldsymbol{A}_1$ and $\boldsymbol{A}_2$?

Exercise 15.9 Continuing the previous exercise, suppose that both Y_{2t} does not Granger-cause Y_{1t}, and Y_{1t} does not Granger-cause Y_{2t}. What are the implications for the VAR coefficient matrices $\boldsymbol{A}_1$ and $\boldsymbol{A}_2$?

Exercise 15.10 Suppose that you have 20 years of monthly observations on $m = 8$ variables. Your advisor recommends $p = 12$ lags to account for annual patterns. How many coefficients per equation will you be estimating? How many observations do you have? In this context, does it make sense to you to estimate a VAR(12) with all eight variables?

Exercise 15.11 Let $\widehat{e}_t$ be the least squares residuals from an estimated VAR, $\widehat{\Sigma}$ be the residual covariance matrix, and $\widehat{\boldsymbol{B}} = \operatorname{chol}(\widehat{\Sigma})$. Show that $\widehat{\boldsymbol{B}}$ can be calculated by recursive least squares using the residuals.

Exercise 15.12 Cholesky factorization

(a) Derive the Cholesky decomposition of the covariance matrix $\begin{bmatrix} \sigma_1^2 & \rho\sigma_1\sigma_2 \\ \rho\sigma_1\sigma_2 & \sigma_1^2 \end{bmatrix}$.

(b) Write the answer for the correlation matrix (the special case $\sigma_1^2 = 1$ and $\sigma_2^2 = 1$).

(c) Find an upper triangular decomposition for the correlation matrix. That is, find an upper-triangular matrix R that satisfies $RR' = \begin{bmatrix} 1 & \rho \\ \rho & 1 \end{bmatrix}$.

(d) Suppose $\Theta_h = \begin{bmatrix} 1 & 0 \\ 1 & 1 \end{bmatrix}$, $\sigma_1^2 = 1$, $\sigma_2^2 = 1$, and $\rho = 0.8$. Find the orthogonalized impulse response OIRF(h) using the Cholesky decomposition.

(e) Suppose that the ordering of the variables is reversed. This is equivalent to using the upper triangular decomposition from part (c). Calculate the orthogonalized impulse response OIRF(h).

(f) Compare the two orthogonalized impulse responses.

Exercise 15.13 You read an empirical paper that estimates a VAR in a listed set of variables and displays estimated OIRFs. No comment is made in the paper about the ordering or the identification of the system, and you have no reason to believe that the order used is "standard" in the literature. How should you interpret the estimated impulse response functions?

Exercise 15.14 Use the quarterly series *gdpc1* (real GDP), *gdpctpi* (GDP price deflator), and *fedfunds* (fed funds interest rate) from `FRED-QD`. Transform the first two into growth rates as in Section 15.13. Estimate the same three-variable VAR(6) using the same ordering. The identification strategy discussed in Section 15.23 specifies the supply shock as the orthogonalized shock to the GDP equation. Calculate the IRF of GDP, the price level, and the Fed funds rate with respect to this supply shock. For the first two variables, this will require calculating the CIRF. (Explain why.) Comment on the estimated functions.

Exercise 15.15 Use the `Kilian2009` dataset, which has the variables *oil* (oil production), *output* (global economic activity), and *price* (price of crude oil). Estimate an orthogonalized VAR(4) using the same ordering as in Kilian (2009), as described in Section 15.24. (As described in that section, multiply "oil" by -1, so that all shocks increase prices.) Estimate the impulse response of output with respect to the three shocks. Comment on the estimated functions.

Exercise 15.16 Use the monthly series *permit* (building permits), *houst* (housing starts), and *realln* (real estate loans) from FRED-MD. The listed ordering is motivated by transaction timing. A developer is required to obtain a building permit before starting to build a house (the latter is known as a "housing start"). A real estate loan is obtained when the house is purchased.

(a) Transform *realln* into growth rates (first difference of logs).

(b) Select an appropriate lag order for the three-variable system by comparing the AIC of VARs of order 1 through 8.

(c) Estimate the VAR model, and plot the IRFs of housing starts with respect to the three shocks.

(d) Interpret your findings.

Exercise 15.17 Consider the quarterly series *gpdic1* (real gross private domestic investment), *gdpctpi* (GDP price deflator), *gdpc1* (real GDP), and *fedfunds* (fed funds interest rate) from `FRED-QD`. Transform the first three into logs (e.g., $gdp = 100\log(gdpc1)$). Consider a structural VAR based on short-run restrictions. Use a structure of the form $\boldsymbol{A}e_t = \varepsilon_t$. Impose the restrictions that the first three variables do not react to the fed funds rate, that investment does not respond to prices, and that prices do not respond to investment. Finally, impose the condition that investment is short-run unit elastic with respect to GDP (in the equation for investment, the $\boldsymbol{A}$ coefficient on GDP is -1).

(a) Write down the matrix $\boldsymbol{A}$ similar to (15.22), imposing the identifying constraints as defined above.

(b) Is the model identified? Is there a condition for identification? Explain.

(c) In this model, are output and price simultaneous, or are they recursive as in the example described in Section 15.23?

(d) Estimate the structural VAR using six lags or a different number of your choosing (justify your choice) and include an exogenous time trend. Report your estimates of the $\boldsymbol{A}$ matrix. Can you interpret the coefficients?

(e) Estimate and report the following three IRFs:
   1. The effect of the fed funds rate on GDP.
   2. The effect of the GDP shock on GDP.
   3. The effect of the GDP shock on prices.

Exercise 15.18 Consider the `Kilian2009` dataset, which has the variables *oil* (oil production), *output* (global economic activity), and *price* (price of crude oil). Consider a structural VAR based on short-run restrictions. Use a structure of the form $\boldsymbol{A}e_t = \varepsilon_t$. Impose the restrictions that oil production does not respond to output or oil prices, and that output does not respond to oil production. The last restriction can be motivated by the observation that supply disruptions take more than a month to reach the retail market, so the effect on economic activity is similarly delayed by one month.

(a) Write down the matrix $\boldsymbol{A}$ similar to (15.22), imposing the identifying constraints as defined above.
(b) Is the model identified? Is there a condition for identification? Explain.
(c) Estimate the structural VAR using four lags or a different number of your choosing (justify your choice). (As described in Section 15.24, multiply "oil" by -1, so that all shocks increase prices.) Report your estimates of the $\boldsymbol{A}$ matrix. Can you interpret the coefficients?
(d) Estimate the impulse response of oil price with respect to the three shocks. Comment on the estimated functions.

Exercise 15.19 Consider the quarterly series *gdpc1* (real GDP), *m1realx* (real M1 money stock), and *cpiaucsl* (CPI) from `FRED-QD`. Create nominal M1 (multiply *m1realx* times *cpiaucsl*), and transform real GDP and nominal M1 to growth rates. The hypothesis of monetary neutrality is that the nominal money supply has no effect on real outcomes, such as GDP. Strict monetary neutrality states that there is no short- or long-term effect. Long-run neutrality states that there is no long-term effect.

(a) To test strict neutrality, use a Granger-causality test. Regress GDP growth on four lags of GDP growth and four lags of money growth. Test the hypothesis that the four money lags jointly have coeffficients of 0. Use robust standard errors. Interpret the results.
(b) To test long-run neutrality, test whether the sum of the four coefficients on money growth equals 0. Interpret the results.
(c) Estimate a structural VAR in real GDP growth and nominal money growth, imposing the long-run neutrality of money. Explain your method.
(d) Report estimates of the impulse responses of the levels of GDP and nominal money to the two shocks. Interpret the results.

Exercise 15.20 Shapiro and Watson (1988) estimate a structural VAR imposing long-run constraints. Replicate a simplified version of their model. Take the quarterly series *hoanbs* (hours worked, nonfarm business sector), *gdpc1* (real GDP), and *gdpctpi* (GDP deflator) from `FRED-QD`. Transform the first two to growth rates, and for the third (GDP deflator) take the second difference of the logarithm (differenced inflation). Shapiro and Watson estimate a structural model imposing the constraints that labor supply hours are long-run unaffected by output and inflation, and GDP is long-run unaffected by demand shocks. This implies a recursive ordering in the variables for a long-run restriction.

(a) Write down the matrix $\boldsymbol{C}$ as in (15.24), imposing the identifying constraints as defined above.
(b) Is the model identified?
(c) Use the AIC to select the number of lags for a VAR.
(d) Estimate the structural VAR. Report the estimated $\boldsymbol{C}$ matrix. Can you interpret the coefficients?
(e) Estimate the structural impulse responses of the level of GDP with respect to the three shocks. Interpret the results.

CHAPTER 16

NONSTATIONARY TIME SERIES

16.1 INTRODUCTION

At the beginning of Chapter 14, we displayed a set of economic time series. Several (real GDP, exchange rate, interest rate, crude oil price) did not appear to be stationary. In Section 14.23, we introduced the nonstationary unit root process, which is an autoregressive process with an autoregressive root at unity. Plots of two simulated examples (Figure 14.5) displayed time-paths with wandering behavior similar to the economic time series. This suggests that perhaps a unit root autoregression is a reasonable model for these series. In this chapter, we explore econometric estimation and inference for nonstationary unit root time series.

16.2 PARTIAL SUM PROCESS AND FUNCTIONAL CONVERGENCE

Consider the multivariate random walk

$$Y_t = Y_{t-1} + e_t$$

where $(e_t, \mathscr{F}_t)$ is a vector MDS with finite covariance matrix Σ. By back-substitution, we find $Y_t = Y_0 + S_t$, where

$$S_t = \sum_{i=1}^{t} e_i$$

is the cumulative sum of the errors up to time t. We call S_t a **partial sum process.**

The time index t ranges from 0 to n. Write[1] $t = \lfloor nr \rfloor$ as a fraction r of the sample size n. This allows us to write $S_{\lfloor nr \rfloor}$ as a function of the fraction r. Divide by $\sqrt{n}$ so that the variance is stabilized. With these modifications, we define the standardized partial sum process:

$$S_n(r) = \frac{1}{\sqrt{n}} S_{\lfloor nr \rfloor} = \frac{1}{\sqrt{n}} \sum_{t=1}^{\lfloor nr \rfloor} e_t.$$

The random process $S_n(r)$ is a scaled version of the time series Y_t and is a function of the sample fraction $r \in [0, 1]$. It is a stochastic process, meaning that it is a random function. For any finite n, $S_n(r)$ is a step function with n jumps.

Consider the behavior of $S_n(r)$ as n increases. Its largest discrete jump equals $n^{-1/2} \max_{1 \le t \le n} \|e_t\|$. Theorem 6.15 shows that this is $o_p(1)$, which suggests that the jumps in $S_n(r)$ asymptotically vanish. We would like to find its asymptotic distribution. We expect the limit distribution to be a stochastic process as well.

[1] The notation $\lfloor x \rfloor$ means "round down to the nearest integer."

To find this distribution, we need to define the asymptotic distribution of a random function. The primary tool is the functional central limit theorem (FCLT) which is a component of empirical process theory (see Chapter 18 of *Probability and Statistics for Economists*). It turns out that the FCLT depends on how we measure the difference between two functions. The most commonly used measure is the **uniform metric**. On the space of functions from $[0, 1]$ to $\mathbb{R}^m$, it is

$$\rho(\nu_1, \nu_2) = \sup_{0\le r\le 1} \|\nu_1(r) - \nu_2(r)\|.$$

Convergence in distribution for random processes (e.g., Definition 18.6 of *Probability and Statistics for Economists*) is defined with respect to a specific metric. I won't repeat the details here, but the important consequence is that continuity is defined with respect to this metric, and this impacts applications such as the continuous mapping theorem (CMT).

The **Functional Central Limit Theorem** (FCLT; Theorem 18.9 of *Probability and Statistics for Economists*) states that $S_n(r) \xrightarrow[d]{} S(r)$ as a function over $r \in [0, 1]$ if two conditions hold:

1. The limit distributions of $S_n(r)$ coincide with those of $S(r)$.
2. $S_n(r)$ is asymptotically equicontinuous.

The first condition means that for any fixed $r_1, \ldots, r_m$, $(S_n(r_1), \ldots, S_n(r_m)) \xrightarrow[d]{} (S(r_1), \ldots, S(r_m))$. The second condition is technical but essentially requires that $S_n(r)$ is approximately continuous with respect to the uniform metric in large samples.

Let now characterize the limit distributions of $S_n(r)$. There are three important properties:

1. $S_n(0) = 0$.
2. For any r, $S_n(r) \xrightarrow[d]{} \mathrm{N}(0, r\Sigma)$.
3. For $r_1 < r_2$, $S_n(r_1)$ and $S_n(r_2) - S_n(r_1)$ are asymptotically independent.

The first property follows from the definition of $S_n(r)$. For the second, set $N = \lfloor nr \rfloor$. For $r > 0$, $N \to \infty$ as $n \to \infty$. The MDS CLT (Theorem 14.11) implies that

$$S_n(r) = \sqrt{\frac{\lfloor nr \rfloor}{n}} \frac{1}{\sqrt{N}} \sum_{t=1}^{N} e_t \xrightarrow[d]{} \sqrt{r}\mathrm{N}(0, \Sigma) = \mathrm{N}(0, r\Sigma)$$

as claimed. For the third property, the assumption that e_t is a MDS implies that $S_n(r_1)$ and $S_n(r_2) - S_n(r_1)$ are uncorrelated. An extension of the previous asymptotic argument shows that they are jointly asymptotically normal with a 0 covariance and hence are asymptotically independent.

The above three limit properties of $S_n(r)$ are asymptotic versions of the definition of Brownian motion.

Definition 16.1 A vector **Brownian motion** $B(r)$ for $r \ge 0$ is defined by the properties:

1. $B(0) = 0$.
2. For any r, $B(r) \sim \mathrm{N}(0, r\Sigma)$.
3. For any $r_1 \le r_2$, $B(r_1)$ and $B(r_2) - B(r_1)$ are independent.

We call Σ the covariance matrix of $B(r)$. If $\Sigma = \boldsymbol{I}_m$, we say that $B(r)$ is a **standard Brownian motion** and denote it by $W(r)$. It satisfies $B(r) = \Sigma^{1/2} W(r)$.

A Brownian motion $B(r)$ is continuous with probability 1 but is nowhere differentiable. In physics, Brownian motion is used to describe the movement of particles. The wandering properties of particles suspended in liquid was described as far back as the Roman poet Lucretius (*On the Nature of the Universe*, 55 BCE). The name "Brownian motion" credits the pioneering observational studies of botanist Robert Brown. The mathematical process is often called a **Wiener process**, crediting the work of Norbert Wiener.

The above discussion has shown that the limit distributions of the partial sum process $S_n(r)$ coincide with those of Brownian motion $B(r)$. In Section 16.22, we demonstrate that $S_n(r)$ is asymptotically equicontinuous (see the proof of Theorem 16.1 in that section). Together with the FCLT, this establishes that $S_n(r)$ converges in distribution to $B(r)$.

Theorem 16.1 Weak Convergence of Partial Sum Process. If $(e_t, \mathscr{F}_t)$ is a strictly stationary and ergodic MDS and $\Sigma = \mathbb{E}\left[e_t e_t'\right] < \infty$, then as a function over $r \in [0,1]$, $S_n(r) \underset{d}{\longrightarrow} B(r)$, a Brownian motion with covariance matrix Σ.

We extend Theorem 16.1 to serially correlated processes in Section 16.4.

Let's connect our analysis of $S_n(r)$ with the random walk series Y_t. Since $Y_t = Y_0 + S_t$, we find

$$\frac{1}{\sqrt{n}} Y_{\lfloor nr \rfloor} = S_n(r) + \frac{1}{\sqrt{n}} Y_0.$$

The second term is $o_p(1)$ when Y_0 is finite with probability 1. Thus under this assumption, $n^{-1/2} Y_{\lfloor nr \rfloor} = S_n(r) + o_p(1) \underset{d}{\longrightarrow} B$. We will frequently implicitly assume $Y_0 = 0$ to simplify the notation, as the case with $Y_0 \neq 0$ does not fundamentally change the analysis.

16.3 BEVERIDGE-NELSON DECOMPOSITION

Section 16.2 focused on random walk processes. A unit root process more broadly is an autoregression with a single root at unity, which means that the differenced process ΔY_t is serially correlated but stationary.

Beveridge and Nelson (1981) introduced a clever way to decompose a unit root process into a permanent (random walk) component and a transitory (stationary) component. This allows a straightforward generalization of Theorem 16.1 to incorporate serial correlation.

Recall that a stationary process has a Wold representation $\Delta Y_t = \Theta(\mathrm{L}) e_t$, where $\Theta(z) = \sum_{j=0}^{\infty} \Theta_j z^j$.

Assumption 16.1 ΔY_t is strictly stationary with no deterministic component, mean 0, and finite covariance matrix Σ. The coefficients of its Wold representation $\Delta Y_t = \Theta(\mathrm{L}) e_t$ satisfy

$$\sum_{j=0}^{\infty} \left\| \sum_{\ell=j+1}^{\infty} \Theta_\ell \right\| < \infty. \tag{16.1}$$

The condition (16.1) on the coefficients is stronger than absolute summability but holds (for example) if ΔY_t is generated by a stationary AR process. It is similar to the condition used for the autoregressive Wold representation (Theorem 14.19).

Consider the following factorization of the lag polynomial,

$$\Theta(z) = \Theta(1) + (1-z)\Theta^*(z) \tag{16.2}$$

where $\Theta(1) = \sum_{\ell=0}^{\infty} \Theta_\ell$, and $\Theta^*(z)$ is the lag polynomial

$$\Theta^*(z) = \sum_{j=0}^{\infty} \Theta_j^* z^j \tag{16.3}$$

$$\Theta_j^* = -\sum_{\ell=j+1}^{\infty} \Theta_\ell. \tag{16.4}$$

At the end of this section we demonstrate (16.2)–(16.4). Assumption (16.1) is the same as $\sum_{j=0}^{\infty} \left\| \Theta_j^* \right\| < \infty$, which implies that $U_t = \Theta^*(\mathrm{L})e_t$ is convergent, strictly stationary, and ergodic (by Theorem 15.4).

The factorization (16.2) means that we can write

$$\Delta Y_t = \xi_t + U_t - U_{t-1}$$

where $\xi_t = \Theta(1)e_t$. This decomposes ΔY_t into the innovation e_t plus the first-difference of the stochastic process U_t. Summing the differences, we find

$$Y_t = S_t + U_t + V_0$$

where $S_t = \sum_{i=1}^{t} \xi_t$ and $V_0 = Y_0 - U_0$. This decomposes the unit root process Y_t into the random walk S_t, the stationary process U_t, and an initial condition V_0.

We have established the following.

Theorem 16.2 Under Assumption 16.1, (16.2)–(16.4) hold with $\sum_{j=0}^{\infty} \left\| \Theta_j^* \right\| < \infty$. The process ΔY_t satisfies

$$\Delta Y_t = \xi_t + U_t - U_{t-1}$$

and

$$Y_t = S_t + U_t + V_0$$

where $S_t = \sum_{i=1}^{t} \xi_t$ is a random walk, ξ_t is white noise with variance $\Theta(1)\Sigma\Theta(1)'$, U_t is strictly stationary, and V_0 is an initial condition.

Beveridge and Nelson (1981) called S_t the **permanent** (trend) component of Y_t and U_t the **transitory** component. They called S_t the permanent component, as it determines the long-run behavior of Y_t.

As an example, take the MA(1) case $\Delta Y_t = e_t + \Theta_1 e_{t-1}$. This has decomposition $\Delta Y_t = (\boldsymbol{I}_m + \Theta_1)e_t - \Theta_1(e_t - e_{t-1})$. In this case, $U_t = -\Theta_1 e_t$.

The Beveridge-Nelson decomposition of a series is unique, but it is not the only way to construct a permanent/transitory decomposition. The Beveridge-Nelson decomposition has the characteristic that the innovations driving the permanent and transitory components S_t and U_t are perfectly correlated. Other decompositions do not use this restriction.

Let us close this section by verifying (16.2)–(16.4). Observe that the right side of (16.2) is

$$\begin{aligned}\sum_{j=0}^{\infty}\Theta_j-\sum_{j=0}^{\infty}\sum_{\ell=j+1}^{\infty}\Theta_\ell z^j(1-z)&=\sum_{j=0}^{\infty}\Theta_j-\sum_{j=0}^{\infty}\sum_{\ell=j+1}^{\infty}\Theta_\ell z^j+\sum_{j=0}^{\infty}\sum_{\ell=j+1}^{\infty}\Theta_\ell z^{j+1}\\&=\Theta_0-\sum_{j=1}^{\infty}\sum_{\ell=j+1}^{\infty}\Theta_\ell z^j+\sum_{j=1}^{\infty}\sum_{\ell=j}^{\infty}\Theta_\ell z^j\\&=\Theta_0+\sum_{j=1}^{\infty}\Theta_j z^j\end{aligned}$$

which is $\Theta(z)$, as claimed.

16.4 FUNCTIONAL CLT

Theorem 16.1 showed that a random walk process converges in distribution to a Brownian motion. We now extend this result to the case of a unit root process with correlated differences. Under Assumption 16.1, a unit root process can be written as $Y_t=S_t+U_t+V_0$, where $S_t=\sum_{i=1}^{t}\xi_t$. Define the scaled processes $Z_n(r)=n^{-1/2}Y_{\lfloor nr\rfloor}$ and $S_n(r)=n^{-1/2}S_{\lfloor nr\rfloor}$. We find

$$Z_n(r)=S_n(r)+\frac{1}{\sqrt{n}}V_0+\frac{1}{\sqrt{n}}U_{\lfloor nr\rfloor}.$$

If the errors e_t are a MDS with covariance matrix Σ, then by Theorem 16.1, $S_n(r)\underset{d}{\longrightarrow}B(r)$, a vector Brownian motion with covariance matrix $\Omega=\Theta(1)\Sigma\Theta(1)'$. The initial condition $n^{-1/2}V_0$ is $o_p(1)$. The third term, $n^{-1/2}U_{\lfloor nr\rfloor}$, is $o_p(1)$ if $\sup_{1\le t\le n}\left|\frac{1}{\sqrt{n}}U_t\right|=o_p(1)$, which holds under Theorem 6.15 if U_t has a finite variance. We now show that this holds under Assumption 16.1. The latter implies that $\sum_{j=0}^{\infty}\left\|\Theta_j^*\right\|<\infty$, as discussed before the statement of Theorem 16.2. Thus,

$$\|\mathrm{var}\,[U_t]\|=\left\|\sum_{j=0}^{\infty}\Theta_j^*\Sigma\Theta_j^{*\prime}\right\|\le\|\Sigma\|\sum_{j=0}^{\infty}\left\|\Theta_j^*\right\|^2\le\|\Sigma\|\max_j\left\|\Theta_j^*\right\|\sum_{j=0}^{\infty}\left\|\Theta_j^*\right\|<\infty$$

as needed.

Combining these results, we find that

$$Z_n(r)=S_n(r)+o_p(1)\underset{d}{\longrightarrow}B(r).$$

The variance of the limiting process is $\Omega=\Theta(1)\Sigma\Theta(1)'$. This is the "long-run variance" of ΔY_t.

Theorem 16.3 Under Assumption 16.1 and in addition assuming that $(e_t,\mathscr{F}_t)$ is a MDS with covariance matrix Σ, then as a function over $r\in[0,1]$, $Z_n(r)\underset{d}{\longrightarrow}B(r)$, a vector Brownian motion with covariance matrix Ω.

Our derivation used the assumption that the linear projection errors are a MDS. This is not essential for the basic result; the FCLT holds under a variety of dependence conditions. A more flexible version can be stated using mixing conditions.

Theorem 16.4 If ΔY_t is strictly stationary, $\mathbb{E}[\Delta Y_t] = 0$, with mixing coefficients $\alpha(\ell)$, and for some $r > 2$, $\mathbb{E}\|\Delta Y_t\|^r < \infty$ and $\sum_{\ell=1}^{\infty} \alpha(\ell)^{1-2/r} < \infty$, then as a function over $r \in [0,1]$, $Z_n(r) \underset{d}{\longrightarrow} B(r)$, a vector Brownian motion with covariance matrix

$$\Omega = \sum_{\ell=-\infty}^{\infty} \mathbb{E}[\Delta Y_t \Delta Y_{t-\ell}]. \tag{16.5}$$

For a proof, see Davidson (1994, theorems 31.5 and 31.15). Interestingly, Theorem 16.4 employs exactly the same assumptions as for Theorem 14.15 (the CLT for mixing processes). Thus we obtain the stronger result (the FCLT) without stronger assumptions.

The covariance matrix Ω appearing in (16.5) is the **long-run covariance matrix** of ΔY_t as defined in Section 14.13. It is useful to observe that we can decompose the long-run variance as $\Omega = \Sigma + \Lambda + \Lambda'$, where $\Sigma = \text{var}[\Delta Y_t]$, and

$$\Lambda = \sum_{\ell=1}^{\infty} \mathbb{E}\left[\Delta Y_t \Delta Y_{t-\ell}'\right].$$

This decomposes the long-run variance of ΔY_t into its static (one-period) variance Σ and a sum of covariances Λ. The matrix Λ is not symmetric.

16.5 ORDERS OF INTEGRATION

Consider a univariate series Y_t. Theorems 16.3 and 16.4 show that if ΔY_t is stationary and mean 0, then the level process Y_t, suitably scaled, is asymptotically a Brownian motion with variance ω^2. For this theory to be meaningful, this variance should be strictly positive definite. To see why this is a potential restriction, suppose that $Y_t = a(\mathrm{L})e_t$, where the coefficients of $a(z)$ are absolutely convergent and e_t is i.i.d. $(0, \sigma^2)$. Then $\Delta Y_t = b(\mathrm{L})e_t$, where $b(z) = (1-z)a(z)$, so $\omega^2 = b(1)^2\sigma^2 = 0$. That is, ΔY_t has a long-run variance of 0. We call the process ΔY_t **over-differenced**, since Y_t is strictly stationary and does not require differencing to achieve stationarity.

To meaningfully differentiate between processes that require differencing to achieve stationarity, we use the following definition.

Definition 16.2 Order of Integration.

1. $Y_t \in \mathbb{R}$ is **Integrated of Order** 0, written $I(0)$, if Y_t is weakly stationary with positive long-run variance.
2. $Y_t \in \mathbb{R}$ is **Integrated of Order** d, written $I(d)$, if $u_t = \Delta^d Y_t$ is $I(0)$.

$I(0)$ processes are stationary processes that are not overdifferenced. $I(1)$ processes include random walks and unit root processes. $I(2)$ processes require double differencing to achieve stationarity. $I(-1)$ processes are stationary, but their cumulative sums are also stationary and are therefore overdifferenced stationary processes.

Many macroeconomic time series in log-levels are potentially $I(1)$ processes. Economic time series that are potentially $I(2)$ are log price indices, because their first differences (inflation rates) are potentially nonstationary proceses. In this textbook, we focus on integer-valued orders of integration, but fractional d are also well defined. In most applications, economists presume that economic series are either $I(0)$ or $I(1)$ and often use the shorthand "integrated" to refer to $I(1)$ series.

The long-run variance of ARMA processes is straightforward to calculate. As we have seen, if $\Delta Y_t = b(\mathrm{L})e_t$, where e_t is white noise with variance σ^2, then $\omega^2 = b(1)^2\sigma^2$. Now suppose $a(\mathrm{L})\Delta Y_t = e_t$, where $a(z)$ is invertible. Then $b(z) = a(z)^{-1}$ and $\omega^2 = \sigma^2/a(1)^2$. For an ARMA process $a(\mathrm{L})\Delta Y_t = b(\mathrm{L})e_t$ with invertible $a(z)$, then $\omega^2 = \sigma^2 b(1)^2/a(1)^2$. Hence, if ΔY_t satisfies the ARMA process $a(\mathrm{L})\Delta Y_t = b(\mathrm{L})e_t$, then Y_t is $I(1)$ if $a(z)$ is invertible and $b(1) \neq 0$.

Consider vector processes. The long-run covariance matrix of $\Delta Y_t = \Theta(\mathrm{L})e_t$ is $\Omega = \Theta(1)\Sigma\Theta(1)'$. The long-run covariance matrix of $\boldsymbol{A}(\mathrm{L})\Delta Y_t = e_t$ is $\Omega = \boldsymbol{A}(1)^{-1}\Sigma\boldsymbol{A}(1)^{-1\prime}$. It is conventional to describe the vector ΔY_t as $I(0)$ if each element of ΔY_t is $I(0)$, but this allows its covariance matrix to be singular. To exclude the latter case, we introduce the following definition.

Definition 16.3 The vector process Y_t is **full rank** $I(0)$ if its long-run covariance matrix Ω is positive definite.

16.6 MEANS, LOCAL MEANS, AND TRENDS

Theorem 16.4 shows that $Z_n(r) \underset{d}{\longrightarrow} B(r)$. The CMT shows that if a function $f(x)$ is continuous,[2] then $f(Z_n) \underset{d}{\longrightarrow} f(B)$. This can be used to obtain the asymptotic distribution of many statistics of interest. Simple examples are $Z_n(r)^2 \underset{d}{\longrightarrow} B(r)^2$ and $\int_0^1 Z_n(r)dr \underset{d}{\longrightarrow} \int_0^1 B(r)dr$. The latter produces the asymptotic distribution for the sample mean, as we now show.

Let $\overline{Y}_n = n^{-1}\sum_{t=1}^n Y_t$ be the sample mean. For simplicity, assume $Y_0 = 0$. Note that for $r \in \left[\frac{t}{n}, \frac{t+1}{n}\right)$,

$$\frac{1}{n^{1/2}} Y_t = Z_n(r) = n\int_{t/n}^{(t+1)/n} Z_n(r)dr.$$

Taking the average for $t = 0$ to $n-1$, we find

$$\frac{1}{n^{1/2}}\overline{Y}_n = \frac{1}{n^{3/2}}\sum_{t=0}^{n-1} Y_t = \sum_{t=0}^{n-1}\int_{t/n}^{(t+1)/n} Z_n(r)dr = \int_0^1 Z_n(r)dr.$$

This is the integral (or average) of $Z_n(r)$ over $[0, 1]$.

The CMT can be applied.[3] The above expression converges in distribution to the random variable $\int_0^1 B(r)dr$. This is the average of the Brownian motion over $[0, 1]$.

Now consider subsample means. Let $\overline{Y}_{1n} = (n/2)^{-1}\sum_{t=0}^{n/2-1} Y_t$ and $\overline{Y}_{2n} = (n/2)^{-1}\sum_{t=n/2}^{n-1} Y_t$ be the sample means on the first half and second half of the sample, respectively. By a similar analysis as for

[2] With respect to the uniform metric ρ.

[3] The integral $f(g) = \int_0^1 g(r)dr$ is a continuous function of g with respect to the uniform metric. (Small changes in g result in small changes in f.)

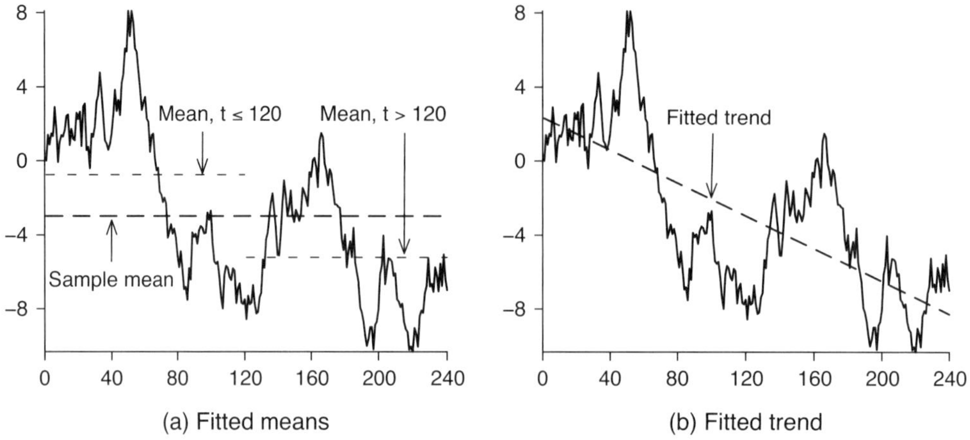

FIGURE 16.1 Random walk with fitted mean, subsample means, and trend

the full-sample mean,

$$\frac{1}{n^{1/2}}\overline{Y}_{1n} = \frac{2}{n^{3/2}}\sum_{t=0}^{n/2-1} Y_t = 2\int_0^{1/2} Z_n(r)dr \underset{d}{\longrightarrow} 2\int_0^{1/2} B(r)dr$$

$$\frac{1}{n^{1/2}}\overline{Y}_{2n} = \frac{2}{n^{3/2}}\sum_{t=n/2}^{n-1} Y_t = 2\int_{1/2}^{1} Z_n(r)dr \underset{d}{\longrightarrow} 2\int_{1/2}^{1} B(r)dr$$

which are the averages of $B(r)$ over the regions $[0, 1/2]$ and $[1/2, 1]$. These are distinct random variables. This gives rise to the prediction that if Y_t is a unit root process, sample averages will not be constant (even in large samples) and will vary across subsamples.

Furthermore, observe that the limit distributions were obtained after dividing by $n^{1/2}$. Thus without this standardization, the sample mean would not be bounded in probability, which implies that the sample mean can be (randomly) large. This leads to the rather peculiar property that sample means will be large, random, and uninformative about population parameters, so interpreting simple statistics such as means is treacherous when the series may be a unit root process.

To illustrate, Figure 16.1(a) displays a simulated random walk with $n = 240$ observations. Also plotted is the sample mean $\overline{Y}_n = -2.98$, along with the subsample means $\overline{Y}_{1n} = -0.75$ and $\overline{Y}_{2n} = -5.21$. As predicted, the mean and subsample means are large, variable, and uninformative regarding the population mean.

Now consider a linear regression of Y_t on a linear time trend. The model for estimation is

$$Y_t = \beta_0 + \beta_1 t + e_t = X_t'\beta + e_t$$

where $X_t = (1, t)'$. Again for simplicity, assume that $Y_0 = 0$. Take the least squares estimator $\widehat{\beta}$. Theorem 14.36 shows that

$$\frac{1}{n^2}\sum_{t=1}^{n} t \to \int_0^1 r dr = \frac{1}{2}$$

$$\frac{1}{n^3}\sum_{t=1}^{n} t^2 \to \int_0^1 r^2 dr = \frac{1}{3}.$$

Define $D_n = \begin{bmatrix} 1 & 0 \\ 0 & n \end{bmatrix}$. We calculate that

$$D_n^{-1}\frac{1}{n}\sum_{t=1}^{n} X_t X_t' D_n^{-1} = \begin{bmatrix} \frac{1}{n}\sum_{t=1}^{n} 1 & \frac{1}{n^2}\sum_{t=1}^{n} t \\ \frac{1}{n^2}\sum_{t=1}^{n} t & \frac{1}{n^3}\sum_{t=1}^{n} t^2 \end{bmatrix} \rightarrow \begin{bmatrix} 1 & \int_0^1 r dr \\ \int_0^1 r dr & \int_0^1 r^2 dr \end{bmatrix} = \int_0^1 X(r)X(r)' dr$$

where $X(r) = (1, r)$.

An application of the CMT and Theorem 16.1 yields

$$D_n^{-1}\frac{1}{n^{3/2}}\sum_{t=1}^{n} X_t Y_t = \int_0^1 X(r) Z_n(r) dr \underset{d}{\longrightarrow} \int_0^1 X(r)B(r)dr.$$

We obtain

$$\begin{aligned} D_n n^{-1/2}\widehat{\beta} &= D_n n^{-1/2}\left(\sum_{t=1}^{n} X_t X_t'\right)^{-1}\left(\sum_{t=1}^{n} X_t Y_t\right) \\ &= \left(D_n^{-1}\frac{1}{n}\sum_{t=1}^{n} X_t X_t' D_n^{-1}\right)^{-1}\left(D_n^{-1}\frac{1}{n^{3/2}}\sum_{t=1}^{n} X_t Y_t\right) \\ &\underset{d}{\longrightarrow} \left(\int_0^1 X(r)X(r)' dr\right)^{-1}\left(\int_0^1 X(r)B(r)dr\right). \end{aligned}$$

Thus the estimator $\widehat{\beta}$ has an asymptotic distribution that is a transformation of the Brownian motion $B(r)$. For compactness we often write the final expression as $\left(\int_0^1 XX'\right)^{-1}\left(\int_0^1 XB\right)$.

To illustrate, Figure 16.1(b) displays the random walk from panel (a) along with a fitted trend line. The fitted trend appears large and substantial. However, it is purely random, a feature only of this specific realization, is uninformative about the underlying parameters, and is dangerously misleading for prediction.

16.7 DEMEANING AND DETRENDING

A common preliminary step in time series analysis is demeaning (subtracting off a mean) and detrending (subtracting off a linear trend). With stationary processes, this does not affect asymptotic inference. In contrast, an important property of unit root processes is that their behavior is altered by these transformations.

Consider demeaning. The demeaned version of Y_t is $Y_t^* = Y_t - \overline{Y}_n$. An important observation is that Y_t^* is invariant to the initial condition Y_0, so without loss of generality, we simply assume $Y_0 = 0$.

The normalized process is

$$Z_n^*(r) = \frac{1}{\sqrt{n}} Y_{\lfloor nr \rfloor} - \frac{1}{\sqrt{n}}\overline{Y}_n = Z_n(r) - Z_n(1) \underset{d}{\longrightarrow} B(r) - \int_0^1 B \overset{\text{def}}{=} B^*(r).$$

$B^*(r)$ is **demeaned Brownian motion**. It has the property that $\int_0^1 B^*(r)dr = 0$.

Now consider linear detrending. Based on least squares estimation of a linear trend, the detrended series is $Y_t^{**} = Y_t - X_t'\widehat{\beta}$, where $X_t = (1, t)'$. Like the demeaned series, the detrended series is invariant to Y_0. The associated normalized process is

$$\begin{aligned}Z_n^{**}(r) &= \frac{1}{\sqrt{n}} Y_{\lfloor nr \rfloor} - \frac{1}{\sqrt{n}} X'_{\lfloor nr \rfloor} \widehat{\beta} \\ &= Z_n(r) - X(\lfloor nr \rfloor / n)' D_n \frac{1}{\sqrt{n}} \widehat{\beta} \\ &\underset{d}{\longrightarrow} B(r) - X(r)' \left(\int_0^1 XX' \right)^{-1} \left(\int_0^1 XB \right) \stackrel{\text{def}}{=} B^{**}(r).\end{aligned}$$

$B^{**}(r)$ is the continuous-time residual of the Brownian motion $B(r)$ projected orthogonal to $X(r) = (1, r)'$. We call $B^{**}(r)$ the **detrended Brownian motion**.

There is another method of detrending through first differencing. Suppose that $Y_t = \beta_0 + \beta_1 t + Z_t$. The first difference is $\Delta Y_t = \beta_1 + \Delta Z_t$. An estimator of β_1 is the sample mean of ΔY_t:

$$\overline{\Delta Y}_n = \frac{1}{n} \sum_{t=1}^{n} \Delta Y_t = \frac{Y_n - Y_0}{n}.$$

The normalization $Z_0 = 0$ implies $Y_0 = \beta_0$, so an estimator of β_0 is Y_0. The detrended version of Y_t is $\widetilde{Y}_t = Y_t - Y_0 - (t/n)(Y_n - Y_0)$. The associated normalized process is

$$\widetilde{Z}_n(r) = Z_n(r) - \frac{\lfloor nr \rfloor}{n} Z_n(1) \underset{d}{\longrightarrow} B(r) - rB(1) \stackrel{\text{def}}{=} V(r).$$

$V(r)$ is called a **Brownian Bridge** or a **tied-down Brownian motion**. It has the property that $V(0) = V(1) = 0$. It is also a detrended version of $B(r)$ but is distinct from the linearly detrended version $B^*(r)$.

We summarize these findings in the following theorem.

Theorem 16.5 Under the conditions of either Theorem 16.3 or Theorem 16.4, then as $n \to \infty$,

1. $Z_n^*(r) \underset{d}{\longrightarrow} B^*(r)$
2. $Z_n^{**}(r) \underset{d}{\longrightarrow} B^{**}(r)$
3. $\widetilde{Z}_n(r) \underset{d}{\longrightarrow} V(r)$.

To illustrate, Figure 16.2 displays two detrended versions of the series from Figure 16.1. Panel (a) shows the linear detrended series Y_t^*. Panel (b) shows the first-difference detrended series $\widetilde{Y}_t$. They are visually similar to one another and to Figure 16.1 except that the strong linear trend has been removed.

16.8 STOCHASTIC INTEGRALS

The distribution of the least squares estimator in the regression model $Y_t = X_t'\beta + e_t$ requires the distribution of the sample moments $n^{-1} \sum_{t=1}^{n-1} X_t e_{t+1}$. When X_t is nonstationary, the limit distribution is nonstandard and equals a **stochastic integral**.

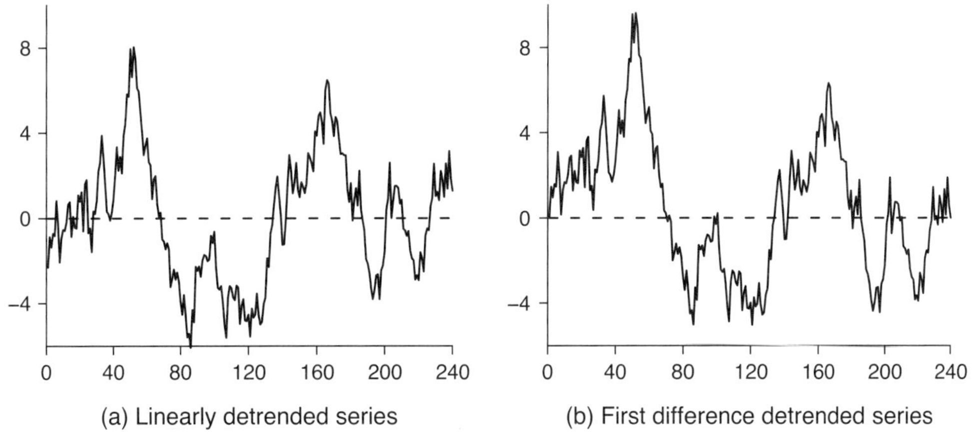

FIGURE 16.2 Detrended random walk

It may help to recall the definition of the Riemann-Stieltijes integral. Over the region [0, 1], the integral of $g(x)$ with respect to $f(x)$ is

$$\int_0^1 g(x)df(x) = \lim_{N\to\infty} \sum_{i=0}^{N-1} g\left(\frac{i}{N}\right)\left(f\left(\frac{i+1}{N}\right) - f\left(\frac{i}{N}\right)\right).$$

A stochastic integral is the case where the function f is random and is defined as a probability limit.

Definition 16.4 The **stochastic integral** of vector-valued $X(r)$ with respect to vector-valued $Z(r)$ over [0, 1] is

$$\int_0^1 XdZ' = \int_0^1 X(r)dZ(r)' = \operatorname*{plim}_{N\to\infty} \sum_{i=0}^{N-1} X\left(\frac{i}{N}\right)\left(Z\left(\frac{i+1}{N}\right) - Z\left(\frac{i}{N}\right)\right)'.$$

Now consider the following setting. Let (X_t, e_t) be vector-valued sequences, where e_t is a MDS with finite variance and X_t is nonstationary. Assume that for some scaling sequence D_n, the scaled process $X_n(r) = D_n^{-1}X_{\lfloor nr \rfloor}$ satisfies $X_n(r) \underset{d}{\longrightarrow} X(r)$ for some deterministic or stochastic process $X(r)$. Examples of X_t sequences include the partial sum process constructed from e_t or another shock, a detrended version of a partial sum process, or a deterministic trend proceses. We desire the asymptotic distribution of $\sum_{t=1}^{n-1} X_t e_{t+1}'$. Define the partial sum process for e_t as $S_n(r) = n^{-1/2}\sum_{t=1}^{\lfloor nr \rfloor} e_t$. From Theorem 16.1, $S_n \underset{d}{\longrightarrow} B$. We calculate that

$$\frac{1}{\sqrt{n}} D_n^{-1} \sum_{t=0}^{n-1} X_t e_{t+1}' = \sum_{t=0}^{n-1} X_n\left(\frac{t}{n}\right)\left(S_n\left(\frac{t+1}{n}\right) - S_n\left(\frac{t}{n}\right)\right)' = \int_0^1 X_n dS_n'.$$

The equalities hold because $S_n(r)$ and $X_n(r)$ are step functions with jumps at $r = t/n$. Since $X_n(r)$ and $S_n(r)$ converge to $X(r)$ and $B(r)$, by analogy, we expect $\int_0^1 X_n dS_n$ to converge to $\int_0^1 XdB$. This is true, but rather tricky to show, since the stochastic integral is not a continuous function of $B(r)$. A general statement of the conditions has been provided by Kurtz and Protter (1991, theorem 2.2). The following is a simplification of their result.

Theorem 16.6 If $(e_t, \mathscr{F}_t)$ is a martingale difference sequence, $\mathbb{E}\left[e_t e_t'\right] = \Sigma < \infty$, $X_t \in \mathscr{F}_t$, and $(X_n(r), S_n(r)) \underset{d}{\longrightarrow} (X(r), B(r))$, then

$$\int_0^1 X_n dS_n' = \frac{1}{\sqrt{n}} D_n^{-1} \sum_{t=1}^{n-1} X_t e_{t+1} \underset{d}{\longrightarrow} \int_0^1 X dB'$$

where $B(r)$ is a Brownian motion with covariance matrix Σ.

The basic application of Theorem 16.6 is to the case $X_n(r) = S_n(r)$. Thus if $S_t = \sum_{i=1}^t e_i$ and e_t is a MDS with covariance matrix Σ, then

$$\frac{1}{n} \sum_{t=1}^{n-1} S_t e_{t+1}' \underset{d}{\longrightarrow} \int_0^1 B dB'.$$

We can extend this result to the case of serially correlated errors.

Theorem 16.7 If Z_t satisfies the conditions of Theorem 16.4 and $S_t = \sum_{i=1}^t Z_i$, then

$$\frac{1}{n} \sum_{t=1}^{n-1} S_t Z_{t+1}' \underset{d}{\longrightarrow} \int_0^1 B dB' + \Lambda$$

where $B(r)$ is a Brownian motion with covariance matrix $\Omega = \Sigma + \Lambda + \Lambda'$, $\Sigma = \mathbb{E}\left[Z_t Z_t'\right]$, and $\Lambda = \sum_{j=1}^{\infty} \mathbb{E}\left[Z_{t-j} Z_t'\right]$.

The proof is presented in Section 16.22.

16.9 ESTIMATION OF AN AR(1)

Consider least squares estimation of the AR(1) parameter α in the model $Y_t = \alpha Y_{t-1} + e_t$. The centered estimator is $\widehat{\alpha} - \alpha = \left(\sum_{t=1}^{n-1} Y_t^2\right)^{-1} \left(\sum_{t=1}^{n-1} Y_t e_{t+1}\right)$. Use the scaling

$$n\left(\widehat{\alpha} - \alpha\right) = \frac{\frac{1}{n} \sum_{t=1}^{n-1} Y_t e_{t+1}}{\frac{1}{n^2} \sum_{t=1}^{n-1} Y_t^2}.$$

Let us examine the denominator and numerator separately under the assumption $\alpha = 1$.

Similarly to our analysis of the sample mean, the denominator can be written as an integral. Thus

$$\frac{1}{n^2} \sum_{t=1}^{n-1} Y_t^2 = \frac{1}{n} \sum_{t=1}^{n-1} \left(\frac{1}{n^{1/2}} Y_t\right)^2 = \int_0^1 Z_n(r)^2 dr \underset{d}{\longrightarrow} \int_0^1 B(r)^2 dr = \sigma^2 \int_0^1 W(r)^2 dr.$$

The convergence is by the CMT.[4] The final equality recognizes that if $B(r)$ has variance σ^2, then $B(r)^2 = \sigma^2 W(r)^2$, where $W(r)$ is standard Brownian motion. For conciseness, we often write the final integral as $\int_0^1 W^2$.

For the numerator, we appeal to Theorem 16.6:

$$\frac{1}{n}\sum_{t=1}^{n-1} Y_t e_{t+1} = \int_0^1 Z_n dS_n \underset{d}{\longrightarrow} \int_0^1 BdB = \sigma^2 \int_0^1 WdW.$$

This limiting stochastic integral is quite famous. It is known as Itô's integral.

Theorem 16.8 Itô's Integral. $\int_0^1 WdW = \frac{1}{2}\left(W(1)^2 - 1\right)$.

If you are not surprised by Itô's integral, take another look. The derivative of $\frac{1}{2}W(r)^2$ is $W(r)dW(r)$. Thus by standard calculus and $W(0) = 0$, you might expect $\int_0^1 WdW = \frac{1}{2}W(1)^2$. The presence of the extra term $-1/2$ is surprising. It arises because $W(r)$ has unbounded variation.

The random variable $W(1)^2$ is χ_1^2, which has expectation 1. Therefore the random variable $\int_0^1 WdW$ is mean 0 but skewed.

The proof of Theorem 16.8 is presented in Section 16.22.

Returning to the least squares estimation problem, we have shown that when $\alpha = 1$,

$$n(\widehat{\alpha} - 1) \underset{d}{\longrightarrow} \frac{\frac{\sigma^2}{2}\left(W(1)^2 - 1\right)}{\sigma^2 \int_0^1 W^2} = \frac{\int_0^1 WdW}{\int_0^1 W^2}.$$

Theorem 16.9 Dickey-Fuller Coefficient Distribution. If $Y_t = \alpha Y_{t-1} + e_t$ with $\alpha = 1$, and $(e_t, \mathscr{F}_t)$ is a strictly stationary and ergodic martingale difference sequence with a finite variance, then

$$n(\widehat{\alpha} - 1) \underset{d}{\longrightarrow} \frac{\int_0^1 WdW}{\int_0^1 W^2}.$$

The limit distribution in Theorem 16.9 is known as the **Dickey-Fuller Distribution** due to the work of Wayne Fuller and David Dickey. Theorem 16.9 shows that the least squares estimator is consistent for $\alpha = 1$ and converges at the "super-consistent" rate $O_p\left(n^{-1}\right)$. The limit distribution is nonstandard and is written as a function of the Brownian motion $W(r)$. There is no closed-form expression for the distribution or density of the statistic. Most commonly it is calculated by simulation.

The density of the Dickey-Fuller coefficient distribution is displayed[5] in Figure 16.3(a) with the label "No Intercept". You can see that the density is highly skewed with a long left tail, and most of the probability mass

[4]The function $g(f) = \int_0^1 f(x)^2 dx$ is continuous with respect to the uniform metric.

[5]The densities in Figure 16.3 were estimated from one million simulation draws of the finite sample distribution for a sample size $n = 10,000$. The densities were estimated using nonparametric kernel methods (see Chapter 17 of *Probability and Statistics for Economists*).

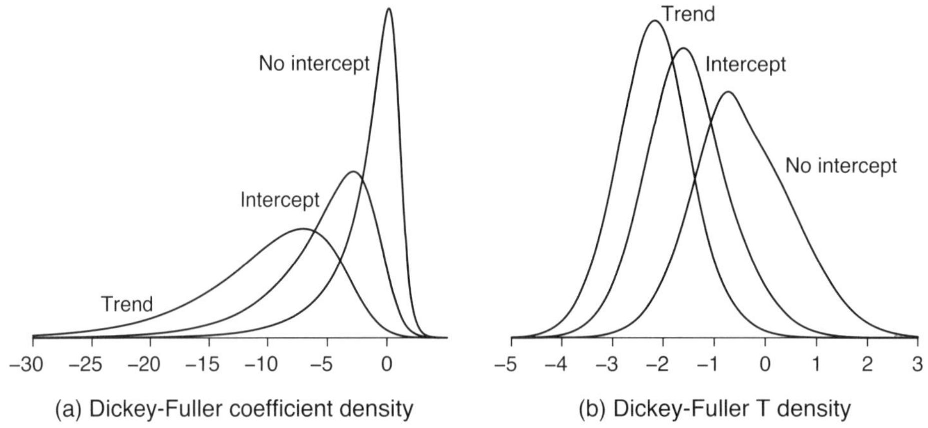

FIGURE 16.3 Unit root distributions

of the distribution is over the negative region. This implies that the density has a negative mean and median. Hence the asymptotic distribution of the least squares estimator is biased negatively, which has the practical implication that when $\alpha = 1$, the least squares estimator is biased away from 1.

We can also examine the limit distribution of the t-ratio. Let $\widehat{e}_t = Y_t - \widehat{\alpha} Y_{t-1}$ be the least squares residual, $\widehat{\sigma}^2 = n^{-1} \sum \widehat{e}_t^2$ the least squares variance estimator, and $s(\widehat{\alpha}) = \widehat{\sigma} / \sqrt{\sum Y_t^2}$ the classical standard error for $\widehat{\alpha}$. The t-ratio for α is $T = (\widehat{\alpha} - 1) / s(\widehat{\alpha})$.

Theorem 16.10 Dickey-Fuller T Distribution. Under the assumptions of Theorem 16.9,

$$T = \frac{\widehat{\alpha} - 1}{s(\widehat{\alpha})} \underset{d}{\longrightarrow} \frac{\int_0^1 W dW}{\left(\int_0^1 W^2\right)^{1/2}}.$$

The limit distribution in Theorem 16.10 is known as the **Dickey-Fuller T distribution**. Theorem 16.10 shows that the classical t-ratio converges to a nonstandard asymptotic distribution. There is no closed-form expression for the distribution or density, so it is typically calculated using simulation techniques. The proof is presented in Section 16.22.

The density of the Dickey-Fuller T distribution is displayed in Figure 16.3(b) with the label "No Intercept". You can see that the density is skewed but much less so than the coefficient distribution. The distribution appears to be a "fatter" version of the conventional student t distribution. An implication is that conventional inference (confidence intervals and tests) will be inaccurate. We discuss testing in Section 16.13.

16.10 AR(1) ESTIMATION WITH AN INTERCEPT

Suppose that Y_t is a random walk, and we estimate an AR(1) model with an intercept. The estimated model is $Y_t = \mu + \alpha Y_{t-1} + e_t$. By the Frisch-Waugh-Lovell Theorem (Theorem 3.5), the least squares estimator $\widehat{\alpha}$ of α can be written as the simple regression using the demeaned series Y_t^*. That is, the normalized estimator is

$$n(\widehat{\alpha}-1)=\frac{\frac{1}{n}\sum_{t=1}^{n-1}Y_t^*e_{t+1}}{\frac{1}{n^2}\sum_{t=1}^{n-1}Y_t^{*2}}$$

where $Y_t^* = Y_t - \overline{Y}$ with $\overline{Y} = \frac{1}{n}\sum_{t=1}^{n-1} Y_t$. By Theorems 16.5 part 1 and 16.6, the calculations from Section 16.9 show that

$$n(\widehat{\alpha}-1)\underset{d}{\longrightarrow}\frac{\int_0^1 W^*dW}{\int_0^1 W^{*2}}.$$

This is similar to the distribution in Theorem 16.9 and is known as the Dickey-Fuller coefficient distribution for the case of an included intercept.

Similarly, if we estimate an AR(1) model with an intercept and trend, the estimated model is $Y_t = \mu + \beta t + \alpha Y_{t-1} + e_t$. By the Frisch-Waugh-Lovell Theorem, this is equivalent to regression on the detrended series Y_t^{**}. Applying Theorems 16.5 part 2 and 16.6, we find

$$n(\widehat{\alpha}-1)\underset{d}{\longrightarrow}\frac{\int_0^1 W^{**}dW}{\int_0^1 W^{**2}}.$$

This is known as the Dickey-Fuller coefficient distribution for the case of an included intercept and linear trend.

Similar results hold for the t-ratios. We summarize the results in the following theorem.

Theorem 16.11 Under the assumptions of Theorem 16.9, for the case of an estimated AR(1) with an intercept,

$$n(\widehat{\alpha}-1)\underset{d}{\longrightarrow}\frac{\int_0^1 W^*dW}{\int_0^1 W^{*2}}$$

$$T\underset{d}{\longrightarrow}\frac{\int_0^1 W^*dW}{\left(\int_0^1 W^{*2}\right)^{1/2}}.$$

For the case of an estimated AR(1) with an intercept and linear time trend,

$$n(\widehat{\alpha}-1)\underset{d}{\longrightarrow}\frac{\int_0^1 W^{**}dW}{\int_0^1 W^{**2}}$$

$$T\underset{d}{\longrightarrow}\frac{\int_0^1 W^{**}dW}{\left(\int_0^1 W^{**2}\right)^{1/2}}.$$

The densities of the Dickey-Fuller coefficient distributions are displayed in Figure 16.3(a), labeled as "Intercept" for the case with an included intercept and "Trend" for the case with an intercept and linear time trend. The densities are considerably affected by the inclusion of the intercept or intercept and trend.

The effect is twofold: (1) the distributions shift substantially to the left; and (2) the distributions substantially widen. Examining the "trend" version, we can see that there is very little probability mass above 0. Thus the asymptotic distribution is not only biased downward, the realization is also nearly always negative. This has the practical implication that the least squares estimator is almost certainly less than the true coefficient value, which is a strong form of bias.

The densities of the Dickey-Fuller T distributions are displayed in Figure 16.3(b). The effect of detrending on the T distributions is quite different from the effect on the coefficient distirbutions. Here we see that the primary effect is a location shift with only a mild impact on dispersion. The strong location shift is a bias in the asymptotic T distribution, implying that conventional inferences will be incorrect.

16.11 SAMPLE COVARIANCES OF INTEGRATED AND STATIONARY PROCESSES

Let (X_t, u_t) be a sequence where X_t is nonstationary and u_t is mean 0 and strictly stationary. Assume that for some scaling sequence D_n, the scaled process $X_n(r) = D_n^{-1} X_{\lfloor nr \rfloor}$ satisfies $X_n(r) \underset{d}{\longrightarrow} X(r)$, where $X(r)$ is continuous with probability 1. Consider the scaled sample covariance

$$C_n = \frac{1}{n} D_n^{-1} \sum_{t=1}^{n} X_t u_t.$$

Theorem 16.12 Assume that $X_n(r) = D_n^{-1} X_{\lfloor nr \rfloor} \underset{d}{\longrightarrow} X(r)$, where $X(r)$ is almost surely continuous. Assume that u_t is mean 0, strictly stationary, ergodic, and $\mathbb{E}|u_t| < \infty$. Then $C_n \underset{p}{\longrightarrow} 0$ as $n \to \infty$.

The proof is presented in Section 16.22.

16.12 AR(P) MODELS WITH A UNIT ROOT

Assume that Y_t satisfies $a(\mathrm{L})\Delta Y_t = e_t$, where $a(z)$ is a $p-1$ order invertible lag polynomial, and e_t is a stationary MDS with finite variance σ^2. Then Y_t can be written as the AR(p) process

$$Y_t = a_1 Y_{t-1} + \cdots + a_p Y_{t-p} + e_t \tag{16.6}$$

where the coefficients satisfy $a_1 + \cdots + a_p = 1$. Let $\widehat{a}$ be the least squares estimator of $a = (a_1, \ldots, a_p)$. We now discuss its sampling distribution.

Let B be the $p \times p$ matrix that transforms $(Y_{t-1}, \ldots, Y_{t-p})$ to $(Y_{t-1}, \Delta Y_{t-1}, \ldots, \Delta Y_{t-p+1})$, for example, when $p = 3$, then $B = \begin{bmatrix} 1 & 0 & 0 \\ 1 & -1 & 0 \\ 0 & 1 & -1 \end{bmatrix}$. Make the partition $B^{-1\prime} a = (\rho, \beta)$, where $\rho \in \mathbb{R}$ and $\beta \in \mathbb{R}^{p-1}$. Then the AR(p) model can be written as

$$Y_t = \rho Y_{t-1} + \beta' X_{t-1} + e_t \tag{16.7}$$

where $X_{t-1} = (\Delta Y_{t-1}, \ldots, \Delta Y_{t-p+1})$. The leading coefficient is $\rho = a_1 + \cdots + a_p = 1$. This transformation separates the regressors into the unit root component Y_{t-1} and the stationary component X_{t-1}.

Consider the least squares estimators $(\widehat{\rho}, \widehat{\beta})$. Assuming a unit root, as they can be written under the

$$\begin{pmatrix} n(\widehat{\rho}-1) \\ \sqrt{n}(\widehat{\beta}-\beta) \end{pmatrix} = \begin{pmatrix} \frac{1}{n^2}\sum_{t=1+p}^{n} Y_{t-1}^2 & \frac{1}{n^{3/2}}\sum_{t=1+p}^{n} Y_{t-1}X_{t-1}' \\ \frac{1}{n^{3/2}}\sum_{t=1+p}^{n} X_{t-1}Y_{t-1} & \frac{1}{n}\sum_{t=1+p}^{n} X_{t-1}X_{t-1}' \end{pmatrix}^{-1} \begin{pmatrix} \frac{1}{n}\sum_{t=1+p}^{n} Y_{t-1}e_t \\ \frac{1}{\sqrt{n}}\sum_{t=1+p}^{n} X_{t-1}e_t \end{pmatrix}.$$

Theorem 16.4 and the CMT show that

$$\frac{1}{n^2}\sum_{t=1+p}^{n} Y_{t-1}^2 \underset{d}{\longrightarrow} \omega^2 \int_0^1 W^2$$

where ω^2 is the long-run variance of ΔY_t, which equals $\omega^2 = \sigma^2/a(1)^2 > 0$.

Theorem 16.12 shows that

$$\frac{1}{n^{3/2}}\sum_{t=1+p}^{n} X_{t-1}Y_{t-1} \underset{p}{\longrightarrow} 0.$$

Theorems 16.4 and 16.6 show that

$$\frac{1}{n}\sum_{t=1+p}^{n} Y_{t-1}e_t \underset{d}{\longrightarrow} \omega\sigma \int_0^1 WdW.$$

The WLLN and the CLT for stationary processes show that

$$\frac{1}{n}\sum_{t=1+p}^{n} X_{t-1}X_{t-1}' \underset{p}{\longrightarrow} \boldsymbol{Q}$$

$$\frac{1}{\sqrt{n}}\sum_{t=1+p}^{n} X_{t-1}e_t \underset{d}{\longrightarrow} \mathrm{N}(0,\Omega)$$

where $\boldsymbol{Q} = \mathbb{E}\left[X_{t-1}X_{t-1}'\right]$ and $\Omega = \mathbb{E}\left[X_{t-1}X_{t-1}'e_t^2\right]$. Together, these results establish the following.

Theorem 16.13 Assume that Y_t satisfies $a(\mathrm{L})\Delta Y_t = e_t$, where $a(z)$ is a $p-1$ order invertible lag polynomial, and $(e_t, \Im_t)$ is a stationary MDS with finite variance σ^2. Then

$$\begin{pmatrix} n(\widehat{\rho}-1) \\ \sqrt{n}(\widehat{\beta}-\beta) \end{pmatrix} \underset{d}{\longrightarrow} \begin{pmatrix} a(1)\dfrac{\int_0^1 WdW}{\int_0^1 W^2} \\ \mathrm{N}(0,V) \end{pmatrix} \tag{16.8}$$

where $V = \boldsymbol{Q}^{-1}\Omega\boldsymbol{Q}^{-1}$.

This theorem provides an asymptotic distribution theory for the least squares estimators. The estimator $(\widehat{a}, \widehat{\beta})$ is consistent, the coefficient $\widehat{\beta}$ on the stationary variables is asymptotically normal, and the coefficient $\widehat{a}$ on the unit root component has a scaled Dickey-Fuller distribution.

The estimator of the representation (16.6) is the linear transformation $B'(\widehat{\rho}, \widehat{\beta}')'$, and therefore its asymptotic distribution is the transformation B' of (16.8). Since the unit root component converges at a faster

$O_p(n^{-1})$ rate than the stationary component, it drops out of the asymptotic distribution. We obtain

$$\sqrt{n}\,(\widehat{a}-a) \underset{d}{\longrightarrow} \mathrm{N}(0, \boldsymbol{G}V\boldsymbol{G}') \tag{16.9}$$

where, in the $p=3$ case,

$$\boldsymbol{G} = \begin{bmatrix} 1 & 0 \\ -1 & 1 \\ 0 & -1 \end{bmatrix}.$$

The asymptotic covariance matrix $\boldsymbol{G}V\boldsymbol{G}'$ is deficient with rank $p-1$. Hence this is only a partial characterization of the asymptotic distribution; equation (16.8) is a complete first-order characterization. The implication of (16.9) is that individual coefficient estimators and standard errors of (16.6) have conventional asymptotic interpretations. This extends to conventional hypothesis tests that do not include the sum of the coefficients. For most purposes (except testing the unit root hypothesis), this means that asymptotic inference on the coefficients of (16.6) can be based on the conventional normal approximation and can ignore the possible presence of unit roots.

16.13 TESTING FOR A UNIT ROOT

The asymptotic properties of the time series process change discontinuously at the unit root $\rho = a_1 + \cdots + a_p = 1$. It is therefore of interest to test the hypothesis of a unit root. We typically express this as the test of $\mathbb{H}_0 : \rho = 1$ against $\mathbb{H}_1 : \rho < 1$. We typically view the test as one-sided, as we are interested in the alternative hypothesis that the series is stationary (not that it is explosive).

The test for $\mathbb{H}_0$ vs. $\mathbb{H}_1$ is the t-statistic for $a_1 + \cdots + a_p = 1$ in the AR(p) model (16.6). It is identical to the t-statistic for $\rho = 1$ in reparameterized form (16.7). Since the latter is a simple t-ratio, this is the most convenient implementation. It is typically called the **augmented Dickey-Fuller** statistic. It equals

$$\mathrm{ADF} = \frac{\widehat{\rho}-1}{s\,(\widehat{\rho})}$$

where $s\,(\widehat{\rho})$ is a standard error for $\widehat{\rho}$. This t-ratio is typically calculated using a classical (homoskedastic) standard error, perhaps for historical reasons, and perhaps because the asymptotic distribution of ADF is invariant to conditional heteroskedasticity. The statistic is called the ADF statistic when the estimated model is an AR(p) model with $p > 1$; it is typically called the Dickey-Fuller statistic if the estimated model is an AR(1).

The asymptotic distribution of ADF depends on the fitted deterministic components. The test statistic is most typically calculated in a model with a fitted intercept or a fitted intercept and time trend, though the theory is also presented for the case with no fitted intercept and extends to any polynomial order trend.

Theorem 16.14 Assume that Y_t satisfies $a(\mathrm{L})\Delta Y_t = e_t$, where $a(z)$ is a $p-1$ order invertible lag polynomial, and $(e_t, \Im_t)$ is a stationary MDS with finite variance σ^2. Then

$$\mathrm{ADF} \underset{d}{\longrightarrow} \frac{\int_0^1 U dW}{\left(\int_0^1 U^2\right)^{1/2}} \stackrel{\text{def}}{=} \xi$$

where W is Brownian motion. The process U depends on the fitted deterministic components:

1. Case 1: No intercept or trend. $U(r) = W(r)$.
2. Case 2: Fitted intercept (demeaned data). $U(r) = W(r) - r\int_0^1 W$.
3. Case 3: Fitted intercept and trend (detrended data). $U(r) = W(r) - X(r)'\left(\int_0^1 XX'\right)^{-1}\left(\int_0^1 XW\right)$, where $X(r) = (1, r)'$.

Let Z_α satisfy $\mathbb{P}[\xi \leq Z_\alpha] = \alpha$. The test "Reject $\mathbb{H}_0$ if ADF $< Z_\alpha$" has asymptotic size α.

Asymptotic critical values are displayed in the first three columns of Table 16.1. The ADF is a one-sided hypothesis test, so rejections occur when the test statistic is less than (more negative than) the critical value. For example, the 5% critical value for the case of a fitted intercept is -2.86. Thus if the ADF t-ratio is more negative than -2.86 (for example, ADF $= -3.0$), then the test rejects the hypothesis of no unit root. But if the ADF t-ratio is greater than -2.86 (for example, ADF $= -2.0$), then the the test does not reject the hypothesis of a unit root.

In most applications, an ADF test is implemented with at least a fitted intercept (the second column in the table). Many are implemented with a fitted linear time trend (which is the third column). The choice depends on the nature of the alternative hypothesis. If $\mathbb{H}_1$ is that the series is stationary about a constant mean, then the case of a fitted intercept is appropriate. Example series for this context are unemployment and interest rates. If $\mathbb{H}_1$ is that the series is stationary about a linear trend, then the case of a fitted trend is appropriate. Examples for this context are levels or log-levels of macroeconomic aggregates.

The ADF test depends on the autoregressive order p. The issue of selection of p is similar to that of autoregressive model selection. In general, if p is too small, then the model is misspecified and the ADF statistic has an asymptotic bias. If p is too large, then the test coefficient $\widehat{\rho}$ is imprecisely estimated, reducing the power of the test. Since $\widehat{\rho}$ is the sum of the p estimated AR coefficients in the levels model, the imprecision can be sensitive to the choice of p. A reasonable selection rule is to use the AIC-selected AR model. Improved rules have been studied by Ng and Perron (2001).

I have argued that it is better to report asymptotic p-values rather than "accept/reject". For this calculation, we need the asymptotic distribution function, but this is not available in closed form. A simple approximation is interpolation of the critical values. For example, suppose ADF $= -3.0$ with a fitted intercept. The two closest critical values are the 10% (-3.13) and 15% (-2.94) values. Linear interpolation between these values yields

$$p = \frac{0.10 \times (3.0 - 2.94) + 0.15 \times (3.13 - 3.0)}{3.13 - 2.94} = 0.13.$$

Thus the asymptotic p-value is approximately 13%. Reporting a p-value instead of the "decision" of a test improves interpretation and communication.

How should unit root tests be used in empirical practice? The answer is subtle. A common mistake is: "We use a unit root test to discover whether or not the series has a unit root." This is a mistake, because a test does not reveal the truth. Instead, it presents evidence for whether or not $\mathbb{H}_0$ can be rejected. If the test fails to reject $\mathbb{H}_0$, this does not mean that "We have found a unit root." Instead, the correct conclusion is "We cannot reject the hypothesis that it has a unit root." Thus we do not know. If the test rejects $\mathbb{H}_0$ (if the p-value is very small), then we can conclude that the series is unlikely to be a unit root process; its behavior is more consistent with a stationary process. Another common mistake is to adopt the rule: "If the ADF test rejects, then we work with Y_t in levels; if the ADF test does not reject, then we work with the differenced series ΔY_t." This is a mistake because it assigns a modeling rule to the result of a statistical test, but the test is only designed to answer the question of whether there is evidence against the hypothesis of a unit root. The choice of Y_t versus ΔY_t is a model selection choice, not a hypothesis testing decision.

Table 16.1
Unit root testing critical values

	ADF			KPSS	
	No intercept	Intercept	Trend	Intercept	Trend
0.01%	−3.92	−4.69	−5.21	1.598	0.430
0.1%	−3.28	−4.08	−4.58	1.176	0.324
1%	−2.56	−3.43	−3.95	0.744	0.218
2%	−2.31	−3.20	−3.73	0.621	0.187
3%	−2.15	−3.06	−3.60	0.550	0.169
4%	−2.03	−2.95	−3.50	0.500	0.157
5%	−1.94	−2.86	−3.41	0.462	0.148
7%	−1.79	−2.72	−3.28	0.406	0.134
10%	−1.62	−2.57	−3.13	0.348	0.119
15%	−1.40	−2.37	−2.94	0.284	0.103
20%	−1.23	−2.22	−2.79	0.241	0.091
30%	−0.96	−1.97	−2.56	0.185	0.076
50%	−0.50	−1.57	−2.18	0.119	0.056
70%	0.05	−1.15	−1.81	0.079	0.041
90%	0.89	−0.44	−1.24	0.046	0.028
99%	2.02	0.60	−0.32	0.025	0.017

Source: Calculated by simulation from one million replications of samples of size $n = 10{,}000$

I believe a reasonable approach is to start with a hypothesis based on theory and context. Does economic theory lead you to treat a series as stationary or nonstationary? Is there a reason to believe that a series should be stationary—thus stable in the mean—or is there reason to believe the series will exhibit growth and change? If you have a clear answer to these questions, that should be your starting point, your default. Use the unit root test to help confirm your assumptions rather than to select a modeling approach. If your assumption is that Y_t has a unit root but the unit root test strongly rejects, then you should reappraise your theory. However, if your assumption is that Y_t is stationary but the unit root test fails to reject the null of a unit root, do not necessarily depart from your theoretical base. Consider the degree of evidence and the sample size, as well as the point estimates. Use all information together to determine your decision.

To illustrate application of the ADF test, let's take the eight series displayed in Figures 14.1 and 14.2 using the variables measured in levels or log-levels. The variables and transformations are listed in Table 16.2. For six of the eight series (all but the interest and unemployment rates), we took the log transformation. We included an intercept and linear time trend in each regression and selected the autoregressive order by minimizing the AIC across AR(p) models with a linear time trend. For the quarterly series, we examined AR(p) models up to $p = 8$, for the monthly series up to $p = 12$. The selected values of p are shown in the table. The point estimate $\widehat{\rho} - 1$, its standard error, the ADF t-statistic, and its asymptotic p-value are shown. What we see is for seven of the eight series (all but the unemployment rate), the p-values are far from the critical region, indicating failure to reject the null hypothesis of a unit root. The p-value for the unemployment rate is 0.01, however, indicating rejection of a unit root. Overall, the results are consistent with the hypotheses that the unemployment rate is stationary and that the other seven variables are possibly (but not decisively) unit root processes.

The ADF test became popular in economics with a seminar paper by Nelson and Plosser (1982). These authors applied the ADF to a set of standard macroeconomic variables (similar to those in Table 16.2) and found that the unit root hypothesis could not be rejected in most series. This empirical finding had a substantial

Table 16.2
Unit root and KPSS test applications

	p	$\widehat{\rho}-1$	ADF	p-value	M	KPSS_2	p-value
log(real GDP)	3	−0.017 (.009)	−1.8	0.71	18	0.23	0.01
log(real consumption)	4	−0.029 (.012)	−2.4	0.37	18	0.113	0.12
log(exchange rate)	11	−0.009 (.004)	−2.2	0.49	26	0.31	< .01
interest rate	12	−0.005 (.004)	−1.5	0.52	26	0.56	< .01
log(oil price)	2	−0.013 (.005)	−2.4	0.35	26	0.23	< .01
unemployment rate	7	−0.014 (.004)	−3.4	0.01	26	0.14	0.06
log(CPI)	11	−0.001 (.001)	−1.0	0.95	26	0.55	< .01
log(stock price)	6	−0.010 (.004)	−2.2	0.47	26	0.30	< .01

effect on applied economic time series. Before this paper, the conventional wisdom was that economic series were stationary (possibly about linear time trends). After their work, it became more accepted to assume that economic time series are better described as autoregressive unit root processes. Nelson and Plosser (1982) used this empirical finding to make a further and stronger claim. They argued that Keynesian macroeconomic models (which were standard at the time) imply that economic time series are stationary, while real business cycle (RBC) models (which were new at the time) imply that economic time series are unit root processes. Nelson-Plosser argued that the empirical finding that the unit root tests do not reject was strong support for the RBC research program. Their argument was influential and was a factor motivating the rise of the RBC literature. In hindsight, we can see that Nelson and Plosser (1982) made a fundamental error in this argument. The unit root behavior in RBC models is not inherent to their structure; instead it is a by-product of the assumptions about the technology process. (If exogenous technology is a unit root process or a stationary process, then macroeconomic variables will also be unit root processes or stationary processes, respectively.) Similarly, the stationary behavior of 1970s Keynesian models was not inherent to their structure but instead a by-product of assumptions about unobservables. Fundamentally, the unit root/stationary distinction says little about the RBC/Keynesian debate.

The ADF test with a fitted intercept can be implemented in Stata by the command `dfuller y, lags(q) regress`. For a fitted intercept and trend, add the option `trend`. The number of lags "q" in the command is the number of first differences in (16.7), hence $q=p-1$, where p is the autoregressive order. The `dfuller` command reports the estimated regression, the ADF statistic, asymptotic critical values, and approximate asymptotic p-value.

16.14 KPSS STATIONARITY TEST

Kwiatkowski, Phillips, Schmidt, and Shin (1992) developed a test of the null hypothesis of stationarity against the alternative of a unit root that has become known as the KPSS test. Many users find this idea attractive as a counterpoint to the ADF test.

The test is derived from what is known as a **local level model**. This is

$$Y_t = \mu + \theta S_t + e_t$$

$$S_t = S_{t-1} + u_t$$

where e_t is a mean 0 stationary process, and u_t is i.i.d. $(0, \sigma_u^2)$. When $\sigma_u^2 = 0$, then Y_t is stationary. When $\sigma_u^2 > 0$, then Y_t is a unit root process. Thus a test of the null of stationarity against the alternative of a unit root is a test of $\mathbb{H}_0 : \sigma_u^2 = 0$ against $\mathbb{H}_1 : \sigma_u^2 > 0$. Add the auxillary assumption that (e_t, u_t) are i.i.d normal. The Lagrange multiplier test can be shown to reject $\mathbb{H}_0$ in favor of $\mathbb{H}_1$ for large values of

$$\frac{1}{n^2 \widehat{\sigma}^2} \sum_{i=1}^{n} \left(\sum_{t=1}^{i} \widehat{e}_t \right)^2$$

where $\widehat{e}_t = Y_t - \overline{Y}$ are the residuals under the null, and $\widehat{\sigma}^2$ is its sample variance. To generalize to the context of serially correlated e_t, KPSS proposed the statistic

$$\text{KPSS}_1 = \frac{1}{n^2 \widehat{\omega}^2} \sum_{i=1}^{n} \left(\sum_{t=1}^{i} \widehat{e}_t \right)^2$$

where

$$\widehat{\omega}^2 = \sum_{\ell=-M}^{M} \left(1 - \frac{|\ell|}{M+1} \right) \frac{1}{n} \sum_{t=1}^{n} \widehat{e}_t \widehat{e}_{t-\ell}$$

is the Newey-West estimator of the long-run variance ω^2 of Y_t.

For contexts allowing for a linear time trend, the local level model takes the form

$$Y_t = \mu + \beta t + \theta S_t + e_t$$

which has null least squares estimator

$$Y_t = \widetilde{\mu} + \widetilde{\beta} t + \widetilde{e}_t.$$

Notice that $\widetilde{e}_t$ is the linearly detrended Y_t. The KPSS test for $\mathbb{H}_0$ against $\mathbb{H}_1$ rejects for large values of

$$\text{KPSS}_2 = \frac{1}{n^2 \widetilde{\omega}^2} \sum_{i=1}^{n} \left(\sum_{t=1}^{i} \widetilde{e}_t \right)^2$$

where $\widetilde{\omega}^2$ is defined as $\widehat{\omega}^2$ but with the detrended residuals $\widetilde{e}_t$.

Theorem 16.15 If Y_t follows Assumption 16.1, then

$$\text{KPSS}_1 \underset{d}{\longrightarrow} \int_0^1 V^2$$

and

$$\text{KPSS}_2 \underset{d}{\longrightarrow} \int_0^1 V_2^2$$

where $V(r) = W(r) - rW(1)$ is a Brownian bridge, and $V_2(r) = W(r) - \left(\int_0^r X(s)ds\right)' \left(\int_0^1 XX'\right)' \int_0^1 X dW$ with $X(s) = (1, s)'$.

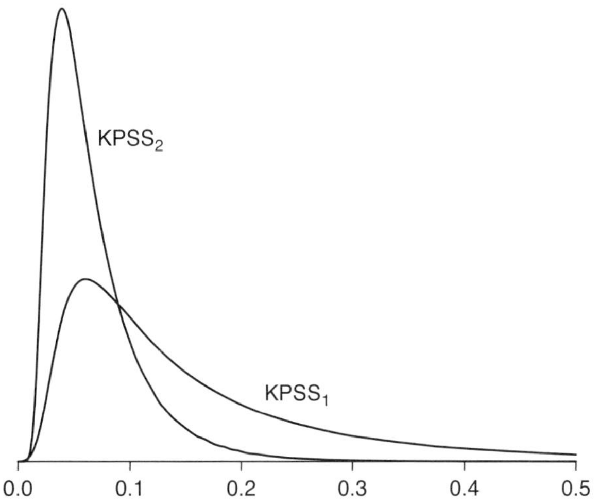

FIGURE 16.4 Density of KPSS distribution

The asymptotic distributions in Theorem 16.15 are nonstandard and are typically calculated by simulation. The process $V_2(r)$ is known as a **second-level Brownian Bridge**. The asymptotic distributions are displayed[6] in Figure 16.4. The densities are skewed with a slowly decaying right tail. The KPSS_2 distribution is substantially shifted toward the origin compared to the KPSS_1 distribution, indicating a substantial effect of detrending.

Asymptotic critical values are displayed in the final two columns of Table 16.1. Rejections occur when the test statistic exceeds the critical value. For example, for a regression with fitted intercept and time trend, suppose that the statistic equals $\text{KPSS}_2 = 0.163$. This exceeds the 4% critical value 0.157 but not the 3% critical value 0.169. Thus the test rejects at the 4% but not the 3% level. An interpolated p-value is 3.5%, which is moderate evidence against the hypothesis of stationarity in favor of the alternative hypothesis of nonstationarity.

The KPSS statistic depends on the lag order M used to estimate the long-run variance ω^2, which is a challenge for test implementation. If Y_t is stationary but highly persistent (for example, an AR(1) with a large autoregressive coefficient), then the lag truncation M needs to be large to accurately estimate ω^2. However, for the alternative that Y_t is a unit root process, the estimator $\widehat{\omega}^2$ will increase roughly linearly with M, so that for any given sample, the KPSS statistic can be made arbitrarily small by selecting M sufficiently large.

Recall that the Andrews (1991b) reference rule (14.51) is

$$M = \left(6\frac{\rho^2}{\left(1-\rho^2\right)^2}\right)^{1/3} n^{1/3}$$

where ρ is the first autocorrelation of Y_t. For the KPSS test, we should not replace ρ with an estimator $\widehat{\rho}$, as the latter converges to 1 under $\mathbb{H}_0$, leading to $M \to \infty$ and rendering the test inconsistent. Instead we can use a default rule based on a reasonable alternative. Suppose we consider the alternative $\rho = 0.8$. The associated Andrews reference rule is $M = 3.1n^{1/3}$, which leads to a simple rule $M = 3n^{1/3}$. An interpretation of this choice

[6]Calculated by simulation from one million simulation draws of samples of size $n = 10,000$.

is that it should approximately control the size of the test when the truth is an AR(1) with coefficient 0.8 but over-reject for more persistent AR processes.

To illustrate, Table 16.2 reports the KPSS_2 statistic for the same eight series as examined in Section 16.13, using $M = 3n^{1/3}$. For the first two quarterly series, $n = 228$, leading to $M = 18$. For the six monthly series, $n = 684$, leading to $M = 26$. For six of the eight series (all but consumption and the unemployment rate), the KPSS statistic equals or exceeds the 1% critical value, leading to a rejection of the null hypothesis of stationarity in favor of the alternative of a unit root. This result is consistent with the ADF test, which failed to reject a unit root for these series.

For the consumption series, the KPSS statistic has a p-value of 12%, which does not reject the hypothesis of stationarity. Recall that the ADF test failed to reject the hypothesis of a unit root. Thus neither test leads to a decisive result; as a pair, the two tests are inconclusive. In this context, I recommend staying with the prediction of economic theory (consumption is a martingale), as it is not rejected by a hypothesis test. The KPSS fails to reject stationarity, but that does not mean that the series is stationary.

An interesting case is the unemployment rate series. It has $\mathrm{KPSS}_2 = 0.14$ with a p-value of 6%, which is borderline significant for rejection of stationarity. However, recall that the ADF test had a p-value of 1%, rejecting the unit root hypothesis. These results are borderline conflicting. To augment our information, we calculate the KPSS_1 test, as the unemployment rate does not appear to be trended. We find $\mathrm{KPSS}_1 = 0.19$ with a p-value of 30%, which is clearly in the nonrejection region, failing to provide evidence against stationarity. As a whole, the ADF test (reject unit root), the KPSS_1 test (accept stationarity), and the KPSS_2 test (borderline reject stationarity) taken together are consistent with the interpretation that the unemployment rate is a stationary process.

The KPSS_2 test can be implemented in Stata using the command[7] `kpss y, maxlag(q)`. For the KPSS_1 test, add the option `notrend`. The command reports the KPSS statistics for $M = 1, \ldots, q$, as well as asymptotic critical values. Approximate asymptotic p-values are not reported.

16.15 SPURIOUS REGRESSION

One of the most empirically relevant discoveries from the theory of nonstationary time series is the phenomenon of spurious regression. This is the finding that two statistically independent series, if both are unit root processes, are likely to fool traditional statistical analysis by appearing to be statistically related by both eyeball scrutiny and traditional statistical tests. The phenomenon was observed[8] and named by Granger and Newbold (1974) and explained using the theory of nonstationary time series by P. Phillips (1986). The primary lesson is that it is easy to be tricked by nonstationary time series, but the problem disappears if we pay suitable attention to dynamic specification.

To illustrate the problem, examine Figure 16.5(a). Displayed are two time series, monthly for 1980–2020. A casual review of the graphs shows that both series are generally increasing over 1980–2010 with a no-growth period around 2000, and the series display a downward trend for the final decade. A more refined perusal may appear to reveal that Series 2 leads Series 1 by about 5 years, in the sense that Series 2 reaches turning points about 5 years before Series 1. A casual observer is likely to deduce based on Figure 16.5(a) that the two time series are strongly related.

---

[7] The command `kpss` is not part of the standard package, but it can be installed by typing `ssc install kpss`.

[8] In numerical simulations.

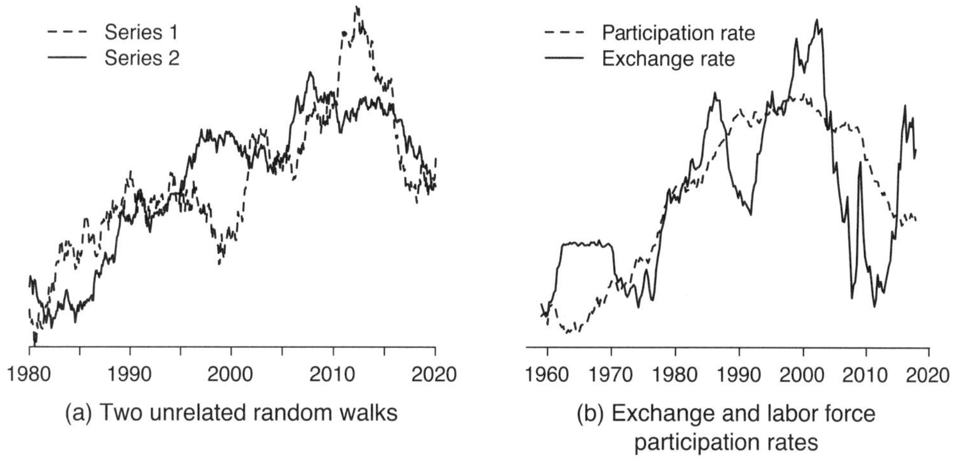

FIGURE 16.5 Plots of empirical series

However, the truth is that Series 1 and Series 2 are statistically independent random walks generated by computer simulation, each standardized to have mean 0 and variance 1 for the purpose of visual comparison. The "fact" that both series are generally upward trended and have "similar" turning points are statistical accidents. Random walks have an uncanny ability to fool casual analysis. Newspaper (and other journalistic) articles containing plots of time series are routinely subject to the tricks displayed in Figure 16.5(a). Economists are also routinely tricked and fooled.

Traditional statistical examination of the series in Figure 16.5(a) can also lead to a false inference of a strong relationship. A linear regression of Series 1 on Series 2 yields a slope coefficient of 0.76 with classical standard error of 0.03. The t-ratio for the test of a zero slope is $T = 26$. The equation R^2 is 0.59. These traditional statistics support the incorrect inference that the two series are strongly related.

Spurious relationships of this form are commonplace in economic time series. An example is shown in Figure 16.5(b), which displays the U.S. labor force participation rate and U.S.-Canada exchange rate, quarterly for 1960–2017. As a visual aid, both series have been normalized to have mean 0 and variance 1. Both series appear to grow at a similar rate from 1960 to 2000, though the exchange rate is more volatile. From 2000 to 2017, they reverse course, with both series declining. The visual evidence is supported by traditional statistics. A linear regression of labor participation on the exchange rate yields a slope coefficient of 0.70 with a clasical standard error of 0.05. The t-ratio for the test of a zero slope is $T = 15$. The equation R^2 is 0.49. The visual and statistical evidence support the inference that the two series are related.

This empirical "finding" that the labor participation and exchange rates are related does not make economic sense. Is this an example of a spurious regression between nonstationary variables? A visual inspection of each series supports the contention that each is nonstationary and may be well characterized as a unit root process. We saw in Sections 16.13 and 16.14 that the ADF and KPSS tests support the hypothesis that the exchange rate is a unit root process. Similar tests reach the same conclusion for labor force participation. Thus the two series are reasonably characterized as unit root processes, and these two series could be an empirical example of a spurious regression.

For a formal framework, assume that the series Y_t and X_t are random walk processes,

$$Y_t = Y_{t-1} + e_{1t} \tag{16.10}$$

$$X_t = X_{t-1} + e_{2t} \tag{16.11}$$

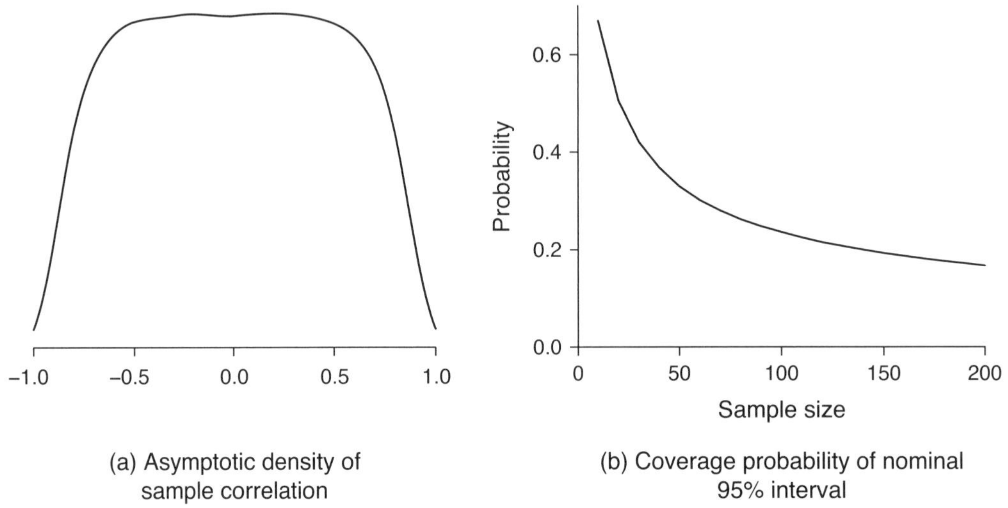

FIGURE 16.6 Properties of spurious regression

where (e_{1t}, e_{2t}) are i.i.d., mean 0, mutually uncorrelated, and normalized to have variance 1. Let Y_t^* and X_t^* denote demeaned versions of Y_t and X_t. From the FCLT, they satisfy

$$\left(\frac{1}{\sqrt{n}}Y^*_{\lfloor nr \rfloor}, \frac{1}{\sqrt{n}}X^*_{\lfloor nr \rfloor}\right) \underset{d}{\longrightarrow} \left(W_1^*(r), W_2^*(r)\right)$$

where $W_1^*(r)$ and $W_2^*(r)$ are demeaned Brownian motions.

Applying the CMT, the sample correlation has the asymptotic distribution

$$\widehat{\rho} = \frac{\frac{1}{n^2}\sum_{i=1}^n Y_i^* X_i^*}{\left(\frac{1}{n^2}\sum_{i=1}^n Y_i^{*2}\right)^{1/2}\left(\frac{1}{n^2}\sum_{i=1}^n X_i^{*2}\right)^{1/2}} \underset{d}{\longrightarrow} \frac{\int_0^1 W_1^* W_2^*}{\left(\int_0^1 W_1^{*2}\right)^{1/2}\left(\int_0^1 W_2^{*2}\right)^{1/2}}.$$

The right-hand side is a random variable. Furthermore it is also nondegenerate (indeed, it is nonzero with probability 1). Thus the sample correlation $\widehat{\rho}$ remains random in large samples.

To understand magnitudes, Figure 16.6(a) displays the asymptotic distributon[9] of $\widehat{\rho}$. The density has most probability mass in the interval $[-0.5, 0.5]$, over which the density is essentially flat. Thus the sample correlation has a diffuse distribution. Earlier in this section, we saw that the two simulated random walks had a sample correlation[10] of 0.76 and the two empirical series a sample correlation of 0.70. We can now see that these results are consistent with the distribution shown in Figure 16.6(a) and are therefore uninformative regarding the underlying relationships.

We can also examine the regression estimators. The slope coefficient from a regression of Y_t on X_t has the asymptotic distribution

$$\widehat{\beta} = \frac{\frac{1}{n^2}\sum_{i=1}^n Y_i^* X_i^*}{\frac{1}{n^2}\sum_{i=1}^n X_i^{*2}} \underset{d}{\longrightarrow} \frac{\int_0^1 W_1^* W_2^*}{\int_0^1 W_2^{*2}}.$$

[9]Calculated by simulation from one million simulation draws of samples of size $n = 10{,}000$.

[10]Since the variables have been standardized to have a unit variance, the sample correlation equals the least squares slope coefficient.

This is a nondegenerate random variable. Thus the slope estimator remains random in large samples and does not converge in probability.

Now consider the classical t-ratio T. It has the asymptotic distribution

$$\frac{1}{n^{1/2}}T = \frac{\frac{1}{n^2}\sum_{i=1}^n Y_i^* X_i^*}{\left(\frac{1}{n^2}\sum_{i=1}^n X_i^{*2}\right)^{1/2}\left(\frac{1}{n^2}\sum_{i=1}^n \left(Y_i^* - X_i^*\widehat{\beta}\right)^2\right)^{1/2}} \underset{d}{\longrightarrow} \frac{\int_0^1 W_1^* W_2^*}{\left(\int_0^1 W_2^{*2}\right)^{1/2}\left(\int_0^1\left(W_1^* - W_2^*\frac{\int_0^1 W_1^* W_2^*}{\int_0^1 W_2^{*2}}\right)^2\right)^{1/2}}.$$

This is nondegenerate. Thus the t-ratio has an asymptotic distribution only after normalization by $n^{1/2}$, meaning that the unnormalized t-ratio diverges in probability!

To understand the utter failure of classical inference theory, observe that the regression equation is

$$Y_t = \alpha + \beta X_t + \xi_t \tag{16.12}$$

with true values $\alpha = 0$ and $\beta = 0$. Thus the error $\xi_t = Y_t$ is a random walk. The latter is considerably more strongly autocorrelated than allowed by stationary regression theory, invalidating conventional standard errors. The latter are too small by an order of magnitude, resulting in t-ratios that are misleadingly large.

What this means in practice is that t-ratios from spurious regressions are random and large, even when there is no relationship. This explains the large t-ratio $T = 26$ for the simulated series and shows that the value $T = 15$ for the empirical series is uninformative. The reason for a large t-ratio is not because the series are related but is instead because the series are unit root processes, so classical standard errors mis-characterize estimation variance.

One of the features of the above theory is that it shows that the magnitude of the distortion of the t-ratio increases with sample size. Interestingly, the original Granger and Newbold (1974) analysis was a simulation study that confined attention to the case $n = 50$. Granger and Newbold found the (then surprising) result that t-tests substantially overreject under the null hypothesis of a zero coefficient. It wasn't until the theoretical analysis by P. Phillips (1986) that it was realized that this distortion *worsened* as sample size increased. These results illustrate the insights—and limitations—of simulation analysis. Using simulation, Granger and Newbold pointed out that there was a problem. But by fixing sample size at a single value, they did not discover the surprising effect of sample size.

That the t-ratio diverges as n increases means that the coverage of classical confidence intervals worses as n increases. To calibrate the magnitude of this distortion, examine Figure 16.6(b), which plots[11] the finite-sample coverage probability of classical nominal 95% confidence intervals for the slope using student t critical values plotted as a function of sample size n. The observations were generated as independent random walks with normal innovations. You can see that the coverage ranges from 0.68 (for $n = 10$) to 0.2 (for $n = 200$). These coverage rates are unacceptably below the nominal coverage level of 0.95.

The above analysis focuses on classical t-ratios and confidence intervals constructed with old-fashioned homoskedastic standard errors. This analysis may seem out-of-date, as we have made the case that old-fashioned standard errors are not used in contemporary econometric practice. However, the problem as described carries over to alternative standard error constructions. The common heteroskedastic standard errors do not fundamentally change the asymptotic distribution. The Newey-West standard errors reduce the undercoverage but only partially. They are designed to consistently estimate the long-run variance of stationary series but fail when the series are nonstationary.

[11] Calculated by simulation on a grid of values for n with one million simulation replications.

At this point, let us summarize what we have learned. If we have two time series that are independent unit root processes, then by using time series plots, correlation analysis, and simple linear regressions, it is easy to make the false inference that they are related. Their sample correlations and regression slope estimates will be random, inconsistent, and uninformative.

Our deduction is that it is inappropriate to use simple inference techniques when handling potentially nonstationary time series. We need to be more careful and use better inference methods.

It turns out that a simple modification is often sufficient to fundamentally alter the inference problem. Again, suppose we observe the independent series (16.10) and (16.11). A linear regression model is (16.12) with error $\xi_t = Y_t$. We can write the latter as $\xi_t = Y_{t-1} + e_t$. Then a correct dynamic specfication of the regression model is

$$Y_t = \alpha + \beta X_t + \delta Y_{t-1} + e_t \tag{16.13}$$

with $\alpha = \beta = 0$ and $\delta = 1$. If equation (16.13) is estimated, the error is no longer a random walk, and inference on β can proceed conventionally! In this simple example, a solution is simply to include the lagged dependent variable Y_{t-1} in the estimated regression. More generally, if a trend component is missing or ΔY_t is serially correlated, it is necessary to include the trend terms and/or sufficient lags of Y_t in the estimated regression.

For example, take the simulated random walk series from Figure 16.5(a). Estimating model (16.13), we find $\widehat{\beta} = 0.004$ with a standard error of 0.005. Thus by adding the lagged dependent variable, the spurious regression relationship has been broken. Now take the empirical series from Figure 16.5(b). Let us estimate an analog of (16.13) augmented with a linear trend. The estimate of β in this model is 0.16 with a standard error of 0.12. Once again, the spurious regression relationship has been broken by a simple dynamic readjustment.

This seems like a straightforward solution. If so, why does the spurious regression problem persist[12] in applied analysis? The reason is partially that nonspecialists find that the simple regression (16.12) is easy to interpret, while the dynamic model (16.13) is challenging to interpret. One of the tasks of a skilled econometrician is to understand this failure of reasoning, to explain the problem to colleagues and users, and to present constructive useful alternative methods of analysis.

16.16 NONSTATIONARY VARS

Let Y_t be an $m \times 1$ time series. Suppose that Y_t satisfies a VAR(p-1) in first differences, and thus $\boldsymbol{D}(\mathrm{L})\Delta Y_t = e_t$, where $\boldsymbol{D}(z)$ is invertible, and $\Sigma = \operatorname{var}[e_t] > 0$. Then ΔY_t has the long-run covariance matrix $\Omega = \boldsymbol{D}(1)^{-1}\Sigma\boldsymbol{D}(1)^{-1\prime} > 0$. In this case, Y_t is a vector $I(1)$ process in the sense that each element of Y_t is $I(1)$, and so are all linear combinations of Y_t.

The model can be written as a VAR in levels as

$$Y_t = \boldsymbol{A}_1 Y_{t-1} + \boldsymbol{A}_2 Y_{t-2} + \cdots + \boldsymbol{A}_p Y_{t-p} + e_t \tag{16.14}$$

where $\boldsymbol{A}_1 + \boldsymbol{A}_2 + \cdots + \boldsymbol{A}_p = \boldsymbol{I}_m$. It can also be written in the mixed format

$$\Delta Y_t = \boldsymbol{A} Y_{t-1} + \boldsymbol{D}_1 \Delta Y_{t-1} + \cdots + \boldsymbol{D}_{p-1}\Delta Y_{t-p+1} + e_t \tag{16.15}$$

where $\boldsymbol{A} = 0$. These are equivalent algebraic representations. Let $d = \operatorname{vec}\left(\left(\boldsymbol{D}_1, \ldots, \boldsymbol{D}_{p-1}\right)'\right)$.

[12] An amusing exercise is to peruse newspaper/magazine articles for time series plots of historical series. More often than not, the displayed series appear to be $I(1)$, and more often than not, the article describes the series as "related" based on a combination of eyeball analysis and simple correlation statistics.

Let $\left(\widehat{\boldsymbol{A}}, \widehat{d}\right)$ be the multivariate least squares estimator of (16.15). Set $X_t = (\Delta Y_{t-1}, \ldots, \Delta Y_{t-p+1})$.

Theorem 16.16 Assume that ΔY_t follows the VAR(p-1) process $\boldsymbol{D}(\mathrm{L})\Delta Y_t = e_t$ with invertible $\boldsymbol{D}(z)$, $\mathbb{E}\left[e_t \mid \mathscr{F}_{t-1}\right] = 0$, $\mathbb{E}\left\|e_t\right\|^4 < \infty$, and $\mathbb{E}\left[e_t e_t'\right] = \Sigma > 0$. Then as $n \to \infty$

$$\begin{pmatrix} n\widehat{\boldsymbol{A}} \\ \sqrt{n}\left(\widehat{d} - d\right) \end{pmatrix} \underset{d}{\longrightarrow} \begin{pmatrix} \Sigma^{1/2} \int_0^1 dWW' \left(\int_0^1 WW'\right)^{-1} \Omega^{-1/2} \\ \mathrm{N}(0, \boldsymbol{V}) \end{pmatrix}$$

where $W(r)$ is vector Brownian motion and

$$\boldsymbol{V} = \left(\boldsymbol{I}_m \otimes \mathbb{E}\left[X_t X_t'\right]\right)^{-1} \Omega \left(\boldsymbol{I}_m \otimes \mathbb{E}\left[X_t X_t'\right]\right)^{-1}$$
$$\Omega = \mathbb{E}\left[e_t e_t' \otimes X_t X_t'\right].$$

The top component of the asymptotic distribution is a multivariate version of the Dickey-Fuller coefficient distribution. The bottom component is a conventional normal distribution. Thus the coefficient estimator $\widehat{\boldsymbol{A}}$ is consistent at the $O_p(n^{-1})$ rate, converges to a non-standard (biased and non-normal) asymptotic distribution, and the coefficient estimator $\widehat{d}$ has a conventional asymptotic normal distribution.

Parameters of interest, including the coefficients of the levels equation (16.14), impulse response functions, and forecast error decompositions, are linear combinations of the estimators $\left(\widehat{\boldsymbol{A}}, \widehat{d}\right)$. For VAR(p) models with $p \geq 2$, unless the linear combination of interest is in the span of $\widehat{\boldsymbol{A}}$, the asymptotic distribution of estimators is dominated by the $O_p(n^{-1/2})$ component $\widehat{d}$. Thus these coefficient estimators have conventional asymptotic normal distributions. Consequently, for most purposes, estimation and inference on a VAR model is robust to the presence of (multivariate) unit roots.

There are two important exceptions. First, inference on the sum of levels coefficients $\boldsymbol{A}_1 + \boldsymbol{A}_2 + \cdots + \boldsymbol{A}_p$ is non-standard, as the estimator of this sum has the multivariate Dickey-Fuller coefficient distribution. This includes questions concerning the presence of unit roots and many questions concerning the long-run properties of the series. Second, the long-run impulse matrix $\boldsymbol{C} = \boldsymbol{A}^{-1} = \left(\boldsymbol{I} - \boldsymbol{A}_1 - \boldsymbol{A}_2 - \cdots - \boldsymbol{A}_p\right)^{-1}$ is a (nonlinear) function of this same sum and thus by the delta method is asymptotically a linear transformation of the multivariate Dickey-Fuller coefficient distribution. Thus the least squares estimator of $\boldsymbol{C}$ is non-standard (biased and non-normal). Because $\boldsymbol{C}$ is the limit of the CIRF as the horizon tends to infinity, estimators of the CIRF at long horizons will be non-standard in finite samples. Consequently, when a VAR model includes variables that are potentially unit root processes, the conventional confidence intervals for the CIRF at long horizons are not trustworthy. This issue is widespread, because macroeconomists routinely estimate VAR models with macroeconomic variables in levels (for example, the Blanchard and Perotti (2002) model presented in Section 15.25).

16.17 COINTEGRATION

Cointegration is a fascinating topic. The idea is due to Granger (1981) and was articulated in detail by Engle and Granger (1987). A pair of unit root processes are **cointegrated** if their difference (or some linear combination) is stationary. This means that the pair "hang together" over the long run.

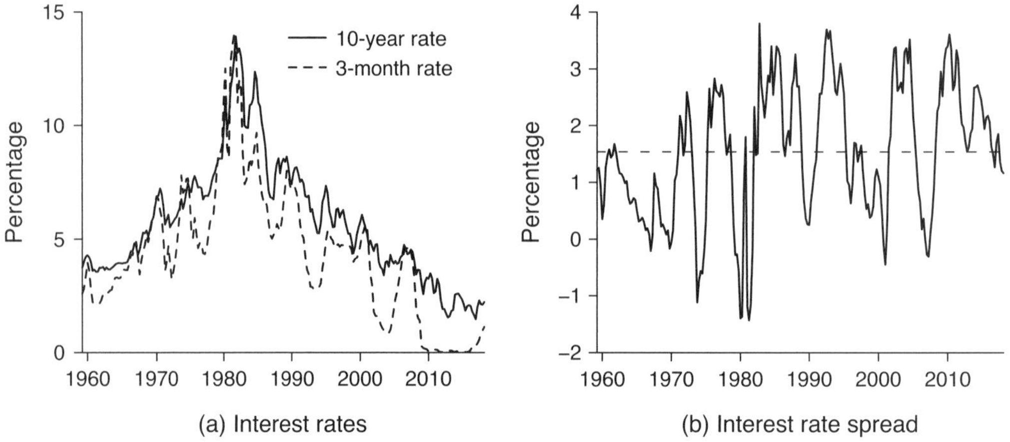

FIGURE 16.7 Cointegration

To visualize, examine Figure 16.7(a), which shows two interest rate series. The solid line is the interest rate (quarterly for 1959–2017) on 10-year U.S. Treasury Bonds.[13] The dashed line is the interest rate on 3-month U.S. Treasury Bonds.[14] Over the 59-year period, the two series move up and down together. The 10-year rate exceeds the 3-month rate in most time periods. For some periods, the two lines pull apart, but they always come together again. Thus the two time series are tightly tied together. From our unit root analysis, we have already determined that the 10-year interest rate is consistent with a unit root process; the same findings apply to the 3-month series. Thus it appears that these are two time series that are individually unit root processes but jointly track each other closely.

To see this, define the **interest rate spread** as the difference between the two interest rates, long (10-year) minus short (3-month). This series is plotted in Figure 16.7(b). The mean of the series is displayed by the dashed line. What we can see is that the spread roughly appears to be mean reverting. With the possible exception of the first decade of the plot, we see that the spread crosses its mean multiple times each decade. The fluctuations appear to be stationary. Applying an ADF unit root test with no trend included to the spread yields ADF $= -4.0$, which is less than the 1% critical value, rejecting the null hypothesis of a unit root. Thus the levels of the two interest rates appear to be nonstationary, while the spread is stationary. This result suggests that the two interest rate series are cointegrated.

This concept is formalized in the following definition.

Definition 16.5 The $m \times 1$ nondeterministic series Y_t is **cointegrated** if there exists a full rank $m \times m$ matrix $[\beta, \beta_\perp]$ such that $\beta' Y_t \in \mathbb{R}^r$ and $\beta_\perp' \Delta Y_t \in \mathbb{R}^{m-r}$ are $I(0)$. The r vectors in β are called the **cointegrating vectors**. The variable $Z_t = \beta' Y_t$ is called the **equilibrium error**.

In the interest rate example of Figure 16.7, there are $m = 2$ series and $r = 1$ cointegrating relationships. Our discussion assumes that the cointegrating vector is $\beta = (1, -1)'$.

[13]From FRED-QD, series *gs10*.

[14]From FRED-QD, series *tb3ms*.

The cointegrating vectors β are not individually identified; only the space spanned by the vectors is identified, so β is typically normalized. When $r=1$, a common normalization is to set one nonzero element equal to 1. Another common normalization is to set β to be orthonormal: $\beta'\beta = \boldsymbol{I}_r$.

Theorem 16.17 Granger Representation Theorem, Part I. If nondeterministic $Y_t \in \mathbb{R}^m$ is cointegrated with $m \times r$ cointegrating vectors β, and (16.1) holds, then

1. The coefficients of the Wold representation
$$\Delta Y_t = \theta + \Theta(\mathrm{L}) e_t \tag{16.16}$$
satisfy $\Theta(1) = \beta_\perp \eta'$ and $\theta = \beta_\perp \gamma$ for some full-rank $m \times (m-r)$ matrix η and some $(m-r) \times 1 \gamma$.
2. The Beveridge-Nelson decomposition of Y_t is
$$Y_t = \beta_\perp \left(\gamma t + \eta' S_t\right) + U_t + V_0 \tag{16.17}$$
where $S_t = \sum_{i=1}^t e_t$, $U_t = \Theta^*(\mathrm{L}) e_t$ is a stationary linear process, and $V_0 = Y_0 - U_0$ is an initial condition.
3. Assume further that (a) all complex solutions to det $(\Theta(z)) = 0$ are either $z=1$ or $|z| \geq 1+\delta$ for some $\delta > 0$; and that (b) $\beta'\Theta^*(1)\eta_\perp$ is full rank, where $\eta_\perp$ is a full rank $m \times r$ matrix such that $\eta'\eta_\perp = 0$. Then Y_t has the (infinite-order) convergent VAR representation
$$\boldsymbol{A}(\mathrm{L}) Y_t = a + e_t \tag{16.18}$$
where the coefficients satisfy $\boldsymbol{A}(1) = -\eta_\perp \left(\beta'\Theta^*(1)\eta_\perp\right)^{-1} \beta'$. All complex solutions to det $(\boldsymbol{A}(z)) = 0$ are either $z=1$ or $|z| \geq 1+\delta$ for some $\delta > 0$.
4. Under the assumptions of part 3 plus $\sum_{j=0}^\infty \left\| \sum_{k=0}^\infty k \Theta_{j+k} \right\|^2 < \infty$, the VAR representation can be written in error-correction form
$$\Delta Y_t = \alpha \beta' Y_{t-1} + \Gamma(\mathrm{L}) \Delta Y_{t-1} + a + e_t \tag{16.19}$$
where $\Gamma(\mathrm{L})$ is a lag polynomial with absolutely summable coefficient matrices and $\alpha = -\eta_\perp \left(\beta'\Theta^*(1)\eta_\perp\right)^{-1}$.
5. If $\theta = 0$ in the Wold representation (16.16) then $\gamma = 0$ in (16.17) so there is no linear trend in (16.17). The intercept in (16.18) and (16.19) equals $a = \alpha\mu$ where μ is $r \times 1$. Equation (16.19) can be written as
$$\Delta Y_t = \alpha \left(\beta' Y_{t-1} + \mu\right) + \Gamma(\mathrm{L}) \Delta Y_{t-1} + e_t. \tag{16.20}$$

The proof is presented in Section 16.22. The Granger Representation Theorem appears in Engle and Granger (1987). The assumption on $\beta'\Theta^*(1)\eta_\perp$ was introduced by Johansen (1995, theorem 4.5).

Part 1 shows that the coefficients of the Wold representation sum to a singular matrix in the null space of the cointegrating vectors.

Part 2 gives the Beveridge-Nelson permanent-transitory representation of Y_t. It shows that the trend $\beta_\perp \left(\gamma t + \eta' S_t\right)$ lies in the null space of the cointegrating vectors. Thus there is no trend in the range space of the cointegrating vectors. So the cointegrated vector Y_t can be thought of as possessing r "unit roots and linear trends" and $m-r$ "stationary processes."

Part 3 provides the VAR representation. It shows that the VAR coefficients sum to a singular matrix that is in the range space of the cointegrating vectors.

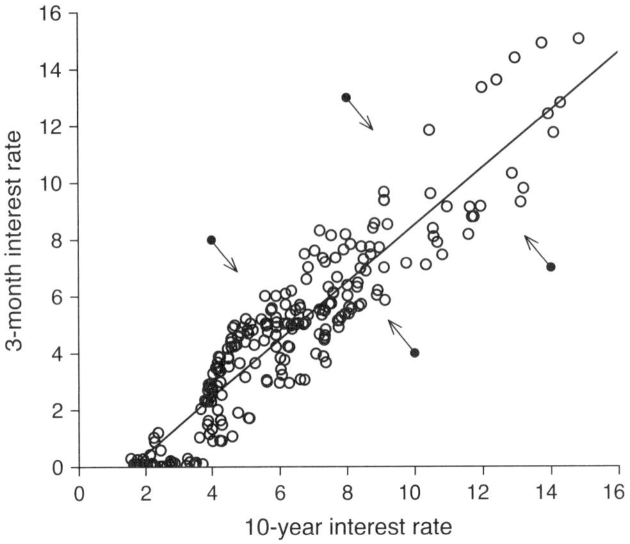

FIGURE 16.8 Error correction effect

Part 4 is perhaps the most famous result. It shows that a cointegrated system satisfies equation (16.19), which is called the **error-correction representation**. Equation (16.19) viewed as a model is called a **vector error correction model** (VECM). The error-correction representation is a regression model in stationary transformations, because the variables ΔY_t and $\beta' Y_{t-1}$ are stationary. The equation shows that the change ΔY_t relates to past changes ΔY_{t-1} (as in a standard VAR) as well as the equilibrium error $\beta' Y_{t-1}$. The full term $\alpha\beta' Y_{t-1}$ is known as the "error-correction term." It is the key component that governs how the cointegrated relationship is maintained.

Part 5 examines the case of no linear trend. The condition $\theta = 0$ arises when the variables ΔY_t are all mean 0. The theorem (unsuprisingly) shows that this implies that the linear trend does not appear in the Beveridge-Nelson decomposition. More interestingly, the theorem shows that this condition implies that the error-correction model can be written to incorporate the intercept.

To understand the error-correction effect, examine Figure 16.8, which shows a scatter plot of the historical values of the two interest rate series from Figure 16.7. Also plotted is an estimate[15] of the linear relation $\beta' Y + \mu$ displayed as the solid line. This is the attractor of the system. For values of Y on this line, $\beta' Y + \mu = 0$. For values to the southeast, $\beta' Y + \mu < 0$, and for values to the northwest, $\beta' Y + \mu > 0$. The components of α dictate how these values impact the expected direction of ΔY. The arrows indicate these directions.[16] When $\beta' Y + \mu > 0$, the error correction decreases the 3-month rate and increases the 10-year rate, pushing Y toward the line of attraction. When $\beta' Y + \mu < 0$, the error correction increases the 3-month rate and decreases the 10-year rate, again pushing Y toward the line of attraction. In this particular example, the two effects are similar in magnitude, so the arrows in Figure 16.8 show that both variables move toward the attractor in response to deviations.

Theorem 16.17 shows that if Y_t is cointegrated, then it satisfies a VECM. The reverse is also the case.

[15]From Table 16.4 in Section 16.20.

[16]From the estimates in Table 16.5 in Section 16.20.

Theorem 16.18 Granger Representation Theorem, Part II. Suppose that Y_t satisfies a VAR(∞) model $\boldsymbol{A}(\mathrm{L})Y_t = a + e_t$ with VECM representation

$$\Delta Y_t = \alpha\beta' Y_{t-1} + \Gamma(\mathrm{L})\Delta Y_{t-1} + a + e_t$$

where β and α are $m \times r$ and full rank. Suppose that (a) All complex solutions to $\det(\boldsymbol{A}(z)) = 0$ are either $z = 1$ or $|z| \geq 1 + \delta$ for some $\delta > 0$; (b) $\sum_{j=0}^{\infty} \left\|\Gamma_j\right\| < \infty$; (c) $\alpha'_{\perp}\left(\boldsymbol{I}_m - \Gamma(1)\right)\beta_{\perp}$ is full rank, where $\alpha_{\perp}$ and $\beta_{\perp}$ lie in the null spaces of α and β. Then Y_t is cointegrated with cointegrating vectors β.

The proof is presented in Section 16.22. This result for a finite-order VAR first appeared in Johansen (1995, theorem 4.2).

The condition that $\alpha'_{\perp}\Gamma(1)\beta_{\perp}$ is full rank is necessary to exclude the (somewhat pathological) possibility that the system is "multi-cointegrated," meaning that a linear combination of $\beta' Y_{t-1}$ and ΔY_{t-1} is of reduced order of integration. Together, Theorems 16.17 and 16.18 show that a VECM representation is necessary and sufficient for a vector time series to be cointegrated.

16.18 ROLE OF INTERCEPT AND TREND

The role of intercepts and trends in cointegrating VECMs gives rise to distinct models. I list some of the major options.

1. **Trend Model 1**. This specification has no intercept or trend terms:

   $$\Delta Y_t = \alpha\beta' Y_{t-1} + \Gamma(\mathrm{L})\Delta Y_{t-1} + e_t.$$

   This model is convenient for pedagogy but is not relevant for empirical applications. In Stata, use option `trend(none)`.
2. **Trend Model 2**. This specification is appropriate for non-trended series, such as interest rates. In this model, the intercept is in the cointegrating relationship

   $$\Delta Y_t = \alpha\left(\beta' Y_{t-1} + \mu\right) + \Gamma(\mathrm{L})\Delta Y_{t-1} + e_t.$$

   In Stata, use option `trend(rconstant)`.
3. **Trend Model 3**. This model is appropriate for series that have possible linear trends. It has an unconstrained intercept

   $$\Delta Y_t = \alpha\beta' Y_{t-1} + \Gamma(\mathrm{L})\Delta Y_{t-1} + a + e_t.$$

   In this model, the level series Y_t is the sum of a linear time trend and a unit root process. The equilibrium error $\beta' Y_t$ is stationary, so this eliminates the linear time trend and the unit root component. In Stata, use option `trend(constant)`.
4. **Trend Model 4**. This model extends the VECM model to allow a linear trend in the cointegrating relationship. This model is

   $$\Delta Y_t = \alpha\left(\beta' Y_{t-1} + \mu t\right) + \Gamma(\mathrm{L})\Delta Y_{t-1} + a + e_t.$$

In this model, the level series Y_t is the sum of a linear time trend and a unit root process. The equilibrium error $\beta' Y_t$ contains a linear time trend and a stationary process. Thus the cointegrating vector β only eliminates the unit root, not the time trend component. In Stata, use option `trend(rtrend)`.

5. **Trend Model 5**. This model is a further extension, allowing an unconstrained trend term

$$\Delta Y_t = \alpha\beta' Y_{t-1} + \Gamma(\mathrm{L})\Delta Y_{t-1} + a + bt + e_t.$$

In this model, the unconstrained trend induces a quadratic time trend into the levels series Y_t. It is not a typical modeling choice for applied economic time series. In Stata, use option `trend(trend)`.

16.19 COINTEGRATING REGRESSION

If Y_t is cointegrated with a single cointegrating vector ($r=1$), then it turns out that β can be estimated by a least squares regression of one component of Y_t on the others. This approach may be fruitfully employed when the major focus is the cointegrating vector, the number of variables m is small (e.g. $m=2$ or $m=3$), and it is known that the number of cointegrating vectors r is at most one.

Partition $Y_t = (Y_{1t}, Y_{2t})$, and reparameterize β as $(1, -\beta)$. Thus the first component of the cointegrating vector has been normalized to 1 (this requires that the true value is nonzero) and the remainder multiplied by -1. The coefficient of interest is β. Least squares is fit either to the equation

$$Y_{1t} = \mu + \beta' Y_{2t} + u_{1t} \tag{16.21}$$

(for Trend Models 1 or 2) or to the equation

$$Y_{1t} = \mu + \theta t + \beta' Y_{2t} + u_{1t} \tag{16.22}$$

(for Trend Models 3 or 4).

Define $u_{2t} = \Delta Y_{2t}$, $u_t = (u_{1t}, u_{2t}')'$, and the long-run covariance matrix $\Omega = \Sigma + \Lambda + \Lambda'$, where $\Sigma = \mathbb{E}\left[u_t u_{t-\ell}'\right]$ and $\Lambda = \sum_{\ell=1}^{\infty} \mathbb{E}\left[u_{t-\ell} u_t'\right]$. Partition the covariance matrices conformably with Y, that is,

$$\Omega = \begin{bmatrix} \Omega_{11} & \Omega_{12} \\ \Omega_{21} & \Omega_{22} \end{bmatrix}.$$

Theorem 16.19 If u_t satisfies the conditions of Theorem 16.4 and $\Omega_{22} > 0$, then the least squares estimator satisfies

$$n\left(\widehat{\beta} - \beta\right) \underset{d}{\longrightarrow} \left(\int_0^1 XX'\right)^{-1} \left(\int_0^1 X dB_1 + \Sigma_{21} + \Lambda_{21}\right)$$

where $B(r) = (B_1(r), B_2(r))$ is a vector Brownian motion with covariance matrix Ω, and $X(r)$ is determined by the model:

Trend Model 1 or 2 estimated by (16.21): $X = B_2^*$ (demeaned $B_2(r)$).
Trend Model 3 or 4 estimated by (16.22): $X = B_2^{**}$ (detrended $B_2(r)$).

The proof is presented in Section 16.22.

Theorem 16.19 shows that the estimator converges at the superconsistent $O_p(n^{-1})$ rate. This was discovered by Stock (1987), and the asymptotic distribution was derived by Park and Phillips (1988b). The asymptotic distribution is non-standard due to the serial correlation terms. Consider our empirical example. A least squares regression of the 3-month interest rate on the 10-year interest rate yields the estimated equation $\widehat{Y}_{1t} = 1.03Y_{2t} - 1.71$.

Modifications to the least squares estimator that eliminate the non-standard components were introduced by P. Phillips and B. Hansen (1990) and Stock and Watson (1993). The Phillips-Hansen estimator, known as Fully Modified OLS (FM-OLS), eliminates the non-standard components through first-stage estimation of the serial correlation terms. The Stock-Watson estimator, known as Dynamic OLS (DOLS), eliminates the non-standard components by estimating an augmented regression including leads and lags of ΔY_{2t}.

We are often interested in testing the hypothesis of no cointegration:

$$\mathbb{H}_0 : r = 0$$

$$\mathbb{H}_1 : r > 0.$$

Under $\mathbb{H}_0$, $Z_t = \beta' Y_t$ is $I(1)$, yet under $\mathbb{H}_1$ Z_t is $I(0)$. When β is known, $\mathbb{H}_0$ can be tested by appying a univariate ADF test on Z_t. Consider the interest rate example from Section 16.17. We already conjectured that the interest rate spread is stationary, which is the same as the hypothesis that $\beta = 1$ is the cointegrating coefficient. Using this value, we computed ADF $= -4.0$ with an asymptotic p-value less than 0.01. Hence we are able to reject the null hypothesis of a unit root in the spread, or equivalently, reject the null hypothesis of no cointegration.

When β is unknown, Engle and Granger (1987) proposed testing the null hypothesis of no cointegration by applying the ADF test to the least squares residual $\widehat{u}_{1t}$ from either (16.21) or (16.22). The asymptotic null distribution is different from the Dickey-Fuller distribution, since under $\mathbb{H}_0$, the estimated regression is spurious, so the least squares estimator is inconsistent. The asymptotic distribution of the statistic was worked out by P. Phillips and Ouliaris (1990) by combining the theory of spurious regression with Dickey-Fuller distribution theory. Let EG_p denote the Engle-Granger ADF statistic with p autoregressive lags in the ADF regression.

Theorem 16.20 Assume that $(\Delta Y_{1t}, \Delta Y_{2t})$ satisfies the conditions of Theorem 16.4, and $\Omega > 0$. If $p \to \infty$ as $n \to \infty$ such that $p^3/n \to 0$, then

$$\mathrm{EG}_p \underset{d}{\longrightarrow} \frac{\left(\int_0^1 V dV\right)}{\left(\int_0^1 V^2\right)^{1/2} (1 + \zeta'\zeta)^{1/2}}$$

where $V(r) = W_1^*(r) - \zeta' W_2^*(r)$ and $\zeta = \left(\int_0^1 W_2^* W_2^{*\prime}\right)^{-1} \left(\int_0^1 W_2^* W_1^*\right)$, $W(r) = (W_1(r), W_2(r))$ is vector standard Brownian motion, and $W^*(r)$ is demeaned $W(r)$ if (16.21) is estimated or it is detrended $W(r)$ if (16.22) is estimated.

For a proof, see P. Phillips and Ouliaris (1990).

An unusual feature of this theorem is that it requires $p \to \infty$ as $n \to \infty$, even if the true process is a finite order AR process, because the first stage spurious regression induces serial correlation into the first-stage residuals, which needs to be handled in the second stage ADF test. Another unusual feature is the component $1 + \zeta'\zeta$ in the denominator. This is due to the variance estimator component, which asymptotically is random because of the first stage spurious regression.

Table 16.3
Engle-Granger cointegration test critical values

	Intercept			Trend		
	$m=2$	$m=3$	$m=4$	$m=2$	$m=3$	$m=4$
0.01%	−5.07	−5.44	−5.81	−5.52	−5.82	−6.12
0.1%	−4.54	−4.93	−5.28	−4.96	−5.28	−5.60
1%	−3.89	−4.29	−4.64	−4.33	−4.66	−4.97
2%	−3.67	−4.07	−4.42	−3.97	−4.44	−4.74
3%	−3.53	−3.93	−4.28	−3.86	−4.30	−4.61
4%	−3.42	−3.82	−4.18	−3.78	−4.20	−4.51
5%	−3.34	−3.74	−4.09	−3.65	−4.12	−4.42
7%	−3.20	−3.61	−3.96	−3.50	−3.98	−4.29
10%	−3.04	−3.45	−3.81	−3.48	−3.83	−4.14
15%	−2.85	−3.26	−3.62	−3.31	−3.65	−3.96
20%	−2.70	−3.11	−3.47	−3.16	−3.50	−3.81
30%	−2.45	−2.86	−3.23	−2.92	−3.26	−3.57
50%	−2.05	−2.47	−2.83	−2.54	−2.87	−3.18
70%	−1.65	−2.08	−2.45	−2.16	−2.49	−2.80
90%	−1.00	−1.48	−1.88	−1.60	−1.94	−2.25
99%	0.09	−0.44	−0.94	−0.69	−1.05	−1.41

Source: Calculated by simulation from one million replications of samples of size $n = 10{,}000$

The asymptotic critical values[17] are displayed in Table 16.3. The EG test is one-sided, so rejections occur when the test statistic is less than (more negative than) the critical value. The critical values are a function of the number of variables m and the detrending method.

Let's summarize the Engle-Granger cointegration test: The null hypothesis is that the series is not cointegrated, or equivalently, that the equilibrium error is $I(1)$. The alternative hypothesis is cointegration. The regression (16.21) or (16.22) is estimated by least squares to obtain the residual. The ADF test is applied to this residual. This is done by fitting an AR(p) model and testing that the sum of the autoregressive coefficients equals 1. Critical values are taken from Table 16.3 according to the trend specification (discussed below) and the number of variables m. If the t-statistic is smaller than the appropriate critical value, the null hypothesis of no cointegration is rejected in favor of the hypothesis of cointegrationd. Otherwise, the hypothesis of no cointegration is not rejected.

An important question is which trend model to fit. If the observations are untrended, then the intercept regression (16.21) should be fit and the "Intercept" critical values used. If the observations are trended and no constraints are imposed, then the trend regression (16.22) should be fit and the "Trend" critical values used. A complication arises in the case of Model 3, which allows the observations to be trended but the trend is excluded from the cointegrating regression. In this case, there are two options. One is to treat the situation as Model 4: estimate regression (16.22) and use the associated critical values. The other option is to estimate (16.21), because the linear trend is not in the cointegrating relationship. In this case, the appropriate critical values are from the "Trend" section of Table 16.3, but with the row corresponding to $m-1$. This is because one of the unit root processes in regression (16.22) is dominated by a linear trend. For example, if there are $m=3$ variables in the system and (16.21) is estimated, then use the critical values for "Trend" and $m=2$. If there are $m=2$ variables, then use the "Case 3" ADF critical values from Table 16.1.

[17] Calculated by simulation from one million simulation draws for a sample of size $n = 10,000$.

To illustrate, consider the interest rate application. These variables are non-trended, so we use model (16.21) with the "Intercept" critical values. The least squares residuals are $\widehat{u}_{1t} = \widehat{Y}_{1t} - 1.03Y_{2t} - 1.7$. Applying an ADF test with $p=8$, we obtain $\mathrm{EG}=-4.0$. This is smaller than the 1% asymptotic critical value of -3.9 from Table 16.3. We therefore reject the hypothesis of no cointegration, supporting the hypothesis that the pair is cointegrated.

16.20 VECM ESTIMATION

The Granger Representation Theorem (Theorems 16.17 and 16.18) showed that Y_t is cointegrated if (and only if) Y_t satisfies an error-correction model. A VECM(p) model is

$$\Delta Y_t = \alpha\beta' Y_{t-1} + \Gamma_1 \Delta Y_{t-1} + \cdots + \Gamma_{p-1}\Delta Y_{t-p+1} + a + e_t. \tag{16.23}$$

This is a reduced rank regression, as introduced in Section 11.11. The standard estimation method is maximum likelihood under the auxilary assumption that e_t is i.i.d. $\mathrm{N}(0,\Sigma)$, as described in Theorem 11.7. I repeat this result here for the VECM model.

Theorem 16.21 The MLE for the VECM (16.23) under $e \sim \mathrm{N}(0,\Sigma)$ is given as follows. First, regress ΔY_t and Y_{t-1} on $\Delta Y_{t-1},\ldots,\Delta Y_{t-p+1}$ and an intercept to obtain the residual vectors $\widehat{u}_{0t}$ and $\widehat{u}_{1t}$, organized in matrices as $\widehat{\boldsymbol{U}}_0$ and $\widehat{\boldsymbol{U}}_1$. The MLE $\widehat{\beta}$ equals the first r generalized eigenvectors of $\frac{1}{n}\widehat{\boldsymbol{U}}_1'\widehat{\boldsymbol{U}}_0\left(\frac{1}{n}\widehat{\boldsymbol{U}}_0'\widehat{\boldsymbol{U}}_0\right)^{-1}\frac{1}{n}\widehat{\boldsymbol{U}}_0'\widehat{\boldsymbol{U}}_1$ with respect to $\frac{1}{n}\widehat{\boldsymbol{U}}_1'\widehat{\boldsymbol{U}}_1$, corresponding to the r largest eigenvalues $\widehat{\lambda}_j$. This uses the normalization $\widehat{\beta}'\frac{1}{n}\widehat{\boldsymbol{U}}_1'\widehat{\boldsymbol{U}}_1\widehat{\beta} = \boldsymbol{I}_r$. The MLE for the remaining coefficients $\widehat{\alpha}, \widehat{\Gamma}_1,\ldots,\widehat{\Gamma}_{p-1}$, and $\widehat{a}$ are obtained by the least squares regression of ΔY_t on $\widehat{\beta}'Y_{t-1}, \Delta Y_{t-1},\ldots,\Delta Y_{t-p+1}$, and an intercept. The maximized log-likelihood function is

$$\ell_n(r) = \frac{m}{2}\left(n\log(2\pi) - 1\right) - \frac{n}{2}\det\left(\frac{1}{n}\widehat{\boldsymbol{U}}_0'\widehat{\boldsymbol{U}}_0\right) - \frac{n}{2}\sum_{j=1}^{r}\log\left(1-\widehat{\lambda}_j\right).$$

This estimation method was developed by Johansen (1988, 1991, 1995) as an extension of the reduced rank regression of Anderson (1951).

The VECM is a constrained VAR, so the VECM estimates can be used for any purpose for which a VAR is used. An advantage of the VECM estimation approach is that it provides a coherent model of the system, is computationally straightforward, and can handle multiple cointegrating vectors. A disadvantage is that when there are multiple cointegrating vectors ($r > 1$), then interpretation of the cointegrating space (the space spanned by β) is difficult.

The VECM model assumes that the VAR order p and cointegrating rank r are known. In practice, data-based selection rules are used. AIC minimization may be used for selection of p. A simple approach is to select p by estimating unrestricted VAR models. Selection of r is typically done by testing methods, which is reviewed in Section 16.21.

We illustrate with the two interest rate series already introduced. AIC selection on levels VARs selects a VAR(8); we report here a VAR(4), as it yields similar results. This implies a VECM with three dynamic lags. Since interest rates are not a trended series, we use Trend Model 2. The estimated model is reported in Tables 16.4 and 16.5.

Table 16.4
VECM cointegrating vector

	β	s.e.
3-month	1	
10-year	−1.01	0.07
Intercept	1.58	0.46

Table 16.5
Vector error correction model

	Δ3-month$_t$	Δ10-year$_t$
Z_{t-1}	−0.09	0.07
	(0.04)	(0.03)
Δ3-month$_{t-1}$	0.37	0.04
	(0.08)	(0.06)
Δ3-month$_{t-2}$	−0.20	−0.08
	(0.08)	(0.06)
Δ3-month$_{t-3}$	0.28	0.07
	(0.08)	(0.06)
Δ10-year$_{t-1}$	0.06	0.21
	(0.07)	(0.08)
Δ10-year$_{t-2}$	−0.19	−0.09
	(0.12)	(0.08)
Δ10-year$_{t-3}$	0.10	0.06
	(0.12)	(0.08)

Table 16.4 reports the estimated cointegrating vector β. The coefficient on the 3-month interest rate is normalized to 1. The estimated coefficient on the 10-year rate is near -1, and the estimated intercept is about 1.6. The latter means that the 3-month rate is on average 1.6 percentage points below the 10-year rate. The coefficients of the estimated VECM are reported in Table 16.5, one column for each variable. The first reported coefficient is $\widehat{\alpha}$, the error-correction term. The coefficient for the 3-month rate is negative and that for the 10-year rate is positive, and they are of similar magnitude. Thus when the 3-month rate exceeds the 10-year rate by more than the typical 1.6, the 3-month rate tends to fall and the 10-year rate tends to rise, moving the two rates closer to the cointegrating relation. The following six coefficients are the dynamic coefficients of the VECM. We can see that each variable tends to respond mostly to its own lagged changes. The 3-month interest rate has considerably larger coefficients than the 10-year rate, indicating that it has stronger serial correlation. The varying signs of the coefficients reveal complicated dynamics.

An asymptotic distribution of the VECM estimator requires a normalization for the cointegrating vectors. A popular choice is $\beta = (\boldsymbol{I}_r, \beta^{*\prime})'$. Johansen (1995, theorem 13.5) shows that under the assumption that the errors e_t are i.i.d. with covariance matrix Σ, the coefficient estimators $\widehat{\theta} = (\widehat{\alpha}, \widehat{\Gamma})$ satisfy

$$\sqrt{n}\left(\widehat{\theta} - \theta\right) \underset{d}{\longrightarrow} \mathrm{N}\left(0, \Sigma \otimes \boldsymbol{Q}^{-1}\right)$$

where $\boldsymbol{Q} = \mathbb{E}\left[X_t X_t'\right]$ with $X_t = (\beta' Y_{t-1}, \Delta Y_{t-1}, \ldots, \Delta Y_{t-p+1})$, the regressors given β. This is a classical (homoskedastic) asymptotic distribution for multivariate regression. This result shows that inference on the coefficients θ can proceed using conventional methods. The homoskedastic covariance matrix is due to the assumption that the errors are homoskedastic. If the latter assumption is relaxed, then the asymptotic distribution generalizes to the case of an unrestricted covariance matrix.

Johansen (1995, theorem 13.3) presents the asymptotic distribution of $\widehat{\beta}$. He shows that the asymptotic distribution is normal with a random covariance matrix. The latter is known as a mixed Gaussian distribution. From a practical point of view, this means that we can treat the asymptotic distribution as normal, because when scaled by an appropriate standard error, the asymptotic distribution is standard normal. For brevity we do not discuss the details.

In Stata, use the command `vec` to estimate a VECM with given cointegrating rank r and VAR order p.

16.21 TESTING FOR COINTEGRATION IN A VECM

Consider the model

$$\Delta Y_t = \Pi Y_{t-1} + \Gamma_1 \Delta Y_{t-1} + \cdots + \Gamma_{p-1} \Delta Y_{t-p+1} + a + e_t. \tag{16.24}$$

The Granger Representation Theorem shows that Y_t is cointegrated with r cointegrating vectors if and only if the rank of Π equals r. Thus testing for cointegration is equivalent to testing hypotheses on the rank of Π. Write the hypothesis that there are r cointegrating vectors as $\mathbb{H}(r) : \operatorname{rank}(\Pi) = r$.

Cointegration is a restriction on the unrestricted model $\mathbb{H}(m)$. A test for r cointegrating vectors against an unrestricted alternative is a test of $\mathbb{H}(r)$ against $\mathbb{H}(m)$. The likelihood ratio statistic for $\mathbb{H}(r)$ against $\mathbb{H}(m)$ is

$$\mathrm{LR}(r) = 2\left(\ell_n(m) - \ell_n(r)\right) = -n \sum_{j=1}^{m} \log\left(1 - \widehat{\lambda}_j\right) + n \sum_{j=1}^{r} \log\left(1 - \widehat{\lambda}_j\right) = -n \sum_{j=r+1}^{m} \log\left(1 - \widehat{\lambda}_j\right)$$

where $\widehat{\lambda}_j$ are the eigenvalues from the estimation problem (16.21). The test accepts $\mathbb{H}(r)$ for small values of $\mathrm{LR}(r)$; the test rejects $\mathbb{H}(r)$ for large values of $\mathrm{LR}(r)$.

The asymptotic distribution theory was developed by Johansen (1988, 1991, 1995).

Theorem 16.22 Assume that the finite-lag VECM (16.24) is correctly specified, the conditions of Theorem 16.18 hold, and the errors e_t are a MDS. Under the hypothesis that Π has rank r,

$$\mathrm{LR}(r) \underset{d}{\longrightarrow} \operatorname{tr}\left[\left(\int_0^1 dWX'\right)\left(\int_0^1 XX'\right)^{-1}\left(\int_0^1 XdW'\right)\right]$$

where $W(r)$ is an $m-r$ dimensional standard Brownian motion, and $X(r)$ is a stochastic process that is a function of $W(r)$ depending on the trend model:

1. Trend Model 1. $X(r) = W(r)$,
2. Trend Model 2. $X(r) = (W(r), 1)$,
3. Trend Model 3. $X(r) = (W_1^*(r), r - 1/2)$,
4. Trend Model 4. $X(r) = (W^*(r), r - 1/2)$,

where $W^*(r) = W(r) - \int_0^1 W$ is demeaned $W(r)$, and $W_1^*(r)$ is the first $m-r-1$ components of $W^*(r)$.

Table 16.6
VECM cointegration rank critical values: Trend model 2

$m-r$	1	2	3	4	5	6	7	8	9	10	11	12
0.01%	22.4	37.3	55.7	78.5	105	135	169	208	250	296	347	402
0.1%	17.6	31.5	48.8	70.1	95.7	125	158	196	237	282	332	385
1%	12.8	25.1	41.3	61.3	85.4	113	146	182	222	266	314	366
2%	11.3	23.1	38.7	58.4	81.9	110	141	177	216	260	308	359
3%	10.4	21.9	37.2	56.5	79.8	107	138	174	213	256	304	355
4%	9.71	21.0	36.1	55.2	78.3	105	136	171	210	254	301	352
5%	9.19	20.3	35.2	54.1	77.0	104	135	170	208	251	298	349
7%	8.42	19.2	33.8	52.5	75.0	102	132	167	205	248	295	345
10%	7.57	18.0	32.3	50.6	72.8	99.0	129	163	202	244	290	341
15%	6.60	16.6	30.4	48.3	70.1	95.9	126	159	197	239	285	335
20%	5.89	15.5	29.0	46.5	67.9	93.4	123	156	194	235	281	330
30%	4.86	13.9	26.8	43.7	64.6	89.5	119	151	188	229	274	323
50%	3.45	11.4	23.4	39.4	59.4	83.4	111	143	179	219	263	312
70%	2.39	9.39	20.4	35.5	54.6	77.6	105	136	171	210	253	300
90%	1.35	6.96	16.7	30.4	48.1	69.9	95.7	125	159	197	239	285

Source: Calculated by simulation from one million replications of samples of size $n = 10{,}000$

A proof of Theorem 16.22 is algebraically tedious. I provide a sketch in Section 16.22. See Johansen (1995, chapter 11) for full details.

Theorem 16.22 provides the asymptotic distribution of the LR test for cointegration rank. Because the asymptotic distribution equals the trace of a multivariate Dickey-Fuller distribution, the statistic LR is often referred to as the "trace test" or "Johansen's trace test." The asymptotic distribution is a function of the stochastic process $X(r)$, which equals the trend components of Y_t (under the hypothesis of r cointegrating vectors) projected orthogonally to the other regressors. For Trend Model 2, the intercept is included in the cointegrating relationship, so it is a component of $X(r)$. For Trend Model 3, the variables are trended, which dominates the other components and so appears in the asymptotic distribution. Since the intercept is excluded from the cointegrating relationship the components of $X(r)$ are all demeaned. For Trend Model 4, the linear trend is included in the cointegrating relationship, so it is added to the trend components while the intercept is excluded, thus the $X(r)$ process is demeaned.

The asymptotic distribution is a function only of $m-r$ and the trend specification. Asymptotic critical values[18] are displayed in Tables 16.6–16.8 for $m-r$ up to 12 for Trend Models 2, 3, and 4. These are upper-tailed tests, so the null hypothesis that the cointegrating rank is r is rejected if the test statistic is larger than the appropriate critical value; otherwise, the null hypothesis is not rejected. For example, the hypothesis of no cointegration is the same as $r=0$. The appropriate critical value is then the table column corresponding to the number of variables m. For example, for Trend Model 2 with $m=4$ variables, the 5% critical value is 54.1. If $\mathrm{LR}(r) > 54.1$, the hypothesis of no coingration is rejected (implying that the series is cointegrated); otherwise, the hypothesis of no cointegration is not rejected.

How are the test statistics $\mathrm{LR}(r)$ used in practice? When the cointegrating rank is unknown, the statistics can be used to determine r. The conventional procedure is a sequential test. Start with $\mathbb{H}(0)$ (the null hypothesis of no cointegration) and the associated statistic $\mathrm{LR}(0)$, which has m degrees of freedom. If the test rejects (i.e., if $\mathrm{LR}(0)$ exceeds the row m critical value), this is evidence that there is at least one cointegrating vector, or $r \geq 1$.

[18]Calculated by simulation from one million simulation draws for a sample of size $n = 10,000$.

Table 16.7
VECM cointegration rank critical values: Trend model 3

$m-r$	1	2	3	4	5	6	7	8	9	10	11	12
0.01%	15.2	31.5	49.0	71.0	96.9	125	159	196	238	283	333	386
0.1%	10.8	25.9	42.8	63.3	87.7	116	148	185	225	269	318	370
1%	6.63	20.0	35.5	54.7	77.9	105	136	171	210	253	300	351
2%	5.42	18.1	33.2	51.9	74.5	101	132	166	205	247	294	345
3%	4.72	17.0	31.7	50.2	72.5	98.9	128	163	202	244	290	341
4%	4.23	16.2	30.7	48.9	71.0	97.1	127	161	199	241	288	338
5%	3.85	15.5	29.8	47.9	69.8	95.7	126	160	197	239	285	335
7%	3.29	14.5	28.5	46.3	67.9	93.6	123	157	194	236	282	331
10%	2.71	13.4	27.1	44.5	65.8	91.1	120	154	191	232	277	327
15%	2.08	12.2	25.3	42.3	63.2	88.1	117	150	187	227	272	321
20%	1.64	11.2	24.0	40.7	61.2	85.7	114	147	183	224	268	317
30%	1.07	9.75	22.0	38.0	58.0	82.0	110	142	178	218	262	310
50%	0.45	7.68	18.9	34.0	53.1	76.2	103	134	169	208	251	298
70%	0.15	5.96	16.2	30.4	48.5	70.7	96.8	127	161	199	241	287
90%	0.02	4.04	12.8	25.7	42.5	63.3	88.1	117	150	187	227	272

Source: Calculated by simulation from one million replications of samples of size $n = 10,000$

Table 16.8
VECM cointegration rank critical values: Trend model 4

$m-r$	1	2	3	4	5	6	7	8	9	10	11	12
0.01%	27.4	44.4	64.6	90.0	117	150	186	226	271	319	372	428
0.1%	22.1	38.1	57.4	81.0	108	139	175	214	258	305	356	412
1%	16.6	31.2	49.4	71.5	97.6	128	162	200	242	288	338	392
2%	14.9	29.0	46.7	68.4	94.0	124	157	195	236	282	332	385
3%	13.9	27.6	45.1	66.4	91.8	121	154	192	233	278	328	381
4%	13.1	26.7	43.9	65.0	90.1	119	152	189	230	275	325	378
5%	12.5	25.9	42.9	63.9	88.8	118	151	187	228	273	322	375
7%	11.7	24.7	41.4	62.1	86.7	115	148	184	225	270	318	371
10%	10.7	23.3	39.8	60.1	84.4	113	145	181	221	266	314	366
15%	9.53	21.7	37.7	57.6	81.5	109	141	177	217	261	309	360
20%	8.70	20.5	36.2	55.7	79.2	107	138	174	213	257	304	356
30%	7.45	18.7	33.8	52.8	75.7	103	134	169	207	250	297	348
50%	5.70	15.9	30.0	48.1	70.2	96.2	126	160	198	240	286	336
70%	4.28	13.5	26.7	43.8	65.0	90.1	119	152	189	231	276	325
90%	2.79	10.5	22.4	38.2	58.0	81.8	110	141	177	217	261	309

Source: Calculated by simulation from one million replications of samples of size $n = 10,000$

Next, take $\mathbb{H}(1)$ (the null hypothesis of one cointegrating vector) and the associated statistic LR(1), which has $m-1$ degrees of freedom. If this test also rejects (i.e., if LR(1) exceeds the row $m-1$ critical value), this is evidence that there are at least two cointegrating vectors, or $r \geq 2$. Continue this sequence of tests until one of them fails to reject.

For example, when there are two variables ($m = 2$) compare the statistic LR(0) against the $m = 2$ critical value. If the test rejects (if the statistic exceeds the critical value), this is evidence that the series are cointegrated. If the test fails to reject, the inference is uncertain.

Table 16.9
Tests for cointegrating rank

	LR(r)	p-value
0	120	< 0.01
1	68.3	< 0.01
2	33.6	0.07
3	10.8	> 0.50
4	2.9	> 0.50

This testing procedure is appealing when m is small (e.g., $m \leq 4$) but is less appealing for large m. For large m, the procedure presents several challenges. Sequential testing requires multiple testing, for which it is difficult to control Type I error. In addition, the test can have low power, implying that the procedure is likely to "identify" an inappropriately low value of r.

An alternative approach is to use cointegration tests to verify a selected specification. Start with economic modeling to motivate the cointegrating rank r. The likelihood ratio $\mathrm{LR}(r)$ can be used to test this assumption against the unrestricted VAR. If the test rejects $\mathbb{H}(r)$, this is evidence that the proposed model is incorrect.

I illustrate using the interest rate series with a VAR(4) and Trend Model 2. Our starting presumption is that the variables are $I(1)$ and cointegrated, implying that the cointegrating rank is $r = 1$. The value of LR(0) is 31.6. To compute the p-value, we use Table 16.6 for Trend Model 2 with $m - r = 2$. The value 31.6 exceeds the 1% critical value of 25.1, so the asymptotic p-value of the test is less than 1%. Thus the null hypothesis of no cointegration is strongly rejected in favor of at least one cointegrating vector. The value of LR(1) is 2.8. The p-value is calculated using $m - r = 1$. The value 2.8 is smaller than the 50% critical value of 3.5, so the p-value is larger than 50%. The statistic does not reject the hypothesis of $\mathbb{H}(1)$. Together the statistics are consistent with the modeling assumption that the series is $I(1)$ and mutually cointegrated.

For a broader application, let us expand to five Treasury interest rates:[19] 3-month, 6-month, 1-year, 5-year, and 10-year. Our starting presumption is that each series is $I(1)$ and the system of variables are cointegrated, so that the cointegrating rank is at least 1. If all four spreads are mutually stationary, then the system will have four coingrating vectors, thus $r = 4$. However, if the the distribution of the spreads change over time, the cointegrating rank could be less than 4. Thus we expect $1 \leq r \leq 4$ but are uncertain of its precise value.

Table 16.9 reports the likelihood ratio tests for cointegration rank. The LR test for $r = 0$ is 120, which exceeds the 1% critical value of 85.4, and the LR test for $r = 1$ is 68.3, which exceeds the 1% critical value of 61.3, so we safely reject the hypotheses of $r = 0$ and $r = 1$. This suggests that $r \geq 2$. The LR test for $r = 2$ is 33.6 with a p-value of 0.07, which is borderline significant. The tests for $r = 3$ and $r = 4$ are insignificant. In sum, we cannot reject the models $\mathbb{H}(2)$, $\mathbb{H}(3)$, or $\mathbb{H}(4)$. $\mathbb{H}(2)$ is doubtful, but the statistical evidence alone cannot distinguish $\mathbb{H}(3)$ versus $\mathbb{H}(4)$. Our recommendation in this context is to use either $\mathbb{H}(3)$ or $\mathbb{H}(4)$.

In Stata, use `vecrank` to calculate the LR tests for cointegrating rank. The output is a table displaying LR(r) for $r = 0, \ldots, m - 1$, along with the asymptotic 5% critical values. The p-value can be calculated from Tables 16.6–16.8.

[19] FRED-MD series TB3MS, TB6MS, GS1, GS5, and GS10.

16.22 TECHNICAL PROOFS*

Proof of Theorem 16.1 In the text we showed that the limit distributions of S_n coincide with those of B. To appeal to the FCLT (Theorem 18.3 of *Probability and Statistics for Economists*), we need to verify that S_n is asymptotically equicontinuous (see Definition 18.7 of *Probability and Statistics for Economists*). For simplicity, we focus on the scalar case $e_t \in \mathbb{R}$.

Assume without loss of generality that $\sigma^2 = 1$. Take any $0 < \eta < 1$ and $0 < \epsilon < 1$. Set $\delta \le \epsilon\eta^4/48^2$. Note that

$$\sup_{|r_2-r_1|\le\delta} |S_n(r_2) - S_n(r_1)| \le 2 \sup_{0\le j\le \lfloor 1/\delta \rfloor} \sup_{0\le r\le\delta} \left|S_n(j\delta + r) - S_n\left(j\delta\right)\right|.$$

Then

$$\begin{aligned}
\mathbb{P}\left[\sup_{|r_2-r_1|\le\delta} |S_n(r_2) - S_n(r_1)| > \eta\right] &\le \mathbb{P}\left[\bigcup_{j=0}^{\lfloor 1/\delta \rfloor} \sup_{0\le r\le\delta} \left|S_n(j\delta + r) - S_n\left(j\delta\right)\right| > \frac{\eta}{2}\right] \\
&\le \sum_{j=0}^{\lfloor 1/\delta \rfloor} \mathbb{P}\left[\sup_{0\le r\le\delta} \left|S_n(j\delta + r) - S_n\left(j\delta\right)\right| > \frac{\eta}{2}\right] \\
&\le \left(\frac{1}{\delta} + 1\right) \mathbb{P}\left[\sup_{0\le r\le\delta} |S_n(r)| > \frac{\eta}{2}\right] \\
&= \left(\frac{1}{\delta} + 1\right) \mathbb{P}\left[\max_{i\le\lfloor n\delta \rfloor} \left|\frac{1}{\sqrt{n}} \sum_{t=1}^{i} e_t\right| > \frac{\eta}{2}\right] \\
&\le 2\left(\frac{1}{\delta} + 1\right) \mathbb{P}\left[\left|\frac{1}{\sqrt{n}} \sum_{t=1}^{\lfloor n\delta \rfloor} e_t\right| > \frac{\eta}{4}\right].
\end{aligned}$$

The final inequality is Billingsley's inequality (B.52), which holds because $\delta < \eta/4\sqrt{2}$ under the assumptions. The statement (B.52) of Billingsley's inequality assumes that e_t is an i.i.d. sequence; the result can be extended to a MDS sequence.

The CLT implies that $n^{-1/2}\sum_{t=1}^{\lfloor n\delta \rfloor} e_t \xrightarrow[d]{} Z_\delta \sim \mathrm{N}(0, \delta)$. For n sufficiently large, the final inequality is bounded by

$$\frac{3}{\delta}\mathbb{P}\left[|Z_\delta| > \frac{\eta}{4}\right] = \frac{3}{\delta}\mathbb{P}\left[Z_\delta^4 > \frac{\eta^4}{16^2}\right] \le \frac{3}{\delta}\frac{16^2}{\eta^4}\mathbb{E}\left[Z^4\right] = \frac{48^2}{\eta^4}\delta = \epsilon. \tag{16.25}$$

The first inequality is Markov's, the following equality $\mathbb{E}\left[Z_\delta^4\right] = 3\delta^2$, and the final equality is the assumption $\delta = \epsilon\eta^4/48^2$. Thus S_n satisfies the definition of asymptotic equicontinuity. ■

Proof of Theorem 16.7 Z_t has the Wold decomposition $Z_t = \Theta(\mathrm{L})e_t$. We add the additional assumption that e_t is a MDS to simplify the proof. By the Beveridge-Nelson decomposition, $Z_t = \xi_t + U_t - U_{t-1}$, where $\xi_t = \Theta(1)e_t$ and $U_t = \Theta^*(\mathrm{L})e_t$. Then

$$\begin{aligned}
\frac{1}{n}\sum_{t=1}^{n} S_{t-1}Z_t' &= \frac{1}{n}\sum_{t=1}^{n} S_{t-1}\xi_t' + \frac{1}{n}\sum_{t=1}^{n} S_{t-1}U_t' - \frac{1}{n}\sum_{t=1}^{n} S_{t-1}U_{t-1}' \\
&= \frac{1}{n}\sum_{t=1}^{n} S_{t-1}\xi_t' - \frac{1}{n}\sum_{t=1}^{n-1} Z_tU_t' + o_p(1).
\end{aligned}$$

The first term converges to $\int_0^1 BdB'$ by Theorem 16.6. The Brownian motion has covariance matrix equal to the long-run variance of Z_t, which is Ω. The second term converges in probability to $\mathbb{E}\left[Z_t U_t'\right]$. Making the substitutions $U_t = \xi_{t+1} + U_{t+1} - Z_{t+1}$ and $\mathbb{E}\left[Z_t \xi_{t+1}'\right] = 0$, this can be written as

$$\begin{aligned}
\mathbb{E}\left[Z_t U_t'\right] &= \mathbb{E}\left[Z_t \xi_{t+1}'\right] + \mathbb{E}\left[Z_t U_{t+1}'\right] - \mathbb{E}\left[Z_t Z_{t+1}'\right] \\
&= \mathbb{E}\left[Z_t U_{t+1}'\right] - \mathbb{E}\left[Z_t Z_{t+1}'\right] \\
&= \mathbb{E}\left[Z_t U_{t+2}'\right] - \mathbb{E}\left[Z_t Z_{t+2}'\right] - \mathbb{E}\left[Z_t Z_{t+1}'\right] \\
&= \cdots \\
&= -\sum_{j=1}^{\infty} \mathbb{E}\left[Z_t Z_{t+j}'\right] = -\sum_{j=1}^{\infty} \mathbb{E}\left[Z_{t-j} Z_t'\right] = -\Lambda.
\end{aligned}$$

The third line makes the substitutions $U_{t+1} = \xi_{t+2} + U_{t+2} - Z_{t+2}$ and $\mathbb{E}\left[Z_t \xi_{t+2}'\right] = 0$, and the substitutions are repeated until infinity. We have shown the result as claimed. ■

Proof of Theorem 16.8 By the definition of the stochastic integral,

$$\int_0^1 WdW = \operatorname*{plim}_{N\to\infty} \sum_{i=0}^{N-1} W\left(\frac{i}{N}\right)\left(W\left(\frac{i+1}{N}\right) - W\left(\frac{i}{N}\right)\right). \tag{16.26}$$

Take any positive integer N and any $j < N$. Observe that

$$W\left(\frac{j+1}{N}\right) = W\left(\frac{j}{N}\right) + \left(W\left(\frac{j+1}{N}\right) - W\left(\frac{j}{N}\right)\right).$$

Squaring, we obtain

$$W\left(\frac{j+1}{N}\right)^2 - W\left(\frac{j}{N}\right)^2 = 2W\left(\frac{j}{N}\right)\left(W\left(\frac{j+1}{N}\right) - W\left(\frac{j}{N}\right)\right) + \frac{1}{N}\chi_{jN}$$

where $\chi_{jN} = N\left(W\left(\frac{j+1}{N}\right) - W\left(\frac{j}{N}\right)\right)^2$. Notice that the χ_{jN} are i.i.d. across j, distributed as χ_1^2, and have expectation 1. Summing over $j = 0$ to $N-1$, we obtain

$$W(1)^2 = 2\sum_{i=0}^{N-1} W\left(\frac{i}{N}\right)\left(W\left(\frac{i+1}{N}\right) - W\left(\frac{i}{N}\right)\right) + \frac{1}{N}\sum_{i=0}^{N-1} \chi_{iN}^2.$$

Rewriting, we have

$$\sum_{i=0}^{N-1} W\left(\frac{i}{N}\right)\left(W\left(\frac{i+1}{N}\right) - W\left(\frac{i}{N}\right)\right) = \frac{1}{2}\left(W(1)^2 - \frac{1}{N}\sum_{i=0}^{N-1} \chi_{iN}^2\right).$$

By (16.26), $\int_0^1 WdW$ is the probability limit of the right side. By the WLLN, this is $\frac{1}{2}\left(W(1)^2 - 1\right)$, as claimed. ■

Proof of Theorem 16.10 We have

$$\widehat{\sigma}^2 = \frac{1}{n}\sum_{t=1}^{n-1}\widehat{e}_{t+t}^2 = \frac{1}{n}\sum_{t=1}^{n-1} e_{t+t}^2 - \frac{1}{n}\frac{\left(\frac{1}{n}\sum_{t=1}^{n-1} Y_t e_{t+1}\right)^2}{\frac{1}{n^2}\sum_{t=1}^{n-1} Y_t^2} = \frac{1}{n}\sum_{t=1}^{n-1} e_{t+t}^2 + o_p(1) \underset{p}{\longrightarrow} \sigma^2.$$

Then

$$T = \frac{\frac{1}{n}\sum_{t=1}^{n-1} Y_t e_{t+1}}{\left(\frac{1}{n^2}\sum_{t=1}^{n-1} Y_t^2\right)^{1/2}\widehat{\sigma}} \underset{d}{\longrightarrow} \frac{\sigma^2 \int_0^1 WdW}{\left(\sigma^2 \int_0^1 W^2\right)^{1/2}\sigma} = \frac{\int_0^1 WdW}{\left(\int_0^1 W^2\right)^{1/2}}.$$

■

Proof of Theorem 16.12 Pick $\eta > 0$ and $\epsilon > 0$. Pick δ such that

$$\mathbb{P}\left(\sup_{|r-s|\leq\delta} |X(r) - X(s)| > \epsilon\right) \leq \eta \tag{16.27}$$

which is possible since $X(r)$ is almost surely continuous. Set $N = \lfloor 1/\delta \rfloor$ and $t_k = kn/N$. Write $X_{nt} = D_n^{-1}X_t$. Then

$$C_n = \frac{1}{n}\sum_{k=0}^{N}\sum_{t=t_k}^{t_{k+1}-1} X_{nt}u_t = \frac{1}{n}\sum_{k=0}^{N} X_{n,t_k}\sum_{t=t_k}^{t_{k+1}-1} u_t + \frac{1}{n}\sum_{k=0}^{N}\sum_{t=t_k}^{t_{k+1}-1}\left(X_{nt} - X_{n,t_k}\right)u_t$$

and

$$|C_n| \leq \sup_{0\leq r\leq 1} |X_n(r)|\, A_n + \sup_{|r-s|\leq\delta} |X_n(r) - X_n(s)|\, B_n$$

where

$$A_n = \frac{N}{n}\max_{k\leq N}\left|\sum_{t=t_k}^{t_{k+1}-1} u_t\right|$$

$$B_n = \frac{1}{n}\sum_{t=1}^{n} |u_t|.$$

Since $X_n \underset{d}{\longrightarrow} X$ and X is continuous,

$$\sup_{0\leq r\leq 1} |X_n(r)| \underset{d}{\longrightarrow} \sup_{0\leq r\leq 1} |X(r)| < \infty$$

almost surely. Thus $\sup_{0\leq r\leq 1} |X_n(r)| = O_p(1)$. Since $X_n \underset{d}{\longrightarrow} X$,

$$\sup_{|r-s|\leq\delta} |X_n(r) - X_n(s)| \underset{d}{\longrightarrow} \sup_{|r-s|\leq\delta} |X(r) - X(s)| \leq \epsilon$$

where the inequality holds with probability exceeding $1 - \eta$ by (16.27). Thus for sufficiently large n, the left side is bounded by 2ϵ with the same probability and hence is $o_p(1)$.

For fixed N, $A_n \underset{p}{\longrightarrow} 0$ by the ergodic theorem (Theorem 14.9). The assumption that $\mathbb{E}|u_t| < \infty$ implies that $B_n = O_p(1)$. This argument shows that

$$|C_n| \le O_p(1)o_p(1) + o_p(1)O_p(1) = o_p(1)$$

as stated. ∎

Proof of Theorem 16.17

Part 1: The definition of cointegration implies that ΔY_t is stationary with a finite covariance matrix. By the multivariate Wold representation (Theorem 15.2), $\Delta Y_t = \theta + \Theta(\mathrm{L})e_t$ with the errors being white noise. Premultiplication by β' yields $\beta'\Delta Y_t = \beta'\theta + \beta'\Theta(\mathrm{L})e_t$, which has long-run variance $\beta'\Theta(1)\Sigma\Theta(1)'\beta$, where Σ is the covariance matrix of e_t. The assumption that $\beta' Y_t$ is $I(0)$ implies that $\beta'\theta = 0$ (else $\beta' Y_t$ will have a time trend). Thus θ lies in the range space of $\beta_\perp$, and hence $\theta = \beta_\perp \gamma$ for some γ. Also, the assumption that $\beta' Y_t$ is $I(0)$ implies that $\beta'\Delta Y_t$ is $I(-1)$, which implies that its long-run covariance matrix equals zero. Thus $\beta'\Theta(1) = 0$, and hence $\Theta(1) = \beta_\perp \eta'$ for some matrix η. The assumption that $\beta_\perp' \Delta Y_t$ is $I(0)$ implies that $\beta_\perp'\Theta(1)\Sigma\Theta(1)'\beta_\perp > 0$, which implies that $\Theta(1)$ must have rank $m - r$ and hence so does the matrix η.

Part 2: The Beveridge-Nelson decomposition plus $\Theta(1) = \beta_\perp\eta'$ implies $\Theta(\mathrm{L}) = \beta_\perp\eta' + \Theta^*(\mathrm{L})(1-\mathrm{L})$. Applied to the Wold representation, we obtain $\Delta Y_t = \beta_\perp\gamma + \beta_\perp\eta' e_t + \Theta^*(\mathrm{L})\Delta e_t$. Summing, we find the stated representation.

Part 3: Without loss of generality, assume that $H = [\beta, \beta_\perp]$ is orthonormal. Also define the orthonormal matrix $H_\eta = [\eta_\perp, \overline{\eta}]$, where $\overline{\eta} = \eta(\eta'\eta)^{-1/2}$. Define $X_t = H' Y_t$. The Wold representation implies $\Delta X_t = \begin{pmatrix} 0 \\ \gamma \end{pmatrix} + \boldsymbol{C}(\mathrm{L})e_t$, where using the Beveridge-Nelson decomposition we have

$$\boldsymbol{C}(\mathrm{L}) = H'\left(\beta_\perp\eta' + \Theta^*(\mathrm{L})(1-\mathrm{L})\right) = \begin{pmatrix} \beta'\Theta^*(\mathrm{L})(1-\mathrm{L}) \\ \eta' + \beta_\perp'\Theta^*(\mathrm{L})(1-\mathrm{L}) \end{pmatrix}.$$

Partition $X_t = (X_{1t}, X_{2t})$ comformably with H. We see that

$$\begin{pmatrix} \Delta X_{1t} \\ \Delta X_{2t} \end{pmatrix} = \begin{pmatrix} \beta'\Theta^*(\mathrm{L})(1-\mathrm{L})e_t \\ \gamma + \eta' e_t + \beta_\perp'\Theta^*(\mathrm{L})(1-\mathrm{L})e_t \end{pmatrix}.$$

Summing the first equation, we obtain

$$\begin{pmatrix} X_{1t} \\ \Delta X_{2t} \end{pmatrix} = \begin{pmatrix} \mu \\ \gamma \end{pmatrix} + \boldsymbol{D}(\mathrm{L})H_\eta' e_t \tag{16.28}$$

where $\mu = X_{1,0} - \beta'\Theta^*(\mathrm{L})e_0$, and

$$\boldsymbol{D}(\mathrm{L}) = \begin{pmatrix} \beta'\Theta^*(\mathrm{L}) \\ \eta' + \beta_\perp'\Theta^*(\mathrm{L})(1-\mathrm{L}) \end{pmatrix} H_\eta = \begin{pmatrix} \beta'\Theta^*(\mathrm{L})\eta_\perp & \beta'\Theta^*(\mathrm{L})\overline{\eta} \\ \beta_\perp'\Theta^*(\mathrm{L})\eta_\perp(1-\mathrm{L}) & (\eta'\eta)^{1/2} + \beta_\perp'\Theta^*(\mathrm{L})\overline{\eta}(1-\mathrm{L}) \end{pmatrix}.$$

This is an invertible matrix polynomial. To see this, first observe that

$$\boldsymbol{D}(1) = \begin{pmatrix} \beta'\Theta^*(1)\eta_\perp & \beta'\Theta^*(1)\overline{\eta} \\ 0 & (\eta'\eta)^{1/2} \end{pmatrix}$$

which is full rank under the assumption that $\beta'\Theta^*(1)\eta_\perp$ is full rank. Then $\det(\boldsymbol{D}(z))$ has no unit roots. Second, (16.28) and the definition of X_t imply that

$$\boldsymbol{D}(z) = \begin{pmatrix} 1-z & 0 \\ 0 & 1 \end{pmatrix} H\Theta(z)H_\eta.$$

Since H and H_η are full rank, this implies that the solutions to $\det(\boldsymbol{D}(z)) = 0$ are solutions to $\det(\Theta(z)) = 0$ and hence satisfy $|z| \geq 1+\delta$ (because $z \neq 1$) by the assumption on $\Theta(z)$. Taken together, we have shown that $\boldsymbol{D}(\mathrm{L})$ is invertible. Thus (16.28) implies

$$H_\eta \boldsymbol{D}(\mathrm{L})^{-1}\begin{pmatrix} X_{1t} \\ \Delta X_{2t}\end{pmatrix} = a + e_t \tag{16.29}$$

where

$$a = H_\eta \boldsymbol{D}(1)^{-1}\begin{pmatrix}\mu \\ \gamma\end{pmatrix}.$$

Equation (16.29) is a VAR representation for $\left(\beta' Y_t, \beta_\perp' \Delta Y_t\right)$ with all roots satisfying $|z| \geq 1+\delta$. This implies a VAR representation for Y_t, which is equation (16.18) with

$$\boldsymbol{A}(z) = H_\eta \boldsymbol{D}(z)^{-1}\begin{pmatrix}\beta' \\ \beta_\perp'(1-z)\end{pmatrix}.$$

By partitioned matrix inversion, we calculate

$$\begin{aligned}
\boldsymbol{A}(1) &= H_\eta \boldsymbol{D}(1)^{-1}\begin{pmatrix}\beta' \\ 0\end{pmatrix} \\
&= [\eta_\perp, \overline{\eta}]\begin{pmatrix}\left(\beta'\Theta^*(1)\eta_\perp\right)^{-1} & -\left(\beta'\Theta^*(1)\eta_\perp\right)^{-1}\beta'\Theta^*(1)\eta \\ 0 & \left(\eta'\eta\right)^{-1/2}\end{pmatrix}\begin{pmatrix}\beta' \\ 0\end{pmatrix} \\
&= \eta_\perp\left(\beta'\Theta^*(1)\eta_\perp\right)^{-1}\beta' \\
&= -\alpha\beta'.
\end{aligned}$$

as claimed.

Part 4. Under the assumption $\sum_{j=0}^{\infty}\left\|\sum_{k=0}^{\infty} k\Theta_{j+k}\right\|^2 < \infty$, Theorem 15.3 implies that the coefficients $\boldsymbol{A}_k^* = \sum_{j=0}^{\infty}\boldsymbol{A}_{j+k}$ are absolutely summable. We can then apply the Beveridge-Nelson decomposition $\boldsymbol{A}(z) = \boldsymbol{A}(1) + \boldsymbol{A}^*(z)(1-z)$. Applying $\boldsymbol{A}(1) = -\alpha\beta'$ and a little rewriting yields

$$\boldsymbol{A}(z) = \boldsymbol{I}_m(1-z) - \alpha\beta' z - \left(\boldsymbol{I}_m + \alpha\beta' - \boldsymbol{A}^*(z)\right)(1-z).$$

Applied to (16.18), we obtain the stated result with $\Gamma(\mathrm{L}) = \boldsymbol{I}_m + \alpha\beta' - \boldsymbol{A}^*(z)$. The coefficients of $\Gamma(\mathrm{L})$ are absolutely summable, because the coefficients $\boldsymbol{A}_k^*$ are.

Part 5. The assumption $\theta = 0$ directly implies $\gamma = 0$. Then

$$\begin{aligned}
a &= H_\eta \boldsymbol{D}(1)^{-1}\begin{pmatrix}\mu \\ 0\end{pmatrix} \\
&= [\eta_\perp, \overline{\eta}]\begin{pmatrix}\left(\beta'\Theta^*(1)\eta_\perp\right)^{-1} & -\left(\beta'\Theta^*(1)\eta_\perp\right)^{-1}\beta'\Theta^*(1)\eta \\ 0 & \left(\eta'\eta\right)^{-1/2}\end{pmatrix}\begin{pmatrix}\mu \\ 0\end{pmatrix} \\
&= \eta_\perp\left(\beta'\Theta^*(1)\eta_\perp\right)^{-1}\mu \\
&= \alpha\mu
\end{aligned}$$

as claimed. ■

Proof of Theorem 16.18 Write the VECM as $\Gamma^*(\mathrm{L})\Delta Y_t - \alpha\beta' Y_{t-1} = a + e_t$, where $\Gamma^*(z) = \boldsymbol{I}_m - \Gamma(z)$. Set $\overline{\alpha} = \alpha\left(\alpha'\alpha\right)^{-1/2}$ and orthonormal $H = [\overline{\alpha}, \alpha_\perp]$. Assume that $[\beta, \beta_\perp]$ is orthonormal. Define $Z_t = \beta' Y_t$ and

$U_t = \beta_\perp' \Delta Y_t$. Our goal is to show that (Z_t, U_t) is $I(0)$, which is the same as showing that Y_t is cointegrated with cointegrating vectors β.

Premultiplying the VECM model by H', we obtain the system

$$H'\left(\Gamma^*(\mathrm{L})\Delta Y_t - \alpha\beta' Y_{t-1}\right) = H'a + H'e_t.$$

Using the identity $\boldsymbol{I}_m = \beta\beta' + \beta_\perp\beta_\perp'$, we see that $\Delta Y_t = \beta\Delta Z_t + \beta_\perp U_t$. Making this substitution and setting $\overline{a} = H'a$ $v_t = H'e_t$, we obtain the system

$$\boldsymbol{D}(\mathrm{L})\begin{pmatrix} Z_t \\ U_t \end{pmatrix} = \overline{a} + v_t$$

where

$$\boldsymbol{D}(z) = \begin{bmatrix} \overline{\alpha}'\Gamma^*(z)\beta(1-z) - \boldsymbol{I}_m & \overline{\alpha}'\Gamma^*(z)\beta_\perp \\ \alpha_\perp'\Gamma^*(z)\beta(1-z) & \alpha_\perp'\Gamma^*(z)\beta_\perp \end{bmatrix}.$$

We now show that this is a stationary system. First, note that

$$\boldsymbol{D}(1) = \begin{bmatrix} -\boldsymbol{I}_m & \overline{\alpha}'\Gamma^*(1)\beta_\perp \\ 0 & \alpha_\perp'\Gamma^*(1)\beta_\perp \end{bmatrix}$$

which is full rank under the assumption that $\alpha_\perp'\Gamma^*(1)\beta_\perp$ is full rank. Thus $\det(\boldsymbol{D}(z)) = 0$ has no solutions $z = 1$. Second, $\boldsymbol{D}(z)$ relates to $\boldsymbol{A}(z)$ by the relationship

$$\boldsymbol{D}(z) = H'\boldsymbol{A}(z)\left[\beta, \beta_\perp(1-z)\right].$$

Thus the solutions $z \neq 1$ to

$$\det(\boldsymbol{D}(z)) = \det(H)\det(\boldsymbol{A}(z))\det([\beta, \beta_\perp(1-z)]) = 0$$

are all solutions to $\det(\boldsymbol{A}(z)) = 0$, which all satisfy $|z| \geq 1 + \delta$ by assumption. Thus $\boldsymbol{D}(z)$ is invertible with summable moving average coefficient matrices. This implies that the VAR system for (Z_t, U_t) is stationary.

As discussed above, this result shows that (Z_t, U_t) is a stationary process and hence Y_t is cointegrated with cointegrating vector β. ■

Proof of Theorem 16.19 Set $Y_{2t}^* = Y_{2t} - \overline{Y}_2$. The estimator satisfies

$$n\left(\widehat{\beta} - \beta\right) = \left(\frac{1}{n^2}\sum_{t=1}^n Y_{2t}^* Y_{2t}^{*\prime}\right)^{-1}\left(\frac{1}{n}\sum_{t=1}^n Y_{2t}^* u_{1t}\right).$$

Set $S_t = \sum_{i=1}^t u_t$. Theorems 16.4 and 16.5 imply $S_{\lfloor nr \rfloor} \underset{d}{\longrightarrow} B(r)$ and $Y_{2\lfloor nr \rfloor}^* \underset{d}{\longrightarrow} B_2^*(r)$. By the CMT,

$$\frac{1}{n^2}\sum_{t=1}^n Y_{2t}^* Y_{2t}^{*\prime} \underset{d}{\longrightarrow} \int_0^1 B_2^* B_2^{*\prime}.$$

By Theorem 16.7 and the WLLN

$$\frac{1}{n}\sum_{t=1}^n Y_{2t}^* u_{1t} = \frac{1}{n}\sum_{t=1}^n Y_{2t-1}^* u_{1t} + \frac{1}{n}\sum_{t=1}^n u_{2t}u_{1t} + o_p(1) \underset{d}{\longrightarrow} \int_0^1 B_2^* dB_1 + \Lambda_{21} + \Sigma_{21}.$$

Combining these we obtain the stated result. ■

Proof of Theorem 16.22 (sketch). For simplicity, abstract from the dynamic and trend coefficients, so that the unconstrained model is

$$\Delta Y_t = \alpha\beta' Y_{t-1} + e_t$$

where e_t is a MDS with covariance matrix Σ. We examine two cases in detail. First, the case $\mathbb{H}(0)$ (which is relatively straightforward) and second, the case $\mathbb{H}(r)$ (which is algebraically more tedious).

First, consider $\mathbb{H}(0)$, in which case the process is $\Delta Y_t = e_t$. The statistic is

$$\begin{aligned}
\mathrm{LR}(0) &= -n\sum_{j=1}^{m}\log\left(1-\widehat{\lambda}_j\right) \simeq n\sum_{j=1}^{m}\widehat{\lambda}_j \\
&= \mathrm{tr}\left[\left(\frac{1}{n}\sum_{t=1}^{n} Y_{t-1}e_t'\right)\left(\frac{1}{n}\sum_{t=1}^{n} e_te_t'\right)^{-1}\left(\frac{1}{n}\sum_{t=1}^{n} e_tY_{t-1}'\right)\left(\frac{1}{n^2}\sum_{t=1}^{n} Y_{t-1}Y_{t-1}'\right)^{-1}\right] \\
&\underset{d}{\longrightarrow} \mathrm{tr}\left[\left(\int_0^1 dBB'\right)\left(\int_0^1 BB'\right)^{-1}\left(\int_0^1 BdB'\right)\right] \\
&= \mathrm{tr}\left[\left(\int_0^1 dWW'\right)\left(\int_0^1 WW'\right)^{-1}\left(\int_0^1 WdW'\right)\right]
\end{aligned}$$

where $B(r)$ is a Brownian motion with covariance matrix Σ, and $W(r) = \Sigma^{-1/2}B(r)$ is standard Brownian motion. This is the stated result.

Second, take $\mathbb{H}(r)$ for $1 < r < m$. Define $Z_t = \beta' Y_t$. The process under $\mathbb{H}(r)$ is $\Delta Y_t = \alpha Z_{t-1} + e_t$. Normalize β so that $\mathbb{E}\left[Z_tZ_t'\right] = \boldsymbol{I}_r$. The test statistic is invariant to linear transformations of Y_t, so we can rescale the data so that $\mathbb{E}\left[\Delta Y_t\Delta Y_t'\right] = \boldsymbol{I}_m$. Notice that $\Sigma = \mathbb{E}\left[e_te_t'\right] = \mathbb{E}\left[\Delta Y_t\Delta Y_t'\right] - \alpha\mathbb{E}\left[Z_tZ_t'\right]\alpha' = \boldsymbol{I}_m - \alpha\alpha'$.

The likelihood ratio statistic is

$$\mathrm{LR}(r) = -n\sum_{j=r+1}^{m}\log\left(1-\widehat{\lambda}_j\right) \simeq \sum_{j=r+1}^{m}\widehat{\rho}_j$$

where the $\widehat{\rho}_j = n\widehat{\lambda}_j$ are the $m-r$ smallest roots of the equation $\det\left(S(\rho)\right) = 0$, and

$$S(\rho) = \rho\frac{1}{n^2}\sum_{t=1}^{n} Y_{t-1}Y_{t-1}' - \frac{1}{n}\sum_{t=1}^{n} Y_{t-1}\Delta Y_t'\left(\frac{1}{n}\sum_{t=1}^{n}\Delta Y_t\Delta Y_t'\right)^{-1}\frac{1}{n}\sum_{t=1}^{n}\Delta Y_tY_{t-1}'.$$

Define a full-rank matrix $H = [\beta, \beta_\perp]$, where $\beta'\beta_\perp = 0$. The roots of $\widehat{\rho}_j$ are the same as those of $\det\left(S^*(\rho)\right) = 0$, where $S^*(\rho) = H'S(\rho)H$, which replaces Y_{t-1} with (Z_{t-1}, X_{t-1}), where $X_t = \beta_\perp' Y_t$. We calculate that

$$\begin{aligned}
S^*(\rho) &= \rho\begin{bmatrix} \frac{1}{n^2}\sum_{t=1}^{n} Z_{t-1}Z_{t-1}' & \frac{1}{n^2}\sum_{t=1}^{n} Z_{t-1}X_{t-1}' \\ \frac{1}{n^2}\sum_{t=1}^{n} X_{t-1}Z_{t-1}' & \frac{1}{n^2}\sum_{t=1}^{n} X_{t-1}X_{t-1}' \end{bmatrix} \\
&\quad - \begin{bmatrix} \frac{1}{n}\sum_{t=1}^{n} Z_{t-1}\Delta Y_t' \\ \frac{1}{n}\sum_{t=1}^{n} X_{t-1}\Delta Y_t' \end{bmatrix}\left(\frac{1}{n}\sum_{t=1}^{n}\Delta Y_t\Delta Y_t'\right)^{-1}\begin{bmatrix} \frac{1}{n}\sum_{t=1}^{n} Z_{t-1}\Delta Y_t' \\ \frac{1}{n}\sum_{t=1}^{n} X_{t-1}\Delta Y_t' \end{bmatrix}'.
\end{aligned}$$

Now apply the asymptotic theory for nonstationary theory to each component. The process $X_t = \beta_\perp' Y_t$ is nonstationary and satisfies the FCLT $n^{-1}X_{\lfloor nr\rfloor} \underset{d}{\longrightarrow} X(r) \sim BM\left(\beta_\perp'\Omega\beta_\perp\right)$, where Ω is the long-run covariance matrix of ΔY_t. The sum of the errors satisfies $n^{-1/2}\sum_{t=1}^{\lfloor nr\rfloor} e_t \underset{d}{\longrightarrow} B(r) \sim BM(\Sigma)$. The process $X(r)$ is a linear function of $B(r)$.

We find that $\frac{1}{n^2}\sum_{t=1}^n X_{t-1}X_{t-1}' \underset{d}{\longrightarrow} \int_0^1 XX'$, $\frac{1}{n^2}\sum_{t=1}^n X_{t-1}e_t \underset{d}{\longrightarrow} \int_0^1 XdB'$, $\frac{1}{n}\sum_{t=1}^n Z_{t-1}Z_{t-1}' \underset{p}{\longrightarrow} \boldsymbol{I}_r$, $\frac{1}{n}\sum_{t=1}^n \Delta Y_t \Delta Y_t' \underset{p}{\longrightarrow} \boldsymbol{I}_m$, $\frac{1}{n}\sum_{t=1}^n Z_{t-1}\Delta Y_t' \underset{p}{\longrightarrow} \alpha'$, $\frac{1}{n}\sum_{t=1}^n X_{t-1}Z_{t-1}' \underset{d}{\longrightarrow} \zeta$ for some random matrix by Theorem 16.7, and $\frac{1}{n}\sum_{t=1}^n X_{t-1}\Delta Y_t' \underset{d}{\longrightarrow} \zeta'\alpha' + \int_0^1 XdB'$. Combining these results, we find that

$$S^*(\rho) \underset{d}{\longrightarrow} \rho\begin{bmatrix} 0 & \\ 0 & \int_0^1 XX' \end{bmatrix} - \begin{bmatrix} \alpha'\alpha & \alpha'\left(\alpha\zeta + \int_0^1 dBX'\right) \\ \left(\zeta'\alpha' + \int_0^1 XdB'\right)\alpha & \left(\zeta'\alpha' + \int_0^1 XdB'\right)\left(\alpha\zeta + \int_0^1 dBX'\right) \end{bmatrix}.$$

Thus $\det(S^*(\rho))$ converges in distribution to the determinant of the right-hand side, which equals (using property 5 of Theorem A.1) $\det(\alpha'\alpha)$ multiplied by the determinant of

$$\begin{aligned} &\rho\int_0^1 XX' - \left(\zeta'\alpha' + \int_0^1 XdB'\right)\left(\boldsymbol{I}_m - \alpha\left(\alpha'\alpha\right)^{-1}\alpha'\right)\left(\alpha\zeta + \int_0^1 dBX'\right) \\ &= \rho\int_0^1 XX' - \int_0^1 XdB'M_\alpha \int_0^1 dBX' \\ &= \rho\int_0^1 XX' - \int_0^1 XdW'H_1' \int_0^1 H_1 dWX' \\ &= \rho\int_0^1 XX' - \int_0^1 XdW' \int_0^1 dWX' \end{aligned} \tag{16.30}$$

where $M_\alpha = \boldsymbol{I}_m - \alpha\left(\alpha'\alpha\right)^{-1}\alpha'$, and

$$M_\alpha B(r) \sim BM\left(M_\alpha\left(\boldsymbol{I}_m - \alpha\alpha'\right)M_\alpha\right) = BM(M_\alpha) = H_1 W(r)$$

where $M_\alpha = H_1H_1'$, $H_1'H_1 = \boldsymbol{I}_{m-r}$, and $W(r) \sim BM(\boldsymbol{I}_{m-r})$.

The determinant of (16.30) has $m-r$ roots, and their sum equals

$$\operatorname{tr}\left[\left(\int_0^1 dWX'\right)\left(\int_0^1 XX'\right)^{-1}\left(\int_0^1 XdW'\right)\right] = \operatorname{tr}\left[\left(\int_0^1 dWW'\right)\left(\int_0^1 WW'\right)^{-1}\left(\int_0^1 WdW'\right)\right]$$

because $X(r)$ is a linear rotation of $W(r)$. This is the stated result. ■

16.23 EXERCISES

Exercise 16.1 Consider $S_t = S_{t-1} + e_t$ with $S_0 = 0$ and e_t i.i.d. $(0, \sigma^2)$.

(a) Calculate $\mathbb{E}[S_t]$ and $\operatorname{var}[S_t]$.

(b) Set $Y_t = (S_t - \mathbb{E}[S_t])/\sqrt{\operatorname{var}[S_t]}$. By construction, $\mathbb{E}[Y_t] = 0$ and $\operatorname{var}[Y_t] = 1$. Is Y_t stationary?

(c) Find the asymptotic distribution of $Y_{\lfloor nr\rfloor}$ for $r \in [\delta, 1]$.

Exercise 16.2 Find the Beveridge-Nelson decomposition of $\Delta Y_t = e_t + \Theta_1 e_{t-1} + \Theta_2 e_{t-2}$.

Exercise 16.3 Suppose $Y_t = X_t + u_t$, where $X_t = X_{t-1} + e_t$ with $(e_t, u_t) \sim I(0)$.

(a) Is Y_t $I(0)$ or $I(1)$?

(b) Find the asymptotic functional distribution of $n^{-1/2} Y_{\lfloor nr \rfloor}$.

Exercise 16.4 Let $Y_t = e_t$ be i.i.d. and $X_t = \Delta Y_t$.

(a) Show that Y_t is stationary and $I(0)$.

(b) Show that X_t is stationary but not $I(0)$.

Exercise 16.5 Let $U_t = U_{t-1} + e_t$, $Y_t = U_t + v_t$ and $X_t = 2U_t + w_t$, where (e_t, v_t, w_t) is an i.i.d. sequence. Find the cointegrating vector for (Y_t, X_t).

Exercise 16.6 Consider the AR(1) model $Y_t = \alpha Y_{t-1} + e_t$ with i.i.d. e_t and the least squares estimator $\widehat{\alpha}$. Chaper 14 showed that the asymptotic distribution when $|\alpha| < 1$ is $\sqrt{n}\,(\widehat{\alpha} - \alpha) \underset{d}{\longrightarrow} \mathrm{N}\left(0, 1 - \alpha^2\right)$. How do you reconcile this with Theorem 16.9, especially for α close to 1?

Exercise 16.7 Consider the VECM(1) model $\Delta Y_t = \alpha\beta' Y_{t-1} + e_t$. Show that $Z_t = \beta' Y_t$ follows an AR(1) process.

Exercise 16.8 An economist estimates the model $Y_t = \alpha Y_{t-1} + e_t$ and finds $\widehat{\alpha} = 0.9$ with $s(\widehat{\alpha}) = 0.05$. She asserts: "The t-statistic for testing $\alpha = 1$ is 2, so $\alpha = 1$ is rejected." Is there an error in this reasoning?

Exercise 16.9 An economist estimates the model $Y_t = \alpha Y_{t-1} + e_t$ and finds $\widehat{\alpha} = 0.9$ with $s(\widehat{\alpha}) = 0.04$. He asserts: "The 95% confidence interval for α is [0.82, 0.98], which does not contain 1. So $\alpha = 1$ is not consistent with the data." Is there an error in this reasoning?

Exercise 16.10 An economist takes Y_t, detrends to obtain the detrended series Z_t, applies an ADF test to Z_t and finds ADF $= -2.5$. She asserts: "Stata provides the 5% critical value -1.9 with p-value less than 1%. Thus we reject the null hypothesis of a unit root." Is there an error in this reasoning?

Exercise 16.11 An economist wants to build an autoregressive model for the number of daily tweets by a prominant politician. For a model with an intercept, he obtains ADF $= -2.0$. He asserts "The number of tweets is a unit root process." Is there an error in this reasoning?

Exercise 16.12 For each of the following monthly series from `FRED-MD`, implement the Dickey-Fuller unit root test. For each, you need to consider the AR order p and the trend specification.

(a) Log real personal income: log(*rpi*).

(b) Industrial production index: *indpro*.

(c) Housing starts: *houst*.

(d) Help-wanted index: *hwi*.

(e) Civilian labor force: *clf16ov*.

(f) Initial claims: *claims*.

(g) Industrial production index (fuels): *ipfuels*.

Exercise 16.13 For each of the series in the previous exercise, implement the KPSS test of stationarity. For each, you need consider the lag truncation M and the trend specification.

Exercise 16.14 For each of the following monthly pairs from `FRED-MD`, test the hypothesis of no cointegration using the Johansen trace test. For each, you need to consider the VAR order p and the trend specification.

(a) 3-month treasury interest rate (*tb3ms*) and 10-year treasury interest rate (*gs10*). Note: In the text, we implemented the test on the quarterly series, not monthly.

(b) interest rate on AAA bonds (*aaa*) and interest rate on BAA bonds (*baa*).

(c) log(industrial production durable consumer goods) and log(industrial production nondurable consumer goods) (i.e., log of *ipdcongd* and *ipncongd*).

CHAPTER 17

PANEL DATA

17.1 INTRODUCTION

Economists traditionally use the term **panel data** to refer to data structures consisting of observations on individuals for multiple time periods. Other fields, such as statistics, typically call this structure **longitudinal data**. The observed "individuals" can be, for example, people, households, workers, firms, schools, production plants, industries, regions, states, or countries. The distinguishing feature relative to cross-sectional datasets is the presence of multiple observations for each individual. More broadly, panel data methods can be applied to contexts with cluster-type dependence.

There are several distinct advantages of panel data relative to cross-section data. One is the possibility of controlling for unobserved time-invariant endogeneity without the use of instrumental variables. A second is the possibility of allowing for broader forms of heterogeneity. A third is modeling dynamic relationships and effects.

Two broad categories of panel datasets are used in economic applications: micro panels and macro panels. Micro panels are typically surveys or administrative records on individuals and are characterized by a large number of individuals (often in the thousands or higher) and a relatively small number of time periods (often 2 to 20 years). Macro panels are typically national or regional macroeconomic variables and are characterized by a moderate number of individuals (e.g., 7–20) and a moderate number of time periods (20–60 years).

Panel data were once relatively esoteric in applied economic practice. Now, they are a dominant feature of applied research.

A typical maintained assumption for micro panels (which we follow in this chapter) is that the individuals are mutually independent, while the observations for a given individual are correlated across time periods. Thus the observations follow a clustered dependence structure. Because of this, current econometric practice is to use cluster-robust covariance matrix estimators when possible. Similar assumptions are often used for macro panels, although the assumption of independence across individuals (e.g., countries) is much less compelling.

The application of panel data methods in econometrics started with the pioneering work of Mundlak (1961) and Balestra and Nerlove (1966). Several excellent monographs and textbooks have been written on panel econometrics, including Arellano (2003), Hsiao (2003), Wooldridge (2010), and Baltagi (2013). This chapter summarizes some of the main themes, but for a more in-depth treatment see these references.

One challenge arising in panel data applications is that the computational methods can require meticulous attention to detail. It is therefore advised to use established packages for routine applications. For most panel data applications in economics, Stata is the standard package.

17.2 TIME INDEXING AND UNBALANCED PANELS

It is typical to index observations by both the individual i and the time period t, thus Y_{it} denotes a variable for individual i in period t. We index individuals as $i = 1, \ldots, N$ and time periods as $t = 1, \ldots T$. Thus N is the number of individuals in the panel, and T is the number of time series periods.

Panel datasets can involve data at any time series frequency, though the typical application involves annual data. The observations in a dataset will be indexed by calendar time, which for the case of annual observations is the year. For notational convenience, it is customary to denote the time periods as $t = 1, \ldots, T$, so that $t = 1$ is the first time period observed and T is the final time period.

When observations are available on all individuals for the same time periods, we say that the panel is **balanced**. In this case, there are an equal number T of observations for each individual, and the total number of observations is $n = NT$.

When different time periods are available for the individuals in the sample, we say that the panel is **unbalanced**. This is the most common type of panel dataset. It does not pose a problem for applications but does make the notation cumbersome and also complicates computer programming.

To illustrate, consider the dataset `Invest1993` on the textbook webpage. This is a sample of 1962 U.S. firms extracted from Compustat, assembled by Bronwyn Hall, and used in the empirical work in B. Hall and R. Hall (1993). Table 17.1 displays a set of variables from the dataset for the first 13 observations. The first variable is the firm code number. The second variable is the year of the observation. These two variables are essential for any panel data analysis. In Table 17.1, you can see that the first firm (#32) is observed for the years 1970 through 1977. The second firm (#209) is observed for 1987 through 1991. You can see that the years vary considerably across the firms, so this is an unbalanced panel.

For unbalanced panels the time index $t = 1, \ldots, T$ denotes the full set of time periods. For example, in the dataset `Invest1993`, there are observations for the years 1960 through 1991, so the total number of time periods is $T = 32$. Each individual is observed for a subset of T_i periods. The set of time periods for individual i is denoted as S_i, so that individual-specific sums (over time periods) are written as $\sum_{t \in S_i}$.

The observed time periods for a given individual are typically contiguous (for example, in Table 17.1, firm #32 is observed for each year from 1970 through 1977), but in some cases are noncontinguous (if, for example, 1973 was missing for firm #32). The total number of observations in the sample is $n = \sum_{i=1}^{N} T_i$.

Table 17.1
Observations from investment dataset

Firm code number	Year	I_{it}	$\bar{I}_i$	$\dot{I}_{it}$	Q_{it}	$\overline{Q}_i$	$\dot{Q}_{it}$	$\widehat{e}_{it}$
32	1970	0.122	0.155	−0.033	1.17	0.62	0.55	—
32	1971	0.092	0.155	−0.063	0.79	0.62	0.17	−0.005
32	1972	0.094	0.155	−0.061	0.91	0.62	0.29	−0.005
32	1973	0.116	0.155	−0.039	0.29	0.62	−0.33	0.014
32	1974	0.099	0.155	−0.057	0.30	0.62	−0.32	−0.002
32	1975	0.187	0.155	0.032	0.56	0.62	−0.06	0.086
32	1976	0.349	0.155	0.194	0.38	0.62	−0.24	0.248
32	1977	0.182	0.155	0.027	0.57	0.62	−0.05	0.081
209	1987	0.095	0.071	0.024	9.06	21.57	−12.51	—
209	1988	0.044	0.071	−0.027	16.90	21.57	−4.67	−0.244
209	1989	0.069	0.071	−0.002	25.14	21.57	3.57	−0.257
209	1990	0.113	0.071	0.042	25.60	21.57	4.03	−0.226
209	1991	0.034	0.071	−0.037	31.14	21.57	9.57	−0.283

17.3 NOTATION

This chapter focuses on panel data regression models whose observations are pairs (Y_{it}, X_{it}), where Y_{it} is the dependent variable, and X_{it} is a k-vector of regressors. These are the observations on individual i for time period t.

It will be useful to cluster the observations at the level of the individual. We borrow the notation from Section 4.21 to write $\boldsymbol{Y}_i$ as the $T_i \times 1$ stacked observations on Y_{it} for $t \in S_i$, stacked in chronological order. Similarly, we write $\boldsymbol{X}_i$ as the $T_i \times k$ matrix of stacked X'_{it} for $t \in S_i$, stacked in chronological order.

We also sometimes use matrix notation for the full sample. To do so, let $\boldsymbol{Y} = (\boldsymbol{Y}'_1, \ldots, \boldsymbol{Y}'_N)'$ denote the $n \times 1$ vector of stacked $\boldsymbol{Y}_i$, and similarly set $\boldsymbol{X} = (\boldsymbol{X}'_1, \ldots, \boldsymbol{X}'_N)'$.

17.4 POOLED REGRESSION

The simplest model in panel regression is pooled regresssion,

$$\begin{aligned} Y_{it} &= X'_{it}\beta + e_{it} \\ \mathbb{E}\left[X_{it}e_{it}\right] &= 0 \end{aligned} \tag{17.1}$$

where β is a $k \times 1$ coefficient vector, and e_{it} is an error. The model can be written at the level of the individual as

$$\begin{aligned} \boldsymbol{Y}_i &= \boldsymbol{X}_i\beta + \boldsymbol{e}_i \\ \mathbb{E}\left[\boldsymbol{X}'_i\boldsymbol{e}_i\right] &= 0 \end{aligned}$$

where $\boldsymbol{e}_i$ is $T_i \times 1$. The equation for the full sample is $\boldsymbol{Y} = \boldsymbol{X}\beta + \boldsymbol{e}$, where $\boldsymbol{e}$ is $n \times 1$.

The standard estimator of β in the pooled regression model is least squares, which can be written as

$$\begin{aligned} \widehat{\beta}_{\text{pool}} &= \left(\sum_{i=1}^{N}\sum_{t\in S_i} X_{it}X'_{it}\right)^{-1}\left(\sum_{i=1}^{N}\sum_{t\in S_i} X_{it}Y_{it}\right) \\ &= \left(\sum_{i=1}^{N}\boldsymbol{X}'_i\boldsymbol{X}_i\right)^{-1}\left(\sum_{i=1}^{N}\boldsymbol{X}'_i\boldsymbol{Y}_i\right) \\ &= \left(\boldsymbol{X}'\boldsymbol{X}\right)^{-1}\left(\boldsymbol{X}'\boldsymbol{Y}\right). \end{aligned}$$

In the context of panel data, $\widehat{\beta}_{\text{pool}}$ is called the **pooled regression estimator**. The vector of residuals for the ith individual is $\widehat{\boldsymbol{e}}_i = \boldsymbol{Y}_i - \boldsymbol{X}_i\widehat{\beta}_{\text{pool}}$.

The pooled regression model is ideally suited for the context where the errors e_{it} satisfy **strict mean independence**:

$$\mathbb{E}\left[e_{it} \mid \boldsymbol{X}_i\right] = 0. \tag{17.2}$$

This occurs when the errors e_{it} are mean independent of all regressors X_{ij} for all time periods $j = 1, \ldots, T$. Strict mean independence is stronger than pairwise mean independence, $\mathbb{E}\left[e_{it} \mid X_{it}\right] = 0$, as well as projection (17.1). Strict mean independence requires that neither lagged nor future values of X_{it} help to forecast e_{it}. It excludes lagged dependent variables (such as $Y_{i,t-1}$) from X_{it} (otherwise, e_{it} would be predictable given $X_{i,t+1}$). It also requires that X_{it} is exogenous in the sense discussed in Chapter 12.

We now discuss some statistical properties of $\widehat{\beta}_{\text{pool}}$ under (17.2). First, notice that by linearity and the cluster-level notation, we can write the estimator as

$$\widehat{\beta}_{\text{pool}} = \left(\sum_{i=1}^{N} \boldsymbol{X}_i'\boldsymbol{X}_i\right)^{-1} \left(\sum_{i=1}^{N} \boldsymbol{X}_i'\left(\boldsymbol{X}_i\beta + \boldsymbol{e}_i\right)\right) = \beta + \left(\sum_{i=1}^{N} \boldsymbol{X}_i'\boldsymbol{X}_i\right)^{-1} \left(\sum_{i=1}^{N} \boldsymbol{X}_i'\boldsymbol{e}_i\right).$$

Using (17.2),

$$\mathbb{E}\left[\widehat{\beta}_{\text{pool}} \mid \boldsymbol{X}\right] = \beta + \left(\sum_{i=1}^{N} \boldsymbol{X}_i'\boldsymbol{X}_i\right)^{-1} \left(\sum_{i=1}^{N} \boldsymbol{X}_i'\mathbb{E}\left[\boldsymbol{e}_i \mid \boldsymbol{X}_i\right]\right) = \beta$$

so $\widehat{\beta}_{\text{pool}}$ is unbiased for β.

Under the additional assumption that the error e_{it} is serially uncorrelated and homoskedastic, the covariance estimator takes a classical form, and the classical homoskedastic variance estimator can be used. If the error e_{it} is heteroskedastic but serially uncorrelated, then a heteroskedasticity-robust covariance matrix estimator can be used.

In general, however, we expect the errors e_{it} to be correlated across time t for a given individual. This does not necessarily violate (17.2), but it does invalidate classical covariance matrix estimation. The conventional solution is to use a cluster-robust covariance matrix estimator that allows arbitrary within-cluster dependence. Cluster-robust covariance matrix estimators for pooled regression equal

$$\widehat{\boldsymbol{V}}_{\text{pool}} = \left(\boldsymbol{X}'\boldsymbol{X}\right)^{-1} \left(\sum_{i=1}^{N} \boldsymbol{X}_i'\widehat{\boldsymbol{e}}_i\widehat{\boldsymbol{e}}_i'\boldsymbol{X}_i\right) \left(\boldsymbol{X}'\boldsymbol{X}\right)^{-1}.$$

As in (4.52), this can be multiplied by a degree-of-freedom adjustment. The adjustment used by the Stata `regress` command is

$$\widehat{\boldsymbol{V}}_{\text{pool}} = \left(\frac{n-1}{n-k}\right)\left(\frac{N}{N-1}\right) \left(\boldsymbol{X}'\boldsymbol{X}\right)^{-1} \left(\sum_{i=1}^{N} \boldsymbol{X}_i'\widehat{\boldsymbol{e}}_i\widehat{\boldsymbol{e}}_i'\boldsymbol{X}_i\right) \left(\boldsymbol{X}'\boldsymbol{X}\right)^{-1}.$$

The pooled regression estimator with cluster-robust standard errors can be obtained using the Stata command `regress cluster(id)`, where `id` indicates the individual.

When strict mean independence (17.2) fails, the pooled least squares estimator $\widehat{\beta}_{\text{pool}}$ is not necessarily consistent for β. Because strict mean independence is a strong and undesirable restriction, it is typically preferred to adopt one of the alternative estimators described in the following sections.

To illustrate the pooled regression estimator, consider the dataset `Invest1993` described in Section 17.2. We consider a simple investment model

$$I_{it} = \beta_1 Q_{i,t-1} + \beta_2 D_{i,t-1} + \beta_3 CF_{i,t-1} + \beta_4 T_i + e_{it} \tag{17.3}$$

where I is investment/assets, Q is market value/assets, D is long-term debt/assets, CF is cash flow/assets, and T is a dummy variable indicating whether the corporation's stock is traded on the NYSE or AMEX. The regression also includes 19 dummy variables indicating an industry code. The Q theory of investment suggests that $\beta_1 > 0$, while $\beta_2 = \beta_3 = 0$. Theories of liquidity constraints suggest that $\beta_2 < 0$ and $\beta_3 > 0$. We will be using this example throughout this chapter. The values of I and Q for the first 13 observations are also displayed in Table 17.1.

Table 17.2
Estimates of investment equation

	Pooled	Random effects	Fixed effects	Two-way	Hausman-Taylor
$Q_{i,t-1}$	0.0024	0.0019	0.0017	0.0016	0.0017
	(0.0010)	(0.0009)	(0.0008)	(0.0008)	(0.0008)
$D_{i,t-1}$	0.0096	−0.0092	−0.0139	−0.0140	0.0132
	(0.0041)	(0.0039)	(0.0049)	(0.0051)	(0.0050)
$CF_{i,t-1}$	0.0261	0.0412	0.0491	0.0476	0.0408
	(0.0111)	(0.0125)	(0.0132)	(0.0129)	(0.0119)
T_i	−0.0167	−0.0181			−0.0348
	(0.0024)	(0.0028)			(0.0048)
Industry dummies	Yes	Yes	No	No	Yes
Time effects	No	No	No	Yes	Yes

Note: Cluster-robust standard errors in parenthesis

Table 17.2 presents the pooled regression estimates of (17.3) in the first column with cluster-robust standard errors.

17.5 ONE-WAY ERROR COMPONENT MODEL

One approach to panel data regression is to model the correlation structure of the regression error e_{it}. The most common choice is an error-components structure. The simplest takes the form

$$e_{it} = u_i + \varepsilon_{it} \tag{17.4}$$

where u_i is an individual-specific effect, and the ε_{it} are idiosyncratic (i.i.d.) errors. This is known as a **one-way error component model**.

In vector notation, we can write $\boldsymbol{e}_i = \mathbf{1}_i u_i + \boldsymbol{\varepsilon}_i$, where $\mathbf{1}_i$ is a $T_i \times 1$ vector of 1's.

The one-way error component regression model is

$$Y_{it} = X_{it}'\beta + u_i + \varepsilon_{it}$$

written at the level of the observation, or $\boldsymbol{Y}_i = \boldsymbol{X}_i\beta + \mathbf{1}_i u_i + \boldsymbol{\varepsilon}_i$, written at the level of the individual.

To illustrate why an error-component structure such as (17.4) might be appropriate, examine Table 17.1. The final column lists the pooled regression residuals $\widehat{e}_{it}$ for these observations. (There is no residual for the first year for each firm because of the lack of lagged regressors for this observation.) What is quite striking is that the residuals for the second firm (#209) are all negative, clustering around −0.25. While informal, this suggests that it may be appropriate to model these errors using (17.4), expecting that firm #209 has a large negative value for its individual effect u.

17.6 RANDOM EFFECTS

The random effects model assumes that the errors u_i and ε_{it} in (17.4) are conditionally mean 0, uncorrelated, and homoskedastic.

Assumption 17.1 Random Effects. Model (17.4) holds with

$$\mathbb{E}\left[\varepsilon_{it} \mid \boldsymbol{X}_i\right] = 0 \tag{17.5}$$

$$\mathbb{E}\left[\varepsilon_{it}^2 \mid \boldsymbol{X}_i\right] = \sigma_\varepsilon^2 \tag{17.6}$$

$$\mathbb{E}\left[\varepsilon_{it}\varepsilon_{js} \mid \boldsymbol{X}_i\right] = 0 \tag{17.7}$$

$$\mathbb{E}\left[u_i \mid \boldsymbol{X}_i\right] = 0 \tag{17.8}$$

$$\mathbb{E}\left[u_i^2 \mid \boldsymbol{X}_i\right] = \sigma_u^2 \tag{17.9}$$

$$\mathbb{E}\left[u_i\varepsilon_{it} \mid \boldsymbol{X}_i\right] = 0 \tag{17.10}$$

where (17.7) holds for all $s \neq t$.

Assumption 17.1 is known as a **random effects** specification. It implies that the vector of errors $\boldsymbol{e}_i$ for individual i has the covariance structure

$$\begin{aligned}
\mathbb{E}\left[\boldsymbol{e}_i \mid \boldsymbol{X}_i\right] &= 0 \\
\mathbb{E}\left[\boldsymbol{e}_i\boldsymbol{e}_i' \mid \boldsymbol{X}_i\right] &= \mathbf{1}_i\mathbf{1}_i'\sigma_u^2 + \boldsymbol{I}_i\sigma_\varepsilon^2 \\
&= \begin{pmatrix} \sigma_u^2+\sigma_\varepsilon^2 & \sigma_u^2 & \cdots & \sigma_u^2 \\ \sigma_u^2 & \sigma_u^2+\sigma_\varepsilon^2 & \cdots & \sigma_u^2 \\ \vdots & \vdots & \ddots & \vdots \\ \sigma_u^2 & \sigma_u^2 & \cdots & \sigma_u^2+\sigma_\varepsilon^2 \end{pmatrix} \\
&= \sigma_\varepsilon^2\Omega_i
\end{aligned}$$

say, where $\boldsymbol{I}_i$ is an identity matrix of dimension T_i. The matrix Ω_i depends on i, because its dimension depends on the number of observed time periods T_i.

Assumption 17.1 parts 1 and 4 state that the idiosyncratic error ε_{it} and individual-specific error u_i are strictly mean independent, so the combined error e_{it} is strictly mean independent as well.

The random effects model is equivalent to an **equi-correlation** model. That is, suppose that the error e_{it} satisfies

$$\begin{aligned}
\mathbb{E}\left[e_{it} \mid \boldsymbol{X}_i\right] &= 0 \\
\mathbb{E}\left[e_{it}^2 \mid \boldsymbol{X}_i\right] &= \sigma^2
\end{aligned}$$

and

$$\mathbb{E}\left[e_{is}e_{it} \mid \boldsymbol{X}_i\right] = \rho\sigma^2$$

for $s \neq t$. These conditions imply that e_{it} can be written as (17.4) with the components satisfying Assumption 17.1 with $\sigma_u^2 = \rho\sigma^2$ and $\sigma_\varepsilon^2 = (1-\rho)\sigma^2$. Thus random effects and equi-correlation are identical.

The random effects regression model is

$$Y_{it} = X_{it}'\beta + u_i + \varepsilon_{it}$$

or $\boldsymbol{Y}_i = \boldsymbol{X}_i\beta + \mathbf{1}_i u_i + \boldsymbol{\varepsilon}_i$, where the errors satisfy Assumption 17.1.

Given the error structure, the natural estimator for β is generalized least squares (GLS). Suppose σ_u^2 and σ_ε^2 are known. The GLS estimator of β is

$$\widehat{\beta}_{\mathrm{gls}}=\left(\sum_{i=1}^{N} X_i'\Omega_i^{-1}X_i\right)^{-1}\left(\sum_{i=1}^{N} X_i'\Omega_i^{-1}Y_i\right).$$

A feasible GLS estimator replaces the unknown σ_u^2 and σ_ε^2 with estimators. See Section 17.15.

Let us now discuss some statistical properties of the estimator subject to Assumption 17.1. By linearity,

$$\widehat{\beta}_{\mathrm{gls}}-\beta=\left(\sum_{i=1}^{N} X_i'\Omega_i^{-1}X_i\right)^{-1}\left(\sum_{i=1}^{N} X_i'\Omega_i^{-1}e_i\right).$$

Thus

$$\mathbb{E}\left[\widehat{\beta}_{\mathrm{gls}}-\beta\mid X\right]=\left(\sum_{i=1}^{N} X_i'\Omega_i^{-1}X_i\right)^{-1}\left(\sum_{i=1}^{N} X_i'\Omega_i^{-1}\mathbb{E}\left[e_i\mid X_i\right]\right)=0.$$

Thus $\widehat{\beta}_{\mathrm{gls}}$ is conditionally unbiased for β. The conditional variance of $\widehat{\beta}_{\mathrm{gls}}$ is

$$V_{\mathrm{gls}}=\left(\sum_{i=1}^{n} X_i'\Omega_i^{-1}X_i\right)^{-1}\sigma_\varepsilon^2. \tag{17.11}$$

Now let's compare $\widehat{\beta}_{\mathrm{gls}}$ with the pooled estimator $\widehat{\beta}_{\mathrm{pool}}$. Under Assumption 17.1, the latter is also conditionally unbiased for β and has conditional variance

$$V_{\mathrm{pool}}=\left(\sum_{i=1}^{n} X_i'X_i\right)^{-1}\left(\sum_{i=1}^{n} X_i'\Omega_i X_i\right)^{-1}\left(\sum_{i=1}^{n} X_i'X_i\right)^{-1}. \tag{17.12}$$

Using the algebra of the Gauss-Markov theorem (Theorem 4.5), we deduce that

$$V_{\mathrm{gls}}\le V_{\mathrm{pool}} \tag{17.13}$$

and thus the random effects estimator $\widehat{\beta}_{\mathrm{gls}}$ is more efficient than the pooled estimator $\widehat{\beta}_{\mathrm{pool}}$ under Assumption 17.1. (See Exercise 17.1.) The two variance matrices are identical when there is no individual-specific effect (when $\sigma_u^2=0$), because then, $V_{\mathrm{gls}}=V_{\mathrm{pool}}=\left(X'X\right)^{-1}\sigma_\varepsilon^2$.

Under the assumption that the random effects model is a useful approximation but not literally true, we can consider a cluster-robust covariance matrix estimator, such as

$$\widehat{V}_{\mathrm{gls}}=\left(\sum_{i=1}^{N} X_i'\Omega_i^{-1}X_i\right)^{-1}\left(\sum_{i=1}^{N} X_i'\Omega_i^{-1}\widehat{e}_i\widehat{e}_i'\Omega_i^{-1}X_i\right)\left(\sum_{i=1}^{n} X_i'\Omega_i^{-1}X_i\right)^{-1} \tag{17.14}$$

where $\widehat{e}_i=Y_i-X_i\widehat{\beta}_{\mathrm{gls}}$. This may be rescaled by a degree of freedom adjustment if desired.

The random effects estimator $\widehat{\beta}_{\mathrm{gls}}$ can be obtained using the Stata command `xtreg`. The default covariance matrix estimator is (17.11). For the cluster-robust covariance matrix estimator (17.14), use the command `xtreg vce(robust)`. (The `xtset` command must be used first to declare the group identifier. For example, `cusip` is the group identifier in Table 17.1.)

To illustrate, the second column of Table 17.2 presents the random effects regression estimates of the investment model (17.3) with cluster-robust standard errors (17.14). The point estimates are reasonably different from the pooled regression estimator. The coefficient on debt switches from positive to negative (the latter consistent with theories of liquidity constraints), and the coefficient on cash flow increases significantly in magnitude. These changes appear to be greater in magnitude than would be expected if Assumption 17.1 were correct. In Section 17.7, we consider a less restrictive specification.

17.7 FIXED EFFECTS MODEL

Consider the one-way error component regression model

$$Y_{it} = X_{it}'\beta + u_i + \varepsilon_{it} \tag{17.15}$$

or

$$\boldsymbol{Y}_i = \boldsymbol{X}_i\beta + \mathbf{1}_i u_i + \boldsymbol{\varepsilon}_i. \tag{17.16}$$

In many applications, it is useful to interpret the individual-specific effect u_i as a time-invariant unobserved missing variable. For example, in a wage regression, u_i may be the unobserved ability of individual i. In the investment model (17.3), u_i may be a firm-specific productivity factor.

When u_i is interpreted as an omitted variable, it is natural to expect it to be correlated with the regressors X_{it}. This is especially the case when X_{it} includes choice variables.

To illustrate, consider the entries in Table 17.1. The final column displays the pooled regression residuals $\widehat{e}_{it}$ for the first 13 observations, which we interpret as estimates of the error $e_{it} = u_i + \varepsilon_{it}$. As described before, what is particularly striking about the residuals is that they are all strongly negative for firm #209, clustering around -0.25. We can interpret this as an estimate of u_i for this firm. Examining the values of the regressor Q for the two firms, we can see that firm #209 has very large values (in all time periods) for Q. (The average value $\overline{Q}_i$ for the two firms appears in the seventh column.) Thus it appears (though we are only looking at two observations) that u_i and Q_{it} are correlated. It is not reasonable to infer too much from these limited observations, but the relevance is that such correlation violates strict mean independence.

In the econometrics literature, if the stochastic structure of u_i is treated as unknown and possibly correlated with X_{it}, then u_i is called a **fixed effect**.

Correlation between u_i and X_{it} will cause both pooled and random effect estimators to be biased. This is due to the classic problems of omitted variables bias and endogeneity. To see this in a generated example, look at Figure 17.1, which shows a scatter plot of three observations (Y_{it}, X_{it}) from three firms. The true model is $Y_{it} = 9 - X_{it} + u_i$. (The true slope coefficient is -1.) The variables u_i and X_{it} are highly correlated, so the fitted pooled regression line through the nine observations has a slope close to $+1$. (The random effects estimator is identical.) The apparent positive relationship between Y and X is driven entirely by the positive correlation between X and u. Conditional on u, however, the slope is -1. Thus regression techniques that do not control for u_i will produce biased and inconsistent estimators.

The presence of the unstructured individual effect u_i means that it is not possible to identify β under a simple projection assumption, such as $\mathbb{E}[X_{it}\varepsilon_t] = 0$. It turns out that a sufficient condition for identification is the following.

Definition 17.1 The regressor X_{it} is **strictly exogenous** for the error ε_{it} if

$$\mathbb{E}[X_{is}\varepsilon_{it}] = 0 \tag{17.17}$$

for all $s = 1, \ldots, T$.

Strict exogeneity is a strong projection condition, meaning that if X_{is} for any $s \neq t$ is added to (17.15), it will have a zero coefficient. Strict exogeneity is a projection analog of strict mean independence:

$$\mathbb{E}[\varepsilon_{it} \mid \boldsymbol{X}_i] = 0. \tag{17.18}$$

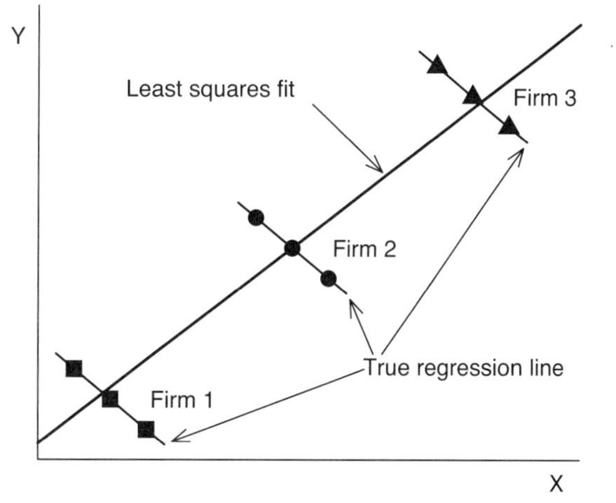

FIGURE 17.1 Scatter plot and pooled regression line

Equation (17.18) implies (17.17) but not conversely. Although (17.17) is sufficient for identification and asymptotic theory, we will also use the stronger condition (17.18) for finite sample analysis.

Although (17.17) and (17.18) are strong assumptions, they are much weaker than (17.2) or Assumption 17.1, which require that the individual effect u_i is also strictly mean independent. In contrast, (17.17) and (17.18) make no assumptions about u_i.

Strict exogeneity (17.17) is typically inappropriate in dynamic models. In Section 17.41, we discuss estimation under the weaker assumption of predetermined regressors.

17.8 WITHIN TRANSFORMATION

In the previous section, we showed that if u_i and X_{it} are correlated, then pooled and random-effects estimators will be biased and inconsistent. If we leave the relationship between u_i and X_{it} fully unstructured, then the only way to consistently estimate the coefficient β is by an estimator that is invariant to u_i. This can be achieved by transformations that eliminate u_i.

One such transformation is the **within transformation**. In this section, we discuss this transformation in detail.

Define the mean of a variable for a given individual as

$$\overline{Y}_i = \frac{1}{T_i} \sum_{t \in S_i} Y_{it}.$$

We call this the **individual-specific mean**, because it is the mean of a given individual. Some authors call this the **time-average** or **time-mean**, because it is the average over the time periods.

Subtracting the individual-specific mean from the variable, we obtain the deviations

$$\dot{Y}_{it} = Y_{it} - \overline{Y}_i.$$

This is known as the **within transformation**. We also refer to $\dot{Y}_{it}$ as the **demeaned values** or **deviations from individual means**. Some authors refer to $\dot{Y}_{it}$ as **deviations from time means**. What is important is that the demeaning has occured at the individual level.

Some algebra may also be useful. We can write the individual-specific mean as $\overline{Y}_i = \left(\mathbf{1}_i'\mathbf{1}_i\right)^{-1} \mathbf{1}_i'\boldsymbol{Y}_i$. Stacking the observations for individual i, we can write the within transformation using the notation

$$\begin{aligned}\dot{\boldsymbol{Y}}_i &= \boldsymbol{Y}_i - \mathbf{1}_i\overline{Y}_i \\ &= \boldsymbol{Y}_i - \mathbf{1}_i\left(\mathbf{1}_i'\mathbf{1}_i\right)^{-1}\mathbf{1}_i'\boldsymbol{Y}_i \\ &= \boldsymbol{M}_i\boldsymbol{Y}_i\end{aligned}$$

where $\boldsymbol{M}_i = \boldsymbol{I}_i - \mathbf{1}_i\left(\mathbf{1}_i'\mathbf{1}_i\right)^{-1}\mathbf{1}_i'$ is the individual-specific demeaning operator. Notice that $\boldsymbol{M}_i$ is an idempotent matrix.

Similarly, for the regressors, we define the individual-specific means and demeaned values:

$$\begin{aligned}\overline{X}_i &= \frac{1}{T_i}\sum_{t\in S_i} X_{it} \\ \dot{X}_{it} &= X_{it} - \overline{X}_i \\ \dot{\boldsymbol{X}}_i &= \boldsymbol{M}_i\boldsymbol{X}_i.\end{aligned}$$

We illustrate demeaning in Table 17.1. The fourth and seventh columns display the firm-specific means $\overline{I}_i$ and $\overline{Q}_i$, and in the fifth and eighth columns, the demeaned values $\dot{I}_{it}$ and $\dot{Q}_{it}$.

We can also define the full-sample in operator. Define $\boldsymbol{D} = \operatorname{diag}\left\{\mathbf{1}_{T_1}, \ldots, \mathbf{1}_{T_N}\right\}$ and $\boldsymbol{M}_{\boldsymbol{D}} = \boldsymbol{I}_n - \boldsymbol{D}\left(\boldsymbol{D}'\boldsymbol{D}\right)^{-1}\boldsymbol{D}'$. Note that $\boldsymbol{M}_{\boldsymbol{D}} = \operatorname{diag}\{\boldsymbol{M}_1, \ldots, \boldsymbol{M}_N\}$. Thus

$$\boldsymbol{M}_{\boldsymbol{D}}\boldsymbol{Y} = \dot{\boldsymbol{Y}} = \begin{pmatrix}\dot{\boldsymbol{Y}}_1 \\ \vdots \\ \dot{\boldsymbol{Y}}_N\end{pmatrix}, \qquad \boldsymbol{M}_{\boldsymbol{D}}\boldsymbol{X} = \dot{\boldsymbol{X}} = \begin{pmatrix}\dot{\boldsymbol{X}}_1 \\ \vdots \\ \dot{\boldsymbol{X}}_N\end{pmatrix}. \tag{17.19}$$

Now apply these operations to equation (17.15). Taking individual-specific averages, we obtain

$$\overline{Y}_i = \overline{X}_i'\beta + u_i + \overline{\varepsilon}_i \tag{17.20}$$

where $\overline{\varepsilon}_i = \frac{1}{T_i}\sum_{t\in S_i}\varepsilon_{it}$. Subtracting from (17.15), we obtain

$$\dot{Y}_{it} = \dot{X}_{it}'\beta + \dot{\varepsilon}_{it} \tag{17.21}$$

where $\dot{\varepsilon}_{it} = \varepsilon_{it} - \overline{\varepsilon}_{it}$. The individual effect u_i has been eliminated!

We can alternatively write this result in vector notation. Applying the demeaning operator $\boldsymbol{M}_i$ to (17.16), we obtain

$$\dot{\boldsymbol{Y}}_i = \dot{\boldsymbol{X}}_i\beta + \dot{\boldsymbol{\varepsilon}}_i. \tag{17.22}$$

The individual-effect u_i is eliminated, because $\boldsymbol{M}_i\mathbf{1}_i = 0$. Equation (17.22) is a vector version of (17.21).

Equation (17.21) is a linear equation in the transformed (demeaned) variables. As desired, the individual effect u_i has been eliminated. Consequently, estimators constructed from (17.21) (or equivalently, (17.22)) will be invariant to the values of u_i. Thus the endogeneity bias described in Section 17.7 will be eliminated.

Another consequence, however, is that all time-invariant regressors are also eliminated. That is, if the original model (17.15) had included any regressors $X_{it} = X_i$ that are constant over time for each individual, then for these regressors, the demeaned values are identically 0. Thus if equation (17.21) is used to estimate

β, it will be impossible to estimate (or identify) a coefficient on any regressor that is time invariant. This is not a consequence of the estimation method but instead a consequence of the model assumptions. In other words, if the individual effect u_i has no known structure, then it is impossible to disentangle the effect of any time-invariant regressor X_i. The two have observationally equivalent effects and cannot be separately identified.

The within transformation can greatly reduce the variance of the regressors. This can be seen in Table 17.1, where you can see that the variation between the elements of the transformed variables $\dot{I}_{it}$ and $\dot{Q}_{it}$ is less than that of the untransformed variables, as much of the variation is captured by the firm-specific means.

It is not typically needed to directly program the within transformation, but if it is desired, the following Stata commands easily do so.

Stata Commands for Within Transformation

```
*     x is the original variable
*     id is the group identifier
*     xdot is the within-transformed variable
egen xmean = mean(x), by(id)
gen xdot = x - xmean
```

17.9 FIXED EFFECTS ESTIMATOR

Consider least squares applied to the demeaned equation (17.21) or equivalently, (17.22):

$$\begin{aligned}\widehat{\beta}_{\text{fe}} &= \left(\sum_{i=1}^{N}\sum_{t\in S_i}\dot{X}_{it}\dot{X}_{it}'\right)^{-1}\left(\sum_{i=1}^{N}\sum_{t\in S_i}\dot{X}_{it}\dot{Y}_{it}\right)\\ &= \left(\sum_{i=1}^{N}\dot{\boldsymbol{X}}_i'\dot{\boldsymbol{X}}_i\right)^{-1}\left(\sum_{i=1}^{N}\dot{\boldsymbol{X}}_i'\dot{\boldsymbol{Y}}_i\right)\\ &= \left(\sum_{i=1}^{N}\boldsymbol{X}_i'\boldsymbol{M}_i\boldsymbol{X}_i\right)^{-1}\left(\sum_{i=1}^{N}\boldsymbol{X}_i'\boldsymbol{M}_i\boldsymbol{Y}_i\right).\end{aligned}$$

This is known as the **fixed effects** or **within** estimator of β. It is called the "fixed effects" estimator, because it is appropriate for the fixed effects model (17.15). It is called the within estimator, because it is based on the variation of the data within each individual.

The above definition implicitly assumes that the matrix $\sum_{i=1}^{N}\dot{\boldsymbol{X}}_i'\dot{\boldsymbol{X}}_i$ is full rank. This requires that all components of X_{it} have time variation for at least some individuals in the sample.

The fixed effects residuals are

$$\begin{aligned}\widehat{\varepsilon}_{it} &= \dot{Y}_{it} - \dot{X}_{it}'\widehat{\beta}_{\text{fe}}\\ \widehat{\boldsymbol{\varepsilon}}_i &= \dot{\boldsymbol{Y}}_i - \dot{\boldsymbol{X}}_i\widehat{\beta}_{\text{fe}}.\end{aligned} \tag{17.23}$$

Let us consider some of the statistical properties of the estimator under strict mean independence (17.18). By linearity and the fact $\boldsymbol{M}_i \mathbf{1}_i = 0$, we can write

$$\widehat{\beta}_{\mathrm{fe}} - \beta = \left(\sum_{i=1}^{N} \boldsymbol{X}_i' \boldsymbol{M}_i \boldsymbol{X}_i\right)^{-1} \left(\sum_{i=1}^{N} \boldsymbol{X}_i' \boldsymbol{M}_i \boldsymbol{\varepsilon}_i\right).$$

Then (17.18) implies

$$\mathbb{E}\left[\widehat{\beta}_{\mathrm{fe}} - \beta \mid \boldsymbol{X}\right] = \left(\sum_{i=1}^{N} \boldsymbol{X}_i' \boldsymbol{M}_i \boldsymbol{X}_i\right)^{-1} \left(\sum_{i=1}^{N} \boldsymbol{X}_i' \boldsymbol{M}_i \mathbb{E}\left[\boldsymbol{\varepsilon}_i \mid \boldsymbol{X}_i\right]\right) = 0.$$

Thus $\widehat{\beta}_{\mathrm{fe}}$ is unbiased for β under (17.18).

Let $\Sigma_i = \mathbb{E}\left[\boldsymbol{\varepsilon}_i \boldsymbol{\varepsilon}_i' \mid \boldsymbol{X}_i\right]$ denote the $T_i \times T_i$ conditional covariance matrix of the idiosyncratic errors. The variance of $\widehat{\beta}_{\mathrm{fe}}$ is

$$\boldsymbol{V}_{\mathrm{fe}} = \operatorname{var}\left[\widehat{\beta}_{\mathrm{fe}} \mid \boldsymbol{X}\right] = \left(\sum_{i=1}^{N} \dot{\boldsymbol{X}}_i' \dot{\boldsymbol{X}}_i\right)^{-1} \left(\sum_{i=1}^{N} \dot{\boldsymbol{X}}_i' \Sigma_i \dot{\boldsymbol{X}}_i\right) \left(\sum_{i=1}^{N} \dot{\boldsymbol{X}}_i' \dot{\boldsymbol{X}}_i\right)^{-1}. \tag{17.24}$$

This expression simplifies when the idiosyncratic errors are homoskedastic and serially uncorrelated:

$$\mathbb{E}\left[\varepsilon_{it}^2 \mid \boldsymbol{X}_i\right] = \sigma_\varepsilon^2 \tag{17.25}$$

$$\mathbb{E}\left[\varepsilon_{ij} \varepsilon_{it} \mid \boldsymbol{X}_i\right] = 0 \tag{17.26}$$

for all $j \neq t$. In this case, $\Sigma_i = \boldsymbol{I}_i \sigma_\varepsilon^2$ and (17.24) simplifies to

$$\boldsymbol{V}_{\mathrm{fe}}^0 = \sigma_\varepsilon^2 \left(\sum_{i=1}^{N} \dot{\boldsymbol{X}}_i' \dot{\boldsymbol{X}}_i\right)^{-1}. \tag{17.27}$$

It is instructive to compare the variances of the fixed effects and pooled estimators under (17.25)–(17.26) and the assumption that there is no individual-specific effect $u_i = 0$. In this case, we see that

$$\boldsymbol{V}_{\mathrm{fe}}^0 = \sigma_\varepsilon^2 \left(\sum_{i=1}^{N} \dot{\boldsymbol{X}}_i' \dot{\boldsymbol{X}}_i\right)^{-1} \geq \sigma_\varepsilon^2 \left(\sum_{i=1}^{N} \boldsymbol{X}_i' \boldsymbol{X}_i\right)^{-1} = \boldsymbol{V}_{\mathrm{pool}}. \tag{17.28}$$

The inequality holds because the demeaned variables $\dot{\boldsymbol{X}}_i$ have reduced variation relative to the original observations $\boldsymbol{X}_i$. (See Exercise 17.5.) This shows the cost of using fixed effects relative to pooled estimation. The estimation variance increases because of reduced variation in the regressors. This reduction in efficiency is a necessary by-product of the robustness of the estimator to the individual effects u_i.

17.10 DIFFERENCED ESTIMATOR

The within transformation is not the only transformation that eliminates the individual-specific effect. Another important transformation that does the same is first differencing.

The **first-differencing** transformation is $\Delta Y_{it} = Y_{it} - Y_{it-1}$. This can be applied to all but the first observation (which is essentially lost). At the level of the individual, this transformation can be written as $\Delta \boldsymbol{Y}_i =$

$\boldsymbol{D}_i \boldsymbol{Y}_i$, where $\boldsymbol{D}_i$ is the $(T_i - 1) \times T_i$ matrix differencing operator:

$$\boldsymbol{D}_i = \begin{bmatrix} -1 & 1 & 0 & \cdots & 0 & 0 \\ 0 & -1 & 1 & & 0 & 0 \\ \vdots & & & \ddots & & \vdots \\ 0 & 0 & 0 & \cdots & -1 & 1 \end{bmatrix}.$$

Applying the transformation Δ to (17.15) or (17.16), we obtain $\Delta Y_{it} = \Delta X_{it}'\beta + \Delta\varepsilon_{it}$ or

$$\Delta \boldsymbol{Y}_i = \Delta \boldsymbol{X}_i \beta + \Delta \boldsymbol{\varepsilon}_i. \tag{17.29}$$

We can see that the individual effect u_i has been eliminated.

Least squares applied to the differenced equation (17.29) is

$$\begin{aligned} \widehat{\beta}_\Delta &= \left(\sum_{i=1}^N \sum_{t\geq 2} \Delta X_{it} \Delta X_{it}'\right)^{-1} \left(\sum_{i=1}^N \sum_{t\geq 2} \Delta X_{it} \Delta Y_{it}\right) \\ &= \left(\sum_{i=1}^N \Delta \boldsymbol{X}_i' \Delta \boldsymbol{X}_i\right)^{-1} \left(\sum_{i=1}^N \Delta \boldsymbol{X}_i' \Delta \boldsymbol{Y}_i\right) \\ &= \left(\sum_{i=1}^N \boldsymbol{X}_i' \boldsymbol{D}_i' \boldsymbol{D}_i \boldsymbol{X}_i\right)^{-1} \left(\sum_{i=1}^N \boldsymbol{X}_i' \boldsymbol{D}_i' \boldsymbol{D}_i \boldsymbol{Y}_i\right). \end{aligned} \tag{17.30}$$

Equation (17.30) is called the **differenced estimator**. For $T = 2$, $\widehat{\beta}_\Delta = \widehat{\beta}_{\text{fe}}$ equals the fixed effects estimator. See Exercise 17.6. They differ, however, for $T > 2$.

When the errors ε_{it} are serially uncorrelated and homoskedastic, then the error $\Delta \boldsymbol{\varepsilon}_i = \boldsymbol{D}_i \boldsymbol{\varepsilon}_i$ in (17.29) has covariance matrix $\boldsymbol{H}\sigma_\varepsilon^2$, where

$$\boldsymbol{H} = \boldsymbol{D}_i \boldsymbol{D}_i' = \begin{pmatrix} 2 & -1 & 0 & 0 \\ -1 & 2 & \ddots & 0 \\ 0 & \ddots & \ddots & -1 \\ 0 & 0 & -1 & 2 \end{pmatrix}. \tag{17.31}$$

We can reduce estimation variance by using GLS. When the errors ε_{it} are i.i.d. (serially uncorrelated and homoskedastic), this is

$$\begin{aligned} \widetilde{\beta}_\Delta &= \left(\sum_{i=1}^N \Delta \boldsymbol{X}_i' \boldsymbol{H}^{-1} \Delta \boldsymbol{X}_i\right)^{-1} \left(\sum_{i=1}^N \Delta \boldsymbol{X}_i' \boldsymbol{H}^{-1} \Delta \boldsymbol{Y}_i\right) \\ &= \left(\sum_{i=1}^N \boldsymbol{X}_i' \boldsymbol{D}_i' \left(\boldsymbol{D}_i \boldsymbol{D}_i'\right)^{-1} \boldsymbol{D}_i \boldsymbol{X}_i\right)^{-1} \left(\sum_{i=1}^N \boldsymbol{X}_i' \boldsymbol{D}_i' \left(\boldsymbol{D}_i \boldsymbol{D}_i'\right)^{-1} \boldsymbol{D}_i \boldsymbol{Y}_i\right) \\ &= \left(\sum_{i=1}^N \boldsymbol{X}_i' \boldsymbol{M}_i \boldsymbol{X}_i\right)^{-1} \left(\sum_{i=1}^N \boldsymbol{X}_i' \boldsymbol{M}_i \boldsymbol{Y}_i\right) \end{aligned}$$

where $\boldsymbol{M}_i = \boldsymbol{D}_i' \left(\boldsymbol{D}_i \boldsymbol{D}_i'\right)^{-1} \boldsymbol{D}_i$. Recall that the matrix $\boldsymbol{D}_i$ is $(T_i - 1) \times T_i$ with rank $T_i - 1$ and is orthogonal to the vector of ones $\mathbf{1}_i$. Thus $\boldsymbol{M}_i$ projects orthogonally to $\mathbf{1}_i$ and so equals the within transformation matrix. Hence $\widetilde{\beta}_\Delta = \widehat{\beta}_{\text{fe}}$, the fixed effects estimator!

What we have shown is that under i.i.d. errors, GLS applied to the first-differenced equation precisely equals the fixed effects estimator. Since the Gauss-Markov theorem shows that GLS has lower variance than least squares, the fixed effects estimator is more efficient than first differencing under the assumption that ε_{it} is i.i.d.

This argument extends to any other transformation that eliminates the fixed effect. GLS applied after such a transformation is equal to the fixed effects estimator and is more efficient than least squares applied after the same transformation under i.i.d. errors. Thus the fixed effects estimator is Gauss-Markov efficient in the class of estimators that eliminate the fixed effect, under these assumptions.

17.11 DUMMY VARIABLES REGRESSION

An alternative way to estimate the fixed effects model is by least squares of Y_{it} on X_{it} and a full set of dummy variables, one for each individual in the sample. It turns out that this is algebraically equivalent to the within estimator.

To see this, start with the error-component model without a regressor:

$$Y_{it} = u_i + \varepsilon_{it}. \tag{17.32}$$

Consider least squares estimation of the vector of fixed effects $u = (u_1, \ldots, u_N)'$. Since each fixed effect u_i is an individual-specific mean and the least squares estimate of the intercept is the sample mean, it follows that the least squares estimate of u_i is $\widehat{u}_i = \overline{Y}_i$. The least squares residual is then $\widehat{\varepsilon}_{it} = Y_{it} - \overline{Y}_i = \dot{Y}_{it}$, the within transformation.

If you prefer an algebraic argument, let d_i be a vector of N dummy variables, where the ith element indicates the ith individual. Thus the ith element of d_i is 1, and the remaining elements are 0. Notice that $u_i = d_i' u$, and (17.32) equals $Y_{it} = d_i' u + \varepsilon_{it}$. This is a regression with the regressors d_i and coefficients u. We can also write it in vector notation at the level of the individual as $\boldsymbol{Y}_i = \mathbf{1}_i d_i' u + \boldsymbol{\varepsilon}_i$ or using full matrix notation as $\boldsymbol{Y} = \boldsymbol{D} u + \boldsymbol{\varepsilon}$, where $\boldsymbol{D} = \operatorname{diag}\left\{\mathbf{1}_{T_1}, \ldots, \mathbf{1}_{T_N}\right\}$.

The least squares estimate of u is

$$\begin{aligned}
\widehat{\boldsymbol{u}} &= \left(\boldsymbol{D}'\boldsymbol{D}\right)^{-1} \left(\boldsymbol{D}'\boldsymbol{Y}\right) \\
&= \operatorname{diag}\left(\mathbf{1}_i'\mathbf{1}_i\right)^{-1} \left\{\mathbf{1}_i'\boldsymbol{Y}_i\right\}_{i=1,\ldots,n} \\
&= \left\{\left(\mathbf{1}_i'\mathbf{1}_i\right)^{-1} \mathbf{1}_i'\boldsymbol{Y}_i\right\}_{i=1,\ldots,n} \\
&= \left\{\overline{Y}_i\right\}_{i=1,\ldots,n}.
\end{aligned}$$

The least squares residuals are

$$\widehat{\boldsymbol{\varepsilon}} = \left(\boldsymbol{I}_n - \boldsymbol{D}\left(\boldsymbol{D}'\boldsymbol{D}\right)^{-1}\boldsymbol{D}'\right)\boldsymbol{Y} = \dot{\boldsymbol{Y}}$$

as shown in (17.19). Thus the least squares residuals from the simple error-component model are the within transformed variables.

Now consider the error-component model with regressors, which can be written as

$$Y_{it} = X_{it}'\beta + d_i'u + \varepsilon_{it} \tag{17.33}$$

since $u_i = d_i'u$ as discussed above. In matrix notation,

$$\boldsymbol{Y} = \boldsymbol{X}\beta + \boldsymbol{D}u + \boldsymbol{\varepsilon}. \tag{17.34}$$

Let us consider estimation of (β, u) by least squares and write the estimates as $\boldsymbol{Y} = \boldsymbol{X}\widehat{\beta} + \boldsymbol{D}\widehat{u} + \widehat{\boldsymbol{\varepsilon}}$. We call this the **dummy variable estimator** of the fixed effects model.

By the Frisch-Waugh-Lovell Theorem (Theorem 3.5), the dummy variable estimator $\widehat{\beta}$ and residuals $\widehat{\boldsymbol{\varepsilon}}$ may be obtained by the least squares regression of the residuals from the regression of $\boldsymbol{Y}$ on $\boldsymbol{D}$ on the residuals from the regression of $\boldsymbol{X}$ on $\boldsymbol{D}$. We learned above that the residuals from the regression on $\boldsymbol{D}$ are the within transformations. Thus the dummy variable estimator $\widehat{\beta}$ and residuals $\widehat{\boldsymbol{\varepsilon}}$ may be obtained from least squares regression of the within transformed $\dot{\boldsymbol{Y}}$ on the within transformed $\dot{\boldsymbol{X}}$. This is exactly the fixed effects estimator $\widehat{\beta}_{\text{fe}}$. Thus the dummy variable and fixed effects estimators of β are identical.

This result is sufficiently important that we state it as a theorem.

Theorem 17.1 The fixed effects estimator of β algebraically equals the dummy variable estimator of β. The two estimators have the same residuals.

This result may be the most important practical application of the Frisch-Waugh-Lovell Theorem. It shows that we can estimate the coefficients either by applying the within transformation or by inclusion of dummy variables (one for each individual in the sample). In some cases, one approach is more convenient than the other, and so it is important to know that the two methods are algebraically equivalent.

When N is large, it is advisable to use the within transformation rather than the dummy variable approach, because the latter requires considerably more computer memory. To see this, consider the matrix $\boldsymbol{D}$ in (17.34) in the balanced case. It has TN^2 elements, which must be created and stored in memory. When N is large, this can be excessive. For example, if $T = 10$ and $N = 10,000$, the matrix $\boldsymbol{D}$ has one billion elements! Whether a package can technically handle a matrix of this dimension depends on several particulars (system RAM, operating system, package version), but even if it can execute the calculation, the computation time is excessive. Hence for fixed effects estimation with large N, it is advisable to use the within transformation rather than the dummy variable regression.

The dummy variable formulation may add insight to how the fixed effects estimator achieves invariance to the fixed effects. Given the regression equation (17.34), we can write the least squares estimator of β using the residual regression formula:

$$\begin{aligned}\widehat{\beta}_{\text{fe}} &= \left(\boldsymbol{X}'\boldsymbol{M}_{\boldsymbol{D}}\boldsymbol{X}\right)^{-1}\left(\boldsymbol{X}'\boldsymbol{M}_{\boldsymbol{D}}\boldsymbol{Y}\right)\\ &= \left(\boldsymbol{X}'\boldsymbol{M}_{\boldsymbol{D}}\boldsymbol{X}\right)^{-1}\left(\boldsymbol{X}'\boldsymbol{M}_{\boldsymbol{D}}\left(\boldsymbol{X}\beta + \boldsymbol{D}u + \boldsymbol{\varepsilon}\right)\right)\\ &= \beta + \left(\boldsymbol{X}'\boldsymbol{M}_{\boldsymbol{D}}\boldsymbol{X}\right)^{-1}\left(\boldsymbol{X}'\boldsymbol{M}_{\boldsymbol{D}}\boldsymbol{\varepsilon}\right)\end{aligned} \tag{17.35}$$

since $\boldsymbol{M}_{\boldsymbol{D}}\boldsymbol{D} = 0$. The expression (17.35) is free of the vector u, and thus $\widehat{\beta}_{\text{fe}}$ is invariant to u. This is another demonstration that the fixed effects estimator is invariant to the actual values of the fixed effects, and thus its statistical properties do not rely on assumptions about u_i.

17.12 FIXED EFFECTS COVARIANCE MATRIX ESTIMATION

Consider estimation of the classical covariance matrix $\boldsymbol{V}^0_{\text{fe}}$ as defined in (17.27):

$$\widehat{\boldsymbol{V}}^0_{\text{fe}} = \widehat{\sigma}^2_{\varepsilon} \left(\dot{\boldsymbol{X}}' \dot{\boldsymbol{X}} \right)^{-1} \tag{17.36}$$

with

$$\widehat{\sigma}^2_{\varepsilon} = \frac{1}{n-N-k} \sum_{i=1}^{n} \sum_{t \in S_i} \widehat{\varepsilon}^2_{it} = \frac{1}{n-N-k} \sum_{i=1}^{n} \widehat{\boldsymbol{\varepsilon}}'_i \widehat{\boldsymbol{\varepsilon}}_i. \tag{17.37}$$

The $N+k$ degree of freedom adjustment is motivated by the dummy variable representation. You can verify that $\widehat{\sigma}^2_{\varepsilon}$ is unbiased for σ^2_{ε} under assumptions (17.18), (17.25), and (17.26). See Exercise 17.8.

Notice that the assumptions (17.18), (17.25), and (17.26) are identical to (17.5)–(17.7) of Assumption 17.1. The assumptions (17.8)–(17.10) are not needed. Thus the fixed effects model weakens the random effects model by eliminating the assumptions on u_i but retaining those on ε_{it}.

The classical covariance matrix estimator (17.36) for the fixed effects estimator is valid when the errors ε_{it} are homoskedastic and serially uncorrelated but is invalid otherwise. A covariance matrix estimator that allows ε_{it} to be heteroskedastic and serially correlated across t is the cluster-robust covariance matrix estimator, clustered by individual:

$$\widehat{\boldsymbol{V}}^{\text{cluster}}_{\text{fe}} = \left(\dot{\boldsymbol{X}}' \dot{\boldsymbol{X}} \right)^{-1} \left(\sum_{i=1}^{N} \dot{\boldsymbol{X}}'_i \widehat{\boldsymbol{\varepsilon}}_i \widehat{\boldsymbol{\varepsilon}}'_i \dot{\boldsymbol{X}}_i \right) \left(\dot{\boldsymbol{X}}' \dot{\boldsymbol{X}} \right)^{-1} \tag{17.38}$$

where the $\widehat{\boldsymbol{\varepsilon}}_i$ are the fixed effects residuals as defined in (17.23). Equation (17.38) was first proposed by Arellano (1987). As in (4.52), $\widehat{\boldsymbol{V}}^{\text{cluster}}_{\text{fe}}$ can be multiplied by a degree-of-freedom adjustment. The adjustment recommended by the theory of C. Hansen (2007) is

$$\widehat{\boldsymbol{V}}^{\text{cluster}}_{\text{fe}} = \left(\frac{N}{N-1} \right) \left(\dot{\boldsymbol{X}}' \dot{\boldsymbol{X}} \right)^{-1} \left(\sum_{i=1}^{N} \dot{\boldsymbol{X}}'_i \widehat{\boldsymbol{\varepsilon}}_i \widehat{\boldsymbol{\varepsilon}}'_i \dot{\boldsymbol{X}}_i \right) \left(\dot{\boldsymbol{X}}' \dot{\boldsymbol{X}} \right)^{-1} \tag{17.39}$$

and that corresponding to (4.52) is

$$\widehat{\boldsymbol{V}}^{\text{cluster}}_{\text{fe}} = \left(\frac{n-1}{n-N-k} \right) \left(\frac{N}{N-1} \right) \left(\dot{\boldsymbol{X}}' \dot{\boldsymbol{X}} \right)^{-1} \left(\sum_{i=1}^{N} \dot{\boldsymbol{X}}'_i \widehat{\boldsymbol{\varepsilon}}_i \widehat{\boldsymbol{\varepsilon}}'_i \dot{\boldsymbol{X}}_i \right) \left(\dot{\boldsymbol{X}}' \dot{\boldsymbol{X}} \right)^{-1}. \tag{17.40}$$

These estimators are convenient, because they are simple to apply and allow for unbalanced panels.

In typical micropanel applications, N is very large and k is modest. Thus the adjustment in (17.39) is minor, while that in (17.40) is approximately $\overline{T}/(\overline{T}-1)$, where $\overline{T} = n/N$ is the average number of time periods per individual. When $\overline{T}$ is small, this can be a very large adjustment. Hence the choice between (17.38), (17.39), and (17.40) can be substantial.

To understand if the degree of freedom adjustment in (17.40) is appropriate, consider the simplified setting where the residuals are constructed with the true β but with estimated fixed effects u_i. This approximation is useful, because the number of estimated slope coefficients β is small relative to the sample size n. Then $\widehat{\boldsymbol{\varepsilon}}_i = \dot{\boldsymbol{\varepsilon}}_i = \boldsymbol{M}_i \boldsymbol{\varepsilon}_i$ so $\dot{\boldsymbol{X}}'_i \widehat{\boldsymbol{\varepsilon}}_i = \dot{\boldsymbol{X}}'_i \boldsymbol{\varepsilon}_i$, and (17.38) equals

$$\widehat{\boldsymbol{V}}^{\text{cluster}}_{\text{fe}} = \left(\dot{\boldsymbol{X}}' \dot{\boldsymbol{X}} \right)^{-1} \left(\sum_{i=1}^{N} \dot{\boldsymbol{X}}'_i \boldsymbol{\varepsilon}_i \boldsymbol{\varepsilon}'_i \dot{\boldsymbol{X}}_i \right) \left(\dot{\boldsymbol{X}}' \dot{\boldsymbol{X}} \right)^{-1}$$

which is the idealized estimator with the true errors rather than the residuals. Since $\mathbb{E}\left[\boldsymbol{\varepsilon}_i\boldsymbol{\varepsilon}_i' \mid \boldsymbol{X}_i\right] = \Sigma_i$, it follows that $\mathbb{E}\left[\widehat{\boldsymbol{V}}_{\text{fe}}^{\text{cluster}} \mid \boldsymbol{X}\right] = \boldsymbol{V}_{\text{fe}}$, and $\widehat{\boldsymbol{V}}_{\text{fe}}^{\text{cluster}}$ is unbiased for $\boldsymbol{V}_{\text{fe}}$! Thus no degree of freedom adjustment is required, even though the N fixed effects have been estimated. While this analysis concerns the idealized case where the residuals have been constructed with the true coefficients β, and so does not translate into a direct recommendation for the feasible estimator, it still suggests that the strong ad hoc adjustment in (17.40) is unwarranted.

This (crude) analysis suggests that for the cluster robust covariance estimator for fixed effects regression, the adjustment recommended by C. Hansen, (17.39) is the most appropriate. It is typically well approximated by the unadjusted estimator (17.38). Based on current theory, there is no justification for the ad hoc adjustment (17.40). The main argument for the latter is that it produces the largest standard errors and is thus the most conservative choice.

In current practice, the estimators (17.38) and (17.40) are the most commonly used covariance matrix estimators for fixed effects estimation.

In Sections 17.22 and 17.23, we discuss covariance matrix estimation under heteroskedasticity but no serial correlation.

To illustrate, Table 17.2 in Section 17.4 presents the fixed effect regression estimates of the investment model (17.3) in the third column with cluster-robust standard errors. The trading indicator T_i and the industry dummies cannot be included, as they are time invariant. The point estimates are similar to the random effects estimates, though the coefficients on debt and cash flow increase in magnitude.

17.13 FIXED EFFECTS ESTIMATION IN STATA

Several methods can be used to obtain the fixed effects estimator $\widehat{\beta}_{\text{fe}}$ in Stata.

The first method is dummy variable regression, which can be obtained by the Stata `regress` command, for example, `reg y x i.id, cluster(id)`, where `id` is the group (individual) identifier. In most cases, as discussed in Section 17.11, this is not recommended because of the excessive computer memory requirements and slow computation. If this command is used, it may be useful to suppress display of the full list of coefficient estimates. To do so, type `quietly reg y x i.id, cluster(id)` followed by `estimates table, keep(x _cons) be se`. The second command will report the coefficient(s) on `x` only, not those on the index variable `id`. (Other statistics can be reported as well.)

The second method is to manually create the within transformed variables as described in Section 17.8, and then use `regress`.

The third method is to use `xtreg fe`, which is specifically written for panel data. This method estimates the slope coefficients using the partialing-out approach. The default covariance matrix estimator is classical, as defined in (17.36). The cluster-robust covariance matrix (17.38) can be obtained using the options `vce(robust)` or `r`.

The fourth method is to use `areg absorb(id)`. This command is an alternative implementation of partialing-out regression. The default covariance matrix estimator is the classical (17.36). The cluster-robust covariance matrix estimator (17.40) can be obtained using the `cluster(id)` option. The heteroskedasticity-robust covariance matrix is obtained when `r` or `vce(robust)` is specified, but this is not recommended unless T_i is large, as discussed in Section 17.22.

An important difference between the Stata `xtreg` and `areg` commands is that they implement different cluster-robust covariance matrix estimators: (17.38) in the case of `xtreg` and (17.40) in the case of `areg`.

As discussed in Section 17.12, the adjustment used by `areg` is ad hoc and not well justified, but it produces the largest and hence most conservative standard errors.

Another difference between the commands is how they report the equation R^2. This difference can be huge and stems from the fact that they are estimating distinct population counterparts. Full dummy variable regression and the `areg` command calculate R^2 the same way: the squared correlation between Y_{it} and the fitted regression with all predictors, including the individual dummy variables. The `xtreg fe` command reports three values for R^2: within, between, and overall. The "within" R^2 is identical to what is obtained from a second stage regression using the within transformed variables. (The second method described earlier in this section.) The "overall" R^2 is the squared correlation between Y_{it} and the fitted regression, excluding the individual effects.

Which R^2 should be reported? The answer depends on the baseline model before regressors are added. If we view the baseline as an individual-specific mean, then the **within** calculation is appropriate. If the baseline is a single mean for all observations, then the full regression (`areg`) calculation is appropriate. The latter (`areg`) calculation is typically much higher than the within calculation, as the fixed effects typically "explain" a large portion of the variance. In any event, as there is no single definition of R^2, it is important to be explicit about the method if it is reported.

In current econometric practice, both `xtreg` and `areg` are used, though `areg` appears to be the more popular choice. Because the latter typically produces a much higher value of R^2, reported R^2 values should be viewed skeptically unless their calculation method is documented by the author.

17.14 BETWEEN ESTIMATOR

The **between estimator** is calculated from the individual-mean equation (17.20):

$$\overline{Y}_i = \overline{X}_i'\beta + u_i + \overline{\varepsilon}_i. \tag{17.41}$$

Estimation can be done at the level of individuals or at the level of observations. Least squares applied to (17.41) at the level of the N individuals is

$$\widehat{\beta}_{\mathrm{be}} = \left(\sum_{i=1}^{N} \overline{X}_i\overline{X}_i'\right)^{-1} \left(\sum_{i=1}^{N} \overline{X}_i\overline{Y}_i\right).$$

Least squares applied to (17.41) at the level of observations is

$$\widetilde{\beta}_{\mathrm{be}} = \left(\sum_{i=1}^{N}\sum_{t\in S_i} \overline{X}_i\overline{X}_i'\right)^{-1} \left(\sum_{i=1}^{N}\sum_{t\in S_i} \overline{X}_i\overline{Y}_i\right) = \left(\sum_{i=1}^{N} T_i\overline{X}_i\overline{X}_i'\right)^{-1} \left(\sum_{i=1}^{N} T_i\overline{X}_i\overline{Y}_i\right).$$

In balanced panels, $\widetilde{\beta}_{\mathrm{be}} = \widehat{\beta}_{\mathrm{be}}$, but they differ on unbalanced panels. $\widetilde{\beta}_{\mathrm{be}}$ equals weighted least squares applied at the level of individuals with weight T_i.

Under the random effects assumptions (Assumption 17.1), $\widehat{\beta}_{\mathrm{be}}$ is unbiased for β and has variance

$$\boldsymbol{V}_{\mathrm{be}} = \operatorname{var}\left[\widehat{\beta}_{\mathrm{be}} \mid \boldsymbol{X}\right] = \left(\sum_{i=1}^{N} \overline{X}_i\overline{X}_i'\right)^{-1} \left(\sum_{i=1}^{N} \overline{X}_i\overline{X}_i'\sigma_i^2\right) \left(\sum_{i=1}^{N} \overline{X}_i\overline{X}_i'\right)^{-1}$$

where

$$\sigma_i^2 = \text{var}\left[u_i + \overline{\varepsilon}_i\right] = \sigma_u^2 + \frac{\sigma_\varepsilon^2}{T_i}$$

is the variance of the error in (17.41). When the panel is balanced, the variance formula simplifies to

$$\boldsymbol{V}_{\text{be}} = \text{var}\left[\widehat{\beta}_{\text{be}} \mid \boldsymbol{X}\right] = \left(\sum_{i=1}^{N} \overline{X}_i \overline{X}_i'\right)^{-1} \left(\sigma_u^2 + \frac{\sigma_\varepsilon^2}{T}\right).$$

Under the random effects assumption, the between estimator $\widehat{\beta}_{\text{be}}$ is unbiased for β but is less efficient than the random effects estimator $\widehat{\beta}_{\text{gls}}$. Consequently, there seems to be little direct use for the between estimator in linear panel data applications.

Instead, its primary application is to construct an estimate of σ_u^2. First, consider estimation of

$$\sigma_b^2 = \frac{1}{N}\sum_{i=1}^{N} \sigma_i^2 = \sigma_u^2 + \frac{1}{N}\sum_{i=1}^{N} \frac{\sigma_\varepsilon^2}{T_i} = \sigma_u^2 + \frac{\sigma_\varepsilon^2}{\overline{T}}$$

where $\overline{T} = N / \sum_{i=1}^{N} T_i^{-1}$ is the harmonic mean of T_i. (In the case of a balanced panel, $\overline{T} = T$.) A natural estimator of σ_b^2 is

$$\widehat{\sigma}_b^2 = \frac{1}{N-k}\sum_{i=1}^{N} \widehat{e}_{bi}^2 \tag{17.42}$$

where $\widehat{e}_{bi} = \overline{Y}_i - \overline{X}_i' \widehat{\beta}_{\text{be}}$ are the between residuals. (Either $\widehat{\beta}_{\text{be}}$ or $\widetilde{\beta}_{\text{be}}$ can be used.)

From the relation $\sigma_b^2 = \sigma_u^2 + \sigma_\varepsilon^2 / \overline{T}$ and (17.42), we can deduce an estimator for σ_u^2. We have already described an estimator $\widehat{\sigma}_\varepsilon^2$ for σ_ε^2 in (17.37) for the fixed effects model. Since the fixed effects model holds under weaker conditions than the random effects model, $\widehat{\sigma}_\varepsilon^2$ is valid for the latter as well. This suggests the following estimator for σ_u^2:

$$\widehat{\sigma}_u^2 = \widehat{\sigma}_b^2 - \frac{\widehat{\sigma}_\varepsilon^2}{\overline{T}}. \tag{17.43}$$

To summarize, the fixed effect estimator is used for $\widehat{\sigma}_\varepsilon^2$, the between estimator for $\widehat{\sigma}_b^2$, and $\widehat{\sigma}_u^2$ is constructed from the two estimators.

It is possible for (17.43) to be negative. It is typical to use the constrained estimator

$$\widehat{\sigma}_u^2 = \max\left[0, \widehat{\sigma}_b^2 - \frac{\widehat{\sigma}_\varepsilon^2}{\overline{T}}\right]. \tag{17.44}$$

Equation (17.44) is the most common estimator for σ_u^2 in the random effects model.

The between estimator $\widehat{\beta}_{\text{be}}$ can be obtained using the Stata command `xtreg be`. The estimator $\widetilde{\beta}_{\text{be}}$ can be obtained by `xtreg be wls`.

17.15 FEASIBLE GLS

The random effects estimator can be written as

$$\widehat{\beta}_{\mathrm{re}}=\left(\sum_{i=1}^{N} \boldsymbol{X}_i'\Omega_i^{-1}\boldsymbol{X}_i\right)^{-1}\left(\sum_{i=1}^{N} \boldsymbol{X}_i'\Omega_i^{-1}\boldsymbol{Y}_i\right)=\left(\sum_{i=1}^{N} \widetilde{\boldsymbol{X}}_i'\widetilde{\boldsymbol{X}}_i\right)^{-1}\left(\sum_{i=1}^{N} \widetilde{\boldsymbol{X}}_i'\widetilde{\boldsymbol{Y}}_i\right) \tag{17.45}$$

where $\widetilde{\boldsymbol{X}}_i=\Omega_i^{-1/2}\boldsymbol{X}_i$, and $\widetilde{\boldsymbol{Y}}_i=\Omega_i^{-1/2}\boldsymbol{Y}_i$. It is instructive to study these transformations.

Define $\boldsymbol{P}_i=\mathbf{1}_i\left(\mathbf{1}_i'\mathbf{1}_i\right)^{-1}\mathbf{1}_i'$, so that $\boldsymbol{M}_i=\boldsymbol{I}_i-\boldsymbol{P}_i$. Thus while $\boldsymbol{M}_i$ is the within operator, $\boldsymbol{P}_i$ can be called the "individual-mean operator," since $\boldsymbol{P}_i\boldsymbol{Y}_i=\mathbf{1}_i\overline{Y}_i$. We can write

$$\Omega_i=\boldsymbol{I}_i+\mathbf{1}_i\mathbf{1}_i'\sigma_u^2/\sigma_\varepsilon^2=\boldsymbol{I}_i+\frac{T_i\sigma_u^2}{\sigma_\varepsilon^2}\boldsymbol{P}_i=\boldsymbol{M}_i+\rho_i^{-2}\boldsymbol{P}_i$$

where

$$\rho_i=\frac{\sigma_\varepsilon}{\sqrt{\sigma_\varepsilon^2+T_i\sigma_u^2}}. \tag{17.46}$$

Since the matrices $\boldsymbol{M}_i$ and $\boldsymbol{P}_i$ are idempotent and orthogonal, we find that $\Omega_i^{-1}=\boldsymbol{M}_i+\rho_i^2\boldsymbol{P}_i$ and

$$\Omega_i^{-1/2}=\boldsymbol{M}_i+\rho_i\boldsymbol{P}_i=\boldsymbol{I}_i-(1-\rho_i)\,\boldsymbol{P}_i. \tag{17.47}$$

Therefore the transformation used by the GLS estimator is

$$\widetilde{\boldsymbol{Y}}_i=(\boldsymbol{I}_i-(1-\rho_i)\,\boldsymbol{P}_i)\,\boldsymbol{Y}_i=\boldsymbol{Y}_i-(1-\rho_i)\,\mathbf{1}_i\overline{Y}_i$$

which is a partial within transformation.

The transformation as written depends on ρ_i, which is unknown. It can be replaced by the estimator

$$\widehat{\rho}_i=\frac{\widehat{\sigma}_\varepsilon}{\sqrt{\widehat{\sigma}_\varepsilon^2+T_i\widehat{\sigma}_u^2}} \tag{17.48}$$

where the estimators $\widehat{\sigma}_\varepsilon^2$ and $\widehat{\sigma}_u^2$ are given in (17.37) and (17.44), respectively. We obtain the feasible transformations

$$\widetilde{\boldsymbol{Y}}_i=\boldsymbol{Y}_i-(1-\widehat{\rho}_i)\,\mathbf{1}_i\overline{Y}_i \tag{17.49}$$

and

$$\widetilde{\boldsymbol{X}}_i=\boldsymbol{X}_i-(1-\widehat{\rho}_i)\,\mathbf{1}_i\overline{X}_i'. \tag{17.50}$$

The feasible random effects estimator is (17.45) using (17.49) and (17.50).

In Section 17.14, we noted that it is possible for $\widehat{\sigma}_u^2=0$. In this case, $\widehat{\rho}_i=1$ and $\widehat{\beta}_{\mathrm{re}}=\widehat{\beta}_{\mathrm{pool}}$.

What this shows is the following. The random effects estimator (17.45) is least squares applied to the transformed variables $\widetilde{\boldsymbol{X}}_i$ and $\widetilde{\boldsymbol{Y}}_i$ defined in (17.50) and (17.49). When $\widehat{\rho}_i=0$, these are the within transformations, so $\widetilde{\boldsymbol{X}}_i=\dot{\boldsymbol{X}}_i$, $\widetilde{\boldsymbol{Y}}_i=\dot{\boldsymbol{Y}}_i$, and $\widehat{\beta}_{\mathrm{re}}=\widehat{\beta}_{\mathrm{fe}}$ is the fixed effects estimator. When $\widehat{\rho}_i=1$, the data are untransformed $\widetilde{\boldsymbol{X}}_i=\boldsymbol{X}_i$, $\widetilde{\boldsymbol{Y}}_i=\boldsymbol{Y}_i$, and $\widehat{\beta}_{\mathrm{re}}=\widehat{\beta}_{\mathrm{pool}}$ is the pooled estimator. In general, $\widetilde{\boldsymbol{X}}_i$ and $\widetilde{\boldsymbol{Y}}_i$ can be viewed as partial within transformations.

Recalling the definition $\widehat{\rho}_i=\widehat{\sigma}_\varepsilon/\sqrt{\widehat{\sigma}_\varepsilon^2+T_i\widehat{\sigma}_u^2}$, we see that when the idiosyncratic error variance $\widehat{\sigma}_\varepsilon^2$ is large relative to $T_i\widehat{\sigma}_u^2$, then $\widehat{\rho}_i\approx 1$ and $\widehat{\beta}_{\mathrm{re}}\approx\widehat{\beta}_{\mathrm{pool}}$. Thus when the variance estimates suggest that the individual effect is relatively small, the random effect estimator simplifies to the pooled estimator. In contrast, when the individual effect error variance $\widehat{\sigma}_u^2$ is large relative to $\widehat{\sigma}_\varepsilon^2$, then $\widehat{\rho}_i\approx 0$ and $\widehat{\beta}_{\mathrm{re}}\approx\widehat{\beta}_{\mathrm{fe}}$. Thus when the variance estimates suggest that the individual effect is relatively large, the random effect estimator is close to the fixed effects estimator.

17.16 INTERCEPT IN FIXED EFFECTS REGRESSION

The fixed effects estimator does not apply to any regressor that is time invariant for all individuals. This includes an intercept. Yet some authors and packages (e.g., Amemiya (1971) and `xtreg` in Stata) report an intercept. To see how to construct an estimator of an intercept, consider the components regression equation adding an explicit intercept

$$Y_{it} = \alpha + X_{it}'\beta + u_i + \varepsilon_{it}.$$

We have already discussed estimation of β by $\widehat{\beta}_{\mathrm{fe}}$. Replacing β in this equation with $\widehat{\beta}_{\mathrm{fe}}$ and then estimating α by least squares, we obtain

$$\widehat{\alpha}_{\mathrm{fe}} = \overline{Y} - \overline{X}'\widehat{\beta}_{\mathrm{fe}}$$

where $\overline{Y}$ and $\overline{X}$ are averages from the full sample. This is the estimator reported by the Stata command `xtreg`.

17.17 ESTIMATION OF FIXED EFFECTS

For most applications, researchers are interested in the coefficients β, not the fixed effects u_i. But in some cases, the fixed effects themselves are interesting. This arises when we want to measure the distribution of u_i to understand its heterogeneity. It also arises in the context of prediction. As discussed in Section 17.11, the fixed effects estimate $\widehat{u}$ is obtained by least squares applied to the regression (17.33). To find their solution, replace β in (17.33) with the least squares minimizer $\widehat{\beta}_{\mathrm{fe}}$ and apply least squares. Since this is the individual-specific intercept, the solution is

$$\widehat{u}_i = \frac{1}{T_i}\sum_{t\in S_i}\left(Y_{it} - X_{it}'\widehat{\beta}_{\mathrm{fe}}\right) = \overline{Y}_i - \overline{X}_i'\widehat{\beta}_{\mathrm{fe}}. \tag{17.51}$$

Alternatively, using (17.34), this is

$$\begin{aligned}
\widehat{u} &= \left(\boldsymbol{D}'\boldsymbol{D}\right)^{-1}\boldsymbol{D}'\left(\boldsymbol{Y} - \boldsymbol{X}\widehat{\beta}_{\mathrm{fe}}\right)\\
&= \operatorname{diag}\left\{T_i^{-1}\right\}\sum_{i=1}^{N} d_i\mathbf{1}_i'\left(\boldsymbol{Y}_i - \boldsymbol{X}_i\widehat{\beta}_{\mathrm{fe}}\right)\\
&= \sum_{i=1}^{N} d_i\left(\overline{Y}_i - \overline{X}_i'\widehat{\beta}_{\mathrm{fe}}\right)\\
&= \left(\widehat{u}_1, \dots, \widehat{u}_N\right)'.
\end{aligned}$$

Thus the least squares estimates of the fixed effects can be obtained from the individual-specific means and does not require a regression with $N+k$ regressors.

If an intercept has been estimated (as discussed in Section 17.16), it should be subtracted from (17.51). In this case, the estimated fixed effects are

$$\widehat{u}_i = \overline{Y}_i - \overline{X}_i'\widehat{\beta}_{\text{fe}} - \widehat{\alpha}_{\text{fe}}. \tag{17.52}$$

With either estimator, when the number of time series observations T_i is small, $\widehat{u}_i$ will be an imprecise estimator of u_i. Thus calculations based on $\widehat{u}_i$ should be interpreted cautiously.

The fixed effects (17.52) may be obtained in Stata after `ivreg, fe` using the `predict u` command or after `areg` using the `predict d` command.

17.18 GMM INTERPRETATION OF FIXED EFFECTS

We can also interpret the fixed effects estimator through the generalized method of moments. Consider the fixed effects model after applying the within transformation (17.21). We can view this as a system of T equations, one for each time period t. It is a multivariate regression model. Using the notation of Chapter 11, define the $T \times kT$ regressor matrix:

$$\overline{\boldsymbol{X}}_i = \begin{pmatrix} \dot{X}_{i1}' & 0 & \cdots & 0 \\ \vdots & \dot{X}_{i2}' & & \vdots \\ 0 & 0 & \cdots & \dot{X}_{iT}' \end{pmatrix}. \tag{17.53}$$

If we treat each time period as a separate equation, we have the kT moment conditions

$$\mathbb{E}\left[\overline{\boldsymbol{X}}_i'\left(\dot{\boldsymbol{Y}}_i - \dot{\boldsymbol{X}}_i\beta\right)\right] = 0.$$

This is an overidentified system of equations when $T \geq 3$, as there are k coefficients and kT moments. (However, the moments are collinear due to the within transformation. There are $k(T-1)$ effective moments.) Interpreting this model in the context of multivariate regression, overidentification is achieved by the restriction that the coefficient vector β is constant across time periods.

This model can be interpreted as a regression of $\dot{\boldsymbol{Y}}_i$ on $\dot{\boldsymbol{X}}_i$ using the instruments $\overline{\boldsymbol{X}}_i$. The 2SLS estimator using matrix notation is

$$\widehat{\beta} = \left(\left(\dot{\boldsymbol{X}}'\overline{\boldsymbol{X}}\right)\left(\overline{\boldsymbol{X}}'\overline{\boldsymbol{X}}\right)^{-1}\left(\overline{\boldsymbol{X}}'\dot{\boldsymbol{X}}\right)\right)^{-1}\left(\left(\dot{\boldsymbol{X}}'\overline{\boldsymbol{X}}\right)\left(\overline{\boldsymbol{X}}'\overline{\boldsymbol{X}}\right)^{-1}\left(\overline{\boldsymbol{X}}'\dot{\boldsymbol{Y}}\right)\right).$$

Notice that

$$\begin{aligned}
\overline{\boldsymbol{X}}'\overline{\boldsymbol{X}} &= \sum_{i=1}^{n} \begin{pmatrix} \dot{X}_{i1} & 0 & \cdots & 0 \\ \vdots & \dot{X}_{i2} & & \vdots \\ 0 & 0 & \cdots & \dot{X}_{iT} \end{pmatrix} \begin{pmatrix} \dot{X}_{i1}' & 0 & \cdots & 0 \\ \vdots & \dot{X}_{i2}' & & \vdots \\ 0 & 0 & \cdots & \dot{X}_{iT}' \end{pmatrix} \\
&= \begin{pmatrix} \sum_{i=1}^{n} \dot{X}_{i1}\dot{X}_{i1}' & 0 & \cdots & 0 \\ \vdots & \sum_{i=1}^{n} \dot{X}_{i2}\dot{X}_{i2}' & & \vdots \\ 0 & 0 & \cdots & \sum_{i=1}^{n} \dot{X}_{iT}\dot{X}_{iT}' \end{pmatrix}
\end{aligned}$$

$$\overline{\boldsymbol{X}}'\dot{\boldsymbol{X}} = \begin{pmatrix} \sum_{i=1}^{n} \dot{X}_{i1}\dot{X}_{i1}' \\ \vdots \\ \sum_{i=1}^{n} \dot{X}_{iT}\dot{X}_{iT}' \end{pmatrix}$$

and

$$\overline{\boldsymbol{X}}'\dot{\boldsymbol{Y}} = \begin{pmatrix} \sum_{i=1}^{n} \dot{X}_{i1}\dot{Y}_{i1} \\ \vdots \\ \sum_{i=1}^{n} \dot{X}_{iT}\dot{Y}_{iT} \end{pmatrix}.$$

Thus the 2SLS estimator simplifies to

$$\begin{aligned}
\widehat{\beta}_{\text{2sls}} &= \left(\sum_{t=1}^{T}\left(\sum_{i=1}^{n}\dot{X}_{it}\dot{X}_{it}'\right)\left(\sum_{i=1}^{n}\dot{X}_{it}\dot{X}_{it}'\right)^{-1}\left(\sum_{i=1}^{n}\dot{X}_{it}\dot{X}_{it}'\right)\right)^{-1} \\
&\quad\times\left(\sum_{t=1}^{T}\left(\sum_{i=1}^{n}\dot{X}_{it}\dot{X}_{it}'\right)\left(\sum_{i=1}^{n}\dot{X}_{it}\dot{X}_{it}'\right)^{-1}\left(\sum_{i=1}^{n}\dot{X}_{it}\dot{Y}_{it}\right)\right) \\
&= \left(\sum_{t=1}^{T}\sum_{i=1}^{n}\dot{X}_{it}\dot{X}_{it}'\right)^{-1}\left(\sum_{t=1}^{T}\sum_{i=1}^{n}\dot{X}_{it}\dot{Y}_{it}\right) \\
&= \widehat{\beta}_{\text{fe}}
\end{aligned}$$

the fixed effects estimator!

Thus if we treat each time period as a separate equation with its separate moment equation so that the system is overidentified, and then estimate by GMM using the 2SLS weight matrix, the resulting GMM estimator equals the simple fixed effects estimator. There is no change by adding the additional moment conditions.

The 2SLS estimator is the appropriate GMM estimator when the equation error is serially uncorrelated and homoskedastic. If we use a two-step efficient weight matrix, which allows for heteroskedasticity and serial correlation, the GMM estimator is

$$\begin{aligned}
\widehat{\beta}_{\text{gmm}} &= \left(\sum_{t=1}^{T}\left(\sum_{i=1}^{n}\dot{X}_{it}\dot{X}_{it}'\right)\left(\sum_{i=1}^{n}\dot{X}_{it}\dot{X}_{it}'\widehat{e}_{it}^{2}\right)^{-1}\left(\sum_{i=1}^{n}\dot{X}_{it}\dot{X}_{it}'\right)\right)^{-1} \\
&\quad\times\left(\sum_{t=1}^{T}\left(\sum_{i=1}^{n}\dot{X}_{it}\dot{X}_{it}'\right)\left(\sum_{i=1}^{n}\dot{X}_{it}\dot{X}_{it}'\widehat{e}_{it}^{2}\right)^{-1}\left(\sum_{i=1}^{n}\dot{X}_{it}\dot{Y}_{it}\right)\right)
\end{aligned}$$

where $\widehat{e}_{it}$ are the fixed effects residuals.

Notationally, this GMM estimator has been written for a balanced panel. For an unbalanced panel, the sums over i need to be replaced by sums over individuals observed during time period t. Otherwise, no changes need to be made.

17.19 IDENTIFICATION IN THE FIXED EFFECTS MODEL

The identification of the slope coefficient β in fixed effects regression is similar to that in conventional regression but is somewhat more nuanced. It is most useful to consider the within-transformed equation, which can be written as $\dot{Y}_{it} = \dot{X}_{it}'\beta + \dot{\varepsilon}_{it}$ or $\dot{\boldsymbol{Y}}_i = \dot{\boldsymbol{X}}_i\beta + \dot{\boldsymbol{\varepsilon}}_i$.

From regression theory, we know that the coefficient β is the linear effect of $\dot{X}_{it}$ on $\dot{Y}_{it}$. The variable $\dot{X}_{it}$ is the deviation of the regressor from its individual-specific mean, and similarly for $\dot{Y}_{it}$. Thus the fixed effects model does not identify the effect of the average level of X_{it} on the average level of Y_{it}, but instead the effect of the deviations in X_{it} on Y_{it}.

In any given sample, the fixed effects estimator is only defined if $\sum_{i=1}^{N} \dot{\boldsymbol{X}}_i'\dot{\boldsymbol{X}}_i$ is full rank. The population analog (when individuals are i.i.d.) is

$$\mathbb{E}\left[\dot{\boldsymbol{X}}_i'\dot{\boldsymbol{X}}_i\right] > 0. \tag{17.54}$$

Equation (17.54) is the identification condition for the fixed effects estimator. It requires that the regressor matrix is full-rank in expectation after application of the within transformation. The regressors cannot contain any variable that does not have time variation at the individual level, nor can it contain a set of regressors whose time variation at the individual level is collinear.

17.20 ASYMPTOTIC DISTRIBUTION OF FIXED EFFECTS ESTIMATOR

In this section, we discuss an asymptotic distribution theory for the fixed effects estimator in balanced panels. Unbalanced panels are considered in Section 17.21.

We use the following assumptions.

Assumption 17.2

1. $Y_{it} = X_{it}'\beta + u_i + \varepsilon_{it}$ for $i = 1, \dots, N$ and $t = 1, \dots, T$ with $T \geq 2$.
2. The variables $(\boldsymbol{\varepsilon}_i, \boldsymbol{X}_i)$, $i = 1, \dots, N$, are i.i.d.
3. $\mathbb{E}\left[X_{is}\varepsilon_{it}\right] = 0$ for all $s = 1, \dots, T$.
4. $\boldsymbol{Q}_T = \mathbb{E}\left[\dot{\boldsymbol{X}}_i'\dot{\boldsymbol{X}}_i\right] > 0$.
5. $\mathbb{E}\left[\varepsilon_{it}^4\right] < \infty$.
6. $\mathbb{E}\left\|X_{it}\right\|^4 < \infty$.

Given Assumption 17.2, we can establish asymptotic normality for $\widehat{\beta}_{\text{fe}}$.

Theorem 17.2 Under Assumption 17.2, as $N \to \infty$, $\sqrt{N}\left(\widehat{\beta}_{\text{fe}} - \beta\right) \underset{d}{\longrightarrow} \mathrm{N}\left(0, \boldsymbol{V}_{\boldsymbol{\beta}}\right)$, where $\boldsymbol{V}_{\beta} = \boldsymbol{Q}_T^{-1}\Omega_T\boldsymbol{Q}_T^{-1}$ and $\Omega_T = \mathbb{E}\left[\dot{\boldsymbol{X}}_i'\boldsymbol{\varepsilon}_i\boldsymbol{\varepsilon}_i'\dot{\boldsymbol{X}}_i\right]$.

This asymptotic distribution is derived as the number of individuals N diverges to infinity while the number of time periods T is held fixed. Therefore the normalization is $\sqrt{N}$ rather than $\sqrt{n}$ (though either could be used, since T is fixed). This approximation is appropriate in the context of a large number of individuals. We could alternatively derive an approximation for the case where both N and T diverge to infinity, but it would not be a stronger result. One way of thinking about this is that Theorem 17.2 does not require T to be large.

Theorem 17.2 may appear to be routine, given our arsenal of asymptotic theory, but in a fundamental sense, it is quite different from any other result we have discussed. Fixed effects regression is effectively estimating $N+k$ coefficients—the k slope coefficients β plus the N fixed effects u—and the theory specifies that $N \to \infty$. Thus the number of estimated parameters is diverging to infinity at the same rate as sample size, yet the the estimator obtains a conventional mean-zero sandwich-form asymptotic distribution. In this sense, Theorem 17.2 is new and special.

We now discuss the assumptions.

Assumption 17.2 part 2 states that the observations are independent across individuals i. This is commonly used for panel data asymptotic theory. An important implied restriction is that it means that we exclude from the regressors any serially correlated aggregate time series variation.

Assumption 17.2 part 3 imposes that X_{it} is strictly exogeneous for ε_{it}. This condition is stronger than simple projection but is weaker than strict mean independence (17.18). It does not impose any condition on the individual-specific effects u_i.

Assumption 17.2 part 4 is the identification condition discussed in Section 17.19.

Assumption 17.2 parts 5 and 6 are needed for the CLT.

Let us now prove Theorem 17.2. The assumptions imply that the variables $(\dot{\boldsymbol{X}}_i, \boldsymbol{\varepsilon}_i)$ are i.i.d. across i and have finite fourth moments. Thus by the WLLN,

$$\frac{1}{N}\sum_{i=1}^{N} \dot{\boldsymbol{X}}_i'\dot{\boldsymbol{X}}_i \underset{p}{\longrightarrow} \mathbb{E}\left[\dot{\boldsymbol{X}}_i'\dot{\boldsymbol{X}}_i\right] = \boldsymbol{Q}_T.$$

Assumption 17.2 part 3 implies

$$\mathbb{E}\left[\dot{\boldsymbol{X}}_i'\boldsymbol{\varepsilon}_i\right] = \sum_{t=1}^{T} \mathbb{E}\left[\dot{X}_{it}\varepsilon_{it}\right] = \sum_{t=1}^{T} \mathbb{E}\left[X_{it}\varepsilon_{it}\right] - \sum_{t=1}^{T}\sum_{j=1}^{T} \mathbb{E}\left[X_{ij}\varepsilon_{it}\right] = 0$$

so they are mean zero. Assumptions 17.2 parts 5 and 6 imply that $\dot{\boldsymbol{X}}_i'\boldsymbol{\varepsilon}_i$ has a finite covariance matrix Ω_T. The assumptions for the CLT (Theorem 6.3) hold, thus

$$\frac{1}{\sqrt{N}}\sum_{i=1}^{N} \dot{\boldsymbol{X}}_i'\boldsymbol{\varepsilon}_i \underset{d}{\longrightarrow} \mathrm{N}\left(0, \Omega_T\right).$$

Taken together, we find

$$\sqrt{N}\left(\widehat{\beta}_{\mathrm{fe}} - \beta\right) = \left(\frac{1}{N}\sum_{i=1}^{N} \dot{\boldsymbol{X}}_i'\dot{\boldsymbol{X}}_i\right)^{-1} \left(\frac{1}{\sqrt{N}}\sum_{i=1}^{N} \dot{\boldsymbol{X}}_i'\boldsymbol{\varepsilon}_i\right) \underset{d}{\longrightarrow} \boldsymbol{Q}_T^{-1}\mathrm{N}\left(0, \Omega_T\right) = \mathrm{N}\left(0, \boldsymbol{V}_\beta\right)$$

as stated.

17.21 ASYMPTOTIC DISTRIBUTION FOR UNBALANCED PANELS

In this section, we extend the theory of Section 17.20 to cover unbalanced panels under random selection. My presentation is built on section 17.1 of Wooldridge (2010).

Think of an unbalanced panel as a shortened version of an idealized balanced panel, where the shortening stems from "missing" observations caused by random selection. Thus suppose that the underlying (potentially latent) variables are $\boldsymbol{Y}_i = (Y_{i1}, \ldots, Y_{iT})'$ and $\boldsymbol{X}_i = (X_{i1}, \ldots, X_{iT})'$. Let $\boldsymbol{s}_i = (s_{i1}, \ldots, s_{iT})'$ be a vector of selection indicators, meaning that $s_{it} = 1$ if the time period t is observed for individual i, and $s_{it} = 0$ otherwise. Then we can describe the estimators algebraically as follows.

Let $\boldsymbol{S}_i = \text{diag}(\boldsymbol{s}_i)$ and $\boldsymbol{M}_i = \boldsymbol{S}_i - \boldsymbol{s}_i \left(\boldsymbol{s}_i'\boldsymbol{s}_i\right)^{-1} \boldsymbol{s}_i'$, which is idempotent. The within transformations can be written as $\dot{\boldsymbol{Y}}_i = \boldsymbol{M}_i\boldsymbol{Y}_i$ and $\dot{\boldsymbol{X}}_i = \boldsymbol{M}_i\boldsymbol{X}_i$. They have the property that if $s_{it} = 0$ (so that time period t is missing) then the tth element of $\dot{\boldsymbol{Y}}_i$ and the tth row of $\dot{\boldsymbol{X}}_i$ are all zeros. The missing observations have been replaced by zeros. Consequently, they do not appear in matrix products and sums.

The fixed effects estimator of β based on the observed sample is

$$\widehat{\beta}_{\text{fe}} = \left(\sum_{i=1}^{N} \dot{\boldsymbol{X}}_i'\dot{\boldsymbol{X}}_i\right)^{-1} \left(\sum_{i=1}^{N} \dot{\boldsymbol{X}}_i'\dot{\boldsymbol{Y}}_i\right).$$

Centered and normalized, it is

$$\sqrt{N}\left(\widehat{\beta}_{\text{fe}} - \beta\right) = \left(\frac{1}{N}\sum_{i=1}^{N} \dot{\boldsymbol{X}}_i'\dot{\boldsymbol{X}}_i\right)^{-1} \left(\frac{1}{\sqrt{N}}\sum_{i=1}^{N} \dot{\boldsymbol{X}}_i'\boldsymbol{\varepsilon}_i\right).$$

Notationally this result appears to be identical to the case of a balanced panel, but the difference is that the within operator $\boldsymbol{M}_i$ incorporates the sample selection induced by the unbalanced panel structure.

To derive a distribution theory for $\widehat{\beta}_{\text{fe}}$, we need to be explicit about the stochastic nature of $\boldsymbol{s}_i$. That is, why are some time periods observed and some not? We could take several approaches:

1. We could treat $\boldsymbol{s}_i$ as fixed (nonrandom). This is the easiest approach but the most unsatisfactory.
2. We could treat $\boldsymbol{s}_i$ as random but independent of $(\boldsymbol{Y}_i, \boldsymbol{X}_i)$. This is known as "missing at random" and is a common assumption used to justify methods with missing observations. It is justified when the reason observations are not observed is independent of the observations. This is appropriate, for example, in panel datasets where individuals enter and exit in "waves." The statistical treatment is not substantially different from the case of fixed $\boldsymbol{s}_i$.
3. We could treat $(\boldsymbol{Y}_i, \boldsymbol{X}_i, \boldsymbol{s}_i)$ as jointly random but impose a condition sufficient for consistent estimation of β. This is the approach we take in this section. The condition turns out to be a form of mean independence. The advantage of this approach is that it is less restrictive than full independence. The disadvantage is that we must use a conditional mean restriction rather than uncorrelatedness to identify the coefficients.

The specific assumptions we impose are as follows.

Assumption 17.3

1. $Y_{it} = X_{it}'\beta + u_i + \varepsilon_{it}$ for $i = 1, \ldots, N$ with $T_i \geq 2$.
2. The variables $(\boldsymbol{\varepsilon}_i, \boldsymbol{X}_i, \boldsymbol{s}_i)$, $i = 1, \ldots, N$, are i.i.d.
3. $\mathbb{E}\left[\varepsilon_{it} \mid \boldsymbol{X}_i, \boldsymbol{s}_i\right] = 0$.
4. $\boldsymbol{Q}_T = \mathbb{E}\left[\dot{\boldsymbol{X}}_i'\dot{\boldsymbol{X}}_i\right] > 0$.
5. $\mathbb{E}\left[\varepsilon_{it}^4\right] < \infty$.
6. $\mathbb{E}\left\|X_{it}\right\|^4 < \infty$.

The primary difference with Assumption 17.2 is that we have strengthened strict exogeneity to strict mean independence, which ensures that the regression model is properly specified and that selection does not affect the mean of ε_{it}. It is less restrictive than full independence, because $\boldsymbol{s}_i$ can affect other moments of ε_{it} and more importantly, it does not restrict the joint dependence between $\boldsymbol{s}_i$ and $\boldsymbol{X}_i$.

Given the above development, it is straightforward to establish asymptotic normality.

Theorem 17.3 Under Assumption 17.3, as $N \to \infty$, $\sqrt{N}\left(\widehat{\beta}_{\text{fe}} - \beta\right) \underset{d}{\longrightarrow} \mathrm{N}\left(0, \boldsymbol{V}_\beta\right)$, where $\boldsymbol{V}_\beta = \boldsymbol{Q}_T^{-1} \Omega_T \boldsymbol{Q}_T^{-1}$ and $\Omega_T = \mathbb{E}\left[\dot{\boldsymbol{X}}_i' \boldsymbol{\varepsilon}_i \boldsymbol{\varepsilon}_i' \dot{\boldsymbol{X}}_i\right]$.

Let us now prove Theorem 17.3. The assumptions imply that the variables $(\dot{\boldsymbol{X}}_i, \boldsymbol{\varepsilon}_i)$ are i.i.d. across i and have finite fourth moments. By the WLLN,

$$\frac{1}{N}\sum_{i=1}^{N} \dot{\boldsymbol{X}}_i' \dot{\boldsymbol{X}}_i \underset{p}{\longrightarrow} \mathbb{E}\left[\dot{\boldsymbol{X}}_i' \dot{\boldsymbol{X}}_i\right] = \boldsymbol{Q}_T.$$

The random vectors $\dot{\boldsymbol{X}}_i' \boldsymbol{\varepsilon}_i$ are i.i.d. The matrix $\dot{\boldsymbol{X}}_i$ is a function of $(\boldsymbol{X}_i, \boldsymbol{s}_i)$ only. Assumption 17.3 part 3 and the law of iterated expectations implies

$$\mathbb{E}\left[\dot{\boldsymbol{X}}_i' \boldsymbol{\varepsilon}_i\right] = \mathbb{E}\left[\dot{\boldsymbol{X}}_i' \mathbb{E}\left[\boldsymbol{\varepsilon}_i \mid \boldsymbol{X}_i, \boldsymbol{s}_i\right]\right] = 0.$$

so that $\dot{\boldsymbol{X}}_i' \boldsymbol{\varepsilon}_i$ is mean zero. Assumption 17.3 parts 5 and 6 and the fact that $\boldsymbol{s}_i$ is bounded imply that $\dot{\boldsymbol{X}}_i' \boldsymbol{\varepsilon}_i$ has a finite covariance matrix, which is Ω_T. The assumptions for the CLT hold, and thus

$$\frac{1}{\sqrt{N}}\sum_{i=1}^{N} \dot{\boldsymbol{X}}_i' \boldsymbol{\varepsilon}_i \underset{d}{\longrightarrow} \mathrm{N}\left(0, \Omega_T\right).$$

Combining these results, we obtain the stated theorem.

17.22 HETEROSKEDASTICITY-ROBUST COVARIANCE MATRIX ESTIMATION

We have introduced two covariance matrix estimators for the fixed effects estimator. The classical estimator (17.36) is appropriate for the case where the idiosyncratic errors ε_{it} are homoskedastic and serially uncorrelated. The cluster-robust estimator (17.38) allows for heteroskedasticity and arbitrary serial correlation. Here and in Section 17.23, we consider the intermediate case where ε_{it} is heteroskedastic but serially uncorrelated.

Assume that (17.18) and (17.26) hold but not necessarily (17.25). Define the conditional variances

$$\mathbb{E}\left[\varepsilon_{it}^2 \mid \boldsymbol{X}_i\right] = \sigma_{it}^2. \tag{17.55}$$

Then $\Sigma_i = \mathbb{E}\left[\boldsymbol{\varepsilon}_i \boldsymbol{\varepsilon}_i' \mid \boldsymbol{X}_i\right] = \operatorname{diag}\left(\sigma_{it}^2\right)$. The covariance matrix (17.24) can be written as

$$\boldsymbol{V}_{\text{fe}} = \left(\dot{\boldsymbol{X}}' \dot{\boldsymbol{X}}\right)^{-1} \left(\sum_{i=1}^{N} \sum_{t \in S_i} \dot{X}_{it} \dot{X}_{it}' \sigma_{it}^2\right) \left(\dot{\boldsymbol{X}}' \dot{\boldsymbol{X}}\right)^{-1}. \tag{17.56}$$

A natural estimator of σ_{it}^2 is $\widehat{\varepsilon}_{it}^2$. Replacing σ_{it}^2 with $\widehat{\varepsilon}_{it}^2$ in (17.56) and making a degree-of-freedom adjustment, we obtain a White-type covariance matrix estimator:

$$\widehat{\boldsymbol{V}}_{\text{fe}} = \frac{n}{n-N-k}\left(\dot{\boldsymbol{X}}'\dot{\boldsymbol{X}}\right)^{-1}\left(\sum_{i=1}^{N}\sum_{t\in S_i}\dot{X}_{it}\dot{X}_{it}'\widehat{\varepsilon}_{it}^2\right)\left(\dot{\boldsymbol{X}}'\dot{\boldsymbol{X}}\right)^{-1}.$$

Following the insight of White (1980), it may seem appropriate to expect $\widehat{\boldsymbol{V}}_{\text{fe}}$ to be a reasonable estimator of $\boldsymbol{V}_{\text{fe}}$. Unfortunately, this is not the case, as discovered by Stock and Watson (2008). The problem is that $\widehat{\boldsymbol{V}}_{\text{fe}}$ is a function of the individual-specific means $\overline{\varepsilon}_i$, which are negligible only if the number of time series observations T_i is large.

We can see this by a simple bias calculation. Assume that the sample is balanced and that the residuals are constructed with the true β. Then

$$\widehat{\varepsilon}_{it} = \dot{\varepsilon}_{it} = \varepsilon_{it} - \frac{1}{T}\sum_{t=1}^{T}\varepsilon_{ij}.$$

Using (17.26) and (17.55), we have

$$\mathbb{E}\left[\widehat{\varepsilon}_{it}^2 \mid \boldsymbol{X}_i\right] = \left(\frac{T-2}{T}\right)\sigma_{it}^2 + \frac{\overline{\sigma}_i^2}{T} \tag{17.57}$$

where $\overline{\sigma}_i^2 = T^{-1}\sum_{t=1}^{T}\sigma_{it}^2$. (You are asked to show this in Exercise 17.10.) Using (17.57) and setting $k=0$, we obtain

$$\begin{aligned}\mathbb{E}\left[\widehat{\boldsymbol{V}}_{\text{fe}} \mid \boldsymbol{X}\right] &= \frac{T}{T-1}\left(\dot{\boldsymbol{X}}'\dot{\boldsymbol{X}}\right)^{-1}\left(\sum_{i=1}^{N}\sum_{t\in S_i}\dot{X}_{it}\dot{X}_{it}'\mathbb{E}\left[\widehat{\varepsilon}_{it}^2 \mid \boldsymbol{X}_i\right]\right)\left(\dot{\boldsymbol{X}}'\dot{\boldsymbol{X}}\right)^{-1}\\ &= \left(\frac{T-2}{T-1}\right)\boldsymbol{V}_{\text{fe}} + \frac{1}{T-1}\left(\dot{\boldsymbol{X}}'\dot{\boldsymbol{X}}\right)^{-1}\left(\sum_{i=1}^{N}\dot{\boldsymbol{X}}_i'\dot{\boldsymbol{X}}_i\overline{\sigma}_i^2\right)\left(\dot{\boldsymbol{X}}'\dot{\boldsymbol{X}}\right)^{-1}.\end{aligned}$$

Thus $\widehat{\boldsymbol{V}}_{\text{fe}}$ is biased of order $O\left(T^{-1}\right)$. Unless $T\to\infty$, this bias will persist as $N\to\infty$. $\widehat{\boldsymbol{V}}_{\text{fe}}$ is unbiased in two contexts. The first is when the errors ε_{it} are homoskedastic. The second is when $T=2$. (To show the latter requires some algebra and so is omitted.)

To correct the bias for the case $T>2$, Stock and Watson (2008) proposed the estimator

$$\widetilde{\boldsymbol{V}}_{\text{fe}} = \left(\frac{T-1}{T-2}\right)\widehat{\boldsymbol{V}}_{\text{fe}} - \frac{1}{T-1}\widehat{\boldsymbol{B}}_{\text{fe}} \tag{17.58}$$

$$\widehat{\boldsymbol{B}}_{\text{fe}} = \left(\dot{\boldsymbol{X}}'\dot{\boldsymbol{X}}\right)^{-1}\left(\sum_{i=1}^{N}\dot{\boldsymbol{X}}_i'\dot{\boldsymbol{X}}_i\widehat{\sigma}_i^2\right)\left(\dot{\boldsymbol{X}}'\dot{\boldsymbol{X}}\right)^{-1}$$

$$\widehat{\sigma}_i^2 = \frac{1}{T-1}\sum_{t=1}^{T}\widehat{\varepsilon}_{it}^2. \tag{17.59}$$

You can check that $\mathbb{E}\left[\widehat{\sigma}_i^2 \mid \boldsymbol{X}_i\right] = \overline{\sigma}_i^2$ and $\mathbb{E}\left[\widetilde{\boldsymbol{V}}_{\text{fe}} \mid \boldsymbol{X}_i\right] = \boldsymbol{V}_{\text{fe}}$, so $\widetilde{\boldsymbol{V}}_{\text{fe}}$ is unbiased for $\boldsymbol{V}_{\text{fe}}$ (see Exercise 17.11).

Stock and Watson (2008) show that $\widetilde{\boldsymbol{V}}_{\text{fe}}$ is consistent with T fixed and $N\to\infty$. In simulations, they show that $\widetilde{\boldsymbol{V}}_{\text{fe}}$ has excellent performance.

Because of the Stock-Watson analysis, Stata no longer calculates the heteroskedasticity-robust covariance matrix estimator $\widehat{\boldsymbol{V}}_{\text{fe}}$ when the fixed effects estimator is calculated using the `xtreg` command. Instead, the cluster-robust estimator $\widehat{\boldsymbol{V}}_{\text{fe}}^{\text{cluster}}$ is reported when robust standard errors are requested. However, the fixed effects estimator is often implemented using the `areg` command, which reports the biased estimator $\widehat{\boldsymbol{V}}_{\text{fe}}$ if robust standard errors are requested. These leads to the practical recommendation that `areg` should be used with the `cluster(id)` option.

At present, the corrected estimator (17.58) has not been programmed as a Stata option.

17.23 HETEROSKEDASTICITY-ROBUST ESTIMATION–UNBALANCED CASE

A limitation with the bias-corrected robust covariance matrix estimator of Stock and Watson (2008) is that it was only derived for balanced panels. In this section, we generalize their estimator to cover unbalanced panels.

The estimator is

$$\widetilde{\boldsymbol{V}}_{\text{fe}} = \left(\dot{\boldsymbol{X}}'\dot{\boldsymbol{X}}\right)^{-1} \widetilde{\Omega}_{\text{fe}} \left(\dot{\boldsymbol{X}}'\dot{\boldsymbol{X}}\right)^{-1} \tag{17.60}$$

$$\widetilde{\Omega}_{\text{fe}} = \sum_{i=1}^{N} \sum_{t\in S_i} \dot{X}_{it}\dot{X}_{it}' \left[\left(\frac{T_i\widehat{\varepsilon}_{it}^2 - \widehat{\sigma}_i^2}{T_i - 2}\right) \mathbb{1}\{T_i > 2\} + \left(\frac{T_i\widehat{\varepsilon}_{it}^2}{T_i - 1}\right) \mathbb{1}\{T_i = 2\}\right]$$

where

$$\widehat{\sigma}_i^2 = \frac{1}{T_i - 1}\sum_{t\in S_i} \widehat{\varepsilon}_{it}^2.$$

To justify this estimator, as in Section 17.22, make the simplifying assumption that the residuals are constructed with the true β. We calculate that

$$\mathbb{E}\left[\widehat{\varepsilon}_{it}^2 \mid \boldsymbol{X}_i\right] = \left(\frac{T_i - 2}{T_i}\right)\sigma_{it}^2 + \frac{\overline{\sigma}_i^2}{T_i} \tag{17.61}$$

$$\mathbb{E}\left[\widehat{\sigma}_i^2 \mid \boldsymbol{X}_i\right] = \overline{\sigma}_i^2. \tag{17.62}$$

You can show that under these assumptions, $\mathbb{E}\left[\widetilde{\boldsymbol{V}}_{\text{fe}} \mid \boldsymbol{X}\right] = \boldsymbol{V}_{\text{fe}}$ and thus $\widetilde{\boldsymbol{V}}_{\text{fe}}$ is unbiased for $\boldsymbol{V}_{\text{fe}}$. (See Exercise 17.12.)

In balanced panels, the estimator $\widetilde{\boldsymbol{V}}_{\text{fe}}$ simplifies to the Stock-Watson estimator (with $k = 0$).

17.24 HAUSMAN TEST FOR RANDOM VS. FIXED EFFECTS

The random effects model is a special case of the fixed effects model. Thus we can test the null hypothesis of random effects against the alternative of fixed effects. The Hausman test is typically used for this purpose. The statistic is quadratic in the difference between the fixed effects and random effects estimators. The statistic is

$$\begin{aligned} H &= \left(\widehat{\beta}_{\text{fe}} - \widehat{\beta}_{\text{re}}\right)' \widehat{\text{var}}\left[\widehat{\beta}_{\text{fe}} - \widehat{\beta}_{\text{re}}\right]^{-1} \left(\widehat{\beta}_{\text{fe}} - \widehat{\beta}_{\text{re}}\right) \\ &= \left(\widehat{\beta}_{\text{fe}} - \widehat{\beta}_{\text{re}}\right)' \left(\widehat{\boldsymbol{V}}_{\text{fe}} - \widehat{\boldsymbol{V}}_{\text{re}}\right)^{-1} \left(\widehat{\beta}_{\text{fe}} - \widehat{\beta}_{\text{re}}\right) \end{aligned}$$

where both $\widehat{\boldsymbol{V}}_{\text{fe}}$ and $\widehat{\boldsymbol{V}}_{\text{re}}$ take the classical (non-robust) form.

The test can be implemented on a subset of the coefficients β. In particular, this needs to be done if the regressors X_{it} contain time-invariant elements, so that the random effects estimator contains more coefficients than the fixed effects estimator. In this case, the test should be implemented only on the coefficients for the time-varying regressors.

An asymptotic $100\alpha\%$ test rejects if H exceeds the $1-\alpha$th quantile of the χ_k^2 distribution, where $k = \dim(\beta)$. If the test rejects, this is evidence that the individual effect u_i is correlated with the regressors, so the random effects model is not appropriate. In contrast, if the test fails to reject, this evidence says that the random effects hypothesis cannot be rejected.

It is tempting to use the Hausman test to select whether to use the fixed effects or random effects estimator. One could imagine using the random effects estimator if the Hausman test fails to reject the random effects hypothesis and using the fixed effects estimator otherwise. This approach is not, however, wise. This procedure—selecting an estimator based on a test—is known as a **pretest estimator** and is biased. The bias arises because the result of the test is random and correlated with the estimators.

Instead, the Hausman test can be used as a specification test. If you are planning to use the random effects estimator (and believe that the random effects assumptions are appropriate in your context), the Hausman test can be used to check this assumption and provide evidence to support your approach.

17.25 RANDOM EFFECTS OR FIXED EFFECTS?

We have discussed the random effects and fixed effects estimators of the regression coefficients. Which should be used in practice? How should we view the difference?

The basic distinction is that the random effects estimator requires the individual errors u_i to satisfy the conditional mean assumption (17.8). The fixed effects estimator does not require (17.8) and is robust to its violation. In particular, the individual effect u_i can be arbitrarily correlated with the regressors. However, the random effects estimator is efficient under random effects (Assumption 17.1).

Current econometric practice is to prefer robustness over efficiency. Consequently, current practice is (nearly uniformly) to use the fixed effects estimator for linear panel data models. Random effects estimators are only used in contexts where fixed effects estimation is unknown or challenging (which occurs in many nonlinear models).

The labels "random effects" and "fixed effects" are misleading. These labels arose in the early literature, and we are stuck with them today. In a previous era, regressors were viewed as "fixed." Viewing the individual effect as an unobserved regressor leads to the label of the individual effect as "fixed." Today, we rarely refer to regressors as "fixed" when dealing with observational data. We view all variables as random. Consequently, describing u_i as "fixed" does not make much sense, and it is hardly a contrast with the "random effect" label, because under either assumption, u_i is treated as random. Once again, the labels are unfortunate but the key difference is whether u_i is correlated with the regressors.

17.26 TIME TRENDS

In general, we expect that economic agents will experience common shocks during the same time period. For example, business cycle fluctations, inflation, and interest rates affect all agents in the economy. Therefore it is often desirable to include time effects in a panel regression model.

The simplest specification is a linear time trend:

$$Y_{it} = X_{it}'\beta + \gamma t + u_i + \varepsilon_{it}.$$

For a introduction to time trends, see Section 14.42. More flexible specifications (such as a quadratic) can also be used. For estimation, it is appropriate to include the time trend t as an element of the regressor vector X_{it} and then apply fixed effects.

In some cases, the time trends may be individual-specific. Series may be growing or declining at different rates. A linear time trend specification only extracts a common time trend. To allow for individual-specific time trends, we need to include an interaction effect, which can be written as

$$Y_{it} = X_{it}'\beta + \gamma_i t + u_i + \varepsilon_{it}.$$

In a fixed effects specification, the coefficients (γ_i, u_i) are treated as possibly correlated with the regressors. To eliminate them from the model, we treat them as unknown parameters and estimate all by least squares. By the FWL theorem (Theorem 3.5), the estimator for β equals least squares of $\dot{\boldsymbol{Y}}$ on $\dot{\boldsymbol{X}}$, where their elements are the residuals from the least squares regressions on a linear time trend fit separately for each individual and variable.

17.27 TWO-WAY ERROR COMPONENTS

In Section 17.26, we discussed inclusion of time trends and individual-specific time trends. The functional forms imposed by linear time trends are restrictive. There is no economic reason to expect the "trend" of a series to be linear. Business cycle "trends" are cyclic, which suggests that it is desirable to be more flexible than is possible with a linear (or polynomial) specification. In this section, we consider the most flexible specification, where the trend is allowed to take any arbitrary shape, but we will require that it is common rather than individual-specific.

The model we consider is the **two-way error component model**:

$$Y_{it} = X_{it}'\beta + v_t + u_i + \varepsilon_{it}. \tag{17.63}$$

In this model, u_i is an unobserved individual-specific effect, v_t is an unobserved time-specific effect, and ε_{it} is an idiosyncratic error.

The two-way model (17.63) can be handled either using random effects or fixed effects. In a random effects framework, the errors v_t and u_i are modeled as in Assumption 17.1. When the panel is balanced, the covariance matrix of the error vector $\boldsymbol{e} = v \otimes \mathbf{1}_N + \mathbf{1}_T \otimes u + \boldsymbol{\varepsilon}$ is

$$\operatorname{var}[\boldsymbol{e}] = \Omega = \left(\boldsymbol{I}_T \otimes \mathbf{1}_N \mathbf{1}_N'\right)\sigma_v^2 + \left(\mathbf{1}_T \mathbf{1}_T' \otimes \boldsymbol{I}_N\right)\sigma_u^2 + \boldsymbol{I}_n \sigma_\varepsilon^2. \tag{17.64}$$

When the panel is unbalanced, a similar but cumbersome expression for (17.64) can be derived. This variance (17.64) can be used for GLS estimation of β.

More typically, (17.63) is handled using fixed effects. The two-way within transformation subtracts both individual-specific means and time-specific means to eliminate both v_t and u_i from the two-way model (17.63). For a variable Y_{it}, we define the time-specific mean as follows. Let S_t be the set of individuals i for which the observation t is included in the sample, and let N_t be the number of these individuals. Then the time-specific mean at time t is

$$\widetilde{Y}_t = \frac{1}{N_t} \sum_{i \in S_t} Y_{it}.$$

This is the average across all values of Y_{it} observed at time t.

For the case of balanced panels, the **two-way within transformation** is

$$\ddot{Y}_{it} = Y_{it} - \overline{Y}_i - \widetilde{Y}_t + \overline{Y} \tag{17.65}$$

where $\overline{Y}=n^{-1}\sum_{i=1}^{N}\sum_{t=1}^{T}Y_{it}$ is the full-sample mean. If Y_{it} satisfies the two-way component model,

$$Y_{it}=v_t+u_i+\varepsilon_{it}$$

then $\overline{Y}_i=\overline{v}+u_i+\overline{\varepsilon}_i$, $\widetilde{Y}_t=v_t+\overline{u}+\widetilde{\varepsilon}_t$ and $\overline{Y}=\overline{v}+\overline{u}+\overline{\varepsilon}$. Hence

$$\begin{aligned}\ddot{Y}_{it}&=v_t+u_i+\varepsilon_{it}-(\overline{v}+u_i+\overline{\varepsilon}_i)-(v_t+\overline{u}+\widetilde{\varepsilon}_t)+\overline{v}+\overline{u}+\overline{\varepsilon}\\&=\varepsilon_{it}-\overline{\varepsilon}_i-\widetilde{\varepsilon}_t+\overline{\varepsilon}=\ddot{\varepsilon}_{it}\end{aligned}$$

so the individual and time effects are eliminated.

The two-way within transformation applied to (17.63) yields

$$\ddot{Y}_{it}=\ddot{X}_{it}'\beta+\ddot{\varepsilon}_{it} \tag{17.66}$$

which is invariant to both v_t and u_i. The **two-way within estimator** is least squares applied to (17.66).

For the unbalanced case, there are two computational approaches to implement the estimator. Both are based on the realization that the estimator is equivalent to including dummy variables for all time periods. Let τ_t be a set of T dummy variables where the tth variable indicates the tth time period. Thus the tth element of τ_t is 1, and the remaining elements are 0. Set $v=(v_1,\ldots,v_T)'$ as the vector of time fixed effects. Notice that $v_t=\tau_t'v$. We can write the two-way model as

$$Y_{it}=X_{it}'\beta+\tau_t'v+u_i+\varepsilon_{it}. \tag{17.67}$$

Equation (17.67) is the dummy variable representation of the two-way error components model.

Model (17.67) can be estimated by one-way fixed effects with regressors X_{it} and τ_t and coefficient vectors β and v. This model can be implemented by standard one-way fixed effects methods, including `xtreg` or `areg` in Stata. It produces estimates of the slopes β as well as the time effects v. To achieve identification, one time dummy variable is omitted from τ_t, so the estimated time effects are all relative to this baseline time period. This is the most common method in practice to estimate a two-way fixed effects model. As the number of time periods is typically modest, the method is a computationally attractive approach.

The second computational approach is to eliminate the time effects by residual regression, which is done by the following steps. First, subtract individual-specific means for (17.67), yielding

$$\dot{Y}_{it}=\dot{X}_{it}'\beta+\dot{\tau}_t'v+\dot{\varepsilon}_{it}.$$

Second, regress $\dot{Y}_{it}$ on $\dot{\tau}_t$ to obtain a residual $\ddot{Y}_{it}$ and regress each element of $\dot{X}_{it}$ on $\dot{\tau}_t$ to obtain a residual $\ddot{X}_{it}$. Third, regress $\ddot{Y}_{it}$ on $\ddot{X}_{it}$ to obtain the within estimator of β. These steps eliminate the fixed effects v_t, so the estimator is invariant to their value. What is important about this two-step procedure is that the second step is not a within transformation across the time index but instead a standard regression.

If the two-way within estimator is used, then the regressors X_{it} cannot include any time-invariant variables X_i or common time series variables X_t. Both are eliminated by the two-way within transformation. Coefficients are only identified for regressors that vary both across individuals and across time.

If desired, the relevance of the time effects can be tested by an exclusion test on the coefficients v. If the test rejects the hypothesis of zero coefficients, then this indicates that the time effects are relevant in the regression model.

The fixed effects estimator of (17.63) is invariant to the values of v_t and u_i, thus no assumptions need to be made concerning their stochastic properties.

To illustrate, the fourth column of Table 17.2 presents fixed effects estimates of the investment equation, augmented to included year dummy indicators, and is thus a two-way fixed effects model. In this example, the coefficient estimates and standard errors are not greatly affected by the inclusion of the year dummy variables.

17.28 INSTRUMENTAL VARIABLES

Consider the fixed effects model:

$$Y_{it} = X_{it}'\beta + u_i + \varepsilon_{it}. \tag{17.68}$$

We say X_{it} is exogenous for ε_{it} if $\mathbb{E}\left[X_{it}\varepsilon_{it}\right] = 0$, and we say X_{it} is endogenous for ε_{it} if $\mathbb{E}\left[X_{it}\varepsilon_{it}\right] \neq 0$. In Chapter 12, we discussed several economic examples of endogeneity, and the same issues apply in the panel data context. The primary difference is that in the fixed effects model, we only need to be concerned if the regressors are correlated with the idiosyncratic error ε_{it}, as correlation between X_{it} and u_i is allowed.

As in Chapter 12, if the regressors are endogenous, then the fixed effects estimator will be biased and inconsistent for the structural coefficient β. The standard approach to handling endogeneity is to specify instrumental variables Z_{it} that are both relevant (correlated with X_{it}) and exogenous (uncorrelated with ε_{it}).

Let Z_{it} be an $\ell \times 1$ instrumental variable where $\ell \geq k$. As in the cross-section case, Z_{it} may contain both included exogenous variables (variables in X_{it} that are exogenous) and excluded exogenous variables (variables not in X_{it}). Let $\boldsymbol{Z}_i$ be the stacked instruments by individual and $\boldsymbol{Z}$ be the stacked instruments for the full sample.

The dummy variable formulation of the fixed effects model is $Y_{it} = X_{it}'\beta + d_i'u + \varepsilon_{it}$, where d_i is an $N \times 1$ vector of dummy variables, one for each individual in the sample. The model in matrix notation for the full sample is

$$\boldsymbol{Y} = \boldsymbol{X}\beta + \boldsymbol{D}u + \boldsymbol{\varepsilon}. \tag{17.69}$$

Theorem 17.1 shows that the fixed effects estimator for β can be calculated by least squares estimation of (17.69). Thus the dummies $\boldsymbol{D}$ should be viewed as included exogenous variables.

Consider 2SLS estimation of β using the instruments $\boldsymbol{Z}$ for $\boldsymbol{X}$. Because $\boldsymbol{D}$ is an included exogenous variable, it should also be used as an instrument. Thus 2SLS estimation of the fixed effects model (17.68) is algebraically 2SLS of the regression (17.69) of $\boldsymbol{Y}$ on $(\boldsymbol{X}, \boldsymbol{D})$ using the pair $(\boldsymbol{Z}, \boldsymbol{D})$ as instruments.

Since the dimension of $\boldsymbol{D}$ can be excessively large, as discussed in Section 17.11, it is advisable to use residual regression to compute the 2SLS estimator, as we now discuss.

Section 12.12 describes several alternative representations for the 2SLS estimator. The fifth representation (equation (12.32)) shows that the 2SLS estimator for β equals

$$\widehat{\beta}_{\text{2sls}} = \left(\boldsymbol{X}'\boldsymbol{M}_{\boldsymbol{D}}\boldsymbol{Z}\left(\boldsymbol{Z}'\boldsymbol{M}_{\boldsymbol{D}}\boldsymbol{Z}\right)^{-1}\boldsymbol{Z}'\boldsymbol{M}_{\boldsymbol{D}}\boldsymbol{X}\right)^{-1}\left(\boldsymbol{X}'\boldsymbol{M}_{\boldsymbol{D}}\boldsymbol{Z}\left(\boldsymbol{Z}'\boldsymbol{M}_{\boldsymbol{D}}\boldsymbol{Z}\right)^{-1}\boldsymbol{Z}'\boldsymbol{M}_{\boldsymbol{D}}\boldsymbol{Y}\right)$$

where $\boldsymbol{M}_{\boldsymbol{D}} = \boldsymbol{I}_n - \boldsymbol{D}\left(\boldsymbol{D}'\boldsymbol{D}\right)^{-1}\boldsymbol{D}'$. The latter is the matrix within operator, thus $\boldsymbol{M}_{\boldsymbol{D}}\boldsymbol{Y} = \dot{\boldsymbol{Y}}$, $\boldsymbol{M}_{\boldsymbol{D}}\boldsymbol{X} = \dot{\boldsymbol{X}}$, and $\boldsymbol{M}_{\boldsymbol{D}}\boldsymbol{Z} = \dot{\boldsymbol{Z}}$. It follows that the 2SLS estimator is

$$\widehat{\beta}_{\text{2sls}} = \left(\dot{\boldsymbol{X}}'\dot{\boldsymbol{Z}}\left(\dot{\boldsymbol{Z}}'\dot{\boldsymbol{Z}}\right)^{-1}\dot{\boldsymbol{Z}}'\dot{\boldsymbol{X}}\right)^{-1}\left(\dot{\boldsymbol{X}}'\dot{\boldsymbol{Z}}\left(\dot{\boldsymbol{Z}}'\dot{\boldsymbol{Z}}\right)^{-1}\dot{\boldsymbol{Z}}'\dot{\boldsymbol{Y}}\right).$$

This is convenient. It shows that the 2SLS estimator for the fixed effects model can be calculated by applying 2SLS to the within-transformed Y_{it}, X_{it}, and Z_{it}. The 2SLS residuals are $\widehat{\boldsymbol{e}} = \dot{\boldsymbol{Y}} - \dot{\boldsymbol{X}}\widehat{\beta}_{2\text{sls}}$.

This estimator can be obtained using the Stata command `xtivreg fe`. It can also be obtained using the Stata command `ivregress` after making the within transformations.

The presentation above focused for clarity on the one-way fixed effects model. There is no substantial change in the two-way fixed effects model

$$Y_{it} = X_{it}'\beta + u_i + v_t + \varepsilon_{it}.$$

The easiest way to estimate the two-way model is to add $T-1$ time-period dummies to the regression model and include these dummy variables as both regressors and instruments.

17.29 IDENTIFICATION WITH INSTRUMENTAL VARIABLES

To understand the identification of the structural slope coefficient β in the fixed effects model, it is necessary to examine the reduced form equation for the endogenous regressors X_{it}. This is

$$X_{it} = \Gamma Z_{it} + W_i + \zeta_{it}$$

where W_i is a $k \times 1$ vector of fixed effects for the k regressors, and ζ_{it} is an idiosyncratic error.

The coefficient matrix Γ is the linear effect of Z_{it} on X_{it} holding the fixed effects W_i constant. Thus Γ has a similar interpretation as the coefficient β in the fixed effects regression model. It is the effect of the variation in Z_{it} about its individual-specific mean on X_{it}.

The 2SLS estimator is a function of the within transformed variables. Applying the within transformation to the reduced form, we find $\dot{X}_{it} = \Gamma \dot{Z}_{it} + \dot{\zeta}_{it}$. Thus Γ is the effect of the within-transformed instruments on the regressors. If there is no time variation in the within-transformed instruments or no correlation between the instruments and the regressors after removing the individual-specific means, then the coefficient Γ will be either not identified or singular. In either case, the coefficient β will not be identified.

Thus for identification of the fixed effects instrumental variables model, we need

$$\mathbb{E}\left[\dot{\boldsymbol{Z}}_i'\dot{\boldsymbol{Z}}_i\right] > 0 \tag{17.70}$$

and

$$\operatorname{rank}\left(\mathbb{E}\left[\dot{\boldsymbol{Z}}_i'\dot{\boldsymbol{X}}_i\right]\right) = k. \tag{17.71}$$

Condition (17.70) is the same as the condition for identification in fixed effects regression – the instruments must have full variation after the within transformation. Condition (17.71) is analogous to the relevance condition for identification of instrumental variable regression in the cross-section context, but it applies to the within-transformed instruments and regressors.

Condition (17.71) shows that to examine instrument validity in the context of fixed effects 2SLS, it is important to estimate the reduced form equation using fixed effects (within) regression. Standard tests for instrument validity (F tests on the excluded instruments) can be applied. However, since the correlation structure of the reduced form equation is in general unknown, it is appropriate to use a cluster-robust covariance matrix, clustered at the level of the individual.

17.30 ASYMPTOTIC DISTRIBUTION OF FIXED EFFECTS 2SLS ESTIMATOR

This section presents an asymptotic distribution theory for the fixed effects estimator. I provide a formal theory for the case of balanced panels and discuss an extension to the unbalanced case.

We use the following assumptions for balanced panels.

Assumption 17.4

1. $Y_{it} = X_{it}'\beta + u_i + \varepsilon_{it}$ for $i = 1, \ldots, N$ and $t = 1, \ldots, T$, with $T \geq 2$.
2. The variables $(\boldsymbol{\varepsilon}_i, \boldsymbol{X}_i, \boldsymbol{Z}_i)$, $i = 1, \ldots, N$, are i.i.d.
3. $\mathbb{E}[Z_{is}\varepsilon_{it}] = 0$ for all $s = 1, \ldots, T$.
4. $\boldsymbol{Q}_{ZZ} = \mathbb{E}\left[\dot{\boldsymbol{Z}}_i'\dot{\boldsymbol{Z}}_i\right] > 0$.
5. $\operatorname{rank}\left(\boldsymbol{Q}_{ZX}\right) = k$, where $\boldsymbol{Q}_{ZX} = \mathbb{E}\left[\dot{\boldsymbol{Z}}_i'\dot{\boldsymbol{X}}_i\right]$.
6. $\mathbb{E}\left[\varepsilon_{it}^4\right] < \infty$.
7. $\mathbb{E}\|X_{it}\|^2 < \infty$.
8. $\mathbb{E}\|Z_{it}\|^4 < \infty$.

Given Assumption 17.4, we can establish asymptotic normality for $\widehat{\beta}_{2\text{sls}}$.

Theorem 17.4 Under Assumption 17.4, as $N \to \infty$, $\sqrt{N}\left(\widehat{\beta}_{2\text{sls}} - \beta\right) \underset{d}{\longrightarrow} \mathrm{N}\left(0, \boldsymbol{V}_\beta\right)$, where

$$\boldsymbol{V}_\beta = \left(\boldsymbol{Q}_{ZX}'\boldsymbol{Q}_{ZZ}^{-1}\boldsymbol{Q}_{ZX}\right)^{-1}\left(\boldsymbol{Q}_{ZX}'\boldsymbol{Q}_{ZZ}^{-1}\Omega_{Z\varepsilon}\boldsymbol{Q}_{ZZ}^{-1}\boldsymbol{Q}_{ZX}\right)\left(\boldsymbol{Q}_{ZX}'\boldsymbol{Q}_{ZZ}^{-1}\boldsymbol{Q}_{ZX}\right)^{-1}$$

$$\Omega_{Z\varepsilon} = \mathbb{E}\left[\dot{\boldsymbol{Z}}_i'\boldsymbol{\varepsilon}_i\boldsymbol{\varepsilon}_i'\dot{\boldsymbol{Z}}_i\right].$$

The proof of the result is similar to Theorem 17.2 and so it is omitted. The key condition is Assumption 17.4 part 3, which states that the instruments are strictly exogenous for the idiosyncratic errors. The identification conditions are Assumption 17.4 parts 4 and 5, which were discussed in Section 17.29.

The theorem is stated for balanced panels. For unbalanced panels, we can modify the theorem as for Theorem 17.3 by adding the selection indicators $\boldsymbol{s}_i$ and replacing Assumption 17.4 part 3 with $\mathbb{E}[\varepsilon_{it} \mid \boldsymbol{Z}_i, \boldsymbol{s}_i] = 0$, which states that the idiosyncratic errors are mean independent of the instruments and selection.

If the idiosyncratic errors ε_{it} are homoskedastic and serially uncorrelated, then the covariance matrix simplifies to

$$\boldsymbol{V}_\beta = \left(\boldsymbol{Q}_{ZX}'\boldsymbol{Q}_{ZZ}^{-1}\boldsymbol{Q}_{ZX}\right)^{-1}\sigma_\varepsilon^2.$$

In this case, a classical homoskedastic covariance matrix estimator can be used. Otherwise, a cluster-robust covariance matrix estimator can be used and takes the form

$$\widehat{\boldsymbol{V}}_{\widehat{\beta}} = \left(\dot{\boldsymbol{X}}'\dot{\boldsymbol{Z}}\left(\dot{\boldsymbol{Z}}'\dot{\boldsymbol{Z}}\right)^{-1}\dot{\boldsymbol{Z}}'\dot{\boldsymbol{X}}\right)^{-1}\left(\dot{\boldsymbol{X}}'\dot{\boldsymbol{Z}}\right)\left(\dot{\boldsymbol{Z}}'\dot{\boldsymbol{Z}}\right)^{-1}\left(\sum_{i=1}^N \dot{\boldsymbol{Z}}_i'\widehat{\boldsymbol{\varepsilon}}_i\widehat{\boldsymbol{\varepsilon}}_i'\dot{\boldsymbol{Z}}_i\right)$$
$$\times\left(\dot{\boldsymbol{Z}}'\dot{\boldsymbol{Z}}\right)^{-1}\left(\dot{\boldsymbol{Z}}'\dot{\boldsymbol{X}}\right)\left(\dot{\boldsymbol{X}}'\dot{\boldsymbol{Z}}\left(\dot{\boldsymbol{Z}}'\dot{\boldsymbol{Z}}\right)^{-1}\dot{\boldsymbol{Z}}'\dot{\boldsymbol{X}}\right)^{-1}.$$

As for the case of fixed effects regression, the heteroskedasticity-robust covariance matrix estimator is not recommended due to bias when T is small, and a bias-corrected version has not been developed.

The Stata command `xtivreg, fe` by default reports the classical homoskedastic covariance matrix estimator. To obtain a cluster-robust covariance matrix, use option `vce(robust)` or `vce(cluster id)`.

17.31 LINEAR GMM

Consider the just-identified 2SLS estimator. It solves the equation $\dot{\boldsymbol{Z}}'\left(\dot{\boldsymbol{Y}}-\dot{\boldsymbol{X}}\beta\right)=0$. These are sample analogs of the population moment condition $\mathbb{E}\left[\dot{\boldsymbol{Z}}_i'\left(\dot{\boldsymbol{Y}}_i-\dot{\boldsymbol{X}}_i\beta\right)\right]=0$. These population conditions hold at the true β, because $\dot{\boldsymbol{Z}}'u=\boldsymbol{Z}'\boldsymbol{M}\boldsymbol{D}u=0$ as u lies in the null space of $\boldsymbol{D}$, and $\mathbb{E}\left[\dot{\boldsymbol{Z}}_i'\boldsymbol{\varepsilon}\right]=0$ is implied by Assumption 17.4 part 3.

The population orthogonality conditions hold in the overidentified case as well. In this case, an alternative to 2SLS is GMM. Let $\widehat{\boldsymbol{W}}$ be an estimator of $\boldsymbol{W}=\mathbb{E}\left[\dot{\boldsymbol{Z}}_i'\boldsymbol{\varepsilon}_i\boldsymbol{\varepsilon}_i'\dot{\boldsymbol{Z}}_i\right]$, for example,

$$\widehat{\boldsymbol{W}}=\frac{1}{N}\sum_{i=1}^{N}\dot{\boldsymbol{Z}}_i'\widehat{\boldsymbol{\varepsilon}}_i\widehat{\boldsymbol{\varepsilon}}_i'\dot{\boldsymbol{Z}}_i \tag{17.72}$$

where the $\widehat{\boldsymbol{\varepsilon}}_i$ are the 2SLS fixed effects residuals. The GMM fixed effects estimator is

$$\widehat{\beta}_{\mathrm{gmm}}=\left(\dot{\boldsymbol{X}}'\dot{\boldsymbol{Z}}\widehat{\boldsymbol{W}}^{-1}\dot{\boldsymbol{Z}}'\dot{\boldsymbol{X}}\right)^{-1}\left(\dot{\boldsymbol{X}}'\dot{\boldsymbol{Z}}\widehat{\boldsymbol{W}}^{-1}\dot{\boldsymbol{Z}}'\dot{\boldsymbol{Y}}\right). \tag{17.73}$$

The estimator (17.72)–(17.73) does not have a Stata command but can be obtained by generating the within transformed variables $\dot{\boldsymbol{X}}$, $\dot{\boldsymbol{Z}}$, and $\dot{\boldsymbol{Y}}$, and then estimating by GMM a regression of $\dot{\boldsymbol{Y}}$ on $\dot{\boldsymbol{X}}$ using $\dot{\boldsymbol{Z}}$ as instruments and a weight matrix clustered by individual.

17.32 ESTIMATION WITH TIME-INVARIANT REGRESSORS

One of the disappointments with the fixed effects estimator is that it cannot estimate the effect of regressors that are time invariant. They are not identified separately from the fixed effect and are eliminated by the within transformation. In contrast, the random effects estimator allows for time-invariant regressors but does so only by assuming strict exogeneity, which is stronger than typically desired in economic applications.

It turns out that we can consider an intermediate case that maintains the fixed effects assumptions for the time-varying regressors but uses stronger assumptions on the time-invariant regressors. For our exposition, I denote the time-varying regressors by the $k\times 1$ vector X_{it} and the time-invariant regressors by the $\ell\times 1$ vector Z_i.

Consider the linear regression model

$$Y_{it}=X_{it}'\beta+Z_i'\gamma+u_i+\varepsilon_{it}.$$

At the level of the individual, this can be written as

$$\boldsymbol{Y}_i=\boldsymbol{X}_i\beta+\boldsymbol{Z}_i\gamma+\boldsymbol{\iota}_iu_i+\boldsymbol{\varepsilon}_i$$

where $\boldsymbol{Z}_i = \boldsymbol{\iota}_i Z_i'$. For the full sample we can write this in matrix notation as

$$\boldsymbol{Y} = \boldsymbol{X}\beta + \boldsymbol{Z}\gamma + \boldsymbol{u} + \boldsymbol{\varepsilon}. \tag{17.74}$$

We maintain the assumption that the idiosyncratic errors ε_{it} are uncorrelated with both X_{it} and Z_i at all time horizons:

$$\mathbb{E}\left[X_{is}\varepsilon_{it}\right] = 0 \tag{17.75}$$

$$\mathbb{E}\left[Z_i\varepsilon_{it}\right] = 0. \tag{17.76}$$

In this section, we consider the case where Z_i is uncorrelated with the individual-level error u_i, thus

$$\mathbb{E}\left[Z_i u_i\right] = 0, \tag{17.77}$$

but the correlation of X_{it} and u_i is left unrestricted. In this context, we say that Z_i is exogenous with respect to the fixed effect u_i, while X_{it} is endogenous with respect to u_i. Note that this is a different type of endogeneity than that considered in the sections on instrumental variables: there endogeneity meant correlation with the idiosyncratic error ε_{it}. Here endogeneity means correlation with the fixed effect u_i.

We consider estimation of (17.74) by instrumental variables and thus need instruments that are uncorrelated with the error $u_i + \varepsilon_{it}$. The time-invariant regressors Z_i satisfy this condition because of (17.76) and (17.77), thus

$$\mathbb{E}\left[\boldsymbol{Z}_i'\left(\boldsymbol{Y}_i - \boldsymbol{X}_i\beta - \boldsymbol{Z}_i\gamma\right)\right] = 0.$$

Although the time-varying regressors X_{it} are correlated with u_i, the within transformed variables $\dot{X}_{it}$ are uncorrelated with $u_i + \varepsilon_{it}$ under (17.75), thus

$$\mathbb{E}\left[\dot{\boldsymbol{X}}_i'\left(\boldsymbol{Y}_i - \boldsymbol{X}_i\beta - \boldsymbol{Z}_i\gamma\right)\right] = 0.$$

Therefore we can estimate (β, γ) by instrumental variable regression using the instrument set $(\dot{\boldsymbol{X}}, \boldsymbol{Z})$. Specifically, we use regression of $\boldsymbol{Y}$ on $\boldsymbol{X}$ and $\boldsymbol{Z}$, treating $\boldsymbol{X}$ as endogenous, $\boldsymbol{Z}$ as exogenous, and using the instrument $\dot{\boldsymbol{X}}$. Write this estimator as $(\widehat{\beta}, \widehat{\gamma})$. This can be implemented using the Stata `ivregress` command after constructing the within transformed $\dot{\boldsymbol{X}}$.

This instrumental variables estimator is algebraically equal to a simple two-step estimator. The first step $\widehat{\beta} = \widehat{\beta}_{\mathrm{fe}}$ is the fixed effects estimator. The second step sets $\widehat{\gamma} = \left(\boldsymbol{Z}'\boldsymbol{Z}\right)^{-1}\left(\boldsymbol{Z}'\widehat{\boldsymbol{u}}\right)$, the least squares coefficient from the regression of the estimated fixed effect $\widehat{u}_i$ on Z_i. To see this equivalence, observe that the instrumental variables estimator solves the sample moment equations

$$\dot{\boldsymbol{X}}'\left(\boldsymbol{Y} - \boldsymbol{X}\beta - \boldsymbol{Z}\gamma\right) = 0 \tag{17.78}$$

$$\boldsymbol{Z}'\left(\boldsymbol{Y} - \boldsymbol{X}\beta - \boldsymbol{Z}\gamma\right) = 0. \tag{17.79}$$

Notice that $\dot{\boldsymbol{X}}_i'\boldsymbol{Z}_i = \dot{\boldsymbol{X}}_i'\boldsymbol{\iota}_i Z_i' = 0$, so $\dot{\boldsymbol{X}}'\boldsymbol{Z} = 0$. Thus (17.78) is the same as $\dot{\boldsymbol{X}}'\left(\boldsymbol{Y} - \boldsymbol{X}\beta\right) = 0$, whose solution is $\widehat{\beta}_{\mathrm{fe}}$. Plugging this into the left side of (17.79), we obtain

$$\boldsymbol{Z}'\left(\boldsymbol{Y} - \boldsymbol{X}\widehat{\beta}_{\mathrm{fe}} - \boldsymbol{Z}\gamma\right) = \boldsymbol{Z}'\left(\overline{\boldsymbol{Y}} - \overline{\boldsymbol{X}}\widehat{\beta}_{\mathrm{fe}} - \boldsymbol{Z}\gamma\right) = \boldsymbol{Z}'\left(\widehat{\boldsymbol{u}} - \boldsymbol{Z}\gamma\right)$$

where $\overline{\boldsymbol{Y}}$ and $\overline{\boldsymbol{X}}$ are the stacked individual means $\boldsymbol{\iota}_i\overline{Y}_i$ and $\boldsymbol{\iota}_i\overline{X}_i'$. Setting equal to 0 and solving, we obtain the least squares estimator $\widehat{\gamma} = \left(\boldsymbol{Z}'\boldsymbol{Z}\right)^{-1}\left(\boldsymbol{Z}'\widehat{\boldsymbol{u}}\right)$, as claimed. This equivalence was first observed by Hausman and Taylor (1981).

For standard error calculation, it is recommended to estimate (β, γ) jointly by instrumental variable regression and use a cluster-robust covariance matrix clustered at the individual level. Classical and heteroskedasticity-robust estimators are misspecified due to the individual-specific effect u_i.

The estimator $(\widehat{\beta}, \widehat{\gamma})$ is a special case of the Hausman-Taylor estimator described in Section 17.33. (For an unknown reason, the above estimator cannot be estimated using Stata's `xthtaylor` command.)

17.33 HAUSMAN-TAYLOR MODEL

Hausman and Taylor (1981) consider a generalization of the previous model. Their model is

$$Y_{it} = X'_{1it}\beta_1 + X'_{2it}\beta_2 + Z'_{1i}\gamma_1 + Z'_{2i}\gamma_2 + u_i + \varepsilon_{it}$$

where X_{1it} and X_{2it} are time-varying, and Z_{1i} and Z_{2i} are time-invariant. Let the dimensions of X_{1it}, X_{2it}, Z_{1i}, and Z_{2i} be k_1, k_2, ℓ_1, and ℓ_2, respectively.

Write the model in matrix notation as

$$\boldsymbol{Y} = \boldsymbol{X}_1\beta_1 + \boldsymbol{X}_2\beta_2 + \boldsymbol{Z}_1\gamma_1 + \boldsymbol{Z}_2\gamma_2 + \boldsymbol{u} + \boldsymbol{\varepsilon}. \tag{17.80}$$

Let $\overline{\boldsymbol{X}}_1$ and $\overline{\boldsymbol{X}}_2$ denote conformable matrices of individual-specific means, and let $\dot{\boldsymbol{X}}_1 = \boldsymbol{X}_1 - \overline{\boldsymbol{X}}_1$ and $\dot{\boldsymbol{X}}_2 = \boldsymbol{X}_2 - \overline{\boldsymbol{X}}_2$ denote the within-transformed variables.

The Hausman-Taylor model assumes that all regressors are uncorrelated with the idiosyncratic error ε_{it} at all time horizons and that X_{1it} and Z_{1i} are exogenous with respect to the fixed effect u_i, so that

$$\mathbb{E}\left[X_{1it}u_i\right] = 0$$

$$\mathbb{E}\left[Z_{1i}u_i\right] = 0.$$

The regressors X_{2it} and Z_{2i}, however, are allowed to be correlated with u_i.

Set $\boldsymbol{X} = (\boldsymbol{X}_1, \boldsymbol{X}_2, \boldsymbol{Z}_1, \boldsymbol{Z}_2)$ and $\beta = (\beta_1, \beta_2, \gamma_1, \gamma_2)$. The assumptions imply the following population moment conditions:

$$\mathbb{E}\left[\dot{\boldsymbol{X}}'_1(\boldsymbol{Y} - \boldsymbol{X}\beta)\right] = 0$$

$$\mathbb{E}\left[\dot{\boldsymbol{X}}'_2(\boldsymbol{Y} - \boldsymbol{X}\beta)\right] = 0$$

$$\mathbb{E}\left[\overline{\boldsymbol{X}}'_1(\boldsymbol{Y} - \boldsymbol{X}\beta)\right] = 0$$

$$\mathbb{E}\left[\boldsymbol{Z}'_1(\boldsymbol{Y} - \boldsymbol{X}\beta)\right] = 0.$$

There are $2k_1 + k_2 + \ell_1$ moment conditions and $k_1 + k_2 + \ell_1 + \ell_2$ coefficients. Identification requires $k_1 \geq \ell_2$: that there are at least as many exogenous time-varying regressors as endogenous time-invariant regressors. (This includes the model of Section 17.32, where $k_1 = \ell_2 = 0$.)

Given the moment conditions, the coefficients $\beta = (\beta_1, \beta_2, \gamma_1, \gamma_2)$ can be estimated by 2SLS regression of (17.80) using the instruments $\boldsymbol{Z} = (\dot{\boldsymbol{X}}_1, \dot{\boldsymbol{X}}_2, \overline{\boldsymbol{X}}_1, \boldsymbol{Z}_1)$ or equivalently, $\boldsymbol{Z} = (\boldsymbol{X}_1, \dot{\boldsymbol{X}}_2, \overline{\boldsymbol{X}}_1, \boldsymbol{Z}_1)$. This is 2SLS regression treating $\boldsymbol{X}_1$ and $\boldsymbol{Z}_1$ as exogenous and $\boldsymbol{X}_2$ and $\boldsymbol{Z}_2$ as endogenous and using the excluded instruments $\dot{\boldsymbol{X}}_2$ and $\overline{\boldsymbol{X}}_1$.

It is recommended to use cluster-robust covariance matrix estimation clustered at the individual level. Neither conventional nor heteroskedasticity-robust covariance matrix estimators should be used, as they are misspecified due to the individual-specific effect u_i.

When the model is just-identified, the estimators simplify as follows. $\widehat{\beta}_1$ and $\widehat{\beta}_2$ are the fixed effects estimator; $\widehat{\gamma}_1$ and $\widehat{\gamma}_2$ equal the 2SLS estimator from a regression of $\widehat{u}_i$ on Z_{1i} and Z_{2i} using $\overline{X}_{1i}$ as an instrument for Z_{2i}. (See Exercise 17.14.)

When the model is over identified the equation can also be estimated by GMM with a cluster-robust weight matrix using the same equations and instruments.

This estimator with cluster-robust standard errors can be calculated using the Stata `ivregress cluster(id)` command after constructing the transformed variables $\dot{\boldsymbol{X}}_2$ and $\overline{\boldsymbol{X}}_1$.

The 2SLS estimator described above corresponds to the Hausman and Taylor (1981) estimator in the just-identified case with a balanced panel.

Hausman and Taylor derived their estimator under the stronger assumption that the errors ε_{it} and u_i are strictly mean independent and homoskedastic. Consequently, they proposed a GLS-type estimator, which is more efficient when these assumptions are correct. Define $\Omega = \operatorname{diag}(\Omega_i)$, where $\Omega_i = \boldsymbol{I}_i + \mathbf{1}_i \mathbf{1}_i' \sigma_u^2/\sigma_\varepsilon^2$, and σ_ε^2 and σ_u^2 are the variances of the error components ε_{it} and u_i, respectively. Define the transformed variables $\widetilde{\boldsymbol{Y}} = \Omega^{-1/2}\boldsymbol{Y}$, $\widetilde{\boldsymbol{X}} = \Omega^{-1/2}\boldsymbol{X}$, and $\widetilde{\boldsymbol{Z}} = \Omega^{-1/2}\boldsymbol{Z}$. The Hausman-Taylor estimator is

$$
\begin{aligned}
\widehat{\beta}_{\mathrm{ht}} &= \left(\boldsymbol{X}'\Omega^{-1}\boldsymbol{Z}\left(\boldsymbol{Z}'\Omega^{-1}\boldsymbol{Z}\right)^{-1}\boldsymbol{Z}'\Omega^{-1}\boldsymbol{X}\right)^{-1}\left(\boldsymbol{X}'\Omega^{-1}\boldsymbol{Z}\left(\boldsymbol{Z}'\Omega^{-1}\boldsymbol{Z}\right)^{-1}\boldsymbol{Z}'\Omega^{-1}\boldsymbol{Y}\right) \\
&= \left(\widetilde{\boldsymbol{X}}'\widetilde{\boldsymbol{Z}}\left(\widetilde{\boldsymbol{Z}}'\widetilde{\boldsymbol{Z}}\right)^{-1}\widetilde{\boldsymbol{Z}}'\widetilde{\boldsymbol{X}}\right)^{-1}\left(\widetilde{\boldsymbol{X}}'\widetilde{\boldsymbol{Z}}\left(\widetilde{\boldsymbol{Z}}'\widetilde{\boldsymbol{Z}}\right)^{-1}\widetilde{\boldsymbol{Z}}'\widetilde{\boldsymbol{Y}}\right).
\end{aligned}
$$

Recall from (17.47) that $\Omega_i^{-1/2} = \boldsymbol{M}_i + \rho_i \boldsymbol{P}_i$, where ρ_i is defined in (17.46). Thus

$$
\begin{aligned}
\widetilde{Y}_i &= Y_i - (1-\rho_i)\,\overline{Y}_i \\
\widetilde{X}_{1i} &= X_{1i} - (1-\rho_i)\,\overline{X}_{1i} \\
\widetilde{X}_{2i} &= X_{2i} - (1-\rho_i)\,\overline{X}_{2i} \\
\widetilde{Z}_{1i} &= \rho_i Z_{1i} \\
\widetilde{Z}_{2i} &= \rho_i Z_{2i} \\
\widetilde{\dot{X}}_{1i} &= \dot{X}_{1i} \\
\widetilde{\dot{X}}_{2i} &= \dot{X}_{2i}.
\end{aligned}
$$

It follows that the Hausman-Taylor estimator can be calculated by 2SLS regression of $\widetilde{\boldsymbol{Y}}_i$ on $(\widetilde{\boldsymbol{X}}_{1i}, \widetilde{\boldsymbol{X}}_{2i}, \rho_i \boldsymbol{Z}_{1i}, \rho_i \boldsymbol{Z}_{2i})$ using the instruments $(\dot{\boldsymbol{X}}_{1i}, \dot{\boldsymbol{X}}_{2i}, \rho_i \overline{\boldsymbol{X}}_{1i}, \rho_i \boldsymbol{Z}_{1i})$.

When the panel is balanced, the coefficients $\rho_i = \rho$ all equal and scale out from the instruments. Thus the estimator can be calculated by 2SLS regression of $\widetilde{\boldsymbol{Y}}_i$ on $(\widetilde{\boldsymbol{X}}_{1i}, \widetilde{\boldsymbol{X}}_{2i}, \rho \boldsymbol{Z}_{1i}, \rho \boldsymbol{Z}_{2i})$ using the instruments $\left(\dot{\boldsymbol{X}}_{1i}, \dot{\boldsymbol{X}}_{2i}, \overline{\boldsymbol{X}}_{1i}, \boldsymbol{Z}_{1i}\right)$.

In practice, ρ_i is unknown. It can be estimated as in (17.48) with the modification that the error variance is estimated from the untransformed 2SLS regression. Under the homoskedasticity assumptions used by Hausman and Taylor, the estimator $\widehat{\beta}_{\mathrm{ht}}$ has a classical asymptotic covariance matrix. When these assumptions are relaxed, the covariance matrix can be estimated using cluster-robust methods.

The Hausman-Taylor estimator with cluster-robust standard errors can be implemented in Stata by the command `xthtaylor vce(robust)`. This Stata command, for an unknown reason, requires that there is at least one exogenous time-invariant variable ($\ell_1 \geq 1$) and at least one exogenous time-varying variable ($k_1 \geq 1$), even when the model is identified. Otherwise, the estimator can be implemented using the instrumental variable method described above.

The Hausman-Taylor estimator was refined by Amemiya and MaCurdy (1986) and Breusch, Mizon and Schmidt (1989), who proposed more efficient versions using additional instruments that are valid under stronger orthogonality conditions. The observation that in the unbalanced case the instruments should be weighted by ρ_i was made by Gardner (1998).

In the overidentified case, it is unclear whether it is preferable to use the simpler 2SLS estimator $\widehat{\beta}_{2\text{sls}}$ or the GLS-type Hausman-Taylor estimator $\widehat{\beta}_{\text{ht}}$. The advantages of $\widehat{\beta}_{\text{ht}}$ are that it is asymptotically efficient under their stated homoskedasticity and serial correlation conditions and that a program is available in Stata. The advantage of $\widehat{\beta}_{2\text{sls}}$ is that it is much simpler to program (if doing so yourself), may have better finite sample properties (because it avoids variance-component estimation), and is the natural estimator from the the modern GMM viewpoint.

To illustrate, the final column of Table 17.2 contains Hausman-Taylor estimates of the investment model treating $Q_{i,t-1}$, $D_{i,t-1}$, and T_i as endogenous for u_i, and $CF_{i,t-1}$ and the industry dummies as exogenous. Relative to the fixed effects models, this allows estimation of the coefficient on the trading indicator T_i. The most interesting change relative to the previous estimates is that the coefficient on the trading indicator T_i doubles in magnitude relative to the random effects estimate. This behavior is consistent with the hypothesis that T_i is correlated with the fixed effect, hence the random effects estimate is biased.

17.34 JACKKNIFE COVARIANCE MATRIX ESTIMATION

As an alternative to asymptotic inference, the delete-cluster jackknife can be used for covariance matrix calculation. In the context of fixed effects estimation, the delete-cluster estimators take the form

$$\widehat{\beta}_{(-i)} = \left(\sum_{j\neq i} \dot{\boldsymbol{X}}_j'\dot{\boldsymbol{X}}_j\right)^{-1}\left(\sum_{j\neq i} \dot{\boldsymbol{X}}_j'\dot{\boldsymbol{Y}}_j\right) = \widehat{\beta}_{\text{fe}} - \left(\sum_{i=1}^{N} \dot{\boldsymbol{X}}_i'\dot{\boldsymbol{X}}_i\right)^{-1} \dot{\boldsymbol{X}}_i'\widetilde{\boldsymbol{e}}_i$$

where

$$\widetilde{\boldsymbol{e}}_i = \left(\boldsymbol{I}_i - \dot{\boldsymbol{X}}_i\left(\dot{\boldsymbol{X}}_i'\dot{\boldsymbol{X}}_i\right)^{-1}\dot{\boldsymbol{X}}_i'\right)^{-1}\widehat{\boldsymbol{e}}_i$$

$$\widehat{\boldsymbol{e}}_i = \dot{\boldsymbol{Y}}_i - \dot{\boldsymbol{X}}_i\widehat{\beta}_{\text{fe}}.$$

The delete-cluster jackknife estimator of the variance of $\widehat{\beta}_{\text{fe}}$ is

$$\widehat{\boldsymbol{V}}_{\widehat{\beta}}^{\text{jack}} = \frac{N-1}{N}\sum_{i=1}^{N}\left(\widehat{\beta}_{(-i)} - \overline{\beta}\right)\left(\widehat{\beta}_{(-i)} - \overline{\beta}\right)'$$

$$\overline{\beta} = \frac{1}{N}\sum_{i=1}^{N}\widehat{\beta}_{(-i)}.$$

The delete-cluster jackknife estimator $\widehat{\boldsymbol{V}}_{\widehat{\beta}}^{\text{jack}}$ is similar to the cluster-robust covariance matrix estimator.

For parameters that are functions $\widehat{\theta}_{\text{fe}} = r(\widehat{\beta}_{\text{fe}})$ of the fixed effects estimator, the delete-cluster jackknife estimator of the variance of $\widehat{\theta}_{\text{fe}}$ is

$$\widehat{\boldsymbol{V}}^{\text{jack}}_{\widehat{\theta}} = \frac{N-1}{N} \sum_{i=1}^{N} \left(\widehat{\theta}_{(-i)} - \overline{\theta}\right) \left(\widehat{\theta}_{(-i)} - \overline{\theta}\right)'$$

$$\widehat{\theta}_{(-i)} = r(\widehat{\beta}_{(-i)})$$

$$\overline{\theta} = \frac{1}{N} \sum_{i=1}^{N} \widehat{\theta}_{(-i)}.$$

The estimator $\widehat{\boldsymbol{V}}^{\text{jack}}_{\widehat{\theta}}$ is similar to the delta-method cluster-robust covariance matrix estimator for $\widehat{\theta}$.

As in the context of i.i.d. samples, one advantage of the jackknife covariance matrix estimator is that it does not require the user to make a technical calculation of the asymptotic distribution. A downside is an increase in computation cost, because N separate regressions are effectively estimated. This can be particularly costly in micro panels with a large number N of individuals.

In Stata, jackknife standard errors for fixed effects estimators are obtained by using either `xtreg fe vce(jackknife)` or `areg absorb(id) cluster(id) vce(jackknife)`, where `id` is the cluster variable. For the fixed effects 2SLS estimator, use `xtivreg fe vce(jackknife)`.

17.35 PANEL BOOTSTRAP

Bootstrap methods can also be applied to panel data by a straightforward application of the pairs cluster bootstrap, which samples entire individuals rather than single observations. In the context of panel data, we call this the "panel nonparametric bootstrap."

The **panel nonparametric bootstrap** samples N individual histories $(\boldsymbol{Y}_i, \boldsymbol{X}_i)$ to create the bootstrap sample. Fixed effects (or any other estimation method) is applied to the bootstrap sample to obtain the coefficient estimates. By repeating B times, bootstrap standard errors for coefficients estimates, or functions of the coefficient estimates, can be calculated. Percentile-type and percentile-t confidence intervals can be calculated. The BC_a interval requires an estimator of the acceleration coefficient a, which is a scaled jackknife estimate of the third moment of the estimator. In panel data, the delete-cluster jackknife should be used for estimation of a.

In Stata, to obtain bootstrap standard errors and confidence intervals, use either `xtreg, vce(bootstrap, reps(#))` or `areg, absorb(id) cluster(id) vce(bootstrap, reps(#))`, where `id` is the cluster variable, and # is the number of bootstrap replications. For the fixed effects 2SLS estimator, use `xtivreg, fe vce(bootstrap, reps(#))`.

17.36 DYNAMIC PANEL MODELS

The models considered so far in this chapter have been static with no dynamic relationships. In many economic contexts, it is natural to expect that behavior and decisions are dynamic, explicitly depending on past behavior. In our investment equation, for example, economic models predict that a firm's investment in any given year will depend on investment decisions from previous years. These considerations lead us to consider explicitly dynamic models.

The workhorse dynamic model in a panel framework is the pth-order autoregression with regressors and a one-way error component structure:

$$Y_{it} = \alpha_1 Y_{i,t-1} + \cdots + \alpha_p Y_{i,t-p} + X_{it}'\beta + u_i + \varepsilon_{it} \tag{17.81}$$

where α_j are the autoregressive coefficients, X_{it} is a k vector of regressors, u_i is an individual effect, and ε_{it} is an idiosyncratic error. It is conventional to assume that the errors u_i and ε_{it} are mutually independent, and the ε_{it} are serially uncorrelated and mean 0. For the present, let us assume that the regressors X_{it} are strictly exogenous (17.17). In Section 17.41, we discuss predetermined regressors.

For many illustrations, we will focus on the AR(1) model:

$$Y_{it} = \alpha Y_{i,t-1} + u_i + \varepsilon_{it}. \tag{17.82}$$

The dynamics should be interpreted individual-by-individual. The coefficient α in (17.82) equals the first-order autocorrelation. When $\alpha = 0$, the series is serially uncorrelated (conditional on u_i). $\alpha > 0$ means Y_{it} is positively serially correlated; $\alpha < 0$ means Y_{it} is negatively serially correlated. An autoregressive unit root holds when $\alpha = 1$, which means that Y_{it} follows a random walk with possible drift. Since u_i is constant for a given individual, it should be treated as an individual-specific intercept. The idiosyncratic error ε_{it} plays the role of the error in a standard time series autoregression.

If $|\alpha| < 1$, the model (17.82) is stationary. By standard autoregressive backward recursion, we calculate that

$$Y_{it} = \sum_{j=0}^{\infty} \alpha^j (u_i + \varepsilon_{it}) = (1-\alpha)^{-1} u_i + \sum_{j=0}^{\infty} \alpha^j \varepsilon_{i,t-j}. \tag{17.83}$$

Thus conditional on u_i, the mean and variance of Y_{it} are $(1-\alpha)^{-1} u_i$ and $\left(1-\alpha^2\right)^{-1} \sigma_\varepsilon^2$, respectively. The kth autocorrelation (conditional on u_i) is α^k. Notice that the effect of cross-section variation in u_i is to shift the mean but not the variance or serial correlation. Thus if we view time series plots of Y_{it} against time for a set of individuals i, the series Y_{it} will appear to have different means but have similar variances and serial correlation.

As for the case with time series data, serial correlation (large α) can proxy for other factors, such as time trends. Thus in applications, it will often be useful to include time effects to eliminate spurious serial correlation.

17.37 THE BIAS OF FIXED EFFECTS ESTIMATION

To estimate the panel autoregression (17.81), it may appear natural to use the fixed effects (within) estimator. Indeed, the within transformation eliminates the individual effect u_i. The trouble is that the within operator induces correlation between the AR(1) lag and the error. The result is that the within estimator is inconsistent for the coefficients when T is fixed. A thorough explanation appears in Nickell (1981). We describe the basic problem in this section, focusing on the AR(1) model (17.82).

Applying the within operator to (17.82), we obtain

$$\dot{Y}_{it} = \alpha \dot{Y}_{i,t-1} + \dot{\varepsilon}_{it}$$

for $t \geq 3$. As expected, the individual effect is eliminated. The difficulty is that $\mathbb{E}\left[\dot{Y}_{i,t-1}\dot{\varepsilon}_{it}\right] \neq 0$, because both $\dot{Y}_{i,t-1}$ and $\dot{\varepsilon}_{it}$ are functions of the entire time series.

To see this clearly in a simple example, suppose we have a balanced panel with $T = 3$. There are two observed pairs $(Y_{it}, Y_{i,t-1})$ per individual, so the within estimator equals the differenced estimator. Applying the differencing operator to (17.82) for $t = 3$, we find

$$\Delta Y_{i3} = \alpha \Delta Y_{i2} + \Delta \varepsilon_{i3}. \tag{17.84}$$

Because of the lagged dependent variable and differencing, there is effectively one observation per individual. Notice that the individual effect has been eliminated.

The fixed effects estimator of α is equal to the least squares estimator applied to (17.84), which is

$$\widehat{\alpha}_{\text{fe}} = \left(\sum_{i=1}^{N} \Delta Y_{i2}^2\right)^{-1} \left(\sum_{i=1}^{N} \Delta Y_{i2} \Delta Y_{i3}\right) = \alpha + \left(\sum_{i=1}^{N} \Delta Y_{i2}^2\right)^{-1} \left(\sum_{i=1}^{N} \Delta Y_{i2} \Delta \varepsilon_{i3}\right).$$

The differenced regressor and error are negatively correlated. Indeed,

$$\begin{aligned}
\mathbb{E}\left[\Delta Y_{i2} \Delta \varepsilon_{i3}\right] &= \mathbb{E}\left[(Y_{i2} - Y_{i1})(\varepsilon_{i3} - \varepsilon_{i2})\right] \\
&= \mathbb{E}\left[Y_{i2}\varepsilon_{i3}\right] - \mathbb{E}\left[Y_{i1}\varepsilon_{i3}\right] - \mathbb{E}\left[Y_{i2}\varepsilon_{i2}\right] + \mathbb{E}\left[Y_{i1}\varepsilon_{i2}\right] \\
&= 0 - 0 - \sigma_\varepsilon^2 + 0 \\
&= -\sigma_\varepsilon^2.
\end{aligned}$$

Using the variance formula for AR(1) models (assuming $|\alpha| < 1$), we calculate that $\mathbb{E}\left[(\Delta Y_{i2})^2\right] = 2\sigma_\varepsilon^2/(1+\alpha)$. It follows that the probability limit of the fixed effects estimator $\widehat{\alpha}_{\text{fe}}$ of α in (17.84) is

$$\operatorname*{plim}_{N\to\infty} \left(\widehat{\alpha}_{\text{fe}} - \alpha\right) = \frac{\mathbb{E}\left[\Delta Y_{i2} \Delta \varepsilon_{i3}\right]}{\mathbb{E}\left[(\Delta Y_{i2})^2\right]} = -\frac{1+\alpha}{2}. \tag{17.85}$$

It is typical to call (17.85) the "bias" of $\widehat{\alpha}_{\text{fe}}$, though it is technically a probability limit.

The bias found in (17.85) is large. For $\alpha = 0$, the bias is $-1/2$ and increases toward 1 as $\alpha \to 1$. Thus for any $\alpha < 1$, the probability limit of $\widehat{\alpha}_{\text{fe}}$ is negative! This is extreme bias.

Now take the case $T > 3$. From Nickell's (1981) expressions and some algebra, we can calculate that the probability limit of the fixed effects estimator for $|\alpha| < 1$ is

$$\operatorname*{plim}_{N\to\infty} \left(\widehat{\alpha}_{\text{fe}} - \alpha\right) = \frac{1+\alpha}{\dfrac{2\alpha}{1-\alpha} - \dfrac{T-1}{1-\alpha^{T-1}}}. \tag{17.86}$$

It follows that the bias is of order $O(1/T)$.

It is often asserted that it is okay to use fixed effects if T is sufficiently large (e.g., $T \geq 30$). However, from (17.86) we can calculate that for $T = 30$, the bias of the fixed effects estimator is -0.056 when $\alpha = 0.5$, and the bias is -0.15 when $\alpha = 0.9$. For $T = 60$ and $\alpha = 0.9$, the bias is -0.05. These magnitudes are unacceptably large, including values for the longer time series encountered in macro panels. Thus the Nickell bias problem applies to both micro and macro panel applications.

The conclusion from this analysis is that the fixed effects estimator should not be used for models with lagged dependent variables, even if the time series dimension T is large.

17.38 ANDERSON-HSIAO ESTIMATOR

Anderson and Hsiao (1982) made an important breakthrough by showing that a simple instrumental variables estimator is consistent for the parameters of (17.81).

The method first eliminates the individual effect u_i by first-differencing (17.81) for $t \geq p+1$:

$$\Delta Y_{it} = \alpha_1 \Delta Y_{i,t-1} + \alpha_2 \Delta Y_{i,t-2} + \cdots + \alpha_p \Delta Y_{i,t-p} + \Delta X_{it}' \beta + \Delta \varepsilon_{it}. \tag{17.87}$$

This eliminates the individual effect u_i. The challenge is that first-differencing induces correlation between $\Delta Y_{i,t-1}$ and $\Delta \varepsilon_{it}$:

$$\mathbb{E}\left[\Delta Y_{i,t-1} \Delta \varepsilon_{it}\right] = \mathbb{E}\left[\left(Y_{i,t-1} - Y_{i,t-2}\right)\left(\varepsilon_{it} - \varepsilon_{i,t-1}\right)\right] = -\sigma_\varepsilon^2.$$

The other regressors are not correlated with $\Delta \varepsilon_{it}$. For $s > 1$, $\mathbb{E}\left[\Delta Y_{i,t-s} \Delta \varepsilon_{it}\right] = 0$, and when X_{it} is strictly exogenous, $\mathbb{E}\left[\Delta X_{it} \Delta \varepsilon_{it}\right] = 0$.

The correlation between $\Delta Y_{i,t-1}$ and $\Delta \varepsilon_{it}$ is endogeneity. One solution to endogeneity is to use an instrument. Anderson and Hsiao pointed out that $Y_{i,t-2}$ is a valid instrument because it is correlated with $\Delta Y_{i,t-1}$ yet uncorrelated with $\Delta \varepsilon_{it}$:

$$\mathbb{E}\left[Y_{i,t-2} \Delta \varepsilon_{it}\right] = \mathbb{E}\left[Y_{i,t-2} \varepsilon_{it}\right] - \mathbb{E}\left[Y_{i,t-2} \varepsilon_{it-1}\right] = 0. \tag{17.88}$$

The Anderson-Hsiao estimator is IV using $Y_{i,t-2}$ as an instrument for $\Delta Y_{i,t-1}$. Equivalently, it is IV using the instruments $(Y_{i,t-2}, \ldots, Y_{i,t-p-1})$ for $(\Delta Y_{i,t-1}, \ldots, \Delta Y_{i,t-p})$. The estimator requires $T \geq p+2$.

To show that this estimator is consistent, for simplicity, assume we have a balanced panel with $T = 3$, $p = 1$, and no regressors. In this case, the Anderson-Hsiao IV estimator is

$$\widehat{\alpha}_{\text{iv}} = \left(\sum_{i=1}^N Y_{i1} \Delta Y_{i2}\right)^{-1} \left(\sum_{i=1}^N Y_{i1} \Delta Y_{i3}\right) = \alpha + \left(\sum_{i=1}^N Y_{i1} \Delta Y_{i2}\right)^{-1} \left(\sum_{i=1}^N Y_{i1} \Delta \varepsilon_{i3}\right).$$

Under the assumption that ε_{it} is serially uncorrelated, (17.88) shows that $\mathbb{E}\left[Y_{i1} \Delta \varepsilon_{i3}\right] = 0$. In general, $\mathbb{E}\left[Y_{i1} \Delta Y_{i2}\right] \neq 0$. As $N \to \infty$,

$$\widehat{\alpha}_{\text{iv}} \underset{p}{\longrightarrow} \alpha - \frac{\mathbb{E}\left[Y_{i1} \Delta \varepsilon_{i3}\right]}{\mathbb{E}\left[Y_{i1} \Delta Y_{i2}\right]} = \alpha.$$

Thus the IV estimator is consistent for α.

The Anderson-Hsiao IV estimator relies on two critical assumptions. First, the validity of the instrument (uncorrelatedness with the equation error) relies on the assumption that the dynamics are correctly specified, so that ε_{it} is serially uncorrelated. For example, many applications use an AR(1). If instead the true model is an AR(2), then $Y_{i,t-2}$ is not a valid instrument and the IV estimates will be biased. Second, the relevance of the instrument (correlatedness with the endogenous regressor) requires $\mathbb{E}\left[Y_{i1} \Delta Y_{i2}\right] \neq 0$. This condition turns out to be problematic and is explored further in Section 17.40. These considerations suggest that the validity and accuracy of the estimator are likely to be sensitive to these unknown features.

17.39 ARELLANO-BOND ESTIMATOR

The orthogonality condition (17.88) is one of many implied by the dynamic panel model. Indeed, all lags $Y_{i,t-2}, Y_{i,t-3}, \ldots$ are valid instruments. If $T > p+2$, these can be used to potentially improve estimation efficiency. This was first pointed out by Holtz-Eakin, Newey, and Rosen (1988) and further developed by Arellano and Bond (1991).

Using these extra instruments has the complication that there are a different number of instruments for each time period. The solution is to view the model as a system of T equations, as in Section 17.18.

It will be useful to first write the model in vector notation. Stack the differenced regressors $(\Delta Y_{i,t-1}, \ldots, \Delta Y_{i,t-p}, \Delta X_{it}')$ into a matrix $\Delta \boldsymbol{X}_i$ and the coefficients into a vector θ. We can write (17.87) as $\Delta \boldsymbol{Y}_i = \Delta \boldsymbol{X}_i \theta + \Delta \boldsymbol{\varepsilon}_i$. Stacking all N individuals, this can be written as $\Delta \boldsymbol{Y} = \Delta \boldsymbol{X} \theta + \Delta \boldsymbol{\varepsilon}$.

For period $t = p+2$, we have $p+k$ valid instruments $\left[Y_{i1} \ldots, Y_{ip}, \Delta X_{i,p+2}\right]$. For period $t = p+3$, there are $p+1+k$ valid instruments $\left[Y_{i1} \ldots, Y_{i,p+1}, \Delta X_{i,p+3}\right]$. For period $t = p+4$, there are $p+2+k$ instruments. In general, for any $t \geq p+2$, there are $t-2$ instruments $\left[Y_{i1}, \ldots, Y_{i,t-2}, \Delta X_{it}\right]$. Similarly to (17.53), we can define the instrument matrix for individual i as

$$\boldsymbol{Z}_i = \begin{bmatrix} \left[Y_{i1}, \ldots, Y_{ip}, \Delta X_{i,p+2}'\right] & 0 & & 0 \\ 0 & \left[Y_{i1}, \ldots, Y_{i,p+1}, \Delta X_{i,p+3}'\right] & & 0 \\ & & \ddots & \\ 0 & 0 & & \left[Y_{i1}, Y_{i2}, \ldots, Y_{i,T-2}, \Delta X_{i,T}'\right] \end{bmatrix}. \tag{17.89}$$

This is $\left(T-p-1\right) \times \ell$, where $\ell = k\left(T-p-1\right) + \left(\left(T-2\right)\left(T-1\right) - \left(p-2\right)\left(p-1\right)\right)/2$. This instrument matrix consists of all lagged values $Y_{i,t-2}, Y_{i,t-3}, \ldots$ that are available in the dataset plus the differenced strictly exogenous regressors.

The ℓ moment conditions are

$$\mathbb{E}\left[\boldsymbol{Z}_i'\left(\Delta \boldsymbol{Y}_i - \Delta \boldsymbol{X}_i \alpha\right)\right] = 0. \tag{17.90}$$

If $T > p+2$, then $\ell > p$ and the model is overidentified. Define the $\ell \times \ell$ covariance matrix for the moment conditions

$$\Omega = \mathbb{E}\left[\boldsymbol{Z}_i' \Delta \boldsymbol{\varepsilon}_i \Delta \boldsymbol{\varepsilon}_i' \boldsymbol{Z}_i\right].$$

Let $\boldsymbol{Z}$ denote $\boldsymbol{Z}_i$ stacked into a $\left(T-p-1\right) N \times \ell$ matrix. The efficient GMM estimator of α is

$$\widehat{\alpha}_{\text{gmm}} = \left(\Delta \boldsymbol{X}' \boldsymbol{Z} \Omega^{-1} \boldsymbol{Z}' \Delta \boldsymbol{X}\right)^{-1} \left(\Delta \boldsymbol{X}' \boldsymbol{Z} \Omega^{-1} \boldsymbol{Z}' \Delta \boldsymbol{Y}\right).$$

If the errors ε_{it} are conditionally homoskedastic, then

$$\Omega = \mathbb{E}\left[\boldsymbol{Z}_i' \boldsymbol{H} \boldsymbol{Z}_i\right] \sigma_\varepsilon^2$$

where $\boldsymbol{H}$ is given in (17.31). In this case set

$$\widehat{\Omega}_1 = \sum_{i=1}^{N} \boldsymbol{Z}_i' \boldsymbol{H} \boldsymbol{Z}_i$$

as a (scaled) estimate of Ω. Under these assumptions, an asymptotically efficient GMM estimator is

$$\widehat{\alpha}_1 = \left(\Delta \boldsymbol{X}' \boldsymbol{Z} \widehat{\Omega}_1^{-1} \boldsymbol{Z}' \Delta \boldsymbol{X}\right)^{-1} \left(\Delta \boldsymbol{X}' \boldsymbol{Z} \widehat{\Omega}_1^{-1} \boldsymbol{Z}' \Delta \boldsymbol{Y}\right). \tag{17.91}$$

Estimator (17.91) is known as the **one-step Arellano-Bond GMM estimator**.

Under the assumption that the error ε_{it} is homoskedastic and serially uncorrelated, a classical covariance matrix estimator for $\widehat{\alpha}_1$ is

$$\widehat{V}_1^0 = \left(\Delta X' Z \widehat{\Omega}_1^{-1} Z' \Delta X\right)^{-1} \widehat{\sigma}_\varepsilon^2 \tag{17.92}$$

where $\widehat{\sigma}_\varepsilon^2$ is the sample variance of the one-step residuals $\widehat{\boldsymbol{\varepsilon}}_i = \Delta \boldsymbol{Y}_i - \Delta \boldsymbol{X}_i \widehat{\alpha}$. A covariance matrix estimator that is robust to violation of these assumptions is

$$\widehat{V}_1 = \left(\Delta X' Z \widehat{\Omega}_1^{-1} Z' \Delta X\right)^{-1} \left(\Delta X' Z \widehat{\Omega}_1^{-1} Z' \widehat{\Omega}_2 Z \widehat{\Omega}_1^{-1} Z' \Delta X\right) \left(\Delta X' Z \widehat{\Omega}_1^{-1} Z' \Delta X\right)^{-1} \tag{17.93}$$

where

$$\widehat{\Omega}_2 = \sum_{i=1}^N Z_i' \widehat{\boldsymbol{\varepsilon}}_i \widehat{\boldsymbol{\varepsilon}}_i' Z_i$$

is a (scaled) cluster-robust estimator of Ω using the one-step residuals.

An asymptotically efficient two-step GMM estimator that allows heteroskedasticity is

$$\widehat{\alpha}_2 = \left(\Delta X' Z \widehat{\Omega}_2^{-1} Z' \Delta X\right)^{-1} \left(\Delta X' Z \widehat{\Omega}_2^{-1} Z' \Delta Y\right). \tag{17.94}$$

Estimator (17.94) is known as the **two-step Arellano-Bond GMM estimator**. An appropriate robust covariance matrix estimator for $\widehat{\alpha}_2$ is

$$\widehat{V}_2 = \left(\Delta X' Z \widehat{\Omega}_2^{-1} Z' \Delta X\right)^{-1} \left(\Delta X' Z \widehat{\Omega}_2^{-1} Z' \widehat{\Omega}_3 Z \widehat{\Omega}_2^{-1} Z' \Delta X\right) \left(\Delta X' Z \widehat{\Omega}_2^{-1} Z' \Delta X\right)^{-1} \tag{17.95}$$

where

$$\widehat{\Omega}_3 = \sum_{i=1}^N Z_i' \widehat{\boldsymbol{\varepsilon}}_i \widehat{\boldsymbol{\varepsilon}}_i' Z_i$$

is a (scaled) cluster-robust estimator of Ω using the two-step residuals $\widehat{\boldsymbol{\varepsilon}}_i = \Delta \boldsymbol{Y}_i - \Delta \boldsymbol{X}_i \widehat{\alpha}_2$. Asymptotically, $\widehat{\boldsymbol{V}}_2$ is equivalent to

$$\widetilde{V}_2 = \left(\Delta X' Z \widehat{\Omega}_2^{-1} Z' \Delta X\right)^{-1}. \tag{17.96}$$

The GMM estimator can be iterated until convergence to produce an iterated GMM estimator.

The advantage of the Arellano-Bond estimator over the Anderson-Hsiao estimator is that when $T > p + 2$, the additional (overidentified) moment conditions reduce the asymptotic variance of the estimator and stabilize its performance. The disadvantage is that when T is large, using the full set of lags as instruments may cause a "many weak instruments" problem. The recommended compromise is to limit the number of lags used as instruments.

The advantage of the one-step Arellano-Bond estimator is that the weight matrix $\widehat{\Omega}_1$ does not depend on residuals and is therefore less random than the two-step weight matrix $\widehat{\Omega}_2$. This can result in better performance by the one-step estimator in small to moderate samples, especially when the errors are approximately homoskedastic. The advantage of the two-step estimator is that it achieves asymptotic efficiency allowing for heteroskedasticity and is thus expected to perform better in large samples with non-homoskedastic errors.

To summarize, the Arellano-Bond estimator applies GMM to the first-differenced equation (17.87) using a set of available lags $Y_{i,t-2}, Y_{i,t-3}, \ldots$ as instruments for $\Delta Y_{i,t-1}, \ldots, \Delta Y_{i,t-p}$.

The Arellano-Bond estimator may be obtained in Stata using either the `xtabond` or `xtdpd` command. The default setting is the one-step estimator (17.91) and non-robust standard errors (17.92). For the two-step estimator and robust standard errors, use the `twostep vce(robust)` options. Reported standard errors in Stata are based on Windmeijer's (2005) finite-sample correction to the asymptotic estimator (17.96). Neither the robust covariance matrix (17.95) nor the iterated GMM estimator are implemented.

17.40 WEAK INSTRUMENTS

Blundell and Bond (1998) pointed out that the Anderson-Hsiao and Arellano-Bond estimators suffer from weak instruments. This can be seen most easily in the AR(1) model with the Anderson-Hsiao estimator, which uses $Y_{i,t-2}$ as an instrument for $\Delta Y_{i,t-1}$. The reduced form equation for $\Delta Y_{i,t-1}$ is

$$\Delta Y_{i,t-1} = Y_{i,t-2}\gamma + v_{it}.$$

The reduced form coefficient γ is defined by projection. Using $\Delta Y_{i,t-1} = (\alpha - 1) Y_{i,t-2} + u_i + \varepsilon_{i,t-1}$ and $\mathbb{E}\left[Y_{i,t-2}\varepsilon_{i,t-1}\right] = 0$, we calculate that

$$\gamma = \frac{\mathbb{E}\left[Y_{i,t-2}\Delta Y_{i,t-1}\right]}{\mathbb{E}\left[Y_{i,t-2}^2\right]} = (\alpha - 1) + \frac{\mathbb{E}\left[Y_{i,t-2}u_i\right]}{\mathbb{E}\left[Y_{i,t-2}^2\right]}.$$

Assuming stationarity so that (17.83) holds,

$$\mathbb{E}\left[Y_{i,t-2}u_i\right] = \mathbb{E}\left[\left(\frac{u_i}{1-\alpha} + \sum_{j=0}^{\infty}\alpha^j\varepsilon_{i,t-2-j}\right)u_i\right] = \frac{\sigma_u^2}{1-\alpha}$$

and

$$\mathbb{E}\left[Y_{i,t-2}^2\right] = \mathbb{E}\left[\left(\frac{u_i}{1-\alpha} + \sum_{j=0}^{\infty}\alpha^j\varepsilon_{i,t-2-j}\right)^2\right] = \frac{\sigma_u^2}{(1-\alpha)^2} + \frac{\sigma_\varepsilon^2}{\left(1-\alpha^2\right)}$$

where $\sigma_u^2 = \mathbb{E}\left[u_i^2\right]$ and $\sigma_\varepsilon^2 = \mathbb{E}\left[\varepsilon_{it}^2\right]$. Using these expressions and a fair amount of algebra, Blundell and Bond (1998) found that the reduced form coefficient equals

$$\gamma = (\alpha - 1)\left(\frac{k}{k + \sigma_u^2/\sigma_\varepsilon^2}\right) \tag{17.97}$$

where $k = (1-\alpha)/(1+\alpha)$.

The Anderson-Hsiao instrument $Y_{i,t-2}$ is weak if γ is close to 0. From (17.97) we see that $\gamma = 0$ when either $\alpha = 1$ (a unit root) or $\sigma_u^2/\sigma_\varepsilon^2 = \infty$ (the idiosyncratic effect is small relative to the individual-specific effect). In either case, the coefficient α is not identified. We know from our earlier study of the weak instruments problem (Section 12.36) that when γ is close to 0 then α is weakly identified and the estimators will perform poorly. Thus when the autoregressive coefficient α is large or the individual-specific effect dominates the idiosyncratic effect, these estimators will be weakly identified, have poor performance, and conventional inference methods will be misleading. Because the value of α and the relative variances are unknown a priori, we should generically treat this class of estimators as weakly identified.

An alternative estimator that has improved performance is discussed in Section 17.42.

17.41 DYNAMIC PANELS WITH PREDETERMINED REGRESSORS

The assumption that regressors are strictly exogenous is restrictive. A less restrictive assumption is that the regressors are predetermined. Dynamic panel methods can be modified to handle predetermined regressors by using their lags as instruments.

Definition 17.2 The regressor X_{it} is **predetermined** for the error ε_{it} if

$$\mathbb{E}\left[X_{i,t-s}\varepsilon_{it}\right]=0 \tag{17.98}$$

for all $s \geq 0$.

The difference between strictly exogenous and predetermined regressors is that for the former, (17.98) holds for all s, not just $s \geq 0$. One way of interpreting a regression model with predetermined regressors is that the model is a projection on the complete past history of the regressors.

Under (17.98), leads of X_{it} can be correlated with ε_{it} (that is, $\mathbb{E}\left[X_{i,t+s}\varepsilon_{it}\right] \neq 0$ for $s \geq 1$), or equivalently, X_{it} can be correlated with lags of ε_{it} (that is, $\mathbb{E}\left[X_{it}\varepsilon_{i,t-s}\right] \neq 0$ for $s \geq 1$). Thus X_{it} can respond dynamically to past values of Y_{it}, as in, for example, an unrestricted vector autoregression.

Consider the differenced equation (17.87):

$$\Delta Y_{it}=\alpha_1 \Delta Y_{i,t-1}+\alpha_2 \Delta Y_{i,t-2}+\cdots+\alpha_p \Delta Y_{i,t-p}+\Delta X_{it}'\beta+\Delta\varepsilon_{it}.$$

When the regressors are predetermined but not strictly exogenous, X_{it} and ε_{it} are uncorrelated, but ΔX_{it} and $\Delta\varepsilon_{it}$ are correlated. To see this, note that

$$\begin{aligned}\mathbb{E}\left[\Delta X_{it}\Delta\varepsilon_{it}\right]&=\mathbb{E}\left[X_{it}\varepsilon_{it}\right]-\mathbb{E}\left[X_{i,t-1}\varepsilon_{it}\right]-\mathbb{E}\left[X_{it}\varepsilon_{i,t-1}\right]+\mathbb{E}\left[X_{i,t-1}\varepsilon_{i,t-1}\right]\\&=-\mathbb{E}\left[X_{it}\varepsilon_{i,t-1}\right]\neq 0.\end{aligned}$$

Thus if we treat ΔX_{it} as exogenous, the coefficient estimates will be biased.

To solve the correlation problem, we can use instruments for ΔX_{it}. A valid instrument is $X_{i,t-1}$, because it is generally correlated with ΔX_{it} yet uncorrelated with $\Delta\varepsilon_{it}$. Indeed, for any $s \geq 1$,

$$\mathbb{E}\left[X_{i,t-s}\Delta\varepsilon_{it}\right]=\mathbb{E}\left[X_{i,t-s}\varepsilon_{it}\right]-\mathbb{E}\left[X_{i,t-s}\varepsilon_{i,t-1}\right]=0.$$

Consequently, Arellano and Bond (1991) recommend the instrument set $\left(X_{i1}, X_{i2}, \ldots, X_{i,t-1}\right)$. When the number of time periods is large, it is advised to limit the number of instrument lags to avoid the many weak instruments problem.

Algebraically, GMM estimation is the same as the estimators described in Section 17.39, except that the instrument matrix (17.89) is modified to

$$\boldsymbol{Z}_i=\begin{bmatrix}\left[Y_{i1},\ldots,Y_{ip},X_{i1}',..,X_{i,p+1}'\right] & 0 & 0\\ 0 & \left[Y_{i1},\ldots,Y_{i,p+1},X_{i1}',..,X_{i,p+2}'\right] & 0\\ & & \ddots\\ 0 & 0 & \left[Y_{i1},\ldots,Y_{i,T-2},X_{i1}',..,X_{i,T-1}'\right]\end{bmatrix}. \tag{17.99}$$

To understand how the model is identified, we examine the reduced form equation for the regressor. For $t=p+2$ and using the first lag as an instrument, the reduced form is

$$\Delta X_{it} = \gamma_1 Y_{i,t-2} + \Gamma_2 X_{i,t-1} + \zeta_{it}.$$

The model is identified if Γ_2 is full rank, which is true (in general) when X_{it} is stationary. Identification fails, however, when X_{it} has a unit root. This indicates that the model will be weakly identified when the predetermined regressors are highly persistent.

The method generalizes to handle multiple lags of the predetermined regressors. To see this, write the model explicitly as

$$Y_{it} = \alpha_1 Y_{i,t-1} + \cdots + \alpha_p Y_{i,t-p} + X_{it}'\beta_1 + \cdots + X_{i,t-q}'\beta_q + u_i + \varepsilon_{it}.$$

In first differences, the model is

$$\Delta Y_{it} = \alpha_1 \Delta Y_{i,t-1} + \cdots + \alpha_p \Delta Y_{i,t-p} + \Delta X_{it}'\beta_1 + \cdots + \Delta X_{i,t-q}'\beta_q + \Delta\varepsilon_{it}.$$

A sufficient set of instruments for the regressors is $(X_{it-1}, \Delta X_{i,t-1}, \ldots, \Delta X_{i,t-q})$ or equivalently, $(X_{i,t-1}, X_{i,t-2}, \ldots, X_{i,t-q-1})$.

In many cases, it is more reasonable to assume that $X_{i,t-1}$ is predetermined but not X_{it}, because X_{it} and ε_{it} may be endogenous. For example, this is the standard assumption in vector autoregressions. In this case, the estimation method is modified to use the instruments $(X_{i,t-2}, X_{i,t-3}, \ldots, X_{i,t-q-1})$. While this weakens the exogeneity assumption, it also weakens the instrument set as now the reduced form uses the second lag $X_{i,t-2}$ to predict ΔX_{it}.

The advantage obtained by treating a regressor as predetermined (rather than strictly exogenous) is that it is a substantial relaxation of the dynamic assumptions. Otherwise the parameter estimates will be inconsistent due to endogeneity.

The major disadvantage of treating a regressor as predetermined is that it substantially reduces the strength of identification, especially when the predetermined regressors are highly persistent.

In Stata, the `xtabond` command by default treats independent regressors as strictly exogenous. To treat the regressors as predetermined, use the option `pre`. By default all regressor lags are used as instruments, but the number can be limited if specified.

17.42 BLUNDELL-BOND ESTIMATOR

Arellano and Bover (1995) and Blundell and Bond (1998) introduced a set of orthogonality conditions that reduce the weak instrument problem discussed in the Section 17.40 and improve performance in finite samples.

Consider the levels AR(1) model with no regressors (17.82). Recall that least squares (pooled) regression is inconsistent, because the regressor $Y_{i,t-1}$ is correlated with the error u_i. This raises the question: Is there an instrument Z_{it} that solves this problem in the sense that Z_{it} is correlated with $Y_{i,t-1}$ yet uncorrelated with $u_{it} + \varepsilon_{it}$? Blundell and Bond propose the instrument $\Delta Y_{i,t-1}$. Clearly, $\Delta Y_{i,t-1}$ and $Y_{i,t-1}$ are correlated, so $\Delta Y_{i,t-1}$ satisfies the relevance condition. Also, $\Delta Y_{i,t-1}$ is uncorrelated with the idiosyncratic error ε_{it} when the latter is serially uncorrelated. Thus the key to the Blundell-Bond instrument is whether

$$\mathbb{E}\left[\Delta Y_{i,t-1} u_i\right] = 0. \tag{17.100}$$

Blundell and Bond (1998) show that a sufficient condition for (17.100) is

$$\mathbb{E}\left[\left(Y_{i1}-\frac{u_i}{1-\alpha}\right)u_i\right]=0. \tag{17.101}$$

Recall that $u_i/(1-\alpha)$ is the conditional mean of Y_{it} under stationarity. Condition (17.101) states that the deviation of the initial condition Y_{i1} from this conditional mean is uncorrelated with the individual effect u_i. Condition (17.101) is implied by stationarity but is somewhat weaker.

To see that (17.101) implies (17.100), by applying recursion to (17.87), we find that

$$\Delta Y_{i,t-1}=\alpha^{t-3}\Delta Y_{i2}+\sum_{j=0}^{t-3}\alpha^j\Delta\varepsilon_{i,t-1-j}.$$

Also,

$$\Delta Y_{i2}=(\alpha-1)\,Y_{i1}+u_i+\varepsilon_{i2}=(\alpha-1)\left(Y_{i1}-\frac{u_i}{1-\alpha}\right)+\varepsilon_{i2}.$$

Hence

$$\begin{aligned}\mathbb{E}\left[\Delta Y_{i,t-1}u_i\right]&=\mathbb{E}\left[\left(\alpha^{t-3}(\alpha-1)\left(Y_{i1}-\frac{u_i}{1-\alpha}\right)+\alpha^{t-3}\varepsilon_{i2}+\sum_{j=0}^{t-3}\alpha^j\Delta\varepsilon_{i,t-1-j}\right)u_i\right]\\&=\alpha^{t-3}(\alpha-1)\,\mathbb{E}\left[\left(Y_{i1}-\frac{u_i}{1-\alpha}\right)u_i\right]\\&=0\end{aligned}$$

under (17.101), as claimed.

Now consider the full model (17.81) with predetermined regressors. Consider the assumption that the regressors have constant correlation with the individual effect

$$\mathbb{E}\left[X_{it}u_i\right]=\mathbb{E}\left[X_{is}u_i\right]$$

for all s. This assumption implies

$$\mathbb{E}\left[\Delta X_{it}u_i\right]=0 \tag{17.102}$$

which means that the differenced predetermined regressors ΔX_{it} can also be used as instruments for the level equation.

Using (17.100) and (17.102), Blundell and Bond propose the following moment conditions for GMM estimation:

$$\mathbb{E}\left[\Delta Y_{i,t-1}\left(Y_{it}-\alpha_1 Y_{i,t-1}-\cdots-\alpha_p Y_{i,t-p}-X_{it}'\beta\right)\right]=0 \tag{17.103}$$

$$\mathbb{E}\left[\Delta X_{i,t}\left(Y_{it}-\alpha_1 Y_{i,t-1}-\cdots-\alpha_p Y_{i,t-p}-X_{it}'\beta\right)\right]=0 \tag{17.104}$$

for $t=p+2,\ldots,T$. Notice that these are for the levels (undifferenced) equation, while the Arellano-Bond (17.90) moments are for the differenced equation (17.87). We can write (17.103)–(17.104) in vector notation if we set $\boldsymbol{Z}_{2i}=\operatorname{diag}\left(\Delta Y_{i2},\ldots,\Delta Y_{i,T-1},\Delta X_{i3},\ldots,\Delta X_{iT}\right)$. Then (17.103)–(17.104) equals

$$\mathbb{E}\left[\boldsymbol{Z}_{2i}\left(\boldsymbol{Y}_i-\boldsymbol{X}_i\theta\right)\right]=0. \tag{17.105}$$

Blundell and Bond proposed combining the ℓ Arellano-Bond moments with the levels moments, which can be done by stacking the moment conditions (17.90) and (17.105). Recall from Section 17.39 the variables $\Delta \boldsymbol{Y}_i$, $\Delta \boldsymbol{X}_i$, and $\boldsymbol{Z}_i$. Define the stacked variables $\overline{\boldsymbol{Y}}_i = \left(\Delta \boldsymbol{Y}_i', \boldsymbol{Y}_i'\right)'$, $\overline{\boldsymbol{X}}_i = \left(\Delta \boldsymbol{X}_i', \boldsymbol{X}_i'\right)'$, and $\overline{\boldsymbol{Z}}_i = \operatorname{diag}\left(\boldsymbol{Z}_i, \boldsymbol{Z}_{2i}\right)$. The stacked moment conditions are

$$\mathbb{E}\left[\overline{\boldsymbol{Z}}_i\left(\overline{\boldsymbol{Y}}_i - \overline{\boldsymbol{X}}_i\theta\right)\right] = 0.$$

The Blundell-Bond estimator is found by applying GMM to this equation. They call this a systems GMM estimator. Let $\overline{\boldsymbol{Y}}$, $\overline{\boldsymbol{X}}$, and $\overline{\boldsymbol{Z}}$ denote $\overline{\boldsymbol{Y}}_i$, $\overline{\boldsymbol{X}}_i$, and $\overline{\boldsymbol{Z}}_i$, respectively, stacked into matrices. Define $\overline{\boldsymbol{H}} = \operatorname{diag}\left(\boldsymbol{H}, \boldsymbol{I}_{T-2}\right)$, where $\boldsymbol{H}$ is from (17.31), and set

$$\widehat{\Omega}_1 = \sum_{i=1}^{N} \overline{\boldsymbol{Z}}_i' \overline{\boldsymbol{H}}\, \overline{\boldsymbol{Z}}_i.$$

The **Blundell-Bond one-step GMM estimator** is

$$\widehat{\theta}_1 = \left(\overline{\boldsymbol{X}}'\overline{\boldsymbol{Z}}\widehat{\Omega}_1^{-1}\overline{\boldsymbol{Z}}'\overline{\boldsymbol{X}}\right)^{-1}\left(\overline{\boldsymbol{X}}'\overline{\boldsymbol{Z}}\widehat{\Omega}_1^{-1}\overline{\boldsymbol{Z}}'\overline{\boldsymbol{Y}}\right). \tag{17.106}$$

The systems residuals are $\widehat{\boldsymbol{\varepsilon}}_i = \overline{\boldsymbol{Y}}_i - \overline{\boldsymbol{X}}_i\widehat{\theta}_1$. A robust covariance matrix estimator is

$$\widehat{\boldsymbol{V}}_1 = \left(\overline{\boldsymbol{X}}'\overline{\boldsymbol{Z}}\widehat{\Omega}_1^{-1}\overline{\boldsymbol{Z}}'\overline{\boldsymbol{X}}\right)^{-1}\left(\overline{\boldsymbol{X}}'\overline{\boldsymbol{Z}}\widehat{\Omega}_1^{-1}\overline{\boldsymbol{Z}}'\widehat{\Omega}_2\overline{\boldsymbol{Z}}\widehat{\Omega}_1^{-1}\overline{\boldsymbol{Z}}'\overline{\boldsymbol{X}}\right)\left(\overline{\boldsymbol{X}}'\overline{\boldsymbol{Z}}\widehat{\Omega}_1^{-1}\overline{\boldsymbol{Z}}'\overline{\boldsymbol{X}}\right)^{-1} \tag{17.107}$$

where

$$\widehat{\Omega}_2 = \sum_{i=1}^{N} \overline{\boldsymbol{Z}}_i'\widehat{\boldsymbol{\varepsilon}}_i\widehat{\boldsymbol{\varepsilon}}_i'\overline{\boldsymbol{Z}}_i.$$

The **Blundell-Bond two-step GMM estimator** is

$$\widehat{\theta}_2 = \left(\overline{\boldsymbol{X}}'\overline{\boldsymbol{Z}}\widehat{\Omega}_2^{-1}\overline{\boldsymbol{Z}}'\overline{\boldsymbol{X}}\right)^{-1}\left(\overline{\boldsymbol{X}}'\overline{\boldsymbol{Z}}\widehat{\Omega}_2^{-1}\overline{\boldsymbol{Z}}'\overline{\boldsymbol{Y}}\right). \tag{17.108}$$

The two-step systems residuals are $\widehat{\boldsymbol{\varepsilon}}_i = \overline{\boldsymbol{Y}}_i - \overline{\boldsymbol{X}}_i\widehat{\theta}_2$. A robust covariance matrix estimator is

$$\widehat{\boldsymbol{V}}_2 = \left(\overline{\boldsymbol{X}}'\overline{\boldsymbol{Z}}\widehat{\Omega}_2^{-1}\overline{\boldsymbol{Z}}'\overline{\boldsymbol{X}}\right)^{-1}\left(\overline{\boldsymbol{X}}'\overline{\boldsymbol{Z}}\widehat{\Omega}_2^{-1}\overline{\boldsymbol{Z}}'\widehat{\Omega}_3\overline{\boldsymbol{Z}}\widehat{\Omega}_2^{-1}\overline{\boldsymbol{Z}}'\overline{\boldsymbol{X}}\right)\left(\overline{\boldsymbol{X}}'\overline{\boldsymbol{Z}}\widehat{\Omega}_2^{-1}\overline{\boldsymbol{Z}}'\overline{\boldsymbol{X}}\right)^{-1} \tag{17.109}$$

where

$$\widehat{\Omega}_3 = \sum_{i=1}^{N} \overline{\boldsymbol{Z}}_i'\widehat{\boldsymbol{\varepsilon}}_i\widehat{\boldsymbol{\varepsilon}}_i'\overline{\boldsymbol{Z}}_i.$$

Asymptotically, $\widehat{\boldsymbol{V}}_2$ is equivalent to

$$\widetilde{\boldsymbol{V}}_2 = \left(\overline{\boldsymbol{X}}'\overline{\boldsymbol{Z}}\widehat{\Omega}_2^{-1}\overline{\boldsymbol{Z}}'\overline{\boldsymbol{X}}\right)^{-1}. \tag{17.110}$$

The GMM estimator can be iterated until convergence to produce an iterated GMM estimator.

Simulation experiments reported in Blundell and Bond (1998) indicate that their systems GMM estimator performs substantially better than the Arellano-Bond estimator, especially when α is close to 1 or the variance ratio $\sigma_u^2/\sigma_\varepsilon^2$ is large. The explanation is that the orthogonality condition (17.103) does not suffer the weak instrument problem in these cases.

The advantage of the Blundell-Bond estimator is that the added orthogonality condition (17.103) greatly improves performance relative to the Arellano-Bond estimator when the latter is weakly identified. A disadvantage of the Blundell-Bond estimator is that their orthogonality condition is justified by a stationarity condition (17.101), and its violation may induce estimation bias.

The advantages and disadvantages of the one-step versus two-step Blundell-Bond estimators are the same as described for the Arellano-Bond estimator in Section 17.39. Also as described there, when T is large, it may be desirable to limit the number of lags used as instruments to avoid the many weak instruments problem.

The Blundell-Bond estimator may be obtained in Stata using either the `xtdpdsys` or `xtdpd` command. The default setting is the one-step estimator (17.106) and non-robust standard errors. For the two-step estimator and robust standard errors, use the `twostep vce(robust)` options. Stata standard errors are Windmeijer's (2005) finite-sample correction to the asymptotic estimate (17.110). Neither the robust covariance matrix estimator (17.109) nor the iterated GMM estimator are implemented.

17.43 FORWARD ORTHOGONAL TRANSFORMATION

Arellano and Bover (1995) proposed an alternative transformation that eliminates the individual-specific effect and may have advantages in dynamic panel models. The **forward orthogonal transformation** is

$$Y_{it}^{*} = c_{it}\left(Y_{it} - \frac{1}{T_i - t}\left(Y_{i,t+1} + \cdots + Y_{iT_i}\right)\right) \tag{17.111}$$

where $c_{it}^2 = (T_i - t)\,/\,(T_i - t + 1)$. This transformation can be applied to all but the final observation (which is lost). Essentially, Y_{it}^{*} subtracts from Y_{it} the average of the remaining values and then rescales so that the variance is constant under the assumption of homoskedastic errors. The transformation (17.111) was originally proposed for time series observations by Hayashi and Sims (1983).

At the level of the individual, (17.111) can be written as $\boldsymbol{Y}_i^{*} = \boldsymbol{A}_i \boldsymbol{Y}_i$, where $\boldsymbol{A}_i$ is the $(T_i - 1) \times T_i$ orthogonal deviation operator

$$\boldsymbol{A}_i = \operatorname{diag}\left(\sqrt{\frac{T_i - 1}{T_i}}, \ldots, \sqrt{\frac{1}{2}}\right)\begin{bmatrix} 1 & -\frac{1}{T_i-1} & -\frac{1}{T_i-1} & \cdots & -\frac{1}{T_i-1} & -\frac{1}{T_i-1} & -\frac{1}{T_i-1} \\ 0 & 1 & -\frac{1}{T_i-2} & \cdots & -\frac{1}{T_i-2} & -\frac{1}{T_i-2} & -\frac{1}{T_i-2} \\ \vdots & \vdots & \vdots & & \vdots & \vdots & \vdots \\ 0 & 0 & 0 & \cdots & 1 & -\frac{1}{2} & -\frac{1}{2} \\ 0 & 0 & 0 & \cdots & 0 & -1 & 1 \end{bmatrix}.$$

Important properties of the matrix $\boldsymbol{A}_i$ are that $\boldsymbol{A}_i \mathbf{1}_i = 0$ (so it eliminates individual effects), $\boldsymbol{A}_i' \boldsymbol{A}_i = \boldsymbol{M}_i$, and $\boldsymbol{A}_i \boldsymbol{A}_i' = \boldsymbol{I}_{T_i - 1}$. These can be verified by direct multiplication.

Applying the transformation $\boldsymbol{A}_i$ to (17.81), we obtain

$$Y_{it}^{*} = \alpha_1 Y_{i,t-1}^{*} + \cdots + \alpha_p Y_{i,t-p}^{*} + X_{it}^{*\prime}\beta + \varepsilon_{it}^{*}. \tag{17.112}$$

for $t = p+1, \ldots, T-1$. This is equivalent to first differencing (17.87) when $T = 3$ but differs for $T > 3$.

What is special about the transformed equation (17.112) is that under the assumption that ε_{it} are serially uncorrelated and homoskedastic, the error vector $\boldsymbol{\varepsilon}_i^{*}$ has variance $\sigma_\varepsilon^2 \boldsymbol{A}_i \boldsymbol{A}_i' = \sigma_\varepsilon^2 \boldsymbol{I}_{T_i - 1}$. Thus $\boldsymbol{\varepsilon}_i^{*}$ has the same covariance structure as $\boldsymbol{\varepsilon}_i$. Thus the orthogonal transformation operator eliminates the fixed effect while preserving the covariance structure, in contrast to (17.87), which has serially correlated errors $\Delta\varepsilon_{it}$.

The transformed error ε_{it}^* is a function of $\varepsilon_{it}, \varepsilon_{i,t+1}, \ldots, \varepsilon_{iT}$. Thus valid instruments are $Y_{i,t-1}, Y_{i,t-2}, \ldots$. Using the instrument matrix $\boldsymbol{Z}_i$ from (17.89) in the case of strictly exogenous regressors or (17.99) with predetermined regressors, the ℓ moment conditions can be written using matrix notation as

$$\mathbb{E}\left[\boldsymbol{Z}_i'\left(\boldsymbol{Y}_i^* - \boldsymbol{X}_i^*\theta\right)\right] = 0. \tag{17.113}$$

Define the $\ell \times \ell$ covariance matrix

$$\Omega = \mathbb{E}\left[\boldsymbol{Z}_i'\boldsymbol{\varepsilon}_i^*\boldsymbol{\varepsilon}_i^{*\prime}\boldsymbol{Z}_i\right].$$

If the errors ε_{it} are conditionally homoskedastic, then $\Omega = \mathbb{E}\left[\boldsymbol{Z}_i'\boldsymbol{Z}_i\right]\sigma_\varepsilon^2$. Thus an asymptotically efficient GMM estimator is 2SLS applied to the orthogonalized equation using $\boldsymbol{Z}_i$ as an instrument. In matrix notation,

$$\widehat{\theta}_1 = \left(\boldsymbol{X}^{*\prime}\boldsymbol{Z}\left(\boldsymbol{Z}'\boldsymbol{Z}\right)^{-1}\boldsymbol{Z}'\boldsymbol{X}^*\right)^{-1}\boldsymbol{Y}^*.$$

This is the one-step GMM estimator.

Given the residuals $\widehat{\boldsymbol{\varepsilon}}_i = \boldsymbol{Y}_i^* - \boldsymbol{X}_i^*\widehat{\theta}_1$, the two-step GMM estimator that is robust to heteroskedasticity and arbitrary serial correlation is

$$\widehat{\theta}_2 = \left(\boldsymbol{X}^{*\prime}\boldsymbol{Z}\widehat{\Omega}_2^{-1}\boldsymbol{Z}'\boldsymbol{X}^*\right)^{-1}\left(\boldsymbol{X}^{*\prime}\boldsymbol{Z}\widehat{\Omega}_2^{-1}\boldsymbol{Z}'\boldsymbol{Y}^*\right)$$

where

$$\widehat{\Omega}_2 = \sum_{i=1}^N \boldsymbol{Z}_i'\widehat{\boldsymbol{\varepsilon}}_i\widehat{\boldsymbol{\varepsilon}}_i'\boldsymbol{Z}_i.$$

Standard errors for $\widehat{\theta}_1$ and $\widehat{\theta}_2$ can be obtained using cluster-robust methods.

Forward orthogonalization may have advantages over first differencing. First, the equation errors in (17.112) have a scalar covariance structure under i.i.d. idiosyncratic errors, which is expected to improve estimation precision. It also implies that the one-step estimator is 2SLS rather than GMM. Second, although no formal analysis has been done of the weak instrument properties of the estimators after forward orthogonalization, it appears that if $T > p + 2$, the method is less affected by weak instruments than is first differencing. The disadvantages of forward orthogonalization are that it treats early observations asymmetrically from late observations, it is less thoroughly studied than first differencing, and it is not available for several popular estimation methods.

The Stata command `xtdpd` includes forward orthogonalization as an option, but not when levels (Blundell-Bond) instruments are included or if there are gaps in the data. An alternative is the downloadable Stata package `xtabond2`.

17.44 EMPIRICAL ILLUSTRATION

I illustrate the dynamic panel methods with the investment model (17.3). Estimates from two models are presented in Table 17.3. Both are estimated by Blundell-Bond two-step GMM with lags 2 through 6 as instruments, a cluster-robust weight matrix, and clustered standard errors.

The first column presents estimates of an AR(2) model. The estimates show that the series has a moderate amount of positive serial correlation but appears to be well modeled as an AR(1), because the AR(2) coefficient is close to 0. This pattern of serial correlation is consistent with the presence of investment projects that span 2 years.

Table 17.3
Estimates of dynamic investment equation

	AR(2)	AR(2) with regressors
$I_{i,t-1}$	0.3191 (0.0172)	0.2519 (0.0220)
$I_{i,t-2}$	0.0309 (0.0112)	0.0137 (0.0125)
$Q_{i,t-1}$		0.0018 (0.0007)
$Q_{i,t-2}$		−0.0000 (0.0003)
$D_{i,t-1}$		−0.0154 (0.0058)
$D_{i,t-2}$		−0.0043 (0.0054)
$CF_{i,t-1}$		0.0400 (0.0091)
$CF_{i,t-2}$		−0.0290 (0.0051)

Note: Two-step GMM estimates. Cluster-robust standard errors in parenthesis.
All regressions include time effects. GMM instruments include lags 2 through 6.

The second column presents estimates of the dynamic version of the investment regression (17.3) excluding the trading indicator. Two lags are included of the dependent variable and each regressor. The regressors are treated as predetermined in contrast to the fixed effects regressions, which treated the regressors as strictly exogenous. The regressors are not contemporaneous with the dependent variable but are lagged one and two periods. This is done so that they are valid predetermined variables. Contemporaneous variables are likely endogenous and so should not be treated as predetermined.

The estimates in the second column of Table 17.3 complement the earlier results. The evidence shows that investment has a moderate degree of serial dependence, is positively related to the first lag of Q, and is negatively related to lagged debt. Investment appears to be positively related to change in cash flow, rather than the level. Thus an increase in cash flow in year $t-1$ leads to investment in year t.

17.45 EXERCISES

Exercise 17.1

(a) Show (17.11) and (17.12).

(b) Show (17.13).

Exercise 17.2 Is $\mathbb{E}[\varepsilon_{it} \mid X_{it}] = 0$ sufficient for $\widehat{\beta}_{\mathrm{fe}}$ to be unbiased for β? Explain why or why not.

Exercise 17.3 Show that $\operatorname{var}\left[\dot{X}_{it}\right] \leq \operatorname{var}\left[X_{it}\right]$.

Exercise 17.4 Show (17.24).

Exercise 17.5 Show (17.28).

Exercise 17.6 Show that when $T=2$, the differenced estimator (17.30) equals the fixed effects estimator.

Exercise 17.7 Section 17.14 describes how to estimate the individual-effect variance σ_u^2 using the between residuals. Develop an alternative estimator of σ_u^2 only using the fixed effects error variance $\widehat{\sigma}_\varepsilon^2$ and the levels error variance $\widehat{\sigma}_e^2 = n^{-1}\sum_{i=1}^N \sum_{t\in S_i} \widehat{e}_{it}^2$, where the $\widehat{e}_{it} = Y_{it} - X_{it}'\widehat{\beta}_{\text{fe}}$ are computed from the levels variables.

Exercise 17.8 Verify that $\widehat{\sigma}_\varepsilon^2$ defined in (17.37) is unbiased for σ_ε^2 under (17.18), (17.25), and (17.26).

Exercise 17.9 Develop a version of Theorem 17.2 for the differenced estimator $\widehat{\beta}_\Delta$. Can you weaken Assumption 17.2 part 3? State an appropriate version that is sufficient for asymptotic normality.

Exercise 17.10 Show (17.57).

Exercise 17.11

(a) For $\widehat{\sigma}_i^2$ defined in (17.59), show that $\mathbb{E}\left[\widehat{\sigma}_i^2 \mid \boldsymbol{X}_i\right] = \overline{\sigma}_i^2$.
(b) For $\widetilde{\boldsymbol{V}}_{\text{fe}}$ defined in (17.58), show that $\mathbb{E}\left[\widetilde{\boldsymbol{V}}_{\text{fe}} \mid \boldsymbol{X}\right] = \boldsymbol{V}_{\text{fe}}$.

Exercise 17.12

(a) Show (17.61).
(b) Show (17.62).
(c) For $\widetilde{\boldsymbol{V}}_{\text{fe}}$ defined in (17.60), show that $\mathbb{E}\left[\widetilde{\boldsymbol{V}}_{\text{fe}} \mid \boldsymbol{X}\right] = \boldsymbol{V}_{\text{fe}}$.

Exercise 17.13 Consider the fixed effects model $Y_{it} = X_{it}\beta_1 + X_{it}^2\beta_2 + u_i + \varepsilon_{it}$. A researcher estimates the model by first obtaining the within transformed $\dot{Y}_{it}$ and $\dot{X}_{it}$ and then regressing $\dot{Y}_{it}$ on $\dot{X}_{it}$ and $\dot{X}_{it}^2$. Is this the correct estimation method? If not, describe the correct fixed effects estimator.

Exercise 17.14 In the model discussed in section 17.33, verify that in the just-identified case, the 2SLS estimator; $\widehat{\beta}_{2\text{sls}}$ simplifies as claimed: $\widehat{\beta}_1$ and $\widehat{\beta}_2$ are the fixed effects estimator. $\widehat{\gamma}_1$ and $\widehat{\gamma}_2$ equal the 2SLS estimator from a regression of $\widehat{\boldsymbol{u}}$ on $\boldsymbol{Z}_1$ and $\boldsymbol{Z}_2$, using $\overline{\boldsymbol{X}}_1$ as an instrument for $\boldsymbol{Z}_2$.

Exercise 17.15 In this exercise, you will replicate and extend the empirical work reported in Arellano and Bond (1991) and Blundell and Bond (1998). Arellano-Bond gathered a dataset of 1,031 observations from an unbalanced panel of 140 U.K. companies for 1976–1984 and is in the datafile `AB1991` on the textbook webpage. The variables you will be using are log employment (N), log real wages (W), and log capital (K). See the description file for definitions.

(a) Estimate the panel AR(1) $K_{it} = \alpha K_{i,t-1} + u_i + v_t + \varepsilon_{it}$ using Arellano-Bond one-step GMM with clustered standard errors. Note that the model includes year fixed effects.
(b) Re-estimate using Blundell-Bond one-step GMM with clustered standard errors.
(c) Explain the difference in the estimates.

Exercise 17.16 This exercise uses the same dataset as the previous exercise. Blundell and Bond (1998) estimated a dynamic panel regression of log employment N on log real wages W and log capital K. The following specification[1] uses the Arellano-Bond one-step estimator, treating $W_{i,t-1}$ and $K_{i,t-1}$ as predetermined:

$$N_{it} = \underset{(.0842)}{.7075} N_{i,t-1} - \underset{(.1171)}{.7088} W_{it} + \underset{(.1113)}{.5000} W_{i,t-1} + \underset{(.1010)}{.4660} K_{it} - \underset{(.0859)}{.2151} K_{i,t-1}. \tag{17.114}$$

This equation also included year dummies, and the standard errors are clustered.

(a) Estimate (17.114) using the Arellano-Bond one-step estimator and treating W_{it} and K_{it} as strictly exogenous.

(b) Estimate (17.114) treating $W_{i,t-1}$ and $K_{i,t-1}$ as predetermind to verify the results in (17.114). What is the difference between the estimates treating the regressors as strictly exogenous versus predetermined?

(c) Estimate the equation using the Blundell-Bond one-step systems GMM estimator.

(d) Interpret the coefficient estimates viewing (17.114) as a firm-level labor demand equation.

(e) Describe the impact on the standard errors of the Blundell-Bond estimates in part (c) if you forget to use clustering. (You do not have to list all the standard errors, but describe the magnitude of the impact.)

Exercise 17.17 Use the datafile `Invest1993` on the textbook webpage. You will be estimating the panel AR(1) $D_{it} = \alpha D_{i,t-1} + u_i + \varepsilon_{it}$ for $D = debt/assets$ (this is *debta* in the datafile). See the description file for definitions.

(a) Estimate the model using Arellano-Bond two-step GMM with clustered standard errors.

(b) Re-estimate using Blundell-Bond two-step GMM.

(c) Experiment with your results, trying two-step versus one-step, AR(1) versus AR(2), number of lags used as instruments, and classical versus robust standard errors. What makes the most difference for the coefficient estimates? For the standard errors?

Exercise 17.18 Use the datafile `Invest1993` on the textbook webpage. You will be estimating the model

$$D_{it} = \alpha D_{i,t-1} + \beta_1 I_{i,t-1} + \beta_2 Q_{i,t-1} + \beta_3 CF_{i,t-1} + u_i + \varepsilon_{it}.$$

The variables are *debta, inva, vala,* and *cfa* in the datafile. See the description file for definitions.

(a) Estimate the above regression using Arellano-Bond two-step GMM with clustered standard errors, treating all regressors as predetermined.

(b) Re-estimate using Blundell-Bond two-step GMM, treating all regressors as predetermined.

(c) Experiment with your results, trying two-step versus one-step, number of lags used as instruments, and classical versus robust standard errors. What makes the most difference for the coefficient estimates? For the standard errors?

[1] Blundell and Bond (1998), table 4, column 3.

CHAPTER 18
DIFFERENCE IN DIFFERENCES

18.1 INTRODUCTION

One of the most popular ways to estimate the effect of a policy change is the method of difference in differences, often called "diff in diffs."Estimation is typically a two-way panel data regression with a policy indicator as a regressor. Clustered variance estimation is generally recommended for inference.

Three key conditions must be met to intrepret a difference in difference estimate as a policy effect. First, the estimated regression must be the correct conditional expectation. In particular, this requires that all trends and interactions are properly included. Second, the policy must be exogenous—it satisfies conditional independence. Third, there are no other relevant unincluded factors coincident with the policy change. If these assumptions are satisfied, the difference in difference estimand is a valid causal effect.

18.2 MINIMUM WAGE IN NEW JERSEY

The best-known application of the difference in difference methodology is Card and Krueger (1994), who investigated the impact of New Jersey's 1992 increase of the minimum hourly wage from \$4.25 to \$5.05. Classical economics teaches that an increase in the minimum wage will lead to decreases in employment and increases in prices. To investigate the magnitude of this impact, the authors surveyed a panel of 331 fast food restaurants in New Jersey during the period February 15, 1992–March 4, 1992 (before the enactment of the minimum wage increase) and then again during November 5, 1992–December 31, 1992 (after the enactment). Fast food restaurants were selected for investigation as they are a major employer of minimum wage employees. Before the change, about 30% of the sampled workers were paid the minimum wage of \$4.25.

The data file `CK1994` is extracted from the original Card-Krueger dataset and is posted on the textbook webpage.

Table 18.1 (first column) displays the mean number[1] of full-time equivalent employees[2] at New Jersey fast food restaurants before and after the minimum wage increase. Before the increase, the average number of employees was 20.4. After the increase the average number of employees was 20.9. Contrary to the predictions of conventional theory, employment slightly increased (by 0.5 employees per restaurant) rather than decreased.

This estimate—the change in employment—could be called a **difference estimator**. It is the change in employment coincident with the change in policy. A difficulty in interpretation is that all employment change is

[1]Our calculations drop restaurants if they were missing the number of full-type equivalent employees in either survey.

[2]Following Card and Krueger, full-time equivalent employees is defined as the sum of the number of full-time employees, managers, and assistant managers, plus one-half of the number of part-time employees.

Table 18.1
Average employment at fast food restaurants

	New Jersey	Pennsylvania	Difference
Before increase	20.43	23.38	2.95
After increase	20.90	21.10	0.20
Difference	0.47	−2.28	**2.75**

attributed to the policy. It does not provide direct evidence of the counterfactual—what would have happened if the minimum wage had not been increased.

A **difference in difference estimator** improves on a difference estimator by comparing the change in the treatment sample with a comparable change in a control sample.

Card and Krueger selected eastern Pennsylvania for their control sample. The minimum wage was constant at \$4.25 an hour in the state of Pennsylvania during 1992. At the beginning of the year, starting wages at fast food restaurants in the two states were similar. The two areas (New Jersey and eastern Pennsylvania) share further similarities. Any trends or economic shocks that affect one state are likely to affect both. Therefore, Card and Krueger argued that it is appropriate to treat eastern Pennsylvania as a control. Thus in the absence of a minimum wage increase, they expected the same changes in employment to occur in both New Jersey and eastern Pennsylvania.

Card and Krueger surveyed a panel of 79 fast food restaurants in eastern Pennsylvania simultaneously while surveying the New Jersey restaurants. The average number of full-time equivalent employees in eastern Pennsylvania is displayed in the second column of Table 18.1. Before the policy change, the average number of employees was 23.4. After the policy change, the average number was 21.1. Thus in Pennsylvania, average employment decreased by 2.3 employees per restaurant.

Treating Pennsylvania as a control means comparing the change in New Jersey (0.5) with that in Pennsylvnia (−2.3). The difference (2.75 employees per restaurant) is the difference in difference estimate of the impact of the minimum wage increase. In complete contradiction to conventional economic theory, the estimate indicates an increase in employment rather than a decrease. This surprising estimate has been widely discussed among economists[3] and in the popular press.

It is constructive to rewrite the estimates in Table 18.1 in regression format. Let Y_{it} denote employment at restaurant i surveyed at time t. Let $State_i$ be a dummy variable indicating the state, with $State_i = 1$ for New Jersey and $State_i = 0$ for Pennsylvania. Let $Time_t$ be a dummy variable indicating the time period, with $Time_t = 0$ for the period before the policy change and $Time_t = 1$ for the period after the policy change. Let D_{it} denote a treatment dummy, with $D_{it} = 1$ if the minimum wage equals \$5.05 and $D_{it} = 0$ if the minimum wage equals \$4.25. In this application, it equals the interaction dummy $D_{it} = State_i Time_t$.

Table 18.1 is a saturated regression in the two dummy variables and can therefore be written as the regression equation

$$Y_{it} = \beta_0 + \beta_1 State_i + \beta_2 Time_t + \theta D_{it} + \varepsilon_{it}. \tag{18.1}$$

Indeed, the coefficients can be written in the terms used in Table 18.1 by the following correspondence:

[3] Most economists do not take the estimate literally—they do not believe that increasing the minimum wage will cause employment increases. Instead it has been interpreted as evidence that small changes in the minimum wage may have only minor impacts on employment levels.

	New Jersey	Pennsylvania	Difference
Before increase	$\beta_0 + \beta_1$	β_0	β_1
After increase	$\beta_0 + \beta_1 + \beta_2 + \theta$	$\beta_0 + \beta_2$	$\beta_1 + \theta$
Difference	$\beta_2 + \theta$	β_2	θ

We see that the coefficients in the regression (18.1) correspond to interpretable difference and difference in difference estimands. β_1 is the difference estimand of the effect of "New Jersey vs. Pennsylvania" in the period before the policy change, and β_2 is the difference estimand of the time effect in the control state. θ is the difference in difference estimand: the change in New Jersey relative to the change in Pennsylvania.

Our estimate of the regression (18.1) is

$$\underset{}{Y_{it}} = \underset{(1.4)}{23.4} - \underset{(1.5)}{2.9}\; State_i - \underset{(1.2)}{2.3}\; Time_t + \underset{(1.34)}{2.75}\; D_{it} + \varepsilon_{it}. \tag{18.2}$$

The standard errors are clustered by restaurant. As expected, the coefficient $\widehat{\theta}$ on the treatment dummy precisely equals the difference in difference estimate from Table 18.1. The coefficient estimates can be interpreted as described. The pre-change difference between New Jersey and Pennsylvania is -2.9, and the time effect is -2.3. The difference in difference effect is 2.75. The t-statistic to test the hypothesis of zero effect is just above 2 with an asymptotic p-value of 0.04.

Because the observations are divided into the groups $State_i = 0$ and $State_i = 1$, and $Time_t$ is equivalent to a time index, this regression is identical to a two-way fixed effects regression of Y_{it} on D_{it} with state and time fixed effects. Furthermore, because the regressor D_{it} does not vary across individuals within the state, this fixed effects regression is unchanged if restaurant-level fixed effects are included instead of state fixed effects. (Restaurant fixed effects are orthogonal to any variable constant across restaurants within the state demeaned at the state level. See Exercise 18.1.) Thus the above regression is identical to the two-way fixed effects regression

$$Y_{it} = \theta D_{it} + u_i + v_t + \varepsilon_{it} \tag{18.3}$$

where u_i is a restaurant fixed effect, and v_t is a time fixed effect. The simplest method to implement this is by using a one-way fixed effects regression with time dummies. The estimates are

$$Y_{it} = \underset{(1.34)}{2.75}\; D_{it} - \underset{(1.2)}{2.3}\; Time_t + u_i + \varepsilon_{it} \tag{18.4}$$

which are identical to the previous regression.

Equation (18.3) is the basic difference in difference model. It is a two-way fixed effects regression of the response Y_{it} on a binary policy D_{it}. The coefficient θ corresponds to the double difference in sample means and can be interpreted as the policy impact (also called the "treatment effect") of D on Y. (We discuss identification in Section 18.3.) The presentation here (and the Card-Krueger example) focuses on the basic case of two aggregate units (states) and two time periods. The regression formulation (18.3) is convenient, as it can be easily generalized to allow for multiple states and time periods. Doing so provides more convincing evidence of an identified policy effect. Equation (18.3) can also be generalized by changing the trend specification and using a continuous treatment variable.

Another common generalization is to augment the regression with controls X_{it}. This model is

$$Y_{it} = \theta D_{it} + X_{it}'\beta + u_i + v_t + \varepsilon_{it}. \tag{18.5}$$

Many empirical studies report estimates both of the basic model and regressions with controls. For example, we could augment the Card-Krueger regression to include the variable *hoursopen*, the number of hours a day the restaurant is open. A restaurant with longer hours will tend to have more employees:

$$\underset{}{Y_{it}} = \underset{(1.31)}{2.84}\ D_{it} - \underset{(1.2)}{2.2}\ Time_t + \underset{(0.4)}{1.2}\ hoursopen_{it} + u_i + \varepsilon_{it}.$$

The estimated effect is that a restaurant employs an additional 1.2 employees for each hour open, and this effect is statistically significant. The estimated treatment effect is not meaningfully changed.

18.3 IDENTIFICATION

Consider the difference in difference equation (18.5) for $i = 1, \ldots, N$ and $t = 1, \ldots, T$. We are interested in conditions under which the coefficient θ is the causal impact of the treatment D_{it} on the outcome Y_{it}. The answer can be found by applying Theorem 2.12 from Section 2.30.

Section 2.30 introduced the potential outcomes framework, which writes the outcome as a function of the treatment, controls, and unobservables. The outcome (e.g., employment at a restaurant) is written as $Y = h(D, X, e)$, where D is treatment (minimum wage policy), X are controls, and e is a vector of unobserved factors. Model (18.5) specifies that $h(D, X, e)$ is separable and linear in its arguments and that the unobservables consist of individual-specific, time-specific, and idiosyncratic effects.

We now discuss sufficient conditions under which the coefficient θ can be interpreted as a causal effect. Recall the two-way within transformation (17.65), and set $\ddot{Z}_{it} = \left(\ddot{D}_{it}, \ddot{X}_{it}'\right)'$.

Theorem 18.1 Suppose the following conditions hold:

1. $Y_{it} = \theta D_{it} + X_{it}'\beta + u_i + v_t + \varepsilon_{it}$.
2. $\mathbb{E}\left[\ddot{Z}_{it}\ddot{Z}_{it}'\right] > 0$.
3. $\mathbb{E}\left[X_{it}\varepsilon_{is}\right] = 0$ for all t and s.
4. Conditional on $X_{i1}, X_{i2}, \ldots, X_{iT}$, the random variables D_{it} and ε_{is} are statistically independent for all t and s.

Then the coefficient θ in (18.5) equals the average causal effect for D on Y conditional on X.

Condition 1 states that the outcome equals the specified linear regression model, which is additively separable in the observables, individual effect, and time effect.

Condition 2 states that the two-way within transformed regressors have a nonsingular design matrix, which requires that all elements of D_{it} and X_{it} vary across time and individuals.

Condition 3 is the standard exogeneity asumption for regressors in a fixed-effects model.

Condition 4 states that the treatment variable is conditionally independent of the idiosyncratic error. This is the conditional independence assumption for fixed effects regression.

To prove Theorem 18.1, apply the two-way within transformation (17.65) to (18.5). We obtain

$$\ddot{Y}_{it} = \theta\ddot{D}_{it} + \ddot{X}_{it}'\beta + \ddot{\varepsilon}_{it}.$$

Under Condition 2, the projection coefficients (θ, β) are uniquely defined, and under Conditions 3 and 4, they equal the linear regression coefficients. Thus θ is the regression derivative with respect to D. Condition

4 implies that conditional on $\ddot{X}_{it}$, the random variables $\ddot{D}_{it}$ and $\ddot{\varepsilon}_{is}$ are statistically independent. Theorem 2.12 shows that the regression derivative θ equals the average causal effect, as stated in Theorem 18.1.

The assumption that D and ε are independent is the fundamental exogeneity assumption. To intrepret θ as a treatment effect, it is important that D is defined as the treatment and not simply as an interaction (time and state) dummy. This requirement is subtle. Examine equation (18.5), recalling that D is defined as the treatment (an increase in the minimum wage). In this equation, the error ε_{it} contains all variables and effects not included in the regression. Thus if there are other changes in New Jersey that coincide with the minimum wage increase, the assumption that D and ε are independent means that those coincident changes are independent of ε and thus do not affect employment. This is a strong assumption. Once again, Condition 4 states that all other effects that are coincident with the minimum wage increase have no effect on employment. Without this assumption, it would not be possible to claim that the difference in difference regression identifies the causal effect of the treatment.

Furthermore, independence of D_{it} and ε_{is} means that neither can be affected by the other. Thus the policy (treatment) was not enacted in response to knowledge about the response variable in either period, and it also means that the outcome (employment) did not change in the first period in anticipation of the upcoming policy change.

It is difficult to know whether the exogeneity of D is a reasonable assumption. It is similar to instrument exogeneity in instrumental variable regression. Its validity hinges on a well articulated structural argument. An empirical investigation based on a difference in difference specification needs to make an explicit case for exogeneity of D similar to that for IV regression.

In the case of the Card-Krueger application, the authors argue that the policy was exogeneous, because it was adopted 2 years before taking effect. At the time of the passage of the legislation, the economy was in an expansion, but by the time of adoption, the economy has slipped into recession. Thus it is credible to assume that the policy decision in 1990 was not affected by employment levels in 1992. Furthermore, concern about the impact of the increased minimum wage during a recession led to a serious discussion about reversing the policy, meaning that there was uncertainty about whether the policy would actually be enacted at the time of the first survey. It thus seems credible that employment decisions at that time were not determined in anticipation of the upcoming minimum wage increase.

The authors do not discuss, however, whether there were other coincident events in the New Jersey or Pennsylvania economies during 1992 that could have affected employment differentially in the two states. It seems plausible that there could have been many such coincident events, which seems to be the greatest weakness in their identification argument.

Identification (the conditions for Theorem 18.1) also requires that the regression model is correctly specified, which means that the true model is linear in the specified variables and all interactions are included. Since the basic 2×2 specification is a saturated dummy variable model, it is necessarily a conditional expectation and thus correctly specified. This is not the case in applications with more than two states or time periods, and thus model specification needs to be carefully considered in such cases.

18.4 MULTIPLE UNITS

The basic difference in difference model has two aggregate units (e.g., states) and two time periods. Additional information can be obtained if there are multiple units or multiple time periods. This section focuses on the case of multiple units. There can be multiple treatment units, multiple control units, or both. In this section,

Table 18.2
Average employment at fast food restaurants

	South NJ	Central NJ	North NJ	PA 1	PA 2
Before increase	16.6	22.0	22.0	24.8	22.2
After increase	17.3	21.4	22.7	21.0	21.2
Difference	0.7	−0.6	0.7	−3.8	−1.0

we suppose that the number of periods is $T=2$. Let $N_1 \geq 1$ be the number of untreated (control) units, and $N_2 \geq 1$ be the number of treated units, with $N=N_1+N_2$.

The basic regression model,

$$Y_{it}=\theta D_{it}+u_i+v_t+\varepsilon_{it}$$

imposes two strong restrictions. First, all units are equally affected by time as v_t is common across i. Second, the treatment effect θ is common across all treated units.

The Card-Krueger dataset only contains observations from two states, but the authors did record additional variables, including the region of the state. They divided New Jersey into three regions (North, Central, and South) and eastern Pennsylvania into two regions (1 for northeast Philadelphia suburbs and 2 for the remainder).

Table 18.2 displays the mean number of full-time equivalent employees by region, before and after the minimum wage increase. We observe that two of the three New Jersey regions had nearly identical increases in employment and all three changes are small. We can also observe that both of the Pennsylvania regions had employment decreases, though of different magnitudes.

We can test the assumption of equal treatment effect θ by a regression exclusion test. This can be done by adding interaction dummies to the regression and testing for the exclusion of the interactions. As there are three treated regions in New Jersey, we include two of the three New Jersey region dummies interacted with the time index. In general, we would include N_2-1 such interactions. These coefficients measure the treatment effect difference across regions. Testing that these two coefficients are 0 we obtain a p-value of 0.60, which is far from significant. Thus we accept the hypothesis that the treatment effect θ is common across the New Jersey regions.

In contrast, when the treatment effect θ varies, we call this a **heterogeneous treatment effect**. It is not a violation of the treatment effect framework, but it can be considerably more complicated to analyze. (A model that incorrectly imposes a homogeneous treatment effect is misspecified and produces inconsistent estimates.)

A more serious problem arises if the control effect is heterogeneous. The control effect is the change in the control group. Table 18.2 breaks down the estimated control effect across the two Pennsylvania regions. Although both estimates are negative, they are somewhat different from each other. If the effects are distinct, there is no homogeneous control effect. We can test the assumption of equal control effects by a regression exclusion test. As there are two Pennsylvania regions, we include the interaction of one of the Pennsylvania regions with the time index. (In general, we would include N_1-1 interactions.) This coefficient measures the difference in the control effect across the regions. We test that this coefficient is 0, obtaining a t-statistic of 1.2 and a p-value of 0.23. It is not statistically significant, meaning that we cannot reject the hypothesis that the control effect is homogeneous.

In contrast, if the control effect were heterogeneous, then the difference in difference estimation strategy is misspecified. The method relies on the ability to identify a credible control sample. Therefore, if a test for

Table 18.3
Number of car thefts by city block

	Same block	Not on same block	Difference
April–June	0.112	0.095	−0.017
August–December	0.035	0.105	0.070
Difference	−0.077	0.010	**−0.087**

equal control effects rejects the hypothesis of homogeneous control effects, this should be taken as evidence against interpretation of the difference in difference parameter as a treatment effect.

18.5 DO POLICE REDUCE CRIME?

DiTella and Schargrodsky (2004) use a difference in difference approach to study the question of whether the street presence of police officers reduces car theft. Rational crime models predict that the the presence of an observable police force will reduce crime rates (at least locally) due to deterrence. The causal effect is difficult to measure, however, as police forces are not allocated exogenously, but instead are allocated in anticipation of need. A difference in difference estimator requires an exogenous event that changes police allocations. The innovation in DiTella-Schargrodsky was to use the police response to a terrorist attack as an exogenous variation.

In July 1994, a horrific terrorist attack was perpetrated on the main Jewish center in Buenos Aires, Argentina. Within 2 weeks, the federal government provided police protection to all Jewish and Muslim buildings in the country. DiTella and Schargrodsky (2004) hypothesized that their presence, while allocated to deter a terror or reprisal attack, would also deter other street crimes, such as automobile theft locally due to the deployed police. The authors collected detailed information on car thefts in selected neighborhoods of Buenos Aires for April–December 1994, resulting in a panel for 876 city blocks. They hypothesized that the terrorist attack and the government's response were exogenous to auto thievery and is thus a valid treatment. They postulated that the deterrence effect would be strongest for any city block that contained a Jewish institution (and thus police protection). Potential car thiefs would be deterred from a burglary due to the enhanced threat of being caught. The deterrence effect was expected to weaken as the distance from the protected sites increased. The authors therefore proposed a difference in difference estimator based on the average number of car thefts per block, before and after the terrorist attack, and between city blocks with and without a Jewish institution. Their sample has 37 blocks with Jewish institutions (the treatment sample) and 839 blocks without an institution (the control sample).

The data file `DS2004` is a slightly revised version of the author's AER replication file and is posted on the textbook webpage.

Table 18.3 displays the average number of car thefts per block, separately for the months before the July attack and the months after the July attack, and separately for city blocks that have a Jewish institution (and therefore received police protection starting in late July) and for other city blocks. We can see that the average number of car thefts dramatically decreased in the protected city blocks, from 0.112 per month to 0.035, while the average number in unprotected blocks was nearly constant, rising from 0.095 to 0.105. Taking the difference in difference, we find that the effect of police presence decreased car thefts by 0.087, which is about 78%.

Table 18.4
Number of car thefts by city block

		Same block	Not on same block	Difference
Pre-attack	April	0.112	0.110	−0.012
	May	0.088	0.100	0.012
	June	0.128	0.076	−0.052
Post-attack	August	0.047	0.111	0.064
	September	0.014	0.099	0.085
	October	0.061	0.108	0.047
	November	0.027	0.100	0.073
	December	0.027	0.106	0.079

A general way to estimate a difference in difference model is a regression of the form (18.3), where Y_{it} is the number of car thefts on block i during month t, and u_i and v_t are block and month fixed effects. This regression[4] yields the same estimate of 0.087, because the panel is balanced and there are no control variables.

The model (18.3) makes the strong assumption that the treatment effect is constant across the five treated months. We investigate this assumption in Table 18.4, which breaks down the car thefts by month. For the control sample, the number of car thefts is near constant across the months. For seven of the eight months, the average number per block ranges from 0.10 to 0.11, with only one month (June) a bit lower at 0.08. In the treatment sample, the average number of thefts per block in the 3 months before the terrorist atack are similar to the averages in the control sample. But in the 5 months following the attack, the number of car thefts is uniformly reduced. The averages range from 0.014 to 0.061. In each month after the attack, the control sample has lower thefts, with averages ranging from 0.047 to 0.085. Given the small sample size (37) of the treatment sample, this is strikingly uniform evidence.

We can formally test the homogeneity of the treatment effect by including four dummy variables for the interactions of four post-attack months with the treatment sample and then testing the exclusion of these variables. The p-value for this test is 0.81, exceedingly far from significant. Thus we find no reason in the data to be suspicious of the homogeneity assumption.

The goal was to estimate the causal effect of police presence as a deterrence for crime. Let us evaluate the case for identification. It seems reasonable to treat the terrorist attack as exogenous. The government response also to be appears to be exogenous. Neither is reasonably related to the auto theft rate. We also observe that the evidence in Tables 18.3 and 18.4 indicates that theft rates were similar in the pre-attack treatment and control samples. Thus the additional police protection seems credibly provided for the purpose of attack prevention rather than as an excuse for crime prevention. The general homogeneity of the theft rate across months, once we allow for the treatment effect, gives credibility to the claim that the police response was a causal effect. The terror attack itself did not reduce car theft rates, as there seems to be no measurable effect outside the treatment sample. Finally, although the paper does not explicitly address whether there was any other coincident event in July 1994 that may have effected these specific city blocks, it is difficult to conceive of an alternative explanation for such a large effect. Our conclusion is that this is a strong identification argument. Police presence greatly reduces the incidence of car theft.

The authors asserted the inference that police presence deters crime more broadly. This extension is tenuous, because the paper does not provide direct evidence of this claim. Although it may seem reasonable, we should be cautious about making generalizations without supporting evidence.

[4] I omit the observations for July, because the car theft data is only for the first half of the month.

Overall, DiTella and Schargrodsky (2004) is an excellent example of a well articulated and credibly identified difference in difference estimate of an important policy effect.

18.6 TREND SPECIFICATION

Some applications (including the two introduced earlier in this chapter) apply to a short period of time, such as 1 year, in which case we may not expect the variables to be trended. Other applications cover many years or decades, in which case the variables are likely to be trended. These trends can reflect long-term growth, business cycle effects, changing tastes, or many other features. If trends are incorrectly specified, then the model will be misspecified, and the estimated policy effect will be inconsistent due to omitted variable bias. Consider the difference in difference equation (18.5). This model imposes the strong assumption that the trends in Y_{it} are entirely explained by the included controls X_{it} and the common unobserved time component v_t. This assumption can be quite restrictive. It is reasonable to expect that trends may differ across units and are not fully captured by observed controls.

One way to think about this problem is in terms of overidentification. For simplicity, suppose there are no controls and the panel is balanced. Then there are NT observations. The two-way model with a policy effect has $N+T$ coefficients. Unless $N=T=2$, this model is overidentified. In addition to considering heterogeneous treatment effects, it is reasonable to consider heterogeneous trends.

One generalization is to include interactions of a linear trend with a control variable. This model is

$$Y_{it} = \theta D_{it} + X_{it}'\beta + Z_i'\delta t + u_i + v_t + \varepsilon_{it}.$$

It specifies that the trend in Y_{it} differs across units, depending on the controls Z_i.

A broader generalization is to include unit-specific linear time trends. This model is

$$Y_{it} = \theta D_{it} + X_{it}'\beta + u_i + v_t + tw_i + \varepsilon_{it}. \tag{18.6}$$

In this model, w_i is a time trend fixed effect that varies across units. If there are no controls, this model has $2N+T$ coefficients and is identified as long as $T \geq 4$.

Estimation of model (18.6) can be done one of three ways. If N is small (e.g., applications with state-level data), the regression can be estimated using the explicit dummy variable approach. Let d_i and S_t be dummy variables indicating the ith unit and tth time period, respectively. Set $d_{it} = d_i t$, the interaction of the individual dummy with the time trend. The equation is estimated by regression of Y_{it} on D_{it}, X_{it}, d_i, S_t, and d_{it}. Equivalently, one can apply one-way fixed effects with regressors D_{it}, X_{it}, S_t, and d_{it}.

When N is large, a computationally more efficient approach is to use residual regression. For each unit i, estimate a time trend model for each variable Y_{it}, D_{it}, X_{it}, and S_t. That is, for each i, estimate

$$Y_{it} = \widehat{\alpha}_0 + \widehat{\alpha}_1 t + \dot{Y}_{it}.$$

This estimator is a generalized within transformation. The residuals $\dot{Y}_{it}$ are used in place of the original observations. Regress $\dot{Y}_{it}$ on $\dot{D}_{it}$, $\dot{X}_{it}$, and $\dot{S}_t$ to obtain the estimates of (18.6).

The relevance of the trend fixed effects v_t can be assessed by a significance test. Specifically, the hypothesis that the coefficients on the period dummies are 0 can be tested using a standard exclusion test. Similarly, trend interaction terms can be tested for significance using standard exclusion tests. If the tests are statistically significant, then their inclusion is relevant for correct specification. Unfortunately, the unit-specific linear time trends cannot be tested for significance when the covariance matrix is clustered at the unit level. This is similar to the problem of testing the significance of a dummy variable with a single observation. The unit-specific time trends can only be tested for significance if the covariance matrix is clustered at a finer level. Otherwise, the covariance matrix estimate is singular and biased downward. Naïve tests will overstate significance.

Our discussion for simplicity has focused on the case of balanced panels. The methods equally apply to unbalanced panels, using standard panel data estimation.

18.7 DO BLUE LAWS AFFECT LIQUOR SALES?

Historically, many U.S. states prohibited or limited the sale of alcoholic beverages on Sundays. These laws are known as "blue laws."In recent years, these laws have been relaxed. Have these changes led to increased consumption of alcoholic beverages? Bernheim, Meer, and Novarro (2016) investigated this question using a detailed panel on alcohol consumption and sales hours. It is possible that observed changes coincident with changes in the law might reflect underlying trends. That different states changed their laws during different years allows for a difference in difference methodology to identify the treatment effect.

The paper focuses on distilled liquor sales, though wine and beer sales are also included in their data. An abridged version of their dataset `BMN2016` is posted on the textbook webpage. Liquor is measured in per capita gallons of pure ethanol equivalent. The data are state-level for 47 U.S. states for the years 1970–2007, unbalanced.

The authors carefully gathered information on the allowable hours that alcohol can be sold on a Sunday. They make a distinction between off-premise sales (liquor stores, supermarkets) where consumption is off premise, and on-premise sales (restaurants, bars) where consumption is on-premise. Let Y_{it} denote the natural logarithm of per capita liquor sales in state i in year t. A simplified version of their basic model is

$$\begin{aligned} Y_{it} = \underset{(0.003)}{0.011} \; OnHours_{it} + \underset{(0.003)}{0.003} \; OffHours_{it} - \underset{(0.004)}{0.013} \; UR_{it} \\ + \underset{(0.008)}{0.029} \; OnOutFlows_{it} - \underset{(0.010)}{0.000} \; OffOutFlows_{it} + u_i + v_t + \varepsilon_{it}. \end{aligned} \tag{18.7}$$

OnHours and OffHours are the number of allowable Sunday on-premises and off-premises sale hours, respectively. UR is the state unemploment rate. OnOutFlows (OffOutFlows) is the weighted number of on(off)-premises sale hours less than neighbor states. These are added to adjust for possible cross-border transactions. The model includes both state and year fixed effects. The standard errors are clustered by state.

The estimates indicate that increased on-premise sale hours lead to a small increase in liquor sales, which is consistent with alcohol being a complementary good in social (restaurant and bar) settings. The small and insignificant coefficient on *OffHours* indicates that increased off-premise sale hours does not lead to an increase in liquor sales. This is consistent with rational consumers who adjust their purchases to known hours. The negative effect of the unemployment rate means that liquor sales are pro-cyclical.

The authors were concerned about whether their dynamic and trend specifications were correctly specified, so they tried some alternative specifications and interactions. To understand the trend issue, Figure 18.1 shows the time series path of the log of per capita liquor sales for three states: California, Iowa, and New York. You can see that all three exhibit a downward trend from 1970 until about 1995 and then an increasing trend. The trend components of the three series, however, are not identical, which suggests that it may be incorrect to treat the trends as common across states.

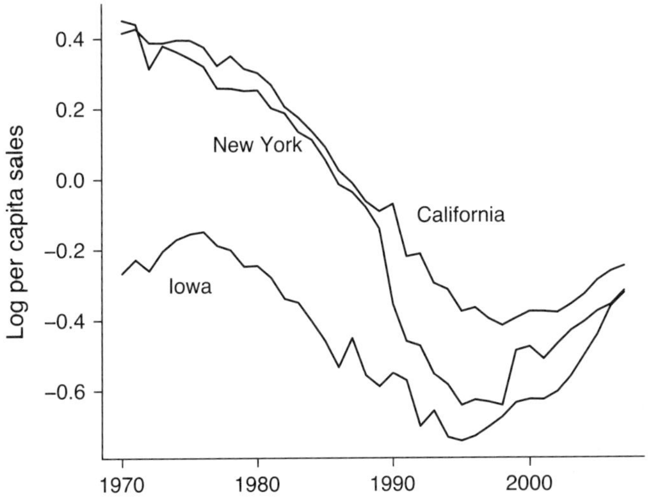

FIGURE 18.1 Liquor sales by state

If we augment the basic model to include state-specific linear trends, the estimates are as follows:

$$\begin{aligned} Y_{it} = \; & \underset{(0.002)}{0.000} \; OnHours_{it} + \underset{(0.002)}{0.002} \; OffHours_{it} - \underset{(0.004)}{0.015} \; UR_{it} \\ & + \underset{(0.005)}{0.005} \; OnOutFlows_{it} - \underset{(0.005)}{0.005} \; OffOutFlows_{it} + tw_i + u_i + v_t + \varepsilon_{it}. \end{aligned} \quad (18.8)$$

The estimated coefficient for *OnHours* drops to 0 and becomes insignificant. The other estimates do not change meaningfully. The authors only discuss this regression in a footnote, stating that adding state-specific trends "demands a great deal from the data and leaves too little variation to identify the effects of interest." This is an unfortunate claim, as actually the standard errors have decreased, not increased, indicating that the effects are better identified. The trouble is that *OnHours* and *OffHours* are trended, and the trends vary by state. Thus these variables are correlated with the state-trend interaction. Omitting the trend interaction induced omitted variable bias. That explains why the coefficient estimates change when the trend specification changes.

Bernheim, Meer, and Novarro (2016) is an excellent example of meticulous empirical work with careful attention to detail and isolating a treatment strategy. It is also a good example of how attention to trend specification can affect results.

18.8 CHECK YOUR CODE: DOES ABORTION IMPACT CRIME?

In a highly discussed paper, Donohue and Levitt (2001) used a difference in difference approach to develop an unusual theory. Crime rates fell dramatically throughout the United States in the 1990s. Donohue and Levitt postulated that one contributing explanation was the landmark 1973 legalization of abortion. The latter might affect the crime rate through two potential channels. First, it reduced the cohort size of young males. Second, it reduced the cohort size of young males at risk for criminal behavior. These observations suggest that the substantial increase in abortions in the early 1970s will translate into a substantial reduction in crime 20 years later.

As you might imagine, this paper was controversial on several dimensions. The paper was also meticulous in its empirical analysis, investigating the potential links by using a variety of tools and differing levels of granularity. The most detailed-oriented regressions were presented at the very end of the paper, where the authors exploited differences across age groups. These regressions took the form

$$\log\left(Arrests_{itb}\right) = \beta Abortion_{ib} + u_i + \lambda_{tb} + \theta_{it} + \varepsilon_{itb}$$

where i, t, and b index state, year, and birth cohort. *Arrests* is the raw number of arrests for a given crime, and *Abortion* is the ratio of abortions to live births. The regression includes state fixed effects, cohort-year interactions, and state-year interactions. By including all these interaction effects, the regression is estimating a triple-difference and is identifying the abortion impact on within-state cross-cohort variation, which is a much stronger identification argument than a simple cross-state difference in difference regression. Donohue and Levitt reported an estimate of β equaling -0.028 with a small standard error. Based on these estimates, Donohue and Levitt suggest that legalizing abortion reduced crime by about 15–25%.

Unfortunately, their estimates contained an error. In an attempt to replicate the Donohue-Levitt work, Foote and Goetz (2008) discovered that Donohue-Levitt's computer code inadvertently omitted the state-year interactions θ_{it}. This omission was important as without θ_{it}, the estimates are based on a mix of cross-state and cross-cohort variation rather than on just cross-cohort variation, as claimed. Foote and Goetz re-estimated the regression and found an estimate of β equaling -0.010. While still statistically different from 0, the reduction in magnitude substantially decreased the estimated impact. Foote and Gootz include more extensive empirical analysis as well.

Regardless of the errors and political ramifications, the Donohue-Levitt paper is a very clever and creative use of the difference in difference method. It is unfortunate that this creative work was somewhat overshadowed by a debate over computer code.

I believe there are two important messages from this episode. First, include the appropriate controls! In the Donohue-Levitt regression, they were correct to advocate for the regression that includes state-year interactions, as this allows the most precise measurement of the desired causal impact. Second, check your code! Computation errors are pervasive in applied economic work. It is very easy to make errors; it is very difficult to clean them out of lengthy code. Errors in most papers are ignored as the details receive minor attention. Important and influential papers, however, are scrutinized. If you ever are so blessed as to write a paper that receives significant attention, you will find it most embarrassing if a coding error is found after publication. The solution is to be proactive and vigilant.

18.9 INFERENCE

Many difference in difference applications use highly aggregate (e.g., state level) data, because they are investigating the impact of policy changes that occur at an aggregate level. It has become customary in the recent literature to use clustering methods to calculate standard errors, with clustering applied at a high level of aggregation.

To understand the motivation for this choice, it is useful to review the traditional argument for clustered variance estimation. Suppose that the error e_{ig} for individual i in group g is independent of the regressors, has variance σ^2, and has correlation ρ across individuals within the group. If the number of individuals in each group is N, then the exact variance of the least squares estimator (recall equation (4.50)) is

$$V_{\widehat{\beta}} = \left(X'X\right)^{-1} \sigma^2 \left(1 + \rho\left(N - 1\right)\right)$$

as originally derived by Moulton (1990). This equation inflates the "usual" variance by the factor $(1 + \rho (N - 1))$. Even if ρ is very small, if N is huge, then this inflation factor can be large as well.

The clustered variance estimator imposes no structure on the conditional variances and correlations within each group. It allows for arbitrary relationships. The advantage is that the resulting variance estimators are robust to a broad range of correlation structures. The disadvantage is that the estimators can be much less precise. Effectively, clustered variance estimators should be viewed as constructed from the number of groups. If you are using U.S. states as your groups (as is commonly seen in applications), then the number of groups is (at most) 51. Thus you are estimating the covariance matrix using 51 observations, regardless of the number of "observations" in the sample. One implication is that if you are estimating more than 51 coefficients, the sample covariance matrix estimator will not be full rank, which can invalidate potentially relevant inference methods.

The case for clustered standard errors was made convincingly in an influential paper by Bertrand, Duflo, and Mullainathan (2004). These authors demonstrated their point by taking the well-known Current Population Survey (CPS) dataset and then adding randomly generated regressors. They found that if non-clustered variance estimators were used, then standard errors would be much too small, and a researcher would inappropriately conclude that the randomly generated "variable" has a significant effect in a regression. The false rejections could be eliminated by using clustered standard errors that are clustered at the state level. Based on the recommendations from this paper, researchers in economics now routinely cluster at the state level.

There are limitations, however. Take the Card and Krueger (1994) example introduced in Section 18.2. Their sample had only two states (New Jersey and Pennsylvania). If the standard errors are clustered at the state level, then only two effective observations are available for standard error calculation, which is much too few. For this application, clustering at the state level is impossible. One implication might be that this casts doubts on applications involving just a handful of states. If we cannot rule out clustered dependence structures, and cannot use clustering methods due to the small number of states, then it may be inappropriate to trust the reported standard errors.

Another challenge arises when treatment ($D_{it} = 1$) applies to only a small number of units. The most extreme case is where there is only one treated unit. This could arise, for example, when you are interested in measuring the effect of a policy that only one state has adopted. This situation is particularly treacherous and is algebraically identical to the problem of robust covariance matrix estimation with sparse dummy variable (see Section 4.16.). As we learned from that analysis, in the extreme case of a single treated unit, the robust covariance matrix estimator is singular and highly biased toward 0. The problem is because the variance of the sub-group is estimated from a single observation.

The same analysis applies to cluster-variance estimators. If there is a single treated unit, then the standard clustered covariance matrix estimator will be singular. If you calculate a standard error for the sub-group mean, it will be algebraically 0 despite being the most imprecisely estimated coefficient. The treatment effect will have a nonzero reported standard error but it will be incorrect and highly biased toward 0. For a more detailed analysis and recommendations for inference, see Conley and Taber (2011).

18.10 EXERCISES

Exercise 18.1 In the text it was claimed that in a balanced sample, individual-level fixed effects are orthogonal to any variable constant across individuals within the state demeaned at the state level.

(a) Prove this claim.

(b) Does this claim hold in unbalanced samples?

(c) Explain why this claim implies that the regressions

$$Y_{it} = \beta_0 + \beta_1 State_i + \beta_2 Time_t + \theta D_{it} + \varepsilon_{it}$$

and

$$Y_{it} = \theta D_{it} + u_i + \delta_t + \varepsilon_{it}$$

yield identical estimates of θ.

Exercise 18.2 In regression (18.1) with $T=2$ and $N=2$, suppose that the time variable is omitted. Thus the estimating equation is

$$Y_{it} = \beta_0 + \beta_1 State_i + \theta D_{it} + \varepsilon_{it}$$

where $D_{it} = State_i Time_t$ is the treatment indicator.

(a) Find an algebraic expression for the least squares estimator $\widehat{\theta}$.

(b) Show that $\widehat{\theta}$ is a function only of the treated subsample and is not a function of the untreated subsample.

(c) Is $\widehat{\theta}$ a difference in difference estimator?

(d) Under which assumptions might $\widehat{\theta}$ be an appropriate estimator of the treatment effect?

Exercise 18.3 Consider the basic difference in difference model

$$Y_{it} = \theta D_{it} + u_i + \delta_t + \varepsilon_{it}.$$

Instead of assuming that D_{it} and ε_{it} are independent, assume we have an instrumental variable Z_{it} that is independent of ε_{it} but is correlated with D_{it}. Describe how to estimate θ.

Hint: Review Section 17.28.

Exercise 18.4 For the specification tests of Section 18.4, explain why the regression test for homogeneous treatment effects includes only $N_2 - 1$ interaction dummy variables rather than all N_2 interaction dummies. Also explain why the regression test for equal control effects includes only $N_1 - 1$ interaction dummy variables rather than all N_1 interaction dummies.

Exercise 18.5 An economist is interested in the impact of Wisconsin's 2011"Act 10" legislation on wages. (For background, Act 10 reduced the power of labor unions.) She computes the following statistics[5] for average wage rates in Wisconsin and the neighboring state of Minnesota for the decades before and after Act 10 was enacted:

[5]These numbers are completely fictitious.

	Years	Average wage
Wisconsin	2001–2010	15.23
Wisconsin	2010–2020	16.72
Minnesota	2001–2010	16.42
Minnesota	2010–2020	18.10

(a) Based on this information, what is her point estimate of the impact of Act 10 on average wages?

(b) The numbers in the above table were calculated as county-level averages. (The economist was given the average wage in each county. She calculated the average for the state by taking the average across the counties.) Now suppose that she estimates the following linear regression, treating individual counties as observations:

$$\text{wage} = \alpha + \beta \text{Act10} + \gamma \text{Wisconsin} + \delta \text{Post2010} + e.$$

The three regressors are dummy variables for "Act 10 in effect in the state," "county is in Wisconsin," and "time period is 2011–2020." What value of $\widehat{\beta}$ does she find?

(c) What value of $\widehat{\gamma}$ does she find?

Exercise 18.6 Use the datafile `CK1994` on the textbook webpage. Classical economics teaches that increasing the minimum wage will increase product prices. You can therefore use the Card-Krueger difference in difference methodology to estimate the effect of the 1992 New Jersey minimum wage increase on product prices. The data file contains the variables *priceentree*, *pricefry*, and *pricesoda*. Create the variable *price* as the sum of these three, indicating the cost of a typical meal.

(a) Some values of *price* are missing. Delete these observations. This will produce an unbalanced panel, as *price* may be missing for only one of the two surveys. Balance the panel by deleting the paired observation, which can be accomplished in Stata by the commands:
- `drop if price == .`
- `bys store: gen nperiods = [_N]`
- `keep if nperiods == 2`

(b) Create an analog of Table 18.1 but with the price of a meal rather than the number of employees. Interpret the results.

(c) Estimate an analog of regression (18.2) with price as the dependent variable.

(d) Estimate an analog of regression (18.4) with state fixed effects and price as the dependent variable.

(e) Estimate an analog of regression (18.4) with restaurant fixed effects and price as the dependent variable.

(f) Are the results of the regressions in parts (c)–(e) the same?

(g) Create an analog of Table 18.2 for the price of a meal. Interpret the results.

(h) Test for homogeneous treatment effects across regions.

(i) Test for equal control effects across regions.

Exercise 18.7 Use the datafile `DS2004` on the textbook webpage. The authors argued that an exogenous police presence would deter automobile theft. The evidence presented in the chapter showed that car theft was reduced for city blocks that received police protection. Does this deterrence effect extend beyond the same block? The dataset has the dummy variable *oneblock*, that indicates whether the city block is one block away from a protected institution.

(a) Calculate an analog of Table 18.3 that shows the difference between city blocks that are one block away from a protected institution and those that are more than one block away from a protected institution.

(b) Estimate a regression with block and month fixed effects that includes two treatment variables: for city blocks on the same block as a protected institution, and for city blocks one block away, both interacted with a post-July dummy. Exclude observations for July.

(c) Comment on your findings. Does the deterrence effect extend beyond the same city block?

Exercise 18.8 Use the datafile `BMN2016` on the textbook webpage. The authors report results for liquor sales. The data file contains the same information for beer and wine sales. For either beer or wine sales, estimate difference in difference models similar to (18.7) and (18.8) and interpret your results. Some relevant variables are *id* (state identification), *year*, *unempw* (unemployment rate). For beer, the relevant variables are *logbeer* (log of beer sales), *beeronsun* (number of hours of allowed on-premise sales), *beeroffsun* (number of hours of allowed off-premise sales), *beerOnOutflows*, *beerOffOutflows*. For wine, the variables have similar names.

PART V

NONPARAMETRIC METHODS

CHAPTER 19
NONPARAMETRIC REGRESSION

19.1 INTRODUCTION

We now turn to nonparametric estimation of the conditional expectation function (CEF):

$$\mathbb{E}[Y \mid X = x] = m(x).$$

Unless an economic model restricts the form of $m(x)$ to a parametric function, $m(x)$ can take any nonlinear shape and is therefore **nonparametric**. In this chapter, we discuss nonparametric kernel smoothing estimators of $m(x)$. These are related to the nonparametric density estimators of Chapter 17 of *Probability and Statistics for Economists*. In Chapter 20 of this textbook, we explore estimation by series methods.

There are many excellent monographs written on nonparametric regression estimation, including Härdle (1990), Fan and Gijbels (1996), Pagan and Ullah (1999), and Li and Racine (2007).

To get started, suppose that there is a single real-valued regressor X. We consider the case of vector-valued regressors later. The nonparametric regression model is

$$\begin{aligned} Y &= m(X) + e \\ \mathbb{E}[e \mid X] &= 0 \\ \mathbb{E}\left[e^2 \mid X\right] &= \sigma^2(X). \end{aligned}$$

Assume that we have n observations for the pair (Y, X). The goal is to estimate $m(x)$ either at a single point x or at a set of points. For most of our theory, we focus on estimation at a single point x that is in the interior of the support of X.

In addition to the conventional regression assumptions, assume that both $m(x)$ and $f(x)$ (the marginal density of X) are continuous in x. For our theoretical treatment, assume that the observations are i.i.d. The methods extend to dependent observations, but the theory is more advanced. See Fan and Yao (2003). We discuss clustered observations in Section 19.20.

19.2 BINNED MEANS ESTIMATOR

For clarity, fix the point x and consider estimation of $m(x)$. This is the expectation of Y for random pairs (Y, X) such that $X = x$. If the distribution of X were discrete, then we could estimate $m(x)$ by taking the average of the subsample of observations Y_i for which $X_i = x$. But when X is continuous, the probability is 0 that X exactly equals x. So there is no subsample of observations with $X = x$, and this estimation idea is infeasible. However, if $m(x)$ is continuous, then it should be possible to get a good approximation by taking the average

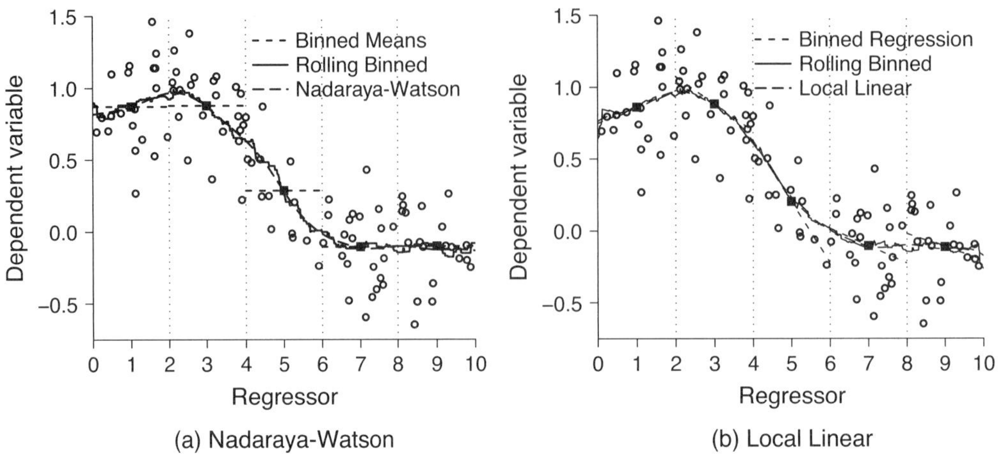

FIGURE 19.1 Nadaraya-Watson and Local Linear regression

of the observations for which X_i is close to x, perhaps for the observations for which $|X_i - x| \leq h$ for some small $h > 0$. As for the case of density estimation, call h a **bandwidth**. This **binned means estimator** can be written as

$$\widehat{m}(x) = \frac{\sum_{i=1}^{n} \mathbb{1}\left\{|X_i - x| \leq h\right\} Y_i}{\sum_{i=1}^{n} \mathbb{1}\left\{|X_i - x| \leq h\right\}}. \tag{19.1}$$

This is an step function estimator of the regression function $m(x)$.

To visualize, Figure 19.1(a) displays a scatter plot of 100 random pairs (Y_i, X_i) generated by simulation. The observations are displayed as open circles. The estimator (19.1) of $m(x)$ at $x = 1$ with $h = 1$ is the average of the Y_i for the observations such that X_i falls in the interval $[0 \leq X_i \leq 2]$. This estimator is $\widehat{m}(1)$ and is shown on Figure 19.1(a) by the first solid square. We repeat the calculation (19.1) for $x = 3$, 5, 7, and 9, which is equivalent to partitioning the support of X into the bins $[0, 2]$, $[2, 4]$, $[4, 6]$, $[6, 8]$, and $[8, 10]$. These bins are shown in Figure 19.1(a) by the vertical dotted lines and the estimates (19.1) by the five solid squares.

The binned estimator $\widehat{m}(x)$ is the step function, which is constant within each bin and equals the binned mean. In Figure 19.1(a), it is displayed by the horizontal dashed lines that pass through the solid squares. This estimate roughly tracks the central tendency of the scatter of the observations (Y_i, X_i). However, the huge jumps at the edges of the partitions are disconcerting, counterintuitive, and clearly an artifact of the discrete binning.

If we take another look at the estimation formula (19.1), there is no reason to evaluate (19.1) only on a course grid. We can evaluate $\widehat{m}(x)$ for any set of values of x. In particular, we can evaluate (19.1) on a fine grid of values of x and thereby obtain a smoother estimate of the CEF. This estimator is displayed in Figure 19.1(a) with the solid line. We call this estimator "Rolling Binned Means." This is a generalization of the binned estimator and by construction passes through the solid squares. It turns out that this is a special case of the Nadaraya-Watson estimator considered in Section 19.3. This estimator, while less abrupt than the Binned Means estimator, is still quite jagged.

19.3 KERNEL REGRESSION

One deficiency of the estimator (19.1) is that it is a step function in x, even when evaluated on a fine grid. That is why its plot in Figure 19.1 is jagged. The source of the discontinuity is that the weights are discontinuous indicator functions. If instead the weights were continuous functions, then $\widehat{m}(x)$ would also be continuous in x. Appropriate weight functions are called kernel functions.

Definition 19.1 A (second-order) **kernel function** $K(u)$ satisfies

1. $0 \le K(u) \le \overline{K} < \infty$.
2. $K(u) = K(-u)$.
3. $\int_{-\infty}^{\infty} K(u)du = 1$.
4. $\int_{-\infty}^{\infty} |u|^r K(u)du < \infty$ for all positive integers r.

Essentially, a kernel function is a bounded probability density function that is symmetric about 0. Assumption 19.1 Part 4 is not essential for most results but is a convenient simplification and does not exclude any kernel function used in standard empirical practice. Some of the mathematical expressions are simplified if we restrict attention to kernels whose variance is normalized to 1.

Definition 19.2 A **normalized kernel function** satisfies $\int_{-\infty}^{\infty} u^2 K(u)du = 1$.

A large number of functions satisfy Definition 19.1, and many are programmed as options in statistical packages. Table 19.1 lists the most important: the Rectangular, Gaussian, Epanechnikov, Triangular, and Biweight kernels. In practice, it is unnecessary to consider kernels beyond these five. For nonparametric regression, I recommend either the Gaussian or Epanechnikov kernel, and either will give similar results. Table 19.1 lists the kernels in normalized form.

For more discussion on kernel functions, see Chapter 17 of *Probability and Statistics for Economists*.

A generalization of (19.1) is obtained by replacing the indicator function with a kernel function:

$$\widehat{m}_{\mathrm{nw}}(x) = \frac{\sum_{i=1}^{n} K\left(\frac{X_i - x}{h}\right) Y_i}{\sum_{i=1}^{n} K\left(\frac{X_i - x}{h}\right)}. \tag{19.2}$$

The estimator (19.2) is known as the **Nadaraya-Watson (NW)** estimator, the **kernel regression** estimator or the **local constant** estimator, and was introduced independently by Nadaraya (1964) and Watson (1964).

The rolling binned means estimator (19.1) is the Nadarya-Watson estimator with the rectangular kernel. The NW estimator (19.2) can be used with any standard kernel and is typically estimated using the Gaussian or Epanechnikov kernel. In general, I recommend the Gaussian kernel, because it produces an estimator $\widehat{m}_{\mathrm{nw}}(x)$ that possesses derivatives of all orders.

The bandwidth h plays a similar role in kernel regression as in kernel density estimation. Namely, larger values of h will result in estimates $\widehat{m}_{\mathrm{nw}}(x)$ that are smoother in x, and smaller values of h will result in estimates that are more erratic. It might be helpful to consider the two extreme cases $h \to 0$ and $h \to \infty$. As $h \to 0$, we can see that $\widehat{m}_{\mathrm{nw}}(X_i) \to Y_i$ (if the values of X_i are unique), so that $\widehat{m}_{\mathrm{nw}}(x)$ is simply the scatter of Y_i on X_i. In contrast, as $h \to \infty$, then $\widehat{m}_{\mathrm{nw}}(x) \to \overline{Y}$, the sample mean. For intermediate values of h, $\widehat{m}_{\mathrm{nw}}(x)$ will smooth between these two extreme cases.

Table 19.1
Common normalized second-order kernels

Kernel	Formula	R_K
Rectangular	$K(u)=\begin{cases}\dfrac{1}{2\sqrt{3}} & \text{if } \lvert u\rvert<\sqrt{3}\\ 0 & \text{otherwise}\end{cases}$	$\dfrac{1}{2\sqrt{3}}$
Gaussian	$K(u)=\dfrac{1}{\sqrt{2\pi}}\exp\left(-\dfrac{u^2}{2}\right)$	$\dfrac{1}{2\sqrt{\pi}}$
Epanechnikov	$K(u)=\begin{cases}\dfrac{3}{4\sqrt{5}}\left(1-\dfrac{u^2}{5}\right) & \text{if } \lvert u\rvert<\sqrt{5}\\ 0 & \text{otherwise}\end{cases}$	$\dfrac{3\sqrt{5}}{25}$
Triangular	$K(u)=\begin{cases}\dfrac{1}{\sqrt{6}}\left(1-\dfrac{\lvert u\rvert}{\sqrt{6}}\right) & \text{if } \lvert u\rvert<\sqrt{6}\\ 0 & \text{otherwise}\end{cases}$	$\dfrac{\sqrt{6}}{9}$
Biweight	$K(u)=\begin{cases}\dfrac{15}{16\sqrt{7}}\left(1-\dfrac{u^2}{7}\right)^2 & \text{if } \lvert u\rvert<\sqrt{7}\\ 0 & \text{otherwise}\end{cases}$	$\dfrac{5\sqrt{7}}{49}$

The estimator (19.2) using the Gaussian kernel and $h=1/\sqrt{3}$ is also displayed in Figure 19.1(a) with the long dashes. As you can see, this estimator appears to be much smoother than the binned estimator but tracks exactly the same path. The bandwidth $h=1/\sqrt{3}$ for the Gaussian kernel is equivalent to the bandwidth $h=1$ for the binned estimator, because the latter is a kernel estimator using the rectangular kernel scaled to have a standard deviation of 1/3.

19.4 LOCAL LINEAR ESTIMATOR

The NW estimator is often called a **local constant** estimator, because it locally (about x) approximates $m(x)$ as a constant function. One way to see this is to observe that $\widehat{m}_{\mathrm{nw}}(x)$ solves the minimization problem

$$\widehat{m}_{\mathrm{nw}}(x)=\underset{m}{\operatorname{argmin}}\sum_{i=1}^{n}K\left(\frac{X_i-x}{h}\right)(Y_i-m)^2.$$

This is a weighted regression of Y on an intercept only. Thus the NW estimator is making the local approximation $m(X)\simeq m(x)$ for $X\simeq x$, which means it is making the approximation

$$Y=m(X)+e\simeq m(x)+e.$$

The NW estimator is a local estimator of this approximate model using weighted least squares.

This interpretation suggests that we can construct alternative nonparametric estimators of $m(x)$ by alternative local approximations. Many such local approximations are possible. A popular choice is the **local linear (LL)** approximation. Instead of the approximation $m(X) \simeq m(x)$, LL uses the linear approximation $m(X) \simeq m(x) + m'(x)\,(X - x)$. Thus

$$Y = m(X) + e \simeq m(x) + m'(x)\,(X - x) + e.$$

The LL estimator then applies weighted least squares similarly as in NW estimation.

One way to represent the LL estimator is as the solution to the minimization problem

$$\left\{\widehat{m}_{\mathrm{LL}}(x), \widehat{m}'_{\mathrm{LL}}(x)\right\} = \underset{\alpha,\beta}{\operatorname{argmin}} \sum_{i=1}^{n} K\left(\frac{X_i - x}{h}\right)(Y_i - \alpha - \beta\,(X_i - x))^2 .$$

Another is to write the approximating model as

$$Y \simeq Z(X, x)'\beta(x) + e$$

where $\beta(x) = \left(m(x), m'(x)\right)'$ and

$$Z(X, x) = \begin{pmatrix} 1 \\ X - x \end{pmatrix}.$$

This is a linear regression with regressor vector $Z_i(x) = Z(X_i, x)$ and coefficient vector $\beta(x)$. Applying weighted least squares with the kernel weights, we obtain the LL estimator

$$\begin{aligned}\widehat{\beta}_{\mathrm{LL}}(x) &= \left(\sum_{i=1}^{n} K\left(\frac{X_i - x}{h}\right) Z_i(x) Z_i(x)'\right)^{-1} \sum_{i=1}^{n} K\left(\frac{X_i - x}{h}\right) Z_i(x) Y_i \\ &= \left(\boldsymbol{Z}'\boldsymbol{K}\boldsymbol{Z}\right)^{-1} \boldsymbol{Z}'\boldsymbol{K}\boldsymbol{Y}\end{aligned}$$

where $\boldsymbol{K} = \operatorname{diag}\{K((X_1 - x)/h), \ldots, K((X_n - x)/h)\}$, $\boldsymbol{Z}$ is the stacked $Z_i(x)'$, and $\boldsymbol{Y}$ is the stacked Y_i. This expression generalizes the NW estimator, as the latter is obtained by setting $Z_i(x) = 1$ or constraining $\beta = 0$. Notice that the matrices $\boldsymbol{Z}$ and $\boldsymbol{K}$ depend on x and h.

The local linear estimator was first suggested by Stone (1977) and came into prominence through the work of Fan (1992, 1993).

To visualize, Figure 19.1(b) displays the scatter plot of the same 100 observations from panel (a) divided into the same five bins. A linear regression is fit to the observations in each bin. These five fitted regression lines are displayed by the short dashed lines. This "binned regression estimator" produces a flexible appromation for the CEF but has large jumps at the boundaries of the partitions. The midpoints of each of these five regression lines are displayed by the solid squares and could be viewed as the target estimate for the binned regression estimator. A rolling version of the binned regression estimator moves these estimation windows continuously across the support of X and is displayed by the solid line. This corresponds to the local linear estimator with a rectangular kernel and a bandwidth of $h = 1/\sqrt{3}$. By construction, this line passes through the solid squares. To obtain a smoother estimator, we can replace the rectangular with the Gaussian kernel (using the same bandwidth $h = 1/\sqrt{3}$). These estimates are displayed with long dashes in the figure. This has the same shape as the rectangular kernel estimate (rolling binned regression) but is visually much smoother. This is called the LL estimator, because it is the standard implementation.

One interesting feature is that as $h \to \infty$, the LL estimator approaches the full-sample least squares estimator $\widehat{m}_{\mathrm{LL}}(x) \to \widehat{\alpha} + \widehat{\beta}x$. That is because as $h \to \infty$, all observations receive equal weight. In this sense, the LL estimator is a flexible generalization of the linear OLS estimator.

Another useful property of the LL estimator is that it simultaneously provides estimates of the regression function $m(x)$ and its slope $m'(x)$ at x.

19.5 LOCAL POLYNOMIAL ESTIMATOR

The NW and LL estimators are both special cases of the **local polynomial estimator**. The idea is to approximate the regression function $m(x)$ by a polynomial of fixed degree p, and then estimate it locally using kernel weights.

The approximating model is a pth order Taylor series approximation

$$\begin{aligned}
Y &= m(X) + e \\
&\simeq m(x) + m'(x)\,(X-x) + \cdots + m^{(p)}(x)\frac{(X-x)^p}{p!} + e \\
&= Z(X,x)'\beta(x) + e_i
\end{aligned}$$

where

$$Z(X,x) = \begin{pmatrix} 1 \\ X-x \\ \vdots \\ \dfrac{(X-x)^p}{p!} \end{pmatrix} \qquad \beta(x) = \begin{pmatrix} m(x) \\ m'(x) \\ \vdots \\ m^{(p)}(x) \end{pmatrix}.$$

The estimator is

$$\begin{aligned}
\widehat{\beta}_{\mathrm{LP}}(x) &= \left(\sum_{i=1}^{n} K\left(\frac{X_i - x}{h}\right) Z_i(x) Z_i(x)'\right)^{-1} \left(\sum_{i=1}^{n} K\left(\frac{Y_i - x}{h}\right) Z_i(x) Y_i\right) \\
&= \left(\boldsymbol{Z}'\boldsymbol{K}\boldsymbol{Z}\right)^{-1} \boldsymbol{Z}'\boldsymbol{K}\boldsymbol{Y}
\end{aligned}$$

where $Z_i(x) = Z(X_i, x)$. Notice that this expression includes the NW and LL estimators as special cases with $p=0$ and $p=1$, respectively.

There is a tradeoff between the polynomial order p and the local smoothing bandwidth h. By increasing p, we improve the model approximation and thereby can use a larger bandwidth h. However, increasing p increases estimation variance.

19.6 ASYMPTOTIC BIAS

Since $\mathbb{E}[Y \mid X = x] = m(x)$, the conditional expectation of the NW estimator is

$$\mathbb{E}\left[\widehat{m}_{\mathrm{nw}}(x) \mid \boldsymbol{X}\right] = \frac{\sum_{i=1}^{n} K\left(\frac{X_i - x}{h}\right) \mathbb{E}[Y_i \mid X_i]}{\sum_{i=1}^{n} K\left(\frac{X_i - x}{h}\right)} = \frac{\sum_{i=1}^{n} K\left(\frac{X_i - x}{h}\right) m(X_i)}{\sum_{i=1}^{n} K\left(\frac{X_i - x}{h}\right)}. \tag{19.3}$$

We can simplify this expression as $n \to \infty$.

The following regularity conditions will be maintained through the chapter. Let $f(x)$ denote the marginal density of X, and let $\sigma^2(x) = \mathbb{E}\left[e^2 \mid X = x\right]$ denote the conditional variance of $e = Y - m(X)$.

Assumption 19.1

1. $h \to 0$.
2. $nh \to \infty$.
3. $m(x), f(x)$, and $\sigma^2(x)$ are continuous in some neighborhood $\mathcal{N}$ of x.
4. $f(x) > 0$.

These conditions are similar to those used for the asymptotic theory for kernel density estimation. The assumptions $h \to 0$ and $nh \to \infty$ mean that the bandwidth gets small yet the number of observations in the estimation window diverges to infinity. Assumption 19.1 Part 3 states are minimal smoothness conditions on the conditional expectation $m(x)$, marginal density $f(x)$, and conditional variance $\sigma^2(x)$. Assumption 19.1 Part 4 specifies that the marginal density is nonzero. This is required, because we are estimating the conditional expectation at x, so there needs to be a nontrivial number of observations for X_i near x.

Theorem 19.1 Suppose Assumption 19.1 holds and $m''(x)$ and $f'(x)$ are continuous in $\mathcal{N}$. Then as $nh \to \infty$ with $h \to 0$,

1. $\mathbb{E}\left[\widehat{m}_{\text{nw}}(x) \mid \boldsymbol{X}\right] = m(x) + h^2 B_{\text{nw}}(x) + o_p\left(h^2\right) + O_p\left(\sqrt{\frac{h}{n}}\right)$ where
$$B_{\text{nw}}(x) = \frac{1}{2} m''(x) + f(x)^{-1} f'(x) m'(x).$$
2. $\mathbb{E}\left[\widehat{m}_{\text{LL}}(x) \mid \boldsymbol{X}\right] = m(x) + h^2 B_{\text{LL}}(x) + o_p\left(h^2\right) + O_p\left(\sqrt{\frac{h}{n}}\right)$ where
$$B_{\text{LL}}(x) = \frac{1}{2} m''(x).$$

The proof for the NW estimator is presented in Section 19.26. For a proof for the local linear estimator, see Fan and Gijbels (1996).

We call the terms $h^2 B_{\text{nw}}(x)$ and $h^2 B_{\text{LL}}(x)$ the **asymptotic bias** of the estimators.

Theorem 19.1 shows that the asymptotic bias of the NW and LL estimators is proportional to the squared bandwidth h^2 (the degree of smoothing) and to the functions $B_{\text{nw}}(x)$ and $B_{\text{LL}}(x)$. The asymptotic bias of the LL estimator depends on the curvature (second derivative) of the CEF function $m(x)$, similarly to the asymptotic bias of the kernel density estimator in Theorem 17.1 of *Probability and Statistics for Economists.* When $m''(x) < 0$, then $\widehat{m}_{\text{LL}}(x)$ is downward biased. When $m''(x) > 0$, then $\widehat{m}_{\text{LL}}(x)$ is upward biased. Local averaging smooths $m(x)$, inducing bias, and this bias is increasing in the level of curvature of $m(x)$. It is called **smoothing bias**.

The asymptotic bias of the NW estimator adds a second term that depends on the first derivatives of $m(x)$ and $f(x)$, because the NW estimator is a local average. If the density is upward sloping at x (if $f'(x) > 0$), then there are (on average) more observations to the right of x than to the left, so a local average will be biased if $m(x)$ has nonzero slope. In contrast, the bias of the local linear estimator does not depend on the local slope

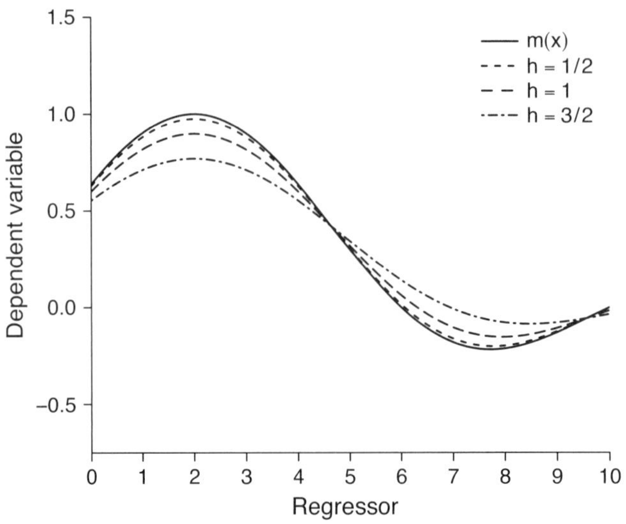

FIGURE 19.2 Smoothing bias

$m'(x)$, because it locally fits a linear regression. That the bias of the LL estimator has fewer terms than the bias of the NW estimator (and is invariant to the slope $m'(x)$) justifies the claim that the local linear estimator has generically reduced bias relative to NW.

Figure 19.2 illustrates asymptotic smoothing bias. The solid line is the true CEF for the data displayed in Figure 19.1. The dashed lines are the asymptotic approximations to the expectation $m(x) + h^2 B(x)$ for bandwidths $h = 1/2$, $h = 1$, and $h = 3/2$. (The asymptotic biases of the NW and LL estimators are the same, because X has a uniform distribution.) You can see that there is minimal bias for the smallest bandwidth but considerable bias for the largest. The dashed lines are smoothed versions of the CEF, attenuating the peaks and valleys.

Smoothing bias is a natural by-product of nonparametric estimation of nonlinear functions. It can only be reduced by using a small bandwidth. As we shall see in Section 19.7, this will result in high estimation variance.

19.7 ASYMPTOTIC VARIANCE

From (19.3) we deduce that

$$\widehat{m}_{\mathrm{nw}}(x) - \mathbb{E}\left[\widehat{m}_{\mathrm{nw}}(x) \mid \boldsymbol{X}\right] = \frac{\sum_{i=1}^{n} K\left(\frac{X_i - x}{h}\right) e_i}{\sum_{i=1}^{n} K\left(\frac{X_i - x}{h}\right)}.$$

Since the denominator is a function only of X_i and the numerator is linear in e_i, we can calculate that the finite sample variance of $\widehat{m}_{\mathrm{nw}}(x)$ is

$$\operatorname{var}\left[\widehat{m}_{\mathrm{nw}}(x) \mid \boldsymbol{X}\right] = \frac{\sum_{i=1}^{n} K\left(\frac{X_i - x}{h}\right)^2 \sigma^2(X_i)}{\left(\sum_{i=1}^{n} K\left(\frac{X_i - x}{h}\right)\right)^2}. \tag{19.4}$$

We can simplify this expression as $n \to \infty$. Let $\sigma^2(x) = \mathbb{E}\left[e^2 \mid X = x\right]$ denote the conditional variance of $e = Y - m(X)$.

Theorem 19.2 Under Assumption 19.1,

1. $\operatorname{var}\left[\widehat{m}_{\mathrm{nw}}(x) \mid \boldsymbol{X}\right] = \dfrac{R_K \sigma^2(x)}{f(x) nh} + o_p\left(\dfrac{1}{nh}\right).$
2. $\operatorname{var}\left[\widehat{m}_{\mathrm{LL}}(x) \mid \boldsymbol{X}\right] = \dfrac{R_K \sigma^2(x)}{f(x) nh} + o_p\left(\dfrac{1}{nh}\right).$

In these expressions,

$$R_K = \int_{-\infty}^{\infty} K(u)^2 du$$

is the **roughness** of the kernel $K(u)$.

The proof for the NW estimator is presented in Section 19.26. For the local linear estimator, see Fan and Gijbels (1996).

We call the leading terms in Theorem 19.2 the **asymptotic variance** of the estimators. Theorem 19.2 shows that the asymptotic variances of the two estimators are identical. The asymptotic variance is proportional to the roughness R_K of the kernel $K(u)$ and to the conditional variance $\sigma^2(x)$ of the regression error. It is inversely proportional to the effective number of observations nh and to the marginal density $f(x)$. This expression reflects the fact that the estimators are local estimators. The precision of $\widehat{m}(x)$ is low for regions where e has a large conditional variance and/or X has a low density (where there are relatively few observations).

19.8 AIMSE

We define the **asymptotic MSE (AMSE)** of an estimator $\widehat{m}(x)$ as the sum of its squared asymptotic bias and asymptotic variance. Using Theorems 19.1 and 19.2 for the NW and LL estimators, we obtain

$$\mathrm{AMSE}\,(x) \stackrel{\mathrm{def}}{=} h^4 B(x)^2 + \frac{R_K \sigma^2(x)}{nhf(x)}$$

where $B(x) = B_{\mathrm{nw}}(x)$ for the NW estimator and $B(x) = B_{\mathrm{LL}}(x)$ for the LL estimator. This is the asymptotic MSE for the estimator $\widehat{m}(x)$ for a single point x.

A global measure of fit can be obtained by integrating AMSE(x). It is standard to weight the AMSE by $f(x)w(x)$ for some integrable weight function $w(x)$. The result is called the **asymptotic integrated MSE (AIMSE)**. Let S be the support of X (the region where $f(x) > 0$):

$$\mathrm{AIMSE} \stackrel{\mathrm{def}}{=} \int_S \mathrm{AMSE}\,(x) f(x) w(x) dx = \int_S \left(h^4 B(x)^2 + \frac{R_K \sigma^2(x)}{nhf(x)} \right) f(x) w(x) dx = h^4 \overline{B} + \frac{R_K}{nh} \overline{\sigma}^2 \tag{19.5}$$

where

$$\overline{B} = \int_S B(x)^2 f(x) w(x) dx$$

$$\overline{\sigma}^2 = \int_S \sigma^2(x) w(x) dx.$$

The weight function $w(x)$ can be omitted if S is bounded. Otherwise, a common choice is $w(x) = \mathbb{1}\{\xi_1 \le x \le \xi_2\}$. An integrable weight function is needed when X has unbounded support to ensure that $\overline{\sigma}^2 < \infty$.

The form of the AIMSE is similar to that for kernel density estimation (Theorem 17.3 of *Probability and Statistics for Economists*). It has two terms (squared bias and variance). The first is increasing in the bandwidth h, and the second is decreasing in h. Thus the choice of h affects AIMSE with a tradeoff between these two components. Similarly to density estimation, we can calculate the bandwidth that minimizes the AIMSE. (See Exercise 19.2.) The solution is given in the following theorem.

Theorem 19.3 The bandwidth that minimizes the AIMSE (19.5) is

$$h_0 = \left(\frac{R_K \overline{\sigma}^2}{4\overline{B}}\right)^{1/5} n^{-1/5}. \tag{19.6}$$

For $h \sim n^{-1/5}$, $\text{AIMSE}\left[\widehat{m}(x)\right] = O\left(n^{-4/5}\right)$.

This result characterizes the AIMSE-optimal bandwidth. This bandwidth satisfies the rate $h = cn^{-1/5}$, which is the same rate as for kernel density estimation. The optimal constant c depends on the kernel $K(x)$, the weighted average squared bias $\overline{B}$, and the weighted average variance $\overline{\sigma}^2$. The constant c is different, however, from that for density estimation.

Inserting (19.6) into (19.5) plus some algebra, we find that the AIMSE using the optimal bandwidth is

$$\text{AIMSE}_0 \simeq 1.65 \left(R_K^4 \overline{B} \overline{\sigma}^8\right)^{1/5} n^{-4/5}.$$

This expression depends on the kernel $K(u)$ only through the constant R_K. Since the Epanechnikov kernel has the smallest value[1] of R_K, it is also the kernel that produces the smallest AIMSE. This is true for both the NW and LL estimators.

Theorem 19.4 The AIMSE (19.5) of the NW and LL regression estimators is minimized by the Epanechnikov kernel.

The efficiency loss by using the other standard kernels, however, is small. The relative efficiency[2] of estimation using the another kernel is $\left(R_K / R_K \left(\text{Epanechnikov}\right)\right)^{2/5}$. Using the values of R_K from Table 19.1, we calculate that the efficiency losses from using the triangle, Gaussian, and rectangular kernels are 1%, 2%, and 3%, respectively, which are minimal. Since the Gaussian kernel produces the smoothest estimates, which is important for estimation of marginal effects, my overall recommendation is the Gaussian kernel.

---

[1] See Theorem 17.4 of *Probability and Statistics for Economists.*

[2] Measured by the square root of AIMSE.

19.9 REFERENCE BANDWIDTH

The NW, LL, and LP estimators depend on a bandwidth, and without an empirical rule for selection of h, the methods are incomplete. It is useful to have a reference bandwith that mimics the optimal bandwidth in a simplified setting and provides a baseline for further investigations.

Theorem 19.3 and a little rewriting reveals that the optimal bandwidth equals

$$h_0 = \left(\frac{R_K}{4}\right)^{1/5}\left(\frac{\overline{\sigma}^2}{n\overline{B}}\right)^{1/5} \simeq 0.58\left(\frac{\overline{\sigma}^2}{n\overline{B}}\right)^{1/5} \tag{19.7}$$

where the approximation holds for all single-peaked kernels by similar calculations,[3] as in Section 17.9 of *Probability and Statistics for Economists.*

A reference approach can be used to develop a rule-of-thumb for regression estimation. In particular, Fan and Gijbels (1996, Section 4.2) develop what they call the ROT (rule of thumb) bandwidth for the local linear estimator. I now describe their derivation.

First, set $w(x) = \mathbb{1}\{\xi_1 \le x \le \xi_2\}$. Second, form a pilot or preliminary estimator of the regression function $m(x)$ using a qth-order polynomial regression

$$m(x) = \beta_0 + \beta_1 x + \beta_2 x^2 + \cdots + \beta_q x^q$$

for $q \ge 2$. (Fan and Gijbels (1996) suggest $q = 4$, but this is not essential.) By least squares, we obtain the coefficient estimates $\widehat{\beta}_0, \ldots, \widehat{\beta}_q$ and implied second derivative $\widehat{m}''(x) = 2\widehat{\beta}_2 + 6\widehat{\beta}_3 x + 12\widehat{\beta}_4 x^2 + \cdots + q(q-1)\widehat{\beta}_q x^{q-2}$. Third, notice that $\overline{B}$ can be written as an expectation:

$$\overline{B} = \mathbb{E}\left[B(X)^2 w(X)\right] = \mathbb{E}\left[\left(\frac{1}{2}m''(X)\right)^2 \mathbb{1}\{\xi_1 \le X \le \xi_2\}\right].$$

A moment estimator is

$$\widehat{B} = \frac{1}{n}\sum_{i=1}^{n}\left(\frac{1}{2}\widehat{m}''(X_i)\right)^2 \mathbb{1}\{\xi_1 \le X_i \le \xi_2\}. \tag{19.8}$$

Fourth, assume that the regression error is homoskedastic $\mathbb{E}\left[e^2 \mid X\right] = \sigma^2$, so that $\overline{\sigma}^2 = \sigma^2(\xi_2 - \xi_1)$. Estimate σ^2 by the error variance estimate $\widehat{\sigma}^2$ from the preliminary regression. Plugging these into (19.7), we obtain the reference bandwidth

$$h_{\text{rot}} = 0.58\left(\frac{\widehat{\sigma}^2(\xi_2 - \xi_1)}{n\widehat{B}}\right)^{1/5}. \tag{19.9}$$

Fan and Gijbels (1996) call this the **Rule-of-Thumb (ROT) bandwidth**.

Fan and Gijbels developed similar rules for higher-order odd local polynomial estimators but not for the local constant (NW) estimator. However, we can derive a ROT for the NW as well by using a reference model for the marginal density $f(x)$. A convenient choice is uniform density, for which $f'(x) = 0$, and the optimal bandwidths for NW and LL coincide. This motivates using (19.9) as a ROT bandwidth for both the LL and NW estimators.

As mentioned above, Fan and Gijbels suggest using a fourth-order polynomial for the pilot estimator, but this specific choice is not essential. In applications, it may be prudent to assess sensitivity of the ROT bandwith

[3]The constant $(R_K/4)^{1/5}$ is bounded between 0.58 and 0.59.

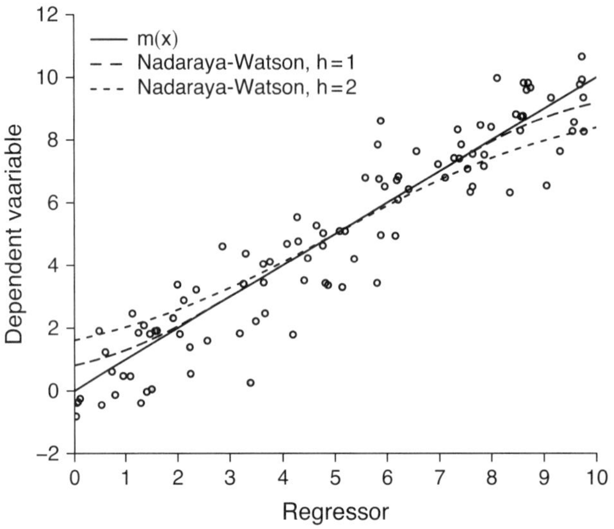

FIGURE 19.3 Boundary bias

to the choice of q and to examine the estimated pilot regression for precision of the estimated higher-order polynomial terms.

Consider the choice of the weight region $[\xi_1, \xi_2]$. When X has bounded support, then $[\xi_1, \xi_2]$ can be set equal to this support. Otherwise, $[\xi_1, \xi_2]$ can be set equal to the region of interest for $\widehat{m}(x)$, or the endpoints can be set to equal fixed quantiles (e.g., 0.05 and 0.95) of the distribution of X.

To illustrate, consider the data shown in Figure 19.1. If we fit a fourth order polynomial, we find $\widehat{m}(x) = .49 + .70x - .28x^2 - .033x^3 - .0012x^4$, which implies $\widehat{m}''(x) = -.56 - .20x - .014x^2$. Setting $[\xi_1, \xi_2] = [0, 10]$ from the support of X, we find $\widehat{B} = 0.00889$. The residuals from the polynomial regression have variance $\widehat{\sigma}^2 = 0.0687$. Plugging these into (19.9), we find $h_{\text{rot}} = 0.551$, which is similar to the value used in Figure 19.1.

19.10 ESTIMATION AT A BOUNDARY

One advantage of the LL over the NW estimator is that the LL has better performance at the boundary of the support of X. The NW estimator has excessive smoothing bias near the boundaries. In many contexts in econometrics, the boundaries are of great interest. In such cases, it is strongly recommended to use the LL estimator (or a local polynomial estimator with $p \geq 1$).

To understand the problem, it may be helpful to examine Figure 19.3. This figure shows a scatter plot of 100 observations generated as $X \sim U[0, 10]$ and $Y \sim \mathrm{N}(X, 1)$, so that $m(x) = x$. Suppose we are interested in the CEF $m(0)$ at the lower boundary $x = 0$. The NW estimator equals a weighted average of the Y observations for small values of $|X|$. Since $X \geq 0$, these are all observations for which $m(X) \geq m(0)$, and therefore $\widehat{m}_{\text{nw}}(0)$ is biased upward. Symmetrically, the NW estimator at the upper boundary $x = 10$ is a weighted average of observations for which $m(X) \leq m(10)$ and therefore, $\widehat{m}_{\text{nw}}(10)$ is biased downward.

In contrast, the LL estimators $\widehat{m}_{\text{LL}}(0)$ and $\widehat{m}_{\text{LL}}(10)$ are unbiased in this example, because $m(x)$ is linear in x. The LL estimator fits a linear regression line. Since the expectation is correctly specified, there is no estimation bias.

The exact bias[4] of the NW estimator is shown in Figure 19.3 by the dashed lines. The long dashes show the expectation $\mathbb{E}\left[\widehat{m}_{\mathrm{nw}}(x)\right]$ for $h=1$, and the short dashes display the expectation $\mathbb{E}\left[\widehat{m}_{\mathrm{nw}}(x)\right]$ for $h=2$. We can see that the bias is substantial. For $h=2$, the bias is visible for all values of x. For the smaller bandwidth $h=1$, the bias is minimal for x in the central range of the support but is still quite substantial for x near the boundaries.

To calculate the asymptotic smoothing bias, let us revisit the proof of Theorem 19.1 Part 1, which calculates the asymptotic bias at interior points. Equation (19.29) calculates the bias of the numerator of the estimator expressed as an integral over the marginal density. Evaluated at a lower boundary, the density is positive only for $u \geq 0$, so the integral is over the positive region $[0,\infty)$. This applies as well to equation (19.31) and the equations that follow. In this case, the leading term of this expansion is the first term in (19.32), which is proportional to h rather than h^2. Completing the calculations, we find the following. Define $m(x+) = \lim_{z\downarrow x} m(z)$, and $m(x-) = \lim_{z\uparrow x} m(z)$.

Theorem 19.5 *Suppose Assumption 19.1 holds. Set $\mu_K = 2\int_0^\infty K(u)du$. Let the support of X be $S=[\underline{x},\overline{x}]$.*

If $m''(\underline{x}+)$, $\sigma^2(\underline{x}+)$ and $f'(\underline{x}+)$ exist, and $f(\underline{x}+)>0$, then

$$\mathbb{E}\left[\widehat{m}_{\mathrm{nw}}(\underline{x}) \mid \boldsymbol{X}\right] = m(\underline{x}) + hm'(\underline{x})\mu_K + o_p(h) + O_p\left(\sqrt{\frac{h}{n}}\right).$$

If $m''(\overline{x}-)$, $\sigma^2(\overline{x}-)$ and $f'(\overline{x}-)$ exist, and $f(\overline{x}-)>0$ then

$$\mathbb{E}\left[\widehat{m}_{\mathrm{nw}}(\overline{x}) \mid \boldsymbol{X}\right] = m(\overline{x}) - hm'(\overline{x})\mu_K + o_p(h) + O_p\left(\sqrt{\frac{h}{n}}\right).$$

Theorem 19.5 shows that the asymptotic bias of the NW estimator at the boundary is $O(h)$ and depends on the slope of $m(x)$ at the boundary. When the slope is positive, the NW estimator is upward biased at the lower boundary and downward biased at the upper boundary. The standard interpretation of Theorem 19.5 is that the NW estimator has high bias near boundary points.

Similarly, we can evaluate the performance of the LL estimator. I summarize the results without derivation (as they are more technically challenging) and instead refer interested readers to Cheng, Fan, and Marron (1997) and Imbens and Kalyanaraman (2012).

Define the kernel moments $\nu_j = \int_0^\infty u^j K(u)du$, $\pi_j = \int_0^\infty u^j K(u)^2 du$, and projected kernel

$$K^*(u) = \begin{bmatrix} 1 & 0 \end{bmatrix} \begin{bmatrix} \nu_0 & \nu_1 \\ \nu_1 & \nu_2 \end{bmatrix}^{-1} \begin{bmatrix} 1 \\ u \end{bmatrix} K(u) = \frac{\nu_2 - \nu_1 u}{\nu_0\nu_2 - \nu_1^2} K(u).$$

Define its second moment

$$\sigma_{K^*}^2 = \int_0^\infty u^2 K^*(u)du = \frac{\nu_2^2 - \nu_1\nu_3}{\nu_0\nu_2 - \nu_1^2}$$

and roughness

$$R_K^* = \int_0^\infty K^*(u)^2 du = \frac{\nu_2^2\pi_0 - 2\nu_1\nu_2\pi_1 + \nu_1^2\pi_2}{\left(\nu_0\nu_2 - \nu_1^2\right)^2}.$$

[4] Calculated by simulation from 10,000 simulation replications.

Theorem 19.6 Under the assumptions of Theorem 19.5, at a boundary point $\underline{x}$,

1. $\mathbb{E}\left[\widehat{m}_{\mathrm{LL}}(\underline{x}) \mid \boldsymbol{X}\right] = m(\underline{x}) + \dfrac{h^2 m''(\underline{x})\sigma_{K*}^2}{2} + o_p\left(h^2\right) + O_p\left(\sqrt{\frac{h}{n}}\right).$
2. $\operatorname{var}\left[\widehat{m}_{\mathrm{LL}}(\underline{x}) \mid \boldsymbol{X}\right] = \dfrac{R_K^* \sigma^2(\underline{x})}{f(\underline{x})nh} + o_p\left(\dfrac{1}{nh}\right).$

Theorem 19.6 shows that the asymptotic bias of the LL estimator at a boundary is $O(h^2)$, the same as at interior points and is invariant to the slope of $m(x)$. The theorem also shows that the asymptotic variance has the same rate as at interior points.

Taking Theorems 19.1, 19.2, 19.5, and 19.6 together, we conclude that the LL estimator has superior asymptotic properties relative to the NW estimator. At interior points, the two estimators have the same asymptotic variance. The bias of the LL estimator is invariant to the slope of $m(x)$, and its asymptotic bias only depends on the second derivative, whereas the bias of the NW estimator depends on both the first and second derivatives. At boundary points, the asymptotic bias of the NW estimator is $O(h)$ which is of higher order than the $O(h^2)$ bias of the LL estimator. For these reasons, I recommend the LL estimator over the NW estimator. A similar argument can be made to recommend the local cubic estimator, but this is not widely used.

The asymptotic bias and variance of the LL estimator at the boundary is slightly different than in the interior. The difference is that the bias and variance depend on the moments of the kernel-like function $K^*(u)$ rather than the original kernel $K(u)$.

An interesting problem is to find the optimal kernel function for boundary estimation. By the same calculations as for Theorem 19.4, we find that the optimal kernel $K^*(u)$ minimizes the roughness R_K^*, given the second moment σ_{K*}^2, and as argued for Theorem 19.4, this is achieved when $K^*(u)$ equals a quadratic function in u. Because $K^*(u)$ is the product of $K(u)$ and a linear function, then $K(u)$ must be linear in $|u|$, implying that the optimal kernel $K(u)$ is the triangular kernel. See Cheng, Fan, and Marron (1997). Calculations similar to those following Theorem 19.4 show that efficiency loss[5] of estimation using the Epanechnikov, Gaussian, and rectangular kernels are 1%, 1%, and 3%, respectively.

19.11 NONPARAMETRIC RESIDUALS AND PREDICTION ERRORS

Given any nonparametric regression estimator $\widehat{m}(x)$, the fitted regression at $x = X_i$ is $\widehat{m}(X_i)$, and the fitted residual is $\widehat{e}_i = Y_i - \widehat{m}(X_i)$. As a general rule (but especially when the bandwidth h is small), it is hard to view $\widehat{e}_i$ as a good measure of the fit of the regression. For the NW and LL estimators, as $h \to 0$, $\widehat{m}(X_i) \to Y_i$ and therefore $\widehat{e}_i \to 0$. This is clearly overfitting, as the true error e_i is not 0. In general, because $\widehat{m}(X_i)$ is a local average that includes Y_i, the fitted value necessarily will be close to Y_i and the residual $\widehat{e}_i$ small, and the degree of this overfitting increases as h decreases.

A standard solution is to measure the fit of the regression at $x = X_i$ by re-estimating the model excluding the ith observation. Let $\widetilde{m}_{-i}(x)$ be the leave-one-out nonparametric estimator computed without observation i. For example, for NW regression, this is

[5] Measured by root AIMSE.

$$\widetilde{Y}_i = \widetilde{m}_{-i}(x) = \frac{\sum_{j \neq i} K\left(\frac{X_j - x}{h}\right) Y_j}{\sum_{j \neq i} K\left(\frac{X_j - x}{h}\right)}.$$

Notationally, the "$-i$" subscript is used to indicate that the ith observation is omitted.

The leave-one-out predicted value for Y_i at $x = X_i$ is $\widetilde{Y}_i = \widetilde{m}_{-i}(X_i)$, and the leave-one-out prediction error is

$$\widetilde{e}_i = Y_i - \widetilde{Y}_i. \tag{19.10}$$

Because $\widetilde{Y}_i$ is not a function of Y_i, there is no tendency for $\widetilde{Y}_i$ to overfit for small h. Consequently, $\widetilde{e}_i$ is a good measure of the fit of the estimated nonparametric regression.

When possible, the leave-one-out prediction errors should be used instead of the residuals $\widehat{e}_i$.

19.12 CROSS-VALIDATION BANDWIDTH SELECTION

The most popular method in applied statistics to select bandwidths is cross-validation. The general idea is to estimate the model fit based on leave-one-out estimation. Here we describe the method as typically applied for regression estimation. The method applies to NW, LL, and LP estimation, as well as to other nonparametric estimators.

To be explicit about the dependence of the estimator on the bandwidth, let us write an estimator of $m(x)$ with a given bandwidth h as $\widehat{m}(x, h)$.

Ideally, we would like to select h to minimize the **integrated mean-squared error (IMSE)** of $\widehat{m}(x, h)$ as a estimator of $m(x)$:

$$\text{IMSE}_n(h) = \int_S \mathbb{E}\left[(\widehat{m}(x, h) - m(x))^2\right] f(x) w(x) dx$$

where $f(x)$ is the marginal density of X, and $w(x)$ is an integrable weight function. The weight $w(x)$ is the same as that used in (19.5) and can be omitted when X has bounded support.

The difference $\widehat{m}(x, h) - m(x)$ at $x = X_i$ can be estimated by the leave-one-out prediction errors (19.10):

$$\widetilde{e}_i(h) = Y_i - \widetilde{m}_{-i}(X_i, h)$$

where we are being explicit about the dependence on the bandwidth h. A reasonable estimator of $\text{IMSE}_n(h)$ is the weighted average mean squared prediction errors:

$$\text{CV}(h) = \frac{1}{n} \sum_{i=1}^{n} \widetilde{e}_i(h)^2 w(X_i). \tag{19.11}$$

This function of h is known as the **cross-validation criterion**. Once again, if X has bounded support, then the weights $w(X_i)$ can be omitted, and this is typically done in practice.

It turns out that the cross-validation criterion is an unbiased estimator of the IMSE plus a constant for a sample with $n - 1$ observations.

Theorem 19.7

$$\mathbb{E}\left[\text{CV}(h)\right] = \overline{\sigma}^2 + \text{IMSE}_{n-1}(h) \tag{19.12}$$

where $\overline{\sigma}^2 = \mathbb{E}\left[e^2 w(X)\right]$.

The proof of Theorem 19.7 is presented in Section 19.26.

Since $\overline{\sigma}^2$ is a constant independent of the bandwidth h, $\mathbb{E}[\mathrm{CV}(h)]$ is a shifted version of $\mathrm{IMSE}_{n-1}(h)$. In particular, the h that minimizes $\mathbb{E}[\mathrm{CV}(h)]$ and $\mathrm{IMSE}_{n-1}(h)$ are identical. When n is large, the bandwidth that minimizes $\mathrm{IMSE}_{n-1}(h)$ and $\mathrm{IMSE}_n(h)$ are nearly identical, so $\mathrm{CV}(h)$ is essentially unbiased as an estimator of $\mathrm{IMSE}_n(h)+\overline{\sigma}^2$. This considerations leads to the recommendation to select h as the value that minimizes $\mathrm{CV}(h)$.

The cross-validation bandwidth h_{cv} is the value that minimizes $\mathrm{CV}(h)$

$$h_{\mathrm{cv}} = \underset{h \geq h_\ell}{\operatorname{argmin}}\, \mathrm{CV}(h) \tag{19.13}$$

for some $h_\ell > 0$. The restriction $h \geq h_\ell$ can be imposed so that $\mathrm{CV}(h)$ is not evaluated over unreasonably small bandwidths.

There is not an explicit solution to the minimization problem (19.13), so it must be solved numerically. One method is grid search. Create a grid of values for h (e.g., $[h_1, h_2, \ldots, h_J]$), evaluate $\mathrm{CV}(h_j)$ for $j = 1, \ldots, J$, and set

$$h_{\mathrm{cv}} = \underset{h \in [h_1, h_2, \ldots, h_J]}{\operatorname{argmin}} \quad \mathrm{CV}(h).$$

Evaluation using a coarse grid is typically sufficient for practical applications. Plots of $\mathrm{CV}(h)$ against h are a useful diagnostic tool to verify that the minimum of $\mathrm{CV}(h)$ has been obtained. A computationally more efficient method for obtaining the solution (19.13) is Golden-Section Search. See Section 12.4 of *Probability and Statistics for Economists*.

It is possible for the solution (19.13) to be unbounded, that is, $\mathrm{CV}(h)$ is decreasing for large h, so that $h_{\mathrm{cv}} = \infty$. This is okay. It simply means that the regression estimator simplifies to its full-sample version. For NW estimator, this is $\widehat{m}_{\mathrm{nw}}(x) = \overline{Y}$. For the LL estimator it is $\widehat{m}_{\mathrm{LL}}(x) = \widehat{\alpha} + \widehat{\beta} x$.

For NW and LL estimation, the criterion (19.11) requires leave-one-out estimation of the conditional mean at each observation X_i. This is different from calculation of the estimator $\widehat{m}(x)$, as the latter is typically done at a set of fixed values of x for purposes of display.

To illustrate, Figure 19.4(a) displays the cross-validation criteria $\mathrm{CV}(h)$ for the NW and LL estimators using the data from Figure 19.1, both estimators using the Gaussian kernel. The CV functions are computed on a grid on $[h_{\mathrm{rot}}/3, 3h_{\mathrm{rot}}]$ with 200 gridpoints. The CV-minimizing bandwidths are $h_{\mathrm{nw}} = 0.830$ for the NW estimator and $h_{\mathrm{LL}} = 0.764$ for the LL estimator. These are somewhat higher than the rule of thumb $h_{\mathrm{rot}} = 0.551$ value calculated earlier. Figure 19.4(a) marks the minimizing bandwidths by the arrows.

The CV criterion can also be used to select between different nonparametric estimators. The CV-selected estimator is the one with the lowest minimized CV criterion. For example, in Figure 19.4(a), you can see that the LL estimator has a minimized CV criterion of 0.0699, which is lower than the minimum 0.0703 obtained by the NW estimator. Since the LL estimator achieves a lower value of the CV criterion, LL is the CV-selected estimator. The difference, however, is small, indicating that the two estimators achieve similar IMSE.

Figure 19.4(b) displays the local linear estimates $\widehat{m}(x)$ using the ROT and CV bandwidths along with the true conditional mean $m(x)$. The estimators track the true function quite well, and the difference between the bandwidths is relatively minor in this application.

19.13 ASYMPTOTIC DISTRIBUTION

We first provide a consistency result.

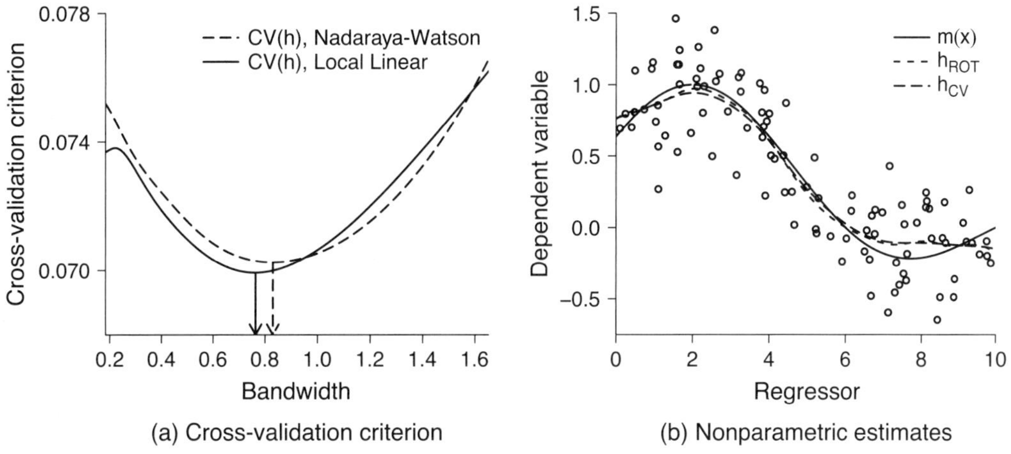

FIGURE 19.4 Bandwidth selection

Theorem 19.8 Under Assumption 19.1, $\widehat{m}_{\mathrm{nw}}(x) \underset{p}{\longrightarrow} m(x)$ and $\widehat{m}_{\mathrm{LL}}(x) \underset{p}{\longrightarrow} m(x)$.

A proof for the NW estimator is presented in Section 19.26. For the LL estimator, see Fan and Gijbels (1996).

Theorem 19.8 shows that the estimators are consistent for $m(x)$ under mild continuity assumptions. In particular, no smoothness conditions on $m(x)$ are required beyond continuity.

We next discuss an asymptotic distribution result. The following shows that the kernel regression estimators are asymptotically normal with a nonparametric rate of convergence, a nontrivial asymptotic bias, and a nondegenerate asymptotic variance.

Theorem 19.9 Suppose Assumption 19.1 holds. Assume in addition that $m''(x)$ and $f'(x)$ are continuous in $\mathscr{N}$, that for some $r > 2$ and $x \in \mathscr{N}$,

$$\mathbb{E}\left[|e|^r \mid X = x\right] \leq \overline{\sigma} < \infty \tag{19.14}$$

and

$$nh^5 = O(1). \tag{19.15}$$

Then

$$\sqrt{nh}\left(\widehat{m}_{\mathrm{nw}}(x) - m(x) - h^2 B_{\mathrm{nw}}(x)\right) \underset{d}{\longrightarrow} \mathrm{N}\left(0, \frac{R_K \sigma^2(x)}{f(x)}\right). \tag{19.16}$$

Similarly,

$$\sqrt{nh}\left(\widehat{m}_{\mathrm{LL}}(x) - m(x) - h^2 B_{\mathrm{LL}}(x)\right) \underset{d}{\longrightarrow} \mathrm{N}\left(0, \frac{R_K \sigma^2(x)}{f(x)}\right).$$

A proof for the NW estimator appears in Section 19.26. For the LL estimator, see Fan and Gijbels (1996).

Relative to Theorem 19.8, Theorem 19.9 requires stronger smoothness conditions on the conditional mean and marginal density. There are also two technical regularity conditions. The first is a conditional moment bound (19.14) (which is used to verify the Lindeberg condition for the CLT), and the second is the bandwidth bound $nh^5 = O(1)$. The latter means that the bandwidth must decline to 0 at least at the rate $n^{-1/5}$ and is used[6] to ensure that higher-order bias terms do not enter the asymptotic distribution (19.16).

Several interesting features of the asymptotic distribution are noticeably different than for parametric estimators. First, the estimators converge at the rate $\sqrt{nh}$, not $\sqrt{n}$. Since $h \to 0$, $\sqrt{nh}$ diverges slower than $\sqrt{n}$, thus the nonparametric estimators converge more slowly than a parametric estimator. Second, the asymptotic distribution contains a nonnegligible bias term $h^2 B(x)$. Third, the distribution (19.16) is identical in form to that for the kernel density estimator (Theorem 17.7 of *Probability and Statistics for Economists*).

The fact that the estimators converge at the rate $\sqrt{nh}$ has led to the interpretation of nh as the "effective sample size." This is because the number of observations being used to construct $\widehat{m}(x)$ is proportional to nh, not n as for a parametric estimator.

It is helpful to understand that the nonparametric estimator has a reduced convergence rate relative to parametric asymptotic theory because the object being estimated—$m(x)$—is nonparametric. This is harder than estimating a finite-dimensional parameter, and thus comes at a cost.

Unlike parametric estimation, the asymptotic distribution of the nonparametric estimator includes a term representing the bias of the estimator. The asymptotic distribution (19.16) shows the form of this bias. It is proportional to the squared bandwidth h^2 (the degree of smoothing) and to the function $B_{\mathrm{nw}}(x)$ or $B_{\mathrm{LL}}(x)$, which depends on the slope and curvature of the CEF $m(x)$. Interestingly, when $m(x)$ is constant, then $B_{\mathrm{nw}}(x) = B_{\mathrm{LL}}(x) = 0$ and the kernel estimator has no asymptotic bias. The bias is essentially increasing in the curvature of the CEF function $m(x)$. This is because the local averaging smooths $m(x)$, and the smoothing induces more bias when $m(x)$ is curved. Because the bias terms are multiplied by h^2, which tends to 0, it might be thought that the bias terms are asymptotically negligible and can be omitted. But this is mistaken, because they are within the parentheses that are mutiplied by the factor $\sqrt{nh}$. The bias terms can only be omitted if $\sqrt{nh}h^2 \to 0$, which is known as an undersmoothing condition and is discussed in Section 19.14.

The asymptotic variance of $\widehat{m}(x)$ is inversely proportional to the marginal density $f(x)$. Thus $\widehat{m}(x)$ has relatively low precision for regions where X has a low density. This makes sense, because these are regions where there are relatively few observations. An implication is that the nonparametric estimator $\widehat{m}(x)$ will be relatively inaccurate in the tails of the distribution of X.

19.14 UNDERSMOOTHING

The bias term in the asymptotic distribution of the kernel density estimator can be technically eliminated if the bandwidth is selected to converge to 0 faster than the optimal rate $n^{-1/5}$, thus $h = o\left(n^{-1/5}\right)$. This is called an **undersmoothing** bandwidth. By using a small bandwidth, the bias is reduced and the variance is increased. Thus the random component dominates the bias component (asymptotically). The following is the technical statement.

---

[6]This could be weakened if stronger smoothness conditions are assumed. For example, if $m^{(4)}(x)$ and $f^{(3)}(x)$ are continuous, then (19.15) can be weakened to $nh^9 = O(1)$, which means that the bandwidth must decline to 0 at least at the rate $n^{-1/9}$.

Theorem 19.10 Under the conditions of Theorem 19.9, and $nh^5 = o(1)$,

$$\sqrt{nh}\,(\widehat{m}_{\mathrm{nw}}(x) - m(x)) \underset{d}{\longrightarrow} \mathrm{N}\left(0, \frac{R_K \sigma^2(x)}{f(x)}\right)$$

$$\sqrt{nh}\,(\widehat{m}_{\mathrm{LL}}(x) - m(x)) \underset{d}{\longrightarrow} \mathrm{N}\left(0, \frac{R_K \sigma^2(x)}{f(x)}\right).$$

Theorem 19.10 has the advantage of no bias term. Consequently, this theorem is popular with some authors. There are also several disadvantages. First, the assumption of an undersmoothing bandwidth does not really eliminate the bias, it simply assumes it away. Thus in any finite sample, there is always bias. Second, it is not clear how to set a bandwidth so that it is undersmoothing. Third, an undersmoothing bandwidth implies that the estimator has increased variance and is inefficient. Finally, the theory is simply misleading as a characterization of the distribution of the estimator.

19.15 CONDITIONAL VARIANCE ESTIMATION

The conditional variance is

$$\sigma^2(x) = \operatorname{var}[Y \mid X = x] = \mathbb{E}\left[e^2 \mid X = x\right].$$

In various contexts, it is desirable to estimate $\sigma^2(x)$, including prediction intervals and confidence intervals for the estimated CEF. In general the conditional variance function is nonparametric, as economic models rarely specify the form of $\sigma^2(x)$. Thus estimation of $\sigma^2(x)$ is typically done nonparametrically.

Since $\sigma^2(x)$ is the CEF of e^2 given X, it can be estimated by nonparametric regression. For example, the ideal NW estimator (if e were observed) is

$$\overline{\sigma}^2(x) = \frac{\sum_{i=1}^{n} K\left(\frac{X_i - x}{h}\right) e_i^2}{\sum_{i=1}^{n} K\left(\frac{X_i - x}{h}\right)}.$$

Since the errors e are not observed, we need to replace them with an estimator. A simple choice is the residuals $\widehat{e}_i = Y_i - \widehat{m}(X_i)$. A better choice is the leave-one-out prediction errors $\widetilde{e}_i = Y_i - \widetilde{m}_{-i}(X_i)$. The latter are recommended for variance estimation, as they are not subject to overfitting. With this substitution, the NW estimator of the conditional variance is

$$\widehat{\sigma}^2(x) = \frac{\sum_{i=1}^{n} K\left(\frac{X_i - x}{h}\right) \widetilde{e}_i^2}{\sum_{i=1}^{n} K\left(\frac{X_i - x}{h}\right)}. \tag{19.17}$$

This estimator depends on a bandwidth h, but there is no reason for this bandwidth to be the same as that used to estimate the CEF. The ROT or cross-validation using $\widetilde{e}_i^2$ as the dependent variable can be used to select the bandwidth for estimation of $\widehat{\sigma}^2(x)$ separately from the choice for estimation of $\widehat{m}(x)$.

There is one subtle difference between CEF and conditional variance estimation. The conditional variance is inherently nonnegative ($\sigma^2(x) \geq 0$), and it is desirable that the estimator satisfy this property. The NW estimator (19.17) is necessarily nonnegative, because it is a smoothed average of the nonnegative squared residuals. The LL estimator, however, is not guaranteed to be nonnegative for all x. Furthermore, the NW estimator has as a special case the homoskedastic estimator $\widehat{\sigma}^2(x) = \widehat{\sigma}^2$ (full sample variance), which may be a relevant selection. For these reasons, the NW estimator may be preferred for conditional variance estimation.

Fan and Yao (1998) derive the asymptotic distribution of the estimator (19.17). They obtain the surprising result that the asymptotic distribution of the two-step estimator $\widehat{\sigma}^2(x)$ is identical to that of the one-step idealized estimator $\overline{\sigma}^2(x)$.

19.16 VARIANCE ESTIMATION AND STANDARD ERRORS

It is relatively straightforward to calculate the exact conditional variance of the NW, LL, or local polynomial estimator. The estimators can be written as

$$\widehat{\beta}(x) = \left(\boldsymbol{Z}'\boldsymbol{K}\boldsymbol{Z}\right)^{-1}\left(\boldsymbol{Z}'\boldsymbol{K}\boldsymbol{Y}\right) = \left(\boldsymbol{Z}'\boldsymbol{K}\boldsymbol{Z}\right)^{-1}\left(\boldsymbol{Z}'\boldsymbol{K}\boldsymbol{m}\right) + \left(\boldsymbol{Z}'\boldsymbol{K}\boldsymbol{Z}\right)^{-1}\left(\boldsymbol{Z}'\boldsymbol{K}\boldsymbol{e}\right)$$

where $\boldsymbol{m}$ is the $n \times 1$ vector of means $m(X_i)$. The first component is a function only of the regressors, and the second is linear in the error $\boldsymbol{e}$. Thus conditionally on the regressors $\boldsymbol{X}$,

$$\boldsymbol{V}_{\widehat{\beta}}(x) = \operatorname{var}\left[\widehat{\beta} \mid \boldsymbol{X}\right] = \left(\boldsymbol{Z}'\boldsymbol{K}\boldsymbol{Z}\right)^{-1}\left(\boldsymbol{Z}'\boldsymbol{K}\boldsymbol{D}\boldsymbol{K}\boldsymbol{Z}\right)\left(\boldsymbol{Z}'\boldsymbol{K}\boldsymbol{Z}\right)^{-1}$$

where $\boldsymbol{D} = \operatorname{diag}\left(\sigma^2(X_1), \ldots \sigma^2(X_n)\right)$.

A White-type estimator can be formed by replacing $\sigma^2(X_i)$ with the squared residuals $\widehat{e}_i^2$ or prediction errors $\widetilde{e}_i^2$:

$$\widehat{\boldsymbol{V}}_{\widehat{\beta}}(x) = \left(\boldsymbol{Z}'\boldsymbol{K}\boldsymbol{Z}\right)^{-1}\left(\sum_{i=1}^{n} K\left(\frac{X_i - x}{h}\right)^2 Z_i(x) Z_i(x)' \widetilde{e}_i^2\right)\left(\boldsymbol{Z}'\boldsymbol{K}\boldsymbol{Z}\right)^{-1}. \tag{19.18}$$

Alternatively, $\sigma^2(X_i)$ could be replaced with an estimator such as (19.17) evaluated at $\widehat{\sigma}^2(X_i)$ or $\widehat{\sigma}^2(x)$.

A simple option is the asymptotic formula

$$\widehat{V}_{\widehat{m}(x)} = \frac{R_K \widehat{\sigma}^2(x)}{nh\widehat{f}(x)}$$

with $\widehat{\sigma}^2(x)$ from (19.17) and $\widehat{f}(x)$ a density estimator, such as

$$\widehat{f}(x) = \frac{1}{nb}\sum_{i=1}^{n} K\left(\frac{X_i - x}{b}\right) \tag{19.19}$$

where b is a bandwidth. (See Chapter 17 of *Probability and Statistics for Economists.*)

In general, I recommend (19.18) calculated with prediction errors, as this is the closest analog of the finite sample covariance matrix.

For local linear and local polynomial estimators, the estimator $\widehat{V}_{\widehat{m}(x)}$ is the first diagonal element of the matrix $\widehat{\boldsymbol{V}}_{\widehat{\beta}}(x)$. For any of the variance estimators, a standard error for $\widehat{m}(x)$ is the square root of $\widehat{V}_{\widehat{m}(x)}$.

19.17 CONFIDENCE BANDS

We can construct asymptotic confidence intervals. A 95% interval for $m(x)$ is

$$\widehat{m}(x) \pm 1.96\sqrt{\widehat{V}_{\widehat{m}(x)}}. \tag{19.20}$$

This confidence interval can be plotted along with $\widehat{m}(x)$ to assess precision.

It should be noted, however, that this confidence interval has two unusual properties. First, it is pointwise in x, meaning that it is designed to have coverage probability at each x, not uniformly across x. Thus they are typically called **pointwise confidence intervals**.

Second, because it does not account for the bias, it is not an asymptotically valid confidence interval for $m(x)$. Instead it is an asymptotically valid confidence interval for the pseudo-true (smoothed) value, for example, $m(x) + h^2 B(x)$. One way of thinking about this is that the confidence intervals account for the variance of the estimator but not its bias. A technical trick that solves this problem is to assume an undersmoothing bandwidth. In this case, the above confidence intervals are technically asymptotically valid. This is only a technical trick, as it does not really eliminate the bias but only assumes it away. The plain fact is that once we honestly acknowledge that the true CEF is nonparametric, it then follows that any finite sample estimator will have finite sample bias, and this bias will be inherently unknown and thus difficult to incorporate into confidence intervals.

Despite these unusual properties, we can still use the interval (19.20) to display uncertainty and as a check on the precision of the estimates.

19.18 THE LOCAL NATURE OF KERNEL REGRESSION

The kernel regression estimators (NW, LL, and local polynomial) are all essentially local estimators in that given h, the estimator $\widehat{m}(x)$ is a function only of the subsample for which X is close to x. The other observations do not directly affect the estimator. This is reflected in the distribution theory as well. Theorem 19.8 shows that $\widehat{m}(x)$ is consistent for $m(x)$ if the latter is continuous at x. Theorem 19.9 shows that the asymptotic distribution of $\widehat{m}(x)$ depends only on the functions $m(x), f(x)$, and $\sigma^2(x)$ at the point x. The distribution does not depend on the global behavior of $m(x)$.

Global features do affect the estimator $\widehat{m}(x)$, however, through the bandwidth h. The bandwidth selection methods described here are global in nature, as they attempt to minimize AIMSE. Local bandwidths (designed to minimize the AMSE at a single point x) can alternatively be employed, but they are less commonly used, in part because such bandwidth estimators have high imprecision. Picking local bandwidths adds extra noise. Furthermore, selected bandwidths may be meaningfully large, so that the estimation window may be a large portion of the sample. In this case, estimation is neither local nor fully global.

19.19 APPLICATION TO WAGE REGRESSION

Let us illustrate the methods with an application to the the CPS dataset. We are interested in the nonparametric regression of log(*wage*) on *experience*. To illustrate, we take the subsample of Black men with 12 years of education (high school graduates). This sample has 762 observations.

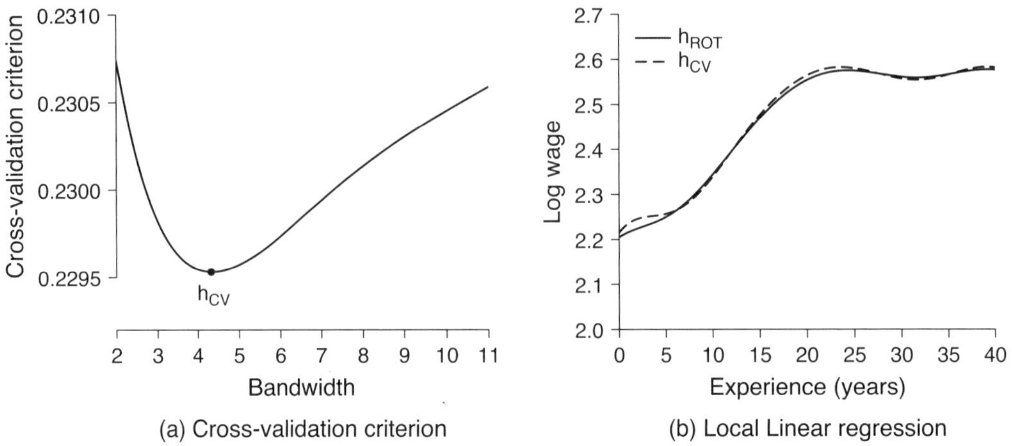

FIGURE 19.5 Log wage regression on experience

We first need to decide on the region of interest (range of *experience*) for which we will calculate the regression estimator. We select the range [0, 40], because most observations (90%) have experience levels below 40 years.

To avoid boundary bias let us use the local linear estimator.

We next calculate the Fan-Gijbels ROT bandwidth (19.9) and find $h_{\mathrm{rot}} = 5.14$. We then calculate the cross-validation criterion using the ROT as a baseline. The CV criterion is displayed in Figure 19.5(a). The minimizer is $h_{\mathrm{cv}} = 4.32$, which is somewhat smaller than the ROT bandwidth.

We calculate the LL estimator using both bandwidths and display the estimates in Figure 19.5(b). The regression functions are increasing for experience levels up to 20 years and then become flat. Although the functions are roughly concave, they are noticeably different from a traditional quadratic specification. Comparing the estimates, the smaller CV-selected bandwidth produces a regression estimate that is a bit too wavy, whereas the ROT bandwidth produces a regression estimate that is much smoother yet captures the same essential features. Based on this inspection, let us select the estimate based on the ROT bandwidth (the solid line in panel (b)).

Next, consider estimation of the conditional variance function. We calculate the ROT bandwidth for a regression using the squared prediction errors and find $h_{\mathrm{rot}} = 6.77$, which is larger than the bandwidth used for conditional mean estimation. We then calculate the cross-validation functions for conditional variance estimation (regression of squared prediction errors on *experience*), using both NW and LL regression. The CV functions are displayed in Figure 19.6(a). The CV plots are quite interesting. For the LL estimator, the CV function has a local minimum around $h = 5$, but the global minimizer is unbounded. The CV function for the NW estimator is globally decreasing with an unbounded minimizer. The NW also achieves a considerably lower CV value than the LL estimator. Thus that the CV-selected variance estimator is the NW estimator with $h = \infty$, which is the simple full-sample estimator $\widehat{\sigma}^2$ calculated with the prediction errors.

Let us compute standard errors for the regression function estimates using formula (19.18). Figure 19.6(b) displays the estimated regression (the same as Figure 19.5 using the ROT bandwidth) along with 95% asymptotic confidence bands computed as in (19.20). By displaying the confidence bands, we can see that there is considerable imprecision in the estimator for low experience levels. We can still see that the estimates and confidence bands show that the experience profile is increasing up to about 20 years of experience and then flattens above 20 years. The estimates imply that for this population (Black men who are high school graduates), the

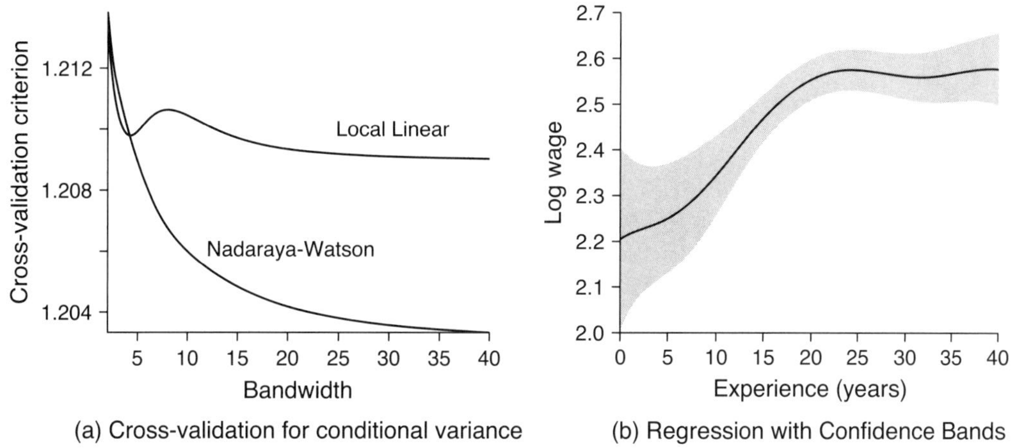

FIGURE 19.6 Confidence band construction

average wage rises for the first 20 years of work experience (from 18 to 38 years of age) and then flattens with no further increases in average wages for the next 20 years of work experience (from 38 to 58 years of age).

19.20 CLUSTERED OBSERVATIONS

Clustered observations are (Y_{ig}, X_{ig}) for individuals $i=1,\ldots,n_g$ in cluster $g=1,\ldots,G$. The model is

$$Y_{ig} = m\left(X_{ig}\right) + e_{ig}$$
$$\mathbb{E}\left[e_{ig} \mid \boldsymbol{X}_g\right] = 0$$

where $\boldsymbol{X}_g$ is the stacked X_{ig}. The assumption is that the clusters are mutually independent. Dependence within each cluster is unstructured.

Write

$$Z_{ig}(x) = \begin{pmatrix} 1 \\ X_{ig} - x \end{pmatrix}.$$

Stack Y_{ig}, e_{ig} and $Z_{ig}(x)$ into cluster-level variables $\boldsymbol{Y}_g$, $\boldsymbol{e}_g$, and $\boldsymbol{Z}_g(x)$, respectively. Let $\boldsymbol{K}_g(x) = \operatorname{diag}\left\{K\left(\frac{X_{ig}-x}{h}\right)\right\}$. The LL estimator can be written as

$$\begin{aligned}\widehat{\beta}(x) &= \left(\sum_{g=1}^{G}\sum_{i=1}^{n_g} K\left(\frac{X_{ig}-x}{h}\right) Z_{ig}(x) Z_{ig}(x)'\right)^{-1} \left(\sum_{g=1}^{G}\sum_{i=1}^{n_g} K\left(\frac{X_{ig}-x}{h}\right) Z_{ig}(x) Y_{ig}\right) \\ &= \left(\sum_{g=1}^{G} \boldsymbol{Z}_g(x)' \boldsymbol{K}_g(x) \boldsymbol{Z}_g(x)\right)^{-1} \left(\sum_{g=1}^{G} \boldsymbol{Z}_g(x)' \boldsymbol{K}_g(x) \boldsymbol{Y}_g\right). \end{aligned} \tag{19.21}$$

The LL estimator $\widehat{m}(x) = \widehat{\beta}_1(x)$ is the intercept in (19.21).

The natural method to obtain prediction errors is by delete-cluster regression. The delete-cluster estimator of β is

$$\widetilde{\beta}_{(-g)}(x) = \left(\sum_{j \neq g} \boldsymbol{Z}_j(x)' \boldsymbol{K}_j(x) \boldsymbol{Z}_j(x) \right)^{-1} \left(\sum_{j \neq g} \boldsymbol{Z}_j(x)' \boldsymbol{K}_j(x) \boldsymbol{Y}_j \right). \tag{19.22}$$

The delete-cluster estimator of $m(x)$ is the intercept $\widetilde{m}_1(x) = \widetilde{\beta}_{1(-g)}(x)$ from (19.22). The delete-cluster prediction error for observation ig is

$$\widetilde{e}_{ig} = Y_{ig} - \widetilde{\beta}_{1(-g)}(X_{ig}). \tag{19.23}$$

Let $\widetilde{\boldsymbol{e}}_g$ be the stacked $\widetilde{e}_{ig}$ for cluster g.

The variance of (19.21), conditional on the regressors $\boldsymbol{X}$, is

$$\boldsymbol{V}_{\widehat{\beta}}(x) = \left(\sum_{g=1}^{G} \boldsymbol{Z}_g(x)' \boldsymbol{K}_g(x) \boldsymbol{Z}_g(x) \right)^{-1} \left(\sum_{g=1}^{G} \boldsymbol{Z}_g(x)' \boldsymbol{K}_g(x) \boldsymbol{S}_g(x) \boldsymbol{K}_g(x) \boldsymbol{Z}_g(x) \right) \left(\sum_{g=1}^{G} \boldsymbol{Z}_g(x)' \boldsymbol{K}_g(x) \boldsymbol{Z}_g(x) \right)^{-1} \tag{19.24}$$

where $\boldsymbol{S}_g = \mathbb{E}\left[\boldsymbol{e}_g \boldsymbol{e}_g' \mid \boldsymbol{X}_g \right]$. The covariance matrix (19.24) can be estimated by replacing $\boldsymbol{S}_g$ with an estimator of $\boldsymbol{e}_g \boldsymbol{e}_g'$. Based on analogy with regression estimation, I suggest using the delete-cluster prediction errors $\widetilde{\boldsymbol{e}}_g$, as they are not subject to over-fitting. This covariance matrix estimator using this choice is

$$\widehat{\boldsymbol{V}}_{\widehat{\beta}}(x) = \left(\sum_{g=1}^{G} \boldsymbol{Z}_g(x)' \boldsymbol{K}_g(x) \boldsymbol{Z}_g(x) \right)^{-1} \left(\sum_{g=1}^{G} \boldsymbol{Z}_g(x) \boldsymbol{K}_g(x) \widetilde{\boldsymbol{e}}_g \widetilde{\boldsymbol{e}}_g' \boldsymbol{K}_g(x) \boldsymbol{Z}_g(x) \right) \left(\sum_{g=1}^{G} \boldsymbol{Z}_g(x) \boldsymbol{K}_g(x) \boldsymbol{Z}_g(x) \right)^{-1}. \tag{19.25}$$

The standard error for $\widehat{m}(x)$ is the square root of the first diagonal element of $\widehat{\boldsymbol{V}}_{\widehat{\beta}}(x)$.

There is no current theory on how to select the bandwidth h for nonparametric regression using clustered observations. The Fan-Ghybels ROT bandwidth h_{rot} is designed for independent observations, so it is likely to be a crude choice in the case of clustered observations. Standard cross-validation has similar limitations. A practical alternative is to select the bandwidth h to minimize a delete-cluster cross-valiation criterion. Although there is no formal theory to justify this choice, it seems like a reasonable option. The delete-cluster CV criterion is

$$\mathrm{CV}(h) = \frac{1}{n} \sum_{g=1}^{G} \sum_{i=1}^{n_g} \widetilde{e}_{ig}^2$$

where $\widetilde{e}_{ig}$ are the delete-cluster prediction errors (19.23). The delete-cluster CV bandwidth is the value that minimizes this function:

$$h_{\text{cv}} = \underset{h \geq h_\ell}{\operatorname{argmin}}\, \mathrm{CV}(h).$$

As for the case of conventional cross-validation, it may be valuable to plot $\mathrm{CV}(h)$ against h to verify that the minimum has been obtained and to assess sensitivity.

19.21 APPLICATION TO TEST SCORES

Let us illustrate kernel regression with clustered observations by using the Duflo, Dupas, and Kremer (2011) investigation of the effect of student tracking on test scores. Recall that the core question was effect of the

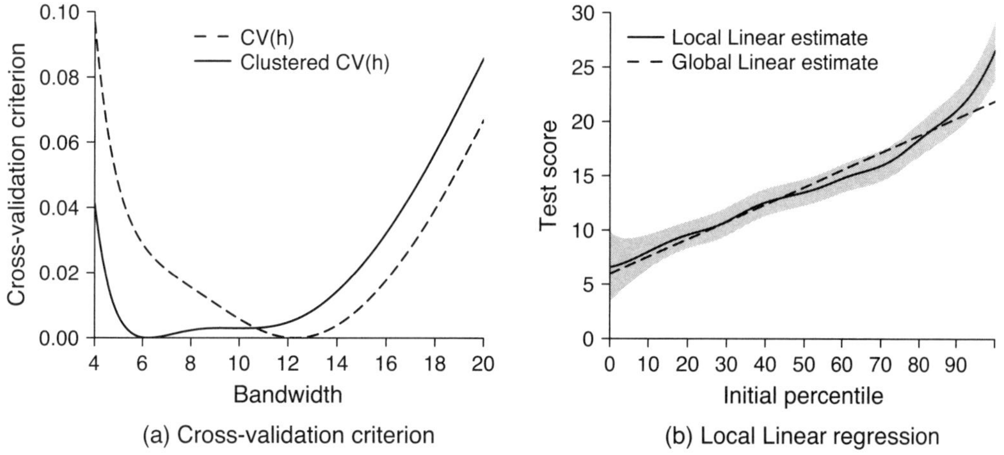

FIGURE 19.7 Test score as a function of initial percentile

dummy variable *tracking* on the continuous variable *testscore*. A set of controls were included including a continuous variable *percentile*, which recorded the student's initial test score (as a percentile). We investigate the authors' specification of this control using local linear regression.

Let us take the subsample of 1,487 girls who experienced tracking and estimate the regression of *testscores* on *percentile*. For this application, we used unstandardized[7] test scores, which range from 0 to about 40. We used local linear regression with a Gaussian kernel.

First consider bandwidth selection. The Fan-Ghybels ROT and conventional cross-validation bandwidths are $h_{\text{rot}} = 6.7$ and $h_{\text{cv}} = 12.3$. We then calculated the clustered cross-validation criterion, which has minimizer $h_{\text{cv}} = 6.2$. To understand the differences, the standard and clustered cross-validation functions are plotted in Figure 19.7(a). To plot on the same graph, we normalize each by subtracting their minimized value (so each is minimized at 0). What we can see from Figure 19.7(a) is that although the conventional CV criterion is sharply minimized at $h = 12.3$, the clustered CV criterion is essentially flat between 5 and 11. Thus the clustered CV criterion has difficulty discriminating between these bandwidth choices.

Using the bandwidth selected by clustered cross-validation, we can calculate the local linear estimator $\widehat{m}_{\text{LL}}(x)$ of the regression function. The estimate is plotted in Figure 19.7(b). We calculate the delete-cluster prediction errors $\widetilde{\boldsymbol{e}}_g$ and use these to calculate the standard errors for the local linear estimator $\widehat{m}_{\text{LL}}(x)$ using formula (19.25). (These standard errors are roughly twice as large as those calculated using the non-clustered formula.) We use the standard errors to calculate 95% asymptotic pointwise confidence bands as in (19.20). These are plotted in Figure 19.7(b) along with the point estimate. Also plotted for comparison is an estimated linear regression line. The local linear estimator is similar to the global linear regression for initial percentiles below 80%. But for initial percentiles above 80%, the two lines diverge. The confidence bands suggest that these differences are statistically meaningful. Students with initial testscores at the top of the initial distribution have higher final testscores on average than predicted by a linear specification.

[7] In Section 4.21, following Duflo, Dupas, and Kremer (2011), the dependent variable was standardized testscores (normalized to have mean 0 and variance 1).

19.22 MULTIPLE REGRESSORS

Our analysis has focused on the case of real-valued X for simplicity, but the methods of kernel regression extend to the multiple regressor case at the cost of a reduced rate of convergence. In this section, we consider the case of estimation of the conditional expectation function $\mathbb{E}[Y \mid X=x]=m(x)$, where

$$X=\begin{pmatrix} X_1 \\ \vdots \\ X_d \end{pmatrix} \in \mathbb{R}^d.$$

For any evaluation point x and observation i, define the kernel weights

$$K_i(x)=K\left(\frac{X_{1i}-x_1}{h_1}\right)K\left(\frac{X_{2i}-x_2}{h_2}\right)\cdots K\left(\frac{X_{di}-x_d}{h_d}\right)$$

which is a d-fold product kernel. The kernel weights $K_i(x)$ assess whether the regressor vector X_i is close to the evaluation point x in the Euclidean space $\mathbb{R}^d$.

These weights depend on a set of d bandwidths, h_j, one for each regressor. Given these weights, the NW estimator takes the form

$$\widehat{m}(x)=\frac{\sum_{i=1}^{n} K_i(x) Y_i}{\sum_{i=1}^{n} K_i(x)}.$$

For the LL estimator, define

$$Z_i(x)=\begin{pmatrix} 1 \\ X_i - x \end{pmatrix}$$

and then the LL estimator can be written as $\widehat{m}(x)=\widehat{\alpha}(x)$, where

$$\begin{aligned}\begin{pmatrix} \widehat{\alpha}(x) \\ \widehat{\beta}(x) \end{pmatrix} &= \left(\sum_{i=1}^{n} K_i(x) Z_i(x) Z_i(x)'\right)^{-1} \sum_{i=1}^{n} K_i(x) Z_i(x) Y_i \\ &= \left(\boldsymbol{Z}'\boldsymbol{K}\boldsymbol{Z}\right)^{-1} \boldsymbol{Z}'\boldsymbol{K}\boldsymbol{Y}\end{aligned}$$

and $\boldsymbol{K}=\operatorname{diag}\{K_1(x),\ldots,K_n(x)\}$.

In multiple regressor kernel regression, cross-validation remains a recommended method for bandwidth selection. The leave-one-out residuals $\widetilde{e}_i$ and cross-validation criterion $\mathrm{CV}(h_1,\ldots,h_d)$ are defined identically as in the single regressor case. The only difference is that now the CV criterion is a function over the d bandwidths $h_1,\ldots,h_d$. Thus numerical minimization needs to be done more efficiently than by a simple grid search.

The asymptotic distribution of the estimators in the multiple regressor case is an extension of the single regressor case. Let $f(x)$ denote the marginal density of X, $\sigma^2(x)=\mathbb{E}\left[e^2 \mid X=x\right]$ denote the conditional variance of $e=Y-m(X)$, and set $|h|=h_1 h_2\cdots h_d$.

Proposition 19.1 Let $\widehat{m}(x)$ denote either the NW or LL estimator of $m(x)$. As $n\to\infty$ and $h_j\to 0$ such that $n|h|\to\infty$,

$$\sqrt{n|h|}\left(\widehat{m}(x)-m(x)-\sum_{j=1}^{d} h_j^2 B_j(x)\right) \underset{d}{\longrightarrow} \mathrm{N}\left(0,\frac{R_K^d \sigma^2(x)}{f(x)}\right).$$

For the NW estimator,

$$B_j(x) = \frac{1}{2}\frac{\partial^2}{\partial x_j^2}m(x) + f(x)^{-1}\frac{\partial}{\partial x_j}f(x)\frac{\partial}{\partial x_j}m(x)$$

and for the LL estimator,

$$B_j(x) = \frac{1}{2}\frac{\partial^2}{\partial x_j^2}m(x).$$

I do not provide regularity conditions or a formal proof but instead refer interested readers to Fan and Gijbels (1996).

19.23 CURSE OF DIMENSIONALITY

The term "curse of dimensionality" is used to describe the phenomenon that the convergence rate of nonparametric estimators slows as the dimension increases.

When X is vector-valued, we define the AIMSE as the integral of the squared bias plus variance, integrating with respect to $f(x)w(x)$, where $w(x)$ is an integrable weight function. For notational simplicity, consider the case that there is a single common bandwidth h. In this case, the AIMSE of $\widehat{m}(x)$ equals

$$\text{AIMSE} = h^4 \int_S \left(\sum_{j=1}^d B_j(x)\right)^2 f(x)w(x)dx + \frac{R_K^d}{nh^d}\int_S \sigma^2(x)w(x)dx.$$

We see that the squared bias is of order h^4, the same as in the single regressor case. The variance, however, is of larger order $(nh^d)^{-1}$.

If we pick the bandwith minimizing the AIMSE, we find that it equals $h = cn^{-1/(4+d)}$ for some constant c. This generalizes the formula for the one-dimensional case. The rate $n^{-1/(4+d)}$ is slower than the $n^{-1/5}$ rate, which effectively means that with multiple regressors, a larger bandwidth is required.

When the bandwidth is set as $h = cn^{-1/(4+d)}$, then the AIMSE is of order $O\left(n^{-4/(4+d)}\right)$. This is a slower rate of convergence than in the one-dimensional case.

Theorem 19.11 For vector-valued X, the bandwidth that minimizes the AIMSE is of order $h \sim n^{-1/(4+d)}$. With $h \sim n^{-1/(4+d)}$, $\text{AIMSE} = O\left(n^{-4/(4+d)}\right)$.

See Exercise 19.6.

We see that the optimal AIMSE rate $O\left(n^{-4/(4+d)}\right)$ depends on the dimension d. As d increases, this rate slows. Thus the precision of kernel regression estimators worsens with multiple regressors. The reason is that the estimator $\widehat{m}(x)$ is a local average of Y for observations such that X is close to x, and when there are multiple regressors, the number of such observations is inherently smaller.

This phenomenon—that the rate of convergence of nonparametric estimation decreases as the dimension increases—is called the **curse of dimensionality**. It is common across most nonparametric estimation problems and is not specific to kernel regression.

The curse of dimensionality has led to the practical rule that most applications of nonparametric regression have a single regressor. Some have two regressors and on occasion, three. More is uncommon.

19.24 PARTIALLY LINEAR REGRESSION

To handle discrete regressors and/or reduce the dimensionality, we can separate the regression function into a nonparametric and a parametric part. Let the regressors be partitioned as (X, Z), where X and Z are d- and k-dimensional, respectively. A **partially linear regression model** is

$$Y = m(X) + Z'\beta + e \tag{19.26}$$
$$\mathbb{E}[e \mid X, Z] = 0.$$

This model combines two elements. One, it specifies that the CEF is **separable** between X and Z (there are no nonparametric interactions). Two, it specifies that the CEF is linear in the regressors Z. These are assumptions that may be true or may be false. In practice, it is best to think of the assumptions as approximations.

When some regressors are discrete (as is common in econometric applications), they belong in Z. The regressors X must be continuously distributed. In typical applications, X is either scalar or two-dimensional. This may not be a restriction in practice, as many econometric applications only have a small number of continuously distributed regressors.

The seminal contribution for estimation of (19.26) is Robinson (1988), who proposed a nonparametric version of residual regression. His key insight was to see that the nonparametric component can be eliminated by transformation. Consider the expectation of equation (19.26) conditional on X:

$$\mathbb{E}[Y \mid X] = m(X) + \mathbb{E}[Z \mid X]' \beta.$$

Subtract this from (19.26), obtaining

$$Y - \mathbb{E}[Y \mid X] = (Z - \mathbb{E}[Z \mid X])' \beta + e.$$

The model is now a linear regression of the nonparametric regression error $Y - \mathbb{E}[Y \mid X]$ on the vector of nonparametric regression errors $Z - \mathbb{E}[Z \mid X]$.

Robinson's estimator replaces the infeasible regression errors by nonparametric counterparts. The result is a three-step estimator.

1. Using nonparametric regression (NW or LL), regress Y_i on X_i, Z_{1i} on X_i, Z_{2i} on X_i, ..., and Z_{ki} on X_i, obtaining the fitted values $\widehat{g}_{0i}, \widehat{g}_{1i}, \ldots$, and $\widehat{g}_{ki}$.
2. Regress $Y_i - \widehat{g}_{0i}$ on $Z_{1i} - \widehat{g}_{1i}, \ldots, Z_{ki} - \widehat{g}_{ki}$ to obtain the coefficient estimate $\widehat{\beta}$ and standard errors.
3. Use nonparametric regression to regress $Y_i - Z_i'\widehat{\beta}$ on X_i to obtain the nonparametric estimator $\widehat{m}(x)$ and confidence intervals.

The resulting estimators and standard errors have conventional asymptotic distributions under specific assumptions on the bandwidths. A full proof is provided by Robinson (1988). Andrews (1994) provides a more general treatment with insight into the general structure of semiparametric estimators.

The most difficult challenge is to show that the asymptotic distribution $\widehat{\beta}$ is unaffected by the first step estimation. Briefly, these are the steps of the argument. First, the first-step error $Z - \mathbb{E}[Z \mid X]$ has 0 covariance with the regression error e. Second, the asymptotic distribution will be unaffected by the first-step estimation if replacing (in this covariance) the expectation $\mathbb{E}[Z \mid X]$ with its first-step nonparametric estimator induces an error of order $o_p\left(n^{-1/2}\right)$. Third, because the covariance is a product, this holds when the first-step estimator has a convergence rate of $o_p\left(n^{-1/4}\right)$. Fourth, this holds under Theorem 19.11 if $h \sim n^{-1/(4+d)}$ and $d < 4$.

The reason that the third step estimator has a conventional asymptotic distribution is a bit simpler to explain. The estimator $\widehat{\beta}$ converges at a conventional $O_p\left(n^{-1/2}\right)$ rate. The nonparametric estimator $\widehat{m}(x)$ converges at a rate slower than $O_p\left(n^{-1/2}\right)$. Thus the sampling error for $\widehat{\beta}$ is of lower order and does not affect the first-order asymptotic distribution of $\widehat{m}(x)$.

Once again, the theory is advanced, so the above two paragraphs should not be taken as a full explanation. The good news is that the estimation method is straightforward.

19.25 COMPUTATION

Stata has two commands that implement kernel regression: `lpoly` and `npregress`. `lpoly` implements local polynomial estimation for any p, including NW (the default) and LL estimation, and it selects the bandwidth using the Fan-Gijbels ROT method. It uses the Epanechnikov kernel by default, but the Gaussian can be selected as an option. The `lpoly` command automatically displays the estimated CEF along with 95% confidence bands with standard errors computed using (19.18).

The Stata command `npregress` estimates LL (the default) or NW regression. By default it selects the bandwidth by cross-validation. It uses the Epanechnikov kernel by default, but the Gaussian can be selected as an option. Confidence intervals may be calculated using the percentile bootstrap. A display of the estimated CEF and 95% confidence bands at specific points (computed using the percentile bootstrap) may be obtained with the postestimation command `margins`.

Several R packages implement kernel regression. One flexible choice is `npreg`, available in the `np` package. Its default method is NW estimation using a Gaussian kernel with bandwidth selected by cross-validation. There are options that allow LL and local polynomial estimation, alternative kernels, and alternative bandwidth selection methods.

19.26 TECHNICAL PROOFS*

All technical proofs make the simplifying assumption that the kernel function $K(u)$ has bounded support, thus $K(u)=0$ for $|u|>a$. The results extend to the Gaussian kernel using additional technical arguments.

Proof of Theorem 19.1 Part 1 Equation (19.3) shows that

$$\mathbb{E}\left[\widehat{m}_{\mathrm{nw}}(x) \mid \boldsymbol{X}\right]=m(x)+\frac{\widehat{b}(x)}{\widehat{f}(x)} \tag{19.27}$$

where $\widehat{f}(x)$ is the kernel density estimator (19.19) of $f(x)$ with $b=h$, and

$$\widehat{b}(x)=\frac{1}{nh}\sum_{i=1}^{n} K\left(\frac{X_i-x}{h}\right)\left(m(x_i)-m(x)\right). \tag{19.28}$$

Theorem 17.6 of *Probability and Statistics for Economists* established that $\widehat{f}(x) \underset{p}{\longrightarrow} f(x)$. The proof is completed by showing that $\widehat{b}(x)=h^2 f(x) B_{\mathrm{nw}}(x)+o_p\left(h^2+1/\sqrt{nh}\right)$.

Since $\widehat{b}(x)$ is a sample average, it has the expectation

$$\begin{aligned}\mathbb{E}\left[\widehat{b}(x)\right] &= \frac{1}{h}\mathbb{E}\left[K\left(\frac{X-x}{h}\right)(m(X)-m(x))\right] \\ &= \int_{-\infty}^{\infty}\frac{1}{h}K\left(\frac{v-x}{h}\right)(m(v)-m(x))f(v)dv \\ &= \int_{-\infty}^{\infty}K(u)\,(m(x+hu)-m(x))f(x+hu)du. \end{aligned} \tag{19.29}$$

The second equality expresses the expectation as an integral with respect to the density of X. The third uses the change-of-variables $v=x+hu$. We next use two Taylor series expansions:

$$m(x+hu)-m(x)=m'(x)hu+\frac{1}{2}m''(x)h^2u^2+o(h^2) \tag{19.30}$$

$$f(x+hu)=f(x)+f'(x)hu+o(h).$$

Inserted into (19.29), we find that (19.29) equals

$$\int_{-\infty}^{\infty}K(u)\left(m'(x)hu+\frac{1}{2}m''(x)h^2u^2+o(h^2)\right)\left(f(x)+f'(x)hu+o(h)\right)du \tag{19.31}$$

$$=h\left(\int_{-\infty}^{\infty}uK(u)\,du\right)m'(x)\left(f(x)+o(h)\right) \tag{19.32}$$

$$+h^2\left(\int_{-\infty}^{\infty}u^2K(u)\,du\right)\left(\frac{1}{2}m''(x)f(x)+m'(x)f'(x)\right)$$

$$+h^3\left(\int_{-\infty}^{\infty}u^3K(u)\,du\right)\frac{1}{2}m''(x)f'(x)+o(h^2)$$

$$=h^2\left(\frac{1}{2}m''(x)f(x)+m'(x)f'(x)\right)+o(h^2)$$

$$=h^2B_{\mathrm{nw}}(x)f(x)+o(h^2).$$

The second equality uses the fact that the kernel $K(x)$ integrates to 1, its odd moments are 0, and the kernel variance is 1. We have shown that $\mathbb{E}\left[\widehat{b}(x)\right]=B_{\mathrm{nw}}(x)f(x)h^2+o(h^2)$.

Now consider the variance of $\widehat{b}(x)$. Since $\widehat{b}(x)$ is a sample average of independent components and the variance is smaller than the second moment, we have

$$\begin{aligned}\operatorname{var}\left[\widehat{b}(x)\right] &= \frac{1}{nh^2}\operatorname{var}\left[K\left(\frac{X-x}{h}\right)(m(X)-m(x))\right] \\ &\le \frac{1}{nh^2}\mathbb{E}\left[K\left(\frac{X-x}{h}\right)^2(m(X)-m(x))^2\right] \\ &= \frac{1}{nh}\int_{-\infty}^{\infty}K(u)^2\,(m(x+hu)-m(x))^2f(x+hu)du \qquad (19.33) \\ &= \frac{1}{nh}\int_{-\infty}^{\infty}u^2K(u)^2\,du\,\left(m'(x)\right)^2f(x)\left(h^2+o(1)\right) \\ &\le \frac{h}{n}\overline{K}\left(m'(x)\right)^2f(x)+o\left(\frac{h}{n}\right). \end{aligned}$$

The second equality writes the expectation as an integral. The third uses (19.30). The final inequality uses $K(u) \le \overline{K}$ from Definition 19.1 Part 1 and the fact that the kernel variance is 1. Thus

$$\operatorname{var}\left[\widehat{b}(x)\right] \le O\left(\frac{h}{n}\right).$$

Combining these results, we conclude that

$$\widehat{b}(x) = h^2 f(x) B_{\mathrm{nw}}(x) + o\left(h^2\right) + O_p\left(\sqrt{\frac{h}{n}}\right)$$

and

$$\frac{\widehat{b}(x)}{\widehat{f}(x)} = h^2 B_{\mathrm{nw}}(x) + o_p\left(h^2\right) + O_p\left(\sqrt{\frac{h}{n}}\right). \tag{19.34}$$

Together with (19.27), this implies Theorem 19.1 Part 1. ∎

Proof of Theorem 19.2 Part 1 Equation (19.4) states that

$$nh \operatorname{var}\left[\widehat{m}_{\mathrm{nw}}(x) \mid \boldsymbol{X}\right] = \frac{\widehat{v}(x)}{\widehat{f}(x)^2}$$

where

$$\widehat{v}(x) = \frac{1}{nh} \sum_{i=1}^{n} K\left(\frac{X_i - x}{h}\right)^2 \sigma^2(X_i)$$

and $\widehat{f}(x)$ is the estimator (19.19) of $f(x)$. Theorem 17.6 of *Probability and Statistics for Economists* established $\widehat{f}(x) \underset{p}{\longrightarrow} f(x)$. The proof is completed by showing $\widehat{v}(x) \underset{p}{\longrightarrow} R_K \sigma^2(x) f(x)$.

First, writing the expectation as an integral with respect to $f(x)$, making the change-of-variables $v = x + hu$, and appealing to the continuity of $\sigma^2(x)$ and $f(x)$ at x,

$$\begin{aligned}
\mathbb{E}\left[\widehat{v}(x)\right] &= \int_{-\infty}^{\infty} \frac{1}{h} K\left(\frac{v-x}{h}\right)^2 \sigma^2(v) f(v) dv \\
&= \int_{-\infty}^{\infty} K(u)^2 \sigma^2(x+hu) f(x+hu) du \\
&= \int_{-\infty}^{\infty} K(u)^2 \sigma^2(x) f(x) + o(1) \\
&= R_K \sigma^2(x) f(x).
\end{aligned}$$

Second, because $\widehat{v}(x)$ is an average of independent random variables and the variance is smaller than the second moment

$$\begin{aligned}
nh \operatorname{var}\left[\widehat{v}(x)\right] &= \frac{1}{h} \operatorname{var}\left[K\left(\frac{X-x}{h}\right)^2 \sigma^2(X)\right] \\
&\le \frac{1}{h} \int_{-\infty}^{\infty} K\left(\frac{v-x}{h}\right)^4 \sigma^4(v) f(v) dv \\
&= \int_{-\infty}^{\infty} K(u)^4 \sigma^4(x+hu) f(x+hu) du \\
&\le \overline{K}^2 R_k \sigma^4(x) f(x) + o(1)
\end{aligned}$$

so $\operatorname{var}\left[\widehat{v}(x)\right] \to 0$.

We deduce from Markov's inequality that $\widehat{v}(x) \underset{p}{\longrightarrow} R_K\sigma^2(x)f(x)$, completing the proof. ■

Proof of Theorem 19.7 Observe that $m(X_i) - \widetilde{m}_{-i}(X_i, h)$ is a function only of $(X_1, \ldots, X_n)$ and $(e_1, \ldots, e_n)$ excluding e_i, and is thus uncorrelated with e_i. Since $\widetilde{e}_i(h) = m(X_i) - \widetilde{m}_{-i}(X_i, h) + e_i$, then

$$
\begin{aligned}
\mathbb{E}\left[\mathrm{CV}(h)\right] &= \mathbb{E}\left(\widetilde{e}_i(h)^2 w(X_i)\right) \\
&= \mathbb{E}\left[e_i^2 w(X_i)\right] + \mathbb{E}\left[\left(\widetilde{m}_{-i}(X_i, h) - m(X_i)\right)^2 w(X_i)\right] \\
&\quad + 2\mathbb{E}\left[\left(\widetilde{m}_{-i}(X_i, h) - m(X_i)\right) w(X_i) e_i\right] \\
&= \overline{\sigma}^2 + \mathbb{E}\left[\left(\widetilde{m}_{-i}(X_i, h) - m(X_i)\right)^2 w(X_i)\right]. \qquad (19.35)
\end{aligned}
$$

The second term is an expectation over the random variables X_i and $\widetilde{m}_{-i}(x, h)$, which are independent as the second is not a function of the ith observation. Thus, taking the conditional expectation given the sample excluding the ith observation, this is the expectation over X_i only, which is the integral with respect to its density:

$$
\mathbb{E}_{-i}\left[\left(\widetilde{m}_{-i}(X_i, h) - m(X_i)\right)^2 w(X_i)\right] = \int \left(\widetilde{m}_{-i}(x, h) - m(x)\right)^2 f(x) w(x) dx.
$$

Taking the unconditional expecation yields

$$
\begin{aligned}
\mathbb{E}\left[\left(\widetilde{m}_{-i}(X_i, h) - m(X_i)\right)^2 w(X_i)\right] &= \mathbb{E}\left[\int \left(\widetilde{m}_{-i}(x, h) - m(x)\right)^2 f(x) w(x) dx\right] \\
&= \mathrm{IMSE}_{n-1}(h)
\end{aligned}
$$

where this is the IMSE of a sample of size $n-1$, because the estimator $\widetilde{m}_{-i}$ uses $n-1$ observations. Combined with (19.35), we obtain (19.12), as desired. ■

Proof of Theorem 19.8 We can write the NW estimator as

$$
\widehat{m}_{\mathrm{nw}}(x) = m(x) + \frac{\widehat{b}(x)}{\widehat{f}(x)} + \frac{\widehat{g}(x)}{\widehat{f}(x)} \qquad (19.36)
$$

where $\widehat{f}(x)$ is the estimator (19.19), $\widehat{b}(x)$ is defined in (19.28), and

$$
\widehat{g}(x) = \frac{1}{nh} \sum_{i=1}^{n} K\left(\frac{X_i - x}{h}\right) e_i. \qquad (19.37)
$$

Since $\widehat{f}(x) \underset{p}{\longrightarrow} f(x) > 0$ by Theorem 17.6 of *Probability and Statistics for Economists*, the proof is completed by showing $\widehat{b}(x) \underset{p}{\longrightarrow} 0$ and $\widehat{g}(x) \underset{p}{\longrightarrow} 0$.

Consider $\widehat{b}(x)$. From (19.29) and the continuity of $m(x)$ and $f(x)$,

$$
\mathbb{E}\left[\widehat{b}(x)\right] = \int_{-\infty}^{\infty} K(u)\left(m(x + hu) - m(x)\right) f(x + hu) du = o(1)
$$

as $h \to \infty$. From (19.33),

$$
nh \operatorname{var}\left[\widehat{b}(x)\right] \leq \int_{-\infty}^{\infty} K(u)^2 \left(m(x + hu) - m(x)\right)^2 f(x + hu) du = o(1)
$$

as $h \to \infty$. Thus $\operatorname{var}\left[\widehat{b}(x)\right] \longrightarrow 0$. By Markov's inequality, we conclude $\widehat{b}(x) \overset{p}{\longrightarrow} 0$.

Now consider $\widehat{g}(x)$. Since $\widehat{g}(x)$ is linear in e_i and $\mathbb{E}[e \mid X] = 0$, we find $\mathbb{E}\left[\widehat{g}(x)\right] = 0$. Since $\widehat{g}(x)$ is an average of independent random variables, the variance is smaller than the second moment, and the definition $\sigma^2(X) = \mathbb{E}\left[e^2 \mid X\right]$, it follows that

$$
\begin{aligned}
nh \operatorname{var}\left[\widehat{g}(x)\right] &= \frac{1}{h} \operatorname{var}\left[K\left(\frac{X-x}{h}\right) e\right] \\
&\leq \frac{1}{h} \mathbb{E}\left[K\left(\frac{X-x}{h}\right)^2 e^2\right] \\
&= \frac{1}{h} \mathbb{E}\left[K\left(\frac{X-x}{h}\right)^2 \sigma^2(X)\right] \\
&= \int_{-\infty}^{\infty} K(u)^2 \sigma^2(x+hu) f(x+hu) du \\
&= R_K \sigma^2(x) f(x) + o(1) \qquad (19.38)
\end{aligned}
$$

where the final equality holds because $\sigma^2(x)$ and $f(x)$ are continuous in x. Thus $\operatorname{var}\left[\widehat{g}(x)\right] \longrightarrow 0$. By Markov's inequality, we conclude $\widehat{g}(x) \underset{p}{\longrightarrow} 0$, completing the proof. ■

Proof of Theorem 19.9 From (19.36), Theorem 17.6 of *Probability and Statistics for Economists*, and (19.34), we have

$$
\begin{aligned}
\sqrt{nh}\left(\widehat{m}_{\mathrm{nw}}(x) - m(x) - h^2 B_{\mathrm{nw}}(x)\right) &= \sqrt{nh}\left(\frac{\widehat{g}(x)}{\widehat{f}(x)}\right) + \sqrt{nh}\left(\frac{\widehat{b}(x)}{\widehat{f}(x)} - h^2 B_{\mathrm{nw}}(x)\right) \\
&= \sqrt{nh}\left(\frac{\widehat{g}(x)}{f(x)}\right)(1 + o_p(1)) + \sqrt{nh}\left(o_p\left(h^2\right) + O_p\left(\sqrt{\frac{h}{n}}\right)\right) \\
&= \sqrt{nh}\left(\frac{\widehat{g}(x)}{f(x)}\right)(1 + o_p(1)) + \left(o_p\left(\sqrt{nh^5}\right) + O_p(h)\right) \\
&= \sqrt{nh}\left(\frac{\widehat{g}(x)}{f(x)}\right) + o_p(1)
\end{aligned}
$$

where the final equality holds because $\sqrt{nh}\widehat{g}(x) = O_p(1)$ by (19.38) and the assumption $nh^5 = O(1)$. The proof is completed by showing $\sqrt{nh}\widehat{g}(x) \underset{d}{\longrightarrow} \mathrm{N}\left(0, R_K \sigma^2(x) f(x)\right)$.

Define $Y_{ni} = h^{-1/2} K\left(\frac{X_i - x}{h}\right) e_i$, which are independent and mean 0. We can write $\sqrt{nh}\widehat{g}(x) = \sqrt{n}\overline{Y}$ as a standardized sample average. We verify the conditions for the Lindeberg CLT (Theorem 6.4). In the notation of Theorem 6.4, set $\overline{\sigma}_n^2 = \operatorname{var}\left[\sqrt{n}\overline{Y}\right] \to R_K f(x) \sigma^2(x)$ as $h \to 0$. The CLT holds if we can verify the Lindeberg condition.

This is an advanced calculation and will not interest most readers. It is provided here for those interested in a complete derivation.

Fix $\epsilon > 0$ and $\delta > 0$. Since $K(u)$ is bounded, we can write $K(u) \leq \overline{K}$. Let nh be sufficiently large so that

$$
\left(\frac{\epsilon nh}{\overline{K}^2}\right)^{(r-2)/2} \geq \frac{\overline{\sigma}}{\delta}.
$$

The conditional moment bound (19.14) implies that for $x \in \mathcal{N}$,

$$\mathbb{E}\left[e^2 \mathbb{1}\left\{e^2 > \frac{\epsilon nh}{\overline{K}^2}\right\} \middle| X = x\right] = \mathbb{E}\left[\frac{|e|^r}{|e|^{r-2}} \mathbb{1}\left\{e^2 > \frac{\epsilon nh}{\overline{K}^2}\right\} \middle| X = x\right]$$
$$\leq \mathbb{E}\left[\frac{|e|^r}{\left(\epsilon nh/\overline{K}^2\right)^{(r-2)/2}} \middle| X = x\right]$$
$$\leq \delta.$$

Since $Y_{ni}^2 \leq h^{-1}\overline{K}^2 e_i^2$, we find

$$\mathbb{E}\left[Y_{ni}^2 \mathbb{1}\left\{Y_{ni}^2 > \epsilon n\right\}\right] \leq \frac{1}{h}\mathbb{E}\left[K\left(\frac{X-x}{h}\right)^2 e^2 \mathbb{1}\left\{e^2 > \frac{\epsilon nh}{\overline{K}^2}\right\}\right]$$
$$= \frac{1}{h}\mathbb{E}\left[K\left(\frac{X-x}{h}\right)^2 \mathbb{E}\left(e^2 \mathbb{1}\left\{e^2 > \frac{\epsilon nh}{\overline{K}^2}\right\} \middle| X\right)\right]$$
$$= \int_{-\infty}^{\infty} K(u)^2 \mathbb{E}\left[e^2 \mathbb{1}\left\{e^2 > \epsilon nh/\overline{K}^2\right\} \middle| X = x + hu\right] f(x+hu)du$$
$$\leq \delta \int_{-\infty}^{\infty} K(u)^2 f(x+hu)du$$
$$= \delta R_K f(x) + o(1)$$
$$= o(1)$$

because δ is arbitrary. This is the Lindeberg condition (6.2). The Lindeberg CLT (Theorem 6.4) shows that

$$\sqrt{nh}\widehat{g}(x) = \sqrt{n}\overline{Y} \underset{d}{\longrightarrow} \mathrm{N}\left(0, R_K \sigma^2(x) f(x)\right).$$

This completes the proof. ■

19.27 EXERCISES

Exercise 19.1 For kernel regression, suppose you rescale Y, for example, replace Y with $100Y$. How should the bandwidth h change? To answer this, first address how the functions $m(x)$ and $\sigma^2(x)$ change under rescaling, and then calculate how $\overline{B}$ and $\overline{\sigma}^2$ change. Deduce how the optimal h_0 changes due to rescaling Y. Does your answer make intuitive sense?

Exercise 19.2 Show that (19.6) minimizes the AIMSE (19.5).

Exercise 19.3 Describe in words how the bias of the LL estimator changes over regions of convexity and concavity in $m(x)$. Does this make intuitive sense?

Exercise 19.4 Suppose the true regression function is linear, $m(x) = \alpha + \beta x$, and you estimate the function using the NW estimator. Calculate the bias function $B(x)$. Suppose $\beta > 0$. For which regions is $B(x) > 0$, and for which regions is $B(x) < 0$? Now suppose that $\beta < 0$ and answer the question. Can you intuitively explain why the NW estimator is positively and negatively biased for these regions?

Exercise 19.5 Suppose $m(x) = \alpha$ is a constant function. Find the AIMSE-optimal bandwith (19.6) for NW estimation. Explain what you find.

Exercise 19.6 Prove Theorem 19.11: Show that when $d \geq 1$, the AIMSE optimal bandwidth takes the form $h_0 = cn^{-1/(4+d)}$, and AIMSE is $O\left(n^{-4/(4+d)}\right)$.

Exercise 19.7 Take the `DDK2011` dataset and the subsample of boys who experienced tracking. As in Section 19.21, use the LL estimator to estimate the regression of *testscores* on *percentile*, but now with the subsample of boys. Plot with 95% confidence intervals. Comment on the similarities and differences with the estimate for the subsample of girls.

Exercise 19.8 Take the `cps09mar` dataset and the subsample of individuals with *education*=20 (professional degree or doctorate), with *experience* between 0 and 40 years.

(a) Use the NW estimator to estimate the regression of log(*wage*) on *experience*, separately for men and women. Plot with 95% confidence intervals. Comment on how the estimated wage profiles vary with experience. In particular, do you think the evidence suggests that expected wages fall for experience levels above 20 for this education group?

(b) Repeat using LL estimator. How do the estimates and confidence intervals change?

Exercise 19.9 Take the `Invest1993` dataset and the subsample of observations with $Q \leq 5$. (In the dataset, Q is the variable *vala*.)

(a) Use the NW estimator to estimate the regression of I on Q. (In the dataset, I is the variable *inva*.) Plot with 95% confidence intervals.

(b) Repeat using the LL estimator.

(c) Is there evidence to suggest that the regression function is nonlinear?

Exercise 19.10 The `RR2010` dataset is from Reinhart and Rogoff (2010). It contains observations on annual U.S. GDP growth rates, inflation rates, and the debt/GDP ratio for the long time span 1791–2009. The paper made the strong claim that GDP growth slows as debt/GDP increases and in particular, that this relationship is nonlinear, with debt negatively affecting growth for debt ratios exceeding 90%. Their full dataset includes 44 countries. Our extract only includes the United States.

(a) Use the NW estimator to estimate the regression of GDP growth on the debt ratio. Plot with 95% confidence intervals.

(b) Repeat using the LL estimator.

(c) Do you see evidence of nonlinearity and/or a change in the relationship at 90%?

(d) Now estimate a regression of GDP growth on the inflation rate. Comment on what you find.

Exercise 19.11 Consider a nonlinear AR(1) model for GDP growth rates:

$$Y_t = m(Y_{t-1}) + e_t$$

$$Y_t = 100\left(\left(\frac{GDP_t}{GDP_{t-1}}\right)^4 - 1\right).$$

(a) Create GDP growth rates Y_t. Extract the level of real U.S. GDP (*gdpc1*) from `FRED-QD`, and make the above transformation to growth rates.

(b) Use the NW estimator to estimate $m(x)$. Plot with 95% confidence intervals.

(c) Repeat using the LL estimator.

(d) Do you see evidence of nonlinearity?

CHAPTER 20
SERIES REGRESSION

20.1 INTRODUCTION

Chapter 19 examined nonparametric regression by kernel smoothing methods. In this chapter, we study an alternative class of nonparametric methods known as series regression.

The basic model is identical to that examined in Chapter 19. We assume that there are random variables (Y, X) such that $\mathbb{E}\left[Y^2\right] < \infty$ and that satisfy the regression model

$$\begin{aligned} Y &= m(X) + e \qquad (20.1) \\ \mathbb{E}\left[e \mid X\right] &= 0 \\ \mathbb{E}\left[e^2 \mid X\right] &= \sigma^2(X). \end{aligned}$$

The goal is to estimate the CEF $m(x)$. We start with the simple setting where X is scalar and consider more general cases later.

A series regression model is a sequence $K = 1, 2, \ldots,$ of approximating models $m_K(x)$ with K parameters. In this chapter, we exclusively focus on linear series models, and in particular polynomials and splines. This is because these models are simple, convenient, and cover most applications of series methods in applied economics. Other series models include trigonometric polynomials, wavelets, orthogonal wavelets, B-splines, and neural networks. For a detailed review, see Chen (2007).

Linear series regression models take the form

$$Y = X_K' \beta_K + e_K \qquad (20.2)$$

where $X_K = X_K(X)$ is a vector of regressors obtained by making transformations of X, and β_K is a coefficient vector. There are multiple possible definitions of the coefficient β_K. Let us define[1] it by projection:

$$\beta_K = \mathbb{E}\left[X_K X_K'\right]^{-1} \mathbb{E}\left[X_K Y\right] = \mathbb{E}\left[X_K X_K'\right]^{-1} \mathbb{E}\left[X_K m(X)\right]. \qquad (20.3)$$

The series regression error e_K is defined by (20.2) and (20.3), is distinct from the regression error e in (20.1), and is indexed by K, because it depends on the regressors X_K. The series approximation to $m(x)$ is

$$m_K(x) = X_K(x)' \beta_K. \qquad (20.4)$$

[1] An alternative is to define β_K as the best uniform approximation as in (20.8). The choice is not critical so long as we are careful to be consistent with our notation.

The coefficient is typically[2] estimated by least squares:

$$\widehat{\beta}_K = \left(\sum_{i=1}^{n} X_{Ki}X_{Ki}'\right)^{-1}\left(\sum_{i=1}^{n} X_{Ki}Y_i\right) = \left(\boldsymbol{X}_K'\boldsymbol{X}_K\right)^{-1}\left(\boldsymbol{X}_K'\boldsymbol{Y}\right). \tag{20.5}$$

The estimator for $m(x)$ is

$$\widehat{m}_K(x) = X_K(x)'\widehat{\beta}_K. \tag{20.6}$$

The difference between specific models arises due to the different choices of transformations $X_K(x)$.

The theoretical issues we will explore in this chapter are: (1) approximation properties of polynomials and splines; (2) consistent estimation of $m(x)$; (3) asymptotic normal approximations; (4) selection of K; and (5) extensions.

For a textbook treatment of series regression, see Li and Racine (2007). For an advanced treatment, see Chen (2007). Two seminal contributions are Andrews (1991a) and Newey (1997). Two recent important papers are Belloni et al. (2015) and Chen and Christensen (2015).

20.2 POLYNOMIAL REGRESSION

The prototypical series regression model for $m(x)$ is a pth order polynomial:

$$m_K(x) = \beta_0 + \beta_1 x + \beta_2 x^2 + \cdots + \beta_p x^p.$$

We can write it in vector notation as (20.4), where

$$X_K(x) = \begin{pmatrix} 1 \\ x \\ \vdots \\ x^p \end{pmatrix}.$$

The number of parameters is $K = p + 1$. Notice that we index $X_K(x)$ and β_K by K, as their dimensions and values vary with K.

The implied **polynomial regression model** for the random pair (Y, X) is (20.2) with

$$X_K = X_K(X) = \begin{pmatrix} 1 \\ X \\ \vdots \\ X^p \end{pmatrix}.$$

The degree of flexibility of a polynomial regression is controlled by the polynomial order p. A larger p yields a more flexible model, while a smaller p typically results in a estimator with a smaller variance.

In general, a **linear series regression model** takes the form

$$m_K(x) = \beta_1\tau_1(x) + \beta_2\tau_2(x) + \cdots + \beta_K\tau_K(x)$$

[2] Penalized estimators have also been recommended. We do not review these methods here.

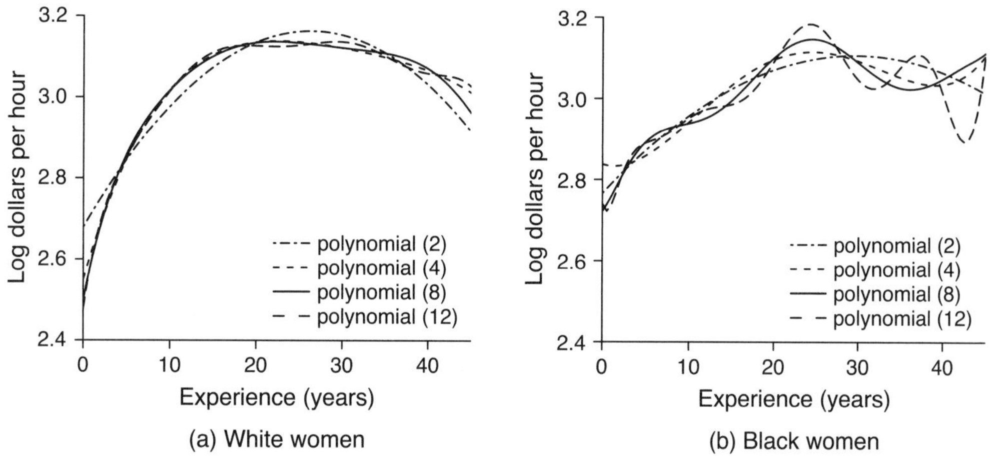

FIGURE 20.1 Polynomial estimates of experience profile

where the functions $\tau_j(x)$ are called the **basis transformations**. The polynomial regression model uses the power basis $\tau_j(x) = x^{j-1}$. The model $m_K(x)$ is called a series regression, because it is obtained by sequentially adding the series of variables $\tau_j(x)$.

20.3 ILLUSTRATING POLYNOMIAL REGRESSION

Consider the `cps09mar` dataset and a regression of log(*wage*) on *experience* for women with a college education (*education*= 16), separately for white women and Black women. The classical Mincer model uses a quadratic in experience. Given the large sample sizes (4,682 for white women and 517 for Black women), we can consider higher-order polynomials. Figure 20.1 plots least squares estimates of the CEFs using polynomials of order 2, 4, 8, and 12.

Examine panel (a), which shows the estimates for the subsample of white women. The quadratic specification appears misspecified with a shape noticeably different from the other estimates. The difference between the polynomials of order 4, 8, and 12 is relatively minor, especially for experience levels below 20.

Now examine panel (b), which shows the estimates for the subsample of Black women. This panel is quite different from panel (a). The estimates are erratic and increasingly so as the polynomial order increases. Assuming we are expecting a concave (or nearly concave) experience profile, the only estimate that satisfies this is the quadratic.

Why the difference between panels (a) and (b)? The most likely explanation is the different sample sizes. The subsample of Black women has far fewer observations, so the CEF is much less precisely estimated, giving rise to the erratic plots. This suggests (informally) that it may be preferred to use a smaller polynomial order p in the second subsample, or equivalently, to use a larger p when the sample size n is larger. The idea that model complexity—the number of coefficients K—should vary with sample size n is an important feature of series regression.

The erratic nature of the estimated polynomial regressions in Figure 20.1(b) is a common feature of higher-order estimated polynomial regressions. Better results can sometimes be obtained by a spline regression, which is described in Section 20.5.

20.4 ORTHOGONAL POLYNOMIALS

Standard implementation of the least squares estimator (20.5) of a polynomial regression may return a computational error message when p is large. (See Section 3.24.) This is because the moments of X^j can be highly heterogeneous across j and because the variables X^j can be highly correlated. These two factors imply in practice that the matrix $\boldsymbol{X}_K'\boldsymbol{X}_K$ can be ill-conditioned (the ratio of the largest to smallest eigenvalue can be quite large), and some packages will return error messages rather than compute $\widehat{\beta}_K$.

In most cases, the condition of $\boldsymbol{X}_K'\boldsymbol{X}_K$ can be dramatically improved by rescaling the observations. As discussed in Section 3.24, a simple method for nonnegative regressors is to rescale each by its sample mean, for example, replace X_i^j with $X_i^j / \left(n^{-1}\sum_{i=1}^n X_i^j\right)$. Even better conditioning can often be obtained by rescaling X_i to lie in $[-1, 1]$ before applying powers. In most applications, one of these methods will be sufficient for a well-conditioned regression.

A computationally more robust implementation can be obtained by using orthogonal polynomials. These are linear combinations of the polynomial basis functions and produce identical regression estimators (20.6). The goal of orthogonal polynomials is to produce regressors that are either orthogonal or close to orthogonal and have similar variances, so that $\boldsymbol{X}_K'\boldsymbol{X}_K$ is close to diagonal and has similar diagonal elements. These orthogonalized regressors $X_K^* = \boldsymbol{A}_K X_K$ can be written as linear combinations of the original variables X_K. If the regressors are orthogonalized, then the regression estimator (20.6) is modified by replacing $X_K(x)$ with $X_K^*(x) = \boldsymbol{A}_K X_K(x)$.

One approach is to use sample orthogonalization. This is done by using a sequence of regressions of X_i^j on the previously orthogonalized variables and then rescaling, which results in perfectly orthogonalized variables. This is what is implemented in many statistical packages under the label "orthogonal polynomials," for example, the function `poly` in R. If done, then the least squares coefficients have no meaning outside this specific sample, and it is not convenient for calculation of $\widehat{m}_K(x)$ for values of x other than sample values. This approach is used for the examples presented in Section 20.3.

Another approach is to use an algebraic orthogonal polynomial. This polynomial is orthogonal with respect to a known weight function $w(x)$. Specifically, it is a sequence $p_j(x), j = 0, 1, 2, \ldots$, with the property that $\int p_j(x)p_\ell(x)w(x)dx = 0$ for $j \neq \ell$. Thus if $w(x) = f(x)$, the marginal density of X, then the basis transformations $p_j(X)$ will be mutually orthogonal (in expectation). Since we do now know the density of X, this is not feasible in practice, but if $w(x)$ is close to the density of X, then we can expect that the basis transformations will be close to mutually orthogonal. To implement an algebraic orthogonal polynomial, you first should rescale your X variable, so that it satisfies the support for the weight function $w(x)$.

The following three choices are most relevant for economic applications.

Legendre Polynomial. These polynomials are orthogonal with respect to the uniform density on $[-1, 1]$ (so they should be applied to regressors scaled to have support in $[-1, 1]$):

$$p_j(x) = \frac{1}{2^j}\sum_{\ell=0}^{j}\binom{j}{\ell}^2 (x-1)^{j-\ell}(x+1)^{\ell}.$$

For example, the first four are $p_0(x) = 1$, $p_1(x) = x$, $p_2(x) = \left(3x^2 - 1\right)/2$, and $p_3(x) = \left(5x^3 - 3x\right)/2$. The best computational method is the recurrence relationship

$$p_{j+1}(x) = \frac{(2j+1)\,xp_j(x) - jp_{j-1}(x)}{j+1}.$$

Laguerre Polynomial. These are orthogonal with respect to the exponential density e^{-x} on $[0, \infty)$ (so they should be applied to nonnegative regressors scaled if possible to have approximately unit mean and/or variance):

$$p_j(x) = \sum_{\ell=0}^{j} \binom{j}{\ell} \frac{(-x)^\ell}{\ell!}.$$

For example, the first four are $p_0(x) = 1$, $p_1(x) = 1 - x$, $p_2(x) = \left(x^2 - 4x + 2\right)/2$, and $p_3(x) = (-x^3 + 9x^2 - 18x + 6)/6$. The best computational method is the recurrence relationship

$$p_{j+1}(x) = \frac{\left(2j + 1 - x\right) p_j(x) - j p_{j-1}(x)}{j+1}.$$

Hermite Polynomial. These are orthogonal with respect to the standard normal density on $(-\infty, \infty)$ (so they should be applied to regressors scaled to have mean 0 and variance 1):

$$p_j(x) = j! \sum_{\ell=0}^{\lfloor j/2 \rfloor} \frac{(-1/2)^\ell x^{\ell - 2j}}{\ell! \left(j - 2\ell!\right)}.$$

For example, the first four are $p_0(x) = 1$, $p_1(x) = x$, $p_2(x) = x^2 - 1$, and $p_3(x) = x^3 - 3x$. The best computational method is the recurrence relationship

$$p_{j+1}(x) = x p_j(x) - j p_{j-1}(x).$$

The R package `orthopolynom` provides a convenient set of commands to compute many orthogonal polynomials, including the above.

20.5 SPLINES

A **spline** is a piecewise polynomial. Typically the order of the polynomial is preselected to be linear, quadratic, or cubic. The flexibility of the model is determined by the number of polynomial segments. The join points between the segments are called **knots**.

To impose smoothness and parsimony, it is common to constrain the spline function to have continuous derivatives up to the order of the spline. Thus a linear spline is constrained to be continuous, a quadratic spline is constrained to have a continuous first derivative, and a cubic spline is constrained to have continuous first and second derivatives.

A simple way to construct a regression spline is as follows. A linear spline with one knot τ is

$$m_K(x) = \beta_0 + \beta_1 x + \beta_2 (x - \tau) \mathbb{1} \{x \geq \tau\}.$$

To see that this is a linear spline, observe that for $x \leq \tau$, the function $m_K(x) = \beta_0 + \beta_1 x$ is linear with slope β_1; for $x \geq \tau$, the function $m_K(x)$ is linear with slope $\beta_1 + \beta_2$; and the function is continuous at $x = \tau$. Note that β_2 is the change in the slope at τ. A linear spline with two knots $\tau_1 < \tau_2$ is

$$m_K(x) = \beta_0 + \beta_1 x + \beta_2 (x - \tau_1) \mathbb{1} \{x \geq \tau_2\} + \beta_3 (x - \tau_2) \mathbb{1} \{x \geq \tau_2\}.$$

A quadratic spline with one knot is

$$m_K(x) = \beta_0 + \beta_1 x + \beta_2 x^2 + \beta_3 (x - \tau)^2 \mathbb{1} \{x \geq \tau\}.$$

To see that this is a quadratic spline, observe that for $x \le \tau$, the function is the quadratic $\beta_0 + \beta_1 x + \beta_2 x^2$ with second derivative $m_K''(\tau) = 2\beta_2$; for $x \ge \tau$, the second derivative is $m_K''(\tau) = 2(\beta_2 + \beta_3)$; so $2\beta_3$ is the change in the second derivative at τ. The first derivative at $x = \tau$ is the continuous function $m_K'(\tau) = \beta_1 + 2\beta_2\tau$.

In general, a pth-order spline with N knots $\tau_1 < \tau_2 < \cdots < \tau_N$ is

$$m_K(x) = \sum_{j=0}^{p} \beta_j x^j + \sum_{k=1}^{N} \beta_{p+k} (x - \tau_k)^p \mathbb{1}\{x \ge \tau_k\}$$

which has $K = N + p + 1$ coefficients.

The implied **spline regression model** for the random pair (Y, X) is (20.2), where

$$X_K = X_K(X) = \begin{pmatrix} 1 \\ X \\ \vdots \\ X^p \\ (X - \tau_1)^p \mathbb{1}\{X \ge \tau_1\} \\ \vdots \\ (X - \tau_N)^p \mathbb{1}\{X \ge \tau_N\} \end{pmatrix}.$$

In practice, a spline will depend critically on the choice of the knots τ_k. When X is bounded with an approximately uniform distribution, it is common to space the knots evenly so that all segments have the same length. When the distribution of X is not uniform, an alternative is to set the knots at the quantiles $j/(N+1)$, so that the probability mass is equalized across segments. A third alternative is to set the knots at the points where $m(x)$ has the greatest change in curvature (see Schumaker (2007), chapter 7). In all cases, the set of knots τ_j can change with K. Therefore a spline is a special case of an approximation of the form

$$m_K(x) = \beta_1 \tau_{1K}(x) + \beta_2 \tau_{2K}(x) + \cdots + \beta_K \tau_{KK}(x)$$

where the **basis transformations** $\tau_{jK}(x)$ depend on both j and K. Many authors call such approximations a **sieve** rather than a series, because the basis transformations change with K. This distinction is not critical to our treatment so for simplicity, we refer to splines as series regression models.

20.6 ILLUSTRATING SPLINE REGRESSION

In Section 20.3, we illustrated regressions of $\log(wage)$ on *experience* for white and Black women with a college education. Now consider a similar regression for Black men with a college education, a subsample with 394 observations.

We use a quadratic spline with four knots at experience levels of 10, 20, 30, and 40. This regression model has seven coefficients. The estimated regression function is displayed in Figure 20.2(a). An estimated sixth order polynomial regression is also displayed for comparison (a sixth order polynomial is an appropriate comparison, because it also has seven coefficients).

While the spline is a quadratic over each segment, you can see that the first two segments (experience levels between 0–10 and 10–20 years) are essentially linear. Most of the curvature occurs in the third and fourth segments (20–30 and 30–40 years), where the estimated regression function peaks and twists into a negative slope. The estimated regression function is smooth.

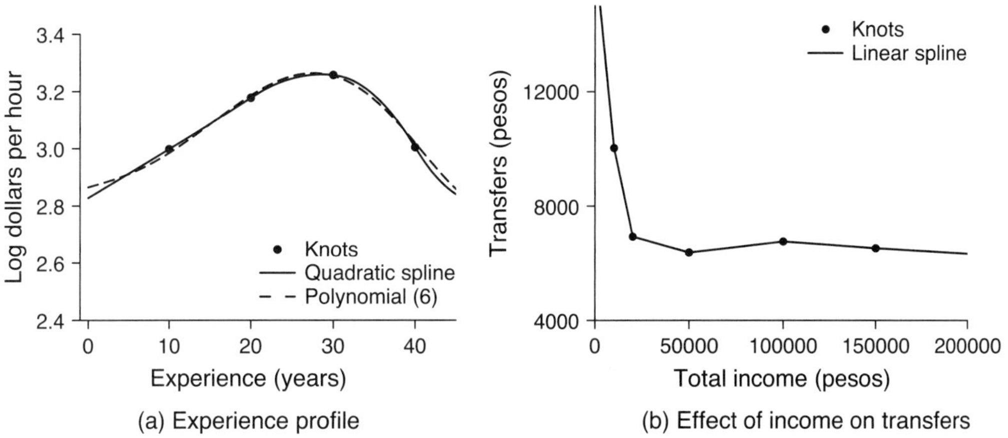

FIGURE 20.2 Spline regression estimates

A quadratic or cubic spline is useful when it is desired to impose smoothness, as in Figure 20.2(a). In contrast, a linear spline is useful when it is desired to allow for sharp changes in slope.

To illustrate, consider the dataset CHJ2004, which is a sample of 8684 urban Philippino households from Cox, B. Hansen, and Jimenez (2004). This paper studied the crowding-out impact of a family's income on nongovernmental (e.g., extended family) income transfers.[3] A model of altruistic transfers predicts that extended families will make gifts (transfers) when the recipient family's income is sufficiently low, but will not make transfers if the recipient family's income exceeds a threshold. A pure altruistic model predicts that the regression of transfers received on family income should have a slope of -1 up to this threshold and be flat above this threshold. We estimated this regression (including the same controls as the authors[4]) using a linear spline with knots at 10,000, 20,000, 50,000, 100,000, and 150,000 pesos. These knots were selected to give flexibility for low income levels, where there are more observations. This model has a total of 22 coefficients.

The estimated regression function (as a function of household income) is displayed in Figure 20.2(b). For the first two segments (incomes levels below 20,000 pesos), the regression function is negatively sloped, as predicted, with a slope about -0.7 from 0 to 10,000 pesos, and -0.3 from 10,000 to 20,000 pesos. The estimated regression function is effectively flat for income levels above 20,000 pesos. This shape is consistent with the pure altruism model. A linear spline model is particularly well suited for this application as it allows for discontinuous changes in slope.

Linear spline models with a single knot have been recently popularized by Card et al. (2015) with the label **regression kink design**.

20.7 THE GLOBAL/LOCAL NATURE OF SERIES REGRESSION

Recall from Section 19.18 that we described kernel regression as inherently local in nature. The NW, LL, and LP estimators of the CEF $m(x)$ are weighted averages of Y_i for observations for which X_i is close to x.

[3]Defined as the sum of transfers received domestically, from abroad, and in-kind, less gifts.

[4]The controls are: age of household head, education (five dummy categories), married, female, married female, number of children (three dummies), size of household, and employment status (two dummies).

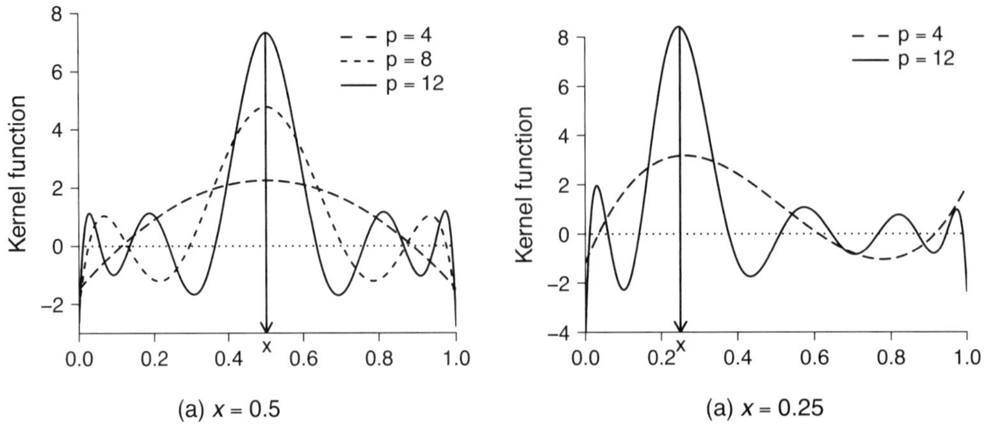

FIGURE 20.3 Kernel representation of polynomial weight function

In contrast, series regression is typically described as global in nature. The estimator $\widehat{m}_K(x) = X_K(x)'\widehat{\beta}_K$ is a function of the entire sample. The coefficients of a fitted polynomial (or spline) are affected by the global shape of the function $m(x)$ and thus affect the estimator $\widehat{m}_K(x)$ at any point x.

Although this description has some merit, it is not a complete description. As we now show, series regression estimators share the local smoothing property of kernel regression. As the number of series terms K increases a series estimator $\widehat{m}_K(x) = X_K(x)'\widehat{\beta}_K$ also becomes a local weighted average estimator.

To see this, observe that we can write the estimator as

$$\begin{aligned}\widehat{m}_K(x) &= X_K(x)'\left(\boldsymbol{X}_K'\boldsymbol{X}_K\right)^{-1}\left(\boldsymbol{X}_K'\boldsymbol{Y}\right)\\ &= \frac{1}{n}\sum_{i=1}^{n} X_K(x)'\widehat{\boldsymbol{Q}}_K^{-1}X_K(X_i)Y_i\\ &= \frac{1}{n}\sum_{i=1}^{n}\widehat{w}_K(x, X_i)Y_i\end{aligned}$$

where $\widehat{\boldsymbol{Q}}_K = n^{-1}\boldsymbol{X}_K'\boldsymbol{X}_K$ and $\widehat{w}_K(x, u) = x_K(x)'\widehat{\boldsymbol{Q}}_K^{-1}x_K(u)$. Thus $\widehat{m}_K(x)$ is a weighted average of Y_i using the weights $\widehat{w}_K(x, X_i)$. The weight function $\widehat{w}_K(x, X_i)$ appears to be maximized at $X_i = x$, so $\widehat{m}(x)$ puts more weight on observations for which X_i is close to x, similarly to kernel regression.

To see this more precisely, observe that because $\widehat{\boldsymbol{Q}}_K$ will be close in large samples to $\boldsymbol{Q}_K = \mathbb{E}\left[X_K X_K'\right]$, $\widehat{w}_K(x, u)$ will be close to the deterministic weight function

$$w_K(x, u) = X_K(x)'\boldsymbol{Q}_K^{-1}X_K(u).$$

Consider the case $X \sim U[0, 1]$. Figure 20.3 plots the weight function $w_K(x, u)$ as a funtion of u for $x = 0.5$ (panel (a)) and $x = 0.25$ (panel (b)) for $p = 4$, 8, 12 in panel (a) and $p = 4$, 12 in panel (b). First, examine panel (a). Here you can see that the weight function $w(x, u)$ is symmetric in u about x. For $p = 4$, the weight function appears similar to a quadratic in u, and as p increases, the weight function concentrates its main weight around x. However, the weight function is not nonnegative. It is quite similar in shape to what are known as higher-order (or bias-reducing) kernels, which were not reviewed in Chapter 19 but are part of the kernel estimation toolkit. Second, examine panel (b). Again the weight function is maximized at x, but now it is asymmetric in u about that point. Still, the general features from panel (a) carry over to panel (b). Namely, as p increases, the polynomial estimator puts most weight on observations for which X is close to x (just as for kernel regression), but is different from conventional kernel regression in that the weight function is not nonnegative. Qualitatively similar plots are obtained for spline regression.

There is little formal theory (of which I am aware) that makes a formal link between series regression and kernel regression, so the comments presented here are illustrative.[5] However, the point is that statements of the form "series regession is a global method; kernel regression is a local method" may not be complete. Both are global in nature when h is large (kernels) or K is small (series), and are local in nature when h is small (kernels) or K is large (series).

20.8 STONE-WEIERSTRASS AND JACKSON APPROXIMATION THEORY

A good series approximation $m_K(x)$ has the property that it gets close to the true CEF $m(x)$ as the complexity K increases. Formal statements can be derived from the mathematical theory of the approximation of functions.

An elegant and famous theorem is the **Stone-Weierstrass Theorem** (Weierstrass, 1885; Stone, 1948), which states that any continuous function can be uniformly well approximated by a polynomial of sufficiently high order. Specifically, the theorem states that if $m(x)$ is continuous on a compact set S, then for any $\epsilon > 0$ there is some K sufficiently large such that

$$\inf_{\beta} \sup_{x\in S} \left| m(x) - X_K(x)'\beta \right| \leq \epsilon. \tag{20.7}$$

Thus the true unknown $m(x)$ can be arbitrarily well approximated by selecting a suitable polynomial.

Jackson (1912) strengthened this result to give convergence rates that depend on the smoothness of $m(x)$. The basic result has been extended to spline functions. The following notation will be useful. Define the β that minimizes the left side of (20.7) as

$$\beta_K^* = \underset{\beta}{\operatorname{argmin}} \sup_{x\in S} \left| m(x) - X_K(x)'\beta \right| \tag{20.8}$$

define the approximation error as

$$r_K^*(x) = m(x) - X_K(x)'\beta_K^* \tag{20.9}$$

and define the minimized value of (20.7) as

$$\delta_K^* \stackrel{\text{def}}{=} \inf_{\beta} \sup_{x\in S} \left| m(x) - X_K(x)'\beta \right| = \sup_{x\in S} \left| m(x) - X_K(x)'\beta_K^* \right| = \sup_{x\in S} \left| r_K^*(x) \right|. \tag{20.10}$$

Theorem 20.1 If for some $\alpha \geq 0$, $m^{(\alpha)}(x)$ is uniformly continuous on a compact set S and $X_K(x)$ is either a polynomial basis or a spline basis (with uniform knot spacing) of order $s \geq \alpha$, then as $K \to \infty$,

$$\delta_K^* \leq o\left(K^{-\alpha}\right). \tag{20.11}$$

Furthermore, if $m^{(2)}(x)$ is uniformly continuous on S and $X_K(x)$ is a linear spline basis, then $\delta_K^* \leq O\left(K^{-2}\right)$.

[5] Similar connections are made in the appendix of Chen, Liao, and Sun (2012).

For a proof for the polynomial case, see theorem 4.3 of Lorentz (1986) or theorem 3.12 of Schumaker (2007) plus his equations (2.119) and (2.121). For the spline case, see theorem 6.27 of Schumaker (2007) plus his equations (2.119) and (2.121). For the linear spline case, see theorem 6.15 of Schumaker, equation (6.28).

Theorem 20.1 is more useful than the classic Stone-Weierstrass theorem, as it gives an approximation rate that depends on the smoothness order α. The rate $o(K^{-\alpha})$ in (20.11) means that the approximation error (20.10) decreases as K increases and decreases at a faster rate when α is large. The standard interpretation is that when $m(x)$ is smoother, it is possible to approximate it with fewer terms.

It will turn out that for our distribution theory, it is sufficient to consider the case that $m^{(2)}(x)$ is uniformly continuous. For this case, Theorem 20.1 shows that polynomials and quadratic/cubic splines achieve the rate $o(K^{-2})$ and linear splines achieve the rate $O(K^{-2})$. For most of of our results, the latter bound will be sufficient.

More generally, Theorem 20.1 makes a distinction between polynomials and splines, as polynomials achieve the rate $o\left(K^{-\alpha}\right)$ adaptively (without input from the user), whereas splines achieve the rate $o\left(K^{-\alpha}\right)$ only if the spline order s is appropriately chosen. This is an advantage for polynomials. However, as emphasized by Schumaker (2007), splines simultaneously approximate the derivatives $m^{(q)}(x)$ for $q<\alpha$. Thus, for example, a quadratic spline simultaneously approximates the function $m(x)$ and its first derivative $m'(x)$. There is no comparable result for polynomials. This is an advantage for quadratic and cubic splines. Because economists are often more interested in marginal effects (derivatives) than in levels, this property may be a good reason to prefer splines over polynomials.

Theorem 20.1 is a bound on the best uniform approximation error. The coefficient β_K^*, which minimizes (20.11), is not, however, the projection coefficient β_K as defined in (20.3). Thus Theorem 20.1 does not directly inform us concerning the approximation error obtained by series regression. It turns out, however, that the projection error can be easily deduced from (20.11).

Definition 20.1 The **projection approximation error** is

$$r_K(x)=m(x)-X_K(x)'\beta_K \tag{20.12}$$

where the coefficient β_K is the projection coefficient (20.3). The realized projection approximation error is $r_K=r_K(X)$. The expected squared projection error is

$$\delta_K^2=\mathbb{E}\left[r_K^2\right]. \tag{20.13}$$

The projection approximation error is similar to (20.9) but is evaluated using the projection coefficient rather than the minimizing coefficient β_K^* (20.8). Assuming that X has compact support S, the expected squared projection error satisfies

$$\begin{aligned}
\delta_K &= \left(\int_S \left(m(x)-X_K(x)'\beta_K\right)^2 dF(x)\right)^{1/2} \\
&\le \left(\int_S \left(m(x)-X_K(x)'\beta_K^*\right)^2 dF(x)\right)^{1/2} \\
&\le \left(\int_S \delta_K^{*2}\, dF(x)\right)^{1/2} \\
&= \delta_K^*.
\end{aligned} \tag{20.14}$$

The first inequality holds because the projection coefficient β_K minimizes the expected squared projection error (see Section 2.25). The second inequality is the definition of δ_K^*. Combined with Theorem 20.1, we have established the following result.

Theorem 20.2 If X has compact support S, for some $\alpha \geq 0$, $m^{(\alpha)}(x)$ is uniformly continuous on S, and $X_K(x)$ is either a polynomial basis or a spline basis of order $s \geq \alpha$, then as $K \to \infty$

$$\delta_K \leq \delta_K^* \leq o\left(K^{-\alpha}\right).$$

Furthermore, if $m^{(2)}(x)$ is uniformly continuous on S and $X_K(x)$ is a linear spline basis, then $\delta_K \leq O\left(K^{-2}\right)$.

The available theory of the approximation of functions goes beyond the results described here. For example, there is a theory of weighted polynomial approximation (Mhaskar, 1996) that provides an analog of Theorem 20.2 for the unbounded real line when X has a density with exponential tails.

20.9 REGRESSOR BOUNDS

The approximation result in Theorem 20.2 assumes that the regressors X have bounded support S. This assumption is conventional in series regression theory, as it greatly simplifies the analysis. Bounded support implies that the regressor function $X_K(x)$ is bounded. Define

$$\zeta_K(x) = \left(X_K(x)' \boldsymbol{Q}_K^{-1} X_K(x)\right)^{1/2} \tag{20.15}$$

$$\zeta_K = \sup_x \zeta_K(x) \tag{20.16}$$

where $\boldsymbol{Q}_K = \mathbb{E}\left[X_K X_K'\right]$ is the population design matrix given the regressors X_K. Then for all realizations of X_K,

$$\left(X_K' \boldsymbol{Q}_K^{-1} X_K\right)^{1/2} \leq \zeta_K. \tag{20.17}$$

The constant $\zeta_K(x)$ is the normalized length of the regressor vector $X_K(x)$. The constant ζ_K is the maximum normalized length. Their values are determined by the basis function transformations and the distribution of X. They are invariant to rescaling X_K or linear rotations.

For polynomials and splines, we have explicit expressions for the rate at which ζ_K grows with K.

Theorem 20.3 If X has compact support S with a strictly positive density $f(x)$ on S, then

1. $\zeta_K \leq O(K)$ for polynomials.
2. $\zeta_K \leq O\left(K^{1/2}\right)$ for splines.

For a proof of Theorem 20.3, see Newey (1997, theorem 4).

Furthermore, when X is uniformly distributed, then we can explicitly calculate for polynomials that $\zeta_K = K$, so the polynomial bound $\zeta_K \leq O(K)$ cannot be improved.

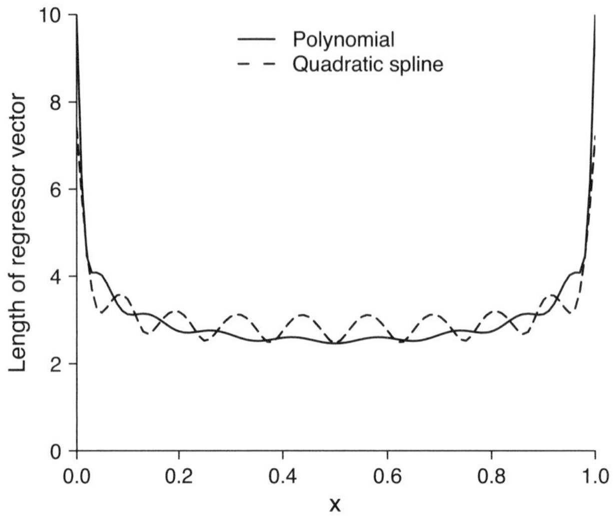

FIGURE 20.4 Normalized regressor length

To illustrate, Figure 20.4 plots the values $\zeta_K(x)$ for the case $X \sim U[0,1]$. The figure plots $\zeta_K(x)$ for a polynomial of degree $p=9$ and a quadratic spline with $N=7$ knots (both satisfy $K=10$). You can see that the values of $\zeta_K(x)$ are close to 3 for both basis transformations and most values of x, but $\zeta_K(x)$ increases sharply for x near the boundary. The maximum values are $\zeta_K=10$ for the polynomial and $\zeta_K=7.4$ for the quadratic spline. Although Theorem 20.3 shows that the two have different rates for large K, for moderate K we see that the differences are relatively minor.

20.10 MATRIX CONVERGENCE

One of the challenges that arises when developing a theory for the least squares estimator is how to describe the large-sample behavior of the sample design matrix

$$\widehat{\boldsymbol{Q}}_K = \frac{1}{n}\sum_{i=1}^{n} X_{Ki}X_{Ki}'$$

as $K \to \infty$. The difficulty is that its dimension changes with K, so we cannot apply a standard WLLN.

It turns out to be convenient if we first rotate the regressor vector so that the elements are orthogonal in expectation. Thus let us define the standardized regressors and design matrix as

$$\widetilde{X}_{Ki} = \boldsymbol{Q}_K^{-1/2} X_{Ki} \tag{20.18}$$

$$\widetilde{\boldsymbol{Q}}_K = \frac{1}{n}\sum_{i=1}^{n} \widetilde{X}_{Ki}\widetilde{X}_{Ki}'.$$

Note that $\mathbb{E}\left[\widetilde{X}_K\widetilde{X}_K'\right] = \boldsymbol{I}_K$. The standardized regressors are not used in practice; they are introduced only to simplify the theoretical derivations.

Our convergence theory will require the following fundamental rate bound on the number of coefficients K.

Assumption 20.1

1. $\lambda_{\min}\left(\boldsymbol{Q}_K\right) \geq \underline{\lambda} > 0$.
2. $\zeta_K^2 \log(K)/n \to 0$ as $n, K \to \infty$.

Assumption 20.1 part 1 ensures that the transformation (20.18) is well defined.[6] Assumption 20.1 part 2 states that the squared maximum regressor length ζ_K^2 grows slower than n. Since ζ_K increases with K, this is a bound on the rate at which K can increase with n. By Theorem 20.2, the rate in Assumption 20.1 part 2 holds for polynomials if $K^2 \log(K)/n \to 0$ and for splines if $K \log(K)/n \to 0$. In either case, this means that the number of coefficients K is growing at a rate slower than n.

We are now in a position to describe a convergence result for the standardized design matrix. The following is lemma 6.2 of Belloni et al. (2015).

Theorem 20.4 If Assumption 20.1 holds, then

$$\left\| \widetilde{\boldsymbol{Q}}_K - \boldsymbol{I}_K \right\| \xrightarrow{p} 0. \tag{20.19}$$

A proof of Theorem 20.4 using a stronger condition than Assumption 20.1 can be found in Section 20.31. The norm in (20.19) is the **spectral norm**

$$\|\boldsymbol{A}\| = \left(\lambda_{\max}\left(\boldsymbol{A}'\boldsymbol{A}\right)\right)^{1/2}$$

where $\lambda_{\max}(\boldsymbol{B})$ denotes the largest eigenvalue of the matrix $\boldsymbol{B}$. For a full description, see Section A.23.

For the least squares estimator what is particularly important is the inverse of the sample design matrix. Fortunately, we can easily deduce consistency of its inverse from (20.19) when the regressors have been orthogonalized as described.

Theorem 20.5 If Assumption 20.1 holds, then

$$\left\| \widetilde{\boldsymbol{Q}}_K^{-1} - \boldsymbol{I}_K \right\| \xrightarrow{p} 0 \tag{20.20}$$

and

$$\lambda_{\max}\left(\widetilde{\boldsymbol{Q}}_K^{-1}\right) = 1/\lambda_{\min}\left(\widetilde{\boldsymbol{Q}}_K\right) \xrightarrow{p} 1. \tag{20.21}$$

The proof of Theorem 20.5 can be found in Section 20.31.

[6] Technically, what is required is that $\lambda_{\min}\left(\boldsymbol{B}_K \boldsymbol{Q}_K \boldsymbol{B}_K'\right) \geq \underline{\lambda} > 0$ for some $K \times K$ sequence of matrices $\boldsymbol{B}_K$, or equivalently, that Assumption 20.1 part 1 holds after replacing X_K with $\boldsymbol{B}_K X_K$.

20.11 CONSISTENT ESTIMATION

In this section, we find conditions for consistent estimation of $m(x)$ by the series estimator $\widehat{m}_K(x) = X_K(x)'\widehat{\beta}_K$.

We know from standard regression theory that for any fixed K, $\widehat{\beta}_K \xrightarrow{p} \beta_K$, and thus $\widehat{m}_K(x) = X_K(x)'\widehat{\beta}_K \xrightarrow{p} X_K(x)'\beta_K$ as $n \to \infty$. Furthermore, from the Stone-Weierstrass theorem, we know that $X_K(x)'\beta_K \to m(x)$ as $K \to \infty$. It therefore seems reasonable to expect that $\widehat{m}_K(x) \xrightarrow{p} m(x)$, as both $n \to \infty$ and $K \to \infty$ together. Making this argument rigorous, however, is technically challenging, in part because the dimensions of $\widehat{\beta}_K$ and its components are changing with K.

Since $\widehat{m}_K(x)$ and $m(x)$ are functions, convergence should be defined with respect to an appropriate metric. For kernel regression, we focused on pointwise convergence (for each value of x separately), as that is the simplest case to analyze. For series regression, it turns out to be simplest to describe convergence with respect to **integrated squared error (ISE)**. Define the latter as

$$\text{ISE}(K) = \int (\widehat{m}_K(x) - m(x))^2 \, dF(x) \tag{20.22}$$

where F is the marginal distribution of X. ISE(K) is the average squared distance between $\widehat{m}_K(x)$ and $m(x)$, weighted by the marginal distribution of X. The ISE is random, depends on both sample size n and model complexity K, and its distribution is determined by the joint distribution of (Y, X). We can establish the following.

> **Theorem 20.6** Under Assumption 20.1 and $\delta_K = o(1)$, then as $n, K \to \infty$,
>
> $$\text{ISE}(K) = o_p(1). \tag{20.23}$$

The proof of Theorem 20.6 can be found in Section 20.31.

Theorem 20.6 shows that the series estimator $\widehat{m}_K(x)$ is consistent in the ISE norm under mild conditions. The assumption $\delta_K = o(1)$ holds for polynomials and splines if $K \to \infty$ and $m(x)$ is uniformly continuous. This result is analogous to Theorem 19.8, which showed that kernel regression estimator is consistent if $m(x)$ is continuous.

20.12 CONVERGENCE RATE

I now give a rate of convergence.

> **Theorem 20.7** Under Assumption 20.1 and $\sigma^2(x) \le \overline{\sigma}^2 < \infty$, then as $n, K \to \infty$,
>
> $$\text{ISE}(K) \le O_p\left(\delta_K^2 + \frac{K}{n}\right) \tag{20.24}$$
>
> where δ_K^2 is the expected squared prediction error (20.13). Furthermore, if $m''(x)$ is uniformly continuous, then for polynomial or spline basis functions,
>
> $$\text{ISE}(K) \le O_p\left(K^{-4} + \frac{K}{n}\right). \tag{20.25}$$

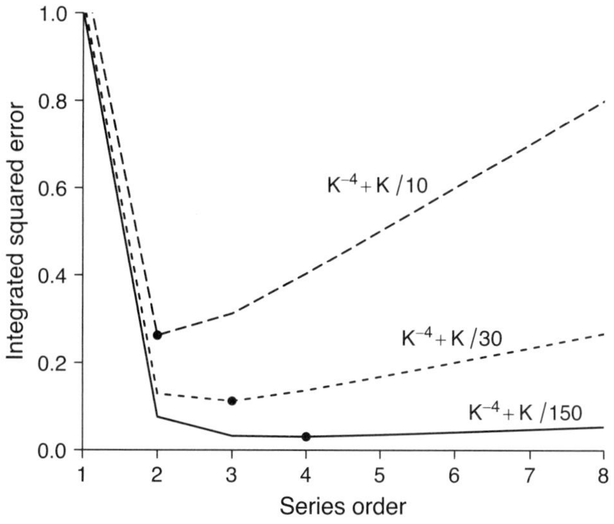

FIGURE 20.5 Integrated squared error

The proof of Theorem 20.7 can be found in Section 20.31. It is based on Newey (1997).

The bound (20.25) is particularly useful, as it gives an explicit rate in terms of K and n. The result shows that the integrated squared error is bounded in probability by two terms. The first, K^{-4}, is the squared bias. The second, K/n, is the estimation variance. This is analogous to the AIMSE for kernel regression (19.5). We can see that increasing the number of series terms K affects the ISE by decreasing the bias but increasing the variance. That the estimation variance is of order K/n can be intuitively explained by the fact that the regression model is estimating K coefficients.

For polynomials and quadratic splines, the bound (20.25) can be written as $o_p\left(K^{-4}\right) + O_p\left(K/n\right)$.

We are interested in the sequence K that minimizes the tradeoff in (20.25). By examining the first-order condition, we find that the sequence that minimizes this bound is $K \sim n^{1/5}$. With this choice, we obtain the optimal integrated squared error $\text{ISE}(K) \leq O_p\left(n^{-4/5}\right)$. This convergence rate is the same as that obtained by kernel regression under similar assumptions.

It is interesting to contrast the optimal rate $K \sim n^{1/5}$ for series regression with $h \sim n^{-1/5}$ for kernel regression. Essentially, one can view K^{-1} in series regression as a "bandwidth" similar to kernel regression, or one can view $1/h$ in kernel regression as the effective number of coefficients.

The rate $K \sim n^{1/5}$ means that the optimal K increases very slowly with the sample size. For example, doubling your sample size implies a 15% increase in the optimal number of coefficients K. To obtain a doubling in the optimal number of coefficients, you would need to multiply the sample size by 32.

To illustrate, Figure 20.5 displays the ISE rate bounds $K^{-4} + K/n$ as a function of K for $n = 10$, 30, 150. The filled circles mark the ISE-minimizing K, which are $K = 2$, 3, and 4 for the three functions. Notice that the ISE functions are steeply downward sloping for small K and nearly flat for large K (when n is large). This is because the bias term K^{-4} dominates for small values of K, while the variance term K/n dominates for large values of K, and the latter flattens as n increases.

20.13 ASYMPTOTIC NORMALITY

Take a parameter $\theta = a(m)$ that is a real-valued linear function of the regression function. This includes the regression function $m(x)$ at a given point x, derivatives of $m(x)$, and integrals over $m(x)$. Given $\widehat{m}_K(x) = X_K(x)'\widehat{\beta}_K$ as an estimator for $m(x)$, the estimator for θ is $\widehat{\theta}_K = a(\widehat{m}_K) = a_K'\widehat{\beta}_K$ for some $K \times 1$ vector of constants $a_K \neq 0$. (The relationship $a(\widehat{m}_K) = a_K'\widehat{\beta}_K$ follows because a is linear in m and $\widehat{m}_K$ is linear in $\widehat{\beta}_K$.)

If K were fixed as $n \to \infty$, then by standard asymptotic theory we would expect $\widehat{\theta}_K$ to be asymptotically normal with variance $V_K = a_K' \boldsymbol{Q}_K^{-1} \Omega_K \boldsymbol{Q}_K^{-1} a_K$, where $\Omega_K = \mathbb{E}\left[X_K X_K' e^2\right]$. The standard justification, however, is not valid in the nonparametric case. This is in part because V_K may diverge as $K \to \infty$, and in part because of the finite sample bias due to the approximation error. Therefore, a new theory is required. Interestingly, it turns out that in the nonparametric case, $\widehat{\theta}_K$ is still asymptotically normal, and V_K is still the appropriate variance for $\widehat{\theta}_K$. The proof is different than the parametric case, because the dimensions of the matrices are increasing with K, and we need to be attentive to the estimator's bias due to the series approximation.

Assumption 20.2 In addition to Assumption 20.1,

1. $\lim_{B \to \infty} \sup_x \mathbb{E}\left[e^2 \mathbb{1}\left\{e^2 > B\right\} \mid X = x\right] = 0.$
2. $\mathbb{E}\left[e^2 \mid X\right] \geq \underline{\sigma}^2 > 0.$
3. $\zeta_K \delta_K = o(1)$ as $K \to \infty$.

Assumption 20.2 part 1 is conditional square integrability. It implies that the conditional variance $\mathbb{E}\left[e^2 \mid X\right]$ is bounded. It is used to verify the Lindeberg condition for the CLT.

Assumption 20.2 part 2 states that the conditional variance is nowhere degenerate. Thus there is no X for which Y is perfectly predictable. This is a technical condition used to bound V_K from below.

Assumption 20.2 part 3 states that approximation error δ_K declines faster than the maximal regressor length ζ_K. For polynomials, a sufficient condition for this assumption is that $m''(x)$ is uniformly continuous. For splines, a sufficient condition is that $m'(x)$ is uniformly continuous.

Theorem 20.8 Under Assumption 20.2, as $n \to \infty$,

$$\frac{\sqrt{n}\left(\widehat{\theta}_K - \theta + a(r_K)\right)}{V_K^{1/2}} \underset{d}{\longrightarrow} \mathrm{N}(0,1). \tag{20.26}$$

The proof of Theorem 20.8 can be found in Section 20.31.

Theorem 20.8 shows that the estimator $\widehat{\theta}_K$ is approximately normal with bias $-a(r_K)$ and variance V_K/n. The variance is the same as in the parametric case. The asymptotic bias is similar to that found in kernel regression.

One useful message from Theorem 20.8 is that the classical variance formula V_K for $\widehat{\theta}_K$ applies to series regression. This justifies conventional estimators for V_K, as discussed in Section 20.18.

Theorem 20.8 shows that the estimator $\widehat{\theta}_K$ has a bias $a(r_K)$. What is this? It is the same transformation of the function $r_K(x)$ as $\theta = a(m)$ is of the regression function $m(x)$. For example, if $\theta = m(x)$ is the regression at a fixed point x, then $a(r_K) = r_K(x)$, the approximation error at the same point. If $\theta = m'(x)$ is the regression derivative, then $a(r_K) = r_K'(x)$ is the derivative of the approximation error.

Thus the bias in the estimator $\widehat{\theta}_K$ for θ shown in Theorem 20.8 is simply the approximation error transformed by the functional of interest. If we are estimating the regression function, then the bias is the error in approximating the regression function; if we are estimating the regression derivative, then the bias is the error in the derivative in the approximation error for the regression function.

20.14 REGRESSION ESTIMATION

A special yet important example of a linear estimator is the regression function at a fixed point x. In the notation of Section 20.13, $a(m) = m(x)$ and $a_K = X_K(x)$. The series estimator of $m(x)$ is $\widehat{\theta}_K = \widehat{m}_K(x) = X_K(x)'\widehat{\beta}_K$. As this is a key problem of interest, let us restate the asymptotic result of Theorem 20.8 for this estimator.

Theorem 20.9 Under Assumption 20.2, as $n \to \infty$,

$$\frac{\sqrt{n}\left(\widehat{m}_K(x) - m(x) + r_K(x)\right)}{V_K^{1/2}(x)} \xrightarrow[d]{} \mathrm{N}(0,1) \tag{20.27}$$

where $V_K(x) = X_K(x)' \boldsymbol{Q}_K^{-1} \Omega_K \boldsymbol{Q}_K^{-1} X_K(x)$.

There are several important features about the asymptotic distribution (20.27).

First, as mentioned in Section 20.13, it shows that the classical variance formula $V_K(x)$ applies for the series estimator $\widehat{m}_K(x)$. Second, (20.27) shows that the estimator has the asymptotic bias $r_K(x)$. This is because the finite order series is an approximation to the unknown regression function $m(x)$, which results in finite sample bias.

There is another fascinating connection between the asymptotic variance of Theorem 20.9 and the regression lengths $\zeta_K(x)$ of (20.15). Under conditional homoskedasticity, we have the simplification $V_K(x) = \sigma^2 \zeta_K(x)^2$. Thus the asymptotic variance of the regression estimator is proportional to the squared regression lengths. From Figure 20.4, we learned that the regression length $\zeta_K(x)$ is much higher at the edge of the support of the regressors, especially for polynomials. Thus the precision of the series regression estimator is considerably degraded at the edge of the support.

20.15 UNDERSMOOTHING

An unpleasant aspect of Theorem 20.9 is the bias term. An interesting trick is that this bias term can be made asymptotically negligible if we assume that K increases with n at a sufficiently fast rate.

Theorem 20.10 Under Assumption 20.2, if in addition $n\delta_K^{*2} \to 0$, then

$$\frac{\sqrt{n}\left(\widehat{m}_K(x) - m(x)\right)}{V_K^{1/2}(x)} \xrightarrow[d]{} \mathrm{N}(0,1). \tag{20.28}$$

The proof of Theorem 20.10 can be found in Section 20.31.

The condition $n\delta_K^{*2} \to 0$ implies that the squared bias converges faster than the estimation variance, so the former is asymptotically negligible. If $m''(x)$ is uniformly continuous, then a sufficient condition for polynomials and quadratic splines is $K \sim n^{1/4}$. For linear splines, a sufficient condition is for K to diverge faster than $K^{1/4}$. The rate $K \sim n^{1/4}$ is somewhat faster than the ISE-optimal rate $K \sim n^{1/5}$.

The assumption $n\delta_K^{*2} \to 0$ is often stated by authors as an innocuous technical condition. This is misleading, as it is a technical trick and should be discussed explicitly. The reason the assumption eliminates the bias from (20.28) is that the assumption forces the estimation variance to dominate the squared bias, so that the latter can be ignored. Thus means that the estimator itself is inefficient.

Because $n\delta_K^{*2} \to 0$ means that K is larger than optimal, we say that $\widehat{m}_K(x)$ is **undersmoothed** relative to the optimal series estimator.

Many authors like to focus their asymptotic theory on the assumptions in Theorem 20.10, as the distribution (20.28) appears to be cleaner. However, it is a poor use of asymptotic theory. There are three problems with the assumption $n\delta_K^{*2} \to 0$ and the approximation (20.28). First, the estimator $\widehat{m}_K(x)$ is inefficient. Second, although the assumption $n\delta_K^{*2} \to 0$ makes the bias of lower order than the variance, it only makes the bias of slightly lower order, meaning that the accuracy of the asymptotic approximation is poor. Effectively, the estimator is still biased in finite samples. Third, $n\delta_K^{*2} \to 0$ is an assumption, not a rule for empirical practice. It is unclear what the statement "Assume $n\delta_K^{*2} \to 0$" means in a practical application. From this viewpoint, the difference between (20.26) and (20.28) is in the assumptions, not in the actual reality or in the actual empirical practice. Eliminating a nuisance (the asymptotic bias) through an assumption is a trick, not a substantive use of theory. My strong view is that the result (20.26) is more informative than (20.28). It shows that the asymptotic distribution is normal but has a nontrivial finite sample bias.

20.16 RESIDUALS AND REGRESSION FIT

The fitted regression at $x = X_i$ is $\widehat{m}_K(X_i) = X_{Ki}'\widehat{\beta}_K$, and the fitted residual is $\widehat{e}_{Ki} = Y_i - \widehat{m}_K(X_i)$. The leave-one-out prediction errors are

$$\widetilde{e}_{Ki} = Y_i - \widehat{m}_{K,-i}(X_i) = Y_i - X_{Ki}'\widehat{\beta}_{K,-i}$$

where $\widehat{\beta}_{K,-i}$ is the least squares coefficient with the ith observation omitted. Using (3.44), we have the simple computational formula

$$\widetilde{e}_{Ki} = \widehat{e}_{Ki}\left(1 - X_{Ki}'\left(\boldsymbol{X}_K'\boldsymbol{X}_K\right)^{-1}X_{Ki}\right)^{-1}. \tag{20.29}$$

As for kernel regression, the prediction errors $\widetilde{e}_{Ki}$ are better estimators of the errors than the fitted residuals $\widehat{e}_{Ki}$, because the former do not have the tendency to over-fit when the number of series terms is large.

20.17 CROSS-VALIDATION MODEL SELECTION

A common method for selection of the number of series terms K is cross-validation. The cross-validation criterion is the sum[7] of squared prediction errors:

$$\mathrm{CV}(K) = \sum_{i=1}^{n} \widetilde{e}_{Ki}^2 = \sum_{i=1}^{n} \widehat{e}_{Ki}^2\left(1 - X_{Ki}'\left(\boldsymbol{X}_K'\boldsymbol{X}_K\right)^{-1}X_{Ki}\right)^{-2}. \tag{20.30}$$

The CV-selected value of K is the integer that minimizes $\mathrm{CV}(K)$.

[7]Some authors define $\mathrm{CV}(K)$ as the average rather than the sum.

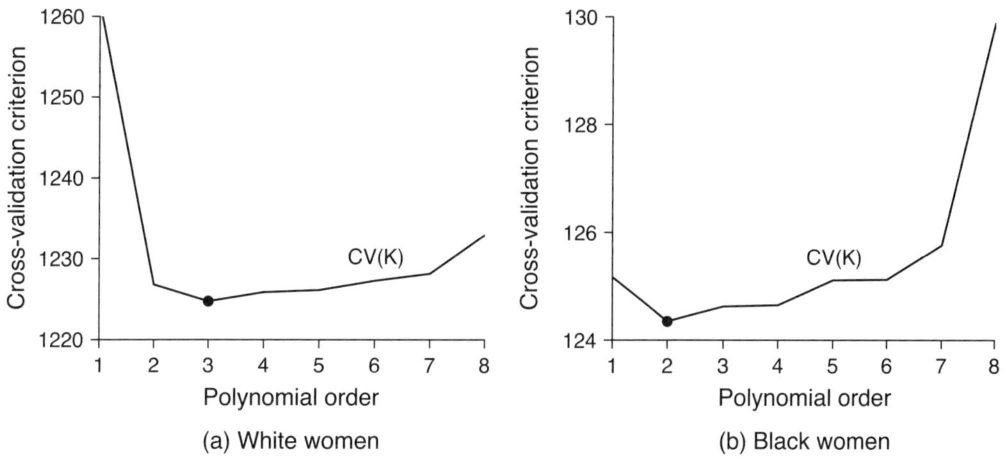

FIGURE 20.6 Cross-validation functions for polynomial estimates of experience profile

As shown in Theorem 19.7, $\mathrm{CV}(K)$ is an approximately unbiased estimator of the integrated mean-squared error (IMSE), which is the expected integrated squared error (ISE). The proof of the result is the same for all nonparametric estimators (series as well as kernels), so it does not need to be repeated here. Therefore, finding the K that produces the smallest value of $\mathrm{CV}(K)$ is a good indicator that the estimator $\widehat{m}_K(x)$ has small IMSE.

For practical implementation, we first designate a set of models (sets of basis transformations and number of variables K) over which to search. (For example, polynomials of order 1 through $K_{\max}$ for some preselected $K_{\max}$.) For each, there is a set of regressors X_K that are obtained by transformations of the original variables X. For each set, we estimate the regression by least squares, and calculate the leave-one-out prediction errors and the CV criterion. Because the errors are a linear operation, this calculation is simple. The CV-selected K is the integer that produces the smallest value of $\mathrm{CV}(K)$. Plots of $\mathrm{CV}(K)$ against K can aid assessment and interpretation. Because the model order K is an integer, the CV criterion for series regression is a discrete function, unlike the case of kernel regression.

If it is desired to produce an estimator $\widehat{m}_K(x)$ with reduced bias, it may be preferable to select a value of K slightly higher than that selected by CV alone.

To illustrate, Figure 20.6 plots the cross-validation functions for the polynomial regression estimates from Figure 20.1. The lowest point marks the polynomial order that minimizes the cross-validation function. Panel (a) plots the CV function for the subsample of white women. Here we see that the CV-selected order is $p = 3$, a cubic polynomial. Panel (b) plots the CV function for the subsample of Black women, which shows that the CV-selected order is $p = 2$, a quadratic. As expected from visual examination of Figure 20.1, the selected model is more parsimonious for panel (b), most likely because it has a substantially smaller sample size. What may be surprising is that even for panel (a), which has a large sample and smooth estimates, the CV-selected model is still relatively parsimonious.

A user who desires a reduced bias estimator might increase the polynomial orders to $p = 4$ or even $p = 5$ for the subsample of white women and to $p = 3$ or $p = 4$ for the subsample of Black women. Both CV functions are relatively similar across these values.

20.18 VARIANCE AND STANDARD ERROR ESTIMATION

The exact conditional variance of the least squares estimator $\widehat{\beta}_K$ under independent sampling is

$$\boldsymbol{V}_{\widehat{\beta}} = \left(\boldsymbol{X}_K'\boldsymbol{X}_K\right)^{-1}\left(\sum_{i=1}^{n} X_{Ki}X_{Ki}'\sigma^2(X_i)\right)\left(\boldsymbol{X}_K'\boldsymbol{X}_K\right)^{-1}. \tag{20.31}$$

The exact conditional variance for the conditional mean estimator $\widehat{m}_K(x) = X_K(x)'\widehat{\beta}_K$ is

$$V_K(x) = X_K(x)'\left(\boldsymbol{X}_K'\boldsymbol{X}_K\right)^{-1}\left(\sum_{i=1}^{n} X_{Ki}X_{Ki}'\sigma^2(X_i)\right)\left(\boldsymbol{X}_K'\boldsymbol{X}_K\right)^{-1} X_K(x).$$

Using the notation of Section 20.7, this equals

$$\frac{1}{n^2}\sum_{i=1}^{n}\widehat{w}_K(x, X_i)^2\sigma^2(X_i).$$

In the case of conditional homoskedasticity, the latter simplifies to

$$\frac{1}{n}\widehat{w}_K(x,x)\sigma^2 \simeq \frac{1}{n}\zeta_K(x)^2\sigma^2$$

where $\zeta_K(x)$ is the normalized regressor length defined in (20.15). Under conditional heteroskedasticty, large samples, and K large (so that $\widehat{w}_K(x, X_i)$ is a local kernel), it approximately equals

$$\frac{1}{n}w_K(x,x)\sigma^2(x) = \frac{1}{n}\zeta_K(x)^2\sigma^2(x).$$

In either case, we find that the variance is approximately

$$V_K(x) \simeq \frac{1}{n}\zeta_K(x)^2\sigma^2(x).$$

Thus the variance of the series regression estimator is a scale of $\zeta_K(x)^2$ and the conditional variance. From the plot of $\zeta_K(x)$ shown in Figure 20.4, we can deduce that the series regression estimator will be relatively imprecise at the boundary of the support of X.

The estimator of (20.31) recommended by Andrews (1991a) is the HC3 estimator

$$\widehat{\boldsymbol{V}}_{\widehat{\beta}} = \left(\boldsymbol{X}_K'\boldsymbol{X}_K\right)^{-1}\left(\sum_{i=1}^{n} X_{Ki}X_{Ki}'\widetilde{e}_{Ki}^2\right)\left(\boldsymbol{X}_K'\boldsymbol{X}_K\right)^{-1} \tag{20.32}$$

where $\widetilde{e}_{Ki}$ is the leave-one-out prediction error (20.29). Alternatives include the HC1 or HC2 estimators.

Given (20.32), a variance estimator for $\widehat{m}_K(x) = X_K(x)'\widehat{\beta}_K$ is

$$\widehat{V}_K(x) = X_K(x)'\left(\boldsymbol{X}_K'\boldsymbol{X}_K\right)^{-1}\left(\sum_{i=1}^{n} X_{Ki}X_{Ki}'\widetilde{e}_{Ki}^2\right)\left(\boldsymbol{X}_K'\boldsymbol{X}_K\right)^{-1} X_K(x). \tag{20.33}$$

A standard error for $\widehat{m}(x)$ is the square root of $\widehat{V}_K(x)$.

20.19 CLUSTERED OBSERVATIONS

Clustered observations are (Y_{ig}, X_{ig}) for individuals $i = 1, \dots, n_g$ in cluster $g = 1, \dots, G$. The model is

$$Y_{ig} = m\left(X_{ig}\right) + e_{ig}$$
$$\mathbb{E}\left[e_{ig} \mid \boldsymbol{X}_g\right] = 0$$

where $\boldsymbol{X}_g$ is the stacked X_{ig}. Stack Y_{ig} and e_{ig} into cluster-level variables $\boldsymbol{Y}_g$ and $\boldsymbol{e}_g$.

The series regression model using cluster-level notation is $\boldsymbol{Y}_g = \boldsymbol{X}_g \beta_K + \boldsymbol{e}_{Kg}$. We can write the series estimator as

$$\widehat{\beta}_K = \left(\sum_{g=1}^{G} \boldsymbol{X}_g' \boldsymbol{X}_g\right)^{-1} \left(\sum_{g=1}^{G} \boldsymbol{X}_g' \boldsymbol{Y}_g\right).$$

The cluster-level residual vector is $\widehat{\boldsymbol{e}}_g = \boldsymbol{Y}_g - \boldsymbol{X}_g \widehat{\beta}_K$.

As for parametric regression with clustered observations, the standard assumption is that the clusters are mutually independent, but dependence within each cluster is unstructured. We therefore use the same variance formulas as used for parametric regression. The standard estimator is

$$\widehat{\boldsymbol{V}}_{\widehat{\beta}}^{\mathrm{CR1}} = \left(\frac{G}{G-1}\right) \left(\boldsymbol{X}_K' \boldsymbol{X}_K\right)^{-1} \left(\sum_{g=1}^{G} \boldsymbol{X}_g' \widehat{\boldsymbol{e}}_g \widehat{\boldsymbol{e}}_g' \boldsymbol{X}_g\right) \left(\boldsymbol{X}_K' \boldsymbol{X}_K\right)^{-1}.$$

An alternative is to use the delete-cluster prediction error $\widetilde{\boldsymbol{e}}_g = \boldsymbol{Y}_g - \boldsymbol{X}_g \widetilde{\beta}_{K,-g}$, where

$$\widetilde{\beta}_{K,-g} = \left(\sum_{j \neq g} \boldsymbol{X}_j' \boldsymbol{X}_j\right)^{-1} \left(\sum_{j \neq g} \boldsymbol{X}_j' \boldsymbol{Y}_j\right)$$

leading to the estimator

$$\widehat{\boldsymbol{V}}_{\widehat{\beta}}^{\mathrm{CR3}} = \left(\boldsymbol{X}_K' \boldsymbol{X}_K\right)^{-1} \left(\sum_{g=1}^{G} \boldsymbol{X}_g' \widetilde{\boldsymbol{e}}_g \widetilde{\boldsymbol{e}}_g' \boldsymbol{X}_g\right) \left(\boldsymbol{X}_K' \boldsymbol{X}_K\right)^{-1}.$$

There is no current theory on how to select the number of series terms K for clustered observations. A reasonable choice is to minimize the delete-cluster cross-validation criterion $\mathrm{CV}(K) = \sum_{g=1}^{G} \widetilde{\boldsymbol{e}}_g' \widetilde{\boldsymbol{e}}_g$.

20.20 CONFIDENCE BANDS

When displaying nonparametric estimators such as $\widehat{m}_K(x)$, it is customary to display confidence intervals. An asymptotic pointwise 95% confidence interval for $m(x)$ is $\widehat{m}_K(x) \pm 1.96 \widehat{V}_K^{1/2}(x)$. These confidence intervals can be plotted along with $\widehat{m}_K(x)$.

To illustrate, Figure 20.7 plots polynomial estimates of the regression of log(*wage*) on *experience* using the selected estimates from Figure 20.1, plus 95% confidence bands. Panel (a) plots the estimate for the subsample of white women using $p = 5$. Panel (b) plots the estimate for the subsample of Black women using $p = 3$. The standard errors are calculated using the formula (20.33). You can see that the confidence bands widen at the boundaries. The confidence bands are tight for the larger subsample of white women, and significantly wider

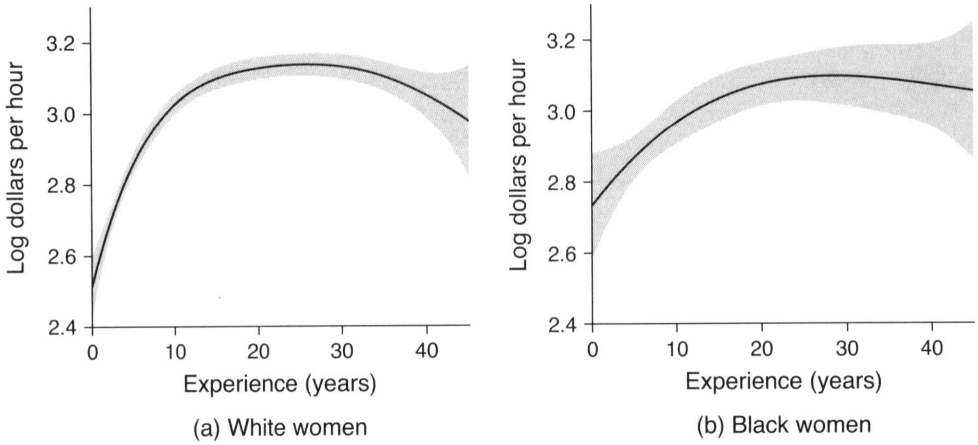

FIGURE 20.7 Polynomial estimates with 95% confidence bands

for the smaller subsample of Black women. Regardless, both plots indicate that the average wage rises for experience levels up to about 20 years and then flattens for experience levels above 20 years.

There are two deficiencies with these confidence bands. First, they do not take into account the bias $r_K(x)$ of the series estimator. Consequently, we should interpret the confidence bounds as valid for the pseudo-true regression (the best finite K approximation) rather than the true regression function $m(x)$. Second, the above confidence intervals are based on a pointwise (in x) asymptotic distribution theory. Consequently, we should interpret their coverage as having pointwise validity and be cautious about interpreting global shapes from the confidence bands.

20.21 UNIFORM APPROXIMATIONS

Since $\widehat{m}_K(x)$ is a function, it is desirable to have a distribution theory that applies to the entire function, not just the estimator at a point. Such a theory can be used, for example, to construct confidence bands with uniform (in x) coverage properties.

For those familiar with empirical process theory, it might be hoped that the stochastic process

$$\eta_K(x) = \frac{\sqrt{n}\left(\widehat{m}_K(x) - m(x)\right)}{V_K^{1/2}(x)}$$

might converge to a stochastic (Gaussian) process, but this is not the case. Effectively, the process $\eta_K(x)$ is not stochastically equicontinuous, so conventional empirical process theory does not apply.

To develop a uniform theory, Belloni et al. (2015) have introduced what are known as strong approximations. Their method shows that $\eta_K(x)$ is equal in distribution to a sequence of Gaussian processes plus a negligible error. Their theory (Theorem 4.4) takes the following form. Under stronger conditions than Assumption 20.2, we have

$$\eta_K(x) =_d \frac{X_K(x)'\left(\boldsymbol{Q}_K^{-1}\Omega_K\boldsymbol{Q}_K^{-1}\right)^{1/2}}{V_K^{1/2}(x)} G_K + o_p(1)$$

uniformly in x, where "$=_d$" means "equality in distribution" and $G_K \sim \mathrm{N}(0, \boldsymbol{I}_K)$.

This shows that the distributional result in Theorem 20.10 can be interpreted as holding uniformly in x. It can also be used to develop confidence bands (different from those in the Section 20.20) with asymptotic uniform coverage.

20.22 PARTIALLY LINEAR MODEL

A common use of a series regression is to allow $m(x)$ to be nonparametric with respect to one variable yet linear in the other variables, which allows flexibility in a particular variable of interest. A partially linear model with vector-valued regressor X_1 and real-valued continuous X_2 takes the form

$$m\left(x_1, x_2\right) = x_1'\beta_1 + m_2(x_2).$$

This model is common when X_1 is discrete (e.g., binary) and X_2 is continuously distributed.

Series methods are convenient for partially linear models, as we can replace the unknown function $m_2(x_2)$ with a series expansion to obtain

$$m\left(X\right) \simeq m_K\left(X\right) = X_1'\beta_1 + X_{2K}(X_2)'\beta_{2K} = X_K'\beta_K$$

where the $X_{2K} = X_{2K}(x_2)$ are basis transformations of x_2 (typically polynomials or splines). After transformation, the regressors are $X_K = (X_1', X_{2K}')$ with coefficients $\beta_K = (\beta_1', \beta_{2K}')'$.

20.23 PANEL FIXED EFFECTS

The one-way error components nonparametric regression model is

$$Y_{it} = m(X_{it}) + u_i + \varepsilon_{it}$$

for $i = 1, \dots, N$ and $t = 1, \dots, T$. It is standard to treat the individual effect u_i as a fixed effect. This model can be interpreted as a special case of the partially linear model from Section 20.22, though the dimension of u_i is increasing with N.

A series estimator approximates the function $m(x)$ with $m_K(x) = X_K(x)'\beta_K$, as in (20.4). This leads to the series regression model $Y_{it} = X_{Kit}'\beta_K + u_i + \varepsilon_{Kit}$, where $X_{Kit} = X_K(X_{it})$.

The fixed effects estimator is the same as in linear panel data regression. First, the within transformation is applied to Y_{it} and to the elements of the basis transformations X_{Kit}. These are $\dot{Y}_{it} = Y_{it} - \overline{Y}_i$ and $\dot{X}_{Kit} = X_{Kit} - \overline{X}_{Kit}$. The transformed regression equation is $\dot{Y}_{it} = \dot{X}_{Kit}'\beta_K + \dot{\varepsilon}_{Kit}$. What is important about the within transformation for the regressors is that it is applied to the transformed variables $\dot{X}_{Kit}$, not to the original regressor X_{it}. For example, in a polynomial regression, the within transformation is applied to the powers X_{it}^j. It is inappropriate to apply the within transformation to X_{it} and then construct the basis transformations.

The coefficient is estimated by least squares on the within transformed variables:

$$\widehat{\beta}_K = \left(\sum_{i=1}^{n}\sum_{t=1}^{T}\dot{X}_{Kit}\dot{X}_{Kit}'\right)^{-1}\left(\sum_{i=1}^{n}\sum_{t=1}^{T}\dot{X}_{Kit}\dot{Y}_{it}\right).$$

Variance estimators should be calculated using the clustered variance formulas, clustered at the level of the individual i, as described in Section 20.19.

For selection of the number of series terms K, there is no current theory. A reasonable method is to use delete-cluster cross-validation, as described in Section 20.19.

20.24 MULTIPLE REGRESSORS

Suppose $X \in \mathbb{R}^d$ is vector-valued and continuously distributed. A multivariate series approximation can be obtained as follows. Construct a set of basis transformations for each variable separately. Take their tensor cross-products. Use these as regressors. For example, a pth-order polynomial is

$$m_K(x) = \beta_0 + \sum_{j_1=1}^{p} \cdots \sum_{j_d=1}^{p} x_1^{j_1} \cdots x_d^{j_d} \beta_{j_1,\ldots,j_d K}.$$

This includes all powers and cross-products. The coefficient vector has dimension $K = 1 + p^d$.

The inclusion of cross-products greatly increases the number of coefficients relative to the univariate case. Consequently, series applications with multiple regressors typically require large sample sizes.

20.25 ADDITIVELY SEPARABLE MODELS

As discussed in section 20.24, when $X \in \mathbb{R}^d$, a full series expansion requires a large number of coefficients, which means that estimation precision will be low unless the sample size is quite large. A common simplification is to treat the regression function $m(x)$ as additively separable in the individual regressors, which means that

$$m(x) = m_1(x_1) + m_2(x_2) + \cdots + m_d(x_d).$$

We then apply series expansions (polynomials or splines) separately for each component $m_j(x_j)$. Essentially, this is the same as the expansions discussed in Section 20.24 but omits the interaction terms.

The advantage of additive separability is the reduction in dimensionality. While an unconstrained pth order polynomial has $1 + p^d$ coefficients, an additively separable polynomial model has only $1 + dp$ coefficients. This is a major reduction. The disadvantage of additive separability is that the interaction effects have been eliminated, which is a substantive restriction on $m(x)$.

The decision to impose additive separability can be based on an economic model that suggests the absence of interaction effects, or it can be a model selection decision similar to the selection of the number of series terms.

20.26 NONPARAMETRIC INSTRUMENTAL VARIABLES REGRESSION

The basic **nonparametric instrumental variables (NPIV)** model takes the form

$$\begin{aligned} Y &= m(X) + e \qquad (20.34) \\ \mathbb{E}[e \mid Z] &= 0 \end{aligned}$$

where Y, X, and Z are real valued. Here, Z is an instrumental variable, and X an endogenous regressor.

In recent years many papers in the econometrics literature have examined the NPIV model, exploring identification, estimation, and inference. Many of these papers are mathematically advanced. Two important and accessible contributions are Newey and Powell (2003) and Horowitz (2011). Here we discuss some of the primary results.

A series estimator approximates the function $m(x)$ with $m_K(x) = X_K(x)'\beta_K$, as in (20.4). This leads to the series structural equation

$$Y = X_K'\beta_K + e_K \tag{20.35}$$

where $X_K = X_K(X)$. For example, if a polynomial basis is used, then $X_K = (1, X, \ldots, X^{K-1})$.

Since X is endogenous, so is the entire vector X_K. Thus we need at least K instrumental varibles. It is useful to consider the reduced-form equation for X. A nonparametric specification is

$$X = g(Z) + u$$
$$\mathbb{E}[u \mid Z] = 0.$$

We can approximate $g(z)$ by the series expansion

$$g(z) \simeq g_L(z) = Z_L(z)'\gamma_L$$

where $Z_L(z)$ is an $L \times 1$ vector of basis transformations, and γ_L is an $L \times 1$ coefficient vector. For example, if a polynomial basis is used, then $Z_L(z) = (1, z, \ldots, z^{L-1})$. For simplicity, most of the literature focuses on the case $L = K$, but this is not essential to the method.

If $L \geq K$, we can then use $Z_L = Z_L(Z)$ as instruments for X_K. The 2SLS estimator $\widehat{\beta}_{K,L}$ of β_K is

$$\widehat{\beta}_{K,L} = \left(\boldsymbol{X}_K'\boldsymbol{Z}_L\left(\boldsymbol{Z}_L'\boldsymbol{Z}_L\right)^{-1}\boldsymbol{Z}_L'\boldsymbol{X}_K\right)^{-1}\left(\boldsymbol{X}_K'\boldsymbol{Z}_L\left(\boldsymbol{Z}_L'\boldsymbol{Z}_L\right)^{-1}\boldsymbol{Z}_L'\boldsymbol{Y}\right).$$

The estimator of $m(x)$ is $\widehat{m}_K(x) = X_K(x)'\widehat{\beta}_{K,L}$. If $L > K$, the linear GMM estimator can be similarly defined.

One way to think about the choice of instruments is to realize that we are actually estimating reduced-form equations for each element of X_K. The reduced-form system is

$$X_K = \Gamma_K' Z_L + u_K$$
$$\Gamma_K = \mathbb{E}\left[Z_L Z_L'\right]^{-1}\mathbb{E}\left[Z_L X_K'\right].$$

For example, suppose we use a polynomial basis with $K = L = 3$. Then the reduced-form system (ignoring intercepts) is

$$\begin{bmatrix} X \\ X^2 \\ X^3 \end{bmatrix} = \begin{bmatrix} \Gamma_{11} & \Gamma_{21} & \Gamma_{31} \\ \Gamma_{12} & \Gamma_{22} & \Gamma_{32} \\ \Gamma_{13} & \Gamma_{13} & \Gamma_{23} \end{bmatrix}\begin{bmatrix} Z \\ Z^2 \\ Z^3 \end{bmatrix} + \begin{bmatrix} u_1 \\ u_2 \\ u_3 \end{bmatrix}. \tag{20.36}$$

This system is modeling the conditional mean of X, X^2, and X^3 as linear functions of Z, Z^2, and Z^3.

To determine whether the coefficient β_K is identified, it is useful to consider the simple reduced-form equation $X = \gamma_0 + \gamma_1 Z + u$. Assume that $\gamma_1 \neq 0$, so that the equation is strongly identified, and assume for simplicity that u is independent of Z with mean 0 and variance σ_u^2. The identification properties of the reduced form are invariant to rescaling and recentering X and Z, so without loss of generality, we can set $\gamma_0 = 0$ and

$\gamma_1 = 1$. Then we can calculate that the coefficient matrix in (20.36) is

$$\begin{bmatrix} \Gamma_{11} & \Gamma_{21} & \Gamma_{31} \\ \Gamma_{12} & \Gamma_{22} & \Gamma_{32} \\ \Gamma_{13} & \Gamma_{13} & \Gamma_{23} \end{bmatrix} = \begin{bmatrix} 1 & 0 & 0 \\ 0 & 1 & 0 \\ 3\sigma_u^2 & 0 & 1 \end{bmatrix}.$$

Notice that this is lower triangular and full rank. It turns out that this property holds for any values of $K = L$, so the coefficient matrix in (20.36) is full rank for any choice of $K = L$. Thus identification of the coefficient β_K is strong if the reduced-form equation for X is strong. Thus to check the identification condition for β_K, it is sufficient to check the reduced-form equation for X. A critically important caveat, however, as discussed in Section 20.27, is that identification of β_K does not mean that the structural function $m(x)$ is identified.

A simple method for pointwise inference is to use conventional methods to estimate $V_{K,L} = \text{var}\left[\widehat{\beta}_{K,L}\right]$ and then estimate $\text{var}\left[\widehat{m}_K(x)\right]$ by $X_K(x)'\widehat{V}_{K,L}X_K(x)$ as in series regression. Bootstrap methods are typically advocated to achieve better coverage. See Horowitz (2011) for details. For state-of-the-art inference methods, see Chen and Pouzo (2015) and Chen and Christensen (2018).

20.27 NPIV IDENTIFICATION

In Section 20.26, we discussed identification of the pseudo-true coefficient β_K. In this section, we discuss identification of the structural function $m(x)$, which is considerably more challenging.

To understand how the function $m(x)$ is determined, apply the expectation operator $\mathbb{E}[\cdot \mid Z = z]$ to (20.34). We find

$$\mathbb{E}[Y \mid Z = z] = \mathbb{E}[m(X) \mid Z = z]$$

with the remainder equal to 0, because $\mathbb{E}[e \mid Z] = 0$. We can write this equation as

$$\mu(z) = \int m(x) f(x \mid z)\, dx \qquad (20.37)$$

where $\mu(z) = \mathbb{E}[Y \mid Z = z]$ is the CEF of Y given $Z = z$, and $f(x \mid z)$ is the conditional density of X given Z. These two functions are identified[8] from the joint distribution of (Y, X, Z). Thus the unknown function $m(x)$ is the solution to the **integral equation** (20.37). Conceptually, you can imagine estimating $\mu(z)$ and $f(x \mid z)$ using standard techniques and then finding the solution $m(x)$. In essence, this is how $m(x)$ is defined, and it is the nonparametric analog of the classical relationship between the structural and reduced forms.

Unfortunately, the solution $m(x)$ may not be unique even in situations where a linear IV model is strongly identified. It is related to what is known as the **ill-posed inverse problem**. The latter means that the solution $m(x)$ is not necessarily a continuous function of $\mu(z)$. Identification requires restricting the class of allowable functions $f(x \mid z)$, which is analogous to the linear IV model, where identification requires restrictions on the reduced-form equations. Specifying and understanding the needed restrictions is more subtle than in the linear case.

The function $m(x)$ is identified if it is the unique solution to (20.37). Equivalently, $m(x)$ is not identified if we can replace $m(x)$ in (20.37) with $m(x) + \delta(x)$ for some nontrivial function $\delta(x)$ and the solution does not change. The latter occurs when

$$\int \delta(x) f(x \mid z)\, dx = 0 \qquad (20.38)$$

[8] Technically, if $\mathbb{E}|Y| < \infty$, the joint density of (Z, X) exists, and the marginal density of Z is positive.

for all z. Equivalently, $m(x)$ is identified if (and only if) (20.38) holds only for the trivial function $\delta(x) = 0$.

Newey and Powell (2003) defined this fundamental condition as **completeness**.

Proposition 20.1 Completeness. $m(x)$ is identified if (and only if) the completeness condition holds: (20.38) for all z implies $\delta(x) = 0$.

Completeness is a property of the reduced-form conditional density $f(x \mid z)$. It is unaffected by the structural equation $m(x)$. This is analogous to the linear IV model, where identification is a property of the reduced-form equations, not a property of the structural equation.

As stated above, completeness may not be satisfied even if the reduced-form relationship is strong. This may be easiest to see by a constructed example.[9] Suppose that the reduced form is $X = Z + u$, $\text{var}[Z] = 1$, u is independent of Z, and u is distributed $U[-1, 1]$. This reduced-form equation has $R^2 = 0.75$ and so is strong. The reduced-form conditional density is $f(x \mid z) = 1/2$ on $[-1 + z, 1 + z]$. Consider $\delta(x) = \sin(x/\pi)$. We calculate that

$$\int \delta(x) f(x \mid z)\, dx = \int_{-1+z}^{1+z} \sin(x/\pi)\, dx = 0$$

for every z, because $\sin(x/\pi)$ is periodic on intervals of length 2 and integrates to 0 over $[-1, 1]$, Thus means that equation (20.37) holds[10] for $m(x) + \sin(x/\pi)$, and so $m(x)$ is not identified. This is despite the fact that the reduced-form equation is strong.

Although identification fails for some conditional distributions, it does not fail for all. Andrews (2017) provides classes of distributions that satisfy the completeness condition and shows that these distribution classes are quite general.

What does this mean in practice? If completeness fails, then the structural equation is not identified and cannot be consistently estimated. Furthermore, by analogy with the weak instruments literature, we expect that if the conditional distribution is close to incomplete, then the structural equation will be poorly identified, and our estimators will be imprecise. Whether or not the conditional distribution is complete is unknown (and is more difficult to assess than in the linear model), which is troubling for empirical research. Effectively, in any given application, we do not know whether or not the structural function $m(x)$ is identified.

A partial answer is provided by Freyberger (2017). He shows that the joint hypothesis of incompleteness and small asymptotic bias can be tested. By applying the test proposed in Freyberger (2017), a user can obtain evidence that their NPIV estimator is well behaved in the sense of having low bias. Unlike Stock and Yogo (2005), however, Freyberger's result does not address inference.

20.28 NPIV CONVERGENCE RATE

As described in Horowitz (2011), the convergence rate of $\widehat{m}_K(x)$ for $m(x)$ is

$$|\widehat{m}_K(x) - m(x)| = O_p\left(K^{-s} + K^r \left(\frac{K}{n}\right)^{1/2}\right) \tag{20.39}$$

[9]This example was suggested by Joachim Freyberger.

[10]In fact, (20.37) holds for $m(x) + \delta(x)$ for any function $\delta(x)$ that is periodic on intervals of length 2 and integrates to 0 on $[-1, 1]$.

where s is the smoothness[11] of $m(x)$, and r is the smoothness of the joint density $f_{XZ}(x,z)$ of (X,Z). The first term K^{-s} is the bias due to the approximation of $m(x)$ by $m_K(x)$ and takes the same form as for series regression. The second term $K^r (K/n)^{1/2}$ is the standard deviation of $\widehat{m}_K(x)$. The component $(K/n)^{1/2}$ is the same as for series regression. The extra component K^r is due to the ill-posed inverse problem (see Section 20.27).

From the rate (20.39), we can calculate that the optimal number of series terms is $K \sim n^{1/(2r+2s+1)}$. Given this rate, the best possible convergence rate in (20.39) is $O_p\left(n^{-s/(2r+2s+1)}\right)$. For $r>0$, these rates are slower than for series regression. If we consider the case $s=2$, these rates are $K \sim n^{1/(2r+5)}$ and $O_p\left(n^{-2/(2r+5)}\right)$, which are slower than the $K \sim n^{1/5}$ and $O_p\left(n^{-2/5}\right)$ rates obtained by series regression.

A very unusual aspect of the rate (20.39) is that smoothness of $f_{XZ}(x,z)$ adversely affects the convergence rate. Larger r means a slower rate of convergence. The limiting case as $r \to \infty$ (for example, joint normality of X and Z) results in a logarithmic convergence rate, which seems very strange. The reason is that when the density $f_{XZ}(x,z)$ is very smooth, the data contain little information about the function $m(x)$. This result is not intuitive and requires a deeper mathematical treatment.

A practical implication of the convergence rate (20.39) is that the number of series terms K should be much smaller than for regression estimation. Estimation variance increases quickly as K increases. Therefore, K should not be taken to be too large. In practice, however, it is unclear how to select the series order K, as standard cross-validation methods do not apply.

20.29 NONPARAMETRIC VS. PARAMETRIC IDENTIFICATION

One of the insights from the nonparametric identification literature is that it is important to understand which features of a model are nonparametrically identified, meaning which are identified without functional form assumptions, and which are only identified based on functional form assumptions. Since functional form assumptions are dubious in most economic applications, the strong implication is that researchers should strive to work only with models that are nonparametrically identified.

Even if a model is determined to be nonparametrically identified, a researcher may estimate a linear (or another simple parametric) model. This approach is valid, because it can be viewed as an approximation to the nonparametric structure. If, however, the model is identified only under a parametric assumption, then it cannot be viewed as an approximation, and it is unclear how to interpret the model more broadly.

For example, in the regression model $Y=m(X)+e$ with $\mathbb{E}[e \mid X]=0$, the CEF is nonparametrically identified by Theorem 2.14. Thus researchers who estimate linear regressions (or other low-dimensional regressions) can interpret their estimated model as an approximation to the underlying CEF.

As another example, in the NPIV model where $\mathbb{E}[e \mid Z]=0$, the structural function $m(x)$ is identified under the completeness condition. Thus researchers who estimate linear 2SLS regressions can interpret their estimated model as an approximation to $m(x)$ (subject to the caveat that it is difficult to know whether completeness holds).

But the analysis can also point out simple yet subtle mistakes. Take the simple IV model with one exogenous regressor X_1 and one endogenous regressor X_2,

$$
\begin{aligned}
Y &= \beta_0+\beta_1 X_1+\beta_2 X_2+e \qquad (20.40)\\
\mathbb{E}[e \mid X_1] &= 0
\end{aligned}
$$

[11]The number of bounded derivatives.

with no additional instruments. Suppose that an enterprising researcher suggests using the instrument X_1^2 for X_2, reasoning that the assumptions imply that $\mathbb{E}\left[X_1^2 e\right]=0$, so X_1^2 is a valid instrument. The trouble is that the basic model is not nonparametrically identified. If we write (20.40) as a partially linear nonparametric IV problem,

$$\begin{aligned} Y &= m(X_1)+\beta_2 X_2+e \\ \mathbb{E}\left[e \mid X_1\right] &= 0 \end{aligned} \tag{20.41}$$

then we can see that this model is not identified. We need a valid excluded instrument Z. Because (20.41) is not identified, (20.40) cannot be viewed as a valid approximation. The apparent identification of (20.40) critically rests on the unknown truth of the linearity in (20.40).

The point of this example is that (20.40) should never be estimated by 2SLS using the instrument X_1^2 for X_2, fundamentally because the nonparametric model (20.41) is not identified.

Another way to describe the mistake is to observe that X_1^2 is a valid instrument in (20.40) only if it is a valid exclusion restriction from the structural equation (20.40). Viewed in the context of (20.41), we can see that this is a functional form restriction. As stated above, identification based on functional form restrictions alone is highly undesirable, because functional form assumptions are dubious.

20.30 EXAMPLE: ANGRIST AND LAVY (1999)

To illustrate nonparametric instrumental variables in practice, let us follow Horowitz (2011) by extending the empirical work reported in Angrist and Lavy (1999). Their paper is concerned with measuring the causal effect on academic achievement of the number of students in an elementary school classroom. They address this issue using a sample of 4,067 Israeli fourth and fifth grade classrooms. The dependent variable is the classroom average score on an achievement test. Here we consider the reading score *avgverb*. The explanatory variables are the number of students in the classroom (*classize*), the number of students in the grade at the school (*enrollment*), and a school-level index of students' socioeconomic status that the authors call percent *disadvantaged*. The variables *enrollment* and *disadvantaged* are treated as exogenous, but *classize* is treated as endogenous, because wealthier schools may be able to offer smaller class sizes.

The authors suggest the following instrumental variable for *classsize*. Israeli regulations specify that class sizes must be capped at 40. Thus *classize* should be perfectly predictable from *enrollment*. If the regulation is followed, a school with up to 40 students will have one classroom in the grade, and schools with 41–80 students will have two classrooms. The precise prediction is that *classsize* equals

$$p=\frac{enrollment}{1+\lfloor 1-enrollment/40\rfloor} \tag{20.42}$$

where $\lfloor a\rfloor$ is the integer part of a. Angrist and Lavy use p as an instrumental variable for *classize*.

They estimate several specifications. We focus on equation (6) from their table VII, which specifies *avgverb* as a linear function of *classize, disadvantaged, enrollment, grade4*, and the interaction of *classize* and *disadvantaged*, where *grade4* is a dummy indicator for fourth grade classrooms. The equation is estimated by instrumental variables, using p and $p\times disadvantaged$ as instruments. The observations are treated as clustered at the level of the school. Their estimates show a negative and statistically significant impact of *classsize* on reading test scores.

Table 20.1
Nonparametric instrumental variable regression for reading test score

Variable	Parameter estimate
classize/40	34.2
	(33.4)
$(classize/40)^2$	−61.2
	(53.0)
$(classize/40)^3$	29.0
	(26.8)
disadvantaged/14	−12.4
	(1.7)
$(disadvantaged/14)^2$	3.33
	(0.54)
$(disadvantaged/14)^3$	−0.377
	(0.078)
(*classize*/40)(*disadvantaged*/14)	0.81
	(1.77)
enrollment	0.015
	(0.007)
grade4	−1.96
	(0.16)
Intercept	77.0
	(6.9)

We are interested in a nonparametric version of their equation. To keep the specification reasonably parsimonious yet flexible, let us use the following equation:

$$\begin{aligned} avgverb = {} & \beta_1\left(\frac{classize}{40}\right) + \beta_2\left(\frac{classize}{40}\right)^2 + \beta_3\left(\frac{classize}{40}\right)^3 \\ & + \beta_4\left(\frac{disadvantaged}{14}\right) + \beta_5\left(\frac{disadvantaged}{14}\right)^2 + \beta_6\left(\frac{disadvantaged}{14}\right)^3 \\ & + \beta_7\left(\frac{classize}{40}\right)\left(\frac{disadvantaged}{14}\right) + \beta_8 enrollment + \beta_9 grade4 + \beta_{10} + e. \end{aligned}$$

This is a cubic equation in *classize* and *disadvantaged*, with a single interaction term, and is linear in *enrollment* and *grade4*. The cubic in *disadvantaged* was selected by a delete-cluster cross-validation regression without *classize*. The cubic in *classize* was selected to allow for a minimal degree of nonparametric flexibility without overparameterization. The variables *classize* and *disadvantaged* were scaled by 40 and 14, respectively, so that the regression is well conditioned. The scaling for *classize* was selected so that the variable essentially falls in [0, 1], and the scaling for *disadvantaged* was selected so that its mean is 1.

The equation is estimated by 2SLS using $(p/40)$, $(p/40)^2$, $(p/40)^3$ and $(p/40) \times (disadvantaged/14)$ as instruments for the four variables involving *classize*. The parameter estimates are reported in Table 20.1. The standard errors are clustered at the level of the school. Most of the individual coefficients do not have interpretable meaning, except that the positive coefficient on *enrollment* shows that larger schools achieve slightly

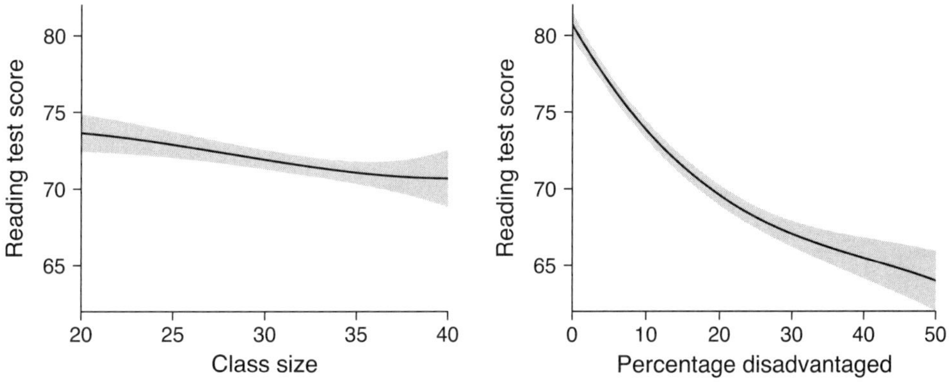

(a) Effect of *classize* (b) Effect of percent *disadvantaged*

FIGURE 20.8 Nonparametric instrumental variables estimates of the effect of *classize* and *disadvantaged* on reading test scores

higher test scores, and the negative coefficient on *grade4* shows that fourth grade students have somewhat lower test scores than fifth grade students.

To obtain a better interpretation of the results, we display the estimated regression functions in Figure 20.8. Panel (a) displays the estimated effect of *classize* on reading test scores. Panel (b) displays the estimated effect of *disadvantaged*. In both panels, the other variables are set at their sample means.[12]

In panel (a) we can see that increasing class size decreases the average test score. This is consistent with the results from the linear model estimated by Angrist and Lavy (1999). The estimated effect is remarkably close to linear.

In panel (b) we can see that increasing the percentage of disadvantaged students greatly decreases the average test score. This effect is substantially greater in magnitude than the effect of *classsize*. The effect also appears to be nonlinear. The effect is precisely estimated with tight pointwise confidence bands.

We can also use the estimated model for hypothesis testing. The question addressed by Angrist and Lavy was whether *classsize* has an effect on test scores. In the nonparametric model estimated here, this hypothesis holds under the linear restriction $\mathbb{H}_0 : \beta_1 = \beta_2 = \beta_3 = \beta_7 = 0$. Examining the individual coefficient estimates and standard errors, it is unclear whether this is a significant effect, as none of these four coefficient estimates is statistically different from 0. This hypothesis is better tested by a Wald test (using cluster-robust variance estimates). This statistic is 12.7, which has an asymptotic p-value of 0.013. This suppports the hypothesis that class size has a negative effect on student performance.

We can also use the model to quantify the impact of class size on test scores. Consider the impact of increasing a class from 20 to 40 students. In the above model, the predicted impact on test scores is

$$\theta = \frac{1}{2}\beta_1 + \frac{3}{4}\beta_2 + \frac{7}{8}\beta_3 + \frac{1}{2}\beta_4.$$

This is a linear function of the coefficients. The point estimate is $\widehat{\theta} = -2.96$ with a standard error of 1.21. (The point estimate is identical to the difference between the endpoints of the estimated function shown in panel (a).) It is a small but substantive impact.

[12]If they are set at other values, it does not change the qualitative nature of the plots.

20.31 TECHNICAL PROOFS*

Proof of Theorem 20.4 I provide a proof under the stronger assumption $\zeta_K^2 K/n \to 0$. (The proof presented by Belloni et al. (2015) requires a more advanced treatment.) Let $\|\boldsymbol{A}\|_F$ denote the Frobenius norm (see Section A.23), and write the jth element of $\widetilde{X}_{Ki}$ as $\widetilde{X}_{jKi}$. Using (A.18),

$$\left\| \widetilde{\boldsymbol{Q}}_K - \boldsymbol{I}_K \right\|^2 \leq \left\| \widetilde{\boldsymbol{Q}}_K - \boldsymbol{I}_K \right\|_F^2 = \sum_{j=1}^{K} \sum_{\ell=1}^{K} \left(\frac{1}{n} \sum_{i=1}^{n} \left(\widetilde{X}_{jKi}\widetilde{X}_{\ell Ki} - \mathbb{E}\left[\widetilde{X}_{jKi}\widetilde{X}_{\ell Ki} \right] \right) \right)^2 .$$

Then

$$\begin{aligned}
\mathbb{E}\left[\left\| \widetilde{\boldsymbol{Q}}_K - \boldsymbol{I}_K \right\|^2 \right] &\leq \sum_{j=1}^{K} \sum_{\ell=1}^{K} \operatorname{var}\left[\frac{1}{n} \sum_{i=1}^{n} \widetilde{X}_{jKi}\widetilde{X}_{\ell Ki} \right] \\
&= \frac{1}{n} \sum_{j=1}^{K} \sum_{\ell=1}^{K} \operatorname{var}\left[\widetilde{X}_{jKi}\widetilde{X}_{\ell Ki} \right] \\
&\leq \frac{1}{n} \mathbb{E}\left[\sum_{j=1}^{K} \widetilde{X}_{jKi}^2 \sum_{\ell=1}^{K} \widetilde{X}_{\ell Ki}^2 \right] \\
&= \frac{1}{n} \mathbb{E}\left[\left(\widetilde{X}_{Ki}'\widetilde{X}_{Ki} \right)^2 \right] \\
&\leq \frac{\zeta_K^2}{n} \mathbb{E}\left[\widetilde{X}_{Ki}'\widetilde{X}_{Ki} \right] = \frac{\zeta_K^2 K}{n} \to 0
\end{aligned}$$

where final lines use (20.17), $\mathbb{E}\left[\widetilde{X}_{Ki}'\widetilde{X}_{Ki} \right] = K$, and $\zeta_K^2 K/n \to 0$. Markov's inequality implies (20.19). ■

Proof of Theorem 20.5 By the spectral decomposition, we can write $\widetilde{\boldsymbol{Q}}_K = \boldsymbol{H}'\Lambda\boldsymbol{H}$, where $\boldsymbol{H}'\boldsymbol{H} = \boldsymbol{I}_K$ and $\Lambda = \operatorname{diag}(\lambda_1, \ldots, \lambda_K)$ are the eigenvalues. Then

$$\left\| \widetilde{\boldsymbol{Q}}_K - \boldsymbol{I}_K \right\| = \left\| \boldsymbol{H}' (\Lambda - \boldsymbol{I}_K) \boldsymbol{H} \right\| = \left\| \Lambda - \boldsymbol{I}_K \right\| = \max_{j \leq K} \left| \lambda_j - 1 \right| \underset{p}{\longrightarrow} 0$$

by Theorem 20.4. This implies $\min_{j \leq K} \left| \lambda_j \right| \underset{p}{\longrightarrow} 1$, which is (20.21). Similarly,

$$\begin{aligned}
\left\| \widetilde{\boldsymbol{Q}}_K^{-1} - \boldsymbol{I}_K \right\| &= \left\| \boldsymbol{H}' \left(\Lambda^{-1} - \boldsymbol{I}_K \right) \boldsymbol{H} \right\| \\
&= \left\| \Lambda^{-1} - \boldsymbol{I}_K \right\| \\
&= \max_{j \leq K} \left| \lambda_j^{-1} - 1 \right| \\
&\leq \frac{\max_{j \leq K} \left| 1 - \lambda_j \right|}{\min_{j \leq K} \left| \lambda_j \right|} \underset{p}{\longrightarrow} 0.
\end{aligned}$$

■

Proof of Theorem 20.6 Using (20.12), we can write

$$\widehat{m}_K(x) - m(x) = X_K(x)' \left(\widehat{\beta}_K - \beta_K \right) - r_K(x). \tag{20.43}$$

Since $e_K = r_K + e$ is a projection error, it satisfies $\mathbb{E}[X_K e_K] = 0$. Since e is a regression error, it satisfies $\mathbb{E}[X_K e] = 0$. We deduce that $\mathbb{E}[X_K r_K] = 0$. Hence $\int X_K(x) r_K(x) f(x) dx = \mathbb{E}[X_K r_K] = 0$. Also observe that $\int X_K(x) X_K(x)' dF(x) = \boldsymbol{Q}_K$ and $\int r_K(x)^2 dF(x) = \mathbb{E}\left[r_K^2\right] = \delta_K^2$. Then

$$\begin{aligned}
\operatorname{ISE}(K) &= \int \left(X_K(x)'\left(\widehat{\beta}_K - \beta_K\right) - r_K(x)\right)^2 dF(x) \\
&= \left(\widehat{\beta}_K - \beta_K\right)' \left(\int X_K(x) X_K(x)' dF(x)\right) \left(\widehat{\beta}_K - \beta_K\right) \\
&\quad - 2\left(\widehat{\beta}_K - \beta_K\right)' \left(\int X_K(x) r_K(x) dF(x)\right) + \int r_K(x)^2 dF(x) \\
&= \left(\widehat{\beta}_K - \beta_K\right)' \boldsymbol{Q}_K \left(\widehat{\beta}_K - \beta_K\right) + \delta_K^2.
\end{aligned} \tag{20.44}$$

We calculate that

$$\begin{aligned}
\left(\widehat{\beta}_K - \beta_K\right)' \boldsymbol{Q}_K \left(\widehat{\beta}_K - \beta_K\right) &= \left(\boldsymbol{e}_K' \boldsymbol{X}_K\right) \left(\boldsymbol{X}_K' \boldsymbol{X}_K\right)^{-1} \boldsymbol{Q}_K \left(\boldsymbol{X}_K' \boldsymbol{X}_K\right)^{-1} \left(\boldsymbol{X}_K' \boldsymbol{e}_K\right) \\
&= \left(\boldsymbol{e}_K' \widetilde{\boldsymbol{X}}_K\right) \left(\widetilde{\boldsymbol{X}}_K' \widetilde{\boldsymbol{X}}_K\right)^{-1} \left(\widetilde{\boldsymbol{X}}_K' \widetilde{\boldsymbol{X}}_K\right)^{-1} \left(\widetilde{\boldsymbol{X}}_K' \boldsymbol{e}_K\right) \\
&= n^{-2} \left(\boldsymbol{e}_K' \widetilde{\boldsymbol{X}}_K\right) \widetilde{\boldsymbol{Q}}_K^{-1} \widetilde{\boldsymbol{Q}}_K^{-1} \left(\widetilde{\boldsymbol{X}}_K' \boldsymbol{e}_K\right) \\
&\leq \left(\lambda_{\max}\left(\widetilde{\boldsymbol{Q}}_K^{-1}\right)\right)^2 \left(n^{-2} \boldsymbol{e}_K' \widetilde{\boldsymbol{X}}_K \widetilde{\boldsymbol{X}}_K' \boldsymbol{e}_K\right) \\
&\leq O_p(1) \left(n^{-2} \boldsymbol{e}_K' \boldsymbol{X}_K \boldsymbol{Q}_K^{-1} \boldsymbol{X}_K' \boldsymbol{e}_K\right)
\end{aligned} \tag{20.45}$$

where $\widetilde{\boldsymbol{X}}_K$ and $\widetilde{\boldsymbol{Q}}_K$ are the orthogonalized regressors as defined in (20.18). The first inequality is the Quadratic Inequality (B.18), the second is (20.21).

Using the fact that $X_K e_K$ are mean 0 and uncorrelated, (20.17), $\mathbb{E}\left[e_K^2\right] \leq \mathbb{E}\left[Y^2\right] < \infty$, and Assumption 20.1 part 2, we have

$$\begin{aligned}
\mathbb{E}\left[n^{-2} \boldsymbol{e}_K' \boldsymbol{X}_K \boldsymbol{Q}_K^{-1} \boldsymbol{X}_K' \boldsymbol{e}_K\right] &= n^{-1} \mathbb{E}\left[X_K' \boldsymbol{Q}_K^{-1} X_K e_K^2\right] \\
&\leq \frac{\zeta_K^2}{n} \mathbb{E}\left[e_K^2\right] \leq o(1).
\end{aligned} \tag{20.46}$$

This shows that (20.45) is $o_p(1)$. Combined with (20.44), we find $\operatorname{ISE}(K) = o_p(1)$, as claimed. ■

Proof of Theorem 20.7 The assumption $\sigma^2(x) \leq \overline{\sigma}^2$ implies that

$$\mathbb{E}\left[e_K^2 \mid X\right] = \mathbb{E}\left[(r_K + e)^2 \mid X\right] = r_K^2 + \sigma^2(X) \leq r_K^2 + \overline{\sigma}^2.$$

Thus (20.46) is bounded by

$$\begin{aligned}
n^{-1} \mathbb{E}\left[X_K' \boldsymbol{Q}_K^{-1} X_K r_K^2\right] + n^{-1} \mathbb{E}\left[X_K' \boldsymbol{Q}_K^{-1} X_K\right] \overline{\sigma}^2 &\leq \frac{\zeta_K^2}{n} \mathbb{E}\left[r_K^2\right] + n^{-1} \mathbb{E}\left[\operatorname{tr}\left(\boldsymbol{Q}_K^{-1} X_K X_K'\right)\right] \overline{\sigma}^2 \\
&= \frac{\zeta_K^2}{n} \delta_K^2 + n^{-1} \operatorname{tr}\left(\boldsymbol{I}_K\right) \overline{\sigma}^2 \\
&\leq o\left(\delta_K^2\right) + \frac{K}{n} \overline{\sigma}^2
\end{aligned}$$

where the inequality is Assumption 20.1 part 2. Thus (20.45) is $o_p\left(\delta_K^2\right)+O_p\left(K/n\right)$. Combined with (20.44) we find $\text{ISE}(K)=O_p\left(\delta_K^2+K/n\right)$, as claimed. ■

Proof of Theorem 20.8 Using (20.12) and linearity,

$$\theta = a\left(m\right) = a\left(Z_K(x)'\beta_K\right)+a\left(r_K\right)=a_K'\beta_K+a\left(r_K\right).$$

Thus

$$\begin{aligned}\sqrt{\frac{n}{V_K}}\left(\widehat{\theta}_K-\theta+a\left(r_K\right)\right) &= \sqrt{\frac{n}{V_K}}a_K'\left(\widehat{\beta}_K-\beta_K\right)\\ &= \sqrt{\frac{1}{nV_K}}a_K'\widehat{\boldsymbol{Q}}_K^{-1}\boldsymbol{X}_K'\boldsymbol{e}_K\\ &= \frac{1}{\sqrt{nV_K}}a_K'\boldsymbol{Q}_K^{-1}\boldsymbol{X}_K'\boldsymbol{e} && (20.47)\\ &\quad+\frac{1}{\sqrt{nV_K}}a_K'\left(\widehat{\boldsymbol{Q}}_K^{-1}-\boldsymbol{Q}_K^{-1}\right)\boldsymbol{X}_K'\boldsymbol{e} && (20.48)\\ &\quad+\frac{1}{\sqrt{nV_K}}a_K'\widehat{\boldsymbol{Q}}_K^{-1}\boldsymbol{X}_K'\boldsymbol{r}_K && (20.49)\end{aligned}$$

where we have used $\boldsymbol{e}_K=\boldsymbol{e}+\boldsymbol{r}_K$. Let us consider the terms in (20.47)–(20.49) separately. We will show that (20.47) is asymptotically normal and (20.48) and (20.49) are asymptotically negligible.

First, consider (20.47). We can write

$$\frac{1}{\sqrt{nV_K}}a_K'\boldsymbol{Q}_K^{-1}\boldsymbol{X}_K'\boldsymbol{e}=\frac{1}{\sqrt{n}}\sum_{i=1}^{n}\frac{1}{\sqrt{V_K}}a_K'\boldsymbol{Q}_K^{-1}X_{Ki}e_i. \tag{20.50}$$

Observe that $a_K'\boldsymbol{Q}_K^{-1}X_{Ki}e_i/\sqrt{V_K}$ are independent across i, mean 0, and have variance 1. Let us apply Theorem 6.4, for which it is sufficient to verify Lindeberg's condition: For all $\epsilon>0$,

$$\mathbb{E}\left[\frac{\left(a_K'\boldsymbol{Q}_K^{-1}X_Ke\right)^2}{V_K}\mathbb{1}\left\{\frac{\left(a_K'\boldsymbol{Q}_K^{-1}X_Ke\right)^2}{V_K}\geq n\epsilon\right\}\right]\to 0. \tag{20.51}$$

Pick $\eta>0$. Set B sufficiently large so that $\mathbb{E}\left[e^2\mathbb{1}\left\{e^2>B\right\}\mid X\right]\leq\underline{\sigma}^2\eta$, which is feasible by Assumption 20.2 part 1. Pick n sufficiently large so that $\zeta_K^2/n\leq\epsilon\underline{\sigma}^2/B$, which is feasible under Assumption 20.1 part 2.

By Assumption 20.2 part 2,

$$\begin{aligned}V_K &= \mathbb{E}\left[\left(a_K'\boldsymbol{Q}_K^{-1}X_K\right)^2e^2\right]\\ &= \mathbb{E}\left[\left(a_K'\boldsymbol{Q}_K^{-1}X_K\right)^2\sigma\left(X^2\right)\right]\\ &\geq \mathbb{E}\left[\left(a_K'\boldsymbol{Q}_K^{-1}X_K\right)^2\underline{\sigma}^2\right]\\ &= a_K'\boldsymbol{Q}_K^{-1}\mathbb{E}\left[X_KX_K'\right]\boldsymbol{Q}_K^{-1}a_K\underline{\sigma}^2\\ &= a_K'\boldsymbol{Q}_K^{-1}a_K\underline{\sigma}^2. && (20.52)\end{aligned}$$

Then by the Schwarz Inequality, (20.17), (20.52), and $\zeta_K^2/n \le \epsilon \underline{\sigma}^2/B$,

$$\frac{\left(a_K' \boldsymbol{Q}_K^{-1} X_K\right)^2}{V_K} \le \frac{\left(a_K' \boldsymbol{Q}_K^{-1} a_K\right)\left(X_K' \boldsymbol{Q}_K^{-1} X_K\right)}{V_K} \le \frac{\zeta_K^2}{\underline{\sigma}^2} \le \frac{\epsilon}{B} n.$$

Then the left side of (20.51) is smaller than

$$\begin{aligned}
\mathbb{E}\left[\frac{\left(a_K' \boldsymbol{Q}_K^{-1} X_K\right)^2}{V_K} e^2 \mathbb{1}\left\{e^2 \ge B\right\}\right] &= \mathbb{E}\left[\frac{\left(a_K' \boldsymbol{Q}_K^{-1} X_K\right)^2}{V_K} \mathbb{E}\left[e^2 \mathbb{1}\left\{e^2 \ge B\right\} \mid X\right]\right] \\
&\le \mathbb{E}\left[\frac{\left(a_K' \boldsymbol{Q}_K^{-1} X_K\right)^2}{V_K}\right] \underline{\sigma}^2 \eta \\
&\le \frac{a_K' \boldsymbol{Q}_K^{-1} a_K}{V_K} \underline{\sigma}^2 \eta \le \eta
\end{aligned}$$

where the final inequality is by (20.52). Since η is arbitrary, this verifies (20.51), and we conclude that

$$\frac{1}{\sqrt{n V_K}} a_K' \boldsymbol{Q}_K^{-1} \boldsymbol{X}_K' \boldsymbol{e} \xrightarrow[d]{} \mathrm{N}(0,1). \tag{20.53}$$

Second, consider (20.48). Assumption 20.2 implies $\mathbb{E}\left[e^2 \mid X\right] \le \overline{\sigma}^2 < \infty$. Since $\mathbb{E}[\boldsymbol{e} \mid \boldsymbol{X}] = 0$, applying $\mathbb{E}\left[e^2 \mid X\right] \le \overline{\sigma}^2$, the quadratic inequality (B.18), (20.52), and Theorems 20.4 and 20.5, we have

$$\begin{aligned}
&\mathbb{E}\left[\left(\frac{1}{\sqrt{n V_K}} a_K' \left(\widehat{\boldsymbol{Q}}_K^{-1} - \boldsymbol{Q}_K^{-1}\right) \boldsymbol{X}_K' \boldsymbol{e}\right)^2 \middle| \boldsymbol{X}\right] \\
&= \frac{1}{n V_K} a_K' \left(\widehat{\boldsymbol{Q}}_K^{-1} - \boldsymbol{Q}_K^{-1}\right) \boldsymbol{X}_K' \mathbb{E}\left[\boldsymbol{e}\boldsymbol{e}' \mid \boldsymbol{X}\right] \boldsymbol{X}_K \left(\widehat{\boldsymbol{Q}}_K^{-1} - \boldsymbol{Q}_K^{-1}\right) a_K \\
&\le \frac{\overline{\sigma}^2}{V_K} a_K' \left(\widehat{\boldsymbol{Q}}_K^{-1} - \boldsymbol{Q}_K^{-1}\right) \widehat{\boldsymbol{Q}}_K \left(\widehat{\boldsymbol{Q}}_K^{-1} - \boldsymbol{Q}_K^{-1}\right) a_K \\
&\le \frac{\overline{\sigma}^2 a_K' \boldsymbol{Q}_K^{-1} a_K}{V_K} \left\| \left(\widehat{\boldsymbol{Q}}_K^{-1} - \boldsymbol{Q}_K^{-1}\right) \widehat{\boldsymbol{Q}}_K \left(\widehat{\boldsymbol{Q}}_K^{-1} - \boldsymbol{Q}_K^{-1}\right) \right\| \\
&= \frac{\overline{\sigma}^2 a_K' \boldsymbol{Q}_K^{-1} a_K}{V_K} \left\| \left(\boldsymbol{I}_K - \widetilde{\boldsymbol{Q}}_K\right) \left(\widetilde{\boldsymbol{Q}}_K^{-1} - \boldsymbol{I}_K\right) \right\| \\
&\le \frac{\overline{\sigma}^2}{\underline{\sigma}^2} \left\| \boldsymbol{I}_K - \widetilde{\boldsymbol{Q}}_K \right\| \left\| \widetilde{\boldsymbol{Q}}_K^{-1} - \boldsymbol{I}_K \right\| \\
&\le \frac{\overline{\sigma}^2}{\underline{\sigma}^2} o_p(1).
\end{aligned}$$

This establishes that (20.48) is $o_p(1)$.

Third, consider (20.49). By the Cauchy-Schwarz inequality, the quadratic inequality, (20.52), and (20.21),

$$\begin{aligned}
\left(\frac{1}{\sqrt{n v_K}} a_K' \widehat{\boldsymbol{Q}}_K^{-1} \boldsymbol{X}_K' \boldsymbol{r}_K\right)^2 &\le \frac{a_K' \boldsymbol{Q}_K^{-1} a_K}{n v_K} \boldsymbol{r}_K' \boldsymbol{X}_K \widehat{\boldsymbol{Q}}_K^{-1} \boldsymbol{Q}_K \widehat{\boldsymbol{Q}}_K^{-1} \boldsymbol{X}_K' \boldsymbol{r}_K \\
&\le \frac{1}{\underline{\sigma}^2} \left(\lambda_{\max} \widetilde{\boldsymbol{Q}}_K^{-1}\right)^2 \frac{1}{n} \boldsymbol{r}_K' \boldsymbol{X}_K \boldsymbol{Q}_K^{-1} \boldsymbol{X}_K' \boldsymbol{r}_K \\
&\le O_p(1) \frac{1}{n} \boldsymbol{r}_K' \boldsymbol{X}_K \boldsymbol{Q}_K^{-1} \boldsymbol{X}_K' \boldsymbol{r}_K.
\end{aligned} \tag{20.54}$$

Note that because the observations are independent, $\mathbb{E}[X_K r_K] = 0$, $X'_{Ki}\boldsymbol{Q}_K^{-1}X_{Ki} \le \zeta_K^2$, and $\mathbb{E}\left[r_K^2\right] = \delta_K^2$,

$$\mathbb{E}\left[\frac{1}{n}\boldsymbol{r}'_K\boldsymbol{X}_K\boldsymbol{Q}_K^{-1}\boldsymbol{X}'_K\boldsymbol{r}_K\right] = \mathbb{E}\left[\frac{1}{n}\sum_{i=1}^{n} r_{Ki}X'_{Ki}\boldsymbol{Q}_K^{-1}\sum_{ij=1}^{n} X_{Kj}r_{Kj}\right]$$
$$= \mathbb{E}\left[X'_K\boldsymbol{Q}_K^{-1}X_K r_K^2\right]$$
$$\le \zeta_K^2\mathbb{E}\left[r_K^2\right] = \zeta_K^2\delta_K^2 = o(1)$$

under Assumption 20.2 part 3. Thus $\frac{1}{n}\boldsymbol{r}'_K\boldsymbol{X}_K\boldsymbol{Q}_K^{-1}\boldsymbol{X}'_K\boldsymbol{r}_K = o_p(1)$, (20.54) is $o_p(1)$, and (20.49) is $o_p(1)$.

Combining those results, we have shown that

$$\sqrt{\frac{n}{V_K}}\left(\widehat{\theta}_K - \theta_K + a(r_K)\right) \underset{d}{\longrightarrow} \mathrm{N}(0,1)$$

as claimed. ■

Proof of Theorem 20.10 It is sufficient to show that

$$\frac{\sqrt{n}}{V_K^{1/2}(x)} r_K(x) = o(1). \tag{20.55}$$

Notice that by Assumption 20.2 part 2,

$$\begin{aligned} V_K(x) &= X_K(x)'\boldsymbol{Q}_K^{-1}\boldsymbol{\Omega}_K\boldsymbol{Q}_K^{-1}X_K(x) \\ &= \mathbb{E}\left[\left(X_K(x)'\boldsymbol{Q}_K^{-1}X_K\right)^2 e^2\right] \\ &= \mathbb{E}\left[\left(X_K(x)'\boldsymbol{Q}_K^{-1}X_K\right)^2 \sigma^2(X)\right] \\ &\ge \mathbb{E}\left[\left(X_K(x)'\boldsymbol{Q}_K^{-1}X_K\right)^2\right]\underline{\sigma}^2 \\ &= X_K(x)'\boldsymbol{Q}_K^{-1}\mathbb{E}\left[X_KX'_K\right]\boldsymbol{Q}_K^{-1}X_K(x)\underline{\sigma}^2 \\ &= X_K(x)'\boldsymbol{Q}_K^{-1}X_K(x)\underline{\sigma}^2 \\ &= \zeta_K(x)^2\underline{\sigma}^2. \end{aligned} \tag{20.56}$$

Using the definitions for β_K^*, $r_K^*(x)$, and δ_K^* from Section 20.8, note that

$$r_K(x) = m(x) - X'_K(x)\beta_K = r_K^*(x) + X'_K(x)\left(\beta_K^* - \beta_K\right).$$

By the triangle inequality, definition (20.10), the Schwarz inequality, and definition (20.15), we have

$$\begin{aligned} |r_K(x)| &\le \left|r_K^*(x)\right| + \left|X'_K(x)\left(\beta_K^* - \beta_K\right)\right| \\ &\le \delta_K^* + \left|X'_K(x)\boldsymbol{Q}_K^{-1}X'_K(x)\right|^{1/2}\left|\left(\beta_K^* - \beta_K\right)'\boldsymbol{Q}_K\left(\beta_K^* - \beta_K\right)\right|^{1/2} \\ &= \delta_K^* + \zeta_K(x)\left|\left(\beta_K^* - \beta_K\right)'\boldsymbol{Q}_K\left(\beta_K^* - \beta_K\right)\right|^{1/2}. \end{aligned}$$

The coefficients satisfy the relationship

$$\beta_K = \mathbb{E}\left[X_KX'_K\right]^{-1}\mathbb{E}\left[X_K m(X)\right] = \beta_K^* + \mathbb{E}\left[X_KX'_K\right]^{-1}\mathbb{E}\left[X_K r_K^*\right].$$

Thus

$$\left(\beta_K^* - \beta_K\right)' \boldsymbol{Q}_K \left(\beta_K^* - \beta_K\right) = \mathbb{E}\left[r_K^* X_K'\right] \mathbb{E}\left[X_K X_K'\right]^{-1} \mathbb{E}\left[X_K r_K^*\right] \leq \mathbb{E}\left[r_K^{2*}\right] \leq \delta_K^{*2}.$$

The first inequality is because $\mathbb{E}\left[r_K^* X_K'\right] \mathbb{E}\left[X_K X_K'\right]^{-1} \mathbb{E}\left[X_K r_K^*\right]$ is a projection. The second inequality follows from the definition (20.10). We deduce that

$$|r_K(x)| \leq (1 + \zeta_K(x))\, \delta_K^* \leq 2\zeta_K(x)\delta_K^*. \tag{20.57}$$

Equations (20.56), (20.57), and $n\delta_K^{*2} = o(1)$ together imply that

$$\frac{n}{V_K(x)} r_K^2(x) \leq \frac{4}{\underline{\sigma}^2} n\delta_K^{*2} = o(1)$$

which is (20.55), as required. ■

20.32 EXERCISES

Exercise 20.1 Consider the estimated model

$$Y = -1 + 2X + 5\,(X-1)\,\mathbb{1}\{X \geq 1\} - 3\,(X-2)\,\mathbb{1}\{X \geq 2\} + e.$$

What is the estimated marginal effect of X on Y for $X = 3$?

Exercise 20.2 Consider the linear spline with three knots:

$$m_K(x) = \beta_0 + \beta_1 x + \beta_2\,(x-\tau_1)\,\mathbb{1}\{x \geq \tau_1\} + \beta_3\,(x-\tau_2)\,\mathbb{1}\{x \geq \tau_2\} + \beta_4\,(x-\tau_3)\,\mathbb{1}\{x \geq \tau_3\}.$$

Find the inequality restrictions on the coefficients β_j so that $m_K(x)$ is non-decreasing.

Exercise 20.3 Using the linear spline from the previous question, find the inequality restrictions on the coefficients β_j so that $m_K(x)$ is concave.

Exercise 20.4 Consider the quadratic spline with three knots:

$$m_K(x) = \beta_0 + \beta_1 x + \beta_2 x^3 + \beta_3\,(x-\tau_1)^2\,\mathbb{1}\{x \geq \tau_1\} + \beta_4\,(x-\tau_2)^2\,\mathbb{1}\{x \geq \tau_2\} + \beta_5\,(x-\tau_3)^2\,\mathbb{1}\{x \geq \tau_3\}.$$

Find the inequality restrictions on the coefficients β_j so that $m_K(x)$ is concave.

Exercise 20.5 Consider spline estimation with one knot τ. Explain why the knot τ must be within the sample support of X. [Explain what happens if you estimate the regression with the knot placed outside the support of X].

Exercise 20.6 You estimate the polynomial regression model:

$$\widehat{m}_K(x) = \widehat{\beta}_0 + \widehat{\beta}_1 x + \widehat{\beta}_2 x^2 + \cdots + \widehat{\beta}_p x^p.$$

You are interested in the regression derivative $m'(x)$ at x.

(a) Write out the estimator $\widehat{m}_K'(x)$ of $m'(x)$.

(b) Is $\widehat{m}_K'(x)$ a linear function of the coefficient estimates?

(c) Use Theorem 20.8 to obtain the asymptotic distribution of $\widehat{m}'_K(x)$.

(d) Show how to construct standard errors and confidence intervals for $\widehat{m}'_K(x)$.

Exercise 20.7 Does rescaling Y or X (multiplying by a constant) affect the $\mathrm{CV}(K)$ function? Does it affect the K that minimizes it?

Exercise 20.8 Consider the NPIV approximating equation (20.35) and error e_K.

(a) Does it satisfy $\mathbb{E}[e_K \mid Z] = 0$?

(b) If $L = K$, can you define β_K so that $\mathbb{E}[Z_K e_K] = 0$?

(c) If $L > K$, does $\mathbb{E}[Z_K e_K] = 0$?

Exercise 20.9 Use the `cps09mar` dataset (full sample), available on the textbook website.

(a) Estimate a sixth-order polynomial regression of $\log(wage)$ on *experience*. To reduce the ill-conditioned problem, first rescale *experience* to lie in the interval $[0, 1]$ before estimating the regression.

(b) Plot the estimated regression function along with 95% pointwise confidence intervals.

(c) Interpret your findings. How do you interpret the estimated function for experience levels above 65?

Exercise 20.10 Continuing the previous exercise, compute the cross-validation function (or alternatively, the AIC) for polynomial orders 1 through 8.

(a) Which order minimizes the function?

(b) Plot the estimated regression function along with 95% pointwise confidence intervals.

Exercise 20.11 Use the `cps09mar` dataset (full sample).

(a) Estimate a sixth-order polynomial regression of $\log(wage)$ on *education*. To reduce the ill-conditioned problem, first rescale *education* to lie in the interval $[0, 1]$.

(b) Plot the estimated regression function along with 95% pointwise confidence intervals.

Exercise 20.12 Continuing the previous exercise, compute the cross-validation function (or alternatively, the AIC) for polynomial orders 1 through 8.

(a) Which order minimizes the function?

(b) Plot the estimated regression function along with 95% pointwise confidence intervals.

Exercise 20.13 Use the `cps09mar` dataset (full sample).

(a) Estimate quadratic spline regressions of $\log(wage)$ on *experience*. Estimate four models: (1) no knots (a quadratic); (2) one knot at 20 years; (3) two knots at 20 and 40; (4) four knots at 10, 20, 30, and 40. Plot the four estimates. Intrepret your findings.

(b) Compare the four-spline models using either cross-validation or AIC. Which is the preferred specification?

(c) For your selected specification, plot the estimated regression function along with 95% pointwise confidence intervals. Intrepret your findings.

(d) If you also estimated a polynomial specification, do you prefer the polynomial or the quadratic spline estimates?

Exercise 20.14 Use the `cps09mar` dataset (full sample).

(a) Estimate quadratic spline regressions of log(*wage*) on *education*. Estimate four models: (1) no knots (a quadratic); (2) one knot at 10 years; (3) three knots at 5, 10, and 15 years; (4) four knots at 4, 8, 12, and 16 years. Plot the four estimates. Intrepret your findings.

(b) Compare the four spline models using either cross-validation or AIC. Which is the preferred specification?

(c) For your selected specification, plot the estimated regression function along with 95% pointwise confidence intervals. Intrepret your findings.

(d) If you also estimated a polynomial specification, do you prefer the polynomial or the quadratic spline estimates?

Exercise 20.15 The `RR2010` dataset (available on the book's website) is from Reinhart and Rogoff (2010). It contains observations on annual U.S. GDP growth rates, inflation rates, and the debt/gdp ratio for the long time span 1791–2009. The paper made the strong claim that GDP growth slows as debt/gdp increases, and in particular that this relationship is nonlinear with debt negatively affecting growth for debt ratios exceeding 90%. Their full dataset includes 44 countries, our extract only includes the United States. Let Y_t denote GDP growth, and let D_t denote debt/gdp. You will estimate the partially linear specification

$$Y_t = \alpha Y_{t-1} + m(D_{t-1}) + e_t$$

using a linear spline for $m(D)$.

(a) Estimate the (1) linear model; (2) linear spline with one knot at $D_{t-1} = 60$; (3) linear spline with two knots at 40 and 80. Plot the three estimates.

(b) For the model with one knot, plot with 95% confidence intervals.

(c) Compare the three spline models using either cross-validation or AIC. Which is the preferred specification?

(d) Interpret your findings.

Exercise 20.16 Consider the `DDK2011` dataset (full sample). Use a quadratic spline to estimate the regression of *testscore* on *percentile*.

(a) Estimate five models: (1) no knots (a quadratic); (2) one knot at 50; (3) two knots at 33 and 66; (4) three knots at 25, 50, and 75; (5) knots at 20, 40, 60, and 80. Plot the five estimates. Intrepret your findings.

(b) Select a model. Consider using leave-cluster-one CV.

(c) For your selected specification, plot the estimated regression function along with 95% pointwise confidence intervals. (Use cluster-robust standard errors.) Intrepret your findings.

Exercise 20.17 The `CHJ2004` dataset is from Cox, Hansen, and Jimenez (2004). As described in Section 20.6, it contains a sample of 8,684 urban Philippino households. This paper studied the crowding-out impact of a family's *income* on non-governmental *transfers*. Estimate an analog of Figure 20.2(b), using polynomial regression. Regress *transfers* on a high-order polynomial in *income*, and possibly a set of regression controls. Ideally, select the polynomial order by cross-validation. You will need to rescale the variable *income* before taking polynomial powers. Plot the estimated function along with 95% pointwise confidence intervals. Comment on the similarities and differences with Figure 20.2(b). For the regression controls, consider the following options: (a) Include no additional controls; (b) Follow the original paper and Figure 20.2(b) by including the variables 12–26 listed in the data description file; (c) Make a different selection, possibly based on cross-validation.

Exercise 20.18 The `AL1999` dataset is from Angrist and Lavy (1999). It contains 4,067 observations on classroom test scores and explanatory variables, including those described in Section 20.30. In Section 20.30 we report a nonparametric instrumental variables regression of reading test scores, (*avgverb*) on *classize*, *disadvantaged*, *enrollment*, and a dummy for *grade=4*, using the Angrist-Levy variable (20.42) as an instrument. Repeat the analysis but instead of reading test scores, use math test scores (*avgmath*) as the dependent variable. Comment on the similarities and differences with the results for reading test scores.

CHAPTER 21

REGRESSION DISCONTINUITY

21.1 INTRODUCTION

One of the core goals in applied econometrics is estimation of treatment effects. A major barrier is that in observational data, treatment is rarely exogenous. Techniques discussed so far in this textbook to deal with potential endogeneity include instrumental variables, fixed effects, and difference in differences. Another important method arises in the context of the regression discontinuity design. This situation is rather special (not at the control of the econometrician), where treatment is determined by a threshold crossing rule. For example: (1) Do political incumbants have an advantage in elections? An incumbant is the winner of the previous election, which means their vote share exceeded a threshold. (2) What is the effect of college attendence? College students are admitted based on an admission exam, which means their exam scores exceeded a specific threshold. In these contexts, the treatment (incumbancy, college attendence) can be viewed as randomly assigned for individuals near the cutoff. (In the examples, for candidates who had vote shares near the winning threshold and for students who had admission exam scores near the cutoff threshold.) This setting is called the **regression discontinuity design (RDD)**. When it applies, there are simple techniques for estimation of the causal effect of treatment.

The first use of regression discontinuity is attributed to Thistlethwaite and Campbell (1960). It was popularized in economics by Black (1999), Ludwig and Miller (2007), and Lee (2008). Important reviews include Imbens and Lemieux (2008), Lee and Lemieux (2010), and Cattaneo, Idrobo, and Titiunik (2020, 2022).

The core model is **sharp regression discontinuity**, where treatment is a discontinuous deterministic rule of an observable. Most applications, however, concern **fuzzy regression discontinuity**, where the probability of treatment is discontinuous in an observable. We start by reviewing sharp regression discontinuity and then cover fuzzy regression discontinuity (Section 21.10).

21.2 SHARP REGRESSION DISCONTINUITY

Consider the potential outcomes framework. An individual is untreated if $D=0$ and is treated if $D=1$. The individual has outcome Y_0 if untreated and Y_1 if treated. The treatment effect for an individual is $\theta = Y_1 - Y_0$, which is random. An observable covariate is X. The conditional **average treatment effect (ATE)** for the subpopulation with $X=x$ is $\theta(x) = \mathbb{E}[\theta \mid X=x]$.

The sharp regression discontinuity design occurs when treatment is determined by a threshold function of X (e.g., $D = \mathbb{1}\{X \geq c\}$). In most applications, the threshold c is determined by policy or rule. The covariate X that determines treatment is typically called the **running variable**. The threshold c is often called the "cutoff."

It may be helpful to discuss a specific example. Ludwig and Miller (2007) used a sharp regression discontinuity design to evaluate a U.S. federal anti-poverty program called **Head Start**. Head Start was established in

1965 to provide preschool, health, and other social services to poor children aged 3–5 years and their families. Head Start funding was awarded to local municipalities through a competitive grant application. Due to a worry that poor regions may not apply at the same rate as well-funded regions, during the spring of 1965, the federal government provided grant-writing assistance to the 300 poorest counties in the United States. The 300 counties were selected based on the poverty rate as measured by the 1960 U.S. census.

As Ludwig and Miller document, the result was a surge in applications from the assisted counties with a resulting surge in program funding: 80% of the 300 treated counties received Head Start support while only 43% of the remaining counties received support. Thus it seems reasonable to conclude that these counties received a substantial exogenous increase in funding.

Ludwig and Miller were interested to see whether this increase in Head Start funding led to measurable changes in outcomes. Their paper examined both mortality and education. (We will focus exclusively on mortality). Specifically, they were interested in the impact on mortality for children in the age range 5–9 years, for deaths they coded as "Head Start Related" (for example, tuberculosis), meaning that a goal of the Head Start program was to reduce these events. They were also interested in the long-term effects of this intervention, and so they so focused on mortality rates in 1973–1983, which is 8 to 18 years after the grant-writing intervention. A subset of their data (assembled by Cattaneo, Titiunik, and Vazquez-Bare (2017)) is posted on the textbook website as `LM2007`.

To summarize, the question addressed by Ludwig and Miller (2007) was whether grant-writing assistance in 1965 to the 300 U.S. counties selected on a poverty index had a measurable effect on childhood mortality 8 to 18 years later in the same counties, relative to counties that did not receive the grant-writing assistance.

In this application, the unit of measurement is a U.S. county. The outcome variable Y is the county mortality rate in 1973–1983. The running variable X is the county poverty rate (percentage of the population below the poverty line) in 1960. The cutoff c is 59.1984. (The later is simply because there were 300 counties with poverty rates equal or above this cutoff.)

21.3 IDENTIFICATION

This section presents the core identification theorem for the regression discontinuity model. Recall that θ is the random individual treatment effect and $\theta(x) = \mathbb{E}[\theta \mid X = x]$ is the conditional ATE. Set $\overline{\theta} = \theta(c)$, the conditional ATE for the subpopulation at the cutoff. This is the subpopulation affected at the margin by the decision to set the cutoff at c. The core identification theorem states that $\overline{\theta}$ is identified by the regression discontinuity design under mild assumptions.

Let $m(x) = \mathbb{E}[Y \mid X = x]$, $m_0(x) = \mathbb{E}[Y_0 \mid X = x]$, and $m_1(x) = \mathbb{E}[Y_1 \mid X = x]$. Note that $\theta(x) = m_1(x) - m_0(x)$. Set $m(x+) = \lim_{z \downarrow x} m(z)$ and $m(x-) = \lim_{z \uparrow x} m(z)$.

The following is the core identification theorem for the regression discontinuity design. It is due to Hahn, Todd, and van der Klaauw (2001).

Theorem 21.1 Assume that treatment is assigned as $D = \mathbb{1}\{X \geq c\}$. Suppose that $m_0(x)$ and $m_1(x)$ are continuous at $x = c$. Then $\overline{\theta} = m(c+) - m(c-)$.

The conditions for Theorem 21.1 are minimal. The continuity of $m_0(x)$ and $m_1(x)$ means that the conditional expectation of the untreated and treated outcomes are continuously affected by the running variable. Take the Head Start example: $m_0(x)$ is the average mortality rate given the poverty rate for counties

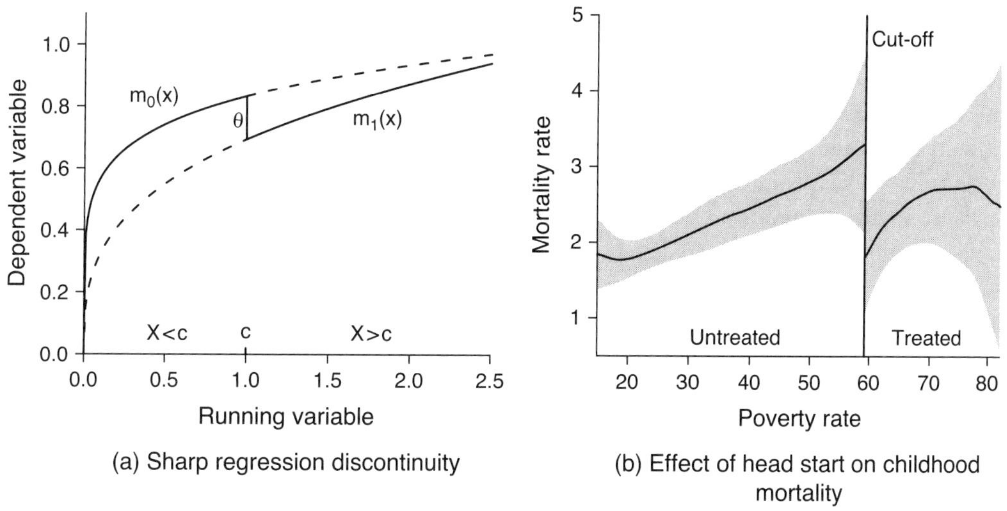

FIGURE 21.1 Sharp RDD

that received no grant-writing assistance, and $m_1(x)$ is the average mortality rate for counties that received grant-writing assistance. There is no reason to expect a discontinuity in either function.

The intuition for the theorem can be seen in Figure 21.1(a). The two continuous functions plotted are the CEFs $m_0(x)$ and $m_1(x)$. The vertical distance between these functions is the conditional ATE function $\theta(x)$. Since the treatment rule assigns all counties with $X \geq c$ to treatment and all counties with $X < c$ to nontreatment, the CEF of the observed outcome $m(x)$ is the solid line, which equals $m_0(x)$ for $x < c$ and $m_1(x)$ for $x \geq 0$. The discontinuity in $m(x)$ at $x = c$ equals the RDD treatment effect $\overline{\theta}$.

The plot in Figure 21.1(a) was designed to mimic what we might expect in the Head Start application. Both $m_0(x)$ and $m_1(x)$ are plotted as increasing functions of x, meaning that the mortality rate is increasing with the poverty rate. The functions are also plotted so that $m_1(x)$ lies below $m_0(x)$, as we expect that grant-writing assistance should reduce mortality.

We know from regression theory that the CEF $m(x)$ is generically identified. Thus so is the RDD treatment effect $\overline{\theta} = m(c+) - m(c-)$. This is the key takeaway from the identification theorem. The regression discontinuity design identifies the conditional ATE at the treatment cutoff. In the Head Start example, this is the ATE for a county with a poverty rate of 59.1984%. Use of $\overline{\theta}$ to infer the ATE for other counties is extrapolation. As displayed in Figure 21.1(a), all that is identified is the solid line; the dashed lines are not identified. Thus a limitation of the RDD approach is that it estimates a narrowly defined treatment effect.

Identification of the RDD treatment effect is intertwined with nonparametric treatment of the functions $m_0(x)$ and $m_1(x)$. If parametric (e.g., linear) forms are imposed, then the best-fitting approximations for $x < c$ and $x \geq c$ will generically have a discontinuity even if the true CEF is continuous. Thus a nonparametric treatment is essential to preclude falsely labeling nonlinearity as a discontinuity.

A formal proof of Theorem 21.1 is simple. We can write the observed outcome as $Y = Y_0 \mathbb{1}\{X < c\} + Y_1 \mathbb{1}\{X \geq c\}$. Taking expectations conditional on $X = x$, we find

$$m(x) = m_0(x)\mathbb{1}\{x < c\} + m_1(x)\mathbb{1}\{x \geq c\}. \tag{21.1}$$

Since $m_0(x)$ and $m_1(x)$ are continuous at $x = c$, we deduce that $m(c+) = m_1(c)$ and $m(c-) = m_0(c)$. Thus $m(c+) - m(c-) = m_1(c) - m_0(c) = \theta(c)$, as claimed.

21.4 ESTIMATION

Our goal is estimation of the conditional ATE $\overline{\theta}$ given observations $\{Y_i, X_i\}$ and known cutoff c. The conditional ATE can be calculated from the CEF $m(x)$. Estimation of the CEF nonparametrically allowing for a discontinuity is the same as separately estimating the CEF for the untreated observations $X_i < c$ and the treated observations $X_i \geq c$. The estimator for $\overline{\theta}$ is the difference between the adjoining estimated endpoints.

Chapters 19 and 20 have study nonparametric kernel and series regression. One of the findings is that for boundary estimation, the preferred method is local linear (LL) regression (Section 19.4). In contrast, the Nadaraya-Watson (NW) estimator is biased at a boundary point (see Section 19.10), and series estimators have high variance at the boundary (see Section 20.14 and Gelman and Imbens (2019)). Consequently, LL estimation is preferred and is the most widely used technique[1] for RDDs.

To describe the estimator, set

$$Z_i(x) = \begin{pmatrix} 1 \\ X_i - x \end{pmatrix}.$$

Let $K(u)$ be a kernel function and h a bandwidth. The LL coefficient estimator for $x < c$ is

$$\widehat{\beta}_0(x) = \left(\sum_{i=1}^n K\left(\frac{X_i - x}{h}\right) Z_i(x) Z_i(x)' \mathbb{1}\{X_i < c\} \right)^{-1} \left(\sum_{i=1}^n K\left(\frac{X_i - x}{h}\right) Z_i(x) Y_i \mathbb{1}\{X_i < c\} \right)$$

and for $x \geq c$ is

$$\widehat{\beta}_1(x) = \left(\sum_{i=1}^n K\left(\frac{X_i - x}{h}\right) Z_i(x) Z_i(x)' \mathbb{1}\{X_i \geq c\} \right)^{-1} \left(\sum_{i=1}^n K\left(\frac{X_i - x}{h}\right) Z_i(x) Y_i \mathbb{1}\{X_i \geq c\} \right).$$

The estimator of the CEF is the first element of the coefficient vectors

$$\widehat{m}(x) = \left[\widehat{\beta}_0(x)\right]_1 \mathbb{1}\{x < c\} + \left[\widehat{\beta}_1(x)\right]_1 \mathbb{1}\{x \geq c\}.$$

The estimator of $\overline{\theta}$ is the difference at $x = c$

$$\widehat{\theta} = \left[\widehat{\beta}_1(c)\right]_1 - \left[\widehat{\beta}_0(c)\right]_1 = \widehat{m}(c+) - \widehat{m}(c-). \tag{21.2}$$

For efficient estimation at boundary points, the triangular kernel is recommended. However, the Epanechnikov and Gaussian have similar efficiencies (see Section 19.10). Some authors have made a case for the rectangular kernel, as this permits standard regression software to be used. There is an efficiency loss (3% in root AMSE) in return for this convenience.

The CEF estimate $\widehat{m}(x)$ should be plotted to allow visual inspection of the regression function and discontinuity. Many authors plot the CEF only over the support near $x = c$ to emphasize the local nature of the estimation. Confidence bands should be calculated and plotted as described in Section 19.17. These are calculated separately for the nontreatment and treatment subsamples but otherwise are identical to those described in Section 19.17.

To illustrate, Figure 21.1(b) displays our estimates of the Ludwig and Miller (2007) Head Start RDD model for childhood mortality due to HS-related causes. We use a normalized[2] triangular kernel and a bandwidth

---

[1] Some authors use polynomials in addition to LL estimation as an appeal to "robustness." This practice should be discouraged, as argued in Gelman and Imbens (2019).

[2] Normalized to have unit variance. Some software implements the triangular kernel scaled to have support on $[-1, 1]$. The results are identical if the bandwidth is multiplied by $\sqrt{6}$. For example, my estimates using $h = 8$ and a normalized triangular kernel are the same as estimates using a $[-1, 1]$ triangular kernel with a bandwidth of $h = 19.6$.

of $h = 8$. This bandwidth choice is described in Section 21.6. The x-axis is the 1960 poverty rate. The cutoff is 59.1984%. Counties below the cutoff did not receive grant-writing assistance; counties above the cutoff received assistance. The mortality rate is on the y-axis (deaths per 100,000). The estimates show that the mortality rate is increasing in the poverty rate (nearly linear) with a substantial downward discontinuity at the 59.1984% cutoff. The discontinuity is about 1.5 deaths per 100,000. The confidence bands indicate that the estimated CEFs have a fair amount of uncertainty at the boundaries. The CEF in the treated sample appears nonlinear, and the confidence bands are very wide.

There is a custom in the applied economics literature to display Figure 21.1(b) somewhat differently. Rather than displaying confidence intervals along with the LL estimates, many applied economists display binned means. The binned means are displayed by squares or triangles and are meant to indicate a raw estimate of the nonparametric shape of the CEF. This custom is a poor choice, a bad habit, and should be avoided. There are two problems with this practice. First, the use of symbols creates the visual impression of a scatter plot of raw data, when in fact what is displayed are binned means. The latter is a nonparametric histogram-shaped estimator and should be displayed as a histogram rather than as a scatter plot. Second, binned means are not really raw data but are instead a different (and inaccurate) nonparametric estimator. Binned means is the same as the NW estimator using a rectangular kernel and only evalutated at a grid of points rather than continuously. LL estimation is superior to the NW, any kernel is superior to the rectangular, and there is no reason to evaluate only on an arbitrary grid. These plots are not best practice; instead they are a bad habit that arose from undisciplined applied practice. The best practice is to plot the best possible nonparametric estimator and to plot confidence intervals to convey uncertainty.

21.5 INFERENCE

As described in Theorems 19.6 and 19.9, the LL estimator $\widehat{m}(x)$ is asymptotically normal under standard regularity conditions. This extends to the RDD estimator $\widehat{\theta}$. It has asymptotic bias

$$\operatorname{bias}\left[\widehat{\theta}\right] = \frac{h^2 \sigma_{K*}^2}{2}\left(m''(c+) - m''(c-)\right)$$

and variance

$$\operatorname{var}\left[\widehat{\theta}\right] = \frac{R_K^*}{nh}\left(\frac{\sigma^2(c+)}{f(c+)} + \frac{\sigma^2(c-)}{f(c-)}\right).$$

The asymptotic variance can be estimated by the sum of the asymptotic variance estimators of the two boundary regression estimators, as described in Section 19.16. Let $\widetilde{e}_i$ be the leave-one-out prediction error, and set

$$Z_i = \begin{pmatrix} 1 \\ X_i - c \end{pmatrix}$$

$$K_i = K\left(\frac{X_i - c}{h}\right).$$

The covariance matrix estimators are

$$\widehat{V}_0 = \left(\sum_{i=1}^n K_i Z_i Z_i' \mathbb{1}\{X_i < c\}\right)^{-1} \left(\sum_{i=1}^n K_i^2 Z_i Z_i' \widetilde{e}_i^2 \mathbb{1}\{X_i < c\}\right) \left(\sum_{i=1}^n K_i Z_i Z_i' \mathbb{1}\{X_i < c\}\right)^{-1}$$

$$\widehat{\boldsymbol{V}}_1 = \left(\sum_{i=1}^{n} K_i Z_i Z_i' \mathbb{1}\{X_i \geq c\}\right)^{-1} \left(\sum_{i=1}^{n} K_i^2 Z_i Z_i' \widetilde{e}_i^2 \mathbb{1}\{X_i \geq c\}\right) \left(\sum_{i=1}^{n} K_i Z_i Z_i' \mathbb{1}\{X_i \geq c\}\right)^{-1}.$$

The asymptotic variance estimator for $\widehat{\theta}$ is the sum of the first diagonal element from these two covariance matrix estimators, $\left[\widehat{\boldsymbol{V}}_0\right]_{11} + \left[\widehat{\boldsymbol{V}}_0\right]_{11}$. The standard error for $\widehat{\theta}$ is the square root of the variance estimator.

Inferential statements about the treatment effect $\overline{\theta}$ are affected by bias, just as they are in any nonparametric estimation context. In general, the degree of bias is uncertain. Two recommendations may help reduce the finite sample bias. First, use a common bandwidth for estimation of the LL regression on each subsample. When $m(x)$ has a continuous second derivative at $x = c$, this will result in a zero first-order asymptotic bias. Second, use a bandwidth that is smaller than the AMSE-optimal bandwidth. This reduces the bias at the cost of increased variance and standard errors. Overall, this leads to more honest inference statements.

To illustrate, Table 21.1 presents the RDD estimate of the Head Start treatment effect (the effect of grant-writing assistance on a county with poverty rate at the policy cutoff). This equals the vertical distance between the estimated CEFs in Figure 21.1(b). The point estimate is -1.51 with a standard error of 0.71. The t-statistic for a test of no effect has a p-value of 3%, consistent with statistical significance at conventional levels. The estimated policy impact is large. It states that federal grant-writing assistance, and the resulting surge in spending on the Head Start program, led to a long-term decrease in targeted mortality by about 1.5 children per 100,000. Given that the estimated untreated mortality rate is 3.3 children per 100,000 at the cutoff, this is a near 50% decrease in the mortality rate.

21.6 BANDWIDTH SELECTION

In nonparametric estimation, the most critical choice is the bandwidth. This is especially important in RDD estimation, as there is no broad agreement on the best bandwidth selection method. It therefore is prudent to calculate several data-based bandwidth rules before estimation. Here I describe two simple approaches based on the global fit of the RDD estimator.

My first suggestion is the rule-of-thumb (ROT) bandwidth (19.9) of Fan and Gijbels (1996), modified to allow for a discontinuity at $x = c$. The method requires a reference model. A modest extension of Fan-Gijbels' approach is a qth-order polynomial plus a level shift discontinuity. This model is

$$m(x) = \beta_0 + \beta_1 x + \beta_2 x^2 + \cdots + \beta_q x^q + \beta_{q+1} D$$

Table 21.1
RDD estimates of the effect of Head Start assistance on childhood mortality

	Baseline	Covariates
$\widehat{\theta}$	-1.51	-1.56
$s(\widehat{\theta})$	(0.71)	(0.71)
% Black		0.027
$s(\widehat{\beta}_1)$		(0.007)
% urban		-0.0094
$s(\widehat{\beta}_2)$		(0.0046)

where $D = \mathbb{1}\{x \geq c\}$. Estimate this model by least squares, and obtain coefficient estimates and the variance estimate $\widehat{\sigma}^2$. From the coefficient estimates, calculate the estimated second derivative:

$$\widehat{m}''(x) = 2\widehat{\beta}_2 + 6\widehat{\beta}_3 x + 12\widehat{\beta}_4 x^2 + \cdots + q(q-1)\widehat{\beta}_q x^{q-2}.$$

The constant $\overline{B}$ in (19.9) is estimated by

$$\widehat{B} = \frac{1}{n}\sum_{i=1}^{n}\left(\frac{1}{2}\widehat{m}''(X_i)\right)^2 \mathbb{1}\{\xi_1 \leq X_i \leq \xi_2\}$$

where $[\xi_1, \xi_2]$ is the region of evaluation (and can be set to equal to the support of X when the latter is bounded). The reference bandwidth (19.9) is then

$$h_{\text{rot}} = 0.58\left(\frac{\widehat{\sigma}^2(\xi_2 - \xi_1)}{\widehat{B}}\right)^{1/5} n^{-1/5}. \tag{21.3}$$

Fan and Gijbels recommend $q = 4$, but other choices can be used for the polynomial order. The ROT bandwidth (21.3) is appropriate for any normalized (variance 1) kernel. For the unnormalized rectangular kernel $K(u) = 1/2$ for $|u| \leq 1$, replace the constant 0.58 with 1.00. For the unnormalized triangular kernel $K(u) = 1 - |u|$ for $|u| \leq 1$, replace the constant 0.58 with 1.42.

Another useful method is cross-validation. CV for the RDD estimator is essentially the same as for any other nonparametric estimator. For each bandwidth, the leave-one-out residuals are calculated and their sum of squares recorded. The bandwidth that minimizes this criterion is the CV-selected choice. Plots of the CV criterion as a function of h can aid in determinining the sensitivity of the fit with respect to the bandwidth.

These two proposals aim to produce a bandwidth h with global accuracy. An alternative is a bandwidth selection rule that aims at accuracy at or near the cutoff. The advantage of the global approach is that it is a simpler estimation problem and thus more accurate and less variable. Bandwidth estimation is a hard problem. Noise in estimation of the bandwidth will translate into estimation noise for the RDD estimate. In contrast, methods that aim at accuracy at the cutoff are targeted at the object of interest. This is a challenging estimation issue, so I will not review it further. For specific proposals, see Imbens and Kalyanaraman (2012), Arai and Ichimura (2018), and Cattaneo, Idrobo, and Titiunik (2020).

A compromise is to calculate the CV criteria with the region of evaluation $[\xi_1, \xi_2]$ being a subset of the full support of X centered close to the cutoff. Several of the early review papers recommended this approach. The challenge with this approach is that the CV criteria is a noisy estimator and by restricting the region of evaluation, we are increasing its estimation variance. This increases noise.

In applications, I recommend that you start by calculating the Fan-Gijbels ROT bandwidth for several values of polynomial order q. When comparing the results, pay attention to the precision of the coefficients in the polynomial regression. If the high-order powers are imprecisely estimated, the bandwidth estimates may be noisy as well. Then find the bandwidth that minimizes the cross-validation criterion. Plot the CV criterion. If it is relatively flat, this informs you that it is difficult to rank bandwidths. Combine the above information to select an AMSE-minimizing bandwidth. Then reduce this bandwidth somewhat (perhaps by 25%) to reduce estimation bias.

Some robustness checking (estimation with alternative bandwidths) is prudent, but narrowly so. A rather odd implication of the robustness craze is to desire results that do not change with bandwidths. Contrariwise, if the true regression function is nonlinear, then results will change with bandwidths. What you should expect is that as you reduce the bandwidth, the estimated function will reveal a combination of shape and noise accompanied by wider confidence bands. As you increase the bandwidth, the estimates will straighten out, and the confidence bands will narrow. The narrowness means that the estimates have reduced variance, but this comes at the cost of increased (and uncertain) bias.

I illustrate using the Ludwig and Miller (2007) Head Start application. I calculated the modified Fan-Gijbels ROT using $q=2$, 3, and 4, obtaining bandwidths of $h_{\text{rot}}(q=2)=24.6$, $h_{\text{rot}}(q=3)=11.0$, and $h_{\text{rot}}(q=4)=5.2$. These results are sensitive to the choice of polynomial. Examining these polynomial regressions, we can see that the third and fourth coefficient estimates have large standard errors and so are noisy. I next evaluated the cross-validation criterion on the region $[1, 30]$ (not shown). The CV criterion is monotonically decreasing with h, though it is quite flat for $h \geq 20$. Essentially the CV criterion recommends an infinite bandwidth, which means using all observations equally weighted. Since we want a bandwidth that is smaller than AMSE-optimal, we should lean toward smaller bandwidths and take a rough average of the ROT bandwidths with $q=3$ and $q=4$ to obtain $h=8$. This is the bandwidth used in the empirical results shown in this chapter.

Larger bandwidths result in flatter (more linear) estimated conditional mean functions and a smaller estimated Head Start effect. Smaller bandwidths result in more curvature in the estimated conditional mean functions, in particular for the section above the cutoff.

21.7 RDD WITH COVARIATES

A powerful implication of Theorem 21.1 is that covariates are not necessary to identify the conditional ATE. Thus augmenting the regression model to include covariates is not necessary for estimation and inference. The precision of estimation, however, will be affected. Inclusion of relevant covariates can reduce the equation error. It is therefore prudent to consider the addition of relevant covariates when available.

Denote the variables as (Y, X, Z), where Z is a vector of covariates. Again consider the potential outcomes framework where Y_0 and Y_1 are the outcome with and without treatment, respectively. Assume that the CEFs take the partially linear form

$$\mathbb{E}\left[Y_0 \mid X=x,\ Z=z\right]=m_0(x)+\beta' z$$

$$\mathbb{E}\left[Y_1 \mid X=x,\ Z=z\right]=m_1(x)+\beta' z.$$

For simplicity, we assume that the linear coefficients are the same in the two equations. This is not essential, but it simplifies the estimation strategy. It follows that the CEF for Y equals

$$m(x, z)=m_0(x) \mathbb{1}\{x, c\}+m_1(x) \mathbb{1}\{x \geq c\}+\beta' z.$$

A minor extension of Theorem 21.1 shows that the conditional ATE is $\bar{\theta}=m(c+, z)-m(c-, z)$.

Different authors have suggested different methods for estimation of the RDD with covariates model. The preferred method is the estimator of Robinson (1988). See Section 19.24. (It is preferred because Robinson demonstrated that it is semiparametrically efficient while the other suggestions have no efficiency justification.) The estimation method is as follows.

1. Use the RDD LL estimator to regress Y_i on X_i to obtain the first-step fitted values $\widehat{m}_i=\widehat{m}(X_i)$.
2. Using LL regression, regress Z_{i1} on X_i, Z_{i2} on $X_i, \ldots,$ and Z_{ik} on X_i, obtaining the fitted values for the covariates, say, $\widehat{g}_{1i}, \ldots, \widehat{g}_{ki}$.
3. Regress $Y_i-\widehat{m}_i$ on $Z_{1i}-\widehat{g}_{1i}, \ldots, Z_{ki}-\widehat{g}_{ki}$ to obtain the coefficient estimate $\widehat{\beta}$ and standard errors.

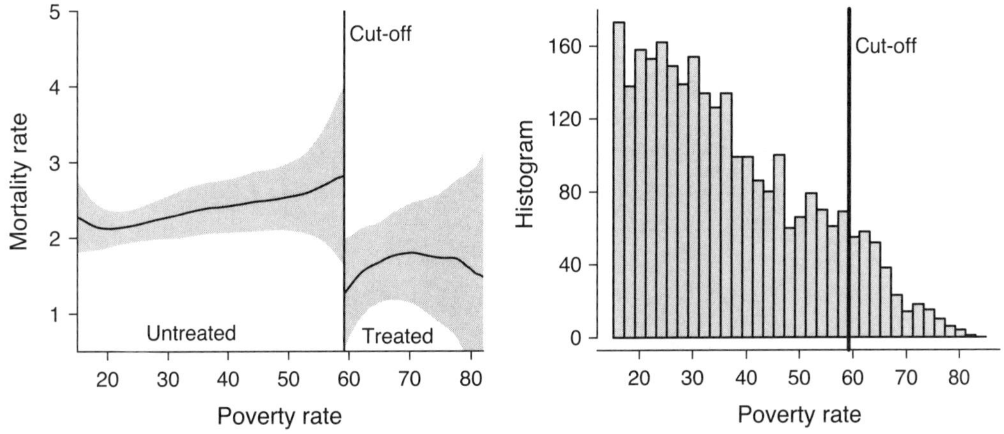

(a) RDD with covariates

(b) Histogram of poverty rate

FIGURE 21.2 RDD diagnostics

4. Construct the residual $\widehat{e}_i = Y_i - Z_i'\widehat{\beta}$.
5. Use the RDD LL estimator to regress $\widehat{e}_i$ on X_i to obtain the nonparametric estimator $\widehat{m}(x)$, conditional ATE $\widehat{\theta}$, and associated standard errors.

As shown by Robinson (1988) and discussed in Section 19.24, the above estimator is semiparametrically efficient, the conventional asymptotic theory is valid, and conventional inference is valid. Thus the estimators can be used to assess the conditional ATE.

As mentioned above, inclusion of covariates does not alter the conditional ATE parameter $\overline{\theta}$ under correct specification. Inclusion of covariates can, however, affect the conditional mean function $m(x)$ at points x away from the discontinuity. Covariates will also affect the precision of the estimator and standard errors.

To illustrate, let us augment the Ludwig-Miller Head Start estimates with two covariates: the county-level Black population percentage, and the county-level urban population percentage. These variables can be viewed as proxies for income. We estimate the model using the Robinson estimator. The estimated nonlinear function $m(x)$ is displayed in Figure 21.2(a) and the coefficient estimates in Table 21.1.

Comparing Figure 21.2(a) with Figure 21.1(b), it appears that the estimated conditional ATE (the treatment effect of the policy) is about the same, but the shape of $m(x)$ is different. With the covariates included, $m(x)$ is considerably flatter. Examining Table 21.1, we can see that the estimated treatment effect is nearly the same as in the baseline model without covariates. We also see that the coefficient on the Black percentage is positive and that on the urban percentage is negative, consistent with the view that these percentages are serving as proxies for income.

21.8 A SIMPLE RDD ESTIMATOR

A simple RDD estimator can be implemented by a standard regression using conventional software. It is equivalent to a LL estimator with an unnormalized rectangular bandwidth. Estimate the regression

$$Y = \beta_0 + \beta_1 X + \beta_3 (X - c) D + \theta D + e \tag{21.4}$$

for the subsample of observations such that $|X - c| \leq h$. The coefficient estimate $\widehat{\theta}$ is the estimated conditional ATE, and inference can proceed conventionally using regression standard errors. The most important choice is the bandwidth. The ROT choice is (21.3) with 1.00 replacing the constant 0.58.

To illustrate, take the Head Start sample. For the normalized triangular kernel, we had used a bandwidth of $h = 8$. This is consistent with a bandwidth of $h = 8\sqrt{3} \simeq 13.8$ for the unnormalized rectangular kernel. Take the subsample of 482 with poverty rates in the interval $59.1984 \pm 13.8 = [45.4, 72.0]$ and estimate equation (21.4) by least squares. The estimates are

$$\widehat{Y} = \underset{(9.13)}{-3.11} + \underset{(0.17)}{0.11}\, X + \underset{(0.23)}{0.18}\, (X - 59.2)D - \underset{(1.06)}{2.20}\, D. \tag{21.5}$$

The point estimate -2.2 of the conditional ATE is larger than those reported in Table 21.1 but is within sampling variation. The standard error for the effect is also larger, consistent with our expectation that the rectangular kernel estimator is less accurate.

21.9 DENSITY DISCONTINUITY TEST

The core identification theorem assumes that the CEFs $m_0(x)$ and $m_1(x)$ are continuous at the cutoff. These assumptions may be violated if the running variable is manipulated by individuals seeking or avoiding treatment. Manipulation to obtain treatment is likely to lead to bunching of the running variable just above or below the cutoff. If there is no manipulation, we expect the density of X to be continuous at $x = c$, but if there is manipulation, we expect there might be a discontinuity in the density of X at $x = c$.

A reasonable specification check is to assess whether the density $f(x)$ of X is continuous at $x = c$. Some care needs to be exercised in implementation, however, as conventional density estimators smooth over discontinuities and they are biased at boundary points (similarly to the bias of the NW estimator at boundary points).

A simple visual check is the histogram of the running variable with narrow bins, carefully constructed so that no bin spans the cutoff. If the histogram bins display no evidence of bunching at one side of the cutoff, this is consistent with the hypothesis that the density is continuous at the cutoff; in contrast, a noticeable spike on either side is inconsistent with the hypothesis of correct specification.

In the Head Start example, it is not credible that the running variable was manipulated by the individual counties, because it was constructed from the 1960 census by a federal agency in 1965. Nevertheless, we can examine the evidence. Figure 21.2(b) displays a histogram of frequency counts for the running variable (county poverty rate), with bins of width 2, constructed so that one of the bin endpoints falls exactly at the cutoff (the solid line). The histogram appears to be continuously decreasing throughout its support. In particular, there is no visual evidence of bunching around the cutoff.

McCrary (2008) implements a formal test for continuity of the density at the cutoff. I only give a brief summary here; see his paper for details. The first step is a fine histogram estimator, similar to Figure 21.2(b) but with more narrow bin widths. The second step is to apply the RDD LL estimator, treating the histogram heights as the outcome variable and the bin midpoints at the running variable. This is a local linear density estimator and is not subject to the boundary bias problems of the conventional kernel density estimator. The RDD conditional ATE is the difference in the density at the cutoff. McCrary derives the asymptotic distribution of the estimator of the density difference and proposes an appropriate t-statistic for testing the hypothesis

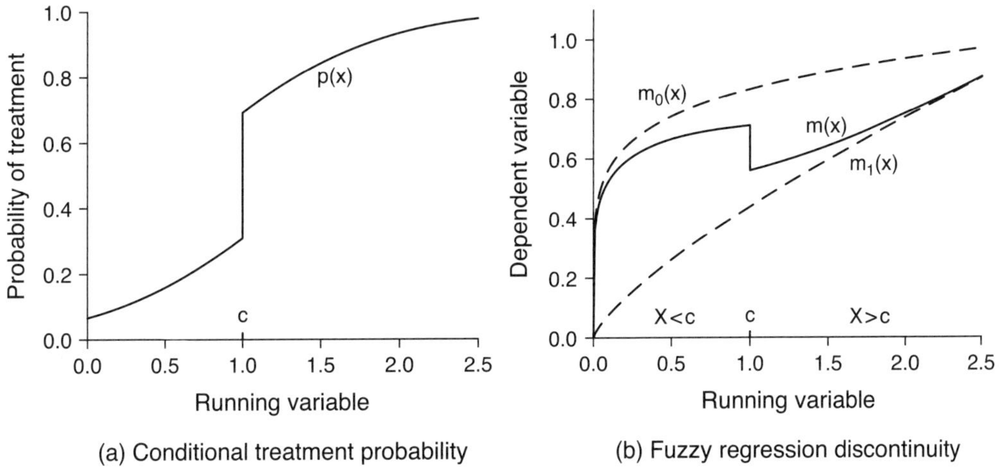

FIGURE 21.3 FRD Design

of a continuous density. If the statistic is large, this is evidence against the assumption of no manipulation, suggesting that the RDD design is not appropriate.

21.10 FUZZY REGRESSION DISCONTINUITY

The sharp regression discontinuity requires that the cutoff perfectly separates treatment from non-treatment. An alternative context is where this separation is imperfect but the conditional probability of treatment is discontinuous at the cutoff. This is called "fuzzy regression discontinuity" (FRD).

Again consider the potential outcomes framework, where Y_0 and Y_1 are the outcomes without treatment and with treatment, respectively; $\theta = Y_1 - Y_0$ is the treatment effect; X is the running variable; the conditional ATE at the cutoff is $\overline{\theta} = \mathbb{E}[\theta \mid X = c]$; and $D = 1$ indicates treatment. Define the conditional probability of treatment

$$p(x) = \mathbb{P}[D = 1 \mid X = x]$$

and the left and right limits at the cutoff $p(c+)$ and $p(c-)$. The FRD applies when $p(c+) \neq p(c-)$.

This siutation is illustrated in Figure 21.3(a), which displays the conditional probability of treatment as a function of the running variable X with a discontinuity at $X = c$.

The following is an identification theorem for the fuzzy regression discontinuity design. It is due to Hahn, Todd, and van der Klaauw (2001).

Theorem 21.2 Suppose that $m_0(x)$ and $m_1(x)$ are continuous at $x = c$, $p(x)$ is discontinuous at $x = c$, and D is independent of θ for X near c. Then

$$\overline{\theta} = \frac{m(c+) - m(c-)}{p(c+) - p(c-)}. \tag{21.6}$$

Theorem 21.2 is a more substantial identification result than Theorem 21.1 as it is inherently surprising. It states that the conditional ATE is identified by the ratio of the discontinuities in the CEF and conditional probability functions under the stated assumptions. This broadens the scope for potential application of the regression discontinuity framework beyond the sharp RDD.

In addition to the discontinuity of $p(x)$, the key additional assumption relative to Theorem 21.1 is that treatment D is independent of the treatment effect θ at $X = x$. This is a strong assumption. It means that treatment is randomly assigned for individuals with X near c. It does not allow, for example, for individuals to select into treatment, because in that case, individuals with high treatment effects θ are more likely to seek treatment than individuals with low treatment effects θ. Hahn, Todd, and van der Klaauw (2001) use the somewhat stronger assumption that treatment effect θ is constant across individuals.

A display of the outcomes is shown in Figure 21.3(b). The two dashed lines are the mean potential outcomes $m_0(x)$ and $m_1(x)$. The realized CEF $m(x)$ is the probability weighted average of these two functions using the probability function displayed in panel (a). Because the probability function is discontinuous at $x = c$, the CEF $m(x)$ also is discontinuous at $x = c$. The discontinuity, however, is not the full conditional ATE $\overline{\theta}$. The important contribution of Theorem 21.2 is that the conditional ATE equals the ratio of the discontinuities in panels (b) and (a).

To prove Theorem 21.2, first note that the observed outcome is

$$\begin{aligned} Y &= Y_0 \mathbb{1}\{D=0\} + Y_1 \mathbb{1}\{D=1\} \\ &= Y_0 + \theta \mathbb{1}\{D=1\}. \end{aligned}$$

Taking expectations conditional on $X = x$ for x near c, we obtain

$$\begin{aligned} m(x) &= m_0(x) + \mathbb{E}\left[\theta \mathbb{1}\{D=1\} \mid X=x\right] \\ &= m_0(x) + \theta(x) p(x) \end{aligned}$$

where the second equality uses the assumption that θ and D are independent for X near c. The left and right limits at c are

$$\begin{aligned} m(c+) &= m_0(c) + \overline{\theta} p(c+) \\ m(c-) &= m_0(c) + \overline{\theta} p(c-). \end{aligned}$$

Taking the difference and rearranging, we establish the theorem.

21.11 ESTIMATION OF FRD

As displayed in (21.2), the LL estimator of the discontinuity $m(c+) - m(c-)$ is obtained by local linear regression of Y on X on the two sides of the cutoff, leading to

$$\widehat{m}(c+) - \widehat{m}(c-) = \left[\widehat{\beta}_1(c)\right]_1 - \left[\widehat{\beta}_0(c)\right]_1.$$

Similarly, an LL estimator $\widehat{p}(c+) - \widehat{p}(c-)$ of the discontinuity $p(c+) - p(c-)$ can obtained by LL regression of Y on D on the two sides of the cutoff. Dividing, we obtain the estimator of the conditional ATE:

$$\widehat{\theta} = \frac{\widehat{m}(c+) - \widehat{m}(c-)}{\widehat{p}(c+) - \widehat{p}(c-)}. \tag{21.7}$$

Equation (21.7) generalizes the sharp RDD estimator, because in that case, $p(c+) - p(c-) = 1$.

This estimator bears a striking resemblance to the Wald expression (12.27) for the structural coefficient and estimator (12.28) in an IV regression with a binary instrument. In fact, $\widehat{\theta}$ can be thought of as a locally weighted IV estimator of a regression of Y on X with instrument D. However, the easiest way to implement estimation is using the expression for $\widehat{\theta}$ above.

The estimator (21.7) requires four LL regressions. It is unclear whether common bandwidths should be used for the numerator and denominator or if different bandwidths is a better choice. Bandwidth selection is critically important. In addition to assessing the fit of the regression of Y on X, it is important to check the fit of the regression of D on X for the estimator $\widehat{p}(x)$. The latter is the reduced form of the IV model. Identification rests on its precision.

The identification of the FRD conditional ATE depends on the magnitude of the discontinuity in the conditional probability $p(x)$ at $x = c$. A small discontinuity will lead to a weak instruments problem.

Standard errors can be calculated similar to IV regression. Let $s(\widehat{\theta})$ be a standard error $\widehat{m}(c+) - \widehat{m}(c-)$. Then a standard error for $\widehat{\theta}$ is $s(\widehat{\theta}) \,/\, \left|\widehat{p}(c+) - \widehat{p}(c-)\right|$.

In FRD applications, it is recommended to plot the estimated functions $\widehat{m}(x)$ and $\widehat{p}(x)$ along with confidence bands to assess precision. You are looking for evidence that the discontinuity in $p(x)$ is real and meaningful, so that the conditional ATE θ is identified. A discontinuity in $m(x)$ is an indicator of whether or not the conditional ATE is nonzero. If there is no discontinuity in $m(x)$, then $\theta = 0$. The estimate of the conditional ATE is the ratio of these two estimated discontinuities.

21.12 EXERCISES

Exercise 21.1 We have discussed the RDD when treatment occurs for $D = \mathbb{1}\{X \geq c\}$. Suppose instead that treatment occurs for $D = \mathbb{1}\{X \leq c\}$. Describe the differences (if any) involved in estimating the conditional ATE $\overline{\theta}$.

Exercise 21.2 Suppose treatment occurs for $D = \mathbb{1}\{c_1 \leq X \leq c_2\}$, where both c_1 and c_2 are in the interior of the support of X. What treatment effects are identified?

Exercise 21.3 Show that (21.1) is obtained by taking the conditional expectation as described.

Exercise 21.4 Explain why equation (21.4) estimated on the subsample for which $|X - c| \leq h$ is identical to an LL regression with a rectangular bandwidth.

Exercise 21.5 Use the datafile `LM2007` on the textbook webpage. Replicate the regresssion (21.5) using the subsample with poverty rates in the interval 59.1984 ± 13.8 (as described in the text). Repeat with intervals of 59.1984 ± 7 and 59.1984 ± 20. Report your estimates of the conditional ATE and standard error. The dependent variable is *mort_age59_related_postHS*. (The running variable is *povrate60*.)

Exercise 21.6 Use the datafile `LM2007` on the textbook webpage. Replicate the baseline RDD estimate as reported in Table 21.1. This uses a normalized triangular kernel with a bandwidth of $h = 8$. (If you use an unnormalized triangular kernel—as used, for example, in Stata—this corresponds to a bandwidth of $h = 19.6$). Repeat with a bandwidth of $h = 4$ and $h = 12$ (or $h = 9.8$ and $h = 29.4$ if an unnormalized triangular kernel is used). Report your estimates of the conditional ATE and standard error.

Exercise 21.7 Use the datafile `LM2007` on the textbook webpage. Ludwig and Miller (2007) show that similar RDD estimates for other forms of mortality do not display similar discontinuities. Perform a similar check. Estimate the conditional ATE using the dependent variable *mort_age59_injury_postHS* (mortality due to injuries in the 5–9 age group).

Exercise 21.8 Do a similar estimation as in the previous exercise but using the dependent variable *mort_age25plus_related_postHS* (mortality due to HS-related causes in the 25+ age group).

Exercise 21.9 Do a similar estimation as in the previous exercise but using the dependent variable *mort_age59_related_preHS* (mortality due to HS-related causes in the 5–9 age group during 1959–1964, before the Head Start program was started).

PART VI
NONLINEAR METHODS

CHAPTER 22
M-ESTIMATORS

22.1 INTRODUCTION

So far in this textbook, we have primarily focused on estimators that have explicit algebraic expressions. However, many econometric estimators need to be calculated by numerical methods. These estimators are collectively described as **nonlinear**. Many fall in a broad class known as **m-estimators**. In this part of the textbook, we discuss a number of m-estimators in wide use in econometrics. They have a common structure, which allows for a unified treatment of estimation and inference.

An m-estimator is defined as a minimizer of a sample average:

$$\widehat{\theta} = \underset{\theta \in \Theta}{\operatorname{argmin}} \, S_n(\theta)$$

$$S_n(\theta) = \frac{1}{n} \sum_{i=1}^{n} \rho\left(Y_i, X_i, \theta\right)$$

where $\rho\left(Y, X, \theta\right)$ is some function of (Y, X) and a parameter $\theta \in \Theta$. The function $S_n(\theta)$ is called the **criterion function** or **objective function**. For notational simplicity, set $\rho_i\left(\theta\right) = \rho\left(Y_i, X_i, \theta\right)$.

M-estimation includes maximum likelihood when $\rho_i\left(\theta\right)$ is the negative log-density function. "m-estimators" are a broader class; the prefix "m" stands for "maximum likelihood-type."

The issues we focus on in this chaper are: (1) identification, (2) estimation, (3) consistency, (4) asymptotic distribution, and (5) covariance matrix estimation.

22.2 EXAMPLES

There are many m-estimators in common econometric usage. Some examples include the following:

1. Ordinary least squares: $\rho_i\left(\theta\right) = \left(Y_i - X_i'\theta\right)^2$.
2. Nonlinear least squares: $\rho_i\left(\theta\right) = \left(Y_i - m\left(X_i, \theta\right)\right)^2$ (Chapter 23).
3. Least absolute deviations: $\rho_i\left(\theta\right) = \left|Y_i - X_i'\theta\right|$ (Chapter 24).
4. Quantile regression: $\rho_i\left(\theta\right) = \left(Y_i - X_i'\theta\right)\left(\tau - \mathbb{1}\left\{\left(Y_i - X_i'\theta\right) < 0\right\}\right)$ (Chapter 24).
5. Maximum likelihood: $\rho_i\left(\theta\right) = -\log f\left(Y_i \mid X_i, \theta\right)$.

The final category—maximum likelihood estimation—includes many estimators as special cases. This includes many standard estimators of limited-dependent-variable models (Chapters 25–27). To illustrate, the **probit model** for a binary dependent variable is

$$\mathbb{P}\left[Y = 1 \mid X\right] = \Phi\left(X'\theta\right)$$

where $\Phi(u)$ is the normal cumulative distribution function. We will study probit estimation in detail in Chapter 25. The negative log-density function is

$$\rho_i(\theta) = -Y_i \log\left(\Phi\left(X_i'\theta\right)\right) - (1 - Y_i)\log\left(1 - \Phi\left(X_i'\theta\right)\right).$$

Not all nonlinear estimators are m-estimators. Examples include method of moments, GMM, and minimum distance.

22.3 IDENTIFICATION AND ESTIMATION

A parameter vector θ is **identified** if it is uniquely determined by the probability distribution of the observations. This is a property of the probability distribution, not of the estimator.

However, when discussing a specific estimator, it is common to describe identification in terms of the criterion function. Assume $\mathbb{E}\left|\rho(Y, X, \theta)\right| < \infty$. Define

$$S(\theta) = \mathbb{E}\left[S_n(\theta)\right] = \mathbb{E}\left[\rho(Y, X, \theta)\right]$$

and its population minimizer

$$\theta_0 = \underset{\theta \in \Theta}{\operatorname{argmin}}\, S(\theta).$$

We say that θ is **identified** (or **point identified**) by $S(\theta)$ if the minimizer θ_0 is unique.

In nonlinear models, it is difficult to provide general conditions under which a parameter is identified. Identification needs to be examined on a model-by-model basis.

An m-estimator $\widehat{\theta}$ by definition minimizes $S_n(\theta)$. When there is no explicit algebraic expression for the solution, the minimization is done numerically. Such numerical methods are reviewed in Chapter 12 of *Probability and Statistics for Economists.*

We illustrate using the probit model of Section 22.2. We use the CPS dataset for Y equal to an indicator that the individual is married,[1] and set the regressors equal to years of education, age, and age squared. We obtain the following estimates:

$$\mathbb{P}\left[married = 1\right] = \Phi\left(\underset{(.002)}{0.031}\ education + \underset{(0.3)}{16.4}\left(\frac{age}{100}\right) - \underset{(0.4)}{16.7}\left(\frac{age}{100}\right)^2 + \underset{(0.07)}{3.73}\right).$$

Standard error calculation will be discussed in Section 22.8. In this application, we see that the probability of marriage is increasing in years of *education* and is an increasing yet concave function of *age*.

22.4 CONSISTENCY

It seems reasonable to expect that if a parameter is identified, then we should be able to estimate the parameter consistently. For linear estimators, we demonstrated consistency by applying the WLLN to the explicit algebraic expressions for the estimators. This is not possible for nonlinear estimators, because they do not have explicit algebraic expressions.

[1] We define $married = 1$ if *marital* equals 1, 2, or 3.

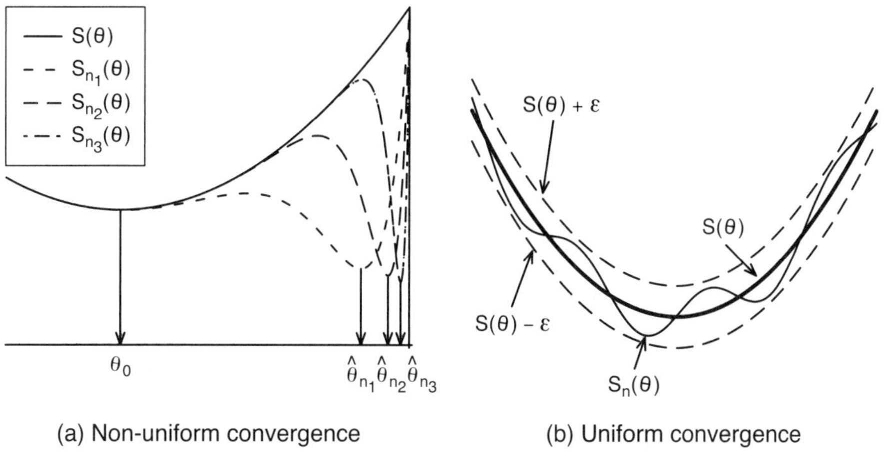

FIGURE 22.1 Non-uniform vs. uniform convergence

Instead, what is available to us is that an m-estimator minimizes the criterion function $S_n(\theta)$, which is itself a sample average. For any given θ, the WLLN shows that $S_n(\theta) \underset{p}{\longrightarrow} S(\theta)$. It is intuitive that the minimizer of $S_n(\theta)$ (the m-estimator $\widehat{\theta}$) will converge in probability to the minimizer of $S(\theta)$ (the parameter θ_0). However, the WLLN by itself is not sufficient to make this extension.

To see the problem, examine Figure 22.1(a). This displays a sequence of functions $S_n(\theta)$ (the dashed lines) for three values of n. What is illustrated is that for each θ, the function $S_n(\theta)$ converges toward the limit function $S(\theta)$. However for each n, the function $S_n(\theta)$ has a steep dip in the right-hand region. The result is that the sample minimizer $\widehat{\theta}_n$ converges to the right-limit of the parameter space. In contrast, the minimizer θ_0 of the limit criterion $S(\theta)$ is in the interior of the parameter space. What we observe is that $S_n(\theta)$ converges to $S(\theta)$ for each θ, but the minimizer $\widehat{\theta}_n$ does not converge to θ_0.

A sufficient condition to exclude this pathological behavior is uniform convergence—uniformity over the parameter space Θ. As we show in Theorem 22.1, uniform convergence in probability of $S_n(\theta)$ to $S(\theta)$ is sufficient to establish that the m-estimator $\widehat{\theta}$ is consistent for θ_0.

Definition 22.1 $S_n(\theta)$ **converges in probability** to $S(\theta)$ **uniformly** over $\theta \in \Theta$ if

$$\sup_{\theta \in \Theta} |S_n(\theta) - S(\theta)| \underset{p}{\longrightarrow} 0$$

as $n \to \infty$.

Uniform convergence excludes erratic wiggles in $S_n(\theta)$ uniformly across θ and n (e.g., what occurs in Figure 22.1(a)). The idea is illustrated in Figure 22.1(b). The heavy solid line is the function $S(\theta)$. The dashed lines are $S(\theta) + \varepsilon$ and $S(\theta) - \varepsilon$. The thin solid line is the sample criterion $S_n(\theta)$. The figure illustrates a situation where the sample criterion satisifes $\sup_{\theta \in \Theta} |S_n(\theta) - S(\theta)| < \varepsilon$. The sample criterion as displayed weaves up and down but stays within ε of $S(\theta)$. Uniform convergence holds if the event shown in Figure 22.1(b) holds with high probability for n sufficiently large, for any arbitrarily small ε.

Theorem 22.1 $\widehat{\theta} \underset{p}{\longrightarrow} \theta_0$ as $n \to \infty$ if

1. $S_n(\theta)$ converges in probability to $S(\theta)$ uniformly over $\theta \in \Theta$.
2. θ_0 uniquely minimizes $S(\theta)$ in the sense that for all $\epsilon > 0$,

$$\inf_{\theta:\|\theta-\theta_0\|\geq\epsilon} S(\theta) > S(\theta_0).$$

Theorem 22.1 shows that an m-estimator is consistent for its population parameter. There are only two conditions. First, the criterion function converges uniformly in probability to its expected value, and second, the minimizer θ_0 is unique. The assumption excludes the possibility that $\lim_j S(\theta_j) = S(\theta_0)$ for some sequence $\theta_j \in \Theta$ not converging to θ_0.

The proof of Theorem 22.1 is provided in Section 22.9.

22.5 UNIFORM LAW OF LARGE NUMBERS

The uniform convergence of Definition 22.1 is a high-level assumption. In this section, we discuss lower level sufficient conditions.

Theorem 22.2 Uniform Law of Large Numbers (ULLN) Assume

1. (Y_i, X_i) are i.i.d.
2. $\rho(Y, X, \theta)$ is continuous in $\theta \in \Theta$ with probability 1.
3. $|\rho(Y, X, \theta)| \leq G(Y, X)$, where $\mathbb{E}[G(Y, X)] < \infty$.
4. Θ is compact.

Then $\sup_{\theta\in\Theta} |S_n(\theta) - S(\theta)| \underset{p}{\longrightarrow} 0$.

Theorem 22.2 is established in Theorem 18.2 of *Probability and Statistics for Economists*.

Assumption 2 holds if $\rho(y, x, \theta)$ is continuous in θ, or if the discontinuities occur at points of 0 probability. This allows for most relevant applications in econometrics. Theorem 18.2 of *Probability and Statistics for Economists* also provides conditions based on finite bracketing or covering numbers, which allow for more generality. Assumption 3 is a slight strengthening of the finite-expectation condition $\mathbb{E}[\rho(Y, X, \theta)] < \infty$. The function $G(Y, X)$ is called an **envelope**.

The ULLN extends to time series and clustered samples. See B. Hansen and Lee (2019) for clustered samples.

Combining Theorems 22.1 and 22.2, we obtain a set of conditions for consistent estimation.

Theorem 22.3 $\widehat{\theta} \underset{p}{\longrightarrow} \theta_0$ as $n \to \infty$ if

1. (Y_i, X_i) are i.i.d.
2. $\rho(Y, X, \theta)$ is continuous in $\theta \in \Theta$ with probability 1.

3. $|\rho(Y,X,\theta)| \le G(Y,X)$, where $\mathbb{E}[G(Y,X)] < \infty$.
4. Θ is compact.
5. θ_0 uniquely minimizes $S(\theta)$.

22.6 ASYMPTOTIC DISTRIBUTION

Let us now establish an asymptotic distribution theory. We start with an informal demonstration, present a general result under high-level conditions, and then discuss the assumptions and conditions. Define

$$\psi(Y,X,\theta) = \frac{\partial}{\partial\theta}\rho(Y,X,\theta)$$
$$\overline{\psi}_n(\theta) = \frac{\partial}{\partial\theta}S_n(\theta)$$
$$\psi(\theta) = \frac{\partial}{\partial\theta}S(\theta).$$

Also define $\psi_i(\theta) = \psi(Y_i, X_i, \theta)$ and $\psi_i = \psi_i(\theta_0)$.

Because the m-estimator $\widehat{\theta}$ minimizes $S_n(\theta)$, it satisfies[2] the first-order condition $0 = \overline{\psi}_n(\widehat{\theta})$. Expand the right-hand side as a first-order Taylor expansion about θ_0. This is valid when $\widehat{\theta}$ is in a neighborhood of θ_0, which holds for n sufficiently large by Theorem 22.1. This expansion yields

$$0 = \overline{\psi}_n(\widehat{\theta}) \simeq \overline{\psi}_n(\theta_0) + \frac{\partial^2}{\partial\theta\partial\theta'}S_n(\theta_0)(\widehat{\theta} - \theta_0). \tag{22.1}$$

Rewriting, we obtain

$$\sqrt{n}(\widehat{\theta} - \theta_0) \simeq -\left(\frac{\partial^2}{\partial\theta\partial\theta'}S_n(\theta_0)\right)^{-1}\left(\sqrt{n}\,\overline{\psi}_n(\theta_0)\right).$$

Consider the two components. First, by the WLLN

$$\frac{\partial^2}{\partial\theta\partial\theta'}S_n(\theta_0) = \frac{1}{n}\sum_{i=1}^{n}\frac{\partial^2}{\partial\theta\partial\theta'}\rho(Y_i,X_i,\theta_0) \underset{p}{\longrightarrow} \mathbb{E}\left[\frac{\partial^2}{\partial\theta\partial\theta'}\rho_i(Y,X,\theta_0)\right] \overset{\text{def}}{=} \boldsymbol{Q}.$$

Second, we have

$$\sqrt{n}\,\overline{\psi}_n(\theta_0) = \frac{1}{\sqrt{n}}\sum_{i=1}^{n}\psi_i. \tag{22.2}$$

Since θ_0 minimizes $S(\theta) = \mathbb{E}[\rho_i(\theta)]$, it satisfies the first-order condition

$$0 = \psi(\theta_0) = \mathbb{E}[\psi(Y,X,\theta_0)]. \tag{22.3}$$

Thus the summands in (22.2) are mean 0. Applying a CLT, this sum converges in distribution to $\mathrm{N}(0,\Omega)$, where $\Omega = \mathbb{E}\left[\psi_i\psi_i'\right]$. We deduce that

$$\sqrt{n}(\widehat{\theta} - \theta_0) \underset{d}{\longrightarrow} \boldsymbol{Q}^{-1}\mathrm{N}(0,\Omega) = \mathrm{N}\left(0, \boldsymbol{Q}^{-1}\Omega\boldsymbol{Q}^{-1}\right).$$

[2]If $\widehat{\theta}$ is an interior solution. Because $\widehat{\theta}$ is consistent, this occurs with probability approaching 1 if θ_0 is in the interior of the parameter space Θ.

The technical hurdle to make this derivation rigorous is justifying the Taylor expansion (22.1), which can be done through smoothness of the second derivative of $\rho_i(\theta_0)$. An alternative (more advanced) argument based on empirical process theory uses weaker assumptions. Set

$$\boldsymbol{Q}(\theta) = \frac{\partial^2}{\partial\theta\partial\theta'} S(\theta)$$

$$\boldsymbol{Q} = \boldsymbol{Q}(\theta_0).$$

Let $\mathscr{N}$ be some neighborhood of θ_0.

Theorem 22.4 Assume that the conditions of Theorem 22.1 hold, plus

1. $\mathbb{E}\|\psi(Y,X,\theta_0)\|^2 < \infty$.
2. $\boldsymbol{Q} > 0$.
3. $\boldsymbol{Q}(\theta)$ is continuous in $\theta \in \mathscr{N}$.
4. For all $\theta_1, \theta_2 \in \mathscr{N}$, $\|\psi(Y,X,\theta_1) - \psi(Y,X,\theta_2)\| \le B(Y,X)\|\theta_1 - \theta_2\|$, where $\mathbb{E}\left[B(Y,X)^2\right] < \infty$.
5. θ_0 is in the interior of Θ.

   Then as $n \to \infty$, $\sqrt{n}\left(\widehat{\theta} - \theta_0\right) \underset{d}{\longrightarrow} \mathrm{N}(0, \boldsymbol{V})$, where $\boldsymbol{V} = \boldsymbol{Q}^{-1}\Omega\boldsymbol{Q}^{-1}$.

The proof of Theorem 22.4 is presented in Section 22.9.

In some cases, the asymptotic covariance matrix simplifies. The leading case is correctly specified maximum likelihood estimation, where $\boldsymbol{Q} = \Omega$, so $\boldsymbol{V} = \boldsymbol{Q}^{-1} = \Omega^{-1}$.

Assumption 1 states that the scores $\psi(Y,X,\theta_0)$ have a finite second moment. This is necessary in order to apply the CLT. Assumption 2 is a full-rank condition and is related to identification. A sufficient condition for assumption 3 is that the scores $\psi(Y,X,\theta)$ are continuously differentiable, but this is not necessary. Assumption 3 is broader, allowing for discontinuous $\psi(Y,X,\theta)$, so long as its expectation is continuous and differentiable. Assumption 4 states that $\psi(Y,X,\theta)$ is Lipschitz-continuous for θ near θ_0. Assumption 5 is required to justify the application of the mean-value expansion.

22.7 ASYMPTOTIC DISTRIBUTION UNDER BROADER CONDITIONS*

Assumption 4 in Theorem 22.4 requires that $\psi(Y,X,\theta)$ is Lipschitz-continuous. Although this holds in most applications, it is violated in some important applications, including quantile regression. In such cases, we can appeal to alternative regularity conditions. These are more flexible but less intuitive.

The following result is a simple generalization of Lipschitz-continuity.

Theorem 22.5 The results of Theorem 22.4 hold if assumption 4 is replaced with the following condition: For all $\delta > 0$ and all $\theta_1 \in \mathscr{N}$,

$$\left(\mathbb{E}\left[\sup_{\|\theta-\theta_1\|<\delta} \|\psi(Y,X,\theta) - \psi(Y,X,\theta_1)\|^2\right]\right)^{1/2} \le C\delta^{\psi} \tag{22.4}$$

for some $C < \infty$ and $0 < \psi < \infty$.

See Theorem 18.5 of *Probability and Statistics for Economists* or theorem 5 of Andrews (1994).

The bound (22.4) holds for many examples with discontinuous $\psi(Y,X,\theta)$ when the discontinuities occur with zero probability.

We next discuss a set of flexible results.

Theorem 22.6 The results of Theorem 22.4 hold if assumption 4 is replaced with the following. First, for $\theta \in \mathcal{N}$, $\|\psi(Y,X,\theta)\| \le G(Y,X)$ with $\mathbb{E}\left[G(Y,X)^2\right] < \infty$. Second, one of the following conditions holds:

1. $\psi(y,x,\theta)$ is Lipschitz-continuous.
2. $\psi(y,x,\theta) = h(\theta'\psi(x))$, where $h(u)$ has finite total variation.
3. $\psi(y,x,\theta)$ is a combination of functions of the form in parts 1 and 2 obtained by addition, multiplication, minimum, maximum, and composition.
4. $\psi(y,x,\theta)$ is a Vapnik-Červonenkis (VC) class.

See Theorem 18.6 of *Probability and Statistics for Economists* or theorems 2 and 3 of Andrews (1994).

The function h in part 2 allows for discontinuous functions, including the indicator and sign functions. Part 3 shows that combinations of smooth (Lipschitz) functions and discontinuous functions satisfying the condition of part 2 are allowed, covering many relevant applications, including quantile regression. Part 4 states a general condition, that $\psi(y,x,\theta)$ is a VC class. As we will not be using this property in this textbook, we will not discuss this further, but I refer the interested reader to any textbook on empirical processes.

Theorems 22.5 and 22.6 provide alternative conditions on $\psi(y,x,\theta)$ (other than Lipschitz-continuity), which can be used to establish asymptotic normality of an m-estimator.

22.8 COVARIANCE MATRIX ESTIMATION

The standard estimator for $\boldsymbol{V}$ takes the sandwich form. We estimate Ω by

$$\widehat{\Omega} = \frac{1}{n}\sum_{i=1}^{n} \widehat{\psi}_i \widehat{\psi}_i'$$

where $\widehat{\psi}_i = \frac{\partial}{\partial\theta}\rho_i\left(\widehat{\theta}\right)$. When $\rho_i(\theta)$ is twice differentiable, an estimator of $\boldsymbol{Q}$ is

$$\widehat{\boldsymbol{Q}} = \frac{1}{n}\sum_{i=1}^{n} \frac{\partial^2}{\partial\theta\partial\theta'}\rho_i\left(\widehat{\theta}\right).$$

When $\rho_i(\theta)$ is not second differentiable, then estimators of $\boldsymbol{Q}$ are constructed on a case-by-case basis.

Given $\widehat{\Omega}$ and $\widehat{\boldsymbol{Q}}$, an estimator for $\boldsymbol{V}$ is

$$\widehat{\boldsymbol{V}} = \widehat{\boldsymbol{Q}}^{-1}\widehat{\Omega}\widehat{\boldsymbol{Q}}^{-1}. \tag{22.5}$$

It is possible to adjust $\widehat{\boldsymbol{V}}$ by multiplying by a degree-of-freedom scaling, such as $n/(n-k)$, where $k = \dim(\theta)$. There is no formal guidance.

For maximum likelihood estimators, the standard covariance matrix estimator is $\widehat{\boldsymbol{V}} = \widehat{\boldsymbol{Q}}^{-1}$. This choice is not robust to misspecification. Therefore, it is recommended to use the robust version (22.5), for example, by using the ", r" option in Stata. This is unfortunately not uniformly done in practice.

For clustered and time series observations, the estimator $\widehat{\boldsymbol{Q}}$ is unaltered, but the estimator $\widehat{\Omega}$ changes. For clustered samples it is

$$\widehat{\Omega} = \frac{1}{n} \sum_{g=1}^{G} \left(\sum_{\ell=1}^{n_g} \widehat{\psi}_{\ell g} \right) \left(\sum_{\ell=1}^{n_g} \widehat{\psi}_{\ell g} \right)'.$$

For time series data, the estimator $\widehat{\Omega}$ is unaltered if the scores ψ_i are serially uncorrelated (which occurs when a model is dynamically correctly specified). Otherwise, a Newey-West covariance matrix estimator can be used and equals

$$\widehat{\Omega} = \sum_{\ell=-M}^{M} \left(1 - \frac{|\ell|}{M+1} \right) \frac{1}{n} \sum_{1 \le t-\ell \le n} \widehat{\psi}_{t-\ell} \widehat{\psi}_t'.$$

Standard errors for the parameter estimates are formed by taking the square roots of the diagonal elements of $n^{-1}\widehat{\boldsymbol{V}}$.

22.9 TECHNICAL PROOFS*

Proof of Theorem 22.1 The proof proceeds in two steps. First, we show that $S\left(\widehat{\theta}\right) \underset{p}{\longrightarrow} S(\theta)$. Second, we show that this implies $\widehat{\theta} \underset{p}{\longrightarrow} \theta$.

Since θ_0 minimizes $S(\theta)$, $S(\theta_0) \le S\left(\widehat{\theta}\right)$. Hence

$$\begin{aligned}
0 &\le S\left(\widehat{\theta}\right) - S(\theta_0) \\
&= S\left(\widehat{\theta}\right) - S_n\left(\widehat{\theta}\right) + S_n(\theta_0) - S(\theta_0) + S_n\left(\widehat{\theta}\right) - S_n(\theta_0) \\
&\le 2 \sup_{\theta \in \Theta} \|S_n(\theta) - S(\theta)\| \underset{p}{\longrightarrow} 0.
\end{aligned}$$

The second inequality uses the fact that $\widehat{\theta}$ minimizes $S_n(\theta)$, so $S_n\left(\widehat{\theta}\right) \le S_n(\theta_0)$ and replaces the other two pairwise comparisons by the supremum. The final convergence is the assumed uniform convergence in probability.

The preceeding argument is illustrated in Figure 22.2. The figure displays the expected criterion $S(\theta)$ with the solid line, and the sample criterion $S_n(\theta)$ is displayed with the dashed line. The distances between the two functions at the true value θ_0 and the estimator $\widehat{\theta}$ are marked by the two dotted lines. The sum of these two lengths is greater than the vertical distance between $S\left(\widehat{\theta}\right)$ and $S(\theta_0)$, because the latter distance equals the sum of the two dotted lines plus the vertical height of the thick section of the dashed line (between $S_n(\theta_0)$ and $S_n\left(\widehat{\theta}\right)$) which is positive because $S_n\left(\widehat{\theta}\right) \le S_n(\theta_0)$. The lengths of the dotted lines converge to 0 under the assumption of uniform convergence. Hence, $S\left(\widehat{\theta}\right)$ converges to $S(\theta_0)$. This completes the first step.

In the second step of the proof, we show that $\widehat{\theta} \underset{p}{\longrightarrow} \theta$. Fix $\epsilon > 0$. The unique minimum assumption implies there is a $\delta > 0$ such that $\|\theta_0 - \theta\| > \epsilon$ implies $S(\theta) - S(\theta_0) \ge \delta$. Thus $\left\|\theta_0 - \widehat{\theta}\right\| > \epsilon$ implies $S\left(\widehat{\theta}\right) - S(\theta_0) \ge \delta$. Hence,

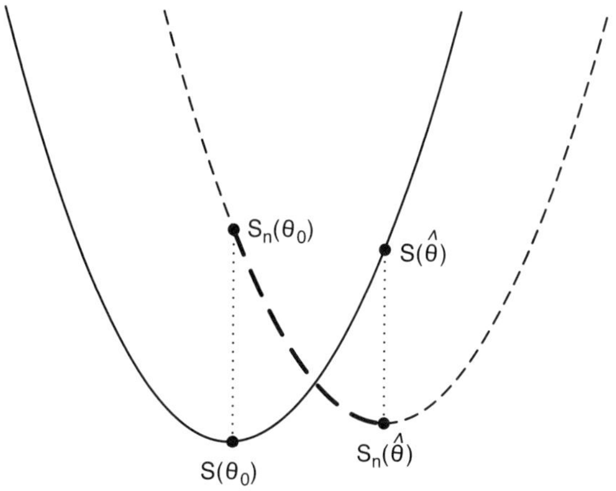

FIGURE 22.2 Consistency of M-estimator

$$\mathbb{P}\left[\left\|\theta_0-\widehat{\theta}\right\|>\epsilon\right]\le\mathbb{P}\left[S\left(\widehat{\theta}\right)-S\left(\theta_0\right)\ge\delta\right].$$

The right-hand side converges to 0 because $S\left(\widehat{\theta}\right)\underset{p}{\longrightarrow}S(\theta)$. Thus the left-hand side converges to 0 as well. Since ϵ is arbitrary, this implies that $\widehat{\theta}\underset{p}{\longrightarrow}\theta$, as stated.

To illustrate, again examine Figure 22.2. We see $S\left(\widehat{\theta}\right)$ marked on the graph of $S(\theta)$. Since $S\left(\widehat{\theta}\right)$ converges to $S\left(\theta_0\right)$, this means that $S\left(\widehat{\theta}\right)$ slides down the graph of $S(\theta)$ toward the minimum. The only way for $\widehat{\theta}$ to not converge to θ_0 would be if the function $S(\theta)$ were flat at the minimum, which is excluded by the assumption of a unique minimum. ■

Proof of Theorem 22.4 Expanding the population first-order condition $0=\psi\left(\theta_0\right)$ around $\theta=\widehat{\theta}$ by using the mean value theorem, we find

$$0=\psi\left(\widehat{\theta}\right)+\boldsymbol{Q}(\theta_n^*)\left(\theta_0-\widehat{\theta}\right)$$

where θ_n^* is intermediate[3] between θ_0 and $\widehat{\theta}$. Solving, we find

$$\sqrt{n}\left(\widehat{\theta}-\theta_0\right)=\boldsymbol{Q}(\theta_n^*)^{-1}\sqrt{n}\psi\left(\widehat{\theta}\right).$$

The assumption that $\psi(\theta)$ is continuously differentiable means that $\boldsymbol{Q}\left(\theta\right)$ is continuous in $\mathscr{N}$. Since θ_n^* is intermediate between θ_0 and $\widehat{\theta}$ and the latter converges in probability to θ_0, it follows that θ_n^* converges in probability to θ_0 as well. Thus by the continuous mapping theorem, $\boldsymbol{Q}\left(\theta_n^*\right)\underset{p}{\longrightarrow}\boldsymbol{Q}\left(\theta_0\right)=\boldsymbol{Q}$.

We next examine the asymptotic distribution of $\sqrt{n}\psi\left(\widehat{\theta}\right)$. Define

$$v_n\left(\theta\right)=\sqrt{n}\left(\overline{\psi}_n\left(\theta\right)-\psi\left(\theta\right)\right).$$

An implication of the sample first-order condition $\overline{\psi}_n\left(\widehat{\theta}\right)=0$ is

$$\sqrt{n}\psi\left(\widehat{\theta}\right)=\sqrt{n}\left(\psi\left(\widehat{\theta}\right)-\overline{\psi}_n\left(\widehat{\theta}\right)\right)=-v_n\left(\widehat{\theta}\right)=-v_n\left(\theta_0\right)+r_n$$

where $r_n=v_n\left(\theta_0\right)-v_n\left(\widehat{\theta}\right)$.

[3]Technically, since $\psi\left(\widehat{\theta}\right)$ is a vector, the expansion is done separately for each element of the vector, so the intermediate value varies by the rows of $\boldsymbol{Q}(\theta_n^*)$. This doesn't affect the conclusion.

Since ψ_i is mean 0 (see (22.3)) and has a finite covariance matrix Ω by assumption, it satisfies the multivariate CLT. Thus,

$$\sqrt{n}\psi_n(\theta) = \frac{1}{\sqrt{n}}\sum_{i=1}^{n}\psi_i \underset{d}{\longrightarrow} \mathrm{N}(0,\Omega).$$

The final step is to show that $r_n = o_p(1)$. Pick any $\eta > 0$ and $\epsilon > 0$. As shown by Theorem 18.5 of *Probability and Statistics for Economists*, Assumption 4 implies that $v_n(\theta)$ is asymptotically equicontinuous, which means that (see Definition 18.7 in *Probability and Statistics for Economists*) given ϵ and η, there is a $\delta > 0$ such that

$$\limsup_{n\to\infty}\mathbb{P}\left[\sup_{\|\theta-\theta_0\|\le\delta}\|v_n(\theta_0) - v_n(\theta)\| > \eta\right] \le \epsilon. \tag{22.6}$$

Theorem 22.1 implies that $\widehat{\theta} \underset{p}{\longrightarrow} \theta_0$, or

$$\limsup_{n\to\infty}\mathbb{P}\left[\left\|\widehat{\theta} - \theta_0\right\| > \delta\right] \le \epsilon. \tag{22.7}$$

We calculate that

$$\begin{aligned}\limsup_{n\to\infty}\mathbb{P}[r_n > \eta] &\le \limsup_{n\to\infty}\mathbb{P}\left[\left\|v_n(\theta_0) - v_n\left(\widehat{\theta}\right)\right\| > \eta, \left\|\widehat{\theta}-\theta_0\right\| \le \delta\right] + \limsup_{n\to\infty}\mathbb{P}\left[\left\|\widehat{\theta}-\theta_0\right\| > \delta\right] \\ &\le \limsup_{n\to\infty}\mathbb{P}\left[\sup_{\|\theta-\theta_0\|\le\delta}\|v_n(\theta_0) - v_n(\theta)\| > \eta\right] + \epsilon \le 2\epsilon.\end{aligned}$$

The second inequality is (22.7) and the final inequality is (22.6). Since η and ϵ are arbitrary, we deduce that $r_n = o_p(1)$. We conclude that

$$\sqrt{n}\psi\left(\widehat{\theta}\right) = -v_n(\theta_0) + r_n \underset{d}{\longrightarrow} \mathrm{N}(0,\Omega).$$

Together, these results show that

$$\sqrt{n}\left(\widehat{\theta}-\theta_0\right) = \boldsymbol{Q}(\theta_n^*)^{-1}\sqrt{n}\psi\left(\widehat{\theta}\right) \underset{d}{\longrightarrow} \boldsymbol{Q}^{-1}\mathrm{N}(0,\Omega) \sim \mathrm{N}\left(0, \boldsymbol{Q}^{-1}\Omega\boldsymbol{Q}^{-1}\right)$$

as claimed. ■

22.10 EXERCISES

Exercise 22.1 Consider the model $Y = X'\theta + e$, where e is independent of X and has known density function $f(e)$, which is continuously differentiable.

(a) Show that the conditional density of Y given $X = x$ is $f\left(y - x'\theta\right)$.

(b) Find the functions $\rho(Y, X, \theta)$ and $\psi(Y, X, \theta)$.

(c) Calculate the asymptotic covariance matrix.

Exercise 22.2 Consider the model $Y = X'\theta + e$. Consider the m-estimator of θ with $\rho(Y, X, \theta) = g\left(Y - X'\theta\right)$, where $g(u)$ is a known function.

(a) Find the functions $\rho(Y, X, \theta)$ and $\psi(Y, X, \theta)$.

(b) Calculate the asymptotic covariance matrix.

Exercise 22.3 For the estimator described in Exercise 22.2, set $g(u) = \frac{1}{4}u^4$.

(a) Sketch $g(u)$. Is $g(u)$ continuous? Differentiable? Second differentiable?

(b) Find the functions $\rho(Y, X, \theta)$ and $\psi(Y, X, \theta)$.

(c) Calculate the asymptotic covariance matrix.

Exercise 22.4 For the estimator described in Exercise 22.2, set $g(u) = 1 - \cos(u)$.

(a) Sketch $g(u)$. Is $g(u)$ continuous? Differentiable? Second differentiable?

(b) Find the functions $\rho(Y, X, \theta)$ and $\psi(Y, X, \theta)$.

(c) Calculate the asymptotic covariance matrix.

CHAPTER 23

NONLINEAR LEAST SQUARES

23.1 INTRODUCTION

A **nonlinear regression model** is a parametric regression function $m(x,\theta) = \mathbb{E}[Y \mid X = x]$ that is nonlinear in the parameters $\theta \in \Theta$. We write the model as

$$
\begin{aligned}
Y &= m(X,\theta) + e \\
\mathbb{E}[e \mid X] &= 0.
\end{aligned}
$$

In nonlinear regression, the ordinary least squares estimator does not apply. Instead the parameters are typically estimated by **nonlinear least squares (NLLS)**. NLLS is an m-estimator that requires numerical optimization.

We illustrate nonlinear regression with three examples.

Our first example is the **Box-Cox regression model**. The Box-Cox transformation (Box and Cox, 1964) for a strictly positive variable $x > 0$ is

$$
x^{(\lambda)} = \begin{cases} \dfrac{x^{\lambda} - 1}{\lambda}, & \text{if } \lambda \neq 0 \\ \log(x), & \text{if } \lambda = 0. \end{cases} \tag{23.1}
$$

The Box-Cox transformation continuously nests linear ($\lambda = 1$) and logarithmic ($\lambda = 0$) functions. Figure 23.1(a) displays the Box-Cox transformation (23.1) over $x \in (0, 2]$ for $\lambda = 2, 1, 0, 0.5, 0$, and -1. The parameter λ controls the curvature of the function.

The Box-Cox regression model is

$$
Y = \beta_0 + \beta_1 X^{(\lambda)} + e
$$

which has parameters $\theta = (\beta_0, \beta_1, \lambda)$. The regression function is linear in (β_0, β_1) but nonlinear in λ.

To illustrate, let us revisit the reduced form regression (12.87) of *risk* on $\log(\textit{mortality})$ from Acemoglu, Johnson, and Robinson (2001). A reasonable question is why the authors specified the equation as a regression on $\log(\textit{mortality})$ rather than on *mortality*. The Box-Cox regression model allows both as special cases, and equals

$$
\textit{risk} = \beta_0 + \beta_1 \textit{mortality}^{(\lambda)} + e. \tag{23.2}
$$

Our second example is a **constant elasticity of substitution (CES)** production function, which was introduced by Arrow, Chenery, Minhas, and Solow (1961) as a generalization of the popular Cobb-Douglass

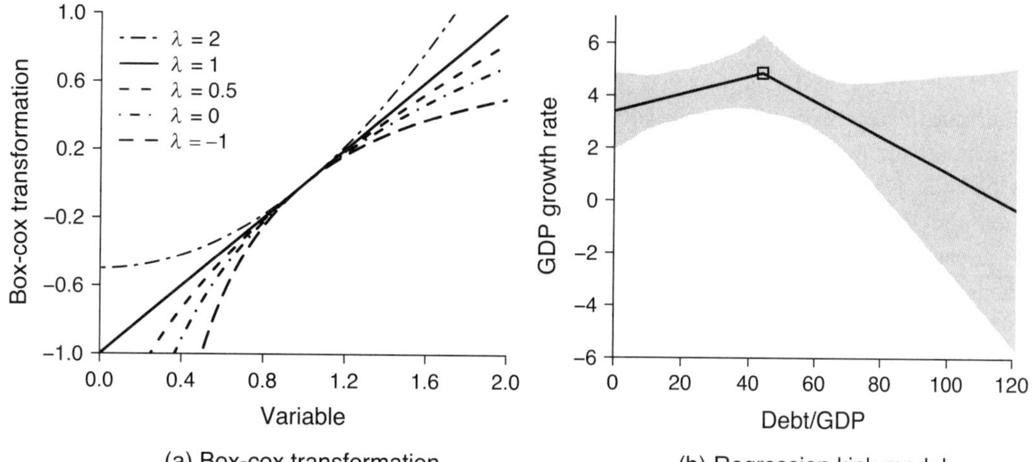

(a) Box-cox transformation
(b) Regression kink model

FIGURE 23.1 Nonlinear regression models

production function. The CES function for two inputs is

$$Y = \begin{cases} A\left(\alpha X_1^{\rho} + (1-\alpha) X_2^{\rho}\right)^{\nu/\rho}, & \text{if } \rho \neq 0 \\ A\left(X_1^{\alpha} X_2^{(1-\alpha)}\right)^{\nu}, & \text{if } \rho = 0. \end{cases}$$

where A is heterogeneous (random) productivity, $\nu > 0$, $\alpha \in (0,1)$, and $\rho \in (-\infty, 1]$. The coefficient ν is the elasticity of scale. The coefficient α is the share parameter. The coefficient ρ is a rewriting[1] of the elasticity of substitution σ between the inputs and satisfies $\sigma = 1/(1-\rho)$. The elasticity satisfies $\sigma > 1$ if $\rho > 0$, and $\sigma < 1$ if $\rho < 0$. At $\rho = 0$, we obtain the unit elastic Cobb-Douglas function. Setting $\rho = 1$ and $\nu = 1$, we obtain a linear production function. Taking the limit $\rho \to -\infty$, we obtain the Leontief production function.

Set $\log A = \beta + e$. The framework implies the regression model

$$\log Y = \beta + \frac{\nu}{\rho} \log\left(\alpha X_1^{\rho} + (1-\alpha) X_2^{\rho}\right) + e \tag{23.3}$$

with parameters $\theta = (\rho, \nu, \alpha, \beta)$.

We illustrate CES production function estimation with a modification of Papageorgiou, Saam, and Schulte (2017). These authors estimate a CES production function for electricity production, where X_1 is generation capacity using "clean" technology and X_2 is generation capacity using "dirty" technology. They estimate the model using a panel of 26 countries for the years 1995 to 2009. Their goal was to measure the elasticity of substitution between clean and dirty electrical generation. The data file `PPS2017` is an extract of the authors' dataset.

Our third example is the **regression kink model**. This is essentially a piecewise continuous linear spline where the knot is treated as a free parameter. The model used in our application is the nonlinear AR(1) model

$$Y_t = \beta_1 (X_{t-1} - c)_- + \beta_2 (X_{t-1} - c)_+ + \beta_3 Y_{t-1} + \beta_4 + e_t \tag{23.4}$$

[1]It is tempting to write the model as a function of the elasticity of substitution σ rather than its transformation ρ. However, this is unadvisable, as it renders the regression function more nonlinear and difficult to optimize.

where $(a)_-$ and $(a)_+$ are the negative-part and positive-part functions, c is the kink point, and the slopes are β_1 and β_2 on the two sides of the kink. The parameters are $\theta = (\beta_1, \beta_2, \beta_3, \beta_4, c)$. The regression function is linear in $(\beta_1, \beta_2, \beta_3, \beta_4)$ and nonlinear in c.

I illustrate the regression kink model with an application from B. E. Hansen (2017), which is a formalization of Reinhart and Rogoff (2010). The data are a time series of annual observations on U.S. real GDP growth Y_t and the ratio of federal debt to GDP X_t for the years 1791–2009. Reinhart and Rogoff were interested in the hypothesis that the growth rate of GDP slows when the level of debt exceeds a threshold. To illustrate, Figure 23.1(b) displays the regression kink function. The kink $c = 44$ is marked by the square. You can see that the function is upward sloped for $X < c$ and downward sloped for $X > c$.

23.2 IDENTIFICATION

The regression model $m(x, \theta)$ is **correctly specified** if there exists a parameter value θ_0 such that $m(x, \theta_0) = \mathbb{E}[Y \mid X = x]$. The parameter is **point identified** if θ_0 is unique. In correctly specified nonlinear regression models, the parameter is point identified if there is a unique true parameter.

Assume $\mathbb{E}[Y^2] < \infty$. Because the conditional expectation is the best mean-squared predictor, it follows that the true parameter θ_0 satisfies the optimization expression

$$\theta_0 = \underset{\theta \in \Theta}{\operatorname{argmin}}\, S(\theta) \tag{23.5}$$

where

$$S(\theta) = \mathbb{E}\left[(Y - m(X, \theta))^2\right]$$

is the expected squared error. This expresses the parameter as a function of the distribution of (Y, X).

The regression model is **misspecified** if there is no θ such that $m(x, \theta) = \mathbb{E}[Y \mid X = x]$. In this case, we define the **pseudo-true value** θ_0 as the best-fitting parameter (23.5). It is difficult to give general conditions under which the solution is unique. Hence, identification of the pseudo-true value under misspecification is typically assumed rather than deduced.

23.3 ESTIMATION

The analog estimator of the expected squared error $S(\theta)$ is the sample average of squared errors:

$$S_n(\theta) = \frac{1}{n} \sum_{i=1}^{n} (Y_i - m(X_i, \theta))^2 .$$

Since θ_0 minimizes $S(\theta)$, its analog estimator minimizes $S_n(\theta)$:

$$\widehat{\theta}_{\text{nlls}} = \underset{\theta \in \Theta}{\operatorname{argmin}}\, S_n(\theta).$$

This is called the **nonlinear least squares (NLLS)** estimator. It includes OLS as the special case when $m(X_i, \theta)$ is linear in θ. It is an m-estimator with $\rho_i(\theta) = (Y_i - m(X_i, \theta))^2$.

As $S_n(\theta)$ is a nonlinear function of θ, in general there is no explicit algebraic expression for the solution $\widehat{\theta}_{\text{nlls}}$. Instead it is found by numerical minimization. Chapter 12 of *Probability and Statistics for Economists* provides an overview. The NLLS residuals are $\widehat{e}_i = Y_i - m\left(X_i, \widehat{\theta}_{\text{nlls}}\right)$.

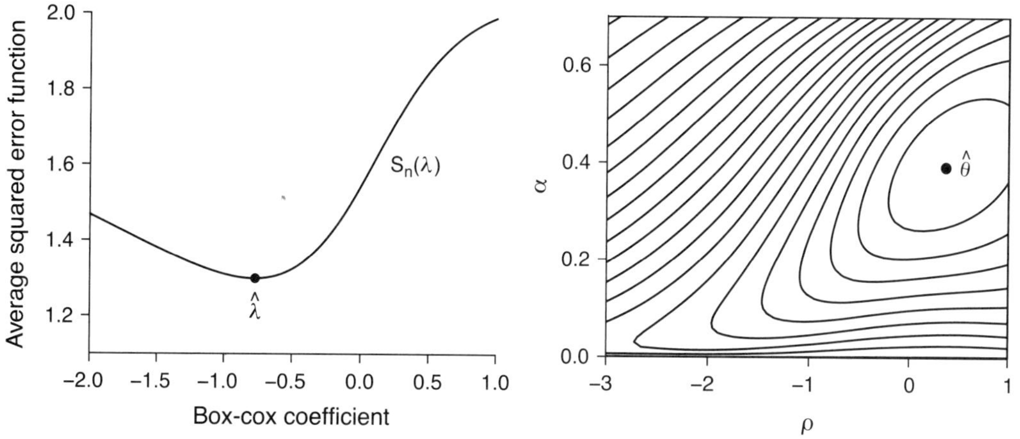

(a) Box-cox regression (b) CES production function

FIGURE 23.2 Average of squared errors functions

In some cases, including our first and third examples in Section 23.1, the model $m(x,\theta)$ is linear in most of the parameters. In these cases, a computational shortcut is to use **nested minimization** (also known as **concentration** or **profiling**). Consider example 1 (Box-Cox regression). Given the Box-Cox parameter λ, the regression is linear. The coefficients (β_0, β_1) can be estimated by least squares, obtaining the residuals and sample concentrated average of squared errors $S_n^*(\lambda)$. The latter can be minimized using one-dimensional methods. The minimizer $\widehat{\lambda}$ is the NLLS estimator of λ. Given $\widehat{\lambda}_{\text{nlls}}$, the NLLS coefficient estimators $\left(\widehat{\beta}_0, \widehat{\beta}_1\right)$ are found by OLS regression of Y_i on a constant and $X_i^{(\widehat{\lambda})}$.

I illustrate with two of our examples.

Figure 23.2(a) displays the concentrated average of squared errors $S_n(\lambda)$ for the Box-Cox regression model applied to (23.2), displayed as a function of the Box-Cox parameter λ. You can see that $S_n(\lambda)$ is neither quadratic nor globally convex but has a well-defined minimum at $\widehat{\lambda} = -0.77$. This parameter value produces a regression model considerably more curved than the logarithm specification used by Acemoglu, Johnson, and Robinson (2001).

Figure 23.2(b) displays the average of squared errors for the CES production function application, displayed as a function of (ρ, α) with the other parameters set at the minimizer. You can see that the minimum is obtained at $(\widehat{\rho}, \widehat{\alpha}) = (.36, .39)$. The function $S_n(\rho, \alpha)$ is displayed by its contour surfaces. A quadratic function has elliptical contour surfaces. You can see that the function appears to be close to quadratic near the minimum but becomes increasingly nonquadratic away from the minimum.

The parameter estimates and standard errors for the three models are presented in Table 23.1. Standard error calculation is discussed in Section 23.5. The standard errors for the Box-Cox and regression kink models were calculated using the heteroskedasticity-robust formula, and those for the CES production function were calculated by the cluster-robust formula, clustering by country.

Consider the Box-Cox regression. The estimate $\widehat{\lambda} = -0.77$ shows that the estimated relationship between *risk* and *mortality* has stronger curvature than the logarithm function, and the estimate $\widehat{\beta}_1 = -17$ is negative, as predicted. The large standard error for $\widehat{\beta}_1$, however, indicates that the slope coefficient is not precisely estimated.

Table 23.1
NLLS estimates of example models

	Parameter	Estimate	Standard error
Box-Cox regression	β_0	27.5	12.4
	β_1	−17.0	15.3
	λ	−0.77	0.28
CES production function	ρ	0.36	0.29
	ν	1.05	0.03
	α	0.39	0.06
	β	1.66	0.31
	σ	1.57	0.46
Regression kink function	β_1	0.033	0.026
	β_2	−0.067	0.046
	β_3	0.28	0.09
	β_4	3.78	0.68
	c	43.9	11.8

Consider the CES production function. The estimate $\widehat{\rho} = 0.36$ is positive, indicating that clean and dirty technologies are substitutes. The implied elasticity of substitution $\sigma = 1/(1-\rho)$ is $\widehat{\sigma} = 1.57$. The estimated elasticity of scale $\widehat{\nu} = 1.05$ is slightly above 1, consistent with increasing returns to scale. The share parameter for clean technology $\widehat{\alpha} = 0.39$ is somewhat less than one-half, indicating that dirty technology is the dominating input.

Now consider the regression kink function. The estimated slope of GDP growth for low debt levels $\widehat{\beta}_1 = 0.03$ is positive, and the estimated slope for high debt levels $\widehat{\beta}_2 = -0.07$ is negative. This is consistent with the Reinhart-Rogoff hypothesis that high debt levels lead to a slowdown in economic growth. The estimated kink point is $\widehat{c} = 44\%$, which is considerably lower than the postulated 90% kink point suggested by Reinhart-Rogoff based on their informal analysis.

Interpreting conventional t-ratios and p-values in nonlinear models should be done thoughtfully. This is a context where the annoying empirical custom of appending asterisks to all "significant" coefficient estimates is particularly inappropriate. For example, consider the CES estimates in Table 23.1. The "t-ratio" for ν is for the test of the hypothesis that $\nu = 0$, which is a meaningless hypothesis. Similarly, the t-ratio for α is for an uninteresting hypothesis. It does not make sense to append asterisks to these estimates and describe them as "significant," because there is no reason to take 0 as an interesting value for the parameter. Similarly in the Box-Cox regression, there is no reason to take $\lambda = 0$ as an important hypothesis. In the regression kink model, the hypothesis $c = 0$ is generally meaningless and could easily lie outside the parameter space.

23.4 ASYMPTOTIC DISTRIBUTION

We first consider the consistency of the NLLS estimator. We appeal to Theorems 22.3 and 22.4 for m-estimators.

Assumption 23.1

1. (Y_i, X_i) are i.i.d.
2. $m(X,\theta)$ is continuous in $\theta \in \Theta$ with probability 1.
3. $\mathbb{E}\left[Y^2\right] < \infty$.
4. $|m(X,\theta)| \le m(X)$ with $\mathbb{E}\left[m(X)^2\right] < \infty$.
5. Θ is compact.
6. For all $\theta \neq \theta_0$, $S(\theta) > S(\theta_0)$.

Assumptions 1–4 are fairly standard. Assumption 5 is not essential but simplifies the proof. Assumption 6 is critical. It states that the minimizer θ_0 is unique.

Theorem 23.1 Consistency of NLLS Estimator
If Assumption 23.1 holds, then $\widehat{\theta} \underset{p}{\longrightarrow} \theta_0$ as $n \to \infty$.

The proof of Theorem 23.1 is in Section 23.10.

We next discuss the asymptotic distribution for differentiable models. I first present the main result, then we discuss the assumptions. Set $m_\theta(x,\theta) = \frac{\partial}{\partial\theta} m(x,\theta)$, $m_{\theta\theta}(x,\theta) = \frac{\partial^2}{\partial\theta\partial\theta'} m(x,\theta)$, and $m_{\theta i} = m_\theta(X_i,\theta_0)$. Define $\boldsymbol{Q} = \mathbb{E}\left[m_{\theta i} m_{\theta i}'\right]$ and $\Omega = \mathbb{E}\left[m_{\theta i} m_{\theta i}' e_i^2\right]$.

Assumption 23.2 For some neighborhood $\mathcal{N}$ of θ_0,

1. $\mathbb{E}[e \mid X] = 0$.
2. $\mathbb{E}\left[Y^4\right] < \infty$.
3. $m(x,\theta)$ and $m_\theta(X,\theta)$ are differentiable in $\theta \in \mathcal{N}$.
4. $\mathbb{E}|m(X,\theta)|^4 < \infty$, $\mathbb{E}\|m_\theta(X,\theta)\|^4 < \infty$, and $\mathbb{E}\|m_{\theta\theta}(X,\theta)\|^4 < \infty$ for $\theta \in \mathcal{N}$.
5. $\boldsymbol{Q} = \mathbb{E}\left[m_{\theta i} m_{\theta i}'\right] > 0$.
6. θ_0 is in the interior of Θ.

Part 1 of Assumption 23.2 imposes that the model is correctly specified. If we relax this assumption, the asymptotic distribution is still normal but the covariance matrix changes. Part 2 is a moment bound that is needed for asymptotic normality. Part 3 states that the regression function is second-order differentiable. This can be relaxed but with a complication of the conditions and derivation. Part 4 states moment bounds on the regression function and its derivatives. Part 5 states that the "linearized regressor" $m_{\theta i}$ has a full rank population design matrix. If this part of the assumption fails, then $m_{\theta i}$ will be multicollinear. Part 6 requires that the parameters are not on the boundary of the parameter space. This is important, as otherwise the sampling distribution will be asymmetric.

Theorem 23.2 Asymptotic Normality of NLLS Estimator
If Assumption 23, parts 1 and 2 hold, then $\sqrt{n}\left(\widehat{\theta}-\theta_0\right) \underset{d}{\longrightarrow} \mathrm{N}(0, \boldsymbol{V})$ as $n \rightarrow \infty$, where $\boldsymbol{V}=\boldsymbol{Q}^{-1} \Omega \boldsymbol{Q}^{-1}$.

The proof of Theorem 23.2 is in Section 23.10.

Theorem 23.2 shows that under general conditions, the NLLS estimator has an asymptotic distribution with similar structure to that of the OLS estimator. The estimator converges at a conventional rate to a normal distribution with a sandwich-form covariance matrix. Furthermore, the asymptotic variance is identical to that in a hypothetical OLS regression with the linearized regressor $m_{\theta i}$. Thus, asymptotically, the distribution of NLLS is identical to a linear regression.

The asymptotic distribution simplifies under conditional homoskedasticity. If $\mathbb{E}\left[e^2 \mid X\right]=\sigma^2$, then the asymptotic variance is $\boldsymbol{V}=\sigma^2 \boldsymbol{Q}^{-1}$.

23.5 COVARIANCE MATRIX ESTIMATION

The asymptotic covariance matrix $\boldsymbol{V}$ is estimated similarly to linear regression with the adjustment that we use an estimate of the linearized regressor $m_{\theta i}$. This estimate is

$$\widehat{m}_{\theta i}=m_\theta\left(X_i, \widehat{\theta}\right)=\frac{\partial}{\partial \theta} m\left(X_i, \widehat{\theta}\right).$$

It is best if the derivative is calculated algebraically, but a numerical derivative (a discrete derivative) can substitute.

Take, for example, the Box-Cox regression model, for which $m(x, \beta_0, \beta_1, \lambda)=\beta_0+\beta_1 x^{(\lambda)}$. We calculate that for $\lambda \neq 0$,

$$m_\theta\left(x, \beta_0, \beta_1, \lambda\right)=\left(\begin{array}{c}\frac{\partial}{\partial \beta_0}\left(\beta_0+\beta_1 x^{(\lambda)}\right) \\ \frac{\partial}{\partial \beta_1}\left(\beta_0+\beta_1 x^{(\lambda)}\right) \\ \frac{\partial}{\partial \beta_\lambda}\left(\beta_0+\beta_1 x_i^{(\lambda)}\right)\end{array}\right)=\left(\begin{array}{c}1 \\ x^{(\lambda)} \\ \dfrac{x^\lambda \log (x)-x^{(\lambda)}}{\lambda}\end{array}\right).$$

For $\lambda=0$, the third entry is $\log^2(x)/2$. The estimate is obtained by replacing λ with the estimator $\widehat{\lambda}$. Hence for $\widehat{\lambda} \neq 0$,

$$\widehat{m}_{\theta i}=\left(\begin{array}{c}1 \\ x^{(\widehat{\lambda})} \\ \dfrac{1-x^{\widehat{\lambda}}+\widehat{\lambda} x^{\widehat{\lambda}} \log (x)}{\widehat{\lambda}^2}\end{array}\right).$$

The covariance matrix components are estimated as

$$\widehat{\boldsymbol{Q}}=\frac{1}{n} \sum_{i=1}^n \widehat{m}_{\theta i} \widehat{m}_{\theta i}^{\prime}$$

$$\widehat{\Omega} = \frac{1}{n}\sum_{i=1}^{n} \widehat{m}_{\theta i}\widehat{m}_{\theta i}'\widehat{e}_i^2$$

$$\widehat{\boldsymbol{V}} = \widehat{\boldsymbol{Q}}^{-1}\widehat{\Omega}\widehat{\boldsymbol{Q}}^{-1} \tag{23.6}$$

where $\widehat{e}_i = Y_i - m\left(X_i, \widehat{\theta}\right)$ are the NLLS residuals. Standard errors are calculated conventionally as the square roots of the diagonal elements of $n^{-1}\widehat{\boldsymbol{V}}$.

If the error is homoskedastic, the covariance matrix can be estimated using the formula

$$\widehat{\boldsymbol{V}}^0 = \widehat{\boldsymbol{Q}}^{-1}\widehat{\sigma}^2$$

$$\widehat{\sigma}^2 = \frac{1}{n}\sum_{i=1}^{n}\widehat{e}_i^2.$$

If the observations satisfy cluster dependence, then a standard cluster variance estimator can be used, again treating the linearized regressor estimate $\widehat{m}_{\theta i}$ as the effective regressor.

To illustrate, standard errors for our three estimated models are displayed in Table 23.1. The standard errors for the first and third models were calculated using the formula (23.6). The standard errors for the CES model were clustered by country.

In small samples, the standard errors for NLLS may not be reliable. An alternative is to use bootstrap methods for inference. The nonparametric bootstrap draws with replacement from the observation pairs (Y_i, X_i) to create bootstrap samples, to which NLLS is applied to obtain bootstrap parameter estimates $\widehat{\theta}^*$. From $\widehat{\theta}^*$, we can calculate bootstrap standard errors and/or bootstrap confidence intervals, for example, by the bias-corrected percentile method.

23.6 PANEL DATA

Consider the nonlinear regression model with an additive individual effect:

$$Y_{it} = m\left(X_{it}, \theta\right) + u_i + \varepsilon_{it}$$

$$\mathbb{E}\left[\varepsilon_{it} \mid X_{it}\right] = 0.$$

To eliminate the individual effect, we can apply the within or first-differencing transformations. Applying the within transformation, we obtain

$$\dot{Y}_{it} = \dot{m}\left(X_{it}, \theta\right) + \dot{\varepsilon}_{it} \tag{23.7}$$

where

$$\dot{m}\left(X_{it}, \theta\right) = m\left(X_{it}, \theta\right) - \frac{1}{T_i}\sum_{t \in S_i} m\left(X_{it}, \theta\right)$$

using the panel data notation. Thus $\dot{m}\left(X_{it}, \theta\right)$ is the within transformation applied to $m\left(X_{it}, \theta\right)$. It is not $m\left(\dot{X}_{it}, \theta\right)$. Equation (23.7) is a nonlinear panel model. The coefficient can be estimated by NLLS. The estimator is appropriate when X_{it} is strictly exogenous, as $\dot{m}\left(X_{it}, \theta\right)$ is a function of X_{is} for all time periods.

An alternative is to apply the first-difference transformation, which yields

$$\Delta Y_{it} = \Delta m\left(X_{it}, \theta\right) + \Delta\varepsilon_{it} \tag{23.8}$$

where $\Delta m(X_{it}, \theta) = m(X_{it}, \theta) - m\left(X_{i,t-1}, \theta\right)$. Equation (23.8) can be estimated by NLLS. Again, this requires that X_{it} be strictly exogenous for consistent estimation.

If the regressors X_{it} contain a lagged dependent variable $Y_{i,t-1}$, then NLLS is not an appropriate estimator. GMM can be applied to (23.8), similar to linear dynamic panel regression models.

23.7 THRESHOLD MODELS

An extreme example of nonlinear regression is the class of threshold regression models. These are discontinuous regression models where the kink points are treated as free parameters. They have been used succesfully in economics to model threshold effects and tipping points. They are also the core tool for the modern machine learning methods of regression trees and random forests. This section provides an overview of these methods.

A threshold regression model takes the form

$$Y = \beta_1' X_1 + \beta_2' X_2 \mathbb{1}\{Q \geq \gamma\} + e$$

$$\mathbb{E}[e \mid X] = 0$$

where X_1 and X_2 are $k_1 \times 1$ and $k_2 \times 1$, respectively, and Q is scalar. The variable Q is called the **threshold variable**, and γ is called the **threshold**.

Typically, both X_1 and X_2 contain an intercept, and X_2 and Q are subsets of X_1. In the latter case, β_2 is the change in the slope at the threshold. The threshold variable Q should be either continuously distributed or ordinal.

In a full threshold specification, $X_1 = X_2 = X$. In this case, all coefficients switch at the threshold. This regression can alternatively be written as

$$Y = \begin{cases} \theta_1' X + e, & Q < \gamma \\ \theta_2' X + e, & Q \geq \gamma \end{cases}$$

where $\theta_1 = \beta_1$ and $\theta_2 = \beta_1 + \beta_2$.

A simple yet full threshold model arises when there is only a single regressor X. The regression can be written as

$$Y = \alpha_1 + \beta_1 X + \alpha_2 \mathbb{1}\{X \geq \gamma\} + \beta_2 X \mathbb{1}\{X \geq \gamma\} + e.$$

This resembles a regression kink model, but it is more general, as it allows for a discontinuity at $X = \gamma$. The regression kink model imposes the restriction $\alpha + \beta\gamma = 0$.

A threshold model is most suitable for a context where an economic model predicts a discontinuity in the CEF. It can also be used as a flexible approximation for a context where it is believed the CEF has a sharp nonlinearity with respect to one variable, or has sharp interaction effects. The regression kink model, for example, does not allow for kink interaction effects.

The threshold model is critically dependent on the choice of threshold variable Q. This variable controls the ability of the regression model to display nonlinearity. In principle, this can be generalized by incorporating multiple thresholds in potentially different variables, but this generalization is limited by sample size and information.

The threshold model is linear in the coefficients $\beta = (\beta_1, \beta_2)$ and nonlinear in γ. The parameter γ is of critical importance, as it determines the model's nonlinearity—the sample split.

Many empirical applications estimate threshold models using ad hoc methods. What you may see is a splitting of the sample into "subgroups" based on regressor characteristics. When the latter split is based on a continuous regressor, the split point is exactly a threshold parameter. When you see such tables, it is prudent to be skeptical. How was this threshold parameter selected? Based on intuition? Or based on data exploration? If the former, do you expect the results to be informative? If the latter, should you trust the reported tests?

To illustrate threshold regression, let us review an influential paper by Card, Mas, and Rothstein (2008). They were interested in the process of racial segregation in U.S. cities. A common hypothesis concerning the behavior of white Americans is that they are only comfortable living in a neighborhood if it has a small percentage of minority residents. A simple model of this behavior (explored in their paper) predicts that this preference leads to an unstable mixed-race equilibrium in the fraction of minorities. They call this equilibrium the **tipping point**. If the minority fraction exceeds this tipping point, the outcome will change discontinuously. The economic mechanism is that if minorities move into a neighborhood at a roughly continuous rate, when the tipping point is reached, there will be a surge in exits by white residents who elect to move due to their discomfort. This model predicts a threshold regression with a discontinuity at the tipping point. The data file `CMR2008` is an abridged version of the authors' dataset.

The authors use a specification similar to the following:

$$\begin{aligned}\Delta W_{cit} &= \delta_0 \mathbb{1}\{M_{cit-1} \geq \gamma\} + \delta_1 (M_{cit-1} - \gamma)\mathbb{1}\{M_{cit-1} \geq \gamma\} \\ &\quad + \beta_1 M_{cit-1} + \beta_2 M_{cit-1}^2 + \theta' X_{cit-1} + \alpha + u_c + e_{cit} \qquad (23.9)\end{aligned}$$

where c is the city MSA,[2] i is a census tract within the city, t is the time period (decade), ΔW_{cit} is the white population percentage change in the tract over the decade, M_{cit} is the fraction of minorties in the tract, u_c is a fixed effect for the city, and X_{cit} are tract-level regression controls. The sample is based on census data, which is collected at 10-year intervals. They estimate models for three decades; we focus on 1970–1980. Thus, ΔW_{cit} is the change in white population over the period 1970–1980, and the remaining variables are for 1970. The controls used in the regression are the unemployment rate, the log mean family income, housing vacancy rate, renter share, fraction of homes in single-unit buildings, and fraction of workers who commute by public transport. This model has $n = 35{,}656$ observations and $N = 104$ cities. This specification allows the relationship between ΔW and M to be nonlinear (a quadratic) with a discontinuous shift in the intercept and slope at the threshold. The authors' major prediction is that δ_0 should be large and negative. The threshold parameter γ is the minority fraction that triggers discontinuous white outward migration.

As the threshold regression model is an explicit nonlinear regression, the appropriate estimation method is NLLS. Because the model is linear in all coefficients except γ, the best computational technique is concentrated least squares. For each γ, the model is linear and the coefficients can be estimated by least squares. This produces a concentrated average of squared errors $S_n^*(\gamma)$ that can be minimized to find the NLLS estimator $\widehat{\gamma}$. To illustrate, the concentrated least squares criterion for the Card-Mas-Rothstein dataset[3] is displayed in Figure 23.3(a). As you can see, the criterion $S_n^*(\gamma)$ is highly nonsmooth. This is typical in threshold applications. Consequently, the criterion needs to be minimized by grid search. The criterion is a step function with a step at each observation. A full search would calculate $S_n^*(\gamma)$ for γ equaling each value of M_{cit-1} in the sample.

---

[2]Metropolitan Statistical Area (MSA). The authors use the 104 MSAs with at least 100 census tracts.
[3]Using the 1970–1980 sample and model (23.9).

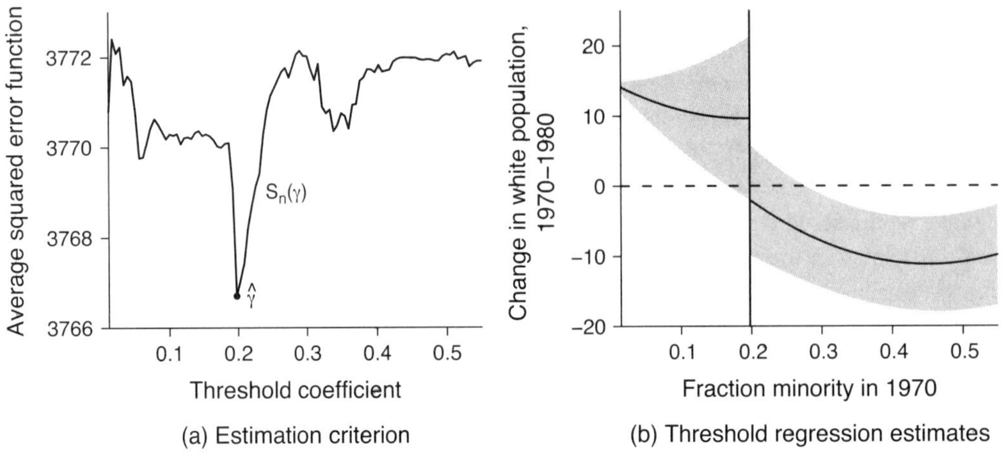

FIGURE 23.3 Threshold regression: Card-Mas-Rothstein (2008) model

A simplification (which we employ) is to calculate the criterion at a smaller number of gridpoints. In this illustration, we use 100 gridpoints equally spaced between the 0.1 and 0.9 quantiles[4] of M_{cit-1}. (These quantiles are the boundaries of the displayed graph.) What you can see is that the criterion is generally lower for values of γ between 0.05 and 0.25, and is especially lower for values of γ near 0.2. The minimum is obtained at $\widehat{\gamma} = 0.198$. This is the NLLS estimator. In the context of the application, this means that the point estimate of the tipping point is 20%, which means that when the neighborhood minority fraction exceeds 20%, white households discontinuously change their behavior. The remaining NLLS estimates are obtained by least squares regression (23.9) setting $\gamma = \widehat{\gamma}$.

Our estimates are reported in Table 23.2. Following Card, Mas, and Rothstein (2008), the standard errors are clustered[5] by city (MSA). Examining Table 23.2, we can see that the estimates suggest that neighborhood declines in the white population were increasing in the minority fraction, with a sharp and accelerating decline above the tipping point of 20%. The estimated discontinuity is −11.6%. This value is nearly identical to the estimate obtained by Card, Mas, and Rothstein (2008) using an ad hoc estimation method.

The white population was also decreasing in response to the unemployment rate, the renter share, and the use of public transportation, but increasing in response to the vacancy rate. Another interesting observation is that even though the sample has a very large (35,656) number of observations, the standard errors for the parameter estimates are rather large, indicating considerable imprecision. This is mostly due to the clustered covariance matrix calculation, as there are only $N = 104$ clusters.

The asymptotic theory of threshold regression is non-standard. Chan (1993) showed that under correct specification, the threshold estimator $\widehat{\gamma}$ converges in probability to γ at the fast rate $O_p(n^{-1})$ and that the other parameter estimators have conventional asymptotic distributions, justifying the standard errors as reported in

[4]It is important that the search be constrained to values of γ that lie well within the support of the threshold variable. Otherwise the regression may be infeasible. The required degree of trimming (away from the boundaries of the support) depends on the individual application.

[5]It is not clear to me whether clustering is appropriate in this application. One motivation for clustering is inclusion of fixed effects, as this induces correlation across observations within a cluster. However in this case, the typical number of observations per cluster is several hundred, so this correlation is near 0. Another motivation for clustering is that the regression error e_{cit} (the unobserved factors for changes in white population) is correlated across tracts within a city. While it may be expected that attitudes toward minorities among whites may be correlated within a city, it seems less clear that we should expect unconditional correlation in population changes.

Table 23.2
Threshold estimates: Card-Mas-Rothstein (2008) model

Variable	Estimate	Standard error
Intercept change	−11.6	3.7
Slope change	−74.1	42.6
Minority fraction	−54.4	28.8
Minority fraction^2	142.3	23.9
Unemployment rate	−81.1	38.8
log (mean family income)	3.4	3.6
Housing vacancy rate	324.9	40.2
Renter share	−62.7	13.6
Fraction single-unit	−4.8	9.5
Fraction public transport	−91.6	24.5
Intercept	14.8	na
MSA fixed effects	yes	
Threshold	0.198	
99% confidence interval	[0.198, 0.209]	
N = number of MSAs	104	
n = number of observations	35,656	

Table 23.2. He also showed that the threshold estimator $\widehat{\gamma}$ has a non-standard asymptotic distribution, which cannot be used for confidence interval construction.

B. Hansen (2000) derived the asymptotic distribution of $\widehat{\gamma}$ and associated test statistics under a "small threshold effect" asymptotic framework for a continuous threshold variable Q. This distribution theory permits simple construction of an asymptotic confidence interval for γ. In brief, he shows that under correct specification, independent observations, and homoskedasticity, the F statistic for testing the hypothesis $\mathbb{H}_0 : \gamma = \gamma_0$ has the asymptotic distribution

$$\frac{n\left(S_n^*(\gamma_0) - S_n^*(\widehat{\gamma})\right)}{S_n^*(\widehat{\gamma})} \xrightarrow[d]{} \xi$$

where $\mathbb{P}[\xi \le x] = \left(1 - \exp(-x/2)\right)^2$. The $1-\alpha$ quantile of ξ can be found by solving $\left(1 - \exp(-c_{1-\alpha}/2)\right)^2 = 1-\alpha$, and equals $c_{1-\alpha} = -2\log(1-\sqrt{1-\alpha})$. For example, $c_{.95} = 7.35$, and $c_{.99} = 10.6$.

Based on test inversion, a valid $1-\alpha$ asymptotic confidence interval for γ is the set of F statistics that are less than $c_{1-\alpha}$ and equals

$$C_{1-\alpha} = \left\{\gamma : \frac{n\left(S_n^*(\gamma) - S_n^*(\widehat{\gamma})\right)}{S_n^*(\widehat{\gamma})} \le c_{1-\alpha}\right\} = \left\{\gamma : S_n^*(\gamma) \le S_n^*(\widehat{\gamma})\left(1 + \frac{c_{1-\alpha}}{n}\right)\right\}.$$

This interval is constructed numerically by grid search. In our example, $C_{0.99} = [0.198, 0.209]$, which is a narrow confidence interval. However, this interval does not take into account clustered dependence. Based on Hansen's theory, we can expect that under cluster dependence, the asymptotic distribution ξ needs to be rescaled. This will result in replacing $(1 + c_{1-\alpha})/n$ in the above formula with $(1 + \rho c_{1-\alpha})/n$ for some adjustment factor ρ, which will widen the confidence interval. Based on the curve shape in Figure 23.3(a), the adjusted confidence interval may not be too wide. However this is a conjecture, as the theory has not been worked out, so we cannot estimate the adjustment factor ρ.

Empirical practice and simulation results suggest that threshold estimates tend to be quite imprecise unless a moderately large sample (e.g., $n \geq 500$) is used. The threshold parameter is identified by observations close to the threshold, not by observations far from the threshold. This requires large samples to ensure a sufficient number of observations near the threshold to pin down its location

Given the coefficient estimates, the regression function can be plotted along with confidence intervals calculated conventionally. Figure 23.3(b) plots the estimated regression function with 95% asymptotic confidence intervals, calculated based on the covariance matrix for the estimates $(\widehat{\beta}_1, \widehat{\beta}_2, \widehat{\delta}_1, \widehat{\delta}_2)$. The estimate $\widehat{\theta}$ does not contribute if the regression function is evaluated at mean values. We ignore estimation of the intercept $\widehat{\alpha}$, because its variance is not identified under clustering dependence, and we are primarily interested in the magnitude of relative comparisons. What we see in Figure 23.3(b) is that the regression function is generally downward sloped, indicating that the change in the white population is generally decreasing as the minority fraction increases, as expected. The tipping effect is visually strong. When the fraction minority crosses the tipping point, there are sharp decreases in both the level and the slope of the regression function. The level of the estimated regression function also indicates that the expected change in the white population switches from positive to negative at the tipping point, consistent with the segregation hypothesis. It is instructive to observe that the confidence bands are quite wide despite the large sample. This is largely due to the decision to use a clustered covariance matrix estimator. Consequently, there is considerable uncertainty in the location of the regression function. The confidence bands are widest at the estimated tipping point.

The empirical results presented in this section are distinct from—yet similar to—those reported in Card, Mas, and Rothstein (2008). This is an influential paper, as it used the rigor of an economic model to give insight into segregation behavior and used a rich, detailed dataset to investigate the strong tipping point prediction.

23.8 TESTING FOR NONLINEAR COMPONENTS

Identification can be tricky in nonlinear regression models. Suppose that

$$m(X, \theta) = X'\beta + X(\gamma)'\delta$$

where $X(\gamma)$ is a function of X and an unknown parameter γ. Examples for $X(\gamma)$ include the Box-Cox transformation and $X\mathbb{1}\{X > \gamma\}$. The latter arises in the regression kink and threshold regression models.

The model is linear when $\delta = 0$. This is often a useful hypothesis (submodel) to consider. For example, in the Card, Mas, and Rothstein (2008) application, this is the hypothesis of no tipping point, which is the key issue explored in their paper.

In this section we consider tests of the hypothesis $\mathbb{H}_0 : \delta = 0$. Under $\mathbb{H}_0$, the model is $Y = X'\beta + e$ and both δ and γ have dropped out. Thus under $\mathbb{H}_0$, the parameter γ is not identified, which renders standard distribution theory invalid. When the truth is $\delta = 0$, the NLLS estimator of (β, δ, γ) is not asymptotically normally distributed. Classical tests excessively over-reject $\mathbb{H}_0$ if applied with conventional critical values.

As an example, consider the threshold regression (23.9). The hypothesis of no tipping point corresponds to the joint hypothesis $\delta_0 = 0$ and $\delta_1 = 0$. Under this hypothesis, the parameter γ is not identified.

To test the hypothesis, a standard test is to reject for large values of the F statistic:

$$\mathrm{F} = \frac{n\left(\widetilde{S}_n - S_n^*(\widehat{\gamma})\right)}{S_n^*(\widehat{\gamma})}$$

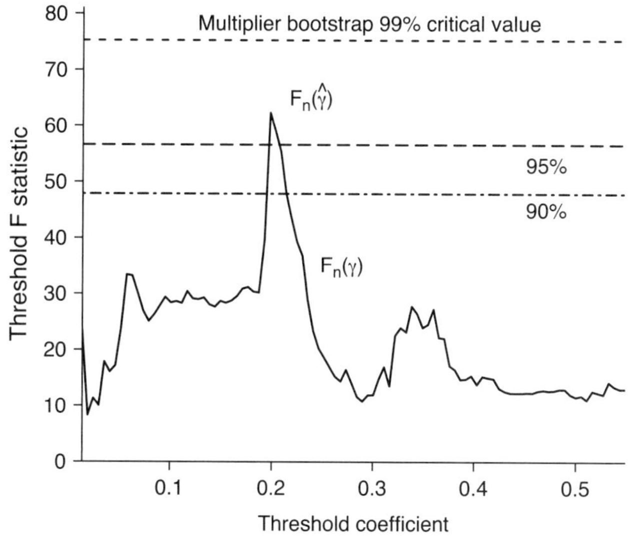

FIGURE 23.4 Test for threshold regression in the Card-Mass-Rothstein model

where $\widetilde{S}_n = n^{-1} \sum_{i=1}^{n} \left(Y_i - X_i'\widehat{\beta}\right)^2$, and $\widehat{\beta}$ is the least squares coefficient from the regression of Y on X. This is the difference between the error variance estimators based on estimates calculated under the null ($\widetilde{S}_n$) and the alternative ($S_n^*(\widehat{\gamma})$).

The F statistic can be written as

$$\mathrm{F} = \max_{\gamma} \mathrm{F}_n(\gamma) = \mathrm{F}_n(\widehat{\gamma})$$

where

$$\mathrm{F}_n(\gamma) = \frac{n\left(\widetilde{S}_n - S_n^*(\gamma)\right)}{S_n^*(\gamma)}.$$

The statistic $\mathrm{F}_n(\gamma)$ is the classical F statistic for a test of $\mathbb{H}_0 : \delta = 0$ when γ is known. We can see from this representation that F is non-standard, as it is the maximum over a potentially large number of statistics $\mathrm{F}_n(\gamma)$.

To illustrate, Figure 23.4 plots the test statistic $\mathrm{F}_n(\gamma)$ as a function of γ. You can see that the function is erratic, similar to the concentrated criterion $S_n^*(\gamma)$. This is sensible, because $\mathrm{F}_n(\gamma)$ is an affine function of the inverse of $S_n^*(\gamma)$. The statistic is maximized at $\widehat{\gamma}$ because of this duality. The maximum value is $\mathrm{F} = \mathrm{F}_n(\widehat{\gamma})$. In this application, we find $\mathrm{F} = 62.4$, which is extremely high by conventional standards.

The asymptotic theory of the test has been worked out by Andrews and Ploberger (1994) and B. Hansen (1996). In particular, Hansen shows the validity of the multiplier bootstrap for calculation of p-values for independent observations. The method is as follows.

1. On the observations (Y_i, X_i), calculate the F test statistic for $\mathbb{H}_0$ against $\mathbb{H}_1$ (or any other standard statistic, such as a Wald or likelihood ratio).
2. For $b = 1, \ldots, B$:
   (a) Generate n random variables ξ_i^* with mean 0 and variance 1 (standard choices are normal and Rademacher).
   (b) Set $Y_i^* = \widehat{e}_i \xi_i^*$, where $\widehat{e}_i$ are the NLLS residuals.
   (c) On $\left(Y_i^*, X_i\right)$, calculate the F statistic F_b^* for $\mathbb{H}_0$ against $\mathbb{H}_1$.

3. The multiplier bootstrap p-value is $p_n^* = \frac{1}{B}\sum_{b=1}^{B} \mathbb{1}\left\{\mathrm{F}_b^* > \mathrm{F}\right\}$.
4. If $p_n^* < \alpha$, the test is significant at level α.
5. Critical values can be calcualted as empirical quantiles of the bootstrap statistics F_b^*.

In step 2b, you can alternatively set $Y_i^* = \widehat{\beta}' Z_i + \widehat{e}_i \xi_i^*$. Tests on δ are invariant to the bootstrap value of δ. What is important is that the bootstrap data satisfy the null hypothesis.

For clustered samples, we need to make a minor modification. Write the regression by cluster as

$$\boldsymbol{Y}_g = \boldsymbol{X}_g \beta + \boldsymbol{X}_g(\gamma)\delta + \boldsymbol{e}_g.$$

The bootstrap method is modified by altering steps 2a and 2b above. Let N denote the number of clusters. The modified algorithm uses the following steps:

2. (a) Generate N random variables ξ_g^* with mean 0 and variance 1.
   (b) Set $\boldsymbol{Y}_g^* = \widehat{\boldsymbol{e}}_g \xi_g^*$.

To illustrate, we apply this test to the threshold regression (23.9) estimated with the Card, Mas, and Rothstein (2008) data. We use $B = 10,000$ bootstrap replications. Applying the first algorithm (suitable for independent observations), the bootstrap p-value is 0%. The 99% critical value is 16.7, so the observed value of $\mathrm{F} = 62.4$ far exceeds this threshold. Applying the second algorithm (suitable under cluster dependence), the bootstrap p-value is 3.1%. The 95% critical value is 56.6 and the 99% is 75.3. Thus the observed value of $\mathrm{F} = 62.4$ is "significant" at the 5% but not the 1% level. For a sample of size $n = 35{,}656$, this is surprisingly mild significance. These critical values are indicated in Figure 23.4 by the dashed lines. The F statistic process breaks the 90% and 95% critical values but not the 99%. Thus despite the visually strong evidence of a tipping effect from Section 23.7, the statistical evidence of this effect is strong but not overwhelming.

23.9 COMPUTATION

Stata has a built-in command `nl` for NLLS estimation. You need to specify the nonlinear equation and give starting values for the numerical search. It is prudent to try several starting values, because the algorithm is not guaranteed to converge to the global minimum.

Estimation of NLLS in R or MATLAB requires a bit more programming but is straightforward. You write a function that calculates the average squared error $S_n(\theta)$ (or concentrated average squared error) as a function of the parameters. You then call a numerical optimizer to minimize this function. For example, in R for vector-valued parameters, the standard optimizer is `optim`. For scalar parameters, use `optimize`.

23.10 TECHNICAL PROOFS*

Proof of Theorem 23.1 We appeal to Theorem 22.3, which holds under five conditions. Conditions 1, 2, 4, and 5 are satisfied directly by Assumption 23.1, parts 1, 2, 5, and 6. To verify condition 3, observe that by the c_r inequality (B.5) and $|m(X,\theta)| \leq m(X)$, we have

$$(Y - m(X,\theta))^2 \leq 2Y^2 + 2m(X)^2.$$

The right side has finite expectation under Assumptions 23.1, parts 3 and 4. We conclude that $\widehat{\theta} \underset{p}{\longrightarrow} \theta_0$, as stated. ■

Proof of Theorem 23.2 We appeal to Theorem 22.4, which holds under five conditions (in addition to consistency, which was established in Theorem 23.1). It is convenient to rescale the criterion so that $\rho_i(\theta) = \frac{1}{2}(Y_i - m(X_i, \theta))^2$. Then $\psi_i = -m_{\theta i} e_i$.

To show condition 1, by the Cauchy-Schwarz inequality (B.32) and Assumption 23.2 parts 2 and 4,

$$\mathbb{E}\|\psi_i\|^2 = \mathbb{E}\|m_{\theta i} e_i\|^2 \le \left(\mathbb{E}\|m_{\theta i}\|^4 \mathbb{E}\left[e_i^4\right]\right)^{1/2} < \infty.$$

We next show condition 3. Using Assumption 23.2 part 1, we calculate that

$$S(\theta) = \mathbb{E}\left[\rho_i(\theta)\right] = \frac{1}{2}\mathbb{E}\left[e^2\right] + \frac{1}{2}\mathbb{E}\left[(m(X,\theta_0) - m(X,\theta))^2\right].$$

Thus

$$\psi(\theta) = \frac{\partial}{\partial \theta} S(\theta) = -\mathbb{E}\left[m_\theta(X,\theta)(m(X,\theta_0) - m(X,\theta))\right]$$

with derivative

$$\begin{aligned} \boldsymbol{Q}(\theta) &= -\frac{\partial}{\partial \theta'}\mathbb{E}\left[m_\theta(X,\theta)(m(X,\theta_0) - m(X,\theta))\right] \\ &= \mathbb{E}\left[m_\theta(X,\theta) m_\theta(X,\theta)'\right] - \mathbb{E}\left[m_{\theta\theta}(X,\theta_0)(m(X,\theta_0) - m(X,\theta))\right]. \end{aligned} \tag{23.10}$$

This exists and is continuous for $\theta \in \mathcal{N}$ under Assumption 23.2 part 4.

Evaluating (23.10) at θ_0, we obtain

$$\boldsymbol{Q} = \boldsymbol{Q}(\theta_0) = \mathbb{E}\left[m_{\theta i} m_{\theta i}'\right] > 0$$

under Assumption 23.2 part 5. This verifies condition 2.

Condition 4 holds if $\psi(Y, X, \theta) = m_\theta(X,\theta)(Y - m(X,\theta))$ is Lipschitz-continuous in $\theta \in \mathcal{N}$. This property holds because both $m_\theta(X,\theta)$ and $m(X,\theta)$ are differentiable in the compact set $\theta \in \mathcal{N}$, and bounded fourth moments (Assumption 23.2 part 2 and 4) imply that the Lipschitz bound for $\psi(Y, X, \theta)$ has a finite second moment.

Condition 5 is implied by Assumption 23.2 part 6.

Together, the five conditions of Theorem 22.4 are satisfied, and the stated result follows. ■

23.11 EXERCISES

Exercise 23.1 Consider the model $Y = \exp(\theta) + e$ with $\mathbb{E}[e] = 0$.

(a) Is the CEF linear or nonlinear in θ? Is this a nonlinear regression model?

(b) Is there a way to estimate the model using linear methods? If so, explain how to obtain an estimator $\widehat{\theta}$ for θ.

(c) Is your answer in part (b) the same as the NLLS estimator or different?

Exercise 23.2 Consider the model $Y^{(\lambda)} = \beta_0 + \beta_1 X + e$ with $\mathbb{E}[e \mid X] = 0$, where $Y^{(\lambda)}$ is the Box-Cox transformation of Y. Is this a nonlinear regression model in the parameters $(\lambda, \beta_0, \beta_1)$? (Careful, this is tricky.)

Exercise 23.3 Consider the model $Y = \dfrac{\beta_1}{\beta_2 + \beta_3 X} + e$ with $\mathbb{E}[e \mid X] = 0$.

(a) Are the parameters $(\beta_1, \beta_2, \beta_3)$ identified?
(b) If not, what parameters are identified? How would you estimate the model?

Exercise 23.4 Consider the model $Y = \beta_1 \exp(\beta_2 X) + e$ with $\mathbb{E}[e \mid X] = 0$.

(a) Are the parameters (β_1, β_2) identified?
(b) Find an expression to calculate the covariance matrix of the NLLS estimators $(\widehat{\beta}_1, \widehat{\beta}_2)$.

Exercise 23.5 Consider the model $Y = m(X, \theta) + e$ with $e \mid X \sim \mathrm{N}(0, \sigma^2)$. Find the MLE for θ and σ^2.

Exercise 23.6 Consider the model $Y = \exp\left(X'\theta\right) + e$ with $\mathbb{E}[Ze] = 0$, where X is $k \times 1$ and Z is $\ell \times 1$.

(a) What relationship between ℓ and k is necessary for identification of θ?
(b) Describe how to estimate θ by GMM.
(c) Describe an estimator of the asymptotic covariance matrix.

Exercise 23.7 Suppose that $Y = m(X, \theta) + e$ with $\mathbb{E}[e \mid X] = 0$, $\widehat{\theta}$ is the NLLS estimator, and $\widehat{\boldsymbol{V}}$ the estimator of $\operatorname{var}\left[\widehat{\theta}\right]$. You are interested in the CEF $\mathbb{E}[Y \mid X = x] = m(x)$ at some x. Find an asymptotic 95% confidence interval for $m(x)$.

Exercise 23.8 The file `PSS2017` contains a subset of the data from Papageorgiou, Saam, and Schulte (2017). For a robustness check they re-estimated their CES production function using approximated capital stocks rather than capacities as their input measures. Estimate the model (23.3) using this alternative measure. The variables for Y, X_1, and X_2 are *EG_total*, *EC_c_alt*, and *EC_d_alt*, respectively. Compare the estimates with those reported in Table 23.1.

Exercise 23.9 The file `RR2010` contains the U.S. observations from Reinhart and Rogoff (2010). The dataset has observations on real GDP growth, debt/GDP, and inflation rates. Estimate the model (23.4), setting Y as the inflation rate and X as the debt ratio.

Exercise 23.10 In Exercise 9.26, you estimated a cost function on a cross-section of electric companies. Consider the nonlinear specification

$$\log TC = \beta_1 + \beta_2 \log Q + \beta_3 \left(\log PL + \log PK + \log PF\right) + \beta_4 \frac{\log Q}{1 + \exp\left(-\left(\log Q - \gamma\right)\right)} + e. \qquad (23.11)$$

This model is called a **smooth threshold** model. For values of $\log Q$ much below γ, the variable $\log Q$ has a regression slope of β_2. For values much above β_7, the regression slope is $\beta_2 + \beta_4$. The model imposes a smooth transition between these regimes.

(a) The model works best when γ is selected so that several values (in this example, at least 10–15) of $\log Q_i$ are both below and above γ. Examine the data, and pick an appropriate range for γ.
(b) Estimate the model by NLLS using a global numerical search over $(\beta_1, \beta_2, \beta_3, \beta_4, \gamma)$.
(c) Estimate the model by NLLS using a concentrated numerical search over γ. Do you obtain the same results as in part (6)?
(d) Calculate standard errors for all the parameter estimates $(\beta_1, \beta_2, \beta_3, \beta_4, \gamma)$.

CHAPTER 24
QUANTILE REGRESSION

24.1 INTRODUCTION

This chapter introduces median regression (least absolute deviations) and quantile regression. An excellent monograph on the subject is Koenker (2005).

A conventional goal in econometrics is estimation of the impact of a variable X on another variable Y. We have discussed projections and conditional expectations, but these are not the only measures of impact. Alternative measures include the conditional median and conditional quantile. In this chapters we focus on the case of continuously distributed Y where quantiles are uniquely defined.

24.2 MEDIAN REGRESSION

Recall that the median of Y is the value $m = \text{med}[Y]$ such that $\mathbb{P}[Y \le m] = \mathbb{P}[Y \ge m] = 0.5$. The median can be thought of the "typical realization." For example, the median hourly wage \$19.23 in the CPS dataset can be interpreted as the wage of a "typical wage-earner." One-half of wage earners have wages less than \$19 and one-half have wages greater than \$19.

When a distribution is symmetric, then the median equals the mean, but when the distribution is asymmetric, they differ.

Throughout this textbook we have primarily focused on conditional relationships. For example, the conditional expectation is the expected value in a subpopulation. Similarly, we define the conditional median as the median of a subpopulation.

Definition 24.1 The **conditional median** of Y given $X = x$ is the value $m(x) = \text{med}[Y \mid X = x]$ such that $\mathbb{P}[Y \le m(x) \mid X = x] = 0.5$.

For example, in the CPS sample, the median hourly wage for men is \$21.15 and that for women is \$16.83. These are the wages of a "typical" man and woman.

We can write the relationship between Y and X as the **median regression model**:

$$Y = m(X) + e$$
$$\text{med}[e \mid X] = 0.$$

As stated, this is simply a definitional framework. $m(X)$ is the conditional median given the random variable X. The error e is the deviation of Y from its conditional median and by definition has a conditional median of 0.

We call $m(x)$ the **median regression function**. In general, it can take any shape. However, for practical convenience, we focus on models that are linear in parameters $m(x) = x'\beta$. (This is not fundamentally restrictive, as it allows series approximations.) These considerations give rise to the **linear median regression model**:

$$Y = X'\beta + e \tag{24.1}$$

$$\text{med}\,[e \mid X] = 0.$$

Equivalently, the model states that $\text{med}\,[Y \mid X] = X'\beta$. As in the case of regression, the true median regression function is not necessarily linear, so the assumption of linearity is a meaningful assumption. The model resembles the linear regression model but is different. The coefficients β in the median and mean regression models are not necessarily equal to one another.

To estimate β, it is useful to characterize β as a function of the distribution. Recall that the least squares estimator is derived from the foundational property that the expectation minimizes the expected squared loss, that is, $\mu = \text{argmin}_\theta\, \mathbb{E}\left[(Y-\theta)^2\right]$. I now present analogous properties of the median.

Define the sign function

$$\frac{d}{dx}|x| = \text{sgn}\,(x) = \begin{cases} \mathbb{1}\{x>0\} - \mathbb{1}\{x<0\}, & x \neq 0 \\ 0 & x = 0. \end{cases}$$

Theorem 24.1 Assume Y is continuously distributed. Then the median m satisfies

$$\mathbb{E}\left[\text{sgn}\,(Y-m)\right] = 0. \tag{24.2}$$

If in addition $\mathbb{E}\,|Y| < \infty$, it satisfies

$$m = \underset{\theta}{\text{argmin}}\, \mathbb{E}\,|Y-\theta|\,. \tag{24.3}$$

If the conditional distribution $F(y \mid x)$ of Y given $X = x$ is continuous in y, the conditional median error $e = Y - m(X)$ satisfies

$$\mathbb{E}\left[\text{sgn}\,(e) \mid X\right] = 0. \tag{24.4}$$

If in addition $\mathbb{E}\,|Y| < \infty$, the conditional median satisfies

$$m(x) = \underset{\theta}{\text{argmin}}\, \mathbb{E}\left[|Y-\theta| \mid X = x\right]. \tag{24.5}$$

If (Y, X) satisfy the linear median regression model (24.1) and $E\,|Y| < \infty$, then the coefficient β satisfies

$$\beta = \underset{b}{\text{argmin}}\, \mathbb{E}\left|Y - X'b\right|. \tag{24.6}$$

The proof is in Section 24.16.

Expression (24.6) is foundational. It shows that the median regression coefficient β minimizes the expected absolute difference between Y and the predicted value $X'\beta$. This is foundational, because it expresses the coefficient as a function of the probability distribution. This result is a direct analog of the property that the mean regression coefficient minimizes the expected squared loss. The difference between the two is the loss function—the measure of the magnitude of a prediction error. To visualize, Figure 24.1(a) displays the two loss functions. Comparing the two, squared loss puts a small penalty on small errors and a large penalty on large errors. Both are symmetric and so treat positive and negative errors identically.

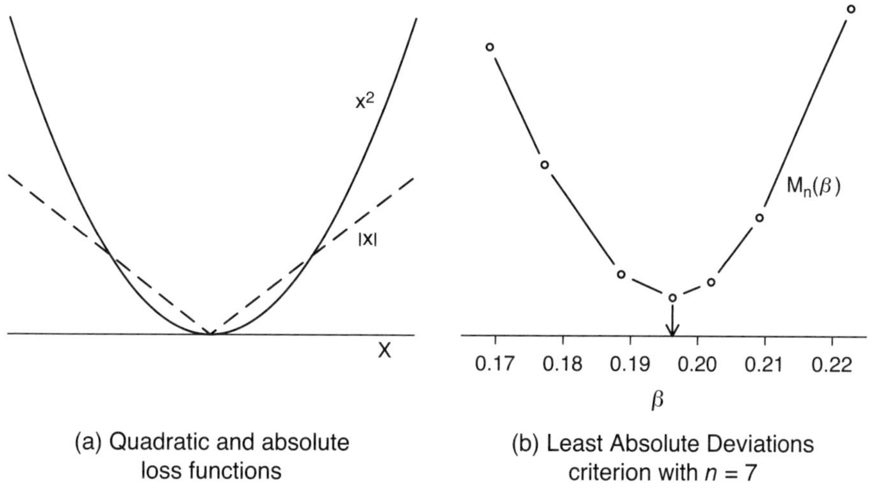

FIGURE 24.1 Least Absolute Deviations criterion

In applications, the linear assumption $X'\beta$ is unlikely to be valid except in a saturated dummy variable regression. Thus in practice, we should view a linear model as a useful approximation, rather than a literal truth. To allow the model to be an approximation, we define the coefficient β as the **best linear median predictor**:

$$\beta \overset{\text{def}}{=} \underset{b}{\operatorname{argmin}}\, \mathbb{E}\left|Y - X'b\right|. \tag{24.7}$$

This equals the true conditional median coefficient when the conditional median is linear but is defined for general distributions satisfying $E|Y| < \infty$. The first-order condition for minimization implies that

$$\mathbb{E}\left[X \operatorname{sgn}(e)\right] = 0. \tag{24.8}$$

That (24.4) holds for median regression and (24.8) for the best linear median predictor are analogs to the relationships $\mathbb{E}[e \mid X] = 0$ and $\mathbb{E}[Xe] = 0$ in the conditional expectation and linear projection models.

24.3 LEAST ABSOLUTE DEVIATIONS

Theorem 24.1 shows that in the linear median regression model, the median regression coefficient minimizes $M(\beta) = \mathbb{E}\left|Y - X'\beta\right|$, the expected absolute error. The sample estimator of this function is the average of absolute errors:

$$M_n(\beta) = \frac{1}{n}\sum_{i=1}^{n}\left|Y_i - X_i'\beta\right|.$$

This is similar to the classical average of squared errors function but instead is the average of absolute errors. By not squaring the errors, $M_n(\beta)$ puts less penalty on large errors relative to the average of squared errors function.

Since β minimizes $M(\beta)$, which is estimated by $M_n(\beta)$, the m-estimator for β is the minimizer of $M_n(\beta)$:

$$\widehat{\beta} = \underset{\beta}{\operatorname{argmin}}\, M_n(\beta).$$

This is called the **least absolute deviations (LAD)** estimator of β, as it minimizes the sum of absolute "deviations" of Y_i from the fitted value $X_i'\beta$. The function $\widehat{m}(x) = x'\widehat{\beta}$ is the **median regression** estimator. The LAD estimator $\widehat{\beta}$ does not has a closed form solution, so it must be found by numerical minimization.

The LAD residuals are $\widehat{e}_i = Y_i - X_i'\widehat{\beta}$. They approximately satisfy the property

$$\frac{1}{n}\sum_{i=1}^{n} X_i \operatorname{sgn}(\widehat{e}_i) \simeq 0.$$

The approximation holds exactly if $\widehat{e}_i \neq 0$ for all i, which can occur when Y is continuously distributed. This is the sample version of (24.8).

The criterion $M_n(\beta)$ is globally continuous and convex. Its surface resembles the surface of an inverted cut gemstone, as it is covered by a network of flat facets. The facets are joined at the n lines where $\operatorname{sgn}\left(Y_i - X_i'\beta\right) = 0$. To illustrate, Figure 24.1(b) displays the LAD criterion $M_n(\beta)$ for seven observations[1] with a single regressor and no intercept. The LAD estimator is the minimizer. As the sample size is small, the criterion $M_n(\beta)$ is visually facetted. In large samples, the facets diminish in size, and the criterion approaches a smooth function.

Because the criterion is faceted, the minimum may be a set. Furthermore, because the criterion has discontinuous derivatives, classical minimization methods fail. The minimizer can be defined by a set of linear constraints, so linear programming methods are appropriate. Fortunately for applications, good estimation algorithms are available and simple to use.

In Stata, LAD is implemented by `qreg`. In R, LAD is implemented by `rq` in the `quantreg` package.

24.4 QUANTILE REGRESSION

The mean and median are measures of the central tendency of a distribution. Measures of the spread of the distribution are its quantiles. Recall that for $\tau \in [0, 1]$, the τth quantile q_τ of Y is defined as the value such that $\mathbb{P}\left[Y \leq q_\tau\right] = \tau$. The median is the special case $\tau = 0.5$. It will be convenient to define the quantile operator $\mathbb{Q}_\tau[Y]$ as the solution to the equation

$$\mathbb{P}\left[Y \leq \mathbb{Q}_\tau[Y]\right] = \tau.$$

As an example, consider the distribution of wages from the CPS dataset. The median wage is \$21.14. This tells us the "typical" wage rate but not the range of typical values. The 0.2 quantile is \$11.65, and the 0.8 quantile is \$31.25. Thus, 20% of wage earners had hourly wages of \$11.65 or below and 20% had wages of \$31.25 and above.

We are also interested in the quantiles of conditional distributions. Continuing the above example, consider the distribution of wages among men and women. The 0.2, 0.5, and 0.8 quantiles are displayed in Table 24.1. We see that the differences between men's and women's wages are increasing by quantile.

> **Definition 24.2** The **conditional quantile** of Y given $X = x$ is the value $q_\tau(x)$ such that $\mathbb{P}\left[Y \leq q_\tau(x) \mid X = x\right] = \tau$.

[1]These are seven of the 20 observations from Table 3.1.

Table 24.1
Quantiles of wage distribution

	$q_{.2}$	$q_{.5}$	$q_{.8}$
All	\$11.65	\$19.23	\$31.25
Men	\$12.82	\$21.14	\$35.90
Women	\$10.58	\$16.83	\$26.44

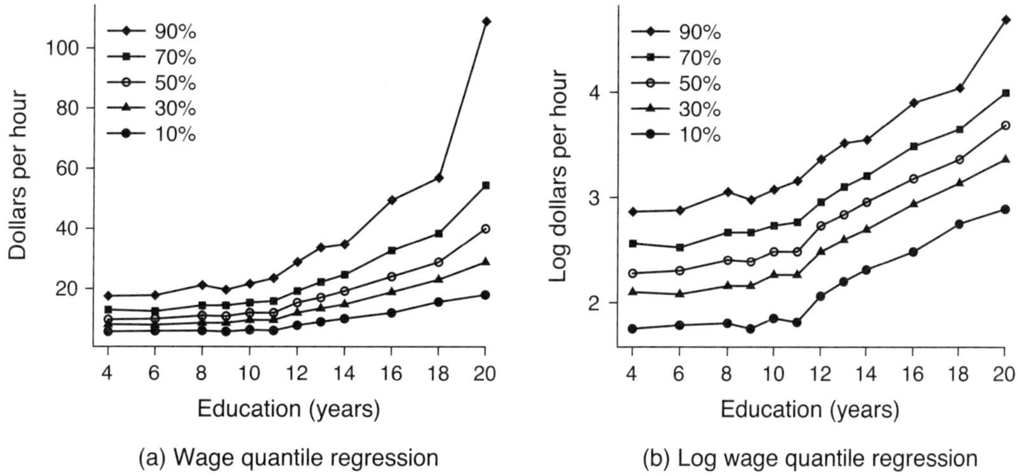

FIGURE 24.2 Quantile regressions

Given this notation, let us define the conditional quantile operators $\mathbb{Q}_\tau[Y \mid X=x]$ and $\mathbb{Q}_\tau[Y \mid X]$. The function $q_\tau(x)$ is also called the **quantile regression function**.

The conditional quantile function $q_\tau(x)$ can take any shape with respect to x. It is monotonically increasing in τ, thus if $\tau_1 < \tau_2$, then $q_{\tau_1}(x) \le q_{\tau_2}(x)$ for all x.

To illustrate, Figure 24.2(a) displays the conditional quantile function of U.S. wages[2] as a function of education for $\tau = 0.1, 0.3, 0.5, 0.7$, and 0.9. The five lines plotted are the quantile regression functions $q_\tau(x)$ with *wage* on the y-axis and *education* on the x-axis. For each level of education, the conditional quantiles $q_\tau(x)$ are strictly ranked in τ, though for low levels of education, they are close to one another. The five quantile regression functions are (generally) increasing in education, though not monotonically. The quantile regression functions also spread out as education increases; thus the gap between the quantiles increases with education. These quantile regression functions provide a summary of the conditional distribution of wages given education.

A useful feature of quantile regression is that it is equivariant to monotone transformations. If $Y_2 = \phi(Y_1)$, where $\phi(y)$ is nondecreasing, then $\mathbb{Q}_\tau[Y_2 \mid X=x] = \phi(\mathbb{Q}_\tau[Y_1 \mid X=x])$. Alternatively, if $q^1_\tau(x)$ and $q^2_\tau(x)$ are the quantile functions of Y_1 and Y_2, then $q^2_\tau(x) = \phi\left(q^1_\tau(x)\right)$. For example, the quantile regression of log wages on education is the logarithm of the quantile regression of wages on education. This is displayed in Figure 24.2(b). Interestingly, the quantile regression functions of log wages are roughly parallel with one another and are roughly linear in education for levels above 12 years.

[2]Calculated using the full `cps90mar` dataset.

Define the **quantile regression model** analogously to the median regression model:

$$Y = q_\tau(X) + e$$
$$\mathbb{Q}_\tau\,[e \mid X] = 0.$$

An important feature of the quantile regression model is that the error e is not centered at 0. Instead, it is centered so that its τth quantile is 0. This is a normalization, but it points out that the meaning of the intercept changes when we move from mean regression to quantile regression and as we move between quantiles. The **linear quantile regression model** is

$$Y = X'\beta_\tau + e \tag{24.9}$$
$$\mathbb{Q}_\tau\,[e \mid X] = 0.$$

Recall that the mean minimizes the squared error loss, and the median minimizes the absolute error loss. There is an analog for the quantile. Define the tilted absolute loss function:

$$\rho_\tau(x) = \begin{cases} -x(1-\tau), & x < 0 \\ x\tau, & x \geq 0 \end{cases} \tag{24.10}$$
$$= x\left(\tau - \mathbb{1}\{x < 0\}\right).$$

For $\tau = 0.5$, this is the scaled absolute loss $\frac{1}{2}|x|$. For $\tau < 0.5$, the function is tilted to the right. For $\tau > 0$, it is tilted to the left. To visualize, Figure 24.3 displays the functions $\rho_\tau(x)$ for $\tau = 0.5$ and $\tau = 0.2$. The latter function is a tilted version of the former. The function $\rho_\tau(x)$ has come to be known as the **check function**, because it resembles a check mark (✓).

Let $\psi_\tau(x) = \frac{d}{dx}\rho_\tau(x) = \tau - \mathbb{1}\{x < 0\}$ for $x \neq 0$. We now discuss some properties of the quantile regression function.

Theorem 24.2 Assume Y is continuously distributed. Then the quantile q_τ satisfies

$$\mathbb{E}\left[\psi_\tau\left(Y - q_\tau\right)\right] = 0. \tag{24.11}$$

If in addition $\mathbb{E}|Y| < \infty$, it satisfies

$$q_\tau = \underset{\theta}{\operatorname{argmin}}\, \mathbb{E}\left[\rho_\tau(Y - \theta)\right]. \tag{24.12}$$

If the conditional distribution $F(y \mid x)$ of Y given $X = x$ is continuous in y, the conditional quantile error $e = Y - q_\tau(X)$ satisfies

$$\mathbb{E}\left[\psi_\tau(e) \mid X\right] = 0. \tag{24.13}$$

If in addition $\mathbb{E}|Y| < \infty$, the conditional quantile function satisfies

$$q_\tau(x) = \underset{\theta}{\operatorname{argmin}}\, \mathbb{E}\left[\rho_\tau(Y - \theta) \mid X = x\right]. \tag{24.14}$$

If (Y, X) satisfy the linear quantile regression model (24.9) and $\mathbb{E}|Y| < \infty$, then the coefficient β satisfies

$$\beta = \underset{b}{\operatorname{argmin}}\, \mathbb{E}\left[\rho_\tau\left(Y - X'b\right)\right]. \tag{24.15}$$

The proof is in Section 24.16.

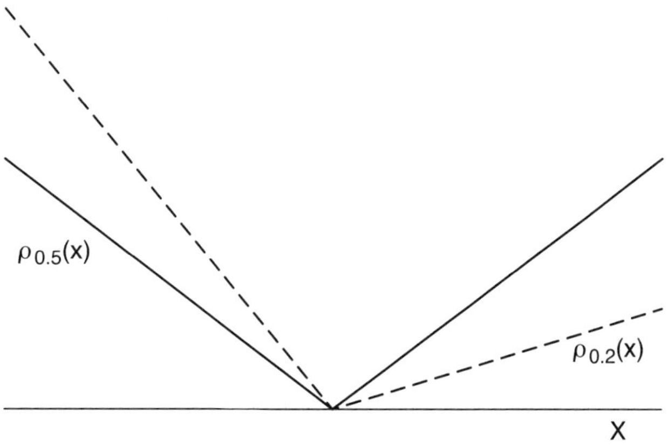

FIGURE 24.3 Quantile loss function

Expression (24.15) shows that the quantile regression coefficient β minimizes the expected check function distance between Y and the predicted value $X'\beta$. This equation connects quantile regression with median and mean regression.

As for mean and median regression, we should think of the linear model $X'\beta$ as an approximation. In general, we therefore define the coefficient β as the **best linear quantile predictor**:

$$\beta_\tau \stackrel{\text{def}}{=} \underset{b}{\operatorname{argmin}} \mathbb{E}\left[\rho_\tau\left(Y - X'b\right)\right]. \tag{24.16}$$

This predictor equals the true conditional quantile coefficient when the true function is linear. The first-order condition for minimization implies that

$$\mathbb{E}\left[X\psi_\tau(e)\right] = 0.$$

Unlike the best linear predictor, we do not have an explicit expression for β_τ. However from its definition, we can see that β_τ will produce an approximation $x'\beta_\tau$ to the true conditional quantile function $q_\tau(x)$ with the approximation weighted by the probability distribution of X.

24.5 EXAMPLE QUANTILE SHAPES

Linear Quantile Functions

The linear quantile regression model implies that the quantile functions $q_\tau(x)$ are linear in x. An example is shown in Figure 24.4(a), which plots linear quantile regression functions for $\tau = 0.1, 0.3, 0.5, 0.7$, and 0.9. In this example, the slopes are positive and increasing with τ.

Linear quantile regressions are convenient as they are simple to estimate and report. Sometimes linearity can be induced by a judicious choice of variable transformation. For example, compare the quantile regressions in Figure 24.2(a) and Figure 24.2(b) in Section 24.4. The quantile regression functions for the level of wages appear to be concave; in contrast, the quantile regression functions for log wages are close to linear for education above 12 years.

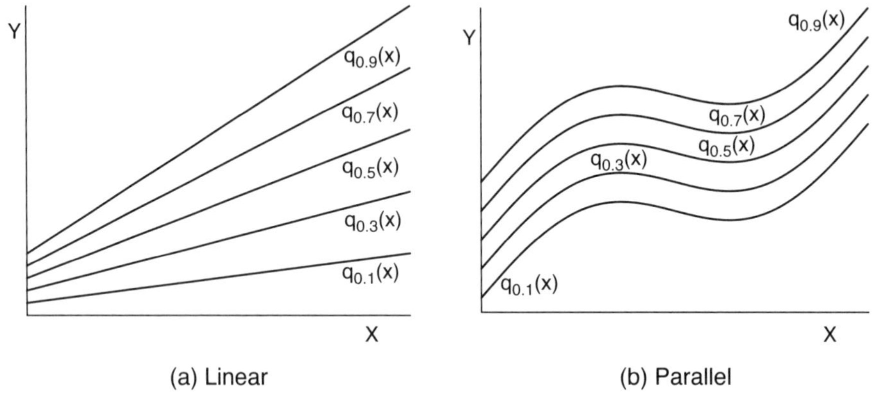

FIGURE 24.4 Quantile shapes

Parallel Quantile Functions

Consider the model $Y = m(X) + e$ with e independent of X. Let z_τ be the τth quantile of e. In this case, the conditional quantile function for Y is $q_\tau(x) = m(x) + z_\tau$. Thus the functions $q_{\tau_1}(x)$ and $q_{\tau_2}(x)$ are parallel, so all of the quantile regression functions are mutually parallel.

An example is shown in Figure 24.4(b), which plots a set of quantile regression functions that are mutually parallel.

In this context—when e is independent of X and/or the quantile regression functions are parallel—there is little to be gained from quantile regression analysis relative to mean regression or median regression. The models have the same slope coefficients and only differ by their intercepts. Furthermore, a regression with e independent of X is a homoskedastic regression. Thus parallel quantile functions is indicative of conditional homoskedasticity.

Once again, examine the quantile regression functions for log wages displayed in Figure 24.2(b). These functions are visually close to being parallel shifts of one another. Thus it appears that the log(wage) regression is close to a homoskedastic regression, and slope coefficients should be relatively robust to estimation by least squares, LAD, or quantile regression. This is a strong motivation for applying the logarithmic transformation to a wage regression.

Coefficient Heterogeneity

Consider the process $Y = \eta' X$, where $\eta \sim \mathrm{N}(\beta, \Sigma)$ is independent of X. I described this in Section 2.29 as a random coefficient model, as the coefficients η are specific to the individual. In this setting, the conditional distribution of Y given $X = x$ is $\mathrm{N}(x'\beta, x'\Sigma x)$, so the conditional quantile functions are $q_\tau(x) = x'\beta + z_\tau \sqrt{x'\Sigma x}$, where z_τ is the τth quantile of $\mathrm{N}(0, 1)$. These quantile functions are parabolic.

24.6 ESTIMATION

Theorem 24.2 shows that in the linear quantile regression model, the coefficient β_τ minimizes $M(\beta;\tau) = \mathbb{E}\left[\rho_\tau\left(Y - X'\beta\right)\right]$, the expected check function distance. The estimator of this function is the sample average

$$M_n(\beta;\tau) = \frac{1}{n}\sum_{i=1}^{n} \rho_\tau\left(Y_i - X_i'\beta\right).$$

Since β_τ minimizes $M(\beta;\tau)$, which is estimated by $M_n(\beta;\tau)$, the m-estimator for β_τ is the minimizer of $M_n(\beta;\tau)$:

$$\widehat{\beta}_\tau = \underset{\beta}{\operatorname{argmin}}\, M_n(\beta;\tau).$$

This is called the **quantile regression** estimator of β_τ. The coefficient $\widehat{\beta}_\tau$ does not have a closed-form solution, so it must be found by numerical minimization. The minimization techniques are identical to those used for median regression; hence, most software packages treat the two together.

The quantile regression residuals $\widehat{e}_i(\tau) = Y_i - X_i'\widehat{\beta}_\tau$ satisfy the approximate property

$$\frac{1}{n}\sum_{i=1}^{n} X_i \psi_\tau\left(\widehat{e}_i(\tau)\right) \simeq 0. \tag{24.17}$$

As for LAD, (24.17) holds exactly if $\widehat{e}_i(\tau) \neq 0$ for all i, which occurs with high probability if Y is continuously distributed.

In Stata, quantile regression is implemented by `qreg`. In R, quantile regression is implemented by `rq` in the `quantreg` package.

24.7 ASYMPTOTIC DISTRIBUTION

I first provide conditions for consistent estimation. Let β_τ be defined as in (24.16), $e = Y - X'\beta_\tau$, and $f_\tau(e \mid x)$ denote the conditional density of e given $X = x$.

Theorem 24.3 Consistency of Quantile Regression Estimator
Assume that (Y_i, X_i) are i.i.d., $\mathbb{E}|Y| < \infty$, $\mathbb{E}\left[\|X\|^2\right] < \infty$, $f_\tau(e \mid x)$ exists and satisfies $f_\tau(e \mid x) \le D < \infty$, and the parameter space for β is compact. For any $\tau \in (0,1)$ such that

$$\boldsymbol{Q}_\tau \overset{\text{def}}{=} \mathbb{E}\left[XX' f_\tau(0 \mid X)\right] > 0 \tag{24.18}$$

then $\widehat{\beta}_\tau \underset{p}{\longrightarrow} \beta_\tau$ as $n \to \infty$.

The proof is provided in Section 24.16.

Theorem 24.3 shows that the quantile regression estimator is consistent for the best linear quantile predictor coefficient under broad assumptions.

A technical condition is (24.18), which is used to establish uniqueness of the coefficient β_τ. One sufficient condition for (24.18) occurs when the conditional density $f_\tau(e \mid x)$ does not depend on x at $e = 0$. Thus $f_\tau(0 \mid x) = f_\tau(e)$ and

$$\boldsymbol{Q}_\tau = \mathbb{E}\left[XX'\right] f_\tau(0). \tag{24.19}$$

In this context, (24.18) holds if $\mathbb{E}\left[XX'\right] > 0$ and $f_\tau(0) > 0$. The assumption that $f_\tau(e \mid x)$ does not depend on x at $e = 0$ (we call this **quantile independence**) is a traditional assumption in the early median regression/quantile regression literature, but it does not make sense outside the narrow context where e is independent of X. Thus we should avoid (24.19) whenever possible, and if not avoidable, view it as a convenient simplification rather than a literal truth. The assumption that $f_\tau(0) > 0$ means that there is a nontrivial set of observations for which the error e is near 0, or equivalently, for which Y is close to $X'\beta_\tau$. These are the observations that provide the decisive information to pin down β_τ.

A weaker way to obtain a sufficient condition for (24.18) is to assume that for some bounded set $\mathscr{X}$ in the support of X, that (a) $\mathbb{E}\left[XX' \mid X \in \mathscr{X}\right] > 0$, and (b) $f_\tau(0 \mid x) \geq c > 0$ for $x \in \mathscr{X}$. This is the same as stating that if we truncate the regressor X to a bounded set, the design matrix is full rank and the conditional density of the error at 0 is bounded away from 0. These conditions are rather abstract but mild.

We now provide the asymptotic distribution.

Theorem 24.4 Asymptotic Distribution of Quantile Regression Estimator
In addition to the assumptions of Theorem 24.3, assume that $f_\tau(e \mid x)$ is continuous in e, and β_τ is in the interior of the parameter space. Then as $n \to \infty$

$$\sqrt{n}\left(\widehat{\beta}_\tau - \beta_\tau\right) \underset{d}{\longrightarrow} \mathrm{N}\left(0, \boldsymbol{V}_\tau\right)$$

where $\boldsymbol{V}_\tau = \boldsymbol{Q}_\tau^{-1} \Omega_\tau \boldsymbol{Q}_\tau^{-1}$ and $\Omega_\tau = \mathbb{E}\left[XX'\psi_\tau^2\right]$ for $\psi_\tau = \tau - \mathbb{1}\left\{Y < X'\beta_\tau\right\}$.

The proof is provided in Section 24.16.

Theorem 24.4 shows that the quantile regression estimator is asymptotically normal with a sandwich asymptotic covariance matrix. Asymptotic normality does not rely on correct model specification, and therefore applies broadly for practical applications where linear models are approximations rather than literal truths. The proof of the asymptotic distribution relies on the theory for general m-estimators (Theorem 22.4). Theorem 24.4 includes the least absolute deviations estimator as the special case $\tau = 0.5$.

The asymptotic covariance matrix in Theorem 24.4 simplifies under correct specification. If $\mathbb{Q}_\tau[Y \mid X] = X'\beta_\tau$, then $\mathbb{E}\left[\psi_\tau^2 \mid X\right] = \tau(1-\tau)$. It follows that $\Omega_\tau = \tau(1-\tau)\boldsymbol{Q}$, where $\boldsymbol{Q} = \mathbb{E}\left[XX'\right]$.

Combined with (24.19) we have three levels of asymptotic covariance matrices:

1. General: $\boldsymbol{V}_\tau = \boldsymbol{Q}_\tau^{-1}\Omega_\tau \boldsymbol{Q}_\tau^{-1}$.
2. Correct specification: $\boldsymbol{V}_\tau^c = \tau(1-\tau)\boldsymbol{Q}_\tau^{-1}\boldsymbol{Q}\boldsymbol{Q}_\tau^{-1}$.
3. Quantile independence: $\boldsymbol{V}_\tau^0 = \dfrac{\tau(1-\tau)}{f_\tau(0)^2}\boldsymbol{Q}^{-1}$.

The quantile independence case $\boldsymbol{V}_\tau^0$ is similar to the homoskedastic least squares covariance matrix.

While $\boldsymbol{V}_\tau$ is the generally appropriate covariance matrix formula, the simplified formula $\boldsymbol{V}_\tau^0$ is easier to interpret and obtain intuition about the precision of the quantile regression estimator. Like the least squares estimator, the covariance matrix is a scale multiple of $\left(\mathbb{E}\left[XX'\right]\right)^{-1}$. Thus it inherits the related properties of the least squares estimator: $\widehat{\beta}_\tau$ is more efficient when X has greater variance and is less collinear. The covariance matrix $\boldsymbol{V}_\tau^0$ is inversely proportional to $f_\tau(0)^2$. Thus $\widehat{\beta}_\tau$ is more efficient when the density is high at 0, which means that there are many observations near the τth quantile of the conditional distribution. If there are few observations near the τth quantile, then $f_\tau(0)$ will be small and $\boldsymbol{V}_\tau^0$ large. We can also express this relationship in terms of the standard deviation σ of e. Let $u = e/\sigma$ be the error scaled to have a unit variance, which has density $g_\tau(x) = \sigma f_\tau(\sigma u)$. Then $\boldsymbol{V}_\tau^0 = \dfrac{\tau(1-\tau)}{g_\tau(0)^2}\sigma^2\left(\mathbb{E}\left[XX'\right]\right)^{-1}$, which is a scale of the homoskedastic least squares covariance matrix.

24.8 COVARIANCE MATRIX ESTIMATION

We have multiple methods for estimating the asymptotic covariance matrix $\boldsymbol{V}_\tau$. The easiest is based on the quantile independence assumption, leading to

$$\widehat{\boldsymbol{V}}_\tau^0 = \tau(1-\tau)\widehat{f_\tau}(0)^{-2}\widehat{\boldsymbol{Q}}^{-1}$$

$$\widehat{\boldsymbol{Q}} = \frac{1}{n}\sum_{i=1}^n X_i X_i'$$

where $\widehat{f_\tau}(0)^{-2}$ is a nonparametric estimator of $f_\tau(0)^{-2}$. For the latter, there are several proposed methods. One uses a difference in the distribution function of Y. A second uses a nonparametric estimator of $f_\tau(0)$.

An estimator of $\boldsymbol{V}_\tau^c$ assuming correct specification is

$$\widehat{\boldsymbol{V}}_\tau^c = \tau(1-\tau)\widehat{\boldsymbol{Q}}_\tau^{-1}\widehat{\boldsymbol{Q}}\widehat{\boldsymbol{Q}}_\tau^{-1}$$

where $\widehat{\boldsymbol{Q}}_\tau$ is a nonparametric estimator of $\boldsymbol{Q}_\tau$. Given a bandwidth h, a feasible choice is

$$\widehat{\boldsymbol{Q}}_\tau = \frac{1}{2nh}\sum_{i=1}^n X_i X_i' \mathbb{1}\left\{|\widehat{e}_i| < h\right\}.$$

An estimator of $\boldsymbol{V}_\tau$ allowing misspecification is

$$\widehat{\boldsymbol{V}}_\tau = \widehat{\boldsymbol{Q}}_\tau^{-1}\widehat{\Omega}_\tau\widehat{\boldsymbol{Q}}_\tau^{-1}$$

$$\widehat{\Omega}_\tau = \frac{1}{h}\sum_{i=1}^n X_i X_i' \widehat{\psi}_{i\tau}^2$$

$$\widehat{\psi}_{i\tau} = \tau - \mathbb{1}\left\{Y_i < X_i'\widehat{\beta}_\tau\right\}.$$

Of the three covariance matrix methods introduced above ($\widehat{\boldsymbol{V}}_\tau^0$, $\widehat{\boldsymbol{V}}_\tau^c$, and $\widehat{\boldsymbol{V}}_\tau$), the classical estimator $\widehat{\boldsymbol{V}}_\tau^0$ should be avoided for the same reasons we avoid classical homoskedastic covariance matrix estimators for least squares estimation. Of the two robust estimators, the better choice is $\widehat{\boldsymbol{V}}_\tau$ (because it does not require correct specification), but unfortunately, it is not programmed in standard packages. Thus in practice, the estimator $\widehat{\boldsymbol{V}}_\tau^c$ is recommended.

The most common method for estimation of quantile regression covariance matrices, standard errors, and confidence intervals is the bootstrap. The conventional nonparametric bootstrap is appropriate for the general model allowing for misspecification, and the bootstrap variance is an estimator for $\widehat{\boldsymbol{V}}_\tau$. As we have learned in our study of bootstrap methods, it is generally advised to use a large number B of bootstrap replications (at least 1,000, with 10,000 preferred). This is somewhat computationally costly in large samples, but its cost should not be a barrier to implementation, as the full bootstrap calculation only needs to be done for the final calculation. Also, as we have learned, for confidence intervals, percentile-based intervals are greatly preferred over the normal-based intervals (which use bootstrap standard errors multiplied by normal quantiles). I recommend the BC percentile intervals, which require changing the default settings in common programs, such as Stata.

In Stata, quantile regression is implemented using `qreg`. The default standard errors are $\widehat{\boldsymbol{V}}_\tau^0$. Use `vce(robust)` for $\widehat{\boldsymbol{V}}_\tau^c$. The covariance matrix estimator $\widehat{\boldsymbol{V}}_\tau$ is not implemented. For bootstrap standard errors and confidence intervals, use `bootstrap, reps(#): qreg y x`. The bootstrap command followed by `estat bootstrap` produces BC percentile confidence intervals.

Table 24.2
Quantile regressions of student test scores on tracking

	$\tau=0.1$	$\tau=0.3$	$\tau=0.5$	$\tau=0.7$	$\tau=0.9$
Tracking	0.069	0.136	0.125	0.185	0.151
Bootstrap standard error	(0.045)	(0.069)	(0.074)	(0.127)	(0.126)
95% confidence interval	[−0.02, .15]	[−0.01, .27]	[−0.01, .28]	[−0.06, .44]	[−0.11, .40]

In R, quantile regression is implemented by the function `rq` in the `quantreg` package. The default standard errors are $\widehat{\boldsymbol{V}}_\tau^c$. The covariance matrix estimator $\widehat{\boldsymbol{V}}_\tau$ is not implemented. For bootstrap standard errors, one method is to use the option `se="boot"` with the `summary` command. At present, the `quantreg` package does not include bootstrap percentile confidence intervals.

24.9 CLUSTERED DEPENDENCE

Under clustered dependence the asymptotic covariance matrix changes. In the formula $\boldsymbol{V}_\tau = \boldsymbol{Q}_\tau^{-1}\Omega_\tau \boldsymbol{Q}_\tau^{-1}$, the matrix $\boldsymbol{Q}_\tau$ is unaltered, but Ω_τ changes to

$$\Omega_\tau^{\text{cluster}} = \lim_{n\to\infty} \frac{1}{n}\sum_{g=1}^{G} \mathbb{E}\left[\left(\sum_{\ell=1}^{n_g} X_{\ell g}\psi_{\ell g\tau}\right)\left(\sum_{\ell=1}^{n_g} X_{\ell g}\psi_{\ell g\tau}\right)'\right]$$

which can be estimated as

$$\widehat{\Omega}_\tau^{\text{cluster}} = \frac{1}{n}\sum_{g=1}^{G} \left[\left(\sum_{\ell=1}^{n_g} X_{\ell g}\widehat{\psi}_{\ell g\tau}\right)\left(\sum_{\ell=1}^{n_g} X_{\ell g}\widehat{\psi}_{\ell g\tau}\right)'\right].$$

This leads to the cluster-robust asymptotic covariance matrix estimator $\widehat{\boldsymbol{V}}_\tau^{\text{cluster}} = \widehat{\boldsymbol{Q}}_\tau^{-1}\widehat{\Omega}_\tau^{\text{cluster}}\widehat{\boldsymbol{Q}}_\tau^{-1}$.

The cluster-robust estimator $\widehat{\boldsymbol{V}}_\tau^{\text{cluster}}$ is not implemented in Stata or in the R `quantreg` package. Instead, the clustered bootstrap (sampling clusters with replacement) is recommended.

In Stata, the clustered bootstrap can be accomplished by: `bootstrap, reps(#) cluster(id): qreg y x`, followed by `estat bootstrap`.

In R, the clustered bootstrap is included as an option in the quantreg package for calculation of standard errors.

The application of clustered quantile regression can be illustrated using the Duflo, Dupas, and Kremer (2011) school tracking application. (See Section 4.21.) Recall that the question was whether *tracking* (separating students into classrooms based on an initial test) influenced average end-of-year scores. Let us repeat the analysis using quantile regression. Parameter estimates and bootstrap standard errors (calculated by clustered bootstrap using 10,000 replications, clustered by school) are reported in Table 24.2.

The results are mixed. The point estimates suggest a stronger effect of tracking at higher quantiles than at lower quantiles. This is consistent with the premise that tracking affects students heterogeneously, has no negative effects, and has the greatest impact on the upper end. The standard errors and confidence intervals, however, are also larger for the higher quantiles, such that the quantile regression coefficients at high quantiles are imprecisely estimated. Using the t test, two of the five slope coefficients are (borderline) statistically

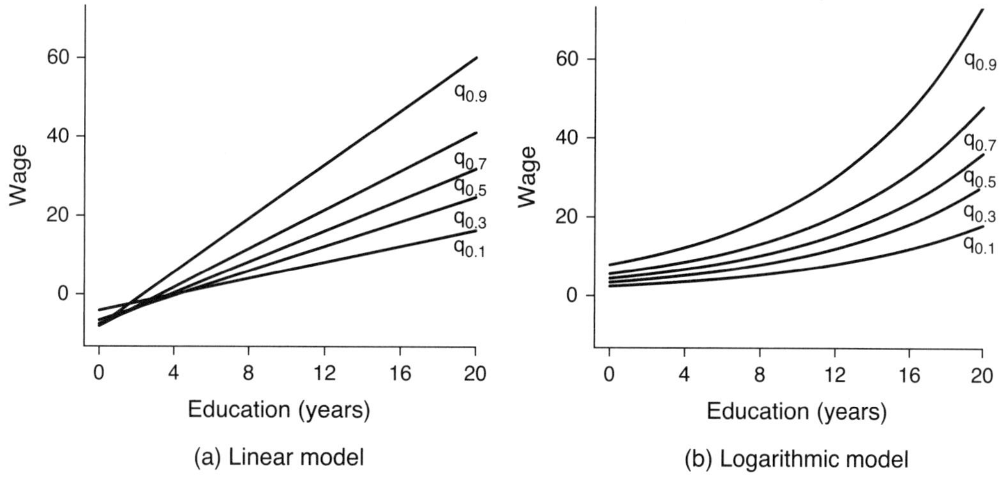

FIGURE 24.5 Quantile crossings

significant at the 5% level and one at the 10% level. In apparent contradiction, all five of the 95% BC percentile intervals include 0. Overall, the evidence that tracking affects student performance is weak.

24.10 QUANTILE CROSSINGS

A property of the quantile regression functions $q_\tau(x)$ is that they are monotonically increasing in τ. Thus quantile functions for different quantiles (e.g., $q_{\tau_1}(x)$ and $q_{\tau_2}(x)$ for $\tau_1 \neq \tau_2$) cannot cross each other. However, a property of linear functions $x'\beta$ with differing slopes is that they will necessarily cross if the support for X is sufficiently large. This is a potential problem in applications, as practical uses of estimated quantile functions may require monotonicity in τ (e.g., if they are to be inverted to obtain a conditional distribution function).

This is only a problem in practical applications if estimated quantile functions actually cross. If they do not, this issue can be ignored. However, when estimated quantile regression functions do cross one another, it can be prudent to address the issue.

To illustrate, examine Figure 24.5(a). This shows estimated linear quantile regressions of *wage* on *education* in the full `cps09mar` dataset. These are linear projection approximations to the plots in Figure 24.2(a). Because the actual quantile regression functions are convex, the estimated linear models cross one another at low education levels. This is the quantile regression crossing phenomenon.

When quantile regressions cross one another there are several possible remedies. First, you could respecify the model. In the example of Figure 24.5(a), the problem arises in part because the true quantile regression functions are convex and are poorly approximated by linear functions. In this example, we know that an improved approximation is obtained by a logarithmic transformation for wages. After a log transformation, the quantile regression functions are much better approximated by linearity. Indeed, such estimates (obtained by quantile regression of log wages on education, and then applying the exponential transformation to return to the original units) are displayed in Figure 24.5(b). These functions are smooth approximations and are strictly monotonic in τ. Problem solved.

Although the logarithmic/exponential transformation works well for a wage regression, it is not a generic solution. If the underlying quantile regressions are nonlinear in X, an improved approximation (and possible elimination of the quantile crossing) may be obtained by a nonlinear or simple series approximation. A visual examination of Figure 24.2(a) suggests that the functions may be piecewise linear with a kink at 11 years of education, which suggests a linear spline with a single knot at $x = 11$. The estimates from fitting this model (not displayed) are strictly monotonic in τ. Problem solved.

A second remedy is to reassess the empirical task. Examining Figure 24.5(a), we see that the crossing phenomenon occurs at very low levels of education (4 years), for which there are very few observations. This may not be viewed as an empirically interesting region. A solution is to truncate the data to eliminate observations with low education levels.

A third remedy is to constrain the estimated functions to satisfy monotonicity. Examine Figure 24.5(a). The five regression functions are increasing with increasing slopes, and the support for X is $[0, 20]$, so it is necessary and sufficient to constrain the five intercepts to be monotonically ranked. This can be imposed on this example by sequentially imposing cross-equation equality constraints. The R function `rq` has an option to impose parameter contraints. This approach may be feasible if the quantile crossing problem is mild.

A final remedy is **rearrangement**. For each x, take the five estimated quantile regression functions as displayed in Figure 24.5(a) and rearrange the estimates so that they satisfy the monotonicity requirement. This does not alter the coefficient estimates, only the estimated quantile regressions. This approach is flexible and works in general contexts without the need for model re-specification. For details, see Chernozhukov, Fernández-Val, and Galichon (2010). The R package `quantreg` includes the option `rearrange` to implement their procedure.

Of these four remedies, my recommendation is to start with a careful and thoughtful re-specification of the model.

24.11 QUANTILE CAUSAL EFFECTS

One question that frequently arises in the study of quantile regression is: "Can we interpret the quantile regression causally?" We can partially answer this question in the treatment response framework by providing conditions under which the quantile regression derivatives equal quantile treatment effects.

Recall that the treatment response model is $Y = h(D, X, U)$, where Y is the outcome, D is the treatment variable, the X are controls, and U is an unobserved structural random error. For simplicity, consider the case that D is binary. For concreteness, let Y be wage, D college attendence, and U unobserved ability.

In this framework, the causal effect of D on Y is

$$C(X, U) = h(1, X, U) - h(0, X, U).$$

In general, this variable is heterogeneous. Although the average causal effect is the expectation of this random variable, the **quantile treatment effect** is its τth conditional quantile

$$Q_\tau(x) = \mathbb{Q}_\tau\left[C(X, U) \mid X = x\right].$$

Section 2.30 presented an example of a population of Jennifers and Georges who had differential wage effects from college attendence. In this example, the unobserved effect U is a person's type (Jennifer or George). The quantile treatment effect Q_τ traces out the distribution of the causal effect of college attendence and is therefore more informative than the average treatment effect alone.

From observational data, we can estimate the quantile regression function

$$q_\tau(d, x) = \mathbb{Q}_\tau\left[Y \mid D = d, X = x\right] = \mathbb{Q}_\tau\left[h(D, X, U) \mid D = d, X = x\right]$$

and its implied effect of D on Y:

$$D_\tau(x) = q_\tau(1,x) - q_\tau(0,x).$$

The question is: Under what condition does $D_\tau = Q_\tau$? That is, when does quantile regression measure the causal effect of D on Y?

Assumption 24.1 Conditions for Quantile Causal Effect

1. The error U is real valued.
2. The causal effect $C(x,u)$ is monotonically increasing in u.
3. The treatment response $h(D,X,u)$ is monotonically increasing in u.
4. Conditional on X, the random variables D and U are independent.

Assumption 24.1 part 1 excludes multidimensional unobserved heterogeneity. Assumption 24.1 part 2 and 3 are known as **monotonicity** conditions. A single monotonicity assumption is not restrictive (it is similar to a normalization), but the two conditions together are a substantive restriction. Consider, for example, the case of the impact of college attendence on wages. Assumption 24.1 part 2 requires that the wage gain from attending college is increasing in latent ability U (given X). Assumption 24.1 part 3 further requires that wages are increasing in latent ability U, regardless of whether an individual attends college. In our Jennifer and George example, these assumptions require that Jennifer receives a higher wage than George if they both are high school graduates, or if they both are college graduates, and that Jennifer's gain from attending college exceeds George's gain. These conditions were satisfied in the example of Section 2.30, but with a tweak, we can change the model so that one of the monotonicity conditions is violated.

Assumption 24.1 part 4 is the traditional conditional independence assumption. This assumption is critical for the causal effect interpretation. The idea is that by conditioning on a sufficiently rich set of variables X, any endogeneity between D and U has been eliminated.

Theorem 24.5 Quantile Causal Effect. If Assumption 24.1 holds, then $D_\tau(x) = Q_\tau(x)$; the quantile regression derivative equals the quantile treatment effect.

The proof is in Section 24.16.

Theorem 24.5 provides conditions under which quantile regression is a causal model. Under the conditional independence and monotonicity assumptions, the quantile regression coefficients are the marginal causal effects of the treatment variable D on the distribution of Y. The coefficients are not the marginal causal effects for specific individuals; instead they are the causal effect for the distribution. Theorem 24.5 shows that under suitable assumptions, we can learn more than just the average treatment effect—we can learn the distribution of treatment effects.

24.12 RANDOM COEFFICIENT REPRESENTATION

For some theoretical purposes, it is convenient to write the quantile regression model using a random coefficient representation. This also provides an alternative interpretation of the coefficients.

Recall that when Y has a continuous and invertible distribution function $F(y)$, the probability integral transformation is $U = F(Y) \sim U[0,1]$. As the inverse of the distribution function is the quantile function, this implies that we can write $Y = q_U$, the quantile function evaluated at the random variable U. The intuition is that U is the "relative rank" of Y.

Similarly, when the conditional distribution $F\left(y \mid x\right)$ of Y given X is invertible, the probability integral transformation is $U = F\left(Y \mid X\right) \sim U[0,1]$, which is independent of X. Here, U is the relative rank of Y in the conditional distribution. Inverting, we obtain $Y = q_U(X)$. There is no additional error term e, because the randomness is captured by U. The equation $Y = q_U(X)$ is a representation of the conditional distribution of Y given X, not a structural model. However, it does imply a mechanism by which we can generate Y. First, draw $U \sim U[0,1]$. Second, draw X from its marginal distibution. Third, set $Y = q_U(X)$.

If we interpret $Y = q_U(X)$ as a structural model (that is, take U as a structural unobservable variable, not merely a derivation based on the probability integral transformation), then we can view U as an individual's latent relative rank, which is invariant to X. Each person is identified with a specific $U = \tau$. In this framework, the quantile slope (the derivative of the quantile regression) is the quantile causal effect of X on Y. This representation satisfies the conditions of Theorem 24.5, because U is independent of X.

In the linear quantile regression model $\mathbb{Q}_\tau\left[Y \mid X\right] = X'\beta_\tau$, the random coefficient[3] representation is $= X'\beta_U$.

24.13 NONPARAMETRIC QUANTILE REGRESSION

As emphasized in Section 24.10, quantile regression functions are undoubtedly nonlinear with unknown functional form and hence nonparametric. Quantile regression functions may be estimated using standard nonparametric methods. This is a potentially extensive subject. We briefly discuss series methods, which have the advantage that they are easily implemented with conventional software.

The nonparametric quantile regression model is

$$Y = q_\tau(X) + e$$
$$\mathbb{Q}_\tau\left[e \mid X\right] = 0.$$

The function $q_\tau(x)$ can be approximated by a series regression, as described in Chapter 20. For example, a polynomial approximation is

$$Y = \beta_0 + \beta_1 X + \beta_2 X^2 + \cdots + \beta_K X^K + e_K$$
$$\mathbb{Q}_\tau\left[e_K \mid X\right] \simeq 0.$$

A spline approximation is defined similarly.

For any K, the coefficients and regression function $q_\tau(x)$ can be estimated by quantile regression. As in series regression, the model order K should be selected to trade off flexibility (bias reduction) and parsimony (variance reduction). Asymptotic theory requires that $K \to \infty$ as $n \to \infty$ but at a slower rate.

An important practical question is how to select K in a given application. Unfortunately, standard information criteria (such as the AIC) do not apply for quantile regression, and it is unclear if cross-validation is an appropriate model selection technique. Undoubtedly these questions are an important topic for future study.

[3]The coefficients depends on U and so are random, but the model is different from the random coefficient model, where each individual's coefficient is a random vector.

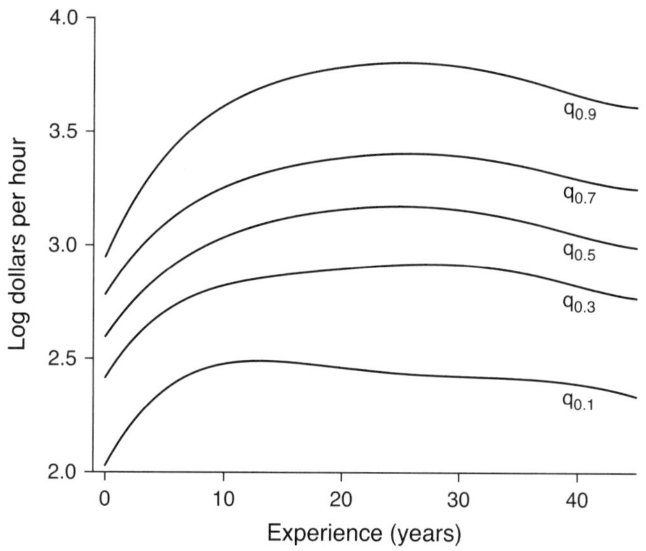

FIGURE 24.6 Log wage quantile regressions

To illustrate, we revisit the nonparametric polynomial estimates of the experience profile for college-educated women displayed in Figure 20.1. We estimate[4] log wage quantile regressions with a fifth-order polynomial in experience and display the estimates in Figure 24.6. The figure displays two notable features. First, the $\tau = 0.1$ quantile function peaks at a low level of experience (about 10 years) and then declines substantially with experience. This is likely an indicator of the wage-path of women on the low end of the pay scale. Second, even though the figure uses a logarithmic scale, the gaps betwen the quantile functions substantially widen with experience. Thus heterogeneity in wages increases more than proportionately as experience increases.

24.14 PANEL DATA

Given a panel data structure $\{Y_{it}, X_{it}\}$, it is natural to consider a panel data quantile regression estimator. A linear model with an individual effect $\alpha_{i\tau}$ is

$$\mathbb{Q}_\tau \left[Y_{it} \mid X_{it}, \alpha_i\right] = X_{it}'\beta_\tau + \alpha_{i\tau}.$$

It seems natural to consider estimation by one of our standard methods: (1) Remove the individual effect by the within transformation; (2) Remove the individual effect by first differencing; or (3) Estimate a full quantile regression model using the dummy variable representation. However, all of these methods fail. The reason methods (1) and (2) fail are the same: The quantile operator $\mathbb{Q}_\tau$ is not a linear operator. The within transformation of $\mathbb{Q}_\tau \left[Y_{it} \mid X_{it}, \alpha_{i\tau}\right]$ does not equal $\mathbb{Q}_\tau \left[\dot{Y}_{it} \mid X_{it}, \alpha_{i\tau}\right]$, and similarly, $\Delta\mathbb{Q}_\tau \left[Y_{it} \mid X_{it}, \alpha_{i\tau}\right] \neq \mathbb{Q}_\tau \left[\Delta Y_{it} \mid X_{it}, \alpha_{i\tau}\right]$. The reason method (3) fails is the incidental parameters problem. A dummy variable model has the number of parameters proportional to sample size, and in this context, nonlinear estimators (including quantile regression) are inconsistent.

[4]The sample is the $n = 5,199$ observations of women with a college degree (16 years of education).

There have been several proposals to deal with this issue, but none are particularly satisfactory. We present here a method due to Canay (2011), which has the advantage of simplicity and wide applicability. The substantive assumption is that the individual effect is common across quantiles: $\alpha_{i\tau} = \alpha_i$. Thus α_i shifts the quantile regressions up and down uniformly. This assumption is sensible when α_i represents omitted time-invariant variables with coefficients that do not vary across quantiles.

Given this assumption, we can write the quantile regression model as

$$Y_{it} = X_{it}'\beta(\tau) + \alpha_i + e_{it}.$$

We can also use the random coefficient representation of Section 24.12 to write

$$Y_{it} = X_{it}'\beta(U_{i\tau}) + \alpha_i$$

where $U_{i\tau} \sim U[0,1]$ is independent of (X_{it}, α_i). Taking conditional expectations, we obtain the model

$$Y_{it} = X_{it}'\theta + \alpha_i + u_{it}$$

where $\theta = \mathbb{E}\left[\beta(U_{i\tau})\right]$, and u_{it} is conditionally mean 0. The coefficient θ is a weighted average of the quantile regression coefficients $\beta(\tau)$.

Canay's estimator takes the following steps:

1. Estimate α_i by fixed effects $\widehat{\alpha}_i$ as in (17.51). [Estimate θ by the within estimator $\widehat{\theta}$, and α_i by taking averages of $Y_{it} - X_{it}'\widehat{\theta}$ for each individual.]
2. Estimate $\beta(\tau)$ by quantile regression of $Y_{it} - \widehat{\alpha}_i$ on X_{it}.

The key to Canay's estimator is the assumption that the fixed effect α_i does not vary across the quantiles τ, which means that the fixed effects can be estimated by conventional fixed effects. Once eliminated, we can apply conventional quantile regression. The primary disadvantage of this approach is that the assumption that α_i does not vary across quantiles is restrictive. In general, panel quantile regression is a potentially important topic for further econometric research.

24.15 IV QUANTILE REGRESSION

As we studied in Chapter 12, in many structural economic models, some regressors are potentially endogenous, meaning that they are jointly dependent with the regression error. This situation also arises in quantile regression models. A standard method for handling endogenous regressors is instrumental variables regression, which relies on a set of instruments Z that satisfy an uncorrelatedness or independence condition. Similar methods can be applied in quantile regression, though the techniques are computationally more difficult, the theory less well developed, and applications limited.

The model is

$$Y = X'\beta_\tau + e$$

$$\mathbb{Q}_\tau\left[e \mid Z\right] = 0$$

where X and β_τ are $k \times 1$, Z is $\ell \times 1$, and $\ell \geq k$. The difference from the conventional quantile regression model is that the second equation is conditional on Z rather than on X.

The assumption on the error implies that $\mathbb{E}\left[\psi_\tau(e) \mid Z\right] = 0$, which holds by the same derivation as for the quantile regression model. This is a conditional moment equation. It implies the unconditional moment equation[5] $\mathbb{E}[Z\psi_\tau(e)] = 0$. It can be written as a function of the observations and parameters:

$$\mathbb{E}\left[Z\psi_\tau\left(Y - X'\beta_\tau\right)\right] = 0.$$

This is a set of ℓ moment equations for k parameters. A suitable estimation method is GMM. A computational challenge is that the moment condition functions are discontinuous in β_τ, so conventional minimization techniques fail.

The method of IV quantile regression was articulated by Chernozhukov and Hansen (2005), which should be consulted for further details.

24.16 TECHNICAL PROOFS*

Proof of Theorem 24.1 Since $\mathbb{P}[Y = m] = 0$,

$$\mathbb{E}\left[\operatorname{sgn}(Y-m)\right] = \mathbb{E}\left[\mathbb{1}\{Y > m\}\right] - \mathbb{E}\left[\mathbb{1}\{Y < m\}\right] = \mathbb{P}[Y > m] - \mathbb{P}[Y < m] = \frac{1}{2} - \frac{1}{2} = 0$$

which is (24.2).

Exchanging integration and differentiation, we have

$$\frac{d}{d\theta}\mathbb{E}\,|Y-\theta| = \mathbb{E}\left[\frac{d}{d\theta}|Y-\theta|\right] = \mathbb{E}\left[\operatorname{sgn}(Y-\theta)\right] = 0,$$

the final equality at $\theta = m$ by (24.2). This is the first-order condition for an optimum. Since $\mathbb{E}\left[\operatorname{sgn}(Y-\theta)\right] = 1 - 2\mathbb{P}[Y < \theta]$ is globally decreasing in θ, the second-order condition shows that m is the unique minimizer. This is (24.3).

Equations (24.4) and (24.5) follow by similar arguments using the conditional distribution. Equation (24.6) follows from (24.5) under the assumption that $\operatorname{med}[Y \mid X] = X'\beta$. ■

Proof of Theorem 24.2 Since $\mathbb{P}\left[Y = q_\tau\right] = 0$,

$$\mathbb{E}\left[\psi_\tau\left(Y - q_\tau\right)\right] = \tau - \mathbb{P}\left[Y < q_\tau\right] = 0$$

which is (24.11).

Exchanging integration and differentiation, we obtain

$$\frac{d}{d\theta}\mathbb{E}\left[\rho_\tau(Y-\theta)\right] = \mathbb{E}\left[\psi_\tau(Y-\theta)\right] = 0,$$

the final equality at $\theta = q_\tau$ by (24.11). This is the first-order condition for an optimum. Since $\mathbb{E}\left[\psi_\tau(Y-\theta)\right] = \tau - \mathbb{P}[Y < \theta]$ is globally decreasing in θ, the second-order condition shows that q_τ is the unique minimizer. This is (24.12).

Equations (24.13) and (24.14) follow by similar arguments using the conditional distribution. Equation (24.15) follows from (24.14) under the assumption that $\mathbb{Q}_\tau[Y \mid X] = X'\beta$. ■

Proof of Theorem 24.3 The quantile regression estimator is an m-estimator, so we appeal to Theorem 22.3, which holds under five conditions. Conditions 1 and 4 are satisfied by assumption, and condition 2

[5] In fact, the assumptions imply $\mathbb{E}[\phi(Z)\psi_\tau(e)] = 0$ for any function ϕ. We assume that the desired instruments have been selected and are incorporated in the vector Z as denoted.

holds because $\rho_\tau\left(Y - X'\beta\right)$ is continuous in β as $\rho_\tau(u)$ is a continuous function. For condition 3, observe that $\left|\rho_\tau\left(Y - X'\beta\right)\right| \leq |Y| + \overline{\beta}\,\|X\|$, where $\overline{\beta} = \sup_{\beta\in B}\|\beta\|$. The right side has finite expectation under the assumptions.

For condition 5, we need to show that β_τ uniquely minimizes $M(\beta;\tau)$. It is a minimizer by (24.16). It is unique, because $M(\beta;\tau)$ is a convex function and

$$\frac{\partial^2}{\partial\beta\partial\beta'}M(\beta_\tau;\tau) = \mathbb{E}\left[XX'f_\tau(0 \mid X)\right] > 0. \tag{24.20}$$

The inequality holds by assumption; we now establish the equality.

Exchanging integration and differentiation, and using $\psi_\tau(x) = \frac{d}{dx}\rho_\tau(x) = \tau - \mathbb{1}\{x < 0\}$, the law of iterated expectations, and the conditional distribution function $F_\tau(u \mid x) = \mathbb{E}\left[\mathbb{1}\{e < u\} \mid X\right]$, we have

$$\begin{aligned}\frac{\partial}{\partial\beta}M(\beta;\tau) &= -\mathbb{E}\left[X\psi_\tau\left(Y - X'\beta\right)\right] \\ &= -\tau\mathbb{E}[X] + \mathbb{E}\left[X\mathbb{E}\left[\mathbb{1}\left\{Y < X'(\beta - \beta_\tau)\right\} \mid X\right]\right] \\ &= -\tau\mathbb{E}[X] + \mathbb{E}\left[XF_\tau\left(X'(\beta - \beta_\tau) \mid X\right)\right].\end{aligned} \tag{24.21}$$

Hence

$$\frac{\partial^2}{\partial\beta\partial\beta'}M(\beta;\tau) = \frac{\partial}{\partial\beta'}\mathbb{E}\left[XF_\tau\left(X'(\beta - \beta_\tau) \mid X\right)\right] = \mathbb{E}\left[XX'f_\tau\left(X'(\beta - \beta_\tau) \mid X\right)\right]. \tag{24.22}$$

The right-hand side of (24.22) is bounded below by $\mathbb{E}\left[XX'\right]D$, which has finite elements under the assumptions. Equation (24.22) is also positive semi-definite for all β, so $M(\beta;\tau)$ is globally convex. Evaluated at β_τ, (24.22) equals (24.20). Thus $M(\beta;\tau)$ is strictly convex at the minimum β_τ, and so the latter is the unique minimizer.

We have established the five conditions of Theorem 22.3, as needed. ■

Proof of Theorem 24.4 Since $\widehat{\beta}_\tau$ is an m-estimator with a discontinuous score, we verify the conditions of Theorem 22.6, which holds under conditions 1, 2, 3, and 5 of Theorem 22.4, $\left\|X\psi_\tau\left(Y - X'\beta\right)\right\| \leq G(Y,X)$ with $\mathbb{E}\left[G(Y,X)^2\right] < \infty$, plus one of the four categories listed in Theorem 22.4.

It is useful to observe that because $\psi_\tau(u) \leq 1$,

$$\left\|X\psi_\tau\left(Y - X'\beta\right)\right\| \leq \|X\|. \tag{24.23}$$

Let us verify conditions 1, 2, 3, and 5 of Theorem 22.4. Condition 1 holds because (24.23) implies that $\mathbb{E}\left[\|X\|^2\psi_\tau^2\right] \leq \mathbb{E}\|X\|^2 < \infty$. Condition 2 holds by (24.18). Equation (24.22) shows that $\frac{\partial^2}{\partial\beta\partial\beta'}M(\beta;\tau)$ is continuous under the assumption that $f_\tau(e \mid x)$ is continuous in e, implying condition 3. Condition 5 holds by assumption.

The upper bound (24.23) satisfies $\mathbb{E}\|X\|^2 < \infty$, as needed. It remains to verify one of the four listed categories of Theorem 22.6. Observe that $\psi_\tau(u)$ is a function of bounded variation, so $\psi_\tau\left(Y - X'\beta\right)$ is in the second category. The score $X\psi_\tau\left(Y - X'\beta\right)$ is the product of the Lipschitz-continuous function X and $\psi_\tau\left(Y - X'\beta\right)$, and thus falls in the third category. This shows that Theorem 22.6 can be applied.

We have verified the conditions for Theorem 22.6, so asymptotic normality follows. For the covariance matrix, we calculate that

$$\mathbb{E}\left[(X\psi_\tau)(X\psi_\tau)'\right] = \mathbb{E}\left[XX'\psi_\tau^2\right] = \Omega_\tau.$$

■

Proof of Theorem 24.5 By the definition of the quantile treatment effect, monotonicity of causal effect (Assumption 24.1 part 2), definition of the causal effect, monotonicity of the treatment response (Assumption 24.1 part 3), and the definition of the quantile regression function, we find that

$$\begin{aligned} Q_\tau(x) &= \mathbb{Q}_\tau\left[C(X,U) \mid X=x\right] \\ &= C(x, \mathbb{Q}_\tau[U \mid X=x]) \\ &= h(1,x,\mathbb{Q}_\tau[U \mid X=x]) - h(0,x,\mathbb{Q}_\tau[U \mid X=x]) \\ &= \mathbb{Q}_\tau[h(1,X,U) \mid X=x] - \mathbb{Q}_\tau[h(0,X,U) \mid X=x] \\ &= q_\tau(1,x) - q_\tau(0,x) \\ &= D_\tau(x) \end{aligned}$$

as claimed. ■

24.17 EXERCISES

Exercise 24.1 Prove (24.4) in Theorem 24.1.

Exercise 24.2 Prove (24.5) in Theorem 24.1.

Exercise 24.3 Define $\psi(x) = \tau - \mathbb{1}\{x < 0\}$. Let θ satisfy $\mathbb{E}\left[\psi(Y-\theta)\right] = 0$. Is θ a quantile of the distribution of Y?

Exercise 24.4 Consider the model $Y = X'\beta + e$, where the distribution of e given X is symmetric about 0.

(a) Find $\mathbb{E}\left[Y \mid X\right]$ and med $\left[Y \mid X\right]$.

(b) Do OLS and LAD estimate the same coefficient β or different coefficients?

(c) Under which circumstances would you prefer LAD over OLS? Under which circumstances would you prefer OLS over LAD? Explain.

Exercise 24.5 You are interested in estimating the equation $Y = X'\beta + e$. You believe the regressors are exogenous, but you are uncertain about the properties of the error. You estimate the equation both by least absolute deviations (LAD) and OLS. A colleague suggests that you should prefer the OLS estimate, because it produces a higher R^2 than the LAD estimate. Is your colleague correct?

Exercise 24.6 Prove (24.13) in Theorem 24.2.

Exercise 24.7 Prove (24.14) in Theorem 24.2.

Exercise 24.8 Suppose X is binary. Show that $\mathbb{Q}_\tau[Y \mid X]$ is linear in X.

Exercise 24.9 Suppose X_1 and X_2 are binary. Find $\mathbb{Q}_\tau[Y \mid X_1, X_2]$.

Exercise 24.10 Show (24.19).

Exercise 24.11 Show under correct specification that $\Omega_\tau = \mathbb{E}\left[XX'\psi_\tau^2\right]$ satisfies the simplification $\Omega_\tau = \tau(1-\tau)\boldsymbol{Q}$.

Exercise 24.12 Consider the treatment response setting of Theorem 24.5. Suppose $h(0, X_2, U) = 0$, meaning that the response variable Y is 0 when there is no treatment. Show that Assumption 24.1 part 3 is not necessary for Theorem 24.5.

Exercise 24.13 In the `cps09mar` dataset, use the sample of Hispanic men with education 11 years or higher. Estimate linear quantile regression functions for log wages on education. Interpret your findings.

Exercise 24.14 In the `cps09mar` dataset, use the sample of Hispanic women with education 11 years or higher. Estimate linear quantile regression functions for log wages on education. Interpret.

Exercise 24.15 Consider the Duflo, Dupas, and Kremer (2011) dataset `DDK2011` and the subsample of students for which *tracking* = 1. Estimate linear quantile regressions of *totalscore* on *percentile* (the latter is the student's test score before the school year). Calculate standard errors by clustered bootstrap. Do the coefficients change meaningfully by quantile? How do you interpret these results?

Exercise 24.16 Using the `cps09mar` dataset, estimate similarly to Figure 24.6 the quantile regressions for log wages on a fifth-order polynomial in experience for college-educated Black women. Repeat for college-educated white women. Interpret your findings.

CHAPTER 25

BINARY CHOICE

25.1 INTRODUCTION

This and the next two chapters treat what are known as **limited dependent variables**. These are variables that have restricted support (a subset of the real line), and this restriction has consequences for econometric modeling. This chapter concerns the simplest case where Y is **binary**, meaning that it takes two values. Without loss of generality, these are taken as 0 and 1, thus Y has support $\{0, 1\}$. In econometrics, we typically call this class of models **binary choice**.

Examples of binary dependent variables include: purchase of a single item; market entry; participation; approval of an application/patent/loan. The dependent variable may be recorded as Yes/No, True/False, or $1/-1$, but it can always be written as $1/0$.

The goal in binary choice analysis is estimation of the conditional or **response probability** $\mathbb{P}[Y=1 \mid X]$, given a set of regressors X. We may be interested in the response probability or some transformation, such as its derivative—the **marginal effect**. A traditional approach to binary choice modeling (and limited dependent variable models in general) is parametric with estimation by maximum likelihood. There is also a substantial literature on semiparametric estimation. In recent years, applied practice has tilted toward linear probability models estimated by least squares.

For more detailed treatments, see Maddala (1983), Cameron and Trivedi (2005), and Wooldridge (2010).

25.2 BINARY CHOICE MODELS

Let (Y, X) be random with $Y \in \{0, 1\}$ and $X \in \mathbb{R}^k$. The **response probability** of Y with respect to X is

$$P(x) = \mathbb{P}[Y=1 \mid X=x] = \mathbb{E}[Y \mid X=x].$$

The response probability completely describes the conditional distribution. The **marginal effect** is

$$\frac{\partial}{\partial x} P(x) = \frac{\partial}{\partial x} \mathbb{P}[Y=1 \mid X=x] = \frac{\partial}{\partial x} \mathbb{E}[Y \mid X=x].$$

This equals the regression derivative. Economic applications often focus on the marginal effect.

To illustrate, consider the probability of marriage given age. We use the `cps09mar` dataset, take the subset of men with a college degree ($n=6{,}441$), set $Y=1$ if the individual is married or widowed but not separated or divorced,[1] and set $Y=0$ otherwise. The regressor is *age*, which takes values in $[19, 80]$. Figure 25.1(a) plots two estimates of $P(x)$. The filled circles are nonparametric estimates—the empirical marriage frequency for each age—and the solid line is our preferred specification (a probit spline model, described

[1] *marital* equals 1, 2, 3, or 4.

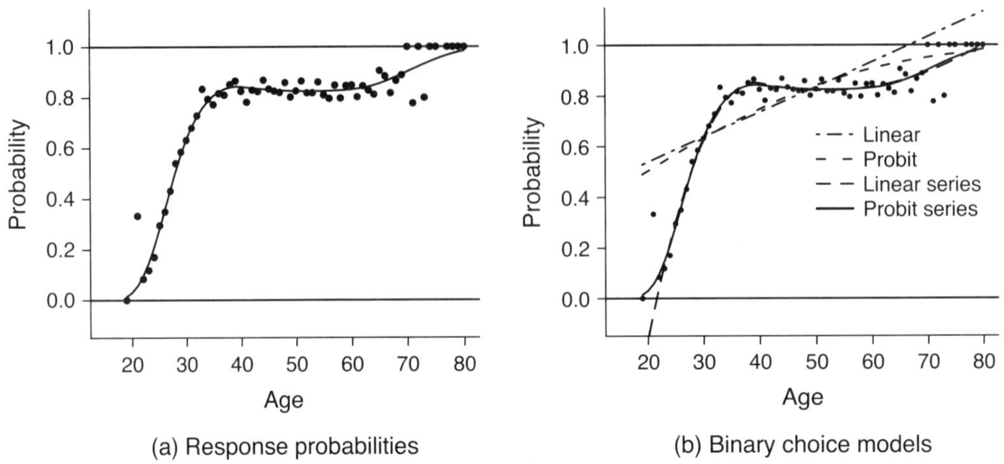

FIGURE 25.1 Probability of marriage given age for college educated men

below). What seems apparant is that the probability of marriage is near 0 for age = 19, increases linearly to 80% around age = 35, remains roughly flat at 80% for ages 40–65, and increases for higher ages.

The variables satisfy the regression framework

$$Y = P(X) + e$$

$$\mathbb{E}[e \mid X] = 0.$$

The error e is not "classical." It has the two-point conditional distribution

$$e = \begin{cases} 1 - P(X), & \text{with probability } P(X) \\ -P(X), & \text{with probability } 1 - P(X). \end{cases} \tag{25.1}$$

It is also highly heteroskedastic with conditional variance:

$$\operatorname{var}[e \mid X] = P(X)(1 - P(X)). \tag{25.2}$$

Regression scatterplots with binary Y are effectively useless, as the Y values do not "scatter" but instead lie exclusively on the lines $y = 0$ and $y = 1$.

25.3 MODELS FOR THE RESPONSE PROBABILITY

We now discuss the most common models used for the response probability $P(x)$.

Linear Probability Model: $P(x) = x'\beta$, where β is a coefficient vector. In this model, the response probability is a linear function of the regressors. The linear probability model has the advantage that it is simple to interpret. The coefficients β equal the marginal effects (when X does not include nonlinear transformations). Because the response probability equals the conditional mean, this model equals the linear regression model. Linearity means that estimation is simple, as least squares can be used to estimate the coefficients. In more complicated settings (e.g., panel data with fixed effects or endogenous variables with instruments), standard estimators can be employed.

A disadvantage of the linear probability model is that it does not respect the [0, 1] boundary. Fitted and predicted values from estimated linear probability models frequently violate these boundaries, producing nonsense results.

To illustrate, Figure 25.1(b) plots with the dash-dotted line the linear probability model fit to the observations in the sample described in Section 25.2. The fitted values are a poor approximation to the response probabilities. They also violate the [0, 1] boundary for men above the age of 67. According to the model, an 80-year-old is married with probability 113%!

Overall, the linear probability model is a poor choice for calculation of probabilities.

Index Models: $P(x) = G(x'\beta)$, where $G(u)$ is a **link** function, and β is a coefficient vector. This framework is also called a **single index** model, where $x'\beta$ is a **linear index** function. In binary choice models, $G(u)$ is a distribution function that respects the probability bounds $0 \leq G(u) \leq 1$. In economic applications, $G(u)$ is typically the normal or logistic distribution function, both of which are symmetric about 0 so that $G(-u) = 1 - G(u)$. We assume throughout this chapter that this symmetry condition holds. Let $g(u) = \frac{\partial}{\partial u}G(u)$ denote the density function of $G(u)$. In an index model, the marginal effect function is

$$\frac{\partial}{\partial x}P(x) = \beta g\left(x'\beta\right).$$

Index models are only slightly more complicated than the linear probability model but have the advantage of respecting the [0, 1] boundary. The two most common index models are the probit and logit.

Probit Model: $P(x) = \Phi(x'\beta)$, where $\Phi(u)$ is the standard normal distribution function. This is a traditional workhorse model for binary choice analysis. It is simple, easy to use, easy to interpret, and is based on the classical normal distribution.

Logit Model: $P(x) = \Lambda(x'\beta)$, where $\Lambda(u) = \left(1 + \exp(-u)\right)^{-1}$ is the logistic distribution function. This is an alternative workhorse model for binary choice analysis. The logistic and normal distribution functions (appropriately scaled) have similar shapes, so the probit and logit models typically produce similar estimates for the response probabilities and marginal effects. One advantage of the logit model is that the distribution function is available in closed form, which speeds computation.

Linear Series Model: $P(x) = x_K'\beta_K$, where $x_K = x_K(x)$ is a vector of transformations of x, and β_K is a coefficient vector. A series expansion has the ability to approximate any continuous function, including the response probability $P(x)$. The advantage of a linear series model is that its linear form allows the application of linear econometric methods. It is not guaranteed, however, to be boundary-respecting.

Index Series Model: $P(x) = G\left(x_K'\beta_K\right)$, where $G(u)$ is a distribution function (either normal or logistic in practice), $x_K = x_K(x)$ is a vector of transformations of x, and β_K is a coefficient vector. A series expansion has the ability to approximate any continuous function, including the transformed response probability $G^{-1}\left(p(x)\right)$. Thus the index series model has the ability to approximate any continuous response probability. In addition, the model is boundary-respecting.

To illustrate the approximating capabilities of the models, view Figure 25.1(b), which plots four estimated response probability functions: (1) linear; (2) probit; (3) linear series; and (4) probit series. The first two models are specified as linear in `age`. The two series models use a quadratic spline in `age` with kinks at 40 and 60.

As discussed earlier, in this application, the linear probability model is a particularly poor fit. It overpredicts the probability for men under 30 and over 50, underpredicts the others, and violates the [0, 1] boundary. The simple probit model is also quite poor. It produces an estimated response probability function that is similar to the linear probability model for ages up to 60. Its advantage is that for ages over 60, it does not violate the [0, 1] boundary. In contrast, the two series models produce excellent fitted response probability functions. The two estimates are nearly identical for ages above 25. The main difference between the estimated functions is that the probit series model provides a globally excellent fit, while the linear series model fails for ages less than 25, severely violating the [0, 1] boundary. The linear series model estimates that a 19-year-old is married with negative probability: −27%!

To summarize, a probit series model has several excellent features. It is simple, based on a popular link function, globally approximates any continuous response probability function, and respects the [0, 1] boundary. A linear series model is also a reasonable candidate, but has the disadvantage of not necessarily respecting the [0, 1] boundary.

Probit and Logit

The intruiging labels *probit* and *logit* have a long history in statistical analysis. The term *probit* was coined by Chester Bliss in 1934 as a contraction of "probability unit." The *logistic function* was introduced by Pierre François Verhulst in 1938 as a modified exponential growth model. It is speculated that he used the term *logistic* as a contrast to *logarithmic*. In 1944, Joseph Berkson proposed a binary choice model based on the logistic distribution function. He motivated the logistic as a convenient computational approximation to the normal. As his model was an analog of the *probit*, Berkson called his model the *logit*.

25.4 LATENT VARIABLE INTERPRETATION

An index model can be interpreted as a latent variable model. Consider

$$\begin{aligned} Y^* &= X'\beta + e \\ e &\sim G(e) \\ Y &= \mathbb{1}\left\{Y^* > 0\right\} = \begin{cases} 1, & \text{if } Y^* > 0 \\ 0, & \text{otherwise.} \end{cases} \end{aligned}$$

In this model, the observables are (Y, X). The variable Y^* is latent, linear in X, and has an error e, with the latter drawn from a symmetric distribution G. The observed binary variable Y equals 1 if the latent variable Y^* exceeds 0 and equals 0 otherwise.

The event $Y = 1$ is the same as $Y^* > 0$, which is the same as

$$X'\beta + e > 0. \tag{25.3}$$

Thus the response probability is

$$P(x) = \mathbb{P}\left[e > -x'\beta\right] = 1 - G\left(-x'\beta\right) = G\left(x'\beta\right).$$

The final equality uses the assumption that $G(u)$ is symmetric about 0. Thus the response probability is $P(x) = G(x'\beta)$, which is an index model with link function $G(u)$.

This latent variable model corresponds to a choice model, where Y^* is an individual's relative utility (or profit) of the options $Y=1$ and $Y=0$, and the individual selects the option with the higher utility. We see that this structural choice model is identical to an index model with link function equaling the distribution of the error. It is a probit model if the error e is standard normal and is a logit model if e is logistically distributed.

You may have noticed that we have discussed cases where the error e is either *standard* normal or *standard* logistic, that is, their scale is fixed. This is because the scale of the error distribution is not identified. To see this, suppose that $e=\sigma\varepsilon$, where ε has a distribution $G(u)$ with unit variance. Then the response probability is

$$\mathbb{P}[Y=1 \mid X=x]=\mathbb{P}\left[\sigma e>-x'\beta\right]=G\left(\frac{x'\beta}{\sigma}\right)=G\left(x'\beta^*\right)$$

where $\beta^*=\beta/\sigma$. This is an index model with coefficient β^*. Thus β and σ are not separately identified; only the ratio $\beta^*=\beta/\sigma$ is identified. The standard solution is to normalize σ to a convenient value. The probit and logit models use the normalizations $\sigma=1$ and $\sigma=\pi/\sqrt{3}\simeq 1.8$, respectively.

Two consequences of the above analysis are that (1) interpretation of the coefficient vector β cannot be separated from the scale of the error; and (2) the coefficients of probit and logit models cannot be compared without rescaling. In general, it is best to interpret the coefficient of a probit model as β/σ, the structural coefficient scaled by the stuctural standard deviation, and to interpret the coefficient of a logit model as β/v, the structural coefficient scaled by the structural logistic scale parameter $v=\sigma\sqrt{3}/\pi$. For a rough comparison[2] of probit and logit coefficients, multiply the probit coefficients by 1.8 or divide the logit coefficients by 1.8.

Although the coefficient β is not identified, the following parameters are identified:

1. Scaled coefficients: $\beta^*=\beta/\sigma$.
2. Ratios of coefficients: $\beta_1/\beta_2=\beta_1^*/\beta_2^*$.
3. Marginal effects: $\frac{\partial}{\partial x}P(x)=\frac{\beta}{\sigma}g\left(\frac{x'\beta}{\sigma}\right)=\beta^*g\left(x'\beta^*\right)$.

These parameters only depend on β^* and so are identified.

Concerning identification, if we take a broader nonparametric view, the error distribution $G(u)$ is not identified. To see this, write the structural equation nonparametrically as $Y^*=m(X)+e$. The response probability is

$$P(x)=1-G(-m(x)). \tag{25.4}$$

The joint distribution identifies $P(x)$. If $G(e)$ and $m(x)$ are nonparametric, they cannot be separately identified from the response probability. Only the composite (25.4) is identified.

An important implication is that there is no loss of generality in setting $G(u)$ equal to a specific parametric distribution, such as the normal, so long as the function $m(x)$ is treated nonparametrically.

25.5 LIKELIHOOD

Probit and logit models are typically estimated by maximum likelihood. To construct the likelihood, we need the distribution of an individual observation. Recall that if Y is Bernoulli, such that $\mathbb{P}[Y=1]=p$ and $\mathbb{P}[Y=0]=1-p$, then Y has the probability mass function

$$\pi(y)=p^y(1-p)^{1-y}, \qquad y=0,1.$$

[2]This produces only a rough comparison, as this normalization only puts the coefficients on the same scale. They are not equal, since the models are different.

In the index model $\mathbb{P}[Y=1 \mid X]=G(X'\beta)$, Y is conditionally Bernoulli, so its conditional probability mass function is

$$\pi(Y \mid X)=G(X'\beta)^{Y}\left(1-G(X'\beta)\right)^{1-Y}=G(X'\beta)^{Y}G(-X'\beta)^{1-Y}=G(Z'\beta) \tag{25.5}$$

where

$$Z=\begin{cases} X, & \text{if } Y=1 \\ -X, & \text{if } Y=0. \end{cases}$$

Taking logs and summing across observations, we obtain the log-likelihood function:

$$\ell_n(\beta)=\sum_{i=1}^{n}\log G(Z_i'\beta).$$

For the probit and logit models this is

$$\ell_n^{\text{probit}}(\beta)=\sum_{i=1}^{n}\log \Phi(Z_i'\beta)$$

$$\ell_n^{\text{logit}}(\beta)=\sum_{i=1}^{n}\log \Lambda(Z_i'\beta).$$

Define the first and (negative) second derivatives of the log distribution function: $h(x)=\frac{d}{dx}\log G(x)$ and $H(x)=-\frac{d^2}{dx^2}\log G(x)$. For the logit model, these equal (see Exercise 25.5)

$$h_{\text{logit}}(x)=1-\Lambda(x)$$

$$H_{\text{logit}}(x)=\Lambda(x)\left(1-\Lambda(x)\right)$$

and for the probit model (see Exercise 25.6),

$$h_{\text{probit}}(x)=\frac{\phi(x)}{\Phi(x)}\stackrel{\text{def}}{=}\lambda(x)$$

$$H_{\text{probit}}(x)=\lambda(x)\left(x+\lambda(x)\right).$$

The function $\lambda(x)=\phi(x)/\Phi(x)$ is known as the **inverse Mills ratio**.

Both the logit and probit have the property that $H(x)>0$. This is easily seen for the logit case, because it is the product of the distribution function and its complement, but is less so for the probit case. Here we make use of a convenient property of **log concave**[3] functions: If a density $f(x)$ is log concave, then the distribution function $F(x)$ is log concave. The standard normal density $\phi(x)$ is log concave,[4] implying that $\Phi(x)$ is log concave, implying $H_{\text{probit}}(x)>0$ as desired.

The likelihood score and Hessian are

$$S_n(\beta)=\frac{\partial}{\partial\beta}\ell_n(\beta)=\sum_{i=1}^{n}Z_i h(Z_i'\beta) \tag{25.6}$$

$$\mathscr{H}_n(\beta)=-\frac{\partial^2}{\partial\beta\partial\beta'}\ell_n(\beta)=\sum_{i=1}^{n}X_iX_i'H(Z_i'\beta). \tag{25.7}$$

---

[3] A function $f(x)$ is **log concave** if $\log f(x)$ is concave.

[4] $\log\phi(x)=-\frac{1}{2}\log(2\pi)-x^2/2$ is concave.

Examining (25.7), we can see that $H(x) > 0$ implies that $\mathscr{H}_n(\beta) > 0$ globally in β. This in turn implies that the log-likelihood $\ell_n(\beta)$ is globally concave. Because both $H_{\text{logit}}(x) > 0$ and $H_{\text{probit}}(x) > 0$, we deduce that the probit and logit log likelihood functions $\ell_n^{\text{probit}}(\beta)$ and $\ell_n^{\text{logit}}(\beta)$ are globally concave in β.

The MLE is the value that maximizes $\ell_n(\beta)$. We write this as

$$\widehat{\beta}^{\text{probit}} = \underset{\beta}{\operatorname{argmax}}\, \ell_n^{\text{probit}}(\beta)$$

$$\widehat{\beta}^{\text{logit}} = \underset{\beta}{\operatorname{argmax}}\, \ell_n^{\text{logit}}(\beta).$$

Because the probit and logit log-likelihoods are globally concave, $\widehat{\beta}^{\text{probit}}$ and $\widehat{\beta}^{\text{logit}}$ are unique. There is no explicit solution, so they need to be found numerically. As the log likelihoods are smooth, concave, with known first and second derivatives, numerical optimization is straightforward.

In Stata, use the commands `probit` and `logit` to obtain the MLE. In R, use the commands

```
glm(Y~X,family=binomial(link="probit"))
glm(Y~X,family=binomial(link="logit")).
```

25.6 PSEUDO-TRUE VALUES

The expected log mass function is

$$\ell(\beta) = \mathbb{E}\left[\log G\left(Z'\beta\right)\right].$$

The model is **correctly specified** if there is a coefficient β_0 such that $\mathbb{P}[Y=1 \mid X] = G\left(X'\beta_0\right)$. When this holds, then β_0 has the property that it maximizes $\ell(\beta)$ and thus satisfies

$$\beta_0 = \underset{\beta}{\operatorname{argmax}}\, \ell(\beta). \tag{25.8}$$

We say that the model is **misspecified** if there is no β such that $\mathbb{P}[Y=1 \mid X] = G\left(X'\beta\right)$. In this case, we view the model $G\left(X'\beta\right)$ as an approximation to the response probability and define the pseudo-true coefficient β_0 as the value that satisfies (25.8). By construction, (25.8) equals the true coefficient when the model is correctly specified and otherwise produces the best-fitting model with respect to the expected log mass function.

When the distribution function $G(x)$ is log concave (as it is for the probit and logit models), then $\ell(\beta)$ is globally concave. To see this, define

$$\boldsymbol{Q}(\beta) = -\frac{\partial^2}{\partial\beta\partial\beta'}\ell(\beta) = \mathbb{E}\left[XX'H\left(Z'\beta\right)\right]$$

and observe that $H(x) > 0$ (by log concavity), which implies $\boldsymbol{Q}(\beta) \geq 0$, which implies that $\ell(\beta)$ is globally concave. Furthermore, the minimizer (25.8) is unique under the full rank condition

$$\mathbb{E}\left[XX'H\left(X'\beta_0\right)\right] > 0. \tag{25.9}$$

It is important to note that the concavity of $\ell(\beta)$ and uniqueness of the maximizer β_0 are properties of the model $G\left(X'\beta\right)$, not of the true distribution.

For specificity, for the probit and logit models, define the population criterions

$$\ell^{\text{probit}}(\beta) = \mathbb{E}\left[\log \Phi\left(Z'\beta\right)\right]$$
$$\ell^{\text{logit}}(\beta) = \mathbb{E}\left[\log \Lambda\left(Z'\beta\right)\right]$$

and the pseudo-true values

$$\beta^{\text{probit}} = \underset{\beta}{\operatorname{argmax}}\, \ell^{\text{probit}}(\beta)$$
$$\beta^{\text{logit}} = \underset{\beta}{\operatorname{argmax}}\, \ell^{\text{logit}}(\beta).$$

Let us now describe the full rank condition (25.9) for the logit and probit models. For the probit model, $H_{\text{logit}}(-x) = H_{\text{logit}}(x)$ is symmetric about 0, so $H_{\text{logit}}\left(Z'\beta\right) = H_{\text{logit}}\left(X'\beta\right) = \Lambda\left(X'\beta\right)\left(1 - \Lambda\left(X'\beta\right)\right)$. We deduce that (25.9) is the same as

$$\boldsymbol{Q}_{\text{logit}} \stackrel{\text{def}}{=} \mathbb{E}\left[XX'\Lambda\left(X'\beta^{\text{logit}}\right)\left(1 - \Lambda\left(X'\beta^{\text{logit}}\right)\right)\right] > 0. \tag{25.10}$$

For the probit model, the condition (25.9) is

$$\boldsymbol{Q}_{\text{probit}} \stackrel{\text{def}}{=} \mathbb{E}\left[XX'H_{\text{probit}}\left(Z'\beta^{\text{probit}}\right)\right] > 0. \tag{25.11}$$

When (25.10) and/or (25.11) hold, the population minimizers β^{probit} and/or β^{logit} are unique.

25.7 ASYMPTOTIC DISTRIBUTION

I first provide conditions for consistent estimation. Let B be the parameter space for β.

Theorem 25.1 Consistency of Logit Estimation. If (1) (Y_i, X_i) are i.i.d.; (2) $\mathbb{E}\|X\| < \infty$; (3) $\boldsymbol{Q}_{\text{logit}} > 0$; and (4) B is compact; then $\widehat{\beta}^{\text{logit}} \underset{p}{\longrightarrow} \beta^{\text{logit}}$ as $n \to \infty$.

Theorem 25.2 Consistency of Probit Estimation. If (1) (Y_i, X_i) are i.i.d.; (2) $\mathbb{E}\|X\|^2 < \infty$; (3) $\boldsymbol{Q}_{\text{probit}} > 0$; and (4) B is compact; then $\widehat{\beta}^{\text{probit}} \underset{p}{\longrightarrow} \beta^{\text{probit}}$ as $n \to \infty$.

The proofs are in Section 25.14. To derive the asymptotic distributions, we appeal to Theorem 22.4 for m-estimators, which shows that the asymptotic distribution is normal with a covariance matrix $\boldsymbol{V} = \boldsymbol{Q}^{-1}\Omega\boldsymbol{Q}^{-1}$, where $\boldsymbol{Q}$ is defined in (25.10) for the logit model and is defined in (25.11) for the probit model. The variance of the score is $\Omega = \mathbb{E}\left[XX'h\left(Z'\beta\right)^2\right]$. In the logit model, we have the simplification

$$\Omega_{\text{logit}} = \mathbb{E}\left[XX'\left(Y - \Lambda\left(X'\beta^{\text{logit}}\right)\right)^2\right] \tag{25.12}$$

(explained below). We do not have a similar simplification for the probit model (except under correct specification, discussed below) and thus define

$$\Omega_{\text{probit}} = \mathbb{E}\left[XX'\lambda\left(Z'\beta^{\text{probit}}\right)^2\right]. \tag{25.13}$$

To see (25.12), with some algebra, you can show that

$$h\left(Z'\beta\right)^2 = \frac{g\left(X'\beta\right)^2}{G\left(X'\beta\right)^2}Y + \frac{g\left(X'\beta\right)^2}{\left(1-G\left(X'\beta\right)\right)^2}(1-Y) = \frac{g\left(X'\beta\right)^2\left(Y-G\left(X'\beta\right)\right)^2}{G\left(X'\beta\right)^2\left(1-G\left(X'\beta\right)\right)^2}. \tag{25.14}$$

In the logit model, the right side simplifies to $\left(Y-\Lambda\left(X'\beta\right)\right)^2$, which implies

$$\Omega_{\text{logit}} = \mathbb{E}\left[XX'h_{\text{logit}}\left(Z'\beta\right)^2\right] = \mathbb{E}\left[XX'\left(Y-\Lambda\left(X'\beta^{\text{logit}}\right)\right)^2\right]$$

as claimed.

Theorem 25.3 If the conditions of Theorem 25.1 hold plus $\mathbb{E}\|X\|^4 < \infty$ and β^{logit} is in the interior of B; then as $n \to \infty$,

$$\sqrt{n}\left(\widehat{\beta}^{\text{logit}} - \beta^{\text{logit}}\right) \underset{d}{\longrightarrow} \mathrm{N}\left(0, \boldsymbol{V}_{\text{logit}}\right)$$

where $\boldsymbol{V}_{\text{logit}} = \boldsymbol{Q}_{\text{logit}}^{-1}\Omega_{\text{logit}}\boldsymbol{Q}_{\text{logit}}^{-1}$.

Theorem 25.4 If the conditions of Theorem 25.2 hold plus $\mathbb{E}\|X\|^4 < \infty$ and β^{probit} is in the interior of B, then as $n \to \infty$,

$$\sqrt{n}\left(\widehat{\beta}^{\text{probit}} - \beta^{\text{probit}}\right) \underset{d}{\longrightarrow} \mathrm{N}\left(0, \boldsymbol{V}_{\text{probit}}\right)$$

where $\boldsymbol{V}_{\text{probit}} = \boldsymbol{Q}_{\text{probit}}^{-1}\Omega_{\text{probit}}\boldsymbol{Q}_{\text{probit}}^{-1}$.

The proofs are in Section 25.14.

Under correct specification, the information matrix equality implies the simplifications $\boldsymbol{V}_{\text{logit}} = \boldsymbol{Q}_{\text{logit}}^{-1}$ and $\boldsymbol{V}_{\text{probit}} = \boldsymbol{Q}_{\text{probit}}^{-1}$. We also have the simplification

$$\Omega_{\text{probit}} = \boldsymbol{Q}_{\text{probit}} = \mathbb{E}\left[XX'\lambda\left(X'\beta^{\text{probit}}\right)\lambda\left(-X'\beta^{\text{probit}}\right)\right]. \tag{25.15}$$

This follows from (25.14), which for the probit model can be written as

$$\lambda\left(Z'\beta\right)^2 = \lambda\left(X'\beta\right)\lambda\left(-X'\beta\right)\frac{\left(Y-\Phi\left(X'\beta\right)\right)^2}{\Phi\left(X'\beta\right)\left(1-\Phi\left(X'\beta\right)\right)}.$$

Under correct specification, $\mathbb{E}\left[Y \mid X\right] = \Phi(X'\beta)$, and $\mathbb{E}\left[\left(Y-\Phi\left(X'\beta\right)\right)^2 \mid X\right] = \Phi(X'\beta)\left(1-\Phi(X'\beta)\right)$. Taking expectations given X, the above expression simplifies to $\lambda\left(X'\beta\right)\lambda\left(-X'\beta\right)$. Inserted into (25.13) it yields (25.15).

25.8 COVARIANCE MATRIX ESTIMATION

For the logit model, define $\widehat{\Lambda}_i = \Lambda\left(X_i' \widehat{\beta}^{\text{logit}}\right)$ and

$$\widehat{\boldsymbol{Q}}_{\text{logit}} = \frac{1}{n}\sum_{i=1}^{n} X_i X_i' \widehat{\Lambda}_i \left(1 - \widehat{\Lambda}_i\right)$$

$$\widehat{\Omega}_{\text{logit}} = \frac{1}{n}\sum_{i=1}^{n} X_i X_i' \left(Y_i - \widehat{\Lambda}_i\right)^2.$$

The sandwich covariance matrix estimator for $\boldsymbol{V}_{\text{logit}}$ is $\widehat{\boldsymbol{V}}_{\text{logit}} = \widehat{\boldsymbol{Q}}_{\text{logit}}^{-1} \widehat{\Omega}_{\text{logit}} \widehat{\boldsymbol{Q}}_{\text{logit}}^{-1}$. Under the assumption of correct specification, we may alternatively use $\widehat{\boldsymbol{V}}^{0}_{\text{logit}} = \widehat{\boldsymbol{Q}}_{\text{logit}}^{-1}$.

For the probit model, define $\widehat{\mu}_i = Z_i' \widehat{\beta}^{\text{probit}}$, $\widehat{\lambda}_i = \lambda\left(\widehat{\mu}_i\right)$, and

$$\widehat{\boldsymbol{Q}}_{\text{probit}} = \frac{1}{n}\sum_{i=1}^{n} X_i X_i' \widehat{\lambda}_i \left(\widehat{\mu}_i + \widehat{\lambda}_i\right)$$

$$\widehat{\Omega}_{\text{probit}} = \frac{1}{n}\sum_{i=1}^{n} X_i X_i' \widehat{\lambda}_i^2.$$

The sandwich covariance matrix estimator for $\boldsymbol{V}_{\text{probit}}$ is $\widehat{\boldsymbol{V}}_{\text{probit}} = \widehat{\boldsymbol{Q}}_{\text{probit}}^{-1} \widehat{\Omega}_{\text{probit}} \widehat{\boldsymbol{Q}}_{\text{probit}}^{-1}$. Under the assumption of correct specification, we may alternatively use

$$\widehat{\boldsymbol{Q}}^{0}_{\text{probit}} = \frac{1}{n}\sum_{i=1}^{n} X_i X_i' \lambda\left(X' \widehat{\beta}^{\text{probit}}\right) \lambda\left(-X' \widehat{\beta}^{\text{probit}}\right)$$

and $\widehat{\boldsymbol{V}}^{0}_{\text{probit}} = \left(\widehat{\boldsymbol{Q}}^{0}\right)^{-1}$.

In Stata and R, the default covariance matrix and standard errors are calculated by $\widehat{\boldsymbol{V}}^{0}_{\text{logit}}$ and $\widehat{\boldsymbol{V}}^{0}_{\text{probit}}$. For the robust covariance matrix estimation and standard errors $\widehat{\boldsymbol{V}}_{\text{logit}}$ and $\widehat{\boldsymbol{V}}_{\text{probit}}$, in Stata use the option `vce(robust)`. In R use the package `sandwich`, which has options for the HC0, HC1, and HC2 (and other) covariance matrix estimators.

25.9 MARGINAL EFFECTS

As mentioned before, it is common to focus on marginal effects rather than on coefficients, as the latter are difficult to interpret. This Section describes marginal effects in more detail and describes common estimators.

Consider the index model $\mathbb{P}[Y=1 \mid X=x] = G\left(x'\beta\right)$ when x does not include nonlinear transformations. In this case, the marginal effects are

$$\delta(x) = \frac{\partial}{\partial x} P(x) = \beta g\left(x'\beta\right).$$

This expression varies with x. For example, in Figure 25.1, we see that the marginal effect of age on marriage probability is about 0.06 per year for ages between 20 and 30, but it is close to 0 for ages above 40.

For reporting, it is typical to calculate an "average" value. There are more than one way to do so. The most common is the **average marginal effect**:

$$\mathrm{AME} = \mathbb{E}\left[\delta(X)\right] = \beta\mathbb{E}\left[g(X'\beta)\right].$$

An estimator of $\delta(x)$ is $\widehat{\delta}(x) = \widehat{\beta}g\left(x'\widehat{\beta}\right)$. An estimator of the AME is

$$\widehat{\mathrm{AME}} = \frac{1}{n}\sum_{i=1}^{n}\widehat{\delta}\left(X_i\right) = \widehat{\beta}\frac{1}{n}\sum_{i=1}^{n}g\left(X_i'\widehat{\beta}\right).$$

When the vector X includes nonlinear transformations, the marginal effects need to be carefully defined. For example, in the model $\mathbb{P}\left[Y=1 \mid X=x\right] = G\left(\beta_0 + \beta_1 x + \cdots + \beta_p x^p\right)$, the marginal effect is

$$\delta(x) = \left(\beta_1 + \cdots + p\beta_p x^{p-1}\right) g\left(\beta_0 + \beta_1 x + \cdots + \beta_p x^p\right).$$

An estimator of $\delta(x)$ is

$$\widehat{\delta}(x) = \left(\widehat{\beta}_1 + \cdots + p\widehat{\beta}_p x^{p-1}\right) g\left(\widehat{\beta}_0 + \widehat{\beta}_1 x + \cdots + \widehat{\beta}_p x^p\right).$$

An estimator of the AME is $\widehat{\mathrm{AME}} = \frac{1}{n}\sum_{i=1}^{n}\widehat{\delta}(X_i)$.

In Stata, marginal effects can be estimated with `margins, dydx(*)`.

25.10 APPLICATION

Let us illustrate these ideas with an application to the probability of marriage using the `cps09mar` dataset, selecting the subsample of men with ages up to 35 ($n = 9137$). We include as regressors an individual's age, education, and indicators for Black, Asian, Hispanic, and three regions. We estimate linear logit and linear probit models, calculate coefficients and average marginal effects, and report robust standard errors. The results are reported in Table 25.1.

Reading the table, you can see that the logit and probit coefficient estimates all have the same signs, but the logit coefficients are larger in magnitude. The probability of marriage is increasing in age, is lower for Black individuals, and varies across geographic regions. The coefficients themselves are difficult to intepret, so it is better to focus on the estimated marginal effects. Doing so, we see that the logit and probit estimates are essentially identical. This is a common finding in empirical applications when both estimates provide good approximations to the response probability. Examining the coefficients further, we see that the probability of marriage increases by about 4.5% for each year of age. The point estimate of the impact of education is 0.3% per year of education, which is a small magnitude. Black men are married with a reduced probability of 15% relative to the omitted category (men who are not Black, Asian, or Hispanic). The estimated marginal effects for Asian and Hispanic men are small (1% and −2%, respectively) relative to the omitted category. Comparing regions, we see that marriage rates are about 6–8% higher in the Midwest, South, and West relative to the Northeast (the omitted category). Equivalently, men in the Northeast have a reduced probability of about 7% relative to the rest of the country.

Two messages from this application are that the choice of logit versus probit is unimportant and that it is better to focus on marginal effects than on coefficients. A hidden message is that (as for all econometric applications) model specification is critically important. The estimates in Table 25.1 are for men aged 19–35. This choice was made so that the response probability would be well modeled with a single linear term in age. If instead the estimates were calculated on the full sample (and still using a linear specification), then the

Table 25.1
Binary choice regressions for marriage

	Logit		Probit	
Variable	Coefficient	AME	Coefficient	AME
age	0.217	0.044	0.132	0.045
	(0.006)	(0.001)	(0.003)	(0.001)
education	0.014	0.003	0.009	0.003
	(0.010)	(0.002)	(0.006)	(0.002)
Black	−0.767	−0.156	−0.454	−0.153
	(0.092)	(0.018)	(0.054)	(0.018)
Asian	0.033	0.007	0.025	0.008
	(0.103)	(0.021)	(0.063)	(0.021)
Hispanic	−0.084	−0.017	−0.048	−0.017
	(0.063)	(0.013)	(0.038)	(0.013)
Midwest	0.272	0.056	0.165	0.056
	(0.074)	(0.011)	(0.045)	(0.015)
South	0.338	0.069	0.203	0.069
	(0.070)	(0.014)	(0.043)	(0.014)
West	0.383	0.078	0.228	0.077
	(0.072)	(0.015)	(0.044)	(0.015)
Intercept	−6.45		−3.93	
	(0.21)		(0.12)	

estimated marginal effect of age would have been 1% per year rather than 4.5%, a large mis-estimate of the effect of age on marriage probability.

25.11 SEMIPARAMETRIC BINARY CHOICE

The semiparametric binary choice model is

$$\mathbb{P}[Y=1 \mid X]=G\left(X'\beta\right)$$

where $G(x)$ is unknown. Interest typically focuses on the coefficient β.

In the latent variable framework, $G(x)$ is the distribution function of a latent error e. As it is not credible that the distribution $G(x)$ is known, the semiparametric model treats $G(x)$ as unknown. The goal is to estimate the coefficient β while remaining agnostic about $G(x)$.

There are many contributions to this literature. Two of the most influential are Manski (1975) and Klein and Spady (1993). Both use the latent variable framework $Y^*=X'\beta+e$.

Manksi (1975) shows that β is identified up to scale if $\operatorname{med}[e \mid X]=0$. He proposes a clever **maximum score estimator** that is consistent for β up to scale under this weak condition. His method, however, does not permit estimation of the response probabilities or marginal effects, because his assumptions are insufficient to identify $G(x)$.

Klein and Spady (1993) add the assumption that e is independent of X, which implies identification of $G(x)$. They propose simultaneous estimation of β and $G(x)$ based on the following two properties: (1) If $G(x)$ is known, then β can be estimated by maximum likelihood; (2) If β is known, then $G(x)$ can be estimated by nonparametric regression of Y on $X'\beta$. Combining these two properties into a nested criterion, they produce a consistent, asymptotically normal, and efficient estimator of β.

Although the ideas of Manski and Klein-Spady are quite clever, the trouble is that the model $G(x'\beta)$ relies on the parametric linear index assumption. Suppose we relax the latter to a nonparametric function $m(x)$ but assume that e is independent of X. Then the response probability is $1-G(-m(x))$. In this case, neither $G(x)$ nor $m(x)$ is identifed; only the composite function $G(-m(x))$ is identified. Thus estimation of $m(x)$, while agnostic about $G(x)$, is impossible without a parametric assumption about $m(x)$. Consequently, the modern view is to take $P(x)=\mathbb{P}[Y=1 \mid X=x]$ as nonparametrically identified. Consistent estimation can be achieved by a series approximation, using a linear, probit, or logit link. From this viewpoint, there is no gain from the restriction to the function form $G(x'\beta)$, and hence no gain from the semiparametric approach.

25.12 IV PROBIT

A latent variable structural equation model is

$$\begin{aligned} Y_1^* &= X'\beta_1 + Y_2\beta_2 + e_1 \\ Y_2 &= X'\gamma_1 + Z'\gamma_2 + e_2 \\ Y_1 &= \mathbb{1}\left\{Y_1^* > 0\right\}. \end{aligned}$$

In this model, Y_2 is scalar, endogenous, and continuously distributed; the X are included exogenous regressors, and the Z are excluded exogenous instruments.

The standard estimation method is maximum likelihood based on the assumption that the errors are jointly normal:

$$\left(\begin{array}{c} e_1 \\ e_2 \end{array}\right)\Bigg| (X,Z) \sim \mathrm{N}\left(\left(\begin{array}{c} 0 \\ 0 \end{array}\right), \left(\begin{array}{cc} 1 & \sigma_{12} \\ \sigma_{21} & \sigma_2^2 \end{array}\right)\right).$$

The likelihood is derived as follows. The regression of e_1 on e_2 equals

$$\begin{aligned} e_1 &= \rho e_2 + \varepsilon \\ \rho &= \frac{\sigma_{12}}{\sigma_2^2} \\ \varepsilon &\sim \mathrm{N}\left(0, \sigma_\varepsilon^2\right) \\ \sigma_\varepsilon^2 &= 1 - \frac{\sigma_{12}^2}{\sigma_2^2}. \end{aligned}$$

Using these relationships, we can write the structural equation as

$$\begin{aligned} Y_1^* &= \mu(\theta) + \varepsilon \qquad (25.16) \\ \mu(\theta) &= X'\beta_1 + Y_2\beta_2 + \rho\left(Y_2 - X'\gamma_1 - Z'\gamma_2\right). \end{aligned}$$

The error ε is independent of e_2 and hence of Y_2. Thus the conditional distribution of Y_1^* is $\mathrm{N}\left(\mu(\theta), \sigma_\varepsilon^2\right)$. It follows that the joint density for (Y_1, Y_2) is

$$\Phi\left(\frac{\mu(\theta)}{\sigma_\varepsilon}\right)^{Y_1}\left(1-\Phi\left(\frac{\mu(\theta)}{\sigma_\varepsilon}\right)\right)^{1-Y_1}\frac{1}{\sigma_2}\phi\left(\frac{Y_2 - X'\gamma_1 - Z'\gamma_2}{\sigma_2}\right).$$

The parameter vector is $\theta = \left(\beta_1, \beta_2, \gamma_1, \gamma_2, \rho, \sigma_\varepsilon^2, \sigma_2^2\right)$.

The joint log-likelihood for a random sample $\{Y_{1i}, Y_{2i}, X_i, Z_i\}$ is

$$\ell_n(\theta) = \sum_{i=1}^{n} \left[Y_{1i} \log \Phi\left(\frac{\mu_i(\theta)}{\sigma_\varepsilon}\right) + (1 - Y_{1i}) \log\left(1 - \Phi\left(\frac{\mu_i(\theta)}{\sigma_\varepsilon}\right)\right)\right]$$

$$- \frac{n}{2}\log(2\pi) - \frac{n}{2}\log\sigma_2^2 - \frac{1}{2\sigma_2^2}\sum_{i=1}^{n}\left(Y_{2i} - X_i'\gamma_1 - Z_i'\gamma_2\right)^2.$$

The maximum likelihood estimator $\widehat{\theta}$ is found by numerically maximizing $\ell_n(\theta)$.

The probit assumption (the treatment of (e_1, e_2) as jointly normal) is important for this derivation, as it allows a simple factorization of the joint distribution into the conditional distribution of Y_1 given Y_2 and the marginal distribution of Y_2. A similar factorization is not easily accomplished in a logit framework.

In Stata, this estimator can be implemented with the `ivprobit` command.

25.13 BINARY PANEL DATA

A binary choice panel model is typically written as

$$Y_{it}^* = X_{it}'\beta + u_i + e_{it}$$

$$Y_{it} = \mathbb{1}\left\{Y_{it}^* > 0\right\}.$$

Here, the observations are (Y_{it}, X_{it}) for $i = 1, \ldots, n$ and $t = 1, \ldots, T$, with Y_{it} binary. For example, Y_{it} could denote the decision of individual i to make a purchase in period t. The individual effect u_i is intended to capture the feature that some individuals i make purchases more (or less) frequently than can be explained by the regressors.

As in linear models, there is a distinction between treating the individual effect u_i as **random** (meaning that it is independent of the regressors) or **fixed** (meaning that it is correlated with the regressors).

Under the random effects assumption, the model can be estimated by maximum likelihood. This is called **random effects probit** or **random effects logit**, depending on the error distribution.

Allowing for fixed effects is more complicated. The individual effect cannot be eliminated by a linear operation, because Y_{it} is a nonlinear function of u_i. For example, the transformation

$$\Delta Y_{it} = \mathbb{1}\left\{Y_{it}^* > 0\right\} - \mathbb{1}\left\{Y_{i,t-1}^* > 0\right\}$$

does not eliminate u_i.

Consequently, there is no fixed effects estimator for the probit model. However, for the logit model, Chamberlain (1980, 1984) developed a fixed effects estimator based on a conditional likelihood. He showed that a feature of the logistic distribution is that the individual effect can be eliminated via odds ratios, allowing the calculation of the likelihood conditional on the sum of the dependent variables.

Let us illustrate the construction of the likelihood for the case $T = 2$. Let Y_{i1}, Y_{i2} denote the outcomes, and $N_i = Y_{i1} + Y_{i2}$ denote their sum. We can calculate the conditional distribution of (Y_{i1}, Y_{i2}) given N_i. This is the distribution of the choices given the total number of choices.

When $N_i = 0$ or $N_i = 2$, the likelihood is trivial. That is,

$$\mathbb{P}\left[Y_{it} = 0 \mid N_i = 0\right] = 0$$

$$\mathbb{P}\left[Y_{it} = 1 \mid N_i = 2\right] = 1.$$

This does not depend on β, so it does not affect estimation. Thus we focus exclusively on the case $N_i = 1$.

The choice probabilities are

$$\mathbb{P}[Y_{it} = 0] = \frac{\exp\left(-X_{it}'\beta - u_i\right)}{1 + \exp\left(-X_{it}'\beta - u_i\right)}$$
$$\mathbb{P}[Y_{it} = 1] = \frac{1}{1 + \exp\left(-X_{it}'\beta - u_i\right)}.$$

Their ratio is

$$\frac{\mathbb{P}[Y_{it} = 0]}{\mathbb{P}[Y_{it} = 1]} = \exp\left(-X_{it}'\beta - u_i\right).$$

Taking a further ratio for $t = 1$ and $t = 2$, we obtain

$$\frac{\mathbb{P}[Y_{i1} = 0]}{\mathbb{P}[Y_{i1} = 1]} \frac{\mathbb{P}[Y_{i2} = 1]}{\mathbb{P}[Y_{i2} = 0]} = \frac{\exp\left(-X_{1t}'\beta - u_i\right)}{\exp\left(-X_{2t}'\beta - u_i\right)} = \exp\left((X_{2t} - X_{1t})'\beta\right).$$

This ratio does not depend on the fixed effect u_i. It is a function only of the change in the regressors $\Delta X_i = X_{i2} - X_{i1}$.

This is effectively a nonlinear within transformation. This odds ratio eliminates dependence on the individual effect, due to the exponential structure of the logistic distribution. This property is special to the logit model and allows construction of a conditional likelihood function that is free of u_i.

Consider the choice probability for period 1 given $N_i = 1$. It is

$$\begin{aligned}
\mathbb{P}[Y_{i1} = 1 \mid N_i = 1] &= \frac{\mathbb{P}[Y_{i1} = 1, Y_{i2} = 0]}{\mathbb{P}[Y_{i1} = 1, Y_{i2} = 0] + \mathbb{P}[Y_{i1} = 0, Y_{i2} = 1]} \\
&= \frac{\mathbb{P}[Y_{i1} = 1]\,\mathbb{P}[Y_{i2} = 0]}{\mathbb{P}[Y_{i1} = 1]\,\mathbb{P}[Y_{i2} = 0] + \mathbb{P}[Y_{i1} = 0]\,\mathbb{P}[Y_{i2} = 1]} \\
&= \frac{1}{1 + \frac{\mathbb{P}[Y_{i1}=0]}{\mathbb{P}[Y_{i1}=1]}\frac{\mathbb{P}[Y_{i2}=1]}{\mathbb{P}[Y_{i2}=0]}} \\
&= \frac{1}{1 + \exp\left(\Delta X_i'\beta\right)} \\
&= 1 - \Lambda\left(\Delta X_i'\beta\right).
\end{aligned}$$

Similarly, $\mathbb{P}[Y_{i1} = 0 \mid N_i = 1] = \Lambda\left(\Delta X_i'\beta\right)$. Combining these results, the log-likelihood function is

$$\ell_n(\beta) = \sum_{i=1}^{n} \mathbb{1}\{N_i = 1\}\left[(1 - Y_{i1})\, Y_{2i} \log \Lambda\left(\Delta X_i'\beta\right) + Y_{i1}\,(1 - Y_{i2}) \log\left(1 - \Lambda\left(\Delta X_{it}'\beta\right)\right)\right].$$

This conditional likelihood is free of the individual effect. Because the conditional likelihood can be computed, it can be maximized to obtain the **conditional likelihood estimator**.

For the likelihood to be a nondegenerate function of β, it is necessary for there to be individuals who are **switchers** (select $Y = 0$ in one period and $Y = 1$ in the other period) and that switchers have time-varying regressors. Coefficients for time-invariant regressors are not identified.

Our derivation focused on $T = 2$. The extension to $T > 2$ is similar but is algebraically complicated.

In Stata, random effects probit is implemented with `xtoprobit` and random effects logit with `xtologit`. Fixed effects probit can be implemented with `xtologit, fe` or `clogit`.

25.14 TECHNICAL PROOFS*

Proof of Theorem 25.1 The MLE $\widehat{\beta}^{\,\text{logit}}$ is an m-estimator, so we appeal to Theorem 22.3, which shows that $\widehat{\beta}^{\text{logit}}$ is consistent under five conditions. Conditions 1 and 4 hold by assumption. Condition 5 (β^{logit} uniquely minimizes $\ell^{\text{logit}}(\beta)$) holds under the assumption $\boldsymbol{Q}_{\text{logit}} > 0$. The log-likelihood components $\log \Lambda\left(Z'\beta\right)$ are continuous over any compact set B, so condition 2 holds. Finally,

$$\left|\log \Lambda(t)\right| = -\log \Lambda(t) = \log\left(1+\exp(-t)\right) \leq \log\left(1+\exp(|t|)\right) \leq \log(2) + |t|\,.$$

Thus,

$$\left|\log \Lambda(Z'\beta)\right| \leq \log(2) + \left|X'\beta\right| \leq \log(2) + \|\beta\|\,\|X\| \leq \log(2) + \overline{\beta}\,\|X\|$$

where $\overline{\beta} = \sup_{\beta\in B}\|\beta\|$. The right side has finite expectation, because $\mathbb{E}\,\|X\| < \infty$ by assumption, which establishes condition 3. Thus, the five conditions of Theorem 22.3 are satisfied. ■

Proof of Theorem 25.2 Following the proof of Theorem 25.1, we need to show that $\left|\log \Phi\left(Z'\beta\right)\right| \leq G(Z)$ with $\mathbb{E}\,|G(Z)| < \infty$.

Theorem 5.7 part 6 of *Probability and Statistics for Economists* states that

$$\frac{d}{dt}\log \Phi(t) = \lambda(t) = \frac{\phi(t)}{\Phi(t)} \leq 1 + |t| \tag{25.17}$$

which implies

$$\left|\log \Phi\,(t)\right| = -\log \Phi\,(t) \leq \log\left(\sqrt{2\pi}\right) + \frac{t^2}{2} + \log(1+|t|) \leq \log\left(\sqrt{2\pi}\right) + \frac{t^2}{2} + |t|\,.$$

Using the Schwarz inequality (B.12)

$$\left|\log \Phi\left(Z'\beta\right)\right| \leq \log\left(\sqrt{2\pi}\right) + \frac{1}{2}\left|X'\beta\right|^2 + \left|X'\beta\right| \leq 2\log\left(\sqrt{2\pi}\right) + \frac{1}{2}\overline{\beta}^2\,\|X\|^2 + \overline{\beta}\,\|X\|$$

where $\overline{\beta} = \sup_{\beta\in B}\|\beta\|$. The right side has finite expectation, because $\mathbb{E}\,\|X\|^2 < \infty$. ■

Proof of Theorem 25.3 Since $\widehat{\beta}^{\text{logit}}$ is an m-estimator, we verify the five conditions for Theorem 22.4.

Conditions 2 and 5 hold by assumption.

Since $\left|h_{\text{logit}}(t)\right| \leq 1$, we see that $\mathbb{E}\left[\left\|Zh_{\text{logit}}\left(Z'\beta^{\text{logit}}\right)\right\|^2\right] \leq \mathbb{E}\,\|X\|^2 < \infty$. Thus condition 1 holds.

The function $\boldsymbol{Q}_{\text{logit}}(\beta)$ is bounded and $\Lambda(x)$ is continuous. Thus $\boldsymbol{Q}_{\text{logit}}(\beta)$ is continuous in β, and condition 3 holds.

As shown in Exercise 25.5(d), $\left|H_{\text{logit}}(t)\right| \leq 1$. Then

$$\mathbb{E}\left[\sup_{\beta}\left\|\frac{\partial}{\partial\beta}Zh_{\text{logit}}\left(X'\beta\right)\right\|^2\right] \leq \mathbb{E}\,\|X\|^4\,\sup_t\left|H_{\text{logit}}\,(t)\right| < \infty$$

which implies condition 4.

We have verified the five conditions for Theorem 22.4, as needed. ■

Proof of Theorem 25.4 The proof follows the same lines as Theorem 25.3, by verifying conditions 1, 3, and 4 of Theorem 22.4.

Using (25.17), we have

$$\mathbb{E}\left\|Z\lambda\left(Z'\beta^{\text{probit}}\right)\right\|^2 \leq \mathbb{E}\left(\|X\|\left(1+\left|X'\beta^{\text{probit}}\right|\right)\right)^2 \leq \mathbb{E}\|X\|^2 + \left\|\beta^{\text{probit}}\right\|^2 \mathbb{E}\|X\|^4 < \infty$$

implying condition 1.

The function $\boldsymbol{Q}_{\text{probit}}(\beta)$ is bounded, and $H_{\text{probit}}(x)$ is continuous. Thus $\boldsymbol{Q}_{\text{probit}}(\beta)$ is continuous in β, and condition 3 holds.

Theorem 5.7 part 7 of *Probability and Statistics for Economists* states that $\left|H_{\text{probit}}(t)\right| \leq 1$. Thus by the same argument as in the proof of Theorem 25.3, we can verify condition 4.

We have verified the conditions for Theorem 22.4, as needed. ■

25.15 EXERCISES

Exercise 25.1 Emily estimates a probit regression setting her dependent variable to equal $Y = 1$ for a purchase and $Y = 0$ for no purchase. Using the same data and regressors, Jacob estimates a probit regression setting the dependent variable to equal $Y = 1$ if there is no purchase and $Y = 0$ for a purchase. What is the difference in their estimated slope coefficients?

Exercise 25.2 Jackson estimates a logit regression where the primary regressor is measured in dollars. Julie estimates a logit regression with the same sample and dependent variable but measures the primary regressor in thousands of dollars. What is the difference in the estimated slope coefficients?

Exercise 25.3 Show (25.1) and (25.2).

Exercise 25.4 Verify (25.5), that $\pi(Y \mid X) = G\left(Z'\beta\right)$.

Exercise 25.5 For the logistic distribution $\Lambda(x) = \left(1+\exp(-x)\right)^{-1}$, verify that

(a) $\frac{d}{dx}\Lambda(x) = \Lambda(x)(1-\Lambda(x))$.
(b) $h_{\text{logit}}(x) = \frac{d}{dx}\log\Lambda(x) = 1-\Lambda(x)$.
(c) $H_{\text{logit}}(x) = -\frac{d^2}{dx^2}\log\Lambda(x) = \Lambda(x)\left(1-\Lambda(x)\right)$.
(d) $\left|H_{\text{logit}}(x)\right| \leq 1$.

Exercise 25.6 For the normal distribution $\Phi(x)$, verify that

(a) $h_{\text{probit}}(x) = \frac{d}{dx}\log\Phi(x) = \lambda(x)$, where $\lambda(x) = \phi(x)/\Phi(x)$.
(b) $H_{\text{probit}}(x) = -\frac{d^2}{dx^2}\log\Phi(x) = \lambda(x)\left(x+\lambda(x)\right)$.

Exercise 25.7

(a) Verify equations (25.6) and (25.7).
(b) Verify the assertion that $H(x) > 0$ implies that $\mathscr{H}_n(\beta) > 0$ globally in β.
(c) Verify the assertion that part (b) implies that $\ell_n(\beta)$ is globally concave in β.

Exercise 25.8 Find the first-order condition for β_0 from the population maximization problem (25.8).

Exercise 25.9 Find the first-order condition for the logit MLE $\widehat{\beta}^{\text{logit}}$.

Exercise 25.10 Find the first-order condition for the probit MLE $\widehat{\beta}^{\text{probit}}$.

Exercise 25.11 Show (25.14). In the logit model, show that the right side of (25.14) simplifies to $\left(Y - \Lambda\left(X'\beta\right)\right)^2$.

Exercise 25.12 Show how to use nonlinear least squares (NLLS) to estimate a probit model.

Exercise 25.13 Consider the endogenous probit model of Section 25.12.

(a) Verify equation (25.16).
(b) Explain why ε is independent of e_2 and Y_2.
(c) Verify that the conditional distribution of Y_1^* is $\mathrm{N}\left(\mu(\theta), \sigma_\varepsilon^2\right)$.

Exercise 25.14 Consider the heteroskedastic nonparametric binary choice model

$$
\begin{aligned}
Y^* &= m(X) + e \\
e \mid X &\sim \mathrm{N}\left(0, \sigma^2(X)\right) \\
Y &= Y^* \mathbb{1}\left\{Y^* > 0\right\}.
\end{aligned}
$$

The observables are $\{Y_i, X_i : i = 1, \ldots, n\}$. The functions $m(x)$ and $\sigma^2(x)$ are nonparametric.

(a) Find a formula for the response probability .
(b) Are $m(x)$ and $\sigma^2(x)$ both identified? Explain.
(c) Find a normalization that achieves identification.
(d) Given your answer to part (c), does it make sense to "allow for heteroskedasticity" in the binary choice model? Explain.

Exercise 25.15 Use the `cps09mar` dataset and the subset of men. Set $Y = 1$ if the individual is a member of a labor union (*union* = 1) and $Y = 0$ otherwise. Estimate a probit model as a linear function of *age*, *education*, and indicators for Black individuals and for Hispanic individuals. Report the coefficient estimates and standard errors. Interpret the results.

Exercise 25.16 Replicate exercise 25.15 but with the subset of women. Interpret the results.

Exercise 25.17 Use the `cps09mar` dataset and the subset of women with a college degree. Set $Y = 1$ if *marital* equals 1, 2, or 3, and set $Y = 0$ otherwise. Estimate a binary choice model for Y as a possibly nonlinear function of *age*. Describe the motivation for the model you use. Plot the estimated response probability. How do the estimates compare with those for men from Figure 25.1?

Exercise 25.18 Use the `cps09mar` dataset and the subset of men. Set Y as in exercise 25.17. Estimate a binary choice model for Y as a possibly nonlinear function of *age*, a linear function of *education*, and including indicators for Black individuals and for Hispanic individuals. Report the coefficient estimates and standard errors. Interpret the results.

Exercise 25.19 Replicate exercise 25.18 but with the subset of women. Interpret the results.

CHAPTER 26
MULTIPLE CHOICE

26.1 INTRODUCTION

This chapter surveys multinomial models, including multinomial response, multinomial logit, conditional logit, nested logit, mixed logit, multinomial probit, ordered response, count data, and the BLP demand model.

For more detailed treatments, see Maddala (1983), Cameron and Trivedi (1998, 2005), Train (2009), and Wooldridge (2010).

26.2 MULTINOMIAL RESPONSE

A **multinomial** random variable Y takes values in a finite set, typically written as $Y \in \{1, 2, \ldots, J\}$. The elements of the set are often called **alternatives**. In most applications, the alternatives are categorical (e.g., car, bicycle, airplane, train) and unordered. When there are no regressors, the model is fully described by the J probabilities $P_j = \mathbb{P}\left[Y = j\right]$.

We typically describe the pair (Y, X) as a **multinomial response** when Y is multinomial and $X \in \mathbb{R}^k$ are regressors. The conditional distribution of Y given X is summarized by the **response probability:**

$$P_j(x) = \mathbb{P}\left[Y = j \mid X = x\right].$$

The response probabilities are nonparametrically identified and can be arbitrary functions of x.

I illustrate by extending the marriage status example of Chapter 25. The CPS variable *marital* records seven categories. Partition these into four alternatives: "married,"[1] "divorced," "separated," and "never married." Let X be *age*. The probability of each marriage status as a function of age is $P_j(x)$ for $j = 1, \ldots, 4$. For our illustration, let us take the population of college-educated women.

Since the response probabilities $P_j(x)$ are nonparametrically identified, a simple estimation method is binary response separately for each category. Figure 26.1(a) plots logit estimates using a quadratic spline in age and a single knot at age 40. The estimates show that the probability of "never married" decreases monotonically with age, the probability for "married" increases until around 38 and then decreases slowly, the probability of "divorced" increases monotonically with age, and the probability of "separated" is low for all age groups.

A defect of the estimates of Figure 26.1(a) is that the sum of the four estimated probabilities (displayed as "Total") does not equal 1, which shows that separate estimation of the response probabilities neglects system information. For the remainder of this chapter, the estimators discussed do not have this defect.

[1] *marital* =1,2,3,4, which includes widowed.

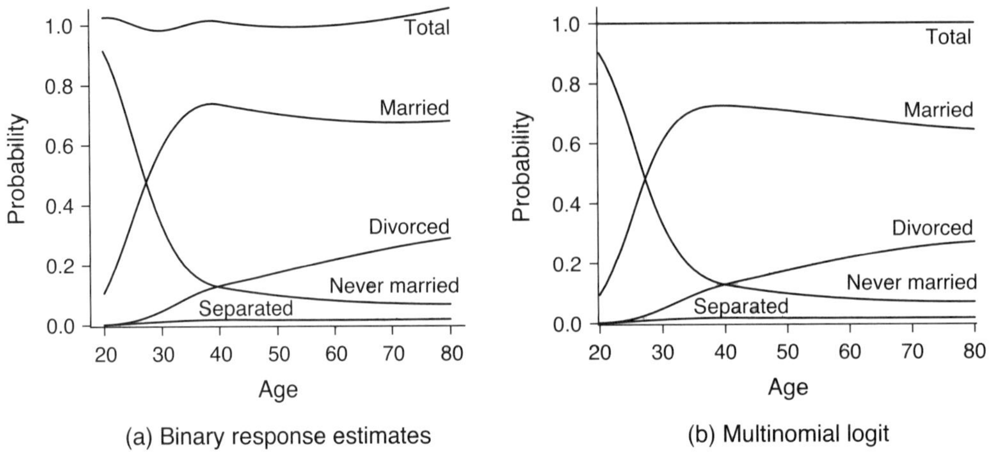

FIGURE 26.1 Probability of marital status given age for college educated women

Multinomial response is typically motivated and derived from a model of latent utility. The utility of alternative j is assumed to equal

$$U_j^* = X'\beta_j + \varepsilon_j \tag{26.1}$$

where β_j are coefficients and ε_j is an alternative-specific error. The coefficients β_j describe how the variable X affects an individual's utility of alternative j. The error ε_j is individual-specific and contains unobserved factors affecting an individual's utility. In the marriage status example (where X is age), the coefficients β_j describe how the utility of each marriage status varies with *age*, and the error ε_j contains the individual factors that are not captured by *age*.

In the latent utility model, an individual is assumed to select the alternative with the highest utility U_j^*. Thus $Y = j$ if $U_j^* \geq U_\ell^*$ for all ℓ. In model (26.1), this choice is unaltered if we add $X'\gamma$ to each utility. Thus the coefficients β_j are not separately identified; at best, the differences between alternatives $\beta_j - \beta_\ell$ are identified. Identification is achieved by imposing a normalization; the standard choice is to set $\beta_j = 0$ for a **base alternative** j, often taken as the last category J. Reported coefficients β_j should be interpreted as differences relative to the base alternative.

The choice is also unchanged if each utility (26.1) is multiplied by a positive constant. Thus the scale of the coefficients β_j is not identified. To achieve identification, it is typical to fix the scale of the errors ε_j. Consequently the scale of the coefficients β_j has no interpretive meaning.

Two classical multinomial response models are logit and probit. We discuss multinomial logit in Section 26.3 and multinomial probit in Section 26.8.

26.3 MULTINOMIAL LOGIT

The **simple multinomial logit** model is

$$P_j(x) = \frac{\exp\left(x'\beta_j\right)}{\sum_{\ell=1}^{J} \exp\left(x'\beta_\ell\right)}. \tag{26.2}$$

The model includes binary logit ($J=2$) as a special case. We call (26.2) the *simple* multinomial logit to distinguish it from the conditional logit model of Section 26.4.

The multinomial logit arises from the latent utility model (26.1) for the following error distributions.

Definition 26.1 The **Type I extreme value** distribution function is

$$F(\varepsilon)=\exp\left(-\exp(-\varepsilon)\right).$$

Definition 26.2 The **generalized extreme value (GEV)** joint distribution is

$$F(\varepsilon_1,\varepsilon_2,\ldots,\varepsilon_J)=\exp\left(-\left[\sum_{j=1}^{J}\exp\left(-\frac{\varepsilon_j}{\tau}\right)\right]^{\tau}\right) \tag{26.3}$$

for $0<\tau\leq 1$.

For $J=1$, the GEV distribution (26.3) equals the Type I extreme value. For $J>1$ and $\tau=1$, the GEV distribution equals the product of independent Type I extreme value distributions. For $J>1$ and $\tau<1$, GEV random variables are dependent with correlation equal to $1-\tau^2$ (see Kotz and Nadarajah (2000)). The parameter τ is known as the **dissimilarity** parameter. The distribution (26.3) is a special case of the "GEV distribution" introduced by McFadden (1981). Furthermore, there is heterogeneity among authors regarding the choice of notation and labeling. The notation used above is consistent with the Stata manual. In contrast, McFadden (1978, 1981) uses $1-\sigma$ in place of τ and calls σ the "similarity parameter." Cameron and Trivedi (2005) use ρ instead of τ and call ρ the "scale parameter."

The following result is due to McFadden (1978, 1981).

Theorem 26.1 Assume that the utility of alternative j is $U_j^*=X'\beta_j+\varepsilon_j$ and the error vector $(\varepsilon_1,\ldots,\varepsilon_J)$ has GEV distribution (26.3). Then the response probabilities equal

$$P_j(X)=\frac{\exp\left(X'\beta_j/\tau\right)}{\sum_{\ell=1}^{J}\exp\left(X'\beta_\ell/\tau\right)}.$$

The proof is in Section 26.13. The response probabilities in Theorem 26.1 are multinomial logit (26.2) with coefficients $\beta_j^*=\beta_j/\tau$. The dissimilarity parameter τ only affects the scale of the coefficients, which is not identified. Thus GEV errors imply a multinomial logit model and τ is not identified.

As discussed above, when $\tau=1$, the GEV distribution (26.3) specializes to i.i.d. Type I extreme value. Thus a special case of Theorem 26.1 is the following: If the errors ε_j are i.i.d. Type I extreme value, then the response probabilities are multinomial logit (26.2) with coefficients β_j. This is the most commonly used and commonly stated implication of Theorem 26.1.

In contemporary choice modeling, a common assumption is that utility is extreme value distributed. This is done so that Theorem 26.1 can be invoked to deduce that the choice probabilities are multinomial logit.

A reasonable deduction is that this assumption is made for algebraic convenience, not because anyone believes that utility is actually extreme value distributed.

The likelihood function given a random sample $\{Y_i, X_i\}$ is straightforward to construct. Write the response probabilities $P_j(X \mid \beta)$ as functions of the parameter vector $\beta = (\beta_1, \ldots, \beta_J)$. The probability mass function for Y is

$$\pi(Y \mid X, \beta) = \prod_{j=1}^{J} P_j(X \mid \beta)^{\mathbb{1}\{Y=j\}}.$$

The log-likelihood function is

$$\ell_n(\beta) = \sum_{i=1}^{n} \sum_{j=1}^{J} \mathbb{1}\left\{Y_i = j\right\} \log P_j(X_i \mid \beta).$$

The maximum likelihood estimator (MLE) is:

$$\widehat{\beta} = \underset{\beta}{\operatorname{argmax}}\, \ell_n(\beta).$$

There is no algebraic solution, so $\widehat{\beta}$ needs to be found numerically. The log-likelihood function is globally concave, so maximization is numerically straightforward.

To illustrate, let us return to the marriage status example of Section 26.2 using multinomial logit. The estimated response probabilities are displayed in Figure 26.1(b). The estimates are similar to the binary choice estimates in panel (a) but by construction sum to 1.

The coefficients of a multinomial choice model can be difficult to interpret. Therefore in applications, it may be useful to examine and report marginal effects. We can calculate[2] that the marginal effects are

$$\delta_j(x) = \frac{\partial}{\partial x} P_j(x) = P_j(x) \left(\beta_j - \sum_{\ell=1}^{J} \beta_\ell P_\ell(x) \right) \tag{26.4}$$

which is estimated by

$$\widehat{\delta}_j(x) = \widehat{P}_j(x) \left(\widehat{\beta}_j - \sum_{\ell=1}^{J} \widehat{\beta}_\ell \widehat{P}_\ell(x) \right).$$

The average marginal effect $\mathrm{AME}_j = \mathbb{E}\left[\delta_j(X)\right]$ can be estimated by

$$\widehat{\mathrm{AME}}_j = \frac{1}{n} \sum_{i=1}^{n} \widehat{\delta}_j(X_i). \tag{26.5}$$

In Stata, multinomial logit can be implemented using the `mlogit` command. Probabilities can be calculated by `predict` and average marginal effects by `margins,dydx`. In R, multinomial logit can be implemented using the `mlogit` command.

[2] See Exercise 26.3.

26.4 CONDITIONAL LOGIT

In the simple multinomial logit model of Section 26.3, the regressors X (e.g., age) are specific to the individual but not the alternative (they do not have a j subscript). In most applications, however, there are regressors that vary across alternatives. A typical example is the price or cost of an alternative. In a latent utility model, it is reasonable to assume that these alternative-specific regressors only affect an individual's utility if that specific alternative is selected. A choice model allowing for regressors that differ across alternatives was developed by McFadden in the 1970s, which he called the **conditional logit** model.

An example will help illustrate the setting. Suppose you (a student) need to select a mode of travel from your apartment to the university. Travel alternatives include walk, bicycle, bus, train, or car. Which will you select? Your choice will undoubtedly depend on a number of factors, and of particular importance is the cost[3] of each alternative. We can model this by specifying that the utility Y_j^* (26.1) of alternative j is a function of its cost X_j.

As a concrete example, consider the dataset `Koppelman` on the textbook webpage. This is an abridged version of the dataset `ModeCanada` distributed with the R package `mlogit` and used in the papers Forinash and Koppelman (1993), Koppelman and Wen (2000), and Wen and Koppelman (2001). The data are responses to a survey[4] of Canadian business travelers concerning their actual travel choices in the Toronto-Montreal corridor. Each observation ($n = 2,779$) is a specific individual making a specific trip. Four travel alternatives were considered: train, air, bus, and car. Available regressors include the *cost* of each alternative, the in-vehicle travel time (*intime*) of each alternative, household *income*, and an indicator if one of the trip endpoints is an *urban* center.

The conditional logit model posits that the utility of alternative j is a function of regressors X_j that vary across alternative j:

$$U_j^* = X_j'\gamma + \varepsilon_j. \tag{26.6}$$

Here, γ are coefficients, and ε_j is an alternative-specific error. Notice that in contrast to (26.1), X_j varies across j while the coefficients γ are common. In the `Koppelman` dataset, the variables *cost* and *intime* are recorded for each individual/alternative pair. (For example, the first observation in the sample is a traveler who could have selected train travel for \$58.25 and a travel time of 215 minutes, air travel for \$142.80 and 56 minutes, bus travel for \$27.52 and 301 minutes, or car travel for \$71.63 and 262 minutes. This traveler selected to travel by air.)

To understand the difference between the multinomial logit and the conditional logit models, (26.1) describes how the utility of a specific alternative (e.g., married or divorced) is affected by a variable such as *age*. This requires a separate coefficient for each alternative to have an impact. In contrast, (26.6) describes how the utility of an alternative (e.g., train or car) is affected by factors such as *cost* and *time*. These variables have common meanings across alternatives, so the restriction that the coefficients are common appears reasonable.

More generally, the conditional logit model allows some regressors X_j to vary across alternatives while other regressors W do not vary across j. This model is

$$U_j^* = W'\beta_j + X_j'\gamma + \varepsilon_j. \tag{26.7}$$

For example, in the `Koppelman` dataset, the variables *cost* and *intime* are components of X_j, while the variables *income* and *urban* are components of W.

[3]Cost can be multidimensional, for example, including monetary cost and travel time.

[4]The survey was conducted by the Canadian national rail carrier to assess the demand for high-speed rail.

In model (26.7), the coefficients γ and coefficient differences $\beta_j - \beta_\ell$ are identified up to scale. Identification is achieved by normalizing the scale of ε_j and setting $\beta_J = 0$ for a base alternative J.

The conditional logit model is (26.6) or (26.7) plus the assumption that the errors ε_j are distributed i.i.d. Type I extreme value.[5] From Theorem 26.1, we deduce that the probability response functions equal

$$P_j(w,x) = \frac{\exp\left(w'\beta_j + x_j'\gamma\right)}{\sum_{\ell=1}^{J} \exp\left(w'\beta_\ell + x_\ell'\gamma\right)}. \tag{26.8}$$

This is multinomial logit but with regressors and coefficients $W'\beta_j + X_j'\gamma$.

Let $\theta = \left(\beta_1, \ldots \beta_J, \gamma\right)$. Given the observations $\{Y_i, W_i, X_i\}$, where $X_i = \{X_{1i}, \ldots, X_{Ji}\}$, the log-likelihood function is

$$\ell_n(\theta) = \sum_{i=1}^{n} \sum_{j=1}^{J} \mathbb{1}\left\{Y_i = j\right\} \log P_j(W_i, X_i \mid \theta).$$

The maximum likelihood estimator (MLE) $\widehat{\theta}$ maximizes $\ell_n(\theta)$. There is no algebraic solution, so $\widehat{\theta}$ needs to be found numerically.

Using the `Koppelman` dataset, we can estimate a conditional logit model. Estimates are reported in Table 26.1. Included as regressors are *cost*, *intime*, *income*, and *urban*. The base alternative is travel by train. The first two coefficient estimates are negative, meaning that the probability of selecting any mode of transport is decreasing in the monetary and time cost of this mode of travel. The income and urban variables are not alternative-specific, so they have coefficients that vary by alternative. The urban coefficient for air is positive and that for car is negative, indicating that the probability of air travel is increased relative to train travel if an endpoint is urban, and conversely for car travel. The income coefficient is positive for air travel and negative for bus travel, indicating that transportation choice is affected by a traveler's income in the expected way.

As discussed previously, coefficient estimates can be difficult to interpret. It may be useful to calculate transformations, such as average marginal effects. The average marginal effects with respect to the input W are estimated as in (26.5) with $\widehat{P}_\ell(X_i)$ replaced by $\widehat{P}_\ell(W_i, X_i)$. For the inputs X_j, we calculate[6] that

$$\delta_{jj}(w,x) = \frac{\partial}{\partial x_j} P_j(w,x) = \gamma P_j(w,x)\left(1 - P_j(w,x)\right) \tag{26.9}$$

and for $j \neq \ell$

$$\delta_{j\ell}(w,x) = \frac{\partial}{\partial x_\ell} P_j(w,x) = -\gamma P_j(w,x) P_\ell(w,x). \tag{26.10}$$

Note that these are double indexed (j and ℓ). For example, for $X =$cost, $j =$train, and $\ell =$air, $\delta_{j\ell}$ is the marginal effect of a change in the cost of air travel on the probability of train travel. In the conditional logit model, calculation (26.10) implies the symmetric response $\delta_{j\ell}(w,x) = \delta_{\ell j}(w,x)$. Thus the marginal effect of (for example) air cost on train travel equals the marginal effect of train cost on air travel.[7] The **average marginal effects** $\text{AME}_{j\ell} = \mathbb{E}\left[\delta_{j\ell}(W,X)\right]$ can be estimated by the analogous sample averages as in (26.5). One useful implication

[5] The model is unaltered if the errors are jointly GEV with dissimilarity parameter τ. However, τ is not identified, so without loss of generality, it is assumed that $\tau = 1$.

[6] See Exercise 26.5.

[7] This symmetry breaks down if nonlinear transformations are included in the model.

Table 26.1
Multinomial models for transportation choice

	Variable	Conditional logit	Nested logit	Mixed logit	Simple multinomial probit	Multinomial probit
	Cost	−0.022	−0.011	−0.023	−0.018	−0.005
		(0.003)	(0.002)	(0.004)	(0.002)	(0.002)
	Intime	−0.015	−0.005	−0.014	−0.011	−0.005
		(0.001)	(0.001)	(0.001)	(0.001)	(0.001)
	σ (Intime)			0.0048		
				(0.0011)		
Air	Income	0.036	0.024	0.040	0.027	0.018
		(0.004)	(0.003)	(0.004)	(0.003)	(0.002)
	Urban	0.29	0.28	0.35	0.29	−0.38
		(0.09)	(0.09)	(0.11)	(0.07)	(0.07)
	Constant	−2.15	−0.46	−2.72	−1.51	0.32
		(0.45)	(0.35)	(0.53)	(0.32)	(0.23)
Bus	Income	−0.051	−0.049	−0.050	−0.019	−0.008
		(0.018)	(0.018)	(0.018)	(0.008)	(0.007)
	Urban	−0.23	−0.21	−0.24	−0.13	−0.14
		(0.44)	(0.45)	(0.44)	(0.21)	(0.17)
	Constant	−1.79	−1.55	−1.82	−1.45	−0.23
		(0.79)	(0.77)	(0.79)	(0.40)	(0.59)
Car	Income	0.008	0.017	0.008	0.006	0.013
		(0.003)	(0.003)	(0.003)	(0.002)	(0.003)
	Urban	−0.99	−0.58	−1.01	−0.73	−0.79
		(0.09)	(0.08)	(0.09)	(0.07)	(0.10)
	Constant	1.86	1.19	1.89	1.44	1.51
		(0.19)	(0.17)	(0.19)	(0.14)	(0.20)
	τ (Car, Air)		0.24			
			(0.05)			
	τ (Train, Bus)		1.00			
			(NA)			
	Log likelihood	−2100.6	−2044.4	−2095.5	−2109.3	−2017.4

of (26.9) and (26.10) is that the components of AME_{jj} have the same signs as the components of γ, and the components of $\text{AME}_{j\ell}$ have the opposite signs. Thus, for example, if the coefficient γ on a cost variable is negative, then the own-price effect is negative and the cross-price effects are positive.

To illustrate, Table 26.2 reports a set of estimated AME of cost and time factors on the probability of train travel. We focus on train travel because the demand for high-speed rail was the focus of the original study. The table shows the calculated AME of the monetary cost and travel time of train, air, and car travel. To convert the AME into approximate elasticities (which may be easier to interpret), divide each AME by the probability of train travel (0.17), and multiply by the sample mean of the factor, reported in the first column. You can calculate that the estimated approximate elasticity of train travel with respect to train cost is −0.9, with respect to train travel time is −2.5, with respect to air cost is 1.0, with respect to air travel time is 0.25, with respect to car cost is 0.6, and with respect to car travel time is 1.5. These estimates indicate that train travel is sensitive to its travel time, is sensitive with respect to its monetary cost and that of airfare, and is sensitive

Table 26.2
AME of cost and time on train travel

Effect of	Mean	Conditional logit	Mixed logit	Simple multinomial probit	Multinomial probit
Train cost ($)	56	−0.27 (0.04)	−0.28 (0.05)	−0.32 (0.04)	−0.08 (0.03)
Train time (min.)	224	−0.19 (0.01)	−0.20 (0.01)	−0.19 (0.01)	−0.09 (0.01)
Air cost ($)	153	0.11 (0.02)	0.11 (0.02)	0.13 (0.02)	0.05 (0.02)
Air time (min.)	54	0.08 (0.01)	0.08 (0.01)	0.08 (0.01)	0.06 (0.01)
Car cost ($)	65	0.16 (0.01)	0.17 (0.03)	0.18 (0.02)	0.02 (0.01)
Car time (min.)	232	0.11 (0.01)	0.12 (0.01)	0.11 (0.01)	0.02 (0.01)

Note: For ease of reading, the reported AME estimates have been multiplied by 100

to the travel time of car travel. We can use the estimated AME to calculate the rough effects of cost and travel time changes. For example, suppose high-speed rail reduces train travel time by 33%—an average reduction of 75 minutes—while price is unchanged. The estimates imply this will increase train travel probability by 0.14, that is, from 17% to 31%, which is close to a doubling of usage.

In many cases, it is natural to expect that the coefficients γ will vary across individuals. We discuss models with random γ in Section 26.7. A simpler specification is to allow γ to vary with the individual characteristic W. For example in the transportation application, the opportunity cost of travel time is likely related to an individual's wage which can be proxied by household income. We can write this as $\gamma = \gamma_1 + \gamma_2 X$. Substituted into (26.7), we obtain the model

$$U_j^* = W\beta_j + X_j\gamma_1 + X_j W\gamma_2 + \varepsilon_j$$

where for simplicity, we assume that W and X_j are scalar. This can be written in the form of (26.7) by redefining X_j as $(X_j, X_j W)$, and the same estimation methods apply. In our application, this model yields a negative estimate for γ_2, indicating that the cost of travel time is indeed increasing in income.

In Stata, model (26.7) can be estimated using `cmclogit`. Probabilities can be calculated by `predict`, and marginal effects by `margins`. In R, use `mlogit`.

26.5 INDEPENDENCE OF IRRELEVANT ALTERNATIVES

The multinomial logit model has an undesirable restriction. For fixed parameters and regressors, the ratio of the probability of two alternatives is

$$\frac{P_j(W,X \mid \theta)}{P_\ell(W,X \mid \theta)} = \frac{\exp\left(W'\beta_j + X_j'\gamma\right)}{\exp\left(W'\beta_\ell + X_\ell'\gamma\right)}. \tag{26.11}$$

This **odds ratio** is a function only of the inputs X_j and X_ℓ, does not depend on any of the inputs specific to the other alternatives, and is unaltered by the presence of other alternatives. This property is called **independence of irrelevant alternatives (IIA)**, meaning that the choice between option j and ℓ is independent of the other alternatives and hence the latter are irrelevant to the bivariate choice. This property is strongly tied to the multinomial logit model, as the latter was derived axiomatically by Luce (1959) from an IIA assumption.

To understand why IIA may be problematic, it is helpful to think through specific examples. Consider the transportation choice problem of Section 26.4. The IIA condition means that the ratio of the probability of selecting train to that of selecting car is unaffected by the price of an airplane ticket. This may make sense if individuals view the set of choices as similarly substitutable, but it does not make sense if train and air are close substitutes. In this latter setting, a cheap airplane ticket may make it highly unlikely that an individual will select train travel while not affecting their likelihood of selecting car travel.

A famous example of this problem is the following setting. Suppose the alternatives are car and bus, and suppose that the probability of the alternatives is split 50%-50%. Now suppose that we can split the bus alternative into "red bus" and "blue bus," so there are a total of three alternatives. Suppose the blue bus and red bus are close equivalents: they have similar schedules, convenience, and cost. In this context, most individuals would be nearly indifferent between the blue and red bus, so these alternatives would receive similar probabilities. It would thus seem reasonable to expect that the probabilities of these three choices would be close to 50%-25%-25%. The IIA condition, however, implies that the ratio of the first two probabilities must remain 1, which implies that the probabilities of the three choices would be 33%-33%-33%. We deduce that the multinomial logit model implies that adding "red bus" to the choice list results in the reduction of car usage from 50% to 33%. This doesn't make sense; it is an unreasonable implication. This example is known as the "red bus/blue bus puzzle."

The source of the problem is that the IIA structure and multinomial logit model exclude differentiated substitutability among the alternatives. This may be appropriate when the alternatives (e.g., bus, train, and car) are clearly differentiated and have reasonably similar degrees of substitutability. It is not appropriate when a subset of alternatives (e.g., red bus and blue bus) are close substitutes.

Part of the problem is due to the restrictive correlation pattern imposed on the errors by the generalized extreme value distribution. To allow for cases such as red bus/blue bus, we require a more flexible correlation structure that allows subsets of alternatives to have differential correlations.

26.6 NESTED LOGIT

The nested logit model circumvents the IIA problem described Section 26.5 by separating the alternatives into groups. Alternatives within groups are allowed to be correlated but are assumed to be uncorrelated across groups.

The model posits that there are J groups each with K_j alternatives. We use j to denote the group, k to denote the alternative within a group, and "jk" to denote a specific alternative. Let W denote individual-specific regressors and X_{jk} denote regressors that vary by alternative. The utility of the jkth alternative is a function of the regressors plus an error:

$$U_{jk}^* = W'\beta_{jk} + X_{jk}'\gamma + \varepsilon_{jk}. \tag{26.12}$$

The model assumes that the individual selects the alternative jk with the highest utility U_{jk}^*.

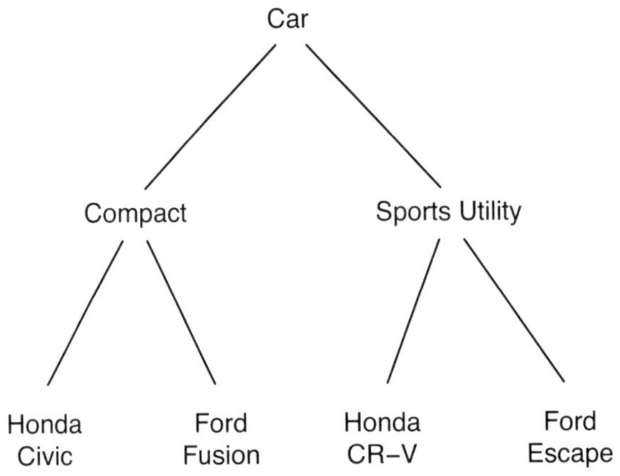

FIGURE 26.2 Nested choice

McFadden's **nested logit** model assumes that the errors have the following GEV joint distribution:

$$F\left(\varepsilon_{11},\ldots,\varepsilon_{JK_J}\right)=\exp\left(-\sum_{j=1}^{J}\left[\sum_{k=1}^{K_j}\exp\left(-\frac{\varepsilon_{jk}}{\tau_j}\right)\right]^{\tau_j}\right). \tag{26.13}$$

This is a generalization of the GEV distribution (26.3). The distribution (26.13) is the product of J GEV distributions (26.3) each with dissimilarity parameter τ_j, which means that the errors in each group are GEV distributed with dissimilarity parameter τ_j. Across groups, the errors are independent. When $\tau_j = 1$ for all j, the errors are mutually independent, and the joint model equals conditional logit. When $\tau_j < 1$ for some j, the errors within group j are correlated but not with the other errors. If a group has a single alternative, its dissimilarity parameter is not identified and so should be set to 1.

The nested logit model (26.12)–(26.13) is structurally identical to the conditional logit model except that the error distribution is (26.13) instead of (26.3). The coefficients β_{jk} and γ have the same interpretation as in the conditional logit model.

As written, (26.12) allows the coefficients β_{jk} to vary across alternatives jk, while the coefficients γ are common across j and k. Other specifications are possible. For example, the model can be altered to allow the coefficients β_j and/or γ_j to vary across groups but not alternatives. The degree of variability is a modeling choice with a flexibility/parsimony tradeoff. It is also possible (but less common in practice) to have variables W_j that vary by group but not by alternative. These can be included in the model with common coefficients.

The partition of alternatives into groups is a modeling decision. Alternatives with a high degree of substitutability should be placed in the same group. Alternatives with a low degree of substitutability should be placed in different groups.

To illustrate, consider a consumer choice of an automobile purchase. For simplicity, suppose there are four choices: Honda Civic, Ford Fusion, Honda CR-V, and Ford Escape. The first two are compact cars and the last two are sports utility vehicles (SUVs). Consequently, it is reasonable to think of the first two as substitutes and the last two as substitutes. This nesting is displayed as a tree diagram in Figure 26.2. This shows the division of the decision "Car" into "Compact" and "Sports Utility Vehicle" and the further division by model.

Only the differences between the coefficients β_{jk} are identified. Identification is achieved by setting one alternative jk as the base alternative. If the coefficients β_j are constrained to vary by group, then identification is achieved by setting a base group. The scale of the coefficients is not identified separately from the scaling of the errors implicit in the GEV distribution (26.13).

Some authors interpret model (26.12) as a nested sequential choice. An individual first selects a group and then selects the best option in the group. For example, in the car choice example, you could imagine first deciding on the style of car (compact or SUV) and then deciding on the specific car within each category (e.g., Civic vs. Fusion or CR-V vs. Escape). The sequential choice interpretation may help structure the groupings. However, sequential choice should be used cautiously, as it is not technically correct. The correct interpretation is the degree of substitutability, not the timing of decisions.

If the coefficients β_j on W are constrained to only vary across groups (this, for example, is the default in Stata), then the effect $W'\beta_j$ in (26.12) shifts the utilities of all alternatives in a group and thus does not affect the choice of an alternative in a group. In this case, the variable W can be described as "affecting the choice of group."

Let us now discuss the nested logit response probabilities.

Theorem 26.2 Assume the utility of alternative jk is $U_{jk}^* = \mu_{jk} + \varepsilon_{jk}$ and the error vector has distribution function (26.13). Then the response probabilities equal $P_{jk} = P_{k|j}P_j$, where

$$P_{k|j} = \frac{\exp\left(\mu_{jk}/\tau_j\right)}{\sum_{m=1}^{K_j} \exp\left(\mu_{jm}/\tau_j\right)}$$

and

$$P_j = \frac{\left(\sum_{m=1}^{K_j} \exp\left(\mu_{jm}/\tau_j\right)\right)^{\tau_j}}{\sum_{\ell=1}^{J}\left(\sum_{m=1}^{K_\ell} \exp\left(\mu_{\ell m}/\tau_\ell\right)\right)^{\tau_\ell}}.$$

The proof of Theorem 26.2 is in Section 26.13. Theorem 26.2 shows that the response probabilities equal the product of two terms: $P_{k|j}$ and P_j. The first, $P_{k|j}$, is the conditional probability of alternative k given the group j and takes the standard conditional logit form. The second, P_j, is the probability of group j.

Let θ be the parameters. The log-likelihood function is

$$\ell_n(\theta) = \sum_{i=1}^{n}\sum_{j=1}^{J}\sum_{k=1}^{K_j} \mathbb{1}\left\{Y_i = jk\right\}\left(\log P_{k|j}(W_i, X_i \mid \theta) + \log P_j(W_i, X_i \mid \theta)\right).$$

The MLE $\widehat{\theta}$ maximizes $\ell_n(\theta)$. There is no algebraic solution, so $\widehat{\theta}$ needs to be found numerically.

Because the probability structure of a nested logit model is more complicated than that of the conditional logit model, it may be difficult to interpret the coefficient estimates. Marginal effects can (in principle) be calculated, but these are complicated functions of the coefficients.

To illustrate, let us estimate a nested logit model of transportation choice using the `Koppelman` dataset. To facilitate comparisons, we estimate the same specification as for conditional logit. The difference is that we use the GEV distribution (26.13) with the groupings {car, air} and {train, bus}. This adds two dissimilarity parameters. The results are reported in the second column of Table 26.1.

The dissimilarity parameter estimate for {car, air} is 0.24, which is small. It implies a correlation of 0.94 between the car and air utility shocks. This suggests that the conditional logit model—which assumes the utility errors are independent—is misspecified. The dissimilarity parameter estimate for {train, bus} is on the boundary[8] 1.00 and so has no standard error.

Nested logit modeling is limited by the necessity of selecting the groupings. Typically there is no unique obvious structure; consequently, any proposed grouping is subject to misspecification.

In this section we have discussed the nested logit model with one nested layer. The model extends to multiple nesting layers. The difference is that the joint distribution (26.13) is modified to allow higher levels of interactions with additional dissimilarity parameters. An applied example is Goldberg (1995), who used a five-level nested logit model to estimate the demand for automobilies. The levels used in her analysis were (1) buy/not buy; (2) new/used; (3) car class; (4) foreign/domestic; and (5) car model.

In Stata, nested logit models can be estimated by `nlogit`.

26.7 MIXED LOGIT

A generalization of the conditional logit model that allows the coefficients γ on the alternative-varying regressors to be random across individuals is known as **mixed logit**. The model is also known as **conditional mixed logit** and **random parameters logit**.

Recall that the conditional logit model is $U_j^* = W'\beta_j + X_j'\gamma + \varepsilon_j$ with ε_j i.i.d. extreme value. Now replace γ with an individual-specific random variable η with distribution $F(\eta \mid \alpha)$ and parameters α. This model is

$$U_j^* = W'\beta_j + X_j'\eta + \varepsilon_j$$
$$\eta \sim F(\eta \mid \alpha).$$

For example, in our transportation choice application, the variables X_j are the cost and travel time of each alternative. The above model allows the effect of cost and time on utility to be heterogeneous across individuals.

The most common distributional assumption for η is $\mathrm{N}(\gamma, D)$ with diagonal covariance matrix D. Other common specifications include $\mathrm{N}(\gamma, \Sigma)$ with unconstrained covariance matrix Σ, and log-normally distributed η to enforce $\eta \geq 0$. (A constraint $\eta \leq 0$ can be imposed by first multiplying the relevant regressor X_j by -1.) It is also common to partition X_j so that some variables have random coefficients and others have fixed coefficients. The reason these constraints may be desirable is parsimony and simpler computation.

Under the normality specifications $\eta \sim \mathrm{N}(\gamma, D)$ and $\eta \sim \mathrm{N}(\gamma, \Sigma)$, the mean γ equals the average random coefficient in the population and has a similar interpretation to the coefficient γ in the conditional logit model. The variances in D or Σ control the dispersion of the distribution of η in the population. Smaller variances mean that η is mildly dispersed; larger variances indicate high dispersion and heterogeneity.

A useful feature of the mixed logit model is that the random coefficients induce correlation among the alternatives. To see this, write $\gamma = \mathbb{E}[\eta]$ and $V_j = X_j'(\eta - \gamma) + \varepsilon_j$. Then the model can be written as

$$Y_j^* = W'\beta_j + X_j'\gamma + V_j$$

[8]The uncontrained maximizer exceeds 1, which violates the parameter space, so the the model is effectively estimated constraining this dissimilarity parameter to equal 1.

which is the conventional random utility framework but with errors V_j instead of ε_j. An important difference is that these errors are conditionally heteroskedastic and correlated across alternatives:

$$\mathbb{E}\left[V_j V_\ell \mid X_j, X_\ell\right] = X_j' \operatorname{var}[\eta] X_\ell.$$

This nonzero correlation means that the IIA property is partially broken, giving the mixed logit model more flexibility than the conditional logit model to capture choice behavior.

Conditional on η, the response probabilities follow from (26.8):

$$P_j(w, x \mid \eta) = \frac{\exp\left(w'\beta_j + x_j'\eta\right)}{\sum_{\ell=1}^{J} \exp\left(w'\beta_\ell + x_\ell'\eta\right)}.$$

The unconditional response probabilities are found by integration:

$$P_j(w, x) = \int P_j(w, x \mid \eta) dF(\eta \mid \alpha). \tag{26.14}$$

The log-likelihood function is

$$\ell_n(\theta) = \sum_{i=1}^{n} \sum_{j=1}^{J} \mathbb{1}\left\{Y_i = j\right\} \log P_j\left(W_i, X_i \mid \theta\right) \tag{26.15}$$

where θ is the list of all parameters including η.

The integral in (26.14) is not available in closed form. A standard numerical implementation[9] is Monte Carlo integration (estimation by simulation). This technique works as follows. Let $\{\eta_1, \ldots, \eta_G\}$ be a set of i.i.d. pseudo-random draws from $F(\eta \mid \alpha)$. The simulation estimator of (26.14) is

$$\widetilde{P}_j(w, x) = \frac{1}{G} \sum_{g=1}^{G} P_j(w, x \mid \eta_g).$$

As G increases, this sum converges in probability to (26.14). Monte Carlo integration is computationally more efficient than numerical integration when the dimension of η is 3 or larger, but it is considerably more computationally intensive than nonrandom conditional logit.

To illustrate, we estimate a mixed logit model for the transportation application, treating the coefficient on travel time as a normal random variable. The coefficient estimates are reported in Table 26.1 with estimated marginal effects in Table 26.2. The results are similar to those for the conditional logit model. The coefficient on travel time has a mean -0.014, which is nearly identical to the conditional logit estimate and a standard deviation of 0.005, which is about one-third of the value of the mean. This suggests that the coefficient is mildly heterogenous among travelers. An interpretation of this random coefficient is that travelers have heterogeneous costs associated with travel time.

In Stata, mixed logit can be estimated by `cmmixlogit`.

---

[9] If the random coefficient η is scalar, a computationally more efficient method is integration by quadrature.

26.8 SIMPLE MULTINOMIAL PROBIT

The **simple multinomial probit** and **simple conditional multinomial probit** models combine the latent utility model

$$U_j^* = W'\beta_j + \varepsilon_j \tag{26.16}$$

or

$$U_j^* = W'\beta_j + X_j'\gamma + \varepsilon_j \tag{26.17}$$

with the assumption that ε_j is i.i.d. $\mathrm{N}(0,1)$. These are identical to the simple multinomial logit model of Section 26.3 and the conditional logit model of Section 26.4, except that the error distribution is normal instead of extreme value.

Simple multinomial probit does not precisely satisfy IIA, but its properties are similar to IIA. The model assumes that the errors are independent and thus does not allow two alternatives (e.g., "red bus" and "blue bus") to be close substitutes. Thus in practice, the simple multinomial probit will produce results that are similar to simple multinomial logit.

Identification is identical to multinomial logit. The coefficients β_j and γ are only identified up to scale, and the coefficients β_j are only identified relative to a base alternative.

The response probability $P_j(W,X)$ is not available in closed form. However, it can be expressed as a one-dimensional integral, as we now show.

Theorem 26.3 In the simple multinomial probit and simple conditional multinomial probit models, the response probabilities equal

$$P_j(W,X) = \int_{-\infty}^{\infty} \prod_{\ell \neq j} \Phi\left(W'\left(\beta_j - \beta_\ell\right) + \left(X_j - X_\ell\right)'\gamma + v\right)\phi(v)\,dv \tag{26.18}$$

where $\Phi(v)$ and $\phi(v)$ are the normal distribution and density functions, respectively.

The proof is presented in Section 26.13. Theorem 26.3 shows that the response probability is a one-dimensional normal integral over the $J-1$-fold product of normal distribution functions. This integral (26.18) is straightforward to numerically evaluate by quadrature methods.

Let $\theta = \left(\beta_1, \ldots \beta_J, \gamma\right)$ denote the parameters. Given the sample $\{Y_i, W_i, X_i\}$, the log-likelihood is

$$\ell_n(\theta) = \sum_{i=1}^{n} \sum_{j=1}^{J} \mathbb{1}\left\{Y_i = j\right\} \log P_j(W_i, X_i \mid \theta).$$

The maximum likelihood estimator (MLE) $\widehat{\theta}$ maximizes $\ell_n(\theta)$.

To illustrate, we estimate a simple conditional multinomial probit model for transportation choice, using the same specification as before. The results are reported in the fourth column of Table 26.1. Average marginal effects are reported in Table 26.2. We see that the estimated AMEs are very close to those of the conditional logit model.

In Stata, simple multivariate probit can be estimated by `mprobit`. The response probabilities and log-likelihood are calculated by applying quadrature to the integral (26.18). Simple conditional multinomial probit can be estimated by `cmmprobit`. The latter uses the method of simulated maximum likelihood (discussed in

Section 26.9) even though numerical calculation could be implemented efficiently using the one-dimensional integral (26.18).

26.9 GENERAL MULTINOMIAL PROBIT

A model that avoids the correlation constraints of multinomial and nested logit is **general multinomial probit**, which is (26.17) with the error vector $\varepsilon \sim \mathrm{N}(0, \Sigma)$ and unconstrained Σ.

Identification of the coefficients is the same as for multinomial logit. The coefficients β_j and γ are only identified up to scale, and the coefficients β_j are only identified relative to a base alternative J.

Identification of the covariance matrix Σ requires more attention. It turns out to be useful to rewrite the model in terms of differenced utility, where differences are taken with respect to the base alternative J. The differenced utilities are

$$U_j^* - U_J^* = W' \left(\beta_j - \beta_J\right) + \left(X_j - X_J\right)' \gamma + \varepsilon_{jJ} \tag{26.19}$$

where $\varepsilon_{jJ} = \varepsilon_j - \varepsilon_J$. Let Σ_J be the covariance matrix of ε_{jJ} for $j = 1, \ldots, J-1$. For example, suppose that the errors ε_j are i.i.d. $\mathrm{N}(0, 1)$. In this case, Σ_J equals

$$\Sigma_J = \begin{bmatrix} 2 & 1 & \cdots & 1 \\ 1 & 2 & \cdots & 1 \\ \vdots & \vdots & \ddots & \vdots \\ 1 & 1 & \cdots & 2 \end{bmatrix}. \tag{26.20}$$

The scale of (26.19) is not identified, so Σ_J is normalized by fixing one diagonal element of Σ_J. In Stata, for example, `cmmprobit` normalizes the variance of one element—the "scale alternative"–to 2, in order to match the case (26.20). Consequently, Σ_J has $(J-1)J/2 - 1$ free covariance parameters.

Multinomial probit with a general covariance matrix Σ_J is more flexible than conditional logit and nested logit. This flexibility allows general multinomial probit to escape the IIA restrictions.

The response probabilities do not have closed-form expressions but can be written as $J-1$ dimensional integrals. Numerical evaluation of integrals in dimensions three and higher is computationally prohibitive. A feasible alternative is numerical simulation. The idea, roughly, is to simulate a large number of random draws from the model and count the fraction that satisfies the desired inequality. This gives a simulation estimate of the response probability. Brute force implementation of this idea can be inefficient, so clever tricks have been introduced to produce computationally efficient estimates. The standard implementation was developed in a series of papers by Geweke, Hajivassiliou, and Keane, and is known as the GHK simulator. See Train (2009) for a description and references. The GHK simulator provides a feasible method to estimate the likelihood function and is known as **simulated maximum likelihood**. Although feasible, simulated maximum likelihood is computationally intensive, so optimizing the likelihood to find the MLE is computationally slow. Furthermore, the likelihood is not concave in the parameters, so convergence can be difficult to obtain in some applications. Consequently it may be prudent to use simpler methods, such as conditional and nested logit for exploratory analysis and multinomial probit for final-stage estimation.

To illustrate, let us estimate the general multinomial probit model for the transportation application of Section 26.4. We set the base alternative to train and the scale alternative to air. The coefficient estimates are reported in Table 26.1 and marginal effects in Table 26.2. We see that the estimated marginal effects with respect to cost and travel time are considerably smaller than in the conditional logit model. This indicates greatly reduced price elasticity (−0.3) and travel time elasticity (−1.1). Suppose (as we considered in Section 26.4) that high-speed rail reduces train travel time by 33%. The multinomial probit estimates imply that this increases train travel from 17% to 24%—about a 40% increase. This is substantial but is one-half of the increase estimated by conditional logit.

A multinomial probit model with four alternatives has five covariance parameters. The estimates for the transportation application are reported in the following 3 × 3 table. The diagonal elements are the variance estimates, the off-diagonal elements are the correlation estimates. One interesting finding is that the estimated correlation between air and car travel is 0.99, which is similar to the estimate from the nested logit model. In both frameworks, the estimates indicate a high correlation between air and car travel, implying that specifications with independent errors are misspecified.

$$\begin{bmatrix} \widehat{\sigma}^2_{\texttt{Air}} = 2 & & \\ \widehat{\rho}_{\texttt{Air,Bus}} = 0.60 & \widehat{\sigma}^2_{\texttt{Bus}} = 0.41 & \\ \widehat{\rho}_{\texttt{Air,Car}} = 0.99 & \widehat{\rho}_{\texttt{Car,Bus}} = 0.60 & \widehat{\sigma}^2_{\texttt{Car}} = 3.8 \end{bmatrix}$$

In Stata, multivariate probit can be estimated by `cmmprobit`. It uses GHK simulated maximum likelihood as described earlier in this section.

26.10 ORDERED RESPONSE

A multinomial Y is **ordered** if the alternatives have an ordinal (ordered) interpretation. For example, a student may be asked to "rate your [econometrics] professor" with possible responses: poor, fair, average, good, or excellent, coded as $\{1, 2, 3, 4, 5\}$. These responses are categorical but are also ordinally related. We could use standard multinomial methods (e.g., multinomial logit or probit), but this ignores the ordinal structure and is therefore inefficient.

The standard approach to ordered response is based on the latent variable framework

$$U^* = X'\beta + \varepsilon$$
$$\varepsilon \sim G$$

where X does not include an intercept. The model specifies that the response Y is determined by U^* crossing a series of ordered thresholds $\alpha_1 < \alpha_2 < \cdots < \alpha_{J-1}$. Thus,

$$\begin{array}{lll} Y = 1 & \text{if} & U^* \leq \alpha_1 \\ Y = 2 & \text{if} & \alpha_1 < U^* \leq \alpha_2 \\ \vdots & \vdots & \vdots \\ Y = J-1 & \text{if} & \alpha_{J-2} < U^* \leq \alpha_{J-1} \\ Y = J & \text{if} & \alpha_{J-1} < U^*. \end{array}$$

Writing $\alpha_0 = -\infty$ and $\alpha_J = \infty$, we can write these J equations more compactly as $Y = j$ if $\alpha_{j-1} < U^* \leq \alpha_j$. When $J = 2$, this model specializes to binary choice.

The standard interpretation is that U^* is a latent continuous response, and Y is a discretized version. Consider again the example of "rate your professor." In the model, U^* is a student's true assessment. The response Y is a discretized version. The threshold crossing model postulates that responses are increasing in the latent variable and are determined by the thresholds.

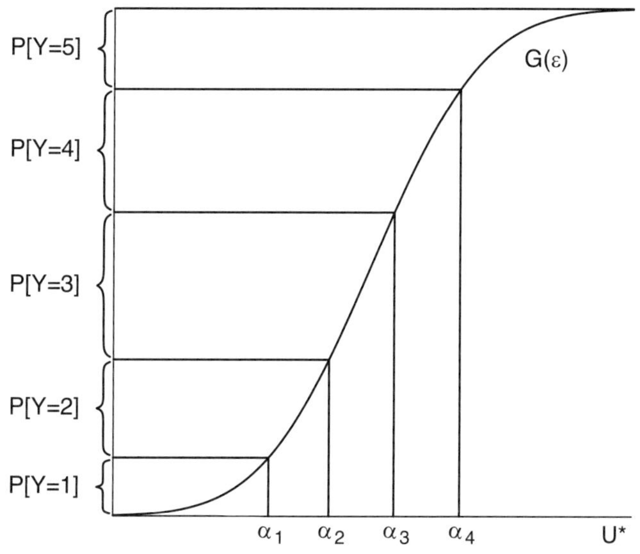

FIGURE 26.3 Ordered choice

In the standard ordered response framework, the distribution $G(x)$ of the error ε is assumed known; in practice, either the normal or logistic distribution is used. When ε is normal, the model is called **ordered probit**. When ε is logistic, the model is called **ordered logit**. The coefficients and thresholds are only identified up to scale; the standard normalization is to fix the scale of the distribution of ε.

The response probabilities are

$$\begin{aligned} P_j(x) &= \mathbb{P}\left[Y = j \mid X = x\right] \\ &= \mathbb{P}\left[\alpha_{j-1} < U^* \le \alpha_j \mid X = x\right] \\ &= \mathbb{P}\left[\alpha_{j-1} - X'\beta < \varepsilon \le \alpha_j - X'\beta \mid X = x\right] \\ &= G\left(\alpha_j - x'\beta\right) - G\left(\alpha_{j-1} - x'\beta\right). \end{aligned}$$

It may be easier to interpret the cumulative response probabilities:

$$\mathbb{P}\left[Y \le j \mid X = x\right] = G\left(\alpha_j - x'\beta\right).$$

The marginal effects are

$$\frac{\partial}{\partial x} P_j(x) = \beta\left(g\left(\alpha_{j-1} - x'\beta\right) - g\left(\alpha_j - x'\beta\right)\right)$$

and marginal cumulative effects are

$$\frac{\partial}{\partial x}\mathbb{P}\left[Y \le j \mid X = x\right] = -\beta g\left(\alpha_j - x'\beta\right).$$

To illustrate, Figure 26.3 displays how the response probabilities are determined. The figure plots the distribution function of latent utility U^* with four thresholds, α_1, α_2, α_3 and α_4, displayed on the x-axis. The response Y is determined by U^* crossing each threshold. Each threshold is mapped to a point on the y-axis. The probability of each outcome is marked on the y-axis as the difference between each probability crossing.

The parameters are $\theta = (\beta, \alpha_1, \ldots \alpha_{J-1})$. Given the sample $\{Y_i, X_i\}$, the log-likelihood is

$$\ell_n(\theta) = \sum_{i=1}^{n} \sum_{j=1}^{J} \mathbb{1}\left\{Y_i = j\right\} \log P_j(X_i \mid \theta).$$

The maximum likelihood estimator (MLE) $\widehat{\theta}$ maximizes $\ell_n(\theta)$.

In Stata, ordered probit and logit can be estimated by `oprobit` and `ologit`, respectively.

26.11 COUNT DATA

Count data refers to situations where the dependent variable is the number of "events" recorded as positive integers $Y \in \{0, 1, 2, \ldots\}$. Examples include the number of doctor visits, the number of accidents, the number of patent registrations, the number of absences, or the number of bank failures. Count data models are typically employed in contexts where the counts are small integers.

A count data model specifies the response probabilities $P_j(x) = \mathbb{P}\left[Y = j \mid x\right]$ for $j = 0, 1, 2, \ldots$, with the property $\sum_{j=0}^{\infty} P_j(x) = 1$.

The baseline model is **Poisson regression**. This model specifies that Y is conditionally Poisson distributed with a Poisson parameter λ written as an exponential link of a linear function of the regressors. The exponential link is used to ensure that the Poisson parameter is strictly positive. This model is

$$P_j(x) = \frac{\exp(-\lambda(x))\,\lambda(x)^j}{j!}$$

$$\lambda(x) = \exp(x'\beta).$$

The Poisson distribution has the property that its mean and variance equal the Poisson parameter λ. Thus,

$$\mathbb{E}[Y \mid X] = \exp(X'\beta)$$

$$\text{var}[Y \mid X] = \exp(X'\beta).$$

The first equation shows that the conditional expectation (e.g., the regression function) equals $\exp(X'\beta)$. This is why the model is called "Poisson regression."

The log-likelihood function is

$$\ell_n(\beta) = \sum_{i=1}^{n} \log P_{Y_i}(X_i \mid \beta) = \sum_{i=1}^{n} \left(-\exp(X_i'\beta) + Y_i X_i'\beta - \log(Y_i!)\right).$$

The MLE $\widehat{\beta}$ is the value of β that maximizes $\ell_n(\beta)$. Its first and second derivatives are

$$\frac{\partial}{\partial \beta}\ell_n(\beta) = \sum_{i=1}^{n} X_i\left(Y_i - \exp(X_i'\beta)\right)$$

$$\frac{\partial^2}{\partial \beta \partial \beta'}\ell_n(\beta) = -\sum_{i=1}^{n} X_i X_i' \exp(X_i'\beta).$$

Since the second derivative is globally negative definite, the log-likelihood function is globally concave. Hence numerical optimization to find the MLE is computationally straightforward.

In general, there is no reason to expect the Poisson model to be correctly specified. Hence we should view the parameter β as the best-fitting pseudo-true value. From the first-order condition for maximization, we find that this value satisfies

$$\mathbb{E}\left[X\left(Y - \exp(X'\beta)\right)\right] = 0.$$

This holds under the conditional expectation assumption $\mathbb{E}[Y \mid X] = \exp(X'\beta)$. If the latter is correctly specified, Poisson regression correctly identifies the coeffiicent β, the MLE is consistent for this value, and the estimated response probabilities are consistent for the true response probabilities.

To explore this concept further, suppose the true CEF is nonparametric. Since it is nonnegative, we can write it using an exponential link[10] as $\mathbb{E}[Y \mid X] = \exp(m(x))$. The function $m(x)$ is nonparametrically identified and can be approximated by a series $x_K'\beta_K$. Thus, $\mathbb{E}[Y \mid X] \simeq \exp\left(X_K'\beta_K\right)$. What this shows is that if Poisson regression is implemented using a flexible set of regressors (as in series regression), the model will approximate the true CEF and hence will consistently estimate the true response probabilities. This is a broad justification for Poisson regression in count data applications, if suitable attention is paid to the functional form for the included regressors.

Because the model is an approximation, however, the conventional covariance matrix estimator will be inconsistent. Consequently, it is advisable to use the robust formula for covariance matrix and standard error estimation.

For a greater degree of flexibility, the Poisson model can be generalized. One approach, similar to mixed logit, is to treat the parameters as random variables, thereby obtaining a mixed probit model. One particular mixed model of importance is the negative binomial model, which can be obtained as a mixed model as follows. Specify the Poisson parameter as $\lambda(X) = V\exp(X'\beta)$, where V is a random variable with a gamma distribution. This is equivalent to treating the regression intercept as random with a log-gamma distribution. Integrating out V, the resulting conditional distribution for Y is negative binomial. The negative binomial is a popular model for count data regression and has the advantage that the CEF and variance are separately varying.

For more detail, see the excellent monograph on count data models by Cameron and Trivedi (1998).

In Stata, Poisson and negative binomial regression can be estimated by `poisson` and `nbreg`. Generalizations to allow truncation, fixed effects, and random effects are also available.

26.12 BLP DEMAND MODEL

A major development in the 1990s was the extension of conditional logit to models of aggregate market demand. Many of the ideas were developed in the seminal papers of Berry (1994) and Berry, Levinsohn, and Pakes (1995). For a review, see Ackerberg, Benkard, Berry, and Pakes (2007). This model—widely known as the **BLP model**—has become popular in applied industrial organization. To discuss implementation, I use as examples the applications in Berry, Levinsohn, and Pakes (1995) and Nevo (2001).

The context is market-level observations. A "market" is typically a time period matched with a location. For example, a market in Berry, Levinsohn, and Pakes (1995) is the United States for one calendar year. A market in Nevo (2001) is one of 65 U.S. cities for one quarter of a year. An observation contains a set of J goods. In Berry, Levinsohn, and Pakes (1995), the goods are 997 distinct automobile models. In Nevo (2001), the goods are 25 ready-to-eat breakfast cereals. Observations typically include the price and sale quantities of

---

[10] Or, equivalently, $m(x) = \log(\mathbb{E}[Y \mid X])$.

each good, a set of characteristics of each good, and possibly information on demographic characteristics of the market population.

The model is derived from a conditional logit specification of individual behavior. The standard assumption is that each individual in the market purchases one of the J goods or makes no purchase (the latter is called the "outside alternative"). This approach requires taking a stand on the number of individuals in the market. For example, in Berry, Levinsohn, and Pakes (1995), the number of individuals is the entire U.S. population. Their assumption is that each individual makes at most one automobile purchase during each calendar year. In Nevo (2001), the population is the number of individuals in each city. He assumes that each individual purchases a one-quarter (91-day) supply of one brand of breakfast cereal, or purchases no breakfast cereal (the outside alternative). By explicitly including the outside option as a choice, these authors model aggregate demand. Alternatively, they could have excluded the outside option and examined choice among the J goods. This approach would have modeled market shares (percentages of total purchases) but not aggregate demand. The tradeoff is the need to take a stand on the number of individuals in the market.

The model is that each individual purchases one of a set of J goods indexed $j=1,\ldots,J$ or an unobserved outside good. The utility from good j takes a mixed logit form:

$$U_j^* = X_j'\eta + \xi_j + \varepsilon_j \tag{26.21}$$

where X_j includes the price and characteristics of good j. The coefficient η is random (specific to an individual), as in the mixed logit model. The variables ξ_j and ε_j are unobserved errors. ξ_j is market-level, and ε_j is specific to the individual.

The market error ξ_j may contain unobserved product characteristics, so it is likely correlated with product price. Identification requires a vector of instruments Z_j that satisfy

$$\mathbb{E}\left[Z_j\xi_j\right]=0. \tag{26.22}$$

Berry, Levinsohn, and Pakes (1995) recommend as instruments the non-price characteristics in X_j, the sum of characteristics of goods sold by the same firm, and the sum of characteristics of goods sold by other firms. Nevo (2001) also includes the prices of goods in other markets, which is valid if demand shocks are uncorrelated across markets. There is considerable attention in the literature given to the choice and construction of instruments.

Write $\gamma=\mathbb{E}[\eta]$, $V=\eta-\gamma$, and assume that V has distribution $F(V\mid\alpha)$ with parameters α (typically $\mathrm{N}(0,\Sigma)$). Set

$$\delta_j = X_j'\gamma + \xi_j. \tag{26.23}$$

Because the model is mixed logit, (26.14) shows that the response probabilities given $\delta=(\delta_1,\ldots,\delta_J)$ are

$$P_j(\delta,\alpha)=\int \frac{\exp\left(\delta_j + X_j'V\right)}{\sum_{\ell=1}^{J}\exp\left(\delta_\ell + X_\ell'V\right)} dF(V\mid\alpha)dV.$$

As discussed in Section 26.7, the integral in (26.14) is typically evaluated by numerical simulation. Let $\{V_1,\ldots,V_G\}$ be i.i.d. pseudo-random draws from $F(V\mid\alpha)$. The simulation estimator is

$$\widetilde{P}_j(\delta,\alpha)=\frac{1}{G}\sum_{g=1}^{G}\frac{\exp\left(\delta_j+X_j'V_g\right)}{\sum_{\ell=1}^{J}\exp\left(\delta_\ell+X_\ell'V_g\right)}. \tag{26.24}$$

In each market, we observe the quantity purchased Q_j of each good, and we are assumed to know the number of individuals M. The **market share** of good j is defined as $S_j=Q_j/M$, which is a direct estimate of the probability P_j. If the number of individuals M is large, then S_j approximately equals P_j by the WLLN. The BLP approach assumes that M is large enough that we can treat these two as equal. This implies the set of J equalities

$$S_j=\widetilde{P}_j(\delta,\alpha) \tag{26.25}$$

where $S=(S_1,\ldots,S_J)$. The left side of (26.25) is the observed market share of good j (that is, the ratio of sales to individuals in the market). The right side is the estimated probability that the good is selected, given the market attributes and parameters. As there are J elements in each of δ and S (and $\widetilde{P}_j(\delta,\alpha)$ is monotonically increasing in each element of δ), there is a one-to-one and invertible mapping between δ and S. Thus given the market shares S and parameters α, we can numerically calculate the elements δ that solve the J equations (26.25). Berry, Levinsohn, and Pakes (1995) show that the solution can be obtained by iterating on

$$\delta_j^i=\delta_j^{i-1}+\log S_j-\log\widetilde{P}_j\left(\delta^{i-1},\alpha\right). \tag{26.26}$$

The solution is an implicit set of J equations $\delta_j=\delta_j(S,\alpha)$.

We can combine $\delta_j=\delta_j(S,\alpha)$ with (26.23) to obtain the regression-like expression $\delta_j(S,\alpha)=X_j'\gamma+\xi_j$. Combined with (26.22), we obtain the moment equations

$$\mathbb{E}\left[Z_j\left(\delta_j(S,\alpha)-X_j'\gamma\right)\right]=0$$

for $j=1,\ldots,J$.

Estimation is by nonlinear GMM. The observations are markets indexed $t=1,\ldots,T$, including quantities Q_{jt}, prices and characteristics X_{jt}, and instruments Z_{jt}. Market shares are $S_{jt}=Q_{jt}/M_t$, where M_t is the number of individuals in the market. Let $S_t=(S_{1t},\ldots,S_{Jt})$. The moment equation is

$$\overline{g}(\gamma,\alpha)=\frac{1}{TJ}\sum_{t=1}^{T}\sum_{j=1}^{J}Z_{jt}\left(\delta_{jt}(S_t,\alpha)-X_{jt}'\gamma\right).$$

The GMM estimator $(\widehat{\gamma},\widehat{\alpha})$ minimizes the criterion $\overline{g}(\gamma,\alpha)'\boldsymbol{W}\,\overline{g}(\gamma,\alpha)$ for a weight matrix $\boldsymbol{W}$.

I mentioned earlier that observations may include demographic information. This can be incorporated as follows. We can add individual characteristics (e.g., income) to the utility model (26.21) as interactions with the product characteristics X_j. Because individual characteristics are unobserved, they can be treated as random but with a known distribution (taken from the known market-level demographic data). For example, Berry, Levinsohn, and Pakes (1995) treat individual income as log-normally distributed. These random variables are then treated jointly with the random coefficients with no effective change in the estimation method.

An asymptotic theory developed by Berry, Linton, and Pakes (2004) shows that this GMM estimator is consistent and asymptotically normal as $J\to\infty$, under certain assumptions. Thus the estimator can be applied in contexts with small T and large J, as well as in contexts with large T.

To estimate a BLP model in Stata, there is an add-on command `blp`. In R, there is a package `BLPestimatoR`. Python has a package `PyBLP`.

26.13 TECHNICAL PROOFS*

Proof of Theorem 26.1 Define $\mu_{j\ell} = X'(\beta_j - \beta_\ell)$. It will useful to observe that

$$P_j(X) = \frac{\exp(X'\beta_j/\tau)}{\sum_{\ell=1}^{J} \exp(X'\beta_\ell/\tau)} = \left(\sum_{\ell=1}^{J} \exp\left(-\frac{\mu_{j\ell}}{\tau}\right)\right)^{-1}.$$

Define

$$\begin{aligned}
F_j(\varepsilon_1, \ldots, \varepsilon_J) &= \frac{\partial}{\partial \varepsilon_j} F(\varepsilon_1, \ldots, \varepsilon_J) \\
&= \exp\left(-\left[\sum_{\ell=1}^{J} \exp\left(-\frac{\varepsilon_\ell}{\tau}\right)\right]^{\tau}\right)\left[\sum_{\ell=1}^{J} \exp\left(-\frac{\varepsilon_\ell}{\tau}\right)\right]^{\tau-1} \exp\left(-\frac{\varepsilon_j}{\tau}\right).
\end{aligned}$$

The event $Y = j$ occurs if $U_j^* \geq U_\ell^*$ for all ℓ, which occurs when $\varepsilon_\ell \leq \varepsilon_j + \mu_{j\ell}$. The probability $\mathbb{P}[Y = j]$ is the integral of the joint density $f(\varepsilon_1, \ldots, \varepsilon_J)$ over the region $\varepsilon_\ell \leq \varepsilon_j + \mu_{j\ell}$. This is

$$\mathbb{P}[Y = j] = \mathbb{P}[\varepsilon_\ell \leq \varepsilon_j + \mu_{j\ell}, \text{all } \ell] = \int_{-\infty}^{\infty}\left[\int_{-\infty}^{\varepsilon_j+\mu_{j1}} \cdots \int_{-\infty}^{\varepsilon_J+\mu_{jJ}} f(\varepsilon_1, \ldots, \varepsilon_J)\, d\varepsilon_1 d\varepsilon_2 \cdots d\varepsilon_J\right] d\varepsilon_j$$

where the outer integral is over ε_j. The $J-1$ inner set of integrals equals $F_j(\varepsilon_j + \mu_{j1}, \ldots, \varepsilon_j + \mu_{jJ})$. Thus,

$$\mathbb{P}[Y = j] = \int_{-\infty}^{\infty} F_j(\varepsilon_j + \mu_{j1}, \ldots, \varepsilon_j + \mu_{jJ})\, d\varepsilon_j. \tag{26.27}$$

Next, we substitute the above expression for F_j and collect terms to find that (26.27) equals

$$\begin{aligned}
&\int_{-\infty}^{\infty} \exp\left(-\left[\sum_{\ell=1}^{J} \exp\left(-\frac{\varepsilon_\ell + \mu_{j\ell}}{\tau}\right)\right]^{\tau}\right)\left[\sum_{\ell=1}^{J} \exp\left(-\frac{\varepsilon_\ell + \mu_{j\ell}}{\tau}\right)\right]^{\tau-1} \exp\left(-\frac{\varepsilon_j}{\tau}\right) d\varepsilon_j \\
&= \int_{-\infty}^{\infty} \exp\left(-\exp(-\varepsilon_j) P_j(X)^{-\tau}\right) P_j(X)^{1-\tau} \exp\left(-\frac{\varepsilon_j}{\tau}\right)^{\tau-1} \exp\left(-\frac{\varepsilon_j}{\tau}\right) d\varepsilon_j \\
&= \int_{-\infty}^{\infty} \exp\left(-\exp\left(-\varepsilon_j - \log P_j(X)^{\tau}\right)\right) P_j(X)^{1-\tau} \exp(-\varepsilon_j)\, d\varepsilon_j \\
&= P_j(X)^{1-\tau} \int_{-\infty}^{\infty} \exp\left(-\exp\left(-\varepsilon_j - \log P_j(X)^{\tau}\right)\right) \exp(-\varepsilon_j)\, d\varepsilon_j \\
&= P_j(X) \int_{-\infty}^{\infty} \exp\left(-\exp(-u)\right) \exp(-u)\, du \\
&= P_j(X).
\end{aligned}$$

The second-to-last equality makes the change of variables $u = \varepsilon_j + \log P_j(X)^{\tau}$. The final uses the fact that $\exp(-\exp(-u))\exp(-u)$ is the Type I extreme value density, which integrates to 1. This derivation shows $\mathbb{P}[Y = j] = P_j(X)$, as claimed. ■

Proof of Theorem 26.2 The proof method is similar to that of Theorem 26.1. The joint distribution of the errors is

$$F\left(\varepsilon_{11},\ldots,\varepsilon_{JK_J}\right)=\exp\left(-\sum_{\ell=1}^{J}\left[\sum_{m=1}^{K_\ell}\exp\left(-\frac{\varepsilon_{\ell m}}{\tau_\ell}\right)\right]^{\tau_\ell}\right).$$

The derivative with respect to ε_{jk} is

$$\begin{aligned}F_{jk}\left(\varepsilon_{11},\ldots,\varepsilon_{JK_J}\right)&=\frac{\partial}{\partial\varepsilon_{jk}}F\left(\varepsilon_{11},\ldots,\varepsilon_{JK_J}\right)\\&=\exp\left(-\sum_{\ell=1}^{J}\left[\sum_{m=1}^{K_\ell}\exp\left(-\frac{\varepsilon_{\ell m}}{\tau_\ell}\right)\right]^{\tau_\ell}\right)\left[\sum_{m=1}^{K_j}\exp\left(-\frac{\varepsilon_{jm}}{\tau_j}\right)\right]^{\tau_j-1}\exp\left(-\frac{\varepsilon_{jk}}{\tau_j}\right).\end{aligned}$$

The event $Y_{jk}=1$ occurs if $U^*_{jk}\geq U^*_{\ell m}$ for all ℓ and m, which occurs when $\varepsilon_{\ell m}\leq\varepsilon_{jk}+\mu_{jk}-\mu_{lm}$. Setting $I_j=\sum_{m=1}^{K_j}\exp\left(\mu_{jm}/\tau_j\right)$ and $I=\sum_{\ell=1}^{J}I_\ell^{\tau_\ell}$, we find that

$$\begin{aligned}\mathbb{P}\left[Y_{jk}=1\right]&=\int_{-\infty}^{\infty}F_{jk}\left(v+\mu_{jk}-\mu_{11},\ldots,v+\mu_{jk}-\mu_{JK_J}\right)dv\\&=\int_{-\infty}^{\infty}\exp\left(-\sum_{\ell=1}^{J}\left[\sum_{m=1}^{K_\ell}\exp\left(-\frac{v+\mu_{jk}-\mu_{\ell m}}{\tau_\ell}\right)\right]^{\tau_\ell}\right)\\&\qquad\left[\sum_{m=1}^{K_j}\exp\left(-\frac{v+\mu_{jk}-\mu_{jm}}{\tau_j}\right)\right]^{\tau_j-1}\exp\left(-\frac{v}{\tau_j}\right)dv\\&=I_j^{\tau_j-1}\left(\exp\left(-\mu_{jk}\right)\right)^{\frac{\tau_j-1}{\tau_j}}\int_{-\infty}^{\infty}\exp\left(-\exp\left(-v-\mu_{jk}\right)\sum_{\ell=1}^{J}I_\ell^{\tau_\ell}\right)\exp\left(-v\right)dv\\&=\frac{\exp\left(\mu_{jk}/\tau_j\right)I_j^{\tau_j-1}}{I}\int_{-\infty}^{\infty}\exp\left(-\exp\left(-v-\mu_{jk}+\log I\right)\right)\exp\left(-v-\mu_{jk}+\log I\right)dv\\&=\frac{\exp\left(\mu_{jk}/\tau_j\right)I_j^{\tau_j-1}}{I}=P_{k|j}P_j\end{aligned}$$

as claimed. ■

Proof of Theorem 26.3 We follow the proof of Theorem 26.1 through (26.27), where in this case, $\mu_{j\ell}=X'\left(\beta_j-\beta_\ell\right)+\left(Z_j-Z_\ell\right)'\gamma$, and

$$F_j\left(\varepsilon_1,\ldots,\varepsilon_J\right)=\frac{\partial}{\partial\varepsilon_j}F\left(\varepsilon_1,\ldots,\varepsilon_J\right)=\prod_{\ell\neq j}\Phi\left(\mu_{j\ell}+\varepsilon_j\right)\phi(\varepsilon_j)$$

Thus

$$\mathbb{P}\left[Y=j\right]=\int_{-\infty}^{\infty}\prod_{\ell\neq j}\Phi\left(\mu_{j\ell}+v\right)\phi(v)dv$$

as claimed. ■

26.14 EXERCISES

Exercise 26.1 For the multinomial logit model (26.2), show that $0 \le P_j(x) \le 1$ and $\sum_{j=1}^{J} P_j(x) = 1$.

Exercise 26.2 Show that $P_j(x)$ in the multinomial logit model (26.2) only depends on the coefficient differences $\beta_j - \beta_J$.

Exercise 26.3 For the multinomial logit model (26.2), show that the marginal effects equal (26.4).

Exercise 26.4 Show that (26.8) holds for the conditional logit model.

Exercise 26.5 For the conditional logit model (26.8), show that the marginal effects are (26.9) and (26.10).

Exercise 26.6 Show that $P_j(w,x)$ in the conditional logit model (26.8) depends only on the coefficient differences $\beta_j - \beta_J$ and variable differences $x_j - x_J$.

Exercise 26.7 In the conditional logit model, find an estimator for AME_{jj}.

Exercise 26.8 Show (26.11).

Exercise 26.9 In the conditional logit model with no alternative-invariant regressors W, show that (26.11) implies $P_j(x)/P_\ell(x) = \exp\left(\left(x_j - x_\ell\right)' \gamma\right)$.

Exercise 26.10 Consider the nested logit model. If k and ℓ are alternatives in the same group j, show that the ratio $P_{jk}/P_{j\ell}$ is independent of variables in the other groups. What does this mean?

Exercise 26.11 Consider the nested logit model. For groups j and ℓ, show that the ratio P_j/P_ℓ is independent of variables in the other groups. What does this mean?

Exercise 26.12 Use the `cps09mar` dataset and the subset of men. Estimate a multinomial logit model for marriage status similar to that shown in Figure 26.1 as a function of *age*. How do your findings compare with those for women?

Exercise 26.13 Use the `cps09mar` dataset and the subset of women with ages up to 35. Estimate a multinomial logit model for marriage status as linear functions of *age* and *education*. Interpret your results.

Exercise 26.14 Use the `cps09mar` dataset and the subset of women. Estimate a nested logit model for marriage status as a function of *age*. Describe how you decide on the grouping of alternatives.

Exercise 26.15 Use the `Koppelman` dataset. Estimate conditional logit models similar to those reported in Table 26.1 but with the following modifications. For each case, report the estimated coefficients and standard errors for the cost and time variables, and the log-likelihood, and describe how the results change.

(a) Replicate the results of Table 26.1 for conditional logit with the same variables. Note: The regressors used in Table 26.1 are *cost*, *intime*, *income*, and *urban*.

(b) Add the variable *outtime*, which is out-of-vehicle time.

(c) Replace *intime* with $time = intime + outtime$.

(d) Replace *cost* and *intime* with log(*cost*) and log(*intime*).

Exercise 26.16 Use the `Koppelman` dataset. Estimate a nested logit model similar to those reported in Table 26.1 but with the following modifications. For each case, report the estimated coefficients and standard errors for the cost and time variables, the log-likelihood, and describe how the results change.

(a) Replicate the results of Table 26.1 for nested logit with the same variables. Note: You will need to constrain the dissimilarity parameter for {train, bus}.

(b) Replace *cost* and *intime* with log(*cost*) and log(*intime*).

(c) Use the groupings {car} and {train, bus, air}. Why (or why not) might this nesting make sense?

(d) Use the groupings {air} and {train, bus, car}.Why (or why not) might this nesting make sense?

Exercise 26.17 Use the `Koppelman` dataset. Estimate a mixed logit model similar to that reported in Table 26.1 but with the following modifications. For each case, report the estimated coefficients and standard errors for the cost and time variables, the log-likelihood, and describe how the results change.

(a) Replicate the results of Table 26.1 for mixed logit with the same variables.

(b) Replace *intime* with $time = intime + outtime$.

(c) Treat the coefficient on *intime* as the negative of a lognormal random variable. (Replace *intime* with $nintime = intime$, and treat the coefficient as lognormally distributed.) How do you compare the results of the estimated models?

Exercise 26.18 Use the `Koppelman` dataset. Estimate a general multinomial probit model similar to that reported in Table 26.1 but with the following modifications. For each case, report the estimated coefficients and standard errors for the cost and time variables, the log-likelihood, and describe how the results change.

(a) Replicate the results of Table 26.1 for multinomial probit with the same variables.

(b) Replace *cost* and *intime* with log(*cost*) and log(*intime*).

CHAPTER 27
CENSORING AND SELECTION

27.1 INTRODUCTION

Censored regression occurs when the dependent variable is constrained, resulting in a pileup of observations on a boundary. Selection occurs when sampling is endogenous. Under either censoring or selection, conventional (e.g., least squares) estimators are biased for the population parameters of the uncensored/unselected distributions. Methods have been developed to circumvent this bias, including the Tobit, censored least absolute deviations (CLAD), and sample selection estimators.

For more detail, see Maddala (1983), Amemiya (1985), Gourieroux (2000), Cameron and Trivedi (2005), and Wooldridge (2010).

27.2 CENSORING

It is common in economic applications for a dependent variable to have a mixed discrete/continuous distribution, where the discrete component is on the boundary of support. Most commonly, this boundary occurs at 0. For example, Figure 27.1(a) displays the density of *tabroad* (transfers from abroad) from the data file `CHJ2004`. This variable is the amount[1] of remittances received by a Philippino household from a foreign source. For 80% of households, this variable equals 0. The associated mass point is displayed by the bar at 0. For 20% of households, *tabroad* is positive and continuously distributed with a thick right tail. The associated density is displayed by the line graph.

Given such observations, it is unclear how to proceed with a regression analysis. Should we use the full sample including the 0's? Should we use only the subsample excluding the 0's? Or should we do something else?

To answer these questions, it is useful to have a statistical model. A classical framework is **censored regression**, which posits that the observed variable is a censored version of a latent continuously distributed variable. Without loss of generality, we focus on the case of **censoring from below** at 0.

The censored regression model was proposed by Tobin (1958) to explain household consumption of durable goods. Tobin observed that in survey data, durable good consumption is zero for a positive fraction of households. He proposed treating the observations as censored realizations from a continuous distribution. His model is

$$\begin{aligned} Y^* &= X'\beta + e \\ e \mid X &\sim \mathrm{N}(0, \sigma^2) \\ Y &= \max\left(Y^*, 0\right). \end{aligned} \tag{27.1}$$

[1] In thousands of Philippino pesos.

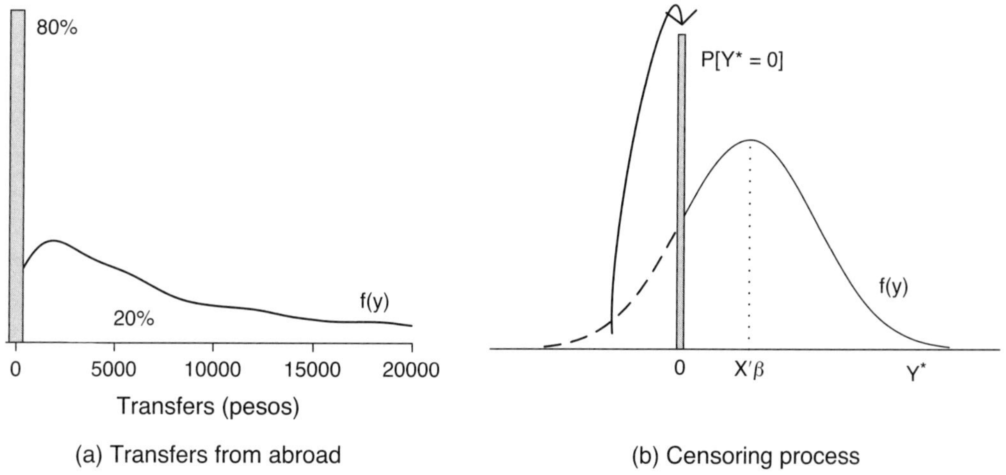

FIGURE 27.1 Censored densities

This model is known as **Tobit regression** or **censored regression**. It is also known as the **Type 1 Tobit model**. The variable Y^* is latent (unobserved). The observed variable Y is censored from below at 0. So positive values are uncensored, and negative values are transformed to 0. This censoring model replicates the observed phenomenon of a pileup of observations at 0.

The Tobit model can be justified by a latent choice framework, where an individual's optimal (unconstrained) continuously distributed choice is Y^*. Feasible choices, however, are constrained to satisfy $Y \geq 0$. (For example, negative purchases are not allowed.) Consequently, the realized value Y is a censored version of Y^*. To justify this interpretation of the model, we need to envisage a context where desired choices include negative values. This may be a strained interpretation for consumption purchases, but it may be reasonable when negative values make economic sense.

The censoring process is depicted in Figure 27.1(b). The latent variable Y^* has a normal density centered at $X'\beta$. The portion for $Y^* > 0$ is maintained, while the portion for $Y^* < 0$ is transformed to a point mass at 0. The location of the density and the degree of censoring are controlled by the conditional mean $X'\beta$. As $X'\beta$ moves to the right, the amount of censoring is decreased. As $X'\beta$ moves to the left, the amount of censoring is increased.

A common "remedy" to the censoring problem is deletion of the censored observations. This creates a **truncated** distribution that is defined by the following transformation:

$$Y^{\#} = \begin{cases} Y, & \text{if } Y > 0 \\ \text{missing}, & \text{if } Y = 0. \end{cases}$$

In Figure 27.1(a) and Figure 27.1(b), the truncated distribution is the continuous portion above 0 with the mass point at 0 omitted.

The censoring and truncation processes are depicted in Figure 27.2(a), which plots 100 random[2] draws (Y^*, X). The uncensored variables are marked by the open circles and squares. The open squares are the realizations for which $Y^* > 0$, and the open circles are the realizations for which $Y^* < 0$. The censored distribution

[2] $X \sim U[-3,3]$, and $Y^* \mid X \sim N(1+X, 1)$.

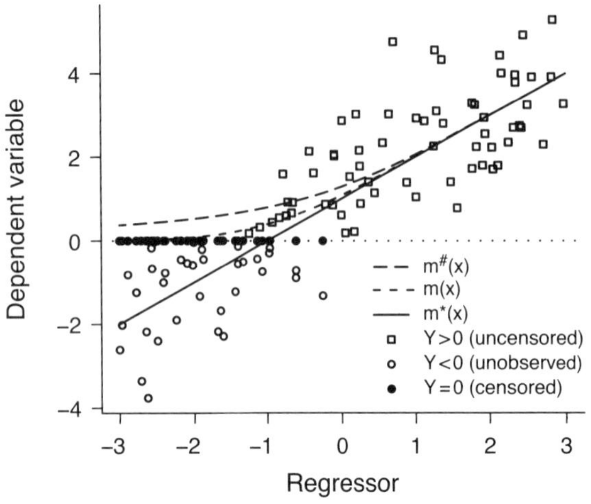

(a) Censored regression functions

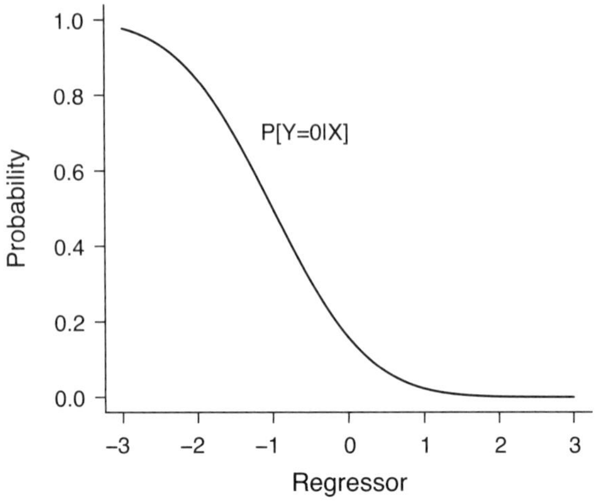

(b) Censoring probability

FIGURE 27.2 Properties of censored distributions

replaces the negative values of Y^* with 0, and replaces the open with the filled circles. The censored distribution thus consists of the open squares and filled circles. The truncated distribution is obtained by deleting the censored observations and so consists of just the open squares.

To summarize: We distinguish between three distributions and variables: **uncensored** (Y^*), **censored** (Y), and **truncated** ($Y^\#$).

The censored regression model (27.1) makes several strong assumptions: (1) linearity of the conditional mean; (2) independence of the error; and (3) normal distribution. The linearity assumption is not critical, as we can interpret $X'\beta$ as a series expansion or similar flexible approximation. The independence assumption, however, is quite important, as its violation (e.g., heteroskedasticity) changes the properties of the censoring process. The normality assumption is also quite important, yet it is difficult to justify from first principles.

27.3 CENSORED REGRESSION FUNCTIONS

We can calculate some properties of the conditional distribution of the censored random variable. The conditional probability of censoring is

$$\mathbb{P}\left[Y^* < 0 \mid X\right] = \mathbb{P}\left[e < -X'\beta \mid X\right] = \Phi\left(-\frac{X'\beta}{\sigma}\right).$$

Figure 27.2(b) plots the censoring probability as a function of X for the example from Figure 27.2(a). The censoring probability is 98% for $X=-3$, 50% for $X=-1$, and 2% for $X=1$.

The conditional mean of the uncensored, censored, and truncated distributions are, respectively,

$$m^*(X) = \mathbb{E}\left[Y^* \mid X\right] = X'\beta,$$

$$m(X) = \mathbb{E}\left[Y \mid X\right] = X'\beta\, \Phi\left(\frac{X'\beta}{\sigma}\right) + \sigma\phi\left(\frac{X'\beta}{\sigma}\right) \tag{27.2}$$

$$m^{\#}(X) = \mathbb{E}\left[Y^{\#} \mid X\right] = X'\beta + \sigma\lambda\left(\frac{X'\beta}{\sigma}\right). \tag{27.3}$$

The function $\lambda(x) = \phi(x)/\Phi(x)$ in (27.3) is called the **inverse Mills ratio**. To obtain (27.2) and (27.3), see Theorem 5.8 parts 4 and 6 of *Probability and Statistics for Economists* and Exercise 27.1.

Since $Y^* \leq Y \leq Y^{\#}$, it follows that

$$m^*(x) \leq m(x) \leq m^{\#}(x)$$

for all x with strict inequality if the censoring probability is positive. Thus the conditional means of the truncated and censored distributions are biased for the uncensored conditional mean.

Figure 27.2(a) illustrates this bias. The uncensored mean $m^*(x)$ is marked by the straight line, the censored mean $m(x)$ is marked by the dashed curve, and the truncated mean $m^{\#}(x)$ is marked by the long dashes. The functions are strictly ranked, with the truncated mean exhibiting the highest bias.

27.4 THE BIAS OF LEAST SQUARES ESTIMATION

If the observations (Y, X) are generated by the censored model (27.1), then least squares estimation using either the full sample (including the censored observations) or the truncated sample (excluding the censored observations) will be biased. Indeed, an estimator that is consistent for the CEF (such as a series estimator) will estimate the censored mean $m(x)$ or truncated mean $m^{\#}(x)$ in the censored and truncated samples, respectively, not the latent CEF $m^*(x)$.

It is also interesting to consider the properties of the best linear predictor of Y on X, which is the estimand of the least squares estimator. In general, this depends on the marginal distribution of the regressors. However, when the regressors are normally distributed, the best linear predicator takes a simple form, as discovered by Greene (1981). Write the model with an explicit intercept as $Y^* = \alpha + X'\beta + e$, and assume that $X \sim \mathrm{N}(0, \Sigma)$. Greene showed that the best linear predictor slope coefficient is

$$\beta_{\mathrm{BLP}} = \beta\,(1 - \pi) \tag{27.4}$$

where $\pi = \mathbb{P}\left[Y = 0\right]$ is the censoring probability. Equation (27.4) is derived at the end of this section.

Greene's formula (27.4) shows that the least squares slope coefficients are shrunk toward 0 proportionately with the censoring percentage. Although Greene's formula is special to normal regressors, it gives a baseline estimate of the bias due to censoring. The censoring proportion π is easily estimated from the sample (e.g., $\pi = 0.80$ in our transfers example), allowing a quick calculation of the expected bias due to censoring. This can be used as a rule of thumb. If the expected bias is sufficiently small (e.g., less than 5%), the resulting expected estimation bias (e.g., 5%) may be acceptable, leading to conventional least squares estimation using the full sample without an explicit treatment of censoring. However, if the censoring proportion π is sufficiently high (e.g., 10%), then estimation methods that correct for censoring bias may be desired.

I close this section by deriving (27.4). The calculation is simplified by a trick suggested by Goldberger (1981). Notice that $Y^* \sim \mathrm{N}(\alpha, \sigma_Y^2)$ with $\sigma_Y^2 = \sigma^2 + \beta'\Sigma\beta$. Using the moments of the truncated normal distribution (see *Probability and Statistics for Economists*, Theorems 5.7 part 6 and 5.7 part 8) and setting $\lambda = \lambda(\alpha/\sigma_Y)$, we can calculate that

$$\begin{aligned}\mathbb{E}\left[\left(Y^* - \alpha\right) Y^* \mid Y^* > 0\right] &= \operatorname{var}\left[Y^* \mid Y^* > 0\right] + \left(\mathbb{E}\left[Y^* \mid Y^* > 0\right] - \alpha\right)\mathbb{E}\left[Y^* \mid Y^* > 0\right] \\ &= \sigma_Y^2\left(1 - \frac{\alpha}{\sigma_Y}\lambda - \lambda^2\right) + \sigma_Y\lambda\left(\alpha + \sigma_Y\lambda\right) = \sigma_Y^2.\end{aligned}$$

The projection of X on Y^* is $X = \mathbb{E}[XY^*]\sigma_Y^{-2}(Y^* - \alpha) + u$, where u is independent of Y^*. Thus we have

$$\begin{aligned}\mathbb{E}\left[XY^* \mid Y^* > 0\right] &= \mathbb{E}\left[\left(\mathbb{E}\left[XY^*\right]\sigma_Y^{-2}\left(Y^* - \alpha\right) + u\right) Y^* \mid Y^* > 0\right] \\ &= \mathbb{E}\left[XY^*\right]\sigma_Y^{-2}\mathbb{E}\left[\left(Y^* - \alpha\right) Y^* \mid Y^* > 0\right] \\ &= \mathbb{E}\left[XY^*\right].\end{aligned}$$

Hence

$$\begin{aligned}\beta_{\mathrm{BLP}} &= \mathbb{E}\left[XX'\right]^{-1}\mathbb{E}\left[XY\right] \\ &= \mathbb{E}\left[XX'\right]^{-1}\mathbb{E}\left[XY^* \mid Y^* > 0\right](1-\pi) \\ &= \mathbb{E}\left[XX'\right]^{-1}\mathbb{E}\left[XY^*\right](1-\pi) \\ &= \beta(1-\pi)\end{aligned}$$

which is (27.4), as claimed.

27.5 TOBIT ESTIMATOR

Tobin (1958) proposed estimation of the censored regression model (27.1) by maximum likelihood. The censored variable Y has a conditional distribution function, which is a mixture of continuous and discrete components:

$$F(y \mid x) = \begin{cases} 0, & y < 0 \\ \Phi\left(\dfrac{y - x'\beta}{\sigma}\right), & y \geq 0. \end{cases}$$

The associated density[3] function is

$$f(y \mid x) = \Phi\left(-\frac{x'\beta}{\sigma}\right)^{\mathbb{1}\{y=0\}}\left[\sigma^{-1}\phi\left(\frac{y - x'\beta}{\sigma}\right)\right]^{\mathbb{1}\{y>0\}}.$$

The first component is the probability of censoring, and the second component is the normal regression density.

The log-likelihood is the sum of the log density functions evaluated at the observations:

$$\begin{aligned}\ell_n\left(\beta, \sigma^2\right) &= \sum_{i=1}^{n} \log f\left(Y_i \mid X_i\right) \\ &= \sum_{i=1}^{n}\left(\mathbb{1}\left\{Y_i = 0\right\}\log f\left(Y_i \mid X_i\right) + \mathbb{1}\left\{Y_i > 0\right\}\log\left[\sigma^{-1}\phi\left(\frac{Y_i - X_i'\beta}{\sigma}\right)\right]\right) \\ &= \sum_{Y_i=0}\log\Phi\left(-\frac{X_i'\beta}{\sigma}\right) - \frac{1}{2}\sum_{Y_i>0}\left(\log\left(2\pi\sigma^2\right) + \frac{1}{\sigma^2}\left(Y_i - X_i'\beta\right)^2\right).\end{aligned}$$

[3] Since the distribution function is discontinuous at $y = 0$, the density is technically the derivative with respect to a mixed continuous/discrete measure.

The first component is the same as in a probit model, and the second component is the same as for the normal regression model.

The MLE $\left(\widehat{\beta}, \widehat{\sigma}^2\right)$ are the values that maximize the log-likelihood $\ell_n\left(\beta, \sigma^2\right)$. This estimator was nicknamed "Tobit" by Goldberger because of its connection with the probit estimator. Amemiya (1973) established its asymptotic normality.

Computation is improved, as shown by Olsen (1978), if we transform the parameters to $\gamma = \beta/\sigma$ and $\nu = 1/\sigma$. Then the reparameterized log-likelihood equals

$$\ell_n(\gamma, \nu) = \sum_{Y_i=0} \log \Phi\left(-X_i'\gamma\right) + \sum_{Y_i>0} \log\left(\nu/\sqrt{2\pi}\right) + \left(-\frac{1}{2}\right) \sum_{Y_i>0} \left(Y_i\nu - X_i'\gamma\right)^2. \tag{27.5}$$

This is the sum of three terms, each of which is globally concave in (γ, ν) (as we now discuss), so $\ell_n(\gamma, \nu)$ is globally concave in (γ, ν), ensuring global convergence of Newton-based optimizers. Indeed, the third term in (27.5) is the negative of a quadratic in (γ, ν), so it is concave. The second term in (27.5) is logarithmic in ν, which is concave. The first term in (27.5) is a function only of γ and has second derivative

$$\frac{\partial^2}{\partial\gamma\partial\gamma'} \sum_{Y_i=0} \log \Phi\left(-X_i'\gamma\right) = \sum_{Y_i=0} X_i X_i' \lambda'\left(-X_i'\gamma\right)$$

which is negative definite, because the Mills ratio satisfies $\lambda'(u) < 0$ (see Theorem 5.7 part 7 in *Probability and Statistics for Economists*). Hence the first term in (27.5) is concave.

In Stata, Tobit regression can be estimated with the `tobit` command. In R there are several options, including the `tobit` command in the `AER` package.

James Tobin

James Tobin (1918–2002) of the United States was one of the leading macroeconomists of the mid-twentieth century and winner of the 1981 Nobel Memorial Prize in Economic Sciences. His 1958 paper introduced censored regression and its MLE, typically called the "Tobit estimator." As a fascinating coincidence, the name "Tobit" also arises in the 1951 novel *The Caine Mutiny*, set on a U.S. Navy destroyer during World War II. At one point in the novel, the author describes a crew member named "Tobit" who had "a mind like a sponge," because of his high intellect. It turns out the author (Herman Wouk) and James Tobin served on the same Navy destroyer during World War II. Go figure!

27.6 IDENTIFICATION IN TOBIT REGRESSION

The Tobit model (27.1) makes several strong assumptions. Which are critical? To investigate this question, consider the nonparametric censored regression framework

$$\begin{aligned} Y^* &= m(X) + e \\ \mathbb{E}[e] &= 0 \\ Y &= \max\left(Y^*, 0\right) \end{aligned}$$

where $e \sim F$ is independent of X, and the regression function $m(x)$ and distribution function $F(e)$ are unknown. What is identified?

Suppose that the random variable $m(X)$ has unbounded support on the real line (as occurs when $m(X) = X'\beta$ and X has an unbounded distribution, such as the normal). Then we can find a set $\mathscr{X} \subset \mathbb{R}^k$ such that for $x \in \mathscr{X}$, $\mathbb{P}[Y=0 \mid X=x] = F(-m(x)) \simeq 0$. We can then imagine taking the subsample of observations for which $X \in \mathscr{X}$. The function $m(x)$ is identified for $x \in \mathscr{X}$, permitting the identification of the distribution $F(e)$. Because the censoring probability $\mathbb{P}[Y=0 \mid X=x] = F(-m(x))$ is globally identified, the function $m(x)$ is globally identified as well. This discussion shows that so long as we maintain the assumption that X and e are independent, the regression function $m(x)$ and distribution function $F(e)$ are nonparametrically identified when the CEF $m(X)$ has full support. These two assumptions, however, are essential, as we now discuss.

Suppose the full support condition fails in the sense that the regression function is bounded $m(X) \le \overline{m}$ at a value such that $\mathbb{P}[Y=0 \mid X=x] = F(-\overline{m}) > 0$. In this case, the error distribution $F(e)$ is not identified for $e \le -\overline{m}$. Then the distribution function can take any shape for $e \le -\overline{m}$, so long as it is weakly increasing. This implies that the expectation $\mathbb{E}[e]$ is not identified, so the location of $m(x)$ (the intercept of the regression) is not identified.

The second important assumption is that e is independent of X. This assumption has been relaxed by Powell (1984, 1986) in the conditional quantile framework. The model is

$$Y^* = q_\tau(X) + e_\tau$$

$$\mathbb{Q}_\tau[e_\tau \mid X] = 0$$

$$Y = \max\left(Y^*, 0\right)$$

for some $\tau \in (0,1)$. This model defines $q_\tau(x)$ as the τth conditional quantile function. Because quantiles are equivariant to monotone transformations, we have the relationship:

$$\mathbb{Q}_\tau[Y \mid X=x] = \max\left(q_\tau(x), 0\right).$$

Thus the conditional quantile function of Y is the censored quantile function of Y^*. The function $\mathbb{Q}_\tau[Y \mid X=x]$ is identified from the joint distribution of (Y, X). Consequently, the function $q_\tau(x)$ is identified for any x such that $q_\tau(x) > 0$. This is an important conceptual breakthrough. Powell's result shows that identification of $q_\tau(x)$ does not require the error to be independent of X or to have a known distribution. The key insight is that quantiles, not means, are nonparametrically identified from a censored distribution.

A limitation of Powell's result is that the function $q_\tau(x)$ is only identifed on subpopulations for which censoring does not exceed τ%.

To illustrate, Figure 27.3(a) displays the conditional quantile functions $q_\tau(x)$ for $\tau = 0.3, 0.5, 0.7$, and 0.9 for the conditional distribution $Y^* \mid X \sim \mathrm{N}\left(\sqrt{x} - \frac{3}{2}, 2 + x\right)$. The portions above 0 (which are identified from the censored distribution) are plotted with solid lines. The portions below 0 (which are not identified from the censored distribution) are plotted with dashed lines. We can see that in this example, the quantile function $q_{.9}(x)$ is identified for all values of x, the quantile function $q_{.3}(x)$ is not identified for any values of x, and the quantile functions $q_{.7}(x)$ and $q_{.5}(x)$ are identified for a subset of values of x. The explanation is that for any fixed value of $X = x$, we only observe the censored distribution Y and so only observe the quantiles above the censoring point. There is no nonparametric information about the distribution of Y^* below the censoring point.

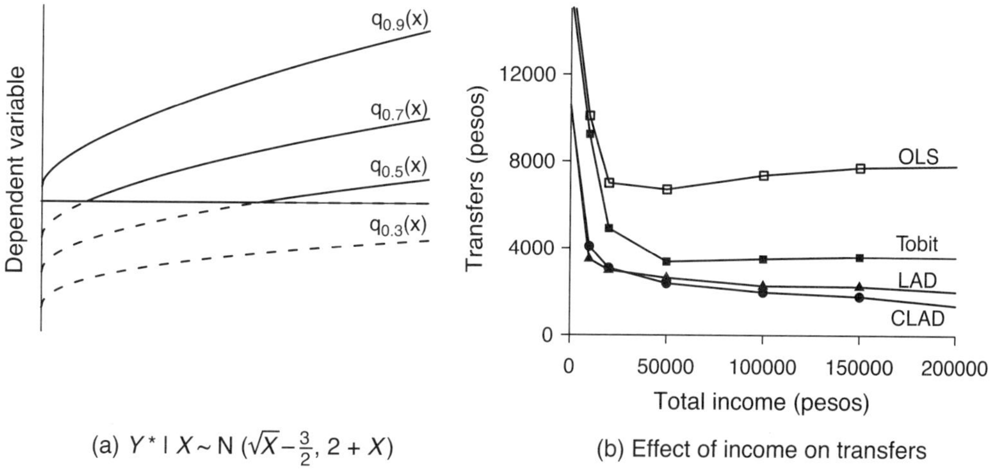

FIGURE 27.3 Censored regression quantiles

27.7 CLAD AND CQR ESTIMATORS

Powell (1984, 1986) applied the quantile identification strategy described in Section 27.6 to develop straightforward censored regression estimators.

The model in Powell (1984) is censored median regression:

$$Y^* = X'\beta + e$$
$$\text{med}\,[e \mid X] = 0$$
$$Y = \max\left(Y^*, 0\right).$$

In this model, Y^* is latent with $\text{med}\,[Y^* \mid X] = X'\beta$, and Y is censored at 0. As described in Section 27.6, the equivariance property of the median implies that the conditional median of Y equals

$$\text{med}\,[Y \mid X] = \max\left(X'\beta, 0\right).$$

This is a parametric but nonlinear median regression model for Y.

The appropriate estimator for median regression is least absolute deviations (LAD). The **censored least absolute deviations (CLAD)** criterion is

$$M_n(\beta) = \frac{1}{n}\sum_{i=1}^{n}\left|Y_i - \max\left(X_i'\beta, 0\right)\right|.$$

The CLAD estimator minimizes $M_n(\beta)$:

$$\widehat{\beta}_{\text{CLAD}} = \underset{\beta}{\operatorname{argmin}}\, M_n(\beta).$$

The CLAD criterion $M_n(\beta)$ has similar properties as the LAD criterion, namely, that it is continuous, faceted, and has discontinuous first derivatives. An important difference, however, is that $M_n(\beta)$ is not globally convex, so minimization algorithms may converge to a local rather than a global minimum.

Powell (1986) extended CLAD to censored quantile regression (CQR). The model is

$$Y^* = X'\beta + e$$
$$\mathbb{Q}_\tau [e \mid X] = 0$$
$$Y = \max(Y^*, 0)$$

for $\tau \in (0, 1)$. The equivariance property implies that the conditional quantile function for Y is

$$\mathbb{Q}_\tau [Y \mid X] = \max(X'\beta, 0).$$

The CQR criterion is

$$M_n(\beta; \tau) = \frac{1}{n} \sum_{i=1}^{n} \rho_\tau \left(Y_i - \max\left(X_i'\beta, 0\right)\right)$$

where $\rho_\tau(u)$ is the check function (24.10). The CQR estimator minimizes this criterion

$$\widehat{\beta}_{\text{CQR}}(\tau) = \underset{\beta}{\operatorname{argmin}}\, M_n(\beta; \tau).$$

As for CLAD, the criterion is not globally concave, so numerical minimization is not guarenteed to converge to the global minimum.

Powell (1984, 1986) shows that the CLAD and CQR estimators are asymptotically normal by similar arguments as for quantile regression. An important technical difference from quantile regression is that the CLAD and CQR estimators require stronger conditions for identification. As we discussed in the Section 27.6, the quantile function $X'\beta$ is only identified for regions where it is positive. Thus we require a positive fraction of the population to satisfy $X'\beta > 0$. Furthermore, the relevant design matrix (24.18) is defined on this subpopulation and must be full rank for conventional inference. Essentially, there must be sufficient variation in the regressors over the region of the sample space where there is no censoring.

CLAD can be estimated in Stata with the add-on package `clad`. In R, CLAD and CQR can be estimated with the `crq` command in the package `quantreg`.

27.8 ILLUSTRATING CENSORED REGRESSION

To illustrate the methods, let us revisit the applications reported in Section 20.6, where we used a linear spline to estimate the impact of income on nongovernmental transfers for a sample of 8,684 Philippino households. The least squares estimates indicated a sharp discontinuity in the conditional mean around 20,000 pesos. The dependent variable is the sum of transfers received domestically, from abroad, and in-kind, less gifts. Each of these four subvariables is nonnegative. If we apply the model to any of these subvariables, there is substantial censoring. To illustrate, we set the dependent variable to equal the sum of transfers received domestically, from abroad, and in-kind, for which the censoring proportion is 18%. This proportion is sufficiently high that we should expect significant censoring bias if censoring is ignored.

We estimate the same model as reported in Section 20.6 and displayed in Figure 20.2(b), which is a linear spline in *income* with five knots and 15 additional control regressors. We estimated the equation using four methods: (a) least squares, (b) Tobit regression, (c) LAD, and (d) CLAD. Figure 27.3(b) displays the estimated regression as a function of income (with remaining regressors set at sample means).

The basic insight—that the regression has a slope close to -1 for low income levels and is flat for high income levels, with a sharp discontinuity at an income level of 20,000 pesos—is remarkably robust across the four estimates. What is noticeably different, however, is the level of the regression function. The least squares estimate is several thousand pesos above the others. The fact that the LAD and CLAD estimates have a meaningfully different level should not be surprising. The dependent variable is highly skewed, so the mean and median are quite different (the unconditional mean and median are 7,700 and 1,200, respectively). This implies a level shift of the regression function. It does not explain, however, why the Tobit estimate is also substantially shifted down. Instead, this shift can be explained by censoring bias. Because the regression function is negatively sloped, the censoring probability is increasing in income, so the bias of the least squares estimator is positive and increasing in the income level. The LAD and CLAD estimates are quite similar, even though the LAD estimates do not account for censoring. Overall, the CLAD estimates are the preferred choice, because they are robust to both censoring and non-normality.

27.9 SAMPLE SELECTION BIAS

Although econometric models typically assume random sampling, actual observations are typically gathered nonrandomly, which can induce estimation bias if selection (presence in the sample) is endogeneous. The following are examples of potential sample selection.

1. **Wage regression**. Wages are only observed for individuals who have wage income, which means that the individual is a member of the labor force and has a wage-paying job. The decision to work may be endogenously related to the person's observed and unobserved characteristics.
2. **Program evaluation**. The goal is to measure the impact of a program, such as workforce training through a pilot program. Endogenous selection arises when individuals volunteer to participate (rather than being randomly assigned). Individuals who volunteer for a training program may have abilities that are correlated with outcomes.
3. **Surveys**. Although a survey may be randomly distributed, the act of completing the survey is nonrandom. Most surveys have low response rates. Endogenous selection arises when the decision to complete and return the survey is correlated with the survey responses.
4. **Ratings**. We are routinely asked to rate products, services, and experiences. Most people do not respond to the request. Endogenous selection arises when the decision to rate the product is correlated with the response.

To understand the effect of sample selection, it is useful to view sampling as a two-stage process. In the first stage, the random variables (Y, X) are drawn. In the second stage, the pair is either selected into the sample $(S=1)$ or unobserved $(S=0)$. The sample then consists of the pairs (Y, X) for which $S=1$. Suppose that the variables satisfy the latent regression model $Y = X'\beta + e$, with $\mathbb{E}[e \mid X] = 0$. Then the CEF in the observed (selected) sample is

$$\mathbb{E}[Y \mid X, S=1] = X'\beta + \mathbb{E}[e \mid X, S=1].$$

Selection bias occurs when the second term is nonzero. To understand this further, suppose that selection can be modeled as $S = \mathbb{1}\left\{X'\gamma + u > 0\right\}$ for some error u, which is consistent with a latent utility framework, where $X'\gamma + u$ is the latent utility of participation. Given this framework, we can write the CEF of Y in the selected sample as

$$\mathbb{E}[Y \mid X, S=1] = X'\beta + \mathbb{E}\left[e \mid u > -X'\gamma\right].$$

Let $e = \rho u + \varepsilon$ be the projection of e on u. Suppose that the errors are independent of X, and u and ε are mutually independent. Then the above expression equals

$$\mathbb{E}[Y \mid X, S=1] = X'\beta + \rho\mathbb{E}\left[u \mid u > -X'\gamma\right] = X'\beta + \rho g\left(X'\gamma\right)$$

for some function $g(u)$. When $u \sim \mathrm{N}(0,1)$, $g(u) = \phi(u)/\Phi(u) = \lambda(u)$ (see Exercise 27.7), so the expression equals

$$\mathbb{E}[Y \mid X, S=1] = X'\beta + \rho\lambda\left(X'\gamma\right). \tag{27.6}$$

This equation is the same as (27.3) in the special case $\rho = \sigma$ and $\gamma = \beta/\sigma$. As shown in Figure 27.2(a), this equation deviates from the latent CEF $X'\beta$.

One way to interpret this effect is that the regression function (27.6) contains two components: $X'\beta$ and $\rho\lambda\left(X'\gamma\right)$. A linear regression on X omits the second term and thus inherits omitted variables bias, because X and $\lambda\left(X'\gamma\right)$ are correlated. The extent of omitted variables bias depends on the magnitude of ρ, which is the coefficient from the projection of e on u. When the errors e and u are independent (when selection is exogenous), then $\rho = 0$ and (27.6) simplifies to $X'\beta$ and there is no omitted term. Thus, sample selection bias arises if (and only if) selection is correlated with the equation error.

Furthermore, the omitted selection term $\lambda\left(X'\gamma\right)$ only impacts estimated marginal effects if the slope coefficients γ are nonzero. In contrast, suppose that $X'\gamma = \gamma_0$, a constant. Then (27.6) equals $\mathbb{E}[Y \mid X, S=1] = X'\beta + \rho\lambda(\gamma_0)$, so the impact of selection is an intercept shift. If our focus is on marginal effects, sample selection bias only arises when the selection equation has nontrivial dependence on the regressors X.

In Figure 27.2(a), we saw that censoring attenuates (flattens) the regression function. Although the selection CEF (27.6) takes a similar form, it is broader and can have a different impact. In contrast to the censoring case, selection can both steepen as well as flatten the regression function. In general, it is difficult to predict the effect of selection on regression functions.

As we have shown, endogenous selection changes the conditional expectation. If samples are generated by endogenous selection, then estimation will be biased for the parameters of interest. Without information on the selection process, little can be done to "correct" the bias other than to be aware of its presence. In the next section, we discuss one approach that corrects for sample selection bias when we have information on the selection process.

27.10 HECKMAN'S MODEL

Heckman (1979) showed that sample selection bias can be corrected if we have a sample that includes the nonselected observations. Suppose that the observations $\{Y_i, X_i, Z_i\}$ are a random sample, where Y is a selected variable (such as wage, which is only observed if a person has wage income). Heckman's approach is to build a joint model of the full sample (not just the selected sample) and use this to estimate the model parameters.

Heckman's model is

$$\begin{aligned}
Y^* &= X'\beta + e \\
S^* &= Z'\gamma + u \\
S &= \mathbb{1}\left\{S^* > 0\right\} \\
Y &= \begin{cases} Y^*, & \text{if } S=1 \\ \text{missing}, & \text{if } S=0 \end{cases}
\end{aligned}$$

with

$$\begin{pmatrix} e \\ u \end{pmatrix} \sim \mathrm{N}\left(0, \begin{pmatrix} \sigma^2 & \sigma_{21} \\ \sigma_{21} & 1 \end{pmatrix}\right).$$

The model specifies that the latent variables Y^* and S^* are linear in regressors X and Z with structural errors e and u. The variable S indicates *selection* and follows a probit equation. The variable Y equals the latent variable Y^* if selected ($S=1$) and otherwise is missing. The model specifies that the errors are jointly normal with covariance σ_{21}. The variance of u is not identified, so it is normalized to equal 1.

In Heckman's classic example, Y^* is the wage (or log(wage)) an individual would receive if they were employed, S is employment status, and Y is observed wage. The coefficients β are those of the wage regression; the coefficients γ are those that determine employment status. The error e is unobserved ability and other unobserved factors that determine an individual's wages; the error u is the unobserved factors that determine employment status; and the two are likely to be correlated.

Based on the same calculations as discussed in Section 27.9, the CEF of Y in the selected sample is

$$\mathbb{E}[Y \mid X, Z, S=1] = X'\beta + \sigma_{21}\lambda\left(Z'\gamma\right) \tag{27.7}$$

where $\lambda(x)$ is the inverse Mills ratio.

Heckman proposed a two-step estimator of the coefficients. The insight is that the coefficient γ is identified by the probit regression of S on Z. Given γ, the coefficients β and σ_{21} are identified by least squares regression of Y on $\left(X, \lambda(Z'\gamma)\right)$ using the selected sample. The steps are as follows:

1. Construct (if necessary) the binary variable S from the observed series Y.
2. Estimate the coefficient $\widehat{\gamma}$ by probit regression of S on Z.
3. Construct the variables $\widehat{\lambda}_i = \lambda\left(Z_i'\widehat{\gamma}\right)$.
4. Estimate the coefficients $(\widehat{\beta}, \widehat{\sigma}_{21})$ by least squares regression of Y_i on $(X_i, \widehat{\lambda}_i)$ using the subsample with $S_i = 1$.

Heckman showed that the estimator $\widehat{\beta}$ is consistent and asymptotically normal. The variable $\widehat{\lambda}_i$ is a generated regressor (see Section 12.26), which affects covariance matrix estimation. The method is sometimes called "Heckit", as it is an analog of probit, logit, and Tobit regressions.

As a by-product, we obtain an estimator of the covariance σ_{21}. This parameter indicates the magnitude of sample selection endogeneity. If selection is exogenous, then $\sigma_{21}=0$. The null hypothesis of exogenous selection can be tested by examining the t-statistic for $\widehat{\sigma}_{21}$.

An alternative to two-step estimation is joint maximum likelihood. The joint density of S and Y is

$$f(s, y \mid x, z) = \mathbb{P}[S=0 \mid x, z]^{1-s} f\left(y, S=1 \mid x, z\right)^s.$$

The selection probability is $\mathbb{P}[S=0 \mid x, z] = 1 - \Phi\left(z'\gamma\right)$. The conditional density component is

$$\begin{aligned} f\left(y, S=1, \mid x, z\right) &= \int_0^\infty f\left(y, s^* \mid x, z\right) ds^* \\ &= \int_0^\infty f\left(s^* \mid y, x, z\right) f\left(y \mid x, z\right) ds^* \\ &= \left(1 - F\left(s^* \mid y, x, z\right)\right) f\left(y \mid x, z\right). \end{aligned}$$

The first equality holds because $S=1$ is the same as $S^* > 0$. The second factors the joint density into the product of the conditional of S^* given Y and the marginal of Y. The marginal density of Y is $\sigma^{-1}\phi\left((y - x'\beta)/\sigma\right)$. The conditional distribution of S^* given Y is $\mathrm{N}\left(Z'\gamma + \frac{\sigma_{21}}{\sigma^2}\left(Y - X'\beta\right), 1 - \frac{\sigma_{21}}{\sigma^2}\right)$. Making these substitutions we obtain the joint mixed density:

$$f(s, y \mid x, z) = \left(1 - \Phi\left(z'\gamma\right)\right)^{1-s}\left[\Phi\left(\frac{z'\gamma + \frac{\sigma_{21}}{\sigma^2}\left(y - x'\beta\right)}{\sqrt{1 - \frac{\sigma_{21}}{\sigma^2}}}\right)\frac{1}{\sigma}\phi\left(\frac{y - x'\beta}{\sigma}\right)\right]^s.$$

Evaluated at the observations, we obtain the log-likelihood function:

$$\begin{aligned}\ell_n\left(\beta, \gamma, \sigma^2, \sigma_{21}\right) &= \sum_{S_i=0} \log\left(1 - \Phi\left(Z_i'\gamma\right)\right)\\ &\quad + \sum_{S_i=1}\left[\log\Phi\left(\frac{Z_i'\gamma + \frac{\sigma_{21}}{\sigma^2}\left(Y_i - X_i'\beta\right)}{\sqrt{1 - \frac{\sigma_{21}}{\sigma^2}}}\right) - \frac{1}{2}\log\left(2\pi\sigma^2\right) - \frac{1}{2\sigma^2}\left(Y_i - X_i'\beta\right)^2\right].\end{aligned}$$

The MLE $\left(\widehat{\beta}, \widehat{\gamma}, \widehat{\sigma}^2, \widehat{\sigma}_{21}\right)$ maximizes the log-likelihood.

The MLE is the preferred estimation method for final reporting. It can be computationally demanding in some applications, however, so the two-step estimator can be useful for preliminary analysis.

In Stata, the two-step estimator and joint MLE can be obtained with the `heckman` command.

27.11 NONPARAMETRIC SELECTION

A nonparametric selection model is

$$\begin{aligned}Y^* &= m(X) + e\\ S^* &= g(Z) + u\\ S &= \mathbb{1}\left\{S^* > 0\right\}\\ Y &= \begin{cases} Y^*, & \text{if } S = 1\\ \text{missing}, & \text{if } S = 0\end{cases}\end{aligned}$$

where the distribution of (e, u) is unknown. For simplicity, we assume that (e, u) are independent of (X, Z).

Selection occurs if $u > -g(Z)$. This is unaffected by monotonically increasing transformations. Therefore, the distribution of u is not separately identified from the function $g(Z)$. Consequently, we can normalize the distribution of u to a convenient form. Here we use the normal distribution: $u \sim \Phi(x)$.

Because the functions $m(X)$ and $g(Z)$ are nonparametric, we can use series methods to approximate them by linear models of the form $m(X) = X'\beta$ and $g(Z) = Z'\gamma$ after suitable variable transformation. We will use the latter notation to link the models to estimation methods.

The conditional probability of selection is

$$p(Z) = \mathbb{P}\left[S = 1 \mid Z\right] = \mathbb{P}\left[u > -Z'\gamma \mid Z\right] = \Phi\left(Z'\gamma\right).$$

The probability $p(Z)$ is known as the **propensity score**; it is nonparametrically identified from the joint distribution of (S, Z), so the function $g(Z) = Z'\gamma$ is identified. The coefficient γ and propensity score can be estimated by binary choice methods, for example, by a series probit regression.

The CEF of Y given selection is

$$\mathbb{E}[Y \mid X, Z, S=1] = X'\beta + h_1\left(Z'\gamma\right) \tag{27.8}$$

where $h_1(x) = \mathbb{E}[e \mid u > -x]$. In general, $h_1(x)$ can take a range of possible shapes. When (e, u) are jointly normal with covariance σ_{21}, then $h_1(x) = \sigma_{21}\lambda(x)$, where $\lambda(x) = \phi(x)/\Phi(x)$ is the inverse Mills ratio. There are two alternative representations of the CEF that are potentially useful. Since $g(Z) = \Phi^{-1}\left(p(Z)\right)$, we have the representation

$$\mathbb{E}[Y \mid X, Z, S=1] = X'\beta + h_2\left(p(Z)\right) \tag{27.9}$$

where $h_2(x) = h_1\left(\Phi^{-1}(x)\right)$. Also, because $\lambda(x)$ is invertible, we have the representation

$$\mathbb{E}[Y \mid X, Z, S=1] = X'\beta + h_3\left(\lambda(Z'\gamma)\right) \tag{27.10}$$

where $h_3(x) = h_1\left(\lambda^{-1}(x)\right)$.

The three equations (27.8)–(27.10) suggest three two-step approaches to nonparametric estimation, which we now discuss. Each is based on a first-step binary choice estimator $\widehat{\gamma}$ of γ.

Equation (27.8) suggests a regression of Y on X and a series expansion in $Z'\widehat{\gamma}$, for example, a low-order polynomial in $Z'\widehat{\gamma}$.

Equation (27.9) suggests a regression of Y on X and a series expansion in the propensity score $\widehat{p} = \Phi\left(Z'\widehat{\gamma}\right)$, for example, a low-order polynomial in $\widehat{p}$.

Equation (27.10) suggests a regression of Y on X and a series expansion in $\widehat{\lambda} = \lambda\left(Z'\widehat{\gamma}\right)$, for example, a low-order polynomial in $\widehat{\lambda}$.

The advantage of expansions based on (27.10) is that they will be first-order accurate in the leading case of the normal distribution. So for distributions close to the normal, series expansions will be accurate even with a small number of terms. The advantage of expansions based on (27.9) is interpretability: The regression is expressed as a function of the propensity score.

Das, Newey, and Vella (2003) provide a detailed asymptotic theory for this class of estimators, focusing on those based on (27.9). They provide conditions under which the models are identified, and the estimators consistent and asymptotically normally distributed.

These nonparametric selection estimators are two-step estimators with generated regressors (see Section 12.26). Therefore, conventional covariance matrix estimators and standard errors are inconsistent. Asymptotically valid covariance matrix estimators can be constructed using GMM. An alternative is to use bootstrap methods. The latter should be implemented as an explicit two-step estimator, so that the first-step estimation is treated by the bootstrap distribution.

A standard recommendation is that the regressors Z in the selection equation should include at least one relevant variable that is a valid exclusion from the regressors X in the main equation. The reason is that otherwise, the series expansions for $m(x)$ and $h(Z'\gamma)$ can be highly collinear and not separately identified. This insight applies to the parametric case as well. One difficulty is that in applications, it may be challenging to identify variables that affect selection S^* but not the outcome Y^*.

27.12 PANEL DATA

A panel censored regression (panel Tobit) model is

$$Y_{it}^* = X_{it}'\beta + u_i + e_{it}$$

$$Y_{it} = \max\left(Y_{it}^*, 0\right).$$

The individual effect u_i can be treated as a random effect (uncorrelated with the errors) or a fixed effect (unstructured correlation).

A random effects estimator can be derived under the assumption of joint normality of the errors. This is implemented in the Stata command `xttobit`. The advantage is that the procedure is simple to implement. The disadvantages are those typically associated with random effects estimators.

A fixed effects estimator was developed by Honoré (1992). His key insight is the following, which is illustrated assuming $T=2$. If the errors (e_{i1}, e_{i2}) are independent of (X_{i1}, X_{i2}, u_i), then the distribution of (Y_{i1}^*, Y_{i2}^*) conditional on (X_{i1}, X_{i2}) is symmetric about the 45 degree line through the point $(\Delta X'\beta, 0)$ in (Y_1, Y_2) space. This distribution does not depend on the fixed effect u_i. From this symmetry and the censoring rules, Honoré derived moment conditions that identify the coefficients β and allow estimation by GMM. Honoré (1992) provides a complete asymptotic distribution theory. Honoré has provided a Stata command `Pantob`, which implements his estimator and is available on his website.

A panel sample selection model is

$$\begin{aligned} Y_{it}^* &= X_{it}'\beta + u_i + e_{it} \\ S_{it}^* &= Z_{it}'\gamma + \eta_i + v_{it} \\ S_{it} &= \mathbb{1}\left\{S_{it}^* > 0\right\} \\ Y_{it} &= \begin{cases} Y_{it}^*, & \text{if } S_{it} = 1 \\ \text{missing}, & \text{if } S_{it} = 0. \end{cases} \end{aligned}$$

A method to estimate this model is presented in Kyriazidou (1997). Again for exposition, let us focus on the $T=2$ case. Her estimator is motivated by the observation that β could be consistently estimated by least squares applied to the subsample where $S_{i1} = S_{i2} = 1$ (both observations are selected) and $Z_{i1}'\gamma = Z_{i2}'\gamma$ (both observations have same probability of selection). The parameter γ is identified up to scale by the selection equation, so it can be estimated as $\widehat{\gamma}$ by the methods described in Section 25.13 (e.g., Chamberlain (1980, 1984)). Given $\widehat{\gamma}$, we estimate β by kernel-weighted least squares on the subsample with $S_{i1} = S_{i2} = 1$, with kernel weights depending on $(Z_{i1} - Z_{i2})'\widehat{\gamma}$. Kyriazidou (1997) provides a complete distribution theory.

27.13 EXERCISES

Exercise 27.1 Derive (27.2) and (27.3). Hint: Use Theorems 5.7 and 5.8 of *Probability and Statistics for Economists.*

Exercise 27.2 Consider the model

$$\begin{aligned} Y^* &= X'\beta + e \\ e &\sim \mathrm{N}\left(0, \sigma^2\right) \\ Y &= \begin{cases} Y^*, & \text{if } Y^* \leq \tau \\ \text{missing}, & \text{if } Y^* > \tau. \end{cases} \end{aligned}$$

In this model, we say that Y is capped from above. Suppose you regress Y on X. Is OLS consistent for β? Describe the nature of the effect of the mismeasured observation on the OLS estimator.

Exercise 27.3 consider the model

$$Y = X'\beta + e$$
$$e \sim \mathrm{N}\left(0, \sigma^2\right).$$

Let $\widehat{\beta}$ denote the OLS estimator for β based on an available sample.

(a) Suppose that an observation is in the sample only if $X_1 > 0$, where X_1 is an element of X. Is $\widehat{\beta}$ consistent for β? Obtain an expression for its probability limit.

(b) Suppose that an observation is in the sample only if $Y > 0$. Is $\widehat{\beta}$ consistent for $\widehat{\beta}$? Obtain an expression for its probability limit.

Exercise 27.4 For the censored conditional mean (27.2), propose an NLLS estimator of (β, σ).

Exercise 27.5 For the truncated conditional mean (27.3), propose an NLLS estimator of (β, σ).

Exercise 27.6 A latent variable Y^* is generated by

$$Y^* = \beta_0 + X\beta_1 + e$$
$$e \mid X \sim \mathrm{N}\left(0, \sigma^2(X)\right)$$
$$\sigma^2(X) = \gamma_0 + X^2\gamma_1$$
$$Y = \max\left(Y^*, 0\right)$$

where X is scalar. Assume $\gamma_0 > 0$ and $\gamma_1 > 0$. The parameters are $\beta, \gamma_0, \gamma_1$. Find the log-likelihood function for the conditional distribution of Y given X.

Exercise 27.7 Consider the model

$$S = \mathbb{1}\left\{X'\gamma + u > 0\right\}$$
$$Y = \begin{cases} X'\beta + e, & \text{if } S = 1 \\ \text{missing}, & \text{if } S = 0 \end{cases}$$
$$\begin{pmatrix} e \\ u \end{pmatrix} \sim \mathrm{N}\left(0, \begin{pmatrix} \sigma^2 & \sigma_{21} \\ \sigma_{21} & 1 \end{pmatrix}\right)$$

Show that $\mathbb{E}\left[Y \mid X, S = 1\right] = X'\beta + \sigma_{21}\lambda\left(X'\gamma\right)$.

Exercise 27.8 Show (27.7).

Exercise 27.9 Use the CHJ2004 dataset. The variables *tinkind* and *income* are household transfers received in-kind and household income, respectively. Divide both variables by 1,000 to standardize. Create the regressor *Dincome*=(*income*-1)$\times\mathbb{1}\left\{\textit{income} > 1\right\}$.

(a) Estimate a linear regression of *tinkind* on *income* and *Dincome*. Interpret the results.

(b) Calculate the percentage of censored observations (the percentage for which *tinkind*$=0$). Do you expect censoring bias to be a problem in this example?

(c) Suppose you try to fix the problem by omitting the censored observations. Estimate the regression on the subsample of observations for which *tinkind* > 0.

(d) Estimate a Tobit regression of of *tinkind* on *income* and *Dincome*.

(e) Estimate the same regression as in part (d) using CLAD.

(f) Interpret and explain the differences between your results in (a)–(e).

Exercise 27.10 Consider the `cps09mar` dataset and the subsample of individuals with at least 12 years of education. Create *wage=earnings/(hours* $\times$ *weeks)* and *lwage*=log(*wage*).

(a) Estimate a linear regression of *lwage* on *education* and $education^2$. Interpret the results.

(b) Suppose the wage data had been capped at about \$30/hour. Create a variable *cwage*, which is *lwage* capped at 3.4. Estimate a linear regression of *cwage* on *education* and $education^2$. How would you interpret these results if you were unaware that the dependent variable was capped?

(c) Suppose you try to fix the problem by omitting the capped observations. Estimate the regression on the subsample of observations for which *cwage* is less than 3.4.

(d) Estimate a Tobit regression of *cwage* on *education* and $education^2$ with upper censoring at 3.4.

(e) Estimate the same regression as in part (d) using CLAD. You may need to impose an upper censoring of 3.3.

(f) Interpret and explain the differences between your results parts in (a)–(e).

Exercise 27.11 Consider the `DDK2011` dataset. Create a variable *testscore* that is *totalscore* standardized to have mean 0 and variance 1. The variable *tracking* is a dummy, indicating that the students were tracked (separated by initial test score). The varible *percentile* is the student's percentile in the initial distribution. For the following regressions, cluster by school.

(a) Estimate a linear regression of *testscore* on *tracking, percentile,* and $percentile^2$. Interpret the results.

(b) Suppose the scores were censored from below. Create a variable *ctest* that is *testscore* censored at 0. Estimate a linear regression of *ctest* on *tracking, percentile,* and $percentile^2$. How would you interpret these results if you were unaware that the dependent variable was censored?

(c) Suppose you try to fix the problem by omitting the censored observations. Estimate the regression on the subsample of observations for which *ctest* is positive.

(d) Interpret and explain the differences between your results in parts (a), (b), and (c).

CHAPTER 28
MODEL SELECTION, STEIN SHRINKAGE, AND MODEL AVERAGING

28.1 INTRODUCTION

This chapter reviews model selection, James-Stein shrinkage, and model averaging. Model selection is a tool for selecting one model (or estimator) out of a set of models. Different model selection methods are distinguished by the criteria used to rank and compare models. Model averaging is a generalization of model selection. Models and estimators are averaged using data-dependent weights. James-Stein shrinkage modifies classical estimators by shrinking toward a reasonable target. Shrinking reduces mean squared error.

Two excellent monographs on model selection and averaging are Burnham and Anderson (1998) and Claeskens and Hjort (2008). James-Stein shrinkage theory is thoroughly covered in Lehmann and Casella (1998). See also Wasserman (2006) and Efron (2010).

28.2 MODEL SELECTION

In the course of an applied project, an economist will routinely estimate multiple models. Indeed, most applied papers include tables displaying the results from different specifications. The question arises: Which model is best? Which should be used in practice? How can we select the best choice? This is the question of model selection.

Take, for example, a wage regression. Suppose we want a model that includes education, experience, region, and marital status. How should we proceed? Should we estimate a simple linear model plus a quadratic in experience? Should education enter linearly, a simple spline as in Figure 2.6(a), or with separate dummies for each education level? Should marital status enter as a simple dummy (married or not) or allowing for all recorded categories? Should interactions be included? Which? How many? In sum, we need to select the specific regressors to include in the regression model.

Model "selection" may be a misnomer. It would be more appropriate to call the issue "estimator selection." When we examine a table containing the results from multiple regressions, we are comparing multiple estimates of the same regression. One estimator may include fewer variables than another; that is a restricted estimator. One may be estimated by least squares and another by 2SLS. Another could be nonparametric. The underlying model is the same; the difference is the estimator. Regardless, the literature has adopted the term "model selection," and we will adhere to this convention.

To gain some basic understanding, it may be helpful to start with a stylzed example. Suppose that we have a $K \times 1$ estimator $\widehat{\theta}$ that has expectation θ and known covariance matrix $\boldsymbol{V}$. An alternative feasible estimator is $\widetilde{\theta} = 0$. The latter may seem like a silly estimator, but it captures the feature that model selection typically concerns exclusion restrictions. In this context, we can compare the accuracy of the two estimators by their **weighted mean-squared error (WMSE)**. For a given weight matrix $\boldsymbol{W}$, define

$$\text{wmse}\left[\widehat{\theta}\right] = \text{tr}\left(\mathbb{E}\left[\left(\widehat{\theta}-\theta\right)\left(\widehat{\theta}-\theta\right)'\right]\boldsymbol{W}\right) = \mathbb{E}\left[\left(\widehat{\theta}-\theta\right)'\boldsymbol{W}\left(\widehat{\theta}-\theta\right)\right].$$

The calculations simplify by setting $\boldsymbol{W} = \boldsymbol{V}^{-1}$, which we will do for our remaining calculations.

For our two estimators, we calculate that

$$\text{wmse}\left[\widehat{\theta}\right] = K \tag{28.1}$$

$$\text{wmse}\left[\widetilde{\theta}\right] = \theta'\boldsymbol{V}^{-1}\theta \stackrel{\text{def}}{=} \lambda. \tag{28.2}$$

(See Exercise 28.1) The WMSE of $\widehat{\theta}$ is smaller if $K < \lambda$, and the WMSE of $\widetilde{\theta}$ is smaller if $K > \lambda$. One insight from this simple analysis is that we should prefer smaller (simpler) models when potentially omitted variables have small coefficients relative to estimation variance, and we should prefer larger (more complicated) models when these variables have large coefficients relative to estimation variance. Another insight is that the ideal choice is infeasible, because λ is unknown.

The comparison between (28.1) and (28.2) is a basic bias-variance tradeoff. The estimator $\widehat{\theta}$ is unbiased but has a variance contribution of K. The estimator $\widetilde{\theta}$ has zero variance but has a squared bias contribution λ. The WMSE combines these two components.

Selection based on WMSE suggests that we should ideally select the estimator $\widehat{\theta}$ if $K < \lambda$ and select $\widetilde{\theta}$ if $K > \lambda$. A feasible implementation replaces λ with an estimator. A plug-in estimator is $\widehat{\lambda} = \widehat{\theta}'\boldsymbol{V}^{-1}\widehat{\theta} = W$, the Wald statistic for the test of $\theta = 0$. However, the estimator $\widehat{\lambda}$ has expectation

$$\mathbb{E}\left[\widehat{\lambda}\right] = \mathbb{E}\left[\widehat{\theta}'\boldsymbol{V}^{-1\prime}\widehat{\theta}\right] = \theta'\boldsymbol{V}^{-1\prime}\theta + \mathbb{E}\left[\left(\widehat{\theta}-\theta\right)'\boldsymbol{V}^{-1}\left(\widehat{\theta}-\theta\right)\right] = \lambda + K$$

so is biased. An unbiased estimator is $\widetilde{\lambda} = \widehat{\lambda} - K$. Notice that $\widetilde{\lambda} > K$ is the same as $W > 2K$. This leads to the model-selection rule: Use $\widehat{\theta}$ if $W > 2K$, and use $\widetilde{\theta}$ otherwise.

This setting is overly simplistic, but it highlights the fundamental ingredients of criterion-based model selection. Comparing the MSE of different estimators typically involves a tradeoff between the bias and variance, with more complicated models exhibiting less bias but increased estimation variance. The actual tradeoff is unknown, because the bias depends on the unknown true parameters. The bias, however, can be estimated, giving rise to empirical estimates of the MSE and empirical model selection rules.

Many model selection criteria have been proposed. I list here those most frequently used in applied econometrics.

I first list selection criteria for the linear regression model $Y = X'\beta + e$ with $\sigma^2 = \mathbb{E}\left[e^2\right]$ and a $k \times 1$ coefficient vector β. Let $\widehat{\beta}$ be the least squares estimator, $\widehat{e}_i$ the least squares residual, and $\widehat{\sigma}^2 = n^{-1}\sum_{i=1}^{n}\widehat{e}_i^2$ the variance estimator. The number of estimated parameters (β and σ^2) is $K = k + 1$.

Bayesian Information Criterion

$$\text{BIC} = n + n\log\left(2\pi\widehat{\sigma}^2\right) + K\log(n). \tag{28.3}$$

Akaike Information Criterion

$$\text{AIC} = n + n\log\left(2\pi\widehat{\sigma}^2\right) + 2K. \tag{28.4}$$

Cross-Validation

$$\text{CV} = \sum_{i=1}^{n}\widetilde{e}_i^2 \tag{28.5}$$

where $\widetilde{e}_i$ are the least squares leave-one-out prediction errors.

I next list two commonly used selection criteria for likelihood-based estimation. Let $f(y,\theta)$ be a parametric density with a $K \times 1$ parameter θ. The likelihood $L_n(\theta) = \prod_{i=1}^{n} f(Y_i,\theta)$ is the density evaluated at the observations. The maximum likelihood estimator $\widehat{\theta}$ maximizes $\ell_n(\theta) = \log L_n(\theta)$.

Bayesian Information Criterion

$$\mathrm{BIC} = -2\ell_n(\widehat{\theta}) + K\log(n). \tag{28.6}$$

Akaike Information Criterion

$$\mathrm{AIC} = -2\ell_n(\widehat{\theta}) + 2K. \tag{28.7}$$

In the following sections, we derive and discuss these and other model selection criteria.

28.3 BAYESIAN INFORMATION CRITERION

The **Bayesian information criterion (BIC)**, also known as the **Schwarz criterion**, was introduced by Schwarz (1978). It is appropriate for parametric models estimated by maximum likelihood and is used to select the model with the highest approximate probability of being the true model.

Let $\pi(\theta)$ be the prior density for θ. The joint density of Y and θ is $f(y,\theta)\pi(\theta)$. The marginal density of Y is

$$p(y) = \int f(y,\theta)\pi(\theta)d\theta.$$

The marginal density $p(Y)$ evaluated at the observations is known as the **marginal likelihood**.

Schwarz (1978) established the following approximation.

> **Theorem 28.1 Schwarz.** If the model $f(y,\theta)$ satisfies standard regularity conditions and the prior $\pi(\theta)$ is diffuse, then
>
> $$-2\log p(Y) = -2\ell_n(\widehat{\theta}) + K\log(n) + O(1)$$
>
> where the $O(1)$ term is bounded as $n \to \infty$.

A heuristic proof for normal linear regression is given in Section 28.32. A "diffuse" prior is one that distributes weight uniformly over the parameter space.

Schwarz's theorem shows that the marginal likelihood approximately equals the maximized likelihood multiplied by an adjustment that depends on the number of estimated parameters and the sample size. The approximation (28.6) is commonly called the **Bayesian Information Criterion** or **BIC**. The BIC is a **penalized log likelihood**. The term $K\log(n)$ can be interpreted as an overparameterization penalty. The multiplication of the log likelihood by -2 is traditional, as it puts the criterion into the same units as a log-likelihood statistic.

In the context of normal linear regression, we have calculated in (5.6) that

$$\ell_n(\widehat{\theta}) = -\frac{n}{2}\left(\log(2\pi) + 1\right) - \frac{n}{2}\log\left(\widehat{\sigma}^2\right)$$

where $\widehat{\sigma}^2$ is the residual variance estimate. Hence BIC equals (28.3) with $K = k+1$.

Since $n\log(2\pi) + n$ does not vary across models, this term is often omitted. It is better, however, to define the BIC as described above, so that different parametric families are comparable. It is also useful to know that some authors define the BIC by dividing the above expression by n (e.g., $\mathrm{BIC} = \log\left(2\pi\widehat{\sigma}^2\right) + K\log(n)/n$), which does not change the rankings of models. However, this is an unwise choice because it alters the scaling, making it difficult to compare the degree of difference between models.

Now suppose that we have two models $\mathscr{M}_1$ and $\mathscr{M}_2$ that have marginal likelihoods $p_1(Y)$ and $p_2(Y)$, respectively. Assume that both models have equal prior probability. Bayes Theorem states that the probability that a model is true given the data is proportional to its marginal likelihood. Specifically,

$$\mathbb{P}[\mathscr{M}_1 \mid Y] = \frac{p_1(Y)}{p_1(Y)+p_2(Y)}$$

$$\mathbb{P}[\mathscr{M}_2 \mid Y] = \frac{p_2(Y)}{p_1(Y)+p_2(Y)}.$$

Bayes selection picks the model with highest probability. Thus if $p_1(Y) > p_2(Y)$, we select $\mathscr{M}_1$. If $p_1(Y) < p_2(Y)$, we select $\mathscr{M}_2$.

Finding the model with highest marginal likelihood is the same as finding the model with the lowest value of $-2\log p(Y)$. Theorem 28.1 shows that the latter approximately equals the BIC. BIC selection picks the model with the lowest[1] value of BIC. Thus, BIC selection is approximate Bayes selection.

The above discussion concerned two models but applies to any number of models. BIC selection picks the model with the smallest BIC. For implementation, you simply estimate each model, calculate its BIC, and compare.

The BIC may be obtained in Stata by using the command `estimates stats` after an estimated model.

28.4 AKAIKE INFORMATION CRITERION FOR REGRESSION

The **Akaike Information Criterion (AIC)** was introduced by Akaike (1973). It is used to select the model whose estimated density is closest to the true density, and is designed for parametric models estimated by maximum likelihood.

Let $\widehat{f}(y)$ be an estimator of the unknown true density $g(y)$ of the observation vector $Y = (Y_1, \dots, Y_n)$. For example, the normal linear regression estimate of $g(y)$ is $\widehat{f}(y) = \prod_{i=1}^n \phi_{\widehat{\sigma}}\left(Y_i - X_i'\widehat{\beta}\right)$.

To measure the distance between the two densities g and $\widehat{f}$, Akaike used the **Kullback-Leibler information criterion (KLIC)**:

$$\mathrm{KLIC}(g,f) = \int g(y)\log\left(\frac{g(y)}{f(y)}\right)dy.$$

Notice that $\mathrm{KLIC}(g,f) = 0$ when $f(y) = g(y)$. By Jensen's inequality,

$$\mathrm{KLIC}(g,f) = -\int g(y)\log\left(\frac{f(y)}{g(y)}\right)dy \geq -\log\int f(y)dy = 0.$$

Thus $\mathrm{KLIC}(g,f)$ is a nonnegative measure of the deviation of f from g, with small values indicating a smaller deviation.

The KLIC distance between the true and estimated densities is

$$\begin{aligned}\mathrm{KLIC}(g,\widehat{f}) &= \int g(y)\log\left(\frac{g(y)}{\widehat{f}(y)}\right)dy \\ &= \int g(y)\log(g(y))\,dy - \int g(y)\log\left(\widehat{f}(y)\right)dy.\end{aligned}$$

[1]When the BIC is negative, this means taking the most negative value.

This is random, as it depends on the estimator $\widehat{f}$. Akaike proposed the expected KLIC distance:

$$\mathbb{E}\left[\mathrm{KLIC}(g,\widehat{f})\right] = \int g(y)\log\left(g\left(y\right)\right)dy - \mathbb{E}\left[\int g(y)\log\left(\widehat{f}\left(y\right)\right)dy\right]. \tag{28.8}$$

The first term in (28.8) does not depend on the model. So minimization of expected KLIC distance is minimization of the second term. Multiplied by 2 (similarly to the BIC), this is

$$T = -2\mathbb{E}\left[\int g(y)\log\left(\widehat{f}(y)\right)dy\right]. \tag{28.9}$$

The expectation is over the random estimator $\widehat{f}$.

An alternative interpretation is to notice that the integral in (28.9) is an expectation over Y with respect to the true data density $g(y)$. Thus we can write (28.9) as

$$T = -2\mathbb{E}\left[\log\left(\widehat{f}\left(\widetilde{Y}\right)\right)\right] \tag{28.10}$$

where $\widetilde{Y}$ is an independent copy of Y. The key to understanding this expression is that both the estimator $\widehat{f}$ and the evaluation points $\widetilde{Y}$ are random and independent. T is the expected log-likelihood fit using the estimated model $\widehat{f}$ of an out-of-sample realization $\widetilde{Y}$. Thus, T can be interpreted as an expected predictive log likelihood. Models with low values of T have good fit based on the out-of-sample log-likelihood.

To gain further understanding, consider the simple case of the normal linear regression model with K regressors. The log density of the model for the observations is

$$\log f(Y,\boldsymbol{X},\theta) = -\frac{n}{2}\log\left(2\pi\sigma^2\right) - \frac{1}{2\sigma^2}\sum_{i=1}^{n}\left(Y_i - X_i'\beta\right)^2. \tag{28.11}$$

The expected value at the true parameter values is $-\frac{n}{2}\log\left(2\pi\sigma^2\right) - \frac{n}{2}$. Thus the idealized value of T is $T_0 = n\log\left(2\pi\sigma^2\right) + n$. This would be the value obtained if there were no estimation error.

To simplify the calculations, let us add the assumption that the variance σ^2 is known.

Theorem 28.2 Suppose $\widehat{f}(y)$ is an estimated normal linear regression model with K regressors and a known variance σ^2. Suppose that the true density $g(y)$ is a conditionally homoskedastic regression with variance σ^2. Then

$$T = n\log\left(2\pi\sigma^2\right) + n + K = T_0 + K \tag{28.12}$$

$$\mathbb{E}\left[-2\ell_n(\widehat{\theta})\right] = n\log\left(2\pi\sigma^2\right) + n - K = T_0 - K. \tag{28.13}$$

The proof is given in Section 28.32.

These expressions are interesting. Expression (28.12) shows that the expected KLIC distance T equals the idealized value T_0 plus K. The latter is the cost of parameter estimation, measured in terms of expected KLIC distance. By estimating parameters (rather than using the true values), the expected KLIC distance increases by K.

Expression (28.13) shows the converse story. It shows that the sample log-likelihood function is smaller than the idealized value T_0 by K. This is the cost of in-sample overfitting. The sample log-likelihood is an in-sample measure of fit and therefore understates the population log-likelihood. The two expressions together show that the expected sample log-likelihood is smaller than the target value T by $2K$. This is the combined cost of overfitting and parameter estimation.

Combining these expressions, we can suggest an unbiased estimator for T. In the normal regression model, we use (28.4). Because $n\log(2\pi)+n$ does not vary across models, it are often omitted. Thus for linear regression, it is common to use the definition $\text{AIC}=n\log\left(\widehat{\sigma}^2\right)+2K$.

Interestingly the AIC takes a similar form to the BIC. Both the AIC and BIC are penalized log-likelihoods, and both penalties are proportional to the number of estimated parameters K. The difference is that the AIC penalty is $2K$ while the BIC penalty is $K\log(n)$. Because $2<\log(n)$ if $n\geq 8$, the BIC uses a stronger parameterization penalty.

Selecting a model by the AIC is equivalent to calculating the AIC for each model and selecting the model with the lowest[2] value.

Theorem 28.3 Under the assumptions of Theorem 28.2, $\mathbb{E}[\text{AIC}]=T$. AIC is thus an unbiased estimator of T.

One of the interesting features of these results are that they are exact—there is no approximation—and they do not require that the true error is normally distributed. The critical assumption is conditional homoskedasticity. If homoskedasticity fails, then the AIC loses its validity.

The AIC may be obtained in Stata by using the command `estimates stats` after an estimated model.

28.5 AKAIKE INFORMATION CRITERION FOR LIKELIHOOD

For the general likelihood context, Akaike proposed the criterion (28.7). Here, $\widehat{\theta}$ is the maximum likelihood estimator, $\ell_n(\widehat{\theta})$ is the maximized log-likelihood function, and K is the number of estimated parameters. The criterion specializes to (28.4) for the case of a normal linear regression model.

As for regression, AIC selection is performed by estimating a set of models, calculating AIC for each, and selecting the model with the smallest AIC.

The advantages of the AIC are that it is simple to calculate, easy to implement, and straightforward to interpret. It is intuitive, as it is a simple penalized likelihood.

The disadvantage is that its simplicity may be deceptive. The proof shows that the criterion is based on a quadratic approximation to the log likelihood and an asymptotic chi-square approximation to the classical Wald statistic. When these conditions fail, then the AIC may not be accurate. For example, if the model is an approximate (quasi) likelihood rather than a true likelihood, then the failure of the information matrix equality implies that the classical Wald statistic is not asymptotically chi-square. In this case, the accuracy of AIC fails. Another problem is that many nonlinear models have parameter regions where parametric identification fails. In these models, the quadratic approximation to the log likelihood function fails to hold uniformly in the parameter space, so the accuracy of the AIC fails. These qualifications point to challenges in interpretation of the AIC in nonlinear models.

The following is an analog of Theorem 28.3.

Theorem 28.4 Under standard regularity conditions for maximum likelihood estimation, plus the assumption that certain statistics (identified in the proof) are uniformly integrable, $\mathbb{E}[\text{AIC}]=T+O\left(n^{1/2}\right)$. AIC is thus an approximately unbiased estimator of T.

[2]When the AIC is negative, this means taking the most negative value.

A sketch of the proof is given in Section 28.32.

This result shows that the AIC is, in general, a reasonable estimator of the KLIC fit of an estimated parametric model. The theorem holds broadly for maximum likelihood estimation, and thus the AIC can be used in a wide variety of contexts.

28.6 MALLOWS CRITERION

The Mallows criterion was proposed by Mallows (1973) and is often called the C_p criterion. It is appropriate for linear estimators of homoskedastic regression models.

Consider the homoskedastic regression framework

$$\begin{aligned} Y &= m + e \\ m &= m(X) \\ \mathbb{E}[e \mid X] &= 0 \\ \mathbb{E}\left[e^2 \mid X\right] &= \sigma^2. \end{aligned}$$

Write the first equation in vector notation for the n observations as $\boldsymbol{Y} = \boldsymbol{m} + \boldsymbol{e}$. Let $\widehat{\boldsymbol{m}} = \boldsymbol{A}\boldsymbol{Y}$ be a linear estimator of $\boldsymbol{m}$, meaning that $\boldsymbol{A}$ is some $n \times n$ function of the regressor matrix $\boldsymbol{X}$ only. The residuals are $\widehat{\boldsymbol{e}} = \boldsymbol{Y} - \widehat{\boldsymbol{m}}$. The class of linear estimators includes least squares, weighted least squares, kernel regression, local linear regression, and series regression. For example, the least squares estimator using a regressor matrix $\boldsymbol{Z}$ is the case $\boldsymbol{A} = \boldsymbol{Z}\left(\boldsymbol{Z}'\boldsymbol{Z}\right)^{-1}\boldsymbol{Z}'$.

Mallows (1973) proposed the criterion

$$C_p = \widehat{\boldsymbol{e}}'\widehat{\boldsymbol{e}} + 2\widetilde{\sigma}^2 \operatorname{tr}(\boldsymbol{A}) \tag{28.14}$$

where $\widetilde{\sigma}^2$ is a preliminary estimator of σ^2 (typically based on fitting a large model). In the case of least squares regression with K coefficients, (28.14) simplifies to

$$C_p = n\widehat{\sigma}^2 + 2K\widetilde{\sigma}^2. \tag{28.15}$$

The Mallows crierion can be used similarly to the AIC. A set of regression models is estimated and the criterion C_p calculated for each. The model with the smallest value of C_p is the Mallows-selected model.

Mallows designed the criterion C_p as an unbiased estimator of the following measure of fit:

$$R = \mathbb{E}\left[\sum_{i=1}^{n}\left(\widehat{m}_i - m_i\right)^2\right].$$

This is the expected squared difference between the estimated and true regressions evaluated at the observations.

An alternative motivation for R is in terms of prediction accuracy. Consider an independent set of observations $\widetilde{Y}_i$, $i = 1, \ldots, n$, which have the same regressors X_i as those in sample. Consider prediction of $\widetilde{Y}_i$ given X_i and the fitted regression. The least squares predictor is $\widehat{m}_i$. The sum of expected squared prediction errors is

$$\mathrm{MSFE} = \sum_{i=1}^{n} \mathbb{E}\left[\left(\widetilde{Y}_i - \widehat{m}_i\right)^2\right].$$

The best possible (infeasible) value of this quantity is

$$\mathrm{MSFE}_0 = \sum_{i=1}^{n} \mathbb{E}\left[\left(\widetilde{Y}_i - m_i\right)^2\right].$$

The difference is the **prediction accuracy** of the estimator:

$$\begin{aligned}\mathrm{MSFE} - \mathrm{MSFE}_0 &= \sum_{i=1}^{n} \mathbb{E}\left[\left(\widetilde{Y}_i - \widehat{m}_i\right)^2\right] - \sum_{i=1}^{n} \mathbb{E}\left[\left(\widetilde{Y}_i - m_i\right)^2\right] \\ &= \mathbb{E}\left[\sum_{i=1}^{n} (\widehat{m}_i - m_i)^2\right] \\ &= R\end{aligned}$$

which equals Mallows' measure of fit. Thus R is a measure of prediction accuracy.

I stated that the Mallows criterion is an unbiased estimator of R. More accurately, the adjusted criterion $C_p^* = C_p - \boldsymbol{e}'\boldsymbol{e}$ is unbiased for R. When comparing models, C_p and C_p^* are equivalent, so this substitution has no consequence for model selection.

Theorem 28.5 If $\widehat{\boldsymbol{m}} = \boldsymbol{AY}$ is a linear estimator, the regression error is conditionally mean 0 and homoskedastic, and $\widetilde{\sigma}^2$ is unbiased for σ^2, then

$$\mathbb{E}\left[C_p^*\right] = R$$

so the adjusted Mallows criterion C_p^* is an unbiased estimator of R.

The proof is given in Section 28.32.

28.7 HOLD-OUT CRITERION

Dividing the sample into two parts, one for estimation and the second for evaluation, creates a simple device for model evaluation and selection. This procedure is often labeled **hold-out evaluation**. In the recent machine learning literature, the data division is typically described as a **training sample** and a **test sample**.

The sample is typically divided randomly, so that the estimation (training) sample has N observations and the evaluation (test) sample has P observations, where $N + P = n$. There is no universal rule for the choice of N and P, but $N = P = n/2$ is a standard choice.

For more complicated procedures, such as the evaluation of model selection methods, it is desirable to make a tripartite division of the sample into (1) training, (2) model selection, and (3) final estimation and assessment. This division can be particularly useful when it is desired to obtain a parameter estimator whose distribution is not distorted by the model selection process. Such divisions are most suited for a context of an extremely large sample.

Take the standard case of a bipartite division, where $1 \le i \le N$ is the estimation sample and $N + 1 \le i \le N + P$ is the evaluation sample. On the estimation sample, we construct the parameter estimates, for example, the least squares coefficients:

$$\widetilde{\beta}_N = \left(\sum_{i=1}^{N} X_i X_i'\right)^{-1} \left(\sum_{i=1}^{N} X_i Y_i\right).$$

Combining this coefficient with the evaluation sample, we calculate the prediction errors $\widetilde{e}_{N,i} = Y_i - X_i'\widetilde{\beta}_N$ for $i \geq N+1$.

In Section 4.12, we defined the mean squared forecast error (MSFE) based on a estimation sample of size N as the expectation of the squared out-of-sample prediction error $\text{MSFE}_N = \mathbb{E}\left[\widetilde{e}_{N,i}^2\right]$. The hold-out estimator of the MSFE is the average of the squared prediction errors:

$$\widetilde{\sigma}_{N,P}^2 = \frac{1}{P} \sum_{i=N+1}^{N+P} \widetilde{e}_{N,i}^2.$$

We can see that $\widetilde{\sigma}_{N,P}^2$ is unbiased for MSFE_N.

When $N = P$, we can improve estimation of the MSFE by flipping the procedure. Exchanging the roles of estimation and evaluation samples, we obtain a second MSFE estimator, say, $\widetilde{\omega}_{N,P}^2$. The global estimator is their average $\widetilde{\sigma}_{N,P}^{*2} = \left(\widetilde{\sigma}_{N,P}^2 + \widetilde{\omega}_{N,P}^2\right)/2$. This estimator also has expectation MSFE_N but has reduced variance.

The estimated MSFE $\widetilde{\sigma}_{N,P}^{*2}$ can be used for model selection. The quantity $\widetilde{\sigma}_{N,P}^{*2}$ is calculated for a set of proposed models. The selected model is the one with the smallest value of $\widetilde{\sigma}_{N,P}^{*2}$. The method is intuitive, general, and flexible, and it does not rely on technical assumptions.

The hold-out method has two disadvantages. First, if our goal is estimation using the full sample, our desired estimate is MSFE_n, not MSFE_N. Hold-out estimation provides an estimator of the MSFE based on estimation using a substantially reduced sample size, and is thus biased for the MSFE based on estimation using the full sample. Second, the estimator $\widetilde{\sigma}_{N,P}^{*2}$ is sensitive to the random sorting of the observations into the estimation and evaluation samples. This affects model selection. Results can depend on the initial sample sorting and are therefore partially arbitrary.

28.8 CROSS-VALIDATION CRITERION

In applied statistics and machine learning, the default method for model selection and tuning parameter selection is cross-validation. We have introduced some of the concepts throughout the book, and review and unify the concepts at this point. Cross-validation is closely related to the hold-out criterion introduced in Section 28.7.

In Section 3.20, we defined the leave-one-out estimator as that obtained by applying an estimation formula to the sample omitting the ith observation. This procedure is identical to the hold-out problem as described previously, where the estimation sample is $N = n-1$ and the evaluation sample is $P = 1$. The estimator obtained omitting observation i is written as $\widehat{\beta}_{(-i)}$. The prediction error is $\widetilde{e}_i = Y_i - X_i'\widehat{\beta}_{(-i)}$. The out-of-sample mean squared error "estimate" is $\widetilde{e}_i^2$. This is repeated n times, once for each observation i, and the MSFE estimate is the average of the n squared prediction errors:

$$\text{CV} = \frac{1}{n} \sum_{i=1}^{n} \widetilde{e}_i^2.$$

The estimator CV is called the **cross-validation** (CV) criterion. It is a natural generalization of the hold-out criterion and eliminates the two disadvantages described in Section 28.7. First, the CV criterion is an unbiased estimator of MSFE_{n-1}, which is essentially the same as MSFE_n. Thus CV is essentially unbiased for model selection. Second, the CV criterion does not depend on a random sorting of the observations. As there is no random component, the criterion takes the same value in any implementation.

In least squares estimation, the CV criterion has a simple computational implementation. Theorem 3.7 shows that the leave-one-out least squares estimator (3.42) equals

$$\widehat{\beta}_{(-i)} = \widehat{\beta} - \frac{1}{(1-h_{ii})}\left(\boldsymbol{X}'\boldsymbol{X}\right)^{-1} X_i \widehat{e}_i$$

where the $\widehat{e}_i$ are the least squares residuals, and the h_{ii} are the leverage values. The prediction error thus equals

$$\widetilde{e}_i = Y_i - X_i'\widehat{\beta}_{(-i)} = (1-h_{ii})^{-1}\widehat{e}_i$$

where the second equality is from Theorem 3.7. Consequently the CV criterion is

$$\mathrm{CV} = \frac{1}{n}\sum_{i=1}^{n}\widetilde{e}_i^2 = \frac{1}{n}\sum_{i=1}^{n}(1-h_{ii})^{-2}\widehat{e}_i^2.$$

Recall as well that in our study of nonparametric regression (Section 19.12), we defined the cross-validation criterion for kernel regression as the weighted average of the squared prediction errors:

$$\mathrm{CV} = \frac{1}{n}\sum_{i=1}^{n}\widetilde{e}_i^2 w(X_i).$$

Theorem 19.7 showed that CV is approximately unbiased for the integrated mean squared error (IMSE), which is a standard measure of accuracy for nonparametric regression. These results show that CV is an unbiased estimator for both the MSFE and IMSE, demonstrating a close connection between these measures of accuracy.

In Section 20.17 and equation (20.30), we defined the CV criterion for series regression as in (28.5). Selecting variables for series regression is identical to model selection. The results as described above show that the CV criterion is an estimator for the MSFE and IMSE of the regression model and is therefore a good candidate for assessing model accuracy. The validity of the CV criterion is much broader than the AIC, because the theorems for CV do not require conditional homoskedasticity. This is not an artifact of the proof method; CV is inherently more robust than AIC or BIC.

Implementation of CV model selection is the same as for the other criteria. A set of regression models is estimated. For each, the CV criterion is calculated. The model with the smallest value of CV is the CV-selected model.

The CV method is also much broader in concept and potential application. It applies to any estimation method so long as a "leave one out" error can be calculated. It can also be applied to other loss functions beyond squared error loss. For example, a CV estimate of absolute loss is

$$\mathrm{CV} = \frac{1}{n}\sum_{i=1}^{n}\left|\widetilde{e}_i\right|.$$

Computationally and conceptually, it is straightforward to select models by minimizing such criteria. However, the properties of applying CV to general criteria is not known.

Stata does not have a standard command to calculate the CV criterion for regression models.

28.9 K-FOLD CROSS-VALIDATION

Two deficiencies with the CV criterion can be alleviated by the closely related **K-fold cross-validation** criterion. The first deficiency is that CV calculation can be computationally costly when sample sizes are very large or the estimation method is other than least squares. For estimators other than least squares, it may be necessary to calculate n separate estimations. This can be computationally prohibitive in some contexts. A second deficiency is that the CV criterion, viewed as an estimator of MSFE_n, has a high variance. The source is that the leave-one-out estimators $\widehat{\beta}_{(-i)}$ have minimal variation across i and are therefore highly correlated.

An alternative is to split the sample into K groups (or "folds") and treat each group as a hold-out sample. This effectively reduces the number of estimations from n to K. (This K is not the number of estimated coefficients. I apologize for the possible confusion in notation, but K is the standard label.) A common choice is $K = 10$, leading to what is known as **10-fold cross-validation**.

The method works by the following steps. This description is for estimation of a regression model $Y = g(X, \theta) + e$ with estimator $\widehat{\theta}$.

1. Randomly sort the observations.
2. Split the observations into **folds** $k = 1, \dots, K$ of (roughly) equal size $n_k \simeq n/K$. Let I_k denote the observations in fold k.
3. For $k = 1, \dots, K$
   (a) Exclude fold I_k from the dataset. This produces a sample with $n - n_k$ observations.
   (b) Calculate the estimator $\widehat{\theta}_{(-k)}$ on this sample.
   (c) Calculate the prediction errors $\widetilde{e}_i = Y_i - g(X_i, \widehat{\theta}_{(-k)})$ for $i \in I_k$.
   (d) Calculate $\text{CV}_k = n_k^{-1} \sum_{i \in I_k} \widetilde{e}_i^2$.
4. Calculate $\text{CV} = K^{-1} \sum_{k=1}^{K} \text{CV}_k$.

If $K = n$, the method is identical to leave-one-out cross validation.

A useful feature of K-fold CV is that we can calculate an approximate standard error. It is based on the approximation $\text{var}[\text{CV}] \simeq K^{-1} \text{var}[\text{CV}_k]$, which is based on the idea that the CV_k are approximately uncorrelated across folds. This leads to the standard error

$$s(\text{CV}) = \sqrt{\frac{1}{K(K-1)} \sum_{k=1}^{K} (\text{CV}_k - \text{CV})^2}.$$

This error formula is similar to a clustered variance formula, where the folds are treated as clusters. The standard error $s(\text{CV})$ can be reported to assess the precision of CV as an estimate of the MSFE.

One disadvantage of K-fold CV is that CV can be sensitive to the initial random sorting of the observations, leading to partially arbitrary results. This problem can be reduced by a technique called **repeated CV**, which repeats the K-fold CV algorithm M times (each time with a different random sorting), leading to M values of CV. These are averaged to produce the repeated CV value. As M increases, the randomness due to sorting is eliminated. An associated standard error can be obtained by taking the square root of the average squared standard errors.

CV model selection is typically implemented by selecting the model with the smallest value of CV. An alternative implementation is known as the **one standard error (1se) rule** which selects the most parsimonious model whose value of CV is within one standard error of the minimum CV. The (informal) idea is that models whose value of CV is within one standard error of one another are not statistically distinguishable, and all else held equal, we should lean toward parsimony. The 1se rule is the default in the popular `cv.glmnet`

R function. The 1se rule is an oversmoothing choice, meaning that it leans toward higher bias and reduced variance. In contrast, for inference, many econometricians recommend undersmoothing bandwidths, which means selecting a less parsimonious model than the CV minimizing choice.

28.10 MANY SELECTION CRITERIA ARE SIMILAR

For the linear regression model, many selection criteria have been introduced. However, many of these alternative criteria are quite similar to one another. In this section, we review some of these connections. The following discussion is for the standard regression model $Y = X'\beta + e$ with n observations, K estimated coefficients, and least squares variance estimator $\widehat{\sigma}_K^2$.

Shibata (1980) proposed the criteria

$$\text{Shibata} = \widehat{\sigma}_K^2 \left(1 + \frac{2K}{n}\right)$$

as an estimator of the MSFE. Recalling the Mallows criterion for regression (28.15), we see that Shibata $= C_p/n$ if we replace the preliminary estimator $\widetilde{\sigma}^2$ with $\widehat{\sigma}_K^2$. Thus the two are quite similar in practice.

Taking logarithms and using the approximation $\log(1+x) \simeq x$ for small x, we have

$$n \log(\text{Shibata}) = n \log\left(\widehat{\sigma}_K^2\right) + n \log\left(1 + \frac{2K}{n}\right) \simeq n \log\left(\widehat{\sigma}_K^2\right) + 2K = \text{AIC}.$$

Thus minimization of Shibata's criterion and AIC are similar.

Akaike (1969) proposed the final prediction error criterion

$$\text{FPE} = \widehat{\sigma}_K^2 \left(\frac{1 + K/n}{1 - K/n}\right).$$

Using the expansions $(1-x)^{-1} \simeq 1 + x$ and $(1+x)^2 \simeq 1 + 2x$, we see that FPE $\simeq$ Shibata.

Craven and Wahba (1979) proposed generalized cross-validation:

$$\text{GCV} = \frac{n\widehat{\sigma}_K^2}{(n-K)^2}.$$

By the expansion $(1-x)^{-2} \simeq 1 + 2x$, we find that

$$n\text{GCV} = \frac{\widehat{\sigma}_K^2}{(1 - K/n)^2} \simeq \widehat{\sigma}_K^2 \left(1 + \frac{2K}{n}\right) = \text{Shibata}.$$

The above calculations show that the WMSE, AIC, Shibata, FPE, GCV, and Mallows criterion are all close approximations to one another when K/n is small. Differences arise in finite samples for large K. However, the above analysis shows that there is no fundamental difference between these criteria. They are all estimating the same target. This is in contrast to BIC, which uses a different parameterization penalty and is asymptotically distinct.

Interestingly there also is a connection between CV and the above criteria. Again using the expansion $(1-x)^{-2} \simeq 1 + 2x$, we find that

$$\text{CV} = \sum_{i=1}^{n} (1 - h_{ii})^{-2} \widehat{e}_i^2$$

$$
\begin{aligned}
&\simeq \sum_{i=1}^{n} \widehat{e}_i^2 + \sum_{i=1}^{n} 2h_{ii}\widehat{e}_i^2 \\
&= n\widehat{\sigma}_K^2 + 2\sum_{i=1}^{n} X_i' \left(\boldsymbol{X}'\boldsymbol{X}\right)^{-1} X_i\widehat{e}_i^2 \\
&= n\widehat{\sigma}_K^2 + 2\operatorname{tr}\left(\left(\boldsymbol{X}'\boldsymbol{X}\right)^{-1}\left(\sum_{i=1}^{n} X_iX_i'\widehat{e}_i^2\right)\right) \\
&\simeq n\widehat{\sigma}_K^2 + 2\operatorname{tr}\left(\left(\mathbb{E}\left[XX'\right]\right)^{-1}\left(\mathbb{E}\left[XX'e^2\right]\right)\right) \\
&= n\widehat{\sigma}_K^2 + 2K\sigma^2 \\
&\simeq \text{Shibata.}
\end{aligned}
$$

The third-to-last line holds asymptotically by the WLLN. The following equality holds under conditional homoskedasiticity. The final approximation replaces σ^2 by the estimator $\widehat{\sigma}_K^2$. This calculation shows that under the assumption of conditional homoskedasticity, the CV criterion is similar to the other criteria. It differs under heteroskedasticity, however, which is one of its primary advantages.

28.11 RELATION WITH LIKELIHOOD RATIO TESTING

Because the AIC and BIC are penalized log-likelihoods, AIC and BIC selection are related to likelihood ratio testing. Suppose we have two nested models $\mathscr{M}_1$ and $\mathscr{M}_2$ with log-likelihoods $\ell_{1n}\left(\widehat{\theta}_1\right)$ and $\ell_{2n}\left(\widehat{\theta}_2\right)$ and $K_1 < K_2$ estimated parameters. AIC selects $\mathscr{M}_1$ if $\text{AIC}(K_1) < \text{AIC}(K_2)$, which occurs when

$$
-2\ell_{1n}\left(\widehat{\theta}_1\right) + 2K_1 < -2\ell_{2n}\left(\widehat{\theta}_2\right) + 2K_2
$$

or

$$
\text{LR} = 2\left(\ell_{2n}\left(\widehat{\theta}_2\right) - \ell_{1n}\left(\widehat{\theta}_1\right)\right) < 2r
$$

where $r = K_2 - K_1$. Thus AIC selection is similar to selection by likelihood ratio testing with a different critical value. Rather than using a critical value from the chi-square distribution, the "critical value" is $2r$. This is not to say that AIC selection is testing (it is not); instead, there is a similar structure in the decision.

There are two useful practical implications. One is that when test statistics are reported in their F form (which divide by the difference in coefficients r), then the AIC "critical value" is 2. The AIC selects the restricted (smaller) model if $F < 2$. It selects the unrestricted (larger) model if $F > 2$.

Another useful implication is in when considering a single coefficient (when $r = 1$). AIC selects the coefficient (the larger model) if $\text{LR} > 2$. In contrast, a 5% significance test "selects" the larger model (rejects the smaller) if $\text{LR} > 3.84$. Thus AIC is more generous in terms of selecting larger models. An equivalent way of seeing this is that AIC selects the coefficient if the t-ratio exceeds 1.41, whereas the 5% significance test selects if the t-ratio exceeds 1.96.

Similar comments apply to BIC selection, though the effective critical values are different. For comparing models with coefficients $K_1 < K_2$, the BIC selects $\mathscr{M}_1$ if $\text{LR} < \log(n)r$. The "critical value" for an F statistic is $\log(n)$. Hence, BIC selection becomes stricter as sample sizes increase.

28.12 CONSISTENT SELECTION

An important property of a model selection procedure is whether it selects a true model in large samples. We call such a procedure **consistent**.

To discuss this further, we need to thoughtfully define what is a "true" model. The answer depends on the type of model. When a model is a parametric density or distribution $f(y,\theta)$ with $\theta \in \Theta$ (as in likelihood estimation), then the model is true if there is some $\theta_0 \in \Theta$ such that $f(y,\theta_0)$ equals the true density or distribution. Notice that it is important in this context that both the function class $f(y,\theta)$ and parameter space Θ are appropriately defined.

In a semiparametric conditional moment condition model that states $\mathbb{E}\left[g(Y,X,\theta) \mid X\right]=0$ with $\theta \in \Theta$, the model is true if there is some $\theta_0 \in \Theta$ such that $\mathbb{E}\left[g(Y,X,\theta_0) \mid X\right]=0$. This includes the regression model $Y=m(X,\theta)+e$ with $\mathbb{E}[e \mid X]=0$, where the model is true if there is some $\theta_0 \in \Theta$ such that $m(X,\theta_0)=\mathbb{E}[Y \mid X]$. It also includes the homoskedastic regression model, which adds the requirement that $\mathbb{E}\left[e^2 \mid X\right]=\sigma^2$ is a constant.

In a semiparametric unconditional moment condition model $\mathbb{E}\left[g(Y,X,\theta)\right]=0$, the model is true if there is some $\theta_0 \in \Theta$ such that $\mathbb{E}\left[g(Y,X,\theta_0)\right]=0$. A subtle issue here is that when the model is just identified and Θ is unrestricted, then this condition typically holds, and so the model is typically true. This includes least squares regression interpreted as a projection and just-identified instrumental variables regression.

In a nonparametric model, such as $Y \sim f \in \mathscr{F}$, where $\mathscr{F}$ is some function class (such as second-order differentiable densities), the model is true if the true density is a member of the function class $\mathscr{F}$.

The complication arises that there may be multiple true models. This cannot occur when models are strictly non-nested (meaning that there is no common element in both model classes), but strictly non-nested models are rare. Most models have nontrivial intersections. For example, the linear regression models $Y=\alpha+X_1'\beta_1+e$ and $Y=\alpha+X_2'\beta_2+e$ with X_1 and X_2 containing no common elements may appear non-nested, but they intersect when $\beta_1=0$ and $\beta_2=0$. As another example, consider the linear model $Y=\alpha+X'\beta+e$ and log-linear model $\log(Y)=\alpha+X'\beta+e$. If we add the assumption that $e \sim \mathrm{N}(0,\sigma^2)$, then the models are non-intersecting. But if we relax normality and instead use the conditional mean assumption $\mathbb{E}[e \mid X]=0$, then the models are intersecting when $\beta_1=0$ and $\beta_2=0$.

The most common type of intersecting models are nested. In regression, this occurs when the two models are $Y=X_1'\beta_1+e$ and $Y=X_1'\beta_1+X_2'\beta_2+e$. If $\beta_2 \neq 0$, then only the second model is true. But if $\beta_2=0$, then both are true models.

In general, given a set of models $\overline{\mathscr{M}}=\{\mathscr{M}_1,\ldots,\mathscr{M}_M\}$, a subset $\overline{\mathscr{M}}^*$ are true models (as described above), and the remainder are not true models.

A model selection rule $\widehat{\mathscr{M}}$ selects one model from the set $\overline{\mathscr{M}}$. We say a method is consistent if it asymptotically selects a true model.

> **Definition 28.1** A model selection rule is **model selection consistent** if $\mathbb{P}\left[\widehat{\mathscr{M}} \in \overline{\mathscr{M}}^*\right] \to 1$ as $n \to \infty$.

This definition states that the model selection rule selects a true model with probability tending to 1 as the sample size diverges.

A broad class of model selection methods satisfy this definition of consistency. To see this, consider the class of information criteria

$$\mathrm{IC}=-2\ell_n\left(\widehat{\theta}\right)+c(n,K).$$

This includes AIC ($c = 2K$), BIC ($c = K\log(n)$), and testing-based selection (c equals a fixed quantile of the χ_K^2 distribution).

> **Theorem 28.6** Under standard regularity conditions for maximum likelihood estimation, selection based on IC is model selection consistent if $c(n,K) = o(n)$ as $n \to \infty$.

The proof is given in Section 28.32.

This result covers AIC, BIC, and testing-based selection. Thus all are model selection consistent.

A major limitation with this result is that the definition of model selection consistency is weak. A model may be true but overparameterized. To understand the distinction, consider the models $Y = X_1'\beta_1 + e$ and $Y = X_1'\beta_1 + X_2'\beta_2 + e$. If $\beta_2 = 0$, then both $\mathscr{M}_1$ and $\mathscr{M}_2$ are true, but $\mathscr{M}_1$ is the preferred model as it is more parsimonious. When two nested models are both true models, it is conventional to think of the more parsimonious model as the correct model. In this context, we do not describe the larger model as an incorrect model but rather as overparameterized. If a selection rule asymptotically selects an overparameterized model, we say that it "over-selects."

> **Definition 28.2** A model selection rule **asymptotically over-selects** if there are models $\mathscr{M}_1 \subset \mathscr{M}_2$ such that $\liminf_{n\to\infty} \mathbb{P}\left[\widehat{\mathscr{M}} = \mathscr{M}_2 \mid \mathscr{M}_1\right] > 0$.

The definition states that over-selection occurs when two models are nested and the smaller model is true (so both models are true models, but the smaller model is more parsimonious) if the larger model is asymptotically selected with positive probability.

> **Theorem 28.7** Under standard regularity conditions for maximum likelihood estimation, selection based on IC asymptotically over-selects if $c(n,K) = O(1)$ as $n \to \infty$.

The proof is given in Section 28.32.

This result includes both AIC and testing-based selection. Thus these procedures over-select. For example, if the models are $Y = X_1'\beta_1 + e$ and $Y = X_1'\beta_1 + X_2'\beta_2 + e$ and $\beta_2 = 0$ holds, then these procedures select the overparameterized regression with positive probability.

Following this line of reasoning, it is useful to draw a distinction between true and parsimonious models. We define the set of **parsimonious models** $\overline{\mathscr{M}}^0 \subset \overline{\mathscr{M}}^*$ as the set of true models with the fewest number of parameters. When the models in $\overline{\mathscr{M}}^*$ are nested, then $\overline{\mathscr{M}}^0$ will be a singleton. In the regression example with $\beta_2 = 0$, then $\mathscr{M}_1$ is the unique parsimonious model among $\{\mathscr{M}_1, \mathscr{M}_2\}$. We introduce a stronger consistency definition for procedures that asymptotically select parsimonious models.

> **Definition 28.3** A model selection rule is **consistent for parsimonious models** if $\mathbb{P}\left[\widehat{\mathscr{M}} \in \overline{\mathscr{M}}^0\right] \to 1$ as $n \to \infty$.

Of the methods we have reviewed, only BIC selection is consistent for parsimonious models, as we now show.

Theorem 28.8 Under standard regularity conditions for maximum likelihood estimation, selection based on IC is consistent for parsimonious models if for all $K_2 > K_1$,

$$c(n, K_2) - c(n, K_1) \to \infty \tag{28.16}$$

as $n \to \infty$, yet $c(n, K) = o(n)$ as $n \to \infty$.

The proof is given in Section 28.32.

The condition includes BIC because $c(n, K_2) - c(n, K_1) = (K_2 - K_1)\log(n) \to \infty$ if $K_2 > K_1$.

Some economists have interpreted Theorem 28.8 as indicating that BIC selection is preferred over the other methods. This is an incorrect deduction. In Section 28.13, we show that the other selection procedures are asymptotically optimal in terms of model fit and in terms of out-of-sample forecasting. Thus, consistent model selection is only one of several desirable statistical properties.

28.13 ASYMPTOTIC SELECTION OPTIMALITY

Regressor selection by the AIC/Shibata/Mallows/CV class turns out to be asymptotically optimal with respect to out-of-sample prediction under quite broad conditions. This may appear to conflict with the results of Section 28.12, but it does not, as there is a critical difference between the goals of consistent model selection and accurate prediction.

Our analysis will use the homoskedastic regression model conditioning on the regressor matrix $\boldsymbol{X}$. Write the regression model as

$$Y = m + e$$

$$m = \sum_{j=1}^{\infty} X_j \beta_j$$

$$\mathbb{E}[e \mid X] = 0$$

$$\mathbb{E}\left[e^2 \mid X\right] = \sigma^2$$

where $X = (X_1, X_2, \ldots)$. We can also write the regression equation in matrix notation as $\boldsymbol{Y} = \boldsymbol{m} + \boldsymbol{e}$.

The Kth regression model uses the first K regressors $X_K = (X_1, X_2, \ldots, X_K)$. The least squares estimates in matrix notation are

$$\boldsymbol{Y} = \boldsymbol{X}_K \widehat{\beta}_K + \widehat{\boldsymbol{e}}_K.$$

As in Section 28.6, define the fitted values $\widehat{\boldsymbol{m}} = \boldsymbol{X}_K \widehat{\beta}_K$ and regression fit (sum of expected squared prediction errors) as

$$R_n(K) = \mathbb{E}\left[(\widehat{\boldsymbol{m}} - \boldsymbol{m})' (\widehat{\boldsymbol{m}} - \boldsymbol{m}) \mid \boldsymbol{X}\right] \tag{28.17}$$

though now we index R by sample size n and model K.

In any sample, there is an optimal model K that minimizes $R_n(K)$:

$$K_n^{\text{opt}} = \underset{K}{\operatorname{argmin}}\, R_n(K).$$

Model K_n^{opt} obtains the minimized value of $R_n(K)$

$$R_n^{\text{opt}} = R_n(K_n^{\text{opt}}) = \min_K R_n(K).$$

Now consider model selection using the Mallow's criterion for regression models:

$$C_p(K) = \widehat{\boldsymbol{e}}_K' \widehat{\boldsymbol{e}}_K + 2\sigma^2 K$$

where we explicitly index by K, and for simplicity, we assume the error variance σ^2 is known. (The results are unchanged if it is replaced by a consistent estimator.) Let the selected model be

$$\widehat{K}_n = \underset{K}{\operatorname{argmin}}\, C_p(K).$$

Prediction accuracy using the Mallows-selected model is $R_n(\widehat{K}_n)$. We say that a selection procedure is **asymptotically optimal** if the prediction accuracy is asymptotically equivalent with the infeasible optimum. This can be written as

$$\frac{R_n(\widehat{K}_n)}{R_n^{\text{opt}}} \underset{p}{\longrightarrow} 1. \tag{28.18}$$

We consider convergence in (28.18) in terms of the risk ratio, because R_n^{opt} diverges as the sample size increases.

Li (1987) established the asymptotic optimality (28.18). His result depends on the following conditions.

Assumption 28.1

1. The observations (Y_i, X_i), $i = 1, \ldots, n$, are i.i.d.
2. $\mathbb{E}[e \mid X] = 0$.
3. $\mathbb{E}\left[e^2 \mid X\right] = \sigma^2$.
4. $\mathbb{E}\left[|e|^{4r} \mid X\right] \leq B < \infty$ for some $r > 1$.
5. $R_n^{\text{opt}} \to \infty$ as $n \to \infty$.
6. The estimated models are nested.

Assumption 28.1 parts 2 and 3 state that the true model is a conditionally homoskedastic regression. Assumption 28.1 part 4 is a technical condition, that a conditional moment of the error is uniformly bounded. Assumption 28.1 part 5 is subtle. It effectively states that there is no correctly specified finite-dimensional model. To see this, suppose that there is a K_0 such that the model is correctly specified, meaning that $m_i = \sum_{j=1}^{K_0} X_{ji}\beta_j$. In this case, we can show that for $K \geq K_0$, $R_n(K) = R_n(K_0)$ does not change with n, violating Assumption 28.1 part 5. Assumption 28.1 part 6 is a technical condition that restricts the number of estimated models. This assumption can be generalized to allow non-nested models, but in this case, an alternative restriction on the number of estimated models is needed.

Theorem 28.9 Assumption 28.1 implies (28.18). Thus Mallows selection is asymptotically equivalent to using the infeasible optimal model.

The proof is given in Section 28.32.

Theorem 28.9 states that Mallows selection in a conditional homoskedastic regression is asymptotically optimal. The key assumptions are homoskedasticity and that all finite-dimensional models are misspecified (incomplete), meaning that there are always omitted variables. The latter means that regardless of the sample size, there is always a tradeoff between omitted variables bias and estimation variance. The theorem as stated is specific for Mallows selection but can be extended to AIC, Shibata, GCV, FPE, and CV with some additional technical considerations. The primary message is that the selection methods discussed in Section 28.12 asymptotically select a sequence of models that are best-fitting in the sense of minimizing the prediction error.

Using a similar argument, Andrews (1991c) showed that selection by CV satisfies the same asymptotic optimality condition without requiring conditional homoskedasticity. The treatment is a bit more technical, so we do not review it here. This result indicates an important advantage for cross-validation selection over the other methods.

28.14 FOCUSED INFORMATION CRITERION

Claeskens and Hjort (2003) introduced the **focused information criterion (FIC)** as an estimator of the MSE of a scalar parameter. The criterion is appropriate in correctly specified likelihood models when one of the estimated models nests the other models. Let $f(y,\theta)$ be a parametric model density with a $K\times 1$ parameter θ.

The class of models (submodels) allowed are those defined by a set of differentiable restrictions $r(\theta)=0$. Let $\widetilde{\theta}$ be the restricted MLE that maximizes the likelihood subject to $r(\theta)=0$.

A key feature of the FIC is that it focuses on a real-valued parameter $\mu=g(\theta)$, where g is some differentiable function. Claeskens and Hjort call μ the **target parameter**. The choice of μ is made by the researcher and is a critical choice. In most applications, μ is the key coefficient in the application (for example, the returns to schooling in a wage regression). The unrestricted MLE for μ is $\widehat{\mu}=g(\widehat{\theta})$, the restricted MLE is $\widetilde{\mu}=g(\widetilde{\theta})$.

Estimation accuracy is measured by the MSE of the estimator of the target parameter, which is the squared bias plus the variance:

$$\operatorname{mse}[\widetilde{\mu}]=\mathbb{E}\left[(\widetilde{\mu}-\mu)^2\right]=(\mathbb{E}[\widetilde{\mu}]-\mu)^2+\operatorname{var}[\widetilde{\mu}].$$

It turns out to be convenient to normalize the MSE by that of the unrestricted estimator. Define this as the **Focus**:

$$\mathrm{F}=\operatorname{mse}[\widetilde{\mu}]-\operatorname{mse}[\widehat{\mu}].$$

The Claeskens-Hjort FIC is an estimator of F. Specifically,

$$\mathrm{FIC}=(\widetilde{\mu}-\widehat{\mu})^2-2\widehat{\boldsymbol{G}}'\widehat{\boldsymbol{V}}_{\widehat{\theta}}\widehat{\boldsymbol{R}}\left(\widehat{\boldsymbol{R}}'\widehat{\boldsymbol{V}}_{\widehat{\theta}}\widehat{\boldsymbol{R}}\right)^{-1}\widehat{\boldsymbol{R}}'\widehat{\boldsymbol{V}}_{\widehat{\theta}}\widehat{\boldsymbol{G}}$$

where $\widehat{\boldsymbol{V}}_{\widehat{\theta}}$, $\widehat{\boldsymbol{G}}$ and $\widehat{\boldsymbol{R}}$ are estimators of $\operatorname{var}\left[\widehat{\theta}\right]$, $\boldsymbol{G}=\frac{\partial}{\partial\theta'}g(\theta)$, and $\boldsymbol{R}=\frac{\partial}{\partial\theta'}r(\theta)$.

In a least squares regression $\boldsymbol{Y}=\boldsymbol{X}\beta+\boldsymbol{e}$ with a linear restriction $\boldsymbol{R}'\beta=0$ and linear parameter of interest $\mu=\boldsymbol{G}'\beta$, the FIC equals

$$\begin{aligned}\mathrm{FIC}=&\left(\boldsymbol{G}'\boldsymbol{R}\left(\boldsymbol{R}'\left(\boldsymbol{X}'\boldsymbol{X}\right)^{-1}\boldsymbol{R}\right)^{-1}\boldsymbol{R}'\left(\boldsymbol{X}'\boldsymbol{X}\right)^{-1}\widehat{\beta}\right)^2\\&-2\widehat{\sigma}^2\boldsymbol{G}'\left(\boldsymbol{X}'\boldsymbol{X}\right)^{-1}\boldsymbol{R}\left(\boldsymbol{R}'\left(\boldsymbol{X}'\boldsymbol{X}\right)^{-1}\boldsymbol{R}\right)^{-1}\boldsymbol{R}'\left(\boldsymbol{X}'\boldsymbol{X}\right)^{-1}\boldsymbol{G}.\end{aligned}$$

The FIC is used similarly to AIC. The FIC is calculated for each submodel of interest, and the model with the lowest value of FIC is selected.

The advantage of the FIC is that it is specifically targeted to minimize the MSE of the target parameter. The FIC is therefore appropriate when the goal is to estimate a specific target parameter. A disadvantage is that it does not necessarily produce a model with good estimates of the other parameters. For example, in a linear regression $Y = X_1\beta_1 + X_2\beta_2 + e$, if X_1 and X_2 are uncorrelated and the focus parameter is β_1, then the FIC will tend to select the submodel without X_2, and thus the selected model will produce a highly biased estimate of β_2. Consequently when using the FIC, it is dubious if attention should be paid to estimates other than those of μ.

Computationally it may be convenient to implement the FIC using an alternative formulation. Define the adjusted focus

$$\mathrm{F}^* = n\left(\mathrm{F} + 2\mathrm{mse}\left[\widehat{\mu}\right]\right) = n\left(\mathrm{mse}\left[\widetilde{\mu}\right] + \mathrm{mse}\left[\widehat{\mu}\right]\right).$$

This adds the same quantity to all models and therefore does not alter the minimizing model. Multiplication by n puts the FIC in units that are easier for reporting. The estimate of the adjusted focus is an adjusted FIC and can be written as

$$\mathrm{FIC}^* = n\left(\widetilde{\mu} - \widehat{\mu}\right)^2 + 2n\widehat{\boldsymbol{V}}_{\widetilde{\mu}} \tag{28.19}$$

$$= n\left(\widetilde{\mu} - \widehat{\mu}\right)^2 + 2ns\left(\widetilde{\mu}\right)^2 \tag{28.20}$$

where

$$\widehat{\boldsymbol{V}}_{\widetilde{\mu}} = \widehat{\boldsymbol{G}}'\left(\boldsymbol{I}_k - \widehat{\boldsymbol{V}}_{\widehat{\theta}}\widehat{\boldsymbol{R}}\left(\widehat{\boldsymbol{R}}'\widehat{\boldsymbol{V}}_{\widehat{\theta}}\widehat{\boldsymbol{R}}\right)^{-1}\widehat{\boldsymbol{R}}'\widehat{\boldsymbol{V}}_{\widehat{\theta}}\right)\widehat{\boldsymbol{G}}$$

is an estimator of $\mathrm{var}\left[\widetilde{\mu}\right]$, and $s\left(\widetilde{\mu}\right) = \widehat{\boldsymbol{V}}_{\widetilde{\mu}}^{1/2}$ is a standard error for $\widetilde{\mu}$.

Thus FIC* can be easily calculated using conventional software without additional programming. The estimator $\widehat{\mu}$ can be calculated from the full model (the long regression) and the estimator $\widetilde{\mu}$ and its standard error $s\left(\widetilde{\mu}\right)$ from the restricted model (the short regression). The formula (28.20) can then be applied to obtain FIC*.

The formula (28.19) also provides an intuitive understanding of the FIC. When we minimize FIC*, we are minimizing the variance of the estimator of the target parameter ($\widehat{\boldsymbol{V}}_{\widetilde{\mu}}$) while not altering the estimate $\widetilde{\mu}$ too much from the unrestricted estimate $\widehat{\mu}$.

When selecting from just two models, the FIC selects the restricted model if $\left(\widetilde{\mu} - \widehat{\mu}\right)^2 + 2\widehat{\boldsymbol{V}}_{\widetilde{\mu}} < 0$, which is the same as $\left(\widetilde{\mu} - \widehat{\mu}\right)^2 / \widehat{\boldsymbol{V}}_{\widetilde{\mu}} < 2$. The statistic to the left of the inequality is the squared t-statistic in the restricted model, which is used for testing the hypothesis that μ equals the unrestricted estimator $\widehat{\mu}$ but ignoring the estimation error in the latter. Thus a simple implementation (when just comparing two models) is to estimate the long and short regressions, take the difference in the two estimates of the coefficient of interest, and compute a t-ratio using the standard error from the short (restricted) regression. If this t-ratio exceeds 1.4, the FIC selects the long regression estimate. If the t-ratio is smaller than 1.4, the FIC selects the short regression estimate.

Claeskens and Hjort motivate the FIC using a local misspecification asymptotic framework. We use a simpler heuristic motivation. First, consider the unrestricted MLE. Under standard conditions, $\widehat{\mu}$ has asymptotic variance $\boldsymbol{G}'\boldsymbol{V}_\theta\boldsymbol{G}$, where $\boldsymbol{V}_\theta = \mathscr{I}^{-1}$. As the estimator is asymptotically unbiased, it follows that

$$\mathrm{mse}\left[\widehat{\mu}\right] \simeq \mathrm{var}\left[\widehat{\mu}\right] \simeq n^{-1}\boldsymbol{G}'\boldsymbol{V}_\theta\boldsymbol{G}.$$

Second, consider the restricted MLE. Under standard conditions, $\widetilde{\mu}$ has asymptotic variance

$$\boldsymbol{G}'\left(\boldsymbol{V}_\theta - \boldsymbol{V}_\theta \boldsymbol{R}\left(\boldsymbol{R}'\boldsymbol{V}_\theta \boldsymbol{R}\right)^{-1} \boldsymbol{R}\boldsymbol{V}_\theta\right)\boldsymbol{G}.$$

$\widetilde{\mu}$ also has a probability limit, say μ_R, which (generally) differs from μ. Taken together, we find that

$$\operatorname{mse}\left[\widetilde{\mu}\right] \simeq B + n^{-1}\boldsymbol{G}'\left(\boldsymbol{V}_\theta - \boldsymbol{V}_\theta \boldsymbol{R}\left(\boldsymbol{R}'\boldsymbol{V}_\theta \boldsymbol{R}\right)^{-1} \boldsymbol{R}\boldsymbol{V}_\theta\right)\boldsymbol{G}$$

where $B = (\mu - \mu_R)^2$. Subtracting, we find that the Focus is

$$\mathrm{F} \simeq B - n^{-1}\boldsymbol{G}'\boldsymbol{V}_\theta \boldsymbol{R}\left(\boldsymbol{R}'\boldsymbol{V}_\theta \boldsymbol{R}\right)^{-1} \boldsymbol{R}\boldsymbol{V}_\theta \boldsymbol{G}.$$

The plug-in estimator $\widehat{B} = (\widehat{\mu} - \widetilde{\mu})^2$ of B is biased, because

$$\begin{aligned}
\mathbb{E}\left[\widehat{B}\right] &= (\mathbb{E}\left[\widehat{\mu} - \widetilde{\mu}\right])^2 + \operatorname{var}\left[\widehat{\mu} - \widetilde{\mu}\right] \\
&\simeq B + \operatorname{var}\left[\widehat{\mu}\right] - \operatorname{var}\left[\widetilde{\mu}\right] \\
&\simeq B + n^{-1}\boldsymbol{G}'\boldsymbol{V}_\theta \boldsymbol{R}\left(\boldsymbol{R}'\boldsymbol{V}_\theta \boldsymbol{R}\right)^{-1} \boldsymbol{R}\boldsymbol{V}_\theta \boldsymbol{G}.
\end{aligned}$$

It follows that an approximately unbiased estimator for F is

$$\widehat{B} - 2n^{-1}\boldsymbol{G}'\boldsymbol{V}_\theta \boldsymbol{R}\left(\boldsymbol{R}'\boldsymbol{V}_\theta \boldsymbol{R}\right)^{-1} \boldsymbol{R}\boldsymbol{V}_\theta \boldsymbol{G}.$$

The FIC is obtained by replacing the unknown $\boldsymbol{G}$, $\boldsymbol{R}$, and $n^{-1}\boldsymbol{V}_\theta$ by estimates.

28.15 BEST SUBSET AND STEPWISE REGRESSION

Suppose that we have a set of potential regressors $\{X_1, \ldots, X_K\}$, and we want to select a subset of the regressors to use in a regression. Let S_m denote a subset of the regressors, and let $m = 1, \ldots, M$ denote the set of potential subsets. Given a model selection criterion (e.g., AIC, Mallows, or CV) the **best subset model** is the one that minimizes the criterion across the M models. This is implemented by estimating the M models and comparing the model selection criteria.

If K is small, it is computationally feasible to compare all subset models. However, when K is large, this approach may not be feasible, because the number of potential subsets is $M = 2^K$, which increases quickly with K. For example, $K = 10$ implies $M = 1{,}024$, $K = 20$ implies $M \geq 1{,}000{,}000$, and $K = 40$ implies M exceeds one trillion. It simply does not make sense to estimate all subset regressions in such cases.

If the goal is to find the set of regressors that produces the smallest selection criterion, it seems likely that we should be able to find an approximating set of regressors at a much reduced computational cost. Some specific algorithms to implement this goal are called stepwise, stagewise, and least angle regression. None of these procedures actually achieve the goal of minimizing any specific selection criterion; instead they are viewed as useful computational approximations. There is also some potential confusion, as different authors seem to use the same terms for somewhat different implementations. We use the terms here as described in Hastie, Tibshirani, and Friedman (2008).

In the following descriptions, $\mathrm{SSE}(m)$ refers to the sum of squared residuals from a fitted model, and $C(m)$ refers to the selection criterion used for model comparison (AIC is most typically used).

Backward Stepwise Regression

1. Start with all regressors $\{X_1, \ldots, X_K\}$ included in the "active set."

2. For $m = 0, \dots, K-1$
   (a) Estimate the regression of Y on the active set.
   (b) Identify the regressor whose omission will have the smallest impact on $C(m)$.
   (c) Put this regressor in slot $K-m$, and delete from the active set.
   (d) Calculate $C(m)$ and store in slot $K-m$.
3. The model with the smallest value of $C(m)$ is the selected model.

Backward stepwise regression requires $K < n$, so that regression with all variables is feasible. It produces an ordering of the regressors from "most relevant" to "least relevant." A simplified version is to exit the loop when $C(m)$ increases. (This may not yield the same result as completing the loop.) For the case of AIC selection, step (b) can be implemented by calculating the classical (homoskedastic) t-ratio for each active regressor and finding the regressor with the smallest absolute t-ratio. (See Exercise 28.3.)

Forward Stepwise Regression

1. Start with the null set $\{\varnothing\}$ as the "active set" and all regressors $\{X_1, \dots, X_K\}$ as the "inactive set."
2. For $m = 1, \dots, \min(n-1, K)$
   (a) Estimate the regression of Y on the active set.
   (b) Identify the regressor in the inactive set whose inclusion will have the largest impact on $C(m)$.
   (b) Put this regressor in slot m, and move it from the inactive to the active set.
   (c) Calculate $C(m)$ and store in slot m.
3. The model with the smallest value of $C(m)$ is the selected model.

A simplified version is to exit the loop when $C(m)$ increases. (This may not yield the same answer as completing the loop.) For the case of AIC selection, step (b) can be implemented by finding the regressor in the inactive set with the largest absolute correlation with the residual from step (a). (See Exercise 28.4.)

There are combined algorithms that check both forward and backward movements at each step. The algorithms can also be implemented with the regressors organized in groups (so that all elements are either included or excluded at each step). There are also old-fashioned versions that use significance testing rather than selection criterion (this is generally not advised).

Stepwise regression based on old-fashioned significance testing can be implemented in Stata using the `stepwise` command. If attention is confined to models that include regressors one at a time, AIC selection can be implemented by setting the significance level equal to $p = 0.32$. Thus the command `stepwise, pr(.32)` implements backward stepwise regression with the AIC criterion, and `stepwise, pe(.32)` implements forward stepwise regression with the AIC criterion.

Stepwise regression can be implemented in R using the `lars` command.

28.16 THE MSE OF MODEL SELECTION ESTIMATORS

Model selection can lead to estimators with poor sampling performance. In this section, we show that the mean squared error of estimation is not necessarily improved—and can be considerably worsened—by model selection.

To keep things simple, consider an estimator with an exact normal distribution and known covariance matrix. Normalizing the latter to the identity, we consider the setting

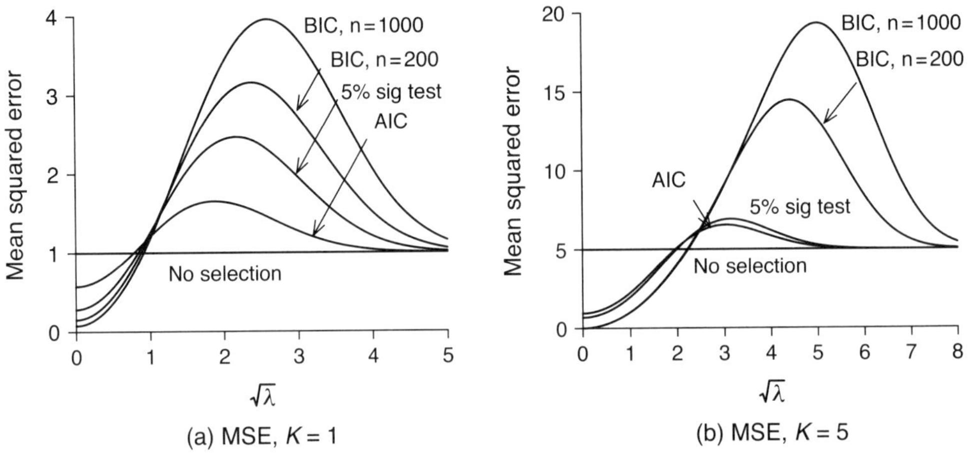

FIGURE 28.1 MSE of post-model-selection estimators

$$\widehat{\theta} \sim \mathrm{N}(\theta, \boldsymbol{I}_K)$$

and the class of model selection estimators

$$\widehat{\theta}_{\text{pms}} = \begin{cases} \widehat{\theta}, & \text{if } \widehat{\theta}'\widehat{\theta} > c \\ 0, & \text{if } \widehat{\theta}'\widehat{\theta} \le c \end{cases}$$

for some c. AIC sets $c = 2K$, BIC sets $c = K\log(n)$, and 5% significance testing sets c to equal the 95% quantile of the χ^2_K distribution. It is common to call $\widehat{\theta}_{\text{pms}}$ a **post-model-selection (PMS)** estimator

We can explicitly calculate the MSE of $\widehat{\theta}_{\text{pms}}$.

Theorem 28.10 If $\widehat{\theta} \sim \mathrm{N}(\theta, \boldsymbol{I}_K)$, then

$$\operatorname{mse}\left[\widehat{\theta}_{\text{pms}}\right] = K + (2\lambda - K)\, F_{K+2}(c,\lambda) - \lambda F_{K+4}(c,\lambda)$$

where $F_r(x,\lambda)$ is the non-central chi-square distribution function with r degrees of freedom and non-centrality parameter $\lambda = \theta'\theta$.

The proof is given in Section 28.32.

The MSE is determined only by K, λ, and c. The parameter $\lambda = \theta'\theta$ turns out to be important for the MSE. As the squared Euclidean length, it indexes the magnitude of the coefficient θ.

We can see the following limiting cases. If $\lambda = 0$, then $\operatorname{mse}\left[\widehat{\theta}_{\text{pms}}\right] = K(1 - F_{K+2}(c,0))$. As $\lambda \to \infty$, then $\operatorname{mse}\left[\widehat{\theta}_{\text{pms}}\right] \to K$. The unrestricted estimator obtains if $c = 0$, in which case, $\operatorname{mse}\left[\widehat{\theta}_{\text{pms}}\right] = K$. As $c \to \infty$, $\operatorname{mse}\left[\widehat{\theta}_{\text{pms}}\right] \to \lambda$. The latter implies that the PMS estimator based on the BIC has MSE $\to \infty$ as $n \to \infty$.

Using Theorem 28.10, we can numerically calculate the MSE. Figure 28.1 plots the MSE of a set of estimators for a range of values of $\sqrt{\lambda}$. Panel (a) is for $K = 1$, panel (b) is for $K = 5$. Note that the MSE of the unselected estimator $\widehat{\theta}$ is invariant to λ, so its MSE plot is a flat line at K. The other estimators plotted are AIC selection ($c = 2K$), 5% significance testing selection (chi-square critical value), and BIC selection ($c = K\log(n)$) for $n = 200$ and $n = 1{,}000$.

In the plots you can see that the PMS estimators have lower MSE than the unselected estimator roughly for $\lambda < K$ but higher MSE for $\lambda > K$. The AIC estimator has MSE that is least distorted from the unselected estimator, reaching a peak of about 1.5 for $K = 1$. The BIC estimators, however, have very large MSE for larger values of λ, and the distortion is growing as n increases. The MSE of the selection estimators increases with λ until it reaches a peak and then slowly decreases and asymptotes back to K. Furthermore, the MSE of BIC is unbounded as n diverges. Thus for very large sample sizes, the MSE of a BIC-selected estimator can be a very large multiple of the MSE of the unselected estimator. The plots show that if λ is small, there are advantages to model selection, as MSE can be greatly reduced. However if λ is large, then MSE can be greatly increased if BIC is used, and moderately increased if AIC is used. A sensible reading of the plots leads to the practical recommendation to not use the BIC for model selection, and use the AIC with care.

The numerical calculations show that MSE is reduced by selection when λ is small but increased when λ is moderately large. What does this mean in practice? λ is small when θ is small, which means the compared models are similar in terms of estimation accuracy. In this context, model selection can be valuable, as it helps select smaller models to improve precision. However when λ is moderately large (which means that θ is moderately large), the smaller model has meaningful omitted variable bias, yet the selection criteria have difficulty detecting which model to use. The conservative BIC selection procedure tends to select the smaller model and thus incurs greater bias, resulting in high MSE. These considerations suggest that it is better to use the AIC when selecting among models with similar estimation precision. Unfortunately it is impossible to known a priori the appropriate models.

The results of this section may appear to contradict Theorem 28.8, which showed that the BIC is consistent for parsimonious models, because for all $\lambda > 0$ in the plots, the correct parsimonious model is the larger model. Yet BIC is not selecting this model with sufficient frequency to produce a low MSE. There is no contradiction. The consistency of the BIC appears in the lower portion of the plots, where the MSE of the BIC estimator is very small, and approaching 0 as $\lambda \to 0$. The fact that the MSE of the AIC estimator somewhat exceeds that of the BIC in this region is due to the over-selection property of the AIC.

28.17 INFERENCE AFTER MODEL SELECTION

Economists are typically interested in inferential questions, such as hypothesis tests and confidence intervals. If an econometric model has been selected by a procedure such as AIC or CV, what are the properties of statistical tests applied to the selected model?

To be concrete, consider the regression model $Y = X_1\beta_1 + X_2\beta_2 + e$ and selection of the variable X_2. That is, we compare $Y = X_1\beta_1 + e$ with $Y = X_1\beta_1 + X_2\beta_2 + e$. It is not too profound a realization that in this context, it is inappropriate to conduct conventional inference for β_2 in the selected model. If we select the smaller model, there is no estimate of β_2. If we select the larger, it is because the t-ratio for β_2 exceeds the critical value. The distribution of the t-ratio, conditional on exceeding a critical value, is not conventionally distributed, and there seems little point to push this issue further.

The more interesting and subtle question is the impact on inference concerning β_1. This indeed is a context of typical interest. An economist is interested in the impact of X_1 on Y, given a set of controls X_2. It is common to select across these controls to find a suitable empirical model. Once it has been obtained, we want to make inferential statements about β_1. Has selection over the controls impacted inference?

I illustrate the issue numerically. Suppose that (X_1, X_2) are jointly normal with unit variances and correlation ρ, e is independent and standard normal, and $n = 30$. Let us estimate the long regression of Y on (X_1, X_2)

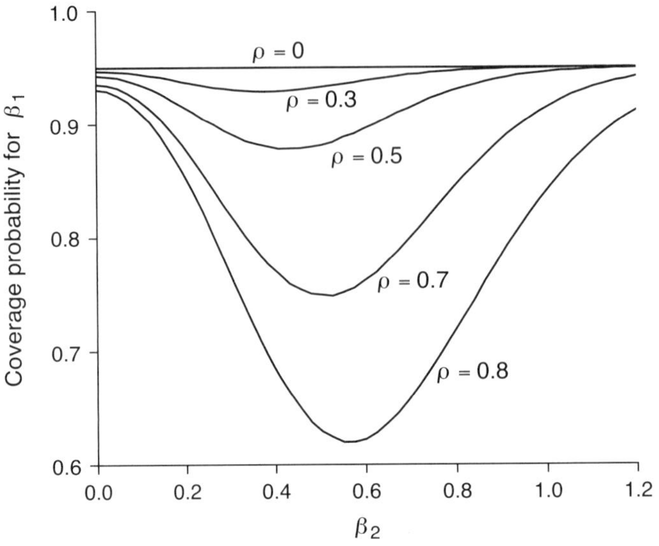

FIGURE 28.2 Coverage probability of post-model selection

and the short regression of Y on X_1 alone. We construct the t-statistic[3] for $\beta_2 = 0$ in the long regression and select the long regression if the t-statistic is significant at the 5% level and select the short regression if the t-statistic is not significant. We construct the standard 95% confidence interval[4] for β_1 in the selected regression. These confidence intervals will have exact 95% coverage when there is no selection and the estimated model is correct, so deviations from 95% are due to model selection and mis-specification. We calculate the actual coverage probability by simulation using one million replications, varying[5] β_2 and ρ.

Figure 28.2 displays the coverage probabilities as a function of β_2 for several values of ρ. If the regressors are uncorrelated ($\rho = 0$), then the actual coverage probability equals the nominal level of 0.95. This is because the t-statistic for β_2 is independent of those for β_1 in this normal regression model, and the coefficients on X_1 in the short and long regression are identical.

This invariance breaks down for $\rho \neq 0$. As ρ increases, the coverage probability of the confidence intervals fall below the nominal level. The distortion is strongly affected by the value of β_2. For $\beta_2 = 0$, the distortion is mild. The reason is that when $\beta_2 = 0$, the selection t-statistic selects the short regression with high probability (95%), which leads to approximately valid inference. Also, as $\beta_2 \to \infty$, the coverage probability converges to the nominal level. The reason is that for large β_2, the selection t-statistic selects the long regression with high probability, again leading to approximately valid inference. The distortion is large, however, for intermediate values of β_2. For $\rho = 0.5$, the coverage probability falls to 88%, and for $\rho = 0.8$, the probability is as low as 62%. The reason is that for intermediate values of β_2, the selection t-statistic selects both models with meaningful probability, and this selection decision is correlated with the t-statistics for β_1. The degree of undercoverage is enormous and greatly troubling.

[3]Using the homoskedastic variance formula and assuming the error variance is known. This is done to focus on the selection issue rather than on covariance matrix estimation.

[4]Using the homoskedastic variance formula and assuming the correct error variance is known.

[5]The coverage probability is invariant to β_1.

Table 28.1
Estimates of return to experience among Asian women

	Model 1	Model 2	Model 3	Model 4	Model 5	Model 6	Model 7	Model 8	Model 9
Return	13%	22%	20%	29%	40%	37%	33%	47%	45%
s.e.	7	8	7	11	11	11	17	18	17
BIC	956	**907**	924	964	913	931	977	925	943
AIC	915	861	858	914	858	**855**	916	860	857
CV	405	387	386	405	385	**385**	406	387	386
FIC	86	48	53	58	**32**	34	86	71	68
Education	College	Spline	Dummy	College	Spline	Dummy	College	Spline	Dummy
Experience	2	2	2	4	4	4	6	6	6

The message from this figure is that inference after model selection is problematic. Conventional inference procedures do not have conventional distributions, and the distortions are potentially unbounded.

28.18 EMPIRICAL ILLUSTRATION

I illustrate the model selection methods with an application. Consider the CPS dataset and the subsample of Asian women, which has $n = 1{,}149$ observations. Consider a log wage regression with primary interest on the return to experience, measured as the percentage difference between expected wages between 0 and 30 years of experience. Let us consider and compare nine least squares regressions. All include an indicator for *married* and three indicators for *region*. The estimated models range in complexity concerning the impact of education and experience.

Terms for experience:

- Models 1–3 include include experience and its square.
- Models 4–6 include powers of experience up to power 4.
- Models 7–9 include powers of experience up to power 6.

Terms for education:

- Models 1, 4, and 7 include a single dummy variable *college*, indicating that years of education is 16 or higher.
- Models 2, 5, and 8 include a linear spline in education with a single knot at education $= 9$.
- Models 3, 6, and 9 include six dummy variables, for education equaling 12, 13, 14, 16, 18, and 20.

Table 28.1 reports key estimates from the nine models. Reported are the estimate of the return to experience as a percentage wage difference, its standard error (HC1), the BIC, AIC, CV, and FIC, the latter treating the return to experience as the focus. What we can see is that the estimates vary meaningfully, ranging from 13% to 47%. Some of the estimates also have moderately large standard errors. (In most models, the return to experience is "statistically significant," but by large standard errors, I mean that it is difficult to pin down the precise value of the return to experience.) We can also see that the most important factors impacting the magnitude of the point estimate are going beyond the quadratic specification for experience and going beyond the simplest specification for education. Another item to notice is that the standard errors are most affected by the number of experience terms.

The BIC picks a parsimonious model with the linear spline in education and a quadratic in experience. The AIC and CV select a less parsimonious model with the full dummy specification for education and a fourth-order polynomial in experience. The FIC selects an intermediate model, with a linear spline in education and a fourth-order polynomial in experience.

When selecting a model by using information criteria, it is useful to examine several criteria. In applications, decisions should be made by a combination of judgment as well as the formal criteria. In this case, the CV criterion selects model 6, which has the estimate 37%, but similar values of the CV criterion are obtained by models 3 and 9, which have the estimates 20% and 45%. The FIC, which focuses on this specific coefficient, selects model 5, which has the point estimate 40%, similar to the CV-selected model. Overall, based on this evidence, the CV-selected model and its point estimate of 37% seems an appropriate choice. However, the uncertainty reflected by the flatness of the CV criterion suggests that uncertainty remains in the choice of specification.

28.19 SHRINKAGE METHODS

Shrinkage methods are a broad class of estimators that reduce variance by moving an estimator $\widehat{\theta}$ towards a pre-selected point, such as the zero vector. In high dimensions, the reduction in variance more than compensates for the increase in bias resulting in improved efficiency when measured by mean squared error. This and the next few sections review material presented in Chapter 15 of *Probability and Statistics for Economists.*

The simplest shrinkage estimator takes the form $\widetilde{\theta}=(1-w)\,\widehat{\theta}$ for some shrinkage weight $w\in[0,1]$. Setting $w=0$, we obtain $\widetilde{\theta}=\widehat{\theta}$ (no shrinkage) and setting $w=1$, we obtain $\widetilde{\theta}=0$ (full shrinkage). It is straightforward to calculate the MSE of this estimator. Assume $\widehat{\theta}\sim(\theta,\boldsymbol{V})$. Then $\widetilde{\theta}$ has bias

$$\operatorname{bias}\left[\widetilde{\theta}\,\right]=\mathbb{E}\left[\widetilde{\theta}\,\right]-\theta=-w\theta \tag{28.21}$$

variance

$$\operatorname{var}\left[\widetilde{\theta}\,\right]=(1-w)^2\,\boldsymbol{V} \tag{28.22}$$

and WMSE (using the weight matrix $\boldsymbol{W}=\boldsymbol{V}^{-1}$)

$$\operatorname{wmse}\left[\widetilde{\theta}\,\right]=K\,(1-w)^2+w^2\lambda \tag{28.23}$$

where $\lambda=\theta'\boldsymbol{V}^{-1}\theta$.

Theorem 28.11 If $\widehat{\theta}\sim(\theta,\boldsymbol{V})$ and $\widetilde{\theta}=(1-w)\,\widehat{\theta}$, then

1. $\operatorname{wmse}\left[\widetilde{\theta}\,\right]<\operatorname{wmse}\left[\widehat{\theta}\,\right]$ if $0<w<2K/(K+\lambda)$.
2. $\operatorname{wmse}\left[\widetilde{\theta}\,\right]$ is minimized by the shrinkage weight $w_0=K/(K+\lambda)$.
3. The minimized WMSE is $\operatorname{wmse}\left[\widetilde{\theta}\right]=K\lambda/(K+\lambda)$.

You are asked to supply the proof, in Exercise 28.6.

Part 1 of the theorem shows that the shrinkage estimator has reduced WMSE for a range of values of the shrinkage weight w. Part 2 of the theorem shows that the WMSE-minimizing shrinkage weight is a simple function of K and λ. The latter is a measure of the magnitude of θ relative to the estimation variance. When λ is large (the coefficients are large), then the optimal shrinkage weight w_0 is small; when λ is small (the coefficients are small), then the optimal shrinkage weight w_0 is large. Part 3 calculates the associated optimal WMSE. This can be substantially less than the WMSE of the original estimator $\widehat{\theta}$. For example, if $\lambda = K$, then $\operatorname{wmse}\left[\widetilde{\theta}\right] = K/2$, one-half the WMSE of the original estimator.

To construct the optimal shrinkage weight, we need the unknown λ. An unbiased estimator is $\widehat{\lambda} = \widehat{\theta}' \boldsymbol{V}^{-1} \widehat{\theta} - K$ (see Exercise 28.7), implying the shrinkage weight

$$\widehat{w} = \frac{K}{\widehat{\theta}' \boldsymbol{V}^{-1} \widehat{\theta}}. \tag{28.24}$$

Replacing K with a free parameter c (which we call the "shrinkage coefficient"), we obtain

$$\widetilde{\theta} = \left(1 - \frac{c}{\widehat{\theta}' \boldsymbol{V}^{-1} \widehat{\theta}}\right) \widehat{\theta}. \tag{28.25}$$

This equation is often called a **Stein-Rule** estimator.

This estimator has many appealing properties. It can be viewed as a smoothed selection estimator. The quantity $\widehat{\theta}' \boldsymbol{V}^{-1} \widehat{\theta}$ is a Wald statistic for the hypothesis $\mathbb{H}_0 : \theta = 0$. Thus when this Wald statistic is large (when the evidence suggests the hypothesis of a zero coefficient is false), the shrinkage estimator is close to the original estimator $\widehat{\theta}$. However, when this Wald statistic is small (when the evidence is consistent with the hypothesis of a zero coefficient), then the shrinkage estimator moves the original estimator toward 0.

28.20 JAMES-STEIN SHRINKAGE ESTIMATOR

James and Stein (1961) made the following discovery.

Theorem 28.12 Assume that $\widehat{\theta} \sim \mathrm{N}(\theta, \boldsymbol{V})$, $\widetilde{\theta}$ is defined in (28.25), and $K > 2$.

1. If $0 < c < 2(K-2)$, then $\operatorname{wmse}\left[\widetilde{\theta}\right] < \operatorname{wmse}\left[\widehat{\theta}\right]$.
2. The WMSE is minimized by setting $c = K - 2$ and equals

$$\operatorname{wmse}\left[\widetilde{\theta}\right] = K - (K-2)^2\, \mathbb{E}\left[Q_K^{-1}\right]$$

where $Q_K \sim \chi_K^2(\lambda)$.

See Theorem 15.3 of *Probability and Statistics for Economists.*

This result stunned the world of statistics. Part 1 shows that the shrinkage estimator has strictly smaller WMSE for all values of the parameters and thus dominates the original estimator. The latter is the MLE, so this result shows that the MLE is dominated and thus inadmissible. This is a stunning result, because it had previously been assumed that it would be impossible to find an estimator that dominates the MLE.

Theorem 28.12 critically depends on the condition $K > 2$, which means that shrinkage achieves uniform improvements only in dimensions three or higher.

The minimizing choice for the shrinkage coefficient $c = K - 2$ leads to what is commonly known as the **James-Stein estimator**:

$$\widetilde{\theta} = \left(1 - \frac{K-2}{\widehat{\theta}' \boldsymbol{V}^{-1} \widehat{\theta}}\right) \widehat{\theta}.$$

In practice, $\boldsymbol{V}$ is unknown, so we substitute an estimator $\widehat{\boldsymbol{V}}$, leading to

$$\widetilde{\theta}_{\mathrm{JS}} = \left(1 - \frac{K-2}{\widehat{\theta}'\widehat{\boldsymbol{V}}^{-1}\widehat{\theta}}\right)\widehat{\theta}$$

which is fully feasible, as it does not depend on unknowns or tuning parameters. The substitution of $\widehat{\boldsymbol{V}}$ for $\boldsymbol{V}$ can be justified by finite sample or asymptotic arguments.

28.21 INTERPRETATION OF THE STEIN EFFECT

The James-Stein Theorem appears to conflict with classical statistical theory. The original estimator $\widehat{\theta}$ is the maximum likelihood estimator. It is unbiased. It is minimum variance unbiased. It is Cramér-Rao efficient. How can it be that the James-Stein shrinkage estimator achieves uniformly smaller MSE?

Part of the answer is that classical theory has caveats. The Cramér-Rao Theorem, for example, restricts attention to unbiased estimators and thus precludes consideration of shrinkage estimators. The James-Stein estimator has reduced MSE, but is not Cramér-Rao efficient, because it is biased. Therefore the James-Stein Theorem does not conflict with the Cramér-Rao Theorem. Instead they are complementary results. On one hand, the Cramér-Rao Theorem describes the best possible variance when unbiasedness is an important property for estimation. On the other hand, the James-Stein Theorem shows that if unbiasedness is not a critical property but instead MSE is important, then there are better estimators than the MLE.

The James-Stein Theorem may also appear to conflict with our results from Section 28.16, which showed that selection estimators do not achieve uniform MSE improvements over the MLE. This may appear to be a conflict, because the James-Stein estimator has a similar form to that of a selection estimator. The difference is that selection estimators are **hard threshold** rules—they are discontinuous functions of the data—while the James-Stein estimator is a **soft threshold** rule—it is a continuous function of the data. Hard thresholding tends to result in high variance; soft thresholding tends to result in low variance. The James-Stein estimator is able to achieve reduced variance because it is a soft threshold function.

The MSE improvements achieved by the James-Stein estimator are greatest when λ is small, which occurs when the parameters θ are small in magnitude relative to the estimation variance $\boldsymbol{V}$. Thus the user needs to choose the centering point wisely.

28.22 POSITIVE PART ESTIMATOR

The simple James-Stein estimator has the odd property that it can "over-shrink." When $\widehat{\theta}'\boldsymbol{V}^{-1}\widehat{\theta} < K-2$, then $\widetilde{\theta}$ has the opposite sign from $\widehat{\theta}$, which does not make sense and suggests that further improvements can be made. The standard solution is to use "positive-part" trimming by bounding the shrinkage weight (28.24) between 0 and 1. This estimator can be written as

$$\begin{aligned}\widetilde{\theta}^{+} &= \begin{cases}\widetilde{\theta}, & \widehat{\theta}'\boldsymbol{V}^{-1}\widehat{\theta} \geq K-2\\ 0, & \widehat{\theta}'\boldsymbol{V}^{-1}\widehat{\theta} < K-2\end{cases}\\ &= \left(1 - \frac{K-2}{\widehat{\theta}'\boldsymbol{V}^{-1}\widehat{\theta}}\right)_{+}\widehat{\theta}\end{aligned}$$

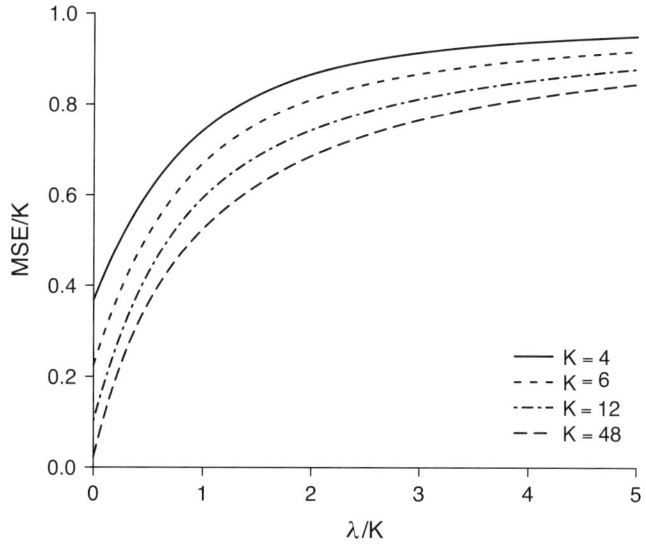

FIGURE 28.3 WMSE of James-Stein estimator

where $(a)_+ = \max[a, 0]$ is the "positive-part" function. Alternatively, it can be written as

$$\widetilde{\theta}^+ = \widehat{\theta} - \left(\frac{K-2}{\widehat{\theta}' \boldsymbol{V}^{-1} \widehat{\theta}}\right)_1 \widehat{\theta}$$

where $(a)_1 = \min[a, 1]$

The positive part estimator simultaneously performs "selection" as well as "shrinkage." If $\widehat{\theta}' \boldsymbol{V}^{-1} \widehat{\theta}$ is sufficiently small, $\widetilde{\theta}^+$ "selects" 0. When $\widehat{\theta}' \boldsymbol{V}^{-1} \widehat{\theta}$ is of moderate size, $\widetilde{\theta}^+$ shrinks $\widehat{\theta}$ toward 0. When $\widehat{\theta}' \boldsymbol{V}^{-1} \widehat{\theta}$ is very large, $\widetilde{\theta}^+$ is close to the original estimator $\widehat{\theta}$.

Consistent with our intuition, the positive part estimator has uniformly lower WMSE than the unadjusted James-Stein estimator.

Theorem 28.13 Under the assumptions of Theorem 28.12,

$$\text{wmse}\left[\widetilde{\theta}^+\right] < \text{wmse}\left[\widetilde{\theta}\right]. \tag{28.26}$$

For a proof, see Theorem 15.6 of *Probability and Statistics for Economists*. Theorem 15.7 of *Probability and Statistics for Economists* provides an explicit numerical evaluation of the MSE for the positive-part estimator.

Figure 28.3 plots $\text{wmse}\left[\widetilde{\theta}^+\right]/K$ as a function of λ/K for $K = 4$, 6, 12, and 48. The plots are uniformly below 1 (the normalized WMSE of the MLE), substantially so for small and moderate values of λ. The WMSE functions fall as K increases, demonstrating that the MSE reductions are more substantial when K is large.

In summary, the positive-part transformation is an important improvement over the unadjusted James-Stein estimator. It is more reasonable and reduces the mean squared error. The broader message is that imposing boundary conditions on shrinkage weights can improve estimation efficiency.

28.23 SHRINKAGE TOWARD RESTRICTIONS

The classical James-Stein estimator does not have direct use in applications, because it is rare that we wish to shrink an entire parameter vector toward a specific point. Instead it is more common to shrink a parameter vector toward a set of restrictions. Here are a few examples:

1. Shrink a long regression toward a short regression.
2. Shrink a regression toward an intercept-only model.
3. Shrink the regression coefficients toward a set of restrictions.
4. Shrink a set of estimates (or coefficients) toward their common mean.
5. Shrink a set of estimates (or coefficients) toward a parametric model.
6. Shrink a nonparametric series model toward a parametric model.

The way to think generally about these applications it that the researcher wants to allow for generality with the large model but believes that the smaller model may be a useful approximation. A shrinkage estimator allows the data to smoothly select between these two options, depending on the strength of information for the two specifications.

Let $\widehat{\theta} \sim \mathrm{N}(\theta, \boldsymbol{V})$ be the original estimator, for example, a set of regression coefficient estimates. The normality assumption is used for the exact theory but can be justified based on an asymtotic approximation as well. The researcher considers a set of $q > 2$ linear restrictions, which can be written as $\boldsymbol{R}'\theta = \boldsymbol{r}$, where $\boldsymbol{R}$ is $K \times q$ and $\boldsymbol{r}$ is $q \times 1$. A minimum distance estimator for θ is

$$\widehat{\theta}_{\boldsymbol{R}} = \widehat{\theta} - \boldsymbol{V}\boldsymbol{R}\left(\boldsymbol{R}'\boldsymbol{V}\boldsymbol{R}\right)^{-1}\left(\boldsymbol{R}'\widehat{\theta} - \boldsymbol{r}\right).$$

The James-Stein estimator with positive-part trimming is

$$\widetilde{\theta}^{+} = \widehat{\theta} - \left(\frac{q-2}{\left(\widehat{\theta} - \widehat{\theta}_{\boldsymbol{R}}\right)' \boldsymbol{V}^{-1}\left(\widehat{\theta} - \widehat{\theta}_{\boldsymbol{R}}\right)}\right)_1 \left(\widehat{\theta} - \widehat{\theta}_{\boldsymbol{R}}\right).$$

The function $(a)_1 = \min[a, 1]$ bounds the shrinkage weight below 1.

Theorem 28.14 Under the assumptions of Theorem 28.12, if $q > 2$, then

$$\mathrm{wmse}\left[\widetilde{\theta}^{+}\right] < \mathrm{wmse}\left[\widetilde{\theta}\right].$$

The shrinkage estimator achieves uniformly smaller MSE if the number of restrictions is three or greater. The number of restrictions q plays the same role as the number of parameters K in the classical James-Stein estimator. Shrinkage achieves greater gains when there are more restrictions q, and it achieves greater gains when the restrictions are close to being satisfied in the population. If the imposed restrictions are far from satisfied, then the shrinkage estimator will have similar performance as the original estimator. It is therefore important to select the restrictions carefully.

In practice the covariance matrix $\boldsymbol{V}$ is unknown, so it is replaced by an estimator $\widehat{\boldsymbol{V}}$. Thus the feasible version of the estimators equal

$$\widehat{\theta}_{\boldsymbol{R}} = \widehat{\theta} - \widehat{\boldsymbol{V}}\boldsymbol{R}\left(\boldsymbol{R}'\widehat{\boldsymbol{V}}\boldsymbol{R}\right)^{-1}\left(\boldsymbol{R}'\widehat{\theta} - \boldsymbol{r}\right)$$

and

$$\widetilde{\theta}^{+} = \widehat{\theta} - \left(\frac{q-2}{J}\right)_1 \left(\widehat{\theta} - \widehat{\theta}_{\boldsymbol{R}}\right) \tag{28.27}$$

where

$$J = \left(\widehat{\theta} - \widehat{\theta}_{\boldsymbol{R}}\right)' \widehat{\boldsymbol{V}}^{-1} \left(\widehat{\theta} - \widehat{\theta}_{\boldsymbol{R}}\right).$$

It is insightful to notice that J is the minimum distance statistic for the test of the hypothesis $\mathbb{H}_0 : \boldsymbol{R}'\theta = \boldsymbol{r}$ against $\mathbb{H}_1 : \boldsymbol{R}'\theta \neq \boldsymbol{r}$. Thus the degree of shrinkage is a smoothed version of the standard test of the restrictions. When J is large (so the evidence indicates that the restrictions are false), the shrinkage estimator is close to the unrestricted estimator $\widehat{\theta}$. When J is small (so the evidence indicates that the restrictions could be correct), the shrinkage estimator equals the restricted estimator $\widehat{\theta}_{\boldsymbol{R}}$. For intermediate values of J, the shrinkage estimator shrinks $\widehat{\theta}$ toward $\widehat{\theta}_{\boldsymbol{R}}$.

We can substitute for J any similar asymptotically chi-square statistic, including the Wald, likelihood ratio, and score statistics. We can also use the F statistic (which is commonly produced by statistical software) if we multiply by q. These substitutions do not produce the identical finite sample distribution but are asymptotically equivalent.

For linear regression, we have some very convenient simplifications available. In general, $\widehat{\boldsymbol{V}}$ can be a heteroskedastic-robust or cluster-robust covariance matrix estimator. However, if the dimension K of the unrestricted estimator is quite large or has sparse dummy variables, then these covariance matrix estimators are ill-behaved, and it may be better to use a classical covariance matrix estimator to perform the shrinkage. If this is done, then $\widehat{\boldsymbol{V}} = \left(\boldsymbol{X}'\boldsymbol{X}\right)^{-1} s^2$, $\widehat{\theta}_{\boldsymbol{R}}$ is the constrained least squares estimator (in most applications, the least squares estimator of the short regression), and J is a conventional (homoskedastic) Wald statistic for a test of the restrictions. We can write the latter in F statistic form:

$$J = \frac{n\left(\widehat{\sigma}_R^2 - \widehat{\sigma}^2\right)}{s^2} \tag{28.28}$$

where $\widehat{\sigma}_R^2$ and $\widehat{\sigma}^2$ are the least squares error variance estimators from the restricted and unrestricted models, respectively. The shrinkage weight $((q-2)/J)_1$ can be easily calculated from standard regression output.

28.24 GROUP JAMES-STEIN

The James-Stein estimator can be applied to groups (blocks) of parameters. Suppose we have the parameter vector $\theta = (\theta_1, \theta_2, \ldots, \theta_G)$ partitioned into G groups, each of dimension $K_g \geq 3$. We have a standard estimator $\widehat{\theta} = \left(\widehat{\theta}_1, \widehat{\theta}_2, \ldots, \widehat{\theta}_G\right)$ (for example, least squares regression or MLE) with covariance matrix $\boldsymbol{V}$. The group James-Stein estimator is

$$\widetilde{\theta} = \left(\widetilde{\theta}_1, \widetilde{\theta}_2, \ldots, \widetilde{\theta}_G\right)$$

$$\widetilde{\theta}_g = \widehat{\theta}_g \left(1 - \frac{K_g - 2}{\widehat{\theta}_g' \boldsymbol{V}_g^{-1} \widehat{\theta}_g}\right)_+$$

where $\boldsymbol{V}_g$ is the gth diagonal block of $\boldsymbol{V}$. A feasible version of the estimator replaces $\boldsymbol{V}$ with $\widehat{\boldsymbol{V}}$ and $\boldsymbol{V}_g$ with $\widehat{\boldsymbol{V}}_g$.

The group James-Stein estimator separately shrinks each block of coefficients. The advantage relative to the classical James-Stein estimator is that this allows the shrinkage weight to vary across blocks. Some parameter blocks can use a large amount of shrinkage, while others use a minimal amount. Because the positive-part trimming is used, the estimator simultaneously performs shrinkage and selection. Blocks with small effects will be shrunk to 0 and eliminated. The disadvantage of the estimator is that the benefits of shrinkage may be reduced, because the shrinkage dimension is reduced. The tradeoff between these factors will depend on how heterogeneous the optimal shrinkage weight varies across the parameters.

The groups should be selected based on two criteria. First, they should be selected so that the groups separate variables by expected amount of shrinkage. Thus coefficients that are expected to be "large" relative to their estimation variance should be grouped together, and coefficients expected to be "small" should be grouped together. This will allow the estimated shrinkage weights to vary according to the group. For example, a researcher may expect high-order coefficients in a polynomial regression to be small relative to their estimation variance. Hence it is appropriate to group the polynomial variables into "low order" and "high order." Second, the groups should be selected so that the researcher's loss (utility) is separable across groups of coefficients. This is because the optimality theory (given below) relies on the assumption that the loss is separable. To understand the implications of these recommendations, consider a wage regression. Our interpretation of the education and experience coefficients are separable if we use them for separate purposes, such as for estimation of the return to education and the return to experience. In this case, it is appropriate to separate the education and experience coefficients into different groups.

For an optimality theory, we define weighted MSE with respect to the block-diagonal weight matrix $\boldsymbol{W} = \operatorname{diag}(\boldsymbol{V}_1^{-1}, \ldots, \boldsymbol{V}_G^{-1})$.

Theorem 28.15 Under the assumptions of Theorem 28.12, if WMSE is defined with respect to $\boldsymbol{W} = \operatorname{diag}(\boldsymbol{V}_1^{-1}, \ldots, \boldsymbol{V}_G^{-1})$ and $K_g > 2$ for all $g = 1, \ldots, G$, then

$$\operatorname{wmse}\left[\widetilde{\theta}\right] < \operatorname{wmse}\left[\widehat{\theta}\right].$$

The proof is a simple extension of the classical James-Stein theory. The block diagonal structure of $\boldsymbol{W}$ means that the WMSE is the sum of the WMSE of each group. The classical James-Stein theory can be applied to each group, finding that the WMSE is reduced by shrinkage group-by-group. Thus the total WMSE is reduced by shrinkage.

28.25 EMPIRICAL ILLUSTRATIONS

I illustrate James-Stein shrinkage with three empirical applications.

The first application is to the sample used in Section 28.18, the CPS dataset with the subsample of Asian women ($n = 1{,}149$) focusing on the return to experience profile. Consider shrinkage of Model 9 (sixth-order polynomial in experience) toward Model 3 (second-order polynomial in experience). The difference in the number of estimated coefficients is 4. Set $\widehat{\boldsymbol{V}}$ to equal the HC1 covariance matrix estimator. The empirically determined shrinkage weight is 0.46, meaning that the Stein Rule estimator is approximately an equal weighted average of the estimates from the two models. The estimated experience profiles are displayed in Figure 28.4(a).

The two least squares estimates are visually distinct. The sixth order polynomial (Model 9) shows a steep return to experience for the first 10 years, then a wobbly experience profile up to 40 years, and declining above that. It also shows a dip at around 25 years. The quadratic specification misses some of these features. The James-Stein estimator is essentially an average of the two profiles. It retains most features of the quartic specification, except that it smooths out the unappealing 25-year dip.

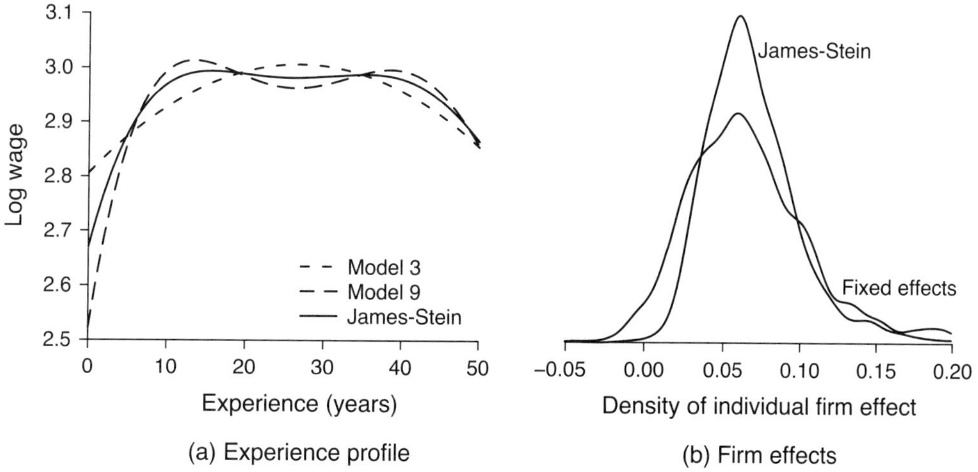

FIGURE 28.4 Shrinkage illustrations

The second application is to the `Invest1993` dataset used in Chapter 17. This is a panel dataset of annual observations on investment decisions by corporations. We focus on the firm-specific effects. These are of interest when studying firm heterogeneity and are important for firm-specific forecasting. Accurate estimation of firm effects is challenging when the number of time series observations per firm is small.

To keep the analysis focused, we restrict attention to firms that are traded on either the NYSE or AMEX and to the last 10 years of the sample (1982–1991). Because the regressors are lagged, there are at most nine time-series observations per firm. The sample has a total of $N = 786$ firms and $n = 5,692$ observations for estimation. Our baseline model is the two-way fixed effects linear regression as reported in the fourth column of Table 17.2. Our restricted model replaces the firm fixed effects with 19 industry-specific dummy variables. This is similar to the first column of Table 17.2, except that the trading dummy is omitted and time dummies are added. The Stein Rule estimator thus shrinks the fixed effects model toward the industry effects model. The latter will do well if most of the fixed effects are explained by industry rather than firm-specific variation.

Because of the large number of estimated coefficients in the unrestricted model, we use the homoskedastic weight matrix as a simplification. This allows the calculation of the shrinkage weight using the simple formula (28.28) for the statistic J. The heteroskedastic covariance matrix is not appropriate, and the cluster-robust covariance matrix will not be reliable due to the sparse dummy specification.

The empirically determined shrinkage weight is 0.35, which means that the Stein Rule estimator puts about 1/3 weight on the industry-effect specification and 2/3 weight on the firm-specific specification.

To report our results let us focus on the distribution of the firm-specific effects. For the fixed effects model, these are the estimated fixed effects. For the industry-effect model, these are the estimated industry dummy coefficients (for each firm). For the Stein Rule estimates, they are a weighted average of the two. We estimate[6] the densities of the estimated firm-specific effects from the fixed-effects and Stein Rule estimators, and plot them in Figure 28.4(b).

You can see that the fixed-effects estimate of the firm-specific density is more dispersed, while the Stein estimator is sharper and more peaked, indicating that the fixed effects estimator attributes more variation in

[6]The two densities are estimated with a common bandwidth to aid comparison. The bandwidth was selected as a compromise between those selected for the two samples.

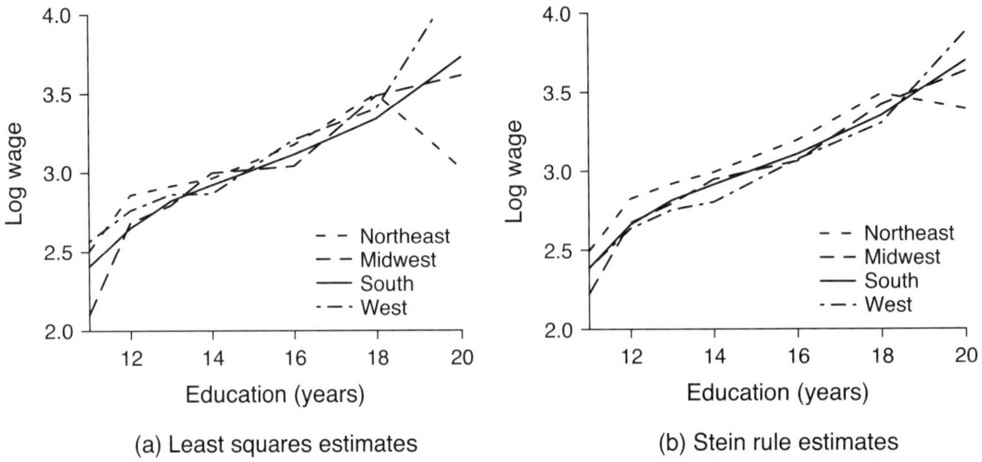

FIGURE 28.5 Stein rule estimation of education profiles across regions

firm-specific factors than the Stein estimator does. The Stein estimator pulls the fixed effects toward their common mean, adjusting for the randomness due to their estimation. Our expectation is that the Stein estimates, if used for an application such as firm-specific forecasting, will be more accurate, because they will have reduced variance relative to the fixed effects estimates.

The third application uses the CPS dataset with the subsample of Black men ($n = 2,413$) focusing on the return to education across U.S. regions (Northeast, Midwest, South, and West). Suppose you are asked to flexibly estimate the return to education for Black men, allowing the return to education to vary across the regions. Given the model selection information from Section 28.18, a natural baseline is model 6 augmented to allow for greater variation across regions. A flexible specification interacts the six education dummy variables with the four regional dummies (omitting the intercept), which adds 18 coefficients and allows the return to education to vary without restriction in each region.

The least squares estimate of the return to education by region is displayed in Figure 28.5(a). For simplicity, we combine the omitted education group (less than 12 years education) as "11 years." The estimates appear noisy due to the small samples. One feature we can see is that the four lines track one another for years of education between 12 and 18. That is, they are roughly linear in years of education with the same slope but different intercepts.

To improve the precision of the estimates, we can shrink the four profiles toward Model 6. So we are shrinking the profiles not toward each other but toward the model with the same effect of education but regional-specific intercepts. Again we use the HC1 covariance matrix estimate. The number of restrictions is 18. The empirically determined shrinkage weight is 0.49, which means that the Stein Rule estimator puts equal weight on the two models.

The Stein Rule estimates are displayed in Figure 28.5(b). The estimates are less noisy than panel (a), and it is easier to see the patterns. The four lines track each other and are approximately linear over 12–18 years. For 20 years of education, the four lines disperse, which seems likely to be due to small samples. In panel (b), it is easier to see the patterns across regions. It appears that the Northeast region has the highest wages (conditional on education), while the West region has the lowest wages. This ranking is constant for nearly all levels of education.

While the Stein Rule estimates shrink the nonparametric estimates toward the common-education-factor specification, it does not impose the latter specification. The Stein Rule estimator has the ability to put nearly 0 weight on the common-factor model. That the estimates put 1/2 weight on both models is the choice selected by the Stein Rule and is data-driven.

The message from these three applications is that the James-Stein shrinkage approach can be constructively used to reduce estimation variance in economic applications. These applications illustrate common forms of potential applications: Shrinkage of a flexible specification toward a simpler specification; shrinkage of heterogeneous estimates toward homogeneous estimates; and shrinkage of fixed effect towards group dummy estimates. These three applications also employed moderately large sample sizes ($n=1{,}149$, 2,413, and 5,692), yet we found shrinkage weights near 50%. Thus the benefits of Stein shrinkage are not confined to "small" samples but instead can be constructively used in moderately large samples with complicated structures.

28.26 MODEL AVERAGING

Recall that the problem of model selection is how to select a single model from a general set of models. The James-Stein shrinkage estimator smooths between two nested models by taking a weighted average of two estimators. More generally, we can take an average of an arbitrary number of estimators. These estimators are known as model averaging estimators. The key issue for estimation is how to select the averaging weights.

Suppose we have a set of M models $\overline{\mathscr{M}}=\{\mathscr{M}_1,\ldots,\mathscr{M}_M\}$. For each model, there is an estimator $\widehat{\theta}_m$ of the parameter θ. The natural way to think about multiple models, parameters, and estimators is the same as for model selection. All models are subsets of a general superset (overlapping) model that which contains all submodels as special cases.

Corresponding to the set of models, we introduce a set of weights $w=\{w_1,\ldots,w_M\}$. It is common to restrict the weights to be nonnegative and to sum to 1. The set of such weights is called the $\mathbb{R}^M$ probability simplex.

Definition 28.4 **The probability simplex** is the set $\mathscr{S}\subset\mathbb{R}^M$ of vectors such that $\sum_{m=1}^{M} w_m=1$ and $w_i\geq 1$ for $i=1,\ldots,M$.

The probability simplex in $\mathbb{R}^2$ and $\mathbb{R}^3$ is shown in the two panels of Figure 28.6. The simplex in $\mathbb{R}^2$ (panel (a)) is the line between the vertices $(1,0)$ and $(0,1)$. An example element is the point $(.7,.3)$ indicated by the point w. This is the weight vector that puts weight 0.7 on model 1 and weight 0.3 on model 2. The vertex (1,0) is the weight vector that puts all weight on model 1, corresponding to model selection, and similarly the vertex (0,1) is the weight vector that puts all weight on model 2.

The simplex in $\mathbb{R}^3$ (panel (b)) is the equilateral triangle formed between $(1,0,0)$, $(0,1,0)$, and $(0,0,1)$. An example element is the point $(.1,.5,.4)$ indicated by the point w. The edges are weight vectors that are averages between two of the three models. For example, the bottom edge consists of weight vectors that divide the weight between models 1 and 2, placing no weight on model 3. The vertices are weight vectors that put all weight on one of the three models and correspond to model selection.

Because the weights on the probability simplex sum to 1, an alternative representation is to eliminate one weight by substitution. Thus we can set $w_M=1-\sum_{m=1}^{M-1} w_m$, and define the set of vectors $w=\{w_1,\ldots,w_{M-1}\}$ that lie in the $\mathbb{R}^{M-1}$ unit simplex, which is the region bracketed by the probability simplex and the origin.

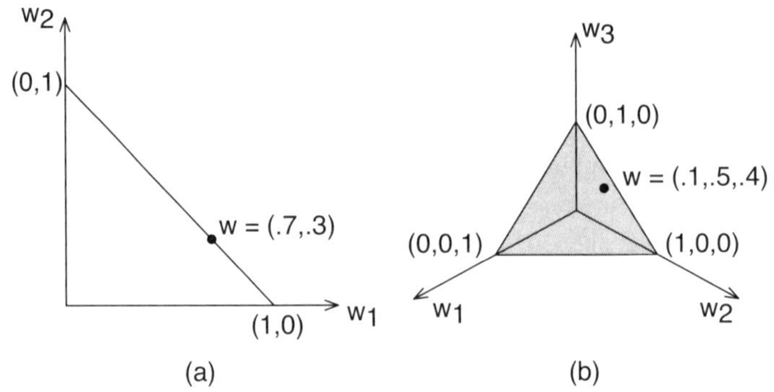

FIGURE 28.6 Probability simplex in $\mathbb{R}^2$ and $\mathbb{R}^3$

Given a weight vector, we define the **averaging estimator**:

$$\widehat{\theta}(w) = \sum_{m=1}^{M} w_m \widehat{\theta}_m. \tag{28.29}$$

Selection estimators emerge as the special case where the weight vector w is a unit vector (e.g., the vertices in Figure 28.6).

It is not absolutely necessary to restrict the weight vector of an averaging estimator to lie in the probability simplex $\mathscr{S}$, but in most cases, it is a sensible restriction that improves performance. The unadjusted James-Stein estimator, for example, is an averaging estimator that does not enforce nonnegativity of the weights. The positive-part version, however, imposes nonnegativity and achieves reduced MSE as a result.

In Section 28.19 and Theorem 28.11, we explored the MSE of a simple shrinkage estimator that shrinks an unrestricted estimator toward the zero vector. This is the same as a model averaging estimator where one of the two estimators is the zero vector. Theorem 28.11 shows that the MSE of the optimal shrinkage (model averaging) estimator is less than that of the unrestricted estimator. This result extends to the case of averaging between an arbitrary number of estimators. The MSE of the optimal averaging estimator is less than the MSE of the estimator of the full model in any given sample.

The optimal averaging weights, however, are unknown. A number of methods have been proposed for selection of the averaging weights.

One simple method is **equal weighting**, which is achieved by setting $w_m = 1/M$ and results in the estimator

$$\widehat{\theta}^* = \frac{1}{M} \sum_{m=1}^{M} \widehat{\theta}_m.$$

The advantages of equal weighting are that it is simple, easy to motivate, and no randomness is introduced by estimation of the weights. The variance of the equal weighting estimator can be calculated because the weights are fixed. Another important advantage is that the estimator can be constructed in contexts where it is unknown how to construct empirical-based weights, for example, when averaging models from completely different probability families. The disadvantages of equal weighting are that the method can be sensitive to the set of models considered, there is no guarantee that the estimator will perform better than the unrestricted estimator, and sample information is inefficiently used. In practice, equal weighting is best used in contexts where the set of models have been pre-screened, so that all are considered "reasonable" models.

From the standpoint of econometric methodology, equal weighting is not a proper statistical method, as it is an incomplete methodology.

Despite these concerns, equal weighting can be constructively employed when summarizing information for a nontechnical audience. The relevant context is when you have a small number of reasonable but distinct estimates typically made using different assumptions. The distinct estimates are presented to illustrate the range of possible results, and the average is taken to represent the "consensus" or "recommended" estimate.

As mentioned above, various methods have been proposed for selection of the averaging weights. The following sections outline four popular methods: smoothed BIC, smoothed AIC, Mallows averaging, and jackknife averaging.

28.27 SMOOTHED BIC AND AIC

Recall that Schwarz's Theorem 28.1 states that for a probability model $f(y, \theta)$ and a diffuse prior, the marginal likelihood $p(Y)$ satisfies

$$-2\log p(Y) \simeq -2\ell_n\left(\widehat{\theta}\right) + K\log(n) = \mathrm{BIC}.$$

This result has been been interpreted to mean that the model with the highest value of the right-hand side approximately has the highest marginal likelihood and is thus the model with the highest probability of being the true model.

There is another interpretation of Schwarz's result. The marginal likelihood is approximately proportional to the probability that the model is true, conditional on the data. Theorem 28.1 implies that this is approximately

$$p(Y) \simeq \exp(-\mathrm{BIC}/2)$$

which is a simple exponential transformation of the BIC. Weighting by posterior probability can be achieved by setting model weights proportional to this transformation. These are known as BIC weights and produce the smoothed BIC estimator.

To describe the method completely, suppose that we have a set of models $\overline{\mathscr{M}} = \{\mathscr{M}_1, \ldots, \mathscr{M}_M\}$. Each model $f_m(y, \theta_m)$ depends on a $K_m \times 1$ parameter vector θ_m, which is estimated by the maximum likelihood. The maximized likelihood is $L_m(\widehat{\theta}_m) = f_m(Y, \widehat{\theta}_m)$. The BIC for model m is $\mathrm{BIC}_m = -2\log L_m(\widehat{\theta}_m) + K_m\log(n)$.

The **BIC weights** are

$$w_m = \frac{\exp(-\mathrm{BIC}_m/2)}{\sum_{j=1}^{M}\exp\left(-\mathrm{BIC}_j/2\right)}.$$

Some properties of the BIC weights are as follows. They are nonnegative, so all models receive positive weight. Some models can receive weight arbitrarily close to 0 and in practice, many estimated models may receive BIC weight that is essentially 0. The model that is selected by BIC receives the greatest weight, and models that have BIC values close to the minimum receive weights closest to the largest weight. Models whose BIC is not close to the minimum receive weight near 0.

The **smoothed BIC (SBIC)** estimator is

$$\widehat{\theta}_{\mathrm{sbic}} = \sum_{m=1}^{M} w_m \widehat{\theta}_m.$$

The SBIC estimator is a smoother function of the data than BIC selection, as there are no discontinuous jumps across models.

An advantage of the smoothed BIC weights and estimator is that they can be used to combine models from different probability families. As for the BIC, it is important that all models are estimated on the same sample. It is also important that the full formula is used for the BIC (no omission of constants) when combining models from different probability families.

Computationally, it is better to implement smoothed BIC with what are called "BIC differences" rather than the actual values of the BIC, because the formula as written can produce numerical overflow problems. The difficulty is due to the exponentiation in the formula. This problem can be eliminated as follows. Let

$$\mathrm{BIC}^* = \min_{1\leq m\leq M} \mathrm{BIC}_m$$

denote the lowest BIC among the models, and define the BIC differences

$$\Delta\mathrm{BIC}_m = \mathrm{BIC}_m - \mathrm{BIC}^*.$$

Then

$$\begin{aligned} w_m &= \frac{\exp\left(-\mathrm{BIC}_m/2\right)}{\sum_{j=1}^M \exp\left(-\mathrm{BIC}_j/2\right)} \\ &= \frac{\exp\left(-\mathrm{BIC}_m/2\right)\exp\left(\mathrm{BIC}^*/2\right)}{\sum_{j=1}^M \exp\left(-\mathrm{BIC}_j/2\right)\exp\left(\mathrm{BIC}^*/2\right)} \\ &= \frac{\exp\left(-\Delta\mathrm{BIC}_m/2\right)}{\sum_{j=1}^M \exp\left(-\Delta\mathrm{BIC}_j/2\right)}. \end{aligned}$$

Thus the weights are algebraically identical whether computed on BIC_m or $\Delta\mathrm{BIC}_m$. Because the $\Delta\mathrm{BIC}_m$ are of smaller magnitude than BIC_m, overflow problems are less likely to occur.

Because of the properties of the exponential, if $\Delta\mathrm{BIC}_m \geq 10$, then $w_m \leq 0.01$. Thus smoothed BIC typically concentrates weight on models whose BIC values are close to the minimum. So in practice, smoothed BIC puts effective nonzero weight on a small number of models.

Burnham and Anderson (1998) follow a suggestion they credit to Akaike that if we make the same transformation to the AIC as to the BIC to obtain the smoothed BIC weights, we obtain frequentist approximate probabilities for the models. Specifically, they propose the **AIC weights**

$$w_m = \frac{\exp\left(-\mathrm{AIC}_m/2\right)}{\sum_{j=1}^M \exp\left(-\mathrm{AIC}_j/2\right)}.$$

They do not provide a strong theoretical justification for this specific choice of transformation, but it seems natural, given the smoothed BIC formula, and it works well in simulations.

The algebraic properties of the AIC weights are similar to those of the BIC weights. All models receive positive weight, though some receive weights that are arbitrarily close to 0. The model with the smallest AIC receives the greatest AIC weight, and models with similar AIC values receive similar AIC weights.

The AIC weights should be computed using AIC differences. Define

$$\mathrm{AIC}^* = \min_{1\leq m\leq M} \mathrm{AIC}_m$$

$$\Delta\mathrm{AIC}_m = \mathrm{AIC}_m - \mathrm{AIC}^*.$$

Algebraically, the AIC weights equal

$$w_m = \frac{\exp\left(-\Delta \mathrm{AIC}_m \mathrm{AIC}_m/2\right)}{\sum_{j=1}^{M} \exp\left(-\Delta \mathrm{AIC}_j/2\right)}.$$

As for the BIC weights, $w_m \leq 0.01$ if $\Delta \mathrm{AIC}_m \geq 10$, so the AIC weights will be concentrated on models whose AIC values are close to the minimum. However, in practice, it commonly happens that the AIC criterion is less concentrated than the BIC criterion, because the AIC puts a smaller penalty on large parameterizations. The AIC weights tend to be more spread out across models than the corresponding BIC weights.

The **Smoothed AIC (SAIC)** estimator is

$$\widehat{\theta}_{\mathrm{saic}} = \sum_{m=1}^{M} w_m \widehat{\theta}_m.$$

The SAIC estimator is a smoother function of the data than is AIC selection.

Recall that both AIC selection and BIC selection are model selections that are consistent in the sense that as the sample size gets large, the probability that the selected model is a true model becomes arbtrarily close to 1 Furthermore, BIC is consistent for parsimonious models, and AIC asymptotically over-selects.

These properties extend to SBIC and SAIC. In large samples, SAIC and SBIC weights will concentrate exclusively on true models; the weight on incorrect models will asymptotically approach 0. However, SAIC will asymptotically spread weight across both parsimonious true models and overparameterized true models, while SBIC asymptotically concentrates weight only on parsimonious true models.

An interesting property of the smoothed estimators is the possibility of asymptotically spreading weight across equal-fitting parsimonious models. Suppose we have two non-nested models with the same number of parameters and the same KLIC value, so they are equal approximations. In large samples, both SBIC and SAIC will be weighted averages of the two estimators rather than simply selecting one of the two.

28.28 MALLOWS MODEL AVERAGING

In linear regression, the Mallows criterion (28.14) applies directly to the model averaging estimator (28.29). The homoskedastic regression model is

$$\begin{aligned} Y &= m + e \\ m &= m(X) \\ \mathbb{E}\left[e \mid X\right] &= 0 \\ \mathbb{E}\left[e^2 \mid X\right] &= \sigma^2. \end{aligned}$$

Suppose that there are M models for $m(X)$, each of which takes the form $\beta_m' X_m$ for some $K_m \times 1$ regression vector X_m. The mth model estimator of the coefficient is $\widehat{\beta}_m = \left(\boldsymbol{X}_m' \boldsymbol{X}_m\right)^{-1} \boldsymbol{X}_m' \boldsymbol{Y}$, and the estimator of the vector $\boldsymbol{m}$ is $\widehat{\boldsymbol{m}}_m = \boldsymbol{P}_m \boldsymbol{Y}$, where $\boldsymbol{P}_m = \boldsymbol{X}_m \left(\boldsymbol{X}_m' \boldsymbol{X}_m\right)^{-1} \boldsymbol{X}_m'$. The corresponding residual vector is $\widehat{\boldsymbol{e}}_m = \left(\boldsymbol{I}_n - \boldsymbol{P}_m\right) \boldsymbol{Y}$.

The model averaging estimator for fixed weights is

$$\widehat{\boldsymbol{m}}_m(w) = \sum_{m=1}^{M} w_m \boldsymbol{P}_m \boldsymbol{Y} = \boldsymbol{P}(w) \boldsymbol{Y}$$

where

$$P(w) = \sum_{m=1}^{M} w_m P_m.$$

The model averaging residual is

$$\widehat{e}(w) = (I_n - P(w))\, Y = \sum_{m=1}^{M} w_m (I_n - P_m)\, Y.$$

The estimator $\widehat{m}_m(w)$ is linear in Y, so the Mallows criterion can be applied. It equals

$$\begin{aligned} C(w) &= \widehat{e}(w)'\widehat{e}(w) + 2\widetilde{\sigma}^2 \operatorname{tr}(P(w)) \\ &= \widehat{e}(w)'\widehat{e}(w) + 2\widetilde{\sigma}^2 \sum_{m=1}^{M} w_m K_m \end{aligned}$$

where $\widetilde{\sigma}^2$ is a preliminary[7] estimator of σ^2.

In the case of model selection, the Mallows penalty is proportional to the number of estimated coefficients. In the model averaging case, the Mallows penalty is the average number of estimated coefficients.

The Mallows-selected weight vector minimizes the Mallows criterion. It equals

$$\widehat{w}_{\text{mma}} = \underset{w \in \mathscr{S}}{\operatorname{argmin}}\, C(w). \tag{28.30}$$

Computationally, it is useful to observe that $C(w)$ is a quadratric function in w. Indeed, defining the $n \times M$ matrix $\widehat{E} = [\widehat{e}_1, \dots, \widehat{e}_M]$ of residual vectors and the $M \times 1$ vector $K = [K_1, \dots, K_M]$, the criterion is

$$C(w) = w'\widehat{E}'\widehat{E}w + 2\widetilde{\sigma}^2 K'w.$$

The probability simplex $\mathscr{S}$ is defined by one equality and $2M$ inequality constraints. The minimization problem (28.30) falls in the category of **quadratic programming**, which means optimization of a quadratic subject to linear equality and inequality constraints. This is a well-studied area of numerical optimization, and numerical solutions are widely available. In R, use the command `solve.QP` in the package `quadprog`. In MATLAB, use the command `quadprog`.

Figure 28.7 illustrates the Mallows weight computation problem. Displayed is the probability simplex $\mathscr{S}$ in $\mathbb{R}^3$. The axes are the weight vectors. The ellipses are the contours of the unconstrained sum of squared errors as a function of the weight vectors projected onto the constrained set $\sum_{m=1}^{M} w_m = 1$. This is the extension of the probability simplex as a two-dimensional plane in $\mathbb{R}^3$. The midpoint of the contours is the minimizing weight vector allowing for weights outside [0, 1]. The point where the lowest contour ellipse intersects the probability simplex is the solution (28.30), the Mallows selected weight vector. The left panel displays an example where the solution is the vertex $(0, 1, 0)$, so the selected weight vector puts all weight on model 2. The right panel displays an example where the solution lies on the edge between $(1, 0, 0)$ and $(0, 0, 1)$, meaning that the selected weight vector averages models 1 and 3 but puts no weight on model 2. Because the contour sets are ellipses and the constraint set is a simplex, solution points tend to be on edges and vertices, meaning that some models receive 0 weight. In fact, where there are a large number of models, a generic feature of the solution is that most models receive 0 weight; the selected weight vector puts positive weight on a small subset of the eligible models.

[7] It is typical to use the bias-corrected least squares variance estimator from the largest model.

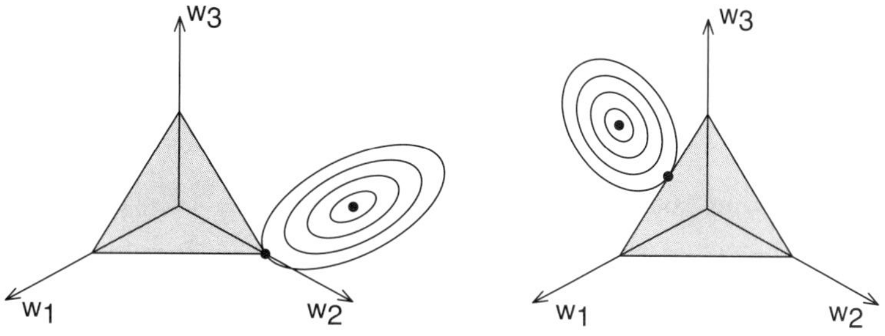

FIGURE 28.7 Mallows weight selection

Once the weights $\widehat{w}$ are obtained, the model averaging estimator of the coefficients is found by averaging the model estimates $\widehat{\beta}_m$ using the weights.

In the special case of two nested models, the Mallows criterion can be written as

$$
\begin{aligned}
C(w) &= (w, 1-w)\begin{pmatrix} \widehat{e}_1'\widehat{e}_1 & \widehat{e}_1'\widehat{e}_2 \\ \widehat{e}_2'\widehat{e}_1 & \widehat{e}_2'\widehat{e}_2 \end{pmatrix}\begin{pmatrix} w \\ 1-w \end{pmatrix} + 2\widetilde{\sigma}^2 (wK_1 + (1-w)K_2) \\
&= (w, 1-w)\begin{pmatrix} \widehat{e}_1'\widehat{e}_1 & \widehat{e}_2'\widehat{e}_2 \\ \widehat{e}_2'\widehat{e}_2 & \widehat{e}_2'\widehat{e}_2 \end{pmatrix}\begin{pmatrix} 1-w \\ w \end{pmatrix} + 2\widetilde{\sigma}^2 (wK_1 + (1-w)K_2) \\
&= w^2\left(\widehat{e}_1'\widehat{e}_1 - \widehat{e}_2'\widehat{e}_2\right) + \widehat{e}_2'\widehat{e}_2 - 2\widetilde{\sigma}^2 (K_2 - K_1)\, w + 2\widetilde{\sigma}^2
\end{aligned}
$$

where we assume $K_1 < K_2$, so that $\widehat{e}_1'\widehat{e}_2 = Y'(I_n - P_1)(I_n - P_2)Y = Y'(I_n - P_2)Y = \widehat{e}_2'\widehat{e}_2$. The minimizer of this criterion is

$$
\widehat{w} = \left(\frac{\widetilde{\sigma}^2 (K_2 - K_1)}{\widehat{e}_1'\widehat{e}_1 - \widehat{e}_2'\widehat{e}_2}\right)_1 .
$$

This is the same as the Stein Rule weight (28.27) with a slightly different shrinkage constant. Thus the Mallows averaging estimator for $M = 2$ is a Stein Rule estimator. Hence for $M > 2$, the Mallows averaging estimator is a generalization of the James-Stein estimator to multiple models.

Based on the latter observation, B. Hansen (2014) shows that the MMA estimator has lower WMSE than the unrestricted least squares estimator when the models are nested linear regressions, the errors are homoskedastic, and the models are separated by 4 coefficients or greater. The latter condition is analogous to the conditions for improvements in the Stein Rule theory.

B. Hansen (2007) showed that the MMA estimator asymptotically achieves the same MSE as the infeasible optimal best weighted average using the theory of Li (1987) under similar conditions. Thus, using model selection tools to select the averaging weights is asymptotically optimal for regression fitting and point forecasting.

28.29 JACKKNIFE (CV) MODEL AVERAGING

A disadvantage of Mallows selection is that the criterion is valid only when the errors are conditionally homoskedastic. In contrast, selection by CV does not require homoskedasticity. Therefore it seems sensible to use CV rather than Mallows to select the weight vectors. It turns out that this is a simple extension with excellent finite sample performance. In the machine learning literature, this method is called **stacking**.

A fitted averaging regression (with fixed weights) can be written as

$$Y_i = \sum_{m=1}^{M} w_m X'_{mi} \widehat{\beta}_m + \widehat{e}_i(w)$$

where $\widehat{\beta}_m$ are the least squares coefficient estimates from model m. The corresponding leave-one-out equation is

$$Y_i = \sum_{m=1}^{M} w_m X'_{mi} \widehat{\beta}_{m,(-i)} + \widetilde{e}_i(w)$$

where the $\widehat{\beta}_{m,(-i)}$ are the least squares coefficient estimates from model m when observation i is deleted. The leave-one-out prediction errors satisfy the simple relationship

$$\widetilde{e}_i(w) = \sum_{m=1}^{M} w_m \widetilde{e}_{mi}$$

where the $\widetilde{e}_{mi}$ are the leave-one-out prediction errors for model m. In matrix notation, $\widetilde{\boldsymbol{e}}(w) = \widetilde{\boldsymbol{E}} w$, where $\widetilde{\boldsymbol{E}}$ is the $n \times M$ matrix of leave-one-out prediction errors.

As a result, the jackknife estimate of variance (or equivalently, the CV criterion) equals

$$\mathrm{CV}(w) = w' \widetilde{\boldsymbol{E}}' \widetilde{\boldsymbol{E}} w$$

which is a quadratic function of the weight vector. The CV choice for the weight vector is the minimizer

$$\widehat{w}_{\mathrm{jma}} = \underset{w \in \mathscr{S}}{\operatorname{argmin}} \, \mathrm{CV}(w). \tag{28.31}$$

Given the weights, the coefficient estimates (and any other parameters of interest) are found by taking weighted averages of the model estimates using the weight vector $\widehat{w}_{\mathrm{jma}}$. B. Hansen and Racine (2012) call this the **jackknife model averaging (JMA)** estimator.

The algebraic properties of the solution are similar to Mallows. Because (28.31) minimizes a quadratic function subject to a simplex constraint, solutions tend to be on edges and vertices, which means that many (or most) models receive 0 weight. Hence JMA weight selection simultaneously performs selection and shrinkage. The solution is found numerically by quadratic programming, which is computationally simple and fast even when the number of models M is large.

B. Hansen and Racine (2012) showed that the JMA estimator is asymptotically equivalent to the infeasible optimal weighted average across least squares estimates based on a regression fit criteria. Their results hold under quite mild conditions, including conditional heteroskedasticity. This result is similar to the Andrews (1991c) generalization of the Li (1987) result for model selection.

The implication of this theory is that JMA weight selection is computationally simple and has excellent sampling performance.

28.30 GRANGER-RAMANATHAN AVERAGING

A method similar to JMA based on hold-out samples was proposed for forecast combination by Granger and Ramanathan (1984) and has emerged as a popular method in the modern machine learning literature.

Table 28.2
Model averaging weights and estimates of return to experience among Asian women

	Model 1	Model 2	Model 3	Model 4	Model 5	Model 6	Model 7	Model 8	Model 9	Return
SBIC	.02	.96	.00	.00	.04	.00	.00	.00	.00	22%
SAIC	.00	.02	.10	.00	.15	.44	.00	.06	.22	38%
MMA	.09	.02	.02	.00	.30	.00	.00	.00	.57	39%
JMA	.17	.00	.08	.00	.57	.01	.00	.00	.17	34%

Randomly split the sample into two parts: an estimation an an evaluation sample. Using the estimation sample, estimate the M regression models, obtaining the coefficients $\widehat{\beta}_m$. Using these coefficients and the evaluation sample, construct the fitted values $\widetilde{Y}_{mi} = X'_{mi}\widehat{\beta}_m$ for the M models. Then estimate the model weights by a least squares regression of Y_i on $\widetilde{Y}_{mi}$ and no intercept, using the evaluation sample. This regression is

$$Y_i = \sum_{m=1}^{M} \widehat{w}_m \widetilde{Y}_{mi} + \widehat{e}_i.$$

The least squares coefficients $\widehat{w}_m$ are the **Granger-Ramanathan weights.**

Based on an informal argument, Granger and Ramanathan (1984) recommended an unconstrained least squares regression to obtain the weights. But this approach is not advised, as it produces extremely erratic empirical weights, especially when M is large. Instead, it is recommended to use constrained regression, imposing the constraints $\widehat{w}_m \geq 0$ and $\sum_{m=1}^{M} \widehat{w}_m = 1$. To impose the nonnegativity constraints, it is best to use quadratic programming.

This Granger-Ramanathan approach is best suited for applications with a very large sample size, where the efficiency loss from the hold-out sample split is not a concern.

28.31 EMPIRICAL ILLUSTRATION

I illustrate the model averaging methods with the empirical application from Section 28.18, which reported wage regression estimates for the CPS subsample of Asian women, focusing on the return to experience between 0 and 30 years.

Table 28.2 reports the model averaging weights obtained using the methods of SBIC, SAIC, Mallows model averaging (MMA), and jackknife model averaging (JMA). Also reported in the final column is the weighted average estimate of the return to experience as a percentage.

The results show that the methods put weight on somewhat different models. The SBIC puts nearly all weight on model 2. The SAIC puts nearly 1/2 of the weight on model 6, with most of the remainder split between models 5 and 9. MMA puts nearly 1/2 of the weight on model 9, 30% on 5, and 9% on model 1. JMA is similar to MMA but places more emphasis on parsimony, with 1/2 of the weight on model 5, 17% on model 9, 17% on model 1, and 8% on model 3. One of the interesting things about the MMA/JMA methods is that they can split weight between quite different models (e.g., models 1 and 9).

The averaging estimators from the non-BIC methods are similar to one another, but SBIC produces a much smaller estimate than the other methods.

28.32 TECHNICAL PROOFS*

Proof of Theorem 28.1 We establish the theorem under the simplifying assumptions of the normal linear regression model with a $K \times 1$ coefficient vector β and known variance σ^2. The likelihood function is

$$L_n(\beta) = \left(2\pi\sigma^2\right)^{-n/2} \exp\left(-\frac{1}{2\sigma^2}\sum_{i=1}^{n}\left(Y_i - X_i'\beta\right)^2\right).$$

Evaluated at the MLE $\widehat{\beta}$, this equals

$$L_n(\widehat{\beta}) = \left(2\pi\sigma^2\right)^{-n/2} \exp\left(-\frac{\sum_{i=1}^{n}\widehat{e}_i^2}{2\sigma^2}\right). \tag{28.32}$$

Using (8.21), we can write

$$\begin{aligned} L_n(\beta) &= \left(2\pi\sigma^2\right)^{-n/2} \exp\left(-\frac{1}{2\sigma^2}\left(\sum_{i=1}^{n}\widehat{e}_i^2 + \left(\widehat{\beta}-\beta\right)' \boldsymbol{X}'\boldsymbol{X}\left(\widehat{\beta}-\beta\right)\right)\right) \\ &= L_n(\widehat{\beta}) \exp\left(-\frac{1}{2\sigma^2}\left(\widehat{\beta}-\beta\right)' \boldsymbol{X}'\boldsymbol{X}\left(\widehat{\beta}-\beta\right)\right). \end{aligned}$$

For a diffuse prior $\pi(\beta) = C$, the marginal likelihood is

$$\begin{aligned} p(Y) &= L_n(\widehat{\beta}) \int \exp\left(-\frac{1}{2\sigma^2}\left(\widehat{\beta}-\beta\right)' \boldsymbol{X}'\boldsymbol{X}\left(\widehat{\beta}-\beta\right)\right) C d\beta \\ &= L_n(\widehat{\beta}) n^{-K/2} \left(2\pi\sigma^2\right)^{K/2} \det\left(\frac{1}{n}\boldsymbol{X}'\boldsymbol{X}\right)^{-1/2} C \end{aligned}$$

where the final equality is the multivariate normal integral. Rewriting and taking logs, we have

$$\begin{aligned} -2\log p(Y) &= -2\log L_n(\widehat{\beta}) + K\log n - K\log\left(2\pi\sigma^2\right) + \log\det\left(\frac{1}{n}\boldsymbol{X}'\boldsymbol{X}\right) + \log C \\ &= -2\ell_n(\widehat{\beta}) + K\log n + O(1). \end{aligned}$$

This is the theorem. ■

Proof of Theorem 28.2 From (28.11), we have

$$\begin{aligned} \int g(y)\log f(y,\widehat{\theta})dy &= -\frac{n}{2}\log\left(2\pi\sigma^2\right) - \frac{1}{2\sigma^2}\sum_{i=1}^{n}\int\left(y - X_i'\widehat{\beta}\right)^2 g\left(y \mid X_i\right)dy \\ &= -\frac{n}{2}\log\left(2\pi\sigma^2\right) - \frac{1}{2\sigma^2}\sum_{i=1}^{n}\left(\sigma^2 + \left(\widehat{\beta}-\beta\right)' X_iX_i'\left(\widehat{\beta}-\beta\right)\right) \\ &= -\frac{n}{2}\log\left(2\pi\sigma^2\right) - \frac{n}{2} - \frac{1}{2\sigma^2}\boldsymbol{e}'\boldsymbol{P}\boldsymbol{e}. \end{aligned}$$

Thus,

$$T = -2\mathbb{E}\left[\int g(y)\log\widehat{f}(y)dy\right] = n\log\left(2\pi\sigma^2\right) + n + \frac{1}{\sigma^2}\mathbb{E}\left[\boldsymbol{e}'\boldsymbol{P}\boldsymbol{e}\right] = n\log\left(2\pi\sigma^2\right) + n + K.$$

This is (28.12). The final equality holds under the assumption of conditional homoskedasticity.

Evaluating (28.11) at $\widehat{\beta}$, we obtain the log likelihood

$$-2\ell_n(\widehat{\beta}) = n\log\left(2\pi\sigma^2\right) + \frac{1}{\sigma^2}\sum_{i=1}^{n}\widehat{e}_i^2 = n\log\left(2\pi\sigma^2\right) + \frac{1}{\sigma^2}\boldsymbol{e}'\boldsymbol{M}\boldsymbol{e}$$

which has expectation

$$-\mathbb{E}\left[2\ell_n(\widehat{\beta})\right] = n\log\left(2\pi\sigma^2\right) + \frac{1}{\sigma^2}\mathbb{E}\left[\boldsymbol{e}'\boldsymbol{M}\boldsymbol{e}\right] = n\log\left(2\pi\sigma^2\right) + n - K.$$

This is (28.13). The final equality holds under conditional homoskedasticity. ■

Proof of Theorem 28.4 The proof uses Taylor expansions similar to those used for the asymptotic distribution theory of the MLE in nonlinear models. We avoid technical details, so this is not a full proof.

Write the model density as $f(y,\theta)$ and the estimated model as $\widehat{f}(y) = f(y,\widehat{\theta})$. Recall from (28.10) that we can write the target T as

$$T = -2\mathbb{E}\left[\log f(\widetilde{Y},\widehat{\theta})\right]$$

where $\widetilde{Y}$ is an independent copy of Y. Let $\widetilde{\theta}$ be the MLE calculated on the sample $\widetilde{Y}$. $\widetilde{\theta}$ is an independent copy of $\widehat{\theta}$. By symmetry, we can write T as

$$T = -2\mathbb{E}\left[\log f(Y,\widetilde{\theta})\right]. \tag{28.33}$$

Define the Hessian $H = -\frac{\partial}{\partial\theta\partial\theta'}\mathbb{E}\left[\log f(Y,\theta)\right] > 0$. Now take a second-order Taylor series expansion of the log likelihood $\log f(Y,\widetilde{\theta})$ about $\widehat{\theta}$:

$$\begin{aligned}\log f(Y,\widetilde{\theta}) &= \log f(Y,\widehat{\theta}) + \frac{\partial}{\partial\theta'}\log f(Y,\widehat{\theta})\left(\widetilde{\theta}-\widehat{\theta}\right) - \frac{1}{2}\left(\widetilde{\theta}-\widehat{\theta}\right)'H\left(\widetilde{\theta}-\widehat{\theta}\right) + O_p\left(n^{-1/2}\right)\\ &= \log f(Y,\widehat{\theta}) - \frac{n}{2}\left(\widetilde{\theta}-\widehat{\theta}\right)'H\left(\widetilde{\theta}-\widehat{\theta}\right) + O_p\left(n^{-1/2}\right).\end{aligned} \tag{28.34}$$

The second equality holds because of the first-order condition for the MLE $\widehat{\theta}$.

If the $O_p(n^{-1/2})$ term in (28.34) is uniformly integrable, (28.33) and (28.34) imply that

$$\begin{aligned}T &= -\mathbb{E}\left[2\log f(Y,\widehat{\theta})\right] + \mathbb{E}\left[n\left(\widetilde{\theta}-\widehat{\theta}\right)'H\left(\widetilde{\theta}-\widehat{\theta}\right)\right] + O\left(n^{-1/2}\right)\\ &= -\mathbb{E}\left[2\log L(\widehat{\theta})\right] + \mathbb{E}\left[n\left(\widetilde{\theta}-\theta\right)'H\left(\widetilde{\theta}-\theta\right)\right] + \mathbb{E}\left[n\left(\widehat{\theta}-\theta\right)'H\left(\widehat{\theta}-\theta\right)\right]\\ &\quad + 2\mathbb{E}\left[n\left(\widetilde{\theta}-\theta\right)'H\left(\widehat{\theta}-\theta\right)\right] + O\left(n^{-1/2}\right)\\ &= -\mathbb{E}\left[2\ell_n(\widehat{\theta})\right] + \mathbb{E}\left[\chi_K^2\right] + \mathbb{E}\left[\widetilde{\chi}_K^2\right] + O\left(n^{-1/2}\right)\\ &= -\mathbb{E}\left[2\ell_n(\widehat{\theta})\right] + 2K + O\left(n^{-1/2}\right)\end{aligned}$$

where χ_K^2 and $\widetilde{\chi}_K^2$ are chi-square random variables with K degrees of freedom. The second-to-last equality holds if

$$n\left(\widehat{\theta}-\theta\right)'H\left(\widehat{\theta}-\theta\right) \underset{d}{\longrightarrow} \chi_K^2 \tag{28.35}$$

and the Wald statistic on the left side of (28.35) is uniformly integrable. The asymptotic convergence (28.35) holds for the MLE under standard regularity conditions (including correct specification). ■

Proof of Theorem 28.5 Using matrix notation, we can write $\widehat{\boldsymbol{m}} - \boldsymbol{m} = -(\boldsymbol{I}_n - \boldsymbol{A})\boldsymbol{m} + \boldsymbol{A}\boldsymbol{e}$. We can then write the fit as

$$\begin{aligned}
R &= \mathbb{E}\left[(\widehat{\boldsymbol{m}} - \boldsymbol{m})'(\widehat{\boldsymbol{m}} - \boldsymbol{m}) \mid \boldsymbol{X}\right] \\
&= \mathbb{E}\left[\boldsymbol{m}'\left(\boldsymbol{I}_n - \boldsymbol{A}'\right)(\boldsymbol{I}_n - \boldsymbol{A})\boldsymbol{m} - 2\boldsymbol{m}'\left(\boldsymbol{I}_n - \boldsymbol{A}'\right)\boldsymbol{A}\boldsymbol{e} + \boldsymbol{e}'\boldsymbol{A}'\boldsymbol{A}\boldsymbol{e} \mid \boldsymbol{X}\right] \\
&= \boldsymbol{m}'\left(\boldsymbol{I}_n - \boldsymbol{A}'\right)(\boldsymbol{I}_n - \boldsymbol{A})\boldsymbol{m} + \sigma^2 \operatorname{tr}\left(\boldsymbol{A}'\boldsymbol{A}\right).
\end{aligned}$$

Notice that this calculation relies on the assumption of conditional homoskedasticity.

Now consider the Mallows criterion. We find that

$$\begin{aligned}
C_p^* &= \widetilde{\boldsymbol{e}}'\widetilde{\boldsymbol{e}} + 2\widetilde{\sigma}^2 \operatorname{tr}(\boldsymbol{A}) - \boldsymbol{e}'\boldsymbol{e} \\
&= (\boldsymbol{m} + \boldsymbol{e})'\left(\boldsymbol{I}_n - \boldsymbol{A}'\right)(\boldsymbol{I}_n - \boldsymbol{A})(\boldsymbol{m} + \boldsymbol{e}) + 2\widetilde{\sigma}^2 \operatorname{tr}(\boldsymbol{A}) - \boldsymbol{e}'\boldsymbol{e} \\
&= \boldsymbol{m}'\left(\boldsymbol{I}_n - \boldsymbol{A}'\right)(\boldsymbol{I}_n - \boldsymbol{A})\boldsymbol{m} + 2\boldsymbol{m}'\left(\boldsymbol{I}_n - \boldsymbol{A}'\right)(\boldsymbol{I}_n - \boldsymbol{A})\boldsymbol{e} + \boldsymbol{e}'\boldsymbol{A}'\boldsymbol{A}\boldsymbol{e} - 2\boldsymbol{e}'\boldsymbol{A}\boldsymbol{e} + 2\widetilde{\sigma}^2 \operatorname{tr}(\boldsymbol{A}).
\end{aligned}$$

Taking expectations and using the assumptions of conditional homoskedasticity and $\mathbb{E}\left[\widetilde{\sigma}^2 \mid \boldsymbol{X}\right] = \sigma^2$, we have

$$\mathbb{E}\left[C_p^* \mid \boldsymbol{X}\right] = \boldsymbol{m}'\left(\boldsymbol{I}_n - \boldsymbol{A}'\right)(\boldsymbol{I}_n - \boldsymbol{A})\boldsymbol{m} + \sigma^2 \operatorname{tr}\left(\boldsymbol{A}'\boldsymbol{A}\right) = R.$$

This is the result as stated. ■

Proof of Theorem 28.6 Take any two models $\mathscr{M}_1$ and $\mathscr{M}_2$, where $\mathscr{M}_1 \notin \overline{\mathscr{M}}^*$ and $\mathscr{M}_2 \in \overline{\mathscr{M}}^*$. Let their information criteria be written as

$$\begin{aligned}
\mathrm{IC}_1 &= -2\ell_1(\widehat{\theta}_1) + c(n, K_1) \\
\mathrm{IC}_2 &= -2\ell_2(\widehat{\theta}_2) + c(n, K_2).
\end{aligned}$$

Model $\mathscr{M}_1$ is selected over $\mathscr{M}_2$ if

$$\mathrm{LR} < c(n, K_2) - c(n, K_1)$$

where $\mathrm{LR} = 2\left(\ell_2(\widehat{\theta}_2) - \ell(\widehat{\theta}_1)\right)$ is the likelihood ratio statistic for testing $\mathscr{M}_1$ against $\mathscr{M}_2$. Since we have assumed that $\mathscr{M}_1$ is not a true model, while $\mathscr{M}_2$ is true, then LR diverges to $+\infty$ at rate n. Thus for any $\alpha > 0$, $n^{-1+\alpha}\mathrm{LR} \underset{p}{\longrightarrow} +\infty$. Furthermore, the assumptions imply $n^{-1+\alpha}\left(c(n, K_1) - c(n, K_2)\right) \longrightarrow 0$. Fix $\epsilon > 0$. There is an n sufficiently large such that $n^{-1+\alpha}\left(c(n, K_1) - c(n, K_2)\right) < \epsilon$. Thus,

$$\begin{aligned}
\mathbb{P}\left[\widehat{\mathscr{M}} = \mathscr{M}_1\right] &\le \mathbb{P}\left[n^{-1+\alpha}\mathrm{LR} < n^{-1+\alpha}\left(c(n, K_2) - c(n, K_1)\right)\right] \\
&\le \mathbb{P}\left[\mathrm{LR} < \epsilon\right] \to 0.
\end{aligned}$$

Since this holds for any $\mathscr{M}_1 \notin \overline{\mathscr{M}}^*$, we deduce that the selected model is in $\overline{\mathscr{M}}^*$ with probability approaching 1. Thus the selection criterion is model selection consistent, as claimed. ■

Proof of Theorem 28.7 Take the setting as described in the proof of Theorem 28.6, but now assume $\mathscr{M}_1 \subset \mathscr{M}_2$, and $\mathscr{M}_1, \mathscr{M}_2 \in \overline{\mathscr{M}}^*$. The likelihood ratio statistic satisfies $\mathrm{LR} \underset{d}{\longrightarrow} \chi_r^2$, where $r = K_2 - K_1$. Let

$$B = \limsup_{n \to \infty} \left(c(n, K_1) - c(n, K_2)\right) < \infty.$$

Letting $F_r(u)$ denote the χ_r^2 distribution function, we have

$$\begin{aligned}\mathbb{P}\left[\widehat{\mathscr{M}}=\mathscr{M}_2\right] &= \mathbb{P}\left[\mathrm{LR} > (c(n,K_2)-c(n,K_1))\right] \\ &\geq \mathbb{P}\left[\mathrm{LR} > B\right] \\ &\to \mathbb{P}\left[\chi_r^2 > B\right] = 1-F_r(B) > 0\end{aligned}$$

because χ_r^2 has support over the positive real line and $B<\infty$. Thus the selection criterion asymptotically over-selects with positive probability. ■

Proof of Theorem 28.8 Since $c(n,K)=o(n)$, the procedure is model selection consistent. Take two models $\mathscr{M}_1, \mathscr{M}_2 \in \overline{\mathscr{M}}^*$ with $K_1<K_2$. Because both models are true, then $\mathrm{LR}=O_p(1)$. Fix $\epsilon>0$. There is a $B<\infty$ such that $\mathrm{LR}\leq B$ with probability exceeding $1-\epsilon$. By (28.16), there is an n sufficiently large such that $c(n,K_2)-c(n,K_1)>B$. Thus,

$$\mathbb{P}\left[\widehat{\mathscr{M}}=\mathscr{M}_2\right] \leq \mathbb{P}\left[\mathrm{LR} > (c(n,K_2)-c(n,K_1))\right] \leq \mathbb{P}\left[\mathrm{LR}>B\right] \leq \epsilon.$$

Since ϵ is arbitrary, $\mathbb{P}\left[\widehat{\mathscr{M}}=\mathscr{M}_2\right] \longrightarrow 0$, as claimed. ■

Proof of Theorem 28.9 First, we examine $R_n(K)$. Write the predicted values in matrix notation as $\widehat{\boldsymbol{m}}_K = \boldsymbol{X}_K\widehat{\beta}_K = \boldsymbol{P}_K\boldsymbol{Y}$, where $\boldsymbol{P}_K = \boldsymbol{X}_K\left(\boldsymbol{X}_K'\boldsymbol{X}_K\right)^{-1}\boldsymbol{X}_K'$. It is useful to observe that $\boldsymbol{m}-\widehat{\boldsymbol{m}}_K = \boldsymbol{M}_K\boldsymbol{m}-\boldsymbol{P}_K\boldsymbol{e}$, where $\boldsymbol{M}_K = \boldsymbol{I}_K - \boldsymbol{P}_K$. We find that the prediction risk equals

$$\begin{aligned}R_n(K) &= \mathbb{E}\left[(\boldsymbol{m}-\widehat{\boldsymbol{m}}_K)'(\boldsymbol{m}-\widehat{\boldsymbol{m}}_K)\mid \boldsymbol{X}\right] \\ &= \mathbb{E}\left[(\boldsymbol{M}_K\boldsymbol{m}-\boldsymbol{P}_K\boldsymbol{e})'(\boldsymbol{M}_K\boldsymbol{m}-\boldsymbol{P}_K\boldsymbol{e})\mid \boldsymbol{X}\right] \\ &= \boldsymbol{m}'\boldsymbol{M}_K\boldsymbol{m} + \mathbb{E}\left[\boldsymbol{e}'\boldsymbol{P}_K\boldsymbol{e}\mid \boldsymbol{X}\right] \\ &= \boldsymbol{m}'\boldsymbol{M}_K\boldsymbol{m} + \sigma^2 K.\end{aligned}$$

The choice of regressors affects $R_n(K)$ through the two terms in the final line. The first term, $\boldsymbol{m}'\boldsymbol{M}_K\boldsymbol{m}$, is the squared bias due to omitted variables. As K increases, this term decreases, reflecting reduced omitted variables bias. The second term, σ^2K, is estimation variance. It is increasing in the number of regressors. Increasing the number of regressors affects the quality of out-of-sample prediction by reducing the bias but increasing the variance.

Next, examine the adjusted Mallows criterion. We find that

$$\begin{aligned}C_n^*(K) &= \widehat{\boldsymbol{e}}_K'\widehat{\boldsymbol{e}}_K + 2\sigma^2K - \boldsymbol{e}'\boldsymbol{e} \\ &= (\boldsymbol{m}+\boldsymbol{e})'\boldsymbol{M}_K(\boldsymbol{m}+\boldsymbol{e}) + 2\sigma^2K - \boldsymbol{e}'\boldsymbol{e} \\ &= \boldsymbol{m}'\boldsymbol{M}_K\boldsymbol{m} + 2\boldsymbol{m}'\boldsymbol{M}_K\boldsymbol{e} - \boldsymbol{e}'\boldsymbol{P}_K\boldsymbol{e} + 2\sigma^2K.\end{aligned}$$

The next step is to show that

$$\sup_K \left|\frac{C_n^*(K)-R_n(K)}{R_n(K)}\right| \underset{p}{\longrightarrow} 0 \qquad (28.36)$$

as $n\to\infty$. To establish (28.36), observe that

$$C_n^*(K)-R_n(K) = 2\boldsymbol{m}'\boldsymbol{M}_K\boldsymbol{e} - \boldsymbol{e}'\boldsymbol{P}_K\boldsymbol{e} + \sigma^2K.$$

Pick $\epsilon > 0$ and some sequence $B_n \to \infty$ such that $B_n/\left(R_n^{\text{opt}}\right)^r \to 0$. (This is feasible by Assumption 28.1 part 5) By Boole's inequality (B.24), Whittle's inequality (B.48), the facts that $\boldsymbol{m}'\boldsymbol{M}_K\boldsymbol{m} \leq R_n(K)$ and $R_n(K) \geq \sigma^2 K$, $B_n/\left(R_n^{\text{opt}}\right)^r \to 0$, and $\sum_{K=1}^{\infty} K^{-r} < \infty$, we have

$$
\begin{aligned}
\mathbb{P}\left[\sup_K \left|\frac{\boldsymbol{m}'\boldsymbol{M}_K\boldsymbol{e}}{R_n(K)}\right| > \epsilon \,\middle|\, \boldsymbol{X}\right] &\leq \sum_{K=1}^{\infty} \mathbb{P}\left[\left|\frac{\boldsymbol{m}'\boldsymbol{M}_K\boldsymbol{e}}{R_n(K)}\right| > \epsilon \,\middle|\, \boldsymbol{X}\right] \\
&\leq \frac{C_{1r}}{\epsilon^{2r}} \sum_{K=1}^{\infty} \frac{\left|\boldsymbol{m}'\boldsymbol{M}_K\boldsymbol{m}\right|^r}{R_n(K)^{2r}} \\
&\leq \frac{C_{1r}}{\epsilon^{2r}} \sum_{K=1}^{\infty} \frac{1}{R_n(K)^r} \\
&= \frac{C_{1r}}{\epsilon^{2r}} \sum_{K=1}^{B_n} \frac{1}{R_n(K)^r} + \frac{C_{1r}}{\epsilon^{2r}} \sum_{K=B_n+1}^{\infty} \frac{1}{R_n(K)^r} \\
&\leq \frac{C_{1r}}{\epsilon^{2r}} \frac{B_n}{\left(R_n^{\text{opt}}\right)^r} + \frac{C_{1r}}{\epsilon^{2r}\sigma^{2r}} \sum_{K=B_n+1}^{\infty} \frac{1}{K^r} \\
&\to 0.
\end{aligned}
$$

By a similar argument but using Whittle's inequality (B.49), $\operatorname{tr}(\boldsymbol{P}_K\boldsymbol{P}_K) = \operatorname{tr}(\boldsymbol{P}_K) = K$, and $K \leq \sigma^{-2}R_n(K)$,

$$
\begin{aligned}
\mathbb{P}\left[\sup_K \left|\frac{\boldsymbol{e}'\boldsymbol{P}_K\boldsymbol{e} - \sigma^2 K}{R_n(K)}\right| > \epsilon \,\middle|\, \boldsymbol{X}\right] &\leq \sum_{K=1}^{\infty} \mathbb{P}\left[\left|\frac{\boldsymbol{e}'\boldsymbol{P}_K\boldsymbol{e} - \mathbb{E}\left(\boldsymbol{e}'\boldsymbol{P}_K\boldsymbol{e}\right)}{R_n(K)}\right| > \epsilon \,\middle|\, \boldsymbol{X}\right] \\
&\leq \frac{C_{2r}}{\epsilon^{2r}} \sum_{K=1}^{\infty} \frac{\operatorname{tr}\left(\boldsymbol{P}_K\boldsymbol{P}_K\right)^r}{R_n(K)^{2r}} \\
&= \frac{C_{2r}}{\epsilon^{2r}} \sum_{K=1}^{\infty} \frac{K^r}{R_n(K)^{2r}} \\
&\leq \frac{C_{1r}}{\epsilon^{2r}\sigma^{2r}} \sum_{K=1}^{\infty} \frac{1}{R_n(K)^r} \\
&\to 0.
\end{aligned}
$$

Together these results imply (28.36).

Finally, we can show that (28.36) implies (28.18). The argument is similar to the standard consistency proof for nonlinear estimators. Expression (28.36) states that $C_n^*(K)$ converges uniformly in probability to $R_n(K)$. Thus the minimizer of $C_n^*(K)$ converges in probability to that of $R_n(K)$. Formally, because K_n^{opt} minimizes $R_n(K)$, we have

$$
0 \leq \frac{R_n(\widehat{K}_n) - R_n(K_n^{\text{opt}})}{R_n(\widehat{K}_n)}
$$

$$
\begin{aligned}
&= \frac{C_n^*(\widehat{K}_n) - R_n(K_n^{\text{opt}})}{R_n(\widehat{K}_n)} - \frac{C_n^*(\widehat{K}_n) - R_n(\widehat{K}_n)}{-R_n(\widehat{K}_n)} \\
&\leq \frac{C_n^*(\widehat{K}_n) - R_n(K_n^{\text{opt}})}{R_n(\widehat{K}_n)} + o_p(1) \\
&\leq \frac{C_n^*(K_n^{\text{opt}}) - R_n(K_n^{\text{opt}})}{R_n(K_n^{\text{opt}})} + o_p(1) \\
&\leq o_p(1).
\end{aligned}
$$

The second inequality is (28.36). The following inequality uses the facts that $\widehat{K}_n$ minimizes $C_n^*(K)$ and K_n^{opt} minimizes $R_n(K)$. The final is (28.36). This is (28.18). ■

Before providing the proof of Theorem 28.10, I present two technical results related to the non-central chi-square density function with degree of freedom K and non-centrality parameter λ, which equals

$$
f_K(x,\lambda) = \sum_{i=0}^{\infty} \frac{e^{-\lambda/2}}{i!} \left(\frac{\lambda}{2}\right)^i f_{K+2i}(x) \tag{28.37}
$$

where

$$
f_r(x) = \frac{x^{r/2-1} e^{-x/2}}{2^{r/2}\Gamma\left(r/2\right))}
$$

is the χ_K^2 density function.

Theorem 28.16 The non-central chi-square density function (28.37) obeys the recursive relationship $f_K(x,\lambda) = \frac{K}{x} f_{K+2}(x,\lambda) + \frac{\lambda}{x} f_{K+4}(x,\lambda)$.

The proof of Theorem 28.16 is a straightforward manipulation of the non-central chi-square density function (28.37).

The second technical result is from Bock (1975, theorems A&B).

Theorem 28.17 If $X \sim \mathrm{N}(\theta, \boldsymbol{I}_K)$, then for any function $h(u)$

$$
\mathbb{E}\left[Xh\left(X'X\right)\right] = \theta \mathbb{E}\left[h\left(Q_{K+2}\right)\right] \tag{28.38}
$$

$$
\mathbb{E}\left[X'Xh\left(X'X\right)\right] = K\mathbb{E}\left[h\left(Q_{K+2}\right)\right] + \lambda \mathbb{E}\left[h\left(Q_{K+4}\right)\right] \tag{28.39}
$$

where $\lambda = \theta'\theta$, and $Q_r \sim \chi_r^2(\lambda)$ is a non-central chi-square random variable with r degrees of freedom and non-centrality parameter λ.

Proof of Theorem 28.17 To show (28.38), we first show that for $Z \sim \mathrm{N}(\mu, 1)$ then for any function $g(u)$

$$
\mathbb{E}\left[Zg\left(Z^2\right)\right] = \mu \mathbb{E}\left[g\left(Q_3\right)\right]. \tag{28.40}
$$

Assume $\mu > 0$. Using the change-of-variables $y = x^2$,

$$\mathbb{E}\left[Zg\left(Z^2\right)\right] = \int_{-\infty}^{\infty} \frac{x}{\sqrt{2\pi}} g\left(x^2\right) \exp\left(-\frac{1}{2}(x-\mu)^2\right) dx$$

$$= \int_0^{\infty} \frac{y}{2\sqrt{2\pi}} e^{-(y+\mu^2)/2} \left(e^{\sqrt{y}\mu} - e^{-\sqrt{y}\mu}\right) g(y)\, dy. \tag{28.41}$$

By expansion and Legendre's duplication formula

$$e^x - e^{-x} = 2\sum_{i=0}^{\infty} \frac{x^{1+2i}}{(1+2i)!} = \sqrt{\pi}\, x \sum_{i=0}^{\infty} \frac{(x^2/2)^i}{2^i i! \Gamma(i+3/2)}.$$

Then (28.41) equals

$$\mu \int_0^{\infty} y e^{-(y+\mu^2)/2} \sum_{i=0}^{\infty} \frac{(\mu^2/2)^i y^{i+1/2}}{2^{3/2+i} i! \Gamma(i+3/2)} g(y)\, dy = \mu \int_0^{\infty} y f_3(y, \mu^2) g(y)\, dy = \mu \mathbb{E}\left[g(Q_3)\right]$$

where $f_3(y, \lambda)$ is the non-central chi-square density (28.37) with three degrees of freedom. This is (28.40).

Consider the jth row of (28.38). Write $X'X = X_j^2 + J$, where $X_j \sim \mathrm{N}(\theta_j, 1)$ and $J \sim \chi^2_{K-1}(\lambda - \theta_j^2)$ are independent. Setting $g(u) = h(u + J)$ and using (28.41), we have

$$\begin{aligned}
\mathbb{E}\left[X_j h\left(X'X\right)\right] &= \mathbb{E}\left[X_j h\left(X_j^2 + J\right)\right] \\
&= \mathbb{E}\left[\mathbb{E}\left[X_j g\left(X_j^2\right) \mid J\right]\right] \\
&= \mathbb{E}\left[\theta_j \mathbb{E}\left[g(Q_3) \mid J\right]\right] \\
&= \theta_j \mathbb{E}\left[h(Q_3 + J)\right] \\
&= \theta_j \mathbb{E}\left[h(Q_{K+2})\right]
\end{aligned}$$

which is (28.38). The final equality uses the fact that $Q_3 + J \sim Q_{K+2}$.

Observe that $X'X$ has density $f_K(x, \lambda)$. Using Theorem 28.16

$$\begin{aligned}
\mathbb{E}\left[X'X\left(X'X\right)\right] &= \int_0^{\infty} x h(x) f_K(x, \lambda) dx \\
&= K \int_0^{\infty} h(x) f_{K+2}(x, \lambda) dx + \lambda \int_0^{\infty} h(x) f_{K+4}(x, \lambda) dx \\
&= K\mathbb{E}\left[h(Q_{K+2})\right] + \lambda \mathbb{E}\left[h(Q_{K+4})\right]
\end{aligned}$$

which is (28.39). ■

Proof of Theorem 28.10 By the quadratic structure, we can calculate that

$$\begin{aligned}
\mathrm{mse}\left[\widehat{\theta}^*\right] &= \mathbb{E}\left[\left(\widehat{\theta} - \theta - \widehat{\theta}\mathbb{1}\left\{\widehat{\theta}'\widehat{\theta} \le c\right\}\right)'\left(\widehat{\theta} - \theta - \widehat{\theta}\mathbb{1}\left\{\widehat{\theta}'\widehat{\theta} \le c\right\}\right)\right] \\
&= \mathbb{E}\left[\left(\widehat{\theta} - \theta\right)'\left(\widehat{\theta} - \theta\right)\right] - \mathbb{E}\left[\widehat{\theta}'\widehat{\theta}\mathbb{1}\left\{\widehat{\theta}'\widehat{\theta} \le c\right\}\right] + 2\mathbb{E}\left[\theta'\widehat{\theta}\mathbb{1}\left\{\widehat{\theta}'\widehat{\theta} \le c\right\}\right] \\
&= K - K\mathbb{E}\left[\mathbb{1}\left\{Q_{K+2} \le c\right\}\right] - \lambda\mathbb{E}\left[\mathbb{1}\left\{Q_{K+4} \le c\right\}\right] + 2\lambda\mathbb{E}\left[\mathbb{1}\left\{Q_{K+2} \le c\right\}\right] \\
&= K + (2\lambda - K) F_{K+2}(c, \lambda) - \lambda F_{K+4}(c, \lambda).
\end{aligned}$$

The third equality uses the two results from Theorem 28.17, setting $h(u) = \mathbb{1}\left\{u \le c\right\}$. ■

28.33 EXERCISES

Exercise 28.1 Verify equations (28.1) and (28.2).

Exercise 28.2 Find the Mallows criterion for the weighted least squares estimator of a linear regression $Y_i = X_i'\beta + e_i$ with weights ω_i (assume conditional homoskedasticity).

Exercise 28.3 Backward stepwise regression. Verify the claim that for the case of AIC selection, step (b) of the algorithm can be implemented by calculating the classical (homoskedastic) t-ratio for each active regressor, and find the regressor, with the smallest absolute t-ratio.

Hint: Use the relationship between likelihood ratio and F statistics and the equality between F and Wald statistics to show that for tests on one coefficient, the smallest change in the AIC is identical to identifying the smallest squared t-statistic.

Exercise 28.4 Forward stepwise regression. Verify the claim that for the case of AIC selection, step (b) of the algorithm can be implemented by identifying the regressor in the inactive set with the greatest absolute correlation with the residual from step (a).

Hint: This is challenging. First show that the goal is to find the regressor that will most decrease $\text{SSE} = \widehat{\boldsymbol{e}}'\widehat{\boldsymbol{e}} = \|\widehat{\boldsymbol{e}}\|^2$. Use a geometric argument to show that the regressor most parallel to $\widehat{\boldsymbol{e}}$ will most decrease $\|\widehat{\boldsymbol{e}}\|$. Show that this regressor has the greatest absolute correlation with $\widehat{\boldsymbol{e}}$.

Exercise 28.5 An economist estimates several models and reports a single selected specification, stating that "the other specifications had insignificant coefficients." How should we interpret the reported parameter estimates and t-ratios?

Exercise 28.6 Verify Theorem 28.11, including (28.21), (28.22), and (28.23).

Exercise 28.7 Under the assumptions of Theorem 28.11, show that $\widehat{\lambda} = \widehat{\theta}'\boldsymbol{V}^{-1}\widehat{\theta} - K$ is an unbiased estimator of $\lambda = \theta'\boldsymbol{V}^{-1}\theta$.

Exercise 28.8 Prove Theorem 28.14 for the simpler case of the unadjusted (not positive part) Stein estimator $\widetilde{\theta}$, $\boldsymbol{V} = \boldsymbol{I}_K$, and $r = 0$.

Extra challenge: Show that under these assumptions,

$$\text{wmse}\left[\widetilde{\theta}\right] = K - (q-2)^2 J_q(\lambda_{\boldsymbol{R}})$$

$$\lambda_{\boldsymbol{R}} = \theta'\boldsymbol{R}\left(\boldsymbol{R}'\boldsymbol{R}\right)^{-1}\boldsymbol{R}'\theta.$$

Exercise 28.9 Suppose you have two unbiased estimators $\widehat{\theta}_1$ and $\widehat{\theta}_2$ of a parameter vector $\widehat{\theta}$ with covariance matrices $\boldsymbol{V}_1$ and $\boldsymbol{V}_2$. The goal is to Minimize the unweighted mean squared error (e.g., $\operatorname{tr}\boldsymbol{V}_1$ for $\widehat{\theta}_1$). Assume that $\widehat{\theta}_1$ and $\widehat{\theta}_2$ are uncorrelated.

(a) Show that the optimal weighted average estimator equals

$$\frac{\frac{1}{\operatorname{tr}\boldsymbol{V}_1}\widehat{\theta}_1 + \frac{1}{\operatorname{tr}\boldsymbol{V}_2}\widehat{\theta}_2}{\frac{1}{\operatorname{tr}\boldsymbol{V}_1} + \frac{1}{\operatorname{tr}\boldsymbol{V}_2}}.$$

(b) Generalize to the case of M unbiased uncorrelated estimators.

(c) Interpret the formulas.

Exercise 28.10 You estimate M linear regressions $Y = X_m'\beta_m + e_m$ by least squares. Let $\widehat{Y}_{mi} = X_{mi}'\widehat{\beta}_m$ be the fitted values.

(a) Show that the Mallows averaging criterion is the same as

$$\sum_{i=1}^{n}\left(Y_i - w_1\widehat{Y}_{1i} - w_2\widehat{Y}_{2i} - \cdots - w_M\widehat{Y}_{Mi}\right)^2 + 2\sigma^2\sum_{m=1}^{M} w_m k_m.$$

(b) Assume that the models are nested, with M being the largest model. If the previous criterion were minimized over w in the probability simplex but the penalty were omitted, what would be the solution? (What would be the minimizing weight vector?)

Exercise 28.11 You estimate M linear regressions $Y = X_m'\beta_m + e_m$ by least squares. Let $\widetilde{Y}_{mi} = X_{mi}'\widehat{\beta}_{m(-i)}$ be the predicted values from the leave-one-out regressions. Show that the JMA criterion equals

$$\sum_{i=1}^{n}\left(Y_i - w_1\widetilde{Y}_{1i} - w_2\widetilde{Y}_{2i} - \cdots - w_M\widetilde{Y}_{Mi}\right)^2.$$

Exercise 28.12 Using the `cps09mar` dataset, perform an analysis similar to that presented in Section 28.18 but instead use the subsample of Hispanic women. This sample has 3,003 observations. Which models are selected by BIC, AIC, CV, and FIC? (The precise information criteria you examine may be limited, depending on your software.) How do you interpret the results? Which model/estimate would you select as your preferred choice?

CHAPTER 29

MACHINE LEARNING

29.1 INTRODUCTION

This chapter reviews machine learning methods for econometrics. This is a large and growing topic, so our treatment is selective. The chapter briefly covers ridge regression, Lasso, elastic net, regression trees, bagging, random forests, ensembling, Lasso IV, double-selection/post-regularization, and double/debiased machine learning.

A classic reference is Hastie, Tibshirani, and Friedman (2008). Introductory textbooks include James, Witten, Hastie, and Tibshirani (2013) and Efron and Hastie (2017). For a theoretical treatment, see Bühlmann and van de Geer (2011). For reviews of machine learning in econometrics see Belloni, Chernozhukov and Hansen (2014a), Mullainathan and Spiess (2017), Athey and Imbens (2019), and Belloni, Chernozhukov, Chetverikov, Hansen, and Kato (2021).

29.2 BIG DATA, HIGH DIMENSIONALITY, AND MACHINE LEARNING

Three interrelated concepts are big data, high dimensionality, and machine learning.

Big data is typically used to describe datasets that are unusually large and/or complex relative to traditional applications. The definition of "large" varies across disciplines and time, but typically refers to datasets with millions of observations. These datasets can arise in economics from household census data, government administrative records, and supermarket scanner data. Some challenges associated with big data are storage, transmission, and computation.

High dimensionality is typically used to describe datasets with an unusually large number of variables. Again the definition of "large" varies across applications, but typically refers to hundreds or thousands of variables. In the theoretical literature, "high dimensionality" is used specifically for the context where $p >> n$, meaning that the number of variables p greatly exceeds the number of observations n.

Machine learning is typically used to describe a set of algorithmic approaches to statistical learning. The methods are primarily focused on point prediction in settings with unknown structure. Machine learning methods generally allow for large sample sizes, large numbers of variables, and unknown structural form. The early literature was algorithmic with no associated statistical theory. This was followed by a statistical literature examining the properties of machine learning methods, mostly providing convergence rates under **sparsity** assumptions. Only recently has the literature expanded to include inference.

Machine learning embraces a large and diverse set of tools for a variety of settings, including **supervised learning** (prediction rules for Y given high-dimensional X), **unsupervised learning** (uncovering structure among high-dimensional X), and **classification** (discrete choice analysis with high-dimensional predictors). In this chapter, we focus on supervised learning, as it is a natural extension of linear regression.

Machine learning arose from the computer science literature and thereby adopted a distinct set of labels to describe familar concepts. For example, this literature speaks of "training" rather than "estimation" and "features" rather than "regressors." In this chapter, however, we will use standard econometric language and terminology.

For econometrics, machine learning can be thought of as highly nonparametric. Suppose we are interested in estimating the conditional mean $m(X) = \mathbb{E}[Y \mid X]$ when the shape of $m(x)$ is unknown. A nonparametric analysis typically assumes that X is low-dimensional. In contrast, a machine learning analysis may allow for hundreds or even thousands of regressors in X, and it does not require prior information about which regressors are most relevant.

Connections between nonparametric estimation, model selection, and machine learning methods arise in tuning parameter selection by CV and evaluation by out-of-sample prediction accuracy. These issues are taken seriously in machine learning applications, frequently with multiple levels of hold-out samples.

29.3 HIGH-DIMENSIONAL REGRESSION

We are familiar with the linear regression model $Y = X'\beta + e$, where X and β are $p \times 1$ vectors.[1] In conventional regression models, we are accustomed to thinking of the number of variables p as small relative to the sample size n. Traditional parametric asymptotic theory assumes that p is fixed as $n \to \infty$, which is typically interpreted as implying that p is much smaller than n. Nonparametric regression theory assumes that $p \to \infty$ but at a much slower rate than n. This is interpreted as p being moderately large but still much smaller than n. **High-dimensional regression** is used to describe the context where p is very large, including the case where p is larger than n. It even includes the case where p is exponentially larger than n.

It may seem shocking to contemplate an application with more regressors than observations. But the situation arises in a number of contexts. First, in our discussion of series regression (Chapter 20), we discussed how a regression function can be approximated by an infinite series expansion in basis transformations of the underlying regressors. Expressed as a linear model, this implies a regression model with an infinite number of regressors. Practical models (as discussed in that chapter) use a moderate number of regressors in estimated regressions, because this provides a balance between bias and variance. This latter models, however, are not the true conditional mean (which has an infinite number of regressors) but rather a low-dimensional best linear approximation. Second, many economic applications involve a large number of binary, discrete, and categorical variables. A saturated regression model converts all discrete and categorical variables into binary variables and includes all interactions. Such manipulations can result in thousands of regressors. For example, ten binary variables fully interacted yields 1,024 regressors. Twenty binary variables fully interacted yields over one million regressors. Third, many contemporary "big" datasets contain thousands of potential regressors. Many of the variables may be low-information, but it is difficult to know a priori which are relevant and which irrelevant.

When $p > n$, the least squares estimator $\widehat{\beta}_{\text{ols}}$ is not uniquely defined, because $\boldsymbol{X}'\boldsymbol{X}$ has deficient rank. Furthermore, for $p < n$ but "large," the matrix $\boldsymbol{X}'\boldsymbol{X}$ can be near-singular or ill-conditioned, so the least squares estimator can be numerically unstable and have high variance. Consequently, we turn to estimation methods other than least squares. In this chapter, we discuss several alternative estimation methods, including ridge regression, Lasso, elastic net, regression trees, and random forests.

---

[1] In most of this textbook, I have denoted the dimension of X as k. In this chapter, I instead denote the dimension of X as p, as this is the custom in the machine learning literature.

29.4 P-NORMS

For the discussion of ridge and Lasso regression, we will be making extensive use of the 1-norm and 2-norm, so it is useful to review the definition of the general p-norm. For a vector $a = (a_1, \ldots, a_k)'$, the p-norm ($p \geq 1$) is

$$\|a\|_p = \left(\sum_{j=1}^{k} |a_j|^p \right)^{1/p}.$$

Important special cases include the 1-norm

$$\|a\|_1 = \sum_{j=1}^{k} |a_j|$$

the 2-norm

$$\|a\|_2 = \left(\sum_{j=1}^{k} a_j^2 \right)^{1/2}$$

and the sup-norm

$$\|a\|_\infty = \max_{1 \leq j \leq k} |a_j|.$$

We also define the "0-norm"

$$\|a\|_0 = \sum_{j=1}^{k} \mathbb{1}\left\{a_j \neq 0\right\}$$

the number of nonzero elements, which is only heuristically labeled as a "norm."

The p-norm satisfies the following additivity property. If $a = (a_0, a_1)$, then

$$\|a\|_p^p = \|a_0\|_p^p + \|a_1\|_p^p.$$

The following inequalities are useful. The Hölder inequality for $1/p + 1/q = 1$ is

$$\left|a'b\right| \leq \|a\|_p \|b\|_q. \tag{29.1}$$

The case $p = 1$ and $q = \infty$ is

$$\left|a'b\right| \leq \|a\|_1 \|b\|_\infty. \tag{29.2}$$

The Minkowski inequality for $p \geq 1$ is

$$\|a + b\|_p \leq \|a\|_p + \|b\|_p. \tag{29.3}$$

The p-norms for $p \geq 1$ satisfy norm monotonicity. In particular,

$$\|a\|_1 \geq \|a\|_2 \geq \|a\|_\infty.$$

Applying Hölder's inequality (29.1), we also have the inequality

$$\|a\|_1 = \sum_{j=1}^{k} |a_j| \, \mathbb{1}\left\{a_j \neq 0\right\} \leq \|a\|_2 \|a\|_0^{1/2}. \tag{29.4}$$

29.5 RIDGE REGRESSION

Ridge regression is a shrinkage-type estimator with similar but distinct properties from the James-Stein estimator (see Section 28.20). There are two competing motivations for using ridge regression. The traditional motivation is to reduce the degree of collinearity among the regressors. The modern motivation (though in mathematics, it pre-dates the "traditional" motivation) is regularization of high-dimensional and ill-posed inverse problems. We discuss both in turn.

As discussed in Section 29.4, when p is large, the least squares coefficient estimate can be numerically unreliable due to an ill-conditioned $\boldsymbol{X}'\boldsymbol{X}$. As a numerical improvement, Hoerl and Kennard (1970) proposed the **ridge regression estimator**:

$$\widehat{\beta}_{\text{ridge}} = \left(\boldsymbol{X}'\boldsymbol{X} + \lambda \boldsymbol{I}_p\right)^{-1} \boldsymbol{X}'\boldsymbol{Y}$$

where $\lambda > 0$ is called the "ridge parameter." This estimator has the property that it is well defined and does not suffer from multicollinearity or ill-conditioning. It even holds if $p > n$! It is, the ridge regression estimator is well defined even when the number of regressors exceeds the sample size.

The ridge parameter λ controls the extent of shrinkage and can be viewed as a tuning parameter. We discuss how to select λ below.

To see how $\lambda > 0$ ensures that the inverse problem is solved, use the spectral decomposition to write $\boldsymbol{X}'\boldsymbol{X} = \boldsymbol{H}'\boldsymbol{D}\boldsymbol{H}$, where $\boldsymbol{H}$ is orthonormal, and $\boldsymbol{D} = \text{diag}\{r_1, \ldots, r_p\}$ is a diagonal matrix with the eigenvalues r_j of $\boldsymbol{X}'\boldsymbol{X}$ on the diagonal. Set $\Lambda = \lambda \boldsymbol{I}_p$. We can write

$$\boldsymbol{X}'\boldsymbol{X} + \lambda \boldsymbol{I}_p = \boldsymbol{H}'\boldsymbol{D}\boldsymbol{H} + \lambda \boldsymbol{H}'\boldsymbol{H} = \boldsymbol{H}'\left(\boldsymbol{D} + \Lambda\right)\boldsymbol{H}$$

which has strictly positive eigenvalues $r_j + \lambda > 0$. Thus all eigenvalues are bounded away from 0 so $\boldsymbol{X}'\boldsymbol{X} + \lambda \boldsymbol{I}_p$ is full rank and well-conditioned.

The second motivation is based on penalization. When $\boldsymbol{X}'\boldsymbol{X}$ is ill-conditioned, its inverse is **ill-posed**. Techniques to deal with ill-posed estimators are called **regularization** and date back to Tikhonov (1943). A leading method is penalization. Consider the sum of squared errors penalized by the squared 2-norm of the coefficient vector:

$$\text{SSE}_2\left(\beta, \lambda\right) = \left(\boldsymbol{Y} - \boldsymbol{X}\beta\right)'\left(\boldsymbol{Y} - \boldsymbol{X}\beta\right) + \lambda \beta'\beta = \|\boldsymbol{Y} - \boldsymbol{X}\beta\|_2^2 + \lambda \|\beta\|_2^2 .$$

The minimizer of $\text{SSE}_2\left(\beta, \lambda\right)$ is a regularized least squares estimator.

The first-order condition for minimization of $\text{SSE}_2\left(\beta, \lambda\right)$ over β is

$$-2\boldsymbol{X}'\left(\boldsymbol{Y} - \boldsymbol{X}\beta\right) + 2\lambda\beta = 0. \tag{29.5}$$

The solution is $\widehat{\beta}_{\text{ridge}}$. Thus the regularized (penalized) least squares estimator equals ridge regression. This shows that the ridge regression estimator minimizes the sum of squared errors subject to a penalty on the squared 2-norm of the regression coefficient. Penalizing large coefficient vectors keeps the latter from being too large and erratic. Hence, one interpretation of λ is as a penalty on the magnitude of the coefficient vector.

Minimization subject to a penalty has a dual representation as constrained minimization. The latter is

$$\min_{\beta'\beta \le \tau} \left(\boldsymbol{Y} - \boldsymbol{X}\beta\right)'\left(\boldsymbol{Y} - \boldsymbol{X}\beta\right)$$

for some $\tau > 0$. To see the connection, the Lagrangian for the constrained problem is

$$\min_{\beta} \left(\boldsymbol{Y} - \boldsymbol{X}\beta\right)'\left(\boldsymbol{Y} - \boldsymbol{X}\beta\right) + \lambda\left(\beta'\beta - \tau\right)$$

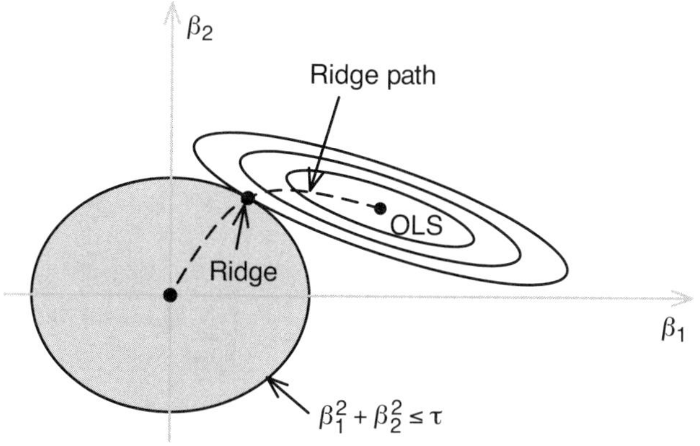

FIGURE 29.1 Ridge regression dual minimization solution

where λ is a Lagrange multiplier. The first-order condition is (29.5), which is the same as the penalization problem. Thus they have the same solution.

The practical difference between the penalization and constraint problems is that in the first, you specify the ridge parameter λ, but in the second, you specify the constraint parameter τ. They are connected because the values of λ and τ satisfy the relationship

$$\boldsymbol{Y}'\boldsymbol{X}\left(\boldsymbol{X}'\boldsymbol{X}+\lambda \boldsymbol{I}_p\right)^{-1}\left(\boldsymbol{X}'\boldsymbol{X}+\lambda \boldsymbol{I}_p\right)^{-1}\boldsymbol{X}'\boldsymbol{Y}=\tau.$$

To find λ given τ, it is sufficient to (numerically) solve this equation.

To visualize the constraint problem, see Figure 29.1, which plots an example in $\mathbb{R}^2$. The constraint set $\beta'\beta \le \tau$ is displayed as the ball about the origin, and the contour sets of the sum of squared errors are displayed as ellipses. The least squares estimator is the center of the ellipses, while the ridge regression estimator is the point on the circle where the contour is tangent. This shrinks the least squares coefficient towards the zero vector. Unlike the Stein estimator, however, it does not shrink along the line segment connecting least squares with the origin; instead it shrinks along a trajectory determined by the degree of correlation between the variables. This trajectory is displayed by the dashed lines, marked as "Ridge Path." This is the sequence of ridge regression coefficients obtained as λ is varied from 0 to ∞. When $\lambda = 0$, the ridge estimator equals least squares. For small λ, the ridge estimator moves slightly toward the origin by sliding along the ridge of the contour set. As λ increases, the ridge estimator takes a more direct path toward the origin. This behaviour is unlike that of the Stein estimator, which shrinks the least squares estimator toward the origin along the connecting line segment.

It is straightforward to generalize ridge regression to allow different penalties on different groups of regressors. Consider the model

$$Y = X_1'\beta_1 + \cdots + X_G'\beta_G + e$$

and minimize the SSE subject to the penalty

$$\lambda_1\beta_1'\beta_1 + \cdots + \lambda_G\beta_G'\beta_G.$$

The solution is

$$\widehat{\beta}_{\text{ridge}} = \left(\boldsymbol{X}'\boldsymbol{X}+\Lambda\right)^{-1}\boldsymbol{X}'\boldsymbol{Y}$$

where

$$\Lambda = \operatorname{diag}\left\{\lambda_1\boldsymbol{I}_{p_1},\ldots,\lambda_G\boldsymbol{I}_{p_G}\right\}.$$

Grouped ridge allows some coefficients to be penalized more (or less) than other coefficients. This added flexibility comes at the cost of selecting the ridge parameters $\lambda = (\lambda_1, \ldots, \lambda_G)$. One important special case is $\lambda_1 = 0$; thus one group of coefficients is not penalized. With $G = 2$, this partitions the coefficients into two groups: penalized and nonpenalized.

The most popular method for selecting the ridge parameter λ is cross-validation. The leave-one-out ridge regression estimator, prediction errors, and CV criterion are

$$\widehat{\beta}_{-i}(\lambda) = \left(\sum_{j \neq i} X_j X_j' + \Lambda\right)^{-1} \left(\sum_{j \neq i} X_j Y_i\right)$$

$$\widetilde{e}_i(\lambda) = Y_i - X_i' \widehat{\beta}_{-i}(\lambda)$$

$$\mathrm{CV}(\lambda) = \sum_{i=1}^{n} \widetilde{e}_i(\lambda)^2.$$

The CV-selected ridge parameter λ_{cv} minimizes $\mathrm{CV}(\lambda)$. The CV ridge estimator is calculated using λ_{cv}.

In practice, it may be tricky to minimize $\mathrm{CV}(\lambda)$. The minimum may occur at $\lambda = 0$ (ridge equals least squares), at $\lambda = \infty$ (full shrinkage), or there may be multiple local minima. The scale of the minimizing λ depends on the scaling of the regressors and in particular on the singular values of $\boldsymbol{X}'\boldsymbol{X}$. It can be important to explore $\mathrm{CV}(\lambda)$ for very small values of λ.

As for least squares, there is a simple formula to calculate the CV criterion for ridge regression, which greatly speeds computation.

Theorem 29.1 The leave-one-out ridge regression prediction errors are

$$\widetilde{e}_i(\lambda) = \left(1 - X_i' \left(\boldsymbol{X}'\boldsymbol{X} + \Lambda\right)^{-1} X_i\right)^{-1} \widehat{e}_i(\lambda) \tag{29.6}$$

where $\widehat{e}_i(\lambda) = Y_i - X_i' \widehat{\beta}_{\mathrm{ridge}}(\lambda)$ are the ridge regression residuals.

For a proof, see Exercise 29.1.

An alternative method for selection of λ is to minimize the Mallows criterion, which equals

$$C(\lambda) = \sum_{i=1}^{n} \widehat{e}_i(\lambda)^2 + 2\widehat{\sigma}^2 \operatorname{tr}\left(\left(\boldsymbol{X}'\boldsymbol{X} + \Lambda\right)^{-1} \left(\boldsymbol{X}'\boldsymbol{X}\right)\right). \tag{29.7}$$

where $\widehat{\sigma}^2$ is the variance estimator from least squares estimation. Exercise 29.2 asks you to derive (29.7). The Mallows-selected ridge parameter λ_{m} minimizes $C(\lambda)$. The Mallows-selected ridge estimator is calculated using λ_{m}. Li (1986) showed that in the normal regression model, the ridge estimator with the Mallows-selected ridge parameter is asymptotically equivalent to the infeasible best ridge parameter in terms of regression fit. I am unaware of a similar optimality result for cross-validated-selected ridge estimation.

An important caveat is that the ridge regression estimator is not invariant to rescaling the regressors or to other linear transformations. Therefore, it is common to apply ridge regression after applying standardizing transformations to the regressors.

Ridge regression can be implemented in R with the `glmnet` command. In Stata, ridge regression is available in the downloadable package `lassopack`.

29.6 STATISTICAL PROPERTIES OF RIDGE REGRESSION

Under the assumptions of the linear regression model, it is straightforward to calculate the exact bias and variance of the ridge regression estimator. Consider the linear regression model

$$Y = X'\beta + e$$
$$\mathbb{E}[e \mid X] = 0.$$

The bias of the ridge estimator with fixed λ is

$$\text{bias}\left[\widehat{\beta}_{\text{ridge}} \mid \boldsymbol{X}\right] = -\lambda\left(\boldsymbol{X}'\boldsymbol{X} + \lambda \boldsymbol{I}_p\right)^{-1}\beta. \tag{29.8}$$

Under random sampling, its covariance matrix is

$$\text{var}\left[\widehat{\beta}_{\text{ridge}} \mid \boldsymbol{X}\right] = \left(\boldsymbol{X}'\boldsymbol{X} + \lambda \boldsymbol{I}_p\right)^{-1}\left(\boldsymbol{X}'\boldsymbol{D}\boldsymbol{X}\right)\left(\boldsymbol{X}'\boldsymbol{X} + \lambda \boldsymbol{I}_p\right)^{-1} \tag{29.9}$$

where $\boldsymbol{D} = \text{diag}\left\{\sigma^2(X_1), \dots, \sigma^2(X_n)\right\}$, and $\sigma^2(X) = \mathbb{E}\left[e^2 \mid X\right]$. Exercise 29.3 asks you to derive (29.8) and (29.9). Under cluster or serial dependence, the central component modifies in the standard way.

We can measure estimation efficiency by the mean squared error (MSE) matrix:

$$\text{mse}\left[\widehat{\beta} \mid \boldsymbol{X}\right] = \mathbb{E}\left[\left(\widehat{\beta} - \beta\right)\left(\widehat{\beta} - \beta\right)' \mid \boldsymbol{X}\right].$$

Define $\underline{\sigma}^2 = \min_{x \in \mathscr{X}} \sigma^2(x)$, where $\mathscr{X}$ is the support of X.

Theorem 29.2 In the linear regression model, if $0 < \lambda < 2\underline{\sigma}^2/\beta'\beta$, then

$$\text{mse}\left[\widehat{\beta}_{\text{ridge}} \mid \boldsymbol{X}\right] < \text{mse}\left[\widehat{\beta}_{\text{ols}} \mid \boldsymbol{X}\right].$$

For a proof, see Section 29.23.

Theorem 29.2 shows that the ridge estimator dominates the least squares estimator, if λ satisfies a specific range of values. This holds regardless of the dimension of β. Because the upper bound $2\underline{\sigma}^2/\beta'\beta$ is unknown, however, it is unclear if feasible ridge regression dominates least squares. The upper bound does not give practical guidance for the selection of λ.

Given (29.9), it is straightforward to construct estimators of $V_{\widehat{\beta}} = \text{var}\left[\widehat{\beta}_{\text{ridge}} \mid \boldsymbol{X}\right]$. I suggest the HC3 analog:

$$\widetilde{V}_{\widehat{\beta}} = \left(\boldsymbol{X}'\boldsymbol{X} + \lambda \boldsymbol{I}_p\right)^{-1}\left(\sum_{i=1}^{n} X_i X_i' \widetilde{e}_i(\lambda)^2\right)\left(\boldsymbol{X}'\boldsymbol{X} + \lambda \boldsymbol{I}_p\right)^{-1} \tag{29.10}$$

where the $\widetilde{e}_i(\lambda)$ are the ridge regression prediction errors (29.6). Alternatively, the ridge regression residuals $\widehat{e}_i(\lambda)$ can be used, but it is unclear how to make an appropriate degree-of-freedom correction. Under clustering or serial dependence, the central component of $\widetilde{V}_{\widehat{\beta}}$ can be modified as usual. If the regressors are highly sparse (as in a sparse dummy variable regression), it may be prudent to use the homoskedastic estimator

$$\widetilde{V}^0_{\widehat{\beta}} = \widetilde{\sigma}^2(\lambda)\left(\boldsymbol{X}'\boldsymbol{X} + \lambda \boldsymbol{I}_p\right)^{-1}\left(\boldsymbol{X}'\boldsymbol{X}\right)\left(\boldsymbol{X}'\boldsymbol{X} + \lambda \boldsymbol{I}_p\right)^{-1}$$

with $\widetilde{\sigma}^2(\lambda) = n^{-1}\sum_{i=1}^{n} \widetilde{e}_i(\lambda)^2$.

Given that the ridge estimator is explicitly biased, there are natural concerns about how to interpret standard errors calculated from these covariance matrix estimators. Confidence intervals calculated the usual way will have deficient coverage due to the bias. One answer is to interpret the ridge estimator $\widehat{\beta}_{\text{ridge}}$ and its standard

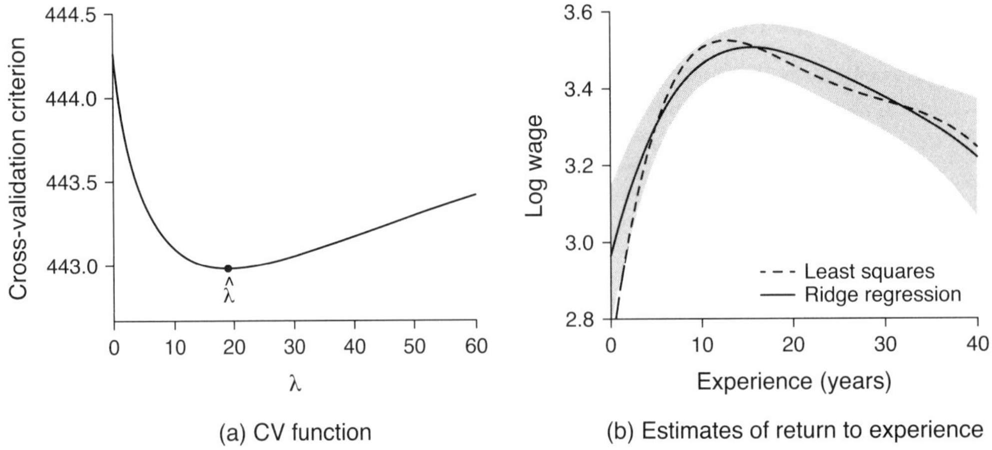

FIGURE 29.2 Least squares and ridge regression estimates of the return to experience

errors similarly to those obtained in nonparametric regression. The estimators and confidence intervals are valid for the pseudo-true projections (e.g., $\beta^* = \left(X'X + \lambda I_p\right)^{-1} X'X\beta$), not the coefficients β themselves. This is the same interpretation as we use for the projection model and for nonparametric regression. For asymptotically accurate inference on the true coefficients β, the ridge parameter λ could be selected to satisfy $\lambda = o\left(\sqrt{n}\right)$ analogously to an undersmoothing bandwidth in nonparametric regression.

29.7 ILLUSTRATING RIDGE REGRESSION

To illustrate ridge regression, let us use the CPS dataset with the sample of Asian men with a college education (16 years of education or more) to estimate the experience profile. Consider a fifth-order polynomial in experience for the conditional mean of log wages. Start by standardizing the regressors. First center experience at its mean, create powers up to order five, and then standardize each to have mean 0 and variance 1. Estimate the polynomial regression by least squares and by ridge regression, the latter shrinking the five coefficients on experience but not the intercept.

Calculate the ridge parameter by CV. The CV function is displayed in Figure 29.2(a) over the interval $[0, 60]$. Because we have standardized the regressors to have zero mean and unit variance, the ridge parameter is scaled comparably with sample size, which in this application is $n = 875$. The CV function is uniquely minimized at $\lambda = 19$. I use this value of λ for the following ridge regression estimation.

Figure 29.2(b) displays the estimated experience profiles. Least squares is displayed by dashes and ridge regression by the solid line. The ridge regression estimate is smoother and more compelling. The gray shaded region indicates the 95% normal confidence bands centered at the ridge regression estimate, calculated using the HC3 covariance matrix estimator (29.10).

29.8 LASSO

In Section 29.7, we learned that ridge regression minimizes the sum of squared errors plus a 2-norm penalty on the coefficient vector. Model selection (e.g., Mallows) minimizes the sum of squared errors plus the 0-norm penalty (the number of nonzero coefficients). An intermediate case uses the 1-norm penalty, which

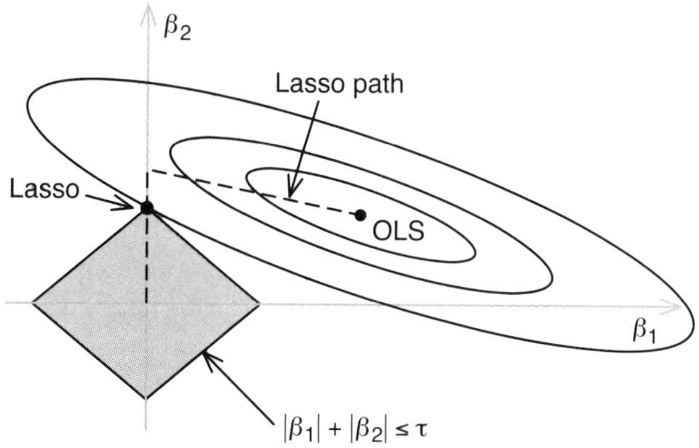

FIGURE 29.3 Lasso dual minimization solution

was proposed by Tibshirani (1996) and is known as the **Lasso** (for **Least Absolute Shrinkage and Selection Operator**). The least squares criterion with a 1-norm penalty is

$$\mathrm{SSE}_1(\beta, \lambda) = (\boldsymbol{Y} - \boldsymbol{X}\beta)'(\boldsymbol{Y} - \boldsymbol{X}\beta) + \lambda \sum_{j=1}^{p} |\beta_j| = \|\boldsymbol{Y} - \boldsymbol{X}\beta\|_2^2 + \lambda \|\beta\|_1 .$$

The Lasso estimator is its minimizer:

$$\widehat{\beta}_{\text{Lasso}} = \underset{\beta}{\operatorname{argmin}}\, \mathrm{SSE}_1(\beta, \lambda).$$

Except for special cases, the solution must be found numerically. Fortunately, computational algorithms are surprisingly simple and fast. An important property is that when $\lambda > 0$, the Lasso estimator is well defined even if $p > n$.

The Lasso minimization problem is equivalent to the dual constrained minimization problem:

$$\widehat{\beta}_{\text{Lasso}} = \underset{\|\beta\|_1 \le \tau}{\operatorname{argmin}}\, \mathrm{SSE}_1(\beta).$$

To see that the two problems are the same, observe that the constrained minimization problem has the Lagrangian

$$\min_{\beta}\, (\boldsymbol{Y} - \boldsymbol{X}\beta)'(\boldsymbol{Y} - \boldsymbol{X}\beta) + \lambda \left(\sum_{j=1}^{p} |\beta_j| - \tau \right)$$

which has first-order conditions

$$-2\boldsymbol{X}_j'(\boldsymbol{Y} - \boldsymbol{X}\beta) + \lambda\, \mathrm{sgn}(\beta_j) = 0.$$

This is the same as those for minimization of the penalized criterion. Thus the solutions are identical.

The constraint set $\{\|\beta\|_1 \le \tau\}$ for the dual problem is a cross-polytope resembling a multifaceted diamond. The minimization problem in $\mathbb{R}^2$ is illustrated in Figure 29.3. The sum of squared error contour sets are the ellipses with the least squares solution at the center. The constraint set is the shaded polytope. The Lasso estimator is the intersection point of the constraint set and the largest ellipse drawn. In this example, it hits a vertex of the constraint set, and so the constrained estimator sets $\widehat{\beta}_1 = 0$. This outcome is typical in Lasso estimation. Because we are minimizing a quadratic subject to a polytope, solutions tend to be at vertices, eliminates a subset of the coefficients.

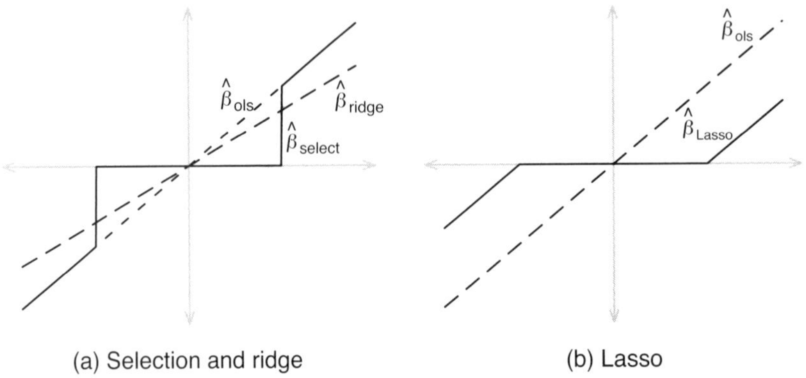

FIGURE 29.4 Transformations of least squares estimates by selection, ridge, and Lasso

The Lasso path is drawn with the dashed line in the figure. This is the sequence of solutions obtained as the constraint set is varied. The solution path has the property that it is a straight line from the least squares estimator to the y-axis (in this example), at which point β_2 is set to 0, and then the solution path follows the y-axis to the origin. In general, the solution path is linear on segments until a coefficient hits 0, at which point that coefficient is eliminated. In this example, the solution path shows β_2 increasing while β_1 decreases. Thus although Lasso is a shrinkage estimator, it does not shrink individual coefficients monotonically.

It is instructive to compare Figures 29.1 and 29.3, which have the same sum of squares contours. The ridge estimator is generically an interior solution with no individual coefficient set to 0, whereas the Lasso estimator typically sets some coefficients equal to 0. However, both estimators follow similar solution paths, following the ridge of the SSE criterion rather than taking a direct path toward the origin.

One case for which we can explicitly calculate the Lasso estimates is when the regressors are orthogonal (i.e., $\boldsymbol{X}'\boldsymbol{X} = \boldsymbol{I}_p$). Then the first-order condition for minimization simplifies to

$$-2\left(\widehat{\beta}_{\mathrm{ols},j} - \widehat{\beta}_{\mathrm{Lasso},j}\right) + \lambda \operatorname{sgn}\left(\widehat{\beta}_{\mathrm{Lasso},j}\right) = 0$$

which has the explicit solution

$$\widehat{\beta}_{\mathrm{Lasso},j} = \begin{cases} \widehat{\beta}_{\mathrm{ols},j} - \lambda/2, & \widehat{\beta}_{\mathrm{ols},j} > \lambda/2 \\ 0, & \left|\widehat{\beta}_{\mathrm{ols},j}\right| \le \lambda/2 \\ \widehat{\beta}_{\mathrm{ols},j} + \lambda/2, & \widehat{\beta}_{\mathrm{ols},j} < -\lambda/2. \end{cases}$$

Thus the Lasso estimate is a continuous transformation of the least squares estimate. For small values of the least squares estimate, the Lasso estimate is set to 0. For all other values, the Lasso estimate moves the least squares estimate toward 0 by $\lambda/2$.

It is constructive to contrast this behavior with ridge regression and selection estimation. When $\boldsymbol{X}'\boldsymbol{X} = \boldsymbol{I}_k$, the ridge estimator equals $\widehat{\beta}_{\mathrm{ridge}} = (1+\lambda)^{-1}\,\widehat{\beta}_{\mathrm{ols}}$ and so shrinks the coefficients toward by a common multiple. A selection estimator (for simplicity, consider selection based on a homoskedastic t-test with $\widehat{\sigma}^2 = 1$ and critical value c) equals $\widehat{\beta}_{\mathrm{select}} = \mathbb{1}\left\{\left|\widehat{\beta}_{\mathrm{ols},j}\right| > c\right\}\widehat{\beta}_{\mathrm{ols},j}$. Thus the Lasso, ridge, and selection estimates are all transformations of the least squares coefficient estimate. We illustrate these transformations in Figure 29.4. Panel (a) displays the selection and ridge transformations, and panel (b) displays the Lasso transformation.

The Lasso and ridge estimators are continuous functions, while the selection estimator is a discontinuous function. The Lasso and selection estimators are thresholding functions, meaning that the function equals 0 for a region about the origin. Thresholding estimators are selection estimators, because they equal 0 when the least squares estimator is sufficiently small. The Lasso function is a "soft thresholding" rule, as it is a continuous function with bounded first derivative. The selection estimator is a "hard thresholding" rule as it is discontinuous. Hard thresholding rules tend to have high variance because of the discontinuous transformation. Consequently, we expect the Lasso to have reduced variance relative to selection estimators, permitting overall lower MSE.

As for ridge regression, Lasso is not invariant to the scaling of the regressors. If you rescale a regressor, then the penalty has a different meaning. Consequently, it is important to scale the regressors appropriately before applying Lasso. It is conventional to scale all the variables to have mean 0 and variance 1.

Lasso is also not invariant to rotations of the regressors. For example, Lasso on $(\boldsymbol{X}_1, \boldsymbol{X}_2)$ is not the same as Lasso on $(\boldsymbol{X}_1 - \boldsymbol{X}_2, \boldsymbol{X}_2)$, despite having identical least squares solutions. This lack of invariance is troubling, as typically there is no default specification.

Applications of Lasso estimation in economics are growing. Belloni, Chernozhukov, and Hansen (2014a) illustrate the method using three applications: (1) the effect of eminent domain on housing prices in an instrumental variables framework, (2) a re-examination of the effect of abortion on crime using the framework of Donohue and Levitt (2001), (3) a re-examination of the the effect of democracy on economic growth using the framework of Acemoglu, Johnson, and Robinson (2001). Mullainathan and Spiess (2017) illustrate machine learning with a prediction model for housing prices using characteristics. Oster (2018) uses household scanner data to measure the effect of a diabetes diagnosis on food purchases.

29.9 LASSO PENALTY SELECTION

Critically important for Lasso estimation is the penalty λ. For λ close to 0 the estimates are close to least squares. As λ increases, the number of selected variables falls. Picking λ induces a tradeoff between complexity and parsimony.

It is common in the statistics literature to see coefficients plotted as a function of λ, which can be used to visualize the tradeoff between parsimony and variable inclusion. It does not, however, provide a statistical rule for selection.

The most common selection method is minimization of K-fold cross-validation (see Section 28.9). Leave-one-out CV is not typically used, as it is computationally expensive. Many programs set the default number of folds as $K = 10$, though some authors use $K = 5$, while others recommend $K = 20$.

K-fold cross-validation is an estimator of out-of-sample mean squared forecast error. Therefore, penalty selection by minimization of the K-fold criterion aims to select models with good forecast accuracy, but not necessarily for other purposes, such as accurate inference.

Conventionally, the value of λ selected by CV is the value that minimizes the CV criterion. Another popular choice is called the "1se" rule, which is the λ that yields the most parsimonious model for λ values within 1 standard error of the minimum. The idea is to select a model similar but more parsimonious than the CV-minimizing choice.

K-fold cross-validation is implemented by first randomly dividing the observations into K groups. Consequently, the CV criterion is sensitive to the random sorting. It is therefore prudent to set the random number seed for replicability and to assess sensitivity across initial seeds. In general, selecting a larger value for K reduces this sensitivity.

Asymptotic consistency of CV selection for Lasso estimation has been demonstrated by Chetverikov, Liao, and Chernozhukov (2021).

29.10 LASSO COMPUTATION

The constraint representation of Lasso is minimization of a quadratic subject to linear inequality constraints. This can be implemented by standard quadratic programming, which is computationally simple. For evaluation of the CV function, however, it is useful to compute the entire Lasso path. For this a computationally appropriate method is the modified LARS algorithm. ("LARS" stands for **least angle regression**.)

The LARS algorithm produces a path of coefficients starting at the origin and ending at least squares. The sequence corresponds to the sequence of constraints τ that can be calculated by the absolute sum of the coefficients, but neither these values nor λ are used by the algorithm. The steps are as follows.

1. Start with all coefficients equal to 0.
2. Find X_j most correlated with Y.
3. Increase β_j in the direction of correlation.
   (a) Compute residuals along the way.
   (b) Stop when some other X_ℓ has the same correlation with the residual as X_j.
   (c) If a nonzero coefficient hits 0, drop from the active set of variables and recompute the joint least squares direction.
4. Increase (β_j, β_ℓ) in their joint least squares direction until some other X_m has the same correlation with the residual.
5. Repeat until all predictors are in model.

This algorithm produces the Lasso path. The equality between the estimator and stated algorithm is not immediately apparent. The demonstration is tedious and so is not shown here.

The most popular computational implementation for Lasso is the R `glmnet` command in the `glmnet` package. Penalty selection by K-fold cross-validation is implmented by the `cv.glmnet` command. The latter by default reports the penalty selected by the "1se" rule and reports the minimizing λ as `lambda.min`. The default number of folds is $K = 10$.

In Stata, Lasso is available with the command `lasso`. By default, it selects the penalty by minimizing the K-fold cross-validation criterion with $K = 10$ folds. Many options are available, including constraining the estimator to penalize only a subset of the coefficients. An alternative downloadable package with many options is `lassopack`.

29.11 ASYMPTOTIC THEORY FOR THE LASSO

The current distribution theory of Lasso estimation is challenging and mostly focused on convergence rates. The results are derived under **sparsity** or **approximate sparsity** conditions, the first restricting the number of nonzero coefficients, and the second restricting how a sparse model can approximate a general parameterization. In this section, we determine a basic convergence rate for the Lasso estimator $\widehat{\beta}_{\text{Lasso}}$ under a mild moment bound on the errors and a sparsity assumption on the coefficients.

The model is the high-dimensional projection framework:

$$Y = X'\beta + e$$

$$\mathbb{E}[Xe] = 0 \tag{29.11}$$

where X is $p \times 1$ with $p >> n$. The true coefficient vector β is assumed to be **sparse** in the sense that only a subset of the elements of β are nonzero.

For some λ, let $\widehat{\beta}_{\text{Lasso}}$ be the Lasso estimator that minimizes $\text{SSE}_1(\beta, \lambda)$. Define the scaled design matrix $\boldsymbol{Q}_n = n^{-1}\boldsymbol{X}'\boldsymbol{X}$ and the **regression fit**

$$\left(\widehat{\beta}_{\text{Lasso}} - \beta\right)' \boldsymbol{Q}_n \left(\widehat{\beta}_{\text{Lasso}} - \beta\right) = \frac{1}{n}\sum_{i=1}^{n}\left(X_i'\left(\widehat{\beta}_{\text{Lasso}} - \beta\right)\right)^2. \tag{29.12}$$

Let us determine provide a bound on the regression fit (29.12), the 1-norm fit $\left\|\widehat{\beta} - \beta\right\|_1$ and the 2-norm fit $\left\|\widehat{\beta} - \beta\right\|_2$.

The regression fit (29.12) is similar to measures of fit we have used before, including the integrated squared error (20.22) in series regression and the regression fit $R_n(K)$ (equation (28.17)) for evaluation of model selection optimality.

When $p > n$, the matrix $\boldsymbol{Q}_n$ is singular. The theory, however, requires that it not be "too singular." What is required is nonsingularity of all submatrices of $\boldsymbol{Q}_n$ corresponding to the nonzero coefficients and not "too many" of the zero coefficients. The specific requirement is rather technical. Partition $\beta = (\beta_0, \beta_1)$, where the elements of β_0 are all 0, and the elements of β_1 are nonzero. (This partition is a theoretical device and is unknown to the econometrician.) Let $b = (b_0, b_1) \in \mathbb{R}^p$ be partitioned conformably. Define the cone $B = \left\{b \in \mathbb{R}^p : \|b_0\|_1 \leq 3\|b_1\|_1\right\}$. This is the set of vectors b such that the subvector b_0 is not "too large" relative to the subvector b_1.

Assumption 29.1 Restricted Eigenvalue Condition (REC)
With probability approaching 1 as $n \to \infty$,

$$\min_{b \in B} \frac{b'\boldsymbol{Q}_n b}{b'b} \geq c^2 > 0. \tag{29.13}$$

To gain some understanding of what the REC means, notice that if the minimum of (29.13) is taken without restriction over $\mathbb{R}^p$, it equals the smallest eigenvalue of $\boldsymbol{Q}_n$. Thus when $p < n$, a sufficient condition for the REC is $\lambda_{\min}\left(\boldsymbol{Q}_n\right) \geq c^2 > 0$. Instead, the minimum in (29.13) is calculated only over the cone B. In this sense, this calculation is similar to a "restricted eigenvalue," which is the source of its name. The REC takes a variety of forms in the theoretical literature; Assumption 29.1 is not the weakest but is the most intuitive. Assumption 29.1 has been shown to hold under primitive conditions on X, including normality and boundedness. See Section 3 of Bickel, Ritov, and Tsybakov (2009) and section 3.1 of Belloni, Chen, Chernozhukov, and Hansen (2012).

I provide a rate for the Lasso estimator under the assumption of normal errors.

Theorem 29.3 Suppose that model (29.11) holds with $p > 1$ and Assumption 29.1 holds. Assume that each regressor has been standardized so that $n^{-1}\boldsymbol{X}_j'\boldsymbol{X}_j = 1$ before applying the Lasso. Suppose that $e \mid X \sim \mathrm{N}\left(0, \sigma^2(X)\right)$, where $\sigma^2(x) \leq \overline{\sigma}^2 < \infty$. For some C sufficiently large, set

$$\lambda = C\sqrt{n \log p}. \tag{29.14}$$

Then there is a $D < \infty$ such that with probability arbitrarily close to 1,

$$\left(\widehat{\beta}_{\text{Lasso}} - \beta\right)' \boldsymbol{Q}_n \left(\widehat{\beta}_{\text{Lasso}} - \beta\right) \leq D\|\beta\|_0 \frac{\log p}{n}, \tag{29.15}$$

$$\left\|\widehat{\beta}_{\text{Lasso}} - \beta\right\|_1 \le D \left\|\beta\right\|_0 \sqrt{\frac{\log p}{n}}, \tag{29.16}$$

and

$$\left\|\widehat{\beta}_{\text{Lasso}} - \beta\right\|_2 \le D \left\|\beta\right\|_0^{1/2} \sqrt{\frac{\log p}{n}}. \tag{29.17}$$

For a proof, see Section 29.23.

Theorem 29.3 presents three convergence rates for the Lasso coefficient estimator $\widehat{\beta}_{\text{Lasso}}$, for the regression fit (29.12), covering the 1-norm and the 2-norm. These rates depend on the number of nonzero coefficients $\|\beta\|_0$, the number of variables p, and the sample size n. Suppose that $\|\beta\|_0$ is fixed. Then the bounds (29.15)–(29.17) are $o(1)$ if $\log p = o(n)$. Thus Lasso estimation is consistent even for an exponentially large number of variables. The rates, however, allow the number of nonzero coefficients $\|\beta\|_0$ to increase with n at the cost of slowing the allowable rate of increase of p.

Earlier in this section we had assumed that the coefficient vector β is sparse, meaning that only a subset of the elements of β are nonzero. This appears in the theory through the 0-norm $\|\beta\|_0$, the number of nonzero coefficients. If all elements of β are nonzero, then $\|\beta\|_0 = p$ and the bound (29.15) is $O\left(p \log p/n\right)$, which is similar to bound (20.24) for series regression obtained in Theorem 20.7. Instead, the assumption of sparsity enables the Lasso estimator to achieve a much improved rate of convergence.

The key to establishing Theorem 29.3 is a maximal inequality applied to $\frac{1}{n}\boldsymbol{X}'\boldsymbol{e}$. Our proof uses the Gaussian tail inequality (B.20), which requires the assumption of normality. This follows the analysis of Bickel, Ritov, and Tsybakov (2009), though these authors impose homoskedastic errors, which (as shown in Theorem 29.3) can be replaced by the assumption of bounded heteroskedasticity. Other papers in the statistics literature (see the monograph of Bühlmann and van de Geer (2011)) use instead the assumption of sub-Gaussian tails, which is weaker than normality.

A theory that allows for non-normal heteroskedastic errors has been developed by Belloni, Chen, Chernozhukov, and Hansen (2012). These authors examine an alternative Lasso estimator that adds regresssor-specific weights to the penalty function, with weights equaling the square roots of $n^{-1}\sum X_{ji}^2\widehat{e}_i^2$. They use a maximal inequality based on self-normalization and obtain rates similar to (29.15)–(29.17), though with considerably more complicated regularity conditions. Although their specific conditions may not be the weakest possible, their theory shows that the assumption of Gaussian or sub-Gaussian errors is not essential to the convergence rates (29.15)–(29.17). I expect that future research will further clarify the needed conditions.

An important limitation of results such as Theorem 29.3 is the sparsity assumption. It is untestable and counterintuitive. Researchers in this field frequently use the phrase "imposing sparsity" as if it were something under the control of the theorist—but sparsity is a property of the true coefficients, not a choice of the researcher. Fortunately, there are alternatives to the sparsity assumption, as we now discuss.

29.12 APPROXIMATE SPARSITY

The theory developed in Section 29.11 uses the strong assumption that the true regression is sparse: Only a subset of the coefficients are nonzero, and the convergence rate depends on the cardinality of the nonzero coefficients. However, as shown by Belloni, Chen, Chernozhukov, and Hansen (2012), strict sparsity is not required. Instead, convergence rates similar to those in Theorem 29.3 hold under the assumption of approximate sparsity.

Once again, consider the high-dimensional regression model (29.11), but do not assume that β necessarily has a sparse structure. Instead, view a sparse model as an approximation. For each integer $K > 0$, let $B_K = \{b \in \mathbb{R}^p : \|b\|_0 = K\}$ be the set of vectors with K nonzero elements. Define the best sparse approximation

$$\beta_K = \underset{b \in B_K}{\operatorname{argmin}} \left\| \boldsymbol{Q}_n (\beta - b) \right\|_\infty$$

with associated approximation error

$$r_K = \left\| \boldsymbol{Q}_n (\beta - \beta_K) \right\|_\infty .$$

Assumption 29.2 Approximate Sparsity. For some $s > 1$, $r_K = O\left(K^{-s}\right)$.

Assumption 29.2 states that the approximation error of the sparse approximation decreases at a power law rate. In Section 20.8 and Theorem 20.1, we learned that approximations similar to Assumption 29.2 hold for polynomial and spline series regressions with bounded regressors, if the true regression function has a uniform sth derivative. The primary difference is that series regression requires that the econometrician knows how to order the regressors, while Assumption 29.2 does not impose a specific ordering. In this sense, Assumption 29.2 is weaker than the approximation conditions of Section 20.8.

Belloni, Chen, Chernozhukov, and Hansen (2012) show that convergence results similar to Theorem 29.3 hold under the approximate sparsity condition of Assumption 29.2. The convergence rates are slowed and depend on the approximation exponent s. As $s \to \infty$, the convergence rates approach those under the assumption of sparsity, because as s increases, the regression function can be approximated with a smaller number K of nonzero coefficients. Belloni et al.'s results show that exact sparsity is not required for Lasso estimation; instead what is needed is approximation properties similar to those used in series regression theory.

The approximate sparsity condition fails when the regressors cannot be easily ordered. Suppose, for example, that $\boldsymbol{Q}_n = \boldsymbol{I}_p$ and all elements of β have common value δ. In this case, $r_K = \delta$, which does not decrease with K. In this context, Assumption 29.2 does not hold, and the convergence results of Belloni, Chen, Chernozhukov, and Hansen (2012) do not apply.

29.13 ELASTIC NET

The difference between Lasso and ridge regression is that the Lasso uses the 1-norm penalty, while ridge uses the 2-norm penalty. Because both procedures have advantages, it seems reasonable that further improvements may be obtained by a compromise. Taking a weighted average of the penalties, we obtain the **Elastic Net** criterion:

$$\operatorname{SSE}(\beta, \lambda, \alpha) = (\boldsymbol{Y} - \boldsymbol{X}\beta)' (\boldsymbol{Y} - \boldsymbol{X}\beta) + \lambda \left(\alpha \|\beta\|_2^2 + (1-\alpha) \|\beta\|_1\right)$$

with weight $0 \le \alpha \le 1$. This expression includes Lasso ($\alpha = 0$) and ridge regression ($\alpha = 1$) as special cases. For small but positive α, the constraint sets are similar to "rounded" versions of the Lasso constraint sets.

Typically the parameters (α, λ) are selected by joint minimization of the K-fold CV criterion. Because the elastic net penalty is linear-quadratic, the solution is computationally similar to Lasso.

Elastic net can be implemented in R with the `glmnet` command. In Stata, use `elasticnet` or the downloadable package `lassopack`.

29.14 POST-LASSO

The Lasso estimator $\widehat{\beta}_{\text{Lasso}}$ simultaneously selects variables and shrinks coefficients. Shrinkage introduces bias into estimation. This bias can be reduced by applying least squares after Lasso selection. This is known as the **post-Lasso** estimator.

The procedure takes two steps. First, estimate the model $Y = X'\beta + e$ by Lasso. Let X_S denote the variables in X that have nonzero coefficients in $\widehat{\beta}_{\text{Lasso}}$. Let β_S denote the corresponding coefficients in β. Second, the coefficient β_S is estimated by least squares, thus $\widehat{\beta}_S = \left(\boldsymbol{X}_S'\boldsymbol{X}_S\right)^{-1}\left(\boldsymbol{X}_S'\boldsymbol{Y}\right)$. This is the post-Lasso least squares estimator. Belloni and Chernozhukov (2013) provide conditions under which the post-Lasso estimator has the same convergence rates as the Lasso estimator.

The post-Lasso is a hard thresholding or post-model-selection estimator. Indeed, when the regressors are orthogonal, the post-Lasso estimator precisely equals a selection estimator, transforming the least squares coefficient estimates by using the hard threshold function displayed in Figure 29.4(a). Consequently, the post-Lasso estimator inherits the statistical properties of PMS estimators (see Sections 28.16 and 28.17), including high variance and non-standard distributions.

29.15 REGRESSION TREES

Regression trees were introduced by Breiman et al. (1984), and are also known by the acronym "CART" for **Classification and Regression Trees**. A regression tree is a nonparametric regression using a large number of step functions. The idea is that with a sufficiently large number of split points, a step function can approximate any function. Regression trees may be especially useful when there are a combination of continuous and discrete regressors, so that traditional kernel and series methods are challenging to implement.

Regression trees can be thought of as a zeroth-order spline with free knots. They are also similar to threshold regression with intercepts only (no slope coefficients) and a very large number of thresholds.

The goal is to estimate $m(x) = \mathbb{E}[Y \mid X = x]$ for scalar Y and vector X. The elements of X can be continuous, binary, or ordinal. If a regressor is categorical, it should be first transformed to a set of binary variables.

The literature on regression trees has developed some colorful language to describe the tools based on the metaphor of a living tree:

1. A subsample is a **branch**.
2. Terminal branches are **nodes** or **leaves**.
3. Increasing the number of branches is **growing** a tree.
4. Decreasing the number of branches is **pruning** a tree.

The basic algorithm starts with a single branch. Grow a large tree by sequentially splitting the branches. Then prune back using an information criterion. The goal of the growth stage is to develop a rich data-determined tree that has small estimation bias. Pruning back is an application of backward stepwise regression with the goal of reducing overparameterization and estimation variance.

The regression tree algorithm makes extensive use of the **regression sample split algorithm**. This is a simplified version of threshold regression (Section 23.7). The method uses NLLS to estimate the model

$$Y = \mu_1 \mathbb{1}\{X_d \leq \gamma\} + \mu_2 \mathbb{1}\{X_d > \gamma\} + e$$

$$\mathbb{E}[e \mid X] = 0$$

with the index d and parameter γ as free parameters.[2] The NLLS criterion is minimized over (d, γ) by grid search. The estimates produce a sample split. The regression tree algorithm applies sequential sample splitting to make a large number of splits, each on a subsample of observations.

The basic growth algorithm is as follows. The observations are $\{Y_i, X_{1i}, \ldots, X_{ki} : i = 1, \ldots, n\}$.

1. Select a minimum node size $N_{\min}$ (e.g., 5). This is the minimal number of observations on each leaf.
2. Sequentially apply regression sample splits.
   (a) Apply the regression sample split algorithm to split each branch into two sub-branches, each with size at least $N_{\min}$.
   (b) On each sub-branch b:
      i. Take the sample mean $\widehat{\mu}_b$ of Y_i for observations on the sub-branch.
      ii. This is the estimator of the regression function on this sub-branch.
      iii. The residuals on the sub-branch are $\widehat{e}_i = Y_i - \widehat{\mu}_b$.
   (c) Select the branch whose split most reduces the sum of squared errors.
   (d) Split this branch into two branches. Make no other split.
   (e) Repeat (a)–(d) until each branch cannot be further split. The terminal (unsplit) branches are the leaves.

After the growth algorithm has been run, the estimated regression is a multidimensional step function with a large number of branches and leaves.

The basic pruning algorithm is as follows.

1. Define the Mallows-type information criterion

$$C = \sum_{i=1}^{n} \widehat{e}_i^2 + \alpha N$$

   where N is the number of leaves, and α is a penalty parameter.
2. Compute the criterion C for the current tree.
3. Use backward stepwise regression to reduce the number of leaves:
   (a) Identify the leaf whose removal most decreases C.
   (b) Prune (remove) this leaf.
   (c) If there is no leaf whose removal decreases C, then stop pruning.
   (d) Otherwise, repeat (a)–(c).

The penalty parameter α is typically selected by K-fold CV. The Mallows-type criterion is used because of its simplicity, but to my knowledge it does not have a theoretical foundation for regression tree penalty selection.

The advantage of regression trees is that they provide a highly flexible nonparametric approximation. Their main use is for prediction. One disadvantage of regression trees is that the results are difficult to interpret, as there are no regression coefficients. Another disadvantage is that the fitted regression $\widehat{m}(x)$ is a discrete step function, which may be a crude approximation when $m(x)$ is continuous and smooth. To obtain a good approximation, a regression tree may require a large number of leaves, which can result in a nonparsimonious model with high estimation variance.

---

[2] If $X_d \in \{0, 1\}$ is binary, then $\gamma = 0$ is fixed.

The sampling distribution of regression trees is difficult to derive, in part because of the strong correlation between the placement of the sample splits and the estimated means. This is similar to the problems associated with post-model-selection. (See Sections 28.16 and 28.17.) A method that breaks this dependence is the **honest tree** proposal of Wager and Athey (2018). Split the sample into two halves A and B. Use the A sample to place the splits and the B sample to do within-leaf estimation. Although reducing estimation efficiency (the sample is effectively halved), the estimated conditional mean will not be distorted by the correlation between the estimated splits and means.

Regression trees algorithms are implemented in the R package `rpart`.

29.16 BAGGING

Bagging (**b**ootstrap **agg**regat**ing**) was introduced by Breiman (1996) as a method to reduce the variance of a predictor. We focus here on its use for estimation of a conditional expectation. The basic idea is simple. You generate a large number B of bootstrap samples, estimate your regression model on each bootstrap sample, and take the average of the bootstrap regression estimates. The average of the bootstrap estimates is the bagging estimator of the CEF.

Bagging is believed to be useful when the CEF estimator has low bias but high variance, which occurs for hard thresholding estimators, such as regression trees, model selection, and post-Lasso. Bagging is a smoothing operation that reduces variance. The resulting bagging estimator can have lower MSE as a result. Bagging is believed to be less useful for estimators with high bias, as bagging may exaggerate the bias.

The estimation algorithm is as follows. Let $m(x) = \mathbb{E}[Y \mid X = x]$ be the CEF and $\widehat{m}(x)$ an estimator, such as a regression tree. Let $\widehat{m}_b^*(x)$ be the same estimator constructed on a bootstrap sample. The bagging estimator of $m(x)$ is

$$\widehat{m}_{\text{bag}}(x) = \frac{1}{B}\sum_{B=1}^{b} \widehat{m}_b^*(x).$$

As B increases, this converges in bootstrap probability to the ideal bagging estimator $\mathbb{E}^*[\widehat{m}^*(x)]$.

To understand the bagging process, consider an example from Bühlmann and Yu (2002). As in Section 28.16, suppose that $\widehat{\theta} \sim \mathrm{N}(\theta, 1)$, and consider a selection estimator based on a 5% test, $\widehat{\theta}_{\text{pms}} = \widehat{\theta}\mathbb{1}\left\{\widehat{\theta}^2 \geq c\right\} = h(\widehat{\theta})$, where $c = 3.84$ and $h(t) = t\mathbb{1}\left\{t^2 \geq c\right\}$. Applying Theorem 28.17, equation (28.38), we can calculate that $\mathbb{E}\left[\widehat{\theta}_{\text{pms}}\right] = g(\theta)$, where $g(t) = t\left(1 - F_3\left(c, t^2\right)\right)$ and $F_r(x, \lambda)$ is the non-central chi-square distribution function.[3] This representation is not intuitive, so it is better to visualize its graph. The functions $h(t)$ and $g(t)$ are plotted in Figure 29.5(a). The selection function $h(t)$ is identical to the plot in Figure 29.4(a). The function $g(t)$ is a smoothed version of $h(t)$, everywhere continuous and differentiable.

Suppose that the bagging estimator is constructed using the parametric bootstrap $\widehat{\theta}^* \sim \mathrm{N}(\widehat{\theta}, 1)$. The bootstrap selection estimator is $\widehat{\theta}^*_{\text{pms}} = h\left(\widehat{\theta}^*\right)$. It follows that the bagging estimator is $\widehat{\theta}_{\text{bag}} = \mathbb{E}^*\left[\widehat{\theta}^*_{\text{pms}}\right] = \mathbb{E}^*\left[h\left(\widehat{\theta}^*\right)\right] = g(\widehat{\theta})$. Thus while the selection estimator $\widehat{\theta}_{\text{pms}} = h(\widehat{\theta})$ is the hard threshold transformation $h(t)$ applied to $\widehat{\theta}$, the bagging estimator $\widehat{\theta}_{\text{bag}} = g(\widehat{\theta})$ is the smoothed transformation $g(t)$ applied to $\widehat{\theta}$. Thus Figure 29.5(a) displays how $\widehat{\theta}_{\text{pms}}$ and $\widehat{\theta}_{\text{bag}}$ are transformations of $\widehat{\theta}$, with the bagging estimator a smooth transformation rather than a hard threshold transformation.

Bühlmann and Yu (2002) argue that smooth transformations generally have lower variances than hard threshold transformations, and thus they argue that $\widehat{\theta}_{\text{bag}}$ will generally have lower variance than $\widehat{\theta}_{\text{pms}}$. This is

[3] Bühlmann and Yu (2002), proposition 2.2, provide an alternative representation using the normal CDF and pdf functions.

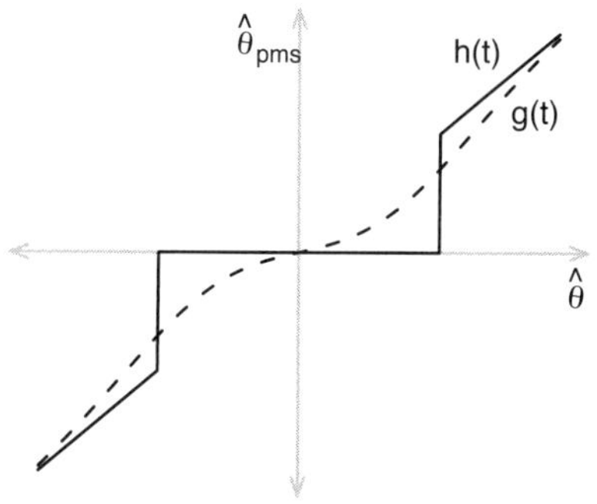

(a) Selection and bagging transformations

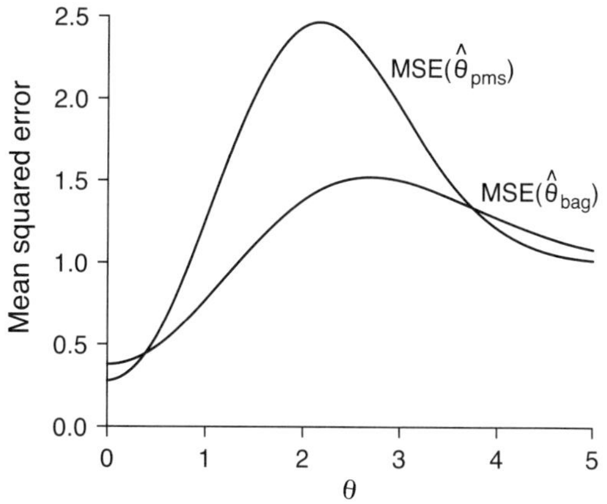

(b) MSE of selection and bagging estimators

FIGURE 29.5 Bagging and selection

difficult to demonstrate as a general principle, but it seems to be satisfied in specific examples. For our example, Figure 29.5(b) displays[4] the MSE of the selection estimator $\widehat{\theta}_{\text{pms}}$ and its bagged verion $\widehat{\theta}_{\text{bag}}$ as functions of θ. As discussed in Section 28.16, the MSE of the selection estimator $\widehat{\theta}_{\text{pms}}$ is a hump-shaped function of θ. In Figure 29.5(b), we can see that the MSE of the bagged estimator is considerably reduced relative to the selection estimator for most values of θ. The reduction in MSE is greatest in the region where the MSE of $\widehat{\theta}_{\text{pms}}$ is greatest. Bühlmann and Yu (2002) also calculate that most of this MSE reduction is due to a reduction in the variance of the bagged estimator.

The most common application of bagging is to regression trees. Trees have a similar structure to our example selection estimator $\widehat{\theta}_{\text{pms}}$ and are therefore expected to have a similar reduction in estimation variance and MSE relative to regression tree estimation.

One convenient by-product of bagging is a CV proxy called the **out-of-bag** prediction error. A typical nonparametric bootstrap sample contains about 63% of the original observations, meaning that about 37% of the observations are not present in that bootstrap sample. Therefore a bootstrap estimate of the regression function $m(x)$ constructed on this bootstrap sample has "left out" about 37% of the observations, meaning that valid prediction errors can be calculated on these "left out" observations. Alternatively, for any given observation i, out of the B bootstrap samples, about $0.63 \times B$ samples will contain this observation, and about $0.37 \times B$ samples will not include this observation. The bagging "leave i out" estimator $\widehat{m}_{-i}(x)$ of $m(x)$ is obtained by averaging just this second set (the 37% that exclude the observation). The **out-of-bag error** is $\widetilde{e}_i = Y_i - \widehat{m}_{-i}(X_i)$. The **out-of-bag CV** criterion is $\sum_{i=1}^{n} \widetilde{e}_i^2$. This can be used as an estimator of out-of-sample MSFE and can be used to compare and select models.

Wager, Hastie, and Efron (2014) propose estimators of $V_n(x) = \operatorname{var}\left[\widehat{m}_{\text{bag}}(x)\right]$. Let N_{ib} denote the number of times observation i appears in the bootstrap sample b and $N_i = B^{-1} \sum_{b=1}^{B} N_{ib}$. The **infinitesimal jackknife** estimator of V_n is

[4]For $\widehat{\theta}_{\text{pms}}$, the MSE is calculated using Theorem 28.10. For $\widehat{\theta}_{\text{bag}}$, the MSE is calculated by numerical integration.

$$\widehat{V}_n(x) = \sum_{i=1}^{n} \mathrm{cov}^* \left(N_i, \widehat{m}_{\mathrm{bag}}(x)\right)^2 = \sum_{i=1}^{n} \left(\frac{1}{B} \sum_{b=1}^{B} (N_{ib} - N_i) \left(\widehat{m}_b^*(x) - \widehat{m}_{\mathrm{bag}}(x)\right) \right)^2 . \tag{29.18}$$

This variance estimator is based on Efron (2014).

Although Breiman's proposal and most applications of bagging are implemented using the nonparametric bootstrap, an alternative is to use subsampling. A subsampling estimator is based on sampling without replacement rather than with replacement, as done in the conventional bootstrap. Samples of size $s < n$ are drawn from the original sample and used to construct the estimator $\widehat{m}_b^*(x)$. Otherwise, the methods are identical. It turns out that it is somewhat easier to develop a distribution theory for bagging under subsampling, so a subsampling assumption is frequently employed in theoretical treatments.

29.17 RANDOM FORESTS

Random forests, introduced by Breiman (2001), are a modification of bagged regression trees. The modification is designed to reduce estimation variance. Random forests are popular in machine learning applications and have effectively displaced simple regression trees.

Consider the procedure of applying bagging to regression trees. Because bootstrap samples are similar to one another, the estimated bootstrap regression trees will also be similar to one another, particularly in the sense that they tend to have the splits based on the same variables. Thus conditional on the sample, the bootstrap regression trees are positively correlated. This correlation means that the variance of the bootstrap average remains high, even when the number of bootstrap replications B is large. The modification proposed by random forests is to *decorrelate* the bootstrap regression trees by introducing extra randomness. This decorrelation reduces the variance of the bootstrap average, thereby reducing its MSE.

The basic random forest algorithm is as follows. The recommended defaults are taken from the description in Hastie, Tibshirani, and Friedman (2008).

1. Pick a minimum leaf size $N_{\min}$ (default $= 5$), a minimal split fraction $\alpha \in [0, 1)$, and a sampling number $m < p$ (default $= p/3$).
2. For $b = 1, \ldots, B$:
   (a) Draw a nonparametric bootstrap sample.
   (b) Grow a regression tree on the bootstrap sample using the following steps:
      i. Select m variables at random from the p regressors.
      ii. Among these m variables, pick the one that produces the best regression split, where each split subsample has at least $N_{\min}$ observations and at least a fraction α of the observations in the branch.
      iii. Split the bootstrap sample accordingly.
   (c) Stop when each leaf has between $N_{\min}$ and $2N_{\min} - 1$ observations.
   (d) Set $\widehat{m}_b(x)$ as the sample mean of Y on each leaf of the bootstrap tree.
3. $\widehat{m}_{\mathrm{rf}}(x) = B^{-1} \sum_{B=1}^{b} \widehat{m}_b(x)$.

Using randomization to reduce the number of variables from p to m at each step alters the tree structure and thereby reduces the correlation between the bootstrapped regression trees. This reduces the variance of the bootstrap average.

The infinitesimal jackknife (29.18) can be used for variance and standard error estimation, as discussed in Wager, Hastie, and Efron (2014).

Although random forests are popular in applications, a distributional theory has been slow to develop. Some of the more recent results have made progress by focusing on random forests generated by subsampling rather than bootstrap (see the discussion at the end of Section 29.16).

A variant proposed by Wager and Athey (2018) is to use **honest trees** (see the discussion at the end of Section 29.15) to remove the dependence between the sample splits and the sample means.

Consistency and asymptotic normality has been established by Wager and Athey (2018). They assume that the conditional expectation and variance are Lipschitz-continuous in x, $X \sim U[0,1]^p$, and p is fixed.[5] They assume that the random forest is created by subsampling, estimated by honest trees, and that the minimal split fraction satisfies $0 < \alpha \leq 0.2$. Under these conditions, they establish that pointwise in x,

$$\frac{\widehat{m}_{\mathrm{rf}}(x) - m(x)}{\sqrt{V_n(x)}} \underset{d}{\longrightarrow} \mathrm{N}(0,1)$$

for some variance sequence $V_n(x) \to 0$. These results justify inference for random forest estimation of the regression function and standard error calculation. The asymptotic distribution does not contain a bias component, indicating that the estimator is undersmoothed. The Wager-Athey conditions for asymptotic normality are surprisingly weak. The theory does not give insight, however, into the convergence rate of the estimator. The essential idea of the result is as follows. The splitting algorithm and restrictions ensure that the regressor space is (in a rough sense) evenly split into $N \sim n^{\gamma}$ leaves which grows at a power rate in n. This ensures that the estimator is asymptotically unbiased. With suitable control over γ, the squared bias can be made smaller than the variance. The assumption that $\alpha > 0$ ensures that the number of observations per leaf increases with n. When combined with the honest tree construction, this ensures asymptotic normality of the estimator.

Furthermore, Wager and Athey (2018) assert (but do not provide a proof) that the variance $V_n(x)$ can be consistently estimated by the infinitesimal jackknife (29.18), in the sense that $\widehat{V}_n(x)/V_n(x) \underset{p}{\longrightarrow} 1$.

The standard computational implementation of random forests is the R `randomForest` command.

29.18 ENSEMBLING

"Ensembling" is the term used in machine learning for model averaging across machine learning algorithms. Ensembling is popular in applied machine learning.

Suppose you have a set of estimators (e.g., CV selection, James-Stein shrinkage, JMA, SBIC, PCA, kernel regression, series regression, ridge regression, Lasso, regression tree, bagged regression tree, and random forest). Which should you use? It is reasonable to expect that one method may work well with some types of data and other methods may work well with other types of data. The principle of model averaging suggests that you can do better by taking a weighted average rather than just selecting one.

We discussed model averaging models in Sections 28.26–28.31. Ensembling for machine learning can use many of the same methods. One popular method known as **stacking** is the same as JMA discussed in Section 28.29. This method selects the model averaging weights by minimizing a CV criterion, subject to the constraint that the weights are nonnegative and sum to 1.

[5]The authors claim that the uniform distribution assumption on X can be replaced by the condition that the joint density is bounded away from 0 and infinity.

Unfortunately, the theoretical literature concerning ensembling is thin. Much of the advice concerning specific methods is based on empirical performance.

29.19 LASSO IV

Belloni, Chen, Chernozhukov, and Hansen (2012) propose Lasso for estimation of the reduced form of an instrumental variables regression.

The model is linear IV:

$$\begin{aligned} Y &= X'\beta + e \\ \mathbb{E}\left[e \mid Z\right] &= 0 \\ X &= \Gamma' Z + U \\ \mathbb{E}\left[U \mid Z\right] &= 0 \end{aligned}$$

where β is $k \times 1$ (fixed), and Γ is $p \times n$, with p large. If $p > n$, the 2SLS estimator equals least squares. If $p < n$ but large, the 2SLS estimator suffers from the "many instruments" problem. The authors' recommendation is to estimate Γ by Lasso or post-Lasso.[6]

The reduced-form equations for the endogenous regressors are $X_j = \gamma_j' Z + U_j$. Each is estimated separately by Lasso, yielding coefficient estimates $\widehat{\gamma}_j$ that are stacked into the matrix $\widehat{\Gamma}_{\text{Lasso}}$ and used to form the predicted values $\widehat{\boldsymbol{X}}_{\text{Lasso}} = \boldsymbol{Z}\widehat{\Gamma}_{\text{Lasso}}$. The Lasso IV estimator is

$$\widehat{\beta}_{\text{Lasso-IV}} = \left(\widehat{\boldsymbol{X}}'_{\text{Lasso}}\boldsymbol{X}\right)^{-1}\left(\widehat{\boldsymbol{X}}'_{\text{Lasso}}\boldsymbol{Y}\right).$$

The paper discusses alternative formulations. One is obtained by split-sample estimation as in Angrist and Krueger (1995) (see Section 12.14). Divide the sample randomly into two independent halves A and B. Use A to estimate the reduced-form equations by Lasso. Then use B to estimate the structural coefficient β. Specifically, using sample A, construct the Lasso coefficient estimate matrix $\widehat{\Gamma}_{\text{Lasso},A}$. Combine this with sample B to create the predicted values $\widehat{\boldsymbol{X}}_{\text{Lasso},B} = \boldsymbol{Z}_B\widehat{\Gamma}_{\text{Lasso},A}$. Finally, using B, construct the estimator

$$\widehat{\beta}_{\text{Lasso},B} = \left(\widehat{\boldsymbol{X}}'_{\text{Lasso},B}\boldsymbol{X}_B\right)^{-1}\left(\widehat{\boldsymbol{X}}'_{\text{Lasso},B}\boldsymbol{Y}_B\right).$$

We can reverse the procedure. Use B to estimate the reduced-form coefficient matrix $\widehat{\Gamma}_{\text{Lasso},B}$ by Lasso, and use A to estimate the structural coefficient, thus $\widehat{\boldsymbol{X}}_{\text{Lasso},A} = \boldsymbol{Z}_A\widehat{\Gamma}_{\text{Lasso},B}$. The moments are averaged to obtain the Lasso SSIV estimator:

$$\widehat{\beta}_{\text{Lasso-SSIV}} = \left(\widehat{\boldsymbol{X}}'_{\text{Lasso},B}\boldsymbol{X}_B + \widehat{\boldsymbol{X}}'_{\text{Lasso},A}\boldsymbol{X}_A\right)^{-1}\left(\widehat{\boldsymbol{X}}'_{\text{Lasso},B}\boldsymbol{Y}_B + \widehat{\boldsymbol{X}}'_{\text{Lasso},A}\boldsymbol{Y}_A\right).$$

In later work (see Section 29.22), the authors describe $\widehat{\beta}_{\text{Lasso},B}$ as a "sample split" and $\widehat{\beta}_{\text{Lasso-SSIV}}$ as a "cross-fit" estimator.

Using the asymptotic theory for Lasso estimation, the authors show that these estimators are equivalent to estimation using the infeasible instrument $W = \Gamma' Z$.

---

[6]As they discuss, any machine learning estimator can be used, though the specific assumptions listed in their paper are for Lasso estimation.

Theorem 29.4 Under the assumptions listed in theorem 3 of Belloni, Chen, Chernozhukov, and Hansen (2012), including

$$\|\Gamma\|_0 \frac{\log p}{\sqrt{n}} \to 0 \tag{29.19}$$

then

$$\left(\boldsymbol{Q}^{-1}\Omega\boldsymbol{Q}^{-1}\right)\sqrt{n}\left(\widehat{\beta}_{\text{Lasso-IV}} - \beta\right) \underset{d}{\longrightarrow} \mathrm{N}\left(0, \boldsymbol{I}_k\right) \tag{29.20}$$

where $\boldsymbol{Q} = \mathbb{E}\left[WW'\right]$, $\Omega = \mathbb{E}\left[WW'e^2\right]$, and $W = \Gamma'Z$. Furthermore, the standard covariance matrix estimators are consistent for the asymptotic covariance matrix. The same distribution result holds for $\widehat{\beta}_{\text{Lasso-SSIV}}$ under the assumptions listed in their theorem 7. In particular, (29.19) is replaced by

$$\|\Gamma\|_0 \frac{\log p}{n} \to 0. \tag{29.21}$$

For a sketch of the proof, see Section 29.23.

Equation (29.19) requires that the reduced-form coefficient Γ is sparse in the sense that the number of nonzero reduced-form coefficients $\|\Gamma\|_0$ grows more slowly than $\sqrt{n}$. This allows p to grow exponentially with n but at a somewhat slower rate than allowed by Theorem 29.3. Condition (29.19) is one of the key assumptions needed for the distribution result (29.20).

For Lasso SSIV, equation (29.21) replaces (29.19). This rate condition is weaker, allowing p to grow at the same rate as for regression estimation. The difference is due to the split-sample estimation, which breaks the dependence between the reduced-form coefficient estimates and the second-stage structural estimates. There are two interpretable implications of the difference between (29.19) and (29.21). First, a direct implication is that Lasso SSIV allows for larger number of variables p. Second, an indirect implication is that for any set of variables, Lasso SSIV will have reduced bias relative to Lasso IV. Both interpretations suggest that Lasso SSIV is the preferred estimator.

Belloni, Chen, Chernozhukov, and Hansen (2012) extend Theorem 29.4 to allow for approximate sparsity (as in Section 29.12) at the cost of more restrictive rate conditions.

An important disadvantage of the split-sample and cross-fit estimators is that they depend on the random sorting of the observations into the samples A and B. Consequently, two researchers will obtain two different estimators. Furthermore, the split-sample estimators use $n/2$ observations rather than n, which may impact finite-sample performance. A deduction is that the split-sample estimators are not appropriate when n is small.

IV Lasso can be implemented in Stata using the downloadable package `ivlasso`.

29.20 DOUBLE SELECTION LASSO

Post-estimation inference is difficult with most machine learning estimators. For example, consider the post-Lasso estimator (least squares applied to the regressors selected by the Lasso). This is a PMS estimator, as discussed in Sections 28.16 and 28.17. As shown in Section 28.17, the coverage probability of standard confidence intervals applied to PMS estimators can be far from the nominal level. Belloni, Chernozhukov, and Hansen (2014b) proposed an alternative estimation and inference method that achives better coverage rates.

Consider the linear model

$$Y = D\theta + X'\beta + e \tag{29.22}$$
$$\mathbb{E}[e \mid D, X] = 0$$

where Y and D are scalar, and X is $p \times 1$. The variable D is the main focus of the regression; the variable X is a control. The goal is inference on θ.

Suppose you estimate model (29.22) by group post-Lasso, only penalizing β. This performs selection on the variable X, resulting in a least squares regression of Y on D and the selected variables in X. This is identical to the model studied in Section 28.17 (except that in that analysis, selection was performed by testing), where Figure 28.2 shows that the coverage probabilities for θ are downward biased, and the distortions are serious. The distortions are primarily affected by (and increasing in) the correlation between D and X.

Belloni, Chernozhukov, and Hansen (2014b) deduce that improved coverage accuracy can be achieved if the variable X is included in the regression (29.22) when X and D are correlated. This gives rise to the practical suggestion to perform what they call **double-selection**. We start by specifying an auxiliary equation for D:

$$D = X'\gamma + V \tag{29.23}$$
$$\mathbb{E}[V \mid X] = 0.$$

Substituting (29.23) into (29.22), we obtain a reduced form for Y:

$$Y = X'\eta + U \tag{29.24}$$
$$\mathbb{E}[U \mid X] = 0$$

where $\eta = \beta + \gamma\theta$, and $U = e + V\theta$. The proposed double-selection algorithm applies model selection (e.g., Lasso selection) separately to equations (29.23) and (29.24), takes the union of the selected regressors, and then estimates (29.22) by least squares using the selected regressors. This method ensures that a variable X is included if it is relevant for the regression (29.22) or if it is correlated with D.

The double-selection estimator as recommended by Belloni, Chernozhukov, and Hansen (2014b) is:

1. Estimate (29.23) by Lasso. Let X_1 be the selected variables from X.
2. Estimate (29.24) by Lasso. Let X_2 be the selected variables from X.
3. Let $\widetilde{X} = X_1 \cup X_2$ be the union of the variables in X_1 and X_2.
4. Regress Y on $(D, \widetilde{X})$ to obtain the double-selection coefficient estimate $\widehat{\theta}_{\mathrm{DS}}$.
5. Calculate a conventional (heteroskedastic) standard error for $\widehat{\theta}_{\mathrm{DS}}$.

Belloni, Chernozhukov, and Hansen (2014b) show that when both (29.22) and (29.23) satisfy an approximate sparsity structure (so that the regressions are well approximated by a finite set of regressors), then the double-selection estimator $\widehat{\theta}_{\mathrm{DS}}$ and its t-ratio are asymptotically normal, so conventional inferernce methods are valid. Their proof is technically tedious and so is not repeated here. The essential idea is that because $\widetilde{X}$ includes the variables in X_2, the estimator $\widehat{\theta}_{\mathrm{DS}}$ is asymptotically equivalent to the regression where D is replaced with the error V from (29.23). Since V is uncorrelated with the regressors in X, the estimator and t-ratio satisfy the conventional nonselection asymptotic distribution.

It should be emphasized that this distributional claim is asymptotic; finite sample inferences remain distorted from nominal levels. Furthermore, the result rests on the adequacy of the approximate sparsity assumption for both the structural equation (29.22) and the auxillary regression (29.23).

The primary advantage of the double-selection estimator is its simplicity and clear intuitive structure.

In Stata, the double-selection Lasso estimator can be computed by the `dsregress` command or with the `pdslasso` add-on package. Double-selection is available in R with the `hdm` package.

29.21 POST-REGULARIZATION LASSO

A potential improvement on double-selection Lasso is the **post-regularization** Lasso estimator of Chernozhukov, Hansen, and Spindler (2015), which is labeled as **partialing-out Lasso** in the Stata manual. The estimator is essentially the same as Robinson (1988) for the partially linear model (see Section 19.24) but is estimated by Lasso rather than kernel regression.

We first transform the structural equation (29.22) to eliminate the high-dimensional component. Take the expected value of (29.22) conditional on X, and subtract from each side. This leads to the equation

$$Y - \mathbb{E}[Y \mid X] = (D - \mathbb{E}[D \mid X])\,\theta + e.$$

Notice that this equation eliminates the regressor X and the high-dimensional coefficient β. The models (29.23)–(29.24) specify $\mathbb{E}[Y \mid X]$ and $\mathbb{E}[D \mid X]$ as linear functions of X. Substituting these expressions, we obtain

$$Y - X'\eta = \left(D - X'\gamma\right)\theta + e. \tag{29.25}$$

If η and γ were known, the coefficient θ could be estimated by least squares. As η and γ are unknown, they need to be estimated. Chernozhukov, Hansen, and Spindler (2015) recommend estimation by Lasso or post-Lasso, separately for Y and D.

The estimator recommended by Chernozhukov, Hansen, and Spindler (2015) is:

1. Estimate (29.23) by Lasso or post-Lasso with Lasso parameter λ_1. Let $\widehat{\gamma}$ be the coefficient estimator and $\widehat{V}_i = D_i - X_i'\widehat{\gamma}$ the residual.
2. Estimate (29.24) by Lasso or post-Lasso with Lasso parameter λ_2. Let $\widehat{\eta}$ be the coefficient estimator and $\widehat{U}_i = Y_i - X_i'\widehat{\eta}$ the residual.
3. Let $\widehat{\theta}_{\mathrm{PR}}$ be the OLS coefficient from the regression of $\widehat{U}$ on $\widehat{V}$.
4. Calculate a conventional (heteroskedastic) standard error for $\widehat{\theta}_{\mathrm{PR}}$.

Chernozhukov, Hansen, and Spindler (2015) introduce the following insight to understand why $\widehat{\theta}_{\mathrm{PR}}$ may be relatively insensitive to post-model-selection. The reason model selection invalidates inference is because when the variables D and X are correlated, the moment condition for θ is sensitive to β. Specifically, the moment condition for θ based on (29.22) is

$$m(\theta, \beta) = \mathbb{E}\left[D\left(Y - D\theta - X'\beta\right)\right] = 0.$$

Its **sensitivity** with respect to β is its derivative evaluated at the true coefficients,

$$\frac{\partial}{\partial \beta} m(\theta, \beta) = -\mathbb{E}\left[DX'\right]$$

which is nonzero when D and X are correlated. Thus inclusion/exclusion of the variable X has an impact on the moment condition for θ and hence its solution.

In contrast, the moment condition for θ based on (29.25) is

$$\begin{aligned} m_{\mathrm{PR}}(\theta,\beta) &= \mathbb{E}\left[\left(D - X'\gamma\right)\left(Y - X'\eta - \left(D - X'\gamma\right)\theta\right)\right] \\ &= \mathbb{E}\left[\left(D - X'\gamma\right)\left(Y - D\theta - X'\beta\right)\right]. \end{aligned}$$

Its sensitivity with respect to β is

$$\frac{\partial}{\partial\beta} m_{\mathrm{PR}}(\theta,\beta) = -\mathbb{E}\left[\left(D - X'\gamma\right)X'\right] = -\mathbb{E}\left[VX'\right] = 0.$$

This equals 0, because V is a regression error as specified in (29.23) and thus is uncorrelated with X. Since the sensitivity of $m_{\mathrm{PR}}(\theta,\beta)$ with respect to β is 0, inclusion/exclusion of the variable X has only a mild impact on the moment condition for θ and its estimator.

These insights are formalized in the following distribution theory.

Theorem 29.5 Suppose model (29.22)–(29.23) holds and Assumption 29.1 holds for both β and γ. Assume that each regressor has been standardized so that $n^{-1}\boldsymbol{X}_j'\boldsymbol{X}_j = 1$. Suppose $e \mid X \sim \mathrm{N}\left(0, \sigma_e^2(X)\right)$ and $V \mid X \sim \mathrm{N}\left(0, \sigma_V^2(X)\right)$, where $\sigma_e^2(x) \le \overline{\sigma}_e^2 < \infty$ and $\sigma_V^2(x) \le \overline{\sigma}_V^2 < \infty$. For some C_1 and C_2 sufficiently large, the Lasso parameters satisfy $\lambda_1 = C_1\sqrt{n\log p}$ and $\lambda_2 = C_2\sqrt{n\log p}$. Assume $p \to \infty$ and

$$\left(\|\beta\|_0 + \|\gamma\|_0\right)\frac{\log p}{\sqrt{n}} = o(1). \tag{29.26}$$

Then

$$\sqrt{n}\left(\widehat{\theta}_{\mathrm{PR}} - \theta\right) \underset{d}{\longrightarrow} \mathrm{N}\left(0, \frac{\mathbb{E}\left[V^2e^2\right]}{\left(\mathbb{E}\left[V^2\right]\right)^2}\right).$$

Furthermore, the standard variance estimator for $\widehat{\theta}_{\mathrm{PR}}$ is consistent for the asymptotic variance.

For a proof, see Section 29.23.

To simplify the proof, Theorem 29.5 uses the assumption of normal errors. This is not essential. Chernozhukov, Hansen, and Spindler (2015) state the same distributional result under weaker regularity conditions.

Theorem 29.5 shows that the post-regularization (partialing-out) Lasso estimator has a conventional asymptotic distribution, allowing conventional inference for the coefficient θ. The key rate condition is (29.26), which is stronger than required for Lasso estimation, and is identical to (29.19) used for Lasso IV. Equation (29.26) requires that both β and γ are sparse. The condition (29.26) can be relaxed to allow approximate sparsity, as in Section 29.12, at the cost of a more restrictive rate condition.

The advantage of the post-regularization estimator $\widehat{\theta}_{\mathrm{PR}}$ over the double-selection estimator $\widehat{\theta}_{\mathrm{DS}}$ is efficiency. The post-regularization estimator uses only the relevant components of X to separately demean Y and D, leading to greater parsimony. Different components of X may be relevant to D and Y. The post-regularization estimator allows such distinctions and estimates each separately. In contrast, the double-selection estimator uses the union of the two regressor sets for estimation of θ, leading to a less parsimonious specification. As a consequence, an advantage of the double-selection estimator is reduced bias and robustness. Regarding the theory, the derivation of the asymptotic theory for the post-regularization estimator is considerably easier than that for the double-selection estimator, as it only involves the manipulation of rates of convergence, whereas the double-selection estimator requires a careful attention to the handling of the union of the regressor sets.

The partialing-out Lasso estimator is available with the `poregress` command in Stata (implemented with post-Lasso estimation only), or with the `pdslasso` add-on package. Partialing-out Lasso is available in R with the `hdm` package.

29.22 DOUBLE/DEBIASED MACHINE LEARNING

The most recent contribution to inference methods for model (29.22) is the **double/debiased machine learning (DML)** estimator of Chernozhukov, Chetverikov, Demirer, Duflo, Hansen, Newey, and Robins (2018). Our description will focus on linear regression estimated by Lasso, though their treatment is considerably more general. This estimation method has received considerable attention among econometricians in recent years and is considered the state-of-the-art estimation method.

The DML estimator extends the post-regularization estimator of Section 29.21 by adding sample-splitting similarly to the split-sample IV estimator (see Section 29.19). The authors argue that this reduces the dependence between the estimation stages and can improve performance.

As presented in Section 29.21, the post-regularization estimator first estimates the coefficients γ and η in the models (29.23) and (29.24) and then estimates the coefficient θ. The split-sample estimator performs these estimation steps using separate samples. The DML estimator takes this a step further by using K-fold partitioning. The estimation algorithm is as follows:

1. Randomly partition the sample into K independent folds A_k, $k=1,\dots,K$, of roughly equal size n/K.
2. Write the data matrices for each fold as $(\boldsymbol{Y}_k, \boldsymbol{D}_k, \boldsymbol{X}_k)$.
3. For $k=1,\dots,K$
   (a) Use all observations except those for fold k to estimate the coefficients γ and η in (29.23) and (29.24) by Lasso or post-Lasso. Write these leave-fold-out estimators as $\widehat{\gamma}_{-k}$ and $\widehat{\eta}_{-k}$.
   (b) Set $\widehat{\boldsymbol{V}}_k = \boldsymbol{D}_k - \boldsymbol{X}_k\widehat{\gamma}_{-k}$ and $\widehat{\boldsymbol{U}}_k = \boldsymbol{Y}_k - \boldsymbol{X}_k\widehat{\eta}_{-k}$. These are the estimated values of V and U for observations in the kth fold using the leave-fold-out estimators.
4. Set $\widehat{\theta}_{\mathrm{DML}} = \left(\sum_{k=1}^K \widehat{\boldsymbol{V}}_k'\widehat{\boldsymbol{V}}_k\right)^{-1}\left(\sum_{k=1}^K \widehat{\boldsymbol{V}}_k'\widehat{\boldsymbol{U}}_k\right)$. Equivalently, stack $\widehat{\boldsymbol{V}}_k$ and $\widehat{\boldsymbol{U}}_k$ into $n\times 1$ vectors $\widehat{\boldsymbol{V}}$ and $\widehat{\boldsymbol{U}}$ and set $\widehat{\theta}_{\mathrm{DML}} = \left(\widehat{\boldsymbol{V}}'\widehat{\boldsymbol{V}}\right)^{-1}\left(\widehat{\boldsymbol{V}}'\widehat{\boldsymbol{U}}\right)$.
5. Construct a conventional (heteroskedastic) standard error for $\widehat{\theta}_{\mathrm{DML}}$.

The authors call $\widehat{\theta}_{\mathrm{DML}}$ a **cross-fit** estimator, because in the $K=2$ case, it performs sample splitting in both directions and is therefore fully asymptotically efficient. The estimator as described above is labeled the "DML2" estimator by the authors. An alternative they label "DML1" is $\widehat{\theta}_{\mathrm{DML1}} = \sum_{k=1}^K \left(\widehat{\boldsymbol{V}}_k'\widehat{\boldsymbol{V}}_k\right)^{-1}\left(\widehat{\boldsymbol{V}}_k'\widehat{\boldsymbol{U}}_k\right)$. These estimators are asymptotically equivalent, but DML2 is preferred.

The estimator requires the selection of the number of folds K. Similarly to K-fold CV, Chernozhukov et al. (2018) recommend $K=10$. Computational cost is roughly proportional to K.

Theorem 29.6 Under the assumptions of Theorem 29.5,

$$\sqrt{n}\left(\widehat{\theta}_{\mathrm{DML}} - \theta\right) \underset{d}{\longrightarrow} \mathrm{N}\left(0, \frac{\mathbb{E}\left[V^2e^2\right]}{\left(\mathbb{E}\left[V^2\right]\right)^2}\right).$$

Furthermore, the standard variance estimator for $\widehat{\theta}_{\mathrm{DML}}$ is consistent for the asymptotic variance.

Theorem 29.6 shows that the DML estimator achieves a standard asymptotic distribution. The proof is a straightforward extension of that for Theorem 29.5 and so is omitted. Weaker (but high-level) regularity conditions are provided by Chernozhukov et al. (2018).

The authors argue that the DML estimator has improved sampling performance due to an improved rate of convergence of certain error terms. If we examine the proof of Theorem 29.5, one of the error bounds is (29.44), which shows that

$$\left|\left(\widehat{\gamma}_{-k}-\gamma\right)' \frac{1}{\sqrt{n}} \boldsymbol{X}_k' \boldsymbol{e}_k\right| \leq O_p\left(\|\gamma\|_0 \frac{\log p}{\sqrt{n}}\right) = o_p(1). \tag{29.27}$$

Under sample splitting, however, we have an improved rate of convergence. The components $\widehat{\gamma}_{-k}$ and $\boldsymbol{X}_k'\boldsymbol{e}_k$ are independent. Thus the left side of (29.27), conditional on $\widehat{\gamma}_{-k}$ and $\boldsymbol{X}_k$, has mean 0 and has conditional variance bounded by $\overline{\sigma}_e^2\left(\widehat{\gamma}_{-k}-\gamma\right)' \frac{1}{n} \boldsymbol{X}_k' \boldsymbol{X}_k\left(\widehat{\gamma}_{-k}-\gamma\right)$. This is $O_p\left(\|\gamma\|_0 \frac{\log p}{n}\right)$ by Theorem 29.3. Hence (29.27) is $O_p\left(\sqrt{\|\gamma\|_0 \frac{\log p}{n}}\right)$, which is of smaller order. This improvement suggests that the deviations from the asymptotic approximation should be smaller under sample splitting and the DML estimator. The improvements, however, do not lead to a relaxation of the regularity conditions. The proof requires bounding the terms (29.42) and (29.43), and these are not improved by sample splititng. Consequently, it is unclear if the distributional impact of sample splitting is large or small.

The advantage of the DML estimator over the post-regularization estimator is that the sample splitting eliminates the dependence between the two estimation steps, thereby reducing post-model-selection bias. The procedure has several disadvantages, however. First, the estimator is random due to the sample splitting. Two researchers with the same dataset but making different random splits will obtain two distinct estimators. This arbitrariness is unsettling. The randomness can be reduced by using a larger value of K, but this increases computation cost. Another disadvantage of sample-splitting is that estimation of γ and η is performed using smaller samples, which reduces estimation efficiency, though this effect is minor if $K \geq 10$. Regardless, these considerations suggest that DML may be most appropriate for settings with large n and $K \geq 10$.

At the beginning of this section, the DML estimator was described as the "state-of-the-art." This field is rapidly developing, so this specific estimator soon may be eclipsed by a further iteration.

In Stata, the DML estimator is available with the `xporegress` command. By default it implements the DML2 estimator with $K = 10$ folds. The coefficients γ and η are estimated by post-Lasso.

29.23 TECHNICAL PROOFS*

Proof of Theorem 29.2 Combining (29.8) and (29.9), we find that

$$\begin{aligned}
\operatorname{mse}\left[\widehat{\beta}_{\text{ridge}} \mid \boldsymbol{X}\right] &= \operatorname{var}\left[\widehat{\beta}_{\text{ridge}} \mid \boldsymbol{X}\right] + \operatorname{bias}\left[\widehat{\beta}_{\text{ridge}} \mid \boldsymbol{X}\right] \operatorname{bias}\left[\widehat{\beta}_{\text{ridge}} \mid \boldsymbol{X}\right]' \\
&= \left(\boldsymbol{X}'\boldsymbol{X} + \lambda \boldsymbol{I}_p\right)^{-1}\left(\boldsymbol{X}'\boldsymbol{D}\boldsymbol{X} + \lambda^2 \beta\beta'\right)\left(\boldsymbol{X}'\boldsymbol{X} + \lambda \boldsymbol{I}_p\right)^{-1}.
\end{aligned}$$

The MSE of the least squares estimator is

$$\begin{aligned}
\operatorname{mse}\left[\widehat{\beta}_{\text{ols}} \mid \boldsymbol{X}\right] &= \left(\boldsymbol{X}'\boldsymbol{X}\right)^{-1}\left(\boldsymbol{X}'\boldsymbol{D}\boldsymbol{X}\right)\left(\boldsymbol{X}'\boldsymbol{X}\right)^{-1} \\
&= \left(\boldsymbol{X}'\boldsymbol{X} + \lambda \boldsymbol{I}_p\right)^{-1}\left(\boldsymbol{X}'\boldsymbol{X} + \lambda \boldsymbol{I}_p\right)\left(\boldsymbol{X}'\boldsymbol{X}\right)^{-1}\left(\boldsymbol{X}'\boldsymbol{D}\boldsymbol{X}\right)\left(\boldsymbol{X}'\boldsymbol{X}\right)^{-1}\left(\boldsymbol{X}'\boldsymbol{X} + \lambda \boldsymbol{I}_p\right)\left(\boldsymbol{X}'\boldsymbol{X} + \lambda \boldsymbol{I}_p\right)^{-1}
\end{aligned}$$

$$= \left(X'X + \lambda I_p\right)^{-1} \Big(X'DX + \lambda \left(X'X\right)^{-1} \left(X'DX\right) + \lambda \left(X'DX\right) \left(X'X\right)^{-1}$$
$$+\lambda^2 \left(X'X\right)^{-1} \left(X'DX\right) \left(X'X\right)^{-1}\Big) \left(X'X + \lambda I_p\right)^{-1}$$
$$\geq \left(X'X + \lambda I_p\right)^{-1} \Big(X'DX + \lambda \left(X'X\right)^{-1} \left(X'DX\right) + \lambda \left(X'DX\right) \left(X'X\right)^{-1}\Big) \left(X'X + \lambda I_p\right)^{-1}.$$

Their difference is

$$\operatorname{mse}\left[\widehat{\beta}_{\mathrm{ols}} \mid X\right] - \operatorname{mse}\left[\widehat{\beta}_{\mathrm{ridge}} \mid X\right] \geq \lambda \left(X'X + \lambda I_p\right)^{-1} A \left(X'X + \lambda I_p\right)^{-1} \tag{29.28}$$

where

$$A = \left(X'X\right)^{-1} \left(X'DX\right) + \left(X'DX\right) \left(X'X\right)^{-1} - \lambda \beta \beta'.$$

The right-hand side of (29.28) is positive definite if $A > 0$. Its smallest eigenvalue satisfies

$$\lambda_{\min}(A) = 2 \min_{\alpha'\alpha=1} \alpha' \left(X'X\right)^{-1/2} \left(X'DX\right) \left(X'X\right)^{-1/2} \alpha - \lambda \beta'\beta \geq 2 \min_{h'h=1} h'Dh - \lambda\beta'\beta = 2\underline{\sigma}^2 - \lambda\beta'\beta$$

which is strictly positive when $0 < \lambda < 2\underline{\sigma}^2/\beta'\beta$, as assumed. This shows that (29.28) is positive definite. ■

Proof of Theorem 29.3 Define $V_{nj} = n^{-1} \sum_{i=1}^{n} X_{ji}^2 \sigma^2(X_i)$. The normality assumption implies that for each j, $\left(nV_{nj}\right)^{-1/2} X_j' e \sim \mathrm{N}(0,1)$. The Gaussian tail inequality (B.39) implies that for any x,

$$\mathbb{P}\left[\left|\frac{1}{\sqrt{nV_{nj}}} X_j' e\right| > x\right] \leq 2 \exp\left(-\frac{x^2}{2}\right). \tag{29.29}$$

By Boole's inequality (B.24); (29.29); Jensen's inequality, $V_{nj} \leq \overline{\sigma}^2$; and (29.14), we have

$$\begin{aligned}
\mathbb{P}\left[\left\|\frac{1}{n} X' e\right\|_\infty > \frac{\lambda}{4n} \,\middle|\, X\right] &= \mathbb{P}\left[\max_{1\leq j\leq p}\left|\frac{1}{n} X_j' e\right| > \frac{\lambda}{4n} \,\middle|\, X\right] \\
&= \mathbb{P}\left[\bigcup_{1\leq j\leq p}\left|\frac{1}{\sqrt{nV_{nj}}} X_j' e\right| > \frac{\lambda}{4\sqrt{nV_{nj}}} \,\middle|\, X\right] \\
&\leq \sum_{j=1}^{p} \mathbb{P}\left[\left|\frac{1}{\sqrt{nV_{nj}}} X_j' e\right| > \frac{\lambda}{4\sqrt{nV_{nj}}} \,\middle|\, X\right] \\
&\leq \sum_{j=1}^{p} 2\exp\left(-\frac{\lambda^2}{16 n V_{nj}}\right) \\
&\leq 2p \exp\left(-\frac{C^2}{16\overline{\sigma}^2} \log p\right) \\
&= 2p^{1-C^2/16\overline{\sigma}^2}.
\end{aligned} \tag{29.30}$$

Since $p > 1$, (29.30) can be made arbitrarily small by selecting C sufficiently large, which shows that

$$\left\|\frac{1}{n} X' e\right\|_\infty \leq \frac{\lambda}{4n} \tag{29.31}$$

holds with arbitrarily large probability. The remainder of the proof is algebraic, based on manipulations of the estimation criterion function, conditional on the event (29.31).

Since $\widehat{\beta}$ minimizes $\mathrm{SSE}_1(\beta,\lambda)$, it satisfies $\mathrm{SSE}_1\left(\widehat{\beta},\lambda\right) \le \mathrm{SSE}_1(\beta,\lambda)$ or

$$\left(\boldsymbol{Y}-\boldsymbol{X}\widehat{\beta}\right)'\left(\boldsymbol{Y}-\boldsymbol{X}\widehat{\beta}\right)+\lambda\left\|\widehat{\beta}\right\|_1 \le \boldsymbol{e}'\boldsymbol{e}+\lambda\|\beta\|_1.$$

Writing out the left side, dividing by n, and rearranging and defining $R_n=\left(\widehat{\beta}-\beta\right)'\boldsymbol{Q}_n\left(\widehat{\beta}-\beta\right)$, this implies

$$\begin{aligned}
R_n+\frac{\lambda}{n}\left\|\widehat{\beta}\right\|_1 &\le \frac{2}{n}\boldsymbol{e}'\boldsymbol{X}\left(\widehat{\beta}-\beta\right)+\frac{\lambda}{n}\|\beta\|_1\\
&\le 2\left\|\frac{1}{n}\boldsymbol{X}'\boldsymbol{e}\right\|_\infty\left\|\widehat{\beta}-\beta\right\|_1+\frac{\lambda}{n}\|\beta\|_1\\
&\le \frac{\lambda}{2n}\left\|\widehat{\beta}-\beta\right\|_1+\frac{\lambda}{n}\|\beta\|_1.
\end{aligned}$$

The second inequality is Hölder's (29.2), and the third holds by (29.31).

Partition $\widehat{\beta}=\left(\widehat{\beta}_0,\widehat{\beta}_1\right)$ conformably with $\beta=(\beta_0,\beta_1)$. Using the additivity property of the 1-norm and the fact $\beta_0=0$, the above expression implies

$$\begin{aligned}
R_n+\frac{\lambda}{2n}\left\|\widehat{\beta}_0-\beta_0\right\|_1 &\le \frac{\lambda}{2n}\left\|\widehat{\beta}_1-\beta_1\right\|_1+\frac{\lambda}{n}\left(\|\beta_1\|_1-\left\|\widehat{\beta}_1\right\|_1\right)\\
&\le \frac{3\lambda}{2n}\left\|\widehat{\beta}_1-\beta_1\right\|_1 \qquad (29.32)
\end{aligned}$$

the second inequality uses the fact $\|\beta\|_1 \le \left\|\widehat{\beta}_1-\beta_1\right\|_1+\left\|\widehat{\beta}_1\right\|_1$, which follows from (29.3).

An implication of (29.32) is $\left\|\widehat{\beta}_0-\beta_0\right\|_1 \le 3\left\|\widehat{\beta}_1-\beta_1\right\|_1$. Thus, $\widehat{\beta}-\beta\in B$. A consequence is that we can apply Assumption 29.1 to obtain

$$R_n=\left(\widehat{\beta}-\beta\right)'\boldsymbol{Q}_n\left(\widehat{\beta}-\beta\right)\ge c^2\left\|\widehat{\beta}-\beta\right\|_2^2. \qquad (29.33)$$

This is the only (but key) point in the proof where Assumption 29.1 is used.

Together with (29.32), (29.33) implies

$$\begin{aligned}
c^2\left\|\widehat{\beta}-\beta\right\|_2^2 &\le \frac{3\lambda}{2n}\left\|\widehat{\beta}_1-\beta_1\right\|_1\\
&\le \frac{3\lambda}{2n}\left\|\widehat{\beta}_1-\beta_1\right\|_2\left\|\widehat{\beta}_1-\beta_1\right\|_0^{1/2}\\
&\le \frac{3\lambda}{2n}\left\|\widehat{\beta}-\beta\right\|_2\|\beta\|_0^{1/2}.
\end{aligned}$$

The second inequality is (29.4). The third is $\left\|\widehat{\beta}_1-\beta_1\right\|_2 \le \left\|\widehat{\beta}-\beta\right\|_2$ and $\left\|\widehat{\beta}_1-\beta_1\right\|_0=\|\beta_1\|_0=\|\beta\|_0$. Rearranging and using (29.14), we obtain

$$\left\|\widehat{\beta}-\beta\right\|_2 \le \frac{3\lambda}{2c^2n}\|\beta\|_0^{1/2}=\frac{3C}{2c^2}\|\beta\|_0^{1/2}\sqrt{\frac{\log p}{n}}$$

which is (29.17) with $D=3C/2c^2$.

Expressions (29.32), (29.4), (29.17), and (29.14) imply

$$
\begin{aligned}
R_n + \frac{\lambda}{2n}\left\|\widehat{\beta}_0 - \beta_0\right\|_1 &\leq \frac{3\lambda}{2n}\left\|\widehat{\beta}_1 - \beta_1\right\|_2 \left\|\widehat{\beta}_1 - \beta_1\right\|_0^{1/2} \\
&\leq \frac{3\lambda}{2n}\left\|\widehat{\beta} - \beta\right\|_2 \|\beta\|_0^{1/2} \\
&\leq \frac{9C}{4c^2}\frac{\lambda}{n}\|\beta\|_0\sqrt{\frac{\log p}{n}} \qquad (29.34) \\
&= \frac{9C^2}{4c^2}\|\beta\|_0 \frac{\log p}{n}.
\end{aligned}
$$

This implies (29.15) with $D = 9C^2/4c^2$.

Equation (29.34) also implies

$$\left\|\widehat{\beta}_0 - \beta_0\right\|_1 \leq \frac{9C}{2c^2}\|\beta\|_0\sqrt{\frac{\log p}{n}}.$$

Using (29.4) and (29.17),

$$\left\|\widehat{\beta}_1 - \beta_1\right\|_1 \leq \left\|\widehat{\beta}_1 - \beta_1\right\|_2 \left\|\widehat{\beta}_1 - \beta_1\right\|_0^{1/2} \leq \left\|\widehat{\beta} - \beta\right\|_2 \|\beta\|_0^{1/2} \leq \frac{3C}{2c^2}\|\beta\|_0\sqrt{\frac{\log p}{n}}.$$

Hence

$$\left\|\widehat{\beta} - \beta\right\|_1 = \left\|\widehat{\beta}_0 - \beta_0\right\|_1 + \left\|\widehat{\beta}_1 - \beta_1\right\|_1 \leq \frac{6C}{c^2}\|\beta\|_0\sqrt{\frac{\log p}{n}}$$

which is (29.16) with $D = 6C/c^2$. ■

Proof of Theorem 29.4 I provide a sketch of the proof. Start with Lasso IV. First, consider the idealized estimator $\widehat{\beta} = \left(\boldsymbol{W}'\boldsymbol{X}\right)^{-1}\left(\boldsymbol{W}'\boldsymbol{Y}\right)$, where $\boldsymbol{W} = \boldsymbol{Z}\Gamma$. If the distribution of W does not change with n (which holds when the nonzero coefficients in Γ do not change with n), then $\widehat{\beta}$ has the asymptotic distribution (29.20) under standard assumptions. To allow the nonzero coefficients in Γ to change with n, Belloni, Chen, Chernozhukov, and Hansen (2012) use a triangular array central limit theory, which requires some additional technical conditions. Given this analysis, (29.20) holds if $\boldsymbol{W}$ can be replaced by the predicted values $\widehat{\boldsymbol{X}}_{\text{Lasso}}$ without changing (29.20). This holds if

$$\frac{1}{n}\left(\widehat{\boldsymbol{X}}_{\text{Lasso}} - \boldsymbol{W}\right)'\boldsymbol{X} \underset{p}{\longrightarrow} 0 \qquad (29.35)$$

$$\frac{1}{\sqrt{n}}\left(\widehat{\boldsymbol{X}}_{\text{Lasso}} - \boldsymbol{W}\right)'\boldsymbol{e} \underset{p}{\longrightarrow} 0. \qquad (29.36)$$

For simplicity, assume that $k = 1$. Theorem 29.3 shows that under the regularity conditions for the Lasso applied to the reduced form,

$$\left|\frac{1}{n}\left(\widehat{\boldsymbol{X}}_{\text{Lasso}} - \boldsymbol{W}\right)'\left(\widehat{\boldsymbol{X}}_{\text{Lasso}} - \boldsymbol{W}\right)\right| = \left(\widehat{\Gamma} - \Gamma\right)'\left(\frac{1}{n}\boldsymbol{Z}'\boldsymbol{Z}\right)\left(\widehat{\Gamma} - \Gamma\right) \leq O_p\left(\|\Gamma\|_0 \frac{\log p}{n}\right) \qquad (29.37)$$

and

$$\left\|\widehat{\Gamma} - \Gamma\right\|_1 \leq O_p\left(\|\Gamma\|_0\sqrt{\frac{\log p}{n}}\right). \qquad (29.38)$$

Similar to (29.30), under sufficient regularity conditions

$$\left\| \frac{1}{\sqrt{n}} \boldsymbol{Z}'\boldsymbol{e} \right\|_\infty = O_p\left(\sqrt{\log p}\right). \tag{29.39}$$

By the Schwarz inequality and (29.37),

$$\begin{aligned}
\left| \frac{1}{n} \left(\widehat{\boldsymbol{X}}_{\text{Lasso}} - \boldsymbol{W}\right)' \boldsymbol{X} \right| &\le \left| \frac{1}{n} \left(\widehat{\boldsymbol{X}}_{\text{Lasso}} - \boldsymbol{W}\right)' \left(\widehat{\boldsymbol{X}}_{\text{Lasso}} - \boldsymbol{W}\right) \right|^{1/2} \left| \frac{1}{n} \boldsymbol{X}'\boldsymbol{X} \right|^{1/2} \\
&\le O_p\left(\|\Gamma\|_0 \frac{\log p}{n} \right)^{1/2} \le o_p(1)
\end{aligned}$$

the final inequality follows from (29.19). This establishes (29.35).

By the Hölder inequality (29.2), (29.38), and (29.39),

$$\begin{aligned}
\left| \frac{1}{\sqrt{n}} \left(\widehat{\boldsymbol{X}}_{\text{Lasso}} - \boldsymbol{W}\right)' \boldsymbol{e} \right| &= \left| \left(\widehat{\Gamma} - \Gamma\right)' \frac{1}{\sqrt{n}} \boldsymbol{Z}'\boldsymbol{e} \right| \\
&\le \left\| \widehat{\Gamma} - \Gamma \right\|_1 \left\| \frac{1}{\sqrt{n}} \boldsymbol{Z}'\boldsymbol{e} \right\|_\infty \\
&\le O_p\left(\|\Gamma\|_0 \sqrt{\frac{\log p}{n}} \right) O_p\left(\sqrt{\log p}\right) \\
&= O_p\left(\|\Gamma\|_0 \frac{\log p}{\sqrt{n}} \right) \\
&\le o_p(1)
\end{aligned} \tag{29.40}$$

the final inequality follows from (29.19). This establishes (29.36).

Now consider Lasso SSIV. The steps are essentially the same except for (29.40). For this we use the fact that $\widehat{\Gamma}_{\text{Lasso},A}$ is independent of $\boldsymbol{Z}_B'\boldsymbol{e}_B$. Let $\boldsymbol{D}_B = \operatorname{diag}\left(\mathbb{E}\left[e_i^2 \mid Z_i\right]\right)$ for sample B, and assume $\mathbb{E}\left[e^2 \mid Z\right] \le \overline{\sigma}^2 < \infty$. Conditionally on A and $\boldsymbol{Z}_B$,

$$\begin{aligned}
\operatorname{var}\left[\frac{1}{\sqrt{n}} \left(\widehat{\boldsymbol{X}}'_{\text{Lasso},B} - \boldsymbol{W}_B\right)' \boldsymbol{e}_B \middle| A, \boldsymbol{Z}_B \right] &= \operatorname{var}\left[\left(\widehat{\Gamma}_{\text{Lasso},A} - \Gamma\right)' \frac{1}{\sqrt{n}} \boldsymbol{Z}_B'\boldsymbol{e}_B \middle| A, \boldsymbol{Z}_B \right] \\
&= \left(\widehat{\Gamma}_{\text{Lasso},A} - \Gamma\right)' \frac{1}{n} \boldsymbol{Z}_B'\boldsymbol{D}\boldsymbol{Z}_B \left(\widehat{\Gamma}_{\text{Lasso},A} - \Gamma\right) \\
&\le \overline{\sigma}^2 \left(\widehat{\Gamma}_{\text{Lasso},A} - \Gamma\right)' \frac{1}{n} \boldsymbol{Z}_B'\boldsymbol{Z}_B \left(\widehat{\Gamma}_{\text{Lasso},A} - \Gamma\right) \\
&= O_p\left(\|\Gamma\|_0 \frac{\log p}{n} \right) \\
&\le o_p(1)
\end{aligned}$$

the final bounds by (29.37) and (29.21). Thus $n^{-1/2}\left(\widehat{\boldsymbol{X}}'_{\text{Lasso},B} - \boldsymbol{W}_B\right)' \boldsymbol{e}_B \underset{p}{\longrightarrow} 0$, as needed. ■

Proof of Theorem 29.5 The idealized estimator $\widehat{\theta}_{\text{PR}} = \left(\boldsymbol{V}'\boldsymbol{V}\right)^{-1}\left(\boldsymbol{V}'\boldsymbol{U}\right)$ satisfies

$$\sqrt{n}\left(\widehat{\theta}_{\text{PR}} - \theta\right) = \left(n^{-1}\boldsymbol{V}'\boldsymbol{V}\right)^{-1}\left(n^{-1/2}\boldsymbol{V}'\boldsymbol{e}\right)$$

which has the stated asymptotic distribution. The theorem therefore holds if replacement of $(\boldsymbol{V}, \boldsymbol{U})$ by $(\widehat{\boldsymbol{V}}, \widehat{\boldsymbol{U}})$ is asymptotically negligible.

Since $\boldsymbol{Y} = \boldsymbol{X}\eta + \widehat{\boldsymbol{V}}\theta + \boldsymbol{X}(\widehat{\gamma} - \gamma)\theta + \boldsymbol{e}$,

$$\sqrt{n}\left(\widehat{\theta}_{\mathrm{PR}} - \theta\right) = \sqrt{n}\frac{\widehat{\boldsymbol{V}}'\widehat{\boldsymbol{U}}}{\widehat{\boldsymbol{V}}'\widehat{\boldsymbol{V}}} = \frac{\frac{1}{\sqrt{n}}\widehat{\boldsymbol{V}}'\left(\widehat{\boldsymbol{V}}\theta + \boldsymbol{X}(\widehat{\gamma} - \gamma)\theta - \boldsymbol{X}(\widehat{\eta} - \eta) + \boldsymbol{e}\right)}{\frac{1}{n}\widehat{\boldsymbol{V}}'\widehat{\boldsymbol{V}}}. \tag{29.41}$$

The denominator equals

$$\frac{1}{n}\widehat{\boldsymbol{V}}'\widehat{\boldsymbol{V}} = \frac{1}{n}\boldsymbol{V}'\boldsymbol{V} - 2(\widehat{\gamma} - \gamma)'\frac{1}{n}\boldsymbol{X}'\boldsymbol{V} + (\widehat{\gamma} - \gamma)'\boldsymbol{Q}_n(\widehat{\gamma} - \gamma).$$

The numerator equals

$$\begin{aligned}\frac{1}{\sqrt{n}}\widehat{\boldsymbol{V}}'\left(\widehat{\boldsymbol{V}}\theta + \boldsymbol{X}(\widehat{\gamma} - \gamma)\theta - \boldsymbol{X}(\widehat{\eta} - \eta) + \boldsymbol{e}\right) &= \frac{1}{\sqrt{n}}\boldsymbol{V}'\boldsymbol{e} - (\widehat{\gamma} - \gamma)'\frac{1}{\sqrt{n}}\boldsymbol{X}'\boldsymbol{e} - (\widehat{\eta} - \eta)'\frac{1}{\sqrt{n}}\boldsymbol{X}'\boldsymbol{V} \\ &\quad + \theta(\widehat{\gamma} - \gamma)'\frac{1}{\sqrt{n}}\boldsymbol{X}'\boldsymbol{V} + \sqrt{n}(\widehat{\gamma} - \gamma)'\boldsymbol{Q}_n(\widehat{\eta} - \eta) \\ &\quad - \theta\sqrt{n}(\widehat{\gamma} - \gamma)'\boldsymbol{Q}_n(\widehat{\gamma} - \gamma).\end{aligned}$$

The terms on the right side beyond the first are asymptotically negligible, because

$$\sqrt{n}(\widehat{\gamma} - \gamma)'\boldsymbol{Q}_n(\widehat{\gamma} - \gamma) \le O_p\left(\|\gamma\|_0\frac{\log p}{\sqrt{n}}\right) = o_p(1) \tag{29.42}$$

$$\sqrt{n}(\widehat{\eta} - \eta)'\boldsymbol{Q}_n(\widehat{\eta} - \eta) \le O_p\left(\|\eta\|_0\frac{\log p}{\sqrt{n}}\right) = o_p(1) \tag{29.43}$$

by Theorem 29.3 and assumption (29.26),

$$\begin{aligned}\sqrt{n}(\widehat{\gamma} - \gamma)'\boldsymbol{Q}_n(\widehat{\eta} - \eta) &\le \left(\sqrt{n}(\widehat{\gamma} - \gamma)'\boldsymbol{Q}_n(\widehat{\gamma} - \gamma)\right)^{1/2}\left(\sqrt{n}(\widehat{\eta} - \eta)'\boldsymbol{Q}_n(\widehat{\eta} - \eta)\right)^{1/2} \\ &\le O_p\left(\|\gamma\|_0^{1/2}\|\eta\|_0^{1/2}\frac{\log p}{\sqrt{n}}\right) = o_p(1)\end{aligned}$$

by the Schwarz inequality and the above results, and

$$\begin{aligned}\left|(\widehat{\gamma} - \gamma)'\frac{1}{\sqrt{n}}\boldsymbol{X}'\boldsymbol{e}\right| &\le \|\widehat{\gamma} - \gamma\|_1\left\|\frac{1}{\sqrt{n}}\boldsymbol{X}'\boldsymbol{e}\right\|_\infty \\ &\le O_p\left(\|\gamma\|_0\sqrt{\frac{\log p}{n}}\right)O_p\left(\sqrt{\log p}\right) = O_p\left(\|\gamma\|_0\frac{\log p}{\sqrt{n}}\right) = o_p(1)\end{aligned} \tag{29.44}$$

by Hölder's inequality (29.2), Theorem 29.3, (29.39), and the assumption (29.26). Similarly,

$$(\widehat{\gamma} - \gamma)'\frac{1}{\sqrt{n}}\boldsymbol{X}'\boldsymbol{V} = o_p(1)$$

$$(\widehat{\eta} - \eta)'\frac{1}{\sqrt{n}}\boldsymbol{X}'\boldsymbol{V} = o_p(1).$$

These results show that in (29.41), the replacement of $(\boldsymbol{V}, \boldsymbol{U})$ by $(\widehat{\boldsymbol{V}}, \widehat{\boldsymbol{U}})$ is asymptotically negligible. ∎

29.24 EXERCISES

Exercise 29.1 Prove Theorem 29.1. Hint: The proof is similar to that of Theorem 3.7.

Exercise 29.2 Show that (29.7) is the Mallows criterion for ridge regression. For a definition of the Mallows criterion, see Section 28.6.

Exercise 29.3 Derive the conditional bias (29.8) and variance (29.9) of the ridge regression estimator.

Exercise 29.4 Show that the ridge regression estimator can be computed as least squares applied to an augmented dataset. Take the original data $(\boldsymbol{Y}, \boldsymbol{X})$. Add p 0's to $\boldsymbol{Y}$ and p rows of $\sqrt{\lambda}\boldsymbol{I}_p$ to $\boldsymbol{X}$, apply least squares, and show that the results equals $\widehat{\beta}_{\text{ridge}}$.

Exercise 29.5 Which estimator produces a higher regression R^2, least squares or ridge regression?

Exercise 29.6 Does ridge regression require that the columns of $\boldsymbol{X}$ be linearly independent? Consider a sample $(\boldsymbol{Y}, \boldsymbol{X})$. Create the augmented regressor set $\widetilde{\boldsymbol{X}} = (\boldsymbol{X}, \boldsymbol{X})$ (add a duplicate of each regressor), and let $(\widehat{\beta}_1, \widehat{\beta}_2)$ be the ridge regression coefficients for the regression of $\boldsymbol{Y}$ on $\widetilde{\boldsymbol{X}}$. Show that $\widehat{\beta}_1 = \widehat{\beta}_2 = \frac{1}{2}\left(\boldsymbol{X}'\boldsymbol{X} + \boldsymbol{I}_p\widetilde{\lambda}\right)^{-1}\left(\boldsymbol{X}'\boldsymbol{Y}\right)$ with $\widetilde{\lambda} = \lambda/2$.

Exercise 29.7 Repeat Exercise 29.6 for Lasso regression. Show that the Lasso coefficient estimates $\widehat{\beta}_1$ and $\widehat{\beta}_2$ are individually indeterminate, but their sum satisfies $\widehat{\beta}_1 + \widehat{\beta}_2 = \widehat{\beta}_{\text{Lasso}}$, the coefficients from the Lasso regression of $\boldsymbol{Y}$ on $\boldsymbol{X}$.

Exercise 29.8 You have the continuous variables (Y, X) with $X \geq 0$, and you want to estimate a regression tree for $\mathbb{E}[Y \mid X]$. A friend suggests adding a quadratic X^2 to the variables for added flexibility. Does this make sense?

Exercise 29.9 USe the `cpsmar09` dataset and the subsample of Asian women ($n = 1{,}149$). Estimate a Lasso linear regression of log(wage) on the following variables: *education*; dummies for *education* equaling 12, 13, 14, 15, 16, 18, and 20; *experience/40* in powers from 1 to 9; dummies for marriage categories married, divorced, separated, widowed, and never married; dummies for the four regions; dummy for union membership. Report the estimated model and coefficients.

Exercise 29.10 Repeat Exercise 29.9 using the subsample of Hispanic men ($n = 4{,}547$).

APPENDIXES

APPENDIX A

MATRIX ALGEBRA

A.1 NOTATION

A **scalar** a is a single number.

A **vector** $\boldsymbol{a}$ is a $k \times 1$ list of numbers typically arranged in a column. We write this as

$$\boldsymbol{a} = \begin{pmatrix} a_1 \\ a_2 \\ \vdots \\ a_k \end{pmatrix}.$$

Equivalently, a vector $\boldsymbol{a}$ is an element of Euclidean k space, written as $\boldsymbol{a} \in \mathbb{R}^k$. If $k = 1$, then $\boldsymbol{a}$ is a scalar.

A **matrix** $\boldsymbol{A}$ is a $k \times r$ rectangular array of numbers, written as

$$\boldsymbol{A} = \begin{bmatrix} a_{11} & a_{12} & \cdots & a_{1r} \\ a_{21} & a_{22} & \cdots & a_{2r} \\ \vdots & \vdots & & \vdots \\ a_{k1} & a_{k2} & \cdots & a_{kr} \end{bmatrix}.$$

By convention, a_{ij} refers to the element in the ith row and jth column of $\boldsymbol{A}$. If $r = 1$, then $\boldsymbol{A}$ is a column vector. If $k = 1$, then $\boldsymbol{A}$ is a row vector. If $r = k = 1$, then $\boldsymbol{A}$ is a scalar.

A standard convention (which is followed in this text when possible) is to denote scalars by lowercase italics a, vectors by lowercase bold italics $\boldsymbol{a}$, and matrices by uppercase bold italics $\boldsymbol{A}$. Sometimes a matrix $\boldsymbol{A}$ is denoted by the symbol (a_{ij}).

A matrix can be written as a set of column vectors or as a set of row vectors. That is,

$$\boldsymbol{A} = \begin{bmatrix} \boldsymbol{a}_1 & \boldsymbol{a}_2 & \cdots & \boldsymbol{a}_r \end{bmatrix} = \begin{bmatrix} \boldsymbol{\alpha}_1 \\ \boldsymbol{\alpha}_2 \\ \vdots \\ \boldsymbol{\alpha}_k \end{bmatrix}$$

where

$$\boldsymbol{a}_i = \begin{bmatrix} a_{1i} \\ a_{2i} \\ \vdots \\ a_{ki} \end{bmatrix}$$

are column vectors, and

$$\boldsymbol{\alpha}_j = \begin{bmatrix} a_{j1} & a_{j2} & \cdots & a_{jr} \end{bmatrix}$$

are row vectors.

The **transpose** of a matrix $\boldsymbol{A}$, denoted $\boldsymbol{A}'$, $\boldsymbol{A}^\top$, or $\boldsymbol{A}^t$, is obtained by flipping the matrix on its diagonal. In most of the econometrics literature, and this textbook, we use $\boldsymbol{A}'$, but in the mathematics literature, $\boldsymbol{A}^\top$ is the convention. Thus

$$\boldsymbol{A}' = \begin{bmatrix} a_{11} & a_{21} & \cdots & a_{k1} \\ a_{12} & a_{22} & \cdots & a_{k2} \\ \vdots & \vdots & & \vdots \\ a_{1r} & a_{2r} & \cdots & a_{kr} \end{bmatrix}.$$

Alternatively, letting $\boldsymbol{B} = \boldsymbol{A}'$, then $b_{ij} = a_{ji}$. Note that if $\boldsymbol{A}$ is $k \times r$, then $\boldsymbol{A}'$ is $r \times k$. If $\boldsymbol{a}$ is a $k \times 1$ vector, then $\boldsymbol{a}'$ is a $1 \times k$ row vector.

A matrix is **square** if $k = r$. A square matrix is **symmetric** if $\boldsymbol{A} = \boldsymbol{A}'$, which requires $a_{ij} = a_{ji}$. A square matrix is **diagonal** if the off-diagonal elements are all 0, so that $a_{ij} = 0$ if $i \neq j$. A square matrix is **upper (lower) diagonal** if all elements below (above) the diagonal equal 0.

An important diagonal matrix is the **identity matrix**, which has 1s on the diagonal. The $k \times k$ identity matrix is denoted as

$$\boldsymbol{I}_k = \begin{bmatrix} 1 & 0 & \cdots & 0 \\ 0 & 1 & \cdots & 0 \\ \vdots & \vdots & & \vdots \\ 0 & 0 & \cdots & 1 \end{bmatrix}.$$

A **partitioned matrix** takes the form

$$\boldsymbol{A} = \begin{bmatrix} \boldsymbol{A}_{11} & \boldsymbol{A}_{12} & \cdots & \boldsymbol{A}_{1r} \\ \boldsymbol{A}_{21} & \boldsymbol{A}_{22} & \cdots & \boldsymbol{A}_{2r} \\ \vdots & \vdots & & \vdots \\ \boldsymbol{A}_{k1} & \boldsymbol{A}_{k2} & \cdots & \boldsymbol{A}_{kr} \end{bmatrix}$$

where the $\boldsymbol{A}_{ij}$ denote matrices, vectors, or scalars.

A.2 COMPLEX MATRICES

Scalars, vectors, and matrices may contain real or complex numbers as entries. (However, most econometric applications exclusively use real matrices.) If all elements of a vector $\boldsymbol{x}$ are real, we say that $\boldsymbol{x}$ is a real vector, and similarly for matrices.

Recall that a complex number can be written as $x = a + b\mathrm{i}$, where where $\mathrm{i} = \sqrt{-1}$, and a and b are real numbers. Similarly, a vector with complex elements can be written as $\boldsymbol{x} = \boldsymbol{a} + \boldsymbol{b}\mathrm{i}$, where $\boldsymbol{a}$ and $\boldsymbol{b}$ are real vectors, and a matrix with complex elements can be written as $\boldsymbol{X} = \boldsymbol{A} + \boldsymbol{B}\mathrm{i}$, where $\boldsymbol{A}$ and $\boldsymbol{B}$ are real matrices.

Recall that the complex conjugate of $x = a + bi$ is $x^* = a - bi$. For matrices, the analogous concept is the conjugate transpose. The conjugate transpose of $\boldsymbol{X} = \boldsymbol{A} + \boldsymbol{B}\mathrm{i}$ is $\boldsymbol{X}^* = \boldsymbol{A}' - \boldsymbol{B}'\mathrm{i}$. It is obtained by taking the transpose and taking the complex conjugate of each element.

A.3 MATRIX ADDITION

If the matrices $\boldsymbol{A} = (a_{ij})$ and $\boldsymbol{B} = (b_{ij})$ are of the same order, we define the sum

$$\boldsymbol{A} + \boldsymbol{B} = (a_{ij} + b_{ij}).$$

Matrix addition follows the commutative and associative laws:

$$\boldsymbol{A} + \boldsymbol{B} = \boldsymbol{B} + \boldsymbol{A}$$

$$\boldsymbol{A} + (\boldsymbol{B} + \boldsymbol{C}) = (\boldsymbol{A} + \boldsymbol{B}) + \boldsymbol{C}.$$

A.4 MATRIX MULTIPLICATION

If $\boldsymbol{A}$ is $k \times r$ and c is real, we define their product as

$$\boldsymbol{A}c = c\boldsymbol{A} = (a_{ij}c).$$

If $\boldsymbol{a}$ and $\boldsymbol{b}$ are both $k \times 1$, then their inner product is

$$\boldsymbol{a}'\boldsymbol{b} = a_1 b_1 + a_2 b_2 + \cdots + a_k b_k = \sum_{j=1}^{k} a_j b_j.$$

Note that $\boldsymbol{a}'\boldsymbol{b} = \boldsymbol{b}'\boldsymbol{a}$. We say that two vectors $\boldsymbol{a}$ and $\boldsymbol{b}$ are **orthogonal** if $\boldsymbol{a}'\boldsymbol{b} = 0$.

If $\boldsymbol{A}$ is $k \times r$ and $\boldsymbol{B}$ is $r \times s$, so that the number of columns of $\boldsymbol{A}$ equals the number of rows of $\boldsymbol{B}$, we say that $\boldsymbol{A}$ and $\boldsymbol{B}$ are **conformable**. In this event, the matrix product $\boldsymbol{AB}$ is defined. Writing $\boldsymbol{A}$ as a set of row vectors and $\boldsymbol{B}$ as a set of column vectors (each of length r), then the matrix product is defined as

$$\boldsymbol{AB} = \begin{bmatrix} \boldsymbol{a}_1' \\ \boldsymbol{a}_2' \\ \vdots \\ \boldsymbol{a}_k' \end{bmatrix} \begin{bmatrix} \boldsymbol{b}_1 & \boldsymbol{b}_2 & \cdots & \boldsymbol{b}_s \end{bmatrix} = \begin{bmatrix} \boldsymbol{a}_1'\boldsymbol{b}_1 & \boldsymbol{a}_1'\boldsymbol{b}_2 & \cdots & \boldsymbol{a}_1'\boldsymbol{b}_s \\ \boldsymbol{a}_2'\boldsymbol{b}_1 & \boldsymbol{a}_2'\boldsymbol{b}_2 & \cdots & \boldsymbol{a}_2'\boldsymbol{b}_s \\ \vdots & \vdots & & \vdots \\ \boldsymbol{a}_k'\boldsymbol{b}_1 & \boldsymbol{a}_k'\boldsymbol{b}_2 & \cdots & \boldsymbol{a}_k'\boldsymbol{b}_s \end{bmatrix}.$$

Matrix multiplication is not commutative: in general, $\boldsymbol{AB} \neq \boldsymbol{BA}$. However, it is associative and distributive:

$$\boldsymbol{A}(\boldsymbol{BC}) = (\boldsymbol{AB})\boldsymbol{C}$$

$$\boldsymbol{A}(\boldsymbol{B} + \boldsymbol{C}) = \boldsymbol{AB} + \boldsymbol{AC}.$$

An alternative way to write the matrix product is to use matrix partitions. For example,

$$\boldsymbol{AB} = \begin{bmatrix} \boldsymbol{A}_{11} & \boldsymbol{A}_{12} \\ \boldsymbol{A}_{21} & \boldsymbol{A}_{22} \end{bmatrix} \begin{bmatrix} \boldsymbol{B}_{11} & \boldsymbol{B}_{12} \\ \boldsymbol{B}_{21} & \boldsymbol{B}_{22} \end{bmatrix} = \begin{bmatrix} \boldsymbol{A}_{11}\boldsymbol{B}_{11} + \boldsymbol{A}_{12}\boldsymbol{B}_{21} & \boldsymbol{A}_{11}\boldsymbol{B}_{12} + \boldsymbol{A}_{12}\boldsymbol{B}_{22} \\ \boldsymbol{A}_{21}\boldsymbol{B}_{11} + \boldsymbol{A}_{22}\boldsymbol{B}_{21} & \boldsymbol{A}_{21}\boldsymbol{B}_{12} + \boldsymbol{A}_{22}\boldsymbol{B}_{22} \end{bmatrix}.$$

As another example,

$$AB = \begin{bmatrix} A_1 & A_2 & \cdots & A_r \end{bmatrix} \begin{bmatrix} B_1 \\ B_2 \\ \vdots \\ B_r \end{bmatrix}$$
$$= A_1 B_1 + A_2 B_2 + \cdots + A_r B_r$$
$$= \sum_{j=1}^{r} A_j B_j.$$

An important property of the identity matrix is that if A is $k \times r$, then $AI_r = A$ and $I_k A = A$.

We say two matrices A and B are **orthogonal** if $A'B = 0$, which means that all columns of A are orthogonal with all columns of B.

The $k \times r$ matrix H, $r \leq k$, is called **orthonormal** if $H'H = I_r$, which means that the columns of H are mutually orthogonal, and each column is normalized to have unit length.

A.5 TRACE

The **trace** of a $k \times k$ square matrix A is the sum of its diagonal elements:

$$\operatorname{tr}(A) = \sum_{i=1}^{k} a_{ii}.$$

Some straightforward properties for square matrices A and B and real c are

$$\operatorname{tr}(cA) = c \operatorname{tr}(A)$$
$$\operatorname{tr}\left(A'\right) = \operatorname{tr}(A)$$
$$\operatorname{tr}(A + B) = \operatorname{tr}(A) + \operatorname{tr}(B)$$
$$\operatorname{tr}(I_k) = k.$$

Also, for $k \times r$ A and $r \times k$ B, we have

$$\operatorname{tr}(AB) = \operatorname{tr}(BA). \tag{A.1}$$

Indeed,

$$\operatorname{tr}(AB) = \operatorname{tr} \begin{bmatrix} a_1'b_1 & a_1'b_2 & \cdots & a_1'b_k \\ a_2'b_1 & a_2'b_2 & \cdots & a_2'b_k \\ \vdots & \vdots & & \vdots \\ a_k'b_1 & a_k'b_2 & \cdots & a_k'b_k \end{bmatrix}$$
$$= \sum_{i=1}^{k} a_i' b_i$$
$$= \sum_{i=1}^{k} b_i' a_i$$
$$= \operatorname{tr}(BA).$$

A.6 RANK AND INVERSE

The rank of the $k \times r$ matrix $(r \leq k)$

$$A = \begin{bmatrix} a_1 & a_2 & \cdots & a_r \end{bmatrix}$$

is the number of linearly independent columns a_j and is written as $\operatorname{rank}(A)$. We say that A has full rank if $\operatorname{rank}(A) = r$.

A square $k \times k$ matrix A is said to be **nonsingular** if it is has full rank (i.e., $\operatorname{rank}(A) = k$). This means that there is no $k \times 1$ $c \neq 0$ such that $Ac = 0$.

If a square $k \times k$ matrix A is nonsingular, then there exists a unique matrix $k \times k$ matrix A^{-1} called the **inverse** of A that satisfies

$$AA^{-1} = A^{-1}A = I_k.$$

For nonsingular A and C, some important properties include

$$AA^{-1} = A^{-1}A = I_k$$

$$\left(A^{-1}\right)' = \left(A'\right)^{-1}$$

$$(AC)^{-1} = C^{-1}A^{-1}$$

$$(A + C)^{-1} = A^{-1}\left(A^{-1} + C^{-1}\right)^{-1} C^{-1}$$

$$A^{-1} - (A + C)^{-1} = A^{-1}\left(A^{-1} + C^{-1}\right)^{-1} A^{-1}.$$

If a $k \times k$ matrix H is orthonormal (so that $H'H = I_k$), then H is nonsingular, and $H^{-1} = H'$. Furthermore, $HH' = I_k$, and $H'^{-1} = H$.

Another useful result for nonsingular A is known as the **Woodbury matrix identity:**

$$(A + BCD)^{-1} = A^{-1} - A^{-1}BC\left(C + CDA^{-1}BC\right)^{-1} CDA^{-1}.$$

In particular, for $C = 1$, $B = b$, and $D = b'$ for vector b, we find the **Sherman-Morrison formula**

$$\left(A + bb'\right)^{-1} = A^{-1} - \left(1 + b'A^{-1}b\right)^{-1} A^{-1}bb'A^{-1}$$

and similarly, using $C = -1$,

$$\left(A - bb'\right)^{-1} = A^{-1} + \left(1 - b'A^{-1}b\right)^{-1} A^{-1}bb'A^{-1}. \tag{A.2}$$

The following fact about inverting partitioned matrices is quite useful:

$$\begin{bmatrix} A_{11} & A_{12} \\ A_{21} & A_{22} \end{bmatrix}^{-1} \stackrel{\text{def}}{=} \begin{bmatrix} A^{11} & A^{12} \\ A^{21} & A^{22} \end{bmatrix} = \begin{bmatrix} A_{11\cdot 2}^{-1} & -A_{11\cdot 2}^{-1}A_{12}A_{22}^{-1} \\ -A_{22\cdot 1}^{-1}A_{21}A_{11}^{-1} & A_{22\cdot 1}^{-1} \end{bmatrix} \tag{A.3}$$

where $A_{11\cdot 2} = A_{11} - A_{12}A_{22}^{-1}A_{21}$, and $A_{22\cdot 1} = A_{22} - A_{21}A_{11}^{-1}A_{12}$. There are alternative algebraic representations for the components. For example, using the Woodbury matrix identity, you can show the following alternative expressions:

$$A^{11} = A_{11}^{-1} + A_{11}^{-1}A_{12}A_{22\cdot 1}^{-1}A_{21}A_{11}^{-1}$$

$$A^{22} = A_{22}^{-1} + A_{22}^{-1}A_{21}A_{11\cdot 2}^{-1}A_{12}A_{22}^{-1}$$

$$A^{12} = -A_{11}^{-1}A_{12}A_{22\cdot 1}^{-1}$$

$$A^{21} = -A_{22}^{-1}A_{21}A_{11\cdot 2}^{-1}.$$

Even if a matrix $\boldsymbol{A}$ does not possess an inverse, we can define the **Moore-Penrose generalized inverse** $\boldsymbol{A}^-$ as the matrix that satisfies

$$\boldsymbol{A}\boldsymbol{A}^-\boldsymbol{A} = \boldsymbol{A}$$

$$\boldsymbol{A}^-\boldsymbol{A}\boldsymbol{A}^- = \boldsymbol{A}^-$$

$$\boldsymbol{A}\boldsymbol{A}^- \text{ is symmetric}$$

$$\boldsymbol{A}^-\boldsymbol{A} \text{ is symmetric.}$$

For any matrix $\boldsymbol{A}$, the Moore-Penrose generalized inverse $\boldsymbol{A}^-$ exists and is unique.

For example, if

$$\boldsymbol{A} = \begin{bmatrix} \boldsymbol{A}_{11} & \boldsymbol{0} \\ \boldsymbol{0} & \boldsymbol{0} \end{bmatrix}$$

and $\boldsymbol{A}_{11}^{-1}$ exists, then

$$\boldsymbol{A}^- = \begin{bmatrix} \boldsymbol{A}_{11}^{-1} & \boldsymbol{0} \\ \boldsymbol{0} & \boldsymbol{0} \end{bmatrix}.$$

A.7 ORTHOGONAL AND ORTHONORMAL MATRICES

We say that two $k \times 1$ vectors $\boldsymbol{h}_1$ and $\boldsymbol{h}_2$ are **orthogonal** if $\boldsymbol{h}_1'\boldsymbol{h}_2 = 0$, which means that they are perpendicular.

We say that a $k \times 1$ vector $\boldsymbol{h}$ is a **unit vector** if $\boldsymbol{h}'\boldsymbol{h} = 1$, which means that it has unit length in $\mathbb{R}^k$.

We say that two $k \times 1$ vectors $\boldsymbol{h}_1$ and $\boldsymbol{h}_2$ are **orthonormal** if they are orthogonal unit vectors.

We say that the $k \times m_1$ and $k \times m_2$ matrices $\boldsymbol{H}_1$ and $\boldsymbol{H}_2$ are **orthogonal** if $\boldsymbol{H}_1'\boldsymbol{H}_2 = 0$.

We say that the $k \times m$ $(k \geq m)$ matrix $\boldsymbol{H}$ is **orthonormal** if $\boldsymbol{H}'\boldsymbol{H} = \boldsymbol{I}_m$, which means that the columns of $\boldsymbol{H}$ are orthonormal. Some call $\boldsymbol{H}$ an "orthogonal matrix."

Typically, an orthonormal matrix is written as $\boldsymbol{H}$.

If $\boldsymbol{H}$ is a $k \times k$ orthogonal matrix, then it has full rank k, $\boldsymbol{H}'\boldsymbol{H} = \boldsymbol{I}_k$, $\boldsymbol{H}\boldsymbol{H}' = \boldsymbol{I}_k$, and $\boldsymbol{H}^{-1} = \boldsymbol{H}'$.

A.8 DETERMINANT

The **determinant** is a measure of the volume of a square matrix. It is written as $\det \boldsymbol{A}$ or $|\boldsymbol{A}|$. In this textbook, we use $\det \boldsymbol{A}$ for clarity.

Although the determinant is widely used, its precise definition is rarely needed. However, I give the definition here for completeness. Let $\boldsymbol{A} = (a_{ij})$ be a $k \times k$ matrix. Let $\pi = (j_1, \ldots, j_k)$ denote a permutation of $(1, \ldots, k)$. There are $k!$ such permutations. There is a unique count of the number of inversions of the indices of such permutations (relative to the natural order $(1, \ldots, k)$. Let $\varepsilon_\pi = +1$ if this count is even and $\varepsilon_\pi = -1$ if the count is odd. Then the determinant of $\boldsymbol{A}$ is defined as

$$\det \boldsymbol{A} = \sum_\pi \varepsilon_\pi a_{1j_1} a_{2j_2} \cdots a_{kj_k}.$$

For example, if $\boldsymbol{A}$ is 2×2, then the two permutations of $(1, 2)$ are $(1, 2)$ and $(2, 1)$, for which $\varepsilon_{(1,2)} = 1$ and $\varepsilon_{(2,1)} = -1$. Thus

$$\det \boldsymbol{A} = \varepsilon_{(1,2)} a_{11} a_{22} + \varepsilon_{(2,1)} a_{21} a_{12}$$
$$= a_{11} a_{22} - a_{12} a_{21}.$$

For a square matrix $\boldsymbol{A}$, the **minor** M_{ij} of the ijth element a_{ij} is the determinant of the matrix obtained by removing the ith row and jth column of $\boldsymbol{A}$. The **cofactor** of the ijth element is $C_{ij} = (-1)^{i+j} M_{ij}$. An important representation, known as **Laplace's expansion**, relates the determinant of $\boldsymbol{A}$ to its cofactors:

$$\det \boldsymbol{A} = \sum_{j=1}^{k} a_{ij} C_{ij}$$

which holds for all $i = 1, \ldots, k$. This representation is often presented as a method for computation of a determinant.

Theorem A.1 Properties of the Determinant.

1. $\det(\boldsymbol{A}) = \det(\boldsymbol{A}')$.
2. $\det(c\boldsymbol{A}) = c^k \det \boldsymbol{A}$.
3. $\det(\boldsymbol{AB}) = \det(\boldsymbol{BA}) = (\det \boldsymbol{A})(\det \boldsymbol{B})$.
4. $\det(\boldsymbol{A}^{-1}) = (\det \boldsymbol{A})^{-1}$.
5. $\det \begin{bmatrix} \boldsymbol{A} & \boldsymbol{B} \\ \boldsymbol{C} & \boldsymbol{D} \end{bmatrix} = (\det \boldsymbol{D}) \det(\boldsymbol{A} - \boldsymbol{B}\boldsymbol{D}^{-1}\boldsymbol{C})$ if $\det \boldsymbol{D} \neq 0$.
6. $\det \begin{bmatrix} \boldsymbol{A} & \boldsymbol{B} \\ \boldsymbol{0} & \boldsymbol{D} \end{bmatrix} = \det(\boldsymbol{A})(\det \boldsymbol{D})$ and $\det \begin{bmatrix} \boldsymbol{A} & \boldsymbol{0} \\ \boldsymbol{C} & \boldsymbol{D} \end{bmatrix} = \det(\boldsymbol{A})(\det \boldsymbol{D})$.
7. If $\boldsymbol{A}$ is $p \times q$ and $\boldsymbol{B}$ is $q \times p$, then $\det(\boldsymbol{I}_p + \boldsymbol{AB}) = \det(\boldsymbol{I}_q + \boldsymbol{BA})$.
8. If $\boldsymbol{A}$ and $\boldsymbol{D}$ are invertible, then $\det(\boldsymbol{A} - \boldsymbol{B}\boldsymbol{D}^{-1}\boldsymbol{C}) = \dfrac{\det(\boldsymbol{A})}{\det(\boldsymbol{D})} \det(\boldsymbol{D} - \boldsymbol{C}\boldsymbol{A}^{-1}\boldsymbol{B})$.
9. $\det \boldsymbol{A} \neq 0$ if and only if $\boldsymbol{A}$ is nonsingular.
10. If $\boldsymbol{A}$ is triangular (upper or lower), then $\det \boldsymbol{A} = \prod_{i=1}^{k} a_{ii}$.
11. If $\boldsymbol{A}$ is orthonormal, then $\det \boldsymbol{A} = \pm 1$.
12. $\boldsymbol{A}^{-1} = (\det \boldsymbol{A})^{-1} \boldsymbol{C}$, where $\boldsymbol{C} = (C_{ij})$ is the matrix of cofactors.

A.9 EIGENVALUES

The **characteristic equation** of a $k \times k$ square matrix $\boldsymbol{A}$ is

$$\det(\lambda \boldsymbol{I}_k - \boldsymbol{A}) = 0.$$

The left side is a polynomial of degree k in λ, so it has exactly k roots, which are not necessarily distinct and may be real or complex. They are called the **latent roots**, **characteristic roots**, or **eigenvalues** of $\boldsymbol{A}$. If λ is an eigenvalue of $\boldsymbol{A}$, then $\lambda \boldsymbol{I}_k - \boldsymbol{A}$ is singular, so there exists a nonzero vector $\boldsymbol{h}$ such that $(\lambda \boldsymbol{I}_k - \boldsymbol{A}) \boldsymbol{h} = 0$ or

$$\boldsymbol{Ah} = \boldsymbol{h}\lambda.$$

The vector $\boldsymbol{h}$ is called a **latent vector**, **characteristic vector**, or **eigenvector** of $\boldsymbol{A}$ corresponding to λ. They are typically normalized so that $\boldsymbol{h}'\boldsymbol{h} = 1$ and thus $\lambda = \boldsymbol{h}'\boldsymbol{A}\boldsymbol{h}$.

Set $H = [h_1 \cdots h_k]$ and $\Lambda = \mathrm{diag}\{\lambda_1, \ldots, \lambda_k\}$. A matrix expression is

$$AH = H\Lambda$$

Some useful properties are as follows.

Theorem A.2 (Properties of Eigenvalues.) Let λ_i and h_i, $i = 1, \ldots, k$, denote the k eigenvalues and eigenvectors, respectively of a square matrix A.

1. $\det(A) = \prod_{i=1}^{k} \lambda_i$.
2. $\mathrm{tr}(A) = \sum_{i=1}^{k} \lambda_i$.
3. A is nonsingular if and only if all its eigenvalues are nonzero.
4. The nonzero eigenvalues of AB and BA are identical.
5. If B is nonsingular, then A and $B^{-1}AB$ have the same eigenvalues.
6. If $Ah = h\lambda$, then $(I - A)h = h(1 - \lambda)$. So $I - A$ has the eigenvalue $1 - \lambda$ and associated eigenvector h.

Many eigenvalue applications in econometrics concern the case where the matrix A is real and symmetric. In this case, all eigenvalues of A are real, and its eigenvectors are mutually orthogonal. Thus H is orthonormal, so $H'H = I_k$ and $HH' = I_k$. When the eigenvalues are all real, it is conventional to write them in decending order: $\lambda_1 \geq \lambda_2 \geq \cdots \geq \lambda_k$.

The following is an important property of real symmetric matrices that follows directly from the equations $AH = H\Lambda$ and $H'H = I_k$.

Theorem A.3 Spectral Decomposition. If A is a $k \times k$ real symmetric matrix, then $A = H\Lambda H'$, where H contains the eigenvectors and Λ is a diagonal matrix with the eigenvalues on the diagonal. The eigenvalues are all real and the eigenvector matrix satisfies $H'H = I_k$.

The spectral decomposition can be alternatively written as $H'AH = \Lambda$.

If A is real, symmetric, and invertible, then by the spectral decomposition and the properties of orthonormal matrices, $A^{-1} = H'^{-1}\Lambda^{-1}H^{-1} = H\Lambda^{-1}H'$. Thus the columns of H are also the eigenvectors of A^{-1}, and its eigenvalues are $\lambda_1^{-1}, \lambda_2^{-1}, \ldots, \lambda_k^{-1}$.

A.10 POSITIVE DEFINITE MATRICES

We say that a $k \times k$ real symmetric square matrix A is **positive semi-definite** if for all $c \neq 0$, $c'Ac \geq 0$. This is written as $A \geq 0$. We say that A is **positive definite** if for all $c \neq 0$, $c'Ac > 0$. This is written as $A > 0$.

Some properties include the following.

Theorem A.4 Properties of Positive Semi-definite Matrices.

1. If $A = G'BG$ with $B \geq 0$ and some matrix G, then A is positive semi-definite. (For any $c \neq 0$, $c'Ac = \alpha' B\alpha \geq 0$, where $\alpha = Gc$.) If G has full column rank and $B > 0$, then A is positive definite.
2. If A is positive definite, then A is nonsingular and A^{-1} exists. Furthermore, $A^{-1} > 0$.
3. $A > 0$ if and only if it is symmetric and all its eigenvalues are positive.

4. By the spectral decomposition, $\boldsymbol{A} = \boldsymbol{H}\Lambda\boldsymbol{H}'$, where $\boldsymbol{H}'\boldsymbol{H} = \boldsymbol{I}_k$ and Λ is diagonal with nonnegative diagonal elements. All diagonal elements of $\boldsymbol{\Lambda}$ are strictly positive if (and only if) $\boldsymbol{A} > 0$.
5. The rank of $\boldsymbol{A}$ equals the number of strictly positive eigenvalues.
6. If $\boldsymbol{A} > 0$, then $\boldsymbol{A}^{-1} = \boldsymbol{H}\Lambda^{-1}\boldsymbol{H}'$.
7. If $\boldsymbol{A} \geq 0$ and $\operatorname{rank}(\boldsymbol{A}) = r \leq k$, then the Moore-Penrose generalized inverse of $\boldsymbol{A}$ is $\boldsymbol{A}^{-} = \boldsymbol{H}\boldsymbol{\Lambda}^{-}\boldsymbol{H}'$, where $\boldsymbol{\Lambda}^{-} = \operatorname{diag}\left(\lambda_1^{-1}, \lambda_2^{-1}, \ldots, \lambda_r^{-1}, 0, \ldots, 0\right)$.

A.11 IDEMPOTENT MATRICES

A $k \times k$ square matrix $\boldsymbol{A}$ is **idempotent** if $\boldsymbol{A}\boldsymbol{A} = \boldsymbol{A}$. When $k = 1$, the only idempotent numbers are 1 and 0. For $k > 1$, there are many possibilities. For example, the following matrix is idempotent:

$$\boldsymbol{A} = \begin{bmatrix} 1/2 & -1/2 \\ -1/2 & 1/2 \end{bmatrix}.$$

If $\boldsymbol{A}$ is idempotent and symmetric with rank r, then it has r eigenvalues that equal 1 and $k - r$ eigenvalues that equal 0. To see this, using the spectral decomposition, we can write $\boldsymbol{A} = \boldsymbol{H}\Lambda\boldsymbol{H}'$, where $\boldsymbol{H}$ is orthonormal and Λ contains the eigenvalues. Then

$$\boldsymbol{A} = \boldsymbol{A}\boldsymbol{A} = \boldsymbol{H}\Lambda\boldsymbol{H}'\boldsymbol{H}\Lambda\boldsymbol{H}' = \boldsymbol{H}\Lambda^2\boldsymbol{H}'.$$

We deduce that $\Lambda^2 = \Lambda$ and $\lambda_i^2 = \lambda_i$ for $i = 1, \ldots, k$. Hence each λ_i must equal either 0 or 1. Because the rank of $\boldsymbol{A}$ is r, and the rank equals the number of positive eigenvalues, it follows that

$$\Lambda = \begin{bmatrix} \boldsymbol{I}_r & 0 \\ 0 & 0_{k-r} \end{bmatrix}.$$

Thus the spectral decomposition of an idempotent matrix $\boldsymbol{A}$ takes the form

$$\boldsymbol{A} = \boldsymbol{H}\begin{bmatrix} \boldsymbol{I}_r & 0 \\ 0 & 0_{k-r} \end{bmatrix}\boldsymbol{H}' \tag{A.4}$$

with $\boldsymbol{H}'\boldsymbol{H} = \boldsymbol{I}_k$. Additionally, $\operatorname{tr}(\boldsymbol{A}) = \operatorname{rank}(\boldsymbol{A})$, and $\boldsymbol{A}$ is positive semi-definite.

If $\boldsymbol{A}$ is idempotent and symmetric with rank $r < k$, then it does not possess an inverse, but its Moore-Penrose generalized inverse takes the simple form $\boldsymbol{A}^{-} = \boldsymbol{A}$. This can be verified by checking the conditions for the Moore-Penrose generalized inverse , for example, $\boldsymbol{A}\boldsymbol{A}^{-}\boldsymbol{A} = \boldsymbol{A}\boldsymbol{A}\boldsymbol{A} = \boldsymbol{A}$.

If $\boldsymbol{A}$ is idempotent, then $\boldsymbol{I} - \boldsymbol{A}$ is also idempotent.

A useful fact is that if $\boldsymbol{A}$ is idempotent, then for any conformable vector $\boldsymbol{c}$,

$$\boldsymbol{c}'\boldsymbol{A}\boldsymbol{c} \leq \boldsymbol{c}'\boldsymbol{c} \tag{A.5}$$

$$\boldsymbol{c}'(\boldsymbol{I} - \boldsymbol{A})\boldsymbol{c} \leq \boldsymbol{c}'\boldsymbol{c}. \tag{A.6}$$

To see this, note that

$$\boldsymbol{c}'\boldsymbol{c} = \boldsymbol{c}'\boldsymbol{A}\boldsymbol{c} + \boldsymbol{c}'(\boldsymbol{I} - \boldsymbol{A})\boldsymbol{c}.$$

Since $\boldsymbol{A}$ and $\boldsymbol{I} - \boldsymbol{A}$ are idempotent, they are both positive semi-definite, so both $\boldsymbol{c}'\boldsymbol{A}\boldsymbol{c}$ and $\boldsymbol{c}'(\boldsymbol{I} - \boldsymbol{A})\boldsymbol{c}$ are nonnegative. Thus they must satisfy (A.5) and (A.6).

A.12 SINGULAR VALUES

The **singular values** σ_j of a $k \times r$ real matrix $\boldsymbol{A}$ are the positive square roots of the eigenvalues of $\boldsymbol{A}'\boldsymbol{A}$. Thus for $j = 1, \ldots, r$,

$$\sigma_j = \sqrt{\lambda_j\left(\boldsymbol{A}'\boldsymbol{A}\right)}.$$

Because $\boldsymbol{A}'\boldsymbol{A}$ is positive semi-definite, its eigenvalues are nonnegative. Thus singular values are always real and nonnegative.

The nonzero singular values of $\boldsymbol{A}$ and $\boldsymbol{A}'$ are the same. The number of nonzero singular values equals the rank of $\boldsymbol{A}$.

When $\boldsymbol{A}$ is positive semi-definite, then the singular values of $\boldsymbol{A}$ correspond to its eigenvalues.

It is convention to write the singular values in decending order: $\sigma_1 \geq \sigma_2 \geq \cdots \geq \sigma_r$.

A.13 MATRIX DECOMPOSITIONS

There are several useful ways to decompose a matrix into the products of simpler matrices. Theorem A.3 in Section A.9 defined spectral decomposition. The definition is repeated here for completeness. The following definitions apply to real matrices $\boldsymbol{A}$.

Spectral Decomposition: If $\boldsymbol{A}$ is $k \times k$ and symmetric, then $\boldsymbol{A} = \boldsymbol{H}\Lambda\boldsymbol{H}'$ where $\boldsymbol{H}'\boldsymbol{H} = \boldsymbol{I}_k$ and Λ is a diagonal matrix with the (real) eigenvalues on the diagonal.

Eigendecomposition: If $\boldsymbol{A}$ is $k \times k$ and has distinct eigenvalues, there exists a nonsingular matrix $\boldsymbol{P}$ such that $\boldsymbol{A} = \boldsymbol{P}\Lambda\boldsymbol{P}^{-1}$ and $\boldsymbol{P}^{-1}\boldsymbol{A}\boldsymbol{P} = \Lambda$. The columns of $\boldsymbol{P}$ are the eigenvectors. The matrix Λ is diagonal with the eigenvalues on the diagonal.

Matrix Square Root: If $\boldsymbol{A}$ is $k \times k$ and positive definite, we can find a matrix $\boldsymbol{B}$ such that $\boldsymbol{A} = \boldsymbol{B}\boldsymbol{B}'$. We call $\boldsymbol{B}$ a **matrix square root** of $\boldsymbol{A}$, and it is typically written as $\boldsymbol{B} = \boldsymbol{A}^{1/2}$.

The matrix $\boldsymbol{B}$ need not be unique. One matrix square root is obtained using the spectral decomposition $\boldsymbol{A} = \boldsymbol{H}\Lambda\boldsymbol{H}'$. Then $\boldsymbol{B} = \boldsymbol{H}\Lambda^{1/2}\boldsymbol{H}'$ is itself symmetric and positive definite and satisfies $\boldsymbol{A} = \boldsymbol{B}\boldsymbol{B}$. Another matrix square root is the Cholesky decomposition, described in Section A.16.

Singular Value Decomposition: If $\boldsymbol{A}$ is $k \times r$, then $\boldsymbol{A} = \boldsymbol{U}\Lambda\boldsymbol{V}'$, where $\boldsymbol{U}$ is $k \times k$, $\boldsymbol{\Lambda}$ is $k \times r$, and $\boldsymbol{V}$ is $r \times r$. $\boldsymbol{U}$ and $\boldsymbol{V}$ are orthonormal ($\boldsymbol{U}'\boldsymbol{U} = \boldsymbol{I}_k$ and $\boldsymbol{V}'\boldsymbol{V} = \boldsymbol{I}_r$). Λ is a diagonal matrix with the singular values of $\boldsymbol{A}$ on the diagonal.

Cholesky Decomposition: If $\boldsymbol{A}$ is $k \times k$ and positive definite, then $\boldsymbol{A} = \boldsymbol{L}\boldsymbol{L}'$ where $\boldsymbol{L}$ is **lower triangular** and full rank. See Section A.16.

QR Decomposition: If $\boldsymbol{A}$ is $k \times r$ with $k \geq r$ and rank r, then $\boldsymbol{A} = \boldsymbol{Q}\boldsymbol{R}$. $\boldsymbol{Q}$ is a $k \times r$ and orthonormal matrix ($\boldsymbol{Q}'\boldsymbol{Q} = \boldsymbol{I}_r$). $\boldsymbol{R}$ is a $r \times r$ full rank **upper triangular** matrix. See Section A.17.

Jordan Matrix Decomposition: If A is $k \times k$, then $A = PJP^{-1}$, where J takes the **Jordan normal form**. The latter is a block diagonal matrix $J = \text{diag}\{J_1, \ldots, J_r\}$, where r is the number of distinct eigenvalues of A. The **Jordan blocks** J_i are $m_i \times m_i$, where m_i is the multiplicity of λ_i (number of eigenvalues equaling λ_i), and take the form

$$J_i = \begin{bmatrix} \lambda_i & 1 & 0 \\ 0 & \lambda_i & 1 \\ 0 & 0 & \lambda_i \end{bmatrix} \tag{A.7}$$

illustrated here for $m_i = 3$.

A.14 GENERALIZED EIGENVALUES

Let A and B be $k \times k$ matrices. The generalized characteristic equation is

$$\det(\mu B - A) = 0.$$

The solutions μ are known as **generalized eigenvalues** of A with respect to B. Associated with each generalized eigenvalue μ is a **generalized eigenvector** v that satisfies

$$Av = Bv\mu.$$

They are typically normalized, so that $v'Bv = 1$ and thus $\mu = v'Av$.

A matrix expression is $AV = BVM$, where $M = \text{diag}\{\mu_1, \ldots, \mu_k\}$.

If A and B are real and symmetric, then the generalized eigenvalues are real.

Suppose in addition that B is invertible. Then the generalized eigenvalues of A with respect to B are equal to the eigenvalues of $B^{-1/2}AB^{-1/2\prime}$. The generalized eigenvectors V of A with respect to B are related to the eigenvectors H of $B^{-1/2}AB^{-1/2\prime}$ which by the relationship $V = B^{-1/2\prime}H$, which implies $V'BV = I_k$. Thus the generalized eigenvectors are orthogonalized with respect to the matrix B.

If $Av = Bv\mu$, then $(B - A)\,v = Bv(1-\mu)$. So a generalized eigenvalue of $B - A$ with respect to B is $1 - \mu$ with associated eigenvector v.

Generalized eigenvalue equations have an interesting dual property. The following is based on lemma A.9 of Johansen (1995).

Theorem A.5 Suppose that B and C are invertible $p \times p$ and $r \times r$ matrices, respectively, and A is $p \times r$. Then the generalized eigenvalue problems

$$\det\left(\mu B - AC^{-1}A'\right) = 0 \tag{A.8}$$

and

$$\det\left(\mu C - A'B^{-1}A\right) = 0 \tag{A.9}$$

have the same nonzero generalized eigenvalues. Furthermore, for any such generalized eigenvalue μ, if v and w are the associated generalized eigenvectors of (A.8) and (A.9), then

$$w = \mu^{-1/2}C^{-1}A'v. \tag{A.10}$$

Proof Let $\mu \neq 0$ be an eigenvalue of (A.8). Using Theorem A.1 Part 8,

$$0 = \det\left(\mu B - AC^{-1}A'\right)$$

$$= \frac{\det(\mu \boldsymbol{B})}{\det(\boldsymbol{C})} \det\left(\boldsymbol{C} - \boldsymbol{A}'(\mu \boldsymbol{B})^{-1}\boldsymbol{A}\right)$$
$$= \frac{\det(\boldsymbol{B})}{\det(\boldsymbol{C})} \det\left(\mu \boldsymbol{C} - \boldsymbol{A}'\boldsymbol{B}^{-1}\boldsymbol{A}\right).$$

Because $\det(\boldsymbol{B}) / \det(\boldsymbol{C}) \neq 0$, this implies that (A.10) holds. Hence μ is an eigenvalue of (A.9), as claimed.

We next show that (A.10) is an eigenvector of (A.9). Note that the solutions to (A.8) and (A.9) satisfy

$$\boldsymbol{B}\boldsymbol{v}\mu = \boldsymbol{A}\boldsymbol{C}^{-1}\boldsymbol{A}'\boldsymbol{v} \tag{A.11}$$

and

$$\boldsymbol{C}\boldsymbol{w}\mu = \boldsymbol{A}'\boldsymbol{B}^{-1}\boldsymbol{A}\boldsymbol{w} \tag{A.12}$$

and are normalized, so that $\boldsymbol{v}'\boldsymbol{B}\boldsymbol{v} = 1$ and $\boldsymbol{w}'\boldsymbol{C}\boldsymbol{w} = 1$. We show that (A.10) satisfies (A.12). Using (A.10), we find that the leftside of (A.12) equals

$$\boldsymbol{C}\left(\mu^{-1/2}\boldsymbol{C}^{-1}\boldsymbol{A}'\right)\mu = \boldsymbol{A}'\mu^{1/2} = \boldsymbol{A}'\boldsymbol{B}^{-1}\boldsymbol{B}\boldsymbol{v}\mu^{1/2} = \boldsymbol{A}'\boldsymbol{B}^{-1}\boldsymbol{A}\boldsymbol{C}^{-1}\boldsymbol{A}'\boldsymbol{v}\mu^{-1/2} = \boldsymbol{A}'\boldsymbol{B}^{-1}\boldsymbol{A}\boldsymbol{w}.$$

The third equality is (A.11), and the final is (A.10). This shows that (A.12) holds and thus, (A.10) is an eigenvector of (A.9), as stated. ■

A.15 EXTREMA OF QUADRATIC FORMS

The extrema of quadratic forms in real symmetric matrices can conveniently be written in terms of eigenvalues and eigenvectors. Let $\boldsymbol{A}$ denote a $k \times k$ real symmetric matrix. Let $\lambda_1 \geq \cdots \geq \lambda_k$ be the ordered eigenvalues of $\boldsymbol{A}$ and $\boldsymbol{h}_1, \ldots, \boldsymbol{h}_k$ the associated ordered eigenvectors.

Let us start with results for the extrema of $\boldsymbol{x}'\boldsymbol{A}\boldsymbol{x}$. Throughout this section, the ısolutionȷ of an extremum problem refers to the solution of the normalized expression:

- $\max_{\boldsymbol{x}'\boldsymbol{x}=1} \boldsymbol{x}'\boldsymbol{A}\boldsymbol{x} = \max_{\boldsymbol{x}} \frac{\boldsymbol{x}'\boldsymbol{A}\boldsymbol{x}}{\boldsymbol{x}'\boldsymbol{x}} = \lambda_1$. The solution is $\boldsymbol{x} = \boldsymbol{h}_1$. (That is, the maximizer of $\boldsymbol{x}'\boldsymbol{A}\boldsymbol{x}$ over $\boldsymbol{x}'\boldsymbol{x} = 1$.)
- $\min_{\boldsymbol{x}'\boldsymbol{x}=1} \boldsymbol{x}'\boldsymbol{A}\boldsymbol{x} = \min_{\boldsymbol{x}} \frac{\boldsymbol{x}'\boldsymbol{A}\boldsymbol{x}}{\boldsymbol{x}'\boldsymbol{x}} = \lambda_k$. The solution is $\boldsymbol{x} = \boldsymbol{h}_k$.

Multivariate generalizations can involve either the trace or the determinant:

- $\max_{\boldsymbol{X}'\boldsymbol{X}=\boldsymbol{I}_\ell} \operatorname{tr}\left(\boldsymbol{X}'\boldsymbol{A}\boldsymbol{X}\right) = \max_{\boldsymbol{X}} \operatorname{tr}\left(\left(\boldsymbol{X}'\boldsymbol{X}\right)^{-1}\boldsymbol{X}'\boldsymbol{A}\boldsymbol{X}\right) = \sum_{i=1}^{\ell} \lambda_i$.
  The solution is $\boldsymbol{X} = [\boldsymbol{h}_1, \ldots, \boldsymbol{h}_\ell]$.
- $\min_{\boldsymbol{X}'\boldsymbol{X}=\boldsymbol{I}_\ell} \operatorname{tr}\left(\boldsymbol{X}'\boldsymbol{A}\boldsymbol{X}\right) = \min_{\boldsymbol{X}} \operatorname{tr}\left(\left(\boldsymbol{X}'\boldsymbol{X}\right)^{-1}\boldsymbol{X}'\boldsymbol{A}\boldsymbol{X}\right) = \sum_{i=1}^{\ell} \lambda_{k-i+1}$.
  The solution is $\boldsymbol{X} = [\boldsymbol{h}_{k-\ell+1}, \ldots, \boldsymbol{h}_k]$.

For a proof, see theorem 11.13 of Magnus and Neudecker (2019).

Suppose as well that $\boldsymbol{A} > 0$ with ordered eigenvalues $\lambda_1 \geq \lambda_2 \geq \cdots \geq \lambda_k$ and eigenvectors $[\boldsymbol{h}_1, \ldots, \boldsymbol{h}_k]$:

- $\max_{\boldsymbol{X}'\boldsymbol{X}=\boldsymbol{I}_\ell} \det\left(\boldsymbol{X}'\boldsymbol{A}\boldsymbol{X}\right) = \max_{\boldsymbol{X}} \frac{\det\left(\boldsymbol{X}'\boldsymbol{A}\boldsymbol{X}\right)}{\det\left(\boldsymbol{X}'\boldsymbol{X}\right)} = \prod_{i=1}^{\ell} \lambda_i$. The solution is $\boldsymbol{X} = [\boldsymbol{h}_1, \ldots, \boldsymbol{h}_\ell]$.

- $\min_{X'X=I_\ell} \det\left(X'AX\right) = \min_X \dfrac{\det\left(X'AX\right)}{\det\left(X'X\right)} = \prod_{i=1}^{\ell} \lambda_{k-i+1}$. The solution is $X = [h_{k-\ell+1}, \ldots, h_k]$.
- $\max_{X'X=I_\ell} \det\left(X'\left(I-A\right)X\right) = \max_X \dfrac{\det\left(X'\left(I-A\right)X\right)}{\det\left(X'X\right)} = \prod_{i=1}^{\ell} \left(1-\lambda_{k-i+1}\right)$.
  The solution is $X = [h_{k-\ell+1}, \ldots, h_k]$.
- $\min_{X'X=I_\ell} \det\left(X'\left(I-A\right)X\right) = \min_X \dfrac{\det\left(X'\left(I-A\right)X\right)}{\det\left(X'X\right)} = \prod_{i=1}^{\ell} \left(1-\lambda_i\right)$. The solution is $X = [h_1, \ldots, h_\ell]$.

For a proof, see theorem 11.15 of Magnus and Neudecker (2019).

We can extend the above results to incorporate generalized eigenvalue equations. Let A and B be $k \times k$ real symmetric matrices with $B > 0$. Let $\mu_1 \geq \cdots \geq \mu_k$ be the ordered generalized eigenvalues of A with respect to B and $v_1, \ldots, v_k$ be the associated ordered eigenvectors:

- $\max_{x'Bx=1} x'Ax = \max_x \dfrac{x'Ax}{x'x} = \mu_1$. The solution is $x = v_1$.
- $\min_{x'Bx=1} x'Ax = \min_x \dfrac{x'Ax}{x'x} = \mu_k$. The solution is $x = v_k$.
- $\max_{X'BX=I_\ell} \operatorname{tr}\left(X'AX\right) = \max_X \operatorname{tr}\left(\left(X'BX\right)^{-1} X'AX\right) = \sum_{i=1}^{\ell} \mu_i$.
  The solution is $X = [v_1, \ldots, v_\ell]$.
- $\min_{X'BX=I_\ell} \operatorname{tr}\left(X'AX\right) = \min_X \operatorname{tr}\left(\left(X'BX\right)^{-1} X'AX\right) = \sum_{i=1}^{\ell} \mu_{k-i+1}$.
  The solution is $X = [v_{k-\ell+1}, \ldots, v_k]$.

Suppose as well that $A > 0$:

- $\max_{X'BX=I_\ell} \det\left(X'AX\right) = \max_X \dfrac{\det\left(X'AX\right)}{\det\left(X'BX\right)} = \prod_{i=1}^{\ell} \mu_i$.
  The solution is $X = [v_1, \ldots, v_\ell]$.
- $\min_{X'BX=I_\ell} \det\left(X'AX\right) = \min_X \dfrac{\det\left(X'AX\right)}{\det\left(X'BX\right)} = \prod_{i=1}^{\ell} \mu_{k-i+1}$.
  The solution is $X = [v_{k-\ell+1}, \ldots, v_k]$.
- $\max_{X'BX=I_\ell} \det\left(X'\left(I-A\right)X\right) = \max_X \dfrac{\det\left(X'\left(I-A\right)X\right)}{\det\left(X'BX\right)} = \prod_{i=1}^{\ell} \left(1-\mu_{k-i+1}\right)$.
  The solution is $X = [v_{k-\ell+1}, \ldots, v_k]$.
- $\min_{X'BX=I_\ell} \det\left(X'\left(I-A\right)X\right) = \min_X \dfrac{\det\left(X'\left(I-A\right)X\right)}{\det\left(X'BX\right)} = \prod_{i=1}^{\ell} \left(1-\mu_i\right)$.
  The solution is $X = [v_1, \ldots, v_\ell]$.

By change-of-variables, we can re-express one eigenvalue problem in terms of another. For example, let $A > 0$, $B > 0$, and $C > 0$. Then

$$\max_X \frac{\det\left(X'CACX\right)}{\det\left(X'CBCX\right)} = \max_X \frac{\det\left(X'AX\right)}{\det\left(X'BX\right)}$$

and

$$\min_X \frac{\det(X'CACX)}{\det(X'CBCX)} = \min_X \frac{\det(X'AX)}{\det(X'BX)}.$$

A.16 CHOLESKY DECOMPOSITION

For a $k \times k$ positive definite matrix $\boldsymbol{A}$, its **Cholesky decomposition** takes the form $\boldsymbol{A} = \boldsymbol{L}\boldsymbol{L}'$, where $\boldsymbol{L}$ is **lower triangular** and full rank. A lower triangular matrix (also known as a **left triangular** matrix) takes the form

$$\boldsymbol{L} = \begin{bmatrix} L_{11} & 0 & \cdots & 0 \\ L_{21} & L_{22} & \cdots & 0 \\ \vdots & \vdots & \ddots & \vdots \\ L_{k1} & L_{k2} & \cdots & L_{kk} \end{bmatrix}.$$

The diagonal elements of $\boldsymbol{L}$ are all strictly positive. The Cholesky decomposition is unique.

The decomposition is useful for a range of computations, especially when a matrix square root is required. Algorithms for computation are available in standard packages (for example, `chol` in either MATLAB or R).

Lower triangular matrices such as $\boldsymbol{L}$ have special properties. One is that its determinant equals the product of the diagonal elements.

Proofs of uniqueness of the Cholesky decomposition (as well as computation) are algorithmic. Here are the details for the case $k = 3$. Write out

$$\begin{bmatrix} A_{11} & A_{21} & A_{31} \\ A_{21} & A_{22} & A_{32} \\ A_{31} & A_{32} & A_{33} \end{bmatrix} = \boldsymbol{A} = \boldsymbol{L}\boldsymbol{L}' = \begin{bmatrix} L_{11} & 0 & 0 \\ L_{21} & L_{22} & 0 \\ L_{31} & L_{32} & L_{33} \end{bmatrix} \begin{bmatrix} L_{11} & L_{21} & L_{31} \\ 0 & L_{22} & L_{32} \\ 0 & 0 & L_{33} \end{bmatrix}$$

$$= \begin{bmatrix} L_{11}^2 & L_{11}L_{21} & L_{11}L_{31} \\ L_{11}L_{21} & L_{21}^2 + L_{22}^2 & L_{31}L_{21} + L_{32}L_{22} \\ L_{11}L_{31} & L_{31}L_{21} + L_{32}L_{22} & L_{31}^2 + L_{32}^2 + L_{33}^2 \end{bmatrix}.$$

There are six equations, six knowns (the elements of $\boldsymbol{A}$), and six unknowns (the elements of $\boldsymbol{L}$). We can solve for the latter by starting with the first column, moving from top to bottom. The first element has the simple solution $L_{11} = \sqrt{A_{11}}$. This has a real solution, because $A_{11} > 0$. Moving down, because L_{11} is known, for the entries beneath L_{11}, we can solve and find

$$L_{21} = \frac{A_{21}}{L_{11}} = \frac{A_{21}}{\sqrt{A_{11}}}$$

$$L_{31} = \frac{A_{31}}{L_{11}} = \frac{A_{31}}{\sqrt{A_{11}}}.$$

Next we move to the second column. Observe that L_{21} is known. Then we can solve for L_{22}:

$$L_{22} = \sqrt{A_{22} - L_{21}^2} = \sqrt{A_{22} - \frac{A_{21}^2}{A_{11}}}.$$

This has a real solution, because $\boldsymbol{A} > 0$. Then because L_{22} is known, we can move down the column to find

$$L_{32} = \frac{A_{32} - L_{31}L_{21}}{L_{22}} = \frac{A_{32} - \frac{A_{31}A_{21}}{A_{11}}}{\sqrt{A_{22} - \frac{A_{21}^2}{A_{11}}}}.$$

Finally, consider the third column. All elements except L_{33} are known. So we solve to find

$$L_{33} = \sqrt{A_{33} - L_{31}^2 - L_{32}^2} = \sqrt{A_{33} - \frac{A_{31}^2}{A_{11}} - \frac{\left(A_{32} - \frac{A_{31}A_{21}}{A_{11}}\right)^2}{A_{22} - \frac{A_{21}^2}{A_{11}}}}.$$

A.17 QR DECOMPOSITION

The QR decomposition is widely used for numerical problems, such as matrix inversion and solving systems of linear equations.

Let $\boldsymbol{A}$ be a $k \times r$ matrix, with $k \geq r$ and rank r. The QR, decomposition of $\boldsymbol{A}$ is $\boldsymbol{A} = \boldsymbol{Q}\boldsymbol{R}$ where $\boldsymbol{Q}$ is a $k \times r$ orthonormal matrix, and $\boldsymbol{R}$ is a $r \times r$ full rank **upper triangular** matrix (also known as a **right triangular** matrix).

To show that the QR decomposition exists, observe that $\boldsymbol{A}'\boldsymbol{A}$ is $r \times r$ and positive definite. Apply the Cholesky decomposition (Section A.16) to find $\boldsymbol{A}'\boldsymbol{A} = \boldsymbol{L}\boldsymbol{L}'$, where $\boldsymbol{L}$ is lower triangular and full rank. We then set $\boldsymbol{Q} = \boldsymbol{A}\left(\boldsymbol{L}'\right)^{-1}$ and $\boldsymbol{R} = \boldsymbol{L}'$. The matrix $\boldsymbol{R}$ is upper triangular by construction. Also,

$$\boldsymbol{Q}'\boldsymbol{Q} = \left(\boldsymbol{L}'\right)^{-1\prime}\boldsymbol{A}'\boldsymbol{A}\left(\boldsymbol{L}'\right)^{-1} = \boldsymbol{L}^{-1}\boldsymbol{L}\boldsymbol{L}'\left(\boldsymbol{L}'\right)^{-1} = \boldsymbol{I}_k$$

so $\boldsymbol{Q}$ is orthonormal, as claimed.

Numerical computation of the QR decomposition does not use the above matrix operations. Instead it is done algorithmically. Standard methods include the **Gram-Schmidt** and **Householder** algorithms. The Gram-Schmidt is simple to describe and implement, but the Householder is numerically more stable and is therefore the standard implementation. Because the algorithm is involved, we do not discuss it here.

A.18 SOLVING LINEAR SYSTEMS

A linear system of k equations with k unknowns is

$$\begin{aligned} a_{11}b_1 + a_{12}b_2 + \cdots + a_{1k}b_k &= c_1 \\ a_{21}b_1 + a_{22}b_2 + \cdots + a_{2k}b_k &= c_2 \\ &\vdots \\ a_{k1}b_1 + a_{k2}b_2 + \cdots + a_{kk}b_k &= c_k \end{aligned}$$

or in matrix notation

$$\boldsymbol{A}\boldsymbol{b} = \boldsymbol{c} \tag{A.13}$$

where $\boldsymbol{A}$ is $k \times k$, and $\boldsymbol{b}$ and $\boldsymbol{c}$ are $k \times 1$. If $\boldsymbol{A}$ is full rank, then the solution $\boldsymbol{b} = \boldsymbol{A}^{-1}\boldsymbol{c}$ is unique. In this section, we discuss three algorithms to numerically find the solution $\boldsymbol{b}$. The first uses Gaussian elimination, the second uses the QR decomposition, and the third uses the Cholesky decomposition.

(1) Solving by **Gaussian elimination**

The solution $\boldsymbol{b}$ in (A.13) is invariant to row operations; including multiplying an equation by nonzero numbers, and adding and subtracting equations from one another. To exploit this insight, combine the known constants $\boldsymbol{A}$ and $\boldsymbol{c}$ into a $k \times (k+1)$ augmented matrix:

$$[\boldsymbol{A} \mid \boldsymbol{c}]. \tag{A.14}$$

The row operations described above are the same as multiplying rows of $[\boldsymbol{A} \mid \boldsymbol{c}]$ by nonzero numbers and adding and subtracting rows of $[\boldsymbol{A} \mid \boldsymbol{c}]$ from one another. Such operations do not change the solution $\boldsymbol{b}$. Gaussian elimination works by applying row operations to $[\boldsymbol{A} \mid \boldsymbol{c}]$ until the left section equals the identity matrix $\boldsymbol{I}_k$ and thus equals

$$[\boldsymbol{I}_k \mid \boldsymbol{d}]. \tag{A.15}$$

Because row operations do not alter the solution, the solution $\boldsymbol{b}$ in (A.13) also satisfies $\boldsymbol{I}_k\boldsymbol{b} = \boldsymbol{d}$, which implies $\boldsymbol{b} = \boldsymbol{d}$. Thus the solution $\boldsymbol{b}$ can be found as the right-most vector $\boldsymbol{d}$ in (A.15).

The Gauss-Jordan algorithm implements a sequence of row operations that obtains the solution for any pair (A.14) such that $\boldsymbol{A}$ is full rank. The algorithm is as follows.

For $r = 1, \dots, k$:

1. Divide the elements of row r by a_{rr}. Thus make the changes
   i. $a_{ri} \mapsto a_{ri}/a_{rr}$ for $i = 1, \dots, k$
   ii. $c_r \mapsto c_r/a_{rr}$.
2. For rows $j \neq r$, subtract a_{jr} times row r from row j. Thus make the changes
   i. $a_{ji} \mapsto a_{ji} - a_{jr}a_{ri}$ for $i = 1, \dots, k$
   ii. $c_j \mapsto c_j - a_{jr}c_r$.

Each pair of operations transforms a column of the matrix $\boldsymbol{A}$ into an column of the identity matrix $\boldsymbol{I}_k$, starting with the first column and working sequentially to the right. The first operation (dividing by a_{rr}) normalizes the rth diagonal element to unity. The second set of operations makes row operations to transform the remaining elements of the rth column to equal 0. Because the previous columns are unit vectors, they are unaffected by these operations.

(2) Solving by **QR Decomposition**
First, compute the QR decomposition $\boldsymbol{A} = \boldsymbol{Q}\boldsymbol{R}$, where $\boldsymbol{Q}$ is a $k \times k$ orthogonal matrix, and $\boldsymbol{R}$ is $k \times k$ and upper triangular. This is is done numerically (typically by the Householder algorithm), as described in Section A.17. Then (A.13) can be written as $\boldsymbol{Q}\boldsymbol{R}\boldsymbol{b} = \boldsymbol{c}$. Premultiplying by $\boldsymbol{Q}'$ and observing $\boldsymbol{Q}'\boldsymbol{Q} = \boldsymbol{I}_k$, we obtain $\boldsymbol{R}\boldsymbol{b} = \boldsymbol{Q}'\boldsymbol{c} \stackrel{\text{def}}{=} \boldsymbol{d}$. This system can be written as

$$\begin{aligned}
r_{11}b_1 + r_{12}b_2 + \cdots + r_{1,k-1}b_{k-2} + r_{1k}b_k &= d_1 \\
r_{22}b_2 + \cdots + r_{2,k-1}b_{k-2} + r_{2k}b_k &= d_2 \\
&\vdots \\
r_{k-1,k-1}b_{k-2} + r_{k-1,k}b_k &= d_{k-1} \\
r_{kk}b_k &= d_k.
\end{aligned}$$

This system can be solved by **backward recursion:**

$$\begin{aligned}
b_k &= d_k/r_{kk} \\
b_{k-1} &= \left(d_{k-1} - r_{k-1,k}b_k\right)/r_{k-1,k-1} \\
&\vdots \\
b_1 &= \left(d_1 - r_{12}b_2 - \cdots - r_{1k}b_k\right)/r_{11}.
\end{aligned}$$

To summarize, the **QR solution method** is

(a) Numerically compute the QR decomposition $\boldsymbol{A}=\boldsymbol{Q}\boldsymbol{R}$.
(b) Calculate $\boldsymbol{d}=\boldsymbol{Q}'\boldsymbol{c}$.
(c) Solve for $\boldsymbol{b}$ by backward recursion.

(3) Solving by **Cholesky Decomposition** for positive definite $\boldsymbol{A}$
First, compute the Cholesky decomposition $\boldsymbol{A}=\boldsymbol{L}\boldsymbol{R}$, where $\boldsymbol{L}$ is $k\times k$ and lower triangular, and $\boldsymbol{R}=\boldsymbol{L}'$ is upper triangular. This is done numerically, as described in Section A.16. Thus that (A.13) can be written as $\boldsymbol{L}\boldsymbol{R}\boldsymbol{b}=\boldsymbol{c}$ or $\boldsymbol{L}\boldsymbol{d}=\boldsymbol{c}$, where $\boldsymbol{d}=\boldsymbol{R}\boldsymbol{b}$. The vector $\boldsymbol{d}$ can be solved from $\boldsymbol{L}$ and $\boldsymbol{c}$ using **forward recursion**. The equation $\boldsymbol{R}\boldsymbol{b}=\boldsymbol{d}$ can then be solved for $\boldsymbol{b}$ by backward recursion.

We have discussed three algorithms. Which should be used in practice? For positive definite $\boldsymbol{A}$, solving by the Cholesky decomposition is the preferred method, as it is numerically most efficient and stable. When $\boldsymbol{A}$ is not positive definite, solving by the QR decomposition is the preferred method, as it is numerically most stable. The advantage of the Gauss-Jordan algorithm is that it is the simplest to program.

A.19 ALGORITHMIC MATRIX INVERSION

Numerical methods for solving linear systems can be used to calculate the inverse of a full-rank $k\times k$ matrix $\boldsymbol{A}$. Let $\boldsymbol{B}=\boldsymbol{A}^{-1}$ be the inverse of $\boldsymbol{A}$. The matrices satisfy $\boldsymbol{A}\boldsymbol{B}=\boldsymbol{I}_k$, which is a matrix generalization of (A.13). The goal is to solve this system to obtain $\boldsymbol{B}$. We describe three methods.

1. Solving by Gaussian elimination:
   Replace $\boldsymbol{c}$ in (A.14) with $\boldsymbol{I}_k$, and apply the Gauss-Jordan elimination algorithm. The solution is $\boldsymbol{B}$.
2. Solving by QR decomposition:
   Numerically compute the QR decomposition $\boldsymbol{A}=\boldsymbol{Q}\boldsymbol{R}$, which implies $\boldsymbol{Q}\boldsymbol{R}\boldsymbol{B}=\boldsymbol{I}_k$. Premultiplying by $\boldsymbol{Q}'$ and observing that $\boldsymbol{Q}'\boldsymbol{Q}=\boldsymbol{I}_k$, we obtain $\boldsymbol{R}\boldsymbol{B}=\boldsymbol{Q}'$. Write $\boldsymbol{B}=[\boldsymbol{b}_1,\dots,\boldsymbol{b}_k]$ and $\boldsymbol{Q}'=[\boldsymbol{q}_1,\dots,\boldsymbol{q}_k]$. For $j=1,\dots,k$, $\boldsymbol{R}\boldsymbol{b}_j=\boldsymbol{q}_j$. Since $\boldsymbol{R}$ is upper triangular, the vector $\boldsymbol{b}_j$ can be found by backward recursion, as described in Section A.18.
3. Solving by Cholesky decomposition for positive definite $\boldsymbol{A}$:
   Compute the Cholesky decomposition $\boldsymbol{A}=\boldsymbol{L}\boldsymbol{R}$, where $\boldsymbol{L}$ is $k\times k$ and lower triangular, and $\boldsymbol{R}=\boldsymbol{L}'$ is upper triangular. This implies $\boldsymbol{L}\boldsymbol{R}\boldsymbol{B}=\boldsymbol{I}_k$ or $\boldsymbol{L}\boldsymbol{C}=\boldsymbol{I}_k$, where $\boldsymbol{C}=\boldsymbol{R}\boldsymbol{B}$. Applying forward recursion one column at a time, we can solve for $\boldsymbol{C}$. We then have $\boldsymbol{R}\boldsymbol{B}=\boldsymbol{C}$. Applying backward recursion one column at a time, we can solve for $\boldsymbol{B}$.

A.20 MATRIX CALCULUS

Let $\boldsymbol{x}=(x_1,\dots,x_k)'$ be $k\times 1$ and $g(\boldsymbol{x})=g(x_1,\dots,x_k):\mathbb{R}^k\to\mathbb{R}$. The vector derivative is

$$\frac{\partial}{\partial \boldsymbol{x}}g(\boldsymbol{x})=\begin{pmatrix}\frac{\partial}{\partial x_1}g(\boldsymbol{x})\\ \vdots\\ \frac{\partial}{\partial x_k}g(\boldsymbol{x})\end{pmatrix}$$

and

$$\frac{\partial}{\partial \boldsymbol{x}'} g(\boldsymbol{x}) = \left(\frac{\partial}{\partial x_1} g(\boldsymbol{x}) \quad \cdots \quad \frac{\partial}{\partial x_k} g(\boldsymbol{x}) \right).$$

Some properties are now summarized.

Theorem A.6 Properties of Matrix Derivatives.

1. $\frac{\partial}{\partial \boldsymbol{x}} \left(\boldsymbol{a}'\boldsymbol{x}\right) = \frac{\partial}{\partial \boldsymbol{x}} \left(\boldsymbol{x}'\boldsymbol{a}\right) = \boldsymbol{a}$.
2. $\frac{\partial}{\partial \boldsymbol{x}} \left(\boldsymbol{x}'\boldsymbol{A}\right) = \boldsymbol{A}$ and $\frac{\partial}{\partial \boldsymbol{x}'} \left(\boldsymbol{A}\boldsymbol{x}\right) = \boldsymbol{A}$.
3. $\frac{\partial}{\partial \boldsymbol{x}} \left(\boldsymbol{x}'\boldsymbol{A}\boldsymbol{x}\right) = \left(\boldsymbol{A} + \boldsymbol{A}'\right)\boldsymbol{x}$.
4. $\frac{\partial^2}{\partial \boldsymbol{x} \partial \boldsymbol{x}'} \left(\boldsymbol{x}'\boldsymbol{A}\boldsymbol{x}\right) = \boldsymbol{A} + \boldsymbol{A}'$.
5. $\frac{\partial}{\partial \boldsymbol{A}} \operatorname{tr}\left(\boldsymbol{B}\boldsymbol{A}\right) = \boldsymbol{B}'$.
6. $\frac{\partial}{\partial \boldsymbol{A}} \log\det\left(\boldsymbol{A}\right) = \left(\boldsymbol{A}^{-}\right)'$.

To show part 1, note that

$$\frac{\partial}{\partial x_j} \left(\boldsymbol{a}'\boldsymbol{x}\right) = \frac{\partial}{\partial x_j} \left(a_1 x_1 + \cdots + a_k x_k\right) = a_j.$$

Thus,

$$\frac{\partial}{\partial \boldsymbol{x}} \left(\boldsymbol{a}'\boldsymbol{x}\right) = \begin{pmatrix} a_1 \\ \vdots \\ a_k \end{pmatrix} = \boldsymbol{a}$$

as claimed.

For part 2, write $\boldsymbol{A} = [\boldsymbol{a}_1, \ldots, \boldsymbol{a}_m]$, so that

$$\frac{\partial}{\partial \boldsymbol{x}} \left(\boldsymbol{x}'\boldsymbol{A}\right) = \frac{\partial}{\partial \boldsymbol{x}} \left[\boldsymbol{x}'\boldsymbol{a}_1, \ldots, \boldsymbol{x}'\boldsymbol{a}_m\right] = \left[\frac{\partial}{\partial \boldsymbol{x}} \left(\boldsymbol{x}'\boldsymbol{a}_1\right), \ldots, \frac{\partial}{\partial \boldsymbol{x}} \left(\boldsymbol{x}'\boldsymbol{a}_m\right)\right] = [\boldsymbol{a}_1, \ldots, \boldsymbol{a}_m] = \boldsymbol{A}$$

using part 1. Then $\frac{\partial}{\partial \boldsymbol{x}'} \left(\boldsymbol{A}\boldsymbol{x}\right) = \boldsymbol{A}$ follows by taking the transpose.

For part 3, notice that $\boldsymbol{x}'\boldsymbol{A}\boldsymbol{x} = \boldsymbol{x}'\boldsymbol{A}'\boldsymbol{x}$ and apply the product rule and then part 2:

$$\frac{\partial}{\partial \boldsymbol{x}} \left(\boldsymbol{x}'\boldsymbol{A}\boldsymbol{x}\right) = \frac{\partial}{\partial \boldsymbol{x}} \left(\boldsymbol{x}'\boldsymbol{I}_k\right)\boldsymbol{A}\boldsymbol{x} + \frac{\partial}{\partial \boldsymbol{x}} \left(\boldsymbol{x}'\boldsymbol{A}'\right)\boldsymbol{x} = \boldsymbol{I}_k\boldsymbol{A}\boldsymbol{x} + \boldsymbol{A}'\boldsymbol{x} = \left(\boldsymbol{A} + \boldsymbol{A}'\right)\boldsymbol{x}.$$

For part 4, applying part 3, we find

$$\frac{\partial^2}{\partial \boldsymbol{x} \partial \boldsymbol{x}'} \left(\boldsymbol{x}'\boldsymbol{A}\boldsymbol{x}\right) = \frac{\partial}{\partial \boldsymbol{x}} \frac{\partial}{\partial \boldsymbol{x}'} \left(\boldsymbol{x}'\boldsymbol{A}\boldsymbol{x}\right) = \frac{\partial}{\partial \boldsymbol{x}} \boldsymbol{x}'\left(\boldsymbol{A} + \boldsymbol{A}'\right) = \boldsymbol{A} + \boldsymbol{A}'.$$

For part 5, recall from Section A.5 that we can write out explicitly

$$\operatorname{tr}\left(\boldsymbol{B}\boldsymbol{A}\right) = \sum_i \sum_j a_{ij} b_{ji}.$$

Thus if we take the derivative with respect to a_{ij}, we find

$$\frac{\partial}{\partial a_{ij}} \operatorname{tr}\left(\boldsymbol{B}\boldsymbol{A}\right) = b_{ji}$$

which is the ijth element of $\boldsymbol{B}'$, establishing part 5.

For part 6, recall Laplace's expansion:

$$\det \boldsymbol{A} = \sum_{j=1}^{k} a_{ij} C_{ij}$$

where C_{ij} is the ijth cofactor of $\boldsymbol{A}$. Set $\boldsymbol{C} = (C_{ij})$. Observe that for $j = 1, \ldots, k$, the C_{ij} are not functions of a_{ij}. Thus the derivative with respect to a_{ij} is

$$\frac{\partial}{\partial a_{ij}} \log \det (\boldsymbol{A}) = (\det \boldsymbol{A})^{-1} \frac{\partial}{\partial a_{ij}} \det \boldsymbol{A} = (\det \boldsymbol{A})^{-1} C_{ij}.$$

Together these results imply

$$\frac{\partial}{\partial \boldsymbol{A}} \log \det (\boldsymbol{A}) = (\det \boldsymbol{A})^{-1} \boldsymbol{C} = \boldsymbol{A}^{-1}$$

where the second equality is Theorem A.1 Part 12.

A.21 KRONECKER PRODUCTS AND THE VEC OPERATOR

Let $\boldsymbol{A} = [\boldsymbol{a}_1 \; \boldsymbol{a}_2 \; \cdots \; \boldsymbol{a}_n]$ be $m \times n$. The **vec** of $\boldsymbol{A}$, denoted by $\operatorname{vec}(\boldsymbol{A})$, is the $mn \times 1$ vector

$$\operatorname{vec}(\boldsymbol{A}) = \begin{pmatrix} \boldsymbol{a}_1 \\ \boldsymbol{a}_2 \\ \vdots \\ \boldsymbol{a}_n \end{pmatrix}.$$

Let $\boldsymbol{A} = \left(a_{ij}\right)$ be an $m \times n$ matrix, and let $\boldsymbol{B}$ be any matrix. The **Kronecker product** of $\boldsymbol{A}$ and $\boldsymbol{B}$, denoted $\boldsymbol{A} \otimes \boldsymbol{B}$, is the matrix

$$\boldsymbol{A} \otimes \boldsymbol{B} = \begin{bmatrix} a_{11}\boldsymbol{B} & a_{12}\boldsymbol{B} & \cdots & a_{1n}\boldsymbol{B} \\ a_{21}\boldsymbol{B} & a_{22}\boldsymbol{B} & \cdots & a_{2n}\boldsymbol{B} \\ \vdots & \vdots & & \vdots \\ a_{m1}\boldsymbol{B} & a_{m2}\boldsymbol{B} & \cdots & a_{mn}\boldsymbol{B} \end{bmatrix}.$$

Some important properties are now summarized. These results hold for matrices for which all matrix multiplications are conformable.

Theorem A.7 Properties of the Kronecker Product.

1. $(\boldsymbol{A} + \boldsymbol{B}) \otimes \boldsymbol{C} = \boldsymbol{A} \otimes \boldsymbol{C} + \boldsymbol{B} \otimes \boldsymbol{C}$.
2. $(\boldsymbol{A} \otimes \boldsymbol{B}) (\boldsymbol{C} \otimes \boldsymbol{D}) = \boldsymbol{AC} \otimes \boldsymbol{BD}$.
3. $\boldsymbol{A} \otimes (\boldsymbol{B} \otimes \boldsymbol{C}) = (\boldsymbol{A} \otimes \boldsymbol{B}) \otimes \boldsymbol{C}$.
4. $(\boldsymbol{A} \otimes \boldsymbol{B})' = \boldsymbol{A}' \otimes \boldsymbol{B}'$.
5. $\operatorname{tr}(\boldsymbol{A} \otimes \boldsymbol{B}) = \operatorname{tr}(\boldsymbol{A}) \operatorname{tr}(\boldsymbol{B})$.
6. If $\boldsymbol{A}$ is $m \times m$ and $\boldsymbol{B}$ is $n \times n$, $\det(\boldsymbol{A} \otimes \boldsymbol{B}) = (\det(\boldsymbol{A}))^n (\det(\boldsymbol{B}))^m$.
7. $(\boldsymbol{A} \otimes \boldsymbol{B})^{-1} = \boldsymbol{A}^{-1} \otimes \boldsymbol{B}^{-1}$.
8. If $\boldsymbol{A} > 0$ and $\boldsymbol{B} > 0$, then $\boldsymbol{A} \otimes \boldsymbol{B} > 0$.
9. $\operatorname{vec}(\boldsymbol{ABC}) = \left(\boldsymbol{C}' \otimes \boldsymbol{A}\right) \operatorname{vec}(\boldsymbol{B})$.
10. $\operatorname{tr}(\boldsymbol{ABCD}) = \operatorname{vec}\left(\boldsymbol{D}'\right)' \left(\boldsymbol{C}' \otimes \boldsymbol{A}\right) \operatorname{vec}(\boldsymbol{B})$.

A.22 VECTOR NORMS

Given a vector space V (such as Euclidean space $\mathbb{R}^m$) a **norm** is a function $\rho : V \to \mathbb{R}$ with the properties:

1. $\rho(c\boldsymbol{a}) = |c|\,\rho(\boldsymbol{a})$ for any complex number c and $\boldsymbol{a} \in V$.
2. $\rho(\boldsymbol{a}+\boldsymbol{b}) \le \rho(\boldsymbol{a}) + \rho(\boldsymbol{b})$.
3. If $\rho(\boldsymbol{a}) = 0$ then $\boldsymbol{a} = 0$.

A **seminorm** on V is a function that satisfies the first two properties. The second property is known as the triangle inequality. It is the one property that typically needs a careful demonstration (as the other two properties typically hold by inspection).

The typical norm used for Euclidean space $\mathbb{R}^m$ is the **Euclidean norm:**

$$\|\boldsymbol{a}\| = \left(\boldsymbol{a}'\boldsymbol{a}\right)^{1/2} = \left(\sum_{i=1}^{m} a_i^2\right)^{1/2}.$$

An alternative norm is the p-norm (for $p \ge 1$)

$$\|\boldsymbol{a}\|_p = \left(\sum_{i=1}^{m} |a_i|^p\right)^{1/p}.$$

Special cases include the Euclidean norm ($p = 2$), the 1-norm

$$\|\boldsymbol{a}\|_1 = \sum_{i=1}^{m} |a_i|$$

and the sup-norm

$$\|\boldsymbol{a}\|_\infty = \max\left(|a_1|, \dots, |a_m|\right).$$

For real numbers ($m = 1$), these norms coincide.

A.23 MATRIX NORMS

Two common norms used for matrix spaces are the **Frobenius norm** and the **spectral norm**. We will use $\|\boldsymbol{A}\|_F$ for the Frobenius and $\|\boldsymbol{A}\|$ for the spectral norm. The spectral norm is more widely used.

The **Frobenius norm** of an $m \times k$ matrix $\boldsymbol{A}$ is the Euclidean norm applied to its elements:

$$\|\boldsymbol{A}\|_F = \|\operatorname{vec}(\boldsymbol{A})\| = \left(\operatorname{tr}\left(\boldsymbol{A}'\boldsymbol{A}\right)\right)^{1/2} = \left(\sum_{i=1}^{m}\sum_{j=1}^{k} a_{ij}^2\right)^{1/2}.$$

When $m \times m$ $\boldsymbol{A}$ is real symmetric, then

$$\|\boldsymbol{A}\|_F = \left(\sum_{\ell=1}^{m} \lambda_\ell^2\right)^{1/2}$$

where λ_ℓ, $\ell = 1, \ldots, m$ are the eigenvalues of $\boldsymbol{A}$. To see this, by the spectral decomposition, $\boldsymbol{A} = \boldsymbol{H}\boldsymbol{\Lambda}\boldsymbol{H}'$ with $\boldsymbol{H}'\boldsymbol{H} = \boldsymbol{I}$ and $\boldsymbol{\Lambda} = \operatorname{diag}\{\lambda_1, \ldots, \lambda_m\}$, so

$$\|\boldsymbol{A}\|_F = \left(\operatorname{tr}\left(\boldsymbol{H}\boldsymbol{\Lambda}\boldsymbol{H}'\boldsymbol{H}\boldsymbol{\Lambda}\boldsymbol{H}'\right)\right)^{1/2} = \left(\operatorname{tr}\left(\boldsymbol{\Lambda}\boldsymbol{\Lambda}\right)\right)^{1/2} = \left(\sum_{\ell=1}^{m} \lambda_\ell^2\right)^{1/2}. \tag{A.16}$$

A useful calculation is for any $m \times 1$ vectors $\boldsymbol{a}$ and $\boldsymbol{b}$, using (A.1), we have

$$\left\|\boldsymbol{a}\boldsymbol{b}'\right\|_F = \operatorname{tr}\left(\boldsymbol{b}\boldsymbol{a}'\boldsymbol{a}\boldsymbol{b}'\right)^{1/2} = \left(\boldsymbol{b}'\boldsymbol{b}\boldsymbol{a}'\boldsymbol{a}\right)^{1/2} = \|\boldsymbol{a}\|\,\|\boldsymbol{b}\|$$

and in particular,

$$\left\|\boldsymbol{a}\boldsymbol{a}'\right\|_F = \|\boldsymbol{a}\|^2. \tag{A.17}$$

The **spectral norm** of an $m \times k$ real matrix $\boldsymbol{A}$ is its largest singular value:

$$\|\boldsymbol{A}\| = \sigma_{\max}(\boldsymbol{A}) = \left(\lambda_{\max}\left(\boldsymbol{A}'\boldsymbol{A}\right)\right)^{1/2}$$

where $\lambda_{\max}(\boldsymbol{B})$ denotes the largest eigenvalue of the matrix $\boldsymbol{B}$. Notice that

$$\lambda_{\max}\left(\boldsymbol{A}'\boldsymbol{A}\right) = \left\|\boldsymbol{A}'\boldsymbol{A}\right\|$$

so

$$\|\boldsymbol{A}\| = \left\|\boldsymbol{A}'\boldsymbol{A}\right\|^{1/2}.$$

If $\boldsymbol{A}$ is $m \times m$ and symmetric with eigenvalues λ_j, then $\|\boldsymbol{A}\| = \max_{j \le m} |\lambda_j|$.

The Frobenius and spectral norms are closely related. They are equivalent when applied to a matrix of rank 1, because $\left\|\boldsymbol{a}\boldsymbol{b}'\right\| = \|\boldsymbol{a}\|\,\|\boldsymbol{b}\| = \left\|\boldsymbol{a}\boldsymbol{b}'\right\|_F$. In general, for $m \times k$ matrix $\boldsymbol{A}$ with rank r,

$$\|\boldsymbol{A}\| = \left(\lambda_{\max}\left(\boldsymbol{A}'\boldsymbol{A}\right)\right)^{1/2} \le \left(\sum_{j=1}^{k} \lambda_j\left(\boldsymbol{A}'\boldsymbol{A}\right)\right)^{1/2} = \|\boldsymbol{A}\|_F. \tag{A.18}$$

Since $\boldsymbol{A}'\boldsymbol{A}$ also has rank at most r, it has at most r nonzero eigenvalues, and hence

$$\|\boldsymbol{A}\|_F = \left(\sum_{j=1}^{k} \lambda_j\left(\boldsymbol{A}'\boldsymbol{A}\right)\right)^{1/2} = \left(\sum_{j=1}^{r} \lambda_j\left(\boldsymbol{A}'\boldsymbol{A}\right)\right)^{1/2} \le \left(r\lambda_{\max}\left(\boldsymbol{A}'\boldsymbol{A}\right)\right)^{1/2} = \sqrt{r}\,\|\boldsymbol{A}\|. \tag{A.19}$$

Given any vector norm $\|\boldsymbol{a}\|$, the **induced matrix norm** is defined as

$$\|\boldsymbol{A}\| = \sup_{\boldsymbol{x}'\boldsymbol{x}=1} \|\boldsymbol{A}\boldsymbol{x}\| = \sup_{\boldsymbol{x}\neq 0} \frac{\|\boldsymbol{A}\boldsymbol{x}\|}{\|\boldsymbol{x}\|}.$$

To see that this is a norm, we need to check that it satisfies the triangle inequality. Indeed,

$$\|\boldsymbol{A}+\boldsymbol{B}\| = \sup_{\boldsymbol{x}'\boldsymbol{x}=1} \|\boldsymbol{A}\boldsymbol{x}+\boldsymbol{B}\boldsymbol{x}\| \le \sup_{\boldsymbol{x}'\boldsymbol{x}=1} \|\boldsymbol{A}\boldsymbol{x}\| + \sup_{\boldsymbol{x}'\boldsymbol{x}=1} \|\boldsymbol{B}\boldsymbol{x}\| = \|\boldsymbol{A}\| + \|\boldsymbol{B}\|.$$

For any vector $\boldsymbol{x}$, by the definition of the induced norm, $\|\boldsymbol{A}\boldsymbol{x}\| \le \|\boldsymbol{A}\|\,\|\boldsymbol{x}\|$, a property that is called **consistent norms.**

Let $\boldsymbol{A}$ and $\boldsymbol{B}$ be conformable and $\|\boldsymbol{A}\|$ an induced matrix norm. Then using the property of consistent norms, we have

$$\|\boldsymbol{AB}\| = \sup_{\boldsymbol{x}'\boldsymbol{x}=1} \|\boldsymbol{ABx}\| \leq \sup_{\boldsymbol{x}'\boldsymbol{x}=1} \|\boldsymbol{A}\| \, \|\boldsymbol{Bx}\| = \|\boldsymbol{A}\| \, \|\boldsymbol{B}\| \, .$$

A matrix norm that satisfies this property is called a **sub-multiplicative norm** and is a matrix form of the Schwarz inequality.

The matrix norm induced by the Euclidean vector norm is the spectral norm. Indeed,

$$\sup_{\boldsymbol{x}'\boldsymbol{x}=1} \|\boldsymbol{Ax}\|^2 = \sup_{\boldsymbol{x}'\boldsymbol{x}=1} \boldsymbol{x}'\boldsymbol{A}'\boldsymbol{Ax} = \lambda_{\max}\left(\boldsymbol{A}'\boldsymbol{A}\right) = \|\boldsymbol{A}\|^2 \, .$$

It follows that the spectral norm is consistent with the Euclidean norm and is sub-multiplicative.

APPENDIX B

USEFUL INEQUALITIES

This Appendix lists a set of inequalities and bounds that are used frequently in econometric theory, predominantly in asymptotic analysis. The proofs are presented in Section B.5.

B.1 INEQUALITIES FOR REAL NUMBERS

Triangle Inequality. For any real numbers x_j,

$$\left|\sum_{j=1}^{m} x_j\right| \leq \sum_{j=1}^{m} \left|x_j\right|. \tag{B.1}$$

Jensen's Inequality. If $g(\cdot):\mathbb{R}\to\mathbb{R}$ is convex, then for any nonnegative weights a_j such that $\sum_{j=1}^{m} a_j = 1$, and any real numbers x_j,

$$g\left(\sum_{j=1}^{m} a_j x_j\right) \leq \sum_{j=1}^{m} a_j g\left(x_j\right). \tag{B.2}$$

In particular, setting $a_j = 1/m$, then

$$g\left(\frac{1}{m}\sum_{j=1}^{m} x_j\right) \leq \frac{1}{m}\sum_{j=1}^{m} g\left(x_j\right). \tag{B.3}$$

If $g(\cdot):\mathbb{R}\to\mathbb{R}$ is concave, then the inequalities in (B.2) and (B.3) are reversed.

Geometric Mean Inequality. For any nonnegative real weights a_j such that $\sum_{j=1}^{m} a_j = 1$, and any nonnegative real numbers x_j,

$$x_1^{a_1} x_2^{a_2} \cdots x_m^{a_m} \leq \sum_{j=1}^{m} a_j x_j. \tag{B.4}$$

Loève's c_r Inequality. For any real numbers x_j, and any $0 < r \leq 1$,

$$\left|\sum_{j=1}^{m} x_j\right|^r \leq \sum_{j=1}^{m} \left|x_j\right|^r \tag{B.5}$$

and if $r \geq 1$,

$$\left| \sum_{j=1}^{m} x_j \right|^r \leq m^{r-1} \sum_{j=1}^{m} |x_j|^r . \tag{B.6}$$

For the important special case $m = 2$, we can combine these two inequalities as

$$|a+b|^r \leq C_r \left(|a|^r + |b|^r \right) \tag{B.7}$$

where $C_r = \max \left[1, 2^{r-1} \right]$.

Norm Monotonicity. If $0 < t \leq s$, and any real numbers x_j,

$$\left| \sum_{j=1}^{m} |x_j|^s \right|^{1/s} \leq \left| \sum_{j=1}^{m} |x_j|^t \right|^{1/t} . \tag{B.8}$$

B.2 INEQUALITIES FOR VECTORS

Triangle Inequality. If $\boldsymbol{a} = (a_1, \ldots, a_m)'$,

$$\|\boldsymbol{a}\| \leq \sum_{j=1}^{m} |a_j| . \tag{B.9}$$

c_2 Inequality. For any $m \times 1$ vectors $\boldsymbol{a}$ and $\boldsymbol{b}$,

$$(\boldsymbol{a}+\boldsymbol{b})' (\boldsymbol{a}+\boldsymbol{b}) \leq 2\boldsymbol{a}'\boldsymbol{a} + 2\boldsymbol{b}'\boldsymbol{b}. \tag{B.10}$$

Hölder's Inequality. If $p > 1$, $q > 1$, and $1/p + 1/q = 1$, then for any $m \times 1$ vectors $\boldsymbol{a}$ and $\boldsymbol{b}$,

$$\left| \boldsymbol{a}'\boldsymbol{b} \right| \leq \|\boldsymbol{a}\|_p \|\boldsymbol{b}\|_q . \tag{B.11}$$

Schwarz Inequality. For any $m \times 1$ vectors $\boldsymbol{a}$ and $\boldsymbol{b}$,

$$\left| \boldsymbol{a}'\boldsymbol{b} \right| \leq \|\boldsymbol{a}\| \|\boldsymbol{b}\| . \tag{B.12}$$

Minkowski's Inequality. For any $m \times 1$ vectors $\boldsymbol{a}$ and $\boldsymbol{b}$, and any $p \geq 1$,

$$\|\boldsymbol{a}+\boldsymbol{b}\|_p \leq \|\boldsymbol{a}\|_p + \|\boldsymbol{b}\|_p . \tag{B.13}$$

Triangle Inequality. For any $m \times 1$ vectors $\boldsymbol{a}$ and $\boldsymbol{b}$,

$$\|\boldsymbol{a}+\boldsymbol{b}\| \leq \|\boldsymbol{a}\| + \|\boldsymbol{b}\| . \tag{B.14}$$

B.3 INEQUALITIES FOR MATRICES

Schwarz Matrix Inequality. For any $m \times k$ and $k \times m$ matrices $\boldsymbol{A}$ and $\boldsymbol{B}$, and for both the Frobenius and spectral norms,

$$\|\boldsymbol{A}\boldsymbol{B}\| \le \|\boldsymbol{A}\| \, \|\boldsymbol{B}\| . \tag{B.15}$$

Triangle Inequality. For any $m \times k$ matrices $\boldsymbol{A}$ and $\boldsymbol{B}$, and for both the Frobenius and spectral norms,

$$\|\boldsymbol{A}+\boldsymbol{B}\| \le \|\boldsymbol{A}\| + \|\boldsymbol{B}\| . \tag{B.16}$$

Trace Inequality. For any $m \times m$ matrices $\boldsymbol{A}$ and $\boldsymbol{B}$ such that $\boldsymbol{A}$ is symmetric and $\boldsymbol{B} \geq 0$,

$$\operatorname{tr}(\boldsymbol{A}\boldsymbol{B}) \le \|\boldsymbol{A}\| \operatorname{tr}(\boldsymbol{B}) . \tag{B.17}$$

Quadratic Inequality. For any $m \times 1$ $\boldsymbol{b}$ and $m \times m$ symmetric matrix $\boldsymbol{A}$,

$$\boldsymbol{b}'\boldsymbol{A}\boldsymbol{b} \le \|\boldsymbol{A}\| \, \boldsymbol{b}'\boldsymbol{b}. \tag{B.18}$$

Strong Schwarz Matrix Inequality. For any conformable matrices $\boldsymbol{A}$ and $\boldsymbol{B}$,

$$\|\boldsymbol{A}\boldsymbol{B}\|_F \le \|\boldsymbol{A}\| \, \|\boldsymbol{B}\|_F . \tag{B.19}$$

Norm Equivalence. For any $m \times k$ matrix $\boldsymbol{A}$ of rank r,

$$\|\boldsymbol{A}\| \le \|\boldsymbol{A}\|_F \le \sqrt{r} \, \|\boldsymbol{A}\| . \tag{B.20}$$

Eigenvalue Product Inequality. For any $m \times m$ real symmetric matrices $\boldsymbol{A} \geq 0$ and $\boldsymbol{B} \geq 0$, the eigenvalues $\lambda_\ell(\boldsymbol{A}\boldsymbol{B})$ are real and satisfy

$$\lambda_{\min}(\boldsymbol{A})\,\lambda_{\min}(\boldsymbol{B}) \le \lambda_\ell(\boldsymbol{A}\boldsymbol{B}) \le \lambda_{\max}(\boldsymbol{A})\,\lambda_{\max}(\boldsymbol{B}) . \tag{B.21}$$

(Zhang and Zhang (2006), corollary 11).

B.4 PROBABILITY INEQUALITIES

Monotone Probability Inequality. For any events A and B such that $A \subset B$,

$$\mathbb{P}[A] \le \mathbb{P}[B] . \tag{B.22}$$

Inclusion-Exclusion Principle. For any events A and B,

$$\mathbb{P}[A \cup B] = \mathbb{P}[A] + \mathbb{P}[B] - \mathbb{P}[A \cap B] . \tag{B.23}$$

Boole's Inequality (Union Bound). For any events A and B,

$$\mathbb{P}[A \cup B] \le \mathbb{P}[A] + \mathbb{P}[B] . \tag{B.24}$$

Bonferroni's Inequality. For any events A and B,

$$\mathbb{P}[A \cap B] \geq \mathbb{P}[A] + \mathbb{P}[B] - 1. \tag{B.25}$$

Expectation Equality. If $X \in \mathbb{R}$ is a nonnegative random variable, then

$$\mathbb{E}[X] = \int_0^\infty \mathbb{P}[X > u]\, du. \tag{B.26}$$

Jensen's Inequality. If $g(x) : \mathbb{R}^m \to \mathbb{R}$ is convex, then for any random vector $X \in \mathbb{R}^k$ for which $\mathbb{E}\|X\| < \infty$ and $\mathbb{E}\left|g(X)\right| < \infty$,

$$g(\mathbb{E}[X]) \leq \mathbb{E}\left[g(X)\right]. \tag{B.27}$$

If $g(\cdot)$ is concave, the inequality is reversed.

Conditional Jensen's Inequality. If $g(x) : \mathbb{R}^m \to \mathbb{R}$ is convex, then for any random variables $(Y, X) \in \mathbb{R}^m \times \mathbb{R}^k$ for which $\mathbb{E}\|Y\| < \infty$ and $\mathbb{E}\left\|g(Y)\right\| < \infty$,

$$g(\mathbb{E}[Y \mid X]) \leq \mathbb{E}\left[g(Y) \mid X\right]. \tag{B.28}$$

If $g(x)$ is concave, the inequality is reversed.

Conditional Expectation Inequality. For any $r \geq 1$ and for any random variables $(Y, X) \in \mathbb{R} \times \mathbb{R}^k$ such that $\mathbb{E}|Y|^r < \infty$,

$$\mathbb{E}|\mathbb{E}(Y \mid X)|^r \leq \mathbb{E}|Y|^r < \infty. \tag{B.29}$$

Expectation Inequality. For any random vector $Y \in \mathbb{R}^m$ with $\mathbb{E}\|Y\| < \infty$,

$$\|\mathbb{E}[Y]\| \leq \mathbb{E}\|Y\|. \tag{B.30}$$

Hölder's Inequality. For any $p > 1$ and $q > 1$ such that $\frac{1}{p} + \frac{1}{q} = 1$, and any random $m \times n$ matrices X and Y,

$$\mathbb{E}\left\|X'Y\right\| \leq \left(\mathbb{E}\|X\|^p\right)^{1/p} \left(\mathbb{E}\|Y\|^q\right)^{1/q}. \tag{B.31}$$

Cauchy-Schwarz Inequality. For any random $m \times n$ matrices X and Y,

$$\mathbb{E}\left\|X'Y\right\| \leq \left(\mathbb{E}\|X\|^2\right)^{1/2} \left(\mathbb{E}\|Y\|^2\right)^{1/2}. \tag{B.32}$$

Matrix Cauchy-Schwarz Inequality. Tripathi (1999). For any random $X \in \mathbb{R}^m$ and $Y \in \mathbb{R}^\ell$,

$$\mathbb{E}\left[YX'\right]\left(\mathbb{E}\left[XX'\right]\right)^- \mathbb{E}\left[XY'\right] \leq \mathbb{E}\left[YY'\right]. \tag{B.33}$$

Minkowski's Inequality. For any random $m \times n$ matrices X and Y,

$$\left(\mathbb{E}\|X + Y\|^p\right)^{1/p} \leq \left(\mathbb{E}\|X\|^p\right)^{1/p} + \left(\mathbb{E}\|Y\|^p\right)^{1/p}. \tag{B.34}$$

Lyapunov's Inequality. For any random $m \times n$ matrix X and any $0 < r \leq p$,

$$\left(\mathbb{E}\,\|X\|^r\right)^{1/r} \leq \left(\mathbb{E}\,\|X\|^p\right)^{1/p}. \tag{B.35}$$

Markov's Inequality (Standard Form). For any random $X \in \mathbb{R}^k$, nonnegative function $g(x) \geq 0$, and any $\epsilon > 0$,

$$\mathbb{P}\left[g(X) > \epsilon\right] \leq \epsilon^{-1}\mathbb{E}\left[g(X)\right]. \tag{B.36}$$

Markov's Inequality (Strong Form). For any random $X \in \mathbb{R}^k$, nonnegative function $g(x) \geq 0$, and any $\epsilon > 0$,

$$\mathbb{P}\left[g(X) > \epsilon\right] \leq^{-1} \mathbb{E}\left[g\,(X)\,\mathbb{1}\left\{g(X) > \epsilon\right\}\right]. \tag{B.37}$$

Chebyshev's Inequality. For any random $X \in \mathbb{R}$ and any $\epsilon > 0$,

$$\mathbb{P}\left[|X - \mathbb{E}\left[X\right]| > \epsilon\right] \leq \epsilon^{-2}\operatorname{var}\left[X\right]. \tag{B.38}$$

Gaussian Tail Inequality (Chernoff Bound). If $X \sim \mathrm{N}(0,1)$, then for any $t > 0$,

$$\mathbb{P}\left[X > t\right] \leq \exp\left(-\frac{t^2}{2}\right). \tag{B.39}$$

Bernstein's Inequality. If $X_i \in \mathbb{R}$ are independent, $\mathbb{E}\left[X_i\right] = 0$, $\overline{\sigma}^2 = \sum_{i=1}^n \mathbb{E}\left[X_i^2\right]$, and $|X_i| \leq M < \infty$, then for all $\epsilon > 0$,

$$\mathbb{P}\left[\left|\sum_{i=1}^n X_i\right| > \epsilon\right] \leq 2\exp\left(-\frac{\epsilon^2}{4\overline{\sigma}^2 + 4M\epsilon}\right). \tag{B.40}$$

Bernstein's Inequality for Vectors. If $X_i = (X_{1i}, \ldots, X_{mi})'$ are independent random vectors, $\mathbb{E}\left[X_i\right] = 0$, $\overline{\sigma}^2 = \max_j \sum_{i=1}^n \mathbb{E}\left[X_{ji}^2\right]$, and $\left|X_{ji}\right| \leq M < \infty$, then for all $\epsilon > 0$,

$$\mathbb{P}\left[\left\|\sum_{i=1}^n X_i\right\| > \epsilon\right] \leq 2m\exp\left(-\frac{\epsilon^2}{4m^2\overline{\sigma}^2 + 4mM\epsilon}\right). \tag{B.41}$$

Bahr-Esseen Inequality. If $X_i \in \mathbb{R}$ are independent and $\mathbb{E}\left[X_i\right] = 0$, then for any $0 < r \leq 2$,

$$\mathbb{E}\left|\sum_{i=1}^n X_i\right|^r \leq 2\sum_{i=1}^n \mathbb{E}\,|X_i|^r. \tag{B.42}$$

Some of the following inequalities make use of **Rademacher** random variables ε, which are two-point discrete variables satisfying

$$\mathbb{P}\left[\varepsilon = 1\right] = \frac{1}{2}$$
$$\mathbb{P}\left[\varepsilon = -1\right] = \frac{1}{2}.$$

Exponential Inequality. If ε_i are independent Rademacher random variables, then for any constants a_i,

$$\mathbb{E}\left[\exp\left(\sum_{i=1}^{n} a_i\varepsilon_i\right)\right] \le \exp\left(\frac{\sum_{i=1}^{n} a_i^2}{2}\right). \tag{B.43}$$

Symmetrization Inequality. If $X_i \in \mathbb{R}$ are independent, $\mathbb{E}[X_i] = 0$, and ε_i are independent Rademacher random variables, then for any $r \ge 1$,

$$\mathbb{E}\left|\sum_{i=1}^{n} X_i\right|^r \le 2^r \mathbb{E}\left|\sum_{i=1}^{n} X_i\varepsilon_i\right|^r. \tag{B.44}$$

Khintchine's Inequality. If ε_i are independent Rademacher random variables, then for any $r > 0$ and any real numbers a_i,

$$\mathbb{E}\left|\sum_{i=1}^{n} a_i\varepsilon_i\right|^r \le K_r\left(\sum_{i=1}^{n} a_i^2\right)^{r/2} \tag{B.45}$$

where $K_r = 1$ for $r \le 2$, and $K_r = 2^{r/2}\Gamma\left((r+1)/2\right)/\pi^{1/2}$ for $r \ge 2$.

Maximal Khintchine Inequality. If ε_i are independent Rademacher random variables and $J \ge 2$, then for any real numbers a_{ji},

$$\mathbb{E}\left[\max_{1\le j\le J}\left|\sum_{i=1}^{n} a_{ji}\varepsilon_i\right|\right] \le 2\left(\log J\right)^{1/2} \max_{1\le j\le J}\left(\sum_{i=1}^{n} a_i^2\right)^{1/2}. \tag{B.46}$$

Marcinkiewicz-Zygmund Inequality. If $X_i \in \mathbb{R}$ are independent and $\mathbb{E}[X_i] = 0$, then for any $r \ge 1$,

$$\mathbb{E}\left|\sum_{i=1}^{n} X_i\right|^r \le M_r \mathbb{E}\left|\sum_{i=1}^{n} X_i^2\right|^{r/2} \tag{B.47}$$

where $M_r = 2^r K_r$ with K_r from the Khintchine inequality.

Whittle's Inequalities. Whittle (1960). Assume $X_i \in \mathbb{R}$ and for some $r \ge 2$, $\mathbb{E}|X_i|^r \le B_{1r} < \infty$. There is a constant $C_{1r} < \infty$ such that for any mutually independent X_i with $\mathbb{E}[X_i] = 0$, and any real numbers a_i,

$$\mathbb{E}\left|\sum_{i=1}^{n} a_i X_i\right|^r \le C_{1r}\left|\sum_{i=1}^{n} a_i^2\right|^{r/2}. \tag{B.48}$$

Furthermore, if $\mathbb{E}|X_i|^{2r} \le B_{2r} < \infty$, then there is a constant $C_{2r} < \infty$ such that for any real $n \times n$ matrix $\boldsymbol{A}$ and setting $X = (X_1, \ldots, X_n)'$,

$$\mathbb{E}\left|X'\boldsymbol{A}X - \mathbb{E}\left[X'\boldsymbol{A}X\right]\right|^r \le C_{2r}\operatorname{tr}\left(\boldsymbol{A}'\boldsymbol{A}\right)^{r/2}. \tag{B.49}$$

The proof in Section B.5 shows that we can set $C_{1r} = M_r B_{1r}$ and $C_{2r} = 4^r K_r C_{1r}^{1/2} B_{2r}^{1/2}$, where M_r and K_r are from the Marcinkiewicz-Zygmund and Khinchine inequalities.

Rosenthal's Inequality. For any $r > 0$ there is a constant $R_r < \infty$ such that if $X_i \in \mathbb{R}$ are independent and $\mathbb{E}[X_i] = 0$,

$$\mathbb{E}\left|\sum_{i=1}^{n} X_i\right|^r \leq R_r \left\{ \left(\sum_{i=1}^{n} \mathbb{E}\left[X_i^2\right]\right)^{r/2} + \sum_{i=1}^{n} \mathbb{E}\left|X_i\right|^r \right\}. \tag{B.50}$$

The proof in Section B.5 establishes that (B.50) holds with $R_r = 2^{r(r-2)/8} M_r$, where M_r is from the Marcinkiewicz-Zygmund inequality.

For a generalization of Rosenthal's inequality to the matrix, case see B. Hansen (2015).

Kolmogorov's Inequality. If X_i are independent, $\mathbb{E}[X_i] = 0$, and $\mathbb{E}\left[X_i^2\right] < \infty$, then for any $\epsilon > 0$,

$$\mathbb{P}\left[\max_{1 \leq j \leq n} \left|\sum_{i=1}^{j} X_i\right| > \epsilon\right] \leq \epsilon^{-2} \sum_{i=1}^{n} \mathbb{E}\left[X_i^2\right]. \tag{B.51}$$

Billingsley's Inequality. If X_i are independent, $\mathbb{E}[X_i] = 0$, $S_i = \sum_{j=1}^{i} X_j$, and $\sigma_n^2 = \text{var}[S_n]$, then for any $\lambda > 2\sqrt{2}$,

$$\mathbb{P}\left[\max_{1 \leq i \leq n} |S_i| > \sigma_n \lambda\right] \leq 2\mathbb{P}\left[|S_n| > \frac{\sigma_n \lambda}{2}\right]. \tag{B.52}$$

Billingsley (1999, lemma 10.7).

B.5 PROOFS*

Proof of Triangle Inequality (B.1) Take the case $m = 2$. Observe that

$$-|x_1| \leq x_1 \leq |x_1|$$
$$-|x_2| \leq x_2 \leq |x_2|.$$

Adding, we find

$$-|x_1| - |x_2| \leq x_1 + x_2 \leq |x_1| + |x_2|$$

which is (B.1) for $m = 2$. For $m > 2$, apply (B.1) $m - 1$ times. ■

Proof of Jensen's Inequality (B.2). See *Probability and Statistics for Economists*, Theorem 2.12.

Proof of Geometric Mean Inequality (B.4). See *Probability and Statistics for Economists*, Theorem 2.13.

Proof of Loève's c_r Inequality (B.5). See *Probability and Statistics for Economists*, Theorem 2.14.

Proof of Norm Monotonicity (B.8). See *Probability and Statistics for Economists*, Theorem 2.15.

Proof of Triangle Inequality (B.9) Apply the c_r inequality (B.5) with $r = 1/2$ to find

$$\|\boldsymbol{a}\| = \left|\sum_{j=1}^{m} a_j^2\right|^{1/2} \leq \sum_{j=1}^{m} \left|a_j\right|.$$ ■

Proof of c_2 Inequality (B.10) By the c_r inequality (B.6) with $r=2$, $(a_j+b_j)^2 \le 2a_j^2 + 2b_j^2$. Thus

$$(\boldsymbol{a}+\boldsymbol{b})'(\boldsymbol{a}+\boldsymbol{b}) = \sum_{j=1}^{m}(a_j+b_j)^2 \le 2\sum_{j=1}^{m} a_j^2 + 2\sum_{j=1}^{m} b_j^2 = 2\boldsymbol{a}'\boldsymbol{a} + 2\boldsymbol{b}'\boldsymbol{b}.$$

■

Proof of Hölder's Inequality (B.11) Without loss of generality, assume $\sum_{j=1}^{m}|a_j|^p = \|\boldsymbol{a}\|_p^p = 1$ and $\sum_{j=1}^{m}|b_j|^q = \|\boldsymbol{b}\|_q^q = 1$. By the geometric mean inequality (B.4),

$$|a_j b_j| \le |a_j|\,|b_j| \le \frac{|a_j|^p}{p} + \frac{|b_j|^q}{q}. \tag{B.53}$$

By the triangle inequality (B.1), (B.53), the assumptions $\sum_{j=1}^{m}|a_j|^p = 1$, $\sum_{j=1}^{m}|b_j|^q = 1$, and $1/p + 1/q = 1$,

$$\begin{aligned}
|\boldsymbol{a}'\boldsymbol{b}| &= \left|\sum_{j=1}^{m} a_j b_j\right| \\
&\le \sum_{j=1}^{m} |a_j b_j| \\
&\le \sum_{j=1}^{m}\left(\frac{|a_j|^p}{p} + \frac{|b_j|^q}{q}\right) \\
&= \frac{1}{p} + \frac{1}{q} = 1
\end{aligned}$$

which is (B.11). ■

Proof of Schwarz Inequality (B.12) This is a special case of Hölder's inequality (B.11) with $p=q=2$:

$$|\boldsymbol{a}'\boldsymbol{b}| \le \sum_{j=1}^{m}|a_j b_j| \le \|\boldsymbol{a}\|\,\|\boldsymbol{b}\|.$$

■

Proof of Minkowski's Inequality (B.13) Set $q = p/(p-1)$, so that $1/p + 1/q = 1$. Using the triangle inequality for real numbers (B.1) and two applications of Hölder's inequality (B.11),

$$\begin{aligned}
\|\boldsymbol{a}+\boldsymbol{b}\|_p^p &= \sum_{j=1}^{m}|a_j+b_j|^p \\
&= \sum_{j=1}^{m}|a_j+b_j|\,|a_j+b_j|^{p-1} \\
&\le \sum_{j=1}^{m}|a_j|\,|a_j+b_j|^{p-1} + \sum_{j=1}^{m}|b_j|\,|a_j+b_j|^{p-1}
\end{aligned}$$

$$\le \|a\|_p \left(\sum_{j=1}^{m} |a_j + b_j|^{(p-1)q} \right)^{1/q} + \|b\|_p \left(\sum_{j=1}^{m} |a_j + b_j|^{(p-1)q} \right)^{1/q}$$

$$= \left(\|a\|_p + \|b\|_p \right) \|a + b\|_p^{p-1} .$$

Solving, we find (B.13). ■

Proof of Triangle Inequality (B.14) This is Minkowski's inequality (B.13) with $p = 2$. ■

Proof of Schwarz Matrix Inequality (B.15) The inequality holds for the spectral norm, because it is an induced norm. Now consider the Frobenius norm. Partition $\boldsymbol{A}' = [\boldsymbol{a}_1, \ldots, \boldsymbol{a}_n]$ and $\boldsymbol{B} = [\boldsymbol{b}_1, \ldots, \boldsymbol{b}_n]$. Then by partitioned matrix multiplication, the definition of the Frobenius norm and the Schwarz inequality (B.12),

$$\|\boldsymbol{AB}\|_F = \left\| \begin{matrix} \boldsymbol{a}_1'\boldsymbol{b}_1 & \boldsymbol{a}_1'\boldsymbol{b}_2 & \cdots \\ \boldsymbol{a}_2'\boldsymbol{b}_1 & \boldsymbol{a}_2'\boldsymbol{b}_2 & \cdots \\ \vdots & \vdots & \ddots \end{matrix} \right\|_F$$

$$\le \left\| \begin{matrix} \|\boldsymbol{a}_1\| \|\boldsymbol{b}_1\| & \|\boldsymbol{a}_1\| \|\boldsymbol{b}_2\| & \cdots \\ \|\boldsymbol{a}_2\| \|\boldsymbol{b}_1\| & \|\boldsymbol{a}_2\| \|\boldsymbol{b}_2\| & \cdots \\ \vdots & \vdots & \ddots \end{matrix} \right\|_F$$

$$= \left(\sum_{i=1}^{m} \sum_{j=1}^{m} \|\boldsymbol{a}_i\|^2 \left\|\boldsymbol{b}_j\right\|^2 \right)^{1/2}$$

$$= \left(\sum_{i=1}^{m} \|\boldsymbol{a}_i\|^2 \right)^{1/2} \left(\sum_{i=1}^{m} \|\boldsymbol{b}_i\|^2 \right)^{1/2}$$

$$= \left(\sum_{i=1}^{k} \sum_{j=1}^{m} \boldsymbol{a}_{ji}^2 \right)^{1/2} \left(\sum_{i=1}^{m} \sum_{j=1}^{k} \left\|\boldsymbol{b}_{ji}\right\|^2 \right)^{1/2}$$

$$= \|\boldsymbol{A}\|_F \|\boldsymbol{B}\|_F .$$ ■

Proof of Triangle Inequality (B.16) The inequality holds for the spectral norm, because it is an induced norm. Now consider the Frobenius norm. Let $\boldsymbol{a} = \text{vec}(\boldsymbol{A})$ and $\boldsymbol{b} = \text{vec}(\boldsymbol{B})$. Then by the definition of the Frobenius norm and the triangle inequality (B.14),

$$\|\boldsymbol{A} + \boldsymbol{B}\|_F = \|\text{vec}(\boldsymbol{A} + \boldsymbol{B})\|_F = \|\boldsymbol{a} + \boldsymbol{b}\| \le \|\boldsymbol{a}\| + \|\boldsymbol{b}\| = \|\boldsymbol{A}\|_F + \|\boldsymbol{B}\|_F .$$ ■

Proof of Trace Inequality (B.17) By the spectral decomposition for symmetric matices, $\boldsymbol{A} = \boldsymbol{H}\Lambda\boldsymbol{H}'$, where Λ has the eigenvalues λ_j of $\boldsymbol{A}$ on its diagonal and $\boldsymbol{H}$ is orthonormal. Define $\boldsymbol{C} = \boldsymbol{H}'\boldsymbol{B}\boldsymbol{H}$, which has non-negative diagonal elements C_{jj}, because $\boldsymbol{B}$ is positive semi-definite. Then

$$\text{tr}(\boldsymbol{AB}) = \text{tr}(\Lambda\boldsymbol{C}) = \sum_{j=1}^{m} \lambda_j C_{jj} \le \max_j |\lambda_j| \sum_{j=1}^{m} C_{jj} = \|\boldsymbol{A}\|_2 \, \text{tr}(\boldsymbol{C})$$

where the inequality uses the fact that $C_{jj} \geq 0$. Note that

$$\operatorname{tr}(\boldsymbol{C}) = \operatorname{tr}\left(\boldsymbol{H}'\boldsymbol{B}\boldsymbol{H}\right) = \operatorname{tr}\left(\boldsymbol{H}\boldsymbol{H}'\boldsymbol{B}\right) = \operatorname{tr}(\boldsymbol{B})$$

because $\boldsymbol{H}$ is orthonormal. Thus $\operatorname{tr}(\boldsymbol{A}\boldsymbol{B}) \leq \|\boldsymbol{A}\|_2 \operatorname{tr}(\boldsymbol{B})$, as stated. ■

Proof of Quadratic Inequality (B.18) In the trace inequality (B.17), set $\boldsymbol{B} = \boldsymbol{b}\boldsymbol{b}'$, and note that $\operatorname{tr}(\boldsymbol{A}\boldsymbol{B}) = \boldsymbol{b}'\boldsymbol{A}\boldsymbol{b}$ and $\operatorname{tr}(\boldsymbol{B}) = \boldsymbol{b}'\boldsymbol{b}$. ■

Proof of Strong Schwarz Matrix Inequality (B.19) By the definition of the Frobenius norm, the property of the trace, the trace inequality (B.17) (noting that both $\boldsymbol{A}'\boldsymbol{A}$ and $\boldsymbol{B}\boldsymbol{B}'$ are symmetric and positive semi-definite), and the Schwarz matrix inequality (B.15),

$$\begin{aligned}
\|\boldsymbol{A}\boldsymbol{B}\|_F &= \left(\operatorname{tr}\left(\boldsymbol{B}'\boldsymbol{A}'\boldsymbol{A}\boldsymbol{B}\right)\right)^{1/2} \\
&= \left(\operatorname{tr}\left(\boldsymbol{A}'\boldsymbol{A}\boldsymbol{B}\boldsymbol{B}'\right)\right)^{1/2} \\
&\leq \left(\left\|\boldsymbol{A}'\boldsymbol{A}\right\|_2 \operatorname{tr}\left(\boldsymbol{B}\boldsymbol{B}'\right)\right)^{1/2} \\
&= \|\boldsymbol{A}\|_2 \|\boldsymbol{B}\|_F .
\end{aligned}$$ ■

Proof of Norm Equivalence (B.20) The first inequality was established in (A.18), and the second in (A.19). ■

Proof of Monotone Probability Inequality (B.22). See *Probability and Statistics for Economists*, Theorem 1.2 Part 4.

Proof of Inclusion-Exclusion Principle (B.23). See *Probability and Statistics for Economists*, Theorem 1.2 Part 5.

Proof of Boole's Inequality (B.5). See *Probability and Statistics for Economists*, Theorem 1.2 Part 6.

Proof of Bonferrroni's Inequality (B.25). See *Probability and Statistics for Economists*, Theorem 1.2 Part 7.

Proof of Expectation Equality (B.26) Let $F^*(u) = \mathbb{P}[X > u] = 1 - F(u)$, where $F(u)$ is the distribution function. By integration by parts,

$$\mathbb{E}[X] = \int_0^\infty u dF(u) = -\int_0^\infty u dF^*(u) = -\left[uF^*(u)\right]_0^\infty + \int_0^\infty F^*(u) du = \int_0^\infty \mathbb{P}[X > u]\, du$$

as stated. ■

Proof of Jensen's Inequality (B.27). See *Probability and Statistics for Economists*, Theorem 2.9.

Proof of Conditional Jensen's Inequality (B.28). Apply Jensen's inequality to the conditional distribution.

Proof of Conditional Expectation Inequality (B.29) As the function $|u|^r$ is convex for $r \geq 1$, the conditional Jensen's inequality (B.28) implies

$$|\mathbb{E}[Y \mid X]|^r \leq \mathbb{E}\left[|Y|^r \mid X\right].$$

Taking unconditional expectations and using the law of iterated expectations, we obtain

$$\mathbb{E}\left[|\mathbb{E}[Y \mid X]|^r\right] \leq \mathbb{E}\left[\mathbb{E}\left[|Y|^r \mid X\right]\right] = \mathbb{E}\left[|Y|^r\right] < \infty$$

as required. ■

Proof of Expectation Inequality (B.30). See *Probability and Statistics for Economists*, Theorem 2.10.

Proof of Hölder's Inequality (B.31). See *Probability and Statistics for Economists*, Theorem 4.15.

Proof of Cauchy-Schwarz Inequality (B.32). See *Probability and Statistics for Economists*, Theorem 4.11.

Proof of Matrix Cauchy-Schwarz Inequality (B.33) Define $e = Y - \mathbb{E}\left[YX'\right]\left(\mathbb{E}\left[XX'\right]\right)^{-} X$. Note that $\mathbb{E}\left[ee'\right] \geq 0$ is positive semi-definite. We can calculate that

$$\mathbb{E}\left[ee'\right] = \mathbb{E}\left[YY'\right] - \left(\mathbb{E}\left[YX'\right]\right)\left(\mathbb{E}\left[XX'\right]\right)^{-} \mathbb{E}\left[XY'\right].$$

Because the left side is positive semi-definite, so is the right side. Thus,

$$\mathbb{E}\left[YY'\right] \geq \mathbb{E}\left[YX'\right]\left(\mathbb{E}\left[XX'\right]\right)^{-} \mathbb{E}\left[XY'\right]$$

as stated. ■

Proof of Minkowski's Inequality (B.34). See *Probability and Statistics for Economists*, Theorem 4.16.

Proof of Lyapunov's Inequality (B.35). See *Probability and Statistics for Economists*, Theorem 2.11.

Proof of Markov's Inequality (B.36) and (B.37). See *Probability and Statistics for Economists*, Theorem 7.3.

Proof of Chebyshev's Inequality (B.38). See *Probability and Statistics for Economists*, Theorem 7.1.

Proof of Gaussian Tail Inequality (B.39) Since $t > 0$, using Markov's inequality (B.36), and the moment generating function of the standard normal (See *Probability and Statistics for Economists*, Theorem 5.3),

$$\mathbb{P}[X > t] = \mathbb{P}\left[\exp(tX) > \exp\left(t^2\right)\right] \leq \frac{\mathbb{E}\left[\exp(tX)\right]}{\exp\left(t^2\right)} = \frac{\exp\left(\frac{t^2}{2}\right)}{\exp\left(t^2\right)}$$

which simplies to (B.39). ■

Proof of Bernsteins's Inequality (B.40) We first show that

$$\mathbb{P}\left[\sum_{i=1}^{n} X_i > \epsilon\right] \leq \exp\left(-\frac{\epsilon^2}{4\overline{\sigma}^2 + 4M\epsilon}\right). \tag{B.54}$$

Set $\sigma_i^2 = \mathbb{E}\left[X_i^2\right]$ and $t = \epsilon / \left(2\overline{\sigma}^2 + 2M\epsilon\right) > 0$. Observe that

$$t^k \leq \frac{\epsilon}{2\overline{\sigma}^2}\left(\frac{1}{2M}\right)^{k-2} t \tag{B.55}$$

and $|X_i| \leq M$ implies

$$\mathbb{E}\left[X_i^k\right] \leq \sigma_i^2 (2M)^{k-2}. \tag{B.56}$$

Using Markov's inequality (B.36), the left side of (B.54) equals

$$\mathbb{P}\left[\exp\left(t\sum_{i=1}^{n} X_i\right) > \exp(t\epsilon)\right] \leq e^{-t\epsilon}\mathbb{E}\left[\exp\left(t\sum_{i=1}^{n_i} X_i\right)\right] = e^{-t\epsilon}\prod_{i=1}^{n}\mathbb{E}\left[\exp(tX_i)\right]. \tag{B.57}$$

Expanding the exponential function, using the assumption $\mathbb{E}[X_i] = 0$, (B.55), and (B.56)

$$\begin{aligned}
\mathbb{E}\left[\exp(tX_i)\right] &= 1 + t\mathbb{E}[x_i] + \sum_{k=2}^{\infty}\frac{t^k\mathbb{E}\left[X_i^k\right]}{k!} \\
&\leq 1 + \frac{\sigma_i^2\epsilon t}{2\overline{\sigma}^2}\sum_{k=2}^{\infty}\frac{1}{k!} \\
&\leq 1 + \frac{\sigma_i^2\epsilon t}{2\overline{\sigma}^2} \\
&\leq \exp\left(\frac{\sigma_i^2\epsilon t}{2\overline{\sigma}^2}\right).
\end{aligned}$$

Thus the right side of (B.57) is less than

$$\exp\left(-t\epsilon + \frac{\epsilon t}{2}\right) = \exp\left(-\frac{\epsilon t}{2}\right) = \exp\left(-\frac{\epsilon^2}{4\overline{\sigma}^2 + 4M\epsilon/3}\right)$$

where the second equality uses the defintion $t = \epsilon / \left(2\overline{\sigma}^2 + 2M\epsilon\right)$. This establishes (B.54).

Replacing X_i with $-X_i$ in the above argument, we obtain

$$\mathbb{P}\left[\sum_{i=1}^{n} X_i < -\epsilon\right] \leq \exp\left(-\frac{\epsilon^2}{4\overline{\sigma}^2 + 4M\epsilon}\right). \tag{B.58}$$

Together, (B.54) and (B.58) establish (B.40). ■

Proof of Bernsteins's Inequality for Vectors (B.41) By the triangle inequality (B.9), Boole's inequality (B.24), and then Bernstein's inequality (B.40),

$$\begin{aligned}
\mathbb{P}\left[\left\|\sum_{i=1}^{n} X_i\right\| > \epsilon\right] &\leq \mathbb{P}\left[\sum_{j=1}^{m}\left|\sum_{i=1}^{n} X_{ji}\right| > \epsilon\right] \\
&\leq \mathbb{P}\left[\bigcup_{j=1}^{m}\mathbb{1}\left\{\left|\sum_{i=1}^{n} X_{ji}\right| > \epsilon/m\right\}\right]
\end{aligned}$$

$$\leq \sum_{j=1}^{m} \mathbb{P}\left[\left|\sum_{i=1}^{n} X_{ji}\right| > \epsilon/m\right]$$

$$\leq 2m \exp\left(-\frac{(\epsilon/m)^2}{4\overline{\sigma}^2 + 4M(\epsilon/m)}\right)$$

which is (B.41). ■

Proof of Bahr-Esseen Inequality (B.42) Our proof is taken from von Bahr and Esseen (1965). For $0 < r \leq 1$, (B.42) holds by the c_r inequality (B.5). For $r = 2$, (B.42) holds by independence and direct calculation. We thus focus on the case $1 < r < 2$.

We start with a characterization of an absolute moment. Define the generalized cosine integral

$$K(r) = \int_0^\infty t^{-(r+1)} (1 - \cos(t))\, dt \tag{B.59}$$

which is finite for $0 < r < 2$. Making the change of variable $t = sx$ and rearranging, we obtain

$$|x|^r = K(r)^{-1} \int_0^\infty t^{-(r+1)} (1 - \cos(tx))\, dt.$$

Let $C_i(t)$ denote the characteristic function of X_i, and let $R_i(t) = \mathbb{E}[\cos(tX_i)]$ denote its real part. Thus for any $0 < r < 2$,

$$\mathbb{E}|X_i|^r = K(r)^{-1} \int_0^\infty t^{-(r+1)} (1 - R_i(t))\, dt. \tag{B.60}$$

Let Y_i be an independent copy of X_i. The characteristic function of $X_i - Y_i$ is $C_i(t)C_i(-t) = |C_i(t)|^2$. The facts $|C_i(t)|^2 \geq |R_i(t)|^2$ and $|R_i(t)| \leq 1$ imply

$$1 - |C_i(t)|^2 \leq 1 - R_i(t)^2 = (1 - R_i(t))(1 + R_i(t)) \leq 2(1 - R_i(t)). \tag{B.61}$$

Using the characterization (B.60), (B.61), and (B.60) again, we find that for $0 < r < 2$,

$$\begin{aligned}
\mathbb{E}|X_i - Y_i|^r &= K(r)^{-1} \int_0^\infty t^{-(r+1)} \left(1 - |C_i(t)|^2\right) dt \\
&\leq 2\sum_{i=1}^{n} K(r)^{-1} \int_0^\infty t^{-(r+1)} (1 - R_i(t))\, dt \\
&= 2\mathbb{E}|X_i|^r.
\end{aligned} \tag{B.62}$$

Let $\mathbb{E}_Y$ denote expectation over Y_i. Since X_i and Y_i have the same distribution, $\mathbb{E}_Y[Y_i] = 0$. Using Jensen's inequality (B.27) because $|u|^r$ is convex for $r \geq 1$,

$$\begin{aligned}
\mathbb{E}\left|\sum_{i=1}^{n} X_i\right|^r &= \mathbb{E}\left|\mathbb{E}_Y \sum_{i=1}^{n} (X_i - Y_i)\right|^r \\
&\leq \mathbb{E}\left[\mathbb{E}_Y \left|\sum_{i=1}^{n} (X_i - Y_i)\right|^r\right] \\
&= \mathbb{E}\left|\sum_{i=1}^{n} Z_i\right|^r
\end{aligned} \tag{B.63}$$

where the final equality sets $Z_i = X_i - Y_i$.

Because the Z_i are mutually independent, the characteristic function of $\sum_{i=1}^{n} Z_i$ is $\prod_{i=1}^{n} |C_i(t)|^2$, which is real. We next employ the following inequality. If $|a_i| \leq 1$, then

$$1 - \prod_{i=1}^{n} a_i \leq \sum_{i=1}^{n} (1 - a_i). \tag{B.64}$$

To establish (B.64) first do so for $n = 2$, and then apply induction. The inequality follows from $0 \leq (1 - a_1)(1 - a_2) = 1 - a_1 - a_2 + a_1 a_2$ and rearranging. Since $|C_i(t)| \leq 1$, (B.64) implies

$$1 - \prod_{i=1}^{n} |C_i(t)|^2 \leq \sum_{i=1}^{n} \left(1 - |C_i(t)|^2\right). \tag{B.65}$$

Recalling the characterization (B.60) and the fact that the characteristic function of $\sum_{i=1}^{n} Z_i$ is $\prod_{i=1}^{n} |C_i(t)|^2$, applying (B.65), and then using (B.60) again,

$$\begin{aligned}
\mathbb{E}\left|\sum_{i=1}^{n} Z_i\right|^r &= K(r)^{-1} \int_0^\infty t^{-(r+1)} \left(1 - \prod_{i=1}^{n} |C_i(t)|^2\right) dt \\
&\leq \sum_{i=1}^{n} K(r)^{-1} \int_0^\infty t^{-(r+1)} \left(1 - |C_i(t)|^2\right) dt \\
&= \sum_{i=1}^{n} \mathbb{E}\,|Z_i|^r \\
&= \sum_{i=1}^{n} \mathbb{E}\,|X_i - Y_i|^r \\
&\leq 2 \sum_{i=1}^{n} \mathbb{E}\,|X_i|^r .
\end{aligned}$$

The final inequality is (B.62). Combined with (B.63), this is (B.42). ■

Proof of Exponential Inequality (B.43) Using the definition of the exponential function and the fact $(2k)! \geq 2^k k!$,

$$\begin{aligned}
\frac{\exp(-u) + \exp(u)}{2} &= \frac{1}{2} \sum_{k=0}^{\infty} \frac{1}{k!} \left((-u)^k + u^k\right) \\
&= \sum_{k=0}^{\infty} \frac{u^{2k}}{(2k)!} \\
&\leq \sum_{k=0}^{\infty} \frac{\left(u^2/2\right)^k}{k!} \\
&= \exp\left(\frac{u^2}{2}\right).
\end{aligned} \tag{B.66}$$

Taking expectations and applying (B.66),

$$\exp\left(a_i\varepsilon_i\right) = \frac{\exp\left(-a_i\right)+\exp\left(-a_i\right)}{2} \leq \exp\left(\frac{\lambda^2 a_i^2}{2}\right). \tag{B.67}$$

Using that the ε_i are independent and applying (B.67),

$$\mathbb{E}\left[\exp\left(\sum_{i=1}^{n} a_i\varepsilon_i\right)\right] = \prod_{i=1}^{n}\mathbb{E}\left[\exp\left(a_i\varepsilon_i\right)\right] \leq \prod_{i=1}^{n}\exp\left(\frac{\lambda^2 a_i^2}{2}\right) = \exp\left(\frac{\lambda^2\sum_{i=1}^{n} a_i^2}{2}\right) \tag{B.68}$$

which is (B.43). ■

Proof of Symmetrization Inequality (B.44) Let Y_{ji} be an independent copy of X_{ji} (a random variable independent of X_{ji} with the same distribution). Let $\mathbb{E}_X$ denote expectation conditional on X_{ji}. Because $\mathbb{E}_X\left[Y_{ji}\right]=0$,

$$\mathbb{E}_X\left[\sum_{i=1}^{n}\left(X_{ji}-Y_{ji}\right)\right] = \sum_{i=1}^{n} X_{ji}. \tag{B.69}$$

Using (B.69) and Jensen's inequality (B.27) (because $|u|^r$ is convex for $r \geq 1$),

$$\max_{1\leq j\leq J}\left|\sum_{i=1}^{n} X_{ji}\right|^r = \max_{1\leq j\leq J}\left|\mathbb{E}_X\left[\sum_{i=1}^{n}\left(X_{ji}-Y_{ji}\right)\right]\right|^r \leq \max_{1\leq j\leq J}\mathbb{E}_X\left|\sum_{i=1}^{n}\left(X_{ji}-Y_{ji}\right)\right|^r \leq \mathbb{E}_X\max_{1\leq j\leq J}\left|\sum_{i=1}^{n}\left(X_{ji}-Y_{ji}\right)\right|^r.$$

Taking unconditional expectations, we obtain

$$\mathbb{E}\left[\max_{1\leq j\leq J}\left|\sum_{i=1}^{n} X_{ji}\right|^r\right] \leq \mathbb{E}\left[\max_{1\leq j\leq J}\left|\sum_{i=1}^{n}\left(X_{ji}-Y_{ji}\right)\right|^r\right]. \tag{B.70}$$

The random variables $X_{ji}-Y_{ji}$ are symmetrically distributed about 0, and therefore have the same distribution as $\left(X_{ji}-Y_{ji}\right)\varepsilon_i$. Making this substitution and applying the c_r inequality (B.6), (B.70) equals

$$\begin{aligned}\mathbb{E}\left[\max_{1\leq j\leq J}\left|\sum_{i=1}^{n}\left(X_{ji}-Y_{ji}\right)\varepsilon_i\right|^r\right] &\leq 2^{r-1}\left(\mathbb{E}\left[\max_{1\leq j\leq J}\left|\sum_{i=1}^{n} X_{ji}\varepsilon_i\right|^r\right]+\mathbb{E}\left[\max_{1\leq j\leq J}\left|\sum_{i=1}^{n} Y_{ji}\varepsilon_i\right|^r\right]\right)\\ &= 2^r\mathbb{E}\left[\max_{1\leq j\leq J}\left|\sum_{i=1}^{n} X_{ji}\varepsilon_i\right|^r\right],\end{aligned}$$

where the final equality holds because the two sums are identically distributed. This is (B.44). ■

Proof of Khintchine's Inequality (B.45) For $r \leq 2$, by Lyapunov's inequality (B.35),

$$\left(\mathbb{E}\left|\sum_{i=1}^{n} a_i\varepsilon_i\right|^r\right)^{1/r} \leq \left(\mathbb{E}\left|\sum_{i=1}^{n} a_i\varepsilon_i\right|^2\right)^{1/2} = \left(\sum_{i=1}^{n}\mathbb{E}\left[a_i^2\varepsilon_i^2\right]\right)^{1/2} = \left(\sum_{i=1}^{n} a_i^2\right)^{1/2}$$

which is (B.45) with $K_r=1$.

Consider $r \geq 2$. Let $b_i = a_i/\left(\sum_{i=1}^{n} a_i^2\right)^{1/2}$, so $\sum_{i=1}^{n} b_i^2 = 1$. Then

$$\mathbb{E}\left|\sum_{i=1}^{n} a_i\varepsilon_i\right|^r = \left(\sum_{i=1}^{n} a_i^2\right)^{r/2}\mathbb{E}\left|\sum_{i=1}^{n} b_i\varepsilon_i\right|^r. \tag{B.71}$$

We show below that the expectation is bounded by replacing the b_i with the common value $n^{-1/2}$. Thus,

$$\mathbb{E}\left|\sum_{i=1}^{n} b_i\varepsilon_i\right|^r \leq \mathbb{E}\left|\frac{1}{\sqrt{n}}\sum_{i=1}^{n}\varepsilon_i\right|^r \tag{B.72}$$

$$\leq \limsup_{n\to\infty}\mathbb{E}\left|\frac{1}{\sqrt{n}}\sum_{i=1}^{n}\varepsilon_i\right|^r$$

$$=\mathbb{E}\left|Z\right|^r = 2^{r/2}\Gamma\left((r+1)/2)\right)/\pi^{1/2}.$$

The second-to-last equality follows from the central limit theorem and the fact that the ε_i are bounded and thus uniformly integrable. The final equality is Theorem 5.1 Part 4. Together with (B.71), this is (B.45) with $K_r = 2^{r/2}\Gamma\left((r+1)/2\right)/\pi^{1/2}$.

The proof is completed by showing (B.72). Without loss of generality, assume that the $b_i \geq 0$ and are ordered ascending, so that b_1 is the smallest and b_n is the largest. The argument below shows that the left side of (B.72) is increased if we replace b_1 and b_n by the common value $\sqrt{\left(b_1^2+b_n^2\right)/2}$ (which does not alter the sum $\sum_{i=1}^n b_i^2$). Iteratively, this implies (B.72).

Set $S=\sum_{i=2}^{n-1} b_i\varepsilon_i$. Then

$$\mathbb{E}\left[\left|\sum_{i=1}^{n} b_i\varepsilon_i\right|^r \middle| S\right] = \mathbb{E}\left[\left|b_1\varepsilon_1+b_n\varepsilon_n+S\right|^r \middle| S\right]$$

$$=\frac{1}{4}\left[\left|b_1+b_n+S\right|^r+\left|b_1-b_n+S\right|^r+\left|-b_1+b_n+S\right|^r+\left|-b_1-b_n+S\right|^r\right]$$

$$=g\left(u_1\right)+g\left(u_2\right) \tag{B.73}$$

where

$$g(u)=\frac{1}{4}\left(\left|S+\sqrt{u}\right|^r+\left|S-\sqrt{u}\right|^r\right)$$

$$u_1=\left(b_1+b_n\right)^2$$

$$u_2=\left(b_n-b_1\right)^2.$$

The function $g(u)$ is convex on $u\geq 0$, because $S\geq 0$ and $r\geq 2$. (For a formal proof, see Whittle (1960, lemma 1.) Set $c=2\left(b_1^2+b_n^2\right)$. We find

$$g\left(u_1\right)+g\left(u_2\right)=g\left(\frac{u_1}{c}w_1+(1-\frac{u_1}{c})0\right)+g\left(\frac{u_2}{c}c+(1-\frac{u_2}{c})0\right)$$

$$\leq\frac{u_1}{c}g(c)+(1-\frac{u_1}{c})g(0)+\frac{u_2}{c}g(c)+(1-\frac{u_2}{c})g(0)$$

$$=g(c)+g(0).$$

The inequality is two applications of Jensen's inequality (B.2), and the final equality is $u_1+u_2=c$. Combined with (B.73) we have shown that

$$\mathbb{E}\left[\left|\sum_{i=1}^{n} b_i\varepsilon_i\right|^r \middle| S\right]\leq g(c)+g(0).$$

The right side is (B.73) when $b_1=b_n=\sqrt{c}/2$.

Thus the left side of (B.72) can be increased by replacing b_1 and b_n by the common value $\sqrt{c}/2$, as described earlier. Iteratively, replace the smallest and largest b_i by their common value, with each step increasing the expectation. In the limit, we obtain (B.72). ■

Proof of Maximal Khintchine Inequality (B.46) Set

$$C = \max_{1\leq j\leq J}\left(\frac{\sum_{i=1}^{n} a_{ji}^2}{2\log(2J)}\right)^{1/2}. \tag{B.74}$$

Since $\exp(x)$ is convex, by Jensen's inequality (B.27),

$$\begin{aligned}\exp\left(\mathbb{E}\left[\frac{1}{C}\max_{1\leq j\leq J}\left|\sum_{i=1}^{n} a_{ji}\varepsilon_i\right|\right]\right) &\leq \mathbb{E}\left[\exp\left(\frac{1}{C}\max_{1\leq j\leq J}\left|\sum_{i=1}^{n} a_{ji}\varepsilon_i\right|\right)\right]\\ &= \mathbb{E}\left[\max_{1\leq j\leq J}\exp\left(\frac{1}{C}\left|\sum_{i=1}^{n} a_{ji}\varepsilon_i\right|\right)\right]\\ &\leq J\max_{1\leq j\leq J}\mathbb{E}\left[\exp\left(\frac{1}{C}\left|\sum_{i=1}^{n} a_{ji}\varepsilon_i\right|\right)\right].\end{aligned} \tag{B.75}$$

The second inequality uses $\mathbb{E}\left[\max_{1\leq j\leq J}|Z_j|\right] \leq \sum_{j=1}^{J}\mathbb{E}|Z_j| \leq J\max_{1\leq j\leq J}\mathbb{E}|Z_j|$.

For a random variable Y symmetrically distributed about 0,

$$\begin{aligned}\mathbb{E}\left[\exp(|Y|)\right] &= \mathbb{E}\left[\exp(Y)\mathbb{1}\{Y>0\}\right] + \mathbb{E}\left[\exp(-Y)\mathbb{1}\{Y<0\}\right]\\ &= 2\mathbb{E}\left[\exp(Y)\mathbb{1}\{Y>0\}\right]\\ &\leq 2\mathbb{E}\left[\exp(Y)\right].\end{aligned}$$

Thus (B.75) is bounded by

$$2J\max_{1\leq j\leq J}\mathbb{E}\left[\exp\left(\frac{1}{C}\sum_{i=1}^{n} a_{ji}\varepsilon_i\right)\right] \leq 2J\max_{1\leq j\leq J}\exp\left(\frac{1}{2C^2}\sum_{i=1}^{n} a_{ji}^2\right) = (2J)^2.$$

The inequality is the exponential inequality (B.43). The equality substitutes (B.74) for C.

We have shown that

$$\exp\left(\mathbb{E}\left[\frac{1}{C}\max_{1\leq j\leq J}\left|\sum_{i=1}^{n} a_{ji}\varepsilon_i\right|\right]\right) \leq (2J)^2.$$

Taking logs, multiplying by C, and substituting (B.74), we obtain

$$\mathbb{E}\left[\max_{1\leq j\leq J}\left|\sum_{i=1}^{n} a_{ji}\varepsilon_i\right|\right] \leq \left(2\log(2J)\right)^{1/2}\max_{1\leq j\leq J}\left(\sum_{i=1}^{n} a_{ji}^2\right)^{1/2}.$$

Using $2 \leq J$ to make the simplification $\left(2\log(2J)\right)^{1/2} \leq 2\left(\log(J)\right)^{1/2}$ we obtain (B.46). ■

Proof of Marcinkiewicz-Zygmund Inequality (B.47) Let ε_i be independent Rademacher random variables. Let $\mathbb{E}_X$ and $\mathbb{E}_\varepsilon$ denote expectations conditional on X_i and ε_i, respectively. By the symmetrization inequality (B.44),

$$\mathbb{E}\left|\sum_{i=1}^{n} X_i\right|^r \le 2^r \mathbb{E}\left|\sum_{i=1}^{n} \varepsilon_i X_i\right|^r = 2^r \mathbb{E}_\varepsilon\left[\mathbb{E}_X\left|\sum_{i=1}^{n} \varepsilon_i X_i\right|^r\right]. \tag{B.76}$$

The expectation $\mathbb{E}_X$ treats X_i as fixed, so we can apply Khintchine's inequality (B.45). Thus (B.76) is bounded by

$$2^r K_r \mathbb{E}_\varepsilon\left(\sum_{i=1}^{n} X_i^2\right)^{r/2} = 2^r K_r \mathbb{E}\left(\sum_{i=1}^{n} X_i^2\right)^{r/2}.$$

This is (B.47). ■

Proof of Whittle's Inequality (B.48) By the Marcinkiewicz-Zygmund inequality (B.47), Minkowski's inequality (B.34), and $\mathbb{E}\,|X_i|^r \le B_{1r}$,

$$\begin{aligned}
\mathbb{E}\left|\sum_{i=1}^{n} a_i X_i\right|^r &\le M_r \mathbb{E}\left|\sum_{i=1}^{n} a_i^2 X_i^2\right|^{r/2} \\
&\le M_r\left(\sum_{i=1}^{n} a_i^2\left(\mathbb{E}\,|X_i|^r\right)^{2/r}\right)^{r/2} \\
&\le B_{1r} M_r\left(\sum_{i=1}^{n} a_i^2\right)^{r/2}.
\end{aligned}$$

which is (B.48) with $C_{1r} = B_{1r} M_r$, as claimed. ■

Proof of Whittle's Inequality (B.49) As shown in (B.63),

$$\mathbb{E}\left|X'\boldsymbol{A}X - \mathbb{E}\left[X'\boldsymbol{A}X\right]\right|^r \le \mathbb{E}\left|X'\boldsymbol{A}X - Y'\boldsymbol{A}Y\right|^r \tag{B.77}$$

where $Y = (Y_1, \ldots, Y_n)'$ is an independent copy of X. We can write

$$(X+Y)'\,\boldsymbol{A}\,(X-Y) = \xi'\,(X-Y)$$

where $\xi = \boldsymbol{A}\,(X+Y)$.

Independence implies exchangeability, which implies the distribution of $X_i - Y_i$ conditional on $X_i + Y_i$ is symmetric about the origin. To see this formally, by exchangeability,

$$\begin{aligned}
\mathbb{P}\left[X_i - Y_i \le u \mid X_i + Y_i = v\right] &= \mathbb{P}\left[Y_i - X_i \le u \mid Y_i + X_i = v\right] \\
&= 1 - \mathbb{P}\left[Y_i - X_i > u \mid Y_i + X_i = v\right] \\
&= 1 - \mathbb{P}\left[X_i - Y_i < -u \mid X_i + Y_i = v\right] \\
&= \mathbb{P}\left[X_i - Y_i \ge -u \mid X_i + Y_i = v\right]
\end{aligned}$$

which is the definition of a symmetric distribution. Thus we can write $X_i - Y_i = \eta_i \varepsilon_i$, where $\eta_i = |X_i - Y_i|$, and ε_i is an independent Rademacher random variable.

Denote the ith element of ξ as $\xi_i = \boldsymbol{a}_i'(X+Y)$, where $\boldsymbol{a}_i'$ is the ith column of $\boldsymbol{A}$. Then $\xi'(X-Y) = \sum_{i=1}^n \xi_i \eta_i \varepsilon_i$. Applying Khintchine's inequality (B.45),

$$\begin{aligned}
\mathbb{E}\left|X'\boldsymbol{A}X - Y'\boldsymbol{A}Y\right|^r &= \mathbb{E}\left|\sum_{i=1}^n \xi_i\eta_i\varepsilon_i\right|^r \\
&\le K_r \mathbb{E}\left[\left(\sum_{i=1}^n \xi_i^2\eta_i^2\right)^{r/2}\right] \\
&\le K_r\left(\sum_{i=1}^n \left(\mathbb{E}\left[|\xi_i|^r |\eta_i|^r\right]\right)^{2/r}\right)^{r/2} \\
&\le K_r\left(\sum_{i=1}^n \left(\mathbb{E}\left[\xi_i^{2r}\right]\right)^{1/r}\left(\mathbb{E}\left[\eta_i^{2r}\right]\right)^{1/r}\right)^{r/2}. \qquad \text{(B.78)}
\end{aligned}$$

The first inequality is Minkowski's (B.34), the second is Cauchy-Schwarz (B.32). Observe that

$$\mathbb{E}\left[\eta_i^{2r}\right] \le 2^{2r}\mathbb{E}\left[X_i^{2r}\right] \le 2^{2r}B_{2r}.$$

By Whittle's first inequality (B.48),

$$\mathbb{E}\left[\xi_i^{2r}\right] = \mathbb{E}\left|\sum_{j=1}^n a_{ji}\left(X_j+Y_j\right)\right|^{2r} \le 2^{2r}C_{1r}\left(\sum_{j=1}^n a_{ji}^2\right)^r.$$

Hence (B.78) is bounded by

$$4^r K_r C_{1r}^{1/2} B_{2r}^{1/2}\left(\sum_{i=1}^n\sum_{j=1}^n a_{ji}^2\right)^{r/2} = 4^r K_r C_{1r}^{1/2} B_{2r}^{1/2}\left(\operatorname{tr}\left(\boldsymbol{A}'\boldsymbol{A}\right)^{r/2}\right)^{r/2}.$$

This is (B.49) with $C_{2r} = 4^r K_r C_{1r}^{1/2} B_{2r}^{1/2}$. ■

Proof of Rosenthal's Inequality (B.50) Define $\mu_s = \sum_{i=1}^n \mathbb{E}|X_i|^s$ for any $s>0$.

Take $0<r\le 2$. By Lyapunov's inequality (B.35),

$$\left(\mathbb{E}\left|\sum_{i=1}^n X_i\right|^r\right)^{1/r} \le \left(\mathbb{E}\left|\sum_{i=1}^n X_i\right|^2\right)^{1/2} = \mu_2^{1/2}.$$

Raising to the power r implies (B.50). For the remainder of the proof, assume $r>2$.

By the Marcinkiewicz-Zygmund inequality (B.47),

$$\mathbb{E}\left|\sum_{i=1}^n X_i\right|^r \le M_r \mathbb{E}\left|S_n\right|^{r/2} \qquad \text{(B.79)}$$

where $S_n = \sum_{i=1}^n X_i^2$. For any i, using the c_r inequality (B.7),

$$|S_n|^{r/2-1} = \left| X_i + \sum_{j \neq i} X_j \right|^{r/2-1} \leq c_{r/2-1} \left(|X_i|^{r/2} + \left| \sum_{j \neq i} X_j \right|^{r/2-1} \right).$$

Thus

$$\begin{aligned}
\mathbb{E}\,|S_n|^{r/2} &= \mathbb{E}\left[S_n\,|S_n|^{r/2-1}\right] \\
&= \sum_{i=1}^{n} \mathbb{E}\left[X_i^2\,|S_n|^{r-2}\right] \\
&\leq c_{r/2-1} \sum_{i=1}^{n} \mathbb{E}\left[X_i^2 \left(|X_i|^{r/2} + \left| \sum_{j \neq i} X_j \right|^{r/2-1} \right)\right] \\
&\leq c_{r/2-1} \left(\sum_{i=1}^{n} \mathbb{E}\,|X_i|^r + \sum_{i=1}^{n} \mathbb{E}\left[X_i^2 \left| \sum_{j \neq i} X_j^2 \right|^{r/2-1} \right] \right) \\
&= c_{r/2-1} \left(\mu_r + \sum_{i=1}^{n} \mathbb{E}\left[X_i^2\right] \mathbb{E} \left| \sum_{j \neq i} X_j^2 \right|^{r/2-1} \right) \\
&\leq c_{r/2-1} \left(\mu_r + \mu_2 \mathbb{E}\,|S_n|^{r/2-1} \right).
\end{aligned} \tag{B.80}$$

The second-to-last line holds because X_i^2 is independent of $\sum_{j \neq i} X_j^2$. The final inequality holds because $\sum_{j \neq i} X_j^2 \leq S_n$ and $\sum_{i=1}^{n} \mathbb{E}\left[X_i^2\right] = \mu_2$.

Suppose $2 \leq r \leq 4$. Then $r/2 - 1 \leq 1$. By Jensen's inequality (B.27), $\mathbb{E}\,|S_n|^{r/2-1} \leq (\mathbb{E}\,|S_n|)^{r/2-1} = \mu_2^{r/2-1}$. Also, $c_{r/2-1} = 1$. Taken together, we can bound (B.80) by $\sum_{i=1}^{n} \mathbb{E}\,|X_i|^r + \mu_2^{r/2}$, which implies

$$\mathbb{E}\,|S_n|^{r/2} \leq \sum_{i=1}^{n} \mathbb{E}\,|X_i|^r + \mu_2^{r/2}. \tag{B.81}$$

We now establish that

$$\mathbb{E}\,|S_n|^{s/2} \leq 2^{s(s-2)/8} \left(\mu_s + \mu_2^{s/2} \right) \tag{B.82}$$

for all $s \geq 2$ by a recursive argument. Inequality (B.81) shows that (B.82) holds for $2 \leq s \leq 4$. We now show that (B.82) for $s = r - 2$ implies (B.82) for $s = r$. Take $r > 4$. Using (B.80), $c_{r/2-1} = 2^{r/2-2}$, and (B.82),

$$\begin{aligned}
\mathbb{E}\,|S_n|^{r/2} &\leq 2^{r/2-2} \left(\mu_r + \mu_2 \mathbb{E}\,|S_n|^{r/2-1} \right) \\
&\leq 2^{r/2-2} \left(\mu_r + \mu_2 2^{(r-2)(r-4)/8} \left(\mu_{r-2} + \mu_2^{(r-2)/2} \right) \right) \\
&\leq 2^{r/2-2} 2^{(r-2)(r-4)/8} \left(\mu_r + \mu_2 \mu_{r-2} + \mu_2^{r/2} \right) \\
&= 2^{r(r-2)/8-1} \left(\mu_r + \mu_2 \mu_{r-2} + \mu_2^{r/2} \right).
\end{aligned}$$

Using Hölder's inequality (B.31), Hölder's inequality for vectors (B.11), and the geometric mean inequality (B.4), we have

$$
\begin{aligned}
\mu_2\mu_{r-2} &\le \mu_2 \sum_{i=1}^{n} \left(\mathbb{E}\left[X_i^2\right]\right)^{2/(r-2)} \left(\mathbb{E}\,|X_i|^r\right)^{(r-4)/(r-2)} \\
&\le \mu_2 \left(\sum_{i=1}^{n} \mathbb{E}\left[X_i^2\right]\right)^{2/(r-2)} \left(\sum_{i=1}^{n} \mathbb{E}\,|X_i|^r\right)^{(r-4)/(r-2)} \\
&= \mu_2^{r/(r-2)} \mu_r^{(r-4)/(r-2)} \\
&\le \frac{2}{r-2}\mu_2^{r/2} + \frac{r-4}{r-2}\mu_r \\
&\le \mu_2^{r/2} + \mu_r.
\end{aligned}
$$

Combining these results, we have

$$
\mathbb{E}\,|S_n|^{r/2} \le 2^{r(r-2)/8}\left(\mu_r + \mu_2^{r/2}\right)
$$

which is (B.82) for $s = r$. This shows that (B.82) holds for all $s \ge 2$. Finally, inequalities (B.79) and (B.82) imply (B.50) for $r > 2$. ■

Proof of Kolmogorov's Inequality (B.51). See *Probability and Statistics for Economists*, Theorem 7.13.

Proof of Billingsley's Inequality (B.52) Without loss of generality, assume $\sigma_n^2 = 1$. Define the events

$$
A_i = \left\{ |S_i| > \lambda, \max_{j<i} \left|S_j\right| \le \lambda \right\}.
$$

These events are disjoint. Their union is

$$
A = \bigcup_{i=1}^{n} A_i = \left\{ \max_{i \le n} |S_i| > \lambda \right\}.
$$

Then

$$
\mathbb{P}[A] = \mathbb{P}\left[\bigcup_{i=1}^{n} A_i\right] \le \mathbb{P}\left[|S_n| > \frac{\lambda}{2}\right] + \mathbb{P}\left[\left\{\bigcup_{i=1}^{n} A_i\right\} \cap \left\{|S_n| \le \frac{\lambda}{2}\right\}\right].
$$

Since the A_i are disjoint, the second term on the right equals

$$
\sum_{i=1}^{n} \mathbb{P}\left[A_i \cap \left\{|S_n| \le \frac{\lambda}{2}\right\}\right] \le \sum_{i=1}^{n} \mathbb{P}\left[A_i \cap \left\{|S_n - S_i| > \frac{\lambda}{2}\right\}\right],
$$

where the inequality, holds because the events $\{|S_i| > \lambda\}$ and $\left\{|S_n| \le \frac{\lambda}{2}\right\}$ imply $\left\{|S_n - S_i| > \frac{\lambda}{2}\right\}$. The events A_i and $\left\{|S_n - S_i| > \frac{\lambda}{2}\right\}$ are independent (because X_i are independent), so the final term equals

$$
\sum_{i=1}^{n} \mathbb{P}[A_i]\,\mathbb{P}\left[|S_n - S_i| > \frac{\lambda}{2}\right] \le \sum_{i=1}^{n} \mathbb{P}[A_i] \frac{4}{\lambda^2} \operatorname{var}[S_n - S_i] \le \sum_{i=1}^{n} \mathbb{P}[A_i] \frac{4}{\lambda^2} \le \frac{\mathbb{P}[A]}{2}.
$$

The first inequality is Chebyshev's, and the second is $\operatorname{var}[S_n - S_i] \le \sigma_n^2 = 1$, and the final is $4/\lambda^2 < 1/2$ when $\lambda > 2\sqrt{2}$. We have shown that $\mathbb{P}[A] \le \mathbb{P}[|S_n| > \lambda/2] + \mathbb{P}[A]/2$, which on rearrangement is (B.52). ■

REFERENCES

Abadir, Karim M., and Jan R. Magnus (2005): *Matrix Algebra*. Cambridge: Cambridge University Press.

Acemoglu, Daron, Simon Johnson, and James A. Robinson (2001): "The colonial origins of comparative development: An empirical investigation," *American Economic Review* 91, 1369–1401.

Acemoglu, Daron, Simon Johnson, and James A. Robinson (2012): "The colonial origins of comparative development: An empirical investigation: Reply," *American Economic Review* 102, 3077–3110.

Ackerberg, Daniel, C. Lanier Benkard, Steven Berry, and Ariel Pakes (2007): "Econometric tools for analyzing market outcomes," in James J. Heckman and Edward E. Leamer (editors), *Handbook of Econometrics*, Volume 6A, 4171–4276. Amsterdam: North-Holland.

Aitken, Alexander C. (1935): "On least squares and linear combinations of observations," *Proceedings of the Royal Statistical Society* 55, 42–48.

Akaike, Hirotugu (1969): "Fitting autoregressive models for prediction," *Annals of the Institute of Statistical Mathematics* 21, 243–247.

Akaike, Hirotugu (1973): "Information theory and an extension of the maximum likelihood principle," in B. Petrov and F. Csaki (editors), *Second International Symposium on Information Theory*, 267–281. Budapest: Akademiai Kiado.

Amemiya, Takeshi (1971): "The estimation of the variances in a variance-components model," *International Economic Review* 12, 1–13.

Amemiya, Takeshi (1973): "Regression analysis when the dependent variable is truncated normal," *Econometrica* 41, 997–1016.

Amemiya, Takeshi (1974): "The nonlinear two-stage least-squares estimator," *Journal of Econometrics* 2, 105–110.

Amemiya, Takeshi (1977): "The maximum likelihood and nonlinear three-stage least squares estimator in the general nonlinear simultaneous equations model," *Econometrica* 45, 955–968.

Amemiya, Takeshi (1985): *Advanced Econometrics*. Cambridge, MA: Harvard University Press.

Amemiya, Takeshi, and Thomas E. MaCurdy (1986): "Instrumental-variable estimation of an error components model. *Econometrica* 54, 869–881.

Anderson, Theodore W. (1951): "Estimating linear restrictions on regression coefficeints for multivariate normal distributions," *Annals of Mathematical Statistics* 22, 327–350.

Anderson, Theodore W. (2003): *An Introduction to Multivariate Statistical Analysis*, Third Edition. Hoboken, NJ: Wiley.

Anderson, Theodore W., and Cheng Hsiao (1982): "Formulation and estimation of dynamic models using panel data," *Journal of Econometrics* 18, 47–82.

Anderson, Theodore W., and H. Rubin (1949): "Estimation of the parameters of a single equation in a complete system of stochastic equations," *Annals of Mathematical Statistics* 20, 46–63.

Andrews, Donald W. K. (1984): "Non-strong mixing autoregressive processes," *Journal of Applied Probability* 21, 930–934.

Andrews, Donald W. K. (1991a): "Asymptotic normality of series estimators for nonparameric and semiparametric regression models," *Econometrica* 59, 307–345.

Andrews, Donald W. K. (1991b): "Heteroskedasticity and autocorrelation consistent covariance matrix estimation," *Econometrica* 59, 817–858.

Andrews, Donald W. K. (1991c): "Asymptotic optimality of generalized C_L, cross-validation, and generalized cross-validation in regression with heteroskedastic errors," *Journal of Econometrics* 47, 359–377.

Andrews, Donald W. K. (1994): "Empirical process methods in econometrics," in *Handbook of Econometrics, Volume 4*, ch 37. Robert F. Engle and Daniel L. McFadden (editors), pp. 2247–2294. Amsterdam: Elsevier.

Andrews, Donald W. K. (2017): "Examples of L^2-complete and boundedly-complete distributions," *Journal of Econometrics* 199, 213–220.

Andrews, Donald W. K., and Werner Ploberger (1994): "Optimal tests when a nuisance parameter is present only under the alternative," *Econometrica* 62, 1383–1414.

Angrist, Joshua D., and Alan B. Krueger (1991): "Does compulsory school attendance affect schooling and earnings?" *Quarterly Journal of Economics* 91, 444–455.

Angrist, Joshua D., and Alan B. Krueger (1995): "Split sample instrumental variables estimates of the return to schooling," *Journal of Business and Economic Statistics* 13, 225–235.

Angrist, Joshua D., and Victor Lavy (1999): "Using Maimonides' rule to estimate the effect of class size on scholastic achievement," *Quarterly Journal of Economics* 114, 533–575.

Angrist, Joshua D., and Jörn-Steffen Pischke (2009): *Mostly Harmless Econometrics: An Empiricists Companion*. Princeton, NJ: Princeton University Press.

Angrist, Joshua D., Guido W. Imbens, and Alan B. Krueger (1999): "Jackknife instrumental variables estimation," *Journal of Applied Econometrics* 14, 57–67.

Angrist, Joshua D., Guido W. Imbens, and Donald B. Rubin (1996): "Identification of causal effects using instrumental variables," *Journal of the American Statistical Association* 55, 650–659.

Arai, Yochi, and Hidehiko Ichimura (2018): "Simultaneous selection of optimal bandwidths for the sharp regression discontinuity estimator," *Quantitative Economics* 9, 441–482.

Arellano, Manuel (1987): "Computing standard errors for robust within-groups estimators," *Oxford Bulletin of Economics and Statistics* 49, 431–434.

Arellano, Manuel (2003): *Panel Data Econometrics*. Oxford: Oxford University Press.

Arellano, Manuel, and Stephen Bond (1991): "Some tests of specification for panel data: Monte Carlo evidence and an application to employment equations," *Review of Economic Studies* 58, 277–297.

Arellano, Manuel, and Olympia Bover (1995): "Another look at the instrumental variable estimation of error-components models," *Journal of Econometrics* 68, 29–51.

Arrow, Kenneth, Hollis Chenery, Bagicha Minhas, and Robert Solow (1961): "Capital-labor substitution and economic efficiency," *Review of Economics and Statistics* 43, 225–250.

Ash, Robert B. (1972): *Real Analysis and Probability*. Cambridge, MA: Academic Press.

Athey, Susan, and Guido W. Imbens (2019): "Machine learning methods economists should know about," manuscript.

Bai, Jushan (2003): "Inferential theory for factor models of large dimensions," *Econometrica* 71, 135–172.

Bai, Jushan, and Serena Ng (2002): "Determining the number of factors in approximate factor models," *Econometrica* 70, 191–221.

Bai, Jushan, and Serena Ng (2006): "Confidence intervals for diffusion index forecasts and inference for factor-augmented regressions," *Econometrica* 74, 1133–1150.

Balestra, Pietro, and Marc Nerlove (1966): "Pooling cross section and time series data in the estimation of a dynamic model: The demand for natural gas," *Econometrica* 34, 585–612.

Baltagi, Badi H. (2013): *Econometric Analysis of Panel Data*, Fifth Edition. Hoboken, NJ: Wiley.

Barro, Robert J. (1977): "Unanticipated money growth and unemployment in the United States," *American Economic Review* 67, 101–115.

Basmann, Robert L. (1957): "A generalized classical method of linear estimation of coefficients in a structural equation," *Econometrica* 25, 77–83.

Basmann, Robert L. (1960): "On finite sample distributions of generalized classical linear identifiability test statistics," *Journal of the American Statistical Association* 55, 650–659.

Baum, Christopher F., Mark E. Schaffer, and Steven Stillman (2003): "Instrumental variables and GMM: Estimation and testing," *Stata Journal* 3, 1–31.

Bekker, Paul A. (1994): "Alternative approximations to the distributions of instrumental variable estimators, *Econometrica* 62, 657–681.

Belloni, Alexandre, Daniel Chen, Victor Chernozhukov, and Christian B. Hansen (2012): "Sparse models and methods for optimal instruments with an application to eminent domain," *Econometrica* 80, 2369–2429.

Belloni, Alexandre, and Victor Chernozhukov (2013): "Least squares after model selection in high-dimensional sparse models," *Bernoulli* 19, 521–547.

Belloni, Alexandre, Victor Chernozhukov, and Christian B. Hansen (2014a): "High-dimensional methods and inference on structural and treatment effects," *Journal of Economic Perspectives* 28, 29–50.

Belloni, Alexandre, Victor Chernozhukov, and Christian B. Hansen (2014b): "Inference on treatment effects after selection among high-dimensional controls," *Review of Economic Studies* 81, 608–650.

Belloni, Alexandre, Victor Chernozhukov, Denis Chetverikov, and Kengo Kato (2015): "Some new asymptotic theory for least squares series: Pointwise and uniform results," *Journal of Econometrics* 186, 345–366.

Belloni, Alexandre, Victor Chernozhukov, Denis Chetverikov, Christian B. Hansen, and Kengo Kato (2021): "High-dimensional econometrics and regularized GMM," in Steven Durlauf, Lars Hansen, James Heckman and Rosa Matzkin (editors), *Handbook of Econometrics*, Volume 7b, forthcoming. Amsterdam: North-Holland.

Bernheim, B. Douglas, Jonathan Meer, and Neva K. Novarro (2016): "Do consumers exploit commitment opportunities? Evidence from natural experiments involving liquor consumption," *American Economic Journal: Economic Policy* 8, 41–69.

Berry, Steven (1994): "Estimating discrete choice models of product differentiation," *RAND Journal of Economics* 25, 242–262.

Berry, Steven, James Levinsohn, and Ariel Pakes (1995): "Automobile prices in market equilibrium," *Econometrica* 63, 841–890.

Berry, Steven, Oliver B. Linton, and Ariel Pakes (2004): "Limit theorems for estimating the parameters of differentiated product demand systems," *Review of Economic Studies* 71, 613–654.

Bertrand, Marianne, Esther Duflo, and Sendhil Mullainathan (2004): "How much should we trust differences-in-differences estimates?" *Quarterly Journal of Economics* 119, 249–275.

Beveridge, Stephen, and Charles R. Nelson (1981): "A new approach to the decomposition of economic time series into permanent and transitory components with particular attention to measurement of the business cycle," *Journal of Monetary Economics* 7, 151–174.

Bickel, Peter J., Ya'acov Ritov, and Alexandre B. Tsybakov (2009): "Simultaneous analysis of Lasso and Dantzig selector," *Annals of Statistics* 37, 1705–1732.

Billingsley, Patrick (1999): *Convergence of Probability Measures*, Second Edition. Hoboken, NJ: Wiley.

Black, Sandra E. (1999): "Do better schools matter? Parental valuation of elementary education," *Quarterly Journal of Economics* 114, 577–599.

Blanchard, Olivier Jean, and Roberto Perotti (2002): "An empirical characterization of the dynamic effects of changes in government spending and taxes on output," *Quarterly Journal of Economics* 117, 1329–1368.

Blanchard, Olivier Jean, and Danny Quah (1989): "The dynamic effects of aggregate demand and supply disturbances," *American Economic Review* 89, 655–673.

Blundell, Richard, and Stephen Bond (1998): "Initial conditions and moment restrictions in dynamic panel data models," *Journal of Econometrics* 87, 115–143.

Bock, Mary Ellen (1975): "Minimax estimators of the mean of a multivariate normal distribution," *The Annals of Statistics* 3, 209–218.

Box, George E. P., and Dennis R. Cox, (1964): "An analysis of transformations," *Journal of the Royal Statistical Society, Series B*, 26, 211–252.

Breiman, Leo (1996): "Bagging predictors," *Machine Learning* 24, 123–140.

Breiman, Leo (2001): "Random forests," *Machine Learning* 45, 5–32.

Breiman, Leo, Jerry Friedman, Richard A. Olshen, and Charles J. Stone (1984): *Classification and Regression Trees*. Abington-on-Thames, UK: Taylor & Francis.

Breusch, Trevor S., Graham E. Mizon and Peter Schmidt (1989): "Efficient estimation using panel data," *Econometrica* 57, 695–700.

Brockwell, Peter J., and Richard A. Davis (1991): *Time Series: Theory and Methods*, Second Edition. New York: Springer-Verlag.

Bühlmann, Peter, and Sara van de Geer (2011): *Statistics for High-Dimensional Data: Methods, Theory and Applications*. New York: Springer-Verlag.

Bühlmann, Peter, and Bin Yu (2002): "Analyzing bagging," *Annals of Statistics* 30, 927–961.

Burnham, Kenneth P., and David R. Anderson (1998): *Model Selection and MultiModel Inference: A Practical Information-Theoretic Approach*, Second Edition. New York: Springer.

Cameron, A. Colin, and Pravin K. Trivedi (1998): *Regression Analysis of Count Data*. Cambridge: Cambridge University Press.

Cameron, A. Colin, and Pravin K. Trivedi (2005): *Microeconometrics: Methods and Applications*. Cambridge: Cambridge University Press.

Cameron, A. Colin, Johan B. Gelbach, and Douglas L. Miller (2008): "Bootstrap-based improvements for inference with clustered errors," *Review of Economics and Statistics* 90, 414–437.

Campbell, John Y., Adrew W. Lo, and A. Craig MacKinlay (1997): *The Econometrics of Financial Markets*. Princeton, NJ: Princeton University Press.

Canay, Ivan A. (2011): "A simple approach to quantile regression for panel data," *Econometrics Journal* 14, 368–386.

Canova, Fabio (1995): "Vector autoregressive models: Specification, estimation, inference, and forecasting," in M. Hashem Peseran and Michael R. Wickens (editors) *Handbook of Applied Econometrics, Volume 1: Macroeconomics*. Hoboken, NJ: Blackwell.

Card, David (1995): "Using geographic variation in college proximity to estimate the return to schooling," in L. N. Christofides, E. K. Grant, and R. Swidinsky (editors) *Aspects of Labor Market Behavior: Essays in Honour of John Vanderkamp*. Toronto: University of Toronto Press.

Card, David, and Alan B. Krueger (1994): "Minimum wages and employment: A case study of the fast-food industry in New Jersey and Pennsylvania." *American Economic Review*. 84, 772–793.

Card, David, Alexandre Mas, and Jesse Rothstein (2008): "Tipping and the dynamics of segregation." *Quarterly Journal of Economics* 123, 177–218.

Card, David, David S. Lee, Zhuan Pei, and Andrea Weber (2015): "Inference on causal effects in a generalized regression kink design," *Econometrica* 57, 695–700.

Cattaneo, Matias D., Nicolás Idrobo, and Rocío Titiunik (2020): *A Practical Introduction to Regression Discontinuity Designs: Foundations*. Cambridge: Cambridge University Press.

Cattaneo, Matias D., Nicolás Idrobo, and Rocío Titiunik (2022): *A Practical Introduction to Regression Discontinuity Designs: Extensions*. Cambridge: Cambridge University Press, to appear.

Cattaneo, Matias D., Rocío Titiunik, and Gonzalo Vazquez-Bare (2017): "Comparing inference approaches for RD designs: A reexamination of the effect of head start on child mortality," *Journal of Policy Analysis and Management* 36, 643–681.

Chamberlain, Gary (1980): "Analysis of covariance with qualitative data," *Review of Economic Studies* 47, 225–238.

Chamberlain, Gary (1984): "Panel Data," in Zvi Griliches and Michael D. Intrilligator (editors) *Handbook of Econometrics*, Volume 2, 1247–1318. Amsterdam: North-Holland.

Chamberlain, Gary (1987): "Asymptotic efficiency in estimation with conditional moment restrictions," *Journal of Econometrics* 34, 305–334.

Chamberlain, Gary, and Michael Rothschild (1983): "Arbitrage, factor structure, and mean-variance analysis on large asset markets," *Econometrica* 51, 1281–1304.

Chan, Kung-Sik (1993): "Consistency and limiting distribution of the least squares estimator of a threshold autoregressive model," *Annals of Statistics* 21, 520–533.

Chang, Pao Li and Shinichi Sakata (2007): "Estimation of impulse response functions using long autoregression," *Econometrics Journal* 10, 453–469.

Chao, John C., Norman R. Swanson, Jerry A. Hausman, Whitney K. Newey, and Tiemen Woutersen (2012):

"Asymptotic distribution of JIVE in a heteroskedastic IV regression with many instruments," *Econometric Theory* 28, 42–86.

Chen, Xiaohong (2007): "Large sample sieve estimation of semi-nonparametric models," in James J. Heckman and Edward E. Leamer, (editors) *Handbook of Econometrics*, Volume 6B, 5549–5632. Amsterdam: North-Holland.

Chen, Xiaohong, and Timothy M. Christensen (2015): "Optimal uniform convergence rates and asymptotic normality for series estimators under weak dependence and weak conditions," *Journal of Econometrics* 188, 447–465.

Chen, Xiaohong, and Timothy M. Christensen (2018): "Optimal sup-norm rates and uniform inference on nonlinear functionals of nonparametric IV regression," *Quantitative Economics* 9, 39–84.

Chen, Xiaohong and Demian Pouzo (2015): "Sieve Wald and QLR inferences on semi/nonparametric conditional moment models," *Econometrica* 83, 1013–1079.

Chen, Xiaohong, Zhipeng Liao, and Yixiao Sun (2012): "Sieve inference on semi-nonparametric time series models." New Haven, CT: Cowles Foundation Discussion Paper #1849.

Cheng, Ming-Yen, Jianqing Fan and J.S. Marron (1997): "On automatic boundary corrections," *Annals of Statistics* 25, 1691–1708.

Chernozhukov, Victor, and Christian B. Hansen (2005): "An IV model of quantile treatment effects," *Econometrica* 73, 245–261.

Chernozhukov, Victor, Iván Fernández-Val, and Alfred Galichon (2010): "Quantile and Probability Curves without Crossing," *Econometrica* 74, 1093–1125.

Chernozhukov, Victor Christian B. Hansen, and Martin Spindler (2015): "Post-selection and post-regularization inference in linear models with many controls and instruments," *American Economic Review Papers and Proceedings* 105, 486–490.

Chernozhukov, Victor, Denis Chetverikov, Mert Demirer, Esther Duflo, Christian B. Hansen, Whitney Newey, and James Robins (2018): "Double/debiased machine learning for treatment and structural parameters," *Econometrics Journal* 21, C1–C68.

Chetverikov, Denis, Zhipeng Liao, and Victor Chernozhukov (2021): "On cross-validated Lasso in high dimensions," *Annals of Statistics* 49, 1300–1317.

Claeskens, Gerda, and Nils Lid Hjort (2003): "The focused information criterion," *Journal of the American Statistical Association* 98, 900–945.

Claeskens, Gerda, and Nils Lid Hjort (2008): *Model Selection and Model Averaging*. Cambridge: Cambridge University Press.

Conley, Timothy G., and Christopher R. Taber (2011): "Inference with 'difference in differences' with a small number of policy changes," *Review of Economics and Statistics* 93, 113–125.

Cox, Donald, Bruce E. Hansen, and Emmanuel Jimenez (2004): "How responsive are private transfers to income? Evidence from a laissez-faire economy," *Journal of Public Economics* 88, 2193–2219.

Cragg, John G., and Stephen G. Donald (1993): "Testing identifiability and specification in instrumental variable models," *Econometric Theory* 9, 222–240.

Craven, Peter, and Grace Wahba (1979): "Smoothing noisy data with spline functions: Estimating the correct degree of smoothing by the method of generalized cross-validation," *Numerische Mathematik* 31, 377–403.

Cunningham, Scott (2021): *Causal Inference: The Mixtape*. New Haven, CT: Yale University Press.

Das, Mitali, Whitney K. Newey, and Francis Vella (2003): "Nonparametric estimation of sample selection models," *Review of Economic Studies* 70, 33–58.

Davidson, James (1994): *Stochastic Limit Theory: An Introduction for Econometricians*. Oxford: Oxford University Press.

Davidson, James (2000): *Econometric Theory*. Hoboken, NJ: Blackwell.

Davidson, Russell, and Emmanuel Flachaire (2008): "The wild bootstrap, tamed at last," *Journal of Econometrics* 146, 162–169.

Davidson, Russell, and James G. MacKinnon (1993): *Estimation and Inference in Econometrics*. Oxford: Oxford University Press.

Davidson, Russell, and James G. MacKinnon (2004): *Econometric Theory and Methods*. Oxford: Oxford University Press.

Davison, A. C., and D. V. Hinkley (1997): *Bootstrap Methods and Their Application*. Cambridge: Cambridge University Press.

De Luca, Giuseppe, Jan R. Magnus, and Franco Peracchi (2018): "Balanced variable addition in linear models" *Journal of Economic Surveys* 31, 1183–1200.

DiTella, Rafael, and Ernesto Schargrodsky (2004): "Do police reduce crime? Estimates using the allocation of police forces after a terrorist attack," *American Economic Review* 94, 115–138.

Donald, Stephen G., and Whitney K. Newey (2001): "Choosing the number of instruments," *Econometrica* 69, 1161–1191.

Donohue, John J. III, and Steven D. Levitt (2001): "The impact of legalized abortion on crime," *Quarterly Journal of Economics* 116, 379–420.

Duflo, Esther, Pascaline Dupas, and Michael Kremer (2011): "Peer effects, teacher incentives, and the impact of tracking: Evidence from a randomized evaluation in Kenya," *American Economic Review* 101, 1739–1774.

Dufour, Jean-Marie (1997): "Some impossibility theorems in econometrics with applications to structural and dynamic models," *Econometrica* 65, 1365–1387.

Durbin, James (1954): "Errors in variables," *Review of the International Statistical Institute* 22, 23–32.

Durbin, James (1960): "The fitting of time-series models," *Revue de l'Institut International de Statistique* 28, 233–244.

Efron, Bradley (1979): "Bootstrap methods: Another look at the jackknife," *Annals of Statistics* 7, 1–26.

Efron, Bradley (1982): *The Jackknife, the Bootstrap, and Other Resampling Plans*. Philadelphia: Society for Industrial and Applied Mathematics.

Efron, Bradley (1987): "Better bootstrap confidence intervals (with discussion)," *Journal of the American Statistical Association* 82, 171–200.

Efron, Bradley (2010): *Large-Scale Inference: Empirical Bayes Methods for Estimation, Testing and Prediction.* Cambridge: Cambridge University Press.

Efron, Bradley (2014): "Estimation and accuracy after model selection," (with discussion), *Journal of the American Statistical Association* 109, 991–1007.

Efron, Bradley, and Trevor Hastie (2017): *Computer Age Statistical Inference: Algorithms, Evidence, and Data Science.* Cambridge: Cambridge University Press.

Efron, Bradley, and Robert J. Tibshirani (1993): *An Introduction to the Bootstrap.* Boca Raton, FL: Chapman & Hall.

Eichenbaum, Martin S., Lars Peter Hansen, and Kenneth J. Singleton (1988): "A time series analysis of representative agent models of consumption and leisure choice," *Quarterly Journal of Economics* 103, 51–78.

Eicker, Friedhelm (1963): "Asymptotic normality and consistency of the least squares estimators for families of linear regressions," *Annals of Mathematical Statistics* 34, 447–456.

Elliott, Graham, and Allan Timmermann (2016): *Economic Forecasting.* Princeton, NJ: Princeton University Press.

Enders, Walter (2014): *Applied Economic Time Series*, Fourth Edition. Hoboken, NJ: Wiley.

Engle, Robert F., and Clive W. J. Granger (1987): "Co-integration and error correction: Representation, estimation and testing," *Econometrica* 55, 251–276.

Fan, Jianqing (1992): "Design-adaptive nonparametric regression," *Journal of the American Statistical Association* 87, 998–1004.

Fan, Jianqing (1993): "Local linear regression smoothers and their minimax efficiency," *Annals of Statistics* 21, 196–216.

Fan, Jianqing, and Irene Gijbels (1996): *Local Polynomial Modelling and Its Applications*, Boca Raton, FL: Chapman & Hall.

Fan, Jianqing, and Qiwei Yao (1998): "Efficient estimation of conditional variance functions in stochastic regression," *Biometrika* 85, 645–660.

Fan, Jianqing and Qiwei Yao (2003): *Nonlinear Time Series: Nonparametric and Parametric Methods.* New York: Springer-Verlag.

Foote, Christopher L., and Christopher F. Goetz (2008): "The impact of legalized abortion on crime: Comment," *Quarterly Journal of Economics* 123, 407–423.

Forinash, Christopher V., and Frank S. Koppelman (1993): "Application and interpretation of nested logit models of intercity mode choice," *Transportation Research Record* 1413, 98–106.

Freyberger, Joachim (2017): "On completeness and consistency in nonparametric instrumental variable models," *Econometrica* 85, 1629–1644.

Frisch, Ragnar (1933): "Editorial," *Econometrica* 1, 1–4.

Frisch, Ragnar, and Frederick V. Waugh (1933): "Partial time regressions as compared with individual trends," *Econometrica* 1, 387–401.

Fuller, Wayne A. (1977): "Some properties of a modification of the limited information estimator," *Econometrica* 45, 939–953.

Gallant, A. Ronald (1977): "Three-stage least-squares estimation for a system of simultaneous, nonlinear, implicit equations," *Journal of Econometrics* 5, 71–88.

Gallant, A. Ronald, and Dale W. Jorgenson (1979): "Statistical inference for a system of nonlinear, implicit equations in the context of instrumental variable estimation," *Journal of Econometrics* 11, 275–302.

Galton, Francis (1886): "Regression towards Mediocrity in Hereditary Stature," *Journal of the Anthropological Institute of Great Britain and Ireland* 15, 246–263.

Gardner, Robert (1998): "Unobservable individual effects in unbalanced panel data," *Economics Letters* 58, 39–42.

Gelman, Andrew, and Guido W. Imbens (2019): "Why high-order polynomials should not be used in regression discontinuity designs," *Journal of Business & Economic Statistics* 37, 447–456.

Godambe, V. P. (1991): *Estimating Functions.* Oxford: Oxford University Press.

Goldberg, Pinelopi Koujianou (1995): "Product differentiation and oligopoly in international markets: The case of the U.S. automobile industry," *Econometrica* 63, 891–951.

Goldberger, Arthur S. (1964): *Econometric Theory.* Hoboken, NJ: Wiley.

Goldberger, Arthur S. (1968): *Topics in Regression Analysis.* New York: Macmillan.

Goldberger, Arthur S. (1981): "Linear regression after selection," *Journal of Econometrics* 15, 357–366.

Goldberger, Arthur S. (1991): *A Course in Econometrics.* Cambridge, MA: Harvard University Press.

Goodnight, James H. (1979): "A tutorial on the SWEEP operator," *American Statistician* 33, 149–158.

Gourieroux, Christian (2000): *Econometrics of Qualitative Dependent Variables.* Cambridge: Cambridge University Press.

Granger, Clive W. J. (1969): "Investigating causal relations by econometric models and cross-spectral methods," *Econometrica* 37, 424–438.

Granger, Clive W. J. (1981): "Some properties of time series data and their use in econometric specification," *Journal of Econometrics* 16, 121–130.

Granger, Clive W. J. (1989): *Forecasting in Business and Economics*, Second Edition. Cambridge, MA: Academic Press.

Granger, Clive W. J., and Paul Newbold (1974): "Spurious regressions in econometrics," *Journal of Econometrics* 2, 111–120.

Granger, Clive W. J., and Paul Newbold (1986): *Forecasting in Business and Economic Time Series*, Second Edition. Cambridge, MA: Academic Press.

Granger, Clive W. J., and Ramu Ramanathan (1984): "Improved methods of combining forecasts," *Journal of Forecasting* 3, 197–204.

Greene, William H. (1981): "On the asymptotic bias of the ordinary least squares estimator of the Tobit model," *Econometrica* 49, 505–513.

Greene, William H. (2018): *Econometric Analysis*, Eighth Edition. London: Pearson.

Gregory, Allan W., and Michael R. Veall (1985): "On formulating Wald tests of nonlinear restrictions," *Econometrica* 53, 1465–1468.

Haavelmo, Trygve (1944): "The probability approach in econometrics," *Econometrica* supplement, 12.

Hahn, Jinyong (1996): "A note on bootstrapping generalized method of moments estimators," *Econometric Theory* 12, 187–197.

Hahn, Jinyong, Petra Todd, and Wilbert van der Klaauw (2001): "Identification and estimation of treatment effects with a regression-discontinuity design," *Econometrica* 69, 201–209.

Hall, Bronwyn H., and Robert E. Hall (1993): "The Value and Performance of U.S. Corporations," *Brookings Papers on Economic Activity* 1–49.

Hall, Peter (1992): *The Bootstrap and Edgeworth Expansion*. New York: Springer-Verlag.

Hall, Peter (1994): "Methodology and theory for the bootstrap," in Robert F. Engle and Daniel L. McFadden (editors) *Handbook of Econometrics*, Volume 4. Amsterdam: Elsevier.

Hall, Peter, and C. C. Heyde (1980): *Martingale Limit Theory and Its Application*. Cambridge, MA: Academic Press.

Hall, Peter, and Joel L. Horowitz (1996): "Bootstrap critical values for tests based on generalized-method-of-moments estimation," *Econometrica* 64, 891–916.

Hall, Robert E. (1978): "Stochastic implications of the life cycle-permanent income hypothesis: Theory and evidence," *Journal of Political Economy* 86, 971–987.

Halmos, Paul R. (1956): *Lectures in Ergodic Theory*. New York: Chelsea Publishing.

Hamilton, James D. (1994) *Time Series Analysis*. Princeton, NJ: Princeton University Press.

Hansen, Bruce E. (1992): "Consistent covariance matrix estimation for dependent heterogeneous processes," *Econometrica* 60, 967–972.

Hansen, Bruce E. (1996): "Inference when a nuisance parameter is not identified under the null hypothesis," *Econometrica* 64, 413–430.

Hansen, Bruce E. (2000): "Sample splitting and threshold estimation," *Econometrica* 68, 575–603.

Hansen, Bruce E. (2006): "Edgeworth expansions for the Wald and GMM statistics for nonlinear restrictions," in Dean Corbae, Steven N. Durlauf, and Bruce E. Hansen (editors) *Econometric Theory and Practice: Frontiers of Analysis and Applied Research*. Cambridge: Cambridge University Press.

Hansen, Bruce E. (2007): "Least squares model averaging," *Econometrica* 75, 1175–1189.

Hansen, Bruce E. (2014): "Model averaging, asymptotic risk, and regressor groups," *Quantitative Economics* 5, 495–530.

Hansen, Bruce E. (2015): "The integrated mean squared error of series regression and a Rosenthal Hilbert-space inequality," *Econometric Theory* 31, 337–361.

Hansen, Bruce E. (2017): "Regression kink with an unknown threshold," *Journal of Business and Economic Statistics* 35, 228–240.

Hansen, Bruce E. (2022a): "A modern Gauss-Markov theorem," *Econometrica*, forthcoming.

Hansen, Bruce E. (2022b): *Probability and Statistics for Economists*. Princeton, NJ: Princeton University Press.

Hansen, Bruce E., and Seojeong Lee (2019): "Asymptotic Theory for Clustered Samples," *Journal of Econometrics* 210, 268–290.

Hansen, Bruce E., and Seojeong Lee (2021): "Inference for iterated GMM under misspecification," *Econometrica* 89, 1419–1447.

Hansen, Bruce E., and Jeffrey Racine (2012): "Jackknife model averaging," *Journal of Econometrics* 167, 38–46.

Hansen, Christian B. (2007): "Asymptotic properties of a robust variance matrix estimator for panel data when T is large," *Journal of Econometrics* 141, 595–620.

Hansen, Lars Peter (1982): "Large sample properties of generalized method of moments estimators, *Econometrica* 50, 1029–1054.

Hansen, Lars Peter, and Robert J. Hodrick (1980): "Forward exchange rates as optimal predictors of future spot rates: An econometric analysis," *Journal of Political Economy* 88, 829–853.

Hansen, Lars Peter, John Heaton, and A. Yaron (1996): "Finite sample properties of some alternative GMM estimators," *Journal of Business and Economic Statistics* 14, 262–280.

Härdle, Wolfgang (1990): *Applied Nonparametric Regression*. Cambridge: Cambridge University Press.

Harvey, Andrew (1990): *The Econometric Analysis of Time Series*, Second Edition. Cambridge, MA: MIT Press.

Hastie, Trevor, Robert Tibshirani, and Jerome Friedman (2008): *The Elements of Statistical Learning: Data Mining, Inference, and Prediction*. New York: Springer.

Hausman, Jerry A. (1978): "Specification tests in econometrics," *Econometrica* 46, 1251–1271.

Hausman, Jerry A., and William E. Taylor (1981): "Panel data and unobservable individual effects," *Econometrica* 49, 1377–1398.

Hausman, Jerry A., Whitney K. Newey, Tiemen Woutersen, John C. Chao, and Norman R. Swanson (2012): "Instrumental variable estimation with heteroskedasticity and many instruments," *Quantitative Economics* 3, 211–255.

Hayashi, Fumio (2000): *Econometrics*. Princeton, NJ: Princeton University Press.

Hayashi, Fumio, and Christopher Sims (1983): "Nearly efficient estimation of time series models with predetermined, but not exogenous, instruments," *Econometrica* 51, 783–798.

Heckman, James (1979): "Sample selection bias as a specification error," *Econometrica* 47, 153–161.

Hinkley, David V. (1977): "Jackknifing in unbalanced situations," *Technometrics* 19, 285–292.

Hoerl, Arthur E., and Robert W. Kennard (1970): "Ridge regression: Biased estimation for non-orthogonal problems," *Technometrics* 12, 55–67.

Holtz-Eakin, Douglas, Whitney Newey, and Harvey S. Rosen (1988): "Estimating vector autoregressions with panel data," *Econometrica* 56, 1371–1395.

Honoré, Bo E. (1992): "Trimmed LAD and least squares estimation of truncated and censored regression models with fixed effects," *Econometrica* 60, 533–565.

Horn, S. D., R. A. Horn, and D. B. Duncan. (1975): "Estimating heteroscedastic variances in linear models," *Journal of the American Statistical Association* 70, 380–385.

Horowitz, Joel (2001): "The bootstrap," in James J. Heckman and Edward E. Leamer (editors) *Handbook of Econometrics*, Volume 5, 3159–3228. Amsterdam: Elsevier.

Horowitz, Joel (2011): "Applied nonparametric instrumental variables estimation," *Econometrica* 79, 347–394.

Hsiao, Cheng (2003): *Analysis of Panel Data*, Second Edition. Cambridge: Cambridge University Press.

Imbens, Guido W., and Joshua D. Angrist (1994): "Identification and estimation of local average treatment effects," *Econometrica* 62, 467–476.

Imbens, Guido W., and Karthik Kalyanaraman (2012): "Optimal bandwidth choice for the regression discontinuity estimator," *Review of Economic Studies* 79, 933–959.

Imbens, Guido W., and Thomas Lemieux (2008): "Regression discontinuity designs: A guide to practice," *Journal of Econometrics* 142, 615–635.

Jackson, Dunham (1912): "On the approximation by trigonometric sums and polynomials with positive coefficients," *Transactions of the American Mathematical Society* 13, 491–515.

James, Gareth, Daniela Witten, Trevor Hastie, Robert Tibshirani (2013): *An Introduction to Statistical Learning: with Applications in R*. New York: Springer.

James, William, and Charles M. Stein (1961): "Estimation with quadratic loss," *Proceedings of the Fourth Berkeley Symposium on Mathematical Statistics and Probability* 1, 361–380.

Johansen, Soren (1988): "Statistical analysis of cointegrating vectors," *Journal of Economic Dynamics and Control* 12, 231–254.

Johansen, Soren (1991): "Estimation and hypothesis testing of cointegration vectors in the presence of linear trend," *Econometrica* 59, 1551–1580.

Johansen, Soren (1995): *Likelihood-Based Inference in Cointegrated Vector Auto-Regressive Models*. Oxford: Oxford University Press.

Johnston, Jack, and John DiNardo (1997): *Econometric Methods*, Fourth Edition. New York: McGraw-Hill.

Jordà, Òscar (2005): "Estimation and inference of impulse responses by local projections," *American Economic Review* 95, 161–182.

Judge, George G., W. E. Griffiths, R. Carter Hill, Helmut Lütkepohl, and Tsoung-Chao Lee (1985): *The Theory and Practice of Econometrics*, Second Edition. Hoboken, NJ: Wiley.

Keating, John W. (1992): "Structural approaches to vector autoregressions," *Federal Reserve Bank of St. Louis Review* 74, 37–57.

Kilian, Lutz (2009): "Not all oil price shocks are alike: Disentangling demand and supply shocks in the crude oil market," *American Economic Review* 99, 1053–1069.

Kilian, Lutz, and Helmut Lütkepohl: (2017): *Structural Vector Autoregressive Analysis*. Cambridge: Cambridge University Press.

Kinal, Terrence W. (1980): "The existence of moments of k-class estimators," *Econometrica* 48, 241–249.

Kleibergen, Frank, and Richard Paap (2006): "Generalized reduced rank tests using the singular value decomposition," *Journal of Econometrics* 133, 97–126.

Klein, Roger W., and Richard H. Spady (1993): "An efficient semiparametric estimator for discrete choice," *Econometrica* 61, 387–421.

Koenker, Roger (2005): *Quantile Regression*. Cambridge: Cambridge University Press.

Koppelman, Frank S., and Chieh-Hua Wen (2000): "The paired combinatorial logit model: Properties, estimation and application," *Transportation Research Part B*, 34, 75–89.

Kotz, Samuel, and Saralees Nadarajah (2000): *Extreme Value Distributions: Theory and Applications*. London: Imperical College Press.

Kurtz, Thomas G., and Phillip Protter (1991): "Weak limit theorems for stochastic integrals and stochastic differential equations," *Annals of Probability* 19, 1035–1070.

Kwiatkowski, Denis, Peter C. B. Phillips, Peter Schmidt, and Yongcheol Shin (1992): "Testing the null hypothesis of stationarity against the alternative of a unit root," *Journal of Econometrics* 54, 159–178.

Kyriazidou, Ekaterini (1997): "Estimation of a panel data sample selection model," *Econometrica* 65, 1335–1364.

Lafontaine, Francine, and Kenneth J. White (1986): "Obtaining any Wald statistic you want," *Economics Letters* 21, 35–40.

Lee, David S. (2008): "Randomized experiments from nonrandom selection in U.S. House elections," *Journal of Econometrics* 142, 675–697.

Lee, David S., and Thomas Lemieux (2010): "Regression discontinuity designs in economics," *Journal of Economic Literature* 48, 281–355.

Lehmann, Erich L., and George Casella (1998): *Theory of Point Estimation*, Second Edition. New York: Springer.

Lehmann, Erich L., and Joseph P. Romano (2005): *Testing Statistical Hypotheses*, Third Edition. New York: Springer.

Li, Ker-Chau (1986): "Asymptotic optimality of C_L and generalized cross-validation in ridge regression with application to spline smoothing," *Annals of Statistics* 14, 1101–1112.

Li, Ker-Chau (1987): "Asymptotic optimality for C_p, C_L, cross-validation and generalized cross-validation: Discrete index set," *Annals of Statistics* 15, 958–975.

Li, Qi, and Jeffrey Racine (2007): *Nonparametric Econometrics*. Princeton, NJ: Princeton University Press.

Liu, Regina Y. (1988): "Bootstrap procedures under some non-I.I.D. models," *Annals of Statistics* 16, 1696–1708.

Lorentz, George G. (1986): *Approximation of Functions*, Second Edition. New York: Chelsea Publishing.

Lovell, Michael C. (1963): "Seasonal adjustment of economic time series," *Journal of the American Statistical Association* 58, 993–1010.

Luce, Robert Duncan (1959): *Individual Choice Behavior: A Theoretical Analysis*. Hoboken, NJ: Wiley.

Ludwig, Jens, and Douglas L. Miller (2007): "Does Head Start improve children's life chances? Evidence from a regression discontinuity design," *Quarterly Journal of Economics* 122, 159–208.

Lütkepohl, Helmut (2005): *New Introduction to Multiple Time Series Analysis*. New York: Springer.

MacKinnon, James G., and Halbert White (1985): "Some heteroskedasticity-consistent covariance matrix estimators with improved finite sample properties," *Journal of Econometrics* 29, 305–325.

Maddala, G. S. (1983): *Limited-Dependent and Qualitative Variables in Econometrics*. Cambridge: Cambridge University Press.

Magnus, Jan R. (2017): *Introduction to the Theory of Econometrics*. Amsterdam: VU University Press.

Magnus, Jan R., and H. Neudecker (2019): *Matrix Differential Calculus with Applications in Statistics and Econometrics*, Third Edition. Hoboken, NJ: Wiley.

Mallows, C. L. (1973): "Some comments on C_p," *Technometrics* 15, 661–675.

Mammen, Enno (1993): "Bootstrap and wild bootstrap for high dimensional linear models," *Annals of Statistics* 21, 255–285.

Mankiw, N. Gregory, David Romer, and David N. Weil (1992): "A contribution to the empirics of economic growth," *Quarterly Journal of Economics* 107, 407–437.

Manski, Charles F. (1975): "The maximum score estimator of the stochastic utility model of choice," *Journal of Econometrics* 3, 205–228.

Mariano, Robert S. (1982): "Analytical small-sample distribution theory in econometrics: The simultaneous equations case," *International Economic Review* 23, 503–534.

McCracken, Michael W., and Serena Ng (2016): "FRED-MD: A Monthly Database for Macroeconomic Research," *Journal of Business and Economic Statistics* 34, 574–579.

McCracken, Michael W., and Serena Ng (2021): "FRED-QD: A quarterly database for macroeconomic research," *Federal Reserve Bank of St. Louis Review*, 1–44.

McCrary, Justin (2008): "Manipulation of the running variable in the regression discontinuity design: A density test," *Journal of Econometrics* 142, 698–714.

McCulloch, J. Huston (1985): "On heteros*edasticity," *Econometrica* 53, 483.

McFadden, Daniel (1978): "Modeling the choice of residential location," in A. Karlgvist (editor) *Spatial Interaction Theory and Residential Location*, 75–96. Amsterdam: North-Holland.

McFadden, Daniel (1981): "Econometric models of probabilistic choice," in Charles Manski and Daniel McFadden (editors) *Structural Analysis of Discrete Data with Econometric Applications*, 198–272. Cambridge, MA: MIT Press.

Mertens, Karel, and Morten O. Ravn (2013): "The dynamic effects of personal and corporate income tax changes in the United States," *American Economic Review* 103, 1212–1247.

Meyer, Marco, and Jens-Peter Kreiss (2015): "On the vector autoregressive sieve bootstrap," *Journal of Time Series Analysis* 36, 377–397.

Mhaskar, Hrushikesh N. (1996): *Introduction to the Theory of Weighted Polynomial Approximation*. Singapore: World Scientific.

Moulton, Brent R. (1990): "An illustration of a pitfall in estimating the effects of aggregate variables on micro units," *Review of Economics and Statistics* 72, 334–338.

Mullainathan, Sendhil, and Jann Spiess (2017): "Machine learning: An applied econometric approach," *Journal of Economic Perspectives* 31, 87–106.

Mundlak, Yair (1961): "Empirical production function free of management bias," *Journal of Farm Economics* 43, 44–56.

Murphy, Kevin M., and Robert H. Topel (1985): "Estimation and inference in two-step econometric models," *Journal of Business and Economic Statistics* 3, 370–379.

Nadaraya, Èlizbar A. (1964): "On estimating regression," *Theory of Probability and Its Applications* 9, 141–142.

Nelson, Charles R., and Charles I. Plosser (1982): "Trends and random walks in macroeconomic time series: Some evidence and implications," *Journal of Monetary Economics* 10, 139–162.

Nerlove, Marc (1963): "Returns to scale in electricity supply," in Carl Christ, Milton Friedman, and Leo A. Goodman (editors), *Measurement in Economics*, 167–198. Redwood City, CA: Stanford University Press.

Nevo, Aviv (2001): "Measuring market power in the ready-to-eat cereal industry," *Econometrica* 69, 307–342.

Newey, Whitney K. (1985): "Generalized method of moments specification testing," *Journal of Econometrics* 29, 229–256.

Newey, Whitney K. (1990): "Semiparametric efficiency bounds," *Journal of Applied Econometrics* 5, 99–135.

Newey, Whitney K. (1997): "Convergence rates and asymptotic normality for series estimators," *Journal of Econometrics* 79, 147–168.

Newey, Whitney K., and James L. Powell (2003): "Instrumental variable estimation of nonparametric models," *Econometrica* 71, 1565–1578.

Newey, Whitney K., and Kenneth D. West (1987a): "Hypothesis testing with efficient method of moments estimation," *International Economic Review* 28, 777–787.

Newey, Whitney K., and Kenneth D. West (1987b): "A simple positive semi-definite, heteroskedasticity and autocorrelation consistent covariance matrix," *Econometrica* 55, 703–708.

Newey, Whitney K., and Kenneth D. West (1994): "Automatic lag selection in covariance matrix estimation," *Review of Economic Studies* 61, 631–654.

Ng, Serena, and Pierre Perron (2001): "Lag length selection and the construction of unit root tests with good size and power,"*Econometrica* 69, 1519–1554.

Nickell, Stephen (1981): "Biases in dynamic models with fixed effects," *Econometrica* 49, 1417–1426.

Olsen, Randall J. (1978): "Note on the uniqueness of the maximum likelihood estimator for the Tobit model," *Econometrica* 46, 1211–1215.

Oster, Emily (2018): "Diabetes and diet: Purchasing behavior change in response to health information," *American Economic Journal: Applied Economics* 10, 308–348.

Pagan, Adrian (1984): "Econometric issues in the analysis of regressions with generated regressors," *International Economic Review* 25, 221–247.

Pagan, Adrian (1986): "Two stage and related estimators and their applications," *Review of Economic Studies* 53, 517–538.

Pagan, Adrian, and Aman Ullah (1999): *Nonparametric Econometrics*. Cambridge: Cambridge University Press.

Papageorgiou, Chris, Marianne Saam, and Patrick Schulte (2017): "Substitution between clean and dirty energy inputs: A macroeconomic perspective," *Review of Economics and Statistics* 99, 281–290.

Park, Joon Y., and Peter C. B. Phillips (1988a): "On the formulation of Wald tests of nonlinear restrictions," *Econometrica* 56, 1065–1083.

Park, Joon Y., and Peter C. B. Phillips (1988b): "Statistical inference in regressions with integrated processes: Part 1," *Econometric Theory* 4, 468–497.

Petersen, Karl E. (1983): *Ergodic Theory*. Cambridge: Cambridge University Press.

Pham, Tuan D., and Lanh T. Tran (1985): "Some mixing properties of time series models," *Stochastic Processes and Their Applications* 19, 297–303.

Phillips, Alban W. (1958): "The relation between unemployment and the rate of change of money wage rates in the United Kingdom 1861–1957," *Economica* 25, 283–299.

Phillips, G. D. A., and C. Hale (1977): "The bias of instrumental variable estimators of simultaneous equation systems," *International Economic Review* 18, 219–228.

Phillips, Peter C. B. (1983): "Exact small sample theory in the simultaneous equations model," in Zvi Griliches and Michael D. Intriligator (editors), *Handbook of Econometrics*, Volume 1. Amsterdam: North-Holland.

Phillips, Peter C. B. (1986): "Understanding spurious regressions in econometrics," *Journal of Econometrics* 33, 311–340.

Phillips, Peter C. B., and Bruce E. Hansen (1990): "Statistical inference in instrumental variables regression with I(1) processes," *Review of Economic Studies* 57, 99–125.

Phillips, Peter C. B., and Sam Ouliaris (1990): "Asymptotic properties of residual based tests for cointegration," *Econometrica* 58, 165–193.

Politis, Dimitris N., and Tucker S. McElroy (2020): *Time Series: A First Course with Bootstrap Starter*. London: Chapman & Hall/CRC Press.

Politis, Dimitris N., Joseph P. Romano, and Michael Wolf (1999): *Subsampling*. New York: Springer.

Powell, James L. (1984): "Least absolute deviations estimation for the censored regression model," *Journal of Econometrics* 25, 303–325.

Powell, James L. (1986): "Censored regression quantiles," *Journal of Econometrics* 32, 143–155.

Quenouille, M. H. (1949): "Approximate tests of correlation in time series," *Journal of the Royal Statistical Society, Series B*, 11, 18–84.

Ramey, Valerie A. (2016): "Macroeconomic shocks and their propagation," in John B. Taylor and Harald Uhlig (editors), *Handbook of Macroeconomics*, Volume 2. Amsterdam: Elsevier.

Ramsey, James B. (1969): "Tests for specification errors in classical linear least-squares regression analysis," *Journal of the Royal Statistical Society, Series B*, 31, 350–371.

Reiersøl, Olav (1945): *Confluence Analysis by Means of Instrumental Sets of Variables*. Uppsala: Almqvist & Wilksell.

Reinhart, Carmen M., and Kenneth S. Rogoff (2010): "Growth in a time of debt," *American Economic Review: Papers and Proceedings* 100, 573–578.

Robinson, Peter R. (1988) "Root-n-consistent semiparametric regression," *Econometrica* 56, 931–954.

Rubin, Donald B. (1974): "Estimating causal effects of treatments in randomized and non-randomized studies," *Journal of Educational Psychology* 66, 688–701

Ruud, Paul A. (2000): *An Introduction to Classical Econometric Theory*. Oxford: Oxford University Press.

Samuelson, Paul A. (1939): "Interactions between the multiplier analysis and the principle of acceleration," *Review of Economic Statistics* 21, 75–78.

Sargan, J. Dennis (1958): "The estimation of economic relationships using instrumental variables," *Econometrica* 26, 393–415.

Schumaker, Larry L. (2007): *Spline Functions: Basic Theory*, Third Edition. Cambridge: Cambridge University Press.

Schwarz, Gideon (1978): "Estimating the dimension of a model," *Annals of Statistics* 6, 461–464.

Shao, Jun, and Dongsheng Tu (1995): *The Jackknife and Bootstrap*. New York: Springer.

Shapiro, Matthew D., and Mark W. Watson (1988): "Sources of business cycle fluctuations," in Stanley Fischer (editor), *NBER Macroeconomics Annual*, 111–148. Cambridge, MA: MIT Press.

Shibata, Ritei (1980): "Asymptotically efficient selection of the order of the model for estimating parameters of a linear process," *Annals of Statistics* 8, 147–164.

Sims, Christopher A. (1972): "Money, income and causality," *American Economic Review* 62, 540–552.

Sims, Christopher A. (1980): "Macroeconomics and reality," *Econometrica* 48, 1–48.

Staiger, Douglas, and James H. Stock (1997): "Instrumental variables regression with weak instruments," *Econometrica* 65, 557–586.

Stock, James H. (1987): "Asymptotic properties of least squares estimators of cointegrating vectors," *Econometrica* 55, 1035–1056.

Stock, James H., and Francesco Trebbi (2003): "Retrospectives: Who invented instrumental variable regression?" *Journal of Economic Perspectives* 17, 177–194.

Stock, James H., and Mark W. Watson (1993): "A simple estimator of cointegrating vectors in higher order integrated systems," *Econometrica* 61, 783–820.

Stock, James H., and Mark W. Watson (2007): "Why has U.S. inflation become harder to forecast?" *Journal of Money, Credit and Banking* 39, 3–33.

Stock, James H., and Mark W. Watson (2008): "Heteroskedasticity-robust standard errors for fixed effects panel data regression," *Econometrica* 76, 155–174.

Stock, James H., and Mark W. Watson (2016): "Factor models and structural vector autoregressions in macroeconomics," in John B. Taylor and Harald Uhlig (editors), *Handbook of Macroeconomics*, Volume 2. Amsterdam: Elsevier.

Stock, James H., and Mark W. Watson (2019): *Introduction to Econometrics*, Fourth Edition. London: Pearson.

Stock, James H., and Jonathan H. Wright (2000): "GMM with weak identification," *Econometrica* 68, 1055–1096.

Stock, James H., and Motohiro Yogo (2005): "Testing for weak instruments in linear IV regression," in Donald W. K. Andrews and James H. Stock (editors), *Identification and Inference for Econometric Models: Essays in Honor of Thomas Rothenberg*, 80–108. Cambridge: Cambridge University Press.

Stone, Charles J. (1977): "Consistent nonparametric regression," *Annals of Statistics* 5, 595–645.

Stone, Marshall H. (1948): "The generalized Weierstrass approximation theorem," *Mathematics Magazine* 21, 167–184.

Stout, William F. (1974): *Almost Sure Convergence*. Cambridge, MA: Academic Press.

Theil, Henri (1953): "Repeated least squares applied to complete equation systems," The Hague, Central Planning Bureau, mimeo.

Theil, Henri (1961): *Economic Forecasts and Policy*. Amsterdam: North-Holland.

Theil, Henri. (1971): *Principles of Econometrics*. Hoboken, NJ: Wiley.

Thistlethwaite, Donald L., and Donald T. Campbell (1960): "Regression-discontinuity analysis: An alternative to the ex-post facto experiment," *Journal of Educational Psychology* 51, 309–317.

Tibshirani, Robert (1996): "Regression shrinkage and selection via the lasso," *Journal of the American Statistical Association, Series B*, 58, 267–288.

Tikhonov, Andrey Nikolayevich (1943): "On the stability of inverse problems," *Doklady Akademii Nauk SSSR* 39, 195–198.

Tobin, James (1958): "Estimation of relationships for limited dependent variables," *Econometrica* 26, 24–36.

Tong, Howell (1990): *Non-linear Time Series: A Dynamical System Approach*. Oxford: Oxford University Press.

Train, Kenneth E. (2009): *Discrete Choice Methods with Simulation*, Second Edition. Cambridge: Cambridge University Press.

Tripathi, Gautam (1999): "A matrix extension of the Cauchy-Schwarz inequality," *Economics Letters* 63, 1–3.

Tukey, John (1958): "Bias and confidence in not quite large samples," *Annals of Mathematical Statistics* 29, 614.

von Bahr, Bengt, and Carl-Gustav Esseen (1965): "Inequalities for the rth absolute moment of a sum of random variables, $1 \leq r \leq 2$," *Annals of Mathematical Statistics* 36, 299–303.

Wager, Stefan, and Susan Athey (2018): "Estimation and inference of heterogeneous treatment effects using random forests," *Journal of the American Statistical Association* 113, 1228–1242.

Wager, Stefan, Trevor Hastie, and Bradley Efron (2014): "Confidence intervals for random forests: The jackknife and the infinitesimal jackknife," *Journal of Machine Learning Research* 15, 1625–1651.

Wald, Abraham (1940): "The fitting of straight lines if both variables are subject to error," *Annals of Mathematical Statistics* 11, 283–300

Wald, Abraham (1943): "Tests of statistical hypotheses concerning several parameters when the number of observations is large," *Transactions of the American Mathematical Society* 54, 426–482.

Walters, Peter (1982): *An Introduction to Ergodic Theory*. New York: Springer-Verlag.

Wasserman, Larry (2006): *All of Nonparametric Statistics*. New York: Springer.

Watson, Geoffrey S. (1964): "Smooth regression analysis," *Sankya* Series A, 26, 359–372.

Watson, Mark W. (1994): "VARs and cointegration," in Robert Engle and Daniel McFadden (editors), *Handbook of Econometrics*, Volume 4. Amsterdam: North-Holland.

Weierstrass, Karl (1885): "Über die analytische Darstellbarkeit sogenannter willkürlicher Functionen einer reellen Veränderlichen," *Sitzungsberichte der Königlich Preuÿischen Akademie der Wissenschaften zu Berlin*.

Wen, Chieh-Hua, and Frank S. Koppelman (2001): "The generalized nested logit model," *Transportation Research, Part B*, 35, 627–641.

White, Halbert (1980): "A heteroskedasticity-consistent covariance matrix estimator and a direct test for heteroskedasticity," *Econometrica* 48, 817–838.

White, Halbert (1982): "Instrumental variables regression with independent observations," *Econometrica* 50, 483–499.

White, Halbert, and Ian Domowitz (1984): "Nonlinear regression with dependent observations," *Econometrica* 52, 143–162.

Whittle, Peter (1960): "Bounds for the moments of linear and quadratic forms in independent variables," *Theory of Probability and Its Applications* 5, 302–305.

Wiener, Nobert, and Pesi R. Masani (1958): "The prediction theory of multivariate stochastic processes, II," *Acta Mathematica* 99, 93–137.

Windmeijer, Frank (2005): "A finite sample correction for the variance of linear efficient two-step GMM estimators," *Journal of Econometrics* 126, 25–51.

Wooldridge, Jeffrey M. (1995): "Score diagnostics for linear models estimated by two-stage least squares," in G. S. Maddala, Peter C. B. Phillips, and T. N. Srinivasan (editors), *Advances in Econometrics and Quantitative Economics: Essays in Honor of Professor C. R. Rao*, 66–87. Cambridge: Blackwell.

Wooldridge, Jeffrey M. (2010): *Econometric Analysis of Cross Section and Panel Data*, Second Edition. Cambridge, MA: MIT Press.

Wooldridge, Jeffrey M. (2020): *Introductory Econometrics: A Modern Approach,* Sixth Edition. La Jolla, CA: Southwestern.

Working, Elmer J. (1927): "What Do Statistical 'Demand Curves' Show?" *Quarterly Journal of Economics* 41, 212–235.

Wright, Philip G. (1915): "Moore's Economic Cycles," *Quarterly Journal of Economics* 29, 631–641.

Wright, Philip G. (1928): *The Tariff on Animal and Vegetable Oils*. New York: Macmillan.

Wright, Sewell (1921): "Correlation and causation," *Journal of Agricultural Research* 20, 557–585.

Wu, De-Min (1973): Alternative tests of independence between stochastic regressors and disturbances," *Econometrica* 41, 733–750.

Zellner, Arnold (1962): "An efficient method of estimating seemingly unrelated regressions, and tests for aggregation bias," *Journal of the American Statistical Association* 57, 348–368.

Zhang, Fuzhen, and Qingling Zhang (2006): "Eigenvalue inequalities for matrix product," *IEEE Transactions on Automatic Control* 51, 1506–1509.

INDEX